AMG All Music Guide to
the Blues

the experts' guide to the BEST BLUES recordings

2nd edition

Edited by

Michael Erlewine, Executive Editor

Vladimir Bogdanov, Database Design

Chris Woodstra, Editor-in-chief

Cub Koda, Blues Editor

Stephen Thomas Erlewine, Senior Editor

Miller Freeman Books

San Francisco

Published by Miller Freeman Books, 600 Harrison Street, San Francisco, CA 94107
Miller Freeman, Inc. is a United News & Media company
Publishers of *Guitar Player, Bass Player,* and *Keyboard* magazines

un Miller Freeman

Distributed to the book trade in the U.S. and Canada by
    Publishers Group West, 1700 Fourth St., Berkeley, CA 94710
Distributed to the music trade in the U.S. and Canada by
    Hal Leonard Publishing, P.O. Box 13819, Milwaukee, WI 53213

ISBN 0-87930-548-7

Library of Congress Cataloging-in-Publication Data
All music guide to the blues : the experts' guide to the best blues
    recordings / edited by Michael Erlewine . . . [et al.]. -- 2nd ed.
        p. cm. -- (AMG all music guide series)
    Includes bibliographical references (p.   ) and index.
    ISBN 0-87930-548-7
    1. Blues (Music)--Discography. 2. Sound recordings--Reviews.
I. Erlewine, Michael. II. Series
ML 156.4.B6A45 1999
016.781643'0266--dc21   98-42564
                                                     CIP
                                                     MN

Cover Design: Nita Ybarra
Cover Photo: Jay Blakesberg

Printed in the United States of America
99 00 01 02 03 04 9 8 7 6 5 4 3 2 1

Contents

How to Use This Book

ARTIST NAME   (Alternate name in parentheses).

VITAL STATISTICS   For indivdual performers, date and place of birth and death, if known.

INSTRUMENT(S) / STYLE   Major instruments for each performer, followed by one or more styles of music associated with each performer or group.

BIOGRAPHY   A quick view of the artist's life and musical career. For major performers, proportionately longer biographies are provided.

ALBUM REVIEWS   These are the albums selected by our editors and contributors.

KEY TO SYMBOLS   ● ☆ ★

☆ ESSENTIAL RECORDINGS   Albums marked with a star should be part of any good collection of the genre. Often, these are also a good first purchase (filled star). By hearing these albums, you can get a good overview of the entire genre. These are must-hear and must-have recordings. You can't go wrong with them.

●★ FIRST PURCHASE   Albums marked with either a filled circle or a filled star should be your first purchase. This is where to begin to find out if you like this particular artist. These albums are representative of the best this artist has to offer. If you don't like these picks, chances are this artist is not for you. In the case of an artist who has a number of distinct periods, you will find an essential pick marked for each period. Albums are listed chronologically when possible.

ALBUM RATINGS: ♦ TO ♦♦♦♦♦   In addition to the stars and circles used to distinguish exceptional noteworthy albums, as explained above, all albums are rated on a scale from one to five diamonds.

ALBUM TITLE   The name of the album is listed in bold as it appears on the original when possible. Very long titles have been abbreviated, or repeated in full as part of the comment, where needed.

DATE   The year of an album's first recording or release, if known.

RECORD LABEL   Record labels indicate the current (or most recent) release of this recording. Label numbers are not included because they change frequently.

REVIEWERS   The name of each review's author are given at the end of the review. "AMG" indicates a review written by the *All Music Guide* staff.

Juke Boy Bonner

b. Mar. 22, 1932, Bellville, TX, **d.** Jun. 29, 1978, Houston, TX
Guitar, Harmonica, Vocals / Electric Texas Blues

One-man bands weren't any too common on the postwar blues scene. Joe Hill Louis and Dr. Ross come to mind as greats who plied their trade all by their lonesome—and so did Juke Boy Bonner, a Texan whose talent never really earned him much in the way of tangible reward.

Born into impoverished circumstances in the Lone Star State during the Depression, Weldon Bonner took up the guitar in his teens. He caught a break in 1947 in Houston, winning a talent contest that led to a spot on a local radio outlet. He journeyed to Oakland in 1956, cutting his debut single for Bob Geddins' Irma imprint ("Rock with Me Baby"/"Well Baby") with Lafayette "Thing" Thomas supplying the lead guitar. Goldband Records boss Eddie Shuler was next to take a chance in 1960; Bonner recorded for him in Lake Charles, LA, with Katie Webster on piano, but once again, nothing happened.

Troubled by stomach problems during the '60s, Bonner utilized his hospital downtime to write poems that he later turned into songs. He cut his best work during the late '60s for Arhoolie Records, accompanying himself on both guitar and racked harmonica as he weaved extremely personal tales of his rough life in Houston. A few European tours ensued, but they didn't really lead to much. Toward the end of his life, he toiled in a chicken processing plant to make ends meet. Bonner died of cirrhosis of the liver in 1978. —*Bill Dahl*

Juke Boy Bonner, 1960-1967 / Mar. 15, 1960-Dec. 12, 1967 / Flyright ♦♦♦
There's a Lightnin' Hopkins-meets-Jimmy Reed sound on these delightfully funky guitar/harp-accompanied blues by this Houstonian, whose ironic lyrics are half the fun. —*Jas Obrecht*

One Man Trio / Feb. 1967 / Flyright ♦♦♦♦

Going Back to the Country / Dec. 20, 1967-Jan.23, 1968 / Arhoolie ♦♦♦♦

● **Life Gave Me a Dirty Deal** / Nov. 30, 1968-May 5, 1969 / Arhoolie ♦♦♦♦
Likely the most consistent and affecting collection you'll encounter by this singular Texas bluesman, whose strikingly personal approach was stunningly captured by Arhoolie's Chris Strachwitz during the late '60s in Houston. Twenty-three utter originals include "Stay Off Lyons Avenue," "Struggle Here in Houston," "I Got My Passport," and the title track. Bonner sang movingly of his painfully impoverished existence for Arhoolie, and the results still resound triumphantly today. —*Bill Dahl*

☆ **The Struggle** / Nov. 30, 1968-May 5, 1969 / Arhoolie ♦♦♦♦♦
Recorded in extreme stereo, with drums on one channel and Bonner's guitar on the other, this is Juke Boy Bonner's most cohesive album. Great songwriting and performances throughout. —*Cub Koda*

Things Ain't Right / Nov. 4, 1969-Nov. 28, 1969 / Sequel ♦♦
This set is somewhat disappointing compared to the Arhoolie sides. —*Bill Dahl*

Legacy of the Blues, Vol. 5 / 1972 / GNP ♦♦♦

Adventures of Juke Boy Bonner / 1980 / Collectables ♦♦

The Texas Blues Troubadours / 1990 / Collectables ♦♦♦

Jumpin with Juke Boy / Sept. 14, 1993 / Collectables ♦♦♦

Blues is root music, always radical–the root or essence of other musics. Many music genres claim they have blues roots–rock, jazz, and rhythm & blues. Blues is pure food for fusion and many musics ground themselves in feelings through their bluesy elements. And yet blues still is fresh–untouched. That is because blues is a singularity rather than itself a fusion with something else. It is indivisible–recursive. The root of blues is the human experience and psyche itself.

We own a great debt to black Americans for delivering this great treasure to the world in the form we have it now, but blues is not a matter of color or form. Its root is the human experience itself–for all times and in all cultures. All people feel the blues in one way or another. You can hear the blues crying from many a proud country tune. And it is all through mountain and folk music. Gospel is its spiritual twin. If you have the ear, you can even hear it in the great classical composers–Bach's oboe lines or Mozart's bass lines. And classical music of the Renaissance period is nothing but blues! Eastern music, with its half and quarter tones, has mastered this form a long time ago. Blues has always been an integral part of us. But most of all you can hear the blues in the music described in this book, the sincere gift of the African American tradition to the world.

I would like to thank the entire All Music Guide staff for working so hard on getting this to you. In particular, editors Chris Woodstra, Stephen Thomas Erlewine, and Richie Unterberger did it the old-fashioned way–working 'til the wee hours of the morning to make sure that we got everyone we could into the number of pages we were allowed. And a very special thanks to our blues editor Cub Koda, who not only watched over the project like a mother hen but also (toward the end of the project) volunteered to work on site for many weeks with our staff to get it just right. We hope you enjoy this book.

Aside from this volume, the All Music Guide series includes our main guide (*All Music Guide*) and the *All Music Guide to Rock*, *All Music Guide to Jazz*, and the *All Music Guide to Country Music*. The complete AMG guide is also available on CD-ROM from Corel Corporation. Also, be sure to visit our home page on the World-Wide Web at http://AllMusic.com. The All-Music Guide is an ongoing database project, the largest collection of substantive album reviews ever assembled. We welcome your feedback.

Perhaps we have left out some of your favorite albums, and/or included ones that you don't consider essential. Let us know about it. We welcome criticism, suggestions, and additions. Perhaps you are an expert on the complete output of a particular artist or group and would like to participate in future editions of this book and/or our larger computer database. We would be glad to hear from you.

Michael Erlewine, Executive Editor
All-Music Guide
407 N. State Street, Big Rapids, MI 49307
Phone (616) 796 3437, Fax (616) 796 1244
E-mail: AMG@AllMusic.com

Contributors

Acknowledgments:
Special thanks to: Cary Wolfson of *Blues Access*, Bill Dahl, Richie Unterberger, Carl Bierling, and the staff of Holland Compact Disc.

Editors
Michael Erlewine
 Executive Editor
Vladimir Bogdanov
 Database Design
Chris Woodstra
 Editor-in-chief
Cub Koda
 Blues Editor
Stephen Thomas Erlewine
 Senior Editor

AMG Production Staff
Jason Ankeny
Jackie Baldwin
Jonathan Ball
Sherry Batchelder
Nancy Beilfuss
Julie Bloem
Melissa Bos
John Bush
Shannon Carmichael
Julie Clark
Tammy Danneels
Dave Datta
Mark Donkers
Brandy Ellison
Jamie Erler
Margaret J. Erlewine
Margaret Louise Erlewine
Kevin Fowler
Beki Friend
Doug Gabert
Yelena German
Tanya Guild
Brenda Haney
Jodi Heffron
April Hinkley
Will Holmes

Steve Huey
Jennifer Hughes
Debbie Kirby
Sarah Kirby
Angel Lake
Jennifer Parke
Forest Ray
Danielle Ruppert
Shey Ryans
Kermit Snelson
Bob Smith
Mike Tinnes

Matrix Staff
Sandra Brennan
Irene Baldwin
Richard Batchelder
Susan Brownlee
Stephanie Clement
Walter Crockett
Tricia Davis
Teresa Swift-Eckert
Phillip Erlewine
Stephen Erlewine
Yuri German
Thomas Goyett
Mary Anne Henry
Mary E. King
Mike King
Madeline Koperski
Linda Lang
Jamie Longstreet
Martin Machnowski
Eleonor Mannikka
Heather Nowlin
Dan Pavlides
Frank Piechoski
Sean Torongeau

Contributors
Jason Ankeny
William AshfordGeorge Bedard
Myles Boisen
Ross Boissoneau
Rob Bowman
Sandra Brennan
Jeff Burger
John Bush
Bil Carpenter
James Chrispell
Rick Clark
Jeff Crooke
Bill Dahl
Hank Davis
Michael P. Dawson
Donna DiChario
Scott Dirks
John Dougan
Bruce Eder
Michael Erlewine
Stephen Thomas Erlewine
John Floyd
Dan Forte
Niles J. Frantz
Richard S. Ginell
Robert Gordon
Bob Gottlieb
Tom Graves
Char Ham
Jeff Hannusch
Craig Harris
Dan Heilman
Alex Henderson
Bob Hinkle
Larry Hoffman
Steve Hoffman
Steve Huey
Mark A. Humphrey
Steve James
Cub Koda

Richard Lieberson
Kip Lornell
John Lowe
David L. Mayers
Steven McDonald
Richard Meyer
Michael G. Nastos
Opal Louis Nations
Jim Newsom
Jim O'Neal
Jas Obrecht
Christine Ohlman
Richard Pack
Roch Parisien
Barry Lee Pearson
Jana Pendragon
Bob Porter
Jim Powers
Greg Prato
Bruce Boyd Raeburn
Chip Renner
John Storm Roberts
William Ruhlmann
Tim Sheridan
Richard Skelly
Chris Slawecki
Leo Stanley
David Szatmary
Jeff Tamarkin
Neal Umphred
Richie Unterberger
Billy C. Wirtz
Cary Wolfson
Jan Mark Wolkin
Chris Woodstra
Jim Worbois
Ron Wynn
Scott Yanow

Michael Erlewine

All Music Guide editor Michael Erlewine helped form the Prime Movers Blues Band in Ann Arbor, Michigan in 1965. He was the lead singer and played amplified harmonica in this pace-setting band (the first of its kind). The original band included a number of now well-known musicians including Iggy Pop (drums), "Blue" Gene Tyranny (piano; now a well-known avant-garde classical composer); Jack Dawson (bass; became bass player for Siegel-Schwall Blues Band); and Michael's brother Dan Erlewine (lead guitar; now monthly columnist for *Guitar Player* magazine). Michael has extensively interviewed blues performers, both in video and audio, and, along with his band, helped to shape the first few Ann Arbor Blues festivals. Today Michael is a systems programmer and director of Matrix Software. Aside from the company's work in music and film data, Matrix is the largest center for astrological programming and research in North America. Michael has been a practicing astrologer for more than 30 years and has an international reputation in that field.

Michael is also very active in Tibetan Buddhism and serves as the director of the Heart Center Karma Thegsum Choling, one of the main centers in North America for the translation, transcription, and publication of psychological texts and teachings of the Karma Kagyu Lineage of Tibetan Buddhism. Michael has been married for 25 years, and he and his wife Margaret live in Big Rapids, Michigan. They have four children.

Vladimir Bogdanov

Russian mathematician and programmer Vladimir Bogdanov has been involved in the design and development of *All Music Guide* databases since 1991. Having experience in many different fields such as nuclear physics, psychology, social studies and ancient chronology he now applies his knowledge to the construction of unique music reference tools utilizing the latest computer technologies. His personal interest lies in applying artificial intelligence and other mathematical methods to areas with complex semantic structures, like music, film, literature. Vladimir's ultimate goal is to provide people with the means to find what they need, even if they don't know what they are looking for.

Chris Woodstra

Chris Woodstra has had a lifelong obsession with music and is an avid record collector. He has worked many years in music retail, he was a DJ, hosting programs in every genre of music, and has been a contributing editor for several local arts and entertainment magazines. Working as an editor for the *All Music Guide* database has given him the opportunity to combine his technical skills, a B.S. in Physics and Mathematics, and his love of music for the first time in his life. Being a perfectionist by nature, Chris makes sure that that any information that goes into the database has been carefully researched and verified.

Cub Koda

Cub Koda is a musician and a journalist with a long and varied career. As a musician, Koda achieved his greatest chart success as a member of the '70s rock 'n' roll band Brownsville Station, who had a number three hit in 1973 with his song, "Smokin' In the Boy's Room." After the breakup of Brownsville in 1979, Cub began a wildly eclectic solo career, during which he played with Hound Dog Taylor's band, the Houserockers, performing a number of concerts and releasing several acclaimed albums during the '80s and '90s. In the late '70s, Koda began writing a monthly music column called "The Vinyl Junkie" for Goldmine, now published in *DISCoveries* magazine. The column established Cub as a lively, knowledgeable music journalist and by the early '90s, he was contributing liner notes to reissues for a variety of labels. In 1996, Koda won the *Living Blues* Magazine's critics poll award for Best Reissue Liner Notes for 1995, based on his work for AVI Records' Excello series.

Stephen Thomas Erlewine

Stephen Thomas Erlewine studied English at the University of Michigan and was the arts editor of the school's newspaper, *The Michigan Daily*. In addition to editing the *All Music Guide*, Erlewine is a freelance writer and musician.

Richie Unterberger

Richie Unterberger is a writer and editor who lives in San Francisco. He was the editor of the travel and music sections of *The Millenium Whole Earth Catalog* (Harper Collins, 1994). Between 1985 and 1991, he was the editor of *Option* magazine, the national publication devoted to coverage of all types alternative and independently produced music. In his professional work, he is dedicated to enhancing the appreciation of the arts, culture, and history in as educational, entertaining, and affordable a fashion as possible, in both multimedia technologies and more traditional print mediums. Since watching *A Hard Day's Night* at the age of four, his favorite group has been the Beatles.

Blues Styles

CLASSIC FEMALE BLUES

The earliest recorded form of the blues. This genre features female vocalists singing material with close connections to pop music of the period (mid-'20s to early '30s) and primarily jazz backings. Main proponents: Mamie Smith, Bessie Smith, Ma Rainey, Lucille Bogan, and Victoria Spivey.

DELTA BLUES

Also known as Mississippi blues, this is the earliest guitar-dominated music to make it onto record. Consisting of performers working primarily in a solo, self-accompanied context, it also embraces the now-familiar string-band/small-combo format, both precursors to the modern-day blues band. Main proponents: Charlie Patton, Robert Johnson, and Son House.

COUNTRY-BLUES

A term that delineates the depth and breadth of the first flowering of guitar-driven blues, embracing all regional styles and variations (Piedmont, Atlanta, early Chicago, ragtime, folk, songster, etc.). Primarily acoustic guitarists, some country-blues performers later switched to electric guitars without changing their style. Major proponents: Henry Thomas, Skip James, Barbecue Bob, Leadbelly, Mississippi John Hurt, Lonnie Johnson, Blind Blake, and Tommy Johnson.

MEMPHIS BLUES

A strain of country-blues all its own, the Memphis style gives us the rise of two distinct forms, the jug band (humorous, jazz-style blues played on homemade instruments) and the beginnings of assigning parts to guitarists for solo (lead) and rhythm, a tradition that is now part-and-parcel of all modern-day blues bands. The later, post-WWII electric version of this genre featured explosive guitar work, thunderous drumming, and declamatory vocals. Main proponents: Cannon's Jug Stompers, Furry Lewis, Memphis Minnie, and the early recordings of B.B. King and Howlin' Wolf.

TEXAS BLUES

A subgenre earmarked by a more relaxed, swinging feel than other styles of blues. The earlier, acoustic version embraced both songster and country-blues traditions, while the post-war electric style featured jazzy, single-string soloing over predominantly horn-driven backing. Main proponents: Blind Lemon Jefferson, Lightnin' Hopkins, Clarence "Gatemouth" Brown, and T-Bone Walker.

CHICAGO BLUES

Delta blues fully amplified and put into a small-band context. Later permutations of the style took their cue from the lead guitar work of B.B. King and T-Bone Walker. Main proponents: Muddy Waters, Howlin' Wolf, Little Walter, Big Walter Horton, Jimmy Rogers, Elmore James, Jimmy Reed, Otis Rush, Magic Sam, and Buddy Guy.

JUMP BLUES

Uptempo, jazz-tinged blues, usually featuring a vocalist in front of a large, horn-driven orchestra with less reliance on guitar work than other styles. Main proponents: Amos Milburn, Johnny Otis, Roy Brown, Wynonie Harris, and Big Joe Turner.

NEW ORLEANS BLUES

Primarily (but not exclusively) piano- and horn-driven, this genre strain is enlivened by Caribbean rhythms, party atmosphere, and the "second-line" strut of the Dixieland music so indigenous to the area. Main proponents: Professor Longhair, Guitar Slim, and Snooks Eaglin.

WEST COAST BLUES

More piano-based and jazz-influenced than anything else, the West Coast style (California in particular) also embraces post-war Texas guitar expatriates and jump-blues practitioners. Main proponents: Charles Brown, Pee Wee Crayton, Lowell Fulson, and Percy Mayfield.

PIANO BLUES

A genre that runs through the entire history of the music itself, this embraces everything from ragtime, barrelhouse, boogie-woogie, and smooth West Coast jazz stylings to the hard-rocking rhythms of Chicago blues. Main proponents: Big Maceo Merriweather, Leroy Carr, Sunnyland Slim, Roosevelt Sykes, Albert Ammons, and Otis Spann.

LOUISIANA BLUES

A looser, more laidback and percussive version of the Jimmy Reed side of the Chicago style. Production techniques on most of the recordings utilize massive amounts of echo, giving the performances a "doomy" sound and feel. Main proponents: Slim Harpo, Lightnin' Slim, and Lazy Lester.

R&B/SOUL BLUES

A more modern form, this fuses elements of Black popular music (the rhythm and blues strain of the '50s and the Southern soul style of the mid-'60s) to a wholly urban blues amalgam of its own.

MODERN ACOUSTIC BLUES

Newer artists reviving the older, more country-derived styles of blues. Main proponents: John Hammond, Rory Block, John Cephas, Taj Mahal, and the earlier recordings of Bonnie Raitt.

MODERN ELECTRIC BLUES

An eclectic mixture, this genre replicates older styles of urban blues while simultaneously recasting them in contemporary fashion. Main proponents: Stevie Ray Vaughan, the Fabulous Thunderbirds, Robert Cray, and Roomful of Blues.

BRITISH BLUES

More than a mere geographical distinction, the British style pays strict adherence to replicating American blues genres, with an admiration for its originators bordering on reverence. Main proponents: Alexis Korner, John Mayall, and the early recordings of Fleetwood Mac and the Rolling Stones.

— Cub Koda

A Note about the Second Edition:

We are proud to introduce the second edition of *The All Music Guide to the Blues*, which *Real Blues* calls "Easily the best blues guide to hit the market both as an encyclopedia and as a tool to help readers pick discs for purchase..." This second edition includes profiles of almost twice as many musicians, as well as reviews and listings of more than twice as many recordings as the first edition. We've also expanded the coverage to include gospel, with profiles of the significant gospel musicians and a new essay on gospel music.

Introduction to the First Edition:

"I live across the street from a juke box, baby– All night long it plays the blues."

I was recently talking to a friend of mine and was telling them about the project you now hold in your hands, the blues entry into the *All Music Guide* series of reference books. As I was explaining to him about the avalanche of information to be checked and crosschecked, the myriad essays highlighting the music's history, the thousands of albums and compilations to be listened to and the blues maps to show how all the different styles came together and who influenced who, my buddy put his index finger up to his pursed lips, like he always does when I'm yammering on and on and he wants me to shut up. Then he smiled and said, "So, is this another blues revival we're going through?" I smiled back and thought to myself, blues *explosion* is more like it.

The blues is big business these days, bigger than ever and if you don't believe me, just turn on your TV set or radio; the sound and style is seemingly everywhere. The blues–in all its myriad strains–has become party music for the millennium. Just look at the short list of irrefutable facts in the last decade of the 20th century: A chain franchise of blues clubs with weekly syndicated TV broadcasts emanating from them? Howlin' Wolf and Muddy Waters' faces emblazoned on the front of t-shirts that you can order out of catalogs? A blues chart in *Billboard* magazine? The Pillsbury Dough Boy selling blueberry muffins on TV with a honking blues riff in the background? Robert Johnson guitar picks and polishing cloths with a facsimile of his autograph on one and his picture on the other?

Instructional videos for aspiring guitarists and harmonica blowers by the carload? John Lee Hooker doing Pepsi commercials? Do you think *any* of this could have happened–or even have been conceivable–30 years ago? No way. The days of the blues as a growth industry have definitely arrived. If you've come to this guide from a rock'n'roll background, we certainly have no intentions of making you feel stupid or ashamed of it, quite the contrary. To be honest, that's where most of us came in. As a matter of fact, one of the really cool things about the blues is its inclu-

sionary nature; there's room for everybody. You don't have to be a walking blues encyclopedia to hear and get its basic message. That rock'n'roll comes straight from the blues is one of the few facts about its history that you can get a room full of critics, musicians or fans to agree on. Now whether you define the moment of its mass acceptance as Elvis cutting loose in the Sun studios or Eric Clapton recycling Robert Johnson for the first time, and whether or not you believe that they (and myriad others) took the music somewhere the originators couldn't have imagined, is usually where the arguments start up.

But the blues are far more than just your standard 'seminal' genre influence, like comparing Louis Armstrong's recordings from the '20s to some contemporary, horn-tooting be-bopper and saying, "*This* is where it came from!" The music is now so interwoven into the fabric of rock and popular music, we take something like hearing the music of Muddy Waters in a TV commercial or a bunch of child actors attempting to sing the blues while extolling the virtues of Kraft Macaroni and Cheese–a couple of notions that would have been unthinkable just a few years back– as nothing out of the ordinary. As rock and country music become more manufactured and fragmented, the blues as a popular music force becomes stronger and stronger. This still surprises some folks, who–while changing channels on their remote control– watch John Lee Hooker picking up Grammy awards while singing duets with Bonnie Raitt, listen to slide guitar and harmonica wailings in beer commercials, gaze at B.B. King and Buddy Guy duking it out on the Tonight Show while ZZ Top does the endless boogie on MTV, then usually say something profound along the lines of, "Wow, the blues are really gettin' popular!" These poor, misguided people react as if the music just pitched a tent in their back yard, moving in while they were asleep. But to quote Lord Chesterfield, "An honest mistake is to be pitied, not ridiculed."

Because the blues has *always* been here. Part of its resiliency stems from it being such a bedrock musical form. The other part of the equation is the fact that blues can run the emotional roller coaster from sounding sad and lonesome one minute to the rockinest party you've ever been to the next, and every place in between. It'll definitely go thru surges of popularity, but it originally found its way onto records (big, clunky 10 inch ones that went around the turntable at 78 RPM and broke in half if you sat on them) because it *was* popular music. It sounded good, it sounded different. It was like hearing the same song over and over again, but all with their own distinct flavor. The familiarity of its basic structure–and how *far* you could go with it–made it sound as comfortable as the music felt. But no matter how familiar the form was, it was always developing, going different places. And like all evolving American art forms infused by commerce (in this case, the recording industry), the blues kept on changing, splintering off into new permutations, reinventing itself to keep pace with the modern world. Of course, like any other self-respecting branch of indigenous American music, it's a genre filled with absolutely great songs. Most of these numbers have stood the test the time, becoming part and parcel of everyone's set list, from the legendary greats that spawned them to the local bar band playing down the street. Now a great song can always come back and find a new audience, sometimes without changing a single note and other times just dressing it up in contemporary clothes, not unlike an audio Mary Kay makeover. If you think this theory doesn't really hold water, then how else do you explain David Lee Roth having a hit with Louis Prima material? (A man who made so many records for so many different labels, by the way, that he could easily qualify for his *own* All Music Guide.) Most of the music's originators didn't live long enough to reap the big paycheck from all this, but it is all of one piece, a taut connecting thread that links it all together. Elmore James may not have lived long enough to jam on M-TV with Eric Clapton and the Rolling Stones, but it all comes from *somewhere*, and Henri Cartier Bresson, famous art photographer from the '40s and '50s, perhaps said it best; "There are no new ideas in the world, only new ways of doing them." That's pretty good, but maybe President Harry S. Truman said it even better; "The only thing new is the history you don't know." And *that*, dear reader, is where this book comes in.

What you are now holding in your hands is a very real collection of American musical history, something that leaps boundaries between blues and its bastard child, rock'n'roll with stops along the way between jazz, jump, New Orleans zydeco and sweet soul music. If you're an old hardliner, who's done more than your fair share of excavating into the dark past of American roots music, most of these artists and their work will be as plain as the nose on your face. If you're coming to this guide with an interest in the blues that outweighs your knowledge of its history (which roughly parallels the history of recorded music), you're fully expected to keep smacking the side of your head and exclaiming, "So *that's* where that came from!" while you wade through it all, using our handy little maps to tie it all together. We'll do our best to turn you on to the good stuff. Then it's up to you to decide which ones *you* want to add to your collection.

But in the final analysis, it really doesn't matter who you are or what you know or don't know, because the blues are for *everybody*, from old hippies who were there when Howlin' Wolf and Son House had their first encounters playing to a sea of White faces to young affluent yuppies to whom Howlin' Wolf is just a Black face on a postage stamp. This volume does not purport to be the 'ultimate' blues book and considering the raft of other books currently out there (a long way down the research highway from 30 years ago when Robert Johnson was more a fictional romantic vision than a set of cold facts with a couple of photographs to go along with it), the notion of there even *being* such an animal is at best subjective. As a famous bluesman once told me backstage at a genre mixed pop festival back in the '70s, "You can't be the best, you just try to be a good 'un" and that's what we have honestly strived for here. A lot of sweat, hard work and a steady diet of warmed over coffee and even colder pizza have gone into these pages. And a lot of love for the music and the people that make it, too. There's no didactic axe to grind out of any of the writers contributing to this book; if there was, their revisionist historical opinions would be promptly filed by the editors into the round file cabinet next to their respective desks, if you get my drift. We've tried to keep the bios and essays unclouded by romantic projection while still being infused with verve, wit and style and we certainly make no apologies for our various contributors' unabashed passion for certain artists. After all, this *is* a music of and about passion and when the blues hits you hard, it's easy to get swept up in that passion, too.

While the book definitely tips its hat to the music's pioneers and originators–the true giants of the blues in a very spiritual sense–we also haven't tried to make too many distinctions about what is and isn't the blues. Long before the Blue Brothers were doing their own brand of minstrel show for folks who thought Lightnin' Slim was a weight loss program, the old critical saw of 'can white men sing the blues?' had been raging at full throttle. We don't make those kind of decisions here, that's somebody else's book. We don't care what color somebody's skin is, their point of ethnic origin or their economic strata. If they can sing and play the blues and sound good doing it, you're going to be reading about it here. While perhaps not quite adopting a 'let it all in and let 'em sort it out later' attitude, we've tried to illustrate the depth and wide breadth of the music, while giving current artists of substantive worth their moment in the sun as well. Just don't expect to find a listing for the *101 Strings Play The Blues* album anywhere between these covers, ok?

What we *have* done is try to assemble the definitive picks on every artist and compilation listed. Walking into any new disc emporium these days can be a fairly daunting task. Most well stocked stores have a decent sized blues section. But there's a hundred Lightnin' Hopkins CDs here; which ones are the *good* ones? Which one do I buy first? That's where we come in; if it's good, we want to steer you straight to it. Also along the way, you'll see the occasional buyer beware alert review listed as well. If it's a stinkburger, no sense in you getting stuck with it. We also realize that not everybody has the financial outlay to go purchasing multi-disc box sets just because that's the definitive statement on a particular artist or genre. So wherever possible we've listed single disc best of's as well. If you're coming to an artist for the very first time, that 12 song mid line priced compilation just might be the perfect one to start with. And if your old favorite moth eaten vinyl album that you've had since Kennedy was President isn't listed here, don't despair. Now that record companies have figured out a way to sell us back our own record collections, eventually *everything* will get reissued on compact disc sooner or later.

So in putting this book to bed, we here at the All Music Guide are struck with the inescapable conclusion that the blues continue to roll on, its history continuing to be rewritten at every turn. While sadly most of the originators are gone (and wouldn't it be nice to watch that Robert Johnson video that never got made right about now?), their achievements have outlasted the vagaries of fads and fashion and will undoubtedly continue to do so into the next century. This is a music of great substance. We've done our best to steer you to the best of it, while giving it a sense of place and time. So please enjoy this book and don't let anybody tell you different; until time travel is perfected and we can all go back and watch Charlie Patton and Son House jamming in a Mississippi juke joint, *these* are the good old days for the music. Just listen to these blues.
—*Cub Koda*

Mick Abrahams

b. Apr. 7, 1943, Luton, Bedfordshire, England
Guitar, Vocals / Singer-Songwriter, Blues-Rock, R&B, Art-Rock/Progressive-Rock

Mick Abrahams was one of the more unfortunate hard-luck stories in rock music. Best known for his work on Jethro Tull's debut album, *This Was*, where he played blues licks that had critics comparing him favorably to Eric Clapton, he left the group, and since then has never managed to achieve lasting success as a recording artist, or the world-class fame of his former bandmates. Leading various incarnations of his best known band, Blodwyn Pig, he has persevered over the last quarter century, and achieved some major cult recognition, especially in England.

Abrahams joined his first band, the Crusaders, in 1964, alongside pianist Graham Waller, drummer (and Screaming Lord Sutch/Cyril Davies veteran) Carlo Little, and bassist Alex Dmochowski, all backing singer Neil Christian. Abrahams' musical hero was Alexis Korner, the man who—with Cyril Davies—brought blues to England. He was one of that legion of young guitarists, which included Brian Jones and Keith Richards, who found their way into music through Korner's groundbreaking work with Blues Incorporated. In 1965, Abrahams and Waller joined the Toggery Five, a septet whose members included drummer Clive Bunker. That group had a momentary brush with the record books when they cut a Mick Jagger-Keith Richards song as a failed single, but otherwise failed to make any lasting impression.

In the summer of 1967, while playing in his next group, McGregor's Engine with Bunker, Abrahams met Ian Anderson and bassist Glenn Cornick, who were playing in a group called the John Evan Smash. After comparing notes on their shared enthusiasm for blues, they decided to form Jethro Tull. Abrahams remained with the group until November of 1968, and his guitar was very prominent in the group's sound during this period, revealing him to be one of the best among England's legions of bluesmen. Evidence of his skill, passion, and persuasiveness are all over their second single, "A Song For Jeffrey," and the album *This Was*. Anderson's voice and flute, however, quickly challenged Abrahams for primacy, and by the fall of 1968 Anderson had won that battle; in November, Abrahams was gone.

Early in 1969, Abrahams formed his own group, Blodwyn Pig, with Jack Lancaster on saxophone, ex-McGregor's Engine member Andy Pyle on bass, and Ron Berg on drums. This was a blues band through-and-through, and even arriving on the scene in a time when London was filled with white blues players, Blodwyn Pig quickly became a critical favorite with its performances and its first album, *Ahead Rings Out*. Considered a classic progressive blues album, the record found a small audience in the United States, while in England it was a top 10 album. The group's second long-player, *Getting To This*, released a year later, was received with enthusiasm as well, and also made the British top 10.

The group was riven by internal conflicts, however, as Lancaster and the other members expressed a desire to go in a somewhat different direction in their music and for Lancaster's sax to become more prominent. Abrahams left the band in 1970, to be replaced by ex-Yes guitarist Peter Banks and guitarist/singer Larry Wallis. The group continued on under the leadership of Lancaster, and it was eventually renamed Lancaster's Bomber. Initially Abrahams formed a new group called Wommet; it was very short-lived, however, so he reorganized his career around the Mick Abrahams Band, with Walter Monaghan on bass, Bob Sargeant on guitar, keyboards and vocals, and Ritchie Dharma on drums. He released two albums on Chrysalis, *Mick Abrahams* and *At Last*, with his former Blodwyn Pig bandmate Lancaster

expanding the lineup to a quintet. Neither sold very well, although Abrahams was never at a loss for paying gigs.

In 1974, Abrahams reformed Blodwyn Pig with his ex-Tull bandmate Bunker, Pyle, and Lancaster, but the group only lasted a few gigs before breaking up. Soon after, Abrahams virtually left the music business, but not before he recorded what proved to be his biggest selling solo album of all, an instruction record entitled *Learning To Play Guitar With Mick Abrahams*. He continued to play occasional shows, but made his living outside of music, working as a driver, lifeguard, and financial consultant. He seemed content to play the odd impromptu show at the local pub, or for causes that mattered to him in his home town of Dunstable.

Finally, in 1988, however, he reformed Blodwyn Pig with Andy Pyle back in the line-up on bass, ex-Bonzo Dog Band member Dick Heckstall-Smith and Bernie Hetherington on saxes, Bruce Boardman on keyboards, and Clive Bunker on drums. The reformed group was a success, releasing a well received album called *All Said And Done*. Their 1993 line-up, including new keyboardist Dave Lennox, Mike Summerland on bass, and Graham Walker on drums, released the album *Lies (A New Day)*, Blodwyn Pig's most accomplished album ever. The group later issued a live recording from their 1993 tour (where Abrahams was reunited with Ian Anderson at one gig), entitled *All Tore Down*. Abrahams continues to play and record regularly, with a following in England and America with Blodwyn Pig. As of the mid-1990s, the group consisted of a quartet of Abrahams, Walker, Lennox, and Summerland, with vocalist Jackie Challoner and sax-player Nick Payne augmenting their membership in the studio. —*Bruce Eder*

● **Mick Abrahams** / 1971 / A&M ✦✦✦
Abrahams' first formal solo album is more focused on blues and blues-rock, and far less on jazz, than his work with Blodwyn Pig, and it is a better record for it. For first time listeners, much of this record will recall Clapton's first post-Cream solo LP, *Eric Clapton*, in its generally laid back sound and the presence of a fairly strong country blues influence. Abrahams' vocals here are a little more mournful than soulful—his playing (especially when he picks up an acoustic guitar) is up to his usual standard, however, and Ritchie Dharma's drumming is dizzying in its speed and complexity. Much of the material is substandard, however, and one number in particular, "Seasons," is especially annoying—evidently Abrahams couldn't decide whether he wanted to invade Yes territory (especially Steve Howe's solo noodlings) or the Allman Bros. turf on this 15-minute extended track (which, as a piece of psychedelia, is several years late), which ultimately goes nowhere. "Winds of Change," an unassuming four-minute acoustic blues, is far more to the point. —*Bruce Eder*

At Last / 1972 / Chrysalis ✦✦

Lies / 1995 / A New Day ✦✦✦

One / 1996 / A New Day ✦✦✦

Mick's Back / Jul. 30, 1996 / Indigo ✦✦✦

Nathan Abshire

b. Jun. 23, 1913, Gueydan, LA, **d.** May 13, 1981, Basile, LA
Vocals, Accordion / Electric Louisiana Blues, Electric Swamp Blues

Nathan Abshire helped bring the blues and honky tonk to Cajun music and re-popularized the accordion with his recordings during the 1950s and '60s, but still never managed a living from his music. Born in Gueydan, LA, on June 23, 1913, Abshire began playing professionally in the 1920s, and he first recorded in the early '30s with Happy Fats & the Rainbow Ramblers.

Abshire went to work at the Basile, LA town dump around that time, and he held the job for most of his working life.

His fortunes began looking bright by 1936, however, when the Rainbow Ramblers began backing him on sides for Bluebird. After serving in World War II, Abshire cut "Pine Grove Blues"—his most famous single and later his signature song—for D.T. Records. He recorded for Khoury/Lyric, Swallow and Kajun during the 1950s and '60s, meanwhile playing local dances and appearing on sessions by the Balfa Brothers. A renewal of interest in Cajun and folk music during the '70s gave Abshire a chance to play several festivals and colleges, and star in the 1975 PBS-TV Cajun documentary, *Good Times Are Killing Me*. The title proved prophetic, however, as Abshire fought alcoholism during his last years. Several sessions for Folkways and La Louisienne followed in the late '70s, but he died on May 13, 1981. —*John Bush*

Cajun Social Music / 1990 / Smithsonian/Folkways ◆◆◆◆
A summit meeting of Cajun stars yields outstanding renditions of classics and originals. —*Ron Wynn*

● **The Cajun Legend: Best of Nathan Abshire** / 1991 / Swallow ◆◆◆◆
With "The Good Times Are Killing Me" emblazoned on his accordion case, Abshire embodied the Cajun musician's ethos. There are 20 two-steps and waltzes here, some with the Balfa Brothers—includes a remake of the great "Pine Grove Blues" and a heartfelt "Tramp Sur La Rue" with wailing vocals from Abshire. —*Mark A. Humphrey*

★ **French Blues** / 1993 / Arhoolie ◆◆◆◆◆
Recorded between 1949 and 1956, this is prime Cajun music. The fidelity is slightly better than the best Cajun discs of the 1930s, but the approach is still satisfyingly raw and spontaneous, with waltzes, boogies, and blues. A steel guitar is present to varying degrees on most of the tracks, giving the fiddle/accordion-dominated arrangements a bit more flavor. This has a great spontaneous feel that stops short (but not that short) of raggedness, highlighted by Abshire's joyous calls and asides. Includes his big "hit," "Pine Grove Blues," although a hit by the standards of this regional style only constituted about three thousand copies sold. With 28 tracks and 78 minutes running time, it's the usual excellent value for an Arhoolie reissue. —*Richie Unterberger*

The Great Cajun Accordianist / Dec. 12, 1995 / Ace ◆◆◆◆

Johnny Ace (John Alexander)

b. Jun. 9, 1929, Memphis, TN, **d.** Dec. 25, 1954, Houston, TX
Vocals, Piano / R&B
The senseless death of young pianist Johnny Ace while indulging in a round of Russian roulette backstage at Houston's City Auditorium on Christmas Day of 1954 tends to overshadow his relatively brief but illustrious recording career on Duke Records. That's a pity, for Ace's gentle, plaintive vocal balladry deserves reverence on its own merit, not because of the scandalous fallout resulting from his tragic demise.

John Marshall Alexander was a member in good standing of the Beale Streeters, a loosely knit crew of Memphis youngbloods that variously included B.B. King, Bobby Bland, and Earl Forest. Signing with local DJ David Mattis' fledgling Duke logo in 1952, the rechristened Ace hit the top of the R&B charts his very first time out with the mellow ballad "My Song." From then on, Ace could do no musical wrong, racking up hit after hit for Duke in the same smooth, urbane style. "Cross My Heart," "The Clock," "Saving My Love for You," "Please Forgive Me," and "Never Let Me Go" all dented the uppermost reaches of the charts. And then, with one fatal gunshot, all that talent was lost forever (weepy tribute records quickly emerged by Frankie Ervin, Johnny Fuller, Varetta Dillard, and the Five Wings).

Ace scored his biggest hit of all posthumously. His haunting "Pledging My Love" (cut with the Johnny Otis orchestra in support) remained atop *Billboard's* R&B lists for ten weeks in early 1955. One further hit, "Anymore," exhausted Duke's stockpile of Ace masters, so they tried to clone the late pianist's success by recruiting Johnny's younger brother (St. Clair Alexander) to record as Buddy Ace. When that didn't work out, Duke boss Don Robey took singer Jimmy Lee Land, renamed him Buddy Ace, and recorded him all the way into the late '60s. —*Bill Dahl*

● **Johnny Ace Memorial Album** / 1974 / MCA ◆◆◆◆
It's downright bizarre that Ace's catalog hasn't enjoyed a fresh reissue in 40 years. This 12-song CD is the exact same package that Don Robey rushed

out following the pianist's death, with all the velvety hits ("Pledging My Love," "My Song," "The Clock," "Never Let Me Go") and a mere two blistering rockers, "How Can You Be So Mean" and "Don't You Know." A more thorough examination of Ace's discography is definitely in order! —*Bill Dahl*

Arthur Adams

Vocals, Guitar / Urban, Electric Memphis Blues
As house bandleader at B.B. King's Los Angeles blues club, Arthur Adams cranks out searing blues for the well-heeled tourists who trod the length of Universal Studios' glitzy City Walk. But the great majority of his transient clientele couldn't begin to imagine the depth and variety of the guitarist's career.

The shaven-headed Tennessee native began playing guitar in the mid-'50s, taking early inspiration from the man whose name adorns the club that now employs him (Howard Carroll, axeman for gospel's Dixie Hummingbirds, also was a principal influence). He studied music at Tennessee State University, playing briefly with the school's resident jazz and blues aggregation.

Touring as a member of singer Gene Allison's band, Adams found himself stranded in Dallas, where he dazzled the locals with his fancy fretwork. Relocating to L.A. in 1964, he began to do session work for jazz great Quincy Jones and cut singles for the Bihari brothers' Kent label and Hugh Masekela's Motown-distributed Chisa imprint. His late-'60s R&B sides for the latter were co-produced by Stewart Levine and featured support from most of the Crusaders. Adams' 1970 debut LP for Blue Thumb, *It's Private Tonight*, was co-produced by Bonnie Raitt and Tommy Lipuma. More recently, Adams wrote two songs for King's *There Is Always One More Time* album. —*Bill Dahl*

It's Private Tonight / 1972 / Blue Thumb ◆◆◆

● **Home Brew** / 1975 / Fantasy ◆◆◆◆
Arthur Adams' second album *Home Brew* may boast a production that's a little too slick, but there's no disguising the fact that the record is an appealing collection of driving blues, distinguished by some unpredictable jazzy flourishes that keep things interesting, even when the songwriting is uneven. —*Thom Owens*

Midnight Serenade / 1977 / Fantasy ◆◆◆

I Love Love Love My Lady / 1979 / A&M ◆◆

Johnny Adams

b. Jan. 5, 1932, New Orleans, LA
Vocals / Soul, R&B, Soul Blues, New Orleans R&B, Retro-Soul
Renowned around his Crescent City homebase as "the Tan Canary" for his extraordinary set of soulfully soaring pipes, veteran R&B vocalist Johnny Adams has tackled an exceptionally wide variety of material for Rounder in recent years—elegantly rendered tribute albums to legendary songwriters Doc Pomus and Percy Mayfield preceded forays into mellow, jazzier pastures. But then, Adams was never particularly into the parade-beat grooves that traditionally define the New Orleans R&B sound, preferring to deliver sophisticated soul ballads draped in strings.

Adams sang gospel professionally before crossing over to the secular world in 1959. Songwriter Dorothy LaBostrie—the woman responsible for cleaning up the bawdy lyrics of Little Richard's "Tutti Frutti" enough for worldwide consumption—convinced her neighbor Adams to sing her tasty ballad "I Won't Cry." The track, produced by a teenaged Mac Rebennack, was released on Joe Ruffino's Ric logo, and Adams was on his way. He waxed some outstanding follow-ups for Ric, notably "A Losing Battle" (the Rebennack-penned gem proved Adams' first national R&B hit in 1962) and "Life Is a Struggle."

After a prolonged dry spell, Adams resurfaced in 1968 with an impassioned R&B revival of Jimmy Heap's country standard "Release Me" for Shelby Singleton's SSS imprint that blossomed into a national hit. Even more arresting was Adams' magnificent 1969 country-soul classic "Reconsider Me," his lone leap into the R&B Top Ten; in it, he swoops effortlessly up to a death-defying falsetto range to drive his anguished message home with fervor.

Despite several worthy SSS follow-ups ("I Can't Be All Bad" was another sizable seller), Adams never traversed those lofty commercial heights again (particularly disappointing was a short stay at Atlantic). But he's found a new extended recording life at Rounder—his 1984 set, *From the Heart*, proved to the world that this Tan Canary can still chirp like a champ. —*Bill Dahl*

I Won't Cry / 1959-1963 / Rounder ♦♦♦♦
Even on his earliest singles, Adams already had developed a velvety crooning style seemingly at odds with his raucous hometown. This 14-track collection of Adams' 1959-63 work for Ric Records contains some stunning stuff, most of it in the big-voiced ballad mode (with an occasional nod to Ray Charles). "I Won't Cry," "A Losing Battle," and "Lonely Drifter" capture Adams' tender, mellifluous delivery beautifully. — *Bill Dahl*

Heart & Soul / 1969 / SSS ♦♦♦♦
This country-soul, containing all his hits from 1962-1968, was produced by Shelby Singleton. — *Richard Pack*

A Tan Nightingale / 1969 / Charly ♦♦♦

● **Reconsider Me** / 1969 / Charly ♦♦♦♦
This 22-song British compilation is the only place to find a decent cross-section of Adams' SSS sides, including his two biggest hits, the stately "Release Me" and the truly stunning "Reconsider Me." Not all of Adams' late-'60s waxings were ballads; "South Side of Soul Street" is a sizzling upbeat workout. But it's as a balladeer that Adams has always excelled; some of his finest soul senders are to be found right here. — *Bill Dahl*

Stand by Me / 1976 / Chelsea ♦♦♦
This is a relaxed, live-in-the-studio recording of standards. — *Richard Pack*

After All the Good Is Gone / 1978 / Ariola ♦♦

From the Heart / 1984 / Rounder ♦♦♦♦
First-class production by Scott Billington, a delicious Crescent City combo led by longtime cohort Walter "Wolfman" Washington on guitar and Red Tyler on tenor sax, and Adams' perennially luxurious pipes tab this as one of his finest contemporary outings. Nice song selection: the pens of Tony Joe White, Percy Mayfield, Sam Cooke, and Doc Pomus were all tapped. Johnny unfurls his "mouth trombone" — an uncanny vocal 'bone imitation — on Mayfield's "We Don't See Eye to Eye." — *Bill Dahl*

After Dark / Jul. 1985 / Rounder ♦♦♦♦
When Adams signed with Rounder in the mid-'80s, few outside the R&B/ soul and blues world were aware of his skills or eclectic range. *After Dark* was Adams' second Rounder session. It included amazing covers of Doc Pomus' "I Don't Know You" and "Give A Broken Heart A Break," John Hiatt's "Lovers Will" and the Dan Penn/Chips Moman soul classic "Do Right Woman — Do Right Man." This was one of the first records on which Adams' wondrous voice, with its extensive range at the top and bottom, was both well-produced and effectively mastered and recorded. — *Ron Wynn*

Room with a View of the Blues / Apr. 1987-May 1987 / Rounder ♦♦♦
Although calling Johnny Adams a blues singer is far too confining, he's certainly among the finest to perform in that idiom. He's equally brilliant at slow or uptempo numbers, can effectively convey irony, heartache or triumph, and is a masterful storyteller. These ten blues numbers covered every emotional base, allowing Adams a chance to show his proficiency. With great support from an instrumental corps that included guitarists Walter "Wolfman" Washington and Duke Robillard, keyboardist Dr. John, and saxophonists Red Tyler and Foots Samuel, plus Ernie Gautreau on valve trombone, Adams didn't just cut a blues album, he made unforgettable blues statements. — *Ron Wynn*

Walking on a Tightrope / Mar. 1989-May 1989 / Rounder ♦♦♦♦
Whenever Johnny Adams does a repertory album, it's as much his own showcase as a forum for the spotlighted composer. Even Percy Mayfield's lyrically brilliant works didn't hamper Adams from displaying his special magic; his treatments on the session's ten tunes ranged from excellent to magnificent. Adams was gripping on "My Heart Is Hangin' Heavy," nicely bemused on "The Lover and the Married Woman" and convincing on the title track and "Danger Zone." Although he's done numerous Rounder vehicles, Adams hasn't yet turned in a dud. — *Ron Wynn*

Johnny Adams Sings Doc Pomus: The Real Me / 1991 / Rounder ♦♦♦♦
The late Doc Pomus was one of the top songwriters in the R&B/blues tradition while Johnny Adams was one of his favorite singers; their eventual matchup was quite logical. Pomus wrote a few new songs and worked with Adams on planning this Rounder CD up until his own death. Fortunately the project was not halted and resulted in an enjoyable set. Pomus' intelligent and universal lyrics perfectly fit Adams' style which features flawless enunciation and an ability to sincerely convey a wide range of emotions. With hornlines arranged by Red Tyler, occasional brief solos contributed by pianist Dr.

John and guitarist Duke Robillard, and top notch singing by Johnny Adams, Doc Pomus' music is well served on a strong set of blues and ballads. — *Scott Yanow*

Good Morning Heartache / 1993 / Rounder ♦♦♦
Adams could sing the phone book and make it sound sweet, so his personalized rendition of the title track and several more jazz standards on this collection shouldn't come as too much of a surprise. Nevertheless, it's a long way from "Reconsider Me," and perhaps a bit too jazzy for some R&B fans. — *Bill Dahl*

The Verdict / 1995 / Rounder ♦♦
Fans of Adams' R&B dusties may not find everything on this jazz-based collection to their taste, but Adams' vocal ease within the jazz idiom is undeniable. Noteworthy sidemen include Harry Connick, Jr., and Houston Person. — *Bill Dahl*

One Foot in the Blues / 1996 / Rounder ♦♦♦♦
Johnny Adams is renowned for his smoky but smooth voice, but *One Foot in the Blues* is as much a showcase for Lonnie Smith's Hammond B-3 organ, which sounds like a living, breathing creature. The spare, mostly live-in-the-studio production allows plenty of wide open sonic space for Smith's expressive organ (including his pulsating bass pedal), Ed Peterson's after-hours tenor sax, and Jimmy Ponder's gentle guitar fills. While Adams' most fervent champions thrill to his every note, others may find his singing mannered on the ballads that dominate this session, and his voice is certainly huskier than in the days when he earned the sobriquet "the Tan Canary." As the title suggests, the CD is only partly blues; Adams' other "foot" here, as on his previous '90s recordings, is placed squarely between the cabaret-jazz crooning of Johnny Hartman and the soul-pop styling of Lou Rawls. — *Steve Hoffman*

Greatest Performances / Ace ♦♦♦
Greatest Performances collects recordings Johnny Adams made for the Hep Me label in the early '80s. Although Adams himself is in fine form, the production is too slick and has dated poorly. For many of the songs, Adams simply sang to pre-recorded rhythm tracks, which gives the material a flat, processed ambience. Furthermore, the material is not suited to his style — though he tries hard, Adams simply can't breathe life into "Feelings." When he does have a song he can sink his teeth into, such as "The Greatest Love," the results are quite good. Unfortunately, he doesn't get enough of those kinds of songs on *Greatest Performances*. — *Thom Owens*

Ray Agee

b. Apr. 10, 1930, Dixons Mills, AL, **d.** 1990
Vocals, Guitar / Electric California Blues, West Coast Blues
Known primarily for his tough 1963 remake of the blues standard "Tin Pan Alley" (featuring the moaning lead guitar of Johnny Heartsman) for the tiny Sahara logo, vocalist Ray Agee recorded for a myriad of labels both large and small during the 1950s and '60s without much in the way of national recognition outside his Los Angeles homebase. That's a pity — he was a fine, versatile blues singer whose work deserves a wider audience (not to mention CD reissue).

Agee was stricken with polio at age four, leaving the Alabama native with a permanent handicap. After moving to Los Angeles with his family, he apprenticed with his brothers in a gospel quartet before striking out in the R&B field with a 1952 single for Eddie Mesner's Aladdin Records (backed by saxist Maxwell Davis' band). From there, his discography assumes daunting proportions; he appeared on far too many logos to list here (Elko, Spark, Ebb, and Cash among them).

Ray Agee slowly slipped away from the music business in the early '70s. Reportedly, he died around 1990. — *Bill Dahl*

● **Tin Pan Alley** / 1960-1968 / Diving Duck ♦♦♦♦
This obscure Dutch LP is the only collection of Agee's vintage singles you're likely to encounter until someone decides to do some serious cross-licensing. Yes, the doom-laden "Tin Pan Alley" is aboard, along with the distinctive "You Hit Me Where It Hurts" and "The Gamble." — *Bill Dahl*

Dave Alexander

b. Mar. 10, 1938, Shreveport, LA
Piano, Bass, Trumpet / Electric West Coast Blues, Piano Blues
Pianist and drummer Dave Alexander is both an effective vocalist and outstanding instrumentalist who's best known for many festival and club ap-

pearances and his Arhoolie albums. Also known as Omar Hakim Khayyam, Alexander's an articulate writer and advocate for the blues and African American music. He's written several articles for *Living Blues*. A self-taught pianist, Alexander's played with LC Robinson, Big Mama Thornton, Jimmy McCracklin, and Lafayette Thomas. *—Ron Wynn*

● **The Rattler / Dirt on the Ground** / Aug. 1, 1972+Dec. 5, 1972 / Arhoolie ✦✦✦✦
The compact disc *The Rattler / Dirt on the Ground* contains two of Dave Alexander's early '70s albums, offering a good portrait of Alexander's eclectic, entertaining blues. *—Thom Owens*

Texas Alexander

b. 1890, Jewett, TX, d. Apr. 16, 1954, Richards, TX
Vocals / Acoustic Texas Blues
A rarity among country bluesmen in that he did not play an instrument on any of his records, Alexander was second in popularity only to Blind Lemon Jefferson among the early Texas blues recording artists. Alexander made over 30 records for OKeh and Vocalion (1927-34), usually accompanied by such gifted musicians as Lonnie Johnson or the Mississippi Sheiks. His blues, like Jefferson's, often had a lonesome, lyrical quality, and bits from a number of his songs have reappeared in the works of other artists. Alexander, who carried a guitar with him but always sought out someone to serve as an accompanist, was either a mentor or a companion to most of the great downhome Texas stylists—his guitarists included Jefferson, Lightnin' Hopkins, Lowell Fulson, and J.T. "Funny Papa" Smith, "The (Original) Howling Wolf."
—Jim O'Neal

● **Texas Alexander, Vol. 1 (1927)** / Dec. 1, 1995 / Document ✦✦✦✦
Texas Alexander, Vol. 1 (1927) is the first installment of Document's multivolume series of his complete recorded works. The first disc contains many of his classics, including a number of recordings with Lonnie Johnson that rank among his very best work. *—Thom Owens*

Texas Alexander, Vol. 2 (1928-9) / Matchbox ✦✦✦✦

Bernard Allison

b. Nov. 26, 1965
Vocals, Guitar / Modern Electric Blues
Bernard Allison is the guitar-playing, singing and songwriting son of the late, legendary blues guitarist Luther Allison. True to form for this chip off the old block, the young Allison injects every bit as much energy into his live shows as his late father did.

Bernard counts among his influences icons like Albert King, Muddy Waters and Freddie King, and later, Stevie Ray Vaughan and Johnny Winter.

Allison began accompanying his famous father to blues festivals in the early 1970s. There, he was introduced to a who's-who of Chicago blues stars: Muddy Waters, Hound Dog Taylor, and Albert King, among others. When he was seven or eight, he began having aspirations of becoming a guitar slinger like his father. Allison's father was more than just a casual record collector, and so Bernard benefited from his father's and brothers' collections of classic blues and gospel.

After graduating from high school, Allison began playing with Koko Taylor in her touring band. He stayed with Taylor's band until 1985, when he left to hustle up his own gigs as Bernard Allison and Back Talk. Allison spent a lot of time in Canada with his first band, and later rejoined Taylor and her Blues Machine for another two years in the late 1980s.

After joining his father in Europe for a live recording, Bernard was asked to join Luther's touring band and become his European bandleader. Allison's father helped his son along with the finer points of showmanship for several years until he was good enough to lead his own trio or quartet. At Christmas, 1989, while both were living together in Paris, the elder Allison arranged to give his son the most precious gift for budding musicians: studio time to record his first album. Allison's debut, *Next Generation,* was recorded for Mondo Records using musicians from his dad's band. His other foreign-label releases include *Hang On, No Mercy,* and *Funkifino.*

In December 1996, Allison was contacted by Cannonball Records founder Ron Levy. Allison was home in Chicago visiting family at Christmas, and hadn't brought any of his guitars or other equipment with him. Levy wanted something based in traditional electric blues, with a few bones for newer

fans of the idiom who have jumped on the blues bandwagon since 1990. Allison released his stunning US debut, *Keepin' the Blues Alive* in early 1997, receiving a great deal of critical acclaim. On his successful tour of clubs around the US in the latter half of 1997, Allison was joined by drummer Ray "Killer" Allison (no relation), and Buddy Guy bassist Greg Rzab, among others. Based in Paris full-time, he has the comfort and security that the multitude of blues clubs and festivals around Europe can provide. *—Richard J. Skelly*

Hang On / Mar. 15, 1994 / Peter Pan ✦✦✦

No Mercy / Feb. 21, 1996 / Inakustik ✦✦✦

● **Keepin' the Blues Alive** / Jul. 1, 1997 / Cannonball ✦✦✦✦
Using a group of hand-picked Chicago musicians he was friendly with, and borrowed equipment, Bernard Allison recorded his stunning US debut, *Keepin' the Blues Alive.* The album was released early in 1997, perfectly blending traditional post-WWII Chicago blues with a few blues-rock riffs from the 1970s and '80s thrown in. Songs like "Young Boy's Blues," "When I'm Lonely," and "Tell Me Why" demonstrate a refreshing approach to blues songwriting reminiscent of Louisiana bluesman Larry Garner. *—Richard Skelly*

Luther Allison

b. Aug. 17, 1939, Widener, AR, d. Aug. 13, 1997
Guitar, Vocals / R&B, Modern Electric Blues, Chicago Blues
An American-born guitarist, singer, and songwriter who lived in France since 1980, Luther Allison was the man to book at blues festivals in the mid-'90s. Allison's comeback into the mainstream was ushered in by a recording contract with an American record company, Chicago-based Alligator Records. After he signed with Alligator in 1994, Allison's popularity grew exponentially and he worked steadily until his death in 1997.

Born August 17, 1939, in Widener, AR, Allison was the fourteenth of 15 children, the son of cotton farmers. His parents moved to Chicago when he was in his early teens, but he had a solid awareness of blues before he left Arkansas, as he played organ in the church and learned to sing gospel in Widener as well. Allison recalled that his earliest awareness of blues came via the family radio in Arkansas, which his dad would play at night. Allison recalls listening to both the Grand Ole Opry and B.B. King on the King Biscuit Show on Memphis' WDIA. Although he was a talented baseball player and had begun to learn the shoemaking trade in Chicago after high school, it wasn't long before Allison began to focus more of his attention on playing blues guitar. Allison had been hanging out in blues clubs all through high school, and with his brother's encouragement, he honed his string bending skills and powerful, soul-filled vocal technique.

It was while living with his family on Chicago's West Side that he had his first awareness of wanting to become a full-time bluesman, and he played bass behind guitarist Jimmy Dawkins, who Allison grew up with. Also in Allison's neighborhood were established blues greats like Freddie King, Magic Sam, and Otis Rush. He distinctly remembers everyone talking about Buddy Guy when he came to town from his native Louisiana. After the Allison household moved to the South Side, they lived a few blocks away from Muddy Waters and Allison and Waters' son Charles became friends. When he was 18 years old, his brother showed him basic chords and notes on the guitar, and the super bright Allison made rapid progress after that. Allison went on to "blues college" by sitting in with some of the most legendary names in blues in Chicago's local venues: Muddy Waters, Elmore James, and Howlin' Wolf among them.

His first chance to record came with Bob Koester's then-tiny Delmark Record label, and his first album, *Love Me Mama,* was released in 1969. But like anyone else with a record out on a small label, it was up to him to go out and promote it, and he did, putting in stellar, show-stopping performances at the Ann Arbor Blues festivals in 1969, 1970, and 1971. After that, people began to pay attention to Luther Allison, and in 1972 he signed with Motown Records. Meanwhile, a growing group of rock 'n' roll fans began showing up at Allison's shows, because his style seemed so reminiscent of Jimi Hendrix and his live shows clocked in at just under four hours!

Although his Motown albums got him to places he'd never been before, like Japan and new venues in Europe, the recordings didn't sell well. He does have the distinction of being one of a few blues musicians to record for Motown. Allison stayed busy in Europe through the rest of the 1970s and 1980s, and recorded *Love Me Papa* for the French Black and Blue label in

1977. He followed with a number of live recordings from Paris, and in 1984 he settled outside of Paris, since France and Germany were such major markets for him. At home in the US, Allison continued to perform sporadically, when knowledgeable blues festival organizers or blues societies would book him.

As accomplished a guitarist as he was, Allison wasn't a straightahead Chicago blues musician. He learned the blues long before he got to Chicago. What he did so successfully is take his base of Chicago blues and add touches of rock, soul, reggae, funk and jazz. Allison's first two albums for Alligator, *Soul Fixin' Man* and *Blue Streak*, are arguably two of his strongest. His talents as a songwriter are fully developed, and he's well recorded and well produced, often with horns backing his band. Another one to look for is a 1992 reissue on Evidence, *Love Me Papa*. In 1996, Motown reissued some of the three albums worth of material he recorded for that label (between 1972 and 1976), on compact disc.

Well into his mid-50s Allison continued to delight club and festival audiences around the world with his lengthy, sweat-drenched, high energy shows, complete with dazzling guitar playing and inspired, soulful vocals. He continued to tour and record until July of 1997, when he was diagnosed with inoperable lung cancer. Just over a month later, he died in a hospital in Madison, Wisconsin—a tragic end to one of the great blues comeback stories. —*Richard Skelly*

Love Me Mama / Jun. 24, 1969-Jun. 25, 1969 / Delmark ♦♦♦
Although it has its moments—particularly on the title track—Luther Allison's debut album, *Love Me Papa*, is on the whole uneven, featuring more mediocre tracks than killer cuts. Nevertheless, it offers intriguing glimpses of the style he would later develop. —*Thom Owens*

Bad News Is Coming / 1973 / Gordy ♦♦

Luther's Blues / 1974 / Gordy ♦♦♦♦
Luther's Blues is where Luther Allison began to come into his own, developing a fluid, gutsy style full of soulful string bending. There are still a few weak spots, but the album remains an effective slice of contemporary Chicago blues. —*Thom Owens*

Night Life / Oct. 1975 / Gordy ♦
On *Night Life*, Luther Allison tried to make a soul crossover album but the slick production fails to provide a suitable bed for his bluesy guitars and vocals. Occasionally, he spits out a good solo, but only the most devoted listeners will be able to dig them out, since they're buried beneath a glossy varnish. —*Thom Owens*

● **Love Me Papa** / Dec. 13, 1977 / Evidence ♦♦♦♦
Luther Allison is the blues' proverbial little boy with the curl; when he's good, he's great. When he's bad, he's awful. Allison was on throughout most of the nine tracks (three bonus cuts) on this 1977 date recently reissued by Evidence on CD, playing with the ferocity, direction, and inventiveness that is often missing from his more uneven efforts. His covers of Little Walter Jacobs' "Last Night" and "Blues With A Feeling" are not reverential or respectful but are launching pads for high-octane, barreling riffs, snappy phrases, and exciting solos. His vocals are not always that keen, but Allison at least stretches them out and adds verbal embellishments, yells, and shouts of encouragement. —*Ron Wynn*

Live in Paris / 1979 / Paris Album ♦♦♦
Live in Paris was recorded in the late '70s, shortly before Luther Allison decided to leave America for France because the US blues scene was faltering. And, as *Live in Paris* attests, Allison was at his best when he played straight blues with a bit of a wild, electric edge. The album isn't perfect by any means, but there's energy and fire to his playing that holds your attention throughout the record. —*Stephen Thomas Erlewine*

Live / 1979 / Blue Silver ♦♦

Gonna Be a Live One in Here Tonight / Apr. 18, 1979-Apr. 19, 1979 / Rumble ♦♦
Gonna Be a Live One in Here Tonight is a solid, no-frills documentation of a late-'70s club show from Luther Allison. Though it's not an exceptional performance, it certainly isn't a disappointing one and dedicated fans will find it worth their time. —*Thom Owens*

Power Wire Blues / Apr. 18, 1979-Apr. 19, 1979 / Charly ♦
Power Wire Blues is a collection of outtakes from his uneven *Rumble* album.

Since the best takes of these sessions were pretty weak, these lesser tracks have even less to distinguish—much less recommend—them. It's one to be avoided. —*Thom Owens*

Life Is a Bitch / 1984 / Encore! ♦♦♦

Here I Come / 1985 / Encore! ♦♦♦

Serious / 1987 / Blind Pig ♦♦♦♦
Serious marks the beginning of Luther Allison's late-'80s/early-'90s hot streak. The more streamlined, rock-oriented approach actually is a benefit, since it gives Allison a shot of energy that makes his guitar simply burn all the way through the record. —*Thom Owens*

Hand Me Down My Moonshine / 1994 / Inakustik ♦♦♦
Hand Me Down My Moonshine is a refreshing all-acoustic session from Allison that demonstrates a previously hidden side of his talent. Though there are some hard-rocking stomps, his playing reveals new grace and subtlety, making it a necessary purchase for all diehard fans. —*Thom Owens*

Soul Fixin' Man / 1994 / Alligator ♦♦♦♦
This new venture, recorded in Memphis, is Allison's finest session since his days at Delmark. He blends blues, soul/R&B and even occasional funk, and his guitar playing is alternately flashy and refined, sometimes explosive, sometimes carefully measured. His vocals are powerful, convincing and earnest on all 12 selections. Luther Allison finally gives American blues fans the definitive portrait they wanted. —*Ron Wynn*

Blue Streak / Oct. 1995 / Alligator ♦♦♦♦
Luther Allison's run of winning contemporary blues albums continues with *Blue Streak*, a typically enjoyable set of hot guitar playing and impassioned singing, hampered only slightly by occasionally perfunctory songwriting. —*Thom Owens*

The Motown Years 1972-1976 / 1996 / Motown ♦♦♦
Allison's reign as Motown's only bluesman saw the guitarist offer competently executed, but basically unmemorable, blues with some soul and rock influences. This 17-track compilation includes selections from all three of the LPs he issued on the label (drawing most heavily from his second, *Luther's Blues*), and adds a previously unreleased live cut from the 1972 Ann Arbor Blues Festival. Pop influences can be heard in the occasional wah-wah guitar and brass-conscious production; Berry Gordy even co-wrote one of the tracks ("Someday Pretty Baby"), and Randy Brecker arranged the horns on Allison's final Motown full-length. —*Richie Unterberger*

Where Have You Been?—Live in Montreux 1976-1994 / 1997 / Ruf ♦♦♦♦
This CD features the exciting blues guitarist/singer Luther Allison on selections taken from four appearances at the Montreux Jazz Festival. Although the title says 1974-94, the earliest numbers are actually from 1976, and these are the most memorable cuts on the CD. Even when sticking to cover tunes throughout the powerhouse performance (such as "Sweet Home Chicago" and "Little Red Rooster"), Allison plays with such enthusiasm and ferocity that he sounds as if he wrote the songs himself. Among the other highlights, Allison is heard on his 1983 set closer "Sky Is Crying," shouting out a Memphis soul-type ballad ("Memories") in 1984 and sounding remarkably close to B.B. King at times during 1994's "Bad Love" (which has background riffs from the Memphis Horns). This is a strong (and easily recommended) all-around overview that can serve as a perfect introduction to the talented Luther Allison. —*Scott Yanow*

Reckless / Mar. 25, 1997 / Alligator ♦♦♦
Luther's third album for Alligator finds the 50-something bluesman truly at the peak of his powers. His superb guitar playing has never been more focused, and his singing shows a fervent shouter in full command. But Allison's songwriting has made giant strides as well, and ten of the 14 tracks aboard feature him as a co-writer as well. The production by Jim Gaines delivers a modern-sounding album that stays firmly in the blues tradition while giving full vent to Luther's penchant for blending soul, rock and funk grooves into his musical stew. There are really no duff tracks aboard, but special attention should be paid to the sloppy but right slide guitar-meets-rock 'n' roll groove of "Low Down And Dirty," Allison's incredibly hot minor key soloing (at full rock volume) on "Drowning At The Bottom," an acoustic duet with his son Bernard on "Playin' A Losing Game," and the grinding social commentary of "Pain In The Streets." If Allison had made albums like this for Motown 20-

some years ago, it would be very interesting to speculate on how the blues history books just might have been rewritten. —*Cub Koda*

Mose Allison (Mose John Allison, Jr.)

b. Nov. 11, 1927, Tippo, MS
Piano, Vocals / Hard Bop, Folk-Jazz, Jazz Blues, Country Blues
Not unlike his namesake, Luther Allison, pianist Mose Allison has suffered from "categorization problem," given his equally brilliant career. Although his boogie woogie and bebop-laden piano style is innovative and fresh sounding when it comes to blues and jazz, it is as a songwriter that Allison really shines. Allison's songs have been recorded by the Who ("Young Man Blues"), Leon Russell ("I'm Smashed"), and Bonnie Raitt ("Everybody's Cryin' Mercy"). Other admirers include Tom Waits, John Mayall, Georgie Fame, the Rolling Stones, and Van Morrison. But because he's always played both blues and jazz, and not one to the exclusion of the other, his career has suffered. As he himself admits, he has a "category" problem that lingers to this day. "There's a lot of places I don't work because they're confused about what I do," he explained in a 1990 interview in *Goldmine* magazine. Despite the lingering confusion, Allison remains one of the finest songwriters in 20th century blues.

Born in Tippo, MS, on November 11, 1927, Allison's first exposure to blues on record was through Louis Jordan recordings, including "Outskirts of Town" and "Pinetop Blues." Allison credits Jordan as being a major influence on him, and also credits Nat "King" Cole, Louis Armstrong, and Fats Waller. He started out on trumpet but later switched to piano. In his youth, he had easy access, via the radio, to the music of Pete Johnson, Albert Ammons, and Meade Lux Lewis. Allison also credits the songwriter Percy Mayfield, "The Poet Laureate of the Blues," as being a major inspiration on his songwriting.

After a stint in college and the Army, Allison's first professional gig was in Lake Charles, LA, in 1950. He returned to college to finish up at Louisiana State University in Baton Rouge, where he studied English and Philosophy, a far cry from his initial path as a chemical engineering major.

Allison began his recording career with the Prestige label in 1956, shortly after he moved to New York City. He recorded an album with Al Cohn and Bobby Brookmeyer, and then in 1957 got his own record contract. A big break was the opportunity to play with Cohn and Zoot Sims shortly after his arrival in New York, but he later became more well known after playing with saxophonist Stan Getz. After leaving Prestige Records, where he recorded now classic albums like *Back Country Suite* (1957), *Young Man Mose* (1958), and *Seventh Son* (1958-59), he moved to Columbia for two years before meeting up with Nesuhi Ertegun of Atlantic Records. He recalled that he signed his contract with Atlantic after about ten minutes in Ertegun's office. Allison spent a big part of his recording career at Atlantic Records, where he became most friendly with Ertegun. After the company saw substantial growth and Allison was no longer working directly with Ertegun, he became discouraged and left. Allison also has recorded for Columbia (before he began his long relationship with Atlantic), and the Epic and Prestige labels.

Allison's discography is a lengthy one, and there are gems to be found on all of his albums, many of which can be found in vinyl shops. His output since 1957 has averaged at least one album a year until 1976, when he finished up at Atlantic with the classic *Your Mind Is On Vacation.* There was a gap of six years before he recorded again, this time for Elektra's Musician subsidiary in 1982, when he recorded *Middle Class White Boy.* Since 1987, he's been with Bluenote/Capitol. His debut for that label was *Ever Since the World Ended.* Allison has recorded some of the most creative material in his career with the Bluenote subsidiary of Capitol Records, including *My Back-yard* (1992) and *The Earth Wants You* (1994), both produced by Ben Sidran. Also in 1994, Rhino Records released a boxed set, *Allison Wonderland.* —*Richard Skelly*

Back Country Suite / Mar. 7, 1957 / Original Jazz Classics ✦✦✦✦
Mose Allison's very first recording finds the 29-year old pianist taking just two vocals (on his "Young Man Blues" and "One Room Country Shack") but those are actually the most memorable selections. The centerpiece of this trio outing with bassist Taylor LaFargue and drummer Frank Isola (which has been reissued on CD) is Allison's ten-part "Back Country Suite," a series of short, concise folk melodies that puts the focus on his somewhat unique piano style which, although boppish, also looked back towards the country blues tradition. Very interesting music. —*Scott Yanow*

Greatest Hits / Mar. 7, 1957-Feb. 13, 1959 / Original Jazz Classics ✦✦✦✦
Basic, no-frills anthology of 13 of his better late-'50s Prestige sides, all of which feature his vocals. It has most of his most famous songs, particularly to listeners from a rock background, including his versions of "The Seventh Son," "Eyesight to the Blind" (covered by The Who on *Tommy*, though Sonny Boy Williamson did it before Allison), "Parchman Farm" (done by John Mayall), and "Young Man's Blues" (also covered by The Who). Were it not for the significant omission of "I'm Not Talking" (retooled by The Yardbirds), this would qualify as the basic collection for most listeners, although more thorough retrospectives are available (particularly Rhino's *Anthology*). *Greatest Hits* does include liner notes by Pete Townshend, originally penned for a 1972 collection. —*Richie Unterberger*

Local Color / Nov. 8, 1957 / Original Jazz Classics ✦✦✦
This CD reissue brings back Mose Allison's second of six Prestige recordings. Allison performs eight instrumentals in a trio with bassist Addison Farmer and drummer Nick Stabulas, displaying his unusual mixture of country blues and bebop and even taking an effective trumpet solo on "Trouble In Mind." However it is his vocals on "Lost Mind" and particularly the classic "Parchman Farm" that are most memorable. —*Scott Yanow*

● **Allison Wonderland: Anthology** / 1957-1989 / Rhino ✦✦✦✦
Only Dave Frishberg and possibly Mark Murphy can rival Mose Allison when it comes to creative use of irony in lyric writing and neither compares as an instrumentalist. He's a fine bop pianist able to play challenging instrumentals and eclectic enough to integrate country blues and gospel elements into his style. Allison's unique mix of down-home and uptown styles has made him a standout since the '50s. He's one of the few jazz musicians on Atlantic's roster ideally suited for Rhino's two-disc anthology format. Allison recorded so many different kinds of songs and was always as much, if not more, a singles than an album artist. In addition, Rhino thankfully sequenced the selected songs—which span over 40 years, from 1957 to 1989, and include all of his best-known songs—chronologically. Allison does reflective duo and trio pieces, moves into uptempo combo numbers with a jump beat, then returns to the intimate small group sound. His ability to highlight key lyrics, delivery, timing, and packing is superb. The set includes such classics as "Back Country Blues," "Parchman Farm," "Western Man," and "Ever Since the World Ended," plus definitive covers of of Willie Dixon's "The Seventh Son" and Sonny Boy Williamson II's "Eyesight to the Blind." It's an essential introduction to Allison's catalog. —*Ron Wynn*

Creek Bank / Jan. 24, 1958+Aug. 15, 1958 / Prestige ✦✦✦✦
When Mose Allison recorded his six early albums for Prestige, he was best-known as a bop-based pianist who occasionally sang. This single CD (which reissues in full *Young Man Mose* and *Creek Bank*) has 15 instrumentals including a rare appearance by Allison on trumpet ("Stroll") but it is his five typically ironic vocals that are most memorable, particularly Allison's classic "The Seventh Son" and "If You Live." His piano playing, even with the Bud Powell influence, was beginning to become original and he successfully performs both revived swing songs and moody originals. —*Scott Yanow*

Autumn Song / Feb. 13, 1959 / Original Jazz Classics ✦✦✦✦
Mose Allison recorded six albums as a leader for Prestige during 1957-59, an era which he was better known as a jazz pianist than as a folk/country blues vocalist and masterful lyricist. On this CD reissue of his final Prestige date, Allison (in a trio with bassist Addison Farmer and drummer Ronnie Free) performs seven instrumentals (including "It's Crazy," "Autumn Song," and "Groovin' High") but it is the three vocals ("Eyesight To The Blind," "That's All Right," and Duke Ellington's "Do Nothin' Till You Hear From Me") that are most memorable. One realizes why Allison was soon emphasizing his vocals; he was a much more distinctive singer than pianist although his piano playing was actually pretty inventive. This is an excellent all-round set. —*Scott Yanow*

Mose Allison Trilogy: High Jinks! / Dec. 21, 1959-May 23, 1961 / Columbia/ Legacy ✦✦✦✦
Three formerly rare Mose Allison albums originally cut for Columbia and Epic (*Transfiguration of Hiram Brown, I Love The Life I Live,* and *V-8 Ford Blues*) are reissued in full on this attractive three-CD set plus six previously unreleased numbers. During this period (which dates between his associations with the Prestige and Atlantic labels), Mose Allison was making the transition from being a pianist-vocalist to a vocalist-pianist. He sings on

roughly half the selections including "Baby, Please Don't Go," "Deed I Do," "Fool's Paradise," and "I Love The Life I Live." The instrumentals (which also feature Addison Farmer, Henry Grimes, Bill Crow, or Aaron Bell on bass and Jerry Segal, Paul Motian, Gus Johnson or Osie Johnson on drums) are highlighted by the interesting eight-song "Hiram Brown Suite." Mose Allison fans will want to go out of their way to get this set. — *Scott Yanow*

I Don't Worry About a Thing / May 15, 1962 / Rhino ++++
Mose Allison was already 34 and had recorded nine records as a leader before cutting his debut for Atlantic (which has been reissued on CD by Rhino) but this was his breakthrough date. One of jazz's greatest lyricists, at the time, Allison was making the transition from being a pianist who occasionally sang to becoming a vocalist who also played his own unusual brand of piano. In addition to the original versions of "Your Mind Is on Vacation," "I Don't Worry About a Thing (Because I Know Nothing Will Turn out Right)," and "It Didn't Turn out That Way," he sings bluish versions of two standards ("Meet Me at No Special Place" and "The Song Is Ended") and plays five instrumentals with his trio. There are only 33 1/2 minutes of music on this straight reissue of the orignal LP, but the set is one of Mose Allison's most significant recordings. — *Scott Yanow*

I Don't Worry About a Thing / May 15, 1962 / Atlantic ++++

The Best of Mose Allison / 1962-1970 / Atlantic ++++
The Mose Allison installment in Atlantic's Jazz Anthology series of 1970 is superior to most in that line simply on the grounds of time. Since Mose's songs were usually brief, Atlantic was able to fit 12 of them onto a single LP and thus provide a wider selection of his output, unlike others in that series which included only five or six tracks. Although this is very short for a CD (about 33 minutes), it still serves as a pretty good capsule introduction to one of American music's most idiosyncratic individualists. Many of his most famous songs are here—"Your Mind Is on Vacation," "New Parchman," "I'm the Wild Man," "I Don't Worry About a Thing," "Your Molecular Structure," etc., along with covers like "Rollin' Stone" and a rushed live remake of his biggest "hit," Willie Dixon's "Seventh Son." For a more comprehensive—and well-packaged—overview of most of his career, turn to the double-CD box *Allison Wonderland* on Rhino/Atlantic. — *Richard S. Ginell*

I 've Been Doin' Some Thinkin' / Jul. 9, 1968 / Atlantic ++++
Unaffected so far by the rock and electronic revolutions, the Mose kept on doing his inimitable thing through the late '60s, developing his chromatic acoustic piano idiom, wryly observing life, covering an occasional standard. This album yielded at least three Allison classics—the clever chemical love song "Your Molecular Structure," his trenchant rebuke to platitude criers of all stripes "Everybody Cryin' Mercy," and the urban warning that probably didn't go over too well with the drug crowd at the time, "If You're Goin' to the City." The standard under consideration this time is Gov. Jimmie Davis's "You Are My Sunshine." Red Mitchell (bass) and Bill Goodwin (drums) provide the backing, and that's all Mose needed for another entertaining, thought-provoking set. — *Richard S. Ginell*

Mose in Your Ear / Apr. 25, 1972-Apr. 26, 1972 / Atlantic ++++
This live session from 1972 features Mose Allison at his best. Performing with his working trio (bassist Clyde Flowers and drummer Eddie Charlton), Allison sounds quite inspired on such tunes as "Fool's Paradise," "I Don't Worry About A Thing," "Hey Good Lookin'," "I Ain't Got Nothin' But The Blues" and "The Seventh Son." Most memorable is his minor-toned downbeat ballad version of "You Are My Sunshine" which casts new meaning on the usually optimistic lyrics. This near-classic set is long overdue to be reissued on CD. — *Scott Yanow*

Your Mind Is on Vacation / Apr. 5, 1976-Apr. 9, 1976 / Atlantic ++++
It seems strange to realize that this was Mose Allison's only recording during the 1973-81 period. In addition to his trio with bassist Jack Hannah and drummer Jerry Granelli, such guests as altoist David Sanborn, Al Cohn and Joe Farrell on tenors, and trumpeter Al Porcino pop up on a few selections. However, Mose Allison is easily the main star, performing ten of his originals (including a remake of the famous title cut, "What Do You Do After You Ruin Your Life" and "Swingin' Machine") plus renditions of the standards "Foolin' Myself" and "I Can't See For Lookin'." This excellent LP has unfortunately not been reissued yet. — *Scott Yanow*

Pure Mose / 1978 / 32 Jazz +++
This 1997 CD features pianist/vocalist/composer Mose Allison on a pre-

viously unreleased live session from San Francisco's legendary Keystone Korner, playing his usual repertoire in a trio with bassist Tom Rutley and drummer Jerry Granelli. Since Allison only recorded one album during 1973-81, this decently recorded live set is quite valuable; the year (1978) is an estimate. Most of the material is fairly familiar, but the singer's spirited delivery and interplay with the audience make this a CD well worth getting by his fans. Highlights include "Wildman on the Loose," "Swinging Machine," "I Live the Life I Love," "I Ain't Got Nothin' But the Blues," and "Your Mind Is on Vacation." — *Scott Yanow*

Middle Class White Boy / Feb. 2, 1982 / Elektra/Musician ++++
This Elektra LP finds the unique Mose Allison well-featured in a sextet also including Joe Farrell on tenor and flute and guitarist Phil Upchurch. Allison's unusual mixture of bop, country-blues and his own eccentric personality have long given him a distinctive sound on piano but it is his ironic vocals and superb lyric-writing abilities that make him a major figure. In addition to such originals as "How Does It Feel? (To Be Good Looking)," "I Don't Want Much," and "I'm Nobody Today," Allison brings new life to such standards as "When My Dreamboat Comes Home," "I'm Just a Lucky So-and-So," and "The Tennessee Waltz." — *Scott Yanow*

Lesson in Living / Jul. 21, 1982 / Elektra +++
On the second of two albums cut in 1982 (which were his only recordings from the 1977-86 period), vocalist-pianist Mose Allison is saddled with an unnecessary and not always complementary all-star group consisting of guitarist Eric Gale, bassist Jack Bruce, drummer Billy Cobham and (on "You Are My Sunshine") altoist Lou Donaldson. However, for this live set (recorded at the Montreux Jazz Festival), Mose is in fine form performing mostly remakes of his songs. Highlights include "Your Mind Is On Vacation," "Lost Mind," "Seventh Son," "I Don't Worry About A Thing," and the definitive rendition of his unusual minor-toned version of "You Are My Sunshine." — *Scott Yanow*

Ever Since the World Ended / May 11, 1987-Jun. 2, 1987 / Blue Note +++
Mose Allison, who was a musical institution long before 1987, had not run out of creative juices after 30 years of major league performances. This set finds him introducing such ironically truthful songs as "Ever Since The World Ended," "Top Forty," "I Looked In The Mirror," and "What's Your Movie." The many guest artists (including altoist Arthur Blythe, tenor-saxophonist Bennie Wallace, Bob Malach on both alto and tenor, and guitarist Kenny Burrell) are unnecessary frivolities but Allison's trio (with bassist Dennis Irwin and drummer Tom Whaley) is tight and ably backs the unique singer-pianist. — *Scott Yanow*

Jazz Profile / May 11, 1987-Sep. 1993 / Blue Note +++
This single CD has highlights from Mose Allison's three Blue Note albums of 1987-93 (*Ever Since the World Ended*, *My Backyard*, and *The Earth Wants You*). Although it would be preferable to acquire the complete records instead (and Allison's greatest material was actually recorded in earlier years), there are plenty of gems on this set, including "Ever Since the World Ended," "I Looked in the Mirror," "Ever Since I Stole the Blues," and "Certified Senior Citizen." Joined by a variety of all-star players (including Bennie Wallace on tenor, altoist Arthur Blythe, and guitarist John Scofield), Allison's singing, witty delivery, piano playing, and insightful (yet humorous) lyrics easily steal the show. — *Scott Yanow*

My Backyard / Dec. 5, 1989-Dec. 7, 1989 / Blue Note +++
For this New Orleans session, vocalist-pianist-lyricist Mose Allison utilized several top local but world-class musicians: tenor-saxophonist Tony Dagradi, guitarist Steve Masakowski, bassist Bill Huntington, and drummer John Vidacovich. Among the new songs introduced at the session were "Ever Since I Stole The Blues," "You Call It Joggin'," "The Gettin' Paid Waltz," and "My Backyard." Allison, who is heard in top form, revived "That's Your Red Wagon" and "Sleepy Lagoon" and sounds in good spirits throughout this enjoyable and typically philosophical outing. — *Scott Yanow*

The Earth Wants You / Sep. 8, 1993-Sep. 9, 1993 / Blue Note ++++
Mose Allison, one of the top lyricists of the '90s, shows throughout this entertaining CD that his powers as a pianist and singer are also very much intact. The album introduces a few new classics in "Certified Senior Citizen," "This Ain't Me," and "Who's in, Who's Out." His voice is still in prime form and his piano playing remains quite unique. It is true that the guests on the set (guitarist John Scofield, altoist Joe Lovano, Bob Malach on tenor, and trumpeter

Randy Brecker) are not all that necessary but Allison's performance makes this an excellent showcase for his music. — *Scott Yanow*

Gimcracks and Gewgaws / 1997 / Blue Note ◆◆◆◆

The older Mose Allison gets, the sharper his mind becomes, the more idiosyncratic his music sounds, and the more pleasure the aficionado gets for spending the better part of an hour with his latest stuff. By this time, the 70-year-old philosopher from Tippo, MS, had sharpened his wit and insight on life to an even keener edge, musing wryly on materialism, technology, aging, death, even his own name ("MJA, Jr."). The tunes seem to have disappeared almost entirely but it doesn't matter; the lyrics are so damned clever and as hilarious as ever, even when they are obviously sequels to previous masterworks like "Your Mind Is On Vacation" ("What's With You") or "Young Man's Blues" ("Old Man Blues"). Mose's piano style by now has been pared down to its unique essentials, a ceaseless, swinging linear flow drawing from the three Bs — Bach, Bartok and bop — and his voice has barely aged since his Prestige days. Mark Shim muses ably on tenor sax now and then, and guitarist Russell Malone ranges all over the stylistic lot between R&B and jazz. At this rate, waiting four years or so between albums in the '90s, Allison has kept his creative batteries fresh every time out. — *Richard S. Ginell*

The Allman Brothers Band

f. 1969, Macon, GA, **db.** 1982
Group / Southern Rock, Blues-Rock

The story of the Allman Brothers Band is one of triumph, tragedy, redemption, dissolution, and a new redemption. Over nearly 30 years, they've gone from being America's single most influential band to a has-been group trading on past glories, to reach the 1990s as one of the most respected rock acts of their era.

For the first half of the 1970s, the Allman Brothers Band was the most influential rock group in America, redefining rock music and its boundaries. The band's mix of blues, country, jazz, and even classical influences, and their powerful, extended onstage jamming altered the standards of concert performance — other groups were known for their onstage jamming, but when the Allman Brothers stretched a song out for 30 or 40 minutes, at their best they were exciting, never self-indulgent. They gave it all a distinctly Southern voice and, in the process, opened the way for a wave of '70s rock acts from south of the Mason-Dixon Line, including the Marshall Tucker Band, Lynyrd Skynyrd, and Blackfoot, whose music, at least initially, celebrated their roots. And for a time, almost single-handedly, they also made Capricorn Records into a major independent label.

The group was founded in 1969 by Duane Allman (Nov. 20, 1946-Oct. 29, 1971) on guitar and Gregg Allman (b. Dec. 8, 1947) on vocals and organ; Forrest Richard ("Dickey") Betts (b. Dec. 12, 1943) on guitar; Berry Oakley (b. Apr. 4, 1948, d. Nov. 12, 1972) on bass; and Butch Trucks and Jaimoe Johnny Johanson (b. July 8, 1944) on drums. Duane and Gregg Allman loved soul and R&B, although they listened to their share of rock 'n' roll, especially as it sounded coming out of England in the mid-1960s. Their first group was a local Daytona Beach garage band called the Escorts, who sounded a lot like the early Beatles and Rolling Stones; they later became the Allman Joys and plunged into Cream-style British blues, and then the Hour Glass, a more soul-oriented outfit. The group landed a contract with Liberty Records with help from the Nitty Gritty Dirt Band, but the company wasted the opportunity on a pair of overproduced albums that failed to capture the Hour Glass' sound. The group split up after Liberty rejected a proposed third LP steeped in blues and R&B.

Duane Allman began working as a session guitarist at Fame Studios in Muscle Shoals, Alabama, and it was there, appearing on records by Wilson Pickett, Aretha Franklin, John Hammond, and King Curtis, among others, that he made his reputation. In 1969, at the coaxing of ex-Otis Redding manager Phil Walden, Allman gave up session work and began putting together a new band — Jaimoe (Johnny Lee Johnson) Johanson came aboard, and then Allman's longtime friend Butch Trucks, and another Allman friend, Berry Oakley joined, along with Dickey Betts, with whom Oakley was playing in a group called Second Coming. A marathon jam session ensued, at the end of which Allman had his band, except for a singer — that came later, when his brother Gregg agreed to join. They were duly signed to Walden's new Capricorn label.

The band didn't record their first album until after they'd worked their

sound out on the road, playing heavily around Florida and Georgia. The self-titled debut album was a solid blues-rock album and one of the better showcases for guitar pyrotechnics in a year with more than its share, amid albums by the Cream, Blind Faith, the Jeff Beck Group, and Led Zeppelin. It didn't sell 50,000 copies on its initial release, but *The Allman Brothers Band* impressed everyone who heard it and nearly everyone who reviewed it. Coming out at the end of the 1960s, it could have passed for a follow-up to the kind of blues-rock coming out of England from acts like Cream, except that it had a sharper edge — the Allmans were American and Southern, and their understanding of blues (not to mention elements of jazz, mostly courtesy of Jaimoe) was as natural as breathing. The album also introduced one of the band's most popular concert numbers, "Whipping Post."

Their debut album attracted good reviews and a cult following with its mix of assured dual lead guitars by Duane Allman and Dickey Betts, soulful singing by Gregg Allman, and a rhythm section that was nearly as busy as the lead instruments, between Oakley's rock-hard bass and the dual drumming of Trucks and Johanson. Their second album, 1970's *Idlewild South*, recorded at Capricorn's studios in Macon, Georgia, was produced by Tom Dowd, who had previously recorded Cream. This was a magical combination — Dowd was completely attuned to the group's sound and goals, and *Idlewild South* broadened that sound, adding a softer acoustic texture to their music and introducing Dickey Betts as a composer (including the original studio version of "In Memory of Elizabeth Reed," an instrumental tribute to Miles Davis that would become a highlight of their shows, in many different forms, for the next 30 years). It also had a Gregg Allman number, "Midnight Rider," which became one of the band's more widely covered originals and the composer's signature tune.

By this time, the band's concerts were becoming legendary for the extraordinarily complex yet coherent interplay between the two guitarists and Gregg Allman's keyboards, sometimes in jams of 40 minutes or more to a single song without wasting a note. And unlike the art rock bands of the era, they weren't interested in impressing anyone with how they played scales, how many different tunings they knew, or which classical riffs they could quote. Rather, the Allmans incorporated the techniques and structures of jazz and classical into their playing. In March of 1971, the band played a series of shows at the Fillmore East that were recorded for posterity and subsequently transformed into their third album, *At Fillmore East*. This double LP, issued in July of 1971, became an instant classic, rivaling the previous blues-rock touchstone cut at the Fillmore, Cream's *Wheels of Fire*. Duane Allman and his band were suddenly the new heroes to millions of mostly older teenage fans. Although it never cracked the Top 10, *At Fillmore East* was certified as a gold record on October 15, 1971.

Fourteen months later, Duane Allman was killed in a motorcycle accident. The band had been midway through work on their next album, *Eat a Peach*, which they completed as a five-piece, with Dickey Betts playing all of the lead and slide guitar parts. Their second double album in a row became another instant classic, and their first album to reach the Top Ten, peaking at number five.

Despite having completed *Eat a Peach*, the group was intact in name only. Rather than try and replace Duane Allman as a guitarist, they contrived to add a second solo instrument in the form of a piano, played by Chuck Leavell. The group had already begun work on a long-delayed follow-up to *Eat a Peach*, when Oakley was killed in a motorcycle accident only a few blocks from Allman's accident site.

Lamar Williams (b. Jan. 15, 1949, d. Jan. 25, 1983) was recruited on bass, and the new lineup continued the group's concert activities, as well as eventually finishing their next album, *Brothers and Sisters*. which was released on August 1, 1973. During the extended gap in releases following *Eat a Peach*, Atco reissued *The Allman Brothers Band* and *Idlewild South* together as the double LP *Beginnings*, which charted higher than either individual release.

Brothers and Sisters marked the beginning of a new era. The album had a more easygoing and freewheeling sound, less bluesy and more countryish. This was partly a result of Capricorn's losing the services of Tom Dowd, who had produced their three previous albums. Additionally, Dickey Betts' full emergence as a songwriter and singer as well as the group's only guitarist, playing all of the lead and slide parts, altered the balance of the group's sound, pushing forth his distinct interest in country-rock. Betts also became the reluctant *de facto* leader of the band during this period, not from a desire for control as much as because he was the only one with the comparative stability and creative input to take on the responsibility.

The record occupied the number one spot for six weeks, spurred by the number two single "Ramblin' Man," and became their most well known album. It was an odd reversal of the usual order of success for a rock band—usually, it was the release of the album that drew the crowds to concerts, but in this case, the months of touring the band had done paved the way for the album. The fact that it kept getting pushed back only heightened the fans' interest.

Ironically, *Brothers and Sisters* was a less challenging record than the group's earlier releases, with a relatively laidback sound, relaxed compared to the groundbreaking work on the group's previous four albums. But all of this hardly mattered; based on the reputation they'd established with their first four albums, and the crowd-pleasing nature of "Ramblin' Man" and the Dickey Betts-composed instrumental "Jessica," the group was playing larger halls and bigger crowds than ever.

An entire range of Southern-based rock acts had started to make serious inroads into the charts in the wake of the Allman Brothers. Labels such as MCA and even Island Records began looking for this same audience, signing acts like Lynyrd Skynyrd and Blackfoot, respectively, among others. For the first time since the mid-1950s, the heyday of the rockabilly era, a major part of the country was listening to rock 'n' roll with a distinctly Southern twang.

The band began showing cracks in 1974, as Gregg Allman and Dickey Betts both began solo careers, recording albums separately from the group. Allman married Cher (twice), an event that set him up in a Hollywood-based lifestyle that created a schism with the rest of the band. They might have survived all of this, but for the increasing strain of the members' other personal habits—drugs and alcohol had always been a significant part of the lives of each of the members, except perhaps for Jaimoe, but as the strain and exhaustion of touring continued, coupled with the need to produce new music, these indulgences began to get out of control, and Betts' leadership of the group created a further strain for him.

The band's difficulties were showcased by their next album, the highly uneven *Win, Lose Or Draw*, which lacked the intensity and sharpness of their prior work. The whole band wasn't present for some of the album, and Gregg Allman's involvement with Cher, coupled with his serious drug problems, prevented him from participating with the rest of the group—his vocals were added separately, on the other side of the country.

The band finally came apart in 1976 when Allman found himself in the midst of a federal drug case against a supplier and agreed to testify against a friend and band employee. Leavall, Johanson, and Williams split to form Sea Level, which became a moderately successful band, cutting four Capricorn over the next four years, while Betts pursued a solo career. All of them vowed never to work with Gregg Allman again.

Amid this split, Capricorn Records, reaching ever deeper into its vaults for anything that could generate income, issued two collections, a double-LP live collection called *Wipe the Windows, Check the Oil, Dollar Gas*, showcasing the *Brothers & Sisters*-era band at various concerts, and a double-LP best-of package, *And the Road Goes On Forever*. *Wipe the Windows* was a modest seller, appearing as it did when the group's sales had already fallen off, and was compared unfavorably with the legendary work on *At Fillmore East*. The studio compilation passed with barely a ripple, however, because most fans already had the stuff on the original albums.

They were all back together by 1978, however, and over the next four years the group issued a somewhat uneven series of albums. *Enlightened Rogues* (1979) somewhat redeemed their reputations—produced by Tom Dowd, who had always managed to get the very best work out of the group, it had more energy than any record they'd issued in at least six years. It also restored the two-guitar lineup, courtesy of Dan Toler (from Dickey Betts' solo band), who was brought in when Chuck Leavell (along with Lamar Williams) refused to return to the Allmans. By that time, however, the Allmans were fighting against time and musical trends. Disco, punk, and power-pop had pretty much stolen a march on the arena acts epitomized by the Allmans; whatever interest they attracted was a matter of nostalgia for their earlier releases. The group was in danger of becoming arena rock's third big oldies act (after the Moody Blues and Paul McCartney's Wings).

Additionally, their business affairs were in a shambles, owing to the bankruptcy of Capricorn Records in late 1979. When the fallout from the Capricorn collapse settled, PolyGram Records, the company's biggest creditor, took over the label's library, and the Allman Brothers were cut loose from their contract.

Their signing to Arista enabled the group to resume recording. What they released, however, was safe, unambitious, routinely commercial pop-rock, closer in spirit to the Doobie Brothers than to their own classic work—a shadow of that work, without any of the invention and daring upon which they'd built their reputations. The group's fortunes hit a further downturn when Jaimoe was fired, breaking up one of the best rhythm sections in rock. For most of the 1980s, the group was on hiatus, while the individual members sorted out their personal and professional situations. During those years, only Dickey Betts seemed to be in a position to do much with his music, and most of that wasn't selling.

In 1989, the band was reactivated again, partly owing to PolyGram's decision to issue the four-CD box set retrospective *Dreams*. That set, coupled with the reissue of their entire Capricorn catalog on compact disc in the years leading up to the box's release, reminded millions of older listeners of the band's greatness, and introduced the group to millions of people too young to have been around for Watkins Glen, much less the Fillmore shows.

They reunited and also restored the band's original double-lead-guitar configuration, adding Warren Haynes on lead guitar alongside Dickey Betts, with Allen Woody playing bass. Chuck Leavell was gone, however, having agreed to join the Rolling Stones on tour as their resident keyboard player, and Lamar Williams had succumbed to cancer in 1983.

The new lineup reinvigorated the band, which signed with Epic Records and surprised everyone with their first release, *Seven Turns*. Issued in 1990, it got some of the best reviews and healthiest sales they'd had in more than a decade. Their subsequent studio albums failed to attract as much enthusiasm, and their two live albums, *An Evening With the Allman Brothers Band* and *2nd Set*, released in 1992 and 1995, respectively, were steady but not massive sellers. Much of this isn't the fault of the material so much as a natural result of the passage of time, which has left the Allmans competing with two decades' worth of successors and rivals.

The group has stayed together since 1989, overcoming continuing health and drug problems which have occasionally battered their efforts at new music. They remain a top concert attraction 25 years-plus after their last historically important album, easily drawing more than 20,000 fans at a time to outdoor venues, or booking 2,000-seat theaters for three weeks at a time. Their back catalog, especially the first five albums, remain consistent sellers on compact disc and recently returned to the reconstituted Capricorn label (still a home for Southern rockers, including the latter-day Lynyrd Skynyrd, as well as reissues of Elmore James and other classic bluesmen), under a 1997 licensing agreement that has resulted in their third round of digital remastering.

Apart from their Arista releases, the Allman Brothers Band has remained remarkably consistent, altering their music only gradually over 30 years. They sound more country than they did in their early days, and they're a bit more varied in the vocal department, but the band still soars at their concerts and on most of their records for the last ten years. —*Bruce Eder*

The Allman Brothers Band / 1969 / Polydor ♦♦♦♦
This might be the best debut album ever delivered by an American blues band, a bold, powerful, hard-edged, soulful essay in electric blues with a native Southern ambience. Some lingering elements of the psychedelic era then drawing to a close can be found in "Dreams," along with the template for the group's onstage workouts with "Whipping Post," and a solid cover of Muddy Waters' "Trouble No More." There isn't a bad song here, and only the fact that the group did even better the next time out keeps this from getting the highest possible rating. —*Bruce Eder*

☆ **Idlewild South** / 1970 / Polydor ♦♦♦♦♦
The best studio album in the group's history, electric blues with an acoustic texture, virtuoso lead, slide, and organ playing, and a killer selection of songs, including "Midnight Rider," "Revival," "Don't Keep Me Wonderin'," and "In Memory of Elizabeth Reed" in its embryonic studio version, which is pretty impressive even at a mere six minutes and change. They also do the best white cover of Willie Dixon's "Hoochie Coochie Man" anyone's ever likely to hear. —*Bruce Eder*

☆ **Live at Fillmore East** / Mar. 1971 / Polydor ♦♦♦♦♦
This is one of rock's greatest live albums, featuring amazing interplay within exceptionally dynamic arrangements. The material ranges from classics like

Blind Willie McTell's "Statesboro Blues" and T-Bone Walker's "Stormy Monday Blues" to solid originals like Dickey Betts' epic "In Memory of Elizabeth Reed" and Gregg Allman's "Whipping Post." Three of the numbers run over ten minutes, with two of them at 20 minutes or more, but it has all aged exceedingly well—this may be the one live album of extended pieces that doesn't seem dated, bloated, or outsized 20+ years later. Contrary to claims that these are untouched performances, *Fillmore East* actually was a skillfully edited amalgam of performances drawn from four shows over two nights and assembled by producer Tom Dowd. In addition to its original double-LP release, *At Fillmore East* has appeared in numerous CD versions—a double-CD from Polydor, a gold-plated audiophile version from Mobile Fidelity, and, most recently, a single CD from Capricorn. The audiophile disc is probably the best sounding, though the Capricorn release is far less expensive and has its own merits. The material was also recompiled and re-edited from the original concert tapes for the double CD *The Fillmore Concerts.* —*Rick Clark & Bruce Eder*

★ **Eat a Peach** / 1972 / Polydor ♦♦♦♦♦
Half of *Eat a Peach* consists of more fiery improvisations and high-wattage blues from the Fillmore dates that comprised *Live at the Fillmore East*, in the form of the 33-minute "Mountain Jam" (based on Donovan's "There Is a Mountain," no less) and "Trouble No More," which have since reappeared on Polydor's 1992 live compilation *The Fillmore Concerts. Eat a Peach* was released after Duane Allman's fatal motorcycle accident, but the studio sides include some tracks showcasing his soaring lead work, as well as the delicate acoustic guitar duo "Little Martha" (credited to Duane Allman as composer), featuring him and Dickey Betts. The band was at its creative peak, with great tracks like "Ain't Wastin' Time No More," "Melissa," "One Way Out," "Stand Back," and "Blue Sky," and this album has been a perennial best-seller, despite the "Mountain Jam"'s appearance elsewhere. This album has been issued in different CD versions, including two from Polydor (the later one is superior), one audiophile edition from Mobile Fidelity, and, in 1997, a newly remastered version licensed to the Capricorn label, on which it originally appeared; the Capricorn CD has a very bright but somewhat brittle sound, different from any of the others. —*Rick Clark & Bruce Eder*

Brothers and Sisters / 1973 / Polydor ♦♦♦♦
The group's first new studio album in two years shows off a leaner brand of musicianship, which, coupled with a pair of serious crowd-pleasers, "Ramblin' Man" and "Jessica," helped drive it to the top of the charts for a month and a half and, platinum record sales. This was the first album to feature the group's new lineup, with Chuck Leavell on keyboards and Lamar Williams on bass, as well as Dickey Betts' emergence as a singer alongside Gregg Allman. The tracks appear on the album in the order in which they were recorded, and the first three, up through "Ramblin' Man," feature Berry Oakley—their sound is rock-hard and crisp. The subsequent songs with Williams have the bass buried in the mix, and an overall muddier sound. The interplay between Leavell and Betts is beautiful on some songs, and Betts' slide on "Pony Boy" is a dazzling showcase that surprised everybody. Despite its sales, *Brothers & Sisters* is not quite a classic album (although it was their best for the next 17 years), especially in the wake of the four that had appeared previously, but it served as a template for some killer stage performances, and it proved that the band could survive the deaths of two key members. Capricorn's 1997 reissue has a brighter sound than the older PolyGram CD, but the Mobile Fidelity audiophile disc has the best sound, a richer, broader tone. —*Bruce Eder*

☆ **Beginnings** / 1973 / Polydor ♦♦♦♦♦
This is where the group's CD release history gets complicated. *Beginnings* was originally put together by Atco as a double-LP to encourage new fans who'd missed them to buy the group's first two albums, and proved so successful that it was kept in print on CD by Polydor when it acquired the group's catalog. Polydor's single-CD version of this double-LP, however, was substandard in audio quality, digitized from an LP production master, and their individual CDs of *The Allman Brothers Band* and *Idlewild South* were far superior. But when Capricorn got the library back in 1997, they remastered *Beginnings* along with the rest of the library, and the Capricorn version of this CD is one of the better bargains going on CD. —*Bruce Eder*

Win, Lose or Draw / 1975 / Polydor ♦♦
An unexpectedly poor showing from the group, considering the two-year lag between albums and what had come before. Despite a good cover of Muddy Waters' "Can't Lose What You Never Had"—highlighted by a great Dickey Betts solo—as an opener, there's not much here that's first-rate. The band sounds lethargic, although they still play decently. The title track and Dickey Betts' instrumental "High Falls" are among the few highlights, decent but unexceptional performances sparked by Betts' playing (which is engaging even on the loser tracks like "Louisiana Lou"). The album's main fault lies not with what it is, but what it could have been, and who it's from—as a debut album from a new band, it would be excusable and acceptable. —*Bruce Eder*

Wipe the Windows, Check the Oil, Dollar Gas / 1976 / Polydor ♦♦♦
This live album was released by Capricorn Records largely as a way of raising money in a hurry, but it fares surprisingly well musically. The 1973-74 Allman Brothers Band featured here is the one that most fans actually saw, since most listeners didn't discover them or get to their concerts until after the deaths of Duane Allman and Berry Oakley. *Wipe the Windows* isn't a landmark release like the Fillmore tapes—a collection of rock's greatest guitar albums could be complete without it. But no Allman Brothers Band fan should pass up *Wipe the Windows*, which is a most solid live album, and, in particular, a better representation of the songs off of *Brothers and Sisters* and *Win, Lose or Draw* than the original studio versions. "Southbound," "Ramblin' Man," "Jessica," and, to a lesser degree, "Wasted Words," come off exceptionally well. This second-generation band, with Dickey Betts as the sole lead guitar and Gregg Allman and Chuck Leavell sharing the keyboards, also performs a reconceived version of "In Memory of Elizabeth Reed"— they could never spark more fire than the version from the Fillmore, so they transform it into a moodier piece with more space for the keyboards to open up. Compiled from shows in New Orleans, San Francisco, Bakersfield, Oakland, and Watkins Glen (New York). —*Bruce Eder*

Enlightened Rogues / 1979 / Polydor ♦♦♦
The group's best studio album since *Brothers & Sisters* is a loud, brash, hard-rocking collection of consistently solid if not first-rate songs. The singing is some of the best since *Idlewild South*, and although they would do better once they brought in Warren Haynes, the dual guitar lineup of Dickey Betts and Dan Toler is a reminder of what the group had been missing since Duane Allman's death. The music isn't earth-shattering, but it is exciting through and through. —*Bruce Eder*

Reach for the Sky / 1980 / Razor & Tie ♦♦
The second album from *Allmans Mach Two* shows them holding their own, wearing their influences (especially gospel) a bit more on their sleeves, and even coming up with a minor single in "Angeline." —*William Ruhlmann*

Brothers of the Road / 1981 / Razor & Tie ♦♦
"Straight From The Heart" (No. 39), written by Dickey Betts and Johnny Cobb and sung by Gregg Allman, is one of the group's better accommodations to pop music, and on the whole, this is an accessible version of their trademark sound: call it Allmans Lite. The ruling influence here may be Arista president Clive Davis, who also oversaw the pop-oriented Grateful Dead albums of the same period. But the main duty of pop music is to sell, and when this album petered out at No. 44, the Allmans called it quits for the second time. —*William Ruhlmann*

Dreams / Jun. 1989 / Polydor ♦♦♦♦
This is a thoughtfully compiled boxed set, containing highlights throughout the Allman Brothers' entire career, as well as solo projects and early pre-Allman recordings. A booklet, with generous annotation and photos, is provided. The remastering is a noticeable improvement over initial CD releases of the Allman catalog. If you've got the bucks for a boxed set, this is a worthwhile acquisition for completists and those looking for a comprehensive introduction. —*Rick Clark*

Seven Turns / Oct. 1990 / Epic ♦♦♦♦
The group's comeback album, their best blues-based outing since *Idlewild South*, and one that restored a lot of their reputation. With Tom Dowd running the session, and the group free to make the music they wanted to, they ended up producing this bold, rock-hard album, made up mostly of songs by Dickey Betts (with contributions by new keyboardman Johnny Neel and lead guitarist Warren Haynes), almost every one of them a winner. Apart from the rippling opening number, "Good Clean Fun," which he co-authored, Gregg Allman's contribution is limited to singing and the organ, but the band seems

more confident than ever, ripping through numbers like "Low Down Dirty Mean," "Shine It On," and "Let Me Ride" like they were inventing blues-rock here, and the Ornette Coleman-inspired "True Gravity" is their best instrumental since "Jessica." — *Bruce Eder*

Live at Ludlow Garage: 1970 / 1991 / Polydor ✦✦✦✦

Ninety-one minutes of the Allman Brothers Band in concert from a Cincinnati venue that they loved, nearly a year before their legendary Fillmore shows. The acoustics are good, though a little shaky—the tape was made at 7 ips, the bare minimum professional standard, which leaves more hiss than one might like, and a bit less clarity than a fully professional live album might show; on the other hand, the group's sound imparts its own punch and clarity, and it was done in stereo, and if not for the existence of the Fillmore tapes, and the fact that the albums they yielded sold a kajillion copies, this show might well have been released in the 1970s. It isn't as intense as the Fillmore shows, but it does capture the group as a little-known working band with but a single album out and building a reputation—and with Dickey Betts yet to emerge as either a singer or composer, and their sound still being worked out ("Statesboro Blues" gets a startlingly subdued performance, anticipating the acoustic version of "In Memory of Elizabeth Reed" from the 1990s' *Second Set*). They build their set on ambitious reinterpretations of songs by Blind Willie McTell, Muddy Waters ("Trouble In Mind"), John Lee Hooker ("Dimples"), and Willie Dixon, whose "Hoochie Coochie Man" is a soaring highlight of this two-disc set, in a version that makes every other white band's cover seem wimpy by comparison, climaxing with a searing, though somewhat disjointed 44-minute version of "Mountain Jam." — *Bruce Eder*

Shades of Two Worlds / Jul. 1991 / Epic ✦✦✦✦

The group's follow-up to their comeback album is a major step forward, with more mature songs, more improvisation than the group had featured in their work since the early 1970s, and more confidence than they'd shown since *Brothers and Sisters*. It's all here, from acoustic bottleneck playing ("Come On In My Kitchen") to jazz improvisation ("Kind of Bird"), with the most reflective songwriting ("Nobody Knows") in their history. — *Bruce Eder*

Decade of Hits 1969-1979 / Oct. 1991 / Polydor ✦✦✦✦

Decade of Hits 1969-1979 collects highlights from the Allman Brothers' first decade of existence and features many of their best-known songs; it provides a solid introduction to the definitive Southern-rock band. — *Stephen Thomas Erlewine*

Evening with the Allman Brothers Band / Mar. 1992 / Epic ✦✦✦✦

A good live album, but not quite the worthy successor to the Fillmore shows in their various forms—the band is on form throughout this more than one-hour distillation of shows in Boston and New York from their 1992 tour, covering old and new repertory, but there are no surprises. The song lineup wastes some opportunities, however, and there isn't any serious new ground covered, which may be par for the course for a band in its 22nd year. On the up side, very much, the crispness of the recording helps one fully appreciate the power and articulation of the playing by everyone, but especially Dickey Betts and Warren Haynes. — *Bruce Eder*

The Fillmore Concerts / Oct. 20, 1992 / Polydor ✦✦✦✦

A good idea that worked out even better, with one small caveat. *The Fillmore Concerts* is made up of performances from the two Fillmore shows that originally comprised *Live at the Fillmore East* and the concert portions of *Eat a Peach*, plus one track ("One Way Out") from a Fillmore show from a couple of months later, the 16-track masters from each show transferred to digital and remixed by original producer Tom Dowd. The sound is sterling, and the two hour-plus running time makes this a dream for fans of the band, as well as an improvement on the original releases of this material. It is also a slightly less honest release, where "In Memory of Elizabeth Reed" is concerned—Dowd edited the version here together from two different performances, first and second shows, the dividing line being where Duane Allman's solo comes in. Not that this is the only concert album where this kind of editing has been done, but the original *Live at the Fillmore* contained a single take of the song, and some purists may prefer that. Otherwise, this set runs circles around more than 99% of the guitar albums ever released, with breathtaking sound (which, unlike the similarly conceived but less effective *Derek and the Dominos Live at the Fillmore*, loses none of its bite), and most fans might as well start here. — *Bruce Eder*

Where It All Begins / May 3, 1994 / Epic ✦✦✦

After a year of personal and personnel problems, the group got back together to record this surprisingly consistent live-in-the-studio venture. It lacks the ambition and stretch of *Seven Turns* or *Shades of Two Worlds*, along with their peaks, but it is still a solidly consistent album, driven by some of the virtues of live spontaneity. Highlights include Gregg Allman's frank drug song "All Night Train," the Bo Diddley-beat-driven "No One to Run With," and the glorious dual guitar workout "Back Where It All Begins." — *Bruce Eder*

2nd Set / 1995 / Epic ✦✦✦✦

The Allman Brothers Band's fifth live release in 25 years, cut during 1994 in Raleigh, NC, and at the Garden State Arts Center in New Jersey, is a high-water mark in their Epic Records catalog. If anything, they're even better here than they were on the earlier *Evening With the Allman Brothers Band*, the old material getting fresh new approaches—the band was *on* for both nights, and presented sets, including an acoustic version of "In Memory of Elizabeth Reed," and "Jessica" (which won a Grammy Award), that soared and flowed, especially Dickey Betts' and Warren Haynes' guitars. What's more, the clarity of the recording and the volume at which it was recorded make this a most rewarding 70 minutes of live music on a purely technical level—you can practically hear the action on the guitars during the acoustic set. It won't replace *Live at the Fillmore* or the live portions of *Eat a Peach*, but it deserves a place on the shelf not very far from them. — *Bruce Eder*

New York City Blues / 1997 / [bootleg] ✦✦✦✦

Made from a live-in-the-studio radio broadcast from August of 1971 (not April as the label says, since they talk about King Curtis' murder, which happened in August), this 70-minute bootleg CD features the classic lineup, some two months after their second major Fillmore appearance. The performance isn't nearly as tight or intense as the Fillmore shows, though Duane, Dickey, and Gregg are spot-on, along with the rest of the band. The songs, eight of them, include "Stormy Monday," "Trouble No More," "Statesboro Blues," "One Way Out," "In Memory of Elizabeth Reed," "Don't Keep Me Wondering," and "You Don't Love Me," the latter featuring a guitar cadenza that stretches it out exquisitely into a nice closing jam (which doesn't get an index point of its own). The sound is stereo and really close and loud, there are no liner notes, and the only flaw is the annoying spots where the sound blanks out over the applause (no music is interfered with, but you'd think they'd have edited out the splices altogether) between songs, where the radio station call letters are mentioned by the deejay. — *Bruce Eder*

Mycology: An Anthology / Jun. 9, 1998 / Sony ✦✦✦✦

Mycology: An Anthology collects highlights from the Allman Brothers' '90s recordings for Epic Records. Although these latter-day recordings didn't quite reach the heights of the group's '70s heyday, they were surprisingly strong and *Mycology* is the best way for the curious fan to discover that. By rounding up the best moments from *Seven Turns*, *Shades of Two Worlds*, *An Evening with the Allman Brothers*, and *Where it All Begins*, the collection offers a good distillation of an underrated portion of the group's career, thereby making it of equal interest to casual and hardcore fans alike. — *Stephen Thomas Erlewine*

Duane Allman

b. Nov. 20, 1946, Nashville, TN, **d.** Oct. 29, 1971, Macon, GA
Guitar, Slide Guitar / Southern Rock, Blues-Rock, Soul, R&B

Duane Allman went from musical unknown to become one of rock's most revered guitar virtuosos, only to die a legend, all in about 24 months. He barely had time to establish his legacy, much less his name—two finished studio albums with his band, a live album and lots of shows with them (some of which, off radio, are starting to surface on bootlegs) and session work in which he played behind other artists, along with songs off of a busted solo album project. The bulk of his reputation and legacy rests, understandably, with the Allman Brothers Band, but there were enough outside projects to justify a pair of anthology collections. Either one is the place to start musically, with the first set also containing a wonderful extended essay on his life and career, but serious fans will obviously want the entire albums from which a lot of those tracks, even the session work, were pulled. — *Bruce Eder*

● **Anthology / 1972 / Polydor ✦✦✦✦**

This double CD/double LP was the first fully annotated rock anthology, complete with biographical essay and song analysis. It probably would have succeeded regardless, but the presence of Derek and the Dominos' "Layla," just at the point that it was becoming a rock standard (which showed up at just about the same time on the *History of Eric Clapton*) helped push the sales even higher. The highlights, electric *and* acoustic, are too numerous to detail—"Goin' Down Slow," a glorious finished fragment from Duane Allman's attempted solo album; the B.B. King medley played by the pre-Allman Brothers Band, The Hour Glass, in one of their few unfettered trips into the studio; and shining moments playing behind others, including "The Weight" by Aretha Franklin and "Hey Jude" by Wilson Pickett, plus work with King Curtis (on whose "Games People Play" we hear Duane playing an electric sitar), Cowboy, Johnny Jenkins ("Rollin' Stone"), John Hammond ("Shake For Me"), Boz Scaggs (the 13-minute epic "Loan Me a Dime"), and Delaney and Bonnie and Friends, rounded out by some great moments with the Allman Brothers Band. —*Bruce Eder*

Anthology, Vol. 2 / 1974 / Polydor ✦✦✦✦
The session work with other players here isn't quite as good as the material on the first anthology, but *Volume Two* does feature a live cut by Delaney & Bonnie, plus a pair of what were then previously unissued Allman Brothers Band live tracks (among them "Hey Jude" from the Fillmore East in June 1971). There's another good Duane Allman solo number and a good Hour Glass track ("Been Gone Too Long"), more session work with Aretha Franklin and King Curtis, Ronnie Hawkins ("Matchbox"), Wilson Pickett ("Born to Be Wild"), Johnny Jenkins, Boz Scaggs, Sam Samudio, and Otis Rush. The annotation here isn't as thorough as it was on the first volume, but anyone who owns the first double-CD set will almost certainly have to own this one as well, and for a mid-priced set there's a lot of very good music. —*Bruce Eder*

Gregg Allman

b. Dec. 8, 1947, Nashville, TN
Organ, Piano, Keyboards, Vocals / Southern Rock, Blues-Rock, R&B, Pop-Soul
Gregg Allman's most visible contribution to rock music is as lead singer, organist, and songwriter within the Allman Brothers Band, founded by his brother Duane (d. 1971) in 1969. He has never threatened to eclipse the band that carries his family name, but he has found occasional success and popularity with his solo work, which is distinctly different, more soulful, and less focused on high-wattage virtuosity.

Allman's instrument is the organ, and he is most effective (when he is in top form) as a singer. His first instrument, ironically enough, was the guitar, which he took up before his older brother Duane did. But Duane learned it better and quickly eclipsed Gregg. Where Gregg did excel was on the organ and as a singer (a role Duane was never comfortable with), which proved important but not at the center of a group that became famous for its 40-minute instrumental jams and three-hour sets. Through their early efforts, in bands like the Allman Joys and the Hour Glass, they shared the spotlight, with Duane taking the lengthy solos and Gregg fronting the band and offering Booker T. Jones-type keyboard playing. Liberty Records signed the Hour Glass and tried making Gregg into the focus of their efforts during the late 1960s, but it never quite worked.

When the Allman Brothers Band was organized, the flashy (and vital) instrumental moments belonged to his brother and Dickey Betts and, later still, Warren Haynes. Gregg's songs, however, including "Whipping Post" and "Midnight Rider," were among the group's notable originals during their classic period, 1969-72. Beginning with *Brothers & Sisters*, Betts' songwriting and singing came to increasing prominence.

It was during the period that *Brothers & Sisters* was burning up the charts that Gregg Allman emerged as a solo artist with his first album, the critically well-received hit *Laid Back*, which put the softer, more serious, soul- and gospel-tinged side of his work in sharper focus. A tour followed, which yielded a live album that was also a success. This first period of solo popularity was interrupted by a combination of professional and personal conflicts; the Allman Brothers Band toured extensively and struggled to come up with a follow-up to *Brothers & Sisters*, and Gregg Allman began a relationship with Cher, the ex-wife and singing partner of Sonny Bono, which resulted in a tumultuous series of marriages and divorces for the two. These activities were played out amid Allman's well-publicized drug problems, which culminated with his testifying against a band employee in a federal drug case,

which, in turn, led to the temporary but extended dissolution of the Allman Brothers Band.

Ironically, it was during this period, in 1977, that he delivered *Playin' Up a Storm*, a pop-soul effort that proved to be his most accomplished and successful album. Alas, this was to be the peak of his career away from the band. His next two albums, *I'm No Angel* and *Just Before the Bullets Fly*, released at the end of the 1980s, were quickly eclipsed by the re-formed and reinvigorated Allman Brothers Band's success on stage and on record. His 1997 release *Searching for Simplicity* and the double-CD anthology *One More Try* had none of the urgency or success of the band's activities. —*Bruce Eder*

Laid Back / 1973 / Polydor ✦✦✦✦
Recorded in the same year as the *Brothers & Sisters* album, this solo debut release is a beautiful amalgam of R&B, folk, and gospel sounds, with the best singing on any of Gregg Allman's solo releases. He covers his own "Midnight Rider" in a more mournful, dirge-like manner, and Jackson Browne's "These Days" gets its most touching and tragic-sounding rendition as well. Although Chuck Leavell and Jaimoe are here, there's very little that sounds like the Allman Brothers Band—prominent guitars, apart from a few licks by Tommy Talton (Cowboy, ex-We The People) are overlooked in favor of gospel-tinged organ and choruses behind Allman's soulful singing. —*Bruce Eder*

Tour / 1974 / Polygram ✦✦
Cut during his first solo tour, complete with an orchestra backing him, this CD (originally two LPs) is almost as good a musical showcase, complete with a honky-tonk arrangement of the Elvis hit "Feel So Bad" and a cover of "Turn On Your Love Light" spread among performances of stuff from *Laid Back* and the Allmans' repertory. —*Bruce Eder*

The Gregg Allman Tour / Mar. 1975 / Polydor ✦✦
In the wake of his debut solo album, *Laid Back*, Gregg Allman assembled a backup band and went on tour, resulting in this two-LP live album, which combines his interests in rock, blues, gospel, and country music and finds him backed by a 24-piece orchestra. But there isn't enough original material to establish the star's identity, and the idea of including tracks by opening act Cowboy smacks of filler and record company manipulation. Given that Allman's reputation was based on live work and The Allman Brothers Band's *At Fillmore East* album, this was especially disappointing. (The lead-off track, a cover of the 1965 Fontella Bass and Bobby McClure hit "Don't Mess Up A Good Thing," hit No.106.) —*William Ruhlmann*

Playin' Up a Storm / 1977 / Razor & Tie ✦✦✦✦
There's weaker material here, but the playing and singing more than compensate. —*Rick Clark*

I'm No Angel / 1986 / Epic ✦✦✦
The title track was a comeback hit. Allman's voice is distanced in the mix by a little too much reverb. The band tracks are particularly hot. —*Rick Clark*

Just Before the Bullets Fly / 1988 / Epic ✦✦
"Demons" is a highlight on this, another solid journeyman outing. As on *I'm No Angel*, the release suffers from overly wet mixes. —*Rick Clark*

● **One More Try: An Anthology** / Sep. 23, 1997 / Polygram ✦✦✦✦
Although it may be a little too comprehensive for some tastes, *One More Try: An Anthology* is the definitive Gregg Allman collection. Spanning two discs and 34 songs, the collection touches upon every phase of his career. Of course, it concentrates on his solo career—all of his hits, key album tracks and AOR staples are here—but it also contains a couple of Allman Brothers cuts for good measure. The end result is a weighty anthology that winds up as the final statement on Gregg Allman's career. —*Thom Owens*

Searching for Simplicity / Nov. 11, 1997 / Sony ✦✦✦
In his initial solo recordings, Gregg Allman tried for a more eclectic pop approach than the Southern blues-rock of his day job with the Allman Brothers Band. His later solo work, done during breaks in the Brothers' career, was much closer to the traditional ABB sound. On his first solo album since the Allmans' reformation in 1989, he again makes what is essentially an Allman Brothers Band record without the other members, except new guitarist Jack Pearson, whose Duane Allman/Dickey Betts-style slide work is all over the disc. Allman signals the same-but-different approach by opening the album with an "unplugged" version of the Allmans' signature song, "Whip-

ping Post," and though he adds horns to some tracks for a more R&B feel, the rest of the album finds him growling through standard-issue blues-rock, some of the songs originals, some covers, among them an excellent version of "Dark End of the Street" and an arrangement of John Hiatt's "Memphis in the Meantime," that makes it sound like a Betts country-rocker. Recovering from personnel changes, the Allman Brothers Band didn't release an album in 1997; this record should help tide their fans over. — *William Ruhlmann*

Albert Ammons (Albert C. Ammons)

b. Sep. 23, 1907, Chicago, IL, **d.** Dec. 2, 1949, Chicago, IL
Piano / Boogie-Woogie, Swing, Piano Blues
Albert Ammons was one of the big three of late-30s boogie-woogie along with Pete Johnson and Meade Lux Lewis. Arguably the most powerful of the three, Ammons was also flexible enough to play swing music. Ammons played in Chicago clubs from the 1920s on although he also worked as a cab driver for a time. Starting in 1934, he led his own band in Chicago and he made his first records in 1936. In 1938 Ammons appeared at Carnegie Hall with Pete Johnson and Meade Lux Lewis, an event that really helped launch the boogie-woogie craze. Ammons recorded with the other pianists in duets and trios, fit right in with the Port of Harlem Jazzmen on their Blue Note session, appeared regularly at Cafe Society, recorded as a sideman with Sippie Wallace in the 1940s, and he even cut a session with his son, the great tenorman Gene Ammons. Albert Ammons worked steadily throughout the 1940s, playing at President Harry Truman's inauguration in 1949; he died later that year. Many of his recordings are currently available on CD. — *Scott Yanow*

☆ **The Complete Blue Note Recordings of Albert Ammons and Meade Lux Lewis** / Nov. 21, 1935-Apr. 22, 1944 / Mosaic ◆◆◆◆◆
This magnificent three-LP box set was issued as part of the first release by the Mosaic label. The out-of-print collection has all of the music recorded during Blue Note's first session (nine piano solos by Albert Ammons, eight including a five-part "The Blues" by Meade Lux Lewis and a pair of Ammons-Lewis duets) plus Lewis' 1935 version of "Honky Tonk Train Blues" and his complete sessions of Oct. 4, 1940, Apr. 9, 1941 (four songs on harpsichord), and Aug. 22, 1944. The music emphasizes boogie-woogie and both Ammons (quite memorable on "Boogie Woogie Stomp") and Lewis are heard in prime form. Incidentally, one of their duets (which is mistakenly titled "The Sheik Of Araby") is actually "Nagasaki." This box is well worth bidding on at an auction. — *Scott Yanow*

1936-1939 / Feb. 13, 1936-Apr. 8, 1939 / Classics ◆◆◆◆

Master of Boogie / Dec. 23, 1938-May 1939 / Milan ◆◆
This is the type of CD that frustrates completists and veteran collectors; the 13 selections are taken from a variety of sessions and the recording dates that are given are often incorrect. The great boogie-woogie pianist Albert Ammons is heard on five of the nine piano solos he recorded at Blue Note's debut session in 1939 along with a solo number apiece that were cut for Columbia and Storyville. In addition Ammons plays "Two And Fews" in duet with Meade Lux Lewis (from the Blue Note date), leads a hot group on two of the four numbers from his relatively rare debut session (dating from 1936, not 1939 as it states on the back cover), and is heard at the famous Spirituals To Swing concert of 1938 backing blues singer-guitarist Big Bill Broonzy and jamming with Meade Lux Lewis and Pete Johnson on three pianos. Great music, inexcusably lousy packaging. — *Scott Yanow*

● **The First Day** / Jan. 6, 1939 / Blue Note ◆◆◆◆
Producer Alfred Lion, who had attended John Hammond's Spiritual to Swing concert of Dec. 23, 1938 which had introduced boogie-woogie pianists Albert Ammons and Meade Lux Lewis to New York audiences, was very impressed. Two weeks later he started the Blue Note label by recording nine Ammons solos, eight by Lewis and a pair of heated duets during a single day. All of the music (except an untitled original by Meade Lux Lewis slated to be issued by Blue Note in the future) is on this single CD. Ammons, the more forceful (relatively speaking) of the two pianists, generally takes honors but there are plenty of rewarding performances including Lewis' five-part "The Blues," Ammons' "Boogie Woogie Stomp," and their duet on "Nagasaki." Highly recommended to collectors who do not already own Mosaic's more extensive three-LP limited-edition Ammons/Lewis set. — *Scott Yanow*

King of Boogie Woogie (1939-1949) / Jan. 6, 1939-Jan. 4, 1948 / Blues Classics ◆◆◆
Albert Ammons is featured on six piano solos from two sessions in 1939, leading a quartet in 1946, and jamming with his sextet during 1947-48 on this LP sampler. His boogie-woogie music is consistently exciting in all the formats even if one regrets that these performances have been reissued in a somewhat hodge-podge fashion; the selections are drawn from the catalogs of Blue Note, Solo Art and Mercury. Highlights include "Boogie Woogie Stomp," "Boogie Woogie at the Civic Opera," "Baltimore Breakdown," and "Swanee River Boogie." — *Scott Yanow*

1939-1946 / Apr. 8, 1939-Apr. 2, 1946 / Classics ◆◆◆◆

Kip Anderson

b. 193?, Anderson, SC
Vocals / R&B, Modern Electric Blues, Soul Blues, Northern Soul
Without benefit of anything resembling a chart hit, Kip Anderson has amassed an impressive Southern soul legacy over the last three-plus decades. And how many other R&B artists were named after Rudyard Kipling, anyway?

Anderson still lives in the same rural region of South Carolina where he grew up. The singer learned his way around his folks' upright piano as a youth, composing his first tune in 1959. Anderson later bounced from label to label, cutting "I Will Cry" for producer Bobby Robinson in 1963; "That's When the Crying Begins" for ABC-Paramount the following year, and several gems for Checker in 1965-66 (including one of his best-known numbers, "A Knife and a Fork," in Muscle Shoals under the supervision of Rick Hall and Gene "Daddy G" Barge). By 1969, Anderson was inked to Nashville-based Excello, where he waxed the impassioned deep soul gem "I Went Off and Cried."

Anderson's hearty vocal talents have popped up most recently on Ichiban Records. He's cut two albums for the Atlanta firm — *A Dog Don't Wear No Shoes* and *A Knife and a Fork* — and contributed the jolliest track of all, "Gonna Have a Merry Christmas," to the label's 1994 anthology *Ichiban Blues at Christmas Volume Three*. — *Bill Dahl*

● **A Dog Don't Wear No Shoes** / 1992 / Ichiban ◆◆◆◆
A Dog Don't Wear No Shoes is an energetic latter-day record from Kip Anderson that proves that the vocalist has lost very little of his power or charisma over the years. All of the music is in the deep soul tradition and he doesn't alter the formula much at all, but with a vocalist as gritty and impassioned as Anderson, that doesn't matter. — *Thom Owens*

A Knife & a Fork / 1993 / Ichiban ◆◆◆
A Knife & a Fork is nearly a carbon copy of its predecessor, *A Dog Don't Wear No Shoes*, but that's not necessarily a bad thing. Though the material is slightly weaker than the previous album, Kip Anderson makes the weakest songs somewhat convincing with his wonderful voice. — *Thom Owens*

Little Willie Anderson

b. May 21, 1920, West Memphis, AR, **d.** Jun. 20, 1991, Chicago, IL
Vocals, Harmonica / Electric Harmonica Blues, Chicago Blues
Some folks called Chicago harpist Little Willie Anderson "Little Walter Jr.," so faithfully did Anderson's style follow that of the legendary harp wizard. But Anderson was already quite familiar with the rudiments of the harmonica before he ever hit the Windy City, having heard Sonny Boy Williamson, Robert Nighthawk, and Robert Jr. Lockwood around West Memphis.

Anderson came to Chicago in 1939, eventually turning pro as a sideman with Johnny Young. Anderson served as Walter's valet, chauffeur, and pal during the latter's heyday, but his slavish imitations probably doomed any recording possibilities for Anderson — until 1979, that is, when Blues on Blues label boss Bob Corritore escorted him into a Chicago studio and emerged with what amounts to Anderson's entire recorded legacy. — *Bill Dahl*

● **Swinging the Blues** / Jul. 1979 / Earwig ◆◆◆◆
Blues on Blues has been defunct for quite some time, but Earwig recently restored Anderson's only album to digital print. It's a loose, informal affair, Anderson's raw vocals and swinging harp backed by an all-star crew: guitarists Robert Jr. Lockwood, Sammy Lawhorn, and Jimmie Lee Robinson; bassist Willie Black, and drummer Fred Below. Anderson only revived one Walter

standard, having brought a sheaf of his own intermittently derivative material to the session (although he does take a stab at bluesifying Lester Young's jazz classic "Lester Leaps In"). — *Bill Dahl*

Pink Anderson

b. Feb. 12, 1900, Spartanburg, SC, **d.** Oct. 12, 1974, Spartanburg, SC
Vocals, Guitar / Acoustic Blues, Piedmont Blues, Prewar Country Blues
A good-natured finger-picking guitarist, Anderson played for about 30 years as part of a medicine show. He did make a couple of sides for Columbia in the late '20s with Simmie Dooley, but otherwise didn't record until a 1950 session, the results of which were issued on a Riverside LP that also included tracks by Gary Davis. Anderson went on to make some albums on his own after the blues revival commenced in the early '60s, establishing him as a minor but worthy exponent of the Piedmont school, versed in blues, ragtime, and folk songs. Anderson also became an unusual footnote in rock history when Syd Barrett, a young man in Cambridge, England, combined Pink's first name with the first name of another obscure bluesman (Floyd Council) to name his rock group, Pink Floyd, in the mid-'60s. — *Richie Unterberger*

● **Carolina Blues Man, Vol. 1** / Apr. 12, 1961 / Prestige/Bluesville ✦✦✦✦
Anderson runs through a number of both blues and folk standards on this relaxed and engaging, if somewhat slight, session. The CD reissue adds the bonus track "Try Some of That," previously available on Bluesville's *Bawdy Blues* compilation. — *Richie Unterberger*

Ballad and Folksinger, Vol. 3 / Aug. 14, 1961 / Prestige/Bluesville ✦✦✦✦
As the title implies, this is more weighted toward folk and ballad material, along the lines of "John Henry" and "The Wreck of the Old 97," than straight traditional blues. Whether you prefer this or the *Carolina Blues Man* CD may thus depend on what your favorite sorts of genres are, though to this reviewer the performances on *Ballad & Folksinger* are more interesting and engaging. — *Richie Unterberger*

Gospel, Blues & Street Songs / 196 / Original Blues Classics ✦✦✦

The Animals

f. 1964, Newcastle, England, **db.** 1968
Group / British Invasion, Psychedelic, Rock 'n' Roll, British Blues, Electric British Blues
One of the most important bands originating from England's R&B scene during the early '60s, the Animals were second only to the Rolling Stones in influence among R&B-based bands in the first wave of the British Invasion. The Animals had their origins in a Newcastle-based group called the Kansas City Five, whose membership included pianist Alan Price, drummer John Steel, and vocalist Eric Burdon. Price exited to join the Kontours in 1962, while Burdon went off to London. The Kontours, whose membership included Bryan "Chas" Chandler, eventually were transmuted into the Alan Price R&B Combo, with John Steel joining on drums. Burdon's return to Newcastle in early 1963 heralded his return to the lineup. The final member of the combo, guitarist Hilton Valentine, joined just in time for the recording of a self-produced EP under the band's new name, the Animals. That record alerted Graham Bond to the Animals; he was likely responsible for pointing impresario Giorgio Gomelsky to the group.

Gomelsky booked the band into his Crawdaddy Club in London, and they were subsequently signed by Mickie Most, an independent producer who secured a contract with EMI's Columbia imprint. A studio session in February 1964 yielded their Columbia debut single, "Baby Let Me Take You Home" (adapted from "Baby Let Me Follow You Down"), which rose to number 21 on the British charts. For years it has been rumored incorrectly that the Animals got their next single, "House of the Rising Sun," from Bob Dylan's first album, but more recently it has been revealed that, like "Baby Let Me Take You Home," the song came to them courtesy of Josh White. In any event, the song—given a new guitar riff by Valentine and a soulful organ accompaniment devised by Price—shot to the top of the UK and US charts early that summer. This success led to a follow-up session that summer, yielding their first long-playing record, *The Animals*. Their third single, "I'm Crying," rose to number eight on the British charts. The group compiled an enviable record of Top Ten successes, including "Don't Let Me Be Misunderstood" and "We've Gotta Get Out of This Place," along with a second album, *Animal Tracks*.

In May of 1965, immediately after recording "We've Gotta Get Out of This

Place," Alan Price left the band, citing fear of flying as the reason; subsequent biographies of the band have indicated that the reasons were less psychological. When "House of the Rising Sun" was recorded, using what was essentially a group arrangement, the management persuaded the band to put one person's name down as arranger. Price came up the lucky one, supposedly with the intention that the money from the arranger credit would be divided later on. The money was never divided, however, and as soon as it began rolling in, Price suddenly developed his fear of flying and exited the band. Others cite the increasing contentiousness between Burdon and Price over leadership of the group as the latter's reason for leaving. In any case, a replacement was recruited in the person of Dave Rowberry.

In the meantime, the group was growing increasingly unhappy with the material they were being given to record by manager Mickie Most. Not only were the majority of these songs much too commercial for their taste, but they represented a false image of the band, even if many were successful. "It's My Life," a number seven British hit and a similar smash in America, caused the Animals to terminate their association with Most and with EMI Records. They moved over to Decca/London Records and came up with a more forceful, powerful sound on their first album for the new label, *Animalisms*. The lineup shifts continued, however—Steel exited in 1966, after recording *Animalisms*, and was replaced by Barry Jenkins, formerly of the Nashville Teens. Chandler left in mid-1966 after recording "Don't Bring Me Down" and Valentine remained until the end of 1966, but essentially "Don't Bring Me Down" marked the end of the original Animals.

Burdon reformed the group under the aegis of Eric Burdon and the New Animals, with Jenkins on drums, John Weider on guitar and violin, Danny McCulloch on bass, and Vic Briggs on guitar. He remained officially a solo act for a time, releasing a collection of material called *Eric Is Here* in 1967. As soon as the contract with English Decca was up, Burdon signed with MGM directly for worldwide distribution, and the new lineup made their debut in mid-1967. Eric Burdon and the New Animals embraced psychedelia to the hilt amid the full bloom of the Summer of Love. By the end of 1968, Briggs and McCulloch were gone, to be replaced by Burdon's old friend, keyboard player/vocalist Zoot Money, and his longtime stablemate, guitarist Andy Summers, while Weider switched to bass. Finally, in 1969, Burdon pulled the plug on what was left of the Animals. He hooked up with a Los Angeles-based group called War, and started a subsequent solo career that continues to this day.

The original Animals reunited in 1976 for a superb album called *Before We Were So Rudely Interrupted*, which picked up right where *Animalisms* had left off a decade earlier and which was well received critically but failed to capture the public's attention. In 1983, a somewhat longer lasting reunion came about between the original members, augmented with the presence of Zoot Money on keyboards. The resulting album, *Ark*, consisting of entirely new material, was well received by critics and charted surprisingly high, and a world tour followed. By the end of the year and the heavy touring schedule, however, it was clear that this reunion was not going to be a lasting event. The quintet split up again, having finally let the other shoe drop on their careers and history, and walked away with some financial rewards, along with memories of two generations of rock fans cheering their every note. — *Bruce Eder*

The Animals [US] / 1964 / MGM ✦✦✦
Early blues-oriented material rounded out by a few more commercial tracks—this album is stronger than the British version, as it includes several more tracks off of their singles. — *Bruce Eder*

The Animals [UK] / 1964 / Columbia ✦✦
The group's British debut long-player in England is a somewhat dry collection of blues and R&B covers, showing the group still trying to gain some confidence within the studio. Note: All material from this album appears on EMI's *Complete Animals* double-CD set. — *Bruce Eder*

The Animals on Tour / 1965 / MGM ✦✦
Lest anyone think this is a live album, don't be fooled by the title—MGM Records used the "On Tour" moniker for an album by Herman's Hermits as well, but that wasn't a live one either. The tracks are good ones, though, showing a lot more flash than their first long-player. — *Bruce Eder*

In the Beginning / 1965 / Sundazed ✦✦✦
Recorded in December of 1963 at a live concert, this CD captures The Ani-

mals at their rawest and most animated on record, ripping ferociously through a bunch of standards (by Chuck Berry, James B. Odom et al.), playing the crowd and making snide comments about their London rivals The Rolling Stones, all with Sonny Boy Williamson II hanging somewhere around the stage. Sundazed has actually found the original master to this oft-bootlegged piece of rock/blues history. —*Bruce Eder*

Animal Tracks [UK] / 1965 / Columbia ++++
The band's second British album displays far more energy and dexterity than its predecessor. Originals such as "For Miss Caulker" are paired up with excellent covers like "Bright Lights Big City," "I Ain't Got You," and "Roadrunner," along with Ray Charles' "Hallelujah I Love Her So" and "I Believe to My Soul." Note: All tracks appearing on this album are available on EMI's *Complete Animals* double CD. —*Bruce Eder*

Animalization / 1966 / Polygram ++++
The best of the group's early albums, mostly sophisticated blues-based rock which, for the first time on a long-player, managed to capture the spontaneity of their live sound while also allowing them a chance to really stretch out in the studio. Around this time in the band's history, however, the albums get confusing: *Animalization*, released in September of 1966 by MGM in America, was simply the British *Animalisms* with three tracks missing, and four other songs ("Don't Bring Me Down," "Cheating," "Inside Looking Out," and "See See Rider") added. But MGM's *Animalism*, released two months later, consisted of tracks recorded in America during the original group's final US tour that never saw the light of day in England. —*Bruce Eder*

Animalism [US] / 1966 / Decca +++
The last gasp of the original Animals, albeit with Barry Jenkins on the drums in place of John Steel and Dave Rowberry on the ivories in lieu of Alan Price. A superb collection of rock numbers, as advanced from the band's early classics as the Stones' *Aftermath* repertory was from "It's All Over Now." Loud, intense, well-focused, hard-rocking blues. —*Bruce Eder*

Animalisms / 1966 / Decca ++++
Very similar in lineup to the American *Animalization*, this is probably the group's best noncompilation album, with a finely developed R&B sound throughout and excellent playing, all yielding an incomparable collection of good, solid, bluesy, ballsy rock numbers, highlighted by "Gin House Blues" and "Don't Bring Me Down." —*Bruce Eder*

Winds of Change / 1967 / One Way +++
This album marked the debut of Eric Burdon and the New Animals, a decidedly looser, more psychedelic outfit than any the blues-singing idol had previously been associated with. "San Franciscan Nights," "Paint It Black," and "Yes I'm Experienced" (Burdon's answer to Jimi Hendrix's "Are You Experienced?") were moody and pulsating, and also fiercely experimental—one can get a glimpse of this band at work in the D.A. Pennebaker movie *Monterey Pop*, doing "Paint It Black" on stage. It was a logical extension of the later work of the original Animals into the Summer of Love. —*Bruce Eder*

Eric Is Here / 1967 / One Way ++
During the months after Eric Burdon and the remaining members of the original Animals split, the singer cut this album backed by an orchestra and doing songs by Randy Newman, Barry Mann and Cynthia Weil, and other pop-music fixtures—quite a turnaround for the blues purist Burdon, and also very effective as mainstream pop music, including the US hit "Help Me Girl." To add to the general confusion surrounding this material, some of it seems to have been recorded with the original Animals, or at sessions conducted while they were still together. Several songs, including "Help Me Girl," show up on Sequel Records' *Inside Looking Out*. —*Bruce Eder*

Every One of Us / 1968 / One Way ++
A rather spare and disappointing album, recorded amid the splintering of the original New Animals. Keyboard player Zoot Money arrived to fill up the lineup even as guitarist Vic Briggs and bassist Danny McCullough prepared to leave. —*Bruce Eder*

The Twain Shall Meet / 1968 / One Way +++
The Twain Shall Meet was a more lopsidedly experimental album—even its major hit, "Sky Pilot," a venture into anti-war politicking on an epic level, marked a new level of sophistication for the band, which played hard and became well-known for their ability to jam on stage. —*Bruce Eder*

Love Is / 1968 / One Way ++
One can get an idea of the confusion that fans must have felt by virtue of the fact that *Love Is* was the third album by Eric Burdon and the Animals to be issued in 1968, even with a major lineup change taking place. Future Police-man Andy Somers (aka Summers) arrived on guitar to join his longtime stablemate Zoot Money, while John Weider moved over to bass. This album marked the end of The Animals as a continuously operating music unit, and betrays an understandable lack of direction and enthusiasm. —*Bruce Eder*

The Best of Eric Burdon & the Animals, Vol. 2 / 1969 / MGM +++
Actually the third Animals hits LP to be released by MGM in the 1960s, this collection is the work of lead singer Eric Burdon with the backup group he assembled upon the breakup of the original Animals. The recordings all come from 1967 and 1968, Burdon's psychedelicized period, when he was penning praises of the Monterey Pop Festival ("Monterey," No.15) and San Francisco ("San Franciscan Nights," No.9). The only other Top 40 hit on the album was the antiwar epic "Sky Pilot" (No.15), in its full seven-and-a-half-minute glory. Burdon had come a long way from his Manchester roots and his blues records, and this was the last album in his second phase; in fact, the New Animals had split by the time it was released. — *William Ruhlmann*

Before We Were So Rudely Interrupted / 1976 / Jet +++
The title says it all—returning to the studio a decade after their break-up, the original group lineup with Alan Price picks up right where *Animalization* and *Animalism* left off, with superb musicianship and a good, if unspectacular, selection of material. —*Bruce Eder*

Ark / 1983 / IRS ++
The group's formal reunion, complete with a new repertory and a well-financed recording. The album has its dark, moody moments, and sometimes bogs down in the sheer heaviness of the sound and sensibilities, but where Burdon is on target as a singer, which is 70% of the time, the group sounds amazingly good. —*Bruce Eder*

Rip It to Shreds: Their Greatest Hits Live / 1984 / IRS ++
A document of the group's 1983 reunion tour. They played better shows along this tour than the one they actually taped—some of the balances (especially on the guitars) are a little off, and the band's sound and overall performance are somewhat creaky and anemic at times, but it is a fair representation of a largely successful attempt at recapturing past glories. —*Bruce Eder*

★ **The Best of the Animals [Abkco]** / 1988 / ABKCO +++++
The original Animals' American hits, including "House of the Rising Sun," "Don't Let Me Be Misunderstood," "It's My Life," and "We Gotta Get Out of This Place," in a compilation originally released in 1965. The lineup of songs is strong, but the sound is indifferent—the British *Complete Animals* covers the same territory and a lot more to much greater effect, at only twice the cost with three times the music and infinitely superior sound and notes. —*Bruce Eder*

Inside Looking Out: The 1965-1966 Sessions / 1990 / Sequel ++++
Together with the double-CD *The Complete Animals, Inside Looking Out* forms a complete retrospective of the great British Invasion band. This 22-song compilation features all of the essential recordings cut by the group in 1965 and 1966 after they broke with their original producer Mickie Most, and before Eric Burdon dissolved the core of the original lineup to pursue solo stardom with an Animals group featuring entirely different musicians. These tracks were perhaps more soul-oriented than their previous recordings, but the group still burns on the hits "Inside Looking Out" and "Don't Bring Me Down." Despite the absence of original keyboardist Alan Price, the group continued to showcase Burdon's passionate vocals and burning, vibrant organ (by Price's replacement Dave Rowberry) on both renowned and obscure R&B tunes, with an occasional original thrown in. Besides the entirety of their final British LP *Animalisms* (from 1966) and the above-mentioned singles, the CD includes the hits "Help Me Girl" and "See See Rider" (credited to "Eric Burdon and the Animals," these were possibly Burdon solo records). The four tracks from their first release, an independently released 1963 EP featuring primitive R&B standards, are small but noteworthy bonus cuts that close this collection. —*Richie Unterberger*

Roadrunners! / 1990 / Raven +++
A 19-track collection of otherwise unavailable live performances from 1966-1968, taken from shows in Melbourne, Stockholm, London, and the 1967

Monterey Pop Festival, as well as radio and television broadcasts. Most of this dates from the psychedelic version of the band, which will disappoint those who are primarily interested in the group's rock/R&B prime. It's quite a good relic, though, with rough and ready execution by both Burdon and the band, and some unusual R&B and psychedelic material alongside the versions of hits like "Inside Looking Out," "Monterey," "San Franciscan Nights," and "When I Was Young." Sound ranges from fair to very good. —*Richie Unterberger*

★ **The Complete Animals** / Jul. 1990 / EMI ✦✦✦✦✦
The title is a bit of a misnomer; this double CD does include the complete sessions that the Animals recorded with producer Mickie Most in 1964 and 1965. The 40 songs capture the band at their peak, including most of their best and biggest hits: "House of the Rising Sun," "Don't Let Me Be Misunderstood," "Bring It on Home to Me," "We Gotta Get Out of This Place," "I'm Crying," "It's My Life," and "Boom Boom." Most of the rest of the tunes don't match the excellence of these smashes, though they're solid. The great majority of them are covers of vintage R&B/rock tunes by Chuck Berry, Fats Domino, and the like, which aren't quite as durable as reinterpretations from the same era by the Stones and Yardbirds. When they hit the mark, though, the Animals produced some great album tracks that have been mostly forgotten by time, such as "I'm Mad Again" (originally by John Lee Hooker), "Worried Life Blues," and "Bury My Body." After leaving Most, the group would maintain their peak for another year or so (this period is represented on the fine import collection *Inside Looking Out*) despite the departure of one of rock's all-time finest organists, Alan Price. This compilation has everything that Price recorded with the group, including four previously unreleased cuts and the non-LP Eric Burdon original on the B-side of "It's My Life," "I'm Gonna Change the World." —*Richie Unterberger*

Fernest Arceneaux

b. Aug. 27, 1940, Lafayette, LA
Accordion / Zydeco
A torch-bearer for the classic zydeco traditions personified by Clifton Chenier, Fernest Arceneaux earned the title "The New Prince of Accordion" for his virtuosic prowess. Born August 27, 1940 to a large sharecropping family based in Lafayette, Louisiana, he first picked up his brother-in-law's accordion while working the fields as a child, and learned his craft by copying his father, himself a rural musician whom the youngster often backed at local house parties. However, by the 1960s, Arceneaux had abandoned his zydeco roots to play guitar in a rock 'n' roll band, a group which originally featured two drummers and created such a mighty racket that they were dubbed Fernest and the Thunders. Only during the late 1970s—and only at the behest of his hero Chenier himself—did Arceneaux return to the accordion, and soon the Thunders made the move from rock to zydeco. Discovered in 1978 by Belgian blues aficionado Robert Sacre, the group—also featuring singer/bassist Victor Walker, guitarist Chester Chevalier and drummer Clarence "Jockey" Etienne—mounted the first of many European tours, and within months they recorded their debut LP *Fernest and the Thunders;* albums like 1979's *Rockin' Pneumonia* and 1981 *Zydeco Stomp!* followed, but shortly after recording the latter, Walker was killed in a barroom brawl. Arceneaux himself then assumed vocal duties, although as a result of asthma his presence failed to pack the same punch; still, the Thunders remained a popular live attraction, especially on the Gulf Coast crawfish circuit, and continued issuing LPs including 1985's *Zydeco Thunder,* 1987's *Gumbo Special* and 1994's *Zydeco Blues Party.* —*Jason Ankeny*

● **Zydeco Stomp!** / 1981 / JSP ✦✦✦✦
Working with his longtime backing band the Thunders, Fernest Arceneaux turns in a wonderful zydeco blues collection with *Zydeco Stomp.* Arceneaux and the Thunders cut the album in London in 1981, playing a set of covers and originals that don't stray far from the zydeco-blues formula. That's hardly a bad thing, however, since the group packs musical muscle, and bassist Victor Walker is a powerful vocalist— he's equally powerful on uptempo rockers and slow blues. Arceneaux isn't as strong vocally, but he's still enjoyable. More importantly, he packs quite a punch on the accordion, driving *Zydeco Stomp* into the realm of ecstatic party music with his propulsive style. —*Thom Owens*

Alphonse "Bois Sec" Ardoin

b. Nov. 16, 1916, Louisiana
Accordion / Creole, Zydeco
The son of a sharecropper, Alphonse "Bois-Sec" Ardoin is one of Cajun music's influential players. His appearance at the Newport Folk Festival in 1966 helped to spread Cajun and Creole music past southwest Louisiana while his 1971 album, *La Musique Creole,* recorded with five of his sons, the Ardoin Brothers, and blues-tinged Cajun fiddler Canray Fontenot, was a major influence on such modern Cajun bands as Beausoleil and File.

Ardoin was given his nickname, "Bois-Sec," which translates as "dry wood," for his youthful knack of seeking shelter from the rain under an old dry wood tree. Although neither of his parents were musicians, they exposed him to Cajun music at house parties that featured his uncle, Amadé Ardoin, who was the first Cajun musician to be recorded. Raised by his mother from the age of four after the death of his father, Ardoin developed an early passion for music. At the age of seven, he was borrowing his brother Houston's accordion and teaching himself to play. By his thirteenth birthday, he was playing the squeeze box at local dances and sitting in on triangle with his uncle's band at a music club in Basile. In order to supplement his work as a musician, Ardoin worked on a small farm, planting corn and raising chickens, pigs, and cows. In 1934, he married Marceline Victorian and started a family that grew to include fourteen children, including the five sons who performed zydeco as the Ardoin Brothers in the late 1960s.

Although Ardoin and Fontenot played together as youngsters, they didn't record their first album until the 1970s. They joined together in 1948 to perform as the Duralde Ramblers. In 1986, they received a National Heritage Fellowship from the National Endowment for the Arts. They continued to collaborate until Fontenot's death in July 1995. —*Craig Harris*

★ **La Musique Creole** / 1974 / Arhoolie ✦✦✦✦✦
The superb *La Musique Creole* is most notable for its inclusion of the rare 1966 Alphonse "Bois Sec" Ardoin and Canray Fontenot LP *Les Blues du Bayou,* the record the duo cut in the wake of their triumphant appearance at that year's Newport Folk Festival. Long renowned among the finest Creole records ever made, its 16 tracks capture Ardoin and Fontenot at the peak of their powers—their interplay on cuts like "Les Blues du Voyager," "Duralde Ramble," and the bluesy instrumental "La Danse de la Misere" borders on the telepathic. The inclusion of eight tracks from a 1971 Arhoolie LP also titled *La Musique Creole,* as well the Ardoin Family Orchestra's previously unreleased "Ardoin Two-Step," is just the icing on the cake—a must for all Creole fans. —*Jason Ankeny*

Amadé Ardoin

b. 1896, L'Anse Rougeau, LA, d. Nov. 4, 1941, Alexandria, LA
Vocals, Accordion / Zydeco, Creole
Amadé Ardoin is to zydeco music as Robert Johnson is to the blues and Buddy Bolden is to jazz. Like Johnson and Bolden, Ardoin not only died under still mysterious conditions, but also shares the potency of their musical influence, having laid the foundation for southwest Louisiana's zydeco music.

The first Creole to be recorded, Ardoin is best remembered for his resonating, high-pitched vocals and sizzling-hot accordion playing. Although he only recorded 30 tunes, his compositions have been included in the repertoire of Cajun and zydeco bands ranging from Austin Pitre and Dewey Balfa to Beausoleil and C.J. Chenier. Iry LeJeune helped to launch a revival in Cajun music in the 1950s, when he recorded twelve of Ardoin's tunes.

The great-grandson of a slave, Ardoin moved, as a child, with his family to work on the Rougeau farm in L'Anse des Rougeau near Basile. While there, he frequented the homes of his friends Adam Fontenot, who played accordion and was later the father of fiddler Canray Fontenot, and Alphonse LaFleur, who played fiddle. Together with LaFleur or Douglas Bellard, a black fiddler from Bellaire Cove, Ardoin became a frequent performer at dances, playing mostly for white audiences who paid him $2.50 per night.

In his teens Ardoin moved frequently, working for room and board. For a while, he worked as a sharecropper on Oscar Comeaux's farm near Chataignier. While there, he met Dennis McGee, a white fiddler from Eunice. One of the first biracial Cajun duos, Ardoin and McGee began to play at house parties, often attended by Ardoin's cousin, Bois-Sec Ardoin. When Comeaux sold the farm, the two musicians moved to Eunice, where they worked at Celestin

Marcantel's farm. A lover of music, Marcantel often transported Ardoin and McGee to performances in his horse-drawn buggy.

Ardoin and McGee's recording debut came on December 9, 1929, when they cut seven tunes at a studio in New Orleans. They returned to the studio to record six songs on November 20 and 21, 1930. On August 8, 1934, they recorded six tunes at the Texas Hotel in San Antonio. Their fourth and final recording session, recorded at a New York studio on December 22, 1934, produced twelve new tunes. Their recordings were issued on the Brunswick, Vocalion, Decca, Melotone, and Bluebird labels.

Ardoin often performed with fiddler Sady Courville of Eunice. In the late 1930s, they played every Saturday night at Abe's Palace in Eunice. Courville's mother, however, prevented them from recording together.

Ardoin's death remains shrouded in mystery. One report has him being brutally beaten after wiping his brow with a handkerchief handed to him by the daughter of a white farm owner. According to McGee, Ardoin was poisoned by a jealous fiddler. More recent studies have concluded that Ardoin died of venereal disease at the Pineville Mental Institution. — *Craig Harris*

★ **Louisiana Cajun Music, Vol. 6: Amade Ardoin—His Original Recordings** / Mar. 1983 / Old Timey ✦✦✦✦

Amadé Ardoin's *His Original Recordings, 1928-1938* is divided between seven songs Ardoin recorded with Dennis McGee and seven solo tracks. The duets with McGee are among the most legendary Cajun recordings; McGee's fiddle perfectly meshes with Ardoin's accordion and raw, bluesy voice. These are the recordings that laid the foundation on contemporary Cajun and Zydeco. Ardoin's solo recordings are nearly as influential and exciting, capturing him alone with his accordion. While these aren't quite as kinetic as the duets, they are nevertheless enjoyable. — *Thom Owens*

☆ **The Roots of Zydeco** / 1995 / Arhoolie ✦✦✦✦✦

Amadé Ardoin was arguably the founder of zydeco music, incorporating blues into French folk. The songs on this collection were recorded in 1930 and 1934. Though the sound might be a bit harsh for some—these were taken from 78s, after all—these are important recordings and they continue to sound fresh and vital. — *Thom Owens*

First Black Cajun Recording Artist / Arhoolie ✦✦✦

Violinist Dennis McGee is featured on this 14-track album, which contains recordings from 1929, 1930, and 1934. — *AMG*

Chris Ardoin

b. 1981, Louisiana
Group / Zydeco

A third generation product of the southwestern Louisiana region's most famed musical dynasty, nouveau zydeco accordionist Chris Ardoin followed in the traditions established by his father, French Zydeco Band frontman Lawrence "Black" Ardoin; his grandfather, Cajun "la la" legend Alphonse "Bois Sec" Ardoin; and his distant cousin, Creole virtuoso Amadé Ardoin. Born in 1981, Chris made his public debut at the age of four, playing with his father at a Texas gumbo cook-off; just five years later, he backed his grandfather during an appearance at Carnegie Hall. The child prodigy also soon joined his father's new band Lagniappe as a full-time member, but like Lawrence before him, Ardoin eventually rejected the confines of traditional zydeco to pursue his own muse; with his older brother Sean, cousin Alphonse, and family friend Peter Jacobs, he formed the band Double Clutchin', the name representative of the kind of repeated bass drum kicks which define the funky "new zydeco" sound. Double Clutchin' debuted with 1994's *That's Da Lick*, recorded when bandleader Ardoin was just 13; *Lick It Up!* followed a year later, and in 1997 the group signed to Rounder for *Gon'be Jus'fine*. — *Jason Ankeny*

That's Da Lick / 1994 / Maison de Soul ✦✦✦

Lick It Up! / 1995 / Maison de Soul ✦✦✦

● **Gon'be Jus'fine** / Jul. 8, 1997 / Rounder ✦✦✦✦

Although only a mere 15 years old at the time of this 1997 release, Chris Ardoin was already somewhat of a veteran of zydeco music with two previous albums for local Louisiana labels to his credit. He's also a member of one of zydeco's most established musical families: he's the grandnephew of Amadé Ardoin—the first Cajun or Creole musician to record in the 1920s—and the grandson of Alphonse "Bois Sec" Ardoin. With his brother Sean on

drums and vocals and Gabriel "Pandy" Perrodin, Jr. on guitar (son of bayou guitarist Gabriel "Fats" Perrodin, aka Guitar Gable, who played the buzzing riff on Slim Harpo's "I'm a King Bee"), Tammy Ledet on rubboard and Derek "Dee" Greenwood on bass, they forge a new chapter in zydeco with a sound that mines new beats and grooves from reggae to hip-hop while keeping all firmly grounded in their Creole roots. The Ardoin brothers' harmony vocals add a fresh twist to the sound as well, sounding especially fine on the title track, "I Don't Want What I Can't Keep," and the blues-rocker "I Believe In You." There are traditional numbers here, including the frantic workout of "Ardoin Two Step" (a version of the family's "Amede Two Step") and the old-time waltz "Dimanche apres midi (Sunday Afternoon Waltz)," which Sean sings in the original French. But the true highlights are the more forward-looking pieces, like the college chant stomp of "We Are the Boys" (which appears in a special "Bad Boys Dance Mix" version at the end as a bonus track), "Lake Charles Connection" (sporting a wild guitar solo from Perrodin), and "When I'm Dead and Gone," perhaps zydeco's first song about the apocalypse. This is dance music of the highest order, wedding modern funk grooves to the basic fun core of the music's roots. If the Ardoin brothers and their band are truly the future of zydeco, then the future is in very good hands and the dance floor was never fuller. — *Cub Koda*

Lawrence "Black" Ardoin

b. 1946, Duralde, Louisiana
Drums / Zydeco

The son of Creole accordion legend Alphonse "Bois Sec" Ardoin, Lawrence "Black" Ardoin not only carried on the family's musical traditions, but he later passed on the torch to his own son Chris, one of the most acclaimed proponents of the nouvelle zydeco sound. Born in Duralde, Louisiana in 1946, Ardoin was the second of Bois Sec's sons, joining his father and siblings Morris and Gustave in the Ardoin Brothers Band; originally a drummer, he took over accordion duties when Gustave was killed in a 1974 auto accident, and upon his father's mid-1970s retirement assumed full leadership of the group. However, over time the confines of traditional Creole music stifled Ardoin, and in the early 1980s he formed a new combo, the French Zydeco Band, which also allowed him to pursue his interests in Cajun and swamp-pop sounds. In 1984, the group debuted with the LP *Lawrence "Black" Ardoin and His French Zydeco Band;* a long recording hiatus preceded the release of 1992's follow-up, *Hot and Spicy Zydeco.* Following its release, Ardoin formed a new group, Lagniappe, which included his son Chris on accordion; as the youngster continued his creative evolution, he began leading his own unit, Double Clutchin', which Lawrence also managed. — *Jason Ankeny*

● **Lawrence "Black" Ardoin & His French Band** / 1984 / Arhoolie ✦✦✦✦

Hot & Spicy Zydeco / 1992 / La Louisianne ✦✦✦✦

Although it doesn't match the heights of Lawrence "Black" Ardoin's 1984 album for Arhoolie, *Hot & Spicy Zydeco* nevertheless cooks, boasting some hot zydeco jams that carry the album through some uneven material. — *Leo Stanley*

James Armstrong

b. Apr. 22, 1957, Los Angeles, CA
Vocals / Modern Electric Blues

Guitarist, singer and songwriter James Armstrong has a bright future in blues music. However, this is in spite of the fact that as of summer 1997, he is still recovering from a brutal stabbing attack by an unknown assailant who broke into his apartment in Sunnyvale, California.

Armstrong's debut album for Hightone Records, *Sleeping with a Stranger,* got him noticed by clubs and festivals around the US and Europe. He was supposed to tour in support of his album in the spring and summer of 1997, but it was canceled owing to his injuries in the brutal attack. (The assailant was arrested.)

Armstrong, the son of a guitarist, began playing guitar at age nine and joined his first band at 13. He began writing and performing his own songs shortly after that. He spent his early childhood in the L.A. area. Jimi Hendrix changed his life, and he credits the *Are You Experienced?* album with having a particularly big impact on his guitar playing. From the time of his first band at 13, Armstrong always insisted he and his bandmates do no covers, only their own tunes; however, later on, his band would work a few Hendrix covers into their sets. Armstrong counts among his other influences more conventional bluesmen like Albert and Freddie King, as well as B.B. King.

Over the years in the Los Angeles area, before he moved to northern California, Armstrong backed up the likes of Big Joe Turner, Sam Taylor, Albert Collins and Rickie Lee Jones. —*Richard Skelly*

● **Sleeping with a Stranger** / Oct. 17, 1995 / Hightone ✦✦✦✦
One listen to his *Sleeping With a Stranger* and one might be inclined to compare James Armstrong with Robert Cray, but the similarities end after the obvious comparison: young, talented black songwriters who believe in incorporating elements of soul and R&B into their blues playing. The truth is, Armstrong is a supremely talented songwriter, a guitarist who has no need to be overly flashy, and a more than adequate singer. As *Sleeping with a Stranger* shows, Armstrong has a bright future, and he'll continue to broaden the parameters of modern blues for some time to come. —*Richard Skelly*

Billy Boy Arnold

b. Sep. 16, 1935, Chicago, IL
Vocals, Harmonica / Electric Chicago Blues, Modern Electric Blues, Chicago Blues, Electric Harmonica Blues, Harmonica Blues
Talk about a comeback! After too many years away from the studio, Chicago harpist Billy Boy Arnold has returned to action in a big way with two fine albums for Alligator: 1993's *Back Where I Belong* and 1995's *Eldorado Cadillac*. Retaining his youthful demeanor despite more than four decades of blues experience, Arnold's wailing harp and sturdy vocals remain in top-flight shape following the lengthy recording layoff.

Born in Chicago rather than Mississippi (as many of his musical forefathers were), young Billy Boy gravitated right to the source in 1948. He summoned up the courage to knock on the front door of his idol, harmonica great John Lee "Sonny Boy" Williamson, who resided nearby. Sonny Boy kindly gave the lad a couple of harp lessons, but their relationship was quickly severed when Williamson was tragically murdered. Still in his teens, Arnold cut his debut 78 for the extremely obscure Cool logo in 1952. "Hello Stranger" went nowhere but gave him his nickname when its label unexpectedly read "Billy Boy Arnold."

Arnold made an auspicious connection when he joined forces with Bo Diddley and played on the shave-and-a-haircut-beat specialist's two-sided 1955 debut smash "Bo Diddley"/"I'm a Man" for Checker. That led, in a roundabout way, to Billy Boy's signing with rival Vee-Jay Records (the harpist mistakenly believed Leonard Chess didn't like him). Arnold's "I Wish You Would," utilizing that familiar Bo Diddley beat, sold well and inspired a later famous cover by the Yardbirds. That renowned British blues-rock group also took a liking to another Arnold classic on Vee-Jay, "I Ain't Got You." Other Vee-Jay standouts by Arnold included "Prisoner's Plea" and "Rockinitis," but by 1958, his tenure at the logo was over.

Other than an excellent Samuel Charters-produced 1963 album for Prestige, *More Blues on the South Side*, Arnold's profile diminished over the years in his hometown (though European audiences enjoyed him regularly). Fortunately, that's changed: *Back Where I Belong* restored this Chicago harp master to prominence, and *Eldorado Cadillac* drove him into the winner's circle a second time. —*Bill Dahl*

Blow the Back off It / 1953-Sep. 1957 / Red Lightnin' ✦✦
Bootleg vinyl collection of the harpist's Vee-Jay stuff suffering from truly rotten sound quality. Its only saving grace is the appearance of Arnold's ultra-rare 1953 debut 78, "Hello Stranger," but its aural reproduction is worst of all (you can barely discern the music from the scratches and noise). —*Bill Dahl*

● **I Wish You Would** / Apr. 1955-Sep. 1957 / Charly ✦✦✦✦
The harpist's indispensable dozen 1955-1957 waxings for Vee-Jay, including the classic "I Wish You Would" and its blues-soaked flip "I Was Fooled" (stinging guitar by Jody Williams), the often-covered (but never bettered, except maybe by Jimmy Reed) "I Ain't Got You," and the vicious "Don't Stay Out All Night" and "You've Got Me Wrong." Also included are a pair of rarities Arnold cut for Chess prior to his exit as Diddley's sideman; "Sweet on You Baby" and "You Got to Love Me" feature big bad Bo on guitar and the ever-dynamic Jerome Green shakin' the maracas. —*Bill Dahl*

Crying and Pleading / Apr. 1955-Sep. 1957 / Charly ✦✦✦✦
This vinyl collection of Arnold's complete Vee-Jay output is mid-'50s Chicago

blues at its best. Includes "I Wish You Would," "I Was Fooled," "Rockinitis," and the original "I Ain't Got You," later covered by The Yardbirds. —*Cub Koda*

More Blues on the South Side / Dec. 30, 1963 / Bellaphon ✦✦✦✦
Over half a decade away from the studio didn't hinder Arnold one bit on this 1963 session. His still-youthful vocals, strong harp, and imaginative songs are very effectively spotlighted, backed by a mean little Chicago combo anchored by guitarist Mighty Joe Young and pianist Lafayette Leake. The CD reissue adds a previously unreleased instrumental, "Playing with the Blues." —*Bill Dahl*

Going to Chicago / Jun. 1966 / Testament ✦✦✦
Uneven but intriguing 1966 collection, most of it previously unreleased. The first half-dozen sides are the best, full of ringing West Side-styled guitar licks by Mighty Joe Young and Jody Williams and Arnold's insinuating vocals (he rocks "Baby Jane" with a Chuck Berry-inspired fury). An odd drumless trio backs Arnold on the next seven selections, which get a little sloppy at times but retain period interest nonetheless. —*Bill Dahl*

King of Chicago Blues, Vol. 3 / 1975 / Vogue ✦✦✦

Sinner's Prayer / 1976 / Red Lightnin' ✦✦✦

Checkin' It Out / 1979 / Red Lightnin' ✦✦

Ten Million Dollars / Dec. 15, 1984 / Evidence ✦✦
Recording opportunities were scarce for Arnold stateside in 1984. But over in France, Black & Blue welcomed the harpist into their studios to cut this set, backed by guitarist Jimmy Johnson's professional outfit. Only a handful of originals here; the set is predominated by hoary standards such as "My Babe," "Just a Little Bit," "Last Night," and "I Done Got Over It" (but at least they're played with a bit more panache than usual). —*Bill Dahl*

Back Where I Belong / 1993 / Alligator ✦✦✦✦
Indeed he is. Recorded in Los Angeles with a crew of young acolytes offering spot-on backing (guitarists Zach Zunis and Rick Holmstrom acquit themselves well), Arnold eases back into harness with a remake of "I Wish You Would" before exposing some fine new originals (the Chuck Berry-styled rocker "Move on Down the Road" is a stomping standout) and an homage to his old mentor Sonny Boy (a romping "Shake the Boogie"). —*Bill Dahl*

Eldorado Cadillac / Nov. 1995 / Alligator ✦✦✦✦
This time around, Arnold recorded in his hometown with another gang of well-seasoned players behind him (guitar duties were ably handled by ex-Muddy Waters bandsman Bob Margolin and the versatile James Wheeler), retaining the same high standards set by his previous offering. Seven impressive new originals are joined by solid covers of Roosevelt Sykes' downbeat "Sunny Road" and Ray Charles' streetwise "It Should Have Been Me." —*Bill Dahl*

Kokomo Arnold (James "Kokomo" Arnold)

b. Feb. 15, 1901, Lovejoys Station, GA, d. Nov. 8, 1968, Chicago, IL
Guitar, Vocals / Acoustic Blues, Acoustic Chicago Blues
A popular recording artist of the '30s, James "Kokomo" Arnold was a left-handed bottleneck guitarist who usually recorded solo, occasionally with piano accompaniment. His first Chicago session (Decca, 1934) produced the widely covered "Milk Cow Blues" and "Old Original Kokomo Blues" (the model for Robert Johnson's "Sweet Home Chicago"), as well as the first appearance on record of the classic "I believe I'll dust my broom" line (in "Sagefield Woman Blues"). Critic Hugues Panassi wrote, "Arnold is one of the greatest blues singers ever recorded." Arnold continued to play for a few years in Chicago after his last session (1938) but later took a job in a steel mill, disillusioned with the music business. Interviewed by two Frenchmen in 1959, Arnold said, "I'm finished with music and that mad way of life." —*Jim O'Neal*

Complete Recorded Works, Vols. 1-4 / May 17, 1930-May 12, 1938 / Document ✦✦✦
The four-volume set *Complete Recorded Works* contains all the material slide guitarist Kokomo Arnold recorded during the '30s. Arnold was one of the most distinctive and influential blues singers of the decade, but his most essential material is compiled on Yazoo's single-disc *Bottleneck Guitar of the '30s*. That leaves this multi-disc set—which is available in four separate volumes—as the province of historians and completists. For those listeners,

Complete Recorded Works is invaluable, featuring a wealth of rare, unreleased material, including several alternate takes. However, casual fans—and listeners that have only a curiosity about solo acoustic blues—will find that Yazoo's compilation is preferable. — *Thom Owens*

King of the Bottleneck Guitar (1934-1937) / 1934-1937 / Black & Blue ◆◆◆◆

Blues Classics by Kokomo Arnold & Peetie Wheatstraw / 1934-1938 / Blues Classics ◆◆◆◆
Eight tracks each by Kokomo Arnold and Peetie Wheatstraw. Includes "Milk Cow Blues." — *Michael Erlewine*

★ **Bottleneck Guitar of the 30's** / 1934-1938 / Yazoo ◆◆◆◆◆
Bottleneck Guitar of the '30s collects all of Kokomo Arnold's classic tracks from the '30s, including the classic "Milk Cow Blues." It's an essential item for a blues library—within these sides lay the groundwork for the Delta and Chicago blues to come, from Robert Johnson to Elmore James. — *Thom Owens*

Asylum Street Spankers

f. 1995, Austin, TX
Group / Americana, Folk-Rock, Acoustic Blues
The Asylum Street Spankers, from Austin, Texas, are a unique band led by blues guitarist and songwriter Guy Forsyth. They're finding a growing cult following for their unique brand of acoustic blues and early jazz. While much of their material is blues from the 1920s and '30s, the band also performs original songs in their live shows and on their debut album for Watermelon Records, *Spanks for the Memories*. The band's live shows are performed without amplifiers or microphones, usually including tunes from Bessie Smith, Robert Johnson and other standard, traditional blues tunes. In addition to Forsyth, who plays harmonicas and guitars and sings, members of the Asylum Street Spankers include guitarist Colonel Josh, banjo and mandolin player Pops Bayless, drummer Jimmie Dean, guitarist and saw player Olivier, kazoo player Mysterious John, vocalist Christina Marrs, and bassist Kevin Smith.

The genesis of the eight-member band occurred in the early 1990s at a hotel outside of Austin. After an all-night acoustic tune swap, the musicians realized they were on to something, getting back to basics and playing acoustic music. After several phone calls and circulated tapes, the band met again for a rehearsal, and the chemistry took over from there.

The band began attracting growing crowds after playing steady Wednesdays at the Electric Lounge, a bar in Austin, and from that following they took the next step and recorded their debut album for a local label, Watermelon Records. While many of the melodies and progressions on *Spanks for the Memories* are old, some of the band's lyrics are straight out of contemporary America. Songs like "Funny Cigarette," "Trade Winds," "Lee Har-

vey," and "Hometown Boy" are funny and entertaining to most audiences. — *Richard Skelly*

● **Live** / Jun. 24, 1997 / Watermelon ◆◆◆◆
Live captures the wackiness and musical acumen of the Asylum Street Spankers equally well. Their humor—which can make the music sound near-parodic—may frustrate some purists, but their talent for folk-blues, string band music and jump blues may win them over yet. There's a bit more energy and flair on *Live* than their studio albums, which helps make it their best record to date. — *Stephen Thomas Erlewine*

Nasty Novelties [EP] / Nov. 4, 1997 / Freedom ◆◆◆

Lynn August

b. Aug. 7, 1948, Lafayette, LA
Accordion, Vocals / Zydeco
One of zydeco's most versatile performers, Lynn August spiked his native southwestern Louisiana sound with elements of pop, gospel and R&B. Born in Lafayette on August 7, 1948, the blind August was encouraged by his mother to pursue a career in music, and he was raised on a steady diet of zydeco, New Orleans rhythm and blues and swamp-pop. After learning to play drums on an old wash basin, at the age of 12 he was recruited to play percussion with the legendary Esquerita, who convinced him to also take up the piano; a few years later, August made the switch to the Hammond B-3 organ as well. During the mid-1960s, he played with a young Stanley "Buckwheat" Dural, later mounting a solo career as well as sitting in with a variety of local swamp-pop combos; he also led a big band, and even directed a church choir. In 1988, August turned to the accordion and began his zydeco career in earnest; forming the Hot August Knights with tenor saxophonist John Hart, he also studied field recordings made in 1934 by archivist Alan Lomax to absorb the original Creole style of "jure" singing into his own contemporary aesthetic. After signing to the Maison de Soul label, August debuted with *It's Party Time*, followed in 1989 by *Zydeco Groove;* a move to Black Top heralded the release of 1992's *Creole Cruiser*, with the acclaimed *Sauce Piquante* appearing a year later. — *Jason Ankeny*

It's Party Time / 1988 / Maison de Soul ◆◆◆

Zydeco Groove / 1989 / Maison de Soul ◆◆◆

● **Creole Cruiser** / Jan. 1992 / Black Top ◆◆◆◆
Creole Cruiser is Lynn August's first effort for Black Top Records, and like his pair of records for Maison de Soul, it's rollicking, energetic zydeco. Backed by a band that features Meters bassist George Porter Jr. and keyboardist Sammy Berfect, August tears through a set of New Orleans standards, augmenting the play list with such fine originals as "'58 Pink Cadillac" and several traditional jures. He and his band really cook up a head of steam during these 16 numbers, making *Creole Cruiser* an excellent party record of neo-traditional New Orleans zydeco. — *Thom Owens*

Sauce Piquante / Jul. 1, 1993 / Black Top ◆◆◆

B

Smoky Babe

b. 1927, Itta Bena, MS, d. 1975
Guitar, Vocals / Acoustic Louisiana Blues
Robert Brown aka Smoky Babe is a shadowy figure from the early days of the '60s folk-blues revival. The scant details of his life read like a prototypical country bluesman's bio; born in Itta Bena, MS, in 1927, raised on a plantation, had a hard life of sharecropping, picked up the guitar along the way, spent several years hoboing throughout the South, moved to the big city, and found life no better there. He apparently only worked sporadically as a semi-pro musician for a spell in New Orleans in the '50s, returning to his adopted home base of Scotlandville to work as a garage mechanic at the time of his discovery. His brief recording career was limited to a pair of album-length releases recorded as "in the field" location sessions in 1960 and 1961 for the Folk Lyric and Bluesville labels. His few recordings display a strong rhythmic sense in his guitar playing with a strong thumping bass line with the occasional foray into slide guitar. His vocals were nothing less than rich, strong and authoritative. After a few years of playing at picnics and local parties for friends around Baton Rouge in the early '60s, he seemingly disappeared, never to be seen or heard from again. His death in 1975 still remains unconfirmed at the time of this writing. — *Cub Koda*

● **Louisiana Country Blues** / 1996 / Arhoolie ◆◆◆◆
A reissue (on compact disc) of a reissue (on Arhoolie) of an album originally released on the Folk Lyric label, this combines two albums of Louisiana country blues material on one CD. Smoky Babe may have been a semi-pro musician, but the feel of the 12 sides suggests that he was full command of his powers when folklorist Dr. Harry Oster hit the "record" button. Combined with another album's worth of material from the equally obscure Herman E. Johnson (who performs four tracks on electric guitar in a most chaotic manner), this is back porch country blues of the highest order. Just because neither is a "famous name," don't let that keep you checking this superlative release out. — *Cub Koda*

Hot Blues / 1997 / Arhoolie ◆◆◆◆

Mildred Bailey (Mildred [Née Rinker] Bailey)

b. 1901, Tekoa, WA, d. Dec. 12, 1951, Pougakeepsie, WA
Vocals / Swing, Standards, Traditional Pop, Classic Female Blues
Although her high-pitched childlike voice (which contrasted with her plump body) takes a bit of getting used to for some, Mildred Bailey was one of the finest jazz singers to emerge during the 1930s. She learned from her predecessors Ethel Waters, Bessie Smith, and Connie Boswell, and developed her own lightly swinging style. After singing locally, Bailey sent a demonstration record to Paul Whiteman in 1929; he immediately added her to his band. During her four years with Whiteman, Bailey mostly sang ballads and became identified with "Rockin' Chair" and "Georgia on My Mind." In 1933 she married Red Norvo and they eventually were known as "Mr. and Mrs. Swing." Mildred Bailey was famous and well-paid throughout the 1930s, appearing regularly on radio and recording some superb small-group jazz dates. She was well-featured with Red Norvo's distinctive big band during 1936-39, a group that often found her vocals enhanced by Eddie Sauter's arrangements. Unfortunately her insecurities about her appearance made her an erratic personality. Bailey's marriage ended in divorce in 1943 although she worked with Norvo on and off in the '40s. After 1945 her health faded and the singer died in 1951 when she was 50. Many of Mildred Bailey's records are currently available and she would probably be shocked to know that she is on a postage stamp! — *Scott Yanow*

Volume One / Oct. 5, 1929-Mar. 2, 1932 / TOM ◆◆◆
The first of two Mildred Bailey CDs from the TOM label contains 21 of the vocalist's first 23 recordings; the two bypassed selections are included on the second volume. The superior swing singer is mostly heard on ballads (some of which are a bit dated) with orchestras led by Eddie Lang ("What Kind O' Man Is You?"), Frankie Trumbauer ("I Like to Do Things for You"), Jimmie Noone, Glen Gray, and Paul Whiteman in addition to her initial sessions as a leader; this release is accurately subtitled "Sweet Beginnings" and the jazz content is generally not all that high. Although there are fairly long liner notes (the same ones are used on both volumes), the personnel for these early recordings are not included. Despite that inexcusable omission, fans of Mildred Bailey should be delighted to have these interesting sides reissued; highlights include "Concentratin' on You," "Home," "All of Me," and her original version of "Georgia on My Mind." — *Scott Yanow*

★ **Her Greatest Performances (1929-1946)** / 1929-1946 / Columbia ◆◆◆◆◆
This three-LP box set (which deserves to be reissued on CD) lives up to its name. Bailey was one of the top singers of the 1930s and this package, which features highlights from her career (mostly dating from 1933-39), shows why. She holds her own with a variety of all-star groups which include such classic players as trumpeters Bunny Berigan, Buck Clayton, Charlie Shavers, and Roy Eldridge (the latter is great on "I'm Nobody's Baby"), trombonist Tommy Dorsey, clarinetist Benny Goodman, altoist Johnny Hodges, tenors Coleman Hawkins and Chu Berry, pianists Teddy Wilson and Mary Lou Williams, and her husband, xylophonist Red Norvo. There are lots of gems on this definitive set. — *Scott Yanow*

The Rockin' Chair Lady / Sep. 15, 1931-Apr. 25, 1950 / Decca ◆◆◆◆
The superior swing singer is heard on 20 studio performances throughout this diverse CD which spans virtually her entire recording career. The best selections are the first four, a complete session from 1935 that has Bailey joined by an all-star quartet comprised of trumpeter Bunny Berigan, altoist Johnny Hodges, pianist Teddy Wilson, and bassist Grachan Moncur. In addition she sings four ballads from 1931 with The Casa Loma Orchestra and is accompanied on ten songs by The Delta Rhythm Boys, a quartet led by pianist Herman Chittison or Harry Sosnick's octet in 1941-42. This interesting CD concludes with Mildred Bailey's final studio session, two numbers ("Cry, Cry, Cry" and "Blue Prelude") from 1950. Some of the material was formerly rare, making this an essential CD for swing collectors. — *Scott Yanow*

Volume 2 / Dec. 1, 1931-Feb. 2, 1934 / TOM ◆◆◆
The second of two CDs from the TOM ("The Old Masters") label finishes the documentation of singer Mildred Bailey's earliest recordings. Bailey is featured with Paul Whiteman, the Dorsey Brothers Big Band, the Casa Loma Orchestra ("Heat Wave"), an all-star group with Benny Goodman (and tenor-great Coleman Hawkins), and on a her few of her own sessions. Although the emphasis is on ballads, the program generally holds on to one's interest (despite a few songs with racist lyrics, notably "Snowball") and the Goodman session (which is rounded off with an instrumental version of "Georgia Jubilee") is a near-classic. Other highlights include "I'll Never Be the Same," "Love Me Tonight," a touching "There's a Cabin in the Pines," and Bailey's earliest version of her future theme song "Rockin' Chair." — *Scott Yanow*

Legendary V-Disc Series / 1940-1951 / Vintage Jazz ◆◆◆◆
Mildred Bailey fans will find this to be a very interesting CD for the talented swing singer is heard on some previously unavailable V-Disc sessions from the war years (including a few false starts) along with some radio appearances. There is a complete radio show with her guests The Delta Rhythm Boys, four duets with pianist Teddy Wilson, three selections with vibraphon-

ist Red Norvo's quintet, a few songs with either Paul Baron's studio orchestra or the Ellis Larkins Trio, one number ("There'll Be a Jubilee") with Benny Goodman's big band, and two selections ("Lover, Come Back to Me" and "It's So Peaceful in the Country") from a 1951 radio aircheck that ended up being her last recordings. Any listener who wonders why Mildred Bailey was awarded her own postage stamp should be required to get this CD. — *Scott Yanow*

Mildred Bailey Radio Show / Nov. 24, 1944-Jan. 1945 / Sunbeam ✦✦✦
These radio performances, taken from three different shows, find singer Mildred Bailey in particularly stirring form. While she sticks mostly to ballads, there are also instrumentals featuring trombonist Trummy Young, the Teddy Wilson Sextet, and the Paul Baron Orchestra; in addition Woody Herman drops by to sing a blues. This hard-to-find LP is easily recommended to those who can find it. — *Scott Yanow*

All of Me [Evergreen] / Dec. 1945 / Monmouth Evergreen ✦✦✦
This difficult-to-find LP features Bailey singing 16 songs recorded during 1945-47 when she is still in her prime. Some feature her former husband, vibraphonist Red Norvo, while the selections on side two include some of her most mature ballad statements. Highpoints include "I've Got the World on a String," "I'm Glad There Is You," "Me and the Blues," and the title cut. — *Scott Yanow*

Majestic Mildred Bailey / Mar. 5, 1946-Nov. 1947 / Savoy ✦✦✦
During 1946-47 Mildred Bailey recorded four sessions for the Majestic record label; these late sides were among her finest recordings. This Savoy LP reissues most of the music from these sessions, including bassist Neil Swainson and drummer Jerry Fuller. This Montreal recording features four of Ballantyne's originals along with the standard "You and the Night and the Music" and is a strong example of modern straightahead jazz. It's well worth picking up. — *Scott Yanow*

American Legends #4 / 1996 / Laserlight ✦✦✦
The almost complete lack of documentation on this low-priced disc (which nevertheless manages to state both the artist's claimed year of birth, 1907, and her actual one, 1901) makes it difficult to place in Mildred Bailey's discography, but the performances, on many of which Bailey is backed by Red Norvo or Ellis Larkins, are typically accomplished. Her hit "Thanks for the Memory" (now remembered as Bob Hope's theme song) is included, as are some excellent offbeat arrangements of such songs as "The Lamp Is Low" and "Smoke Dreams" (the latter featuring a delightful Norvo xylophone solo). Sound quality is adequate, and with a running time for the 12 tracks of over 36 minutes, you will get what you pay for if you only pay in the vicinity of $5 for this disc. — *William Ruhlmann*

Etta Baker

b. Mar. 31, 1913, Caldwell County, NC
Banjo, Fiddle, Guitar, Piano, Vocals / Country Blues, Piedmont Blues
Guitarist Etta Baker quietly enjoyed one of the blues' most enduring careers, working in almost total obscurity and recording only on the rarest of occasions while honing her craft throughout the greater part of the 20th century. Born in Caldwell County, NC, on March 31, 1913, she was the product of a musical family, taking up the guitar as a child and learning from her father and other relatives traditional blues and folk songs. Over time, Baker emerged among the foremost practitioners of acoustic Piedmont guitar finger-picking, an open-tuned style not far removed from bluegrass banjo picking; however, for decades only relatives and friends ever heard her play, as she confined her performances solely to family gatherings and parties. She finally made her initial recordings in 1956, joining her father and other family members on a field recording titled *Instrumental Music of the Southern Appalachians;* she again faded into willful obscurity, however, raising her nine children and toiling in a textile mill. Finally, while in her sixties — at an age at which most performers consider retirement — Baker finally began pursuing music professionally, hitting the folk and blues festival circuit. In 1991 — 35 years after her debut recording — she issued the album *One-Dime Blues,* and continued performing live throughout the decade to follow. — *Jason Ankeny*

● **One-Dime Blues** / Oct. 1988-Jul. 1990 / Rounder ✦✦✦✦
Guitarist/vocalist Etta Baker hadn't made any recordings or even been in a studio since 1956 before making the 20 numbers comprising this CD. But

judging from the arresting vocals, prickly accompaniment and commanding presence she displayed on each song, it seemed as if she had been cutting tracks daily. Baker moved from sassy and combative blues tunes like "Never Let Your Deal Go Down" and "But On The Other Hand Baby" to chilling numbers like "Police Dog Blues," novelty tunes, double-entendre cuts, folk pieces, and even country-flavored material. Singing and playing in vintage Piedmont style with a two- and three-finger technique, Etta Baker offered timeless, memorable performances. — *Ron Wynn*

LaVern Baker

b. Nov. 11, 1929, Chicago, IL, **d.** Mar. 10, 1997, Manhattan, New York, NY
Vocals / R&B, Jump Blues
LaVern Baker was one of the sexiest divas gracing the mid-'50s rock 'n' roll circuit, boasting a brashly seductive vocal delivery tailor-made for belting the catchy novelties "Tweedlee Dee," "Bop-Ting-a-Ling," and "Tra La La" for Atlantic Records during rock's first wave of prominence.

Born Delores Williams, she was singing at the Club DeLisa on Chicago's south side at age 17, decked out in raggedy attire and billed as "Little Miss Sharecropper" (the same handle that she made her recording debut under for RCA Victor with Eddie "Sugarman" Penigar's band in 1949). She changed her name briefly to Bea Baker when recording for OKeh in 1951 with Maurice King's Wolverines, then settled on the first name of LaVern when she joined Todd Rhodes' band as featured vocalist in 1952 (she fronted Rhodes' aggregation on the impassioned ballad "Trying" for Cincinnati's King Records).

LaVern signed with Atlantic as a solo in 1953, debuting with the incendiary "Soul on Fire." The coy, Latin-tempoed "Tweedlee Dee" was a smash in 1955 on both the R&B and pop charts, although her impact on the latter was blunted when squeaky-clean Georgia Gibbs covered it for Mercury. An infuriated Baker filed suit over the whitewashing, but she lost. By that time, though, her star had ascended: Baker's "Bop-Ting-A-Ling," "Play It Fair," "Still," and the rocking "Jim Dandy" all vaulted into the R&B Top Ten over the next couple of years.

Baker's statuesque figure and charismatic persona made her a natural for TV and movies. She co-starred on the historic R&B revue segment on Ed Sullivan's TV program in November of 1955 and did memorable numbers in Alan Freed's rock movies *Rock, Rock, Rock* and *Mr. Rock & Roll.* Her Atlantic records remained popular throughout the decade — she hit big in 1958 with the ballad "I Cried a Tear," adopted a pseudosanctified bellow for the rousing Leiber & Stoller-penned gospel sendup "Saved" in 1960, and cut a Bessie Smith tribute album before leaving Atlantic in 1964. A brief stop at Brunswick Records (where she did a sassy duet with Jackie Wilson, "Think Twice") preceded a late-'60s jaunt to entertain the troops in Vietnam. She became seriously ill after the trip and was hospitalized, eventually settling far out of the limelight in the Philippines. She remained there for 22 years, running an NCO club on Subic Bay for the US government.

Finally, in 1988, Baker returned stateside to star in Atlantic's 40th anniversary bash at New York's Madison Square Garden. That led to a soundtrack appearance in the film *Dick Tracy,* a starring role in the Broadway musical *Black & Blue* (replacing her ex-Atlantic labelmate Ruth Brown), a nice comeback disc for DRG (*Woke Up This Mornin'*), and a memorable appearance at the Chicago Blues Festival. Baker died on March 3, 1997. — *Bill Dahl*

Sings Bessie Smith / Jan. 27, 1958 / Atlantic ✦✦✦✦
This is an album that should not have worked. LaVern Baker (a fine R&B singer) was joined by all-stars from mainstream jazz (including trumpeter Buck Clayton, trombonist Vic Dickenson, tenor-saxophonist Paul Quinichette, and pianist Nat Pierce) for twelve songs associated with the great '20s blues singer Bessie Smith. Despite the potentially conflicting styles, this project is quite successful and often exciting. The arrangements by Phil Moore, Nat Pierce, and Ernie Wilkins do not attempt to re-create the original recordings, Baker sings in her own style (rather than trying to emulate Bessie Smith), and the hot solos work well with her vocals. — *Scott Yanow*

Precious Memories / Jun. 4, 1959 / Atlantic ✦✦✦
LaVern Baker sang gospel with passion, exuberance, and reverence on this '59 session. She was backed by a small combo with the Alex Bradford singers and sounded more magnificent and moving than at any time she had done jazz, blues or R&B. This one is very hard to find and has not as of yet been reissued on CD. — *Ron Wynn*

★ **Soul on Fire: The Best of LaVern Baker** / 1991 / Rhino ✦✦✦✦✦
The cream of this vivacious 1950s R&B belter's Atlantic catalog comprises this 20-track hits collection. Includes Baker's bouncy "Tweedlee Dee," the storming rockers "Jim Dandy" and "Bop-Ting-a-Ling," the pseudo-gospel raveup "Saved," and Baker's torchy blues ballads "Soul on Fire" and "I Cried a Tear." She imparts "See See Rider" with a lighthearted reading that contrasts starkly with Chuck Willis' Atlantic smash of a few years before. — *Bill Dahl*

Blues Side of Rock 'n' Roll / 1993 / Star Club ✦✦✦
This import may be of slightly dubious origins (sounds like everything was dubbed from vinyl, though the sound quality is quite acceptable), but it delves a lot deeper into LaVern Baker's Atlantic discography (26 cuts) and picks up a few essential sides ignored by Atlantic's own CD: "Tra La La," "Voodoo Voodoo," "Hey Memphis" (Baker's sequel to Elvis' "Little Sister"), and a hellacious version of "He's a Real Gone Guy" sporting a vicious King Curtis sax break. — *Bill Dahl*

Long John Baldry

b. Jan. 12, 1941, London, England
Harmonica, Vocals / Electric British Blues, Blues-Rock, British Invasion, British Blues
Like Cliff Richard, Chris Farlowe, Slade, Blur, and eel pie, Long John Baldry is one of those peculiarly British phenomenons that doggedly resists American translation. As a historical figure, he has undeniable importance. When he began singing as a teenager in the 1950s, he was one of the first British vocalists to perform folk and blues music. In the early '60s, he sang in the band of British blues godfather Alexis Korner, Blues Incorporated, which also served as a starting point for future rock stars Mick Jagger, Jack Bruce, and others. As a member of Blues Incorporated, he contributed to the first British blues album, *R&B at the Marquee* (1962). He then joined the Cyril Davies R&B All Stars, taking over the group (renamed Long John Baldry and His Hoochie Coochie Men) after Davies' death in early 1964. This band featured Rod Stewart as a second vocalist, and also employed Geoff Bradford (who had been in an embryonic version of the Rolling Stones) on guitar.

In the mid-'60s, he helped form Steampacket, a proto-supergroup that also featured Stewart, Julie Driscoll, and Brian Auger. When Steampacket broke up, he fronted Bluesology, the band that gave keyboardist Reg Dwight—soon to become Elton John—his first prestigious gig. He was a well-liked figure on the London club circuit, and in fact the Beatles took him on as a guest on one of their 1964 British TV specials, at a time when the Fab Four could have been no bigger, and Baldry was virtually unknown.

All of these famous assocations, alas, don't change the hard fact that Baldry wasn't much of a singer. His dry-as-dust, charmless croak approximated what Manfred Mann's Paul Jones (whom Baldry resembled slightly physically) may have sounded like while recovering from a tonsillectomy. His greatest commercial success came not with blues, but unbearably gloppy orchestrated pop ballads that echoed Engelbert Humperdinck. The 1967 single "Let the Heartaches Begin" reached number one in Britain, and Baldry had several other small British hits in the late '60s, the biggest of which was "Mexico" (1968). (None of these made an impression in the US.)

The commercial success of his ballads led Baldry to forsake the blues on record for a few years. Cruel as it may be to say, it wasn't much of a loss to the blues world; Baldry's early blues recordings don't hold a candle even to second-tier acts like Graham Bond, let alone the Stones or the Bluesbreakers. He returned to blues and rock in 1971 on *It Ain't Easy*, for which Rod Stewart and Elton John shared the production duties. The album contained a tiny American chart item, "Don't Try to Lay No Boogie-Woogie on the King of Rock 'n' Roll," and Stewart and John split the production once again on the 1972 follow-up, *Everything Stops for Tea*. Baldry never caught on as an international figure, though, and by 1980 had become a Canadian citizen. If he was heard at all after that, it was usually via commercial voiceovers, or as the voice of Captain Robotnick in children's cartoons. — *Richie Unterberger*

Long John's Blues/Looking at Long John / 1964 / BGO ✦✦✦✦
Beat Goes On combined Long John Baldry's first two albums—*Long John's Blues* and *Looking at Long John*—on a single CD in 1995. Even if Baldry's music never quite lives up to his historical reputation, this remains the best place for the curious to become acquainted with his restrained British blues, since it has his bluesiest album (*Long John's Blues*). But British blues fans

should be forewarned that his second record is more pop-soul than blues. — *Thom Owens*

● **Long John's Blues** / Aug. 1964 / Ascot ✦✦✦✦
Stacked up against other British blues/R&B albums of the time, this is a distinctly lower-echelon effort, much stiffer and more routine than the recordings of The Stones, John Mayall, Graham Bond, Duffy Power, and others. What made early British efforts in this style exciting was the sense of risk-taking, even recklessness. Baldry and the Hoochie Coochie Men are totally lacking in that department, displaying a by-the-numbers approach in arrangements (particuarly in the trad piano rolls) and material selection, which consists almost entirely of overdone standards like "My Babe," "Got My Mojo Working," and "Goin' Down Slow." Stacked up against *Baldry's* own work, though, this qualifies as his most "essential" effort, if only because it is for his contributions to the British blues scene that he is most remembered. This is the most accurate reflection of his work in that field, and Baldry is in better voice here than he is on much of his later '60s work. The album is still mediocre or worse, although it does feature Geoff Bradford (who played in a very early precursor to The Rolling Stones) on guitar. The BGO CD reissue combines *Long John's Blues* and the 1966 LP *Looking at Long John* on one disc. — *Richie Unterberger*

Looking at Long John / 1966 / United Artists ✦✦✦
Baldry's move from blues into pop/soul for his second album may have been viewed as something of a loss in integrity, given his purist blues stance on his debut. Maybe it wasn't such a bad idea, though, given that a) the debut LP wasn't very good, and b) the British blues-rock field was crowded with many greater talents in the mid-'60s. *Looking at Long John*, with a sub-Righteous Brothers sort of approach, is certainly a change in style, but the result really isn't any better. Baldry's vocal limitations are a big handicap whether applied to white-boy blues or blue-eyed soul, and the production is thin in comparison with the American soul/pop it's clearly trying to emulate. If you wanted this kind of stuff, The Righteous Brothers did it many times better. Not only that, if you were British at the time and weren't aware of The Righteous Brothers, you weren't about to turn to John Baldry; the Walker Brothers (American, but based in Britain) also did this kind of stuff much better. The BGO CD reissue combines this and the 1964 LP *Long John's Blues* on one disc. — *Richie Unterberger*

Let the Heartaches Begin / 1968 / Pye ✦✦
With "Let the Heartaches Begin," Baldry abandoned all pretenses at blues or soul for treacly MOR pop of the worst sort. The marketplace did not respond with the emphatic veto that cosmic justice demanded; on the contrary, the single went to number one in Britain, and was the singer's greatest commercial success by far. The album offered material in the same vein: over-orchestrated, sentimental ballads with female backup vocals supporting Long John's hoarse wall of gravel, many written by the same Tony Macaulay-John Macleod team that was responsible for "Heartaches." Even if you've got a yen for MOR British pop of the period, you're much better off with Tom Jones, or even Engelbert Humperdinck. The BGO CD reissue combines this and the 1969 LP *Wait for Me* on one disc. — *Richie Unterberger*

Let There Be Long John / 1969 / Pye ✦✦

Wait for Me / 1969 / Janus ✦✦✦
For his last album of the '60s, Baldry took a marginally more soulful approach than he had on *Let the Heartaches Begin*, although Tony Macaulay (co-writer of the "Let the Heartaches Begin" single) was still around to feed him a few mainstream pop tunes. The result was more bearable than the previous effort, but not much. No one's going to highly value Baldry's soul-revue interpretations of "Sunshine of Your Love," "Cry Like a Baby," or other soul and rock hits of the period, even for camp or nostalgia value. The more pop-oriented selections are still the sort of cabaret-ish hack jobs that induce grimaces, and Baldry's vocals are still lacking in basic chops. The CD reissue adds the bonus tracks "Mexico" and "When the Sun Comes Shining Thru," which were both British Top 30 hits for Baldry in the late '60s. The BGO CD reissue combines *Wait for Me* and the 1967 LP *Let the Heartaches Begin* on one disc. — *Richie Unterberger*

Baldry's Out / 1979 / EMI ✦✦✦
On Stage Tonight—Baldry's Out! nicely rectifies a 30-year oversight: the gentleman has never previously released a live recording. Captured in Germany, the disc blends the strongest tracks from Baldry's *It Still Ain't Easy* comeback

album with updated past greats. And it just wouldn't be Baldry (especially live) without the ferocious backing of longtime soulmate Kathi McDonald. While Baldry's blues can sometimes be a tad too "polite," *On Stage Tonight* captures that unique smoky growl in top form. — *Roch Parisien*

It Still Ain't Easy / 1991 / Stony Plain ✦✦✦✦
Baldry's deep, rough-edged vocals have not changed over the years. The band is tight, with Mike Kalanj's Hammond B-3 and Bill Rogers' sax standing out. There are no flaws on this one, just great music. — *Chip Renner*

Let the Heartaches Begin/Wait for Me / 1995 / BGO ✦✦✦

A Thrill's a Thrill: The Canadian Years / 1996 / EMI ✦✦✦
Two-CD set *A Thrill's a Thrill—The Canadian Years* distills the best from Baldry's seven Canadian releases, recorded between 1979 and 1993. I would have been happier with a complete career retrospective, but the highlights here hold up elegantly in their own right: "Baldry's Out," "It Still Ain't Easy," and a definitive cover of Tim Hardin's "Morning Dew" among them. Besides, an eight-minute live rendition of signature song "Don't Try to Lay No Boogie Woogie on the King of Rock 'n' Roll" captures the old days nicely. — *Roch Parisien*

Right to Sing the Blues / 1996 / Stony Plain ✦✦✦
One of the founding fathers of the '60s British Blues scene, Long John Baldry owns one of the great white blues voices, a power that remains undiminished for *Right To Sing The Blues*. The disc forms another consistent Baldry primer visiting the rich diversity of blues styles, from the quiet folk-blues of "Whoa Back Buck" (longtime colleague Papa John King tearing up his slide guitar) to jump blues party tunes like opener "They Raided the Joint." Vocal sidekick Kathi McDonald also carries the torch, especially on an incendiary title track already highlighted by a scorching Colin James guitar riff. On occasion, the tall one is too much the mannered gentleman for the good of his muse. I would love to hear him bust loose more frequently—as he does on "I'm Shakin'," his pipes sounding like gargled nails with an Irish Cream chaser. It would also be nice to find him writing again. While mostly recognized as a judicious interpreter, Baldry has proven his capability over the years, and the complete absence of self-penned material strikes one as borderline laziness. He even dips back to a tune already covered on a previous release—Bonnie Dobson's classic "Morning Dew"—albeit giving it a fresh Cajun/Zydeco coat of paint. In case dependable, honorable music isn't enough incentive on its own, the disc earns bonus points by concluding with a 23-minute interview in which Baldry recounts his take on the British Blues scene. Not exactly flashy multimedia, but a nice addition for fans of pop music history. — *Roch Parisien*

Marcia Ball

b. Mar. 20, 1949, Orange, TX
Piano, Vocals / Modern Electric Blues, Piano Blues, Electric Texas Blues
Pianist, singer and songwriter Marcia Ball is a living example of how east Texas blues meets southwest Louisiana swamp rock. Ball was born March 20, 1949, in Orange, TX, but grew up across the border in Vinton, LA. That town is squarely in the heart of "the Texas triangle," an area that includes portions of both states and that has produced some of our country's greatest blues talents: Janis Joplin, Johnny and Edgar Winter, Queen Ida Guillory, Lonnie Brooks, Zachary Richard, Clifton Chenier, and Kenny Neal, to name a few. Ball's earliest awareness of blues came over the radio, where she heard people like Irma Thomas, Professor Longhair. and Etta James, all of whom she now credits as influences. She began playing piano at age five, learning from her grandmother and aunt and also taking formal lessons from a teacher.

Ball entered Louisiana State University in the late '60s as an English major. In college, she played in a psychedelic rock 'n' roll band, Gum. In 1970, Ball and her first husband were headed west in their car to San Francisco, but the car needed repairs in Austin, where they had stopped off to visit one of their former bandmates. After hearing, seeing and tasting some of the music, sights and food in Austin, the two decided to stay there. Ball has been based in Austin since then.

Her piano style, which mixes equal parts boogie-woogie with zydeco and Louisiana swamp rock, is best exemplified on her series of excellent recordings for the Rounder label. They include *Soulful Dress* (1983), *Hot Ta-*

male Baby (1985), *Gatorhythms* (1989), and *Blue House* (1994). Also worthy of checking out is her collaboration with Angela Strehli and Lou Ann Barton on the Antone's label, *Dreams Come True* (1990). Ball, like her peer Angela Strehli, is an educated business woman, fully aware of all the realities of the record business. Ball never records until she feels she's got a batch of top-notch, quality songs. Most of the songs on her albums are her own creations, so songwriting is a big part of her job description.

Although Ball is a splendid piano player and a more than adequate vocalist, "the songwriting process is the most fulfilling part of the whole deal for me," she said in a 1994 interview, "so I always keep my ears and eyes open for things I might hear or see.... I like my songs to go back to blues in some fashion." As much a student of the music as she is a player, some of Ball's albums include covers of material by O.V. Wright, Dr. John, Joe Ely, Clifton Chenier, and Shirley and Lee.

Ball, who's established herself as an important player in the club scenes in both New Orleans and Austin, continues to work at festivals and clubs throughout the US, Canada and Europe. — *Richard Skelly*

Soulful Dress / 1983 / Rounder ✦✦✦
Marcia Ball got things started in a celebratory fashion on her debut Rounder release, doing the title track in a taunting, challenging manner aided by flashy guitar riffs from Stevie Ray Vaughan. From there, she artfully displayed other sides of her personality, from dismayed to defiant and assured. Her rendition of "Soul On Fire" was heartfelt, but didn't approach the majestic quality of LaVern Baker's original. She did much better on "I Don't Want No Man," striking the air of disdain and dissatisfaction that Bobby "Blue" Bland immortalized on "I Don't Want No Woman"; guitarist Kenny Ray even got the Wayne Bennett licks down perfectly. — *Ron Wynn*

Hot Tamale Baby / Apr. 1985 / Rounder ✦✦✦✦
Marcia Ball solidified the favorable impression made with her debut Rounder effort with this rousing second outing. She dedicated it to the late King of Zydeco, Clifton Chenier, and was backed by a fine band of veteran pros that included saxophonist Alvin Tyler. Ball ripped through Booker T. Jones' soul gem "Never Like This Before" and Chenier's title composition, while also demonstrating her own facility with R&B on "That's Enough of That Stuff" and "Love's Spell." She came close, but didn't quite hit the mark on O.V. Wright's "I'm Gonna Forget About You," turning in a more than acceptable rendition that still didn't approach the original. But other than that one misstep, which she compensated for with a charged version of "I Don't Know," Marcia Ball proved that her debut was no fluke. — *Ron Wynn*

● **Gatorhythms** / 1989 / Rounder ✦✦✦✦
Marcia Ball explored R&B and honky-tonk country on this album, keeping her blues chops in order while expanding her repertoire. She included a pair of tunes by country vocalist Lee Roy Parnell, "What's A Girl To Do" and "Red Hot," doing both in a feisty, attacking fashion. She also was challenging and upbeat on Dr. John's "How You Carry On" and "Find Another Fool." Her third Rounder album was her most entertaining and dynamic, as Ball became less of an interpreter and more of an individualist. — *Ron Wynn*

Dreams Come True / 1990 / Antone's ✦✦✦
Dreams Come True is an all-star session by vocalists Marcia Ball, Lou Ann Barton and Angela Strehli. The three women sing with a band led by Dr. John and the session features guest appearances by such luminaries as David "Fathead" Newman and Jimmie Vaughan. The music is straight out of the Texas school of roadhouse R&B and blues boogie but it's delivered with a gritty, heartfelt edge, particularly on the part of the three vocalists. *Dreams Come True* may follow formula, but it's followed with style and affection, which makes it a very enjoyable listen. — *Thom Owens*

Blue House / 1994 / Rounder ✦✦✦

Let Me Play with Your Poodle / Jun. 24, 1997 / Rounder ✦✦✦✦
This album of snaky swamp rock is one of Ball's best recordings. Great choice of songs (she wrote 5 of the 13) that let her show all her talents, both vocally and instrumentally. Slow-tempo songs display the force of her voice, as in "I Still Love You," and another of the many gems, "For the Love of a Man." Meanwhile, the playfulness of the title cut and "The Right Tool for the Job" allow her to have fun and let the band air it out. Then there is the perfect song to end the disc and an absolute tour de force, Randy Newman's "Louisiana 1927." Ball has again assembled another top-notch cast of characters who

more than hold up their end of the bargain. A few of the many who shine are George Rains on drums, Mark Kazanoff, who does double duty as a co-producer and excels on various saxes, and Derek O'Brien, who also co-produced and shares much of the guitar work with Steve Williams. If you don't know Marcia Ball, this is a fantastic introduction, and if you liked her past work this is a gem you won't want to miss. — *Bob Gottlieb*

Sing It! / Jan. 13, 1998 / Rounder ✦✦✦
Bringing together solo singers in any genre to work as a unit is always a dicey proposition. Sometimes egos get in the way, but mostly it comes down to voices that have been the lead for so many years suddenly finding themselves unable or unwilling to blend with others. What starts out as a spirited session turns into a hog-calling contest. Fortunately, none of the above happens on this disc, teaming Irma Thomas with two of her acolytes, Marcia Ball and Tracy Nelson. With a crack staff of Memphis and Louisiana players behind them, the ladies cherry-pick a raft of great songs without relying too heavily on old soul gems, and the results are simply splendid. The solo-turn highlights include Marcia on "Love Maker," Tracy on "Please No More," and Irma on "People Will Be People," and the trio blends effortlessly on "I Want to Do Everything for You," Sarah Brown's "If I Know You," and the title track. This is one spirited session and proof that star collaborations sometimes work quite effectively. — *Cub Koda*

Chico Banks

Guitar, Vocals / Modern Electric Blues, Contemporary Blues
Along with Bernard Allison, Melvin Taylor, and a handful of others, guitarist, singer and songwriter Chico Banks is part of the new generation of Chicago blues players who are expanding the boundaries of this often maligned, misunderstood music. Like Allison and Taylor, and even older Southern musicians like Larry Garner and Sherman Robertson, Banks focuses on good-time, upbeat blues.

Banks' music may not impress blues purists—he freely mixes in elements of soul, funk and rock—but when a musical form remains too static, as the late Luther Allison would say, it loses its vibrancy. He credits influences from a mixed bag of artists from the 1960s and '70s: "Magic Sam" Maghett, Buddy Guy, Albert King, Jimi Hendrix, Otis Clay, George Benson, and Tyrone Davis. But his playing also reflects the contribution of jazz pianist Ahmad Jamal, and the funk of Prince, the Isley Brothers, the Ohio Players and Parliament/Funkadelic. Also not to be overlooked is his father, Jesse Banks, who played with the gospel group the Mighty Clouds of Joy.

Since joining his first band, a Top 40 cover group, at 14, Banks has performed with Johnny Christian, Evidence labelmate Melvin Taylor, Buddy Guy, Otis Clay, James Cotton, Artie "Blues Boy" White, Little Milton, Magic Slim, Big Time Sarah, Chick Rogers, and, most recently, Mavis Staples. Banks' sessionography includes albums by Willie Kent, Freddie Roulette, and Pops Staples.

On his 1997 debut, *Candy Lickin' Man,* Banks is joined by the great gospel singer Mavis Staples, who also contributes liner notes. Although only in his 20s, Banks is already a veteran song interpreter; he covers classics like "Groove Me," "Got to Be Some Changes Made," and "The Sky Is Crying," putting his own individual stamp on each tune. — *Richard J. Skelly*

Candy Lickin' Man / Oct. 14, 1997 / Evidence ✦✦✦✦
When Chico Banks played guitar with the Staple Singers, his playing was hard, uncluttered, and straight to the point, yet it was tempered to fit right in with the Staples' sound. Banks' father Jessie was with the Mighty Clouds of Joy and also a bluesman. Banks' brother Stanley Banks is a keyboardist, with whom he co-wrote two of these songs. His playing is influenced by blues, rhythm & blues, gospel, and the psychedelia of Jimi Hendrix, especially on his tasty, never burdensome use of the wah-wah pedal. His voice is more than adequate for the job, but the cuts that stand out are those on which he concentrates his guitar. On "It Must Be Love," Mavis Staples does the vocals, and you can feel the electricity between the two born of a mutual respect for excellence. On "All Your Love," he has "Big James" Montgomery handling the vocals and lets loose some fine playing through that wah-wah pedal. This is one of the finest guitar players to come down the avenue in a good stretch, and he can only mature from here. This is no throwaway first album, with one good cut and lots of dross; its nearly 70 minutes are filled with some mighty fine playing. — *Bob Gottlieb*

Barbecue Bob (Robert Hicks)

b. Sep. 11, 1902, Walnut Grove, GA, **d.** Oct. 21, 1931, Lithonia, GA
Guitar, Vocals / Country Blues, Prewar Country Blues
Barbecue Bob may be a familiar name to some blues fans today because at least two young White musicians have adopted the name, but back in the '20s the original Barbecue Bob (Robert Hicks) was a big name on the Black "race-records" scene. Recording for Columbia from 1927 to 1930, Hicks was the most popular of the Atlanta blues guitarists of his time, and Columbia's best-selling bluesman. But Barbecue Bob died of pneumonia at the age of 29, and some of his contemporaries like Blind Willie McTell are much better known to modern-day audiences. Most of Bob's recordings were solo outings featuring rhythmic 12-string bottleneck-guitar work and original lyrical themes. In historian Stephen Calt's opinion, "For sheer musical verve and punch, Hicks easily rivals Charley Patton." — *Jim O'Neal*

Complete Recorded Works, Vols. 1-3 / Mar. 25, 1927-Dec. 8, 1930 / Document ✦✦✦
Over the course of three CDs, Document Records compiled every note Barbecue Bob recorded in the late '20s. The first volume covers everything he cut between March 25, 1927 and April 13, 1928; the second, April 21, 1928 to November 3, 1929; and the third November 6, 1929 to December 8, 1930. In between the first song on the set—which has been issued as individual volumes—and the last song, there is some incredible country blues; there was a reason why he was among the most popular bluesmen of his time. Although there is too much music here for anyone not dedicated country blues fans to be able to digest and the sound quality isn't terrific (which isn't surprising, considering that the series had to be mastered from 78s), Document's *Complete Recorded Works in Chronological Order* is an excellent historical document that happens to contain music that still sounds fresh and vital decades after it was recorded. — *Thom Owens*

Brownskin Gal / 1927-1930 / Agram ✦✦✦
A boxed import set with a variety of blues, hokum, and comedy routines. Includes an 80-page bio and transcription book. Unfortunately, this compilation is marred by weak sound quality. — *Barry Lee Pearson*

● **Chocolate to the Bone** / 1927-1930 / Yazoo ✦✦✦✦
Although Robert "Barbecue Bob" Hicks recorded over 65 extant sides (three are not known to have survived) in a three-year stretch starting in 1927 up to his death in 1931, the 20 collected here make a perfect introduction to the work of this Atlanta-based artist. He may have played a big-city acoustic 12-string guitar, but Hicks' playing was provincial, down-home, and often modal, reducing any chord progression down to one or two chords. He also played embellishments on this instrument with a bottleneck, a rarity then and a rarity now. Usually tuned to an open chord, Barbecue Bob's playing nonetheless shows great diversity and musical flexibility. The 20 sides collected here (all of them old, scratchy 78s and cleaned up as well as can be expected) gives a nice cross-section of that diversity as a solo artist, along with a pair of sides showcasing Bob in a small band context with Buddy Moss on harmonica and Curley Weaver on second guitar and another with Hicks backing up former gal pal Nellie Florence on a raucous "Jacksonville Blues." Of special merit for collectors are the inclusion of two previously unissued sides struck from slightly better sounding test pressings, "Twistin' Your Stuff" and "She Shook Her Gin." This expanded collection replaces the 14-track vinyl collection of the same name. — *Cub Koda*

John Henry Barbee

b. Nov. 14, 1905, Henning, TN, **d.** Nov. 3, 1964, Chicago, IL
Guitar, Vocals / Country Blues, Delta Blues, Prewar Country Blues
A strong storyteller and good guitarist, John Henry Barbee learned music playing in various homes throughout Henning, Tennessee as a youth. He worked for a short time with John Lee Williamson (Sonny Boy Williamson I) in 1934, then began playing with Sunnyland Slim. They made appearances across the Mississippi Delta. Barbee later moved to Chicago, where he recorded for Vocalion in 1938. He played with Moody Jones' group on Maxwell Street in the '40s, but then left the music business for several years. Barbee recorded for Spivey and Storyville in the mid-'60s, and toured Europe as part of the American Folk Blues Festival. A portion of the tour's concert in Hamburg, Germany was issued by Fontana. Barbee was involved in an auto accident in 1964, and suffered a heart attack while in jail waiting for the case to come to court. — *Ron Wynn*

● **Blues Masters, Vol. 3: I Ain't Gonna Pick No More Cotton** / Oct. 8, 1964 / Storyville ✦✦✦✦

Storyville recorded a session from John Henry Barbee during the blues revival of the early '60s, which was released as *Blues Masters, Vol. 3: I Ain't Gonna Pick No More Cotton*. The country bluesman hauled out several of his old songs, plus a handful of classics, ranging from "John Henry" and "That's Alright Mama" to "Dust My Broom." Barbee's performances are direct and unadorned, similar in style to his late-'20s/early-'30s recordings but, if anything, they're a little bit better. His playing may not be quite as raw, but his voice has grown deeper and more powerful with age, giving the music an unexpected resonance. Barbee wasn't much more than a minor country-blues player, but his music was quite enjoyable, and this 16-track collection is the best way to hear his modest talents. — *Thom Owens*

Barkin' Bill

b. Mississippi

Vocals / Electric Chicago Blues

Blessed with a lush, deeply burnished baritone that's seemingly the antithesis of the rough-hewn Chicago blues sound, Barkin' Bill Smith finally broke through in 1994 with his own debut album for Delmark. Influenced by the likes of Joe Williams (Count Basie's smooth crooner, not the gruff nine-string guitarist), Brook Benton, and Jimmy Witherspoon, the natty dresser grew up in Mississippi and stopped off to sing in East St. Louis and Detroit before settling in the Windy City.

Slide guitarist Homesick James anointed Bill with his enduring stage handle in 1958 when the two shared a stage. After scuffling for decades on the South and West sides, Smith finally hooked up with young guitarist Dave Specter & the Bluebirds and made his recorded debut on the band's 1991 Delmark release, *Bluebird Blues*. After leaving Specter's employ, Smith's own album bow *Gotcha!* emerged three years later. — *Bill Dahl*

● **Gotcha!** / 1994 / Delmark ✦✦✦✦

The veteran vocalist wraps his suave, bottomless pipes around a well-chosen cross-section of covers, from Duke Henderson's jump blues "Get Your Kicks" and Johnny "Guitar" Watson's "I Love to Love You" to tougher straightforward blues originally cut by Freddy King, Guitar Slim, Jimmy Rogers, and Little Walter. A cadre of local session aces provides fine support, especially guitarist Steve Freund (who receives a couple of instrumental showcases). — *Bill Dahl*

Roosevelt "Booba" Barnes

b. Sep. 25, 1936, Longwood, MS, **d.** Apr. 2, 1996, Chicago, IL

Guitar, Vocals / Electric Delta Blues

"Booba" Barnes and his Playboys band rocked the hardest of all the juke-joint combos in the Mississippi delta during the '80s, and after the release of his debut album (*The Heartbroken Man*, 1990), Booba took his act and his band north to Chicago, following the trail of his idols Howlin' Wolf and Little Milton. In a *Guitar Player* review, Jas Obrecht called Barnes "a wonderfully idiosyncratic guitar player and an extraordinary vocalist by any standard."

Roosevelt Booba Barnes began playin music professionally in 1960, playing guitar in a Mississippi band named the Swinging Gold Coasters. Four years later, he moved to Chicago, where he performed in blues clubs whenever he could get work. Barnes returned to his home state of Mississippi in 1971, where he began playing bars and clubs around Greenville.

Barnes continued to play the juke joints of Mississippi for the next decade. In 1985, he opened his own joint, the Playboy Club. With Barnes and his backing band, the Playboys, acting as the house band, the bar became one of the most popular in the Delta. Soon, the band was popular enough to have a record contract with Rooster Blues. Their first album, *The Heartbroken Man*, was released in 1990. After its release, Barnes and the Playboys toured the United States and Europe. They continued to tour, as well as occasionally record, until Barnes died of cancer in April 1996. — *Jim O'Neal & Stephen Thomas Erlewine*

★ **The Heartbroken Man** / 1990 / Rooster Blues ✦✦✦✦✦

Roosevelt "Booba" Barnes didn't record his first album, *Heartbroken Man*, until 1990. By that point, he had become a seasoned bluesman, and was well-known in the South as a tough, hard-rocking guitarist. *Heartbroken Man* delivers on the promise of his reputation. It's an astonishing record, filled with gutsy vocals and gnarled, unpredictable guitar. Unlike most mod-

ern blues, it's teeming with life, and its raw, unvarnished production is a welcome bracing contrast to the sterile atmosphere of most modern blues records. But what really counts is the music itself, and Barnes proves to be the heir to such classic bluesmen as Howlin' Wolf and Slim Harpo (both of whom he covers here), as both a performer and songwriter. An instant modern classic. — *Thom Owens*

The Barrett Sisters

Vocals / Black Gospel

Delois, Billie, and Rodessa Barrett began singing in the Chicago-based Morning Star Baptist Church in the '40s as children. Under the direction of their aunt, Mattie Dacus, they were originally known as The Barrett and Hudson Singers before becoming The Barrett Sisters. Delois was recruited for The Roberta Martin Singers while a high school senior at Englewood High. After graduation, she joined Martin's group full time and remained a member for 18 years. Rodessa Barrett became a choral director of Galileo Baptist church and Billie Barrett became a church soloist after taking voice lessons at the American Music Conservatory. They formed The Barrett Sisters in 1962 and have remained together ever since. Their first LP was recorded for Savoy in 1963. They currently record for I Am Records in Chicago. — *Ron Wynn*

What Shall I Render Unto God / Dec. 1, 1995 / Sony Special Products ✦✦✦✦

Best of the Barrett Sisters [Intersound] / Jun. 25, 1996 / Intersound ✦✦✦✦

Nobody Does It Better / Word ✦✦✦✦

One of the hottest gospel albums ever from this great trio. Their shimmering voices and precise yet spontaneous-sounding interaction on every tune expertly convey gospel's hypnotic charm. They're particularly inspiring on "Christ Is All," "Rapture," "All My Help," and "Nobody But Jesus." They haven't de-emphasized the overt religious base of the songs or tried to hedge the themes and lyrics. Anyone who doubted whether a trio could sustain the same clout and drive as a quartet or large group should hear "Walk and Talk" or "Fly Away"; The Barretts can sing up a storm. — *Ron Wynn*

What a Wonderful World / I Am ✦✦✦

A more contemporary production, geared toward fans of a modern approach. — *Ron Wynn*

● **What Will You Do with Your Life** / Savoy ✦✦✦✦

What Will You Do with Your Life is a fine collection of the Barrett Sisters' Savoy recordings that showcases the gospel group at their very best. — *Leo Stanley*

The Best of the Barrett Sisters [MCA] / MCA ✦✦✦✦

Great sides by one of today's leading female aggregations. Nashboro sides. — *Opal Louis Nations*

Sweet Emma Barrett

b. Mar. 25, 1897, New Orleans, LA, **d.** Jan. 28, 1983, New Orleans, LA

Piano, Vocals / New Orleans Jazz

Sweet Emma Barrett, who was at her most powerful in the early '60s, became a symbolic figure with the Preservation Hall Jazz Band, playing in a joyous but obviously weakened and past-her-prime style on world tours. Barrett spent most of her career living and playing in New Orleans, including gigs with Oscar "Papa" Celestin in the 1920s and later with Armand Piron. Sweet Emma, who gained the nickname of "the bell gal" because she wore red garters with bells that made sounds while she played, was purely a local figure until 1961, when she made her finest recording, a Riverside set with the future members of the Preservation Hall Jazz Band. Ironically, as Barrett (through the group's well-received tours) became better known, her playing and singing swiftly declined due to her age, and after a 1967 stroke, she continued to perform, despite having a largely paralyzed left hand. In addition to the recommended Riverside set (reissued on CD), Barrett led less significant sessions for GHB (1963-64), Preservation Hall, Nobility and a 1978 album for Smoky Mary. — *Scott Yanow*

● **New Orleans: The Living Legends** / Jan. 1961 / Original Jazz Classics ✦✦✦✦

This CD reissue of the future members of The Preservation Hall Jazz Band is at such a high level it makes one wonder why this group had so many erratic recordings. Pianist Emma Barrett (who also takes four vocals) is in fine form and trombonist Jim Robinson was always a major asset to any New Orleans jazz band but it is the performances of trumpeter Percy Humphrey (who never sounded better on record) and his brother, clarinetist Willie, that really makes this music special. Together the septet plays such songs as "Bill Bailey," "Just a Little While to Stay Here," and "The Saints" with drive, enthusiasm and surprising musicianship. It's essential music for all New Orleans jazz fans. — *Scott Yanow*

Sweet Emma Barrett and Her New Orleans Music / Sep. 1963 / Southland ✦✦✦

For her second LP as a leader, pianist Sweet Emma Barrett (who sings on four of the eight songs) heads two overlapping groups. While she is joined throughout by banjoist Emanuel Sayles, bassist Placide Adams, and drummer Paul Barbarin, the frontlines change, with four songs featuring trumpeter Alvin Alcorn, trombonist Jim Robinson and clarinetist Louis Cottrell; the remaining four numbers have trumpeter Don Albert, trombonist Frog Joseph, and clarinetist Raymond Burke. Overall, this set gives listeners a good sampling of the state of New Orleans jazz circa 1963 and is one of the few recordings of Barrett mostly without the regular members of what would become the Preservation Hall Jazz Band (Robinson and Sayles excepted). The ensemble-oriented renditions of such numbers as "Big Butter and Egg Man," "Bogalusa Strut," and "Take Me Out to the Ball Game" are fun and joyful. — *Scott Yanow*

Sweet Emma and Her Preservation Hall Jazz Band / Oct. 18, 1964 / Preservation Hall ✦✦✦

This LP features The Preservation Hall Jazz Band in its early days, when pianist/vocalist Sweet Emma Barrett was the leader. Clarinetist Willie Humphrey and trumpeter Percy Humphrey, although not up to the level they attained on the Riverside CD, are in better than usual form, and trombonist Jim Robinson is his usual consistent self. This band clearly enjoys themselves jamming mostly on warhorses, making this a high-spirited set of New Orleans jazz. — *Scott Yanow*

New Orleans Traditional Jazz Legends / 1992 / Mardi Gras ✦✦✦

A '92 reissue featuring noted classic blues and traditional New Orleans jazz vocalist Sweet Emma Barrett. She lived up to her reputation, belting out the one-liners, double entendres, and innuendo with gusto, then turning poignant or bemused when necessary. Her fine vocals were backed by fairly routine support, but hearing Sweet Emma Barrett made everything worthwhile. — *Ron Wynn*

Dave Bartholomew

b. Dec. 24, 1940, Edgard, LA
Trumpet / New Orleans R&B, R&B

A major contributor to New Orleans R&B, Dave Bartholomew was a pivotal figure as a writer, arranger, producer, and A&R man for Imperial. It was Bartholomew's productions that helped make Fats Domino a major player in R&B and rock 'n' roll, and he assembled the great house band that backed Domino, Little Richard, Lloyd Price, Smiley Lewis, and several other Crescent City greats. This band included pianist Allen Toussaint, bassist Frank Fields, saxophonists Lee Allen, Alvin "Red" Tyler, and Herb Hardesty, and drummer Earl Palmer. Bartholomew recorded as a solo artist for King and others prior to taking over at Imperial, but his fame came from that stint. Bartholomew greatly reduced his activities after Domino left Imperial in the early '60s, but occasionally resurfaced to conduct his band. — *Ron Wynn*

In the Alley / 1991 / Charly ✦✦✦

Early work for King (1949-52) spotlighting his vocals and trumpet. — *Bill Dahl*

★ **The Spirit of New Orleans: The Genius of Dave Bartholomew** / 1993 / Capitol ✦✦✦✦✦

A two-disc set featuring 50 tracks and several different artists (including Fats Domino, Smiley Lewis, T-Bone Walker, Shirley and Lee, and Earl King), *The Spirit of New Orleans* effectively conveys Bartholomew's groundbreaking achievements in R&B and rock 'n' roll. — *Stephen Thomas Erlewine*

Lou Ann Barton

b. Feb. 17, 1954, Fort Worth, TX
Vocals / Blues-Rock, Electric Texas Blues

Although she doesn't tour nearly as much as she probably could, Austin-based vocalist Lou Ann Barton is one of the finest purveyors of raw, unadulterated roadhouse blues from the female gender that you'll ever hear. Like Delbert McClinton, she can belt out a lyric so that she can be heard over a two-guitar band with horns. Born February 17, 1954, in Fort Worth, she's a veteran of thousands of dance hall and club shows all over Texas. Barton moved to Austin in the 1970s and later performed with the Fabulous Thunderbirds and Stevie Ray Vaughan and Double Trouble.

Although she has a few great recordings out, notably *Old Enough* (1982, Asylum Records), produced by Jerry Wexler and Glenn Frey, Barton has to be seen live to be fully appreciated. She belts out her lyrics in a twangy voice so full of Texas that you can smell the barbecue sauce. She swaggers confidently about the stage, casually tossing her cigarette to the floor as the band kicks in on its first number. The grace, poise and confidence she projects on stage is part of a long tradition for women blues singers. The blues world still needs more good female blues singers like Barton to help to broaden the appeal of the music to diverse audiences and to further its evolution.

Barton has several other excellent albums out on the Austin-based Antone's Records, *Read My Lips* (1989) and her cooperative effort with fellow Texas blues women Marcia Ball and Angela Strehli, *Dreams Come True* (1990). *Old Enough* was reissued on compact disc in 1992 on the Antone's label. The only criticism one could level at Barton—and it may be unfair because of business complications—is that she hasn't recorded much. Here's hoping that this premier interpreter of Texas roadhouse blues will be well recorded through the rest of the 1990s. — *Richard Skelly*

● **Old Enough** / 1982 / Discovery ✦✦✦✦

Lou Ann Barton arrived fully formed with her debut album, *Old Enough*. It was clear from the outset that she was a magnificent singer, full of bold, gritty sensuality. Though there are a few hints of gloss on the album, Barton tears through any pretense and delivers a scorching first album. — *Thom Owens*

Forbidden Tones / 1986 / Spindletop ✦✦✦

Read My Lips / 1989 / Antone's ✦✦✦✦

Barton's lascivious delivery of roadhouse R&B chestnuts by Hank Ballard, Slim Harpo, and others is hotter than four-alarm chili on a Texas summer night. Members from The Fabulous Thunderbirds, Stevie Ray Vaughan's band, and other Austin heavy-hitters ensure that songs like "Sexy Ways," "Shake Your Hips," "You Can Have My Husband," "Sugar Coated Love," and "Rocket in My Pocket" have the right amount of grease. — *Rick Clark*

Dreams Come True / 1990 / Antone's ✦✦✦

Dreams Come True is an all-star session by vocalists Marcia Ball, Lou Ann Barton and Angela Strehli. The three women sing with a band led by Dr. John and the session features guest appearances by such luminaries as David "Fathead" Newman and Jimmie Vaughan. The music is straight out of the Texas school of roadhouse R&B and blues boogie but it's delivered with a gritty, heartfelt edge, particularly on the part of the three vocalists. *Dreams Come True* may follow formula, but it's followed with style and affection, which makes it a very enjoyable listen. — *Thom Owens*

Paul Bascomb

b. Feb. 12, 1912, Birmingham, AL, **d.** Dec. 2, 1986, Chicago, IL
Sax (Tenor) / Swing, Early R&B Jazz, Jump Blues

It is easy to divide Paul Bascomb's career into two for he was a top soloist with Erskine Hawkins' swing orchestra and later on recorded a popular series of early rhythm & blues records. The brother of trumpeter Dud Bascomb (another star of the Hawkins band), the tenorman was one of the founding members of the 'Bama State Collegians (which eventually became the Erskine Hawkins Big Band) in the early '30s and, except for a period in 1938-39 when he replaced the late Herschel Evans with Count Basie's Orchestra, he was with Hawkins until 1944. Bascomb co-led groups with Dud (1944-47) and in the early '50s recorded extensively for the United label; the accessible performances have been partially reissued by Delmark. Paul Bascomb was active (if maintaining a low profile) into the mid-'80s. — *Scott Yanow*

● **Bad Bascomb!** / Mar. 3, 1952-Aug. 30, 1952 / Delmark ✦✦✦✦

This CD collects together tenor-saxophonist Paul Bascomb's United recordings of 1952. The material is pretty basic and R&Bish but fun with the highlights including "Blues and the Beat," "Pink Cadillac," "Soul and Body" and "Indiana." The backup group includes trumpeter Eddie Lewis and pianist

Duke Jordan and the CD reissue adds four alternate takes to the original 13 selections. Recommended. — *Scott Yanow*

Johnny Bassett

b. Oct. 9, 1935, Marianna, FL

Guitar, Vocals / Modern Electric Blues

Guitarist, singer and songwriter Johnny Bassett grew up with blues music all around him in his native Florida. His unique ability to combine jump blues and Delta stylings gives his playing a distinctive sound.

The self-taught guitarist recalls seeing Tampa Red, Arthur "Big Boy" Crudup and other classic blues artists at fish fries in his grandmother's backyard. Bassett cites Aaron "T-Bone" Walker as a major influence, as well as B.B. and Albert King, Tiny Grimes and Billy Butler.

After Bassett's family moved to Detroit in 1944, he made his debut as a guitarist with Joe Weaver and the Bluenotes, a teenage R&B band. The group won local talent contests and were hired to back up Big Joe Turner, Ruth Brown and others on their tour stops in Detroit. Bassett went into the Army in 1958 and played in a country & western group while stationed in Washington state.

After returning to Detroit, he found work as a session guitarist for Fortune Records by day and in nightclubs at night. In the studios, he played backup to musicians and groups like Nolan Strong and the Diablos, Andre Williams and the Don Juans, and the Five Dollars. He also played guitar on the first recording by Smokey Robinson and the Miracles while traveling to Chicago to record as a session man for the Chess Records label. During his Detroit days, he also accompanied John Lee Hooker, Eddie Burns, Alberta Adams, Lowell Fulson, and the T.J. Fowler Band at their live shows, as well as Dinah Washington.

In the '60s, Bassett moved to Seattle, where he backed up Tina Turner, Little Willie John and others. Jimi Hendrix was a frequent guest at the bluesman's club gigs around Seattle. Before the decade ended, he moved back to Detroit, where he's been based ever since.

In 1994, Bassett received a lifetime achievement award from the Detroit Blues Society. He later recorded an album for the Dutch Black Magic label, *I Gave My Life to the Blues* (1996). Bassett and his band, the Blues Insurgents—which he's been fronting since the early '90s—have made several US, Canadian and European tours in support of LPs including 1997's *Bassett Hound* and 1998's *Cadillac Blues.* — *Richard Skelly*

● **Cadillac Blues** / Jan. 20, 1998 / Cannonball ◆◆◆◆

A veteran of the '50s Detroit blues scene, Johnnie Bassett brings his big hollow-body guitar and supple voice to this, his debut album. Produced by Ron Levy, Bassett's big-voiced guitar lines exhibit both swing and restraint, while his voice shows little, if any, of the ravages of time. The horn parts dart in and out around his regular band, the Blues Insurgents, who manage to keep the groove simple and straightforward throughout. There's more a hint of jump in this album, with "I Can't Get It Together," "Raise the Roof, Raise the Rent," and the swinging "Walk On Baby" being particular standouts. An impressive, well-produced debut. — *Cub Koda*

Chris Beard

Guitar, Vocals / Modern Electric Blues

Guitarist, singer and songwriter Chris Beard is the son of Rochester-area blues guitarist Joe Beard. He has been patiently paying his dues on the club circuit around the Northeast for the last 20 years. Beard, who goes by the nickname "Prince of the Blues," is one of the young lions of blues in the '90s. He can be safely grouped with other idiom-expanding artists like Larry Garner, Tutu Jones and Michael Hill.

Beard began playing guitar at age five, inspired by all the blues talent his father had over to the house—artists like Buddy Guy and Matt "Guitar" Murphy. He learned to play "Green Onions" as a 6-year-old, and at 15 he began playing with a local classic rhythm & blues ensemble. He continued playing in local bands and sitting in with his father's band through high school. After graduation, he began fronting his own group and writing his own songs, taking inspiration from people like Albert King and Johnny "Guitar" Watson.

Beard's debut album, *Barwalkin',* for the London-based JSP Records, is a 12-track showcase of style and songwriting virtuosity. Produced by Johnny Rawls, who also plays guitar on the recording, Beard is accompanied by Hammond B-3 organist Brian Charettte, former Johnny Copeland Band bass-

ist Randy Lippincott, and drummer Barry Harrison. The Nutmeg Horns, consisting of Bruce and Robert Feiner on saxophones and Jim Hunt on trumpet, add body to some songs. — *Richard Skelly*

Barwalkin' / Jun. 24, 1997 / JSP ◆◆◆

Joe Beard

b. Feb. 4, 1938, Ashland, MS

Guitar / Modern Electric Blues

Born and raised in Ashland, Mississippi, guitarist Joe Beard grew up with the Murphy brothers, one of whom later found an international following as Matt "Guitar" Murphy. Guitarist Nathan Beauregard lived with Beard's cousin, so he was surrounded by aspiring and veteran blues musicians while growing up, and he began singing at an early age. Beard became interested in playing guitar via the Murphy brothers, who sat in with a young B.B. King when he played at the Roosevelt Lake Club. Beard began to learn guitar at age 17 from Ernest Scruggs, a neighbor, before heading to Chicago.

Beard moved to Rochester, N.Y., and from time to time would visit one of his brothers in Chicago. He quickly became enamored of the blues being played in clubs there by people like Jimmy Reed and Sonny Boy Williamson. Beard sat in with John Lee Hooker one night and received encouraging words from Hooker, and also later sat in with his idol, Muddy Waters.

While in Rochester, he formed the Soul Brothers Six, playing bass and singing, but he didn't perform in public on guitar until 1965. Beard befriended classic blues guitarist Son House, who was a neighbor in Rochester, and played a concert for students at the University of Rochester in 1968. Beard worked as an electrician by day and would occasionally play out at night and on weekends for most of the '60s on through to the '80s. He has a reputation as one of the best local players around Rochester, and though he may not be a household name in other parts of the US, he toured Europe in 1983 and did studio and stage work that same year with Buster Benton, Lafayette Leake and Memphis Slim. At the famed BK Lounge, Beard and his backing bands opened for Bobby Bland, Albert King and others. More recently, Beard performed at President George Bush's inaugural gala. In 1990, he recorded an album for Kingsnake Records, *No More Cherry Rose,* which was well received by the blues radio community.

Beard recently recorded an album with Ronnie Earl's band for the California-based AudioQuest label, *Blues Union* (1996). Accompanying him are Hammond B-3 organist Bruce Katz and tenor saxophonist David "Fathead" Newman. — *Richard Skelly*

● **Blues Union** / Aug. 18, 1995-Aug. 19, 1995 / AudioQuest ◆◆◆◆

Although Joe Beard is a country-based bluesman and fellow guitarist Ronnie Earl (who brought along his Broadcasters for this set) is strictly city, they work together quite well. The emphasis is often on Beard's expressive vocals (which sometimes look towards John Lee Hooker and Lightnin' Hopkins but display their own personality). Beard and Earl contribute contrasting guitar solos, pianist-organist Bruce Katz fuels a grooving rhythm section, tenor saxophonist David "Fathead" Newman has a couple of cameos and the harmonica of Joe Dubuc is a strong asset on three songs. Even with its nods towards the past, this release is a fine example of blues in the mid-'90s. — *Scott Yanow*

No More Cherry Rose / 1996 / Ichiban ◆◆◆

For Real / Mar. 24, 1998 / AudioQuest ◆◆◆

This well-presented variations of old-style blues, from acoustic ("Dirty Groundhog"), to slow burners ("Elem"), to Chicago/Muddy Waters style ("Who's Using Who"). Duke Robillard graciously acts in his role as a team player, although he stands out with a hip solo on "If That's What Pleases Her." Portney's harp on "She's Wonderful" is slow and easy, reminiscent of a hot summer's day in the country. — *Char Ham*

Jeff Beck

b. Jun. 24, 1944, Wallington, Surrey, England

Guitar, Bass / Rock 'n' Roll, Hard Rock, Fusion, Electric British Blues

While he was as innovative as Jimmy Page, as tasteful as Eric Clapton and nearly as visionary as Jimi Hendrix, Jeff Beck never achieved the same commercial success as any of his contemporaries, primarily because of the haphazard way he approached his career. After Rod Stewart left the Jeff Beck Group in 1971, Beck never worked with a charismatic lead singer who could have helped sell his music to a wide audience. Furthermore, he was simply too idiosyncratic, moving from heavy metal to jazz-fusion within a blink of an eye. As his career progressed, he became more fascinated by automobiles than guitars, releasing only one album during the course of the '90s. All the while, Beck retained the respect of fellow guitarists, who found his reclusiveness all the more alluring.

Jeff Beck began his musical career following a short stint at London's Wimbledon Art College. He earned a reputation by supporting Lord Sutch, which helped him land the job as the Yardbirds' lead guitarist following the departure of Eric Clapton. Beck stayed with the Yardbirds for nearly two years, leaving in late in 1966 with the pretense that he was retiring from music. He returned several months later with "Love Is Blue," a single he played poorly because he detested the song. Later in 1967, he formed the Jeff Beck Group with vocalist Rod Stewart, bassist Ron Wood and drummer Aynsley Dunbar, who was quickly replaced by Mickey Waller; keyboardist Nicky Hopkins joined in early 1968. With their crushingly loud reworkings of blues songs and vocal and guitar interplay, the Jeff Beck Group established the template for heavy metal. Neither of the band's records, *Truth* (1968) or *Beck-Ola* (a 1969 album which was recorded with new drummer Tony Newman), were particularly successful, and the band tended to fight regularly, especially on their frequent tours of the US. In 1970, Stewart and Wood left to join the Faces, and Beck broke up the group.

Beck had intended to form a power trio with Vanilla Fudge members Carmine Appice (drums) and Tim Bogert (bass), but those plans were derailed when he suffered a serious car crash in 1970. By the time he recuperated in 1971, Bogert and Appice were playing in Cactus, so the guitarist formed a new version of the Jeff Beck Group. Featuring keyboardist Max Middleton, drummer Cozy Powell, bassist Clive Chaman, and vocalist Bobby Tench, the new band recorded *Rough and Ready* (1971) and *The Jeff Beck Group* (1972). Neither album attracted much attention. Cactus dissolved in late 1972, and Beck, Bogert and Appice formed a power trio the following year. The group's lone studio album—a live record was released in Japan but never in the UK or US—was widely panned due to its plodding arrangements and weak vocals, and the group disbanded the following year.

For about 18 months, Beck remained quiet, re-emerging in 1975 with *Blow By Blow*. Produced by George Martin, *Blow By Blow* was an all-instrumental jazz-fusion album that received strong reviews. Beck collaborated with Jan Hammer, a former keyboardist for the Mahavishnu Orchestra, for 1976's *Wired*, and supported the album with a co-headlining tour with Hammer's band. The tour was documented on the 1977 album, *Jeff Beck with the Jan Hammer Group—Live*.

After the Hammer tour, Beck retired to his estate outside of London and remained quiet for three years. He returned in 1980 with *There and Back*, which featured contributions from Hammer. Following the tour for *There and Back*, Beck retired again, returning five years later with the slick, Nile Rodgers-produced *Flash*. A pop-rock album recorded with a variety of vocalists, *Flash* featured Beck's only hit single, the Stewart-sung "People Get Ready," and also boasted "Escape," which won the Grammy for Best Rock instrumental. During 1987, he played lead guitar on Mick Jagger's second solo album, *Primitive Cool*. There was another long wait between *Flash* and 1989's *Jeff Beck's Guitar Shop with Terry Bozzio and Tony Hymas*. Though the album sold only moderately well, *Guitar Shop* received uniformly strong reviews and won the Grammy for Best Rock Instrumental. Beck supported the album with a tour, this time co-headlining with guitarist Stevie Ray Vaughan. Again, Beck entered semi-retirement upon the completion of the tour.

In 1992, Beck played lead guitar on Roger Waters' comeback album, *Amused to Death*. A year later, he released *Crazy Legs*, a tribute to Gene Vincent and his lead guitarist Cliff Gallup, which was recorded with the Big Town Playboys. Beck remained quiet after the album's release. — *Stephen Thomas Erlewine*

Truth / Aug. 1968 / Epic ✦✦✦✦

Possibly Jeff Beck's most influential recording, *Truth* takes the amped-up blues-rock of the Yardbirds and the guitarist's psychedelicized sonic experimentation to the next level. Beck enlisted a powerful hard rock band featuring Rod Stewart on vocals, Ron Wood on bass, and Mick Waller on drums; the interplay between all the musicians is tremendous, especially Stewart and Beck trading vocal and guitar lines, respectively, a motif that would later become a heavy metal staple. The repertoire is quite varied, composed of heavy, loud blues standards ("You Shook Me," "I Ain't Superstitious"), folk

songs, largely instrumental guitar showcases (including the shattering "Beck's Bolero"), and a few originals, plus a reworked "Shapes of Things." *Truth* laid down the blueprint for early heavy metal, foreshadowing Led Zeppelin in particular, and Beck's inventive guitar playing and hard-rocking band have kept it a rich, rewarding listen today. — *Steve Huey*

Beck-Ola / Jun. 1969 / Epic ✦✦✦✦

A year after Jeff Beck recorded *Truth*, he came back with the even heavier *Beck-Ola*. Although the songwriting seems diluted, and the addition of Nicky Hopkins on piano added spice in all the wrong places, *Beck-Ola* is still a gut-slamming good time. Notable tracks include "Spanish Boots" and "Plynth (Water Down the Drain)." — *Tom Graves*

Rough & Ready / Oct. 1971 / Epic ✦✦✦

After Jeff Beck nearly died in a car crash, he came back in 1971 with a new group and a new sound, reflecting his more introspective state of mind. Although the firepower and guitar blasts are still there, he burns cooler. With the help of the jazzy Max Middleton on piano, Beck created one of rock's most haunting set pieces, "Raynes Park Blues." Other highlights include the dynamic ballad "Jody" and the hard grinding rock groove of "I've Been Used." — *Tom Graves & Rick Clark*

Jeff Beck Group / Apr. 1972 / Epic ✦✦✦

Continuing with the same group lineup as on *Rough & Ready*, *Jeff Beck Group* was slagged off by critics for Steve Cropper's admittedly lazy production. However, several of the songs hold up masterfully, including the skronky "Ice Cream Cakes," the superlative redo of Don Nix's "Going Down," and the beautifully sad and wistful instrumental, "Definitely Maybe." Beware of early, poor-sounding versions. — *Tom Graves*

Blow by Blow / Mar. 1975 / Epic ✦✦✦✦

When Jeff Beck announced that he was working on an all-instrumental album, few but his legion of guitar fans could have predicted the far-reaching impact of this pivotal jazz-rock fusion album. Teamed with the Beatles' ex-producer George Martin, Beck singlehandedly created a new subtext for rock 'n' roll. With his virtuosity and taste at an all-time peak, Beck let loose with such unforgettable tracks as the Roy Buchanan-inspired "Cause We've Ended as Lovers" and the percolating "Freeway Jam." This is one of rock's great instrumental works. — *Tom Graves*

Wired / May 1976 / Epic ✦✦✦✦

Nearly *Blow by Blow*'s equal, although Beck doesn't venture any further musically. Charles Mingus's "Goodbye Pork Pie Hat" is worth the price alone. (Available on Mobile Fidelity's Ultradisc) — *Tom Graves*

Live With the Jan Hammer Group / Mar. 1977 / Epic ✦✦

Jeff Beck toured to promote *Wired*, backed by a jazz-fusion group led by synthesizer player Jan Hammer. This straightforward live souvenir combines songs from *Blow by Blow* and *Wired*, plus a few other things, and while it features typically fiery playing from Beck, the backup is a bit too heavy-handed and the occasional vocals (by Hammer and drummer Tony Smith) are embarrassing. — *William Ruhlmann*

There & Back / Jun. 1980 / Epic ✦✦✦

Jeff Beck's first new studio album in four years found him moving from old keyboard partner Jan Hammer (three tracks) to new one Tony Hymas (five), which turned out to be the difference between competition and support. Hence, the second side of this instrumental album is more engaging and less of a funk-fusion extravaganza than most of the first. If it were anybody else, you'd say that this was a transitional album, but this was the only studio album Beck released between 1976 and 1985, which makes it more like an unexpected Christmas letter from an old friend: "Everything's fine, still playing guitar." — *William Ruhlmann*

Flash / Jul. 1985 / Epic ✦✦✦

Produced by Nile Rodgers and Arthur Baker, *Flash* is Beck's surprisingly successful stab at a pop album, featuring a fine performance with Rod Stewart on "People Get Ready." — *Stephen Thomas Erlewine*

Jeff Beck's Guitar Shop / Oct. 1989 / Epic ✦✦✦✦

A guitar hero in his prime, he's full of fury and finesse, with top-notch support from Terry Bozzio and Tony Hymas. — *Jas Obrecht*

Beckology / Nov. 19, 1991 / Epic ✦✦✦✦

Covering everything from his earliest (and terrific) tracks with the Tridents through his spot-on interpretation of Santo & Johnny's "Sleep Walk," *Beckol-*

ogy features great remastering, smart packaging (resembling a vintage Fender tweed guitar case), and the essential Yardbirds and solo years material. The set (55 tracks in all) also collects the best material from weaker albums such as *Flash* and *There & Back*. A definitive overview of Beck's career would have included his work as a sideman with artists like Stevie Wonder, Rod Stewart, and Donovan; nevertheless, *Beckology* is as comprehensive a collection as one will find on this innovative guitarist. — *Tom Graves & Rick Clark*

Frankie's House / Jan. 5, 1992 / Epic ♦♦
Beck fans will find his playing here mesmerizing, surpassing the technical mastery of *Guitar Shop*. Apart from a sizzling instrumental version of "High Heeled Sneakers," less devoted listeners will find *Frankie's House* as captivating as most other incidental film music. — *Stephen Thomas Erlewine*

Crazy Legs / Jun. 29, 1993 / Epic ♦♦
Jeff Beck has made many strange albums, but none were ever quite as strange as this. With the Big Town Playboys offering support, Beck rips through 15 Gene Vincent numbers (not "Be-Bop-a-Lula," however), paying tribute to Vincent's guitarist, Cliff Gallup. Beck sounds terrific as he reconstructs Gallup's parts, but he doesn't add anything to the originals. Still, *Crazy Legs* is a fun listen and offers many insights into Beck's playing, if not Gallup's. — *Stephen Thomas Erlewine*

● **The Best of Beck [Epic]** / Aug. 15, 1995 / Columbia ♦♦♦♦
Basically this record exists because the record company wanted to have some product on the shelf while Beck was touring. The 14 tracks do contain some of his most often-played (by radio, at any rate) recordings, including "Shapes of Things," "Plynth," and "Beck's Bolero" from the original Jeff Beck Group days in the late '60s, and the vocoder showcase "She's a Woman" and fusion landmark "Freeway Jam" from *Blow by Blow*. It may do for casual listeners who only want one Beck CD, although more serious fans would be better off with the *Beckology* box. — *Richie Unterberger*

Best of Jeff Beck [Columbia Import] / Epic ♦♦
The chief appeal of this European import, a skimpy nine-song survey of Beck's late-'60s work, is the inclusion of three tracks from rare solo singles that weren't featured on the first two Jeff Beck Group albums: "Hi Ho Silver Lining," "Tallyman," and "Love Is Blue." Beck takes lead vocals on the first two of these, and though "Hi Ho Silver Lining" actually made the British Top 20, Beck and/or those around him quickly realized that a strong lead vocal presence (i.e., someone other than Beck) was in order. These are typical British pop-rock tunes of the era, but the real curiosity is "Love Is Blue," a cheesy rendition of the Paul Mauriat megasmash that sets Beck's stinging guitar against a near-muzak arrangement. — *Richie Unterberger*

Carey Bell

b. Nov. 14, 1936, Macon, MS
Harmonica, Vocals, Bass, Drums, Guitar / Electric Chicago Blues, Modern Electric Chicago Blues
His place on the honor roll of Chicago blues harpists long ago assured, Carey Bell has truly come into his own during the last few years as a bandleader with terrific discs for Alligator and Blind Pig. He learned his distinctive harmonica riffs from the Windy City's very best (both Walters — Little *and* Big — as well as Sonny Boy Williamson No. 2), adding his own signature effects for good measure (an other-worldly moan immediately identifies many of his more memorable harp rides).

Born Carey Bell Harrington in the blues-fertile state of Mississippi, he was already playing the harp when he was eight and working professionally with his godfather, pianist Lovie Lee, at 13. The older and more experienced Lee brought Carey with him to Chicago in search of steady musical opportunities in 1956. Gigs frequently proved scarce, and Carey eventually took up electric bass, playing behind Robert Nighthawk, Johnny Young, and his mentor Big Walter Horton. Finally, in 1969, Bell made his debut album (on harp) for Delmark, and he was on his way.

Bell served invaluable early-'70s stints in the bands of Muddy Waters and Willie Dixon, touring extensively and recording with both legends. Alligator Records has been responsible for much of Bell's best recorded work as a leader, beginning with a joint venture with Horton back in 1972. Four cuts by Bell on the first batch of Alligator's *Living Chicago Blues* anthologies in 1978 preceded his participation in the 1990 harmonica summit meeting

Harp Attack!, which brought him into the studio with fellow greats James Cotton, Junior Wells, and Billy Branch. His recent solo set for Alligator, *Deep Down*, rates as his finest album to date. Bell has sired a passel of blues-playing progeny; best-known of the brood is mercurial guitarist Lurrie Bell. — *Bill Dahl*

Carey Bell's Blues Harp / Feb. 12, 1969 + May 6, 1969 / Delmark ♦♦♦
It's a mite ragged around the edges, but Bell's 1969 debut session certainly sports the proper ambience — and no wonder, with guitarists Eddie Taylor and Jimmy Dawkins and pianist Pinetop Perkins on hand to help out. No less than four Little Walter covers and two more from Muddy Waters' songbook dot the set, but many of the best moments occur on the original numbers. Delmark's CD reissue includes three previously unissued items. — *Bill Dahl*

Last Night / 1973 / One Way ♦♦♦
Nothing flashy or outrageous here, just a meat-and-potatoes session produced by Al Smith that satisfyingly showcases Bell's charms. Once again, there are hearty tributes to Little Walter ("Last Night") and Muddy Waters ("She's 19 Years Old"), but there's some original stuff too, backed by a combo that boasted a daunting collective experience level: Taylor and Perkins return, along with bassist David Myers and drummer Willie "Big Eyes" Smith. — *Bill Dahl*

Heartaches and Pain / 1977 / Delmark ♦♦♦
Legendary producer Ralph Bass supervised this quickie session back in 1977, but it failed to see the light of day domestically until Delmark rescued it from oblivion. They did the blues world a favor: it's a worthwhile session, Bell storming through a mostly original setlist (the omnipresent Little Walter cover this time is "Everything's Gonna Be Alright"). Aron Burton and Sam Lay comprise the rhythm section, and son Lurrie contributes lead guitar. — *Bill Dahl*

Son of a Gun / May 27, 1983-Jun. 2, 1982 / Rooster Blues ♦♦♦
The raucous pairing of this harpist and his guitarist son Lurrie creates some sparks. — *Bill Dahl*

Harpslinger / 1988 / JSP ♦♦

Dynasty! / 1990 / JSP ♦♦

Harp Attack! / 1990 / Alligator ♦♦♦♦
Four of Chicago's preeminent blues harpists — Bell, James Cotton, Junior Wells, and relative newcomer Billy Branch — gathered in a downtown studio to wax this historic summit meeting. Bell's vocal showcases include two originals, "Hit Man" and "Second Hand Man," and a Muddy Waters cover, "My Eyes Keep Me in Trouble." — *Bill Dahl*

Mellow Down Easy / 1991 / Blind Pig ♦♦♦♦
The harpist hooked up with a young Maryland-based band called Tough Luck for this disc, certainly one of his better outings. The traditional mindset of the combo pushed Bell back to his roots, whether on the originals "Just like You" and the Horton homage "Big Walter Strut" or revivals of Muddy Waters' "Short Dress Woman" and "Walking Thru the Park" and the classic Little Walter title cut. — *Bill Dahl*

Goin' on Main Street / 1994 / Evidence ♦♦♦

● **Deep Down** / 1995 / Alligator ♦♦♦♦
More than a quarter century after he cut his debut album, Bell recently made his finest disc to date. Boasting superior material and musicianship (guitarists Carl Weathersby and Lurrie Bell and pianist Lucky Peterson are all stellar) and a goosed-up energy level that frequently reaches incendiary heights, the disc captures Bell outdoing himself vocally on the ribald "Let Me Stir in Your Pot" and a suitably loose "When I Get Drunk" and instrumentally on the torrid "Jawbreaker." For a closer, Bell settled on the atmospheric Horton classic "Easy"; he does it full justice. — *Bill Dahl*

Good Luck Man / Oct. 7, 1997 / Alligator ♦♦♦
Chicago harp wizard Carey Bell comes back for his second Alligator album, which is even stronger than his last effort, *Deep Down*. With blistering lead guitar support from Steve Jacobs, Bell explores and invests in some more modern grooves this time around ("My Love Strikes Like Lightning," "Brand New Deal," and the title track) while still exhibiting a tone on his harp as big as a Mack truck on tracks like "Bell Hop" and a fine version of Big Walter Horton's "Hard Hearted Woman." Carey's fine chromatic harp work is featured nicely on "Going Back to Mississippi" and the romping instrumental

"Double Cross," and there isn't a dull moment anywhere to be found on this disc. A very strong effort. — *Cub Koda*

Brought up the Hard Way / Mar. 10, 1998 / JSP ✦✦✦✦
Brought Up the Hard Way compiles a selection of Carey Bell's best JSP sides; featured guests are Lefty Dizz and Louisiana Red. — *Steve Huey*

Lurrie Bell

b. Dec. 13, 1958, Chicago, IL
Guitar, Vocals / Modern Electric Chicago Blues, Modern Electric Chicago Blues, Electric Chicago Blues
Lurrie Bell was born to play the blues. His famous father, harpist Carey Bell, had him working out on guitar as a wee lad. By 1977, he was recording with his dad and playing behind a variety of established stars, tabbed by many observers at the time as a sure star on the rise. But personal problems took their toll on his great potential; Bell's recorded output and live performances have been inconsistent over the last decade or so.
    Among the highlights of Lurrie's discography: three tracks in tandem with harpist Billy Branch under the Sons of Blues banner (Lurrie was a founding member of the still-thriving band) from Alligator's first batch of 1978 *Living Chicago Blues* anthologies and a 1984 collaboration with his old man for Rooster Blues, *Son of a Gun* (the latter remains unavailable on CD). Then there's his recent set for Delmark, *Mercurial Son*, as bizarre a contemporary blues album as you're likely to encounter. Bell followed *Mercurial Son* with the more straightforward *700 Blues* in the spring of 1997. — *Bill Dahl*

● **Son of a Gun** / May 27, 1982-Jun. 2, 1982 / Rooster Blues ✦✦✦✦
Lurrie and his dear old dad democratically split the vocals and most of the solo space on this LP to generally winning effect. Nothing overly polished or endlessly rehearsed; just solid mainstream Chicago blues. — *Bill Dahl*

Everybody Wants to Win / 1989 / JSP ✦✦✦

Mercurial Son / Oct. 3, 1995 / Delmark ✦✦
Don't blame Lurrie for the overbearingly weird vibe of this album. Producer/drummer Steve Cushing supplied much of the material, which is delivered by Bell so incomprehensibly that the printed lyrics inside the booklet are the only way to decipher them (once you read up on the misogynistic "Your Daddy Done Tripped the Trigger" and the bizarre "Blues in the Year One-D-One," you'll wish you hadn't). Big Time Sarah was recruited to belt "Your Wild Thing Ain't Wild Enough," one of the dirtiest and most childish diatribes ever recorded in the name of blues. Bell's guitar work, however, remains sharp, and when he sings something of his own—"Lurrie's Cool Groove," or "Tell Me About Your Love"—the magic temporarily returns. — *Bill Dahl*

700 Blues / Apr. 29, 1997 / Delmark ✦✦✦

Young Man's Blues: The Best of the JSP Sessions (1989-1990) / Nov. 18, 1997 / JSP ✦✦✦✦

Fred Below

b. Sep. 16, 1926, Chicago, IL, **d.** Aug. 14, 1988, Chicago, IL
Drums / Chicago Blues, Modern Electric Blues
Fred Below was born in Chicago on September 16, 1926. Below played drums in high school and went on to study percussion at the Roy C. Knapp School of Percussion. Primarily a jazz drummer at the time, he played bebop and joined the Army as part of the 427th Army band. After the service, he returned to Chicago in 1951 to find that blues gigs were what was happening. Jazz was in a lull.
    Then Muddy Waters drummer Elgin Evans introduced Below to a group called the Three Aces—Junior Wells (vocals, harp), Louis Myers (guitar), and Dave Myers (bass)—who needed a drummer. As a jazz drummer, Below did not know blues drumming and it was a rough fit at first. The next big event came when Little Walter (on the sudden success of his instrumental "Juke") quit the Muddy Waters band and was replaced by Junior Wells. Little Walter then joined the Three Aces which he had been itching to do because Muddy Waters did not play in the up-tempo style that Walter was into. Little Walter and the Four Aces (later renamed the Jukes) were a perfect fit and this four-piece electric blues combo became the hottest band in Chicago.
    It is hard to estimate the effect of this band on Chicago music scene, and a large part of this success is due to the refined and elegant drumming of Below. He plays on almost all of Walter's greatest hits. He was in total demand for recording sessions. Everyone wanted him and he recorded for

Muddy Waters, Willie Dixon, Chuck Berry, Otis Rush, Elmore James, Junior Wells, Buddy Guy, Dinah Washington, John Brim, the Platters, the Moonglows, the Drifters, Bo Diddley, John Lee Hooker, Howlin' Wolf, and many more. Fred Below and the Aces pretty much created the standard for the blues shuffle beat. Below also was known for his use of the ride cymbal, the wood block, tom-tom fills, and many other embellishments. Just check out his drum solo on Little Walter's classic tune "Off the Wall." — *Michael Erlewine*

Duster Bennett (Anthony Bennett)

b. 1940, **d.** Mar. 25, 1976
Guitar, Harmonica, Drums, Vocals / Blues-Rock, Electric British Blues, British Blues
Duster Bennett was a British blues singer and harmonica player. He signed to Mike Vernon's Blue Horizon label in 1967 and was backed on his debut album, *Smiling Like I'm Happy* (1968), by members of Fleetwood Mac. He was a session harmonica player and a member of John Mayall's Bluesbreakers. He was killed in a car accident in 1976. — *William Ruhlmann*

Out in the Blue / 1966-1976 / Indigo ✦✦✦✦
Odds and ends, mostly from 1966-68, with a few tracks from 1975 and 1976, the year Bennett was killed in a car wreck. Two tracks feature fine lead guitar by Duster's longtime friend (and original Yardbird) Top Topham—home tapes worthy of inclusion if only for Top's amazing and expressive vibrato. Five tracks feature Peter Green, including a demo of his "Trying So Hard to Forget" that's especially moody and the fascinating snippet "Two Harps" instrumental duet (unaccompanied harmonicas, as the title implies), showing the similarity in the pair's harp styles. The final cut, "Everyday," from 1976, sets one of Bennett's finest vocal performnces against a string backdrop. What a contrast to the one-man band shouting "Worried Mind"—and it works. — *Dan Forte*

● **Smiling Like I'm Happy** / Jul. 8, 1968-Sep. 9, 1968 / Blue Horizon ✦✦✦✦
One of the unsung heroes of British blues, this one-man band was a fine harmonica player and singer, a decent guitarist, and a soulful enough singer to make one overlook his distinctly *unbluesy* high voice. The opening "Worried Mind"—just Duster on harp, guitar, voice, high-hat and kick drum—is a marvelously sloppy shuffle romp that holds its own with the Fabulous Thunderbirds' work ten years hence. On other tracks Bennett is backed by three-fourths of the original Fleetwood Mac, who provide simple, effective support without stealing any limelight; solos are kept to a minimum. Originals "My Lucky Day" (with chromatic harmonica) and "Jumping at Shadows" which Mac would later cover) are absolutely outstanding, and Duster does justice to Magic Sam's "My Love Is Your Love." — *Dan Forte*

Bright Lights / 1969 / Blue Horizon ✦✦✦

12 Dbs / 1970 / Blue Horizon ✦✦✦

Bennett / 1970 / Blue Horizon ✦✦✦

Justa / 1970 / Blue Horizon ✦✦✦

Jumpin' at Shadows / 1995 / Indigo ✦✦✦

Blue Inside / 1996 / Indigo ✦✦✦

Tab Benoit

b. Nov. 17, 1967, Baton Rouge, LA
Guitar, Vocals / Electric Louisiana Blues
Guitarist, singer and songwriter Tab Benoit makes his home south of New Orleans in Houma, LA. Born November 17, 1967, he's one of a handful of bright rising stars on the modern blues scene. For most of the 1990s, he's been working each of his records the old fashioned way, by playing anywhere and everywhere he and his band can play. Unlike so many others before him, Benoit understands that blues is not a medium in favor with 50,000 watt commercial rock radio stations, so as a consequence, he's worked each of his releases with as many shows as he can possibly play. Since the release of his first album for Justice, Benoit has taken his brand of Cajun-influenced blues all over the US, Canada, and Europe. *Nice and Warm*, his debut album for Houston-based Justice Records, prompted some critics to say he's reminiscent, at times, of three blues guitar gods: Albert King, Albert Collins, and Jimi Hendrix.
    Although the hardworking, modest guitarist scoffs at those comparisons,

and doesn't think he sounds like them (and doesn't try to sound like them), Benoit doesn't appear to be one who's easily led into playing rock 'n' roll in favor of his downhome blend of swamp blues and east Texas guitar-driven blues. Talk to Tab at one of his shows, and he'll tell you about his desire to "stay the course," and not water down his blues by playing items that could be interpreted as "alternative" rock. Despite the screaming guitar licks he coaxes from his Telecaster and his powerful songwriting and singing abilities, Benoit's laidback, down-to-earth personality off stage is the exact opposite of his live shows.

Benoit's releases include *Nice and Warm* (1992), *What I Live For* (1994), *Standing On The Bank* (1995) and *Swampland Jam: Live* (1997). All have sent shock waves through the blues community: How can a guy who's so young be so powerful? And since each of Benoit's records has surpassed the 50,000 mark (impressive numbers for an independent record label), he's well on his way to a career that could rival the kind of popularity that the late Stevie Ray Vaughan enjoyed in the late '80s. — *Richard Skelly*

● **Nice & Warm** / 1992 / Justice ✦✦✦✦
Tab Benoit's debut album *Nice & Warm* is a startlingly fresh debut. The guitarist has a gutsy, fuel-injected style that adds real spice to his swampy blues. Benoit draws equally from the Louisiana and Texas traditions and *Nice & Warm* proves it; not only does he carry on the tradition, he offers a fresh take on it as well. — *Thom Owens*

Benoit Freeman Project / 1994 / GRP ✦✦✦

What I Live For / 1994 / Justice ✦✦✦
What I Live For is a white-hot sophomore effort by Tab Benoit, showcasing a more assured and confident guitarist. Although he hasn't changed his basic musical approach—it's all hard-driving Southern blues—his sound is fuller and more direct this time around, proving that his debut was no fluke. — *Thom Owens*

Standing on the Bank / 1995 / Justice ✦✦✦
On his third album, Tab Benoit stripped his sound to its bare essentials by recording live, directly to a two-track. Naturally, the process gives *Standing on the Bank* a startling immediacy, as the guitarist shreds a number of originals to pieces with his piercing solos. — *Thom Owens*

Swampland Jam: Live / Sep. 16, 1997 / Justice ✦✦✦✦
This is by far the best album this Louisiana blues/swamp-rocker has come up with to date. Benoit is playing with basically a three-piece, with Doug Therrien on bass and Allyn Robinson on drums. The rest of the sound is filled in by various guests, some exceedingly strong Louisiana players. Therein lives both the problem and the strength of this disc—the sound is a bit thin when there's no guest taking up some space. Only on the slow burner "Heart of Stone" and "Gone Too Long" does the basic band fill up the airwaves. The music is good, but without that fourth player, it doesn't have enough density. When there is another player, the sound is as gritty and raw as they come—Cajun-based blues with a swampy sensuality. Benoit's singing and guitar playing have taken giant steps forward and are up there with the best. — *Bob Gottlieb*

Buster Benton

b. Jul. 19, 1932, Texarkana, AR, **d.** Jan. 20, 1996, Chicago, IL
Guitar, Vocals / Electric Blues
Despite the amputation of parts of both his legs during the course of his career, Chicago guitarist Buster Benton never gave up playing his music— an infectious hybrid of blues and soul that he dubbed at one point "disco blues" (an unfortunate appellation in retrospect, but useful in describing its danceability). In the late '70s, when blues was at low ebb, Benton's waxings for Ronn Records were a breath of fresh air.

Inspired by the music of Sam Cooke and B.B. King, the gospel-bred Benton began playing the blues during the mid-'50s while living in Toledo, OH. By 1959, he was leading his own band in Chicago. During the '60s, he cut a series of soul-slanted singles for local concerns (Melloway, Alteen, Sonic, Twinight) before hooking up with the great Willie Dixon in 1971.

Benton was a member of Dixon's Blues All-Stars for a while, and Dixon is credited as songwriter of Benton's best-known song, the agonized slow blues "Spider in My Stew." Its release on Stan Lewis' Shreveport-based Jewel Records gave Benton a taste of fame; its follow-up, "Money Is the Name of the Game," solidified his reputation. A 1979 LP for Jewel's Ronn subsidiary

(logically titled *Spider in My Stew*) stands as one of the most engaging Chicago blues LPs of its era, its contemporary grooves abetting Benton's tasty guitar work and soulful vocals.

Benton cut three albums later on for Ichiban, but compared to his Ronn output, they were disappointing. On the Chicago circuit, Benton's extreme courage in the face of physical adversity will long be cited. He was on kidney dialysis for the last few years of his life as a result of diabetes, and a portion of his right leg was amputated in 1993 due to poor circulation (he had already lost part of the other a decade earlier). Still, he continued to play his brand of uplifting blues until the end. — *Bill Dahl*

● **Spider in My Stew** / Jul. 21, 1978 / Ronn ✦✦✦✦
Without a doubt, this album, originally released on Ronn in 1979, stands as the best place to begin an in-depth examination of Benton's legacy. "Spider in My Stew," obviously, is here, along with the wonderful Cooke-influenced R&B outing "Lonesome for a Dime," an irresistibly funky "Sweet 94" (Ron Scott's gurgly electric saxophone gives this cut and several others a unique feel), a driving "Funny About My Money," and the mournful minor-key blues "Sorry." Ronn has beefed the CD program up still further with three additions: the doomy, Bobby Bland-styled "Money Is the Name of the Game," a shuffling "Dangerous Woman," and Benton's happy-go-lucky cover of David Dee's "Going Fishin'." — *Bill Dahl*

Blues Buster / 1979 / Red Lightnin' ✦✦✦✦

Buster Benton Is the Feeling / 1980 / Ronn ✦✦✦
The guitarist's 1980 follow-up didn't pack quite the same knockout punch as its predecessor, but it's a decidedly solid encore effort nonetheless, with tight backup from a talented unit (harpist Carey Bell, pianist Lafayette Leake, rhythm guitarist Jimmy Johnson, and saxist Scott). — *Bill Dahl*

Sweet 94 / 1980 / Charly ✦✦✦

Buster Benton [Blue Phoenix] / 1983 / Blue Phoenix ✦✦✦

Blues at the Top / Nov. 22, 1983-May 2, 1985 / Evidence ✦✦✦✦
A compilation of the two albums Benton made for the French Black & Blue label in 1983 and 1985, this 15-song collection rates with his best. Two separate bands are involved, and the sound changes with them: backed by harpist Billy Branch's Sons of Blues, Benton exercises his R&B-laced chops, while the older hands behind him on "Honey Bee," "The Hawk Is Coming," and "Hole in My Head" (guitarist Johnny Littlejohn, pianist Leake, drummer Odie Payne) assure that the grooves stay more in the mainstream. — *Bill Dahl*

First Time in Europe / 1985 / Blue Phoenix ✦✦

Why Me / 1988 / Ichiban ✦✦
The pleading title track is a worthy addition to the Benton canon, but this album isn't nearly as consistent as the guitarist's superior Ronn output. — *Bill Dahl*

I Like to Hear My Guitar Sing / 1991 / Ichiban ✦✦
Ironically, Benton's axe doesn't have much room to sing on this disappointing outing. — *Bill Dahl*

That's the Reason / May 15, 1997 / Ronn ✦✦✦

Eric Bibb

b. Aug. 16, 1951, New York, NY
Modern Electric Blues, Modern Blues
Eric Bibb's music is a rich blend of the blues with elements of folk, country, gospel, and soul, thanks in part to his being the son of New York folk singer Leon Bibb, which afforded young Eric exposure to a wide variety of music and opportunities to meet performers like Pete Seeger and Bob Dylan. Bibb launched his career in Europe, performing at blues and folk festivals in London, Cambridge, and Dublin, sometimes with a full band and sometimes with slide guitarist Gorn Wennerbrandt; he eventually settled permanently in Sweden, where he works as a music and voice teacher when not performing. Bibb's debut album, *Good Stuff*, was released in Europe in 1997 and the US a year later; it was followed by *Shakin' a Tailfeather* in 1998, which featured producer Linda Tillery and a guest appearance by Taj Mahal. — *Steve Huey*

● **Good Stuff** / Apr. 15, 1997 / Opus 3 ✦✦✦✦
Eric Bibb's debut album, *Good Stuff*, is a clever fusion of contemporary folk and classic country-blues and classic gospel that emphasizes the guitarist's skill at fusing genres, as well as his flair for writing solid bluesy songs. Not

all of the material really catches hold, but it all shows promise, and the very best moments on the record confirm that he's one of the more intriguing new bluesmen in the late '90s. — *Thom Owens*

Me to You / 1998 / Code Blue ✦✦✦

Big Brother & the Holding Company

f. 1965, San Francisco, CA, **db.** 1972
Group / Blues-Rock, Psychedelic
Big Brother are primarily remembered as the group that gave Janis Joplin her start. There's no denying both that Joplin was by far the band's most striking asset, and that Big Brother would never have made a significant impression if they hadn't been fortunate enough to add her to their lineup shortly after forming. But Big Brother also occupy a significant place in the history of San Francisco psychedelic rock, as one of the bands that best captured the era's loosest, reckless, and indulgent qualities in its high-energy mutations of blues and folk-rock.

Big Brother were formed in 1965 in the Haight-Ashbury; by the time Joplin joined in mid-1966, the lineup was Sam Andrews and James Gurley on guitar, Peter Albin on bass, and David Getz on drums. Joplin, a recent arrival from Texas, entered the band at the instigation of Chet Helms, who (other than Bill Graham) was the most important San Francisco rock promoter. Big Brother, like the Grateful Dead and Quicksilver Messenger Service, were not great songwriters or singers. They didn't entirely welcome Joplin's presence at first, though, and Joplin did not dominate the group right away, sharing the lead vocals with other members.

It soon became evident to both band and audience that Joplin's fiery wail—mature and emotionally wrenching, even at that early stage—had to be spotlighted to make Big Brother a contender. But Big Brother weren't superfluous to the effort, interpreting folk and blues with an inventive (if sometimes sloppy) eclecticism that often gave way to distorted guitar jamming, and matching Joplin's passion with a high-spirited, anything-goes ethos of their own.

Big Brother catapulted themselves into national attention with their performance at the Monterey Pop Festival in June 1967, particularly with Joplin's galvanizing interpretation of "Ball and Chain" (which was a highlight of the film of the event). High-powered management and record label bids rolled in immediately, but unfortunately the group had tied themselves up in a bad contract with the small Mainstream label, at a time where they were stranded on the road and needed cash. Their one Mainstream album (released in 1967) actually isn't bad at all, containing some of their stronger cuts, such as "Down on Me" and "Coo Coo." It didn't fully capture the band's strengths, and with the help of new high-powered manager Albert Grossman (also handler of Bob Dylan, the Band, and Peter, Paul & Mary), they extricated themselves from the Mainstream deal and signed with Columbia.

The one Big Brother album for Columbia that featured Joplin, *Cheap Thrills* (1968), wasn't completed without problems of its own. John Simon found the band so difficult to work with that he withdrew his production credit from the final LP, which was assembled from both studio sessions and live material (recorded for an aborted concert album). *Cheap Thrills* nonetheless went to number one when it was finally released, and though it too was an erratic affair, it contained some of the best moments of acid rock's glory days, including "Ball and Chain," "Summertime," "Combination of the Two," and "Piece of My Heart."

Cheap Thrills made Big Brother superstars, a designation that was short-lived. By the end of 1968, Joplin had decided to go solo, a move from which neither she nor Big Brother ever fully recovered. That's putting matters too simply: Joplin never found a backing band as sympathetic, but did record some excellent material in the remaining two years of her life. Big Brother, on the other hand, had the wind totally knocked out of their sails. Although they did re-form for a while in the early '70s with different singers (indeed, they continue to perform in watered-down variations today), nothing would ever be the same. — *Richie Unterberger*

Big Brother & the Holding Company / 1967 / Columbia ✦✦✦
Big Brother's debut LP was a low-budget quickie, but it included a Joplin classic in Top 50 hit "Down on Me" and was a good example of San Francisco psychedelia. — *William Ruhlmann*

★ **Cheap Thrills** / Aug. 1968 / Columbia ✦✦✦✦✦
Cheap Thrills, the major-label debut of Janis Joplin, was one of the most eagerly anticipated, and one of the most successful, albums of 1968. Joplin and Big Brother had earned extensive press notice ever since they played the Monterey Pop Festival in June 1967, but their only recorded work was a poorly produced, self-titled Mainstream album, and they spent a year getting out of their contract with Mainstream in order to sign with Columbia while demand built. When *Cheap Thrills* appeared in August 1968, it shot into the charts, reaching No.1 and going gold within a couple of months, while "Piece of My Heart" became a Top 40 hit. Joplin, with her ear- (and vocal cord-) shredding voice, was the obvious standout. Nobody had ever heard singing as emotional, as desperate, as determined, as loud as Joplin's, and *Cheap Thrills* was her greatest moment. Big Brother's backup, typical of the guitar-dominated sound of San Francisco psychedelia, made up in enthusiasm what it lacked in precision. But everybody knew who the real star was, and Joplin played her last gig with Big Brother while the album was still on top of the charts. Neither she nor the band would ever equal it. Heard today, *Cheap Thrills* is a musical time capsule and remains a showcase for one of rock's most distinctive singers. — *William Ruhlmann*

Be a Brother / Oct. 1970 / Columbia ✦✦
Big Brother comes back as a sextet with the additions of guitarist David Schallock and singer-songwriter/producer Nick Gravenites. Of course, it's a different band without Janis Joplin, but that psychedelic sound is still in place, albeit with a Chicago blues edge courtesy of Gravenites. There's also an amusing reply to Merle Haggard's "Okie From Muskogee," "I'll Change Your Flat Tire, Merle." — *William Ruhlmann*

Cheaper Thrills / 1984 / Made to Last ✦✦
Recorded on July 28, 1966, before the band had cut any studio material, this performance was one of Janis Joplin's first gigs with Big Brother. The sound is decent, with several famous staples of their repertoire already in place—"Down on Me," "Coo-Coo," "Ball and Chain." Yet in comparison with their best studio and live recordings from 1967 and 1968, this is a bit limp. Big Brother were never noted for their polish, but made up for that with reckless bravado; however, that's largely missing at this juncture in their development, which finds them sounding somewhat tentative in their adaptation of R&B and garage-band ethos to heavy guitar arrangements. Big Brother were never noted for their songwriting ability either, and this set is pretty reliant on R&B staples like "Let the Good Times Roll" and "I Know You Rider"; the unabashedly psychedelic workout "Gutra's Garden" hasn't aged well at all. Joplin's vocals are fairly strong, but these early versions of "Down on Me" and, especially, "Ball and Chain" don't hold a candle to her performances of the same tunes at the 1967 Monterey Pop Festival. Other members of the band take the lead vocal on a few numbers, emphatically proving—as they always did when given a chance—that Joplin was necessary to put them on the map. This recording is an interesting glimpse into the group's formative days, though, and features eight songs not on their late-'60s albums. — *Richie Unterberger*

Live at Winterland '68 / 1998 / Columbia ✦✦✦
Recorded live in San Francisco on April 12 and April 13, this set is a snapshot of the band—with fine sound—reaching the peak of their form. All of the well-known songs from their first two albums are present: "Ball and Chain," "Down on Me," "Piece of My Heart," "Summertime," "Combination of the Two," and "Light Is Faster Than Sound," for starters. There isn't a single song that isn't available in some form on either the *Janis* box or the *Farewell Song* compilation, though. Also, these versions aren't remarkably different or better than the familiar ones, although they tend to run longer, particularly on the seven-minute "Light Is Faster Than Sound" and the ten-minute "Ball and Chain." A treat for fans to hear, with a 24-page booklet that has lots of comments from the band. — *Richie Unterberger*

Big Maceo Merriweather (Major Merriweather)

b. Mar. 31, 1905, Atlanta, GA, **d.** Feb. 26, 1953, Chicago, IL
Piano, Vocals / Piano Blues, Chicago Blues, Electric Blues
The thundering 88s of Big Maceo Merriweather helped pave the way for the great Chicago blues pianists of the '50s—men like Johnny Jones, Otis Spann, and Henry Gray. Unfortunately, Merriweather wouldn't be around to enjoy their innovations—he died a few years after suffering a debilitating stroke in 1946.

Major Merriweather was already a seasoned pianist when he arrived in Detroit in 1924. After working around the Motor City scene, he ventured to

Chicago in 1941 to make his recording debut for producer Lester Melrose and RCA Victor's Bluebird subsidiary. His first day in the studio produced 14 tracks—six of his own and eight more as accompanist to renowned Chicago guitarist Tampa Red. One of his initial efforts, "Worried Life Blues," has passed into blues standard status (Chuck Berry was hip to it, covering it for Chess).

Merriweather remained Tampa Red's favorite pianistic accompanist after that, gigging extensively with him and Big Bill Broonzy on Chicago's South side. The pianist cut a series of terrific sessions as a leader for Bluebird in 1941-42 and 1945 (the latter including his tour de force, "Chicago Breakdown") before the stroke paralyzed his right side. He tried to overcome it, cutting for Victor in 1947 with Eddie Boyd assuming piano duties and again for Specialty in 1949 with Johnny Jones, this time at the stool. His health fading steadily after that, Merriweather died in 1953. —*Bill Dahl*

☆ **Chicago Breakdown** / Oct. 1975 / Bluebird ✦✦✦✦✦
Chicago Breakdown is worth searching out since it contains seven extra songs that aren't on the similiar Arhoolie release *King of Chicago Blues Piano, Vol. 1-2*, including "It's All Up to You," "Why Should I Hang Around," "Come on Home," and "It's All Over Now." Mike Rowe's fascinating liner notes are utilized for both *Chicago Breakdown* and *King of Chicago Blues Piano* packages, so there's no clear-cut advantage in that department. —*Bill Dahl*

Volume One / 1976 / RCA ✦✦✦✦
Chicago Blues is synonymous with Muddy Waters to most, but the 1930s saw the growth of a superb style based on piano and acoustic guitar. Leroy Carr and Scrapper Blackwell were two of the giants. Big Maceo Merriweather and Tampa Red matched them in a slightly more robust style with greater country links. These are some of the blues' greatest moments. —*John Storm Roberts, Original Music*

Big Maceo / 1984 / RCA ✦✦✦✦

The King of Chicago Blues Piano / 1984 / Blues Classics ✦✦✦✦

The King of Chicago Blues Piano, Vol. 2 / 1984 / Arhoolie ✦✦✦✦

★ **The King of Chicago Blues Piano, Vol. 1-2** / 1992 / Arhoolie ✦✦✦✦✦
A slightly truncated CD version of the RCA two-record set that first anthologized the thundering 1940s RCA Bluebird sides of pianist Big Maceo (25 cuts on the CD, 32 on the vinyl). The CD opens with Maceo's immortal blues "Worried Life Blues," closes with his instrumental tour de force "Chicago Breakdown," and boasts a great deal of blues piano magic in between. —*Bill Dahl*

The Best of Big Maceo: The King of Chicago Blues Piano / 1992 / Arhoolie ✦✦✦✦
The title *The King of Chicago Blues Piano* is no joke—while never achieving the level of fame won by many of his contemporaries, Big Maceo was indeed a major force behind the development of the Windy City sound, and these '40s sides, cut in collaboration with guitarist Tampa Red, remain his most enduring legacy. Combining startling instrumental proficiency with a traditional blues sensibility, Maceo was also a powerful vocalist; despite recording just 28 sides—all but three of which are included here—he was still a pivotal figure, bridging the country-blues of the 1920s with the urbanized electric sound of the '50s. Among the highlights: the instrumental closer "Chicago Breakdown," an instrumental tribute to his incredible prowess, and "Worried Life Blues," later covered by Chuck Berry. —*Jason Ankeny*

Bluebird Recordings 1941-1942 / Jan. 30, 1996 / BMG ✦✦✦
Bluebird Recordings 1941-42 contains all 16 tracks Big Maceo Merriweather recorded for the label during that year, including the classic "Worried Life Blues." Merriweather was one of the most influential barrelhouse blues pianists, and these Bluebird recordings form the core of his legacy. While these recordings are available in more thorough anthologies, this single disc remains an excellent introduction to his best work. —*Thom Owens*

★ **Victor/Bluebird Recordings 1945-1947** / Apr. 29, 1997 / RCA ✦✦✦✦✦
Victor/Bluebird Recordings 1945-47 contains all the music Big Maceo Merriweather recorded for the label in those two years.

Big Maybelle (Maybelle Smith)
b. May 1, 1924, Jackson, TN, d. Jan. 23, 1972, Cleveland, OH
Vocals / Jump Blues, R&B, New York Blues
Her mountainous stature matching the sheer soulful power of her massive vocal talent, Big Maybelle was one of the premier R&B chanteuses of the

'50s. Her deep, gravelly voice was as singular as her recorded output for OKeh and Savoy, which ranged from down-in-the-alley blues to pop-slanted ballads. In 1967, she even covered ? & the Mysterians' "96 Tears" (it was her final chart appearance). Alleged drug addiction leveled the mighty belter at the premature age of 47, but Maybelle packed a lot of living into her shortened lifespan.

Born Mabel Louise Smith, the singer strolled off with top honors at a Memphis amateur contest at the precocious age of eight. Gospel music was an important element in Maybelle's intense vocal style, but the church wasn't big enough to hold her talent. In 1936, she hooked up with Memphis bandleader Dave Clark; a few years later, Maybelle toured with the International Sweethearts of Rhythm. She debuted on wax with pianist Christine Chatman's combo on Decca in 1944 before signing with Cincinnati's King Records in 1947 for three singles of her own backed by trumpeter Hot Lips Page's band.

Producer Fred Mendelsohn discovered Smith in the Queen City, rechristened her Big Maybelle, and signed her to Columbia's OKeh R&B subsidiary in 1952. Her first OKeh platter, the unusual "Gabbin' Blues" (written by tunesmith Rosemarie McCoy and arranger Leroy Kirkland) swiftly hit, climbing to the upper reaches of the R&B charts. "Way Back Home" and "My Country Man" made it a 1953 hat trick for Maybelle and OKeh. In 1955, she cut a rendition of "Whole Lot of Shakin' Goin' On" a full two years before Louisiana piano pumper Jerry Lee Lewis got his hands and feet on it. Mendelsohn soon brought her over to Herman Lubinsky's Savoy diskery, where her tender rendition of the pop chestnut "Candy" proved another solid R&B hit in 1956. Maybelle rocked harder than ever at Savoy, her "Ring Dang Dilly," "That's a Pretty Good Love," and "Tell Me Who" benefitting from blistering backing by New York's top sessioneers. Her last Savoy date in 1959 reflected the changing trends in R&B; Howard Biggs' stately arrangements encompassed four violins. Director Bert Stern immortalized her vivid blues-belting image in his documentary *Jazz on a Summer's Day*, filmed in color at the 1958 Newport Jazz Festival.

Maybelle persevered throughout the '60s, recording for Brunswick, Scepter (her "Yesterday's Kisses" found her coping admirably with the uptown soul sound), Chess, Rojac (source of "96 Tears"), and other labels. But the good years were long gone when she slipped into a diabetic coma and passed away in a Cleveland hospital in 1972. —*Bill Dahl*

● **The Complete OKeh Sessions 1952-'55** / Oct. 8, 1952-Mar. 21, 1955 / Epic/Legacy ✦✦✦✦
Maybelle's entire OKeh output—26 tracks—including her three R&B chart items, "Whole Lotta Shakin' Goin' On," and the risque slow blues "I'm Getting 'Long Alright." "Gabbin' Blues," her 1952 OKeh debut smash, is a humorous dialog between Maybelle and gossiping rival Rosemarie McCoy, the tune's co-writer. Maybelle was no mere copyist; her sandpapery vocals stood in sharp contrast to the many interchangeable thrushes then populating the R&B world. Great support from New York session wizards such as tenor saxist Sam "The Man" Taylor and guitarist Mickey Baker throughout. —*Bill Dahl*

Candy / May 14, 1956-Nov. 26, 1957 / Savoy Jazz ✦✦✦✦
The belter moved over to Newark, NJ-based Savoy midway through the decade and continued to prosper: "Candy," "Ramblin' Blues," and the intense "Blues Early, Early" rate with her finest cuts. "Ring Dang Dilly" and "Tell Me Who" rock with the seemingly effortless swing peculiar to New York's R&B scene at the time, thanks to the presence of saxists Warren Lucky and Jerome Richardson and guitarists Baker and Kenny Burrell, among others. —*Bill Dahl*

Blues, Candy and Big Maybelle / 1956-1957 / Savoy ✦✦✦
Sixteen tracks of late '50s R&B from the Savoy label. Mickey Baker appears on guitar. —*Bill Dahl*

Big Maybelle Sings / 1958 / Savoy ✦✦✦✦

Saga of the Good Life and Hard Times / 1966-1969 / Rojac ✦✦✦
A mix of soul and blues from her last sessions is sung with despair. —*Richard Pack*

Big Maybelle [Savoy] / 1988 / Savoy ✦✦✦✦

Very Best of Big Maybelle: That's All / Jan. 5, 1998 / Collectables ✦✦✦
Collectables' *The Very Best of Big Maybelle: That's All* features 12 songs that she recorded for Sceptor Records in the '60s. This wasn't the most particu-

larly distinguished period of Maybelle's career, and this collection doesn't put it in perspective, leaving out some of the best records she made for the label, including the minor hit "Yesterday's Kisses." That said, this does have its moments—enough to make it worthwhile to dedictated soul collectors willing to sort the wheat from the chaff. It just isn't a definitive collection, not even of her Scepter recordings. —*Stephen Thomas Erlewine*

The Big Three Trio

f. 1946, Chicago, IL, **db.** 1952
Group / Acoustic Chicago Blues

For the legendary Willie Dixon, the Big Three Trio was an important launching pad for a fantastic career. Pianist Leonard "Baby Doo" Caston and guitarist Bernardo Dennis (replaced after a year by Ollie Crawford) joined upright bassist Dixon to form the popular trio in 1946. Caston was just out of the service (where he'd played on USO tours during World War II); Dixon had been a conscientious objector. Dixon had previously worked with Caston in the Five Breezes and with Dennis in the Four Jumps of Jive.

Sharing vocal (they specialized in three-part harmonies) and writing duties democratically, the trio signed with Jim Bulleit's Bullet imprint in 1946 for a solitary session before making a giant jump in stature to Columbia Records in 1947. Their polished, pop-oriented presentation resulted in one national hit, "You Sure Look Good to Me," in 1948, and a slew of other releases that stretched into 1952 (toward the end, they were shuttled over to the less prestigious OKeh subsidiary).

Incidentally, Dixon dusted off two songs the trio waxed for OKeh, "Violent Love" and "My Love Will Never Die," and handed them to Otis Rush a few years later when the burly bassist was working as a producer at Eli Toscano's Cobra Records. Rush's tortured "My Love Will Never Die" was a postwar masterpiece; the corny "Violent Love" may be the worst thing the southpaw guitarist ever committed to tape.

Caston split at the end of 1952, effectively breaking up the trio. But Dixon's destiny was at Chess Records, where he was already making inroads as a session bassist and songwriter. Pretty soon, he'd be recognized as one of the most prolific and invaluable figures on the Windy City scene. —*Bill Dahl*

I Feel Like Steppin' Out / 1946-Jun. 16, 1952 / Dr. Horse ♦♦♦
I Feel Like Steppin' Out compliments the Columbia release *The Big Three Trio*, gathering most of the material that was left off that disc and only duplicating "Signifying Monkey." The Big Three played the blues very loosely, adding bits of jazz and pop to their sound—unlike most blues groups of their time, they all sang in unison. Though this compilation isn't quite as strong as the Columbia disc, it's worthwhile for dedicated fans. —*Thom Owens*

● **The Willie Dixon: The Big Three Trio** / 1990 / Columbia/Legacy ♦♦♦♦
The only domestic compilation celebrating this trio's accomplishments is a 21-track affair containing Dixon's "dozens" diatribe "Signifying Monkey," the catchy "Tell That Woman" (later covered by Peter, Paul & Mary as "Big Boat Up the River"), and several crackling instrumentals ("Big 3 Boogie," "Hard Notch Boogie Beat") that show what fine musicianship this triumvirate purveyed. Points off, though, for not including their only legit hit, "You Sure Look Good to Me." —*Bill Dahl*

Big Time Sarah

b. Jan. 31, 1953, Coldwater, MS
Vocals / Electric Chicago Blues

A rousing vocalist and dynamic entertainer, "Big Time" Sarah Streeter's among the more enterprising contemporary blues performers. She moved to Chicago from Coldwater, MS, as a child, and sang in South Side gospel choirs before debuting as a blues vocalist on stage at Morgan's Lounge at 14. She later worked with Buddy Guy and Junior Wells, Johnny Bernard and Sunnyland Slim. A single on Slim's Airways label helped launch her solo career. Streeter's been a featured performer at many North Side clubs since the late '70s, and appeared at several blues festivals. She formed the Big Time Express in 1989, and Delmark issued her most recent recording, *Lay It On 'Em*, in 1993. *Blues in the Year One-D-One* followed in 1996. —*Ron Wynn*

Blues with the Girls / 1982 / EPM ♦♦♦
● **Lay It on 'em Girls** / 1993 / Delmark ♦♦♦♦
Big Time Sarah Streeter has the power, struttin' tone and booming voice

ideal for stomping, sassy numbers. This CD spotlights the band Streeter formed in 1989, the BTS Express. Streeter's songs explore the familiar battle between the sexes, with Streeter sometimes angry, sometimes confused and often confrontational in the "classic" blues style. She covers three numbers by Willie Dixon, as well as material from Bill Withers, George Gershwin and Leonard Feather, and displays both a vibrant style and more versatility than might be expected. —*Ron Wynn*

Blues in the Year One-D-One / Jun. 4, 1996 / Delmark ♦♦♦

Big Twist & the Mellow Fellows

f. 1937, Terre Haute, IN, **db.** Mar. 14, 1990, Broadview, IL
Group / Electric Chicago Blues

Larry "Big Twist" Nolan heartily epitomized the image "300 pounds of heavenly joy." Based in Chicago, the huge singer and his trusty R&B band, the Mellow Fellows, were one of the hottest draws on the midwestern college circuit during the '80s with a slickly polished sound modeled on the soul-slanted approach of Bobby Bland, Little Milton, and Tyrone Davis.

Twist started out singing and playing drums in rough-and-tumble country bars in downstate Illinois during the late '50s and early '60s (chicken wire-enclosed stages were a necessity on this raucous scene). Young saxist Terry Ogolini jammed often with the big man at a joint called Junior's in a Prairie State burg called Colp. Ogolini and guitarist Pete Special spearheaded the nucleus of the first edition of the Mellow Fellows in the college town of Carbondale during the early '70s, with Twist doubling on drums. After taking southern Illinois by storm, the unit relocated en masse to Chicago in 1978.

Their eponymous 1980 debut album for Flying Fish accurately captured the group's slick sound, while the 1982 follow-up, *One Track Mind*, attempted to be somewhat more contemporary without losing the band's blues/R&B base. A move to Alligator in 1983 elicited an album co-produced by Gene "Daddy G" Barge, whose sax solos previously enlivened R&B classics by Chuck Willis, Gary (US) Bonds, Little Milton, and countless more. The group's final album with Twist up front was the *Live from Chicago!—Bigger Than Life!!*

Numerous personnel changes over the years failed to scuttle the band, and neither did the death of Twist in 1990 from diabetes and kidney failure. Martin Allbritton, an old singing buddy of Twist's from downstate who had previously gigged around Chicago as front man for Larry & the Ladykillers, had already been deputizing for the ailing Twist, so it fell to Allbritton to assume the role full-time. Barge shared the singing duties at selected gigs and on the band's 1990 album *Street Party*.

Special left the organization not long after that, taking the name Mellow Fellows with him when he hit the door. That's when the remaining members adopted the handle of the Chicago Rhythm & Blues Kings. With Ogolini and longtime trumpeter Don Tenuto comprising a red-hot horn section, they're still a popular, dance-friendly fixture around the Chicago scene. —*Bill Dahl*

Big Twist & The Mellow Fellows / 1980 / Flying Fish ♦♦♦♦
The upbeat rhythms and charismatic persona of Big Twist always afforded this group an accessibility greater than that of most hardcore Chicago blues acts. This debut set followed the same formula, mixing time-tested favorites such as Tyrone Davis' "Turn Back the Hands of Time" with the inevitable crowd-pleaser "The Sweet Sound of Rhythm & Blues." —*Bill Dahl*

One Track Mind / Aug. 1981-Dec. 1981 / Flying Fish ♦♦♦
A slicker affair than their first album, highlighted by a revival of Albert King's "Cold Women" and the rousing "Living It Up." —*Bill Dahl*

● **Playing for Keeps** / 1983 / Alligator ♦♦♦♦
Twist's adopted theme song, the Willie Dixon-penned "300 Pounds of Heavenly Joy," hails from this goodtime collection, co-produced by tenor-sax legend Gene "Daddy G" Barge. —*Bill Dahl*

Live from Chicago! Bigger Than Life! / Jan. 31, 1987-Feb. 2, 1987 / Alligator ♦♦♦♦
Recorded live in 1987 at Biddy Mulligan's, a longtime Chicago blues institution that fell on hard times not too long thereafter, this disc showcases the Mellow Fellows' strengths in front of a rabidly devoted crowd. "300 Pounds of Heavenly Joy," "Turning Point," and the playful "Too Much Barbeque" rate among the highlights, as Twist's onstage charisma makes the show go. —*Bill Dahl*

Big Wheeler

b. Georgia

Harmonica, Vocals / Electric Chicago Blues, Modern Electric Blues

He's been part of the Chicago circuit for four decades, but Golden "Big" Wheeler waited until 1993 to release his debut album on Delmark. As befits such a veteran, Wheeler's sturdy harmonica style is a throwback to the '50s and his idol, Little Walter.

Wheeler was first turned onto the harp while driving a cab by one of his regular fares, Buster Brown. Brown's shot at "Fannie Mae"-fired stardom was still a few decades down the line, but Wheeler's was even further off. He left Georgia in 1941, eventually settling in Chicago, where he met Little Walter. The two became friends, Walter acting as something of a mentor. Wheeler began fronting his own combo in 1956 but never really sustained a musical career (he worked as a mechanic to pay the bills).

In 1993, Delmark unleashed the harpist's debut disc, *Big Wheeler's Bone Orchard,* which found him backed by a young local outfit, the Ice Cream Men. *Jump In* followed in 1997. Wheeler's brother, guitarist James Wheeler, is also a longtime denizen of the Windy City scene; he's currently a mainstay of Mississippi Heat after spending an extended stint behind Otis Rush. —*Bill Dahl*

● **Bone Orchard** / 1993 / Delmark ◆◆◆◆

The veteran Chicago harpist's long-overdue debut album is quite credible, but you can't help but think he's got a far more satisfying set within him yet. Dreary backing by the overly cautious Ice Cream Men is the prime reason the set only occasionally soars—with a less derivative combo, Wheeler could come up with something special before he's through. —*Bill Dahl*

Jump In / 1997 / Delmark ◆◆◆

On his second LP, Wheeler is joined by his brother James on guitar, pianist Allen Batts, bassist Bob Stroger and drummer Baldhead Pete for a traditionally minded set featuring a number of the singer/harmonica player's original compositions. —*Jason Ankeny*

Chicago Blues Session, Vol. 14 / 1998 / Wolf ◆◆◆◆

Elvin Bishop

b. Oct. 21, 1942, Glendale, CA

Guitar, Vocals / Blues-Rock, Southern Rock, Modern Electric Blues, Modern Electric Chicago Blues

Elvin Bishop was born in Glendale, CA, on October 21, 1942. He grew up on a farm in Iowa with no electricity and no running water. His family moved to Oklahoma when he was ten. Raised in an all-White community, he had no exposure to Blacks or their music except though the radio where he would listen to sounds from far away Mexico and blues stations in Shreveport, LA, in particular, the piercing sound of Jimmy Reed's harmonica got his attention. Bishop says it was like a crossword puzzle that he had to figure out. What is this music? Who makes it? Where and how do Black people live? What is this music all about? He put the pieces together.

But it was not until he won a National Merit Scholarship to the University of Chicago in 1959 that he found the real answers to his questions. Suddenly, there he was right in the heart of the Chicago blues scene. Live. It was a dream come true. "The first thing I did when I got there was to make friends with the black guys working in the cafeteria. They took me to all the clubs. I sunk myself totally in the blues life as quick as I could," says Bishop.

After two years of college, he just dropped out and was into music full time. Howlin' Wolf guitarist Smokey Smothers befriended Bishop and taught him the basics of blues guitar. In the early '60s he met and teamed up with Paul Butterfield to become the core of the Butterfield Blues Band. Although only playing guitar for a few years, he practiced day and night on the blues music that he loved. He and Butterfield played together in just about every place possible—campuses, houses, parks, and clubs. They began to become well known in 1963 when they took a job at Big John's on Chicago's North Side and the Paul Butterfield Blues Band was born. Bishop helped to create and played on the first several Butterfield albums. (The Pigboy Crabshaw is Bishop's countrified persona referred to in the title of the third Butterfield album.)

When he left the Butterfield band after the *In My Own Dream* album (1968), Bishop relocated to and settled in the San Francisco area where he appeared often at the Filmore with artists like Eric Clapton, B. B. King, and Jimi Hendrix. He recorded for Epic (four albums) and later signed with Capricorn in 1974. His recording of "Traveling Shoes" (from the album *Let It Flow*) hit the charts, but he scored big with the lovely tune "Fooled Around and Fell in Love" (from his album *Struttin' My Stuff*) in 1976. He was (and is) famous for having fun on stage (putting on a great show) and letting the good times roll. Over the next few years the Elvin Bishop Group dissolved. He released his album *Best Of* in 1979, and was not heard from much until he signed with Alligator in 1988.

Bishop then released *Big Fun* (1988) and *Don't Let the Bossman Get You Down* (1991), which were well received. He also participated in Alligator's 1992 20th Anniversary cross-country tour. His latest release is *Ace in the Hole* (1995). Over the years, Bishop has graced the albums of many great bluesmen including Clifton Chenier and John Lee Hooker. He toured with B.B. King in 1995. Bishop is known for his sense of humor, his unique style of slide guitar, and fusion of blues, gospel, R&B, and country flavors. He lives with his wife and family in the San Francisco area, is a prodigious gardener, and continues to play dates in the US and abroad. —*Michael Erlewine*

The Elvin Bishop Group / Oct. 1969 / Fillmore ◆◆

The Best of Elvin Bishop: Tulsa Shuffle / 1969-1972 / Epic/Legacy ◆◆◆◆

In his first manifestation as a band leader (1969-1972), Elvin Bishop lived in Marin County, California, and performed under the auspices of promoter Bill Graham. Not surprisingly, the three albums he cut in that period fit into the soul-blues-rock style of post-psychedelic San Francisco, even to the point of featuring an extended instrumental, "Hogbottom," on which Bishop takes Carlos Santana's place fronting the Santana percussion section. This 18-track compilation selects from the albums *The Elvin Bishop Group, Feel It!,* and *Rock My Soul,* effectively summarizing this phase in Bishop's career. The only thing wrong with it is that it would be easy to make the mistake of thinking that it covers all of his solo career rather than only the first four years, especially because there have now been four different albums released with the title *The Best Of Elvin Bishop.* —*William Ruhlmann*

Feel It! / Oct. 1970 / Fillmore ◆◆◆

● **Sure Feels Good: The Best of Elvin Bishop** / 1970-1972 / Polygram ◆◆◆◆

A fine collection of the blues-rock guitarist's best moments, which covers more material than the earlier compilation, *Best of Elvin Bishop/Crabshaw Rising.* —*Stephen Thomas Erlewine*

The Best of Elvin Bishop: Crabshaw Rising / 1970-1972 / Epic ◆◆◆

In his first manifestation as a band leader (1969-1972), Elvin Bishop lived in Marin County, CA, and performed under the auspices of promoter Bill Graham. Not surprisingly, the three albums he cut in that period, two for Graham's Fillmore label and the third for its parent, Epic, fit into the soul-blues-rock style of post-psychedelic San Francisco, even to the point of featuring an extended instrumental, "Hogbottom," on which Bishop takes Carlos Santana's place fronting the Santana percussion section. This ten-track compilation selects from the albums *The Elvin Bishop Group, Feel It!,* and *Rock My Soul,* effectively summarizing this phase in Bishop's career. Long out of print, it was superseded in 1994 by the 18-track CD *The Best of Elvin Bishop: Tulsa Shuffle,* which contained nine of its selections. Then, oddly enough, it was reissued in 1996! —*William Ruhlmann*

Rock My Soul / Sep. 1972 / Epic ◆◆◆

Let It Flow / May 1974 / One Way ◆◆◆◆

For his fourth album, Elvin Bishop organized a new backup group and switched to Capricorn Records. Capricorn was known as the standard bearer of the Southern rock movement—the Allman Brothers Band, The Marshall Tucker Band, etc.—and Bishop was able to emphasize the country/blues aspects of his persona and his music in the move from Marin County, CA, to Macon, GA. The guest artists included the Allmans' Dickey Betts, Marshall Tucker's Toy Caldwell, Charlie Daniels, and Sly Stone, and Bishop turned in one of his best sets of songs, including "Travelin' Shoes" (with its Allmans-like twin lead guitar work), which became his first charting single, just as the album was his first to make the Top 100 LPs. —*William Ruhlmann*

Juke Joint Jump / Apr. 1975 / One Way ◆◆◆

Elvin Bishop's Macon Takeover continued on his second Capricorn album, which had a slightly less country feel than *Let It Flow* but continued to be dominated by twin guitar playing (courtesy of Bishop and Johnny "V" Vernazza) and honky tonk piano playing (from Phil Aaberg). The song quality wasn't quite as consistent this time, but "Sure Feels Good" became Bishop's second singles chart entry. — *William Ruhlmann*

Struttin' My Stuff / Dec. 1975 / Capricorn ✦✦✦
Features the hit single "Fooled Around and Fell in Love," sung by Mickey Thomas. — *William Ruhlmann*

Hometown Boy Makes Good! / Oct. 1976 / Capricorn ✦✦
Elvin Bishop broke the bank with the success of "Fooled Around And Fell In Love" in the spring of 1976, so when he returned with this album in the fall, he turned up on the cover holding bags of money. The question, of course, was whether the hit would turn out to be a breakthrough or a fluke. The nearest thing to a follow-up to "Fooled Around" was "Spend Some Time," a ballad on which Mickey Thomas again sang soulfully. But it barely scraped into the charts, and the rest was typical Bishop good-time boogie (along with trendy tastes of disco and reggae), the relatively thin songwriting reflecting a rushed recording schedule—this was Bishop's fourth new album in just over two-and-a-half years. — *William Ruhlmann*

Raisin' Hell / Jul. 1977 / One Way ✦✦

Hog Heaven / 1978 / Capricorn ✦✦✦
Capricorn Records, having switched distribution from Warner Brothers to Phondisc, was on its way out by the time it released this, its sixth Elvin Bishop album, which may help explain why, only two years after he was in the Top 10 with "Fooled Around And Fell In Love," he didn't even reach the charts with this album. It's also true that lead singer Mickey Thomas had decamped to join Jefferson Starship, leaving Bishop to reestablish his country blues boy persona. But Maria Muldaur had signed on (she sings lead on "True Love"), and with two years between studio albums, Bishop had found the time to write some good vehicles for his guitar work and Southern rock backup band. — *William Ruhlmann*

Big Fun / 1988 / Alligator ✦✦✦
In the 10 years between the release of *Hog Heaven* and this comeback record, Elvin Bishop was represented in record stores by a *Best Of* on Capricorn and an album released only in Germany (*Is You Is Or Is You Ain't My Baby?* on Line Records). Then he signed with Bruce Iglauer's independent blues label Alligator and made this record, which, naturally, emphasizes his more blues-oriented guitar playing, although without sacrificing his country boy identity. Dr. John tickles some of the ivories, and harmonica player Norton Buffalo (of Commander Cody and His Lost Planet Airmen) also guests. — *William Ruhlmann*

Don't Let the Bossman Get You Down! / Jul. 1, 1991 / Alligator ✦✦✦✦
On *Don't Let the Bossman Get You Down,* Bishop projects a good-natured, humorous persona in the extended spoken-word sections of his songs, but still finds time to play a lot of tasty blues guitar. — *William Ruhlmann*

Ace in the Hole / Jul. 25, 1995 / Alligator ✦✦✦
On Elvin Bishop's third Alligator release, *Ace in the Hole,* his guitar playing remains as fiery as ever, but the overall quality of the songwriting has slipped somewhat, making it his least-consistent effort on the label. — *Thom Owens*

Billy Bizor

b. 1917, Centerville, TX, d. Apr. 4, 1969, Houston, TX
Harmonica, Vocals / Texas Blues
The blues revival of the '60s allowed the spotlight to finally fall on performers like Billy Bizor, an otherwise obscure harpist best known in conjunction with his recordings in support of his cousin, the renowned Lightnin' Hopkins. Born in Centerville, Texas in 1917, Bizor (also, variously, Bizer and Biser) dwelled in almost total obscurity prior to the '60s, developing a spare, haunted sound largely unaffected by the passage of time, making him a prime candidate for rediscovery by purists. Among his first recordings were a series of unheralded early-'60s dates backing Hopkins; between 1968 and 1969, Bizor cut his only solo session in Houston with producer Roy Ames, revealing him to be an intense, emotionally charged singer. Eventually issued as *Blowing My Blues Away,* the end result went unreleased for several years; tragically, Bizor himself never saw the recordings come to light—he died April 4, 1969. — *Jason Ankeny*

Blowing My Blues Away / 1968-1969 / Collectables ✦✦✦✦
Blowing My Blues Away was recorded in 1968 and 1969, at the height of the blues revival. Billy Bizor wasn't very well known before the blues revival

and that's part of the reason why his style didn't change very much from the '30s and '40s—his blues is still deeply indebted to the stripped-down sounds of Lightnin' Hopkins, who happens to be Bizor's cousin. All of the material on *Blowing My Blues Away* was previously unreleased, so it's designed for hardcore blues collectors, but for those listeners that are interested, this is an entertaining curiosity. — *Thom Owens*

Black Ace

f. Dec. 21, 1907, Hughes Springs, TX, **db.** Nov. 7, 1972, Fort Worth, TX
Guitar, Vocals / Acoustic Texas Blues
A solid guitarist and vocalist, Babe Turner AKA Black Ace built his own guitar as a child, then taught himself to play. He was also in a gospel choir in Hughes Springs, TX. Turner honed his skills playing at community functions during the '20s, then worked with Smokey Hogg at dances in Greenville, TX in the '30s. Hogg and Buddy Woods were frequent partners for Turner, who made several solo tours in the '30s and '40s. He appeared in the 1941 film *The Blood of Jesus* and 1962 movie *The Blues.* Turner had a show on Fort Worth radio station KFJZ from 1936—1941. He recorded for Decca in 1937. After a stint in the army during the early '40s, Turner's jobs were mostly non-musical, except for his film stints. He did make a 1960 LP for Arhoolie. Turner took his nickname from the 1936 recording "Black Ace." — *Ron Wynn*

● **I'm the Boss Card in Your Hand, 1937-1960** / 1937-1960 / Arhoolie ✦✦✦✦
I Am the Boss Card in Your Hand stands as the definitive Black Ace collection to date—not only does Arhoolie's CD reissue include the entirety of their original 1960 release, but it also appends previously unissued material from the same session and even tosses in a half dozen tracks from his 1937 Decca label debut. Thanks largely to its steadfast refusal to fit easily into any kind of regional genre pigeonhole, Ace's music possesses a beautifully timeless quality; though he's a poignant vocalist, the real treat here is his slide guitar mastery, as instrumentals like "Ace's Guitar Blues" and "Bad Times Stomp" reveal a unique hybrid sound successfully bridging the gap between the Delta and Hawaiian styles. — *Jason Ankeny*

Black Ace / 1960 / Arhoolie ✦✦✦

Otis Blackwell

b. 1931, Brooklyn, NY
Piano / R&B, Rock & Roll, Urban Blues, East Coast Blues
Few '50s rock 'n' roll tunesmiths were as prolifically talented as Otis Blackwell. His immortal compositions include Little Willie John's "Fever," Elvis Presley's "Don't Be Cruel" and "All Shook Up," Jerry Lee Lewis' "Great Balls of Fire" and "Breathless," and Jimmy Jones' "Handy Man" (just for starters).

Though he often collaborated with various partners on the thriving '50s New York R&B scene (Winfield Scott, Eddie Cooley and Jack Hammer, to name three), Blackwell's songwriting style is as identifiable as that of Willie Dixon or Jerry Leiber & Mike Stoller. He helped formulate the musical vocabulary of rock 'n' roll when the genre was barely breathing on its own.

Befitting a true innovator, Blackwell's early influences were a tad out of the ordinary. As a lad growing up in Brooklyn, he dug the Westerns that his favorite nearby cinema screened. At that point, Tex Ritter was Otis' main man. Smooth blues singers Chuck Willis and Larry Darnell also made an impression. By 1952, Blackwell parlayed a victory at an Apollo Theater talent show into a recording deal with veteran producer Joe Davis for RCA, switching to Davis' own Jay-Dee logo the next year. He was fairly prolific at Jay-Dee, enjoying success with the throbbing "Daddy Rollin' Stone" (later covered by the Who). From 1955 on, though, Blackwell concentrated primarily on songwriting (Atlantic, Date, Cub, and MGM later issued scattered Blackwell singles).

"Fever," co-written by Cooley, was Blackwell's first winner (he used the pen name of John Davenport, since he was still contractually obligated to Jay-Dee). Blackwell never met Elvis in person, but his material traveled a direct pipeline to the rock icon; "Return to Sender," "One Broken Heart for Sale," and "Easy Question" also came from his pen. Dee Clark ("Just Keep It Up" and "Hey Little Girl"), Thurston Harris, Wade Flemons, Clyde McPhatter, Brook Benton, Ben E. King, the Drifters, Bobby Darin, Ral Donner, Gene Vincent, and plenty more of rock's primordial royalty benefitted from Blackwell's compositional largesse before the British Invasion forever altered the Brill Building scene.

In 1976, Blackwell returned to recording with a Herb Abramson-produced set for Inner City comprised of his own renditions of the songs that made him famous. A 1991 stroke paralyzed the legendary songscribe, but his influence remains so enduring that it inspired *Brace Yourself!*, an all-star 1994 tribute album that included contributions by Dave Edmunds, Joe Ely, Deborah Harry, Chrissie Hynde, Kris Kristofferson, Graham Parker, and bluesman Joe Louis Walker. — *Bill Dahl*

● **Otis Blackwell 1953-55** / 1953-Feb. 9, 1955 / Flyright ++++
The British Flyright logo has neatly compiled all 17 known titles that Blackwell cut for Jay-Dee, including "Daddy Rollin' Stone," the equally ominous "On That Power Line," and four sides with a killer New York combo featuring tenor sax wailer Sam "The Man" Taylor and guitarist Mickey Baker. — *Bill Dahl*

All Shook Up / Oct. 14, 1976-Oct. 27, 1976 / Shanachie ++
If only Blackwell was supported by his classic '50s combo when he recorded his own songbook for producer Herb Abramson in October of 1976. Instead, a graceless rock group named Grande Union, apparently Blackwell's band of choice at the time, was used, and the results are disappointing. "Back Trail," one of the few new compositions Blackwell brought to the party, was redone in superior fashion by Chicago bluesman Lonnie Brooks on his 1983 Alligator LP *Hot Shot*. Shanachie has added a handful of rare vintage Blackwell demos at the end of the CD that outshine anything from the original *Inner City* album; especially valuable is Blackwell's original treatment of "One Broken Heart for Sale" (Presley's phrasing, as usual, faithfully mirrored Blackwell's). — *Bill Dahl*

Scrapper Blackwell (Francis Blackwell)

b. Feb. 21, 1903, Syracuse, NC, **d.** Oct. 27, 1954, Indianapolis, IN
Guitar, Vocals / Acoustic Chicago Blues, Piedmont Blues
Scrapper Blackwell was best known for his work with pianist Leroy Carr during the early and mid-'30s, but he also recorded many solo sides between 1928 and 1935. A distinctive stylist whose work was closer to jazz than blues, Blackwell was an exceptional player with a technique, built around single-note picking, that anticipated the electric blues of the '40s and '50s. He abandoned music for more than 20 years after Carr's death in 1935, but re-emerged at the end of the '50s and began his career anew, before his life was taken in an apparent robbery attempt.

Francis Hillman "Scrapper" Blackwell was of part-Cherokee Indian descent, one of 16 children born to Payton and Elizabeth Blackwell in Syracuse, NC. His father played the fiddle, and Blackwell himself was a self-taught guitarist, having started out by building his own instrument out of cigar boxes, wood, and wire. He also took up the piano, an instrument that he played professionally on occasion. By the time he was a teenager, Blackwell was working as a part-time musician, and traveled as far away as Chicago. By most accounts, as an adult Blackwell had a withdrawn personality, and could be difficult to work with, although he had an exceptionally good working relationship with Nashville-born pianist Leroy Carr, whom he met in Indianapolis in the mid-'20s. They made a natural team, for Carr's piano playing emphasized the bass, and liberated Blackwell to explore the treble strings of his instrument to the fullest.

Carr and Blackwell performed together throughout the midwest and parts of the south, including Louisville, St. Louis, Cincinnati, and Nashville, and were notably successful. With Blackwell's help, Carr became one of the top blues stars of the early '30s, and the two recorded well over 100 sides together between 1928 and 1935. They might've had major success going into the war years and beyond. It was not to be, however, as Carr's heavy drinking and a nephritis condition caused his death in Indianapolis on April 29, 1935.

Blackwell also recorded without Carr, both as a solo and also occasionally with other partners, including Georgia Tom Dorsey and an obscure singer named Black Bottom McPhail, and had occasionally worked with blues bands such as Robinson's Knights of Rest. His biggest success and greatest effectiveness, however, lay in his work with Carr, and after the latter's death he continued working long enough to cut a tribute to his late partner. His withdrawn personality didn't lend itself to an extended solo career, and he gave up the music business before the end of the '30s.

Blackwell's career might've ended there, preserved only in memory and a hundred or so sides recorded mostly with Carr. At the end of the '50s, however, with the folk/blues revival gradually coming into full swing, he was rediscovered living in Indianapolis, and prevailed upon to resume playing

and recording. This he did, for the Prestige/Bluesville label, at least one album's worth of material that showed his singing and playing unmarred by age or other abuse. Blackwell appeared ready to resume his career without missing a beat, and almost certainly would've been a prime candidate for stardom before the burgeoning young White audience of college students and folk enthusiasts that embraced the likes of Furry Lewis, the Rev. Gary Davis, and Mississippi Fred McDowell. In 1962, however, soon after finishing his work on his first Prestige/Bluesville long-player (which, for reasons best understood by the label's current parent company, Fantasy Records, has never been re-released on CD), Blackwell was shot to death in a back alley in Indianapolis, the victim of a mugging. The crime was never solved.

Scrapper Blackwell was one of the most important guitar players of the '20s and early '30s, with a clean, dazzlingly articulate style that anticipated the kind of prominent solo work that would emerge in Chicago as electric blues in the '40s and '50s, in the persons of Robert Nighthawk and the young Muddy Waters. His "string-snapping" solos transcend musical genres and defy the limitations of his period. Although Blackwell's recordings were done entirely on acoustic guitar, the playing on virtually every extant track is — and this is no joke — electrifying in its clarity and intensity. Along with Tampa Red (who also had some respect in jazz circles, and who was a more derivative figure, especially as a singer), Blackwell was one of a handful of pre-war blues guitarists whose work should be known by every kid who thinks it all started with Chuck Berry or even Muddy Waters.

Note: In addition to the albums credited to Scrapper Blackwell, his recordings can also be found on collections of Leroy Carr's work (virtually all of which features Blackwell) including such releases as Magpie Records' *The Piano Blues: Leroy Carr 1930-35;* and one Carr/Blackwell duet, "Papa's on the Housetop," which is not on *The Virtuoso Guitar of Scrapper Blackwell*, but shows up on Yazoo's *Uptown Blues: Guitar Piano Duets* anthology. — *Bruce Eder*

★ **Virtuoso Guitar 1925-1934** / 1925-1934 / Yazoo +++++
It's for recordings like this that a lot of blues guitar fans started listening to the music in the first place. The definitive Blackwell collection to date, featuring not only his best extant solo sides, but also his work in association with Leroy Carr, Black Bottom McPhail, and Tommy Bradley. The 14 songs here all have something to offer in the playing — and generally the singing as well — that will give the listener pause, a run, an arpeggio, a solo passage that makes you say, "Whoa, what was that?" The sound is surprisingly good, and one only wishes there were more than 14 songs here, although it's hard to imagine anything that could follow the last track, Leroy Carr's "Barrelhouse Woman No. 2." — *Bruce Eder*

1928-1939, Vol. 1 / Jun. 16, 1928+Mar. 17, 1939 / Document ++++

Blues Before Sunrise / Jan. 1962 / 77 +++

Mr. Scrapper's Blues / Sep. 1962 / Prestige +++

Scrapper Blackwell, Vol. 2 (1934-1958) / 1994 / RST ++++
The second volume of Scrapper Blackwell sides features material he cut solo in 1934, accompanying himself on the piano, and as a solo guitarist from 1935 ("D Blues," "A Blues"), as well as songs cut as part of Pinewood Tom and His Blues Hounds, teamed as a guitarist with Josh White (on vocals and guitar) and pianist Leroy Carr; under the name Frankie Black accompanied by pianist Dot Rice, and some in association with Bumble Bee Slim. These are all first-rate sides, equal to the best of his work with Leroy Carr and among the finest guitar playing in any category of music that you're ever likely to hear. Among the songs, "My Old Pal Blues (Dedicated to the Memory of Leroy Carr)" is a beautiful and poignant piece of personal, topical blues songwriting dealing with Carr's death in April of 1935, with Dot Rice providing excellent, fluid piano accompaniment to Blackwell's voice and guitar. Rice and Blackwell are teamed together again, backing Bumble Bee Slim on "Hey Lawdy Mama," the song that Willie Dixon later transformed into the classic "Meet Me in the Bottom" for Howlin' Wolf. The real treat, however, is the first release on CD of the four songs that Blackwell recorded in 1958, at the outset of his comeback — these little-known tracks are dark, moody, and utterly dazzling. Most of the masters are in surprisingly good condition ("Mean Mistreater Mama" and "She's Alright with Me" from 1934, and "Hey Lawdy Mama" from 1935 are notable and unfortunate exceptions), and this is an indispensable release for any serious fan of blues guitar, or guitar-piano duets. Neither gets any better than this. — *Bruce Eder*

Scrapper Blackwell, Vol. 3 (1959-1960) / 1994 / Document ✦✦✦✦
Austria's Document Records apparently had this 22-track, 75-minute CD out in 1994, but it only started coming into the US in 1996, and doesn't even show up in some reference sources. Scrapper Blackwell's all-too-brief comeback at the end of the 1950s is well represented by a dozen songs from a live concert at Indianapolis' "1444 Gallery" from September 20, 1959, some teaming Blackwell with singer Brooks Berry, paired off with ten tracks from Blackwell's 1960 British-only album on Dave Dobell's 77 label. Blackwell's technique on the guitar had not suffered at all from his nearly 20-year layoff from performing—he finesses sounds from his acoustic instrument that are soft and glittering, utilizing melody notes and carefully varied rhythms, and six of the tracks here are guitar solos, all of which are fascinating on repeated listening. Even the one song that is repeated between the two sets, "Shady Lane Blues," is so well played and so different, that there is no feeling of repetition. His piano playing is also represented on one track. Blackwell's voice lacks some of the resonance that it had on his 1930s recordings, and if anything the sadness in his persona is even more pronounced this late in his career, but he imbues his work with an intense passion that makes it compelling to hear. The worth of these performances makes his death, during an apparent mugging in 1962, all the more tragic, for more than almost any blues figure—including Memphis Minnie and Big Bill Broonzy—who almost made it to the folk/blues revival, Blackwell shows here how he could have reached millions with his work, had he lived only a couple of years longer. Oh, and the apology made by the producers for the sound quality of the 1959 concert tape (provided by Duncan Schmidt, who also appears on a track or two) is utterly unnecessary. —*Bruce Eder*

Bobby "Blue" Bland

b. Jan. 27, 1930, Rosemark, TN
Vocals / Soul, R&B, Soul Blues, Electric Texas Blues, Electric R&B, Texas Blues
Bobby Bland earned his enduring blues superstar status the hard way: without a guitar, harmonica, or any other instrument to fall back upon. All Bland had to offer was his magnificent voice, a tremendously powerful instrument in his early heyday, injected with charisma and melisma to spare. Just ask his legion of female fans, who deem him a sex symbol to this day.

For all his promise, Bland's musical career ignited slowly. He was a founding member of the Beale Streeters, the fabled Memphis aggregation that also included B.B. King and Johnny Ace. Singles for Chess in 1951 (produced by Sam Phillips) and Modern the next year bombed, but that didn't stop local deejay David Mattis from cutting Bland on a couple of 1952 singles for his fledgling Duke logo.

Bland's tormented crying style was still pretty rough around the edges before he entered the Army in late 1952. But his progress upon his 1955 return was remarkable; with saxist Bill Harvey's band (featuring guitarist Roy Gaines and trumpeter Joe Scott) providing sizzling support, Bland's assured vocal on the swaggering "It's My Life Baby" sounds like the work of a new man. By now, Duke was headed by hard-boiled Houston entrepreneur Don Robey, who provided top-flight bands for his artists. Scott soon became Bland's mentor, patiently teaching him the intricacies of phrasing when singing sophisticated fare (by 1962, Bland was credibly crooning "Blue Moon," a long way from Beale Street).

Most of Bland's savage Texas blues sides during the mid-to-late '50s featured the slashing guitar of Clarence Hollimon, notably "I Smell Trouble," "I Don't Believe," "Don't Want No Woman," "You Got Me (Where You Want Me)," and the torrid "Loan a Helping Hand" and "Teach Me (How To Love You)." But the insistent guitar riffs guiding Bland's first national hit, 1957's driving "Farther up the Road," were contributed by Pat Hare, another vicious picker who would eventually die in prison after murdering his girlfriend and a cop. Later, Wayne Bennett took over on guitar, his elegant fretwork prominent on Bland's Duke waxings throughout much of the '60s.

The gospel underpinnings inherent to Bland's powerhouse delivery were never more apparent than on the 1958 outing "Little Boy Blue," a vocal tour de force that wrings every ounce of emotion out of the grinding ballad. Scott steered his charge into smoother material as the decade turned—the seminal mixtures of blues, R&B and primordial soul "I Pity the Fool," the Brook Benton-penned "I'll Take Care of You," and "Two Steps from the Blues" were tremendously influential to a legion of up-and-coming southern soulsters.

Scott's blazing brass arrangements upped the excitement ante on Bland's

frantic rockers "Turn on Your Love Light" in 1961 and "Yield Not to Temptation" the next year, but the vocalist was learning his lessons so well that he sounded just as conversant on soulful R&B rhumbas (1963's "Call on Me") and polished ballads ("That's the Way Love Is," "Share Your Love with Me") as with an after-hours blues revival of T-Bone Walker's "Stormy Monday Blues" that proved a most unlikely pop hit for him in 1962. With "Ain't Nothing You Can Do," "Ain't Doing Too Bad," and "Poverty," Bland rolled through the mid-'60s, his superstar status diminishing not a whit.

In 1973, Robey sold his labels to ABC Records, and Bland was part of the deal. Without Scott and his familiar surroundings to lean on, Bland's releases grew less consistent artistically, though *His California Album* in 1973 and *Dreamer* the next year boasted some nice moments (there was even an album's worth of country standards). The singer reteamed with his old pal B.B. King for a couple of mid-'70s albums that broke no new ground but further heightened Bland's profile, while his solo work for MCA teetered closer and closer to MOR (Bland has often expressed his admiration for ultra-mellow pop singer Perry Como).

Since the mid-'80s, Bland has recorded for Jackson, MS's Malaco Records. His pipes undeniably reflect the ravages of time, and those phlegm-flecked "snorts" he habitually emits become annoying in large doses. But Bobby "Blue" Bland endures as a blues superstar of the loftiest order. —*Bill Dahl*

The 3b Blues Boy—The Blues Years: 1952-59 / Jul. 21, 1952-1959 / Ace ✦✦✦
25-track compilation of bluesy material that Bland recorded for Duke between 1952 and 1959. Bland had previously released a few sides for Chess and Modern in the early '50s, but these sides represent the era in which he began to find his voice. It still catches him at a relatively early stage in his development, concentrating on jump blues-oriented material, sometimes with horn sections, showing the considerable influence of B.B. King. There's some sharp guitar on these sides (including some by Roy Gaines, who also played with Chuck Willis and Hound Dog Thornton), and the vocals are full and confident, if a bit overripe. But neophytes should begin with his early and mid-'60s sides, when his blend of blues and soul reached a much higher level of maturity. —*Richie Unterberger*

★ **I Pity the Fool: The Duke Recordings, Vol. 1** / Jul. 21, 1952-1960 / MCA ✦✦✦✦✦
Everything the young Bland waxed for Duke between 1952 and the 1960 date that produced "Cry, Cry, Cry" and the R&B-laced "Don't Cry No More." From 1955 on, this is uniformly seminal stuff, Bland's vocal confidence growing by the session and buttressed by the consistently innovative riffs and solos of guitarists Clarence Hollimon, Wayne Bennett (he's amazing on a torrid "You Did Me Wrong"), Roy Gaines and Pat Hare. "Farther up the Road," the exotic ballad "Hold Me Tenderly," "Little Boy Blue," and the title track are but few of the two-disc collection's many standouts. No blues fan should be minus this set! —*Bill Dahl*

Blues Consolidated / May 1958 / Duke/MCA ✦✦✦✦
An album split between Bland and his Blues Consolidated touring partner Junior Parker, featuring great early-'50s sides by these two Houston-based performers. —*Cub Koda & Hank Davis*

The Voice: Duke Recordings 1959-69 / 1959-1969 / Ace ✦✦✦✦
A 26-track compilation of Duke sides from Bland's peak decade (1959-1969). MCA's two-volume *The Duke Recordings* covers this period in greater depth, and will be more readily available to most North American consumers. On its own terms, though, it's an excellent collection. Contains most of his biggest R&B hits ("Turn on Your Love Light," "Stormy Monday Blues," "Call on Me," "Ain't Nothing You Can Do"), as well as some cuts that didn't make it onto *The Duke Recordings*. —*Richie Unterberger*

Like Er Red Hot / 1960 / Duke ✦✦✦
This anthology presents a cross-section of early Duke/Peacock hits. —*Bill Dahl*

☆ **Turn on Your Love Light/The Duke Recordings, Vol. 2** / 1960-1964 / MCA ✦✦✦✦✦
Picking up right where the first volume left off and continuing into 1964, this two-disc compilation (50 tracks!) showcases one of Bland's most appealing periods at Duke. Joe Scott was experimenting boldly with his protégé's repertoire, his brass-powered arrangements urging Bland to increased heights of incendiary energy on "Turn on Your Love Light" and "Yield Not to

Temptation" (driven by future James Brown drummer Jabo Starks' funky traps) and advanced sophistication levels for the honey-smooth "Share Your Love with Me" and "That's the Way Love Is." Bennett's crackling blues licks invest "Stormy Monday Blues," "The Feeling Is Gone," and "Black Night" with T-Bone-derived tradition, while Bland handles Charlie Rich's "Who Will the Next Fool Be" with just the right amount of bluesy resignation. — *Bill Dahl*

☆ **Two Steps from the Blues** / 1961 / Duke/MCA ♦♦♦♦♦
Including classics like "Don't Cry No More," "I Pity The Fool," and "Little Boy Blue," this early-'60s set captures Bland at the point where his sound had just fully matured into a horn-punctuated blend of blues, gospel, and early soul. All 12 of the songs are included on MCA's *Duke Recordings* series, though, making this unnecessary if you're building a complete collection of Bland on CD. — *Richie Unterberger*

Call on Me / 1963 / MCA ♦♦♦♦
A near-perfect collection of early-'60s sides documents the man at his best. — *Hank Davis*

Ain't Nothing You Can Do / 1964-1965 / MCA ♦♦♦
Fine soulful mid-'60s sides, including the title track, "Loneliness Hurts," and a cathartic reading of the soul classic "Blind Man." — *Cub Koda & Hank Davis*

The Soul of the Man / 1966 / MCA ♦♦♦

Touch of the Blues / 1967 / Duke ♦♦♦♦
During his Duke tenure, Bobby "Blue" Bland's rich, creamy voice was at its stark, dramatic peak. Like his other label releases, even when he got overly sentimental or just plain corny material, or the songs were overarranged, Bland's smashing leads made everything work. — *Ron Wynn*

Touch of the Blues/Spotlighting The Man / 1967 / Mobile Fidelity ♦♦♦♦
Two of Bland's better albums for Duke coupled on one great-sounding CD. Both LPs were issued originally in 1969 but contained tracks from as far back as his 1967 Top Ten R&B hit "That Did It" and its immediate follow-up, "Touch of the Blues." Bland never turned his back on the style that brought him to prominence (he digs into Charles Brown's "Driftin' Blues" aggressively, Bennett providing luscious chording behind him), even if his stately reading of Joe Turner's "Chains of Love" is sweetened considerably by strings. On the other hand, the husky singer's unwise whack at Anthony Newley's Broadway showstopper, "Who Can I Turn To," is about as far removed from blues tradition as is imaginable. — *Bill Dahl*

The Best of Bobby Bland, Vol. 2 / Mar. 1968 / Duke ♦♦♦

Spotlight on the Man / 1969 / Duke ♦♦♦

Here's the Man! / 1969 / Duke ♦♦♦
The soulful vocals are backed by superb jazzy arrangements by Joe Scott. — *Hank Davis*

★ **The Best of Bobby Blue Bland** / 196 / MCA ♦♦♦♦♦
Excellent compilation of the sides that made the legend. Includes "Call on Me," "Farther up the Road," "I Pity the Fool," and "Turn on Your Love Light." — *Cub Koda*

Barefoot Rock & You Got Me / 196 / Duke ♦♦♦
Half Jr. Parker, half Bobby Bland, and all classic '50s R&B. — *Bill Dahl*

If Loving You Is Wrong / 1970 / Duke ♦♦♦

His California Album / 1973 / MCA ♦♦♦
And his first for ABC-Dunhill in 1973 after more than two decades with Duke (Robey's still represented, though, under his songwriting alias of Deadric Malone on four cuts, including the album's biggest hit, "This Time I'm Gone for Good"). Producer Steve Barri contemporized Bland by having him cover Leon Russell's "Help Me Make It Through the Day," Luther Ingram's "(If Loving You Is Wrong) I Don't Want to Be Right," and Gladys Knight & the Pips' "I've Got to Use My Imagination." — *Bill Dahl*

Woke up Screaming / 1974 / Duke ♦♦♦♦
This is a 16-track import anthology of Bland's earliest Duke sides from 1952 to 1957, at which point the *Blues Consolidated* album takes over. — *Hank Davis*

Introspective of the Early Years / 1974 / Duke ♦♦♦

Dreamer / 1974 / MCA ♦♦♦
Barri's slightly antiseptic production style and Michael Omartian's arrange-

ments weren't the equivalent of Joe Scott's immaculate collaborations with Bland, but this 1974 album's "Ain't No Love in the Heart of the City" and a meaty "I Wouldn't Treat a Dog (The Way You Treated Me)" were both huge hits. — *Bill Dahl*

Together for the First Time . . . Live / 1974 / MCA ♦♦♦
Although the duo of Bobby Blue Bland and B.B. King was one of the most popular touring acts of the '70s and '80s, their first duet album—appropriately titled *Together for the First Time . . . Live*—doesn't quite live up to expectations. Both musicians are in fine form, but rarely do any sparks fly. Occasionally, King turns out a good solo and Bland sings with passion, but usually the vibe of the record is too relaxed to be truly engaging. It's a pleasant record, just not the essential listening that it should have been. — *Thom Owens*

Get on Down with Bobby Bland / 1975 / ABC ♦♦♦

Together Again . . . Live / 1976 / MCA ♦♦
This not-so-exciting second Bobby "Blue" Bland and B.B. King pairing was recorded in Los Angeles Coconut Grove. There are more show business theatrics and less solid, soulful blues vocalizing than on their acclaimed debut, but there are still enough good moments to make it acceptable. — *Ron Wynn*

Reflections in Blue / 1977 / MCA ♦♦♦

Come Fly with Me / 1978 / MCA ♦♦

Greatest Hits / 1979 / Fairway ♦♦♦♦

I Feel Good, I Feel Fine / 1979 / MCA ♦♦♦

Sweet Vibrations / 1980 / MCA ♦♦♦
Slick and smooth. — *Bill Dahl*

Tell Mr. Bland / 1983 / MCA ♦♦
Laidback and slickly produced. — *Bill Dahl*

Members Only / 1985 / Malaco ♦♦♦
After some fairly soporific early-'80s releases for MCA, this album re-energized Bland's recording fortunes. The Larry Addison-penned title track caught on with blues-soul fans, making it to the middle reaches of the R&B charts as a single. — *Bill Dahl*

After All / 1986 / Malaco ♦♦

1st Class Blues / 1987 / Malaco ♦♦♦♦

Blues You Can Use / 1987 / Malaco ♦♦

Midnight Run / 1989 / Malaco ♦♦♦

☆ **The Best of Bobby Blue Bland, Vol. 2** / 198 / MCA ♦♦♦♦♦
Features the classics "It's My Life Baby," "Queen for a Day," and "Two Steps from the Blues." — *Cub Koda*

Portrait of the Blues / 1991 / Malaco ♦♦♦

Years of Tears / 1993 / Malaco ♦♦♦♦
Perhaps no artist has flourished at Malaco more than Bobby "Blue" Bland. Bland's animated, raw voice, though not as wide-ranging, still has a character and quality unmatched in blues, soul, or vintage R&B. This CD is his finest for the label since *Members Only*. The opening number, "Somewhere Between Right & Wrong," has a simmering track, Bland's mournful, explosive leads, tasty organ, tight drumming, and on-the-money lyrics from composers Johnny Barranco and Jackson. It sets the stage for nine additional country-tinged and bluesy soul tunes, including three from Frederick Knight, who also produced his compositions. It's not his Duke material, but it's close enough to satisfy. — *Ron Wynn*

Sad Street / Oct. 24, 1995 / Malaco ♦♦
Malaco's well-oiled, violin-enriched studio sound fits Bland's laidback, contemporary approach just fine these days (even if his voice admittedly ain't what it used to be). With top-flight songwriters George Jackson, Robert Johnson, and Sam Mosley contributing material to the project, the results are agreeable if less than earthshaking. Why Bland chose to cover Rod Stewart's "Tonight's the Night" remains a mystery, however. — *Bill Dahl*

That Did It!: The Duke Recordings 3 / Jun. 18, 1996 / MCA ♦♦♦
That Did It! is the third and final installment in MCA's series of double-disc compilations of Bobby Blue Bland's Duke recordings. This set collects everything he recorded between 1965 and 1972, including two unreleased tracks and several alternate takes. Although the music on *That Did It!* isn't quite as strong as the songs on the first two installments of the series, it does

collect a full 16 singles that have never appeared on an album before, as well as featuring several top-notch album tracks. For Bland fans, the collection remains a necessary purchase—this is Bland's final set of essential recordings. — *Thom Owens*

Live on Beale Street / Feb. 17, 1998 / Malaco ✦✦✦
Recorded live at the New Daisy Theater with Bland's regular working road band, this captures him in fine form, bringing together old favorites with some other numbers for a heady blend. When called for, the old Joe Scott heavy horn-laden arrangements are summoned up on tunes like "St. James Infirmary," "Farther on up the Road," "That's the Way Love Is," "I Pity the Fool," and "I'll Take Care of You," with consumate ease. But even more telling is how effortlessly and seamlessly material like Buddy Ace's "Love of Mine," "Members Only," "Soon as the Weather Breaks," and Bill Withers' "Ain't No Sunshine" and "Get Your Money Where You Spend Your Time" meshes with the old standbys. A lengthy, slow-blues medley brings guest appearances from Johnnie Taylor and Bobby Rush on "Stormy Monday," but the real star here is Bland himself. He's in good voice and good humor, and this makes a fine addition to his stack of latter-day recordings. — *Cub Koda*

The Blazers

f. 1990, Fullerton, CA
Group / Roots-Rock
The Blazers, who play a guitar-heavy blend of blues, surf-rock, country, rocked-up norteno, cumbia, and other Mexican styles, are often compared their East Los Angeles counterparts, Los Lobos. Like Los Lobos, the Gourds, or Doug Sahm's Texas Tornados, the Blazers perform a rousing, danceable mix of North American musical styles. The group is driven by two guitarist-singers, Manuel Gonzales and Ruben Guaderrama, who have been playing together since high school, rocking the beer joints of East L.A. Their fiery guitar playing and bluesy, soulful singing are given a strong, driving beat by bassist Lee Stuart and drummer Raul Medrano. The Blazers' infectious Ameri-Mex rock grooves and dual guitar action have prompted comparisons with Santana, the Kinks, the Rolling Stones, Chuck Berry and the Allman Brothers. Their 1994 debut album, *Short Fuse*, was hailed as one of the best rock records of the year by many critics. Already the group has made several overseas tours and been well-received by roots-starved European audiences.

The band's albums, all for Rounder Records, also include *East Side Soul* (1995) and *Just for You* (1997). All of them should find favor with any fan of hard-driving blues-rock and rockabilly. — *Richard Skelly*

Short Fuse / 1994 / Rounder ✦✦✦
The Blazers come out of the same milieu—indeed, the same Los Angeles neighborhood—as Los Lobos, and they share the same mixture of '50s rock, blues, and country styles in their music. *Short Fuse*, their debut album, was produced by Cesar Rosas of Los Lobos, and that's appropriate because the Blazers lean toward his more traditional side of Los Lobos' music. There's nobody in the band who writes songs with the depth and imaginativeness of Los Lobos' team of David Hidalgo and Louis Perez, but that doesn't keep them from playing up a storm on a combination of English-language rock ravers and Spanish-language folk-based tunes. If you love Los Lobos, you will at least like the Blazers. — *William Ruhlmann*

● **East Side Soul** / Oct. 17, 1995 / Rounder ✦✦✦✦

Just for You / Aug. 5, 1997 / Rounder ✦✦✦

Blind Blake (Arthur Phelps)

b. 189?, Jacksonville, FL, d. 1933
Guitar, Vocals / Country Blues, Piedmont Blues, Prewar Country Blues, Piano Blues, Acoustic Chicago Blues
What happened to Blind Blake? His disappearance in 1932 from the Chicago blues scene, where he was undisputed king of the string and recorded 81 solo sides for Paramount, is one of the unresolved mysteries of early blues. Similarly mysterious is Blake's prodigious fingerstyle guitar technique which has plank spankers to this day asking: "How the hell did he do that!?"

Like many early blues recording artists, Blake was regionally well-known, if not legendary, before he began making records. His peregrinations through the Southeast and Midwest were those of the itinerant songster; his repertoire included everything from blues to rags to music hall novelties. On Paramount records he broke out in 1926 with his debut release, a finger-buster called "West Coast Blues." Through the late '20s he performed and recorded with banjoists Papa Charlie Jackson and Gus Cannon, chanteuses Ma Rainey and Ida Cox, pianist Charlie Spand and a host of others as first-call guitar on Paramount's studio A-team. His best playing, however, was reserved for solo outings like "Diddie-Wah-Diddie" or "Police Dog Blues." On these he spun off guitar variations so dense they were dubbed "piano sounding" by his label. The hot licks framed lyrics often laced with suggestive double entendre. His hypermetabolic instrumentals were full of diffident spoken asides in an accent that gave credence to his supposed Southern seaboard origins.

Blake spent part of 1930 and 1931 touring with the vaudeville show "Happy-Go-Lucky" and returned to the Paramount studios in Grafton, WI, for his final session in 1932. His subsequent whereabouts, including rumors of his murder or death by mishap, have never been substantiated. It's commonly supposed that, as the Depression knocked the bottom out of the race record industry, Blake simply moved back to the South so beloved in his song lyrics, and died there soon after.

Blake's influence, especially in the folk/blues revival, was pervasive. His brilliant playing was touted by guitar godfathers like Josh White and Gary Davis; his songs covered by contemporary acousticians including Dave Van Ronk, Leon Redbone and Ry Cooder. On guitar, he's still the one to beat ... probably always will be. As he says himself, "Here's somethin' gonna make you feel good!" — *Steve James*

Complete Recorded Works, Vols. 1-4 / Aug. 1926-Jan. 1932 / Document ✦✦✦
Over the course of four discs—which are all sold individually—Document Records presents everything Blind Blake recorded in the late '20s and early '30s for Paramount Records. During that time, he was one of the most popular bluesmen in Chicago, and these 80-plus sides show why. Blake had a unique guitar style that influenced a number of successive generations. For that reason alone, *Complete Recorded Works in Chronological Order* would be of interest, but the music itself is compelling and gripping. However, the length and comprehensiveness of the set makes it a collection that only musicologists and dedicated fans would find necessary. For more casual listeners, Yazoo's *Ragtime Guitar's Foremost Fingerpicker* is a better purchase, since it distills all of his classic tracks to one disc. — *Thom Owens*

★ **Ragtime Guitar's Foremost Fingerpicker** / Nov. 1926-Oct. 1931 / Yazoo ✦✦✦✦✦
Ragtime Guitar's Foremost Fingerpicker contains a total of 28 prime tracks from Blind Blake. Alternating between solo acoustic numbers and songs recorded with a string band, the set demonstrates how exceptionally gifted the guitarist was—he's playing arrangements and rhythms that several subsequent generations were never able to figure out completely. Blind Blake was one of the finest acoustic guitarists of the '20s and '30s and this is the definitive compilation. — *Thom Owens*

Complete Recorded Works, Vol. 1 (1926-1927) / 1991 / Document ✦✦✦
Can't get enough of that stuff, yas, yas, yas! — *Jas Obrecht*

Complete Recorded Works, Vol. 2 (1927-1928) / 1991 / Document ✦✦✦
Document's *Complete Recorded Works, Vol. 2 (1927-1928)* continues the exhaustive overview of Blind Blake's early recordings. For less dedicated listeners, the long running time, exacting chronological sequencing, poor fidelity (all cuts are transferred from original acetates and 78s), and number of performances are hard to digest. The serious blues listener will find all these factors to be positive, but enthusiasts and casual listeners will find that the collection is of marginal interest for those very reasons, even in spite of the fine music to be found here. — *Thom Owens*

Complete Recorded Works, Vol. 4 (1929-1932) / 1991 / Document ✦✦✦
The fourth and final volume in Document's series assembles a wide range of Blind Blake material, from sides cut under the name Blind Arthur ("Guitar Chimes" and "Blind Arthur's Breakdown"), collaborations with vaudeville singer Chocolate Brown (a.k.a. Irene Scruggs), and even his sole two-part blues, the morbid "Rope Stretchin' Blues." Among the final pair of tracks, from mid-1932, the first, "Champagne Charlie Is My Name," is so atypical that some question whether it is even Blake at all; however, his last known side, "Depression's Gone from Me Blues," is a career-capping triumph—just why he never recorded again is just one of the many mysteries which continue to swirl about this legendary figure. — *Jason Ankeny*

Complete Recorded Works, Vol. 3 (1928-1929) / 1991 / Document ◆◆◆
The third volume in the series opens with a pair of mid-1928 tracks featuring Blind Blake in the role of sideman, lending his brilliant guitar leads in support of Elzadie Robinson on "Elzadie's Policy Blues" and "Pay Day Daddy Blues." Blake's next session, from later that same year, returns him to the fore, yielding the mesmerizing "Notoriety Woman," one of the most menacingly violent tracks he ever cut; the same date also produced the comparatively lighthearted "Sweet Papa Low Down," a seeming attempt to cash in on the Charleston dance craze. The real jewel of the set, however, is a 1929 session teaming him with pianist Charlie Spand; "Hastings St." is a lively, swinging guitar and piano duet, while "Police Dog Blues" is among Blake's most vividly lyrical efforts, further galvanized by his haunting instrumental work. — *Jason Ankeny*

The Master of Ragtime Guitar: The Essential Recordings / 1996 / Indigo ◆◆◆◆

Rory Block

b. Nov. 6, 1949, New York, NY
Guitar, Vocals / Modern Acoustic Blues
Rory Block is one of the brightest stars among a galaxy of modern-day country-blues interpreters. Rory's superb renderings of classic songs by Robert Johnson, Tommy Johnson, Charley Patton, and others display her deep passion and instinct for historic preservation, but seldom are her covers mere mimics. With its body-pounds, potent bass-string snaps, and precision rhythms, her fierce acoustic-guitar attack recalls the great Willie Brown. Rory's originals are often as strong as her covers, a standout being the title track from *Mama's Blues*. Her urgent, soulful voice is in a class of its own. As Taj Mahal says, "She's very simply the best there is."

Born and raised in New York's Greenwich Village, Rory Block began playing music as child. When she was ten years old, she became infatuated with the Village's folk music scene and she began playing guitar, taking classical guitar lessons. While she was a teenager she heard the blues and fell in love with the music. She played and took lessons from bluesmen like Rev. Gary Davis, Mississippi John Hurt, and Son House. In her mid-teens, Block left New York for California with fellow blues guitarist Stefan Grossman. After she arrived in California, she played clubs and coffeehouses; but she soon stopped performing, choosing to raise a family instead.

In the mid-'70s, Rory returned to performing, landing a record contract with the independent label Blue Goose in 1975, That same year, the label released her debut album, *Rory Block (I'm in Love)*. After its release, she was signed by Chrysalis Records, who released *Intoxication So Bitter Sweet* and *You're the One* in 1977 and 1978, respectively. During the late '70s, her music was spiked with contemporary R&B and pop production techniques in an ill-fated attempt to reach a mass audience.

Block didn't come into her own until she signed with Rounder Records in 1981. Beginning with *High Heeled Blues*, her first album for the label, she returned to her roots—solo acoustic country blues. Featuring a mixture of standards and originals, *High Heeled Blues* received positive reviews from both blues-oriented and mainstream publications. The positive reviews paved the way for popular success—throughout the '80s and '90s, Block was one of the most popular attractions on the blues circuit. Toward the beginning of the '90s, she expanded her sonic palette somewhat, recording with other musicians and occasionally a full band. However, the bulk of her work remains straightforward, traditional Delta acoustic blues and she is one of the artists that brought the genre to a mass audience in the '80s. Rory Block remained a popular artist in the '90s, selling numerous albums and concert tickets. — *Jas Obrecht & Stephen Thomas Erlewine*

The Early Tapes 1975-1976 / 1975-1976 / Alcazar ◆◆
On *The Early Tapes 1975-1976*, Rory Block is still trying to find a distinctive style. She samples from her idols—Robert Johnson, Charley Patton, and several others—adding slight blues and folk influences to her solo acoustic blues. However, she hasn't arrived at an original sound on any of these takes. Consequently, *Early Tapes* is of interest to historians and Rory Block completists, but few other listeners. — *Thom Owens*

Intoxication So Bitter Sweet / 1977 / Chrysalis ◆◆

You're the One / 1978 / Chrysalis ◆◆

High Heeled Blues / 1981 / Rounder ◆◆◆◆
This was the most blues-oriented release of the three sessions Block issued

in 1989 for Rounder; it was also the most concentrated and successful. There were none of the experimental or tentative qualities that sometimes marred the other two dates; Block was in command from the opening moments of her cover of "Walkin' Blues" to the final bars of "Uncloudy Day." Her voice had fire, soul and grit, and she never sounded maudlin or unconvincing, whether doing "Hilarity Rag" or "Devil Got My Man." Her playing was also dynamic and focused, and John Sebastian obviously made a good production partner, as Block got back on track after making records that contained some good cuts but weren't as consistent. — *Ron Wynn*

● **Best Blues & Originals** / 1981-1987 / Rounder ◆◆◆◆
Best Blues & Originals collects the highlights from Rory Block's '80s albums for Rounder, saving a bunch of fine tracks from otherwise spotty releases. It's a nice overview and, consequently, a solid introduction to her catalog. — *Thom Owens*

Blue Horizon / 1983 / Rounder ◆◆◆
Block bounced all over the musical lot on this session. She did vintage folk tunes such as "Frankie and Johnny" effectively and covered Rev. Gary Davis' "Feel Just Like Goin' On" and the spiritual "Swing Low" with vigor, but wasn't as compelling on "Catastrophe Rag" or the bittersweet/satiric "Just Like a Man." Block's voice and talents are versatile enough to handle multiple styles, but she remains first and foremost a fine interpreter of classic blues and gospel. When she opts for the singer-songwriter bit or folk/country mode, she's professional enough to bring it off, but lacks the flair or distinctiveness to make it sound anything except competent. — *Ron Wynn*

Rhinestones & Steel Strings / 1983 / Rounder ◆◆◆◆
Guitarist/vocalist Rory Block's mix of traditional blues covers, originals, satirical and folk/country material was featured on this album mixing mid-'80s and early-'90s tracks. Her versions of Robert Wilkins' "No Way for Me to Get Along" and Rev. Gary Davis' "Sit Down on the Banks" were among the high points, as well as Block's "Dr. Make it Right" and "I Might Find a Way." For the most part, the songs were nicely performed and varied between upbeat and somber themes. Block's vocals were frequently outstanding and never less than convincing, while her playing was strong and steady. — *Ron Wynn*

I've Got a Rock in My Sock / 1986 / Rounder ◆◆
Rory Block was combative, poignant, energetic, and laidback on this record. She did a good cover of Charley Patton's "Moon's Going Down," which changed things considerably from the strident mood established on the opening selection, "Send the Man Back Home." She handled the melancholy title track, was playful on "Lovin' Whiskey," and introspective on the final song "Highland Overture," a guitar/synthesizer duet that almost, but didn't quite plunge into the New Age/background music abyss. This seemed like an experimental/searching session for Block, who sometimes was enjoyable, but overall didn't fare as well as on most of her other releases. — *Ron Wynn*

House of Hearts / 1987 / Rounder ◆◆◆
A somber, morose mood permeated this album dedicated to Block's son, guitarist Thiele David Biehusen, who died in a car crash at age 20 and whose voice can be heard on the answering machine in the lengthy final cut "House of Hearts." There are also other equally gripping tunes, like "Farewell Young Man," "Heavenly Bird" and "Bonnie Boy." Block's voice was at its most mournful, and this is both a deeply moving work and a downer of an album. It's impossible not to be affected hearing Block's singing or these lyrics; anyone who's been through any remotely similar experience will feel the pain, and even those who haven't can't help but share in her sadness. — *Ron Wynn*

Color Me Wild: Inside Your Own Mind You Are Perfectly Free / 1990 / Alacazam!/Alcazar ◆◆◆◆
There's a wonderful sense of communication with children, particularly mid-childhood. Ages four to five. — *Bob Hinkle*

Mama's Blues / 1991 / Rounder ◆◆◆◆
Rory Block is quite impressive. Ignoring the fact that she is a white woman singing older-style blues in the 1990s, Block compares favorably to many of the top country-blues artists of the 1930s. Highlights of her very enjoyable set include Robert Johnson's "Terraplane Blues," a pair of Tommy Johnson classics and two songs recorded by Bessie Smith ("Do Your Duty" and "Weepin' Willow Blues"). Block's own originals (which have intelligent lyrics) sound more contemporary (with the influences of R&B, pop and gospel being felt), which alters the general mood of the release a bit. However, even with

its brief playing time (38 minutes), her CD is highly recommended as a fine example of the work of this talented blues performer. — *Scott Yanow*

Ain't I a Woman / 1992 / Rounder ✦✦✦✦
Rory Block's 11th album marked both a personal and professional milestone. Now a thoroughly experienced singer, Block sounded much more confident and assured doing traditional blues tunes. Her performance on the title cut was both assertive and definitive, while she also displayed her customary versatility, doing country and folk-flavored numbers such as "Silver Wings" and "Rolling Log" in addition to a stunning gospel number, "Walk in Jerusalem." Block's vocals and guitar work have blossomed, toughened and greatly improved over her career, and were in prime form here. — *Ron Wynn*

Angel of Mercy / Feb. 28, 1994 / Rounder ✦✦✦
Block moves completely away from the blues form on this release, doing original pieces that evoke the familiar themes of alienation, anguish and romantic conflicts, but in a production climate geared more toward folk and singer-songwriter arrangements than 12-bar settings. She still plays excellent guitar solos and accompaniment, but her vocals are now powerful or mournful, questioning or declarative, and she's unconcerned with trying to capture the quality of someone else's compositions. The disc's final selection, the nine-minute-plus "A Father and Two Sons," reworks the biblical Prodigal son tale with a contemporary focus, featuring wonderful vocal interaction between Block and her son Jordan. This album showcases Rory Block's own sound and vision and deserves widespread praise and attention. — *Ron Wynn*

When a Woman Gets the Blues / 1995 / Rounder ✦✦✦

Turning Point / 1996 / Munich ✦✦
Recorded in 1989, this wasn't released in the United States until 1996. Block sounds like she's trying to capture the AOR market on most of this all-original set, in somewhat the same vein as Bonnie Raitt, but less effectively so. Glimpses of her acoustic and blues roots are no more than fleeting, as on "Leavin' Here" or the acoustic guitar instrumental, "Down the Hiway." It's not arresting enough to capture the pop audience, and Block fans who like her bluesy stuff the best might find the slick approach downright alienating. — *Richie Unterberger*

Tornado / Mar. 19, 1996 / Rounder ✦✦✦
After establishing her blues credentials with the traditional "Mississippi Bottom Blues," Rory Block turns to a set of original folk-rock songs on which she is joined by a band and such guests as David Lindley (who plays a guitar solo on "Pictures of You") and Mary-Chapin Carpenter (who sings harmony on "You Didn't Mind"). Block brings a blues simplicity and directness to her music and lyrics, which helps ease her transition from folk-blues interpreter to folk-rock singer-songwriter. — *William Ruhlmann*

Gone Woman Blues / 1997 / Rounder ✦✦✦✦
Subtitled "The Country Blues Collection," Rory Block sticks to what she may do better than any other contemporary player around. These cuts have all been heard scattered about on various other albums going back to *High Heeled Blues* from 1989; here they are pulled together into one comprehensive whole. She explores the wide variety of country-blues, and even at 69-plus minutes this disc never gets repetitive. Except for five cuts, she is unaccompanied, and when she is, it only enhances what she does. Her youngest son, Jordan Block Valdina, helps out by doing the male vocal on a stunning a cappella version of "Be Ready When He Comes." The harmonica backing by Little Annie Raines (a frequent collaborator with Paul Rishell) just perfectly walks that line of being enhancing without intruding. If you like country-blues, this is one you don't want to miss. — *Bob Gottlieb*

Best Blues & Originals, Vol. 2 / Aug. 19, 1997 / Munich ✦✦✦

Blodwyn Pig

f. 1968, England
Group / Blues-Rock
A quirky detour of late-'60s British progressive/blues-rock, Blodwyn Pig was founded by former Jethro Tull guitarist Mick Abrahams, who left Tull after the *This Was* album. Abrahams was joined by bassist Andy Pyle, drummer Ron Berg, and Jack Lancaster, who gave the outfit their most distinctive colorings via his saxophone and flute. On their two albums, they explored a jazz/blues/progressive style somewhat in the mold of (unsurprisingly) Jethro Tull, but with a lighter feel. They also bore some similarities to John Mayall's jazzy

late-'60s versions of the Bluesbreakers, or perhaps Colosseum, but with more eclectic material. Both of their LPs made the British Top Ten, though the players' instrumental skills were handicapped by thin vocals and erratic (though oft-imaginative) material. The group were effectively finished by Abrahams' departure after 1970's *Getting to This*. They briefly reunited in the mid-'70s, and Abrahams was part of a different lineup that reformed in the late '80s; they have since issued a couple of albums in the 1990s. — *Richie Unterberger*

● **Ahead Rings Out** / Aug. 1969 / A&M ✦✦✦✦
A nifty, if often drifting, fusion of blues-rock with jazzy instrumentation, the material varying from riff-based instrumental passages to contemplative, acoustic-flavored bluesy bits. "Dear Jill" and "The Change Song" are their best tunes, showing a more subtle side of the band than the numbers emphasizing their instrumental flash. — *Richie Unterberger*

Getting to This / Apr. 1970 / A&M ✦✦✦
On their follow-up, the group explored similar avenues as they did on *Ahead Rings Out*. It took a more pile-driving approach than their first effort, but the material wasn't as strong. — *Richie Unterberger*

Lies / 1993 / Viceroy ✦✦✦✦
The reconstituted Blodwyn Pig, consisting of Mick Abrahams (lead vocals, guitars), Graham Walker (drums), Dave Lennox (keyboards, vocals), and Mike Summerland (bass, vocals), with Jackie Challoner (backing vocals), and Nick Payne (harmonica, saxes). This is more of a soul band than the original Blodwyn Pig, and thankfully they've left jazz and progressive rock behind on this album. Apart from the superb title track, there's a ton of R&B-styled material here, all played and sung hard but well, with a level of maturity that only adds to the depth of the performances. In addition to originals by Abrahams, there are covers of songs by Doc Pomus and Dr. John ("The Victim") and Alexis Korner ("I Wonder Who"), the latter one of a pair of live tracks reuniting Abrahams with his former bandmates Clive Bunker and Andy Pyle. — *Bruce Eder*

All Tore Down (Blodwyn Pig Live) / 1994 / Indigo ✦✦✦✦
It would be difficult to imagine a better live album coming from the likes of the Blodwyn Pig. The music is pure R&B—mid-'60s British style, only more soulful than most of those bands ever got. Abrahams and company perform dazzling, passionate renditions of their best songs, including "Lies," a tribute to Alexis Korner ("I Wonder Who"), and even an extended (17 minutes, no less) version of "Cat's Squirrel," a song that Abrahams brought to Jethro Tull's *This Was* back in 1968. One of those rare cases—you might say a unique example—of a revamped, reformed sixties/seventies band outdoing its original incarnation on every count. — *Bruce Eder*

Modern Alchemist / May 5, 1997 / Indigo ✦✦✦

Live at the Lafayette / Mar. 4, 1998 / Indigo ✦✦✦

Michael Bloomfield

b. Jul. 28, 1943, Chicago, IL, d. Feb. 15, 1981, San Francisco, CA
Guitar, Keyboards, Vocals / Blues-Rock, Electric Chicago Blues
Michael Bloomfield was born July 28, 1943, in Chicago, IL. An indifferent student and self-described social outcast, Bloomfield immersed himself in the multicultural music world that existed in Chicago in the 1950s.

He got his first guitar at age 13. Initially attracted to the roots-rock sound of Elvis Presley and Scotty Moore, Bloomfield soon discovered the electrified big-city blues music indigenous to Chicago. At the age of 14 the exuberant guitar *wunderkind* began to visit the blues clubs on Chicago's South Side with friend Roy Ruby in search of his new heroes: players such as Muddy Waters, Otis Spann, Howlin' Wolf, and Magic Sam. Not content with viewing the scene from the audience, Bloomfield was known to leap onto the stage, asking if he could sit in as he simultaneously plugged in his guitar and began playing riffs.

Bloomfield was quickly accepted on the South Side, as much for his ability as for the audiences' appreciation of seeing a young White player in a part of town where few Whites were seen. Bloomfield soon discovered a group of like-minded outcasts. Young White players such as Paul Butterfield, Nick Gravenites, Charlie Musselwhite, and Elvin Bishop were also establishing themselves as fans who could hold their own with established bluesmen, many of whom were old enough to be their fathers.

In addition to playing with the established stars of the day, Bloomfield began to search out older, forgotten bluesmen, playing and recording with Sleepy John Estes, Yank Rachell, Little Brother Montgomery, and Big Joe Williams, among others. By this time he was managing a Chicago folk music club, the Fickle Pickle, and often hired older acoustic blues players for the Tuesday night blues sessions. Big Joe Williams memorialized those times in the song "Pick a Pickle" with the line "You know Mike Bloomfield ... will always treat you right ... come to the Pickle, every Tuesday night." Bloomfield's relationship with Big Joe Williams is documented in "Me and Big Joe," a moving short story detailing Bloomfield's adventures on the road with Williams.

Bloomfield's guitar work as a session player caught the ear of legendary CBS producer and talent scout John Hammond, Sr., who flew to Chicago and immediately signed him to a recording contract. However CBS was unsure of exactly how to promote their new artist, declining to release any of the tracks recorded by Bloomfield's band, which included harp player Charlie Musselwhite.

With a contract but not much else, Bloomfield returned to playing clubs around Chicago until he was approached by Paul Rothchild, the producer of the Paul Butterfield Blues Band albums. Bloomfield was recruited to play slide guitar and piano on early recordings (later released as *The Lost Elektra Sessions*) which were rejected for not fully capturing the sound of the band. Although more competitors than friends ("I knew Paul, was scared of him," remembered Mike), the addition of Bloomfield to the Butterfield Band provided Paul Butterfield with a musician of equal caliber—Paul and Michael inspired and challenged each other as they traded riffs and musical ideas, one establishing a pattern and the other following it, extending it, and handing it back.

In between recording sessions with the Butterfield Band, Bloomfield backed up Bob Dylan on the classic *Highway 61 Revisited* album, and appeared with him at the Newport Folk Festival in 1965 when Dylan stunned the purist "folk" crowd by playing electric rock 'n' roll. Declining an offer from Dylan to join his touring band, Bloomfield and the Butter Band returned to the studio; with the addition of pianist Mark Naftalin they finally captured their live sound on vinyl.

The first two Butterfield Blues Band albums, the Dylan sessions, and the live appearances by the Butterfield Band firmly established Bloomfield as one of the most talented and influential guitar players in America. The second album featured the Bloomfield composition "East-West" which ushered in an era of long instrumental psychedelic improvisations.

Bloomfield left the Butterfield Blues Band in early 1967, ostensibly to give original guitarist Elvin Bishop, in Mike's words, "a little space." Undoubtedly he had also become uncomfortable with Paul Butterfield's position as bandleader and was anxious to lead his own band.

That band, The Electric Flag, included Bloomfield's old friends from Chicago, organist Barry Goldberg and singer-songwriter Nick Gravenites, as well as bass player Harvey Brooks and drummer Buddy Miles. The band was well received at its official debut at the Monterey Pop Festival but quickly fell apart due to drugs, egos, and poor management.

Bloomfield, weary of the road, suffering from insomnia, and uncomfortable in the role of guitar superstar, returned to San Francisco to score movies, produce other artists, and play studio sessions. One of those sessions was a day of jamming in the studio with keyboardist Al Kooper, who had previously worked with Bloomfield on the 1965 Dylan sessions.

Super Session, the resultant release, with Bloomfield on side one and guitarist Stephen Stills on side two, once again thrust Bloomfield into the spotlight. Kooper's production and the improvisational nature of the recording session captured the quintessential Bloomfield sound: the fast flurries of notes, the incredible string bending, the precise attack, and his masterful use of tension and release.

Although *Super Session* was the most successful recording of his career, Bloomfield considered it to be a "scam," more of an excuse to sell records than a pursuit of musical goals. After a followup live album, he "retired" to San Francisco and lowered his visibility.

In the '70s, Bloomfield played gigs in the San Francisco area and infrequently toured as Bloomfield and Friends, a group which usually included Mark Naftalin and Nick Gravenites. Bloomfield also occasionally helped out friends by lending his name to recording projects and business propositions,

such as the ill-fated Electric Flag reunion in 1974 and the KGB album in 1976. In the mid-'70s Bloomfield recorded a number of albums with a more traditional blues focus for smaller record labels. He also recorded an instructional album of various blues styles for *Guitar Player* magazine.

By the late '70s, Bloomfield's continuing drug and health problems caused erratic behavior and missed gigs, alienating a number of his old associates. Bloomfield continued playing with other musicians, including Dave Shorey and Jonathan Cramer. In the summer of 1980, he toured Italy with classical guitarist Woody Harris and cellist Maggie Edmondson. On November 15, 1980, Bloomfield joined Bob Dylan on stage at the Warfield Theater in San Francisco and jammed on "Like a Rolling Stone," the song they had recorded together 15 years earlier.

Michael Bloomfield was found dead in his car of a drug overdose in San Francisco, CA, on February 15, 1981.

Nick Gravenites remembers Michael Bloomfield this way: "I thought he was a huge giant of a person. I think the totality of his character is the thing that impressed me most. People forget how charismatic he was. He had a certain charisma about him, people wanted to be around him, touch the hem of his garment, that sort of thing. I think it was the totality of his character I was impressed with, not only his musical ability but also his intellect, his sense of humor, his compassion, his generosity, all those things that make up a human being. And those are my fondest memories, of character.

"He was quite a forceful personality. He was quite a wit. And also had a very deep character—was very generous, very soulful. The effect that he had on me and people around him, people that knew him and loved his music and stuff was profound.

"Michael's friends, the ones that were closest to him, really loved the guy. And they did it for a lot of reasons. He helped them live their lives, make something out of their lives in many ways, very profoundly. I can still think in terms of those major, those big terms, when I think about Michael." —*Jan Mark Wolkin*

Don't Say That I Ain't Your Man / 1964-1969 / Sony ♦♦♦♦

15 tracks covering the pioneering blues-rock guitarist's '60s work, which was by far his best and most influential. Bloomfield worked with a bunch of bands during the decade, and the compilation flits rather hurriedly from his contributions to The Paul Butterfield Blues Band and Electric Flag to his collaborations with Al Kooper and some late-'60s solo tracks (none of his groundbreaking mid-'60s work with Dylan is here). Collectors will be interested in the first five songs, which date from previously unreleased sessions produced by John Hammond in late 1964 and early 1965. Featuring Charlie Musselwhite on harmonica, this pre-Butterfield Blues Band outfit plays convincingly, but the material is standard-issue, and Bloomfield's vocals are thin and weak (they didn't improve much over time). As befits Bloomfield's considerable but erratic talent, this is an interesting but erratic compilation; seek out the first two Paul Butterfield albums for a more cohesive showcase of his skills. —*Richie Unterberger*

● Super Session / 1968 / Columbia ♦♦♦♦

Al Kooper was the mastermind behind this appropriately named album, one side of which features his "spontaneous" studio collaboration with Mike Bloomfield and the other a session with Stephen Stills. The recordings have an off-the-cuff energy that displays the inventiveness of the two guitarists to best advantage. The best-selling recording of Bloomfield's career, it inspired the follow-up *The Live Adventures of Mike Bloomfield and Al Kooper.* —*Jeff Tamarkin*

Live at Bill Grahams Fillmore West / 1969 / Columbia ♦♦♦♦

This session from early 1969 featured Nick Gravenites, Mark Naftalin, John Kahn and Snooky Flowers (among others), with cameos from Taj Mahal and Jesse Ed Davis, but it's clear from the opening notes who the real star is. Over the years, Bloomfield's titanic solos on "Blues on a Westside" have dwarfed the rest of the album in my memory, but the truth is his playing just burns across every track. (More of Michael's great guitar work from these shows is on Nick Gravenites' *My Labors* on Columbia.) —*Cary Wolfson*

The Live Adventures of Mike Bloomfield and Al Kooper / 1969 / Columbia ♦♦

Recorded over three nights in 1968 at the Fillmore Auditorium in San Francisco, the follow-up to the acclaimed *Super Session* has its moments, but is mostly long on '60s noodly grooviness and lacking in focus and inspiration. It's notable (sort of) for Bloomfield's singing debut. — *Cary Wolfson*

It's Not Killing Me / 1969 / Columbia ♦♦
Let's see. For his first solo album, take a brilliant young guitarist who can barely sing and put the emphasis on … his vocals. Well, somebody thought it was a good idea; too bad they were wrong. There are just a few examples of that B.B. King-inflected guitar style among the rock and country-flavored throwaways. — *Cary Wolfson*

Triumvirate / 1973 / Columbia ♦♦♦
In 1973 someone at Columbia evidently decide to try and recoup some of the investment the label made in Bloomfield and John Hammond — they were thrown into a recording studio along with Dr. John, who had recently scored a hit with "Right Place, Wrong Time." It probably sounded like a good idea at the time, but the results were uninspired. Pass by this CD and pick up any one of their solo recordings instead. — *Jan Mark Wolkin*

Try It Before You Buy It / 1975 / One Way ♦♦
Try It Before You Buy It is one of Michael Bloomfield's neglected albums, and there's a reason why — although there's some very fine playing scattered throughout the album, the performances are uneven and unfocused. Furthermore, the album leans too close to a straight rock 'n' roll direction for blues purists. If you dig hard, there are some rewards on *Try It Before You Buy It*, but on the whole, it's one that should be left on the shelf. — *Thom Owens*

The Root of Blues / 1976 / Laserlight ♦♦♦
A budget-label reissue of the instructional blues LP released by *Guitar Player* magazine in 1976, this CD includes most of the songs but omits Michael's spoken passages about each track. Bloomfield pays tribute to his influences and favorites: acoustic and electric, solo and with a band. Standout tracks include "Death in My Family," played in the style of Guitar Slim, "WDIA," a tribute to B.B. King, "City Girl," dedicated to T-Bone Walker, and an acoustic version of "Kansas City," played, in Bloomfield's words, "in a style I would call 'Travis Picking,' after Merle Travis. It seems an anomaly to use a modern style for such an old song, but the method of syncopated contrapuntal fingerpicking is well suited to the song because the key of E has so many open strings." — *Jan Mark Wolkin*

I'm with You Always / 1977 / Demon ♦♦♦
This release, recorded at McCabe's Guitar Shop in Santa Monica, CA, in 1977, captures a superb live show, with Bloomfield in top form as he performs before an appreciative audience in an intimate setting. Michael's singing is spirited and his guitar playing is precise and inventive as he plays favorite songs from his repertoire. Highlights include solo acoustic performances of two songs written by Shelton Brooks in the early 1900s, a piano/guitar duet demonstrating the rapport he had with pianist Mark Naftalin, and hot performances by Bloomfield, Naftalin and a rhythm section of Buddy Helm on drums and Buell Neidlinger on bass. Bloomfield shows what he had been doing all those years out of the spotlight — refining his technique and researching the music he loved. — *Jan Mark Wolkin*

Best of Michael Bloomfield / 1978-1980 / Takoma ♦♦♦♦
By the time the majority of these 12 tracks from various solo projects were recorded, Bloomfield was already well established as America's first official guitar slinger of the baby boomer generation. The selections on this CD come from the later stages of his career, and as such are a marvelous showcase for his wide ranging versatility. They run the gamut from Mississippi John Hurt-style fingerpicking ("Frankie and Johnny"), Scrapper Blackwell acoustic style flat-picking and Lonnie Johnson slide playing (with "Mr. Johnson and Mr. Dunn," "Effiona Rag," "See That My Grave Is Kept Clean" featuring him on acoustic slide, piano, accordion and tipple, and two duets with Little Brother Montgomery, "Pleading Blues" and "Michigan Water Blues") to the red-hot electric solo work he's best noted for. Other highlights include "Between the Hard Place and the Ground" and a stray track with the Woody Herman big band, "Hitch-Hike on the Possum Trot Line." — *Cub Koda*

Between the Hard Place and The Ground / 1979 / Takoma ♦♦
Bloomfield and friends have always been able to get it together on record, and this effort is one more example of seasoned pros putting out music which appears to magically flow from them. "Big Chief from New Orleans" and "Lights Out" show Bloomfield in a lighter frame of mind. Of course, by this time, the public was generally ignoring his output, which is a shame, because *Between the Hard Place and the Ground* is well worth seeking out

to experience Mike Bloomfield in the later stages of his career. — *James Chrispell*

Living in the Fast Lane / 1980 / AJK ♦♦♦
Michael Bloomfield was a pioneer in blues-rock, one of the performers who found a way to maintain his own sound while paying tribute to the blues greats that created the music he idolized. The 10 tracks presented on *Living in the Fast Lane* weren't as vital as his earlier material, but were done with the same intensity and passion that marked all his numbers. They were backed on several cuts by Duke Tito and the Marin Country Playboys, while on "When I Get Home," the Singers of the Church of God in Christ joined lead vocalist Roger Troy for a rousing, spirit-filled performance that was the album's high point. — *Ron Wynn*

Sugar Blue

b. New York, NY
Harmonica / Contemporary Blues
Sugar Blue grew up in Harlem listening to Billie Holiday, James Brown and all the acts playing at the Apollo Theatre. After much session work (including the Rolling Stones' *Some Girls*, *Emotional Rescue* and *Tattoo You*), the bluesy harmonica player finally earned a solo album in 1980, when *Crossroads* appeared on the Blue Silver label. *Chicago to Paris* followed two years later, and after playing with Syl Johnson, Willie Dixon and Paul Schaffer, Sugar Blue released two more solo albums on Alligator: *Blue Blazes* (1994) and *In Your Eyes* (1995). — *John Bush*

Crossroads / 1980 / Tol ♦♦♦

● **Blue Blazes** / Mar. 1994 / Alligator ♦♦♦♦
Harmonica player and vocalist Sugar Blue isn't a singer who doubles on harp; he's an extraordinary instrumentalist who's also a quality vocalist. Blue covers tunes by Willie Dixon, Muddy Waters, James Cotton, and Sonny Boy Williamson (II) classics, presents a decent, if disposable version of the Rolling Stones' "Miss You," and adds the good-natured original, "Country Blues," co-written with his guitarist Motoaoki Makino. But it's those harmonica lines and phrases that make the CD. One of Alligator's best contemporary albums in a long time. — *Ron Wynn*

Blues Boy Willie (Willie McFalls)

b. Nov. 28, 1946, Memphis, TX
Harmonica, Vocals / R&B, Modern Electric Blues, Contemporary Blues
Willie McFalls, a native Memphian from Texas, not Tennessee, took the chitlin circuit by surprise in 1990 when the comical blues dialog of "Be-Who?" put his second album on the *Billboard* charts and his act on the road. Blues Boy Willie came to Ichiban Records courtesy of his boyhood friend from Texas, bluesman-producer Gary B.B. Coleman. Willie's three albums to date all bear the typical Coleman touch — competent but predictable blues tracks with a small studio band. It has been the spunky spoken repartee between Willie and his wife Miss Lee on the novelty numbers that has earned Willie an unexpected niche on the Southern soul-blues scene. — *Jim O'Neal*

● **Strange Things Happening** / 1989 / Ichiban ♦♦♦♦
Blues Boy Willie's debut album, *Strange Things Happening*, is an excellent collection of classic Southern soul and electric blues, given a modern edge. While the production may be a little too slick for fans of classic '60s grit, there's no doubting that Willie's heart is in the right place, and he keeps things engaging even when the material gets a little predictable. — *Thom Owens*

Be Who? 2 / 1990 / Ichiban ♦♦♦

I Got the Blues / 1992 / Ichiban ♦♦♦

Don't Look Down / 1993 / Ichiban ♦♦

Juke Joint Blues / 1995 / Ichiban Blues ♦♦♦♦

The Blues Project

f. 1965, New York, NY, **db.** 1972
Group / Blues-Rock, Folk-Rock, Modern Electric Blues
One of the first album-oriented, "underground" groups in the United States, the Blues Project offered an electric brew of rock, blues, folk, pop, and even some jazz, classical, and psychedelia during their brief heyday in the mid-'60s. It's not quite accurate to categorize them as a blues-rock group, although

they did plenty of that kind of material; they were more like a Jewish-American equivalent to British bands like the Yardbirds, who used a blues and R&B base to explore any music that interested them. Erratic songwriting talent and a lack of a truly outstanding vocalist prevented them from rising to the front line of '60s bands, but they recorded plenty of interesting material over the course of their first three albums, before the departure of their most creative members took its toll.

The Blues Project was formed in Greenwich Village in the mid-'60s by guitarist Danny Kalb (who had played sessions for various Elektra folk and folk-rock albums), Steve Katz (a guitarist with Elektra's Even Dozen Jug Band), flutist/bassist Andy Kulberg, drummer Roy Blumenfeld, and singer Tommy Flanders. Al Kooper, in his early twenties a seasoned vet of rock sessions, joined after sitting in on the band's Columbia Records audition, although they ended up signing to Verve, an MGM subsidiary. Early member Artie Traum (guitar) dropped out during early rehearsals; Flanders would leave after their first LP, *Live at the Cafe Au-Go-Go* (1966).

The eclectic resumes of the musicians, who came from folk, jazz, blues, and rock backgrounds, was reflected in their choice of material. Blues by Muddy Waters and Chuck Berry tunes ran alongside covers of contemporary folk-rock songs by Eric Anderson and Patrick Sky, as well as the group's own originals. These were usually penned by Kooper, who had already built songwriting credentials as the co-writer of Gary Lewis' huge smash "This Diamond Ring," and established a reputation as a major folk-rock shaker with his contributions to Dylan's mid-'60s records. Kooper also provided the band's instrumental highlights with his glowing organ riffs.

The live debut sounds rather tame and derivative; the group truly hit their stride on *Projections* (late 1966), which was, disappointingly, their only full-length studio recording. While they went through straight blues numbers with respectable energy, they really shone best on the folk and jazz-influenced tracks, like "Fly Away," Katz's lilting "Steve's Song," Kooper's jazz instrumental "Flute Thing" (an underground radio standard that's probably their most famous track), and Kooper's fierce adaptation of an old Blind Willie Johnson number, "I Can't Keep from Crying." A non-LP single from this era, the pop-psychedelic "No Time Like the Right Time," was their greatest achievement and one of the best "great hit singles that never were" of the decade.

The band's very eclecticism didn't augur well for their long-term stability, and in 1967 Kooper left in a dispute over musical direction (he has recalled that Kalb opposed his wishes to add a horn section). Then Kalb mysteriously disappeared for months after a bad acid trip, which effectively finished the original incarnation of the band. A third album, *Live at Town Hall*, was a particularly half-assed project given the band's stature, pasted together from live tapes and studio outtakes, some of which were overdubbed with applause to give the impression that they had been recorded in concert.

Kooper got to fulfill his ambitions for soulful horn rock as the leader of the original Blood, Sweat & Tears, although he left that band after their first album; BS&T also included Katz (who stayed onboard for a long time). Blumenfeld and Kulberg kept the Blues Project going for a fourth album before forming Seatrain, and the group re-formed in the early '70s with various lineups, Kooper rejoining for a live 1973 album, *Reunion in Central Park*. The first three albums from the Kooper days are the only ones that count, though; the best material from these is on Rhino's best-of compilation. *— Richie Unterberger*

Live at the Cafe Au-Go-Go / May 1966 / Verve/Forecast ◆◆◆
Although Tommy Flanders (who'd already left the band by the time this debut hit the streets) is credited as sole vocalist, four of the then-sextet's members sang; in fact, Danny Kalb handles as many leads as Flanders (four each), Steve Katz takes center stage on Donovan's "Catch the Wind," and Al Kooper is featured on "I Want to Be Your Driver." The band could be lowdown when appropriate (Kalb's reading of "Jelly, Jelly"), high-energy (Muddy Waters' "Goin' Down Louisiana" sounds closer to Chuck Berry or Bo Diddley), and unabashedly eclectic (tossing in Donovan or Eric Andersen with no apologies). Kalb's moody take on "Alberta" is transcendent, and the uptempo arrangement of "Spoonful" is surprisingly effective. *— Dan Forte*

Projections from the Past / Sep. 1, 1966 / Hablabel ◆◆◆
A double album of dubious legality, but fairly easy availability. This captures the Blues Project's best lineup—Kooper, Katz, Kalb, Kulberg, and Blumenfeld—live at the Matrix club in San Francisco on September 1, 1966. If there's

any revelation to be had from these fair-quality tapes, it's that there's not much of a revelation at all. The group performs a lot of the stronger material from their first and second albums in versions very close to the records. They shine brightest on the more adventurous material with jazz and folk tangents, like "Steve's Song," "Flute Thing," "Catch the Wind," and "Cheryl's Going Home." Most of the rest is competent, but not especially brilliant, white-boy blues renditions of numbers like "Hoochie Coochie Man," "You Can't Catch Me," and "You Can't Judge a Book by the Cover"; the swaggering "Shake That Baby" is about the best of these. Essential only for serious collectors. Be warned that there are a few (not many) clumsy edits, and that the entire fourth side is simply tracks lifted from their *Live at Town Hall* LP. *— Richie Unterberger*

Projections / Nov. 1966 / Verve/Forecast ◆◆◆◆
Produced by Tom Wilson (Dylan, Zappa), the Blues Project's second effort was their finest hour. In less than a year the enthusiastic live band had matured into a seasoned studio ensemble. Steve Katz's features are lightweight folk but Al Kooper reworks two gospel themes ("Wake Me, Shake Me," "I Can't Keep from Crying") into ambitious blues-rock compositions, and Danny Kalb proves he's no mere folkie on extended versions of "Two Trains Running" and "Caress Me Baby." Bassist Andy Kulberg switches to flute and Kalb gets psychedelic on the jazzy "Flute Thing," penned by Kooper. *— Dan Forte*

The Best of the Blues Project [Rhino] / 1966-1967 / Rhino ◆◆◆◆
With the exception of a live version of "Flute Thing" from the Blues Project's 1973 reunion concert included only on the CD version, this compilation is culled entirely from the albums *Live at the Cafe Au-Go-Go, Projections,* and *The Blues Project Live at Town Hall,* all recorded and released in the period 1966-1967. Just as those individual albums do, it confirms the acclaim accorded the Blues Project at the time. The group's sophistication and ability to create a hybrid of musical styles keeps the music from sounding dated. In fact, this music not only stands as among the best of its time, but it continues to appeal where much of the music made simultaneously fails to escape its era. (Not to be confused with *Best of the Blues Project,* Verve Forecast FTS 3077 [1969 07], which is an earlier compilation with a different selection of songs.) *— William Ruhlmann*

Live at Town Hall / Sep. 1967 / One Way ◆◆◆
Released just after Al Kooper left the band, one imagines that neither he nor the other members of the group were pleased with this LP. According to Kooper, it was a pastiche of studio outtakes and a few live performances, and only one of the songs was actually recorded at New York City's Town Hall. Anyway, this has a meandering, ten-minute "Flute Thing" and decent live versions of "Wake Me, Shake Me" and "I Can't Keep from Crying" which, despite a somewhat rawer feel, are not necessary supplements to the fine studio takes. "Where There's Smoke, There's Fire" and the great "No Time Like the Right Time" had already been released as singles; to hear them without canned applause, you only need to turn to Rhino's first-rate *Best of the Blues Project* instead. That compilation also contains the other cut of note on this album, an outtake-sounding cover of Patrick Sky's "Love Will Endure." *— Richie Unterberger*

Planned Obsolescence / Dec. 1968 / One Way ◆◆◆

Lazarus / 1971 / Capitol ◆◆◆

The Blues Project / 1972 / Capitol ◆◆◆

Original Blues Project Reunion in Central Park / 1973 / One Way ◆◆◆
Considering that the original lineup had broken up six years earlier, this ranks as one of the most artistically successful reunions in blues or rock. If there were any ego problems, they don't show; typically Kalb and Kooper shine, but all five are playing as a team. Most important, the members seem to respect their own past—and re-create it with spontaneity and energy. *— Dan Forte*

Anthology / Jan. 28, 1997 / Polygram ◆◆◆◆
The most complete Blues Project collection ever assembled, the two-disc *Anthology* compiles 36 tracks taken from their three albums on Verve and their two records on Capitol as well as rare singles, previously unreleased songs and alternate versions, and material from solo projects. *— Jason Ankeny*

Lucille Bogan (Lucille Armstrong)

b. Apr. 1, 1897, Amory, MS, **d.** Aug. 10, 1948, Los Angeles, CA
Vocals / Classic Female Blues, Prewar Country Blues
The big-voiced Bogan made some important sides in the classic female blues tradition throughout the the mid-'20s and early '30s. Singing with astonishing forthrightness about abusive men, prostitution, and predilections for both whiskey and sex, her recorded work is all solidly imbued with proto-feminist outlooks, all the more surprising given the time frame in which her best work exists. After scoring a "race" hit in 1927 with "Sweet Petunia," she changed her name (and her vocal style with it) to Bessie Jackson. Her best known tune, the salacious "Shave 'Em Dry," has shown up on numerous compilations of bawdy blues material and is always the track everyone plays first, as its X-rated lyrical content has cross-generational appeal. Unlike other women singers from the genre, she seldom strayed into pop-style music, remaining essentially a straight-ahead blues stylist with a rock solid sense of time and a big old heart. — *Cub Koda*

Lucille Bogan (1923-1935) / 1923-1935 / Story of Blues ◆◆◆◆
A solid 18-track compilation of Lucille's best sides from her peak period. — *Cub Koda*

● **Lucille Bogan & Walter Roland, 1927-1935** / Mar. 1927-Mar. 7, 1935 / Yazoo ◆◆◆◆
14-track compilation split evenly down the middle between Bogan and her main piano accompanist, Roland, who also doubles on guitar on some tracks. The Bogan sides are a particular delight, featuring a version of "Barbecue Bess" that is nothing short of sublime. As all of these tracks are rescued off highly battered 78s, the fidelity is about what you would expect. But that's no reason to deter you from enjoying this timeless music. — *Cub Koda*

Complete Recorded Works, Vol. 1 / Jun. 2, 1994 / Document ◆◆◆

Complete Recorded Works, Vol. 2 (1930-1933) / Jun. 2, 1994 / Document ◆◆◆

Complete Recorded Works, Vol. 3 (1934-1935) / Jun. 2, 1994 / Document ◆◆◆

Deanna Bogart

b. 1960, Detroit, MI
Piano, Saxophone, Vocals / Jump Blues, Piano Blues, Modern Electric Blues
Drawing on a variety of musical sources ranging from boogie-woogie to New Orleans R&B to swing to rock 'n' roll, singer and barrelhouse pianist Deanna Bogart emerged as one of the most eclectic performers in contemporary blues. Born in Detroit in 1960, she cut her teeth on the Maryland blues circuit, developing a crowd-pleasing style which often found her leaping up from her piano bench to chat with the audience; clad in her trademark black fedora, Bogart was also known to blow a mean tenor saxophone. A gifted composer as well, her debut LP *Out to Get You* appeared in 1991, followed in 1992 by *Crossing Borders;* a four-year hiatus preceded the release of *New Address.* — *Jason Ankeny*

● **Out to Get You** / May 1991 / Blind Pig ◆◆◆◆
Debut album by this delightful two-fisted boogie-woogie pianist, saxophonist, and songster. Highlights abound everywhere, but of particular note is her striking originals "Over Thirty" and "Morning Glory." — *Cub Koda*

Crossing Borders / 1992 / Flying Fish ◆◆◆
The follow-up album to Bogart's debut effort is chock full of the kind of wonderful cross-breeding of styles this artist brings to her work. "Don't Know a Thing about Love" is a slice of low-down funk 'n' nasty while the kickoff track, "Tell Me", rocks as hard as anything on the album. Of course, Deanna's specialty—the piano boogie—is represented nicely by the tracks "Eclectic Boogie" and "Backstage Boogie." — *Cub Koda*

New Address / Oct. 29, 1996 / Viceroy ◆◆◆

Spencer Bohren

b. Wyoming
Vocals, Guitar / Folk-Blues
Guitarist, singer and songwriter Spencer Bohren is from Wyoming but is often associated with the Crescent City, as he lived there for a number of years and continues to prove a popular club attraction there. Brought up in a strict Baptist family, Bohren sang harmonies in church, and it was his

passion for gospel music that led him to become an equally diligent student of blues. He left Wyoming in 1968 for the folk scene around Denver. At the Denver Folklore Center and in coffeehouses, he learned acoustic folk-blues firsthand from people like Reverend Gary Davis before moving to Seattle, where he played with a series of blues bands and continued to hone his songwriting abilities. In 1973, he moved back to Colorado to play with folk-blues singer Judy Roderick, and after talking extensively with Dr. John (Mac Rebennack) one night, he decided to move to New Orleans, where Rebennack was born and raised. Bohren spent a decade there, playing clubs like Tipitinas and the Absinthe Bar. In 1983, Bohren and his family began a seven-year journey on the road in an Airstream RV; Bohren performed all over the US, and later began to tour extensively in Europe and Japan. In 1989, Bohren had a Top 40 hit in Sweden. Although his discography is quite extensive and Bohren has been presented at many large festivals around the US and Europe, a major-label deal in the US still eludes him. Bohren's albums include *Born in a Biscayne* (1984) for Great Southern Records, *Down in Mississippi* (1986) for New Blues Records, 1989's *Live in New Orleans* for Great Southern Records, *Snap Your Fingers* for Loft Records (a French label), and *Totta and Hot 'n' Tots* (a Swedish group featuring Bohren); *Spencer Bohren* for Alpha Records of Japan in 1991, *Full Moon* for Virgin Records of France in 1992, and *Present Tense* for Loft Records in France, a 1995 release. His most recent recordings on US labels include *Vintage*, a 1994 release for New Blues of New Orleans, and *Dirt Roads*, a 1996 release on his own Zephur label out of Caspar, Wyoming. In 1990, Bohren moved back to Caspar and has been based there ever since. Bohren continues to tour Europe three or four times a year, and as of 1996, Bohren's album *Present Tense* was available in Europe on Sony and on his own Zephur label here in the US. — *Richard Skelly*

Down in Mississippi / 1986 / New Blues ◆◆◆

● **Live in New Orleans** / Mar. 5, 1989 / Great Southern ◆◆◆◆
Spencer Bohren, a folk-blues singer and guitarist who was 39 at the time of this recording, gives life and vitality to some older styles throughout *Live in New Orleans.* In some ways a throwback to the early 1960s, Bohren explores country blues, Bo Diddley's "Hoodoo You Love," a few folk songs, a brief throwaway version of "Maple Leaf Rag," and even an a cappella version of the gospel song "This Body Is a Prison." His duo partner, Jab Wilson, gives the date a little extra color with his harmonica and Bohren's guitar is particularly expressive on "Mindin' My Business" and "The Sky Is Crying," but the emphasis here is on Spencer Bohren the singer and storyteller. This is a pleasing set that should satisfy fans of the folkish side of the blues legacy. — *Scott Yanow*

Vintage / 1994 / Zephur Artists ◆◆◆◆

Dirt Roads / Nov. 26, 1996 / Zephur Artists ◆◆◆

Zuzu Bollin

b. Sep. 5, 1922, Frisco, TX, **d.** Oct. 2, 1990
Guitar, Vocals / Jump Blues, Electric Blues, Electric Texas Blues, Texas Blues
Two 78s in the early '50s and a 1989 rediscovery album don't add up to much of a recorded legacy. But Zuzu Bollin's contribution to the Texas blues legacy shouldn't be overlooked—his T-Bone Walker-influenced sound typified postwar Lone Star blues guitar.

Born A.D. Bollin, Zuzu listened to everyone from Blind Lemon Jefferson and Leroy Carr (on records) to Joe Turner and Count Basie. He picked up his nickname while in the band of Texan E.X. Brooks; seems he had a sweet tooth for a brand of ginger snap cookies called ZuZus! Bollin formed his own combo in 1949, featuring young saxist David "Fathead" Newman. After a stint with Percy Mayfield's band, Bollin resumed playing around Dallas. In late 1951, he made his recording debut for Bob Sutton's Torch logo. Newman and saxist Leroy Cooper, both future members of Ray Charles' band, played on Bollin's "Why Don't You Eat Where You Slept Last Night" and "Headlight Blues." A Torch follow-up, "Stavin' Chain"/"Cry, Cry, Cry," found Bollin backed by Jimmy McCracklin's combo.

No more recording ensued after that, though Bollin toured with bandleaders Ernie Fields and Joe Morris before chucking the music biz in 1964 to go into a more stable profession: dry cleaning. Bollin's 1987 rediscovery was the Dallas Blues Society's doing: they engineered a series of gigs and eventually a fine 1989 album, *Texas Bluesman*, that beautifully showcased Bollin's approach. Their efforts were barely in time—Bollin died in 1990. — *Bill Dahl*

● **Texas Bluesman** / 1989 / Antone's ♦♦♦♦
Zuzu's principal contribution to Texas blues history is an immaculately realized collection that includes remakes of both sides of his debut 78 (the original version of "Why Don't You Eat Where You Slept Last Night" is available
on *Vol. 3* of Rhino's *Blues Masters* series, "Texas Blues") and a uniformly
tasty lineup of jump blues goodies. The sterling band includes guitarist Duke
Robillard (who co-produced), drummer George Rains, and saxists David
Newman and Kaz Kazanoff. — *Bill Dahl*

Graham Bond (Graham John Clifton Bond)

b. Oct. 28, 1937, Romford, Essex, England, **d.** May 8, 1974, London, England
Saxophone, Organ, Vocals / British Invasion, Blues-Rock, British Blues
An important, underappreciated figure of early British R&B, Graham Bond
is known in the US, if at all, for heading the group that Jack Bruce and
Ginger Baker played in before they joined Cream. Originally an alto sax
player—in fact, he was voted "Britain's New Jazz Star" in 1961—he met
Bruce and Baker in 1962 after joining Alexis Koerner's Blues Incorporated,
the finishing school for numerous British rock and blues musicians. By the
time he, Bruce, and Baker split to form their own band in 1963, Bond was
mostly playing the Hammond organ, as well as handling the lion's share of
the vocals. John McLaughlin was a member of the Graham Bond Organization in the early days for a few months, and some live material that he recorded with the group was eventually issued after most of its members had
achieved stardom in other contexts. Saxophonist Dick Heckstall-Smith completed Bond's most stable lineup, which cut a couple decent albums and a
few singles in the mid-'60s.

In its prime, the Graham Bond Organization played rhythm and blues
with a strong jazzy flavor, emphasizing Bond's demonic organ and gruff vocals. The band arguably would have been better served to feature Bruce as
its lead singer—he is featured surprisingly rarely on their recordings. Nevertheless, their best records were admirably tough British R&B-rock-jazz-soul,
and though Bond has sometimes been labeled as a pioneer of jazz-rock, in
reality it was much closer to rock than jazz. The band performed imaginative
covers and fairly strong original material, and Bond was also perhaps the
very first rock musician to record with the Mellotron synthesizer. Hit singles,
though, were necessary for British bands to thrive in the mid-'60s, and Bond's
group began to fall apart in 1966, when Bruce and Baker joined forces with
Eric Clapton to form Cream. Bond attempted to carry on with the Organization for a while with Heckstall-Smith and drummer Jon Hiseman, both of
whom went on to John Mayall's Bluesbreakers and Colosseum.

Bond never recaptured the heights of his work with the Organization. In
the late '60s, he moved to the US, recording albums with musicians including
Harvey Brooks, Harvey Mandel, and Hal Blaine. Moving back to Britain, he
worked with Ginger Baker's Airforce, the Jack Bruce Band, and Cream lyricist Pete Brown, as well as forming the band Holy Magick, who recorded a
couple albums. Bond's demise was more tragic than most: he developed serious drug and alcohol problems and an obsession with the occult, and it has
even been posthumously speculated (in the British Bond biography *Mighty
Shadow*) that he sexually abused his stepdaughter. He committed suicide
by throwing himself into the path of a London Underground train in 1974.
— *Richie Unterberger*

● **The Sound of 65** / Mar. 1965 / Edsel ♦♦♦♦
Although the Organization's first album was recorded a mere year or two
before Cream's debut, it bears little resemblance to Cream's pioneering hard
blues-rock. Instead, it's taut British R&B with a considerable jazz influence.
That influence comes not so much from the rhythm section as saxophonist
Dick Heckstall-Smith and lead singer/organist Bond himself. This LP is not
as exciting or rock-oriented as those of contemporaries like the Rolling
Stones or John Mayall, but is respectably gritty, mostly original material,
with an occasionally nasty edge. There are some obscure treasures of the
British R&B explosion to be found here, including the original version of
"Train Time" (later performed by Cream), the thrilling bass runs on "Baby Be
Good To Me," and the group's hardboiled rearrangements of such traditional
standards as "Wade in the Water" and "Early in the Morning." Even their
blatant stab at commerciality (the ballad "Tammy") has its charm. — *Richie
Unterberger*

There's a Bond Between Us / Nov. 1965 / Edsel ♦♦♦♦
Bond's second album stakes out similar territory as his debut in a more

polished but slightly less exciting fashion. Some of the covers are a bit routine and hackneyed, and the original material isn't quite as strong (or frequent) as on the first effort. On a few tunes, the group expands from raveups
to mellower, jazzier ballads that retain an R&B base. Highlights include the
early Jack Bruce composition "Hear Me Calling Your Name" (to which he
also contributes a fine lead vocal) and the excellent Bond tune "Walkin' in
the Park," which holds up to the best early British R&B numbers. The album
is also notable for being one of the very first rock LPs to feature the Mellotron, which Bond uses subtly and well. — *Richie Unterberger*

Mighty Grahame Bond / 1969 / Pulsar ♦♦
Despite the presence of high-profile musicians Harvey Brooks and Harvey
Mandel, Bond's second album from his stay in the US in the late '60s was a
lukewarm, half-inspired affair. It's average blues-rock with light gospel and
funk overtones, and a few of the songs are pretty shapeless. It's best when
Bond brings out the demonic tones of both his organ (or, occasionally, mellotron) and vocals, but these are flashed infrequently. The label made it clear
that Graham was not a top priority in their promotion department by misspelling his first name on the record itself. — *Richie Unterberger*

Solid Bond / May 1970 / Warner Brothers ♦♦♦

Graham Bond Organization / 1984 / Charly ♦♦
This live 1964 gig is one of Giorgio Gomelsky's innumerable tapes of British
club acts of the period, several of which would be released many years later
in attempts to cash in on some big names who were present. These historical
documents, never intended for release, ranged from superb to wretched. This
LP (which, like most of these Gomelsky projects, has been reissued under
numerous different covers and titles) falls about right in the middle of this
scale. Bond led an erratic, interesting group that incorporated elements of
jazz and improvisation into its blend of blues, R&B, and rock. Future Cream
members Jack Bruce and Ginger Baker were his rhythm section in his prime,
and Dick Heckstall-Smith handled horns; this is the lineup featured on this
set. But it's not deathless stuff. The fidelity, for one, is muddy, especially the
bottom, Bruce's bass suffering the most. The better tunes—"Wade in the Water," "Early in the Morning," "Train Time," and "Spanish Blues"—are available
in better performances and much clearer fidelity on the group's first studio
album, *The Sound of 65*. The rest is routine, even below average in spots,
early British R&B. The Organization may have been among the most accomplished players on the scene, but they couldn't hold a candle to the Stones
or Yardbirds in terms of imagination and excitement. A better introduction
to the sound of this lineup is the fine Edsel reissue of *The Sound of 65* and
There's a Bond Between Us, which have been combined into one package.
— *Richie Unterberger*

Son Bonds

b. Mar. 16, 1909, Brownsville, TN, **d.** Aug. 31, 1947, Dyersburg, TN
Guitar, Kazoo, Vocals / Country Blues
An associate of Sleepy John Estes and Hammie Nixon, Bonds played very
much in the same rural Brownsville style that the Estes-Nixon team popularized in the '20s and '30s. Curiously, either Estes or Nixon (but never both of
them together) played on all of Bonds' recordings. The music to one of Bonds'
songs, "Back and Side Blues" (1934), became a standard blues melody when
John Lee "Sonny Boy" Williamson from nearby Jackson, TN, used it in his
classic "Good Morning, (Little) School Girl" (1937). According to Nixon,
Bonds was shot to death, while sitting on his front porch, by a nearsighted
neighbor who mistook him for another man. — *Jim O'Neal*

Complete Recorded Works in Chronological Order / Sep. 6, 1934-Sep. 24,
1941 / Wolf ♦♦♦♦
This is an above average collection from Wolf Records in Vienna, both in
terms of audio quality and content. The 18 songs by "Brownsville" Son
Bonds, recorded between 1934 and 1941, are in surprisingly decent sound,
for the most part, with no horrendous flaws to mar the collection. The songs
are all good and the playing generally inspired, especially on the later tracks,
where Bonds adds a kazoo to his sound and really takes off, in a more rocking and freewheeling way than even Tampa Red. The diversity of the material is also a surprise—four of the songs are rough, fervent gospel numbers,
including the extraordinarily beautiful "I Want to Live So God Can Use Me,"
"Ain't That News," and "Give Me That Old Time Religion," cut by Bonds working as "Brother Son Bonds" (with Hammie Nixon backing him up on vocals

and jug). They fit in well with their raw quality amid the lusty country blues numbers ("All Night Long," "She Walks Like My Woman," etc.) that make up the rest of this disc. The guitar-harmonica duets between Bonds and Nixon are especially pleasing, but Bonds' voice, surging and soaring, is the real show, especially on the early numbers, where the recordings really don't do justice to his guitar. The last four songs on this disc feature Charlie Pickett on vocals and guitar, and were recorded in 1937, with Nixon linking one of Pickett's songs with the rest of this collection. — *Bruce Eder*

Juke Boy Bonner

b. Mar. 22, 1932, Bellville, TX, **d.** Jun. 29, 1978, Houston, TX
Guitar, Harmonica, Vocals / Electric Texas Blues, Texas Blues, West Coast Blues
One-man bands weren't any too common on the postwar blues scene. Joe Hill Louis and Dr. Ross come to mind as greats who plied their trade all by their lonesome—and so did Juke Boy Bonner, a Texan whose talent never really earned him much in the way of tangible reward.

Born into impoverished circumstances in the Lone Star State during the Depression, Weldon Bonner took up the guitar in his teens. He caught a break in 1947 in Houston, winning a talent contest that led to a spot on a local radio outlet. He journeyed to Oakland in 1956, cutting his debut single for Bob Geddins' Irma imprint ("Rock with Me Baby"/"Well Baby") with Lafayette "Thing" Thomas supplying the lead guitar. Goldband Records boss Eddie Shuler was next to take a chance in 1960; Bonner recorded for him in Lake Charles, LA, with Katie Webster on piano, but once again, nothing happened career-wise.

Troubled by stomach problems during the '60s, Bonner utilized his hospital downtime to write poems that he later turned into songs. He cut his best work during the late '60s for Arhoolie Records, accompanying himself on both guitar and racked harmonica as he weaved extremely personal tales of his rough life in Houston. A few European tours ensued, but they didn't really lead to much. Toward the end of his life, he toiled in a chicken processing plant to make ends meet. Bonner died of cirrhosis of the liver in 1978. — *Bill Dahl*

Juke Boy Bonner, 1960-1967 / Mar. 15, 1960-Dec. 12, 1967 / Flyright ✦✦✦
There's a Lightnin' Hopkins-meets-Jimmy Reed sound on these delightfully funky guitar/harp-accompanied blues by this Houstonian, whose ironic lyrics are half the fun. — *Jas Obrecht*

One Man Trio / Feb. 1967 / Flyright ✦✦✦✦

Going Back to the Country / Dec. 20, 1967-Jan. 23, 1968 / Arhoolie ✦✦✦✦

● **Life Gave Me a Dirty Deal** / Nov. 30, 1968-May 5, 1969 / Arhoolie ✦✦✦✦
Likely the most consistent and affecting collection you'll encounter by this singular Texas bluesman, whose strikingly personal approach was stunningly captured by Arhoolie's Chris Strachwitz during the late '60s in Houston. Twenty-three stark originals include "Stay off Lyons Avenue," "Struggle Here in Houston," "I Got My Passport," and the title track. Bonner sang movingly of his painfully impoverished existence for Arhoolie, and the results still resound triumphantly today. — *Bill Dahl*

☆ **The Struggle** / Nov. 30, 1968-May 5, 1969 / Arhoolie ✦✦✦✦✦
Recorded in extreme stereo, with drums on one channel and Bonner's guitar on the other, this is Juke Boy Bonner's most cohesive album. Great songwriting and performances throughout. — *Cub Koda*

Things Ain't Right / Nov. 4, 1969-Nov. 28, 1969 / Sequel ✦✦
This set is somewhat disappointing compared to the Arhoolie sides. — *Bill Dahl*

Legacy of the Blues, Vol. 5 / 1972 / GNP ✦✦✦

Adventures of Juke Boy Bonner / 1980 / Collectables ✦✦

The Texas Blues Troubadours / 1990 / Collectables ✦✦✦

Jumpin' with Juke Boy / Sep. 14, 1993 / Collectables ✦✦✦

Boogie Woogie Red

b. Oct. 18, 1925, Rayville, LA, **d.** 1985, Detroit, MI
Piano, Vocals / Piano Blues
Though a Louisiana native, Vernon Harrison has been associated with the Detroit blues sound as long as anyone. A Motor City resident since 1927, he began performing in the local clubs as a teenager. As a sideman he worked

locally with Sonny Boy Williamson, Baby Boy Warren, and John Lee Hooker. Despite Red's renown for the blues and boogie-woogie style that earned him his nickname, he has recorded only a few times as a featured artist, and aside from a bit of European touring in the '70s, he has remained a local Detroit treasure, rarely appearing outside the area. — *Jim O'Neal*

● **Live at the Blind Pig** / 1974 / Blind Pig ✦✦✦✦
A crudely recorded but fun live album, it captures the somewhat demented 80-proof charm of this Detroit pianist. Recorded in the basement of the Blind Pig in Ann Arbor, MI, this album features guest appearances by John Nicholas, Fran Christina, and Bill Heid. — *George Bedard*

Red Hot / 1977 / Blind Pig ✦✦✦✦

Roy Book Binder

b. Oct. 5, 1941, New York, NY
Guitar, Vocals / Modern Acoustic Blues
An often stirring folk/blues guitarist and vocalist, Roy Book Binder's been playing country blues since the mid-'60s, when he began recording for Blue Goose. Greatly influenced by Rev. Gary Davis and Pink Anderson, Book Binder played in East Coast coffeehouses in the early '60s, then began accompanying Rev. Davis on tours in the mid-'60s. He also played with Larry Johnson, Arthur "Big Boy" Crudup and Homesick James. Besides constant concerts and tours, Book Binder's made additional recordings for Blue Goose, as well as Adelphi and Rounder.

Book Binder began playing blues guitar while he was enlisted in the navy. Following his discharge from the military, he enrolled in Rhode Island Junior College. After a brief spell there, he attended New York's New School for Social Research. Book Binder quit school in 1967, after he met the Rev. Gary Davis. Roy became Davis' chauffeur, during which he took extensive lessons from the blind guitarist. Book Binder started his recording career slowly, cutting some singles for Kicking Mule and Blue Goose in 1968. In 1969, he toured England with Arthur "Big Boy" Crudup and Homesick James. The following year, he released his first album, *Travelin' Man*, on Adelphi. After the release of *Travelin' Man*, he began touring America extensively.

Book Binder began playing with fiddler Fats Kaplin in 1973, recording *Git Fiddle Shuffle* the same year. Roy and Fats were a duo for three years, playing numerous concerts and recording a second album, *Ragtime Millionaire* in 1976. Following the release of *Ragtime Millionaire*, the duo stopped performing together and Book Binder bought a motor home, which became his permanent residence. Live performances became his primary concern after the release of *Goin' Back to Tampa* in 1979. For nearly ten years, he toured the country in the motor home, driving himself from club to club, hitting numerous coffeehouses and festivals along the way.

Book Binder returned to recording in 1988, releasing *Bookaroo!* on Rounder Records. During the '80s, he recorded regularly—releasing an album every two to four years—in addition to his constant touring. — *Ron Wynn & Stephen Thomas Erlewine*

Travelin' Man / 1970 / Adelphi ✦✦✦

Git Fiddle Shuffle / 1976 / Blue Goose ✦✦✦

Goin' Back to Tampa / Mar. 1979 / Flying Fish ✦✦✦
Although Roy Book Binder doesn't put a new spin on acoustic Delta blues, he is passionate about the music and, as his debut *Goin' Back to Tampa* proves, he can replicate the sound of the genre exactly. *Goin' Back to Tampa* didn't exactly launch his recording career—it would take him a decade to release another album—but it captured the spirit of his music quite effectively. — *Thom Owens*

Bookeroo! / 1988 / Rounder ✦✦✦
The line between sincere appreciation and blind imitation is a thin one, and too often contemporary blues or country musicians cross it when covering classic songs. Roy Book Binder avoids the problem by refusing to become overwhelmed by idolatry, and instead enjoying himself while doing vintage material. That was evident on the 12 songs that comprised this session. While Book Binder's convivial vocals made his versions of Jesse Thomas' "Friend Like Me," Merle Haggard's "Nobody Knows I'm Hurtin'," or Jimmie Rodgers' "Waiting for a Train" appealing, his guitar solos and band interaction gave the songs a vital, modern kick. — *Ron Wynn*

● **The Hillbilly Blues Cats** / Jun. 15, 1992 / Rounder ✦✦✦✦
Roy Book Binder and his Hillbilly Blues Cats band expertly convey the ur-

gency of vintage blues by performing them with a brash rockabilly attitude. They cover classic songs in a manner that's neither reverential nor disrespectful, putting their own spin on such numbers as Blind Willie McTell's "Statesboro Blues" or Happy Traum's "Mississippi John." Book Binder's vocals are joyous, exuberant, and sometimes comical, while his trio provides stomping backgrounds and harmonies. Although Book Binder and the band can't improve upon the originals, they do nothing to detract from an appreciation of them. — *Ron Wynn*

Live Book . . . Don't Start Me Talkin' . . . / May 2, 1994 / Rounder ◆◆◆
Live Book . . . Don't Start Me Talkin' . . . captures Roy Book Binder in concert, playing a selection of standards and originals with conviction and energy. In fact, the record is frequently more compelling and exciting than his studio efforts, which tend to sound a bit too clean and studied. Here, he just plays the blues and the results are always engaging. — *Thom Owens*

Polk City Ramble / Jan. 13, 1998 / Rounder ◆◆◆◆
The laidback blues of Roy Book Binder sounds like a cross between Rev. Gary Davis and Leon Redbone. This collection finds Binder strumming a National steel guitar through a mix of blues classics, originals, and a hybrid of the two. While his style won't tear out your heart, it will set your foot tapping and leave a pleasant mellow feeling. — *Tim Sheridan*

James Booker (James Carroll Booker III)

b. Dec. 17, 1939, New Orleans, LA, **d.** Nov. 8, 1983, New Orleans, LA
Piano, Vocals / R&B, Piano Blues, Boogie-Woogie, Acoustic New Orleans Blues
Certainly one of the most flamboyant New Orleans pianists in recent memory, James Carroll Booker, III was a major influence on the local rhythm & blues scene in the '50s and '60s. Booker's training included classical instruction until age 12, by which time he had already begun to gain recognition as a blues and gospel organist on radio station WMRY every Sunday. By the time he was out of high school he had recorded on several occasions, including his own first release, "Doing the Hambone," in 1953. In 1960 he made the national charts with "Gonzo," an organ instrumental, and over the course of the next two decades played and recorded with artists as varied as Lloyd Price, Aretha Franklin, Ringo Starr, the Doobie Brothers, and B.B. King. In 1967 he was convicted of possession of heroin and served a one-year sentence at Angola Penitentiary (referred to as the "Ponderosa," which took the momentum out of an otherwise promising career. The rediscovery of "roots" music by college students during the '70s (focusing primarily on "Fess"—Professor Longhair) provided the opportunity for a comeback by 1974, with numerous engagements at local clubs like Tipitina's, The Maple Leaf, and Snug Harbor. As with "Fess," Booker's performances at the New Orleans Jazz & Heritage Festivals took on the trappings of legendary "happenings," and he often spent his festival earnings to arrive in style, pulling up to the stage in a rented Rolls-Royce and attired in costumes befitting the "Piano Prince of New Orleans," complete with a cape. Such performances tended to be unpredictable: he might easily plant some Chopin into a blues tune or launch into a jeremiad on the CIA with all the fervor of a "Reverend Ike-meets-Moms Mabley" tag-team match.

Booker's left hand was simply phenomenal, often a problem for bass players who found themselves running for cover in an attempt to stay out of the way; with it he successfully amalgamated the jazz and rhythm & blues idioms of New Orleans, adding more than a touch of gospel thrown in for good measure. His playing was also highly improvisational, reinventing a progression (usually his own) so that a single piece would evolve into a medley of itself. In addition, he had a plaintive and seering vocal style which was equally comfortable with gospel, jazz standards, blues, or popular songs. Despite his personal eccentricities, Booker had the respect of New Orleans' best musicians, and elements of his influence are still very much apparent in the playing of pianists like Henry Butler and Harry Connick, Jr. — *Bruce Boyd Raeburn*

King of the New Orleans Keyboard / 1976 / Junco Partner ◆◆◆◆
Spectacular date by a great New Orleans pianist whose personal difficulties prevented him from both long life and sustained career achievement. Booker was cited as inspiration by everyone from Dr. John to Harry Connick, Jr., and played with an array of performers, from Lloyd Price to Aretha Franklin, B.B. King, Ringo Starr, and the Doobie Brothers. He seamlessly fused a blues

base, jazz touches, and R&B/gospel feeling, and this was among his best (and few) recordings. — *Ron Wynn*

Junco Partners / Oct. 22, 1976 / Hannibal ◆◆◆◆
A superb effort from a premier New Orleans piano master who made far too few recordings. The rumbling licks, often astonishing technique, and variety of rhythms and styles that Booker fused were always matched by his energy and exuberance. These sessions have since been reissued on CD. — *Ron Wynn*

New Orleans Piano Wizard: Live! / Nov. 27, 1977 / Rounder ◆◆◆◆
Why so much of what pianist/vocalist James Booker recorded in the 1970s didn't surface until the '90s is a mystery, but that's secondary compared to the greatness routinely presented on this CD. It contains nine Booker selections which he performed at the 1977 Boogie Woogie and Ragtime Piano Contest held in Zurich. His relentless, driving style, ability to switch from a hard-hitting tune to a light, soft one without skipping a beat, and wild mix of sizzling keyboard licks and bemused, manic vocals is uniformly impressive. It's a bit short for a CD at 37 minutes, but it has so much flamboyant music and singing that it shouldn't be missed. — *Ron Wynn*

Resurrection of the Bayou Maharajah / 1977-1982 / Rounder ◆◆◆◆
For a man of such talent and influence, New Orleans piano legend James Booker is amazingly underrecorded. This disc, along with its partner (*Spiders on the Keys*) offer up some measure of what the folks of the Big Easy might have heard if they caught James Booker on one of his "on" nights (he was a known drug user and inconsistent in his playing). He is at his best here (recorded at the Maple Leaf between 1972-1982), focused and intense in his playing, wildly passionate on both keyboards and vocals. Some songs are repeated on the companion disc, but each treatment makes the songs new again, so that even his standards are always fresh and vital. Sheer genius at the keyboards and unrestrained, heartfelt vocals on such highlights as Fats Domino's "All by Myself," "The Fat Man," and "St. James Infirmary." — *Bob Gottlieb*

★ **Classified** / Oct. 18, 1982 + Oct. 20, 1982 / Rounder ◆◆◆◆◆
While there has suddenly been a flood of CDs featuring masterful New Orleans keyboard wizard and vocalist James Booker, his best release arguably remains *Classified*. The 12-track set, recently issued on CD, was a landmark album, as Booker displayed every facet of his distinctive style. He did uptempo blues, quasi-classical, rock, and R&B, making them all sound easy while performing frequently awesome keyboard feats. His "Professor Longhair Medley: Bald Head/Tipitina" pays homage to a legend while also demonstrating how much farther Booker's pianistic skills had developed. While his vocals sometimes aren't the equal of his brilliant playing, they're never less than effective and are sometimes almost frightening in their intensity. — *Ron Wynn*

King of the New Orleans Keyboard, Vol. 1 / 1984 / JSP ◆◆◆◆

King of the New Orleans Keyboard, Vol. 2 / 1985 / JSP ◆◆◆◆

Spiders on the Keys / 1993 / Rounder ◆◆◆
This aptly named disc showcases James Booker's piano playing; his stretches and runs are breathtaking in their fluidity. This disc (along with its Rounder partner, *Resurrection of the Bayou Maharajah*) was culled from some 60 or so hours of tapes that John Parsons recorded at the Maple Leaf Bar from 1977 to 1982. The main difference in the music on the two discs is that this one is purely instrumental. In fact listen to this version of "Papa Was a Rascal," and then listen to the rendition on *Resurrection*, and what you have is two almost entirely different entities. This disc is made up roughly of what might be called piano bar standards, such as "Sunny Side of the Street" and "Eleanor Rigby," but regardless of how many times you have heard this fare, Booker manages to make each song sound fresh and vital. A special debt of gratitude must go to both Scott Billington and John Parsons for the care taken with this recorded legacy. — *Bob Gottlieb*

Gonzo: More Than All the 45's / Jun. 11, 1996 / Night Train ◆◆◆◆

Lost Paramount Tapes / Mar. 11, 1997 / DJM ◆◆◆
This is a disc made by one of the best piano players to come out of New Orleans, James Booker, playing with an all-star band of New Orleans musicians, most of whom Booker befriended during his days with Dr. John. The music sparkles, all the more amazing because it was recorded live in the Los Angeles area with no overdubs in 1973, and is just being released in 1997

because it was lost for 20 years. This disc hits a groove and does not quit, shifting from straight-ahead blues to an R&B beat, drifting into some complex Caribbean rhythms, moving off into some jazz riffs, but all the time maintaining the original blues feel it started with. All the players get to shine, but it is definitely James Booker's disc. —*Bob Gottlieb*

Lillian Boutte (Lillian Boutté)

b. Aug. 6, 1949, New Orleans, LA
Vocals / Standards
An often electrifying singer whose tastes, delivery and approach lean toward the blues/R&B/gospel side of the traditional jazz equation. She was once part of the Golden Voices Choir, then studied music at Xavier University. She turned professional in 1973, working with area New Orleans musicians like Allen Toussaint. She later was the star of the musical "One Mo' Time." Boutte toured Europe in 1981 and 1982, then formed an international group called the Music Frieds, with saxophonist Thomas l'Etienne. The two eventually married, and she's recorded many times with the group. Boutte has also toured the United States frequently, appearing at various festivals. —*Ron Wynn*

● **Lipstick Traces** / Apr. 27, 1992 / Enja ✦✦✦✦
Lillian Boutte's debut album, *Lipstick Traces*, is an appealing blend of classy New Orleans R&B, Southern soul, classic female blues, and jazzy pop, all performed with a signature sense of swing. Boutte doesn't belt these songs out—she caresses them and delivers them with style. Her phrasing is closer to jazz than blues, but her music is inarguably blues, which means that her singing, her music, and her album have a classy, sophisticated flavor that is quite alluring. —*Leo Stanley*

Jazz Book / Feb. 1993 / Blues Beacon ✦✦✦

Gospel Book / Dec. 16, 1993 / Blues Beacon ✦✦✦

But . . . Beautiful / 1995 / Dinosaur ✦✦✦
Lillian Boutte is a versatile singer who can swing. This particular CD is really more of a middle-of-the-road soulful pop recording than a jazz date (no real improvising takes place) but Boutte's appealing voice and easygoing style sound fine throughout the diverse program, even if the background musicians are given little to do. Highlights include "Be Glad You Ain't Dead" (which has a guest vocal from the date's producer, Dr. John), "You'd Be So Nice to Come Home To," "When Sunny Gets Blue" and "Tomorrow Night." —*Scott Yanow*

Pat Boyack

b. Jun. 26, 1967, Helper, UT
Guitar / Contemporary Blues
Like so many guitarists of his generation, Pat Boyack traced his initial fascination with the blues back to his early admiration of Stevie Ray Vaughan. Born June 26, 1967, in Helper, Utah, Boyack's tastes as a teen originally ran more along the lines of Van Halen and Kiss, but soon he became so immersed in the contemporary Texas blues sound that he eventually relocated to Dallas to pursue a musical career of his own. In 1993, he relocated to the Phoenix area, where he formed the bar band Rocket 88s with vocalist/harpist Jimmy Morello; after the group dissolved, Boyack returned to Dallas, where he eventually formed the blues-rock unit the Prowlers with bassist John Garza and drummer Doug Swancy. After issuing their debut effort, *Armed and Dangerous*, in 1993, the Prowlers welcomed Morello into their ranks, and *Breakin' In* followed in late 1994. After 1996's *On the Prowl*, the band fell apart, and Boyack assembled a new supporting cast for his 1997 solo debut, *Super Blue and Funky*. —*Jason Ankeny*

Breakin' In / 1994 / Bullseye Blues ✦✦✦

On the Prowl / Mar. 19, 1996 / Bullseye Blues ✦✦✦
Overall, this is not quite in the top echelon but is a solid entry in the increasingly crowded sub-genre of greasy, white-hipster, roadhouse blues—a retro-blend of Texas and Chicago blues sensibilities with dirty-toned guitar, danceable jump and shuffle rhythms, and soul-inflected vocals. The band is a guitar-bass-drums trio, plus singer Jimmy Morello (who brings to mind Kim Wilson and Sugar Ray Norcia, sans harp). Boyack displays flashes of wit on guitar. Producer Ron Levy thickens the sound with his own Hammond B-3, although mixed very much in the background, and with horns on a few cuts. The tunes are all originals, a majority written or co-written by Morello (who

has since left the band). Best cuts are the upbeat "Sugar," with its catchy "wo-wo-wo-wo" hook; the minor key "I Know It's Over"; and the Albert King-style "Cleanin' Out My Closet." —*Steve Hoffman*

● **Super Blue & Funky** / Jul. 8, 1997 / Bullseye Blues ✦✦✦✦
Pat Boyack shows up with a new and different sound from his previous efforts on this, his third album for the Bullseye Blues label. When the nucleus of the Prowlers fell apart after the release of their second album, *On the Prowl*, it left Boyack without a band. But producer Mark Kazanoff encouraged him to keep honing his craft, and the result is a disc that shows much growth, both in the writing and the playing. Boyack penned ten of the 14 songs on this, and catchy numbers like "I'll Be the Joker" and the two ballads, "Sweet Redemption" and "Why Must I Suffer?," show a real maturation of his tunesmithing skills. Departing vocalist Jimmy Morello is ably replaced by new singer Spencer Thomas, who brings a mellower and more relaxed feel to the band on tracks like "Think (Before You Do)," Jimmy Nolan's "The Way You Do" and "Can't You See?" W.C. Clark also contributes guest vocals on "Righteous Love" and "Why Must I Suffer?," while Boyack literally blazes on guitar showcases like "Poppa Stoppa," "Mexican Vodka," and his own "Longwallin'." With great tunes, solid playing, and crisp production all in place, this is Boyack's most realized effort to date. —*Cub Koda*

Eddie Boyd (Edward Riley Boyd)

b. Nov. 25, 1914, Stovall, MS, **d.** Jul. 13, 1994, Helsinki, Finland
Piano, Vocals / Chicago Blues, Piano Blues, Electric Chicago Blues
Few postwar blues standards have retained the universal appeal of Eddie Boyd's "Five Long Years." Cut in 1951, Boyd's masterpiece has attracted faithful covers by B.B. King, Muddy Waters, Jimmy Reed, Buddy Guy, and too many other bluesmen to recount here. But Boyd's discography is filled with evocative compositions, often full of after-hours ambience.

Like so many Chicago blues stalwarts, Boyd hailed from the fertile Mississippi Delta. The segregationist policies that had a stranglehold on much of the South didn't appeal to the youngster, so he migrated up to Memphis (where he began to play the piano, influenced by Roosevelt Sykes and Leroy Carr). In 1941, Boyd settled in Chicago, falling in with the "Bluebird beat" crowd that recorded for producer Lester Melrose. He backed harp legend Sonny Boy Williamson on his 1945 classic "Elevator Woman," also accompanying Bluebird stars Jazz Gillum, Tampa Red, and Jazz Gillum on wax. Melrose produced Boyd's own 1947 recording debut for RCA as well; the pianist stayed with Victor through 1949.

Boyd reportedly paid for the date that produced "Five Long Years" himself, peddling the track to JOB Records (where the stolid blues topped the R&B charts during 1952). Powerful deejay Al Benson signed Boyd to a contract with his Parrot imprint and promptly sold the pact to Chess, inaugurating a stormy few years with Chicago's top blues outlet. There he waxed "24 Hours" and "Third Degree," both huge R&B hits in 1953, and a host of other Chicago blues gems. But Boyd and Leonard Chess were often at loggerheads, so it was on to Narvel "Cadillac Baby" Eatmon's Bea & Baby imprint in 1959 for eight solid sides with Robert Jr. Lockwood on guitar and a slew of lesser labels after that. A serious auto wreck in 1957 had stalled his career for a spell.

Sick of the discrimination he perceived towards African Americans in this country, Boyd became enamored of Europe during his tour with the 1965 American Folk Blues Festival, so he moved to Belgium. The recording opportunities long denied him in his native land were plentiful overseas; Boyd cut prolifically during the late '60s, including two LPs for producer Mike Vernon. In the early '70s, he settled in Helsinki, Finland, where he played often and lived comfortably until his death. —*Bill Dahl*

Rattin' and Running Around / 1947-1956 / Crown Prince ✦✦✦✦
Import vinyl containing a nice cross-section of Boyd's RCA and Chess efforts, including three sides from 1947 with Bill Casimir on tenor sax; the doomy Chess entries "The Nightmare Is Over," a rocking "Driftin'," and "Life Gets to Be a Burden," and the bouncy 1956 rhumba "Don't." —*Bill Dahl*

● **Third Degree** / 1951-1959 / Charly ✦✦✦✦
Amazingly, the only comprehensive overview of Boyd's 1951-1959 Chess stint available on CD. Both "Third Degree" and "24 Hours" are aboard this 20-track compilation, along with the lesser-known standouts "I Got the Blues," "Nothing but Trouble," and "Cool Kind Treatment." Boyd's sturdy, concise piano work and darkly introspective vocals were brilliantly captured

on tape by Leonard Chess, even if the two weren't exactly the best of pals. —*Bill Dahl*

Five Long Years / Oct. 20, 1965 / Evidence ++++
One of the first and best of Boyd's many overseas recordings, cut while he was in the midst of that auspicious 1965 American Folk Blues Festival tour of Europe. While the caravan was ensconced in London, young producer Mike Vernon spirited Boyd and a rhythm section (guitarist Buddy Guy, bassist Jimmie Lee Robinson, and drummer Fred Below) off to the studio, where Boyd ran through some of his classics ('I'm Comin' Home," "24 Hours," the title track) and a few less familiar items while alternating between piano and organ. —*Bill Dahl*

Eddie Boyd & His Blues Band / 1967 / Decca +++

Live / 1968 / Storyville +++

7936 South Rhodes / Jan. 25, 1968 / BGO +++
Recorded in London in January 1968 with three members of the early lineup of Fleetwood Mac (the one that played blues, not pop-rock): Peter Green (guitar), John McVie (bass), and Mick Fleetwood (drums). It's an adequate setting for Boyd's straight Chicago piano blues, going heavier on the slow-to-midtempo numbers than the high-spirited ones, though Green is a far more sympathetic accompanist than the rhythm section. —*Richie Unterberger*

Legacy of the Blues, Vol. 10 / 1974 / GNP +++

Vacation from the Blues / 1976 / Jefferson +++

Lovers Playground / 1985 / Stockholm ++

Live in Switzerland / May 30, 1995 / Storyville +++

Ishmon Bracey

b. Jan. 9, 1901, Byram, MS, **d.** Feb. 12, 1970, Jackson, MS
Vocals, Guitar / Delta Blues, Prewar Country Blues
One of the early giants of the Delta blues, Ishmon Bracey often worked with local Jackson, MS, legends like Tommy Johnson, Son Spand and Charlie Mc-Coy. He cut a small handful of sides for the Paramount label in 1930, some of the most coveted discs in blues history. Bracey's best work is marked by a tremulous vibrato to his largely nasal voice and simple, but effective, guitar work. As a parenthetical note, when Bracey was trying to be coaxed out of retirement to record in the '60s, to get researchers off his back he directed them to the whereabouts of another Delta legend—Skip James. —*Cub Koda*

● **Complete Recorded Works (1928-1929)** / Feb. 4, 1928-Dec. 1929 / Document ++++
Bracey's complete recorded works (1928-1929) are presented in chronological order on this single disc, with the bonus of four tracks by the elusive Charley Taylor. Since Bracey only recorded a handful of sides, this compilation is far more accessible than most of Document's *Complete Recorded Works* discs. Furthermore, Bracey was one of the best Delta blues artists of the '20s and his work is consistently engaging. *Complete Recorded Works (1928-1929)* is the best compilation available on Bracey—not only does it work as a concise introduction, it has everything completists will need. —*Cub Koda & Stephen Thomas Erlewine*

Prof. Alex Bradford

b. 1926, Bessemer, AL, **d.** Feb. 15, 1978, Newark, NJ
Vocals, Piano / Black Gospel, Traditional Gospel
Professor Alex Bradford was among the truly pivotal figures of gospel's golden era; the author of more standards than any other gospel composer of his generation, his music was both reverently traditional and restlessly innovative, true to its spiritual roots but never out of step with the advances of contemporary pop and jazz. A master showman renowned for his theatrical flamboyance, he was not only a gifted singer and songwriter but also a noted pianist, arranger, and group and choral director; like Ray Charles, Little Richard and Sam Cooke—all of whom acknowledged Bradford as a key influence—he walked the tightrope between religious and secular music with rare skill, and through his later compositions for the great LaVern Baker pioneered the fusion of gospel and pop which later evolved into the classic soul sound.

Born in Bessemer, Alabama in 1926, Bradford was something of a child prodigy, taking dance and music lessons from jazz pianist Martha Belle Hall and making his vaudeville stage debut at the age of four. Gospel remained

his true passion, however, and he grew up singing in his mother's Baptist church; a cappella quartets were the dominant gospel sound of the Depression era, but even at the outset, Bradford preferred the piano-based music of the sanctified church, and as a teen he regularly traveled to New York and Chicago to seek out the new urban sound, drawing heavily on its trademark harmonies, colorful robes and dramatic showmanship. While in New York during the late 1930s, he directed his own group, the Bronx Gospelaires; upon returning to Alabama, he briefly taught school—hence the "Professor" nickname—and flirted with the notion of singing blues before plunging fully into gospel, becoming an ordained minister in no less than three churches.

Still, Bradford maintained his ties to the secular music world; during World War II, he sang at Army Camp Shows, and after settling in Chicago upon his discharge from duty he often supplemented his income by working as a bar pianist. By 1950, he was widely regarded as the Windy City's most promising new soloist, and that year he signed on with the Willie Webb Singers, with whom he made his first recordings. Already a singular stylist, Bradford was the first imporant male gospel performer to absorb the lessons of the whooping falsetto popularized by Marion Williams; he made his first solo recordings for the Apollo label in 1951, and among his earliest releases were "He's a Wonder," "Who Can I Blame," and "God Is Good to Me," all original songs which quickly became favorites with choirs across the country. These early efforts also teamed Bradford with high tenor Charles Campbell, who remained a fixture of his group backgrounds for decades to follow.

With Campbell, Bradford also soon formed his own all-male group, the Bradford Specials, with tenor Jonathan Jackson and baritone Louis Gibson. With this group in support, in 1953 he made his first recordings for Specialty; his debut for the label, "Too Close to Heaven," was an instant classic, becoming the company's biggest gospel hit. Other Bradford smashes—"He Lifted Me," "Lord, Lord, Lord," "He'll Wash You Whiter Than Snow"—soon followed, all refining a unique style typified by his titanic vocals and fluid piano as well as celeste and bongos, a pair of instruments his music helped popularize; within months, he was the highest-paid male performer on the gospel circuit. As his popularity soared, Bradford's stage act rose to the occasion, and began featuring outrageously elaborate choreography verging on the cartoonish; regardless, his music remained deeply rooted in tradition, and for all of its pop overtures was embraced by gospel purists as well.

Bradford continued recording for Specialty through 1958; he eventually settled in Newark, NJ, where for two decades he acted as minister of music for the Abyssinian Baptist Church. In 1961, he co-starred with Marion Williams in *Black Nativity*, the first-ever gospel musical; the production toured the US and Europe for four years, during which time Bradford also became a mentor to a number of young singers whose church backgrounds served as a springboard to pop success, among them LaVern Baker and Dionne Warwick (both alumni of his ensembles). After *Black Nativity* closed, he spent the next several years out of sight before co-starring with wife Alberta Carter Bradford in *Don't Bother Me I Can't Cope*, followed by an appearance in *Your Arms Too Short to Box with God*. While working on another musical, *Don't Cry Mary*, Bradford suffered a stroke and died on February 15, 1978. —*Jason Ankeny*

Too Close / 1953-1958 / Specialty ++++
Rev. Alex Bradford was an amazing singer, prolific composer, and outstanding pianist whose work in the '50s was extremely influential. His flamboyant, exuberant manner and slashing style were imitated by many secular singers and served as a blueprint for the emergence of a sound that would eventually be labeled "soul." This 29-song package includes his biggest hits, particularly the incredible "Too Close to Heaven," a remarkable three-minute piece that merges theatrics, lyrical metaphors, and fire-breathing vocals into a transcendent tour-de-force. There are also seven newly released numbers, including "Move Upstairs," a 1958 duet between Bradford and Bessie Griffin. —*Ron Wynn*

● **The Best of Alex Bradford** / 1982 / Specialty ++++
A comprehensive selection of his fiery, stomping cuts with the Bradford Specials all-male quintet on Specialty Records. —*Ron Wynn*

Rainbow in the Sky / 1992 / Specialty ++++
A broad range of formats and self-penned songs by one of gospel's greatest writers, producers, and soloists, some are issued for the first time here (circa 1954-58). —*Opal Louis Nations*

One Step/Angel on Vacation / 1993 / Vee-Jay ✦✦✦✦
Prof. Alex Bradford announced his arrival on the Vee-Jay label with 1962's *One Step*, which is paired with its follow-up *Angel on Vacation* for this fine two-fer release. While Bradford, who's in peak form throughout, remains the focal point on the majority of these 26 tracks, he also allows the other members of his group to grab the spotlight, typically yielding interesting results; tenor Kenneth Washington lends his coarse voice for a series of duets including "Left My Sins Behind Me," "He Always Keeps His Promises" and "Nothing but the Holy Ghost," while organist Willie James McPhatter takes a solo vocal on "I Made God a Promise" and "Oh My Good Lord." However, the clear standout is Madeline Bell, the Bradford group's first full-time female member; her stunning contralto, heard to powerful effect on "What About You," "Daniel Is a Prayin' Man" and "Just to Know I Made It In," made the leap to secular material a year later, scoring the hit "I'm Gonna Make You Love Me." —*Jason Ankeny*

Too Close to Heaven / Sep. 1, 1995 / Charly ✦✦✦✦
Fine 1960s Vee-Jay collection with Bradford and his singers. —*Opal Louis Nations*

He Lifted Me / Specialty ✦✦✦
A good "hard gospel" outing, spiced with animated leads from Bradford. —*Ron Wynn*

Walking with the King / Savgos ✦✦✦
Prof. Alex Bradford delivered a series of smashing, aggressive, animated hard gospel anthems here, singing with the fire and fury normally associated with Golden Age material, yet also incorporating some elements of modern production. While not quite as majestic as Brother Joe May, Bradford could moan, shout, and holler with almost any singing evangelist, and he demonstrated that on these numbers. —*Ron Wynn*

Tiny Bradshaw

b. Sep. 23, 1905, Youngstown, OH, **d.** Nov. 26, 1958, Cincinnati, OH
Piano, Drums, Vocals / Jump Blues, R&B
Tiny Bradshaw was one of the most prominent bandleaders of the '30s and '40s who led groups of essentially jazz-trained musicians into the developing (and more commercial) field that came to be known as rhythm & blues. A vocalist with other bands early in his career, Bradshaw formed his own band in 1934 and kept it going through the early '50s, enjoying five *Billboard* hits (and also recording the original "Train Kept A-Rollin'") with King Records (where he was a labelmate to many of the other leading jump blues performers of the era). Bradshaw's band produced such saxophone stars as Sonny Stitt, Red Prysock, and Sil Austin; among the vocalists to record with the group were Roy Brown, Arthur Prysock, Lonnie Johnson, and Tiny Kennedy. —*Jim O'Neal*

Off and On / 1950-1952 / King ✦✦✦✦

● **Breakin' Up the House** / 1950-1952 / Charly ✦✦✦✦
Sixteen of Tiny Bradshaw's biggest and hardest-swinging King label waxings from 1950-52, notably "The Train Kept A-Rollin'," "Well, Oh Well," "Two Dry Bones on the Pantry Shelf," "Walkin' the Chalk Line," and the jiving title item. Unfortunately, the torrid big band-styled instrumental arrangements that also defined Bradshaw's output are nowhere to be found on this collection. —*Bill Dahl*

Selections / 1957 / King ✦✦✦✦

Great Composer / 1959 / King ✦✦✦
Domestic CD collection that duplicates one of the popular jump blues bandleader's early albums from the King catalog. —*Bill Dahl*

24 Great Songs / 1966 / King ✦✦✦

Doyle Bramhall

b. Feb. 17, 1949, Dallas, TX
Guitar, Vocals, Drums / Electric Texas Blues
Born in Dallas in 1949, this singer-songwriter/drummer grew up listening to Dallas radio (with heavy doses of Jimmy Reed, Ray Charles and Bobby Blue Bland on rock 'n' roll stations) and locals the Nightcaps, one of the country's first White electric blues bands. In high school he joined the Chessmen, which soon included a young Jimmie Vaughan on guitar; they opened in Dallas on Jimi Hendrix's first US tour. Moving to Austin in 1970, he and

Vaughan formed Texas Storm, which later shortened its name to Storm and occasionally included Jimmie's younger brother Stevie on bass. Doyle next formed the Nightcrawlers with Stevie (now on lead guitar), who later credited Bramhall as a primary vocal influence. During this time the two also co-wrote "Dirty Pool," which Vaughan included on his debut, *Texas Flood*. Doyle wrote or co-wrote seven more songs on subsequent Stevie Ray albums, and collaborated on three for *Family Style* by the Vaughan Brothers (which also featured Bramhall on drums). While drumming with Marcia Ball and Mason Ruffner in the early '80s, Bramhall began stockpiling solo recordings, which eventually comprised his long-awaited debut on CD, featuring both Vaughan's and Doyle's son, guitarist Doyle Bramhall, II, formerly of the Arc Angels. Recently he began a collaboration that should prove interesting—with pop singer Jennifer Warnes. —*Dan Forte*

● **Birdnest on the Ground** / 1994 / Discovery ✦✦✦✦
Well, they say the best things in life are worth waiting for—drummer Bramhall started recording this tasty blues-rock album in 1980, wrapping it up in 1992—here it is, out on Antone's in 1994. Not a shabby effort, either—Bramhall has that big smoky Bob Seger kind of voice, and the music is muscular and warm, a friendly, welcome bar-rock kind of sound. Good stuff, I say. —*Steven McDonald*

Doyle Bramhall II / Sep. 9, 1996 / Geffen ✦✦✦
With his second album, bluesman Doyle Bramhall continues to move deeper into soul, which isn't surprising considering that Wendy & Lisa, Prince's collaborators during the mid-'80s, produced *Vol. 2*. While there is stilll a distinct bluesy bent to his guitar playing, the material is more soul-oriented and polished than before, which will initially alienate some of his contemporary blues fans. However, *Vol. 2* shows considerable musical invention and skill, particularly during its instrumental passages. It's just unfortunate that it loses momentum due to inconsistent songwriting. —*Thom Owens*

Billy Branch (William Earl Branch)

b. Oct. 3, 1951, Great Lakes, IL
Harmonica, Vocals / Modern Electric Blues, Chicago Blues
If blues harmonica has a longterm future on the Chicago circuit, Billy Branch will likely play a leading role in shaping its direction. Educator as well as musician, Branch has led the Sons of Blues, his skin-tight quartet, since the late '70s. Despite numerous personnel changes, the SOBs have never wavered in their dedication to pure, unadulterated Chicago blues.

Although he was born just north of the Windy City, Branch grew up in Los Angeles, only to return to Chicago in 1969 to attend the University of Illinois. Spurred on by the entrancing riffs of mouth organ masters Carey Bell, Big Walter Horton, and Junior Wells, Branch began to make a name for himself. He replaced Bell in Willie Dixon's Chicago Blues All-Stars, recording with the prolific legend and touring extensively.

The SOBs really were dominated by second-generation talent at the start—guitarist Lurrie Bell was Carey Bell's son, while bassist Freddie Dixon was the offspring of Willie Dixon. They contributed three tunes to Alligator's first batch of *Living Chicago Blues* anthologies in 1978. The SOBs waxed *Where's My Money?*, their Red Beans Records LP, in 1984; by then, personnel included guitarist Carlos Johnson, bassist J.W. Williams, and drummer Moses Rutues. Shortly after that album was completed, guitarist Carl Weathersby was installed as co-front man, where he remains (as does Rutues; bass is now handled by Nick Charles).

Other than co-headlining Alligator's 1990 summit meeting *Harp Attack!* with fellow harp masters Junior Wells, Carey Bell, and James Cotton, Branch largely busied himself with extensive sideman work (he's first-call session harpist around the Windy City) and teaching an innovative "Blues in the Schools" program until 1995, when Verve issued his *The Blues Keep Following Me Around*, an impressive showcase for his gravelly vocals and spellbinding harp.

A lot is expected of Billy Branch in the near future. He'll have to usher Chicago's proud blues harp tradition into the next century—a task he's eminently capable of pulling off. —*Bill Dahl*

Where's My Money? / 1984 / Evidence ✦✦✦
Slightly scattershot 1984 LP, originally released on the now-defunct Red Beans logo, that hits more than it misses. At its best—the sardonic title track, a couple of vocals by veteran pianist Jimmy Walker, a stunning "Son of Juke"

that spotlights Branch's harp wizardry—it's a fine introduction to the SOBs' multi-faceted attack. —*Bill Dahl*

Harp Attack! / 1990 / Alligator ✦✦✦✦
Four of the Windy City's undisputed harmonica masters in the same studio, trading solos and vocals with good-natured abandon. Billy's showcases are the apt original "New Kid on the Block" and a deft cover of Little Walter's "Who." —*Bill Dahl*

Mississippi Flashback / Jan. 1992 / GBW ✦✦✦

Live '82 / 1994 / Evidence ✦✦✦

• **The Blues Keep Following Me Around** / 1995 / Verve ✦✦✦✦
Branch and Carl Weathersby ventured down to Maurice, LA, to cut this impressive disc with a home-grown rhythm section, but only Branch's name appears on its front. Certainly the harpist is the star of the show, growling covers of dusties by Sonny Boy Williamson, Willie Dixon, and Howlin' Wolf. Nevertheless, guitarist Weathersby provides two of the set's highlights, passionately singing his own "Should Have Been Gone" and "Should Have Known Better." —*Bill Dahl*

Billy Branch & Hubert Sumlin / Wolf ✦✦✦✦
This disc is a fine portrait of Chicago blues—past and present. Award-winning harpist Billy Branch and legendary giant of the famed Howlin' Wolf Band, Hubert Sumlin, here join hands with some of the finest contemporary musicians in the Windy City—among them: Willie Kent, John Primer, Johnny B. Moore, and Carl Weathersby. Sumlin offers two superb band tracks as well as five acoustic duets with guitarist John Primer. In addition, there are four Billy Branch numbers that recast the work of Jimmy Rogers, Jimmy Reed, and Little Walter without ever becoming slavish. The dual-guitar work of Johnny B. Moore and John Primer is exceptional. —*Larry Hoffman*

Jackie Brenston

b. Aug. 15, 1930, Clarksdale, MS, **d.** Dec. 15, 1979, Memphis, TN
Vocals, Saxophone / Jump Blues, Electric Memphis Blues
Determining the first actual rock 'n' roll record is a truly impossible task. But you can't go too far wrong citing Jackie Brenston's 1951 Chess waxing of "Rocket 88," a seminal piece of rock's fascinating history with all the prerequisite elements firmly in place: practically indecipherable lyrics about cars, booze, and chicks; Raymond Hill's booting tenor sax, and a churning, beat-heavy rhythmic bottom.

Sam Phillips, then a fledgling in the record business, produced "Rocket 88," Brenston's debut waxing, in Memphis. The singer/saxist was backed by Ike Turner's Kings of Rhythm, an aggregation that Brenston had joined the previous year. Turner played piano on the tune; Willie Kizart supplied dirty, distorted guitar. Billed as by Jackie Brenston & His Delta Cats, "Rocket 88" drove up to the top slot on the R&B charts and remained there for more than a month. But none of his Chess follow-ups sported the same high-octane performance, though "Real Gone Rocket" was certainly a deserving candidate.

Brenston's slide from the spotlight was swift. After a few more Chess singles stiffed (including a duet with Edna McRaney, "Hi-Ho Baby"), Brenston reunited with Turner in 1955, holding down the baritone sax chair until 1962. He cut a series of terrific sides fronting Turner's Kings of Rhythm along the way: "Gonna Wait for My Chance" and "Much Later" for Federal in 1956, "You've Got to Lose" for Chicago's Cobra label in 1958 (also doing session work there with Otis Rush and Buddy Guy), and "You Ain't the One" for Sue in 1961. After a final single for Mel London's Mel-Lon imprint, Brenston was through—he worked as a truck driver and showed little interest in reliving his glory years. —*Bill Dahl*

• **Rocket 88** / Mar. 5, 1951-Apr. 17, 1953 / Charly ✦✦✦✦
If Brenston's "Rocket 88" was in actuality the very first rock 'n' roll record, as many experts claim, the rest of his brief Chess legacy adds up to quite a definitive rockin' statement. Among these 16 sides dating from 1951-53 are his amazing sequel "My Real Gone Rocket," which probably rocks even harder than "Rocket 88" as Ike Turner pounds the keys; "Tuckered Out," the evocative "Fat Meat Is Greasy" (one of several items only out in Japan before the advent of this British CD), and seven sides Brenston cut in Chicago without Sam Phillips to guide him, nor Turner's Kings of Rhythm to back him up. Great stuff deserving of domestic release! —*Bill Dahl*

John Brim

b. Apr. 10, 1922, Hopkinsville, KY
Vocals, Guitar, Harmonica / Electric Chicago Blues
One of the last still-active links to the classic 1950s Chicago blues sound that once thrived at Chess Records (only one of Brim's several label associations during the 1950s), John Brim may be best-known for writing and cutting the original "Ice Cream Man" that David Lee Roth and Van Halen covered on their first album. That's a pity, for the seriously underrecorded Brim made some exceptionally hard-nosed waxings.

Brim picked up his early guitar licks from the 78s of Tampa Red and Big Bill Broonzy before venturing first to Indianapolis in 1941 and Chicago four years later. He met his wife Grace in 1947; fortuitously, she was a capable drummer who played on several of John's records. In fact, she was the vocalist on a 1950 single for Detroit-based Fortune Records that signaled the beginning of her hubby's discography.

John recorded for Random, JOB, Al Benson's Parrot logo (the socially aware "Tough Times"), and Chess ("Rattlesnake," his answer to Big Mama Thornton's "Hound Dog," was pulled from the shelves by Chess for fear of a plagiarism suit). Cut in 1953, the suggestive "Ice Cream Man" had to wait until 1969 to enjoy a very belated release. Brim's last Chess single, "I Would Hate to See You Go," was waxed in 1956 with a stellar combo consisting of harpist Little Walter, guitarist Robert Jr. Lockwood, bassist Willie Dixon, and drummer Fred Below (clearly, Chess had high hopes for Brim, but to no avail).

After a hiatus of a few decades, Brim made a welcome return to studio action with a recent set for Tone-Cool Records, *The Ice Cream Man*. He still plays occasionally around Chicago. —*Bill Dahl*

• **Whose Muddy Shoes** / 1991 / MCA/Chess ✦✦✦✦
First unleashed back in 1969 on vinyl as part of the Chess Vintage Series, this hard-hitting disc couples six of Brim's meanest Parrot and Chess sides with nine Elmore James gems. Brim is at his toughest on the threatening "Be Careful" and "Lifetime Baby." —*Bill Dahl*

Ice Cream Man / 1994 / Tone-Cool ✦✦✦
Brim's vocals don't quite possess the same snap, crackle, and pop that they did in the mid-'50s, but thanks to a savvy song selection and sympathetic backing by the likes of guitarist Bob Margolin and harpist Jerry Portnoy, Brim's comeback album is a generally successful project. —*Bill Dahl*

Brooklyn All-Stars

f. 1950
Group / Traditional Gospel, Black Gospel
The Brooklyn All-Stars are an internationally recognized male gospel group who have been performing since 1950. Over their long, fruitful careers, they have won numerous awards and racked up two gold albums. Original members include the group's founder, Thomas J. Spann, Hardie Clifton, and Sam Thomas. They recorded several cuts for Peacock in 1959, including "Rest Awhile" and "Meet Me in Galilee." Their early years were difficult ones; with little money for touring, they often traveled to engagements stuffed into a single car, relying on parishioners' hospitality for food and lodging because they were not permitted inside restaurants and motels. Things improved over the '60s, and they established themselves as a fine traditional gospel act. Between 1971 and 1978, they were annually voted the number one gospel group in the US. Their biggest-selling hits are "When I Stood on the Banks of Jordan" and "He Touched Me and Made Me Whole," on Jewel, the label they have been with since 1971. During the '80s, the All-Stars embarked upon a series of world tours. —*Sandra Brennan*

Family Prayer / 1964 / Hob ✦✦✦✦
Tight harmonies, fine lead work from Hardie Clifton and Thomas Spann. —*Opal Louis Nations*

The Best of the Brooklyn Allstars / 1995 / Nashboro ✦✦✦✦
As the title suggests, truly the quartet's finest moments on Nashboro. —*Opal Louis Nations*

• **Our Greatest Hits** / Nashboro ✦✦✦✦
Powerful material drawn from a variety of '60s and '70s Nashboro albums, it's led principally by the soaring tenor of the underrated Hardie Clifton. —*Opal Louis Nations*

I've Got My Ticket / Jewel ++++
Good strong quartet singing with power-packed delivery. —*Opal Louis Nations*

Hadda Brooks

b. Oct. 29, 1916, Los Angeles, CA
Piano, Vocals / Piano Blues
In the mid-to-late '40s, Black popular music began to mutate from swing jazz and boogie-woogie into the sort of rhythm & blues that helped lay the foundation for rock 'n' roll. Singer and pianist Hadda Brooks was one of the many figures who were significant in aiding that transition, although she's largely forgotten today. While her torch song delivery was rooted in the big-band era, her boogie-woogie piano looked forward to jump blues and R&B. Ironically, the same qualities that made her briefly successful—her elegant vocals and jazzy arrangements—left her ill-equipped to compete when harder-driving forms of rhythm & blues, and then early rock 'n' roll, began to dominate the marketplace in the early '50s.

Brooks got a recording deal through a chance meeting with jukebox operator Jules Bihari, who was looking to record some boogie-woogie. The Los Angeles-based Bihari, along with his brother Joe, would become major players in early R&B via their Modern label, which issued sides by B.B. King, John Lee Hooker, Etta James, Jesse Belvin, and other stars. Brooks actually preferred ballads to boogie-woogies, but worked up her style by listening to Pete Johnson, Albert Ammons, and Meade Lux Lewis records. Her first record, the pounding "Swingin' the Boogie," was a sizable regional hit in 1945. Joe Bihari would later tell author Arnold Shaw that the single was instrumental in establishing the Biharis in the record business.

Brooks' first records were instrumental, but by 1946 she was singing as well. She had a fair amount of success for Modern in the late '40s, reaching the R&B Top Ten with "Out of the Blue" and her most famous song, "That's My Desire" (which was covered for a big pop hit by Frankie Laine). Her success on record led to some roles in films, most notably in a scene from *In a Lonely Place*, which starred Humphrey Bogart.

Brooks briefly left Modern for an unsuccessful stint with major label London in 1950. After a similarly unrewarding return to Modern in the early '50s, and a brief stay at OKeh, she largely withdrew from recording into the nightclub circuit. For most of the 1960s, in fact, she was based in Australia, where she hosted her own TV show. Her profile was boosted in the mid-'90s by her induction into the Rhythm & Blues Foundation Hall of Fame, and by the inclusion of her recording of "Anytime, Anyplace, Anywhere" in the film *The Crossing Guard.* A new album on Pointblank, *Time Was When,* was released in early 1996. —*Richie Unterberger*

● **That's My Desire** / 1945-1950 / Virgin ++++
25 tracks from her prime, recorded for Modern in the 1940s and 1950s, including her hits "That's My Desire" and "Out of the Blue," as well as "Anytime, Anyplace, Anywhere." While Brooks was an important figure of the Los Angeles 1940s R&B scene, latter-day listeners may find this rather tame. Vocally she owed much more to pop-jazz stylings than gritty R&B influences. Her most durable and influential performances were her instrumental ones at the piano bench, especially on the pounding "Swingin' the Boogie," which leads off this collection. —*Richie Unterberger*

Femme Fatale / 1956 / Modern +++

Boogie / 1958 / Crown +++

Sings & Swings / 1963 / Crown +++

Anytime, Anyplace, Anywhere / Sep. 25, 1994 / DRG ++++

Time Was When / Feb. 20, 1996 / Virgin +++

Jump Back Honey: Complete OKeh Sessions / Feb. 11, 1997 / Sony ++++
She was best known as a boogie-woogie piano player in the late 1940s, but this first-time CD reissue focuses on Hadda Brooks' brilliantly sophisticated, laidback vocal material in the 1950s. These songs don't carry the dirgelike sentiments of most blues, but more of a euphoric look at life and love. There are rocking dancers such as "Jump Back Honey" and "Brooks Boogie" among tasteful ballads such as "I Went To Your Wedding" and saucy midtempos like "Time Was When." —*Bill Carpenter*

Lonnie Brooks

b. Dec. 18, 1933, Dubuisson, LA
Guitar, Vocals / Modern Electric Blues, Modern Electric Chicago Blues, Electric Chicago Blues
Having forged a unique Louisiana/Chicago blues synthesis unlike anyone else's on the competitive Windy City scene, charismatic guitarist Lonnie Brooks has long reigned as one of the town's top bluesmen. A masterful showman, the good-natured Brooks puts on a show equal to his recordings (and that's saying a lot, considering there's four decades of wax to choose from).

Born Lee Baker, Jr., in Louisiana, Lonnie took his time when choosing his vocation—he didn't play guitar seriously until he was in his early 20s and living in Port Arthur, TX. Rapidly assimilating the licks of B.B. King and Long John Hunter, he landed a gig with zydeco pioneer Clifton Chenier (not a bad way to break into the business) before inaugurating his own recording career in 1957 with the influential swamp-pop ballad "Family Rules" for Eddie Shuler's Lake Charles, LA-based Goldband Records. The young rock 'n' roller—then billed as Guitar Junior—enjoyed more regional success on Goldband with the rocking dance number "The Crawl" (much later covered by the Fabulous Thunderbirds). Mercury also issued two 45s by Guitar Junior.

When Sam Cooke offered the young rocker a chance to accompany him to Chicago, he gladly accepted. But two problems faced him once he arrived: there was another Guitar Junior in town (precipitating the birth of Lonnie Brooks), and the bayou blues that so enthralled Gulf Coast crowds didn't cut it up north. Scattered session work (he played on Jimmy Reed's Vee-Jay classic "Big Boss Man") and a series of R&B-oriented 45s for Midas, USA, Chirrup, and Chess ensued during the '60s, as Lonnie learned a new style of blues. The Guitar Junior sobriquet was dusted off briefly in 1969 for his Capitol album debut, *Broke an' Hungry,* but its lack of success buried the alias for good.

By the late '70s, Brooks was gaining a deserved reputation as an exceptionally dynamic Chicago bluesman with a fresh perspective. He cut four outstanding sides for Alligator's first batch of *Living Chicago Blues* anthologies in 1978 that quickly led to his own 1979 debut LP, *Bayou Lightning,* the next year. Five more albums of his own for the firm and extensive touring have cemented Brooks' standing as a Chicago blues giant. Son Ronnie Baker Brooks is a chip off the proverbial block, playing rhythm guitar in his old man's band and duetting on "Like Father, Like Son" on Lonnie's 1991 album *Satisfaction Guaranteed.* —*Bill Dahl*

The Crawl / 1955-1959 / Charly ++++
Lonnie Brooks' pervasive 1950s bayou blues roots, laid bare and rocking hard. "Family Rules" was highly influential to the blossoming swamp-pop movement soon sweeping southern Louisiana; "The Crawl," "I Got It Made (When I Marry Shirley Mae)," "Roll, Roll, Roll," and "Knocks Me Out" (the latter one of his Mercury singles) drive with youthful abandon. The youngster's ears were wide-open—he even covered Harlan Howard's country ditty "Pick Me Up on Your Way Down," investing it with serious swamp angst. —*Bill Dahl*

Live at Pepper's 1968 / 1968 / Black Top +++
Lonnie Brooks in his jukebox bluesman mode, playing the hits of the day for an appreciative crowd at one of Chicago's legendary blues joints. First issued on the European Black Magic label, the set captures his showmanship effectively as he attacks "You Don't Have to Go," "Sweet Little Angel," "Hide Away," and Johnnie Taylor's soul workout "Who's Making Love." Even in 1968, he was stockpiling originals—a rocking "Shakin' Little Mama" and a distinctive "The Train & the Horse" are all his. —*Bill Dahl*

Broke & Hungry / Oct. 6, 1969 + Oct. 8, 1969 / Capitol +++
A momentary 1969 return to the Guitar Junior monicker—for Capitol Records, no less—was produced by Eddie Shuler's son Wayne and focuses on Lonnie Brooks' enduring swamp blues roots (long after he'd jettisoned the style). Unavailable on CD (Crosscut reissued it on vinyl), the LP consists of interpretations of oldies first rendered by Guitar Slim, Lightnin' Slim, Elton Anderson, Larry Davis, Hop Wilson, and Professor Longhair (along with Brooks' own "The Train and the Horse"). —*Bill Dahl*

Sweet Home Chicago / Dec. 8, 1975 / Evidence ++
The French Black & Blue label was savvy enough to spirit Brooks into a studio when he was touring the continent in 1975 as part of Chicago Blues

Festival '75. As befits the jam-session ambience of the date (pianist Willie Mabon, harpist Mack Simmons, and two-thirds of the Aces are on hand), hoary standards predominate: "Crosscut Saw," "Things I Used to Do," "Mama Talk to Your Daughter," and the ubiquitous title track (which remains a signature song). The omnipresent "The Train and the Horse" returns as well. — *Bill Dahl*

Let's Talk It Over / Mar. 24, 1977 / Delmark ✦✦✦
Of all the quickie dates produced by Ralph Bass in 1977 for a project that never came to real fruition, Lonnie Brooks' contribution to the series is likely the most satisfying—thanks to a tight band (his working unit at the time) and a sheaf of imaginative originals (notably "Crash Head on into Love," "Greasy Man," and the title cut). An ingenious reworking of Lowell Fulson's "Reconsider Baby" doesn't hurt either. — *Bill Dahl*

● **Bayou Lightning** / Mar. 1979 / Alligator ✦✦✦✦
All the promise that Lonnie Brooks possessed was realized on this album, his finest and most consistent to date. The churning bayou groove of "Voodoo Daddy," a soul-steeped "Watch What You Got," a bone-chilling remake of Junior Parker's "In the Dark," rollicking covers of Tommy Tucker's "Alimony" and Brooks' own "Figure Head," and the swaggering originals "You Know What My Body Needs" and "Watchdog" are among the set's many incendiary highlights. — *Bill Dahl*

Turn on the Night / 1981 / Alligator ✦✦✦
Inconsistent in comparison to its illustrious predecessor, his encore Alligator offering still contains some goodies. Chief among them are the infectious originals "Eyeballin'" and "Don't Go to Sleep on Me," along with a delicious revival of Bobby "Blue" Bland's "I'll Take Care of You." — *Bill Dahl*

Hot Shot / 1983 / Alligator ✦✦✦✦
A return to rollicking good-time form, boasting the roaring "Don't Take Advantage of Me" and "I Want All My Money Back," relentless rocking revivals of Otis Blackwell's "Back Trail" and J.B. Lenoir's "One More Shot," and a faithful remake of Lonnie Brooks' own "Family Rules" from the Guitar Junior era. — *Bill Dahl*

Live at Pepper's / 1985 / Black Magic ✦✦✦
This excellent 1968 live recording came from Chicago. — *Bill Dahl*

Wound Up Tight / 1986 / Alligator ✦✦✦
More energetic efforts with a decidedly rocked-up edge. Johnny Winter, long an ardent admirer of Brooks back to the Guitar Junior days, drops by with a passel of fiery guitar licks for the title track and "Got Lucky Last Night." — *Bill Dahl*

Live from Chicago / Nov. 5, 1987-Nov. 7, 1987 / Alligator ✦✦✦
Cut live at Chicago's B.L.U.E.S. Etcetera nightclub, the disc captures the high-energy excitement of Lonnie Brooks' live show. Many familiar titles from his Alligator catalog, along with a handful of never-before released tunes and a marathon "Hide Away" where Brooks pulls out all the guitaristic tricks at his command. — *Bill Dahl*

Satisfaction Guaranteed / 1991 / Alligator ✦✦
Only intermittently satisfying, contrary to its title: a little more subtlety would have benefitted drummer Kevin Mitchell, and some of the material is a bit makeweight. Nevertheless, there are some nice moments, especially on the tunes Brooks penned himself. "Like Father, like Son," the duet between Lonnie and son Ronnie, seems a mite contrived. — *Bill Dahl*

Roadhouse Rules / Feb. 27, 1996 / Alligator ✦✦✦
Lonnie Brooks' music comes from the R&B side of the blues. Brooks is a passionate singer with an intense rockish guitar style. With the exception of "Roll of the Tumbling Dice" (a relaxed duet featuring the harmonica of Sugar Blue), the music on this CD is generally unrelenting in its ferocity, blues-oriented but also quite open to the influences of Stax-type soul and rock. The impressive musicianship and sincerity of Lonnie Brooks' music is probably easier to respect than to love; this release gives listeners a good sampling of his playing. — *Scott Yanow*

● **Deluxe Edition** / Oct. 28, 1997 / Alligator ✦✦✦✦
Deluxe Edition rounds up 15 highlights from Lonnie Brooks' late-'70s and '80s recordings for Alligator. Like many Alligator artists, Brooks made records that were just a little too slick to demonstrate the depth of his talents and the grittiness of his playing, yet they still remained solid, rock-inflected contemporary blues albums. The bulk of the highlights from his records

are here, making it a fine introduction to Brooks' most popular recordings. — *Stephen Thomas Erlewine*

Big Bill Broonzy (William Lee Conley Broonzy)

b. Jun. 26, 1893, Scott, MS, **d.** Aug. 15, 1958, Chicago, IL
Guitar, Vocals, Mandolin / Country Blues, Acoustic Chicago Blues, Blues Revival

In terms of his musical skill, the sheer size of his repertoire, the length and variety of his career and his influence on contemporaries and musicians who would follow, Big Bill Broonzy is among a select few of the most important figures in recorded blues history. Among his hundreds of titles are standards like "All by Myself" and "Key to the Highway." In this country he was instrumental in the growth of the Chicago Blues sound, and his travels abroad rank him as one of the leading blues ambassadors.

Literally born on the banks of the Mississippi, he was one of a family of 17 who learned to fiddle on a homemade instrument. Taught by his uncle, he was performing by age ten at social functions and in church. After brief stints on the pulpit and in the Army, he moved to Chicago where he switched his attention from violin to guitar, playing with elders like Papa Charlie Jackson. Broonzy began his recording career with Paramount in 1927. In the early '30s he waxed some brilliant blues and hokum and worked Chicago and the road with great players like pianist Black Bob, guitarist Will Weldon, and Memphis Minnie.

During the Depression years, Big Bill Broonzy continued full steam ahead, doing some acrobatic label-hopping (Paramount to Bluebird to Columbia to OKeh!). In addition to solo efforts, he contributed his muscular guitar licks to recordings by Bumble Bee Slim, John Lee (Sonny Boy) Williamson and others who were forging a powerful new Chicago sound.

In 1938, Broonzy was at Carnegie Hall (ostensibly filling in for the fallen Robert Johnson) for John Hammond's revolutionary Spirtuals to Swing Series. The following year he appeared with Benny Goodman and Louis Armstrong in George Seldes' film production *Swingin' the Dream*. After his initial brush with the East Coast cognoscenti, however, Broonzy spent a good part of the early '40s barnstorming the South with Lil Green's road show or kicking back in Chicago with Memphis Slim.

He continued alternating stints in Chicago and New York with coast-to-coast road work until 1951 when live performances and recording dates overseas earned him considerable notoriety in Europe and led to worldwide touring. Back in the States he recorded for Chess, Columbia and Folkways, working with a spectrum of artists from Blind John Davis to Pete Seeger. In 1955, *Big Bill Blues*, his life as told to Danish writer Yannick Bruynoghe, was published.

In 1957, after one more British tour, the pace began to catch up with Broonzy. He spent the last year of his life in and out of hospitals and succumbed to cancer in 1958. He survives though; not only in his music, but in the remembrances of people who knew him ... from Muddy Waters to Studs Terkel. A gentle giant they say ... tough enough to survive the blues world ... but not so tough he wouldn't give a struggling young musician the shirt off his back. His music, of course, is absolutely basic to the blues experience. — *Steve James*

★ **The Young Big Bill Broonzy (1928-35)** / 1928-1935 / Yazoo ✦✦✦✦✦
The young Bill Broonzy was as far removed from his later folk blues posturings as you could imagine. If you're only familiar with his later work, these early sides will come as quite a jolt. Big Bill whips off some fleet-fingered single note leads and his rhythmic drive is never less than spot on. Great stuff. — *Cub Koda*

☆ **Do That Guitar Rag (1928-1935)** / 1928-1935 / Yazoo ✦✦✦✦
This is a marvelous little companion piece to *Young Big Bill Broonzy (1928-35)* on Yazoo. Broonzy's ragtime guitar picking is textbook in its scope and his vocals are as warm as can be. Dubbed from old 78s, the ultra-high quality of the music makes any audiophile nitpicking a moot point indeed. Broonzy at his youngest and full of pep. — *Cub Koda*

★ **Good Time Tonight** / 1930-1940 / Columbia/Legacy ✦✦✦✦✦
If you're following the 30-plus year career of Bill Broonzy and already have the two early compilations available on Yazoo, here's where you go next. These are basically ensemble works covering the time frame between 1930 to 1940 and Broonzy sounds very comfortable in the company of Blind John Davis and Joshua Altheimer. The 20 tracks compiled here (culled from vari-

ous Vocalion, ARC and Columbia sessions) sound pretty great, benefitting mightily from modern sound restoration devices. — *Cub Koda*

Blues in the Mississippi Night / 1946 / Rykodisc ✦✦✦✦
In 1946, the day after a successful Town Hall concert was given by guitarist Big Bill Broonzy, pianist Memphis Slim, and harmonica wizard Sonny Boy Williamson, Alan Lomax met the trio at the Decca studios in New York. Armed with just a single microphone and a disc recorder, Lomax persuaded Memphis Slim to play a blues and then he said, "Listen, you all have lived with the blues all your life, but nobody here understands them. Tell me what the blues are all about." For the next two hours the three bluesmen talked about their lives, the day-to-day struggles with racism, and the constant battle to avoid prisons and lynch mobs in the South. Broonzy did the majority of the storytelling and there are many interesting (and sometimes scary) anecdotes, some dark humor, and demonstrations about how anger towards the White man could be safely expressed in music. After hearing the playback of the candid conversations, the bluesmen begged Lomax not to release them because they were fearful that their families and relatives in the South would be murdered if their frank comments ever came out. One hour of the discussions was finally released in 1991 on this single CD along with an accompanying booklet which contains the complete transcription of the meeting. Although there are only three brief songs on this set, the important release (recorded 19 years before the Civil Rights Act made anti-racism protests a bit safer) should be of great interest to blues historians and those concerned with the history of race relations. — *Scott Yanow*

Big Bill Broonzy & Washboard Sam / 1953 / MCA ✦✦✦
Although Chess didn't bother to anthologize these sides into album form until the early '60s, this marvelous collection actually dates from 1953. Broonzy and Sam are both in great form here, sharing the vocals throughout and recalling their earlier days as Bluebird label and session mates. The sound is fleshed out by the addition of guitarist Lee Cooper (who at times almost sounds a bit too modern for the genre being explored here, throwing in what can only be described as Chuck Berry licks) and Big Crawford on upright bass. — *Cub Koda*

Big Bill Broonzy Sings Folk Songs / 1956 / Smithsonian/Folkways ✦✦✦✦
Two different sessions provided the material for this collection of folk songs, spirituals, and blues standards. Half the disc is previously unreleased material from Broonzy's final Folkways recording session. The other half of the disc was recorded at a live broadcast with Pete Seeger for radio station WFMT Chicago in front of an audience of friends; Seeger joins Broonzy during "John Henry." Although his vocal range is not quite what it used to be, Bill sings with authority and vibrance, using the occasional strained notes for effect. His fluid guitar technique remains unhampered. Unlike many of his peers, Big Bill Broonzy was able to utilize the late-'50s folk boom as an opportunity to be recognized while he was still alive. This disc shows Broonzy in his element as one of the classic blues masters. — *Jim Powers*

☆ **Big Bill's Blues** / 198_ / Portrait ✦✦✦✦✦
If you're going to sweat a Big Bill Broonzy collection down to only one disc, this is the one to keep in the collection. It's really his most representative work, highlighting most of the best-known numbers from his extensive repertoire and the highlights (including a hilarious "When I've Been Drinkin'," in which he supposedly downs several shots on microphone during the take) are numerous. — *Cub Koda*

1955 London Sessions / 1990 / Castle ✦✦✦

In Chronological Order / 1991 / Document ✦✦✦
If having it *all* is your ultimate goal as a blues collector, this 11-CD set will certainly aid and abet in that pursuit. On this exhaustive collection from 1927-1942 you *will* find a plethora of great sides, including "C-C Rider," "Milkcow Blues," and his finest instrumental, "House Rent Stomp." Collecting up 15 years of recorded works and running them in strict chronological order is a most laudable effort, but this certainly is not the place to start in building up a great Big Bill Broonzy collection. For completists only. — *Cub Koda*

Complete Recorded Works, Vol. 1 (1927-1932) / 1991 / Document ✦✦✦
Document's eleven-volume *Complete Recorded Works* features everything Broonzy recorded between 1927 and 1942; for hardcore Big Bill Broonzy collectors, it's essential. — *AMG*

Complete Recorded Works, Vol. 2 (1932-1934) / 1991 / Document ✦✦✦
By early 1932, the point at which this second volume in Document's series begins, Big Bill Broonzy was well established on the Chicago music scene; although his music was beginning to take on an urbanized flavor, his forté was still country-blues, and the opening tracks here—"Mr. Conductor Man," "Too-Too Train Blues," and "Bull Cow Blues" among them—are among his finest examples of the form. Of equal interest are the sides he subsequently recorded with his Jug Busters, a rather mysterious group which yielded just two tracks—"Rukus Juice Blues" and "M and O Blues"—but which pushed Broonzy further away from his rural roots; in all likelihood, the group also inaugurated his collaboration with the enigmatic yet renowned Black Bob, with whom he would cut a series of classic guitar and piano duets in the months to follow. — *Jason Ankeny*

Complete Recorded Works, Vol. 3 (1934-1935) / 1991 / Document ✦✦✦
Big Bill Broonzy's absorption of the urbanized Chicago blues style was essentially complete by the time of the 1934-35 recordings assembled here. The highlight is a highly productive session featuring the State Street Boys, a group featuring Broonzy alongside harpist Jazz Gillum, guitarist Carl Martin, pianist Black Bob and violinist Zeb Wright, whose dissonant, scraping style lends the combo a highly distinctive sound; their material is fascinatingly diverse, ranging from the train songs "Midnight Special" and "Mobile and Western Line" to the saucy "She Caught the Train," and the much-covered "Don't Tear My Clothes." Also with Black Bob, Broonzy continued recording more simplified guitar/piano duets—their "Southern Blues" is a lovely and nostalgic reminiscence about life on the other side of the Mason-Dixon line, while "Good Jelly" ranks among his most lyrically inventive efforts. — *Jason Ankeny*

Unissued Test Pressings / 1992 / Milan ✦✦✦
Unissued Test Pressings compiles 15 alternate versions of Big Bill Broonzy classics like "WPA Blues," "Married Life Is a Pain," and "Unemployed Stomp," released here with their spoken introductions intact; that alone makes these sides invaluable for scholars, as the intros not only run down the other musicians on the session but also provide additional track information. Unfortunately, scholars and Broonzy fanatics are about the only listeners to whom the collection will appeal—the overall sound quality is simply too poor for casual fans to endure. — *Jason Ankeny*

Complete Recorded Works, Vol. 4 (1935-1936) / 1992 / Document ✦✦✦

Complete Recorded Works, Vol. 5 (1936-1937) / 1992 / Document ✦✦✦

Complete Recorded Works, Vol. 6 (1937) / 1992 / Document ✦✦✦
Primarily for completists, specialists and academics, Document's *Complete Recorded Works, Vol. 6 (1937)* continues the exhaustive overview of Big Bill Broonzy's recordings. For less dedicated listeners, the long running time, exacting chronological sequencing, poor fidelity (all cuts are transferred from original acetates and 78s), and number of performances will be hard to digest. The serious blues listener will find all these factors to be positive, as well as a wealth of classic performances, but others are advised to find a less comprehensive overview. — *Thom Owens*

Complete Recorded Works, Vol. 11 (1940-1942) / 1992 / Document ✦✦✦
For completists, specialists and academics, Document's *Complete Recorded Works, Vol. 11 (1940-1942)* is invaluable, offering an exhaustive overview of Big Bill Broonzy's recordings. Like the other volumes, it contains some absolutely wonderful performances, long running time, exacting chronological sequencing, poor fidelity (all cuts are transferred from original acetates and 78s), and quite a large number of performances. The serious blues listener will find all these factors to be positive, but enthusiasts and casual listeners will find that the collection is of marginal interest for those very reasons. — *Thom Owens*

I Feel So Good / 1995 / Indigo ✦✦✦✦

Complete Recorded Works, Vol. 12 (1945-1947) / Sep. 1, 1995 / Document ✦✦✦

The Complete Bluebird Recordings, 1934-1935 / Oct. 1995 / Bluebird ✦✦✦✦

Treat Me Right / Feb. 6, 1996 / Rykodisc Tradition ✦✦✦

Sings Folk Songs / Smithsonian/Folkways ✦✦✦✦
Big Bill Broonzy was a narrative genius; someone who could take lyrics,

situations, and themes and make them resonate with pain, sadness, anger, or joy. This 11-song set takes a slightly different tack. It's a compilation with Broonzy doing his renditions of well-known (some obscure) folk songs. From the woeful laments of "Backwater Blues" and "Tell Me Who" to the assertive strains of "This Train" and "I Don't Want No Woman (To Try to Be My Boss)," Broonzy puts his own stamp on every number, even shopworn items like "John Henry" and "Bill Bailey." — *Ron Wynn*

Andrew Brown

b. Feb. 25, 1937, Jackson, MS, **d.** Dec. 11, 1985
Guitar, Vocals / Electric Chicago Blues, Modern Electric Chicago Blues
Tragically underrecorded until late in his career, Chicago blues guitarist Andrew Brown still had time enough to wax a handful of great singles during the mid-'60s and two 1980s albums (unfortunately, both of them were only available as imports) that beautifully showcased his fluid, concise lead guitar and hearty vocals.

The Mississippi native moved to Chicago in 1946. With Earl Hooker teaching him a few key licks, Brown matured quickly; he was playing in south suburban clubs—his main circuit—by the early '50s. His 45s for USA (1962's "You Better Stop") and 4 Brothers (the mid-'60s sides "You Ought to Be Ashamed" and "Can't Let You Go") were well-done urban blues. But it wasn't until 1980, when Alligator issued three of his songs on its second batch of *Living Chicago Blues* anthologies, that Brown's name began to resonate outside the Windy City.

Producer Dick Shurman was responsible for Brown's only two albums: the Handy Award-winning *Big Brown's Chicago Blues* for Black Magic in 1982 and *On the Case* for Double Trouble three years later. But Brown was already suffering from lung cancer when the second LP emerged. He died a short time later. — *Bill Dahl*

● **Big Brown's Chicago Blues** / Oct. 5, 1981+Oct. 25, 1981 / Black Magic ✦✦✦✦
Quite an impressive full-length debut, even if American audiences were hard-pressed to locate a copy. Well-chosen covers—Joe Tex's "I Want To (Do Everything for You)," Betty Everett's "Your Love Is Important to Me," Bobby Rush's "Mary Jane"—mingle with six attractive originals. — *Bill Dahl*

On the Case / Aug. 9, 1983-Oct. 26, 1984 / Double Trouble ✦✦✦✦
Another classy contemporary blues album that frustratingly still awaits domestic CD reissue, just like its predecessor. Once again, the tasty guitarist exhibits intriguing taste in covers, reviving Donna Hightower's "Right Now," Little Milton's "Losing Hand," and the immortal Birdlegs & Pauline's "Spring." But the majority of the set consists of well-conceived originals. Jimmy Johnson is on board as rhythm guitarist. — *Bill Dahl*

Buster Brown

b. Aug. 15, 1911, Cordele, GA, **d.** Jan. 31, 1976, Brooklyn, NY
Harmonica, Vocals / R&B, Electric Blues, Electric Harmonica Blues
Whooping blues harpists nearing the age of 50 with number one R&B hits to their credit were predictably scarce in 1959. Nevertheless, that's the happy predicament Buster Brown found himself in when his infectious "Fannie Mae" paced the charts. Even more amazingly, the driving number made serious inroads on the pop airwaves as well.

The Georgian, whose harp style was clearly influenced by Sonny Terry, had never made a professional recording (there was a 1943 Library of Congress session that laid unissued at the time) before Fire Records boss Bobby Robinson brought the short, stockily built Brown into a New York studio in June of 1959 to wax "Fannie Mae."

Brown's reign as an unlikely star was short-lived. He managed minor follow-up hits on Fire with a rather ragged 1960 revival of Louis Jordan's "Is You Is or Is You Ain't My Baby" and his 1962 farewell bow, the effervescent rocker "Sugar Babe." A subsequent 1964 stop at Chicago's Checker Records produced a glistening update of the old blues "Crawlin' Kingsnake" that sank without a trace. — *Bill Dahl*

● **The New King of the Blues** / 1960-1961 / Collectables ✦✦✦✦
Best of the Fire sessions, including No. 1 hit "Fannie Mae" and "Is You Is or Is You Ain't My Baby?" — *Barry Lee Pearson*

Raise a Ruckus Tonight / 1960-1961 / DJM ✦✦✦✦
Twenty-one Fire Records masters by the whooping harmonica ace, including his classic "Fannie Mae" (in crystal-clear stereo), the irresistible "Sugar Babe," and a load of similar stompers that should have been hits but weren't—"Good News," "Doctor Brown," the previously unissued "No More," "Lost in a Dream." Brown occasionally made an unwise stab at something other than 12-bar fare; "Blueberry Hill," "St. Louis Blues," and the Moonglows' "Sincerely" definitely didn't suit Brown's raucous, untutored approach. — *Bill Dahl*

Good News / 1996 / Charly ✦✦✦

Charles Brown

b. Sep. 13, 1922, Texas City, TX
Piano, Vocals / R&B, Electric West Coast Blues, West Coast Blues, Acoustic West Coast Blues, Urban Blues, Piano Blues
How many blues artists remain at the absolute top of their game after more than a half century of performing? One immediately leaps to mind: Charles Brown. His incredible piano skills and laidback vocal delivery remain every bit as mesmerizing today as they were way back in 1945, when his groundbreaking waxing of "Drifting Blues" with guitarist Johnny Moore's Three Blazers invented an entirely new blues genre for sophisticated postwar revelers—an ultra-mellow, jazz-inflected sound perfect for sipping a late-night libation in some hip after-hours joint. Brown's smooth trio format was tremendously influential to a host of high-profile disciples—Ray Charles, Amos Milburn, and Floyd Dixon, for starters.

Classically trained on the ivories, Brown earned a degree in chemistry before moving to Los Angeles in 1943. He soon hooked up with the Blazers (Moore and bassist Eddie Williams), who modeled themselves after Nat "King" Cole's trio but retained a bluesier tone within their ballad-heavy repertoire. With Brown installed as their vocalist and pianist, the Blazers' "Drifting Blues" for Philo Records remained on *Billboard's* R&B charts for 23 weeks, peaking at number two. Follow-ups for Exclusive and Modern (including "Sunny Road," "So Long," "New Orleans Blues," and their immortal 1947 Yuletide classic "Merry Christmas Baby") kept the Blazers around the top of the R&B listings from 1946 through 1948, until Brown opted to go solo.

If anything, Brown was even more successful on his own. Signing with Eddie Mesner's Aladdin logo, he visited the R&B Top Ten no less than ten times from 1949 to 1952, retaining his mournful, sparsely arranged sound for the smashes "Get Yourself Another Fool," the chart-topping "Trouble Blues" and "Black Night," and "Hard Times." Despite a 1956 jaunt to New Orleans to record with the Cosimo's studio band, Brown's mellow approach failed to make the transition to rock's brasher rhythms, and he soon faded from national prominence (other than when his second holiday perennial, "Please Come Home for Christmas," hit in 1960 on the King label).

Occasionally recording without causing much of a stir during the '60s and '70s, Brown began to regroup by the mid-'80s. *One More for the Road*, a set cut in 1986 for the short-lived Blue Side logo, announced to anyone within earshot that Brown's talents hadn't diminished at all while he was gone (the set later reemerged on Alligator). Bonnie Raitt took an encouraging interest in Brown's comeback bid, bringing him on tour with her as her opening act (thus introducing the blues vet to a whole new generation of fans). His recording career took off too, with a series of albums for Bullseye Blues (the first entry, 1990's *All My Life*, is especially pleasing), and more recently, a disc for Verve.

Today, touring extensively with a terrific combo in tow headed by guitarist Danny Caron, Charles Brown is finally receiving at least a portion of the recognition he's deserved for so long as a genuine rhythm and blues pioneer. But the suave, elegant Brown is by no means a relic, as anyone who's witnessed his thundering boogie piano style will gladly attest! — *Bill Dahl*

1944-1945 / 1944-Sep. 11, 1945 / Classics ✦✦✦✦
This Classics CD features pianist/vocalist Charles Brown on his first 22 recordings, when he was a sideman with guitarist Johnny Moore's Three Blazers. Brown already sounded quite distinctive, and as it turned out, the 21st song ("Drifting Blues") was his biggest hit. The music, due to the instrumentation (a trio/quartet with bassist Eddie Williams and sometimes Oscar Moore on second guitar), is a bit reminiscent at times of the Nat King Cole

Trio, but it had a special soul and feeling of its own. Frankie Laine makes a couple of early appearances, but Brown takes care of the bulk of the vocals, and there are also eight excellent instrumentals. Recommended. — *Scott Yanow*

☆ **The Complete Aladdin Recordings of Charles Brown** / Sep. 11, 1945-Sep. 4, 1956 / Mosaic ✦✦✦✦✦
Every single brilliant side—some 109 in all—that this elegant, tremendously influential pianist cut for the Mesner brothers' Philo and Aladdin imprints from 1945 to 1956 is housed in this lavishly produced five-disc boxed set. Mosaic's customary attention to detail is evident in the packaging and the sound; Brown's brilliance makes the entire box a delight, from his earliest sessions with the Three Blazers through his hitmaking run as a solo star during the late '40s and early '50s. The genesis of the entire West Coast "club blues" style resides in this box; its expense is well worth it. — *Bill Dahl*

Snuff Dippin' Mama / 1946-1947 / Night Train ✦✦✦✦
Even with the above box, you won't own all of Brown's seminal work. In 1946, he and the Blazers landed at Exclusive Records, which is the era that this collection examines via 19 fine sides including the jivey "Juke Box Lil" and "C.O.D.," a mournful "Sunny Road," and the jazzy "B-Sharp You'll See." Guitarist Johnny Moore and bassist Eddie Williams were indeed sharp in smooth support. — *Bill Dahl*

★ **Driftin' Blues: The Best of** / 1948-1956 / EMI America ✦✦✦✦✦
If your budget only allows the acquisition of a single CD of Brown's Aladdin material, let it be this one. It sports most of the truly important hits that inspired so many West Coasters—"Driftin' Blues," "Black Night," "Trouble Blues," and many others. — *Bill Dahl*

Driftin' Blues / 1963 / DCC ✦✦
Brown's balladeer leanings come heavily to the fore on these lushly arranged 1963 sides, originally produced by Bob Shad for issue on his Mainstream logo. He croons Steve Lawrence's "Go Away Little Girl," Ruby & the Romantics' "Our Day Will Come," and Henry Mancini's "Days of Wine and Roses" in his mellowest supper-club style—which simply doesn't match up to what came before. Charles plays organ on this album, contributing to the lounge-like ambience. — *Bill Dahl*

The Boss of the Blues / 1963 / Mainstream ✦✦
More 1963-64 Mainstream sides with some duplication—the first six tracks here also appear on the DCC compilation. Tracks seven through sixteen find Brown surrounded by strings as he smoothly intones "Pledging My Love," "Blueberry Hill," and "Cottage for Sale" (they didn't even let him sit down at the keyboard at all for these dates!). — *Bill Dahl*

Sunny Land / 1979 / Route 66 ✦✦✦✦
This is a nice cross-section of the pianist's smooth early work for a variety of labels. — *Bill Dahl*

One More for the Road / Aug. 6, 1986-Aug. 8, 1986 / Alligator ✦✦✦
One of the first comeback salvos that the veteran pianist fired after suffering the slings and arrows of anonymity for much too long. Typically delectable in a subtle, understated manner, Brown eases through a very attractive program. — *Bill Dahl*

All My Life / 1990 / Bullseye Blues ✦✦✦✦
By far Brown's best contemporary effort (and the set that really got his recording career back in high gear). Cameos by Dr. John and Ruth Brown certainly didn't hurt the set's chances, but it's the eternally suave pianist and his excellent road band (especially guitarist Danny Caron and saxist Clifford Solomon) that make this such a delightful collection. — *Bill Dahl*

Someone to Love / 1992 / Bullseye Blues ✦✦✦
Bonnie Raitt, who played such an integral role in Brown's successful comeback, guests on two tracks on the pianist's Bullseye Blues encore, which isn't quite the tour de force that his previous outing was but is eminently solid nonetheless. Caron and Solomon once again shine in support of their leader. — *Bill Dahl*

Cool Christmas Blues / 1994 / Rounder ✦✦✦
Long recognized as the perennial top contender when it comes to Yuletide R&B, Brown salutes the holiday season in his own inimitable manner. Naturally, there's the umpteenth remake of his seminal "Merry Christmas Baby," along with several more that he's been crooning every December since before most of us were born. But nobody does 'em better! — *Bill Dahl*

Just a Lucky So and So / Jan. 24, 1994 / Bullseye Blues ✦✦
Charles Brown's casual, yet stunning phrasing, inventive voicings and piano accompaniment are wonderfully presented on this 10-song set. Ron Levy's production and the arrangements of Wardell Quezergue and Brown are tasteful, breezy and geared for his carefully constructed, teasing solos and rich, creamy leads. Such numbers as Brown's classic "Drifting Blues," as well as "Gloomy Sunday" and "I Won't Cry Anymore," convey despair and hurt, yet retain a certain appeal and charm. Brown keeps making fine records, sounding as convincing in the 1990s as he did at the start of his career. — *Ron Wynn*

Honey Dripper / Nov. 5, 1996 / Verve ✦✦✦✦
"Soothing" is not a word normally associated with blues, but it's the word that best captures the experience of listening to Charles Brown, and *Honey Dripper* is no exception. Listening to it is like sipping a fine bottle of cognac. Seventy-two years old at the time of this recording session, Brown sounds agile, almost ageless. Indeed, time seems to stand still when he plays and sings in that same understated, urbane manner he popularized with Johnny Moore's Three Blazers back in the 1940s. Like his other recordings this decade, *Honey Dripper* features Brown's regular working combo, led by guitarist Danny Caron and including saxophonist Clifford Solomon. The songs range from straight-ahead blues to jazz ballads, with some straddling the line. — *Steve Hoffman*

Clarence "Gatemouth" Brown

b. Apr. 18, 1924, Vinton, LA
Guitar, Mandolin, Violin, Drums, Vocals, Bass, Harmonica / Texas Blues
Whatever you do, don't refer to multi-instrumentalist Clarence "Gatemouth" Brown as a bluesman, although his imprimatur on the development of Texas blues is enormous. You're liable to get him riled. If you must pigeonhole the legend, just call him an eclectic Texas musical master whose interests encompass virtually every roots genre imaginable.

Brown learned the value of versatility while growing up in Orange, TX. His dad was a locally popular musician who specialized in country, cajun, and bluegrass—but not blues. Later, Brown was entranced by the big bands of Count Basie, Lionel Hampton, and Duke Ellington (a torrid arrangement of "Take the 'A' Train" remains a centerpiece of Brown's repertoire). Tagged with the "Gatemouth" handle by a high school instructor who accused Brown of having a "voice like a gate," Brown has used it to his advantage throughout his illustrious career. (His older brother, James "Widemouth" Brown, recorded "Boogie Woogie Nighthawk" for Jax in 1951.)

In 1947, Gate's impromptu fill-in for an ailing T-Bone Walker at Houston entrepreneur Don Robey's Bronze Peacock nightclub convinced Robey to assume control of Brown's career. After two singles for Aladdin stiffed, Robey inaugurated his own Peacock label in 1949 to showcase Gate's blistering riffs, which proved influential to a legion of Houston string-benders (Albert Collins, Johnny Copeland, Johnny "Guitar" Watson, Cal Green, and many more have pledged allegiance to Brown's riffs). Peacock and its sister label Duke prospered through the '50s and '60s.

Gate stayed with Peacock through 1960. The R&B charts didn't reflect Brown's importance (he hit only once nationwide with 1949's two-sided smash "Mary Is Fine"/"My Time Is Expensive"). But his blazing instrumentals ("Boogie Uproar," "Gate Walks to Board," 1954's seminal "Okie Dokie Stomp"), horn-enriched rockers ("She Walked Right In," "Rock My Blues Away") and lowdown Lone Star blues ("Dirty Work at the Crossroads") are a major component of the rich Texas postwar blues legacy. Brown broke new ground often—even in the '50s, he insisted on sawing his fiddle at live performances, although Robey wasn't interested in capturing Gate's violin talent until "Just Before Dawn" (his final Peacock platter in 1959).

The '60s weren't all that kind to Brown. His cover of Little Jimmy Dickens' country novelty "May the Bird of Paradise Fly Up Your Nose" for tiny Hermitage Records made a little noise in 1965 (and presaged things to come stylistically). But the decade was chiefly memorable for Brown's 1966 stint as house bandleader for *The!!!!Beat*, a groundbreaking syndicated R&B television program out of Dallas hosted by WLAC deejay Bill "Hoss" Allen.

When Gate began to rebuild his career in the '70s, he was determined to do things his way. Country, jazz, even calypso now played a prominent role in his concerts; he's as likely to launch into an oldtime fiddle hoedown as a swinging guitar blues. He turned up on *Hee Haw* with pickin' and grinnin' pal Roy Clark after they cut a sizzling 1979 duet album for MCA, *Makin' Music*. Acclaimed discs for Rounder, Alligator, and Verve over the last 15 years have proven that Gatemouth Brown is a steadfastly unclassifiable American original. —*Bill Dahl*

San Antonio Ballbuster / Dec. 1948-Sep. 1959 / Red Lightnin' ◆◆◆◆
Considering how sub-par the sound quality is on this disc (it's a CD reproduction of an old Red Lightnin' bootleg), it wouldn't rate a recommendation if the material therein were otherwise available. But many of these Peacock masters aren't obtainable anywhere else—the stunning 1953 instrumental "Boogie Uproar," storming rockers "Win with Me Baby," "You Got Money," and "Just Got Lucky," and the after-hours hit "I've Been Mistreated," for starters. So until something better comes along.... —*Bill Dahl*

★ **The Original Peacock Recordings** / 1948-1959 / Rounder ◆◆◆◆◆
Only 12 songs long, this collection remains the best place to begin appreciating why so many young Texas blues guitarists fell in love with Gatemouth Brown's style (until MCA decides to compile the ultimate Brown package, anyway). Listen to the way his blazing axe darts and weaves through trombonist Pluma Davis' jazzy horn chart on 1954's "Okie Dokie Stomp," or the stratospheric licks drenching "Dirty Work at the Crossroads." Brown proves that a violin can adapt marvelously to the blues (in the right hands, anyway) on "Just Before Dawn," and blows a little atmospheric harp on "Gate's Salty Blues." —*Bill Dahl*

San Antonio Ballbuster [Charly] / 1965 / Charly ◆◆◆
It's 1965, and Gate's guitar sound is different—not so brash and trebly but smoother, with more of a jazz and occasional country kick. Most of these sides were never issued after being acquired by Chess. There are two takes of Little Jimmy Dickens' C&W novelty hit "May the Bird of Paradise," both of 'em swinging easy. Gate was in a Sonny Boy Williamson mood that day, reviving three of the harpist's oldies along with a few of his own and the ominous blues "Long Way Home," which threatens mayhem most charmingly. —*Bill Dahl*

The Blues Ain't Nothin' / 1972 / Black & Blue ◆◆◆

Just Got Lucky / Mar. 22, 1973-Jul. 1, 1973 / Evidence ◆◆◆◆
More goodies from the same French 1973 dates (originally issued on Black & Blue). Lots of Jordan covers, along with Brown's own "Here Am I" and "Long Way Home," three Peacock remakes, and a sizzling revival of Bill Doggett's "Honey Boy." The last three titles date from a 1977 session, again cut in France, and are all Brown originals. —*Bill Dahl*

Sings Louis Jordan / Jul. 22, 1973-Jul. 24, 1973 / Black & Blue ◆◆◆
Enjoyable foray thru Jordan's songbook by a master guitarist. —*Bill Dahl*

Pressure Cooker / Jul. 23, 1973-Aug. 1, 1973 / Alligator ◆◆◆◆
Before Gate was able to rebuild a following stateside, he frequently toured Europe. He recorded the contents of this inexorably swinging set in France in 1973 with all-star backing by keyboardists Milt Buckner and Jay McShann, saxists Arnett Cobb and Hal Singer, among others. Brown indulges his passion for Louis Jordan by ripping through "Ain't That Just like a Woman" and "Ain't Nobody Here but Us Chickens" and exhibits his immaculate fretwork on the torrid title item. —*Bill Dahl*

Cold Strange / Jul. 31, 1973-Aug. 1, 1973 / Black & Blue ◆◆◆
Swinging guitar and tasty vocals. —*Bill Dahl*

Gate's on the Heat / 1975 / Barclay ◆◆
The worst Brown album currently on the shelves. Cut back in the '70s with a band that wouldn't know how to swing if it were permanently marooned on a playground (the rhythm guitarist is particularly abominable), this one's a must to avoid. —*Bill Dahl*

Black Jack / 1975 / Music Is Medicine ◆◆◆
It may not be the strongest LP in his catalog, but Gate's first domestic album offerred more than a hint of things to come with its daring mixture of country, jazz, and blues numbers. —*Bill Dahl*

Bogalusa Boogie Man / 1976 / Barclay ◆◆

Makin' Music [Roy Clark] / Oct. 31, 1978-Nov. 2, 1978 / MCA ◆◆◆◆
Surround two of the most versatile guitar pickers on the planet in a studio with a cadre of world-class sidemen and what do you get? This irresistible duet album by Gate and Roy Clark, first out on MCA. Good vibes abound as the fun-loving pair blast out "Caldonia," "Take the 'A' Train," "The Drifter,"

"Justice Blues," and more, trading licks, vocals, and quips with a jam session-oriented looseness. —*Bill Dahl*

Alright Again! / Jun. 2, 1981-Jun. 8, 1981 / Rounder ◆◆◆◆
One of the most satisfying contemporary Brown discs of all for the discerning blues fan. Nothing but swinging, horn-abetted blues adorn this album, as Gate pays tribute to an influence and a protege by covering T-Bone Walker's "Strollin' with Bones" and Albert Collins' "Frosty." Brown jauntily revives Junior Parker's "I Feel Alright Again" and Percy Mayfield's "Give Me Time to Explain," while his own numbers—a funky "Dollar Got the Blues," the luxurious blues "Sometimes I Slip"—are truly brilliant. —*Bill Dahl*

One More Mile / Oct. 1982 / Rounder ◆◆◆
Considerably more varied than its predecessor, with nods toward the Louisiana swamp ("Sunrise Cajun Style," complete with pedal steel guitar), sentimental ballads (Cecil Gant's "I Wonder"), and jazz ("Big Yard"). Blues purists will perk up for revivals of Junior Parker's "Stranded" and Roy Milton's "Information Blues." —*Bill Dahl*

Atomic Energy / 1984 / Blues Boy ◆◆◆◆
Another cross-section of old Peacock efforts, there is some sound quality. —*Bill Dahl*

More Stuff / 1985 / Black & Blue ◆◆◆

Real Life (Live) / Sep. 4, 1985-Sep. 7, 1985 / Rounder ◆◆◆
Live set cut in Fort Worth, TX, that presents an accurate depiction of the breadth and scope of a Gatemouth Brown concert. Switching between guitar and violin, Gate offers everything from a reprise of "Okie Dokie Stomp" to a tender "Please Send Me Someone to Love" from Percy Mayfield's songbook and personalized renditions of "St. Louis Blues" and "Frankie and Johnny." —*Bill Dahl*

Texas Swing / 1988 / Rounder ◆◆◆◆

Standing My Ground / 1989 / Alligator ◆◆◆◆
A delightfully eclectic program spotlighting nearly all of Gate's musical leanings—blues, jazz, country, even a hearty taste of "Louisiana Zydeco"—and a revealing glimpse of his multi-instrumental abilities: he plays guitar, violin, drums, and piano! There's a tender remake of the Chuck Willis R&B ballad and a funk-tinged update of "Got My Mojo Working," but everything else is from Brown's own pen. —*Bill Dahl*

No Looking Back / 1992 / Alligator ◆◆◆
Clarence "Gatemouth" Brown was one of the most jazz-oriented of bluesmen, a colorful guitarist and a primitive but swinging fiddler. On this release he includes many instrumental sections in his performances including four all-out boppish jazz jams ("Digging New Ground," "C-Jam Blues," "The Peeper," and the stomping "We're Outta Here"). Brown's vocals, which feature consistently intelligent lyrics ("Better Off with the Blues" is particularly memorable), are part of the music rather than the entire show; he even gives his obscure backup horns chances to solo. The set is a particularly strong example of Gatemouth Brown's music with each of the 11 selections (except perhaps for "I Will Be Your Friend," a poppish vocal duet with Michelle Shocked) being well worth hearing. —*Scott Yanow*

Live 1980 / Dec. 6, 1994 / Charly ◆◆◆

Man / 1995 / Verve ◆◆◆
Brown made the big jump to major-label stature for this typically unclassifiable set, which feistily sweeps through zydeco ("Big Mammou"), country ("Up Jumped the Devil"), Louis Jordan ("Early in the Morning"), and even a little blues along its unpredictable course. Cajun accordionist Jo-El Sonnier receives several solos in a guest-starring role. —*Bill Dahl*

The Best of Clarence Gatemouth Brown, A Blues Legend / Oct. 1995 / Verve ◆◆◆

A Long Way Home / Apr. 1996 / Verve ◆◆
One of the few lousy recordings of this determinedly eclectic multi-instrumentalist's lengthy career. He's stuck going the superstar cameo route à la John Lee Hooker (there's less Gate on this disc than on any other Gate set), welcoming Eric Clapton aboard for some amazingly generic guitar solos; vocally duetting with frog-voiced Leon Russell and chirpy Maria Muldaur, and backing Loudermilk as he sings his own composition "Tobacco Road" (where's Lou Rawls when you need him?). A handful of acoustic numbers

add depth, but there's not much here at all that's likely to satisfy Gate's legion of blues fans. — *Bill Dahl*

Gate Swings / Jul. 15, 1997 / Verve ◆◆◆

J.T. Brown

b. Apr. 2, 1918, MS, **d.** Nov. 24, 1969, Chicago, IL
Vocals, Sax (Tenor) / Chicago Blues, Electric Blues
His braying tenor sax tone earned J.T. Brown the dubious distinction of being told his horn sounded like a "nanny goat." That didn't stop the likes of Elmore James from hiring Brown for some of his most important sessions for Meteor and Modern, though; Brown's style was truly distinctive.

Mississippi-born John T. Brown was a member of the Rabbit Foot Minstrels down South before arriving in the Windy City. By 1945, Brown was recording behind pianist Roosevelt Sykes and singer St. Louis Jimmy Oden, later backing Eddie Boyd and Washboard Sam for RCA Victor. He debuted on wax as a bandleader in 1950 on the Harlem label, subsequently cutting sessions in 1951 and 1952 for Chicago's United logo as well as JOB.

Brown's sideman credentials included wailing riffs beside slide guitarist Elmore James and pianist Little Johnny Jones for the Bihari brothers' Meteor and Flair logos in 1952 and 1953. Meteor issued a couple of singles under Brown's own name (well, sort of) during the same timeframe: "Round House Boogie"/"Kickin' the Blues Around" was credited to the Bep Brown Orchestra, while "Sax-ony Boogie" was listed as by Saxman Brown and its flip, the vocal "Dumb Woman Blues," as by J.T. "Big Boy" Brown! All four are available on Flair's four-disc James box set, incidentally.

After a final 1956 date for United that laid unissued at the time, Brown's studio activities were limited to sideman roles. In January of 1969, he was part of Fleetwood Mac's *Blues Jam at Chess* album, even singing a tune for the project, but he died before the close of that year. — *Bill Dahl*

Rockin' with J.T. / 1950-Oct. 1952 / Krazy Kat ◆◆◆◆
Rockin' with J.T. collects a number of tracks J.T. Brown recorded during the late '40s and early '50s. Unfortunately, many of these songs—some of which were changed upon the 1984 reissue, so that the collection could feature songs that weren't on *Windy City Boogie*—feature Brown only as a sideman, working with the likes of Washboard Sam, Roosevelt Sykes, and Booker T. Washington. That said, the cuts with him as a sideman positively smoke, and his jumping saxophone is a good reason why. There are also a handful of songs he cut with his own band that round out this imperfect but quite valuable collection. — *Thom Owens*

● **Windy City Boogie** / Jul. 12, 1951-1956 / Pearl ◆◆◆◆
Inexplicably still unavailable on CD, this LP showcases Brown's hearty vocals and "nanny goat horn" in a bandleading role. With frequent cohort Little Brother Montgomery deftly tinkling the ivories, Brown delivers "Blackjack Blues" and "When I Was a Lad." Storming boogie instrumentals were an integral part of Brown's repertoire; this set (spanning 1951-1956) boasts a host of stellar houserockers. — *Bill Dahl*

Nappy Brown

b. Oct. 12, 1929, Charlotte, NC
Vocals / Jump Blues, R&B, Modern Electric Blues
Nobody sounded much like Nappy Brown during the mid-'50s. Exotically rolling his consonants with sing-song impugnity (allegedly, Savoy Records boss Herman Lubinsky thought Brown was singing in Yiddish), bellowing the blues with gospel-inspired ferocity, Brown rode rock 'n' roll's first wave for a few glorious years before his records stopped selling. But a dozen years ago or thereabouts, Brown seemingly rose from the dead to stage a comeback bid. Now he's ensconced once again as a venerable blues veteran who'll stop at nothing (including rolling around the stage in sexual simulation) to enthrall his audience.

Napoleon Brown's sanctified screams come naturally—he grew up in Charlotte, NC, singing gospel as well as blues. He was fronting a spiritual aggregation, the Heavenly Lights, who were signed to the roster of Newark, NJ's Savoy Records when Lubinsky convinced the leather-lunged shouter to cross the secular line in 1954. Voila! Nappy Brown the R&B singer was born.

Brown brought hellfire intensity to his blues-soaked Savoy debut, "Is It True," but it was "Don't Be Angry" the next year that caused his fortunes to skyrocket. The sizzling rocker sported loads of Brown's unique vocal gimmicks and a hair-raising tenor sax solo by Sam "the Man" Taylor, becoming his first national smash. Those onboard New York session aces didn't hurt the overall ambience of Brown's Savoy dates—Taylor's scorching horn further enlivened "Open up That Door," while Budd Johnson or Al Sears took over on other equally raucous efforts. Novelty-tinged upbeat items such as "Little by Little" and "Piddily Patter Patter" defined Nappy's output, but his throat-busting turn on the 1957 blues "The Right Time" (borrowed by Ray Charles in short order!) remains a highlight of Brown's early heyday.

After decades away from the limelight, Nappy resurfaced in 1984 with a very credible album for Landslide Records, *Tore Up*, with guitarist Tinsley Ellis' band, the Heartfixers. Since then, he's recorded a fine set for Black Top (*Something Gonna Jump Out the Bushes*) with Anson Funderburgh, Ronnie Earl, and Earl King sharing guitar duties, and some not-so-fine CDs for other logos. — *Bill Dahl*

That Man / Mar. 31, 1954-Aug. 21, 1961 / Swift ◆◆◆◆
That Man collects 17 songs Nappy Brown recorded for Savoy Records between 1954 and 1961, including "The Right Time," "Down in the Alley," and "Is It True." The compilation spotlights his lesser-known recordings, not his hits, but these songs are every bit as good as his more popular material from the same era. — *Thom Owens*

Nappy Brown Sings / 1955 / Savoy ◆◆◆◆
Scorching N.Y. R&B from the '50s. — *Bill Dahl*

★ **Don't Be Angry!** / Feb. 1, 1955-Oct. 4, 1956 / Savoy ◆◆◆◆◆
Rolling his consonants like a crazed cantor, shouter Nappy Brown brought a gospel-imbued fervor to his rocking mid-'50s output that few of his peers could match. Backed by some of New York's finest sessioneers, Brown roars 16 of his best early Savoy sides on this essential purchase. "Don't Be Angry," "Just a Little Love," "Open Up That Door," and "Bye Bye Baby" rate with his hottest jump efforts. "I Cried like a Baby" and "It's Really You" are hair-raising blues, and "Little by Little" rides a bouncy, pop-accessible groove. Now where's volume two?? — *Bill Dahl*

The Right Time / 1958 / Savoy ◆◆◆◆
Scorching N.Y. R&B from the '50s. — *Bill Dahl*

I Done Got Over / Feb. 26, 1983-Apr. 1983 / Stockholm ◆◆
I Done Got Over features some good vocal performances from Nappy Brown, but this album—which essentially runs through his '50s hits, with a couple new tracks thrown in for good measure—is one of his lesser works. Brown is supported by the Roosters, a stiff Swedish band that can't get the music cooking. Consequently, Brown never puts forth much of an effort. The result is a disappointingly uninspired record. — *Thom Owens*

Tore Up / Aug. 1984 / Alligator ◆◆◆
After too many years during which he was missing and presumed forever lost in action, Brown returned to prominence with this very credible album, cut with backing by guitarist Tinsley Ellis and the Heartfixers and originally issued on the tiny Landslide logo. He reprises his salacious blues in "Lemon Squeezin' Daddy" and rolls his R's like the good old days on dusties by Little Walter, the Midnighters, Howlin' Wolf, and even Bob Dylan and the Allmans. — *Bill Dahl*

Something Gonna Jump out the Bushes / Apr. 1987 / Black Top ◆◆◆◆
Ultra-solid support from guitarists Anson Funderburgh, Eugene Ross, Ronnie Earl, and Earl King, and Black Top's superb house horn section make this Dallas-cut set Brown's best contemporary album to date. His lusty shouting style works well on covers of the Dominoes' "Have Mercy Baby," the "5" Royales' title track, a pair of Earl King-penned numbers, and Robert Ward's "Your Love Is Real." — *Bill Dahl*

Just for Me / 1988 / JSP ◆◆

Deep Sea Diver / 1989 / Meltone ◆◆
Deep Sea Diver is a competent, but not particularly inspiring, live album recorded in 1989. Occasionally, Nappy Brown turns in a fiery performance—particularly on "Things Have Changed" and the title track—but just as often, his singing is workmanlike. There are enough good moments to make the album worthwhile for fans, but it is not an essential purchase. — *Thom Owens*

Apples & Lemons / 1990 / Ichiban ◆◆◆
Early-'90s jump blues, shouting R&B, and gospel-edged soul from Nappy Brown, who made his finest material in the '50s and '60s, but has done some

exuberant material during the '80s and '90s. While his voice doesn't have the swagger or ferocity it did in its heyday, it's still impressive enough to give this the residue of authenticity. — *Ron Wynn*

Aw! Shucks / Jan. 1991-Feb. 1991 / Ichiban ♦♦

Aw! Shucks is one of Nappy Brown's most uninspired efforts. Out of the nine songs, only one was written by Brown; the remaining eight were written by various songwriters, including members of the Ichiban staff. None of the songs are engaging and they're made even worse by flat, uninspired performances. The musicians may be accomplished professionals, but they can't breathe life into any of these songs. — *Thom Owens*

I'm a Wild Man / Jun. 1, 1995 / New Moon ♦♦♦

Who's Been Foolin' You / May 20, 1997 / New Moon ♦♦♦

Roy Brown

b. Sep. 10, 1925, New Orleans, LA, **d.** May 25, 1981, San Fernando, CA
Piano, Vocals / R&B, Rock 'n' Roll, Jump Blues, West Coast Blues
When you draw up a short list of the R&B pioneers who exerted a primary influence on the development of rock 'n' roll, respectfully place singer Roy Brown's name near its very top. His seminal 1947 DeLuxe Records waxing of "Good Rockin' Tonight" was immediately ridden to the peak of the R&B charts by shouter Wynonie Harris and subsequently covered by Elvis Presley, Ricky Nelson, Jerry Lee Lewis, and many more early rock icons (even Pat Boone!). In addition, Brown's melismatically pleading, gospel-steeped delivery impacted the vocal styles of B.B. King, Bobby Bland, and Little Richard (among a plethora of important singers). Clearly, Roy Brown was an innovator—and from 1948-1951, an R&B star whose wild output directly presaged rock's rise.

Born in the Crescent City, Brown grew up all over the place: Eunice, LA (where he sang in church and worked in the sugarcane fields), Houston, TX, and finally Los Angeles by age 17. Back then, Bing Crosby was Roy's favorite singer—but a nine-month stint at a Shreveport, LA, nightclub exposed him to the blues for the first time. He conjured up "Good Rockin' Tonight" while fronting a band in Galveston, TX. Ironically, Harris wanted no part of the song when Brown first tried to hand it to him. When pianist Cecil Gant heard Brown's knockout rendition of the tune in New Orleans, he had Roy sing it over the phone to a sleepy DeLuxe boss, Jules Braun, in the wee hours of the morning! Though Brown's original waxing (with Bob Ogden's band in support) was a solid hit, Harris' cover beat him out for top chart honors.

Roy didn't have to wait long to dominate the R&B lists himself. He scored 15 hits from mid-1948 to late 1951 for DeLuxe, ranging from the emotionally wracked crying blues "Hard Luck Blues" (his biggest seller of all in 1950) to the party-time rockers "Rockin' at Midnight," "Boogie at Midnight," "Miss Fanny Brown," and "Cadillac Baby." Strangely, his sales slumped badly from 1952 on, even though his frantic "Hurry Hurry Baby," "Ain't No Rockin' No More," "Black Diamond," and "Gal from Kokomo" for Cincinnati's King Records rate among his hottest houserockers.

Brown was unable to cash in on the rock 'n' roll idiom he helped to invent, though he briefly rejuvenated his commercial fortunes at Imperial Records in 1957. Working with New Orleans producer Dave Bartholomew, then riding high with Fats Domino, Brown returned to the charts with the original version of "Let the Four Winds Blow" (later a hit for Fats) and cut the sizzling sax-powered rockers "Diddy-Y-Diddy-O," "Saturday Night," and "Ain't Gonna Do It." Not everything was an artistic triumph; Brown's utterly lifeless cover of Buddy Knox's "Party Doll"—amazingly, a chart entry for Brown—may well be the worst thing he ever committed to wax (rivaled only by a puerile "School Bell Rock" cut during a momentary return to King in 1959).

After a long dry spell, Brown's acclaimed performance as part of Johnny Otis' troupe at the 1970 Monterey Jazz Festival and a 1973 LP for ABC-Blues-Way began to rebuild his long-lost momentum. But it came too late—Brown died of a heart attack in 1981 at age 56, his role as a crucial link between postwar R&B and rock's initial rise still underappreciated by the masses. — *Bill Dahl*

★ **Good Rocking Tonight: The Best of Roy Brown** / 1947-1957 / Rhino ♦♦♦♦♦

An unassailable 18-cut cross-section of the monstrously popular and influential New Orleans jump blues shouter's sides for DeLuxe, King, and Imperial labels that spans 1947-57 and takes in his seminal "Good Rocking To-

night" (where it all began!), "Rockin' at Midnight," "Boogie at Midnight," and "Love Don't Love Nobody"; the almost unbearably tortured "Hard Luck Blues," and the unbelievably raunchy two-parter "Butcher Pete." Looking for the origins of rock? Here they are! — *Bill Dahl*

Mighty Mighty Man! / 1953-1959 / Ace ♦♦♦♦

Another British import that really delivers the rocking goods! This time zeroing in on Brown's 1953-59 King sides exclusively, the 22-cut CD shows that Brown actually picked up his tempos to meet rock's rise head on. The clever sequel "Ain't No Rocking No More," "Black Diamond," "Gal from Kokomo," and "Shake 'Em Up Baby" rate with his hottest rockers, with great support from a crew of Crescent City stalwarts. — *Bill Dahl*

The Complete Imperial Recordings / Sep. 27, 1956-Mar. 6, 1958 / Capitol ♦♦♦

In the mid-'50s Brown, like many other early R&B pioneers, was a bit lost at sea amid the rock 'n' roll explosion. From 1956 to 1958, he recorded these 20 tracks for Imperial under the direction of legendary New Orleans R&B producer Dave Bartholomew. Brown and Bartholomew were attempting to update Brown's jump blues/R&B hybrid with a lot of Fats Domino-type Crescent City influence on these sides. The results weren't bad, but with Bartholomew co-writing most of the tunes and using local musicians like saxophonist Lee Allen, Brown sounded more like a journeyman New Orleans R&B singer than an innovative, bluesy forefather of rock 'n' roll. There were a couple of commercial successes; his cover of Buddy Knox's "Party Doll" made the R&B Top 20, and "Let the Four Winds Blow" actually made the pop Top 40, although Fats Domino would have much greater success with the same song when he covered it a few years later. Diluted by occasional pop and rock influences, as well as a substandard variation of "Good Rockin' Tonight," this compilation shouldn't be the first Brown on your shelf. But for those who want to go a little further, it's packaged very well, with thorough liner notes and seven previously unissued cuts. — *Richie Unterberger*

☆ **Blues Deluxe** / 1991 / Charly ♦♦♦♦♦

More tracks (two dozen in all) from Brown's voluminous DeLuxe and King catalogs make this British import well worth searching around for. Hellacious jumps—"Cadillac Baby," "Good Rockin' Man"—and plenty of rarities distinguish this collection by one of the true pioneers of R&B. — *Bill Dahl*

Ruth Brown

b. Jan. 30, 1928, Portsmouth, VA
Vocals / R&B, Jump Blues
They called Atlantic Records "the house that Ruth built" during the 1950s, and they weren't referring to the Sultan of Swat. Ruth Brown's regal hitmaking reign from 1949 to the close of the '50s helped tremendously to establish the New York label's predominance in the R&B field. Later, the business all but forgot her—she was forced to toil as domestic help for a time—but she's back on top now, her status as a postwar R&B pioneer (and tireless advocate for the rights and royalties of her peers) recognized worldwide.

Young Ruth Weston was inspired initially by jazz chanteuses Sarah Vaughan, Billie Holiday, and Dinah Washington. She ran away from her Portsmouth home in 1945 to hit the road with trumpeter Jimmy Brown, whom she soon married. A month with bandleader Lucky Millinder's orchestra in 1947 ended abruptly in Washington, D.C., when she was canned for delivering a round of drinks to members of the band. Cab Calloway's sister Blanche gave Ruth a gig at her Crystal Caverns nightclub and assumed a managerial role in the young singer's life. DJ Willis Conover dug Brown's act and recommended her to Ahmet Ertegun and Herb Abramson, bosses of a fledgling imprint named Atlantic.

Unfortunately, Brown's debut session for the firm was delayed by a nine-month hospital stay caused by a serious auto accident en route to New York that badly injured her leg. When she finally made it to her first date in May of 1949, she made up for lost time by waxing the torch ballad "So Long" (backed by guitarist Eddie Condon's band), which proved to be her first hit.

Brown's seductive vocal delivery shone incandescently on her Atlantic smashes "Teardrops in My Eyes" (an R&B chart-topper for 11 weeks in 1950), "I'll Wait for You" and "I Know" in 1951, 1952's "5-10-15 Hours" (another number one rocker), the seminal "(Mama) He Treats Your Daughter Mean" in 1953, and a tender Chuck Willis-penned "Oh What a Dream" and the timely "Mambo Baby" the next year. Along the way, Frankie Laine tagged her "Miss Rhythm" during an engagement in Philly. Brown belted a series of her hits on the groundbreaking TV program "Showtime at the Apollo" in 1955, exhibiting delicious comic timing while trading sly one-liners with emcee Willie Bryant (ironically, ex-husband Jimmy Brown was a member of the show's house band!).

After an even two dozen R&B chart appearances for Atlantic that ended in 1960 with "Don't Deceive Me" (many of them featuring hell-raising tenor sax solos by then-hubby Willis "Gator" Jackson), Brown faded from view. After raising her two sons and working a nine-to-five job, Brown began to rebuild her musical career in the mid-'70s. That comedic sense served her well during a TV sitcom stint co-starring with McLean Stevenson in *Hello, Larry;* in a meaty role in director John Waters' 1985 sock-hop satire film *Hairspray,* and during her 1989 Broadway starring turn in *Black and Blue* (which won her a Tony Award).

There have been more records for Fantasy in recent years (notably 1991's jumping *Fine and Mellow*), and a lengthy tenure as host of National Public Radio's "Harlem Hit Parade" and "BluesStage." Brown's nine-year ordeal to recoup her share of royalties from all those Atlantic platters led to the formation of the nonprofit Rhythm & Blues Foundation, an organization dedicated to helping others in the same frustrating situation.

Factor in all those time-consuming activities, and it's a wonder Ruth Brown has time to sing anymore. But she does (quite royally, too), her pipes mellowed but not frayed by the ensuing decades that have seen her rise to stardom not once, but twice. —*Bill Dahl*

Sweet Baby of Mine (1949-1956) / Apr. 6, 1949-Mar. 2, 1956 / Route 66 ✦✦✦✦
Excellent collection covering blues and R&B songs Brown did prior to becoming a huge hit artist for Atlantic in the late '50s. These were R&B gems, but such artists as Patti Page and Georgia Gibbs were covering them for the White market and Brown was locked out until 1957. But she enjoyed 11 Top 10 R&B hits, which are contained on this anthology. —*Ron Wynn*

★ **The Best of Ruth Brown [Rhino]** / May 25, 1949-May 1959 / Rhino ✦✦✦✦✦
For those who want a cheaper and more concise collection of her best Atlantic cuts than the two-CD *Miss Rhythm,* this superb 23-track CD has the cream of her '50s work, including no less than 19 Top Ten R&B singles. Charting her evolution from her jazzy debut, "So Long," through jump blues and early rock 'n' roll, it also adds a bonus of two previously unissued live cuts from 1959. —*Richie Unterberger*

★ **Miss Rhythm (Greatest Hits and More)** / 1949-1960 / Rhino ✦✦✦✦✦
Before Aretha Franklin was exalted as the Queen of Soul, Ruth Brown was dubbed "Miss Rhythm"—and with good reason. A gritty, aggressive belter with an impressive range and a powerhouse of a voice, Brown was the top female R&B singer of the early-to-mid-'50s, and would directly or indirectly have an influence such greats as Etta James and LaVern Baker. A two-CD set ranging from Brown's early hits to engaging obscurities and rarities, *Miss Rhythm* offers a fine overview of her Atlantic years. Early hits like "Mama, He Treats Your Daughter Mean," "Teardrops from My Eyes," "Mambo Baby," and "5-10-15 Hours" point to the fact that a lot of early R&B was essentially blues at a fast tempo. The set also reminds us of early R&B's connection to jazz—in fact, classics like 1949's "So Long" (her first single) and "Have a Good Time" are examples of first-class torch singing. There are numerous Brown albums that are well worth acquiring, but for those interested in exploring her early music for the first time, *Miss Rhythm* is an excellent place to start. —*Alex Henderson*

Ruth Brown Sings Favorites / 1956 / Atlantic ✦✦✦
Ruth Brown had extensive gospel and jazz roots, which Atlantic honed to perfection, turning her into an R&B queen. These songs aren't quite the same, but they show her full stylistic range and also how powerful and strong her voice was in the '50s. —*Ron Wynn*

Ruth Brown / 1957 / Atlantic ✦✦✦
Ruth Brown at her stinging, assertive, bawdy best, doing the sizzling, innuendo-laden R&B that helped make Atlantic the nation's prime independent during the early days of rock and roll. There's also plenty of equally fiery, hot musical accompaniment, with then-husband Willis Jackson sometimes featured on tenor sax. —*Ron Wynn*

Late Date with Ruth Brown / Jan. 27, 1959-Feb. 5, 1959 / Atlantic ✦✦✦✦
Good after-hours, smoky blues and R&B session featuring Ruth Brown in prime form. Nobody, male or female, sang with more spirit, sass, and vigor

than Brown during the '50s, and this session reminded those who had forgotten that Brown could also hold her own with sophisticated material as well as sexy stuff. —*Ron Wynn*

Have a Good Time / Jun. 10, 1988-Jun. 11, 1988 / Fantasy ✦✦✦✦
Ruth Brown, a top-selling artist in the 1950s, endured over two decades of relative obscurity before she began to be noticed again in 1988. Recorded live at the Cinegrill in Hollywood, Brown is assisted by a fine quintet (which includes tenor great Red Holloway, altoist Charles Williams and organist Bobby Forrester) for fresh remakes of some of her hits, along with some newer material. All of Brown's Fantasy CDs feature a mature singer still in her prime. Highlights of this particular release (her debut for the label) include "Gee Baby, Ain't I Good to You," "Teardrops From My Eyes," "When I Fall in Love," and "Mama He Treats Your Daughter Mean." —*Scott Yanow*

Blues on Broadway / Jun. 12, 1989-Jun. 13, 1989 / Fantasy ✦✦✦✦
Ruth Brown was starring on Broadway in *Black and Blue* when she recorded her second Fantasy set. The emphasis is on ancient standards (mostly from the 1920s) that predated Brown's rise as an R&B star in the 1950s. Assisted by trumpeter Spanky Davis, tenorman Red Holloway, trombonist Britt Woodman, a rhythm section led by pianist/organist Bobby Forrester and (on three numbers) altoist Hank Crawford, Brown makes such songs as "Nobody Knows You When You're Down and Out," "If I Can't Sell It, I'll Keep Sittin' on It," and "Am I Blue" sound as if they were written for her. —*Scott Yanow*

Fine and Mellow / Apr. 1, 1991-Aug. 13, 1991 / Fantasy ✦✦✦✦
Nice contemporary effort with a strongly swinging R&B flavor running throughout. Ruth Brown goes back to the '40s (Louis Jordan's "Knock Me a Kiss," Dinah Washington's "Salty Papa Blues") and '50s (Brook Benton's "It's Just a Matter of Time," Jackie Wilson's "I'll Be Satisfied," the Lula Reed/Ray Charles dirge "Drown in My Own Tears") for much of the disc, paying loving tribute to her main lady Billie Holiday with the tasty title cut and delivering a pair of Duke Ellington numbers along the way. —*Bill Dahl*

Songs of My Life / Mar. 1993 / Fantasy ✦✦✦
Before Ruth Brown became an R&B and rock legend in the '50s, she was a jazz, blues, and gospel stylist. She shows that aspect of her talent on *The Songs of My Life,* a fine set produced by guitarist Rodney Jones, who also did the arrangements and conducted the backing band. While she displays her timing, interpretive skills, and still-impressive delivery and enunciation throughout, Brown also demonstrates on her rendition of Eric Clapton's "Tears In Heaven" that she retains an interest in and awareness of contemporary songs that fit her style. Ruth Brown proves that it's not the song or the lyric but the singer who makes a tune work. —*Ron Wynn*

R+B = Ruth Brown / Jan. 20, 1997-Feb. 28, 1997 / Bullseye Blues ✦✦✦✦
This is laidback New Orleans rhythm & blues that packs more into what it doesn't do than most discs are able to capture on tape. Ruth Brown has a voice that has been honed to the sharpness of a microfine edge, as well as the timing and phrasing most singers only wish they could have. Listen to what she does with the Doc Pomus-George Fishhoff tune "Destination Heartbreak," a lesson in timing, phrasing, and intimation that would benefit most R&B singers. Then listen to the control and latent power of her voice on "Too Little Too Late." It's not just her voice and presence which shine here; it's also the musicianship of the stellar cast of New Orleans musicians backing her. The arrangers deserve special mention here—six songs are arranged and conducted by Wardell Quezergue, Victor Goines arranged four tunes, and Bobby Forrester did one. It may take a couple of listenings to get used to Ruth Brown's power in this laidback New Orleans style, but one is able to see all the subtle nuances under the pure power she normally sings with. —*Bob Gottlieb*

Walter Brown

b. Aug. 1917, Dallas, TX, **d.** Jun. 1956, Lawton, OK
Vocals / Jazz Blues, Jump Blues
Blues singer Walter Brown fronted the roaring Jay McShann Orchestra (which included young alto saxist Charlie Parker) in 1941, when the roaring Kansas City aggregation cut their classic "Confessin' The Blues" and "Hootie Blues" for Decca. The Dallas native remained with McShann from 1941 to '45 before going solo (with less successful results). —*Bill Dahl*

● **Confessin' the Blues** / Apr. 22, 1949-Nov. 1, 1949 / Affinity ✦✦✦✦
Confessin' the Blues collects a number of tracks Walter Brown recorded with

Jay McShann during 1949. Although this is an imperfect collection, spot-lighting only a small portion of Brown's recorded legacy, it nevertheless is a terrific jump blues record that proves Brown was a fine blues shouter. —*Leo Stanley*

Willie Brown

b. Aug. 6, 1900, Clarksdale, MS, **d.** Dec. 30, 1952, Tunica, MS
Guitar / Delta Blues, Prewar Country Blues
One of the most influential of the early Delta blues guitarists, Willie Brown was arguably the quintessential accompanist of his era, most notably back-ing legends including Charley Patton and Son House. Born August 6, 1900 in Clarksdale, MS, Brown was an affecting singer and extraordinary guitarist, but spent the vast majority of his career as a sideman, with his ability to "second" other players much celebrated among his peers. In addition to per-forming alongside Robert Johnson, he appeared on many of the seminal sides cut by Patton between 1929 and 1934, including a legendary 1930 Paramount label session which also yielded two of the three existing Brown solo cuts, "M & O Blues" and "Future Blues," as well as material with bar-relhouse pianist Louise Johnson. His final solo performance, "Make Me a Pallet on the Floor," originated from a 1941 Alan Lomax Library of Congress field recording; during the same session, Brown also backed Son House. (In regards to Brown's own discography, it should be noted that among blues scholars there is some debate over the origins of a 1929 track called "Rowdy Blues"; credited to one Kid Bailey, it's believed in some quarters that it is in fact Brown under an assumed name, while others contend that he merely played second guitar on the date instead.) Little to nothing is known of Brown's later years, and he died in Tunica, MS, on December 30, 1952. —*Jason Ankeny*

Bob Brozman

b. Mar. 8, 1954, New York, NY
Guitar, Ukulele, Vocals / Electric Blues, Country Blues
Multi-instrumentalist, historian and educator Bob Brozman was born in New York on March 8, 1954. His uncle, Barney Josephson, was a prominent clu-bowner who ran Cafe Society in Greenwich Village, one of the first places in New York, or anywhere, where Black and White musicians played on stage together.

Brozman studied music and ethnomusicology at Washington University in St. Louis. Brozman is not only a master of classic blues from the '20s and '30s, but also a competent performer of early jazz and ragtime. In the mid-'70s while still in college, he would make trips down South to find, interview and play with the older blues artists from the 1920s and '30s whom he ad-mired.

Brozman recorded several fine albums in the early and mid-'80s for the Kicking Mule and Rounder labels, and though they may not have been reis-sued on compact disc, for students of early, vintage blues and vintage guitar afficianados, they're well worth digging out of the vinyl shops. Brozman's albums include *Blue Hula Stomp* (1981) and *Snapping the Strings* (1983), both for the California-based Kicking Mule label. In 1985, he recorded *Hello Central, Give Me Dr. Jazz* for the Massachusetts-based Rounder label and followed up in 1988 with *Devil's Slide*. For die-hard blues fans who seek an album devoid of any of the other genres Brozman so easily interprets (like ragtime and calypso), the album to get is *A Truckload of Blues*, a 1992 Rounder release. —*Richard Skelly*

Blue Hula Stomp / 1981 / Kicking Mule ♦♦♦

Hello Central: Give Me Dr. Jazz / Sep. 1985 / Rounder ♦♦♦
Bob enlists George Winston and others to faithfully re-create the 78-rpm era, focusing on early-jazz standards, hokum, and blues. —*Myles Boisen*

● **Devil's Slide** / 1988 / Rounder ♦♦♦♦
Blues, Hawaiian, calypso, hot jazz—slide-wizard Bob can do it all with star-tling authenticity and humor. This CD compilation has five cuts from his *Hello Central* album to boot. —*Myles Boisen*

A Truckload of Blues / 1992 / Rounder ♦♦♦♦
Guitarist Bob Brozman's long-awaited all-blues album covers similar terri-tory as others who have turned in heartfelt treatments of traditional and Delta blues tunes. But the difference between Brozman and many of his predecessors is that he has fun doing these songs. He's wise enough to under-

stand that there are only so many ways one can sing "Old Dog Blues" or "Kitchen Man," and that many of the great veterans really enjoyed what they sang. Brozman is also a technical marvel, particularly on bottleneck. But just as his vocals aren't simply replications, he doesn't merely whip out licks and display flash; there's thought in the soloing, creativity in the riffs and plenty of heart in the grooves. Brozman emerges with one of the better and more memorable repertory projects, one that seems more like his take on tradi-tional blues rather than one more museum piece. —*Ron Wynn*

Kika Kila Meets Ki Ho' Alu / Apr. 15, 1997 / Windham Hill ♦♦♦
This is one of the better and livelier entries in Dancing Cat's extensive slack-key guitar series, for reasons of variety alone. The title of the album is roughly translated as Hawaiian acoustic steel meets slack-key, and the disc, logically, is comprised of duets between steel player Brozman and slack gui-tarist Kaapana. Brozman, noted as both a Hawaiian-style steel virtuoso and archivist of vintage Hawaiian recordings, tends to dominate the arrange-ments, with Kaapana acting more as a second foil. Brozman goes for a circa 1920 sound, reminiscent of the time when the Hawaiian guitar was in transi-tion from its purely acoustic origins to the louder sound created by resonator guitars. The pair mostly cover Hawaiian songs from the late 19th and early 20th centuries, often from early Hawaiian recording artists such as Tau Moe, Sol Hoopii, and Kalama's Quartet. —*Richie Unterberger*

Jack Bruce (John Symon Asher Bruce)

b. May 14, 1943, Glasgow, Scotland
Bass, Vocals, Harmonica, Keyboards / Art-Rock/Progressive-Rock, Electric British Blues
Although some may be tempted to call multi-instrumentalist, songwriter and composer Jack Bruce a rock 'n' roll musician, blues and jazz are what this innovative musician really loves. As a result, these two genres are at the base of most of the recorded output from a career that goes back to the beginning of London's blues scene in 1962. In that year, he joined Alexis Korner's Blues Incorporated.

Bruce's most famous songs are, in essence, blues tunes: "Sunshine of Your Love," "Strange Brew," "Politician," and "White Room." Bruce's best-known songs remain those he penned for Cream, the legendary blues-rock trio he formed with drummer Ginger Baker and guitarist Eric Clapton in July, 1966. Baker and Bruce played together for five years before Clapton came along, and although their trio only lasted until November 1968, the group is cred-ited with changing the face of rock 'n' roll and bringing blues to a worldwide audience. Through their creative arrangements of classic blues tunes like Robert Johnson's "Crossroads," Skip James' "I'm So Glad," Willie Dixon's "Spoonful," and Albert King's "Born Under a Bad Sign," the group helped popularize blues-rock and led the way for similar groups that came about later on, like Led Zeppelin.

Bruce was born May 14, 1943, in Lanarkshire, near Glasgow, Scotland. His father was a big jazz fan, and so he credits people like Louis Armstrong and Fats Waller among his earliest influences. He grew up listening to jazz and took up bass and cello as a teen. After three months at the Royal Scottish Academy of Music, he left, disgusted with the politics of music school. After travelling around Europe for a while, he settled into the early blues scene in 1962 in London, where he eventually met drummer Ginger Baker. He played with British blues pioneers Alexis Korner and Graham Bond before leaving in 1965 to join John Mayall's Bluesbreakers, whose guitarist was Eric Clapton. This gave him time to get his chops together without having to practice. With Manfred Mann, who he also played with before forming Cream, Bruce learned about the business of making hit songs. The group's reputation for long, extended blues jams began at the Fillmore in San Fran-cisco at a concert organized by impressario Bill Graham. Bruce later realized that Cream gave him a chance to succeed as a musician, and admitted that if it weren't for that group, he might never have escaped London. After Cream split up in November 1968, Bruce formed Jack Bruce and Friends with drummer Mitch Mitchell and guitarist Larry Coryell. Recording-wise, Bruce took a different tack away from blues and blues-rock, leaning more in a folk-rock direction with his solo albums *Songs for a Tailor* (1969), *Har-mony Row* (1971), and *Out of the Storm* (1974).

In 1970 and 1971, he worked with Tony Williams Lifetime before putting together another power trio with guitarist Leslie West and drummer Corky Laing in 1972, simply called West, Bruce and Laing. After working with

Frank Zappa on his album *Apostrophe* in 1974, Bruce was at it again in '75 with the Jack Bruce Band, where members included keyboardist Carla Bley and guitarist Mick Taylor. Again on the road in 1980 with Jack Bruce and Friends, the latter version of the group included drummer Billy Cobham, keyboardist David Sancious and guitarist Clem Clempson, formerly of Humble Pie. In the early '80s, he formed another trio, BLT, this time with guitarist Robin Trower before working with Kip Hanrahan on his three solo albums.

Through three and a half decades, Bruce has always been a supreme innovator, pushing himself into uncharted waters with his jazz and folk-rock compositions. Bruce's bluesiest albums would have to include all of his work with Cream, the albums *BLT* and *Truce* with Robin Trower, some of his West, Bruce and Laing recordings, and several of his albums from the 1980s and early '90s. These include *Willpower* (PolyGram, 1989), *A Question of Time* (Epic Records, 1989), which includes guest performances by Albert Collins, Nicky Hopkins and Baker, as well as his CMP Records live career retrospective album, recorded in Cologne, France, *Cities of the Heart* (1993). Bruce's most recent release is 1995's *Monkjack*, an album of his jazz piano compositions, which he performs with organist Bernie Worrell, issued on the CMP Record label. —*Richard Skelly*

Songs for a Tailor / 1969 / Atco ♦♦♦♦
There's not a weak song on this first and most accessible solo album. "Theme for an Imaginary Western" (also made popular by Mountain) is one of the finest songs Bruce has ever recorded. Musically, this is more subdued and keyboard-oriented than Bruce's work with Cream. —*Rick Clark*

Things We Like / 1970 / Atco ♦♦

Harmony Row / 1971 / Atco ♦♦♦
Bruce's third effort is a much more challenging listen, possessing more complicated arrangements and impenetrable lyrics than *Songs for a Tailor*. Among the album's many highlights are the aggressive multi-time-signature rock of "You Burned the Tables on Me" and the haunting "Victoria Sage." —*Rick Clark*

Out of the Storm / 1974 / RSO ♦♦♦

How's Tricks / 1977 / RSO ♦♦♦♦

I've Always Wanted to Do This / 1980 / Epic ♦♦♦

Truce / 1982 / One Way ♦♦♦

● **Willpower: A Twenty-Year Retrospective** / 1989 / Atco ♦♦♦♦
Willpower is a well-compiled overview of Bruce's entire solo output, with choice unreleased tracks. This is the place to start if you are budgeting one disc of his music for your collection. Otherwise, get *Songs for a Tailor*. —*Rick Clark*

Roy Buchanan

b. Sep. 23, 1939, Ozark, AL, **d.** Aug. 14, 1988, Fairfax, VA
Guitar, Vocals / Blues-Rock
Buchanan's reputation as a hot-shot guitarist extends back to the beginnings of rock 'n' roll itself. On the road and recording with Dale Hawkins by his teens, Buchanan became the law of the land around the Washington, D.C., area by the mid-to-late '60s. His use of the Fender Telecaster, using high harmonic squeals in place of feedback and distortion, was part and parcel of rock guitar's vocabulary by the early '70s. A reluctant superstar, Buchanan later became more unfocused as his career waned, but his unique stylings remain etched into his best records.

Sadly, when Buchanan seemed on the verge of a comeback in 1988, he hung himself in a police cell after he was arrested on a drunk-driving charge. He left behind a number of records which testify that he was a consummate guitarist, capable of tones and techniques that other guitarists only dream of. —*Cub Koda*

Roy Buchanan / Aug. 1972 / Polydor ♦♦♦♦
His debut album, with a skunk-hot stage band. Buchanan's guitar sizzles on tracks like "Haunted House," "Sweet Dreams," and "The Messiah Will Come Again." —*Cub Koda*

Second Album / 1973 / Polydor ♦♦♦
More blues-based than his debut, with great stretched-out jams showcasing some of his best playing. —*Cub Koda*

That's What I Am Here For / Feb. 1974 / Polydor ♦♦♦
Excellent blues-rock guitar, it includes the riveting Hendrix tribute "Hey Joe." —*David Szatmary*

Live Stock / Aug. 1975 / Polydor ♦♦♦♦
Brilliant live blues-rock guitar by the legend who turned down a spot in the Rolling Stones. A must for guitar-hero fans. —*David Szatmary*

A Street Called Straight / Apr. 1976 / Atlantic ♦♦

Loading Zone / May 1977 / Atlantic ♦♦

You're Not Alone / Apr. 1978 / Atlantic ♦♦♦
Piercing guitar solos explode in a spacey atmosphere. —*David Szatmary*

My Babe / 1981 / AJK ♦♦
Buchanan was a terrific guitarist, but *My Babe* is not the place to hear him in his glory. Too often, the album is dragged down by slick production and Paul Jacobs' overbearing vocals. Buchanan's playing is fairly good, but he sounds a little uninspired, which is understandable, considering his surroundings. —*Stephen Thomas Erlewine*

When a Guitar Plays the Blues / Jul. 1985 / Alligator ♦♦♦
This is an excellent example of the blues-rock guitar virtuoso's recent work. —*David Szatmary*

Dancing on the Edge / Jun. 1986 / Alligator ♦♦♦

Hot Wires / 1987 / Alligator ♦♦♦
Another stinging effort. —*David Szatmary*

● **Sweet Dreams: The Anthology** / Sep. 22, 1992 / Polydor ♦♦♦♦
Over two CDs, *Sweet Dreams* collects the finest moments from Buchanan's '70s albums, including nine unreleased tracks; as a career retrospective, it's the finest collection available. —*Stephen Thomas Erlewine*

Guitar on Fire: Atlantic Sessions / Apr. 20, 1993 / Rhino ♦♦♦

Buckwheat Zydeco (Stanley Dural)

b. Nov. 14, 1947, Lafayette, LA
Accordion, Keyboards / Zydeco
Contemporary zydeco's most popular performer, accordionist Stanley "Buckwheat" Dural was the natural successor to the throne vacated by the death of his mentor Clifton Chenier; infusing his propulsive party music with strains of rock and R&B, his urbanized sound—complete with touches of synthesizer and trumpet—married traditional and contemporary zydeco with uncommon flair, in the process reaching a wider mainstream audience than any artist before him. Dural was born in Lafayette, LA, on November 14, 1947; with his braided hair, he soon acquired the nickname "Buckwheat" (an homage to the *Our Gang* character), and by the age of four was already touted as a piano prodigy. Although often exposed to traditional zydeco as a child, he preferred R&B, and by the mid-1950s was playing professionally with Lynn August; Dural's notoriety as a keyboardist quickly spread, and he also backed notables including Joe Tex and Clarence "Gatemouth" Brown.

In 1971, Dural founded Buckwheat and the Hitchhikers, a 16-piece funk band which he led for the next half-decade; however, in 1976 he finally fell under zydeco's sway when recruited to back Chenier—a friend of his father—on tour. Originally brought on as an organist, Dural picked up the accordion within two years and began learning from the master himself; rechristening himself Buckwheat Zydeco, he formed his own combo by 1979, the Ils Sont Partis Band (translated as "They're off!," so named in honor of the cry heard at the beginning of each horse race at the Lafayette track). Upon signing to the Blues Unlimited label, the group debuted in 1979 with *One for the Road*, followed in 1980 by *Take It Easy Baby*. After 1983's *100% Fortified Zydeco*, the group moved to the Rounder label, where they issued the Grammy-nominated *Turning Point*; its 1985 follow-up, *Waitin' for My Ya Ya*, was similarly honored.

In 1986, New York-based music critic Ted Fox helped Buckwheat Zydeco land a deal with Island Records, in the process becoming the first zydeco act ever signed to a major label; Fox subsequently acted as their producer as well. The group made their Island debut in 1987 with the acclaimed *On a Night Like This*, another Grammy nominee; that same year they also appeared in the hit movie *The Big Easy*, further increasing their public visibility. *Taking It Home* followed in 1988, but after 1990's *Where There's Smoke There's Fire*, Buckwheat Zydeco was dropped by Island, signing to Charisma for 1992's *On Track*. The years to follow saw the band drifting from one label to another, signing to Warner for 1994's *Choo Choo Boogaloo*, then hopping to Atlantic for 1997's *Trouble;* although their commercial fortunes may have dipped, they remained hugely popular as a live attraction, despite purists' charges of commercialism. — *Jason Ankeny*

★ **100% Fortified Zydeco** / 1983 / Black Top ♦♦♦♦♦
Currently the most visible zydeco artist nationally, this mid-'80s effort is his best, as the material recorded is more inventive. The sound is great and the song selection is superior. — *Jeff Hannusch*

Turning Point / 1983 / Rounder ♦♦♦
This is a good sampling of modern zydeco. — *Jeff Hannusch*

Waitin' for My Ya-Ya / 1985 / Rounder ♦♦♦
Buckwheat Zydeco came closest on this 1985 session to balancing his R&B and pop tendencies with a zydeco authenticity missing from his releases on other labels. The Ils Sont Partis Band, especially guitarist Jimmy Reed, rubboard man Elijah Cudges and trumpeter Calvin Landry put some spark and drive behind the arrangements on the covers of Fats Domino's "Walkin' to New Orleans" and Percy Sledge's "Warm and Tender Love," while Zydeco's singing on these and other numbers like "Lache Pas La Patate" and "Tee Nah Nah" was more focused, less gimmicky and more on target than at any time before or since. Although he never was as talented as some of his supporters claimed, Buckwheat Zydeco was closer to a serious zydeco performer than merely another copyist here. — *Ron Wynn*

Buckwheat's Party / 1987 / Rounder ♦♦♦♦

On a Night Like This / 1987 / Island ♦♦♦
Not bad, it's still not as good as his Black Top or Rounder label work. — *Jeff Hannusch*

Taking It Home / 1988 / PolyGram ♦♦♦
On his second album for Island Records, Buckwheat Zydeco continues to mix things up, adding some rock and pop covers to his trademark zydeco gumbo. Like its predecessor, *On a Night Like This,* the results on *Taking It Home* are a little mixed—the production is a little slick, covers like Derek & the Dominos' "Why Does Love Got to Be So Sad" (featuring none other than Eric Clapton on guitar) are ill-advised, and there simply isn't the fire that distinguished his independent work. That said, no Buckwheat Zydeco album is a complete waste, and hearing him run through gritty, funky originals like "These Things You Do" and "Down Dallas Alley" makes *Taking It Home* worthwhile for long-term fans. — *Thom Owens*

On Track / 1992 / Charisma ♦♦♦
When Buckwheat Zydeco laces on the accordion, you can bet that it's well past Lawrence Welk's bedtime. *On Track* is party-time zydeco, the indigenous dance music of southwest Louisiana's black Creoles spiced with contemporary rock, soul, and blues. Dural throws just about everything into the gumbo, from the funky bass and driving horns of "Won't You Let Me Go?" to the bayou lullaby "There Will Always Be Tomorrow." The most soulful version ever of "The Midnight Special" is also well worth checking out. Lovers of down-to-earth, good-time music will find themselves right *On Track* with Buckwheat's latest. — *Roch Parisien*

● **Menagerie: The Essential Zydeco Collection** / 1993 / Mango ♦♦♦♦
Menagerie: The Essential Zydeco Collection collects highlights from Buckwheat Zydeco's three albums for Island Records between 1987 and 1990. There are a number of really good songs here ("Ma 'Tit Fille," "Hey Good Lookin'," "Where There's Smoke There's Fire"), and the compilation actually distills his uneven Island albums into a strong single-disc collection. However, if you're looking for Buckwheat at his best, stick to the Rounder and Black Top releases. — *Thom Owens*

Trouble / Apr. 29, 1997 / Atlantic ♦♦♦

Norton Buffalo

b. Sep. 28, 1951, Oakland, CA
Harmonica, Vocals / Modern Electric Blues
One of the most versatile harpists in contemporary music, Norton Buffalo earned his greatest success in blues circles, but also proved himself adept in areas ranging from rock to country to even new age. Born September 28, 1951 in Oakland, California, he earned perhaps his greatest success as a member of the Steve Miller Band, a position he held for over two decades beginning in the mid-1970s; as a session player, Buffalo also lent his harmon-

ica skills to records from performers including the Doobie Brothers, Bonnie Raitt, Johnny Cash and Elvin Bishop. He issued his solo debut, *Lovin' in the Valley of the Moon,* on Capitol in 1977, followed a year later by *Desert Horizon.* After spending the 1980s primarily as a sideman, Buffalo teamed with blues slide guitarist Roy Rogers in 1991 for *R&B,* which earned a Grammy nomination for the track "Song for Jessica"; the duo's follow-up, *Travellin' Tracks,* appeared a year later. Additionally, Buffalo led his own band, the Knockouts. — *Jason Ankeny*

Lovin' in the Valley of The Moon / 1977 / Capitol ♦♦

Desert Horizon / 1978 / Capitol ♦♦♦

● **Lovin' in the Valley of the Moon/Desert Horizon** / Nov. 1995 / Edsel ♦♦♦♦
Lovin' in the Valley of the Moon/Desert Horizon combines Norton Buffalo's two late-'70s albums on one compact disc. While both albums are quite uneven, Buffalo has some fine solos on each record, and this is a nice bargain for diehard blues-rock collectors and serious harp fans. — *Stephen Thomas Erlewine*

George "Mojo" Buford

b. Nov. 10, 1929, Hernando, MS
Harmonica / Electric Chicago Blues, Harmonica Blues
When Muddy Waters deemed a harp player talented enough to follow Little Walter and James Cotton into his peerless combo, he must have been someone special. Mojo Buford spent several stints in the employ of the Chicago blues legend, and was his harpist of choice in the final edition of the Waters band.

George Buford left Mississippi for Memphis while still young, learning his early blues lessons there. He relocated to Chicago in 1952, eventually forming a band called the Savage Boys that mutated into the Muddy Waters Jr. Band (no, they weren't fronted by a Waters imitator; they subbed for their mighty sponsor at local clubs when he was on the road). Buford played with Muddy as early as 1959, but a 1962 uprooting to Minneapolis in front of his own combo and cut a couple of solid but extremely obscure LPs for Vernon and Folk-Art removed him from the Windy City scene for a while. Buford returned to Muddy's combo in 1967 for a year, put in a longer stint with Waters during the early '70s, and came back for the last time after Jerry Portnoy exited with the rest of his mates to form the Legendary Blues Band. Buford has recorded as a bandleader for Mr. Blues (later reissued on Rooster Blues) and the British JSP logo, never drifting far from his enduring Chicago blues roots. — *Bill Dahl*

Exciting Harmonica Sound of Mojo Buford / 1963 / BluesRecordSoc ♦♦♦
One of his best and earliest LPs. — *Bill Dahl*

● **Mojo Buford's Blues Summit** / Feb. 17, 1979 / Rooster Blues ♦♦♦♦
Buford in the company of guitarists Little Smokey Smothers, Pee Wee Madison, Sammy Lawhorn, and Sonny Rogers, with a rhythm section pounding it out like crazy. — *Cub Koda*

Built For Comfort Blues Band

f. Syracuse, NY
Group / Modern Electric Blues
Built for Comfort was a short-lived Syracuse, NY, group featuring two brothers on guitar and harmonica/vocals. But the real stars were the rhythm section of Mark Tiffault on drums and Paul "Big Daddy" LaRonde on bass, the two most in-demand musicians in that area of the country. Adept in a number of styles, LaRonde and Tiffault are currently the rhythm section for the New Orleans-inspired group Lil Georgie & the Shuffling Hungarians. — *AMG*

Be Cool / 1992 / Blue Wave ♦♦♦
Local Syracuse blues quartet running through a typical set of Chicago standards. No new ground broken here, but the rhythm section of Paul LaRonde and drummer Mark Tiffault swings admirably. — *AMG*

● **Keep Cool** / Nov. 1992 / Blue Wave ♦♦♦♦
Central New York bar band blues is what BFC serves up on this 14-track set, featuring members of local groups the Kingsnakes and the Corvairs. The song lineup is split down the middle between genre-faithful originals and bar staples like Little Walter's "Too Late" and Jimmy Reed's "I Ain't Got You." — *Cub Koda*

High Ballin' / Jun. 16, 1996 / Blue Wave ♦♦♦

Bull City Red

Group / East Coast Blues, Country Blues

Bull City Red, whose real name was George Washington, is best known as a sometimes sideman on washboard to the likes of Blind Boy Fuller, Sonny Terry, and Blind Gary Davis. He was a partial albino, and he came from Durham, NC, a town best known for W.T. Blackwell's "Genuine Durham Smoking Tobacco," which carried a bull trademark image. The town earned the nickname of "Bull City," which became attached to guitarist/washboard man George Washington. He wasn't an especially gifted guitarist, his strongest skill being his ability to imitate Blind Boy Fuller.

His strongest talent lay with the washboard, which he played extremely well, backing up any number of other players. Red led an otherwise blind group that included Fuller, Sonny Terry and, for a time, Blind Gary Davis as well, and with help from their manager, department store owner J.B. Long, landed a contract with Vocalion. At one point in their history, Red, Fuller, Terry, and guitarist Sonny Jones performed together as "Brother George and His Sanctified Singers," and made several recordings of gospel-themed material.

Red was later responsible for hooking Terry up with Brownie McGhee, whom he met while on a trip to Burlington. McGhee was partnered with a blues harpist and one-man band named Jordan Webb at the time, and Red introduced the two to Fuller and Terry as well as their manager. Eventually a musical relationship developed between Terry and McGhee, and following Fuller's death during surgery in 1941, Long began recording McGhee with Webb, Terry, washboard man Robert Young (who had previously played with McGhee), and Red.

Between 1935 and 1939, he cut more than a dozen sides, showing off his skills as a singer and guitarist as well as on the washboard. The material as such wasn't too impressive, at least as far as Red's guitar work, but his performance on washboard was lively and his singing most expressive. *— Bruce Eder*

1935-1939 / 1935+1939 / Story of Blues ✦✦✦

Not a bad compilation—13 songs cut by Bull City Red over a four-year stretch, which include gospel-tinged songs as well as country-blues in the Blind Boy Fuller mode. The sound is reasonably good throughout, given the rarity of some of the records, and the analog-to-digital transfer fairly clean given the age of the source material—Red's guitar comes through in startling clarity, and surface noise is generally held in check, or at least to manageable levels. Among the highlights here is Red's version of "I Saw the Light," which, in another form, entered the repertory of Hank Williams, among others. His singing, however, is actually much better on more traditional blues numbers like "I Won't Be Dogged Around" and the grimly amusing "Pick and Shovel Blues." The last five numbers here, from July of 1939 (four years later than the next oldest cuts), were credited to "Brother George and His Sanctified Singers," and have a strong religious content, although they still play out okay as blues. Sonny Terry also sings on those, and Sonny Jones plays some of the guitar, while Red goes back to washboard. *— Bruce Eder*

Bumble Bee Slim (Amos Easton)

b. May 7, 1905, Brunswick, GA, **d.** 1968, Los Angeles, CA

Guitar, Vocals / Country Blues, Acoustic Chicago Blues, Piedmont Blues, Prewar Country Blues

Popular and prolific, Bumble Bee Slim parlayed a familiar but rudimentary style into one of the earliest flowerings of the Chicago style. Much of what he performed he adapted from the groundbreaking duo Leroy Carr and Scrapper Blackwell—Slim built on Carr's laconic, relaxed vocal style and Blackwell's guitar technique. During the mid-'30s, Bumble Bee Slim recorded a number of sides for a variety of labels, including Bluebird, Vocalion, and Decca, becoming one of the most-recorded bluesmen of the decade.

Born in Georgia, Bumble Bee Slim left his home when he was a teenager. He joined a circus and travelled throughout the South and the Midwest for much of his adolescence and early adulthood. Eventually, he made a home in Indianapolis, where he played local parties and dance halls.

Bumble Bee Slim moved to Chicago in the early '30s. After a few years in the city, he began a recording career; his first singles appeared on Bluebird. Slim wrote and recorded frequently during the mid-'30s, selling more records than most of his contemporaries. In addition to cutting his own sides, he

played on records by Big Bill Broonzy and Cripple Clarence Lofton, among others.

Bumble Bee Slim moved back to Georgia in the late '30s. After a few years, he left the state once again, relocating to Los Angeles in the early '40s. During the '50s, Slim cut some West Coast blues for Specialty and Pacific Jazz, which failed to gain much interest. For the rest of his career, he kept a low profile, playing various California clubs. Bumble Bee Slim died in 1968. *— Cub Koda & Stephen Thomas Erlewine*

● **1931-1937** / 1931-1937 / Document ✦✦✦✦

Document's *1931-1937* rounds up 18 of Bumble Bee Slim's best sides. The collection highlights Slim's easygoing style—even when the tempo starts rocking, his vocals are relaxed—which he had based on Leroy Carr and Scrapper Blackwell. He found great success because he was happy to follow expectations, turning in side after side of laidback country-blues. These 18 songs contain many of his best—including "No Woman No Nickel," "Bye Bye Baby Blues," "Deep Bass Boogie," "Can't You Trust Me No More," "I Done Lost My Baby," "Steady Roll Mama Blues," "How Long, How Long Blues," and "Going Back to Florida"—making it the best available overview of his peak years. *— Thom Owens*

Bumble Bee Slim (1931-1937) / Mar. 1991 / Story of Blues ✦✦✦✦

Released on CD as part of DA Music's *Story of the Blues* series, this CD features Bumble Bee Slim (aka Amos Easton), one of the more popular blues vocalists of the 1930s. This is an excellent overview of his early work. With the assistance of pianists Jimmy Gordon, Myrtle Jackson and Black Bob, guitarist Big Bill Broonzy and many unknown musicians, Slim (who also plays guitar on the solo "No Woman No Nickel") dispalys a likable delivery and an easy-to-understand enunciation on the set of vintage acoustic Chicago blues. A fine sampling. *— Scott Yanow*

Complete Recorded Works, Vol. 1: (1931-1934) / Sep. 1, 1994 / Document ✦✦✦✦

The first of nine releases devoted to Slim's music. As with many Document releases, the sound is pretty uneven. But considering that "Rough Rugged Road Blues," recorded in October of 1931, was one of the last sides ever issued by Paramount, and that no copies were known to exist until 1992, one has to live with the considerable surface noise on that number, and on "Honey Bee Blues," and the even worse sound on "Stumbling Block Blues" and "Yo Yo String Blues" (on which one can barely tell that a song is there beneath the scratchiness). "Chain Gang Bound," by comparison, sounds almost like a modern recording, despite dating from exactly the same era. The six Paramount sides here are the only recordings here on which Slim played his own guitar, and his style is clean and engaging, with some very deft slide playing in evidence. The other cuts, mostly for Vocalion, generally sound considerably better and were recorded with piano accompaniment, or a band with piano and guitars, and they have a more sophisticated urban sound, anticipating R&B more than they resemble Slim's earlier rural-style songs. His vocals are also considerably more expressive and show a far greater range. Slim's Vocalion debut, "Greasy Greens" and "I'm Waiting On You," cut in New York, are remarkable performances for 1932. His subsequent sides were all cut in Chicago, and are more readily identifiable with that city's then-burgeoning blues tradition—none of the Chicago sides are quite as unexpected as the four New York sides, but they're all eminently listenable. The eight sides cut by Bumble Bee Slim & His Three Sharks—a pretty fair band featuring piano, guitar, and mandolin—features "Someday Things Will Be Breaking My Way," a song more familiar to modern listeners as "Sitting On Top of the World" and immortalized by Albert King and Cream. "Runnin' Drunk Blues" is a delightful, sprightly rag; and on the latest songs on this volume, the guitar returns to the fore, most notably on "Dead and Gone Mother," which features three guitars. *— Bruce Eder*

Complete Recorded Works, Vol. 2: (1934) / Sep. 1, 1994 / Document ✦✦✦✦

Complete Recorded Works, Vol. 3: (1934-1935) / Sep. 1, 1994 / Document ✦✦✦✦

The opening six songs on this volume, which covers the period from November 1934 until April 1935, are decidedly different in texture from much of the material that preceded them in Slim's output. With no more than a guitar or two and perhaps a mandolin backing him up, his music leans less toward the kind of urban R&B sound that his early Vocalion tracks did. The playing is superb, with Carl Martin and Ted Bogan showing off a special virtuosity, while Slim's vocals are brilliantly expressive. The sound is rather rough on some of the material here, leading one to believe that there aren't many copies around of several of these songs—"Way Down In Georgia" and "There You Stand" would not pass muster for release on most labels, being nearly inaudible amid their extreme surface noise. When Slim resumed his piano-based recording in early 1935, he took on a more sophisticated and less rural sound, and his voice became stronger in this mode, far more expressive and involved, alternately playful, sly, or mournful. The guitar accompaniment on some of the late February 1935 tracks, however, are notable as they include Big Bill Broonzy in the session—one of these, "Milk Cow Blues," will prove a major frustration, a magnificent, classic piece of Chicago blues with great playing all around, but almost unlistenable because of the surface noise on the master source, which, one assumes, was irreplaceable. But "Everybody's Fishin'," which follows, is so clean and delightful that it almost makes up for the sonic sins of the earlier song. —*Bruce Eder*

Complete Recorded Works, Vol. 4: (1935) / Sep. 1, 1994 / Document ◆◆◆◆

Complete Recorded Works, Vol. 5: (1935-1936) / Sep. 1, 1994 / Document ◆◆◆◆

Complete Recorded Works, Vol. 6: (1936) / Sep. 1, 1994 / Document ◆◆◆◆

Complete Recorded Works, Vol. 7: (1936-1937) / Sep. 1, 1994 / Document ◆◆◆◆

Complete Recorded Works, Vol. 8: (1937-1951) / Sep. 1, 1994 / Document ◆◆◆◆

Complete Recorded Works, Vol. 9: (1934-1951) / Jan. 2, 1998 / Document ◆◆◆◆

Eddie "Guitar" Burns

b. Feb. 8, 1928, Belzoni, MS
Guitar, Vocals, Harmonica / Modern Electric Blues
Detroit boasted a vibrant blues scene during the postwar era, headed by John Lee Hooker and prominently featuring Eddie Burns, who hit the Motor City in 1948 and musically flourished there. While still in Mississippi, Burns picked up his early blues training from the 78s of Sonny Boy Williamson, Tommy McClennan, and Big Bill Broonzy. When he hit Detroit, Burns was exclusively a harp player. He cut "Notoriety Woman," his first single for Holiday in 1948, with partner John T. Smith on guitar. Burns added guitar to his personal arsenal the next year, cutting sessions with Hooker. Burns' own discography was slim but select—he cut singles for DeLuxe in 1952 ("Hello Miss Jessie Lee"), Checker in 1954 ("Biscuit Baking Mama"), JVB and Chess in 1957 ("Treat Me Like I Treat You"). In 1961, Burns waxed the slashing "Orange Driver" and several more R&B-slanted sides for Harvey Fuqua's Harvey Records.

More recently, Burns made a fine album for Blue Suit Records, *Detroit*, that showed his versatility on two instruments to good advantage. Incidentally, blues talent runs in the Burns family: brother Jimmy is a blues-soul performer based in Chicago, with his own impressive discography stretching back to the '60s. —*Bill Dahl*

• **Treat Me Like I Treat You** / 1948-1965 / Moonshine ◆◆◆◆
With everything dubbed from vinyl onto vinyl, the sound quality on this LP won't be top-notch—but as it contains Burns' rough-edged 1948-1965 Detroit blues and boogies, it's the best cross-section of his early work compiled thus far. The guitarist/harpist's first few singles were marvelously raw affairs—"Treat Me like I Treat You" and "Biscuit Baking Mama" drip Hastings Street ambience—while Burns' 1961 sides for Harvey Fuqua's Harvey logo—"Messin' with My Bread," "Orange Driver"—are driving R&B. —*Bill Dahl*

Bottle up & Go / 1972 / Action Replay ◆◆

Detroit / 1989 / Evidence ◆◆◆◆
Impressive contemporary outing that captures Burns' traditional leanings very effectively. Backed by a mean little combo that includes ex-Motown staff pianist Joe Hunter, Burns revives his classic "Orange Driver" and offers a few fresh compositions as well. Originally issued on Toledo, OH-based Blue Suit Records. —*Bill Dahl*

Eddie Burns / 1989 / Blue Suit ◆◆◆◆
Eddie Burns features solid, contemporary backing against Burns' impassioned vocals. —*Cub Koda*

Eddie Burns Blues Band / 1993 / Evidence ◆◆◆
Eddie Burns is not an especially attractive vocalist, but when you listen closely to his weary sighs, straining delivery, and anguished inflections, it's hard not to be swayed by his expressiveness. His playing is not loaded with catchy hooks, spinning lines, distorted fills, or other rock-blues devices, but is simple, tight, and nicely executed. Burns' band includes keyboardist Joe Hunter, bassist Frank Bryant, and drummer Bobby Smith, all of whom are also straightforward, no-frills types. These are lean, direct, unsophisticated tunes. Burns' music won't appeal to those seeking innovation or flair, but it is a good outing of conventional, often derivative blues material. —*Ron Wynn*

Jimmy Burns

b. Feb. 27, 1943, Dublin, MS
Guitar, Vocals / Modern Electric Blues
The younger brother of bluesman Eddie Burns, singer/guitarist Jimmy Burns followed in the family tradition, becoming a staple of Chicago's West Side club circuit after a long absence from the spotlight. Born February 27, 1943 in Dublin, MI, he cut a handful of singles early in his career, but upon marrying and starting a family, he largely applied the brakes to his musical aspirations to focus on domestic life. Burns performed only rarely in the decades to follow; however, with his children all grown in the early 1990s, he rekindled his career, following up a hard day of operating his barbecue stand by cutting loose with a set of soulful blues at the Smokedaddy, his regular venue. In 1996, at the age of 53, Burns finally issued his long-awaited full-length debut, *Leaving Here Walking*. —*Jason Ankeny*

Leaving Here Walking / Nov. 26, 1996 / Delmark ◆◆◆

R.L. Burnside

b. Nov. 23, 1926, Oxford, MS
Vocals, Guitar / Electric Delta Blues, Delta Blues
North Mississippi guitarist R.L. Burnside is one of the paragons of state-of-the-art Delta juke joint blues. The guitarist, singer and songwriter was born November 23, 1926 in Oxford, MS, and makes his home in Holly Springs, in the hill country above the Delta. He's lived most of his life in the Mississippi hill country, which, unlike the Delta region, consists mainly of a lot of small farms. He learned his music from his neighbor, Fred McDowell, and the highly rhythmic style that Burnside plays is evident in McDowell's recording as well. Despite the otherworldly country-blues sounds put down by Burnside and his family band, known as the Sound Machine, his other influences are surprisingly contemporary: Muddy Waters, John Lee Hooker, and Lightnin' Hopkins. But Burnside's music is pure country Delta juke joint blues, heavily rhythm-oriented and played with a slide.

It's only recently that he's been hitting full stride with his tours and his music, thanks to the efforts of Fat Possum Records. In recent years, the label has issued recordings made by a group of Burnside's peers, including Junior Kimbrough, Dave Thompson, and others.

Up until the mid-'80s, Burnside was primarily a farmer and fisherman. After getting some attention in the late '60s via folklorists David Evans and George Mitchell (Mitchell recorded him for the Arhoolie label), he recorded for the Vogue, Swingmaster, and Highwater record labels. Although he had done short tours, it wasn't until the late '80s that he was invited to perform at several European blues festivals. In 1992, he was featured alongside his friend Junior Kimbrough (whose Holly Spings juke joint Burnside lives next to), in a documentary film, *Deep Blues*. His debut recording, *Bad Luck City*, was recorded and released the following year on Fat Possum Records. Burnside has a second record out on the Oxford-based Fat Possum label, *Too Bad Jim* (1994).

Both recordings showcase the raw, barebones electric guitar stylings of Burnside, and on both recordings he's accompanied by a small band, which includes his son Dwayne on bass and son-in-law Calvin Jackson on drums, as well as guitarist Kenny Brown. Both recordings also adequately capture the feeling of what it must be like to be in Junior Kimbrough's juke joint, where both men have been playing this kind of raw, unadulterated blues for over 30 years. This is the kind of downhome, backporch blues played today as it has been for many decades. —*Richard Skelly*

• **Bad Luck City** / May 1991 / Fat Possum ◆◆◆◆
Welcome to Mississippi. This is the sound you would be likely to hear in any juke joint hosting the talents of the real-life Burnside family band. What you

can't see on this disc is the picture of them grinning ear-to-ear as they play— or the sight of R.L.'s son Dwayne duck-walking while his dad smiles and nods to friends across the floor. His other son, Joseph, would likely be pounding out the solid bass line, while his son-in-law Calvin Jackson proudly presided over the drums. No, you can't see it but you can hear it if you listen closely. This set was recorded live at Syd's in Oxford, MS. As for the music, it's rough, real, and one-of-a-kind … the way blues should be. — *Larry Hoffman*

Too Bad Jim / 1994 / Fat Possum ✦✦✦✦
Too Bad Jim is cut from the same cloth as its predecessor, *Bad Luck City*. It features R.L. Burnside fronting a small juke joint combo, tearing through some greasy blues. However, *Too Bad Jim* is the better album, simply from a performance standpoint. Burnside sounds more relaxed and the band steps back from the spotlight slightly, letting the guitarist burn brightly on his own, showcasing his deep blues roots. — *Thom Owens*

A Ass Pocket O' Whiskey / Jun. 25, 1996 / Matador ✦✦✦✦
Although he had been playing for years, it wasn't until the '90s that R.L. Burnside's raw electrified Delta blues was heard by a wide audience. His new fans celebrated his wild, unbridled energy, so it made sense for him to team with the Jon Spencer Blues Explosion, the warped indie-rock band that's all about energy. However, the very purists who celebrate Burnside hate Spencer, believing that he mocks the blues. As the blistering *A Ass Pocket O' Whiskey* proves, Spencer may not treat the blues with reverence, but he and his band capture the wild essence of juke-joint blues. And that makes them the perfect match for Burnside, who knows his history but isn't burdened by it. Together, Burnside and the Blues Explosion make raw, scintillating, unvarnished blues that positively burns. — *Thom Owens*

Mr. Wizard / Mar. 11, 1997 / Fat Possum/Epitaph ✦✦✦
While it's not quite as relentlessly exciting as *A Ass Pocket o' Whiskey*, primarily because the Jon Spencer Blues Explosion isn't along to provide support, *Mr. Wizard* is another set of blistering electric blues from R.L. Burnside, highlighted by his stomping guitar, powerful voice and cheerfully vulgar lyrics. — *Thom Owens*

Sound Machine Groove / Jul. 22, 1997 / HMG ✦✦✦
Recorded by folklorist David Evans in 1979 and 1980, these are Burnside's first recordings with electric guitar and also his first with a band. That band was the Sound Machine, a band he literally created himself out of members of his own family, blending raw Mississippi blues with soul, funk, R&B and other urban flavors to make a marvelous amalgam of his own. Contemporary beats and modern themes like "Bad Luck City," "Searching for My Baby," "Can't Let You Go," and "Sound Machine Groove" sit nicely alongside slower, traditional material like "Going Down South" and "Begged for a Nickel," while R.L.'s duets with drummer Calvin Jackson on "Goin' Away Baby" and "Long Haired Doney" show a marvelous empathy and interplay. Especially notable is a version of "Sitting on Top of the World" with Burnside on slide guitar that, with Jackson's help, neatly evokes the sound and feel of a fife and drum band. Although R.L. is presently the darling of the blues crowd and hailed as something of an overnight success, one listen to this disc tells you he was already forging a new chapter in the Mississippi blues tradition with these recordings. — *Cub Koda*

Acoustic Stories / Sep. 23, 1997 / M.C. ✦✦✦
R.L. Burnside was notorious for his gritty, greasy Delta blues, as each of his records since his 1991 discovery have been blistering electric recordings. That's what makes *Acoustic Stories* so refreshing. Recorded at New York City in 1988 with harp player John Neremberg, the album balances originals with a handful of well-selected covers, including three John Lee Hooker tunes: "When My First Wife Left Me," "Hobo Blues," and "Meet Me in the Bottom." Burnside is more exciting when he's electric, but these are unexpectedly haunting recordings that prove he's not just about rocking the joint. — *Thom Owens*

Rollin Tumblin / May 4, 1998 / Bong Load ✦✦✦✦

Harold Burrage

b. Mar. 30, 1931, Chicago, IL, **d.** Nov. 26, 1966, Chicago, IL
Piano, Vocals / R&B, Soul, Electric R&B
Pianist Harold Burrage started out singing blues and R&B during the 1950s and ended up as a linchpin of the emerging Chicago soul sound of the '60s; he made recordings in both styles and more than a few idiomatic shades in between. Burrage mentored young soul singers Otis Clay and Tyrone Davis but never had a chance to see them fully blossom; he died young in 1966.

Burrage debuted on wax in 1950 with a jumping "Hi-Yo Silver" for Decca with Horace Henderson's band in support. Singles for Aladdin and States preceded one of his most prolific studio periods with Eli Toscano's Cobra imprint. In 1956, Burrage cut the amusing "You Eat Too Much" for Cobra, backed by a solid combo featuring guitarist Wayne Bennett and bassist Willie Dixon. Jody Williams added stinging guitar to Burrage's 1957 Cobra offering "Messed Up," while "Stop for the Red Light," his third Cobra 45, was a novelty complete with auto wreck sound effects. "Betty Jean," his last Cobra single, is unabashed rock 'n' roll, with Otis Rush on guitar. Burrage also served as a session pianist for the firm, backing up Magic Sam and Charles Clark.

After a romping 1960 effort for Vee-Jay, "Crying for My Baby," Burrage revamped his vocal approach considerably when recording rather prolifically for One-derful's M-Pac! subsidiary during the early-to-mid-'60s. There he sang in a very credible soul style, enjoying his only national R&B hit in 1965 with the driving "Got to Find a Way" (later revived by one of Burrage's protégés, Otis Clay). — *Bill Dahl*

She Knocks Me Out! / 1956-1958 / Flyright ✦✦✦✦
Only showcases one facet of the late piano-playing singer's multi-faceted discography, but it's one of the most fascinating—his 1956-1958 stay at Chicago's Cobra Records. Under Willie Dixon's supervision, Burrage recorded in a variety of styles—rockin' blues ("Satisfied," the amusing "You Eat Too Much"), novelty stuff ("Stop for the Red Light," complete with crashing sound effects reminiscent of Nervous Norvus), and straightahead rock 'n' roll ("Betty Jean"). — *Bill Dahl*

Aron Burton

b. Jun. 15, 1938, Senatobia, MS
Bass, Vocals / Electric Chicago Blues
Long recognized as a rock-solid bassist (and a master landscaper for the Chicago Park District), Aron Burton has begun to emphasize his vocal talents more prominently of late. His 1993 Earwig album *Past, Present and Future* showcased both of Burton's specialties, eastablishing him as bandleader instead of bandsman. Burton left Mississippi for Chicago in 1955. He got his feet wet as a singer and bassist in the late '50s with Freddy King at Walton's Corner on the West side (King bought Aron his first bass). He got drafted in 1961, came out four years later, and got back into playing with various rock (notably Baby Huey & the Babysitters) and blues (Junior Wells, Fenton Robinson) groups. Burton did sessions with Wild Child Butler, Jackie Ross, Carey Bell, and a 45 of his own for Eddy Clearwater's Cleartone logo ("Garbage Man"), but it was his signing on as a charter member of Albert Collins' Icebreakers in 1978 (Aron's brother Larry was the band's rhythm guitarist) that catapulted him into the spotlight. He played on Collins' landmark Alligator LP *Ice Pickin'* and toured extensively with the Master of the Telecaster before getting restless and leaving the band. Burton did sessions with Johnny Littlejohn, James Cotton, and Fenton Robinson before taking a three-year European hiatus in the late '80s. That's where he cut his debut LP, *Usual Dangerous Guy*, with Champion Jack Dupree guesting on piano. Since returning to Chicago, Burton has picked up where he left off—he's playing, singing, and leading his own band instead of backing others. — *Bill Dahl*

● **Past, Present, & Future** / 1993 / Earwig ✦✦✦✦
A compendium of tracks cut back in the 1980s (some with the late pianist Champion Jack Dupree) over in Europe (the "past" part of the title) and a few more recent sides waxed in his Chicago hometown, this collection effectively spotlights bassist Aron Burton's talents as a front man. — *Bill Dahl*

Aron Burton Live / 1996 / Earwig ✦✦✦✦
Veteran bassist Aron Burton, after nearly four decades as a greatly in-demand sideman in the blues world, finally put together his own band in the early 1990s. This CD, his third recording as a leader, is very much a blues revue in the spirit of Johnny Otis. Burton sings on six of the 13 songs, sharing the vocal mike with guitarist Michael Dotson, keyboardist Allen Batts, drummer Kenny Smith, the fine harmonica player Lester Davenport, and (on extroverted versions of "Fever" and "Hound Dog") Liz Mandville-Greeson. Instrumentally, Burton sounds quite happy to liberally feature his sidemen and play a supportive role. Although all of the players fare well, each one displaying a strong musical personality, the high-powered guitarist Dotson often takes honors, demonstrating that he is a highly expressive and up-and-

coming bluesman. Whether it be warhorses or newer material, the Aron Burton show keeps moving and never loses one's interest. Recommended. — *Scott Yanow*

The Butler Twins

f. Detroit, MI
Group / Modern Electric Blues
Clarence and Curtis Butler are two longtime beacons on the Detroit-area blues scene, and with two recently recorded albums for the London-based JSP Records, they may finally begin to garner a wider following outside of Detroit. The brothers' albums for JSP include *Pursue Your Dreams* (1996) and *Not Gonna Worry About Tomorrow* (1995).

Guitarist Clarence and harmonica player Curtis Butler grew up near W.C. Handy's birthplace of Florence, AL, about 30 miles from the Mississippi Delta. They took their earliest musical cues from their father, guitarist Willie "Butch" Butler, who was famous in the region but never recorded.

The twins moved to Detroit in the 1960 and quickly found work in Motor City auto plants. The club scene at the time was booming, with the music of John Lee Hooker, Little Sonny, Bo Collins, Bobo Jenkins, and dozens of others spilling out of the city's juke joints. The twins continued working and sitting in as much as they could, but by the late 1960s, the blues scene in Detroit had dried up. Civil unrest and the rise of the Motown sound didn't leave much room for a flourishing blues scene, but by the early 1980s, when the blues began a resurgence again nationally, the Butler Twins were still on the scene. More importantly, they were celebrated as survivors and veterans.

The twins' two JSP releases may allow them to tour more extensively in the US, Canada and Europe. — *Richard Skelly*

● **Not Gonna Worry About Tomorrow** / May 2, 1995 / JSP ◆◆◆◆
The Butler Twins turned in a fine debut with *Not Gonna Worry About Tomorrow*. The pair specialize in hard-driving urban blues, straight out of the '60s. There are no innovations here, but there don't need to be, since the duo slams home this blistering electric blues with passion and energy. — *Thom Owens*

Pursue Your Dreams / May 7, 1996 / JSP ◆◆◆

George "Wild Child" Butler

b. Oct. 1, 1936, Hernando, MS
Harmonica, Vocals, Guitar / Electric Chicago Blues
From all accounts, George Butler was indeed a "wild child." But he found time between the youthful shenanigans that inspired his mom to bestow his descriptive nickname to learn some harp basics at age 12. He was gigging professionally as a bandleader by the late '50s, but Butler's recording career didn't blossom until he moved to Chicago in 1966 and signed with Shreveport, LA-based Jewel Records (his sidemen on these sessions included bassist Willie Dixon and guitarist Jimmy Dawkins).

The harpist didn't have much luck in the recording wars — his 1969 Mercury album sank with little trace, while a 1976 LP for T.K., *Funky Butt Lover*, did equally little for his fortunes (it was later reissued in slightly altered form on Rooster Blues as *Lickin' Gravy*). Around 1981, Butler moved up north to Ontario, Canada, and continued his career. A decade later, he cut the first of two albums for British producer Mike Vernon; *These Mean Old Blues* was an engaging set of original material cut in London. *Stranger,* the fruits of another English session, emerged in 1994. — *Bill Dahl*

● **Open up Baby** / 1966-1967 / Charly ◆◆◆◆
Charly's *Open Up Baby* rounds up several singles George "Wild Child" Butler recorded for Jewel between 1966 and 1968. All of the sessions were produced by Willie Dixon, and the great majority of the songs were written either by Butler or Dixon. Some of the material has dated a bit ("Hippy Playground," for instance), but there's no denying the down-and-dirty grit in Butler's performances, as he's backed by such well-known musicians as Big Walter Horton and Jimmy Dawkins. Butler rarely did straightahead Chicago blues any better than he did here. — *Thom Owens*

Keep on Doing What You're Doing / Nov. 11, 1969 / Mercury ◆◆◆

Lickin' Gravy / Feb. 7, 1976 / Rooster Blues ◆◆◆
Before it finally saw the light of day, this 1976 album had to undergo some overdubbing touchups a full decade later that replaced certain guitar tracks with Pinetop Perkins' keyboards. Not the best way to make an album, but

the results are nevertheless pretty decent, as Butler dishes up a set of his own material, a couple of Willie Dixon copyrights, and Lightnin' Slim's "Rooster Blues." — *Bill Dahl*

These Mean Old Blues / Apr. 24, 1991-Apr. 25, 1991 / Bullseye Blues ◆◆◆◆
Considering his nickname and near-anonymity at the time, it is surprising to realize that Wild Child Butler was already 55 when he made this CD. Although he had recorded very few released sessions before this album, Butler had been active most of the time since settling in Ontario, Canada. A talented harmonica player, he also possesses a deep and very expressive voice. With a first-rate combo that features the intense guitar of Pete Boss, Butler performs most of his best material for his Bullseye Blues debut. Among the highpoints are the title cut, the topical "Crack House Woman," an unaccompanied "Walkin' The Little Girl Home" and the minor-toned "It's A Pity." Recommended. — *Scott Yanow*

Stranger / 1994 / Bullseye Blues ◆◆◆◆
Another set of impressive originals cut in England and produced by Mike Vernon with the same attention to traditional detail as their fine previous collaboration. Butler's understated approach reeks of an authenticity that grows harder to find with every passing year, whether on his own "Weak in the Knees" and "Face It Baby" or the Vernon-generated "High I.Q." and "I'm Not Guilty." — *Bill Dahl*

Henry Butler

b. New Orleans, LA
Piano, Vocals / Blues, R&B, Post-Bop
Henry Butler's blues-based, New Orleans funk-style piano playing is not for every blues fan, to be sure. Butler is a local legend in New Orleans, but rarely tours other parts of the country; most any time of the year, he can be found playing in one of New Orleans' famous nightspots. It's not an exaggeration to say Butler is a piano genius who has yet to be discovered by the masses. His recordings demonstrate that he can do it all: he writes his own songs, does his own arrangements of classic tunes by Professor Longhair and others, and can play with as much passion as a soloist as he can with a band. What makes him great — but admittedly difficult for record companies to market — is that he constantly pushes himself in new directions as a musician. He can't be pigeonholed as blues, jazz, or even rock 'n' roll, though he performs all three genres with impeccable taste, depth of understanding and freshness of appreciation. Butler's playing also reflects influences like gospel and classic R&B.

Butler was born in New Orleans and first began playing piano at a neighbor's house when he was six. While attending the Louisiana State School for the Blind in Baton Rouge, he began taking piano lessons, also studying drums, baritone saxophone and valve trombone. He began playing professionally when he was 14 in Baton Rouge clubs, and then attended college at Southern University in Baton Rouge. He later did post-graduate work at Michigan State University. Before graduating from college, Butler received a National Endowment for the Arts grant to study with Cannonball Adderley and his group of veteran musicians; he learned a lot from all of them, including pianist George Duke.

In the mid-1970s, he returned to New Orleans and found work as a voice teacher at the New Orleans Center for the Creative Arts. Butler then lived in Los Angeles and New York City for several periods of time, pursuing record deals.

Butler credits jazz clarinetist Alvin Batiste with being a major influence on his career. When Butler was listening to Jimi Hendrix and Chicago, Batiste advised him to begin studying the music of John Coltrane and Charlie Parker, which enabled Butler to develop the great improvisational abilities he demonstrates in his performances today.

Butler has several albums to his credit: *Fivin' Around* (MCA/Impulse!, 1986), *The Village* (MCA/Impulse!, 1988), *Orleans Inspiration* (1990,) album for the now-defunct Windham Hill Jazz label; a 1992 independent release, *Blues & More, Vol. 1;* and 1996's *For All Seasons* on the Atlantic Jazz label. Butler continues to support himself through private lessons and performances around the Crescent City. — *Richard J. Skelly*

Fivin' Around / 1985-1986 / MCA ◆◆◆
Pianist Henry Butler's recording debut as a leader was also the first record released by the "new" Impulse label. Cut in the mid-'80s when MCA was directly involved with Impulse, the program features Butler with some rather

notable musicians—bassist Charlie Haden, drummer Billy Higgins, trumpeter Freddie Hubbard and tenorman Azar Lawrence plus occasional color provided by flutist Steve Kujala and the oboe of Jeff Clayton. Two selections (including "Giant Steps") add a string quartet, and Butler sings "I Want Jesus to Walk With Me." The wide-ranging repertoire (which also has seven diverse originals and the standard "Old Folks") and the inventive frameworks make this a memorable and very successful set. — *Scott Yanow*

The Village / Feb. 1987-Mar. 1987 / MCA ♦♦♦♦
Henry Butler's second Impulse recording is a two-LP set (not yet reissued on CD) that is essentially a post-bop performance. The influence of the pianist's New Orleans heritage (which is partly felt on his version of Scott Joplin's "The Entertainer") and gospel music would be explored more fully in the future. Butler is joined by bassist Ron Carter, drummer Jack DeJohnette and occasionally by clarinetist Alvin Batiste, John Purcell (on soprano, flute, oboe and English horn) and (for "The Entertainer") Bob Stewart on tuba. Butler sings "Music Came," but essentially this is an advanced trio set that shows how fine a pianist he is. — *Scott Yanow*

● **Orleans Inspiration** / Jul. 27, 1989-Jul. 28, 1989 / Windham Hill ♦♦♦♦
Henry Butler, who had recorded a pair of post-bop sets for MCA/Impulse, switches to New Orleans R&B on this spirited program, cut live at Tipitina's in New Orleans. Assisted by guitarist Leo Nocentelli, bassist Chris Severin, drummer Herman Jackson, and the synthesizer of Michael Goods, Butler puts on a fine show. He plays and sings (in a gospellish baritone voice) a variety of originals, plus Leonard Bernstein's "Somewhere," "Goin' Down Slow," and Professor Longhair's "Tipitina's" and "Mardi Gras in New Orleans." — *Scott Yanow*

Blues & More, Vol. 1 / 1992 / Windham Hill ♦♦♦
A versatile pianist with a passionate voice, Henry Butler emphasizes the bluesy side of his musical personality throughout this CD of unaccompanied solos. Most of the selections on the date (other than "Down by the Riverside," "That Lucky Old Sun," and "Jamaica Farewell") are his own and Butler puts plenty of feeling and soulful swing into the music. An accessible and generally creative outing. — *Scott Yanow*

For All Seasons / Jun. 14, 1995-Jun. 16, 1995 / Atlantic ♦♦♦
On some of his recordings, Henry Butler has performed gospel music and/ or New Orleans funk, taken soulful vocals, and played some electric keyboard. This trio album, however, is purely acoustic and mostly in the straight ahead vein. With assistance from bassist Dave Holland and drummer Herman Jackson (trombonist Steve Turre dropped by to play the romantic melody on "Souvenir d'un Amour"), Butler explores such numbers as "St. Louis Blues," "How Insensitive," "Without a Song," and several of his originals. This is one of Butler's strongest jazz dates and finds him displaying his individuality on basic but viable chord structures. — *Scott Yanow*

Blues After Sunset / Apr. 21, 1998 / Black Top ♦♦♦
The New Orleans piano tradition of Professor Longhair and Allan Toussaint is carried on by this veteran ivory tickler. Joined here on many tracks by axeman Snooks Eaglin and Mark Kazanoff on harmonica, Butler belts out soulful original tunes and a number of covers. The best thing about the disc is the essential quality of the soul: unfettered by overproduction, Butler gets down to the business of the blues. — *Tim Sheridan*

Paul Butterfield

b. Dec. 17, 1942, Chicago, IL, d. May 4, 1987, Hollywood, CA
Harmonica, Guitar, Vocals, Flute / Blues-Rock, Electric Chicago Blues, Blues Revival, Harmonica Blues
Butterfield grew up in Chicago's Hyde Park, and according to his brother Peter, "There was a lot of music around. Hyde Park, a place unique in Chicago because it was an island in the Southside ghetto, and a bastion of liberal politics. When we grew up there was a crime problem—mostly due to scattered groups of Puerto Ricans and poor White trash—but no one made a connection to the Black community as a source of crime. We grew up about half a block from something called the International Houses and you would see people from all over the world in the immediate area. "
Butterfield was culturally sophisticated. His father was a well-known attorney in the Hyde Park area, and his mother was an artist—a painter. Butterfield took music lessons (flute) from an early age and by the time he reached high school, was studying with the first-chair flutist of the Chicago

Symphony. He was exposed to both classical music and jazz from an early age. Butterfield ran track in high school and was offered a running scholarship to Brown University, which he had to refuse after a serious knee injury. From that point onward, he turned toward the music scene around him. He began learning the guitar and harmonica.

He met singer Nick Gravenites and started hanging around outside of the Chicago blues clubs, listening. He and Gravenites began to play together at various campuses—Ann Arbor, University of Wisconsin, and the University of Chicago. His parents sent him off to the University of Illinois, but he would put in a short academic week, return home early (but not check in) and instead play and hang out at the blues clubs. Soon, he was doing this six or seven days a week with no school at all. When this was discovered by his parents, he then dropped out of college and turned to music full time.

Butterfield practiced long hours by himself—just playing all the time. His brother Peter writes, "He listened to records, and he went places, but he also spent an awful lot of time, by himself, playing. He'd play outdoors. There's a place called The Point in Hyde Park, a promontory of land that sticks out into Lake Michigan, and I can remember him out there for hours playing. He was just playing all the time ... It was a very solitary effort. It was all internal, like he had a particular sound he wanted to get and he just worked to get it. "

In the meantime, Elvin Bishop had come from Oklahoma to the University of Illinois on a scholarship and had discovered the various blues venues for himself. Elvin remembers, "One day I was walking around the neighborhood and I saw a guy sitting on a porch drinking a quart of beer—White people that were interested in blues were very few and far between at that time. But this guy was singing some blues and singing it good. It was Butterfield. We gravitated together real quick and started playing parties around the neighborhood, you know, just acoustic. He was playing more guitar than harp when I first met him. But in about six months, he became serious about the harp. And he seemed to get about as good as he ever got in that six months. He was just a natural genius. And this was in 1960 or 1961."

Butterfield and Bishop began going down to the clubs, sitting in, and playing with all the great Black blues players—then in their prime—players like Otis Rush, Magic Sam, Howlin' Wolf, Junior Wells, Little Walter, and especially Muddy Waters. They often were the only Whites there, but were soon accepted because of their sincerity, their sheer ability, and the protection of players like Muddy Waters, who befriended them.

An important event in the history of introducing blues to White America came in 1963 when Big John's, a club located on Chicago's White North Side invited Butterfield to bring his band there and play on a regular basis. He said "sure," and Butterfield and Bishop set about putting such a band together. They pulled Jerome Arnold (bass) and Sam Lay (drums) from Howlin' Wolf's band (with whom they had worked for the past six years!), by offering them more money. Butterfield and Bishop (the core team), Arnold, and Lay were all about the same age, and these four became the Butterfield Blues Band. They had been around for a long time and knew the Chicago blues scene and its repertoire cold. This new racially-mixed band opened at Big John's, was very successful, and made a first great step to opening up the blues scene to White America.

When the new group thought about making an album, they looked around for a lead guitarist. Michael Bloomfield, who was known to Butterfield from his appearances at Big Johns, joined the band early in 1965. Bloomfield, somewhat cool at first to Butterfield's commanding manner, warmed to the group as Butterfield warmed to his guitar playing. It took a while for Bloomfield to fit in, but by the summer of that year, the band was cookin'. Mark Naftalin, another music student, joined the band as the first album was being recorded, in fact while they were actually in the studio creating that first album on Elektra. He sat in (playing the Hammond organ for the first time!), Butterfield liked the sound, and Naftalin recorded eight of the 11 tracks on the first album during that first session. After the session, Paul invited Naftalin to join the band and go on the road with them. These six, then, became the Paul Butterfield Blues Band.

The first two Butterfield Blues albums are essential from an historical perspective. While *East-West*, the second album, with its Eastern influence and extended solos (See: Michael Bloomfield) set the tone for psychedelic rockers, it was that incredible first album that alerted the music scene as to what was coming.

Although it has been perhaps over-emphasized in recent years, it is important to point out that the release of *The Paul Butterfield Blues Band* on Elektra in 1965, had a huge effect on the White music culture of the time. Used to hearing blues covered by groups like the Rolling Stones, that first album had an enormous impact on young (and primarily White) rock players. Here is no deferential imitation of Black music by Whites, but a racially-mixed hard-driving blues album that, in a word, rocked. It was a signal to White players to stop making respectful tributes to Black music, and just play it. In a flash the image of blues as old-time music was gone. Modern Chicago-style urban blues was out of the closet and introduced to mainstream White audiences, who loved it. The Butterfield band appeared at the Newport Folk Festival late in 1965 to rave reviews.

Perhaps the next major event in the Butterfield band came when drummer Sam Lay became ill, late in 1965. Jazz drummer Billy Davenport was called in and soon became a permanent member of the group. Davenport was to become a key element in the development of the second Butterfield Blues Band album, *East-West* (See: Mark Naftalin), in particular the extended solo of the same name.

Fueled by Bloomfield's infatuation with Eastern music and Indian ragas at the time and aided by Davenport's jazz-driven sophistication on drums, there arose in the group a new music form that was to greatly affect rock music—the extended solo. There is little question that here is the root of psychedelic (acid) rock—a genuine fusion between East and West.

Those first two albums served as a wakeup call to an entire generation of White would-be blues musicians. Speaking as one who was on the scene, that first Butterfield album stopped us in our tracks, and we were never the same afterward. It changed our lives.

The third album (released in 1967), *The Butterfield Blues Band; The Resurrection of Pigboy Crabshaw* is the last album that preserves any of the pure blues direction of the original group. By this time, Bloomfield had left to create his own group, The Electric Flag and, with the addition of a horn section (including a young David Sandborn), the band was drifting more toward an R&B sound. Mark Naftalin left the group soon after this album, and the Butterfield band took on other forms.

Aside from these first three albums, later Butterfield material somehow misses the mark. He never lost his ferocity or integrity, but the synergy of that first group was special. There has been some discussion in the literature about the personal transformation of Butterfield as his various bands developed. It is said that he went from being a self-centered bandleader (shouting orders to his crew à la Howlin' Wolf) to a more democratic style of leadership, providing his group with musical freedom (like Muddy Waters). For what it's worth, it is clear that the best music is in those first two (maybe three) albums. Subsequent albums, although also interesting, have not gotten as much attention then or now from reviewers.

When I knew Butterfield (during the first three albums), he was always intense, somewhat remote, and even, on occasion, downright unfriendly. Although not much interested in other people, he was a compelling musician and a great harp player. Bloomfield and Naftalin, also great players, were just the opposite—always interested in the other guy. They went out of their way to inquire about you, even if you were a nobody. Naftalin, well known around the San Francisco Bay Area, continues to this day to support blues projects and festivals (Marin County Blues Festival, etc.) in the San Francisco Bay area.

After Bloomfield and Naftalin left the group, Butterfield spun off on his own more and more. The next two albums, *In My Own Dream* (1968) and *Keep on Moving* (1969) moved still farther away from the blues roots until, in 1972, Butterfield dissolved the group, forming the group Better Days. This new group recorded two albums, *Paul Butterfield's Better Days* and *It All Comes Back*. After that, Butterfield faded into the general rock scene, with an occasional appearance here and there, as in the documentary *The Last Waltz* (1976)—a farewell concert from The Band. The albums *Put It in Your Ear* (1976) and *North South* (1981) were attempts to make a comeback, but both failed. Paul Butterfield died of a drug-related heart failure in 1987.

Even to this day, Butterfield remains as one of the only White harmonica players to develop his own style (another is William Clarke)—one respected by Black players. Butterfield has no real imitators. Like most Chicago-style amplified harmonica players, Butterfield played the instrument like a horn—a trumpet. Although he sometimes used a chromatic harmonica, Butterfield mostly played the standard Hohner Marine Band in the standard cross position. Remember, he was left-handed and held the harp in his left hand, but

in the standard position with the low notes facing to the left. He tended to play single notes rather than bursts of chords. His harp playing is always intense, understated, concise, and serious—only Big Walter Horton has a better sense of note selection.

The effect of the Butterfield Blues Band on aspiring White blues musicians was enormous, and the impact of the band on live audiences was stunning. Butterfield the performer was always intense, serious, and definitive—no doubt about this guy. Blues purists sometimes like to quibble about Butterfield's voice and singing style, but the moment he picked up a harmonica, that was it. He is one of the finest harp players (period).

Butterfield and the six members of the original Paul Butterfield Blues Band made a huge contribution to modern music, turning a whole generation of White music lovers onto the blues as something other than a quaint piece of music history. The musical repercussions of the second Butterfield album, *East-West* continue to echo through the music scene even today! (See: Michael Bloomfield, Mark Naftalin)

We would like to thank *Blues Access* magazine for permission to use the quotes by Peter Butterfield and Elvin Bishop from the excellent article by Tom Ellis. —*Michael Erlewine*

Offer You Can't Refuse / 1963 / Red Lightnin' ♦♦♦

An album released on the Red Lightnin' label in 1972 consisting of one side of Big Walter Horton and the other side with very early Paul Butterfield (1963) (See: Big Walter Horton). Contains six tracks with Butterfield, Smokey Smothers on guitar, Jerome Arnold on bass, and Sam Lay on drums. This was recorded at Big John's, the North Side Chicago club where the Butterfield Band first played in 1963—some two years before the material on the first Paul Butterfield Blues Band album, which was released in 1965. The six tracks include two instrumentals, "Got My Mojo Working" and the Butterfield-authored tune "Loaded." Although this is very early Butterfield, the harp playing is excellent and already in his own unique style. The singing is a little rough and heavy sounding. Butterfield fans will want to find this rare vinyl for musical and historical reasons. —*Michael Erlewine*

The Original Lost Elektra Sessions / Dec. 1964 / Rhino ♦♦♦♦

All but one of these 19 tracks were recorded in December, 1964, as Butterfield's projected first LP; the results were scrapped and replaced by their official self-titled debut, cut a few months later. With both Bloomfield and Bishop already in tow, these sessions rank among the earliest blues-rock ever laid down. Extremely similar in feel to the first album, it's perhaps a bit rawer in production and performance, but not appreciably worse or different than what ended up on the actual debut LP. Dedicated primarily to electric Chicago blues standards, Butterfield fans will find this well worth acquiring, as most of the selections were never officially recorded by the first lineup (although different renditions of five tracks showed up on the first album and the *What's Shakin'* compilation). —*Richie Unterberger*

☆ Paul Butterfield Blues Band / 1965 / Elektra ♦♦♦♦♦

Butterfield's unique amplified harmonica style is already present on this classic first album—a wakeup call for a generation of young White players used to hearing blues filtered through covers by groups like the Rolling Stones or as a part of music history. Here was a racially mixed group of brilliant young players that rocked—an historic album. Great guitar from Michael Bloomfield and Elvin Bishop. With Mark Naftalin (organ), Jerome Arnold (bass), and Sam Lay (drums). —*Michael Erlewine*

★ East-West / 1966 / Elektra ♦♦♦♦♦

The second Butterfield album had an even greater effect on music history, paving the way for experimentation that is still being explored today. This came in the form of an extended blues-rock solo (some 13 minutes)—a real fusion of jazz and blues inspired by the Indian raga. This ground-breaking instrumental was the first of its kind and marks the root from which the acid rock tradition emerged. —*Jeff Tarmarkin and Michael Erlewine*

East-West Live / 1966-1967 / Winner ♦♦♦♦

The tune "East-West" from the second Butterfield Blues Band album of the same name made music history. It is arguably the first extended rock solo, a fusing of blues-rock with Eastern scales and tone. Here is the root of psychedelic—acid rock. Now, thanks to Mark Naftalin (the original Butterfield keyboardist), we have three live recordings of "East-West" recorded in 1966-1967 that capture the origin and development of this classic tune. The first example (some 12 minutes) was taped prior to the edited studio version; the second (16 minutes) and third (28 minutes) were recorded after the album cut. There is some great music (and music history) here. — *Michael Erlewine*

The Resurrection of Pigboy Crabshaw / 1967 / Elektra ✦✦✦
In his third album, Butterfield adds a horn section and the direction of the group has started to veer away from straight Chicago-style blues toward a sound more influenced by R&B. By this time, Bloomfield has left the group and Elvin Bishop (a.k.a. Pigboy Crabshaw) takes over on lead guitar. A lot of great tunes here, like "Driftin' and Driftin." — *Michael Erlewine*

Strawberry Jam / 1996 / Winner ✦✦✦
These nine cuts are from various live performances of the Paul Butterfield Blues Band during their heyday in the middle-to-late '60s. This album was put together by Mark Naftalin, who played keyboards on those first few incredible Butterfield albums. Don't look for the clearest sound (it's adequate) because these are live tunes recorded at clubs, often with minimal equipment. It is the music that is in focus here—a window into that incredible band at a time when they were hot. Those of us who were on the scene at the time know that, although the original Butterfield albums are great, the band was a total knockout when heard live. Featuring Butterfield's harmon-

ica, here are glimpses into that time and music. Most of the tunes have appeared elsewhere, but the extended instrumental "Strawberry Jam" (written by Naftalin) is unique to this album—worth hearing. It features great guitar by Elvin Bishop. — *Michael Erlewine*

Anthology—The Elektra Years / Oct. 28, 1997 / Elektra/Asylum ✦✦✦✦
An Anthology—The Elektra Years is a double-disc, 33-song set that offers a comprehensive overview of Paul Butterfield's eight years with the label. His first two albums, *Paul Butterfield Blues band* and *East-West*, were seminal, groundbreaking records that blurred the boundaries between blues, jazz and rock, suggesting everything from blues-rock to psychedelia. They were stunning achievements which proved to be difficult to match, but Butterfield's remaining albums for the label all had a few good cuts. *An Anthology* does a nice job of rounding up those highlights, picking the best moments from uneven records; consequently, it's quite a valuable package for listeners who simply want a sampling from those later albums instead of purchasing them individually. Butterfield's first two albums remain necessary listens in their own right, but this set offers an excellent summary of his entire stint with Elektra. — *Stephen Thomas Erlewine*

Shirley Caesar

b. Oct. 13, 1938, Durham, NC
Vocals / Black Gospel, Contemporary Gospel, Traditional Gospel
Born in Durham, NC, Caesar sang with the Caravans in the early '60s before going solo in 1966. She is a strict traditionalist known for her shouting style and evangelizing messages. — *Bil Carpenter*

The Best of Shirley Caesar with the Caravans / 1966 / Savoy ◆◆◆◆
This anthology covers Caesar's Savoy material during the initial period after she left The Caravans. It's mostly traditional gospel, often superbly performed, though not as well produced or engineered as her later releases for Word. — *Ron Wynn*

First Lady / 1977 / Hob ◆◆◆
Secular songs and Christian themes are mixed here. — *Bil Carpenter*

Shirley Caesar Sings Her Gospel Favorites, Vol. 2 / 1978 / Spire ◆◆◆◆
More fervent singing with Caesar Singers & Choirs. — *Opal Louis Nations*

Live in Chicago with Rev. Milton Brunson & the Thompson Community Singers / 1988 / Word ◆◆◆
Including traditional Black gospel testifying, singing, and storytelling, this album was recorded with the Thompson Community Singers and Albertina Walker. — *Bil Carpenter*

Celebration / 1990 / Myrrh ◆◆◆
Like all the great gospel singers, Shirley Caesar is a survivor; she began with the Caravans, and she's still a star. Sheer vocal talent aside, and as this fine pop-gospel hit album from a couple of years ago confirms, she has always managed to steer a course between conservatism and selling out, in the enduring gospel tradition of drawing on the secular music of its time. — *John Storm Roberts, Original Music*

● **Her Very Best** / 1991 / Word ◆◆◆◆
Her Very Best collects highlights from four of Shirley Caesar's albums for Word in the '80s, selecting two from each album and adding two unreleased cuts as incentives for hardcore fans that already have the original albums. The result is a representative introduction to her latter-day recordings. These aren't necessarily her best work, but they're nevertheless strong, offering further proof that Shirley Caesar is one of the great voices in recorded gospel history. — *Leo Stanley*

I Remember Mama / Feb. 25, 1992 / Word ◆◆◆◆
Shirley Caesar's poignant rembrances of her mother set the stage for this album that mixed sentimental fare with rocking evangelism and surging performances. No Golden Age gospel artists have been more successful at retaining their zeal while adapting to contemporary production and arranging tendencies than Caesar. She doesn't compromise her lyrical message, but will hold still for electronics, strings, and even an occasional funk backbeat. This resulted in another hit LP for a gospel legend. — *Ron Wynn*

Jesus, I Love Calling Your Name / Apr. 28, 1992 / Word ◆◆◆
More fervent lyrical material from Shirley Caesar, backed by both choral and contemporary production and arrangements. The results weren't always successful, but when they clicked, they were masterful. The title track was a sizable hit on gospel radio, and Caesar continued her string of successful LPs that blended traditional vocals and modern/mainstream voicings and backing. — *Ron Wynn*

Sailin' / Apr. 28, 1992 / Word ◆◆◆◆
Shirley Caesar and Rev. Al Green made a magnificent team on the title track, which helped win each a Grammy. Caesar's evocative leads and Green's

shimmering harmonies and equally spectacular leads were a session highlight, although there were some other fine numbers spotlighting Caesar as well. — *Ron Wynn*

No Charge / Mar. 14, 1995 / Hob ◆◆◆◆
More gospel pyrotechnics from this queen of the revival circuit. — *Opal Louis Nations*

Don't Drive Your Mama Away / Oct. 24, 1995 / Hob ◆◆◆◆
Some of Caesar's finest work was cut for Hob, and this collection proves it. — *Opal Louis Nations*

Just a Word / Jul. 1996 / Sony ◆◆◆◆
Not strictly a Shirley Caesar album, *Just a Word* nevertheless is a good showcase of mid-'90s contemporary gospel music. Recorded on the final day of the Outreach Convention, *Just A Word* features four songs with Caesar's lead vocals and a host of other gospel vocalists and musicians, singing both standards and new gospel songs. The performances are energetic and invigorating, demonstrating that traditional gospel is nearly always best heard in a live setting. Makes you wish you were there.... — *Leo Stanley*

Rejoice / Myrrh ◆◆◆◆
The title track featured Shirley Caesar in peak form, soaring, shouting, and declaring her love for God. The LP overall wasn't quite as strong as some other Caesar releases, lacking consistent material or top performances. Still, Caesar often managed to salvage things solely with her vocal power and personality. — *Ron Wynn*

Faded Rose / Hob ◆◆◆◆
More memorable moments by this ex-Caravan soloist. — *Opal Louis Nations*

Chris Cain

b. Nov. 19, 1955, San Jose, CA
Guitar, Vocals / Modern Electric Blues
Chris Cain's crisp lead guitar and gravelly vocals have brought him national recognition. Influenced by B.B. and Albert King as well as various jazz players, Cain has cooked up a jumping sound on the Bay Area circuit.

A native of San Jose, CA, Cain began playing California blues clubs in the mid-'80s, most notable the JJ's Cafe and JJ's Lounge South Bay circuit. Soon, his following was large enough to earn him a contract with an independent record label, Blue Rock'it. Cain's debut album, *Late Night City Blues,* was released in 1987. By this time, his backing band featured lead tenor saxophonist Noel Catura, bassist Ron Torbensen, saxophonist Mark Whitney, and drummer Robert Higgins. The album received good reviews, which led to national bookings for Cain and his band, as well as several European dates. In 1988, Cain and his band received a handful of WC Handy Award nominations, including Blues Band of the Year and Guitarist of the Year. Cain signed to Blind Pig in 1990, releasing his second album, *Cuttin' Loose,* the same year. The guitarist stayed at Blind Pig for the next few years, releasing *Can't Buy A Break* in 1992 and *Somewhere Along the Way* in 1995. Cain and his band remained a popular concert attraction throughout the '90s. — *Bill Dahl & Stephen Thomas Erlewine*

Late Night City Blues / 1987 / Blue Rock'it ◆◆◆
This debut album was rewarded with four Handy Award nominations. — *Bill Dahl*

● **Cuttin' Loose** / 1990 / Blind Pig ◆◆◆◆
This is a wonderful, big-voiced, contemporary West Coast bluesman and superb guitar player. There are several horns in the band, giving it a great, huge sound. Even better things will be coming. — *Niles J. Frantz*

Can't Buy a Break / 1992 / Blind Pig ✦✦✦✦

Can't Buy a Break is a slow-burning, laidback contemporary blues record that positively swings. Cain's licks are clean, warm and fluid—he's able to seamlessly bounce back and forth between R&B, funk, jazz, jump blues, and Chicago blues. Furthermore, he proves himself to be an adept saxophonist, keyboardist, and vocalist, as well as songwriter—the album is a true tour-de-force. His backing band is tight and sympathetic, giving the impression that Cain is fronting a much larger band than he is. It's a refreshing, diverse, and relaxed record that shows there is more to contemporary blues than wailing blues-rock. — *Thom Owens*

Somewhere Along the Way / Nov. 1995 / Blind Pig ✦✦✦

Unscheduled Flight / Nov. 18, 1997 / Blue Rock'it ✦✦✦

J.J. Cale

b. Dec. 5, 1938, Oklahoma City, OK
Guitar, Vocals / Singer-Songwriter, Blues-Rock, Pop-Rock

Notorious for his laidback, rootsy style, J.J. Cale (born Jean Jacques Cale) is best known for writing "After Midnight" and "Cocaine," songs that Eric Clapton later made into hits. But Cale's influence wasn't only through songwriting—his distinctly loping sense of rhythm and shuffling boogie became the blueprint for the adult-oriented roots-rock of Clapton and Mark Knopfler, among others. Cale's refusal to vary the sound of his music over the course of his career caused some critics to label him as a one-trick pony, but he managed to build a dedicated cult following with his sporadically released recordings.

Born in Oklahoma City but raised in Tulsa, OK, Cale played in a variety of rock 'n' roll bands and Western swing groups as a teenager, including one outfit that also featured Leon Russell. In 1959, at the age of 21, he moved to Nashville, where he was hired by the Grand Ole Opry's touring company. After a few years, he returned to Tulsa, where he reunited with Russell and began playing local clubs. In 1964, Cale and Russell moved to Los Angeles with another local Oklahoma musician, Carl Radle.

Shortly after he arrived in Los Angeles, Cale began playing with Delaney and Bonnie. He only played with the duo for a brief time, beginning a solo career in 1965. That year, he cut the first version of "After Midnight," which would become his most famous song. Around 1966, Cale formed the Leathercoated Minds with songwriter Roger Tillison. One group released a psychedelic album called *A Trip Down Sunset Strip* the same year.

Deciding that he wouldn't be able to forge a career in Los Angeles, Cale returned to Tulsa in 1967. Upon his return, he set about playing local clubs. Within a year, he had recorded a set of demos. Radle obtained a copy of the demos and forwarded it to Denny Cordell, who was founding a record label called Shelter with Leon Russell. Shelter signed Cale in 1969. The following year, Eric Clapton recorded "After Midnight," taking it to the American Top 20 and thereby providing Cale with needed exposure and royalties. In December of 1971, Cale released his debut album, *Naturally*, on Shelter Records; the album featured the Top 40 hit "Crazy Mama," as well as a re-recorded version of "After Midnight," which nearly reached the Top 40, and "Call Me the Breeze," which Lynyrd Skynyrd later covered. Cale followed *Naturally* with *Really*, which featured the minor hit "Lies," later that year.

Following the release of *Really*, J.J. Cale adopted a slow work schedule, releasing an album every other year or so. *Okie*, his third album, appeared in 1974. Two years later, he released *Troubadour*, which yielded "Hey Baby," his last minor hit, as well as the original version of "Cocaine," a song that Clapton would later cover. By this point, Cale had settled into a comfortable career as a cult artist and he rarely made any attempt to break into the mainstream. One more album on Shelter Records, *Number Five*, appeared in 1979 and then he switched labels, signing with MCA in 1981. MCA only released one album (1981's *Shades*) and Cale moved to Mercury Records the following year, releasing *Grasshopper*.

In 1983, Cale released his eighth album, *No. 8*. The album became his first not to chart. Following its release, Cale left Mercury and he entered a long period of seclusion, reappearing in late 1989 with *Travel-Log*, which was released on the British independent label Silvertone; the album appeared in America the following year. *Number 10* was released in 1992. The album failed to chart, but it re-established his power as a cult artist. He moved to

the major label Virgin in 1994, releasing *Close to You* the same year. It was followed by *Guitar Man* in 1996. — *Stephen Thomas Erlewine*

Naturally / Dec. 1971 / Mercury ✦✦✦

J.J. Cale's debut album, *Naturally*, was recorded after Eric Clapton made "After Midnight" a huge success. Instead of following Slowhand's cue and constructing a slick blues-rock album, Cale recruited a number of his Oklahoma friends and made a laid-back country-rock record that firmly established his distinctive, relaxed style. Cale included a new version of "After Midnight" on the album, but the true meat of the record lay in songs like "Crazy Mama," which became a hit single, and "Call Me the Breeze," which Lynyrd Skynyrd later covered. On these songs and many others on *Naturally*, Cale effortlessly captured a lazy, rolling boogie that contradicted all the commerical styles of boogie, blues, and country-rock at the time. Where his contemporaries concentrated on solos, Cale worked the song and its rhythm, and the result was a pleasant, engaging album that was in no danger of raising anybody's temperature. — *Thom Owens*

Really / Dec. 1972 / Mercury ✦✦✦

Cale's guitar work manages to be both understated and intense here. The same is true of his seemingly offhand singing, which finds him drawling lines like "You get your gun, I'll get mine" with disarming casualness. But he has trouble coming up with original material as strong as that on his debut, and for some, his approach will be too casual; there are many times, when the band is percolating along and Cale is muttering into the microphone, that the music seems to be all background and no foreground. You may find yourself waiting for a payoff that never comes. — *William Ruhlmann*

Okie / May 1974 / Mercury ✦✦✦

Cale moves toward country and gospel on some songs here, but since those are two of his primary influences, the movement is slight. And on some songs, longtime producer Audie Ashworth attempts to place more emphasis on Cale's vocals by double-tracking them and pushing them up in the mix. But much of this is still low-key and bluesy in what was becoming Cale's patented style. — *William Ruhlmann*

Troubadour / Sep. 1976 / Mercury ✦✦✦✦

Producer Audie Ashworth introduced some different instruments, notably vibes and what sound like horns (although none are credited), for a slightly altered sound here. But Cale's albums are so steeped in his introspective style that they become interchangeable. If you like one of them, chances are you'll want to have them all. This one is notable for introducing "Cocaine," which Eric Clapton covered on his *Slowhand* album a year later. — *William Ruhlmann*

5 / Aug. 1979 / Mercury ✦✦

As Cale's influence on others expanded, he just continued to turn out the occasional album of bluesy, minor-key tunes. This one was even sparer than usual, with the artist handling bass as well as guitar on many tracks. Listened to today, it sounds so much like a Dire Straits album, it's scary. (Mark Knopfler & Co. had appeared in 1978, seven years after Cale.) — *William Ruhlmann*

Shades / Feb. 1981 / Mercury ✦✦

Grasshopper / Mar. 1982 / Mercury ✦✦

J.J. Cale drifts toward a more pop approach on this album, starting with the lead-off track, "City Girls," which could almost but not quite be a hit single. The usual blues and country shuffle approach is in effect, but Audie Ashworth's production is unusually sharp, the playing has more bite than usual, and Cale, whose vocals are for the most part up in the mix, sounds more engaged. It's not clear, however, that this is an improvement over his usual laidback approach, and, in any case, it shouldn't be over-emphasized—this is still a J.J. Cale album, with its cantering tempos and single-note guitar runs. It's just that, when you have a style as defined as Cale's, little movements in style loom larger. — *William Ruhlmann*

8 / 1983 / Mercury ✦✦

Twelve years and eight albums into his recording career, Cale's approach has changed little, and here is another collection of groove tunes that act as platforms for the artist's intricate guitar playing. He is sometimes accompanied by a female vocalist, co-writer Christine Lakeland. — *William Ruhlmann*

Special Edition / 1984 / Mercury ✦✦✦✦

Sinuous rhythms, conversational singing, and, most of all, intricate, bluesy guitar playing characterize Cale's performances of his own songs. This compilation, covering 11 years of recording, includes the songs Eric Clapton, who borrowed heavily from Cale's style in his 1970s solo work, made famous: "After Midnight" and "Cocaine." — *William Ruhlmann*

Travel-Log / Feb. 1990 / Silvertone ✦✦✦✦

Cale's first album in six years finds him taking a more aggressive stance in terms of tempos and playing, although he remains a man with a profound sense of the groove, and especially as a singer, a minimalist. But as he says, "Shuffle or die." — *William Ruhlmann*

10 / Nov. 10, 1992 / Silvertone ✦✦✦

There are no major surprises on Cale's tenth outing; fans get the same dependable, unassuming, comfy results, like a well-worn but form-fitting pair of slippers. Subtle licks percolate and resonate from the front-porch jam session on "Jailer," "Low Rider," "Lonesome Train" and "Shady Grove" choogle along, as amiable as they are hypnotic. The closest thing to a twist comes with the phased vocals and spiraling guitar runs of "Digital Blues." It would be easy to imagine *Number 10* getting completely buried behind a wash of '90s white noise, but for those prepared to kick off their boots and sit a spell, Cale's latest offers up some seductive rewards. — *Roch Parisien*

Closer to You / Aug. 23, 1994 / Virgin ✦✦

Guitar Man / Jun. 25, 1996 / Virgin ✦✦✦

J.J. Cale's albums usually sound interchangeable, and his twelfth release, *Guitar Man*, is no exception. Although he has recorded *Guitar Man* as a one-man band effort, it sounds remarkably relaxed and laidback, like it was made with a seasoned bar band. That doesn't mean there's much excitement on the album, but Cale's music has never been about excitement—it's more about laying back and letting the music flow. Of course, that approach results in remarkably uneven records, and *Guitar Man* is no exception. There's a handful of very good songs, but there's nothing on the level of his previous classics. It's just another pleasant J.J. Cale album, nothing more but nothing less, either. — *Thom Owens*

● **Anyway the Wind Blows: The JJ Cale Anthology** / Jun. 17, 1997 / Polygram ✦✦✦✦

Although it is a little too extensive for casual fans, the double-disc, 50-track *Anyway the Wind Blows—The JJ Cale Anthology* is a definitive retrospective of J.J. Cale's career, featuring all the highlights from his career. Cale's albums often sounded similar, but they were remarkably uneven in terms of quality, which is what makes *Anyway the Wind Blows* essential for both neophytes and collectors. Not only is it a perfect introduction, containing such essentials as "Cocaine," "Call Me the Breeze" and "After Midnight," but it is one of his most consistently listenable and enjoyable discs. — *Stephen Thomas Erlewine*

The Very Best of J.J. Cale / Jun. 9, 1998 / Polygram ✦✦✦✦

In 1984, the year after J.J. Cale completed his contractual obligation to Mercury Records, the label released the compilation *Special Edition* on LP, sampling his first eight albums, released between 1972 and 1983. A mere 13 years later comes this CD compilation of the same material, which contains all 12 tracks from *Special Edition* plus an additional eight, among them the previously unreleased "Midnight in Memphis." Curiously for an artist best known for the covers of his songs, Cale is more of a player than a songwriter, and his intricate fingerpicking style, weaving in and out of the shuffles that constitute most of his tunes, is his real signature. (Those of you who haven't heard it have probably heard Cale's chief disciple, Mark Knopfler of Dire Straits.) The difference in his work between the best and the rest is thus subtle and consists mainly in a slightly greater craft and, inescapably, familiarity—you just know such songs as "After Midnight," "Cocaine," and "Call Me the Breeze" better. This collection demonstrates that Cale has a clutch of other songs just as good, and includes the songwriter's versions of the hit covers, too.— *William Ruhlmann*

Blind James Campbell

b. Sep. 17, 1906, Nashville, TN
Modern Electric Blues
Among the last of a dying breed of Southern street musicians, bluesman Blind James Campbell and his Friendly Five were a staple of the Nashville

musical landscape for decades. Campbell was born in Music City on September 17, 1906; although he played guitar from the age of 13, he did not pursue performing as a livelihood until the age of 30, when he was left permanently blind following an accident at the fertilizer plant where he worked. He then formed a group dubbed the Nashville Washboard Band, a loose-knit aggregation which consisted of himself on vocals and guitar, mandolin, lard can (or tub bass), and a washboard; they honed their skills not only on the streets but also at area parties, typically playing to white audiences but also sitting in at black roadhouses. Campbell followed much the same path in the years and decades which followed, later informally rechristening the band the Friendly Five; in 1962 he was discovered by Arhoolie Records chief Chris Strachwitz, who recorded him with a backing group consisting of multi-instrumentalist Beauford Clay, trumpeter George Bell, second guitarist Bell Ray and tuba player Ralph Robinson. Unhappy with the quality of the recordings, Strachwitz returned to Nashville a year later and recorded Campbell again; the best selections were then assembled for release as the LP *Blind James Campbell and His Nashville Street Band.* —*Jason Ankeny*

● **Blind James Campbell & His Nashville Street Band** / 1995 / Arhoolie ✦✦✦✦

On their lone release, Blind James Campbell and His Nashville Street Band serve up a singular blend of blues, jazz, old-time, skiffle, and jug band music; while their material is traditional, the presentation is anything but, with a tuba taking the place of bass guitar and Campbell's gravelly voice going lower and deeper than either. —*Jason Ankeny*

Eddie C. Campbell

b. May 6, 1939, Duncan, MS
Guitar, Vocals / Modern Electric Blues, Modern Electric Chicago Blues
Happily, Eddie C. Campbell is currently back in Chicago after spending a decade entrenched in Europe. His shimmering West Side-styled guitar style and unusually introspective songwriting have been a breath of fresh air on the Windy City circuit, reuniting the veteran bluesman with fans he left behind in 1984.

Campbell left rural Mississippi for the bright lights of Chicago at age ten, sneaking a peek at Muddy Waters at the 1125 Club soon after he arrived and jamming with his idol when he was only 12. He fell in with some West side youngbloods—Luther Allison, Magic Sam—and honed a guitar attack rooted deep in the ringing style. Campbell paid his sideman dues on the bandstand with everyone from Howlin' Wolf and Little Walter to Little Johnny Taylor and Jimmy Reed. Koko Taylor recommended Campbell to Willie Dixon, who hired him as a Chicago Blues All-Star in 1976.

Campbell cut his own debut album, the rousing *King of the Jungle*, in 1977 for the Steve Wisner's short-lived Mr. Blues logo (now available on Rooster Blues, it includes the guitarist's lighthearted Yuletide perennial "Santa's Been Messin' with the Kid"). But he split the country for calmer European climates, recording a nice 1984 album with a Dutch group, *Let's Pick It!*, that first came out on Black Magic and now adorns the Evidence catalog.

When Campbell finally returned stateside for the birth of his son, he made up for lost time by gigging steadily around Chicago and making a comeback album for Blind Pig, *That's When I Know*, that contained some very distinctive originals. Hopefully, he'll stay put for a while. — *Bill Dahl*

● **King of the Jungle** / 1977 / Rooster Blues ✦✦✦✦

Flamboyant West Side-styled guitarist's debut album, first issued on the short-lived Mr. Blues logo, remains his best, with his slashing guitarist and lowdown vocals beautifully presented on covers of material by Magic Sam, Muddy Waters, Percy Mayfield, Willie Mabon, and his own Yuletide perennial "Santa's Messin' with the Kid." Great band, too: harpist Carey Bell, pianist Lafayette Leake, bassist Bob Stroger, and drummer Clifton James. — *Bill Dahl*

Let's Pick It / Oct. 1984 / Evidence ✦✦✦✦

Recorded while Eddie Campbell was on a European sojourn that lasted a decade or so, this disc, cut back in 1984 for Black Magic with an overseas combo, is a very convincing effort mixing Campbell's own "Cold and Hungry," "Dream," and "Messin' with My Pride" with songs by Albert King, Jimmy Reed, Jimmie Lee Robinson, and Magic Sam. — *Bill Dahl*

The Baddest Cat on the Block / 1985 / JSP ✦✦
This is not his best album. — *Bill Dahl*

Mind Trouble / 1988 / Double Trouble ✦✦✦

That's When I Know / 1994 / Blind Pig ✦✦✦✦

During that long decade away from home, Campbell's skills as a unique blues songwriter certainly blossomed. His triumphant homecoming set contains some highly distinctive material—a homespun "Sister Taught Me Guitar," the incandescent title track, a forceful "Sleep," and "Busted," and a decidedly mystical "Son of Sons." —*Bill Dahl*

John Campbell

b. Jan. 20, 1952, Shreveport, LA, **d.** Jun. 13, 1993

Guitar / Cool, Modern Electric Blues

Guitarist, singer, and songwriter John Campbell had the potential of turning a whole new generation of people onto the blues in the 1990s, much the same way Stevie Ray Vaughan did in the 1980s. His vocals were so powerful and his guitar playing so fiery, you couldn't help but stop what you were doing and pay attention to what you were hearing. But unfortunately, because of frail health and a rough European tour, he suffered a heart attack while sleeping on June 13, 1993, at the age of 41.

Campbell was born in Shreveport, LA, on January 20, 1952, and grew up in Center, TX. Although he got his own guitar at age eight and began playing professionally when he was 13, he didn't get serious about playing blues for a living until he was involved in a near-fatal drag racing accident that broke several ribs, collapsed a lung, and took his right eye. In his teens, Campbell opened for people like Clarence "Gatemouth" Brown, Albert Collins, and Son Seals, but he later got sidetracked by drag racing, and it was while he was recuperating from his near-death drag racing accident that he re-learned guitar, developing his own distinctive, rhythm and slide-heavy style, based in some measure on the music of Lightnin' Hopkins.

In 1985, after playing a variety of clubs between east Texas and New Orleans, Campbell moved to New York. One night in New York, guitarist Ronnie Earl happened upon Campbell in a club, playing with Johnny Littlejohn. Earl was so impressed that he offered to produce an album by Campbell, and the result was *A Man and His Blues* (Crosscut 1019), a Germany-only release that has since been made available in the US. That album earned Campbell a W.C. Handy Award nomination in 1989, and not long after that, the rock 'n' roll world started to take notice of him. Although he never sent a tape to a record company in his life, after drawing ever-growing crowds to the downtown New York clubs where he played, executives at Elektra Records took notice of him and signed him to a contract. Both of his albums for Elektra, *One Believer* (1991) and *Howlin' Mercy* (1993) are brilliant, well-produced recordings, yet they only hint at Campbell's potential for greatness, had he lived longer. —*Richard Skelly*

One Believer / 1991 / Elektra ✦✦✦✦

A ten-tune program of mostly original compositions, it was co-written with Dennis Walker, who co-produced it. The Robert Cray Band rhythm section is on hand for half of this very impressive album. —*Bob Porter*

● **Howlin' Mercy** / 1993 / Elektra ✦✦✦✦

There are plenty of fine performers who do credible, down-and-dirty, swampy blues. John Campbell is the whole swamp. *Howlin' Mercy* is contemporary blues at its most powerful. On the whole, the album is anchored by a thundering rhythm section and Campbell's grinding, cement-mixer voice—a riveting instrument that expresses the torment of a life experience you really only want to know about second hand. —*Roch Parisien*

Canned Heat

f. 1966, Los Angeles, CA, **db.** 1981

Group / Blues-Rock, Modern Electric Blues, Boogie Rock

A hard-luck blues band of the '60s, Canned Heat was founded by blues historians and record collectors Al Wilson and Bob Hite. They seemed to be on the right track and played all the right festivals (including Monterey and Woodstock, making it very prominently into the documentaries about both) but somehow never found a lasting audience.

Certainly their hearts were in the right place. Their debut album—released shortly after their appearance at Monterey—was every bit as deep into the roots of the blues as any other combo of the time mining similar turf, with the exception of the original Paul Butterfield band. Hite was nicknamed "The Bear" and stalked the stage in the time-honored tradition

of Howlin' Wolf and other large-proportioned bluesmen. Wilson was an extraordinary harmonica player, with a fat tone and great vibrato. His work on guitar, especially in open tunings (he played on Son House's rediscovery recordings of the mid-'60s, incidentally) gave the band a depth and texture that most other rhythm players could only aspire to. Henry Vestine—another dyed-in-the-wool record collector—was the West Coast's answer to Michael Bloomfield and capable of fretboard fireworks at a moment's notice. Their breakthrough moment occurred with the release of their second album, establishing them with hippie ballroom audiences as the "kings of the boogie." As a way of paying homage to the musician they got the idea from in the first place, they later collaborated on an album with John Lee Hooker that was one of the elder bluesman's most successful outings with a young White (or Black, for that matter) combo backing him up. After two big chart hits with "Goin' up the Country" and an explosive version of Wilbert Harrison's "Let's Work Together," Wilson died under mysterious (probably drug-related) circumstances in 1970, and Hite carried on with various reconstituted versions of the band until his death just before a show in 1981, from a heart seizure. —*Cub Koda & Bruce Eder*

Hooker 'n' Heat / 1971 / EMI ✦✦✦

John Lee Hooker's simple boogie was something Canned Heat mastered early on in their career. It could be argued that it was the only thing they mastered—they simply knew how to amplify it really loudly. They never found the subtle variations that Hooker did, but that doesn't mean they were a hindrance to the legend on this jam session. If anything, Hooker spurs the group to some of their grittiest, low-down boogie on record. The jams get a little lethargic and lengthy at times, especially since the album meanders its way through two discs, but this is certainly some of the best blues Canned Heat ever recorded. —*Stephen Thomas Erlewine*

● **The Best of Canned Heat** / 1972 / EMI America ✦✦✦✦

All of Canned Heat's best tracks and biggest hits ("Goin' up the Country," "On the Road Again") are included on this single-disc collection. —*Stephen Thomas Erlewine*

On the Road / 1989 / EMI ✦✦✦✦

On the Road is a compilation concentrating entirely on Canned Heat's earliest recordings, hitting all the highlights ("On the Road Again," "Goin' up the Country") from their biggest albums and offering most casual fans a definitive—if not a little too comprehensive—overview. —*Stephen Thomas Erlewine*

Uncanned! The Best of Canned Heat / May 17, 1994 / EMI America ✦✦✦✦

Uncanned! The Best of Canned Heat is exactly what it claims to be—the definitive portrait of the blues-soaked hippie boogie band. Spreading 41 tracks (including numerous rarities, alternate takes, and Levi commercials) over two CDs, the set is perfect for the hardcore Canned Heat collector. For casual fans, the collection simply contains too much music; they would be better served by the single-disc collection, *The Best of Canned Heat*. —*Stephen Thomas Erlewine*

Cannon's Jug Stompers (Gus Cannon)

Vocals, Banjo, Guitar, Jug, Kazoo, Piano / Acoustic Memphis Blues, Prewar Country Blues

Gus Cannon was the best known of all the jugband musicians and a seminal figure on the Memphis blues scene. His recollections have also provided us with much of our knowledge of the earliest days of the blues in the Mississippi Delta. Cannon led his Jug Stompers on banjo and jug in a historic series of dates for the Victor label in 1928-1930. The ensemble usually included a second banjoist or guitarist, one of whom often doubled on kazoo, and the legendary Noah Lewis on harmonica. The jug-band style enjoyed a revival during the folk boom of the '50s and '60s, resulting in an ultra-rare Gus Cannon album on Stax, of all labels, after his "Walk Right In" became the nation's best-selling record for the Rooftop Singers in 1963. Cannon's Victor output was also a favorite source of early blues material for the Grateful Dead. —*Jim O'Neal*

Legendary 1928-30 Recordings / 1994 / JSP ✦✦✦✦

● **The Complete Recordings** / Yazoo ✦✦✦✦

This innocent and exuberant Memphis good-time blues was the inspiration for '50s British skiffle and Greenwich Village folkies alike. —*Mark A. Humphrey*

Gus Cannon

b. Sep. 12, 1885, Bed Banks, MS, **d.** Oct. 15, 1979, Memphis, TN
Banjo, Fiddle, Guitar, Jug, Kazoo, Piano / Acoustic Blues, Acoustic Memphis
Blues, Prewar Country Blues

A remarkable musician (he could play five-string banjo and jug simultaneously!), Gus Cannon bridged the gap between early blues and the minstrel and folk styles which preceded it. His band of the '20s and '30s, Cannon's Jug Stompers, represents the apogee of jug band style. Songs they recorded, notably the raggy "Walk Right In," were staples of the folk repertoire decades later; and Cannon himself continued to record and perform into the 1970s.

Self-taught on an instrument made from a frying pan and a raccoon skin, he learned early repertoire in the 1890s from older musicians, notably Mississipian Alec Lee. The early 1900s found him playing around Memphis with songster Jim Jackson and forming a partnership with Noah Lewis whose harmonica wizardry would be basic to the Jug Stompers sound. In 1914, Cannon began work with a succession of medicine shows which would continue into the 1940s, and where he further developed his style and repertoire.

His recording career began with Paramount sessions in 1927. He continued to record into the '30s as a soloist and with his incredible trio which included Noah Lewis along with guitarists Hosea Wood and Ashley Thompson. (Side projects included duets with Blind Blake and the first ever recordings of slide banjo!) Often obliged to find employment in other fields than music, Cannon continued to play anyway, mostly around Memphis. He resumed his stalled recording efforts in 1956 with sessions for Folkways. Subsequent sessions paired him with other Memphis survivors like Furry Lewis. Advancing age curtailed his activities in the '70s, but he still played the occasional cameo, sometimes from a wheelchair, until shortly before his death. *— Steve James*

Walk Right In / 1962 / Stax ♦♦

Complete Recorded Works, Vol. 2 (1929-1930) / 1990 / Document ♦♦♦
Highlighted by Gus Cannon's signature "Walk Right In"—popularized in the early '60s by the Rooftop Singers—the second volume in Document's series is a jumble of prime recordings by Cannon and longtime partner Noah Lewis, collecting both solo sides and various group outings. The first tracks come from the Beale Street Boys, a duo comprising Cannon and vocalist/banjoist Hosea Woods, and are followed by a handful of solo harmonica recordings by Lewis; despite their extracurricular activities, by the time all three come together as Cannon's Jug Stompers they're in peak form, shifting easily from the ribald "Tired Chicken" to the plaintive "Going to Germany." With an ad hoc jug band including guitarist Sleepy John Estes and mandolinist Yank Rachell, Lewis then headlines four more sides before rejoining Cannon for one final session which brought their recording career together to a close. *— Jason Ankeny*

Complete Recorded Works, Vol. 1 (1927-1928) / 1990 / Document ♦♦♦

Complete Recorded Works, Vols. 1-2 / Document ♦♦♦
All of the recordings Gus Cannon—both as a solo artist and with his band the Jug Stompers—made between 1927 and 1930 are collected on the two-volume set *Complete Recorded Works* (each disc is sold seperately). For historians and completists, this set is essential, but casual fans will find Yazoo's *Complete Works* more manageable. *— Thom Owens*

★ **Complete Works** / Yazoo ♦♦♦♦♦
Complete Works compiles all of the recordings Cannon's Jug Stompers made in the late '20s. Gus Cannon and the Jug Stompers were the definitive jug band and all of their classic tracks, including "Walk Right In," are featured on this essential single-disc collection. *— Thom Owens*

The Caravans

f. 1952, Chicago, IL
Group / Traditional Gospel, Black Gospel

During the period stretching from the late '50s to the mid-'60s, the Caravans went unrivaled as the nation's most popular touring gospel group; acclaimed as one of the greatest female acts ever to arrive on the spiritual music front, their fluctuating roster was unparalleled as a launching pad for future superstars—Shirley Caesar, Inez Andrews, Bessie Griffin, and James Cleveland were just a few of the ensemble's alumni who later went on to solo fame. The Caravans were formed in Chicago in 1952 by contralto Albertina Walker and other onetime members of the Robert Anderson Singers, among them

Ora Lee Hopkins, Elyse Yancey, and Nellie Grace Daniels; virtually from the outset, their lineup shifted regularly, but in addition to longtime mainstay Walker, the recordings the group made for the States label between 1952 and 1956 include Griffin, Dorothy Norwood, and Cassietta George, who enlisted in 1954. Also present was Cleveland, who not only accompanied the group on piano but also narrated hymns, his relaxed monologues a stark contrast to the fervent group vocals behind him.

By 1956, the Caravans were among the most popular acts in all of gospel music, famed for their uncanny—almost telepathic—teamwork. They moved to Savoy in 1958, where their lineup now included both Andrews and Caesar as well as Dolores Washington; the combination of the young soprano phenom Caesar and the shrieking contralto Andrews was a powerhouse one-two punch, and as the decade drew to a close, the Caravans were the queens of the gospel circuit. Although Andrews had exited by 1962, the group continued to ride high, signing to Vee-Jay to record the LP *Seek Ye the Lord*. Their Vee-Jay tenure proved their most stable, with a consistent roster of Walker, Caesar, George, Washington, Josephine Howard, and pianist James Herndon appearing on all of their output for the label. However, when Caesar exited in 1966 to go solo, the Caravans' run at the top ended, and within months only Walker remained. She set about forming a new edition which included future disco diva Loleatta Holloway, but the venture proved short-lived; Caravans reunion concerts, however, were common in the years to follow. *—Jason Ankeny*

The Best of the Caravans / 1977 / Savoy ♦♦♦
This doesn't necessarily contain their best material, only those songs that garnered either chart success or radio airplay during the 1950s and early '60s. Like all Savoy releases, there's almost no discographical information, although Walker, Andrews, and Caesar are the artists featured most prominently. *—Ron Wynn*

Soul Salvation / 1978 / Fairway ♦♦♦♦
More soul-searing songs led by Cassietta George, Inez Andrews, Albertina Walker, and Shirley Caesar. *— Opal Louis Nations*

Seek Ye the Lord/The Soul of the Caravans / Oct. 1993 / Vee-Jay ♦♦♦♦
1962's *Seek Ye the Lord* and the following year's *The Soul of the Caravans*, the group's first two LPs for the Vee-Jay label, are compiled on this fine two-fer set featuring the incendiary vocals of Shirley Caesar. It's Caravans leader Albertina Walker, however, who most frequently commands the spotlight, taking over the first five tracks for solo performances; while Caesar chimes in with scorching originals including "Jesus Will Save," "One of These Old Days," and "I'm Going Thru," Cassietta George also assumes control for typically elegant readings of "I'm Ready to Save the Lord," "Lord, Don't Leave Us Now," and "My Religion." *—Jason Ankeny*

Amazing Grace / May 30, 1995 / Charly ♦♦♦♦
Best of the Vee-Jay output with Albertina Walker, Shirley Caesar, and Inez Andrews. *—Opal Louis Nations*

Carry Me Home / Oct. 24, 1995 / Hob ♦♦♦♦
Fabulous gospel from the golden age. *— Opal Louis Nations*

Jesus & Me: The Very Best of the Caravans / Mar. 3, 1998 / Collectables ♦♦♦
Fine Vee-Jay sides led by one of today's major soloists. *— Opal Louis Nations*

★ **Till I Meet the Lord** / ♦♦♦♦♦
The collection here is taken from the two Vee-Jay albums recorded in the early '60s between two lengthy contracts with Herman Lubinsky's Savoy label. Featured singers include founder, manager, and lead Albertina ("Tina") Walker, ably supported by Cassietta George, the great Shirley Caesar, and Josephine Howard, supported by James Herndon and Kenneth Woods on organ and piano. There are some fine high-spirited moments with Walker's raspy wails and Caesar's amazing glissandos. *— Opal Louis Nations, Roots & Rhythm Newsletter*

Chuck Carbo

Vocals / New Orleans R&B, R&B

The mellifluous vocal tones of Chuck Carbo were a principal ingredient in the success of the Spiders, the premier R&B vocal group around New Orleans during the 1950s. He's mounted a strong comeback bid of late as a smooth solo artist, cutting two albums for Rounder: *Drawers Trouble* in 1993 and 1996's *The Barber Blues*.

The gospel-steeped Carbo (whose actual first name is Hayward) and his brother Chick (real first name: Leonard) shared frontman duties for the Spiders, whose hits for Imperial included the two-sided smash "I Didn't Want to Do It"/"You're the One" and a ribald "I'm Slippin' In" in 1954 and "Witchcraft" (later covered by Elvis Presley) the next year. Imperial's main man in the Crescent City, Dave Bartholomew, produced the quintet's 1954-56 output, as well as writing many of their best numbers (notably a risqué "The Real Thing"). Carbo cut a few 45s under his own name for Imperial, Rex, and Ace after going solo; Chick waxed 45s of his own for Atlantic, Vee-Jay, and Instant.

Chuck Carbo never stopped performing entirely, although he made his living as a lumber truck driver when gigs got scarce. In 1989, he scored a local hit with his cover of Jeannie and Jimmy Cheatham's "Meet Me with Your Black Drawers On." It was reprised on *Drawers Trouble*, a comeback set reuniting Carbo with pianists Mac "Dr. John" Rebennack and Edward Frank. *The Barber's Blues* ensured Carbo's return to the spotlight with two more Cheatham copyrights and a second-line "Hey, Mardi Gras! (Here I Am)." — *Bill Dahl*

● **Drawers Trouble** / 1993 / Rounder ✦✦✦✦
Veteran New Orleans R&B singer Carbo proves he's a capable front man even without the presence of his '50s vocal group, the Spiders, on this infectious comeback set. With Crescent City vet Edward Frank handling piano and arranging duties, Carbo smoothly intones a mostly original lineup of songs (Jeannie & Jimmy Cheatham's lascivious standard "Meet Me with Your Black Drawers On" being one of the few exceptions). Dr. John contributes his considerable skills on keyboard and guitar to the project. — *Bill Dahl*

The Barber's Blues / 1996 / Rounder ✦✦✦
Ex-Spiders lead Carbo returns with a Rounder encore that eschews Dr. John but brings back Edward Frank as co-producer and pianist. Some of the selections are a little on the hackneyed side (a permanent moratorium on "Everyday I Have the Blues," please!), but Carbo's second line-based "Hey, Mardi Gras! (Here I Am)," the title item, and a easy-on-the-ears reprise of the Cheathams' "Don't Boogie with Your Black Drawers On" hit the spot. — *Bill Dahl*

Barbara Carr

b. Jan. 9, 1941, St. Louis, MO
Vocals / Soul, Blues, Electric R&B
Folks only familiar with her more recent work may be mildly surprised that alluring singer Barbara Carr recorded for Chess back in 1966. Carr's "Don't Knock Love" was a delicious slice of Chicago soul arranged by Phil Wright that got dusted off and released by Chess a second time in 1970 when she came back to the company and cut "Think About It Baby" (written, arranged, and produced by St. Louis saxist Oliver Sain). After a lengthy fallow period, Carr returned with an infectious "Good Woman Go Bad" for (presumably) her own Bar-Car logo. Carr also did a credible job on "Messin' with My Mind," a George Jackson number that both Otis Clay and Clarence Carter have also cut. Stan Lewis' Shreveport-based Paula Records recently issued an album of Carr material from this era that deftly mixes blues and soul genres. — *Bill Dahl*

Footprints on the Ceiling / Mar. 4, 1997 / Ecko ✦✦✦✦

Bone Me Like You Own Me / May 5, 1998 / Ecko ✦✦✦

● **Good Woman Go Bad** / Paula ✦✦✦✦
Barbara Carr had a number of good Chess singles during the late '60s, but she never received the opportunity to record a full album for the label. She didn't make a full-length album until the '90s, when all kinds of underappreciated blues veterans were given a second chance. Carr was one of the more deserving of that breed, as *Good Woman Go Bad* proves. She's a dynamic, energetic vocalist who invests true passion to even mediocre songs. Unfortunately, there are a few too many average tunes on the record, but Carr saves the day with her storming performances. — *Thom Owens*

Leroy Carr

b. Mar. 27, 1905, Nashville, TN, **d.** Apr. 29, 1935, Indianapolis, IN
Piano, Vocals / Piano Blues
The term "urban blues" is usually applied to post-World War II blues-band music, but one of the forefathers of the genre in its pre-electric format was pianist Leroy Carr. Teamed with the exemplary guitarist Scrapper Blackwell

in Indianapolis, Carr became one of the top blues stars of his day, composing and recording almost 200 sides during his short lifetime, including such classics as "How Long, How Long," "Prison Bound Blues," "When the Sun Goes Down," and "Blues Before Sunrise." His blues were expressive and evocative, recorded only with piano and guitar, yet as author Sam Charters has noted, Carr was "a city man" whose singing was never as rough or intense as the country bluesmen's; and as reissue producer Francis Smith put it, "He, perhaps more than any other single artist, was responsible for transforming the rural blues patterns of the '20s into the more city-oriented blues of the '30s."

Born in Nashville, Leroy Carr moved to Indianapolis as a child. While he was still in his teens, he taught himself how to play piano. Carr quit school in his mid-teens, heading out for a life on the road. For the next few years, he would play piano at various parties and dances in the midwest and south. During this time, he held a number of odd jobs—he joined a circus, he was in the army for a while, and he was briefly a bootlegger. In addition to his string of jobs, he was married for a short time.

Carr wandered back toward Indianapolis, where he met guitarist Scrapper Blackwell in 1928. The duo began performing and shortly afterward they were recording for Vocalion, releasing "How Long How Long Blues" before the year was finished. The song was an instant, surprise hit. For the next seven years, Carr and Blackwell would record a number of classic songs for Vocalion, including "Midnight Hour Blues," "Blues Before Sunrise," "Hurry Down Sunshine," "Shady Lane Blues" and many others.

Throughout the early '30s, Carr was one of the most popular bluesmen in America. While his professional career was successful, his personal life was spinning out of control, as he sunk deeper and deeper into alcoholism. His addiction eventually cut his life short—he died in April 1935. Carr left behind an enormous catalog of blues and his influence could be heard throughout successive generations of blues musicians, as evidenced by artists like T-Bone Walker, Otis Spann, and Champion Jack Dupree. — *Jim O'Neal & Stephen Thomas Erlewine*

Complete Recorded Works, Vols. 1-3 (1928-1932) / 1928-1932 / Document ✦✦✦
Over the course of three discs—which are all sold separately—Document has collected every song Leroy Carr cut in the late '20s and early '30s. For completists, the compilation is ideal, but there is too much music for casual fans of Carr or pre-war blues. There's important material here, but it is presented elsewhere on better, more manageable collections. — *Thom Owens*

Leroy Carr & Scrapper Blackwell (1929-1935) / 1929-1935 / Story of Blues ✦✦✦

1930-1935 / 1930-1935 / Magpie ✦✦✦✦
It's an incomplete collection, but *1930-1935* collects the great majority of Leroy Carr and Scrapper Blackwell's duets from the early '30s and provides a good introduction to one of the seminal Chicago blues guitar and piano duos. — *Thom Owens*

★ **Blues Before Sunrise** / 1962 / Portrait ✦✦✦✦✦
Despite minimal sound quality, this reissue contains some prime Leroy Carr/ Scrapper Blackwell material. They were arguably the greatest piano and guitar duo to emerge in the late '20s and early '30s. You can find these tracks on other import collections, but this was among the first reissues available on a domestic label. — *Ron Wynn*

Singin' the Blues / 1973 / Biograph ✦✦✦✦
This is late period Carr, superb material done in 1934. It's hard to believe, considering the depth of his piano playing and the vocal quality, that by the end of the next year, Carr's career would be finished. The sound quality is good enough to convey the range and might in Carr's piano fills and delivery. — *Ron Wynn*

☆ **Naptown Blues (1929-1934)** / 1988 / Yazoo ✦✦✦✦✦
A seminal piano/guitar duo, Leroy Carr was among the most influential early blues singer/pianists, and Scrapper Blackwell was a remarkably fluid guitarist. — *Mark A. Humphrey*

The Piano Blues, Vol. 2 / 1992 / Magpie ✦✦✦

Southbound Blues / 1994 / Drive ✦✦✦
With or without the great guitarist Scrapper Blackwell, pianist Carr remains among the greatest 1930s Chicago bluesmen. This re-release includes two of

his best numbers, "Midnight Hour Blues" and "Hurry Down Sunshine." At last here it is: an expensive German import worth twice the price for those two classics alone. —*John Storm Roberts, Original Music*

Complete Recorded Works, Vol. 4 (1932-34) / Jan. 10, 1996 / Document ++++

Complete Recorded Works, Vol. 5 (1934) / Jan. 10, 1996 / Document ++++

Complete Recorded Works, Vol. 6 (1934-35) / Jan. 10, 1996 / Document ++++

Unissued Test Pressings & Alternate Takes (1934-37) / Sep. 10, 1996 / Document ++++

How Long Blues 1928-1935 / Feb. 1998 / EPM +++

Sister Wynona Carr

b. Aug. 23, 1924, Cleveland, OH, d. May 12, 1976, Cleveland, OH
Vocals / R&B, Jump Blues
Though largely unrecognized during her own lifetime, singer and composer Sister Wynona Carr was among the truly pioneering artists of gospel's golden era; while her music—sophisticated and sensual, distinguished by lyrics of rare metaphorical depth and a progressive sound drawing heavily on jazz and blues—was simply too radical for contemporary listeners, in hindsight she stands as one of the great innovators of her day. Born in Cleveland, OH, on August 23, 1924, Carr began learning piano at the age of eight; at 13, she entered the Cleveland Music College to study voice, harmony, and arranging, and a short time later began performing in Baptist churches across the region. In 1944, she relocated to Detroit to direct a local choir, and in the months to follow also formed her own group, the Carr Singers, to tour the Midwest and the South.

While touring with the Wilson Jubilee Singers, an offshoot of Cleveland's renowned Wings Over Jordan Choir, Carr caught the attention of the Pilgrim Travelers' J.W. Alexander, who was so impressed by her talents that he funded her first demo recording and sent it to Specialty Records founder Art Rupe. The label quickly snapped her up, and in early 1949 Carr traveled to Los Angeles to record her first session, backed by a jump combo helmed by ace session pianist Austin McCoy. Her debut 78, pairing the swinging "Each Day" with the torch-like ballad "Lord Jesus," served as an immediate indication of her versatility; produced in the vein of Sister Rosetta Tharpe's recordings of the era, Rupe sought to further emphasize the comparisons between the two vocalists by appending "Sister" to Carr's name, a ploy which reportedly made her bristle.

Carr's next studio date followed in Philadelphia later in 1949; a revolutionary session, it yielded "I'm a Pilgrim Traveler," a reworking of the blues standard "St. James Infirmary," as well as "I Heard the News (Jesus Is Coming Again)," which updated the 1948 Roy Brown and Wynonie Harris hit "Good Rockin' Tonight." Other material, like the Carr original "Our Father," suggested a strong jazz influence; however, while all of the tracks recorded during the session promised to push the singer into new stylistic directions, Rupe apparently felt the songs were all too daring, and none of them were released. Carr's next return to the studio, in 1950, was far more traditional, and included a new rendition of "Our Father," recorded as a duet with Brother Joe May; it too went unreleased, although the song was later covered as a May solo side as well as in a version by the Five Blind Boys of Mississippi.

Despite all of the frustration and setbacks, Carr forged on; she toured relentlessly, but did not go back into the studio until mid-1952. With "The Ball Game," a vividly metaphorical tale of a showdown between Jesus and Satan, she finally scored a major gospel hit, yet her career continued to flounder—another two years passed prior to her next Specialty session, recorded in Detroit (where she was serving as choir director at the New Bethel Baptist Church under the Rev. C.L. Franklin). Although she recorded rarely, Carr nevertheless remained a highly prolific songwriter, composing poetic, topical material often inspired by headlines of the day; she cut dozens of demos for Specialty, and ironically enough earned more money from sales of her sheet music than from her actual recordings.

After successfully touring white nightclubs in 1954 with Sister Rosetta Tharpe and Marie Knight, Carr finally broke her ties with gospel to pursue a career singing R&B; in 1957, she scored with the hit ballad "Should I Ever Love Again," but again fate was against her—at the same time the record

was rising on the chart, she was stricken with tuberculosis, and spent the next two years on the sidelines, convalescing at her parents' home. A number of booking agencies sought Carr out, but she was simply too ill to perform; her career never recovered from the loss of momentum, and after leaving Specialty in 1959 she briefly signed to Reprise before spending the remainder of the 1960s performing on the Cleveland supper club circuit. As the 1970s dawned, Carr went into seclusion; her health continued to decline, and she died on May 12, 1976. —*Jason Ankeny*

Jump Jack Jump! / 1985 / Specialty ++++
This 24-track set covers Carr's R&B tunes, with many unissued but fine tunes such as "If These Walls Could Speak," "Finders Keepers," and "Weather Man" finally getting out of the vault. The CD also includes her trademark upbeat, sassy songs, "Jump Jack Jump," "Boppity Bop (Boogity Boop)," "Ding Dong Daddy," and "Nursery Rhyme Rock." Thematic variety wasn't her label's strong suit when it came to material, and they might have done better with more numbers like "Please Mr. Jailer" and "It's Raining Outside" and a few less boogies and jump pieces. —*Ron Wynn*

★ **Dragnet for Jesus** / 1992 / Specialty ++++++
This is a long-overlooked gospel writer, producer, and soloist: the "Billie Holiday" of gospel. The priceless material on this album is circa 1949-1954. —*Opal Louis Nations*

Chubby Carrier (Roy Carrier)

Accordion, Vocals / Zydeco, Contemporary Blues
While remaining steeped in the zydeco traditions of his native Louisiana, Chubby Carrier also infused his music with driving rock beats and bold arrangements to create a lively, contemporary sound. The son of Cajun accordionist Roy Carrier, he was still a child when he began playing drums in his father's band, and learned accordion at the age of 12. Influenced by the modernized zydeco of Clifton Chenier, he formed his own group, the Bayou Swamp Band, at the age of 18, but in 1987 returned to the drums to play with Terrance Simien's Mallet Playboys on tour. Carrier reassembled the Bayou Swamp Band in 1990, installing his brother Tony on drums and his cousin Kevin on washboard, in addition to bassist Rodney Dural (the nephew of Buckwheat Zydeco) and guitarist David LeJeune; after just six months on the road, the group signed to the Flying Fish label, where they issued *Boogie Woogie Zydeco* in 1991. With 1993's *Dance All Night* they moved to Blind Pig, where they remained for 1996's *Who Stole the Hot Sauce*. —*Jason Ankeny*

★ **Boogie Woogie Zydeco** / 1991 / Flying Fish +++++
After building a resume in zydeco circles playing with Terrance Simien & the Mallot Playboys, singer/accordion player Chubby Carrier struck out on his own in 1990 and soon signed with the Chicago-based Flying Fish label as a solo artist. *Boogie Woogie Zydeco* may have been recorded in the Chicago suburb of Evanston, but sweaty, exuberant originals like "Allons Dancez," "Hey Barbariba," and "Bernadette" are pure Louisiana. Carrier slows down the tempo for the 1960s-type soul numbers "Be Fair to the People" and "Sherrie," both of which are so appealing that they make one wish he embraced slower tempos more often. On the whole, however, the Louisiana native favors zydeco that is unrelenting in its energy. Zydeco fans should make a point of hunting for this CD. —*Alex Henderson*

Roy Carrier

Accordion / Zydeco
While not as well known as his son Chubby, accordionist Roy Carrier enjoyed a successful zydeco career in his own right. A native of Lawtell, Louisiana, he learned to play in the traditional Cajun style from his own father, and later formed his own band which he fronted when not working as an offshore oil-driller or operating his own small farm. At the age of 12, Chubby Carrier joined the band as a drummer, later going on to significant success as a solo performer; Roy continued on as a popular regional attraction, eventually opening his own Lawtell area zydeco club, the Offshore Lounge. During the late '80s, he signed to the Lanor Records label, scoring a pair of local hits with "I Found My Woman Doing the Zydeco" and "I'm Coming Home to Stay"; in 1991 he recorded *The Soulful Side of Zydeco* (a split release with Joe Walker), followed in 1995 by *Zydeco Strokin'.* —*Jason Ankeny*

Zydeco Strokin' / Nov. 1995 / Paula ◆◆◆

Soulful Side of Zydeco / Nov. 21, 1995 / Zane ◆◆◆◆

● **At His Best** / Feb. 20, 1996 / Zane ◆◆◆◆
At His Best collects many of Roy Carrier's greatest songs, even if they're not necessarily in their original versions. Nevertheless, these are really good versions of such staples as "You Better Watch Out," "Strokin'," "She's Naked," and "Leaving Lawtell," making it an excellent introduction to the zydeco accordionist. —*Thom Owens*

Karen Carroll

b. Jan. 30, 1958, Chicago, IL
Vocals / Chicago Blues
Blues singer Karen Carroll was seemingly destined for a career in music: not only was her mother Jeanne Carroll a blues and jazz vocalist as well, but her godparents were guitarist George Freeman and singer Bonnie Lee. Born in Chicago on January 30, 1958, Carroll started performing at the age of nine, joining her mother's band as a guitarist five years later; at 18 she struck out on her own, cutting her teeth in tiny South Side blues joints and developing a deep vocal style heavily influenced by jazz phrasing as well as the intensity of gospel. She made her recorded debut on Carey Bell's 1984 outing *Son of a Gun,* followed by the 1989 Eddie Lusk LP *Professor Strut;* Carroll made her solo debut with 1995's *Had My Fun,* returning two years later with *Talk to the Hand.* —*Jason Ankeny*

● **Had My Fun** / Oct. 3, 1995 / Delmark ◆◆◆◆
Karen Carroll has plenty of opportunity to strut her stuff on her debut, *Had My Fun.* Unlike many contemporary blues albums, which are highly polished blasts of blues-rock, *Had My Fun* takes its time. Many of the songs are torchy slow blues or down-and-dirty Chicago blues—either way, they sound natural, never forced. That's appropriate, since Carroll sings like a natural, carressing the ballads and growling the nastier numbers. Best of all, there's actual grit in the production—four of the songs were recorded live—and that allows Carroll to achieve her full potential on this impressive debut. —*Thom Owens*

Talk to the Hand / 1997 / Delmark ◆◆◆
While her debut *Had My Fun* featured Carroll's thunderous, gospel-influenced vocals in a live setting, this studio recording also spotlights her burgeoning songwriting skills. —*Jason Ankeny*

Bo Carter (Armenter Chatmon)

b. Mar. 21, 1893, Bolton, MS, d. Sep. 21, 1964, Memphis, TN
Banjo, Bass, Clarinet, Guitar, Vocals / Delta Blues, Acoustic Blues, Country Blues
Bo Carter (Armenter "Bo" Chatmon) had an unequaled capacity for creating sexual metaphors in his songs, specializing in such ribald imagery as "Banana in Your Fruit Basket," "Pin in Your Cushion," and "Your Biscuits Are Big Enough for Me." One of the most popular bluesmen of the '30s, he recorded enough material for several reissue albums, and he was quite an original guitar picker, or else three of those albums wouldn't have been released by Yazoo. (Carter employed a number of different keys and tunings on his records, most of which were solo vocal and guitar performances.) Carter's facility extended beyond the risqué business to more serious blues themes, and he was also the first to record the standard "Corrine Corrina" (1928). Bo and his brothers Lonnie and Sam Chatmon also recorded as members of the Mississippi Sheiks with singer/guitarist Walter Vinson. —*Jim O'Neal*

Bo Carter, Vols. 1-5 (1928-1940) / 1928-1940 / Document ◆◆◆
Document's five-disc series—sold individually, not as a package—cover everything Bo Carter recorded between 1928-1940. Although there is plenty of fine music on these discs, only a historian or a completist needs to listen to the entire series—any of Carter's single-disc collections give a better, more concise overview of his music. However, musicologists and diehard fans will find each of the five essential. —*Stephen Thomas Erlewine*

● **Greatest Hits, 1930-1940** / Feb. 1970 / Yazoo ◆◆◆◆
With mostly solo selections by Carter, plus a couple of Mississippi Sheiks songs, it features very fine and distinctive country-blues guitar playing and singing. Most of the songs are of the double-entendre variety—a possible reason why he's not as well known as he deserves to be, since some blues researchers did not deem his material worthy. As with most Yazoo releases,

the liner notes include various guitar tunings and chord progressions for each song—fascinating for guitarists. —*George Bedard*

Twist It Babe / 1974 / Yazoo ◆◆◆

Banana in Your Fruit Basket / 1978 / Yazoo ◆◆◆◆
Some of Carter's best double-entendre material, including the salacious "I Got Ants in My Pants." —*Cub Koda*

Bo Carter, Vol. 2 (1931-1934) / 1991 / Document ◆◆◆
22 songs (with three still missing) cut by Carter, solo with guitar or with Lonnie Chatmon on fiddle, over a three-year period. Document has had unusual luck with the quality on this release, as there's relatively little surface noise on much of it. This helps bring out the richness, dexterity, and playfulness of Carter's playing, as well as the expressiveness of his voice in extraordinary detail. Perhaps the most surprising element of these sides are the two unissued OKeh tracks from 1931, "The Law Is Gonna Step On You" and "Pig Meat Is What I Crave," which are the equal of anything that the label did put out from those same sessions, and show Carter's playing to great advantage and in extraordinarily high-quality sound. His music was probably closest in spirit to the early work of Tampa Red and Georgia Tom Dorsey, with its mixture of double-entendre lyrics and hokum influences. The three-year gap in Carter's recordings, caused by the crunch that hit the blues business with the Great Depression, show him re-emerging at the end (for Bluebird) with a more sophisticated sound, less stripped-down than his early sides but just as playful in its risqué way ("Banana in Your Fruit Basket," etc.). —*Bruce Eder*

Goree Carter

b. Dec. 31, 1930, Houston, TX, d. Dec. 29, 1990, Houston, TX
Guitar, Vocals / Electric Texas Blues
T-Bone Walker inspired a legion of young Texas blues guitarists during the years following World War II with his elegant electrified riffs and fat chords. Among his legion of disciples was Houston's Goree Carter, whose big break came when Solomon Kahal signed him to Houston's Freedom Records circa 1949.
Carter's best-known waxing, the torrid "Rock Awhile" (billed to Goree Carter & His Hepcats) emerged not long thereafter, its sizzling opening lick sounding quite a bit like primordial Chuck Berry. Freedom issued plenty of Carter platters over the next few years, and he later recorded for Imperial/Bayou, Sittin' in With, Coral, Jade, and Modern without denting the national charts. Eventually, he left music behind altogether. —*Bill Dahl*

● **Unsung Hero** / 1992 / Collectables ◆◆◆◆
Houston guitarist Goree Carter's slashing late-'40s/early-'50s sides for Freedom display a strong T-Bone Walker influence, though his best-known effort, the storming "Rock Awhile," kicks a lot harder than Walker's elegant output. These 14 sides are fine examples of the horn-leavened Lone Star sound of the early '50s; while derivative, Carter was a very competent axe-handler. —*Bill Dahl*

Joe Carter

b. Nov. 6, 1927, Midland, GA
Vocals, Slide Guitar / Blues-Rock, Electric Chicago Blues, Harmonica Blues
One of the truly great unsung heroes of the Chicago club scene of the 1950s, Joe Carter was a slide-playing twin disciple of Elmore James and Muddy Waters. Born in Georgia, Carter came under the early tutelage of local player Lee Willis, who showed the youngster various tunings and how to use a thumb pick. Arriving in Chicago by 1952, Joe made a beeline to the area's club scene to see his idols Muddy Waters and Elmore James. It was Muddy who lent Carter the money to purchase his first electric guitar. Shortly thereafter, Joe started up his first group with guitarist Smokey Smothers and Lester Davenport on harmonica, quickly establishing himself as a club favorite throughout Chicago. Sadly, Carter never recorded with this group—or any other configuration—during his heyday. A contract with Cobra Records was offered (with a young Freddie King being added in the studio to his regular group), but Joe declined as he felt the money would in no way equal what he was pulling down in club work. A true shame and a moment of blues history forever lost as Carter didn't end up being documented until he returned to active playing in the '70s, recording his lone album for the Barrelhouse label in 1976. The intervening years hadn't changed his approach

one bit, still full of biting guitar and hoarse, shouted vocals over a bedrock simple foundation. The hoarseness of the vocals, unfortunately, were a portent of the future, as Carter retired from playing in the '80s after a bout with throat cancer. Joe Carter clearly worked in the mode of Elmore and Muddy—seldom contributing much in the way of original material—but it was all delivered with a passion that was 100% genuine, easily making him an emblematic figure of '50s-style Chicago blues in its heyday. —*Cub Koda*

● **Mean & Evil Blues** / Jan. 1978 / Barrelhouse ◆◆◆◆
Joe Carter's lone recorded effort for the tiny Barrelhouse label remains to this day one of the great lost blues albums of the '70s, if not at the top of the list. On the surface, its content could not be more at odds with the standard blues album of that decade; a two guitars-drums-no bass combo running through a set of Chicago staples largely plucked from the repertoires of Muddy Waters and Elmore James, minus any modern embellishments, recorded in studio environs that could best be described as crude. But the intensity and emotional commitment radiates off of Carter like laser beams on every single track, making the starkness of this album all the more appealing. With a guitar tone from his massive Epiphone hollow body that cuts like a knife coupled with a voice that wavers between phlegmatic, stentorian and utterly agonized (the second verse of "Treat Me the Way You Do"), Carter creates a mood on these sides so loaded with ambience that the listener is immediately sucked in from beginning to end. As real as any Hound Dog Taylor Alligator album of the period minus the good time slant, this is eerie, late-night, juke-joint music of the highest order. Currently MIA on compact disc (as of press time), its non-appearance is one of the great tragedies of the reissue field, considering the dearth of lesser albums from this period being re-released. Needless to say, its appearance in any form is a worthwhile addition to any blues collection. —*Cub Koda*

Original Chicago Blues / 1982 / JSP ◆◆◆

Tommy Castro

b. 1955, San Jose, CA
Slide Guitar / Blues-Rock, Soul Blues, Contemporary Blues
According to all the press and hype and hoopla, Tommy Castro is pegged as the next big star of the blues. Long a favorite among Bay Area music fans, Castro—in the space of two album releases—has taken his music around the world and back again with a sheaf of praise from critics and old-time blues musicians alike. His music is a combination of soul-inflected rockers with the occasional slow blues or shuffle thrown into the mix to keep it honest. His vocals are laidback and always a hair behind the beat, while his scorching guitar tone is Stevie Ray Stratocaster-approved. Currently working as the house band on NBC's *Comedy Showcase*, airing after *Saturday Night Live*, should only boost his visibility and name value. Crossover success does not seem out of the question.

Born and raised in San Jose, CA, Castro started playing guitar at the tender age of ten. Initially inspired by Mike Bloomfield, Eric Clapton, and Elvin Bishop, he started the inevitable journey into the roots of his heroes and discovered and quickly became enamored of B.B. King, Buddy Guy, Elmore James, Muddy Waters, and Freddie King. His vocal styling came from constant listening to Ray Charles, Wilson Pickett, James Brown, and Otis Redding. After playing with numerous Bay Area groups honing his chops, he landed a gig playing guitar for the San Francisco band the Dynatones, who were then signed to Warner Brothers. The two-year stint augured well for Castro, playing to the biggest crowds he had seen up to that point and backing artists as diverse as Carla Thomas and Albert King.

Returning back to San Francisco, Castro formed his own group and released his first self-produced album in 1993, *No Foolin',* on the dime-sized Saloon label. That same year also saw him winning the Bay Area Music Award for best club band, an honor he duplicated the following year. In 1997, he won "Bammies" for Outstanding Blues Musician and for Outstanding Blues Album for his debut release on Blind Pig Records, *Exception to the Rule.* With everyone from industry insiders to B.B. King singing his praises, Castro appears to be headed for bigger and better things. —*Cub Koda*

Exception to the Rule / 1995 / Blind Pig ◆◆◆

● **Can't Keep a Good Man Down** / May 5, 1997 / Blind Pig ◆◆◆◆
There's a clean San Francisco sheen to Tommy Castro's second album for

Blind Pig, and it's not just the glossy production work of Jim Gaines (Santana, Huey Lewis, and Stevie Ray Vaughan) that's responsible for it. Castro and his band have long been local favorites of the Bay area bar crowd, and his blues-rock/soul-pop synthesis with the occasional slow blues thrown in makes him another young contender for the yuppie throne of modern bluesdom. From the opening rock strut of "Can't Keep a Good Man Down" and "You Knew the Job Was Dangerous," Castro lays down lazy, in-the-pocket vocals (the only time he hits scream territory is on the closer, Albert King's "Can't You See What You're Doing to Me") pitted against in your face guitar blasts a la Stevie Ray Vaughan. These Texas-approved Stratocaster tones reach their apex on a five-minute-plus workout of Buddy Guy's "My Time After Awhile," where Castro literally wrenches every textbook tone and volume setting out of his instrument and makes this perhaps the most blues-approved moment of the set. A large quotient of varied originals abound, and the soulful strut of "I Want to Show You," "Take the Highway Down," and the funk-jive of "High on the Hog" and "You Gotta Do What You Gotta Do" play off against the simplistic shuffle "You Only Go Around Once" and the lowdown blues instrumental "Hycodan," an atmospheric duet between Castro's guitar and saxophonist Keith Crossan's late-night mood blowing. But the real blues moments are few and far between here—this is blues-rock, no doubt about it, and the end result is music with crossover written all over it. If Huey Lewis and the News were to cut a blues album with a hotter guitar player in tow, it might end up sounding very much like this. —*Cub Koda*

Cephas & Wiggins

f. 1984
Group / Modern Acoustic Blues
The duo of acoustic guitarist John Cephas and harpist Phil Wiggins enjoyed a partnership spanning across several decades, during which time they emerged among contemporary music's most visible exponents of the Piedmont blues tradition. Both were born in Washington, D.C., although Wiggins was a quarter century younger than his partner; they met at a jam session in 1977, and both performed as regular members of Wilbert "Big Chief" Ellis' Barrelhouse Rockers for a time prior to Ellis' death. Their music, rooted in the rural African-American dance music of Virginia and North Carolina, showed the influence of Blind Boy Fuller, Gary Davis, and Sonny Terry, with a broad repertoire consisting of Piedmont blues standards as well as an eclectic sampling of Delta stylings, R&B, ballads, ragtime, gospel, and country & western; from their 1984 debut onward, *Sweet Bitter Blues*, Cephas and Wiggins' sound applied sophisticated instrumentation and modern gospel-edged vocals to both traditional standards and their own hard-hitting compositions, offering a soulful acoustic option to electric blues. A popular festival act, they also issued LPs including 1986's W.C. Handy Award-winning *Dog Days of August*, 1988's *Walking Blues*, 1992's *Flip, Flop and Fly*, and 1996's *Cool Down*. —*Barry Lee Pearson & Richard Skelly*

Sweet Bitter Blues / 1984 / L&R ◆◆◆
This German import, released by Evidence Music in 1994 on compact disc, is notable for seven live tracks, the rest being studio cuts, many from previous releases. While the live recording quality is a little muddy at times, the stage energy of this Piedmont acoustic blues duo is unmistakable on such tracks as their own "Burn Your Bridges" and an inspired version of Jimmy Reed's "Running and Hiding." —*Jeff Crooke*

Let It Roll: Bowling Green / 1985 / Marimac ◆◆◆
Similar to *Dog Days of August*, but includes five other cuts. —*Barry Lee Pearson*

● **Dog Days of August** / 1986 / Flying Fish ◆◆◆◆
Handy Award-winning acoustic guitar and harmonica Piedmont blues. Includes ballads "John Henry," "Staggerlee," and ten original compositions. —*Barry Lee Pearson*

Guitar Man / 1987 / Flying Fish ◆◆◆◆
Their second Handy Award winner includes slide guitar, Piedmont fingerpicking, and wonderful harmonica. —*Barry Lee Pearson*

Walking Blues / 1988 / Marimac ◆◆◆◆
A fine assortment of Piedmont blues, ragtime, and country. Includes "Walking Blues." —*Barry Lee Pearson*

Flip, Flop, & Fly / 1992 / Flying Fish ◆◆◆

Bluesmen / 1993 / Chesky ◆◆◆

Cool Down / Jan. 30, 1996 / Alligator ◆◆◆◆
Cool Down is the first album the acoustic blues duo Cephas & Wiggins have recorded for Alligator Records and it ranks among their best. The spirit of the session is laidback and eclectic, as the pair draws on everyone from Blind Lemon Jefferson and Blind Boy Fuller to Fats Domino and Merle Travis. There are also a half-dozen originals that might not be as captivating as the covers, but they certainly elicit engaging performances from the pair. Throughout *Cool Down*, Cephas dominates the music but Wiggins' harmonica steals the show whenever he pops through the cracks. *Cool Down* is the kind of album that demonstrates how some blues musicians simply get better with age. — *Thom Owens*

Ray Charles (Ray Charles Robinson)

b. Sep. 23, 1930, Albany, GA
Piano, Vocals / Soul, R&B, Jazz Blues, Country-Soul, Pop, Bop, Urban Blues, Piano Blues, Soul-Jazz
Ray Charles was the musician most responsible for developing soul music. Singers like Sam Cooke and Jackie Wilson also did a great deal to pioneer the form, but Charles did even more to devise a new form of Black pop by merging '50s R&B with gospel-powered vocals, adding plenty of flavor from contemporary jazz, blues, and (in the '60s) country. Then there is his singing—his style is among the most emotional and easily identifiable of any 20th-century performer, up there with the likes of Elvis and Billie Holiday. He's also a superb keyboard player, arranger, and bandleader. The brilliance of his 1950s and 1960s work, however, can't obscure the fact that he's made few classic tracks since the mid-'60s, though he's recorded often and tours to this day.

Blind since the age of six (from glaucoma), Charles studied composition and learned many instruments at the St. Augustine School for the Deaf and the Blind. His parents had died by his early teens, and he worked as a musician in Florida for a while before using his savings to move to Seattle in 1947. By the late '40s, he was recording in a smooth pop/R&B style derivative of Nat "King" Cole and Charles Brown. He got his first Top Ten R&B hit with "Baby, Let Me Hold Your Hand" in 1951. Charles' first recordings have come in for their fair share of criticism, as they are much milder and less original than the classics that would follow, although they're actually fairly enjoyable, showing strong hints of the skills that were to flower in a few years.

In the early '50s, Charles' sound started to toughen as he toured with Lowell Fulson, went to New Orleans to work with Guitar Slim (playing piano on and arranging Slim's huge R&B hit, "The Things That I Used to Do"), and got a band together for R&B star Ruth Brown. It was at Atlantic Records that Ray truly found his voice, consolidating the gains of recent years and then some with "I Got a Woman," a number two R&B hit in 1955. This is the song most frequently singled out as his pivotal performance, on which Charles first truly let go with his unmistakable gospelish moan, backed by a tight, bouncy horn-driven arrangement.

Throughout the '50s, Charles ran off a series of R&B hits that, although they weren't called "soul" at the time, did a lot to pave the way for soul by presenting a form of R&B that was sophisticated without sacrificing any emotional grit. "This Little Girl of Mine," "Drown in My Own Tears," "Hallelujah I Love Her So," "Lonely Avenue," and "The Right Time" were all big hits. But Charles didn't really capture the pop audience until "What'd I Say," which caught the fervor of the church with its pleading vocals, as well as the spirit of rock 'n' roll with its classic electric piano line. It was his first Top Ten pop hit, and one of his final Atlantic singles, as he left the label at the end of the '50s for ABC.

One of the chief attractions of the ABC deal for Charles was a much greater degree of artistic control of his recordings. He put it to good use on early-'60s hits like "Unchain My Heart" and "Hit the Road Jack," which solidified his pop stardom with only a modicum of polish attached to the R&B he had perfected at Atlantic. In 1962, he surprised the pop world by turning his attention to country & western music, topping the charts with the "I Can't Stop Loving You" single, and making a hugely popular album (in an era in which R&B/soul LPs rarely scored high on the charts) with *Modern Sounds in Country and Western Music.* Perhaps it shouldn't have been so surprising; Charles had always been eclectic, recording quite a bit of straight jazz at

Atlantic, with noted jazz musicians like David "Fathead" Newman and Milt Jackson.

Charles remained extremely popular through the mid-'60s, scoring big hits like "Busted," "You Are My Sunshine," "Take These Chains from My Heart," and "Crying Time," although his momentum was slowed by a 1965 bust for heroin. This led to a year-long absence from performing, but he picked up where he left off with "Let's Go Get Stoned" in 1966. Yet by this time Charles was focusing increasingly less on rock and soul, in favor of pop tunes, often with string arrangements, that seemed aimed more at the easy-listening audience than anyone else. Charles' influence on the rock mainstream was as apparent as ever; Joe Cocker and Steve Winwood in particular owe a great deal of their style to him, and echoes of his phrasing can be heard more subtly in the work of greats like Van Morrison.

One approaches sweeping criticism of Charles with hesitation; he's an American institution, after all, and his vocal powers have barely diminished over the years. The fact remains, though, that his work since the late '60s on record has been very disappointing. Millions of listeners yearned for a return to the all-out soul of his 1955-1965 classics, but Charles had actually never been committed to soul above all else. Like Aretha Franklin and Elvis Presley, his focus is more upon all-around pop than many realize; his love of jazz, country, and pop standards is evident, even if his more earthy offerings are the ones that truly broke ground and will stand the test of time. He's dented the charts (sometimes the country ones) occasionally, and can command devoted international concert audiences whenever he feels like it. For good or ill, he's ensured his imprint upon the American mass consciousness in the 1990s by singing several ads for Diet Pepsi. The CD era has seen several excellent packages that focus on various chronological/thematic phases of the legend's career. — *Richie Unterberger*

Genius & Soul: The 50th Anniversary Collection / Feb. 1949-1993 / Rhino ◆◆◆◆
As the first comprehensive, multi-label box set assembled on Ray Charles, the five-disc, 101-song *Genius & Soul: The 50th Anniversary Collection* is an extensive overview of one of the greatest musicians of the 20th century. Charles produced a body of work so rich and diverse that even five CDs only scratches the surface of his accomplishments. None of his instrumentals are on *Genius & Soul*, nor are his jazz and traditional pop efforts spotlighted. Instead, the box traces the evolution of his career, as he moves from an R&B pioneer to a mainstream pop crooner to a country-pop vocalist to a contemporary soul singer. Charles was a gripping, captivating vocalist, capable of making even bland music sound vital, but the fact is, his '70s and '80s recordings pale in comparison to his seminal '50s and '60s sides. Which means that the set becomes less compelling as it reaches the fifth disc, but the first three and a half discs are filled with timeless music that remains exciting, vital, and altogether wondrous. — *Stephen Thomas Erlewine*

Blues & Jazz / May 26, 1950-Jun. 26, 1959 / Rhino/Atlantic ◆◆◆◆
Another easy access point for Charles' seminal Atlantic catalog. This two-disc set is evenly split between his bluesiest sides on the first disc and a selection of his greatest jazz sides on disc two (gorgeously showcasing the sax work of David "Fathead" Newman on several pieces). Charles was a masterful blues purveyor; his "I Believe to My Soul" is simultaneously invested with heartbreak and humor, while the earlier "Sinner's Prayer," "The Sun's Gonna Shine Again," and the gospel-based "A Fool for You" emanate both hope and deep pain. — *Bill Dahl*

The Great Ray Charles / 1956 / Atlantic ◆◆◆
This set is rather unusual, for it is strictly instrumental, allowing Ray Charles a rare opportunity to be a jazz-oriented pianist. Two selections are with a trio (bassist Oscar Pettiford joins Charles on "Black Coffee"), while the other six are with a septet taken from his big band of the period. Key among the sidemen are David Newman (soloing on both tenor and alto) and trumpeter Joseph Bridgewater; highlights include Quincy Jones' "The Ray," "My Melancholy Baby," "Doodlin'," and "Undecided." Ray Charles should have recorded in this setting more often in his later years. — *Scott Yanow*

Ray Charles [Atlantic] / Jul. 1957 / Atlantic ◆◆◆
These are animated soul and R&B recordings, although the rock 'n' roll links are pretty obvious as well. The songs, vocals, arrangements, and production are great; only the sound quality falters. But they can also be obtained on many other anthologies with far superior sound. — *Ron Wynn*

Ray Charles at Newport / Oct. 1958 / Atlantic ♦♦♦♦
For his appearance at the Newport Jazz Festival on July 5, 1958, Charles pulled out all the stops, performing raucous versions of "The Right Time," "I Got a Woman," and "Talkin' 'bout You." (This album was reissued in 1973 as a two-record set, packaged with *Ray Charles in Person* under the title *Ray Charles Live* [Atlantic SD 2-503].) — *William Ruhlmann*

The Genius of Ray Charles / 1959 / Atlantic ♦♦♦♦
Some players from Ray Charles' big band are joined by many ringers from the Count Basie and Duke Ellington bands for the first half of this program, featuring Charles belting out six songs arranged by Quincy Jones. "Let the Good Times Roll" and "Deed I Do" are highlights, and there are solos by tenorman David "Fathead" Newman, trumpeter Marcus Belgrave and (on "Two Years of Torture") tenor Paul Gonsalves. The remaining six numbers are ballads, with Charles backed by a string orchestra arranged by Ralph Burns (including "Come Rain or Come Shine" and "Don't Let the Sun Catch You Cryin'"). Ray Charles' voice is heard throughout in peak form, giving soul to even the veteran standards. — *Scott Yanow*

What'd I Say / Sep. 1959 / Atlantic ♦♦♦
At a concert held at Herndon Stadium in Atlanta on May 28, 1959, Ray Charles turns in a blistering version of "What'd I Say" and takes on the big band era with versions of Tommy Dorsey's "Yes Indeed!" and Artie Shaw's "Frenesi," not to mention performances of "The Right Time" and "Tell the Truth." (This album was reissued in 1960 under the title *Ray Charles in Person* and again in 1973 as a part of a two-record set, packaged with *Ray Charles at Newport* under the title *Ray Charles Live* (Atlantic 503). — *William Ruhlmann*

The Genius Hits the Road / Jul. 1960 / ABC/Paramount ♦♦♦
In keeping with his jazz/pop crossover ambitions, Charles decided to record a concept album of sorts with a dozen songs devoted to various parts of the US—"Alabamy Bound," "Georgia On My Mind," "Moonlight in Vermont," "California, Here I Come," "Blue Hawaii," etc. The crossover vibe is further heightened by the brassy big-band arrangements, and material from the likes of Al Jolson and Hoagy Carmichael. It sounds a bit corny now, with an in-your-face gung-ho cheer. But it did what Charles wanted it to do, reaching the Top Ten of the album charts, and spinning off a big hit with "Georgia On My Mind." The 1997 CD reissue on Rhino adds seven bonus tracks from 1956-1972 that also had a travel/geographic theme, and the best of these are actually the highlights of the record, most notably "Hit the Road Jack," "Lonely Avenue," and his cover of Hank Snow's "I'm Movin' On." — *Richie Unterberger*

Genius + Soul = Jazz/My Kind of Jazz / Dec. 26, 1960-1970 / Rhino ♦♦♦♦
Single-disc CD reissue combines two of Charles' more jazz-oriented outings, though *Genius + Soul* (from 1961) enjoys a much more sterling reputation than the comparatively obscure *My Kind of Jazz* (1970). Question: if genius plus soul equals jazz, does that mean genius minus soul equals fusion? — *Richie Unterberger*

The Genius After Hours / 1961 / Rhino ♦♦♦♦
Taken from the same three sessions as *The Great Ray Charles* but not duplicating any of the performances, this set casts Charles as a jazz-oriented pianist in an instrumental setting. Brother Ray has five numbers with a trio (three songs have Oscar Pettiford on bass) and jams three other tunes ("Hornful Soul," "Ain't Misbehavin'" and "Joy Ride") with a septet arranged by Quincy Jones; solo space is given to David "Fathead" Newman on tenor and alto and trumpeter Joseph Bridgewater. Fine music, definitely a change of pace for Ray Charles. — *Scott Yanow*

Dedicated to You / Jan. 1961 / ABC/Paramount ♦♦♦
Rhino's reissue of Ray Charles' 1961 duet album with Betty Carter, *Dedicated to You*, combined the terrific original album with their other great duet album, *Ray Charles and Betty Carter*. Both records were recorded the same year and were produced by Sid Feller and arranged by Marty Paitch. Both are stellar albums, showcasing their astonishing range and wonderful, empathetic interplay. — *Leo Stanley*

Genius + Soul = Jazz / Mar. 1961 / DCC ♦♦♦
One of the best early-'60s examples of soul/jazz crossover, this record, like several of his dates from the period, featured big-band arrangements (played by the Count Basie band). This fared better than some of Charles' similar outings, however, if only because it muted some of his straight pop aspira-

tions in favor of some pretty mean and lean, cut-to-the-heart-of-the-matter B-3 Hammond organ licks. Most of the album is instrumental and swings pretty vivaciously, although Charles does take a couple of vocals with "I'm Gonna Move to the Outskirts of Town" and "I've Got News for You." Yet one of those instrumentals, a cover of the Clovers' "One Mint Julep," would give Charles one of his most unpredictable (and best) early-'60s hits. In 1997, it was combined with the much later *My Kind of Jazz* album (from 1970) onto a single-disc CD reissue by Rhino. — *Richie Unterberger*

Ray Charles & Betty Carter / Jun. 13, 1961-1966 / ABC/Paramount ♦♦♦♦
This pairing of two totally idiosyncratic vocalists acquired legendary status over the decades in which it had been out of print. But the proof is in the listening, and frankly it doesn't represent either artist's best work. There is certainly a powerful, often sexy rapport between the two—Charles in his sweet balladeering mode, Carter with her uniquely keening, drifting high register—and they definitely create sparks in the justly famous rendition of "Baby, It's Cold Outside." The main problem is in Marty Paich's string/choir arrangements, which too often cross over the line into treacle, whereas his charts for big band are far more listenable. Moreover, Charles' sweetness can get a bit cloying too, although some of the old grit emerges on "Takes Two To Tango." On the CD reissue—remixed by Charles himself—Dunhill adds the great, rare B-side to the "Unchain My Heart" single, "But On The Other Hand Baby," and two excellent if unrelated album cuts, "I Never See Maggie Alone" (1964) and "I Like To Hear It Sometime" (1966). — *Richard S. Ginell*

The Genius Sings the Blues / Oct. 1961 / Atlantic ♦♦♦♦
Down-home, anguished laments and moody ballads were turned into triumphs by Ray Charles. He sang these songs with the same conviction, passion, and energy that made his country and soul vocals so majestic. This has not as of yet turned up in the reissue bins, but is probably headed in that direction. — *Ron Wynn*

☆ **Modern Sounds in Country & Western Music** / Jan. 1962 / Rhino ♦♦♦♦♦
Modern Sounds in Country & Western Music is historically important, and considered by most critics to be a classic, but some have mixed feelings about it. Charles' interpretations of songs previously recorded by Hank Williams, Eddy Arnold, Floyd Tillman, and Don Gibson are superb, but so often the arrangements by Marty Paich, Gerald Wilson, and Gil Fuller threaten to drown him in a sea of lachrymose bric-a-brac. "I Can't Stop Loving You" and "You Don't Know Me" were Top Ten pop and R&B. — *Rob Bowman*

☆ **Modern Sounds in Country & Western, Vol. 2** / Oct. 1962 / Rhino ♦♦♦♦♦
Charles' second installment of *Modern Sounds in Country & Western Music* is every bit as essential as the first, containing stellar interpretations of "Your Cheatin' Heart" and "You Are My Sunshine." — *Stephen Thomas Erlewine*

Ingredients in a Recipe for Soul / Jul. 1963 / DCC ♦♦♦♦
Although it was a big commercial success, reaching number two on the LP charts, this record would typify the erratic nature of much of Charles' '60s output. It's too eclectic for its own good, really, encompassing pop standards, lowdown blues, Mel Torme songs, and after-hours ballads. The high points are very high—"Busted," his hit reworking of a composition by country songwriter Harlan Howard, is jazzy and tough, and one of his best early-'60s singles. And the low points are pretty low, especially when he adds the snow-white backup vocals of the Jack Halloran Singers to "Over the Rainbow" and "Ol' Man River." A number of the remaining cuts are pretty respectable, like the tight big-band arrangement of "Ol' Man Time" and the ominously urbane "Where Can I Go?" In 1997, it was paired with the 1964 LP *Have a Smile with Me* on a two-for-one CD reissue on Rhino, with the addition of historical liner notes. — *Richie Unterberger*

Sweet & Sour Tears / Mar. 1964 / Rhino ♦♦♦
One of a series of ultra-loose concept albums Charles cut in the '60s, this one dedicated entirely to songs with titles or lyrical references to crying and tears. It's an excuse for Ray to choose his usual varied menu of upbeat jumpers, slow countrified weepers, and proudly saccharine pop standards. The production, as one might fear, also tends to the lachrymose side on the slow tunes, with the thick strings and backup vocals straight out of TV variety shows. One is almost tempted to think that Charles was toying with audience expectations by mixing unabashedly sentimental slow tunes with the far more bluesy, satisfying, and upbeat numbers, such as "Don't Cry, Baby" and "Baby, Don't You Cry," as well as his surprisingly brassy, punchy treatment of "Cry Me a River." These outings have always played much better with

critics than the gloppy pop tunes, and for good reason—they are much better. The Rhino CD reissue adds seven bonus tracks from throughout his early career (1956-71) that also tapped into the "crying" motif. These threaten to steal the show from the *Sweet & Sour Tears* album it's supposedly embellishing, including the Bacharach-David penned 1964 single "I Wake Up Crying," the smoldering 1966 album track "No Use Crying," and the 1956 R&B chart-topper "Drown in My Own Tears," next to which much of the rest of the program sounds positively hokey. —*Richie Unterberger*

Have a Smile with Me / Jun. 1964 / ABC/Paramount ◆◆
The idea behind this LP was to offer a lighthearted sequel to its quasi-concept predecessor, *Sweet and Sour Tears*. There's nothing wrong with the idea of letting Ray just kick back and have fun, but "The Thing" and "The Man with the Weird Beard" transcend the boundaries of humor into silliness and, worse, stupidity. On the other hand, he also turns out a good jazzy version of Hank Williams' "Move It On Over" (the record's highlight), and manages to swing through fairly superficial fare like "Ma (She's Making Eyes at Me)" and "Two Ton Tessie" with solid flair. It was another inconsistent '60s set, the shortage of top-notch tunes disguised by a flimsy concept, though he elevates the material with soulful vocals and good arrangements, particularly when the Raeletts back him up (as they do on half the tracks). In 1997, it was paired with the 1963 LP *Ingredients in a Recipe for Soul* on a two-for-one CD reissue on Rhino, with the addition of historical liner notes. —*Richie Unterberger*

Country & Western Meets Rhythm & Blues / Aug. 1965 / ABC/Paramount ◆◆◆
A partially successful revisiting by Charles of his country sessions of the early '60s. These songs weren't quite as transcendent as those on the prior dates, but he showed once again that the lines between country, R&B, and soul weren't as rigid as many in the various camps thought. —*Ron Wynn*

My Kind of Jazz / Apr. 1970 / Tangerine ◆◆◆◆
This LP came seemingly out of the blue as a showcase for the Ray Charles big band, spawning two little-known sequels later on in the '70s. It's a roaring, solid band, too, playing jazz standards like "This Here," "The Sidewinder," "Bluesette," and "Senor Blues," comfortable at slow, loping tempos as well as in the rousers, with excellent mainstream soloists (none of whom are identified) and good conventional charts (also uncredited). The sole exception to the pattern—and a hit single in its own right—is a catchy, funky, Charles gospel/blues called "Booty Butt," where Ray adds multi-tracked gospel moans for his sole vocal contribution, and the band chimes in only on the very last chord. Clearly, the title and the appalling lack of credits say volumes about Charles' reputation as a control freak; this is his kind of jazz and nobody else's. In 1997, it was combined with the much earlier *Genius + Soul* album onto a single-disc CD reissue by Rhino. —*Richard S. Ginell & Richie Unterberger*

Greatest Hits, Vol. 1 / 1987 / DCC ◆◆◆◆
The first of two DCC compilations to collect the best of Brother Ray's 1960s stint at ABC-Paramount Records, when he flew off in a dozen different stylistic directions. Included on this 20-track disc are Charles' immortal rendering of "Georgia on My Mind," the sinuously bluesy "Unchain My Heart," the Latin-beat instrumental "One Mint Julep," personalized remakes of the country standards "Born to Lose," "Your Cheating Heart," and "Crying Time," and his exultant rendition of the soulful "Let's Go Get Stoned." —*Bill Dahl*

Greatest Hits, Vol. 2 / 1987 / DCC ◆◆◆◆
More seminal performances from the '60s ABC catalog of the Genius (DCC split the classics evenly between the two discs, making both of them indispensable). His beloved "Hit the Road Jack" (one of several Percy Mayfield copyrights dotting Charles' repertoire), the daring country crossover "I Can't Stop Loving You," an electric-piano powered "Sticks and Stones," a wise "Them That Got," and a wonderfully mellow "At the Club" rank with the 20-song disc's standouts (though versions of the Beatles' "Yesterday" and the corny "Look What They Done to My Song, Ma" end the set on a bummer note). —*Bill Dahl*

☆ **Greatest Country Western Hits** / 1988 / DCC ◆◆◆◆◆
Collecting the highlights from Charles' two *Modern Sounds in Country & Western Music* albums, *Greatest Country Western Hits* features some of the most essential country-soul material ever recorded. —*Stephen Thomas Erlewine*

Soul Brothers/Soul Meeting / 1989 / Atlantic ◆◆◆◆
A great two-disc package that combined the pivotal Ray Charles sessions with Milt Jackson. The special release even had some bonus tracks, while the remastering and annotation were marvelous. There was no question about the quality of the tracks; Charles and Jackson were instantly compatible, with Jackson getting to display blues elements he normally suppressed when playing with the Modern Jazz Quartet, and Charles getting space to present his jazz and improvising skills. —*Ron Wynn*

☆ **The Birth of Soul** / Oct. 1, 1991 / Rhino ◆◆◆◆◆
The title isn't just hype—this absolutely essential three-disc box is where soul music first took shape and soared, courtesy of Ray Charles' church-soaked pipes and bedrock piano work. Brother Ray's formula for inventing the genre was disarmingly simple: he brought gospel intensity to the R&B world with his seminal "I Got a Woman," "Hallelujah I Love Her So," "Leave My Woman Alone," "You Be My Baby," and the primal 1959 call-and-response classic "What'd I Say." There's plenty of brilliant blues content within these 53 historic sides: Charles' mournful "Losing Hand," "Feelin' Sad," "Hard Times," and "Blackjack" ooze after-hours desperation. No blues collection should be without this boxed set, which comes with well-researched notes by Robert Palmer, a nicely illustrated accompanying booklet, and discographical info aplenty. —*Bill Dahl*

The Birth of a Legend / 1992 / Ebony ◆◆◆◆
Of all the countless compilations that have been stitched together of Ray Charles' early sides for Jack Lauderdale's Swing Time Records, this two-disc box is the only CD package that treats these enormously important works with the reverent respect that they deserve (meaning decent mono sound quality instead of murky electronic reprocessed stereo dubbed from vinyl, cogent liner notes, and full discographical annotation). This is where the Genius began, imitating Charles Brown at the very start (1949) and sounding like nobody but Brother Ray by 1952 (when he defected to Atlantic and hit the real big time). Forty-one tracks in all. —*Bill Dahl*

The Early Years [Tomato] / 1994 / Tomato ◆◆◆
In the late '40s and early '50s, Charles recorded several dozen sides for the Swingtime/Downbeat label, 30 of which are presented here. As has been noted many times by critics, these usually found Charles in a Nat "King" Cole swing-blues groove that was much smoother than the gritty R&B/soul he'd record for Atlantic in the later '50s; the influence of urban blues balladeer Charles Brown was also evident. Some critical essays, in fact, may lead you to believe that this work is trivial, but while it's undeniably derivative, it's enjoyable on its own terms, and not without strong hints of the searing soulfulness that was to come. Some of the selections are delivered with such refined polish that it doesn't even sound like Charles. But on the more anguished and fast-tempoed cuts in particular, you can hear him starting to arrive at the phrasing and emotion that would flower in the mid-'50s. Unfortunately, like most Tomato reissues, the sound is substandard; even assuming that the master tapes can't be located, a better job was probably possible, and a couple of cuts even duplicate skips from the vinyl. Exact dates and songwriting credits are also missing, although Pete Welding's essay does at least discuss the material on the discs in some detail, unlike many of Tomato's liner notes. —*Richie Unterberger*

★ **The Best of Atlantic** / Jul. 19, 1994 / Rhino ◆◆◆◆◆
The 20-track compilation (only 12 tracks on cassette), *The Best of Atlantic*, compiles all of Ray Charles' Top Ten R&B hits for Atlantic Records, from "I've Got A Woman" and "This Little Girl of Mine" to "Drown in My Own Tears," "Hallelujah I Love Her So," "Lonely Avenue," "(Night Time Is) The Right Time," and "What'd I Say (Part 1)." In addition to the big hits, there are minor hits that nevertheless showcase Charles at his peak, like "Swanee River Rock" and "Just for a Thrill." For fans that only want the hits and don't want to invest in the splendid three-disc set, *The Birth of Soul, The Best of Atlantic* is an essential purchase. —*Stephen Thomas Erlewine*

Berlin 1962 / 1996 / Fantasy ◆◆◆
An hour of previously unreleased live music from Ray Charles in his prime. During this era he was touring with a big band including saxophonists David "Fathead" Newman and Hank Crawford, as well as background singers the Raelettes. The fidelity is excellent, and the set includes Charles standards like "One Mint Julep," "I Got a Woman," "Georgia on My Mind," "Hallelujah I Love

Her So," "I Believe to My Soul," "Hit the Road, Jack," "Unchain My Heart," and "What'd I Say." Yet most fans will probably much prefer the more compact, small-combo arrangements of the studio versions. The horn charts offer an interesting contrast, but these live performances may be a little too stagey for optimum results, with some detours from hard R&B into popular standards. — *Richie Unterberger*

Complete Swing Time & Down Beat Recordings 1949-52 / Feb. 21, 1997 / Night Train ◆◆◆

Ingredients in a Recipe for Soul/Have a Smile with Me / Aug. 19, 1997 / Rhino ◆◆◆

A two-for-one pairing of albums from 1963 (*Recipe for Soul*) and 1964 (*Have a Smile with Me*), with the addition of historical liner notes. Neither rate among his better albums—both are inconsistent mixtures of hard-edged jazz/pop/soul and mainstream pop standards. Each, though, has some fine cuts, notably the Top Ten hit "Busted" (on *Recipe*) and a jazzy cover of Hank Williams' "Move It On Over" (on *Smile*). The CD also adds two bonus tracks: both parts of the orchestral pop "Without a Song" single from 1965. — *Richie Unterberger*

Standards / Mar. 3, 1998 / Rhino ◆◆◆◆

Standards is a 17-track collection of Ray Charles' versions of classic pop songs, culled recordings he made for Atlantic, ABC/Paramount, ABC/TRC and Crossover/Atlantic between 1959 and 1977. There are a handful of hits— "Georgia on My Mind," "Ruby," "That Lucky Old Sun," "Without Love (There Is Nothing)," "Makin' Whoopee"—but the collection concentrates on little-known album tracks and live cuts. Although the steady stream of repackages from Rhino can be a little overwhelming, the idea behind *Standards* is attractive, and it's executed well—it's nice to have all these songs on one collection, even if the live cuts can be a little distracting. Certainly, anyone looking for a collection of mellow ballads from Charles will not be disappointed by this set. — *Stephen Thomas Erlewine*

Rockie Charles

b. Nov. 14, 1942, Boothville, LA
Guitar, Vocals / Modern Electric Blues
Although a longtime veteran of the music industry, singer/guitarist Rockie Charles and his soulful blues sound only began attracting attention during the mid-1990s. Born Charles Merick in Boothville, LA on November 14, 1942, he first emerged during the early 1960s in a series of New Orleans R&B bands, taking inspiration from Earl King and Chuck Berry; auditions for the Minit and Imperial labels went nowhere, but during the middle of the decade Charles cut a handful of sides for Black Patch, including "Sinking Like a Ship." He soon relocated to Nashville, where he backed performers including O.V. Wright, Little Johnny Taylor and Roscoe Shelton. Upon returning to New Orleans in 1970, Charles established his own label, Soulgate, scoring a local hit with the single "The President of Soul"; however, with the rise of disco, his fortunes dwindled, and he spent the better part of the next two decades working as a tugboat captain and oyster fisherman. In 1994, however, Orleans Records producer Carlo Ditta responded to an advertisement Charles had placed in a local entertainment magazine, and two years later the singer finally released his debut solo LP, *Born for You.* — *Jason Ankeny*

Born For You / Dec. 17, 1996 / Orleans ◆◆◆

Sam Chatmon

b. Jan. 10, 1897, Boltmon, MS, **d.** Feb. 2, 1983, Hollandale, MS
Guitar, Vocals / Country Blues, Delta Blues
A product of the prodigious Chatmon family that included not only Lonnie of the famous Mississippi Sheiks but also the prolific Bo Carter and several other blues-playing brothers, Sam Chatmon survived to be hailed as a modern-day blues guru when he began performing and recording again in the '60s. Sam continued brother Bo's tradition of sly double-entendre blues to entertain a new generation of aficionados, but he also showed a more serious side on songs like the title track of the early Arhoolie anthology *I Have to Paint My Face.*

Chatmon began playing music as a child, occasionally with his family's string band, as well as the Mississippi Sheiks. Sam launched his own solo career in the early '30s. While he performed and recorded as a solo act, he

would still record with the Mississippi Sheiks and with his brother Lonnie. Throughout the '30s, Sam travelled throughout the south, playing with a variety of minstrel and medicine shows. He stopped travelling in the early '40s, making himself a home in Hollandale, Mississippi, where he worked on plantations.

For the next two decades, Sam Chatmon was essentially retired from music and only worked on the plantations. When the blues revival arrived in the late '50s, he managed to capitalize on the genre's resurgent popularity. In 1960, he signed a contract with Arhoolie and he recorded a number of songs for the label. Throughout the '60s and '70s, he recorded for a variety of labels, as well as playing clubs and blues and folk festivals across America. Chatmon was an active performer and recording artist until his death in 1983. — *Jim O'Neal & Stephen Thomas Erlewine*

Mississippi Sheik / 1970 / Blue Goose ◆◆◆◆

● **Sam Chatmon's Advice** / 1979 / Rounder ◆◆◆◆
Sam Chatmon's Advice is an excellent collection that features many of his greatest sides from the early '30s, making it the best available distillation of Chatmon's numerous solo recordings. — *Thom Owens*

Sam Chatmon & His Barbecue Boys / 1987 / Flying Fish ◆◆◆
An excellent set of trio recordings by this underrated performer. — *Ron Wynn*

Rev. Julius Cheeks

b. Aug. 7, 1929, Spartanburg, SC, **d.** Jan. 27, 1981, Miami, FL
Vocals / Black Gospel
At the peak of his career, the Reverend Julius Cheeks was the definitive hard gospel singer, famed for a gritty, powerful baritone which influenced not only the next generation of gospel performers but also secular stars including James Brown and Wilson Pickett. Born into abject poverty on August 7, 1929 in Spartanburg, South Carolina, as a child Cheeks was enamored of the recordings of the Dixie Hummingbirds, the Soul Stirrers and others; he began singing in the second grade, quitting school that same year to pick cotton. Later joining a local gospel group dubbed the Baronets, in 1946 he was spotted by the Rev. B.L. Parks, a former Dixie Hummingbird in the process of forming a new group called the Nightingales; upon Cheeks' arrival, he became infamous across the gospel circuit for playing the clown, while each night pushing his voice to its breaking point.

The Nightingales enjoyed considerable success on the road, but they made virtually no money; to make ends meet Cheeks briefly joined the Soul Stirrers, rejoining the Nightingales during the early '50s. Upon signing to Peacock, the group rattled off a string of hits, among them "Somewhere to Lay My Head" and "The Last Mile of the Way"; they were in fact so popular, and so often the subject of acclaim, that they eventually rechristened themselves the Sensational Nightingales. In 1954, Cheeks offically became a preacher, but he remained a performer, emerging as a gifted writer and arranger as well; a temperamental man, he left the group on numerous occasions, finally quitting for good in 1960 and going into semi-retirement. He soon returned to action with a new group, the Sensational Knights. Cheeks died in Miami on January 27, 1981. — *Jason Ankeny*

How Far is Heaven / Jul. 1, 1991 / Savoy ◆◆◆◆
A collection of the best Knights sides headed by this great, late dynamic lead singer. — *Opal Louis Nations*

Family / Savoy ◆◆◆
Nice vocals and more mid-tempo song sermons. — *Ron Wynn*

● **Somebody Left on That Morning Train** / Savoy ◆◆◆◆
Marvelous leads and a good production. This is the best album Cheeks has made as a solo singer. — *Ron Wynn*

We'll Lay Down Our Lives / Savoy ◆◆◆
Representative, but a cut below his best single sessions. — *Ron Wynn*

Clifton Chenier

b. Jun. 25, 1925, Opelousas, LA, **d.** Dec. 12, 1987, Lafayette, LA
Accordion, Vocals / Zydeco
Clifton Chenier was a master Louisiana musical chef of the highest order. On a good night with a crowd in high spirits, Chenier's musical gumbo had Cajun two-steps and waltzes sitting right next to slow blues or a scorching

rendition of "Bon Ton Roulet," which was Clifton's version of Louis Jordan's "Let the Good Times Roll" sung in French. The musical hybrid that he helped to create—zydeco, or "zodico," its spelling variant and superior phonetic pronunciation—is as rich and as deep as the area from which it sprang. Chenier may not have invented the form—an accordion-driven, blues-inspired variant of Cajun music played for dancing—but he single handedly helped give it shape and define the form as we know it today. In his own words, "What I did was to put a little rock 'n' roll into the zydeco to mix it up a bit. You see, people been playing zydeco for a long time, old style, like French music. But I was the first one to put the pep to it." Chenier had taken a backwoods art form, mixed it up with rock 'n' roll, country, R&B, and blues, put a heavier beat to it, and ended up bringing this spicy gumbo concoction to the world. Of course, it also helps that Clifton put this Creole hybrid over with personality to spare, singing and playing his squeeze box with a high energy approach that made the music damn near impossible to ignore. While the crown for the king of the blues sits uneasily on a number of heads, merely ask anyone in the South who was there during his reign and there's absolutely no doubt that Clifton *was* the King of Zydeco, and had the crown to prove it.

Chenier was born in 1925 near Opelousas, LA, to a sharecropping family who played music on the side. Early inspirations for him included his father, John Chenier, who played accordion and fiddle and his guitar-playing uncle, Maurice "Big" Chenier, as well as local player Izeb Laza, who gave him his first accordion. But the musician who really turned Clifton's head around came with his early exposure to the records of Amadé Ardoin, the first Black Creole musician to play the blues on an accordion.

Ardoin was the Charley Patton of the music, king of the Louisiana dance music being dispensed as far back as 1928—then called French lala's—making the sounds on the front porch, loose, rough and informal. The accordion was usually accompanied by a triangle, a washboard, and a fiddle. It was homegrown music, based on the two steps and waltzes of Cajun music, and when Ardoin became the first to put blues licks to ancient French melodies, a livelier version of the form immediately existed. Once Clifton heard Ardoin's records, he was hooked; here was a dance music that was elastic enough in form to be able to change, update and expand its vocabulary. Yet at the same time that Chenier was learning Ardoin's lively versions of the old French-Cajun dance tunes, Chenier learned his very first tune on the accordion, the Joe Liggins jump blues hit, "The Honeydripper."

By the age of 17, Chenier was already working weekend gigs in nearby Lake Charles, with his older brother Cleveland playing the rubboard. Their good-time party music was perfectly suited for the numerous "joys" (little dance halls, which were usually nothing more than a shack) that dotted the coastal region, and they worked a lot at their uncle Big Chenier's club. Soon the duo expanded and by the early '50s, Clifton had his first electric band together, the Hot Sizzling Band (aka the Hot Sizzlers), a perfect description of the sound that the seven-piece combo was laying down. With electric guitar, piano, tenor saxophone, bass, and drums fleshing out the sound of the two Chenier brothers, this was clearly a long ways away from a triangle player tinging along with a squeeze box in the backyard. With a piece of the Louisiana club and outdoor frolic circuit clearly in his back pocket, how Clifton came to make records in 1954 out in California is still a matter of speculation. But the conventional wisdom is that Beaumont, TX-bluesman Clarence Garlow—who had been booking Chenier at his Bon Ton Drive-In for three years in a row—put in the good word to Los Angeles record man J.R. Fullbright. Legend has it that when Garlow put the telephone up to Clifton's amplifier and J.R. heard the sound of the music, he told Clarence, "I'm coming to get him."

With Fullbright behind the controls, Chenier and his band cut seven sides at a Lake Charles radio station. The first single issued ("Louisiana Stomp") kicked up enough noise on J.R.'s Elko label that four more sides from the session were quickly issued on an Imperial subsidiary, Post.

By the following year, Fullbright had hooked Clifton up with Specialty Records in Hollywood; the 1955 sessions that he cut for the label is where his success story—and that of the music—truly begins. After quickly signing in April, a session in Los Angeles was immediately set up with Bumps Blackwell (who would later produce Little Richard) in charge. Legend has it that Blackwell pulled half of the band—which included Philip Walker and later, Cornelius "Lonesome Sundown" Green on guitar—off of the session to give greater focus to Chenier's accordion in the mix. A quick listen to the two sessions reveals that this appears to been have a track-by-track decision; but

some feature the full band and players drift in and out of the lineup on other tracks while most are just Clifton and the rhythm section vainly trying to keep up with him on boogie woogie instrumentals that jump time every chorus and a third. But Clifton's first Specialty single—"Ay-Te Te Fee" and "Boppin' the Rock," released a month after it was cut—became a left field R&B charter, moving enough copies to get him booked on package shows with the likes of Etta James and Jimmy Reed. But rock 'n' roll was also coming in strong and with Richard's "Tutti Frutti" outselling everyone else in the Specialty catalog *combined*, Chenier suddenly found himself without a recording contract. But he quickly signed for a short stint with Chess, resulting in two excellent singles and a couple of years later became a part of Crowley, LA producer Jay Miller's stable, recording for his Zynn label between 1958 and 1960.

Meanwhile, Chenier stayed a hot road attraction, playing all through Texas and Louisiana, for dances, picnics, nightclubs and anyplace else that was ready to party down and hear the real thing on a Saturday night. It was after relocating to Houston's Frenchtown quarter in 1960 that his next (and longest) recording partnership came about. A young California-based folklorist and record label owner was in town, and after Lightnin' Hopkins hooked the two of them up, Chenier was quickly signed to Chris Strachwitz's fledgling Arhoolie label.

Not that everything was always an easy road to travel between the two men. Strachwitz wanted to keep the music as close as possible to the rubboard, drums, and accordion format of the old-time French lala material, while Clifton wanted to rip through a set of the tunes that people danced to on a live gig. Though Chenier stayed with Strachwitz for several albums and singles into the '70s, he was also recording during the same period for Floyd Soileau's Bayou label, with both men later leasing material to labels like Bell and Blue Thumb. In addition to Arhoolie and Bayou, Clifton would also record for Crazy Cajun, Blue Star, GNP Crescendo, Jin, Caillier, Maison de Soul, and his final stop, Alligator Records in 1982.

After the release of the Arhoolie albums, Europe came a-calling and in 1969 Chenier was bowling over crowds on the American Folk Blues Festival tour, staying overseas and adding extra play dates to his already crowded calendar. By the '70s, Clifton and his Red Hot Louisiana Band seemingly covered the globe, touring Stateside and abroad, bringing the sound of the bayou to places as far away from the hot sauce capital of New Iberia, LA, as anyone could have possibly imagined.

Unfortunately by the dawn of the following decade, Clifton was slowly becoming a very sick man. Diagnosed with diabetes and with a road schedule that was unrelenting, the ravages of the disease—failing kidneys that needed dialysis treatment every third day and a partially amputated foot—started to take its toll. In 1984 he played the White House and didn't bother to look back, but his health finally gave out on December 12, 1987. However, in the numerous recordings he left behind and especially in the modern day work of his many disciples, the music lives on. Bon Ton Roulet, indeed. —*Cub Koda*

Zodico Blues & Boogie / 1955 / Specialty ✦✦✦✦
Clifton Chenier's mid-'50s singles for Specialty were among his rawest and simplest; they were short ditties with rippling accordion and gritty vocals on top and driving rhythms and surging instrumental accompaniment underneath. That's the formula displayed on this 20-cut presentation of Chenier's early work, where he was often backed by guitarists Phillip Walker or Cornelius Green (Lonesome Sundown), with his brother Cleveland handling rubboard duties. This is Chenier in his stylistic infancy, building and nurturing what ultimately became a signature sound. —*Ron Wynn*

Louisiana Blues & Zydeco / 1965 / Arhoolie ✦✦✦
Featured is excellent small-combo zydeco. —*Jeff Hannusch*

Bayou Blues / 1970 / Specialty ✦✦✦✦
Bayou Blues compiles a selection of 12 tracks Clifton Chenier cut for Specialty Records in 1955, including the original versions of "Boppin' the Rock," "Eh, Petite Fille," "I'm On My Way," and "Zodico Stomp." It may not be a definitive retrospective, but it's an entertaining and necessary sampler of Chenier at the beginning of his career. —*Thom Owens*

Out West / 1974 / Arhoolie ✦✦✦✦
Special guests Elvin Bishop and Steve Miller joined Chenier for an excellent outing blending blues and rock influences with zydeco. Chenier's vocals were

tough and convincing, while Bishop and Miller, along with saxophonist Jon Hart, were outstanding. —*Ron Wynn*

In New Orleans / 1979 / GNP ✦✦✦
In New Orleans was recorded in the late '70s with one of Clifton Chenier's classic bands, which featured his brother on washboard, saxophonist John Hart, and guitarist Paul Senegal, among others. The album is textbook Chenier—it rocks & rolls, wails and shouts. It's may be a typical record for the king of zydeco, but that means it's very, very enjoyable. —*Thom Owens*

Bon Ton Roulet / May 1981 / Arhoolie ✦✦✦✦
Great rock'em-sock'em zydeco. —*Jeff Hannusch*

I'm Here! / May 1982 / Alligator ✦✦✦
Although not so good as his Arhoolie albums, this won Chenier a Grammy. —*Jeff Hannusch*

The King of Zydeco Live at Montreux / 1984 / Arhoolie ✦✦✦
This is a nice concert set. —*Mark A. Humphrey*

Live! / 1985 / Arhoolie ✦✦✦
The 19 selections on this disc were done in the early '80s, when Chenier was past his romping prime but still keeping the zydeco engine running. He has done them all before on other releases, but keeps them entertaining and enjoyable through sheer will and personality. —*Ron Wynn*

Sings the Blues / 1987 / Arhoolie ✦✦✦
Lots of great accordion and unique vocals come from the blues side of the bayou. —*Jeff Hannusch & Mark A. Humphrey*

Bogalusa Boogie / Jul. 1987 / Arhoolie ✦✦✦
Backed by a fuller band on this release, he sounds great. Here's the hottest of the red-hot Louisiana bands, and they're feelin' frisky. —*Jeff Hannusch & Mark A. Humphrey*

Live at St. Mark's / 1988 / Arhoolie ✦✦✦
Live at St. Mark's captures a rollicking concert performed in San Francisco. Chenier leads the band through a blend of zydeco and blues, singing with gusto and spice all along. Furthermore, he plays to the audience, telling jokes and stories, which give the album a special, intimate feel. With all the wonderful music and joy that *Live at St. Marks* radiates, there's little question that it is one of Chenier's finest live albums. —*Thom Owens*

60 Minutes with the King of Zydeco / 1988 / Arhoolie ✦✦✦✦
Zydeco at its best, it compiles his greatest hits from the Arhoolie label. —*Jeff Hannusch*

★ **Zydeco Dynamite: The Clifton Chenier Anthology** / 1993 / Rhino ✦✦✦✦✦
Clifton Chenier was to zydeco what Elvis Presley was to rockabilly, only more so—the genre's founding father and tireless ambassador. Rhino has done an admirable job of collecting the accordionist's important work for this two-disc, 40-track set, harking back to a wonderfully chaotic "Louisiana Stomp" that he waxed in Lake Charles, LA in 1954 for J.R. Fullbright's tiny Elko label. Whether you're in the market for one zydeco collection to summarize the entire genre or ready to delve deeply into the legacy of the idiom's pioneer, this is precisely where to begin. —*Bill Dahl*

We're Gonna Party / Oct. 25, 1994 / Collectables ✦✦✦

The Chicago Blue Stars

f. Chicago, IL
Group / Electric Chicago Blues
This was in actuality Charlie Musselwhite's band circa 1969, but because of his Vanguard contract he could not sing or be pictured on the sextet's only LP—although his harp playing is credited. Boasting perhaps the greatest Chicago rhythm section ever (drummer Fred Below and bass monster Jack Myers), the group showcased steel guitarist Freddie Roulette, pianist Skip Rose, and Aces guitarist Louis Myers. —*Dan Forte*

Coming Home / Mar. 1970 / Blue Thumb ✦✦✦
Because Musselwhite's contract forbade him to sing and Roulette had yet to develop into a strong vocalist, Louis Myers bears most of the vocal weight, and Rose and Below make one rather weak attempt each. But instrumentally—two Roulette spotlights and Musselwhite's jazzy arrangement of the title track—the group backed up their legendary status. As welcome as this "group" effort is, it's a shame the unit never recorded in the context it was formed—as Musselwhite's stellar backup band. —*Dan Forte*

Chicken Shack

f. 1966, Birmingham, England, **db.** 1973
Group / Blues-Rock, British Blues
This British blues-rock group is remembered mostly for their keyboard player, Christine Perfect, who would join Fleetwood Mac after marrying John McVie and changing her last name. Although they were one of the more pedestrian acts of the British blues boom, Chicken Shack were quite popular for a time in the late '60s, placing two albums in the British Top 20. The frontperson of Chicken was not Perfect/McVie, but guitarist Stan Webb, who would excite British audiences by entering the crowds at performances, courtesy of his 100-meter-long guitar lead. They were signed to Mike Vernon's Blue Horizon label, a British blues pillar that had its biggest success with early Fleetwood Mac.

Chicken Shack were actually not far behind Mac in popularity in the late '60s, purveying a more traditional brand of Chicago blues, heavily influenced by Freddie King. Although Webb took most of the songwriting and vocal duties, Christine Perfect also chipped in with occasional compositions and lead singing. In fact, she sang lead on their only British Top 20 single, "I'd Rather Go Blind" (1969). But around that time, she quit the music business to marry John McVie and become a housewife, although, as the world knows, that didn't last too long. Chicken Shack never recovered from Christine's loss, commercially or musically. Stan Webb kept Chicken Shack going, with a revolving door of other musicians, all the way into the 1980s, though he briefly disbanded the group to join Savoy Brown for a while in the mid-'70s. —*Richie Unterberger*

Forty Blue Fingers, Freshly Packed and Ready to Serve / 1968 / Epic ✦✦✦✦
If one can overlook Stan Webb's hyperventilating vocal excesses (which ain't easy), this is a promising debut, especially noteworthy for Webb's Freddie King-inspired guitar sting and Christine Perfect's understated vocals (only two, unfortunately compared to Webb's six). Webb does justice to his mentor with two instrumentals, King's "San-Ho-Zay" and his own "Webbed Feet." and Perfect proves the ideal counterpart—one of the few pianists paying homage to King's longtime collaborator Sonny Thompson. Nice spare sound, typical of Mike Vernon's Blue Horizon Label. —*Dan Forte*

O.K. Ken? / 1969 / BGO ✦✦
This was Chicken Shack's most popular album, making the British Top Ten. If you're looking for relics of the British Blues Boom, however, you'd be much better off with Ten Years After, to say nothing of legitimate artists such as Fleetwood Mac and John Mayall. British blues at its best could be exciting (if usually derivative), but it's difficult to fathom how this relentlessly plodding, monotonous effort met with such success. Stan Webb took most of the songwriting and vocal chores, emulating the slow-burning Chicago boogie with little skill or subtlety (though he wasn't a bad guitarist). Christine Perfect did write and sing a few songs, but these unfortunately found both her compositional and vocal chops at a most callow stage of development. To nail the coffin, most of the songs were preceded by excruciating comic dialog that made Cheech & Chong sound sophisticated in comparison. —*Richie Unterberger*

● **Collection** / 1988 / Castle ✦✦✦✦
Collection contains the cream of Chicken Shack's uneven albums and provides a perfect introduction to the British blues band. —*Thom Owens*

On Air / May 1998 / Strange Fruit ✦✦✦

Chosen Gospel Singers

f. 1950, Houston, TX
Group / Traditional Gospel, Black Gospel
Despite notching a series of hits between the early 1950s and early 1960s, the Chosen Gospel Singers remain one of the most elusive groups of gospel's golden era—plagued by constant lineup changes, the ensemble's proper history remains sketchy at best, and even the exact involvement of their most famous alumnus, Lou Rawls, is something of a mystery. It's known that the Chosen Gospel Singers were formed in Houston in 1950, and originally consisted of J.B. Randall, Aaron Wyatt, Willie Rose, and two shadowy figures later recalled by their surnames of Sheridan and Files. On the advice of manager Joe Johnson, himself a founding member of the Pilgrim Travelers, the group soon relocated to Los Angeles; upon arriving on the West Coast,

the first of countless roster fluctuations struck, and in seemingly no time Randall was the only surviving original member.

Tenors E.J. Blumfeld, George Butler, and Fred Sims, in addition to baritone Oscar Cook, were soon recruited to flesh out the Chosen lineup, and in November 1952 this quintet made their first recordings for the Specialty label, yielding the hit single "One-Two-Three." (Ted Taylor, later a soul singer of some renown, was also briefly a member during this same period, although he did not appear on record.) The steady personnel shifts have been attributed in large part to the group's status as a semi-professional venture—the Chosen's grueling weekend touring schedules played havoc with the individual members' day jobs, and for many the frustrations of constant firings ultimately ended in rejecting music in favor of finding steady work. Additionally, many had family commitments which made touring outside of the West Coast impossible.

When the Chosen went back into the studio in mid-1953, then, only Randall remained from the previous incarnation; his new collaborators included low tenor John Evans, tenors J.T. "Rattler" Ratley and Preston Whitted, and baritone Sam Thomas. During a subsequent tourstop in Chicago, they recruited 17-year-old lead vocalist Lou Rawls, already a gospel veteran through his work with the Teenage Kings of Harmony, the Holy Wonders, and the Highway QC's. In February 1954, Rawls made his first recordings as a Chosen Gospel Singer; another session followed just two months later, but in the interim both Evans and Ratley apparently exited the ranks. Also gone was Randall, the sole remaining link to the group's origins; he was replaced by Raeford Blair. There is some evidence that E.J. Booker, later of the Pilgrim Travelers, was also in the group at this juncture, although other accounts deny such a claim.

Rawls joined the Army prior to the Chosen's final Specialty session, recorded in early 1955; he was replaced by Brooklyn native Bob Crutcher for the studio date, which generated the hit "Prayer for the Doomed." Later that year, the Chosen signed with the Nashboro label; Crutcher remained in the lead slot, with Tommy Ellison of the Harmonizing Four soon joining him at the helm. Rawls resurfaced on their fourth Nashboro single, "Walk with Me," which may or may not have been first cut prior to his military tenure; both Sims and Brumfeld definitely returned to action, however, with the latter fronting the final incarnation of the Chosen, a lineup which also included the members of a Tyler, Texas quartet led by singer Willie Neal Johnson known as the Gospel Keynotes. When Brumfield quit soon after, he handed the reins to Johnson, who restored the name to the Gospel Keynotes, bringing the Chosen's convoluted story to a close. —*Jason Ankeny*

● **The Lifeboat** / 1954 / Specialty ✦✦✦✦
Featured are previously unreleased tracks, alternate takes, and long-out-of-print gems by this major gospel quartet, led at times by Lou Rawls. —*Opal Louis Nations*

Meet the Selah Jubilees / ✦✦✦
The Chosen Gospel Singers were a spiritual group in the sanctified style fronting such vocalists as the sing-and-preach Bob Crutcher, Joe Johnson from the Trumpeteers, jazz-soul singer Lou Rawls, and the hard-working Tommy Ellison, who later went on to form the Five Singing Stars. These are exciting selections from various labels, recorded between 1952 and 1963. Side B features the great Thermon Ruth and the Selah Singers, who sang both R&B and gospel under various aliases during the '40s and '50s. The material here from their postwar Arista, Continental, Gotham, and Mercury period is entirely gospel—close jubilee harmonies with sparse accompaniment. The songs are taken from rare 45s and 78s. There's good overall sound quality (cassette only). —*Opal Louis Nations, Roots & Rhythm Newsletter*

Popa Chubby

b. Bronx, NY
Vocals / Modern Electric Blues, Contemporary Blues
Born Ted Horowitz in the Bronx, N.Y., Popa Chubby was the son of a candy store owner. At 13, Chubby began playing drums; shortly thereafter, he discovered the music of the Rolling Stones and began playing guitar. Although he grew up in the 1970s, Chubby took his cue from artists of the 1960s, including Sly and the Family Stone, Jimi Hendrix, and Eric Clapton, among others. By the time he was in his early 20s, he enjoyed and played blues music, but also worked for a while backing up punk poet Richard Hell. Chub-

by's first big break was winning a national blues talent search sponsored by KLON, a public radio station in Long Beach, CA. He won New Artist of the Year Award and opened at the Long Beach Blues Festival in 1992. Chubby has continued to play more than 200 club dates a year through the 1990s. His Sony/OKeh debut, *Booty and the Beast*, was produced by longtime Atlantic Records engineer/producer Tom Dowd, whose recordings by Aretha Franklin, Ray Charles, Wilson Pickett, and others are legendary. In 1994, Chubby released several albums on his own Laughing Bear label, *It's Chubby Time* and *Gas Money*, before landing his deal with Sony Music/OKeh Records for *Booty and the Beast*, his major label debut, released in 1995. In 1996, the 1-800-Prime CD label released a live recording of Chubby's, *Hit the High Hard One*. Two years later, *One Million Broken Guitars* was released on Lightyear Records. —*Richard Skelly*

Gas Money / 1994 / 1-800-Prime ✦✦✦

It's Chubby Time / 1994 / 1-800-Prime ✦✦✦✦

● **Booty and the Beast** / 1995 / OKeh/550 Music ✦✦✦✦
Popa Chubby's debut album is an inspiring set of energetic, gut-bucket blues-rock, filled with exceptional playing. Chubby has soul, even if he doesn't quite cut it as a songwriter; there aren't many songs that are inventive or memorable. But as an instrumental workout, *Booty and the Beast* is terrific. Using the blues as a basic foundation, Popa Chubby spins off into new directions, incorporating bits of rock and jazz to his forceful playing. His guitar playing is what makes the album a promising debut. —*Stephen Thomas Erlewine*

Hit the High Hard One / 1996 / Prime/Laughing Bear ✦✦✦

One Million Broken Guitars / Jun. 2, 1998 / Lightyear ✦✦✦

Eric Clapton (Eric Patrick Clapp)

b. Mar. 30, 1945, Ripley, England
Guitar, Vocals / Pop-Rock, Blues-Rock, Rock 'n' Roll, Adult Contemporary, British Blues, Electric British Blues
By the time Eric Clapton launched his solo career with the release of his self-titled debut album in August 1970, he was long established as one of the world's major rock stars due to his group affiliations—the Yardbirds, John Mayall's Bluesbreakers, Cream, and Blind Faith—affiliations that had demonstrated his claim to being the best rock guitarist of his generation. That it took Clapton so long to go out on his own, however, was evidence of a degree of reticence unusual for one of his stature. And his debut album, though it spawned the Top 40 hit "After Midnight," was typical of his self-effacing approach: It was, in effect, an album by the group he had lately been featured in, Delaney & Bonnie & Friends.

Not surprisingly, before his solo debut had even been released, Clapton had retreated from his solo stance, assembling from the D&B&F ranks the personnel for a group, Derek & the Dominos, with which he played for most of 1970. Clapton was largely inactive in 1971 and 1972, due to heroin addiction, but he performed a comeback concert at the Rainbow Theatre in London on January 13, 1973, resulting in the album *Eric Clapton's Rainbow Concert* (September 1973).

But Clapton did not launch a sustained solo career until July 1974, when he released *461 Ocean Boulevard*, which topped the charts and spawned the No. 1 single "I Shot the Sheriff."

The persona Clapton established over the next decade was less that of guitar hero than arena rock star with a weakness for ballads. The follow-ups to *461 Ocean Boulevard, There's One in Every Crowd* (March 1975), the live *E.C. Was Here* (August 1975), and *No Reason to Cry* (August 1976), were less successful. But *Slowhand* (November 1977), which featured both the powerful "Cocaine" (written by J.J. Cale, who had also written "After Midnight") and the hit singles "Lay Down Sally" and "Wonderful Tonight," was a million-seller, and its follow-ups, *Backless* (November 1978), featuring the Top Ten hit "Promises," the live *Just One Night* (April 1980), and *Another Ticket* (February 1981), featuring the Top Ten hit "I Can't Stand It," were all big sellers.

Clapton's popularity waned somewhat in the first half of the '80s, as the albums *Money and Cigarettes* (February 1983), *Behind the Sun* (March 1985), and *August* (November 1986) indicated a certain career stasis. But he was buoyed up by the release of the boxed set retrospective *Crossroads* (April

1988), which seemed to remind his fans of how great he was. *Journeyman* (November 1989) was a return to form.

It would be his last new studio album for nearly five years, though in the interim he would suffer greatly and enjoy surprising triumph. On March 20, 1991, Clapton's four-year-old son was killed in a fall. While he mourned, he released a live album, *24 Nights* (October 1991), culled from his annual concert series at the Royal Albert Hall in London, and prepared a movie soundtrack, *Rush* (January 1992). The soundtrack featured a song written for his son, "Tears in Heaven," that became a massive hit single.

In March 1992, Clapton recorded a concert for *MTV Unplugged* that, when released on an album in August, became his biggest-selling record ever. Two years later, Clapton returned with a blues album, *From the Cradle*, which became one of his most successful albums, both commerically and critically. *Crossroads 2: Live in the '70s*, a box set chronicling his live work from the '70s, was released to mixed reviews. In early 1997, Clapton, billing himself by the pseudonym "x-sample," collaborated with keyboardist/producer Simon Climie as the ambient new-age and trip-hop duo T.D.F. The duo released *Retail Therapy* to mixed reviews in early 1997.

Clapton retained Climie as his collaborator for *Pilgrim*, his first album of new material since 1989's *Journeyman*. *Pilgrim* was greeted with decidedly mixed reviews upon its spring 1998 release, but the album debuted at number four and stayed in the Top Ten for several weeks on the success of the single "My Father's Eyes." — *William Ruhlmann*

Eric Clapton / Jul. 1970 / Polydor ✦✦✦✦
Eric Clapton's eponymous solo debut was recorded after he completed a tour with Delaney & Bonnie. Clapton used the core of the duo's backing band and co-wrote the majority of the songs with Delaney Bramlett—accordingly, *Eric Clapton* sounds more laidback and straightforward than any of the guitarist's previous recordings. There are still elements of blues and rock 'n' roll, but they're hidden beneath layers of gospel, R&B, country, and pop flourishes. And the pop element of the record is the strongest of the album's many elements—"Blues Power" isn't a blues song and only "Let It Rain," the album's closer, features extended solos. Throughout the album, Clapton turns out concise solos that de-emphasize his status as guitar god, even when they display astonishing musicality and technique. That is both a good and a bad thing—it's encouraging to hear him grow and become a more fully rounded musician, but too often the album needs the spark that some loud guitar solos would have given it. In short, it needs a little more of Clapton's personality. — *Stephen Thomas Erlewine*

461 Ocean Boulevard / Jul. 1974 / Polydor ✦✦✦✦
461 Ocean Boulevard is Eric Clapton's second studio solo album, arriving after his side project of Derek & the Dominos and a long struggle with heroin addiction. Although there are some new reggae influences, the album doesn't sound all that different from the rock, pop, blues, country, and R&B amalgam of *Eric Clapton*. However, *461 Ocean Boulevard* is a tighter, more focused outing that enables Clapton to stretch out instrumentally. Furthermore, the pop concessions on the album—the sleek production, the concise running times—don't detract from the rootsy origins of the material, whether it's Johnny Otis's "Willie and the Hand Jive," the traditional blues "Motherless Children," Bob Marley's "I Shot the Sheriff," or Clapton's emotional originals, "Better Make It Through Today" and "Let It Grow." With its relaxed, friendly atmosphere and strong bluesy roots, *461 Ocean Boulevard* set the template for Clapton's '70s albums. Though he tried hard to make an album exactly like it, he never quite managed to replicate its charms. — *Stephen Thomas Erlewine*

There's One in Every Crowd / Mar. 1975 / Polydor ✦✦
Having stayed out of the recording studio for four years prior to making his comeback album, *461 Ocean Boulevard*, Eric Clapton returned to recording only a few months later to make its follow-up, *There's One in Every Crowd*. Perhaps he hadn't had time to write or gather sufficient material to make a similarly effective album, since the result is a scattershot mixture of styles, leading off with two gospel tunes, one a reggae version of "Swing Low, Sweet Chariot." Clapton and his second guitarist, George Terry, had written a sequel to "I Shot the Sheriff," "Don't Blame Me," which Clapton sang in his best impersonation of Bob Marley's voice. The album's best track, naturally, was the blues cover, Clapton's take on Elmore James' "The Sky Is Crying." But *There's One in Every Crowd* was a disappointing follow-up to *461 Ocean*

Boulevard, and fans let Clapton know it: While the former album had topped the charts and gone gold, the latter didn't even make the Top Ten. — *William Ruhlmann*

E.C. Was Here / Aug. 1975 / Polydor ✦✦✦
Since Eric Clapton and his longtime fans have always thought of him primarily as a bluesman, it is curious that this live album, which is devoted to extended guitar solos on blues standards like "Have You Ever Loved a Woman," "Rambling on My Mind," and "Further on up the Road," didn't become a massive hit. Maybe it was that the once reclusive Clapton was now spitting out new albums every six months, but *E.C. Was Here* did not achieve the renown it deserved upon release, and Clapton, who had been reluctant to put out a straight blues album to begin with, didn't try anything similar again for almost 20 years, instead making sure to keep his records within a pop framework that usually diluted their effectiveness. In its CD reissue, with "Drifting Blues" extended out to its full 11 minutes, the album is even more impressive. — *William Ruhlmann*

No Reason to Cry / Aug. 1976 / Polydor ✦✦✦
When he gave a speech inducting the Band into the Rock & Roll Hall of Fame, Eric Clapton said that after he heard their debut album, *Music from Big Pink*, he wanted to join the group, the fact that they already had a guitarist in Robbie Robertson notwithstanding. In the winter of 1975-1976, when he cut *No Reason to Cry* at the Band's Shangri-la Studio in Malibu, CA, he came as close as he ever would to realizing that desire. Clapton is a musical chameleon; though some of *No Reason to Cry* is identifiable as the kind of pop-rock Clapton had been making since the start of his solo career (the best of it being "Hello Old Friend," which became his first Top 40 single in two years), the most memorable music on the album occurs when Clapton is collaborating with members of the Band and other guests. He duets with Band bassist Rick Danko on Danko's "All Our Past Times," and with Bob Dylan on Dylan's "Sign Language," as Robertson's distinctive lead guitar is heard rather than Clapton's. As a result, the album is a good purchase for fans of Bob Dylan and the Band, but not necessarily for those of Eric Clapton. (The CD reissue adds a bonus track, "Last Night," which is a traditional 12-bar blues song credited to Clapton.) — *William Ruhlmann*

Slowhand / Nov. 1977 / Polydor ✦✦✦✦
After the all-star *No Reason to Cry* failed to make much of an impact commerically, Eric Clapton returned to using his own band for *Slowhand*. The difference is substantial—where *No Reason to Cry* struggled hard to find the right tone, *Slowhand* opens with the relaxed, bluesy shuffle of J.J. Cale's "Cocaine" and sustains it throughout the course of the album. Alternating between straight blues ("Mean Old Frisco"), country ("Lay Down Sally"), mainstream rock ("Cocaine," "The Core") and pop ("Wonderful Tonight"), *Slowhand* doesn't sound schizophrenic because of the band's grasp of the material. This is laidback virtuosity—although Clapton and his band are never flashy, their playing is masterful and assured. That assurance and the album's eclectic material makes *Slowhand* rank with *461 Ocean Boulevard* as Eric Clapton's best album. — *Stephen Thomas Erlewine*

Backless / Nov. 1978 / Polydor ✦✦✦
Having made his best album since *461 Ocean Boulevard* with *Slowhand*, Eric Clapton followed with *Backless*, which took the same authoritative, no-nonsense approach. If it wasn't quite the masterpiece, or the sales monster, that *Slowhand* had been, this probably was because of that usual Clapton problem—material. Once again, he returned to those Oklahoma hills for another song from J.J. Cale, but "I'll Make Love to You Anytime" wasn't quite up to "Cocaine" or "After Midnight." Bob Dylan contributed two songs, but you could see why he hadn't saved them for his own album, and Clapton's own writing contributions were mediocre. Clapton did earn a Top Ten hit with Richard Feldman and Roger Linn's understated pop shuffle "Promises," but it was not one of his more memorable recordings. Of course, Clapton's blues playing on the lone obligatory blues cut, "Early in the Morning" (presented in its full eight-minute version on the CD reissue), was stellar. (*Backless* was his last album to feature the backup group that had been with him since 1974.) — *William Ruhlmann*

Just One Night / Apr. 1980 / Polydor ✦✦✦✦
Although Eric Clapton has released a bevy of live albums, none of them have ever quite captured the guitarist's raw energy and dazzling virtuosity. The

double-live album *Just One Night* may have gotten closer to that elusive goal than most of its predecessors, but it is still lacking in many ways. The most notable difference between *Just One Night* and Clapton's other live albums is his backing band. Led by guitarist Albert Lee, the group is a collective of accomplished professionals that have managed to keep some grit in their playing. They help push Clapton along, forcing him to spit out crackling solos throughout the album. However, the performances aren't consistent on *Just One Night*—there are plenty of dynamic moments like "Double Trouble" and "Rambling on My Mind," but they are weighed down by pedestrian renditions of songs like "All Our Past Times." Nevertheless, more than any other Clapton live album, *Just One Night* suggests the guitarist's in-concert potential. It's just too bad that the recording didn't occur on a night when he *did* fulfill all of that potential. — *Stephen Thomas Erlewine*

Another Ticket / Feb. 1981 / Polydor ✦✦✦
Now, here's a star-crossed album. Polydor rejected the first version of it, produced by Glyn Johns, and Eric Clapton was forced to cut it all over again with Tom Dowd. Then, a few dates into a US promotional tour coinciding with its release, Clapton collapsed and was found to be near death from ulcers due to his alcoholism. Finally, it turned out to be the final record of his 15-year association with Polydor, which therefore had no reason to promote it. Nevertheless, the album made the Top Ten, went gold, and spawned a Top Ten single in "I Can't Stand It." And the rest of it wasn't too shabby, either. The first and last Clapton studio album to feature his all-British band of the early '80s, it gave considerable prominence to second guitarist Albert Lee and especially to keyboard player/singer Gary Brooker (formerly leader of Procol Harum), and they gave it more of a blues-rock feel than the country-funk brewed up by the Tulsa shuffle crew Clapton had used throughout the 1970s. Best of all, Clapton had taken the time to write some songs—he's credited on six of the nine selections—and tunes such as the title track and "I Can't Stand It" held up well. This wasn't great Clapton, but it was good, and it deserved more recognition that conditions allowed it at the time. — *William Ruhlmann*

Time Pieces: Best of Eric Clapton / May 1982 / Polydor ✦✦✦✦
Time Pieces is a good single-disc collection of Eric Clapton's solo hits—including "I Shot the Sheriff," "After Midnight," "Wonderful Tonight," Derek & the Domino's "Layla," and "Cocaine"—that has since been supplanted by the more thorough *The Cream of Eric Clapton*, which combines his solo work with selections of his Cream and Blind Faith work. Nevertheless, the compilation still provides a good introduction for neophyte Clapton fans, especially those that just want copies of his '70s hits. — *Stephen Thomas Erlewine*

Money and Cigarettes / Feb. 1983 / Reprise ✦✦✦✦
Recorded with some old friends—including Ry Cooder, Duck Dunn, and Albert Lee—*Money and Cigarettes* is one of Clapton's finest albums. Instead of being an empty exercise in studio professionalism, the record is an appealing, low-key effort featuring some of the smoothest blues Clapton has ever played. — *Stephen Thomas Erlewine*

Time Pieces II/Live in the '70s / 1985 / Polydor ✦✦✦
Neither a career retrospective nor a rarities collection, *Time Pieces II: Live in the '70s* is an odd record. Featuring a selection of material recorded in concert at various points in the '70s, the album never gives an accurate impression of Clapton's progression as a guitarist —it's sequenced haphazardly, with tracks falling outside of strict chronological order. Nevertheless, there are a number of fine performances here, especially on album tracks like "Tulsa Time" and "If I Don't Be There by Morning," as well as the extended solos of "Rambling on My Mind." Diehard fans will find things of interest on *Time Pieces II*, but the album can be safely ignored by most listeners. — *Stephen Thomas Erlewine*

Behind the Sun / Mar. 1985 / Reprise ✦✦✦
Clapton's career was in decline in the early '80s when he switched record labels from Polydor to Warner Bros. and his debut Warner album, *Money and Cigarettes*, became his first to fall below gold-record status in more than six years. As a result, Warner looked critically at his follow-up, the Phil Collins-produced *Behind the Sun*, in the fall of 1984 and rejected the first version submitted, insisting that he record several new songs written by Jerry Williams, backed by Los Angeles session players under the auspices of company producers Lenny Waronker and Ted Templeman. Warner then emphasized the new tracks, releasing two of them, "Forever Man" (which reached

the Top 40) and "See What Love Can Do," as singles. The resulting album, not surprisingly, was somewhat schizophrenic, though the company may have been correct in thinking that the album as a whole was competent without being very exciting. The added tracks were not bad, but they were not the surefire hits they were supposed to be. As usual, there was some effective guitar soloing (notably on "Same Old Blues"), but despite the tinkering, *Behind the Sun* was not one of Clapton's better albums. (It went gold after nearly two years in release.) — *William Ruhlmann*

August / Nov. 1986 / Reprise ✦✦
Eric Clapton adopted a new, tougher, hard R&B approach on *August*, employing a stripped-down band featuring keyboard player Greg Phillinganes, bassist Nathan East, and drummer/producer Phil Collins, plus, on several tracks, a horn section and, on a couple of tracks, backup vocals by Tina Turner, and performing songs written by old Motown hand Lamont Dozier, among others. The excellent, but incongruous, leadoff track, however, was "It's in the Way That You Use It," which Clapton and Robbie Robertson had written for Robertson's score to the film *The Color of Money*. Elsewhere, Clapton sang and played fiercely on songs like "Tearing Us Apart," "Run," and "Miss You," all of which earned AOR radio play. That radio support may have helped the album to achieve gold status in less than six months, Clapton's best commercial showing since 1981's *Another Ticket*, despite the album's failure to generate a hit single. The title commemorates the birth in August 1986 of Clapton's son Conor. (The CD version of the album contains the bonus track "Grand Illusion.") — *William Ruhlmann*

☆ Crossroads / Apr. 1988 / Polydor ✦✦✦✦✦
A four-disc box set spanning Eric Clapton's entire career—running from the Yardbirds to his '80s solo recordings—*Crossroads* not only revitalized Clapton's commerical standing, but it established the rock 'n' roll multi-disc box set retrospective as a commercially viable proposition. Bob Dylan's *Biograph* was successful two years before the release of *Crossroads*, but Clapton's set was a bonafide blockbuster. And it's easy to see why. *Crossroads* manages to sum up Clapton's career succinctly and thoroughly, touching upon all of his hits and adding a bevy of first-rate unreleased material (most notably selections from the scrapped second Derek & the Dominos album). Although not all of his greatest performances are included on the set—none of his work as a session musician or guest artist is included, for instance—every truly essential item he recorded is present on these four discs. No other Clapton album accurately explains why the guitarist was so influential, or demonstrates exactly what he accomplished. — *Stephen Thomas Erlewine*

Journeyman / Nov. 1989 / Reprise ✦✦✦✦
For most of the '80s, Eric Clapton seemed rather lost, uncertain of whether he should return to his blues roots or pander to AOR radio. By the mid-'80s, he appeared to have made the decision to revamp himself as a glossy mainstream rocker, working with synthesizers and drum machines. Instead of expanding his audience, it only reduced it. Then came the career retrospective *Crossroads*, which helped revitalize his career, not only commercially, but also creatively, as *Journeyman*—the first album he recorded after the success of *Crossroads*—proved. Although *Journeyman* still suffers from an overly slick production, Clapton sounds more convincing than he has since the early '70s. Not only is his guitar playing muscular and forceful, his singing is soulful and gritty. Furthermore, the songwriting is consistently strong, alternating between fine mainstream rock originals ("Pretending") and covers ("Before You Accuse Me," "Hound Dog"). Like any of Clapton's best albums, there is no grandstanding to be found on *Journeyman*—it's simply a laidback and thoroughly engaging display of Clapton's virtuosity. On the whole, it's the best studio album he's released since *Slowhand*. — *Stephen Thomas Erlewine*

Rush / Aug. 1991 / Reprise ✦✦✦
An excellent dark blues score written by Clapton (with help on the three songs) and performed by an augumented version of his band. This soundtrack album produced one big hit for Clapton with "Tears In Heaven," but it's a wonderfully intense piece of work all the way through, with some terrific guitar work from Clapton himself. Buddy Guy turns up to add lead vocals and guitar on the 11-minute version of Willie Dixon's "Don't Know Which Way to Go," and that's more than all right too. There's a very good chance that the dark intensity of this music was as much informed by the tragedies in Clapton's life ("Tears In Heaven" is about his son) as the film itself. What-

ever the cause, this album has far more impact than you might expect from the score to a movie—there's a sense of the music here working something out in Clapton's heart, a sense given a lot of power thanks to the intense, heart-wrenching passion invoked by some of the turns taken here. At its best, Clapton's music can speak of the pain he feels—and Clapton has rarely been better than he is here. — *Steven McDonald*

24 Nights / Oct. 8, 1991 / Reprise ✦✦✦
Eric Clapton, who had not released a live album since 1980, had several good reasons to release one in the early '90s. For one thing, his spare backup band of keyboardist Greg Phillinganes, bassist Nathan East, and drummer Steve Ferrone, was his best live unit ever, and its powerful live versions of Cream classics like "White Room" and "Sunshine of Your Love" deserved to be documented. For another, since 1987, Clapton had been playing an annual series of concerts at the Royal Albert Hall in London, putting together various special shows—blues nights, orchestral nights, etc. *24 Nights*, a double album, was culled from two years of such shows, 1990 and 1991, and it demonstrated the breadth of Clapton's work, from his hot regular band to assemblages of bluesmen like Buddy Guy and Robert Cray to examples of his soundtrack work with an orchestra led by Michael Kamen. The result was an album that came across as a lavishly constructed retrospective and a testament to Clapton's musical stature. But it made little impact upon release (though it quickly went gold), perhaps because events overcame it—three months later, Clapton's elegy for his baby son, "Tears In Heaven," was all over the radio, and a few months after that he was redefining himself on *MTV Unplugged*—a live show as austere as *24 Nights* was grand. Still, it would be hard to find a more thorough demonstration of Clapton's abilities than the one presented here. — *William Ruhlmann*

Unplugged / Aug. 18, 1992 / Reprise ✦✦✦✦
Clapton's *Unplugged* was responsible for making acoustic-based music, and *Unplugged* albums in particular, a hot trend in the early '90s. Clapton's concert was not only one of the finest *Unplugged* episodes, but was also some of the finest music he had recorded in years. Instead of the slick productions that tainted his '80s albums, the music was straightforward and direct, alternating between his pop numbers and traditional blues songs. The result was some of the most genuine, heartfelt music the guitarist has ever committed to tape. And some of his most popular—the album sold over seven million copies in the US and won several Grammies. — *Stephen Thomas Erlewine*

From the Cradle / Sep. 13, 1994 / Reprise ✦✦✦✦
For years, fans craved an all-blues album from Clapton; he waited until 1994 to deliver *From the Cradle*. The album manages to recreate the ambience of postwar electric blues, right down to the bottomless thump of the rhythm section. If it wasn't for Clapton's labored vocals, everything would be perfect. As long as he plays his guitar, he can't fail—his solos are white-hot and evocative, original and captivating. When he sings, Clapton loses that sense of originality, choosing to mimic the vocals of the original recordings. At times, his overemotive singing is painful; he doesn't have the strength to pull off Howlin' Wolf's growl or the confidence to replicate Muddy Waters' assured phrasing. Yet, whenever he plays, it's easier to forget his vocal shortcomings. Even with its faults, *From the Cradle* is one of Clapton's finest moments. — *Stephen Thomas Erlewine*

● **The Cream of Clapton** / Mar. 7, 1995 / Polydor ✦✦✦✦
Eric Clapton was contracted to Polydor Records from 1966 to 1981, first as a member of Cream, then Blind Faith, and later as a solo artist and as the leader of Derek & the Dominos. This 19-track, 79-minute disc surveys his career, presenting an excellent selection from the period, including the Cream hits "Sunshine of Your Love," "White Room," and "Crossroads"; "Presence of the Lord," Clapton's finest moment with Blind Faith; "Bell Bottom Blues" and "Layla" from Derek & the Dominos; and 11 songs from Clapton's solo work, among them the hits "I Shot The Sheriff," "Promises," and "I Can't Stand It." The selection is thus broader and better than that found on 1982's *Time Pieces* collection, and with excellent sound and liner notes by Clapton biographer Ray Coleman, *The Cream of Clapton* stands as the single-disc best-of to own for Clapton's greatest recordings. (Not to be confused with the popular 1987 Polydor [UK] compilation *The Cream of Eric Clapton*, which has since been retitled *The Best of Eric Clapton*.) — *William Ruhlmann*

Eric Clapton's Rainbow Concert [Expanded] / Jul. 25, 1995 / Polydor ✦✦✦
In these days of CD expansion, it is not unusual for a record company to reissue an old album with a bonus track or two. This reconstruction of the January 13, 1973, comeback concert by Eric Clapton is something else again, however. The original six-track LP ran less than 27 minutes; the new 14-track CD runs almost 74 minutes. The eight additions—"Layla," "Blues Power," "Bottle of Red Wine," "Bell Bottom Blues," "Tell the Truth," "Key to the Highway," "Let It Rain," and "Crossroads"—make the disc an effective recapitulation of Clapton's career over the previous seven years, including his solo work and his appearances with John Mayall's Bluesbreakers, Cream, and Derek and the Dominos. Despite the addiction that had kept him largely homebound for almost two years, Clapton played well, though the all-star backup band was as ragged as it was spirited. The loose feel of the evening was brought out in the stage announcements, many by Pete Townshend, who even mentioned a social disease just before introducing "Presence of the Lord." This still isn't a great Eric Clapton show, but it has been transformed from a historical curiosity to a historical document. — *William Ruhlmann*

Crossroads 2: Live in the '70s / Apr. 2, 1996 / Polydor/Chronicles ✦✦✦
Crossroads was a box set that appealed to both beginners and fanatics. *Crossroads 2: Live in the '70s* appeals only to fanatics. Spanning four discs and consisting almost entirely of live material (there are a handful of studio outtakes), this is music that will enthrall only completists and archivists. For those listeners, there is a wealth of fascinating, compelling performances here, as well as a fair share of mediocre, uninspired tracks. The key word for the entire album is detail—it is an album for studying the intricacies of Clapton's playing and how it evolved. For example, it's easy to hear the differences and progressions between the four versions of Robert Johnson's "Rambling on My Mind." And it is Clapton that evolves, not his supporting band—although they are proficient, they are hardly exciting. However, their static, professional support provides a nice bed to chart Slowhand's growth over the course of the decade, simply because he is *always* the focal point. *Crossroads 2* may be only for a collector, but for those collectors it is a treasure, even if some of the tracks are fool's gold. — *Stephen Thomas Erlewine*

Pilgrim / Mar. 10, 1998 / Warner Brothers ✦✦
Eric Clapton reached the peak of his popularity in the '90s, as the back-to-back No. 1 albums *Unplugged* and *From the Cradle* combined for a total of over 13 million sales in the US alone. One strange thing about his success is that it relied almost entirely on covers and new versions of classic hits; he released no albums of new material between 1989's *Journeyman* and 1998's *Pilgrim*. In the decade between the two albums, he had two new hits—his moving elegy to his deceased son, "Tears in Heaven," and the slick contemporary soul of the Babyface-written "Change the World"—and *Pilgrim* tries to reach a middle ground between these two extremes, balancing tortured lyrics with smooth sonic surfaces. Working with producer Simon Climie, his collaborator on the TDF side project, Clapton has created a numbingly calm record that, for all of its lyrical torment, displays no emotion whatsoever. Much of the problem lies in the production, which relies entirely on stiff mechanical drumbeats, gauzy synthesizers, and meandering instrumental interludes. These ingredients could result in a good record, as "Change the World" demonstrated, but that's not the case here. Whether it's soul, blues, or pop, all the songs on *Pilgrim* suffer from this monotonous production. Unfortunately, Clapton doesn't want to shake things up—his singing is startlingly mannered, even on emotionally turbulent numbers like "My Father's Eyes" or "Circus." Even worse, he's content to settle back instrumentally, playing slight solos and fills that are as colorless as the electronic backdrops. The deadened sonics would make *Pilgrim* a chore even if there were strong songs on the record; but only a handful of tunes break through the murk. Considering that his previous studio record, *Journeyman*, was a fine workmanlike effort and that *From the Cradle* and *Unplugged* crackled with vitality, the blandness of *Pilgrim* makes it all the more disappointing. — *Stephen Thomas Erlewine*

W.C. Clark
....

b. Nov. 16, 1939, Austin, TX
Guitar, Vocals / Modern Electric Blues, Texas Blues, Retro-Soul
Guitarist, singer, and songwriter W.C. Clark was one of Austin's original blues musicians, and is considered the godfather of that city's blues scene.

Wesley Curley Clark was born and raised in Austin and grew up surrounded by music, since his father was a guitar player and his mother and grandmother sang in the choir at St. John's College Baptist Church. By the time he was 16, he played his first show at Victory Grill and was introduced to local legends T.D. Bell and Erbie Bowser. He began playing bass with Bell's band, honing his blues chops on guitar on his own time. While East Austin's club scene flourished in the late '50s and early '60s, white students from the nearby University of Texas began to patronize the blues clubs, and after taking a regular gig at Charlie's Playhouse, Clark made music his full-time occupation. After six years at the playhouse, he met R&B singer Joe Tex and joined his band as guitarist.

After leaving Tex's band and returning to Austin, Clark was surprised and encouraged by the infusion of young white blues players on the local scene. Bill Campbell, Angela Strehli, Lewis Cowdrey, and Paul Ray and the Vaughan brothers were attracting growing crowds to their shows and forming close bonds with the Black blues players who had already been on the scene.

In the early '70s, Clark teamed up with guitarist and piano player Denny Freeman and vocalist Angela Strehli to form a group called Southern Feeling. With this group Clark was able to blossom as a songwriter, but after a record deal fell apart, he took a job as a mechanic at a local Ford dealership. However, a young guitarist named Stevie Ray Vaughan kept visiting him at the garage. Vaughan was putting his own band together and insisted that Clark be a part of it. Calling themselves the Triple Threat Revue, they eventually took to the road with Lou Ann Barton as lead vocalist. Clark and keyboardist Mike Kindred wrote "Cold Shot," which went on to become one of Vaughan's biggest hits in the mid-1980s.

Clark has recorded three albums—*Something for Everybody* (1986), released independently on his own label, and two albums for the New Orleans-based BlackTop label, 1994's *Heart of Gold* and 1996's *Texas Soul*. On *Texas Soul*, Clark is accompanied by a band of Austin-area blues veterans, including Chris Layton and Tommy Shannon of Vaughan's Double Trouble, producer and guitarist Derek O'Brien, and saxophonist Mark "Kaz" Kazanoff.

In March 1997, Clark and his band had an accident while returning to Austin in their van; he lost his fiancee and drummer. Clark was uninjured, but the experience slowed him down for awhile. However, Clark continues to be active on the Austin blues scene, of which he is affectionately referred to as "the godfather." *—Richard Skelly*

● **Heart of Gold** / May 2, 1994 / Black Top ✦✦✦✦
Heart of Gold is an impressive showcase for W.C. Clark's deep talents, giving him the opportunity to flaunt his chops and prove that he can play nearly anything. Clark's foundation is in greasy roadhouse Texas blues and while there's a number of wonderful cuts in that style here, he doesn't limit himself to Texas shuffles. Instead, he turns out some sweaty soul—including a seductive, passionate reading of Latimore's "Let's Straighten It Out"—and some organ-drenched Tex-Mex workouts which not only give the album diversity, but also give the album depth. And that's the reason why *Heart of Gold* is the definitive W.C. Clark release—it's the first (and arguably only) time he's gotten it completely right on record. *—Thom Owens*

Texas Soul / Sep. 1995 + Nov. 1995 / Black Top ✦✦✦
Although W.C. Clark does perform a few blues, this CD is essentially an R&B/soul session which puts the emphasis on Clark's calm but emotional vocals (some of the lyrics are somewhat philosophical) and stinging guitar. The five-piece Kamikaze Horns are restricted to ensemble fills and riffs. Even if a certain predictability pervades the set, Clark (who in spots reminds one slightly of both Ray Charles and B.B. King) is a skilled performer in the idiom, making this a date recommended to fans of the Stax sound of the 1960s. *—Scott Yanow*

Lover's Plea / May 5, 1998 / Black Top ✦✦✦
The spirit of Stax is alive and well in the bright, brassy blues of W.C. Clark. His high, reedy tenor (sometimes flying into a sweet falsetto) is the perfect center to these blues-pop tunes. The cover of this disc proudly proclaims this is "genuine Texas blues," which goes to show that there's more to the Lone Star State than the attack of Stevie Ray Vaughan and the lowdown chug of Lightnin' Hopkins. *—Tim Sheridan*

William Clarke

b. Mar. 29, 1951, Inglewood, CA, **d.** Nov. 2, 1996, Fresno, CA
Harmonica, Vocals / Modern Electric Blues, Modern Electric Chicago Blues, Electric Chicago Blues, Harmonica Blues
I have had the very good fortune to hear great Chicago harp (harmonica) players like Little Walter, Junior Wells, Big Walter Horton, and many others

playing live in the clubs of Chicago during the mid-'60s. Those days are gone and I had given up hope of ever hearing a new voice on amplified blues harp again in my lifetime. Then came William Clarke. Technically, Clarke is a master of both the cross and chromatic harps. He takes blues on the chromatic up to and well beyond where Little Walter left it years ago. But far more important than the technique is the music. Clarke plays straight-ahead blues that is music to the ears—and it rocks.

William Clarke was born March 29, 1951, in Inglewood, CA, and became turned onto blues during the 1960s, oddly enough by hearing covers of blues tunes by groups like the Rolling Stones. Although he had played some guitar and drums, Clarke started playing the harmonica in 1967. He states that his main early influences were Big Walter Horton, James Cotton, Junior Wells, and Sonny Boy Williamson II. In mid-1968, Clarke began listening to jazz organists such as Jack McDuff, Jimmy McGriff, Shirley Scott, and Richard "Groove" Holmes. "This had a huge influence on my playing," says Clarke. "Along with jazz saxophonists Eddie Lockjaw Davis, Gene Ammons, Lyne Hope, and Willis Jackson, the combination of listening and absorbing the grooves of tenor sax-led organ trios had an everlasting effect on my direction in music. For my style, I incorporated the hardcore attitude and tone of the classic Chicago harmonica players along with the swinging and highly rhythmic grooves of the organ trios, and to this I add my style and ideas, and you have the William Clarke sound."

By the middle of 1969, Clarke was spending a lot of time in the Los Angeles ghetto clubs—South-Central Los Angeles. There he met T-Bone Walker, Pee Wee Crayton, Shakey Jake Harris, Big Joe Turner, Ironing Board Sam, J.D. Nicholson, and George "Harmonica" Smith, who would later become his greatest influence on the chromatic harp. Clarke would go from one club until it closed at 2 a.m., switch to an after-hours club from 2 a.m. to 6 a.m., and then go to jam sessions that could last until 11 a.m.—and still hold down a day job! Clarke spent 20 years working as a machinist and family man before launching his blues career.

Then Clarke began to see and listen more to George Harmonica Smith—a veteran of the Muddy Waters band. Clarke says, "To me George was bigger than life. I was always afraid to start up a conversation with him, not because I thought he was mean, but because I thought of him like a god on the harmonica." Around 1977, they became friends and started performing together. They worked together until Smith passed away in 1983. Clarke was George Smith's protégé, and Smith became the godfather to Clarke's son Willie. Clarke says, "George and me were very close friends and in a lot of ways he was like a father to me."

Clarke recorded a number of albums prior to releasing his first CD. They are *Hittin' Heavy* (Good Times, 1978), *Blues from Los Angeles* (1980), *Can't You Hear Me Calling* (Watch Dog, 1983), *Tip of the Top* (Satch, 1987—nominated for a Handy award) and *Rockin' the Boat* (Rivera, 1988). He won the 1991 Handy award for Blues Song of the Year, "Must Be Jelly," and also received six W.C. Handy Award nominations.

In the early- to mid-'90s, Clarke recorded a string of albums for Alligator, all of which are worth a listen. For my ears, the real legacy of William Clarke can be found on those first two Alligator albums, *Blowin' Like Hell* and *Serious Intentions. Blowin' Like Hell,* in particular, is one of those classic blues album, that everyone should own.

Clarke wrote most of his own songs, and many of them are real ear-catchers. He has a working-class background, and songs like "Gambling for My Bread" and "Pawnshop Bound" are right on the money—just great tunes.

Like all too many of the blues greats before him, William Clarke played hard and lived hard. He and his band traveled by car a lot, alternating between the West Coast and the Midwest in an endless road trip of one-night stands, short gigs, staying in cheap hotels, eating on the run, and probably drinking too much. William Clarke died on an operating table in Fresno, CA, on November 2, 1996. He was only 45 years old. His presence in the blues world is missed.

William Clarke (along with Big Walter Horton and Paul Butterfield) had an almost impeccable sense of which notes to play. There are a lot of players out there (White and Black) who basically play what's on the records of the great Chicago artists. Nothing wrong with this, but no news there either. Clarke was an original. Having heard him play live a number of times, I can testify that here is the real thing—an extension of the classic Chicago-style amplified harp tradition into the present. Just listen to those first two Alligator albums—it's all on the CDs. *—Michael Erlewine*

Hittin' Heavy / 1978 / Good Times ✦✦

Blues from Los Angeles / 1980 / Hittin' Heavy ✦✦

Can't You Hear Me Calling / 1983 / Rivera ✦✦✦
Can't You Hear Me Calling only gives a glimmer of what's to come from this new genius of the blues, but it is enjoyable nonetheless. —*Cub Koda*

Tip of the Top / 1987 / Satch ✦✦✦
Tip of the Top is a loose tribute to William Clarke's mentor, George Harmonica Smith, who taught Clarke many of his tricks. Clarke plays a selection of tracks that were staples in Smith's catalog (including a version of "Hard Times," which features Smith himself), as well as newer songs written in the same style. But what really makes *Tip of the Top* notable is how William Clarke begins to develop his distinctive, idosyncratic sound on the record. Unlike his debut *Can't You Hear Me Calling*, *Tip of the Top* explores some new sounds, which would come to fruition in his next few albums. —*Thom Owens*

Rockin' the Boat / 1988 / Rivera ✦✦✦✦
Recorded live in 1987, this features Clarke and his regular working band on a wide variety of material showcasing his formidable talents as a vocalist and harmonica man extraordinaire. —*Cub Koda*

★ **Blowin' Like Hell** / 1990 / Alligator ✦✦✦✦✦
The title says it all. William Clarke cooks on this one, his first CD. And these are new sounds. Songs like "Lollipop Mama," "Gambling for My Bread," and "Lonesome Bedroom Blues" (all written by Clarke) are just great tunes. "Must Be Jelly" won Clarke a W.C. Handy Award for Blues Song of the Year in 1991. I find myself humming them. Clarke's timing and music are right on the money, with the great Alex Schultz on lead guitar. There is no doubt that Clarke is one of the few modern bluesmen who are exploring and extending the amplified blues harp tradition without violating any of its principles. No one plays chromatic blues harp with this kind of passion and sheer conviction. Hear for yourself. —*Michael Erlewine*

☆ **Serious Intentions** / 1992 / Alligator ✦✦✦✦✦
His follow-up to *Blowin' Like Hell* burns with a ferocious intensity, particularly for his groundbreaking work on chromatic harp and his ability to cover all styles with remarkable elan. Again, he wrote most of the songs, and "Pawnshop Bound," "Trying to Stretch My Money," and "With a Tear in My Eye" are real songs. Instrumentals like "Chasin' the Gator" feature Clarke with Alex Schultz on lead guitar. —*Cub Koda and Michael Erlewine*

Groove Time / 1994 / Alligator ✦✦✦✦
Here is Clarke, hot again. This time he has added a horn section on some cuts for this recording. No problem. Alex Schultz is there on lead guitar to make sure that this album rocks. Clarke once again writes most of the songs—all 15 fat tracks. By this time, his Alligator albums have a style and feel (all his own) that one looks forward to. Plenty of high-impact amplified chromatic harmonica here of the push-the-band-hard variety that Clarke does so well, plus some tasty acoustic thrown in, too. —*Michael Erlewine*

The Hard Way / 1996 / Alligator ✦✦✦✦
His fourth CD from Alligator is his jazziest and bluesiest recording to date. Clarke has written half of the compositions and put his own sound and style on those he did not write. Highlights include "The Boss" (inspired by saxophonist Willis Jackson) which is a fast jump that finds chromatic harp riffing along with a horn section—some interesting ideas. Other tunes are the Benny Moten tune "Moten Swing," "My Mind is Working Overtime," (a Latin-tinged tune written by Clarke), and "Letter from Home." —*Michael Erlewine*

Francis Clay
b. Nov. 16, 1923, Rock Island, IL
Drums / Chicago Blues
Drummer Francis Clay was born in Rock Island, IL, on November 16, 1923. Learning music from his family, Clay was playing some guitar and entering amateur contests at the age of five. But it was drums that fascinated him, and he would create his own drum set from things around the house. He turned professional when he was 15 years old. In 1941 Clay formed his first band—Francis Clay and His Syncopated Rhythm—playing behind acts like Gypsy Rose Lee, in circuses, on riverboats, etc. This lasted until around 1944. He returned to his home in 1946 and ran a booking office and recording studio, and taught drums. Around 1947 Clay was playing with George "Har-

monica" Smith in Chicago. In the early '50s he toured with jazz organist Jack McDuff.

In 1957, Clay took a fill-in job with Muddy Waters and, since he had only played jazz, had no idea how to play the blues. Muddy Waters taught him, and in several days they had the thing together. Waters asked him to stay on and Clay was there for the next four years.

In 1962, Clay left Muddy Waters and formed a band with James Cotton, which lasted about a year. Clay then worked with Otis Rush, Buddy Guy, Bobby Fields, and others. In 1965, Clay rejoined Muddy Waters for a stint of almost two years.

In the late '60s, Clay worked and recorded with a number of artists including James Cotton, Muddy Waters, Lightnin' Hopkins, John Lee Hooker, Big Mama Thornton, Victoria Spivey, George Harmonica Smith, Shakey Jake Harris, Sunnyland Slim, and others. Due to knee problems, Clay has not done much playing in recent years. Clay has been called "the definitive Muddy Waters drummer." He resides in San Francisco. —*Michael Erlewine*

Willie Clayton
b. Mar. 29, 1955, Indianola, MS
Vocals / Soul, Chicago Blues
As long as he's been recording (since 1969), one might think that Willie Clayton is an old geezer. No way—he's barely past the age of 40 and is just hitting his commercial stride with a couple of recent blues-soul albums for Ace that have sold well to the Southern market (where the two interrelated idioms have never been deemed mutually exclusive).

After his debut single for Duplex, "That's the Way Daddy Did," went nowhere, Clayton left Mississippi for Chicago in 1971. Like his older Windy City compatriots Otis Clay and Syl Johnson, the young singer ended up contracted to Hi Records in Memphis, where he worked with producer Willie Mitchell and the vaunted Hi rhythm section. Hi issued a series of fine Clayton efforts on its Pawn subsidiary, including "I Must Be Losin' You," "It's Time You Made Up Your Mind," and "Baby You're Ready," but none of them hit. Finally, in 1984, Clayton enjoyed a taste of soul success when his "Tell Me" (produced by General Crook) and "What a Way to Put It" for Compleat Records nudged onto the R&B charts.

Let's Get Together, Clayton's 1993 album for Johnny Vincent's Ace logo, was a smooth soul-blues hybrid dominated by originals but titled after Al Green's immortal hit. *Simply Beautiful,* his Ace follow-up, found Clayton mixing dusties by Rev. Al, Aretha Franklin, and Arthur Crudup with his own stuff. —*Bill Dahl*

Feels Like Love / 1992 / Ichiban ✦✦✦

Let's Get Together / 1993 / Ace ✦✦✦
Contemporary Southern deep soul with a strong taste of blues underlying. The clever "Three People (Sleeping in My Bed)" and "Back Street Love Affair," along with the self-penned "Feels like Love" and "Let Me Love You," are attractive showcases for Clayton's warm, assured vocal delivery. —*Bill Dahl*

Simply Beautiful / 1994 / Ace ✦✦✦
More of the same—Clayton's intimate, confident vocals framed in terms midway between deep soul and contemporary blues. His own "Lose What You Got" and "Crazy for You" rate highly, along with Frank Johnson's "Love Stealing Ain't Worth Stealing" and the singer's delicate revival of Al Green's title cut. —*Bill Dahl*

No Getting over Me / 1995 / Ichiban ✦✦✦✦
Worth the price of admission for Clayton's soulful remake of country crooner Ronnie Milsap's title track alone—but there's plenty more contemporary deep soul to be found on this exceptionally solid set. —*Bill Dahl*

● **Chicago Soul Greats** / Jul. 18, 1995 / Hi ✦✦✦✦

At His Best / Nov. 21, 1995 / Ichiban ✦✦✦

Ace in the Hole / Feb. 13, 1996 / Ace ✦✦✦✦
The most consistent and satisfying of Clayton's contemporary output for Johnny Vincent's reactivated Ace imprint, thanks to top-flight soul-blues items like "Hurt by Love" and "My Baby's Cheating on Me," the Bob Jones-penned "Equal Opportunity" and "Bartender's Blues," and the singer's own "Happy." —*Bill Dahl*

Chapter One / Apr. 22, 1997 / Gamma ✦✦✦

Never Too Late / Mercury ✦✦✦✦
Underrated soul/R&B vocals. —*Ron Wynn*

Tell Me / Polydor ◆◆◆
Southern soul singer Willie Clayton shortened his first name and cut one late '80s album for Polydor. It was a well-produced and nicely sung date, but the songs, focus, and approach were so "deep" soul oriented that it didn't get any attention from the urban contemporary types at major record companies. Nor did the company pick a single and push it. Clayton soon returned to the Kirstee label. —*Ron Wynn*

Eddy Clearwater

b. Jan. 10, 1935, Macon, MS
Guitar, Vocals / Modern Electric Blues, Chicago Blues, Electric Chicago Blues
Once dismissed by purists as a Chuck Berry imitator (and an accurate one at that), tall, lean, and lanky Chicago southpaw Eddy Clearwater is now recognized as a prime progenitor of West Side-style blues guitar. That's not to say he won't liven up a gig with a little duck-walking or a frat party rendition of "Shout"; after all, Clearwater brings a wide array of influences to the party. Gospel, country, '50s rock, and deep-down blues are all incorporated into his slashing guitar attack. But when he puts his mind to it, "The Chief" (a nickname accrued from his penchant for donning native American headdresses on stage) is one of the Windy City's finest bluesmen.

Eddy Harrington split Birmingham, AL, for Chicago in 1950, initially billing himself on the city's South and West sides as Guitar Eddy. His uncle, Rev. Houston H. Harrington, handed his nephew his initial recording opportunity—the good reverend operated a small label, Atomic-H. Eddy made the most of it, laying down a shimmering minor-key instrumental, "A-Minor Cha Cha" and the Berry-derived "Hillbilly Blues" (both on Delmark's *Chicago Ain't Nothin' but a Blues Band* anthology).

Drummer Jump Jackson invented Eddy's stage monicker as a takeoff on the name of Muddy Waters. As "Clear Waters," he waxed another terrific Berry knockoff, "Cool Water," for Jackson's LaSalle logo. By the time he journeyed to Cincinnati in 1961 to cut the glorious auto rocker "I Was Gone," a joyous "A Real Good Time," and the timely "Twist Like This" for Federal Records producer Sonny Thompson, he was officially Eddy Clearwater. Things were sparse for quite a while after that; Clearwater occasionally secured a live gig dishing out rock and country ditties when blues jobs dried up.

But Rooster Blues' 1980 release of *The Chief,* an extraordinarily strong album by any standards, announced to the world that Eddy Clearwater's ascendancy to Chicago blues stardom was officially underway. Two encores for Rooster Blues, a set for Blind Pig (1992's *Help Yourself*), and *Mean Case of the Blues,* released in 1996 on his reactivated Cleartone Records, along with consistently exciting live performances, have cemented Clearwater's reputation as a masterful blues showman whose principal goal is to provide his fans with a real good time. —*Bill Dahl*

● **The Chief** / 1980 / Rooster Blues ◆◆◆◆
This was the charismatic southpaw's debut album back in 1980, and remains his best to date. He rocks like Chuck Berry used to (but no longer can) on "I Wouldn't Lay My Guitar Down," tears up the West Side-based "Bad Dream" and "Blues for a Living," imparts a hard-driving Chi-town shuffle to "Find You a Job" and "I'm Tore Up," and gives "Lazy Woman" a decidedly un-lazy Latin tempo. One of the best Chicago blues LPs of the 1980s. —*Bill Dahl*

Two Times Nine / 1981 / New Rose ◆◆◆
Recorded originally for Clearwater's own Cleartone label and later leased to Ron Bartolucci's Baron imprint, these late-'70s sides were potent indicators of his maturing blues style. These weren't homemade sessions; all-star sidemen include drummer Casey Jones, guitarist Jimmy Johnson, and saxist Abb Locke. The title cut is a blistering Chuck Berry-styled rocker, "Came Up the Hard Way" displays a firm grasp of the West Side sound, and "A Little Bit of Blues, a Little Bit of Rock & Roll" utilizes a funky groove to foot-stomping advantage. —*Bill Dahl*

Flimdoozie / 1986 / Rooster Blues ◆◆◆
As yet unavailable on compact disc, Clearwater's encore LP for Rooster Blues wasn't quite the equal of its predecessor, but registered as a solid enough outing nonetheless. The Chief coined a new term for the rollicking title track, engaged in some harrowing blues during a lengthy "Black Night" medley, and rocked the house with a '50s-styled "Do This Town Tonight." —*Bill Dahl*

Blues Hang Out / Dec. 3, 1989 / Evidence ◆◆◆
Eddy Clearwater has had a tough time shaking his "Chuck Berry imitator" label, and he includes Berry-tinged numbers at the halfway point and end of this nice, if thoroughly derivative, urban blues set recorded in 1989 for Black and Blue and recently reissued by Evidence on CD, with the familiar country boogie shuffle and tinkling licks. Clearwater could not do a set without the signature "Lay My Guitar Down," and this rendition is surging and enjoyable although inferior to the definitive one. Otherwise, it is a pile-driving and urgently performed date; Clearwater and Will Crosby swap slashing lines, crackling phrases, and answering fills. Clearwater's session contains several robust, entertaining passages, even if there is absolutely nothing you have not heard before. —*Ron Wynn*

Real Good Time: Live! / 1990 / Rooster Blues ◆◆◆◆
Eddy Clearwater delivers on the promise of this set's title on his best concert recording to date, recorded at a couple of Indiana nightspots. Those enduring (and endearing) Berry roots surface anew on a storming medley of "A Real Good Time" and "Cool Water," and there are more '50s-style rockers in "Hi-Yo Silver" and "Party at My House." But he exhibits a social conscience on the decided departure "Tear Down the Wall of Hate." —*Bill Dahl*

Help Yourself / 1992 / Blind Pig ◆◆◆
Clearwater wrote the lion's share of this well-produced collection, reaching back for material by Jimmy Reed, Otis Rush, and Willie Mabon to round it out. It has the usual infectious mix of shimmering West Side blues, hauling rockabilly, and even a touch of funk on "Little Bit of Blues." Guitarist Will Crosby shares lead chores with his boss, and Carey Bell (Clearwater's cousin) handles the harp work. —*Bill Dahl*

Boogie My Blues Away / 1995 / Delmark ◆◆◆
Veteran producer Ralph Bass produced this collection back in 1977 for a blues LP series that never materialized; Delmark finally brought it to domestic light recently. Solid, unpretentious package that shows both Clearwater's West Side-styled southpaw guitar sound and his Chuck Berry-oriented capacity for rocking the house. —*Bill Dahl*

Mean Case of the Blues / 1996 / Cleartone ◆◆◆
Clearwater comes up with a compelling mix of tunes on this 10-track outing, his first for the Bullseye Blues imprint. The southpaw guitarist covers a wide range of styles (as befitting a true West Side guitarist, where versatility is a badge of merit) including Magic Sam's "Look Whatcha Done," Nat King Cole's "Send for Me," Gene Allison's "You Can Make It If You Try," and Clearwater originals like "Party at My House," "Don't Take My Blues," "Hard Way to Make an Easy Living," "Love Being Loved By You," and the title track. Produced by Clearwater and utilizing his regular working band with guest appearances from Jerry Soto on keyboards, Mike Peavey on saxophone, Steven Frost on trumpet, and Billy Branch on harmonica, this is the Chief just laying it down simple and hard, doing what he does best—delivering taut and shimmering West Side guitar and vocals with a vengeance. —*Cub Koda*

Chicago Blues Session, Vol. 23 / Wolf ◆◆
This okay live set isn't the equivalent of his later *Rooster Blues* concert set, though. —*Bill Dahl*

Rev. James Cleveland

b. Dec. 5, 1932, Chicago, IL, **d.** Feb. 9, 1991, Culver City, CA
Vocals, Piano, Trombone / Black Gospel, Traditional Gospel
The visionary behind the contemporary gospel sound, the Reverend James Cleveland was a pioneering composer and choral director whose progressive arrangements—jazzy and soulful, complete with odd time signatures—helped push the music past the confines of the traditional Baptist hymnal into new and unexpected directions, infusing elements of the sanctified church style and secular pop to alter the face of gospel forever. Born in Chicago on December 5, 1932, Cleveland was a boy soprano at Pilgrim Baptist Church, the home of minister of music Thomas A. Dorsey; as his parents were unable to afford a piano, he crafted a makeshift keyboard out of a windowsill, somehow learning to play without ever producing an actual note. When his voice changed, becoming gruff and harsh, Cleveland continued singing, developing into an expressive crooner; for the most part, however, he focused on piano, becoming a top-notch accompanist.

In 1950, Cleveland signed on as a pianist and occasional third lead with the Gospelaires, a trio led by Norsalus McKissick and Bessie Folk; although the group was short-lived, it brought him to the attention of pianist Roberta Martin, for whom he began composing. Even his earliest material reflects a bluesy, funkified style well ahead of its time, while his arrangements of traditional spirituals like "Old Time Religion" and "It's Me O Lord" were highly stylized, almost unrecognizable from their usual interpretations. By the mid-1950s, Cleveland was a member of the Caravans, not only playing piano but also narrating hymns in his rough yet relaxing voice; despite the group's success, however, he kept quitting and rejoining their ranks, earning a reputation as a highly temperamental character. He also played briefly with groups including the Meditation Singers and the Gospel All-Stars; in 1959, he also cut a rendition of Ray Charles' "Hallelujah I Love Her So," his first overt attempt to bridge gospel and R&B.

Although Cleveland kept drifting from group to group, his reputation continued to grow—with the Gospel Chimes, he cut a series of records which veered sharply from pop-inflected ballads to fiery shouters, arranging harmonies which straddled the line between the current group style and the rapidly developing choir sound. By 1960, he was clearly well ahead of the pack; "The Love of God," a cover of a Soul Stirrers number he cut with the Detroit choir the Voices of Tabernacle, was a breakthough hit, his fusion of pop balladry and choir spirit finally reaching its apotheosis. After years of struggle, Cleveland was now a major star, and across the country, choir directors began mimicking his style; he soon signed to Savoy, where he recorded with the All-Stars and Chimes as well as his own group, the Cleveland Singers, which featured on organ a young Billy Preston. His third Savoy LP, 1962's live *Peace Be Still*, made history, selling an astonishing 800,000 copies to an almost exclusively black audience without the benefit of mainstream promotion.

The success of *Peace Be Still* established Cleveland as arguably the most crucial figure to emerge in gospel since Mahalia Jackson; throughout the 1960s, when his status for spiritual records typically reflected sales of five thousand copies, his LPs regularly sold five times that amount. Additionally, his annual Gospel Singers Workshop Convention—an outgrowth of his organization the Gospel Workshop of America—helped launch the careers of numerous younger talents, a generation of artists largely inspired by the modernized sound pioneered by Cleveland himself. During the 1970s he remained a towering figure, leading his latest creation, the Southern California Community Choir, and recording prolifically; although his pace began to slow in the decade that followed—and despite his death on February 9, 1991—Cleveland's shadow continues to loom large across the gospel landscape. —*Jason Ankeny*

☆ **The Best of James Cleveland [Hob]** / 1960 / Hob ✦✦✦✦✦
Great material with the Voices of the Tabernacle of Detroit. —*Opal Louis Nations*

★ **Peace Be Still** / 1962 / Savoy ✦✦✦✦✦
A set of original Cleveland tunes and traditional hymns done in the choir format he pioneered with The Angelic Choir of New Jersey. This live recording, done with crude technology, is helped somewhat by the high-fidelity pressing. It includes "I Had a Talk with God" and "I'll Wear a Crown." Cleveland's gruff vocals appear on most cuts. —*Bil Carpenter*

I Stood on the Banks of The Jordan / 1964 / Savoy ✦✦✦✦
Some of his finest live in-church sides. —*Opal Louis Nations*

Lord Let Me Be an Instrument / 1966 / Savoy ✦✦
Amazing vocal acrobatics from soloist Rosetta Davis. —*Opal Louis Nations*

In the Beginning / 1978 / Kenwood ✦✦✦
Great early-'50s Apollo sides with the Gospelaires and the Gospel All Stars. —*Opal Louis Nations*

Having Church / 1991 / Savoy Gospel ✦✦✦✦
There are those who claim Cleveland's later recordings with The Southern California Community Choir don't quite match those with the group from Nutley, NJ. Perhaps—even probably. He's also lost some power as he's gotten older. But whether led by Cleveland or by other singers (notably the magisterial Lavora Wilson) the material on this CD is powerful and joyous enough to make that kind of distinction irrelevant. —*John Storm Roberts, Original Music*

Victory Shall Be Mine / 1991 / Savoy ✦✦✦
This is among Cleveland's best later works. —*Kip Lornell*

King & Queen of Gospel / 1992 / Hob ✦✦✦
Fine examples of good gospel by both soloists at budget price. —*Opal Louis Nations*

Crown Price of Gospel / Nov. 19, 1993 / Hob ✦✦✦✦
Some of Cleveland's finest moments. —*Opal Louis Nations*

Old Time Religion / 1994 / Hob ✦✦✦✦
Good, best-selling collection of this important innovator's work. —*Opal Louis Nations*

In Times Like This / Mar. 14, 1995 / Hob ✦✦✦✦
More classic material by this singer, composer, arranger, and choirmaster of immense influence. —*Opal Louis Nations*

Get Right Church / Jul. 18, 1996 / Hob ✦✦✦✦
More joy and live church feeling from the man who revolutionized choral singing. —*Opal Louis Nations*

Great Day: The Very Best of Rev. James Cleveland / Mar. 3, 1998 / Collectables ✦✦✦
Rev. James Cleveland changed the sound of gospel music. Some of his best sides. —*Opal Louis Nations*

Climax Blues Band

f. 1969, Stafford, England
Group / Roots-Rock, Blues-Rock, Soft Rock, Pop-Rock
Led by Colin Cooper, the former frontman of the R&B unit the Hipster Image, the Stafford, England-based Climax Chicago Blues Band was one of the leading lights of the late-1960s blues boom. A sextet also comprised of guitarists Derek Holt and Peter Haycock, keyboardist Arthur Wood, bassist Richard Jones and drummer George Newsome, the group debuted in 1969 with a self-titled effort recalling the work of John Mayall.

Prior to the release of 1969's *Plays On*, Jones left the group, prompting Holt to move to bass. In 1970 the Climax Chicago Blues Band moved to the Harvest label, at the same time shifting towards a more rock-oriented sound on the LP *A Lot of Bottle*. Around the release of 1971's *Tightly Knit*, Newsome was replaced by drummer John Holt; upon Wood's exit in the wake of 1972's *Rich Man*, the unit decided to continue on as a quartet, also dropping the "Chicago" portion of their name to avoid confusion with the American band of the same name.

In 1974 the Climax Blues Band issued *FM Live*, a document of a New York radio concert. 1975's *Stamp* was their commercial breakthrough, and 1976's *Gold Plated* fared even better, spurred on by the success of the hit "Couldn't Get It Right." However, the rise of punk effectively stopped the group in their tracks, although they continued recording prolifically well into the 1980s; after 1988's *Drastic Steps*, the Climax Blues Band was silent for a number of years, but resurfaced in 1994 with *Blues From the Attic*. —*Jason Ankeny*

The Climax Chicago Blues Band / 1969 / See For Miles ✦✦✦
The debut album of the Climax Chicago Blues Band (they'd later drop the "Chicago" part of the name) was recorded on two days separated by a couple of months in 1968. As British blues revivalists, Climax was better than most, featuring strong playing from guitarist Peter Haycock and keyboardist Arthur Wood. The selections run the gamut from Chicago retreads ("Mean Old World," "Insurance," "Wee Baby Blues," "Don't Start Me to Talkin'") to band originals like "And Lonely," "Looking for My Baby," "Going Down This Road" and "You've Been Drinking." If one can make it past Colin Cooper's mannered vocals, there's much for Brit blues fans to enjoy here. —*Cub Koda*

Plays On / 1969 / Sire ✦✦✦
The second album by the group showed the band starting to expand from their strictly blues format and taking on more pronounced rock affectations. Haycock's guitar is more to the fore, and Cooper's harmonica takes a back seat to this saxophone work. This album also marks the band dabbling in crediting songs to themselves that were actually written by other older, Blacker blues musicians, a common practice with many British blues groups. —*Cub Koda*

● **Couldn't Get It Right** / 1987 / See For Miles ✦✦✦✦
Couldn't Get It Right contains all of the Climax Blues Band's big hits from 1974 on, which means that it bypasses their earliest material—which was the closest they ever came to the blues. But it does contain all their big hits,

from the title track to "I Love You," making it a near-definitive retrospective. —*Stephen Thomas Erlewine*

25 Years 1968-1993 / 1994 / Repertoire ✦✦✦✦
Most casual fans know the Climax Blues Band through "Couldn't Get It Right" and "I Love You," a pair of slick pop and soft-rock hits from the late '70s and early '80s. Those two songs are a little misleading, in a way, since they arrived halfway through a career that spanned over 25 years. Anyone who heard those two hits probably were puzzled by the "Blues" in the group's name, since they were in no way bluesy. As the double-disc, 32-track set *25 Years* proves, they started out as a British blues band in the late '60s. Unfortunately, they just weren't very good, slogging through the same three chords without much inspiration for nearly ten years. That decade is represented on the first disc, and while the group does show signs of improvement over those 16 songs, the music is still unbelievably dull and, in the case of "Shoot Her if She Runs," offensive), despite titles like "Mole on the Dole," "Losing the Humbles" and "Shopping Bag People." By the late '70s, the band was in desperate need of a hit in order to survive, so they changed their tune, incorporating pop, disco and soft-rock into their sound. "Couldn't Get It Right" was an excellent song, far catchier than any of their early blues tunes, and it deservedly became a Top Ten hit. Following that success, the group turned out a number of songs that tried to replicate the hit, but they couldn't get it right until 1981, when the appealingly schmaltzy "I Love You" almost went Top Ten. Afterward, they played soft-rock until they broke down and decided to return to the blues. Along the way, there was only a handful of memorable songs, which means that *25 Years* is a little tedious to anyone who just wants the hits. Unfortunately, it's the only readily available compilation from the group, so casual fans are stuck with more music than they need. *25 Years* will suit the purpose of anyone who really wants to dig into the Climax Blues Band's career, since it accurately sketches the progression of their career, but unfortunately, it doesn't have enough good music to warrant such an extensive compilation. —*Stephen Thomas Erlewine*

Harvest Years 1969-1972 / Apr. 29, 1998 / See For Miles ✦✦✦✦

Dorothy Love Coates

b. 1930, Birmingham, AL
Vocals / Black Gospel, Traditional Gospel
Born in Birmingham, AL, Coates started singing in the '40s with the Original Gospel Harmonettes, who had the hits "I'm Sealed" and "Get Away." —*Bil Carpenter*

☆ **Get on Board** / 1956 / Specialty ✦✦✦✦✦
With The Original Gospel Harmonettes, here are 24 exciting songs (circa 1951-56) supported by Herbert "Pee Wee" Pickard, gospel's organist supreme. —*Opal Louis Nations*

★ **The Best of Dorothy Love Coates, Vol. 1-2** / 1957 / Specialty ✦✦✦✦✦
Reissue of the two specialty albums containing the group's best-known songs and hit recordings. —*Opal Louis Nations*

The Original Gospel, Vols. 1 & 2 / 1970 / Specialty ✦✦✦
Dorothy singing ragged with the group on fire circa 1951-57. —*Opal Louis Nations*

The Best of Dorothy Love Coates & the Orig. Gospel Harmonettes, Vol. 2 / 1991 / Specialty ✦✦✦
Picking up where the first compilation left off, *Best of Dorothy Love Coates/ Orig. Gospel Harmonettes, Vol. 2* collects 12 of the gospel group's greatest performances from the '50s—including "Jesus Knows It All," "These Are They," "Every Day Will Be Sunday," "There's a God Somewhere," "Just to Behold His Face," and "Am I a Soldier"—making it an excellent complement to its predecessor. The album was later combined with *Vol. 1* on a 1991 CD reissue. —*Leo Stanley*

Best of Dorothy Love Coates / Jan. 31, 1995 / Nashboro ✦✦✦✦
Probably the best of the group's later sides. Strong singing. Nashboro material. —*Opal Louis Nations*

Willie Cobbs

b. Jul. 15, 1932, Monroe, AR
Harmonica, Vocals / Modern Electric Blues
If for nothing else, the name of Willie Cobbs will always ring immortal for the prominence of his composition "You Don't Love Me," covered by every-

one from Junior Wells to the Allman Brothers. But Cobbs' own discography is dotted with other triumphs, including a 1994 album for Rooster Blues, *Down to Earth*, that made it clear that Cobbs was alive, well, and committed to playing the blues.

Cobbs decided the prospect of rice farming didn't appeal to him enough to stick around his native Arkansas, so he migrated to Chicago in 1947. He hung out with Little Walter and Eddie Boyd while honing his harp chops on Maxwell Street. But Cobbs' recording career didn't fully blossom until 1960, when his waxing of "You Don't Love Me" for Billy Lee Riley's Memphis-based Mojo logo made him something of a regional star (one previous 45 for Joe Brown's Ruler imprint back in Chicago had stiffed instantly). "You Don't Love Me" eventually was leased to Vee-Jay—no doubt warming Cobbs' heart, since Vee-Jay boss Jimmy Bracken had once turned down Cobbs' audition, explaining that he sounded too much like Vee-Jay breadwinner Jimmy Reed.

Throughout the '60s, '70s, and '80s, Cobbs recorded a slew of obscure singles, often for his own labels (Riceland, Ricebelt, C&F), and operated nightclubs in Arkansas and Mississippi before cutting his long-overdue album for Rooster Blues (backed by labelmates Johnny Rawls and L.C. Luckett). He's also managed to slip in a little cinematic action into his schedule, appearing in the films *Mississippi Masala* and *Memphis.* —*Bill Dahl*

Hey Little Girl / 1991 / Wilco ✦✦✦
Underrated blues and soul composer and vocalist Willie Cobbs got rare time in the spotlight with this early-'90s release. Although things were erratic production and sound quality-wise, Cobbs' warm, soulful delivery made it consistently entertaining, if not always satisfying. —*Ron Wynn*

● **Down to Earth** / 1994 / Rooster Blues ✦✦✦✦
The only CD widely available by the Arkansas harpist whose chief claim to blues fame resides with his classic composition "You Don't Love Me" (later revived by Junior Wells and the Allman Brothers, among many others). With tasty backing by labelmates Johnny Rawls and L.C. Luckett adding luster to Cobbs' sturdy vocals and harp, the disc is a strong reminder that blues is alive and well in its southern birthplace. And yes, there's an accurate remake of his hit (segued with another of his gems, "Hey Little Girl"). —*Bill Dahl*

Porky Cohen

b. Jun. 2, 1924, Springfield, MA
Trombone / R&B, Swing
Best known for his years as trombonist with Roomful of Blues, Porky Cohen finally had his recording debut as a leader in 1996, a highly enjoyable outing for Bullseye Blues with many of the members of the group. He started playing trombone at 13 and considers Jack Teagarden his most important early influence. Cohen worked local engagements from age 15 and took lessons from Miff Mole after graduating from high school in 1941. After a tryout with Benny Goodman, Cohen played with Tony Pastor's band, Charlie Barnet (off and on during 1943-48), the Casa Loma Orchestra, Lucky Millinder, Tommy Dorsey, Boyd Raeburn, Artie Shaw (1949-50), with a variety of Dixieland bands in the 1950s, Bob Wilber and the Six, and the Jewels of Dixie (from the late 1950s to the late '70s). Porky Cohen was a strong asset to Roomful of Blues from 1979-86 before choosing to semi-retire. —*Scott Yanow*

● **Rhythm & Bones** / 1996 / Bullseye Blues ✦✦✦✦
Although trombonist Porky Cohen has played in the jazz major leagues since the early 1940s (including periods with Tony Pastor, Charlie Barnet, the Casa Loma Orchestra, Lucky Millinder, Boyd Raeburn, Tommy Dorsey, Artie Shaw, Bobby Hackett, The Six with Bob Wilber, and various dixieland bands) and toured regularly with Roomful of Blues during 1979-87, this CD was his first opportunity to lead his own date. Seventy at the time, Cohen is heard in prime form leading a romping session featuring some of the members of Roomful Of Blues along with his successor trombonist Carl Querfurth. The joyous music, which only has two vocals among the 13 numbers (updates of Jimmy Rushing and Bessie Smith songs featuring Sugar Ray Norcia and Michelle Willson), mixes together heated swing and 1950s style R&B blues to exhilarating effect; Illinois Jacquet would feel quite comfortable in this setting. There are plenty of opportunities for not only Cohen to solo but all of the other horn players. An added plus are the lengthy and definitive liner notes which fully relate (along with many photos) the Porky Cohen story. Highly recommended. —*Scott Yanow*

Deborah Coleman

b. Oct. 3, 1956, Portsmouth, VA
Vocals / Contemporary Blues
Although she's a powerful blues guitarist, songwriter and singer, Deborah Coleman got her first inspiration from an unlikely place: seeing the pop group the Monkees on TV. Born in Portsmouth, VA, and raised in a military family, Coleman took to music easily enough, since her dad played piano, two brothers played guitar, and a sister played guitar and keyboards. She picked up the guitar at age eight after seeing the Monkees and began to play professionally at 15, playing bass with a series of Portsmouth-area R&B and rock bands. She later switched to guitar after hearing Jimi Hendrix, also taking to James Brown and the Beatles. Coleman began buying records by blues-rock groups like Cream and Led Zeppelin, and slowly followed the music's origins back to basic blues. When she was 25, she got married and focused on raising her daughter while working day jobs as a nurse and electrician. After her daughter grew old enough to leave home alone, Coleman began to play out again, locally at first. In 1985, she began working with an all-female group, Moxxie. When that group split up in 1988, she got her blues chops together as part of an R&B trio. After two years of touring with the trio, Coleman did some woodshedding, seeing as many blues acts as she could live and studying blues recordings. Coleman got the break she was looking for in 1993 when she entered the Charleston (S.C.) Blues Festival's National Talent Search. Leading her own band, she took first place. She immediately put together her own touring group, the Thrillseekers, beginning a solo career as a bandleader. Coleman used her contest prize of free studio time to record a demo and secure a record deal with New Moon Records out of Chapel Hill, N.C. Her debut, *Takin' A Stand*, was released in 1995 on that label, and she followed it up two years later with *I Can't Lose*, her first album for Blind Pig. — *Richard Skelly*

Takin' a Stand / Jun. 1, 1995 / New Moon ♦♦♦

● **I Can't Lose** / 1996 / Blind Pig ♦♦♦♦
Deborah Coleman's Blind Pig debut, *I Can't Lose*, is a powerful album of great ballads and blues stories, and of course, great guitar playing and singing. Her version of Billie Holiday's "Fine and Mellow" got her a lot of airplay on college and public radio stations around the US — *Richard Skelly*

Gary B.B. Coleman

b. 1947, Paris, TX
Bass, Guitar, Keyboards, Vocals / Modern Electric Blues
After a career as a local bluesman and blues promoter in Texas and Oklahoma, Gary Coleman found his niche when he signed over his first album, a self-produced outing originally issued on his own label, to the fledgling Ichiban company out of Atlanta in 1986. Since that time, both Coleman and Ichiban have made their marks in the blues field — not only has Coleman released half a dozen of his own albums, he has also overseen production of the bulk of Ichiban's hefty blues catalog, bringing to the studio a number of artists he'd booked or toured with in his previous career (Chick Willis, Buster Benton, and Blues Boy Willie, among others). A singer/guitarist onstage, Coleman has often taken on a multi-instrumentalist's role in the studio. His music remains true to the blues and to the King legacy saluted in his "B.B." moniker and in his acknowledged debt to fellow-Texan Freddie King.

Coleman began listening to the blues as a child and by the time he was 15, he was working with Freddie King. Following his association with King, Coleman supported Lightnin' Hopkins and formed his own band, which played around Texas. Coleman also began booking blues musicians into clubs in Texas, Oklahoma, and Colorado. He continued to play gigs and book concerts for nearly two decades. In 1985, he formed Mr. B's Records, his own independent label. Coleman released his debut album *Nothin' But the Blues* the following year. The album was popular and gained the attention of Ichiban Records, who signed Coleman and re-released *Nothin' But the Blues* in 1987.

If You Can Beat Me Rockin', Coleman's second album, was released in 1988. That same year, he began producing albums for a number of other artists, as well as writing songs for other musicians and acting as an A&R scout for Ichiban. Between 1988 and 1992, he released six records and produced another 30, including albums for Little Johnny Taylor and Buster Benton. Coleman continued to be active in the mid-'90s, both as a performing

and recording artist, and as a producer. — *Jim O'Neal & Stephen Thomas Erlewine*

Nothin' But the Blues / 1987 / Ichiban ♦♦♦♦
With a darker overall tone, it's sadder and more introspective, and one of his more consistent records. It includes two very good slow blues, "Let Me Love You Baby" and "Shame on You." — *Niles J. Frantz*

If You Can Beat Me Rockin' ... / 1988 / Ichiban ♦♦♦♦
He was influenced by Jimmy Reed, T-Bone Walker, B.B. King, and Lightnin' Hopkins, along with country & western, cajun, and early rock 'n' roll. — *Niles J. Frantz*

One Night Stand / 1989 / Ichiban ♦♦♦

Dancin' My Blues Away / 1990 / Ichiban ♦♦♦

● **The Best of Gary B. B. Coleman** / 1991 / Ichiban ♦♦♦♦
This is a good career overview, though it does expose a certain lack of originality and diversity. — *Niles J. Frantz*

Romance Without Finance Is a Nuisance / 1991 / Ichiban ♦♦♦
It was no coincidence that Gary Coleman had "B.B." in his name. One of Coleman's main influences was B.B. King, and he was happy to acknowledge King's inspiration (although he's also learned a thing or two from Bobby "Blue" Bland, Jimmy Reed, and the late Albert Collins). *Romance Without Finance* underscores the fact that while Coleman may not be the most original artist in the world, his Ichiban output has been consistent and enjoyable. The singer/electric guitarist's sense of humor serves him quite well on such amusing cuts as "Food Stamp Annie," "If You See My One-Eyed Woman," and "She Ain't Ugly (She Just Don't Look Like Nobody Else)." But he's equally appealing when embracing a somber minor-key groove *a la* Bland, and "Dealing From the Bottom of the Deck" is a fine example of Coleman's brooding side. Whether Coleman is being remorseful or humorous, this CD is a welcome addition to his catalogue. — *Alex Henderson*

Too Much Weekend / 1992 / Ichiban ♦♦♦

Cocaine Annie / Apr. 1996 / Priority ♦♦

Jaybird Coleman

b. May 20, 1896, Gainesville, AL, **d.** Jan. 28, 1950, Tuskegee, AL
Guitar, Vocals, Harmonica, Jug / Delta Blues, Prewar Country Blues, Piedmont Blues
Jaybird Coleman was an early blues harmonica player. Although he only recorded a handful of sides and his technique wasn't particularly groundbreaking, his music was strong and a good representation of the sound of country-blues harmonica in the early '30s.

Coleman was the son of sharecroppers. As a child, he taught himself how to play harmonica. He would perform at parties, both for his family and friends. Coleman served in the Army during World War I. After his discharge, he moved to the Birmingham, AL, area. While he lived in Birmingham, he would perform on street corners and occasionally play with the Birmingham Jug Band.

Jaybird made his first recordings in 1927 — the results were released on Gennett, Silvertone, and Black Patti. For the next few years, he simply played on street corners. Coleman cut his final sessions in 1930, supported by the Birmingham Jug Band. These recordings appeared on the OKeh record label.

During the '30s and '40s, Coleman played on street corners throughout Alabama. By the end of the '40s, he had disappeared from the state's blues scene. In 1950, Jaybird Coleman died of cancer. — *Stephen Thomas Erlewine*

● **1927-1930** / 1993 / Document ♦♦♦♦
Jaybird Coleman wasn't one of the most distinctive early country-blues harmonica players, but he nevertheless made engaging, entertaining music. All of his recordings — which only totalled 11 sides — are collected on Document's *1927-1930*. For fans of the genre, there are some cuts of interest here, but the music doesn't have enough weight to be of interest to anyone but country-blues fanatics. — *Thom Owens*

Albert Collins (Al Collins)

b. Oct. 3, 1932, Leona, TX, **d.** Nov. 24, 1993, Las Vegas, NV
Guitar, Vocals / Post-Bop, R&B, Electric Texas Blues, Texas Blues
Albert Collins — "The Master of the Telecaster," "The Iceman," and "The Razor Blade" — was robbed of his best years as a blues performer by a bout with

liver cancer that ended with his premature death on November 24, 1993. He was just 61 years old. The highly influential, totally original Collins, like the late John Campbell, was on the cusp of a much wider worldwide following via his deal with Virgin Records' Pointblank subsidiary. However, unlike Campbell, Collins had performed for many more years, in obscurity, before finally finding a following in the mid-'80s.

Collins was born October 1, 1932, in Leona, TX. His family moved to Houston when he was seven. Growing up in the city's Third Ward area with the likes of Johnny "Guitar" Watson and Johnny "Clyde" Copeland, Collins started out taking keyboard lessons. His idol when he was a teen was Hammond B-3 organist Jimmy McGriff. But by the time he was 18 years old, he switched to guitar, and hung out and heard his heroes—Clarence "Gatemouth" Brown, John Lee Hooker, T-Bone Walker and Lightnin' Hopkins (his cousin)—in Houston-area nightclubs. Collins began performing in these same clubs, going after his own style, characterized by his use of minor tunings and a capo, by the mid-'50s. It was also at this point that he began his "guitar walks" through the audience, which made him wildly popular with the younger White audiences he played for years later in the 1980s. He led a ten-piece band, the Rhythm Rockers, and cut his first single in 1958 for the Houston-based Kangaroo label, "The Freeze." The single was followed by a slew of other instrumental singles with catchy titles, including "Sno-Cone," "Icy Blue," and "Don't Lose Your Cool." All of these singles brought Collins a regional following. After recording "De-Frost" b/w "Albert's Alley" for Hall-Way Records of Beaumont, TX, he hit it big in 1962 with "Frosty," a million-selling single. Teenagers Janis Joplin and Johnny Winter, both raised in Beaumont, were in the studio when he recorded the song. According to Collins, Joplin correctly predicted that the single would become a hit. The tune quickly became part of his ongoing repertoire, and was still part of his live shows more than 30 years later, in the mid-'80s. Collins' percussive, ringing guitar style became his trademark, as he would use his right hand to pluck the strings. Blues-rock guitarist Jimi Hendrix cited Collins as an influence in any number of interviews he gave.

Through the rest of the 1960s, Collins continued to work day jobs while pursuing his music with short regional tours and on weekends. He recorded for a other small Texas labels, including Great Scott, Brylen, and TFC. In 1968, Bob "The Bear" Hite from the blues-rock group Canned Heat took an interest in the guitarist's music, traveling to Houston to hear him live. Hite took Collins to California, where he was immediately signed to Imperial Records. By later 1968 and 1969, the '60s blues revival was still going on, and Collins got wider exposure opening for groups like the Allman Brothers at the Fillmore West in San Francisco. Collins based his operations for many years in Los Angeles before moving to Las Vegas in the late '80s.

He recorded three albums for the Imperial label before jumping to Tumbleweed Records. There, several singles were produced by Joe Walsh, since the label was owned by Eagles' producer Bill Szymczyk. The label folded in 1973. Despite the fact that he didn't record much through the 1970s and into the early '80s, he had gotten sufficient airplay around the US with his singles to be able to continue touring, and so he did, piloting his own bus from gig to gig until at least 1988, when he and his backing band were finally able to use a driver. Collins' big break came about in 1977, when he was signed to the Chicago-based Alligator Records, and he released his brilliant debut for the label in 1978, *Ice Pickin'.* Collins recorded six more albums for the label, culminating in 1986's *Cold Snap,* on which organist Jimmy McGriff performs. It was at Alligator Records that Collins began to realize that he could sing adequately, and working with his wife Gwynn, he co-wrote many of his classic songs, including items like "Mastercharge," and "Conversation with Collins."

His other albums for Alligator include *Live in Japan, Don't Lose Your Cool, Frozen Alive!* and *Frostbite.* An album he recorded with fellow guitarists Robert Cray and Johnny "Clyde" Copeland for Alligator in 1985, *Showdown!* brought a Grammy award for all three musicians. His *Cold Snap,* released in 1986, was nominated for a Grammy award.

In 1989, Collins signed with the Pointblank subsidiary of major label Virgin Records, and his debut, *Iceman,* was released in 1991. The label released the compilation *Collins Mix* in 1993. Other compact-disc reissues of his early recordings were produced by other record companies who saw Collins' newfound popularity on the festival and theater circuit, and they include *The Complete Imperial Recordings* on EMI Records (1991) and *Truckin' with Albert Collins* (1992) on MCA Records. Collins' sessionography is also quite extensive. The albums he performs on include David Bowie's *Labyrinth,* John Zorn's *Spillane,* Jack Bruce's *A Question of Time,* John Mayall's *Wake Up Call,* B.B. King's *Blues Summit,* Robert Cray's *Shame and a Sin,* and Branford Marsalis' *Super Models in Deep Conversation.*

Although he'd spent far too much time in the 1970s without recording, Collins could sense that the blues were coming back stronger in the mid-'80s, with interest in Stevie Ray Vaughan at an all-time high. Collins enjoyed some media celebrity in the last few years of his life, via concert appearances at Carnegie Hall, on *Late Night with David Letterman,* in the Touchstone film *Adventures in Babysitting,* and in a classy Seagram's Wine Cooler commercial with Bruce Willis. The blues revival that Collins, Vaughan, and the Fabulous Thunderbirds helped bring about in the mid-'80s has continued into the mid-'90s. But sadly, Collins has not been able to take part in the ongoing evolution of the music. —*Richard Skelly*

The Cool Sound of Albert Collins / 1965 / TCF Hall ++++

Love Can Be Found Anywhere / 1969 / Imperial +++

Trash Talkin' / 1969 / Imperial +++

Truckin' with Albert Collins / 1969 / MCA ++++
Truckin' with Albert Collins is a 1969 Blue Thumb reissue of *The Cool Sound of Albert Collins,* which was originally released on TCF Hall Records in 1965. These are the earliest recordings that Collins made and already his trademark sound is in place—his leads are stinging, piercing, and direct. The album features a set of blistering instrumentals (with the exception of the vocal "Dyin' Flu") that would eventually become his signature tunes, including "Frosty" and "Frostbite." Collins doesn't just stick to blues, he adds elements of surf, rock, jazz, and R&B. These songs may not have been hits at the time, but they helped establish his reputation as the Master of the Telecaster. —*Thom Owens*

The Complete Albert Collins / 1970 / Imperial +++
This inconsistent set is worthwhile nonetheless. —*Bill Dahl*

There's Gotta Be a Change / 1971 / Tumbleweed ++
Although this probably isn't Albert Collins' best album, it is significant for several reasons. Producer Bill Szymczyk, who had great commercial success with B.B. King on *Indianola Mississippi Seeds* obviously hoped to duplicate that for his own Tumbleweed label. To that end, an all-star assemblage of players were present for these sessions at the famed Record Plant West in Los Angeles. Highlights include a slashing guitar duel between Collins and Jessie Ed Davis. —*William Ashford*

Alive & Cool / 1971 / Red Lightnin' +

★ **Ice Pickin'** / 1978 / Alligator +++++
Ice Pickin' is the album that brought Albert Collins directly back into the limelight, and for good reason, too. The record captures the wild, unrestrained side of his playing that had never quite been documented before. Though his singing doesn't quite have the fire or power of his playing, the album doesn't suffer at all because of that—he simply burns throughout the album. *Ice Pickin'* was his first release for Alligator Records and it set the pace for all the albums that followed. No matter how much he tried, Collins never completely regained the pure energy that made *Ice Pickin'* such a revelation. —*Thom Owens*

With Barrelhouse Live / 1978 / Munich ++

Frostbite / 1980 / Alligator +++
Frostbite was the first indication that Albert Collins' Alligator albums were going to follow something of a formula. The album replicated all of the styles and sounds of *Ice Pickin',* but the music lacked the power of its predecessor. Nevertheless, there was a wealth of fine playing on the album, even if the quality of the songs themselves is uneven. —*Thom Owens*

Frozen Alive! / 1981 / Alligator +++
Frozen Alive! demonstrates the exuberant power of Albert Collins in concert and contains enough first-rate solos to make it a worthwhile listen for fans of his icy style. —*Thom Owens*

Don't Lose Your Cool / 1983 / Alligator +++
This fourth Alligator Records effort is consistently satisfying. —*Bill Dahl*

Live in Japan / 1984 / Alligator +++
Compared to *Frozen Alive!, Live in Japan* is a little more drawn-out and funky, featuring extended jamming on several songs. That isn't necessarily

a bad thing—Collins and his bandmates can work a groove pretty damn well. Of course, the main reason to listen to an Albert Collins album is to hear the man play. And play he does throughout *Live in Japan*, spitting out piercing leads with glee. On the whole, it's not quite as consistent as *Frozen Alive!*, but that's only by a slight margin. — *Thom Owens*

Showdown / 1985 / Alligator ✦✦✦
A summit meeting between Texas guitar veterans Collins and Johnny Copeland and newcomer Robert Cray, the set is scorching all the way. — *Bill Dahl*

Cold Snap / 1986 / Alligator ✦✦✦
Cold Snap has a stronger R&B direction than Collins' previous Alligator releases, most notably in the presence of a slicker production. That approach doesn't suit him particularly well—he's at his best when he's just playing the blues, not when he's trying to sing. Nevertheless, he turns out a number of gripping solos, and that is what prevents *Cold Snap* from being too much of a disappointment. — *Thom Owens*

Ice Cold Blues / 1986 / Charly ✦✦✦

★ The Complete Imperial Recordings / 1991 / EMI ✦✦✦✦✦
Texan Albert Collins was in the very first rank of post-war blues guitarists. This two-CD set is a reissue of all 36 sides he cut for Imperial from 1968 to 1970—representing this artist's second major recording stint. Instrumentals comprise roughly three-fourths of the material. They frame his distinctive guitar work with a tight ensemble of organ, bass, and drums, adding at times a piano and/or second guitar, punctuated by a horn section. About ten of these tunes are as great as anything Collins ever did. They are riddled with the biting, incisive, dramatic, and economical playing that made him a legend. There are also some outstanding vocals. Although this set is not without its clinkers, it is a solid package and a must for any Collins fan. — *Larry Hoffman*

Iceman / 1991 / Capitol ✦✦✦
Albert Collins doesn't change anything for his major label debut, *Iceman*. Like its predecessors, it is slick and professional, featuring a variety of shuffles, R&B tunes, and slow blues, all stamped with Collins' trademark icy wail. None of the songs or performances are particularly noteworthy, but *Iceman* is a solid set that delivers the goods for fans of his style. — *Thom Owens*

Molten Ice / 1992 / Red Lightnin' ✦✦✦
Reissued domestically in 1998, *Molten Ice* captures Albert Collins live in Toronto in 1973 with backing by that city's Moe Peters Band. — *Steve Huey*

Collins Mix: The Best / Oct. 5, 1993 / Pointblank ✦✦✦✦
This provided fresh looks at 11 Collins classics, among them such epic numbers as "Don't Lose Your Cool," "Frosty," "Honey Hush," and "Tired Man." There were slow, wailing ballads with blistering solos, electrifying uptempo wailers with a great horn section answering Collins' phrases with their own bleats, and first-rate mastering and production. Guest stars included B.B. King, Branford Marsalis, Kim Wilson, and Gary Moore, while Collins injected vitality into numbers he'd already made standards years ago. This set is a wonderful tribute to an incredible guitarist and musician. — *Ron Wynn*

Live 92/93 / Sep. 12, 1995 / Pointblank ✦✦✦
Compiling a number of performances recorded shortly before Albert Collins' death, *Live 92-93* offers definitive proof that the guitarist remained vital until his last days. — *Thom Owens*

Live [Munich] / 1996 / Munich ✦✦✦
Collins is backed by a Dutch band on this recording of a December 1978 show in Alkmaar, Holland. Dividing his attention between originals and covers of tunes by the likes of Lowell Fulson and Guitar Slim, it's a typically energetic set with long solos, the backup musicians playing competently, and female singer Tineke Schoemaker taking the vocals on "Blue River Rising." But it's not particularly an essential addition, or preferable, to his more widely known live albums of the 1980s and '90s. — *Richie Unterberger*

Deluxe Edition / 1997 / Alligator ✦✦✦✦
Deluxe Edition is a solid, albeit imperfect, 13-track collection of highlights from Albert Collins' latter-day recordings for Alligator. There are only a handful of genuine classics, but there are a lot of great performances that spotlight Collins' stinging guitar work and impassioned vocals. Nevertheless, it's only adequate as an introduction, since *Ice Pickin'* remains the place

to become acquainted with Collins' blistering blues. — *Stephen Thomas Erlewine*

Sam Collins

b. Aug. 11, 1887, Louisiana, **d.** Oct. 20, 1949, Chicago, IL
Guitar, Vocals / Country Blues, Delta Blues, Prewar Country Blues
One of the earliest generation of blues performers, Collins developed his style in South Mississippi (as opposed to the Delta). His recording debut single ("The Jail House Blues," 1927) predated those of legendary Mississippians such as Charley Patton and Tommy Johnson, and was advertised as "Crying Sam Collins and his Git-Fiddle." Collins did not become a major name in blues—in fact his later records appeared under several different pseudonyms, most notably the name Jim Foster —but his rural bottleneck guitar pieces were among the first to be compiled on LP when the country-blues reissue era was just beginning. Sam Charters wrote in *The Bluesmen:* "Although Collins was not one of the stylistic innovators within the Mississippi blues idiom, he was enough part of it that, in blues like 'Signifying Blues' and 'Slow Mama Slow,' he had some of the intensity of the Mississippi blues music at its most creative level." — *Jim O'Neal*

Complete Recorded Works (1927-1931) / 1927-1931 / Document ✦✦✦
Every track that Sam Collins recorded at the end of the '20s and early in the '30s is included on Document's *Complete Recorded Works (1927-1931)*. Although the comprehensiveness of the set is a little intimidating for casual listeners—they should stick with the better-sequenced *Jailhouse Blues*—historians will find the collection invaluable. — *Thom Owens*

• Jailhouse Blues / 1990 / Yazoo ✦✦✦✦
One of the '20s most fascinating, eccentric obscurities, although a little Collins goes a long way. — *Mark A. Humphrey*

King of the Blues 11 / 1992 / Pea Vine ✦✦✦✦
22 songs, mostly clean and well transferred, make this one of the better bargains among Japanese imports, especially at a $14 list price. The first 15 songs date from 1927, and most of them feature Collins solo, playing some lively and dexterous blues accompanied by some very expressive vocals. "Lion's Den Blues," "Yellow Dog Blues," "Riverside Blues," and "I'm Still Sitting On Top of the World" (just two of the songs that refer to more familiar later songs) are highlights on this very fine disc, which includes some major surprises—on "Lovely Lady Blues," for instance, one actually gets a real sense of room ambience from the 1927 disc, done for the Gennett label; and there are places where Collins' playing is so animated that it sounds like two guys. The notes are in Japanese, but it's the music that counts here. — *Bruce Eder*

Joanna Connor

b. Sep. 13, 1962, Brooklyn, NY
Guitar, Vocals / Modern Electric Blues, Blues-Rock
What sets Joanna Connor apart from the rest of the pack of guitar-playing female blues singers is her skill on the instrument. Even though Connor has become an accomplished singer over time, her first love was guitar playing, and it shows in her live shows and on her recordings.

Brooklyn-born, Massachusetts-raised Joanna Connor was drawn to the Chicago blues scene like a bee to a half-full soda can. Connor, a fiery guitarist raised in the 1970s—when rock 'n' roll was all over the mass media—just wanted to play blues. She was born August 13, 1962, in Brooklyn, NY, and raised by her mother in Worcester, MA. She benefitted from her mother's huge collection of blues and jazz recordings, and a young Connor was taken to see people like Taj Mahal, Bonnie Raitt, Ry Cooder, and Buddy Guy in concert.

Connor got her first guitar at age seven. When she was 16, she began singing in Worcester-area bands, and when she was 22, she moved to Chicago. Soon after her arrival in 1984, she began sitting in with Chicago regulars like James Cotton, Junior Wells, Buddy Guy, and A.C. Reed. She hooked up with Johnny Littlejohn's group for a short time before being asked by Dion Payton to join his 43rd Street Blues Band. She performed with Payton at the 1987 Chicago Blues Festival. Later that year, she was ready to put her own band together.

Her 1989 debut for the Blind Pig label, *Believe It!*, got her out of Chicago clubs and into clubs and festivals around the US, Canada, and Europe. Her other albums include 1992's *Fight* for Blind Pig (the title track a Luther Allison tune), *Living on the Road* (1993), and *Rock and Roll Gypsy* (1995), the latter two for the Ruf Records label.

In the 1990s, Connor, still in her early '30s, has blossomed into a gifted blues songwriter. Her songwriting talents, strongly influenced by greats like Luther Allison, will insure that she stays in the blues spotlight for years to come. — *Richard Skelly*

● **Believe It!** / 1989 / Blind Pig ✦✦✦✦
On the surface, *Believe It!* is standard-issue bar-band blues-rock, but it is distinguished by Joanna Connor's passion for the music. Connor believes in the music so much, it can't help but appear in the grooves every once in a while. In particular, her guitar playing is noteworthy—it's tough, greasy, and powerful. *Believe It!* suffers from a lack of memorable songs—she's still trying to develop a distinctive songwriting voice—but Connor's strong performances carry the album through any weak moments. — *Thom Owens*

Fight / 1992 / Blind Pig ✦✦✦
To date, Joanna Connor's studio work has not lived up the live-wire energy of her personal performances. *Fight* takes a major step towards setting this right. This stuff wails, especially Robert Johnson's "Walking Blues" which Connor reinvents courtesy of some stinging slidework. While Connor's lack of dependence on cover material rates bonus points, not all her songs are memorable—even if the guitar playing is. — *Roch Parisien*

Living on the Road / 1993 / Inak ✦✦✦

Rock & Roll Gypsy / Oct. 17, 1995 / RFR ✦✦✦

Big Girl Blues / 1996 / Ruf ✦✦✦✦
The comparison of Connor to Bonnie Raitt is unavoidable, considering the similarities of their vocal style and skill at slide guitar. But Connor offers a more savage guitar approach, akin to George Thorogood, and she comes on as a bit nastier. The album is filled with impressive guitar work, but the bad-girl pose wears thin after a while. — *Tim Sheridan*

Slidetime / May 19, 1998 / Blind Pig ✦✦✦
Joanna Connor's fourth album for Blind Pig finds her still working solidly in blues-rock territory with plenty of her blistering slide guitar work well to the fore. Connor penned all 11 of the tunes here, co-writing one of them with guitarist Ron Johnson and the other with drummer Boyd Martin; her songwriting chops show considerable added depth and improvement on this go round. She is still keeping her sound in the time-honored road-band format of two guitars, bass, and drums. She brings aboard background vocals on "Slide It In," "Got To Have You," and "Pea Vine Blues," the latter also featuring some nice fingerpicked guitar from Ron Johnson. Connors' guitar positively blisters on "My Man," "Free Free Woman," and others, making this one of her strongest outings. — *Cub Koda*

Ry Cooder

b. Mar. 15, 1947, Los Angeles, CA
Guitar, Vocals, Mandolin / Blues-Rock, Country-Rock, Roots-Rock, Ethnic Fusion, Modern Electric Blues, Modern Acoustic Blues
Whether serving as a session musician, solo artist, or soundtrack composer, Ry Cooder's chameleon-like fretted instrument virtuosity, songwriting, and choices of material encompass an incredibly eclectic range of North American musical styles, including rock 'n' roll, blues, reggae, Tex-Mex, Hawaiian, Dixieland jazz, country, folk, R&B, gospel, and vaudeville. The 16-year-old Cooder began his career in 1963 in a blues band with Jackie DeShannon and then formed the short-lived Rising Sons in 1965 with Taj Mahal and Spirit drummer Ed Cassidy. Cooder met producer Terry Melcher through the Rising Sons and was invited to perform at several sessions with Paul Revere and the Raiders. During his subsequent career as a session musician, Cooder's trademark slide guitar work graced the recordings of such artists as Captain Beefheart (*Safe as Milk*), Randy Newman, Little Feat, Van Dyke Parks, the Rolling Stones (*Let It Bleed, Sticky Fingers*), Taj Mahal, and Gordon Lightfoot. He also appeared on the soundtracks of *Candy* and *Performance.*

Cooder made his debut as a solo artist in 1970 with a self-titled album featuring songs by Leadbelly, Blind Willie Johnson, Sleepy John Estes, and Woody Guthrie. The follow-up, *Into the Purple Valley,* introduced longtime cohorts Jim Keltner on drums and Jim Dickinson on bass, and it and *Boomer's Story* largely repeated and refined the syncopated style and mood of the first. In 1974, Cooder produced what is generally regarded as his best album, *Paradise and Lunch,* and its follow-up, *Chicken Skin Music,* showcased a

potent blend of Tex-Mex, Hawaiian, gospel, and soul music, and featured contributions from Flaco Jimenez and Gabby Pahinui. In 1979, *Bop till You Drop* was the first major-label album to be recorded digitally. In the early '80s, Cooder began to augment his solo output with soundtrack work on such films as *Blue Collar, The Long Riders,* and *The Border;* he has gone on to compose music for *Southern Comfort, Goin' South, Paris, Texas, Streets of Fire, Bay, Blue City, Crossroads, Cocktail, Johnny Handsome, Steel Magnolias,* and *Geronimo. Music by Ry Cooder* (1995) compiled two discs' worth of highlights from Cooder's film work.

In 1992, Cooder joined Keltner, John Hiatt, and renowned British tunesmith Nick Lowe, all of whom had played on Hiatt's *Bring the Family,* to form Little Village, which toured and recorded one album. Cooder next turned his attention to world music, recording the album *A Meeting by the River* with Indian musician V.M. Bhatt. Cooder's next project, a duet album with renowned African guitarist Ali Farka Toure titled *Talking Timbuktu,* won the 1994 Grammy for Best World Music Recording. — *Steve Huey*

Ry Cooder / 1970 / Reprise ✦✦✦
His debut serves as a neat prototype, with its Sleepy John Estes and Woody Guthrie covers. It also introduces a most talented musician in its leader. But it's still a prototype; the best was yet to come. — *Jeff Tamarkin*

Into the Purple Valley / 1971 / Reprise ✦✦✦✦
First there are no other credits for musicians; because of his reputation for honesty in music, I will assume that he plays all the instruments, including the ones with no strings. He is known as a virtuoso on almost every stringed instrument and on this CD he demonstrates this ability on a wide variety of instruments. The main focus of the music here is on the era of the Dust Bowl, and what was happening in America at the time, socially and musically. Songs by Woody Guthrie, Leadbelly, and a variety of other people show Ry's encyclopedic knowledge of the music of this time, combined with an instinctive feel for the songs. "Phenomenal" is the descriptive word to describe his playing, whether it is on guitar, Hawaiian "slack key" guitar, mandolin, or more arcane instruments he has found. This is a must for those who love instrumental virtuosity, authentic reworkings of an era, or just plain good music. — *Bob Gottlieb*

Boomer's Story / 1972 / Reprise ✦✦✦✦
Largely laidback and bluesy, this album features a number of paeans to an America long lost. — *Jeff Tamarkin*

● **Paradise & Lunch** / 1974 / Reprise ✦✦✦✦
Working with an intriguing collection of veteran musicians, the master musician and archivist turns in a stunning set of timeless remakes and new compositions. — *Jeff Tamarkin*

Chicken Skin Music / 1976 / Reprise ✦✦✦✦
Hawaiian traditional music meets Leadbelly and Ben E. King on Cooder's gospelization of rock & soul. — *Jeff Tamarkin*

Showtime / 1976 / Warner Brothers ✦✦✦
Recorded live in 1976, Cooder cooks and struts his stuff on this grand tour of his abilities. The great Flaco Jimenez is on accordion. — *Jeff Tamarkin*

Jazz / 1978 / Warner Brothers ✦✦✦
A tribute to Dixieland, with a stopover at the blues hotel. Joseph Byrd's arrangements on tunes by Bix Beiderbecke, Joseph Spence, et al., are inspired. — *Jeff Tamarkin*

Bop Till You Drop / 1979 / Warner Brothers ✦✦
Cooder has disowned this early digital recording, and he's right; not only is the sound dry, but the music is rather lifeless. Although it has some bright moments, it's not his best. — *Jeff Tamarkin*

Long Riders / 1980 / Reprise ✦✦

Borderline / 1980 / Warner Brothers ✦
Ry is off track here on covers of old rock 'n' roll songs. The warmth of the earlier recordings is missing, and his already indistinguished vocals are hopeless here. — *Jeff Tamarkin*

The Slide Area / 1982 / Warner Brothers ✦✦
This CD opens with an outrageous and exceedingly funky "UFO Has Landed in the Ghetto," which seems so out of place with the other material. Yes, it is R&B—bordering at times on funk—album, and rap is one direction R&B took, but.... Listen to the groove on "Which Came First," and try to keep your body from bobbing to the strong rhythm laid down by Jim Keltner, Tim

Drummond, and the background vocalists. While we are on the subject of vocals, this is one of Ry Cooder's best efforts, and his backup vocalists are key here and deserve special recognition: Bobby King, John Hiatt, Willie Greene, and Herman Johnson for most of the CD. The two gems on this are the phenomenal treatments of both "Blue Suede Shoes" and Bob Dylan's "I Need a Woman." Two songs as different in the original forms as pigs and gerbils are converted to R&B hit status. Both contain some memorable slide guitar work, but isn't that what we expect from this master of the guitar family. The album is very good but those two songs make it a gem. — *Bob Gottlieb*

Ry Cooder Live / 1982 / Warner Brothers ✦✦✦

Crossroads [O.S.T.] / 1986 / Warner Brothers ✦✦✦
The ersatz blues story of the film gives Ry Cooder leeway to turn in an impressive blues-derived soundtrack featuring Sonny Terry along with his usual collaborators Van Dyke Parks, Jim Keltner, Nathan East, and others. But it's Cooder's guitar playing that highlights the album. — *William Ruhlmann*

Get Rhythm / 1987 / Warner Brothers ✦✦✦
"The Musician's Musician." "The Master of the Eclectic." There are probably a dozen more titles by which this "guitar player" is known. To even refer to him as a guitar player is probably a gross mislabeling of this musician. He defies any sort of categorization; this is his greatest strength and for some his weakness. The theme for these nine cuts is rhythm of all different ilk. I won't even give the parameters because he seems to have none. I wondered how many different instruments he played on this album (I thought I counted five different types of guitar); it only says guitar and vocal for his credits. Listen to his version of "All Shook Up," more bop and rhythm than Elvis could put into four of his songs. It seems musicians line up to play with him, and they feel he did them a favor by letting them play on his albums. He always gives them plenty of space to do what they do. This CD will make the dead start tapping their toes. — *Bob Gottlieb*

Music by Ry Cooder / Jul. 11, 1995 / Warner Brothers ✦✦✦✦
Since he's a limited vocalist with erratic songwriting skills, one could justifiably argue that the soundtrack medium is the best vehicle for Cooder's talents, allowing him to construct eclectic, chiefly instrumental pieces drawing upon all sorts of roots music and ethnic flavors (often, but not always, employing his excellent blues and slide guitar). This two-CD, 34-song compilation gathers excerpts from eleven of the soundtracks he worked on between 1980 and 1993 (three of the cuts, from the 1981 film *Southern Comfort*, are previously unreleased). As few listeners (even Cooder fans) are dedicated enough to go to the trouble of finding all of his individual soundtracks, this is a good distillation of many of his more notable contributions in this idiom, although it inevitably leaves out some fine moments. Still, it's well programmed and evocative, often conjuring visions of ghostly landscapes and funky border towns. — *Richie Unterberger*

Buena Vista Social Club / Sep. 16, 1997 / Elektra/Asylum ✦✦✦
With *Buena Vista Social Club*, Ry Cooder dives deeply into the culture and music of Cuba. Specifically, he concentrates on folk songs that have been passed down throughout the years. Most of these originated in the first half of the 20th century and have been played by Cuban sextets throughout the decades. There are spirited dances, hymns, and ballads that capture the sound and culture of Cuba, mainly because Cooder has assembled a band that is comprised of seasoned Cuban musicians. As a result, *Buena Vista Social Club* is a vital record that is simultaneously provocative and entertaining. — *Thom Owens*

Johnny Copeland

b. Mar. 27, 1937, Haynesville, LA, **d.** Jul. 3, 1997
Guitar, Vocals / R&B, Electric Texas Blues, Texas Blues
Considering the amount of time he spent steadily rolling from gig to gig, Johnny "Clyde" Copeland's rise to prominence in the blues world in the early '90s isn't all that surprising. A contract with the PolyGram/Verve label put his '90s recordings into the hands of thousands of blues lovers around the world. It's not that Copeland's talent changed all that much since he recorded for Rounder Records in the 1980s; it's just that major companies began to see the potential of great, hardworking blues musicians like Copeland. Unfortunately, Copeland was forced to slow down in 1995-96 by heart-related

complications, yet he continued to perform shows until his death in July of 1997.

Johnny Copeland was born March 27, 1937, in Haynesville, LA, about 15 miles south of Magnolia, AR (formerly Texarkana, a hotbed of blues activity in the 1920s and '30s). The son of sharecroppers, his father died when he was very young, but Copeland was given his father's guitar. His first gig was with his friend Joe "Guitar" Hughes. Soon after, Hughes "took sick" for a week and the young Copeland discovered he could be a front man and deliver vocals as well as anyone else around Houston at that time.

His music, by his own reasoning, fell somewhere between the funky R&B of New Orleans and the swing and jump blues of Kansas City. After his family (sans his father) moved to Houston, Copeland was exposed, as a teen, to musicians from both cities. While he was becoming interested in music, he also pursued boxing, mostly as an avocation, and it is from his days as a boxer that he got his nickname "Clyde."

Copeland and Hughes fell under the spell of T-Bone Walker, whom Copeland first saw perform when he was 13 years old.

As a teenager he played at locales such as Shady's Playhouse—Houston's leading blues club, host to most of the city's best bluesmen during the 1950s—and the Eldorado Ballroom. Copeland and Hughes subsequently formed the Dukes of Rhythm, which became the house band at the Shady's Playhouse. After that, he spent time playing on tour with Albert Collins (himself a fellow T-Bone Walker devotee) during the 1950s, and also played on stage with Sonny Boy Williamson, II, Big Mama Thornton, and Freddie King. He began recording in 1958 with "Rock 'n' Roll Lily" for Mercury, and moved between various labels during the 1960s, including All Boy and Golden Eagle in Houston, where he had regional successes with "Please Let Me Know" and "Down on Bending Knees," and later for Wand and Atlantic in New York. In 1965, he displayed a surprising prescience in terms of the pop market by cutting a version of Bob Dylan's "Blowin' in the Wind" for Wand.

After touring around the "Texas triangle" of Louisiana, Texas, and Arkansas, he relocated to New York City in 1974, at the height of the disco boom. It seems moving to New York City was the best career move Copeland ever made, for he had easy access to clubs in Washington, D.C., New York, Philadelphia, New Jersey, and Boston, all of which still had a place for blues musicians like him. Meanwhile, back in Houston, the club scene was hurting, owing partly to the oil-related recession of the mid-'70s. Copeland took a day job at a Brew 'n' Burger restaurant in New York and played his blues at night, finding receptive audiences at clubs in Harlem and Greenwich Village.

Copeland recorded seven albums for Rounder Records, beginning in 1981 and including *Copeland Special, Make My Home Where I Hang My Hat, Texas Twister, Bringin' It All Back Home, When the Rain Starts a Fallin', Ain't Nothing But a Party* (live, nominated for a Grammy) and *Boom Boom;* he also won a Grammy award in 1986 for his efforts on an Alligator album, *Showdown!,* with Robert Cray and the late Albert Collins. Although Copeland had a booming, shouting voice and was a powerful guitarist and live performer, what most people don't realize is just how clever a songwriter he was. His latter-day releases for the PolyGram/Verve/Gitanes label, including *Flyin' High* (1992) and *Catch up with the Blues,* provide ample evidence of this on "Life's Rainbow (Nature Song)" (from the latter album) and "Circumstances" (from the former album).

Because Copeland was only six months old when his parents split up and he only saw his father a few times before he passed away, Copeland never realized he had inherited a congenital heart defect from his father. He discovered this in the midst of another typically hectic tour in late 1994, when he had to go into the hospital in Colorado. After he was diagnosed with heart disease, he spent the next few years in and out of hospitals, undertaking a number of costly heart surgeries. Early in 1997, he was waiting for a heart transplant at Columbia Presbyterian Medical Center in New York City. As he was waiting, he was put on the L-VAD, a recent innovation for patients suffering from congenital heart defects. In 1995, Copeland appeared on CNN and ABC-TV's *Good Morning America*, wearing his L-VAD, offering the invention valuable publicity.

Despite his health problems, Copeland continued to perform and his always spirited concerts did not diminished all that much. After living 20 months on the L-VAD—the longest anyone had lived on the device—he received a heart transplant on January 1, 1997, and for a few months, the heart worked fine and he continued to tour. However, the heart developed a defective valve, necessitating heart surgery in the summer. Copeland died of complications during heart surgery on July 3, 1997. —*Richard Skelly & Bruce Eder*

● **Copeland Special** / 1981 / Rounder ✦✦✦✦
This immaculate collection put the veteran Houston axeman among the blues elite; it features searing guitar and soulful vocals. —*Bill Dahl*

Make My Home Where I Hang My Hat / 1982 / Rounder ✦✦✦
This second Rounder Records album has its share of incendiary moments. —*Bill Dahl*

Texas Twister / 1983 / Rounder ✦✦✦✦
Johnny Copeland's tenure on Rounder Records was mostly productive. He made several albums that ranged from decent to very good, increased his audience and name recognition and got better recording facilities and company support than at most times in his career. The 15 numbers on this anthology cover four Rounder sessions, and include competent renditions of familiar numbers. But what makes things special are the final three selections; these were part of Copeland's superb and unjustly underrated *Bringin' It Back Home* album, recorded in Africa, which matched Texas shuffle licks with swaying, riveting African rhythms. —*Ron Wynn*

I'll Be Around / 1984 / Mr. R&B ✦✦✦✦
Exceptional collection of Copeland's primordial work. —*Bill Dahl*

Showdown [A Collins & R Cray] / 1985 / Alligator ✦✦✦✦
A summit meeting between Texas guitar veterans Collins and Johnny Copeland and newcomer Robert Cray, the set is scorching all the way. —*Bill Dahl*

Down on Bending Knee / 1985 / Mr. R&B ✦✦✦✦
This second volume of his early sides is equally impressive. —*Bill Dahl*

Bringin' It All Back Home / 1986 / Rounder ✦✦✦✦
Imaginative hybrid of blues and African idioms. —*Bill Dahl*

Houston Roots / 1988 / Ace ✦✦✦✦

Ain't Nothing But a Party [Live] / 1988 / Rounder ✦✦✦
Texas guitarist and vocalist Johnny Copeland didn't turn in a formula job on these six tunes recorded live at the 1987 Juneteenth festival. Indeed, the concert setting seems to put some juice in Copeland's singing; his voice isn't raspy or detached, and he actually seems exuberant about doing the umpteenth version of "Big Time" and "Baby, Please Don't Go." His band, especially saxophonist Bert McGowan, also seem to get new life from the crowd reaction and dig in behind Copeland with renewed vigor. Even Copeland's shuffle licks and patterns, which can become awfully predictable, were executed with some sharp twists and surprising turns. —*Ron Wynn*

Collection, Vol. 1 / 1988 / Collectables ✦✦✦
Fifteen mostly early Johnny Copeland sides, originally released on the Golden Eagle, All Boy, Paradise, and Suave labels, recorded between 1960 and the summer of 1967, including the hit singles "Please Let Me Know" and "Down On Bending Knees" (from 1960 and 1963, respectively). Some of the previously unissued numbers, such as the instrumental "Late Hours," are showcases for Copeland (and especially for his guitar) as good as the released stuff. A close listen reveals Copeland developing great confidence, mostly as a singer but also as a guitarist, between 1960 and 1963 on sides like "Working Man's Blues," while other songs, such as "There's a Blessing," show him turning into a top soul shouter, in keeping with the changing times—"It Must Be Love" and "I've Gotta Go Home" are two great unheralded jewels in the latter category on this collection. The B-side "Wella Wella Baby" clocks in at a near-epic-length five minutes, none of it wasted. His heart-stopping vocal workout on the 1967 Paradise single "(The Night Time Is) The Right Time" is also some of the most worthwhile music from this decade of Copeland's career. His never-issued solo acoustic demo of Arthur Crudup's "That's All Right Mama" is followed by the finished single—on electric instruments, with a girl chorus and a full piano and rhythm section—released on Suave in late 1964. All pretty cool, and good sound all the way through, too. —*Bruce Eder*

When the Rain Starts Fallin' / 1988 / Rounder ✦✦✦
More highlights from his Rounder Records material. —*Bill Dahl*

Boom Boom / 1990 / Rounder ✦✦
Sometimes Copeland's Texas shuffle blues just don't have any bite. He came perilously close on this set to having to depend on gimmicks and experience.

Copeland couldn't find any way to refresh material like "Beat the Boom Boom Baby" and "Pie in the Sky," although he tried hard with shouts, cries, and moans. He was more successful on "Nobody But You," "I Was Born All Over," and "Blues Ain't Nothin'," where his soul and gospel roots helped inject some life into the lyrics. His band tried to help matters, but really couldn't elevate the proceedings. If you're only a warm to casual fan, this wasn't one of Copeland's greatest. —*Ron Wynn*

Collection, Vol. 2 / 1990 / Collectables ✦✦✦
Another 14 Johnny Copeland sides, filling in more holes in his history from before and even during his Rounder Records tenure. "Love Song," which opens the set, is from 1990 and shows him in exceptionally good vocal and instrumental form, while "Daily Bread" dates from 1984. All of the rest is attributed to the late '60s and early '70s (although there's an unreleased version of his 1963 single "Please Let Me Know" here as well), which sounds about right. "May the Best Man Win" is a fine piece of late-'60s soul, with a few dissonant edges and a very active horn section that make it doubly interesting. "Heebie Jeebies" is one of the best dance tunes in Copeland's entire output, while his raunchy cover of B.B. King's "Rock Me Baby" is a killer guitar/piano workout, clocking in at over five minutes and worth every second. The rest lurches between '60s soul influences ("Mama Told Me," "Soul Power") and a slicker '70s sound, but it's all enjoyable if one can adjust to the sudden shifts in style and sound. —*Bruce Eder*

Flyin' High / Sep. 1992 / Verve ✦✦
Johnny Copeland's patented "Texas twister" style isn't as flamboyant or forceful on this 10-cut CD as on past occasions (at least instrumentally), but his vocals were in fairly good shape. Copeland was at his best on tunes where the emphasis was on style rather than lyric meaning and elaboration. He seemed ill at ease on other tunes, notably the cover of "Jambalaya," where he never got comfortable with the bayou beat and plowed on through, concluding the number competently, but never offering anything distinctive. The album doesn't cook or boil like Copeland's regional singles, or even his best Alligator material. Instead, it simmers, but winds up just slightly missing the mark. —*Ron Wynn*

Further Up the Road / 1993 / Aim ✦✦✦
This live Australian import is a no-frills Texas guitar feast. —*Bill Dahl*

Catch up with the Blues / 1994 / Polygram ✦✦✦

Jungle Swing / May 1996 / Verve ✦✦
Johnny Copeland's eclectic nature is on display on *Jungle Swing*, an ambitious collaboration with jazz pianist Randy Weston. Weston brings a selection of African rhythms and melodic textures to the table, which are incorporated subtly into the rhythmic underpinnings of each song. In no sense is *Jungle Swing* a worldbeat experiment—it's just a small, affectionate tribute. Even so, the African flourishes don't dominate the sound of the record. Like always, Copeland takes center stage with his clean, precise licks. At this point in his career, he knows exactly what to play and the guitarist never overplays throughout the course of the disc. There are a few weak moments on the disc, but the sheer strength of Copeland's musicianship—and his willingness to stretch out ever so slightly—make it worth the time for any of his fans. —*Thom Owens*

Live in Australia 1990 / Mar. 18, 1997 / Black Top ✦✦✦
This is no hastily assembled disc to cash in on the late Johnny Copeland's unfortunately early demise, but one of his finest recordings. Whether in the studio or live, Copeland always pours a lot of sweat into his playing and singing. The band is tight behind him, giving him the freedom to soar. From the devastation of "Cut Off My Right Arm" to the joy in Nappy Brown's signature tune "Wella Wella Baby," all of the songs are filled with amazingly good vocals and tasteful guitar fills. This album is a fitting tribute to a man who gave his all to every performance. —*Bob Gottlieb*

Ike Cosse

Guitar, Vocals / Modern Electric Blues
Guitarist and vocalist Issac "Ike" Cosse has been leading a band called the Coldbloods around the San Francisco Bay area for the last 20 years. Cosse took his earliest musical inspiration from guitarists like Eric Clapton, Jimmy Page, and Jimi Hendrix, and he played jazz and fusion for some time before settling on the blues.

Cosse joined the band of saxophonist Joe Puttley in 1983 and learned the finer points of blues playing from him, as well as the need to be an entertainer when on the bandstand. After working with Puttley for a number of years, Cosse was given the chance to sing; "Crosscut Saw" and "Further On Up the Road" were the first two blues songs he performed on stage.

After forming his own band, Ike and the Coldbloods, in 1987, he began to work the clubs around the San Francisco Bay area, where he had relocated some years earlier. Ike and the Colbloods played at Slim's in San Francisco, Moe's Alley in Santa Cruz, and other venues around the Bay area. After several years of interpreting cover songs in Bay area clubs, Cosse realized if he was going to take his music anywhere, he would need to perform original compositions.

After dropping a copy of his self-released album off at B.B. King's Club in Los Angeles, Cosse got a booking there, opening for Coco Montoya and Johnny Johnson. Cosse's first album, *The Spot Is Hot,* was released on his own label in 1995. Since then, he's recorded an album for JSP Records of London, *The Lowdown Throwdown.* Cosse currently lives in Santa Clara, California. — *Richard Skelly*

Lowdown Throwdown / Apr. 8, 1997 / JSP ✦✦✦

Elizabeth Cotten

b. 1893, Chapel Hill, NC, **d.** Jun. 29, 1987, Syracuse, NY
Guitar, Vocals / Chicago Blues, Traditional Folk, Folksongs
Elizabeth Cotten was among the most influential guitarists to surface during the roots music revival era, her wonderfully expressive and dexterous fingerpicking style a major inspiration to the generations of players who followed in her wake. Cotten was born in Chapel Hill, NC in the early weeks of 1893; after first picking up the banjo at the age of eight, she soon moved on to her brother's guitar, laying it flat on her lap and over time developing her picking pattern and eventually her chording. By the age of 12 she was working as a domestic, and three years later gave birth to her first child; upon joining the church, she gave up the guitar, playing it only on the rarest of occasions over the course of the next quarter century. By the early 1940s, Cotten had relocated to Washington, D.C., where she eventually began working for the legendary Charles Seeger family and caring for children Pete, Peggy, and Mike.

When the Seegers learned of Cotten's guitar skills a decade later, they recorded her for Folkways, and in 1957 she issued her debut LP, *Folksongs & Instrumentals.* The track "Freight Train," written when she was 12, became a Top Five hit in the UK, and its success ensured her a handful of concert performances. The great interest in her music spurred her to write new material, which appeared on her second album, *Shake Sugaree.* As Cotten became increasingly comfortable performing live, her presentation evolved, and in addition to playing guitar she told stories about her life and even led her audiences in singing her songs; over the years, she recalled more and more tunes from her childhood, and in the course of tours also learned new material. Cotten did not retire from domestic work until 1970, and did not tour actively until the end of the decade; the winner of a National Endowment for the Arts National Heritage Fellowship Award as well as a Grammy—both earned during the final years of her life—she died on June 29, 1987. — *Jason Ankeny*

★ **Folksongs & Instrumentals** ... / 1957 / Smithsonian/Folkways ✦✦✦✦✦
Folksongs & Instrumentals with Guitar. This first LP collection by a widely influential guitarist includes her classic "Freight Train." — *William Ruhlmann*

Freight Train & Other North Carolina Folk Songs and Tunes / 1989 / Smithsonian/Folkways ✦✦✦✦
Recorded in 1957 and early 1958 by Mike Seeger, *Freight Train and Other North Carolina Folk Songs and Tunes* collects the influential debut sides cut by a then-62-year-old Elizabeth Cotten; even decades after their first release, they remain a veritable primer in the art of finger-picked style guitar playing. The quaint, homespun quality of the material—much of it recorded at Cotten's home with her grandchildren looking on in silence—adds immensely to its intimacy and warmth; the sound quality varies wildly from track to track, but the amazing instrumental work shines through regardless on tracks like the opening "Wilson Rag" and the now-standard "Freight Train." — *Jason Ankeny*

James Cotton

b. Jul. 1, 1935, Tunica, MS
Harmonica, Vocals, Drums, Guitar / Electric Chicago Blues, Modern Electric Chicago Blues, Modern Electric Blues, Delta Blues
At his high-energy 1970s peak as a bandleader, James Cotton was a bouncing, sweaty, whirling dervish of a bluesman, roaring his vocals and all but sucking the reeds right out of his defenseless little harmonicas with his prodigious lungpower. Due to throat problems, Cotton's vocals are no longer what they used to be, but he remains a masterful instrumentalist.

Cotton had some gargantuan shoes to fill when he stepped into Little Walter's slot as Muddy Waters' harp ace in 1954, but for the next dozen years, the young Mississippian filled the integral role beside Chicago's blues king with power and precision. Of course, Cotton prepared for such a career move for a long time, having learned how to wail on harp from none other than Sonny Boy Williamson himself.

Cotton was only a child when he first heard Williamson's fabled radio broadcasts for *King Biscuit Time* over KFFA out of Helena, AR. So sure was Cotton of his future that he ended up moving into Williamson's home at age nine, soaking up the intricacies of blues harpdom from one of its reigning masters. Six years later, Cotton was ready to unleash a sound of his own.

Gigging with area notables Joe Willie Wilkins and Willie Nix, Cotton built a sterling reputation around West Memphis, following in his mentor's footsteps by landing his own radio show in 1952 over KWEM. Sam Phillips, whose Sun label was still a fledgling operation, invited Cotton to record for him, and two singles commenced: "Straighten Up Baby" in 1953 and "Cotton Crop Blues" the next year. Legend has it Cotton played drums instead of harp on the first platter.

When Waters rolled through Memphis minus his latest harpist (Junior Wells), Cotton hired on with the legend and came to Chicago. Unfortunately for the youngster, Chess Records insisted on using Little Walter on the great majority of Waters' waxings until 1958, when Cotton blew behind Waters on "She's Nineteen Years Old" and "Close to You." At Cotton's instigation, Waters had added an Ann Cole tune called "Got My Mojo Working" to his repertoire. Walter played on Muddy Waters' first studio crack at it, but that's Cotton wailing on the definitive 1960 reading (cut live at the Newport Jazz Festival).

By 1966, Cotton was primed to make it on his own. Waxings for Vanguard, Prestige, and Loma preceded his official full-length album debut for Verve Records in 1967. His own unit then included fleet-fingered guitarist Luther Tucker and hard-hitting drummer Sam Lay. Throwing a touch of soul into his eponymous debut set, Cotton ventured into the burgeoning blues-rock field as he remained with Verve through the end of the decade.

In 1974, Cotton signed with Buddah and released *100% Cotton,* one of his most relentless LPs, with Matt "Guitar" Murphy sizzlingly backing him up. A decade later, Alligator issued another standout Cotton LP, *High Compression,* that was split evenly between traditional-style Chicago blues and funkier, horn-driven material. *Harp Attack!,* a 1990 summit meeting on Alligator, paired Cotton with three exalted peers: Wells, Carey Bell, and comparative newcomer Billy Branch. Antone's Records was responsible for a pair of gems: a live 1988 set reuniting the harpist with Murphy and Tucker and a stellar 1991 studio project, *Mighty Long Time.*

Cotton still commands a huge following, even though serious throat problems (he sometimes sounds as though he's been gargling Drano) have tragically robbed him of his once-ferocious roar. That malady ruined parts of his last Grammy-nominated album for Verve, *Living the Blues;* only when he stuck to playing harp was the customary Cotton energy still evident. — *Bill Dahl*

Chicago/The Blues/Today!, Vol. 2 / 1964 / Vanguard ✦✦✦✦
Classic compilation, also starring Otis Rush and Homesick James. — *Bill Dahl*

The James Cotton Blues Band / 1967 / Verve ✦✦✦
Upbeat, soul-influenced mid-'60s work by Cotton's initial solo aggregation. — *Bill Dahl*

Cut You Loose! / 1967 / Vanguard ✦✦✦
One of Cotton's earlier solo efforts. — *Bill Dahl*

Pure Cotton / 1968 / Verve ✦✦✦

Cotton in Your Ears / 1968 / Verve ✦✦✦

Taking Care of Business / 1970 / Capitol ✦✦

100% Cotton / Mar. 1974 / One Way ✦✦✦✦
The ebullient, roly-poly Chicago harp wizard was at his zenith in 1974, when this cooking album was issued on Buddah. Matt "Guitar" Murphy matched Cotton note for zealous note back then, leading to fireworks aplenty on the non-stop "Boogie Thing," a driving "How Long Can a Fool Go Wrong," and the fastest "Rocket 88" you'll ever take a spin in. —*Bill Dahl*

High Energy / 1975 / One Way ✦✦
Shipping Cotton off to New Orleans during the mid-'70s to work with producer Allen Toussaint wasn't a good idea at all. The end result can for the most part be described as disco blues with a Crescent City funk tinge, without much to recommend it on any level. —*Bill Dahl*

Live & on the Move / 1976 / One Way ✦✦✦
Originally released on two vinyl platters in 1976 by Buddah, this set was digitally unleashed anew by the British Sequel label. It faithfully captures the boogie-burning capabilities of the mid-'70s Cotton outfit, fired by its leader's incendiary harp wizardry and Murphy's scintillating licks. —*Bill Dahl*

Dealing with the Devil / 1984 / Aim ✦✦✦✦

Two Sides of the Blues / 1984 / Intermedia ✦✦✦

● **High Compression** / 1984 / Alligator ✦✦✦✦
This is the best contemporary Cotton album gracing the shelves today, thanks to its ingenious formatting: half the set places Cotton in a traditional setting beside guitarist Magic Slim and pianist Pinetop Perkins, and a solid rhythm section; the other half pairs him with a contemporary combo featuring guitarist Michael Coleman's swift licks and a three-piece horn section. Both combinations click on all burners. Includes scorching theme song, "Superharp." —*Bill Dahl*

Live on the Move, Vol. 2 / 1986 / Buddah ✦✦✦

Live from Chicago Mr. Superharp Himself / 1986 / Alligator ✦✦
Thoroughly disappointing live collection taped at a Chicago nightspot called Biddy Mulligan's. Band is sloppy (especially horn section), and the harpist himself sounds uninspired. —*Bill Dahl*

Take Me Back / 1987 / Blind Pig ✦✦✦
Another back-to-the-roots campaign for the powerhouse harmonica ace, powered by guitarists Sammy Lawhorn and John Primer and piano patriarch Pinetop Perkins. Cotton attacks nothing but covers, largely of the Chicago subspecies: Little Walter's "My Babe," Jimmy Reed's "Take Out Some Insurance" and "Honest I Do," Muddy Waters' "Clouds in My Heart." Hardly indispensable, but heartfelt. —*Bill Dahl*

Live at Antone's / 1988 / Antone's ✦✦✦✦
Reuniting Cotton with his former guitarists Matt Murphy and Luther Tucker, pianist Pinetop Perkins, and Muddy Waters' ex-rhythm section (bassist Calvin Jones and drummer Willie Smith) looks like a great idea on paper, and it worked equally well in the flesh, when this set was cut live at Antone's Night Club in Austin, TX. —*Bill Dahl*

Harp Attack! / 1990 / Alligator ✦✦✦✦
Four Chicago harmonica greats, one eminently solid album. Teamed with Junior Wells, Billy Branch, and Carey Bell, Cotton sings Willie Love's Delta classic "Little Car Blues" and Charles Brown's "Black Night" and plays along with his cohorts on most of the rest of the set. —*Bill Dahl*

Mighty Long Time / 1991 / Antone's ✦✦✦✦
Although the titles are all familiar (most of them a little too much so), Cotton and his all-star cohorts (guitarists Jimmie Vaughan, Matt Murphy, Luther Tucker, Hubert Sumlin, and Wayne Bennett, the omnipresent Perkins on keys) pull the whole thing off beautifully. Cotton's cover of Wolf's "Moanin' at Midnight" is remarkably eerie in its own right, and he romps through Muddy Waters' "Blow Wind Blow" and "Sugar Sweet" with joyous alacrity. —*Bill Dahl*

3 Harp Boogie / 1994 / Tomato ✦✦
The music on this set is actually all right; it gets a low rating because of its odd patchwork assembly. Five of the tracks come from a 1963 acoustic session recorded at an apartment on the South Side, featuring Elvin Bishop on guitar, Cotton on vocals and harmonica, Paul Butterfield on harmonica, and Billy Boy Arnold on harmonica (hence the title *3 Harp Boogie*). The other four selections are taken from his 1967 Verve album *James Cotton Blues*

Band, available in its entirety on the *Best of the Verve Years* compilation. That means you probably only want this for the rarer acoustic cuts, which are good, but short value for a CD purchase, unless you're a very big Cotton fan. —*Richie Unterberger*

Living the Blues / 1994 / Verve ✦✦
All the guest stars in the world (Joe Louis Walker, Dr. John, Lucky Peterson, Larry McCray) can't mask the simple fact that Cotton's voice was thoroughly shot when he made this disc (apparently the Grammy nominating committee gratuitously overlooked this). The instrumentals, obviously, aren't affected by this malady; they're typically rousing. But whenever Cotton opens his mouth, he sounds as though he's been gargling Drano. —*Bill Dahl*

The Best of the Verve Years / 1995 / Polygram ✦✦✦✦
Taken from the high-energy harpist's first three albums for Verve following his split from Muddy Waters (including the entirety of his fine eponymous 1967 debut), this 20-track anthology is a fine spot to begin any serious Cotton collection. In those days, Cotton was into soul as well as blues—witness his raucous versions of "Knock on Wood" and "Turn on Your Lovelight," backed by a large horn complement. Compiler Dick Shurman has chose judiciously from his uneven pair of Verve follow-ups, making for a very consistent compilation. —*Bill Dahl*

Deep in the Blues / Aug. 1996 / Verve ✦✦✦
Deep in the Blues is a fascinating jam session between James Cotton, guitarist Joe Louis Walker, and jazz bassist Charlie Haden. The trio runs through a number of classic blues songs written by Muddy Waters, Percy Mayfield, and Sonny Boy Williamson and a few originals by Walker and Cotton. The sound is intimate and raw, which is a welcome change from Cotton's usual overproduced records. —*Thom Owens*

Robert Covington

b. Dec. 13, 1941, Yazoo City, MS, d. Jan. 17, 1996, Chicago, IL
Drums, Vocals / Modern Electric Blues
Robert Covington, born in Yazoo City, MS, on December 13, 1941, grew up taking music and voice lessons. Active as a teenager in drum and bugle corps, Covington played in a number of bands, including Little Melvin and the Downbeats. About to go to college (what became Alcorn State University in Lorman, MS), he chose instead to join Big Joe Turner's group when that player passed through town looking for a drummer. Turner's stage presence and vocal technique became a major inspiration and mentor for him, and they toured the South all that summer and fall.

In 1962, Covington had some small success with the Lee Covington Review and his single, "I Know." His group had a horn section, female backup signers, and backed groups like Ernie K-Doe and Ted Taylor.

Covington moved to Chicago in 1965 and played with Little Walter, Buddy Guy, Fenton Robinson, Junior Wells, and Lonnie "Guitar Junior" Brooks. He sat in with Sunnyland Slim at the Flying Fox and they began to work together on a regular basis. In 1983 he became a full-time member of the Sunnyland Slim Band. As Slim's frequency of performing declined (in his later years), Covington fronted his own band and established his own reputation. He was a hot act at Kingston Mines in Chicago, where he served as the swing singer; he even headlined one night a week. Covington's smooth delivery and big-band style voice has earned him the nickname, "golden voice." Robert Covington died on January 17, 1996, in Chicago. —*Michael Erlewine*

The Golden Voice of Robert Covington / 1988 / Evidence ✦✦✦✦
Covington wrote six of the nine songs on this album (formerly released in 1988 on Red Beans). Covington's strong reassuring voice is in good form, in particular on "Trust in Me." With Carl Weathersby on guitar. —*Michael Erlewine*

Ida Cox (Ida [Née Prather] Cox)

b. Feb. 25, 1896, Toccoa, GA, d. Nov. 10, 1967, Knoxville, TN
Vocals / Classic Female Blues
One of the finest classic blues singers of the '20s, Ida Cox was singing in theaters by the time she was 14. She recorded regularly during 1923-29 (her "Wild Woman Don't Have the Blues" and "Death Letter Blues" are her best-known songs). Although she was off record during much of the 1930s, Cox was able to continue working and in 1939 she sang at Cafe Society, appeared at John Hammond's "Spirituals to Swing" concert and made some new re-

cords. Ida Cox toured with shows until a 1944 stroke pushed her into retirement; she came back for an impressive final recording in 1961.

Cox left her hometown of Toccoa, GA as a teenager, travelling the south in vaudeville and tent shows, performing both as a singer and a comedienne. In the early '20s, she performed with Jelly Roll Morton, but she had severed her ties with the pianist by the time she signed her first record contract with Paramount in 1923. Cox stayed with Paramount for six years, recording 78 songs, which usually featured accompaniment by Love Austin and trumpeter Tommy Ladnier. During that time, she also cut tracks for a variety of labels, including Silvertone, using several different pseudonyms, including Velma Bradley, Kate Lewis, and Julia Powers.

During the '30s, Cox didn't record often, but she continued to perform frequently, highlighted by an appearance at John Hammond's 1939 "Spirituals to Swing" concert at Carnegie Hall. The concert increased her visibility, particularly in jazz circles—following the concert, she recorded with a number of jazz artists, including Charlie Christian, Lionel Hampton, Fletcher Henderson, and Hot Lips Page. She toured with a number of different shows in the early '40s until she suffered a stroke in 1944. Cox was retired for most of the '50s, but she was coaxed out of retirement in 1961 to record a final session with Coleman Hawkins. In 1967, Ida Cox died of cancer. — *Scott Yanow & Stephen Thomas Erlewine*

● **The Uncrowned Queen of the Blues** / Jun. 1923-Aug. 1924 / Black Swan ♦♦♦♦
Ida Cox was one of the most talented of the classic blues singers of the '20s. This Black Swan CD has 20 of her first 32 recordings and, although one regrets that it is not a "complete" series (hopefully the dozen other titles will be reissued by Black Swan eventually), the music is consistently enjoyable and timeless. In fact, quite a few of the lyrics (many of which were written by Cox) were later permanently "borrowed" by Jimmy Rushing and Joe Williams; the first stanza of "Goin' to Chicago" was taken from "Chicago Monkey Man Blues" and "Bear-Mash Blues" has a couple of Williams' best lines. When one considers that the music on this CD is taken from 1923-24, it can certainly be considered ahead of its time! Most of the musicians backing Ida Cox are excellent, particularly pianist Lovie Austin and (on five numbers) cornetist Tommy Ladnier and clarinetist Jimmy O'Bryant. The recording quality (even with some surface noise) has been greatly cleaned up for this reissue and Cox's singing is very easy to understand. Although uncrowned, Ida Cox (who after retiring in 1945 came back for a final recording in 1961) can still communicate to today's listeners, something that can be said about very few other singers from 1923. — *Scott Yanow*

★ **Blues for Rampart Street** / 1961 / Original Jazz Classics ♦♦♦♦♦
Classic blues singer Ida Cox had not recorded since 1940 nor performed regularly since the mid-'40s when she was coaxed out of retirement to record a date for Riverside in 1961. At 65 years old (some books list her as being 72), Cox's voice was a bit rusty and past its prime but she still had the feeling, phrasing and enough tricks to perform a strong program. With assistance from trumpeter Roy Eldridge, tenor saxophonist Coleman Hawkins, pianist Sammy Price, bassist Milt Hinton, and drummer Jo Jones (swing-era veterans who came up after Cox was already a major name), the singer does her best on such numbers as "Wild Women Don't Have the Blues," "Blues for Rampart Street," "St. Louis Blues," and "Death Letter Blues." Since she passed away in 1967, this final effort (reissued on CD) was made just in time and is well worth acquiring by 1920s jazz and blues collectors. — *Scott Yanow*

Wild Women Don't Have the Blues / Apr. 11, 1961-Apr. 12, 1961 / Rosetta ♦♦♦♦
Ida Cox's *Wild Women Don't Have the Blues* was recorded at the end of her career. Surprisingly, Cox's voice hadn't faded away—she could belt out a song with nearly as much power as she did in her early career. In fact, *Wild Women Don't Have the Blues* ranks as one of her finest albums. Not only is Cox in fine voice, the support Coleman Hawkins and his small group lends is strong and sympathetic, making this album one to treasure. — *Thom Owens*

Complete Recorded Works, Vol. 1 (1923) / Apr. 1, 1997 / Document ♦♦♦♦

Harry Crafton
Guitar, Vocals / Jump Blues
Not much is known about this Philadelphia-based guitarist and blues shouter. He produced some tasty jump blues and R&B in the early 50s for the Philly-based Gotham label with his band, the Jivetones (later, the Craft Tone). Later he recorded for various labels with the Nite Riders Orchestra, featuring blues pianist Harry Van Walls. Evidently influenced by guitarists T-Bone Walker and Tiny Grimes and vocalists Eddie "Cleanhead" Vinson and Jimmy Witherspoon. — *Niles J. Frantz*

Harry Crafton / 1987 / Collectables ♦♦

Robert Cray
b. Aug. 1, 1953, Columbus, GA
Guitar, Vocals / Modern Electric Blues, Contemporary Blues
Tin-eared critics have frequently damned him as a yuppie blues wanna-be whose slickly soulful offerings bear scant resemblance to the real downhome item. In reality, Robert Cray is one of a precious few young (at this stage, that translates to under 50 years of age) blues artists with the talent and vision to successfully usher the idiom into the 21st century without resorting either to slavish imitation or simply playing rock while passing it off as blues. Just as importantly, his immensely popular records helped immeasurably to jump-start the contemporary blues boom that still holds sway to this day.

Blessed with a soulful voice that sometimes recalls '60s-great O.V. Wright and a concise lead guitar approach that never wastes notes, Cray's rise to international fame was indeed a heartwarming one. For a guy whose 1980 debut album for Tomato, *Who's Been Talkin',* proved an instantaneous cut-out, his ascendancy was amazingly swift—in 1986 his breakthrough *Strong Persuader* album for Mercury (containing "Smoking Gun") won him a Grammy and shot his asking price for a night's work skyward.

An Army brat who grew up all over the country before his folks settled in Tacoma, WA, in 1968, Cray listened intently to soul and rock before becoming immersed in the blues (in particular, the icy Telecaster of Albert Collins, who played at Cray's high-school graduation!). Cray formed his first band with longtime bassist Richard Cousins in 1974. They soon hooked up with Collins as his backup unit before breaking out on their own.

The cinematic set caught a brief glimpse of Cray (even if they weren't aware of it) when he anonymously played the bassist of the frat party band Otis Day & the Knights in *National Lampoon's Animal House.* Cray's Tomato set, also featuring the harp of Curtis Salgado, was an excellent beginning, but it was the guitarist's 1983 set for HighTone, *Bad Influence,* that really showed just how full of talent Cray was.

Another HighTone set, *False Accusations,* preceded the emergence of the Grammy-winning 1985 guitar summit meeting album *Showdown!* for Alligator, which found the relative newcomer more than holding his own alongside Collins and Texan Johnny Copeland. *Strong Persuader* made it two Grammys in two years and made Cray a familiar face even on video-driven MTV.

Unlike too many of his peers, Cray continues to experiment within his two presiding genres, blues and soul. Sets such as *Midnight Stroll, I Was Warned,* and *Shame + a Sin* for Mercury show that the "bluenatics" (as he amusedly labels his purist detractors) have nothing to fear and plenty to anticipate from this innovative, laudably accessible guitarist. — *Bill Dahl*

Who's Been Talkin' / 1980 / Atlantic ♦♦♦♦
The Pacific Northwest-based blues savior's first album in 1980 boded well for his immediate future. Unfurling a sterling vocal delivery equally conversant with blues and soul, Cray offers fine remakes of the Willie Dixon-penned title tune, O.V. Wright's deep soul romp "I'm Gonna Forget About You," and Freddy King's "The Welfare (Turns Its Back on You)," along with his own "Nice as a Fool Can Be" and "That's What I'll Do." — *Bill Dahl*

☆ **Bad Influence** / 1983 / Hightone ♦♦♦♦♦
One of Cray's best albums ever, and the one that etched him into the consciousness of blues aficionados prior to his mainstream explosion. Produced beautifully by Bruce Bromberg and Dennis Walker, the set sports some gorgeous originals ("Phone Booth," "Bad Influence," "So Many Women, So Little Time") and two well-chosen covers, Johnny "Guitar" Watson's "Don't Touch Me" and Eddie Floyd's Stax-era "Got to Make a Comeback." Few albums portend greatness the way this one did. — *Bill Dahl*

False Accusations / 1985 / Hightone ♦♦♦♦
If its predecessor hadn't been so powerful, this collection might have been a little more striking in its own right. As it is, a solid if not overwhelming album sporting the memorable "Playin' in the Dirt" and "I've Slipped Her Mind." — *Bill Dahl*

Showdown [A Collins & J Copeland] / 1985 / Alligator ◆◆◆◆
Cray found himself in some pretty intimidating company for this Grammy-winning blues guitar summit meeting, but he wasn't deterred, holding his own alongside his idol Albert Collins and Texas great Johnny Copeland. Cray's delivery of Muddy Waters' rhumba-rocking "She's into Something" was one of the set's many highlights. —*Bill Dahl*

★ **Strong Persuader** / 1986 / Mercury ◆◆◆◆◆
The set that made Cray a pop star, despite its enduring blues base. Cray's smoldering stance on "Smoking Gun" and "Right Next Door" rendered him the first sex symbol to emerge from the blues field in decades, but it was his innovative expansion of the genre itself that makes this album a genuine 1980s classic. "Nothing but a Woman" boasts an irresistible groove pushed by the Memphis Horns and some metaphorically inspired lyrics, while "I Wonder" and "Guess I Showed Her" sizzle with sensuality. —*Bill Dahl*

Don't Be Afraid of the Dark / 1988 / Mercury ◆◆
A followup to *Strong Persuader,* this suffers from weak songs, but is worthwhile for fans. —*John Floyd*

Midnight Stroll / Jun. 1990 / Mercury ◆◆◆
Cray went into a more soul-slanted direction for this solid collection, coarsening his vocal cords for "The Forecast (Calls for Pain)" and the rest of the set. —*Bill Dahl*

Too Many Cooks / Sep. 1990 / Tomato ◆◆◆◆
Bluesman Robert Cray has occasionally been critized for mixing pop and funk elements in his music but no such criticism can be made about this CD reissue of his recording debut. It seems obvious in hindsight from the music that Cray would become a star for his appealing voice and strong guitar playing evident to both update and reinforce the blues tradition. This superior if brief (under 36-minute) session is recommended to all lovers of the blues. —*Scott Yanow*

I Was Warned / Apr. 1992 / Mercury ◆◆◆
Heavy on Southern-soul influence, Cray has the voice to pull it off. —*Bill Dahl*

Shame + a Sin / Oct. 5, 1993 / Mercury ◆◆◆◆
This time, Cray veered back toward the blues (most convincingly, too), even covering Albert King's "You're Gonna Need Me" and bemoaning paying taxes on the humorous "1040 Blues." Unlike his previous efforts, Cray produced this one himself. Also, longtime bassist Richard Cousins was history, replaced by Karl Sevareid. —*Bill Dahl*

Some Rainy Morning / May 9, 1995 / Mercury ◆◆◆
Typically well-produced and well-played outing—mostly originals, with smoldering covers of Syl Johnson's "Steppin' Out" and Wilson Pickett's "Jealous Love" for good measure. Cray's crisp, concise guitar work and subtly soulful vocals remain honed to a sharp edge. —*Bill Dahl*

Sweet Potato Pie / May 5, 1997 / Polygram ◆◆◆
Robert Cray always flirted with gritty Southern soul, but it wasn't until *Sweet Potato Pie* that he made a full-fledged soul-blues record in Memphis. Cray hasn't abandoned blues, but he's woven punchy horns and sexy rhythms into the mix, resulting in one of his stronger records of the '90s. The material remains a bit uneven, but his taste is impeccable—few blues guitarists are as succinct and memorable as he, and the soul settings of *Sweet Potato Pie* only confirm that fact. —*Thom Owens*

Pee Wee Crayton

b. Dec. 18, 1914, Rockdale, TX, **d.** Jun. 25, 1985, Los Angeles, CA
Guitar, Vocals / R&B, Electric West Coast Blues, West Coast Blues, Texas Blues
Although he was certainly inexorably influenced by the pioneering electric guitar conception of T-Bone Walker (what axe-handler wasn't during the immediate postwar era?), Pee Wee Crayton brought enough daring innovation to his playing to avoid being labeled as a mere T-Bone imitator. Crayton's recorded output for Modern, Imperial, and Vee-Jay contains plenty of dazzling, marvelously imaginative guitar work, especially on stunning instrumentals such as "Texas Hop," "Pee Wee's Boogie," and "Poppa Stoppa," all far more aggressive performances than Walker usually indulged in.

Like Walker, Connie Crayton was a transplanted Texan. He relocated to

Los Angeles in 1935, later moving north to the Bay Area. He signed with the Bihari brothers' L.A.-based Modern logo in 1948, quickly hitting paydirt with the lowdown instrumental "Blues After Hours" (a kissin' cousin to Erskine Hawkins' anthem "After Hours"), which topped the R&B charts in late 1948. The steaming "Texas Hop" trailed it up the lists shortly thereafter, followed the next year by "I Love You So." But Crayton's brief hitmaking reign was over, through no fault of his own.

After recording prolifically at Modern to no further commercial avail, Crayton moved on to Aladdin and, in 1954, Imperial. Under Dave Bartholomew's savvy production, Crayton made some of his best waxings in New Orleans—"Every Dog Has His Day," "You Know Yeah," and "Runnin' Wild" found Crayton's guitar turned up to the boiling point over the fat cushion of saxes characterizing the Crescent City sound.

From there, Crayton tried to regain his momentum at Vee-Jay in Chicago; 1957's "I Found My Peace of Mind," a Ray Charles-tinged gem, should have done the trick, but no dice. After one-off 45s for Jamie, Guyden, and Smash during the early '60s, Crayton largely faded from view until Vanguard unleashed his LP, *Things I Used to Do,* in 1971. After that, Pee Wee Crayton's profile was raised somewhat—he toured and made a few more albums prior to his passing in 1985. —*Bill Dahl*

☆ **Pee Wee Crayton** / 1959 / Crown ◆◆◆◆◆
An ancient but indispensable collection of his Modern label output, it includes the instrumentals "Texas Hop" and "Blues After Hours." —*Bill Dahl*

The Things I Used to Do / 1971 / Vanguard ◆◆◆◆
Pee Wee Crayton, a popular L.A.-based blues singer and guitarist, recorded frequently between 1947-57 but this 1970 session (reissued on CD) was his first LP and ended an eight-year drought in the studios. At 55, Crayton performed some country-flavored tunes and soul ballads but is at his best on the simpler straightahead blues such as a spirited "Let the Good Times Roll," the atmospheric instrumental "Blues After Hours," "Things I Used to Do," and "S.K. Blues" which at 6:24 is easily the longest performance of the brief 41-minute set. Although not a major stylist, Crayton is in good form throughout his date. —*Scott Yanow*

Rocking Down on Central Avenue / 1982 / Ace ◆◆◆◆
Nice vinyl selection of Crayton's Modern output, split between mellow vocals and blistering instrumentals. —*Bill Dahl*

● **Blues After Hours** / 1993 / P-Vine ◆◆◆◆
Regrettably, this is the only compact disc available of Crayton's brilliant early sides for Modern—and it's expensive, make no mistake. But it's worth it (until Pointblank sees fit to anoint us with a domestic collection, anyway)—its 19 sides include the essential instrumentals "Blues After Hours" and "Texas Hop," along with a variety of fine vocal efforts by this California blues guitar mainstay of the late '40s and early '50s. —*Bill Dahl*

Complete Aladdin & Imperial Recordings / Mar. 19, 1996 / Capitol ◆◆◆◆
Crayton was fading fast commercially by the time he cut these sides in the 1950s, though his vocal and instrumental skills, particularly his stinging guitar, were undimmed. Aside from two 1951 tracks cut for Aladdin in 1951, this 20-song compilation is devoted to his mid-'50s hitch with Imperial. The label had him record in New Orleans with Dave Bartholomew and other local musicians, giving many of these sides a hybrid jump blues/New Orleans R&B feel (Imperial would use the same approach with Roy Brown around this time). It's not his very best work, but even at its slightest this is pleasant. It's most effective, however, when the Crescent City touches are muted in favor of slicing straight-ahead blues riffing, as on the instrumental "Blues Before Dawn." Another obscure cut, "Do Unto Others," is nothing less than a revelation, boasting a light-years-ahead-of-its-time opening riff that sounds almost identical—we kid you not—to the blast of notes that opens the Beatles' "Revolution," cut nearly 15 years later. —*Richie Unterberger*

Cream

f. 1966, London, England, **db.** 1968
Group / Blues-Rock, Hard Rock, Psychedelic, Electric British Blues
Although Cream were only together for a little more than two years, their influence was immense, both during their late-'60s peak and in the years following their breakup. Cream were the first top group to truly exploit the

power-trio format, in the process laying the foundation for much blues-rock and hard rock of the 1960s and 1970s. It was with Cream, too, that guitarist Eric Clapton truly became an international superstar. Critical revisionists have tagged the band as overrated, citing the musicians' emphasis upon flash, virtuosity, and showmanship at the expense of taste and focus. This was sometimes true of their live shows in particular, but in reality the best of their studio recordings were excellent fusions of blues, pop, and psychedelia, with concise original material outnumbering the bloated blues jams and overlong solos.

Cream could be viewed as the first rock supergroup to become superstars, although none of the three members were that well known when the band formed in mid-1966. Eric Clapton had the biggest reputation, having established himself as a guitar hero first with the Yardbirds, and then in a more blues-intensive environment with John Mayall's Bluesbreakers. (In the States, however, he was all but unknown, having left the Yardbirds before "For Your Love" made the American Top Ten.) Bassist/singer Jack Bruce and drummer Ginger Baker had both been in the Graham Bond Organisation, an underrated British R&B combo that drew extensively upon the jazz backgrounds of the musicians. Bruce had also been, very briefly, a member of the Bluesbreakers along Clapton, and also briefly a member of Manfred Mann when he became especially eager to pay the rent.

All three of the musicians yearned to break free of the confines of the standard rock/R&B/blues group, in a unit that would allow them greater instrumental and improvisational freedom, somewhat in the mold of a jazz outfit. Eric Clapton's stunning guitar solos would get much of the adulation, yet Bruce was at least as responsible for shaping the group's sound, singing most of the material in his rich voice. He also wrote their best original compositions, sometimes in collaboration with outside lyricist Pete Brown.

At first Cream's focus was electrified and amped-up traditional blues, which dominated their first album, *Fresh Cream*, which made the British Top Ten in early 1967. Originals like "N.S.U." and "I Feel Free" gave notice that the band were capable of moving beyond the blues, and they truly found their voice on *Disraeli Gears* in late 1967, which consisted mostly of group-penned songs. Here they fashioned invigorating, sometimes beguiling hard-driving psychedelic pop, which included plenty of memorable melodies and effective harmonies along with the expected crunching riffs. "Strange Brew," "Dance the Night Away," "Tales of Brave Ulysses," and "S.W.L.A.B.R." are all among their best tracks, and the album broke the band bigtime in the States, reaching the Top Five. It also generated their first big US hit single, "Sunshine of Your Love," which was based around one of the most popular hard-rock riffs of the '60s.

With the double album *Wheels of Fire*, Cream topped the American charts in 1968, establishing themselves alongside the Beatles and Hendrix as one of the biggest rock acts in the world. The record itself was a more erratic affair than *Disraeli Gears*, perhaps dogged by the decision to present separate discs of studio and live material; the concert tracks in particular did much to establish their reputation, for good or ill, for stretching songs way past the ten-minute mark on stage. The majestically doomy "White Room" gave Cream another huge American single, and the group were firmly established as one of the biggest live draws of any kind. Their decision to disband in late 1968—at a time when they were seemingly on top of the world—came as a shock to most of the rock audience.

Cream's short lifespan, however, was in hindsight unsurprising given the considerable talents, ambitions, and egos of each of its members. Clapton in particular was tired of blowing away listeners with sheer power, and wanted to explore more subtle directions. After a farewell tour of the States, the band broke up in November 1968. In 1969, however, they were in a sense bigger than ever—a posthumous album featuring both studio and live material, *Goodbye*, made number two, highlighted by the haunting Eric Clapton-George Harrison composition "Badge," which remains one of Cream's most beloved tracks.

Clapton and Baker would quickly resurface in 1969 as half of another short-lived supergroup, Blind Faith, and Clapton of course went on to one of the longest and most successful careers of anyone in the rock business. Bruce and Baker never attained nearly as high a profile after leaving Cream, but both have kept busy in the ensuing decades with various interesting projects in the fields of rock, jazz, and experimental music. —*Richie Unterberger*

Fresh Cream / Dec. 1966 / Polydor ✦✦✦
Cream's debut album was largely rooted in the blues, and included here highly charged versions of such standards as Willie Dixon's "Spoonful," Muddy Waters' "Rollin' and Tumblin'," and bassist Jack Bruce's "N.S.U."—which took on a whole new life on stage. On this record they sound somewhat flat and uninspired. —*Rob Bowman*

Disraeli Gears / Nov. 1967 / Polydor ✦✦✦✦
Cream's sophomore effort was a substantial step forward. Interestingly, part of the reason seems to be that they stopped covering American blues musicians and started writing their own psychedelic blues-based hybrids. "Sunshine of Your Love" was the big AM radio hit and "Tales of Brave Ulysses," "Strange Brew," and "S.W.L.A.B.R." received substantial FM play. —*Rob Bowman*

Wheels of Fire / Jun. 1968 / Polydor ✦✦✦✦
Wheels of Fire was a two-album set, one disc recorded in the studio, the second disc recorded on stage in San Francisco. Side Three contains the definitive live version of what became Clapton's signature piece, Robert Johnson's "Crossroads," plus a version of "Spoonful" that clocks in just short of 17 minutes. On such pieces, Cream approached blues-based rock with a jazz aesthetic, using the song as a framework to begin and end a performance. The strength of the performance is in the improvisation. When it worked, as it does on "Spoonful," they were brilliant. When it didn't, as on "Traintime" and "Toad," the band became excess incarnate. The studio disc contained their second Top Ten single, Jack Bruce's "White Room," as well as a stunning cover of Albert King's "Born Under a Bad Sign." Other tracks, particularly those written by Ginger Baker, do not hold up. —*Rob Bowman*

Goodbye / Jan. 1969 / Polydor ✦✦✦
As the title implies, this is Cream's farewell. By the time it was issued, the band had broken up. Three studio recordings that were left were coupled with extended live versions of "I'm So Glad," "Politician," and "I'm Sitting on Top of the World." The live tracks burn. Clapton, Bruce, and Baker each take credit for one of the studio tracks. Clapton's cut, "Badge," was co-written by George Harrison and remains what was surely the prettiest melody to ever grace a Cream recording. —*Rob Bowman*

Live Cream, Vol. 1 / Apr. 1970 / Polydor ✦✦✦
Cream was a band born to the stage. This is their most consistently brilliant album. Four of the five cuts appeared on *Fresh Cream*. The fifth, "Lawdy Mama," is a traditional blues piece that makes its first appearance here. All but "Lawdy Mama" are given extended jazz-based treatment. The dialog among the three musicians as the jams develop is fascinating. Foreground and background seem to dissolve as all three musicians take charge, using the full range of their instruments. Performances like this single-handedly raised the stakes of musicianship in rock. —*Rob Bowman*

Live Cream, Vol. 2 / Mar. 1972 / Polydor ✦✦✦
More live Cream concentrating on material from their *Disraeli Gears* and *Wheels of Fire* albums plus an extended workout on Freddie King's "Hideaway." —*Rob Bowman*

Klook's Kleet '66 / 1995 / [bootleg] ✦✦✦✦
A significant addition to the pool of unreleased Cream material, this has eight alternate versions/outtakes from their earliest sessions in the summer of '66, as well as a different version of "Lawdy Mama" from '67, a Falstaff Beer commercial, and seven songs recorded live at the Klook's Kleet club in 1966. It's the studio outtakes that you'd want this for; the fidelity is phenomenal, at the same level of an official release. Contains alternate versions of many of the songs from their first album, with differences ranging from minor to major. "Sweet Wine," with a long extended feedback solo from Clapton, is particularly noteworthy, and "You Make Me Feel," an odd and frankly none too impressive bit of English pop, is an original that would never be released by the group. The liner notes say that the Kloots Kleet acetates were recorded for consideration as a live album, but it's hard to see how that would have happened, as the fidelity is tinny and the vocals muffled. More in line with the standards of typical live bootlegs of the era, it does offer serious fans the chance to hear (approximately) how they sounded onstage at their inception, with a few staples of their early repertoire ("N.S.U.," "Crossroads") and a couple less done-to-death numbers ("Meet Me In The Bottom," "Steppin' Out"). —*Richie Unterberger*

★ **The Very Best of Cream** / May 9, 1995 / Chronicles ♦♦♦♦♦
There have been many compilations drawn from the four albums Cream originally released between 1966 and 1969. But the one most commonly available since the early 1980s was the ten-track *Strange Brew: The Very Best of Cream* (1983) (Polydor 811 639), a bare-bones collection focusing on the group's hit singles. Note, then, that this album, despite the similar title, is a newly compiled 1995 CD/cassette containing all of the recordings on *Strange Brew*, plus ten more. It is thus the most comprehensive Cream anthology on the market, including all the group's essential tracks on a single disc with superior sound in a package containing good annotations. — *William Ruhlmann*

Those Were the Days / Sep. 23, 1997 / Polygram ♦♦♦♦
Those Were the Days is an ambitious four-disc, 63-track box set that divides Cream's career into two halves. The first two discs feature every studio track the group ever released, plus a handful of unreleased cuts, alternate takes and rarities. The other two discs are devoted to live material, which is segued together in an attempt to recreate the "ideal" Cream concert. It's a remarkably comprehensive collection, complete with an extensive booklet and remastered sound, yet it doesn't reveal any new insights about Cream, nor does it offer any invaluable rarities. Therefore, it's only for diehard collectors or listeners wanting to acquire the entire Cream catalog at once; casual fans will be satisfied with individual albums or greatest-hits collections. — *Stephen Thomas Erlewine*

Steppin' Out [bootleg] / Invasion Unlimited ♦♦♦
The best unreleased Cream to circulate widely, this collects 18 performances for the BBC between 1966 and 1968. Mostly very good sound, these fine straightahead renditions include most of the best tracks from their early albums, with the notable absence of their two biggest hits, "White Room" and "Sunshine Of Your Love." The two versions of the instrumental title track, one of Clapton's prime showcases in his Bluesbreakers days, are special highlights. These BBC sessions are available under a number of different guises; this particular package is the most thorough. — *Richie Unterberger*

Arthur "Big Boy" Crudup

b. Aug. 24, 1905, Forest, MS, **d.** Mar. 28, 1974, Nassawadox, VA
Guitar, Vocals / R&B, Electric Blues, Delta Blues, Electric Delta Blues
Arthur Crudup may well have been Elvis Presley's favorite bluesman. The swivel-hipped rock god recorded no less than three of Big Boy's Victor classics during his seminal rockabilly heyday — "That's All Right Mama" (Elvis' Sun debut in 1954), "So Glad You're Mine," and "My Baby Left Me." Often lost in all the hubbub surrounding Presley's classic covers are Crudup's own contributions to the blues lexicon. He didn't sound much like anyone else, and that makes him an innovator, albeit a rather rudimentary guitarist (he didn't even pick up the instrument until he was 30 years old).

Around 1940, Crudup migrated to Chicago from Mississippi. Times were tough at first — he was playing for spare change on the streets and living in a packing crate underneath an elevated train track when powerful RCA/Bluebird producer Lester Melrose dropped a few coins in Crudup's hat. Melrose hired Crudup to play a party that 1941 night at Tampa Red's house attended by the cream of Melrose's stable — Big Bill Broonzy, Lonnie Johnson, Lil Green. A decidedly tough crowd to impress — but Crudup overcame his nervousness with flying colors. By September of 1941, he was himself an RCA artist.

Crudup pierced the uppermost reaches of the R&B lists during the mid-'40s with "Rock Me Mama," "Who's Been Foolin' You," "Keep Your Arms Around Me," "So Glad You're Mine," and "Ethel Mae." He cut the original "That's All Right" in 1946 backed by his usual rhythm section of bassist Ransom Knowling and drummer Judge Riley, but it wasn't a national hit at the time. Crudup remained a loyal and prolific employee of Victor until 1954, when a lack of tangible rewards for his efforts soured Crudup on Nipper (he had already cut singles in 1952 for Trumpet disguised as Elmer James and for Checker as Percy Lee Crudup).

In 1961, Crudup surfaced after a long layoff with an album for Bobby Robinson's Harlem-based Fire logo dominated by remakes of his Bluebird hits. Another lengthy hiatus preceded Delmark boss Bob Koester's following the tip of Big Joe Williams to track down the elusive legend (Crudup had drifted into contract farm labor work in the interim). Happily, the guitarist's sound hadn't been dimmed by Father Time: his late-'60s work for Delmark rang true as he was reunited with Knowling (Willie Dixon also handled bass duties on some of his sides). Finally, Crudup began to make some decent money, playing various blues and folk festivals for appreciative crowds a few years prior to his 1974 death. — *Bill Dahl*

That's Allright Mama [Relic] / 1961 / Relic ♦♦♦
After a long studio hiatus, Crudup re-entered the studio in 1961 at the behest of producer Bobby Robinson of Fire/Fury Records. The results of their brief liaison show that Crudup hadn't altered his approach one whit during the layoff — these remakes of his RCA classics sound amazingly similar to the originals. There are a few unfamiliar titles aboard this 18-song collection to make it all the more worthwhile. — *Bill Dahl*

Mean Ol' Frisco / 1962 / Collectables ♦♦♦♦
These are his '60s Fire sessions. It fits into the second stage of his recording career, with *Look on Yonder's Wall* and *Coal Black Mare*. — *Barry Lee Pearson*

Look on Yonder's Wall / 1969 / Delmark ♦♦♦
This late-'60s Delmark session represents the third stage of his career history. — *Barry Lee Pearson*

☆ **The Father of Rock & Roll** / 1972 / RCA ♦♦♦♦♦
The best collection of Crudup's seminal '40s and '50s Bluebird recordings, including the original version of "That's All Right Mama." — *Barry Lee Pearson*

★ **That's Allright Mama** / 1992 / RCA ♦♦♦♦♦
This may not have been where rock 'n' roll all started, but it's very likely where Elvis Presley's knowledge of blues began: 22 tracks dating from 1941 to 1954 by the guitarist whose "That's All Right" proved Presley's ticket to Sun Records stardom. Crudup was fairly limited on guitar — his accompaniment is rudimentary at best — but his songs were uncommonly sturdy (Elvis also covered "So Glad You're Mine" and "My Baby Left Me," both here in their original incarnations) and his vocals strong. — *Bill Dahl*

Meets the Master Blues Bassists / 1994 / Delmark ♦♦♦
Delmark boss Bob Koester brought Crudup back from obscurity one more time during the late '60s, and by golly, he still sounded pretty much the same. The 1968-69 waxings comprising this disc date from 1968-69 and team the veteran guitarist with two upright bassists of legendary status: Willie Dixon and Crudup's longtime cohort Ransom Knowling. A few remakes are aboard, but plenty of new material as well. — *Bill Dahl*

Complete Recorded Works, Vol. 1 / Jun. 2, 1994 / Document ♦♦♦

Complete Recorded Works, Vol. 2 (1946-1949) / Jun. 2, 1994 / Document ♦♦♦

Complete Recorded Works, Vol. 3 (1949-1952) / Jun. 2, 1994 / Document ♦♦♦

Complete Recorded Works, Vol. 4 (1952-1954) / Jun. 2, 1994 / Document ♦♦♦

After Hours / 1997 / Camden ♦♦♦
After Hours is an uneven collection that combines Crudup's RCA material (recorded between 1941 and 1954) with material he recorded for Fire in the '60s. There's a few essential items here, but in general it's an ill-conceived collection that doesn't serve as a good overview of Crudup's career. — *Stephen Thomas Erlewine*

Cuby & the Blizzards

f. 1965, Grollo, Holland
Group / Blues-Rock
Although unknown to the English-speaking market, Cuby & the Blizzards have been one of Holland's top blues bands since the mid-'60s. Some of their early singles had a beat/punk orientation, particularly "Stumble & Fall" and "Your Body Not Your Soul," both of which would be reissued on various Dutch beat compilations a few decades later. They quickly settled into a straighter blues groove, however. Their claims to fame in the larger rock/pop world are that they briefly backed Van Morrison in the gap between his departure from Them and the beginning of his solo career, although details of the association remain murky; also, at one point lead guitarist Eelco Gel-

ling was asked to join John Mayall's Bluebreakers, although he declined. —*Richie Unterberger*

Desolation / 1966 / Philips ✦✦✦

By the time of their first LP, the group were already sliding toward a straighter blues outlook than had been explored on their more R&B/pop-flavored early singles. For that reason, it might disappoint mid-'60s beat fans looking for something wilder and catchier. As a blues group they were com-

petent, but the execution here is kind of lugubrious, and not up to the level of the best British blues acts with a similar repertoire. —*Richie Unterberger*

● **Best of 66-68** / 1968 / Philips ✦✦✦✦

The Best of 66-68 is a solid collection of Cuby & the Blizzards' best material from the mid-'60s. Although the material was fairly uneven, lead guitarist Eelco Gelling often shines, and the collection may be of interest to hardcore British blues fans. —*Thom Owens*

Larry Dale

b. 1923, Texas
Guitar / Electric Blues, R&B, East Coast Blues
A New York session guitarist who's backed some of the city's top artists, Larry Dale also made a handful of fine singles as a singer during the 1950s and early '60s.

Taking initial inspiration on his guitar from B.B. King during the early '50s, Dale made some solid sides as a leader for Groove in 1954 (including "You Better Heed My Warning"/"Please Tell Me") with a band that included another local guitar great, Mickey Baker, and pianist Champion Jack Dupree. Dale was a frequent studio cohort of the rollicking pianist, playing his axe on all four of Dupree's 1956-58 sessions for RCA's Groove and Vik subsidiaries and, under his legal handle of Ennis Lowery, on the definitive Dupree LP, 1958's *Blues from the Gutter,* for Atlantic. Dale also recorded with saxist Paul Williams during the mid-'50s for Jax, providing the vocal on "Shame Shame Shame."

Dale worked the New York club circuit during the '50s with pianist Bob Gaddy, who had a fairly successful single for Old Town in 1955, "Operator." From 1956 to 1958, Dale played with bandleader Cootie Williams before rejoining Gaddy. At last report, the two still played together.

Dale made most of his best sides as a leader when the decade turned. For Glover Records, he waxed the storming party blues "Let the Doorbell Ring" and an equally potent "Big Muddy" in 1960, then revived Stick McGhee's "Drinkin'-Wine-Spo-Dee-O-Dee" in 1962 on Atlantic. Alas, none of those worthy sides made much of a splash. *— Bill Dahl*

Billy Davenport

b. 1933, Chicago, IL
Drums / Modern Electric Blues, Chicago Blues
Drummer Billy Davenport was born April 23, 1931, in Chicago. His parents were sharecroppers from rural Alabama that migrated to Chicago in 1928. He began learning drums at the age of six, after finding an old pair of drumsticks in an alley behind the Twin Door Lounge on the South Side of Chicago. A natural musician, his parents soon recognized his gift and encouraged him. He started out playing on tin cans after seeing a movie about Gene Krupa. He also admired Sid Catlett. He took drum lessons while in the Boy Scouts and went on to play jazz in high school, in the R.O.T.C., in swing bands, and various venues in the Chicago area. In 1949, he studied music for one year at Midwestern School of Music in Chicago. He played with Bob Hadley, Leo Parker, Slam Stewart, Neal Anderson, Tampa Red, Sonny Stitt, and others. He got to hear everyone live—Billie Holiday, Charlie Parker, Billy Eckstine, Gene Ammons—all the greats. His drum influences included Art Blakey, Louis Bellson, and Max Roach.

From 1951 to 1955, Davenport was in the US Navy, in the Mechanic Drum and Bugle Corps. In the middle 1950s, the jazz scene was on the decline and Davenport turned to blues gigs to pay the rent. In the late '50s, he played with Billy Boy Armond, Dusty Brown, and Freddy King. In 1960 he played with the Ernie Fields Orchestra and joined Otis Rush in 1961, working with him for about a year. He also worked with harp player Little Mack Simmons, Syl Johnson, Junior Wells, Mighty Joe Young, James Cotton, Muddy Waters, and Howlin' Wolf.

He met Paul Butterfield at Pepper's Lounge in 1964 and sat in with them at their gig at Big Johns on Chicago's North Side. When Butterfield's drummer Sam Lay became ill late in 1965, Butterfield called on Davenport to join the group and tour with them. Davenport's jazz background brought a different quality to the Butterfield group. It was at this time that Bloomfield was absorbing Eastern scales and with the more sophisticated drumming of Davenport, they began to work on a tune they called "The Raga." This resulted in the tune "East/West," the extended tune that was to have such an impact on rock music history. Much of this success was due to Davenport's ability to add color and tone to the composition, something not generally found in straightahead blues drummers.

Davenport retired from music in 1968 due to illness, but was playing again from 1972-1974 with Jimmy Dawkins, Willie Dixon, and Buster Benton. He again retired from 1974 to 1981, after which he joined the Pete Baron Jazztet, with whom he still works. Davenport describes his own drumming as a combination of his two idols: the two base drums of Louis Bellson and the unique drum roll of Art Blakey. *—Michael Erlewine*

Charles "Cow Cow" Davenport
(Charles Edwards Davenport)

b. Apr. 23, 1894, Anniston, AL, **d.** Dec. 3, 1955, Cleveland, OH
Piano, Organ / Piano Blues
Charles "Cow Cow" Davenport is one of those seldom remembered names in the annals of early blues history. But a little investigation will unearth the salient fact that he played an important part in developing one of the most enduring strains of the music; yes, "Cow Cow" Davenport was one hell of a boogie-woogie piano player. Davenport worked on numerous vaudeville tours on the TOBA circuit in the '20s and early '30s, usually in the company of vocalist Dora Carr. While he's principally noted as the composer of his signature tune, "The Cow Cow Boogie," which would be revived by jazz band vocalist Ella Mae Morse during the boogie-woogie craze of the early '40s, he also claimed to have written Louis Armstrong's "I'll Be Glad When You're Dead, You Rascal You," selling the tune outright and receiving no royalties or composer credits. He recorded for a variety of labels from 1929 to 1946, eventually settling in Cleveland, Ohio, where he died in 1955 of hardening of the arteries. *— Cub Koda*

● **Charles "Cow Cow" Davenport 1926-1938** / 1926-1938 / Best of Blues ◆◆◆◆
The material ranges from magnificent Cow Cow Davenport solo tunes to good and not-so-good duets with a host of performers. Ivy Smith and Dora Carr are the artists with whom Davenport works best. Since these were dubbed from 78s, don't expect pristine sound. *—Ron Wynn*

Alabama Strut / 1979 / Magpie ◆◆◆◆
Alabama Strut largely consists of solo instrumental tracks Cow Cow Davenport recorded in the late '20s and early '30s. The centerpiece of the collection are three different versions of "Cow Cow Blues"—including a vocal with Dora Carr and one with a cornet—but what really captivates is the fluidity of Davenport's infectious boogie-woogie style. This is one of the best places to hear him play, but unfortunately it's a difficult record to find. *— Thom Owens*

Accompanist / Jun. 2, 1994 / Document ◆◆◆

Complete Recorded Works, Vol. 1 / Jun. 2, 1994 / Document ◆◆◆◆

Complete Recorded Works, Vol. 2 (1929-1945) / Jun. 2, 1994 / Document ◆◆◆◆

Complete Recorded Works, Vol. 3 / Mar. 2, 1998 / Document ◆◆◆◆

Lester Davenport

b. Jan. 16, 1932, Tchula, MS
Harmonica, Vocals / Electric Chicago Blues
Until 1992, Lester Davenport's chief claims to blues fame were the 1955 Bo Diddley Chess session he played harp on (it produced "Pretty Thing" and "Bring It to Jerome") and a lengthy, much more recent stint holding down the harmonica slot with the multi-generational Gary, IN band, the Kinsey Report. That instantly changed with the issue of Davenport's own album for Earwig, *When the Blues Hit You;* now this Chicago blues veteran has something on the shelves to call his very own.

Davenport hit Chicago in 1945 at age 14. He quickly soaked up the sights and sounds so prevalent on the local blues scene, checking out Arthur "Big Boy" Spires, Snooky Pryor, and Homesick James, who invited the youngster to jam sessions and tutored him on the intricacies of the idiom. Gigs with Spires and James preceded his brief hookup with Bo Diddley (which included a booking behind Diddley at New York's famous Apollo Theater). Davenport led his own band while holding down a day job as a paint sprayer during the 1960s, remaining active on the West side prior to joining forces with the Kinseys during the 1980s.

Now, about that "Mad Dog" handle: it seems that Davenport liked to prowl the stage while playing a few notes on every instrument on the bandstand during his younger days. The schtick earned him the name; his tenacious playing did the rest. *— Bill Dahl*

● **When the Blues Hit You** / Aug. 1991 / Earwig ◆◆◆◆
Although he'd been on the Chicago scene since the 1950s, backing Bo Diddley on some of his earliest Chess waxings, this was harpist "Mad Dog" Lester Davenport's long-overdue debut album. And a fine one it was, too, filled with mainstream Windy City blues immersed in the '50s tradition. His band for the project included pianist Sunnyland Slim and guitarist John Primer. *— Bill Dahl*

Cyril Davies

b. 1932, Denham, Buckinghamshire, England, **d.** Jan. 7, 1964, England
Harmonica, Vocals / Electric British Blues, British Blues
The Cyril Davies R&B All-Stars were, after the Rolling Stones, the best British blues band of the early '60s—and if they'd gotten to stay together a little longer under Davies, they might even have given Mick Jagger, Brian Jones, and company a real run for their money. This regrettably short-lived blues band was assembled by harpist/singer Cyril Davies (1932-1964) in 1963, following his exit from Blues Incorporated. The group's original lineup, featuring Davies on harp and vocals, featured Bernie Watson on guitar, Nicky Hopkins on piano, Ricky Brown playing bass, and Carlo Little on the drums—all four had been recruited from the ranks of Screaming Lord Sutch's Savages. This quintet recorded an initial single, "Country Line Special," driven by Davies' wailing harp and vocals, that was sufficiently authentic to get it placed alongside the British releases of songs by Muddy Waters, Howlin' Wolf, and the rest of the Chess Record luminaries in England's Pye Records catalog.

Watson and Brown went their separate ways during the summer of 1963, and Jeff Bradford and Cliff Barton came in on guitar and bass, respectively, with Long John Baldry—another Blues Incorporated alumnus—occasionally sitting in on vocals. Their second single, "Preachin' the Blues," was released in September to modest but promising success, and for a time it looked like Davies and company were going to be a major force on the burgeoning R&B scene. But Davies collapsed late in 1963, and was diagnosed as suffering from acute leukemia; he died in January of 1964.

Long John Baldry kept Hopkins, Bradford, Barton, and Little together as his back-up band, the Hoochie Coochie Men, but the moment had passed. Davies' vocals, though hardly overly impressive, had a character to them that made the group's records competitive during the early blues boom of 1962-63, and his harp playing was second to no one in England, a powerful, alternately mournful or exultant sound. Baldry, by contrast, never became more than a middle-level success in England, though it wasn't for lack of talent—he was a good singer, but by 1966 the audience for British blues was looking for flash along with the talent, and guitar players with charisma were more important than vocalists; witness the talent that Eric Clapton parlayed into international super-stardom, while John Mayall was left behind as a cult figure. Ironically, Baldry's biggest single exposure on record to international

audiences may have been as the speaker introducing the Rolling Stones on their 1966 concert album *Got Live If You Want It.* Nicky Hopkins subsequently emerged as a star session player in his own right, recording and performing with various bands (including the Rolling Stones) during the late '60s and '70s, and members of the All-Stars/Hoochie Coochie Men also turned up on Screaming Lord Sutch's recordings during this period, most notably his *Heavy Friends* album.

The Cyril Davies R&B All-Stars remain an impressive footnote in the history of British blues, however, for their handful of recordings, including "Country Line Special," "Preachin' the Blues," and a hard-rocking rendition of Buddy Holly's "Not Fade Away." They never recorded an album, but their songs appear on numerous anthologies including: *A Shot of Rhythm and Blues* (Sequel Records), *Stroll On* (Sony Music), and *Dealing with the Devil* (Sony Music). *— Bruce Eder*

The Legendary Cyril Davies / 1970 / Folklore ◆◆◆
Early acoustic sides by Davies and Korner, reissued in 1970 on the Folklore label. The two hadn't found their way yet, and while the playing is raw and interesting, the work is a little too unfinished to be truly representative of either artist. The Marquee Club album is more representative. *— Bruce Eder*

● **R&B from the Marquee** / 1971 / Decca ◆◆◆◆
The most important of Blues Incorporated's albums, this record features Davies all over it, and is his one reasonably representative album. He may be the best thing here, his blues harp the most accomplished and authentic sounding instrument, and his vocals are quite convincing and natural as well. *— Bruce Eder*

Dealing with the Devil: Immediate Blues, Vol. 2 / 1972 / Immediate ◆◆◆◆
A multi-artist compilation that includes Davies' and the All-Stars' cover of "Someday Baby." The rest ain't bad, neither. *— Bruce Eder*

Stroll On / 1992 / Sony ◆◆◆◆
Another compilation, this time featuring "Not Fade Away" and worthwhile on that basis alone. *— Bruce Eder*

Debbie Davies

b. Aug. 22, 1952, Los Angeles, CA
Guitar, Vocals / Modern Electric Blues
Like Joanna Connor and Sue Foley, Debbie Davies' first love was playing guitar. Writing good songs and developing her vocal chops came about later for this Los Angeles native now living in Connecticut. Born August 22, 1952, to musician parents in Los Angeles, Davies cut her teeth in the San Francisco Bay area, playing blues and rock 'n' roll for a time in college. Back in Los Angeles in 1986, she joined Maggie Mayall and the Cadillacs, an all-female R&B band led by John Mayall's wife before joining Albert Collins' Icebreakers in the late '80s. Collins used Davies to open his shows, and as part of Collins' band for three years, she got to travel throughout the US, Europe and Canada, playing dueling guitars nightly with Collins.

In 1991, Davies became lead guitarist for Fingers Taylor and the Ladyfingers Revue, a band made up with many of the nation's best female musicians. This group opened for Jimmy Buffett's "Outpost Tour."

Davies takes most of her inspiration from two blues guitar masters she's paid the most attention to, her late boss Albert Collins and Eric Clapton. A talented songwriter, vocalist, and most importantly, ensemble guitar player, Davies has been leading her own band since September, 1991. She has two excellent albums for the San Francisco-based Blind Pig label, *Picture This* (1993) and *Loose Tonight* (1994). *— Richard Skelly*

● **Picture This** / 1993 / Blind Pig ◆◆◆◆
Debbie Davies played with Albert Collins and that experience carries her through her debut album, *Picture This.* All the way through the album, she plays and sings with a barely restrained energy, spitting out burning leads and positively wailing her vocals. The album is a mixture of solid originals and classic covers, including a version of "I Wonder Why" that features a cameo from Collins. On the whole, *Picture This* is an exciting debut. *— Thom Owens*

Loose Tonight / 1994 / Blind Pig ◆◆◆
Davies' second album, *Loose Tonight,* contains the same high-octane blues, R&B and rock 'n' roll as her first, only delivered with a slightly rougher edge.

The roughness kick-starts the record into high gear, which means *Loose Tonight* delivers just as much thrills as *Picture This.* — *Thom Owens*

I Got That Feeling / 1996 / Blind Pig ✦✦✦✦
Davies' third album finds this artist moving in a much more "pop" direction, proving that she can both stretch her wings artistically and has far more to offer than merely recycled riffs and motifs filtered through a women's perspective. Her social consciousness raising quickly comes up for air on the opening track, "Howlin' at the Moon," one of only three Davies originals aboard this outing. But her interpretations of gospel pop ballad material like Lenny McDaniel's beautiful "Tired Angels," and duets with Coco Montoya on Albert Collins' title track and Tab Benoit on "Let the Heartaches Begin" are every bit as strong, her vocal skills showing more maturity and assuredness with each album. Her solo work is spot on, always paying homage to a wide variety of stylistic lessons well learned and solidly in the blues pocket with no added rock affectations to bog it down. But tracks like "Homework" (not the Otis Rush classic) make it clear that this is Debbie Davies being mainstreamed into Bonnie Raitt territory and she doesn't sound uncomfortable there at all, making this a most ambitious effort. — *Cub Koda*

Blind John Davis

b. Dec. 7, 1913, Hattiesburg, MS, **d.** Oct. 12, 1985, Chicago, IL
Piano, Vocals / Piano Blues
The piano work of John Davis was featured on blues records by the score during the '30s and '40s. His accompaniments to Tampa Red, Sonny Boy Williamson, Big Bill Broonzy, and others brought him fame as a blues musician, but like his piano compatriot Little Brother Montgomery, Davis did not care to be typecast as such and often expressed a preference for the sweet, sentimental favorites he played in countless piano lounges. But as with Montgomery, most of Davis' own recording opportunities came from blues companies, and he never failed to acquit himself well when it came to blues and boogie-woogie. He was the first pianist to do a European blues tour (with Broonzy in 1952), returning to the continent frequently as a solo act during the '70s and '80s. With blues-piano appreciation in Europe being what it is and has been, it's not surprising that most of the albums of Blind John Davis were recorded there and not in Chicago, his home from the age of two until his death. — *Jim O'Neal*

1938 / 1938 / Story of Blues ✦✦✦✦

Alive "Live" and Well / 1976 / Chrischaa ✦✦✦

● **Stompin' on a Saturday Night** / 1978 / Alligator ✦✦✦✦
Stompin' on a Saturday Night is a propulsive live set recorded in Germany in 1976 that captures the pianist late in his career. While he may be past his prime, he remains a terrific, instinctive pianist, and the record goes a long way towards proving his influence. — *Thom Owens*

You Better Cut That Out / 1985 / Red Beans ✦✦✦
His final session, with hot piano licks and failing vocals. — *Ron Wynn*

Blind John Davis / 1994 / Story of Blues ✦✦✦

Cedell Davis

b. Jun. 11, 1927, Helena, AR
Guitar, Vocals / Blues-Rock, Contemporary Blues
Cedell Davis was born in 1927 in Helena, AR. His right hand was crippled by polio at the age of ten, so he switched his guitar to a left-handed bottleneck style, which makes for a unique, atonal sound. He played locally throughout the 1950s and '60s, with friends such as Robert Nighthawk, Big Joe Williams, and Charlie Jordan. After a series of compilation appearances and several live dates in New York, Fat Possum Records signed Davis. Noted blues journalist Robert Palmer produced his debut, *Feel like Doin' Something Wrong* (1994). *The Best Of …* (1995) was also released, with help from Col. Bruce Hampton & the Aquarium Rescue Unit. — *John Bush*

Feel like Doin' Something Wrong / 1994 / Fat Possum ✦✦✦✦
Produced by blues historian and journalist Robert Palmer, *Feel like Doin' Something Wrong* captures the haunted, otherworldly blues of Cedell Davis. Using a knife for a guitar slide, Davis creates strange, unpredictable sounds and matches them with his gnarled voice. Even better, there's hardly a bad song in the bunch, and his versions of "Murder My Baby," "Boogie Chillen,"

"Every Day Every Way," and "If You Like Fat Women" rank among the finest contemporary blues in the '80s. — *Stephen Thomas Erlewine*

Cedell Davis / 1994 / Capricorn ✦✦✦

● **The Best of Cedell Davis** / Jan. 24, 1995 / Fat Possum ✦✦✦✦
Cedell Davis' guitar tunings are quite unique—he seems to have some sort of internal scale that makes for brilliant blues guitar and very difficult band performances (for this album he's backed up by Col. Bruce Hampton and members of the Aquarium Rescue Unit). What's amazing is that the sometimes atonal result works beautifully—it's a razorlike mix in that it's cutting and makes for tense social situations, but it's a standout blues album, with Davis' busted-up voice being pushed along by the ARU/Davis music train. A quirky surprise. — *Steven McDonald*

Horror of It All / May 19, 1998 / Epitaph ✦✦✦

Reverend Gary Davis

b. Apr. 30, 1896, Laurens, SC, **d.** May 5, 1972, Hammonton, NJ
Guitar, Vocals / Country Blues, Piedmont Blues, Blues Gospel, Prewar Country Blues
In his prime of life, which is to say the late '20s, the Reverend Gary Davis was one of the two most renowned practitioners of the East Coast school of ragtime guitar; 35 years later, despite two decades spent playing on the streets of Harlem in New York, he was still one of the giants in his field, playing before thousands of people at a time, and an inspiration to dozens of modern guitarist/singers including Bob Dylan, Taj Mahal, Donovan, Jorma Kaukonen, David Bromberg, and Ry Cooder, who studied with Davis.

Davis was partially blind at birth, and lost what little sight he had before he was an adult. He was self-taught on the guitar, beginning at age six, and by the time he was in his 20s he had one of the most advanced guitar techniques of anyone in blues—his only peers among ragtime-based players were Blind Arthur Blake, Blind Lemon Jefferson, and Blind Willie Johnson. Davis himself was a major influence on Blind Boy Fuller.

Davis' influences included gospel, marches, ragtime, jazz, and minstrel hokum, and he integrated them into a style that was his own. In 1911, when Davis was a still teenager, the family moved to Greenville, SC, and he fell under the influence of such local guitar virtuosi as Willie Walker, Sam Brooks, and Baby Brooks. Davis moved to Durham in the mid-'20s, by which time he was a full-time street musician, and celebrated not only for the diversity of styles that his playing embraced, but also for his skills with the guitar, which were already virtually unmatched in the blues field.

Davis went into the recording studio for the first time in the '30s with the backing of a local businessman. Davis cut a mixture of blues and spirituals for the American Record Company label, but there was never an equitable agreement about payment for the recordings, and following these sessions, it was 19 years before he entered the studio again. During that period, he went through many changes. Like many other street buskers, Davis always interspersed gospel songs amid his blues and ragtime numbers, to make it harder for the police to interrupt him. He began taking the gospel material more seriously, and in 1937 he became an ordained minister. After that, he usually refused to perform any blues.

Davis moved to New York in the early '40s and began preaching and playing on streetcorners in Harlem. He recorded again at the end of the 1940s, with a pair of gospel songs, but it wasn't until the mid-'50s that a real following for his work began developing anew. His music, all of it now of a spiritual nature, began showing up on labels such as Stinson, Folkways, and Riverside, where he recorded seven songs in early 1956. Davis was "rediscovered" by the folk revival movement, and after some initial reticence, he agreed to perform as part of the budding folk music revival, appearing at the Newport Folk Festival, where his raspy voiced sung sermons, most notably his transcendent "Samson and Delilah (If I Had My Way)"—a song most closely associated with Blind Willie Johnson—and "Twelve Gates to the City," were highlights of the proceedings for several years. He also recorded a live album for the Vanguard label at one such concert, as well as appearing on several Newport live anthology collections. He was also the subject of two television documentaries, one in 1967 and one in 1970.

Davis became one of the most popular players on the folk revival and blues revival scenes, playing before large and enthusiastic audiences—most of the songs that he performed were spirituals, but they weren't that far removed from the blues that he'd recorded in the 1930s, and his guitar technique was intact. Davis' skills as a player, on the jumbo Gibson acoustic models that he favored, were undiminished, and he was a startling figure to hear, picking and strumming complicated rhythms and countermelodies. Davis became a teacher during this period, and his students included some very prominent White guitar players, including David Bromberg and the Jefferson Airplane's Jorma Kaukonen (who later recorded Davis' "I'll Be Alright" on his acclaimed solo album *Quah!*).

The Reverend Gary Davis left behind a fairly large body of modern (i.e. post-World War II) recordings, well into the 1960s, taking the revival of his career in his stride as a way of carrying the message of the gospel to a new generation. He even recorded anew some of his blues and ragtime standards in the studio, for the benefit of his students. — *Bruce Eder*

American Street Songs / Aug. 8, 1956 / Riverside ◆◆◆

Pure Religion & Bad Company / 1957 / Smithsonian/Folkways ◆◆◆◆
Moses Asch became the first producer to record Davis in a full-length album release, showcasing his dazzling guitar style more fully than ever before. — *Bruce Eder*

Say No to the Devil / 1958 / Bluesville ◆◆◆◆
Say No to the Devil is Rev. Gary Davis' third Bluesville album and it was originally released in 1961. Davis was in fine form throughout the session, playing some startlingly intricate 12-string guitar licks, blowing some rootsy harp, and singing with conviction. Between the songs, Davis tells some rambling stories, which are just as gripping and fascinating as the music itself. — *Thom Owens*

At Newport / 1959 / Vanguard ◆◆◆◆
One of the finest single artist albums to come out of Newport, not quite in the league of Muddy Waters' performance but a superb introduction to the range of his repertory, from ragtime and novelty tunes to gospel numbers. — *Bruce Eder*

☆ **1935-1949** / 1960 / Yazoo ◆◆◆◆◆
Davis' first recordings, encompassing his short-lived 1930s studio career and a pair of sides from after the war. The 1930s material is the real article, Davis in his prime as a singer and player. — *Bruce Eder*

Harlem Street Singer / Aug. 1960 / Bluesville ◆◆◆◆

Gospel, Blues, & Street Songs / Jul. 1961 / Riverside ◆◆◆◆
Eight of Davis' best-known gospel songs, cut in 1956 in New York, and among the most glowing sides of his career. Paired up with seven tracks cut by Pink Anderson for Riverside in 1950. — *Bruce Eder*

At "Al Matthes," / 1966 / ◆◆◆
At "Al Matthes" is taken from a collection of private acetates from 1966 and the sound suffers somewhat, but not the performances. Rev. Gary Davis runs through a selection of blues and rags — his performances are divided equally between instrumentals and vocals. Davis is relaxed and engaging, making this a small rough gem in his catalog. — *Thom Owens*

Rev. Gary Davis at Newport / 1967 / Vanguard ◆◆◆◆

New Blues & Gospel / 1971 / ◆◆◆
As the title suggests, *New Blues & Gospel* is equally divided between blues and gospel recordings. Recorded in 1971, Gary Davis was past his prime when these tracks were cut, but he still manages to invest the songs with grit and passion. It's a minor entry in his catalog, but completists will find the album of interest. — *Thom Owens*

From Blues to Gospel / Mar. 1971 / Biograph ◆◆◆
This particular set was recorded one year before Davis' death, when he was 76 years old. Producer Arnold Caplin has combined two LPs to create this package and believes these to be the artist's very last recordings. Although the master-picker pulls off some prodigious playing here — on both the six-and 12-string guitars — he is no match for his own earlier work recorded between 1935-60. Listeners already familiar with the younger Davis' playing will feel great affection and gratitude for these last recordings. — *Larry Hoffman*

When I Die I'll Live Again / 1972 / Fantasy ◆◆◆
This two-fer offers Davis' best work of the '60s. — *Richard Lieberson*

At the Sign of the Sun / 1973 / Gospel Heritage ◆◆◆
Fine later performances are included on this CD. — *Richard Lieberson*

Blind Gary Davis / 1974 / Document ◆◆◆◆
All of Davis' stunning early recordings (1935-1949). — *Kip Lornell*

O Glory / Jan. 1974 / Adelphi ◆◆

Blues & Ragtime / 1993 / Shanachie ◆◆◆◆
The Rev. Gary Davis forsook his gospel calling for a little while between 1962 and 1966 to set down formal studio versions of many of his most important blues and ragtime repertory. Some of the material here runs over ten minutes, as Davis lays out his best playing and singing voice. The booklet includes a fairly detailed biography as well as musical annotation. — *Bruce Eder*

Complete Works (1935-1949) / 1994 / Document ◆◆◆◆
The multi-volume series *Rev. Blind Gary Davis: Complete Works (1935-1949)* presents every track the guitarist recorded during the late '30s and '40s. Although there is a staggering amount of brilliant music here, it is presented in a way that makes it of interest only to historians and completists. Most of the best material here is available on more concise collections, and the majority of blues fans will find those albums, particularly Yazoo's *Complete Early Recordings*, preferable to this massive series. — *Thom Owens*

★ **Complete Early Recordings** / 1994 / Yazoo ◆◆◆◆◆
Complete Early Recordings collects the highlights of Rev. Gary Davis' work from the late '30s, presented in an intelligent and wisely-sequenced fashion. This is country blues at its purest and finest, and a necessary addition to nearly any blues collection. — *Thom Owens*

O, Glory: The Apostolic Studio Sessions / 1996 / Genes ◆◆◆
Recorded in 1969, *O, Glory: The Apostolic Studio Sessions* is the Rev. Gary Davis' final studio LP, but he went out in style, working under the most state-of-the-art studio conditions of his career. The result is perhaps the best-sounding record in his catalog, even if the performances don't quite capture all the fire of his peak period; equally interesting is another break in tradition — rarely recorded with other artists (outside of a few early-'50s sides cut with Sonny Terry), here Davis is backed by vocalist Sister Annie Davis, harpist Larry Johnson, and the Apostolic Family Chorus. Also worth noting is that Davis performs on a pair of instruments he'd never before recorded with, the piano and the five-string banjo. The cumulative result makes *O Glory* a must for historians, but casual fans will undoubtedly be better served by his earlier material. — *Jason Ankeny*

Guy Davis

b. May 12, 1952, Manhattan, New York, NY
Guitar, Vocals / Modern Acoustic Blues
Updating the rural blues tradition for the modern era, Guy Davis was among the most prominent ambassadors of African-American art and culture of his generation, additionally winning great acclaim for his work in the theater. The son of the noted actors, directors, and activists Ossie Davis and Ruby Dee, he was born in New York City on May 12, 1952; though raised in the city, Davis was frequently regaled with stories of Southern country life as a child, and over time became so enamored of the music of Blind Willie McTell, Skip James, Mississippi John Hurt, and others that he taught himself guitar. As a 13-year-old experiencing his first Buddy Guy concert, Davis' own fate as a bluesman was sealed, especially after he learned his distinctive fingerpicking style from a nine-fingered guitarist he met on a train traveling from Boston to New York some years later.

In 1978, Davis recorded his debut LP *Dreams About Life*, produced for the Folkways label with the assistance of the legendary Moses Asch; around the same time he also began pursuing a career as an actor, landing a recurring role on the daytime soap *One Life to Live* and also appearing in the 1984 hip-hop film *Beat Street*. Long seeking to combine his shared love of music and acting, in 1991 Davis finally found a project that fulfilled all of his ambitions — *Mulebone*, the Broadway production of a Zora Neale Hurston and Langston Hughes collaboration which included a score by Taj Mahal. Two years later, Davis earned rave reviews for his work in the title role of the off-Broadway production *Robert Johnson: Trick the Devil*, with his portrayal later winning the Blues Foundation's W.C. Handy "Keeping the Blues Alive" Award.

In 1994, Davis wrote and starred in the one-man show *In Bed with the Blues: The Adventures of Fishy Waters*, another blues-based off-Broadway drama which played to strong critical notice. A year later, he collaborated with his parents on *Two Hah Hahs and a Homeboy*, which combined original material with African-American folklore and history. Around the same time, he also composed the music for the PBS series *The American Promise;* his score for an earlier telefilm, *To Be a Man*, won an Emmy. During the fall of 1995, Davis returned to writing and performing in the acoustic country-blues tradition with renewed force, issuing the live LP *Stomp Down Rider* on the Red House label; a year later, he returned with *Call Down the Thunder. You Don't Know My Mind* followed in 1998. — *Jason Ankeny*

● **Stomp Down the Rider** / Oct. 17, 1995 / Red House ◆◆◆◆
Guy Davis' debut, *Stomp Down the Rider*, is a surprisingly fresh collection of acoustic blues, entirely comprised of original material. Davis already sounds like a seasoned pro, delivering crisp, intelligent, and passionate songs that suggest he's only beginning to achieve his potential. — *Thom Owens*

Call Down the Thunder / Oct. 15, 1996 / Red House ◆◆◆
From the infectious opening notes of "Georgia Jelly Roll" through the stomping sounds of the closing "New Shoes," this is honest, raw, from-the-gut blues music, imbued with the joy of a gospel meeting. Guy Davis is a master storyteller, penning ten of the 13 songs included here. His slide playing is exceptional and at times very reminiscent of Robert Johnson. — *Bob Gottlieb*

You Don't Know My Mind / Apr. 21, 1998 / Red House ◆◆◆
Davis continues his exploration of blues-pop, mixing Delta styles with a more polished AOR sound, similar to Taj Mahal's *Like Never Before* album. While blues purists may not appreciate this blend, the music is accessible and Davis has a gutsy growl that gives the songs extra bite. — *Tim Sheridan*

James Davis

b. Nov. 10, 1938, Prichard, AL, **d.** Jan. 24, 1992, St. Paul, MN
Vocals / Modern Electric Blues, Texas Blues
James Davis went out the way entertainers often dream of. While performing at the Blues Saloon in St. Paul, MN, he suffered a fatal heart attack in mid-set and died onstage. The tragic event ended a comeback bid that warmed the heart of blues aficionados; Davis' whereabouts were so unknown prior to his triumphant reemergence that he was rumored to be dead.

His melismatic vocal delivery betraying strong gospel roots, Davis secured his first pro gig in 1957 as opening act for Guitar Slim. The flamboyant guitarist was responsible for tagging Davis with his "Thunderbird" moniker. Davis lost a drinking contest to his boss that sent him to the hospital; the singer's libation of choice that fateful day was Thunderbird wine (which Davis swore off for life).

Davis signed on with Don Robey's Houston-based Duke Records in 1961. Robey utilized his new discovery as a demo singer for Bobby Bland when Davis wasn't cutting his own singles. Two of Davis' Duke offerings, the tortured blues "Blue Monday" and "Your Turn to Cry," rank with finest blues 45s of the early '60s but did little for Davis at the time. He left Duke in 1966, opening for Joe Tex and O.V. Wright on the road before settling down.

After just about giving up entirely on show biz, Davis was tracked down in Houma, LA, by Black Top Records boss Hammond Scott and two cohorts. A 1989 album called *Check Out Time* was the happy result; sidemen on the date included two former cohorts, bassist Lloyd Lambert (Guitar Slim's bandleader) and guitarist Clarence Hollimon. The resultant acclaim catapulted Davis back into the limelight for the last years of his life. — *Bill Dahl*

Check Out Time / 1989 / Black Top ◆◆◆◆
Thought by many to be deceased, singer James Davis returned from musical invisibility to make this sparkling comeback set for Black Top. His hearty pipes sounding anything but over-the-hill, Davis roared a combination of his own fine tunes and remakes of songs first done by Bobby Bland, James Carr, and Wynonie Harris in front of a terrific combo (guitarists Anson Funderburgh and Clarence Hollimon, saxist Grady Gaines). A revival of his own slow blues "Your Turn to Cry" recalled Davis' early-'60s glory days. — *Bill Dahl*

Larry Davis

b. Dec. 4, 1936, Kansas City, MO, **d.** Apr. 19, 1994, Los Angeles, CA
Guitar, Vocals / Soul Blues, Modern Delta Blues, Electric Texas Blues, Texas Blues
Anyone who associates "Texas Flood" only with Stevie Ray Vaughan has never auditioned Larry Davis' version. Davis debuted on vinyl in 1958 with

the song, his superlative Duke Records original remaining definitive to this day despite Vaughan's impassioned revival many years down the road.

Davis grew up in Little Rock, AR, giving up the drums to play bass. Forging an intermittent partnership with guitarist Fenton Robinson during the mid-'50s, the pair signed with Don Robey's Duke label on the recommendation of Bobby Bland. Three Davis 45s resulted, including "Texas Flood" and "Angels in Houston," before Robey cut Davis loose. From there, Davis was forced to make the most of limited opportunities in the studio. He lived in St. Louis for a spell and took up the guitar under Albert King's tutelage while playing bass in King's band.

A handful of singles for Virgo and Kent and a serious 1972 motorcycle accident that temporarily paralyzed Davis' left side preceded an impressive 1982 album for Rooster Blues, *Funny Stuff*, produced by Gateway City mainstay Oliver Sain. But follow-up options remained hard to come by: few blues fans could find a copy of the guitarist's 1987 Pulsar LP *I Ain't Beggin' Nobody*.

Finally, in 1992, Ron Levy's Bulleye Blues logo issued a first-class Davis set, *Sooner or Later*, that skillfully showcased his rich, booming vocals and concise, Albert King-influenced guitar. Unfortunately, it came later rather than sooner—Davis died of cancer in the spring of 1994. — *Bill Dahl*

Funny Stuff / 1982 / Rooster Blues ◆◆◆◆
Larry Davis didn't record all that often, but when he did, he certainly made it count. That's the case with this fine St. Louis recording, not available yet on CD but well worth searching for at your favorite used vinyl emporium. Produced by Oliver Sain (who handled all sax work) and featuring Billy Gayles on drums and pianist Johnnie Johnson, the set is a ringing endorsement of Davis' slashing, tremolo-enriched guitar and booming vocals. — *Bill Dahl*

I Ain't Beggin' Nobody / 1987 / Evidence ◆◆◆◆
Only bad luck and the follies of the record industry have prevented Larry Davis from being the well-known blues star he should be. Davis has never received either sustained label support or concentrated marketing and thus is only a footnote when he should be a full chapter. His playing is energetic and varied, while his vocals are animated, soulful, and expressive. He recorded the nine tracks on this '85 date (newly reissued on CD by Evidence) with longtime blues and soul producer and instrumentalist Oliver Sain at the controls, and Davis demonstrated his convincing appeal on Sain's title track, as well as the defiant "I'm a Rolling Stone" (another Sain original), Davis' own anguished "Giving Up On Love," and "Please Don't Go," a Chuck Willis composition. — *Ron Wynn*

● **Sooner or Later** / 1992 / Bullseye Blues ◆◆◆◆
Unless someone has the ultimate Larry Davis album still awaiting release somewhere, the late guitarist's final album also looks to be his best. Sumptuously produced by organist/Bullseye Blues boss Ron Levy with the Memphis Horns providing punchy interjections, Davis roars a finely conceived concoction of covers and his own material ("Goin' Out West," "Little Rock") that represent contemporary blues at its finest. — *Bill Dahl*

Blues Knights / 1994 / Evidence ◆◆◆
Two underrated blues guitarists for the price of one. — *Bill Dahl*

Little Sammy Davis

b. Mississippi
Harmonica, Vocals / Electric Harmonica Blues, Delta Blues, Piedmont Blues
No, he never hung out with the Rat Pack on the martini-stained Vegas strip, and it's highly doubtful that he honors requests for "The Candy Man." This Little Sammy Davis is a veteran harp blower with a discography dating back to 1952 and a fine new debut album on Delmark, *I Ain't Lyin'.*

Where's he been all these years? Poughkeepsie, New York, of course!

Davis learned his way around a harmonica at age eight. He eventually exited Mississippi for Florida, where he worked in the orange groves and met immaculate guitarist Earl Hooker. Davis cut four sides in 1952 for Henry Stone's Rockin' label in Miami as Little Sam Davis (with Hooker providing classy accompaniment) that comprised the bulk of his discography until recently. He visited Chicago in 1953, hanging out with harp genius Little Walter, Jimmy Reed, and Muddy Waters. But Davis rambled on, eventually settling in Poughkeepsie.

Other than a 45 for Pete Lowry's Trix logo, things were pretty quiet for our hero until a few years back, when he joined forces with guitarist Fred Scribner and got back into playing. Now, he's a favorite guest of popular New York morning radio personality Don Imus, he has his own band and an album on the shelves, and with any luck at all, nobody will mistake him for another diminutively proportioned entertainer by the same name. —*Bill Dahl*

I Ain't Lyin / Oct. 3, 1995 / Delmark ✦✦✦✦
From out of nowhere came Little Sam Davis with this sterling set, making it clear that at least a few blues harpists of post-war vintage are still roaming around out there, just waiting to be rediscovered. Backed by a sharp rhythm section, Davis shows that he's been keeping his ear to the ground over the decades. His harp mastery and enthusiastic vocals are equally arresting. —*Bill Dahl*

Maxwell Davis

b. Jan. 14, 1916, Independence, KS, **d.** Sep. 18, 1970, Los Angeles, CA
Sax (Tenor) / Electric West Coast Blues
As a prolific all-purpose producer/songwriter/sideman, tenor saxman Maxwell Davis filled some of the same pivotal roles on the 1950s Los Angeles R&B scene that Willie Dixon handled so skillfully in Chicago. Davis arranged and produced a myriad of West Coast sessions for Modern, Aladdin, and other postwar R&B indies from the late '40s on, lending his husky sax to scads of waxings.

Davis left Kansas for L.A. in 1937, working in Fletcher Henderson's orchestra before being bitten by the R&B bug. Modern/Kent probably kept him employed the steadiest throughout the '50s and '60s; he worked with Pee Wee Crayton, Etta James, Johnny "Guitar" Watson, Lowell Fulson, Z.Z. Hill, and plenty more on the Bihari brothers' star-studded roster. Over at Aladdin, he worked closely with Amos Milburn and Peppermint Harris, among others. Davis didn't have much luck recording as a bandleader, although his instrumentals "Look Sharp—Be Sharp" (an R&B adaptation of the Gillette march) for Aladdin and "Tempo Rock"/"Cool Diggin'" on RPM packed a wallop. —*Bill Dahl*

● **Father of West Coast R&B** / Ace ✦✦✦✦
Ace's *Father of West Coast R&B* is an excellent 14 track collection of the tenor saxophonist's '50s and '60s records. There are several solo sides, plus cuts featuring him with Lloyd Glenn and Gene Phillips' orchestras. Since it features Maxwell Davis as both a leader and a sideman, the collection is a nice overview of his peak years. — *Thom Owens*

Maxwell Street Jimmy Davis

b. Mar. 2, 1925, Tippo, Mississippi, **d.** Dec. 28, 1995
Guitar, Vocals / Modern Electric Blues
A protégé of John Lee Hooker, Maxwell Street Jimmy Davis was a Chicago blues institution throughout the latter half of the 20th century. Born Charles W. Thompson on March 2, 1925 in Tippo, Mississippi, he learned to play guitar from Hooker while still a teenager, developing an insistent single-chord technique similar to that of his mentor; Davis and Hooker regularly gigged together in Detroit throughout the 1940s, with the former settling in Chicago early the next decade. There he became a fixture of the West Side's Maxwell Street marketplace area, performing his distinctive brand of traditional Mississippi blues amidst the daily hustle-and-bustle of local merchants and shoppers; in the wake of the folk-blues revival of the early '60s, he recorded the LP *Maxwell Street Jimmy Davis* for Elektra, and although a fine showcase for his powerful guitar skills and provocative vocals, it failed to make much impact outside of purist circles. Davis continued to record sporadically in the decades that followed, and remained a constant West Side presence prior to his death on December 28, 1995. —*Jason Ankeny*

Chicago Blues Session, Vol. 11 / Jul. 29, 1994 / Wolf ✦✦✦✦

Walter Davis

b. Mar. 1, 1912, Grenada, MS, **d.** Oct. 22, 1963, St. Louis, MO
Piano / Piano Blues
While never a contemporary superstar or latter-day legend on a par with many of his peers, singer/pianist Walter Davis was among the most prolific blues performers to emerge from the pre-war St. Louis scene, cutting over 150 sides between 1930 and 1952. Born March 1, 1912 in Grenada, MS,

Davis' two-fisted piano style bore the heavy influence of Leroy Carr, although he was better known for his funereal vocal style; he first attracted attention upon relocating to St. Louis during the mid-1920s, and soon made the first of his many recordings for the Victor label. Despite its abundance, his work—much of it recorded in conjunction with guitarist Henry Townsend—was solid but unspectacular, eclipsed by the likes of associates including Roosevelt Sykes and Peetie Wheatstraw; still, he enjoyed a fair amount of success before a stroke prompted him to move from music to the ministry during the early '50s. Davis was still preaching at the time of his death on October 22, 1963. —*Jason Ankeny*

First Recordings (1930-1932) / 1930-1932 / JSP ✦✦✦

● **The Bullet Sides** / 1986 / Krazy Kat ✦✦✦✦
Simply the best collection available, including the incredible "Tears Came Rollin' Down," one of Davis's best. (Import) —*Cub Koda*

Complete Works in Chronological Order, Vol. 1 (1933-35) / Feb. 15, 1995 / Document ✦✦✦

Complete Works in Chronological Order, Vol. 2 (1935-37) / Feb. 15, 1995 / Document ✦✦✦

Complete Works in Chronological Order, Vol. 3 (1937-38) / Feb. 15, 1995 / Document ✦✦✦

Complete Works in Chronological Order, Vol. 4 (1938-39) / Feb. 15, 1995 / Document ✦✦✦

Complete Works in Chronological Order, Vol. 5 (1939-40) / Feb. 15, 1995 / Document ✦✦✦

Complete Works in Chronological Order, Vol. 6 (1940-46) / Feb. 15, 1995 / Document ✦✦✦

Complete Works in Chronological Order, Vol. 7 (1946-52) / Feb. 15, 1995 / Document ✦✦✦

Jimmy Dawkins

b. Oct. 24, 1936, Tchula, MS
Guitar, Vocals / Modern Electric Blues, Chicago Blues
Chicago guitarist Jimmy Dawkins would just as soon leave his longtime nickname "Fast Fingers" behind. It was always something of a stylistic misnomer anyway; Dawkins' West Side-styled guitar slashes and surges, but seldom burns with incendiary speed. Dawkins' blues are generally of the brooding, introspective variety—he doesn't engage in flashy pyrotechnics or outrageous showmanship.

It took a long time for Dawkins to progress from West Side fixture to nationally known recording artist. He rode a Greyhound bus out of Mississippi in 1955, dressed warm to ward off the Windy City's infamous chill factor. Only trouble was, he arrived on a sweltering July day! Harpist Billy Boy Arnold offered the newcomer encouragement, and he eventually carved out a niche on the competitive West Side scene (his peers included Magic Sam and Luther Allison).

Sam introduced Dawkins to Delmark Records boss Bob Koester. *Fast Fingers*, Dawkins' 1969 debut LP for Delmark—still his best album to date—was a taut, uncompromising piece of work that won the Grand Prix du Disque de Jazz from the Hot Club of France in 1971 as the year's top album. Andrew "Big Voice" Odom shared the singing and Otis Rush the second guitar duties on Dawkins' 1971 encore *All for Business*. But after his Delmark LP *Blisterstring*, Dawkins' subsequent recordings lacked intensity until 1991's oddly titled *Kant Sheck Dees Bluze* for Chicago's Earwig Records. Since then, Dawkins has waxed a pair of discs for Ichiban and continues to tour extensively. —*Bill Dahl*

● **Fast Fingers** / 1969 / Delmark ✦✦✦✦
Still his toughest and most satisfying album to date, and still criminally not available on CD. Dawkins burst onto the blues scene with this album at the dawn of the '70s, his slashing, angular guitar lines and reserved vocal style beautifully captured throughout the set. —*Bill Dahl*

All for Business / 1971 / Delmark ✦✦✦
This time around, Dawkins handed the majority of the vocal duties to Andrew "Big Voice" Odom and concentrated on his guitar (actually, he had some potent help in that department, too: Otis Rush was on second guitar). A generally solid but not overly enthralling set, with two bonus cuts and an alternate take of "Moon Man" added to the CD version. —*Bill Dahl*

Tribute to Orange / Nov. 30, 1971-Nov. 2, 1974 / Black & Blue ✦✦✦
Jimmy Dawkins' infrequent albums are always a joy, and that was the case when he made his first sojourn to Europe in 1970 and recorded LPs for Black & Blue, Vogue, and Excello in France and England. This disc features eight numbers pairing Dawkins and the great Gatemouth Brown and another four matching him with equally sensational Otis Rush. The Brown/ Dawkins tandem duel, match, and challenge each other as Dawkins' sometimes enigmatic, sometimes bemused, and often compelling vocals set the stage for their instrumental encounters. The same holds true on the Rush/ Dawkins cuts. While Rush provides searing licks and twisting solos, Dawkins' singing sets the tone with its urgent inflections and weary, resigned quality. — *Ron Wynn*

Blisterstring / Jun. 1977 / Delmark ✦✦✦
Not as impressive as either of his previous outings for Delmark, but still a great deal better than some of what would follow over the course of the next few years. — *Bill Dahl*

Hot Wire / 1981 / Isabel ✦✦
Low key, but still worthwhile. — *Bill Dahl*

Hot Wire 81 / Mar. 1981 / Evidence ✦✦
Actually, more like tepid—Dawkins wasn't exactly tearing up the strings on this low-key set, which positively pales in comparison to his previous Delmark releases. — *Bill Dahl*

Feel the Blues / 1985 / JSP ✦✦

All Blues / 1986 / JSP ✦✦

Kant Sheck Dees Bluze / Jun. 1991 / Earwig ✦✦✦✦
Incredibly weird title (many of the songs sport equally bizarre spellings), but a major step back in the right direction for the guitarist, whose dirty, distorted tone won't thrill the purists. — *Bill Dahl*

Blues & Pain / 1994 / Wild Dog ✦✦✦
Dawkins is back on the right track now, making solid if less than earthshaking recordings that at least hint at why he once was billed "Fast Fingers." — *Bill Dahl*

B Phur Real / 1995 / Wild Dog ✦✦✦
Here we go again with the off-the-wall spellings ... more listenable modern work from the Chicago guitarist, who's found his groove again after quite a few years of less than enthralling releases. — *Bill Dahl*

Blues from Iceland / 1995 / Evidence ✦✦✦

Me, My Gitar & the Blues / Aug. 26, 1997 / Ichiban ✦✦✦

Geno Delafose

b. 1972, Eunice, Louisiana, **d.** 1994
Drums, Vocals / Zydeco
The son of the great accordionist John Delafose, Geno Delafose carried on the family name with his own distinctive sound spanning from traditional Creole and Cajun music to contemporary R&B. Born in Eunice, Louisiana, in 1972, he began his career at the age of eight, playing rubboard and drums in his father's band, the Eunice Playboys; he eventually adopted the accordion as well, and was among the few zydeco performers of his era to play both the button and piano models of the instrument. Over the years Delafose's prominence in the group grew, and he and his father often traded lead vocals; when John retired in the months prior to his 1994 death, Geno took over the band, and that same year he recorded his debut LP *French Rockin' Boogie; That's What I'm Talkin' About!* followed in 1996. — *Jason Ankeny*

French Rockin' Boogie / 1994 / Rounder ✦✦✦✦

● **That's What I'm Talking About!** / Jun. 1996 / Rounder ✦✦✦✦
This will stand as one of the finest zydeco albums of the decade. Young Geno (age 24) plays in a more tuneful and traditional style than competitors on the 1990s South Louisiana zydeco circuit like Beau Jocque and Keith Frank, whose thumping dance-beats, one-chord riffs, and profane lyrics constitute a sort of zydeco/hip-hop synthesis. Geno instead draws inspiration from the older Creole songs of his father, John Delafose. But he hasn't merely followed in his father's footsteps; he's outpaced him. His music has just the right combination of lilt and kick to it, thanks in large part to his cousin Jermaine Jack's drum work. *That's What I'm Talking About!* is like a zydeco carousel

that whirls you delightedly round and round. Geno handles button and piano-accordion proficiently, and his voice, used to better advantage here than on his 1994 debut album *French Rockin' Boogie*, possesses that lovely "key of heartbreak" quality that characterizes the best South Louisiana music. — *Steve Hoffman*

John Delafose

b. Apr. 16, 1939, Duralde, LA, **d.** Sep. 17, 1994, Lawtell, LA
Vocals, Accordion / Zydeco
John Delafose and his band the Eunice Playboys bridged the gap between zydeco's roots and its contemporary sound with a mastery matched by few of their peers; despite an affinity for early Creole styles, French lyrics, and two-step waltz rhythms, they played with all of the fiery intensity demanded by modern-day audiences, tapping into a wide array of sources—blues, Cajun, even country—to forge a propulsive traditionalist sound all their own. Born April 16, 1939 in Duralde, Louisiana, Delafose as a child crafted fiddles and guitars out of old boards and cigar boxes fitted with window-screen wire; he eventually took up the harmonica, and at the age of 18 learned the button accordion. He soon turned to farming, and as a result did not seriously pursue music until during the early '70s, at which time he served as an accordionist and harpist with a variety of local zydeco bands. By the middle of the decade his formed his own combo, the Eunice Playboys; originally featuring guitarist Charles Prudhomme and his bassist brother Slim, the group's lineup swelled over time to also include Delafose's sons John "T.T." on rubboard and Tony on drums. Another son, Geno, later joined as well, trading vocal and accordion leads with his father. Delafose and the Eunice Playboys debuted in 1980 with the regional hit "Joe Pete Got Two Women," from the LP *Zydeco Man; Uncle Bud Zydeco* followed in 1982, and as interest in traditional Creole culture swelled, the group became one of the hottest attractions on the Gulf Coast circuit. They returned in 1984 with *Heartaches & Hot Steps*, a year later issuing *Zydeco Excitement;* after a lengthy hiatus from the studio, Delafose resurfaced in 1992 with *Pere et Garcon Zydeco.* 1993's *Blues Stay Away from Me* was his final album; failing health forced him to curtail his touring schedule soon after, and on September 17, 1994, Delafose died. Geno succeeded his father as bandleader. — *Jason Ankeny*

Zydeco Man / 1980 / Arhoolie ✦✦✦✦

Uncle Bud Zydeco / 1982 / Arhoolie ✦✦✦

Heartaches & Hot Steps / 1984 / Maison de Soul ✦✦✦✦
Explosive arrangements, powerhouse vocals and accordion playing, and good band support make this a first-rate contemporary zydeco date. — *Ron Wynn*

Zydeco Excitement! / 1984 / Maison de Soul ✦✦✦

● **Joe Pete Got Two Women** / 1988 / Arhoolie ✦✦✦✦
Delafose's best contains his popular saga of Joe Pete. Zydeco fundamentalism from this singer/accordionist, who's so down-home, his music clearly echoes African hypnotic grooves. — *Jeff Hannusch & Mark A. Humphrey*

Pere Et Garcon Zydeco / 1992 / Rounder ✦✦✦
While zydeco and Cajun-influenced hybrids have been the norm in many circles during the 1980s and '90s, John Delafose & the Eunice Playboys have remained true to the classic style. This session featured predominantly hardcore material, emphasizing the two-steps, waltzes, and French lyrics at the heart of zydeco/Cajun. Delafose and his son Geno alternated lead vocals and accordion support, each singing and playing with vigor, conviction and authenticity. Meanwhile, the band backed them with equal electricity, and while such tunes as "Watch That Dog," "Morning Train" and "Go Back Where You Been" were lyrical departures, they were as fully in the zydeco framework as "Mon Coeur Fait Mal" or "Grand Mamou." — *Ron Wynn*

Paul deLay

b. Jan. 31, 1952, Portland, OR
Harmonica, Vocals / Modern Electric Blues
Paul deLay was born in Portland, OR, on January 31, 1952, but grew up in Milwaukie, OR—a suburb of Portland. He grew up listening to classical, jazz (big band), Dixieland, barrelhouse piano, and barbershop quartets. He came to blues through rock and the various blues covers of British artists. When he discovered Chess Records and the original blues recordings, he had found his vocation.

DeLay joined the band Brown Sugar in 1970, and the band played a combination of blues, soul, and R&B. They stayed together for about ten years working the local bar scene, dances, and coffeehouses. In 1979, deLay formed his own four-piece Chicago-style blues band. This became the Paul deLay Band. DeLay took Paul Butterfield as his model early on but says of his playing, "I guess, more or less, what I've ended up sounding like is a combination between Big Walter, George Smith, Sonny Boy II, and Toots Thielemans."

In 1990, deLay was arrested on cocaine-related charges and spent three years in federal prison. In the early '90s, the band released two CDs *The Other One* (1990), and *Paulzilla* (1992), both now available on one CD from Evidence. Almost all the songs on these CDs were written by deLay.

While deLay was serving time, his band teamed up with singer Linda Hornbuckle, calling themselves the "No Delay Band" and waited for Paul to return. Upon Paul's release, they reformed as the "Paul deLay Band" and released their first post-prison album, *Ocean of Tears*, in September of 1996. The main (long standing) members of the deLay band include Peter Dammann (lead guitar), Louis Pain (keyboards), and Dan Fincher (sax). Dammann was raised in Chicago and traces his musical roots to the blues scene there.

DeLay has an excellent voice—an apologist-style singer in the manner of Bobby Bland and Junior Parker. As a harp player, he is superb. Not just another White guy playing the records of other bluesmen, deLay is expert on both the standard Marine Band Hohner and the chromatic. He (along with William Clarke) has taken the blues chromatic to new heights. DeLay has received a number of awards, including a Handy Award nomination, and appeared at many blues and jazz festivals.

DeLay's music shows R&B, jazz, and gospel influence, but still hangs more or less in the blues groove. He has written some excellent songs in the apologetic style of singers like Bobby "Blue" Bland. He claims, "I'm really a frustrated Dixieland saxophone player." — *Michael Erlewine*

Teasin' / 1970 / Criminal ♦♦
The deLay band's first recording gave birth to Criminal Records. — *Michael Erlewine*

Other One / 1984 / Criminal ♦♦♦
All 11 songs written by deLay plus plenty of fine harp playing. With Peter Dammann on guitar and Louis Pain on keyboards. — *Michael Erlewine*

The Blue One / 1985 / Criminal ♦♦
Six tunes with the earlier band, including "Something's Got a Hold on Me." — *Michael Erlewine*

The Best of Paul deLay: You're Fired / 1990 / Red Lightnin' ♦♦♦♦
A collection of deLay material released by the British label Red Lightnin' in May of 1990. — *Michael Erlewine*

Paulzilla / 1992 / Criminal ♦♦♦♦
Declared the album of the year by the Cascades Blues Association, this was completed just days before deLay's three-year visit to the pen. DeLay wrote most of the songs and there is plenty of first-rate chromatic harp playing here. With Peter Dammann on guitar and Louis Pain on keyboards. — *Michael Erlewine*

● **Take It from the Turnaround** / 1996 / Evidence ♦♦♦♦
Combining the best of two albums (1991's *Just This One* and 1992's *Paulzilla*) on one CD, *Take It from the Turnaround* heralds the arrival of a harp player who's been a certified blues legend in his native region of Portland, OR. DeLay blows with authenticity and a full command of his instrument and way more than a hint of reckless abandon. Traditional blues, even by modern bar-band standards, this ain't, but the high creative level of deLay's songwriting on numbers like "Second Hand Smoke," "Merry Way," and the heartfelt "Just This One" heralds the arrival of a new way of looking at things and bodes well for future recordings. As a parenthetical note, the liner notes that accompany this release are superlative, telling deLay's story in a way that's both horrifying and inspiring. The man has lived a life in the blues and not only lived to tell the tale, but has triumphed over the worst elements a road musician has to suffer through. — *Cub Koda*

Ocean of Tears / Sep. 1996 / Evidence ♦♦♦♦
This 1996 release features deLay after he was released from prison with his original band doing ten tunes, all written by deLay either by himself or as coauthor. Features the title cut "Ocean of Tears," "What Went Wrong," and a

duet with Linda Hornbuckle, "Maybe Our Luck Will Change." — *Michael Erlewine*

Nice & Strong / Feb. 3, 1998 / Evidence ♦♦♦♦
Nice & Strong finds Paul deLay at the top of his form, turning out a set of hard-driving Chicago-style blues. Not only does deLay sound tougher than ever, his songs are simply stunning, displaying a devilish humor and a new vulnerability. It's another winning record from one of the great contemporary blues musicians and harp players of the '90s. — *Stephen Thomas Erlewine*

American Voodoo / Criminal ♦♦♦
The standout album from the early material, this second deLay album reached No.2 on the Italian blues charts. Worth seeking out. — *Michael Erlewine*

Burnin' / Criminal ♦♦♦♦
Reached No. 20 on the *Living Blues* chart. This album was the debut of guitarist Peter Dammann. Includes hornwork by ex-Mayall sax player Chris Mercer. — *Michael Erlewine*

Paul Delay / Criminal ♦♦♦♦

Derek & the Dominos

f. 1970, New York, NY, **db.** 1972
Group / Blues-Rock, Rock & Roll
Derek & the Dominos was a group formed by guitarist/singer Eric Clapton (born Eric Patrick Clapp, Mar. 30, 1945, Ripley, Surrey, England) with other former members of Delaney & Bonnie & Friends, in the spring of 1970. The rest of the lineup was Bobby Whitlock (b. 1948, Memphis, TN) (keyboards, vocals), Carl Radle (b. 1942, Oklahoma City, OK,—d. May 30, 1980) (bass), and Jim Gordon (b. 1945, Los Angeles) (drums). The group debuted at the Lyceum Ballroom in London on June 14 and undertook a summer tour of England. From late August to early October, they recorded the celebrated double album *Layla and Other Assorted Love Songs* (November 1970) with guitarist Duane Allman sitting in. They then returned to touring in England and the US, playing their final date on December 6.

The *Layla* album was successful in the US, where "Bell Bottom Blues" and the title song charted as singles in abbreviated versions, but it did not chart in the UK. The Dominos reconvened to record a second album in May 1971, but split up without completing it. Clapton then retired from the music business, nursing a heroin addiction.

In his absence, and in the wake of Allman's death in a motorcycle accident on October 29, 1971, the Dominos and *Layla* gained in stature. Re-released as a single at its full, seven-minute length in connection with the compilation album *History of Eric Clapton* (Atco 803) (March 1972), "Layla" hit the Top Ten in the US and the UK in the summer of 1972. (It would return to the UK Top Ten in 1982.) A live album, *Derek and the Dominos in Concert* (January 1973), taken from the 1970 US tour, was also a strong seller.

Time has only added to the renown for the group, which is now rated among Eric Clapton's most outstanding achievements. The 1988 Eric Clapton boxed set retrospective *Crossroads* featured material from the abortive second album sessions. *The Layla Sessions* was a 1990 boxed set expanding that album across three CDs/cassettes. *Live at the Fillmore* (1994) offered an expanded version of the *In Concert* album. — *William Ruhlmann*

★ **Layla & Other Assorted Love Songs** / Nov. 1970 / Polydor ♦♦♦♦♦
Wishing to escape the superstar expectations that sank Blind Faith before it was launched, Eric Clapton retreated with several sidemen from Delaney & Bonnie to record the material that formed *Layla & Other Assorted Love Songs*. From these meager beginnings grew his greatest album. Duane Allman joined the band shortly after recording began, and his spectacular slide guitar pushed Clapton to new heights. Then again, Clapton may have gotten there without him, considering the emotional turmoil he was in during the recording. He was in hopeless, unrequited love with Patti Boyd, the wife of his best friend George Harrison, and that pain surges throughout *Layla*, especially on its epic title track. But what really makes *Layla* such a powerful record is that Clapton, ignoring the traditions that occasionally painted him into a corner, simply tears through these songs with burning, intense emotion. He makes standards like "Have You Ever Loved a Woman" and "Nobody Knows You (When You're Down and Out)" into his own, while his collaborations with Bobby Whitlock, including "Anyday" and "Why Does Love Got To Be So Sad?," teem with passion. And, considering what a personal album

Layla is, it's somewhat ironic that the lovely coda "Thorn Tree in the Garden" is a solo performance by Whitlock, and that the song sums up the entire album as well as "Layla" itself. — *Stephen Thomas Erlewine*

Derek & the Dominos in Concert / Jan. 1973 / Polydor ✦✦✦
While it isn't nearly as intense as *Layla, Derek & the Dominos In Concert* offers some fine playing by Clapton and his band and easily ranks among his best live albums. — *Stephen Thomas Erlewine*

The Layla Sessions / Sep. 1990 / Polydor ✦✦✦
Featuring two discs of outtakes and jams, the three-CD box *The Layla Sessions* manages to detract from the original by surrounding it with endless, dull instrumentals. Then again, all the unreleased material proves what a well-constructed album *Layla* is. — *Stephen Thomas Erlewine*

Live at the Fillmore / Feb. 22, 1994 / Polydor ✦✦✦
In his liner notes, Anthony DeCurtis calls *Live at the Fillmore* "a digitally remixed and remastered version of the 1973 Derek and the Dominos double album *In Concert*, with five previously unreleased performances and two tracks that have only appeared on the four-CD Clapton retrospective, *Crossroads*." But this does not adequately describe the album. *Live at the Fillmore* is not exactly an expanded version of *In Concert;* it is a different album culled from the same concerts that were used to compile the earlier album. *Live at the Fillmore* contains six of the nine recordings originally released on *In Concert*, and three of its five previously unreleased performances are different recordings of songs also featured on *In Concert*—"Why Does Love Got to Be So Sad?," "Tell the Truth," and "Let It Rain." The other two, "Nobody Knows You When You're Down and Out" and "Little Wing," have not been heard before in any concert version. Even when the same recordings are used on *Live at the Fillmore* as on *In Concert*, they have, as noted, been remixed and, as not noted, re-edited. In either form, Derek and the Dominos' October 1970 stand at the Fillmore East, a part of the group's only US tour, finds them a looser aggregation than they seemed to be in the studio making their only album, *Layla and Other Assorted Love Songs*. A trio backing Eric Clapton, the Dominos leave the guitarist considerable room to solo on extended numbers, five of which run over ten minutes each. Clapton doesn't show consistent invention, but his playing is always directed, and he plays more blues than you can hear on any other Clapton live recording. — *William Ruhlmann*

Detroiters

f. Detroit, MI
Group / Traditional Gospel
One of the most successful gospel groups of the late '40s, the Detroiters were led by Oliver Green, a native of Texas who began his career during the Depression era as a member of the Southern Wonders. Upon settling in the Motor City in 1938, he formed the Evangelist Singers of Detroit, a quartet which hosted their own local radio and earned some measure of national popularity as a result of their frequent tours with Sister Rosetta Tharpe. The Evangelists were also the first group to cut the hit topical song "Tell Me Why You Like Roosevelt," which was composed by their booking manager Otis Jackson; after signing on with the Detroit radio station WGC, bandleader Horace Heidt insisted they change their name to the Detroiters, a more secular moniker which by extension would allow the addition of pop and folk material to their repertoire. Their frequent radio appearances led to a steady schedule of live bookings, and in addition to high lead Green, their ranks grew to include lower lead Leroy Barnes, first tenor Dempsey Harrison, baritone Bill Johnson, bass Robert Thomas, and pianist Nathaniel Howard. It was this Detroiters lineup which entered the studio on August 14, 1951 to record the first of three singles for the Specialty label, "Let Jesus Lead You"; the same session also yielded a follow-up, combining "I Trust in Jesus" with "Ride On King Jesus." A second date from 1952 spawned a rousing "Old Time Religion," but it was their last Specialty effort; for reasons unknown, label chief Art Rupe did not take a shine to the group, and they were soon dropped. Although Barnes later exited to join the Flying Clouds, the Detroiters continued touring regionally into the early '60s. — *Jason Ankeny*

Old Time Religion / 1992 / Specialty ✦✦✦✦
Old Time Religion showcases two great gospel vocal quartets from the '40s and '50s: the Detroiters and the Golden Echoes. The first half of the disc features 15 cuts from the Detroiters, 11 of which are previously unreleased

songs recorded at United Sound. The Golden Echoes are represented with 11 songs recorded in 1949, ten of which have never been released. Usually, large sections of unreleased material would mean that the disc is primarily of interest to collectors, but that's not necessarily the case here. Both quartets are excellent examples of impassioned, moving, and plain entertaining classic gospel, blessed with remarkable voices—the Detroiters' lineup boasted Oliver Green and Leroy Barnes, while the Golden Echoes featured Paul Foster, Sr., and Wilmer "Little Axe" Broadnax—and true spirit; it's a pleasure to hear them in any setting. Granted, some tastes may find the preponderance of alternate takes a little tedious, but if you program them out, you're left with a sterling collection of classic gospel. — *Leo Stanley*

Big John Dickerson

Vocals / R&B, Soul Blues
Vocalist Big John Dickerson is no stranger to blues and soul music. Dickerson's current backing band, Blue Chamber, have long been the house band at Famous Dave's BBQ and Blues in uptown Minneapolis.

The 60-something Dickerson has been singing for decades; he began his career in Detroit as a session drummer for Motown Records, and worked with classic R&B singers Jerry Butler and Bettye Swann on their respective tours in the 1960s. His session credits include drumming for the Temptations, Five Sharps, Marvin Gaye, James Brown, and Bobby "Blue" Bland, among others.

Dickerson recorded two independently released albums with the regional band Down Right Tight prior to his 1997 debut for Cannonball. — *Richard J. Skelly*

● **Big John Dickerson & Blue Chamber** / Sep. 30, 1997 / Cannonball ✦✦✦✦
Vocalist Big John Dickerson is no stranger to blues and soul music, and his self-titled debut for the Minneapolis-based Cannonball Records proves that point. *Big John Dickerson and Blue Chamber* finds him working with a seven-piece group that includes horns. Produced by organist Ron Levy, the record showcases his vocals and the band's take on classic R&B and blues like "Mother-In-Law Blues," "Homework," "Oh Pretty Woman," and the instrumentals "Okie Dokie Stomp" and "Blues In D Natural." — *Richard Skelly*

Bo Diddley (Ellas Otha Bates McDaniels)

b. Dec. 30, 1928, McComb, MS
Guitar, Violin, Vocals / Rock 'n' Roll, R&B
He only had a few hits in the 1950s and early '60s, but as Bo Diddley sang, "You Can't Judge a Book by Its Cover." You can't judge an artist by his chart success, either, and Diddley produced greater and more influential music than all but a handful of the best early rockers. The Bo Diddley beat—bomp, ba-bomp-bomp, bomp-bomp—is one of rock 'n' roll's bedrock rhythms, showing up in the work of Buddy Holly, the Rolling Stones, and even pop-garage knockoffs like the Strangeloves' 1965 hit "I Want Candy." Diddley's hypnotic rhythmic attack and declamatory, boasting vocals stretched back as far as Africa for their roots, and looked as far into the future as rap. His trademark otherwordly vibrating, fuzzy guitar style did much to expand the instrument's power and range. But even more important, Bo's bounce was fun and irresistibly rocking, with a wisecracking, jiving tone that epitomized rock 'n' roll at its most humorously outlandish and freewheeling.

Before taking up blues and R&B, Diddley had actually studied classical violin, but shifted gears after hearing John Lee Hooker. In the early '50s, he began playing with his longtime partner, maraca player Jerome Green, to get what Bo called "that freight train sound." Billy Boy Arnold, a fine blues harmonica player and singer in his own right, was also playing with Diddley when the guitarist got a deal with Chess in the mid-'50s (after being turned down by rival Chicago label Vee-Jay). His very first single, "Bo Diddley"/"I'm a Man" (1955), was a double-sided monster. The A-side was soaked with futuristic waves of tremolo guitar, set to an ageless nursery rhyme; the flip was a bump-and-grind, harmonica-driven shuffle, based around a devastating blues riff. But the result was not exactly blues, or even straight R&B, but a new kind of guitar-based rock 'n' roll, soaked in the blues and R&B, but owing allegiance to neither.

Diddley was never a top seller on the order of his Chess rival Chuck Berry, but over the next half-dozen or so years, he'd produce a catalog of classics that rival Berry's in quality. "You Don't Love Me," "Diddley Daddy," "Pretty Thing," "Diddy Wah Diddy," "Who Do You Love?," "Mona," "Road Runner,"

"You Can't Judge a Book by Its Cover"—all are stone-cold standards of early, riff-driven rock 'n' roll at its funkiest. Oddly enough, his only Top 20 pop hit was an atypical, absurd back-and-forth rap between him and Jerome, "Say Man," that came about almost by accident as the pair were fooling around in the studio.

As a live performer, Diddley was galvanizing, using his trademark square guitars and distorted amplification to produce new sounds that anticipated the innovations of '60s guitarists like Jimi Hendrix. In Great Britain, he was revered as a giant on the order of Chuck Berry and Muddy Waters. The Rolling Stones in particular borrowed a lot from Bo's rhythms and attitude in their early days, although they only officially covered a couple of his tunes, "Mona" and "I'm Alright." Other British R&B groups like the Yardbirds, Animals, and Pretty Things also covered Diddley standards in their early days. Buddy Holly covered "Bo Diddley" and used a modified Bo Diddley beat on "Not Fade Away"; when the Stones gave the song the full-on Bo treatment (complete with shaking maracas), the result was their first big British hit.

The British Invasion helped increase the public's awareness of Diddley's importance, and ever since then he's been a popular live act. Sadly, though, his career as a recording artist—in commercial and artistic terms—was over by the time the Beatles and Stones hit America. He'd record with ongoing and declining frequency, but after 1963, he'd never write or record any original material on par with his early classics. Whether he'd spent his muse, or just felt he could coast on his laurels, is hard to say. But he remains a vital part of the collective rock 'n' roll consciousness, occasionally reaching wider visibility via a 1979 tour with the Clash, a cameo role in the film *Trading Places*, a late-'80s tour with Ronnie Wood, and a 1989 television commercial for sports shoes with star athlete Bo Jackson. —*Richie Unterberger*

Bo Diddley / 1958 / Checker ++++

Have Guitar, Will Travel / 1960 / Chess ++++

Amazingly, Bo Diddley's third album—containing classics such as "Cops and Robbers," "Run Diddley Daddy" and "Mona (I Need You Baby)"—has only been reissued on vinyl, and even that's out-of-print. More than one British Invasion band learned what they needed to know about American rock 'n' roll from the songs on this record (the Stones cut "Cops and Robbers" at their earliest recording session, and later released a killer version of "Mona," though the most interesting British version of the latter was done by an all-girl band with an attitude called the Liverbirds). This record is every bit as raunchy as Bo's first two albums (the guitars may even be crunchier, and the singing shows more range), and has more than enough to recommend it to collectors and fans. This is the album that began the funny cover photos on Bo's records. —*Bruce Eder*

Bo Diddley in the Spotlight / 1960 / Chess ++++

As with of Bo Diddley's first five albums (except *Have Guitar Will Travel*), the most important cuts (but not all the good ones) off of this album have been included on *The Chess Box* from MCA, which doesn't mean that this record isn't a good separate issue, just somewhat redundant if you have the box. There are surprises from these 1960-vintage recordings, including the languid, Caribbean-sounding "Limber," the soft, romantic "Love Me," the doo-wop style "Deed and Deed I Do," the loping "Walkin' and Talkin'," and upbeat, gospel-tinged rockers such as "Let Me In," interspersed with the hot and raunchy "Road Runner," "The Story of Bo Diddley," "Craw-Dad" (a genuine diamond-in-the-rough), and "Signifying Blues," and solid instrumentals like "Scuttle Bug" (really "Live My Life" with the vocals removed and Otis Spann overdubbed on piano), that make this record more than worthwhile. —*Bruce Eder*

Bo Diddley Is a Lover / 1961 / Checker ++++

There's not a bad song on this long-forgotten album—in fact, it's all good, and so little of it has been reissued that it's a crime. There are a lot of familiar moments here: Bo slips most effectively into his "Say Man" groove on "Bo's Vacation," plays some serious Chicago blues on "Call Me (Bo's Blues)," and makes it count; invades Chuck Berry territory by way of Howlin' Wolf on the window-rattling "Hong Kong Mississippi" (a track so riveting and funny, and so rippling in superb guitar work, it makes this album worthwhile on its own); bounces back to his signature beat on the title song, the hysterically funny autobiographical "Bo Diddley Is Loose," "Quick Draw," "Back Home," and "Not Guilty" (a song that deserves enshrinement as one of Bo's best); and slips into a romantic groove on "You're Looking Good." Find it, buy it, and savor it—though MCA could help by reissuing it on CD! —*Bruce Eder*

Bo Diddley Is a Lover ... Plus / 1961 / See For Miles ++++

Very welcome digital British import reissue of Bo's 1961 Checker album, bolstered by a handful of bonus tracks (including his rendering of Willie Dixon's "My Babe"). On second guitar for many of these sides is Peggy Jones, one of Diddley's prize pupils. Some of the better-known titles include "Not Guilty," "Hong Kong, Mississippi," and the bragadocious title cut. —*Bill Dahl*

Bo Diddley Is a Twister / 1962 / Checker +++

A lot of the material on this record was rushed out in half-finished form, in order to get an album out that cashed in on the "twist" craze of early 1962. There may well have been words intended to the opening track, "Detour," which came out of the 1961 session featuring Peggy "Lady Bo" Jones that produced the excellent "Pills" and the rather perfunctory reading of Willie Dixon's "My Babe," and some lackluster earlier instrumental material, "Shank" and "The Twister." This record also featured "Here 'Tis," the soulful Bo original that would serve the Eric Clapton-era Yardbirds in very good stead on stage—Bo's version blows theirs completely away—as well as the classics "Road Runner" and "Who Do You Love." In all, it isn't half-bad for an album that nobody intended as such, though most of the best (except "Here 'Tis") has been included on various hits compilations. —*Bruce Eder*

Bo Diddley & Company / 1962 / Checker ++++

This album is almost worth owning just for the cover photo of Bo and the Duchess, aka Norma-Jean Wofford, each with their axe. What makes it really cool, though, is the music, which is among the best of Bo's 1960s output. "Bo's A Lumberjack" is one of the most ferociously sexual and funny signature songs Bo ever cut, "(Extra, Read All About It) Ben" is a sort of sideways version of "Say Man," with a rollicking beat and very effective use of piano in the backing band, with a grim subject matter handled in a humorous manner, and "Help Out" is one of Bo's better guitar workouts, with the man getting lots of help from the Duchess. It was records like this that helped keep Bo's reputation alive in England when Americans stopped buying his stuff. "Met You On a Saturday" is an unusual slow, romantic number from Bo, very much in a late-'50s style that was probably a few years late to capture anyone's imagination. Other material, like "Diana" (a reworking of "Hey Bo Diddley") and "Little Girl" is less compelling but still solid rock 'n' roll, as are "Gimme Gimme," "Same Old Thing," "Met You On a Saturday," "Put the Shoes On Willie" (written by Earl Hooker), and "Pretty Girl." The latter has a great chorus, and turned up in the repertories of several British Invasion bands. —*Bruce Eder*

Hey Bo Diddley / 1962 / Chess +++

Bo's music was beginning to slip in sales—though he remained a popular concert act—when Chess released this album in the summer of 1962. "I Can Tell," written by Samuel Smith, showed Bo trying out a slower, more seductively soulful sound, a whole four-and-half-minutes long—it is different, though not very distinguished. "Bo's Twist" isn't much more impressive, a fairly standard instrumental with an unusually grungy (like you were expecting Julian Bream) guitar sound, with the first prominent appearance of an organ in the backing of a Bo Diddley record; "Sad Sack" is a somewhat more successful instrumental. "Mr. Kruschev" is one of the funniest, most delightfully nonsensical pieces of topical songwriting Bo ever engaged in, writing about wanting to go into the army and go over to see the Soviet leader and get him to stop nuclear testing, to a background of "Hut, two—three four!" "You All Green" is first-rate Bo, and deserved to be anthologized somewhere. "You Can't Judge a Book by Its Cover" was the one standard from the album, but other tracks deserving of better exposure include "Bo's Bounce" and "Who May Your Lover Be," which takes off from Howlin' Wolf's "Moaning at Midnight," recasting it in a Bo Diddley beat, with Bo sounding a lot like Wolf here, and "Give Me a Break (Man)," which is a very animated impromptu guitar jam. The album filler tracks include "Mama Don't Allow No Twistin'," Bo's take on "Mama Don't Like Music," a song that was old when country-and-western/novelty singer Smiley Burnette covered it successfully in the 1930s, "Babes in the Woods" (featuring a backing chorus mimicking the doo-wop parody "Get a Job") and "Diddling," a routine Bo instrumental. —*Bruce Eder*

Bo Diddley Is a Gunslinger / 1963 / Chess ++++

Not only does it sport one of the most striking album covers of its era (Diddley decked out in cowboy finery, about to get the drop on some unfortunate varmint with one of his fieriest guitars lying at his feet), this 1963 album contains some fine music. The title track continues the legend of you-know-who, while "Ride on Josephine" and "Cadillac" rock like hell (and Ed Sullivan must have been glad to see that Diddley finally learned "Sixteen Tons"). Two bonus cuts, "Working Man" and "Do What I Say," make this one a must. —*Bill Dahl*

Bo Diddley's Beach Party / 1963 / Checker ✦✦✦✦
A blistering live album, especially in genuine mono (the rechanneled stereo is barely passable)—and quite simply the finest live rock 'n' roll album of its era, cut live by Bo and band at Myrtle Beach, South Carolina on July 5 and 6, 1963. From the opening track (erroneously listed as "Memphis" and credited to Chuck Berry as composer) to the final note, this is some of the loudest, raunchiest guitar-based rock 'n' roll ever preserved. It also bears an uncanny resemblence to the sound that the Rolling Stones achieved on their own *Got Live If You Want It*, which only shows how much the Stones learned from Bo. Highlights include "Gunslinger," "Hey Bo Diddley," "Road Runner," and "I'm All Right." The sound doesn't necessarily translate ideally to compact disc, but that shouldn't dissuade anyone. Currently out-of-print but well worth the search. —*Bruce Eder & Cub Koda*

Surfin' with Bo Diddley / 1963 / Checker ✦✦
This is where Bo—or, more properly, Chess Records—really took a wrong step, starting with the fact that The Originator himself is actually on only about half of the cuts here, the balance having been recorded by organist Jimmy Lee Riley and his group the Megatons. The idea wasn't as bad as it sounded, at least on paper—Bo had been an indirect influence on tons of surf bands, with his signature grunge guitar sound, but the surf music world wasn't ready for a Bo-style instrumental rendition of the Jerome Kern/Oscar Hammerstein II *Showboat* standard "Ol' Man River," and Bo's own inspiration behind songs like "Surfer's Love Call" was muted, to say the least. Almost as bad—although more entertaining—is "Low Tide," Bo's rewrite of Bill Justis' "Raunchy." The best tracks are "Cookie Headed Diddley" and "Surf, Sink, or Swim," which come close to matching some of Bo's solid material from earlier albums and singles. —*Bruce Eder*

Two Great Guitars / 1964 / Chess ✦✦
Diddley shared this 1964 Chess album with his labelmate Chuck Berry. They duel it out on a pair of incredibly lengthy instrumentals (brilliantly titled "Chuck's Beat" and "Bo's Beat") that get tiresome long before they run their full course. Better (and briefer) are two numbers where they don't cross paths—Diddley's rendering of "When the Saints Go Marching In" and Berry's amazing country breakdown "Liverpool Drive." A couple of bonus Bo Diddley sides ("Stay Sharp" and "Stinkey") also make this digital re-incarnation worth acquiring. —*Bill Dahl*

500% More Man / 1965 / Checker ✦✦✦✦
By the end of 1965, Bo was making a conscious effort to recapture both the Black listenership that had deserted him and the White audience that was buying all of those soul records. Unfortunately, neither he nor Chess knew exactly how to go about it, and the result was another good album largely unheard by the public. The title track marks Bo's return to the Muddy Waters beat that he appropriated for "I'm a Man" (and that Muddy took back in "Mannish Boy") a decade earlier, and is one of Bo's greatest '60s sides. "Greasy Spoon" mentions Muddy amid its comical description of the offerings of a particularly unclean eatery (it's amazing when you think of it—ten years recording in Chicago, and longer than that living there, and Bo was still nearly as much a country blues artist as he was when he started). "Let Me Pass" is a hot number with an infectious beat and some very funny lyrics, and Bo playing some delectable guitar. "Stop My Monkey," featuring Bo backed by the singing group the Cookies, has him again trying for a commercial soul sound in a Motown vein, and "Tonight Is Ours" is one of Bo's most heartfelt romantic numbers, with the Cookies singing their hearts out while Bo tries his hand at a song that might've fit well on either of the first two albums by the Miracles, while "Hey, Red Riding Hood" brought back the Bo Diddley beat for another go around, this time with delightfully raunchy lyrics amid crisper textures and a much finer sound than ever before. "Hey's So Mad" is pretty lackluster except for the guitar break, but "Root Hoot" should've been more widely heard than it was, being one of Bo's more infectious chant-based songs. "Corn Bread" has a neatly stinging, Slim Harpo-type lead guitar sound, and is overall an okay instrumental. And then there's "Soul

Food," another great Bo Diddley rocker lost in the middle of the 1960s soul boom—Bo is so smooth, impassioned, sexy, and raw, and the Cookies sound so good backing him to one of his best instrumental tracks ever, that the fact this song was never a hit is a crime. By 1965, however, nobody in America was buying his records, even ones like this filled to bursting with good music and good humor, and even the British were beginning to lose interest in Bo's latest records. This was among Bo's last sessions with the Duchess, and the group he's using is more or less the studio equivalent of the band he's seen with in *The Big TNT Show (aka That Was Rock)*. —*Bruce Eder*

Hey, Good Lookin' / Apr. 1965 / Checker ✦✦✦
One of Bo's least known albums, mostly recorded in April of 1964 and released a year later, at the point when none of his records were selling in America. With an edgy, raunchy sound and modern record techniques (it's in stereo), Bo and band come up with a solid '60s version of his original sound. The title track is a real jewel, featuring Jerome Green on the maracas and Lafayette Leake on the piano. "Mama Keep Your Big Mouth Shut" isn't a bad soul-styled number, with Bo abandoning his standard beat in favor of a smoother, more Motown-like sound. He tries for a similar sound on "I Wonder Why (People Don't Like Me)" and "Brother Bear." In addition to the title track (which is NOT the Hank Williams tune), the Bo Diddley beat gets a workout on "La La La," "Rain Man," and "Bo Diddley's Hoot'nanny." Bo gets to have some real fun on "London Stomp," his commentary on the sudden fashionability of British rock 'n' roll, parodying the accents and attitudes of most of the bands that he encountered on his visit to England in October of 1963. Other tracks sound like they'd have worked well as part of extended jams of the kind that Bo did on stage—"Yeah Yeah Yeah," in particular, could've come from the middle of one of Bo's 15-minute shuffle-and-chant workouts, and would've been great in such a setting, although here, as a freestanding 2:25 track it's a little weak. There is some filler here, most notably "Let's Walk a While" and "Rooster Stew," but that can be forgiven in view of the strength of the rest of the material. —*Bruce Eder*

The Originator / 1966 / Checker ✦✦✦✦
By 1966, Bo Diddley was a long way from chart success in America, and *The Originator* was to be his last official album for four years (in the interim he would appear on the two Chess "Super Blues" all-star jam albums). Strangely enough, this is also one of his best albums, mostly comprised of rare early 1960s singles ("Pills") and B-sides and filled out with some fun new recordings ("Yakky Doodle"). This record is a bit of a throwback compared with *500% More Man*, which preceded it by nearly a year, representing the Bo Diddley of the early '60s—all of the material has the signature beat and guitar, or other virtues to recommend it, including some very high spirits. —*Bruce Eder*

The Black Gladiator / Jun. 1970 / Checker ✦✦
It was four years between the release of Bo's last album of all new cuts, *500% More Man*, and this album, during which time he'd spent time recording with Chess' top bluesmen, Muddy Waters and Howlin' Wolf. The death of Leonard Chess in October of 1969 resulted in the sale of the label to the GRT corporation, and cost the company what little artistic guidance it had. The result was *The Black Gladiator*, an attempt to reshape Bo into a funk artist, in the manner of Sly and the Family Stone. As an experiment it's understandable, and Bo tries very hard (even making another song-length sexual boast on "You, Bo Diddley," which also ends with a great guitar/organ duet between Bo and Bobby Alexis), but he finally fails to find a groove that works. Despite some good guitar here and there, this record falls into the same category as Muddy's *Electric Mud* and *After the Rain* albums and Howlin' Wolf's *New Album*, attempts to transform each into a psychedelic rocker. "Power House" is a pretty good cut, using a modified Muddy Waters-"I'm a Man"/"Mannish Boy" beat and lyrics. Much of the rest is for absolute completists only, however. —*Bruce Eder*

Another Dimension / 1971 / Chess ✦✦
By the end of 1970, most of Bo Diddley's income was derived from his concert work, primarily as an "oldies" act in rock 'n' roll revival shows such as the Toronto concert where he shared a stage with the Plastic Ono Band. But he and Chess believed there was still a way for him to try and reach a wider, more contemporary audience. This album was the result, a valiant effort to update Bo Diddley's sound and image, somewhat in the vein of Muddy Wa-

ters' *Electric Mud* only a few years later and very slightly more successful in that quest, in the sense of yielding one lasting addition to Bo's repertory. Relevance was the key word, not only in the song selection, which includes three John Fogerty songs ("Lodi," "Bad Moon Rising," "Down on the Corner") and covers of numbers by the Band and Elton John, but a new song entitled "Pollution" that tries hard to integrate the Bo Diddley beat into a message piece—it's a good try, but nothing on this record (including "Pollution") was going to challenge Marvin Gaye's *What's Goin' On* for primacy or effectiveness. The record starts off well enough, with a superb, deeply soulful cover of Al Kooper's "I Love You More Than You'll Ever Know," and a decent rendition of "The Shape I'm In." But two of the Fogerty covers ("Lodi" is the only one that sort of works) are embarrassing, with the girlie chorus killing "Bad Moon Rising." And "Bad Side of the Moon" was a waste of studio time. One song from this album has remained part of Bo's concert set for decades, however—"I Said Shutup Woman," which has the most traditional sound of anything on *Another Dimension*. —*Bruce Eder*

Where It All Began / 1972 / Chess ♦♦♦
Johnny Otis and Pete Welding produced this surprisingly successful soul effort by Bo, which succeeded in reshaping his sound, not as a Sly Stewart wannabe or a lounge act covering Creedence Clearwater Revival hits. Bo at least sounds comfortable and natural doing songs like "Look at Grandma" and "Woman," and the latter is a pretty damn good song—Bo finally emerged as a soul singer in his own right, and it worked, artistically at least. "Hey Jerome" even recalled tracks like "Say Man" in a not unflattering light. Unfortunately, none of this mattered to the people who still cared about Bo Diddley—they wanted the beat and the old sound, which was present here, on "I've Had It Hard" and the extraordinary "Bo Diddley-itis," but not in the kind of quantity they craved, amid the more modern sounds; and they wanted the old songs, which he gave them in concert. And it all came so late in the day, not only in terms of Bo's identification as anything but an oldies act but the history of Chess Records (now subsumed into the GRT corporate operation, the Chess imprint having no meaning or significance), that *Where It All Began* vanished from sight leaving scarcely a trace or a ripple on the charts. —*Bruce Eder*

Got Another Bag of Tricks / 1972 / Chess ♦♦♦♦
For a lot of years, this double album compilation—sort of the Bo Diddley equivalent to Chuck Berry's *The Great 28* or the first two Chuck Berry *Golden Decade* sets—was the best collection of Bo's stuff on the market, containing all of his best known songs and some of the best of his album tracks up through the mid-'60s. After it was deleted in America, it was available as an import from Canada and then Europe for a long time. On vinyl it is one place to start, although the double-CD *Chess Box* has supplanted it in many respects. —*Bruce Eder*

The London Bo Diddley Sessions / 1973 / Chess ♦♦♦
After Howlin' Wolf made the Billboard album charts in 1970 with his *London Sessions* release, Chess duly began preparing similarly titled albums by its remaining roster of stars—Muddy Waters and Chuck Berry followed the Wolf, and in 1973 this Bo Diddley release came along. Actually, a lot of it was done in Chicago, with the London portion of the sessions added, seemingly to justify the title. And it did sell better than Bo's other original albums of this era, and it remains in print on compact disc, one of a handful of his albums so released. As with Muddy Waters' *London Sessions* album, Bo's presence was somewhat overwhelmed by the massive number of session musicians involved (well-meaning though they may have been) and more so, because Bo was still looking for a new sound, where Muddy knew what he was about. The songs are pretty fair, a mix of soul and funk, with elements of his old sound, and this is probably the best compromise he achieved during this phase of his career, between the old and the new. —*Bruce Eder*

Big Bad Bo / 1974 / Chess ♦♦
Having tried everything else in his search for a new sound, Bo moved into a jazz vein on this record, and the results are not bad, but not really Bo either! His cover of Van Morrison's "I've Been Workin'" and the rendition of "Hit or Miss" aren't half-bad, but they're just not really Bo—just Bo fronting some really good jazzmen in New York. For the first time the Bo Diddley beat appears nowhere on one of his albums. There is one good blues here, however, in "Evelee," the only Bo original on *Big Bad Bo*, featuring a powerful

performance by The Originator, working for most of its length with a relatively stripped down band on this one number, which should've been the model for the whole album. —*Bruce Eder*

☆ **Bo Diddley/Go Bo Diddley** / 1986 / Chess ♦♦♦♦♦
There are precious few weak tracks on this combination of Bo Diddley's first two late-'50s albums for Chess/Checker, which boasts a plethora of classics ("Bo Diddley," "I'm a Man," "Before You Accuse Me," "Crackin' Up," "Little Girl," even his electric violin workout "The Clock Struck Twelve"). The only drawback: someone failed to notice that "Dearest Darling" was on both LPs, so...it's on here twice! —*Bill Dahl*

☆ **The Chess Years** / Jul. 1990 / MCA ♦♦♦♦♦
Not every single track you'll ever want or need by the legendary shave-and-a-haircut rhythm R&B/rock pioneer, but a great place to begin. Two discs (45 songs) in a great big box with a nice accompanying booklet contain the groundbreaking introduction "Bo Diddley" (never again would he be referred to as Ellas McDaniel), its swaggering flipside "I'm a Man," the killer follow-ups "Diddley Daddy," "I'm Looking for a Woman," "Who Do You Love?," and "Hey Bo Diddley;" signifying street-corner humor ("Say Man"), piledriving rockers ("Road Runner," "She's Alright," "You Can't Judge a Book by Its Cover"), and numerous stunning examples of his daringly innovative guitar style. —*Bill Dahl*

Rare & Well Done / Sep. 10, 1991 / Chess ♦♦♦♦
Sixteen extreme rarities from the deepest recesses of the Chess vaults that date from 1955-1968. The grinding "She's Fine, She's Mine" and snarling "I'm Bad" are comparatively well known, at least to collectors; far more obscure are the previously unissued "Heart-O-Matic Love," "Cookie-Headed Diddley," and "Moon Baby." —*Bill Dahl*

Bo's Blues / 1993 / Ace ♦♦♦♦
Twenty-two of Bo Diddley's best blues-oriented sides from the Chess catalog, including some rare stuff—the rip-roaring 1959 outing "Run Diddley Daddy," a jive-loaded "Cops and Robbers" from 1956 that features maraca shaker Jerome Green more than Diddley, and a surging "Down Home Special." If you think that everything Bo Diddley ever made has that same shave-and-a-haircut beat, this collection will set you straight! —*Bill Dahl*

Let Me Pass . . . Plus / 1994 / See For Miles ♦♦♦
Another British import version of a vintage Checker album, with a few highly desirable bonus cuts at the end to further recommend it. Most of the CD mirrors Diddley's 1965 *500% More Man* LP (the title track obviously being a sequel to his "I'm a Man"), but the extra items include the amusing "Mama, Keep Your Big Mouth Shut" and a danceable "We're Gonna Get Married." —*Bill Dahl*

Hey Bo Diddley/In Concert / Nov. 2, 1994 / Aim ♦♦♦

Hey! Bo Diddley/Bo Diddley / 1996 / BGO ♦♦♦♦
Beat Goes On reissued Bo Diddley's eponymous debut and his 1962 effort *Hey! Bo Diddley* on one compact disc in 1996. Although these two records don't necessarily sit well together—the first is sublime, the second notoriously uneven—it's still a nice way to pick them up on CD, especially since the sound and packaging are first-rate. However, the Chess issue that combines *Bo Diddley* and *Go Bo Diddley* on one CD is a better bet, since those two records—his first two—work better together. —*Stephen Thomas Erlewine*

A Man Amongst Men / May 21, 1996 / Code Blue ♦♦♦
Bo Diddley's major-label '90s comeback effort *A Man Amongst Men* is overflowing with guest stars, but it rarely gets into something distinctive. The presence of such heavyweights as Keith Richards, Ron Wood, and Jimmie Vaughan actually weighs down the set, preventing Diddley from digging deep into the grooves. The band never quite rocks hard enough and no one tears off an inspired solo—*A Man Amongst Men* is pleasant, but it never approaches compelling listening. —*Stephen Thomas Erlewine*

★ **His Best (Chess 50th Anniversary Collection)** / Apr. 8, 1997 / MCA ♦♦♦♦♦
With his various hits and anthology packages all out of print and the multi-disc deluxe box set out of pocketbook reach for most casual consumers, MCA finally comes up with a 20-track compilation that hits the bullseye and makes this rock pioneer's best and most influential work available to everyone. The song list reads like a primer for '60s British rhythm & blues and

'90s blues bands: "Bo Diddley," "I'm a Man," "Diddley Daddy," "Pretty Thing," "Before You Accuse Me," "Hey! Bo Diddley," "Who Do You Love," "Mona," and "Roadrunner" are the tracks that made the legend and put his sound on the map worldwide. The transfers used on this set are exemplary, the majority of them utilizing masters that have a few extra seconds (or more) appended to the fades, which will cause even hardliners to hear these old standards with fresh ears; especially revelatory are the "long versions" of "I Can Tell" and "You Can't Judge a Book by Its Cover." If the box set is too big a trigger to pull and you want all of Bo's influential sides in one package, this one should be first-stop shopping of the highest priority. — *Cub Koda*

The Dirty Dozen Brass Band

f. 1975, New Orleans, LA
Group / New Orleans R&B, New Orleans Brass Bands
The Dirty Dozen Brass Band in its prime successfully mixed together R&B with the instrumentation of a New Orleans brass band. Featuring Kirk Joseph on sousaphone playing with the agility of an electric bassist, the group revitalized the brass band tradition, opening up the repertoire and inspiring some younger groups to imitate their boldness. Generally featuring five horns (two trumpets, one trombone, and two saxes) along with the sousaphone, a snare drummer, and a bass drummer, the DDBB was innovative in its own way, making fine recordings for Rounder, Columbia, and the George Wein Collection (the latter released through Concord); guest artists have included Dr. John, Dizzy Gillespie, and Danny Barker. Unfortunately, in recent years the group has become much more conventional, still using R&B riffs but now with a standard (and less distinctive) rhythm section. — *Scott Yanow*

● **My Feet Can't Fail Me Now** / 1984 / Concord ◆◆◆◆
The Dirty Dozen Brass Band's *My Feet Can't Fail Me Now* is a rollicking, infectious set that captures the spirit of classic New Orleans R&B and jazz because it isn't enslavened to those traditions. The group is willing to play around and have fun, adding different rock, pop, and R&B influences to their sound. The result is a wonderful, unpredictable album that is as wild and rich as New Orleans itself. — *Leo Stanley*

Live: Mardi Gras in Montreux / Jul. 1985 / Rounder ◆◆◆
Not at the same level as their debut (*My Feet Can't Fail Me Now*), this second outing by the Dirty Dozen Brass Band (taken from a couple sets performed at the 1985 Montreux Jazz Festival) is overly loose in spots and has some lightweight material that was better heard live than on record. The party music does have its strong moments, the mightily sousaphone playing of Kirk Joseph (who simulates an electric bass) pushes the group and the joy of the band is not to be denied, but "The Flintstones Meets the President" is only worth hearing once. — *Scott Yanow*

Voodoo / Aug. 1987-Sep. 1987 / Columbia ◆◆◆
The Dirty Dozen Brass Band certainly knew how to have a good time while playing their music. Their spirited blending of New Orleans jazz parade rhythms with R&Bish horn riffs made them flexible enough to welcome guests Dr. John (who sings and play piano on "It's All Over Now"), Dizzy Gillespie ("Oop Pop A Dah"), and Branford Marsalis ("Moose the Mooche") to their Columbia debut without altering their music at all. With Gregory Davis and Efrem Towns playing strong trumpet in the ensembles and occasional solos, and with sousaphonist Kirk Joseph not letting up for a moment, this is a typically spirited set by the unique DDBB. — *Scott Yanow*

New Orleans Album / Aug. 1989-Dec. 1989 / Columbia ◆◆◆
A bit of a hodge-podge, this CD features the Dirty Dozen Brass Band (comprised of two trumpets, two saxes, sometimes one trombone, the sousaphone of Kirk Joseph, snare drum, and bass drum) welcoming such guests as singer Eddie Bo, guitarist-vocalist Danny Barker (showcased on "Don't You Feel My Leg"), trumpeter Dave Bartholomew (heard on "The Monkey"), and rock singer Elvis Costello. However it is the R&Bish parade band that is the main star, romping through group originals plus Cannonball Adderley's "Inside Straight" and "Kidd Jordan's Second Line." — *Scott Yanow*

Open Up: Whatcha Gonna Do for the Rest of Your Life? / Jan. 1991-Apr.
     1991 / Columbia ◆◆◆◆
The Dirty Dozen Brass Band sticks to originals (except for Johnny Dyani's "Eyomzi") on this fairly adventurous set. The octet (which consists of two trumpets, two saxes, one trombone, sousaphone, snare drum, and bass drum)

still had a unique sound in 1991 but three songs on the date only used part of the unit and the DDBB seemed to be trying to escape the sound of the brass band tradition (they had long had a more modern repertoire). Not all of the pieces work although the music in general is pretty colorful and somewhat unpredictable, even if it falls short of essential. — *Scott Yanow*

Jelly / Aug. 1992-Jan. 1993 / Columbia ◆◆◆
The Dirty Dozen Brass Band, an innovative group that combines R&B with New Orleans parade rhythms, pays tribute to the great Jelly Roll Morton on this CD. Actually the DDBB mostly ignores Morton's original recordings (and leaves out some of his themes) in an unusual set that does not find them neglecting their own individuality. A few Danny Barker monologues add to the authenticity of this music, which takes great liberties with Morton's compositions. Trumpeter Gregory Davis (who duets with guest pianist Eddie Bo on "Dead Man Blues") is the most impressive soloist, though it is the sound of the rollicking ensembles (propelled by the sousaphone of Keith Anderson) that gives this set its sense of purpose. Purists, however, should avoid this one. — *Scott Yanow*

The Dixie Hummingbirds

f. 193?, Greenville, South Carolina
Group / Black Gospel, Southern Gospel, Traditional Gospel
A pioneering force behind the evolution of the modern gospel quartet sound, the Dixie Hummingbirds were among the longest-lived and most successful groups of their era; renowned for their imaginative arrangements, progressive harmonies, and all-around versatility, they earned almost universal recognition as the greatest Southern quartet of their generation, and their influence spread not only over the world of spiritual music but also inspired secular artists ranging from Jackie Wilson to Bobby "Blue" Bland to the Temptations. Formed in Greenville, South Carolina by James B. Davis, the Dixie Hummingbirds began their career during the late '30s as a jubilee-styled act; joined in 1938 by 13-year-old baritone phenom Ira Tucker and bass singer extraordinaire Willie Bobo, a former member of the Heavenly Gospel Singers, the group made their recorded debut a year later on Decca, where they issued singles including "Soon Will Be Done with the Troubles of This World," "Little Wooden Church" and "Joshua Journeyed to Jericho."

Upon relocating to Philadelphia in 1942, the Hummingbirds' popularity began to grow — Tucker, in particular, wowed audiences with his flamboyant theatrics, rejecting the long tradition of "flat-footed" singers rooted in place on stage in favor of running up the aisles and rocking prayerfully on his knees. By 1944, he was even regularly jumping off stages — indeed, the frenetic showmanship of soul music may have had its origins in Tucker's manic intensity, itself an emulation of country preaching. At the same time, the Hummingbirds' harmonies continued to grow more sophisticated; the addition of Paul Owens completed the quartet's development, and together he and Tucker honed a style they dubbed "trickeration," a kind of note-bending distinguished by sensual lyrical finesse and staggering vocal intricacy. Their virtuosity did not go unnoticed by audiences, and throughout the mid-'40s — an acknowledged golden age of a cappella quartet singing — the group regularly played to packed houses throughout the south.

Under names like the Swanee Quintet and the Jericho Boys, the Dixie Hummingbirds also regularly appeared on Philadelphia radio station WCAU; it was as the Jericho Boys that they auditioned for the legendary producer John Hammond, who in 1942 booked them into the Cafe Society Downtown, then the Greenwich Village area's preeminent showcase for black talent. By 1946, the Hummingbirds were again recording, cutting sides for labels including Apollo and, later in the decade, Gotham and Hob. In 1952, what many consider the group's definitive lineup — a roster of Tucker, Davis, Bobo, Beachey Thompson, James Walker (replacing Owens), and ace guitarist Howard Carroll, a roster which held intact for close to a quarter century — signed to the Peacock label, where over the course of the following decade they recorded a series of masterpieces, including 1952's "Trouble in My Way," 1953's "Let's Go to the Program," 1954's "Christian's Testimonial," 1957's "Christian's Automobile," and 1959's "Nobody Knows the Trouble I See."

After earning a standing ovation for their performance at the 1966 Newport Folk Festival (captured on the *Gospel at Newport* LP), the Hummingbirds essentially retired from mainstream appearances to focus solely on the church circuit. They did, however, burst back into the popular consciousness in 1973, backing Paul Simon on his pop smash "Loves Me Like a Rock." The death of Willie Bobo in 1976 brought to a sad end a lengthy chapter of the Hummingbirds' history—his membership in their ranks dated back to the late '30s—but the surviving members forged on; just two years later, *Ebony* Magazine named them "The World's Greatest Gospel Group." After Davis retired in 1984, Tucker was the last remaining link to the quartet's formative years; despite the subsequent deaths of Walker in 1992 and Thompson in 1994, Tucker continued leading the group at the century's end, recruiting new blood to keep the Dixie Hummingbirds' spirit alive for years to follow. —*Jason Ankeny*

Christian Testimonial / 1959 / MCA ✦✦✦
Great Peacock sides led by James Walker and Ira Tucker. —*Opal Louis Nations*

Prayer for Peace / 1964 / Peacock ✦✦✦
More great material from this seminal group. —*Opal Louis Nations*

In the Morning / 1964 / Peacock ✦✦✦✦
More fine harmony and tough singing. —*Opal Louis Nations*

The Best of the Dixie Hummingbirds / 1973 / MCA ✦✦✦✦
Terrific collection of the group's best 1950s-'60s Peacock sides. —*Opal Louis Nations*

★ **Live** / 1976 / Mobile Fidelity ✦✦✦✦✦
With 75 minutes of fine performances, good sound quality, and a varied repertoire, this the one to buy. —*Kip Lornell*

The Dixie Hummingbirds [Gospel Heritage] / 1988 / Gospel Heritage ✦✦✦✦
Choice Gotham material with and without Margaret Allison and the Angelic Gospel Singers of Philadelphia. —*Opal Louis Nations*

In the Storm Too Long / 1991 / Gospel Jubilee ✦✦✦✦
Essential Regis, Apollo, & Decca sides from the '40s. —*Opal Louis Nations*

In These Changing Times / 1991 / MCA ✦✦✦
Choice selections from the best on the Peacock label. Great quartet. —*Opal Louis Nations*

We Love You Like a Rock/Every Day and Every Hour / 1991 / Mobile Fidelity ✦✦✦✦

Complete Recorded Works (1939-1947) / Apr. 8, 1997 / Document ✦✦✦✦
Essential early sides by this seminal group. —*Opal Louis Nations*

Up in Heaven: The Very Best of the Dixie Hummingbirds & the Angelics / Mar. 3, 1998 / Collectables ✦✦✦✦
Peacock/ABC Paramount sides by this leading group from Philadelphia. —*Opal Louis Nations*

Love Me Like a Rock / MCA ✦✦✦✦
More fine selections from the Peacock catalog. Seminal quartet material. —*Opal Louis Nations*

Floyd Dixon

b. Feb. 8, 1929, Marshall, TX
Piano, Vocals / R&B, Electric West Coast Blues, Acoustic West Coast Blues, West Coast Blues, Piano Blues, Jump Blues

Floyd Dixon was an unabashed admirer of Charles Brown's mellow "club blues" sound, but he added a more energetic, aggressive jump blues edge to his sound during the early '50s—a formula that made the L.A.-based pianist an R&B star.

A Texas emigre, like so many of his postwar California contemporaries, Dixon hit the City of Angels at age 13. Influenced by Louis Jordan and Amos Milburn along with Brown, Dixon was swept up in the late-'40s R&B boom, recording for Supreme in 1947 and signing with Modern Records in 1949. He nudged into the R&B Top Ten with "Dallas Blues" and just missed similar lofty stature with "Mississippi Blues" later in 1949. After cutting prolifically for Modern, he switched over to Eddie Mesner's Aladdin logo and hit in 1950 with "Sad Journey Blues" (also issued on Peacock), "Telephone Blues" the next year (backed by Johnny Moore's Three Blazers, the same crew that catapulted Charles Brown to stardom), and the mournful "Call Operator 210" in 1952.

But there was a playfully ribald side to Dixon, too. The double-entendre

"Red Cherries," a storming "Wine, Wine, Wine," and the two-sided 1951 live waxing "Too Much Jelly Roll" (penned by a young Jerry Leiber and Mike Stoller) and "Baby, Let's Go Down to the Woods" showcased his more raucous leanings. The hits ceased, but Dixon's West Coast R&B odyssey continued with dates for Specialty in 1953, Atlantic's Cat subsidiary in 1954 (where he waxed the rollicking "Hey Bartender," likely his best-known tune thanks to covers by Koko Taylor and the execrable Blues Brothers), Ebb (where he challenged Little Richard's galvanic energy levels on the torrid "Oooh Little Girl" in 1957), and Checker.

The self-proclaimed "Mr. Magnificent" is still at it today—during the mid-'90s, he secured a contract with Alligator Records and released *Wake Up and Live!* in 1996. —*Bill Dahl*

Opportunity Blues / 1976 / Route 66 ✦✦✦✦
Vinyl-only examination of the pianist's early sides for several West Coast R&B indies that spans 1948-1961. Dixon's ballad style was quite reminiscent of Charles Brown's but his jump blues leanings—here typified by "Wine, Wine, Wine" and "Real Lovin' Mama"—were all his own. —*Bill Dahl*

Rockin' This Joint Tonite / 1978 / JSP ✦✦✦

Houston Jump / 1979 / Route 66 ✦✦✦✦
Another cross-section of Dixon's 1947-1960 output that hasn't made the jump to the digital age as of yet. Surveys a wide array of labels, including a 1954 date for Atlantic's short-lived Cat subsidiary that produced "Roll Baby Roll" and "Is It True." —*Bill Dahl*

Marshall Texas Is My Home / 1991 / Specialty ✦✦✦✦
Dixon landed at Art Rupe's Specialty label in 1953, his music jumping harder than ever. These 22 tracks rate with his best; the collection is full of rarities and previously unissued items, many featuring the wailing tenor sax of Carlos Bermudez in lusty support of the pianist. By 1957, when he momentarily paused at Ebb Records, Dixon could do a pretty fair breathless imitation of Little Richard, as the scorching "Oooh Little Girl" definitively proves. Also includes Dixon's best-known number, the often-covered rocker "Hey Bartender" (first out on Atlantic's Cat subsidiary in 1954). —*Bill Dahl*

● **Complete Aladdin Recordings** / Mar. 19, 1996 / Capitol ✦✦✦✦
It's a matter of opinion as to whether Dixon's Aladdin output was his peak; many would give his Specialty sides (available on the *Marshall Texas Is My Home* compilation) the nod. Still, his late-'40s and early-'50s work for the label included some of his most popular and best tracks, such as "Wine, Wine, Wine," "Call Operator 210," "Tired, Broke and Busted," "Let's Dance," "Telephone Blues," and "Too Much Jelly Roll" (the last of which was one of Leiber-Stoller's first recorded compositions). This two-CD, 48-track compilation is geared more toward the completist collector than the average fan, especially with the inclusion of five Sonny Parker sides (which Dixon now says he didn't play on, despite some reports to the contrary) and about ten songs that feature Mari Jones on vocals. The best stuff is jump blues at its best, though, with good guitar work by Johnny and Oscar Moore (the latter of whom had played with Nat King Cole), Dixon's fine piano playing, and witty, knowing vocals and lyrics. —*Richie Unterberger*

Wake up and Live! / May 21, 1996 / Alligator ✦✦✦✦
There was a time when swing-oriented jazz, R&B, and blues overlapped to form an accessible yet intelligent style of music. In the late '40s Louis Jordan, Charles Brown, and Amos Milburn were popular figures and Floyd Dixon (although a bit in their shadow) was not far behind. When rock 'n' roll suddenly took over pop music in the mid-'50s, the middle-aged black performers were tossed off the charts in favor of their younger white imitators and work began to become scarce. Fortunately Floyd Dixon survived the lean years and, as with Charles Brown, he made a "comeback." This CD is a definitive Floyd Dixon release, mixing together older hits (including his signature tune "Hey Bartender") with newer originals; all 16 selections were written or co-composed by Dixon. Joined by a jumping band that features a liberal amount of solo space for guitarist Port Barlow, tenor saxophonist Eddie Synigal and the old-time styled trombone of Danny Weinstein (plus a couple of spots for Charles Owens' baritone), Dixon sounds in excellent shape. His voice had not aged much, his enthusiasm is very much intact, and his piano playing (whether on slow blues, medium-tempo novelties or the closing instrumental blues "Gettin' Ready") is quite jazz-oriented. Chip Deffaa's liner notes are an added plus. Highly recommended. —*Scott Yanow*

Willie Dixon

b. Jul. 1, 1915, Vicksburg, MS, **d.** Jan. 29, 1992, Burbank, CA
Bass, Guitar, Vocals / Acoustic Chicago Blues, Electric Chicago Blues, Chicago Blues

Willie Dixon's life and work was virtually an embodiment of the progress of the blues, from an accidental creation of the descendants of freed slaves to a recognized and vital part of America's musical heritage. That Dixon was one of the first professional blues songwriters to benefit in a serious, material way—and that he had to fight to do it—from his work also made him an important symbol of the injustice that still informs the music industry, even at the end of this century. A producer, songwriter, bassist and singer, he helped Muddy Waters, Howlin' Wolf, Little Walter, and others find their most commercially successful voices.

By the time he was a teenager, Dixon was writing songs and selling copies to the local bands. He also studied music with a local carpenter, Theo Phelps, who taught him about harmony singing. With his bass voice, Dixon later joined a group organized by Phelps, the Union Jubilee Singers, who appeared on local radio. Dixon eventually made his way to Chicago, where he won the Illinois State Golden Gloves Heavyweight Championship. He might've been a successful boxer, but he turned to music instead, thanks to Leonard "Baby Doo" Caston, a guitarist who had seen Dixon at the gym where he worked out and occasionally sang with him. The two formed a duo playing on streetcorners, and later Dixon took up the bass as an instrument. They later formed a group, the Five Breezes, who recorded for the Bluebird label. The group's success was halted, however, when Dixon refused induction into the armed forces as a consciencious objector. Dixon was eventually freed after a year, and formed another group, the Four Jumps of Jive. In 1945, however, Dixon was back working with Caston in a group called the Big Three Trio, with guitarist Bernardo Dennis (later replaced by Ollie Crawford).

During this period, Dixon would occasionally appear as a bassist at late-night jam sessions featuring members of the growing blues community, including Muddy Waters. Later on when the Chess brothers—who owned a club where Dixon occasionally played—began a new record label, Aristocrat (later Chess), they hired him, initially as a bassist on a 1948 session for Robert Nighthawk. The Chess brothers liked Dixon's playing, and his skills as a songwriter and arranger, and during the next two years he was working regularly for the Chess brothers. He got to record some of his own material, but generally Dixon was seldom featured as an artist at any of these sessions.

Dixon's real recognition as a songwriter began with Muddy Waters' recording of "Hoochie Coochie Man." The success of that single, "Evil" by Howlin' Wolf, and "My Babe" by Little Walter saw Dixon establish as Chess' most reliable tunesmith, and the Chess brothers continually pushed Dixon's songs on their artists. In addition to writing songs, Dixon continued as bassist and recording manager of many of the Chess label's recording sessions, including those by Lowell Fulson, Bo Diddley, and Otis Rush. Dixon's remuneration for all of this work, including the songwriting, was minimal—he was barely able to support his rapidly growing family on the $100 a week that the Chess brothers were giving him, and a short stint with the rival Cobra label at the end of the '50s didn't help him much.

During the mid-'60s, Chess gradually phased out Dixon's bass work, in favor of electric bass, thus reducing his presence at many of the sessions. At the same time, a European concert promoter named Horst Lippmann had begun a series of shows called the American Folk-Blues Festival, for which he would bring some of the top blues players in America over to tour the continent. Dixon ended up organizing the musical side of these shows for the first decade or more, recording on his own as well and earning a good deal more money than he was seeing from his work for Chess. At the same time, he began to see a growing interest in his songwriting from the British rock bands that he saw while in London—his music was getting covered regularly by artists like the Rolling Stones and the Yardbirds, and when he visited England, he even found himself cajoled into presenting his newest songs to their managements. Back at Chess, Howlin' Wolf and Muddy Waters continued to perform Dixon's songs, as did newer artists such as Koko Taylor, who had her own hit with "Wang Dang Doodle." Gradually, however, after the mid-'60s, Dixon saw his relationship with Chess Records come to a halt. Partly this was a result of time—the passing of artists such as Little Walter and Sonny Boy Williamson was part of the problem, and the death of Leonard Chess and the sale of the company called a halt to Dixon's involvement.

By the end of the 1960s, Dixon was eager to try his hand as a performer again, a career that had been interrupted when he'd gone to work for Chess as a producer. He recorded an album of his best-known songs, *I Am the Blues*, for Columbia Records, and organized a touring band, the Chicago Blues All-Stars, to play concerts in Europe. Suddenly, in his 50s, he began making a major name for himself on stage for the first time in his career. Around this time, Dixon began to have grave doubts about the nature of the songwriting contract that he had with Chess' publishing arm, Arc Music. He was seeing precious little money from songwriting, despite the recording of hit versions of such Dixon songs as "Spoonful" by Cream. He had never seen as much money as he was entitled to as a songwriter, but during the 1970s he began to understand just *how much* money he'd been deprived of, by design or just plain negligence on the part of the publisher doing its job on his behalf.

Arc Music had sued Led Zeppelin for copyright infringement over "Bring It on Home" on *Led Zeppelin II*, saying that it was Dixon's song, and won a settlement that Dixon never saw any part of until his manager did an audit of Arc's accounts. Dixon and Muddy Waters would later file suit against Arc Music to recover royalties and the ownership of their copyrights. Additionally, many years later Dixon brought suit against Led Zeppelin for copyright infringement over "Whole Lotta Love" and its resemblance to Dixon's "You Need Love." Both cases resulted in out-of-court settlements that were generous to the songwriter.

The 1980s saw Dixon as the last survivor of the Chess blues stable and he began working with various organizations to help secure song copyrights on behalf of blues songwriters who, like himself, had been deprived of revenue during previous decades. In 1988, Dixon became the first producer/songwriter to be honored with a boxed-set collection, when MCA Records released *Willie Dixon: The Chess Box* that included several rare Dixon sides as well as the most famous recordings of his songs by Chess' stars. The following year, Dixon published *I Am the Blues* (Da Capo Press), his autobiography, written in association with Don Snowden.

Dixon continued performing, and was also called in as a producer on movie soundtracks such as *Gingerale Afternoon*, and *La Bamba*, producing the work of his old stablemate Bo Diddley. By that time, Dixon was regarded as something of an elder statesman, composer, and spokesperson of American blues. Dixon had suffered from increasingly poor health in recent years, and lost a leg to diabetes several years earlier, which didn't slow him down very much. He died peacefully in his sleep early in 1992. —*Bruce Eder*

Willie's Blues / 1959 / Bluesville ✦✦✦
This is a tasty, understated 1959 session with singer/pianist Memphis Slim and bassist/singer-songwriter Willie Dixon. —*Mark A. Humphrey*

I Am the Blues / 1970 / Mobile Fidelity ✦✦✦
The material is superb, consisting of some of Dixon's best-known songs of the 1960s, and the production is smoothly professional, but none of the performances here are likely to make you forget the hits by Howlin' Wolf, Muddy Waters et al. Reissued on CD by Mobile Fidelity and more recently by Sony Music—unfortunately, none of the unreleased tracks from the session seem to have survived. —*Bruce Eder*

Catalyst / 1973 / Ovation ✦✦✦✦
One of his better latter-day efforts. —*Bill Dahl*

Willie Dixon's Peace? / 197 / Yambo ✦✦
This unexciting set appeared on Dixon's own label. —*Bill Dahl*

Mighty Earthquake & Hurricane / 1983 / Chase Music ✦✦✦
Decent modern album by the prolific legend. —*Bill Dahl*

Willie Dixon: Live (Backstage Access) / 1985 / PA/USA ✦✦
Adequate but not earthshaking. —*Bill Dahl*

Hidden Charms / Sep. 28, 1988 / Bug ✦✦✦

★ **The Chess Box** / 1989 / MCA/Chess ✦✦✦✦✦
There are a few holes in this collection, but not many. As it is, the material is virtually a best-of-Chess collection, featuring some of the best tracks in the respective outputs of Muddy Waters, Howlin' Wolf, Little Walter, Sonny Boy Williamson, Bo Diddley, Lowell Fulsom, Koko Taylor et al. —*Bruce Eder*

The Big Three Trio / 1990 / Columbia/Legacy ✦✦✦
The Big Three Trio was Dixon's post-World War II blues vocal trio. His songwriting talent was still developing, and there isn't much relationship between

this material and his subsequent work on Chess. The smooth vocals, however, will recall the Ink Spots, among other vocal groups of the era. —*Bruce Eder*

The Original Wang Dang Doodle / 1995 / MCA/Chess ✦✦✦✦
This is a good collection of hard-to-find and previously unreleased Dixon sides, although there are several Chess tracks that were left off that would have made it much more valuable. The title track is especially worthwhile, as is "Tail Dragger," but it is also easy to see from this collection why Dixon was never quite a star in his own right as a performer—he has a good voice, but not a very memorable or powerful one, compared with Muddy Waters, Howlin' Wolf et al. —*Bruce Eder*

Lefty Dizz

b. Apr. 29, 1937, Osceola, AR, **d.** Sep. 7, 1993, Chicago, IL
Guitar, Vocals / Electric Chicago Blues
In a town like Chicago, where the competition in blues clubs was tough and keen (and still is on a hot night), certain musicians quickly learned that sometimes red-hot playing and singing didn't always get the job done by themselves. You had to entertain, put on a show, because there was *always* someone looking to take your gig away from you. Only those willing to protect their bandstand—and their livelihood in the long run—by generally peppering their presentation with a small to large dollop of showmanship were smart enough to hang in for the long run, keeping both their hometown audience and their turf intact. Although blues revisionist history always seems to overlook this, the show that T-Bone Walker, Guitar Slim, Howlin' Wolf, Muddy Waters, Little Walter, Buddy Guy, and others did in front of a Black audience was wilder and far more audacious than the one a more reserved White audience *ever* got to see. For wild-ass showmen in blues history, though, one would certainly have to go a far piece to beat Walter Williams, known to blues fans in Chicago and Europe as Lefty Dizz.

A regular fixture of the Chicago scene from the mid-'60s into the early '90s, Lefty was quite a sight back in those days; fronting his band, Shock Treatment, playing and singing with an unbridled enthusiasm while simultaneously putting on a show that would have oldtimers guffawing in appreciation while scaring White patrons out of their wits. As an entertainer, he was simply nothing less than a modern day Guitar Slim informed with the outrage of a Hendrix, pulling out every trick in the book to win over an audience, whether he was protecting his home turf bandstand or stealing the show while sitting in somewhere else. It was nothing for him to play a slow blues, bring the band down, and start walking through the crowd dragging his beat-up Stratocaster behind him like a sack of potatoes, playing it with one hand the entire time. Or take on some young Turk axeman gunning for his scalp (and gig) by kicking off Freddie King's "Hideaway" at an impossibly fast tempo, calling for break after break while infusing all of them with so many eye-popping gags that the young Turk in question was merely reduced to becoming another member of the audience. As a bluesman, he was nothing less than deep and 100% for real. Nobody messed with Lefty Dizz.

Born in Arkansas in 1937, Dizz (the nickname was bestowed on him by Hound Dog Taylor and the HouseRockers, appropriating it from drummer Ted Harvey, who used the name when he was "playing jazz in the alley") started playing guitar at age 19 after a four-year hitch in the Air Force. Entirely self-taught, he played a standard right-handed model flipped upside down, without reversing the strings. His sound was raw and distorted and his style owed more to the older bluesmen than to the hipper West Side players like Otis Rush and Buddy Guy working in the B.B. King mode. By the time he came to Chicago, he had honed his craft well enough to become a member of Junior Wells' band in 1964, recording and touring Africa, Europe, and Southeast Asia with him until the late '60s. At various times during the '60s and early '70s, he'd also moonlight as a guitarist with Chicago stalwarts J.B. Lenoir and Hound Dog Taylor, while sitting in everywhere and playing with seemingly everyone. While being well known around town as a "head cutter," Lefty Dizz was always welcome on anyone's bandstand. His personality, while seemingly carefree and humorous, masked a deep, highly intelligent individual who had also earned a degree in economics from Southern Illinois University.

He kept soldiering on in the blues trenches through the '90s when he was diagnosed with cancer of the esophagus. While chemotherapy helped, Lefty went back to work far too soon and far too hard to stay on top of his game for much longer. The unflappable Dizz, who could seemingly make the best out of any given situation without complaint and had friends in the blues community by the truckload, finally passed away on September 7, 1993. And with his passing, the blues lost perhaps its most flamboyant showman. —*Cub Koda*

Ain't It Nice to Be Loved / 1995 / JSP ✦✦
Dizz recorded his final outing at Sotosound studios in Evanston, IL, surrounded with a collection of players who knew his style. Therefore, that this effort falls so short of the mark is all the more puzzling. If anyone truly needed a producer, Dizz was the man. The arrangements meander, the mix (such as it is) buries Lefty's guitar and evidently nobody bothered to tune up before or during the session. JSP has never been much noted for quality releases on either audio or artistic levels, but this is just plain embarrassing. —*Cub Koda*

Lefty Dizz with Big Moose Walker / Black and Blue ✦✦
It has been argued by more than one blues critic that for all his performing acumen, Lefty Dizz never recorded an album that captured even a smidgeon of his live intensity. This poorly produced album, recorded for the French Black and Blue imprint, would certainly support that claim. While the performances are workmanlike enough, Dizz's guitar sound (apparently routed direct to the board, bypassing his amp) gives new meaning to the words flabby and lifeless. Out of print for the time being and perhaps deservedly so. —*Cub Koda*

• Somebody Stole My Christmas / Isabel ✦✦✦✦
Dizz fares much better on this sophomore outing. Featuring a nice take on the title cut and fairly solid playing from all parties concerned, this certainly falls short of the fervor he could produce live but is still the best of the bunch. —*Cub Koda*

Dr. John

b. Nov. 21, 1940, New Orleans, LA
Piano, Vocals, Guitar, Keyboards / R&B, Rock 'n' Roll, New Orleans R&B, Piano Blues
Although he didn't become widely known until the 1970s, Dr. John had been active in the music industry since the late '50s, when the teenager was still known as Mac Rebennack. A formidable boogie and blues pianist with a lovable growl of a voice, his most enduring achievements have fused New Orleans R&B, rock, and Mardi Gras craziness to come up with his own brand of "voodoo" music. He's also quite accomplished and enjoyable when sticking to purely traditional forms of blues and R&B. On record, he veers between the two approaches, making for an inconsistent and frequently frustrating legacy that often makes the listener feel as if the Night Tripper (as he's nicknamed himself) has been underachieving.

In the late '50s, Rebennack gained prominence in the New Orleans R&B scene as a session keyboardist and guitarist, contributing to records by Professor Longhair, Frankie Ford, and Joe Tex. He also did some overlooked singles of his own, and by the 1960s had expanded into production and arranging. After a gun accident damaged his hand in the early '60s, he gave up the guitar to concentrate on keyboards exclusively. Skirting trouble with the law and drugs, he left the increasingly unwelcome environs of New Orleans in the mid-'60s for Los Angeles, where he found session work with the help of fellow New Orleans expatriate Harold Battiste.

Rebennack renamed himself Dr. John the Night Tripper when he recorded his first album, *Gris-Gris*. According to legend, this was hurriedly cut with leftover studio time from a Sonny & Cher session, but it never sounded hastily conceived. In fact, its mix of New Orleans R&B with voodoo sounds and a tinge of psychedelia was downright enthralling, and may have resulted in his greatest album. He began building an underground following with both his music and his eccentric stage presence, which found him conducting ceremonial-type events in full Mardi Gras costume.

Dr. John was nothing if not eclectic, and his next few albums were granted mixed critical receptions because of their unevenness and occasional excess. They certainly had their share of admirable moments, though, and Eric Clapton and Mick Jagger helped out on *The Sun Moon and Herbs* in 1971. The following year's *Gumbo*, produced by Jerry Wexler, proved Dr. John was a master of traditional New Orleans R&B styles, in the mold of one of his heroes, Professor Longhair. In 1973, he got his sole big hit, "In the Right Place," which was produced by Allen Toussaint, with backing by the Meters.

In the same year, he also recorded with Mike Bloomfield and John Hammond, Jr. for the *Triumvirate* album.

The rest of the decade, unfortunately, was pretty much a waste musically. Dr. John could always count on returning to traditional styles for a good critical reception, and he did so constantly in the 1980s. There were solo piano albums, sessions with Chris Barber and Jimmy Witherspoon, and *In a Sentimental Mood* (1989), a record of pop standards. These didn't sell all that well, though. A more important problem was that he's capable of much more than recastings of old styles and material. In fact, by this time he was usually bringing in the bacon not through his own music, but via vocals for numerous commercial jingles.

It's continued pretty much in the same vein throughout the 1990s: New Orleans supersessions for the *Bluesiana* albums, another outing with Chris Barber, an album of New Orleans standards, and *another* album of pop standards. In 1994, *Television* did at least offer some original material. However, at this point it seems like he will usually rely upon cover versions for the bulk of his recorded work, though his interpretive skills will always ensure that these are more interesting than most such efforts. His autobiography, *Under a Hoodoo Moon*, was published by St. Martin's Press in 1994, and in 1998 he resurfaced with *Anutha Zone*, which featured collaborations with latter-day performers including Spiritualized, Paul Weller, Supergrass, and Ocean Colour Scene. — *Richie Unterberger*

Gris Gris / 1968 / Repertoire ✦✦✦✦
The most exploratory and psychedelic outing of Dr. John's career, a one-of-a-kind fusion of New Orleans Mardi Gras R&B and voodoo mysticism. Great rasping, bluesy vocals, soulful backup singers, and eerie melodies on flute, sax, and clarinet, as well as odd Middle Eastern-like chanting and mandolin runs. It's got the setting of a strange religious ritual, but the mood is far more joyous than solemn. — *Richie Unterberger*

Babylon / 1969 / Atco ✦✦✦
Dr. John's ambition remained undiminished on his second solo album, *Babylon*, released shortly after the groundbreaking voodoo-psychedelia-New Orleans R&B fusion of his debut, *Gris-Gris*. The results, however, were not nearly as consistent or impressive. Coolly received by critics, the album nonetheless is deserving of attention, though it pales a bit in comparison with *Gris-Gris*. The production is sparser and more reliant on female backup vocals than his debut. Dr. John remains intent on fusing voodoo and R&B, but the mood is oddly bleak and despairing, in comparison with the wild Mardi Gras-gone-amok tone of his first LP. The hushed, damned atmosphere and afterhours R&B sound a bit like Van Morrison on a bummer trip at times, as peculiar as that might seem. "The Patriotic Flag-Waiver" (sic), in keeping with the mood of the late '60s, damns social ills and hypocrisy of all sorts. An FM underground radio favorite at the time, its ambitious structure remains admirable, though its musical imperfections haven't worn well. To a degree, you could say the same about the album as a whole. But it has enough of an eerie fascination to merit investigation. — *Richie Unterberger*

Remedies / 1970 / Atco ✦✦

Sun Moon & Herbs / Sep. 1971 / Atco ✦✦✦

Dr. John / 1972 / Springboard ✦✦
Dr. John did a lot of sessions during his years of obscurity in New Orleans, and after he achieved national recognition in 1971 with the release of the *Dr. John, The Night Tripper (The Sun, Moon & Herbs)* album on Atco/Atlantic, those early sessions began turning up on low-budget labels. This album contains nine tracks, three of them alternate versions of other tracks, two of them apparently not featuring Dr. John at all (they are credited to "The Night Trippers"), and it still runs less than 24 minutes. Needless to say, it is not representative of later Dr. John material and should be avoided by all but completists. — *William Ruhlmann*

Gumbo / Apr. 1972 / Atco ✦✦✦✦
Gumbo bridged the gap between post-hippie rock and early rock 'n' roll, blues, and R&B, offering a selection of classic New Orleans R&B, including "Tipitina" and "Junko Partner," updated with a gritty, funky beat. There aren't as many psychedelic flourishes as there were on his first two albums, but the ones that are present enhance his sweeping vision of American roots music. And that sly fusion of styles makes *Gumbo* one of Dr. John's finest albums. — *Stephen Thomas Erlewine*

In the Right Place / Mar. 1973 / Atco ✦✦✦
Triumvirate / May 1973 / Columbia ✦✦✦
These three have a common background of blues, but in very differing styles. This could have led to each cut being a centerpiece for the player featured. Or, as is evidenced by what our ears hear, a mix of the styles, and probably most importantly, the setting aside of egos of these three who are used to being "the" leader. So we get to hear the acoustic rural blues of John Hammond, mixed with the city blues of Mike Bloomfield, and the funky New Orleans rhythm & blues of Dr. John. Just listen to the tightness of the band on "Cha-Dooky-Doo," the stretching on "Just to Be with You." You don't get the blending of the three styles but a mixture of players stretching themselves in other related grooves. — *Bob Gottlieb*

Desitively Bonaroo / Apr. 1974 / Atco ✦✦✦
Hollywood Be Thy Name / 1975 / One Way ✦✦
City Lights / Feb. 1978 / Horizon ✦✦✦
Tango Palace / 1979 / Horizon ✦✦
Dr. John's second and final album for the Horizon jazz subsidiary of A&M Records finds him working with producers Tommy LiPuma and Hugh McCracken on a rollicking set that emphasizes his New Orleans roots while attempting to update his sound with '70s effects such as deep, plucked bass notes and occasional disco rhythms. The album leads off with "Keep That Music Simple," a somewhat caustic admonishment to musicians and the music business whose message is disregarded elsewhere on the record, as LiPuma and McCracken seek to cover all stylistic bases from funk to fusion to second line. Dr. John emerges from the production intact, but he is not quite as swampy as when heard at his best. — *William Ruhlmann*

Dr. John Plays Mac Rebennack / 1981 / Clean Cuts ✦✦✦✦
Dr. John was always respected as a consummate pianist, but he didn't make a solo, unaccompanied piano record until 1981's *Dr. John Plays Mac Rebennack*. The wait was well worth it. His music had always been impressive, but this is the first time that his playing had been put on full display, and it reveals that there's even more depth and intricacies to his style than previously expected. More importantly, the music simply sounds good and gritty, as he turns out a set of New Orleans R&B (comprised of both originals and classics) that is funky, swampy and real. — *Thom Owens*

Brightest Smile in Town / 1983 / Clean Cuts ✦✦✦
Doctor John's second solo piano album finds him combining country, blues, and New Orleans standards with originals, half of them instrumentals and half of them containing vocals that sound like they were recorded off the piano microphone. This is not a high-tech recording, by any means, but in its unadorned way it does capture the flavor of Doctor John as directly as any record he's made. — *William Ruhlmann*

The Ultimate Dr. John / 1987 / Warner Brothers ✦✦✦✦
This collection is drawn from Dr. John's years on the Atlantic label. Drawing from the albums *Gris-Gris*, *Gumbo*, *Remedies*, *Desitively Bonnaroo*, and *In the Right Place* it puts his early years as the band leader in perspective. It takes us from the Hoodo-Voodoo sounds of "I Walk on Guilded Splinters" and "Iko Iko," to the more polished tunes like "Such a Night." It is a good sampling of New Orleans rhythm & blues of this phase of his recorded years. His long years as a studio musician earned him the respect of the many great "sidemen" (a virtual who's who of New Orleans musicians) that he has playing with him on this album. If you don't have early Dr. John this is a necessity. He is at his best here. — *Bob Gottlieb*

In a Sentimental Mood / Apr. 1989 / Warner Brothers ✦✦✦
On Dr. John's first major-label effort and first vocal studio album in ten years, he performs a set of pop standards including Cole Porter's "Love for Sale" and Johnny Mercer's "Accentuate the Positive." After starting out with a wild stage act and unusual costumes, Dr. John has evolved into a vocal stylist and piano virtuoso, which makes the idea of doing this sort of material appealing. And he does it well, turning out a leisurely duet with Rickie Lee Jones on "Makin' Whoopee" that won a Grammy (Best Jazz Vocal Performance, Duo or Group) and giving sad feeling to "My Buddy." Maybe he has changed since the *Gris Gris* days, but even a mellowed Dr. John is a tasty one. — *William Ruhlmann*

On a Mardi Gras Day / 1990 / Great Southern ✦✦✦
On a Mardi Gras Day is a live recording from 1983, capturing Dr. John at

London's Marquee with Chris Barber and his 11-piece band. The presence of Barber and his big band gives the music a greater sense of swing, which makes this record—which basically consists of such familiar items as "Iko Iko," "Right Place, Wrong Time," "Li'l Liza Jane," "Stack-A-Lee," and "Such a Night"—something special in Mac Rebennack's catalog. It gives longtime fans the opportunity to hear him stretch out, play with the tempo and flash his jazz chops, which are considerable. Not the definitive or most representative Dr. John live set, but a rewarding one nonetheless. — *Thom Owens*

Dr. John and His New Orleans Congregation / 1990 / Ace ✦✦✦
Ace's *Dr. John and His New Orleans Congregation* isn't a Dr. John compilation in the strictest sense of the term—in other words, if you're looking for nothing but his funky hippie gumbo, you'd better look elsewhere. This disc is actually a great collection of cuts Mac Rebennack either played on or produced during the late '50s. all of which were released on Ace Records. Only "Storm Warning" is a genuine Rebennack song; the rest are New Orleans R&B at its funkiest. Not all of the songs are classics—in fact, only a handful, such as Earl King's "Let the Good Times Roll" come close to that status—but many of them are quite entertaining, especially for hardcore New Orleans R&B fanatics, making this a nice addition to either Dr. John or serious New Orleans R&B collections. — *Stephen Thomas Erlewine*

Bluesiana II / 1991 / Windham Hill ✦✦✦
Previously, Windham Hill Records released *Bluesiana Triangle*, a jazz trio album by drummer Art Blakey, pianist Dr. John, and reed man David "Fathead" Newman. Blakey passed away in 1990, but in the spring of 1991, Dr. John and Newman organized this second Bluesiana session, featuring trombonist Ray Anderson, drummer Will Calhoun, bassists Essiet Okon Essiet and Jay Leonhart (on different tracks), and percussionist Joe Bonadio. The resulting music again justifies the name, blues played in a funky Louisiana style with plenty of room for extended jazzy soloing. Though much of the material was written by Dr. John and he does sing occasionally, this is not a conventional Dr. John vocal album. It does contain some excellent playing, however. — *William Ruhlmann*

Goin' Back to New Orleans / Jun. 23, 1992 / Warner Brothers ✦✦✦
Having cut an album of standards on his first Warner Brothers album, *In a Sentimental Mood* (1989), Dr. John turned for its follow-up to a collection of New Orleans standards. On an album he described in the liner notes as "a little history of New Orleans music," Dr. John returned to his hometown and set up shop at local Ultrasonic Studios, inviting in such local musicians as Pete Fountain, Al Hirt, and the Neville Brothers and addressing the music and styles of such local legends as Jelly Roll Morton, Huey "Piano" Smith, Fats Domino, James Booker, and Professor Longhair. The geography may have been circumscribed, but the stylistic range was extensive, from jazz and blues to folk and rock. And it was all played with festive conviction—Dr. John is the perfect archivist for the music, being one of its primary popularizers, yet he had never addressed it quite as directly as he did here. — *William Ruhlmann*

Mos' Scocious: Anthology / Oct. 19, 1993 / Rhino ✦✦✦✦
Over his 35 years of recording, Mac "Dr. John" Rebennack has worn many hats, from '50s greasy rock 'n' roller to psychedelic '70s weirdo to keeper of the New Orleans music flame. All of these modes, plus more, are excellently served up on this two-disc anthology. From the early New Orleans sides featuring Rebennack's blistering guitar work ("Storm Warning" and "Morgus the Magnificent") to the fabled '70s sides as the Night Tripper to his present day status as repository of the Crescent City's noble musical tradition, this is the one you want to have for the collection. — *Cub Koda*

Television / Mar. 29, 1994 / GRP ✦✦
Dr. John's debut for GRP doesn't deviate from any release he's made for several other labels. It's still his chunky, humorous take on New Orleans funk; these are his songs, visions and performances, and there's none of the elevator material or laidback, detached fare that's a customary GRP byproduct. Such songs as "Witchy Red," "Spaceship Relationship," and the title selection are a delicate mix of seemingly outrageous but actually quite sharp commentary and excellent musical performances from Dr. John on keyboards, Hugh McCracken on guitar, and several other veterans, among them the great Red Tyler on tenor sax. While not quite as fiery as his classic sessions for Atlantic, if anyone can bring the funk to a company that's famous for avoiding it, it's Dr. John. — *Ron Wynn*

Cut Me While I'm Hot: The Sixties Sessions / 1995 / Magnum ✦✦✦
The liner notes for this 19-song compilation are brief, but at least have the honesty to admit that "the precise details of the circumstances surrounding these recordings may be lost forever." It speculates that the first half of the outtake-sounding program was cut in New Orleans during the first half of the 1960s, while the latter part dates from L.A. sessions from 1965-67. It actually sounds like much of this postdates the mid-'60s, with a feeling not unlike his early-'70s work. Most of the titles are self-penned, and there are also a few Professor Longhair covers. The material isn't really up to the level of his better early records, and the earlier tracks boast muffled audio (though fidelity is listenable throughout). At the same time, if you like vintage Dr. John, this is not much worse than the official stuff, the jiving throaty vocals, humorous songwriting, and distinctive keyboard playing all in place. It's low on outstanding compositions, but isn't bad at all, meaning there's no need to rush out and buy it, but also that committed fans won't mind having it around. — *Richie Unterberger*

Afterglow / Feb. 7, 1995-Feb. 9, 1995 / Blue Thumb ✦✦✦
Producer and GRP Records president Tommy LiPuma, a longtime associate of Dr. John's, revived his old Blue Thumb label as an imprint of GRP/MCA with this album, which served as something of a sequel to the last Dr. John/Tommy LiPuma collaboration, *In a Sentimental Mood*. On that earlier album, the two had covered pop standards. Here, they again turned to evergreens by the likes of Irving Berlin and Duke Ellington. But if *Sentimental Mood* was stylistically linked to the '20s and '30s, *Afterglow* was more a recreation of the late '40s and early '50s, with its big-band arrangements and the inclusion of jump blues numbers like Louis Jordan's "I Know What I've Got." Such songs allowed Dr. John plenty of room to play his trademark New Orleans piano solos, and, in the second half of the record, some of the Doctor's own compositions were snuck in among the classics without disturbing the mood. Of course, the dominant sound remained Dr. John's gravel-and-honey voice, an even more appropriate instrument for these bluesier standards than it was for the *Sentimental* ones. — *William Ruhlmann*

● **The Very Best of Dr. John** / Apr. 25, 1995 / Rhino ✦✦✦✦
The Very Best of Dr. John compiles the best moments from the comprehensive double-disc *Anthology*, making it a more effective, and cheaper, introduction for casual fans. — *Stephen Thomas Erlewine*

Crawfish Soiree / Feb. 11, 1997 / Aim ✦✦✦

Doctor Ross

b. Oct. 21, 1925, Tunica, MS
Guitar, Harmonica, Vocals / Country Blues, Electric Blues, Delta Blues
A triple-threat guitarist, harp blower, and vocalist, Dr. Ross decided to fire his sidemen over thirty years ago and carry on as a one-man band, a tradition that also includes Joe Hill Louis, Daddy Stovepipe, and Jesse Fuller. Ross' music does not depend on novelty effect, yet it has a distinctly recognizable sound, in part because he learned to play his own way and essentially plays everything backwards. His guitar is tuned to open G (like John Lee Hooker and other Delta artists), but Ross plays it left-handed and upside-down. He also plays harmonica in a rack, but it is turned around with the low notes to the right. As an instrumentalist, Ross has perfected the interplay between guitar and harmonica. Unlike other Delta artists who tune in G, Ross doesn't use slide, preferring a series of banjo-like strummed riffs, a percussive approach reminiscent of Atlanta twelve-string guitarist Barbecue Bob. A strong vocalist and excellent songwriter, Ross gained early experience playing Delta jukes and eventually radio shows in Clarksdale and Memphis, where he also recorded for Sam Phillips' Sun label.

At the peak of Ross' career, he quit Sun, concerned that his royalties were being used to promote Elvis Presley's recordings. Relocating in Michigan, he recorded for his own label and for several Detroit labels, while working for General Motors. Returning to music as a recording artist, he recently worked the festival circuit. To the present day, Ross' music retains the spirit of his live radio and juke-joint work. I feel the sides he recorded with a band for Sun produced his best material, including classics like "Chicago Breakdown" and "Boogie Disease." As Dr. Ross put it in an interview ten years ago, "I'm kind of like the little boy from the West; I'm different from the rest." Different, yes, but very good. — *Barry Lee Pearson*

● **Boogie Disease** / 1954 / Arhoolie ✦✦✦✦
This one will make your teeth rattle. A veteran of the early '50s Sun Studio

in Memphis, Ross became known as the "one-man band," a routine gleaned from his mentor Joe Hill Louis. He plays both fine harp (out of the Sonny Boy I mold) and exciting rhythm guitar characterized by churning, mesmerizing rhythms spiced by treble fills. These 22 infectious tracks are the good doctor's very first recordings, and they present him with rhythm section—a style that pre-dates his "one-man" days. —*Larry Hoffman*

Call the Doctor / Jun. 1965 / Testament ✦✦✦✦
If you're looking for one-man blues, this is one of the better efforts in that vein available. Ross is in fine form and strong voice on his first full-length album, sometimes pulling out as many stops as his limbs allow for all-out stompers, at other times just accompanying himself on harmonica. The tracks are largely adaptations of well-worn material like "Good Morning, Little Schoolgirl," "32-20," and "Going to the River"; the opening blast of "Cat Squirrel" is especially good. The one-man band approach gets a bit wearing over the course of 17 songs, though, unless you're a sucker for the style. The CD reissue adds the previously unissued bonus track "Jivin' Blues." —*Richie Unterberger*

I'd Rather Be an Old Woman's Baby / 1971 / Fortune ✦✦✦
A wild, chaotic session, featuring the title cut, "Good Things Come to My Remind," and the original version of "Cat Squirrel." —*Cub Koda*

His First Recordings / 1972 / Arhoolie ✦✦✦✦
His best material, originally recorded for the Sun label in the '50s. Outstanding Delta blues in the unique Dr. Ross guitar-and-harmonica style. —*Barry Lee Pearson*

Doctor Ross, the Harmonica Boss / 1972 / Fortune ✦✦✦✦

One Man Band / 1981 / Takoma ✦✦✦
'60s recordings by Norman Dayron. —*Barry Lee Pearson*

Fats Domino (Antoine Domino)

b. Feb. 26, 1928, New Orleans, LA
Vocals, Piano / Rock 'n' Roll, New Orleans R&B, R&B, Piano Blues
The most popular exponent of the classic New Orleans R&B sound, Fats Domino sold more records than any other Black rock 'n' roll star of the 1950s. His relaxed, lolling boogie-woogie piano style and easygoing, warm vocals anchored a long series of national hits from the mid-'50s to the early '60s. Through it all, his basic approach rarely changed. He may not have been one of early rock's most charismatic, innovative, or threatening figures, but he was certainly one of its most consistent.

Domino's first single, "The Fat Man" (1949), is one of the dozens of tracks that have been consistently singled out as a candidate for the first rock 'n' roll record. As far as Fats was concerned, he was just playing what he'd already been doing in New Orleans for years, and would continue to play and sing in pretty much the same fashion even after his music was dubbed "rock 'n' roll."

The record made number two on the R&B charts, and sold a million copies. Just as important, it established a vital partnership between Fats and Imperial A&R man Dave Bartholomew. Bartholomew, himself a trumpeter, would produce Domino's big hits, co-writing many of them with Fats. He would also usually employ New Orleans session greats like Alvin Tyler on sax and Earl Palmer on drums—musicians who were vital in establishing New Orleans R&B as a distinct entity, playing on many other local recordings as well (including hits made in New Orleans by Georgia native Little Richard).

Domino didn't cross over into the pop charts in a big way until 1955, when "Ain't That a Shame" made the Top Ten. Pat Boone's cover of the song stole some of Fats' thunder, going all the way to number one (Boone was also bowdlerizing Little Richard's early singles for pop hits during this time). Domino's long-range prospects weren't damaged, however; between 1955 and 1963, he racked up an astonishing 35 Top 40 singles. "Blueberry Hill" (1956) was probably his best (and best-remembered) single; "Walking to New Orleans," "Whole Lotta Loving," "I'm Walking," "Blue Monday," and "I'm in Love Again" were also huge successes.

After Fats left Imperial for ABC-Paramount in 1963, he would only enter the Top 40 one more time. The surprise was not that Fats fell out of fashion, but that he'd maintained his popularity so long while the essentials of his style remained unchanged. This was during an era, remember, when most of rock's biggest stars had their careers derailed by death or scandal, or were

made to soften up their sound for mainstream consumption. Although an active performer in the ensuing decades, his career as an important artist was essentially over in the mid-'60s. He did stir up a bit of attention in 1968 when he covered the Beatles' "Lady Madonna" single, which had been an obvious homage to Fats' style. —*Richie Unterberger*

★ **My Blue Heaven: The Best of Fats Domino** / Jul. 30, 1990 / EMI America ✦✦✦✦✦
For the budget-minded fan, this 20-track single disc compilation of Fats Domino's Imperial smashes will serve nicely. Not much of his early pre-rock stuff—"The Fat Man" and "Please Don't Leave Me" are all that's here—but there's plenty of his hit-laden output from 1955 on—"Ain't It a Shame," "Blue Monday," "I'm in Love Again," "Blueberry Hill," "I'm Ready," etc. One small but substantial difference between this set and the larger packages: it uses non-sped-up masters of his mid-'50s material (some of his hits from this era were mastered slightly faster than true pitch). Even if they're not historically correct, these versions actually sound better! —*Bill Dahl*

☆ **They Call Me the Fat Man: The Legendary Imperial Recordings** / Oct. 22, 1991 / EMI America ✦✦✦✦
If you can't quite finance the Bear Family box, this four-disc compilation is the next best thing; an even 100 of the best Imperial sides, including a great many from 1958 on that turn up in crystal-clear stereo (as they also do on the Bear Family package). All the hits are aboard, along with a nice cross-section of the important non-hits. The saxes (usually including Herb Hardesty and sometimes Lee Allen) roar with typical Crescent City power, Fats rolls the ivories, and magic happens—over and over again! Another nice booklet with plenty of photos (but a less detailed discography without sideman credits). —*Bill Dahl*

Out of New Orleans / 1993 / Bear Family ✦✦✦✦
An amazing piece of work—a massive eight-disc boxed set that contains every one of Fats Domino's 1949-1962 Imperial waxings. That's a tremendous load of one artist, but the legacy of Domino and his partner Dave Bartholomew is so consistently innovative and infectious that it never grows tiresome for a second. From the clarion call of "The Fat Man," Domino's 1949 debut, to the storming "Dance with Mr. Domino" in 1962, he typified everything charming about Crescent City R&B, his Creole patois and boogie-based piano a non-threatening vehicle for the rise of rock 'n' roll. A thick, photo-filled book accompanies the disc, and there's an exhaustive discography that makes sense of Domino's many visits to Cosimo Matassa's studios. If you care about Fats Domino, this is the package to purchase! —*Bill Dahl*

Fat Man: 25 Classic Performances / Aug. 20, 1996 / Capitol ✦✦✦✦
Ostensibly replacing the compact disc *My Blue Heaven* as the definitive single-disc collection of Fats Domino's biggest hits singles, *Fat Man: 25 Classic Performances* features most of Fats Domino's biggest hits, but it inexplicably neglects such hits as "Walking to New Orleans," "Be My Guest," and "I'm Gonna Be a Wheel Someday." The only justification for the omission of so many hits is that the intent of the collection is to portray Fats Domino as the R&B heavyweight that he undoubtedly is, but seldom receives credit for being. Nevertheless, *Fat Man* masquerades as a greatest hits collection, billing itself as "25 Classic Performances," which leads you to believe that it is simply another hits collection. As an R&B compilation, *Fat Man* is strong—and, like any proper R&B collection, it presents the singles at the speed they were recorded at, not the sped-up versions that became hits—but because it lacks these hits, *My Blue Heaven* remains a preferable collection and introduction to Fats. —*Stephen Thomas Erlewine*

Thomas A. Dorsey

b. Jul. 1, 1899, Villa Rica, GA, **d.** Jan. 23, 1993, Chicago, IL
Piano, Vocals, Guitar / Acoustic Chicago Blues, Piano Blues
The acknowledged father of gospel music, Thomas A. Dorsey remains arguably the most influential figure ever to impact the genre. A versatile composer whose material shifted easily from energetic hard gospel to gossamer hymns, he penned many of the best-known songs in the gospel canon, among them "Take My Hand, Precious Lord" and "Peace in the Valley"; the founder of the National Convention of Gospel Choirs and Choruses, he was also a pioneering force in the renowned Chicago gospel community, where he helped launch the careers of legends including Mahalia Jackson and Sallie Martin. Dorsey was born in Villa Rica, Georgia on July 1, 1899 and raised in

the Atlanta area; there, in addition to the traditional Dr. Watts hymns, he also absorbed early blues and jazz. A child prodigy, he taught himself a wide range of instruments, and was playing blues and ragtime while still in his teens; under the stage name Georgia Tom, he was a prolific composer, authoring witty, slightly racy blues songs like the underground hit "It's Tight Like That."

Dorsey settled in Chicago in 1918, where he briefly enrolled at the city's College of Composition and Arranging; within months of his arrival, he began playing with area jazz bands including Les Hite's Whispering Serenaders. Dorsey also formed his own group, the Wildcats Jazz Band, which traveled in support of Ma Rainey. He later collaborated in a duo with Tampa Red, but in 1928, after suffering his second nervous breakdown in as many years, he opted to retire from the music business. A two-year recovery period followed, during which time a minister convinced Dorsey to return to music, albeit to move from the blues to the church. His first attempt at writing a gospel song, 1921's "If I Don't Get There," had met with some success, and he now returned with a renewed sense of purpose, renouncing secular music to devote all of his talents to the church circuit. Initially, Dorsey met with little success—forced to reject blues jobs and with no gospel offers forthcoming, he soon resorted to peddling song sheets to make a living.

Dorsey's luck appeared to be on the upswing by 1932, the year he organized one of the first gospel choirs at Chicago's Pilgrim Baptist Church; his pianist, Roberta Martin, would in a few years emerge among the top talents on the church circuit. That same year, he also founded the first publishing house devoted exclusively to selling music by black gospel composers. However, a few months later—while traveling with Theodore R. Frye to organize a choir in St. Louis—tragedy struck when Dorsey discovered that his wife had died while giving birth to their son, who himself died two days later. Devastated, Dorsey locked himself inside his music room for three straight days, emerging with a completed draft of "Take My Hand, Precious Lord," a song whose popularity in the gospel community is rivaled perhaps only by "Amazing Grace." Setting his loss behind him, he enjoyed his most prolific period in the years that followed, authoring dozens of songs with a distinctively optimistic sensibility for audiences held in the grip of the Depression.

During that same fateful year of 1932, Dorsey also hired a singer named Sallie Martin to join his group at the Ebenezer Baptist Church. Despite her unrefined vocal style, she instantly connected with audiences; over time Dorsey became increasingly aware of her value not only as a performer but also as an entrepreneur, as she took over his music store and within a few months was turning a tidy profit. In 1933, Dorsey and Martin—along with Frye, Magnolia Lewis Butts, and Beatrice Brown—organized the annual National Convention of Gospel Choirs and Choruses, where they introduced new songs to choir directors from across the nation. By now, Dorsey's songs were enormously popular, not only among black churchgoers but also among White Southerners; by 1939, even the leading White gospel publishers were anthologizing his music. That year, he composed "Peace in the Valley"; although written for Mahalia Jackson, his demo singer at the time, its greatest success was in the White market—both Elvis Presley and Red Foley, among others, scored major hits with the song.

After breaking through with the Singers Covention, Dorsey and Martin next hit the so-called "gospel highway," a touring circuit previously restricted to a cappella quartets. Between the early 1930s and mid-1940s, he toured the nation under the banner "Evenings with Dorsey," training young singers to perform his material; between 1939 and 1944, he also toured regularly with Jackson. By the 1950s, with the rise of hard gospel, Dorsey's influence began to slip a bit, although the popularity of his greatest material held on; during the middle of the decade, with the rise of R&B, his melodies began to resurface in many of the era's secular hits. As James Cleveland emerged as the undisputed king of contemporary gospel, Dorsey began to curtail his writing and traveling, essentially retiring from active duty during the 1960s; however, he continued spearheading the annual NCGGG event for years to follow, and remained among the most revered figures in spiritual music until his death on January 23, 1993. —*Jason Ankeny*

★ **Precious Lord: The Great Gospel Songs of Thomas A. Dorsey** / 1994 / Columbia/Legacy ♦♦♦♦♦
Precious Lord collects 18 of Georgia Thomas Dorsey's greatest songs, offering a terrific introduction to one of the greatest gospel country blues singers of the '30s. —*Thom Owens*

K.C. Douglas

b. Nov. 21, 1913, Sharon, MS, **d.** Oct. 18, 1975, Berkeley, CA
Guitar, Vocals / Electric Country Blues, West Coast Blues, Piedmont Blues
K.C. Douglas was a Mississippi bluesman who transplanted himself and his music, not to Chicago but to the San Francisco Bay Area in 1945. He became one of the rare Californians with such a down-home rural style, as many of his recordings were remakes of old blues he knew from Mississippi. (His first album, an obscure item on the Cook label, was entitled *K.C. Douglas, a Dead Beat Guitar and the Mississippi Blues*.) His re-creations of Tommy Johnson's blues were of particular interest to fans of pre-war blues, but his own compositions attracted attention as well (K.C.'s music was introduced to rock listeners when his "Mercury Boogie" was redone by The Steve Miller Band.) —*Jim O'Neal*

Road Recordings / 1956 / Cook ♦♦♦

Big Road Blues / 1961 / Ace ♦♦♦

● **K.C.'s Blues** / 1961 / Bluesville ♦♦♦♦
Like *Big Road Blues*, *K.C.'s Blues* was recorded in 1961 during the peak of the blues revival. Unlike that record, which contained a number of songs he learned through Tommy Johnson, *K.C.'s Blues* consists primarily of original compositions that showcase Douglas' easy-rolling, relaxed style perfectly. —*Thom Owens*

Mercury Boogie / 1975 / Oldie Blues ♦♦♦

Country Boy / 1981 / Arhoolie ♦♦♦

Driftin' Slim

b. Feb. 24, 1919, Keo, AR, **d.** Sep. 15, 1977, Los Angeles, CA
Harmonica, Guitar, Drums, Vocals / Electric Blues
Elmon "Driftin' Slim" Mickle was a harmonica player from Keo, AR, a stone's throw away from Little Rock. He got his early harmonica training when he saw John Lee "Sonny Boy" Williamson and Yank Rachell perform and approached Sonny Boy to teach him the rudiments of the instrument. By the mid-'40s, he was playing the local juke joint circuit with Sonny Boy Williamson II and King Biscuit Boy drummer Peck Curtis while doing radio stints with stations KDRK and KGHI. In 1951, he had formed his first band with locals Baby Face Turner and Junior Brooks and recorded his first sides for the Modern label. By 1957, he had moved to Los Angeles, refurbishing his act as a one-man band, adding drums and guitar to his neck rack harmonica work. He recorded sporadically, issuing singles on his own and other labels through the early '60s. In the flush of the "folk-music boom" of the mid-'60s, Slim was rediscovered and recorded for a number of collectors' labels. By the turn of the decade, ill health had forced him to retire from music and when he passed away in 1977, a chapter of American music—that of the one-man band—had virtually died with him. —*Cub Koda*

● **Driftin' Slim and His Blues Band** / Dec. 1969 / Milestone ♦♦♦♦
Slim's only full album (his earlier recordings show up on several compilations) is one of the great "rediscovery" albums of the genre. Five of the 15 tracks here are with a full band, but the real treasure trove is the remaining solo performances. These range from full-stops-out one-man-band numbers ("I'm Hunting Somebody" is a true classic) to unaccompanied harmonica pieces ("Mama Blues," "Jonah") to autobiographical recitations like "A Dip of Snuff and a Narrow Escape" that are utterly charming in their simplicity. As of press time, this album was still unavailable on compact disc, but it is still well worth seeking out as it's a true gem with loads of folkish charm. —*Cub Koda*

Chris Duarte

b. Feb. 16, 1963, San Antonio, TX
Guitar, Vocals / Modern Electric Blues
Austin-based guitarist, songwriter, and singer Chris Duarte is such a promising young upstart in the world of modern blues that he's already been compared with the late Stevie Ray Vaughan. It's heady stuff for the musician, who plays a rhythmic style of Texas blues-rock that is at times reminiscent of Vaughan's sound, and at other times reminiscent of Johnny Winter. The truth is, Duarte has his own sound that draws on elements of jazz, blues, and rock 'n' roll. Although he is humbled by the comparisons with the late

Vaughan, the San Antonio-raised musician began playing out in clubs there when he was 15 years old.

After Duarte moved to Austin when he was 16, he began taking his guitar playing much more seriously, and at that time, Vaughan was still around playing in Austin-area clubs. Duarte was one of those lucky few thousand who got to see Vaughan at the Continental Club before the late guitarist got his first break with David Bowie. After a short stint in an Austin jazz band, Duarte joined Bobby Mack and Night Train, and began getting heavily into blues at that point. He traveled all over Texas with that band before a big break came his way in 1994, when New York-based Silvertone Records released his critically praised debut album, *Texas Sugar/Strat Magik. Tailspin Headwhack* followed in 1997. — *Richard Skelly*

● **Texas Sugar Strat Magic** / 1994 / Jive/Novus ✦✦✦✦
Guitarist Chris Duarte's *Texas Sugar Strat Magik* is an impressive debut album, showcasing his fiery, Stevie Ray Vaughan-derived blues-rock. As a songwriter, Duarte is still developing—he fails to come up with any memorable songs, although he does contribute several competent, unexceptional genre pieces—but as an instrumentalist, he's first-rate, spitting out solos with a blistering intensity or laying back with gentle, lyrical phrases. And that's what makes *Texas Sugar Strat Magik* a successful record—it's simply a great guitar album, full of exceptional playing. — *Stephen Thomas Erlewine*

Tailspin Headwhack / Aug. 26, 1997 / Jive ✦✦✦✦
Chris Duarte's debut album, *Texas Sugar Strat Magik*, promised great things, and his second album, *Tailspin Headwhack*, doesn't fail to deliver. Like its predecessor, it's a dynamic collection of hot Texas blues-rock powered by Duarte's muscular, tasteful playing. There's still a lack of distinctive original material, but that doesn't matter, because he infuses each song, from the single "Cleopatra" to a cover of B.B. King's "The Thrill Is Gone," with energy and passion. Most importantly, Duarte is beginning to break away from his Stevie Ray and Hendrix influences and establish himself as a talented stylist in his own right, and that's what makes *Tailspin Headwhack* a successful second record. — *Thom Owens*

Champion Jack Dupree

b. Jul. 4, 1910, New Orleans, LA, **d.** Jan. 21, 1992, Hanover, Germany
Guitar, Piano, Drums, Vocals / Piano Blues, Acoustic Chicago Blues, New Orleans Blues, Electric Louisiana Blues, Electric Swamp Blues, East Coast Blues
A formidable contender in the ring before he shifted his focus to pounding the piano instead, Champion Jack Dupree often injected his lyrics with a rowdy sense of down-home humor. But there was nothing lighthearted about his rock-solid way with a boogie; when he shouted "Shake Baby Shake," the entire room had no choice but to acquiesce.

Dupree was notoriously vague about his beginnings, claiming in some interviews that his parents died in a fire set by the Ku Klux Klan, at other times saying that the blaze was accidental. Whatever the circumstances of the tragic conflagration, Dupree grew up in New Orleans' Colored Waifs' Home for Boys (Louis Armstrong also spent his formative years there). Learning his trade from barrelhouse 88's ace Willie "Drive 'em Down" Hall, Dupree left the Crescent City in 1930 for Chicago and then Detroit. By 1935, he was boxing professionally in Indianapolis, battling in an estimated 107 bouts.

In 1940, Dupree made his recording debut for Chicago A&R man extraordinaire Lester Melrose and OKeh Records. Dupree's 1940-41 output for the Columbia subsidiary exhibited a strong New Orleans tinge despite the Chicago surroundings; his driving "Junker's Blues" was later cleaned up as Fats Domino's 1949 debut, "The Fat Man." After a stretch in the Navy during World War II (he was a Japanese POW for two years), Dupree decided tickling the 88s beat pugilism any old day. He spent most of his time in New York and quickly became a prolific recording artist, cutting for Continental, Joe Davis, Alert, Apollo, and Red Robin (where he cut a blasting "Shim Sham Shimmy" in 1953), often in the company of Brownie McGhee. Contracts meant little—Dupree masqueraded as Brother Blues on Abbey, Lightnin' Jr. on Empire, and the truly imaginative Meat Head Johnson for Gotham and Apex.

King Records corralled Dupree in 1953 and held onto him through 1955 (the year he enjoyed his only R&B chart hit, the relaxed "Walking the Blues"). Dupree's King output rates with his very best—the romping "Mail Order

Woman," "Let the Doorbell Ring," and "Big Leg Emma's" contrasting with the rural "Me and My Mule" (Dupree's vocal on the latter emphasizing a harelip speech impediment for politically incorrect pseudo-comic effect).

After a year on RCA's Groove and Vik subsidiaries, Dupree made a masterpiece LP for Atlantic. 1958's *Blues from the Gutter* is a magnificent testament to Dupree's barrelhouse background, boasting marvelous readings of "Stack-O-Lee," "Junker's Blues," and "Frankie & Johnny" beside the risque "Nasty Boogie."

Dupree was one of the first bluesmen to leave his native country for a less racially polarized European existence in 1959. He lived in a variety of countries overseas, continuing to record prolifically for Storyville, British Decca (with John Mayall and Eric Clapton lending a hand at a 1966 date), and many other firms.

Perhaps sensing his own mortality, Dupree returned to New Orleans in 1990 for his first visit in 36 years. While there, he played the Jazz & Heritage Festival and laid down a zesty album for Bullseye Blues, *Back Home in New Orleans*. Two more albums of new material were captured by the company the next year prior to the pianist's death in January of 1992. Jack Dupree was a champ to the very end. — *Bill Dahl*

★ **Blues from the Gutter** / 1958 / Atlantic ✦✦✦✦✦
The 1958 masterwork album of Dupree's long and prolific career. Cut in New York (in stereo!) with a blasting band that included saxist Pete Brown and guitarist Larry Dale, the Jerry Wexler-produced Atlantic collection provides eloquent testimony to Dupree's eternal place in the New Orleans blues and barrelhouse firmament. There's some decidedly down-in-the-alley subject matter—"Can't Kick the Habit," "T.B. Blues," a revival of "Junker's Blues"—along with the stomping "Nasty Boogie" and treatments of the ancient themes "Stack-O-Lee" and "Frankie & Johnny." — *Bill Dahl*

Natural & Soulful Blues / 1961 / Atlantic ✦✦✦

Champion of the Blues / 1961 / Atlantic ✦✦✦

Sings the Blues / 1961 / King ✦✦✦✦
A domestic no-frills collection of Champion Jack Dupree's aforementioned King label material, albeit containing fewer tracks and little in the way of annotation—but you can't argue with the wonderful music therein! — *Bill Dahl*

Blues at Montreux / 1973 / Atlantic ✦✦✦
Rough around the edges, this set, caught live (and lively) at the 1971 Montreux Jazz Festival, teams Texas-born sax great King Curtis with the irrepressible Dupree. Curtis' young band copes reasonably well with Dupree's unpredictable sense of time, and despite their age differences, everyone has a good time. Only three months later, Curtis would tragically be stabbed to death on his New York doorstep. — *Bill Dahl*

Blues for Everybody / 1990 / Charly ✦✦✦✦
Although Dupree seldom paused at any one label for very long, the piano pounder did hang around at Cincinnati-based King Records from 1951 to 1955—long enough to wax the 20 sides comprising this set and a few more that regrettably aren't aboard. By this time, Dupree was a seasoned R&B artist, storming through "Let the Doorbell Ring" and "Mail Order Woman" and emphasizing his speech impediment on "Harelip Blues" (one of those not-for-the-politically correct numbers). Most of these tracks were done in New York; sidemen include guitarist Mickey Baker and saxist Willis Jackson. — *Bill Dahl*

Back Home in New Orleans / 1990 / Bullseye Blues ✦✦✦✦
By far the best of Dupree's three albums for Bullseye Blues, this collection was cut during the pianist's first trip home to the Crescent City in 36 long years. With his longtime accompanist Kenn Lending on guitar, Dupree sounds happy to be back in his old stomping grounds throughout the atmospheric set. — *Bill Dahl*

Forever & Ever / 1991 / Bullseye Blues ✦✦✦
Dupree's Bullseye Blues encore partly misses the mark compared to his previous effort—the material isn't quite as strong as before. — *Bill Dahl*

New Orleans Barrelhouse Boogie (The Complete Champion Jack Dupree) / 1993 / Columbia/Legacy ✦✦✦✦
The New Orleans barrelhouse boogie piano specialist's earliest sides for OKeh, dating from 1940-1941 and in a few cases sporting some fairly groundbreaking electric guitar runs by Jesse Ellery. Dupree rocks the house

like it's a decade later on two takes of "Cabbage Greens" and "Dupree Shake Dance," while his drug-oriented "Junker Blues" was later cleaned up a bit by a chubby newcomer named Fats Domino for his debut hit 78 "The Fat Man." — *Bill Dahl*

One Last Time / 1993 / Bullseye Blues ✦✦✦
Dupree's last album for the label, slightly more consistent than his last but not the equivalent of his first. — *Bill Dahl*

Won't Be a Fool No More ... Plus / 1993 / See for Miles ✦✦✦✦
Mike Vernon brought Dupree into the studio alongside Eric Clapton (electric guitar) and John Mayall (harmonica) — two months before they recorded the classic *Bluesbreakers* album — plus Tony McPhee (acoustic guitar), Bill Short (washboard), Malcolm Pool (bass), and Keef Hartley (drums), to cut this album, originally issued by English Decca under the title *From New Orleans to Memphis*. Two additional tracks, "Calcutta Blues" and "24 Hours," cut at the same sessions and issued separately, have been added. The disc includes rocking piano boogie like "He Knows the Rules" (with killer bottleneck by Clapton) and "Shim-Sham-Shimmy," as well as New Orleans influences ("T.V. Mama," "Pigfoot and a Bottle of Beer," "Ooh-La-La"), an extraordinary piece of spoken blues ("Big Leg Emma's"), worth the price of the CD by itself, and country blues ("Ain't That a Shame"). Dupree is in excellent vocal form and even takes a turn on acoustic guitar on one track, in addition to his trade-

mark piano blues. The new notes by Roger Dopson include one of the most detailed and entertaining accounts of Dupree's career. — *Bruce Eder*

Dynatones

f. San Francisco, CA
Group / Rock 'n' Roll, Blues-Rock, Roots-Rock
The Dynatones are a San Francisco-based blues/soul band, a mainstay of the local circuit. The group worked and recorded as solid backup behind Charlie Musslewhite in the early '80s, then made the transition to a more R&B-oriented format with numerous personnel changes by the mid-'80s. Continuing to write, record, and tour to this day, The Dynatones are probably best experienced live, but all their recordings are worth checking out. — *Cub Koda*

Curtain Call Live / 1982 / War Bride ✦✦✦

Shameless / 1983 / Warner Brothers ✦✦✦

● **Tough to Shake** / 1985 / Rounder ✦✦✦✦
Propelled by gutsy guitar work and hard-driving rhythms, *Tough to Shake* may be the finest album the Dynatones made. Even though the songwriting is a little uneven, it captures the essence of their greasy bar-room boogie better than any of their other records. — *Thom Owens*

Live It Up! / 1986 / Rounder ✦✦✦

Chopped & Channeled / 1991 / Rhino ✦✦✦

Snooks Eaglin

b. Jan. 21, 1936, New Orleans, LA
Guitar, Vocals / Acoustic New Orleans Blues, Electric New Orleans Blues, New Orleans Blues, Electric Louisiana Blues, Electric Swamp Blues, Piedmont Blues

When they refer to consistently amazing guitarist Snooks Eaglin as a human jukebox in his New Orleans hometown, they're not dissing him in the slightest. The blind Eaglin is a beloved figure in the Crescent City, not only for his gritty, Ray Charles-inspired vocal delivery and wholly imaginative approach to the guitar, but for the seemingly infinite storehouse of oldies that he's liable to pull out on stage at any second (often confounding his bemused band in the process!).

Born Ford Eaglin, Jr., and blind since very early childhood due to glaucoma and a brain tumor, the lad (named after radio character Baby Snooks, who shared his mischievious ways) picked up the guitar at age six and commenced to mastering every style imaginable. Gospel, blues, jazz—young Snooks Eaglin could play it all. He spent time with a Crescent City band, the Flamingoes, whose members also included pianist Allen Toussaint, played around town as Little Ray Charles, and recorded for Chess as accompanist to Sugar Boy Crawford before going it alone on the streets of the French Quarter.

His earliest recordings in 1958 for Folkways presented Eaglin as a solo acoustic folk-blues artist with an extremely eclectic repertoire. His dazzling finger-picking was nothing short of astonishing, but Eaglin really wanted to be making R&B with a band. Imperial Records producer Dave Bartholomew granted him the opportunity in 1960, and the results were sensational. Eaglin's fluid, twisting lead guitar on the utterly infectious "Yours Truly" (a Bartholomew composition first waxed by Pee Wee Crayton) and its sequel "Cover Girl" was unique on the New Orleans R&B front, while his brokenhearted cries on "Don't Slam That Door" and "That Certain Door" were positively mesmerizing. Eaglin stuck with Imperial through 1963, when the firm closed up shop in New Orleans, without ever gaining national exposure.

There followed a dry period for the guitarist, but he came back first as accompanist to Professor Longhair (who was in the midst of a rather remarkable comeback bid himself) and then on his own. Eaglin has reasserted his brilliance in recent years with a series of magnificent albums for hometown Black Top Records (notably *Teasin' You* and *Soul's Edge*). — *Bill Dahl*

Country Boy Down in New Orleans / 1958 / Arhoolie ✦✦✦✦
Country Boy Down in New Orleans collects 23 tracks Snooks Eaglin recorded in the '50s. During this time, he was a street musician, playing with just one guitar or as a one-man band. On these tracks, he is accompanied by a couple of washboard players and a harpist. As expected, the sound is stripped-down, but it is exciting. Eaglin's early repertoire included a broad variety of blues, folk, and gospel songs and all of these genres are covered thoroughly on this delightful single disc. It may not be the ripping electric blues of his best-known records, but it is just as enjoyable. — *Thom Owens*

New Orleans Street Singer / 1958 / Smithsonian/Folkways ✦✦✦✦

Possum up a Simmon Tree / Oct. 1960 / Arhoolie ✦✦✦

That's All Right / 1961 / Prestige ✦✦✦
Recorded during the time in which Eaglin was doubling as a blues/folk singer and a commercial R&B artist (for Imperial). He addresses the acoustic folk and blues side of his repertoire, performing everything solo on six and 12-string guitars. Time will probably judge these not to be as interesting as his full-band New Orleans R&B recordings. But this is warm, good-natured acoustic blues, with interpretations of traditional tunes, early blues by Robert Johnson, and then-recent R&B hits by Ray Charles, Arthur Crudup, and Amos Milburn. — *Richie Unterberger*

Down Yonder / 1978 / GNP ✦✦✦✦
Sam Charters produced this marvelously funky collection of oldies rendered Eaglin-style with an all-star Crescent City combo: pianist Ellis Marsalis, saxist Clarence Ford, and the French brothers as rhythm section. Eaglin's revisit of "Yours Truly" floats over a rhythmic bed so supremely second-line funky that it's astonishing, while he personalizes the New Orleans classics "Oh Red," "Down Yonder," and "Let the Four Winds Blow" as only Snooks Eaglin can. — *Bill Dahl*

Baby, You Can Get Your Gun / 1987 / Black Top ✦✦✦✦
The first of the masterful guitarist's amazing series of albums for Black Top is an earthly delight; his utterly unpredictable guitar weaves and darts through supple rhythms provided by New Orleans vets Smokey Johnson on drums and Erving Charles, Jr. on bass (David Lastie is on sax). Few artists boast Eaglin's "human jukebox" capabilities; his amazingly vast knowledge of eclectic numbers takes in the Four Blazes' "Mary Jo," Tommy Ridgley's "Lavinia," and the Ventures' version of "Perfidia." — *Bill Dahl*

Out of Nowhere / 1988 / Black Top ✦✦✦✦
Another wonderful lineup of Eaglinized oldies ranging from Crescent City standbys by Tommy Ridgley, Benny Spellman, and Smiley Lewis to the always unexpected (Nappy Brown's "Wella Wella Baby-La," the Isleys' "It's Your Thing," the Falcons' "You're So Fine"). Guitarist Anson Funderburgh's band is utilized for backup on half the set; a combo sporting saxist Grady Gaines on most of the rest (Eaglin goes it alone on "Kiss of Fire"). — *Bill Dahl*

New Orleans 1960-1961 / 1988 / Sundown ✦✦✦✦
Great R&B sides for Imperial with full band. — *Bill Dahl*

☆ **Teasin' You** / 1992 / Black Top ✦✦✦✦✦
The best of Eaglin's terrific series of Black Top efforts so far—song selection is absolutely unassailable (lots of savage New Orleans covers, from Lloyd Price and Professor Longhair to Willie Tee and Earl King), the band simmers and sizzles with spicy second-line fire (bassist George Porter, Jr. and drummer Herman Ernest III are a formidable pair indeed), and Eaglin's churchy, commanding vocals and blistering guitar work are nothing short of mind-boggling throughout the entire disc. — *Bill Dahl*

Soul's Edge / 1995 / Black Top ✦✦✦✦
Give this New Orleans master enough studio time, and he'll redo the entire history of post-war R&B his own way. Here he lays his mind to Joe Simon's powerhouse soul ballad "Nine Pound Steel," the Midnighters' "Let's Go, Let's Go, Let's Go," even Bill Haley & the Comets' "Skinny Minnie," and the Five Keys' loopy "Ling Ting Tong," giving each the same singular treatment that he's always brought to his recordings. Porter and Ernest return to lay down their immaculate grooves, and Fred Kemp blows sturdy sax on Eaglin's parade-beat "I Went to the Mardi Gras." — *Bill Dahl*

● **Complete Imperial Recordings** / Oct. 24, 1995 / Capitol ✦✦✦✦
These days, Eaglin is apt to be classified as a blues singer with considerable New Orleans R&B influences. This collection of his early-'60s recordings for the Imperial label would be much more appropriately categorized as exactly the opposite. Produced by Dave Bartholomew (who also wrote over half of the material), the thrust of these recordings is most definitely in the classic-'50s/early-'60s New Orleans R&B mold, though Eaglin's vocal delivery may be bluesier than some other practitioners of the sound. It doesn't suffer for this in the least; it's solid stuff betraying the influence of Guitar Slim and Ray Charles (though Eaglin's style is sometimes compared to the latter, it

isn't extremely similar, with sparer arrangements and a distinct creole vocal slur). This compiles 26 tracks (seven previously unreleased) that he cut between 1960 and 1963, none of which were hits, perhaps because the commercial peak of classic New Orleans R&B had already passed. But it's well worth looking into if you like records from the same period by the likes of Bartholomew, Lee Dorsey, and the early Nevilles. —*Richie Unterberger*

Live in Japan / 1997 / Black Top ✦✦✦
Snooks Eaglin has always maintained a wide, eclectic, freewheeling approach to his music, and with a good band in support, that outlook can subsequently turn into a night of truly fine music, and this is one of those times. Culled from two nights of recording at the Park Tower Hall in Tokyo in December of 1995, this album clearly illustrates what an astonishing breadth and depth there is to the music Snooks Eaglin chooses to interpret in the course of a single evening. His guitar chops are impeccable, his tone clean without being thin and his ability to whip off lick after astonishing lick in a variety of styles (his first solo on "I Went to the Mardi Gras" is jaw-dropping, but so is the second one) while still being his own man puts him at the forefront alongside any new breed innovators you'd care to name. With solid swinging support from George Porter, Jr.'s bass, Jeffrey Alexander's drums and the keyboard work of John Austin, Eaglin sounds relaxed and totally in command. His sideways spins on old chestnuts like "Hello Josephine" sound refreshing (not merely change for change's sake), while his nod to Smiley Lewis on "Down Yonder (We Go Ballin')" and "Lillie Mae" are spot-on treatments imbued with a lot of respect for an old New Orleans running buddy. His soulful reading of Dan Penn's "Nine Pound Steel" sets the stage for a couple of strange (on the surface) choices, the Isley Brothers' "It's Your Thing" and Stevie Wonder's "(Boogie On) Reggae Woman," which Snooks totally stamps with the full-bore charm of his own personality. But if anyone truly doubts that Eaglin is not a serious bluesman to be reckoned with, one listen to the almost seven minutes of "Black Night" will dispel any such notions, even before the guitar solo hits. While many live albums exude a "guess you had to be there" quality to them, this one makes you wish you *had* been there. —*Cub Koda*

Robert Ealey

b. Dec. 6, 1925, Texarkana, TX
Vocals / Texas Blues
Dallas-based vocalist and songwriter Robert Ealey began singing in his local church at age 15 with a quartet group in his native Texarkana. Influenced by the likes of Lightnin' Hopkins, Lil' Son Jackson, Frankie Lee Sims, and Aaron "T-Bone" Walker, he began singing blues professionally at 20 after he moved to Dallas. In nearby Fort Worth, he joined the Boogie Chillen Boys and became a featured vocalist at the Blue Bird Club there. After singing there for 20 years, Ealey bought the Blue Bird Club and ran it for another ten years.

In 1990, Ealey hooked up with guitarist Tone Sommer and began touring outside of Texas. The band quickly found an audience for their authentic Texas urban blues in Europe, where they have toured more than a dozen times since 1990. Sommer and Ealey also did TV commercial work that made use of their music. Every September, Ealey performs in his own blues festival, held in Sundance Square, Fort Worth.

After BlackTop Records purchased several master tapes from the Top Cat label in Dallas, they released Ealey's *Turn Out the Lights*. On the album, he is accompanied by a bevy of the D/FW area's best blues accompanists, including Mike Morgan and Sommer on guitars, Ty Grimes on drums and Mark Rybiski on saxophones. *I Like Music When I Party* followed in 1997. —*Richard Skelly*

Texas Bluemen / Sep. 2, 1994 / Topcat ✦✦✦✦

If You Need Me / 1995 / Topcat ✦✦✦

● **Turn out the Lights** / Jun. 1996 / Black Top ✦✦✦✦
Turn Out the Lights is Robert Ealey's best album to date, not because he's tried anything new, but because he has his best set of songs and performances to date. Supported by such luminaries as drummer Ty Grimes and guitarists Mike Morgan and Tone Summer, Ealey storms through a set of originals making them sound like classic juke-joint rockers. A few of the songs fall a little flat, but *Turn Out the Lights* is nevertheless a roaring good time. —*Thom Owens*

I Like Music When I Party / Mar. 18, 1997 / Black Top ✦✦✦
Robert Ealey is no spring chicken. After singing in local Texas bands for years, he finally started recording in the '90s—*I Like Music When I Party* was the fourth album he cut after starting his recording career. Like the others, it's a greasy collection of Texas blues, spiked with a bit of soul. Ealey's voice may be gravelly with age, but it's by no means gone, and with the support of his youthful backing band, he can really bring it home. There's nothing deep here—just party music, played good and simple. Sometimes, that's enough. —*Thom Owens*

Ronnie Earl

b. Mar. 10, 1953, New York, NY
Guitar / R&B, Modern Electric Blues
Guitarist Ronnie Earl (born Ronald Horvath) was born March 10, 1953, in New York City, but later moved to Boston. In 1975, while attending a Muddy Waters concert, he was so moved by what he heard that he decided to learn the guitar and dedicate himself to mastering the blues tradition. He was soon playing in clubs in and around the Boston area as well as backing various blues artists on tour. He claims that his main influences were T-Bone Walker, B.B. King, Magic Sam, and Robert Jr. Lockwood. In 1980, he replaced Duke Robillard in Roomful of Blues and worked with that band for eight years, helping to take the band to national acclaim.

In the 1980s, Earl recorded three solo albums with his band the Broadcasters that were very well received: *Smokin'* (Black Top, 1983), *They Call Me Mr. Earl* (Black Top, 1984), and *I Like It When It Rains* (Antone's, 1990). Earl left Roomful of Blues in 1988 and continues to perform and record. His intense guitar style, somewhat in the style of T-Bone Walker, has made him one of the most respected young players in the business—much in demand as a backup musician for recording dates. —*Michael Erlewine*

Smokin' / 1983 / Black Top ✦✦✦

They Call Me Mr. Earl / 1984 / Black Top ✦✦✦

Deep Blues / 1985 / Black Top ✦✦✦

Soul Searchin' / 1988 / Black Top ✦✦

I Like It When it Rains / 1990 / Antone's ✦✦✦✦

Peace of Mind / Nov. 1990 / Black Top ✦✦✦✦
Peace of Mind features some nice, swinging stuff. —*Bill Dahl*

Surrounded by Love / May 1991 / Black Top ✦✦✦
Ronnie Earl recorded *Surrounded by Love* with a new version of the Broadcasters. The most notable factor of the new lineup is the reappearance of Sugar Ray Norcia, the finest vocalist/harpist Earl ever recorded with. The band sounds tight and energetic, especially on the three tracks they cut with Robert Jr. Lockwood. Parts of the album are a little slow, but the album is very entertaining, even with its minor flaws. —*Thom Owens*

● **Test of Time** / 1992 / Black Top ✦✦✦✦
Test of Time collects the highlights from Ronnie Earl's six Black Top albums. The 18-song compilation showcases one of the finest blues guitarists of the '80s, picking nearly all of his finest material, which happen to include duets with Robert Jr. Lockwood and Hubert Sumlin. The album is an excellent introduction to Earl, as well as his most consistently entertaining release. —*Thom Owens*

Still River / 1994 / AudioQuest ✦✦

Language of the Soul / 1994 / Bullseye Blues ✦✦✦✦
Language of the Soul is a wonderful change of pace for guitarist Ronnie Earl. The record is the first all-instrumental album Earl has recorded and, if anything, it's even more successful than his full-fledged, band-oriented records. Working without vocals has given him the freedom to try all sorts of new things, whether it's the jazzy interludes of "Indigo Burrell" or the gospel-flavored "I Am With You." Earl's compositions aren't memorable in and of themselves (he wrote all but two of the cuts), yet they give him the opportunity to play freely. He comes up with some truly remarkable solo passages, offering definitive proof that he's one of the best contemporary blues guitarists of the '90s. —*Thom Owens*

Blues and Forgiveness / 1995 / Bullseye Blues ✦✦✦

Guitar Virtuoso Live in Europe / 1995 / Bullseye Blues ✦✦

Eye to Eye / 1996 / AudioQuest ◆◆◆◆
This CD is a fine showcase for guitarist Ronnie Earl, who is teamed with three members of the Legendary Blues Band (pianist Pinetop Perkins, bassist Calvin Jones, and drummer Willie "Big Eyes" Smith), plus organist Bruce Katz. Although pianist Perkins takes vocals on most of the songs and bassist Jones sings on two of the numbers, nearly each selection has plenty of solo space for Earl and Perkins. Sticking exclusively to the blues at a variety of tempos, the fine program (which has superior instrumental playing that overshadows the personable vocals) should be of strong interest to both blues and jazz collectors. — *Scott Yanow*

Grateful Heart: Blues and Ballads / Mar. 19, 1996 / Bullseye Blues ◆◆◆◆
Perhaps the smartest move a non-singing guitar-playing virtuoso like Mister Earl could make was ditching the lame singers who permeate most of his earlier efforts and go with an all-instrumental program. On this outing, he surrounds himself with an excellent quartet of players in David "Fathead" Newman on tenor sax, Per Hanson on drums, Rod Carey on bass, and Bruce Katz on keyboards, and the results are simply sublime. Instead of a bunch of Chicago retreads, we are treated to a heady mixture of blues, jazz, soul, swing, you name it, all of it infused with taste, tone, and economy. When Ronnie burns, the results are jaw dropping; when he slows it down, his choice of notes is exquisite. "Welcome Home," "Still Soul Searching," "Drown in My Own Tears," and "Skyman (For Duane Allman)" are just a few of the highlights, but there really isn't a wasted note on this record to be found. Anywhere. — *Cub Koda*

Plays Big Blues / Feb. 4, 1997 / Black Top ◆◆◆

The Colour of Love / Jun. 24, 1997 / Polygram ◆◆◆
The continuing musical saga of bluesman Ronnie Earl ventures further into jazz territory with this, his first release on the Verve imprint. As always, Earl is ably and tightly backed by the Broadcasters, featuring solid and empathetic playing from drummer Per Hanson, bassist Rod Carey, and keyboardist and co-collaborator Bruce Katz. It's Katz's "Hippology" that opens the album with a swinging bang, sporting guest appearances on alto sax from Hank Crawford and Allman Brothers alumni Jaimoe on drums. Crawford also shows up again on "Anne's Dream," while Jaimoe joins Marc Quinones for a two-drummer rhythm section guest turn on "Bonnie's Theme" and "Mother Angel." Gregg Allman plays Hammond B-3 organ and contributes the album's only vocal on "Everyday Kinda Man." But guest stars aside, this is clearly Ronnie Earl's show to direct, and his playing, as always, sports exquisite taste, economy, and tone for days. His nine-minute-plus soliloquy on Thelonious Monk's "'Round Midnight" (the only cover on this album) blasts the venerable jazz standard into new territory as Earl's passages take on almost trumpet-like tonalities, while his "I Like That Thing You Did" (dedicated to Jimmie Vaughan) creates an organ-like sound with tons of ultra-shimmering Leslie vibrato. Since adopting an all-instrumental format several albums back, Earl's music has blossomed in a multitude of directions, embracing jazz, soul, and the rockier aspects of guitarists like Carlos Santana (the title track) and Peter Green ("Heart of Glass"), and bringing new life to the organ jazz combo format ("Deep Pockets") while remaining true to his deep blues roots, like in his closing tribute to Albert Collins, "O'Yeah." This release pushes the envelope even further and breaks new ground, wrapped in the velvet glove of Tom Dowd's production. — *Cub Koda*

David Honeyboy Edwards

b. Jun. 28, 1915, Shaw, MS
Guitar, Vocals, Harmonica / Delta Blues
Living links to the immortal Robert Johnson are few. There's Robert Jr. Lockwood, of course—and David "Honeyboy" Edwards. Until relatively recently, Edwards was something of an underappreciated figure, but no longer—his slashing, Delta-drenched guitar and gruff vocals are as authentic as it gets.

Edwards had it tough growing up in Mississippi, but his blues prowess (his childhood pals included Tommy McClennan and Robert Petway) impressed Big Joe Williams enough to take him under his wing. Rambling around the south, Honeyboy experienced the great Charley Patton and played often with Robert Johnson. Musicologist Alan Lomax came to Clarksdale, MS, in 1942 and captured Edwards for Library of Congress-sponsored posterity.

Commercial prospects for the guitarist were scant, however—a 1951 78 for Artist Record Co., "Build a Cave" (as Mr. Honey), and four 1953 sides for

Chess that laid unissued until "Drop Down Mama" turned up 17 years later on an anthology constituted the bulk of his early recorded legacy, although Edwards was in Chicago from the mid-'50s on.

The guitarist met young harpist/blues aficionado Michael Frank in 1972. Four years later, they formed the Honeyboy Edwards Blues Band to break into Chicago's then-fledgling North side club scene; they also worked as a duo (and continue to do so on occasion). When Frank inaugurated his Earwig label, he enlisted Honeyboy and his longtime pals Sunnyland Slim, Big Walter Horton, Floyd Jones, and Kansas City Red to cut a rather informal album, *Old Friends*, as his second release in 1979. In 1992, Earwig assembled *Delta Bluesman*, a stunning combination of unexpurgated Library of Congress masters and recent performances that show Honeyboy Edwards has lost none of his blues fire. — *Bill Dahl*

White Windows / Sep. 1988 / Evidence ◆◆◆◆
David "Honeyboy" Edwards is one of the last surviving Delta blues warriors and is among the originators of a musical style as evocative and vibrant as any this nation has ever experienced. Edwards' voice, with its ironic, colorful, weary tonal qualities and cutting, keen delivery are contrasted by a crisp, slicing guitar approach. Edwards does not rely on slickness, inventiveness, or niceties; his riffs, lines, phrases, and licks are as aggressive and fiery as his vocals. He showed what real traditional blues singing was all about when he recorded for Blue Suit in 1988. Evidence has reissued that 13-song session in splendid digital glory, as Edwards' triumphant, resounding voice rings through each number. — *Ron Wynn*

● **Delta Bluesman** / 1992 / Earwig ◆◆◆◆
This fascinating disc combines the vintage Library of Congress recordings made by Alan Lomax in 1942 with recordings made in the 1990s with Carey Bell, Floyd Jones, and Sunnyland Slim. While not a best-of collection, the CD does a fine job of tracing the development of a great bluesman who started as an acoustic country blues player and became equally adept at electric Chicago blues. To paraphrase Sam Phillips, this is where the soul of man never dies. — *Tim Sheridan*

I've Been Around / 1995 / Trix ◆◆

Crawling Kingsnake / Jul. 22, 1997 / Testament ◆◆◆◆
Any fan of Delta blues should grab this reissue as fast they can get to it. These are vintage recordings, mostly from 1967, made by scholar-producer Pete Welding when Edwards was 51 years old. Edwards' itinerant lifestyle resulted in his missing many opportunities to record, so that this was only the fifth session he'd had in over 30 years in music, performing solo, with an acoustic guitar on eight of the 13 cuts here. Edwards cuts a daunting figure on the guitar, making the strings sing in several voices at once (check out the playing on "Love Me Over Slow"), and his singing is a match for his playing. The eight solo numbers, dating from 1967, feature the music he was most familiar with, including Robert Johnson's "Sweet Home Chicago" and the title track of this collection. The rest date from a March 1964 session on which Edwards shares the spotlight with singer-harpist John Lee Henley. As a bonus, the last track is an interview from his 1967 solo session in which Edwards talks about Robert Johnson and Tommy Johnson, both of whom he knew personally. The background ambient sound does nothing to detract from the worth of the music, which has a wonderful raw quality. — *Bruce Eder*

The World Don't Owe Me Nothing / Dec. 24, 1997 / Earwig ◆◆◆
Released to coincide with Edwards' autobiography of the same name, *The World Don't Owe Me Nothing* captures a live date features harmonica player Carey Bell; among the performances is a reading of Freddie King's "Hideaway." — *Jason Ankeny*

Willie Edwards

Guitar, Vocals / Modern Electric Blues
Guitarist, singer, and songwriter Willie Edwards was one of the many white kids who first discovered blues and folk music in the 1960s. He began playing guitar in tenth grade and became a fan of 1960s soul, as well as blues and folk music, buying albums by artists like Solomon Burke and Otis Redding. From the mid-1960s, he led a bevy of soul, R&B, and blues bands around his native Connecticut, always playing rhythm guitar. It wasn't until later that he began playing lead guitar, and with his smoky, throaty vocals and Albert King-inspired guitar riffs, his various bands found audiences in clubs

around Connecticut and Massachusetts. Edwards' songwriting and vocals are what set him apart from other blues bands, aside from the fact that he's been leading his own bands since 1965.

Edwards recorded a strong debut album for the London-based JSP Records, *Everlastin' Tears*. The album, released in 1997 and produced by Johnny Rawls, showcases his unique songwriting voice. Edwards sings songs like "Dollar In," "Company Store," "'90s Blues," and "Read Between the Lines," that contain social commentary as well as some ferocious guitar playing. He's accompanied by Johnny Rawls on guitar and the Nutmeg Horns. —*Richard Skelly*

Everlastin' Tears / Feb. 25, 1997 / JSP ◆◆◆

Willie Egan

Piano / Rock 'n' Roll, Piano Blues, Boogie-Woogie
Known by true aficionados for the handful of great boogie rockers that he cut for the L.A.-based Mambo and Vita imprints during the mid-'50s, pianist Willie Egan should have enjoyed a considerably larger share of fame than he did.

Born on the bayou outside of Shreveport, Egan was lucky to escape his rustic existence for Los Angeles at the age of nine. Piano swiftly became his passion, as he listened to and learned from the recordings of Amos Milburn, Hadda Brooks, and Camille Howard. A 1954 single for John R. Fullbright's Elko label preceded a series of 1955-56 gems for Larry Mead's Mambo and Vita labels, notably "Wow Wow," "What a Shame," "Come On," "She's Gone Away, But," and "Wear Your Black Dress." Egan's surname was frequently misspelled on these platters as Eggins or Egans. After a stint as one of Marvin Phillips' several duet partners (billed as Marvin & Johnny), Egan largely hung it up (a 1983 European tour got him back in the studio for one fresh album, anyway). —*Bill Dahl*

Going Back to Louisiana / 1984 / Ace ◆◆◆

Willie Egan & His Friends / 1985 / Relic ◆◆◆

Rock & Roll Fever / 1988 / Krazy Kat ◆◆

● **Come on** / 1993 / Relic ◆◆◆◆
The R&B boogie pianist waxed some rip-roaring rockers for the tiny Los Angeles-based Vita and Mambo logos during the mid-'50s. Fourteen of his best are collected here for a long-overdue airing. This guy deserved a lot more respect than he got, judging from the jumping Louisiana-tinged "Wow Wow," "Come On," and "She's Gone Away, But..." Also aboard: 11 more obscure goodies from the same labels' vaults, notably four tracks by Harmonica Slim (including "Drop Anchor") and Big Boy Groves' lament "You Can't Beat the Horses." —*Bill Dahl*

Electric Flag

f. 1967, Chicago, IL, **db.** 1974
Group / Blues-Rock
When guitarist Mike Bloomfield left the Paul Butterfield Blues Band in 1967, he wanted to form a band that combined blues, rock, soul, psychedelia, and jazz into something new. The ambitious concept didn't come off, despite some interesting moments; maybe it was *too* ambitious to hold all that weight. Bloomfield knew for sure that he wanted a horn section in the band, which he began forming with a couple of friends, keyboardist Barry Goldberg and singer Nick Gravenites. Although the trio were all veterans of the Chicago music scene, the group based themselves in the San Francisco area. They were in turn bolstered by a rhythm section of bassist Harvey Brooks (who had played on some of Bob Dylan's mid-'60s records) and drummer Buddy Miles; on top of them came a horn section.

Oddly, before even playing any live concerts, the group recorded the soundtrack for the 1967 psychedelic exploitation movie, *The Trip,* which afforded them the opportunity to experiment with some of their ideas without much pressure. Their live debut was at the 1967 Monterey Pop Festival (although they didn't make it into the documentary film of the event), but their first proper studio album didn't come out until the spring of 1968.

A Long Time Comin' was an erratic affair, predating Blood, Sweat & Tears and Chicago as a sort of attempt at a big band rock sound. Calling it an early jazz-rock outing is not exactly accurate; it was more like late '60s soul-rock-psychedelia that sometimes (but not always) employed prominent horns. Indeed, it sometimes didn't always sound like the work of the same band—or,

at least, you could say that it seemed torn between blues-rock, soul-rock, and California psychedelic influences. The album's success is even harder to judge in light of the facts that Gravenites really wasn't a top-notch vocalist, and that the band's instrumental skills outshone their songwriting ones.

There was enough promise on the album to merit further exploration, but it had hardly been released before the Flag began to droop. Goldberg left, followed shortly by Bloomfield, the most important component of the group's vision. A fragmented band recorded an inferior follow-up, but by 1969 they had split up. They did reunite (with Bloomfield) in 1974 for a Jerry Wexler-produced album that got little notice. —*Richie Unterberger*

The Trip / 1967 / Edsel ◆◆◆
Before the Electric Flag had recorded their first album or even played live, they composed and performed the soundtrack to *The Trip,* the 1967 psychedelic exploitation film starring Peter Fonda, directed by Roger Corman, and written by Jack Nicholson. This odd but worthwhile relic is entirely instrumental, and as befits the subject matter, wildly eclectic, veering from ragtime and hurdy-gurdy music to basic soul-rock and sweeping, spacey psychedelia and harsh electronics. One of the funkiest snippets, "Flash, Bam, Pow," was later used by Fonda in *Easy Rider.* —*Richie Unterberger*

A Long Time Comin' / 1968 / Columbia ◆◆◆◆
Ex-Butterfield Band guitarist/drummer Miles and others put this soul-rock band together in 1967. This debut is a testament to their ability to catch fire and keep on burnin'. —*Jeff Tamarkin*

Electric Flag / 1969 / Columbia ◆◆

Band Kept on Playing / 1974 / Atlantic ◆◆◆

● **Old Glory: The Best of Electric Flag** / Oct. 1995 / Columbia/Legacy ◆◆◆◆
A near-definitive anthology, including almost all of the debut LP (but not every last item), key songs from the second album, and some previously unissued demos, alternate takes, and performances from the 1967 Monterey Pop Festival. —*Richie Unterberger*

Robert "Mojo" Elem

b. Itta Bena, MS
Bass, Vocals, Guitar / Electric Chicago Blues
When talking about deep bluesmen who are also great entertainers, the conversation will eventually get around to the coolest bassman/singer/showman the Windy City has in its blues arsenal, Big Mojo Elem. As a singer, he possesses a relatively high-pitched voice that alternately drips with honey and malice. As a bassist, his unique approach to the instrument makes him virtually one of a kind. Unlike most bass players, Elem seldom plays standard walking bass patterns, instead using a single-note groove that lends to any band he's a part of a decidedly juke-joint groove. And as a showman, he possesses an energy that makes other performers half his age look like they're sitting down. Born in Itta Bena, MS, Elem grew up in fertile blues territory. Originally a guitarist, he soaked up licks and ideas by observing masters like Robert Nighthawk and a young Ike Turner first-hand. By his 20th birthday he had arrived in Chicago and was almost immediately pressed into professional service playing rhythm guitar behind Arthur "Big Boy" Spires and harmonica man Lester Davenport. By 1956 Elem had switched over to the newly arrived (in Chicago) electric bass, simply to stand out from the pack of guitar players searching the clubs looking for work. He formed a band with harp player Earl Payton and signed on a young Freddie King as their lead guitarist, playing on King's very first single for the El-Bee label in late 1956. After Freddie's success made him the bandleader, Big Mojo stayed with King off and on for the next eight years. The '50s and '60s also found him doing club work—mostly on the West side—with Magic Sam, Junior Wells, Shakey Jake Harris, Jimmy Dawkins, and Luther Allison with a short stint in Otis Rush's band as well. Aside from a stray anthology cut and a now out-of-print album for a tiny European label, Elem's career has not been documented in much depth, but he remains one of the liveliest players on the scene. —*Cub Koda*

Mojo Boogie / 1978 / MCM ◆◆◆◆
Blessed with a sweet growl of a voice and grinding out a single-note groove heavier than any ZZ Top record you've got, this thing romps like nobody's business, and is the perfect showcase for Elem's hard driving, bare-bones honest singing and bass-pumping talents. Studebaker John Grimaldi plays some nice lead, even nicer slide and blows some fine amplified harp when

needed, while Twist Turner's no-frills drumming slots in nice with Mojo's bass hunch. A nice balance between old favorites and original material, most of it co-written with producer George Paulus. — *Cub Koda*

Big Chief Ellis

b. Nov. 10, 1914, Birmingham, AL, **d.** Dec. 20, 1977, Birmingham, AL
Piano, Vocals / Piano Blues
Prickly insights and sensitive accompaniment were the stock-in-trade of pianist and vocalist Wilbert Thirkield "Big Chief" Ellis. A self-taught player, Ellis performed at house parties and dances during the '20s, then left his native Alabama. He traveled extensively for several years, working mostly in non-musical jobs. After a three-year army stint from 1939—1942, Ellis settled in New York. He accompanied many blues musicians during their visits to the New York area. He started recording for Lenox in 1945, and also did sessions for Sittin' In and Capitol in the '40s and '50s, playing with Sonny Terry and Brownie McGhee for Capitol. Though Ellis reduced his performance schedule after moving from New York to Washington D.C., his career got a final boost in the early '70s. He recorded for Trix and appeared at several folk and blues festivals until his death in 1977. — *Ron Wynn*

● **Big Chief Ellis Featuring Tarheel Slim, Brownie M** / Jun. 1977 / Trix ◆◆◆◆
Some rare late-period blues from two very underrated New York musicians. Big Chief Ellis and Tarheel Slim weren't the greatest technical singers, but each was a fine interpreter, and that makes this late-'70s session quite instructive. — *Ron Wynn*

Tinsley Ellis

b. Jun. 4, 1957, Atlanta, GA
Guitar, Vocals / Modern Electric Blues
A fiery guitarist and talented songwriter, Tinsley Ellis plays a unique blend of Memphis R&B, Southwest blues, and urban funk. Born in Atlanta, Ellis was raised in South Florida and got his first guitar around age seven. Primary influences for Ellis include Elmore James, B.B. King, Freddie King and Gatemouth Brown. While attending Emory University in Atlanta, Ellis worked in a few local bands, including the Alley Cats along with Preston Hubbard, who became a bassist for the Fabulous Thunderbirds. In the early '80s, Ellis and harpman Bob Nelson founded the Heartfixers, a rather eclectic club band that played blues, rockabilly, R&B, and early rock. They became popular on the Southeast club circuit and by 1986 had recorded four albums. Early on, Ellis was compared to Johnny Winter and Stevie Ray Vaughan, but although he had a healthy following in his region, his name was largely unknown to the mainstream. He left the Heartfixers in 1987 and began recording as a solo artist. Though recorded for Landslide, his debut, *Georgia Blue*, was distributed by Alligator Records the following year to good response. Subsequent albums, all for Alligator, include *Trouble Time* (1992) and *Storm Warning* (1994). A tireless live performer, Tinsley and his eponymous band tour constantly and log over 200 performances per year. — *Sandra Brennan*

Live at the Moon Shadow / 1983 / Landslide ◆◆◆
Atlanta blues/rockers Tinsley Ellis and the Heartfixers hit in concert with vocalist Chicago Bob Nelson. — *Michael G. Nastos*

Cool on It / 1986-1991 / Alligator ◆◆◆◆
High-energy roadhouse-rock and blues-rock with the Heartfixers. — *Niles J. Frantz*

Georgia Blue / 1989 / Alligator ◆◆
Like most of Tinsley Ellis' albums, *Georgia Blue* is filled with hot, blistering guitar, mediocre songs, and flat vocals. For fans of blues guitar, there's plenty to hear on the album—the licks and solos burn with a wild, uncontrolled fury. Others might find the album a little tedious, but not without virtue. — *Thom Owens*

● **Fanning of the Flames** / 1989 / Alligator ◆◆◆◆
Fanning of the Flames is an erratic but impressive set from Tinsley Ellis. While his basic sound is indebted to Stevie Ray Vaughan, the guitarist borrows from every other major blues artist. Furthermore, he has a tendency to overplay his licks, giving the album a feeling of unfocused fury. However, that sound can be overwhelming—his technique is impressive, even if he doesn't know when to reign it in. As a consequence, *Fanning of the Flames*

is of interest only to guitar fans, not general listeners, but for guitar fans, there's plenty of music to treasure here. — *Thom Owens*

Trouble Time / 1992 / Alligator ◆◆
Storm Warning / 1994 / Alligator ◆◆◆
A powerful blues guitarist and an excellent vocalist, Tinsley Ellis dominates his fourth Alligator CD as a leader. His backup band (guitarist Oliver Wood, bassist James Ferguson, drummer Stuart Gibson, and occasional organist/pianist Stuart Grimes) does a fine job of inspiring the leader, while slide guitarist Derek Trucks and Albey Scholl on harmonica make notable guest appearances. While Ellis often plays quite passionately and hints at rock, he also performs an occasional quieter piece that shows his more traditional and introspective side. There is plenty of spirit on this generally rousing set. — *Scott Yanow*

Fire It Up / May 27, 1997 / Alligator ◆◆◆
With each successive album, Ellis has moved further and further away from mainstream blues grooves and closer and closer to hard rock. While his guitar playing is as explosive as ever, it also remains unfocused, the end result being soloing that never reaches a musical climax, but is nonetheless played with an unrelenting energy that music fans who like their blues with rock muscles will appreciate. Tracks like "Diggin' My Own Grave," "One Sunny Day," "Soulful," "Just Dropped In (To See What Condition My Condition Was In)," and "I Walk Alone" sound like they could be on anybody's blues-rock/roots-rock album, and even legendary producer Tom Dowd can't do much with Ellis' consistently flat and generally lifeless vocals. Only the slow blues "Are You Sorry," the soul ballad "Change Your Mind," the Buddy Guy/Junior Wells-inspired "Break My Rule," and the laidback set closer, "Everyday," reach for higher musical goals than the mundane. Someone special to look and listen for on this album is former Booker T. and the MGs bassist, Donald "Duck" Dunn. Duck appears on seven of the 12 songs, contributing simple, unobtrusive lines that speak in their own quiet way and underpin the tracks with a groove that's beyond rock-solid. This is a well played, well produced—if unexceptional—set of modern blues-rock, and fans of the genre will find much here to celebrate. — *Cub Koda*

John Ellison

b. Aug. 11, 1941, Montgomery, WV
Vocals / R&B, Soul
The sky-high level of soulful intensity John Ellison brought to his lead vocals with the Soul Brothers Six came straight from the church. No surprise there, since he grew up in a religious household. But the way Ellison harnessed that sanctified passion on the group's secular sides was anything but common.

Leaving the coal mines of West Virginia for a more musically opportune Rochester, NY at age 18, Ellison sang soul and styled hair before hooking up with four brothers named Armstrong (Sam, Charles, Harry, and Moses) and bassist Vonell Benjamin. The Soul Brothers Six were a completely self-contained unit—they played their own instruments in addition to singing. Their first 45s on Fine (1965's "Move Girl") and Lyndell ("Don't Neglect Your Baby" the following year) veritably dripped gospel-soaked inspiration but went nowhere.

The sextet decided to relocate to Philadelphia. On the way there, Ellison wrote the magnificent "Some Kind of Wonderful," the song that put the group on the map. Atlantic Records issued the irresistible soul workout in 1967, and it slipped onto the pop charts (becoming their only hit). Deserving encores on Atlantic didn't recapture the 45's success, and the original lineup broke up in 1969. Ellison assembled another band by the same name and soldiered on at Phil L.A. of Soul Records during 1972-73. Meanwhile, Grand Funk Railroad's graceless cover of "Some Kind of Wonderful" proved a gigantic pop smash in 1974.

The John Ellison story might have ended there (he's mostly been ensconced in Canada since then). But not too long ago, After Hours Records bosses Marty Duda and Gregory Townson happened upon the long-lost legend sitting in at a Rochester ginmill with bluesman Joe Beard. The upshot was a 1993 solo Ellison disc, *Welcome Back*, that reintroduced the singer to the American market. Two tracks, including a remade "Some Kind of Wonderful," even reunited the singer with the Armstrong brothers. Pretty wonderful, eh? — *Bill Dahl*

Welcome Back / 1993 / After Hours/Ichiban ◆◆◆
John Ellison was once a member of the Soul Brothers Six, a fine group who

didn't score many hits, but made one unforgettable number, the anthemic "Some Kind Of Wonderful." Ellison's gritty, crisp voice doesn't sound any softer or less soulful in the 1990s than it did in the 1960s. This includes a good, if not quite transcendent, remake of "Some Kind Of Wonderful," and also contains some heartfelt ballads, a quasi-country number in "You Ain't Ready," and a couple of decent mid-tempo and dance-flavored tunes. The production, sensibility, and mood are vintage 1960s, which will limit its appeal and possibilities. But it's good to hear John Ellison again, even if his disc is more a nod to the past than a beacon to the future. — *Ron Wynn*

● **The Very Best of John Ellison and the Soul Brothers Six** / 1995 / Forevermore ✦✦✦✦

Well, not quite all their best: this gospel-rooted R&B group enjoyed one real hit in 1967 for Atlantic, the glorious "Some Kind of Wonderful." Alas, a recent remake of the tune, albeit a nice one, graces this 20-track collection. The best stuff is the chronologically earliest—a previously unissued 1966 outing "(You're Gonna) Be by Yourself" and obscure mid-'60s 45s "Move Girl" and "Don't Neglect Your Baby" that soar to the heavens with rich sanctified harmonies. Ten 1972-73 Soul Brothers Six items for Phil L.A. of Soul are also aboard, as are five items from Ellison's recent comeback disc for After Hours. — *Bill Dahl*

Billy "The Kid" Emerson

b. Dec. 21, 1925, Tarpon Springs, FL
R&B, Modern Electric Blues, Soul Blues
Slashing blues, infectious R&B, formulaic rock 'n' roll, moving gospel—keyboardist Billy "The Kid" Emerson played all those interrelated styles during a lengthy career that began in Florida and later transported him up to Memphis and Chicago.

Emerson had already learned his way around a piano when he entered the Navy in 1943. After the war, he began playing around Tarpon Springs, attending Florida A&M during the late '40s and early '50s. He picked up his nickname while playing a joint in St. Petersburg; the club owner dressed the band up in cowboy duds that begged comparison with a certain murderous outlaw.

A 1952-53 stint in the Air Force found Emerson stationed in Greenville, MS. That's where he met young bandleader Ike Turner, who whipped Emerson into shape as an entertainer while he sang with Turner's Kings of Rhythm. Turner also got Emerson through the Sun Records in 1954, playing guitar on The Kid's debut waxing "No Teasing Around."

Emerson's songwriting skills made him a valuable commodity around Sun—but more as a source for other performers' material later on. His bluesy 1955 outing "When It Rains It Pours" elicited a cover from Elvis a few years later at RCA, while Emerson's "Red Hot" (a takeoff on an old cheerleaders chant from Emerson's school days) became a savage rockabilly anthem revived by Billy Lee Riley for Sun and Bob Luman on Imperial.

After his "Little Fine Healthy Thing" failed to sell, Emerson exited Sun to sign with Chicago's Vee-Jay Records in late 1955. Despite first-rate offerings such as the jumping "Every Woman I Know (Crazy 'Bout Automobiles)" and a sophisticated "Don't Start Me to Lying," national recognition eluded Emerson at Vee-Jay too.

It was on to Chess in 1958, recording "Holy Mackerel Baby" and the unusual novelty "Woodchuck" (a remake of an earlier Sun single) during his year or so there. 45s for Mad, USA, M-Pac! (where he waxed the dance workout "The Whip"), and Constellation preceded the formation of Emerson's own logo, Tarpon, in 1966. In addition to Emerson's own stuff, Tarpon issued Denise LaSalle's debut single.

A prolific writer, Emerson penned songs for Junior Wells, Willie Mabon, Wynonie Harris, and Buddy Guy during the early '60s, often in conjunction with Willie Dixon. When recording opportunities slowed, Emerson played jazzy R&B in lounges and supper clubs (guitarist Lacy Gibson was a member of his trio for a while). Emerson took Europe by surprise with a dynamic segment on the American Blues Legends 1979 tour. More recently, he's rumored to have reverted to playing gospel in his native state of Florida. — *Bill Dahl*

● **Little Healthy Thing** / 1980 / Charly ✦✦✦✦

Since no CD reissues are easily accessible by this important Florida-born R&B pianist, this vinyl compendium of his 1954-55 Sun catalog will have to suffice for now. Emerson's jumping proto-rock style at Sun supplied notable

rockabillies with killer material—"Red Hot," as first cut by Emerson, was later done full justice by Billy Lee Riley, while Elvis found the hip-grinding "When It Rains It Pours" to his liking. Emerson's bluesy "No Teasing Around" (with Ike Turner on guitar) and the upbeat "Something for Nothing" and the title cut are among the many highlights of this enjoyable LP. — *Bill Dahl*

Crazy 'bout Automobiles / 1982 / Charly ✦✦✦✦

Another vinyl-only collection, this one a ten-incher with only ten songs, covering Emerson's 1955-57 stay at Chicago's Vee-Jay label. Emerson bonded well with Vee-Jay's house bands, especially on the romping "Every Woman I Know (Crazy 'Bout Automobiles)" and a sophisticated "Don't Start Me to Lying." As with his Sun Stuff, the big-voiced Emerson was a captivating performer. — *Bill Dahl*

Sleepy John Estes (John Adams Estes)

b. Jan. 25, 1899, Ripley, TN, **d.** Jun. 5, 1977, Brownville, TN
Guitar, Vocals / Country Blues, Piedmont Blues, Prewar Country Blues
Big Bill Broonzy called John Estes' style of singing "crying" the blues because of its overt emotional quality. Actually his vocal style harks back to his tenure as a work-gang leader for a railroad maintenance crew, where his vocal improvisations and keen, cutting voice set the pace for work activities. Nicknamed "Sleepy" John Estes, supposedly because of his ability to sleep standing up, he teamed with mandolinist Yank Rachell and harmonica player Hammie Nixon to play the houseparty circuit in and around Brownsville in the early '20s. Forty years later, the same team reunited to record for Delmark and play the festival circuit. Never an outstanding guitarist, Estes relied on his expressive voice to carry his music, and the recordings he made from 1929 on have enormous appeal and remain remarkably accessible today.

Despite the fact that he worked to mixed Black and White audiences in string band, jug band, or medicine show format, his music retains a distinct ethnicity and has a particularly plaintive sound. Astonishingly, he recorded during six decades for Victor, Decca, Bluebird, Ora Nelle, Sun, Delmark, and others. Over the course of his career, his music remained simple yet powerful, and despite his sojourns to Memphis or Chicago he retained a traditional down-home sound. Some of his songs are deeply personal statements about his community and life, such as "Lawyer Clark" or "Floating Bridge." Other compositions have universal appeal ("Drop Down Mama" or "Someday Baby") and went on to become mainstays in the repertoires of countless musicians. One of the true masters of his idiom, he lived in poverty, yet was somehow capable of turning his experiences and the conditions of his life into compelling art. — *Barry Lee Pearson*

The Legend of Sleepy John Estes / 1962 / Delmark ✦✦✦✦
The best of his Delmark rediscovery recordings. — *Barry Lee Pearson*

1929-1940 / 1967 / Smithsonian/Folkways ✦✦✦✦
Sleepy John Estes' finest period vocally was the prewar era. This LP includes several expressive and delightful numbers in which Estes' narrative skills are especially strong. He was never a great guitarist, but the accompaniment works here because it's sparse and limited. — *Ron Wynn*

Jazz Heritage—Down South Blues (1935-1940) / 1970 / MCA ✦✦✦
Part of an '80s MCA budget blues series, this album includes "Drop Down Mama" and "Someday Baby." With Hammie Nixon on harmonica. — *Barry Lee Pearson*

Complete Works, Vols. 1-2 / 1990 / Document ✦✦✦
Document's two-volume collection of Sleepy John Estes' recordings contains everything the bluesman cut between 1929 and 1941, presented in chronological order. Although there is plenty of fine music on the collection, the presentation is overwhelming for anyone but completists and historians. If you're neither, stick with Yazoo's single-disc collection, *I Ain't Gonna Be Worried No More*. — *Thom Owens*

★ **Sleepy John Estes 1929-1940: I Ain't Gonna Be Worried No More** / 1992 / Yazoo ✦✦✦✦✦
I Ain't Gonna Be Worried No More compiles 23 songs Sleepy John Estes recorded between 1929 and 1941, capturing the bluesman at the height of his creative powers. Unlike many Delta bluesmen of his era, Estes worked with a full jug band, which gave his music a greater variety of textures. His music swings, with a loose, relaxed feel that isn't heard on many Delta blues records. Furthermore, his songs are inventive, featuring pseudo-autobio-

graphical lyrics loaded with evocative imagery. Nearly all of his best material is included on *I Ain't Gonna Be Worried No More*, making it as close to a definitive retrospective of Estes' music as possible. — *Thom Owens*

Goin' to Brownsville / Feb. 24, 1998 / Testament ✦✦✦

Sleepy John Estes never really changed or altered his style during the 50-year period he recorded. The records he made for Victor in the 1920s didn't sound much different than the ones he made in the late 1960s and 1970s for various collector's labels. This collection features 21 previously unissued solo performances from 1962 capped with a lengthy interview with Sleepy John conducted by producer Pete Welding. Estes is in fine form throughout, particularly effective on "Lost My Eyesight," "Run Around," "Floating Bridge," "Vernita's Blues," and Big Bill Broonzy's "It Was a Dream." In the 18-minute interview that closes this disc, Estes discusses making records for Decca, Victor, and other labels, coming to Chicago and losing his eyesight. Compelling music and even more compelling conversation, all of it loaded with realism and ambience galore. — *Cub Koda*

The Fabulous Thunderbirds

f. 1974, Austin, TX

Group / Blues-Rock, Electric Texas Blues, Rock 'n' Roll, Modern Electric Blues, Modern Electric Texas Blues, Harmonica Blues

With their fusion of blues, rock 'n' roll, and R&B, the Fabulous Thunderbirds helped popularize roadhouse Texas blues with a mass audience in the '80s and, in the process, they helped kick-start a blues revival during the mid-'80s. During their heyday in the early '80s, they were the most popular attraction on the blues bar circuit, which eventually led to a breakthrough to the pop audience in 1986 with their fifth album, *Tuff Enuff.* The mass success didn't last too long, and founding member Jimmie Vaughan left in 1990, but the Fabulous Thunderbirds remained one of the most popular blues concert acts in America during the '90s.

Guitarist Jimmie Vaughan formed the Fabulous Thunderbirds with vocalist/harpist Kim Wilson in 1974; in addition to Vaughan and Wilson, the band's original lineup included bassist Keith Ferguson and drummer Mike Buck. Initially, the group also featured vocalist Lou Ann Barton, but she left the band shortly after its formation. Within a few years, the Thunderbirds became the house band for the Austin club Antone's, where they would play regular sets and support touring blues musicians. By the end of the decade, they had built a strong fan base, which led to a record contract with the local Takoma Records.

In 1979, the Fabulous Thunderbirds released their eponymous debut on Takoma. The record was successful enough to attract the attention of major labels and Chrysalis signed the band the following year. *What's the Word,* the group's second album, was released in 1980 and it was followed in 1981 by *Butt Rockin'.* By the time the Thunderbirds recorded their 1982 album *T-Bird Rhythm,* drummer Mike Buck was replaced by Fran Christina, a former member of Roomful of Blues.

Although the Fabulous Thunderbirds had become favorites of fellow musicians—they opened shows for the Rolling Stones and Eric Clapton—and had been critically well-received, their records didn't sell particularly well. Chrysalis dropped the band following the release of *T-Bird Rhythm,* leaving the band without a record contract for four years. While they were in limbo, they continued to play concerts across the country. During this time, bassist Keith Ferguson left the band and was replaced by Preston Hubbard, another former member of Roomful of Blues. In 1985, they finally landed another record contract, signing with Epic/Associated.

After the deal with Epic/Associated was complete, the T-Birds entered a London studio and recorded their fifth album with producer Dave Edmunds. The resulting album, *Tuff Enuff,* was released in the spring of 1986 and, unexpectedly, became a major crossover success. The title track was released as a single and its accompanying video received heavy play on MTV, which helped the song reach the American Top Ten. The success of the single sent the album to number 13 on the charts; *Tuff Enuff* would eventually receive a platinum record. "Wrap It Up," a cover of an old Sam & Dave song, was the album's second single and it became a Top Ten album rock track. Later in 1986, the T-Birds won the W.C. Handy Award for best blues band.

The Fabulous Thunderbirds' follow-up to *Tuff Enuff, Hot Number,* arrived in the summer of 1987. Initially, the album did fairly well—peaking at number 49 on the charts and spawning the Top Ten album rock hit "Stand Back"—but it quickly fell off the charts. Furthermore, its slick, radio-ready sound alienated their hardcore following of blues fans. "Powerful Stuff," a single from the soundtrack of the Tom Cruise film *Cocktail,* became a number-three-album rock hit in the summer of 1988. It was included on the fol-lowing year's *Powerful Stuff* album, which proved to be a major commercial disappointment—it only spent seven weeks on the charts.

After the two poorly received follow-ups to *Tuff Enuff,* Jimmie Vaughan left the band to play in a duo with his brother, Stevie Ray Vaughan; following Stevie Ray's death in the summer of 1990, Jimmie pursued a full-time solo career. The Fabulous Thunderbirds replaced Vaughan with two guitarists, Duke Robillard and Kid Bangham. The first album from the new lineup, *Walk That Walk, Talk That Talk,* appeared in 1991. Following the release of *Walk That Walk, Talk That Talk,* Epic/Associated dropped the Fabulous Thunderbirds from their roster.

During the early '90s, the Fabulous Thunderbirds were in limbo, as Kim Wilson recorded a pair of solo albums—*Tigerman* (1993) and *That's Life* (1994). Wilson re-assembled the band in late 1994 and the band recorded their ninth album, *Roll of the Dice,* which was released on Private Music in 1995. Following its release, the band returned to actively touring the United States. —*Stephen Thomas Erlewine*

The Fabulous Thunderbirds / 1979 / Chrysalis ♦♦♦♦
Their debut album, with the original lineup of Wilson, Vaughn, Buck, and Ferguson stompin' through a roadhouse set of covers and genre-worthy originals. One of the few White blues albums that works. —*Cub Koda*

What's the Word / 1980 / Chrysalis ♦♦♦♦
Second album, equally powerful. Some of their best, including the off-kilter "Los Fabulosos Thunderbirds" and "Running Shoes." —*Cub Koda*

Butt Rockin' / 1981 / Chrysalis ♦♦♦

T-Bird Rhythm / 1982 / Chrysalis ♦♦♦

Tuff Enuff / 1986 / Epic ♦♦♦
Their breakthrough success. The title track and soul covers point the band in a new, more mainstream direction. —*Cub Koda*

Hot Number / 1987 / Epic ♦♦

Powerful Stuff / 1989 / Epic ♦♦
Like the previous *Hot Number, Powerful Stuff* is a weak collection of watered-down blues-rock that makes too many concessions to the commerical constraints of AOR radio stations. Occasionally, the band works up some energy or Jimmie Vaughan or Kim Wilson turn out a good solo, but for the most part, *Powerful Stuff* is bland, faceless mainstream rock 'n' roll. —*Thom Owens*

The Essential / Jun. 18, 1991 / Chrysalis ♦♦♦♦
Nice compilation of the early Chrysalis albums on one CD. —*Cub Koda*

Walk That Walk, Talk That Talk / Dec. 1991 / Epic ♦♦♦
Walk That Walk, Talk That Talk is the first album the Fabulous Thunderbirds recorded without Jimmie Vaughan. It takes two guitarists—two good guitarists, by the way—to fill his place and even with Duke Robillard and Kid Bangham on board, there is something missing. Though the T-birds have returned to straightahead blues-rock, abandoning the overly commercial production of their previous three albums, they don't sound as distinctive as they did with Vaughan. Kim Wilson blows some good harp, Robillard throws out a few stellar solos, and Bangham can almost keep up with him, but on the whole, the album is a disappointment. —*Thom Owens*

● **Hot Stuff: The Greatest Hits** / Aug. 25, 1992 / Epic ♦♦♦♦
The best tracks from the Fabulous Thunderbirds' more rock-oriented years at CBS Associated Records are collected on this single-disc compilation. —*Stephen Thomas Erlewine*

Roll of the Dice / Aug. 1, 1995 / Private Music ♦♦♦
The Fabulous T-Birds' second album without Jimmie Vaughan is an improvement over *Walk That Walk, Talk That Talk*, featuring a tighter, more focused band and hotter playing. Nevertheless, the band takes a couple of missteps, particularly with a limp version of "Zip-a-Dee-Doo-Dah." — *Stephen Thomas Erlewine*

Different Tacos / 1996 / Country Town Music ♦♦♦
For Fabulous Thunderbirds fanatics, or anyone longing for the raw gutbucket blues-rock of their early recordings, *Different Tacos* is something of a godsend. Essentially, the disc is a rarities collection, boasting nine outtakes from their first four studio albums, a couple of live cuts from various UK tours, and a nearly complete set from an Austin club gig in the late '70s. Each track is straightforward, take-no-prisoners Texas blues, played with astonishing fervor and grit. There are alternate takes and live versions of familiar T-Birds items, plus covers and songs that were reworked or abandoned for the original albums. Certainly, the nature of this live-and-rarities set makes *Different Tacos* primarily of interest to hardcore fans, but those fans will find it a most welcome addition to their Thunderbirds collection. — *Stephen Thomas Erlewine*

Best of the Fabulous Thunderbirds / 1997 / EMI ♦♦♦♦
The Best of the Fabulous Thunderbirds is a terrific 22-track UK collection hitting all the highlights of the group's first four albums and offering a nearly flawless overview of the band's bluesiest period. — *Stephen Thomas Erlewine*

High Water / Aug. 12, 1997 / Highstreet ♦♦♦
Although credited to the Fabulous Thunderbirds, *High Water* was written and performed by bandleader Kim Wilson with guitarist Danny Kortchmar and percussionist Steve Jordan, who produced the album, and it does not feature the rest of the current T-Birds lineup, which, in any case, has long since devolved into a backup band for Wilson. Kortchmar and Jordan are not exactly authentic bluesmen, of course, but instead high-priced sessionmen, and they provide a tightly arranged, somewhat antiseptic accompaniment to Wilson, whose vocals and harmonica playing are the focus. Longtime fans may miss the prominent guitar work and band feel that characterized earlier releases. — *William Ruhlmann*

The Fairfield Four

f. Nashville, TN
Group / Traditional Gospel, Black Gospel, Hymns
During the 1940s, the Fairfield Four were among the top-ranked gospel quartets, along with the Dixie Hummingbirds, Five Blind Boys, and Soul Stirrers. Originally a gospel duet created in the early '20s by the pastor of Fairfield Baptist Church in Nashville to occupy his sons, Harry and Rufus Carrethers, they became a gospel trio with the addition of John Battle. The group was transformed into a jubilee quartet by the '30s and began the first of numerous personnel changes. They recorded for RCA Victor and Columbia during the decade and were known for their reinterpretations of standard hymns, featuring bright, close baritone and tenor harmonies. When the Fairfield Four sang, they utilized the full extent of their voices, moving easily from deep, rolling basslines to the staccato upper peaks of the tenor range, all executed with precise, intricate harmonies and ever-shifting leads.

The Fairfield Four reached their broadest audience when the Sunway Vitamin Company sponsored a nationally broadcast radio show for them daily at 6:45 a.m. on WLAC, Nashville. At the same time, they also continued touring; it was a grueling schedule, especially with the drive to Nashville, and often the group would be missing a member or two on the show. In 1942, the quartet recorded for the Library of Congress, but by 1950, it all became too much. Coupled with some financial trouble and a dwindling radio audience, the Fairfield Four broke up, though one member, Reverend Sam McCary, used the group name to perform with other quartets. In 1980, the Fairfield Four from the '40s was reunited for a concert in Birmingham, Alabama, by Black gospel specialist Doug Seroff. In 1989, they were designated as National Heritage Fellows by the National Endowment for the Arts. They continue to perform, though the original members are either deceased or retired. — *Sandra Brennan & Bil Carpenter*

The Famous Fairfield Four / 1960 / Old Town ♦♦♦♦
More fine singing recorded at the RCA Studios. — *Opal Louis Nations*

One Religion / 1980 / ♦♦♦
This is a prize collection of some of Nashville's Fairfield Four Dot recordings spanning the years 1951 through 1953. The group on these sides is composed of Rev. Sam McCrary—lead, Willie Love—second tenor, James Hill—baritone, and Willie Frank Lewis—bass. Some of these cuts are thought to be alternate takes of earlier Bullet recordings made during the late '40s. Its classic a cappella singing is reminiscent of early Spirit of Memphis material. There's excellent notes by gospel researcher Tony Heilbut. — *Opal Louis Nations, Roots & Rhythm Newsletter*

★ **Angels Watching over Me** / 1981 / P-Vine ♦♦♦♦♦
Angels Watching Over Me is a remarkable collection of classic material the Fairfield Four recorded in the early '50s. Each of the 26 tracks are performed a cappella, yet there's a lot of variety within the music, since the quartet positioned themselves between the classic sound of gospel choirs and the bluesier, harder-edged sound of small vocal combos. The results are stunning and moving, making *Angels Watching Over Me* an essential addition to any serious gospel library. — *Leo Stanley*

Standing in the Safety Zone / 1992 / Warner Alliance ♦♦♦♦
The Fairfield Four were once among the finest hard gospel ensembles around. Unfortunately, they didn't stay together as long as their comrades, disbanding in 1950 due to business problems. They reunited 30 years later, then received a National Heritage Fellowship award in 1989. This wonderful '92 release features awesome harmonies, a guest appearance from The Nashville Bluegrass Band on "Roll, Jordan Roll," and soaring, magnificent lead vocals from Walter Settles, Isaac Freeman, and W.L. Richardson. Old-time gospel at its best, vividly presented via contemporary technology. — *Ron Wynn*

Standing on the Rock / 1995 / Nashboro/AVI ♦♦♦♦
Essential recordings of this leading influential quartet. Dot and Bullet sides. — *Opal Louis Nations*

I Couldn't Hear Nobody Pray / Sep. 9, 1997 / Warner Brothers ♦♦♦
Around the time of this album's release, the Fairfield Four reached a new peak in mainstream visibility, complete with an appearance backing Elvis Costello on *The David Letterman Show*. Elvis Costello-led cut ("That Day Is Done") appears here, and there are odd guest appearances by country singer Pam Tillis and Prairie Home Companion narrator Garrison Keillor. But the focus is usually on the singers, who perform a cappella on most of the cuts. They sing full-bodied vocal arrangements with dignified conviction; the low parts are especially vibrant. — *Richie Unterberger*

Fairfield Four / ♦♦♦♦
Here's 33 cuts by the exciting Jubilee quartet, still performing (after more than 68 years) in a cappella. This contains long-out-of-print Dot (Bullet purchases) and Old Town material from out-of-print Nashboro and Athens album collections, plus two by Joe Henderson, the group's basso in 1960. It's close harmony '50s singing at its best with the legendary Sam McCrary "hard tenor" lead and the unbeatable Isaac "Dickie" Freeman occasional bass lead. This is one of today's best traditional quartets. It has very good sound quality (cassette only). — *Opal Louis Nations, Roots and Rhythm Newsletter*

Dietra Farr

b. Aug. 1, 1957, Chicago, IL
Modern Electric Blues
Chicago vocalist Dietra Farr is so versatile, it's a misnomer to call her singing soul-blues. She's equally comfortable with ballads, pop music, soul, and blues, and she presents a delightful combination of all these styles on her debut record, *The Search Is Over* (1997, JSP Records).

Farr spent her childhood listening to the radio and the soul music of the late '60s and early '70s. She began singing in the choir at the Catholic grade school she attended, and by the time she was a senior in high school, she was singing with her uncle's band. Farr also sang with another local band for fun, but music was still an avocation for her.

Farr first stepped into the recording studio when she was 18 as a vocalist for Jimmy Mayes' band, Mill Street Depot. The single, "You Won't Support

Me," got airplay around Chicago and sparked her enthusiasm for a career as a singer.

After she graduated from Columbia College (in Chicago) with a degree in journalism, Farr met piano player Erwin Helfer. Helfer had learned from and played with people like Willie Mabon, Little Brother Montgomery, and Sunnyland Slim. Farr began sitting in with Helfer's trio before landing a gig of her own at Kingston Mines in Chicago. She began drawing crowds to her shows, helped in no small measure by the fact that she had legendary names sitting with her, people like Homesick James, Louis Meyers, and Sunnyland Slim.

Farr sang on Dave Spector's debut, *Bluebird Blues,* in 1991, and a Japanese record company, DIW, included her on a compilation of Chicago blues artists called *Chicago Blues Nights.* She also can be heard on *Chicago's Finest Blues Ladies,* a compilation for the Wolf Records label, which got her noticed overseas and allowed her to tour in Europe.

Farr's career shifted into high gear after she hooked up with the band Mississippi Heat in 1993 and recorded two albums with them, *Learned the Hard Way* (1993) and *Thunder In My Heart* (1995). Her debut for the London-based JSP Records, *The Search Is Over,* produced by guitarist/impresario Johnny Rawls, was released in 1997. Her vocals were smooth and confident, and her songs covered a broad thematic landscape. — *Richard Skelly*

The Search Is Over / May 20, 1997 / JSP ◆◆◆

H-Bomb Ferguson

b. 1929, Charleston, SC
Piano, Vocals / Jump Blues, Modern Electric Blues
His extroverted antics and multi-colored fright wig might invite the instant dismissal of Cincinnati-based singer Robert "H-Bomb" Ferguson as some sort of comic lightweight. In reality, he's one of the last survivors of the jump blues era whose once-slavish Wynonie Harris imitations have mellowed into a highly distinctive vocal delivery of his own.

Ferguson's dad, a reverend, paid for piano lessons for his son, demanding he stick to sacred melodies on the 88s. Fat chance—by age 19, Bobby Ferguson was on the road with Joe Liggins & the Honeydrippers. When they hit New York, Ferguson branched off on his own. Comedian Nipsey Russell, then emcee at Harlem's Baby Grand Club, got the singer a gig at the nightspot. Back then, Ferguson was billed as "The Cobra Kid."

Singles for Derby, Atlas, and Prestige preceded a 1951-52 hookup with Savoy Records that produced some of Ferguson's best waxings. Most of them were obvious Harris knockoffs, but eminently swinging ones with top-flight backing (blasting saxists Purvis Henson and Count Hastings were aboard the dates). Drummer Jack "The Bear" Parker, who played on the Savoy dates, allegedly bestowed the singer with his explosive monicker. Other accounts credit Savoy producer Lee Magid with coining H-Bomb's handle; either way, his dynamite vocals fulfilled the billing.

Ferguson eventually made Cincinnati his home, recording for Finch, Big Bang, ARC, and the far more prestigious Federal in 1960. H-Bomb terminated his touring schedule in the early '70s. When he returned from premature retirement, his unique wig-wearing shtick (inspired by Rick James' coiffure) was in full bloom. Backed by his fine young band, the Medicine Men, Ferguson waxed his long-overdue debut album, *Wiggin' Out,* for Chicago's Earwig logo in 1993. It showed him to be as wild as ever (witness the gloriously sleazy "Meatloaf"), a talented pianist to boot, and more his own man than ever before. — *Bill Dahl*

Life Is Hard / Nov. 1987 / Savoy ◆◆◆◆
The atomic one in his early-'50s jump blues mode, when he made a living as an unabashed Wynonie Harris clone (and a damned good one at that). Swinging New York bands and Ferguson's hearty vocals make the similarities entirely forgivable. Hopefully, this LP will be available digitally before too long. — *Bill Dahl*

● **Wiggin' Out** / Feb. 1993 / Earwig ◆◆◆◆
Somewhere over the last 40 years or so, this purple wig-wearing R&B pioneer dropped his slavish Wynonie Harris imitations and became his own man, learning how to play piano to boot. His long-overdue debut album joyously recalls the heyday of jump blues via salacious rockers like "Meatloaf" and "Shake Your Apple Tree." Ferguson's young band, the Medi-

cine Men, do a fine job of laying down exciting grooves behind the singer. — *Bill Dahl*

Thomas "Big Hat" Fields

b. 1947, Rayne, Lousiana
Accordion / Zydeco
One of the many new faces to arrive on the zydeco scene during the 1990s, accordionist Thomas "Big Hat" Fields was born in Rayne, Lousiana in 1947. Already well known to his fellow performers for running a zydeco club in the Grand Coteau area, he did not even pick up the accordion until the the late 1980s, soon after forming the Foot Stompin' Zydeco Band with his bassist wife Geneva. Fields debuted in 1994 with *The Big Hat Man; Come to Louisiana* followed in 1995. — *Jason Ankeny*

Louisiana Is the Place to See / 1997 / Lanor ◆◆◆◆
This is zydeco music as it is meant to be played—alive and jumping, getting you out on the dance floor. Fortunately, the most competently performed songs are in English; "Bald Headed Men" is a great example of his sense of humor. Thomas Fields' music reflects a devil-may-care, fun-loving nature. This man didn't pick up an accordion until he was about 48, then taught his wife to play bass so he had the nucleus for his band. They may not be the most innovative band, nor the best on their instruments yet, but reflect the heart and soul of a bright, happy future for traditional zydeco, playing with a heart, a passion, and a joy that makes up for a lot of shortcomings. — *Bob Gottlieb*

The Five Blind Boys of Alabama

f. 1937, Talladega, AL
Group / Black Gospel, Traditional Gospel
Evolving out of the Happyland Jubilee Singers, this traditional Black gospel quartet was formed in 1937 at the Talladega Institute for the Deaf and Blind in Alabama. By the '40s they became "The Blind Boys" and recorded for Specialty, Vee-Jay, Savoy, Elektra, and other labels. Their first hit was "I Can See Everybody's Mother but Mine" in 1949. Current lineup: Joe Watson, Jimmy Carter, Sam & Bobby Butler, Curtis Foster, Johnny Fields, and Clarence Fountain. They appeared on Broadway in *Gospel at Colonus.* — *Bil Carpenter*

★ **The Sermon** / 1953-1956 / Specialty ◆◆◆◆◆
The Five Blind Boys of Alabama were among the most dynamic, energetic gospel quartets to emerge during the '50s "Golden Age." Led by the exuberant Clarence Fountain, they were more open to musical experimentation than most of their contemporaries, something quite evident on this 27-track compilation featuring cuts done during the mid-'50s for Specialty. Besides Fountain's smashing voice, the set is distinguished by the contributions of four singing preachers (Paul Exkano, Samuel K. Lewis, George W. Warren, and Percell Perkins) and the insertion of jazz, Latin, and comedic elements into the musical mix. — *Ron Wynn*

★ **The Sermon** / 1953-1956 / Specialty ◆◆◆◆◆
Soul-searing alternates and previously unreleased songs by this powerhouse quartet; lead alternating between four preachers. — *Opal Louis Nations*

Original Five Blind Boys of Alabama / 1959 / Savoy ◆◆◆◆
Fire and fury from the late '50s. — *Opal Louis Nations*

Church Concert in New Orleans / 1967 / Hob ◆◆◆◆
Pew-burning live recording. — *Opal Louis Nations*

Will Jesus Be Waiting / 1969 / MCA ◆◆◆
Great recordings lead by the magnificent Archie Brownlee. 1950s and '60s Peacock selections. — *Opal Louis Nations*

Oh Lord, Stand by Me / 1970 / Specialty ◆◆◆◆
High voltage quartet led by the fiery Fountain, circa 1952-56. — *Opal Louis Nations*

Marching Up to Zion / 1970 / Specialty ◆◆◆◆
Essential Blind Boys circa 1952-56. — *Opal Louis Nations*

Precious Memories / 1974 / MCA ◆◆◆◆
Impassioned vocals matched against stinging guitar and forthright chorus. — *Opal Louis Nations*

The Five Blind Boys of Alabama / 1987 / Gospel Heritage ✦✦✦✦
An excellent 16-track anthology, it predates their Specialty recordings by four years, with leads shared by Clarence Fountain and the legendary Paul Excano. With scholarly notes and photos, it's a must for collectors. —*Hank Davis*

Oh Lord, Stand by Me/Marching up to Zion / 1991 / Specialty ✦✦✦✦
Reissue of the quartet's two early 1970s albums full of grit and sanctification. —*Opal Louis Nations*

Deep River / 1992 / Elektra/Nonesuch ✦✦✦✦
On their umpteenth release, the Five Blind Boys mix some modern blues and R&B into their core gospel sound. The rhythm section, led by the organ of the legendary Booker T. Jones, keeps the accompaniment simple as the group soars through some traditional material ("Closer Walk with Thee," "Every Time I Feel the Spirit,"), a few originals by lead vocalist Clarence Fountain, and a transcendent version of Bob Dylan's "I Believe in You." —*Jason Ankeny*

Swing Low, Sweet Chariot / Oct. 17, 1994 / Jewel ✦✦✦✦
Good hard-singing collection. —*Opal Louis Nations*

1948-1951 / Dec. 12, 1995 / Flyright ✦✦✦✦
Initial recordings by this leading post-war traditional quartet. —*Opal Louis Nations*

Have Faith: The Very Best of the Five Blind Boys of Alabama / Mar. 3, 1998 / Collectables ✦✦✦✦
Pew-burning Vee-Jay sides by Clarence Fountain and the boys. —*Opal Louis Nations*

The Five Blind Boys of Mississippi

f. 193?, Jackson, MS
Group / Black Gospel, Traditional Gospel
The Five Blind Boys of Mississippi are among the greatest singing groups in popular music history. Their smashing harmonies and the leads of Archie Brownlee not only influenced numerous gospel ensembles, but such secular artists as Ray Charles. Their origins date back to the '30s, when Archie Brownlee (Brownley in some accounts), Joseph Ford, Lawrence Abrams, and Lloyd Woodard formed a quartet. They were students at the Piney Woods School near Jackson, Mississippi. They began as the Cotton Blossom Singers, and did both spiritual and secular material. The quartet sang on the school grounds in 1936, then were recorded in 1937 by Alan Lomax for the Library of Congress. After graduation, they decided to become professional singers and for a time performed under dual identities; they were the Cotton Blossom Singers for popular songs and the Jackson Harmoneers for gospel. They became a quintet when Melvin Henderson joined. When Percell Perkins replaced Henderson in the mid-'40s, they became the Five Blind Boys. Oddly, Perkins, who doubled as their manager, was not blind. They made their recording debut for Excelsior in 1946, after meeting label owner Leon Rene in Cleveland. They recorded for Coleman in 1948, the same year Joseph Ford was replaced by J.T. Clinkscales. But when they joined Don Robey's Peacock label in 1950, the Five Blind Boys became superstars. The single "Our Father" was a Top Ten R&B hit, and they became a prolific ensemble, recording 27 singles and five albums for Peacock through the '60s. Brownlee died in New Orleans in 1960. His riveting, chilling screams and yells were among gospel's most amazing. Perkins left the group soon after becoming a minister. The list of replacements included Revs. Sammy Lewis and George Warren, as well as Tiny Powell. Roscoe Robinson took over for Brownlee, and was assisted by second lead Willmer Broadnax, who was also a masterful singer. The Five Blind Boys continued through the '70s and '80s and into the '90s, though Woodard died in the mid-'70s, and Lawrence Abrams in 1982. —*Ron Wynn*

Soon I'll Be Done / Apr. 1952 / Chess ✦✦✦
Reissue of the group's stunning Chess album with Little Axe and Roscoe Robinson at the helm. —*Opal Louis Nations*

The Great Lost Album / 1957 / Vee-Jay ✦✦✦✦
The Five Blind Boys of Mississippi brought theatrical flair and improvisational fervor to a height equaled by few others in quartet and gospel fare. The original group, led by the searing shouts of Archie Brownlee, were a smashing ensemble, whose voices didn't just sing lyrics, but actually elevated

them, turning every number into a testifying masterpiece. This release contains 17 songs from the late '50s, some of them newly issued, others being part of an album initially titled *The Original Five Blind Boys* and later reissued as *In Memoriam*. —*Ron Wynn*

● **The Original Five Blind Boys** / 1959 / Vee-Jay ✦✦✦✦
Considered the finest post-war quartet album ever made. From Peacock singles, 1951-59. —*Opal Louis Nations*

I'll Go / 1960 / Checker ✦✦✦✦
Archie's soaring tenor and the group's tight harmony make this album one of the best ever released. From Vee-Jay singles, 1956-57. —*Opal Louis Nations*

Father I Stretch My Hands to Thee / 1965 / Peacock ✦✦✦✦
Strong readings by the quartet led by Little Ax and Roscoe Robinson. —*Opal Louis Nations*

The Best of the Five Blind Boys, Vol. 2 / 1973 / MCA ✦✦✦✦
More fine hard gospel from Archie Brownlee or Roscoe Robinson and the boys. —*Opal Louis Nations*

★ **The Best of the Five Blind Boys of Mississippi, Vol. 1** / 1973 / MCA ✦✦✦✦✦
These Specialty recordings truly represent some of the best by this popular group. Arguably the greatest "quartet" ever. Featuring the wondrous Archie Brownlee. —*Kip Lornell & Ron Wynn*

My Desire/There's a God Somewhere / 1974 / Mobile Fidelity ✦✦✦
My Desire/There's a God Somewhere combines two fine albums from the Peacock vaults. Also known as The Original Five Blind Boys and the Jackson Harmoneers. The lead vocals by Archie Brownlee have been known to slay souls and reduce grown men to tears. Powerful material! —*Hank Davis*

The Tide of Life / 1979 / Paula ✦✦✦
Just about the best set recorded by the quartet on this label. —*Opal Louis Nations*

The Best of the Five Blind Boys of Mississippi, Vol. 2 / 1983 / MCA ✦✦✦
More gems from this seminal ensemble. —*Ron Wynn*

In the Hands of the Lord / 1987 / MCA ✦✦
Choice Peacock selections by this shouting quartet led by Archie Brownlee, Big Henry Johnson, and Roscoe Robinson. —*Opal Louis Nations*

★ **Great Lost Blind Boys Album** / 1992 / Vee-Jay ✦✦✦✦✦
The Great Lost Blind Boys Album combines two original Vee-Jay albums from the late '50s, adding a handful of alternate takes, aborted takes and chatter to the mix. While those snippets distract from the music itself, that's not enough to stop the disc from being the definitive Five Blind Boys of Mississippi collection. All of the group's greatest numbers—"My Robe Will Fit Me," "Jesus Love Me," "No Need to Cry," "Let's Have Church," and "Leave You in the Hands of the Lord," among many others—are here in their best versions, making it essential listening for any gospel fan, or anyone who wants to know the roots of doo wop. —*Thom Owens*

Counting on Jesus / 1993 / Soul Potion ✦✦✦
The name may be the same, but these are not the Original Five Blind Boys of Mississippi; Archie Brownlee has been dead for many years, and others have departed. No roster list is included here. They still harmonize with exuberance, and the eight numbers on their most recent release are steadfastly traditional in lyrics, production structure, and feel; no huge backing choirs, synthesized backdrops or bombastic settings, but simple stories about spiritual fulfillment and release. —*Ron Wynn*

I Never Heard a Man / Apr. 16, 1996 / Jewel ✦✦✦

In Concert Live in Europe / Jan. 13, 1998 / Munich ✦✦✦

You Done What the Doctor Couldn't Do / Jubilee ✦✦✦✦
Quintessential "hard" gospel singing from the late '40s and early '50s. Brownlee performs most of the lead chores, with vital dynamism and occasional lead singing from Rev. Percell Perkins and Vance "Tiny" Powell. —*Kip Lornell*

The Best of the Five Blind Boys / MCA Special Products ✦✦✦
MCA's *Best of the Blind Boys* is a good, but not exceptional, collection of 12 highlights from the group's Peacock material. There are a number of wondrous performances here—including "Love Lifted Me," "Jesus Satisfied," and "Speak for Jesus"—but in general, the recordings aren't quite as strong as their recordings for Vee-Jay. Furthermore, the album feels a little skimpy in

these days of extensive reissues, making it more of interest for completists and serious fans than listeners seeking out good values or representative collections. — *Leo Stanley*

Meet the Blind Boys / Jewel ♦♦♦
Good collection by the quartet before breaking up and regrouping around Sandy Foster. — *Opal Louis Nations*

Fleetwood Mac

f. 1967, London, England
Group / Blues-Rock, Pop-Rock, British Blues, Electric British Blues
To most people watching VH-1 reruns these days, Fleetwood Mac is that group of bell-bottomed, sunny Californians fronted by the chirpy vocal talents of Stevie Nicks, whose pop hits dominated the airwaves and sales charts for over a decade, making them the '70s version of Hootie & the Blowfish. *That* story is writ large in the annals of rock history books. But in the beginning—though you'd never know it by listening to any of their greatest hits—the original Fleetwood Mac was one hell of a blues band. Fueled by a driving rhythm section (Mick Fleetwood on drums and John McVie on bass), sporting two lead guitar players (single string wizard Peter Green and slideman Jeremy Spencer)—and eventually three (Danny Kirwan)—and a show that spiraled from dazzling originals, full-throttle Chicago blues to outrageous send-ups of '50s rock 'n' roll, the original Fleetwood Mac was one hell of a band, period.

Their British blues credentials couldn't come any higher up on the food chain; the nucleus of the group met while playing as members of John Mayall's Bluesbreakers, with Peter Green having the unenviable task of replacing Eric Clapton. The young guitarist, whom everyone affectionately called "Greenie," quickly established himself on the next release (*A Hard Road*) and Mayall showed his appreciation by donating some free studio time to the guitarist as a birthday present in 1967. Greenie grabbed Fleetwood and McVie for the rhythm section and went in and cut three songs that day; "It Hurts Me Too" by Elmore James, "Double Trouble" by Otis Rush and an untitled instrumental he had composed. When pressed by the engineer for a title, Green leaned over the recording console and scrawled "Fleetwood Mac" across the tape box. Of such events, legends are born and bands are named.

Greenie and Fleetwood left Mayall at about the same time, but McVie didn't want to give up the steady paycheck that working in the Bluesbreakers provided him with and Bob Brunning "replaced" him until McVie could be coaxed into the new band, odd behavior considering that it was partially named after him to begin with. Green, who loathed all kinds of guitar hero worship, felt that the trio format was too limited and also wanted someone in the band to take part of the singing and performing load off his shoulders. Enter the diminutive Jeremy Spencer and Greenie had found exactly what he wanted and needed for the new combo to take flight. Spencer played a hollow-body guitar almost as big as he was and had the slashing slide wailings of his hero, Elmore James, down cold. Blues history revisionists like to downplay Spencer's credentials, but what he was accomplishing was something more on the level of recreated art than merely copying his record collection and strangling his Midlands voice to sound like James. With Spencer aboard to provide the boogie, Green felt that the band was ready and on August of 1967, they played their debut gig in front of 30,000 people at the prestigious Windsor Jazz and Blues Festival, blasting out a red-hot 30-minute set in front of John Mayall's Bluesbreakers. Fleetwood Mac made a strong enough impression that Sunday to quickly become the talk of English blues circles, especially when John McVie left Mayall three weeks later to join them permanently.

They cut their first album, basically a re-creation of their live show, in only three days. With Green's moody, introspective takes on the B.B. King style juxtaposed against Spencer's Elmore James slide boogie, the mixture proved irresistible to 1968 British audiences and the debut stayed on the pop charts for 17 weeks. Their instant success caused them to not really change their music so much (at first), but to definitely start monkeying around with its presentation in a live format. Tired of the pious-faced, staid British blues band facade that seemed to have begun with Blues Incorporated and handed down to each new band that wanted to be considered *authentic*, Fleetwood Mac—this time led by the mischievous Jeremy Spencer—began to rebel.

Suddenly the band was like some high-voltage, drunken vaudeville English music-hall show gone terribly awry that played stone solid blues while condoms filled with milk dangled off the tuning pegs of their guitars. Reportedly in love with '50s rock 'n' roll music while being simultaneously disgusted with its then-current-day revivalists, the band would leave the stage, grease their hair up into pompadours and with Spencer as a drunk Elvis front man goading them on, Britain's most respected new blues band mutated into a '50s lunatic factory called Earl Vince and the Valiants. It was exactly these kind of drunken hijinks that got them banned from the prestigious Marquee Club in London, but make no mistake about it, it *was* a regular fixture in the original band's stage presentation, both in the UK and on original tours in the US as well.

They began to get further away from the blues format with each successive release; the first single attempt, Green's "Black Magic Woman," flopped in the UK but became a belated hit for Santana, a band that had opened for then in the US Green grew more restless; he wanted a bigger sound and was displeased at Spencer's limitations, both as a performer and as a non-contributing songwriter. Enter guitarist Danny Kirwan, who grew up enthralled with Peter Green the way Greenie was with Eric Clapton. Late in 1968, the band caught its first taste of global chart success with the release of Green's instrumental, "The Albatross." But they hadn't forgot their blues roots and in January of 1969 stood assembled in the Chess studios with some of the city's blues greats, including Big Walter Horton, Otis Spann, J.T. Brown, and Willie Dixon for a marathon blues recording session. The band was getting bigger and bigger everyday; in Europe they were outselling the Beatles and the Rolling Stones and were on the verge of their American breakthrough on the ballroom and festival circuit.

But all of this success didn't make Peter Green very happy at all. As a combination of psychedelic drugs and cult religion made him want to play all future gigs for nothing, effectively giving all the band's money away, his departure to eventually become a grave digger signaled the beginning of the end for the original group. With Kirwan and Spencer attempting to front the band in Greenie's absence, the strain proved to be too much for little Jeremy Spencer. In February of 1971, on the eve of a West Coast tour, Spencer left his Hollywood hotel room to go for a walk, never to return. A few days later, he was found—his head shaved bald—in a locked and guarded warehouse run by the religious cult, the Children of God. With a six-week tour ahead of them and half their act gone, the band coaxed Peter Green back into the fold to finish out the remaining dates. When it was over, he left again, never to return, effectively ending the days of Fleetwood Mac, kings of British blues-rock. The rest, as they say, is rock 'n' roll. — *Cub Koda*

● **Peter Green's Fleetwood Mac** / Feb. 1968 / Blue Horizon ♦♦♦♦
Fleetwood Mac's debut LP was a highlight of the late '60s British blues boom. Green's always inspired playing, the capable (if erratic) songwriting, and the general panache of the band as a whole placed them leagues above the overcrowded field. Elmore James is a big influence on this set, particularly on the tunes fronted by Jeremy Spencer ("Shake Your Moneymaker," "Got to Move"). Spencer's bluster, however, was outshone by the budding singing and songwriting skills of Green. The guitarist balanced humor and vulnerability on cuts like "Looking for Somebody" and "Long Grey Mare," and with "If I Loved Another Woman," he offered a glimpse of the Latin-blues fusion that he would perfect with "Black Magic Woman." The album was an unexpected smash in the UK, reaching No. 4 on the British charts. — *Richie Unterberger*

English Rose / Jan. 1969 / Epic ♦♦♦♦
Under the direction of Peter Green, Fleetwood Mac is heard as a British blues group, although its most notable performances are on Green's original tunes "Black Magic Woman" and "Albatross," both British hits. — *William Ruhlmann*

Pious Bird of Good Omen / Aug. 1969 / Blue Horizon ♦♦♦♦
This is a compilation of Fleetwood Mac's early period, 1967-1968, featuring both sides of its debut single, "I Believe My Time Ain't Long"/"Rambling Pony" and many blues covers, as well as the hits "Albatross" and "Black Magic Woman." — *William Ruhlmann*

Then Play On / Oct. 1969 / Reprise ♦♦♦
The most diverse and accomplished album by the Peter Green-led lineup. Features some wrenching, introspective originals that draw from both blues

and progressive rock, highlighted by the doomy British hit single "Oh Well."
— *Richie Unterberger*

Kiln House / Sep. 1970 / Reprise ✦✦✦

Fleetwood Mac's first album after the departure of their nominal leader, Peter Green, finds the remaining members, Mick Fleetwood, John McVie, Jeremy Spencer, and Danny Kirwan (plus McVie's wife, Christine) trying to maintain the band's guitar-heavy, blues-rock approach, with the burden falling on Spencer and Kirwan. They don't embarrass themselves, but none of this is of the caliber of Green's work. — *William Ruhlmann*

Fleetwood Mac in Chicago / 1975 / Warner Brothers ✦✦

A two-record set culled from sessions the Peter Green/Danny Kirwan/Mick Fleetwood/John McVie edition of the band held at Chess Studios in Chicago in January 1969 with such blues legends as Otis Spann and Willie Dixon. Despite their awe, the Brits hold their own on a set of standards. (Reissued on CD under the title *In Chicago 1969* on April 26, 1994.) — *William Ruhlmann*

Original Fleetwood Mac / 1977 / Sire ✦✦

This collection of outtakes from the group's early days probably dates from 1967-68, and finds the band at their most reverently bluesy. Peter Green wrote most of the material on this set, which is quite similar to the band's first couple of albums in its purist British take on traditional electric blues forms. The material, however, isn't nearly as strong as the best early Fleetwood Mac; not that the band should be faulted for that, as this is an outtake collection, after all. A couple of the tunes featuring Jeremy Spencer are actually taken from an audition that Spencer's pre-Fleetwood Mac outfit, the Levi Set, recorded for the Blue Horizon label in England. The best track is the driving instrumental "Fleetwood Mac," and has been rumored to be an outtake from Green's days with John Mayall's Bluesbreakers. — *Richie Unterberger*

Jumping at Shadows / 1985 / Varrick ✦✦✦

Recorded live in Boston in 1969, this finds the Peter Green-era Mac at their best on seven lengthy but focused cuts. Includes versions of "Black Magic Woman" and "Oh Well," as well as a couple of straight blues covers and some Danny Kirwan material. — *Richie Unterberger*

Cerulean / 1985 / Shanghai ✦✦✦

From the same 1969 Boston gigs that produced *Jumping at Shadows*, this double album's appeal is more limited, with a heavier emphasis on straight blues boogie and eccentric fifties rock 'n' roll parodies that featured Jeremy Spencer. Highlights are the 16-minute version of the British hit "Green Manalishi" and the 24-minute version of "Rattlesnake Shake." — *Richie Unterberger*

Peter Green's Fleetwood Mac Live at the BBC / Oct. 1995 / Castle ✦✦

A substantial (and official) supplement to the band's recorded legacy with Peter Green, this double CD features 36 songs broadcast between 1967 and 1971, in mostly superlative sound (and the few numbers that aren't 100% clean are certainly of listenable fidelity). The title, though, isn't 100% accurate; half a dozen tracks were recorded shortly after Green left the band, and since Green is still listed as part of the lineup for all but one of these in the liner notes, Castle Communications either has the dates or personnel wrong. Anyway, the music gives a good idea of the range of the band in their earliest, and by many accounts, best incarnation. It is not, however, all blues-rock by any means; quite a few of these are given over to Jeremy Spencer-dominated parodies of '50s rock, and while these are entertaining in a modest fashion, the best moments, unsurprisingly, are when guitarists Danny Kirwan and (more particularly) Green play their own material. Some of Green's most well-known compositions from the era are here ("Man of the World," "Albatross," "Rattlesnake Shake," and "Oh Well"), and in the usual BBC tradition these have a sparer and rougher feel than the studio versions, though they don't either match or redefine them. Of most interest to early Mac fans will be the inclusion of several numbers that they never recorded in the studio (although some, like "Sandy Mary" and "Only You," did appear on live albums that weren't issued until the 1980s). "Preachin'," "Preachin' Blues," and "Early Morning Come" are otherwise unavailable showcases for Spencer, Green, and Kirwan respectively that demonstrate their facility with no-nonsense, down-home blues when they got in a serious mood. While this isn't as essential a collection as *Then Play On* or the numerous best-of anthologies covering the Peter Green era, it presents more solid evidence of the band's skills in both blues-rock and surpisingly straight rock (a cover of Tim Har-

din's "Hang on to a Dream" is the surprise find of the set), though some may find the detours into comedy and '50s rock irksome. — *Richie Unterberger*

Mary Flower

b. 1949, Delphi, IN
Dobro, Guitar, Vocals / Acoustic Blues, Folk-Blues

Chances are that you'll find Mary Flower in the folk section of your local record shop. She did found a folk-cum-jazz based ensemble called Mother Folkers in Denver 20-odd years ago, which was the mile-high city's leading women's folk collective; and she could look the part of a folkie "Earth mother" type. Flower moved seriously into blues over the last decade, however, and hasn't looked back since.

Born in Delphi, Indiana, Flower made her way to Denver at the beginning of the 1970s, when she was in her twenties, and set up shop in the city's folk community; her gigs made her a name locally, and she established Mother Folkers. She always appreciated the blues, but it was a two-week period of study with Jim Schwall and Steve James at a blues workshop in West Virginia that transformed her.

Flower described herself as "consumed" by the experience, and made the decision to devote herself to the blues. She restarted her career, but initially encountered resistance, partly because she was a white blueswoman who didn't conform to expectations—ever since Janis Joplin, white female blues performers have been expected to sound like Big Mama Thornton, which Flower didn't, Scrapper Blackwell being more of a role model. Since the early 1990s, however, she has gradually achieved acceptance, and has played places like Buddy Guy's club in Chicago as well as various festivals, where she has been well received, and tours regionally and nationally.

As a folk artist, Flower played alongside Geoff Muldaur, David Bromberg, and Ramblin' Jack Elliot. Her work in blues, however, has been strongly influenced by Scrapper Blackwell, Henry Glover, and Robert Johnson, but especially Blind Lemon Jefferson. She plays with passion, none of it forced or posed, and she has a husky voice to go with the kind of stuff she covers— she could sing prettier than she does, but what she does seems honest. She also writes originals with a cutting, clever edge. Flower has been around about as long as Bonnie Raitt, only without the major-label record contracts, the arena and movie appearances, or the Grammy, and deserves to be known by at least as many people. — *Bruce Eder*

High Heeled Blues / 1991 / RER ✦✦✦

● **Blues Jubilee** / 1994 / Resounding ✦✦✦✦

This record will probably be found in the folk section of your store, but don't let that fool you—it's a dazzling piece of modern acoustic blues, with its feet in the '90s and the '30s and no stretch evident. Flower covers Scrapper Blackwell's "Memphis Town," Memphis Minnie's "Me and My Chauffeur Blues," and, most impressively, Robert Johnson's "Walking Blues" and Blind Lemon Jefferson's "Six White Horses" (which, in a fairer reality, would be the single off this album). Her playing, backed by Steve James, is dexterous and punchy, with some beautiful and subtle flourishes (Scrapper Blackwell will come to mind), and her singing is hard and deep, with none of the softness that normally betrays folkies who try to go this route. Her originals are strong, too, with "Long-Legged Daddy" the standout. She's a blueswoman and she means it. — *Bruce Eder*

Rosewood & Steel / 1996 / Bluesette ✦✦✦

Not quite as strong as it predecessor but definitely worth hearing, *Rosewood & Steel* has Flower putting her own special spin on music by Junior Parker ("Mystery Train"), Charlie Patton ("Pony Blues"), Skip James ("Cypress Grove Blues"), and Brooks Berry ("Can't Sleep For Dreaming"), along with a bunch of originals. Geoff Muldaur, Amos Garrett, Steve James, and Paul Geremia all contribute to various songs. Flower's singing is rich and husky, and her originals exploit the various sides of her musical personality, from playful to dark and moody (check out "Cock-A-Doodle Blues" and "Two Days Straight"), and all but one slots in perfectly with the covers on this collection. Her "Midnite Blue" vaguely recalls CSN's "4+20," with some gorgeous slide by Steve James, while she impresses then and some with her lap steel playing on the delightful "Roll On, Mississippi, Roll On" and Patton's searing "Pony Blues" (which also features Geremia's slide). The real surprise is "Mystery Train," which gets about the slowest, most lyrical treatment ever on record here. — *Bruce Eder*

Sue Foley

b. Mar. 29, 1968, Ottawa, Ontario, Canada
Guitar, Vocals / Modern Electric Blues

This highly touted vocalist/guitarist originally hails from Ottawa, Canada, although her homebase shifted to Austin, Texas when she signed with Antone's Records and cut her debut set, *Young Girl Blues,* in 1992 (an encore, *Without a Warning,* quickly followed). Foley's wicked lead guitar makes her a rarity among blueswomen.

When she was a child in Ottawa, Foley listened to rock 'n' roll and blues-rock groups like the Rolling Stones. Although these bands sowed the seeds of her affection for the blues, her love for the music didn't blossom until she witnessed James Cotton in concert when she was 15 years old. Cotton inspired Foley to pick up the electric guitar. During her late teens and early 20s, she jammed with local Ottawa bar bands—she didn't form her own group until she moved to Vancouver in the mid-'80s.

Foley sent a demo tape of herself to Antone's Records in 1990. Impressed, the label arranged an audition for the guitarist. Sue moved to Austin and soon signed a recording contract with Antone's. In 1992, her debut album, *Young Girl Blues,* was released. It was acclaimed by a number of blues publications. Two years later she released her second album, *Without A Warning.* It was followed by *Big City Blues* in 1995. *— Bill Dahl & Stephen Thomas Erlewine*

● **Young Girl Blues** / 1992 / Antone's ◆◆◆◆
Sue Foley's debut album, *Young Girl Blues,* is an impressive effort. Not only is Foley a wild, adventurous guitarist, she can write songs that don't merely rehash standard blue clichés. Her songs have an intense passion that is heightened by her array of gutsy guitar textures, which are rooted in blues tradition but never tied down to it. *— Thom Owens*

Without a Warning / 1994 / Discovery ◆◆◆

Big City Blues / 1995 / Antone's ◆◆◆◆

Walk in the Sun / Jul. 9, 1996 / Discovery ◆◆◆◆
Walk in the Sun isn't quite typical Sue Foley. With her first three albums, the guitarist demonstrated that she had a firm grasp on searingly electric Chicago blues and high-voltage blues-rock. With *Walk in the Sun,* she expands her sonic palette somewhat, taking in gritty R&B, reverb-drenched surf, and down-home country, among other styles of blues and roots music. Throughout the album, she demonstrates that she is gifted enough to effortlessly bring in these other styles without losing her distinctive identity. The result is her best album since her stellar debut, *Young Girl Blues.* *— Thom Owens*

Ten Days in November / Apr. 21, 1998 / Shanachie ◆◆◆◆
This blond blues belter serves up some soulful original tunes on her fifth album. While her voice is a bit thin, the disc makes a strong impression with sturdy songs and a great backing band. At the forefront are Foley's fluid lead guitar lines. *— Tim Sheridan*

The Ford Blues Band

f. 196?, Ukiah, CA, **db.** 1971
Group / Electric West Coast Blues

After leaving Ukiah, CA, and moving south to San Francisco to form the Charles Ford Band (named for their father) in the late '60s with harmonica player Gary Smith, brothers Pat (drums) and Robben (guitar) were enlisted by Charlie Musselwhite and were pivotal members of one of the best aggregations the harpist ever led. Leaving Musselwhite after recording Arhoolie's *Takin' My Time,* they recruited bassist Stan Poplin and younger brother Mark, then age 17, on harmonica and played under the name the Real Charles Ford Band. Heavily influenced by the original Butterfield Blues Band and the Chess catalog, the quartet was famous for their live jazz explorations—often jamming for 30 minutes or more on a John Coltrane and George Benson tune—and hear-a pin-drop dynamics (with Mark abandoning mike and amp to play acoustically into the room or Robben turning the volume all the way off on his fat-body Gibson L-5). Muddy Waters sat in with and praised the young band, and Chess Records even came courting, but the brothers split on New Year's Eve, 1971, recording their sole LP posthumously, as it were. Robben went on to major cult status via session work and sporadic solo releases, and after lengthy hiatuses Mark and Pat continue to gig around the Bay Area and Europe (Pat founding his own Blue Rock'it label). Twenty-

five years after their dissolution, the band's influence in Northern California is still enormous, particularly among guitar players who continue to ape licks Robben forgot two decades ago. *—Dan Forte*

● **Here We Go!** / 1990 / Crosscut ◆◆◆◆
Here We Go!, the first album from the Ford Blues Band, is a propulsive, energetic collection of Chicago blues with a twist. The twist is the group's passion for improvisation, where they can turn standard three-chord progressions into unexpectedly jazzy interludes which add real meat to their music. The result is a thrilling, exciting debut from a fresh, promising combo. *— Thom Owens*

The Ford Blues Band / 1991 / Blue Rock'it ◆◆◆

Live at Breninale 92 / Nov. 10, 1993 / Blue Rock'it ◆◆◆◆

Hotshots / Nov. 15, 1994 / Blue Rock'it ◆◆◆

Fords & Friends / Sep. 3, 1996 / Blue Rock'it ◆◆◆

Robben Ford

b. Dec. 16, 1951, Ukiah, CA
Guitar / Fusion, Crossover Jazz, Modern Electric Blues

Robben Ford has had a diverse career. He taught himself guitar when he was 13 and considered his first influence to be Mike Bloomfield. At 18 he moved to San Francisco to form the Charles Ford Band (named after his father who was also a guitarist) and was soon hired to play with Charles Musselwhite for nine months. In 1971 the Charles Ford Blues Band was re-formed and recorded for Arhoolie in early 1972. Ford played with Jimmy Witherspoon (1972-73), the L.A. Express with Tom Scott (1974), George Harrison and Joni Mitchell. In 1977 he was a founding member of the Yellowjackets which he stayed with until 1983, simultaneously having a solo career and working as a session guitarist. In 1986 Ford toured with Miles Davis and he had two separate periods (1985 and 1987) with Sadao Watanabe but he seemed to really find himself in 1992 when he returned to his roots, the blues. Robben Ford formed a new group, the Blue Line, and has since recorded a couple of blues-rock dates for Stretch that are among the finest of his career. *— Scott Yanow*

Talk to Your Daughter / 1988 / Warner Brothers ◆◆◆
Efficient, sometimes electrifying playing but detached, uneven material. *—Ron Wynn*

Robben Ford & the Blue Line / 1992 / Stretch ◆◆◆
The debut set by guitarist Robben Ford with his Blue Line trio (a blues band with bassist Roscoe Beck and drummer Tom Brechtlein) finds Ford returning to his roots and playing the music that best fits his style. An effective singer, it is for Ford's powerful guitar playing that this CD (which has seven originals among the nine numbers) is most highly recommended to blues collectors. *— Scott Yanow*

Mystic Mile / 1993 / Stretch ◆◆◆◆

● **Handful of Blues** / Sep. 12, 1995 / Blue Thumb ◆◆◆◆
On *Handful of Blues,* Robben Ford strips his sound back to the basics, recording a set of blues with only a bassist and a drummer. The group runs through a handful of standards, including "Don't Let Me Be Misunderstood" and "I Just Want to Make Love to You," and a number of made-to-order originals. Throughout the album, the musicians play well, but Ford's voice is never commanding. However, this is a minor flaw, since his guitar speaks for itself. *— Stephen Thomas Erlewine*

Blues Connection / Oct. 15, 1996 / ITM ◆◆◆

Discovering the Blues / Feb. 18, 1997 / Rhino ◆◆◆
Discovering the Blues is culled from a series of concerts Robben Ford gave in the early '70s at Huntington Beach's Golden Bear and Ash Grove in Hollywood. At the time, Ford was just beginning his career, and his style wasn't nearly as accomplished as it would later be. Instead, he simply burns, tearing through blues classics with a passion and vigor—there is a joy of discovery in his playing which makes the music nearly transcendent, even with its flaws. *Discovering the Blues* is rawer than most records in Ford's catalog, but any serious fan will find it a necessary addition to their collection. *— Thom Owens*

Tiger Walk / Aug. 12, 1997 / Blue Thumb ◆◆◆

The Authorized Bootleg / Mar. 24, 1998 / Blue Thumb ◆◆◆

Forest City Joe

b. Jul. 10, 1926, Hughes, Arkansas, **d.** Apr. 3, 1960
Vocals, Harmonica / Chicago Blues, Country Blues, Electric Chicago Blues, Delta Blues

Blues harpist Forest City Joe was heavily influenced by John Lee "Sonny Boy" Williamson. He not only played like him, but sang like him as well. Unlike his idol, however, who was murdered on June 1, 1948, Joe lived long enough to record for the Chess brothers in the early days of their activities, when Chess was known as Aristocrat. Joe was remembered as a "great harp player" by Muddy Waters, who only missed playing at Joe's one major Chess Recording session on December 2, 1948, when Joe was only 21. Joe had more of a country sound than most Chicago artists of the period, so it's surprising that the Chess brothers paired him up with J.C. Coles, a jazz guitarist of no seeming special account, who added little to a session but a few barely audible chords.

Joe Bennie Pugh was born in Hughes, Arkansas, on July 10, 1926 to Moses Pugh and Mary Walker. He was raised in the area around Hughes and West Memphis, Arkansas, and even as a boy played the local juke joints in the area. He hoboed his way through the state working road houses and juke joints during the 1940s, and late in the decade hooked up with Big Joe Williams, playing with him around St. Louis, Missouri. Beginning in 1947, he also began working the Chicago area, and a year later had his one and only session for the Chess brothers' Aristocrat label. He also appeared with Howlin' Wolf and Sonny Boy "Rice Miller" Williamson (aka Sonny Boy II) on radio shows in the West Memphis area.

When he returned to Chicago in 1949, he began working with the Otis Spann Combo, appearing at the Tick Tock Lounge and other clubs in the city until the mid-'50s. Pugh returned to Arkansas and gave up music, except for occasional weekend shows with Willie Cobbs, playing in pool rooms and on street corners, beginning in 1955. Pugh recorded for Atlantic Records in 1959, and was still performing until his death in 1960, in a truck accident while returning home from a dance.

Had Muddy played Forest City Joe's one and only Chess Records session, as was intended, chances are more of Joe's work would've seen the light of day, if only in an effort to scrounge up every note that Muddy ever played. But as it was, only "Memory of Sonny Boy" and "A Woman on Every Street" ever saw the light of day, and at this writing only the former has ever appeared on an American CD.

As to his extant music, "Memory of Sonny Boy" was among the first postwar tribute records from one bluesman to another (Scrapper Blackwell had done as much for Leroy Carr in the 1930s), starting a trend that continued for decade. And it's a great record, at least as far as the harp playing and the singing go. Joe's playing mimicks Sonny Boy Williamson I's call-and-response harp playing, performing dazzling volume acrobatics, and his singing is also highly expressive. None of the rest is as strong, but "Shady Lane Woman" is a good, bluesy romantic lament, while "A Woman on Every Street" is the other side of the coin, and a better workout on the harp. "Sawdust Bottom" should have seen release, and "Ash Street Boogie" could've seen action if the accompaniment had been better realized. Alas, J.C. Coles was seemingly content to strum along almost inaudibly in the background—ah, what Muddy might've done....—*Bruce Eder*

Guy Forsyth

Guitar, Vocals / Texas Blues, Blues-Rock

Austin, Texas-based guitarist, singer, interpreter, and songwriter Guy Forsyth is like a lot of Austin musicians. He leads his own band, as well as a group called the Asylum Street Spankers; when he's not performing with either of these groups locally, you can find Forsyth sitting in with someone else just for kicks. Forsyth is a rare combination: he's a talented guitarist, singer, and songwriter, but also a diligent, conscientious student of blues, blues-rock, and other indigenous folk musics.

The Guy Forsyth Band has one album out on the Discovery/Warner Bros. label, *Needle Gun*. On it, his quartet reinvigorates the blues-rock form, taking the music into uncharted waters. Forsyth is accompanied in his band on *Needle Gun* by Gil T. on bass, Keith Bradley on guitar and Rich Chilleri on drums. The music on their debut is equal parts blues, rock 'n' roll, and Americana. Forsyth sings with conviction and plays harmonica and some smoldering guitar. Live, the band is what you'd expect from any good blues-rock conglomeration: loud, raw and raucous. —*Richard Skelly*

● **High Temperature** / 1994 / Lizard Disc ✦✦✦
Guy Forsyth's debut album, *High Temperature*, suffers a bit from his unfortunate tendency to deliver lyrics as if they were jokes, but there's a lot of merit to his music. Forsyth and his backing band have real energy and can turn his originals (plus a handful of covers, like Jimmy Reed's "Mr. Luck" and Elmore James' "Done Somebody Wrong") into real barn-burners. It takes a little work to get beyond the feeling that this is all a parody, however, so this may try the patience of some hardline purists. Those that can take the bad with good, however, will hear some sturdy roadhouse boogie. —*Thom Owens*

Needle Gun / Oct. 17, 1995 / Antone's ✦✦✦
Guy Forsyth's approach to the blues is a little campy—occasionally, he sounds like he's sending up the genre, not paying tribute to it. Nevertheless, he's formed a skunk-hot backing band that brings a twisted, manic energy to the tracks. Sometimes, Forsyth's kitschy "wildman" schtick makes it hard to listen to his band, or his own gut-ripping guitar leads, but if you just concentrate on the music, *Needle Gun* can be engaging. Just try to shut out those ridiculous vocals. —*Thom Owens*

Jesse Fortune

b. Feb. 28, 1930, Macon, MS
Vocals / Electric Chicago Blues

Chicago vocalist Jesse Fortune's voice is as large as his discography is small. A mere handful of 45s headed by his 1963 classic "Too Many Cooks" and a 1993 album on Delmark constitute his entire catalog—but as an active artist on the Windy City circuit, he still has time to fatten it up.

Fortune grew up in Hattiesburg, Mississippi, influenced by the pleading blues vocals of B.B. King. He arrived in Chicago in 1952 and started singing professionally with guitarist Little Monroe. He also worked with Otis Rush and Buddy Guy before the prodigious Willie Dixon officially discovered him. In April of 1963, Fortune waxed four sides for USA Records under Dixon's supervision, including the Dixon-penned minor-key rhumba "Too Many Cooks" (his sidemen at the session included Guy, Big Walter Horton on harp, and pianist Lafayette Leake). Robert Cray revived the tune for his 1980 debut album on Tomato, *Who's Been Talkin'.*

Dissatisfied with the monetary return on his date, Fortune shied away from recording (he made his living as a barber) until young guitarist Dave Specter began working the club circuit with the powerful singer. The upshot was *Fortune Tellin' Man*, the singer's debut disc for Delmark, with swinging support from Specter and his Bluebirds. —*Bill Dahl*

Fortune Tellin' Man / 1993 / Delmark ✦✦✦✦
Team one of the criminally overlooked blues vocalists inhabiting Chicago's West Side with a tight young combo sporting a decidedly retro approach and you get this fine album, veteran singer Jesse Fortune's debut set. Guitarist Dave Specter & the Bluebirds admirably back the big-voiced Fortune as he recuts his Willie Dixon-penned USA label classic "Too Many Cooks," and shouts some lesser-known B.B. King gems and a few new items. Definitely a case of better late than never! —*Bill Dahl*

Leroy Foster

b. Feb. 1, 1923, Algoma, MS, **d.** May 26, 1958, Chicago, IL
Vocals, Drums, Guitar / Electric Chicago Blues

As a charter member of the Headhunters, the brash crew that also included Muddy Waters and Jimmy Rogers (so named because of their penchant for entering nightclubs featuring other musicians and blowing them off the stage with their superior musicianship), "Baby Face" Leroy Foster was on hand to help develop the postwar Chicago blues idiom. Unfortunately, he wasn't around long enough to enjoy the fruits of his labors.

The Mississippi native came to Chicago in 1945 in the star-crossed company of harpist Little Walter and pianist Johnny Jones. He worked with Sunnyland Slim and Sonny Boy Williamson before hooking up with the young and hungry Waters aggregation. Foster played drums on 1948 dates for Tempo-Tone that produced Floyd Jones' brooding "Hard Times," Little Walter's "Blue Baby," and a Sunnyland Slim-fronted "I Want My Baby."

He switched to rhythm guitar to accompany Waters on several of his 1948-

49 Aristocrat 78s, notably "You're Gonna Miss Me (When I'm Dead and Gone)," "Mean Red Spider," and "Screamin' and Cryin'," as well as Johnny Jones' rolling "Big Town Playboy." Foster also recorded for Aristocrat as a front man: "Locked Out Boogie" and "Shady Grove Blues" were done at a 1948 date that produced six Muddy masters.

Waters got in some hot water with the Chess brothers when he moonlighted on Foster's rip-roaring eight-song session for Parkway in January of 1950. Though Foster's crashing drums are prominent throughout, Muddy's slashing slide and mournful moans are clearly heard on Foster's two-part "Rollin' and Tumblin'"—enough so that Waters was forced to wax his own version for Aristocrat to kill sales on Foster's rendition by his bosses.

Those Parkway masters had amazing resiliency—Foster's raunchy "Red Headed Woman" re-emerged on Savoy in 1954 ("Boll Weevil" had turned up on Herald the previous year). Two singles for JOB—1950's "My Head Can't Rest Anymore"/"Take a Little Walk with Me" (with Muddy and Rogers in support, it was later released on Chess) and 1952's "Pet Rabbit"/"Louella" (with Sunnyland and guitarist Robert Jr. Lockwood lending a hand)—round out his slim vinyl legacy. Alcoholism brought Baby Face down early—he was only 35 years old when he died in 1958. —*Bill Dahl*

The Four Aces

f. Chicago, IL
Group / Chicago Blues
Common wisdom says that Muddy Waters was the man responsible for turbo charging the Delta blues and creating what we now call Chicago Blues. Muddy's importance is inestimable, but to lay all the credit at his feet is to ignore the contributions of those who quite literally used Muddy's music as a jumping off point, and blazed historical trails of their own. Of all the great musicians who passed through Muddy's bands, perhaps the most important of all was harmonica player and singer Little Walter Jacobs. Jacobs left Muddy's band at the age of 22 already a seasoned veteran of the road and the recording studio. He quickly recruited his own superb band, and came very close to eclipsing his former boss' success during the heyday of Chicago Blues in the 1950s, with two number one hits among his ten appearances on the nationwide *Billboard* R&B charts; Muddy himself had 12 songs reach the *Billboard* charts but never scored a number one hit. Much of Little Walter's success can be attributed to the fact that he was doing something new, different, and thoroughly urban; where Muddy's appeal lay heavily with southern emigres longing for familiar sounds, Walter's swinging, modern, jazz-inflected style found favor with a younger generation of city blues fans not so closely tied to the "down-home" sounds of the south.

But Little Walter couldn't have done it alone—he needed accompanists who shared his desire to push the edge of the blues envelope, so he recruited his band from among the most accomplished and forward-thinking blues musicians available in Chicago. His first recording and touring band in 1952 was a band that he'd sometimes sat in with while still with Muddy—The Aces, featuring brothers David and Louis Myers on guitars. The Myers brothers were born in Byhalia, MS, and had learned the rudiments of guitar from their father before the family relocated to Chicago in the early '40s while both brothers were still in their early teens. There their musical tastes were formed by equal doses of the big band swing that was popular at the time, pop ballads they heard on the radio, and the blues that was being played all around their south side neighborhood. By the late '40s they had assumed the roles they'd play for much of their musical careers: older brother Dave providing bass lines and chords into which Louis wove his tastefully jazzy blues riffing. Their rock-solid musical foundation provided the perfect base for the veteran bluesman they soon found themselves backing, but their musical precociousness drove them to eventually form the Aces, which incorporated some of the more modern and sophisticated influences that had raised eyebrows with the older blues crowd. The Aces were rounded out by schooled jazz drummer Fred Below, a Chicago native for whom the rough southern blues rhythms were almost completely foreign; after his first gig with the group he was so musically disoriented that he decided to quit the band, but was persuaded to stick it out and adapt his jazz techniques to the blues, ultimately becoming the most in-demand blues drummer in Chicago (in addition to putting the beat to many of rock and roll pioneer Chuck Berry's early hits). Little Walter approached his harmonica like a jazz saxophone

player, and the Aces provided the propulsive backing of a swinging big band. It would have been near impossible at the time to find three musicians who were better suited to providing the solid foundation for Walter's musical innovations than the Aces, who had the musical and dynamic range, swing sensibilities, and melding of individual strengths that made them the standard by which all of Little Walter's later ensembles—and most harp-led blues bands since—have been measured.

Unfortunately this band was not to last; the Aces had been establishing their own name around town, but when their first records with Little Walter were released by the Chess Records subsidiary Checker as by "Little Walter and His Night Caps" or "… and His Jukes" (to capitalize on the popularity of his first hit "Juke," recorded during a session while he was still with Muddy), there was dissension in the ranks. The first to leave was Louis, who was replaced by Robert Jr. Lockwood in 1954. Almost 40 years old at the time, Lockwood's roots were in the Delta; as Robert Johnson's stepson, he had a firm handle on the deepest of blues, but had been studying jazz guitarists since at least the 1930s, and had been recording since before WWII. He proved to be an adept foil for Walter's harp excursions, and many of Walter's jazziest adventures were supported and driven by Lockwood's sophisticated guitar riffing.

Dave Myers was the next to leave, joining his brother Louis in 1955 in a reformed Aces that featured Junior Wells (who had played with them pre-Walter) and later Otis Rush. Dave was replaced by 19-year-old guitar prodigy Luther Tucker, who had been hanging around the band and occasionally sitting in with them, as well as with other local blues acts. Although Tucker's role was initially the same as Dave's—thumping out bass lines on his guitar and providing chordal fills behind Lockwood—he soon distinguished himself as one of the flashiest of the new breed of guitarists in Chicago. When given the chance to take the lead, Tucker's fleet-fingered bursts of nervous energy helped push Little Walter's music in new and exciting directions. The first wave of rock and roll was cresting, aggressively played electric guitar was moving to the forefront of popular music, and Luther Tucker was among the blues guitarists at the leading edge.

It was around this time that Fred Below vacated the drum seat, although as was the custom at Chess/Checker Records, he continued to be brought in for recording sessions for the next several years. Replacing him on the road for a time was his old drum school classmate Odie Payne, Jr., who had been playing and recording in Chicago since the late '40s with the likes of Tampa Red, Memphis Minnie, Memphis Slim and Elmore James, and later worked as the house drummer at Cobra Records, playing behind Buddy Guy, Magic Sam, Otis Rush and others. Payne's slightly more orthodox but still distinctly jazzy style was by all accounts ideally suited to Walter's music, although there's no documentation of him ever appearing on any of Walter's records.

After a short time with a still young and rambunctious Little Walter and the even younger Luther Tucker, Lockwood was began to tire of the grind, and he left Walter's band, although he continued to appear on records with him (and also notably with Sonny Boy Williamson) until the late '50s. In 1956 Jimmie Lee Robinson joined Little Walter's band, pushing Luther Tucker into the lead role that Lockwood had vacated. Robinson was another Chicago native, who had grown up around the blues-rich Maxwell Street Market area, and knew Walter from his escapades there during his earliest years in Chicago. Robinson's formative years included musical apprenticeship on Maxwell Street, followed by formal music lessons for a time, and then time spent with guitarists Freddie King, Elmore James, Eddie Taylor and others in the early '50s. His guitar style had similarities to Tucker's, and eventually their roles carrying the top and bottom of the music melded to the point where they would trade back and forth even during songs. Unfortunately there are only a few examples of Jimmie Lee's years with Walter on record, due to the record label's insistence on not tampering with the successful studio formula that had been established by the Tucker/Lockwood/Below ensemble (usually augmented by Willie Dixon on string bass).

By the end of the 1950s, Little Walter's hit-making days were behind him, and his bands soon became a revolving door through which a number of local musicians passed. In 1959 guitarist Freddie Robinson joined the band for a time (replacing Jimmie Lee Robinson, a move that has caused much confusion among discographers over the years), during which he sometimes played electric bass. Odie Payne left the band after a short time to be replaced by the solid if less musically adventurous George Hunter. During sessions over the next few years the drum throne (on sessions, at least) was also occupied by Billy Stepney, session ace Al Duncan, and even the return of Fred Below for a 1960 session. But blues tastes were changing, and his great ensembles of the past had all scattered and moved on to other pursuits with varying degrees of success. —*Scott Dirks*

Carol Fran

b. Oct. 23, 1933, Lafayette, LA
Vocals, Piano / Modern Electric Blues, Electric Louisiana Blues, Swamp Blues
Just call Carol Fran and her husband Clarence Hollimon the new sweethearts of the blues. Not only are they a coosome twosome offstage, the pair share uncommon empathy onstage as well.

The couple first met in 1957 in New Orleans. Fran was a winsome Louisiana chanteuse with a Gulf Coast hit on Excello, "Emmitt Lee," to her credit; Hollimon was a fiery young guitar slinger who had backed Big Mama Thornton on the road before playing sizzling solos on many of Bobby "Blue" Bland's classic waxings for Duke. But love wasn't in the cards just then. In 1983, fate brought the pair back together at a Houston nightclub, and they've been a romantic item ever since. Two albums on Black Top, *Soul Sensation* in 1992 and *See There!* two years later, have cemented their musical bonds.

Fran toured with bandleader Joe Lutcher when she was a mere 15 years old in 1949. Famed producer J.D. Miller was behind the board when Carol Fran cut "Emmitt Lee" in Crowley, LA, in 1957. Her later waxings for Port and other diskeries tended toward the R&B side of the stylistic tracks. Fran's soulful 1965 reading of "Crying in the Chapel" was crushed by Elvis Presley's competing version. Meanwhile, Hollimon became a studio stalwart, playing on sides by Bland, Junior Parker, Joe Hinton, and a host of others.

Nothing substantial had been heard from Fran or Hollimon prior to their hooking up with Black Top only a few years ago. Lucky in music and in love, they are a versatile duo—she sings jazzy ballads as convincingly as swinging R&B, and Hollimon's fleet fingers are conversant with virtually any chord progression known to man. —*Bill Dahl*

Soul Sensation / 1992 / Black Top ◆◆◆◆
The new sweethearts of the blues' debut for Black Top is an uncommonly varied affair, the pair performing blues, jazz, and every stylistic stripe in between. Hollimon's red-hot licks are seldom short of amazing (his instrumental showcase "Gristle" is a stunner), and Fran's full-throated vocals shine on everything from a Gulf Coast-styled "My Happiness" and a reprise of Mitty Collier's emotionally charged "I Had a Talk with My Man" to the lounge-slanted "Anytime, Anyplace, Anywhere" and the rousing sanctified closer "This Little Light." —*Bill Dahl*

● **See There!** / 1994 / Black Top ◆◆◆◆
The duo's Black Top encore was a slightly more focused effort than their debut. They still exhibit considerable versatility on a highly infectious dance number, the Louisiana-rooted "Daddy, Daddy, Daddy," and soulful remakes of Tyrone Davis' "Are You Serious" and Gladys Knight & the Pips' earthy "I Don't Want to Do Wrong," but there's a more satisfying context overall. The album was waxed in New Orleans and Texas with two entirely different bands, lending laudable variety to the selections. —*Bill Dahl*

Panama Francis (David Albert Francis)

b. Dec. 21, 1918, Miami, FL
Drums / Early R&B Jazz, Swing, Jump Blues
Panama Francis has had a long and versatile career, equally at home in swing and R&B sessions. Playing for church revival meetings were among his earliest gigs and he also gigged with George Kelly's group the Cavaliers in Florida (1934-38) before moving to New York. The following year he worked with Roy Eldridge (making his recording debut) and this was followed by a long period at the Savoy with the Lucky Millinder big band (1940-46) and an association with Cab Calloway (1947-52). Francis then became a busy studio drummer, performing anonymously on many pop and rock 'n' roll records. In 1979 when he was in danger of being forgotten, Francis formed the Savoy Sultans, a group based on the small unit that used to play opposite Millinder at the Savoy. The Sultans recorded a steady stream of exciting hot swing records for Black & Blue and Stash during 1979-83. Since that time Panama Francis has continued freelancing including recording and touring with the Statesmen of Jazz (1994-95). —*Scott Yanow*

All-Stars 1949 / 1949 / Collectables ◆◆◆◆
Collectables' *All Stars 1949* is a storming swing set that drummer Panama Francisco led in 1949. —*Leo Stanley*

● **Savoy Sultans** / Jan. 31, 1979-Feb. 11, 1979 / Classic Jazz ◆◆◆◆
Although their recordings do not always show it, the Savoy Sultans in the late '30s were considered one of the hottest small swing groups in existence. Decades later, drummer Panama Francis decided to revive the group's concept by putting together a new Savoy Sultans, using occasional alumni but mostly utilizing other surviving veteran players. This Classic Jazz LP finds the group at its best, cooking on such numbers as "Song of the Islands," "Frenzy," "Little John Special," and "Clap Hands, Here Comes Charlie." With George Kelly contributing the arrangements as well as his tenor and such other fine soloists as trumpeters Francis Williams and Irv Stokes, altoists Norris Turney and Howard Johnson, and pianist Red Richards, this is a hot band that could outswing the original group. This LP deserves to be reissued on CD. —*Scott Yanow*

Everything Swings / Oct. 3, 1983+Oct. 10, 1983 / Stash ◆◆◆
Panama Francis' Savoy Sultans was one of the most mainstream jazz combos of the late '70s and early '80s, reviving the joy of small-group swing with its riffing and concise but heated solos. This excellent effort, its fourth and thus far final recording, finds the group expanding to ten pieces and featuring hot solos from the likes of trumpeters Irv Stokes and Spanky Davis, veteran tenor George Kelly, and (in a bit of a surprise) the modern but flexible altoist Bobby Watson. Sticking mostly to swing standards, the Savoy Sultans uplift and bring joy to such songs as "Air Mail Special," "Stomping at the Savoy," "In the Mood," and "Just You, Just Me." —*Scott Yanow*

Keith Frank

b. 1972, Soileau, LA
Vocals / Zydeco
One of the leading lights of the "nouveau zydeco" movement, accordionist Keith Frank—the son of zydeco great Preston Frank—fused the traditional sound of his father's generation with latter-day influences ranging from James Brown to Bob Marley to forge his own urbanized and infectiously danceable style. Born in Soileau, LA in 1972, Frank began playing professionally at the age of four, sitting in on a variety of instruments with his father's combo the Family Zydeco Band; despite focusing on the accordion from the age of six onward, he initially loathed zydeco and the pressures of performing, but in high school finally gave in to the music's pull and formed his own group. As Preston Frank began to ease into retirement, Keith gradually assumed leadership duties of the family band, which now also included his sister Jennifer on bass and brother Brad on drums; as he gained confidence, he began adding elements of rap to his music, a move which dismayed purists but met with wide approval from younger listeners. Frank made his debut in 1994 with *What's His Name?; Movin' on Up!* followed a year later. —*Jason Ankeny*

What's His Name? / 1994 / Maison de Soul ◆◆◆◆

Movin' on Up! / 1995 / Maison de Soul ◆◆◆

Only the Strong Survive / Jul. 20, 1996 / Maison de Soul ◆◆◆

● **Get on Boy** / Jul. 25, 1996 / Zydeco Hound ◆◆◆◆

You'd Be Surprised / Apr. 22, 1997 / Maison de Soul ◆◆◆

Calvin Frazier

b. Feb. 16, 1915, Osceola, AR, **d.** Sep. 23, 1972, Detroit, MI
Guitar / Prewar Country Blues
An associate of Robert Johnson, Calvin Frazier never attained the notoriety of other Johnson protégés like Johnny Shines, Robert Jr. Lockwood, or Honeyboy Edwards, but his scant recorded legacy reveals a performer whose take on prewar-era blues is as unique and distinctive as any in the canon. Born February 16, 1915 in Osceola, AR, Frazier began his career performing alongside his brothers, and in the company of Shines, he traveled to Helena, AR in 1930; there they met Johnson, and together the three men slowly journeyed north to Detroit, where they sang hymns on area gospel broadcasts. Upon returning south, Frazier and Johnson also joined with drummer Peck Curtis in a string-band combo. However, in 1935 Frazier was wounded in a Memphis shootout which left another man dead; he fled back to Detroit,

marrying Shines' cousin and settling into a life of quiet anonymity. Apart from gigs supporting the likes of Big Maceo Merriweather, Rice Miller and Baby Boy Warren, he resurfaced in 1938 long enough to cut a session for folklorist Alan Lomax; while the spectre of Johnson undeniably haunts renditions of songs including "Lily Mae" (a rewrite of "Honeymoon Blues") and "Highway 51" (lifted from "Dust My Broom"), Frazier's incomprehensible vocals, menacingly surreal lyrics and exquisite slide guitar are the hallmarks of a total original. He did not record again until a 1951 date with T.J. Fowler's jump band, and entered the studio one last time in 1954 with Warren and Miller; Frazier continued performing in the Detroit area to little notice until his death on September 23, 1972. — *Jason Ankeny*

This Old World's in a Tangle / 1993 / Laurie ✦✦✦✦
1938 Library of Congress field recordings, influenced by Robert Johnson. — *Bill Dahl*

Denny Freeman
b. Aug. 7, 1944, Orlando, FL
Guitar, Piano / Electric Texas Blues
This Dallas native and Austin fixture was co-lead guitarist in the Cobras with Stevie Vaughan, before joining Angela Strehli (cutting two solo LPs during his stint with the songstress), contributing to *Big Guitars from Texas*, and recording with Lou Ann Barton. More original and out-on-a-limb than most textbook-blues players, he co-wrote "Baboom/Mama Said" on the Vaughan Brothers' *Family Style* and played guitar and piano on tour with Jimmie Vaughan following the latter's *Strange Pleasure*. — *Dan Forte*

Blues Cruise / 1986 / Amazing ✦✦✦✦
"Rockin' with B.B." and "Steelin' Berry's" not only reveal two of Freeman's major influences but do justice to Mr. King and Chuck Berry—the latter featuring a fine steel guitar turn by Jimmie Vaughan. The melodic "Denny's Blues" is also a standout. Three lackluster vocal numbers (one each by Angela Strehli, Kim Wilson, and Bill Carter) detract from the continuity (and level) of Freeman's instrumental set. — *Dan Forte*

Out of the Blue / 1987 / Amazing ✦✦✦✦
All instrumental this time, and a bit more varied, with gospel, jazz ("My Dominique"), exotica (Freeman's "Lost Incas" from the *Big Guitars from Texas* album), and even a nod to Billy Gibbons on "Z." Jimmie Vaughan cameos again, on steel and 6-string bass, along with the usual Austin crew (George Rains, Sarah Brown, Mel Brown, Derek O'Brien, Kaz Kazanoff, etc.). — *Dan Forte*

● **Denny Freeman** / 1991 / Amazing ✦✦✦✦
Freeman's two LPs wedged onto one CD, with three tunes unfortunately hitting the editing room floor. Two vocals interrupt the all-instrumental proceedings, and somehow Jimmie Vaughan's steel work on "Louisiana Luau" (from *Blues Cruise*) got the axe. — *Dan Forte*

Blues Cruise / Out of the Blue / 1997 / Amazing ✦✦✦✦
Two of Denny Freeman's mid-'80s albums—*Blues Cruise* (1986) and *Out of the Blues* (1987)—are combined on this single disc. On these albums, Freeman has a chance to stretch out and flaunt his amazing array of Texas blues licks—he rarely plays it safe. The disc was recorded with Antone's house band and features guest vocals by Angela Strehli and Kim Wilson. — *Thom Owens*

A Tone for My Sins / Nov. 11, 1997 / Dallas Blues Society ✦✦✦

Frank Frost (Frank Otis Frost)
b. Apr. 15, 1936, Auvergne, AR
Guitar, Harmonica, Vocals, Piano / R&B, Electric Delta Blues, Soul Blues
The atmospheric juke joint blues of Frank Frost remain steeped in unadulterated Delta funk. But his ongoing musical journey has taken him well outside his Mississippi homebase.

He moved to St. Louis in 1951, learning how to blow harp first from Little Willie Foster and then from the legendary Sonny Boy Williamson who took him on the road—as a guitar player—from 1956 to 1959. Drummer Sam Carr, a longtime Frost ally, was also part of the equation, having enticed Frost to front his combo in 1954 before hooking up with Sonny Boy.

Leaving Williamson's employ in 1959, Frost and Carr settled in Lula, MS. Guitarist Jack Johnson came aboard in 1962 after sitting in with the pair at the Savoy Theatre in Clarksdale. The three meshed perfectly—enough to

interest Memphis producer Sam Phillips in a short-lived back-to-the-blues campaign that same year. *Hey Boss Man!*, issued on Sun's Phillips International subsidiary as by Frank Frost and the Nighthawks, was a wonderful collection of uncompromising Southern blues (albeit totally out of step with the marketplace at the time).

Elvis Presley's ex-guitarist Scotty Moore produced Frost's next sessions in Nashville in 1966 for Jewel Records. Augmented by session bassist Chip Young, the trio's tight downhome ensemble work was once again seamless. "My Back Scratcher," Frost's takeoff on Slim Harpo's "Baby Scratch My Back," even dented the R&B charts on Shreveport-based Jewel for three weeks.

Chicago blues fan Michael Frank sought out Frost in 1975. He located Frost, Johnson, and Carr playing inside Johnson's Clarksdale tavern, the Black Fox. Mesmerized by their sound, Frost soon formed his own record label, Earwig, to capture their raw, charismatic brand of blues. 1979's *Rockin' the Juke Joint Down*, billed as by the Jelly Roll Kings (after one of the standout songs on that old Phillips International LP), showcased the trio's multifaceted approach—echoes of R&B, soul, even Johnny & the Hurricanes permeate their Delta-based attack.

In the years since, Frost has waxed his own Earwig album (1988's *Midnight Prowler*) and appeared on Atlantic's 1992 *Deep Blues* soundtrack—an acclaimed film that reinforced the fact that blues still thrives deep in its southern birthplace. Frost returned in 1996 with *Keep Yourself Together*. — *Bill Dahl*

● **Hey Boss Man** / 1962 / Philips ✦✦✦✦
One of the last great blues recordings produced by the legendary Sam Phillips. Frost and his Mississippi cohorts Jack Johnson and Sam Carr played Southern juke joint blues rough and ready in the classic mold, with plenty of dynamic interplay and nasty, lowdown grooves. — *Bill Dahl*

Frank Frost / 1973 / Paula ✦✦✦
More down-home eclectic blues from the harpist/keyboardist. — *Bill Dahl*

Ride with Your Daddy Tonight / 1985 / Charly ✦✦✦✦
Frost's best sides for the Jewel label. Some of the most down-home '60s blues ever recorded. — *Cub Koda*

Midnight Prowler / 1988 / Earwig ✦✦✦
Frost is front-and-center with a program that's decidedly downhome. This is what modern Mississippi blues sounds like—tough, uncompromising, still rooted mainly in the 1950s with a few modern touches. — *Bill Dahl*

Jelly Roll King / 1990 / Charly ✦✦✦

Jelly Roll Blues / 1991 / Paula ✦✦✦✦
Same band, different producer: this time it was Elvis Presley's legendary guitarist, Scotty Moore, behind the glass as Frost and his pals dished out the lowdown sounds during the mid-'60s for Stan Lewis' Jewel logo. "My Back Scratcher" owes a stylistic debt to Slim Harpo but feels mighty good all the same. The entire 13-song disc reeks of steamy juke-joint ambience. — *Bill Dahl*

Deep Blues / 1992 / Appaloosa ✦✦✦
Harmonica wizard and veteran blues vocalist Frank Frost has plenty left in his harp and voice. His venerable, still vibrant sound fortifies this album, as Frost again takes the spotlight with biting, rolling harmonica riffs, extended lines, wailing refrains and wise, often ironic and bittersweet vocals. This time he's backed by Freddie & The Screamers, a sympathetic unit able to supply both hot uptempo support and low-down assistance. Maybe he did it better years ago, but Frank Frost hasn't slipped all that far in the 1990s. — *Ron Wynn*

Screamers / Sep. 2, 1994 / Appaloosa ✦✦✦

Keep Yourself Together / 1996 / Evidence ✦✦✦
This is a nicely put together—if rather unexceptional—set with Frost's vocal and harp ably supported by his long-time drummer Sam Carr, producer Fred James on guitar, and Bob Kommersmith on string bass. While nothing on here burns with the smoldering intensity of his early Sun-Phillips International sides or his later sessions for Jewel, a pair of Little Walter tunes ("Everything's Gonna Be Alright," "Just a Feeling") a remake of one of his Sun-P.I. sides ("Come on Home") and a version of Jimmy Rushing's "Going to Chicago" make this an album more than worthy of a spin or two in the CD player. — *Cub Koda*

Blind Boy Fuller

b. Jul. 10, 1908, Wadesboro, NC, **d.** Feb. 13, 1941, Durham, NC
Guitar, Vocals / Country Blues, Piedmont Blues, East Coast Blues, Prewar Country Blues

Unlike blues artists like Big Bill or Memphis Minnie who recorded extensively over three or four decades, Blind Boy Fuller recorded his substantial body of work over a short, six-year span. Nevertheless, he was one of the most recorded artists of his time and by far the most popular and influential Piedmont blues player of all time. Fuller could play in multiple styles: slide, ragtime, pop, and blues were all enhanced by his National steel guitar. Fuller worked with some fine sidemen, including Davis, Sonny Terry, and washboard player Bull City Red. Initially discovered and promoted by Carolina entrepreneur H. B. Long, Fuller recorded for ARC and Decca. He also served as a conduit to recording sessions, steering fellow blues musicians to the studio.

In spite of Fuller's recorded output, most of his musical life was spent as a street musician and house party favorite, and he possessed the skills to reinterpret and cover the hits of other artists as well. In this sense, he was a synthesizer of styles, parallel in many ways to Robert Johnson, his contemporary who died three years earlier. Like Johnson, Fuller lived fast and died young in 1941, only 33 years old. Fuller was a fine, expressive vocalist and a masterful guitar player best remembered for his uptempo ragtime hits "Rag Mama Rag," "Trucking My Blues Away," and "Step It Up and Go." At the same time he was capable of deeper material, and his versions of "Lost Lover Blues" or "Mamie" are as deep as most Delta blues. Because of his popularity, he may have been overexposed on records, yet most of his songs remained close to tradition and much of his repertoire and style is kept alive by North Carolina and Virginia artists today. — *Barry Lee Pearson*

Complete Recorded Works, Vol. 5 (1938-1940) / 1938-1940 / Document ♦♦♦♦

Volume five in Document's Blind Boy Fuller series is comprised primarily of two prolific sessions, the first recorded in Columbia, South Carolina on October 29, 1938 with harpist Sonny Terry and washboard player Bull City Red, the second a Memphis date from July 12, 1939 with Terry, Bull City Red (now going as Oh Red) and second guitarist Sonny Jones. The latter is perhaps the most impressive, yielding the signature song "I Want Some of Your Pie" as well as "You've Got Something There" (a rewrite of Buddy Moss' "Daddy Don't Care") and Fuller's immortal rendition of J.B. Long's "Step It Up and Go." — *Jason Ankeny*

Complete Recorded Works, Vol. 6 (1940) / 1940 / Document ♦♦♦♦

The sixth and final volume in the series assembles the fruits of Blind Boy Fuller's final studio sessions, all dating to the first half of 1940. Despite failing health, Fuller is at his most incendiary on these sides—"Shake It, Baby" is among his most galvanizing dance tunes, while "Little Woman You're So Sweet" stands as one of his finest originals. Most energetic, however, are the sanctified songs, including "No Stranger Now," "Jesus Is a Holy Man" and "Twelve Gates to the City"—with his death less than a year away, Fuller burns with spiritual intensity, clearly yearning for some kind of redemption in his final months. — *Jason Ankeny*

★ **Truckin' My Blues Away** / 1978 / Yazoo ♦♦♦♦♦

For most listeners, Yazoo's *Truckin' My Blues Away* may be a better bet than Columbia/Legacy's *East Coast Piedmont Style*, since it actually has a higher concentration of strong material, capturing the influential bluesman at his peak. All of the 14 tracks were recorded between 1935 and 1938, and there are a number of exceptional performances here, including "Homesick and Lonesome Blues," "Truckin' My Blues Away," "I Crave My Pig Meat," "Walking My Troubles Away" and "Sweet Honey Hole." It's a nice, concise introduction and, best of all, there's no duplication between this disc and *East Coast Piedmont Style*, making the two discs wonderful, complementary collections that tell a comprehensive story when taken together. — *Thom Owens*

East Coast Piedmont Style / Aug. 1991 / Columbia/Legacy ♦♦♦♦

Blind Boy Fuller, who died in 1940 when he was only 33, recorded extensively during 1935-40. HIs guitar playing was in the tradition of the ragtime-influenced Blind Blake and Blind Willie McTell while his singing was simple and direct. The music on this CD reissue becomes a bit repetitive after awhile for Fuller generally lacked variety but, taken in small doses (as if one were listening to the original 78s and treasuring individual songs), Blind Boy Full-

er's performances were often memorable. The reissue is a cross section of his work with the emphasis on his earliest recordings. Guitarist Blind Gary Davis, Bull City Red on washboard and harmonica wiz Sonny Terry help out on a few numbers; five of the 20 selections were previously unreleased. — *Scott Yanow*

Complete Recorded Works, Vol. 1-4 / 1992 / Document ♦♦♦♦

The finest collection ever of blues and ragtime. Fuller is here both solo and with Gary Davis, Sonny Terry, and Bull City Red. This is Piedmont blues at its best (1935-1940), a must for anyone interested in down-home blues. — *Barry Lee Pearson*

Jesse Fuller

b. Mar. 12, 1896, Jonesboro, GA, **d.** Jan. 29, 1976, Oakland, CA
Guitar, Harmonica, Kazoo, Vocals / Country Blues, Acoustic West Coast Blues, Prewar Country Blues, Blues Revival

Equipped with a bandful of instruments operated by various parts of his anatomy, Bay Area-legend Jesse Fuller was a folk-music favorite in the '50s and '60s. His infectious rhythm and gentle charm graced old folk tunes, spirituals, and blues alike. One of his inventions was a homemade, foot-operated instrument called the "footdella" or "fotdella." Naturally, Fuller never needed other accompanists to back his one-man show. His best-known songs include "San Francisco Bay Blues" and "Beat It on Down the Line" (the first one covered by Janis Joplin, the second by the Grateful Dead).

Born and raised in Georgia, Jesse Fuller began playing guitar when he was a child, although he didn't pursue the instrument seriously. In his early 20s, Fuller wandered around the southern and western regions of the United States, eventually settling down in Los Angeles. While he was in southern California, he worked as a film extra, appearing in *The Thief of Bagdad, East of Suez, Hearts in Dixie,* and *End of the World.* After spending a few years in Los Angeles, Fuller moved to San Francisco. While he worked various odd jobs around the Bay Area, he played on street corners and parties.

Jesse's musical career didn't properly begin unitl the early '50s, when he decided to become a professional musician—he was 55 years old at the time. Performing as a one-man band, he began to get spots on local television shows and nightclubs. However, Fuller's career didn't take off until 1954, when he wrote "San Francisco Bay Blues." The song helped him land a record contract with the independent Cavalier label and in 1955, he recorded his first album, *Folk Blues: Working on the Railroad with Jesse Fuller.* The albums was a success and soon he was making records for a variety of labels, including Good Time Jazz and Prestige.

In the late '50s and early '60s, Jesse Fuller became one of the key figures of the blues revival, helping bring the music to a new, younger audience. Throughout the '60s and '70s, he toured America and Europe, appearing at numerous blues and folk festivals, as well as countless coffeehouse gigs across the US Fuller continued performing and recording until his death in 1976. — *Jim O'Neal & Stephen Thomas Erlewine*

Jazz, Folk Songs, Spirituals & Blues / Apr. 1958 / Good Time Jazz ♦♦♦♦

Jesse Fuller was among the greatest one-man bands in blues history. The title of this 1958 date adequately described the session's musical width and depth; Fuller handled everything from old spirituals such as as "I'm Going To Meet My Loving Mother" to the rollicking "Memphis Boogie" and "Fingerbuster" and the concluding "Hesitation Blues." As sole performer, melodic, rhythmic and performing focus, Fuller's energy never wanes through the CD's 11 numbers. He nicely conveys the varying moods, themes and sentiments, knowing which lyrics to emphasize, when to intensify the pace and when to lower his voice and let the music make the point. — *Ron Wynn*

Brother Lowdown / 1959 / Fantasy ♦♦

The Lone Cat Sings and Plays Jazz, Folk Songs, Spirituals and Blues / Aug. 1961 / Good Time Jazz ♦♦♦

Lone Cat Sings and Plays Jazz, Folk Songs, Spirituals and Blues features a selection of oldtime blues, ragtime, and string band songs, all performed by the one-man band Jesse Fuller. With his 12-string guitar, harmonica, kazoo, cymbals, and six-string bass (which he played with his foot), Fuller created a very unique sound that surprisingly didn't sound particularly jokey—instead, it sounded like it was part of a tradition. None of his best-known songs are included on *Lone Cat,* but there is an abundance of strange, wonderful music on the record. — *Thom Owens*

● **San Francisco Bay Blues** / 1963 / Good Time Jazz ◆◆◆◆
By the time *San Francisco Bay Blues* was released in 1963, the title track had long been established as a classic and Jesse Fuller's career had been revived. Nevertheless, the album may be his finest, containing wonderful versions of "San Francisco Bay Blues," "Jesse's New Midnight Special," "John Henry," "I Got a Mind to Ramble," and "Crazy About a Woman," that find Fuller at his easygoing best. — *Thom Owens*

Favorites / 1965 / Prestige ◆◆◆
Jesse Fuller's *Favorites* is a highly enjoyable collection of the singer's favorite blues standards. Performing everything as a solo piece, he runs through classics like "Key to the Highway," "The Midnight Special," and "Brownskin Gal" with humor and warmth. It's a small, but entertaining, gem. — *Thom Owens*

Blues, Jazz, Spirituals. . . / 1965 / Good Time Jazz ◆◆◆

Frisco Bound / 1968 / Arhoolie ◆◆◆◆
A one-man band with guitar, harmonica, kazoo, and "footdella" bass, these are some of his first recordings, circa 1955. Innocent echoes of turn-of-the-century rural America. — *Mark A. Humphrey*

Johnny Fuller

b. Apr. 20, 1929, Edwards, MS, **d.** May 20, 1985, Oakland, CA
Guitar, Vocals, Organ, Piano / Electric West Coast Blues, West Coast Blues
Johnny Fuller was a West Coast bluesman who left behind a spate of 1950s recordings that jumped all kinds of genre fences with seemingly no trace of his Mississippi born roots. He was equally at home with low down blues, gospel, R&B, and rock 'n' roll, all of it imbued with strong vocals and a driving guitar style. Although his Mississippi roots were never far below the surface of his best work, Johnny is usually categorized as a West Coast bluesman. Making the Bay Area his home throughout his career, Fuller turned in classic sides for Heritage, Aladdin, Specialty, Flair, Checker, and Hollywood; all but one of them West Coast-based concerns. His two biggest hits, "All Night Long" and the original version of "The Haunted House," improbably found him in the late '50s on rock 'n' roll package shows, touring with the likes of Paul Anka and Frankie Avalon! By and large retiring from the music scene in the '60s (with the exception of one excellent album in 1974), Fuller worked as a garage mechanic until his passing in 1985. — *Cub Koda*

● **Fuller's Blues** / 1974 / Diving Duck ◆◆◆◆
Recorded in 1974, *Fuller's Blues* was Johnny Fuller's much-belated full-length debut, and it also turned out to be his last record. That's too bad, because it certainly illustrates what he was capable of achieving. He runs the gauntlet here, pulling out jumping R&B numbers and acoustic blues with equal aplomb. It's an exhilarating listen—it's just too bad there weren't more like it. — *Thom Owens*

Fools Paradise / 1984 / Diving Duck ◆◆◆

Lowell Fulson

b. Mar. 31, 1921, Tulsa, OK
Guitar, Vocals / R&B, Acoustic West Coast Blues, Electric West Coast Blues, West Coast Blues, Texas Blues, Piedmont Blues
Lowell Fulson has recorded every shade of blues imaginable. Polished urban blues, rustic two-guitar duets with his younger brother Martin, funk-tinged grooves that pierced the mid-'60s charts, even an unwise cover of the Beatles' "Why Don't We Do It in the Road!" Clearly, the veteran guitarist, who's been at it now for more than half a century, isn't afraid to experiment. Perhaps that's why his last couple of discs for Rounder are so vital and satisfying—and why he's been an innovator for so long.
Exposed to the western swing of Bob Wills as well as indigenous blues while growing up in Oklahoma, Fulson joined up with singer Texas Alexander for a few months in 1940, touring the Lone Star state with the veteran bluesman. Fulson was drafted in 1943. The Navy let him go in 1945; after a few months back in Oklahoma, he was off to Oakland, CA, where he made his first 78s for fledgling producer Bob Geddins. Soon enough, Fulson was fronting his own band and cutting a stack of platters for Big Town, Gilt Edge, Trilon, and Down Town (where he hit big in 1948 with "Three O'Clock Blues," later covered by B.B. King).
Swing Time records prexy Jack Lauderdale snapped up Fulson in 1948, and the hits really began to flow: the immortal "Every Day I Have the Blues" (an adaptation of Memphis Slim's "Nobody Loves Me"), "Blue Shadows," the

two-sided holiday perennial "Lonesome Christmas," and a groovy mid-tempo instrumental "Low Society Blues" that really hammers home how tremendously important pianist Lloyd Glenn and alto saxist Earl Brown were to Fulson's maturing sound (all charted in 1950!).
Fulson toured extensively from then on, his band stocked for a time with dazzling pianist Ray Charles (who later covered Lowell's "Sinner's Prayer" for Atlantic) and saxist Stanley Turrentine. After a one-off session in New Orleans in 1953 for Aladdin, Fulson inked a longterm pact with Chess in 1954. His first single for the firm was the classic "Reconsider Baby," cut in Dallas under Stan Lewis' supervision with a sax section that included David "Fathead" Newman on tenor and Leroy Cooper on baritone.
The relentless mid-tempo blues proved a massive hit and perennial cover item—even Elvis Presley cut it in 1960, right after he got out of the Army. But apart from "Loving You," the guitarist's subsequent Checker output failed to find widespread favor with the public. Baffling, since Fulson's crisp, concise guitar work and sturdy vocals were as effective as ever. Most of his Checker sessions were held in Chicago and L.A. (the latter his home from the turn of the '50s).
Fulson stayed with Checker into 1962, but a change of labels worked wonders when he jumped over to Los Angeles-based Kent Records. 1965's driving "Black Nights" became his first smash in a decade, and "Tramp," a loping funk-injected workout co-written by Fulson and Jimmy McCracklin, did even better, restoring the guitarist to R&B stardom, gaining plenty of pop spins, and inspiring a playful Stax cover by Otis Redding and Carla Thomas only a few months later that outsold Fulson's original.
A couple of lesser follow-up hits for Kent ensued before the guitarist was reunited with Stan Lewis at Jewel Records. That's where he took a crack at that Beatles number, though most of his outings for the firm were considerably closer to the blues bone. Fulson has never been absent for long on disc; 1992's *Hold On* and its 1995 follow-up *Them Update Blues*, both for Ron Levy's Bullseye Blues logo, are among his most recent efforts, both quite solid.
Few bluesmen have managed to remain contemporary the way Lowell Fulson has for more than five decades. And fewer still will make such a massive contribution to the idiom. — *Bill Dahl*

★ **Hung Down Head** / 1954 / MCA/Chess ◆◆◆◆◆
The most indispensable collection in Fulson's vast discography. He was hitting on all burners during the mid-'50s when he was with Chess, waxing the immortal "Reconsider Baby," swinging gems like "Check Yourself," "Do Me Right," and "Trouble, Trouble," and the supremely doomy "Tollin' Bells," here in many truncated false takes before he and the band finally jell. — *Bill Dahl*

Lowell Fulson [Chess] / 1959 / Chess ◆◆◆
The rest of Fulson's 1955-62 Chess output is classic stuff. — *Bill Dahl*

Back Home Blues / 1959 / Night Train ◆◆◆
Back Home Blues collects several tracks Lowell Fulson cut early in his career for Swing Time, when he was performing jump blues. This is high-energy, enjoyable blues—even though Fulsom doesn't sound as comfortable with jump blues as he does with postwar Chicago and Southern blues, he is completely creditable on these performances. It's an essential purchase for Fulson fans that want to dig deep into his roots. — *Thom Owens*

Soul / 1966 / United ◆◆◆◆
Funky, uncompromising guitar blues. — *Bill Dahl*

Tramp / 1967 / United ◆◆◆◆
Led by one of his biggest hits, this is one of Fulson's best and funkiest. — *Bill Dahl*

Now / 1969 / United ◆◆◆
More funky blues with lots of covers. — *Bill Dahl*

In a Heavy Bag / 1970 / Jewel ◆◆
Too rock oriented for comfort. — *Bill Dahl*

Let's Go Get Stoned / 1971 / United ◆◆

I've Got the Blues / 1973 / Jewel ◆◆
I've Got the Blues is as simple and straightforward as its title as Lowell Fulson lays down tracks like "Teach Me," "Crying Won't Help," and "Stoned to the Bone" in his inimitable West Coast style. — *Jason Ankeny*

Lowell Fulson (Early Recordings) / 1975 / Arhoolie ◆◆◆
Mostly the country blues roots of the Oklahoma-born guitarist. The first ten

tracks, duets with brother Martin on second guitar, are worlds apart from the swinging horn-powered R&B efforts that Fulson is famous for. The last four numbers, though, revert to that attractive format—especially the scorching instrumental closer "Lowell Jumps One." —*Bill Dahl*

Ol' Blues Singer / 1975 / Granite ♦♦

Blues Masters / 1977 / Chess ♦♦♦♦

Lovemaker / 1978 / Big Town ♦♦♦

Man of Motion / 1981 / Charly ♦♦
Vinyl collection of Fulson's late-'60s stint at Shreveport's Jewel Records. In truth, not the guitarist's shining hour—some of this stuff is competent blues (some backed by the Muscle Shoals house band of the era), others abominable attempts at cracking the blues-rock market (his rendering of the Beatles' "Why Don't We Do It in the Road" stands as the worst thing Fulson ever committed to tape). —*Bill Dahl*

Everyday I Have the Blues / 1984 / Night Train ♦♦♦♦
The first of two extremely solid compilations of the guitarist's late-'40s/early-'50s output for Jack Lauderdale's Los Angeles-based Swing Time imprint. You'll need 'em both, since the essentials are spread across 'em evenly—Fulson's smashes "Every Day," "Lonesome Christmas," and "Blue Shadows" regally inhabit this 20-cut disc. —*Bill Dahl*

Lowell Fulson [Chess Compilation] / 1984 / Chess ♦♦♦

Think Twice Before You Speak / 1984 / JSP ♦♦♦

One More Blues / Mar. 11, 1984 / Evidence ♦♦♦
Fulson hasn't been as prolific over the last couple of decades as he was during the 1950s, but when he does get a chance to enter a studio, he usually emerges with some pretty impressive work. This 1984 album, first out on Black & Blue over in France, is no exception—the band is tight (Phillip Walker is rhythm guitarist), and Fulson came prepared with a sheaf of solid originals. —*Bill Dahl*

The Blues Got Me Down / 1985 / Diving Duck ♦♦♦♦

Blue Days, Black Nights / 1986 / Ace ♦♦♦
Blues Days, Black Nights collects 15 tracks Lowell Fulson recorded in the late '60s, including the classic "Tramp." During this era, he was playing Chicago blues and Southern soul, with the occasional flourish of laidback, Western blues. Although this material is first-rate, it is available on better collections, including Flair's two-fer of *Tramp* and *Soul*. —*Thom Owens*

I Don't Know My Mind / 1987 / Bear Family ♦♦♦♦

Giant of Blues Guitar 1946/57 / 1987 / Blues Boy ♦♦♦♦
Fulson's country-blues roots are the focus on this set of recordings from his postwar-era peak. —*Jason Ankeny*

San Francisco Blues / 1988 / Black Lion ♦♦♦♦
Guitarist and vocalist Lowell Fulson helped establish his reputation with a string of fine songs for the Swingtime label in the late '40s and early '50s. Fulson showed he could belt out hard-hitting blues, do sentimental ballads, double-entendre novelty pieces or irony-filled laments, and also play riveting solos. This '92 CD reissue collects 16 early Fulson numbers, all original compositions, and features Fulson leading a group with Lloyd Glenn, King Solomon, or Rufus J. Russell on piano, Ralph Hamilton, Billy Hadnott or Floyd Montgomery on bass, and Bob Harvey or Asal Carson on drums. —*Ron Wynn*

Chicago Golden Years / 1988 / Vogue ♦♦♦♦

It's a Good Day / 1988 / Rounder ♦♦♦
While no one was anticipating longtime blues great Lowell Fulson to equal or even approach his masterful 1950s work on this session, he turned in a pleasantly competent date of both heartache numbers and more upbeat tunes. Fulson's leads were clear and nicely phrased, his guitar work still tasty and clever. He interspersed some swamp-pop, Texas shuffle and urban blues riffs into his material, and on "Blues and My Guitar" displayed the fluidity and performance magic that made his classic sides unforgettable. —*Ron Wynn*

Tramp/Soul / 1991 / Flair ♦♦♦♦
The veteran guitarist's two best mid-'60s albums for Kent Records on one packed-to-the-gills CD. Fulson cannily made the leap into soul-slanted grooves while at Kent, scoring a major R&B smash with "Tramp." Also

aboard is Fulson's classic "Black Nights;" "Talkin' Woman" (later revived most memorably by Albert Collins as "Honey Hush"), and a fine version of Smokey Hogg's enduring "Too Many Drivers." —*Bill Dahl*

Hold On / May 1992 / Bullseye Blues ♦♦♦♦
Nothing dated about this fine album, produced by organist Ron Levy—Fulson sounds at once both contemporary and timeless, slashing through a mostly original set with Jimmy McCracklin helping out on piano and the sax section including Bobby Forte and Edgar Synigal. —*Bill Dahl*

Reconsider Baby / 1993 / Charly ♦♦♦♦
A more in-depth assessment of Fulson's Chess years (20 titles), minus a few of the most important sides nestled on *Hung Down Head* but boasting a few others of nearly equal import: "Lonely Hours," "Rollin' Blues," "Don't Drive Me Baby," and especially the insane 1957 rocker "Rock This Morning," where Fulson does his best Little Richard imitation as Eddie Chamblee blows up a tenor sax hurricane. —*Bill Dahl*

Them Update Blues / 1995 / Bullseye Blues ♦♦♦
A half century after he made his debut waxings, Fulson is still going strong—and not as some museum piece, either. Still a vital blues artist who refuses to rest on his massive laurels, Fulson's latest is a fine addition to his vast discography, comprised mostly of fresh originals and featuring his customary biting guitar and insinuating vocals. —*Bill Dahl*

Sinner's Prayer / 1995 / Night Train ♦♦♦♦
20 more Swing Time essentials, notably Lowell Fulson's original reading of the mournful "Sinner's Prayer" (soon revived by his onetime band pianist Ray Charles), the exultant instrumental "Low Society" (featuring Earl Brown's sturdy alto sax), and one of Fulson's wildest rockers, "Upstairs." —*Bill Dahl*

Tramp/Soul / Jul. 23, 1996 / Alliance ♦♦♦♦
Led by one of his biggest hits, *Tramp* is one of Fulson's best and funkiest, while uncompromising guitar blues is the order of the day on *Soul*, the second half of this two-fer release. —*Bill Dahl*

My First Recordings / Jan. 21, 1997 / Arhoolie ♦♦♦♦
Twenty-six tracks that Fulson cut between 1946 and 1951 for the Swing Time, Big Town, and Down Town labels. This is far more sparsely produced, and less urbane in feel, than the material Lowell would record for Chess throughout the 1950s. Indeed, on ten of the cuts, he's supported only by his brother Martin on rhythm guitar; there's a small combo on the remainder of the cuts, but a fairly subdued one. Those who prefer their blues down-home might like this better than the more polished sound that Fulson moved into for the rest of his career. It's city blues just out of the country, with Fulson's high, pleading vocals and sharp, countrified electric licks to the fore. The most famous song, by far, is the original version of "Three O'Clock Blues," which was covered for a huge R&B hit by B.B. King in the early '50s. —*Richie Unterberger*

The Complete Chess Masters (50th Anniversary Collection) / Nov. 4, 1997 / MCA ♦♦♦♦
Two-CD, 45-song compilation covers Fulson's Chess years, which spanned 1954 to 1963. Fulson didn't have a great deal of commercial success at Chess (the big exception being "Reconsider Baby," which leads off this set), and his jazzy West Coast form of R&B/blues was considerably more polished than the electrified Delta blues for which Chess is most renowned. Most of this, in fact, was recorded not in Chicago, but in Los Angeles, where Fulson could work with combos more sympathetic to his style. You'd have to consider this Fulson's peak, however, and the two discs' worth of material is not excessive, due to the consistency of his material and vocal confidence throughout the decade. It's not without its weird moments of rawness, either, as in "Blues Rhumba," the Bo Diddleyesque guitar that opens "Please Don't Go," Willie Dixon's classic dirge moaning blues "Tollin' Bells," and the (deliberately?) out-of-tune guitar licks that open "K.C. Bound" with a bang. "Smokey Room" and "Be On Your Merry Way" were previously unreleased in the US; "Father Time" and the alternate takes of "Lonely Hours" and "Check Yourself" were previously unreleased anywhere. —*Richie Unterberger*

My Baby / 1998 / Jewel ♦♦♦♦
Lowell Fulson always moved with the times, evidenced by the fact that one of his best known tunes was the mid-'60s soul number, "Tramp." This 11-

track collection of sides recorded in the late '60s for the Shreveport, LA-based Jewel label finds him moving into blues-rock territory with an eye toward a piece of B.B. and Albert King's turf to call his own. With the Muscle Shoals rhythm section in place on most of the tracks here (appearing here uncredited, as this disc features no liner notes, recording dates or personnel, songwriter and publishing information whatsoever), the accent is more on commercial breakthrough than down-home blues. From the opening slide guitar riff on "Look at You Baby," it's clear that Lowell Fulson is in full command of his blues powers when he needs them. But his stomp down, noisy version of the Beatles' "Why Don't We Do It in the Road" shares the same seemed-like-a-good-idea-at-the-time territory as Muddy Waters' version of "Let's Spend the Night Together" and is totally devoid of any blues content whatsoever. Fulson plugs in a wah-wah on a couple of tunes and on "Don't Destroy Me," comes up with a solo that recalls both Hendrix and Stevie Ray, a long stretch from Oklahoma. While his potent slide and lead guitar work pop up here and there, this is mostly Fulson letting the band do the lion's share of the work and setting the pace. Certainly not the place to start with this prolific artist, but an interesting chapter in his career nonetheless. — *Cub Koda*

Anson Funderburgh

b. Nov. 15, 1954, Plano, TX
Guitar / Electric Texas Blues, Modern Electric Blues
In recent years, Dallas-based guitarist Anson Funderburgh has taken his band the Rockets out of the clubs and onto the festival stages with his critically acclaimed recordings for the BlackTop label out of New Orleans. With Jackson, MS-native Sam Myers delivering the vocals and harmonica treatments, this band mixes up a powerful gumbo of Texas jump blues and Delta blues that can't be found anywhere else. Funderburgh and his Rockets are a particularly hard working band, performing across the US and Europe nearly 300 nights a year.

Funderburgh was born November 15, 1954, and got hooked on the blues when he got his first guitar at age seven or eight. His first musical experiences happened in the clubs in Dallas. He developed his team approach to blues music while learning from the likes of Freddie King, Jimmy Reed, and Albert Collins when these great bluesmen were passing through Dallas-area clubs, but Funderburgh had already taught himself guitar mostly from listening to classic blues records. He never had the chance to see Muddy Waters, but he did get to play with Lightnin' Hopkins in the late '70s. Funderburgh formed the Rockets in 1978, but didn't meet Sam Myers until 1982.

Funderburgh recorded with the Fabulous Thunderbirds on their *Butt Rockin'* album, and went solo in 1981, when the New Orleans-based Black-Top label released *Talk to You by Hand,* the label's first release. Funderburgh added Myers on harmonica and lead vocals in 1986. Myers had traveled for years on the chitlin circuit, where he had the chance to accompany people like Elmore James and Robert Junior Lockwood. Funderburgh admits that adding Myers on vocals and harmonica was a turning point for the Rockets, partly because of the image they project from the stage, a big towering Black man and three White guys backing him up.

The endlessly creative Funderburgh is just coming into his prime by way

of his songwriting talents, so his career deserves close watching in the coming years. The best is yet to come from this guitarist and bandleader. — *Richard Skelly*

Talk to You by Hand / 1981 / Black Top ♦♦

She Knocks Me Out! / 1985 / Black Top ♦♦

Knock You Out / 1985 / Spindrift ♦♦♦

My Love Is Here to Stay / 1986 / Black Top ♦♦♦
This is the first record where Sam Myers (who had been performing with Robert Jr. Lockwood, Myers' latest gig in a professional career that began in the mid-'50s) joined Funderburgh's band. This successful coupling has here and since made some truly wonderful music. — *Niles J. Frantz*

Sins / 1987 / Black Top ♦♦♦♦
Sins is a good fusion of Texas and Delta blues, alternating between rocking shuffles and laidback ballads. Funderburgh's playing is tasteful—he has an enticing sound, but he never falls into grandstanding—and Sam Myers' voice is rich and his harp playing intoxicating. Furthermore, the selection of material is first-rate, featuring sharp originals and well-chosen covers from the likes of Percy Mayfield and Elmore James. The result? One of Anson Funderburgh's best albums. — *Thom Owens*

Black Top Blues a Rama Live / 1988 / Black Top ♦♦♦

Rack 'em Up / 1989 / Black Top ♦♦♦
Rack 'em Up is a straightforward blues album that demonstrates Anson Funderburgh's affection for the Texas shuffle. Nobody on the album, whether it's Funderburgh or the Kamikaze Horns, overplays their hand and it delivers the goods efficiently although without flair. — *Thom Owens*

Tell Me What I Want to Hear / 1991 / Black Top ♦♦♦♦
First-rate, contemporary Texas shuffle and blues with tasteful, biting guitar comes from Funderburgh and great vocals and harp from Mississippian Sam Myers. This is their most varied and ambitious release to date (the band seems to get better with each album). The title track was used in the movie *China Moon.* "Rent Man Blues" is a humorous dialog between Myers and guest-vocalist Carol Fran. Myers also adds an "answer" song to the blues classic "Sloppy Drunk." — *Niles J. Frantz*

● **Thru the Years: A Retrospective (1981-1992)** / 1992 / Black Top ♦♦♦♦
Thru the Years: A Retrospective (1981-1992) collects the highlights from Funderburgh's albums for Black Top, drawing from all the different bands he fronted in that decade or so. The best tracks remain his cuts with Sam Myers or Darrell Nulisch, but the finest songs from his lesser bands are included, making *Thru the Years* an excellent way to get acquainted with the modern blues guitar hero. — *Thom Owens*

Live at Grand Emporium / Jan. 17, 1995 / Black Top ♦♦♦

That's What They Want / Apr. 15, 1997 / Black Top ♦♦♦
While the name Funderburgh may not be evocative of the blues tradition, this axe-wielder can bend a string with some of the best. In fact, his prowess makes up for a weak vocal performance by Sam Myers. But the good spirit of the entire effort makes it a fun listen. Standouts include the title track and a smoking instrumental called "Mudslide." — *Tim Sheridan*

G. Love & Special Sauce

f. 1992, Philadelphia, PA

Group / Alternative Pop-Rock, Alternative Rap, Blues-Rock, Hip Hop

G. Love & Special Sauce is a trio from Philadelphia, PA. Their laidback, sloppy blues sound is quite unique, as it encompasses the sound/production of classic R&B and recent rap artists (the Beastie Boys, in particular). The group—G. Love (born Garrett Dutton) on guitar/vocals/harmonica, Jeff Clemens on drums, and Jim Prescott on upright bass—released their self-titled debut in 1994 on OKeh/Epic. It received enthusiastic reviews and nearly went gold on the strength of the MTV-spun video for "Cold Beverage." The group toured heavily, also landing a subsequent spot on the H.O.R.D.E. tour, and found a receptive young audience. They followed up this success with the more mature *Coast to Coast Motel* in 1995. Although it didn't sell as well as the debut, it was definitely a stronger album. On tour, the group nearly broke up due to bickering over finances. They decided to take a break from each other, while G. Love worked on a new album with three different bands (All Fellas Band, Philly Cartel, and King's Court) and special guest Dr. John. Soon, though, G. Love & Special Sauce made amends, and the next album featured Special Sauce plus combinations of the three other groups. *Yeah, It's That Easy* was released in October of 1997, and it turned out to be a soul-inflected effort, more similar to the debut than their second album. G. Love & Special Sauce soon embarked on another world tour. *— Greg Prato*

G. Love & Special Sauce / 1994 / Epic/OKeh ♦♦♦

Although this is G. Love & Special Sauce's most popular album (approaching gold status), it is not their best. Although there are quite a few musical surprises, the overall sound and quality of the compositions are neither as focused nor as rewarding as future releases would be. "Cold Beverage" became the band's signature tune and a fan favorite, featuring lighthearted jive lyrics and funky musical accompaniment, and its popular MTV video putting them on the map. "This Ain't Living" is a precursor to the comforting Philly soul style that would be explored more thoroughly on 1997's *Yeah, It's That Easy*. "Town to Town" adds variety to the album with its slow-as-molasses blues style. Most of the other tracks tend to blend into each other after awhile, because of their similar sound and feel ("Rhyme for the Summertime," "Shooting Hoops," etc.). Even with its mishaps, G. Love & Special Sauce's debut serves as the musical foundation on which the group would build their future sound. *— Greg Prato*

● **Coast to Coast Motel** / Sep. 19, 1995 / Epic/OKeh ♦♦♦♦

Although not as commercially successful as their self-titled debut, *Coast to Coast Motel* is a definite improvement. The band keeps their hip-hop influence (much more prevalent on the debut) in check here, concentrating more on creating a mighty instrumental groove. It's also more of a traditional rock 'n' roll approach for the band, with the results quite often being successful. The opening "Sweet Sugar Mama" is bass-driven and funky; other highlights include the smooth "Nancy," the uplifting "Chains No.3," and the startling Led Zeppelin attack (musically, anyway) of "Small Fish." "Kiss and Tell" is an obvious attempt at a hit single, while some may consider the lyrics to "Soda Pop" a bit too foolish. As mentioned earlier, however, the group achieves some great, groovy interplay which can easily suck the listener in. Jimmy Prescott's upright bass playing and Jeff Clemens' drumming are tight and locked together, as G. Love adds his scratchy blues guitar on top. These guys have found the groove. *— Greg Prato*

Yeah, It's That Easy / Oct. 28, 1997 / Epic/OKeh ♦♦♦♦

On G. Love's third release, he's joined by his trusty band, Special Sauce, as well as combinations of three others: The All Fellas Band, Philly Cartel, and King's Court. The reason for the joint effort was that prior to the writing/recording of *Yeah, It's That Easy,* the group split up. G. Love soldiered on with the three other bands, but there was a reconciliation with Special Sauce during the album's recording. Hence, others (including the legendary Dr. John on piano and organ) join in with Special Sauce. The group sheds its raw rock 'n' roll vibe, gloriously present in 1995's *Coast to Coast Motel,* and replaces it with the soothing sounds of early-'70s Philly soul. The album's approach resembles their 1994 self-titled debut more than their last release, which seems like a step back for the group. Still, the band presents plenty of compositions worthy of the G. Love & Special Sauce name, and there is more consistency and maturity with the lyrics, which deal with such heavy topics as drug abuse and senseless violence, among other things. One of the best songs, "You Shall See," sports a tribal feel, with the drums and guitar playing together percussively. And "Stepping Stones," "Lay Down the Law," and "Take You There" do a good job of introducing the listener to the band's new soul-oriented approach. The words to "I-76" are about G. Love's hometown of Philadelphia, and the title track preaches harmony between races. A solid album, but not quite as satisfying as their last. Now if the band could just mix the groove-laden music of their second album with the thoughtful lyrics of this record.... *— Greg Prato*

Bob Gaddy

b. Feb. 4, 1924, Vivian, WV

Piano, Vocals / Electric East Coast Blues

Both as a session man and featured recording artist, pianist Bob Gaddy made his presence known on the New York blues scene during the 1950s. He's still part of that circuit today. Gaddy was drafted in 1943, and that's when he began to take the 88s seriously. He picked up a little performing experience in California clubs while stationed on the West Coast before arriving in New York in 1946. Gaddy gigged with Brownie McGhee and guitarist Larry Dale around town, McGhee often playing on Gaddy's waxings for Jackson (his 1952 debut, "Bicycle Boogie"), Jax, Dot, Harlem, and from 1955 on, Hy Weiss' Old Town label. There Gaddy stayed the longest, waxing the fine "I Love My Baby," "Paper Lady," "Rip and Run," and quite a few more into 1960. Sidemen on Gaddy's Old Town sessions included guitarists Joe Ruffin and Wild Jimmy Spruill and saxist Jimmy Wright.

Since then, Gaddy hasn't recorded anything of note for domestic consumption, but like his longtime cohort Larry Dale, he remains active around New York. *— Bill Dahl*

Harlem Blues Operator / Dec. 12, 1995 / Ace ♦♦♦

Grady Gaines

b. May 14, 1934, Waskom, TX

Sax (Tenor) / Electric Texas Blues

Some of the atomic energy that Little Richard emitted nightly during the mid-'50s must have spilled onto Grady Gaines. As the hardy tenor sax blaster with Richard's road band, the Upsetters, Gaines all but blew the reed out of his horn with his galvanic solos. He wails with the same unquenchable spirit today.

The perpetually ebullient Louis Jordan was Grady's main saxman while growing up in Houston (in particular, Gaines loved his "Caldonia"). Grady wasn't the only musician in the Gaines household—brother Roy was an excellent guitarist who supplied the stinging solo on Bobby Bland's 1955 Duke waxing "It's My Life Baby" before leaving to do his own thing.

Grady was working as a session saxist at Don Robey's Duke/Peacock Records (soloing like a man possessed on Big Walter Price's "Pack Fair and Square" and proudly populating the reed section on Gatemouth Brown's searing "Dirty Work at the Crossroads") prior to getting a fateful 1955 call from Little Richard to head up his newly formed band.

Gaines recorded with the piano-pounding rock icon only sparingly—that's his storming wail on "Keep a Knockin'" and "Ooh! My Soul"—but you wouldn't know it from watching Richard's show-stopping appearances in the films *Don't Knock the Rock, The Girl Can't Help It,* and *Mr. Rock and Roll.* In every flick, Gaines is seen on screen, horn-syncing Lee Allen's sax solos!

The Upsetters remained intact long after Richard flipped out and joined the ministry in 1957. They hit the road with Dee Clark (then a Richard clone himself), Little Willie John, Sam Cooke, James Brown, Jackie Wilson, and Joe Tex. The band recorded for Vee-Jay in 1958 behind Clark and with Upsetters vocalist/saxist Wilbert Smith, who went by the name of Lee Diamond and hailed from New Orleans. More sessions at Vee-Jay, Gee, Fire, and Little Star (where they briefly reunited with Richard) followed.

After the Upsetters broke up, Grady hit the road with a variety of R&B luminaries, including Millie Jackson and Curtis Mayfield, before retiring in 1980. Fortunately, he decided to strap his horn back on in 1985, playing in Houston until Black Top Records cajoled him into cutting *Full Gain,* a veritable Houston blues motherlode, in 1988. Brother Roy Gaines, pianist Teddy Reynolds, guitarist Clarence Hollimon, and singer Joe Medwick were all involved in the project. *Horn of Plenty* followed on Black Top in 1992. Gaines and his entourage continue to blow up a Texas-sized storm wherever they touch down. —*Bill Dahl*

● **Full Gain** / 1988 / Black Top ◆◆◆◆
A meeting of Houston-based all-stars that scorches from the first track to the last. Tenor saxman Grady Gaines is in charge of the proceedings, wailing on the instrumentals "There Is Something on Your Mind" and "Soul Twist," while pianist Teddy Reynolds, Gaines' guitar-wielding brother Roy Gaines, and Joe Medwick divvy up the vocals. Outstanding guitarist Clarence Hollimon is also on board. —*Bill Dahl*

Horn of Plenty / 1992 / Black Top ◆◆◆
Gaines is surrounded by more vocal talent this time—Carol Fran, Teddy Reynolds, and Gaines' Texas Upsetters pals Big Robert Smith and Paul David Roberts. Hollimon and Anson Funderburgh are the guitar heroes this time, as Gaines whips up another Lone Star-size sax storm with his lusty tenor. —*Bill Dahl*

The Gales Brothers

f. Memphis, TN
Group / Modern Electric Blues
The Gales Brothers, all born and raised in the same house in Memphis, have all forged their own musical paths in the blues world, but when the three get together for a live performance or a studio outing, a treat is in store for the blues guitar aficionado. Eric and Eugene formed the Eric Gales Band, while Manuel (b. Dec. 4, 1968) took the stage name Little Jimmy King (after Jimi Hendrix and Albert King). King has recorded two albums for the Bullseye Blues/Rounder label, *Little Jimmy King and the Memphis Soul Survivors* and *Something Inside of Me.* Eric, however, was the first family member to break out; at age 15, he signed his first recording contract and released two albums, *The Eric Gales Band* and *Picture of a Thousand Faces.* By 1991, the critics were calling him the next guitar prodigy; Gales won a poll in *Guitar World* magazine as "Best New Talent," appeared several times on *The Arsenio Hall Show,* and found some prominent fans in Eric Clapton, Keith Richards, and Mick Jagger. As a unit, the Gales Brothers released one album, *Left Hand Brand,* on the House of Blues/Private Music label in March, 1995. Although House of Blues has since formed an alliance with another label and Private Music was consolidated into another unit of BMG, the record should still be available. While the Gales brothers have played together all of their lives, this remains the first time they've ever recorded together in a good studio. Recorded at House of Blues Studios in Memphis, it was produced by David Z., who has also worked with Prince, the Fine Young Cannibals, and Big Head Todd and the Monsters. —*Richard Skelly*

Left Hand Brand / Mar. 26, 1995 / House of Blues ◆◆◆

Rory Gallagher

b. Mar. 2, 1949, Ballyshannon, Ireland, **d.** Jun. 14, 1995, London, England
Guitar, Vocals, Harmonica / Blues-Rock, British Blues
For a career that was cut short by illness and a premature death, guitarist, singer, and songwriter Rory Gallagher sure accomplished a lot in the blues music world. Although Gallagher didn't tour the US nearly enough, spending most of his time in Europe, he was known for his no-holds-barred, marathon live shows at clubs and theaters around the United States.

Gallagher was born in Ballyshannon, County Donegal, Irish Republic on March 2, 1949. He passed away from complications owing to liver transplant surgery on June 14, 1995, at age 46. Shortly after his birth, his family moved to Cork City in the south, and at age nine, he became fascinated with American blues and folk singers he heard on the radio. An avid record collector, he had a wide range of influences including Leadbelly, Buddy Guy, Freddie King, Albert King, Muddy Waters, and John Lee Hooker. Gallagher would always try to mix some simple country blues songs onto his recordings.

Gallagher began his recording career after moving to London, when he formed a trio called Taste. The group's self-titled debut album was released in 1969 in England and later picked up for US distribution by Atco/Atlantic. Between 1969 and 1971, with producer Tony Colton behind the board, Gallagher recorded three albums with the group before they split up. Gallagher began performing under his own name in 1971, after recording his 1970 debut, *Rory Gallagher* for Polydor Records in the UK. The album was picked up for US distribution by Atlantic Records, and later that year he recorded *Deuce,* also released by Atlantic in the US.

His prolific output continued, as he followed up *Deuce* with *Live in Europe* (1972) and *Blueprint* and *Tatoo,* both in 1973. *Irish Tour 1974,* like *Live in Europe,* did a good job of capturing the excitement of his live shows on tape, and he followed that with *Calling Card* for Chrysalis in 1976, and *Photo Finish* and *Jinx* for the same label in 1978 and 1982. By this point Gallagher had made several world tours, and he took a few years rest from the road. He got back into recording and performing live again with the 1987 release of *Defender.* His last album, *Fresh Evidence,* was released in 1991 on the Capo/I.R.S. label. Capo was his own record and publishing company that he set up in the hopes of eventually exposing other great blues talents.

Some of Gallagher's best work on record wasn't under his own name, it's stuff he recorded with Muddy Waters on *The London Sessions* (Chess, 1972) and with Albert King on *Live* (RCA/Utopia). Gallagher made his last US tours in 1985 and 1991, and admitted in interviews that he'd always been a guitarist who fed off the instant reaction and feedback a live audience can provide.

In a 1991 interview, he told this writer: "I try to sit down and write a Rory Gallagher song, which generally happens to be quite bluesy. I try to find different issues, different themes and different topics that haven't been covered before... I've done songs in all the different styles... train blues, drinking blues, economic blues. But I try to find a slightly different angle on all these things. The music can be very traditional, but you can sort of creep into the future with the lyrics."

For a good introduction to Gallagher's unparalleled prowess as a guitarist, singer and songwriter, pick up *Irish Tour 1974, Calling Card* or *Fresh Evidence,* all available on compact disc. —*Richard Skelly*

Deuce / 1971 / Atlantic ◆◆
On *Deuce,* Rory Gallagher was just beginning to develop a distinctive style. He doesn't quite have all of the elements mastered yet—his concentration seems to slip on certain tracks, while other cuts aren't particularly strong songs—but it's fascinating to hear him forge something new out of his Chicago blues roots. —*Thom Owens*

Rory Gallagher / 1971 / Atlantic ◆◆◆
Rory Gallagher's eponymous debut is an entertaining, but relatively undistinguished collection of blues-rock, highlighted by his flash slide guitar. —*Thom Owens*

Live in Europe/Stage Struck / 1972 / IRS ◆◆◆
The live album *Live in Europe/Stage Struck* captures Rory Gallagher at his finest, as he tears his way through many of his very best songs. Though the performance quality is a little uneven, there are gems scattered throughout the record, including smoking versions of "Messin' with the Kid" and "Laundromat." —*Thom Owens*

Blueprint / 1973 / Polydor ♦♦

Tattoo / 1973 / Castle ♦♦♦

Rory Gallagher forges a distinctive style on *Tattoo,* one of his strongest albums. Working with a tight quartet, he's given a solid foundation for his terrific solos—it's especially exciting to hear him supported by a piano. All of the players deliver with conviction and studied passion, which makes the record an exciting listen. —*Thom Owens*

Irish Tour '74 / 1974 / IRS ♦♦♦♦

With *Irish Tour '74,* Rory Gallagher hit his highwater mark. Recorded live on his successful 1973 tour, Gallagher displays a remarkable empathy with his band, as they both churn out crunching riffs and fluid, soulful solos. Many of his best songs are included on the set and these versions far eclipse the studio versions. —*Thom Owens*

Calling Card / 1976 / IRS ♦♦♦♦

Following the excellent live set *Irish Tour '74,* Rory Gallagher delivered his best studio album, *Calling Card.* The record captures the dynamic interplay between the guitarist and his band—they burn with a roaring intensity. It also doesn't hurt that the songs are the best batch that Gallagher ever came up with for a record. The combination of top-notch performances and first-rate songs equals the hardest-edged and most rewarding studio set the guitarist ever cut. —*Thom Owens*

Photo-Finish / 1978 / Chrysalis ♦♦

Gallagher was coasting with this record, which doesn't mean that it's a particularly bad record—just a little more laidback than usual. Features some good stuff, with standouts including "Brute Force and Ignorance." —*Steven McDonald*

Top Priority / 1979 / IRS ♦♦

● **Edged in Blue** / 1992 / Edsel ♦♦♦♦

Edged in Blue is a solid, if not exactly definitive, retrospective of Rory Gallagher's career that offers a fine introduction to the British blues star. —*Thom Owens*

Calling Hard (Pts. 1 & 2) / 1992 / Castle ♦♦

Tattoo/Blueprint / Jul. 1, 1992 / Castle ♦♦♦

Cecil Gant

b. Apr. 4, 1913, Nashville, TN, **d.** Feb. 4, 1951, Nashville, TN
Vocals, Piano / R&B, Piano Blues, West Coast Blues
Pianist Cecil Gant seemingly materialized out of the wartime mist to create one of the most enduring blues ballads of the 1940s. Gant was past age 30 when he burst onto the scene in a most unusual way—he popped up in military uniform at a Los Angeles war bonds rally sponsored by the Treasury Department. Private Gant proceeded to electrify the assembled multitude with his piano prowess, leading to his imminent 1944 debut on Oakland's Gilt-Edge Records: the mellow pop-slanted ballad "I Wonder," which topped the R&B charts despite a wartime shellac shortage that hit tiny independent companies like Gilt-Edge particularly hard. Its flip, the considerably more animated "Cecil's Boogie," was a hit in its own right.

Pvt. Gant shot to the upper reaches of the R&B charts for Gilt-Edge like a guided missile with his "Grass Is Getting Greener Every Day" and "I'm Tired" in 1945, recording prolifically for the imprint before switching over to the Bullet label for the 1948 smash "Another Day—Another Dollar" and 1949's "I'm a Good Man but a Poor Man" (in between those two, Gant also hit with "Special Delivery" for Four Star). Urbane after-hours blues, refined ballads, torrid boogies—Gant ran the gamut during a tumultuous few years in the record business (he also turned up on King, Imperial, Dot, and Swing Time/Down Beat), but it didn't last. His "We're Gonna Rock" for Decca in 1950 (as Gunter Lee Carr) presaged the rise of rock 'n' roll later in the decade, but Gant wouldn't be around to view its ascendancy; the one-time "G.I. Sing-Sation" died in 1952 at the premature age of 38. —*Bill Dahl*

Cecil Gant / 1958 / King ♦♦♦

● **Rock Little Baby** / 1976 / Flyright ♦♦♦♦

British record collectors were hip to 1940s boogie and blues pianist Cecil Gant long before American aficionados were (not that there's much recognition of him here even now). Flyright assembled this vinyl slab of Gant goodies in loving tribute, with titles like "Screwy Boogie," "Owl Stew," and the stinging "Rock Little Baby" among the upbeat highlights. Gant's "I'm a Good

Man, But a Poor Man" has been adapted by many blues artists since the pianist waxed this one. —*Bill Dahl*

Cecil Boogie / 1976 / Flyright ♦♦♦♦

A second generous helping of boogies and blues by "the G.I. Sing-Sation," as Pvt. Gant was billed on his earliest mid-'40s sides for Gilt-Edge. His thundering boogie piano style on "We're Gonna Rock," "Nashville Jumps," and "Cecil Boogie" presaged the rise of rock 'n' roll. —*Bill Dahl*

Killer Diller Boogie / 1979 / Magpie ♦♦♦

Cecil Gant / Oct. 7, 1997 / Flyright ♦♦♦

I'm Still Singing the Blues Today / Oldie Blues ♦♦♦♦

Gant only recorded during the immediate postwar era, but he was remarkably prolific during those years. Here we have 20 more gems in the pianist's inimitable style—boogies, blues, ballads, even his personalized rendition of "Coming Round the Mountain!" —*Bill Dahl*

Terry Garland

b. Jun. 3, 1953, Johnson City, TN
Guitar / Modern Acoustic Blues
A country-blues interpreter who plays a National steel-body guitar, often with a slide, in the style of Bukka White and Fred McDowell. —*Niles J. Frantz*

● **Trouble in Mind** / 1991 / First Warning ♦♦♦♦

Garland's National guitar sounds great on this CD. Mark Wenner backs him up on harmonica. Garland can sing the blues, and he chose some big-time blues artists' songs to cover (Willie Dixon, Willie McTell, Johnny Winter, Jimmy Reed). —*Chip Renner*

Edge of the Valley / 1992 / First Warning ♦♦♦

One to Blame / Aug. 20, 1996 / Demon ♦♦♦♦

Like Terry Garland's two albums for RCA, *The One to Blame* is an engaging collection of contemporary country-blues and rock 'n' roll reconfigured to sound like country-blues. Among the highlights are "Stagger Lee," "Closer Walk with Thee," "Rollin' and Tumblin'," and "It'll Be Me." —*Stephen Thomas Erlewine*

Larry Garner

b. Jul. 8, 1952, New Orleans, LA
Guitar, Vocals / Electric Louisiana Blues
Folks in Europe were hip to Larry Garner long before most blues fans in the states. The Baton Rouge guitarist had already toured extensively overseas, with two British albums to his credit, before Verve issued his stunning domestic debut, *You Need to Live a Little,* in 1995. Rooted in the swamp blues tradition indigenous to his Baton Rouge environs, Garner brings a laudable contemporary sensibility and witty composing skills to his craft.

Inspired by local swamp bluesmen Silas Hogan and Clarence Edwards, Larry Garner learned how to play guitar from his uncle and a couple of gospel-playing elders. After completing his military service in Korea, he returned to Baton Rouge and embarked on a part-time musical career (he worked at a Dow chemical plant for almost two decades until his recent retirement).

The British JSP label released Garner's first two albums: *Double Blues* and *Too Blues* (the latter an ironic slap at an unidentified tin-eared US blues label boss who deemed Garner's demo tape "too blues"). With the emergence of *You Need to Live a Little,* where Garner delivers creative originals detailing the difficulty of keeping "Four Cars Running" and the universal pain of suffering through "Another Bad Day," Larry Garner is poised for 21st-century blues stardom. —*Bill Dahl*

Too Blues / Oct. 31, 1994 / JSP ♦♦♦♦

● **You Need to Little a Little** / 1995 / Polygram ♦♦♦♦

A witty, imaginative songwriter, crisply concise guitarist, and convincing singer, Baton Rouge Larry Garner is the proverbial triple threat—and a good bet to rise to blues stardom in the immediate future. His major-label debut is a wondrous collection filled with songs that don't embrace simple cliches ("Four Cars Running," "Another Bad Day," and "Shak Bully" are anything but routine). "Miracles of Time" is almost pop-soul in its structure, while "Rats and Roaches in My Kitchen," Garner's lowdown tribute to swamp blues pioneer Silas Hogan, benefits from Sonny Landreth's burrowing slide guitar. —*Bill Dahl*

Double Dues / 1995 / JSP ✦✦✦

Standing Room Only / May 5, 1998 / A&M ✦✦✦

Although his songwriting slips a little here ("PMS" was an idea that should have never been executed), *Standing Room Only* confirms Larry Garner's position as a tough blues guitarist and dynamic performer. Despite a few weak cuts, there's still a number of very strong songs, and Garner's flair for gritty, swampy performances makes the album quite enjoyable—it just falls a little short of the high quality of his previous masterworks. — *Thom Owens*

J. Geils Band

f. 1967, Boston, MA, db. 1985
Group / Blues-Rock, Rock 'n' Roll, Pop-Rock

The J. Geils Band were one of the most popular touring rock 'n' roll bands in America during the '70s. Where their contemporaries were influenced by the heavy boogie of British blues-rock and the ear-splitting sonic adventures of psychedelia, the J. Geils Band were a bar band pure and simple, churning out greasy covers of obscure R&B, doo-wop, and soul tunes, cutting them with healthy dose of Stonesy swagger. While their muscular sound and the hyper jive of frontman Peter Wolf packed arenas across America, it only rarely earned them hit singles. Seth Justman, the group's main songwriter, could turn out catchy R&B-based rockers like "Give It To Me" or "Must of Got Lost," but these hits never led to stardom, primarily because the group had trouble capturing the energy of their live sound in the studio. In the early '80s, the group tempered their driving rock with some pop, and the makeover paid off with the massive hit single "Centerfold," which stayed at number one for six weeks. By the time the band prepared to record a followup, tensions between Justman and Wolf had grown considerably, resulting in Wolf's departure, which quickly led to the band's demise. After working for years to reach to top of the charts, the J. Geils couldn't stay there once they finally achieved their goal.

Guitarist Jerome Geils, bassist Danny Klein, and harpist Magic Dick (born Richard Salwitz) began performing as an acoustic blues trio sometime in the mid-'60s. In 1967, drummer Stephen Jo Bladd and vocalist Peter Wolf joined the group, and the band went electric. Before joining the J. Geils Band, Bladd and Wolf played together in the Boston-based rock revivalist band the Hallucinations. Both musicians shared a love of arcane doo-wop, blues, R&B and rock 'n' roll, and Wolf had become well-known by spinning such obscure singles as a jive-talking WBCN DJ called Woofuh Goofuh. Wolf and Bladd's specialized tastes became a central force in the newly revamped J. Geils Band, who positioned themselves as tough, '50s greasers in opposition to the colorful psychedelic rockers that dominated the East Coast in the late '60s. Soon, the band had earned a sizable local following, including Seth Justman, an organist who was studying at Boston University. Justman joined the band in 1968, and the band continued to tour for the next few years, landing a record contract with Atlantic in 1970.

The J. Geils Band was a regional hit upon its early 1970 release, and it earned favorable reviews, especially from *Rolling Stone*. The group's second album, *The Morning After*, appeared later that year and, thanks to the Top 40 hit "Looking for a Love," the album expanded their following. However, the band continued to win new fans primarily through their concerts, so it was no surprise that their third album, 1972's *Full House*, was a live set. It was followed by *Bloodshot*, a record that climbed into the Top 10 on the strength of the Top 40 hit, "Give It To Me." Following the relative failure of 1973's *Ladies Invited*, the band had another hit with 1974's *Nightmares*, which featured the number 12 single "Must of Got Lost." While their live shows remained popular throughout the mid-'70s, both *Hot Line* (1975) and the live *Blow Your Face Out* (1976) were significant commercial disappointments. The band revamped their sound and shortened their name to "Geils" for 1977's *Monkey Island*. While the album received good reviews, the record failed to bring the group increased sales.

In 1978, the J. Geils Band left Atlantic Records for EMI, releasing *Sanctuary* later that year. *Sanctuary* slowly gained a following, becoming their first gold album since *Bloodshot*. *Love Stinks* (1980) expanded the group's following even more, peaking at number 18 in the charts and setting the stage for 1981's *Freeze-Frame*, the band's highwater mark. Supported by the infectious single "Centerfold"—which featured a memorable video that received heavy MTV airplay—and boasting a sleek, radio-ready sound, *Freeze-Frame* climbed to number one. "Centerfold" shot to the top of the charts late in

1981, spending six weeks at number one; its followup, "Freeze-Frame," was nearly as successful, reaching number four in the spring of 1982. The live album *Showtime!* became a gold album shortly after its late 1982 release. While the band was experiencing the greatest commercial success of their career, relationships between the members, particularly writing partners Justman and Wolf, were volatile. When the band refused to record material Wolf had written with Don Covay and Michael Jonzun, he left the band in the middle of a 1983 recording session. Justman assumed lead vocals, and the group released *You're Gettin' Even While I'm Gettin' Odd* in late 1984, several months after Wolf's successful solo debut, *Lights Out*. The J. Geils Band's record was a failure, and the band broke up in 1985. Magic Dick and Geils, calling himself Jay instead of Jerome, reunited in 1993 to form the contemporary blues band, Bluestime. — *Stephen Thomas Erlewine*

The J. Geils Band / 1970 / Atlantic ✦✦✦✦

Their debut paid homage to the likes of Otis Rush, John Lee Hooker, and Motown through blistering covers, but originals such as "Wait" and "What's Your Hurry" more than hold their own. Magic Dick steals the show on this one. — *John Floyd*

The Morning After / 1971 / Atlantic ✦✦✦

It's rare when a group's sophomore effort is as good as their debut. *The Morning After* by the J. Geils Band is that, and in some ways, even better. Tighter and more focused than their debut, the band found success on the singles charts with "Looking for a Love." Again, they laid original material alongside blues covers, but the sound was always their own—exciting, enjoyable rocking blues. — *James Chrispell*

Full House Live / 1972 / Atlantic ✦✦✦

Live is the way the J. Geils Band should be experienced; they put on a show like few others, and *Full House* is the proof. From start to finish, there is not one bad cut. From the opener, "First I Look at the Purse" right on through "Looking for a Love," these guys don't give up an inch. — *James Chrispell*

Bloodshot / 1973 / Atlantic ✦✦

More hot, rockin' rhythm & blues from these guys out of Boston. *Bloodshot* includes their Top 40 hit "Give It To Me," as well as the great opener, "(Ain't Nothin' But A) House Party," plus soulful struts and bluesy shuffles in between. It's a wonder these guys could tour almost constantly and still turn out great albums one after another. On *Bloodshot*, the J. Geils Band make it appear easy. — *James Chrispell*

Ladies Invited / 1973 / Atlantic ✦✦✦

On this, their first album of all original material, something appeared to be amiss. Perhaps it was road fatigue—only the band knows for sure, but *Ladies Invited* didn't burn up the charts like their previous efforts, nor did it have that all-important hit single. It's well done and worthwhile, but lacks spark. — *James Chrispell*

Nightmares. . . and Other Tales from the Vinyl Jungle / 1974 / Atlantic ✦✦✦

After a brief sidestep, the J. Geils Band came roaring back with a very urban-jungle sort of album which percolates with beat and rocks with enthusiastic excitement. Here lies the reggae-ish "Give It To Me," as well as the concert staple "Detroit Breakdown." A fertile release from some of the hardest rockers of the seventies. — *James Chrispell*

Hotline / 1975 / Atlantic ✦✦

It appears that with *Hotline* the J. Geils Band backtracked a bit by including a few new originals alongside proven R&B workouts in what one is tempted to call a formula. But *Hotline* is still well worth listening to; it includes "Love-itis," which is entirely worth the price of the rest. — *James Chrispell*

Blow Your Face Out / 1976 / Atlantic ✦✦✦

If you're looking to put on a party record from the mid-seventies, grab a hold of *Blow Your Face Out* and crank up the volume. Always known as a great live band, J. Geils and Co. stomp through one of the most exciting live sets put on vinyl (and tape and CD). The title says it all. — *James Chrispell*

Monkey Island / 1977 / Atlantic ✦✦✦✦

One of the great lost albums, *Monkey Island* is where the Geils Band make the blues their own. It's an elaborately produced, adventurous set that analyzes their commerical failure and looks for answers to hard-to-ask questions. Unlike their 1972 live album *Full House*, *Monkey Island* refuses to pander to blues conservatists or boogie-rock hammerheads; the album is steeped in the kind of pathos and bitterness that infuse the Stones' *Sticky*

Fingers. The album flopped, but it remains the group's most personal statement. —*John Floyd*

Sanctuary / 1978 / EMI America ✦✦✦
The Geils sound is retooled into a streamlined shuffle that owes much to production and songwriting floriation of keyboardist Seth Justman. Their soul and blues chops are still apparent, but they've worked them into a sound that manages to elaborate on the experiments of *Monkey Island* while still paying homage to their early days. —*John Floyd*

The Best of the J. Geils Band / 1979 / Atlantic ✦✦✦✦
Pulling the decent material from these otherwise unspectacular mid-'70s albums makes this an adequate overview of the band's achievements. It's the best place to sample such minor hits as "Must of Got Lost" and "Give It To Me." —*John Floyd*

Love Stinks / 1980 / EMI America ✦✦✦
The title cut brought the band an across-the-board hit, and the near new wave production touches don't get in the way of the crack rhythm section or Geils' tasty leads. A new sound for a new decade. —*John Floyd*

Freeze Frame / 1981 / EMI America ✦✦✦✦
Tempering their bar-band R&B with a touch of new wave pop production, the J. Geils Band finally broke through into the big leagues with *Freeze Frame.* Fans of the hard-driving rock of the group's '70s albums will find the sleek sound of *Freeze Frame* slightly disorienting, but the production gives the album cohesion. Good-time rock 'n' roll remains at the core of the group's music, but the sound of the record is glossier, shining with synthesizers and big pop hooks. With its sing-along chorus, "Centerfold" exemplifies this trend, but it's merely the tip of the iceberg. "Freeze Frame" has a great stopstart chorus, "Flamethrower" and "Piss on the Wall" rush along on hardboogie riffs, and "Angel in Blue" is terrific neo-doo wop. There's still a handful of throwaways, but even the filler has a stylized, synthesized flair that makes it enjoyable, and the keepers are among the band's best. —*Stephen Thomas Erlewine*

Showtime! / 1982 / EMI America ✦✦

You're Gettin' Even While I'm Gettin' Odd / 1984 / EMI ✦✦

Flashback / 1988 / EMI America ✦✦✦
Flashback is a brief but entertaining overview of the J. Geils Band's early '80s hits, featuring the hit singles "Centerfold," "Freeze Frame," "Flamethrower," "Love Stinks," "I Do," and "Just Can't Wait." —*Stephen Thomas Erlewine*

● **Houseparty: Anthology** / 1992 / Rhino ✦✦✦✦
The superb two-disc anthology *Houseparty* concentrates on the rousing, fullthrottle blues-boogie of their heyday, including a full album's worth of live material (ten songs from their three live albums). The pop success of *Love Stinks* and *Freeze Frame* makes sense in the context of the set, but the songs that cut the deepest are the blues-rock numbers on the first disc and the live songs. Thankfully, the compilers (*Trouser Press* editor Ira Robbins and band members Peter Wolf and Seth Justman) end *Houseparty* with three songs from *Sanctuary,* helping secure the image of the J. Geils Band as one of America's top rock 'n' roll groups. —*Stephen Thomas Erlewine*

Clifford Gibson

b. Apr. 17, 1901, Louisville, KY, **d.** Dec. 21, 1963, St. Louis, MO
Guitar, Vocals / Prewar Country Blues, Acoustic Memphis Blues
Though not a particularly great singer, Clifford "Grandpappy" Gibson was an excellent guitarist, among the finest pure players in country blues. Gibson moved from Kentucky to St. Lous in the '20s, where he lived the remainder of his life. He frequently played St. Louis clubs during the '20s and '30s, and began recording for QRS and Victor in 1929. Greatly influenced by Lonnie Johnson, Gibson also accompanied Jimmie Rodgers on a Victor single in 1931, then spent parts of the next three decades playing in the streets around St. Louis. Gibson resurfaced on recordings in 1960 with a Bobbin date, and worked another three years in St. Louis' Gaslight Square before his death in 1963. —*Ron Wynn*

● **Beat You Doing It** / 1972 / Yazoo ✦✦✦✦
Beat You Doing It contains all of the prime tracks Clifford Gibson recorded, offering an excellent, concise overview of the country blues guitarist. —*Thom Owens*

Complete Recorded Works (1929-1931) / 1991 / Document ✦✦✦✦
Document's 23-track collection *Complete Recorded Works* presents everything Clifford Gibson recorded between 1929-1931. Since Gibson was a fine guitarist but not an exceptional vocalist, this is primarily of interest only to diehard country-blues fans. And those casual fans who do want a taste of Gibson are better served by Yazoo's more concise collection, *Beat You Doing It.* —*Thom Owens*

Lacy Gibson

b. May 1, 1936, South Carolina
Guitar, Vocals / Electric Chicago Blues, Modern Electric Chicago Blues
Slowly returning to musical action following major surgery, guitarist Lacy Gibson has been an underappreciated figure on the Windy City circuit for decades.

Lacy and his family left North Carolina for Chicago in 1949. It didn't take long for Gibson to grow entranced by the local action—he learned from veterans Sunnyland Slim and Muddy Waters and picked up pointers from immaculate axemen Lefty Bates, Matt "Guitar" Murphy, and Wayne Bennett. Gibson made a name for himself as a session player in 1963, assuming rhythm guitar duties on sides by Willie Mabon for USA, Billy "The Kid" Emerson for M-Pac!, and Buddy Guy on Chess. Gibson made his vocal debut on the self-penned blues ballad "My Love Is Real" at Chess the same year, though it wasn't released at the time (when it belatedly emerged, it was mistakenly attributed to Guy).

A couple of bargain basement 45s for the remarkably obscure Repeto logo (that's precisely where they were done—in Lacy Gibson's basement!) preceded Gibson's inconsistent album debut for then-brother-in-law Sun Ra's El Saturn label. Ralph Bass produced an album by Gibson in 1977, but the results weren't issued at the time (Delmark is currently releasing the set domestically).

A stint as Son Seals' rhythm axeman (he's on Seals' *Live and Burning* LP) provided an entree to Alligator Records, which included four fine sides by Gibson on its second batch of *Living Chicago Blues* anthologies in 1980. Best of all was a Dick Shurman-produced album for the Dutch Black Magic logo in 1982, *Switchy Titchy,* that brilliantly spotlighted Gibson's clean fretwork and hearty vocals. After he regained his health in the mid-'90s, Lacy Gibson entered the studio and recorded *Crying for My Baby,* which was released in 1996. —*Bill Dahl*

● **Switchy Titchy** / 1982 / Black Magic ✦✦✦✦
Switchy Titchy is the best record Lacy Gibson has recorded to date. Gibson's variation on Chicago blues includes some horns pinched from Southern soul-blues records, and it's a little bit more laidback than the pile-driving sound often associated with the style. He makes up for the relaxed pace with his round, clean guitar tones and big, powerful vocals, both of which are spotlighted throughout *Switchy Titchy.* Best of all, that playing is married to a strong song selection, featuring a couple of originals and a lot of forgotten classics. That unpredictable song selection makes the entire album sound fresh and lifts the record above many of its modern blues peers. —*Thom Owens*

Crying for My Baby / 1996 / Delmark ✦✦✦

Jazz Gillum (William McKinley Gillum)

b. Sep. 11, 1904, Indianola, MS, **d.** Mar. 29, 1966, Chicago, IL
Harmonica, Vocals / Urban, Chicago Blues, Acoustic Chicago Blues
Next to John Lee "Sonny Boy" Williamson, no harmonica player was as popular or as much in demand on recording sessions during the '30s as Jazz Gillum. His high, reedy sound meshed perfectly on dozens of hokum sides on the Bluebird label, both as a sideman and as a leader.

Born in Indianola, MS (B.B. King's birthplace as well) in 1904, Gillum was evidently teaching himself how to play harmonica by the tender age of six. After running away from home in 1911 to live with relatives in Charleston, MS, Jazz spent the next dozen or so years working a day job and spending his weekends playing for tips on local streetcorners. When he visited Chicago in 1923, he found the environment very much to his liking and put down roots there.

There he met guitarist Big Bill Broonzy and the two of them started working club dates around the city as a duo. By 1934, Gillum started popping up on recording dates for ARC and later Bluebird, RCA Victor's budget label.

This association would prove to be a lasting as Chicago producer Lester Melrose frequently called on Gillum as a sideman—as well as cutting sides on his own—as part of the "Bluebird beat" house band. His career seemed to screech to a halt when the label folded in the late '40s and aside from a Memphis Slim session in 1961, he seems to have been largely inactive throughout the '50s until his death from a gunshot wound as a result of an argument in 1966. —*Cub Koda*

Roll Dem Bones 1938-49 / 1938-1949 / Wolf ✦✦✦✦
Roll Dem Bones 1938-49 rounds up a number of sides not issued on the Document series, offering good insight into the final days of Jazz Gillum's career. While it isn't the first place to go—RCA's concise and comprehensive *Bluebird Recordings 1934-1938* holds that title—it nevertheless is a welcome addition to any serious blues historian that has all the Document reissues. —*Thom Owens*

Complete Recorded Works, Vol. 1 (1936-1938) / Jun. 2, 1994 / Document ✦✦✦

Complete Recorded Works, Vol. 2 / Jun. 2, 1994 / Document ✦✦✦

Complete Recorded Works, Vol. 3 / Jun. 2, 1994 / Document ✦✦✦

Complete Recorded Works, Vol. 4 / Jun. 2, 1994 / Document ✦✦✦

● **The Bluebird Recordings 1934-1938** / Feb. 25, 1997 / RCA ✦✦✦✦
The Bluebird Recordings 1934-1938 is the best CD retrospective yet assembled of Jazz Gillum's peak years, offering 22 tracks—including such songs as "Early in the Morning," "Don't Scandalize My Name," "Alberta Blues," "Just Like Jessie James," "Reefer Head Woman," "Worried and Bothered," and "Good Old 51 Highway"—that find him at his easygoing best. Document's multi-volume series may be a more complete overview of his works, but this remains the best summation of his strengths and talents. —*Thom Owens*

Lloyd Glenn

b. Nov. 21, 1909, San Antonio, TX, **d.** May 23, 1985, Los Angeles, CA
Piano / Piano Blues, West Coast Blues, Jump Blues
As an integral behind-the-scenes fixture on the L.A. postwar blues scene, pianist/arranger/A&R man Lloyd Glenn had few equals. His rolling ivories anchored many of Lowell Fulson's best waxings for Swing Time and Checker, and he scored his own major hits on Swing Time with the imaginative instrumentals "Old Time Shuffle Blues" in 1950 and "Chica Boo" the next year. Glenn was already an experienced musician when he left the Lone Star state for sunny California in 1942. His early sessions there included backing T-Bone Walker at the 1947 Capitol date that produced the guitarist's immortal "Call It Stormy Monday." Glenn recorded for the first time under his own name the same year for Imperial with his band, the Joymakers, which included guitarist Gene Phillips, saxist Marshall Royal, and singer Geraldine Carter.

Massively constructed guitarist Tiny Webb introduced Glenn to Swing Time owner Jack Lauderdale in 1949, inaugurating a five-year stint as A&R man at the firm for Glenn. After Swing Time's demise, the pianist moved to Aladdin Records, issuing more catchy instrumentals for Eddie Mesner's firm through 1959. There was also an isolated session for Imperial in 1962 that produced "Twistville" and "Young Date." The pianist remained active into the 1980s, often touring as Big Joe Turner's accompanist. —*Bill Dahl*

After Hours / 1957 / Oldie Blues ✦✦✦✦
Solid collection of instrumentals recorded mid-'70s. In and out of print. —*AMG*

Piano Styling / 1957 / Score ✦✦✦✦
Glenn's tasty piano ticklings were to the fore on this 1950s sides for the Mesners' Aladdin logo. The dozen instrumentals on this LP (still not on CD) include remakes of "Chica-Boo" and "Old Time Shuffle" and the engaging workouts "Tiddleywinks," "Glenn's Glide," "Nite-Flite," "Footloose," and "Southbound Special." —*Bill Dahl*

Honky Tonk Train / 1983 / Night Train ✦✦✦✦
In addition to waxing his own bouncy instrumentals during his late-'40s/early-'50s stay at Swing Time Records (an unissued take of "Old Time Shuffle," one of his own hits, graces this disc), pianist Lloyd Glenn also arranged and played behind several of the firm's veteran vocalists—explaining the presence of exceptional blues outings by Joe Pullum and Jesse Thomas. —*Bill Dahl*

● **Chica Boo** / 1988 / Night Train ✦✦✦✦
Quite a bit of duplication between this 18-song collection and Night Train's previous disc—but since this one contains both of his hits—"Old Time Shuffle" and "Chica Boo"—it wins hands down. Pullum and Thomas are back as guest vocalists on these 1947-1952 waxings. This is lightly swinging West Coast blues with an elegant, understated edge, Glenn's tasty approach to the 88s always in the pocket. —*Bill Dahl*

Lloyd Glenn / 198 / Swingtime ✦✦✦

Old Time Shuffle / Black & Blue ✦✦✦
European sessions from the late '70s. Swinging piano throughout, showing off Glenn's patented Texas-cum-West-Coast lope to good advantage. —*Cub Koda*

Barry Goldberg

b. 1941, Chicago, IL
Piano, Organ, Keyboards, Vocals / Electric Chicago Blues
Barry Goldberg was a regular fixture in the White blues firmament of the mid-'60s that seemed to stretch from Chicago to New York. A keyboardist (organ seemed to be his specialty), Barry was an in-demand session man—he appears with Michael Bloomfield on a Mitch Ryder album, for instance—along with Al Kooper, and his blues playing contemporary from the original Butterfield band, Mark Naftalin. Goldberg was a member of Charlie Musselwhite's first band, contributing great piano and organ lines to the *Stand Back!* album (his work on "Cristo Redentor" is moody and introspective, with a strong jazz-inflected feel, while still retaining strong blues roots) and a handful of others throughout the decade. —*Cub Koda*

Blowing My Mind / 1966 / Epic ✦✦✦

The Barry Goldberg Reunion / 1968 / One Way ✦✦✦✦

● **Two Jews Blues** / 1969 / One Way ✦✦✦✦
This is one of those late-'60s collaborations where I expected the world to explode when I put it on, and felt disappointed when it didn't. However, when you get past looking at players in the band, and listen to the music, there are a number of wonderful cuts. Enough of them for me to replace the vinyl with the CD. "Blues for Barry And. .." is Bloomfield at his best with a solid band behind him cranking out this slow blues you wish wouldn't end. Barry Goldberg has always played a solid organ, whether with Harvey Mandel, Charlie Musselwhite, or out on his own. This is his chance to be the leader of an all-star lineup. My regrets are that it is only 35 minutes, and most importantly I would have liked to put all the guitar players together for a cut or two; they never get to play off one another. —*Bob Gottlieb*

Streetman / 1970 / Buddah ✦✦✦✦

Ivar Avenue Reunion (N Merryweather) / 1970 / RCA ✦✦✦

Barry Goldberg & Friends Recording Live / 1976 / Buddah ✦✦✦

● **Reunion/Two Jews Blues** / Mar. 3, 1994 / Kama Sutra ✦✦✦✦
Two of Barry Goldberg's best albums from the late '60s, *Reunion* and *Two Jews Blues*, are combined on this single disc. There's some very hot playing on these two albums, particularly from Mike Bloomfield on *Two Jews Blues*, but they sound a little dated and don't quite burn as hot as some blues-rock albums from the late '60s. Nevertheless, this does capture Goldberg's two best records, which makes it both a good summary of his peak and a good introduction to his sound. —*Stephen Thomas Erlewine*

Golden Echoes

f. 194?, Los Angeles, CA
Group / Traditional Gospel, Traditional Gospel
One of the first gospel groups signed to the legendary Specialty label, the Los Angeles-based Golden Echoes were led by brothers William "Big Axe" and Wilmer "Little Axe" Broadnax, Houston natives who after relocating to the West Coast during the mid-'40s joined the ranks of the Southern Gospel Singers, an act led by onetime Soul Stirrers member A.L. Johnson. The group was primarily a weekends-only concern, however, and soon the Broadnax brothers' restlessness prompted them to form their own full-time vehicle, the Golden Echoes; a series of lineup changes followed as the decade drew to a close, and eventually William exited to settle in Atlanta, where he joined the Five Trumpets. At the time of the group's one and only Specialty session, recorded in Hollywood on April 5, 1949, their roster included co-leads Wil-

mer Broadnax and Paul Foster, tenor Eldridge Bostic, baritone Jimmy Copeland, and bass James Ricks, a longtime veteran of the gospel circuit whose career included tenures with the Birmingham Jubilees, the Famous Blue Jays, and the Flying Clouds of Detroit. The session yielded the Golden Echoes' lone Specialty single, "When the Saints Go Marching In"; for reasons unknown, label chief Art Rupe dropped the group soon after, and despite a growing reputation on the live circuit they disbanded a few months later. While Foster went on to join the Soul Stirrers, Broadnax later signed on with the likes of the Spirit of Memphis, the Fairfield Four, and the Five Blind Boys of Mississippi; during the mid-'60s, he also led a short-lived new group dubbed Little Ax and the Golden Echoes. —*Jason Ankeny*

Golden Gate Quartet

f. Virginia
Group / Black Gospel, Traditional Gospel, Spirituals
Pioneer Virginia gospel/pop quartet of the '30s and '40s. Calling their innovative approach to sacred hymns "jubilee" singing, the Golden Gate Quartet, propelled by Willie Johnson and William Langford, enjoyed massive acceptance far outside the church. Their smooth Mills Brothers-influenced harmonies made the Gates naturals for pop crossover success, and they began recording for Victor in 1937. National radio broadcasts and an appearance on John Hammond's 1938 "Spirituals to Swing" concert at Carnegie Hall made them coast-to-coast favorites. By 1941 the Gates were recording for Columbia minus Langford, and movie appearances were frequent: *Star Spangled Rhythm, Hollywood Canteen*, and *Hit Parade of 1943*, to name a few. Some experiments with R&B material didn't pan out during the late '40s, and Johnson defected to the Jubilaires in 1948. The group emigrated to France in 1959; led by veteran bass singer Orlando Wilson, the Golden Gate Quartet's vocal blend is as powerful as ever. —*Bill Dahl*

Golden Years (1949-1952) / 1949-1952 / EPM ++++
Gems taken from four important OKeh/Columbia sessions. —*Opal Louis Nations*

The Golden Gate Quartet [Columbia] / 1975 / Columbia ++++
20 of the best post-war Columbia 78s. —*Opal Louis Nations*

Gospel 1937-1941 / 1992 / F&A ++++
Classic early sides by this group who changed the style of quartet. —*Opal Louis Nations*

★ **Travelin' Shoes** / Sep. 1992 / Bluebird +++++
Bluebird's *Travelin' Shoes* is a terrific collection that contains 25 tracks the Golden Gate Quartet recorded between 1937 and 1939. During those years, the group was at their peak, and their a cappella harmonies proved to be quite influential on successive generations of gospel singers, as they had enough foresight to add jazz and blues inflections to their harmonies. There's no better place to judge their greatness than this splendid collection. —*Leo Stanley*

Gospel Train / Apr. 26, 1994 / JSP ++++
First known sides by this group who started out singing barbershop (1937-39). —*Opal Louis Nations*

Meet Me at the Golden Gate / Aug. 1, 1996 / Collector's Edition ++++
Memorable Columbia and OKeh sides from the 1940s when the group was at its peak. —*Opal Louis Nations*

Kings of Gospel / Dec. 26, 1996 / Pmf Music Factory ++++
Repertoire of Gates' golden hits and best-known songs. —*Opal Louis Nations*

The Very Best of the Golden Gate Quartet / Apr. 8, 1997 / Capitol ++++
The Very Best of the Golden Gate Quartet is a terrific collection of songs the group recorded in France for EMI Pathe between 1955 and 1969, including versions of "Shadrack" and "Oh Happy Day." Although these aren't the versions that made them stars, they are nevertheless quite good and offer a good sense of what the group is about. —*Thom Owens*

★ **35 Historic Recordings** / RCA +++++
These breathtaking sides from 1937-1939 are largely a cappella, with both gospel and pop music. The album also includes a landmark version of "Stormy Weather" that is at the root of doo wop. —*Hank Davis*

Nobody Knows / Ibach +++
Another adequate recording by this once-mighty group. —*Kip Lornell*

Spirituals to Swing / Jazz Time ++++
An inspired effort, recorded between 1955 and 1969. —*Kip Lornell*

☆ **Swing Down, Chariot** / Columbia/Legacy +++++
The most influential "jubilee" quartet of the late '30s and '40s, in inspired and deftly syncopated performances, is an archetype. —*Mark A. Humphrey*

The Golden Gate Quartet [Carrere] / Carrere +++
Carrere's *The Golden Gate Quartet* is an odd record from a latter-day version of the classic gospel quartet. By this time, the original version of the group was long gone, but the new incarnation still sounded quite good. However, the choice of songs was strange. Half of the album consisted of classic gospel songs, and half was comprised of classic pop songs like "The Great Pretender," "Blue Suede Shoes," and "Only You." Granted, the group sounds quite good on those songs, but it would have been better if they had recorded an album devoted entirely to pop instead of doing it halfheartedly. As a result, the record is only fitfully entertaining, when it could have been nothing but fun. —*Leo Stanley*

Good Rockin' Charles (Charles Edwards)

b. Mar. 4, 1933, Pratts, AL, d. May 17, 1989, Chicago, IL
Harmonica / Electric Chicago Blues, Chicago Blues
Harpist Good Rockin' Charles is best-known for a solo he didn't play. Suffering from a bad case of studio fright, Charles chickened out of playing on guitarist Jimmy Rogers' 1956 Chess waxing of "Walking by Myself"—leaving the door wide-open for Big Walter Horton to blow a galvanic solo that rates among his very best. Charles' domestic solo discography consists of one nice album for Steve Wisner's short-lived Mr. Blues logo in 1975.

Inspired by both Sonny Boys and Little Walter, Charles Edwards began playing harp shortly after hitting Chicago in 1949. He played with a plethora of local luminaries—Johnny Young, Lee Jackson, Arthur Spires, Smokey Smothers—before joining Rogers' combo in 1955. Cobra Records also tried and failed to corral him for a session in 1957.

Bassist Hayes Ware was instrumental in finally convincing the elusive Good Rockin' into a studio for Mr. Blues, where he shook the walls with revivals of classics by both Sonny Boys, Rogers, and Jay McShann. Unfortunately, it would prove the extent of the mysterious harpist's recorded legacy. —*Bill Dahl*

Good Rockin' Charles / 1976 / Rooster Blues ++++
The elusive Chicago harpist's one and only full-length album, originally issued on Steve Wisner's short-lived Mr. Blues logo and later picked up by Rooster Blues (but not available on CD as yet). Cut in 1975, this set shows that Charles never left the 1950s stylistically—backed by a nails-tough combo, he pays tribute to both Sonny Boys and his ex-boss Jimmy Rogers while betraying more than a hint of Little Walter influence. —*Bill Dahl*

Gov't Mule

f. 1994
Group / Southern Rock, Blues-Rock, Hard Rock
The leaders of Gov't Mule, Warren Haynes and Allen Woody, should be well-known to Allman Brothers fans for their stint in Southern rock's most famous native sons. In 1989, Haynes became the second replacement for Duane Allman, providing a good foil for Gregg Allman and Dickey Betts on guitar and vocals; Woody filled out the Allman sound on bass. Five years after their debut, the duo joined drummer Matt Abts in the side project Gov't Mule, a band in which the Allman Brothers' influence is apparent but complicated with the psychedelic, bluesy power-trio feel of Cream. Gov't Mule debuted in 1995 with a self-titled album on Capricorn Records, followed by the stellar concert date *Live at Roseland Ballroom*. The studio follow-up *Dose* appeared in early 1998. —*John Bush*

● **Gov't Mule** / Oct. 1995 / Relativity ++++
Gov't Mule's self-titled debut is a scorching set of heavy blues-rockers. Although they have some difficulty coming up with memorable original material, the band is loose, funky, gritty, and real. They have enough burning licks to make the record a worthwhile listen for guitar fanatics. —*David Jehnzen*

Live at Roseland Ballroom / Oct. 22, 1996 / Foundation ✦✦✦✦

Dose / Feb. 24, 1998 / Capricorn ✦✦✦✦
Gov't Mule's second album, *Dose*, confirms that their debut was no fluke. Sticking to the basics, the trio bashes out another set of gutsy, hard-hitting heavy blues-rock. There are no surprises here—the songs are simple, three-chord rockers and ballads—but what counts is how they're played, and Gov't Mule is fiery, passionate and committed. Warren Haynes sounds better than ever, spitting out some of his best solos ever, adding another layer of muscle to a set of strong songs. Anyone that thrilled to the group's debut won't be let down by this, and if you love loud Southern blues-rock and haven't checked out Gov't Mule, there's no reason to wait any longer. —*Stephen Thomas Erlewine*

Blind Roosevelt Graves

Guitar, Vocals / Delta Blues, Country Blues, Prewar Country Blues
Blind Roosevelt Graves was a Mississippi guitarist and singer who mixed secular and sacred material and cut some entertaining, celebratory party tunes as well as reverential spirituals in the '20s and '30s. He played with pianists Will Ezell and Cooney Vaughn, clarinetist Baby Jay. Graves was also a member of the Mississippi Jook Band, along with his brother—singer and tambourine player Uaroy Graves—and Vaughn.
Very few biographical details of Blind Roosevelt Graves' life are known. He and his brother Uaroy began playing juke joints in the Mississippi Delta in the early '20s. In 1929, the two brothers cut a number of sides for the Paramount and American Record Companies, which all appeared under Blind Roosevelt's name. They would continue to record until 1936. In the mid-'30s, the pair formed the Mississippi Jook Band with pianist Cooney Vaughn. The band recorded for the American Record Company in the mid- and late '30s.
After leaving behind these handful of recordings, Graves disappeared in the early '40s. It is not known where he settled, nor is his death date known. —*Ron Wynn & Stephen Thomas Erlewine*

● **Complete Recorded Works (1929-1936)** / 1929-1936 / Document ✦✦✦✦
For completists, specialists and academics, Document's *Complete Recorded Works (1929-1936)* is invaluable, offering an exhaustive overview of Blind Roosevelt Graves' career. For less dedicated listeners, the disc is a mixed blessing—the long running time, exacting chronological sequencing, poor fidelity (all cuts are transferred from original acetates and 78s), and number of performances tend to make it inaccessible to all but the serious blues listener. —*Thom Owens*

Henry Gray

b. Jan. 19, 1925, Kenner, LA
Piano, Vocals / Electric Chicago Blues, Piano Blues
Henry Gray was among the Chicago blues piano elite during the 1950s. Unlike most of his contemporaries there, he was from Louisiana rather than Mississippi—and since 1968, he's been living there once again, a stalwart on the swamp blues circuit.
Gray rolled into Chicago in 1946 after fighting for his country during World War II in the Philippines. The formidable Big Maceo was a primary influence on Gray's two-fisted playing. He procured steady gigs with Little Hudson's Red Devil Trio and guitarist Morris Pejoe before moving into extensive work as a session musician behind Jimmy Reed, Little Walter, Bo Diddley, Jimmy Rogers, Billy Boy Arnold, and Pejoe. In 1956, he joined the combo of the great Howlin' Wolf, digging in for a dozen-year run.
The pianist retreated to his homebase outside Baton Rouge after leaving Wolf's employ. In 1988, he returned to Chicago long enough to cut his debut domestic album, *Lucky Man*, for Blind Pig Records. Guitarist Steve Freund produced and played on the set, an alluring combination of Windy City blues and bayou boogie. —*Bill Dahl*

● **Lucky Man** / 1988 / Blind Pig ✦✦✦✦
Renowned as a piano-rippling sideman on the 1950s Chicago scene, Henry Gray returned to his native Louisiana in 1968 before anyone recorded him too prolifically as a leader. This album at least partially makes up for the oversight; backed by a solid Chicago combo, Gray alternates his own stuff

with classics by Big Maceo, Little Walter, and Jimmy Reed, his ruminative voice and rumbling ivories prowess nicely spotlighted. —*Bill Dahl*

Louisiana Swamp Blues, Vol. 2 / 1990 / Wolf ✦✦✦

Cal Green

b. Jun. 22, 1937, Dayton, TX
Guitar / Modern Electric Blues
Few blues guitarists can boast the varied résumé of Texas native Cal Green. From blues to doo wop to jazz, Green has played 'em all—and done each idiom proud in the process.
Green's idol as a teenager was Lone Star wonder Clarence "Gatemouth" Brown. So pervasive was Gate's sway that Green and his ninth-grade pal Roy Gaines used to stage mock guitar battles imitating their idols (Gaines was a T-Bone Walker disciple) at various Houston bars. Cal didn't have to leave the house to find worthy competition; his older brother Clarence was also an accomplished picker who cut a load of killer instrumentals (notably 1962's "Red Light") for small Lone Star diskeries.
Cal Green played on RPM Records releases by Quinton Kimble and pianist Connie McBooker, but his main claim to fame is as the guitarist for Hank Ballard & the Midnighters, who roared through Houston in 1954 looking to replace their just-drafted axeman Arthur Porter, scooped up teenaged Green, and went on their way.
Green received plenty of solo space during his Midnighters stint. His ringing guitar provided a sturdy hook for the group's rocker "Don't Change Your Pretty Ways" and figured prominently on "Tore Up Over You" (later revived in blistering fashion by rockabilly giant Sleepy LaBeef) and "Open Up the Back Door." The Midnighters' label, Cincinnati-based Federal Records, thought enough of Green's slashing Texas licks to cut a couple of 45s on him in 1958: the double-sided instrumental "The Big Push"/"Green's Blues" and a pair of vocals, "I Can Hear My Baby Calling"/"The Search Is All Over."
A 1959 marijuana bust sent Green to a Texas slammer for 21 months, but he briefly rejoined the Midnighters in 1962. After that, jazz became Green's music of choice. He gigged with organist Brother Jack McDuff and then singer Lou Rawls, eventually settling in L.A.
An acclaimed but tough-to-find 1988 album for Double Trouble, *White Pearl*, showed conclusively that Cal Green still knows his way around the blues on guitar. —*Bill Dahl*

● **White Pearl** / 1988 / Double Trouble ✦✦✦✦
After years as a sideman for Texas blues musicians and a session man for Los Angeleno jazz-pop musicians, guitarist Cal Green finally had the opportunity to record a solo album in 1988. Fortunately, the resulting record, *White Pearl*, is closer to his Texas roots than his jazz-pop aspirations. There are still some slick surfaces scattered throughout the album, but almost all of the record is nothing but the blues, giving Green chance to flaunt his chops. His voice isn't particularly strong, but his tasteful playing makes up for any vocal weakness and his stylish, sophisticated playing alone is reason for blues guitar nuts to check out this record. —*Thom Owens*

Clarence Green

b. 1937, Houston, TX, **d.** Mar. 13, 1997, Houston, TX
Guitar, Vocals / Electric Texas Blues, Texas Blues
Though not one of the best known of the modern Texas blues guitarists, Clarence Green is regarded by his peers as one of the best. Green (not to be confused with the late Clarence "Candy" Green, a Texas blues pianist) did session work for Duke Records in the '60s with Junior Parker, Bobby Bland, and others, and performed with stars from Fats Domino to Johnny Nash. His own recordings have mostly been for small Houston labels. As Marcel Vos from Double Trouble Records wrote, "The Clarence Green of today plays a brand of Texas blues that is mixed with soul, jazz, and funk, not unlike the music of fellow Texans such as Roy Gaines, Cornell Dupree, and of course, his brother Cal Green." —*Jim O'Neal*

● **Green's Blues** / 1991 / Collectables ✦✦✦✦
A CD reissue of Texas blues, R&B, and pop, it's all very danceable and very enjoyable. The recordings are from 1958 to 1965. —*Niles J. Frantz*

Lil Green

b. Dec. 22, 1919, Clarksdale, MS, **d.** Apr. 14, 1954, Chicago, IL
Classic Female Blues
Like so many Chicago blues artists Lil Green first learned her craft in the church and country jukes down in Mississippi. After moving to Chicago in the 1930s, she teamed up with Chicago mainstay Big Bill Broonzy and they worked the club circuit together. Her composition "Romance in the Dark" was a 1940 Bluebird hit and in 1941 she followed it with a best selling version of fellow Mississippi Joe McCoy's minor key blues novelty "Why Don't You Do Right?" By then she had outgrown Big Bill and the tavern scene and moved east to work as a rhythm and blues band vocalist. For the next ten years she enjoyed a successful career touring theaters and clubs and recording for RCA, Aladdin and Atlantic, all major R&B labels. When she died in Chicago in 1954 she was only thirty-five years old. Her experiences parallelled those of her male contemporaries and she made it bigger than most. From southern jukes to Chicago clubs and on to the Apollo theater, she participated in the major blues institutions of her time during the golden age of blues history. She was no stranger to trouble. According to R. H. Harris, the leader of the legendary gospel Soul Stirrers, she served time in prision because of her involvement in a juke-joint killing. He also remembered that she sang religious songs beautifully. Her former partner, Big Bill, remembered her in his autobiography as a deeply religious woman who neither smoked nor drank and as a warm-hearted friend. Today, however few people remember her or her fine work though they may be familiar with Peggy Lee's cover of her big hit "Why Don't You Do Right?" We can only wonder why she has been overlooked while more obscure male guitar players with lesser output have received substantially more critical attention. Perhaps the answer is sexism or maybe its resentment of her ability to work with the more successful musicians of her era. Whatever the case, during her brief career, she proved to be one of the best blues vocalists of her time and her contemporary African American audience appreciated her art. She deserves her place in history and today's listener would do well to listen to her music. —*Barry Lee Pearson*

● **1940-1942** / Mar. 6, 1995 / Blues Collection ◆◆◆◆
Blues Collection's *1940-1942* is an excellent collection featuring everything Lil Green cut during those two years. While Rosetta's *Chicago 1940-1947* is a more comprehensive collection, it's difficult to find and never been available on disc. Consequently, this disc is the best available compilation, even if it could have cast its net a little wider. —*Thom Owens*

Big John Greer

Saxophone, Sax (Tenor), Vocals / East Coast Blues
Never attaining the same glistening level of fame that fellow New York sax blasters Sam "The Man" Taylor and King Curtis enjoyed, Big John Greer nevertheless blew strong and sang long on a terrific series of waxings for RCA Victor and its Groove subsidiary from 1949 to 1955.

Greer was a childhood pal of future King Records producer Henry Glover. The pair attended high school together in Hot Springs and progressed to Alabama A&M College. Glover moved up quickly, playing trumpet and arranging for popular bandleader Lucky Millinder by 1948; when Millinder saxist Bull Moose Jackson split the aggregation to promote his blossoming solo career, Glover called his pal Big John Greer to fill Moose's chair. Greer's first record date as a leader was for Bob Shad's fledgling Sittin' in With label, but the great majority of his discography lies in Victor's vaults.

Initially recording as a singer/saxist with Millinder's unit for RCA, Greer stayed put when Millinder defected to King in 1950. That worked out nicely for Greer, who blew scorching tenor sax behind King stars Wynonie Harris (on "Mr. Blues Is Coming to Town" and "Bloodshot Eyes") and Bull Moose Jackson (on the incredibly raunchy "Nosey Joe"). Greer enjoyed his biggest hit as a vocalist in 1952 with the tasty blues ballad "Got You On My Mind" for RCA. The Howard Biggs-Joe Thomas composition attracted covers over the years from a mighty disparate lot, notably the Big Three Trio, Cookie & the Cupcakes, and Jerry Lee Lewis.

Greer's RCA and (from 1954 on) Groove platters were of uncommonly high standards, even for the polished New York scene. But no more hits ensued ("Bottle It Up and Go" and "Come Back Maybelline" certainly deserved a wider audience) for the powerful saxist. Glover brought him over to King in 1955, but a year there didn't slow his slide. Booze was apparently

taking its toll on Greer's employment prospects; by 1957, he was back in Hot Springs, through as anything but a local attraction. He died at age 48, forgotten by all but the most dedicated R&B fans. —*Bill Dahl*

● **Rockin' with Big John** / 1992 / Bear Family ◆◆◆◆
Three discs' worth of an R&B saxist with only one legit R&B hit to his everlasting credit? Yep, and this 92-track examination of Greer's 1949-1955 stay at RCA Victor virtually never grows stale, either, thanks to the torrid jump blues tempos Greer often favored. "Got You on My Mind," the often-covered blues ballad that proved Greer's lone hit, is here, as are rocking renditions of "Bottle It Up and Go," "Come Back Maybelline," and "Clambake Boogie." Guest vocalists include the Du Droppers, Annisteen Allen, and Damita Jo. Typically exhaustive liner notes and discographical info in the Bear Family tradition. —*Bill Dahl*

Grey Ghost

Piano / Big Band, Texas Blues
Sparse and poorly recorded sessions are unfortunately the basis of Grey Ghost's (born Roosevelt Thomas Williams) fame. An exciting, if erratic, Texas barrelhouse pianist who's been active since the '20s, Grey Ghost has enjoyed a slight career boost in the '90s. Other than older fans who'd seen him playing around Austin and hardcore collectors, few people knew anything about The Ghost until the LP *Grey Ghost* surfaced on Catfish. A reissue of '65 field recordings, its horrendous recording quality obscured the often captivating rhythms and his spirited vocals. But since its appearance, The Ghost has been featured at several festivals, and was heard on a "Bluestage" show for National Public Radio in '94. —*Ron Wynn*

● **Grey Ghost** / Oct. 30, 1992 / Spindletop ◆◆◆◆
Although he's been playing around Austin and throughout the Southwest and nation since the '20s, even much of the blues hardcore was unaware of Grey Ghost. Despite some rambling sections and others where rhythmic organization isn't a strong point, there's plenty of vintage boogie and good-natured barrelhouse playing and singing on this set. He's not among the greatest in the genre, but certainly belongs in the group close to the top. —*Ron Wynn*

Mike Griffin

b. Lawton, OK
Guitar, Vocals / Modern Electric Blues
Nashville's aptly named Big Mike Griffin (6'10", 350 lbs.) is a no-holds-barred blues guitarist new to the 1990s blues scene. Griffin grew up in Lawton, OK, and regularly traveled 125 miles as a teen to hear blues in Dallas and Fort Worth clubs. Griffin was influenced by the second generation of blues artists, like Albert King, Mike Bloomfield, Albert Collins, and the Paul Butterfield Blues Band. After the local economy turned sour, he left for Nashville. Initially, he did session guitar work for country artists and played anywhere he could, eventually building his own Unknown Blues Band. After releasing a self-produced album that sold well in Nashville, the band signed with Malaco/Waldoxy Records in 1992. They had already earned a reputation beyond Nashville's city limits, playing at such prestigious festivals as the W.C. Handy Blues Festival in Memphis and the King Biscuit Blues Festival in Arkansas. The band toured incessantly and developed East and West Coast followings before recording *Gimme What I Got Comin'* in 1993, which was a hit among blues fans and DJs. Griffin played a month-long tour of Europe that year with labelmates Denise LaSalle, Little Milton, and Artie "Blues Boy" White. Griffin's unique, economical guitar style can also be heard on White's *Different Shades of Blue* album and James Peterson's *Don't Let the Devil Ride*. His three albums for Malaco include *Back On The Streets Again* (1992), *Gimme What I Got Comin'* (1993), and *Sittin' Here with Nothing* (1995). All are outstanding efforts that incorporate Griffin's gift for humorous storytelling and blend elements of jazz, funk, and swamp rock into his arrangements. —*Richard Skelly*

● **Back on the Streets Again** / Jun. 24, 1992 / Waldoxy ◆◆◆◆
Back on the Streets Again is perhaps the definitive Big Mike Griffin album, a record that showcases his knack for idiosyncratic guitar, soulful vocals, and skewed humor. Most of the album consists of originals, with a few great covers—"Driving Wheel," "I'd Rather Go Blind"—thrown in for good measure. Throughout it all, he spits out terse, biting solos and invests true passion

into his playing. It's a fine debut illustrating that Griffin is in a different class from the average modern bluesman. —*Thom Owens*

Gimme What I Got Comin' / Aug. 15, 1993 / Waldoxy ◆◆◆

Sittin' Here with Nothing / 1995 / Waldoxy ◆◆◆

Throughout *Sittin' Here with Nothing*, Mike Griffin demonstrates his considerable skill as a lead blues guitarist. While his songwriting abilities don't quite match his instrumental prowess, the two Little Milton cuts here positively burn. —*Stephen Thomas Erlewine*

The Griswalds

f. Toledo, OH
Group / Modern Electric Blues
Toledo, OH-based brothers Art and Roman Griswald began playing blues together in 1959. In 1997, they released *All the Way Down*, their third studio album and the only one widely available to date, for the London-based JSP Records. On the recording, Art Griswald plays guitar and sings, while Roman contributes vocals and Hammond B-3 organ.

Both Art and Roman grew up surrounded by the sounds of bent guitar strings and wailing harmonicas. Art got his first guitar at age 17 after a motorcycle wreck laid him up for a few months. He moved to Little Rock, AR and began sitting in with people like Big Moose Walker and others. After moving to Toledo, OH, he became the guitarist for Little Walter Mitchell and honed his craft at a variety of Toledo blues clubs.

Both brothers began their musical education with gospel music, listening to the radio and ordering the latest recordings by Elmore James, Muddy Waters, and others. By 1959, Art was joined in Toledo by his older brother Roman, who had completed a hitch in the armed forces, usually made his mark as a harmonica player. Roman hooked up with Art's band and the Griswalds landed a job at the club Hines Farm, where they had the opportunity to polish their chops backing up touring musicians like Jimmy Ricks, vocalist Little Esther Phillips, Freddie King and Jimmy McCracklin. Finally, by 1965, Art Griswald opened his own tavern and made his own band the house band, playing six days a week. At this point, Roman began to pick up keyboards, since the lengthy jam sessions were taking their toll on him.

The Griswalds first entered the recording studio in the mid-1960s for the Fortune label in Detroit, where they recorded singles including "Pretty Mama" and "What the Judge Man Did to Me." Their singles found some airplay on R&B-oriented radio stations, and they began to tour regionally in Detroit, Houston, Memphis, and New Orleans.

The Griswalds continued to record (mostly singles) for small labels through the 1970s disco boom, but by the 1980s, they recorded and released their first full-length album, *Two Aces and a Jack*, with Toledo blues singer Big Jack Reynolds; the resulting airplay for the release brought them the chance to jam with Lee Atwater at a fund-raiser for President Reagan.

In 1990, the band, by this point paragons of the Toledo blues scene, recorded a live album, *Full Time Blues*, for the Highball label. Also in the early 1990s, they released a studio album, *The Reel Deal*, for the same label. Saxophonist Rick "Big Daddy Cool" Schefdore joined the band in 1991, and he brought a wealth of experience to the group. He wrote two of the songs on *All the Way Down* and produced the band's first widely distributed album. —*Richard Skelly*

All the Way Down / Feb. 25, 1997 / JSP ◆◆◆

The Groundhogs

f. 1963, db. 1975
Group / Hard Rock, Heavy Metal, Blues-Rock, Art-Rock/Progressive-Rock
The Groundhogs were not British blues at their most creative; nor were they British blues at their most generic. They were emblematic of some of the genre's most visible strengths and weaknesses. They were prone to jam too long on basic riffs, they couldn't hold a candle to American blues singers in terms of vocal presence, and their songwriting wasn't so hot. On the other hand, they did sometimes stretch the form in unexpected ways, usually at the hands of their creative force, guitarist/songwriter/vocalist T.S. (Tony) McPhee. For a while they were also extremely popular in Britain, landing three albums in that country's Top Ten in the early '70s.

The Groundhogs' roots actually stretch back to the mid-'60s, when McPhee helped form the group, named after a John Lee Hooker song (the band was

also known briefly as John Lee's Groundhogs). In fact, the Groundhogs would back Hooker himself on some of the blues singer's mid-'60s British shows, and also back him on record on an obscure LP. They also recorded a few very obscure singles with a much more prominent R&B/soul influence than their later work.

In 1966, the Groundhogs evolved into Herbal Mixture, which (as if you couldn't guess from the name) had more of a psychedelic flavor than a blues one. Their sole single, "Machines," would actually appear on psychedelic rarity compilations decades later. The Groundhogs/Herbal Mixture singles, along with some unreleased material, has been compiled on a reissue CD on Distortions.

After Herbal Mixture folded, McPhee had a stint with the John Dummer Blues Band before reforming the Groundhogs in the late '60s at the instigation of United Artists A&R man Andrew Lauder. Initially a quartet (bassist Pete Cruickshank also remained from the original Groundhogs lineup), they'd stripped down to a trio by the time of their commercial breakthrough, *Thank Christ for the Bomb*, which made the UK Top Ten in 1970.

The Groundhogs' power-trio setup, as well as McPhee's vaguely Jack Bruce-like vocals, bore a passing resemblance to the sound pioneered by Cream. They were blunter and less inventive than Cream, but often strained against the limitations of conventional 12-bar blues with twisting riffs and unexpected grinding chord changes. McPhee's lyrics, particularly on *Thank Christ for the Bomb*, were murky, sullen anti-establishment statements that were often difficult to decipher, both in meaning and actual content. They played it straighter on the less sophisticated follow-up, *Split*, which succumbed to some of the period's blues-hard-rock indulgences, putting riffs and flash over substance.

McPhee was always at the very least an impressive guitarist, and a very versatile one, accomplished in electric, acoustic, and slide styles. *Who Will Save the World? The Mighty Groundhogs!* (1972), their last Top Ten entry, saw McPhee straying further from blues territory into somewhat progressive realms, even adding some mellotron and harmonium (though the results were not wholly unsuccessful). The Groundhogs never became well-known in the US, where somewhat similar groups like Ten Years After were much bigger. Although McPhee and the band have meant little in commercial or critical terms in their native country since the early '70s, they've remained active as a touring and recording unit since then, playing to a small following in the UK and Europe. —*Richie Unterberger*

Scratching the Surface / 1968 / World Pacific ◆◆◆

The Groundhogs with John Lee Hooker and John Mayall / 1968 / Cleve ◆◆◆

Blues Obituary / 1969 / Imperial ◆◆◆

● **Thank Christ for the Bomb** / 1970 / BGO ◆◆◆◆
Their most popular album, and probably their most representative, although *Who Will Save the World?* may be more imaginative. McPhee's guitar playing is impressive, and the songs, if not terribly compelling, at least take some lyrical and instrumental chances, building off of a blues-rock base instead of being a slave to it. McPhee seems to be struggling with some very ambitious concepts here, but lacks the clarity and vision to fashion a truly out-of-the-ordinary statement. —*Richie Unterberger*

Split / 1971 / BGO ◆◆◆
Closer to the British blues norm than some of their previous work, this boasts some of the lesser crowd-pleasing annoyances of the age—basic bluesy thumpers and extended, not-terribly-brilliant riffing. McPhee's songwriting suffered, and the band devoted half of the eight-song record to the four-part title track. That didn't prevent the album from being a big hit in Britain, but it hasn't dated well, unless you have an uncritical yen for middling 1970-era blues-rock/hard-rock hybrids. —*Richie Unterberger*

Who Will Save the World? The Mighty Groundhogs! / 1972 / United Artists ◆◆◆◆
McPhee took the unusual step of adding progressive rock elements on this album, especially in his use of mellotron and harmonium. Blues-rock and progressive rock is not exactly a fashionable combination among critics these days, but McPhee at least deserved credit for trying something a little bit different, instead of endlessly recycling the blues-rock cliches he'd mastered. Lyrically, he reached back to the socially conscious (if not terribly clear) musings on war, peace, and philosophy that had preoccupied him on the

Thank Christ for the Bomb album. It wasn't gripping enough to add up to something notable, and the band were still prone to wander off into headache inducing extended riffs, as on the closing track, "The Grey Maze." — *Richie Unterberger*

Hogwash / 1972 / United Artists ✦✦✦

Groundhog Night ... Groundhog Live / 1994 / Gopaco ✦✦
Anyone who feels a big gap in their life not having Cream around to perform and record will love *Groundhog Night*. But for anyone else, this double CD is problematic, capturing as it does McPhee's latter-day, re-formed Groundhogs live in concert in the 1990s. The sound is very heavy, and heavily electric, with amplification more suited to late '60s/early '70s arena rock than mid-1960s blues-rock. Thus, the covers of standards like Muddy Waters' "Still a Fool," "No More Doggin'," and "I Want You to Love Me," and Willie Dixon's "Shake For Me" won't be to every taste, although McPhee's own established showcases, such as "Split Pts. 1 and 2" and "Thank Christ for the Bomb," fare reasonably well, and we even get a pleasing, restrained run through of "Groundhog Blues." There's lots of feedback and sustain, and it seems like McPhee and company try to turn "Still a Fool" into something akin to Cream's version of "Spoonful"—this isn't entirely successful, unless one is very much a fan of that brand of psychedelic or white electric blues. — *Bruce Eder*

Groundhogs Best 1969-72 / 1996 / One Way ✦✦✦✦

Guitar Shorty

b. Sep. 8, 1939, Houston, TX
Guitar, Vocals / West Coast Blues
When he's not turning somersaults, doing backwards flips, and standing on his head—all while playing, of course—Guitar Shorty is prone to cutting loose with savagely slashing licks on his instrument. Live, he's simply amazing—and after some lean years, his two recent albums for Black Top have proven that all that energy translates vividly onto tape.

At age 17, David Kearney was already gigging steadily in Tampa, FL. One night, he was perched on the bandstand when he learned that the mysterious "Guitar Shorty" advertised on the club's marquee was none other than he! His penchant for stage gymnastics was inspired by the flamboyant Guitar Slim, whose wild antics are legendary. In 1957, Shorty cut his debut single, "You Don't Treat Me Right," for Chicago's Cobra Records under Willie Dixon's astute direction. Three superb 45s in 1959 for tiny Pull Records in Los Angeles (notably "Hard Life") rounded out Shorty's discography for quite a while.

During the '60s, he married Jimi Hendrix's stepsister and lived in Seattle, where the rock guitar god caught Shorty's act (and presumably learned a thing or two about inciting a throng) whenever he came off the road. Shorty's career had its share of ups and downs—once he was reduced to competing on Chuck Barris' zany *The Gong Show*, where he copped first prize for delivering "They Call Me Guitar Shorty" while balanced on his noggin.

Los Angeles had long since reclaimed Shorty by the time things started to blossom anew with the 1991 album *My Way on the Highway* for the British JSP logo (with guitarist Otis Grand in support). From there, Black Top signed Shorty; 1993's dazzling *Topsy Turvy* and 1995's *Get Wise to Yourself* have been the head-over-heels results so far. — *Bill Dahl*

My Way on the Highway / 1991 / JSP ✦✦✦✦
Until he joined forces with British guitarist Otis Grand's band and waxed this very credible comeback set, David "Guitar Shorty" Kearney's legacy was largely limited to a solitary single for Cobra and a handful of great but legendarily obscure followups for Los Angeles-based Pull Records during the late '50s. The acrobatic guitarist informed everyone he was alive and lively with this one, exhibiting his Guitar Slim roots on "Down Thru the Years" and slashing with a vengeance on "No Educated Woman" and the title cut (but shouldn't it have read "or the highway?"). — *Bill Dahl*

● **Topsy Turvy** / 1993 / Black Top ✦✦✦✦
More impressive than Shorty's British venture thanks to superior production values and a better handle on his past (there's a stellar remake of "Hard Life"), *Topsy Turvy* made it clear that Guitar Shorty was back to stay stateside. Black Top assembled a fine New Orleans combo for the majority of the album, as Shorty proved that his act translates beautifully to record minus the crowd-pleasing acrobatic antics. — *Bill Dahl*

Get Wise to Yourself / 1995 / Black Top ✦✦✦✦
No sophomore jinx for this veteran L.A. blues guitar wildman. Other than the discordant pseudo-New Orleans number "A Fool Who Wants to Stay," this is non-stop red-hot blues axe with a funky Crescent City twist and a skin-tight horn section led by saxist Kaz Kazanoff. — *Bill Dahl*

Guitar Slim (Eddie Jones)

b. Dec. 10, 1926, Greenwood, MS, **d.** Feb. 7, 1959, New York, NY
Guitar, Vocals / Electric New Orleans Blues, New Orleans Blues
No 1950s blues guitarist even came close to equalling the flamboyant Guitar Slim in the showmanship department. Armed with an estimated 350 feet of cord between his axe and his amp, Slim would confidently stride onstage wearing a garishly hued suit of red, blue, or green—with his hair usually dyed to match! It's rare to find a blues guitarist hailing from Texas or Louisiana who doesn't cite Slim as one of his principal influences; Buddy Guy, Earl King, Guitar Shorty, Albert Collins, Chick Willis, and plenty more have enthusiastically testified to Slim's enduring sway.

Born Eddie Jones in Mississippi, Slim didn't have long to make such an indelible impression. He turned up in New Orleans in 1950, influenced by the atomic guitar energy of Gatemouth Brown. But Slim's ringing, distorted guitar tone and gospel-enriched vocal style were his alone. He debuted on wax in 1951 with a mediocre session for Imperial that barely hinted at what would soon follow. A 1952 date for Bullet produced the impassioned "Feelin' Sad," later covered by Ray Charles (who would arrange and play piano on Slim's breakthrough hit the next year).

With the emergence of the stunning "The Things That I Used to Do" on Art Rupe's Specialty logo, Slim's star rocketed to blazing ascendancy nationwide. Combining a swampy ambience with a churchy arrangement, the New Orleans-cut track was a monster hit, pacing the R&B charts for an amazing 14 weeks in 1954. Strangely, although he waxed several stunning follow-ups for Specialty in the same tortured vein—"The Story of My Life," "Something to Remember You By," "Sufferin' Mind"—as well as the blistering rockers "Well I Done Got Over It," "Letter to My Girlfriend," and "Quicksand," Slim never charted again.

The guitar wizard switched over to Atlantic Records in 1956. Gradually, his waxings became tamer, though "It Hurts to Love Someone" and "If I Should Lose You" summoned the old fire. But Slim's lifestyle was as wild as his guitar work. Excessive drinking and life in the fast lane took its inevitable toll over the years, and he died in 1959 at age 32. Only in recent years has his monumental influence on the blues lexicon begun to be fully recognized and appreciated.

Incidentally, one of his sons bills himself as Guitar Slim, Jr. around the New Orleans circuit, his repertoire heavily peppered with his dad's material. — *Bill Dahl*

The Things That I Used to Do / 1964 / Specialty ✦✦
Great stuff, but irreparably changed by organ and guitar overdubs in an ill-advised attempt to update the classic New Orleans sound. — *Bill Dahl*

Battle of the Blues / 1987 / Ace ✦✦✦

Atco Sessions / Jul. 1988 / Atlantic ✦✦✦
Sometimes a bit subdued compared to his bone-chilling output for Specialty, these 1956-1958 sides for Atco still possess considerable charm, especially the tough "It Hurts to Love Someone" and "If I Should Lose You," which conjure up the same hellfire and brimstone intensity as Slim's earlier work. — *Bill Dahl*

★ **Sufferin' Mind** / 1991 / Specialty ✦✦✦✦✦
His guitar fraught with manic high-end distortion and his vocals fried over church-fired intensity, Eddie "Guitar Slim" Jones influenced a boatload of disciples while enjoying the rewards that came with his 1954 R&B chart-topper "The Things That I Used to Do." This 26-song survey of Slim's seminal 1953-1955 Specialty catalog rates with the best New Orleans blues ever cut—besides the often-imitated but never-duplicated smash, his "Story of My Life," "Sufferin' Mind," and "Something to Remember You By" are overwhelming in their ringing back-alley fury. Slim could rock, too: "Well I Done Got Over It," "Quicksand," "Certainly All," and the raucous introduction "Guitar Slim" drive with blistering power (saxist Joe Tillman was a worthy foil for the flamboyant guitarist in the solo department). — *Bill Dahl*

Carolina Blues NYC 1944 / Nov. 18, 1997 / Arhoolie ✦✦✦✦

Guitar Slim, Jr. (Rodney Armstrong)

b. 1951, New Orleans, LA

Guitar, Vocals / Electric New Orleans Blues

Despite the fact that his first album earned a Grammy nomination, Guitar Slim Jr. remains a somewhat shadowy figure to the blues public. The son of Eddie "Guitar Slim" Jones, his real name is Rodney Armstrong. According to New Orleans-historian Jeff Hannusch's notes on Slim's 1988 album, he "has been a fixture on the Black New Orleans club circuit for the better part of 20 years… [but] doesn't get to play the posher uptown clubs." His Orleans album featured mostly covers of his father's inspirational blues, which he was loath to play earlier in life, but Slim is also known for his extensive soul repertoire. *—Jim O'Neal*

● **Story of My Life** / 1988 / Orleans ◆◆◆◆

Contemporary blues, blues-rock, and soul comes from the son of the late blues/R&B legend. With mostly credible covers of his father's tunes, it was a Grammy nominee. *— Niles J. Frantz*

Nothing Nice / Jul. 30, 1996 / Warehouse Creek ◆◆◆

Buddy Guy

b. Jul. 30, 1936, Lettsworth, LA

Guitar, Vocals / Electric Chicago Blues, Chicago Blues, Modern Electric Blues, Modern Electric Chicago Blues, Electric Blues

He's Chicago's blues king today, ruling his domain just as his idol and mentor Muddy Waters did before him. Yet there was a time, and not all that long ago either, when Buddy Guy couldn't even negotiate a decent record deal. Times sure have changed for the better—Guy's first three albums for Silvertone in the '90s all earned Grammys. Eric Clapton unabashedly calls Buddy Guy his favorite blues axeman, and so do a great many adoring fans worldwide.

High-energy guitar histrionics and boundless onstage energy have always been Guy trademarks, along with a tortured vocal style that's nearly as distinctive as his incendiary rapid-fire fretwork. He's come a long way from his beginnings on the 1950s Baton Rouge blues scene—at his first gigs with bandleader "Big Poppa" John Tilley, the young guitarist had to chug a stomach-jolting concoction of Dr. Tichenor's antiseptic and wine to ward off an advanced case of stage fright. But by the time he joined harpist Raful Neal's band, Guy had conquered his nervousness.

Guy journeyed to Chicago in 1957, ready to take the town by storm. But times were tough initially, until he turned up the juice as a showman (much as another of his early idols, Guitar Slim, had back home). It didn't take long after that for the new kid in town to establish himself. He hung with the city's blues elite: Freddy King, Muddy Waters, Otis Rush, and Magic Sam, who introduced Buddy Guy to Cobra Records boss Eli Toscano. Two searing 1958 singles for Cobra's Artistic subsidiary were the result: "This Is the End" and "Try to Quit You Baby" exhibited more than a trace of B.B. King influence, while "You Sure Can't Do" was an unabashed homage to Guitar Slim. Willie Dixon produced the sides.

When Cobra folded, Guy wisely followed Rush over to Chess. With the issue of his first Chess single in 1960, Guy was no longer aurally indebted to anybody. "First Time I Met the Blues" and its follow-up, "Broken Hearted Blues," were fiery, tortured slow blues brilliantly showcasing Guy's whammy-bar-enriched guitar and shrieking, hellhound-on-his-trail vocals.

Although he's often complained that Leonard Chess wouldn't allow him to turn up his guitar loud enough, the claim doesn't wash: Guy's 1960-1967 Chess catalog remains his most satisfying body of work. A shuffling "Let Me Love You Baby," the impassioned downbeat items "Ten Years Ago," "Stone Crazy," "My Time After Awhile," and "Leave My Girl Alone," and a bouncy "No Lie" rate with the hottest blues waxings of the '60s. While at Chess, Guy worked long and hard as a session guitarist, getting his licks in on sides by Waters, Howlin' Wolf, Little Walter, Sonny Boy Williamson, and Koko Taylor (on her hit "Wang Dang Doodle").

Upon leaving Chess in 1967, Guy pacted with Vanguard. His first LP for the firm, *A Man and the Blues*, followed in the same immaculate vein as his Chess work and contained the rocking "Mary Had a Little Lamb," but *This Is Buddy Guy* and *Hold That Plane!* proved somewhat less consistent. Guy and harpist Junior Wells had long palled around Chicago (Guy supplied the guitar work on Wells' seminal 1965 Delmark set *Hoodoo Man Blues*, initially

billed as "Friendly Chap" because of his Chess contract); they recorded together for Blue Thumb in 1969 as *Buddy and the Juniors* (pianist Junior Mance being the other Junior) and Atlantic in 1970 (sessions co-produced by Eric Clapton and Tom Dowd) and 1972 for the solid album *Buddy Guy & Junior Wells Play the Blues*. Buddy and Junior toured together throughout the '70s, their playful repartee immortalized on *Drinkin' TNT 'n' Smokin' Dynamite*, a live set cut at the 1974 Montreux Jazz Festival.

Guy's reputation among rock guitar gods such as Eric Clapton, Jimi Hendrix, and Stevie Ray Vaughan was unsurpassed, but prior to his Grammy-winning 1991 Silvertone disc *Damn Right, I've Got the Blues*, he amazingly hadn't issued a domestic album in a decade. That's when the Buddy Guy bandwagon really picked up steam—he began selling out auditoriums and turning up on network television (David Letterman, Jay Leno, etc.). *Feels Like Rain*, his 1993 encore, was a huge letdown artistically, unless one enjoys the twisted concept of having one of the world's top bluesmen duet with country hat act Travis Tritt and hopelessly overwrought rock singer Paul Rodgers. By comparison, 1994's *Slippin' In*, produced by Eddie Kramer, was a major step back in the right direction, with no hideous duets and a preponderance of genuine blues excursions.

A Buddy Guy concert can sometimes be a frustrating experience. He'll be in the middle of something downright hair-raising, only to break it off abruptly in mid-song, or he'll ignore his own massive songbook in order to offer imitations of Clapton, Vaughan, and Hendrix. But Guy, whose club remains the most successful blues joint in Chicago (you'll likely find him sitting at the bar whenever he's in town), is without a doubt the Windy City's reigning blues artist—and he rules benevolently. *—Bill Dahl*

I Left My Blues in San Francisco / 1967 / Chess ◆◆◆◆

Featuring such classic Buddy Guy performances as "Buddy's Groove" and "She Suits Me to a Tee," *I Left My Blues in San Francisco* ranks as one of the guitarist's finest albums. All of this material is also available on the double-disc set, *The Complete Chess Recordings*. *— Thom Owens*

A Man and His Blues / 1968 / Vanguard ◆◆◆◆

The guitarist's first album away from Chess—and to be truthful, it sounds as though it could have been cut at 2120 S. Michigan, with Guy's deliciously understated guitar work and a tight combo anchored by three saxes and pianist Otis Spann laying down tough grooves on the vicious "Mary Had a Little Lamb," "I Can't Quit the Blues," and an exultant cover of Mercy Dee's "One Room Country Shack." *— Bill Dahl*

This Is Buddy Guy [Live] / 1968 / Vanguard ◆◆◆

Coming at You / 1968 / Vanguard ◆◆◆

Blues Today / 1968 / Vanguard ◆◆◆

Buddy and the Juniors / 1970 / MCA ◆◆

Strange, off-the-cuff set originally issued on Blue Thumb pairing Buddy Guy and Junior Wells with jazz pianist Junior Mance and no rhythm section. Guy plays acoustic guitar, Wells plays amplified harp, and the hoary setlist includes "Hoochie Coochie Man," "Five Long Years," and "Rock Me Mama." *—Bill Dahl*

In the Beginning (1958/64) / 1971 / Red Lightnin' ◆

Bootleg-quality LP of Guy's early work. *—Bill Dahl*

Buddy Guy & Junior Wells Play the Blues / 1972 / Rhino ◆◆◆

Considering the troubled background of this album (Eric Clapton, Ahmet Ertegun, and Tom Dowd only ended up with eight tracks at a series of 1970 sessions in Miami; two years later, the J. Geils Band was brought in to cut two additional songs to round out the long-delayed LP for 1972 release), the results were pretty impressive. Guy contributes dazzling lead axe to their revival of "T-Bone Shuffle;" Wells provides a sparkling remake of Sonny Boy's "My Baby She Left Me," and Guy is entirely credible in a grinding Otis Redding mode on the southern soul stomper "A Man of Many Words." *—Bill Dahl*

Hold That Plane / 1972 / Vanguard ◆◆

Lackluster set comprised of only seven lengthy workouts, including Guy's renditions of "I'm Ready," "Watermelon Man," and Sugar Pie DeSanto's "Hello San Francisco." Jazzman Junior Mance is pianist for the somewhat underwhelming album. *—Bill Dahl*

I Was Walkin' through the Woods / 1974 / MCA/Chess ◆◆◆◆

Ten of the mercurial guitarist's best recordings ever for Chess, cut during his early-'60s peak. "First Time I Met the Blues" and "Broken Hearted Blues" are harrowing downbeat blues of enormous power, Guy's shrieks and tremolo-rich guitar bursts boasting an intensity level he's only achieved intermittently ever since. Even better, they're here in stereo—unlike virtually every other Chess collection to follow. —*Bill Dahl*

Live in Montreux / Jul. 9, 1977 / Evidence ♦♦♦
No blues tandem in recent memory has given more alternately brilliant and infuriating performances as the duo of Junior Wells and Buddy Guy. They can inspire or anger, stimulate or disgust, amaze or bore. They were in a great groove during the selections recorded at this '79 concert for Isabel. They have been recently reissued with two bonus cuts as part of Evidence's huge cache of blues material. Wells' often rambling, sometimes disjointed and unorganized vocals were not only focused on this occasion but delivered with verve, direction, and intensity. Guy stayed in the background, but when summoned, played with less flair and more power, dispensing with distortion and feedback gimmicks and providing neat fills, slashing lines, and meaty riffs. Fine Wells/Guy material that is close, if not completely equal to, their best. —*Ron Wynn*

Pleading the Blues / Oct. 1979 / Evidence ♦♦♦♦
Recorded on Halloween night in 1979, this pairs up Wells and Guy in a fashion that hasn't been heard since *Hoodoo Man Blues*, their first, and best collaboration. Solid backing by the Philip Guy band (Buddy's brother) makes this album a rare treat. —*Cub Koda*

Stone Crazy! [Alligator] / 1981 / Alligator ♦♦♦
Buddy Guy mostly indulges his histrionic side throughout this high-energy set, first issued in France and soon picked up for domestic consumption by Alligator. It's a particularly attractive proposition for rock-oriented fans, who will no doubt dig Guy's non-stop incendiary, no-holds-barred guitar attack and informal arrangements. Purists may want to look elsewhere. —*Bill Dahl*

Drinkin' TNT 'n' Smokin' Dynamite / 1982 / Blind Pig ♦♦♦
Cut at the 1974 Montreux Jazz Festival with Stones' bassist Bill Wyman anchoring the rhythm section, the set captures some of the ribald musical repartee that customarily distinguished the pairing of Buddy Guy and Junior Wells, though they certainly break no new ground as they roll through their signature songs. —*Bill Dahl*

DJ Play My Blues / 1982 / JSP ♦

Buddy Guy / 1983 / Chess ♦♦♦
This is some of his best from Chess. —*Mark A. Humphrey*

The Original Blues Brothers Live / 1983 / Magnum ♦♦♦

Chess Masters / 1987 / Chess ♦♦♦♦
This anthology's value has been supplanted by the more intelligently sequenced, mastered and annotated two-disc *Complete Studio Recordings* issued in 1992. It's also out of print. —*Ron Wynn*

Complete DJ Play My Blues Session / 1987 / JSP ♦

Breakin' Out / 1988 / JSP ♦

Alone & Acoustic / 1991 / Alligator ♦♦♦
Although it is not obvious from the outside of this 1992 CD, the music was originally released in France in the early 1980s. The unusual set teams together the longtime musical partners Buddy Guy and Junior Wells (famous for their many electric Chicago blues performances) in a relaxed and purely acoustic guitar-harmonica duo setting. The rather informal session has surprisingly few rough moments and lots of similar but highly enjoyable performances. Although Buddy Guy and Junior Wells split the vocal duties right down the middle (taking six songs apiece and singing together on three others), Guy emerges as the main star due to his aggressive and very sturdy guitar work. —*Scott Yanow*

Damn Right, I've Got the Blues / 1991 / Silvertone ♦♦♦♦
Grammy-winning comeback set that brought Guy back to prominence after a long studio hiatus. Too many clichéd cover choices—"Five Long Years," "Mustang Sally," "Black Night," "There Is Something on Your Mind"—to earn unreserved recommendation, but Guy's frenetic guitar histrionics ably cut through the superstar-heavy proceedings (Eric Clapton, Jeff Beck, and Mark Knopfler all turn up) on the snarling title cut and a handful of others. —*Bill Dahl*

☆ **The Complete Chess Studio Sessions** / 1992 / MCA/Chess ♦♦♦♦♦
Here's everything that fleet-fingered Buddy Guy waxed for Chess from 1960 to 1966, including numerous unissued-at-the-time masters, offering the most in-depth peek at his formative years imaginable. Stone Chicago blues classics ("Ten Years Ago," "My Time After Awhile," "Let Me Love You Baby," "Stone Crazy"), rockin' oddities ("American Bandstand," "$100 Bill," "Slop Around"), even a cut that features guitarist Lacy Gibson's vocal rather than Guy's ("My Love Is Real")—some 47 sizzling songs in all. —*Bill Dahl*

● **The Very Best of Buddy Guy** / 1992 / Rhino ♦♦♦♦
Credible attempt to digitally summarize Guy's entire pre-Silvertone career on a single 18-song disc. Encompasses the guitarist's 1957 demo "The Way You Been Treating Me," two killer Cobras, four of his hottest Chess sides, a couple notable Vanguards, a pair of alluring Atlantics, and three tremendously unsubtle 1981 items from Guy's days with the British JSP label. —*Bill Dahl*

My Time After Awhile / 1992 / Vanguard ♦♦♦♦
My Time After Awhile is the best selection from Guy's Vanguard catalog. —*Bill Dahl*

Feels Like Rain / 1993 / Jive/Novus ♦♦♦
Hideous duets with the likes of Paul Rodgers (talk about some bad company!) and lame country hat act Travis Tritt render this the weakest contemporary disc by far in Guy's massive catalog. Duetless revivals of Ray Charles' "Mary Ann," Guitar Slim's "Sufferin' Mind," and Muddy Waters' "She's Nineteen Years Old" are among the set's precious few highlights. —*Bill Dahl*

Slippin' In / 1994 / Silvertone ♦♦♦♦
Now this is more like it: no sign of any superfluous duets, and far fewer hoary standards to contend with (only the Z.Z. Hill title track, in fact). Lots of high-energy guitar fireworks and vocal intensity from the perpetually eager-to-please blues superstar, as he drives through well-chosen numbers first rendered by Bobby Bland, Jimmy Reed, Charles Brown, and Fenton Robinson and Guy's own impassioned "Cities Need Help" and "Little Dab-A-Doo." —*Bill Dahl*

Southern Blues 1957-63 / 1994 / Paula ♦♦♦
Kind of a thrown-together hodgepodge, but still a worthwhile add to your CD collection. Guy's four indispensable 1958 sides for Cobra are here (along with alternates of "This Is the End" and the Guitar Slim-influenced "You Sure Can't Do"), while Guy provides crackling lead guitar on four 1963 outings by singer Jesse Fortune (notably the minor-key rhumba "Too Many Cooks"). Finally, there are two demos that Guy cut at a Baton Rouge radio station back in 1957—or they're supposed to be here, anyway: the crudely engaging "The Way You Been Treatin' Me" is definitely Buddy Guy, but "I Hope You Come Back Home" isn't (no guesses from this corner on exactly who it may be, either). —*Bill Dahl*

Live! The Real Deal / Apr. 1996 / Silvertone ♦♦♦♦
As close as Buddy Guy's ever likely to come to recapturing the long-lost Chess sound. Cut live at his popular Chicago nightspot, Buddy Guy's Legends, with guitarist G.E. Smith's horn-leavened Saturday Night Live Band and pianist Johnnie Johnson in lush support, Guy revisits his roots on sumptuous readings of "I've Got My Eyes on You," "Ain't That Lovin' You," "My Time After Awhile," and "First Time I Met the Blues." No outrageous rock-based solos or Cream/Hendrix/Stevie Ray homages; this is the Buddy Guy album that purists have salivated for the last quarter century or so. —*Bill Dahl*

Buddy's Blues (Chess 50th Anniversary Collection) / Apr. 8, 1997 / MCA ♦♦♦♦
As part of MCA's Chess Records 50th Anniversary series, this sweats his multi-disc retrospective, *The Complete Chess Studio Recordings*, down to a scintillating 15-track package and comes up with a bare-bones winner. There's loads of great guitar on classics like "First Time I Met The Blues," "Let Me Love You Baby," "Pretty Baby," "My Time After Awhile," "Stone Crazy," and Buddy's voice is at its whiplash exuberant best. Unexpected bonuses pop up in the comp's kickoff track, a full-length version of "Worried Mind," that's issued here without the overdubbed applause and crowd noises that accompanied its original release on *Folk Festival Of The Blues* (see Muddy Waters entry). Also noteworthy is Junior Wells' appearance on chromatic harp on "Ten Years Ago," and Guy's stellar guitar behind Lacy Gibson's vocal on a

Buddy Guy original, "My Love Is Real." And special note must also be made of the spacious stereo mixes used on this compilation, making these 30-year-old-plus tracks shine like diamonds coming off the laser beam. We also experience all the stylistic turns toward a kinship with the burgeoning soul and rock scenes that Buddy would make toward the end of his Chess tenure, along with the smoking slow burners that are his trademark, some of which clock in at four to six minutes here. With his very best tracks compiled on one disc and with beautiful transfers of them to enhance the listening experience, this should be one of your very first stops in absorbing the sides that made Buddy's reputation among blues fans and guitar aficionados the world over. —*Cub Koda*

As Good as It Gets / Mar. 10, 1998 / Vanguard ✦✦✦

Phil Guy

b. Apr. 28, 1940, Lettsworth, LA
Guitar / Modern Electric Blues, Chicago Blues
No, Phil Guy's never going to eclipse his older brother Buddy's status as a blues superstar. And in reality, Phil's funky brand of blues has yet to be captured correctly for posterity. But he remains an active attraction on the Chicago circuit, following in his sibling's footsteps and patiently waiting for his own star to rise.

Like his sibling, Phil Guy played with harpist Raful Neal (for a decade) before leaving the Baton Rouge scene for Chicago in 1969. There he played with his brother's high-energy organization as well as behind harpist Junior Wells (Phil handles guitar duties with Sammy Lawhorn on Wells' underrated mid-'70s Delmark album, *On Tap*). Phil Guy has cut albums of his own for JSP; they've generally been lacking in originality if not spirit. —*Bill Dahl*

● **Bad Luck Boy** / 1983 / JSP ✦✦✦✦
Phil Guy never was able to establish an identity separate from his older brother Buddy, but as his debut album *Bad Luck Boy* shows, he didn't really try, either. Guy's stock-in-trade is Chicago blues, and while he doesn't perform with much imagination, he's hardly incompetent, either. The problem may be that he's simply competent, unwilling to shake things up even a tiny bit, but competency can be entertaining as well. That's the case on *Bad Luck Boy*. Guy never really got better than he did here, as he's supported by a number of Chicago veterans and he turns out a likeable, albeit predictable, set of Chicago blues, balancing covers with originals. There's not necessarily much passion here, but it's well-done music, and it illustrates that Guy can deliver the goods on occasion. —*Thom Owens*

It's a Real Mutha Fucka / 1985 / JSP ✦✦
Weak, cover-heavy album by Buddy's little brother. —*Bill Dahl*

Tough Guy / 1989 / Red Lightnin' ✦✦✦

Tina Nu / 1989 / JSP ✦✦
This set offers conclusive proof as to why Buddy's little brother may never shed his long-standing journeyman status—weak covers, done not particularly persuasively, with a mediocre band. —*Bill Dahl*

All Star Chicago Blues Session / Oct. 31, 1994 / JSP ✦✦✦

Breaking Out on Top / Sep. 5, 1995 / JSP ✦✦✦

Travis Haddix

b. Walnut, MS
Vocals, Guitar / Modern Electric Blues, R&B
A native of Walnut, MS, "Moonchild" Haddix was inspired in his early years by B.B. King's broadcasts on WDIA out of Memphis. In Cleveland, OH, where he has lived since 1959, Haddix developed into a fine modern bluesman and songwriter with an original and soulful touch. His albums for Ichiban contain some of the best blues material that label has released. —*Jim O'Neal*

Wrong Side Out / 1988 / Ichiban ◆◆◆
Impressive debut for this Cleveland-based vocalist. —*Bill Dahl*

● **Winners Never Quit** / 1991 / Ichiban ◆◆◆◆
Travis Haddix perfected his blend of Southern soul and contemporary blues on his second album, *Winners Never Quit.* While the production may be a little too clean for some tastes, Haddix has hit upon a winning formula, one that has a bit of grit and a bit of polish and just enough soul to keep things interesting. Chances are you won't mistake this for a Stax or Chess production, but there's enough passion and heart within Haddix as he balances gutsy blues interludes with kicking soul progressions to make this a thoroughly appealing record. —*Thom Owens*

What I Know Right Now / 1992 / Ichiban ◆◆◆◆

I Got a Sure Thing / 1993 / Ichiban ◆◆◆◆

Big Ole Goodun' / 1994 / Ichiban ◆◆◆

Larry Hamilton

Bass / New Orleans Blues, R&B
Crescent City blues and R&B vocalist Larry Hamilton had a revelatory experience at age five when he first heard the Mardi Gras beats of Shriners bands. He took up drums, but his grandmother arranged for him to take piano lessons. He began singing at age 9 and wrote his first lyrics when he was 12. By the time he was 15, he began singing professionally with David Batiste and the Gladiators. His influences include Ray Charles, Nat "King" Cole, Sam Cooke, Big Joe Turner, and Otis Redding. Hamilton sang with the Gladiators from 1965 until the mid-1970s, but also toured with Curtis Mayfield, Betty Swan, Jimmy Hughes, Jackie Wilson, Percy Sledge, Little Johnny Taylor, David Ruffin, Major Lance, Z.Z. Hill, and Al Green. As a songwriter, Hamilton composed "Get On Your Job" for Etta James, "Feel Like Dynamite" for King Floyd, "She's Taking My Part" for Irma Thomas, and "The Feeling" for Albert King. He has also written tunes for Jean Knight, Wayne Cochran, and Johnny Adams.

At a recording session in the late 1970s, Hamilton met producer/songwriter and impresario Allen Toussaint. He joined Toussaint's group and did some touring with him. The two remained close friends, and in 1996, Toussaint signed Hamilton to record for his own NYNO (New York/New Orleans) Records label. Hamilton has one album, *Larry Hamilton* (1997), out on the label. Although many of the songs on Hamilton's debut are Toussaint compositions, future recordings will likely showcase more of Hamilton's original material. —*Richard Skelly*

Larry Hamilton / Apr. 8, 1997 / NYNO ◆◆◆◆
Larry Hamilton's music is R&B in its smooth incarnation, going along the path blazed by the likes of Lou Rawls; it isn't the grit-infused R&B of Bobby Evans and Terry King or the Holmes Brothers. He has the benefit of being produced by Allen Toussaint and singing in front of the Sea-Saint House Band, a superb aggregation of New Orleans musicians. They seem to flow as one, providing exactly what is needed to highlight the lead instrument—that is, Larry Hamilton's rich, powerful voice—and let it take the spotlight. A powerful first effort on NYNO Records for Larry Hamilton. —*Bob Gottlieb*

John Hammond, Jr. (John Paul Hammond)

b. Nov. 13, 1942, New York, NY
Guitar, Vocals, Drums / R&B, Modern Acoustic Blues, Blues-Rock, Folk Revival
With a career that now spans in excess of three decades, John Hammond is one of handful of White blues musicians who was on the scene at the beginning of the first blues renaissance of the mid-'60s. That revival, brought on by renewed interest in folk music around the US, brought about career boosts for many of the great classic blues players, including Mississippi John Hurt, Rev. Gary Davis, and Skip James. Some critics have described Hammond as a White Robert Johnson, and Hammond does justice to classic blues by combining powerful guitar and harmonica playing with expressive vocals and a dignified stage presence. Within the first decade of his career as a performer, Hammond began crafting a niche for himself that is completely his own: the solo guitar man, harmonica slung in a rack around his neck, reinterpreting classic blues songs from the 1930s, '40s, and '50s. Yet, as several of his mid-'90s recordings for the Pointblank label demonstrate, he's also a capable bandleader who plays wonderful electric guitar. This guitar-playing and ensemble work can be heard on *Found True Love* and *Got Love If You Want It,* both for the Pointblank/Virgin label.

Born November 13, 1942, in New York City, Hammond is the son of the famous Columbia Records talent scout, John Hammond, Sr. What most people don't know is that young Hammond didn't grow up with his father. His parents split when he was young, and he would see his father several times a year. He first began playing guitar while attending a private high school, and he was particularly fascinated with slide guitar technique. He saw his idol, Jimmy Reed, perform at New York's Apollo Theatre, and he's never been the same since.

After attending Antioch College in Ohio on a scholarship for a year, he left to pursue a career as a blues musician. By 1962, with the folk revival starting to heat up, Hammond had attracted a following in the coffeehouse circuit, performing in the tradition of the classic country blues singers he loved so much. By the time he was just 20 years old, he had been interviewed for the *New York Times* before one of his East Coast festival performances, and he was a certified national act.

When Hammond was living in the Village in 1966, a young Jimi Hendrix came through town, looking for work. Hammond offered to put a band together for the guitarist, and got the group work at the Cafe Au Go Go. By that point, the coffeehouses were falling out of favor and instead the bars and electric guitars were coming in with folk-rock. Hendrix was approached there by Chas Chandler, who took him to England to record. Hammond recalls telling the young Hendrix to take Chandler up on his offer. "The next time I saw him, about a year later, he was a big star in Europe," Hammond recalled in a 1990 interview. In the late '60s and early '70s, Hammond continued his work with electric blues ensembles, recording with people like Band guitarist Robbie Robertson (and other members of the Band when they were still known as Levon and the Hawks), Duane Allman, Dr. John, harmonica wiz Charlie Musselwhite, Michael Bloomfield, and David Bromberg.

As with Dr. John and other blues musicians who've recorded more than two dozen albums, there are many great recordings that provide a good introduction to the man's body of work. His self-titled debut for the Vanguard label has now been reissued on compact disc by the company's new owners, the Welk Music Group, and other good recordings to check out (on vinyl and/ or compact disc) include *I Can Tell*, (recorded with Bill Wyman from the Rolling Stones), *Southern Fried* (1968), *Sourcepoint* (1970, Columbia), and his most recent string of early- and mid-'90s albums for Pointblank/Virgin Records, *Got Love If You Want It*, *Trouble No More* (both produced by J.J. Cale), and *Found True Love*.

He didn't know it when he was 20, and he may not realize it now, but Hammond deserves special commendation for keeping many of the classic blues songs alive. When fans see Hammond perform them, as Dr. John has observed many times with his music and the music of others, the fans often want to go back further, and find out who did the original versions of the songs Hammond now plays.

Although he's a multi-dimensional artist, one thing Hammond has never professed to be is a songwriter. In the early years of his career, it was more important to him that he bring the art form to a wider audience by performing classic—in some cases forgotten—songs. Now, more than 30 years later, Hammond continues to do this, touring all over the US, Canada, and Europe from his base in northern New Jersey. Anything can happen at a John Hammond concert, and he selects tunes from his vast repertoire like buckets of water from a well.

Whether it's with a band or by himself, Hammond can do it all. Seeing him perform live, one still gets the sense that some of the best is still to come from this energetic bluesman. —*Richard Skelly*

Big City Blues / 1964 / Vanguard ✦✦✦✦
Hammond's second effort was one of the first electric white blues recordings, and one of the very first that could be said to be blues-rock. Covering a variety of Chess Records classics and electrifying some older tunes, the playing, featuring Hammond, Billy Butler, and James Spruill on electric guitar, is first-rate. But Hammond's vocals are overly mannered and overwrought, and although he would improve, these flaws would keep him from rising to the top rank of White bluesmen. —*Richie Unterberger*

Country Blues / 1964 / Vanguard ✦✦✦✦
Although Hammond had already recorded electric material, he went back to a solo acoustic format for his fourth album, accompanying himself on guitar and harmonica on faithful interpretations of standards by Robert Johnson, Blind Willie McTell, John Lee Hooker, Sleepy John Estes, Jimmy Reed, Willie Dixon, and Bo Diddley. If it sounds a bit unimaginative and routine today, one has to remember that the general listening audience was much less aware of these artists and songs in the mid-'60s. Hammond did a commendable job of rendering them here, with fine guitar work and vocals that were a considerable improvement over his earliest efforts. —*Richie Unterberger*

So Many Roads / 1965 / Vanguard ✦✦✦✦
One of young Hammond's better early albums. —*Bill Dahl*

I Can Tell / 1967 / Atlantic ✦✦✦✦
I Can Tell boasts an all-star backing band of rock 'n' roll stars, featuring everyone from Bill Wyman to Robbie Robertson. Hammond leads the band through a set of Chicago blues standards, reaching deep into the catalogs of Willie Dixon, Elmore James, Howlin' Wolf, and many others. Although the performances can occasionally sound too studied, the album is by and large an unadulterated delight—the affection Hammond and his band have for the material is quite clear. The CD reissue includes four cuts from his 1970 album, *Southern Fried*, which feature Duane Allman on slide guitar. —*Thom Owens*

Hot Tracks / 1978 / Vanguard ✦✦✦✦
In September of 1979, John Hammond went into Vanguard Records' 23rd Street Studio in New York with the Nighthawks—Jimmy Thackeray, guitar; Mark Wenner, harmonica; Jan Zukowski, bass; Pete Ragusa, drums—and cut this record, one of his best (and which might've sold better with maybe some better cover art). The sounds are alternately hot and soulful on the ten-song collection, featuring covers of songs by Little Walter ("You Better Watch Yourself," "Last Night"), Chuck Berry ("Nadine"), Jimmy Reed ("Caress Me Baby," one of Hammond's slowest, most seductive numbers), and Robert Johnson ("Sweet Home Chicago"). Highlights include a stunningly beautiful rendition of Howlin' Wolf's "Who's Been Talkin'," a wailing reconsideration of John Lee Hooker's "Sugar Mama," with a really searing guitar break, a very powerful version of "Howlin' For My Darling," and even the best cover of Dixon's

"Pretty Thing" this side of Bo Diddley himself, where Hammond and company manage to be raunchy and smooth at the same time. Nothing's going to make anyone forget Walter, Wolf, or Willie, but this ain't a bad way to spend 40 minutes, especially given the really crunchy guitar sound achieved by Jeff Zaraya and the uncredited producer. A real diamond in the rough, and one of Hammond's best albums. —*Bruce Eder*

Live / 1983 / Rounder ✦✦✦✦
John Hammond has dealt with issues of authenticity and origin, both musical and personal, and moved beyond them. This 18-song session, recorded live in 1983 and recently reissued on CD, may have been his definitive session. It was certainly a masterpiece, with Hammond doing confident, thoroughly distinctive versions of signature Delta and Chicago blues classics by Robert Johnson, Muddy Waters, Willie Dixon, Son House, and others. While "Dust My Broom," "Drop Down Mama," "Wang Dang Doodle," and all the rest have certainly been done to death, Hammond's spirited vocals, riveting guitar work on acoustic or bottleneck and his overall charismatic performances made them seem like fresh discoveries. —*Ron Wynn*

Nobody But You / 1988 / Flying Fish ✦✦✦
Hammond usually performs solo, but here he is backed by a five-piece band, including pianist Gene Taylor. It's good to hear him in this context. All the numbers are blues classics or standards written by John Lee Hooker, Muddy Waters, Arthur Crudup, Little Walter, and B.B. Fuller. —*Michael G. Nastos*

● **The Best of John Hammond** / 1989 / Vanguard ✦✦✦✦
Vanguard's *The Best of John Hammond* is an excellent collection that features 22 highlights from his early albums, balancing acoustic and electric material, including "My Babe," "Milk Cow Calf's Blues," "Big Boss Man," "See That My Grave Is Kept Clean," "Stones in My Passway," "Key to the Highway," and "Who Do You Love," among others. While his first albums hold up quite well as individual records, this collection does a good job of summarizing his strengths, making it a nice introduction to Hammond's peak years. —*Thom Owens*

Got Love If You Want It / 1992 / Charisma ✦✦✦
In many ways, *Got Love If You Want It* is standard-issue John Hammond, Jr. The album is filled with covers by great bluesmen like Son House and Slim Harpo, as well as rock 'n' rollers like Chuck Berry. The difference is ability—Hammond is a professional and is able to pull off convincing performances of these warhorses. Backed by Little Charlie and the Nightcats—who have rarely sounded better, incidentally—Hammond tears through these songs with passion, which makes even the oldest songs sound rather fresh. —*Thom Owens*

John Hammond Live / Jan. 15, 1992 / Rounder ✦✦✦✦
A definitive live set featuring Hammond on guitar and harmonica. —*Michael G. Nastos*

Trouble No More / Jan. 25, 1994 / Pointblank ✦✦✦
John Hammond, Jr., made the leap to the Virgin blues division Pointblank with *Got Love If You Want It* in 1992, but he truly made an artistic comeback with its follow-up, *Trouble No More*, an excellent collection split between solo acoustic numbers and storming electric blues. For the electric numbers, he's supported by Little Charlie & the Nightcats, who give Hammond a surprisingly gritty and flexible support. But the heart of the album is in the acoustic cuts, where he proves that he has absorbed the Delta blues completely. These are among his finest acoustic work, and they're what makes *Trouble No More* such an impressive effort. —*Thom Owens*

Found True Love / Jan. 23, 1996 / Virgin ✦✦✦
Found True Love offers the usual highly proficient replication of classic electric and acoustic blues one has come to expect from John Hammond. Although he can more than hold his own on both guitar and harp, he often prefers to collaborate with other bluesmen on recordings; here, he shares the spotlight even more than usual. Hammond blows harp on only five cuts and plays guitar on only four, leaving most of the fretwork to co-producer Duke Robillard (who brings along his regular rhythm section) and letting Charlie Musselwhite handle harp on a couple of tunes. Still, it is Hammond's alluring, leathery vocals that distinguish the recording. Hammond is an interpreter, not an originator, and on *Found True Love* he covers two each by Little Walter and Howlin' Wolf, and one each by Jimmy Reed, Leroy Carr,

Willie McTell, Baby Boy Warren, Lonnie Johnson, Little Brother Montgomery, Cousin Joe, and Sleepy John Estes. — *Steve Hoffman*

W.C. Handy

b. Nov. 16, 1873, Muscle Shoals, AL, **d.** Mar. 28, 1958
Piano, Bandleader / Blues, Early American Blues

Often referred to as the "father of the blues," William Christopher Handy was born on November 16, 1873, in Muscle Shoals, AL. He studied music early on, starting with the cornet in a brass band, working with a vocal quartet, and eventually playing throughout the South in minstrel and tent shows. It was during his many travels that he began to notate the music he heard, including Delta blues. He would adapt these tunes and sounds to his own performance, in this way popularizing the music he heard, the blues in particular. He was the first to add flatted thirds and sevenths (so-called "blue notes") to published compositions.

He became music director of Mahara's Minstrels in 1896, a group that played rags, popular dance numbers, and even some light classical compositions. They toured the South in the late 1800s and early 1900s. He recorded in New York in 1917 with his Memphis Orchestra.

Handy was the first to compose and publish a tune with the word "blues" in it, "Memphis Blues" in 1912. He composed and published many classic blues tunes including "St. Louis Blues," "Beale Street Blues," "Ole Miss," and "Yellow Dog Blues." Handy's foray into writing and publishing blues songs inspired other writers, including Perry Bradford, the author of "Crazy Blues"—the first blues song ever recorded (1920).

Handy moved himself and his Memphis Orchestra to New York in 1917, started the Handy Record Company (a failure) in 1922, and recorded with his own band until 1923. Throughout the later 1920s and 1930s Handy, who had developed eye problems, was forced to work less. Still, he continued working with many orchestras. He was on recording sessions with Red Allen and Jelly Roll Morton. His autobiography *Father of the Blues* was written in 1938, the same year that he was given a tribute concert in Carnegie Hall. In his later years, Handy was not very active. He died on March 28, 1958. The movie *St. Louis Blues* was released in 1958, starring Nat King Cole. It is not considered to be very reflective of the facts of Handy's life. A legend in Memphis, Handy has a park named after him there containing a statue of himself. The W.C. Handy Award is the most prestigious honor currently awarded to blues artists. Handy, along with Duke Ellington, appears on a US postage stamp.

Although no one person is the father of the blues, and Handy was not by temperament or cultivation what we might call a bluesman, W.C. Handy did much to popularize and publicize what had been until that time a very personal and local phenomenon. Handy helped to broadcast the blues form to the world. — *Michael Erlewine*

W.C. Handy's Memphis Blues Band / Sep. 21, 1917-May 1923 / Memphis Archives ♦♦♦

● **Father of the Blues** / 1923-1962 / DRG ♦♦♦♦

In addition to the nine performances of Handy songs included on this Blues Foundation of Memphis-produced document, there is also a wealth of interview excerpts from 1950 to 1955. The music is wide-ranging, from a 1923 instrumental "Memphis Blues" cut by Handy's Orchestra up to a 1962 Louis Armstrong remote. Also included is a 1934 aircheck vocal take of the aforementioned "Memphis Blues" sung by Mae West with the Duke Ellington Orchestra, as well as the 1929 film soundtrack to Bessie Smith's *St. Louis Blues*. — *Jason Ankeny*

Pat Hare

b. Dec. 20, 1930, Cherry Valley, AR, **d.** Sep. 26, 1980, St. Paul, MN
Guitar, Vocals / Electric Memphis Blues

If highly distorted guitar played with a ton of aggression and just barely suppressed violence is your idea of great blues, then Pat Hare's your man. Born with the improbable name of Auburn Hare (one of those biographical oddities that even the most fanciful blues historian couldn't make up in a million years), he worked the '50s Memphis circuit, establishing his rep as a top-notch player with a scorching tone only rivaled by Howlin' Wolf's guitarist, Willie Johnson. Our first recorded glimpse of him occurs when he showed up at Sam Phillips' Memphis Recording Service sometime in 1953 to play on James Cotton's debut session for the Sun label. His aggressive, biting

guitar work on both sides of that oft-anthologized single—"Cotton Crop Blues" and "Hold Me in Your Arms"—featured a guitar sound so overdriven that with the historical distance of several decades, it now sounds like a direct line to the coarse, distorted tones favored by modern rock players. But what is now easily attainable by 16-year-old kids on modern day effects pedals just by stomping on a switch, Hare was accomplishing with his fingers and turning the volume knob on his Sears & Roebuck cereal-box-sized amp all the way to the right until the speaker was screaming.

After working with Cotton and numerous others around the Memphis area, Hare moved North to Chicago and by the late '50s was a regular member of the Muddy Waters band, appearing on the legendary *Live at Newport, 1960* album. By all accounts Pat was a quiet, introspective man when sober, but once he started drinking the emotional tables turned in the opposite direction. After moving to Minneapolis in the '60s to work with fellow Waters bandmate Mojo Buford, Hare was convicted of murder after a domestic dispute, spending the rest of his life behind bars. In one of the great ironies of the blues, one of the unissued tracks Pat Hare left behind in the Sun vaults was an original composition entitled, "I'm Gonna Murder My Baby." — *Cub Koda*

Mystery Train / Rounder ♦♦♦

Pat Hare only has two of the cuts on this 14-track compilation, which also has nine songs by Junior Parker and three by James Cotton; Hare does play on two of the Cotton selections ("Cotton Crop Blues" and "Hold Me in Your Arms") and one of Parker's ("Sittin' Drinkin' and Thinkin'"). Hare's solo cuts are the infamous "I'm Gonna Murder My Baby," which features his trademark super-distorted tone and an intense, raw vocal, and the more uptempo but less distinguished "Bonus Pay." Most people will want this CD primarily for the Parker material (his classics "Mystery Train" and "Feelin' Good" are both here). But regardless of whether you want the disc for one or all three of the performers, it's a good roundup of mid-'50s Sun blues that also features some of Pat Hare's most notable moments. — *Richie Unterberger*

Harlem Hamfats

f. 1936
Group / East Coast Blues, Acoustic Chicago Blues

The Harlem Hamfats were a crack studio band formed in 1936 by black talent scout Mayo "Ink" Williams. Its main function was backing jazz and blues singers such as Johnny Temple, Rosetta Howard, and Frankie "Half Pint" Jackson for Decca Records; The Hamfats' side career began when its first record "Oh Red" became a hit. Despite its name, none of the band's members came from Harlem, and none were hamfats, a disparaging term referring to indifferent musicians. Brothers Joe (g, v) and Charlie McCoy (g, m) were blues players from Mississippi; leader Herb Morand (tpt, v), Odell Rand (cl), and John Lindsay (b) were from New Orleans; Horace Malcolm (p) and drummers Pearlis Williams and Freddie Flynn were from Chicago. This territorial disparity created a sound which blended various blues styles with New Orleans, Dixieland, and swing jazz. The band's high-spirited playing and excellent musicianship compensated for what some critics have called lack of improvisational skill. The Hamfats' music has been somewhat neglected over the years. The vocalists tended to be derivative of other popular singers of the day such as Louis Armstrong, Fats Waller, and various blues singers. The lyrical content of their songs often revolved around subjects like drinking and sex, leading some to dismiss them as a lightweight novelty act. Although it is not seen as an innovative group, The Harlem Hamfats' riff-based style was influential to Louis Jordan, early Muddy Waters, and what would eventually become rhythm and blues and rock 'n' roll. — *Jim Powers*

Hot Chicago Jazz, Blues and Jive: 1936-1937 / Oct. 2, 1936-Oct. 6, 1937 / Folklyric ♦♦♦♦

Hot Chicago Jazz, Blues and Jive: 1936-1937 collects 17 tracks the Harlem Hamfats recorded in those two years, featuring the band on their own, as well as accompanists. Most of these performances are quite good, and many of them have never been released on LP before, yet the presence of the sidemen tracks makes this more of interest to collectors than the curious. — *Thom Owens*

● **Harlem Hamfats (1936-1939)** / Oct. 1936-Sep. 1939 / Document ♦♦♦♦

Document's *Harlem Hamfats (1936-1939)* is an excellent 20-track collection that contains many of the group's greatest singles, thereby offering a nearly ideal summation of their career. — *Thom Owens*

Keep It Swinging Round and Round / Dec. 1936-Sep. 1939 / Blues Document ✦✦✦

Harlem Hamfats, Vol. 1 / Nov. 4, 1994 / Document ✦✦✦✦

Harlem Hamfats, Vol. 2 / Nov. 4, 1994 / Document ✦✦✦✦

Harlem Hamfats, Vol. 3 / Nov. 4, 1994 / Document ✦✦✦✦

Harlem Hamfats, Vol. 4 / Nov. 4, 1994 / Document ✦✦✦✦

James Harman

b. Jun. 8, 1946, Anniston, AL

Harmonica, Vocals / Modern Electric Blues

James Harman is a California-based blues singer, harmonica player, songwriter, and bandleader with an agenda that definitely distances him from the rest of the pack. A veteran of the blues roadhouse circuit, he has led various combinations of the James Harman Band over the years, most featuring top-notch talent (like guitarists Hollywood Fats and Kid Ramos) to match his own. With roots in the deepest of blues harmonica sources (Little Walter, Walter Horton, Sonny Boy Williamson), Harman scores consistently both live and on record. His most recent recorded efforts show a genuine flair for writing original material (always more important to Harman than just regurgitating his record collection), all of it laced with a generous dollop of wisecracking good humor. Always willing to stretch the boundaries and conceptions of what a good bar band should be capable of, Harman combines rich traditons and beatnik craziness for a blend that's mighty hard to resist.—*Cub Koda*

Those Dangerous Gentlemen / 1987 / Rhino ✦✦✦

Extra Napkins / 1988 / Rivera ✦✦✦

Originally released on Rivera Records in 1988, this is the first of a projected series of compact discs chronicling the recording sessions that went into the making of James Harman's first fully formed studio endeavor. Harman approached the entire recording as if each song was a single, using whatever personnel were right for the song—his regular band on some tunes, horns and other guest artists on others. This initial volume in the set collects the 12 songs that appeared on the original album, which laid the groundwork for Harman's later recorded efforts. As some 53 tunes were recorded in that fertile two-year period between 1985 and the album's final lineup here, this batch is apparently just the tip of iceberg. —*Cub Koda*

Live in '85, Vol. 1 / 1990 / Rivera ✦✦✦

Consisting of tapes recorded live over two nights in March of 1985 at the Belly Up Tavern in Soldano Beach, California, this captures Harman and one of his best bands in full cry, warts and all. Kicking off with a James Brown-announcer-on-acid introduction from fellow harp maestro John "Juke" Logan, Harman and the boys kick hard and heavy through half a dozen of his better known numbers, including an earlier and electric version of "Goatman Holler." The guitar interplay between Hollywood Fats and Kid Ramos is textbook in its accuracy and passion, and the rock-steady rhythm section of Stephen Hodges on drums and William Campbell keeps things totally in groove territory every beat of the way. In this live setting, things get brought down and stretched out, but never unnecessarily so, and even the almost nine-minute shuffle "You're Gone" is worth every second the boys put into it. Although nowhere as wiseass or beatnik-cool as his current persona, Harman nonetheless blows with chops galore, and his vocals (and asides to the crowd between songs) here seem to come with their own built-in smirk. Worth more than a listen or two just for the late Hollywood Fats' stellar solo work and the rarity of being a live album that actually rocks without having to rely on shop-worn cover material. Certainly one of Harman's best efforts and very deserving of a much wider hearing. —*Cub Koda*

● **Do Not Disturb** / 1991 / Black Top ✦✦✦✦

James Harman's *Do Not Disturb* is a first-rate blues album, one that captures all the different sides of postwar blues. At its core, *Do Not Disturb* is Chicago blues, but Harman touches on swing, jump, and Texas roadhouse blues, banging out gritty, greasy harp licks with intensity. His band is up to the challenge of keeping up with him—they tear through the uniformly excellent songs with abandon. *Do Not Disturb* establishes Harman as one of the most exciting blues traditionalists of the '90s. —*Thom Owens*

Two Sides to Every Story / Jun. 1, 1993 / Black Top ✦✦✦✦

Cards on the Table / May 28, 1994 / Black Top ✦✦✦

Black & White / 1995 / Black Top ✦✦

Harmonica Fats

b. Sep. 8, 1927, McDade, LA

Harmonica, Vocals / Modern Electric Blues, Modern Acoustic Blues

Harmonica Fats is actually Harvey Blackston, a former Louisianan who learned the blues growing up on his grandfather's farm; his longtime partner, Bernie Pearl, is a native Angeleno who learned the blues from the musicians who frequented the fabled Ash Grove (a folk and blues club run by Pearl's brother Ed), including Lightnin' Hopkins and Mance Lipscomb.

In the early '50s, Fats took up harmonica as self-prescribed therapy while recuperating from an auto accident. Once confident, he formed a band, playing clubs around Los Angeles, and was known then as "Heavy Juice." Just as carefully, he perfected his songwriting, scoring on the R&B charts in 1961 with the self-penned single "Tore Up." After changing his name to its current incarnation, this success led to work as a studio musician, playing dates with performers as diverse as Bill Cosby, Ringo Starr, and Lou Rawls. He even did a stint as a traveling solo musician, seeking gigs as he drove in a station wagon around the country.

Pearl, through the Ash Grove, backed artists Big Mama Thornton, Bukka White, Mississippi Fred McDowell, Freddie King, and more. In the late '60s, '80s and early '90s, he was a blues DJ, not only entertaining but educating with the knowledge he acquired during the Ash Grove days. Perhaps his best known accomplishment was founding one of the West Coast's top blues events, the Long Beach Blues Festival, and since 1993 he has been the promoter of the Big Time Blues Festival, also held in Long Beach.

The Bernie Pearl Blues Band originated in 1984, with Robert Lucas on harmonica. Fats replaced Lucas in 1986. Fats' witty songs and onstage magnetism is captured on *Live at Cafe Lido*, an album originally intended as a demo. The high demand for that album led Fats and Pearl to form Bee Bump Records, with its first release being *I Had to Get Nasty*. Pearl convinced Fats to work as an acoustic duo, releasing *Two Heads Are Better* in 1995. The following year, they released *Blow Fat Daddy Blow!*, dedicated to the memory of Fats' wife and civil rights activist Johnnie Tillman. —*Char Ham*

Live at Cafe Lido / 1990 / Pearl Til-Blac Prod ✦✦✦✦

Despite the muddiness in the recording, Fats punches it in with 320 pounds of high-energy, gut-wrenching blues. Listen to Fats' harmonica as he leads the band's rhythm section on "Boogie All the Way." Guesting on the Ray Charles hit "Georgia On My Mind," Papa John Creach wails a romantic treatment coupled with Hollis Gilmore's soulful sax. It's little wonder "Tore Up" was such a big hit for Fats—he roars life into the Hank Ballard penning. You can feel the fans filled with heightened vibes in "Harmonica Fats Blows," making one wish he or she were dancing along with Fats. However, on the finale, Robert Johnson would cringe if he heard the vocals on "Walkin' Blues." —*Char Ham*

● **I Had to Get Nasty** / 1991 / Bee Bump ✦✦✦✦

Fats is backed up by the Bernie Pearl Blues Band on this mostly electric effort, though hints of Fats' country origins stick out. On the fast-tempo numbers, Fats' driving, in-your-face energy comes out full bore, and on these songs the wit and humor of his lyrics stand out best. Pearl's attempt at lead vocals on Lightnin' Hopkins' "Automobile Blues" would have been better left off to allow Fats to expand his showman capabilties. —*Char Ham*

Two Heads Are Better Than One / 1995 / Bee Bump ✦✦✦

Fats and Pearl change settings by turning acoustic, but if the album were mixed with more balance between the harmonica and guitar, it would more fittingly show their partnership. Perhaps Fats' greatest asset is the wit and humor in his songwriting, well illustrated in "Just Like Richard Nixon," a rollicking ode to the pre-Presidential days of Nixon interplayed with Fats' dilemma of being constantly hounded by girls. Funnier is "Blabbermouth Man," a supposed confessional about a tongue-wagging, testesterone-laced gossiper. Fats can sing about mundane aspects of life and turn them into curiosities, whether it be the virtues of soul food (what else but "Soul Food"?) or how making small wages isn't enough to spring the boss out of jail in "Everyday's a Working Day for Me." The downside is that the album lacks consistently high-quality material, such as "Vampire Blues," which is dosed with overt corniness. —*Char Ham*

Blow, Fat Daddy, Blow! / Mar. 19, 1996 / Bee Bump ✦✦✦✦

On their third album, the duo of Harmonica Fats and Bernie Pearl turn in a typically engaging set of acoustic blues. All of the songs on *Blow, Fat Daddy,*

Blow! are originals, and it is to the duo's credit that they manage to sound respectful to tradition without being enslaved to it. Certainly, the quality of the material fluctuates somewhat—not every song cuts as deep as the rootsy "Why Should I Holler?" or the powerful "Blues Kaddish"—but the interaction between the two musicians is stellar. Pearl's guitar playing is subtly impressive and Harmonica Fats simply wails, making the set worthwhile for fans of good-humored, stripped-down blues. —*Thom Owens*

Harmonica Slim

b. Dec. 21, 1934, Douglassville, TX
Harmonica, Vocals / Texas Blues
Over the history of the blues, there's been at least three different people plying their wares as Harmonica Slim, with one of them being far better known as Slim Harpo. But *this* Harmonica Slim was born Travis L. Blaylock down in Texas. He picked up the instrument around the age of 12 and was soon working as part of the Sunny South Gospel Singers gospel group, broadcasting over radio station KCMC in his hometown of Texarkana from the mid-'40s on. By 1949, he moved to Los Angeles, ingratiating himself into the burgeoning blues community, working package shows with Lowell Fulson and the like. He first recorded as a sideman on a group of dates in the mid-'50s for West Coast labels like Aladdin, Spry, and Vita. After spending most of the '60s working dates with Percy Mayfield, Harmonica Fats, B.B. King, T-Bone Walker and others, Slim finally got to record a full album under his own name for the Bluestime label in 1969. —*Cub Koda*

● **Back Bottom Blues** / Oct. 1995 / Trix ♦♦♦♦

Give Me My Shotgun / Sep. 23, 1997 / Fedora ♦♦♦

The Harmonizing Four

f. Richmond, VA
Group / Black Gospel, Southern Gospel, Traditional Gospel
One of the top gospel quartets of the postwar era, the Harmonizing Four was also a relative anomaly of the period; as their contemporaries raced to modernize their sound, rejecting the traditional jubilee style in favor of the intensity of the burgeoning "hard gospel" movement, the Four remained true to their roots, focusing instead on the spirituals and hymns of a time gone by. For all of their renown, little is known about the group's formative years—their leader and manager, Joseph "Gospel Joe" Williams, forbade any of the members to agree to interviews unless they were paid in advance, and as a result the anecdotal information that does exist is sketchy and incomplete. Records have indicated that the Four made their formal debut at a grammar school in their native Richmond, VA on October 27, 1927; founding members included Thomas "Goat" Johnson and Levi Handly, with Williams signing on in 1933 and Lonnie Smith—the father of jazz pianist Lonnie Liston Smith—joining four years later.

The Harmonizing Four made their recorded debut on Decca in 1943; in all likelihood they came to the label at the behest of Sister Rosetta Tharpe, whom they frequently backed both on record and in concert. After World War II, they landed on the tiny Coleman label; included in the roster during much of this period was Tommy Ellison, later of the Chosen Gospel Singers. A brief tenure on Gotham followed, and after 1952, the Harmonizing Four cut only one record, a single for the Religious Recordings label, prior to arriving at Vee-Jay in 1957. There, the group—Williams, Smith, Thomas Johnson, and Jimmy Jones—finally began earning the fame long due them, honing their close harmony style to mellow perfection; Jones, in particular, earned renown as perhaps the greatest basso in gospel history, his canyon-deep voice distinguishing hits like "Motherless Child." After leaving Vee-Jay during the early 1960s, the Harmonizing Four recorded for Nashboro, slowly easing into retirement in the years that followed. —*Jason Ankeny*

The Harmonizing Four / 1959 / Vee-Jay ♦♦♦♦
A collection of this close harmony quartet's singles circa 1957-59. —*Opal Louis Nations*

God Will Take Care of You / 1960 / Vee-Jay ♦♦♦♦
More beautiful hymn-like renditions from 1958-59 sessions. —*Opal Louis Nations*

Singing Is Our Life / 1965 / Buddah/Vee Jay ♦♦♦♦
The group's last really great album. —*Opal Louis Nations*

★ **Gospel in My Soul** / 1974 / Chameleon ♦♦♦♦♦
This truly fine collection of 11 close-quartet gospel songs is from Vee-Jay sessions conducted during the late '50s and issued on a Vee-Jay LP in the early '60s. This is one of the few worthwhile Vee-Jay quartet albums that has never been reissued over the ensuing years. The Richmond group is led here by Thomas Johnson (first tenor) and his son Ellis Johnson (bass). Other members of long standing include Lonnie Smith and Joe Williams... This is an excellent collection. —*Opal Louis Nations, Roots & Rhythm Newsletter*

Think of God / 1974 / Vee-Jay ♦♦♦♦
More strong material from 1958-59 sessions. —*Opal Louis Nations*

The Harmonizing Four/God Will Take Care of You / Apr. 1993 / Vee-Jay ♦♦♦♦
While the occasional contemporary gospel song like Thomas A. Dorsey's "When I've Done My Best" occasionally rears its head, the focus on this two-fer from the Harmonizing Four remains the traditional spirituals and hymns of an era gone by, all brought back to life by some of the finest and most exacting harmonies in all of spiritual music. The most immediately distinctive component of the group's sound is bass singer Jimmy Jones, who in a break with convention takes the lead on six of these 23 tracks; his breathtakingly deep voice is widely considered the greatest basso in gospel, and on sides like "Farther Along," "Motherless Child," and "His Eye Is on the Sparrow," it's not difficult to understand why. —*Jason Ankeny*

I Shall Not Be Moved / Sep. 1, 1995 / Charly ♦♦♦♦
Essential 1950s Vee-Jay cuts, some with gospel's premier basso, Jimmy Jones. —*Opal Louis Nations*

1950-1955 / Dec. 7, 1995 / Heritage ♦♦♦♦
The quartet's most devout and touching Gotham sides. —*Opal Louis Nations*

When Day Is Done: The Very Best of the Harmonizing 4 / Mar. 3, 1998 / Collectables ♦♦♦♦
The best of the Vee-Jay sides featuring Ellis Johnson and Gospel Joe Williams. —*Opal Louis Nations*

The Best of the Harmonizing Four / Capitol ♦♦♦
Featured is the bass voice of Ellis Johnson or the legendary Jimmy Jones. —*Opal Louis Nations*

Working for the Lord / Jewel ♦♦♦♦
One of the finer, later collections by this seminal group. —*Opal Louis Nations*

Slim Harpo (James Moore)

b. Jan. 11, 1924, Lobdell, LA, **d.** Jan. 31, 1970, Baton Rouge, LA
Guitar, Harmonica, Vocals / Electric Louisiana Blues, Electric Swamp Blues, Swamp Blues, Harmonica Blues, Blues Revival
In the large stable of blues talent that Crowley, LA producer Jay Miller recorded for the Nashville-based Excello label, no one enjoyed more mainstream success than Slim Harpo. Just a shade behind Lightnin' Slim in local popularity, Harpo played both guitar and neck-rack harmonica in a more down-home approximation of Jimmy Reed, with a few discernible, and distinctive, differences. Slim's music was certainly more laid-back than Reed's, if such a notion was possible. But the rhythm was insistent and overall, Harpo was more adaptable than Reed or most other bluesmen. His material not only made the national charts, but also proved to be quite adaptable for White artists on both sides of the Atlantic, including the Rolling Stones, Yardbirds, Kinks, Dave Edmunds with Love Sculpture, Van Morrison with Them, Sun rockabilly Warren Smith, Hank Williams, Jr., and the Fabulous Thunderbirds.

A people-pleasing club entertainer, he certainly wasn't above working rock 'n' roll rhythms into his music, along with hard-stressed, country & western vocal inflections. Several of his best tunes were co-written with his wife Lovelle and show a fine hand for song construction, appearing to have arrived at the studio pretty well-formed. His harmonica playing was driving and straightforward, full of surprising melodicism, while his vocals were perhaps best described by writer Peter Guralnick as "if a Black country and western singer or a White rhythm and blues singer were attempting to impersonate a member of the opposite genre." And here perhaps was Harpo's true genius, and what has allowed his music to have a wider currency. By the time his first single became a Southern jukebox favorite, his songs were being adapted and played by White musicians left and right. Here was good-time Saturday night blues that could be sung by elements of the Caucasian persuasion with a straight face. Nothing resembling the emotional investment of a Howlin' Wolf or a Muddy Waters was required; it all came natural and easy, and its influence has stood the test of time.

He was born James Moore just outside of Baton Rouge, LA. After his parents died, he dropped out of school to work every juke joint, street corner, picnic and house rent party that came his way. By this time he had acquired the alias of Harmonica Slim, which he used until his first record was released. It was fellow bluesman Lightnin' Slim who first steered him to local record man J.D. Miller. The producer used him as accompanist to Hopkins on a half dozen sides before recording him on his own. When it came time to release his first single ("I'm a King Bee"), Miller informed him that there was another Harmonica Slim recording on the West Coast, and a new name was needed before the record could come out. Moore's wife took the slang word for harmonica, added an 'o' to the end of it, and a new stage name was the result, one that would stay with Slim Harpo the rest of his career.

Harpo's first record became a double-sided R&B hit, spawning numerous follow-ups on the "King Bee" theme, but even bigger was "Rainin' in My Heart," which made the *Billboard* Top 40 pop charts in the summer of 1961. It was another perfect distillation of Harpo's across-the-board appeal, and was immediately adapted by country, Cajun, and rock 'n' roll musicians; anybody could play it and sound good doing it. In the wake of the Rolling Stones covering "I'm a King Bee" on their first album, Slim had the biggest hit of his career in 1966 with "Baby, Scratch My Back." Harpo described it "as an attempt at rock 'n' roll for me," and its appearance in *Billboard's* Top 20 pop charts prompted the dance-oriented follow-ups "Tip on In" and "Tee-Ni-Nee-Ni-Nu," both R&B charters. For the first time in his career, Harpo appeared in such far-flung locales as Los Angeles and New York City. Flush with success, he contacted Lightnin' Slim, who was now residing outside of Detroit, MI. The two reunited and formed a band, touring together as a sort of blues mini-package to appreciative White rock audiences until the end of the decade. The new year beckoned with a tour of Europe (his first ever) all firmed up, and a recording session scheduled when he arrived in London. Unexplainably, Harpo—who had never been plagued with any ailments stronger than a common cold—suddenly succumbed to a heart attack on January 31, 1970. —*Cub Koda*

Rainin' in My Heart / 1961 / Excello ◆◆◆◆
The original 12-song Excello album with the addition of six extra tracks, all of which were originally issued as singles only. With the exception of "Dream Girl," "My Home Is A Prison" and "What A Dream," everything on here also appears on the AVI double disc collection. —*AMG*

I'm a King Bee / 1989 / Flyright ◆◆◆◆
Very generous (24 songs) collection emphasizing the laconic harpist's early (1957-1964) Excello output. The British import boasts the required "I'm a King Bee," "I Got Love If You Want It," and "Rainin' in My Heart," but also the more obscure and previously unissued (including Slim's take on John Lee Hooker's "Boogie Chillun"). —*Bill Dahl*

★ **Scratch My Back: The Best of Slim Harpo** / 1989 / Rhino ◆◆◆◆◆
All the hits, including the original "I'm a King Bee," "Baby, Scratch My Back," "I Got Love If You Want It," "Shake Your Hips," "Rainin' in My Heart," "Tip on In," and "Strange Love." A best-of that really is, with top-flight sound as a bonus. —*Cub Koda*

Shake Your Hips [ACE] / 1995 / Ace ◆◆◆◆
The second installment in Ace's overview of Harpo's swamp blues career, spanning 1962-1966 and including all four of the harpist's rare 1962 sides for Imperial (cut during a brief rift with his producer Jay Miller). More rarities and unissued gems, including a few tracks that exhibit slight soul tendencies (a genre that Harpo took to surprisingly well). —*Bill Dahl*

☆ **Hip Shakin': The Excello Collection, Vol. 2** / 1995 / Excello/AVI ◆◆◆◆◆
A shapely two-disc retrospective, *Hip Shakin'* is the definitive Slim Harpo package. Collecting up all of his hits ("I'm A King Bee," "Got Love If You Want It," "Baby, Scratch My Back") along with other defining moments from his stay with the label, this 44 track compilation also includes three live recordings from a 1961 fraternity dance. —*AMG*

Tip on In / 1996 / Excello ◆◆◆
During the last few years of the '60s (which, as it turned out, were the last few years of his life), Harpo's records took a turn for the slightly more com-

mercial, although they retained a great deal of continuity with his early work. This has 25 tracks recorded between 1967 and 1969, and while it's not quite as good as his prime stuff, it's pretty respectable, retaining his trademark vibrato-laden guitar, relaxed nasal vocals, and shaky harmonica. At this point he had terminated his relationship with longtime producer Jay Miller; rock and soul influences, and even occasional brass and lyrical references to the counterculture, update his sound slightly. But only slightly—although he milks his "Baby, Scratch My Back" riff over and over, the groove is so consistently solid that it makes for listening that's more comfortably dependable than unduly repetitious. Highlighted by the modest R&B hits "Tip on In" and "Te-Ni-Nee-Ni-Nu," as well as one of his best originals, "I'm Gonna Keep What I've Got." —*Richie Unterberger*

The Scratch: Rare & Unissued / Feb. 1996 / AVI-Excello ◆◆◆◆
A 25-track single-disc compilation loaded with previously unissued sides and alternate takes (the title track is an interesting variant of his hit, "Baby, Scratch My Back"), making it the perfect companion volume to *Hip Shakin'.* This also has the added bonus of more (and even wilder) live recordings from the infamous 1961 frat party dance in Alabama. Dodgy sound on the live sides, but performances too great to leave in the can either way. —*AMG*

The Best of Slim Harpo [Hip-O] / Nov. 4, 1997 / Hip-O ◆◆◆◆
There have been many Slim Harpo best-ofs available over the years, some frustratingly incomplete. This one gets all the chart hits together with several of the obscure singles like "Wonderin' and Worryin'," "Strange Love," "One More Day," and "You'll Be Sorry One Day," along with album tracks like "Snoopin' Around" and "Blues Hangover." Transfers are clean and exemplary, and this makes as good an introduction into his music as any currently available. —*Cub Koda*

Corey Harris

b. Feb. 21, 1969, Denver, CO
Guitar, Vocals / Modern Electric Blues, Acoustic Country Blues
Corey Harris is a deliberate musical anachronism. In 1994 at the age of 25, he cut his first album, *Between Midnight and Day,* displaying a style of acoustic playing that crossed paths with Charley Patton and Robert Johnson, the Delta slide of Son House and Bukka White, and the Piedmont-style rags of Blind Boy Fuller. His music also reflects some of the influence of his New Orleans residence. And he makes it all work under one cover. In contrast to most of the White players (excepting John Hammond, who is a unique figure) who have adopted these or other antique blues styles, Harris' approach to the blues is more inspirational than scholarly, which lends a certain honest, direct urgency and emotional involvement to his music, whether he is performing songs by Patton, White, Fred McDowell, or Sleepy John Estes, or presenting an original of his own. He also has one of the richest and most expressive voices of any bluesman working today. —*Bruce Eder*

Between Midnight and Day / Nov. 1995 / Alligator ◆◆◆
An astonishingly good record, covering a multitude of Delta-based styles and songs from Charley Patton to Muddy Waters, as well as a few originals. It's just Harris and his acoustic guitar, some dazzling finger work and a voice that's about as good as you're going to hear from anyone doing blues and still walking around at the end of the 20th century. The material alternately surges and broods, and once in a while does both at the same time, and it's all worth hearing. —*Bruce Eder*

● **Fish Ain't Bitin'** / Mar. 25, 1997 / Alligator ◆◆◆◆
Corey Harris' second outing for Alligator shows that he's no one-album flash in the pan, with this sophomore effort moving his modern-day acoustic Delta blues vision into even broader territory with delightful results. While his debut effort illustrated Harris' absolute mastery of older Delta styles, both instrumentally and vocally, *Fish Ain't Bitin'* charts new terrain using his first album as a stylistic building block. The big news here is that over half of the 17 songs are from Corey's own pen and compositions like "High Fever Blues" (heard here in two versions), "5-0 Blues," "Berry Owen Blues," and "If You Leave Me" show that he's more than adept in wedding contemporary influences to his down-home country sound. Adding to that are his takes on Son House's "Preaching Blues," Memphis Minnie's "Bumble Bee Blues," Big Maceo's "Worried Life Blues," and Blind Lemon Jefferson's "Jack O'Diamonds," all of them rendered in the proper spirit and context and all of them sounding nothing like the originals—a tough feat to pull off, but one that

Harris does with consummate ease, imbuing these warhorses with the stamp of his personality. Several tracks also feature a trombone and tuba or string bass working in tandem with Corey's National steel-bodied guitar, making a Mississippi-New Orleans musical connection that sounds perfectly natural. No sophomore jinx here, as Corey Harris has turned in one great little album that examines the music's past while looking forward to the future for more input. — *Cub Koda*

Peppermint Harris (Harrison Nelsom)

b. Jul. 17, 1925, Texarkana, TX
Guitar, Vocals / Jump Blues, West Coast Blues
The contemporary blues boom has resuscitated the career of many a veteran blues artist who's been silent for ages. Take guitarist Peppermint Harris, who in 1951 topped the R&B charts with his classic booze ode "I Got Loaded." Nobody expected a new Peppermint Harris CD in 1995, but Home Cooking producer Roy C. Ames coaxed one out of old Pep for Collectables nonetheless. *Texas on My Mind* may not be as enthralling as Harris' early '50s output, but it's nice to have him back in circulation.

By the time he was in his early 20s, Harrison Nelson, Jr., was lucky enough to have found a mentor and friend on the Houston blues front: Lightnin' Hopkins took an interest in the young man's musical development. When Harris was deemed ready, Lightnin' accompanied him to Houston's Gold Star Records. Nothing came of that jaunt, but Harris eventually recorded his debut 78 for the company in 1948 (as Peppermint Nelson).

Bob Shad's Sittin' in With label was the vehicle that supplied Harris' early work to the masses—especially his first major hit, "Raining in My Heart," in 1950. These weren't exactly formal sessions—legend has it one took place in a Houston bordello! Nor was Shad too cognizant of Pep's surname—when he couldn't recall it, he simply renamed our man Harris.

Harris moved over to Eddie Mesner's Aladdin Records in 1951, cutting far tighter sides for the firm in Los Angeles (often with the ubiquitous Maxwell Davis serving as bandleader and saxist). After "I Got Loaded" lit up the charts in 1951, Harris indulged in one booze ode after another: "Have Another Drink and Talk to Me," "Right Back On It," "Three Sheets in the Wind." But try as they might, the bottle let Harris down as a lyrical launching pad after that.

He drifted from Money and Cash to RCA's short-lived subsidiary "X" and Don Robey's Duke logo (where he allegedly penned "As the Years Go Passing By" for Fenton Robinson) after that, but it wasn't until a long-lasting association with Stan Lewis' Shreveport, LA-based Jewel Records commenced in 1965 that Harris landed for longer than a solitary single.

Later, Harris worked various day jobs around Houston, including one at a record pressing plant, before retiring to Sacramento, CA (until recently, anyway). — *Bill Dahl*

Peppermint Harris / 1962 / Time ✦✦✦
Nice early-'50s Texas R&B. — *Bill Dahl*

Sittin' in With / 1979 / Mainstream ✦✦✦✦
Fifteen well-chosen 1950-1951 masters from Bob Shad's Sittin' in With label by Houston bluesman Peppermint Harris, including his hit "Rainin' in My Heart." Rowdy little bands behind the powerful singer sometimes included Goree Carter on guitar. — *Bill Dahl*

● **I Got Loaded** / 1987 / Route 66 ✦✦✦✦
Harris hit his full stride after signing with Aladdin Records in 1951 and moving his recording base to Los Angeles. Under saxist Maxwell Davis' direction, Harris waxed his smash "I Got Loaded" and a few more potent rounds after that ("Three Sheets in the Wind," "Have Another Drink and Talk to Me"). Unfortunately not yet available on CD, these sides comprise Pep's chief claim to fame. — *Bill Dahl*

Texas on My Mind / Dec. 1995 / Collectables ✦✦✦
From the late '40s through the early '60s Peppermint Harris recorded for a variety of labels to moderate success. Although he had a few records in the '70s, he was basically retired until 1995, when he recorded *Texas on My Mind* at the age of 72. Although the songs on the album are quite good (most of the numbers are originals), Harris' abilities have dwindled; with his limited voice and guitar skills, he simply doesn't have the power to captivate an audience. — *Thom Owens*

Penthouse in the Ghetto / Oct. 21, 1997 / M.I.L. Multimedia ✦✦✦
Penthouse in the Ghetto features 20 tracks from Texas bluesman Peppermint Harris, including some of his famed "blues drinking songs." — *Steve Huey*

Being Black Twice / Collectables ✦✦✦
These are '60s and '70s sides from the Jewel label. A good vocalist with some unusual material. — *Hank Davis*

Shakey Jake Harris

b. Apr. 12, 1921, Earle, AR, **d.** Mar. 2, 1990
Harmonica, Vocals / Chicago Blues
Jake Harris knew how to shake a pair of dice in order to roll a lucrative winner. He also realized early on that his nephew, guitarist Magic Sam, was a winner as a bluesman. Harris may have not been a technical wizard on his chosen instrument, but his vocals and harp style were proficient enough to result in a reasonably successful career (both with Sam and without).

Born James Harris, the Arkansas native moved to Chicago at age seven. Admiring the style of Sonny Boy Williamson, Harris gradually learned the rudiments of the harp but didn't try his hand at entertaining professionally until 1955. Harris made his bow on vinyl in 1958 for the newly formed Artistic subsidiary of Eli Toscano's West Side-based Cobra Records. His only Artistic 45, "Call Me If You Need Me"/"Roll Your Moneymaker," was produced by Willie Dixon and featured Sam and Syl Johnson on guitars.

The uncompromising Chicago mainstream sound of that 45 contrasted starkly with Jake Harris' next studio project. Prestige's Bluesville subsidiary paired him with a pair of jazzmen—guitarist Bill Jennings and organist Jack McDuff—in 1960 for a full album, *Good Times* (the unlikely hybrid of styles working better than one might expect). The harpist encored later that year with *Mouth Harp Blues*, this time with a quartet including Chicagoan Jimmie Lee Robinson on guitar and a New York rhythm section (both of his Bluesville LPs were waxed in New Jersey).

Jake Harris and Magic Sam remained running partners for much of the 1960s. They shared bandstands at fabled West Side haunts such as Sylvio's—where he was captured on tape in 1966 singing "Sawed Off Shotgun" and "Dirty Work Goin' On" (now available on a Black Top disc by Sam)—and Big Bill Hill's Copacabana before Harris moved to Los Angeles in the late '60s. He recorded for World Pacific and briefly owned his own nightclub and record label before returning to Arkansas (where he died in 1990). — *Bill Dahl*

Good Times / 1961 / Bluesville ✦✦✦✦
Chicago harpist Shakey Jake Harris journeyed all the way to New Jersey to make his debut album in 1960. It was a huge stylistic departure for Harris—he was paired with jazz mainstays Brother Jack McDuff on simmering Hammond organ and blues-tinged guitarist Bill Jennings. The trio located some succulent common ground even without a drummer, Harris keeping his mouth organ phrasing succinct and laying out when his more accomplished session mates catch fire. — *Bill Dahl*

● **Mouth Harp Blues** / 1962 / Bluesville ✦✦✦✦
When Harris returned to New Jersey later that same year to wax his Bluesville encore, he brought along fellow Chicagoan Jimmie Lee Robinson as his guitarist. A full rhythm section was used this time (New York cats all), but the overall approach was quite a bit closer to what he was used to hearing on Chicago's West side. — *Bill Dahl*

Further on Up the Road / 1968 / World Pacific ✦✦✦
The Devil's Harmonica / 1972 / Polydor ✦✦✦✦

William Harris

b. Glendora, MS
Vocals / Delta Blues, Prewar Country Blues
Virtually nothing is known about bluesman William Harris; as a result of the rhythmic intricacy of the guitar work in evidence on the nine songs which comprise his recorded legacy, historians have placed him as a product of the Mississippi Delta, although the geographic references scattered among his music also suggest an Alabama background. Birmingham, AL, was certainly the location of his first recording session, cut on July 18, 1927; accounts suggest that at the time Harris was a performer with F.S. Wolcott's Rabbit Foot Minstrels. Theories that he traveled the medicine show circuit are lent further credence by his second recording date, which occured over a three-day period in October 1928 in Richmond, IN; among the tracks cut by Harris was "Kansas City Blues," previously recorded by Jim Jackson, another medicine show entertainer. Additionally, two other staples of the circuit, Frank Stokes and Papa Charlie Jackson, previously recorded "Take Me Back," up-

dated by Harris as "Hot Time Blues." In all likelihood, these are mysteries which will never be solved—his trail ends after this final session. —*Jason Ankeny*

• **Complete Recorded Works (1927-1929)** / 1991 / Document ++++
Document's *Complete Recorded Works (1927-1929)* is an exhaustive, chronologically sequenced William Harris & Buddy Boy Hawkins collection intended primarily for completists, specialists and academics. Casual listeners will find that the poor fidelity and sheer number of performances make the collection of marginal interest. — *Thom Owens*

Wynonie Harris

b. Aug. 24, 1915, Omaha, NE, **d.** Jun. 14, 1969, Los Angeles, CA
Drums, Vocals / Jump Blues, R&B
No blues shouter embodied the rollicking good times that he sang of quite like raucous shouter Wynonie Harris. "Mr. Blues," as he was not-so-humbly known, joyously related risque tales of sex, booze, and endless parties in his trademark raspy voice over some of the jumpingest horn-powered combos of the postwar era.

Those wanton ways eventually caught up with Harris, but not before he scored a raft of R&B smashes from 1946 to 1952. Harris was already a seasoned dancer, drummer, and singer when he left Omaha for Los Angeles in 1940 (his main influences being Big Joe Turner and Jimmy Rushing). He found plenty of work singing and appearing as an emcee on Central Avenue, the bustling nightlife strip of the Black community there. Wynonie Harris' reputation was spreading fast—he was appearing in Chicago at the Rhumboogie Club in 1944 when bandleader Lucky Millinder hired him as his band's new singer. With Millinder's orchestra in brassy support, Harris made his debut on shellac by boisterously delivering "Who Threw the Whiskey in the Well" that same year for Decca. By the time it hit in mid-1945, Harris was long gone from Millinder's organization and back in Los Angeles.

The shouter debuted on wax under his own name in July of 1945 at an Los Angeles date for Philo with backing from drummer Johnny Otis, saxist Teddy Edwards, and trumpeter Howard McGhee. A month later, he signed on with Apollo Records, an association that provided him with two huge hits in 1946: "Wynonie's Blues" (with saxist Illinois Jacquet's combo) and "Playful Baby." Harris' own waxings were squarely in the emerging jump blues style then sweeping the West Coast. After scattered dates for Hamp-Tone, Bullet, and Aladdin (where he dueled it out with his idol Big Joe on a two-sided "Battle of the Blues"), Harris joined the star-studded roster of Cincinnati's King Records in 1947. There his sales really soared.

Few records made a stronger seismic impact than Harris' 1948 chart-topper "Good Rockin' Tonight." Ironically, Harris shooed away its composer, Roy Brown, when he first tried to hand it to the singer; only when Brown's original version took off did Wynonie cover the romping number. With Hal "Cornbread" Singer on wailing tenor sax and a rocking, socking backbeat, the record provided an easily followed blueprint for the imminent rise of rock 'n' roll a few years later (and gave Elvis Presley something to place on the A side of his second Sun single).

After that, Harris was rarely absent from the R&B charts for the next four years, his offerings growing more boldly suggestive all the time. "Grandma Plays the Numbers," "All She Wants to Do Is Rock," "I Want My Fanny Brown," "Sittin' on It All the Time," "I Like My Baby's Pudding," "Good Morning Judge," "Bloodshot Eyes" (a country tune that was first released on King by Hank Penny), and "Lovin' Machine" were only a portion of the ribald hits Harris scored into 1952 (13 in all)—and then his personal hit parade stopped dead. It certainly wasn't Harris' fault—his King output rocked as hard as ever under Henry Glover's supervision—but changing tastes among fickle consumers that accelerated Wynonie Harris' sobering fall from favor.

Sides for Atco in 1956, King in 1957, and Roulette in 1960 only hinted at the raunchy glory of a short few years earlier. The touring slowed accordingly. In 1963, his chauffeur-driven Cadillacs and lavish New York home a distant memory, Harris moved back to Los Angeles, scraping up low-paying local gigs whenever he could. Chess gave him a three-song session in 1964, but sat on the promising results. Throat cancer silenced him for good in 1969, ending the life of a bigger-than-life R&B pioneer whose ego matched his tremendous talent. — *Bill Dahl*

Everybody Boogie! / Aug. 2, 1945-Dec. 1945 / Delmark ++++
This is one marvelous collection of 1945 recordings made for Apollo Records

with Harris' powerhouse vocals backed by jump blues bands led by jazz greats Illinois Jacquet, Oscar Pettiford and Jack McVea. No real honking and bar walking going on here; quite the opposite, as the Pettiford have bop lines creeping in throughout. But Harris seems oblivious to it all as tracks like "Time to Change Your Town," "Here Come the Blues," "Stuff You Gotta Watch," and "Somebody Changed the Lock on My Door" are on an equal par for sheer bravado and intensity with the best of his later work for King. A welcome compilation. — *Cub Koda*

☆ **Good Rocking Tonight** / 1990 / Charly +++++
Equally splendid compilation of the raspy shouter's King label output from the British Charly logo. Contains 20 sides, including a few essentials that Rhino didn't bother with: a roaring "Rock Mr. Blues" that grants Harris vocal group backing; the lascivious rocker "I Want My Fanny Brown" and "Lollipop Mama," and a celebratory "Mr. Blues Is Coming to Town." Harris and King always used inexorably swinging bands—saxists include Red Prysock, David Van Dyke (who duel it out on the amazing "Quiet Whiskey"), Big John Greer, Hal Singer, and Tom Archia. — *Bill Dahl*

★ **Bloodshot Eyes: The Best of Wynonie Harris** / 1993 / King/Rhino +++++
Wynonie Harris was a hard-living, rousing R&B shouter who made some of the most sexually explicit songs in modern popular music history. Harris didn't leave much to the imagination, but he also possessed a booming voice with wonderful tone and range, and the comedic skill to execute these tunes without becoming raunchy. There are many hilarious cuts on this 18-track anthology, among them "I Like My Baby's Pudding," "Grandma Plays the Numbers," and "Good Morning Judge." Harris roars, struts and wails over equally feverish arrangements, and earns a draw with Joe Turner on "Battle of the Blues." These songs give a good portrait of a delightful, often spectacular vocalist who could be both provocative and compelling. — *Ron Wynn*

Women, Whiskey & Fish Tails / 1993 / Ace ++++
British compiler Ray Topping focuses on Harris' 1952-1957 King output on this 21-song collection, when he was undeniably on the downslide as far as making hits. But there was still plenty of wind in the shouter's sails, judging from "Greyhound," "Christina," "Shake That Thing" (an update of an ancient blues theme), "Git to Gittin' Baby," and "Mr. Dollar." Harris even supplied a savvy sequel to one of his immortal numbers with "Bad News Baby (There'll Be No Rockin' Tonite)." — *Bill Dahl*

Wilbert Harrison

b. Jan. 5, 1929, Charlotte, NC, **d.** Oct. 26, 1994, Spencer, NC
Vocals, Piano, Guitar, Drums / R&B, Soul, Rock 'n' Roll, East Coast Blues
Perceived by casual oldies fans as a two-hit wonder (his 1959 chart-topper "Kansas City" and a heartwarming "Let's Work Together" a full decade later), Wilbert Harrison actually left behind a varied body of work that blended an intriguing melange of musical idioms into something quite distinctive.

Country and gospel strains filtered into Wilbert Harrison's consciousness as a youth in North Carolina. When he got out of the Navy in Miami around 1950, he began performing in a calypso-based style. Miami entrepreneur Henry Stone signed Harrison to his Rockin' logo in 1953; his debut single, "This Woman of Mine," utilized the very same melody as his later reading of "Kansas City" (the first rendition of the Jerry Leiber/Mike Stoller composition by pianist Little Willie Littlefield came out in 1952, doubtless making an impression). Its flip, a country-tinged "Letter Edged in Black," exhibited Harrison's eclectic mindset.

After moving to Newark, NJ, Harrison wandered by the headquarters of Savoy Records one fortuitous day and was snapped up by producer Fred Mendelsohn. Harrison recorded several sessions for Savoy, beginning with a catchy cover of Terry Fell's country tune "Don't Drop It." Top New York sessioneers—arranger Leroy Kirkland, saxist Buddy Lucas and guitarists Mickey Baker and Kenny Burrell—backed Harrison on his 1954-56 Savoy output, but hits weren't forthcoming.

That changed instantly when Harrison waxed his driving "Kansas City" for Harlem entrepreneur Bobby Robinson in 1959. With a barbed-wire guitar solo by Wild Jimmy Spruill igniting Harrison's no-frills piano and clenched vocal, "Kansas City" paced both the R&B and pop charts soon after its issue on Fury Records (not bad for a $40 session). Only one minor problem: Harrison was still technically under contract to Savoy (though label head Herman Lubinsky had literally run him out of his office some years earlier!), leading to all sorts of legal wrangles that finally went Robinson's way. Momentum for any Fury follow-ups had been fatally blunted in the interim, despite fine attempts with "Cheatin' Baby," the sequel "Goodbye Kansas City," and the original "Let's Stick Together."

Harrison bounced from Neptune to Doc to Constellation to Port to Vest with little in the way of tangible rewards before unexpectedly making a comeback in '69 with his infectious "Let's Work Together" for Juggy Murray's Sue imprint. The two-part single proved a popular cover item—Canned Heat revived it shortly thereafter, and Brian Ferry chimed in with his treatment later on. Alas, it was an isolated happenstance—apart from "My Heart Is Yours," a bottom-end chart entry on SSS International in '71, no more hits were in Wilbert's future. But Harrison soldiered on, sometimes as a one-man band, for years to come. —*Bill Dahl*

Let's Work Together / 1969 / Sue ♦♦♦
Quickie album supervised by Juggy Murray to cash in on the unexpected success of Harrison's "Let's Work Together," but not a bad effort all the same. Harrison brings his unique vocal delivery to oldies such as "Blue Monday," "Stagger Lee," "Louie Louie," and "Stand by Me," imparting his own personal stamp to each. This LP deserves digital reissue somewhere down the line. —*Bill Dahl*

Small Labels / 1986 / Krazy Kat ♦♦♦♦
Vinyl survey of Harrison's forays away from the famous indie diskeries, both before and after his hit with "Kansas City." Weirdly, his 1953 effort "This Woman of Mine" uses the same melody as "Kansas City," some six years prior to his hitting big with it. Harrison was liable to try anything to land a hit—he brands himself a "Calypso Man," tries a hillbilly tack on "Letter Edged in Black," and offers a salute to the 1964 "New York World's Fair"—all in that distinctive slurred voice of his. —*Bill Dahl*

Listen to My Song / 1987 / Savoy ♦♦♦♦
Harrison's first label association of any endurance commenced when he signed with Herman Lubinsky's Savoy logo in 1954 for a two-year stretch. Top New York sessioneers like guitarists Mickey Baker and Kenny Burrell and saxists Buddy Lucas and Budd Johnson help out on these 16 Savoy tracks (still unavailable on CD). He liked that C&W; Terry Fell's "Don't Drop It" is a tremendously catchy hillbilly tune given an R&B flavor by the young singer. —*Bill Dahl*

Greatest Classic R&B Hits / 1989 / Grudge ♦♦♦♦
This is the only available CD for Harrison's late-'60s material, long after his 1959 classic "Kansas City." —*Bill Dahl*

● **Kansas City** / 1992 / Relic ♦♦♦♦
Finally, paydirt! Harrison smashed the charts in 1959 with his massive hit "Kansas City" for Bobby Robinson's Fury logo. Here we have 22 fine sides from the Fury hookup, some in stereo and many with Wild Jimmy Spruill on lead guitar. "Cheatin' Baby," "C.C. Rider," "1960," and the inevitable sequel "Goodbye Kansas City" are prime examples of Harrison's slightly off-kilter approach to his craft, while this infectious "Let's Stick Together" developed into the more worldly "Let's Work Together" toward the end of the decade. —*Bill Dahl*

Alvin Youngblood Hart

b. Mar. 2, 1963, Oakland, CA
Guitar / Modern Acoustic Blues
Guitarist, singer, and songwriter Alvin Youngblood Hart is continuing in the path laid down by acoustic blues practitioners like Taj Mahal, Guy Davis, and other 1990s blues revivalists, but his roots go back much further than that, to the classic stylings of Bukka White, Charley Patton, Leadbelly and Blind Willie McTell.

Born in Oakland, CA, Hart accompanied his parents on summer trips to his grandparents' home in the hills of northern Mississippi, and it was there that his passion for acoustic blues was first sparked. On visits to his grandmother's house, he saw people as they lived in the 19th century, without the luxuries of indoor plumbing or phones, and often saw horse-drawn wagons in place of cars. Although there was not a lot of music around the hills of Carrollton, MS, where his grandmother lived, his uncle sparked his interest by playing guitar and telling him stories about Charley Patton. His grandmother also played blues piano, furthering his knowledge and interest.

Despite the trips back to his roots, Hart cites recordings by Jimi Hendrix and the Rolling Stones with helping him along in his blues guitar studies.

His father worked as a salesman for General Electric, so the Hart family moved a lot. He adopted the nickname "Alvin" from the harmonica-playing frontman for the TV cartoon group the Chipmunks. His parents had a good record collection, and he began playing guitar in his early teens, studying the recordings of Jimmy Reed, B.B. King, and Jimmy Witherspoon.

After his parents settled in Schaumburg, IL, he began frequenting Maxwell Street in nearby Chicago. He eventually became known to the regular musicians there as "Youngblood." After attending a nearby community college, Hart's family moved again, to southern California. After becoming fed up with the politics of the local blues club scene there, he began finding his own voice, independent of any groups, playing acoustic blues by himself.

After signing up with the Coast Guard in 1986, he was stationed on a riverboat at Natchez, MS. There, he furthered his blues education by playing in local bars on his off-duty hours. After finishing his seven years in the Coast Guard in Berkeley, he befriended Joe Louis Walker, who invited Hart to open some of his shows in the area. His first big break came about in February 1995 while opening for Taj Mahal at an Oakland jazz club. Mahal's longtime road manager invited Hart to Grateful Dead guitarist Bob Weir's studio for an impromptu jam session. Hart was signed to a management contract and recorded a demo that caught the ears of some executives at the OKeh subsidiary of Epic Records. OKeh was at one time the home of many of Hart's long-gone musical heroes, artists like Blind Boy Fuller, Brownie McGhee and Lonnie Johnson. In the summer of 1996, Hart was tapped for the Further Festival, which continued the spirit of the Grateful Dead after the death of guitarist/bandleader Jerry Garcia in the summer of 1995. Hart found himself exposed to a huge new audience while sandwiched between acts like Bruce Hornsby, Hot Tuna, and Los Lobos on the Further Festival tour.

His brilliant 1996 debut, *Big Mama's Door,* for the OKeh division of Epic Records, received widespread critical acclaim and got his career as an international touring artist off the ground. He offers up blues-tinged covers of well-known folk songs like "When the Boys Were On the Western Plain" and "Gallows Pole." He also covers traditional classic blues tunes like "Hillbilly Willie's Blues" from Blind Willie McTell and "Pony Blues" from Charley Patton.

Based on the strength of his major-label debut and his live shows, Hart received five nominations at the 1997 W.C. Handy Blues Awards, tying him with Luther Allison. Hart was nominated for Best New Artist, Best Acoustic Artist, and Best Traditional Blues Artist, and Hart's album was nominated for both Acoustic Album of the Year and Traditional Album of the Year.

A talented songwriter, interpreter, guitarist, and vocalist, Hart is also an expert at restoring old musical instruments. He has restored many formerly unplayable instruments from the 1920s, '30s, and '40s to playable condition.

When he is not on the road, Hart makes his home in Berkeley, CA. Expect more magic from this multi-talented, multi-faceted practitioner of modern acoustic blues. —*Richard Skelly*

★ **Big Mama's Door** / Apr. 1996 / OKeh/550 Music ♦♦♦♦♦
The debut recording of 33-year-old Hart is extraordinarily simple and simply extraordinary. Except for three cuts on which he's joined by Taj Mahal, *Big Mama's Door* is just Hart on acoustic guitar and vocals, and he's not doing anything fancy—just playing prewar-style blues, mostly in a percussive Delta manner, recorded live to two-track. Yet he succeeds so well in blending technique and feeling, structure and spontaneity, tradition and freshness that he produces a minor gem of a blues record, evocative of the blues masters of the 1920s and '30s. He covers Leadbelly, Blind Willie McTell, Charley Patton, and the Mississippi Sheiks and does originals that replicate older blues idioms, not just in the notes but in the nuances, and in the personal commitment he brings to the material. —*Steve Hoffman*

Buddy Boy Hawkins

Guitar, Vocals / R&B, Acoustic Blues
The scant discography of Walter "Buddy Boy" Hawkins reveals one of the most distinctive country-blues performers of the pre-war era, a gifted vocalist whose taste for slow, dirge-like songs was ideally suited to his intricate guitar work. Almost nothing is known about the singer; various attempts to determine his date and place of birth have resulted in countless chronological and geographical inconsistencies, although the consensus places him as a product of either Alabama or the northern Delta region. Between 1927 and 1929,

Hawkins recorded a dozen tracks for Paramount, many of them portraits of trains and life on the railroad (another possible piece of the puzzle); in any case, these sessions are the only surviving document of his music, and his subsequent activities remain a mystery. — *Jason Ankeny*

Buddy B Hawkins and His Buddies / Yazoo ✦✦✦✦
This is somewhat deceptive packaging, as Hawkins only has half of the selections and the "buddies" have the other half. But since the buddies include Texas Alexander, their contributions are worth close scrutiny. Hawkins' fine vocals and distinctive guitar are still dominant, though. — *Ron Wynn*

Roy Hawkins

Piano, Vocals / R&B, West Coast Blues, Piano Blues
Not only was Roy Hawkins dogged by bad luck during his career (at the height of his popularity, the pianist lost the use of an arm in a car wreck), he couldn't even cash in after the fact. When B.B. King blasted up the charts in 1970 with Roy Hawkins' classic "The Thrill Is Gone," the tune was mistakenly credited to the wrong composers on early pressings.

Little is known of Hawkins' early days. Producer Bob Geddins discovered Hawkins playing in an Oakland, CA nightspot and supervised his first 78s for Cavatone and Downtown in 1948. Modern Records picked up the rights to several Downtown masters before signing Hawkins to a contract in 1949. Two major R&B hits resulted: 1950's "Why Do Things Happen to Me" and "The Thrill Is Gone" the following year. Hawkins recorded for the Bihari brothers' Modern and RPM imprints into 1954. After that, a handful of 45s for Rhythm and Kent were all that was heard of the Bay Area pianist on vinyl. He's rumored to have died in 1973. — *Bill Dahl*

Highway 59 / 1984 / Ace ✦✦✦✦
Early-'50s rarities from the vaults of the Bihari brothers' Modern label, with a good amount of unissued masters recommending this 16-song LP (no CD equivalent yet). Hawkins' cool California blues piano blends well with the tasty little combos Modern provided; of special interest are the title cut and "Would You," a pair of 1952 gems that feature T-Bone Walker's incomparable guitar work. — *Bill Dahl*

● **Why Do Everything Happen to Me** / Route 66 ✦✦✦✦
A cross-section of the West Coast pianist's best-known early-'50s output, including the often-covered title item. Hawkins has been an unjustly overlooked figure for far too long, and this material is no exception—it has yet to make it to CD. — *Bill Dahl*

Screamin' Jay Hawkins

b. Jul. 18, 1929, Cleveland, OH
Vocals, Piano / R&B, Rock 'n' Roll, Jump Blues
Screamin' Jay Hawkins was the most outrageous performer extant during rock's dawn. Prone to emerging out of coffins onstage, a flaming skull named Henry his constant companion, Screamin' Jay was an insanely theatrical figure long before it was even remotely acceptable.

Hawkins' life story is almost as bizarre as his onstage shtick. Originally inspired by the booming baritone of Paul Robeson, Hawkins was unable to break through as an opera singer. His boxing prowess was every bit as lethal as his vocal cords; many of his most hilarious tales revolve around Jay beating the hell out of a musical rival!

Hawkins caught his first musical break in 1951 as pianist/valet to veteran jazz guitarist Tiny Grimes. He debuted on wax for Gotham the following year with "Why Did You Waste My Time," backed by Grimes and his Rockin' Highlanders (they donned kilts and tam o' shanters on stage). Singles for Timely ("Baptize Me in Wine") and Mercury's Wing subsidiary (1955's otherworldly "[She Put The] Wamee [On Me]," a harbinger of things to come) preceded Hawkins' immortal 1956 rendering of "I Put a Spell on You" for Columbia's OKeh imprint.

Hawkins originally envisioned the tune as a refined ballad. After he and his New York session aces (notably guitarist Mickey Baker and saxist Sam "The Man" Taylor) had imbibed to the point of no return, Hawkins screamed, grunted, and gurgled his way through the tune with utter drunken abandon. A resultant success despite the protests of uptight suits-in-power, "Spell" became Screamin' Jay's biggest seller ("Little Demon," its rocking flip, is a minor classic itself).

Hawkins cut several amazing 1957-58 follow-ups in the same crazed

vein—"Hong Kong," a surreal "Yellow Coat," the Jerry Leiber/Mike Stoller-penned "Alligator Wine"—but none of them clicked the way "Spell" had. Deejay Alan Freed convinced Screamin' Jay that popping out of a coffin might be a show-stopping gimmick by handing him a $300 bonus (long after Freed's demise, Screamin' Jay Hawkins is still benefiting from his crass brainstorm).

Hawkins' next truly inspired waxing came in 1969 when he was contracted to Philips Records (where he made two albums). His gross "Constipation Blues" wouldn't garner much airplay, but remains an integral part of his legacy to this day.

The cinema has been a beneficiary of Screamin' Jay's larger-than-life persona in recent years. His featured roles in *Mystery Train* and *A Rage in Harlem* have made Hawkins a familiar visage to youngsters who've never even heard "I Put a Spell on You." Hawkins remains musically active, though his act doesn't seem all that bizarre anymore. — *Bill Dahl*

Frenzy / 1982 / Edsel ✦✦✦✦
Screamin' Jay Hawkins was a truly demented R&B shouter, as evidenced by the classic "I Put a Spell on You." It wasn't long before his camp schtick overshadowed his musical abilities, but for a brief while he had a certain warped genius. Most of these tracks were recorded for OKeh, and the 14-track compilation *Frenzy* contains most of the best of these recordings. Nothing ever quite touched "I Put a Spell on You," but the songs that came the closest are here. *Frenzy* may not be a comprehensive collection, but for anyone that wants more of the sound that made "I Put a Spell on You" a hit, this will suffice. — *Stephen Thomas Erlewine*

Real Life / 1983 / Charly ✦✦✦
An uneven batch of R&B and blues tracks from Screamin' Jay Hawkins cut in the mid-'80s. Hawkins never had that great a voice to begin with, and years of shouting and hollering have affected it even more. But you've got to admire his spirit and personality, which are the strong points of this session. — *Ron Wynn*

Live & Crazy / 1989 / Evidence ✦✦
While Screamin' Jay Hawkins can't really shout with the force or volume of the past and doesn't have the energy to keep a whole set moving briskly, he gets off enough good one-liners to make things a bit interesting. His band plays routine blues shuffles, workouts, R&B covers, and Hawkins originals such as "The Whammy," "Constipation Blues," and of course "I Put A Spell On You." While nearly an hour of this eventually becomes tedious, Hawkins' fans will still enjoy it, and others can satisfy themselves with the occasional nuggets. — *Ron Wynn*

● **Voodoo Jive: The Best of Screamin' Jay Hawkins** / Feb. 1990 / Rhino ✦✦✦✦
Some maintain that Hawkins was a one-hit fluke and a one-dimensional performer with a limited singing voice and no other discernible skills. Others insist that Hawkins was a decent R&B and blues singer and an excellent entertainer and personality whose real talents were overshadowed by the success of "I Put a Spell on You." This anthology doesn't convincingly answer the argument, but it does collect 17 Hawkins singles from OKeh, Enrica, and Phillips, including all of his major hits. The high (or low) point is perhaps 1969's "Constipation Blues." — *Ron Wynn*

Cow Fingers & Mosquito Pie / 1991 / Epic ✦✦✦✦
Magically weird 19-song collection of the bizarre shouter's mid-'50s OKeh/Epic output, when he was at the height of his strange and terrifying vocal powers. In addition to the prerequisite "I Put a Spell on You" and the surreal rockers "Yellow Coat," "Hong Kong," "Alligator Wine," and "Little Demon," there's the amusing "There's Something Wrong with You," a previously unissued "You Ain't Foolin' Me," and a deranged takeoff on the cowboy ditty "Take Me Back to My Boots and Saddle" (and what Jay does to the formerly stately "I Love Paris" and "Orange Colored Sky" is truly indescribable!). — *Bill Dahl*

Spellbound! 1955-74 / 1991 / Bear Family ✦✦✦
Bear Family's *Spellbound! 1955-74* is a double-disc set that captures highlights from Screamin' Jay Hawkins' recordings for Wing, Decca, Phillips and RCA. It's not quite the bargain it seems. Half of the 48 tracks were already issued on two Phillips albums, which were combined on one Edsel CD. Furthermore, most of these songs date from the '60s, with only a handful coming from Hawkins' '50s peak. Strangely, of those songs, not one of them is the original "I Put a Spell On You," which makes this hardly the definitive over-

view that it should be. Instead of focusing on the best of Screamin' Jay Hawkins' best material, it has the campy, silly stuff from the '60s, which will try the patience of anyone outside devoted fans—and those devoted fans will prefer more complete compilations than this strangely scattershot effort from Bear Family. There are some good moments here, but overall, it has to rank as a disappointment. — *Stephen Thomas Erlewine*

Stone Crazy / 1993 / Rhino ◆◆◆
Stone Crazy is a latter-day album from Screamin' Jay Hawkins, recorded with his touring band the Chickenhawks. Musically, the album sounds surprisingly good, since the Chickenhawks are a tight little backing band, but Hawkins' schtick gets a little tiresome after a while, and there aren't many great songs on the album. Only the tribute to the *Twin Peaks* vixen "Sherilyn Fenn" really hits home, but dedicated fans will be pleased that the record does have sporadic fits of energetic playing. — *Stephen Thomas Erlewine*

Somethin' Funny Goin On / Apr. 16, 1995 / Bizarre/Straight ◆◆◆
Former Beat Farmer guitarist Buddy Blue sits in with Screamin' Jay Hawkins' on *Somethin' Funny Goin' On.* It's a fairly predictable set, with the traditional Screamin' antics and spooky blues, without any real standouts. There aren't any dogs on the album, either—it's just a mediocre record, one that fails to capture the wildness of Screamin' Jay or to deliver any memorable songs. — *Stephen Thomas Erlewine*

At Last / Mar. 10, 1998 / Last Call ◆◆
At Last is a collection of all-new material from Screamin' Jay Hawkins, featuring 12 of his originals and a suitably deranged cover of "I Shot the Sheriff." — *Steve Huey*

Portrait of a Man / Edsel ◆◆◆
Portrait of a Man is a collection of rarities and obscurities from a man whose very career was filled with arcania. Of course, it contains the original version of "I Put a Spell on You," but what Screamin' Jay Hawkins collection doesn't? The main point of the disc is rarities that aren't anywhere else, whether it's a remake of "I Put a Spell on You" or his freak English hit "Heart Attack and Vine." There are more interesting things here than the average Screamin' album, which is both good ("Mountain Jive") and bad ("Armpit No. 6"). Either way, it's one of the handful of Hawkins compilations that aren't strict hits collections but are worth hearing. — *Stephen Thomas Erlewine*

Ted Hawkins

b. Oct. 28, 1936, Biloxi, MS, **d.** Jan. 1, 1995, Los Angeles, CA
Guitar, Vocals / Soul, Modern Acoustic Blues, Singer-Songwriter, Soul Blues, Modern Country Blues
Overseas, he was a genuine hero, performing to thousands. But on his Los Angeles hometurf, sand-blown Venice Beach served as Ted Hawkins' makeshift stage. He'd deliver his magnificent melange of soul, blues, folk, gospel, and a touch of country all by his lonesome, with only an acoustic guitar for company. Passersby would pause to marvel at Hawkins' melismatic vocals, dropping a few coins or a greenback into his tip jar on the way by.

That was the way Ted Hawkins kept body and soul together until 1994, when DGC/Geffen Records issued *The Next Hundred Years,* his breakthrough album. Suddenly, Hawkins was poised on the precipice of stardom. And then, just after Christmas that same year, in a bout of cruel irony, he died of a stroke.

Ted Hawkins' existence was no day in the park. Born into abject poverty in Mississippi, an abused and illiterate child, Hawkins was sent to reform school when he was 12 years old. He encountered his first musical inspiration there from New Orleans pianist Professor Longhair, whose visit to the school moved the lad to perform in a talent show. But it wasn't enough to keep him out of trouble. At age 15, he stole a leather jacket and spent three years at Mississippi's infamous state penitentiary at Parchman Farm.

Roaming from Chicago to Philadelphia to Buffalo after his release, Hawkins left the frigid weather behind in 1966, purchasing a one-way ticket to Los Angeles. Suddenly, music beckoned; he bought a guitar and set out to locate the ex-manager of Sam Cooke (one of his idols). No such luck, but he did manage to cut his debut 45, the soul-steeped "Baby"/"Whole Lot Of Women," for Money Records. When he learned no royalties were forthcoming from its sales, Hawkins despaired of ever making a living at his music and took to playing on the streets.

Fortunately, producer Bruce Bromberg was interested in Hawkins' wel-

fare, recording his delightfully original material in 1971 both with guitarist Phillip Walker's band ("Sweet Baby" was issued as a single on the Joliet label) and in a solo acoustic format (with Ted's wife Elizabeth occasionally adding harmonies). The producer lost touch with Hawkins for a while after recording him, Hawkins falling afoul of the law once again. In 1982, those tapes finally emerged on Rounder as *Watch Your Step,* and Hawkins began to receive some acclaim (*Rolling Stone* gave it a five-star review). Bromberg corralled him again for the 1986 encore album *Happy Hour,* which contained the touching "Cold & Bitter Tears."

At the behest of a British deejay, Hawkins moved to England in 1986 and was treated like a star for four years, performing in Great Britain, Ireland, France, even Japan. But when he came home, he was faced with the same old situation. Once again, he set up his tip jar on the beach, donned the black leather glove he wore on his fretting hand, and played for passersby—until DGC ever so briefly propelled him into the major leagues.

Ted Hawkins was a unique talent, unclassifiable and eminently soulful. For a year or so, he was even a star in his own country. — *Bill Dahl*

Watch Your Step / 1982 / Rounder ◆◆◆
Guitarist/vocalist Ted Hawkins was an instant sensation when this session was originally released in 1982. At a time when slick, heavily produced urban contemporary material was establishing its domination on the R&B scene, Hawkins' hard-edged, rough, cutting voice, plus his crisp acoustic guitar accompaniment and country blues roots, seemed both dated and extremely fresh. This 15-track CD includes four numbers with Hawkins backed by Phillip Walker and his band, and others ranging from the humorous "Who Got My Natural Comb?" to the poignant "If You Love Me" and two versions of the title track. He also teamed with his wife Elizabeth on "Don't Lose Your Cool" and "I Gave It All I Had" for moving duets. — *Ron Wynn*

On the Boardwalk / 1986 / Unamerican ◆◆◆

● **Happy Hour** / 1986 / Rounder ◆◆◆◆
Guitarist/vocalist Ted Hawkins' second Rounder record enhanced his reputation. *Happy Hour* features Hawkins' memorable compositions, plus a wonderful version of Curtis Mayfield's "Gypsy Woman." Hawkins' vocals were even more gritty and striking, as was his acoustic guitar backing and chording. He teamed with his wife Elizabeth on "Don't Make Me Explain It," "My Last Goodbye," and "California Song," and with guitarist Night Train Clemons on "Gypsy Woman" and "You Pushed My Head Away." Hawkins blended soul and urban blues stylings with country and rural blues inflections and rhythms, making another first-rate release. — *Ron Wynn*

The Next Hundred Years / Mar. 29, 1994 / DGC ◆◆◆
The former L.A. street musician's major label breakthrough was in a great many ways a far weaker outing than what came before, largely due to a plodding band unwisely inserted behind Hawkins that tends to distract rather than enhance his impassioned vocals and rich acoustic guitar strumming. Mostly originals ("There Stands the Glass" returns, as does "Ladder of Success") that would have sounded so much better in an intimate solo context. — *Bill Dahl*

Songs from Venice Beach / Oct. 1995 / Evidence ◆◆◆◆
Blending every form of roots music imaginable into his own singular soulful stew, the incomparable Ted Hawkins stuck mostly to R&B covers on this splendid 1985 solo outing—songs by Sam Cooke (his idol), Jerry Butler, Bobby Bland, the Temptations, and Garnet Mimms receive gorgeous readings by the acoustic guitarist. But even though he only contributed one original, the touching "Ladder of Success," to the set, Hawkins wasn't content to remain in one genre—his commanding revival of Webb Pierce's hillbilly weeper "There Stands the Glass" ranks with the disc's very best moments (of which there are many). — *Bill Dahl*

● **The Ted Hawkins Story: Suffer No More** / Jan. 13, 1998 / Rhino ◆◆◆◆
Taken individually, Hawkins' albums didn't measure up to his critical reputation, due to uneven material, occasionally inappropriate production, and overreliance upon covers. More than most best-ofs, this 20-song compilation is a revelation of sorts. By focusing on his best moments, it's much easier to make a convincing case for Hawkins as a major, if erratic, roots-music performer who sounded like a coarsened, acoustic-oriented Sam Cooke. The set goes all the way back to both sides of his rare (and good) 1966 soul single on the Money label, and highlights the best originals from the '70s and '80s sessions released on Rounder, wisely selecting sparsely from his cover-

dominated albums of the mid-'80s. The songs from his major-label finale *The Next Hundred Years* can veer towards production slickness, but there's a pleasing bonus in three acoustic, previously unreleased cuts from the early 1990s. It's an intelligently selected, well-rounded disc, presenting several sides of this idiosyncratic artist: composer, folky interpreter of material by Sam Cooke and Brook Benton, and country-tinged soul artist. —*Richie Unterberger*

The Final Hour / Jan. 13, 1998 / Evidence ✦✦✦✦
Ted Hawkins' story is one of the most interesting—and tragic—in the history of R&B. Who'd have thought that a fifty-something street singer who performed 1960s-type soul in Venice Beach, CA would have signed with Geffen's DGC label after decades of obscurity? That's exactly what happened, but tragically, a 58-year-old Hawkins died from a diabetes-related stroke just when things were really looking up for him. Recorded live at three 1994 concerts and released in 1998, *The Final Hour* shows how great Hawkins was sounding during the last months of his life. Nothing slick or elaborate happens on this album—it's just the charismatic Hawkins and his acoustic guitar, drawing on Sam Cooke's influence but always sounding like his own man. Those familiar with Hawkins' Rounder output will be familiar with heartfelt originals like "Bad Dog," "Bring It on Home, Daddy," and "Revenge of Scorpio," all of which demonstrate that he was as superb a composer as he was a singer. Hawkins is equally captivating on interpretations of Brook Benton's "I Got What I Wanted" and "All I Have to Offer You Is Me," a hit for country great Charley Pride that easily lends itself to Hawkins' brand of acoustic R&B. Soul lovers who haven't experienced the joys of Hawkins' music should make a point of obtaining this magnificent album. —*Alex Henderson*

Clifford Hayes

Violin / Classic Jazz, Jazz Blues, Prewar Country Blues
A shadowy figure in jazz and blues history, Clifford Hayes was an okay violinist but more significant as a leader of recording sessions. He recorded with Sara Martin (1924) and often teamed up with banjoist Cal Smith in early jug bands including the Old Southern Jug Band, Clifford's Louisville Jug Band, the well-known Dixieland Jug Blowers (1926-7), and Hayes' Louisville Stompers (1927-29). One of the Dixieland Jug Blowers' sessions featured the great clarinetist Johnny Dodds while pianist Earl Hines was a surprise star with the otherwise primitive Louisville Stompers (a jugless group with a frontline of Hayes' violin and Hense Grundy's trombone). Clifford Hayes' last recordings were in 1931 and all of his sessions (plus those of some other jug bands) are available on four RST CDs. —*Scott Yanow*

Clifford Hayes & the Louisville Jug Bands, Vol. 1 / Sep. 16, 1924-Dec. 10, 1926 / RST ✦✦✦✦
The first of four volumes from the Austrian RST label that reissue the complete output from several historic jug bands from Louisville features violinist Clifford Hayes in several contexts. In 1924 he led the first jug band on record, backing blues singer Sara Martin on some exuberant performances that overcome the primitive recording quality. In addition this CD has Hayes leading the Old Southern Jug Band, Clifford's Louisville Jug Band, and the Dixieland Jug Blowers; all of the groups greatly benefit from the exciting playing of Earl McDonald on jug. The CD is rounded out by four selections from Whistler's Jug Band. Historic and generally enjoyable music, it's recommended to 1920s collectors. —*Scott Yanow*

● **Clifford Hayes & the Louisville Jug Bands, Vol. 2** / Dec. 10, 1926-Apr. 30, 1927 / RST ✦✦✦✦
The second of four CDs in a very valuable series from the Austrian RST label has 12 selections from the Dixieland Jug Blowers (a very spirited sextet with violinist Clifford Hayes, the colorful jug blowing of Earl McDonald, and on six numbers, clarinetist Johnny Dodds as a guest), eight from Earl McDonald's Original Louisville Jug Band, and four by Whistler's Jug Band (its leader Buford Threlked doubles on guitar and nose whistle). The monologue on the former group's "House Rent Rag" is quite memorable and still humorous. Of the four CDs, this is the most essential one for it finds these historic groups in their prime. —*Scott Yanow*

Clifford Hayes & the Louisville Jug Bands, Vol. 3 / Jun. 6, 1927-Feb. 6, 1929 / RST ✦✦✦✦
The third of four CDs from the Austrian RST label has the final ten selections

from the Dixieland Jug Blowers along with 14 by Clifford Hayes' Louisville Stompers. Although the former no longer had the powerful jug playing of Earl McDonald, the mysterious H. Clifford was a good substitute and the three-horn septet (which features two guest vocalists) certainly had plenty of spirit. The Louisville Stompers is essentially a stripped-down jugless version of the Jug Blowers, a jazz-oriented quartet comprised of violinist Clifford Hayes, trombonist Hense Grundy, pianist Johnny Gatewood, and the impressive guitarist Cal Smith who makes "Blue Guitar Stomp" a classic. The final seven Stompers performances are a bit surprising, for the pianist is the great Earl Hines who has a few short solos although mostly in a supporting role. All four of the CDs are easily recommended to collectors of the era, for on a whole they contain the complete output of these unusual groups. —*Scott Yanow*

Dixieland Jug Blowers / Jun. 7, 1927-Jun. 1, 1928 / Yazoo ✦✦✦✦
Jug band material in the hokum and country blues variety. This one goes about as far to the margin as any jug band ever journeyed, thanks to Clifford Hayes' violin and Earl McDonald's jug. —*Ron Wynn*

Clifford Hayes & the Louisville Jug Bands, Vol. 4 / Feb. 6, 1929-Jun. 17, 1931 / RST ✦✦✦✦
The fourth and final CD in this brief but important series from the Austrian RST label features jug bands in a variety of roles. There are the three last performances by Clifford Hayes' Louisville Stompers (the two versions of "You're Ticklin' Me" have Earl Hines on piano while "You Gonna Need My Help" features the classic blues singer Sippie Wallace). The Kentucky Jazz Babies (a quartet with violinist Clifford Hayes and trumpeter Jimmy Strange) does a good job on two numbers, and Phillips' Louisville Jug Band (an odd quartet with Hooks Tifford on C-melody sax and Charles "Cane" Adams playing what is called "walking cane flute") performs eight songs. In addition, Whistler and His Jug Band play two primitive numbers while violinist Clifford Hayes backs the minstrel singer Kid Coley and reunites with the great jug player Earl McDonald behind the vocals of country pioneer Jimmie Rodgers, Ben Ferguson, and John Harris. An interesting set to say the least. All four CDs in this series are recommended to fans of the era. —*Scott Yanow*

Patrick Hazell & Mother Blues Band

Piano, Drums, Harmonica, Vocals / Modern Electric Blues
Patrick Hazell is a White, one-man band (piano, neck rack harmonica, and drums) from Washington, IA. But skin color and point of origin hardly matter, as Hazell sounds like a complete throwback to the recordings of the late '40s and early '50s. His rhythmic drive is superlative while his sound and style are highly reminiscent of Memphis one-man-band star Joe Hill Louis. His raspy harp and vocals (sung into the same distorted microphone he plays through) are fortified with strong material, an unrelenting beat, and sensational ambience as he ekes out a piece of blues turf that hasn't been occupied in a very long time. In the current White-boy blues community—where seemingly every street corner has five people on it with shades, pleated pants, and beat-up Stratocasters in hand—Patrick Hazell stands out as something very unique and cool. —*Cub Koda*

Back Country Shuffle / 1978 / Blue Rhythm ✦✦
Patrick Hazell / 1980 / Blue Rhythm ✦✦✦
After Hours / 1981 / Blue Rhythm ✦✦✦
● **Blues on the Run** / 1995 / Blue Rhythm ✦✦✦✦
Hazell's opus has all the portents of an album you'll find yourself still listening to ten years from now, both for its content and its sheer uniqueness. The title track is five minutes of nasty modal shouting and honking while the opener, "Here I Go Again," answers the question, "What would it have sounded like if Joe Hill Louis had cut a rock 'n' roll record at Sun?" Hazell sounds his best when interpreting his own material, but even his take on a time-worn favorite like "Wang Dang Doodle" is well worth the listen. That he manages to pull off his one-man-band turn without the use of overdubbing makes the performances on this album all the more amazing. —*Cub Koda*

Blue Blood / 1996 / Blue Rhythm ✦✦✦✦
Hazell jettisons part of his one-man band approach for his second album and, despite the loss of autonomy, loses none of the raw feel that has made his previous recordings so enjoyable. Enlisting fellow Iowa blues heads

C-Boy James and Chris McCurdy to keep rudimentary time on drums and assorted lo-fi percussion throughout, Hazell turns in a multitude of great original performances on this disc. All 14 selections are written by him, and that same gritty vocal/Joe Hill Louis overamplified harmonica/boogie piano style that made his debut album so much fun is taken even further here. The opening track, "Here We Go Again" is an update of the first album's "Here I Go Again," recasting its lyrics this time toward the bar patron. There's a real ambient feel on several tracks, with the whole thing sounding like an old Trumpet 78 recorded at a deserted VFW hall, most notably on "Movin' Time," the minor-key "Walkin' on a Tightrope," the solo piano instrumental "Easy Time Blues," "Time Goes by So Quickly," and the set closer, "Avenue Called the Blues." That trademark one-man band feel of Hazell's comes to the fore on "All Mixed Up" and "Hot Cakes," while new territory is mined on the atmospheric "Unspoken Words," a drifting minor-key instrumental that almost veers into jazz territory. A superb harpist and an even better piano man (check out his work on "Washington Boogie" and the aforementioned "Easy Time Blues"), Hazell flexes his muscles beyond the novelty of one-man-band territory on this one, and the results are very fine, indeed. — *Cub Koda*

Jeff Healey

b. Mar. 25, 1966, Toronto, Ontario, Canada
Guitar, Vocals / Blues-Rock
What makes Jeff Healey different from other blues-rockers is also what keeps some listeners from accepting him as anything other than a novelty—the fact that the blind guitarist plays his Fender Stratocaster on his lap, not standing up. With the guitar in his lap, Healey can make unique bends and hammer-ons, making his licks different and more elastic than most of the competition. Unfortunately, his material leans toward standard AOR blues-rock which rarely lets him cut loose, but when he does, his instrumental prowess can be shocking.

Healey lost his sight at the age of one, after developing eye cancer. He began playing guitar when he was three years old and began performing with his band Blues Direction at the age of 15. Healey formed the Jeff Healey trio in 1985, adding bassist Joe Rockman and drummer Tom Stephen. The trio released a handful of self-released singles on their Forte record label, which led to a contract with Arista Records. The Jeff Healey Trio released their debut album, *See the Light,* in 1988 and the guitarist immediately developed a devoted following in blues-rock circles. Featuring the hit single "Angel Eyes," the record went platinum in the US. While the Jeff Healey Trio's subsequent records have been popular, none have been as successful as the debut. — *Stephen Thomas Erlewine*

● **See the Light** / 1988 / Arista ✦✦✦✦
Jeff Healey's debut album *See the Light* may be similar to Stevie Ray Vaughan's high-octane blues-rock, but in blues and blues-rock, it's often the little things that count, such as guitar styles, and there's no denying that Healey has a distinctive style. Healey plays his Stratocaster flat on his lap, allowing him to perform unusual long stretches that give his otherwise fairly predictable music real heart and unpredictability. Throughout the album, his guitar work keeps things interesting, even on slow ballads like "Angel Eyes" (one of two John Hiatt songs, by the way, along with the ripping "Confidence Man"). That's what keeps *See the Light* interesting, and it's what makes it an intriguing, promising debut. Unfortunately, Healey has never quite fulfilled that promise, but it's still exciting to hear the first flowerings of his talent. — *Thom Owens*

Hell to Pay / 1990 / Arista ✦✦✦
A solid follow-up to Healey's impressive debut, *Hell To Pay* features some of the guitarist's hottest playing to date. — *Stephen Thomas Erlewine*

Feel This / Aug. 1992 / Arista ✦✦✦✦
Third time up for sightless guitar wunderkid Jeff Healey and gang; *Feel This* offers the power trio's meatiest and most satisfying outing. JHB's brand of roadhouse rock can be somewhat bland on disc; here the group captures much more of its trademark live intensity than in the past. The unobtrusive addition of keyboards adds a more expansive dimension to several tracks. Boogie fans will want to check out the ZZ Top-like "Cruel Little Number"; blues-rockers will come away satisfied with the likes of "House That Love Built." Hip-hop connoisseurs, on the other hand, will likely want to avoid JHB's rap spoof on "If You Can't Feel Anything Else." — *Roch Parisien*

Cover to Cover / Jun. 13, 1995 / Arista ✦✦
Jeff Healey's collection of cover songs is fitfully entertaining, but his choice of material is predictable and when he does take a chance, such as on Stealer's Wheel's "Stuck in the Middle with You," he spends too much time trying to make it fit into his trademark stomping blues-rock style. — *Stephen Thomas Erlewine*

Johnny Heartsman

b. Feb. 9, 1937, San Fernando, CA, d. Dec. 27, 1996, Sacramento, CA
Bass, Flute, Guitar, Keyboards, Vocals / Modern Electric Blues
Shaven-headed Johnny Heartsman did so many musical things so well that he's impossible to pigeonhole. His low-moaning lead guitar work greatly distinguished a myriad of Bay Area blues recordings during the '50s and '60s, and he still played his axe with delicious dexterity and dynamics into the '90s. But Heartsman was just as likely to cut loose on organ or blow a titillating solo on flute (perhaps the unlikeliest blues instrument imaginable). He possessed a mellow, richly burnished voice to boot.

Through one of his principal influences, guitarist Lafayette "Thing" Thomas, a teenaged Heartsman hooked up with Bay Area producer Bob Geddins. Heartsman played bass on Jimmy Wilson's 1953 rendition of "Tin Pan Alley," handling guitar or piano at other Geddins-supervised dates. He cut his own two-part instrumental, the "Honky Tonk"-inspired "Johnny's House Party," for Ray Dobard's Music City imprint and watched it become a national R&B hit in 1957.

The early '60s brought a lot more session work—Heartsman played on Tiny Powell's "My Time After Awhile" (soon covered by Buddy Guy) and Al King's remake of Lowell Fulson's "Reconsider Baby." By then, Heartsman's imaginative twiddling of the volume knob with his finger to produce an eerie moan had become his guitaristic trademark.

Stints in show bands, jazzy cocktail lounge gigs, and a stand as soul singer Joe Simon's trusty organist came prior to the inauguration of Heartsman's edifying back-to-the-blues campaign. In 1991, Dick Shurman produced Heartsman's most satisfying set to date for Alligator, *The Touch.* He remained a versatile performer until his death in December of 1996. — *Bill Dahl*

Sacramento / 1987 / Crosscut ✦✦✦

Music of My Heart / 1989 / Cat 'n Hat ✦✦✦
Solid LP that catches up with all of Heartsman's varied musical interests: blues, jazz, R&B, and all points in between. "Goose Grease" is a humorous Heartsman vocal outing, while powerful singer Frankie Lee guests on a remake of "My Time After Awhile," and harpist Curtis Salgado takes over behind the mike on "My First Mind." — *Bill Dahl*

● **The Touch** / 1991 / Alligator ✦✦✦✦
The Bay Area multi-instrumentalist assuredly put it all together on this sumptuous release, produced by Dick Shurman. It's a superlative showcase for Heartsman's deeply burnished vocals, moaning guitar, jazzy keyboard skills, and lilting flute work. — *Bill Dahl*

Made in Germany / Jul. 31, 1995 / Inakustik ✦✦✦

Jessie Mae Hemphill

b. 1934, Senatobia, MS
Guitar, Vocals / Delta Blues
A Mississippi singer/guitarist, Jesse Mae Hemphill weaves strong Delta traditions into her idiosyncratic style. Hemphill comes from a musical background—reportedly, her grandfather was recorded in the fields by Alan Lomax in the '40s. Jesse Mae learned how to play guitar as a child by watching her relatives perform. Throughout the '60s and '70s, she sang with various Mississippi bar bands. In the early '80s, she decided to pursue a solo career.

Hemphill began playing solo dates, supporting herself only with an acoustic guitar and percussion. In 1981, she released her debut album, *She-Wolf,* on the European record label, Vogue. In 1987, her first American record, *Feelin' Good,* was released. In 1987 and 1988, she won the W.C. Handy Award for best tradtional female blues artist. Hemphill abandoned a recording career after the late '80s, but she continued to perform into the '90s. — *Cub Koda & Stephen Thomas Erlewine*

She-Wolf / 1981 / Vogue ✦✦✦
This compact disc reissue gathers up all the original tracks from Jessie Mae's 1980 debut album for the French Vogue label along with four remixed bonus

tracks, all seeing their first domestic release. Recorded by folklorist Dr. David Evans (who also contributes second guitar on 13 of the 15 tracks here) in various locales around Memphis and Mississippi, the music stays down-home and primal throughout. There's a strong sense of rhythm that permeates this record, whether it comes from the fife and drum-derived percussion work of Calvin Jackson and Joe Hicks or simply Jessie Mae's own foot-operated tambourine driving the beat home. Highlights include "Jessie's Boogie" and "Standing in My Doorway Crying" (both sides of her first 45 single, underwritten by the National Endowment for the Arts), "Honey Bee," "Boogie Side of the Road," "Crawdad Hole," "Lovin' in the Moonlight," "Married Man Blues," and the title track. The blues, real and raw. — *Cub Koda*

● **Feelin' Good** / 1987 / High Water ✦✦✦✦
Feelin' Good was the first album Jessie Mae Hemphill released in the United States and it differs from its predecessor *She-Wolf* in that it captures her at her rawest. Half of the record features her supported only by a rhythm guitar and drums, while the other half has Hemphill wailing away at her guitar and percussion simultaneously. The result is a hypnotic, mesmerizing record that successfully updates Delta blues, making the covers sound as fresh as the originals. — *Thom Owens*

Duke Henderson

Vocals / West Coast Blues
For a guy with as voluminous a discography as Los Angeles shouter Duke Henderson, one would think someone might possess concrete biographical information about the guy. No such luck.

Henderson got his start as a recording artist with Apollo Records, a New York firm that sent a rep to Los Angeles in 1945 with the intention of recording blues. Tenor saxist Jack McVea recommended Henderson, who ended up cutting three Apollo dates that year with backing from some of Los Angeles' finest sessioneers: saxists Wild Bill Moore, Lucky Thompson, and McVea, guitarist Gene Phillips, bassists Shifty Henry and Charlie Mingus, and drummers Lee Young and Rabon Tarrant.

Swinging as they were, Henderson's Apollo platters failed to sell in sufficient quantities to extend his contract. Thus began a label-hopping odyssey from Globe to Down Beat/Swing Time to Specialty to Modern to Imperial and finally to Flair, where he exhibited a knowledge of then-current sexual trends with his "Hey Mr. Kinsey" (issued as by Big Duke in 1953). Later, Henderson renounced his wicked blues-shouting past, sending the Los Angeles sanctified set as Brother Henderson, a minister and gospel deejay broadcasting for a time over XERB (the same powerful south-of-the-border frequency that Wolfman Jack dominated). — *Bill Dahl*

● **Get Your Kicks** / 1994 / Delmark ✦✦✦✦
Blues shouter Henderson was quite a popular jump blues shouter on the postwar Los Angeles scene. His 1945 output for Apollo, collected here, rates with his best; backed by top-drawer sidemen including saxists Lucky Thompson, Wild Bill Moore, and Jack McVea and guitarist Gene Phillips, Henderson's pipes convey the proper party spirit on these 20 swinging sides. — *Bill Dahl*

Jimi Hendrix

b. Nov. 27, 1942, Seattle, WA, **d.** Sep. 18, 1970, London, England
Guitar, Vocals / Rock 'n' Roll, Blues-Rock, Hard Rock, Psychedelic
In his brief four-year reign as a superstar, Jimi Hendrix expanded the vocabulary of the electric rock guitar more than anyone before or since. Hendrix was a master at coaxing all manner of unforeseen sonics from his instrument, often with innovative amplification experiments that produced astral-quality feedback and roaring distortion. His frequent hurricane blasts of noise, and dazzling showmanship — he could and would play behind his back and with his teeth, and set his guitar on fire — has sometimes obscured his considerable gifts as a songwriter, singer, and master of a gamut of blues, R&B, and rock styles.

When Hendrix became an international superstar in 1967, it seemed as if he'd dropped out of a Martian spaceship, but in fact he'd served his apprenticeship the long, mundane way in numerous R&B acts on the chitlin circuit. During the early and mid-'60s, he worked with such R&B/soul greats as Little Richard, the Isley Brothers, and King Curtis as a backup guitarist. Occasionally he recorded as a session man (the Isley Brothers' 1964 single "Testify" is the only one of these early tracks that offers even a glimpse of his future

genius). But the stars didn't appreciate his show-stealing showmanship, and Hendrix was straightjacketed by sideman roles that didn't allow him to develop as a soloist. The logical step was for Hendrix to go out on his own, which he did in New York in the mid-'60s, playing with various musicians in local clubs, and joining White blues-rock singer John Hammond, Jr.'s band for a while.

It was in a New York club that Hendrix was spotted by Animals bassist Chas Chandler. The first lineup of the Animals was about to split, and Chandler, looking to move into management, convinced Hendrix to move to London and record as a solo act in England. There a group was built around Jimi, also featuring Mitch Mitchell on drums and Noel Redding on bass, that was dubbed the Jimi Hendrix Experience. The trio became stars with astonishing speed in the UK, where "Hey Joe," "Purple Haze," and "The Wind Cries Mary" all made the Top 10 in the first half of 1967. These tracks were also featured on their debut album, *Are You Experienced?*, a psychedelic meisterwerk that became a huge hit in the US after Hendrix created a sensation at the Monterey Pop Festival in June of 1967.

Are You Experienced? was an astonishing debut, particularly from a young R&B veteran who had rarely sung, and apparently never written any own material, before the Experience formed. What caught most people's attention at first was his virtuosic guitar playing, which employed an arsenal of devices, including wah-wah pedals, buzzing feedback solos, crunching distorted riffs, and lightning, liquid runs up and down the scales. But Hendrix was also a first-rate songwriter, melding cosmic imagery with some surprisingly pop-savvy hooks and tender sentiments. He was also an excellent blues interpreter and passionate, engaging singer (although his gruff, throaty vocal pipes were not nearly as great assets as his instrumental skills). *Are You Experienced?* was psychedelia at its most eclectic, synthesizing mod pop, soul, R&B, Dylan, and the electric guitar innovations of British pioneers like Jeff Beck, Pete Townshend, and Eric Clapton.

Amazingly, Hendrix would only record three fully conceived studio albums in his lifetime. *Axis: Bold as Love* and the double-LP *Electric Ladyland* were more diffuse and experimental than *Are You Experienced?*. On *Electric Ladyland* in particular, Hendrix pioneered the use of the studio itself as a recording instrument, manipulating electronics and devising overdub techniques (with the help of engineer Eddie Kramer in particular) to plot uncharted sonic territory. Not that these albums were perfect, as impressive as they were; the instrumental breaks could meander, and Hendrix's songwriting was occasionally half-baked, never matching the consistency of *Are You Experienced?* (although he exercised greater creative control over the later albums).

The final two years of Hendrix's life were turbulent ones musically, financially, and personally. He was embroiled in enough complicated management and record company disputes (some dating from ill-advised contracts he'd signed before the Experience formed) to keep the lawyers busy for years. He disbanded the Experience in 1969, forming the Band of Gypsies with drummer Buddy Miles and bassist Billy Cox to pursue funkier directions. He closed Woodstock with a sprawling, shaky set, redeemed by his famous machine-gun interpretation of "The Star-Spangled Banner." The rhythm section of Mitchell and Redding were underrated keys to Jimi's best work, and the Band of Gypsies ultimately couldn't measure up to the same standard, although Hendrix did record an erratic live album with them. In early 1970, the Experience re-formed again — and disbanded again shortly afterwards. At the same time, Hendrix felt torn in many directions by various fellow musicians, record-company expectations, and management pressures, all of whom had their own ideas of what Hendrix should be doing. Coming up on two years after *Electric Ladyland*, a new studio album had yet to appear, although Hendrix was recording constantly during the period.

While outside parties did contribute to bogging down Hendrix's studio work, it also seems likely that Jimi himself was partly responsible for the stalemate, unable to form a permanent lineup of musicians, unable to decide what musical direction to pursue, unable to bring himself to complete another album despite jamming endlessly. A few months into 1970, Mitchell — Hendrix's most valuable musical collaborator — came back into the fold, replacing Miles in the drum chair, although Cox stayed in place. It was this trio that toured the world during Hendrix's final months.

It's extremely difficult to separate the facts of Hendrix's life from rumors and speculation. Everyone who knew him well, or claimed to know him well, has different versions of his state of mind in 1970. Critics have variously mused that he was going to go into jazz, that he was going to get deeper into the blues, that he was going to continue doing what he was doing, or that he was too confused to know what he was doing at all. The same confusion holds true for his death: contradictory versions of his final days have been given by his closest acquaintances of the time. He'd been working intermittently on a new album, tentatively titled *First Ray of the New Rising Sun*, when he died in London on September 18, 1970, from drug-related complications.

Hendrix recorded a massive amount of unreleased studio material during his lifetime. Much of this (as well as entire live concerts) was issued posthumously; several of the live concerts were excellent, but the studio tapes have been the focus of enormous controversy for over 20 years. These initially came out in haphazard drabs and drubs (the first, *The Cry of Love*, was easily the most outstanding of the lot). In the mid-'70s, producer Alan Douglas took control of these projects, posthumously overdubbing many of Hendrix's tapes with additional parts by studio musicians. In the eyes of many Hendrix fans, this was sacrilege, destroying the integrity of the work of a musician known to exercise meticulous care over the final production of his studio recordings. Even as late as 1995, Douglas was having ex-Knack drummer Bruce Gary record new parts for the typically misbegotten compilation *Voodoo Soup*. After a lengthy legal dispute, the rights to Hendrix's estate, including all of his recordings, returned to Al Hendrix, the guitarist's father, in July of 1995. —*Richie Unterberger*

☆ **Are You Experienced?** / 1967 / MCA ✦✦✦✦✦
One of the most stunning debuts in rock history, and one of the definitive albums of the psychedelic era. On *Are You Experienced?*, Hendrix synthesized various elements of the cutting edge of 1967 rock into music that sounded both futuristic and rooted in the best traditions of rock, blues, pop, and soul. It was his mind-boggling guitar work, of course, that got most of the ink, building upon the experiments of British innovators like Jeff Beck and Pete Townshend to chart new sonic territories in feedback, distortion, and sheer volume. It wouldn't have meant much, however, without his excellent material, whether psychedelic frenzy ("Foxy Lady," "Manic Depression," "Purple Haze"), instrumental freakout jams ("Third Stone from the Sun"), blues ("Red House," "Hey Joe"), or tender, poetic compositions ("The Wind Cries Mary") that demonstrated the breadth of his songwriting talents. Not to be underestimated were the contributions of drummer Mitch Mitchell and bassist Noel Redding, who gave the music a rhythmic pulse that fused parts of rock and improvised jazz. Many of these songs are among Hendrix's very finest; it may be true that he would continue to develop at a rapid pace throughout the rest of his brief career, but he would never surpass his first LP in terms of consistently high quality. The British and American versions of the album differed substantially when they were initially released in 1967; MCA's 17-song CD reissue does everyone a favor by gathering all of the material from the two records in one place, adding a few B-sides from early singles as well. —*Richie Unterberger*

☆ **Axis: Bold as Love** / 1967 / MCA ✦✦✦✦✦
When the Experience recorded their second album, they were in the process of solidfying their international stardom. That meant access to more studio time and more sophisicated technology, but not, alas, a great deal of time to write the material. That may be why *Axis* isn't quite as much of a tour de force as *Are You Exerienced?*, but it's nevertheless another major effort, showing Hendrix continue to grow, particularly in his increasing mastery of the studio and more sophisticated lyrics. Soul and R&B influences are more prominent here than on his debut, though psychedelic experimentalism ran rampant (to great effect) on "If 6 Was 9." "Spanish Castle Magic," "Up from the Skies," "You Got Me Floatin'," and "Castles Made of Sand," all had funky grooves that gave the spiraling guitars and crunchy rhythm section a much-needed buoyancy. The best song, though, might have been the mellowest: "Little Wing" was Hendrix at his most delicate, and perhaps his most personal. —*Richie Unterberger*

☆ **Electric Ladyland** / Oct. 1968 / MCA ✦✦✦✦✦
With *Electric Ladyland*, Hendrix took psychedelic experimentation as far as he could within the original Experience trio format. That meant pushing the barriers of late '60s studio technology as far as they could bend, particularly with regard to multitracking and effects that could only be achieved through certain treatments and manipulation of the tape itself. It also meant greater freedom and looseness in the playing and the songwriting, which could be

both a plus and a drawback, as the compositions became both less constricted and less concise. Not all of the material here is top-of-the-line, but certainly much of this is Hendrix at his best: the dreamy wah-wah guitars of "Rainy Day, Dream Away" were only matched by the dreaminess of the lyrics, and "Have You Ever Been (To Electric Ladyland)" and "Gypsy Eyes" were also standouts. "1983 (A Merman I Should Turn to Be)" and "Voodoo Chile" were lengthy cuts dominated by jam-like instrumental passages; "Crosstown Traffic" and a cover of Dylan's "All Along the Watchtower," by contrast, were two of his catchiest and most pop-friendly tunes. "Voodoo Chile," "Voodoo Child (Slight Return)," and a cover of Earl King's "Come On" are three of his most determined forays into the blues, albeit the blues as fed through a nearly avant-garde filter. Originally released as a double album, the CD reissue fits the entire recording onto one 75-minute disc. —*Richie Unterberger*

Smash Hits / Jul. 1969 / Reprise ✦✦✦✦
Smash Hits is a solid collection of his most popular radio tracks, as well as featuring the bluesy "Red House" and "Stone Free," which were not found on previous albums. —*Rick Clark*

Band of Gypsies / 1970 / Capitol ✦✦✦✦
Hendrix, sans the Experience, hooked up with bassist Billy Cox and drummer Buddy Miles to record this hard electric funk outing live at the Fillmore East in New York on December 31, 1969. While the rhythm section may have lacked the chops for wild free-form excursions, they provided Hendrix with a no-nonsense groove for his funkier R&B experiments. "Machine Gun," the album's highlight, features some of Hendrix's greatest playing. His dramatically violent soundscapes convey the horror of the war experience, with brilliantly controlled use of feedback and rapid-fire bursts of notes. —*Rick Clark*

The Cry of Love / 1971 / Reprise ✦✦✦✦
The posthumously released *The Cry of Love* revealed Hendrix turning toward a more subdued, less psychedelic style, with songs like "Night Bird Flying" and "Angel." Hendrix does deliver a few strong rockers with "Freedom," "Ezy Ryder," and "Astro Man." —*Rick Clark*

Plays Monterey / 1986 / Reprise ✦✦✦✦
Hendrix's show at the 1967 Monterey Pop Festival was the performance that broke him in the United States. While half of this was previously available as one side of an LP that also featured a side of live Otis Redding from the same event, this has his whole performances. Jimi and the Experience were in fine, lean, fiery form on this nine-song set, which showcased the most well-known tunes from the *Are You Experienced?* album and covers of "Killing Floor," "Like a Rolling Stone," "Rock Me Baby," and "Wild Thing." —*Richie Unterberger*

Live at Winterland / 1987 / Rykodisc ✦✦✦✦
Jimi Hendrix's sonic assaults and attacks hypnotized, frightened, and amazed audiences in the late '60s. His studio recordings helped him attain his reputation, but his live works validated it. That's the case on the 13 songs from a 1968 Winterland concert that made their way onto CD in 1987. Whether he was doing short, biting songs like "Fire" or stretching out for sprawling blues statements like "Red House" and "Killing Floor," Jimi Hendrix turned the guitar into a battering ram, forcing everyone to notice and making every solo and note a memorable one. —*Ron Wynn*

Radio One / 1989 / Rykodisc ✦✦✦✦
Seventeen songs from 1967 BBC broadcasts, when the Experience had yet to burn out from the wheel of constant touring, management hassles, and internal strife. They're in good, enthusiastic form as they run through early gems like "Hey Joe," "Foxy Lady," "Fire," and "Stone Free," the lack of studio polish giving these versions a loose feel. The Experience studio albums are still considerably superior to this set, but it's certainly worth acquiring by any serious Hendrix fan, not least because it has several covers that didn't make it onto the three proper Experience LPs. Several of these ("Hoochie Koochie Man," "Killing Floor," "Catfish Blues") reveal his sometimes overlooked affinity for Chicago-style electric blues; there are also a couple of surprises ("Hound Dog" and "Day Tripper"). With good sound, it's a solid addition to the Hendrix library, demonsrating his versatility in various rock, soul, and blues styles. —*Richie Unterberger*

Stages / 1991 / Reprise ✦✦✦
What more could a Hendrix fanatic searching for the ultimate live Jimi experience ask for? The 1991 box set *Stages* contains a total of 4 CDs, each containing one full concert from the years 1967 (in Stockholm), '68 (Paris), '69

(San Diego), and '70 (recorded in Atlanta just two months before his death). Many Hendrix fans already owned bootlegged copies of these concerts, but this was the first time that they were released officially, in crystal clear sound and with informative liner notes. The four discs are an obviously interesting musical journey, showing the rapid musical transformation of Hendrix from showman to serious virtuoso. And although there is a bit of overlap on the discs ("Purple Haze" rears its head on all four), the versions of the repeated songs are strikingly different. Disc 1 (Stockholm '67) features the Jimi Hendrix Experience in their formative stage, and contains the only official release of the Experience's raw cover of the Beatles' "Sgt. Pepper's Lonely Hearts Club Band." This disc is the shortest of the four (barely over 30 minutes in length), containing no-nonsense (and almost 100% jam-less) versions of such standards as "Fire" and "Burning of the Midnight Lamp." The second disc (Paris '68) shows the group starting to stretch out musically (near nine-minute cover versions of both Muddy Waters' "Catfish Blues" and Curtis Knight's "Drivin' South" are the proof), and includes an absolutely gorgeous version of the electric ballad "Little Wing." Disc 3 (San Diego '69) catches the Experience on one of their final tours with original bassist Noel Redding. The group is dedicated to jamming, combining a red-hot version of their "Spanish Castle Magic" with an explosive cover of Cream's "Sunshine of Your Love." Also included is a long take of "Voodoo Child (Slight Return)," which ends the show on a highly energetic and inspired note. By the final disc (Atlanta '70), Hendrix had assembled the Band of Gypsies, with Hendrix's army buddy Billy Cox replacing the ousted Noel Redding on bass (with Mitch Mitchell still behind the drums). Jimi had completely shunned his early concert gimmickry (lighting his guitar on fire, etc.), and by 1970 was making a conscious attempt at forcing his audience to listen to the music, without any distractions. This disc has three songs that were not released while Hendrix was alive ("Lover Man," "Straight Ahead," and "Room Full of Mirrors"), intended for his never really completed *First Rays of the New Rising Sun* album. You'll also be treated to a rare live version of "Stone Free," with its tempo sped up a notch. Admittedly, *Stages* may be too much to take for the new Jimi fan, but for diehards, it simply can't be beat. — *Greg Prato*

● **The Ultimate Experience** / Apr. 27, 1993 / MCA ✦✦✦✦
As a single-disc compilation, *The Ultimate Experience* is hard to beat. Drawing from all of the original Jimi Hendrix Experience albums, the 20-track collection hits all of the major highpoints — "Purple Haze," "All Along the Watchtower," "Little Wing," "Red House," "The Wind Cries Mary," "Highway Chile," "Angel" — and gives an accurate impression of why Hendrix was so revolutionary and influential. All three of Hendrix's completed studio albums are mandatory listening, but *The Ultimate Experience* is a terrific introduction to the guitarist. — *Thom Owens*

Jimi Hendrix: Blues / Apr. 26, 1994 / MCA ✦✦✦✦
While Hendrix remains most famous for his hard rock and psychedelic innovations, more than a third of his recordings were blues-oriented. This CD contains eleven blues originals and covers, eight of which were previously unreleased. Recorded between 1966 and 1970, they feature the master guitarist stretching the boundaries of electric blues in both live and studio settings. Besides several Hendrix blues-based originals, it includes covers of Albert King and Muddy Waters classics, as well as a 1967 acoustic version of his composition "Hear My Train A-Comin'." — *Richie Unterberger*

Jimi Hendrix: Woodstock / Aug. 2, 1994 / MCA ✦✦✦
Hendrix's entire legendary set at Woodstock is featured on this set for the first time. Hardcore Hendrix fans may enjoy this good-sounding set, but it's a lot of endless jamming and general noodling for even the average fan to ingest. Besides his incendiary reading of "The Star Spangled Banner" and moments where the playing really comes together, better live Hendrix sets can be found elsewhere, like *Jimi Hendrix in the West*. — *Rick Clark*

Jimi by Himself: The Home Recordings / 1995 / Berkshire Studio ✦✦✦
This CD is only available (quite legitimately) with the hardback comic/graphic biography *Voodoo Child: The Illustrated Legend Of Jimi Hendrix*. Be warned that if you're primarily (or only) interested in this half-hour disc of previously unreleased material, it only comes at a high price ($35 or so). If you want to take the plunge, you'll find the music — recorded unaccompanied by Hendrix in New York around April of 1968 — quite worthwhile. The guitar is electric, but this is basically *Hendrix Unplugged*, with much quieter, reflective, and personal versions of songs that would get the full-on electric

treatment on *Electric Ladyland* and other albums. "1983," "Gypsy Eyes," "Voodoo Chile," and "Angel" are particularly fascinating to experience in this context, as we hear Jimi tentatively working out (and sometimes fumbling through) skeletal versions of these compositions, with some different lyrics appearing on occasion. What this lacks in typical Hendrix firepower, it makes up for in poetic delicacy. In some respects, these performances bring us closer to the tender heart of his work than the famous official versions of these classics. — *Richie Unterberger*

Voodoo Soup / Apr. 1995 / MCA ✦✦✦
Voodoo Soup was supposed to be the outtake album that got it right. Instead, it was another in a line of botched attempts to recreate Jimi Hendrix's unfinished final studio album. For most fans, the re-recorded drum tracks by the drummer of the Knack was the most unforgivable sin, yet the album is also poorly sequenced and lacks several important tracks. The sound is polished to a disturbingly bright sheen, while the cover art is garishly retro. — *Stephen Thomas Erlewine*

● **Experience Hendrix: The Best of Jimi Hendrix** / 1997 / MCA ✦✦✦✦
Experience Hendrix: The Best of Jimi Hendrix is a terrific 20-track collection that features all of Hendrix's most essential material, from "Purple Haze" and "Hey Joe" to "All Along the Watchtower" and "Star Spangled Banner." There are a few fine moments missing, but everything a casual fan needs is here, making it a great introduction to the groundbreaking guitarist. — *Stephen Thomas Erlewine*

First Rays of the New Rising Sun / Apr. 22, 1997 / MCA ✦✦✦✦
Because Hendrix's death in September 1970 occurred before his work on these tunes was completed, the questions still abound as to what Jimi's ultimate vision for this double album would have been. Minus the worthless — though well intentioned — overdubs and remix manipulation that occurred when this material was issued piecemeal over the years on *The Cry of Love* ("Night Bird Flying," "Angel," "Ezy Rider," "Drifting," "My Friend," "Freedom," "Straight Ahead," "Astro Man," "In From the Storm," and "Belly Button Window"), *War Heroes* ("Izabella," "Beginnings," and "Stepping Stone"), *Rainbow Bridge* ("Room Full of Mirrors," "Dolly Dagger," and "Hey Baby [New Rising Sun]") and the disappointing *Voodoo Soup*, this collection finally gets us back to the master tapes residing in the Electric Ladyland vaults. This gets the listener as close to what Hendrix had in mind as possible, as subject to change as these versions obviously were, and also places the tunes in their original context as an album. Because this collection utilizes mixes that Hendrix and engineer Eddie Kramer were working on at the time, the tracks perhaps lack the sonic wallop of the first three Experience albums, but have much more to offer than the stripped-away and redubbed versions that have been on the market until now. If one views *First Rays of the New Rising Sun* as an almost-completed work in progress, then it becomes obvious that Jimi was heading into a new direction and sound, one rife with funk and rhythm & blues as a bedrock foundation. The psychedelic workouts got more jamlike and experimental, and the ballads got prettier and even more dreamlike in their background soundscapes. What he would have eventually come up with and released as his next musical statement is anyone's guess, but this gets us as close to that answer — and that vision — as we're ever likely to get. — *Cub Koda*

South Saturn Delta / Oct. 7, 1997 / MCA ✦✦✦
Shortly after the Hendrix family reacquired the rights to Jimi's catalog, they signed a long-term deal with MCA Records and pulled many of the compilations of unreleased material and rarities off the shelves, with the intent of re-releasing the material in better collections. *First Rays of the New Rising Sun*, an attempt at assembling Hendrix's uncompleted last album, was the first release from Experience Hendrix, and it was followed months later by *South Saturn Delta*, a collection of rarities — all but one of the 15 tracks were never officially released in the US — that spans his entire career. Its intent is to capture the full range of Hendrix's music through an alternate history, and it works pretty well. Among the highlights are tracks from the *War Heroes* and *Rainbow Bridge* albums ("Look Over Yonder," "Tax Free," "Midnight," "Pali Gap," "Bleeding Heart"), "Sweet Angel" (an early version of "Angel"), an instrumental "Little Wing," a solo take on "Midnight Lightning," and a studio version of "Message to the Universe (Message to Love)." There are also alternate mixes of "All Along the Watchtower," "Power of Soul," "Drifter's Escape," "South Saturn Delta," and "The Stars That Play with Laughing Sam's Dice."

It's an intelligently sequenced, listenable collection of some of the very best outtakes and rarities from Hendrix, and is another sign that Experience Hendrix's restoration of Jimi's catalog will be smart, stylish and logical. *— Stephen Thomas Erlewine*

Clarence "Frogman" Henry

b. Mar. 19, 1937, Algiers, LA
Piano, Trombone, Vocals / New Orleans R&B, R&B
He could sing like a girl, and he could sing like a frog. That latter trademark croak, utilized to the max on his 1956 debut smash "Ain't Got No Home," earned good-natured Clarence Henry his nickname and jump-started a rewarding career that endures to this day around the Crescent City.

Naturally, Fats Domino and Professor Longhair were young Clarence Henry's main influences while growing up in the Big Easy. He played piano and trombone with Bobby Mitchell & the Toppers from 1952 to 1955 before catching on with saxist Eddie Smith's band. Henry improvised the basic idea behind "Ain't Got No Home" on the bandstand one morning in the wee hours; when the crowd responded favorably, he honed it into something unique. Paul Gayten (New Orleans A&R man for Chess Records) concurred, hustling Henry into Cosimo Matassa's studio in September of 1956. Local deejay Poppa Stoppa laid the "Frogman" handle on the youngster when he spun the 45 (issued on the Chess subsidiary Argo), and it stuck.

Despite some fine follow-ups—"It Won't Be Long," "I'm in Love," the inevitable sequel "I Found a Home"—Frog sank back into the marsh sales-wise until 1960, when Allen Toussaint's updated arrangement melded beautifully with a country-tinged Bobby Charles composition called "(I Don't Know Why) But I Do." Henry's rendition of the tune proved a huge pop smash in early 1961, as did a Domino-tinged "You Always Hurt the One You Love" later that year.

Frogman continued to record a variety of New Orleans-styled old standards and catchy originals for Argo (Chess assembled a Henry album that boasted what may be the worst cover art in the history of rock 'n' roll), even recording at one point with Nashville saxist Boots Randolph and pianist Floyd Cramer. But the hits dried up for good after 1961. Henry opened 18 concerts for the Beatles across the US and Canada in 1964, but his main source of income came from the Bourbon Street strip, where he played for 19 years. You'll likely find him joyously reviving his classics at the New Orleans Jazz & Heritage Festival every year come spring—and his croak remains as deep and melodious as ever. *— Bill Dahl*

● **Ain't Got No Home: The Best of Clarence "Frogman" Henry** / 1994 / MCA ✦✦✦✦
The New Orleans R&B singer with the joyous frog's croak in his voice is served well by this 18-song collection of his 1956-1964 output for the Chess subsidiary Argo Records. It begins with his definitive "Ain't Got No Home," follows with his vicious Crescent City rockers "Troubles, Troubles," "It Won't Be Long," and "I'm in Love," and visits his comeback hits "(I Don't Know Why) But I Do" and "You Always Hurt the One You Love." *— Bill Dahl*

But I Do / 1994 / Charly ✦✦✦✦
Twenty Argo waxings by the roly-poly pianist—much duplication with the easier-to-locate MCA disc as far as the hits go, though the inclusion of the sequel "I Found a Home" and the lesser-known rockers "Steady Date," "Oh Why," and "Live It Right" certainly make this one worth looking for. *— Bill Dahl*

The Highway Q.C.'s

f. 194?
Group / Black Gospel, Southern Gospel, Traditional Gospel
Not only among the top gospel groups of the postwar era, the Highway Q.C.'s were also the launching pad for such major secular pop stars as Lou Rawls, Johnnie Taylor and the immortal Sam Cooke. The group was formed in 1945 at Chicago's Highway Baptist Church by a number of teenagers that included Cooke, Creadell Copeland and two pairs of brothers, Marvin & Charles Jones and Curtis & Lee Richardson. Cooke exited in 1951 to join the ranks of hometown heroes the Soul Stirrers; his replacement was Rawls, himself an alumnus of another young Windy City group, the Holy Wonders. In time all of the Wonders' other members—Spencer Taylor, James Walker, and Chris Flowers among them—would join the Highway Q.C.'s as well. Rawls remained for just two years, leaving at that time to join the Los Angeles-based Chosen

Gospel Singers; his substitute was Johnnie Taylor, previously of the Kansas City group the Melody Kings. The group made their debut on the Vee-Jay label in 1955; in 1956 Spencer Taylor joined, and a year later Johnnie Taylor (no relation) quit to join the Soul Stirrers, ironically enough filling the gap created by the exit of Sam Cooke. Spencer Taylor remained the Highway Q.C.'s leader throughout the decades which followed, continuing to helm the group into the 1990s. *— Jason Ankeny*

Spencer Taylor & the Highway Q.C.'s / 1959 / Vee-Jay ✦✦✦✦
Soul-stirring group, has some tracks led by Johnnie Taylor. *— Opal Louis Nations*

● **Jesus Is Waiting** / 1960 / Vee-Jay ✦✦✦✦
The Highway Q.C.'s were considered gospel's greatest farm team, the place where aspiring quartet lead singers would hone their skills before joining an "A-list" group. But that doesn't mean the group made inferior music; the songs on *Jesus Is Waiting*, a single-disc collection combining two albums they cut in the mid-'50s and early '60s, can stand with any issued by the better name ensembles. A youthful Johnnie Taylor soars, whoops, and moans through songs done from 1955-1957, while Spencer Taylor comes on with equal might and ferocity on the later material. They may not have had the reputations or kept their members as long, but at times The Highway Q.C.'s made music that resounded with as much fury as anyone on the gospel trail. *— Ron Wynn*

The Lord Is Sweet / 1965 / Peacock ✦✦✦
Best of the group's late-'60s sides. Includes "Changes at the End" and "Rock Me." *— Opal Louis Nations*

Count Your Blessings / Sep. 1, 1995 / Charly ✦✦✦✦
Essential Vee-Jay tracks with and without Johnnie Taylor. *— Opal Louis Nations*

Nearer My God: The Very Best of the Highway QC's / Mar. 3, 1998 / Collectables ✦✦✦✦
The best of the Vee-Jay sides featuring Johnnie and Spencer Taylor. *— Opal Louis Nations*

The Best of the Highway QC's / Chameleon ✦✦✦✦
A respectable collection for the group that acted as a feeder for The Soul Stirrers and other first-echelon groups. Prior editions included Johnnie Taylor and the unrecorded Sam Cooke and O.V. Wright. *— Ron Wynn*

Blind Joe Hill

Vocals, Guitar, Harmonica / Electric Chicago Blues
A good one-man band performer in the tradition of Joe Hill Louis and Dr. Ross, Blind Joe Hill accompanies his craggy vocals on guitar, bass and drums. He's among the last in the tradition, and that adds some value to his recordings, despite a derivative playing style and erratic compositional skills. *— Ron Wynn*

Boogie in the Dark / Jan. 1978 / Barrelhouse ✦✦✦✦
Opinions vary regarding the quality of Blind Joe Hill's one-man band recordings. He certainly wasn't the greatest in the genre, but he was a creditable exponent. There's nothing especially exciting here, but it was done with sincerity and energy. *— Ron Wynn*

King Solomon Hill

b. 1897, McComb, MS, **d.** 1949, Sibley, LA
Guitar, Vocals / Acoustic Texas Blues, Delta Blues, Prewar Country Blues
One of the more fascinating footnotes in blues history, King Solomon Hill's scant recorded legacy suggests a singer and guitarist of considerable originality and primitive force. Born Joe Holmes circa 1897 in McComb, MS, he first attracted attention in the Lousiana area, becoming a constant at parties and juke joints; most certainly a self-taught guitarist, he is rumored to have roamed the Delta and Panhandle regions playing alongside Sam Collins, Ramblin' Thomas, Oscar "Lone Wolf" Woods, and possibly Blind Lemon Jefferson. Hill signed to the Paramount label in 1932, soon travelling to Grafton, WI to record the six tracks—two of them alternate takes—which comprise his known discography; songs like the eerie "Gone Dead Train" and "Down on Bended Knee" feature apocalyptic, seemingly alien vocals certainly unique to their time and place, accompanied by a raw guitar sound distinguished by irregular rhythms and notes said to be stretched out by a

cow bone. After this lone session, Hill returned to the juke joint circuit, eventually vanishing from sight; reputedly a heavy drinker, he died of a massive brain hemorrhage in Sibley, LA in 1949. — *Jason Ankeny*

Michael Hill

b. 1952, New York, NY
Guitar, Vocals / Contemporary Blues, Modern Electric Blues

Michael Hill, a Bronx-raised guitarist, singer, and songwriter, took his earliest inspiration from the sounds of Jimi Hendrix. His other songwriting influences include socially conscious artists like Marvin Gaye, Bob Marley, and Curtis Mayfield.

Hill has recorded two albums for Alligator Records of Chicago, *Have Mercy* (1996) and *Bloodlines* (1994), which both contain extensive social commentary. Both releases have gotten good reviews from critics and sold respectably, yet he's still considered too "heavy" for some US festivals and clubs. Despite this, Hill has made tours of clubs and festivals around Germany, France, Scandinavia, Austria, England, Italy, Brazil, and Australia.

The 45-year-old Hill argues that his political songs follow the true blues tradition, which includes sounding off on societal problems. Blues songs of the 1920s and '30s by Leadbelly, Mance Lipscomb, and other classic blues artists often dealt head on with society's ills. Hill sees himself as following this tradition. Songs like "Falling Through the Cracks," "Bluestime In America," "Why We Play the Blues," "Evil In the Air," and "Presumed Innocent" reveal another side of life to 1990s fans of blues music, most of whom are middle class, suburban and White.

Hill, based in Brooklyn, NY, since 1988, was born in the Bronx in 1952. The Bronx that Hill remembers was a working-class community with families who looked after one another's kids. Hill comes from a close-knit family, and his brother Kevin began playing bass with him when he formed his first band in 1973.

After seeing Jimi Hendrix play on five occasions around New York City, including at the Woodstock Festival, Hill knew what he wanted to do with the rest of his life. He began playing guitar in 1970, and was soon playing out in rock and soul bands by 1972. He took cues from guitar players including B.B. King, Buddy Guy, Albert King, and Carlos Santana, and his style is a comfortable mesh of all these, plus his own touch. Reading the books of Toni Morrison, James Baldwin, and other Black novelists, Hill began writing songs that spoke about socially relevant subjects as well as more traditional blues topics.

By the mid-1970s, Hill was working as a sideman or session player with the likes of Little Richard, Archie Bell, Harry Belafonte, and Carla Thomas. In the mid-1980s, working with Living Colour's Vernon Reid, he helped establish the Black Rock Coalition, a New York City-based group of Black rock 'n' roll bands, craftspersons, and artists. He caught the attention of Alligator Records in 1993, and in 1994, the label released *Bloodlines*, which was hailed by some critics as the best debut blues album of the year.

Hill's range on his Steinberger guitar is awe-inspiring, and he'll often follow up a slow blues ballad with a fiery blues-rock shuffle that shows off his rock influences, people like Jeff Beck, Hendrix, and Santana. Backed by a trio known as the Blues Mob, which consists of keyboards, bass, and drums, Hill's live shows are an artful blend of originals and a few interpretive covers.

Combine great guitar playing with a strong voice and thinking man's lyrics, and you've got all the ingredients for major blues stardom, and Michael Hill's Blues Mob are helping the idiom continue its evolution. — *Richard Skelly*

Bloodlines / 1994 / Alligator ✦✦✦
If it's possible to label anything "new," Michael Hill's Blues Mob are taking a new approach to the blues. Hill and his associates incorporate numerous musical influences and elements into contemporary material with a blues feel and sound. Hill's slashing slide guitar mixes rock, funk, and reggae as well as blues inflections, and is consistently creative and engaging. The group's compositions feature lyrics which discuss issues and ideas as much as romantic situations and dilemmas, and Hill's vocals aren't pleading, but defiant, triumphant, and aggressive. If you're seeking standard fare, this isn't your cup of tea, but those interested in music that expands the blues vocabulary and range will find Michael Hill's Blues Mob the ticket. — *Ron Wynn*

● **Have Mercy!** / 1996 / Alligator ✦✦✦✦
Michael Hill's primary attribute is his ambition. Where many contemporary

bluesmen are content to turn out standard shuffles and boogies, he wants to bring it all together—Hendrix blues-rock, Chicago blues, soul-blues, jazz, and reggae. It's a difficult task, so it isn't entirely surprising that he and his band the Blues Mob don't quite achieve his dreams on his second album, *Have Mercy!*. What is surprising is how close they come. When Hill and the Blues Mob have everything working right, their music is a heady fusion with real passion and heart. These moments—including "Women Make the World Go Round," "Africa in Her Name," and a reworking of "Stagolee"—are powerful enough to make the failed fusions forgivable, and they suggest that Hill could develop into a distinctive talent in his own right. — *Thom Owens*

Z.Z. Hill (Arzell Hill)

b. Sep. 30, 1935, Naples, TX, **d.** Apr. 27, 1984, Dallas, TX
Vocals / Soul Blues, Soul, R&B, Modern Electric Blues

Texas-born singer Z.Z. Hill managed to resuscitate both his own semi-flagging career and the entire genre at large when he signed on at Jackson, MS's Malaco Records in 1980 and began growling his way through some of the most uncompromising blues to be unleashed on Black radio stations in many a moon.

His impressive 1982 Malaco album *Down Home Blues* remained on *Billboard*'s soul album charts for nearly two years, an extraordinary run for such a blatantly bluesy LP. His songs "Down Home Blues" and "Somebody Else Is Steppin' In" have graduated into the ranks of legitimate blues standards (and there haven't been many of those come along over the last couple of decades).

Arzell Hill started out singing gospel with a quintet called the Spiritual Five, but the output of B.B. King, Bobby Bland, and especially Sam Cooke made a more indelible mark on his approach. He began gigging around Dallas, fashioning his distinctive initials after those of B.B. King. When his older brother Matt Hill (a budding record producer with his own label, M.H.) invited Z.Z. to go west to southern California, the young singer did.

His distinct single on M.H., the gutsy shuffle "You Were Wrong" (recorded in an L.A. garage studio), showed up on *Billboard*'s pop chart for a week in 1964. With such a relatively successful showing his first time out, Hill's fine subsequent singles for the Bihari brothers' Kent logo should have been even bigger. But "I Need Someone (To Love Me)," "Happiness Is All I Need," and a raft of other deserving Kent 45s (many produced and arranged by Maxwell Davis) went nowhere commercially for the singer.

Excellent singles for Atlantic, Mankind, and Hill (another imprint operated by brother Matt, who served as Z.Z.'s producer for much of his career) preceded a 1972 hookup with United Artists that resulted in three albums and six R&B chart singles over the next couple of years. From there, Z.Z. moved on to Columbia, where his 1977 single "Love Is So Good When You're Stealing It" became his biggest-selling hit of all.

Hill's vocal grit was never more effective than on his blues-soaked Malaco output. From 1980 until 1984, when he died suddenly of a heart attack, Z.Z. bravely led a personal back-to-the-blues campaign that doubtless helped to fuel the current contemporary blues boom. It's a shame he couldn't stick around to see it blossom. — *Bill Dahl*

Lot of Soul / 1969 / Kent ✦✦✦

Brand New Z.Z. Hill / 1971 / Mankind ✦✦✦
This is a '70s Swamp Dogg-produced concept album. — *Richard Pack*

Dues Paid in Full / 1972 / Kent ✦✦✦
Z.Z. Hill's second album for Kent, *Dues Paid in Full*, collects a number of singles that he recorded for the label between 1964 and 1965. Hill pretty much played in a straight Texas style during these days, turning out a series of stinging high-octane singles during those two years. Granted, there wasn't much in the way of originality, but there were strong signs of individuality, which makes *Dues Paid in Full* worth investigation for both Hill fans and anyone with a fondness for electric Texas blues. — *Thom Owens*

The Best Thing That's Happened to Me / 1972 / United Artists ✦✦✦

Keep on Loving You / 1975 / United Artists ✦✦✦
Soul material predominates here. — *Bill Dahl*

Let's Make a Deal / 1978 / Columbia ✦✦✦
One of the most commercial of Hill's albums, this disco-tinged release included the minor hits "This Time They Told the Truth" and "Love Is So Good When You're Stealing It." — *Richie Unterberger*

The Mark of Z.Z. Hill / 1979 / Columbia ✦✦✦

Hill's second and final Columbia LP was essentially a continuation of the first. On both, Hill sounds like a journeyman Southern soul singer embellished with period disco/mainstream R&B production, which neither added to the quality of the music nor made it unlistenable. — *Richie Unterberger*

Z.Z. Hill / 1981 / Malaco ✦✦✦✦

The initial step in Hill's amazing rebirth as a contemporary blues star, courtesy of Jackson, MS's Malaco Records and producers Tommy Couch and Wolf Stephenson. The vicious blues outings "Bump and Grind" and "Blue Monday" were the first salvos fired by Hill at the blues market, though much of the set—"Please Don't Make Me (Do Something Bad to You)," "I'm So Lonesome I Could Cry"—was solidly in the Southern soul vein. — *Bill Dahl*

The Rhythm & The Blues / 1982 / Malaco ✦✦✦✦

Led by Hill's second immediate standard—the Denise LaSalle-penned "Someone Else Is Steppin' In"—Hill's third Malaco album was another consistent effort, if not quite the blockbuster that his previous effort was. Hill again dipped into the Little Johnny Taylor songbook for a humorous slow blues, "Open House at My House," while relying on talented songwriters George Jackson and Frank Johnson for most of his tailor-made material. — *Bill Dahl*

☆ **Down Home** / 1982 / Malaco ✦✦✦✦✦

One of the very few classic blues albums of the 1980s. Hill revitalized the genre among African-American listeners with his "Down Home Blues," which earned instant standard status. But the entire album is tremendously consistent, with the percolating R&B workouts "Givin' It Up for Your Love" and "Right Arm for Your Love" contrasting with an intimate "Cheatin' in the Next Room" and the straightahead blues "Everybody Knows About My Good Thing" and "When It Rains It Pours." — *Bill Dahl*

I'm a Blues Man / 1983 / Malaco ✦✦✦✦

Fueled by more impressive material from the pens of Jackson, Johnson, and LaSalle, Hill was in an amazing groove during the years prior to his untimely demise, and the crack Malaco house band was certainly up to the task. Just like the title track ably demonstrated, Z.Z. Hill had indeed rechristened himself as a blues man of the first order. — *Bill Dahl*

Bluesmaster / 1984 / Malaco ✦✦✦

Issued the year he died, *Bluesmaster* boasted more competent soul-blues hybrids by the man who reenergized the blues idiom with his trademark growl. LaSalle's "You're Ruining My Bad Reputation," "Friday Is My Day" (written by legendary Malaco promo man Dave Clark), and a nice reading of Paul Kelly's slinky "Personally" rate with the standouts. — *Bill Dahl*

★ **In Memorium (1935-1984)** / 1985 / Malaco ✦✦✦✦✦

Most of the highlights of Hill's glorious blues-singing stint at Malaco, although the individual albums possess more than their share of worthwhile moments that aren't here. But with hallowed titles like "Down Home Blues," "Someone Else Is Slippin' In," and "Everybody Knows About My Good Thing," this stunning collection neatly summarizes Hill's heartwarming rise to blues power. — *Bill Dahl*

Whoever Is Thrilling You / 1986 / Stateside ✦✦✦

Greatest Hits / 1986 / Malaco ✦✦✦✦

When he died in 1984 at the relatively young age of 48, Z.Z. Hill went down in history as a great blues singer. But he was also an excellent soul singer, and this 1990 CD reminds us that he had as much to do with earthy, gospel-drenched southern soul as he did with B.B. King-influenced electric blues. Focusing on Hill's Malaco output, *Greatest Hits* contains some inspired 12-bar numbers (including "Open House at My House," "Shade Tree Mechanic," and Denise LaSalle's "Someone Else Is Steppin' In") but is just as heavy in its R&B content. "Right Arm for Your Love," "Get a Little, Give a Little," and "Cheatin' In the Next Room" serve as fine examples of his unpretentious approach to Stax-influenced soul. And, of course, the CD boasts what became Hill's signature song, the infectious "Down Home Blues." For those who haven't experienced the impressive material Hill was delivering during the last years of his life, this CD would be the appropriate starting point. — *Alex Henderson*

● **The Best of Z.Z. Hill** / 1987 / Malaco ✦✦✦✦

While it isn't flawless like the similar *In Memorium (1935-1984)*, Malaco's *The Best of Z.Z. Hill* is a solid ten-track sampler of Hill's contemporary blues

recordings for the label. The other collection is more comprehensive, but this offers the bare basics, making it a nice, concise introduction. — *Thom Owens*

The Down Home Soul of Z.Z. Hill / 1992 / Kent ✦✦✦✦

Before Hill made his sensational 1980s comeback as a blues growler, he sang a slightly sweeter brand of West Coast soul during the mid-'60s at Kent. Under saxist Maxwell Davis' supervision, Hill waxed a series of magnificent R&B ballads—"Happiness Is All I Need," "I Need Someone (To Love Me)"—that should have hit but inexplicably didn't. Gathered on one 22-track import disc, they sound terrific in retrospect. — *Bill Dahl*

The Complete Hill/UA Recordings / Mar. 19, 1996 / Capitol ✦✦✦✦

The gritty singer made three albums for United Artists (mostly under his brother Matt's supervision) from 1972 to 1975, and they were an idiomatically mixed bag. All three LPs are housed in their entirety on this two-disc set, its selections ranging from the deep soul sincerity of "I've Got to Get You Back" and "Your Love Makes Me Feel Good" and the country-soul hybrids "You're Killing Me (Slowly But Surely)" and "Country Love" to the funky Lamont Dozier-produced "I Created a Monster" and an Allen Toussaint-supervised "I Keep on Lovin' You." — *Bill Dahl*

Love is So Good When You're Stealing It / Mar. 26, 1996 / Ichiban Soul Classics ✦✦✦

Although Hill is often classified as a soul/blues crossover artist, his late-'70s albums for Columbia are more properly pigeonholed as soul/disco crossover efforts. This is an 18-track anthology of material from his *Let's Make a Deal* (1978) and *The Mark of Z.Z. Hill* (1979) LPs, including the minor hits "This Time They Told the Truth" and "Love Is So Good When You're Stealing It." Certainly Hill is in good voice, but you can't help wondering if this wouldn't have sounded much better with straightforward Southern soul production. And if you appreciate Hill as a soul or soul/blues singer, there are far rootsier efforts to check out than this one. — *Richie Unterberger*

This Time They Told the Truth: The Columbia Years / Feb. 17, 1998 / Sony ✦✦✦✦

The best of Hill's late-'70s stay at Columbia Records, *This Time They Told the Truth* might be a bit of a shock to listeners not familiar with the period, for Hill's always smooth vocals are embellished with a very disco-fied production, not always disturbing, but definitely obtrusive in several places. The songs themselves are quite good (distilled from 1978's *Let's Make a Deal* and 1979's *The Mark of Z.Z. Hill*), including "Stop by and Love Me Sometime," "A Message to the Ladies," and the title track. — *John Bush*

The Hoax

Group / Blues-Rock, British Blues

British blues-rock group the Hoax consists of Jon Amor on guitar, Hugh Coltman on vocals and harmonica, Jess Davey on guitar, Robin Davey on bass, and Dave Raeburn on drums. The members are all young students of the blues and have been playing together since they were in their teens; songwriting and arrangements are worked out together by all five members. The Hoax began to attract attention while on tour with the Smokin' Joe Kubek Band around England, and Code Blue Records label chief Mike Vernon signed them to a deal. Vernon, a veteran producer who has worked with John Mayall, Eric Clapton, Ten Years After, Savoy Brown, and David Bowie, was impressed with the maturity in the band's playing. Critics in England were also impressed with the band's prowess and heaped praise on the Hoax, comparing them to the Yardbirds, John Mayall's Bluesbreakers and the Rolling Stones. Their debut album, *Sound Like This*, was released in 1995 on the Code Blue/Atlantic label (although Code Blue has since been jettisoned by Atlantic), and the recording is a good reflection of their live shows. On it, the band pays tribute to its influences, such as Albert Collins, Albert King, the Fabulous Thunderbirds, Robben Ford, and Stevie Ray Vaughan. — *Richard Skelly*

Sound Like This / 1995 / Code Blue/Atlantic ✦✦✦✦

Hodges Brothers

f. Memphis, TN

Group / R&B

Hi Records producer Willie Mitchell constructed his vaunted house rhythm section around three talented Hodges brothers during the late '60s: guitarist Mabon (nicknamed "Teenie"), bassist Leroy, and organist Charles. With drummer Howard Grimes (and on some of Al Green's sides, MG's trapsman Al Jackson, Jr.) rounding out the lineup, this skin-tight Memphis quartet laid down surging, simmering grooves behind the entire Hi stable during the label's 1970s heyday: Green, Ann Peebles, Otis Clay, Syl Johnson, and Mitchell himself, to name but a few. Mitchell had patiently molded the unit from when the Hodges brothers were in their teens (Grimes was a bit older, having worked as a sideman over at rival Stax during the early '60s).

As the succinctly monickered Hi Rhythm, they remain a cohesive unit today, providing luxurious backing on Syl Johnson's wonderful 1994 comeback set for Delmark, *Back in the Game*. Meanwhile, the Hodges Brothers released a 1994 disc called *Perfect Gentlemen* on the tiny Velvet Recordings of America logo that also featured a fourth brother—Fred—on keys and veteran soul singer Percy Wiggins on several tracks. — *Bill Dahl*

Watermelon Hangin' on the Vine / 1990 / Arhoolie ✦✦✦

Rob Hoeke

Piano / Blues-Rock
A good boogie-woogie-styled pianist, Hoeke led the Rob Hoeke Rhythm and Blues group in the mid-'60s, which had some success in Holland, although they were unknown elsewhere. Hoeke's outfit was probably the most accomplished of the numerous Dutch acts that tried to play blues-rock during the period (such as Cuby & the Blizzards). This was due in large measure to Hoeke's skill as an instrumentalist, and a sense that he had actually familiarized himself with the idiom for a few years, as opposed to some of the sloppier Dutch bands, which seemed to have leaped into R&B after hearing one Rolling Stones hit. Hoeke was also a good singer, with a pinched, hurt phrasing that was less affected than most '60s Continental rock singers performing in English.

Like most blues-rock groups of the time, Dutch or otherwise, Hoeke's band was most interesting when they brought a pop/R&B sensibility to their original material. They did this best on the sullen 1966 single "When People Talk"/"Rain, Snow, Misery," both sides of which have been reissued on compilations of '60s Dutch beat music. Their 1967 album *Save Our Souls*, by contrast, was more focused on straight blues than one might have expected, with a few instrumentals showcasing Hoeke's boogie chops. — *Richie Unterberger*

• **Save Our Souls** / 1967 / Philips ✦✦✦✦
This doesn't quite measure up to the forceful, moody, defiant R&B of their 1966 singles, Hoeke using the LP format to indulge himself in a few piano-dominated instrumentals that stick to straight blues. It's just an okay album, with occasional more satisfying tracks in a scruffy R&B/rock style more akin to the Animals, Them, or early Stones, like "Drinking on My Bed" and "Let's Get Out of Here." — *Richie Unterberger*

Free and Easy / 1980 / Universe ✦✦✦

Rob Hoeke & The Real Boogie Woogie / 1987 / Down South ✦✦✦

Silas Hogan

b. Sep. 15, 1911, Westover, LA, **d.** Jan. 9, 1994, Scotlandville, LA
Vocals, Guitar / Electric Louisiana Blues, Electric Swamp Blues, Swamp Blues
In the collection of local Louisiana blues stars that made their mark on phonograph records bearing the Excello imprint under the aegis of Crowley producer Jay Miller, Silas Hogan was a local phenom who finally had a chance to record at a time when the commercial appeal of his sound was waning in the national marketplace. Hogan recorded for Excello from 1962 to early 1965, seeing the last of his single releases issued late that year.

Sometime in the late '20s Silas learned the basics of the guitar from his two uncles, Robert and Frank Murphy, who later went on to influence the idiosyncratic style of Robert Pete Williams. Learning his trade by playing assorted house parties and picnics in the local vicinity, by the late '30s Hogan was working regularly with guitarist Willie B. Thomas and fiddler Butch Cage, making the local juke-joint circuit his new found home. A move to the Baton Rouge area in the early '50s brought changes to his music. Armed with a Fender electric guitar and amp, Hogan formed his first electric combo—the Rhythm Ramblers—becoming one of the top drawing cards on the Louisiana juke-joint circuit. In 1962, at the ripe old age of 51, Hogan was introduced by Slim Harpo to producer Jay Miller and his recording career finally began in earnest. The recordings he produced in the Crowley studio were solid, no-

frills performances that mirrored the many variants of the "sound of the swamp." After a few singles, Hogan's recording career came to an abrupt halt when Miller clashed with the new owners in 1966, ending the flow of Crowley product on the label. No longer an Excello recording artist, Hogan disbanded his group, going back to his day job at the Exxon refinery near Baton Rogue. The chance to record came around again in the 1970s, with Hogan cutting sides for labels like Arhoolie and Blue Horizon while remaining active on the Southern blues festival circuit for pretty much the rest of the decade. With as little fanfare as his Excello singles were greeted in the marketplace, Silas Hogan quietly passed away in February of 1994, seven months shy of his 83rd birthday. —*AMG*

So Long Blues / 1995 / Ace ✦✦✦

• **Trouble: The Best of the Excello Masters** / 1995 / AVI-Excello ✦✦✦✦
This 26-track single-disc retrospective may not have every last alternate take extant on it, but you'll never need a better compilation mirroring Hogan's stay at the label. "Trouble At Home Blues," "I'm Gonna Quit You Pretty Baby," and "Here They Are Again" are just about as low down as Louisiana swamp blues gets and Jay Miller's studio sorcery is clearly on hand. —*AMG*

Willie "Smokey" Hogg (Willie Anderson Hogg)

b. Jan. 27, 1914, Westconnie, TX, **d.** May 1, 1960, McKinney, TX
Vocals, Guitar, Piano / Texas Blues
Smokey Hogg was a rural bluesman navigating a postwar era infatuated by R&B, but he got along quite nicely nonetheless, scoring a pair of major R&B hits in 1948 and 1950 and cutting a thick catalog for a slew of labels (including Exclusive, Modern, Bullet, Macy's, Sittin' in With, Imperial, Mercury, Recorded in Hollywood, Specialty, Fidelity, Combo, Federal, and Showtime).

During the early '30s, Hogg, who was influenced by Big Bill Broonzy and Peetie Wheatstraw, worked with slide guitarist Black Ace at dances around Greenville, TX. Hogg first recorded for Decca in 1937, but it was an isolated occurrence—he didn't make it back into a studio for a decade. Once he hit his stride, though, Hogg didn't look back. Both his chart hits—1948's "Long Tall Mama" and 1950's "Little School Girl"—were issued on Modern, but his rough-hewn sound seldom changed a whole lot no matter what Los Angeles logo he was appearing on. Hogg's last few sides were cut in 1958 for Lee Rupe's Ebb label.

Smokey's cousin John Hogg also played the blues, recording for Mercury in 1951. —*Bill Dahl*

Sittin' in with / 1949-1950 / Mainstream ✦✦✦✦
A compilation of 14 tracks Willie Smokey Hogg recorded for the Sittin' in With label between 1949 and 1950, this record doesn't offer any of his big hits, but it's an enjoyable slice of postwar Texas blues. —*Thom Owens*

Sings / 1961 / Crown ✦✦✦✦
Smokey Hogg was a fine guitarist and good vocalist, better at mid-tempo and slower material than uptempo numbers. These are some of his best early-'60s cuts; the sound quality is good, but not exceptional. —*Ron Wynn*

Smokey Hogg / 1962 / Time ✦✦✦
Early-'50s Texas blues. —*Bill Dahl*

Original Folk Blues / 1965 / United ✦✦✦✦
Some of Hogg's best early-'50s sides for Modern are here. —*Bill Dahl*

Sings the Blues / 1973 / Ember ✦✦✦

John Lee Hooker, Lightnin Hopkins / 1973 / Specialty ✦✦✦

U Better Watch That Jive / 1974 / Specialty ✦✦✦

Going Back Home / 1984 / Krazy Kat ✦✦✦

• **Angels in Harlem** / 1992 / Specialty ✦✦✦✦
Angels in Harlem is a wonderful compilation of Smokey Hogg's early-'50s recordings for Specialty Records, containing 22 tracks, including "I Want a Roller," "Nobody Treats Me Right," "Evil Mind Blues," "I Ain't Gonna Put You Down," "Born on the 13th," and "Good Mornin' Baby." —*Thom Owens*

Penitentiary Blues / Feb. 28, 1995 / Collectables ✦✦✦✦

Dave Hole

b. Mar. 30, 1948, Heswall, Cheshire, England
Guitar, Vocals / Modern Electric Blues, Contemporary Blues
Australian slide guitarist Dave Hole is noted for his energetic, high-volume rock 'n' roll/blues music and unusual playing style. Though left-handed, Hole

plays guitar right-handed, and developed a technique to compensate for a finger injury in which he places his fingers over the top of the neck. He also uses a pick for a slide, and utilizes finger picking when playing normally.

Born in England, but raised from age four in Perth, Australia, Hole became interested in blues guitar around age six after hearing a schoolmate's Muddy Waters album. He received his first guitar at age 12, but became discouraged trying to learn it by himself (teachers were in short supply in isolated Perth) and abandoned it until he was 16. This time, he began picking up riffs and techniques from records. Primary influences include Eric Clapton, Jimi Hendrix, Robert Johnson, Elmore James, and Mississippi Fred McDowell. Hole became a professional in 1972 working with a band in London. Returning to Perth in 1974, he began his long stint touring the western Australian club circuit, playing 20 years in remote towns before making *Short Fuse Blues*, an album he financed, produced and recorded with his band, Short Fuse, in three days in 1990. He then hawked the album during club performances, and on a whim sent a copy to *Guitar Player* magazine in the US. The editor listened to it, liked it, wrote a praise-filled article hailing him as the newest guitar wizard and comparing him to such greats as Stevie Ray Vaughan and Albert King. He then helped Hole land a distribution deal with Alligator Records. The American debut of *Short Fuse Blues* earned Hole considerable praise from other sources and was well-received by the public. Although best known in Australia, Hole, with the release of his second and third albums, *Working Overtime* (1993) and *Steel on Steel* (1995 both for Alligator), have garnered him a respectable following in the US and Europe. — *Sandra Brennan*

Short Fuse Blues / 1992 / Alligator ✦✦✦
Dave Hole's American debut album is a stunning display of slide guitar pyrotechnics. Hole runs through a dizzying array of licks and solos, pulling out a variety of different tones and textures from his guitar. He can play it straight and greasy or spooky, tough, and gritty or subtle and melodic—his technique is quite impressive. Although the songs themselves are occasionally weak, *Short Fuse Blues* is essentially a guitar record, so the songs don't matter as much as the playing. And the playing is superb throughout *Short Fuse Blues*. — *Thom Owens*

● **Working Overtime** / 1993 / Alligator ✦✦✦✦
Hole's second disc features nine original compositions and covers of Muddy Waters and Big Bill Broonzy, rendered in a vocal and guitar style somewhat similar to Johnny Winter's best blues work but with an edge of youthful vigor. "Biting slide guitar work" is an understatement. Hole can also play the thoughtful Roy Buchanan card on the likes of "Berwick Road." — *Roch Parisien*

Steel on Steel / 1995 / Alligator ✦✦✦
With his third album, *Steel on Steel*, Dave Hole turns in another set of ready-made originals and covers, all highlighted by his sizzling slide guitar work. — *Stephen Thomas Erlewine*

Ticket to Chicago / Feb. 11, 1997 / Alligator ✦✦✦✦
Australian slide guitarist Hole finally comes to the United States and records his first record in the supporting company of several of the Alligator house band stalwarts; Billy Branch on harp, Tony Z. on keys, Johnny B. Gayden on bass, Ray Allison drums, and Gene Barge in charge of the horn arrangements. The change in sidemen is a good one for Hole, who has a tendency to come across as too much of a White blues-rock guy. Although his penchant for over-the-top, intonation-be-damned, playing is still well to the fore, the surroundings seem to bring out a new dimension to his work. Thirteen originals on board, with a closing cover of "Bullfrog Blues" just to round things out. — *Cub Koda*

Billie Holiday (Eleanora Fagan)

b. Apr. 7, 1915, Baltimore, MD, **d.** Jul. 17, 1959, New York, NY
Vocals / Swing, Classic Female Blues, Ballads
Billie Holiday remains (four decades after her death) the most famous of all jazz singers. "Lady Day" (as she was named by Lester Young) had a small voice and did not scat but her innovative behind-the-beat phrasing made her quite influential. The emotional intensity that she put into the words she sang (particularly in later years) was very memorable and sometimes almost scary; she often really did live the words she sang.

Her original name and birthplace have been wrong for years but are listed

correctly above thanks to Donald Clarke's definitive Billie Holiday biography *Wishing on the Moon*. Holiday's early years are shrouded in legend and rumors due to her fanciful ghostwritten autobiography *Lady Sings the Blues* but it is fair to say that she did not have a stable life. Her father Clarence Holiday (who never did marry her mother) played guitar with Fletcher Henderson and abandoned his family early on while her mother was not a very good role model. Billie essentially grew up alone, feeling unloved and gaining a lifelong inferiority complex that led to her taking great risks with her personal life and becoming self-destructive.

Holiday's life becomes clearer after she was discovered by John Hammond singing in Harlem clubs. He arranged for her to record a couple of titles with Benny Goodman in 1933 and although those were not all that successful, it was the start of her career. Two years later she was teamed with a pickup band led by Teddy Wilson and the combination clicked. During 1935-42 she would make some of the finest recordings of her career, jazz-oriented performances in which she was joined by the who's who of swing. Holiday sought to combine together Louis Armstrong's swing and Bessie Smith's sound; the result was her own fresh approach. In 1937 Lester Young and Buck Clayton began recording with Holiday and the interplay between the three of them was timeless.

Lady Day was with Count Basie's Orchestra during much of 1937 but, because they were signed to different labels, all that exists of the collaboration are three songs from a radio broadcast. She worked with Artie Shaw's Orchestra for a time in 1938 but the same problem existed (only one song was recorded) and she had to deal with racism, not only during a Southern tour but in New York too. She had better luck as a star attraction at Cafe Society in 1939. Holiday made history that year by recording the horribly picturesque "Strange Fruit," a strong anti-racism statement that became a permanent part of her repertoire. Her records of 1940-42 found her sidemen playing a much more supportive role than in the past, rarely sharing solo space with her.

Although the settings were less jazz-oriented than before (with occasional strings and even a background vocal group on a few numbers) Billie Holiday's voice was actually at its strongest during her period with Decca (1944-49). She had already introduced "Fine and Mellow" (1939) and "God Bless the Child" (1941) but it was while with Decca that she first recorded "Lover Man" (her biggest hit), "Don't Explain," "Good Morning Heartache," and her renditions of "Ain't Nobody's Business If I Do," "Them There Eyes," and "Crazy He Calls Me." Unfortunately it was just before this period that she became a heroin addict and she spent much of 1947 in jail. Due to the publicity she became a notorious celebrity and her audience greatly increased. Lady Day did get a chance to make one Hollywood movie (*New Orleans*) in 1946 and, although she was disgusted at the fact that she was stuck playing a maid, she did get to perform with her early idol Louis Armstrong.

Billie Holiday's story from 1950 on is a gradual downhill slide. Although her recordings for Norman Granz (which started in 1952) placed her once again with all-star jazz veterans (including Charlie Shavers, Buddy DeFranco, Harry "Sweets" Edison, and Ben Webster), her voice was slipping fast. Her unhappy relationships distracted her, the heroin use and excessive drinking continued and by 1956 she was way past her prime. Holiday had one final burst of glory in late 1957 when she sang "Fine and Mellow" on *The Sound of Jazz* telecast while joined by Lester Young (who stole the show with an emotional chorus), Ben Webster, Coleman Hawkins, Gerry Mulligan, and Roy Eldridge, but the end was near. Holiday's 1958 album *Lady in Satin* found the 43-year old singer sounding 73 (barely croaking out the words) and the following year she collapsed; in the sad final chapter of her life she was placed under arrest for heroin possession while on her deathbed!

Fortunately Billie Holiday's recordings have been better treated than she was during her life and virtually all of her studio sides are currently available on CD. — *Scott Yanow*

☆ **The Quintessential Billie Holiday, Vol. 1 (1933-1935)** / Nov. 27, 1933-Dec. 3, 1935 / Columbia ✦✦✦✦✦
After years of reissuing her recordings in piecemeal fashion, Columbia finally got it right with this nine-CD *Quintessential* series. All of Lady Day's 1933-42 studio recordings (although without the alternate takes) receive the treatment they deserve in this program. *Vol. 1* has Holiday's first two tentative performances from 1933 along with her initial recordings with Teddy Wilson's all-star bands. Highpoints include "I Wished On the Moon," "What

a Little Moonlight Can Do," "Miss Brown to You," and "Twenty-Four Hours a Day." — *Scott Yanow*

Billie Holiday: The Legacy Box 1933-1958 / Nov. 27, 1933-Feb. 19, 1958 / Columbia ✦✦✦

The logic behind this sampler is puzzling. Rather than reissue the very best of Billie Holiday's Columbia recordings on a three-CD box set or a package of her rare alternate takes, CBS tries it both ways by including 60 common selections already available in the *Quintessential* series along with 10 rarities that were either unissued or alternates. This otherwise attractive box (which includes a colorful booklet) will drive completists and veteran collectors crazy. The music (mostly from 1933-42 with three weaker performances from 1957-58) is often classic but duplicates more coherent reissues. — *Scott Yanow*

Lady Day / Jul. 2, 1935-Jun. 15, 1937 / Columbia ✦✦✦✦

This LP, whose contents have since been reissued on CD, used to be the one definitive set to acquire of early Billie Holiday. The 12 selections are all classics (particularly "What a Little Moonlight Can Do," "If You Were Mine," "Billie's Blues," "I Must Have That Man," "Easy Living," "Me, Myself and I," and "I Cried for You") and find Lady Day joined by such all-stars as pianist Teddy Wilson, trumpeters Roy Eldridge, Bunny Berigan, and Buck Clayton, clarinetist Benny Goodman, the tenors of Lester Young and Ben Webster, and altoist Johnny Hodges among others. Wonderful music that is essential to acquire in one form or another. — *Scott Yanow*

If You Were Mine / Jul. 2, 1935-Nov. 28, 1938 / Drive Archive ✦✦

Fourteen of Billie Holiday's studio sides from 1935-38 (most of which were originally under the leadership of pianist Teddy Wilson) are reissued on this Drive Archive CD. Some of the titles are classics (particularly "What a Little Moonlight Can Do" and "Miss Brown to You") while a few are quite obscure. The music is fine but the sound quality is not as good as one would hope, plus these important performances have already been reissued in more definitive fashion on CD by Columbia. This CD does serve as a budget sampler for listeners not yet familiar with Billie Holiday. — *Scott Yanow*

★ **The Quintessential Billie Holiday, Vol. 2 (1936)** / Jan. 30, 1936-Oct. 21, 1936 / Columbia ✦✦✦✦✦

The second of nine volumes in this essential series (all are highly recommended) continues the complete reissue of Billie Holiday's early recordings (although the alternate takes are bypassed). This set is highlighted by "I Cried for You" (which has a classic alto solo from Johnny Hodges), "Billie's Blues" (from Holiday's first session as a leader), "A Fine Romance," and "Easy to Love." Holiday's backup crew includes such greats as pianist Teddy Wilson, baritonist Harry Carney, trumpeters Jonah Jones and Bunny Berigan, and clarinetist Artie Shaw. There's lots of great small-group swing. — *Scott Yanow*

Don't Explain / Sep. 29, 1936-Jul. 25, 1958 / Audio Fidelity ✦✦

This three-LP box set is one of the more bizarre Billie Holiday reissues with virtually all of the discographical information given on its back cover being completely inaccurate. A hodgepodge collection of live performances along with a few (presumably illegal) studio cuts, the recordings jump all over the place, from broadcasts with Count Basie in 1937 to TV appearances, concert performances in the 1950s, and the 1936 studio version of "I Can't Pretend"; the latter has dubbed in phony applause. The recording quality varies from decent to barely listenable. — *Scott Yanow*

★ **The Quintessential Billie Holiday, Vol. 3 (1936-1937)** / Oct. 28, 1936-Feb. 18, 1937 / Columbia ✦✦✦✦✦

The third of nine CDs that document all of Billie Holiday's studio recordings of 1933-42 for Columbia has classic versions of "Pennies from Heaven," "I Can't Give You Anything but Love" (on which she shows the influence of Louis Armstrong), and "My Last Affair," along with Lady Day's first meeting on record with tenor-saxophonist Lester Young. Their initial encounter resulted in four songs including "This Year's Kisses" and "I Must Have That Man." All nine volumes in this admirable series (if only the alternate takes had been included!) are highly recommended. — *Scott Yanow*

☆ **The Quintessential Billie Holiday, Vol. 4 (1937)** / Mar. 31, 1937-Jun. 15, 1937 / Columbia ✦✦✦✦✦

The fourth of nine CDs in this essential series of Billie Holiday's studio recordings of 1933-42 features the great tenor Lester Young on eight of the 16 performances. Prez and Lady Day make a perfect match on "I'll Get By" (although altoist Johnny Hodges steals the honors on that song), "Mean to

Me," "Easy Living," "Me Myself and I," and "A Sailboat in the Moonlight." Other strong selections without Young include "Moanin' Low," "Let's Call the Whole Thing Off," and "Where Is the Sun." It's highly recommended along with all of the other CDs in this perfectly done Billie Holiday reissue program. — *Scott Yanow*

★ **The Quintessential Billie Holiday, Vol. 5 (1937-1938)** / Jun. 15, 1937-Jan. 27, 1938 / Columbia ✦✦✦✦

The fifth of nine CDs in the complete reissue of Billie Holiday's early recordings (sans alternate takes), this great set has 18 selections, all but four featuring tenor-saxophonist Lester Young and trumpeter Buck Clayton. Among the classics are "Getting Some Fun out of Life," "Trav'lin' All Alone," "He's Funny That Way," "My Man," "When You're Smiling" (on which Prez takes a perfect solo), "If Dreams Come True," and "Now They Call It Swing." All nine volumes in this series are highly recommended, but if one can only acquire a single entry, this is the one. — *Scott Yanow*

☆ **The Quintessential Billie Holiday, Vol. 6 (1938)** / May 11, 1938-Nov. 9, 1938 / Columbia ✦✦✦✦✦

The sixth of nine CDs in this very worthy series traces Billie Holiday's recording career throughout much of 1938. Although not containing as many true classics as *Vol. 5*, most of these 18 seletions are quite enjoyable, particularly "You Go to My Head," "Having Myself a Time," "The Very Thought of You," and "They Say." All of the sets in this reissue program are recommended, featuring Lady Day when she was youthful and still optimistic about life. — *Scott Yanow*

The Quintessential Billie Holiday, Vol. 7 (1938-1939) / Nov. 28, 1938-Jul. 5, 1939 / Columbia ✦✦✦✦

By 1939 when the bulk of these 17 selections were recorded, Billie Holiday was dominating her own recordings, allocating less space for her sidemen to solo. This was not really a bad thing since Lady Day's voice was getting stronger each year. On the seventh of nine CD volumes that reissue all of Holiday's 1933-42 Columbia recordings (other than the alternate takes which have been bypassed), Holiday sounds at her best on "More than You Know, Sugar" (featuring a superb Benny Carter alto solo), "Long Gone Blues," and "Some Other Spring." It's recommended along with all of the other entries in the *Quintessential* series. — *Scott Yanow*

Billie Holiday [Commodore] / Apr. 20, 1939-Apr. 8, 1944 / Commodore ✦✦✦✦

This CD includes all of Billie Holiday's Commodore recordings (the master takes but no alternates): four titles from 1939 (including the still haunting "Strange Fruit" and "Fine and Mellow") and the remainder dating from 1944 when Holiday's voice was at its peak. The latter sessions are highlighted by "I'll Get By," "Billie's Blues," "He's Funny That Way," and "I'm Yours." Pianist Eddie Heywood has many sparkling solos on the 1944 selections. This definitive single CD contains music essential for every jazz collection. — *Scott Yanow*

The Complete Commodore Recordings / Apr. 20, 1939-Apr. 8, 1944 / GRP ✦✦✦

Billie Holiday recorded on four occasions for the Commodore label: once in 1939 (a date that resulted in "Fine and Mellow" and "Strange Fruit") and three sessions in 1944 (dates highlighted by "I Cover the Waterfront," "I'm Yours," "He's Funny That Way," "Billie's Blues," and "On the Sunny Side of the Street"). While the former session has Lady Day joined by a background octet that includes trumpeter Frankie Newton, the Eddie Heywood Sextet forms the nucleus of the later dates. This two-CD set has all 18 selections and no less than 27 alternate takes. Since the great majority of the performances are ballads, and with the exception of pianist Heywood, there are very few instrumental solos, there are no significant differences between the versions. Therefore, this set (as opposed to a single CD of the master takes), even though it is well-conceived, is strictly for completists. — *Scott Yanow*

☆ **The Quintessential Billie Holiday, Vol. 8 (1939-1940)** / Jul. 5, 1939-Sep. 12, 1940 / Columbia ✦✦✦✦✦

The eighth of nine volumes that feature all of the master takes from Billie Holiday's Columbia recordings of 1933-42 is one of the better sets although all nine CDs are recommended. Highpoints include "Them There Eyes," "Swing, Brother, Swing," "The Man I Love," "Ghost of Yesterday," "Body and Soul," "Falling in Love Again," and "I Hear Music." Among the variety of all-stars backing her, tenor-saxophonist Lester Young makes his presence known on eight of the 18 numbers. — *Scott Yanow*

Control Booth Series, Vol. 1 / Sep. 12, 1940-Mar. 21, 1941 / Jazz Unlimited ◆◆◆
Strictly for completists, this Storyville CD has 25 performances but just ten separate songs; 15 are alternate takes. Slightly more complete than an Affinity box set that covered the 1940 selections, this release surprisingly leaves out one version of "Loveless Love." The music, particularly the originally released versions, is excellent; Lady Day is in fine form, and there are some solos from trumpeter Roy Eldridge, Benny Carter (on clarinet), tenorman Georgie Auld, pianist Teddy Wilson and (on the final session) tenor saxophonist Lester Young. Among the tunes are "I Hear Music," "St. Louis Blues," "Let's Do It," and "Romance in the Dark." Most collectors would be satisfied with just having the regular versions, but one can appreciate slight differences in each rendition, particularly from the soloists. — *Scott Yanow*

The Quintessential Billie Holiday, Vol. 9 (1940-1942) / Oct. 15, 1940-Feb. 10, 1942 / Columbia ◆◆◆◆
The final volume in this nine-CD series contains all of Billie Holiday's recordings from her final 16 months with the label. Highlights include "St. Louis Blues," "Loveless Love," "Let's Do It," "All of Me" (arguably the greatest version ever of this veteran standard), "Am I Blue," "Gloomy Sunday," and "God Bless the Child." All 153 of Lady Day's Columbia recordings (even the occasional weak item) are well worth hearing and savoring. — *Scott Yanow*

Billie's Blues [Blue Note] / 1942-1954 / Capitol ◆◆◆◆
Most of this excellent CD features one of Billie Holiday's finest concert recordings of the 1950s. Recorded in Europe before an admiring audience, this enjoyable set finds Lady Day performing seven of her standards with her trio and joining in for jam session versions of "Billie's Blues" and "Lover Come Back to Me" with an all-star group starring clarinetist Buddy DeFranco, vibraphonist Red Norvo, and guitarist Jimmy Raney. These performances (which find Holiday in stronger voice than on her studio recordings of the period) have also been included in Verve's massive CD box set. This program concludes with Holiday's four rare sides for Aladdin in 1951 (between her Decca and Verve periods) which are highlighted by two blues and "Detour Ahead," and her 1942 studio recording of "Trav'lin' Light" with Paul Whiteman's Orchestra. — *Scott Yanow*

Masters of Jazz, Vol. 3 / Jan. 18, 1944-1949 / Storyville ◆◆◆
This very interesting CD has a variety of mostly rare Billie Holiday live performances from 1944-49. In addition to two selections with the 1944 Esquire All-Stars, Lady Day is heard with Hot Lips Page, accompanied by pianist Teddy Wilson on a 1947 version of "The Man I Love," backed by Percy Faith's string orchestra on "You Better Go Now," and joined by a Red Norvo-led band in 1949 that also includes trumpeter Neal Hefti and the reeds of Herbie Steward. Collectors are advised to search for this set. — *Scott Yanow*

Fine and Mellow [Collectables] / Jan. 18, 1944-Apr. 15, 1959 / Collectables ◆◆◆
This CD contains 20 selections featuring Billie Holiday in a variety of live performances covering a 15-year period. Starting with two songs in 1944 in which she was backed by the Esquire All-Stars and continuing through TV appearances and club dates, one can hear the gradual aging and decline of Lady Day's voice which definitely took a turn for the worse between 1955-56. And yet oddly enough the last five numbers, which were performed April 15, 1959 (making them Holiday's final recordings), actually find her sounding stronger than she had in a few years, perhaps in a final gasp of energy. Of great historical value, this set has plenty of strong moments to justify its acquisition. — *Scott Yanow*

★ **The Complete Decca Recordings** / Oct. 4, 1944-Mar. 8, 1950 / Decca ◆◆◆◆◆
Billie Holiday is heard at her absolute best on this attractive two-CD set. During her period on Decca, Lady Day was accompanied by strings (for the first time), large studio orchestras and even background vocalists, so jazz solos from her sidemen are few. But her voice was at its strongest during the 1940s (even with her personal problems) and to hear all 50 of her Decca performances (including alternate takes and even some studio chatter) is a real joy. Among the highpoints of this essential set are her original versions of "Lover Man" (Holiday's biggest selling record), "Don't Explain," "Good Morning Heartache," " 'Tain't Nobody's Business if I Do," "Now or Never,"

"Crazy He Calls Me," and remakes of "Them There Eyes" and "God Bless the Child." — *Scott Yanow*

☆ **The Complete Billie Holiday on Verve 1945-1959** / Feb. 12, 1945-Mar. 1, 1959 / Verve ◆◆◆◆◆
This is a rather incredible collection, ten CDs enclosed in a tight black box that includes every one of the recordings that Verve owns of Billie Holiday, not only the many studio recordings of 1952-57 (which feature Lady Day joined by such jazz all-stars as trumpeters Charlie Shavers and Harry "Sweets" Edison, altoist Benny Carter, and the tenors of Flip Phillips, Paul Quinichette and Ben Webster) but prime performances at Jazz at the Philharmonic concerts in 1945-7, an enjoyable European gig from 1954, her "comeback" Carnegie Hall concert of 1956, Holiday's rather sad final studio album from 1959 and even lengthy tapes from two informal rehearsals. It's a perfect purchase for the true Billie Holiday fanatic. — *Scott Yanow*

Lady in Autumn: The Best of the Verve Years / Apr. 1946-Mar. 1959 / Verve ◆◆◆

Billie Holiday at Storyville / Oct. 29, 1951-1953 / Black Lion ◆◆◆
Billie Holiday is in generally good form for this club appearance. On most of the selections she is accompanied by the Carl Drinkard Trio, but six others find her joined by Buster Harding's Trio; the great tenor Stan Getz sits in on three of these numbers, making one wish that he and Lady Day had collaborated more extensively. This set of standards (most of which had been recorded previously by Holiday) are not up to the quality of her Decca output but are enjoyable nevertheless. — *Scott Yanow*

The Billie Holiday Songbook / 1952-1958 / Verve ◆◆◆
Excellent play on the songbook trend, with Holiday doing her own material. — *Ron Wynn*

Lady Sings the Blues / 1954-1956 / Verve ◆◆◆
Immaculate 1954 and 1956 recordings with an all-star lineup and smashing Holiday cuts. One of her last great dates. — *Ron Wynn*

Songs for Distingue Lovers / Jun. 6, 1956-Jun. 7, 1956 / Verve ◆◆◆
During the six days and four sessions covered by this 1997 CD (which in its original form consisted of six songs), Billie Holiday recorded 18 titles; a dozen of the best are here, although "Comes Love" is unaccountably missing. This was the last series of extensive small-group recordings that Lady Day would make in the studios. Although her voice was largely shot at this point, she puts so much feeling into some of the lyrics that one can often overlook her dark sound. The all-star cast (trumpeter Harry "Sweets" Edison, tenor saxophonist Ben Webster, pianist Jimmie Rowles, guitarist Barney Kessel, bassist Red Mitchell, and Alvin Stoller or Larry Bunker on drums) is a major asset, and there are plenty of short solos for Edison, Webster and Kessel. Holiday does her best on such numbers as "A Foggy Day," "One for My Baby," "Just One of Those Things," and "I Wished on the Moon," and there are plenty of haunting moments, even if one could tell (even at the time) that the end was probably drawing near for the singer. The music is still well worth having, although completists will prefer a collection with all 18 songs, while beginners should sample Holiday's Columbia and Decca output first. — *Scott Yanow*

The Essential Billie Holiday Carnegie Hall Concert / Nov. 1956 / Verve ◆◆◆
An excellent live set. Holiday in wonderful form. — *Ron Wynn*

Lady in Satin / Feb. 19, 1958-Feb. 21, 1958 / Columbia ◆◆◆◆
This is the most controversial of all Billie Holiday records. Lady Day herself said that this session (which finds her accompanied by Ray Ellis' string orchestra) was her personal favorite, and many listeners have found her emotional versions of such songs as "I'm a Fool to Want You," "You Don't Know What Love Is," "Glad to Be Unhappy," and particularly "You've Changed" to be quite touching. But Holiday's voice was essentially gone by 1958, and although not yet 43, she could have passed for 73. Ellis' arrangements do not help, veering close to Muzak; most of this record is very difficult to listen to. Late in life, Billie Holiday expressed the pain of life so effectively that her croaking voice had become almost unbearable to hear. The 1997 CD reissue adds two alternate takes of "I'm a Fool to Want You," part of which were used for the original released rendition, plus the stereo version of "The End of a Love Affair" (only previously released in mono) and examples of Lady Day

rehearsing the latter song, including a long unaccompanied stretch. There is certainly a wide range of opinion as to the value of this set. —*Scott Yanow*

The Monterey Jazz Festival with Buddy DeFranco / Oct. 5, 1958 / Black Hawk ✦
Appearing at the first Monterey Jazz Festival, Billie Holiday tried gamely to succeed, but during this live set she often sounds a bit out of it. Accompanied by the Mal Waldron Trio (and on the final few numbers baritonist Gerry Mulligan, altoist Benny Carter, and clarinetist Buddy DeFranco), Lady Day struggles through the half-hour set, performing old favorites but often sounding quite weak. The results, as heard on this LP (recorded nine months before her death), are historic but often rather sad. —*Scott Yanow*

Stay with Me / 1959 / Verve ✦✦✦✦
A '91 reissue from late in Billie Holiday's career. She was fading, but hadn't lost the dramatic quality in her delivery, nor her ability to project and tell a shattering story. She's backed by trumpeter Charlie Shavers, pianist Oscar Peterson, guitarist Herb Ellis, bassist Ray Brown, and drummer Ed Shaughnessy. The CD reissue has three bonus cuts. —*Ron Wynn*

Last Recordings / Mar. 3, 1959-Mar. 11, 1959 / Verve ✦✦
In many ways, a sad event. 1988 reissue of an album with Ray Ellis and his orchestra. It's poignant in a tragic way. —*Ron Wynn*

Verve Jazz Masters 47: Sings Standards / Oct. 1995 / Verve ✦✦✦
Of Verve's countless number of Billie Holiday samplers, this one—which is actually a second helping from the *Jazz Masters* series—is as good as any of them artistically. Like many of its cousins on the shelves, this one takes in the whole cross-section of Holiday's recordings for Norman Granz from an exuberant 1945 JATP concert all the way to her last poignant sessions with the Ray Ellis string orchestra in 1959. Unlike them, this one does not contain songs with which Billie is inextricably tied, but all of the well-worn standards are given the inimitable Holiday stamp, often in league with many of Granz's legendary soloists. Of course, this is the most troubling period for Holiday scholars, for her voice was going downhill fast in the 1950s, yet one has to admit that her Verve recordings often pack an emotional wallop that eclipse most of the earlier ones. A few random highlights: the JATP "All of Me" and "Body and Soul" from the mid-'40s, with Holiday in fresh voice and a whole bunch of star horns wailing in tangled contrapuntal splendor underneath; and a "When It's Sleepy Time Down South" from the Ray Ellis sessions where the combination of Holiday's broken-down voice and exquisite phrasing will break your heart. Verve's thorough discographical entries, here and in the entire Jazz Masters series, are exemplary for what is, after all, an inexpensive sampler for newcomers to jazz. —*Richard S. Ginell*

Control Booth Series, Vol. 2 / Dec. 12, 1995 / Jazz Unlimited ✦✦✦
This Jazz Unlimited CD (available through Storyville) features multiple takes of Billie Holiday during the last four sessions from her early prime years. Strangely enough, three of the takes, including two masters, are not included on this otherwise complete set. Holiday is heard on such numbers as "All of Me," "God Bless the Child," "Am I Blue," "Gloomy Sunday," and a swinging arrangement of "It's a Sin to Tell a Lie"; other than short spots for trumpeter Emmett Berry and pianist Teddy Wilson (in addition to tenorman Lester Young on "All of Me"), the focus is entirely on Lady Day's voice. The many versions (which include eight that were previously unissued) should greatly interest collectors, but the missing renditions are quite unfortunate. —*Scott Yanow*

Tony Hollins

b. 1900, Clarksdale, MS **b.** 1959, Chicago, IL
Guitar, Vocals / Acoustic Blues
Cited as a major influence by no less than John Lee Hooker, Delta blues singer/guitarist Tony Hollins was born in Clarksdale, MS around the turn of the century. Few details are known of Hollins' life; he cut his first recordings for OKeh in 1941, with his fluid, insistent performance of "Crawlin' King Snake" serving as the blueprint for Hooker's own later rendition. His "Traveling Man Blues" was also later appropriated by Hooker for his "When My Wife Quit Me." Clearly admired by his peers, Hollins never caught on as a popular favorite, and after another session in 1951, he gradually drifted out of music, focusing instead on his day job as a barber. He died in Chicago in 1959. —*Jason Ankeny*

The Holmes Brothers

f. 1980, New York, NY
Group / Soul, R&B, Modern Electric Blues
The Holmes Brothers' unique synthesis of gospel-inflected blues harmonies, accompanied by good drumming and rhythm-based guitar playing, gives them a down-home rural feeling that no other touring blues group can duplicate.

Brothers Sherman and Wendell Holmes, along with drummer Popsy Dixon (the falsetto voice), are the group's core members, although they occasionally tour with extra musicians. All three harmonize well together. The Holmes Brothers are so versatile, they're booked solid every summer at folk, blues, gospel, and jazz festivals, as they play a style of music that is a gumbo of church tunes, blues, and soul. Although people like Bo Diddley and especially Jimmy Reed were early influences on Wendell and Sherman, gospel music also played an important role in their respective upbringings.

Although they'd been performing in Harlem for years, the Holmes Brothers—originally from Christchurch, VA—have only recently become international blues touring stars. Thanks to a fair deal at Rounder Records, the group has released three recordings for that label, beginning with a 1989 release, *In the Spirit*. When this album made waves and got them off and running on the festival and club circuit around the US and Europe, they followed it up two years later with *Where It's At* (1991), *Soul Street* (1993), and *Promised Land* (1997).

The group's career has been aided by the interest of people like Peter Gabriel, who recruited them for his WOMAD (world music) Festivals in England and who also recorded them in a gospel context on the album *Jubilation*, for his Real World subsidiary of Virgin Records in 1992. —*Richard Skelly*

In the Spirit / 1990 / Rounder ✦✦✦✦
The Holmes Brothers' voices are too potent, their harmonies too smashing and their love of vintage sounds too immense for them to be content with producer-dominated, softer urban contemporary sounds. This set included some riveting gospel tunes like "None But The Righteous" and "Up Above My Head," plus a credible (if a little lengthy) version of "When Something Is Wrong With My Baby" and the tighter, hard-hitting tunes "Please Don't Hurt Me," "Ask Me No Questions," and "The Final Round." If straight-ahead, rousing shared leads and booming harmonies interest you, The Holmes Brothers do it the way they used to throughout the South in the '60s and '70s. —*Ron Wynn*

Where It's at / 1991 / Rounder ✦✦✦✦
Their second release contained 11 more wonderful tunes that easily moved from surging R&B to rousing blues with an occasional venture into gospel or country. They covered "Drown In My Own Tears" and "High Heel Sneakers" and had the requisite qualities for each one down pat, as well as "Never Let Me Go," "The Love You Save," and "I Saw The Light." But their own numbers, like "I've Been A Loser" and the title track, were even better, displaying a contemporary sensibility and classic style and sound. —*Ron Wynn*

Jubilation / 1992 / Real World ✦✦✦
Jubilation is a revealing, wonderful collection of the Holmes Brothers' distinctive soul. The brothers tie together a seemingly disconnected array of styles—everything from straightforward blues, R&B, and gospel to worldbeat and country—and come up with a cohesive whole. Even when the group delves into soukous or works with a Chinese flutist, it manages to retain the pure qualities of American blues and R&B. —*Thom Owens*

● **Soul Street** / 1993 / Rounder ✦✦✦✦
This album continued The Holmes Brothers' tradition of doing tremendous covers ("You're Gonna Make Me Cry," "Down In Virginia," and "Fannie Mae"), authentic originals ("I Won't Hurt You Anymore," "Dashboard Bar") and adding gospel ("Walk In The Light") and honky-tonk ("There Goes My Everything") into their blend. There's little to criticize about The Holmes Brothers; their sound, vocals, and harmonies aren't laid-back or restrained, and everything they sing is done with exuberance and integrity. It may not be commercially viable, but it's musically sound. —*Ron Wynn*

Promised Land / Apr. 1996-Jun. 1996 / Rounder ✦✦✦

Earl Hooker (Earl Zebedee Hooker)

b. Jan. 15, 1930, Clarksdale, MS, **d.** Apr. 21, 1970, Chicago, IL

Guitar, Vocals / Electric Chicago Blues, Delta Blues

If there was a more immaculate slide guitarist residing in Chicago during the 1950s and '60s than Earl Hooker, his name has yet to surface. Boasting a fretboard touch so smooth and clean that every note rang as clear and precise as a bell, Hooker was an endlessly inventive axeman who would likely have been a star had his modest vocal abilities matched his instrumental prowess and had he not been dogged by tuberculosis (it killed him at age 41).

Born in the Mississippi Delta, Hooker arrived in Chicago as a child. There he was influenced by another slide wizard, veteran Robert Nighthawk. But Hooker never remained still for long. He ran away from home at age 13, journeying to Mississippi. After another stint in Chicago, he rambled back to the Delta again, playing with Ike Turner and Sonny Boy Williamson. Hooker made his first recordings in 1952 and 1953 for Rockin', King, and Sun. At the latter, he recorded some terrific sides with pianist Pinetop Perkins (Sam Phillips inexplicably sat on Hooker's blazing rendition of "The Hucklebuck").

Back in Chicago again, Hooker's dazzling dexterity was intermittently showcased on singles for Argo, C.J., and Bea & Baby during the mid-to-late '50s before he joined forces with producer Mel London (owner of the Chief and Age logos) in 1959. For the next four years, he recorded both as sideman and leader for the producer, backing Junior Wells, Lillian Offitt, Ricky Allen, and A.C. Reed and cutting his own sizzling instrumentals ("Blue Guitar," "Blues in D-Natural"). He also contributed pungent slide work to Muddy Waters' Chess waxing "You Shook Me." Opportunities to record grew sparse after Age folded; Hooker made some tantalizing sides for Sauk City, WI's Cuca Records from 1964 to 1968 (several featuring steel guitar virtuoso Freddie Roulette).

Hooker's amazing prowess (he even managed to make the dreaded wah-wah pedal a viable blues tool) finally drew increased attention during the late '60s. He cut LPs for Arhoolie, ABC-BluesWay, and Blue Thumb that didn't equal what he'd done at Age, but they did serve to introduce Hooker to an audience outside Chicago and wherever his frequent travels deposited him. But tuberculosis halted his wandering ways permanently in 1970. *—Bill Dahl*

Two Bugs and a Roach / 1966 / Arhoolie ✦✦✦✦

A nice representative sample from Chicago's unsung master of the electric guitar, it includes the title track, "Anna Lee," and the atmospheric instrumental, "Off the Hook." *—Bary Lee Pearson*

Sweet Black Angel / 1970 / One Way ✦✦✦

Ike Turner co-produced this set with Blue Thumb Records boss Bob Krasnow. It's a wide-ranging collection, as its oddly generic song titles ("Country and Western," "Shuffle," "Funky Blues") would eloquently indicate. *—Bill Dahl*

There's a Fungus Amung Us / 1972 / Red Lightnin' ✦✦✦

Do You Remember the Great Earl Hooker / 1973 / Bluesway ✦✦✦

Hooker 'n Steve / 1975 / Arhoolie ✦✦✦

Two Bugs & a Roach/Hooker 'n Steve / 1976 / Arhoolie ✦✦✦✦

Leading Brand / 1978 / Red Lightnin' ✦✦✦✦

Hooker's best early-'60s instrumentals for Mel London, along with a few sides that feature his guitar by Ricky Allen, Lillian Offett, etc. Also featured are several equally memorable workouts by guitarist Jody Williams. *—Bill Dahl*

● **Blue Guitar** / 1981 / Paula/Flyright ✦✦✦✦

The slide guitar wizard's immaculate fretwork was never captured more imaginatively than during his early-'60s stay with Mel London's Age/Chief labels. 21 fascinating tracks from that period include Hooker's savage instrumentals "Blue Guitar," "Off the Hook," "The Leading Brand," "Blues in D Natural," and "How Long Can This Go On," along with tracks by A.C. Reed, Lillian Offitt, and Harold Tidwell that cast Hooker as a standout sideman. *—Bill Dahl*

Play Your Guitar Mr Hooker / 1985 / Black Top ✦✦✦

1964-1967 output by the guitarist that was largely done for the tiny Cuca logo of Sauk City, WI. The normally tight-lipped Hooker proves that he could sing on this romping version of "Swear to Tell the Truth," while A.C. Reed, Little Tommy, Frank Clark, and Muddy Waters, Jr., help out behind the mike

elsewhere. A pair of live cuts from 1968 find Hooker stretching out in amazing fashion. *—Bill Dahl*

John Lee Hooker

b. Aug. 17, 1920, Clarksdale, MS

Guitar, Vocals / Delta Blues, Electric Delta Blues, Country Blues, Blues Revival

He's beloved worldwide as the king of the endless boogie, a genuine blues superstar whose droning, hypnotic one-chord grooves are at once both ultra-primitive and timeless. But John Lee Hooker has recorded in a great many more styles than that over a career that stretches back more than half a century.

The Hook is a Mississippi native who became the top gent on the Detroit blues circuit in the years following World War II. The seeds for his eerily mournful guitar sound were planted by his stepfather, Will Moore, while Hooker was in his teens. Hooker had been singing spirituals before that, but the blues took hold and simply wouldn't let go. Overnight visitors left their mark on the youth, too—legends like Blind Lemon Jefferson, Charley Patton, and Blind Blake, who all knew Moore.

Hooker heard Memphis calling while he was still in his teens, but he couldn't gain much of a foothold there. So he relocated to Cincinnati for a seven-year stretch before making the big move to the Motor City in 1943. Jobs were plentiful, but Hooker drifted away from day gigs in favor of playing his unique free-form brand of blues. A burgeoning club scene along Hastings Street didn't hurt his chances any.

In 1948, the aspiring bluesman hooked up with entrepreneur Bernie Besman, who helped him hammer out his solo debut sides, "Sally Mae" and its seminal flip, "Boogie Chillen." This was blues as primitive as anything on the market; Hooker's dark, ruminative vocals were backed only by his own ringing, heavily amplified guitar and insistently pounding foot. Their efforts were quickly rewarded. Los Angeles-based Modern Records issued the sides and "Boogie Chillen"—a colorful, unique travelogue of Detroit's blues scene—made an improbable jaunt to the very peak of the R&B charts.

Modern released several more major hits by the Boogie Man after that: "Hobo Blues" and its raw-as-an-open wound flip, "Hoogie Boogie"; "Crawling King Snake Blues" (all three 1949 smashes), and the unusual 1951 chart-topper "I'm in the Mood," where Hooker overdubbed his voice three times in a crude early attempt at multi-tracking.

But Hooker never, ever let something as meaningless as a contract stop him for making recordings for other labels. His early catalog is stretched across a roadmap of diskeries so complex that it's nearly impossible to fully comprehend (a vast array of recording aliases don't make things any easier).

Along with Modern, Hooker recorded for King (as the geographically challenged Texas Slim), Regent (as Delta John, a far more accurate handle), Savoy (as the wonderfully surreal Birmingham Sam and his Magic Guitar), Danceland (as the downright delicious Little Pork Chops), Staff (as Johnny Williams), Sensation (for whom he scored a national hit in 1950 with "Huckle Up, Baby"), Gotham, Regal, Swing Time, Federal, Gone (as John Lee Booker), Chess, Acorn (as the Boogie Man), Chance, DeLuxe (as Johnny Lee), JVB, Chart, and Specialty before finally settling down at Vee-Jay in 1955 under his own name. Hooker became the point man for the growing Detroit blues scene during this incredibly prolific period, recruiting guitarist Eddie Kirkland as his frequent duet partner while still recording for Modern.

Once tied in with Vee-Jay, the rough-and-tumble sound of Hooker's solo and duet waxings was adapted to a band format. Hooker had recorded with various combos along the way before, but never with sidemen as versatile and sympathetic as guitarist Eddie Taylor and harpist Jimmy Reed, who backed him at his initial Vee-Jay date that produced "Time Is Marching" and the superfluous sequel "Mambo Chillun."

Taylor stuck around for a 1956 session that elicited two genuine Hooker classics, "Baby Lee" and "Dimples," and he was still deftly anchoring the rhythm section (Hooker's sense of timing was his and his alone, demanding big-eared sidemen) when the Boogie Man finally made it back to the R&B charts in 1958 with "I Love You Honey."

Vee-Jay presented Hooker in quite an array of settings during the early '60s. His grinding, tough blues "No Shoes" proved a surprisingly sizable hit in 1960, while the storming "Boom Boom," his top seller for the firm in 1962 (it even cracked the pop airwaves), was an infectious R&B dance number benefiting from the reported presence of some of Motown's house musicians.

But there were also acoustic outings aimed squarely at the blossoming folk-blues crowd, as well as some attempts at up-to-date R&B that featured highly intrusive female background vocals (allegedly by the Vandellas) and utterly unyielding structures that hemmed Hooker in unmercifully.

British blues bands such as the Animals and Yardbirds idolized Hooker during the early '60s; Eric Burdon's boys cut a credible 1964 cover of "Boom Boom" that outsold Hooker's original on the American pop charts. Hooker visited Europe in 1962 under the auspices of the first American Folk Blues Festival, leaving behind the popular waxings "Let's Make It" and "Shake It Baby" for foreign consumption.

Back home, Hooker cranked out gems for Vee-Jay through 1964 ("Big Legs, Tight Skirt," one of his last offerings on the logo, was also one of his best), before undergoing another extended round of label-hopping (except this time, he was waxing whole LPs instead of scattered 78s). Verve-Folkways, Impulse, Chess, and BluesWay all enticed him into recording for them in 1965-66 alone! His reputation among hip rock cognoscenti in the states and abroad was growing exponentially, especially after he teamed up with blues-rockers Canned Heat for the massively selling album *Hooker 'n' Heat* in 1970.

Eventually, though, the endless boogie formula grew incredibly stagnant. Much of Hooker's 1970s output found him laying back while plodding rock-rooted rhythm sections assumed much of the work load. A cameo in the 1980 movie *The Blues Brothers* was welcome, if far too short.

But Hooker wasn't through—not by a long shot. With the expert help of slide guitarist extraordinaire/producer Roy Rogers, the Hook waxed *The Healer*, an album that marked the first of his guest star-loaded albums (Carlos Santana, Bonnie Raitt, and Robert Cray were among the luminaries to cameo on the disc, which picked up a Grammy).

Major labels were just beginning to take notice of the growing demand for blues records, and Pointblank snapped Hooker up, releasing *Mr. Lucky* (this time teaming Hooker with everyone from Albert Collins and John Hammond to Van Morrison and Keith Richards). Once again, Hooker was resting on his laurels by allowing his guests to wrest much of the spotlight away from him on his own album, but by then, he'd earned it. Another Pointblank set, *Boom Boom,* soon followed.

Happily, Hooker is now enjoying the good life. He's in semi-retirement, splitting his relaxation time between several houses he's acquired up and down the California coast. Baseball also takes up much of his interest during the summer months; he's an inveterate Dodger fan. When the right offer comes along, though, he takes it, as that amusing TV commercial for Pepsi indicates.

The King of the Boogie is also one of the last living links to the pre-war blues tradition. He's a true original. —*Bill Dahl*

Everybody's Blues / 1950-1954 / Specialty ✦✦✦
John Lee Hooker reissues abound, as might be expected of a singer and guitarist who's recorded hundreds of songs for countless labels since the late '40s. What makes the 20 tracks on *Everybody's Blues* different from the mountain of other Hooker material available is the fact that seven of them are newly issued, and most were done in the studio with Hooker wailing and accompanying himself on guitar minus any backing chorus or production armada. Even the cuts with a supporting combo are animated and loose, with the vocal trademarks that are now established Hooker cliches sounding fresh and genuine. —*Ron Wynn*

That's My Story/John Lee Hooker Sings the Blues / 1960 / Riverside ✦✦✦✦
Hooker's earliest Riverside albums presented him playing solo acoustic guitar, in a conscious effort to direct his work to listeners outside the R&B audience. Opinions differ on the matter, but I find this outing more interesting than his solo acoustic Riverside records, due to the presence of a supporting rhythm section on most of the tracks. The liner notes (in the fashion of the day) are almost apologetic about this, emphasizing that it's not to create R&B rhythms, but "to free Hooker from the burden of carrying the full rhythm load." To make matters more palatable for the purists, maybe that's why a couple of jazz players were chosen for the job (bassist Sam Jones and drummer Louis Hayes, who formed the rhythm section for Cannonball Adderley at the time). What's important is not how pure the music is, but that it's a decent album, striking a good midpoint between his acoustic and electric sound. —*Richie Unterberger*

House of the Blues / 1960 / MCA/Chess ✦✦✦✦
Verbatim CD reissue of a 1959 Chess album that collected 1951-1954 efforts

by the Hook. Some important titles here: an ominous "Leave My Wife Alone," the stark "Sugar Mama" and "Ramblin' by Myself," and with Eddie Kirkland on second guitar, "Louise" and "High Priced Woman." —*Bill Dahl*

I'm John Lee Hooker / 1960 / Vee-Jay ✦✦✦✦
Some of The Boogie Man's best stuff for Vee-Jay. —*Bill Dahl*

Travelin' / 1960 / Vee-Jay ✦✦✦✦

The Country Blues of John Lee Hooker / Jan. 1960 / Riverside ✦✦✦
Hooker was still churning out R&B-influenced electric blues with a rhythm section for Vee-Jay when he recorded this, his first LP packaged for the folk/traditional blues market. He plays nothing but acoustic guitar, and seems to have selected a repertoire with old-school country blues in mind. It's unimpressive only within the context of Hooker's body of work; in comparison with other solo outings, the guitar sounds thin, and the approach restrained. —*Richie Unterberger*

John Lee Hooker Sings the Blues / 1961 / King ✦✦✦✦

☆ **John Lee Hooker Plays and Sings the Blues** / 1961 / MCA/Chess ✦✦✦✦✦
A 1961 Chess album restored to digital print by MCA that's filled with 1951-1952 gems from the Hook's heyday. Chess originally bought "Mad Man Blues" and "Hey Boogie" from the Gone label; the rest first came out on Chess during Hooker's frenzied early days of recording, when his platters turned up on nearly every R&B indie label existant at the time. —*Bill Dahl*

Don't Turn Me from Your Door / 1963 / Atlantic ✦✦✦
Don't Turn Me from Your Door comprises a set of 1953 sessions that were originally released in 1963 and later with the title *Detroit Special*. Despite its twisted historical background, this is fine, first-rate Hooker. A few tracks feature the support of guitarist/vocalist Eddie Kirkland, a few others an unnamed bassist, but this is pretty much pure John Lee Hooker—just him and a guitar, running through a set of spare, haunting blues that include such tracks as "Blue Monday" and "Stuttering Blues." There are none of his best-known tracks on the album, but it's one of his most consistent original records. —*Thom Owens*

Burning Hell / 1964 / Original Blues Classics ✦✦✦
In April 1959, Hooker recorded a couple of solo acoustic albums for Riverside that were his first efforts geared toward the folk/acoustic blues audience, rather than the commercial R&B one. One of these albums (*The Country Blues of John Lee Hooker*) was issued at the time; the other, *Burning Hell*, wasn't issued until 1964, and then only in England (in 1992, it finally came out in the US on CD). This is very similar to *Country Blues*, mixing originals with covers of tunes by Muddy Waters, Howlin' Wolf, Lightnin' Hopkins, and Big Bill Broonzy. To my ears it has a slight edge—the singing and performances sound a little more committed. But anyone who likes one LP will like the other, though neither ranks among the best of Hooker's one-man recordings. —*Richie Unterberger*

John Lee Hooker at Newport / 1964 / Vee-Jay ✦✦✦✦
Arguably his finest live date, this was John Lee Hooker minus the self-congratulatory mugging now an almost mandatory part of his sets. Instead, there's just lean, straight, defiant Hooker vocals and minimal, but effective backing. —*Ron Wynn*

The Real Folk Blues / 1966 / MCA/Chess ✦✦✦
Although the great majority of the albums in Chess' *Real Folk Blues* series were vintage compilations, this disc was cut in 1966 with longtime cohort Eddie Burns on second guitar and an uncredited band behind him. Not exactly essential in Hooker's personal pantheon, but decent nonetheless. —*Bill Dahl*

Live at Cafe Au Go-Go (And Soledad Prison) / 1966 / MCA ✦✦✦
This reissue contains the entirety of Hooker's 1966 *Cafe Au Go-Go* set, and adds five bonus tracks from his 1972 LP *Live at Soledad Prison*. Luther Tucker is one of the guitarists for the Soledad portion, which has a somewhat more electric, rock-oriented sound than the Au Go-Go material. The disc only has five of the seven cuts from the original *Soledad* album, but that's okay, as the two missing items featured John Lee Hooker, Jr. on lead vocals, rather than Hooker himself. —*Richie Unterberger*

Live at Cafe Au Go Go / 1966 / BGO ✦✦✦
A decent if somewhat low-key electric set, recorded in August of 1966. One of his better live bands, featuring support from Otis Spann and other members of Muddy Waters' group. The eight songs include Hooker standbys like

"One Bourbon, One Scotch, One Beer" and "I'll Never Get out of These Blues Alive." — *Richie Unterberger*

Urban Blues / 1967 / MCA ✦✦✦
The Boogie Man's 1967 ABC-BluesWay album in its entirety, with three bonus numbers from a couple of years later added on the end. Hooker's Chicago sidemen (including Eddie Taylor, Wayne Bennett, and Louis Myers) deftly handle Hooker's eccentricities on "Mr. Lucky," the harrowing "The Motor City Is Burning," and a sprightly remake of "Boom Boom." — *Bill Dahl*

Simply the Truth / 1969 / One Way ✦✦✦
Overseen by noted jazz producer Bob Thiele, this session had Hooker backed by some of his fullest arrangements to date, with noted session drummer Pretty Purdie and keyboards in addition to supplementary guitar and bass. The slightly modernized sound was ultimately neither here nor there, the center remaining Hooker's voice and lyrics. His words nodded toward contemporary concerns with "I Don't Wanna Go to Vietnam" and "Mini Skirts," but the songs were mostly consistent with his usual approaches. Another of his many characteristically solid efforts, although it's not one of his more interesting albums. — *Richie Unterberger*

That's Where It's At! / 1969 / Stax ✦✦✦
A characteristic solo outing with moody compositions and that doomy one-electric-guitar-and-stomping-foot ambience. One of his sparer and more menacing post-'50s outings, highlighted by "Two White Horses" and a seven-minute "Feel So Bad," which features extended verbal sparring with an unidentified male partner. — *Richie Unterberger*

Get Back Home / Nov. 30, 1969 / Evidence ✦✦✦✦
John Lee Hooker's greatness lies in his ability to perform the same songs the same way yet somehow sound different and memorable in the process. He operates at maximum efficiency in minimal surroundings with little production or assistance. That was the case on a 1969 session for Black and Blue; it was just Hooker and his guitar moaning, wailing, and narrating on 10 tracks which included familiar ditties "Boogie Chillen," "Love Affair," "Big Boss Lady," and "Cold Chills." Evidence has now not only reissued these 10 but has added another six bonus cuts, bringing the CD total to 16. If you have ever heard any Hooker, you will not be surprised or stunned by these renditions; you will simply enjoy hearing him rework them one more time, finding a new word, phrase, line, or riff to inject. — *Ron Wynn*

Boogie Chillun / 1972 / Fantasy ✦✦✦✦
Recorded live in November 1962 in San Francisco, this dates from the period in which Hooker often presented himself as a sort of blues/folk singer for the coffeehouse crowd, toning down his volume and aggressiveness somewhat. There's something of a muted "unplugged" feel to these solo performances (though an electric guitar *is* used). It's not ineffective, though not among his best work; it's the kind of Hooker you might want to put on past midnight, just before going to sleep. Hooker's never been bashful about recycling songs, and "Boogie Chillun" appears here in one of its many versions, as does "Dimples" (retitled as "I Like to See You Walk"). He also tackles the rock/soul standard "Money," changing the title to "I Need Some Money," for which he also somehow gets awarded the songwriting credit on the sleeve. — *Richie Unterberger*

Alone / 1976 / Rhino ✦✦✦
Because he's so loose and improvisatory—and because he loves to twist the 12-bar format into so many different shapes and sizes—John Lee Hooker can present a major challenge to sidemen. More than a few times, Hooker has done without sidemen altogether and gone it alone with thrilling results. That's exactly what happens on *Alone*, an outstanding two-CD set containing live performances at New York's Hunter College from 1976. Not having to concern himself with the needs of a drummer or a bassist, the singer/guitarist is especially introspective and doesn't hesitate to let loose and improvise on such familiar tunes as "Boogie Chillen," "Boom Boom" and "One Bourbon, One Scotch, One Beer." Hooker enjoys improvisation as much as a jazz musician, and on these magnificent recordings, he is at his most uninhibited and takes one liberty after another. — *Alex Henderson*

The Cream / Oct. 1978 / Rhino ✦✦
Joined by a full band that includes two other guitarists (John Garcia, Jr., on lead and Ron Thompson on rhythm), John Lee Hooker is passionately rockin' on this live date (recorded at the Keystone in Palo Alto, CA in 1978). Hooker has always been known for taking quite a few liberties with his material,

something that could easily throw some musicians off. Without a doubt, Hooker keeps a sideman on his toes—and he presents even more of a challenge on stage because there are no second and third takes. But this is a band that, although not in a class with Canned Heat, obviously understands (and even thrives on) his sense of spontaneity, and rises to the occasion on such familiar gems as "One Room Country Shack," "When My First Wife Left Me," and "Tupelo," as well as the invigorating "Boogie On" (one of the many variations of "Boogie Chillen" Hooker has provided over the years). Hooker doesn't do as much improvising as he did when playing unaccompanied at New York's Hunter College the previous year, but he never ceases to be confidently soulful. Although not quite essential, *The Cream* is an engaging CD that definitely has a lot going for it. — *Alex Henderson*

Detroit Blues / 1987 / Flyright ✦✦✦
Interesting collection of old 78s that Hooker recorded under various pseudonyms (Johnny Williams, John Lee) in 1950. Along with the original version of "House Rent Boogie" and five others that ended up on the Philadelphia Gotham label, we have the bonus of a half dozen tracks by Hooker sideman Eddie Burns and Detroit bluesman Baby Boy Warren's first single. The sound is rough in the extreme, but the music's great. — *Cub Koda*

Jealous / May 1987 / Chase Music ✦✦✦
While *Jealous* is propelled by the scarily spare stomp of Hook's guitar, it has few standout moments. Instead, it is a consistent record, with few highs or lows—it's a standard contemporary blues album, without many peaks or valleys. *Jealous* may be a grittier record than its successor, *The Healer*, but it tends to fade into the background, making it one of his more undistinguished albums. — *Thom Owens*

40th Anniversary Album / 1989 / DCC ✦✦✦
Fourteen rarities from the seemingly bottomless 1948-1952 stash of Detroit producer Bernie Besman, joined by a 1961 stereo "Blues for Abraham Lincoln" that's painfully out-of-tune. Includes "Boogie Chillen" and an alternate version of "I'm in the Mood." — *Bill Dahl*

The Healer / 1989 / Chameleon ✦✦
The Healer was a major comeback for John Lee Hooker. Featuring a wide array of guest stars, including Bonnie Raitt, Keith Richards, Johnnie Johnson, and Los Lobos, *The Healer* captured widespread media attention because of all the superstar musicians involved in its production. Unfortunately, that long guest list is what makes the album a fairly unengaging listen. Certainly there are moments were it clicks, but that's usually when the music doesn't greatly expand on his stripped-down boogie. The other moments are professional, but not exciting. It's a pleasant listen, but never quite an engaging one. — *Thom Owens*

The Hook: 20 Years of Hits / 1989 / Chameleon ✦✦✦
John Lee Hooker's excellent Vee-Jay material of the 1950s and '60s has been reissued time and time again, both in the US and in Europe. *The Hook* is a 16-song CD that Chameleon released in 1989 for its Vee-Jay Hall of Fame series. As was the case with other Chameleon reissues of Vee-Jay material, *The Hook's* liner notes are inadequate—neither personnel nor recording dates are listed. But the disc's sound quality and content are nothing to complain about. Many of his essential Vee-Jay recordings are here (including "Boom Boom," "Whiskey and Women," "Dimples," "Crawling Kingsnake," and one of his many remakes of "Boogie Chillen"), along with rare versions of "House Rent Boogie," "Nightmare," and "Big Legs, Tight Skirt." Because hits and rarities are combined, *The Hook* isn't really a best-of collection—and, in fact, Chameleon also reissued a CD titled *The Best of John Lee Hooker*. — *Alex Henderson*

Boogie Awhile / 1990 / Krazy Kat ✦✦✦✦
This was originally issued as a 31-track, double LP full of Hooker's earliest and rarest sides, almost all of it taken from goodly hacked up acetates and 78 pressings. The compact disc deletes 11 of the most chewed up and attempts to clean up the rest with varying results. But this is one time when audiophile concerns don't count for much because this is quite simply Hooker at his earliest, his rarest and his very best. — *Cub Koda*

The Best of John Lee Hooker [JCI] / 1991 / JCI ✦✦✦✦
This was hardly the first collection titled *The Best of John Lee Hooker*, and it certainly wouldn't be the last. JCI released this particular CD in 1990 as part of its Masters of the Blues series, and the collection shows just how poorly executed the series was. The liner notes are embarrassing—neither person-

nel nor recording dates are listed, and there is no mention of the labels the material was recorded for (which included Vee-Jay and Chess). JCI does both CD buyers and Hooker a disservice by not being more informative. The label does offer a generous helping of material. Eighteen songs are provided, including celebrated versions of "Boom Boom," "Whiskey and Women," and "Baby Lee." The digital remastering isn't terrible, but it could have been better. Consumers would do better to look for a best-of that isn't so carelessly assembled. — *Alex Henderson*

Mr. Lucky / 1991 / Pointblank ♦♦♦
His latest for Virgin's blues division, contains some entertaining material. It's not a classic, but it's not half-bad either. — *Ron Wynn*

★ **The Ultimate Collection (1948-1990)** / 1991 / Rhino ♦♦♦♦♦
The single best place to begin appreciating the Boogie Man's incredible contributions to the blues lexicon, since it surveys a wide cross-section of labels and eras. Disc one contains "Boogie Chillen," "Sally Mae," "Huckle Up Baby," "I'm in the Mood," "Dimples," and "It Serves Me Right." The second spottier CD sports "Boom Boom," "One Bourbon, One Scotch, One Beer," a snarling "I'm Bad like Jesse James," and an utterly superfluous finale with Bonnie Raitt from a Showtime TV program. At only 31 songs, it could unequivocally be longer, but this anthology serves as a convenient spot for the neophyte to delve into Hookerology. — *Bill Dahl*

More Real Folk Blues: The Missing Album / Sep. 10, 1991 / MCA/Chess ♦♦♦
Produced by Ralph Bass in 1966 but not issued by Chess at the time, *More Real Folk Blues* was unearthed by MCA only a few years back. It's no masterpiece, but certainly deserved release in its day — backed by Burns and a Chicago rhythm section that copes as well as can be expected with Hooker's singular sense of timing, the Boogie Man answers Sir Mack Rice with his "Mustang Sally & GTO" and keeps things way lowdown on several other cuts. — *Bill Dahl*

Hooker & Heat / Oct. 28, 1991 / EMI America ♦♦♦
Probably no other White blues band took John Lee Hooker's boogie rhythms and made a career out of it as much as Canned Heat. It was certainly inevitable that the two forces would unite for a joint recording project and this double CD package (recorded in 1970 and originally a double album) is the delightful result. Canned Heat certainly knew what they were going after, as Hooker brandishes a mean guitar tone that hadn't surfaced since his early Detroit recordings. Surprisingly, Canned Heat hangs back a bit as over half the material are riveting solo recordings, with the full band only coming in as support on the second half. Compare this with most of his '70s recordings for Bluesway (now MCA) and you'll quickly realize that these sides contain some of his most cohesive work with a band, ever. — *Cub Koda*

Boom Boom / 1992 / Pointblank ♦♦
Another guest-heavy collection. — *Bill Dahl*

The Best of John Lee Hooker 1965—1974 / 1992 / MCA ♦♦♦
MCA's *The Best of John Lee Hooker* has a misleading title. All of the 16 selections are taken from his recordings for ABC, which were made at the end of the '60s and beginning of the '70s. During this time, his producers were experimenting with his sound, adding contemporary sonic touches like funk rhythms and wah-wah pedals. Needless to say, this sound didn't sit particularly well with Hooker's lean, haunting blues. However, these songs do take the best material from generally poor albums — anyone who wants to sample his ABC material should turn here first and they'll realize that they don't need to explore much further. — *Thom Owens*

Graveyard Blues [Specialty Reissue Series] / 1992 / Specialty ♦♦♦♦
At the beginning of his career, Hooker's sides were leased to several different labels. This 20-song anthology of material from the late '40s and early '50s was originally released on the Sensation and Specialty labels; while the track listings indicate a timespan of 1948-50, the liner notes say that much of it was recorded in 1954. Doesn't anyone proofread these things? Anyway, this was mostly recorded solo, and boasts his characteristic spooky electric minimalist boogie sound. *The Legendary Modern Recordings*, covering the same era, is a better place to start for this kind of thing due to its stronger content. If you want more of the same, though, this (and Capitol's *Alternative Boogie*) is the next stop. — *Richie Unterberger*

1965 London Sessions / 1993 / Sequel ♦♦♦
Considering how these dates were done — first, Hooker was backed by a Brit-

ish band, Tony McPhee and the Groundhogs; later horns were overdubbed for American consumption — the results aren't too shabby at all. — *Bill Dahl*

John Lee Hooker on Vee-Jay, 1955-1958 / Jul. 1993 / Vee-Jay ♦♦♦♦
Some of Hooker's finest recordings with a band were also some of his first recordings with a band. The unpredictable guitarist seemed to mesh well with guitarist Eddie Taylor, harpist Jimmy Reed, and the rest of the sidemen he was given on his 1955-58 Vee-Jay output. Includes the classic "Baby Lee" and "Dimples," along with 20 more that crackle with electricity. — *Bill Dahl*

★ **The Legendary Modern Recordings 1948-1954** / 1994 / Virgin ♦♦♦♦♦
From the beginning of his career, Hooker recorded prolifically, sometimes for several labels at once, sometimes under a number of pseudonyms. That makes his discography a bit difficult for the collector to sort out, but if you want just one document of his early years, this is the anthology of choice, containing 24 sides from 1948 to 1954 that were issued on the Modern label. These, more than any other, are the recordings that did the most to establish the Hooker prototype — the overamplified electric guitar, the moody boogies, the stomping foot rhythms, performed without a rhythm section (some sides feature accompaniment by Eddie Kirkland on second guitar). Contains his two most massive early hits, "Boogie Chillen" and "I'm in the Mood," as well as his oft-covered "Crawling Kingsnake." This one can get a bit similar-sounding over the course of two dozen tracks, but little other post-war electric blues can match the stark power here. — *Richie Unterberger*

☆ **The Early Years** / 1994 / Tomato ♦♦♦♦♦
Hooker's voluminous output for Vee-Jay Records is scattered across numerous compilations. This double CD contains 31 songs spanning the mid-'50s to the mid-'60s, and is probably the most extensive and satisfying retrospective of his Vee-Jay work (at least domestically). That's not to say it's perfectly assembled; Tomato, as usual, declines to include trimmings like songwriter credits, although Pete Welding's liner notes do (unlike most Tomato releases) provide dates and discuss the sessions in some detail. Hooker's Vee-Jay material was in most ways the most commercially-minded of his early efforts, often employing a rhythm section and R&B-influenced arrangements, and occasionally using horns. It's sometimes been said that this approach diluted Hooker's strengths, but one listen to this collection refutes that notion soundly. This is by and large prime Hooker, with some of his best (and best-selling) songs, like "Boom Boom," "Dimples," "I'm So Excited," and "One Bourbon, One Scotch, One Beer." Hooker may have sometimes sounded a bit ill at ease with a band, but he usually worked with backing musicians very well. Non-purists will find these tracks to be some of his most accessible and dynamic performances. — *Richie Unterberger*

Chill Out / 1995 / Pointblank ♦♦
Chill Out isn't the superstar blowout of John Lee Hooker's late-'80s albums, yet it retains that flavor. Featuring some extended soloing from Carlos Santana, *Chill Out* is filled with long blues workouts, all captured in pristine, state-of-the-art technology. Nothing on the disc captures the raw vitality of Hooker's prime material — it's all relaxed blues-rock jams. The clean, sterile production doesn't help the basically directionless music. Certainly nothing on *Chill Out* is outright bad; in fact, most of it is pleasant, yet few of the songs on the album warrant repeated listens. — *Stephen Thomas Erlewine*

★ **The Very Best of John Lee Hooker [Rhino]** / Apr. 25, 1995 / Rhino ♦♦♦♦♦
The Very Best of John Lee Hooker provides a definitive introduction to the seminal bluesman, presenting over 15 classic tracks in their original hit versions. — *Stephen Thomas Erlewine*

Alternative Boogie: Early Studio Recordings 1948-1952 / Oct. 24, 1995 / Capitol ♦♦♦♦
A whopping three CDs, and 56 songs, from Hooker's early sessions that were unreleased at the time, although they were available for a while in the early 1970s on some United Artists LPs. Like his more widely-known material of the period, it mostly features Hooker unaccompanied, though he's aided by piano and second guitarists on a few tracks. Some of these are alternates of songs that were released in different versions, or embryonic renditions of compositions that evolved into somewhat different shapes. Especially interesting are early versions of his big hit "I'm in the Mood for Love." It's too much at once, though, and too unvarying in approach, for anyone but Hooker specialists. General fans are advised to stick with *The Legendary Modern Recordings*, which has 24 more renowned, and somewhat more accomplished tracks from the same era. It's certainly a well-done package, though,

containing a 38-page insert with detailed liner notes and session information. — *Richie Unterberger*

The Best of Hooker 'n Heat / 1996 / EMI ✦✦✦
These ten songs were originally released as part of a 1971 album (on Liberty 35002); this reissue, despite the lack of historical liner notes, isn't exactly short value, clocking in at 56 minutes. Canned Heat gets top billling, but really it's Hooker's show, as he sings all the tracks and takes all the songwriting credits for the material, which includes remakes of classics like "Dimples," "Boogie Chillen," "Burning Hell," and "Bottle Up and Go." With Hooker fronting a White blues-rock-boogie group, this doesn't offer the optimum circumstances to hear the man. But it's not bad either, Canned Heat playing with spirit and relative economy, although the 11-minute "Boogie Chillen" is excessive. — *Richie Unterberger*

Alone: The First Concert / May 21, 1996 / Blues Alliance ✦✦✦
Reissued by Concord's Blues Alliance label in 1996, this single CD boasts everything on Disc One of Tomato's two-CD set *Alone*, including heartfelt performances of "Boogie Chillen," "Boom Boom," "I'll Never Get Out of This Room Alive" and "One Bourbon, One Scotch, One Beer." The Tomato package contains two sets from Hooker's Hunter College engagement in 1996, whereas this CD focuses only on the first one. The format is just Hooker and his electric guitar, and in this intimate setting, the blues veteran has plenty of room to stretch out, improvise and say what needs to be said. Of course, those who already own the Tomato set don't need this reissue, which contains insightful liner notes by blues critic Kent Cooper. But because the Tomato set is out of print, it would be easier to find this disc and its companion CD *Alone: The Second Concert*. Either way, you're treated to some compelling blues. — *Alex Henderson*

Don't Look Back / Mar. 4, 1997 / Virgin ✦✦✦
With new John Lee Hooker songs, new versions of old Hooker songs, four duets with and a new song by Van Morrison, *Don't Look Back* continues the venerable bluesman's string of excellent albums in his 1990s renaissance. Produced by Morrison, it also celebrates the 25th anniversary of their first recording together, as Van guested on Hooker's seminal *Never Get Out of These Blues Alive* in 1972. *Don't Look Back* hits the ground running with a rowdy, thumpin' remake of "Dimples" with Los Lobos; "Spellbound" pounds out more of Hooker's stylistic trademark—throbbing, raw, hard-driving boogie. The Morrison tracks include the ruminative title cut and his haunting "The Healing Game." Hooker also gives Hendrix's classic blues "Red House" his own rough-hewn, distinctive treatment. — *Chris Slawecki*

Alone: The Second Concert / Apr. 29, 1997 / Blues Alliance ✦✦✦✦
Not just the boogie, but some *serious* blues too. This 1976 concert recording caught Hooker up close, giving both voice and guitar a lot of force. A candidate for best John Lee Hooker live album, complete with Hooker standards like "Boogie Chillen", "Hobo Blues" and "Crawling King Snake" (which comes equipped with a phantom harmonica player), it suffers only from being on the short side at forty-four minutes or so, dropping the listener into a silent void just as things are getting *really* warmed up. — *Steven McDonald*

His Best Chess Sides (Chess 50th Anniversary Collection) / Jun. 17, 1997 / MCA ✦✦✦
Hooker, as anyone with a decent-sized blues collection knows, recorded for a virtual parade of labels early in his career, including Chess, although his stays with the company were fairly brief. Hooker's best early recordings, most would agree, were issued on Modern and Vee-Jay, not Chess. Still, if the only Hooker extant was his Chess sides, his greatness would be readily apparent. Approached not as a best-of but simply as one of many Hooker compilations, this 15-song disc is fine, leaning heavily on early-'50s material (the source for eleven of the songs). This is typical of his early work in its stress on his great guitar work, walking rhythms, and drumless arrangements (most of it is played solo). It's good stuff, even if much of it is derivative of things he recorded elsewhere, and the mike plainly catches him coughing on "Bluebird." The solo on "Leave My Wife Alone" is almost avant-garde in conception, a series of plucked runs up and down the scale with little relation to convention, even by blues standards. Closing the set are four much more modern-sounding cuts from the mid-'60s, comprising the "I'm in the Mood"/ "Let's Go Out Tonight" single and a couple of cuts from the *Real Folk Blues* LP (including his standard "One Bourbon, One Scotch, One Beer"). — *Richie Unterberger*

The Complete 50's Chess Recordings / Jan. 13, 1998 / MCA ✦✦✦
Hooker bounced around between label affiliations like crazy in the 1950s, recording under almost as many fake names as he did labels during that decade. His two lasting record company hookups occurred with Chess in the early 1950s and Vee-Jay later on in the decade. All of Hooker's Chess masters from that decade (he would later record in the '60s for them as well) are here on this two-disc, 31-track collection. Unlike other Chess artists, Hooker did little of his recording in Chicago, preferring to work out of his Detroit home base, where he continued to record for other labels under a variety of pseudonyms. His 1951 Chicago session excepted, the rest of the tracks emanate from Detroit sessions that also saw issuance on the local Gone, H-Q, and Fortune labels. This is early John Lee at his solo-guitar, foot-stomping best, featuring boogies and introspective, slow blues that rival his best work. Some of the Detroit tracks reveal inbred distortion that can't be overcome even with modern day noise reduction techniques, but don't let that deter you from sampling some of the best John Lee Hooker available on compact disc for a second. — *Cub Koda*

Detroit Lion / Demon ✦✦✦
Demon's *The Detroit Lion* is a fine 15-track collection of material John Lee Hooker recorded for Modern Records between 1948 and 1952. By no means complete, the collection concentrates on songs that are off the beaten path. Sure, there's "Boogie Chillen" and "I'm in the Mood," but such singles as "Sally Mae," "Hobo Blues," "Hoogie Blues," and "Crawling King Snake Blues" are passed by in favor of "Hey's, the House Rent Boogie," "Baby How Can You Do It?," "Four Women in My Life," "This Is 19 and 52 Blues," and "Blues for Abraham Lincoln." The result is a disc that's aimed more at the fanatic and collector than the casual fan, and while these recordings are available on more comprehensive collections, this is still a nice way to acquire some of this material. — *Stephen Thomas Erlewine*

Hoosegow

f. 1995
Group / Blues-Rock, Modern Electric Blues
Guitarist Elliott Sharp is most known for experimental outings that are characteristic of the late-20th century "downtown" New York scene, but he has also expressed a deep love for the blues. Even so, Hoosegow—which features Sharp on guitars and Queen Esther on vocals—will surprise much of his audience. Queen Esther and Sharp wrote all but one of the songs on their debut *Mighty*, which is rooted in the classic Chicago electric blues sound, although there is no instrumentation except for Sharp's guitars and Esther's vocals. Sharp proves himself to be quite the virtuoso on stinging blues guitar, and Esther a capable (though not thrilling) singer. The material is more restless and impressionistic than much contemporary blues, refusing to fall into good-timey cliches. It's just off-kilter enough to confuse traditional blues fans, and may be too traditional and accessible for Sharp's usual constituency. On top of that, it's being marketed by an alternative rock label, which means it could well fall between the cracks. That would be unfortunate, as it's a more interesting release than the usual contemporary blues fare, though hardly brilliant. — *Richie Unterberger*

Mighty / 1996 / Homestead ✦✦✦
Sharp may not have much street cred (or even name recognition) among the listeners that usually buy blues records, but there's no denying his impressive skills in the idiom. The songs, too, are interestingly offbeat, being more absorbed with a sort of spiritual, questing attitude than the more mundane cliches of much modern blues. Queen Esther, however, is no more than an average vocalist, sounding as if she may be more at home with jazz than blues. — *Richie Unterberger*

Lightnin' Hopkins (Sam Hopkins)

b. Mar. 15, 1912, Centerville, TX, **d.** Jan. 30, 1982, Houston, TX
Organ, Guitar, Piano, Vocals / Acoustic Texas Blues, Electric Texas Blues, Texas Blues, Country Blues, Blues Revival
Sam Hopkins was a Texas country bluesman of the highest caliber whose career began in the 1920s and stretched all the way into the 1980s. Along the way, Hopkins watched the genre change remarkably, but he never appreciably altered his mournful Lone Star sound, which translated onto both acoustic and electric guitar. Hopkins' nimble dexterity made intricate boogie

riffs seem easy, and his fascinating penchant for improvising lyrics to fit whatever situation might arise made him a beloved blues troubadour.

Hopkins' brothers John Henry and Joel were also talented bluesmen, but it was Sam that became a star. In 1920, he met the legendary Blind Lemon Jefferson at a social function, and even got a chance to play with him. Later, Hopkins served as Jefferson's guide. In his teens, Hopkins began working with another pre-war great, singer Texas Alexander, who was his cousin. A mid-'30s stretch in Houston's County Prison Farm for the young guitarist interrupted their partnership for a time, but when he was freed, Hopkins hooked back up with the older bluesman.

The pair was dishing out their lowdown brand of blues in Houston's Third Ward in 1946 when talent scout Lola Anne Cullum came across them. She had already engineered a pact with Los Angeles-based Aladdin Records for another of her charges, pianist Amos Milburn, and Cullum saw the same sort of opportunity within Hopkins' dusty country blues. Alexander wasn't part of the deal; instead, Cullum paired Hopkins with pianist Wilson "Thunder" Smith, sensibly rechristened the guitarist Lightnin', and presto! Hopkins was very soon an Aladdin recording artist.

"Katie May," cut on November 9, 1946, in Los Angeles with Smith lending a hand on the 88s, was Lightnin' Hopkins' first regional seller of note. He recorded prolifically for Aladdin in both Los Angeles and Houston into 1948, scoring a national R&B hit for the firm with his "Shotgun Blues." "Short Haired Woman," "Abilene," and "Big Mama Jump," among many Aladdin gems, were evocative Texas blues rooted in an earlier era.

A load of other labels recorded the wily Hopkins after that, both in a solo context and with a small rhythm section—Modern/RPM (his uncompromising "Tim Moore's Farm" was an R&B hit in 1949), Gold Star (where he hit with "T-Model Blues" that same year), Sittin' in With ("Give Me Central 209" and "Coffee Blues" were national chart entries in 1952) and its Jax subsidiary, the major labels Mercury and Decca, and in 1954, a remarkable batch of sides for Herald where Hopkins played blistering electric guitar on a series of blasting rockers ("Lightnin's Boogie," "Lightnin's Special," the amazing "Hopkins' Sky Hop") in front of drummer Ben Turner and bassist Donald Cooks (who must have had bleeding fingers, so torrid were some of the tempos).

But Hopkins' style was apparently too rustic and old-fashioned for the new generation of rock 'n' roll enthusiasts (they should have checked out "Hopkins' Sky Hop"). He was back on the Houston scene by 1959, largely forgotten. Folklorist Mack McCormick rediscovered the guitarist, who was dusted off and presented as a folk-blues artist—a role that Hopkins was born to play. Pioneering musicologist Sam Charters produced Hopkins in a solo context for Folkways Records that same year, cutting an entire LP in Hopkins' tiny apartment (on a borrowed guitar). The results helped introduced his music to an entirely new audience.

Lightnin' Hopkins went from gigging at back-alley gin joints to starring at collegiate coffeehouses, appearing on TV programs and touring Europe to boot. His once-flagging recording career went right through the roof, with albums for World Pacific, Vee-Jay, Bluesville, Bobby Robinson's Fire label (where he cut his classic "Mojo Hand" in 1960), Candid, Arhoolie, Prestige, Verve, and in 1965, the first of several LPs for Stan Lewis' Shreveport-based Jewel logo.

Hopkins generally demanded full payment before he'd deign to sit down and record, and seldom indulged a producer's desire for more than one take of any song. His singular sense of country time befuddled more than a few unseasoned musicians; from the 1960s on, his solo work is usually preferable to band-backed material.

Filmmaker Les Blank captured the Texas troubadour's informal lifestyle most vividly in his acclaimed 1967 documentary, *The Blues Accordin' to Lightnin' Hopkins*. As one of the last great country bluesmen, Hopkins was a fascinating figure who bridged the gap between rural and urban styles. —*Bill Dahl*

Lightnin' Hopkins, 1946-1960 / Nov. 4, 1946-Jan. 25, 1960 / DA Music ◆◆◆
21 songs from, as the title indicates, 1946 to 1960, mostly Lightnin' solo on guitar, although there are occasional additional instruments. This rather scattershot anthology isn't the best way to collect Hopkins. On the other hand, if you're not concerned with building a comprehensive discography, it's not a bad pickup, including an hour of decent music. —*Richie Unterberger*

Blues Train / 1951 / Mainstream ◆◆◆◆
Classic sides from Hopkins' 1950-1951 stint with Bobby Shad's Sittin' in With logo. The disc's 15 selections include two of his biggest hits, "Hello Central" and "Coffee Blues." —*Bill Dahl*

Lightnin' Hopkins [Smithsonian/Folkways] / 1959 / Smithsonian/Folkways ◆◆◆◆
Originally released as *The Roots of Lightnin' Hopkins*, Smithsonian/Folkways' *Lightnin' Hopkins* was recorded in 1959. Upon its initial release, it was a pivotal part of the blues revival and helped re-spark interest in Hopkins. Before it was recorded, the bluesman had disappeared from sight; after a great deal of searching, Sam Charters found Hopkins in a rented one-room apartment in Houston. Persuading Lightnin' with a bottle of gin, Charters convinced Hopkins to record ten songs in that room, using only one microphone. The resulting record was one of the greatest albums in Hopkins' catalog, a skeletal record that is absolutely naked in its loneliness and haunting in its despair. These unvarnished performances arguably capture the essence of Lightnin' Hopkins better than any of his other recordings, and it is certainly one of the landmarks of the late-'50s/early-'60s blues revival. —*Thom Owens*

Country Blues / 1960 / Tradition ◆◆◆
While Hopkins in his prime could crank out as many albums as there were days in the week (and sometimes more), some dates were more inspired than others and this casual recording is happily one of those times. In 1959, armed with nothing more than a single microphone mono tape recorder, folklorist Mack McCormick recorded Hopkins in an informal setting in hopes of catching some rough-edged performances that he felt were lacking from the bluesman's then-recent studio efforts. That he succeeded mightily is evidenced in this 15-song collection, almost casual in the way Lightnin' tosses off themes, lyrics, and emotion in a most cavalier fashion. Even with a thorough Sonic Solution No Noise process cleansing, these tapes still contain vocal and instrument distortion in spots where Hopkins got too close to the microphone. But none of it matters in the end, for here is Lightnin' truly in his element, playing for his friends and his own enjoyment, minus the commercial overlay of the times or the imposed "folk blues" posturing of his later acoustic recordings. Not the place to start, but a real good place to visit along the way. —*Cub Koda*

Lightnin' / 1961 / Original Blues Classics ◆◆◆
Recorded for Prestige's Bluesville subsidiary in 1960 and reissued on CD for Fantasy's Original Blues Classics (OBC) series in 1990, *Lightnin'* is among the rewarding acoustic dates Lightnin' Hopkins delivered in the early '60s. The session has an informal, relaxed quality, and this approach serves a 48-year-old Hopkins impressively well on both originals like "Thinkin' 'Bout an Old Friend" and the familiar "Katie Mae," and on enjoyable interpretations of Sonny Terry & Brownie McGhee's "Back to New Orleans" and Arthur "Big Boy" Crudup's "Mean Old Frisco." Hopkins' only accompaniment consists of bassist Leonard Gaskin and drummer Belton Evans, both of whom play in an understated fashion and do their part to make this intimate setting successful. From the remorseful "Come Back Baby" to more lighthearted, fun numbers like "You Better Watch Yourself" and "Automobile Blues," *Lightnin'* is a lot like being in a small club with Hopkins as he shares his experiences, insights and humor with you. —*Alex Henderson*

How Many More Years I Got / 1962 / Fantasy ◆◆◆
Repackaging of three earlier albums, *Walkin' This Road by Myself, Lightnin' & Co.*, and *Smokes like Lightnin'*. Lightnin' plays electric with small band support on these sides, which probably come the closest to what he sounded like in the juke joints around Houston in the early '60s. —*Cub Koda*

Mojo Hand / 1962 / Collectables ◆◆◆◆
This album, recorded for Fire Records, is especially interesting because it casts Hopkins in a more R&B-flavored environment. This obvious effort to get a hit makes for some excellent blues; moody and powerful performances play throughout. There's even a charming novelty Christmas blues, "Santa." —*Tim Sheridan*

Goin' Away / 1963 / Original Blues Classics ◆◆◆
For the 1963 album *Goin' Away*, Lightnin' Hopkins was backed by a spare rhythm section—bassist Leonard Gaskin and drummer Herb Lovelle—who managed to follow his ramshackle, instinctual sense of rhythm quite dexter-

ously, giving Hopkins' skeletal guitar playing some muscle. Still, the spotlight remains Hopkins, who is in fine form here. There are no real classics here, but everything is solid, particularly "Stranger Here" and "You Better Stop Her," making it worth investigation by serious fans of Hopkins' classic material. — *Stephen Thomas Erlewine*

Hopkins Brothers: Lightnin', Joel, & John Henry / Feb. 1964 / Arhoolie ✦✦✦
This family reunion was committed to tape. — *Bill Dahl*

Hootin' the Blues / 1965 / Prestige ✦✦✦
The most important part of Lightnin' Hopkins' career was spent in juke joints in Houston, but during the early 1960s, he also became a star along the folk circuit, playing clubs that catered mostly to college students eager to hear authentic acoustic blues. Several of those shows were recorded over the years to capitalize, and while the albums don't have the same importance as Hopkins' classic blues sides of the 1940s and 1950s, they do show another side of the man, and one he seemed to take to very naturally. *Hootin' The Blues* is one of Hopkins' better folk club concerts, capturing him in an intense performance on acoustic guitar, rapping (in the sense of talking) about the blues and what it means as he introduces some powerful songs: "Blues Is a Feeling," "In the Evenin'," and "Meet Me in the Bottom," among others. The best moment, though, is his reinvention of Ray Charles' "What'd I Say" as an acoustic guitar number (trust me, it works), which displays the kind of fingering that must've made a young Eric Clapton want to sit down and cry. — *Bruce Eder*

Lightnin'! / 1967 / Arhoolie ✦✦✦✦
Lightnin'! is a fine introduction to Hopkins' electric blues material, and features performances of "Mojo Hand," "Rock Me Baby," and "Hold Up Your Head." — *Jason Ankeny*

The Herald Material 1954 / 1988 / Collectables ✦✦✦✦
Lightnin' Hopkins in a heavily amplified mode (especially for 1954!) and tearing it up with some of the wildest licks of his long and storied career! It's hard to fathom a more torrid tempo than the one he employs for "Hopkins' Sky Hop," and "Flash Lightnin'," "Lightnin's Boogie," and "Lightnin' Stomp" aren't far behind. Alas, Hopkins' Herald waxings didn't sell particularly well—though they're downright astonishing in retrospect. — *Bill Dahl*

Po' Lightnin' / 1988 / Arhoolie ✦✦✦
On these recordings cut between 1961 and 1969, Hopkins exhibits the full scope of his music, picking up his electric guitar for a raw rendition of "Ice Storm Blues," sitting at the piano for a compelling version of "Jesus Will You Come By Here" and moving to the organ for an ethereal "My Baby's Gone." — *Jason Ankeny*

Drinkin' in the Blues: Golden Classics, Pt. 1 / 1989 / Collectables ✦✦✦✦
Almost 70 minutes of Lightnin' Hopkins, some live (no date or location listed) and some studio, but all pretty well indispensable for any fan, from the first words of the extraordinary opening monologue ("Big Black Cadillac Blues") on. He's playing acoustic live, and this sounds like one of his coffee-house gigs along the folk circuit from the early 1960s, except that the quality is better than on many of those shows, with a close sound on the guitar—the studio stuff is electric, natch. — *Bruce Eder*

The Herald Recordings, Vol. 2 / 1989 / Collectables ✦✦✦✦
Hopkins left a ton of tapes behind at New York-based Herald Records—enough to support this second volume of 1954 gems. — *Bill Dahl*

The Lost Texas Tapes, Vol. 1 / 1990 / Collectables ✦✦✦
First in a series of five albums, cut at informal studio and live sessions in Houston, by Sam "Lightnin'" Hopkins with producer Aubrey Mayhew. Most of these sides, which were never intended for commercial release, and never before appeared anywhere, add immeasurably to the body of Hopkins' work, capturing as they do some of Hopkins' best solo electric blues playing at a time when he was more active doing acoustic "folk blues." — *Bruce Eder*

The Lost Texas Tapes, Vol. 2 / 1990 / Collectables ✦✦✦
Clocking in at just over 23 minutes, this CD is on the short side, containing seven songs recorded on this particular day in an informal studio session. At his best here for about half of the the disc, Hopkins is in great form, coaxing several voices out of his single electric guitar while holding a beat very nicely. "Gonna Move Off This Street" is the best track here, but "Help Yourself (Christmastime)" is a close second—the solo guitar is captured close

and crunchy. It's all very solid, despite the brevity of the proceedings. — *Bruce Eder*

The Lost Texas Tapes, Vol. 3 / 1990 / Collectables ✦✦✦
The material here is among the best of Hopkins' later recording career, a good rival to his return to blues on Jewel after years of catering to acoustic folk audiences—recorded before a live audience, he plays his electric guitar down and dirty, getting it to "talk" in some surprisingly crisp and articulate tones. Most of the material ("I Heard My Baby Crying," "My Baby Laid Out All Night," "Rock Me Late At Night," etc.) is extended to four or five minutes or more, and it's all in duophonic stereo, with voice on one channel and guitar on the other, which makes it really cool for anyone who just wants to concentrate on the playing. — *Bruce Eder*

The Lost Texas Tapes, Vol. 4 / 1990 / Collectables ✦✦✦

The Lost Texas Tapes, Vol. 5 / 1990 / Collectables ✦✦
Billed as "Lightnin' Hopkins & Friends," this is the least engaging of this series of five volumes, partly because of its brevity (26 minutes), and because Hopkins, according to producer Aubrey Mayhew, was drinking on the night that the live material here was recorded, and spent long stretches staring at the floor. But when he played "Back In My Mother's Arms," the sound was as hot as ever. He only does two solo live numbers, and the rest is studio stuff, supported by singer Curley Lee, who joins him variously on "Goodnight Irene," "One Meat Ball," and "Sorrow to My Heart," and is also represented—as is folk singer Irish O'Malley—on separate featured numbers. The sources and quality of the recordings vary from song to song, with some disc source material in evidence. — *Bruce Eder*

Texas Blues / 1990 / Arhoolie ✦✦✦
Recorded between 1961 and 1969, *Texas Blues* gets to the essence of Lightnin' Hopkins' music, delivering a fine sampling of his guitar work as well as the superior sense of humor which sends cuts like "Bald Headed Woman" and "Meet You at the Chicken Shack" over the top. — *Jason Ankeny*

Gold Star Sessions, Vol. 1 / 1991 / Arhoolie ✦✦✦✦
The first of two discs devoted to Hopkins' extensive recording activities during the late '40s for Bill Quinn's Gold Star logo. — *Bill Dahl*

Gold Star Sessions, Vol. 2 / 1991 / Arhoolie ✦✦✦✦
More wonderfully sparse ruminations by the Texas blues troubadour for Quinn's Gold Star label. Hopkins was amazingly prolific during his first few years of recording, and nearly everything he did back then has great artistic merit. — *Bill Dahl*

☆ **The Complete Aladdin Recordings** / 1991 / Aladdin/EMI ✦✦✦✦✦
This is where it all began for the Houston troubadour: 43 solo sides, as evocative and stark as any he ever did, from 1946-1948. The first 13 sides find the guitarist in tandem with pianist Wilson "Thunder" Smith (who handles the vocals on a few tracks), but after that, old Lightnin' Hopkins went the solo route. "Katie May," "Short Haired Woman," "Abilene," "Shotgun"—all these and more rate with his seminal performances. — *Bill Dahl*

Complete Prestige/Bluesville Recordings / 1991 / Bluesville ✦✦✦✦
This is a seven-CD box set that repackages all 11 LPs that Lightnin' Hopkins recorded for Bluesville and Prestige during the first half of the 1960s: *Last Night Blues, Lightnin', Blues in My Bottle, Walkin' This Road By Myself, Lightnin' and Co., Smokes Like Lightning, Hootin' the Blues, Goin' Away, Down Home Blues, Soul Blues* and *My Life in the Blues*. The very prolific Hopkins (who was never loyal to any one label) also recorded for Candid, Arhoolie, Fire and Vee-Jay during the period! The bulk of *My Life in the Blues* is actually a lengthy and rather historic interview that Samuel Charters conducted with Hopkins. A special bonus of the set is 13 often exciting tracks from a previously unissued concert at the Swarthmore College Folk Festival. The music throughout the box covers quite a variety of moods and subject matter (with Hopkins being unaccompanied on 34 of the tracks) and definitively sums up the veteran bluesman's later period. — *Scott Yanow*

Sittin' in With / 1992 / Mainstream ✦✦✦✦
The second installment of Sittin' in With masters, some with bassist Donald Cooks and drummer Connie Kroll providing rock-solid support (L.C. Williams takes over as vocalist for two cuts). Supple boogies and dusty rural blues, all woven expertly by the Texas guitarist. — *Bill Dahl*

It's a Sin to Be Rich / 1993 / Polygram ✦✦
It's a sin that these sloppy, uninspired 1972 tapes ever saw the light of day.

Hopkins and his cohorts (including John Lee Hooker, who also should have known better) stumble and bumble their way through some of the most disposable performances the guitarist ever knocked off. —*Bill Dahl*

Houston Bound / 1993 / Relic ◆◆◆◆

Thirteen of the last sides he cut for his former R&B audience. Under Bobby Robinson's tutelage, Hopkins' 1960 Fire sides rank with his finest—especially his boogie-based "Mojo Hand," a title he subsequently remade early and often. —*Bill Dahl*

★ Mojo Hand: The Anthology / May 18, 1993 / Rhino ◆◆◆◆◆

As with its John Lee Hooker two-disc set, Rhino offers a very pleasant way to begin serious appreciation of Hopkins' humongous recorded legacy with this 41-track anthology. His Aladdin, Gold Star, RPM, Sittin' in With, and Mercury output are all liberally sampled on disc one, and there are a half dozen of those electrifying 1954 Herald sides that verged on rock 'n' roll. Disc two is a less exciting affair, those 1960s folk-blues and later efforts usually paling in comparison to seminal early efforts. Still, for a cogent overview of the guitarist's daunting discography, this is the place to start. —*Bill Dahl*

Blue Lightnin' / 1995 / Jewel ◆◆◆

After a slew of albums aimed primarily at the folk-blues audience that resuscitated his flagging career during the early '60s, Hopkins attempted to regain his original fan base with these unpretentious 1965 sessions for Stan Lewis' Jewel logo. Pretty convincingly, too, with the two-part "Move on Out" and a down-in-the-alley "Back Door Friend" among the standouts. Elmore Nixon, another Houston mainstay, plays piano on several cuts. —*Bill Dahl*

Blues Hoot / 1996 / Horizon ◆◆◆

Lightnin' Hopkins is the star of this live recording, made at an August 1961 concert at the Ash Grove in Hollywood featuring Hopkins, Sonny Terry, and Brownie McGhee (with Big Joe Williams sitting in on three numbers). It isn't remotely unique, joining a long list of club recordings by all three, although the original LP (on the Davon and Horizon labels) was obscure enough that collectors may welcome this CD. The sound is excellent, and the original master tape has yielded one extra Terry/McGhee track ("Po' Boy") and one extra Hopkins/Terry/McGhee song ("Early Morning Blues") from the same show—the producers have also added on two more songs ("I'm A Stranger Here," "Trouble In Mind") from a Los Angeles Troubador show by Terry and McGhee, bringing the running time up to 60 minutes. The sound is excellent, the performances are spirited enough, and the addition of the ominous "Early Morning Blues" shifts the record more toward blues than the folk/hootenanny orientation of the released Hopkins/Terry/McGhee tracks. "Blues For the Lowlands" is the best of the Terry/McGhee tracks, beautifully showcasing their harmonica/guitar interplay. It is difficult to say, however, anything distinguishes this set from the other folk club recordings that Hopkins, Terry, and McGhee left behind on other labels. —*Bruce Eder*

Big Walter "Shakey" Horton

b. Apr. 6, 1917, Horn Lake, MS, **d.** Dec. 8, 1981, Chicago, IL
Harmonica, Vocals / Electric Blues, Electric Chicago Blues, Chicago Blues, Electric Memphis Blues

Big Walter "Shakey" Horton is one of the all-time great blues harp (harmonica) players. Along with Little Walter, Horton defined modern amplified Chicago-style harmonica. There is no harp player (and that includes Little Walter) with Horton's big tone and spacious sense of time. Horton (who is said to have been somewhat shy) was not a natural group leader and therefore has produced few solo albums. His best work is as a sideman; his backup harmonica and virtuoso harp solos have graced many great Chicago blues recordings—turning an otherwise good cut into a dynamite jam.

Walter is the master of the single note and his characteristic walking bass line (usually with a deep tone and selection of notes that is unsurpassed) is instantly recognizable. As an accompanist, he has few equals. His backup harp is always unobtrusive yet bright and fresh—enhancing whatever else is going on. Give Big Walter a chance to solo and you are in for some of the most tasteful lines Chicago-style harp has ever produced. He made a specialty of playing entire tunes (often in blues style) on the harmonica ("La Cucaracha," "Careless Love," "I Almost Lost My Mind," etc.). This might sound trite, but give them a listen. You'll see.

As for harmonicas, he used Hohner's Marine Band. He was just as comfort-

able playing first position (A harp in the key of A) as with the more standard cross harp (D harp in the key of A). He did not do much with chromatic harmonicas. Although Big Walter could play in the style of other harp players (and was often asked to do so), he has no credible imitators. He is one of a kind.

Walter Horton was born in Horn Lake, MS (April 6, 1917), but his mother soon moved to Memphis where Walter taught himself how to play the harmonica at five years of age. He later learned more about his instrument by working with harp players Will Shade and Hammie Nixon.

In the late '20s, he performed and recorded with the Memphis Jug Band (1927) and generally worked the Southern dance and juke-joint circuit as well as Memphis street corners. Horton moved to Chicago in the late '40s, but was often to be found back in Memphis for recording dates with Sun and Modern/RPM labels. He claimed to be blowing amplified harp as early as 1940, which would make him the first. Johnny Shines recalls that Sonny Boy Williamson (Rice Miller) used to come to Walter for lessons. He also says that he used the name "Little Walter" before the Little Walter Jacobs did, but gave it up to Jacobs. Jacobs acknowledges that he "ran" with Big Walter in Memphis during the 1940s. Horton later called himself "Big Walter" to distinguish himself. The term "Shakey" came from the way he moved his head while playing.

He recorded four sides in 1951 for the Modern/RPM label under the name "Mumbles," but was not fond of that moniker. It was not until 1953 that he really left Memphis and relocated to Chicago to work as a sideman with his friend Eddie Taylor. He soon joined the Muddy Waters band (replacing Junior Wells, who had been drafted into the military) and played with Muddy for about a year.

Over the next few years, Horton worked with Chicago blues artists such as Johnny Shines, Jimmy Rogers, and Otis Rush—both in the Chicago blues clubs and at record studios. He recorded with Chess, Cobra, and States throughout the 1950s. During the 1960s, Horton continued to work with Jimmy Rogers, Shines, Tampa Red, Big Mama Thornton, Robert Nighthawk, Johnny Young, and Howlin' Wolf. In the 1970s, Walter was active in the blues clubs, in recording studios, and also began to appear at blues and folk festivals—primarily with Willie Dixon's Blues All-Stars. He died in Chicago on Dec. 8, 1981, and was inducted into the Blues Foundation's Hall of Fame in 1982.

While his early acoustic recordings in Memphis (1951-1954) are excellent, it is the recordings from the late '50s and mid-'60s that are unrivaled. When Horton's music is discussed in print, often the reference is to his later albums on Blind Pig (*Can't Keep Lovin' You* and *Fine Cuts*) and Alligator (*Big Walter Horton with Carey Bell*). I don't want to take anything away from these albums, but this is not what has made Walter a legend. Here is what has:

The recording of "Easy" with guitarist Jimmy DeBerry (recorded by Sam Phillips of Sun Records in the early '50s) is a striking harp instrumental that remains unrivaled for sheer power. For a superb example of Big Walter playing behind Muddy Waters (and soloing), try the cut "Mad Love (I Want You to Love Me)" that was recorded in 1953. Walter also plays on the classic Jimmy Rogers tune "Walking by Myself," on the Otis Rush tune "I Can't Quit You Baby," and many others. Also hear great Walter on the Flyright album, *Johnny Shines & Robert Lockwood, Joe Hill Louis: The Be-bop Boy* on Bear Family, *Memphis Harmonica 1951-1954* on Sun, and *The Blues Came Down from Memphis* on Charly. This last album contains the incredible instrumental, "Easy."

Walter's singing is seldom mentioned except in an apologetic way. This is something I have never understood. I love to hear Walter sing and his singing style has all the elements of his harp playing, in particular, sincerity and (above all) humor. Make a point to listen to some Big Walter songs like "Need My Baby," "Everybody's Fishin'," and "Have a Good Time." They are priceless. His original recording of "Hard Hearted Woman" on the album *Chicago Blues—the Early Fifties* (Blues Classics) never fails to raise the hair on the back of my neck. His hard-to-find first album for Chess, *The Soul of Blues Harmonica*, is also worth a listen, although not definitive.

But if you want to hear Walter at his best, pick up the Vanguard CD *Chicago/The Blues/Today!, Volume 3* and listen to the music Walter lays down. Both as backup harp and in solos, this is not only classic Big Walter, but Chicago blues at its finest—not to be missed. The music on this album is incredible—Horton's contrapuntal backup harp seems to float in the background, loping along, always stretching and opening up the time. And

Horton's taste in notes and depth of tone is unparalleled in the history of amplified Chicago-style harmonica. As Willie Dixon says, "Big Walter is the best harmonica player I ever heard." I agree. He was the man. *—Michael Erlewine*

The Soul of Blues Harmonica / Jan. 13, 1964 / MCA/Chess ✦✦✦
Big Walter's first album and with an all star cast—Buddy Guy (guitar), Jack Myers (bass), Willie Dixon (vocals), and Willie Smith (drums). Although not definitive, this album is worth seeking out for Horton fans. It features Walter in a variety of musical styles, including a good rendition of "Hard Hearted Woman" and a wild version of "La Cucaracha" *—Michael Erlewine*

★ **Chicago/The Blues/Today!, Vol. 3** / 1967 / Vanguard ✦✦✦✦✦
One of the all-time great blues albums. Period. It features Big Walter with the Johnny Shines Blues Band, the Johnny Young South Side Blues Band, and Big Walter Horton's Blues Harp Band (with Charlie Musselwhite). The timing and sense of musical spaciousness is incredible. Walter's backup harp and harmonica solos mark a high point in his career. A must hear. *—Michael Erlewine*

Southern Comfort / 1969 / Sire ✦✦

Offer You Can't Refuse [1 Side] / 1972 / Red Lightnin' ✦✦✦
An album released on the Red Lightnin' label in 1972 consisting of one side of Big Walter Horton and the other side with very early Paul Butterfield (1963). The Horton side consists of eight tracks of Horton with guitarist Robert Nighthawk (no bass or drums). Nighthawk is playing pure backup here, very little else. It is not clear when these were recorded. Perhaps not classic Walter, but any Big Walter is worth a listen. There are three instrumentals that make for good listening, including a version of "Easy" (not up to the original Walter recording). The instrumental "West Side Blues" has some interesting Walter harp licks that I have not heard elsewhere. The other five cuts are Walter singing. Of these, there is a great version of "Louise" and Walter singing "Tin Pan Alley" which never fails to raise the hair on the back of my neck. If you can find this album, it is good to have. *—Michael Erlewine*

Live at the El Mocambo / 1973 / Red Lightnin' ✦
Recorded at the El Mocambo Club in Toronto on July 25, 1973, this is not vintage Horton. *—Michael Erlewine*

Big Walter Horton with Carey Bell / Jan. 1973 / Alligator ✦✦✦✦
The teacher/pupil angle might be a bit unwieldy here—Bell was already a formidable harpist in his own right by 1972, when Horton made this album—but there's no denying that a stylistic bond existed between the two. A highly showcase for the often recalcitrant harp master, and only his second domestic set as a leader. *—Bill Dahl*

Fine Cuts / Apr. 1979 / Blind Pig ✦✦✦✦
This is perhaps the best of the later Horton material from the late '70s when he was working with John Nicholas. Horton reworks many of his earlier classics including "Everybody's Fishin'," "Need My Baby," and "La Cucaracha." Not as riveting as the originals, but any Big Walter is worth a listen. *—Michael Erlewine*

Little Boy Blue / 1980 / JSP ✦✦✦
A 1980 live recording in Boston. Working with a pickup band consisting of Ronnie Earl on guitar, Mudcat Ward on bass, and Ola Dixon on drums, Horton catches fire and quite simply blows his heart out. The album features some of Horton's best late-period playing. *—Cub Koda*

Harmonica Blues Kings / May 1987 / Pearl Flapper ✦✦✦✦
Six cuts (one side) of an album shared with Alfred Harris. This is very early amplified Walter, recorded in the fall of 1954 for the Black-owned United/States labels. On four of the cuts, Big Walter is playing backup harp and solos for singer Tommy Brown; the other two cuts represent Big Walter's first Chicago record under his own name. Includes the definitive recording of the classic Walter tune "Hard Hearted Woman." *—Michael Erlewine*

Mouth Harp Maestro / 1988 / Ace ✦✦✦✦
These 16 cuts are from the Sam Phillips recordings from the early '50s. Features Walter on acoustic harp. Contains many of the same cuts on the Kent/Crown album, but lacks the amplified songs given there. *—Michael Erlewine*

Can't Keep Lovin' You / 1989 / Blind Pig ✦✦✦
Probably from the mid-'70s, this is later Horton, with John Nicholas on guitar

and Ron Levy on piano. The album features a variety of material, including a good version of "Hard Hearted Woman." Not vintage, but worth a listen. *—Michael Erlewine*

Memphis Recordings 1951 / 1991 / Kent ✦✦✦✦
These are the Modern/Cobra masters—17 cuts from the sessions Walter did with Sam Phillips in 1951, including several alternate takes. This is mostly great acoustic harp, but it does contain the songs "Have a Good Time," and "Need My Baby" with Walter playing amplified harp—and great songs and solos these are! Worth finding. *—Michael Erlewine*

Son House

b. Mar. 21, 1902, Riverton, MS, **d.** Oct. 19, 1988, Detroit, MI
Guitar, Vocals / Delta Blues, Modern Electric Blues, Acoustic Blues, Blues Revival, Work Songs, Prewar Blues

Son House's place, not only in the history of Delta blues, but in the overall history of the music, is a very high one indeed. He was a major innovator of the Delta style, along with his playing partners Charley Patton and Willie Brown. Few listening experiences in the blues are as intense as hearing one of Son House's original 1930s recordings for the Paramount label. Entombed in a hailstorm of surface noise and scratches, one can still be awestruck by the emotional fervor House puts into his singing and slide playing. Little wonder then, that the man became more than just an influence on some White English kid with a big amp; he was the main source of inspiration to both Muddy Waters and Robert Johnson, and it doesn't get much more pivotal than *that*. Even after his rediscovery in the mid-'60s, House was such a potent musical force that what would have been a normally genteel performance by any other bluesmen in a "folk" setting, turned into a night in the nastiest juke joint you could imagine, scaring the daylights out of young White enthusiasts expecting something far more prosaic and comfortable. Not out of Son House, no sir. When the man hit the downbeat on his National steel bodied guitar and you saw his eyes disappear into the back of his head, you *knew* you were going to hear some blues. And when he wasn't shouting the blues, he was singing spirituals, a cappella. Right up to the end, no bluesman was torn between the sacred and the profane more than Son House.

He was born Eddie James House, Jr., on March 21, 1902, in Riverton, MS. By the age of 15, he was preaching the gospel in various Baptist churches as the family seemingly wandered from one plantation to the next. He didn't even bother picking up a guitar until he turned 25; to quote House, "I didn't like no guitar when I first heard it; oh gee, I couldn't stand a guy playin' a guitar. I didn't like *none* of it." But if his ambivalence to the instrument was obvious, even more obvious was the simple fact that Son hated plantation labor even more and had developed a taste for corn whiskey. After drunkenly launching into a blues at a house frolic in Lyon, MS, one night and picking up some coin for doing it, the die seemed to be cast; Son House may have been a preacher, but he was part of the blues world now.

If the romantic notion that the blues life is said to be a life full of trouble is true, then Son found a barrel of it one night at another house frolic in Lyon. He shot a man dead that night and was immediately sentenced to imprisonment at Parchman Farm. He ended up only serving two years of his sentence, with his parents both lobbying hard for his release, claiming self defense. Upon his release—after a Clarksdale judge told him never to set foot in town again—he started a new life in the Delta as a full-time man of the blues.

After hitchhiking and hoboing the rails, he made it down to Lula, MS, and ran into the most legendary character the blues had to offer at that point, the one and only Charley Patton. The two men couldn't have been less similar in disposition, stature and in musical and performance outlook if they had purposely planned it that way. Patton was described as a funny, loud mouthed little guy, who was a noisy, passionate showman, using every trick in the book to win over a crowd. The tall and skinny House was by nature a gloomy man, with a saturnine disposition who still felt extremely guilt-ridden about playing the blues and working in juke joints. Yet when he ripped into one, Son imbued it with so much raw feeling that the performance *became* the show itself, sans gimmicks. The two of them argued and bickered constantly, and the only thing these two men seemed to have in common was a penchant for imbibing whatever alcoholic potable came their way. Though House would later refer in interviews to Patton as a "jerk" and other unprintables, it was Patton's success as a bluesman—both live and especially on record—that got Son's foot in the door as a recording artist. He followed Patton up to Grafton, WI, and recorded a handful of sides for the Paramount label. These records today (selling scant few copies in their time, and the few that did surviving a life of huge steel needles, even bigger scratches and generally lousy care) are some of the most highly prized collector's items of Delta blues recordings, much tougher to find than, say, a Robert Johnson or even a Charley Patton 78. Paramount used a pressing compound for their 78 singles that was so noisy and inferior sounding, that should someone actually come across a clean copy of any of Son's original recordings, it's a pretty safe bet that the listener would still be greeted with a blizzard of surface noise once the needle made contact with the disc.

But audio concerns aside, the absolutely demonic performances House laid down on these three two-part 78s ("My Black Mama," "Preachin' the Blues," and "Dry Spell Blues," with an unreleased test acetate of "Walkin' Blues" showing up decades later) cut through the hisses and pops like a brick through a stained glass window.

It was those recordings that led Alan Lomax to his door in 1941 to record him for the Library of Congress. Lomax was cutting acetates on a "portable" recording machine weighing over 300 pounds. Son was still playing (actually at the peak of his powers, some would say), but had backed off of it a bit since Charley Patton died in 1934. House did some tunes solo, as Lomax asked him to do, but also cut a session backed by a rocking little string band. As the band laid down long and loose (some tracks went on for over six minutes) versions of their favorite numbers, all that was missing was the guitars being plugged in and a drummer's back beat and you were getting a glimpse of the future of the music.

But just as House had gone a full decade without recording, this time after the Lomax recordings, he just as quickly disappeared, moving to Rochester, NY. When folk blues researchers finally found him in 1964, he was cheerfully exclaiming that he hadn't touched a guitar in years. One of the researchers, a young guitarist named Alan Wilson (later of the blues-rock group Canned Heat) literally sat down and retaught Son House how to play like Son House. Once the old master was up to speed, the festival and coffeehouse circuit became his oyster. He recorded again, the recordings becoming an important introduction to his music and for some, a lot easier to take than those old Paramount 78s from a strict audio standpoint. In 1965, he played Carnegie Hall and four years later found himself the subject of an eponymously-titled film documentary, all of this another world removed from Clarksdale, MS, indeed. Everywhere he played, he was besieged by young fans, asking him about Robert Johnson, Charlie Patton and others. For young White blues fans, these were merely exotic names from the past, heard only to them on old, highly prized recordings; for Son House they were flesh and blood contemporaries, not just some names on a record label. Hailed as the greatest living Delta singer still actively performing, nobody dared call themselves the king of the blues as long as Son House was around.

He fell into ill health by the early '70s; what was later diagnosed as both Alzheimer's and Parkinson's disease first affected his memory and his ability to recall songs onstage and later, his hands, which shook so bad he finally had to give up the guitar and eventually live performing altogether by 1976. He lived quietly in Detroit, MI, for another 12 years, passing away on October 19, 1988. His induction into the Blues Foundation's Hall of Fame in 1980 was no less than his due. Son House *was* the blues. — *Cub Koda*

☆ **Masters of the Delta Blues: The Friends of Charlie Patton** / 1930 / Yazoo ◆◆◆◆◆
If you've only heard Son House's 1965 rediscovery recordings for Columbia (or his excellent 1941-1942 Library of Congress sessions), boy, are you in for a shock. This various artists compilation collects up House's original 1930 recordings for the Paramount label, some of the rarest and hardest-to-find 78s in blues history. Recorded in Grafton, WI, House sounds positively demonic on the six issued titles (all of them two-part numbers, each being a separate take, rather than a single performance spread over both sides of a single) and with the inclusion of a previously unissued test acetate of "Walking Blues," this is the most complete document of his first recordings that has survived on this important Delta bluesman. The original Paramount 78s were always considered of inferior pressing quality even back in the days

when turntables were called victrolas and the hailstorm of surface noise on these sides seems by and large resistant to all forms of modern noise reduction devices employed here. But House's performances here cut through the crackles, pops and hisses like slicing up a cold stick of butter with a soldering iron. Absolutely indispensable. — *Cub Koda*

The Legendary Son House: Father of the Folk Blues / 1965 / Columbia ◆◆◆◆
Although not at his strongest during the "rediscovery" phase, Son House could still sing and play riveting country blues in the mid-'60s. This features him doing well-known and obscure material in nearly the same manner as when he was defining the genre during the 1930s. — *Ron Wynn*

At Home: Complete 1969 / 1969 / Document ◆◆◆◆
Document's *At Home: Complete 1969 Recorded Works* is a fascinating look at Son House in an intimate setting, and serious fans will find it necessary, but many of these performances aren't as strong as similar sets he recorded in the '60s. In other words, it's one for the completist. — *Thom Owens*

☆ **Son House & The Great Delta Blues Singers** / 1990 / Document ◆◆◆◆◆
Son House & The Great Delta Blues Singers isn't entirely devoted to Son House—there are cuts by several other musicians, including Willie Brown, Garfield Akers, Rube Lacy and Joe Calicott—but this disc, which contains a complete 1930 session, is the best place to get his earliest songs ("My Black Mama," "Preachin' the Blues," "Dry Spell Blues"), which are among his masterworks. — *Thom Owens*

★ **Delta Blues** / 1991 / Biograph ◆◆◆◆◆
All of the recordings Alan Lomax made of Son House in 1941 and 1942 are collected on this essential CD. — *Stephen Thomas Erlewine*

Father of the Delta Blues: The Complete 1965 Sessions / 1992 / Columbia ◆◆◆◆
After being rediscovered by the folk-blues community in the early '60s, Son House rose to the occasion and recorded this magnificent set of performances. Allowed to stretch out past the shorter running time of the original 78s, House turns in wonderful, steaming performances of some of his best-known material. On some tracks, House is supplemented by folk-blues researcher/musician Alan Wilson, who would later become a member of the blues-rock group Canned Heat and here plays some nice second guitar and harmonica on several cuts. This two-disc set features alternate takes, some unissued material and some studio chatter from producer John Hammond, Sr., that occasionally hints at the chaotic nature inherent to some of these '60s "rediscovery" sessions. While not as overpowering as his earlier work (what could be?), all of these sides are so power packed with sheer emotional involvement from House, they're an indispensable part of his canonade. — *Cub Koda*

Legendary 1969 Rochester Sessions / 1992 / Document ◆◆◆◆
Recorded at his home in September of 1969 by blues enthusiast Steve Lobb, Son House turns in one of the most vital and compelling performances available from his late career comeback. While the 1965 Columbia Records sessions require explanations about his age and extended retirement, there is no excuse necessary for the contents of this CD. Opening with the 20-minute long "Son's Blues," he radiates explosive power, his voice surging and his guitar strings snapping against the fretboard in a slow, fiery performance. The tension and sustained strength of this one piece makes this CD far more valuable as a specimen of Son's best work than any of the CBS material—this is the perfect companion to his inimitable Alan Lomax and Paramount recordings of the 1930s and early 1940s. Nothing else here quite matches the opening track, although Son still seems in far better form than he did on some of his better-known comeback recordings. — *Bruce Eder*

Bee Houston (Edward Wilson Houston)

b. Apr. 19, 1938, San Antonio, TX, **d.** Mar. 19, 1991, Los Angeles, CA
Guitar, Vocals / Texas Blues
Guitarist/vocalist Edward Wilson "Bee" Houston's an exciting performer whose style blends elements of Texas shuffle blues and Southern gospel-tinged soul. Houston played in a high school drum and bugle corps as a youngster in San Antonio, and played in the backing bands of Little Willie John, Junior Parker, Bobby "Blue" Bland and others in the late '50s and early '60s. After a two-year army stint, Houston moved to the West Coast. He

toured and recorded frequently with Big Mama Thornton in the '60s, and also accompanied several visiting blues players during West Coast visits. Houston recorded for Arhoolie in the '60s and '70s, and also made several festival appearances and club dates. — *Ron Wynn*

● **Bee Houston: His Guitar & Band** / 1981 / Arhoolie ◆◆◆◆
While not an instrumental giant, Bee Houston made many delightful and very explosive recordings. He seldom did covers, and this collection has several enjoyable originals. — *Ron Wynn*

Hustler / Nov. 18, 1997 / Arhoolie ◆◆◆◆

Joe Houston

b. Austin, TX
Vocals, Sax (Tenor) / Rock 'n' Roll, Groove, Jump Blues
Joe Houston is a honking R&B saxman of wallpaper-peeling potency who recorded for virtually every major independent R&B label in Los Angeles during the 1950s. When the jump blues tradition faded, he segued right into rock 'n' roll, even cutting budget "twist" and "surf" albums for Crown that didn't sound very different from what he was doing a decade before.

Houston played around Houston (Texas, that is) with the bands of Amos Milburn and Joe Turner during the late '40s. It was Turner who got the young saxist his first deal with Freedom Records in 1949. Houston found his way to the West Coast in 1952 and commenced recording for labels big and small: Modern, RPM, Lucky, Imperial, Dootone, Recorded in Hollywood, Cash, and Money (as well as the considerably better-financed Mercury, where he scored his only national R&B hit, "Worry, Worry, Worry," in 1952).

Houston's formula was simple and savagely direct—he'd honk and wail as hard as he could, from any conceivable position: on his knees, lying on his back, walking the bar, etc. His output for the Bihari brothers' Crown label (where he was billed "Wild Man of the Tenor Sax") is positively exhilarating: "All Nite Long," "Blow Joe Blow," and "Joe's Gone" are herculean examples of single-minded sax blasting.

Houston remains active musically, emphasizing his blues vocal talent more than he used to. — *Bill Dahl*

● **Cornbread and Cabbage Greens** / 1952 / Specialty ◆◆◆◆
Los Angeles was a mecca for honking, wailing R&B tenor saxmen during the 1950s, and Joe Houston was one of the wildest in town. Twenty-six blasting workouts from the early-to-mid-'50s mark this CD as the best digital indication of Houston's sax-sational wailing now available (pretty much the only vintage one on the shelves, in fact). "All Night Long," "Celebrity Club Drag," and "Rockin' and Boppin'" are among the highlights, taken from the archives of John Dolphin's Recorded in Hollywood and Cash labels. — *Bill Dahl*

Rockin' at the Drive In / 1984 / Ace ◆◆◆◆
Fourteen characteristic sax-driven R&B tunes, most instrumental, from the '50s. There's no duplication with the Specialty *Cornbread and Cabbage Greens* CD, except for the well-known "All Night Long," so it's worth finding if you want more than one Houston collection. — *Richie Unterberger*

The Blues & Nothin' Else / Shattered ◆◆◆◆
Of all the honkers who worked the table tops out on the West Coast, one of the very best was "Big" Joe Houston. Able to jump from big band to small combo blues and R&B with consummate ease, Houston was one of the first to test the waters of the newly emerging style that would become known as rock 'n' roll. Cutting one brilliant single after another for a variety of labels— and seeing his early work among the first to be anthologized on a myriad of budget label albums—Houston was the California version of the tenor men who honked and walked the bars in the Big Apple, often outdoing his New York contemporaries with sides of fervent blasting that could not be denied. Fortunately for us, that fervent blasting is alive and well and beating right alongside Houston's big heart on this, his first new album in a good number of years. The most notable fact is that Joe is singing on everything, relegating his tenor work to no more than a couple of choruses on each tune, framing it in proper perspective as another soloist in the very rockin' band that backs him here. The really good news is that Houston's voice is every bit as rough hewn as his sax playing, making you wonder why it took this long to get it properly documented on record. The final track lets you know that the man still has it and really isn't rationing *anything*; the set closer, "Full of Misery," is eight minutes and twenty-five seconds of Joe making a rarely heard ap-

pearance on alto sax, playing the blues all by his lonesome, and making it sound oh so sweet. — *Cub Koda*

Frank Hovington

b. Jan. 9, 1919, Reading, PA, **d.** Jun. 21, 1982, Felton, DE
Vocals, Guitar, Ukulele, Banjo / Country Blues, Piedmont Blues
A tremendous country blues musician who was singing vividly and playing with flair well after the genre's heyday, Franklin "Frank" Hovington started on ukulele and banjo as a child. He teamed with Willliam Walker in the late '30s and '40s playing at house parties and dances in Frederica, PA. Hovington moved to Washington D.C. in the late '40s, and backed such groups as Stewart Dixon's Golden Stars and Ernest Ewin's Jubilee Four. He also worked with Billy Stewart's band. Hovington moved to Delaware in 1967, then was recorded by Flyright in 1975. His '75 LP was a masterpiece, and alerted many in the blues community to his abilities. — *Ron Wynn*

Lonesome Road Blues / 1975 / Rounder ◆◆◆◆
By the time Frank Hovington got a chance to record, the folk/blues boom had passed and there was almost no interest in country blues except among academics. But that didn't stop him from making a definitive album, which compared favorably to the genre's classics done in a different era. It's a textbook case of the right stuff at the wrong time. — *Ron Wynn*

Camille Howard

b. Mar. 29, 1914, Galveston, TX, **d.** Mar. 10, 1993, Los Angeles, CA
Piano, Vocals / Jump Blues, Classic Female Blues
Piano-tinkling chanteuses were quite the rage during the war years. But Camille Howard's two-fisted thundering boogie style, much like her Los Angeles contemporary, Hadda Brooks, was undoubtedly the equivalent of any 88s ace, male or female.

Howard was part of the great migration from Texas to the West Coast. She was installed as pianist with drummer Roy Milton & the Solid Senders sometime during World War II, playing on all their early hits for Art Rupe's Juke Box and Specialty labels (notably the groundbreaking "R.M. Blues" in 1945).

Sensing her potential following the success of Milton's 1947 hit "Thrill Me" (with Howard's vocal), Rupe began recording her as a featured artist at the end of the year. Legend has it that Howard's biggest hit, the roaring instrumental "X-Temporaneous Boogie," was improvised at the tail end of her first date as a leader (its flip, the torch ballad "You Don't Love Me," was a hit in its own right).

Howard's vocal abilities were pretty potent too. Her "Fiesta in Old Mexico" was a hit in 1949, while "Money Blues," credited to Camille Howard & Her Boyfriends, registered strong coin in 1951. Howard cranked out storming boogies and sultry ballads for Specialty through 1953, then jumped from Federal to Vee-Jay before landing in Los Angeles for good. Howard's strong religious ties put a stop to her secular music career long ago. — *Bill Dahl*

● **Rock Me Daddy, Vol. 1** / 1993 / Specialty ◆◆◆◆
25-song reissue of her 1947-52 Specialty material, about half previously unreleased. Includes "You Don't Love Me" and "Money Blues," but not the chart items "Fiesta In Mexico" and "XTemporaneous Boogie." Perhaps too suave and refined for the R&B/rock era, and as comfortable with jazzy ballads as boogies, Howard was nonetheless an important, and nowadays overlooked, star of the transitional era between jump blues and R&B. — *Richie Unterberger*

X-Temporaneous Boogie, Vol. 2 / Feb. 13, 1996 / Specialty ◆◆◆◆
Twenty of these 25 sides, recorded for Specialty between 1947 and 1952, were previously unissued. But there's no difference in quality between these and the better-known ones presented on volume one; the label's decision on what to release was based more on marketing strategies than the level of the performances. Divided between instrumentals and pop-influenced vocal numbers, Howard again proves herself the master of boogie and jump blues piano styles, sometimes slowing things down into a jazzier mode. In addition to the storehouse of vault material, this compilation also includes a couple of late-'40s Top Ten R&B hits, "Thrill Me" and "X-Temporaneous Boogie." — *Richie Unterberger*

Peg Leg Howell

b. Mar. 5, 1888, Eatonton, GA, **d.** Aug. 11, 1966, Atlanta, GA
Guitar, Vocals / Acoustic Blues, Country Blues

One of the first recorded products of the Atlanta blues community of the pre-war era, Peg Leg Howell bridged the gap between the early country-blues sound and the 12-bar stylings to follow, with his guitar work evolving over time to include finger-picking and slide techniques. Born Joshua Barnes Howell in Eatonton, GA on March 5, 1888, he was a self-taught guitarist who acquired his nickname after a 1916 run-in with an irate brother-in-law which ended in a shotgun wound to the leg and, ultimately, amputation. Unable to continue working as a farmhand, he migrated to Atlanta, where he began pursuing music full-time; in addition to playing street corners for passing change, Howell supplemented his income by bootlegging liquor, an offense which led to a one-year prison sentence in 1925. Soon after his release, he signed to Columbia; his first session for the label yielded the menacing "New Prison Blues," a song he'd learned while serving time. Having amassed a huge repertory of songs over the years, Howell recorded prolifically over the following months, his work ranging from traditional ballads ("Skin Game Blues") to dance numbers (the minor hit "Beaver Slide Rag") to even jazz ("New Jelly Roll Blues"); while some of his sides comprised solo performances, others featured the backing of his street group, the Gang (guitarist Henry Williams and fiddler Eddie Anthony). Columbia pulled the plug in 1929, at which time Howell returned to playing Atlanta's famed Decatur Street district; Williams was himself imprisoned not long after, and following Anthony's 1934 death, Howell gradually disappeared from the area blues circuit. He spent the next several decades clouded in obscurity, with diabetes claiming his other leg in 1952. Howell was 75 when the Testament label sought him out in 1963 to record his first new material in over 40 years; he died in Atlanta on August 11, 1966. —*Jason Ankeny*

Howlin' Wolf (Chester Arthur Burnett)

b. Jun. 10, 1910, West Point, MS, **d.** Jan. 10, 1976, Hines, IL
Guitar, Harmonica, Vocals / R&B, Electric Chicago Blues, Chicago Blues, Electric Blues

In the history of the blues, there has never been anyone quite like the Howlin' Wolf. Six foot three and close to 300 pounds in his salad days, the Wolf was the primal force of the music spun out to its ultimate conclusion. A Robert Johnson may have possessed more lyrical insight, a Muddy Waters more dignity, and a B.B. King certainly more technical expertise, but no one could match him for the singular ability to rock the house down to the foundation while simultaneously scaring its patrons out of its wits.

He was born in West Point, MS, and named after the 21st President of the United States. His father was a farmer and Wolf took to it as well until his 18th birthday, when a chance meeting with Delta blues legend Charley Patton changed his life forever. Though he never came close to learning the subtleties of Patton's complex guitar technique, two of the major components of Wolf's style (Patton's inimitable growl of a voice and his propensity for entertaining) were learned first-hand from the Delta blues master. The main source of Wolf's hard-driving, rhythmic style on harmonica came when Aleck "Rice" Miller (Sonny Boy Williamson) married his half-sister Mary and taught him the rudiments of the instrument. He first started playing in the early '30s as a strict Patton imitator, while others recall him at decade's end rocking the juke joints with a neck-rack harmonica and one of the first electric guitars anyone had ever seen. After a four-year stretch in the Army, he settled down as a farmer and weekend player in West Memphis, AR, and it was here that Wolf's career in music began in earnest.

By 1948, he had established himself within the community as a radio personality. As a means of advertising his own local appearances, Wolf had a 15-minute radio show on KWEM in West Memphis, interspersing his down-home blues with farm reports and like-minded advertising that he sold himself. But a change in Wolf's sound that would alter everything was soon in coming because when listeners tuned in for Wolf's show, the sound was up-to-the-minute electric. Wolf had put his first band together, featuring the explosive guitar work of Willie Johnson, whose aggressive style not only perfectly suited Wolf's sound, but aurally extended and amplified the violence and nastiness of it as well. In any discussion of Wolf's early success-both live, over the airwaves, and on record-the importance of Willie Johnson cannot be overestimated.

Wolf finally started recording in 1951, when he caught the ear of Sam Phillips, who first heard him on his morning radio show. The music Wolf made in the Memphis Recording Service studio was full of passion and zest and Phillips simultaneously leased the results to the Bihari brothers in Los Angeles and Leonard Chess in Chicago. Suddenly Howlin' Wolf had two hits at the same time on the R&B charts with two record companies claiming to have him exclusively under contract. Chess finally won him over and as Wolf would proudly relate years later, "I had a four thousand dollar car and $3,900 in my pocket. I'm the onliest one drove out of the South like a gentleman." It was the winter of 1953 and Chicago would be his new home.

When Wolf entered the Chess studios the next year, the violent aggression of the Memphis sides was being replaced with a Chicago backbeat and, with very little fanfare, a new member in the band. Hubert Sumlin proved himself to be the Wolf's longest-running musical associate. He first appears as a rhythm guitarist on a 1954 session, and within a few years' time his style had fully matured to take over the role of lead guitarist in the band by early 1958. In what can only be described as an "angular attack," Sumlin played almost no chords behind Wolf, sometimes soloing right through his vocals, featuring wild skitterings up and down the fingerboard and biting single notes. If Willie Johnson was Wolf's second voice in his early recording career, then Hubert Sumlin would pick up the gauntlet and run with it right to the end of the howler's life.

By 1956, Wolf was in the R&B charts again, racking up hits with "Evil" and "Smokestack Lightnin'." He remained a top attraction both on the Chicago circuit and on the road. His records, while seldom showing up on the national charts, were still selling in decent numbers down South. But by 1960, Wolf was teamed up with Chess staff writer Willie Dixon and for the next five years, he would record almost nothing but songs written by Dixon. The magic combination of Wolf's voice, Sumlin's guitar and Dixon's tunes sold a lot of records and brought the 50-year-old bluesman roaring into the next decade with a considerable flourish. The mid-'60s saw him touring Europe regularly with "Smokestack Lightnin'" becoming a hit in England some eight years after its American release. Certainly any list of Wolf's greatest sides would have to include "I Ain't Superstitious," "The Red Rooster," "Shake for Me," "Back Door Man," "Spoonful," and "Wang Dang Doodle," Dixon compositions all. While almost all of them would eventually become Chicago blues standards, their greatest cache occurred when rock bands the world over started mining the Chess catalog for all it was worth. One of these bands was the Rolling Stones, whose cover of "The Red Rooster" became a number one record in England. At the height of the British Invasion, the Stones came to America in 1965 for an appearance on ABC-TV's rock music show, *Shindig.* Their main stipulation for appearing on the program was that Howlin' Wolf would be their special guest. With the Stones sitting worshipfully at his feet, the Wolf performed a storming version of "How Many More Years," being seen on his network-TV debut by an audience of a few million. Wolf never forgot the respect the Stones paid him, and he spoke of them highly right up to his final days.

Dixon and Wolf parted company by 1964 and Wolf was back in the studio doing his own songs. One of the classics to emerge from this period was "Killing Floor," featuring a modern backbeat and a incredibly catchy guitar riff from Sumlin. Catchy enough for Led Zeppelin to appropriate it for one of their early albums, cheerfully crediting it to themselves in much the same manner as they had done with numerous other blues standards. By the end of the decade, Wolf's material was being recorded by artists including the Doors, the Electric Flag, the Blues Project, Cream, and Jeff Beck. The result of all these covers brought Wolf the belated acclaim of a young, White audience. Chess' response to this was to bring him into the studio for a "psychedelic" album, truly the most dreadful of his career. His last big payday came when Chess sent him over to England in 1970 to capitalize on the then-current trend of *London Session* albums, recording with Eric Clapton on lead guitar and other British superstars. Wolf's health was not the best, but the session was miles above the earlier, ill-advised attempt to update Wolf's sound for a younger audience.

As the '70s moved on, the end of the trail started coming closer. By now Wolf was a very sick man; he had survived numerous heart attacks and was suffering kidney damage from an automobile accident that sent him flying through the car's windshield. His bandleader Eddie Shaw firmly rationed Wolf to a meager half-dozen songs per set. Ocassionally some of the old fire would come blazing forth from some untapped wellspring and his final live and studio recordings show that he could still tear the house apart when the spirit moved him. He entered the Veterans Administration Hospital in 1976 to be operated on, but never survived it, finally passing away on January 10th of that year.

But his passing did not go unrecognized. A life-size statue of him was erected shortly after in a Chicago park. Eddie Shaw kept his memory and music alive by keeping his band, the Wolf Gang, together for several years afterward. A child-education center in Chicago was named in his honor and in 1980 he was elected to the Blues Foundation Hall of Fame. In 1991, he was inducted into the Rock and Roll Hall of Fame. A couple of years later, his face was on a United States postage stamp. Live performance footage of him exists in the CD-ROM computer format. Howlin' Wolf is now a permanent part of American history. — *Cub Koda*

The Real Folk Blues / 1966 / MCA/Chess ✦✦✦✦
This was originally released by Chess in 1966 to capitalize on the then-current folk music boom. The music, however—a collection of Wolf singles from 1956 to 1966—is full-blown electric featuring a nice sampling of Wolf originals with a smattering of Willie Dixon tunes. Some of the man's best middle period work is aboard here; "Killing Floor," "Louise," the hair-raisingly somber "Natchez Burning," and Wolf's version of the old standard "Sitting on Top of the World," which would become his set closer in later years. The Mobile Fidelity version sounds as sonically sharp as anything you've ever heard on this artist and its heftier price tag is somewhat justified by the inclusion of two bonus cuts. But those on a budget who just want the music minus the high-minded audiophile concerns will be happy to note that this is also available as a Chess budget reissue. — *Cub Koda*

More Real Folk Blues / 1967 / MCA/Chess ✦✦✦✦
This companion volume to the *Real Folk Blues* album was issued in 1967 (after the Wolf had appeared on network television with the Rolling Stones, alluded to in the original liner notes) and couldn't be more dissimilar in content to the first one if you had planned it that way. Whereas the previous volume highlighted middle period Wolf, this one goes all the way back to his earliest Chess sessions, many of which sound like leftover Memphis sides. The chaotic opener, "Just My Kind," sets a familiar Wolf theme to a "Rollin' & Tumblin'" format played at breakneck speed and what the track lacks in fidelity is more than made up in sheer energy. For a classic example of Wolf's ensemble Chicago sound, it's pretty tough to beat "I Have a Little Girl" where the various members of his band seem to be all soloing simultaneously—not unlike a Dixieland band—right through Wolf's vocals. For downright scary, the demonic sounding "I'll Be Around" is an absolute must-hear. Wolf's harp solo on this slow blues is one of his best and the vocal that frames it sounds like the microphone is going to explode at any second. As soul singer Christine Ohlman commented upon hearing this track for the first time, "Boy, I'd sure hate to be the woman he's singing that one to." — *Cub Koda*

The London Howlin' Wolf Sessions / 1971 / MCA/Chess ✦✦
For the casual blues fan with a scant knowledge of the Wolf, this 1971 pairing, with Eric Clapton, Bill Wyman, and Charlie Watts from the Rolling Stones, Ringo Starr and other British superstars, appears on the surface to be one hell of a super session. But those lofty notions are quickly dispelled once you slip this disc into the player and hit play. While it's nowhere near as awful as some blues purists make it out to be, the disparity of energy levels between the Wolf and his UK acolytes is not only palpable but downright depressing. Wolf was a very sick man at this juncture and Norman Dayron's non-production idea of just doing remakes of earlier Chess classics is wrongheaded in the extreme. The rehearsal snippet of Wolf trying to teach the band how to play Willie Dixon's "Little Red Rooster" shows just how far off the mark the whole concept of this rock superstar melange truly is. Even Eric Clapton, who usually welcomes *any* chance to play with one of his idols, has criticized this album repeatedly in interviews, which speaks volumes in and of itself. The rest of the leftover tracks are collected up on the 1974 hodgepodge *London Revisited*, later repackaged for compact disc consumption as *Muddy & the Wolf*. Avoid both of these turkeys like the plague they are. — *Cub Koda*

Live & Cookin' at Alice's Revisited / 1972 / Chess ✦✦✦
A compact-disc reissue of Wolf's 1972 live album with the addition of two stellar bonus cuts. The first one, "Big House," first showed up on a hodgepodge Wolf bootleg album from the '70s. Its non-appearance on the original

abum is somewhat of a mystery since it's arguably one of the best performances here. Set at a medium tempo, Wolf stretches out comfortably for over seven minutes, singing certain verses he likes two or three times as the band locks in with deadly authority. Certainly any list of great Howlin' Wolf vocal performances would have to include this one. The second bonus track, "Mr. Airplane Man," is Wolf working his one-riff-fits-all voodoo for all it's worth. You can tell from note one of his vocal entrance that the pilot light of inspiration is fully lit and the ensuing performance is the Wolf at his howlin' best. Also of special note are the wild and wooly takes on "I Had a Dream," "I Didn't Know," and Muddy Waters' "Mean Mistreater." There are mistakes galore out of the band and some p.a. system feedback here and there, both of which only add to the charm of it all. A great document of Wolf toward the end, still capable of bringing the heat and rocking the house down to the last brick. — *Cub Koda*

Change My Way / 1975 / Chess ✦✦✦
Originally compiled and issued in 1975 as a vinyl album in the original Chess Blues Masters Series, this 19-tracker is some of Wolf's best middle-period (1959-1963) material. Surprisingly, many of the tracks were cut in stereo and their appearance on compact disc does much to enhance their sonic ambience. Although some of this material surfaces on the three-disc Howlin' Wolf box set ("I Ain't Superstitious," "Just Like I Treat You"), this single disc stands mightily on its own. If you really want to hear Hubert Sumlin rip up the fretboard, this an excellent place to start. — *Cub Koda*

★ **Howlin' Wolf/Moanin' in the Moonlight** / 1986 / MCA/Chess ✦✦✦✦✦
Wolf's first and second Chess albums, released in 1959 and 1962 respectively, are essential listening of the highest order. Compiled—as were all early blues albums—from various single sessions (not necessarily a bad thing, either), blues fans will probably debate endlessly about which of these two albums is the perfect introduction to his music. But the MCA-Chess CD issue renders all arguments moot as both albums appear on one disc, making this one of the true best buys around today. Wolf's debut opus—curiously tacked on here *after* his second album—features all of his early hits ("How Many More Years," "Moanin' at Midnight," "Smokestack Lightning," "Forty Four," "Evil," and "I Asked for Water [She Gave Me Gasoline]") and is a pretty potent collection in its own right. But it is the follow-up (always referred to as 'the rocking chair album' because of Don Bronstein's distinctive cover art) where the equally potent teaming of Willie Dixon and Wolf produced one Chicago Blues classic ("Spoonful," "The Red Rooster," "Back Door Man," and "Wang Dang Doodle") after another. It's also with this marvelous batch of sides that one can clearly hear lead guitarist Hubert Sumlin coming into his own as a blues picking legend. The number of blues acolytes, both Black and White, who wore the grooves down to mush learning the songs and guitar licks off these two albums would fill a book all by itself. If you have to narrow it down to just one Howlin' Wolf purchase for the collection, this would be the one to have and undoubtedly the place to start. This and *The Best of Muddy Waters* are the essential building blocks of any Chicago Blues collection. And seldom does the music come with this much personality and brute force. — *Cub Koda*

☆ **Cadillac Daddy** / 1989 / Rounder ✦✦✦✦
Great compendium of pre-Chess tracks produced by Sam Phillips. The sheer power of Wolf's voice and Willie Johnson's guitar work never cease to amaze. — *Bill Dahl*

Memphis Days: Definitive Edition, Vol. 1 / 1989 / Bear Family ✦✦✦✦
These are Wolf's earliest and rarest sides recorded at the Sun studios, as raw and explosive as blues records come. Much of this was issued on various European albums during the '70s, always transferred off of muffled-sounding copy tapes. These 21 tracks (all but two of them off the master tapes) feature the amp-on-11 guitar work of Willie Johnson and the cave-man drumming of Willie Steele; they're loose and somewhat chaotic, with Wolf sounding utterly demonic. The real bonus on this volume is the first time inclusion of both sides of the only known acetate of Wolf's first session at Sam Phillip's 706 Union Avenue studio from 1951. With only Johnson and Steele in support (no bass, no piano), these early versions of "How Many More Years" and "Baby Ride with Me (Riding in the Moonlight)" are Wolf at his most primitive. — *Cub Koda*

The Memphis Days: Definitive Edition, Vol. 2 / 1990 / Bear Family ✦✦✦✦
The second volume in this series collects up all the known Memphis re-

cordings that were either issued or originally offered to Chess. As such, it stands as a marvelous collection of Wolf's early 78s for that label. But what truly puts it over is the added bonus of a newly discovered acetate featuring several unissued versions of "How Many More Years" and "Baby Ride With Me (Riding in the Moonlight)." Much of this volume is pulled from discs, but the overall sound is good and the performances make it yet another must-have. — *Cub Koda*

☆ **The Chess Box** / 1991 / MCA/Chess ✦✦✦✦✦
This three-CD box set currently rates as the best—and most digestible—overview of Wolf's career. Disc one starts with the Memphis sides that eventually brought him to the label, including hits like "How Many More Years," but also compiling unissued sides that had previously only been available on vinyl bootlegs of dubious origin and fidelity. The disc finishes with an excellent cross section of early Chicago sessions including classic Wolf tracks like "Evil," "Forty Four," "I'll Be Around," and "Who Will Be Next." Disc two picks it up from there guiding us from mid- to late-'50s barnburners like "The Natchez Burnin'" and "I Better Go Now" to the bulk of the Willie Dixon classics. The final disc runs out the last of the Dixon sessions into mid-'60s classics like "Killing Floor" taking us to a nice selection of his final recordings. A really nice bonus on this box set is the inclusion on the first two discs of snippets from a 1968 Howlin' Wolf interview and two performances of Wolf playing solo acoustic. If you've heard the sound of the Wolf, here's where you go to get a lot of it in one place. Definitely *not* the place to start (unless you have money to burn), but maybe just the perfect place to end up. — *Cub Koda*

☆ **Howlin' Wolf Rides Again** / 1993 / Flair/Virgin ✦✦✦✦✦
While both Bear Family sets deal with a largely unissued wealth of material, this collection is devoted in the main to all the Memphis recordings from 1951 and 1952 that saw the light of day on a number of Los Angeles-based labels owned by the Bihari brothers, being issued and reissued and reissued again on a plethora of $1.98 budget albums. Featuring recordings done in Sam Phillips' Memphis Recording Service and surreptitious sessions recorded by a young Ike Turner in makeshift studios, these 18 sides are the missing piece of the puzzle in absorbing Wolf's early pre-Chess period. It also helps that this just happens to be some of the nastiest sounding blues ever recorded. With no tracks being duplicated from the two Bear Family *Memphis Days* volumes, and sonics far surpassing all previous issues of this material (every last one of them horribly marred by an annoying 60 cycle hum), this is an essential part of any Wolf collection. Alternate take freaks will revel in the inclusion of two extra takes of "Riding in the Moonlight" from an earlier and different session than the issued version also included. While not *quite* as essential as his first two Chess albums (and if we were making a judgement call on just passionate perfomances alone, even *that* would be debatable), this is definitely the next stop along the way in absorbing the raw genius of Howlin' Wolf. — *Cub Koda*

☆ **Ain't Gonna Be Your Dog** / 1994 / MCA/Chess ✦✦✦✦✦
This double-disc set features 42 rare and unissued performances, effectively cleaning out the Chess vaults of all but alternate takes of alternate takes. But these are no bottom-of-the-barrel scrapings here, quite the opposite. The first 14 tunes collect up the remainder of his Memphis recordings for Sam Phillips while the rest does the bootleggers one better, compiling masters that were previously only available on bad-sounding '70s vinyl albums. There's another snippet from his 1968 interview along with four more acoustic numbers from that same session (done, it turns out, as a promotional piece of sorts to preview his "soon-to-be-released psychedelic album," which Wolf always dismissed as "birds**t"), sadly the only time Chess ever tried to record him as a solo artist. A wonderful companion piece to any other Wolf collection you might own. — *Cub Koda*

Rockin' the Blues / 1996 / Collectables ✦✦✦
Collectables could probably do a better job of selling this nine-song CD if they'd indicate somewhere on the outside that it's a live performance by Wolf, from Germany in 1964. That puts it about seven years nearer to Wolf's prime than Chess' official live album (*At Alice's Revisited*) and makes this 1996 release an indispensable part of any serious blues or classic rock collection. Wolf and his band—Hubert Sumlin, guitar; Sunnyland Slim, piano; and Clifton James, drums (no credit for the bass player, but he's there)—open by easing into the title track, an easy, loose-limbed instrumental jam that gives lots of prominence to Slim's piano and Sumlin's guitar. Wolf starts to build

up a head of steam on "All My Life," which also features Wolf's harmonica, but it isn't until "Howlin' for My Darlin'" that they hit their stride, picking up speed and tension as that voice cuts across the stage and through the electronic replication, rasping and moaning in a musical mating call—there are enough wrong notes to notice, but enough intensity not to care. And when Wolf starts that otherworldly howl from the stage, it's a reminder of just how little Sam Phillips had to do back in 1951 to coax that opening howl in "Moaning at Midnight" from him. "Dust My Broom" must've been something to see on stage, because it sure sounds from the tape like there's a lot of motion going on, and not just from James' jackhammer drumming—Wolf must've been all over the place, while Sumlin and the anonymous bassist made like John Entwistle, anchoring the whole performance. The recording of "Going Down Slow" is the best of several live versions left behind by Wolf, for sound as well as performance quality. It'll never replace the wonderful theater of the studio piece with its Howlin' Wolf/Willie Dixon duet, but Wolf's most savage-sounding, knowing spoken-sung performance is a wonder to behold. It's on performances like this that one can hear what Jimi Hendrix learned from listening to Hubert Sumlin—Sumlin and Slim more than manage to keep up with Wolf's narrative/song and drive the piece to new heights of intensity. And just when it seems this disc couldn't get any better, along comes "Shake It for Me," a stage blow-out that's sort of Wolf's answer to Muddy's "Got My Mojo Workin'." The 48 minutes of material here is some of best live Howlin' Wolf available, and forms a superb companion to his official Chess live releases while covering completely different material. It's also sort of compensation for the fact that Wolf's 1966 Newport set has never been released, except for one song in a documentary movie. The sound is exceptionally good, far superior to such recent live Wolf releases as the 1966 Massachusetts show that's a lot more expensive (this disc is mid-priced). Only Collectables can say why they don't tell people it's a live recording, but it is out there and worth at least twice as much as they're asking. — *Bruce Eder*

★ **His Best (Chess 50th Anniversary Collection)** / Apr. 8, 1997 / MCA ✦✦✦✦✦
With the exception of a vinyl compilation issued in the early 1980s (*His Greatest Sides, Volume 1*), there's never really been a single-disc Howlin' Wolf best-of package available. That all changes with this entry in MCA-Chess' 50th Anniversary series, a 20-track retrospective that serves as the perfect introduction to the man and his music, some of the very best the blues has to offer. While some naysayers will always decry the exclusion—or inclusion—of any given number of tracks on any artists' best-of compilation, it's pretty hard to fault what's been collected here. Starting with the two-sided smash that brought him from Memphis to Chicago ("Moanin' At Midnight" b/w "How Many More Years"), this compilation hits all the high points and essential tracks, illustrating how his music developed into the mid-1960s. 11 of the 20 tunes on here are either written or co-written by Willie Dixon, and Wolf's original takes on "Back Door Man," "Spoonful," "The Red Rooster," "Wang Dang Doodle," and "I Ain't Superstitious" are truly the definitive ones, a place where personality and material symbiotically become as one. Even if you have already have this material, diehard Wolf fans—and audiophiles in particular—will want to investigate this package as the master transfers used here are absolutely stunning, with stereo mixes of "Killing Floor," "Built For Comfort," "Hidden Charms" (with the full-length Hubert Sumlin guitar solo), "Shake For Me," and the long version of "Going Down Slow" being particular standouts. This is a set so essential that it should on everyone's Top Ten first purchases in building the perfect blues collection. While Wolf's music will take you to many places (both musically and spiritually), here's where you start to absorb it all. — *Cub Koda*

Walk That Walk / Peavine-Chess ✦✦✦
Subtitled "Wolfman at the Chess Studio, 1957-'59," this documents at least one complete alternate take of eight titles along with a plethora of breakdowns, false starts, and studio chitchat from Leonard Chess, Wolf, and some of the sidemen on the various dates. Actually, the "Chess studio" appellation is somewhat misleading, as the majority of these sides were either cut at Sheldon or Universal, two of Chicago's best equipped and busiest studios, where the Chess brothers did much of their early recording. The real joy, of course, is hearing how all these classic tracks came together in the studio, most of them shaped into finished form by the watchful eye and ear of label owner Leonard Chess. Chess always knew what he was looking for in a great blues performance, and the opening track, "I've Been Abused," sets the tone for this collection of wonderful fly-on-the-wall recordings. "I'm Leaving You"

shows Chess working with Hubert Sumlin to nail a proper intro while getting the best out of Wolf and the rest of the band to get a finished take. "Howlin' for My Baby" is the furthest afield from the released version, as Wolf completely ignores Willie Dixon's lyrics and melody line for "Howlin' for My Darlin'," coming up with his own lyrics and tune to the riff. As Leonard Chess finally gets the drummer to lock in on a groove, he next goes after Wolf to get him back on course with middling results out of the cantankerous bluesman. "Nature" features studio chat between Wolf and one of the session players as he gets plenty steamed over the course of seven failed attempts at the song. "Moaning For My Baby" more or less comes off without a hitch, while the previously unissued instrumental "Wolf In the Mood" prompts Wolf into another altercation with Chess over the title. More nasty talk occurs on "Mr. Airplane Man" where Chess admonishes Wolf for screwing up the lyrics on the first take ("Uh Wolf, an airplane man flies, he don't sail! If he's an airplane man, he's got to fly. A boat man sails.") before starting up another attempt at the tune. The closer for this collection is the original run through of "I Better Go Now," which is followed by the first attempt to get it down on tape, a great raw moment of pure feeling. Although the practice of serving up alternate takes is a somewhat suspect one and listening to songs fall apart at a moment's notice while producer and artist cuss each other out—and it does get pretty raunchy at times—is not for everybody, hardcore Wolf (and Chess) fans will want to go the extra mile to seek this out to add to the collection anyway. Comes with a complete lyric sheet that also documents the studio chatter as well. *—Cub Koda*

Johnny Hoy

b. Connecticut
Harmonica, Vocals / Blues-Rock, Modern Electric Blues
Harmonica player, stone mason and former commercial fisherman Johnny Hoy had good reason to call his band the Bluefish. The group, based in Martha's Vineyard, are all fishing fanatics, and they decided that the basic fighting characteristics of the typical bluefish suited the personalities of everyone in the band at the time.

Hoy was born in Connecticut and raised in New England and southern California. Unlike a lot of more straightahead blues harp player/singers, he has an eclectic set of musical and songwriting influences. They include Tom Waits, James Cotton, Ellen McIlvaine, and Muddy Waters. Waters frequented a club called the Shaboo Inn in Willimantic, CT in the 1970s, and Hoy was there at every show, jaws hanging agape at the sheer musical wizardry of the band of Chicago blues veterans.

Hoy and the Bluefish play a wide range of American roots music, not just Chicago blues, and this is reflected on their two albums for the Boston-based ToneCool Records. Hoy describes his band as a house-rockin' ensemble that enjoys playing clubs as much as it does theaters. Hoy and the Bluefish sneak zydeco music, some early rock 'n' roll, some jump/swing blues, New Orleans funk, and rockabilly into their live shows.

The band cut their collective musical teeth in the greater Boston area, playing numerous functions on Martha's Vineyard, where Hoy has lived for the last two decades. On several occasions, they have played private parties for President Clinton and other Democratic party leaders.

The band's two releases on ToneCool have titles that are both clever references to bluefishing jargon, *Trolling the Hootchy* (1995) and *You Gonna Lose Your Head* (1996). Their raw, garage band sounds are sure to delight fans of roadhouse blues and blues-rock for years to come. *—Richard Skelly*

Trolling the Hootchy / 1995 / Tone-Cool ✦✦✦✦
The official blues party band of Martha's Vineyard steps up to the plate with this debut disc featuring 13 tunes from the band's voluminous set list, including four originals from the pen of bandleader/harmonica man Johnny Hoy. Johnny's wife Barbara plays a rock-solid, nuthin'-fancy bass that drives the rhythm section, even with no less than three different players occupying the drum stool during the recording of this session. Jeremy Berlin's boogie piano is exceptionally fine, and he just may be the secret weapon on this album. Co-producer Danny Kortchmar contributes great guitar on six tracks, while Buck Shank provides a twangier approach on "Little Upsetter," "Johnny McEldoo," "Young and Restless," "Hidden Charms," and a duet between the Hoys on Willie Dixon's "Howlin' for My Darling." The originals stand up nicely against the set staples, and the singing is fresh and invigorating (particularly

compelling is Hoy's chromatic turn on "Tennessee Waltz"), making this one potent party album. *— Cub Koda*

● **You Gonna Lose Your Head** / 1996 / Tone-Cool ✦✦✦✦
The Hoys (singer-songwriter/harmonica ace Johnny and his rock-solid bass-playing partner, Barbara Puciul Hoy) get way more adventurous on their second album with a brace of fresh tunes and finely picked covers. Johnny wrote nine of the 14 tracks on here and demonstrates a big jump forward in the songwriting department with "Beer Bellied Man," "Red Door," and "Made for One Another," heading the band into new waters this time around. Great covers of Lazy Lester's "You Better Listen," John Lee "Sonny Boy" Williamson's "Mellow Chick Swing," and Muddy Waters' "Just to Be With You" are worthy additions to the track lineup. While Jeremy Berlin's fine piano is still aboard, the infusion of new blood in the ranks (Slim Bob Berosh on guitar for five tracks and Tauras Biskis kicking the drums around steadily) makes this second effort far more fun and interesting than the debut disc, showing that here's a band in it for the long haul. The party just keeps getting better. *—Cub Koda*

Walk the Plank / Apr. 7, 1998 / Tone-Cool ✦✦✦✦
Martha's Vineyard's favorite party band comes back to the table with another strong album. As usual, Hoy brings a wide variety of blues to the party, ranging from the cut shuffle "If You Love Me" (which features a duet vocal with wife/Bluefish bassist Barbara Puciul Hoy) to the slow-grind shuffle of Roosevelt Sykes' "I'm Tired" to the driving boogie of "You, You, You." There's a strong preponderance of original material emanating from Hoy's pen on this (ten of the songs are his), and the playing is top notch throughout. *—Cub Koda*

Joe Hughes

b. 1938, Houston, TX
Guitar, Vocals / Electric Texas Blues, Texas Blues
Houston was homebase to a remarkable cadre of red-hot blues guitarists during the 1950s. Joe Hughes may not be known as widely as his peers Albert Collins and Johnny Copeland but he's a solid journeyman with a growing discography.

Another of his Houston neighbors, Johnny "Guitar" Watson, lit a performing fire in a 14-year-old Hughes. Lone Star stalwarts T-Bone Walker and Gatemouth Brown also exerted their influence on Hughes' playing. His path crossed Copeland's circa 1953, when the two shared vocal and guitar duties in a combo called the Dukes of Rhythm. Hughes served as bandleader at a local blues joint known as Shady's Playhouse from 1958 through 1963, cutting a few scattered singles of his own in his spare time ("I Can't Go On This Way," "Ants in My Pants," "Shoe Shy") In 1963, Hughes hit the road with the Upsetters, switching to the employ of Bobby "Blue" Bland in 1965 (he also recorded behind the singer for Duke) and Al "T.N.T." Braggs from 1967 to 1969.

A long dry spell followed, but Hughes finally came back to the spotlight with a fine set for Black Top in 1989, *If You Want to See These Blues* (by that time, he'd inserted a "Guitar" as his middle name, much like his old pal Watson). Hughes' latest set for Bullseye Blues, 1996's *Texas Guitar Slinger,* is a slashing blend of blues and soul with tightly arranged horns and more than enough axe to fulfill Hughes' adopted nickname. *—Bill Dahl*

Texas Guitar Master Craftsman / 1988 / Double Trouble ✦✦✦

Craftsman / 1988 / Double Trouble ✦✦✦

● **If You Want to See These Blues** / 1989 / Black Top ✦✦✦✦
This contemporary of Albert Collins and Johnny Copeland only recently began accruing his own share of immortality—and it really started with this fine album, recorded in both New Orleans and Houston. Hughes' clean, crisp guitar work and hearty vocals may not be quite as distinctive as those of his Houston pals, but he's an authentic Texas blues guitarist all the way. *—Bill Dahl*

Texas Guitar Slinger / Mar. 1996 / Bullseye Blues ✦✦✦✦
The versatile Hughes at times slips a little soul influence into his Lone Star blues conception on this satisfying album. He stakes his undeniable claim as a "Texas Guitar Slinger" on one of the set's best songs, a gent who deserves enshrinement right alongside Johnny Copeland and Albert Collins. No argument there—he was there when they all got started. *—Bill Dahl*

Helen Humes

b. Jun. 23, 1913, Louisville, KY, d. Sep. 9, 1981, Santa Monica, CA
Vocals / Swing, Piedmont Blues, Jump Blues, Classic Female Blues, Prewar Country Blues

Helen Humes was a versatile singer equally skilled on blues, swing standards, and ballads. Her cheerful style was always a joy to hear. As a child she played piano and organ in church and made her first recordings (ten blues in 1927) when she was only 13 and 14. In the 1930s she worked with Stuff Smith and Al Sears, recording with Harry James in 1937-38. In 1938 Humes joined Count Basie's Orchestra for three years. Since Jimmy Rushing specialized in blues, Helen Humes mostly got stuck singing pop ballads but she did a fine job. After freelancing in New York (1941-43) and touring with Clarence Love (1943-44), Humes moved to Los Angeles. She began to record as a leader and had a hit in "Be-ba-ba-le-ba"; her 1950 original "Million Dollar Secret" is a classic. Humes sometimes performed with Jazz at the Philharmonic but was mostly a single in the 1950s. She recorded three superb albums for Contemporary during 1959-61 and had tours with Red Norvo. She moved to Australia in 1964, returning to the US in 1967 to take care of her ailing mother. Humes was out of the music business for several years but made a full comeback in 1973 and stayed busy up until her death. Throughout her career Helen Humes recorded for such labels as Savoy, Aladdin, Mercury, Decca, Dootone, Contemporary, Classic Jazz, Black & Blue, Black Lion, Jazzology, Columbia, and Muse. — *Scott Yanow*

1927-1945 / Apr. 30, 1927-1945 / Classics ✦✦✦✦
When she was just 13 and 14 years old, Helen Humes made her recording debut, cutting ten risque, double-entendre-filled blues, naughty tunes that she later claimed to understand at the time. Until the release of this Classics CD in 1996, those numbers (which have backup in various settings by either De Loise Searcy or J.C. Johnson on piano and Lonnie Johnson or the guitar duo team of Sylvester Weaver and Walter Beasley) had never been reissued on the same set before. Humes sounds fairly mature on the enjoyable blues sides. Her next session as a leader would not take place until 15 years later, when she was 28 and a veteran of Count Basie's Orchestra. The singer is heard here with groups in 1942 and 1944-45, performing three numbers with altoist Pete Brown's sextet (a band including trumpeter Dizzy Gillespie, who unfortunately does not solo), Leonard Feather's Hiptet (which has some rare solos from trumpeter Bobby Stark) and Bill Doggett's spirited octet. The latter date is highlighted by classic renditions of "He May Be Your Man" and "Be-Baba-Leba." Highly recommended. — *Scott Yanow*

Be-Baba-Leba / Nov. 20, 1944-Nov. 20, 1950 / Savoy ✦✦✦✦
Subtitled "The Rhythm and Blues Years," this highly enjoyable LP features the underrated and always cheerful singer Helen Humes in 1944 for four songs with Leonard Feather's Hip-tet (swing-oriented tunes that have been reissued on a Classics CD) and in 1950 with bands led by altoist Marshall Royal, drummer Roy Milton (a live date), and tenor great Dexter Gordon. Humes had a flexible style that could sound quite credible on blues, ballads, swing, and early R&B. Among the many superior numbers heard from the 1950 dates are "This Love of Mine," "He May Be Your Man," "Be-Baba-Leba" and "Helen's Advice." Hopefully, all of this music will be reissued on CD. — *Scott Yanow*

1947 / Aug. 1947-1948 / Trip ✦✦✦✦
The three sessions on this 1970s Trip LP were originally cut for Mercury but have not yet been reissued on CD by Polygram. That is a pity, for the dozen selections feature Helen Humes in prime form, backed by the type of groups that accompanied Billie Holiday a decade earlier. Trumpeter Buck Clayton, tenor saxophonist John Hardee, and (on one session) pianist Teddy Wilson all make their presence known, but Humes is the main star. Able to sing anything from lowdown blues to ballads and swinging stomps with equal skill, Humes is particularly memorable on "Jet Propelled Papa," "They Raided the Joint," "Flippity Flop Flop," and "Married Man Blues." Although it will be difficult to find, this album is worth tracking down. — *Scott Yanow*

'Tain't Nobody's Biz-Ness If I Do / Jan. 5, 1959-Feb. 10, 1959 / Original Jazz Classics ✦✦✦✦
Helen Humes had not recorded as a leader in seven years when she made the first of three albums for Contemporary, all of which have been reissued on CD in the OJC series. Humes, 45 at the time, was at the peak of her

powers, although she never really made a bad record. Accompanied by Benny Carter (on trumpet), trombonist Frank Rosolino, tenor saxophonist Teddy Edwards, pianist Andrew Previn, bassist Leroy Vinnegar, and either Shelly Manne or Mel Lewis on drums, the singer is typically enthusiastic, exuberant, and highly appealing on such numbers as "You Can Depend on Me," "When I Grow Too Old to Dream," and " 'Tain't Nobody's Biz-Ness If I Do." She even sings credible versions of "Bill Bailey" and "When the Saints Go Marching In" on this easily recommended CD. — *Scott Yanow*

★ **Songs I Like to Sing** / Sep. 6, 1960-Sep. 8, 1960 / Original Jazz Classics ✦✦✦✦✦
One of the high points of Helen Humes' career, this Contemporary set (reissued on CD) features superior songs, superb backup and very suitable and swinging arrangements by Marty Paich. Humes' versions of "If I Could Be With You," "You're Driving Me Crazy," and "Million Dollar Secret," in particular, are definitive. On four songs, she is backed by tenor great Ben Webster, a rhythm section, and a string quartet; the other numbers find her joined by a 14-piece band that includes Webster and Teddy Edwards on tenors, along with altoist Art Pepper. This classic release is essential and shows just how appealing a singer Helen Humes could be. — *Scott Yanow*

Swingin' with Humes / Jul. 27, 1961-Jul. 29, 1961 / Original Jazz Classics ✦✦✦✦
The third of Helen Humes' three memorable Contemporary releases, all of which are out on CD, features the distinctive singer on a dozen standards that she had missed documenting thus far. With fine backup work by trumpeter Joe Gordon, tenor saxophonist Teddy Edwards, pianist Wynton Kelly, guitarist Al Viola, bassist Leroy Vinnegar, and drummer Frank Butler, Humes is in top form on such tunes as "When Day Is Done," "There'll Be Some Changes Made," "Pennies From Heaven," and "The Very Thought of You." One of her better albums. — *Scott Yanow*

Sneakin' Around / Mar. 16, 1974 / Classic Jazz ✦✦✦✦
Helen Humes did both bawdy, double-entendre-laden blues and R&B, and more sophisticated, jazz-tinged numbers during her career. This set, done with Gerald Badini, Gerry Wiggins, Major Holley, and Ed Thigpen, had a little of both, and was spiced up by Humes, singing with equal parts sass and grace. It was originally done for the Black and Blue label and was recently on CD. — *Ron Wynn*

On the Sunny Side of The Street / Jul. 2, 1974 / Black Lion ✦✦✦✦
Several major jazz personalities are heard on this Black Lion reissue CD, recorded live at the 1974 Montreux Jazz Festival. The fine singer Helen Humes sticks to standards and blues while accompanied by either Earl Hines or Jay McShann on piano, tenor-saxophonist Buddy Tate, bassist Jimmy Woode, and drummer Ed Thigpen. Although Hines and McShann are not the ideal accompanists, Humes fares quite well, winning the audience over with her enthusiasm and sincerity. — *Scott Yanow*

Helen Humes [Audiophile] / 1974 / Audiophile ✦✦✦✦
This lesser-known Helen Humes album features the veteran singer in an intimate setting with pianist Connie Berry, guitarist Charlie Howard, and bassist Al Autry. Because she primarily sticks to ballads on the set (including "Wrap Your Troubles In Dreams," "Embraceable You," "A Hundred Years From Today," and a wonderful version of "More Than You Know"), this date lacks the excitement of her best albums. However, Helen Humes fans are well aware that she never made an indifferent or uninteresting record and will want this obscure effort too. — *Scott Yanow*

Talk of the Town / Feb. 18, 1975 / Columbia ✦✦✦✦
Two years into her return from a six-year retirement, Helen Humes was at the height of her fame when she reunited with producer John Hammond to make her lone Columbia album. Joined by Buddy Tate (doubling on tenor and clarinet), guitarist George Benson (a Hammond discovery a decade earlier), pianist Ellis Larkins, bassist Major Holley, and drummer Oliver Jackson, Humes is in fine form for a fairly typical mixture of blues, standards, and ballads. She sounds particularly inspired during "He May Be Your Man," "Every Now and Then," "If I Could Be With You," and "Deed I Do." — *Scott Yanow*

● **Helen Humes and the Muse All Stars** / Oct. 5, 1979 + Oct. 8, 1978 / Muse ✦✦✦✦
Helen Humes' return to an active singing career was one of the happier events in jazz of the late '70s. Able to give great feeling and sensitivity to

ballads but also a superb lowdown blues singer, Humes flourished musically during her last years. On this excellent release (the CD reissue adds two alternate takes to the original program), Humes matches wits with altoist/ singer Eddie "Cleanhead" Vinson on "I'm Gonna Move to the Outskirts of Town" and is in top form throughout. Tenors Arnett Cobb and Buddy Tate (along with a fine rhythm section led by pianist Gerald Wiggins) don't hurt either. An enthusiastic "Loud Talking Woman" and "My Old Flame" are highpoints. — *Scott Yanow*

Helen / Jun. 17, 1980 + Jun. 19, 1980 / Muse ♦♦♦♦
Helen Humes was one of the most appealing jazz singers of the late '30s, and of the late '70s. Her comeback in her last few years was a welcome event, and all of her recordings for Muse are recommended. This one finds her backed by a veteran sextet including tenorman Buddy Tate, trumpeter Joe Wilder, and pianist Norman Simmons. Her versions of "There'll Be Some Changes Made," "Easy Living," and "Draggin' My Heart Around" are particularly memorable. — *Scott Yanow*

Let the Good Times Roll / Aug. 1981 / Classic Jazz ♦♦♦♦
Helen Humes had been retired for several years (and off record since 1961) when she began her comeback with this set. Recorded for the French Black & Blue label and made available domestically on a Classic Jazz LP, the album mostly features the veteran swing singer doing remakes, some of which top her earlier versions. Louis Jordan's "They Raided the Joint" is an exciting opener and is matched by "That Old Feeling," "Be-Baba-Leba," "He May Be Your Man," and Humes' classic "A Million Dollar Secret." Particularly strong assets in her notable backup group are tenorman Arnett Cobb, guitarists Al Casey and Clarence "Gatemouth" Brown, pianist Jay McShann, and organist Milt Buckner. Wonderful music that deserves to be made widely available. — *Scott Yanow*

Mark Hummel

b. Dec. 15, 1955, New Haven, CT
Harmonica, Harp, Vocals / Modern Electric Blues, Blues-Rock, Electric Harmonica Blues
Harmonica player, songwriter and singer Mark Hummel is a practitioner of the West Coast blues style, which typically includes elements of jazz and swing. A seasoned bandleader, Hummel is finally beginning to achieve wider recognition through nearly constant touring. Hummel was born in New Haven, CT, but raised in Los Angeles, CA. He became fascinated with the blues-rock of Cream, Jimi Hendrix, Big Brother and the Holding Company, and the Rolling Stones. After seeing songwriter credits on the albums, he began to dig further back into those bands' blues roots. He began playing harmonica in his teens in order to be different from the huge pack of guitar players in his high school. Hummel studied the styles of the Chicago-based players, including James Cotton, Sonny Boy Williamson, Big Walter "Shakey" Horton, and Little Walter Jacobs. Hummel moved to Berkeley, CA, in 1972 and played with local bluesmen there, including Boogie Jake, Cool Papa, Johnny Waters, and Sonny Lane. After graduating high school, he hitchhiked around the country for three years, making stops in New Orleans, Boston, and Chicago to learn from those cities' top players. In 1980, he formed the Blues Survivors, who have since performed at numerous blues festivals around the US, including the Chicago Blues Festival and the San Francisco Blues Festival. Hummel has released a number of self-produced albums around his Oakland, CA, home, including *Playing In Your Town* (1985, Rockinitis Records), *Up & Jumpin'* (with Canadian guitarist Sue Foley, 1989-90), and *Hard Lovin'* (1992, Double Trouble Records). His widely available albums include *Feel Like Rockin'* (1994, Flying Fish Records), *Married To The Blues* (1995, Flying Fish), and most recently, *Heart of Chicago* (1997, Tone-Cool/Rounder), an album recorded in Chicago on which Hummel is accompanied by some veteran Chicago sidemen, including drummer Willie "Big Eyes" Smith, guitarist Dave Myers, and producer/guitarist Steve Freund. Considered one of the top harmonica players in the US, Hummel has also judged and played in the Hohner Harmonica World Championships, held in Germany. — *Richard Skelly*

Hard Lovin' 90's / 1992 / Double Trouble ♦♦♦♦
Harmonica Party / 1993 / Double Trouble ♦♦♦
Feel Like Rockin' / 1994 / Flying Fish ♦♦♦
● **Married to the Blues** / Oct. 1995 / Flying Fish ♦♦♦♦
Married to the Blues is one of Mark Hummel's finest releases, since it gives

him ample opportunity to showcase his greasy, overdriven harmonica. The songs themselves aren't particularly distinctive, but they are good vehicles for him to strut his stuff, and that alone makes it a thoroughly enjoyable record. — *Thom Owens*

Heart of Chicago / Jan. 14, 1997 / Tone-Cool ♦♦♦
This collection of harmonica workouts gets rather tedious after a short while. Only devoted fans of harmonica blues will be able to stomach the onslaught of honking, as well as Hummel's thin voice, which is not suited to the task at hand. — *Tim Sheridan*

Alberta Hunter

b. Apr. 1, 1895, Memphis, TN, d. Oct. 17, 1984, Roosevelt, NY
Vocals / Standards, Classic Female Blues
An early blues vocalist in the 1920s, a sophisticated supper club singer in the 1930s, and a survivor in the 1980s, Alberta Hunter had quite a career. Hunter actually debuted in clubs as a singer as early as 1912, starting out in Chicago. She made her first recording in 1921, wrote "Down Hearted Blues" (which became Bessie Smith's first hit) and used such sidemen on her recordings in the 1920s as Fletcher Henderson, Eubie Blake, Fats Waller, Louis Armstrong, and Sidney Bechet. She starred in *Showboat* with Paul Robeson at the London Palladium (1928-29), worked in Paris, and recorded straight ballads with John Jackson's Orchestra. After returning to the US, Hunter worked for the USO during World War II and Korea, singing overseas. She retired in 1956 to become a nurse (she was 61 at the time) and continued in that field (other than a 1961 recording) until she was forced to retire in 1977 when it was believed she was 65; actually Hunter was 82! She then made a startling comeback in jazz, singing regularly at the Cookery in New York until she was 89, writing the music for the 1978 film *Remember My Name* and recording for Columbia. After the 1920s, Alberta Hunter recorded on an infrequent basis but her dates from 1935, 1939, 1940, and 1950 have been mostly reissued by Stash, her Bluesville album (1961) is out in the OJC series and her Columbia sets are still available. — *Scott Yanow*

The Twenties / 1921-1925 / Stash ♦♦♦♦

Classic Alberta Hunter: The Thirties / 1933-1950 / Stash ♦♦♦♦
After returning to the United States from England in 1935, Alberta Hunter continued working as a jazz-oriented singer in the US although she maintained a lower profile than in the 1920s. She just had three recording sessions during 1935-40 (all of the music is included on this valuable LP) and eight numbers in 1950 (two of which are here) prior to retiring from music in the mid-'50s to become a nurse. Among the highlights of these 15 selections by the timeless singer are "You Can't Tell the Difference After Dark," a remake of "Downhearted Blues," "Someday, Sweetheart," and "My Castle's Rockin'." In the backup groups on some numbers are trumpeter Charlie Shavers, clarinetist Buster Bailey, and either Lil Armstrong or Eddie Heywood on piano among others. Recommended. — *Scott Yanow*

The Legendary Alberta Hunter: '34 London Sessions / Sep. 24, 1934-Nov. 2, 1934 / DRG ♦♦
This handsome LP is a bit of an oddity. Alberta Hunter, famous as a jazz-oriented blues singer in the 1920s, reinvented herself as a sophisticated stage singer in London. Her 11 recordings with Jack Jackson's society dance orchestra in 1934 are very straight, outside of jazz and somewhat dated today. Whether it be "Two Cigarettes in the Dark," "Miss Otis Regrets," or "Two Little Flies on a Lump of Sugar," Hunter interprets the romantic ballads like a cabaret singer. So, although this reissue was perfectly done (with extensive liner notes), there is little here to interest jazz listeners. — *Scott Yanow*

Songs We Taught Your Mother / Aug. 1961 / Original Blues Classics ♦♦♦
Although Alberta Hunter, who had briefly come out of retirement, gets first billing on this CD reissue, in reality she shares the spotlight with two other veterans of the 1920s: Lucille Hegamin and Victoria Spivey. Each of the singers is featured on four songs apiece while backed by such top players as clarinetist Buster Bailey, trombonist J.C. Higginbottham, and Cliff Jackson or Willie "The Lion" Smith on piano. Hunter is in superior form on such numbers as "You Gotta Reap What You Sow" and "I Got a Mind to Ramble," although she would soon be out of music for another 15 years, continuing her work as a nurse. Hegamin (who had not recorded since 1932) was having a brief last hurrah, despite sounding good, and Spivey, reviving her "Black Snake Blues," would soon be launching her own Spivey label. This is a his-

toric and enjoyable set recommended to both classic jazz and blues collectors. — *Scott Yanow*

Chicago: The Living Legends / Aug. 16, 1961 / Riverside ◆◆◆
This CD reissue is notable for two main reasons. It finds Alberta Hunter (who had retired from music in 1954 to become a nurse and who in the interim had only recorded once, two weeks earlier) in peak form on such numbers as "St. Louis Blues," "Downhearted Blues," and "You Better Change." In addition, it was pianist Lovie Austin's first recording in a couple decades; she was nearly 74 at the time and working as pianist at a Chicago dancing school. Austin's "Blues Serenaders" (a quintet also including trombonist Jimmy Archey, clarinetist Darnell Howard, bassist Pops Foster and drummer Jasper Taylor) has some concise solo space on the vocal pieces, and takes three numbers (including Austin's "Gallion Stomp") as instrumentals. A well-conceived and historic set. — *Scott Yanow*

Remember My Name / 1977 / Columbia ◆◆◆◆
Although the cover on this album makes it look as if this is a soundtrack album (the singer had written several songs for the film "Remember My Name"), this is actually an important studio set. Alberta Hunter, a veteran of the 1920s who was 82 at the time, was at the beginning of a remarkable comeback after having been out of music for 20 years (working as a nurse). The singer is absolutely delightful and often saucy on such numbers as "You Gotta Reap What You Sow," "I've Got A Mind To Ramble," "My Castle's Rockin'," and "Downhearted Blues," making this her definitive late-period album. In addition to Hunter and a fine rhythm section (pianist Gerald Cook, guitarist Wally Richardson, bassist Al Hall, and either Connie Kay or Jackie Williams on drums), three veteran horn players (trumpeter Doc Cheatham, trombonist Vic Dickenson, and tenorman Budd Johnson) help out with short solos. Highly recommended. — *Scott Yanow*

Amtrack Blues / 1978 / Columbia ◆◆◆
Alberta Hunter's second recording since launching her remarkable comeback (she was 83 when this album was cut) finds the veteran blues singer (a survivor of the 1920s) still in surprisingly strong form and full of spirit. Such songs as "Darktown Strutters' Ball," "My Handy Man," "Old Fashioned Love," and "I've Got a Mind To Ramble" are given fine treatment by Hunter who is joined by the Gerald Cook quartet, trombonist Vic Dickenson, trumpeter Doc Cheatham, and tenorman Frank Wess on various tracks. Unfortunately none of Alberta Hunter's four Columbia albums have yet been reissued on CD but all are worth searching for. — *Scott Yanow*

Glory of Alberta Hunter / 1981 / Columbia ◆◆◆◆
Alberta Hunter's comeback after 20 years off the music scene was quite inspiring. She was (along with Sippie Wallace) virtually the only classic blues singer of the 1920s still active during part of the 1980s, and her four Columbia albums (of which this was the third) are surprisingly strong. With able backing by the Gerald Cook quartet, trumpeter Doc Cheatham, trombonist Vic Dickenson, and tenor-saxophonist Budd Johnson, Alberta Hunter sings some standards ("Some of These Days," "The Glory of Love," and "I Cried for You"), a few religious hymns ("Ezekiel Saw the Wheel" and "Give Me That Old Time Religion"), the Yiddish tune "Ich Hob Dich Tzufil Lieba" and her own "Alberta's Blues" and "The Love I Have for You." — *Scott Yanow*

Look for the Silver Lining / 1982 / Columbia ◆◆◆◆
Classic blues singer Alberta Hunter's final recording (made when she was 87, two years before her death) is as powerful as her previous three Columbia albums. The legendary delightful singer puts plenty of feeling into "Look for the Silver Lining," "He's Funny That Way," "Somebody Loves Me," and four of her originals. As was true of each of her final sets, Hunter is joined by the Gerald Cook quartet and several veteran horn players (trumpeters Doc Cheatham and Jonah Jones, trombonist Vic Dickenson, and tenorman Budd Johnson), all of whom sound quite happy to be supporting the ancient yet ageless singer. — *Scott Yanow*

Complete Recorded Works, Vol. 1 (1921-1923) / Feb. 15, 1996 / Document ◆◆◆
For completists, specialists and academics, Document's *Complete Recorded Works, Vol. 1 (1921-1923)* is an invaluable overview of Alberta Hunter's early recordings. For less dedicated listeners, the long running time, exacting chronological sequencing, and poor fidelity (all cuts are transferred from original acetates and 78s) will be hard to digest. The serious blues listener will find

all these factors to be positive, but casual listeners will find that the collection is of marginal interest for those very reasons. — *Thom Owens*

Complete Recorded Works, Vol. 2 (1923-24) / Mar. 5, 1996 / Document ◆◆◆

Complete Recorded Works, Vol. 3 (1924-27) / Apr. 9, 1996 / Document ◆◆◆

Complete Recorded Works, Vol. 4 (1927-46) / Apr. 9, 1996 / Document ◆◆◆

Alternate Takes (1921-1924) / Sep. 23, 1997 / Document ◆◆◆

● **Young Alberta Hunter: The Twenties** / Vintage Jazz ◆◆◆◆
This LP gives listeners a strong sampling of singer Alberta Hunter's work in the 1920s. The 14 selections find her joined by such major jazz names as pianists Fletcher Henderson and Eubie Blake, cornetist Louis Armstrong, soprano-saxophonist Sidney Bechet, and Fats Waller (on organ). Although best-known during the era as a classic blues singer, Hunter was always flexible and able to sing a wide variety of material. The best way to acquire all of her 1920s recordings are through her Document CDs but this LP sampler is excellent with the highlights including "Down Hearted Blues" (her composition which Bessie Smith would make into a big hit in 1923), "Nobody Knows The Way I Feel Dis Morning," "If You Can't Hold the Man You Love," and "I'm Going to See My Ma." — *Scott Yanow*

Ivory Joe Hunter

b. Oct. 10, 1914, Kirbyville, TX, **d.** Nov. 8, 1974, Memphis, TN
Piano, Vocals / R&B, West Coast Blues, Piano Blues
Bespectacled and velvet-smooth in the vocal department, pianist Ivory Joe Hunter appeared too much mild-mannered to be a rock 'n' roller. But when the rebellious music first crashed the American consciousness in the mid-'50s, there was Ivory Joe, deftly delivering his blues ballad "Since I Met You Baby" right alongside the wildest pioneers of the era.

Hunter was already a grizzled R&B vet by that time who had first heard his voice on a 1933 Library of Congress cylinder recording made in Texas (where he grew up). An accomplished tunesmith, he played around the Gulf Coast region, hosting his own radio program for a time in Beaumont before migrating to California in 1942. It was a wise move; Hunter (whose real name was Ivory Joe, incidentally—perhaps his folks were psychic!) found plenty of work pounding out blues and ballads in wartime California. He started his own label, Ivory Records, to press up his "Blues at Sunrise" (with Johnny Moore's Three Blazers backing him), and it became a national hit when leased to Leon Rene's Exclusive imprint in 1945. Another Hunter enterprise, Pacific Records, hosted a major hit in 1948 when the pianist's "Pretty Mama Blues" topped the R&B charts for three weeks.

At whatever logo Hunter paused from the mid-'40s through the late '50s, his platters sold like hotcakes. For Cincinnati-based King in 1948-49, he hit with "Don't Fall in Love with Me," "What Did You Do to Me," "Waiting in Vain," and "Guess Who." At MGM, then new to the record biz, he cut his immortal "I Almost Lost My Mind" (another R&B chart-topper in 1950), "I Need You So" (later covered by Elvis), and "It's a Sin." Signing with Atlantic in 1954, he hit big with "Since I Met You Baby" in 1956 and the two-sided smash "Empty Arms"/"Love's A Hurting Game" in 1957.

Hunter's fondness for country music reared its head in 1958. Upon switching to Dot Records, he scored his last pop hit with a cover of Bill Anderson's "City Lights." Hunter's Dot encores went nowhere; neither did typically mellow outings for Vee-Jay, Smash, Capitol, and Veep. Epic went so far as to recruit a simmering Memphis band (including organist Isaac Hayes, trumpeter Gene "Bowlegs" Miller, and saxist Charles Chalmers) for an LP titled *The Return of Ivory Joe Hunter* that hoped to revitalize his career, but it wasn't meant to be. The album's cover photo—a closeup of Hunter's grinning face with a cigarette dangling from his lips—seems grimly ironic in the face of his death from lung cancer only a few years later. — *Bill Dahl*

16 of His Greatest Hits / 1958 / King ◆◆◆
Other than ruining his 1949 smash "Guess Who" entirely with hideous stereo overdubs, King has done pretty well by the pianist on this collection of his post-war output for the Cincinnati firm. Hunter was primarily in a sentimental blues ballad bag back then, some of his hits displaying a tinge of country influence. Sound quality is okay if not superlative. — *Bill Dahl*

The Return of Ivory Joe Hunter / 1971 / Epic ♦♦♦

Commendable attempt to update Ivory Joe Hunter's sound for early-'70s consumption, with an all-star Memphis aggregation that included Isaac Hayes on organ, saxist Charlie Chalmers, and a sax section lifted from the Hi studios. The ploy worked reasonably well, producing updated remakes of Hunter's hits and tasty versions of Don Covay's "I'm Coming Down with the Blues" and Chuck Willis' "What Am I Living For." — *Bill Dahl*

7th Street Boogie / 1980 / Route 66 ♦♦♦♦

These are wonderful mid-'40s and early-'50s sides from an extremely versatile vocalist and sorely neglected composer and pianist. Ivory Joe Hunter could sing everything from blues to soul to gospel to country magnificently; this is predominantly blues and R&B fare. — *Ron Wynn*

● **Since I Met You Baby: The Best of Ivory Joe Hunter** / Oct. 19, 1994 / Razor & Tie ♦♦♦♦

Bespectacled pianist Ivory Joe Hunter's crooning blues balladry made him a hot commodity from the late '40s through the late '50s, but he could rock reasonably convincingly hard too. He does both on this wonderful survey of his 1949-1958 MGM and Atlantic sides—"I Need You So," "I Almost Lost My Mind," and the title item are sophisticated and mellow, while "Rockin' Chair Boogie," "Love Is a Hurting Game," and "Shooty Booty" find the pianist in decidedly unsentimental moods. — *Bill Dahl*

Jumping at the Dew Drop / Route 66 ♦♦♦

A European import slab of vinyl offering an overview of Hunter's 1947-1952 pre-Atlantic days. Emphasis on jump entries ("Are You Hep?," "She's a Killer," "We're Gonna Boogie," "Old Man's Boogie") is a welcome change-of-pace from Hunter's better-known propensity for velvety blues ballads. — *Bill Dahl*

Long John Hunter

b. 1931, LA

Guitar, Vocals / Texas Blues

For much too long, the legend of Long John Hunter has largely been a local one, limited to the bordertown region between El Paso, Texas and Juarez, Mexico. That's where the guitarist reigned for 13 years (beginning in 1957) at Juarez's infamous Lobby Bar. Its riotous, often brawling clientele included locals, cowboys, soldiers from nearby Fort Bliss, frat boys, and every sort of troublemaking tourist in between. Hunter kept 'em all entertained with his outrageous showmanship and slashing guitar riffs.

The Louisiana native got a late start on his musical career. When he was 22 and toiling away in a Beaumont, TX box factory, he attended a B.B. King show and was instantly transfixed. The next day, he bought a guitar. A year later, he was starring at the same bar that B.B. had headlined.

Hunter's 1954 debut single for Don Robey's Houston-based Duke label, "She Used to Be My Woman"/"Crazy Baby," preceded his move to El Paso in 1957. Along the way, Phillip Walker and Lonnie Brooks both picked up on his licks. But Hunter's recording output was slim—a few hot but obscure singles waxed from 1961 to 1963 for the tiny Yucca logo out of Alamogordo, NM (standouts include "El Paso Rock," "Midnight Stroll," and "Border Town Blues"). Perhaps he was just too busy—he held court at the Lobby seven nights a week from sundown to sunup.

Fortunately, Hunter's reputation is finally outgrowing the Lone Star state. His 1992 set for the now-shuttered Spindletop imprint, *Ride With Me*, got the ball rolling. Now, his 1996 disc for Alligator, *Border Town Legend*, should expose this Texas blues great to a far wider (if not wilder) audience than ever before. — *Bill Dahl*

Texas Border Town Blues / 1988 / Double Trouble ♦♦♦

Ride with Me / 1992 / Spindletop ♦♦♦♦

After too many years of being a dusty, distant Texas blues rumor, Long John Hunter happily sprang to life with this 1993 comeback effort for short-lived Spindletop Records. While not as polished or as gloriously consistent as his recent Alligator disc, which should finally catapult him to national recognition, the album does an impressive job of showcasing Hunter's ringing, angular guitar work and twangy vocals. — *Bill Dahl*

Smooth Magic / Dec. 20, 1994 / Double Trouble ♦♦♦♦

● **Border Town Legend** / Jan. 30, 1996 / Alligator ♦♦♦♦

For many years Long John Hunter played in clubs without much attention, but that time sweating it out in roadhouses has paid off. During that time, he developed a gutsy, forceful technique that was fully evident on his belated 1993 debut, *Ride With Me*. Although his second album, *Border Town Legend*, is a slicker, more accessible effort, Hunter hasn't lost any of his spicy, distinctive flavor. Working with a horn section, he still manages to make himself the most powerful element on the record—both his guitar playing and his heated vocals ensure that. Furthermore, Hunter's songwriting is growing stronger. Out of the nine songs he has written or co-written for the album, he has contributed some first-rate tunes that might not stretch beyond generic conventions, but still are mighty fine. — *Stephen Thomas Erlewine*

Swinging from the Rafters / Sep. 2, 1997 / Alligator ♦♦♦♦

Long John's second album for the Alligator imprint is even more potent than his first, *Texas Border Legend*. This time around, Hunter's sly, drawling vocals and stinging clusters of guitar are well to the fore, keeping the spotlight firmly in place on this Texas guitar legend. The record was cut in Austin and Abilene, TX, and as such boasts Lone Star talent like Derek O'Brien, who plays rhythm guitar on this disc and solos on "I Don't Care" and "V-8 Ford." Mark "Kaz" Kazanoff blows saxophone on eight tunes and harmonica on "Locksmith Man." For his part, Hunter contributes 10 of the 14 tunes, co-writing with various members of his Walking Catfish Band or his co-producers, Tary Owens and John Foose. Long John's no-holds-barred approach literally screams Texas blues, letting you know you're listening to an originator, not an imitator. — *Cub Koda*

Mississippi John Hurt

b. Jul. 3, 1893, Teoc, MS, **d.** Nov. 2, 1966, Grenada, MS

Guitar, Harmonica, Vocals / Acoustic Blues, Country Blues, Prewar Country Blues, Delta Blues, Blues Revival

The history of Mississippi John Hurt reads like a real Cinderella story. Born John Smith Hurt on July 3, 1893, in Teoc (Carroll Co.), MS, his family moved to Avalon, MS (where he grew up) when he was two years of age. One of ten children (who all played music of one sort or another), Hurt was the most into it and taught himself how to play. Years later, when his White landlord asked how he came up with his melodies, he replied, "Well sir, I just make it sound like I think it should."

Although he learned to read and write, he did not attend school past the fourth grade. As a young adult, he became a sharecropper or tenant farmer for many years, but finally gave that up and switched to day labor. For fun and extra cash, Hurt joined other local guitarists and fiddlers for church suppers and town dances in surrounding towns. Hurt soon became a popular favorite at these local functions.

In the late '20s, a well-known fiddler named Willie Narmour, with whom Hurt often played, was spotted by a talent scout for OKeh Phonograph, a division of Columbia Records. When asked about other talented local musicians, Narmour gave them the name of John Hurt and directions on how to find him. OKeh found and interviewed Hurt, had him play a few songs, and decided to record him, provided he was willing to travel to Memphis and New York.

Hurt recorded two songs in February of 1928 while in Memphis, "Frankie" and "Nobody's Dirty Business," and these were released by OKeh. That December, Hurt traveled to New York City to record five more sides. During that visit he met Lonnie Johnson, but made a point of declaring that he cribbed nothing from that great guitarist. Hurt's records did not sell in great numbers, perhaps in the hundreds. After his short musical excursion, John returned to Avalon and went back to sharecropping and playing music just about every Saturday night in the towns surrounding his home.

That could have been the end of Hurt's national career had two young blues musicians from Washington, DC, Tom Hoskins and Mike Stewart, not come across the original OKeh recording of "Avalon Blues." This was in 1963. Intrigued by John's intricate finger-picking style, they came up with the idea of trying to locate some of the original artists, should they still be alive. They checked the Mississippi maps, but no town named Avalon could be found. However, after locating an 1878 atlas, sure enough, there was an Avalon marked on a rural road running between Greenwood and Grenada. On a hope and a whim, the two blues archivists headed south armed with a tape recorder. With the help of the old map, they found Avalon with its single gas station/store and inquired about John Hurt.

They were floored to see the attendant point down the road and say that Hurt's house was "about a mile down that road, third mail box up the hill. Can't miss it." Hurt, at 71 years of age, was waiting for them, alive and still able to sing and play about as well as he had before. They recorded John and returned to Washington with the precious taped results and the rediscovery of Mississippi John Hurt. He was a complete and instant success in the folk/blues scene.

From the Spring of 1963, when he was brought to Washington, DC, to perform, until his death in 1966, Hurt played all over the Northeast at clubs and many folk festivals, including twice at the Newport Folk Festival. Much admired by his new-found audience, Hurt loved his late success and gave as much as he got. He was befriended by fellow performers like Doc Watson, Fred McDowell, and Elizabeth Cotten. In the end, he retired to a small home in Granada, MS, not far from his home town of Avalon. So much for a great story; the music is just as good.

Mississippi John Hurt is an exquisite country-blues singer/guitarist with a subtle voice and refined finger-picking guitar style. As mentioned, he recorded in the '20s and again in the '60s, and both periods are well worth hearing. Here is acoustic country-blues with real technical clarity that is also comforting and easy to listen to. There is a gospel flavor in Hurt's blues. Mississippi John Hurt projects a sense of dignity and kindness through all of his recordings. If you have trouble with the occasional heaviness of many blues players, you may find Hurt refreshing. — *Michael Erlewine*

Avalon Blues / Apr. 1963 / Rounder ✦✦✦✦
Recorded in April of 1963, these are part of the legacy of Hurt after his rediscovery. Contains "Avalon Blues" and "Candyman Blues"—11 cuts in all. Great. — *Michael Erlewine*

Worried Blues / Apr. 1963 / Rounder ✦✦✦✦
This is some of the Vanguard material recorded in April of 1963, not long after Hurt's rediscovery. It contains ten tracks with "Worried Blues," and "Oh Mary Don't You Weep." — *Michael Erlewine*

Memorial Anthology / Dec. 1964 / Genes ✦✦✦✦
Mississippi John Hurt's mid-'60s performances were usually distinctive and sometimes staggering. His guitar work was crisp, attractive and frequently brilliant, although his vocals were the real hook. Hurt's narratives, storytelling ability and general communicative powers were at their peak on this two-CD set, which has languished in a vault for nearly 30 years. Hurt covers such traditional numbers as "C.C. Rider" and "Staggerlee" with vigor, plays several originals, sometimes shifts to gospel, and does everything in an unassuming way that nevertheless grabs your attention. The set's treasure is a 31-minute interview with Pete Seeger in which Hurt lays bare his life, times and personality, doing so in the same steady, casual, gripping fashion that underscored his singing and playing. — *Ron Wynn*

The Best of Mississippi John Hurt [Vanguard] / 1965 / Vanguard ✦✦✦✦
Contrary to what its title would make one believe, this record is not a collection of previously available recordings by Mississippi John Hurt—rather, it is a complete concert from Oberlin College on April 15, 1965. Regardless, the title is justified, as the concert features Hurt in excellent form doing most of his best known classic songs from the 1920s as well as newer compositions. — *Bruce Eder*

Today! / 1966 / Vanguard ✦✦✦✦
This is material recorded after his rediscovery in 1963. Includes classic Hurt tunes like "Candy Man" and "Coffee Blues." Wonderful listening. — *Michael Erlewine*

Last Sessions / Feb. 1966-Jul. 1966 / Vanguard ✦✦✦✦
Recorded in New York during February and July of 1966, the 17 songs on this collection represent Mississippi John Hurt's final studio efforts. It is astonishing that this man, in the final months of his life, could do 17 songs that were the equal of anything he had done at his first sessions 45 years earlier, his playing (supported on some tracks with producer Patrick Sky on second guitar) as alluringly complex as ever and his voice still in top form. Hurt is brilliant throughout, his voice overpowering in its mixture of warmth, gentleness, and power, and in addition to the expected crop of standards and originals, he covers songs by Bukka White ("Poor Boy, Long Ways from Home") and Leadbelly ("Goodnight Irene")—all of it is worthwhile, with some tracks, such as "Let the Mermaids Flirt with Me" especially haunting. — *Bruce Eder*

The Immortal / 1967 / Vanguard ✦✦✦✦
This is the best of Hurt's '60s "rediscovery-era" recordings. — *Mark A. Humphrey*

The Mississippi John Hurt / 1968 / Vanguard ✦✦✦
A great double-album collection of '60s Hurt. — *Michael Erlewine*

1928 Sessions / 1988 / Yazoo ✦✦✦✦
The 13 original 1928 recordings of Hurt. Justifiably legendary, with gentle grace and power on these understated vocal and fingerpicking masterpieces. These are the ones to hear, although all Hurt is worth listening to. — *Michael Erlewine*

The Greatest Songsters: Complete Works (1927-1929) / 1990 / Document ✦✦✦✦
You can get a lot of arguments started about which Mississippi blues musician is the best, so let's just say that this is first-rate Mississippi John Hurt material and leave it at that. — *Ron Wynn*

★ **Avalon Blues: The Complete 1928 OKeh Recordings** / Oct. 8, 1996 / Sony ✦✦✦✦✦
Hurt's latter day recordings after his rediscovery have somewhat obscured the importance of these debut sides, the ones that made his rediscovery an idea initially worth pursuing. They are the collector's items that made his rep in the first place and stand as some of the most poetic and beautiful of all country blues recordings. Hurt's playing is sheer musical perfection, with a keen sense of chord melody structure to make his bouncy, rhythmic execution of it sound both elegant and driving. Mississippi John's voice—he was 36 at the time of these recordings—was already a warm and friendly one, imbued with the laidback wistfulness that would earmark his rediscovery recordings half a lifetime later. His best known songs—his adaptions of "Frankie (& Johnny)" and "Stack O' Lee," "Avalon Blues," "Nobody's Dirty Business," "Candy Man Blues"—are all accounted for in their original incarnations here and the NoNoiser remastering on this collection is superb. Mississippi John Hurt would go on to re-record this material for other labels in the 60s with fine results, but these are the originals and the ones that much of his justifiable reputation rests on. — *Cub Koda*

Legend / Oct. 7, 1997 / Rounder ✦✦✦
These 14 songs were recorded in 1963 and 1964; material from these sessions appeared briefly on Canada's Rebel label, as well as Piedmont. The mood is late-night informal, although there's little, if anything, in the Hurt catalog that could *not* be called informal. Hurt's originals are dotted with standards like "See See Rider," "Do Lord Remember Me," "Casey Jones, "and a seven-minute "Stack-O-Lee." It's not as forceful, perhaps, as his best-known recordings, and some of the songs are duplicated on other releases, but the sound quality (despite the destruction of the master tape) is okay, and Hurt fans will almost certainly find it to their liking. — *Richie Unterberger*

J.B. Hutto (Joseph Benjamin Hutto)

b. Apr. 26, 1926, Blackville, SC, **d.** Jun. 12, 1983, Harvey, IL
Guitar, Vocals / Electric Chicago Blues, Modern Electric Blues, Chicago Blues

J.B. Hutto—along with Hound Dog Taylor—was one of the last great slide guitar disciples of Elmore James to make it into the modern age. Hutto's huge voice, largely incomprehensible diction and slash and burn playing was Chicago blues with a fierce, raw edge all its own. He entered the world of music back home in Augusta, GA, singing in the family-oriented group the Golden Crowns Gospel Singers. He came north to Chicago in the mid-'40s, teaching himself guitar and eventually landing his first paying job as a member of Johnny Ferguson and His Twisters. His recording career started in 1954 with two sessions for the Chance label supported by his original combo the Hawks (featuring George Mayweather on harmonica, Porkchop Hines on washboard traps, and Joe Custom on rhythm guitar), resulting in six of the nine songs recorded being issued as singles to scant acclaim. After breaking up the original band, Hutto worked outside of music for a good decade, part of it spent sweeping out a funeral parlor! He resurfaced around 1964 with a stripped down, two guitars-drums-no bass trio version of the Hawks, working regularly at Turner's Blue Lounge and recording blistering new sides for the first time in as many years. From there, he never looked back and once again became a full-time bluesman. For the next 12 years Hutto gigged and recorded with various groups of musicians—always billed as the Hawks—working with electric bass players for the first time and recording for small labels, both here and overseas. After fellow slide man Hound Dog Taylor's death in 1976, J.B. "inherited" his backup band, the Houserockers.

Although never formally recorded in a studio, this short-lived collaboration of Hutto with guitarist Brewer Phillips and drummer Ted Harvey produced live shows that would musically careen in a single performance from smolderingly intense to utter chaos. Within a year, Hutto would be lured to Boston where he put together a mixed group of "New Hawks," recording and touring America and Europe right up until his death in the mid-'80s. Hutto was an incredibly dynamic live performer, dressed in hot pink suits with headgear ranging from a shriner's fez to high-plains-drifters' hats, snaking through the crowd and dancing on tabletops with his 50-foot guitar cord stretched to the max. And this good-time approach to the music held sway on his recordings as well, giving a loose, barroom feel to almost all of them, regardless of who was backing him. — *Cub Koda*

☆ **Chicago/The Blues/Today!, Vol. 1** / 1967 / Vanguard ✦✦✦✦✦
Hutto only has five tracks on this album, sharing it with great solo turns by Junior Wells and Otis Spann, but it's truly the place to start, because it doesn't get much better than this; "Too Much Alcohol," "Please Help," "Going Ahead," and "That's the Truth" are all classics and Hutto is in perfect form throughout with swinging support from the Turner's Blue Lounge version of the Hawks, bass-rhythm guitarist Herman Hassell and former Bo Diddley drummer Frank Kirkland. Sound is crystal clear. — *Cub Koda*

● **Hawk Squat!** / 1968 / Delmark ✦✦✦✦
The raw-as-an-open-wound Chicago slide guitarist outdid himself throughout an outrageously raucous album (most of it waxed in 1966) anchored by an impossible-to-ignore "Hip-Shakin'," the blaring title cut, and savage renditions of "20% Alcohol" and "Notoriety Woman." Sunnyland Slim augments Hutto's Hawks on organ, rather than his customary piano. — *Bill Dahl*

Slidewinder / 1973 / Delmark ✦✦✦
Disappointing Delmark encore from 1972 suffers from Bombay Carter's frequently out-of-tune electric bass and a comparatively uninspired song selection. — *Bill Dahl*

Slideslinger / Apr. 1, 1982 / Evidence ✦✦✦
While he was not in top shape during the early '80s, J.B. Hutto could still bend strings, churn out whiplash chords, and offer exuberant shouts, which he did on this '82 set, reissued on a '92 CD with two bonus cuts. He did not always hit every note on the fretboard or maintain his vocal depth, but his spirit never flagged. Hutto's jagged lines, energized vocals, and inspiring presence made his originals standouts, while his covers of Little Walter Jacobs' "Tell Me Mama" and Elmore James' "Look at the Yonder Wall" resonated with the quality that only a genuine blues survivor could provide. The backing band of guitarist Steve Coveney, bassist Kenny Krumbholz, and drummer Leroy Pina gave Hutto good support, wisely yielding him the spotlight, where he belongs. — *Ron Wynn*

Slippin' & Slidin' / 1983 / Varrick ✦✦✦
Much smoother production by Scott Billington than was normal for Hutto's scathing output, but not alarmingly so. With pianist Ron Levy and the Roomful of Blues horn section augmenting Hutto's New Hawks, the slide guitarist did himself proud on covers of Fenton Robinson's "Somebody Loan Me a Dime" and Junior Parker's "Pretty Baby," alongside a passel of his own distinctive compositions. — *Bill Dahl*

And the Houserockers Live 1977 / 1991 / Wolf ✦✦✦
Culled from a couple of nights in a Boston jazz club and recorded on a cassette deck with two microphones, this stunning document of Hutto with Hound Dog Taylor's band in support gives new meaning to the phrase raw'n'-steamy. Although the trio is fleshed out at this point by the addition of a fairly obtrusive bass player (Mark Harris) and a guest piano man on a couple of tracks, the sheet metal tone of Phillips' and Hutto's twin Telecaster attack cuts through the murkiest of mixes and Ted Harvey swings mightily. — *Cub Koda*

Masters of Modern Blues / 1995 / Testament ✦✦✦✦
1966 was a banner year for Hutto and his Hawks—in addition to laying down the lion's share of his killer Delmark album, the slide master also waxed a similarly incendiary set for Pete Welding's Testament logo. Vicious versions of "Pet Cream Man," "Lulubelle's Here," and "Bluebird" are but a few of its charms, with Big Walter Horton's unmistakable harp winding through the proceedings. — *Bill Dahl*

Roy Hytower & Motif

f. Mobile, AL
Guitar / Modern Electric Blues, R&B
Well-regarded as a blues guitarist and soulful singer around Chicago, Roy Hytower has carved out an equally impressive niche as an actor in various Windy City musical productions. Among his starring roles: portraying Muddy Waters and Otis Redding.

After picking up some experience singing around Mobile, Hytower came to Chicago in 1962, replacing Mighty Joe Young as rhythm guitarist for Otis Rush. Often adopting a soul-slanted sound, Hytower cut 45s for Avin, Expo, Brainstorm, and Mercury's Blue Rock subsidiary (where he sang the fine "I'm in Your Corner" and "Undertaker" in 1969). Hytower's 1988 album *Root Doctor* (with his band, Motif) was issued on Diamond Gem Records. He still performs locally. — *Bill Dahl*

Root Doctor / 1988 / Urgent! ✦✦✦
Hytower is a very competent blues guitarist, but you'll find too little proof of that on this synthesizer-heavy set, cut with his band, Motif. Earthier production values would have greatly benefitted the stop-time title cut, and blues content elsewhere is only intermittent and overly derivative. — *Bill Dahl*

Jabo (Donald Glenn)

b. Texas
Vocals / Zydeco
The self-proclaimed "Texas Prince of Zydeco," Jabo was among the Houston area's most prominent contemporary performers. Born Donald Glenn, he drew early influence from Clifton Chenier and Buckwheat Zydeco, basing his sound as much in the blues as in zydeco proper; in 1990, Jabo issued his debut LP *Texas Prince of Zydeco*. —*Jason Ankeny*

● **Texas Prince of Zydeco** / 1990 / Maison de Soul ♦♦♦♦
Jabo is Donald Glenn, a bluesman whose affection for zydeco music inspired him to fuse the two on *Texas Prince of Zydeco*. Since the music is Lone Star State-oriented rather than from New Orleans, the resulting hybrid is intriguingly odd; saxophonist Leon Childs appears on every cut, and Glenn's own accordion sounds bluesy even on the most manic zydeco number. An inventive, worthwhile release. —*Jason Ankeny*

Bull Moose Jackson (Benjamin Joseph Jackson)

b. Apr. 22, 1919, Cleveland, OH, **d.** Jul. 31, 1989, Cleveland, OH
Saxophone, Vocals / Jump Blues, R&B, Dirty Blues
Allegedly, Benjamin Jackson resembled a bullmoose. At least, that's what a few wags in Lucky Millinder's band thought—and the colorful monicker stuck. Up until then, he was Benjamin Jackson, but it was as Bull Moose that he lit up the R&B charts repeatedly during the late '40s and early '50s. Jackson had a split musical personality—he sang "I Love You, Yes I Do" and "All My Love Belongs to You" like a pop crooner, then switched gears to belt out the double-entendre naughties "I Want a Bowlegged Woman" and "Big Ten Inch Woman" with total abandon. Record buyers loved both sides of the Moose.

Jackson was a childhood violinist prior to taking up the sax. He proved accomplished on the latter, blowing jazz in a variety of situations before latching on with Millinder's outfit in 1944 as both singer and saxist. His first 78 under his own name for Syd Nathan's fledgling Queen logo was "I Know Who Threw the Whiskey in the Well," an answer to a popular Millinder tune from the year before that became a smash in its own right. Jackson dubbed his combo the Buffalo Bearcats due to his frequent gigs at a Buffalo nitery.

Moose hit big for Nathan's King diskery in 1947 with "I Love You, Yes I Do"; in 1948 with "Sneaky Pete," "All My Love Belongs to You," "I Want a Bowlegged Woman," "I Can't Go On Without You," and two more; and in 1949 with "Little Girl, Don't Cry" and "Why Don't You Haul Off and Love Me" (the latter a cover of Wayne Raney's hillbilly hit, a popular cross-fertilizing practice at King). He also made an appearance in the 1948 film *Boarding House Blues* with Millinder's band.

Some of Jackson's hilariously risqué stuff—"Big Ten Inch Record" and the astonishingly raunchy "Nosey Joe" (penned by the young but obviously streetwise Jerry Leiber and Mike Stoller), both from 1952—were probably too suggestive to merit airplay, but they're stellar examples of jump blues at its craziest.

Jackson stayed at King into 1955. Six years later, he briefly reentered the charts by remaking "I Love You, Yes I Do" for 7 Arts, but it was an isolated occurrence (catering kept the bills paid during the lean years in Washington, D.C.). There was a belated outbreak of *Moosemania!* in 1985 when his LP of that name emerged in conjunction with a Pittsburgh band called the Flashcats, but Moose's heartwarming comeback was short—lung cancer felled him in 1989. —*Bill Dahl*

Big Fat Mamas Are Back in Style Again / 1980 / Route 66 ♦♦♦♦
A solid reissue of Jackson's best sides from 1945-1956. —*Cub Koda*

● **Badman Jackson That's Me** / 1991 / Charly ♦♦♦♦
The best representation of saxist Jackson's jump blues activities for King Records during the late '40s and early '50s. The Moose was a smooth ballad crooner, too, but you'll find none of his mellow stuff on this 22-tracker—just horn-leavened blasters, often with hilariously risque lyrics. "Big Ten Inch Record" (here in two takes), "I Want a Bowlegged Woman," the country-rooted "Why Don't You Haul Off and Love Me," and most of all the Leiber & Stoller-penned sleaze-o "Nosey Joe" are party records guaranteed to excite any gathering! —*Bill Dahl*

Final Recordings / 1992 / Bogus ♦♦
This attempt to recreate jump blues style succeeds intermittently. —*Bill Dahl*

Cordell Jackson

b. Jul. 15, 1923, Memphis, TN
Modern Electric Blues
Born in 1923, Cordell Jackson, "Guitar Granny," started performing in the 1930s with her father's band, the Pontiac Ridge Runners. She founded her own Moon Records, the oldest continuously operating label in Memphis, in 1956, to release her own recordings as well as those of other Memphis-based rock 'n' roll artists. Although Moon Records didn't see a lot of activity in the intervening years, when she devoted her attentions more to selling houses, the label still existed. She would act as engineer, arranger and producer, using her living room as a studio. She started Moon Records to issue her "Beboppers Christmas" and "Rock and Roll Christmas" and then began releasing 45 rpm singles by other musicians. In 1980, she brought the label back to release an anthology of Moon Records recordings and began to record her own songs again.

Guitarist Jackson began writing and recording her own songs in the late 1940s. She started performing at age 12 with her father's band, and later played on the radio in Tupelo, Miss. During World War II, she moved to Memphis and began doubling on bass as well. The singles she released on Moon Records were mostly rockabilly and instrumental boogie recordings, and Allen Page was among the artists whose careers she tried to boost.

Although she spent much of her career selling real estate and running the label part-time, trying to promote the careers of other musicians, in the mid-1980s Jackson again moved her own career into the limelight, performing at music conventions and nightclubs. In 1986, she performed at New York's Lone Star Cafe and got a response that stunned her. She went back to the club again in 1988.

Although she doesn't hit the clubs all that often, Jackson still performs around Memphis and occasionally goes on forays around the country, playing wherever she's asked to. In 1983, Jackson released the instrumental, "Knockin' 60," the same song she later performed on a commercial for Budweiser beer, in which she appears with ex-Stray Cat guitarist Brian Setzer. Jackson, a Southern Baptist who doesn't let her religious beliefs interfere with her music, has two sons and 11 grandchildren.

Spurred by the notoriety the beer commercial gave her career, Jackson appeared in 1991 on the TV programs *Arsenio Hall, Late Night with David Letterman, Nashville Now,* and *Entertainment Tonight.* She told people, "If I want to wang dang rock 'n' roll at 69 years old all dressed up in an antebellum dress, it ain't nobody's business but mine."

Compact disc reissues of much of Jackson's early material should be available in the coming years, either on her own Moon Records label or through a deal with another company. —*Richard Skelly*

Live in Chicago / Jun. 24, 1997 / Bug House ♦♦♦

George Jackson

b. Memphis, TN
Guitar / Soul, Soul Blues
This Mississippi songwriter has been one of the most consistent composers in both R&B and pop circles. He initially recorded for Pram in 1963 and later sang with The Ovations, writing "It's Wonderful To Be In Love," which reached No. 22 in 1965. He also recorded for Decca in 1968 as "Bart" Jackson. But it's his compositions that have earned Jackson fame; they include "Too Weak To Fight" for Clarence Carter, "A Man And A Half" for Wilson Pickett, "Down Home Blues" for Z.Z. Hill, "One Bad Apple" for The Osmond Brothers, and "Old Time Rock & Roll" for Bob Seger. He has been a staff writer for Malaco since the early '80s, and has provided songs to Hill, Bobby "Blue" Bland, Latimore, Denise LaSalle, and Johnnie Taylor, among others. *—Ron Wynn*

● **Sweet Down Home Delta Blues** / Amblin' ◆◆◆
George Jackson's lone album *Sweet Down Home Delta Blues* is a straight-ahead collection of Delta blues. Considering that he's a house writer for Malaco Records, where he specialized in merging contemporary blues with soul, that comes as a little bit of a surprise. Unfortunately, he doesn't do the Delta as well as he does soul-blues, and *Sweet Down Home Delta Blues* suffers from predictability and perfunctory performances. Occasionally, the music comes to life, either through inspired playing or a solid song, but that only serves to remind the listeners of what this could have been. *—Thom Owens*

Jim Jackson

b. 1890, Hernando, MS, **d.** 1937, Hernando, MS
Guitar, Keyboards, Vocals / Acoustic Memphis Blues, Prewar Country Blues
Coming from the rich medicine-show tradition of the Memphis area, Jim Jackson veered toward a more pronounced blues feel than most of his song-ster and jug band contemporaries. Born in Hernando, Mississippi in 1890, Jackson took an interest in music early on, learning the rudiments of guitar from his father. By the age of 15, he was already steadily employed in local medicine shows, and by his 20s was working the country frolic and juke joint circuit, usually in the company of Gus Cannon and Robert Wilkins. After joining up with the Silas Green Minstrel Show, he settled in Memphis, working clubs with Furry Lewis, Cannon, and Will Shade. The entire decade known as the "roaring '20s" found him regularly working with his Memphis cronies, finally recording his best known tune, "Kansas City Blues" (one of the great classics of the idiom), and a batch of other classics by the end of the decade. He also appeared in one of the early talkies, *Hallelujah!*, in 1929. While Jackson's best work may seem a bit quaint by modern standards, he was a major influence on Chicago bluesman J.B. Lenoir and his "Kansas City Blues" was a regular fixture of Robert Nighthawk's set list. *—Cub Koda*

● **Kansas City Blues** / 1980 / Agram ◆◆◆◆
Kansas City Blues collects 16 tracks Jim Jackson recorded between 1927 and 1929. This music is country music that has strong ties to minstrel and medicine show music, and may sound dated to some listeners. Nevertheless, the title track is one of the first great blues singles, and that alone makes the collection necessary listening for serious blues fans, even if Document's three-volume set will be of greater interest to historians. The curious will be better served by this concise compilation. *—Thom Owens*

Complete Recorded Works, Vol. 1 (1927-1928) / 1992 / Document ◆◆◆◆
Whew—any collection that opens up with both sides of "Jim Jackson's Kansas City Blues" in its original October 1927 recording (predating RCA's recording of the same number by Jackson by three months) is asking for trouble, because how do you follow up the best double-sided solo blues single this side of Furry Lewis' "Casey Jones, Pts. 1 & 2"? Well, you put on a 1928 rendition of "He's In the Jailhouse Now" that's as soulful as any ever done, and a version of "Old Dog Blue" from January 1928 that could be the earliest blues incarnation of what later became the Bo Diddley beat. And somewhere in there you throw in Jackson's subsequent version of "Kansas City Blues" (the earlier one is better). And the stuff gets better from there on one of the finest solo artist compilations in the Document line, mostly with good sound, too. In contrast to Furry Lewis and almost any other blues great you'd care to name, Jackson's playing on the guitar was pretty basic (check out "Mobile-Central Blues," a great, bitter, topical song about the blues, that benefits from

his repetitive playing), but the success of his work is proof that a smooth style matters more than technical skill, if the voice and the words are there. His playing fit his expressive voice, not too obtrusive, and gave his voice just the little bit of accompaniment it needed, even embellishing the beat (as on "Old Dog Blue") when required. The sound is generally good, and it's hard to complain about the notes being a little sketchy, given the relatively little hard information known about Jackson. Seventy minutes of pure, sweet, golden acoustic blues, highlighted—with Document's usual thoroughness—by two different takes each of "I Heard the Voice of a Pork Chop," "Policy Blues," and "The Morning She Was Gone." *—Bruce Eder*

Complete Recorded Works, Vol. 2 (1928-1930) / 1992 / Document ◆◆◆◆

John Jackson (John H. Jackson)

b. Feb. 25, 1924, Woodville, VA
Banjo, Guitar, Vocals / Country Blues, Piedmont Blues, Prewar Country Blues
For much of his life, John Jackson played for country houseparties in Virginia, or around the house for his own amusement. Then in the '60s he encountered the folk revival, and since that time he has been the Washington, DC area's best-loved blues artist. Undoubtedly the finest traditional Piedmont guitarist active today, Jackson exemplifies the songster tradition at its best. His eclectic repertoire embraces the music of his guitar heroes Willie Walker (who once visited his father's house), Blind Boy Fuller, and—most notably—Blind Blake. Besides the blues, rags, and dance tunes associated with these masters, Jackson plays ballads, country songs, and what he terms "old folk songs," such as "The Midnight Special." His confident finger-picking, down-home Virginia accent, and contagious good humor mark his performances, live or on record, as something special. A world-class storyteller and party-thrower as well as a National Heritage Award-winning musician, Jackson has recorded a half-dozen albums and toured the world as often as he has wanted to. Today he often performs with his son James. *—Barry Lee Pearson*

Blues and Country Dance Tunes from Virginia / 1965 / Arhoolie ◆◆◆◆
John Jackson was an excellent country blues musician whose repertoire also included reels, mountain music, and folk tunes. This was an outstanding collection of vintage material done in what was about as contemporary a fashion as you could get in that genre in the mid-'60s. *—Ron Wynn*

● **Don't Let Your Deal Go Down** / 1970 / Arhoolie ◆◆◆◆
Twenty-six tracks running over 70 minutes, recorded by John Jackson between 1965 and 1969, and featuring the rural blues legend at the very top of his form on vocals, guitar, and even banjo on one instrumental ("If Hattie Wants to Lu, Let Her Lu like a Man"). Jackson's repertory here includes standards like "John Henry" (in one of the most exciting versions ever done, with some killer slide), and "Muleskinner Blues," established parts of other bluesmen's repertories (Blind Boy Fuller's "Rattlesnakin' Daddy," Blind Arthur Blake's "Police Dog Blues," and "Early Morning Blues"), as well as originals, such as the dazzling acoustic pyrotechnic displays on "John's Rag," "Graveyard Blues," and "Knife Blues" (the latter a slide guitar showcase worth the price of the disc by itself), and adaptations of popular songs ("Blind Blake's Rag," which borrows at one point from "Has Anybody Seen My Gal"). Good as his playing is, Jackson's singing is also to be admired, as his baritone voice surges with a quiet power and forcefulness, and a rich tone. "Boats up the River," a children's song adapted from various traditional sources, is probably the vocal standout on this collection. The fidelity is excellent, these being modern recordings, and overall this CD is the best single overview of John Jackson's music, its value enhanced by the presence of detailed notes that have been updated to the 1990s. It's records like this that humble lots of young white bluesmen. *—Bruce Eder*

Step It up & Go / 1979 / Rounder ◆◆◆◆
Virginia ragtime, blues, and hillbilly from this amiable singer/guitarist. *—Mark A. Humphrey*

Mahalia Jackson

b. Oct. 16, 1911, New Orleans, LA, **d.** Jan. 27, 1972, Evergreen Park, IL
Vocals / Black Gospel, Traditional Gospel, Spirituals
General critical consensus holds Mahalia Jackson as the greatest gospel singer ever to live; a major crossover success whose popularity extended across racial divides, she was gospel's first superstar, and even decades after

her death remains for many listeners a defining symbol of the music's transcendent power. With her singularly expressive contralto, Jackson continues to inspire the generations of vocalists who follow in her wake; among the first spiritual perfomers to introduce elements of blues into her music, she infused gospel with a sensuality and freedom it had never before experienced, and her artistry rewrote the rules forever. Born in one of the poorest sections of New Orleans on October 16, 1911, Jackson made her debut in the children's choir of the Plymouth Rock Baptist Church at the age of four, and within a few years was a prominent member of the Mt. Moriah Baptist's junior choir. Raised next door to a sanctified church, she was heavily influenced by their brand of gospel, with its reliance on drums and percussion over piano; another major inspiration was the blues of Bessie Smith and Ma Rainey.

By the time she reached her mid-teens, then, Jackson's unique vocal style was fully formed, combining the full-throated tones and propulsive rhythms of the sanctified church, and the deep expressiveness of the blues with the note-bending phrasing of her Baptist upbringing. After quitting school during the eighth grade, Jackson relocated to Chicago in 1927, where she worked as a maid and laundress; within months of her arrival, she was singing leads with the choir at the Greater Salem Baptist Church, where she joined the three sons of her pastor in their group, the Johnson Brothers. Although other small choir groups had cut records in the past, the Johnson Brothers might have been the first professional gospel unit ever; the first organized group to play the Chicago church circuit, they even produced a series of self-written musical dramas in which Jackson assumed the lead role. Her provocative performing style—influenced by the Southern sanctified style of keeping time with the body, and distinguished by jerks and steps for physical emphasis—enraged many of the more conservative Northern preachers, but few could deny her fierce talent.

After the members of the Johnson Brothers went their separate ways during the mid-1930s, Jackson began her solo career accompanied by pianist Evelyn Gay, who herself later went on to major fame as one half of gospel's Gay Sisters. During the week, Jackson also went to beauty school, and soon opened her own salon. As her reputation as a singer grew throughout the Midwest, in 1937 she made her first recordings for Decca, becoming the first gospel artist signed to the label; curiously, none of the tracks she recorded during her May 21 session was by Thomas A. Dorsey, the legendary composer for whom she began working as a song demonstrator around that same time. (He even wrote "Peace in the Valley" with her in mind.) While her Decca single "God's Gonna Separate the Wheat from the Tares" sold only modestly, prompting a lengthy studio hiatus, Jackson's career continued on the upswing—she soon began peforming live in cities as far away as Buffalo, New Orleans, and Birmingham, becoming famous in churches throughout the country for not only her inimitable voice but also her flirtatious stage presence and spiritual intensity.

Jackson did not record again until 1946, signing with Apollo Records; although her relations with the label were often strained, the work she produced during her eight-year stay on their roster was frequently brilliant. While her first Apollo recordings, including "I Want to Rest" and "He Knows My Heart," fared poorly—so much so, in fact, that the label almost dropped her—producer Art Freeman insisted Jackson record W. Herbert Brewster's "Move on Up a Little Higher"; released in early 1948, the single became the best-selling gospel record of all time, selling in such great quantities that stores could not even meet the demand. Virtually overnight, Jackson became a superstar; beginning in 1950, she became a regular guest on journalist Studs Terkel's Chicago television series, and among white intellectuals and jazz critics, she acquired a major cult following based in large part on her eerie similarities to Bessie Smith. In 1952, her recording of "I Can Put My Trust in Jesus" even won a prize from the French Academy, resulting in a successful tour of Europe—her rendition of "Silent Night" even became one of the all-time best-selling records in Norway's history.

Jackson's success soon reached such dramatic proportions that in 1954, she began hosting her own weekly radio series on CBS, the first program of its kind to broadcast the pure, sanctified gospel style over national airwaves. The show surrounded her with a supporting cast, which included not only pianist Mildred Falls and organist Ralph Jones, but also a white quartet led by musical director Jack Halloran; although her performances with Halloran's group moved Jackson far away from traditional gospel towards an odd hybrid which crossed the line into barbershop quartet singing, they proved

extremely popular with white audiences, and her transformation into a true crossover star was complete. Also in 1954, she signed to Columbia, scoring a Top 40 hit with the single "Rusty Old Halo," and two years later made her debut on *The Ed Sullivan Show*. However, with Jackson's success came the inevitable backlash—purists decried her music's turn towards more pop-friendly production, and as her fame soared, so did her asking price, so much so that by the late 1950s, virtually no black churches could afford to pay her performance fee.

A triumphant appearance at the 1958 Newport Jazz Festival solidified Jackson's standing among critics, but her records continued moving her further away from her core audience—when an LP with Percy Faith became a smash, Columbia insisted on more recordings with orchestras and choirs; she even cut a rendition of "Guardian Angels" backed by comic Harpo Marx. In 1959, she appeared in the film *Imitation of Life*, and two years later, sang at John F. Kennedy's Presidential inauguration. During the 1960s, Jackson was also a confidant and supporter of Dr. Martin Luther King, and at his funeral, sang his last request, "Precious Lord"; throughout the decade she was a force in the civil rights movement, but after 1968, with King and the brothers Kennedy all assassinated, she retired from the political front. At much the same time, Jackson went through a messy and very public divorce, prompting a series of heart attacks, and the rapid loss of over a hundred pounds; in her last years, however, she recaptured much of her former glory, concluding her career with a farewell concert in Germany in 1971. She died January 27, 1972. — *Jason Ankeny*

Live at Newport 1958 / Jan. 1958 / Columbia ✦✦✦✦
Stunning live performances from the 1958 Newport Jazz Festival. — *Opal Louis Nations*

The Power & The Glory / 1960 / Sony ✦✦✦
With orchestra conducted by Percy Faith, Jackson sings 12 of her favorite hyms, including "Onward Christian Soldiers," "Just as I Am," and "Rock of Ages," among others. Though the accompaniment is not what listeners would expect from a Mahalia Jackson album, Faith is for the most part sympathetic. — *John Bush*

In the Upper Room / 1965 / Vogue ✦✦✦✦
Supported by Mildred Falls, the Southern Harmonaires, and the Melody Echoes (the two vocal groups are on different tracks), Mahalia Jackson turns in a typically rousing effort with *In the Upper Room*. All of the songs are classic spirituals and sacred songs, and while this was recorded a little later in her career, Jackson nonetheless sings with an incendiary passion that rivals her classic '40s recordings. Anyone looking to round out their Mahalia Jackson collection should look here, as *In the Upper Room* is one of her finest latter-day efforts. — *Leo Stanley*

A Mighty Fortress / 1968 / Sony ✦✦✦✦
Included are ten tracks of Mahalia Jackson's genius, originally recorded in 1968 and reissued on CD 20 years later. Aside from the title track, Jackson also sings "It Is Well with My Soul," "Power in the Blood," "Sweet Hour of Prayer," and "Be Still My Soul." — *John Bush*

The World's Greatest Gospel Singer / May 4, 1975 / Columbia ✦✦✦✦
Moving performances, tastefully supported by the Falls-Jones Ensemble. — *Opal Louis Nations*

Sings America's Favorite Hymns / 1977 / Columbia ✦✦✦
Another cross-section of Jackson's '50s and '60s work. — *Kip Lornell*

Amazing Grace / 1989 / Sony ✦✦✦✦
A nice sampling of Jackson's later recordings. — *Kip Lornell*

★ **Gospels, Spirituals & Hymns** / 1991 / Columbia/Legacy ✦✦✦✦✦
Although it's missing some of her classic performances, the double-disc set *Gospels, Spirituals & Hymns* is nonetheless an excellent introduction to Mahalia Jackson, arguably the greatest gospel singer of all time. The box set features 36 performances she recorded for Columbia between 1954 and 1969, offering a comprehensive, but by no means exhaustive, introduction to Jackson and her most popular work. — *Leo Stanley*

☆ **Mahalia Jackson, Vol. 2** / Jul. 28, 1992 / Columbia/Legacy ✦✦✦✦✦
With its excellent sound and liner notes, the second box set of Mahalia Jackson's Columbia recordings is just as essential as the first. — *AMG*

Go Tell It on the Mountain / 1993 / Arrival ✦✦✦
This disc features 10 of the original Apollo tracks by the great Mahalia Jack-

son. In addition to the title track, the disc also includes "Nobody Knows," "Just As I Am," and "Amazing Grace." If you like gospel music, this is the real thing! — *Jim Worbois*

☆ **Live at Newport** / 1994 / Sony ✦✦✦✦✦
Live at Newport is a wonderful reissue of the *Newport 1958* album, containing all 15 songs that were on the original record. Jackson was at the peak of her career, and she gave a stunning performance at this show, lifting such songs as "He's Got the Whole World in His Hands," "Lord's Prayer," "Evening Prayer," "I'm on My Way," "Walk over God's Heaven," and "His Eye is on the Sparrow" to glorious heights. It's not only one of the great live gospel albums, it's simply one of the great gospel albums. — *Leo Stanley*

The Apollo Sessions 1946-1951 / 1994 / Pair ✦✦✦✦
Her best sides with vocal group backing and simple rhythm accompaniment. — *Opal Louis Nations*

The Best of Mahalia Jackson / 1995 / Columbia/Legacy ✦✦✦✦
The Best of Mahalia Jackson is a 16-track collection featuring many of Jackson's very best recordings—"God Put a Rainbow in the Sky," "He's Got the Whole World in His Hands," "Walk in Jerusalem," "God is So Good (To Me)," "Just a Little While to Stay Here"—thereby offering a long overdue single-disc introduction to one of the greatest gospel singers in history. — *Stephen Thomas Erlewine*

The Apollo Sessions, Vol. 2 / 1995 / Pair ✦✦✦
More of her finest work with piano/organ and quartet backgrounds. — *Opal Louis Nations*

★ **16 Most Requested Songs** / Aug. 20, 1996 / Columbia ✦✦✦✦✦
If you're looking for something a little less comprehensive and pricey than one of the Mahalia Jackson box sets, this is the best single-disc compilation of her Columbia recordings, spanning the years 1954-1967 in 66 1/2 minutes. It features some amazing performances, including an April 1961 take of "How I Got Over," recorded live in Sweden, a few selections from the 1958 Newport Jazz Festival, and several tracks featuring Billy Preston on organ, among them the seven-minute 1963 version of "In the Upper Room." Jackson is uniformly excellent, and this sampler gives a good sense of the different approaches she took to her music during the Columbia years. Start here, and go on to the more extensive collections. — *William Ruhlmann*

The Apollo Years / Nov. 5, 1996 / Collectables ✦✦✦✦
Indispensable Apollo sides, early 1950s (two-CD set). — *Opal Louis Nations*

Queen of Gospel / May 20, 1997 / Music Club ✦✦✦
These 16 tracks recorded for Bess Berman's Apollo Records from 1947 to 1954 mark the debut recordings of Mahalia Jackson, and the first gospel records to reach a mass audience. The single release from her second session in September of 1947, "Move On Up a Little Higher," was the first gospel record to sell over a million copies, eventually doubling that figure and making her a household name. Never had anyone heard gospel sung quite like this. Simplicity was at the root of her presentation and her eventual success: put Mahalia in the company of her lifelong accompanist, pianist Mildred Falls, and surround her with little more than an organ sustaining chords, an occasional drummer or jazz guitarist and—on even rarer occasions—a vocal group. This kept the focus on Jackson's incredible vocal range and interpretive skills, coming up with sides like "His Eye Is on the Sparrow," "Poor Pilgrim of Sorrow," and her versions of "Silent Night" and "Amazing Grace," which were drenched in gospel fervor and vocal majesty. Mahalia generally preferred to hear her voice unencumbered by backing choirs and such, but superb vocal backing from the Southern Harmonaires—later to record secularly for Apollo as the Larks—is present on "He's My Light," "In the Upper Room (Part 1)," and "Said He Would," while the Melody Echoes sound equally wonderful behind her on "Up In Jerusalem" and "Beautiful Tomorrow." Although she would go on to make more successful and better-produced records when she later moved to Columbia in 1954, she made no greater music than these first recordings for Apollo. And here are 16 of the very best. — *Cub Koda*

20 Greatest Hits / Pentagon ✦✦✦✦
Fine selection of her early Apollo sides circa 1948-53. — *Opal Louis Nations*

Melvin "Lil'" Son Jackson (Melvin Jackson)

b. Aug. 16, 1915, Tyler, TX, **d.** May 30, 1976, Dallas, TX
Vocals, Guitar / Electric Texas Blues
Lil' Son Jackson was a stylistic throwback from the moment he first turned up during the immediate postwar era. He was a Texas country bluesman of the highest order, whose rustic approach appealed wholeheartedly to the early '50s blues marketplace.

Melvin Jackson's dad loved blues, while his mother played gospel guitar. Their son's initial experience came with a spiritual aggregation called the Blue Eagle Four. A mechanic by trade, he served in the Army during World War II before giving up the idea of being a professional blues musician a shot.

In 1946, he shipped off a demo to Bill Quinn, who owned a Houston diskery called Gold Star Records. Quinn was suitably impressed, inking Jackson and enjoying a national R&B hit, "Freedom Train Blues," in 1948 for his modest investment. It would prove Jackson's only national hit, although his 1950-1954 output for Imperial Records must have sold consistently, judging from how many sides the L.A. firm issued by the Texas guitarist.

Jackson's best Imperial work was recorded solo. Later attempts to squeeze his style into a small band format (his idea, apparently) tended to emphasize his timing eccentricities. His "Rockin' and Rollin'," cut in December of 1950, became better-known through a raft of subsequent covers as "Rock Me Baby." He gave up the blues during the mid-'50s after an auto wreck, resuming work as a mechanic. Arhoolie Records boss Chris Strachwitz convinced Jackson to cut an album in 1960, but his comeback proved fleeting. — *Bill Dahl*

● **Lil' Son Jackson** / Mar. 1962 / Arhoolie ✦✦✦✦
Arhoolie's *Lil' Son Jackson* is a good collection of material Jackson recorded for the label in the early '60s, during the height of the blues revival. In many ways, these recordings are better than his original '40s sessions, since they capture him in a clean, well-recorded setting performing his best songs quite powerfully. The result is a minor gem and an excellent country-blues record. — *Leo Stanley*

Blues Come to Texas / 1981 / Arhoolie ✦✦✦✦
Melvin "Lil' Son" Jackson could present stunning, poignant, ironic or gripping stories, and his vocals were ideal for the slow-paced, dramatic storytelling mode. Jackson scored several regional and jukebox hits in the 1950s with his stories of woe, fame, misfortune, tribulation, and perseverance. These were consistent themes emerging throughout the 20 cuts on this CD reissue from a 1960 session. It includes three unreleased cuts and a song ("Johnnie Mae") from another album. Jackson wrote (or adapted) all of the songs, and this disc is a fine portrait of an often overlooked, but significant Texas blues performer. — *Ron Wynn*

Complete Imperial Recordings / 1995 / Capitol ✦✦✦
Two-disc, 55-track compilation of material from the first half of the 1950s. This is blues in the transition from the country to the city, and indeed, much of the first disc lacks a rhythm section, although electric guitar is present. Jackson actually sounds considerably more comfortable when working in a Lightnin' Hopkins mode. In fact, the sides with full accompaniment sometimes sound like the *band* is uncomfortable with band arrangements. On some sides, the drummer seems to have his mind on another session; others boast tentative saxophone that borders on the haphazard. Jackson's subdued, countrified approach actually sounded a bit anachronistic even when these cuts were laid down, though the sloppiness does suit the atypical "Drinkin' Wine Spo-Dee-O-Dee" knockoff "Get High Everybody." At any rate, it's acceptable but somewhat journeyman stuff with a lack of variation that gets tiresome over the course of several dozen tracks, although some of the bandless sides, like "Thrill Me Baby" (with dreamy slide guitar licks) and "Movin' to the Country," hit a very good groove. — *Richie Unterberger*

Papa Charlie Jackson (Charlie Carter)

b. 1885, New Orleans, LA, **d.** 1938, Chicago, IL
Banjo, Guitar, Ukulele, Vocals / Country Blues, Prewar Country Blues
Papa Charlie Jackson was the first bluesman to record, beginning in 1924 with the Paramount label, playing a hybrid banjo-guitar (six strings tuned like a guitar but with a banjo body that gave it a lighter resonance) and ukelele. And apart from his records and their recording dates, little else is known for sure about this pioneering blues performer, other than his prob-

able city of birth, New Orleans—even his death in Chicago during 1938 is more probable than established fact.

Jackson spent his teen years as a singer/performer in minstrel and medicine shows, picking up a repertory of bawdy but entertaining songs that would serve him well for decades. He is known to have busked around Chicago in the early '20s, playing for tips on Maxwell Street, as well as the city's West Side clubs beginning in 1924. In August of that year, Jackson made his first record, "Papa's Lawdy Lawdy Blues" and "Airy Man Blues," for a Paramount label. He followed this up a month later with "Salt Lake City Blues" and "Salty Dog Blues," which became one of his signature tunes—he later re-recorded this number as a member of Freddie Keppard's Jazz Cardinals, also for the Paramount label, a common practice in those days as the notion of contracts and exclusivity was almost unknown in blues recording. Jackson made his first duet records in 1925, "Mister Man, Parts 1 and 2," with singer Ida Cox, again for Paramount, and later cut duets with Ma Rainey and future Oscar-winning actress Hattie McDaniel.

He was already regarded as one of the Paramount label's more successful recording artists, and all but a handful of his recordings were done for Paramount over the next decade. Jackson had a wide diversity of material and voices in which he recorded—"Good Doing Papa Blues" and "Jungle Man Blues" presented Jackson as a ladies' man in playful settings, while "Ma and Pa Poorhouse Blues," cut in a duet with Ma Rainey, was a far more serious song, dealing with poverty and its attendant miseries. "Don't Break Down," by contrast, was a seductive love song with pop elements, while "Baby Please Loan Me Your Heart"—with its exquisite banjo strumming—is a sweetly romantic piece that could've come out of vaudeville. Whether he was strumming or finger-picking, his music was always of interest for its structure, content, and execution.

Jackson reached a musical peak of sorts in September of 1929 when he got to record with his longtime idol, Blind (Arthur) Blake, often known as the king of ragtime guitar during this period. "Papa Charlie and Blind Blake Talk About It" parts one and two are among the most unusual sides of the late '20s, containing elements of blues jam session, hokum recording, and ragtime, containing enough humor to make it the 1920s rival of tracks such as Bo Diddley's "Say Man" as well. More is the pity that better sources haven't survived for both sides, but what is here is beyond price—there may not be a dozen guitar records in any genre that are more important or more fascinating.

Jackson switched to guitar on some of his late '20s recordings, and occasionally played the ukelele as well, although he was back to using the five-string hybrid in 1934, when he cut his final sessions. For reasons that nobody has ever established, he parted company with Paramount after 1930, and never recorded for the label again, even though Paramount lasted another two years before going under amid the hardships of the Great Depression. His last sides for the label, "You Got That Wrong" and "Self Experience," were highly personal songs dealing with romance and an apparent brush with the law, after which he disappeared from recording for four years. Jackson continued performing, however, and he returned to the recording studio again in November of 1934 for sessions on the Okey label, including three songs cut with his friend Big Bill Broonzy, which were never issued. Jackson was an important influence on Broonzy, who outlived his mentor by 20 years.

Papa Charlie Jackson remains a shadowy figure, considered a highly influential figure in the blues, though not quite a major blues figure, apart from the fact that he was the first male singer/guitarist who played the blues to get to record. His recordings are all eminently listenable, although most are not blues, but fall into such related areas as ragtime and hokum. At this writing, the only extant collections consist of three Austrian produced CDs. —*Bruce Eder*

● **Fat Mouth** / 1970 / Yazoo ✦✦✦✦

Yazoo's *Fat Mouth* is the best overview of Papa Charlie Jackson's best recordings, offering 14 tracks he recorded between 1924 and 1927. While a few important songs didn't make it to this set, most of his very best did, and for many listeners this concise compilation is a preferable alternative to the exhaustive multi-volume Document series. — *Thom Owens*

Papa Charlie Jackson / 1972 / Biograph ✦✦✦✦

Jackson's mid-'20s material blended topical fare with hokum hilarity and blues laments, and Jackson's four and six-string banjo accompaniment was

among country blues' most striking. His guitar work wasn't bad either. —*Ron Wynn*

Complete Recorded Works, Vol. 1: (1924-1926) / 1991 / Document ✦✦✦✦

The first 27 of Papa Charlie Jackson's recorded works is, on about ten counts, one of the most important blues documents you can find, dating all the way back to August of 1924, before there was even electrical recording or a true definition to "blues." Indeed, the popular highlight is a dance number called "Shake That Thing," which fairly overwhelmed a lot of Jackson's truer blues records with its beat. The opening number, "Papa's Lawdy Lawdy Blues," shows a kind of formative blues, with it and its B-side "Airy Man (aka "Hairy Man") Blues," closer in spirit to comic novelty numbers. The hybrid banjo-guitar that Jackson played was an absolute necessity on these and his other early records, for it was more audible than any guitar of the era would have been, and serves to keep a beat as well as provide full accompaniment. "Salt Lake City Blues" is closer to our modern definition of blues, a romantic lament that's as honest and cheerful as it is sexist. Jackson's first version of "Salty Dog Blues" is here, along with what is probably the earliest reference to Chicago's outdoor blues Mecca in "Maxwell Street Blues," dating from September of 1925. Other topical references to the future blues capital city can be heard in "Jackson's Blues," dealing with a local politician, and also worth checking out in that regard is "Mama Don't Allow It," telling of a country girl's descent into prostitution after coming to the big city. Also here is one of the earliest known source records for Willie Dixon's composition "Spoonful," entitled "All I Want Is a Spoonful" (though anyone only familiar with the versions by Cream won't really recognize it), and a primordial incarnation of "I'm Alabama Bound" (later immortalized by Leadbelly). The audio quality is amazingly good throughout this disc (the only big exceptions, unfortunately, being the two duets with Ida Cox and the two takes of "Texas Blues," which are really in rough shape), and the sessionography and annotation are reasonably thorough, given how little we actually know about Jackson. —*Bruce Eder*

Complete Recorded Works, Vol. 2: (1926-1928) / 1991 / Document ✦✦✦

Twenty-six of Papa Charlie Jackson's recordings dating between February 1926 and September 1928, and an extraordinary volume this is. Now firmly ensconced in the electrical recording era, the sound on these records brings out the rich texture of Jackson's banjo playing, and his singing is thoroughly enjoyable, as he runs through thinly veiled topical songs ("Judge Cliff Davis Blues"), playful romantic pieces ("Butter and Egg Man Blues"), bouncy rags ("Look Out Papa Don't Tear Your Pants"), and more ambitious remakes of his early songs, most notably an outtake of "Salty Dog," cut with Freddie Keppard's Jazz Cardinals (with New Orleans jazz great Johnny Dodds on clarinet). The two-part "Up the Way Bound," dating from the spring of 1926, isn't quite as well recorded as some of the rest, featuring Jackson on guitar, but his vocal performance carries the song well enough—unfortunately, the second half of this piece, from side two of the original Paramount release, is neither as well recorded nor as well preserved as the first half. There's lots of little slice-of-Black-urban-life material here worth noting as well, including Jackson's homage to the numbers racket, "Four Eleven Forty Four." Jackson's vocal skills are vividly displayed in his extraordinarily impassioned singing on "Bad Luck Woman Blues," one of his finest performances. We also get his first version of "Skoodle-Um-Skoo," an upbeat dance number reminiscent of his earlier "Shake That Thing," which he recut some seven years later—this record also demonstrates better than almost any other side, the full measure of advantage that the banjo had over the guitar in those days of blues recording, with a solo that fairly leaps out at the listener. —*Bruce Eder*

Complete Recorded Works, Vol. 3: (1928-1934) / 1991 / Document ✦✦✦

Papa Charlie Jackson's last 25 recordings, dating from September of 1928 through November of 1934, and doing more proper blues here than on either previous volume. By the time of the release of the material here, Jackson was one of the most seasoned of studio bluesmen, with nearly half a decade recording experience behind him—his vocal presence on all of these records is extraordinary, and he knows how to get the most out of his instrument, guitar or banjo. "Ma and Pa Poorhouse Blues" and "Big Feeling Blues," both duets with Ma Rainey, present him at his most mature and naturally expressive vocally, in sharp contrast to the almost perfunctory vocals on volume one of this set. The Hattie McDaniel's duets, two halves of "Dentist Chair

Blues," are also extremely worthwhile as far more than novelty numbers. In addition to some priceless topical songs, such as "You Got That Wrong," there are some notable re-recordings here, including a killer 1934 remake of Jackson's earlier hit "Skoodle-Um-Skoo" (which by then had entered the repertory of Big Bill Broonzy, who was taught guitar by Jackson), and his last follow-up to "Shake That Thing," "What's That Thing She's Shakin'." The delightfully risqué-sounding "You Put It In, I'll Take It Out" closes this collection. The only drawback to any of this is that, despite the fact that it consists of material recorded much later than anything on volumes one or two, the sound quality on this disc is far lower, with lots of distracting surface noise on many of the sources used for individual songs—the most disappointing of these are the two sides that Jackson cut with Blind (Arthur) Blake, who was very much an influence on Jackson; two of the greatest blues/ragtime guitarists and songsters of the early blues era together on record, and the scratchiness is nearly maddening. Only the four final 1934 sides really come up to the level one would wish on this stuff. —*Bruce Eder*

Colin James (Colin Munn)

b. Aug. 17, 1964, Regina, Saskatchewan, Canada
Guitar, Vocals, Mandolin / Modern Blues
This Canadian guitarist, singer and songwriter is Canada's answer to the US's Chris Duarte or Kenny Wayne Shepherd. Colin Munn grew up in Saskatchewan, listening to folk and blues. After learning the pennywhistle and mandolin, he quit school and worked with a succession of bands, among them, the Hoo Doo Men.

When he was 19 years old, he moved to Vancouver and joined the Night Shades. About two years later, performing under his changed name, Colin James, he was lucky enough to be noticed by the folks at Virgin Records, who signed him. James' 1988 self-titled debut was the fastest-selling album in Canadian history, and he followed that in 1990 with *Sudden Stop*, and *Colin James and the Little Big Band* in 1993. In 1995, James switched over to Warner Music Canada, and released *Bad Habits*. On *Bad Habits*, James is teamed with some good company: Bobby King and Terry Evans, Mavis Staples, guitarist Waddy Wachtel, Lenny Kravitz, and former Stevie Ray Vaughan and Double Trouble keyboardist Reese Wynans.

All of James' albums are well-recorded affairs. The only problem is, he doesn't tour the US very much, and spends most of his time in Canada. In 1988, he toured with Steve Winwood, Little Feat, and Keith Richards, but if he's ever going to become a truly international blues musician, he's going to have to start touring the US a whole lot more. —*Richard Skelly*

Colin James / 1988 / Virgin ✦✦✦✦
Although it's a little short on originality—at times you could swear Stevie Ray Vaughan showed him exactly what to play—Colin James' eponymous debut is an impressive collection of high-octane blues-rock that, at its best, explodes with the intensity of a keg of dynamite. James' forté is his speedy, accomplished guitar playing, which is breathtaking at times, and that's enough to excuse the occasionally awkward originals and predictable covers that pepper the album. After all, good guitarists—even ones that borrow heavily from old masters—aren't all that easy to find, and sometimes you have to accept their flaws in order to embrace them. —*Thom Owens*

Sudden Stop / Oct. 1990 / Virgin ✦✦✦
A solid, stylistically varied follow-up by this Canadian guitarist. —*David Szatmary*

Colin James & The Little Big Band / 1993 / Virgin ✦✦✦
A tasty hybrid of rock 'n' roll, jive, and blues, James' eponymous recording—a collection of standards from the late '40s-early '50s recorded live from the floor—takes a swingin' jump approach with horns and organ given equal billing to smooth, hollow-body guitar tones. Highlights: the finger-snapping, fedora-over-one-eye cool of "Evening," and a bopping, knockout version of "Train Kept A-Rollin'." —*Roch Parisien*

● **Bad Habits** / 1995 / Elektra ✦✦✦✦
Canadian blues guitarist Colin James turns in a fine set of both original and cover material. Paring back the sound of his previous effort to the basic guitar, bass and drums, James uses horns and keyboards to color and accentuate certain tracks rather than overwhelm. He works his blues magic on such covers as Robert Johnson's "Walkin' Blues" and Jerry Williams' "Standing on

The Edge of Love," while proving his own song writing capabilities on cuts like "Freedom" and "Better Days." A great return to form. —*James Chrispell*

Elmore James

b. Jan. 27, 1918, Richland, MS, **d.** May 24, 1963, Chicago, IL
Guitar, Vocals / Electric Chicago Blues, Chicago Blues
No two ways about it, the most influential slide guitarist of the postwar period was Elmore James, hands down. Although his early demise from heart failure kept him from enjoying the fruits of the '60s blues revival as his contemporaries Muddy Waters and Howlin' Wolf did, James left a wide influential trail behind him. And that influence continues to the present time—in approach, attitude, and tone—in just about every guitar player who puts a slide on his finger and wails the blues. As a guitarist, he wrote the book, his slide style influencing the likes of Hound Dog Taylor, Joe Carter, his cousin Homesick James, and J.B. Hutto, while his seldom-heard single-string work had an equally profound effect on B.B. King and Chuck Berry. His signature lick—an electric updating of Robert Johnson's "I Believe I'll Dust My Broom" and one that Elmore recorded in infinite variations from day one to his last session—is so much a part of the essential blues fabric of guitar licks that no one attempting to play slide guitar can do it without being compared to Elmore James. Others may have had more technique—Robert Nighthawk and Earl Hooker immediately come to mind—but Elmore had the sound and all the feeling.

A radio repairman by trade, Elmore reworked his guitar amplifiers in his spare time, getting them to produce raw, distorted sounds that wouldn't resurface until the advent of heavy rock amplification in the late '60s. This amp on 11 approach was hot-wired to one of the strongest emotional approaches to the blues ever recorded. There is never a time when you're listening to one of his records that you feel—no matter how familiar the structure—that he's phoning it in just to grab a quick session check. Elmore James always gave it everything he had, everything he could emotionally invest in a number. This commitment of spirit is something that shows up time and again when listening to multiple takes from his session masters. The sheer repetitiveness of the recording process would dim almost anyone's creative fires, but Elmore always seemed to give it 100% every time the red light went on. Few blues singers had a voice that could compete with James'; it was loud, forceful, prone to "catch" or break up in the high registers, almost sounding on the verge of hysteria at certain moments. Evidently the times back in the mid-'30s when Elmore had first-hand absorption of Robert Johnson as a playing companion had deep influence on him, not only in his choice of material, but also in his presentation of it.

Backing the twin torrents of Elmore's guitar and voice was one of the greatest—and earliest—Chicago blues bands. Named after James' big hit, the Broomdusters featured Little Johnny Jones on piano, J.T. Brown on tenor sax, and Elmore's cousin, Homesick James, on rhythm guitar. This talented nucleus was often augmented by the likes of a second saxophone on occasion, while the drumming stool changed frequently. But this was the band that could go toe to toe in a battle of the blues against the bands of Muddy Waters or Howlin' Wolf and always hold their own, if not walk away with the show. Utilizing a stomping beat, Elmore's slashing guitar, Jones' two-fisted piano delivery, Homesick's rudimentary boogie bass rhythm, and Brown's braying nanny-goat sax leads, the Broomdusters were as loud and powerful and popular as any blues band the Windy City had to offer.

But as urban as their sound was, it all had roots in Elmore's hometown of Canton, MS. He was born there on January 27, 1918, the illegitimate son of Leola Brooks and later given the surname of his stepfather, Joe Willie James. He adapted to music at an early age, learning to play bottleneck on a homemade instrument fashioned out of a broom handle and a lard can. By the age of 14, he was already a weekend musician, working the various country suppers and juke joints in the area under the names "Cleanhead" or Joe Willie James. Although he confined himself to a home base area around Belzoni, he would join up and work with traveling players coming through like Robert Johnson, Howlin' Wolf, and Sonny Boy Williamson. By the late '30s he had formed his first band and was working the Southern state area with Sonny Boy until the Second World War broke out, spending three years stationed with the Navy in Guam. When he was discharged, he picked up where he left off, moving for a while to Memphis, working in clubs with Eddie Taylor and his cousin, Homesick James. Elmore was also one of the first "guest stars" on the popular *King Biscuit Time* radio show on KFFA in Helena, AR, also doing stints on the *Talaho Syrup* show on Yazoo City's WAZF, and the *Hadacol* show on KWEM in West Memphis.

Nervous and unsure of his abilities as a recording artist, Elmore was surreptitiously recorded by Lillian McMurray of Trumpet Records at the tail end of a Sonny Boy session, doing his now signature tune, "Dust My Broom." The legend has it that James didn't even stay around long enough to hear the playback, much less record a second side. Mrs. McMurray stuck a local singer (Bo Bo Thomas) on the flip side and the record became the surprise R&B hit of 1951, making the Top Ten and conversely making a recording star out of Elmore. With a few months left on his Trumpet contract, Elmore was recorded by the Bihari brothers for their Modern label subsidiaries, Flair and Meteor, but the results were left in the can until James' contract ran out. In the meantime, Elmore had moved to Chicago and cut a quick session for Chess, which resulted in one single being issued, and just as quickly being yanked off the market, as the Biharis swooped in to protect their investment. This period of activity found Elmore assembling the nucleus of his great band the Broomdusters, and several fine recordings were issued over the next few years on a plethora of Bihari-owned labels, with several of them charting and most all of them becoming certified blues classics.

By this time, James had established a beach-head in the clubs of Chicago as one of the most popular live acts, and regularly broadcasting over WPOA under the aegis of disc-jockey Big Bill Hill. In 1957, with his contract with the Biharis at an end, he recorded several successful sides for Mel London's Chief label, all of them later being issued on the larger Vee-Jay label. His health—always in a fragile state due to a recurring heart condition—would send him back home to Jackson, MS, where he temporarily set aside his playing for work as a disc jockey or radio repair man. He came back to Chicago to record a session for Chess, then just as quickly, broke the contract to sign with Bobby Robinson's Fire label, producing the classic "The Sky Is Crying" and numerous others. Running afoul with the Chicago musician's union, he returned back to Mississippi, doing sessions in New York and New Orleans while waiting for Big Bill Hill to sort things out. In August of 1963, Elmore returned to Chicago, ready to resume his on-again off-again playing career—his records were still being regularly issued and reissued on a variety of labels—when he suffered his final heart attack. His wake was attended by over 400 blues luminaries before his body was shipped back to Mississippi. He was elected to the Blues Foundation's Hall of Fame in 1980, and was later elected to the Rock & Roll Hall of Fame as a seminal influence. Elmore James may not have lived to reap the rewards of the blues revival, but his music and influence continues to resonate. — *Cub Koda*

Whose Muddy Shoes / 1969 / MCA/Chess ♦♦♦♦
Elmore had recorded a session for Chess in 1953 before settling down with the Bihari brothers, and again in 1960, shortly before starting his final recordings for Bobby Robinson's Fire, Fury, and Enjoy labels. This collects all of them on CD with the bonus addition of an alternate take of "The Sun Is Shining," which can be interpreted as a precursor to his later hit "The Sky Is Crying." The earlier sides from 1953 lack his inimitable slide, but the 1960 session produced classics like "Talk to Me Baby," "Madison Blues," and a powerful reading of T-Bone Walker's "Stormy Monday." These tracks of Elmore working with the Chess production team are delightfully fleshed out with a half dozen gems by the highly underrated John Brim, some of which include stellar harp work by Little Walter ("Rattlesnake," "Be Careful"—on which Walter stops playing in several spots to become an ad-lib backup vocalist—and "You Got Me"), as well as the original version of "Ice Cream Man," better known to rock fans from Van Halen's cover version of it from their debut album. — *Cub Koda*

☆ **The Original Meteor & Flair Sides** / 1984 / Ace ♦♦♦♦♦
The best of James' early-'50s sides with stunning slide and driving band support. At the top of his form, this is a perfect introduction to his music. — *Cub Koda*

Let's Cut It: The Very Best of Elmore James / 1991 / Flair ♦♦♦♦
Let's Cut It: The Very Best of Elmore James rounds up 18 tracks from his Modern, Flair and Meteor recordings. These are generally considered to be some James' greatest recordings, and there's no denying that there are incendiary performances throughout the record that more than prove James' legendary status. A few alternate takes are thrown in that are more

noteworthy for collectors than general listeners. Then again, fans who only want one disc of Elmore will be best served by Rhino's *The Sky Is Crying*, which selects highlights from all of his many labels. This, in turn, is for fans who want to dig a little deeper than that set, since this contains the best of one of his best periods. — *Stephen Thomas Erlewine*

Rollin' & Tumblin': The Best of Elmore James / 1992 / Relic ♦♦♦♦
Although the Capricorn box set does a great job of rounding at least one take of everything James cut for Bobby Robinson's Fire & Enjoy labels, if you want (or need) to sweat it down to bare essentials, this is the one to grab out of the blues bin and take home. The remastering by Little Walter Devenne on this single disc is exemplary, and for late period Elmore, this truly is the best of the best. — *Cub Koda*

☆ **King of the Slide Guitar** / 1992 / Warner Brothers ♦♦♦♦♦
Elmore's last great recordings occurred in the 1960s when he was signed by New York producer/label-owner Bobby Robinson. Unlike many of his contemporaries, James seemingly got *better* as the years went by, and while none of the sides feature a slide guitar anywhere near as nasty as his early Modern and Flair recordings, he's still obviously giving it all on each and every side. These recordings are the ones most commonly issued on James and have surfaced on so many different compilations—all with varying levels of sound quality—that it would be futile to list them all here. Fortunately, to make things easier, we have this two-disc 50-song box set rounding up at least one extant take of everything Elmore recorded with Robinson at the helm. While some of the material are recuts of his best known tunes ("Dust My Broom" resurfaces here in two versions from two different sessions, and the version of "It Hurts Me Too" included here—it was originally cut for Chief in the late '50s—became a posthumous hit for him), the majority of it breaks new ground and stands as some of Elmore's most emotion-laden work. Nice essays in the booklet make up for the disgusting art work that adorns the box. — *Cub Koda*

Dust My Broom: The Best of Elmore James, Vol. 2 / 1992 / Relic ♦♦♦♦
A second Relic volume of classics from the Fire/Fury/Enjoy vaults that picks up where the company's first one left off. Even if you already own Capricorn's definitive two-disc collection of his Bobby Robinson-produced sides, you're missing one gem here: "Poor Little Angel Child," which features the robust vocal talent of harpist Sam Myers. Great sound quality throughout, with many stereo items. — *Bill Dahl*

★ **The Sky Is Crying: The History of Elmore James** / 1993 / Rhino ♦♦♦♦♦
With the confusing plethora of Elmore James discs out on the market, this is truly the place to start, featuring the best of his work culled from several labels. Highlights include James' original recording of "Dust My Broom," "It Hurts Me Too," "T.V. Mama" (with Elmore backing Big Joe Turner), and the title track, one of the best slow blues ever created. Slide guitar doesn't get much better than this, making this particular compilation not only a perfect introduction to Elmore's music, but an essential piece for any blues collection. — *Cub Koda*

☆ **The Classic Recordings** / 1993 / Flair/Virgin ♦♦♦♦♦
After Elmore hit the national charts with his Trumpet recording of "Dust My Broom," he came to record for the Bihari brothers, first for their Meteor subsidiary, then later for their Flair and Modern labels. This multi-disc retrospective rounds up every existing master Elmore recorded for the Biharis, plus his backup work behind band members Johnny Jones and J.T. Brown. James' guitar tone is distorted and overamped to the extreme; *this* is the sound that changed the face of slide guitar forever, influencing everyone from Hound Dog Taylor to J.B. Hutto to George Thorogood and everybody in between. The intensity of James' vocals are nothing short of riveting, and the material collected here (along with breakdowns, studio chat, etc.) is simply the best of Elmore's early-'50s sides and a box set well worth saving up for. — *Cub Koda*

The Best of Elmore James: Early Years / 1995 / Ace ♦♦♦
This breaks down Elmore's Modern recordings into a single disc retrospective, and a damn fine one it is, too. This compiles the A and B sides of every single recorded for the Bihari brothers, with the original Trumpet recording of "Dust My Broom" standing in the place of "1839 Blues." If you really want to hear Elmore at his wildest and most unfettered, and don't want to wade

through a pile of alternate takes to get to it, we heartily suggest adding this one to the collection. Import. — *Cub Koda*

Etta James (Etta James Hawkins)

b. Jan. 25, 1938, Los Angeles, CA
Vocals / Soul, R&B, Soul Blues, Classic Female Blues

Few R&B singers have endured tragic travails on the monumental level that Etta James has and remain on earth to talk about it. The lady's no shrinking violet; her recent autobiography, *Rage to Survive,* describes her past (including numerous drug addictions) in sordid detail.

But her personal problems have seldom affected her singing. James has hung in there from the age of R&B and doo wop in the mid-'50s, through soul's late-'60s heyday, and right up to today (where her 1994 disc *Mystery Lady* paid loving jazz-based tribute to one of her idols, Billie Holiday). Etta James' voice has deepened over the years, coarsened more than a little, but still conveys remarkable passion and pain.

Jamesetta Hawkins was a child gospel prodigy, singing in her Los Angeles Baptist church choir (and over the radio) when she was only five years old under the tutelage of Professor James Earle Hines. She moved to San Francisco in 1950, soon teaming with two other girls to form a singing group. When she was 14, bandleader Johnny Otis gave the trio an audition. He particularly dug their answer song to Hank Ballard & the Midnighters' "Work with Me Annie."

Against her mother's wishes, the young singer embarked for L.A. to record "Roll with Me Henry" with the Otis band and vocalist Richard Berry in 1954 for Modern Records. Otis inverted her first name to devise her stage handle and dubbed her vocal group the Peaches (also Etta's nickname). "Roll with Me Henry," renamed "The Wallflower" when some radio programmers objected to the original title's connotations, topped the R&B charts in 1955.

The Peaches dropped from the tree shortly thereafter, but Etta James kept on singing for Modern throughout much of the decade (often under the supervision of saxist Maxwell Davis). "Good Rockin' Daddy" also did quite well for her later in 1955, but deserving follow-ups such as "W-O-M-A-N" and "Tough Lover" (the latter a torrid rocker cut in New Orleans with Lee Allen on sax) failed to catch on.

James landed at Chicago's Chess Records in 1960, signing with their Argo subsidiary. Immediately, her recording career kicked into high gear; not only did a pair of duets with her then-boyfriend (Moonglows lead singer Harvey Fuqua) chart, but her own sides (beginning with the tortured ballad "All I Could Do Was Cry") chased each other up the R&B lists as well. Leonard Chess viewed James as a classy ballad singer with pop crossover potential, backing her with lush violin orchestrations for 1961's luscious "At Last" and "Trust in Me." But James' rougher side wasn't forsaken—the gospel-charged "Something's Got a Hold on Me" in 1962, a kinetic 1963 live LP (*Etta James Rocks the House*) cut at Nashville's New Era Club, and a blues-soaked 1966 duet with childhood pal Sugar Pie De Santo, "In the Basement," ensured that.

Although Chess hosted its own killer house band, James traveled to Rick Hall's Fame studios in Muscle Shoals in 1967 and emerged with one of her all-time classics. "Tell Mama" was a searing slice of upbeat southern soul that contrasted markedly with another standout from the same sessions, the spine-chilling ballad "I'd Rather Go Blind." Despite the death of Leonard Chess, Etta James remained at the label into 1975, experimenting toward the end with a more rock-based approach.

There were some mighty lean years, both personally and professionally, for Miss Peaches. But she got back on track recording-wise in 1988 with a set for Island, *Seven Year Itch,* that reaffirmed her southern soul mastery. Her last few albums have been a varied lot—1990's *Sticking to My Guns* was contemporary in the extreme; 1992's Jerry Wexler-produced *The Right Time* for Elektra was slickly soulful, and her most recent outings have explored jazz directions.

In concert, Etta James is a sassy, no-holds-barred performer whose suggestive stage antics sometimes border on the obscene. She's paid her dues many times over as an R&B and soul pioneer; long may she continue to shock the uninitiated. — *Bill Dahl*

Second Time Around / 1961 / MCA/Chess ✦✦✦✦
Etta James' second album isn't what you pull off the shelf when you want to hear her belt some soul. Like her debut, it found Chess presenting her as more or less a pop singer, using orchestration arranged and conducted by

Riley Hampton, and mostly tackling popular standards of the '40s. If you're not a purist, this approach won't bother you in the least; James sings with gusto, proving that she could more than hold her own in this idiom as well. R&B isn't entirely neglected either, with the rousing "Seven Day Fool" (co-written by Berry Gordy, Jr.) a standout; "Don't Cry Baby" and "Fool That I Am" were R&B hits that made a mild impression on the pop charts as well. — *Richie Unterberger*

★ **At Last** / 1961 / MCA/Chess ✦✦✦✦✦
Most of these are also on *Greatest Sides.* Those that are not are well worth hearing. — *George Bedard*

Sings for Lovers / 1962 / Cadet ✦✦✦
Smooth and mellow. — *Bill Dahl*

Etta James Sings / 1962 / United ✦✦✦
A collection of her '50s hits, it includes "Roll with Me, Henry" (the answer song to Hank Ballard's "Work with Me, Annie"). Out of print. — *George Bedard*

☆ **Rocks the House** / 1964 / MCA/Chess ✦✦✦✦✦
Simply one of the greatest live blues albums ever captured on tape. Cut in 1963 at the New Era Club in Nashville, the set finds Etta James in stellar shape as she forcefully delivers her own "Something's Got a Hold on Me" and "Seven Day Fool," interspersed with a diet of sizzling covers ("What'd I Say," "Sweet Little Angel," "Money," "Ooh Poo Pah Doo"). The CD incarnation adds three more great titles, including an impassioned reprise of her "All I Could Do Is Cry." Guitarist David T. Walker is outstanding whenever he solos. — *Bill Dahl*

Call My Name / 1966 / Cadet ✦✦✦✦
Still unavailable digitally, James' 1966 LP is dynamite Chicago soul, with the vaunted Chess house band in uplifting support. Among the many standouts are "I'm So Glad (I Found Love in You)," "It Must Be Your Love," and "Don't Pick Me for Your Fool." — *Bill Dahl*

Tell Mama / 1968 / MCA/Chess ✦✦✦✦
Leonard Chess dispatched Etta James to Muscle Shoals in 1967, and the move paid off with one of her best and most soul-searing Cadet albums. Produced by Rick Hall, the resultant album boasted a relentlessly driving title cut, the moving soul ballad "I'd Rather Go Blind," sizzling covers of Otis Redding's "Security," and Jimmy Hughes' "Don't Lose Your Good Thing," and a pair of fine Don Covay copyrights. The skin-tight session aces at Fame Studios really did themselves proud behind Miss Peaches. — *Bill Dahl*

Losers Weepers / 1971 / Cadet ✦✦✦
Another vinyl-only LP from her Chess stint produced by Ralph Bass that traverses a wide range of material. Chess saxist Gene "Daddy G" Barge penned "I Think It's You," but his presence is matched by that of Duke Ellington ("I Got It Bad and That Ain't Good") and J. Fred Coots ("For All We Know") in the composers' credits. — *Bill Dahl*

Come a Little Closer / 1974 / Chess ✦✦✦
James was fighting serious substance-abuse problems when this record was recorded, commuting to the sessions from a rehab center. It was a triumph simply to complete the record at all. But although James' life may have been in rough shape outside of the studio, she delivered a fairly strong set that fused forceful '70s soul arrangements with some rock (Randy Newman and John Kay both contribute compositions), jazz, and New Orleans R&B. Some of the material is routine, but there are some very strong cuts here, like a rousing "Sookie Sookie," and "Out on the Street Again," with its slightly sinister funk groove. "Feeling Uneasy," in fact, counts as one of the unsung highlights of her career, with a wrenching, near-wordless scat-moan vocal over a suitably languorous, melancholy blues-jazz arrangement. The CD reissue adds a couple of interesting bonus tracks: the 1975 single "Lovin' Arms," a good rootsy ballad, and a single edit of one of the tracks from the album, "Out on the Street Again." — *Richie Unterberger*

Deep in the Night / 1978 / Bullseye Blues ✦✦✦✦
Originally released on Warners Brothers to scant acclaim in 1978, this Jerry Wexler-produced masterpiece finds James in astounding voice with a batch of great material to apply her massive interpretive powers to. The band, including the cream of the late-'70s Los Angeles session hot-shots (Cornell Dupree, Jeff Porcaro, Chuck Rainey, Plas Johnson, Jim Horn), lays it down soulful and simple, and the result is a modern-day R&B classic. Highlights

abound throughout, but special attention must be turned to James' takes on "Only Women Bleed" and the Eagles' "Take It to the Limit." — *Cub Koda*

R&B Dynamite / 1987 / Virgin ◆◆◆◆
The singer in her precocious formative years, headed by her 1955 R&B smash "Roll with Me Henry" (aka "The Wallflower"). James' followups included the driving "Good Rockin' Daddy," a bluesy "W-O-M-A-N," and the New Orleans raveup "Tough Lover," which found her backed by the gang at Cosimo's (notably saxman Lee Allen). Even though her tenure at Modern Records only produced a handful of hits, these 22 cuts are delightful artifacts of the belter's earliest days. — *Bill Dahl*

The Sweetest Peaches/Chess Years / 1988 / Chess ◆◆◆◆
A good 20-track survey of her Chess work on this double LP. All but two of the songs, however, are now available on the much more extensive CD *The Essential Etta James*, making this collection redundant. — *Richie Unterberger*

The Right Time / 1992 / Elektra ◆◆
A myriad of big names came together for the making of this album. Jerry Wexler produced it; sidemen include Steve Cropper and Lucky Peterson — but the final product is a disappointment. It's just too slickly rendered to come close to the knockout punch of her vintage Chess material. — *Bill Dahl*

How Strong Is a Woman: The Island Sessions / 1993 / 4th & Broadway ◆◆◆
How Strong Is a Woman collects the highlights from Etta James' late '80s and early '90s stint at Island Records. Although she didn't record any new classics while she was at the label, she demonstrated time and time again that she hadn't lost much of her vocal power and that she remained vital 40 years after she began recording. *How Strong Is a Woman* offers positive proof of that and is a good sampling of her work for Island. — *Thom Owens*

★ **The Essential Etta James** / 1994 / MCA/Chess ◆◆◆◆◆
Forty-four tracks summarizing the long and brilliant Chess tenure of Miss Peaches, opening with her 1960 smash "All I Could Do Was Cry," encompassing her torchy, fully orchestrated ballads "At Last," "My Dearest Darling," and "Trust in Me," and continuing on through her 1962 gospel rocker "Something's Got a Hold on Me," the Chicago soul standouts "I Prefer You," and "842-3089," and her 1967 Muscle Shoals-cut smash "Tell Mama." A few of the '70s sides that conclude the two-disc set seem makeweight when compared to what preceded them, but most of the essentials are aboard. — *Bill Dahl*

Live from San Francisco / 1994 / On The Spot ◆◆◆◆
Commercially, the 1970s weren't nearly as kind to Etta James as the 1950s and '60s had been. The sleekness that characterized northern "uptown" soul and disco didn't appeal to the big-voiced belter, who stuck to her guns and continued to embrace the type of gritty, hard-hitting Southern soul and down-home blues that had earned her so devoted a following. Though absent from Black radio playlists, she had no problem attracting enthusiastic live audiences. At 41, James sounds like she's very much in her prime on this live recording from 1981. Whether tearing into an Otis Redding medley, her hit "Tell Mama" or Chicago blues staples like Willie Dixon's "I Just Want to Make Love to You," and Jimmy Reed's "Baby, What You Want Me to Do," the earthy singer clearly excels by sticking with what she does best. One of the CD's most pleasant surprises is a version of the Eagles' "Take It to the Limit," which works remarkably well in an R&B setting. — *Alex Henderson*

Something's Got a Hold / 1994 / Charly ◆◆◆
It's not that the contents of this 20-song disc aren't terrific; until the last four songs, anyway, they are. After all, this is Etta James' Chess legacy we're talking about here. But compared to MCA's superior-sounding (and annotated) anthologies, this disc falls a bit flat. — *Bill Dahl*

Mystery Lady: Songs of Billie Holiday / Mar. 1, 1994 / Private Music ◆◆◆
The popular Etta James usually performs raunchy single-entendre blues, so this surprisingly subtle outing is a real change of pace. She sounds quite laidback on a set of ballads associated with Billie Holiday, and utilizes a jazz rhythm section led by pianist Cedar Walton plus three horn players, including the great Red Holloway on tenor and alto. James makes no attempts at exploring uptempo material or scatting, sticking to soulful interpretations of the classic ballads. Despite the lack of variety in tempos, the music is quite satisfying. — *Scott Yanow*

These Foolish Things / 1995 / MCA/Chess ◆◆◆◆
James has long been a masterful blues balladeer — a talent spotlighted throughout the course of this 14-song collection. Some tracks are cushioned by string-enriched arrangements, others — notably 1965's passionate "Only Time Will Tell" — are melodic Chicago soul. Four tracks are previously unreleased, including her reading of Billie Holiday's "Lover Man." — *Bill Dahl*

★ **Her Best** / 1997 / Chess ◆◆◆◆◆
While several best-ofs from Etta's Chess period have been available over the years — with the two-disc, 44-track *Essential Etta James* at the top of the list in giving the big picture — this 20-track collection sweats *that* bigger picture down to bare essentials. For those wishing to finally sample Etta's classic period at Chess without opening the wallet for box set-anthology expense, this single-disc retrospective will fill the bill quite nicely. Featuring 20 of the tracks that appear on the double-disc *Essential* anthology without anything literally essential left off, this scintillating little disc now officially becomes the one-stop, first-time purchase in connecting with the emotional greatness inherent in Etta's siren song. There's plenty more after this to discover, but *this* is absolutely where you start. — *Cub Koda*

Love's Been Rough on Me / Apr. 29, 1997 / Private Music ◆◆◆
Love's Been Rough on Me is a terrific latter-day album from Etta James, capturing her at the peak of her powers. James' voice has diminished only slightly over the course of her career, and she knows how to make such warhorses as "I've Been Loving You Too Long" sound fresh. She also invests contemporary music, including John Berry's contemporary country hit "If I Had Any Pride Left at All," with real soul. The result is a record that delivers the real goods with grace and style. — *Leo Stanley*

Skip James (Nehemiah Curtis James)

b. Jun. 21, 1902, Bentonia, MS, **d.** Oct. 3, 1969, Philadelphia, PA
Guitar, Vocals, Kazoo, Organ, Piano / Delta Blues, Country Blues, Piano Blues, Prewar Country Blues, Blues Revival
Among the earliest and most influential Delta bluesmen to record, Skip James was the best known proponent of the so-called Bentonia school of blues players, a genre strain invested with as much fanciful scholarly "research" as any. Coupling an oddball guitar tuning set against eerie, falsetto vocals, James' early recordings could make the hair stand up on the back of your neck. Even more surprising was when blues scholars rediscovered him in the '60s and found his singing and playing skills intact. Influencing everyone from a young Robert Johnson (Skip's "Devil Got My Woman" became the basis of Johnson's "Hellhound on My Trail") to Eric Clapton (who recorded James' "I'm So Glad" on the first Cream album), Skip James' music, while from a commonly shared regional tradition, remains infused with his own unique personal spirit. — *Cub Koda*

Greatest of the Delta Blues Singers / 1964 / Biograph ◆◆◆◆
Shortly after his triumphant resurrection at the 1964 Newport Folk Festival, Skip James returned to the recording studio for the first time in over three decades to cut the 12 sides which comprise the superb *Greatest of the Delta Blues Singers*, a career-capping overview which reprises some of the songs from his 1931 Paramount sessions, and introduces a half-dozen new compositions as well. Although his guitar skills have lost a step in the intervening years, the passage of time has only made James' vocals that much more expressive; his new material is especially devastating, in particular "Sick Bed Blues" and "Washington D.C. Hospital Center Blues," both detailing the fight with cancer that eventually led to his death. — *Jason Ankeny*

She Lyin' / 1964 / Genes ◆◆◆◆
By the time James had been rediscovered in the 1960s, he was still capable of playing entrancing, dynamic music, but was much less consistent and not as striking a vocalist. It was a testimony to his greatness that he still managed to make compelling records, and he was among the best storytellers and dramatic singers in the traditional realm. This mid-'60s CD features songs James recorded for the Adelphi label in 1964 that were never issued. It's hard to understand why this wasn't issued at the time it was recorded; it's just as solid as the albums James recorded for Columbia during the same period. — *Ron Wynn*

☆ **Skip James Today!** / 1965 / Vanguard ◆◆◆◆◆
As quiet as it was kept then, Skip James might have made the best music of anyone who resurfaced during the mid-'60s "rediscovery" era for Mississippi

country blues types. Certainly, there weren't many albums made during that time as good as this one; wonderful vocals, superb guitar, and a couple of tunes with tasty piano make this essential. — *Ron Wynn*

Devil Got My Woman / Mar. 22, 1966 + Mar. 24, 1966 / Vanguard ◆◆◆
Skip James made his original reputation with 17 recordings that he cut during February 1931 when he was 28. Although fluent on both the guitar and (to a lesser extent) the piano, James was most notable for his storytelling lyrics, his haunting high pitched voice, and his distinctive interpretations of the Delta blues. Thirty-three years after his early recordings, James was rediscovered in time to appear at the 1964 Newport Folk Festival. He was quite active during 1964-66, making the music on this solo CD (his last record) three years before his death in 1969. One can easily hear the influence that Skip James' music had on the then flourishing folk music movement, and he still sang his country blues with great intensity. — *Scott Yanow*

☆ **Complete 1931 Session** / 1986 / Yazoo ◆◆◆◆◆
A magnificent sampler of the '30s repertoire of a major Mississippi artist. Blues, ballads, and religious songs are included among the major songs from this idiosyncratic musical genius who has influenced current artists such as John Cephas. — *Barry Lee Pearson*

Complete Recorded Works (1931) / 1990 / Document ◆◆◆◆
For completists, specialists and academics, Document's *Complete Recorded Works (1931)* is invaluable, offering an exhaustive overview of Skip James' recordings. There are some absolutely wonderful, classic performances on the collection, but the long running time, exacting chronological sequencing, poor fidelity (all cuts are transferred from original acetates and 78s), and number of performances will probably appeal only the serious blues listener; casual listeners will find that the collection is of marginal interest. — *Thom Owens*

★ **Complete Early Recordings** / 1994 / Yazoo ◆◆◆◆◆
Complete Early Recordings collects 18 tracks Skip James recorded in the early '30s. The single-disc compilation features all of his classic songs in their original versions, including "I'm So Glad." It's a concise and thorough collection and it's essential to any blues library. — *Thom Owens*

Live: Boston 1964 / Jun. 2, 1994 / Document ◆◆◆

Steve James

b. Jul. 15, 1950, Manhattan, New York, NY
Vocals, Guitar, Mandolin / Modern Acoustic Blues
A native of New York City (born 1950), James got into the blues via his father's guitar (at age 13) and phonograph (thanks to his father's 78s by Leadbelly and Josh White). He was primarily self-taught, although he received tutelage from veterans such as Furry Lewis, Sam McGee, and Lum Guffin, after moving to Tennessee in the early '70s. He also trained in luthiery at Gurian Guitars (1970-71) and was a deejay at WEVL in Memphis. In 1977 he settled in San Antonio, where he played solo and sometimes with R&B sax legend Clifford Scott. After moving to Austin he signed with Antone's Records in 1991. In addition to his solo CDs like 1993's *Two Track Mind*, 1994's *American Primitive*, and 1996's *Art and Grit*, he has backed blues singers Gary Primich and Angela Strehli on record, as well as singer-songwriter James McMurtry and others. He is currently a contributing editor to *Acoustic Guitar* magazine. — *Dan Forte*

Two Track Mind / 1993 / Discovery ◆◆◆
A rarity in today's field of acoustic blues pickers; a guitarist with encyclopedic knowledge who never sounds academic. James embraces a wide scope of fingerpicking styles—Piedmont school ragtime, hokum ("Huggin' and Chalkin'"), country (Sam McGee is the source of two tunes here), and slide (his showstopping take on Sylvester Weaver's "Guitar Rag") with super technique, humor, and a relaxed ease that borders on cockiness. Only one original here, but that situation was to be rectified on Steve's follow-up. — *Dan Forte*

● **American Primitive** / 1994 / Antone's ◆◆◆◆
Utilizing a jug band of fellow Austinites Danny Barnes (tenor guitar and banjo), and Mark Rubin (stand-up bass and Sousaphone—both of the Bad Livers), and harpist Gary Primich on some tracks, James sounds more mature here, evidenced by six originals (the John Hurt-esque "Talco Girl" is particularly nice) and one collaboration with bassist/songwriter Sarah Brown ("My Last Good Car") and effective rather than affected vocals. Stellar

guitar throughout, with an added treat: James' blues mandolin on "Midnight Blues." — *Dan Forte*

Art & Grit / Sep. 9, 1996 / Discovery ◆◆◆◆
James' first album was a solo effort; his second added a small combo. *Art and Grit*, his third, is a virtual celebration of acoustic string instruments. The Austin "jug band" of *American Primitive*—James, Danny Barnes, Mark Rubin, and Gary Primich—reunites on three cuts and forms the nucleus of three others. Guitar virtuoso Rob Brozman and Asleep at the Wheel's Cindy Cashdollar make guest appearances, and all told, there are no fewer than eleven different instrument lineups on the disc, with guitars of many types (standard, slide, Hawaiian, and tenor), banjos (6- and 4-string), and mandolins presented solo and in various combinations. Most memorable cuts are James' delightfully archaic banjo rendition of the century-old "Buddy Bolden's Blues," and the joyfully clanging triple guitar attack on "Downbound Train" (an obscure Chuck Berry album cut, based on an old temperance song). Recording quality is exceptionally vivid, capturing the distinctive timbre of each instrument and making *Art and Grit* an old-timey blues lovers' delight. — *Steve Hoffman*

Blind Lemon Jefferson

b. Jul. 11, 1897, Couchman, TX, **d.** Dec. 1929, Chicago, IL
Guitar, Vocals / Texas Blues, Acoustic Blues
One of the first blues-guitar stars, Blind Lemon Jefferson became the most famous bluesman of the Roaring Twenties. His 78s shattered racial barriers, becoming popular from coast to coast and influencing a generation of musicians. His best songs forged original, imagistic themes with inventive arrangements and brilliantly improvised solos. He was a serious showman, balancing a driving, unpredictable guitar style with a booming, two-octave voice. His guitar became a second voice that complemented rather than repeated his lyrics. He often halted rhythm at the end of vocal lines to launch into elaborate solo flourishes, and he could play in unusual meters with a great deal of drive and flash. A man well acquainted with booze, gambling, and heavy-hipped mamas, Blind Lemon lived the rough-and-tumble themes that dominate his songs. Portraits of Afro-American life during the early 1900s, his lyrics create a unique body of poetry—humorous and harrowing, jivey and risqué, a stunning view of society from the perspective of someone at the bottom. To this day, he ranks among the most gifted and individualistic artists in blues history. — *Jas Obrecht*

Blind Lemon Jefferson / Mar. 1961 / Milestone ◆◆◆◆
Solid collection (73 minutes' worth) of some of Lemon's best. "Jack O'Diamond Blues," "Match Box Blues," and "That Black Snake Moan" are all on board, and with the Sonic Solutions System employed on the audio restoration end, the result is about the best these surviving 60-year-old 78s have ever sounded. — *Cub Koda*

★ **King of the Country Blues** / 1985 / Yazoo ◆◆◆◆◆
King of the Country Blues compiles 28 of Blind Lemon Jefferson's finest songs, all presented in the original '20s versions. It is the finest introduction to the guitarist—as well as the most effective, concise retrospective—ever assembled. — *Thom Owens*

Complete Recorded Works, Vol. 1-4 / Document ◆◆◆
For completists, specialists and academics, Document's *Complete Recorded Works*—available as four separate volumes—is invaluable, offering an exhaustive overview of Blind Lemon Jefferson's early recordings. For less dedicated listeners, the long running time, exacting chronological sequencing, poor fidelity (all cuts are transferred from original acetates and 78s), and number of performances will be hard to digest. — *Thom Owens*

The Jelly Roll Kings

Group / Contemporary Blues
The Jelly Roll Kings are a trio of state-of-the-art Mississippi Delta bluesmen who play their music raw and unvarnished, complete with lilting rhythms, dreamily atmospheric keyboards, dance-shuffle drums, and soul-drenched vocals. Led by guitarist Big Jack Johnson, the band includes two veterans of the Delta juke joint scene—Frank Frost on keyboards and harmonica, and Sam Carr, the son of legendary blues musician Robert Nighthawk, on drums. Johnson, the group's guitarist, chief songwriter and lead vocalist, is the youngest of the three.

Carr began dancing at his father's gigs when he was eight and later took up drums. Harmonica player and keyboardist Frank Frost's background includes playing guitar for Sonny Boy Williamson II, recording in Nashville with Elvis Presley guitarist Scotty Moore, and releasing his own album on the Appaloosa label, *Frank Frost with Freddie and the Screamers*, in 1992. Frost also recorded an album for the British Charly label, *Frank Frost, Jelly Roll King: Charly Blues Masterworks Vol. 36.*

The Jelly Roll Kings have recorded one album for the Fat Possum/Capricorn label, 1997's *Off Yonder Wall*. Produced by author/impresario Robert Palmer, the album does a superb job of capturing the complex interplay between Johnson, Carr, and Frost. The recording is suitably raw and stripped down, with a remarkable live club sound to it. The trio puts a fresh spin on old familiar blues standards like "That's Alright Mama" and "Baby Please Don't Go," while their originals remain true to the spirit of 1990s-era Delta juke joint blues. The result is one of the most unique-sounding albums of the year. —*Richard Skelly*

● **Rockin the Juke Joint Down** / 1979 / Earwig ♦♦♦♦
Michael Frank inaugurated his Earwig imprint with this 1979 album reteaming Frost, Johnson, and Carr in all their glory. Frank was mesmerized by the trio's almost telepathic musical interplay, a trait captured vividly by the album itself. This trio's repertoire was varied—the no-holds-barred "Slop Jar Blues" is offset by the bubbly instrumental "Sunshine Twist." Frost and Johnson share vocal duties. —*Bill Dahl*

Johnny Jenkins

b. 1939, Macon, Georgia
Guitar / R&B
Guitarist, singer and songwriter Johnny Jenkins may have had a long pause between records, but his heart, ears, and mind were always close to blues music. Jenkins never wanted to be a professional musician, and always worked day jobs, including digging wells, logging, and mechanic work. Jenkins' style is at times reminiscent of Elmore James, and at other times, one can hear echoes of Jimi Hendrix in Jenkins' guitar playing—probably because Jenkins was a seminal influence on Hendrix.

Jenkins, born in Macon, GA, in 1939, grew up in a rural area called Swift Creek. He listened to a battery-powered radio and first heard the sounds of blues and classic R&B, artists like Bill Doggett, Bullmoose Jackson, and others. Jenkins built his first guitar out of a cigar box and rubber bands when he was nine, and began playing at a gas station for tips. He played it left-handed and upside down, and this practice continued after his older sister bought him a real guitar a couple of years later.

Capricorn Records founder Phil Walden first heard Jenkins on a local radio talent show in 1959. Walden began to book Jenkins' band, the Pinetoppers, which included Otis Redding on lead vocals. Redding got his first big break in 1962 when he drove Jenkins to the Stax Studios in Memphis to record a follow-up to Jenkins' regional hit, "Love Twist." The producer encouraged the young Redding to take a turn at singing in the studio, and he recorded "These Arms Of Mine" with some extra studio time. Redding's career began to take off and Jenkins was asked to become part of his band, but Jenkins refused, ironically because of his fear of airline travel.

Following Redding's untimely demise in an airplane crash, Jenkins stayed close to home, playing regionally and working day jobs to support his family. His unorthodox guitar style left lasting marks on the young, impressionable Jimi Hendrix, who came out to see Jenkins play while visiting relatives in the Macon area. Later, in 1969, Jenkins and Hendrix teamed up to play together at The Scene, a club owned by Steve Paul in New York. In 1970, Walden put Jenkins into the studio with several members of the Allman Brothers Band to record his debut album, *Ton Ton Macoute*, one of the fledgling Capricorn label's first releases. Although *Ton Ton Macoute* was finally released to high critical praise in 1972, the then-small label had other priorities to deal with, including the newly successful Allman Brothers.

In 1996, Capricorn founder Walden convinced Jenkins to record a "comeback" album, *Blessed Blues*. He's backed by a stellar cast of musicians, including Chuck Leavell on keyboards and Muscle Shoals percussionist Mickey Buckins. Capricorn also has plans to reissue Jenkins' now-legendary *Ton Ton Macoute* on compact disc. —*Richard Skelly*

● **Ton Ton Macoute** / 1970 / Atco ♦♦♦♦
This timeless gem, originally recorded in 1969-70, from the much neglected

Johnny Jenkins, should be a must for anyone who enjoys solid Southern swamp-rock, filtered through the intensity of gospel and blues. The band is a combination of a Capricorn Studios house band and members of the Allman Brothers; there is an added bonus in that you get some of Duane Allman's most intense slide and dobro work. This is a raw, biting album with not a throwaway or weak cut, not even the two CD-reissue bonus tracks. Highlights include "I Walk on Gilded Splinters" and "Rollin' Stone." —*Bob Gottlieb*

Blessed Blues / Aug. 13, 1996 / Capricorn ♦♦♦♦
Twenty-six years after releasing *Ton Ton Macoute*, Johnny Jenkins—a local legend around Macon, GA—released his second album, *Blessed Blues*. Featuring a selection of new songs, classic covers, and a new version of his 1962 hit "Miss Thing (also known as "Love Twist"), *Blessed Blues* gives a good idea why Jenkins is revered in his home state. His playing is swampy, dirty and impassioned—it is soaked in the sounds of the deep South. *Blessed Blues* doesn't clean up his sound at all, preferring to showcase Jenkins in all of his gritty glory. On the whole, it isn't quite as searing as *Ton Ton Macoute*—after all, that featured support by Duane Allman—but *Blessed Blues* proves that good things are worth waiting for. —*Thom Owens*

Beau Jocque

b. 1957, Kinder, Louisiana
Accordion, Vocals / Zydeco
Easily the biggest new zydeco star of the 1990s, Beau Jocque heralded the rise of the genre's new, urbanized style; infusing his high-octane sound with elements of rock, soul, hip-hop, and even reggae, he bridged the gap between traditional Creole culture and contemporary music to create a funky, bass-heavy hybrid calculated for maximum mainstream appeal. Born Andrus Espre in Kinder, Louisiana in 1957, Jocque spent his early adult years working as an electrician, but in 1987 he suffered a serious back injury which left him paralyzed from the waist down for over a year; during his recovery period he picked up his father's Cajun accordion, but always bored by traditional zydeco, he set about updating the music more to his own contemporary tastes. Jocque and his wife Michelle then spent the next five years painstakingly researching zydeco clubs, discovering which kinds of songs earned the greatest response from patrons; at the same time he absorbed the music of Boozoo Chavis, drawn by his propulsive rhythms. Finally, in 1991, he formed the Zydeco Hi-Rollers; the band was an immediate smash in the New Orleans circuit, drawing huge audiences—many of them new to the Creole dancehall scene—captivated by their hard-edged rhythms and Jocque's primal, cavernous vocals. A friendly rivalry with Chavis also increased his notoriety, and in 1993, the Hi-Rollers debuted with *Beau Jocque Boogie*, one of the best-selling zydeco records of all time. *Pick Up on This!* followed in 1994, and a year later they released the explosive live effort *Git It, Beau Jocque!*, which featured the hit "Give Him Cornbread." *Gonna Take You Downtown* appeared in 1996. —*Jason Ankeny*

Beau Jocque Boogie / 1993 / Rounder ♦♦♦
Beau Jocque and the Zydeco Hi-Rollers represent the genre's new school; hip-hop and rap are an element of their style, as well as blues and R&B. Beau Jocque's music has the requisite kick and edge, with his vocals and non-stop excitement spilling out through such songs as "Richard's Club" and "Beau Jocque Boogie." Where he may raise eyebrows is his embrace of sampling technology alongside standard instrumentation. Jocque also speaks fluent French and covers some traditional songs, but puts more emphasis on his own music. This debut disc includes nine originals out of 14 numbers, with Jocque providing arrangements of classic tunes like "Oh Bye Moreau" and "Chere Allien" and establishing this band as prime challengers for honors as the top zydeco ensemble in the 1990s. —*Ron Wynn*

My Name is Beau Jocque / 1994 / Paula/Flyright ♦♦♦♦

● **Pick Up on This!** / Mar. 30, 1994 / Rounder ♦♦♦♦
Beau Jocque's first album for Rounder Records, *Pick Up on This!*, is arguably his best effort to date. The key is in the groove—there might not be much variety on the album, but he keeps the zesty zydeco rhythms pumping throughout. Jocque isn't the only one who shines, however. Every member of the band keeps things cooking, doing their best to ensure that *Pick Up on This!* is a first-rate party album. And that's exactly what it is. —*Thom Owens*

Git It, Beau Jocque! / 1995 / Rounder ✦✦✦

Nursery Rhyme / Nov. 28, 1995 / Beau Jocque ✦✦

Gonna Take You Downtown / 1996 / Rounder ✦✦✦✦

Beau Jocque & The Zydeco Hi-Rollers / Rounder ✦✦✦
This is a dynamite recording, squarely in the zydeco tradition that's fleshed out with touches of this and that—electric blues, a hint of rap— without losing any of the classic go-for-the-feet dancing beat. —*John Storm Roberts, Original Music*

Big Jack Johnson

b. Jul. 30, 1940, Lambert, MS
Guitar, Vocals / Modern Electric Blues, Delta Blues
Contemporary Mississippi blues doesn't get any nastier than in Big Jack Johnson's capable hands. The ex-oil truck driver's axe cuts like a rusty machete, his rough-hewn vocals a siren call to Delta passion. But he's a surprisingly versatile songwriter; *Daddy, When Is Mama Comin Home?*, his ambitious 1990 set for Earwig, found him tackling issues as varied as AIDS, wife abuse, and Chinese blues musicians in front of slick, horn-leavened arrangements!

Big Jack Johnson was a chip off the old block musically. His dad was a local musician playing both blues and country ditties at local functions; by the time he was 13 years old, Johnson was sitting in on guitar with his dad's band. At age 18, Johnson was following B.B. King's electrified lead. His big break came when he sat in with bluesmen Frank Frost and Sam Carr at the Savoy Theatre in Clarksdale. The symmetry between the trio was such that they were seldom apart for the next 15 years, recording for Phillips International and Jewel with Frost, the bandleader.

Chicago blues aficionado Michael Frank was so mesmerized by the trio's intensity when he heard them playing in 1975 at Johnson's Mississippi bar, the Black Fox, that Frank Frost eventually formed Earwig just to capture their steamy repertoire. That album, *Rockin' the Juke Joint Down,* came out in 1979 (as by the Jelly Roll Kings) and marked Johnson's first recordings as a singer.

Johnson's subsequent 1987 album for Earwig, *The Oil Man,* still ranks as his most intense and moving, sporting a hair-raising rendition of "Catfish Blues." The '90s have been good to Big Jack Johnson. In addition to *Daddy, When Is Mama Comin Home?,* he released a live record and two studio albums—1996's *We Got to Stop This Killing* and 1998's *All the Way Back.* He also appeared in the acclaimed film documentary *Deep Blues* and on its resulting soundtrack. —*Bill Dahl*

● **The Oil Man** / 1987 / Earwig ✦✦✦✦
With his barbed-wire guitar work and hearty vocal on a marathon rendition of "Catfish Blues," Johnson hauls the time-honored Delta tradition into contemporary blues. The entire album is an eminently solid, doggedly downhome affair, though nothing else quite measures up to the powerhouse attack of that one vicious workout. —*Bill Dahl*

Daddy, When Is Mama Comin' Home? / 1991 / Earwig ✦✦✦
The precise opposite of the Mississippi guitarist's previous Earwig release. This one's slick, horn-leavened, and full of downhome ruminations on everything from AIDS and spousal abuse to Chinese blues musicians. Too weird for some purists, but definitely engaging in its singular approach. —*Bill Dahl*

We Got to Stop This Killin' / Jun. 18, 1996 / M.C. ✦✦✦✦
Since many modern blues musicians are loath to break away from the norm, Big Jack Johnson can come as a shock. Johnson is determined to keep the blues a vital, living form, so he doesn't simply spit out the old standards again—he writes new songs about modern times, whether it's social commentary or love songs. Not only are his subjects fresh, but he makes sure that his music is fresh too, bringing funk and soul influences to his electrified Delta blues. In short, it fulfills the promise of *Daddy, When Is Mama Coming Home?* by keeping its ambition and adding the grit of *Oil Man.* —*Thom Owens*

Live in Chicago / Dec. 24, 1997 / Earwig ✦✦✦✦
Big Jack Johnson's celebrated live show is documented on this raw set recorded with the Aron Burton Blues Band. —*Jason Ankeny*

All the Way Back / Mar. 31, 1998 / M.C. ✦✦✦✦
For *All the Way Back,* Big Jack Johnson decided to tame the instinct for social

commentary and concentrate on what his audience loves—hard-hitting, electrified Delta blues. The result is a monster of a record, filled with great songs and unbridled, earth-shaking playing from Johnson. The key to his music is that he knows how to write a great song, one that adheres to blues traditions without being a slave to them. The funk and soul flourishes he brings to the blues don't compromise the form, but bring it into fresh new territory; that's what makes *All the Way Back* a terrific listen. —*Thom Owens*

Blind Willie Johnson

b. Feb. C. 1, Temple, TX, **d.** 1947
Guitar, Vocals / Blues Gospel, Acoustic Texas Blues
A guitar-playing evangelist with a scary, emotion-charged voice, Blind Willie Johnson played some of the most exquisite slide guitar ever heard. Void of frivolity or uncertainty, his 78s were clearly the work of a pained believer seeking street-corner redemption with a guitar and a tin cup. He was gifted with an incomparable sense of timing and tone, using his pocketknife slide to duplicate his vocal inflections or to produce an unforgettable phrase from a single strike of a string. With its wide, rough vibrato, his voice was as fierce as Charles Patton's or Son House's, but much easier to understand.

Little is known about his background, but thanks largely to the research of author Samuel Charters, who interviewed Johnson's widow and second wife Angeline Johnson, and an old Texas preacher, Adam Booker, during the late '50s, some sketchy facts were unearthed. He was born around 1902 on the outskirts of Temple, Texas. While still an infant, he and his father, George Johnson, moved to Marlin, where the elder probably worked as a sharecropper. When Willie was about five, he told his father he wanted to become a preacher and made his first guitar out of a cigar box. Following the death of his mother, Johnson's father remarried. One day, George Johnson caught her with another man and beat her up; she retaliated by throwing lye into the face of seven-year-old Willie to deliberately blind him. Later, when his father got a job in Hearne, a town about 35 miles from Marlin, he would take young Johnson to town, where he would sing religious songs and play his guitar every Saturday with a tin cup around his neck for tips.

As a young man, he lived in Marlin, where he married Willie B. Harris in the mid-'20s and attended services at the Marlin Church of God in Christ on Commerce Street, where he often performed. Their marriage apparently dissolved in the early '30s. In 1927, Johnson became one of the first gospel guitarists on 78. Among his 30 recorded songs is the landmark instrumental "Dark Was the Night, Cold Was the Ground," described by Ry Cooder as "the most transcendent piece in all American music." Johnson spent most of his life singing for the Baptist Church or playing for tips on the streets of Beaumont, Texas. He died of pneumonia in the late '40s after his wife made him sleep on wet bedding following a house fire. Decades later, his music echoed in the styles of Mississippi Fred McDowell and Mance Lipscomb. Still, he remains a slide guitarist without parallel, a player so perfect he's impossible to adequately imitate. —*Jas Obrecht & Sandra Brennan*

Praise God I'm Satisfied / 1989 / Yazoo ✦✦✦✦
Yazoo's *Praise God I'm Satisfied* is an excellent collection of 14 tracks Blind Willie Johnson recorded in the '30s, including such numbers as "Jesus Make Up My Dying Bed," "Praise God I'm Satisfied," "Rain Don't Fall on Me," and "Jesus Is Coming Soon." These are excellent, haunting recordings, boasting some stellar guitar work, but everything that's on this disc and its companion, *Sweeter as the Years Go By,* is included on Columbia/Legacy's *The Complete Recordings of Blind Willie Johnson,* which makes this unnecessary for any serious listener. —*Stephen Thomas Erlewine*

Sweeter as the Years Go By / 1990 / Yazoo ✦✦✦✦
Blind Willie Johnson was perhaps the finest singing evangelist of all time. While the 16 tracks on this CD aren't as striking as those on the seminal *Praise God I'm Satisfied,* they're still invigorating and a vital part of his legacy. Johnson played acoustic rather than slide on several cuts, and didn't take flamboyant solos or add slashing counterpoint. But he demonstrated a skillful use of repetition and outstanding rhythmic and melodic skills. Johnson teamed with Willie B. Harris on several songs, and her rough, cutting voice proved an ideal match with his equally ragged sound. —*Ron Wynn*

★ **Complete Recordings of Blind Willie Johnson** / Apr. 27, 1993 / Columbia ✦✦✦✦✦
If you've never heard Blind Willie Johnson, you are in for one of the great, bone-chilling treats in music. Johnson played slide guitar, and sang in a rasp-

ing, false bass that could freeze the blood. But no bluesman was he; this was gospel music of the highest order, full of emotion and heartfelt commitment. Of all the guitar-playing evangelists, Blind Willie Johnson may have been the very best. Though not related by bloodlines to Robert Johnson, comparisons in emotional commitment from both men cannot be helped. This two-CD anthology collects everything known to exist, and that's a lot of stark, harrowing emotional commitment no matter how you slice it. Not for the faint of heart, but hey, the good stuff never is. —*Cub Koda*

Buddy Johnson (Woodrow Wilson Johnson)

b. Jan. 10, 1915, Darlington, SC, **d.** Feb. 9, 1977, New York, NY
Piano / R&B, Big Band, Rock & Roll, Jump Blues, Swing, New York Blues
With his sister Ella seductively serving for decades as his primary vocalist, pianist Buddy Johnson led a large jump blues band that enjoyed tremendous success during the 1940s and '50s. The suave bandleader spotlighted a series of talented singers, including balladeers Arthur Prysock, Nolan Lewis, and Floyd Ryland, but it was Ella's understated delivery (beautifully spotlighted on the sumptuous ballad "Since I Fell for You") and Buddy's crisply danceable "Walk-Em Rhythm" that made the aggregation so successful for so long.

Buddy began taking piano lessons at age four. Although he specialized professionally in tasty R&B, classical music remained one of his passions. In 1939, Buddy Johnson waxed his first 78 for Decca, "Stop Pretending (So Hep You See)." Shortly thereafter, Ella joined her older brother; her delicious vocal on "Please Mr. Johnson" translated into long-term employment.

Buddy had assembled a nine-piece orchestra by 1941 and visited the R&B charts often for Decca during wartime with "Let's Beat Out Some Love," "Baby Don't You Cry," the chart-topping "When My Man Comes Home," and "That's the Stuff You Gotta Watch." Ella cut her beloved rendering of "Since I Fell for You" in 1945, a year after Buddy waxed his jiving gem "Fine Brown Frame."

In addition to their frequent jaunts on the R&B hit parade, the Johnson organization barnstormed the country to sellout crowds throughout the '40s. Buddy moved over to Mercury Records in 1953 and scored two smashes with Ella's "Hittin' on Me" and "I'm Just Your Fool," the latter a 1954 standout that was later purloined by Chicago harpist Little Walter.

Rock 'n' roll eventually halted Buddy Johnson's momentum, but his band (tenor saxophonist Purvis Henson was a constant presence in the reed section) kept recording for Mercury through 1958, switched to Roulette the next year, and bowed out with a solitary session for Hy Weiss' Old Town label in 1964.

Singer Lenny Welch ensured the immortality of "Since I Fell for You" when his velvety rendition of the Johnson-penned ballad reached the uppermost reaches of the pop charts in 1963. It was a perfect match of song and singer; Welch's smooth, assured delivery would have fit in snugly with the Johnson band during its heyday a couple of decades earlier. —*Bill Dahl*

1939-1942 / Nov. 16, 1939-Feb. 26, 1942 / Classics ◆◆◆◆
Pianist Buddy Johnson is best-known for leading a swinging R&B-oriented big band in the late 1940's and 1950's that, with his sister Ella Johnson as the main star, introduced "Since I Fell For You." On this CD from the European Classics label, Johnson's first 24 numbers recorded as a leader are reissued and most of the tracks were formerly quite rare. At the time Buddy Johnson was an Earl Hines-influenced pianist who was searching for his own sound. A few numbers feature vocals by the so-so Mack Sisters and various bandmembers including the leader himself, but it is the songs with Ella Johnson (particularly "Please, Mister Johnson" and "It's the Gold") that stand out. During the two-year period covered by this CD, Buddy Johnson's band grew from a septet to a nonet, but the glory years were still in the future. —*Scott Yanow*

Buddy Johnson Wails / 1957 / Mercury ◆◆◆
This is first-rate music, but is really vintage instrumental R&B with swing foundation. Johnson was a tremendous, energetic saxophonist who had some hit records with his sister, vocalist Ella Johnson, and also had some sessions produced by Quincy Jones. He is a different player from the veteran jazz saxophonist Budd Johnson. —*Ron Wynn*

● **Go Ahead and Rock and Roll** / 1958 / Roulette ◆◆◆◆
Buddy Johnson was one of the top R&B bandleaders and composers in the '50s, as well as being an above-average vocalist. This was prototype '50s material, an era when swing-derived R&B was being mixed with country

and gospel and rock was emerging from the stew. The songs are either raw, stirring uptempo tunes or steamy ballads, and they're done at a powerhouse pace. Johnson, like most great R&B acts, was a singles artist, but the songs featured here are good at worst, and often magical despite clearly being from another era. —*Ron Wynn*

Buddy and Ella Johnson 1953-1964 / 1992 / Bear Family ◆◆◆◆
Four discs (104 tracks in all) that exhaustively document the Mercury, Roulette, and Old Town output of big-band veteran Buddy Johnson, whose eternally swinging outfit was seductively fronted by his sister Ella (along with several interchangeable male crooners). Buddy's band wasn't as big as it once was during his Mercury tenure (tenor saxman Purvis Henson was at the core of the blazing horn section), but the tightly arranged New York-style sizzle remained. —*Bill Dahl*

Walk 'em: Decca Sessions / Jul. 2, 1996 / Ace ◆◆◆◆
A fine 24-track distillation of Johnson's lengthy career for Decca, during which he and his musicians served as a key link between Harlem big bands, jump blues, and R&B. Spanning 1941 to 1952, the focus is on the bluesier and/or more uptempo sides credited to either Buddy or sister Ella, as well as tracks with Johnson associations cut by Arthur Prysock and Harold "Geezil" Minerve. Several of the Johnson clan's most celebrated performances are here: "Walk 'em" (a sort of signature tune for Buddy), Ella's original version of "Since I Fell For You," Ella's huge R&B hits "That's the Stuff You Gotta Watch," and "When My Man Comes Home," and Buddy's 1949 Top 20 pop hit, "Did You See Jackie Robinson Hit That Ball?" (surely one of the greatest baseball/pop novelties ever). Some of the raunchy sax breaks are signposts for a style that would become prevalent in R&B and early rock 'n' roll; the gritty instrumental "Shake 'Em Up," for instance, anticipates the sound of Bill Doggett's "Honky Tonk" by four years. —*Richie Unterberger*

Ella Johnson

b. Jun. 22, 1923, Darlington, SC
Vocals / Ballads, R&B, Classic Female Blues, East Coast Blues, Jump Blues
Vocalist Ella Johnson was the sister of bandleader Buddy Johnson and also a good uptempo R&B vocalist. She was the featured vocalist on several huge hits that Buddy Johnson's band scored for Decca and Mercury during the '40s and '50s. Ella Johnson was lead singer on the number one R&B hit "When My Man Comes Home" in 1944, and the number two R&B single "That's the Stuff You Gotta Watch." She later was featured on the Top Ten singles "Hittin' on Me" and "I'm Just Your Fool" in 1953 and 1954, and "Bring It Home to Me" in 1956. Bear Family issued a two-disc set of material featuring Ella and Buddy Johnson in 1992. —*Ron Wynn*

Swing Me / 1956 / Verve ◆◆◆◆
It's good to get these 20 tracks, most previously available only as singles, back into circulation; hopefully, they'll enable Johnson to be "discovered" once more. —*Ron Wynn*

● **Say Ella** / 1983 / Juke Box Lil ◆◆◆◆
Juke Box Lil's *Say Ella* contains 16 songs Ella Johnson recorded with her brother Buddy's big band for Decca and Mercury between 1942 and 1957. In other words, these 16 songs are among her very best recordings, containing such classics as "I Don't Care Who Knows," "You Got to Walk That Chalk Line," "Somehow, Somewhere," " 'Til My Baby Comes Back," "That's How I Feel About You," "One More Time," and "Mush Mouth." In other words, it's an excellent single-disc introduction to one of the finest female R&B vocalists of her era. —*Thom Owens*

Ernest Johnson

b. Winnsboro, LA
Bass / Soul Blues
Ernie Johnson continues in the soul-blues singing path forged by artists like Bobby "Blue" Bland, Z.Z. Hill, Little Milton and R.L. Griffin. Born in Winnsboro, LA, Johnson didn't begin singing professionally until after moving to Dallas. His vocal influences included Nat King Cole, Dee Clark, Clyde McPhatter, Jackie Wilson, and especially Bobby "Blue" Bland; he recalled that hearing Bland sing "Further On Up The Road" was a revelatory experience. Johnson had a chance to open for Miss Lavelle White and Guitar James in Mexia, Texas, and stole the show. At that point, he quit his day job with the Dallas parks department and formed a band, the Soul Blenders. He recorded

his first single, "Lovin You" b/w "Cold Cold Heart," for Fats Washington's Movin' Records in 1968. Johnson recorded other singles before his first album for Ronn Records, *Just In Time*. Johnson has played the blues festivals in San Francisco and Monterey, and his first compact disc, *It's Party Time*, was released on the Louisiana-based Paula Records label in 1993. Johnson financed and produced the album himself, and wrote all the songs except for his rendition of Otis Redding's "Dreams To Remember." In 1995, Malaco Records released another album, *In the Mood*. Although he doesn't tour that widely, Johnson does get around on the blues festival circuit. —*Richard Skelly*

● **It's Party Time** / 1993 / Paula/Flyright ✦✦✦✦
Although he doesn't show much imagination anywhere on the disc, Ernie Johnson's debut album, *It's Party Time*, is a fine collection of contemporary soul-blues. Most of the record is devoted to originals, which are solid numbers in the classic Chicago and Stax traditions, even if they're not particularly memorable. They do give Johnson an opportunity to spill his guts out vocally, and he proves to be a good vocalist in the tradition of Bobby Bland, Little Milton and Z.Z. Hill, even if he doesn't quite reach their heights. He is good enough, however, to make *It's Party Time* an enjoyable record for fans of that style. — *Thom Owens*

In the Mood / Oct. 3, 1995 / Waldoxy ✦✦✦

Hot & Steamy / May 5, 1998 / Waldoxy ✦✦✦

Herman E. Johnson

b. Louisiana, d. Feb. 2, 1975, Scotlandville, LA
Vocals / Louisiana Blues, Acoustic Country Blues
Another of the many performers briefly illuminated by the spotlight of the folk-blues revival of the 1960s, Louisiana-born country bluesman Herman E. Johnson was the product of a highly religious family environment, a background which heavily informed the spiritual imagery which was a hallmark of his later work as a performer. His early adult years were spent in a fruitless search for steady work which led him from the country to the city and back again; he picked up the guitar around 1927 as a respite from jobs ranging from picking cotton to pouring concrete to working at a scrap metal yard. Eventually, Johnson landed work at the Esso refinery in Baton Rouge, where he worked for 15 years before being unexpectly fired; scrambling to find work—an experience memorably recalled in his song "Depression Blues"— he finally was hired as a janitor at Southern University in nearby Scotlandville. He held the same job at the time of his lone recording session, cut in Baton Rouge by Dr. Harry Oster in 1961; after suffering a stroke in 1970, Johnson went into retirement, and died on February 2, 1975. —*Jason Ankeny*

Louisiana Country Blues / 1981 / Arhoolie ✦✦✦

Jimmy Johnson

b. Nov. 25, 1928, Holly Springs, MS
Guitar, Harmonica, Keyboards, Vocals / Modern Electric Blues, Chicago Blues, Electric Chicago Blues
Chicago guitarist Jimmy Johnson didn't release his first full domestic album until he was 50 years old. He's determinedly made up for lost time ever since, establishing himself as one of the Windy City's premier blues artists with a twisting, unpredictable guitar style and a soaring, soul-dripping vocal delivery that stand out from the pack.

Born into a musical family (younger brother Syl Johnson's credentials as a soul star are all in order, while sibling Mack Thompson was Magic Sam's first-call bassist), Jimmy Thompson moved to Chicago with his family in 1950. But his guitar playing remained a hobby for years—he toiled as a welder while Syl blazed a trail on the local blues circuit. Finally, in 1959, Jimmy Thompson started gigging with harpist Slim Willis around the West Side. Somewhere down the line, he changed his surname to Johnson (thus keeping pace with Syl).

Since there was more cash to be realized playing R&B during the 1960s, Jimmy Johnson concentrated on that end of the stylistic spectrum for a while. He led polished house bands on the South and West sides behind Otis Clay, Denise LaSalle, and Garland Green, cutting an occasional instrumental 45 on the side. Johnson found his way back to the blues in 1974 as Jimmy Dawkins' rhythm guitarist. He toured Japan behind Otis Rush in 1975 (the journey that produced Rush's album *So Many Roads—Live in Concert*).

With the 1978 release of four stunning sides on Alligator's first batch of *Living Chicago Blues* anthologies and the issue of *Johnson's Whacks*, his first full domestic set on Delmark the next year, Jimmy Johnson's star began ascending rapidly. *North/South*, the guitarist's 1982 Delmark follow-up, and the 1983 release of *Bar Room Preacher* by Alligator continued to propel Johnson into the first rank of Chicago bluesdom. Then tragedy struck: on December 2, 1988, Johnson was driving his band van when it swerved off the road in downstate Indiana, killing bassist Larry Exum and keyboardist St. James Bryant.

Understandably, Johnson, himself injured in the wreck, wasn't too interested in furthering his career for a time after the tragedy. But he's back in harness now, cutting a solid set for Verve in 1994, *I'm a Jockey*, that spotlights his blues-soul synthesis most effectively. —*Bill Dahl*

Jimmy Johnson & Luther Johnson / 1977 / MCM ✦✦

Tobacco Road / 1978 / MCM ✦✦

Johnson's Whacks / 1979 / Delmark ✦✦✦✦
Uncommon wit runs through the lyrics of this varied set, certainly one of the more intriguing Chicago blues albums of the late '70s. Johnson's high-pitched vocals are particularly soulful on the impassioned "I Need Some Easy Money" and "Ashes in My Ashtray," while "The Twelve Bar Blues" and "Poor Boy's Dream" are upbeat entries that don't sound as comfortable for the guitarist. Johnson gets away with a honky-tonk reprise of Ernest Tubb's country classic "Drivin' Nails in My Coffin," but his rehash of Dave Brubeck's "Take Five" should have stayed on the bandstand. —*Bill Dahl*

North/South / 1982 / Delmark ✦✦✦
Another lyrically challenging effort from Johnson (unfortunately not on CD yet), though some of the most daring musical aspects of his previous efforts have been smoothed off (for better or worse). Bassist Larry Exum was a bedrock of funky grooves for the guitarist's band. —*Bill Dahl*

● **Bar Room Preacher** / 1983 / Alligator ✦✦✦✦
Unlike his Delmark sets, almost everything on this set (first issued in France on Black & Blue) is a cover (only the observant "Heap See" boasts original lyrics). Still, "Barroom Preacher" stands as the Chicago guitarist's most satisfying and consistent album, as he deals out gorgeous, shimmering versions of "Little by Little," "Cold, Cold Feeling," and "You Don't Know What Love Is" tailored to his soaring vocals and twisting guitar riffs (ominous minor keys often play a role in his rearrangements). —*Bill Dahl*

I'm a Jockey / 1995 / Verve ✦✦✦✦
It shouldn't have taken Johnson a full decade to find his way back into a studio, but such are the injustices of the record business. The wait was worth it, though—backed by his touring trio of the timeframe, Johnson mixes blues and soul, originals (a heartfelt "Black & White Wall" and the soaring ballad "My Ring") and covers (his takes on McKinley Mitchell's "End of a Rainbow" and Wilson Pickett's "Engine Number 9" hit home), in decidedly solid contemporary form. —*Bill Dahl*

Johnnie Johnson

b. Jul. 8, 1924, Fairmont, WV
Piano / R&B, Rock 'n' Roll, Piano Blues
Legendary piano player Johnnie Johnson isn't exactly a household name, even among followers of blues music. That's because for 28 years, he worked as a sideman to one of rock 'n' roll's most prominent performers, Chuck Berry. Berry joined Johnson's band, the Sir John Trio, on New Year's Eve, 1953, and afterward, Berry took over as the group's songwriter and frontman/guitar player. On the strength of a recommendation from Muddy Waters and an audition, Berry got a deal with Chess Records. Johnson's rhythmic piano playing was a key element in all of Berry's hit singles, a good number of which Johnson arranged. The pair's successful partnership lasted a lot longer than most rock 'n' roll partnerships last these days.

Johnson was born July 8, 1924, in Fairmont, WV, and he began playing piano at age five, thanks to his mother, who provided the funds to purchase one and encouraged the young Johnson's interest. His parents had a good collection of 78-rpm records, including items by Bessie Smith and Ethel Waters. In his teens, he listened to the radio broadcasts of big bands, and taught himself based on what he heard from the likes of Art Tatum, Earl "Fatha" Hines, and Meade "Lux" Lewis. Johnson's goal in all of this listening and playing in his teenage years was to come up with his own distinctive style.

His own somewhat ailing career got a shot in the arm with the Chuck Berry concert film, *Hail! Hail! Rock 'n' Roll*, and by his involvement in Keith Richards' solo release with Richards' band, the X-Pensive Winos.

In a 1995 interview, Johnson explains his abilities with a piano as his mother did, as a gift from God. "I can hear something and keep it in my mind until such point as I can get to a piano, and then I'll play it... that is a gift, the ability to do that."

Johnson's albums under his own name include *Blue Hand Johnnie* for the St. Louis-based Pulsar label in 1988; *Johnnie B. Bad* in 1991 for the Elektra American Explorer label; *That'll Work* in 1993 for the same label, and most recently, *Johnnie Be Back* for the New Jersey-based MusicMasters label in 1995. All four are winners, and all are available on compact disc. — *Richard Skelly*

● **Blue Hand Johnnie** / 1988 / Evidence ◆◆◆◆
Johnnie Johnson's rolling, barreling licks are as enticing as ever on this reissued Evidence CD of cuts from '90, but there are some other things that are not so grand. These include barely tolerable vocalists Barbara Carr and Stacy Johnson, whose enthusiasm is commendable, but whose vocals often get in the way. Johnson's covers of Fats Washington's "O.J. Blues" and "Black Nights" are great, as are his versions of "Honky Tonk" and "See See Rider." But he falters on "Baby, What You Want Me To," in part because he does not convey either the original's loping stride or laconic quality, and also because it is not the kind of peppy arrangement and backbeat suited to his style. A decent effort that might have been a superior one with a couple of added touches. — *Ron Wynn*

Rockin' Eighty Eight / Apr. 1990 / Modern Blues ◆◆◆◆
Three underrated pianists, Clayton Love, Johnnie Johnson, and Jimmy Vaughn, typify the St. Louis Blues piano tradition on this solid sender. — *Bill Dahl*

Johnnie B. Bad / 1991 / Elektra/Nonesuch ◆◆◆◆
Keith Richards, Eric Clapton, and various NRBQ members guest on this pianist's inconsistent major-label debut. — *Bill Dahl*

Johnnie Be Back / Oct. 1995 / Music Masters ◆◆◆

L.V. Johnson

b. 1946, Chicago, IL, d. Nov. 22, 1994, Chicago, IL
Vocals, Guitar / Soul, Modern Electric Blues, Chicago Blues, Retro-Soul
A mournful, often gripping singer and a good guitarist, Chicago performer L.V. Johnson actually did better as a writer than a lead artist. His songs "Are You Serious" and "True Love Is Hard to Find" were big hits for Tyrone Davis, while "Country Love" did moderately well for Bobby "Blue" Bland, and "Give Your Baby a Standing Ovation" was among the Dells' finest soul performances. Johnson played with Davis before going on his own in the '80s. The nephew of Elmore James, Johnson learned guitar from B.B. King. Besides working with Davis, Johnson was a staff guitarist at Stax, playing on sessions for the Bar-Kays, Johnnie Taylor, and the Soul Children. He recorded for ICA, Phono, and Ichiban, although his sound and approach to soul were far too deep for the Urban marketplace. Johnson was also part-owner of a steakhouse and nightclub in Chicago. — *Ron Wynn*

● **Cold & Mean** / 1991 / Ichiban ◆◆◆◆
From Clarence Carter to Curtis Mayfield, the Atlanta-based Ichiban Records has been a safe haven for soul veterans the majors lost interest in. In the late 1980s and '90s, one of Ichiban's brightest lights was L.V. Johnson, who joined the label with the outstanding *Cold & Mean*. Instead of aiming for the urban contemporary market, the gruff, big-voiced soul shouter excels with an unapologetically '70s-sounding approach. Combining a silky production style with hard-edged, gospel-influenced vocals, gems like "It's So Cold and Mean (The Drug Scene)," "It's Not My Time," and "Make You Mine" sound like they could have been recorded 15 years earlier. Another high point is "One In a Million You," originally recorded by Larry Graham in 1980. On these confident, soaring performances, the R&B veteran lets us know that he's still at the height of his powers. — *Alex Henderson*

I Got the Touch / 1991 / Ichiban ◆◆◆
I Got The Touch found L.V. Johnson making a few concessions to urban contemporary tastes, but only a few. Despite some new jack moves here and there, this CD leaves no doubt that classic soul is where his heart lies. While the title song is a new jack-oriented number with a pedestrian cameo by

rapper Styles, silky medium-tempo songs like "Are You Serious," "Take a Little Time to Know Her," and "I Am Missing You" could have easily been recorded in 1972. Tina Turner fans will be surprised by "What Do You Mean Love Ain't Got Nothing to Do with It," a clever response to her 1984 smash "What's Love Got to Do with It." Though it falls short of the excellence of *Cold and Mean*, *Touch* definitely has a lot going for it. — *Alex Henderson*

Unclassified / 1992 / Ichiban ◆◆◆
After going for a few urban contemporary touches on *I Got the Touch*, L.V. Johnson returns to a consistently soul-oriented approach on his third Ichiban release *Unclassified*. Stronger than its predecessor and every bit as impressive as *Cold and Mean*, *Unclassified* sounds like an album the deep-voiced singer wanted very much to make. Recalling the smooth northern soul coming out of Chicago, Detroit and Philadelphia in the 1970s, slow and medium-tempo gems like "Voodoo Woman," "Four Walls," and "Whatever Happened" are retro in the best sense of the word. For fans of classic '70s soul, this heartfelt CD is something to savor. — *Alex Henderson*

Lonnie Johnson (Alonzo Johnson)

b. Feb. 8, 1899, New Orleans, LA, d. Jun. 16, 1970, Toronto, Ontario, Canada
Guitar, Vocals / Classic Jazz, Jazz Blues, Acoustic Blues, Country Blues, Piedmont Blues, Prewar Country Blues
Blues guitar simply would not have developed in the manner that it did if not for the prolific brilliance of Lonnie Johnson. He was there to help define the instrument's future within the genre and the genre's future itself at the very beginning, his melodic conception so far advanced from most of his pre-war peers as to inhabit a plane all his own. For more than 40 years, Johnson played blues, jazz, and ballads his way; he was a true blues originator whose influence hung heavy on a host of subsequent blues immortals.

Johnson's extreme versatility doubtless stemmed in great part from growing up in the musically diverse Crescent City. Violin caught his ear initially, but he eventually made the guitar his passion, developing a style so fluid and inexorably melodic that instrumental backing seemed superfluous. He signed up with OKeh Records in 1925 and commenced to recording at an astonishing pace—between 1925 and 1932, he cut an estimated 130 waxings. The red-hot sides he recorded with White jazz guitarist Eddie Lang (masquerading as Blind Willie Dunn) in 1928-29 were utterly groundbreaking in their ceaseless invention. Johnson also recorded pioneering jazz efforts in 1927 with no less than Louis Armstrong's Hot Five and Duke Ellington's orchestra.

After enduring the Depression and moving to Chicago, Johnson came back to recording life with Bluebird for a five-year stint beginning in 1939. Under the ubiquitous Lester Melrose's supervision, Johnson picked up right where he left off, selling quite a few copies of "He's a Jelly Roll Baker" for old Nipper. Johnson went with Cincinnati-based King Records in 1947, and promptly enjoyed one of the biggest hits of his uncommonly long career with the mellow ballad "Tomorrow Night," which topped the R&B charts for seven weeks in 1948. More hits followed posthaste: "Pleasing You (As Long as I Live)," "So Tired," and "Confused."

Time seemed to have passed Johnson by during the late '50s. He was toiling as a hotel janitor in Philadelphia when banjo player Elmer Snowden alerted Chris Albertson to his whereabouts. That rekindled a major comeback, Johnson cutting a series of albums for Prestige's Bluesville subsidary during the early '60s and venturing to Europe under the auspices of Horst Lippmann and Fritz Rau's American Folk Blues Festival banner in 1963. Finally, in 1969, Johnson was hit by a car in Toronto and died a year later from the effects of the accident.

Johnson's influence was massive, touching everyone from Robert Johnson, whose seminal approach bore strong resemblance to that of his older namesake, to Elvis Presley, and Jerry Lee Lewis, who each paid heartfelt tribute with versions of "Tomorrow Night" while at Sun. — *Bill Dahl*

He's a Jelly Roll Baker / Nov. 2, 1939-Dec. 14, 1944 / Bluebird ◆◆◆◆
This 20-song collection covers 1930s and '40s material in which Johnson primarily performs blues tunes, doing salty, sassy, mournful and suggestive numbers in a distinctive, memorable fashion. His vocals on "Rambler's Blues," "In Love Again," the title cut and several others are framed by brilliant, creative playing and excellent support from such pianists as Blind John Davis, Lil Hardin Armstrong, and Joshua Altheimer. This is tight, intuitive music in which Johnson set the tone and dominated the songs. If you're un-

aware of Lonnie Johnson's brilliant blues material, here's an excellent introduction. —*Ron Wynn*

Losing Game / 1960 / Bluesville ++++
Johnson recorded prolifically for Prestige's Bluesville during his early-'60s comeback; this 1960 set is a typically gorgeous solo outing that ranges from torchy standards of the Tin Pan Alley species ("What a Difference a Day Makes," "Summertime") to bluesier pursuits of his own creation. —*Bill Dahl*

★ **Blues & Ballads** / Apr. 5, 1960 / Bluesville +++++
Later Johnson, doing blues and ballads with jazz guitarist Elmer Snowden. Johnson's vocals are refined and sensitive. It is hard to hear him sing his own composition "I Found a Dream" and remain unmoved. Such a lovely album. —*Michael Erlewine*

Idle Hours / Jul. 1961 / Bluesville ++++
Johnson and Victoria Spivey had known one another for decades (they duetted on the ribald "Toothache Blues" way back in 1928), so it's no surprise that their musical repartee on 1961's *Idle Hours* seems so natural and playful. Spivey guests on three tracks (including the title number) and plays piano on her one solo entry. Johnson does the majority of the disc without her, benefitting from pianistic accompaniment by Cliff Jackson. —*Bill Dahl*

Another Night to Cry / Apr. 6, 1962 / Bluesville +++
Lonnie Johnson, a talented vocalist and guitarist who chose to spend much of his life playing blues (although in the 1920s he recorded with some of the top jazz stars), had his fifth recording for Prestige/Bluesville (a solo set) reissued on this CD. "Blues After Hours" is an instrumental that shows off his jazz roots and many of the 11 songs (all of which are Johnson originals) have spots for his guitar. Since there is only around 34 minutes on this set (which could have been combined on one CD with the music from another LP), and none of the individual songs even reach four minutes, this is not one of the more essential Lonnie Johnson releases, but it does have its strong moments. —*Scott Yanow*

The Complete Folkways Recordings / 1967 / Smithsonian/Folkways ++++
An even two dozen solo performances from late in the legendary guitarist's amazing career (1967), but chock full of stellar moments all the same. Artists of Johnson's versatility were rare even then—he brings a multitude of shadings to "My Mother's Eyes" and "How Deep Is the Ocean," then delivers a saucy "Juice Headed Baby" with the same stunning complexity. —*Bill Dahl*

Tomorrow Night / 1976 / Gusto ++++
Here's a two-LP collection just begging for digital reissue. Its 22 sides from Johnson's King stay include the immortal blues ballad "Tomorrow Night," his definitive renditions of "Careless Love" and "Jelly Roll Baker," and the lightly jumping "Trouble Ain't Nothin' but the Blues"—none of which grace Charly's CD compilation by the late blues great. —*Bill Dahl*

Blues by Lonnie Johnson / 1979 / Bluesville ++++
After four years off records and in obscurity, Lonnie Johnson launched his final comeback with this release, which has been reissued on CD. Teamed with tenor saxophonist Hal Singer, pianist Claude Hopkins, bassist Wendell Marshall, and drummer Bobby Donaldson, Johnson sings and plays guitar on a variety of blues, showing that the layoff (he was working at the time as a janitor) had not hurt his abilities in the slightest. —*Scott Yanow*

Mr. Johnson's Blues / 197 / Mamush +++
Fourteen cuts from the late '20s to early '30s, with Eddie Lang, Victoria Spivey, Texas Alexander, Mooch Richardson, Katherine Baker, and Violet Green. Highlights include "Uncle Ned Don't Use Your Head" and "Winnie the Wailer." —*Barry Lee Pearson*

The Originator of Modern Guitar Blues / 1980 / Blues Boy ++++
Later Lonnie Johnson, demonstrating his proficiency on everything from pop to blues and R&B. It's excellently remastered, sequenced and presented, covering 1940s and '50s cuts. —*Ron Wynn*

Blues Roots, Vol. 8 (Swingin' with Lonnie) / Apr. 1983 / Storyville +++
Backed by pianist Otis Spann, singer/guitarist Lonnie Johnson performs blues and ballads on this well-rounded set. Included are such numbers as his old hit "Tomorrow Night," "See See Rider," "Jelly, Jelly," and a lone instrumental, "Swingin' with Lonnie." An above-average outing by the veteran bluesman. —*Scott Yanow*

★ **Steppin' on the Blues** / 1990 / Columbia/Legacy +++++
Groundbreaking guitar work of dazzling complexity that never fails to amaze—and this stuff was cut in the 1920s!! Johnson's astonishingly fluid guitar work was massively influential (Robert Johnson, for one, was greatly swayed by his waxings), and his no-nonsense vocals (frequently laced with threats of violence—"Got the Blues for Murder Only" and "She's Making Whoopee in Hell Tonight" are prime examples on this 19-cut collection) are scarcely less impressive. Johnson's torrid guitar duets with jazzman Eddie Lang retain their sense of legend nearly seven decades after they were cut. —*Bill Dahl*

Me & My Crazy Self / 1991 / Charly ++++
With a firm emphasis on the less schmaltzy side of Johnson's 1947-1952 stint at Cincinnati's King Records, this 20-tracker finds the blues pioneer coming into the age of electric blues and R&B quite adroitly. His dignified vocal style similarly weathered the ensuing decades nicely—"You Can't Buy Love," "Friendless Blues," and the title track are bittersweet outings sporting multiple levels of subtlety. —*Bill Dahl*

Stompin' at the Penny / 1995 / Columbia/Legacy ++
This set (reissued on CD) is a bit unusual, for it features bluesman Lonnie Johnson with a Canadian Dixieland band, McHarg's Metro Stompers. In addition to including a few Johnson vocals, he takes credible solos on some trad jazz standards, including "China Boy." Six of the 13 numbers do not have the guitarist, putting the focus on the fine Dixieland band, which includes cornetist Charlie Gall, and clarinetist Eric Neilson in addition to the leader on bass. The original LP only sold 1,000 copies, so this reissue brings back music heard by very few at the time; this was Lonnie Johnson's last regular recording, although he did cut a series of numbers for Smithsonian in 1967. —*Scott Yanow*

Playing with the Strings / JSP +++
Maybe because his singing was more powerful than raw and his superb guitar-playing straddled jazz and blues, Johnson is vastly underrated. Yet aside from his fine solo recordings and his partnership with Eddie Lang, he recorded with jazzmen from Oliver through Armstrong to Duke Ellington. All are present here along with his brilliant fiddle and banjo, in acceptable dubbings from rare 78s. —*John Storm Roberts, Original Music*

Complete Recorded Works, Vols. 1-7 / Document +++
A fantastic seven-CD collection of Johnson's earliest works. Includes "Bed of Sand," "Treat 'Em Right," "Woke Up with the Blues in My Fingers," "When a Man Is Treated like a Dog," "Have to Change Keys to Play These Blues," "Blues Is Only a Ghost," "Not the Chump I Used to Be," and the romantic "She's Making Whoopee in Hell Tonight." —*Cub Koda*

Luther "Guitar Jr." Johnson

b. Aug. 30, 1934, Itta Bena, MS, **d.** Mar. 18, 1976, Boston, MA
Guitar, Vocals / Electric Blues, Modern Electric Blues
Of the three blues guitarists answering to the name of Luther Johnson, this West side-styled veteran is probably the best-known. Adding to the general confusion surrounding the triumvirate: like Luther "Georgia Boy" Johnson, "Guitar Junior" spent a lengthy stint in the top-seeded band of Muddy Waters (1972-1979).

Gospel and blues intersected in young Luther Johnson's life while he was still in Mississippi. But after he moved to Chicago in the mid-'50s, blues was his main passion, working with Ray Scott and Tall Milton Shelton before taking over the latter's combo in 1962. Magic Sam was a major stylistic inspiration to Johnson during the mid-'60s (Johnson spent a couple of years in Sam's band). The West side approach remains integral to Johnson's sound today, even though he moved to the Boston area during the early '80s.

Johnson's 1976 debut album, *Luther's Blues*, was cut during a European tour with Muddy Waters. By 1980, he was on his own, recording with the Nighthawks as well as four tracks on Alligator's second series of *Living Chicago Blues* anthologies. With his own band, the Magic Rockers, and the Roomful of Blues horn section, Johnson released *Doin' the Sugar Too* on Rooster Blues in 1984. Since 1990, Johnson has been signed to Ron Levy's Bullseye Blues logo; his three albums for the firm have been sizzling, soul-tinged blues (with a strong West Side flavor often slicing through). —*Bill Dahl*

Luther's Blues / Nov. 1, 1976 / Evidence ✦✦✦
The confidence that ex-Muddy Waters sideman Luther "Guitar Junior" Johnson exudes on his contemporary albums wasn't quite there in abundance yet
when the French Black & Blue imprint produced this album in 1976, with
the rest of his Waters bandmates in tow. A few too many hoary covers
("Sweet Home Chicago," "Mother-In-Law Blues") also grate. But as his first
solo album, it's an important chapter in his development. —Bill Dahl

With Muddy Waters Band / 197 / Muse ✦✦✦

Doin' the Sugar Too / 1984 / Rooster Blues ✦✦✦
A step in the right direction—much better production, savvier song selection,
including a few snappy originals, and the five-piece Roomful of Blues horn
section in staunch support. The guitarist's Magic Rockers include keyboardist
Ron Levy, who would go on to produce Johnson's Bullsye Blues output.
—Bill Dahl

I Want to Groove with You / 1990 / Bullseye Blues ✦✦✦✦
Now this is more like it. Johnson and his New England-based Magic Rockers
sizzle the hide off the genre with tough West Side-styled grooves redolent of
Johnson's Chicago upbringing, but up-to-the-minute in their execution. With
this set, Johnson fully came into his own as a recording artist. —Bill Dahl

It's Good to Me / 1992 / Bullseye Blues ✦✦✦✦
Another barn-burner mixing the guitarist's West-side roots with soul and
blues shadings to present some of the fieriest contemporary blues on the
market. Saxist Gordon Beadle and keyboardist Joe Krown distinguish themselves behind Johnson. —Bill Dahl

Country Sugar Papa / Mar. 30, 1994 / Bullseye Blues ✦✦✦✦
Johnson's third and final album for producer Ron Levy's Bullseye Blues diskery is every bit as spellbinding as the prior pair. Whether fronting his latest
batch of Magic Rockers or going it alone, Johnson is totally convincing.
—Bill Dahl

● **Slammin' on the West Side** / Apr. 1996 / Telarc ✦✦✦✦
Lousy album title, great album. Johnson hasn't been based out of Chicago in
years, but that sound remains at the heart of his approach—even when he's
recording in Louisiana with a funky New Orleans rhythm section (bassist
George Porter, Jr., and drummer Herman Ernest). Jump blues in the form of
Buddy Johnson's "A Pretty Girl (A Cadillac and Some Money)," the Magic
Sam tribute "Hard Times (Have Surely Come)," the solo acoustic "Get Up
and Go," a soul-slanted "Every Woman Needs to Be Loved"—Johnson smokes
'em all. —Bill Dahl

Luther "Houserocker" Johnson

b. Jul. 15, 1939, Atlanta, GA
Guitar, Vocals / Modern Electric Blues
The latest Luther Johnson to add his name to the blues directory is an adept
singer/guitarist who is a current favorite on the Atlanta blues scene. Proficient in various shadings of the electric blues idiom, Johnson has recently
extended his repertoire from covers of blues standards to his own material,
performed with the same '50s/'60s flavor.

Johnson taught himself how to play guitar when he was a teenager in
Atlanta by listening to records. Soon, he began playing guitar in pickup
bands, which gave him the opportunity to support such touring musicians
as Johnny Winter. After several years playing in bar bands, Johnson formed
his own group, the Houserockers.

The Houserockers played bars and clubs around Georgia for several years,
eventually landing a record contract with Ichiban in 1989. The next year
Johnson released his debut album, *Takin' A Bite Outta the Blues.* Two years
later, his second record, *Houserockin' Daddy,* appeared. Luther "Houserocker" Johnson continued to tour the US throughout the '90s. —Jim
O'Neal & Stephen Thomas Erlewine

Takin' a Bite Outta the Blues / 1990 / Ichiban ✦✦✦
This tough, direct, small-group blues sounds hardened by years in bars, "giv-
ing people what they want." Included are covers of B.B. King, Jimmy Reed,
Ray Charles, Charles Brown. —Niles J. Frantz

● **Houserockin' Daddy** / 1991 / Ichiban ✦✦✦✦
Johnson is a traditional electric bluesman (now living and working in the
Atlanta area) who was heavily influenced by Jimmy Reed. The album in-
cludes covers of Jimmy Reed, Lightnin' Slim, Howlin' Wolf, and Guitar Slim

tunes. It's simple, driving, to the point, streamlined, no-frills blues. —Niles
J. Frantz

Luther Snake Boy Johnson

b. Aug. 30, 1934, Davisboro, GA, **d.** Mar. 18, 1976
Guitar, Vocals / Chicago Blues
The confusing plethora of artists working under the name of Luther (nickname here) Johnson can leave even those with a decent knowledge of blues
in a major state of confusion. But in this biographical entry, we concern
ourselves with the life and times of Luther "Georgia Boy/Snake Boy" Johnson who, to make matters even *more* confusing, also worked and recorded
under the names Little Luther and Luther King.

He was born in 1934 in Davisboro, GA, which explains at least one of his
nicknames, but it turns out his real name wasn't even Luther, but Lucius.
One of ten children working on a farm, he started playing at the tender age
of seven. He soon ran away from home and was placed in a reform school
by 1947. A three-year stint in the Army followed. Upon his military discharge,
he picked guitar as a member of the Milwaukee Supreme Angels gospel
group, working the local church circuit. But the blues bug hit and he soon
had his own little blues trio together, eventually settling in Chicago by the
early '60s. He played for a while with Elmore James and was a regular fixture
in the Muddy Waters band by the mid-'60s. He recorded as Little Luther
for Chess in the mid-'60s ("The Twirl," available on the Ace anthology,
Houserockin' Blues, listed in the compilation section) and by 1970 was relocated to Boston, MA, working as a solo artist. The next five years found
him working steadily on the college and blues festival circuit before cancer
overtook him on March 18, 1976, at a mere 41 years of age. —Cub Koda

Come on Home / 1969 / Douglas ✦✦✦

The Muddy Waters Blues Band / Dec. 1969 / Douglas ✦✦

Born in Georgia / 1972 / Black & Blue ✦✦✦

Chicken Shack / 1974 / Muse ✦✦✦✦

● **Lonesome in My Bedroom** / Dec. 18, 1975 / Evidence ✦✦✦✦
This was Johnson's final album before his death in 1976, and it was originally
cut for Black and Blue (now reissued with three bonus tracks). While various
tracks reflect the influence of Muddy Waters, Jimmy Reed and John Lee
Hooker, Johnson's own inimitable vocals, raspy lines, and tart guitar eventually create his own aura. He is nicely backed by drummer Fred Below, bassist
Dave Myers, guitar burner Lonnie Brooks, and the solid rhythm work of
Hubert Sumlin. This was a fine session for a good, occasionally outstanding
blues artist. —Ron Wynn

On the Road Again / 1976 / Black & Blue ✦✦✦
On the Road Again, an early-'70s outing, shows Johnson in fine form, assisted
by a tough backing band. Cut in France. —Bill Dahl

Get Down to the Nitty Gritty / 1976 / New Rose ✦✦✦
Culled from a radio broadcast made for a Rochester, NY, radio station in
1976, *Get Down to the Nitty Gritty* is a nifty set of hard-edged Chicago blues.
Luther Johnson pays homage to his mentor and employer, Muddy Waters,
throughout the album, playing classics like "Hoochie Coochie Man" and originals in the same vein. Although the sound quality of the recording is poor—
there are dropouts and tape hiss all over the place—the performance is stellar. Johnson sings with passion and his guitar solos are blistering. *Get Down
to the Nitty Gritty* is a rough gem that is worthwhile to any fan of Johnson
or Muddy Waters. —Thom Owens

Pete Johnson (Peter Johnson)

b. May 23, 1967, Kansas City, MO, **d.** Mar. 23, 1967, Buffalo, NY
Piano / Boogie-Woogie, Blues Jazz
Pete Johnson was one of the three great boogie-woogie pianists (along with
Albert Ammons and Meade Lux Lewis) whose sudden prominence in the
late '30s helped make the style very popular. Originally a drummer, Johnson
switched to piano in 1922. He was part of the Kansas City scene in the 1920s
and '30s, often accompanying singer Big Joe Turner. Producer John Hammond discovered him in 1936 and got him to play at the Famous Door in
New York. After taking part at Hammond's 1938 *Spirituals to Swing* Carnegie Hall concert in 1938, Johnson started recording regularly and appeared
on an occasional basis with Ammons and Lewis as the Boogie Woogie Trio.

He also backed Turner on some classic records. Johnson recorded often in the 1940s and spent much of 1947-49 based in Los Angeles. He moved to Buffalo in 1950 and, other than an appearance at the 1958 Newport Jazz Festival, he was in obscurity for much of the decade. A stroke later in 1958 left him partially paralyzed. Johnson made one final appearance at John Hammond's January 1967 *Spirituals to Swing* concert, playing the right hand on a version of "Roll 'Em Pete" two months before his death. *— Scott Yanow*

1938-1939 / Dec. 30, 1938-Dec. 1938 / Classics ✦✦✦✦
This superlative CD reissue features boogie-woogie pianist Pete Johnson on two classic numbers with singer Big Joe Turner (the original versions of "Goin' Away Blues" and "Roll 'Em Pete"), with inspiring trumpeter Harry James ("Boo Woo" and "Home James"), with his Boogie Woogie Boys (a sextet that includes Turner and trumpeter Hot Lips Page), interacting with fellow pianists Albert Ammons and Meade Lux Lewis (joining Big Joe on "Café Society Rag"), and on a pair of trio numbers. However, it is Johnson's ten unaccompanied piano solos (mostly released previously by Solo Art) that are the rarest and most notable. Taken as a whole, this is Pete Johnson's definitive release, showing that he was much more than just a one-dimensional (although powerful) boogie-woogie specialist. *— Scott Yanow*

The Boogie Woogie Boys / Feb. 1939-Jan. 1953 / Storyville ✦✦✦✦

King of Boogie / Apr. 16, 1939-May 8, 1939 / Milan ✦✦✦
This sampler of pianist Pete Johnson's 1939-41 recordings has somewhat crummy packaging, which claims that the selections were recorded "at various concerts in France"; actually, these are all studio sides cut in the United States. The music—trio and solo performances except for a band number, "627 Stomp"—is excellent, but the 17 numbers are all readily available elsewhere. Fine music which, if found at a budget price, could act as an introduction to the boogie-woogie/blues pianist. *— Scott Yanow*

Master of Blues and Boogie Woogie, Vol. 3 / Dec. 19, 1939-Apr. 1949 / Oldie Blues ✦✦✦
This Dutch LP features pianist Pete Johnson in four different settings spanning a decade of time. Six titles are trio and solo numbers taken from his 1939 Blue Note dates (bassist Abe Bolar is mistakenly listed as playing drums). Much rarer are three songs from a 1946 quintet set with organist Bill Gooden and guitarist Jimmy Shirley, and three songs with a rollicking R&B-ish sextet in 1949. But overall, collectors will prefer to get these performances in complete versions with their original sessions. Good music, but this LP is not essential. *— Scott Yanow*

Boogie Woogie Mood (1940-1944) / Nov. 11, 1940-Feb. 17, 1944 / MCA ✦✦✦
This 1980 LP was quite valuable when it was released, although it has been largely superseded by later CDs. Pianist Pete Johnson is heard jamming with a Kansas City band on "627 Stomp," taking four numbers with a trio (including "Death Ray Boogie" and "Just For You"), and on eight unaccompanied piano solos. The emphasis, as usual, is on boogie-woogie although Johnson could also play very credible swing and blues. *— Scott Yanow*

Central Avenue Boogie / Apr. 18, 1947-Nov. 29, 1947 / Delmark ✦✦✦
Boogie-woogie pianist Pete Johnson is in excellent form on these selections, but this complete reissue of his Apollo recordings does not have much meat. Johnson only cut eight sides for the label so three alternate takes are included plus two titles (and an alternate) from pianist Arnold Wiley's only Apollo session. The results are enjoyable (particularly Johnson's versions of "Margie" and "Swanee River"), although few surprises or real highpoints occur. *— Scott Yanow*

● **1944-1946** / Jul. 15, 1997 / Classics ✦✦✦✦
The third "complete" Pete Johnson CD put out by the European Classics label features the great boogie-woogie pianist in three different settings. There are eight formerly rare piano solos from 1944 that cover a variety of moods, five selections with a hot Kansas City octet which includes trumpeter Hot Lips Page, tenorman Budd Johnson and two vocals from the young Etta Jones, and eight intriguing numbers in which Johnson is gradually joined by an additional musician on each track. "Page Mr. Trumpet" is an exciting outing for Hot Lips, and the other top players include clarinetist Albert Nicholas, trombonist J.C. Higginbotham, and tenorman Ben Webster. A particularly exciting release. *— Scott Yanow*

Robert Johnson

b. May 8, 1911, Hazlehurst, MS, **d.** Aug. 16, 1938, Greenwood, MS
Guitar, Vocals / Delta Blues, Prewar Country Blues

If the blues has a truly mythic figure, one whose story hangs over the music the way a Charlie Parker does over jazz or a Hank Williams does over country, it's Robert Johnson, certainly the most celebrated figure in the history of the blues. Of course, his legend is immensely fortified by the fact that Johnson also left behind a small legacy of recordings that are considered the emotional apex of the music itself. These recordings have not only entered the realm of blues standards ("Love in Vain," "Crossroads," "Sweet Home Chicago," "Stop Breaking Down"), but have been adapted by rock 'n' roll artists as diverse as the Rolling Stones, Steve Miller, Led Zeppelin, and Eric Clapton. While there are historical naysayers who would be more comfortable downplaying his skills and achievements (most of whom have never made a convincing case as where the source of his apocalyptic visions emanates from), Robert Johnson remains a potent force to be reckoned with. As a singer, a composer, and as a guitarist of considerable skills, he produced some of the genre's best music and the ultimate blues legend to deal with. Doomed, haunted, driven by demons, a tormented genius dead at an early age, all of these add up to making him a character of mythology who—if he hadn't actually existed—would have to be created by some biographer's overactive romantic imagination.

The legend of his life—which by now, even folks who don't know *anything* about the blues can cite to you chapter and verse—goes something like this: Robert Johnson was a young Black man living on a plantation in rural Mississippi. Branded with a burning desire to become great blues musician, he was instructed to take his guitar to a crossroad near Dockery's plantation at midnight. There he was met by a large Black man (the Devil) who took the guitar from Johnson, tuned it and handed it back to him. Within less than a year's time, in exchange for his everlasting soul, Robert Johnson became the king of the Delta blues singers, able to play, sing, and create the greatest blues anyone had ever heard.

As success came with live performances and phonograph recordings, Johnson remained tormented, constantly haunted by nightmares of hellhounds on his trail, his pain and mental anguish finding release only in the writing and performing of his music. Just as he was to be brought to Carnegie Hall to perform in John Hammond's first Spirituals to Swing concert, the news had come from Mississippi; Robert Johnson was dead, poisoned by a jealous girlfriend while playing a jook joint. Those who were there swear he was last seen alive foaming at the mouth, crawling around on all fours, hissing and snapping at onlookers like a mad dog. His dying words (either spoken or written on a piece of scrap paper) were, "I pray that my redeemer will come and take me from my grave." He was buried in a pine box in an unmarked grave, his deal with the Devil at an end.

Of course, Johnson's influences in the real world were far more disparate than the legend suggests, no matter how many times it's been retold or embellished. As a teenage plantation worker, Johnson fooled with a harmonica a little bit, but seemingly had no major musical skills to speak of. Every attempt to sit in with local titans of the stature of Son House, Charley Patton, Willie Brown, and others brought howls of derision from the older bluesmen. Son House: "We'd all play for the Saturday night balls, and there'd be this little boy hanging around. That was Robert Johnson. He blew a harmonica then, and he was pretty good at that, but he wanted to play a guitar. He'd sit at our feet and play during the breaks and such another racket you'd never heard." He married young and left Robinsonville, wandering the Delta and using Hazelhurst as base, determined to become a full-time professional musician after his first wife died during childbirth. Johnson returned to Robinsonville a few years later and when he encountered House and Willie Brown at a juke joint in Banks, MS, according to House, "When he finished, all our mouths were standing open. I said, 'Well, ain't that fast! He's gone now!'" To a man, there was only one explanation as how Johnson had gotten *that* good, *that* fast; he had sold his soul to the Devil.

But Johnson's skills were acquired in a far more conventional manner, born more of a concentrated Christian work ethic than a Faustian bargain with old Scratch. He idolized the Delta recording star Lonnie Johnson—sometimes introducing himself to newcomers as "Robert Lonnie, one of the Johnson brothers"—and the music of Scrapper Blackwell, Skip James, and Kokomo Arnold were all inspirational elements from which he drew his unique style. His slide style certainly came from hours of watching local stars like Charley Patton and Son House, among others. Perhaps the biggest influence, however, came from an unrecorded bluesman named Ike Zinneman. We'll never really know what Zinneman's music sounded like (we do know from various reports that he liked to practice late at night in the local graveyard, sitting on tombstones while he strummed away), or how much of his personal muse he imparted to Johnson, if any. What *is* known is that after a year or so under Zinneman's tutelage, Johnson returned with an encyclopedic knowledge of his instrument, an ability to sing and play in a multiplicity of styles, and a very carefully worked-out approach to song construction, keeping his original lyrics with him in a personal digest. As an itinerant musician, playing at country suppers as well as on the street, his audience demanded someone who could play and sing everything from blues pieces to the pop and hillbilly tunes of the day. Johnson's talents could cover all of that and more. His most enduring contribution, the boogie bass line played on the bottom strings of the guitar (adapted from piano players), has become part and parcel of the sound most people associate with down-home blues. It is a sound so very much of a part of the music's fabric that the listener cannot imagine the styles of Jimmy Reed, Elmore James, Eddie Taylor, Lightnin' Slim, Hound Dog Taylor, or a hundred lesser lights existing without that essential component part. As his playing partner Johnny Shines put it, "Some of the things that Robert did with the guitar affected the way everybody played. He'd do rundowns and turnbacks. He'd do repeats. None of this was being done. In the early '30s, boogie on the guitar was rare, something to be heard. Because of Robert, people learned to complement theirselves, carrying their own bass as their own lead with this one instrument." While his music can certainly be put in context as part of a definable tradition, what he did with it and where he took it was another matter entirely.

Although Robert Johnson never recorded near as much as Lonnie Johnson, Charley Patton, or Blind Lemon Jefferson, he certainly traveled more than all of them put together. After his first recordings came out and "Terraplane Blues" became his signature tune (a so-called "race" record selling over three or four thousand copies back in the early to mid-'30s was considered a hit), Johnson hit the road, playing anywhere and everywhere he could. Instilled with a seemingly unquenchable desire to experience new places and things, his wandering nature took him up and down the Delta and as far afield as St. Louis, Chicago, and Detroit (where he performed over the radio on the *Elder Moten Hour*), places Son House and Charley Patton had only seen in the movies, if that. But the end came at a Saturday-night dance at a juke joint in Three Forks, Mississippi, in August of 1938. Playing with Honeyboy Edwards and Sonny Boy Williamson (Rice Miller), Johnson was given a jug of moonshine whiskey laced with either poison or lye, presumably by the husband of a woman the singer had made advances toward. He continued playing into the night until he was too sick to continue, then brought back to a boarding house in Greenwood, some 15 miles away. He lay sick for several days, successfully sweating the poison out of his system, but caught pneumonia as a result and died on August 16th. The legend was just beginning.

In the mid-'60s, Columbia Records released *King of the Delta Blues Singers*, the first compilation of Johnson's music and one of the earliest collections of pure country blues. Rife with liner notes full of romantic speculation, little in the way of hard information and a painting standing for a picture, this for years was the world's sole introduction to the music and the legend, doing much to promote both. A second volume—collecting up the other master takes and issuing a few of the alternates—was released in the '70s, giving fans a first-hand listen to music that had been only circulated through bootleg tapes and albums or cover versions by English rock stars. Finally in 1990—after years of litigation—a complete two-CD box set was released with every scrap of Johnson material known to exist plus the holy grail of the blues; the publishing of the only two known photographs of the man himself. Columbia's parent company, Sony, was hoping that sales would maybe hit 20,000. The box set went on to sell over a million units, the first blues recordings ever to do so.

In the intervening years since the release of the box set, Johnson's name and likeness has become a cottage growth merchandising industry. Posters, postcards, t-shirts, guitar picks, strings, straps, and polishing cloths—all bearing either his likeness or signature (taken from his second marriage certificate)—have become available, making him the ultimate blues commodity with his image being reproduced for profit far more than any contemporary

bluesman, dead or alive. Although the man himself (and his contemporaries) could never have imagined it in a million years, the music and the legend both live on. — *Cub Koda*

☆ **King of the Delta Blues Singers** / 1966 / Columbia ♦♦♦♦♦
Reading about the power inherent in Robert Johnson's music is one thing, but actually *experiencing* it is another matter entirely. Here's where you go to find it. If there is such a thing as a "greatest hits" package available on Johnson, this landmark album would come very close indeed. The majority of Johnson's best-known tunes are aboard; "Crossroads," "Terraplane Blues," "Me and the Devil Blues," "Come on in My Kitchen," and the apocalyptic visions contained in "Hellhound on My Trail" are the blues as its finest, the lyrics sheer poetry. If you are starting your blues collections, be sure to make this your first purchase. — *Cub Koda*

★ **King of the Delta Blues Singers, Vol. 2** / 1970 / Columbia ♦♦♦♦♦
This second volume—although made somewhat superfluous by the arrival two decades later of the box set—contains the rest of the issued takes and some, but not all, of the alternate takes. The music is excellent, featuring the first album appearance of "Love in Vain." — *Cub Koda*

★ **The Complete Recordings** / 1990 / Columbia/Legacy ♦♦♦♦♦
A double-disc box set containing everything Robert Johnson ever recorded, *The Complete Recordings* is essential listening, but it is also slightly problematic. The problems aren't in the music itself, of course, which is stunning and the fidelity of the recordings is the best it ever has been or ever will be. Instead, it's in the track sequencing. As the title implies, *The Complete Recordings* contains all of Johnson's recorded material, including a generous selection of alternate takes. All of the alternates are sequenced directly after the master, which can make listening to the album a little intimidating and tedious for novices. Certainly, the alternates can be programmed out with a CD player, but the set would have been more palatable if the alternate takes were presented on a separate disc. Nevertheless, this is a minor complaint—Robert Johnson's music retains its power no matter what context it is presented in. He, without question, deserves this kind of deluxe box-set treatment. — *Stephen Thomas Erlewine*

King of the Electric Blues Singers [Bootleg] / 1996 / [bootleg] ♦♦
One can either view this bootleg, lo-fi six song cassette as a multi-track experiment gone terribly wrong, the ultimate bad taste commercialization and bastardization of Johnson's music, or a practical joke of the highest order—take your pick. The accompanying "press release" (everything on this homemade "package'" has been Xeroxed again and again) claims that in the early 1970s an executive at Columbia Records requisitioned the Johnson masters from the company vaults, then surreptitiously booked a session with a blues-rock band signed to the label overdubbing themselves on top of them. The idea (supposedly) was to make Johnson more accessible to rock audiences by doing a "Buddy Holly" on him (modern-day backings dubbed onto solo tapes). The end result would then be marketed via album (hence the goofy title) and singles, getting further mileage out of the slim Johnson catalog. However, as the six songs clearly prove, the band doing the overdubbing was no match for Johnson's irregular time and chord changes, and the whole project was abandoned after the one session. While the players (highly amplified and very distorted lead guitar, bass, and drums) lock in here and there—"Sweet Home Chicago" and "Walkin' Blues" are the best-*played* examples of what they were attempting to do—they frequently stumble and lose the beat, lay in wait for the next change to come, or just merely blast away, seemingly oblivious to what is happening on the original recording. While most blues fans will find this whole experiment blues heresy of the highest order (the audio equivalent of painting a headband on the Mona Lisa, not to mention the trashiest, cash-grabbing corruption of Robert's art imaginable), those with a nose for the perverse, the odd, and the just plain weird will want to hear this cheezoid collection at least *once*. — *Cub Koda*

★ **King of the Delta Blues** / Oct. 7, 1997 / Sony ♦♦♦♦♦
This 16-track single-disc compilation gathers up the best-known tracks from the two original volumes of *King of the Delta Blues Singers* for a nice entry-level collection of Robert's best. Utilizing the latest in remastering technology, these recordings have never sounded quite this clear and full-bodied before, and the difference between this and the first pressing of the *Complete Recordings* box set is quite noticeable. While sweating down Johnson's best to a 16-track selection is an arbitrary choice at best, it's hard to fault the

selection here. It's also a focused set that isn't hampered by the inclusion of the more collector-oriented alternate takes that bog down much of the box set's listenability. — *Cub Koda*

Tommy Johnson

b. 1896, Terry, MS, **d.** Nov. 1, 1956, Crystal Springs, MS
Guitar, Kazoo, Vocals / Delta Blues, Country Blues, Prewar Country Blues
Next to Son House and Charley Patton, no one was more important to the development of pre-Robert Johnson Delta blues than Tommy Johnson. Armed with a powerful voice that could go from a growl to an eerie falsetto range, and a guitar style that had all of the early figures and licks of the Delta style clearly delineated, Johnson only recorded for two years — from 1928 to 1930 — but left behind a body of work that's hard to ignore.

The legend of Tommy Johnson is even harder to ignore. The stories about his live performances — where he would play the guitar behind his neck in emulation of Charley Patton's showboating while hollering the blues at full throated level for hours without a break — are part of it. So is his uncontrolled womanizing and alcoholism, both of which constantly got him in trouble. Johnson's addiction to spirits was so pronounced that he was often seen drinking Sterno-denatured alcohol used for artificial heat — or shoe polish strained through bread for the kick each could offer when whiskey wasn't affordable or available in dry counties throughout the South. Then there's the crossroads story. Yes, years before the deal with the Devil at a deserted Delta crossroad was being used as an explanation of the other-worldly abilities of young Robert Johnson, the story was being told repeatedly about Tommy, often by the man himself to reinforce his abilities to doubting audiences.

Then there's the music. His "Cool Water Blues" got amped up in the '50s by one of his early admirers, Howlin' Wolf, and became "I Asked for Water (She Brought Me Gasoline)." Another signature piece, his "Maggie Campbell," came with a chord progression that was used for infinite variations by blues players dating all the way back to his contemporary Charley Patton through Robert Nighthawk. Two of his best-known numbers have survived into modern times; "Big Road Blues" is probably best known to contemporary blues fans from adaptions by Floyd Jones and others, while his "Canned Heat Blues" — a bone-chilling account of his complete addiction to alcohol and his slavish attempts to score it by whatever means necessary — was the tune that gave a California blues-rock band their name. After a while, all of the above starts adding up, no matter how you slice it. Tommy Johnson was one tough hombre, and a real piece of work.

He was born in 1896 in Hinds County, MS, on the George Miller plantation. Once the family moved to Crystal Springs in 1910, Tommy picked up the guitar, learning from his older brother, LeDell. By age 16, Johnson had run away from home to become a "professional" musician, largely supporting himself by playing on the street for tips. By the late teens-early '20s, Tommy was frequently playing the company of rising local stars Charley Patton, Dick Bankston, and Willie Brown, their collective ouevre planting seed, later becoming the first greening of the Mississippi Delta blues. Johnson spent most of the '20s drinking, womanizing, gambling, and playing in the company of Rubin Lacy, Charley McCoy, Son Spand, Walter Vincent, and Ishmon Bracey when the money got low and apparently, only when the mood struck him. By all acounts, Tommy felt no particular drive to relentlessly promote himself and — while he played music for pay until the very end of his life — he certainly wasn't as serious about his career as he was about his drinking. He cut his first records for the Victor (later RCA Victor, now BMG) label at sessions held in Memphis, TN, in 1928. Johnson's first releases hit the area hard, inspiring a raft of up-and-comers that reads like the proverbial who's who list; you could easily count Howlin' Wolf, Robert Nighthawk, Houston Stackhouse, Floyd Jones, Boogie Bill Webb, K.C. Douglas, Johnny "Geechie" Temple, and Otis Spann among his many disciples.

He cut one more stack of great records for the Paramount label in 1930, largely through the maneuvering of fellow drinking buddy Charley Patton. Then the slow descent into alcoholism started taking its toll, the one too many nights of Sterno and shoe polish buzzes reducing his once prodigious talents to small, sporadic flickerings of former genius. He worked on a medicine show with Ishmon Bracey in the '30s, but mostly seemed to be a mainstay of the juke and small party dance circuit the rest of his days. He was playing just such a local house party in November of 1956 when he suffered a fatal heart attack and went out in probably the exact fashion he wanted to.

Whether the story about the deal with the Devil at the crossroads was something he truly believed or just something Johnson said to drum up local interest in himself, it seems odd that you'll find him buried at the Warm Springs Methodist Church Cemetery in Crystal Springs. Maybe he mellowed out towards the end, maybe he found God. Some things about the blues you'll never know, no matter how many computers you hook up to it. — *Cub Koda*

Tommy Johnson (1928-1930) / 1928-1930 / Wolf ✦✦✦✦
Austria-based Wolf Records has done a masterful job on this 12-song collection (missing only two of Johnson's works, which have never turned up), much of it surprisingly clean and crisp. Most of the best sounding material here has already appeared on RCA/BMG's *Canned Heat Blues* compilation, which seems to be headed out-of-print at this writing. "Cool Drink of Water Blues" and "Canned Heat Blues" are by far the best known of Johnson's works, but they've got a lot of worthy pieces surrounding them. "Big Road Blues" is a fine showcase for Johnson's and Charlie McCoy's paired guitars, playing two complex, interwoven figures. And "Bye Bye Blues" and "Maggie Campbell Blues" show off his unique vocal qualities, not the dark heaviness typical of bluesmen at the time, but a more flexible, lighter toned, relaxed instrument that, coupled with his and McCoy's guitars, made his music as "busy" as it was beautiful. The songs featuring only Johnson's guitar are no less intriguing, if only for his ability to get a lot of sound from some surprisingly simple strumming and picking. The later songs, "I Wonder to Myself," "Slidin' Delta," "Lonesome Home Blues," and "Black Mare Blues," leave something to be desired in terms of sound, but at least they're represented here. — *Bruce Eder*

Wallace Johnson

b. 1937, Louisiana
Vocals / Modern Electric Blues
Vocalist Wallace Johnson last sang around New Orleans clubs more than 20 years ago. But it's only recently that his singing has been recorded and made available to a larger public outside of New Orleans, thanks to New Orleans-based pianist/songwriter/arranger/producer Allen Toussaint. Best described as a soul-blues singer, Johnson's album, *Whoever's Thrilling You*, was the debut for Toussaint's NYNO (New York/New Orleans) label, released in 1996.

Born on a plantation in 1937, Johnson got married and joined the Army at age 17. He first performed in public during his term in the Army in the mid-'50s, and after singing around Thibodeaux, LA, in the early '60s, he recorded four singles for AFO Records in 1962, a label Harold Battiste, Toussaint, Dr. John and other New Orleans-based musicians founded. With a growing family and a wife, Johnson reached a crossroads of sorts, and decided to put his singing career on the back burner for a number of years. But fortunately for us, Toussaint stayed in touch with Johnson and recorded eight more singles with him between 1965 and 1972 at Toussaint's home studios.

Between 1972 and 1992, Johnson put show business aside, working as a longshoreman and running a music club, Mr. J's, in Thibodeaux for a number of years. Johnson stayed in touch with Toussaint, though, and would go and visit the producer from time to time.

After being urged to go back on stage and sing by his fiancee and bassist Alonzo Johnson (Rockin' Dopsie), he sang in public once again in April, 1993 at the New Orleans French Quarter Festival. Since then, Johnson has been making regular appearances in Crescent City clubs and in late 1995, he returned to Toussaint's studios to record his first full-length album.

The release of *Whoever's Thrilling You* in the spring of 1996 coincided with his performance at the 1996 New Orleans Jazz and Heritage Festival. Toussaint wrote nine of the album's twelve songs specifically with Johnson in mind. On the album, Johnson sings songs with a wide variety of tempos. His gospel-influenced, soul-drenched vocals are unique, powerful and moving. Now at 60, it appears Johnson is ready to retire from his day job in sanitation and make a go of being a full-time blues singer. — *Richard Skelly*

Whoever's Thrilling You / May 7, 1996 / NYNO ✦✦✦

Andrew "Jr. Boy" Jones

Guitar, Vocals / Modern Electric Blues
Guitarist, songwriter and singer Andrew "Jr. Boy" Jones began working professionally at age 16 with Freddie King's backing band, the Thunderbirds. He

got his first guitar from his uncle, jazz musician Adolphus Sneed. Jones cites an eclectic array of influences: Freddie King, Cornell Dupree, and Larry Carlton. For many years, he's backed various Dallas-area vocalists on guitar, but in the mid-1990s, he came into his own as a vocalist with an album for JSP Records, *I Need Time* (1997), which showcases his crafty songwriting, great guitar playing, and powerful singing.

In 1967, Jones joined Dallas-area vocalist Bobby Patterson's outfit, the Mustangs. Through most of the 1970s, Jones backed various artists, including Patterson, Johnnie Taylor, and Charlie Robertson. In late 1987, he went to California and joined the Solid Partners with bassist Russell Jackson and drummer Tony Coleman, the latter of whom is best known for his work with B.B. King's orchestra. Jones recorded with Bay-area piano player and singer Katie Webster on her critically praised Alligator Records album, *Swamp Boogie Queen*.

Jones met harmonica player Charlie Musselwhite at a Sonny Rhodes recording session, and Musselwhite persuaded him to stay in California and join his band. Jones played guitar on Musselwhite's three late-1980s/early-1990s albums for Alligator Records (*Ace of Harps*, *In My Time*, and *Signature*). He also had the chance to do some extensive world touring with the harmonica master.

Jones left Musselwhite's band amicably in the mid-1990s and is now back in Dallas, where he accompanies Dallas-area blues singers like R.L. Griffin, Hal Harris and the Lowlifers, and others. —*Richard Skelly*

I Need Time / Feb. 25, 1997 / JSP ✦✦✦

Casey Jones

b. Jul. 26, 1939, Nitta Yuma, MS
Drums / Electric Chicago Blues
Long recognized as one of the Chicago circuit's premier drummers, charismatic Casey Jones has moved out in front of his band over the last decade instead of hiding behind his kit. Casey discovered that beating his way through the world was fun while drilling with his high school marching band back in Greenville. He moved to Chicago in 1956. Before the end of the year, he was drumming professionally with an outfit called Otis Luke & the Rhythm Bombers (for a whopping five bucks a night). One auspicious 1959 night, Jones was forced to sing live for the first time when the pianist leading his band was tossed in jail. He found screaming like Little Richard was pretty enjoyable too. Early '60s session work behind Earl Hooker, A.C. Reed, McKinley Mitchell, and Muddy Waters (1962's "You Need Love") kept Jones busy, as did playing on the South and West Sides with the likes of Otis Rush and Freddy King. His profile rose markedly in 1978 when he slid into the drum chair within Albert Collins' hand-picked combo, the Icebreakers. His impeccable timekeeping powered the band for six-and-a-half years, and he played on Collins' first six Alligator albums (notably *Ice Pickin'* and the '85 summit meeting *Showdown!* with Robert Cray and Johnny Copeland).

Casey Jones has been holding down Sunday nights at Chicago's popular Kingston Mines nightclub for nearly a decade—a period that's seen his own discography grow steadily. 1987's *Solid Blue* for Rooster Blues preceded the formation of his own label, Airwax Records (source of his last few CDs, including 1993's *The Crowd Pleaser* and *[I-94] On My Way to Chicago* in 1995). —*Bill Dahl*

Solid Blue / 1987 / Rooster Blues ✦✦✦✦
One of the Chicago drummer's best solo outings, still not yet available on CD. Eight originals, all of them well-done (especially the chunky "Mr. Blues" and a rocking "Hip Hip Hooray"). Jones' vocals are enthusiastic and his backing is expert—sidemen include harpist Billy Branch, guitarist Maurice Vaughn, and bassist Johnny B. Gayden (the latter Jones' former cohort in Albert Collins' band, the Icebreakers). —*Bill Dahl*

Crowd Pleaser / 1993 / Airwax ✦✦✦✦
A very enjoyable collection of new and recent (three songs, including "Tribute to the Boogie Men" and "Mr. Blues," stem from "Solid Blue") numbers on Jones' own Airwax logo. Of course, he handles his own timekeeping throughout. —*Bill Dahl*

● **(I-94) on My Way to Chicago** / 1995 / Airwax ✦✦✦✦
As good a place to begin your Casey Jones collection as any, since his vocals remain strong and his songwriting is as pleasing as ever. The title cut, "I Know I Got a Good Woman," and the sinuous "She Treats Me Right" all make highly favorable impressions. —*Bill Dahl*

Curtis Jones

b. Aug. 18, 1906, Naples, TX, **d.** Sep. 11, 1971, Munich, Germany
Piano, Vocals / Electric Chicago Blues, Piano Blues
The origins of the blues standard "Tin Pan Alley" can be traced directly back to pianist Curtis Jones, who also enjoyed considerable success in 1937 with his "Lonesome Bedroom Blues" for Vocalion (a song inspired by a breakup with his wife).

Jones started out on guitar but switched to the 88s after moving to Dallas. He arrived in Chicago in 1936 and recorded for Vocalion, Bluebird, and OKeh from 1937 to 1941. But the war ended his recording career until 1953, when powerful deejay Al Benson issued a one-off single by Jones, "Wrong Blues"/ "Cool Playing Blues," on his Parrot label with L.C. McKinley on guitar. In 1960, Jones waxed his debut album, *Trouble Blues*, for Prestige's Bluesville subsidiary with a classy crew of New York session aces and Chicagoan Johnny "Big Moose" Walker on guitar. By then, his audience was shifting drastically, as he became a fixture on the Chicago folk circuit. His next LP, *Lonesome Bedroom Blues*, was a 1962 solo affair for Delmark offering definitive renditions of the title cut and "Tin Pan Alley." Jones left Chicago permanently in January of 1962, settling in Europe and extensively touring the continent until his 1971 death. —*Bill Dahl*

● **Trouble Blues** / 1960 / Original Blues Classics ✦✦✦✦
The taciturn pianist in the company of a fine New York rhythm section and Johnny "Big Moose" Walker (but on guitar, not piano) made for a winning combination on this 1960 album. Jones delivers his downbeat "Suicide Blues," "Low Down Worried Blues," "Lonesome Bedroom Blues"... well, you get the picture. Jones wasn't exactly an upbeat kind of guy. The compilers did unearth a bonus for the CD version: Jones' treatment of "Pinetop Boogie." —*Bill Dahl*

Lonesome Bedroom Blues / 1962 / Delmark ✦✦✦✦
Jones, solo and at the top of his powers on piano and vocally, on a set produced by Bob Koester. The pianist was an exceptional lyricist, evidenced by his classic "Tin Pan Alley" and several lesser-known numbers on this album (which awaits digital re-emergence). —*Bill Dahl*

Now Resident in Europe / 1968 / Blue Horizon ✦✦✦

Complete Works, Vol. 1 (September 1937-May 1938) / Feb. 15, 1995 / Document ✦✦✦

Complete Works, Vol. 2 (June 1938-June 1939) / Feb. 15, 1995 / Document ✦✦✦

Complete Works, Vol. 3 (June 1939-September 1940) / Feb. 15, 1995 / Document ✦✦✦

Complete Works, Vol. 4 (January 1941-May 1953) / Feb. 15, 1995 / Document ✦✦✦

Eddie "One String" Jones-Edward Hazelton

b. Dec. 10, 1926
Guitar / Acoustic Blues
In most blues reference books, the name Eddie Jones refers to the given handle of the New Orleans guitarist better known as "Guitar Slim." But this time, we take pause to relate what little information exists on another Eddie Jones, this one a street musician situated in Los Angeles' Skid Row.

Eddie "One String" Jones was, by no stretch of the imagination, a professional musician. Nor, like his more famous namesake, was he even a guitar player. Had it not been for his chance discovery by folklorist and ethnic musicologist Frederick A. Usher in February of 1960, it's a pretty safe bet that no recorded document of him would probably exist.

Usher was in Los Angeles' Skid Row section on business with an associate when he was accosted by two panhandlers. One of those two men (Jones) was holding a rough cut 2'x4' plank, a homemade one-stringed instrument of the crudest construction. After a bit of cajoling from Usher, Jones reached into his pocket and fished out the other two working tools he used to make music with the board—a half pint whiskey bottle to slide with and a carefully whittled stick to bang the single string with, in place of a guitar pick. The sound was raw, jangly, and chaotic, as far removed from normal slide or bottleneck techniques as Usher (or anyone else) had ever heard. This was evidently a direct tie to the African instrument known as the "diddleybow," but Jones' technique with the stick gave the music an otherworldly edge, multiple tones to be derived from a single note, and a total departure from what most folklorists had previously known about the instrument. Sensing that Jones was a modern day link to an African art form long since dissipated, Usher was bowled over and ran back home as fast as he could to grab his portable tape recorder. After hooking up to a nearby store's electricity in a deserted back alley, Usher made the first recordings of Eddie "One String" Jones. But Jones' lifestyle as a homeless person made all attempts by Usher to mainstream him into folk music circles a virtual impossibility. "One String" was most secretive about his technique, the origin of the instrument, even his given name, which—it turns out—could have been Eddie Jones or Jessie Marshall. After scheduling two more informal recording sessions (one of which appears to be a no-show) and a chance to play for a group of Usher's friends in Hollywood, Jones slipped back into obscurity and has eluded all modern day blues detective work to even try and append his bio with a date of his death. If there's a romantic, mystery figure in blues history, Eddie "One String" Jones would certainly be at the top of the list. — *Cub Koda*

One String Blues / 1993 / Gazelle Documents ♦♦♦♦
Jones shares this 15-track compilation with harmonica street player Edward Hazelton, another one of Frederick Usher's elusive Skid Row discoveries, who contributes a half dozen sides featuring a stripped down Sonny Terry style. The first nine tracks by Jones are primitive in the extreme, untouched by any commercial considerations whatsoever. His instrument—described on the front cover as "a home-made African derived Zither-Monochord"— delivers tones that border on somewhere between keening, rhythmic, and downright eerie. Even repeated listening to any of the early Delta blues slide greats will not prepare you for the sound on this recording, which is trebly, bordering on metallic. Blues as folklore, but a whole lot of fun to explore as well. — *Cub Koda*

Floyd Jones

b. Jul. 21, 1917, Marianna, AR, d. Dec. 19, 1989, Chicago, IL
Guitar, Vocals / Chicago Blues, Electric Chicago Blues, Acoustic Chicago Blues
His sound characteristically dark and gloomy, guitarist Floyd Jones contributed a handful of genuine classics to the Chicago blues idiom during the late '40s and early '50s, notably the foreboding "Dark Road" and "Hard Times."

Born in Arkansas, Jones grew up in the blues-fertile Mississippi Delta (where he picked up the guitar in his teens). He came to Chicago in the mid-'40s, working for tips on Maxwell Street with his cousin Moody Jones and Baby Face Leroy Foster, and playing local clubs on a regular basis. Floyd was right there when the postwar Chicago blues movement first took flight, recording with harpist Snooky Pryor for Marvel in 1947; pianist Sunnyland Slim for Tempo Tone the next year (where he cut "Hard Times"), JOB and Chess in 1952-53, and Vee-Jay in 1955 (where he weighed in with a typically downcast "Ain't Times Hard").

Jones remained active on the Chicago scene until shortly before his 1989 death, although electric bass had long since replaced the guitar as his main axe. He participated in Earwig Records' *Old Friends* sessions in 1979, sharing a studio with longtime cohorts Sunnyland Slim, Honeyboy Edwards, Big Walter Horton, and Kansas City Red. — *Bill Dahl*

Elmore James-John Brim-Floyd Jones / 1986 / Vogue ♦♦♦♦
Both the artwork and the first two-thirds of this 20-track CD partially overlap the Chess Records release on Elmore James and John Brim. The last six songs are by Floyd Jones and include his classic "Dark Road" and "You Can't Live Long," cut on December 29, 1951 and September 17, 1952. All of the tracks feature Little Walter on harmonica, and the four 1951 songs also feature Jimmy Rogers. The sound is okay, and in the absence of any official Floyd Jones release from Chess, this is worth tracking down. — *Bruce Eder*

● **Masters of Modern Blues** / 1994 / Testament ♦♦♦♦
Eight priceless 1966 tracks by tragically underrecorded guitarist Floyd Jones are paired for this CD with eight more by sessionmate Eddie Taylor. Produced in both cases by Testament boss Pete Welding with Big Walter Horton on harp, pianist Otis Spann, and drummer Fred Below lending their collective hands, Jones recreates his dour, uncompromising "Dark Road," "Hard Times," and "Stockyard Blues" with an early-'50s sense of purpose. — *Bill Dahl*

Masters of Modern Blues, Vol. 3 / Testament ♦♦♦♦
Don't be put off by the murky sound on this one, because it features Jones, guitarist Eddie Taylor, harmonica wizard Walter Horton, pianist Otis Spann, and drummer Fred Below playing their hearts out. — *Cub Koda*

Johnny Jones

b. Nov. 1, 1924, Jackson, MS, d. Nov. 19, 1964, Chicago, IL
Piano, Vocals / Piano Blues, Chicago Blues, Electric Chicago Blues
In 40 short years on earth, Johnny Jones established himself as one of the greatest piano players ever to inhabit the Chicago blues scene. Best known for his rock-solid accompaniment to slide guitarist Elmore James both in the studio and as an onstage member of James' Broomdusters, "Little Johnny" also waxed a handful of terrific sides as a leader.

Jones arrived in Chicago from Mississippi in 1946 well-versed on the 88s. Influenced greatly by pianist Big Maceo Merriwether, Jones followed him into Tampa Red's band in 1947 after Maceo suffered a stroke. Johnny Jones' talents were soon in demand as a sideman—in addition to rolling the ivories behind Tampa Red for RCA Victor from 1949 to 1953, he backed Muddy Waters on his 1949 classic "Screamin' and Cryin'" and later appeared on sides by Howlin' Wolf.

But it's Elmore James that he'll forever be associated with; the indispensable pianist played on James' halcyon 1952-56 Chicago sessions for the Bihari brothers' Meteor, Flair, and Modern logos, as well as dates for Checker, Chief, and Fire. The Broomdusters (rounded out by saxist J.T. Brown and drummer Odie Payne, Jr.) held down a regular berth at the West Side blues club Sylvio's for five years.

When he got the chance to sit behind a microphone, Jones' insinuating vocal delivery was equally enthralling. Muddy Waters, Jimmy Rogers, and Leroy Foster backed Jones on his 1949 Aristocrat label classic "Big Town Playboy" (later revived by Eddie Taylor, another unsung Chicago hero), while Elmore James and saxist J.T. Brown were on hand for Jones' 1953 Flair coupling "I May Be Wrong"/"Sweet Little Woman" (the latter a wonderfully risqué "dozens" number). The rocking "Hoy Hoy," his last commercial single, was done in 1953 for Atlantic and also featured James and his group in support. Jones continued to work in the clubs (with Wolf, Sonny Boy Williamson, Syl Johnson, Billy Boy Arnold, and Magic Sam, among others) prior to his 1964 death of lung cancer.

Ironically, Jones was reportedly the first cousin of another Chicago piano great, Otis Spann. — *Bill Dahl*

● **Live in Chicago with Billy Boy Arnold** / 1979 / Alligator ♦♦♦♦
Thank heaven Norman Dayron had the presence of mind to capture these sides by Chicago pianist Johnny Jones when he played at the Fickle Pickle in 1963—as little as remains on tape of his talents as a singer, we're eternally indebted to Dayron's actions. Jones' insinuating vocals and bedrock 88s are abetted by harpist Billy Boy Arnold on these performances, and that's it—he had no rhythm section to fall back on. — *Bill Dahl*

Little Sonny Jones

b. Apr. 15, 1931, New Orleans, LA, d. Dec. 17, 1989, New Orleans, LA
Vocals / New Orleans Blues
When Black Top reissued Little Sonny Jones' 1975 album *New Orleans R&B Gems* recently, even some true blues fans probably shook their heads and wondered, "Who?" But rest assured: folks in the Crescent City recall Jones with great affection. He was born there and he died there, making some fine music in between.

Born Johnny Jones, the singer picked up his enduring nickname from his pal Fats Domino when they were both playing at the Hideaway Club in the ninth ward during the late '40s. Domino hit it big, but Jones' vinyl fortunes weren't as lucky: a 1953 single on Specialty ("Do You Really Love Me"/"Is Everything Allright") preceded a four-song session for Imperial the next year under Dave Bartholomew's direction (songs included "I Got Fooled" and "Winehead Baby"). All three 45s stiffed, but Fats kept him employed as a warmup act until 1961.

After seven years back home singing with the band of brothers David and Melvin Lastie, Jones retired until his 1975 album (first issued on Black Magic Records overseas). The set accurately recreated the Crescent City R&B sound of the '50s, thanks to Little Sonny Jones' rich singing and the efforts of veterans Dave "Fat Man" Williams on piano and vocals, saxists Clarence Ford and David Lastie, guitarist Justin Adams, bassist Frank Fields, and drummer Robert French.

Jones came out to play the annual Jazz & Heritage Festival until his 1989 death of heart failure. — *Bill Dahl*

● **New Orleans R&B Gems** / 1975 / Black Magic ◆◆◆◆
Little Sonny Jones was a minor New Orleans R&B legend, performing as Fats Domino's opening act for several years and releasing a series of unheralded singles. After achieving no success of his own, he retired in 1968, but he was coaxed out of retirement in 1975 by the Dutch label Black Magic to record *New Orleans R&B Gems*. It was the first opportunity he had to lead a full session, and he took advantage of it, turning in a wonderful record that captured the rich, rollicking tradition of New Orleans R&B. Throughout it all, his warm, rich voice is in fine form and the music is beyond funky. Serious Crescent City collectors will definitely want to check this one out. — *Thom Owens*

Paul "Wine" Jones

Guitar, Vocals / Modern Electric Blues
Like Big Jack Johnson, Sam Carr and his other labelmates at Fat Possum/ Capricorn, guitarist, singer, and songwriter Paul "Wine" Jones grew up with blues all around him. He learned to play guitar at his father's feet at age four, taking his earliest inspiration from his father's playing. Jones' brother, Casey, is the in-demand Chicago blues drummer who's backed Albert Collins, Koko Taylor, and dozens of others. Jones played music as an avocation for many years, working farming jobs until 1971, when he became a professional welder in Belzoni, MS. He's been based in Belzoni ever since.

In 1995 and 1996, as part of Fat Possum's Mississippi Juke Joint Caravan, he had the opportunity to perform for the first time outside of Mississippi. His 1995 debut for the Fat Possum/Capricorn label, *Mule*, is deeply rooted in the rural juke joint tradition of the Delta, and his style is totally original, a combination of synchronized guitar and vocal phrasings and electric country blues. He's joined on the album by drummer Sam Carr and guitarist Big Jack Johnson. *Mule* was produced by blues scholar/impresario Robert Palmer, author of the book *Deep Blues*. — *Richard Skelly*

Mule / 1995 / Fat Possum ◆◆◆
Jones' vocals and guitar pace a rough-and-ready quartet, which offers modern electric blues at its most spontaneous. The album was granted a very positive critical reception, but it must be noted that the songs themselves have an unfinished (as opposed to merely unpolished) feel. That, combined with the similar-sounding material and arrangements, means that the album tends to drag after a while. — *Richie Unterberger*

Tutu Jones

b. Sep. 9, 1967, Dallas, TX
Guitar, Vocals / Modern Electric Blues, Electric Blues, Country Blues
The son of Dallas-based R&B guitarist John Jones, Tutu Jones was truly a product of his environment — growing up in a house frequently populated by guests including Freddie King, Little Joe Blue, and Ernie Johnson, his own future as a bluesman was never in doubt. Born John Jones Jr., on September 9, 1966, he became a professional drummer while still a teen, backing his uncles Curly "Barefoot" Miller and L.C. Clark before moving on to work with the likes of Z.Z. Hill and R.L. Burnside. At the same time, however, Jones was also honing his guitar and songwriting skills, and eventually began fronting bands of his own; he cut his solo debut *I'm for Real* in 1994, followed by *Blue Texas Soul* in 1996. Two years later, he released *Staying Power*. — *Jason Ankeny*

I'm for Real / Jul. 29, 1994 / JSP ◆◆◆

Blue Texas Soul / 1996 / Bullseye Blues ◆◆◆
This Dallas-based guitarist-singer has an impressive resume, having served as sideman as drummer, guitarist, and warm-up singer for a number of Texas-based bluesmen and soul men like Z.Z. Hill and Little Joe Blue, and having grown up with the blues (his dad and two uncles were active on the local Dallas scene). But on the basis of this and his prior CD (*I'm For Real* on JSP), he has yet to forge his own distinctive sound. His guitar solos, which rely on heavily plucked, long sustained notes, tend toward monotony over the 45

minutes length of the disc, although fans of contemporary blues guitar will be impressed by their muscular quality. — *Steve Hoffman*

● **Staying Power** / May 5, 1998 / Bullseye Blues ◆◆◆◆
Tutu Jones may still be in debt to his influences, particularly Z.Z. Hill, on his third album *Staying Power*, but he's beginning to break away from the soul-blues pack. Jones has a bigger sound than many of his peers, and his guitar can sound positively gigantic at times. Vocally, he follows a similar path, belting out his Texas blues with abandon. That power is what distinguishes Jones, and he's never sounded more powerful than he does on *Staying Power*. He may still be a little lacking in strong material, and the production may be a little too clean to truly be gritty, but it's clear that he's on the right path. — *Thom Owens*

Janis Joplin

b. Jan. 19, 1943, Port Arthur, TX, **d.** Oct. 4, 1970, Los Angeles, CA
Vocals / Blues-Rock, Rock 'n' Roll
The greatest White female rock singer of the 1960s, Janis Joplin was also a great blues singer, making her material her own with her wailing, raspy, supercharged emotional delivery. First rising to stardom as the frontwoman for San Francisco psychedelic band Big Brother & the Holding Company, she left the group in the late '60s for a brief and uneven (though commercially successful) career as a solo artist. Although she wasn't always supplied with the best material or most sympathetic musicians, her best recordings, with both Big Brother and on her own, are some of the most exciting performances of her era. She also did much to redefine the role of women in rock with her assertive, sexually forthright persona and raunchy, electrifying onstage presence.

Joplin was raised in the small town of Port Arthur, Texas, and much of her subsequent personal difficulties and unhappiness has been attributed to her inability to fit in with the expectations of the conservative community. She'd been singing blues and folk music since her teens, playing on occasion in the mid-'60s with future Jefferson Airplane guitarist Jorma Kaukonen. There are a few live pre-Big Brother recordings (not issued until after her death), reflecting the inspiration of early blues singers like Bessie Smith, that demonstrate she was well on her way to developing a personal style before hooking up with the band. She had already been to California before moving there permanently in 1966, when she joined a struggling early San Francisco psychedelic group, Big Brother & the Holding Company.

Big Brother's story is told in more detail in their own entry. Although their loose, occasionally sloppy brand of bluesy psychedelia had some charm, there can be no doubt that Joplin — who initially didn't even sing lead on all of the material — was primarily responsible for lifting them out of the ranks of the ordinary. She made them a hit at the 1967 Monterey Pop Festival, where her stunning version of "Ball and Chain" (perhaps her very best performance) was captured on film. After a debut on the Mainstream label, Big Brother signed a management deal with Albert Grossman, and moved on to Columbia. Their second album, *Cheap Thrills*, topped the charts in 1968, but Joplin left the band shortly afterwards, enticed by the prospects of stardom as a solo act.

Joplin's first album, *I Got Dem Ol' Kozmic Blues Again Mama!*, was recorded with the Kozmic Blues Band, a unit that included horns, and retained just one of the musicians that had played with her in Big Brother (guitarist Sam Andrew). Although it was a hit, it wasn't her best work; the new band, though more polished musically, were not nearly as sympathetic accompanists as Big Brother, purveying a soul-rock groove that could sound forced. That's not to say it was totally unsuccessful, boasting one of her signature tunes in "Try (Just a Little Bit Harder)."

For years, Joplin's life had been a roller coaster of drug addiction, alcoholism, and volatile personal relationships, documented in several biographies. Musically, however, things were on the upswing shortly before her death, as she assembled a better, more versatile backing outfit, the Full Tilt Boogie Band, for her final album, *Pearl* (ably produced by Paul Rothschild). Joplin was sometimes criticized for screeching at the expense of subtlety, but *Pearl* was solid evidence of her growth as a mature, diverse stylist who could handle blues, soul, and folk-rock. "Mercedes Benz," "Get It While You Can," and Kris Kristofferson's "Me and Bobby McGee" are some of her very best tracks. Tragically, she died before the album's release, overdosing on heroin in a

Hollywood hotel in October 1970. "Me and Bobby McGee" became a posthumous No. 1 single in 1971, and thus the song with which she is most frequently identified. — *Richie Unterberger*

I Got Dem Ol' Kozmic Blues Again Mama / 1969 / Columbia ✦✦✦
Joplin's only solo album to be released during her lifetime heavily employs horns and an R&B band feel, but the dominant sound remains Joplin's impassioned singing on such songs as "Try." — *William Ruhlmann*

☆ **Pearl** / Feb. 1971 / Columbia ✦✦✦✦✦
Joplin's second masterpiece (after *Cheap Thrills*), *Pearl* was designed as a showcase for her powerhouse vocals, stripping down the arrangements that had often previously cluttered her music or threatened to drown her out. Thanks also to a more consistent set of songs, the results are magnificent — given room to breathe, Joplin's trademark rasp conveys an aching, desperate passion on funked-up, bluesy rockers, ballads both dramatic and tender, and her signature song, the posthumous number one hit "Me and Bobby McGee." The unfinished "Buried Alive In the Blues" features no Joplin vocals — she was scheduled to record them on the day after she was found dead. Its incompleteness mirrors Joplin's career; *Pearl's* power leaves the listener to wonder what else Joplin could have accomplished, but few artists could ask for a better final statement. — *Steve Huey*

In Concert / May 1972 / Columbia ✦✦✦
About half of this two-record set features Janis Joplin with Big Brother and the Holding Company in 1968, performing songs like "Down on Me" and "Piece of My Heart." The rest, recorded in 1970, finds her with her backup group, Full Tilt Boogie, mostly performing songs from *I Got Dem Ol' Kozmic Blues Again Mama!* Joplin puts herself out on stage, both in terms of singing until her voice is raw and describing her life to her audiences. Parts of this album are moving, parts are heartbreaking, and the rest is just great rock 'n' roll. — *William Ruhlmann*

● **Janis Joplin's Greatest Hits** / Jul. 1973 / Columbia ✦✦✦✦
A solid, if skimpy, ten-track best-of that gathers the most important songs from Joplin's solo career, as well as her stint with Big Brother and the Holding Company. The more recent *18 Essential Songs* offers a wider selection, but does not include the original version of "Me and Bobby McGee," which makes *Greatest Hits* the better purchase for those who only want one Janis Joplin disc, even if it isn't definitive. — *Steve Huey*

Farewell Song / 1983 / Columbia ✦✦✦
A ragtag collection of odds and ends, live and studio, from both the Big Brother and solo era. The best cuts are on the *Janis* box in different versions, but serious fans will find some interesting items here, especially the *Cheap Thrills*-era outtakes and live performances; "Misery 'N," "Farewell Song," and "Catch Me Daddy" were easily good enough to have qualified for inclusion on that album. — *Richie Unterberger*

Janis [Box] / Nov. 23, 1993 / Columbia/Legacy ✦✦✦✦
This 3-CD box set is the most thorough and valuable retrospective of Janis Joplin's career. Besides including all of her most essential recordings with and without Big Brother and the Holding Company, this 49-song package features quite a few enticing rarities; 18 of the tracks were previously unissued. These include a 1962 home recording of the Joplin original "What Good Can Drinkin' Do," which marked the first time her singing was captured on tape; a pair of acoustic blues tunes from 1965 with backup guitar by future Jefferson Airplane star Jorma Kaukonen, an acoustic demo of "Me and Bobby McGee," a 1970 birthday song for John Lennon, and live performances from her appearance on "The Ed Sullivan Show" in 1969. The real showstopper is the previously unissued, eight-minute version of "Ball and Chain" from Big Brother's first set at the 1967 Monterey Pop Festival (the cut on the *Monterey Pop* box set is from their second set). The more forgettable tracks from her solo albums are wisely excised, as are the Big Brother songs which did not feature her vocals. This is the rare multidisc set of a major artist which manages to cover all the official milestones and present a bounty of worthwhile rarities at the same time. — *Richie Unterberger*

18 Essential Songs / Jan. 24, 1995 / Legacy/Columbia ✦✦✦✦
18 Essential Songs is a one-disc distillation of the triple-disc *Janis* box set. Running 70 minutes, it is a more extensive best-of than the ten-track 1973 *Janis Joplin's Greatest Hits* album. But it is denied "first pick" status because, unlike that album, it does not contain the hit version of Joplin's only number

one single, "Me and Bobby McGee." (It does, however, contain an alternate demo version of that song.) — *William Ruhlmann*

Charley Jordan
....
b. 1890, Mabelville, AR, **d.** Nov. 15, 1954, St. Louis, MO
Guitar, Vocals / Acoustic Blues, Acoustic Memphis Blues, Prewar Country Blues
A fine St. Louis guitarist and vocalist, Charley Jordan teamed with many blues luminaries for some fine recordings in the '20s, '30s and '40s. After traveling throughout the Southeast as a hobo in the '30s, Jordan settled in St. Louis. He played with Memphis Minnie, Roosevelt Sykes, Casey Bill Weldon, Peetie Wheatstraw, and many others. Jordan overcame a permanent spine injury he suffered during a shooting incident in 1928. He recorded for Vocalion and Decca in the '30s, and also doubled as a talent scout for both labels. Jordan worked often with Big Joe Williams in the late '30s and the '40s. — *Ron Wynn*

● **Charley Jordan Vol. 1, 1930-31** / 1992 / Document ✦✦✦✦
A fine St. Louis singer and guitarist, this was the first volume of songs Charley Jordan did in the early '30s. He could be very humorous or cuttingly poignant, and there are examples in both veins on this anthology. The sound quality ranges from good to awful. — *Ron Wynn*

Charley Jordan Vol. 2, 1931-34 / 1992 / Document ✦✦✦
As good as the Charley Jordan material here is, the real find of this disc is Hi Henry Brown's recording of "Titanic Blues" and its guitar duet between Brown and Jordan. As a piece of belated topical blues, it is an extraordinary song, but the exciting interplay between two guitars really makes the record and, coupled with Brown's rough-hewn voice, makes it a track to own—the additional Brown/Jordan tracks "Preacher Blues" and "Nut Factory Blues" constitute a good bonus. This volume of Charley Jordan's material covers the period from his brief stay at Victor Records (four sides cut in September of 1931) to his first session with a full band on Decca Records in the summer of 1934. The four Victor sides (which were cut in Chicago) have a peculiar, authentic "live" ambience that, coupled with their good fidelity, makes them especially vibrant; Peetie Wheatstraw's piano accompaniment has a certain distance and echo that evokes a true club atmosphere. Jordan's subsequent Vocalion sides give much greater prominence to the guitar and Wheatstraw's piano isn't nearly as vivid. As a solo player, Jordan was more laidback, but he still manages to impress as a virtuoso. The four Decca sides are the best recordings here on a technical level—"It Ain't Clean" is amazingly crisp—but two of them, "Lost Airship Blues" (what a title, and what a phallic image) and "Rolling Moon Blues," are particularly notable for the presence of a full band, complete with sax and violin. Their sound is completely different (although Jordan still makes himself felt on guitar) from Jordan's earlier output, but both find him able to work well in this more sophisticated idiom. The overall audio quality is good, apart from the barely listenable "Brown Skin Angel"—a few sides, like "Hell Bound Boy Blues" and the wonderful "Rolling Moon Blues," are a little noisy, but that's par for the course. — *Bruce Eder*

Charley Jordan Vol. 3, 1935-37 / 1992 / Document ✦✦✦
This volume is somewhat less compelling than the other two in the series, if only because even the producers themselves acknowledge that eight of the 23 songs here, credited to "The Two Charlies," probably don't feature the St. Louis-based Charley Jordan at all, but another artist of the same name, while four others, credited to Leroy Henderson, *may* feature Jordan. On other songs, Jordan sings duets with Verdi Lee and Mary Harris (possibly also Verdi Lee working under a pseudonym), and those are great tracks, to be recommended without reservation, except perhaps for the fact that the guitar is a bit muted on these numbers, compared with Jordan's solo stuff. "Signifying at You" is a great piece of female-sung blues, raw, angry, defiant, and funny. The Two Charlies tracks, featuring a Charley Jordan working with a guitarist/singer named Charlie Manson, are fine acoustic blues, all good songs (especially "Don't Put Your Dirty Hands on Me") and even better guitar duets, including the surprisingly dissonant "Pork Chop Blues," but they sound much more like Atlanta blues than St. Louis material—their inclusion here adds nothing to the St. Louis Charley Jordan's reputation, but they make an enjoyable interlude. — *Bruce Eder*

Louis Jordan

b. Jul. 8, 1908, Brinkley, AR, **d.** Feb. 4, 1975, Los Angeles, CA

Saxophone, Vocals, Sax (Alto) / Swing, Early R&B Jazz, Jump Blues, Urban Blues, East Coast Blues

Effervescent saxophonist Louis Jordan was one of the chief architects and prime progenitors of the R&B idiom. His pioneering use of jumping shuffle rhythms in a small combo context was copied far and wide during the 1940s.

Jordan's sensational hit-laden run with Decca Records contained a raft of seminal performances, featuring inevitably infectious backing by his band, the Tympany Five, and Jordan's own searing alto sax and street corner jive-loaded sense of humor. Jordan was one of the first Black entertainers to sell appreciably in the pop sector; his Decca duet mates included Bing Crosby, Louis Armstrong, and Ella Fitzgerald.

The son of a musician, Jordan spent time as a youth with the Rabbit Foot Minstrels and majored in music later on at Arkansas Baptist College. After moving with his family to Philadelphia in 1932, Jordan hooked up with pianist Clarence Webb. He joined the orchestra of drummer Chick Webb in 1936 and remained there until 1938. Having polished up his singing abilities with Webb's outfit, Jordan was ready to strike out on his own.

The saxist's first 78 for Decca in 1938, "Honey in the Bee Ball," billed his combo as the Elks Rendezvous Band (after the Harlem nightspot that he frequently played at). From 1939 on, though, Jordan fronted the Tympany Five, a sturdy little aggregation often expanding over quintet status that featured some well-known musicians over the years: pianists Wild Bill Davis and Bill Doggett, guitarists Carl Hogan and Bill Jennings, bassist Dallas Bartley, and drummer Chris Columbus all passed through the ranks.

From 1942 to 1951, Jordan scored an astonishing 57 R&B chart hits (all on Decca), beginning with the humorous blues "I'm Gonna Leave You on the Outskirts of Town" and finishing with "Weak Minded Blues." In between, he drew up what amounted to an easily followed blueprint for the development of R&B (and for that matter, rock 'n' roll—the accessibly swinging shuffles of Bill Haley & the Comets were directly descended from Jordan; Haley often pointed to his Decca labelmate as profoundly influencing his approach).

"G.I. Jive," "Caldonia," "Buzz Me," "Choo Choo Ch' Boogie," "Ain't That Just like a Woman," "Ain't Nobody Here but Us Chickens," "Boogie Woogie Blue Plate," "Beans and Cornbread," "Saturday Night Fish Fry," and "Blue Light Boogie"—every one of those classics topped the R&B lists, and there were plenty more that did precisely the same thing. Black audiences coast-to-coast were breathlessly jitterbugging to Jordan's jumping jive (and one suspects, more than a few Whites kicked up their heels to those same platters as well).

The saxist was particularly popular during World War II. He recorded prolifically for the Armed Forces Radio Service and the V-Disc program. Jordan's massive popularity also translated onto the silver screen—he filmed a series of wonderful short musicals during the late '40s that were decidedly short on plot but long on visual versions of his hits (*Caldonia*, *Reet Petite & Gone*, *Look Out Sister*, and *Beware*, along with countless soundies) that give us an enlightening peek at just what made him such a beloved entertainer. Jordan also cameoed in a big-budget Hollywood wartime musical, *Follow the Boys*.

A brief attempt at fronting a big band in 1951 proved an ill-fated venture, but it didn't dim his ebullience. In 1952, tongue firmly planted in cheek, he offered himself as a candidate for the highest office in the land on the amusing Decca outing "Jordan for President."

Even though his singles were still eminently solid, they weren't selling like they used to by 1954. So after an incredible run of more than a decade-and-a-half, Jordan moved over to the Mesner brothers' Los Angeles-based Aladdin logo at the start of the year. Alas, time had passed the great pioneer by—"Dad Gum Ya Hide Boy," "Messy Bessy," "If I Had Any Sense," and the rest of his Aladdin output sounds great in retrospect, but it wasn't what young R&B fans were searching for at the time. In 1955, he switched to RCA's short-lived "X" imprint, where he tried to remain up-to-date by issuing "Rock 'N' Roll Call."

A blistering Quincy Jones-arranged date for Mercury in 1956 deftly updated Jordan's classics for the rock 'n' roll crowd, with hellfire renditions of "Let the Good Times Roll," "Salt Pork, West Virginia," and "Beware" benefiting from the blasting lead guitar of Mickey Baker and Sam "The Man" Taylor's muscular tenor sax. There was even time to indulge in a little torrid jazz

at Mercury; "The JAMF," from a 1957 LP called *Man, We're Wailin'*, was a sizzling indication of what a fine saxist Jordan was.

Ray Charles had long cited Jordan as a primary influence (he lovingly covered Jordan's "Don't Let the Sun Catch You Crying" and "Early in the Morning"), and paid him back by signing Jordan to the Genius' Tangerine label. Once again, the fickle public largely ignored his worthwhile 1962-64 offerings.

Lounge gigs still offered the saxman a steady income, though, and he adjusted his onstage playlist accordingly. A 1973 album for the French Black & Blue logo found Jordan covering Mac Davis' "I Believe in Music" (can't get much loungier than that!). A heart attack silenced this visionary in 1975, but not before he acted as the bridge between the big-band era and the rise of R&B.

His profile continues to rise posthumously, in large part due to the recent acclaimed Broadway musical *Five Guys Named Moe*, based on Jordan's bubbly, romping repertoire and charismatic persona. — *Bill Dahl*

At the Swing Cats' Ball / Jan. 15, 1937-Nov. 1937 / JSP ✦✦✦✦
This very interesting collector's CD features altoist/singer Louis Jordan at the beginning of his career, tracing his progress until right before he hit it big. Jordan is heard in 1937 taking three almost unrecognizable ballad vocals with Chick Webb's Orchestra, backing singer Rodney Sturgis on three tunes, performing two selections from late 1938 with his Elks Rendez-Vous Band (including a hot instrumental, "Honey In the Bee Ball"), and jamming a dozen numbers from his two sessions in 1939 with his recently formed Tympani Five. Of the latter, highlights include "Flat Face," "At the Swing Cat's Ball," and "Honeysuckle Rose." Louis Jordan fans will really want this British CD if they do not already have the Classics release 1934-1940. — *Scott Yanow*

☆ **Let the Good Times Roll: The Complete Decca Recordings 1938-54** / 1938-1954 / Bear Family ✦✦✦✦✦
The price of this multi-disc import boxed set is indeed a hefty one, but it contains every track the pioneering saxman waxed for Decca—the multitude of hits that inexorably influenced the future of R&B and eventually rock 'n' roll. Bear Family's attention to detail in its presentation is always immaculate, and sound quality follows suit. — *Bill Dahl*

1940-1941 / Mar. 13, 1940+Nov. 15, 1941 / Classics ✦✦✦✦
The second in the Classics label's CD series that reissues all of Louis Jordan's early recordings features the masterful entertainer with his Tympani Five in the period that directly preceded his great commercial successes. Although most of these 26 selections (including "Somebody Done Hoodooed the Hoodoo Man," "After School Swing Session," "Saxa-Woogie," and "De Laff's on You") are quite obscure, the playing by the group is quite infectious and enjoyable. Singers Daisy Winchester and Mabel Robinson are heard on the Mar. 13, 1940 session for a song apiece, but otherwise, the focus is on Jordan and his fine band, which features tenor saxophonist Kenneth Hollon and several trumpeters, including (on one date) Freddy Webster. Recommended to listeners who want to hear more Louis Jordan than just his hit records. — *Scott Yanow*

1941-1943 / Nov. 15, 1941-Nov. 1943 / Classics ✦✦✦✦
During the era covered by this Classics CD (the third in their "complete" Louis Jordan series), Jordan and his Tympani Five became major successes. Among the 24 selections are such hits as "Knock Me a Kiss," "I'm Gonna Move to the Outskirts of Town," "Five Guys Named Moe," and "Is You Is or Is You Ain't My Baby." In addition to the regular Decca recordings, the set includes four numbers originally rejected, plus six Jordan V-Disc performances. Louis Jordan's music (featuring his alto and vocals, plus hot backup work from trumpeter Eddie Roane and a swinging rhythm section) acted as a bridge between small-group swing and early R&B. Highly recommended. — *Scott Yanow*

Five Guys Named Moe: Original Decca Recordings, Vol. 2 / Jul. 21, 1942-May 8, 1952 / Decca ✦✦✦✦
Another 18 of the saxist's Decca label classics (although "Five Guys Named Moe" turns up again, in deference to the hit Broadway production). "Is You Is or Is You Ain't (My Baby)," "Jack, You're Dead," "Texas and Pacific," "Boogie Woogie Blue Plate," and "G.I. Jive" are high on the list of gems this time, along with his persuasive 1952 campaign "Jordan for President." — *Bill Dahl*

The Just Say Moe!: Mo' of the Best of Louis Jordan / Jul. 21, 1942-1973 / Rhino ◆◆◆◆
A nice across-the-board compilation spanning his Decca, Aladdin, RCA, Mercury, and Tangerine label stints. The Decca standouts include "Don't Worry 'Bout That Mule" and the often-covered "Ain't That Just like a Woman," while his Mercury output includes "Big Bess" and "Cat Scratchin.'" Could have done without the live "I Believe in Music" at the end, though—that isn't the way we want to remember this wonderful performer. — *Bill Dahl*

Five Guys Named Moe [MCA] / Aug. 1943-1946 / MCA ◆◆◆◆
Included on this CD are 27 formerly rare performances by altoist/singer Louis Jordan and his famous Tympani Five. Consisting of radio appearances, plus specially recorded V-discs, the release has quite a few songs not otherwise recorded by Jordan, along with different versions of "Five Guys Named Moe," "Outskirts of Town," and "Caldonia." A special bonus is hearing clarinetist Barney Bigard jam "Rose Room" with the band. The front cover of the CD proclaims "The Father of Rock 'n' Roll," and in ways that is true, although ironically the rise of rock in the mid-1950s knocked Louis Jordan permanently off the pop charts. Recommended. — *Scott Yanow*

1943-1945 / Nov. 22, 1943-Jul. 12, 1945 / Classics ◆◆◆◆
Although Louis Jordan's greatest hits are continually reissued, this Classics CD (the fourth in the series) gives listeners an opportunity to hear many of his lesser-known recordings, quite a few of which sound as if they could have been hits too. Jordan, a fine R&Bish altoist who was an underrated singer and a brilliant comedic talent who knew a good line when he heard one (there are many memorable ones throughout this program), is heard in peak form. The 23 performances are Decca sides (including five not originally released), some V-Discs and the privately recorded "Louis' Oldsmbile Song." Bing Crosby sings duets with Jordan on "My Baby Said Yes" and "Your Socks Don't Match." There are two major hits ("G.I. Jive" and "Caldonia") and among the sidemen are the fine trumpeter Eddie Roane, the forgotten but talented pianist Tommy Thomas, trumpeter Idrees Sulieman (on the January 19, 1945 session) and (for the final two songs), pianist Wild Bill Davis. Other highlights include "You Can't Get That No More," "I Like 'em Fat like That," "Deacon Jones," and "They Raided the House." Highly recommended. — *Scott Yanow*

1944-1945 / 1944-1945 / Circle ◆◆◆◆
This interesting album features altoist/vocalist Louis Jordan and three versions of his Tympani Five during 1944-45, when he was reaching the peak of his popularity. With such sidemen as either Eddie Roane, Idrees Sulieman, or Aaron Izenhall on trumpet and (on a few numbers) pianist Wild Bill Davis, Jordan and his group are heard recording radio transcriptions for World Broadcasting. Other than "G.I. Jive," the music emphasizes lesser-known tunes and contains plenty of fine solos from Jordan, including the surprisingly advanced "Re-Bop." — *Scott Yanow*

1945-1946 / Jul. 16, 1945-Oct. 10, 1946 / Classics ◆◆◆◆
Louis Jordan was at the top of his fame when the 23 recordings reissued on this Classics CD were cut. The influential altoist/singer/entertainer during this era led a version of his Tympani Five that also featured trumpeter Aaron Izenhall, Josh Jackson on tenor, and pianist Wild Bill Davis (years before he switched to organ). Among the hits included on the set are "Beware," "Don't Let The Sun Catch You Cryin'," "Choo-Choo Ch'Boogie," "Ain't Nobody Here but us Chickens," "Let the Good Times Roll," and "Jack You're Dead," but even the lesser-known tracks are entertaining. In addition, a couple of unlikely duets with Ella Fitzgerald ("Stone Cold Dead in the Market" and "Petootie Pie") are quite fun. Recommended to listeners not satisfied with owning only Louis Jordan's hits. — *Scott Yanow*

One Guy Named Louis / Jan. 1954-Apr. 1954 / Blue Note ◆◆◆
It is a strange fact that as rock 'n' roll began to catch on, one of the artists who helped influence its birth was dropping rapidly in popularity. Singer/altoist Louis Jordan, who had had dozens of hits with his Tympani Five while on Decca, recorded 21 songs for Aladdin in 1954 (all of which are included on this CD) and none of them sold well. The strange part is that there is nothing wrong with the music. It compares quite well artistically with his earlier performances; it was just out of style. That fact should not trouble latter-day Jordan fans, for the formerly rare music on this set is witty, swinging, and eternally hip. — *Scott Yanow*

Rock 'n' Roll Call / 1955 / RCA ◆◆◆◆
Only a dozen numbers on this disc, but that's all the saxist made during his 1955-1956 pause at RCA's Vik and "X" subsidiaries. The saxist tried hard to keep up with the times, waxing a stomping title track written by Jack Hammer and Rudy Toombs, and a Winfield Scott-penned "Slow, Smooth and Easy" and "Let's Do It Up Baby," but the teenagers just weren't buying. No reason we shouldn't! — *Bill Dahl*

Rock 'n' Roll / Oct. 22, 1956-Aug. 28, 1957 / Verve ◆◆◆
Twenty-one-track French import that contains the best of Jordan's 1956-1957 stay at Mercury. Here are the rockin' remakes of his timeless hits, cut with a New York mob, including Sam "The Man" Taylor on tenor sax and guitarist Mickey Baker, as well as fresh nuggets like "Big Bess," "Cat Scratchin'," and "Rock Doc." "The JAMF" is a scorching jazz showcase for Jordan's alto, and he does a nice easy-swinging job on "Got My Mojo Working." — *Bill Dahl*

No Moe!—Greatest Hits / Oct. 22, 1956-Aug. 1956 / Verve ◆◆◆
With the exception of four numbers taken from a 1957 set in which he heads a quintet co-starring organist Jackie Davis, this CD consists of a dozen songs taken from a 1956 date already reissued (with additional material) on the previously issued CD *Rock 'n' Roll*. Louis Jordan, who had not had a new hit since 1951 (and unfortunately none were in the future) is mostly heard remaking his earlier triumphs such as "Saturday Night Fish Fry," "Ain't Nobody Here but Us Chickens," and "Choo Choo Ch'Boogie." The music is spirited but the earlier CD is the better purchase. — *Scott Yanow*

Louis Jordan & Chris Barber / 1962 / Black Lion ◆◆◆
It seems strange that by 1962, altoist/singer Louis Jordan was thought of as a has-been, for he was actually still in his prime. However, Jordan had run out of new hits and seemed very much passé to some listeners. Most of this CD reissue features Jordan sounding quite exuberant and creative on a 1962 set with trombonist Chris Barber's flexible Dixieland band. The nine selections include four remakes (including "Choo Choo Ch'Boogie" and "Is You Is or Is You Ain't My Baby"), a few newer songs, and bright renditions of "Sister Kate" and "Indiana"; Jordan, Barber, trumpeter Pat Halcox, and clarinetist Ian Wheeler form a potent frontline. Also on the CD are five selections taken from unrelated Barber sessions, including three Duke Ellington songs. Recommended to fans of Dixieland, small-group swing and Louis Jordan. — *Scott Yanow*

Look Out Sister / 1983 / Krazy Kat ◆◆◆
Louis Jordan checks into a sanitarium for a rest, then dreams himself out West to a dude ranch in this all-Black 1948 musical. Like all of Jordan's low-budget features, there's plenty of hot music by the alto saxman. — *Bill Dahl*

Complete Recordings 1938-1941 / 1992 / Affinity ◆◆◆◆
Just what it says—two discs' worth of Jordan's earliest Decca work, filled with jivey novelties and lusty sax work by the leader of the Tympany Five. Ends with a couple of his earliest hits, "Knock Me a Kiss" and "I'm Gonna Move to the Outskirts of Town." Forty-nine tracks in all. — *Bill Dahl*

I Believe in Music / Aug. 18, 1992 / Evidence ◆◆◆
Louis Jordan's final recording (he died 15 months later) has been reissued on this CD, along with six previously unreleased selections. Although Jordan had not been a hitmaker in around 20 years and had been somewhat neglected during the decade before the set, he was still in his musical prime both vocally and instrumentally. The altoist is teamed with tenorman Irv Cox and a rhythm section led by pianist Duke Burrell. There are a few remakes of past hits (including "Caldonia," "Is You Is or Is You Ain't My Baby," "Saturday Night Fish Fry," and "I'm Gonna Move to the Outskirts of Town"), along with newer jump material. Jordan is in good form and high spirits throughout this date. Recommended. — *Scott Yanow*

G.I. Jive / Aug. 27, 1996 / Charly Budget ◆◆◆
Nearly all of the music on this European LP has since been reissued on CD, but it did give listeners a fine sampling of the lesser-known recordings of Louis Jordan's Tympani Five. Jordan, who is well showcased on both vocals and alto, is heard on 16 selections taken from 11 sessions spanning nearly an eight-year period. Such obscurities as his renditions of "Pompton Turnpike," "T-Bone Blues," "I Know What You're Puttin' Down," and "Chicky-Mo

Craney Crow" are on this album, along with two hits: "Deacon Jones" and "G.I. Jive." But get the more complete CDs instead. — *Scott Yanow*

★ The Best of Louis Jordan [MCA] / MCA ♦♦♦♦♦

This is a best-of CD collection that actually lives up to its name. Virtually all of Louis Jordan's hits, which musically bridged the gap between small-group swing, R&B, and rock 'n' roll, are on this single CD, including "Choo Choo Ch'Boogie," "Let the Good Times Roll," "Ain't Nobody Here but Us Chickens," "Saturday Night Fish Fry," "Caldonia," "Five Guys Named Moe," and "Don't Let the Sun Catch You Cryin'." Serious collectors will want to explore a more complete series, particularly the one put out by Classics, but for a single acquisition, this is the Louis Jordan set to get. Jordan's very likable and good-humored vocals, as well as his hot alto, and the playing of the Tympani Five, belong in everyone's music collection. — *Scott Yanow*

Keb' Mo'

b. Oct. 3, 1951, Los Angeles, CA
Guitar, Vocals / Modern Blues, Modern Country Blues, Contemporary Blues, Contemporary Acoustic Blues
Keb' Mo' draws heavily on the old-fashioned country blues style of Robert Johnson, but keeps his sound contemporary with touches of soul and folksy storytelling. He writes much of his own material and has applied his acoustic, electric, and slide guitar skills to jazz and rock-oriented bands in the past as well. Born Kevin Moore in Los Angeles to parents of Southern descent, he was exposed to gospel music at a young age. At 21, Moore joined an R&B band later hired for a tour by Papa John Creach and played on three of Creach's albums. Opening for jazz and rock artists such as the Mahavishnu Orchestra, Jefferson Starship, and Loggins & Messina helped broaden Moore's horizons and musical abilities. Moore cut an R&B-based solo album, *Rainmaker*, in 1980 for Casablanca, which promptly folded. In 1983, he joined Monk Higgins' band as a guitarist and met a number of blues musicians who collectively increased his understanding of the music. He subsequently joined a vocal group called the Rose Brothers and gigged around L.A. 1990 found Moore portraying a Delta bluesman in a local play called *Rabbit Foot* and later playing Robert Johnson in a docudrama called *Can't You Hear the Wind Howl?* He released his self-titled debut album as Keb' Mo' in 1994, featuring two Robert Johnson covers, eleven songs written or co-written by Moore, and his guitar and banjo work. Keb' Mo' performed a well-received set at the 1995 Newport Folk Festival. Keb' Mo's second album, *Just Like You*, was equally well received. — *Steve Huey*

● **Keb' Mo'** / Jun. 3, 1994 / OKeh/550/Epic ◆◆◆◆
Keb' Mo's self-titled debut is an edgy, ambitious collection of gritty country blues. Keb' Mo' pushes into new directions, trying to incorporate some of the sensibilies of the slacker revolution without losing touch of the tradition that makes the blues the breathing, vital art form it is. His attempts aren't always successful, but his gutsy guitar playing and impassioned vocals, as well as his surprisingly accomplished songwriting, make *Keb' Mo'* a debut to cherish. — *Thom Owens*

Just Like You / Jun. 18, 1996 / OKeh/550/Epic ◆◆◆
On his second album, Keb' Mo' begins to expand the borders of his Delta blues by recording with a full band on a couple of tracks and attempting more expansive, rock-based song structures. The attempts aren't entirely successful, and it's ironic that he decided to try rock-oriented material after he received such praise for his traditionalist debut. Still, there are a few songs on the album that rank with the best on his first album, which suggests that *Just Like You* is merely a sophomore slump. — *Thom Owens*

Jack Kelly

d. 1960, Memphis, TN
Drums / Acoustic Memphis Blues, Prewar Country Blues
Singer/guitarist Jack Kelly was the frontman of the South Memphis Jug Band, a popular string band whose music owed a heavy debt to the blues as well as minstrel songs, vaudeville numbers, reels, and rags. Little is known of the hoarse-voiced Kelly's origins; he led the group in tandem with fiddler Will Batts, and they made their first recordings in 1933, followed in 1939 by a second and final session. Although the South Memphis Jug Band's lineup changed frequently, Kelly remained a constant, leading the group in various incarnations until as late as the mid-1950s; he died in Memphis in 1960. — *Jason Ankeny*

● **Complete Recorded Works (1933-1939)** / 1990 / Document ◆◆◆◆
Document's *Complete Recorded Works (1933-1939)* is an exhaustive overview of Jack Kelly's career. However, for all but completists and academics, the disc is a mixed blessing due to its exacting chronological sequencing, poor fidelity (all cuts are transferred from original acetates and 78s), and sheer number of performances. Casual fans are better off with a less comprehensive package. — *Thom Owens*

Vance Kelly

b. Jan. 24, 1954, Chicago, IL
Guitar, Vocals / Modern Electric Blues, Chicago Blues
Already a Chicago blues institution for over a quarter century, Vance Kelly finally began raising his international profile during the mid-1990s. Born January 24, 1954, he began making waves on the South Side club circuit while still a teenager, performing both as a solo artist and as a sideman; over time he developed a ringing guitar sound, and a 1987-1990 tenure as a member of A.C. Reed's Sparkplugs also profoundly influenced his supple vocal style. A favorite among his peers, Kelly and his Backstreet Blues Band still failed to attract record company attention prior to 1992, when he signed with Wolf; his acclaimed debut *Call Me* appeared in 1994, followed a year later by *Joyriding on the Subway*. — *Jason Ankeny*

Chicago Blues Session, Vol. 31 / Jul. 29, 1994 / Wolf ◆◆◆

● **Joyriding in the Subway** / 1995 / Wolf ◆◆◆◆
On his second album *Joyriding in the Subway*, Vance Kelly pushes into new directions, blending funk and soul into traditional Chicago blues. Armed with a sturdy set of originals and covers, Kelly storms through the album, spitting out hot solos and singing with an abandon. His band provides supple support, giving him the freedom to branch into new areas with both his guitar and voice. The production may be a little too pristine for some tatstes, but there's no arguing that Kelly provides enough grit on his own. — *Thom Owens*

Tiny Kennedy

b. Dec. 20, 1925, Chattanooga, TN
Vocals / Jump Blues, East Coast Blues
Tiny Kennedy was anything but diminutive, either in stature or vocal range. "Big and fat" was how Trumpet Records boss Lillian McMurry vividly described him, and she should know: Trumpet recorded the shouter in 1951 and again in 1952.

The vocalist, born Jesse Kennedy, Jr., had recorded with the great Kansas City pianist Jay McShann for Capitol in 1949 prior to joining Tiny Bradshaw's jumping band as one of its featured front men. After a session with Elmore James in 1951 didn't result in anything releasable, McMurry sent Kennedy up to Sam Phillips' fledgling Memphis Recording Service in September of 1952. Musicians on the session, which produced the fine "Strange Kind of Feelin'," "Early in the Mornin', Baby" (with overdubbed crowing by "Elmer, the Disc Jockey Rooster"), and "Blues Disease," included guitarist Calvin Newborn and saxist Richard Sanders. After a 1955 date for RCA's Groove subsidiary, Kennedy disappeared permanently from the R&B scene. — *Bill Dahl*

● **Strange Kind of Feeling** / 1993 / Trumpet ◆◆◆◆
Three of the unsung heroes on Lillian McMurry's Trumpet label fill this anthology with their early-'50s work. Kennedy's sides were cut in Memphis

under Sam Phillips' supervision in 1952. "Strange Kind of Feelin'" and "Blues Disease" rate with the best things the rotund shouter waxed. — *Bill Dahl*

Willie Kent

b. Sep. 24, 1936, Sunflower County, MS
Bass, Vocals / Modern Electric Blues

Bassist Willie Kent and his band, the Gents, are among the last of a dying breed around Chicago: a combo that intuitively knows the meaning of ensemble playing, rather than functioning as a generic backdrop for endless guitar solos. The Mississippi-born Kent has been laying down bedrock bass lines for decades, and his uncommonly powerful vocals make him even more of a standout.

Kent hit Chicago during the '50s, weaned on Muddy Waters, John Lee Hooker, and Robert Nighthawk. He apprenticed long and hard on the West side, playing with the Hudson brothers, Ralph & the Red Tops, Eddie Taylor, Little Walter, Fenton Robinson, and plenty more before folks started taking notice of his bandleading skills. A 1987 heart bypass operation forced him to abandon his day job as a truck driver; from then on, music has been his full-time vocation. Two outstanding albums for Delmark, 1991's *Ain't It Nice* (with a guest vocal by frequent cohort Bonnie Lee), 1994's *Too Hurt to Cry* and 1996's *Long Way to Ol' Miss* have solidified Kent's reputation. — *Bill Dahl*

● **Ain't It Nice** / 1991 / Delmark ◆◆◆◆
West-side bassist Kent and his Gents serve up Chicago blues the way it was meant to be played (but too often isn't nowadays): with tight ensemble passages that greatly enhance the power of Kent's gruff vocals. His first album for Delmark beautifully typifies his groove-heavy approach; whether digging into a slow grinding blues or an upbeat soul-inflected item, he and his comrades keep their business together. — *Bill Dahl*

Too Hurt to Cry / 1994 / Delmark ◆◆◆
There's little newness anyone should expect to hear on a contemporary blues record. The only thing that makes them valuable is if the performer has his or her own notion of the blues and can state it in a distinctive manner. Willie Kent certainly can; his mournful, often powerful vocals are frequently memorable, even when he's mining the reliable formula of heartache and anguish. If his compositions aren't lyrically transcendent, Kent's rendering of the words elevates them. You never tire of hearing him sing, and he makes you feel and believe his messages, even as his backing band plugs in familiar progressions and lines behind him. Indeed, it's only when Kent covers someone else's music that things become less interesting. — *Ron Wynn*

The King of Chicago's West Side Blues . . . / 1996 / Wolf ◆◆◆

Long Way to Ol' Miss / Nov. 26, 1996 / Delmark ◆◆◆

Everybody Needs Somebody / May 12, 1998 / Wolf ◆◆◆◆

Junior Kimbrough

b. Jul. 28, 1930, Hudsonville, MS, d. Jan. 17, 1998
Guitar, Vocals / Modern Delta Blues

Cited as a prime early influence by rockabilly pioneer Charlie Feathers, Mississippi Delta bluesman Junior Kimbrough's modal, hypnotic blues vision remained a regional sensation for most of his career. He finally transcended the confines of his region in the early '90s, when he appeared in the 1991 movie *Deep Blues* and on its Anxious/Atlantic soundtrack, leading to his own debut for Fat Possum Records, *All Night Long.*

Junior Kimbrough was born and raised in Hudsonville, Mississippi, where he learned how to play guitar by listening to records by Delta bluesmen. In 1968, he cut his first single, "Tramp," for the local Philwood label. For the next two decades, Kimbrough didn't have the opportunity to record frequently—he recorded a single, "Keep Your Hands Off Her," for High Water and his "All Night Long" was available on the various artists compilation *National Downhome Festival, Vol. 2* released on Southland Records.

During the '70s and '80s, Kimbrough played juke joints throughout Mississippi, which is where music journalist Robert Palmer discovered him in the late '80s. Palmer featured Kimbrough in his documentary film *Deep Blues.* The exposure in the movie led to a national record contract for Kimbrough—he signed with Fat Possum and released his first full-length album, *All Night Long,* in 1992. The record was critically acclaimed by both blues and main-

stream publications, as was *Deep Blues* and its accompanying soundtrack. All of the media attention led to performances outside of the Delta, including a few shows in England. After the flurry of activity in 1992, Junior Kimbrough returned to playing juke joints in the Delta, recording occasionally—he released his second album, *Sad Days, Lonely Nights,* in 1993. *Most Things Haven't Worked Out* followed in 1997. — *Bill Dahl & Stephen Thomas Erlewine*

● **All Night Long** / 1992 / Fat Possum ◆◆◆◆
A beautifully packaged edition of Junior Kimbrough's first album, recorded live in the converted church that replaced Kimbrough's original wooden shack juke joint. The lineup is Kimbrough on vocals and guitar, Garry Burnside on bass, and Kenny Malone on drums (it's a family business around this area, and you'll find Burnsides and Malones all over Fat Possum's releases). *All Night Long* is a big, scruffy racket of an electric blues album, and it's fantastic material, a mix of charging, biting rhythms, intense slow blues, hollerin', stompin', and moanin'. The lack of studio polish is a big plus here—producer Robert Palmer was absolutely right to give this to us flubs and all—and the energy is wonderful. A great electric blues portrait that's getting widespread attention at last—and deserves it all. — *Steven McDonald*

Sad Days, Lonely Nights / 1993 / Fat Possum ◆◆
If *All Night Long* was a great electric blues portrait, this sophomore release, given more widespread distribution via Fat Possum's deal with Capricorn, is an extension of the portrait, but with a lot more grit and grind thrown in, given a darker, deeper sound by a change in location (still Kimbrough's joint, but a different building). The vocals are further back, buried in the thick, heavy electric mix—some of this music here is Southern electric blues sounding about the way it might when the apocalypse is just around the corner. Forget the fancy stuff, the polished edges, the studio touches—there are no second takes, no overdubs, no last chances. It's terrifyingly compelling at times. Junior Kimbrough plays the blues with a raw edge, and it's brilliant, dark, and mesmerizing—and it's on CD, with nothing buried, nothing hidden, and nothing safe, all the sharp edges intact. — *Steven McDonald*

Most Things Haven't Worked Out / Mar. 25, 1997 / Capricorn ◆◆◆

Do the Rump / Aug. 12, 1997 / HMG ◆◆◆

King Curtis (Curtis Ousley)

b. Feb. 7, 1934, Fort Worth, TX, d. Aug. 14, 1971, New York, NY
Sax (Tenor) / R&B, Groove, East Coast Blues, Southern Soul, Hard Bop

King Curtis was the last of the great R&B tenor sax giants. He came to prominence in the mid-'50s as a session musician in New York, recording, at one time or another, for most East Coast R&B labels. A long association with Atlantic/Atco began in 1958, especially on recordings by the Coasters. He recorded singles for many small labels in the '50s—his own Atco sessions (1958-1959), then Prestige/New Jazz and Prestige/TruSound for jazz and R&B albums (1960-1961). Curtis also had a No. 1 R&B single with "Soul Twist" on Enjoy Records (1962). He was signed by Capitol (1963-1964), where he cut mostly singles, including "Soul Serenade." Returning to Atlantic in 1965, he remained there for the rest of his life. He had solid R&B single success with "Memphis Soul Stew" and "Ode to Billie Joe" (1967). Beginning in 1967, Curtis started to take a more active studio role at Atlantic—leading and contracting sessions for other artists, producing with Jerry Wexler and later on his own. He also became the leader of Aretha Franklin's backing unit, the Kingpins. He compiled several albums of singles during this period. All aspects of his career were in full swing at the time he was murdered in 1971. — *Bob Porter*

The New Scene of King Curtis / 1960 / Original Jazz Classics ◆◆◆◆
At first glance, this would appear to be a CD reissue well worth picking up. R&B tenor saxophonist King Curtis is heard in a rare jazz outing, holding his own with cornetist Nat Adderley (in prime form), pianist Wynton Kelly, bassist Paul Chambers, and drummer Oliver Jackson on four originals and "Willow Weep for Me." But the single-CD *Soul Meeting* not only contains this entire session, but another related six-song set as well. Only get this particular release if it is found at a budget price. — *Scott Yanow*

● **Soul Meeting** / Sep. 18, 1960 / Prestige ◆◆◆◆
King Curtis, an influential and greatly in-demand R&B tenorman, made relatively few jazz dates in his career. This CD has two of the best, complete

albums originally called *The New Scene of King Curtis* and *Soul Meeting;* the former is also available as a separate CD but should be skipped in favor of this one. Curtis teams up with the passionate cornetist Nat Adderley, pianist Wynton Kelly, either Paul Chambers or Sam Jones on bass, and Oliver Jackson or Belton Evans on drums. The music is blues-based bop, with seven basic Curtis originals and four standards. Highly recommended, this set serves as proof that King Curtis could have been a viable jazz player. —*Scott Yanow*

Old Gold / Sep. 19, 1961 / Tru ◆◆◆
King Curtis with Jack McDuff on the Hammond organ, Billy Butler and Eric Gale on guitar. Funky renditions of standards like "Honky Tonk" and "Fever." —*Michael Erlewine*

Country Soul / 1962 / Capitol ◆◆
This album of country standards was intended to be King Curtis' answer to Ray Charles' *Modern Sounds in Country and Western Music.* It never sold remotely as well as Charles' album, primarily because of Curtis' more perfunctory singing and some unwise choices of music to cover—"Night Train to Memphis," "Raunchy" (which *is* an instrumental), and "I'm Movin' On" work as R&B instrumentals, with the latter benefiting from some sizzling interplay between the guitars, the trumpets, and Curtis' sax. But "High Noon" and "Home On the Range" are a lot less convincing, conceptually as well as in execution. There are a few surprises, however, such as a version of "Your Cheatin' Heart" that tries desperately to transform itself into "Stand By Me." (out of print) —*Bruce Eder*

Blow Man, Blow! / May 22, 1962-Mar. 12, 1965 / Bear Family ◆◆◆◆
71 songs spread among three CDs, covering King Curtis' tenure at Capitol from 1962 until 1965. This wasn't the most productive period in Curtis' career, but it was his first chance to make records on more than a piecemeal basis under his own name; the result is a dazzling array of sounds and songs. Hidden among the country covers and abortive early sides on Disc One is a lot of gold, most notably "Slow Drag" and the previously unreleased "New Dance," which features some killer guitar; the early unissued material is superb, including the Curtis original "Frisky," a slow version of "Alexander's Ragtime Band," the beguiling "Sukiyaki," and a gorgeous bossa nova called "Amorosa." (Many of these tracks feature guitarist Cornell Dupree, who was to figure in Curtis' most successful records for Capitol.) Disc Two is where things start to cook: from "More Soul" on through to the previously unreleased "Hung Over," there's not a note of filler on the disc, which encompasses all of the *Soul Serenade* album as well as a brace of unreleased songs and some very fine singles, including a dazzling cover of the Acker Bilk standard "Stranger on the Shore," and a soulful recomposition of Jackie Gleason's "Melancholy Serenade." Disc Three comprises material ranging from reinterpretations of pop standards like "Moon River" and "The Girl from Ipanema" through a dozen covers of Sam Cooke songs, all worthwhile. —*Bruce Eder*

The Best of King Curtis [Capitol] / Aug. 23, 1962-Mar. 11, 1965 / Capitol ◆◆◆◆
Best of King Curtis collects the bulk of King Curtis' singles for Capitol, plus selected album tracks. Although he didn't have many hits while on Capitol—only "Soul Serenade" hit the charts—this collection demonstrates the depths of Curtis' talents, showcasing his stabs at jazz and blues in addition to his trademark R&B. *Instant Soul* remains a stronger introduction, but for fans that want to dig a little deeper, *The Best of King Curtis* is an excellent purchase. —*Stephen Thomas Erlewine*

Soul Serenade / 1964 / Capitol ◆◆◆◆
Curtis' second Capitol album is a triumph on every level. The tragedy is that, apart from the hit title track, almost nothing off of this superb album was heard by the public—most of the singles he cut doing were very different from this material. The album featured Curtis' covers of songs like the Bill Doggett co-authored "Honky Tonk," Chuck Berry's "Memphis," the hottest, most soulful version of the Champs' old hit "Tequila" ever recorded, and Herbie Hancock's "Watermelon Man," as well as a re-recording of his hit "Soul Twist," and a version of his "Night Train," a big hit for Jimmy Forrest. Maybe the biggest surprise here is the cover of the blues standard "Hide Away," written by Curtis' old friend Freddie King. Sharing the spotlight with Curtis' sax throughout this record is Cornell Dupree on lead guitar, adding just the right accompaniment variously as a lead and rhythm instrument—the two make the oft-heard cover of "Hide Away" by John Mayall and Eric

Clapton sound like a poor demo. There's not a wrong or wasted note. —*Bruce Eder*

Plays Hits Made by Sam Cooke / Mar. 9, 1965+Mar. 11, 1965 / Capitol ◆◆◆◆
This is about the only Sam Cooke tribute record—other than individual songs cut by Otis Redding—that one could imagine Cooke himself not only would have approved of fully, but might have enjoyed himself, had it been recorded under other circumstances. One could even visualize him dancing to the versions of "Shake," which does have a few echoes of "Night Train" in it, or "Twistin' The Night Away" or "Good Times." Curtis had known and worked with Cooke, and the singer's shooting death late in 1964 affected the saxophonist deeply, as it did millions of people. This album was the result, a dozen covers that blow away most any other Sam Cooke tribute album (including the still highly collectible Supremes' *We Remember Sam Cooke*). (out of print) —*Bruce Eder*

Blues at Montreux / 1971 / Atlantic ◆◆◆
This live set from the 1971 Montreux Jazz Festival was co-led by tenor saxophonist King Curtis (who tragically would be killed three months later) and veteran blues pianist/vocalist Champion Jack Dupree. With guitarist Cornell Dupree (in excellent form), bassist Jerry Jemmott and drummer Oliver Jackson laying down the foundation, Curtis and Dupree find a great deal of common musical ground. Dupree has quite a few witty vocals (particularly the near-classic "Junker's Blues") while taking choruses of irregular length that keep his sidemen continually guessing. Curtis' distinctive tenor is also heard from, making one truly regret both that this was his final recording and that this LP's music has yet to be reissued on CD. —*Scott Yanow*

Didn't He Play / 1988 / Red Lightnin' ◆◆
Drawn from Curtis' peak during the late '50s and '60s, this collection, while diverse, is shaky at best. It contains none of his most familiar soul and R&B hits (although an early run-through of "Memphis Soul Stew" is included), and is a prime example of how record producers of the era (in this case, Atlantic Records co-founder Herb Abramson) would surround great players like Curtis with sub-par singers, session men and material. As a result, Curtis' excellent sax playing wound up sharing grooves with a one-note, 20-second guitar solo on "Soul Groove Part II," or cutting songs like Jimmy Breedlove's "Don't Be Cruel" rehash "Jealous Fool"—hardly material fit for King. —*Jason Ankeny*

Trouble in Mind / Jul. 1988 / Tru-Sound ◆◆◆
This CD reissue brings back a very unusual King Curtis set. Rather than playing R&B-ish tenor as usual, Curtis switches to alto, plays effective guitar on a few numbers, and sings most of the tunes. Joined by guitarists Al Casey and Mac Pierce, pianist Paul Griffin, bassist Jimmy Lewis, drummer Belton Evans, and three female vocalists, Curtis sticks mostly to veteran blues songs (including "Nobody Knows You When You're Down and Out," "Bad Bad Whiskey," and "Ain't Nobody's Business") and lets the band stretch out on the eight-minute "Deep Fry." A fun (if temporary) departure in King Curtis' career. —*Scott Yanow*

● **Instant Soul: The Legendary King Curtis** / Oct. 19, 1994 / Razor & Tie ◆◆◆◆
King Curtis has never been served with a comprehensive collection until *Instant Soul,* which features the best instrumental singles the distinctive, soulful, and influential tenor saxophonist ever recorded. —*Stephen Thomas Erlewine*

The Complete Enjoy Sessions / 1995 / Relic ◆◆◆◆
King Curtis never officially "joined" Bobby Robinson's Enjoy label. Rather, he came aboard only provisionally, willing to cut a couple of sides and see if they hit, and once they did, he would sign. Robinson ran the session for "Soul Twist" and got Curtis to feature the guitar, the organ, and the piano alternating with his sax—the record became Curtis' first hit, and an album followed, but Curtis never signed to Enjoy, choosing to go with Capitol Records instead in May 1962. The 15 songs here were all that came of his early 1962 association with Robinson, bold numbers mostly featuring very prominent guitar (played by Billy Butler and Joe Richardson) and organ (by Ernie Hayes)—check out "What'd I Say Pts. 1 and 2"—and even a harmonica solo by the King himself on "Harmonica Twist," along with the expected sax breaks. Robinson's big discovery was that Curtis blew all the way through his previous records, rather than using his band for contrast. The sound is

excellent, and the notes, though a little sketchy, tell us a lot about how these records, among Curtis' best (certainly superior to the country & western venture Capitol threw him into) were made. —*Bruce Eder*

King Ernest

b. May 30, 1939, Natchez, MS
Vocals / Chicago Blues

Vocalist King Ernest came up singing in the lively Chicago blues club scene of the 1950s and '60s, sharing stages with the likes of Tyrone Davis, Syl Johnson, and Little Milton Campbell.

Born and raised in Natchez, Mississippi, he learned basic blues from his father, a sharecropper who used to play guitar at local juke joints. After a year at Southern University in Baton Rouge, he moved to Chicago, where he found his inspiration in clubs that hosted the likes of Muddy Waters and Chester Burnett, better known as Howlin' Wolf. His first professional shows in Chicago were with guitarist Byther Smith. Later, he discovered the soul-blues stylings of singers like Syl Johnson and Tyrone Davis. These singers made a bigger impact on his own singing style, and he established a reputation in Chicago's club scene in the early 1960s as Good Rockin' Ernie.

In 1964, Baker left Chicago for New York City, where a new band he formed there gave him the nickname "King" for his wild dancing antics on stage. In 1965, Baker recorded his first single, "I Feel Alright" b/w "I'm So Tired," for the Old Town label, and enjoyed modest success through the 1960s on the East Coast's R&B club circuit until returning to Chicago in 1967. He remained in Chicago for another ten years, recording a number of singles for Chicago labels, including Sonic, Barry, and his own Blue Soul Records. But recognition on a national level still eluded Baker, who moved to Los Angeles in 1980. After a record deal he had there failed to come to fruition, he dropped out and took a job with the L.A. County Sheriff's Department, doing most of his singing in church as a member of the Crenshaw Christian Center Choir.

After retiring from his day job, he began playing shows again at L.A. nightclubs, and his powerful vocals and still-energetic stage persona quickly attracted a small legion of dedicated fans to his club shows. After being discovered by promoter and producer Randy Chortkoff, he began touring up and down the California coast and into Canada.

His debut album for Evidence Records, *King of Hearts*, released in 1997, has helped to expand his audience from a regional following in New York, Chicago and Los Angeles to an international following. On his recording, Baker offers up his interpretations of songs by Charlie Musselwhite, Hound Dog Taylor, Junior Parker, and Harold Burrage. He also tackles "Better Days," a track co-written by guitarist Jimmy Rip and vocalist Mick Jagger of the Rolling Stones. Appropriately, Rip accompanies King Ernest on this track on the album. —*Richard Skelly*

King of Hearts / Jan. 21, 1997 / Evidence ✦✦✦✦
The title is descriptive of why Ernest deserves a royal title, as his punchy vocals are blues laden with a splash of soul. Also, the title serves as the central theme of the material which runs the gamut of emotions ranging from heartbreak ("Tell Me the Reason," "Better Days," and "Cryin' for My Baby"), doubt ("I'm Not the One"), preference to escape life's problems ("Black Bag Blues"), disgust ("I Resign"), jealousy ("In the Dark"), desire ("Sadie"), and remorse ("Forgive Me"). Ernest's musicians are proven blue(s) bloods, some of them being Paul Bryant (Robert Lucas), "Jimmy Rip" (Mick Jagger), and Lester Butler. Jagger's contribution, "Better Days," was originally slated for one of Jagger's solo albums, but then rightfully deeded to Ernest's pipes. Other well-chosen royal subjects come from songwriters/artists Junior Parker, Charlie Musselwhite, and Hound Dog Taylor. Hats go off to producer Randy Chortkoff, whose bold moves to record Ernest rightfully grants him the throne that's been denied him for far too long. —*Char Ham*

Albert King

b. Apr. 25, 1923, Indianola, MS, **d.** Dec. 21, 1992, Memphis, TN
Guitar, Vocals / Soul, R&B, Modern Electric Blues, Soul Blues

Albert King is truly a "King of the Blues," although he doesn't hold that title (B.B. does). Along with B.B. and Freddie King, Albert King is one of the major influences on blues and rock guitar players. Without him, modern guitar music would not sound as it does—his style has influenced both Black and White blues players from Otis Rush and Robert Cray to Eric Clapton and

Stevie Ray Vaughan. It's important to note that while almost all modern blues guitarists seldom play for long without falling into a B.B. King guitar cliché, Albert King never does—he's had his own style and unique tone from the beginning.

Albert King plays guitar left-handed, without re-stringing the guitar from the right-handed setup; this "upside-down" playing accounts for his difference in tone, since he pulls down on the same strings that most players push up on when bending the blues notes. King's massive tone and totally unique way of squeezing bends out of a guitar string has had a major impact. Many young White guitarists—especially rock 'n' rollers—have been influenced by King's playing, and many players who emulate his style may never have heard of Albert King, let alone heard his music. His style is immediately distinguishable from all other blues guitarists, and he's one of the most important blues guitarists to ever pick up the electric guitar.

Born in Indianola, MS, but raised in Forrest City, AR, Albert King (born Albert Nelson) taught himself how to play guitar when he was a child, building his own instrument out of a cigar box. At first, he played with gospel groups—most notably the Harmony Kings—but after hearing Blind Lemon Jefferson, Lonnie Johnson, and several other blues musicians, he solely played the blues. In 1950, he met MC Reeder, who owned the T-99 nightclub in Osceola, AR. King moved to Osceloa shortly afterward, joining the T-99's house band, the In The Groove Boys. The band played several local Arkansas gigs besides the T-99, including several shows for a local radio station.

After enjoying success in the Arkansas area, King moved to Gary, IN, in 1953, where he joined a band that also featured Jimmy Reed and John Brim. Both Reed and Brim were guitarists, which forced King to play drums in the group. At this time, he adopted the name Albert King, which he assumed after B.B. King's "Three O'Clock Blues" became a huge hit. Albert met Willie Dixon shortly after moving to Gary, and the bassist/songwriter helped the guitarist set up an audition at Parrot Records. King passed the audition and cut his first session late in 1953. Five songs were recorded during the session and only one single, "Be On Your Merry Way"/"Bad Luck Blues," was released; the other tracks appeared on various compilations over the next four decades. Although it sold respectably, the single didn't gather enough attention to earn him another session with Parrot. In early 1954, King returned to Osceola and re-joined the In the Groove Boys; he stayed in Arkansas for the next two years.

In 1956, Albert moved to St. Louis, where he initially sat in with local bands. By the fall of 1956, King was headlining several clubs in the area. King continued to play the St. Louis circuit, honing his style. During these years, he began playing his signature Gibson Flying V, which he named Lucy. By 1958, Albert was quite popular in St. Louis, which led to a contract with the fledgling Bobbin Records in the summer of 1959. On his first Bobbin recordings, King recorded with a pianist and a small horn section, which made the music sound closer to jump blues than Delta or Chicago blues. Nevertheless, his guitar was taking a center stage and it was clear that he had developed a unique, forceful sound. King's records for Bobbin sold well in the St. Louis area, enough so that King Records leased the "Don't Throw Your Love on Me So Strong" single from the smaller label. When the single was released nationally late in 1961, it became a hit, reaching number 14 on the R&B charts. King Records continued to lease more material from Bobbin—including a full album, *The Big Blues*, which was released in 1963—but nothing else approached the initial success of "Don't Throw Your Love on Me So Strong." Bobbin also leased material to Chess, which appeared in the late '60s.

Albert King left Bobbin in late 1962 and recorded one session for King Records in the spring of 1963, which were much more pop-oriented than his previous work; the singles issued from the session failed to sell. Within a year, he cut four songs for the local St. Louis independent label Coun-Tree, which was run by a jazz singer named Leo Gooden. Though these singles didn't appear in many cities—St. Louis, Chicago, and Kansas City were the only three to register sales—they foreshadowed his coming work with Stax Records. Furthermore, they were very popular within St. Louis, so much so that Gooden resented King's success and pushed him off the label.

Following this stint at Coun-Tree, Albert King signed with Stax Records in 1966. Albert's records for Stax would bring him stardom, both within blues and rock circles. All of his '60s Stax sides were recorded with the label's house band, Booker T. & the MG's, which gave his blues a sleek, soulful sound. That soul underpinning gave King crossover appeal, as evidenced by his R&B chart hits—"Laundromat Blues" (1966) and "Cross Cut Saw" (1967) both went Top 40, while "Born Under a Bad Sign" (1967) charted in the Top 50. Furthermore, King's style was appropriated by several rock 'n' roll players, most notably Jimi Hendrix and Eric Clapton, who copied Albert's "Personal Manager" guitar solo on the Cream song, "Strange Brew." Albert King's first album for Stax, 1967's *Born Under a Bad Sign*, was a collection of his singles for the label and became one of the most popular and influential blues albums of the late '60s. Beginning in 1968, Albert King was playing not only to blues audiences, but also to crowds of young rock 'n' rollers. He frequently played at the Fillmore West in San Francisco and he even recorded an album, *Live Wire/Blues Power*, at the hall in the summer of 1968.

Early in 1969, King recorded *Years Gone By*, his first true studio album. Later that year, he recorded a tribute album to Elvis Presley (*King Does the King's Things*) and a jam session with Steve Cropper and Pops Staples (*Jammed Together*), in addition to performing a concert with the St. Louis Symphony Orchestra. For the next few years, Albert toured America and Europe, returning to the studio in 1971, to record the *Lovejoy* album. In 1972, he recorded *I'll Play the Blues for You*, which featured accompaniment from the Bar-Kays, the Memphis Horns, and the Movement. The album was rooted in the blues, but featured distinctively modern soul and funk overtones.

By the mid-'70s, Stax was suffering major financial problems, so King left the label for Utopia, a small subsidiary of RCA Records. Albert released two albums on Utopia, which featured some concessions to the constraints of commercial soul productions. Although he had a few hits at Utopia, his time there was essentially a transitional period, where he discovered that it was better to follow a straight blues direction and abandon contemporary soul crossovers. King's subtle shift in style was evident on his first albums for Tomato Records, the label he signed with in 1978. Albert stayed at Tomato for several years, switching to Fantasy in 1983, releasing two albums for the label.

In the mid-'80s, Albert King announced his retirement, but it was short-lived—Albert continued to regularly play concerts and festivals throughout America and Europe for the rest of the decade. King continued to perform until his sudden death in 1992, when he suffered a fatal heart attack on December 21. The loss to the blues was a major one—although many guitarists have tried, no one can replace King's distinctive, trailblazing style. Albert King is a tough act to follow. —*Daniel Erlewine & Stephen Thomas Erlewine*

The Big Blues / 1962 / King ✦✦✦✦
Searing early-'60s sides. —*Bill Dahl*

Travelin' to California / 1967 / Polydor ✦✦✦✦

★ **Born Under a Bad Sign** / 1967 / Stax ✦✦✦✦✦
One day this southpaw was playing little clubs in Osceola, AR, the next he was headlining rock ballrooms like the Fillmore. This is the album that changed everything—including seemingly 90% of the blues and rock guitarists on the landscape. Backed by Booker T. & the MG's and the Memphis Horns, Albert proved he was every bit as hip as they, not to mention flexible. In fact, as throughout his career, he used a relatively small vocabulary of licks, but gave them slightly different timing and English, depending on the groove and the surroundings. The result was a whole new language. This LP is one big classic from top to bottom. "Crosscut Saw," "Oh, Pretty Woman," "The Hunter," "As the Years Go Passing By," "Personal Manager," the title tune—every track is a must-have. —*Dan Forte*

Live Wire/Blues Power / 1968 / Stax ✦✦✦✦
Live Wire/Blues Power is one of Albert King's definitive albums. Recorded live at the Fillmore Auditorium in 1968, the guitarist is at the top of his form throughout the record—his solos are intense and piercing. The band is fine, but ultimately it's King's show—he makes Herbie Hancock's "Watermelon Man" dirty and funky and wrings out all the emotion from "Blues at Sunrise." —*Thom Owens*

Years Gone By / 1969 / Stax ✦✦✦✦
Years Gone By features typically inspired Stax work from the King of the Flying V. —*Bill Dahl*

★ **King of the Blues Guitar** / 1969 / Atlantic ✦✦✦✦✦
Atlantic's original vinyl edition of this was comprised of Albert's Stax singles—a few from *Born Under a Bad Sign*, along with "Cold Feet," "I Love Lucy" (two of King's patented monologues), and the beautiful "You're Gonna Need Me." Great stuff. Even greater, though, is the CD reissue, which includes

those singles (which didn't appear on any other LPs) and *all* of *Born Under a Bad Sign*. Need I say more? —*Dan Forte*

Jammed Together / 1969 / Stax ✦✦✦

Blues for Elvis: Albert King Does the King's Things / 1970 / Stax ✦✦✦
A silly but surprisingly listenable Presley tribute. —*Bill Dahl*

The Lost Session / 1971 / Stax ✦✦
Lost Session is an interesting historical curiosity, but it is rather unsuccessful musically. John Mayall produced the record and he tried to move Albert King towards jazz. First of all, King's style isn't quite suited for jazz—he's too direct and forceful. Furthermore, the songs are simply skeletons—their only function is to let the band solo. And there are a couple of good solos, all of them from King. But ultimately, it's a forgettable exercise that should have been left in the vault. —*Thom Owens*

Lovejoy / 1971 / Stax ✦✦✦
Lovejoy is a rock-tinged departure from his usual Memphis sound. —*Bill Dahl*

I'll Play the Blues for You / 1972 / Stax ✦✦✦✦
A moody, R&B-influenced set with plenty of intensity. —*Bill Dahl*

Blues at Sunset / 1973 / Stax ✦✦✦

I Wanna Get Funky / 1974 / Stax ✦✦✦
Another very solid, early-'70s outing. —*Bill Dahl*

Montreux Festival / 1974 / Stax ✦✦✦

Albert / 1976 / Tomato ✦✦
Gilded by strings and horns, keyboards and flutes, and driven by a propulsive disco beat, *Albert* is about as slick as Albert King ever got, but he manages to turn in a few strong performances on the album. On the whole, the songs aren't particularly distinctive, and the instrumental support is way too anonymous, but hardcore Albert fans may find a couple solos, a couple of phrases worth hearing beneath all the heavy-handed production and thumping beats. —*Thom Owens*

Truckload of Lovin' / 1976 / Tomato ✦✦✦
The best of King's mid-'70s, slightly disco-fied period. —*Bill Dahl*

Tomato Years / 1976-1977 / Rhino/Tomato ✦✦✦
Albert King enjoyed an erratic but memorable reign at Tomato in the 1970s. The label aimed to continue the success King had enjoyed at Stax mixing blues backing and vocals with pop/soul arrangements and lyrics. He recorded six LPs for Tomato; this anthology culls 14 cuts from his Tomato releases, among them the slashing numbers "Blues At Sunrise" and "I'm Gonna Call You Soon As The Sun Goes Down," which vividly illustrated King's guitar prowess. Others, like "Truckload Of Lovin'" and "We All Wanna Boogie," show how he skillfully crammed moments of inspiration into formulaic outings. —*Ron Wynn*

King Albert / 1977 / Tomato ✦✦
Rebounding slightly from the nadir of *Albert*, Albert King delivered *King Albert*, a record that at least sticks to the tough, soul-inflected blues that made his reputation. Granted, the sound of the album is entirely too polished, but there is genuine grit in the performances and some strong songs, such as "You Upset Me Baby" and "Good Time Charlie," on the record. That may be enough for some hardcore fans to give a listen, but they should be fore-warned that even those inspired moments aren't enough to make *King Albert* a worthwhile release. —*Thom Owens*

The Pinch / 1977 / Stax ✦✦✦
One of King's more soul-oriented efforts, from sessions recorded in 1973 and 1974. It's been retitled as *The Blues Don't Change* for its CD reissue. —*Richie Unterberger*

New Orleans Heat / 1978 / Rhino ✦✦
Allen Toussaint is one of the greatest R&B producers ever to grace New Orleans, but his touch as a blues producer is shaky at best. This attempt to update King's early classics is a snooze. —*Bill Dahl*

Chronicle (With Little Milton) / 1979 / Stax ✦✦✦
This compilation has a leftover feel; the liner notes provide no sources and dates, admitting only that these are "Stax recordings, some never before available on LP." If you're a big fan of one or both of the artists involved, though, it's not bad, with a quality that's generally consistent with their fully-

baked, Stax-era albums, though the King half of the program is somewhat superior to the Milton tracks. —*Richie Unterberger*

Albert Live / 1979 / Tomato ♦♦♦

Albert King Live was in some ways the finest live blues album King ever made, although it wasn't as successful as the recordings he made at the Fillmore West. But it featured numerous spectacular solos, with King showing his complete guitar technique. Rhino's recent CD reissue unfortunately opted to trim the superb, lengthy cut, "Jam In A-Flat," which featured blistering solos by King, Rory Gallagher and Louisiana Red. That dubious decision doesn't negate the CD's value, but certainly casts a pall over it, particularly since they retained Robert Palmer's exhaustive original notes and convey the impression that you're getting the total session intact. Still, King's versions of "Stormy Monday," "Kansas City," "Watermelon Man," and "I'll Play the Blues For You" are marvelous, as are "Matchbox Holds My Clothes," "As the Years Go Passing By," and "Don't Burn Down the Bridges." —*Ron Wynn*

San Francisco '83 / 1983 / Fantasy ♦♦♦

Early-'80s studio LP, reissued in its entirety on CD under the title *Crosscut Saw: Albert King in San Francisco*. As that reissue adds two extra previously unreleased tracks, it's the recommended alternative to the original vinyl edition. —*Richie Unterberger*

In San Francisco-Crosscut Saw / Mar. 1983 / Stax ♦♦♦

A reissue of King's 1983 LP *San Francisco '83* (a studio album, not a live one), with the addition of two previously unreleased cuts. His first new release in five years, it wasn't one of King's better records. But it did represent a return to a basic five-piece sound, an improvement upon his over-produced outings of the late '70s. —*Richie Unterberger*

I'm in a Phone Booth, Baby / 1984 / Stax ♦♦♦

King's most recent studio album shows he is still tough. —*Bill Dahl*

The Best of Albert King, Vol. 1 / 1986 / Stax ♦♦♦♦

"The best of Albert King"? More like the best material that he happened to record for Stax between 1968 and 1973. Even that's debatable, the 13 tracks including covers such as "Honky Tonk Woman," "Sky Is Crying," and "Hound Dog." It does present a reasonable cross-section of his soul-inflected work of the period, drawing from over a half-dozen LPs and a couple of singles, though you might be as well or better off with his more focused individual titles. And for the true "best of Albert King," Rhino's *Ultimate Collection* remains the hands-down winner. —*Richie Unterberger*

Blues at Sunrise: Live at Montreux / 1988 / Stax ♦♦♦

Recorded at Albert King's appearance at the 1973 Montreux Jazz Festival, *Blues at Sunrise: Live at Montreux* is a typically engaging live record from the guitarist. King is in good form and the set list is a little unpredictable, featuring standards like "Blues at Sunrise" and "I'll Play the Blues for You" as well as lesser-known items like "Little Brother (Make a Way)" and "Don't Burn Down the Bridge." —*Thom Owens*

Let's Have a Natural Ball / 1989 / Modern Blues ♦♦♦♦

Great compilation of King's Bobbin sides of the late '50s and early '60s. —*Bill Dahl*

Wednesday Night in San Francisco: Recorded Live at the Fillmore Auditorium / 1990 / Stax ♦♦♦

Wednesday Night in San Francisco: Recorded Live at the Fillmore Auditorium was recorded in June of 1968—it's culled from the very same dates as *Live Wire/Blues Power*. It's slightly weaker than *Live Wire*, which isn't surprising since it consists of outtakes. Nevertheless, Albert King is in fine form throughout the record, throwing out stinging solos with passion. It's a necessary purchase for any King fan. —*Thom Owens*

Thursday Night in San Francisco: Recorded Live at the Fillmore Auditorium / 1990 / Stax ♦♦♦

Like *Wednesday Night*, *Thursday Night in San Francisco: Recorded Live at the Fillmore Auditorium* consists of outtakes from a 1968 Fillmore show that are just as scorching as the *Live Wire* album. —*Bill Dahl*

Door to Door / 1990 / MCA/Chess ♦♦♦

Half of *Door to Door* is devoted to early-'60s King, the other half to Otis Rush Chess efforts of the same era. —*Bill Dahl*

The Blues Don't Change / 1992 / Stax ♦♦♦

Previously titled *The Pinch* when it was issued on LP in 1977, this material was actually recorded in 1973 and 1974. These are some of King's most soul-

oriented sessions, with contributions from the Memphis Horns and a couple of the MG's. Blues-oriented fans may find this one of his lesser efforts, putting less emphasis on King's guitar work than usual, and more on the vocals and arrangements. This approach has its merits, though, as it's one of the more relaxed items in the King catalog, with none of the occasional excess that creeped into his blues guitar solos. —*Richie Unterberger*

★ **The Ultimate Collection** / 1993 / Rhino ♦♦♦♦♦

This two-disc set covers a few early songs, but concentrates on the inspired blend of soul, blues, and rock that King made famous in the 1960s and '70s. Many songs, such as "Laundromat Blues," "Crosscut Saw," "I'll Play The Blues For You," and of course "Born Under a Bad Sign," featured simple riffs, catchy lyrics, and solid grooves parlayed into memorable performances through King's confident vocals and soaring solos. To be sure, there were formulaic numbers, and after a time King's solos and note choices were as much show biz effect as they were exciting, but the anthology's live cuts show that King was always capable of surprise and invention on the bandstand. The later numbers aren't quite as powerful, but King's rendition of "Phone Booth" shows his successors and imitators what legitimate blues playing is all about. —*Ron Wynn*

Hard Bargain / Feb. 1996 / Stax ♦♦♦

A collection of B-sides, alternate takes, and previously unissued outtakes from King's Stax prime (1966-1972), some instrumental. It's not as good as King's best Stax material, but it's not far behind, often benefiting from house players like Booker T. & the MGs, Isaac Hayes, and the Bar-Kays. —*Richie Unterberger*

B.B. King (Riley B. King)

b. Sep. 16, 1925, Indianola, MS
Guitar, Vocals / R&B, Modern Electric Blues, Soul Blues

Universally hailed as the reigning king of the blues, the legendary B.B. King is without a doubt the single most important electric guitarist of the last half century. A contemporary blues guitar solo without at least a couple of recognizable King-inspired bent notes is all but unimaginable, and he remains a supremely confident singer capable of wringing every nuance from any lyric (and he's tried his hand at many an unlikely song—anybody recall his version of "Love Me Tender"?).

Yet B.B. King remains an intrinsically humble superstar, an utterly accessible icon who welcomes visitors into his dressing room with self-effacing graciousness. Between 1951 and 1985, King notched an amazing 74 entries on *Billboard's* R&B charts, and he was one of the few full-fledged blues artists to score a major pop hit when his 1970 smash "The Thrill Is Gone" crossed over to mainstream success (engendering memorable appearances on *The Ed Sullivan Show* and *American Bandstand!*).

The seeds of King's enduring talent were sown deep in the blues-rich Mississippi Delta. That's where Riley B. King was sired—in Itta Bena, to be exact. By no means was his childhood easy. Young Riley was shuttled between his mother's home and his grandmother's residence. The youth put in long days working as a sharecropper and devoutly sang the Lord's praises at church before moving to Indianola—another town located in the very heart of the Delta—in 1943.

Country and gospel music left an indelible impression on King's musical mindset as he matured, along with the styles of blues greats T-Bone Walker and Lonnie Johnson and jazz geniuses Charlie Christian and Django Reinhardt. In 1946, B.B. King set off for Memphis to look up his cousin, rough-edged country blues guitarist Bukka White. For ten invaluable months, White taught his eager young relative the finer points of playing blues guitar. After returning briefly to Indianola and the sharecropper's eternal struggle with his wife Martha, King arrived in Memphis once again in late 1948. This time, he stuck around for a while.

King was soon broadcasting his music live via Memphis radio station WDIA, a frequency that had only recently switched to a pioneering all-Black format. Local club owners preferred that their attractions also held down radio gigs so they could plug their nightly appearances on the air. When WDIA deejay Maurice "Hot Rod" Hulbert exited his airshift, King took over his record-spinning duties. At first tagged "The Peptikon Boy" (an alcohol-loaded elixir that rivaled Hadacol) when WDIA put him on the air, King's on-air handle became the "Beale Street Blues Boy," later shortened to Blues Boy and then a far snappier B.B.

1949 was a four-star breakthrough year for King. He cut his first four tracks for Jim Bulleit's Bullet Records (including a number entitled "Miss Martha King" after his wife), then signed a contract with the Bihari brothers' Los Angeles-based RPM Records. King cut a plethora of sides in Memphis over the next couple of years for RPM, many of them produced by a relative newcomer named Sam Phillips (whose Sun Records was still a distant dream at that point in time). Phillips was independently producing sides for both the Biharis and Chess; his stable also included Howlin' Wolf, Rosco Gordon, and fellow WDIA personality Rufus Thomas.

The Biharis also recorded some of King's early output themselves, erecting portable recording equipment wherever they could locate a suitable facility. King's first national R&B chart-topper in 1951, "Three O'Clock Blues" (previously waxed by Lowell Fulson), was cut at a Memphis YMCA. King's Memphis running partners included vocalist Bobby Bland, drummer Earl Forest, and ballad-singing pianist Johnny Ace. When King hit the road to promote "Three O'Clock Blues," he handed the group, known as the Beale Streeters, over to Ace.

It was during this era that King first named his beloved guitar "Lucille." Seems that while he was playing a joint in a little Arkansas town called Twist, fisticuffs broke out between two jealous suitors over a lady. The brawlers knocked over a kerosene-filled garbage pail that was heating the place, setting the room ablaze. In the frantic scramble to escape the flames, King left his guitar inside. He foolishly ran back in to retrieve it, dodging the flames and almost losing his life. When the smoke had cleared, King learned that the lady who had inspired such violent passion was named Lucille. Plenty of Lucilles have passed through his hands since; Gibson has even marketed a B.B.-approved guitar model under the name.

The 1950s saw King establish himself as a perennially formidable hitmaking force in the R&B field. Recording mostly in L.A. (the WDIA airshift became impossible to maintain by 1953 due to King's endless touring) for RPM and its successor Kent, King scored 20 chart items during that musically tumultuous decade, including such memorable efforts as "You Know I Love You" (1952); "Woke Up This Morning" and "Please Love Me" (1953); "When My Heart Beats like a Hammer," "Whole Lotta' Love," and "You Upset Me Baby" (1954); "Every Day I Have the Blues" (another Fulson remake), the dreamy blues ballad "Sneakin' Around," and "Ten Long Years" (1955); "Bad Luck," "Sweet Little Angel," and a Platters-like "On My Word of Honor" (1956); and "Please Accept My Love" (first cut by Jimmy Wilson) in 1958. King's guitar attack grew more aggressive and pointed as the decade progressed, influencing a legion of up-and-coming axemen across the nation.

In 1960, King's impassioned two-sided revival of Joe Turner's "Sweet Sixteen" became another mammoth seller, and his "Got a Right to Love My Baby" and "Partin' Time" weren't far behind. But Kent couldn't hang onto a star like King forever (and he may have been tired of watching his new LPs consigned directly into the 99-cent bins on the Biharis' cheapo Crown logo). King moved over to ABC-Paramount Records in 1962, following the lead of Lloyd Price, Ray Charles, and before long, Fats Domino.

In November of 1964, the guitarist cut his seminal *Live at the Regal* album at the fabled Chicago theater and excitement virtually leaping out of the grooves. That same year, he enjoyed a minor hit with "How Blue Can You Get," one of his many signature tunes. 1966's "Don't Answer the Door" and "Paying the Cost to Be the Boss" two years later were Top Ten R&B entries, and the socially charged and funk-tinged "Why I Sing the Blues" just missed achieving the same status in 1969.

Across-the-board stardom finally arrived in 1969 for the deserving guitarist, when he crashed the mainstream consciousness in a big way with a stately, violin-drenched minor-key treatment of Roy Hawkins' "The Thrill Is Gone" that was quite a departure from the concise horn-powered backing King had customarily employed. At last, pop audiences were convinced that they should get to know King better: not only was the track a No. 3 R&B smash, it vaulted to the upper reaches of the pop lists as well.

King was one of a precious few bluesmen to score hits consistently during the 1970s, and for good reason: he wasn't afraid to experiment with the idiom. In 1973, he ventured to Philadelphia to record a pair of huge sellers, "To Know You Is to Love You" and "I Like to Live the Love," with the same silky rhythm section that powered the hits of the Spinners and the O'Jays. In 1976, he teamed up with his old cohort Bland to wax some well-received duets. And in 1978, he joined forces with the jazzy Crusaders to make the gloriously funky "Never Make Your Move Too Soon" and an inspiring "When It All

Comes Down." Occasionally, the daring deviations veered off-course — *Love Me Tender*, an album that attempted to harness the Nashville country sound, was an artistic disaster.

Although his concerts have long been as consistently satisfying as anyone's now working in the field (and he remains a road warrior of remarkable resiliency who used to gig an average of 300 nights a year), King has tempered his studio activities somewhat. Still, his 1993 MCA disc *Blues Summit* was a return to form, as King duetted with his peers (John Lee Hooker, Etta James, Fulson, Koko Taylor) on a program of standards.

King's immediately recognizable guitar style, utilizing a trademark trill that approximates the bottleneck sound shown him by cousin Bukka White all those decades ago, has long set him apart from his contemporaries. Add his patented pleading vocal style and you have the most influential and innovative bluesman of the post-war period. There can be little doubt that B.B. King will reign as the genre's undisputed king (and goodwill ambassador) for as long as he lives. — *Bill Dahl*

Singin' the Blues / 1956 / Crown ✦✦✦✦
Absolutely seminal material; his classic hits. — *Bill Dahl*

Sing Spirituals / 1960 / Crown ✦✦✦

The Blues / 1960 / Crown ✦✦✦✦
More invaluable sides. — *Bill Dahl*

The Great B.B. King (B. B. King and His Orchestra) / 1960 / Crown ✦✦✦
This collection of singles (1954-1961) includes R&B hits "Sweet Sixteen," "Someday Baby," and "Sneaking Around." — *George Bedard*

B.B. King Wails / 1960 / Crown ✦✦✦

My Kind of Blues / 1961 / Crown ✦✦✦
According to his biographer, Charles Sawyer, this is King's personal favorite among his recordings. Unlike most of his albums from this period (which are mostly collections of singles), this was recorded in one session and takes him out of his usual big-band setting, using only bass, drums, and piano for accompaniment. The result is a masterpiece: a sparse, uncluttered sound with nothing to mask King's beautiful guitar and voice. "You Done Lost Your Good Thing Now" (its unaccompanied guitar intro is a pure distillation of his style), "Mr. Pawn Broker," "Someday Baby" (R&B Top Ten, 1961), "Walkin' Dr. Bill," and a great version of "Drivin' Wheel" are highlights. (Out of print) — *George Bedard*

King of the Blues [Crown] / Jul. 1961 / Crown ✦✦✦✦
Included are R&B hits from 1960—among them, "I've Got a Right to Love My Baby" and "Good Man Gone Bad." — *George Bedard*

I Love You So / 1962 / Crown ✦✦✦
More vintage King from the '50s, its highlights include: "The Woman I Love," "We Can't Make It," "I've Got Papers on You Baby." — *George Bedard*

Mr. Blues [ABC] / 1963 / ABC ✦✦✦✦
Has some very nice moments. — *Bill Dahl*

★ **Live at the Regal** / 1965 / ABC/MCA ✦✦✦✦✦
This is one of the all-time classic live albums. Recorded in 1964, it captures King in his prime playing to a *very* enthusiastic Black audience. He stretches out on guitar in a way he doesn't on his studio recordings—his guitar sound (it's a joy to hear him switching around and playing with different settings and guitar tones) has a vibrancy and, sometimes, a wild edge that doesn't get captured in the studio. This is a must for B.B. King fans. — *George Bedard*

Blues Is King [MCA] / 1967 / MCA ✦✦✦✦

Blues on Top of Blues / 1968 / BGO ✦✦✦✦
This isn't his most well-known stuff, but it's a very solid late '60s set. Featuring brassy arrangements by Johnny Pate (who also worked with many prominent Chicago soul acts during the '60s), it presents King's sound at its fullest without sacrificing any of his grit or sophisticated swing. No famous classics here, but the material is very strong throughout. — *Richie Unterberger*

His Best: The Electric B.B. King / 1968 / Bluesway ✦✦✦
Although this collection has "Don't Answer the Door," "Paying the Cost to Be the Boss," and a nice live re-cut of "Sweet Sixteen" to highly recommend it, this 1968 issue is hardly King's best, and the "electric" part of the title makes it sound like there's an acoustic B.B. King album lurking around somewhere that you and I somehow missed in the last 40 years. To be sure, these are rock solid performances all recorded between 1965 to '68, just as King's music was

getting slicker and more urban. But this was one of the albums that helped introduce King to a more modern audience (it's gone on to sell over a million copies in 30 years' time), heading straight to the timeline of "The Thrill Is Gone" putting him on the map worldwide. This 1998 CD reissue also includes three bonus tracks, studio versions of "Waitin' On You" and "Night Life," plus "Messy but Good" from the motion picture soundtrack *For the Love of Ivy*. Not his best, certainly *electric*, and ultimately, a good one to add to the collection after you've gotten about five or six others first. — *Cub Koda*

Lucille / 1968 / MCA ✦✦✦✦
A decent but short (nine songs) late '60s set, with somewhat sparser production than he'd employ with the beefier arrangements of the "Thrill Is Gone" era. Brass and stinging guitar plays a part on all of the songs, leading off with the eight-minute title track, a spoken narrative about his famous guitar. — *Richie Unterberger*

Live & Well / 1969 / BGO ✦✦✦
Although *Live & Well* wasn't a landmark album in the sense of *Live at the Regal*, it was a significant commercial breakthrough for King, as it was the first of his LPs to enter the Top 100. That may have been because recognition from rock stars such as Eric Clapton had finally boosted his exposure to the White pop audience, but it was a worthy recording on its own merits, divided evenly between live and studio material. King's always recorded well as a live act, and it's the concert tracks that shine brightest, although the studio ones (cut with assistance from studio musicians like Al Kooper and Hugh McCracken) aren't bad. — *Richie Unterberger*

Completely Well / 1969 / MCA ✦✦✦✦
This was King's breakthrough album in 1969, which finally got him the long-deserved acclaim that was no less than his due. It contained his signature number, "The Thrill Is Gone," and eight other tunes, six of them emanating from King's pen, usually in a co-writing situation. Hardliners point to the horn charts and the overdubbed strings as the beginning of the end of King's old style that so identifiably earmarked his early sides for the Bihari brothers and his later tracks for ABC, but this is truly the album that made the world sit up and take notice of B.B. King. The plus points include loose arrangements and a small combo behind him that never dwarfs the proceedings or gets in the way. King, for his part, sounds like he's having a ball, playing and singing at peak power. This is certainly not the place to start your B.B. King collection, but it's a nice stop along the way before you finish it. — *Cub Koda*

Anthology of the Blues: B.B. King / 1969 / Kent ✦✦✦✦
Some of King's very first records are included—some possibly unreleased, as they don't appear on the singles chart included in his biography. Although kind of crude compared to the later stuff, these are still some fine spirited recordings—a fascinating look at his young developing style. — *George Bedard*

Back in the Alley / 1970 / MCA ✦✦✦✦

Indianola Mississippi Seeds / 1970 / MCA ✦✦✦
B.B. King hasn't made many better pop-flavored albums than this. Besides making Leon Russell's "Hummingbird" sound like his own composition, King showed that you can put the blues into any situation and make it work. Carole King was one of several pop luminaries who did more than just hang on for the ride. — *Ron Wynn*

Live in Cook County Jail / 1971 / MCA ✦✦✦✦
B.B. King has cut a lot of albums since the success of *Live at the Regal*. And, like the live shows they document, none of them are any less than solid and professional, hallmarks of King's work aesthetic. But every so often B.B. truly catches fire; his playing and singing comes up an extra notch or two, and the result is a live album with some real sparks to it. *Live in Cook County Jail* is one of those great concerts that the record company was smart enough to be there to capture, documenting King firing on all cylinders in front of an audience that's just damn happy for him to be there. Possibly the best live version of "The Thrill Is Gone" of all its many incarnations, and rock solid renditions of classics like "Everyday I Have the Blues," "How Blue Can You Get?," "Sweet Sixteen," and a great medley of "3 O'Clock Blues" and "Darlin' You Know I Love You." *Live at the Regal* is still the champ of King's live output, but many say this runs a close second, and they just may be right. — *Cub Koda*

In London / 1971 / ABC ✦✦
The plodding rhythms laid down by a coterie of British rock stars for this set make one long for King's road-tested regular band. But it was the fashion in 1971 to dispatch American blues legends to London to record mediocre LPs with alleged rock royalty (the lineup here includes Ringo Starr, Peter Green, Alexis Korner, and Klaus Voorman). — *Bill Dahl*

Guess Who / 1972 / MCA ✦✦✦
When B.B. King is cajoled into covering the Lovin' Spoonful's "Summer in the City," you know material's in dangerously short supply. It's the lead number on this rather undistinguished album, cut with most of his road band of the time. One staple of his live show, the sentimental blues ballad "Guess Who," came from this set. — *Bill Dahl*

To Know You Is to Love You / 1973 / MCA ✦✦✦
The combination of King and the well-oiled Philly rhythm section that powered hits by the O'Jays, Spinners, and Stylistics proved a surprisingly adroit one. Two huge hits came from this album, the Stevie Wonder/Syreeta Wright-penned title track and "I Like to Live the Love," both of them intriguing updates of King's tried-and-true style. — *Bill Dahl*

Together for the First Time . . . Live / 1974 / Dunhill ✦✦
This collaboration mostly works quite well. Singer/guitarist B.B. King and blues ballad vocalist Bobby Bland split the program fairly evenly, sharing the stage for 11 songs, plus a 14-minute, ten-tune hits medley. It is particularly interesting hearing King perform Bland songs and vice versa. Unfortunately, the backup group is not fully identified, and Bland is often not quite on King's level, but their historic meeting is generally a success. — *Scott Yanow*

Midnight Believer / 1978 / MCA ✦✦✦
Another collaboration that worked a lot better than one might have expected. King and the Crusaders blended in a marginally funky, contemporary style for the buoyant "Never Make Your Move Too Soon" and an uplifting "When It All Comes Down." — *Bill Dahl*

Take It Home / 1979 / MCA ✦✦
This 1979 effort finds King interpreting a number of pop-blues tunes, many of them co-written by Will Jennings and co-producer Joe Sample, with King co-writing two of the songs aboard. Even with a large, contemporary backdrop (including a seven-piece horn section and female backup singers), there's still plenty of room for King's stinging guitar and stentorian vocals in the mix. Highlights include the gospel-tinged "Better Not Look Down," "Same Old Story (Same Old Song)," "Happy Birthday Blues," "The Beginning of the End," and the title track. As one of King's more pop-oriented offerings, this succeeds admirably. — *Cub Koda*

Live "Now Appearing" at Ole Miss / 1980 / MCA ✦✦
Surely the worst, most lethargic live album that King ever made. Rumor has long had it that after-the-fact enhancements were added to the live tapes to make them more palatable—if so, it didn't work! — *Bill Dahl*

Great Moments with B.B. King / 1981 / MCA ✦✦✦✦
Very solid 23-track package culled from some of King's best mid-to-late-'60s ABC-Paramount and BluesWay LPs. Some of the best cuts stem from a sizzling live album; "Gambler's Blues," "Waitin' on You," and a stunning "Night Life" find his reverb level rising to the boiling point. A brassy "That's Wrong Little Mama," "Dance with Me," and "Heartbreaker" connect like consecutive right hooks, and his rousing smash "Paying the Cost to Be the Boss" is also on board. — *Bill Dahl*

There Must Be a Better World Somewhere / 1981 / MCA ✦✦✦
During his decade recording for MCA, B.B. King was generally teamed with overblown accompaniment rather than his regular (and perfectly complementary) traveling band. This CD finds the masterful vocalist/guitarist joined by a more logical backup group than usual (with altoist Hank Crawford, tenor saxophonist David "Fathead" Newman and baritonist Ronnie Cuber in the tentet). The two most basic selections ("There Must Be a Better World Somewhere" and "The Victim") are easily the most successful while the other four are funky, more R&B-oriented and overly commercial; it sounds like B.B. was consciously trying for a hit record. Despite some fine solos by Newman and Crawford, this session was rather erratic, brief (under 36 minutes) and far from essential. — *Scott Yanow*

Memphis Masters / 1982 / Ace ✦✦✦✦
Only the absence of substantial or even minimal recording information keeps this from being a showcase release. The songs, culled from early-'50s sessions, are formative King material and should be closely studied by the

hordes who only know King from overarranged major-label LPs and *Tonight Show* appearances. — *Ron Wynn*

Love Me Tender / 1982 / MCA ✦✦
B.B. King's extremely ill-advised foray into mushy Nashville cornpone. Hearing him croon the title track in front of an array of Music Row's most generic pickers is enough to drive one screaming into his or her record collection for a surefire antidote: some 1950s King on RPM! Ahh … — *Bill Dahl*

Blues 'n' Jazz / Aug. 1983 / MCA ✦✦✦
Swinging session that plays to King's strengths. — *Bill Dahl*

Why I Sing the Blues / 1985 / MCA ✦✦✦✦

Completely Live & Well / 1986 / Charly ✦✦✦✦
Here's much of the material that helped B.B. King make his move into the hearts and minds of mainstream America. Whether you think that was ultimately good or bad, it's still necessary to hear it. — *Ron Wynn*

☆ **The Best of B.B. King, Vol. 1** / 1988 / Ace ✦✦✦✦✦
Ace's *The Best of B.B. King, Vol. 1* is a fine 33-track collection of B.B. King's earliest recordings for Crown. While these might not necessarily be the definitive versions, there are some terrific performances scattered throughout the disc, making it worth tracking down for hardcore King fans. — *Leo Stanley*

Six Silver Strings / 1988 / MCA ✦✦
Too slick, MOR-styled disappointment. — *Bill Dahl*

Do the Boogie! B.B. King's Early '50s Classics / 1988 / Flair ✦✦✦✦
20 killer tracks from B.B. King's 1950s heyday, including quite a few alternate takes and a few tough-to-locate items ("Bye Bye Baby," "Dark Is the Night," "Jump with You Baby"). Many of the titles are familiar ones—"Woke Up This Morning," "Every Day," "Please Love Me," "Whole Lotta Love"—but often as not, compiler Ray Topping unearthed contrasting versions from the same sessions that shed new, fascinating light on King's studio techniques. — *Bill Dahl*

King of Blues: 1989 / Nov. 14, 1988 / MCA ✦✦

Do the Boogie / 1989 / Ace ✦✦✦✦
Great early sides from Modern vaults. — *Bill Dahl*

Live at the Apollo / Nov. 1990 / GRP ✦✦✦
There are both good and bad points to this CD. Of the latter, the Phillip Morris "Super Band" is confined to background work with—other than a few spots for Plas Johnson's tenor—no soloists being heard from. As an ensemble, the all-star orchestra performs well, but is essentially anonymous. Also, despite the backing, B.B. King does not attempt to play jazz, a wasted opportunity. But, switching to the good points, *Live at the Apollo* is an excellent example of a strong B.B. King live performance. Somehow he always makes his combination of blues and familiar hits sound fresh. With a liberal amount of space set aside for his guitar solos, King is in top form throughout the well-paced set, which is far superior to most of his overproduced studio sessions for MCA. Even if the big band is mostly irrelevant, this CD is recommended for B.B. King's singing and playing. — *Scott Yanow*

The Best of B.B. King, Vol. 1 / 1991 / Flair ✦✦✦
A 20-track hits compilation that should have been a great deal better than it is. The disc embarrassingly uses an inferior remake of King's classic "Whole Lotta Love" instead of the original, while drums and electric bass have been clumsily overdubbed on the original takes of "You Upset Me Baby," "Every Day," and "Please Love Me," absolutely ruining them. What a shame, since two-thirds of the collection is just fine. — *Bill Dahl*

Spotlight on Lucille / 1991 / Flair ✦✦✦✦
From the contemporary-looking cover, this would appear to be recently recorded material. But wait—these are all 1950s/early-'60s instrumentals from the Modern/Kent vaults, spotlighting B.B. King's pristine lead guitar in an often jazzier mode than he usually adopted in the studio. His workout on Louis Jordan's "Just like a Woman" is a tour de force that's been reissued often, but much of the compilation is rare stuff that gives Lucille her full due. — *Bill Dahl*

The Fabulous B.B. King / 1991 / Flair ✦✦
The Best of B.B. King, Vol. 1, also on Flair, has 20 tracks from the same era covered by this collection, which only has 12. So you should really stick with the other Flair compilation, even if it's a bit more expensive. Which doesn't

mean that this CD is bad; the 12 songs, all from the early and mid-'50s, include some of his most famous early classics, such as "Three O'Clock Blues," "Everyday I Have the Blues," and "Sweet Little Angel." — *Richie Unterberger*

Live at San Quentin / Jun. 1991 / MCA ✦✦

☆ **King of the Blues [Box]** / 1992 / MCA ✦✦✦✦✦
No way can a mere four discs cover every facet of the blues king's amazing recording career, but MCA makes a valiant stab at it. The first two discs, as expected, are immaculate: opening with his Bullet Records debut ("Miss Martha King"), the box continues with a handful of pivotal RPM/Kent masters before digging into his 1960s ABC-Paramount material ("I'm Gonna Sit in 'Til You Give In" and "My Baby's Comin' Home" are little-recalled gems). The hits—"The Thrill Is Gone," "Why I Sing the Blues," "To Know You Is to Love You"—are all here, and if much of the fourth disc is pretty disposable, it only mirrors King's own winding down in the studio. — *Bill Dahl*

There Is Always One More Time / 1992 / MCA ✦✦✦
Most of B.B. King's studio albums of the 1980s and '90s tend to de-emphasize his guitar playing and consist largely of forgettable originals and obvious attempts at pop hits. However this CD (which was cut in the studios) is on a higher level and is quite rewarding. Most of the tunes were co-written by pianist Joe Sample and Will Jennings and the majority are quite catchy and memorable. Certainly it is easy to sing along with the refrains of "I'm Moving On," "Back In L.A.," and "Roll, Roll, Roll." On the date King usually overdubbed his guitar to play along with his vocals (somehow the interplay does not sound spontaneous) but it does not detract from the final results. The intelligent and philosophical lyrics fit King's style very well and his voice is very much in prime form. Well worth acquiring. — *Scott Yanow*

☆ **Singin' the Blues/The Blues** / 1992 / Flair ✦✦✦✦✦
Two great original Crown albums from the '50s appear on one import CD, including most of King's Top Ten R&B hits from the period: "3 O'Clock Blues," "Please Love Me," "You Upset Me Baby," "You Know I Love You," "Woke Up This Morning," and "Sweet Little Angel," plus one of his best, "Crying Won't Help You." This is the stuff that was so hugely influential to other blues guitarists and singers in its original recorded version. Here is lots of the real early, gritty stuff: "That Ain't the Way to Do It," "When My Heart Beats like a Hammer," "Don't You Want a Man like Me?" The guitar intro to "Early in the Morning" is one of the finest examples of King in a jazzy mode. Great guitar! — *George Bedard*

Heart & Soul / 1992 / Pointblank ✦✦✦
The Biharis harbored dreams of crossing the rich-voiced King over into the pop market during the '50s, trying him out on some of the dreariest ballads imaginable. Many of those limp outings turn up on this collection—hearing the king of the blues croon "On My Word of Honour" and "My Heart Belongs to You" like a refugee from the Platters ain't a good time by any means! Fortunately, not everything is so dire: "Story from My Heart and Soul," "Lonely and Blue," and the delicious "Sneakin' Around" sport a more edifying mix of blues and balladry. — *Bill Dahl*

Blues Summit / 1993 / MCA ✦✦✦
On this release, King comes close to equaling his past triumphs on small independent labels in the '50s and '60s. He's ditched the psuedo-hip production fodder and cut a 12-song set matching him with blues peers. His duets with Buddy Guy, John Lee Hooker, and Albert Collins are especially worthy, while the songs with Koko Taylor, Ruth Brown, and Irma Thomas have some good-natured banter and exchanges, as well as tasty vocals. The master gives willing pupils Joe Louis Walker and Robert Cray valuable lessons on their collaborations. There's also a medley in which King invokes the spirit of his chitlin circuit days, taking the vocal spotlight while his Orchestra roars along underneath. — *Ron Wynn*

My Sweet Little Angel / Oct. 5, 1993 / Flair ✦✦✦✦
Another 21-track anthology chock full of alternate takes and previously unreleased masters from B.B. King's 1950s stint at RPM/Kent. A wild cross-section of material—signature items like "Sweet Little Angel" and "Please Accept My Love," an off-the-wall reading of Tony Bennett's "In The Middle of an Island," and best of all, a torrid jazzy instrumental called "String Bean" that finds King pulling some astounding guitar tricks out of a seemingly bottomless bag. — *Bill Dahl*

☆ **Early Blues Boy Years, Vol. 1: 1949-51** / 1995 / Opal ◆◆◆◆◆
MCA has anthologized B.B. King's ABC-Paramount years with *King of the Blues*, and Flair/Virgin has issued some of his 1950's work for the Bihari brothers' various labels (Modern, Kent, etc.). In the absence of a boxed set devoted to those '50s sides, however, this disc and its companion volumes from the Barcelona-based Opal label are the best you're likely to do in assembling the best of B.B. King's work from that era. The sound is okay, and the sessionography is pretty fair, though a proper boxed set would probably be more thorough. — *Bruce Eder*

Early Blues Boy Years, Vol. 2: 1952-54 / 1995 / Opal ◆◆◆◆
This 20-song collection continues B.B. King's mid-'50s history on the Bihari brothers' various labels (Modern, Kent etc.), including his "big band" work, including "When My Heart Beats like a Hammer," "Woke Up This Morning," and "I Love You." There's lots of fiery guitar on this volume, opening on "You Upset Me Baby" and "Blind Love." The material is all first rate, from rollicking rave-ups like "Boogie Woogie Woman" to moody, mournful blues numbers like "Past Day." Unlike the first volume, however, there are no musician or session credits included, partly because they may not exist for much of his work during this period. The sound is quite good through, with lots of bite to the brass and a sense that his guitar and voice could be in the same room with you. Many of these cuts have been issued by Flair/Virgin, but this is still the best comprehensive collection. — *Bruce Eder*

How Blue Can You Get: Classic Live 1964-94 / Jun. 18, 1996 / MCA ◆◆◆
The double-disc collection *How Blue Can You Get: Classic Live 1964-94* covers 30 years of B.B. King's remarkably popular and groundbreaking career, picking out choice live performances from a variety of sources. King has always been acknowledged as one of the most electrifing blues guitarists, as well as one of the best all-around entertainers that the genre has to offer, so it stands to reason that the compilation is filled with terrific music. And it certainly is — from his astonishing performance at the Regal to recent performances in Japan, B.B. shines throughout the set. Despite all of the fine music this has to offer, it doesn't capture the spark of one of his live shows, where he interacts brilliantly with the audience; you still have to pick up *Live At the Regal* to experience that. Even though *How Blue Can You Get* lacks the kinetic energy of a live concert, there's enough prime material to make it an essential addition to any B.B. King fan's library. — *Thom Owens*

Deuces Wild / Nov. 4, 1997 / MCA ◆◆◆
This is King's celebrity duet album, and a straightahead blues album this is not. But longtime fans who are aware of King's genre-stretching capabilities will find much to savor here. Kicking off with King playing some beautiful fills and solo work behind Van Morrison on "If You Love Me," the superstars start lining up to jam with the King, with Tracy Chapman ("The Thrill Is Gone"), Eric Clapton (a funkified "Rock Me Baby"), the Rolling Stones ("Paying the Cost to Be the Boss," with a fine harp solo from Mick Jagger), Willie Nelson (his "Nightlife," long a standard in King's set list), Bonnie Raitt ("Baby I Love You"), and Marty Stuart ("Confessin' the Blues") all turning in fine efforts. The only clinker aboard here is an ill-advised attempt to make a rap record with Heavy D, the execrable "Keep It Coming." — *Cub Koda*

King Biscuit Flower Hour Presents B.B. King / Apr. 28, 1998 / King Biscuit ◆◆
B.B. King's *King Biscuit Flower Hour* captures the legendary blues guitarist in concert in the '80s. The presence of George Benson on "I Got Some Help I Don't Need" and "Just a Little Love," and Johnny & Edgar Winter on "Goin' Down Slow," suggests that the concert was more special than it actually was. In reality, it was simply an average concert with King running through average material; the only classics were "How Blue Can You Get" and "The Thrill Is Gone." The performances are competent, but not inspired, making the disc really of interest to hardcore King collectors, especially since there's a lot of better live King on the market. — *Stephen Thomas Erlewine*

Earl King

b. Feb. 7, 1934, New Orleans, LA
Guitar, Vocals / Soul, R&B, Electric New Orleans Blues, New Orleans R&B
Unilaterally respected around his Crescent City homebase as both a performer and a songwriter, guitarist Earl King has been a prime New Orleans R&B force for more than four decades — and he shows no signs of slowing down.

Born Earl Johnson, the youngster considered the platters of Texas guitarists T-Bone Walker and Gatemouth Brown almost as fascinating as the live performances of local luminaries Smiley Lewis and Tuts Washington. King met his major influence and mentor, Guitar Slim, at the Club Tiajuana, one of King's favorite haunts (along with the Dew Drop, of course), the two becoming fast friends. Still billed as Earl Johnson, the guitarist debuted on wax in 1953 on Savoy with "Have You Gone Crazy" (with pal Huey "Piano" Smith making the first of many memorable supporting appearances on his platters).

Johnson became Earl King upon signing with Specialty the next year (label head Art Rupe intended to name him King Earl, but the typesetter reversed the names!). "A Mother's Love," Earl's first Specialty offering, was an especially accurate Guitar Slim homage produced by Johnny Vincent, who would soon launch his own label, Ace Records, with King one of his principal artists. King's first Ace single, the seminal two-chord south Louisiana blues "Those Lonely, Lonely Nights," proved a national R&B hit (despite a sounda-like cover by Johnny "Guitar" Watson). Smith's rolling piano undoubtedly helped make the track a hit.

King remained with Ace through the rest of the decade, waxing an unbroken string of great New Orleans R&B sides with the unparalleled house band at Cosimo's studio. But he moved over to Imperial in 1960, cutting the classic "Come On" (also known as "Let The Good Times Roll") and 1961's humorous "Trick Bag" and managing a second chart item in 1962 with "Always a First Time." King wrote standout tunes for Fats Domino, Professor Longhair, and Lee Dorsey during the '60s.

Although a potential 1963 pact with Motown was scuttled at the last instant, King admirably rode out the rough spots during the late '60s and '70s. Since signing with Black Top, his performing career has been rejuvenated; 1990's *Sexual Telepathy* and *Hard River to Cross* three years later were both superlative albums. — *Bill Dahl*

Street Parade / 1981 / Charly ◆◆◆
Funky 1972 tracks that should have fueled a comeback for the Crescent City mainstay but didn't (a lease deal with Atlantic fell through). Allen Toussaint was apparently in charge of the sessions, which produced updates of "Mama and Papa" and "A Mother's Love" as well as a bevy of fresh nuggets (notably the fanciful "Medieval Days," later revived by King on Black Top), and the two-part title item. — *Bill Dahl*

● **Trick Bag** / 1983 / EMI America ◆◆◆◆
Here's an extremely hard-to-find French LP that remains the only place where King's wonderful early-'60s Imperial Records catalog was gathered in one place (a handful grace EMI's two-disc Dave Bartholomew set; he produced them). Earl changed his sound to fit the funkier Crescent City sound of the time on the two-part "Come On," the humorous "Trick Bag" and "Mama and Papa," and a passionate "You're More to Me than Gold." — *Bill Dahl*

Glazed / 1988 / Black Top ◆◆◆
The coupling of funky Crescent City guitarist Earl King with the East Coast-based Roomful of Blues wasn't exactly made in heaven (the band excels at jump blues; at second-line beats, they're fairly clueless), but it did mark the beginning of King's heartwarming comeback as a recording artist. King's songwriting skills were certainly in fine shape: "It All Went Down the Drain," "Iron Cupid," and "Love Rent" were typically well-observed originals. — *Bill Dahl*

Sexual Telepathy / 1990 / Black Top ◆◆◆◆
Reunited with a more sympathetic New Orleans rhythm section (bassist George Porter, Jr., and drummer Kenny Blevins) and a funkier horn section, King excelled handsomely on this uncommonly strong outing. As we've come to expect from him, he brought a sheaf of new originals to the sessions, from a saucy "Sexual Telepathy" to a heartwarming "Happy Little Nobody's Waggy Tail Dog." Remakes of his "Always a First Time" and "A Weary Silent Night" were welcome inclusions (especially since we can't easily lay our hands on the originals!). — *Bill Dahl*

Hard River to Cross / 1993 / Black Top ◆◆◆◆
The quirky guitarist with the endlessly wavy hair made it two winners in a row with this one. Snooks Eaglin guests on guitar for three tracks (including the hilarious "Big Foot" and a joyous "No City like New Orleans," while Porter and drummer Herman Ernest III lay down scintillating grooves behind King's ringing axe and wise vocals. — *Bill Dahl*

Those Lonely, Lonely Nights / 1993 / P-Vine ✦✦✦✦
Why must New Orleans guitarist Earl King's 1950s material be so difficult to
locate on CD? This expensive Japanese import does the job handily, if you
can find it—all eight of King's Guitar Slim-influenced Specialty sides (including "A Mother's Love" and its rocking flip, "I'm Your Best Bet Baby") and 17
of his terrific efforts for Ace, notably the hit title track, the equally moving
"My Love Is Strong," and the jumping "Everybody's Carried Away," "Little
Girl," and "I'll Take You Back Home." —*Bill Dahl*

New Orleans Street Talkin' / Mar. 18, 1997 / Black Top ✦✦✦

Earl's Pearls / May 5, 1998 / Westside ✦✦✦✦
This top-notch collection brings together 25 tracks from King's 1955-1960
tenure with Ace Records in Jackson, Mississippi. Classic '50s New Orleans
music doesn't come much finer than this, and Earl's contributions to the
genre are plentiful on this disc, starting with his big hit, the original "Those
Lonely, Lonely Nights." A real treat is hearing Huey "Piano" Smith soloing
with complete abandon on tracks like "Nobody Cares," "Little Girl," "I'll Take
You Back Home," and "Baby You Can Get Your Gun." Earl's guitar playing is
equally fine and his Guitar Slim-derived style is well to the fore on "My Love
Is Strong" and "I'm Packing Up." Although King's discography encompasses
many labels and sessions, this is a great place to start absorbing this Crescent
City genius. —*Cub Koda*

Eddie King

b. Apr. 1, 1938, New York, NY
Guitar / Modern Electric Blues, Electric Chicago Blues
Back in 1957, Eddie "King" Milton was one of the young Turks of the West
Side school of guitar, in the company of Windy City guitarslingers Magic
Sam, Luther Allison, Freddie King, and Eddie C. Campbell. From the mid-
1950s through the '60s, he worked every famous blues club and hole-in-
the-wall joint in Chicago and the surrounding areas, honing his craft while
developing a reputation as a "head cutter" with it came time to jam. Eddie's
talents were picked up on by Willie Dixon, who used his guitar to back up
Sonny Boy Williamson at a Chess recording session. Whether backing up
artists like Little Mack Simmons, Detroit Jr., Willie Cobbs, or fronting his
own group, King kept putting in his time in the trenches, waiting for his big
break and any small ones that came along in the meantime. He recorded for
Joe Brown's JOB label, yielding the single "Shakin' Inside," and Dixon again,
one side from the latter session turning up on a Spivey album miscredited
to J.B. Lenoir. A local 45 on the Conduc label with his sister Mae ("Are You
Pushed to Love") caught the attention of Duke/Peacock label chief Don Robey. What *could* have happened at that juncture is lost to history simply
because a quarrel with the irascible Robey made the release of any of the
sessions a moot point. But King hung in for the next decade, gigging so hard
that when European labels came calling in the 1970s and early '80s, Eddie
was never at home to take the call. In 1973, Koko Taylor hired King as her
lead guitarist/bandleader, an off and on affair that lasted for over 20 years.
Recording again for the Dutch Double Trouble label in 1985, King came up
with a brilliant album that too few got to hear. Back with Koko in the early
'90s, he caught the ear of Joe and Sable Roesch of Roesch Records, who
decided to record him, issuing *Another Cow's Dead* in 1997. Once again,
Eddie King is ready to take on the blues community, still playing and performing at full strength. —*Cub Koda*

Another Cow's Dead / Apr. 8, 1997 / Roesch ✦✦✦✦
King's recorded output is slight bordering on criminal, so these 12 tracks
from the West Side Chicago bluesman are a welcome addition to his scant
discography indeed. King sports a strong, gospel-tinged voice and a nasty,
thick-toned guitar style that never grates, and both are well served here.
Featuring the Blues Brothers-plus horn section of Birch "Slide" Johnson, Alan
Rubin, and "Blue" Lou Marini, abetted by Ronnie Cuber on baritone saxo-
phone, the originals veer between soul and straight blues with "Kitty Kat,"
"Walk Right On In," "How Long Are You Going to Be Gone," "Pocketful of
Blues," "Never Loved a Woman," and the set closer "Hey Mr. Bluesman." The
covers mine the same genre turf with Luther Ingram's "If Lovin' Is Wrong,"
Albert King's "Angel Of Mercy," Eddy Giles' "Losin' Boy," and Elmore James'
"Yonders Wall" being notable highlights. This album just makes you want to
hear more from this highly overlooked artist. —*Cub Koda*

Freddie King (Freddy King)

b. Sep. 3, 1934, Gilmer, TX, **d.** Dec. 28, 1976, Dallas, TX
Guitar, Vocals / Modern Electric Blues
Guitarist Freddie King rode to fame in the early '60s with a spate of catchy
instrumentals which became instant bandstand fodder for fellow bluesmen
and White rock bands alike. Employing a more down-home (thumb and finger picks) approach to the B.B. King single-string style of playing, King enjoyed success on a variety of different record labels. Furthermore, he was
one of the first bluesmen to employ a racially integrated group onstage behind him. Influenced by Eddie Taylor, Jimmy Rogers, and Robert Jr. Lockwood, King went on to influence the likes of Eric Clapton, Mick Taylor, Stevie
Ray Vaughan, and Lonnie Mack, among many others.
   Freddie King (who was originally billed as "Freddy" early in his career)
was born and raised in Gilmer, Texas, where he learned how to play guitar
as a child; his mother and uncle taught him the instrument. Initially, King
played rural acoustic blues, in the vein of Lightin' Hopkins. By the time he
was a teenager, he had grown to love the rough, electrified sounds of Chicago
blues. In 1950, when he was 16 years old, his family moved to Chicago,
where he began frequenting local blues clubs, listening to musicians like
Muddy Waters, Jimmy Rogers, Robert Jr. Lockwood, Little Walter, and Eddie
Taylor. Soon, the young guitarist formed his own band, the Every Hour Blues
Boys, and was performing himself.
   In the mid-'50s, King began playing on sessions for Parrott and Chess
Records, as well as playing with Earlee Payton's Blues Cats and the Little
Sonny Cooper Band. Freddie King didn't cut his own record until 1957, when
he recorded "Country Boy" for the small independent label El-Bee. The single
failed to gain much attention.
   Three years later, King signed with Federal Records, a subsidiary of King
Records, and recorded his first single for the label, "You've Got to Love Her
with a Feeling," in August of 1960. The single appeared the following month
and became a minor hit, scraping the bottom of the pop charts in early 1961.
"You've Got to Love Her with Feeling" was followed by "Hide Away," the
song that would become Freddie King's signature tune and most influential
recording. "Hide Away" was adapted by King and Magic Sam from a Hound
Dog Taylor instrumental and named after one of the most popular bars in
Chicago. The single was released as the B-side of "I Love the Woman" (his
singles featured a vocal A-side and an instrumental B-side) in the fall of 1961
and it became a major hit, reaching number five on the R&B charts and
number 29 on the pop charts. Throughout the '60s, "Hide Away" was one of
the necessary songs blues and rock 'n' roll bar bands across America and
England had to play during their gigs.
   King's first album, *Freddy King Sings*, appeared in 1961 and it was followed later that year by *Let's Hide Away and Dance Away with Freddy King:
Strictly Instrumental*. Throughout 1961, he turned out a series of instrumentals—including "San-Ho-Zay," "The Stumble," and "I'm Tore Down"—which
became blues classics; everyone from Magic Sam and Stevie Ray Vaughan to
Dave Edmunds and Peter Green covered King's material. "Lonesome Whistle
Blues," "San-Ho-Zay," and "I'm Tore Down" all became Top Ten R&B hits
that year.
   Freddie King continued to record for King Records until 1968, with a second instrumental album (*Freddy King Gives You a Bonanza of Instrumentals*) appearing in 1965, although none of his singles became hits. Nevertheless, his influence was heard throughout blues and rock guitarists
throughout the '60s—Eric Clapton made "Hide Away" his showcase number
in 1965. King signed with Atlantic/Cotillion in late 1968, releasing *Freddie
King is a Blues Masters* the following year and *My Feeling for the Blues* in
1970; both collections were produced by King Curtis. After their release, King
and Atlantic/Cotillion parted ways.
   King landed a new record contract with Leon Russell's Shelter Records in
the fall of 1970. King recorded three albums for Shelter in the early '70s, all
of which sold well. In addition to respectable sales, his concerts were also
quite popular with both blues and rock audiences. In 1974, he signed a contract with RSO Records—which was also Eric Clapton's record label—and he
released *Burglar*, which was produced and recorded with Clapton. Following
the release of *Burglar*, King toured America, Europe, and Australia. In 1975,
he released his second RSO album, *Larger than Life*.
   Throughout 1976, Freddie King toured America, even though his health
was beginning to decline. On December 29, 1976, King died of heart failure.

Although his passing was premature—he was only 42 years old—Freddie King's influence could still be heard in blues and rock guitarists 20 years after his death. — *Stephen Thomas Erlewine & Cub Koda*

Let's Hide Away and Dance Away / 1961 / King ♦♦♦♦
The classic first, all-instrumental Freddy King album, it was monstrously influential to succeeding generations of great artists. — *Bill Dahl*

Freddy King Sings / 1961 / Modern Blues ♦♦♦♦
Great stuff from this influential Texas Bluesman—the haunting "Lonesome Whistle Blues," "I'm Tore Down," and other classics. From the B.B. King school, but with his own searing style of singing and playing, it's a must for fans of modern blues. — *George Bedard*

Boy Girl Boy / 1962 / King ♦♦♦
Lula Reed duets with Freddy here. — *Bill Dahl*

Bossa Nova & Blues / 1962 / King ♦♦♦
Inconsistent but worthwhile. — *Bill Dahl*

Freddie King Goes Surfin' / 1963 / King ♦♦
Fake live crowd makes this a wipeout. — *Bill Dahl*

A Bonanza of Instrumentals / 1965 / King ♦♦♦♦
Exceptional all-instrumental set. — *Bill Dahl*

Vocals & Instrumentals: 24 Great Songs / 1966 / King ♦
Avoid these edited King sides. — *Bill Dahl*

Hide Away / 1969 / Starday ♦♦♦♦
Fine retrospective of early work. — *Bill Dahl*

Freddie King Is a Blues Master / 1969 / Atlantic ♦♦♦
This solid set emphasizes King's vocals. — *Bill Dahl*

My Feeling for the Blues / 1970 / Atlantic ♦♦♦
Another vocal heavy set. — *Bill Dahl*

Getting Ready / Apr. 1971 / Shelter ♦♦♦
The first of King's three albums for Leon Russell's Shelter label set the tone for his work for the company: competent electric blues with a prominent rock/soul influence. King sings and plays well, but neither the sidemen nor the material challenge him to scale significant heights. Part of the problem is that Freddie himself wrote none of the songs, which are divided between Chicago blues standards and material supplied by Leon Russell and Don Nix. The entire album is included on the compilation *King of the Blues*. — *Richie Unterberger*

The Texas Cannonball / May 1972 / Shelter ♦♦♦
Similar to his first Shelter outing (*Getting Ready*), but with more of a rock feel. That's due as much to the material as the production. Besides covering tunes by Jimmy Rogers, Howlin' Wolf, and Elmore James, King tackles compositions by Leon Russell and, more unexpectedly, Bill Withers, Isaac Hayes-David Porter, and John Fogerty (whose "Lodi" is reworked into "Lowdown in Lodi"). King's own pen remained virtually in retirement, as he wrote only one of the album's tracks. Reissued in its entirety on *King of the Blues*. — *Richie Unterberger*

Woman Across the River / Jun. 1973 / Shelter ♦♦♦
King's last Shelter album was his most elaborately poduced, with occasional string arrangements and female backups vocals, although these didn't really detract from the end result. Boasting perhaps heavier rock elements than his other Shelter efforts, it was characteristically divided between blues standards (by the likes of Willie Dixon and Elmore James), Leon Russell tunes, and more R&B/soul-inclined material by the likes of Ray Charles and Percy Mayfield. It's been reissued, along with his other Shelter albums, on the *King of the Blues* anthology. — *Richie Unterberger*

Burglar / 1974 / BGO ♦♦♦
This even more rock-oriented album is still quite powerful. — *Bill Dahl*

Just Pickin' / 1986 / Modern Blues ♦♦♦♦
Both of Freddy's all-instrumental albums for the King label (*Let's Hide Away and Dance Away with Freddy King* and *Freddy King Gives You a Bonanza of Instrumentals*) on one compact disc. "Hide Away," "The Stumble," and "San-Ho-Zay" are the numbers that made King's rep and influenced guitarists on both sides of the Atlantic. — *Cub Koda*

★ **Hide Away: The Best of Freddie King** / 1993 / Rhino ♦♦♦♦♦
Although not always placed in the upper echelon of blues performers along-

side the other Kings (B.B. and Albert), Freddie King was a dynamo. He was both a powerhouse, imaginative guitarist and a glorious, soulful vocalist who could belt out come-ons, shout with gusto, or wail in anguish. His instrumentals were also catchy, usually simply structured but vigorous and vividly articulated. This tremendous 20-cut sampler includes familiar hits like "Going Down" and the title cut, plus the shattering "Have You Ever Loved A Woman" and the poignant "Lonesome Whistle Blues." The tracks are exquisitely remastered and intelligently sequenced, and the notes are informative and thorough without being academic or fawning. — *Ron Wynn*

King of the Blues / 1995 / EMI/Shelter ♦♦♦
Double-CD compilation that includes all three of the albums King recorded for Leon Russell's Shelter label in the early 1970s, as well as some other cuts (half a dozen of which were previously unissued) recorded around the same period. King's vocal and guitar-playing skills remained intact when he joined Shelter, but these recordings aren't among his best. That's partially because he was playing with rock-oriented sidemen, and partially because the material—divided between covers of blues standards, contemporary rock and soul items, and songs written by Leon Russell—wasn't especially exciting or sympathetic. Most crucial was the near-total absence of material from the pen of King himself. Although this set isn't bad, when you want to turn to classic King, you'll go elsewhere, particularly to the sides he recorded for the King label in the '60s. — *Richie Unterberger*

Live at the Electric Ballroom, 1974 / Feb. 20, 1996 / Black Top ♦♦♦
An Atlanta concert that wasn't issued for two decades. Archival releases of this sort tend to be for collectors only, but this is a cut above the standard. The sound is very good, the band is pretty tight, and King solos with fire and sings with conviction, sticking mostly to covers of warhorses like "Dust My Broom," "Key to the Highway," and "Sweet Home Chicago." It's a better deal, in fact, than his studio albums for Shelter in the early '70s, boasting a far more suitable, no-frills small combo approach. As a neat bonus, it also contains two solo acoustic performances recorded at a Dallas radio station in the 1970s. — *Richie Unterberger*

Little Jimmy King (Manuel Gales)

b. Dec. 4, 1968, Memphis, TN
Guitar, Vocals / Modern Electric Blues

Memphis-based, left-handed guitar player Little Jimmy King is certainly one of the most exciting of the new crop of blues players to emerge on the scene in the 1990s. King was born December 4, 1968, as Manuel Gales but renamed himself for his two favorite guitar heroes, Jimi Hendrix and Albert King. He got started as a rock 'n' roller, but by the mid-'80s had switched to blues. By 1988, he had left the Memphis blues scene to go on the road with his hero as part of Albert King's band. The late Albert King called Little Jimmy King his grandson, and the late Stevie Ray Vaughan also had high praise for the young guitarist. In a moment King will never forget, Vaughan reportedly told him: "Play on, brother, you've got it. Don't stop playing for nobody."

King's self-titled debut was released in 1991 on the Rounder Bullseye Blues label, and he followed it up in 1994 with *Something Inside of Me*, on which he's accompanied by former Double Trouble bassist Tommy Shannon and drummer Chris "Whipper" Layton. King can also be heard playing guitar on Ann Peebles' *Full Time Love* and Otis Clay's *I'll Treat You Right*.

Little Jimmy King's live shows, like his two highly praised recordings for Bullseye Blues, are full of fire and fury, passionate guitar playing within the context of his band, the Memphis Soul Survivors, great vocals and clever songs. When you realize this guy still hasn't hit 30, you know why he's being called "the future of blues guitar." King is taking the idiom to a whole new generation of younger fans, and he's also a key link in the music's required, ongoing evolution. — *Richard Skelly*

● **Little Jimmy King & the Memphis Soul Survivors** / 1991 / Bullseye Blues ♦♦♦♦
Hailing from the Jimi Hendrix and Stevie Ray Vaughan school of blues-rock, Little Jimmy King turns in a promising eponymous debut. Though he leans a little to heavily toward rock 'n' roll for some tastes—at his rootsiest, he sounds like Albert King—there's no denying his skill. King runs through a number of rollicking uptempo tracks, shuffles, R&B grinders, smoldering slow blues and even funk in the form of a cover of Sly Stone's "Sex Machine." Though his songwriting isn't quite up to par, his conviction carries him

through the weakest moments and he shows signs of developing into a more distinctive songwriter. On the whole, it's an exciting, promising debut. — *Thom Owens*

Something Inside of Me / Mar. 30, 1994 / Bullseye Blues ✦✦✦
Little Jimmy King's second Bullseye/Rounder session matches the slashing guitarist with the rhythm section that once backed Stevie Ray Vaughan. King soars on these 11 cuts; while he lacks Vaughan's speed and is more a straight blues technician, he plays with more imagination and drive than on his debut. He contributes six originals and does a competent job of reworking material by Elmore James, Albert King, and even Phil Collins. While there's nothing here startling or surprising, King effectively teams with Chris Layton and Tommy Shannon, and producer/organist Ron Levy crafts an entertaining program of contemporary blues-rock with vintage sensibilities and overtones. — *Ron Wynn*

Soldier for the Blues / Jun. 24, 1997 / Bullseye Blues ✦✦✦
Little Jimmy King's third album finds him in the well-placed hands of Memphis producing and arranging legend Willie Mitchell. With Mitchell's publishing branch supplying six of the 12 selections here, there's a much more pronounced soul/blues feeling to this album than his two previous efforts, spelled out in a most contemporary manner on the confessional opening track, "Living In the Danger Zone" and "We'll Be Together Again." As always, Little Jimmy tips his hat to his mentor, the late Albert King with every note he hits on his Flying V, squeezing strings over several frets to get those classic Albert microtonal bends on tracks like "I Don't Need Nobody That Don't Need Me," "Drawers" and the title track. This is a thoroughly contemporary blues album that could—and should—expand King's audience beyond the usual blues circles. — *Cub Koda*

Shirley King

b. Oct. 26, 1949, West Memphis, AR
Modern Electric Chicago Blues
The daughter of the legendary B.B. King, vocalist Shirley King carried on the family tradition to become a favorite among Chicago's North Side blues club denizens. Born September 26, 1949 in West Memphis, AR, she pursued a career as an exotic dancer before turning to the blues in 1991; a year later she and harpist Chicago Beau recorded her debut LP, *Jump Through My Keyhole*, a showcase for her husky wail. — *Jason Ankeny*

Jump through My Keyhole / GBW ✦✦✦

Kinsey Report

f. 1984, Gary, IN
Group / Modern Electric Blues, Chicago Blues, Modern Electric Chicago Blues
This family band consists of Donald Kinsey (b. May 12, 1953, Gary, IN), (vocal, guitar); Ralph "Woody" Kinsey, (drums); Kenneth Kinsey, (bass); Ronald Prince, (guitar). Solidly based in the blues as a result of lifelong training in The Big Daddy Kinsey household, The Kinsey scions are also versed in a broad range of music. The older brothers Donald and Ralph had an early blues-rock trio (White Lightnin') in the mid-'70s, long before they regrouped as The Kinsey Report in 1984 and began to launch new excursions into rock. Donald also recorded and toured with Albert King and with Bob Marley, and the influence of those giants (as well as that of Big Daddy Kinsey, naturally) show through in the music of The Kinsey Report. The band expertly covers all the bases from Chicago blues through reggae, rock, funk, and soul, and their recordings are also distinguished by the songwriting talents and self-contained production approach of The Kinseys. — *Jim O'Neal*

● **Edge of the City** / 1987 / Alligator ✦✦✦✦
The Kinsey Report's debut album, *Edge of the City*, crackles with excitement, illustrating that it is possible to unite electric Chicago blues with rock and funk. There's a kinetic energy to the group's interaction that carries the group over occasionally undistinguished songwriting. Instead of sounding forced, the fusions are organic and unpredictable, resulting in some truly compelling music. The Kinsey Report never quite captured that thrilling balance of power ever again, but it's fortunate that they got the mix right at least once. — *Thom Owens*

Midnight Drive / 1989 / Alligator ✦✦✦
With *Midnight Drive,* Big Daddy Kinsey attempts to expand the sonic palette

of blues by adding elements of funk and hard rock. Although there are some interesting moments—primarily in the skillful solos—the music often falls flat and the songwriting isn't distinctive. Kinsey's attempts at diversity are admirable, but ultimately unsuccessful. — *Thom Owens*

Powerhouse / 1991 / Pointblank ✦✦✦
This hard-rock album is spiced (lightly) with blues. — *Niles J. Frantz*

Crossing Bridges / May 4, 1993 / Capitol ✦✦
Crossing Bridges is a disappointing set of rock meanderings. — *Bill Dahl*

Big Daddy Kinsey (Lester Kinsey)

b. Mar. 18, 1927, Pleasant Grove, MS
Guitar, Harmonica, Vocals / Modern Electric Blues, Chicago Blues
Long before Lester "Big Daddy" Kinsey and his clan hit the international blues circuit, he established himself as the modern-day blues patriarch of Gary, IN, and as the Steeltown's answer to Muddy Waters. A slide guitarist and harp blower with roots in both the Mississippi Delta and post-war Chicago styles, Kinsey worked with local bands only long enough for his sons to mature into top-flight musicians, and since 1984 (when Big Daddy recorded his debut album, *Bad Situation*) the family act has become one of the hottest attractions in contemporary blues. Big Daddy's material ranges from deep blues in the Muddy Waters vein to hard-rocking blues with touches of funk and even reggae, courtesy of sons Donald and Ralph (who venture even further afield in their own outings as The Kinsey Report). — *Jim O'Neal*

Bad Situation / 1985 / Rooster Blues ✦✦✦
Crisp, funky and modern, *Bad Situation* shows Big Daddy and the band in fine form. — *Bill Dahl*

● **Can't Let Go** / 1990 / Blind Pig ✦✦✦✦
When the Kinsey Report signed on to back their father for *Can't Let Go*, the group was at their peak, so it would have made commercial sense for the boys to move their direction. Fortunately, they went the other way, choosing to stick to Chicago blues. The Kinseys don't play it straight, however; they rock it hard, which energizes Big Daddy and makes *Can't Let Go* a thoroughly enjoyable collection of hard-rocking contemporary Chicago blues. — *Thom Owens*

I Am the Blues / Jan. 1993 / Verve ✦✦
On this disappointingly pompous set, Kinsey seems to want to occupy Muddy Waters' shoes, even recruiting his old band here; it didn't work! — *Bill Dahl*

Ramblin' Man / Dec. 12, 1995 / Polygram ✦✦✦

Eddie Kirkland

b. Aug. 16, 1928, Jamaica
Guitar, Harmonica, Vocals / Modern Electric Blues, Electric Blues, Soul Blues, Piedmont Blues
How many Jamaican-born bluesmen have recorded with John Lee Hooker and toured with Otis Redding? It's a safe bet there's only one: Eddie Kirkland, who's engaged in some astonishing onstage acrobatics over the decades (like standing on his head while playing guitar on TV's *Don Kirshner's Rock Concert*).

But you won't find any ersatz reggae grooves cluttering Kirkland's work. He was brought up around Dothan, AL, before heading north to Detroit in 1943. There he hooked up with Hooker five years later, recording with him for several firms as well as under his own name for RPM in 1952, King in 1953, and Fortune in 1959. Tru-Sound Records, a Prestige subsidiary, invited Kirkland to Englewood Cliffs, NJ, in 1961-62 to wax his first album, *It's the Blues Man!* The polished R&B band of saxist King Curtis crashed head on into Kirkland's intense vocals, raucous guitar, and harmonica throughout the exciting set.

Exiting the Motor City for Macon, GA, in 1962, Kirkland signed on with Otis Redding as a sideman and show opener not long thereafter. Redding introduced Kirkland to Stax/Volt co-owner Jim Stewart, who flipped over Eddie's primal dance workout "The Hawg." It was issued on Volt in 1963, billed to Eddie Kirk. By the dawn of the 1970s, Kirkland was recording for Pete Lowry's Trix label; he also waxed several CDs for Deluge in the '90s. — *Bill Dahl*

It's the Blues Man! / 1961 / Original Blues Classics ✦✦✦✦
Wildman guitarist/harpist Kirkland brought his notoriously rough-hewn attack to this vicious 1962 album for Tru-Sound, joined by a very accomplished combo led by saxman extraordinaire King Curtis and including guitarist Bill Doggett. As the crew honed in on common stylistic ground, the energy levels soared sky-high, Kirkland roaring "Man of Stone," "Train Done Gone," and "I Tried" with ferocious fervor. — *Bill Dahl*

The Devil & Other Blues Demons / Apr. 1975 / Trix ✦✦✦
Eddie Kirkland has long straddled the fence between bluesy soul and soulful blues. He was at a low point when he recorded for Trix in 1973, but this session recharged him musically, if not sales-wise. It is great to have it available again; whether Kirkland is doing silly numbers, offering taut blues licks, or giving examples of his philosophy, he finds creative ways to utilize the standard 12-bar scheme. — *Ron Wynn*

Have Mercy / 1988 / Evidence ✦✦✦
Kirkland's roaring guitar and garbled, gospel-tinged vocals are pretty much submerged in the mix here, a hodge podge of standard blues readymades and hyperactive funk-blues workouts. — *Cub Koda*

● **Three Shades of the Blues** / 198 / Original Blues Classics ✦✦✦✦
Kirkland's eight sides on this compilation are as hard-driving and intense as you could possibly ask for. It also includes four sides each from B.B. King-disciple Mr. Bo and the Ohio Untouchables, with dazzling guitar work from Robert Ward on the latter. — *Cub Koda*

All Around The World / 1992 / Deluge ✦✦
All Around the World is a comparatively lackluster set. — *AMG*

Some Like It Raw / Sep. 1993 / Deluge ✦✦✦
Recorded live at a blues bar in Vancouver, British Columbia, this finds Kirkland in typical latter day form, full of buzzy guitar, garbled vocals, and loads of intensity. Alternating between original material (most of it in a soul-funk vein) and blues classics (few of which bear much likeness to their original counterparts), Kirkland gets solid support from the young, white backing band here and the recording quality is quite good. — *Cub Koda*

Where You Get Your Sugar / Nov. 7, 1995 / Deluge ✦✦✦
Kirkland remains an amazingly raucous entertainer whose freeform sense of blues convention remains elusive to capture on records; perhaps he's best experienced live. This album's no exception—fiery at times, meandering and frustrating at others. To his credit, Kirkland's no moldy fig, mixing thoroughly contemporary rhythms and unusual chord changes into his rowdy musical stew. — *Bill Dahl*

Lonely Street / Nov. 18, 1997 / Telarc ✦✦✦
Jamaican-born bluesman Kirkland has always stretched the boundaries of his music and on this outing moves further into contemporary waters. Guest stars abound on this album, and Kirkland's idiosyncratic guitar work is answered and abetted by appearances from Tab Benoit, Sonny Landreth, Kenny Neal, Cub Koda, Christine Ohlman, and C.E. Smith, as well as driving work from drummer Jaimoe and organist Richard Bell. The material is all over the road, but particularly noteworthy as highlights are Kirkland's take on Elmore James' "Done Somebody Wrong," "Snake in the Grass," "Nightgirl," and the title track. — *AMG*

Bob Kirkpatrick

b. Jan. 1, 1934, Haynesville, LA
Guitar, Vocals / Texas Blues, Modern Electric Blues
Dallas-based guitarist, singer and songwriter Bob Kirkpatrick may not be a household name, but he's been quietly building an audience for the last 30 years in clubs around Texas, Mississippi and Louisiana. Although he hadn't recorded in 23 years prior to 1996's *Going Back To Texas*, Kirkpatrick has long been a regional star in the Texas triangle, but since he has always made family his first priority, his recording/blues career fell somewhere down the ladder. Kirkpatrick, born in 1934 in Haynesville, TX, became interested in music at age six, starting out on piano and switching to guitar. Kirkpatrick worked with Ivory Joe Hunter while attending school at Grambling, doing some road dates, but it wasn't until he saw B.B. King in 1958 that he became a true convert to the blues. When Kirkpatrick's doctors recommended that he take some time off from school after an illness, Kirkpatrick went to Dallas and played in clubs while holding down several different day jobs over the years. In 1968, he was offered the chance to go on the road as a substitute

guitarist for Bobby "Blue" Bland's regular guitarist, but Kirkpatrick chose to stay home with his young children. Kirkpatrick's brother was involved with the Newport Folk Festival and was able to book him several times, beginning in 1970. In 1973, he recorded *Feeling the Blues* for Moses Asch's Folkways Records (now marketed through the Smithsonian Institution). Kirkpatrick stayed in Dallas, raising his children and playing at the Elks Lodge in south Dallas on weekends for 16 years. After retiring in 1986, Kirkpatrick was urged to get back on the bandstand at area blues clubs by a friend who owned a club. Since the mid-1980s, he has been writing new songs and playing regionally again. Collectors may want to look around vinyl shops for his Folkways album, but easier to find is his 1996 JSP album *Going Back To Texas*, which shows B.B. King's influence on his vocals and guitar playing. — *Richard Skelly*

● **Going Back to Texas** / May 7, 1996 / JSP ✦✦✦✦
Bob Kirkpatrick's comeback album *Going Back to Texas* is a charming record. Kirkpatrick has a classy, jazzy guitar style, and he leads his band through a set of originals and covers, putting an attractive, swinging spin on the music. Even if a couple of tracks fall flat, *Going Back to Texas* is an engaging album of swinging Texas blues. — *Thom Owens*

Feeling the Blues / Smithsonian/Folkways ✦✦✦

Cub Koda

b. Oct. 1, 1948, Detroit, MI
Guitar, Vocals, Harmonica / Rock 'n' Roll, Blues-Rock, Rockabilly, Electric Chicago Blues
Best known as the leader of Brownsville Station and composer of their hit, "Smokin' in the Boys Room," Cub Koda has proven that his roots went far deeper, both before the band's formation, during its days in the sun, and long after its demise. His high school band, the Del-Tinos, was dipping into blues and rockabilly as far back as 1963—not only pre-Butterfield, but pre-Beatles. Similarly, he recorded legendary home tapes during his off hours from Brownsville, before the rockabilly revival had uttered its first hiccup, and later teamed with Hound Dog Taylor's former rhythm section, the Houserockers, to play the blues in the '80s. Along the way he cranked out a monthly column ("The Vinyl Junkie") and recorded a series of albums that kept roots music of all kinds alive without ever treating it like a museum piece.

Originally a drummer at age five, Koda switched over to guitar when he formed his first band, the Del-Tinos, a teenage garage combo equally influenced by rock 'n' roll, blues, and rockabilly. The group cut their first single—Roy Orbison's "Go Go Go"—in the fall of 1963, and released two more 45s independently before they disbanded in 1966. By this time, Koda had become so immersed in the blues, that the last Del-Tinos' single had the trio doing Muddy Waters' "I Got My Mojo Workin'" on one side and Robert Johnson's "Ramblin' on My Mind" on the other.

After a couple of bands in the late '60s that largely went unrecorded, Koda formed Brownsville Station in early 1969. After playing local Midwest gigs and releasing a handful of singles, the band released their first album in 1970. But it wasn't until "Smokin' in the Boys Room" that Brownsville had a genuine hit. Released as a single in the fall of 1973, "Smokin'" climbed all the way to No. 3, eventually selling over two million copies.

But Koda began to back away from the group's loud, overdriven rock sound—at least in private. He purchased a multi-track tape recorder and started producing one-man-band tapes, where he overdubbed all the instruments and vocals. For the next several years, Koda made home recordings of rockabilly, blues, R&B, country, jazz, and early rock 'n' roll—the exact opposite of Brownsville's heavy rock stance; the rockabilly tapes were eventually released as *That's What I Like about the South* in the early '80s, with other tracks showing up on compilations as late as 1993.

When Brownsville disbanded in 1979, Cub began writing a column called "The Vinyl Junkie" for *Goldmine* magazine, now being published in *DISCoveries*. Through the column's success, Koda established himself as an expert record collector and critic—eventually, Cub would compile and write liner notes for a number of projects, including three volumes in Rhino's acclaimed *Blues Masters* series.

In 1980, Koda worked with Hound Dog Taylor's backing band, the Houserockers. Over the next 15 years, Koda, guitarist Brewer Phillips, and drummer Ted Harvey performed and recorded together, with their first album, *It's the Blues*, appearing in 1981 and their latest, *The Joint Was Rockin'*, being released in 1996.

Throughout the '80s and '90s, Koda has continued to divide his time equally between touring, recording, and writing. 1993 saw the twin release of *Smokin' in the Boy's Room: The Best of Brownsville Station* on Rhino and *Welcome to My Job*, a retrospective of his non-Brownsville material on Blue Wave, followed a year later by *Abba Dabba Dabba: A Bananza of Hits* on Schoolkids' Records. — *Stephen Thomas Erlewine*

Cub Koda & the Points / 1980 / Fan Club ✦✦✦✦
Koda's first solo album after Brownsville Station. Highlights include "Jail Bait" and "Welcome to My Job." — *Stephen Thomas Erlewine*

It's the Blues / 1981 / Fan Club ✦✦✦
The addition of bass and special guests Left Hand Frank and Lefty Dizz only distract from the chemistry beween Cub and the Houserockers (even more obvious on their belated live follow-up), but this is a strong session, with the ex-stadium boogie boy sounding totally at home with these blues veterans. His vocal duet with Brewer Phillips on J.B. Lenoir's "Talk to Your Daughter" is a joy, and thankfully not every note is perfectly in place — in the case of Brewer's guitar, in tune. Added treats: Koda's big-toned harp on "Rockin' This Joint Tonight" and humorous dialog with Frank on "Dirty Duck Blues." — *Dan Forte*

Cub Digs Chuck / 1989 / Garageland ✦✦✦
Koda's tribute album to Chuck Berry, featuring blistering versions of "Johnny B. Goode," "Maybellene," and others. — *Stephen Thomas Erlewine*

Live at B.L.U.E.S. 1982 / 1991 / Wolf ✦✦✦✦
What's wrong with this picture? The sawed-off bespectacled singer/guitarist from Brownville Station fronting the late Hound Dog Taylor's ex-rhythm section, the Houserockers — blasphemy, you say? Get a life. Koda smokes like he's: 1) out to dispel any doubts about his legitimacy, and 2) having the time of his life. Opening with Howlin' Wolf's "Highway 49" (a rather tall order), the Cubmaster grabs the Chicago crowd by its collective neck and shakes it into submission. His guitar trade-offs with Brewer Phillips (no bass in this band) are a delight, and by "You Can't Sit Down" drummer Ted Harvey is blowing his police whistle — signalling that things be rockin'! Eddie Clearwater sits in on one tune, and Koda tips his hat to the guitarist with a stellar rendition of Eddie's "Hillbilly Blues." This is worthy of wider release, not to mention an encore. — *Dan Forte*

Cub Digs Bo / 1991 / Garageland ✦✦✦✦
Koda's tribute album to Bo Diddley, including powerhouse renditions of "Mumblin' Guitar," "Roadrunner," and "Background to a Music." — *Stephen Thomas Erlewine*

● Welcome to My Job: The Cub Koda Collection 1963-93 / 1993 / Blue Wave ✦✦✦✦
Covering everything from his pre-Brownsville Station days to two brand-new songs, *Welcome to My Job* is the definitive collection of Cub Koda's versatile solo career. — *Stephen Thomas Erlewine*

Abba Dabba Dabba: A Bonanza of Hits / Jul. 19, 1994 / Schoolkids ✦✦✦✦
Cub Koda's first album for Schoolkids' Records is his wildest, funniest, and simply best album in years. — *Stephen Thomas Erlewine*

The Joint Was Rockin' / 1996 / Deluxe ✦✦✦✦
The Joint Was Rockin' is a raw, rowdy, and deliriously fun record capturing Cub Koda live with the Houserockers in the early '80s. The Houserockers bash away like they were supporting Hound Dog Taylor, and Cub proves that he can play the blues with true passion and feeling. More than anything, however, *The Joint Was Rockin'* is a bracing jolt of energy and fun that's just as good as *Live at B.L.U.E.S. 1982*, his previous live set with the Houserockers. — *Stephen Thomas Erlewine*

Box Lunch / 1997 / J-Bird ✦✦✦✦
Cub Koda has tried a lot of different things in his long career, but he has never made anything close to *Box Lunch*. It's not just that the album consists of nothing but acoustic material; he has never been this open with his emotions. There are a few rockers — "Double Barrel Hell" is menacing and "Gimme Trash" is a tongue-in-cheek kitsch celebration — but the heart of the record is in the ballads, whether it's the nostalgic "We Were Crazy Back Then," the yearning "Runaway Heart," or the lovely "How Could Life Turn Out This Way," which evokes the spirit of Hank Williams. Cub has rarely been this

naked with his feelings and the results are frequently moving. And, to cap it all off, he throws out "Susan Hayward's Diary," a charming finger-picked instrumental. Moments like this make you hope that it's not the last acoustic album Cub will make — *Box Lunch* is so good, you wish there were seconds. — *Stephen Thomas Erlewine*

Koerner, Ray & Glover

f. 196?, Minneapolis, MN
Group / Acoustic Blues

In today's climate of a blues band seemingly on every corner with "the next Stevie Ray Vaughan" being touted every other minute, it's hard to imagine a time when being a White blues singer was considered kind of a novelty. But in those heady times of the early '60s and the folk and blues revival, that's *exactly* how it was. But into this milieu came three young men who knew it, understood it, and could play and sing it; their names were Koerner, Ray, and Glover. They were folkies, to be sure, but the three of them did a lot — both together and separately — to bring the blues to a White audience and in many ways, set certain things in place that have become standards of the Caucasian presentation of the music over the years.

The three of them were college students attending the University of Minnesota, immediately drawn together by their common interests in the music and by the close-knit folk community that existed back then. As was their wont, they all decided to append their names with colorful nicknames; there was "Spider" John Koerner, the Jesse Fuller and Big Joe Williams of the group, Dave "Snaker" Ray, a 12-string playing Leadbelly aficionado, and Tony "Little Sun" Glover on harmonica, holding up the Sonny Terry end of things. This simple little act of reinvention resonates up to the present day, with myriads of White practitioners throwing their mundane appellations out the window to recast themselves as something along the lines of Juke Joint Slim and the Boogie Blues Blasters.

They worked in various configurations within the trio unit, often doing solo turns and duets, but seldom all three of them together. Their breakthrough album, *Blues, Rags, and Hollers*, released in 1963, sent out a clarion call that this music was just as accessible to White listeners — and especially players — as singing and strumming several choruses of "Aunt Rhody." While recording two excellent follow-ups for Elektra, both Koerner and Ray released equally fine solo albums. Tony Glover, for his part, put together one of the very first instructional books on how to play blues harmonica (*Blues Harp*) around this time, and its excellence and conciseness still make it the how-to book of choice for all aspiring harmonica players. Both Koerner and Ray still maintain an active performing schedule, and every so often the three of them get back together for a one-off concert. — *Cub Koda*

● Blues Rags and Hollers / 1963 / Red House ✦✦✦✦
Blues Rags and Hollers, the first album from Koerner Ray & Glover, follows through on the folk and country-blues leanings of the blues revival. The result is a strong, catchy album that nevertheless sounds closer to folkies than the typical British blues record. — *Thom Owens*

Lots More Blues Rags & Hollers / 1964 / Elektra ✦✦✦✦
Not surprisingly, *Lots More Blues Rags and Hollers* follows in the tradition of Koerner Ray & Glover's debut, *Blues Rags and Hollers*, which means that it leans toward the folk elements of the blues revival. That means it's a little clean and folky, but there's a certain charm to the album — not to mention the high quality of the songs — that makes it a worthy follow-up. — *Thom Owens*

Return of Koerner, Ray & Glover / 1966 / Elektra ✦✦
Good Old Koerner, Ray & Glover / 1972 / Mill City ✦✦✦

Al Kooper

b. Feb. 5, 1944, Brooklyn, NY
Vocals, Guitar, Keyboards, Organ / Rock 'n' Roll, Blues-Rock

Even though Al Kooper has been a productive artist in his own right, his solo career has often been overshadowed by his accomplishments as a sideman, session musician, and producer. In particular, Kooper played a major behind-the-scenes role in the development of both blues-rock and jazz-rock as a founding member of both the Blues Project and Blood, Sweat and Tears. Kooper joined the Royal Teens as a guitarist in 1959, a year after their hit "Short Shorts," and found work as a session man and songwriter; he co-wrote Gary Lewis and the Playboys' No. 1 hit "This Diamond Ring." In 1965, producer Tom Wilson invited Kooper to one of Bob Dylan's *Highway 61 Revisited* sessions, but since Mike Bloomfield was already playing guitar, Kooper sat down at an organ, an instrument he barely knew how to play. He played along during the recording of "Like a Rolling Stone," figuring out the chord changes as he went and often hitting them behind the beat; Dylan liked the effect so much that he kept it on the track. Kooper backed Dylan at the 1965 Newport Folk Festival and guested on several Dylan albums in later years, including *Blonde on Blonde, New Morning,* and *Under the Red Sky.*

Later that year, Kooper was invited to join the Blues Project, which began the 1960s blues-rock movement along with the Paul Butterfield Blues Band, as an organist. In spite of the group's success, Kooper and Steve Katz left in 1967 to form Blood, Sweat, and Tears, another seminal combo that was among the first to mix jazz and rock. Kooper produced the band's 1968 debut, *Child Is Father to the Man,* but left that year owing to internal dissension. He signed on as a Columbia staff producer, guested on the Rolling Stones' *Let It Bleed* and Jimi Hendrix's *Electric Ladyland,* and released 1968's *Super Session,* an informal jam with Mike Bloomfield and Stephen Stills. Most of his inconsistent solo output was released over the next four years, and Kooper became better known for his production talents. He discovered Lynyrd Skynyrd and produced their first three albums, and also worked on the debuts of the Tubes and Nils Lofgren. In addition to production work, Kooper participated in several Blues Project reunions and toured with Bob Dylan. Kooper has continued to tour, record, and produce occasionally, and did extensive electronic soundtrack work in the '80s and '90s. *— Steve Huey*

I Stand Alone / 1969 / Columbia ✦✦✦

Al Kooper's first solo effort following his split from Blood, Sweat, & Tears finds him mining the same vein of musical gold he had with that band, only this time he didn't have to worry about group democracy getting in the way of his creativity. Covering a wide and varied field of musical tastes, Kooper added various sound effects to the mix, with sometimes comical results. This didn't detract from the music, though, as Kooper went from covering "Blue Moon of Kentucky" to "One" (from Harry Nilsson) to Gamble & Huff's "Hey, Western Union Man," carefully injecting originals along the way. A fine testament from a creative eccentric. *—James Chrispell*

You Never Know Who Your Friends Are / 1969 / Columbia ✦✦

Live Adventures / 1969 / Edsel ✦✦✦

More jamming, this time at the Fillmore, with guest appearances by Elvin Bishop and Carlos Santana. *— Cub Koda*

New York City (You're a Woman) / 1971 / Columbia ✦✦✦

A rather apocalyptic view of the times greets you upon entering Al Kooper's *New York City.* Religious overtones crop up here and there, such as on "John the Baptist" and the finale, "The Warning (Someone's on the Cross Again)," as well as hints at madness ("Going Quietly Mad"). All in all, *New York City (You're a Woman)* has more of a standard rock feel to it, as Kooper didn't employ as many orchestral fanfares or horn charts on these tunes. Kooper even gives us his take on the Elton John song "Come Down In Time." *New York City (You're a Woman)* is yet another glimpse of Al Kooper's world. *—James Chrispell*

Naked Songs / 1973 / Columbia ✦✦✦✦

Much more soulful and blues-influenced than previous efforts, *Naked Songs* finds Al Kooper reflecting the influences he'd soaked up by working with the Atlanta Rhythm Section, who appear on the record, and Lynyrd Skynyrd. Kooper covers John Prine's "Sam Stone" to chilling effect, and his take on the blues "As the Years Go Passing By" is worth the price alone. *Naked Songs* finds Al Kooper baring his soul to his audience, and it works. *—James Chrispell*

● ### Al's Big Deal (Unclaimed Freight) / 1975 / Columbia ✦✦✦✦

Act Like Nothing's Wrong / 1976 / One Way ✦✦✦

Kooper's sixth solo release opens daringly enough, with his own funky version of "This Diamond Ring," which he transforms completely from its Drifters-inspired origins. Most of the album is in a mid-1970s soul-funk vein, with Tower of Power turning up elsewhere and Kooper trying (with considerable success) to sound soulful on songs like "She Don't Ever Lose Her Groove" and "I Forgot to Be Your Lover." The playing throughout is excellent, with guitars by Kooper himself (who also plays sitar, Mellotron, organ, and synthesizer) as well as Little Beaver and Reggie Young, with Joe Walsh sitting in on one song, and horn arrangements by Kooper and veteran soundtrack com-

poser Dominic Frontiere. The real centerpiece is the epic-length "Hollywood Vampire," which can't quite sustain its seven-minute length. The funkier numbers work, but some of the rest, like "In My Own Sweet Way," don't come off so well. This is two-thirds of a pretty fair album, and only lacks consistency. *— Bruce Eder*

Alexis Korner (Alexis Koerner)

b. Apr. 19, 1928, Paris, France, **d.** Jan. 1, 1984, London, England
Guitar, Vocals / R&B, Electric British Blues, British Blues, Electric Blues, Blues Revival

Without Alexis Korner, there still might have been a British blues scene in the early 1960s, but chances are that it would have been very different from the one that spawned the Rolling Stones, nurtured the early talents of Eric Clapton, and made it possible for figures such as John Mayall to reach an audience. Born of mixed Turkish/Greek/Austrian descent, Alexis Korner spent the first decade of his life in France, Switzerland, and North Africa, and arrived in London in May of 1940, just in time for the German blitz, during which Korner discovered American blues. One of the most vivid memories of his teen years was listening to a record of bluesman Jimmy Yancey during a German air raid. "From then on," he recalled in an interview, "all I wanted to do was play the blues."

After the war, Korner started playing piano and then guitar, and in 1947 he tried playing electric blues, but didn't like the sound of the pick-ups that were then in use, and returned to acoustic playing. In 1949 he joined Chris Barber's Jazz Band, and in 1952 he became part of the much larger Ken Colyer Jazz Group, which had merged with Barber's band. Among those that Korner crossed paths with during this era was Cyril Davies, a guitarist and harmonica player. The two found their interests in American blues completely complementary, and in 1954 they began making the rounds of the jazz clubs as an electric blues duo. They started the London Blues and Barrelhouse Club, where, in addition to their own performances, Korner and Davies brought visiting American bluesmen to listen and play. Very soon they were attracting blues enthusiasts from all over England.

Korner and Davies made their first record in 1957, and in early 1962, they formed Blues Incorporated, a "supergroup" (for its time) consisting of the best players on the early '60s British blues scene. Korner (guitar, vocals), Davies (harmonica, vocals), Ken Scott (piano), and Dick Heckstall-Smith (saxophone) formed the core, with a revolving membership featuring Charlie Watts or Graham Burbridge on drums, Spike Heatley or Jack Bruce on bass, and a rotating coterie of guest vocalists including Long John Baldry, Ronnie Jones, and Art Wood (older brother of Ron Wood). Most London jazz clubs were closed to them, so in March of 1962 they opened their own club, which quickly began attracting large crowds of young enthusiasts, among them Mick Jagger, Keith Richards, and Brian Jones, all of whom participated at some point with the group's performances—others included Ian Stewart, Steve Marriott, Paul Jones, and Manfred Mann. In May of 1962, Blues Incorporated was invited to a regular residency at London's Marquee Club, where the crowds grew even bigger and more enthusiastic. John Mayall later credited Blues Incorporated with giving him the inspiration to form his own Bluesbreakers group.

Record producers began to take notice, and in June of 1962 producer Jack Good arranged to record a live performance by the band. The resulting record, *R&B from the Marquee,* the first full-length album ever made by a British blues band, was released in November of 1962. The album consisted of largely of American standards, especially Willie Dixon numbers, rounded out with a few originals. At virtually the same time that Blues Incorporated's debut was going into stores, Cyril Davies left the group over Korner's decision to add horns to their sound. Korner soldiered on, but the explosion of British rock in 1963, and the wave of blues-based rock bands that followed, including the Rolling Stones, the Animals, and the Yardbirds undercut any chance he had for commercial success. His more studied brand of blues was left stranded in a commercial backwater—there were still regular gigs and recordings, but no chart hits, and not much recognition. While his one-time acolytes the Rolling Stones and the Cream made the front pages of music magazines all over the world, Korner was relegated to the blues pages of England's music papers, and, though not yet 40, to the role of "elder statesman."

For a time, Korner hosted *Five O'Clock Club,* a children's television show that introduced a whole new generation of British youth to American blues and jazz. He also wrote about blues for the music papers, and was a detractor of the flashy, psychedelic and commercialized blues-rock of the late 1960s, which he resented for its focus on extended solos and its fixation on Chicago blues. He continued recording as well, cutting a never-completed album with future Led Zeppelin vocalist Robert Plant in early 1968. Korner's performing career in England was limited, but he could always play to large audiences in Europe, especially in Scandinavia, and there were always new Korner records coming out. It was while touring Scandinavia that he first hooked up with vocalist Peter Thorup, who became Korner's collaborator over the next several years in the band New Church. After his dismissal from the Rolling Stones, Brian Jones considered joining New Church; Korner, however, rejected the idea, because he didn't want his new band to be caught up in any controversy. In 1972, he became peripherally involved in the breakup of another band, inheriting the services of Boz Burrell, Mel Collins, and Ian Wallace when they quit King Crimson.

It was during the 1970s that Korner had his only major hit, as leader (with Peter Thorup) of the 25-member big band ensemble CCS. Their version of Led Zeppelin's "Whole Lotta Love" charted in England, and led to a tour and television appearances. In response, Korner released *Bootleg Him*, a retrospective compiled from tapes in his personal collection, including recordings with Robert Plant, Mick Jagger, and Charlie Watts. Korner played on the "supersession" album *B.B. King in London*, and cut his own, similar album, *Get off My Cloud*, with Keith Richards, Peter Frampton, Nicky Hopkins, and members of Joe Cocker's Grease Band. When Mick Taylor left the Rolling Stones in 1975, Korner was mentioned as a possible replacement, but the spot eventually went to Ron Wood. In 1978, for Korner's 50th birthday, an all-star concert was held featuring Eric Clapton, Paul Jones, Chris Farlowe, and Zoot Money, which was later released as a video.

In 1981, Korner formed the last and greatest "supergroup" of his career, Rocket 88, featuring himself on guitar, Jack Bruce on upright bass, Ian Stewart on piano, and Charlie Watts on drums, backed by trombonists and saxmen, and one or two additional keyboard players. They toured Europe and recorded several gigs, the highlights of which were included on a self-titled album released by Atlantic Records. In contrast to the many blues-rock fusion records with which Korner had been associated, *Rocket 88* mixed blues with boogie-woogie jazz, the group's repertory consisting largely of songs written by W. C. Handy and Pete Johnson.

After a well-received appearance at the Cambridge Folk Festival in the early 1980s, there were rumors afterward that he intended to become more active musically, but his health was in decline by this time. A chain smoker all of his life, Korner died of lung cancer at the beginning of 1984. *— Bruce Eder*

R&B from the Marquee / 1962 / Mobile Fidelity ◆◆◆◆
Alexis Korner's Blues Incorporated's early, raw, unpretentious British take on American blues. The album shows a multitude of influences, from rural, country blues to the electric sounds of Chess Records, Sleepy John Estes to Willie Dixon and Muddy Waters. Note: The British Decca CD from the late '80s has four bonus tracks not on the original album, but the American Mobile Fidelity CD reissue from 1996 has yet another previously unreleased bonus track, a cover of Willie Dixon's "Built for Comfort," that Decca missed on its CD. *— Bruce Eder*

At the Cavern / 1964 / Oriole ◆◆◆
The group is still called Blues Incorporated, but without Cyril Davies or Long John Baldry, who were present on the first record. Recording at Liverpool's Cavern Club was more a gimmick than anything else, and the music is not as well made or exciting as the group's first album. This record shows Korner's more big-band type blues work, favoring horns. A good album, but not one that was going to make much noise amid the work of the Rolling Stones, the Animals, the Yardbirds et al. *— Bruce Eder*

Red Hot from Alex / 1964 / Transatlantic ◆◆

Blues Incorporated / 1964 / Polydor ◆◆◆

Sky High / 1966 / Spot ◆◆◆

I Wonder Who / 1967 / BGO ◆◆
Recorded in a mere two sessions, this had the potential to be a decent, if hardly innovative, effort. At this point, Korner's group was in one its most stripped-down phases, featuring just Alexis on guitar, Danny Thompson on bass, and Terry Cox on drums. Very shortly after this disc, Thompson and

Cox would form the rhythm section of Pentangle, so these cuts are somewhat akin to hearing the bare bones of Pentangle in a much more blues/jazz-based context. The musical backing is not the problem, nor is the material, divided between Korner originals and blues standards by the likes of Jimmy Smith, Percy Mayfield, Ma Rainey, and Jelly Roll Morton. The problem is that Korner elected to sing these himself in his gruff, scraggly croak. It's not like listening to Dylan or Buffy Sainte-Marie, who take some getting used to, but have considerable, idiosyncratic talent—Korner simply cannot, objectively speaking, sing. (His butchering of Herbie Hancock's "Watermelon Man" has to be heard to be believed.) And that makes this album downright difficult to bear, despite the fine, spare musical arrangements (the instrumental cover of Jimmy Smith's "Chicken Shack Back Home" is a major standout in this context). If Korner had the wisdom to employ even a minor-league British bluesman like, say, Duffy Power (who guested with him occasionally during this time) as his singer for these sessions, the results would have been immeasurably better. *— Richie Unterberger*

New Generation of Blues / 1968 / Beat Goes On ◆◆◆
A basically competent, though hardly enthralling, effort from the British bluesman that alternates between minimal, acoustic-flavored production and fuller arrangements with jazzy touches of flute and upright bass. Korner wrote about half of the material, leaving the rest of the space open for R&B/blues covers and adaptations of traditional standards. "The Same For You" has a strange, ever-so-slight psychedelic influence, with its swirling flute, fake fadeout, and odd anti-establishment lyrics. Korner's voice is (and always would be) a tuneless bark, but it sounds better here than it did on the first album to prominently feature his vocals (*I Wonder Who*, 1967). As such, this album is one of the best representations of Korner as a frontman. *— Richie Unterberger*

Bootleg Him! / 1972 / Warner Brothers ◆◆◆◆
The best of all the Korner anthologies, boasting unreleased tapes and a lot of interesting one-off recordings from the various nooks and crannies of his career. *— Bruce Eder*

Get Off of My Cloud / 1975 / See for Miles ◆◆◆
The lineup makes this album virtually an offshoot of Korner's participation on *B.B. King In London* from four years earlier, including Steve Marriott, Peter Frampton etc., with Keith Richards making a guest appearance. Songs include the Rolling Stones title hit, and a cover of the Doors' "The Wasp (Texas Radio)." Nothing to make anyone forget the originals, nor is the new material terribly memorable, but everyone sounds like they're having fun here. *— Bruce Eder*

Rocket 88 / 1981 / Atlantic ◆◆◆◆
This was the best record Korner had made since 1962, and featured a core membership of former acolytes—Charlie Watts, Jack Bruce, and Ian Stewart. The sound is as much jazz as blues-influenced, it was all cut live on tour of Europe, and nobody involved ever sounded better, happier, or more relaxed. Not yet released on CD, and worth its weight in gold on vinyl, this was both Korner's and Stewart's final efforts. *— Bruce Eder*

● **The Alexis Korner Collection** / 1988 / Castle ◆◆◆◆
Castle's *Alexis Korner Collection* is a good single-disc collection that does a nice job of summarizing Korner and his various supporting bands throughout his career. Along the way, most of his popular songs and a healthy selection of his best material are showcased, making this an excellent introduction to his prodigious body of work. *— Thom Owens*

1961-1972 / Jul. 30, 1996 / Castle ◆◆◆◆

Smokin' Joe Kubek

b. Texas
Guitar, Vocals / Electric Texas Blues
Another young Texas axeman from the old school, Smokin' Joe Kubek issued his band's debut disc in 1991 on Bullseye Blues, *Steppin' Out Texas Style*. Kubek was already playing his smokin' guitar on the Lone State chitlin circuit at age 14, supporting such musicians as Freddie King. Soon, he formed his own band and began playing a number of bars across Dallas. In the '80s he met guitarist/vocalist B'nois King, a native of Monroe, LA, and the duo formed the first edition of the Smokin' Joe Kubek Band. The Smokin' Joe Kubek Band began playing the rest of the southwest in the late '80s. In 1991 they signed to Bullseye Blues, releasing their debut *Steppin' Out Texas Style*

the same year. Following its release, the band launched their first national tour. For the rest of the '90s, the Smokin' Joe Kubek Band toured the United States and toured frequently and issued records like 1993's *Texas Cadillac* and 1996's *Got My Mind Back.* — *Bill Dahl & Stephen Thomas Erlewine*

● **Steppin' Out Texas Style** / 1991 / Bullseye Blues ◆◆◆◆
Smokin' Joe Kubek's debut album is a delight. Kubek leads his band through a set of smoking hot Texas and Memphis blues, delivered with passion— they can play this music with precision, but they choose to be looser and more fun than most traditionalists. Kubek's a skillful guitarist and B'Nois King, his vocalist and rhythm guitarist, can play nearly as well and their duels are the high watermark of an already wonderful album. — *Thom Owens*

Chain Smokin' Texas Style / 1992 / Bullseye Blues ◆◆◆
Smokin' Joe Kubek is pure Texas blues—he's a forceful guitarist and his band rocks with a loose, greasy vibe. What makes the album so much fun is the combination of solid material and piledriving performances—it may follow a tradition, but it manages to be unpredictable. — *Thom Owens*

Texas Cadillac / 1993 / Bullseye Blues ◆◆◆◆
Smokin' Joe Kubek's third Rounder album juggles blues-rock originals with faithful, exuberant covers of Jimmy Reed, Willie Dixon, Muddy Waters, and Little Walter Jacobs, among others. Kubek is a good, sometimes captivating guitarist and entertaining singer, if not the greatest pure vocalist, and the band rips through the 11 cuts in a relaxed, yet passionate fashion. But it's hard for any longtime blues fan to get excited over hearing another version of "Little Red Rooster" or "Mean Old World"; it's impossible to reinvent Delta, urban, Texas, or West Coast blues. The solution is probably to make the best music you can and hope you hook those willing to listen to contemporary blues rather than spurn it for the originals. — *Ron Wynn*

Keep Comin' Back / 1995 / Bullseye Blues ◆◆◆
Got My Mind Back / 1996 / Bullseye Blues ◆◆◆◆
There is no need for guest musicians when Smokin' Joe Kubek is around, for the explosive guitarist completely fills up the ensembles with distortions worthy of acid rock. Kubek is a fairly well-rounded player who occasionally leaves space and during at least two songs ("All the Love There Is" and "She's It") on this CD creates some surprising tones on his instrument (sounding like a keyboard on the former and playing 1970s-style wah-wah notes during the latter). With B'nois King contributing smooth but emotional vocals and bassist Paul Jenkins and drummer Mark Hays supporting Kubek, this is a tight group that probably puts on a killer live show. — *Scott Yanow*

Take Your Best Shot / Apr. 7, 1998 / Bullseye Blues ◆◆◆
Kubek's fiery Stratocaster and King's streetwise vocals are well to the fore on this, their sixth album. Guest turns by Little Milton (playing fine guitar on "You Said 'I Love You' First") and Jimmy Thackery (contributing his usual blazing guitar work on "Worst Heartache") and an album of solid original material make this one of the duo's best outings. Highlights include "Roll of the Dice," the playful "Damn Traffic," "Spanish Trace," and the title track. — *Cub Koda*

Lady Bianca

b. Aug. 8, 1953, Kansas City, MO
Vocals / Modern Electric Blues
While primarily a blues vocalist, Lady Bianca first earned notice as a session singer on a wide range of projects including recordings from Van Morrison, Frank Zappa and Merle Haggard. Born Bianca Thornton in Kansas City, MO, on August 8, 1953, she studied at the San Francisco Conservatory of Music before lending her contralto to the role of Bessie Smith in an acclaimed production of Jon Hendrick's *Evolution of the Blues;* in the early 1980s, she appeared on Morrison LPs including *Beautiful Vision* and *Inarticulate Speech of the Heart,* and also backed blues legends like John Lee Hooker and Willie Dixon. In the late 1980s, Lady Bianca teamed with songwriter Stanley Lippitt, an alliance which yielded a number of tracks that grabbed the attention of Joe Louis Walker and in turn resulted in a record deal; she made her solo debut in 1995 with *Best Kept Secret. — Jason Ankeny*

Best Kept Secret / Oct. 1995 / Telarc ✦✦✦

Sonny Landreth

b. Feb. 1, 1951, Caton, MS
Guitar, Vocals, Dobro, Slide Guitar / Modern Electric Blues
Southwest Louisiana-based guitarist, songwriter and singer Sonny Landreth is a musician's musician. The blues slide guitar playing found on his two Zoo Entertainment releases, *Outward Bound* (1992) and *South of I-10* (1995) is distinctive and unlike anything else you've ever heard. His unorthodox guitar style comes from the manner in which he simultaneously plays slide and makes fingering movements on the fret board. Landreth, who has an easygoing personality, can play it all, like any good recording-session musician. His distinctive guitar playing can be heard on recordings by John Hiatt, Leslie West and Mountain, and other rock 'n' rollers.

Landreth was born February 1, 1951, in Canton, MS, and his family lived in Jackson, MS, for a few years before settling in Lafayette, LA. Landreth, who still lives in southwest Louisiana, began playing guitar after a long tenure with the trumpet. His earliest inspiration came from Scotty Moore, the guitarist from Elvis Presley's band, but as time went on, he learned from the recordings of musicians and groups like Chet Atkins and the Ventures. As a teen, Landreth began playing out with his friends in their parents' houses.

"They would ping-pong us from one house to another, and though we were all awful at first, as time went on we got pretty good. It's an evolutionary process, just like songwriting is," Landreth explained in an interview on his 44th birthday in 1995. After his first professional gig with accordionist Clifton Chenier in the 1970s (where he was the only White guy in the Red Beans and Rice Revue for awhile), Landreth struck out on his own, but not before he recorded two albums for the Blues Unlimited label out of Crowley, LA, *Blues Attack* in 1981 and *Way Down in Louisiana* in 1985. If anyone is living proof of the need to press on in spite of obstacles, it is Landreth.

The second of those two albums got him noticed by some record executives in Nashville, which in turn led to his recording and touring work with John Hiatt. That led to still more work with John Mayall, who recorded Landreth's radio-ready "Congo Square." More recently, he's worked with New Orleans bandleader and pianist Allen Toussaint (who guests on several tracks on *South of I-10,* as does Dire Straits guitarist Mark Knopfler).

On Landreth's brilliant albums for Zoo, the lyrics draw the listener in to the sights, sounds, smells and heat of southwest Louisiana, and a strong sense of place is evident in many of Landreth's songs. Although his style is completely his own and his singing is more than adequate, Landreth admits that writers like William Faulkner have had a big influence on his lyric writing. The fact that it's taken so long for academics at American universities to recognize the great body of poetry that blues is concerns Landreth as well. Robert Johnson is Landreth's big hero when it comes to guitar playing. "When I finally discovered Robert Johnson, it all came together for me," Landreth said, noting that he also closely studied the recordings of Skip James, Mississippi John Hurt and Charley Patton. — *Richard Skelly*

Outward Bound / 1992 / Zoo ✦✦
Sonny Landreth is the Louisiana-based slide-guitar master known for his work with John Hiatt and B.C.'s Sue Medley (both make backup vocal appearances here). Like fellow ace Ry Cooder, Landreth's playing sizzles and slashes on his debut solo outing *Outward Bound* without idle wanking. There's lots of space where what isn't played is just as important as what is. "Back to Bayou Teche" echoes the performer's early days backing some of Louisiana's best known Cajun musicians; aboriginal rhythms grace "Sacred Ground"; commercial pop meets Southern boogie on "New Landlord"; Landreth borrows a lick or two from buddy Hiatt for "Common-Law Love." — *Roch Parisien*

Down In Louisiana / Mar. 23, 1993 / Epic ✦✦✦
This is the music from the Saturday-night dances in Louisiana. The hot and sweaty have a good time dancing, drinking, and looking at all the people. Do not look for the Royal Albert Hall production in this CD, as in his stunning *South of I-10,* with its myriad "guest artists." The feel for this music is shown by someone who grew up with it. Listen to the respect and feeling he gives to Clifton Chenier's "If I Ever Get Lucky." Try and keep your body and feet from bouncing to the beat of "Sugar Cane" or "Little Linda." Doesn't your eye just start to look around for a dance partner, even though you're in your living room? There is solid playing throughout even though the sound is at times a bit thin, and the big name "guest artists" are nowhere to be found on this CD. It is a solid effort that spans the musical boundaries of all of Louisiana. Cajun, zydeco, blues, and country are all blended together so they are no longer confining, but a homogenous mix. A solid effort. — *Bob Gottlieb*

● **South of I-10** / 1995 / Praxis/Zoo ✦✦✦✦
Screaming slide guitar plowing right into you and carrying you along on its feral journey into deeper recesses. This CD opens going for your guts and it never quits, though at times its touch is more caressing than careening, as in "Cajun Waltz." This CD got a lot of airplay yet never got tiring, the true test of good music. It stopped me in my tracks the first time I heard a cut come ripping out of speakers. I stopped at the first phone and called the station and demanded to know who it was. I remembered seeing him as a member of John Hiatt's band years ago and liking what I heard. A wide variety of slide guitar styles, backed by an extremely tight rhythm section and various other New Orleans musicians adds to the pleasure of the album. This music combines the best of zydeco, New Orleans R&B, Cajun, and rock 'n' roll into one mood-elevating experience. Listen to "Mojo Boogie" next to "C'est Chaud," then go on to "Shootin' for the Moon," there is no letdown, but there is great variety. A must-buy. — *Bob Gottlieb*

Blues Attack / 1996 / AVI ✦✦✦

Jonny Lang

b. Jan. 29, 1981, Minneapolis, MN
Guitar, Vocals / Modern Electric Blues, Contemporary Blues
Modern blues in the '90s had a weird phenomenon of teenage blues guitarists rocketing to popularity with their first album. The entire trend culminated with Jonny Lang, a guitarist from Fargo, North Dakota, who released

his solo debut album *Lie to Me* when he was 15. At the age of 12, he attended a show by the Bad Medicine Blues Band and began playing with the group. Several months later he had become the leader, and the newly re-named Kid Jonny Lang & the Big Bang relocated from Fargo to Minneapolis and released their debut album, *Smokin*, in 1995. The LP became a regional hit, leading to a major-label bidding war and culminating in Lang's signing to A&M Records in 1996. Early in 1997, his major-label debut, *Lie to Me*, was released to mixed reviews. — *Thom Owens*

Smokin / 1995 / Oarfin ♦♦

● **Lie to Me** / Jan. 28, 1997 / A&M ♦♦♦
Like his peers Kenny Wayne Shepherd and Chris Duarte, Jonny Lang is a technically gifted blues guitarist, capable of spitting out accomplished licks and riffs at an astonishingly rapid rate. That doens't necessarily mean the album has much emotional weight—Lang can deliver the style, but not the substance, simply because he still needs to grow as a musician. Lang does boast an impressive array of licks and instrumental technique, but he needs something more to make *Lie to Me* a substantive record. — *Stephen Thomas Erlewine*

Denise LaSalle
· ·

b. Jul. 16, 1939, LeFlore County, MS
Vocals / R&B, Soul, Soul Blues, Northern Soul
Unlike so many other blues vocalists who just re-interpret material given to them by songwriters, LaSalle is a seriously talented songwriter. Although her soul blues style has strong urban contemporary overtones at times, it's best to think of LaSalle as a modern-day Bessie Smith, because that's really what she is. She writes funny songs full of sassy attitude, and it's an attitude she carries with her on stage. Off stage, LaSalle accommodates all autograph seekers and gladly obliges journalists and radio disc jockeys.

The Jackson, TN-based LaSalle was raised in Belzoni, MS, (also home to Joe Willie "PineTop" Perkins some years earlier), but she got started singing in local churches around LeFlore County. She was born July 16, 1939 as Denise Craig. Growing up, she listened to the Grand Ole Opry radio broadcasts and then in Belzoni, lived across the street from a jukejoint. LaSalle's early influences, from the jukeboxes around Belzoni and over the radio, included Ruth Brown, Dinah Washington and Lavern Baker. LaSalle moved north to Chicago when she was in her early 20s, and would attend shows at the Regal Theatre, always returning home to write songs. She got to know blues musicians and began giving her songs to them, until one day a Chess Records executive stopped by at Mixer's Lounge, where LaSalle was working as a bar maid. He listened to one of her songs and took it down to Chess Records, and the company later signed her as a vocalist, but never recorded her. Two years later, LaSalle recorded and produced her own record with the help of Billy "The Kid" Anderson, the Chess executive who'd originally shown an interest in her. After the record made some waves on local radio, Chess stepped in and purchased the master and took it to Europe. Meanwhile, La-Salle continued writing songs and sitting in with blues musicians around the Chicago clubs.

LaSalle's first big hit came about in 1971 when her "Trapped by a Thing Called Love" broke on the radio in Chicago and then Detroit. That record was for the Westbound label, and then she signed with ABC Records in 1975, cutting three albums in three years, until the label was sold to MCA. After MCA dropped her because of the label's "difficulty in promoting black acts" at that time, she continued performing as much as she could in Chicago and Memphis. In 1980, a Malaco executive called to ask her to write a song for Z.Z. Hill. She's been with Malaco ever since; "they pay their royalties on time" she said, and her Malaco sides are probably her most important recordings, other than the original of her early-'70s hit, "Trapped."

At Malaco, LaSalle hasn't slowed down a bit, and her specialty remains Southern soul-blues. Her records for the label include *Still Trapped, Lady in the Street, Right Place, Right Time, Love Talkin', Hittin' Where It Hurts*, and *Love Me Right*. — *Richard Skelly*

● **On the Loose** / 1973 / Westbound ♦♦♦♦
A prime example of her Memphis work, with Bowlegs Miller arrangements, this set features "Man Sized Job" and "Breaking up Somebody's Home." — *Bil Carpenter*

Hittin' Where It Hurts / 1986 / Malaco ♦♦♦♦
When high-tech urban contemporary sounds became R&B's norm in the

1980s, the small Jackson, Mississippi-based Malaco Records continued to specialize in traditional, southern-style soul music. One of Malaco's best sellers has been Denise LaSalle, a big-voiced soul shouter with a gospel-influenced delivery along the lines of Millie Jackson, Betty Wright, and Laura Lee. One of LaSalle's strongest Malaco releases, *Hittin' Where It Hurts* was recorded in 1988, but often sounds like it could have been recorded in 1967. LaSalle sounds as inspired as ever on such gritty, horn-laden fare as "If You Can't Do Me Right," "Eee Tee" and the bluesy "Caught in Your Own Mess," all of which recall the splendor of Stax Records. Many soul veterans have gone unrecorded in the 1980s and '90s, but thankfully, LaSalle isn't one of them. — *Alex Henderson*

Lady in the Street / 1986 / Malaco ♦♦♦
The title track was among LaSalle's best Malaco tunes, a stomping, urgently sung, sassy bit that walked the line between confrontation, invitation, and remorse. The other tunes weren't quite as inspired, but were equally well performed. Few performers have ever staked out an area and remained loyal to it like LaSalle, who's been doing country/blues soul since the early '70s and seldom strayed from the path, despite numerous trends and changes on the black music scene. Some would call that suicidal; others would say it's commendable. — *Ron Wynn*

Still Trapped / 1990 / Malaco ♦♦♦♦
Still Trapped found Denise LaSalle entering the 1990s without having changed her approach very much since the '70s. Rejecting slick, technology-driven urban contemporary music, the gritty singer continued to excel by pretty much sticking with the type of southern-style soul and blues Stax Records was recording 20 and 25 years earlier. LaSalle had long since disappeared from Black radio playlists, but still commanded a loyal following (especially in the Deep South). A welcome addition to her catalogue, *Still Trapped* is state-of-the-art LaSalle—earthy, humorous, and sassy as hell. From an inspired cover of Al Green's "Love and Happiness" to such hard-edged LaSalle originals as "Chain Letter," "Drop That Zero," and "Wild Thing (All Night Long)," this CD makes listeners grateful that LaSalle has remained true to herself. — *Alex Henderson*

On the Loose/Trapped by a Thing Called Love / 1992 / Westbound ♦♦♦♦
This British import contains much of her best work, including "Trapped By a Thing Called Love," "Now Run and Tell That," and "A Man Sized Job." — *John Lowe*

It's Lying Time Again / Malaco ♦♦♦
Denise LaSalle's Malaco albums have all been fine productions, usually featuring some sassy love songs, heartfelt bluesy ballads, and one or two numbers complete with spoken interludes in which the woman tells off the man. Unfortunately, none of them have matched her Westbound or ABC/MCA releases, mainly because soul no longer gets the same kind of widespread airplay outside the South. LaSalle has the kind of rough, tough, yet vulnerable sound ideal for these songs, and her delivery has as much country and blues influence as soul and gospel. Her style and Malaco's productions may be dated, but they're the kind of vintage sound that anyone who grew up in the '50s and '60s will always revere. — *Ron Wynn*

Love Talkin' / Malaco ♦♦♦
As with all her Malaco albums, Denise LaSalle mixes things up nicely, going from hard-hitting, trash-talking tunes to heartfelt ballads, bluesy numbers, and country/soul wailers. She's had a string of regionally successful releases since joining Malaco in the '80s, but has never been able to break the embargo on Southern soul. She's been around too long to change at this point, and really shouldn't anyway. Her albums are reliable and enjoyable, even if they're a throwback. — *Ron Wynn*

Rain and Fire / Malaco ♦♦
Denise LaSalle has drawn some fire at times for her frank, no-holds-barred dialogues and album cuts. She also has remained loyal to vintage soul and blues/country-tinged songs that will never get urban contemporary airplay and attention because they're thoroughly Southern in style, sound, and production values. Thus, each Malaco album is almost doomed from the beginning, other than as a regional proposition. That said, here's another one right in that same vein, and it's as fine as all the rest in what it does. — *Ron Wynn*

Right Place, Right Time / Malaco ♦♦♦
The title cut came close to getting Denise LaSalle a little attention beyond the standard Southern boundaries. The rest of the album is her familiar

litany of terse, crusty dialogues, country and blues-tinged wailers, and hard-hitting soul tunes. At times, LaSalle and others of her generation seem like illogical warriors, fighting to keep alive a sound that's long since faded as a viable commercial proposition. But as long as she keeps making records and putting her heart and soul into them, they deserve a listen by fans of the genre. — *Ron Wynn*

Booker T. Laury

b. Sep. 2, 1914, Memphis, TN, **d.** Sep. 23, 1995, Memphis, TN
Piano / Modern Electric Blues, Electric Blues, New Orleans Blues
Booker T. Laury grew up with Memphis Slim and the two were good friends. Consequently, his piano style has much of the same barrelhouse sound as Slim's. Laury stayed in Memphis, however, playing in the same clubs his entire life. Although some foreign albums were released, he had no domestic full-length. Therefore, Bullseye Blues released *Nothin' but the Blues*, with Laury's voice and piano the only instruments on the record. — *John Bush*

● **Nothin' But the Blues** / 1993 / Bullseye Blues ✦✦✦✦
A veteran of the old Beale Street scene and once a partner of the legendary Memphis Slim, Laury never got his shot at fame and fortune, or even the opportunity to cut a record. Approaching his 80th birthday, Laury finally made his debut and shows on this rollicking, highly delightful CD that his boisterous voice and piano skills remained in good shape. Every number is an original, as Laury opens the session with some uncensored remembrances about old Southern sanitary habits. From there, you get terse, spirited singing, powerful left and right hand piano lines, and a percussive, pounding attack that features octave-jumping forays and furious phrasing. One record can't correct a lifetime of being unfairly overlooked, but it can go a long way. — *Ron Wynn*

Sammy Lawhorn

b. Jul. 12, 1935, Little Rock, AR, **d.** Apr. 29, 1990, Chicago, IL
Guitar / Chicago Blues
Guitarist Sammy Lawhorn was born Samuel David Lawhorn on July 12, 1935, in Little Rock, AR. He was raised in the South by his grandparents after his mother and stepfather moved to Chicago. He first heard live guitar from blind guitar players on the street and soon was learning the instrument. Starting with a ukulele, graduating to an acoustic (Stella), and finally getting an electric (Supro), Lawhorn learned to play the guitar in about two years.

As a teenager he worked as a King Biscuit Boy for Sonny Boy Williamson II and learned slide guitar from Houston Stackhouse. After a stint in the service, Lawhorn returned to Arkansas and played and/or recorded with Willie C. Cobbs, the Five Royals, Eddie Boyd, and Roy Brown.

He moved to Chicago in the early '60s and became part of the house band at Theresa's, one of Chicago's main blues clubs. He worked on and off with Muddy Waters for about ten years and toured with that band. Lawhorn became best known as the resident guitarist at Theresa's club, where he played behind just about any great blues artist you could name. His influences were T-Bone Walker, Lightnin' Hopkins, Pee Wee Crayton, Lowell Fulson, and Muddy Waters. He was especially drawn to slide and Hawaiian-style guitar, and became well known for his use of the tremolo bar. He is considered as one of finest examples of postwar style Chicago blues guitar. He can be heard on recordings of Muddy Waters, Big Mama Thornton, Otis Spann, Junior Wells, John Lee Hooker, Eddie Boyd, and many others. Lawhorn died on April 29, 1990, in Chicago. — *Michael Erlewine*

Johnny Laws

b. Jul. 12, 1943, Chicago, IL
Vocals / Chicago Blues
While a fixture of Chicago's South Side blues community since the mid-1960s, singer/guitarist Johnny Laws long remained unknown outside of his native Windy City, and did not make his debut recordings for another three decades. Born July 12, 1943, he garnered considerable local attention as a result of his aching falsetto voice, in addition to a vast and eclectic repertoire of songs; still, Laws remained little more than a cult favorite until the release of his 1995 Wolf label debut *My Little Girl* finally made his music available to a wider audience. — *Jason Ankeny*

My Little Girl / 1995 / Wolf ✦✦✦

Sam Lay

b. Mar. 20, 1935, Birmingham, AL
Drums, Vocals / Chicago Blues
Sam Lay was born March 20, 1935, in Birmingham, AL, and began his career as a drummer in Cleveland in 1954, working with the Moon Dog Combo. In 1957 he joined the Original Thunderbirds and stayed with that group until 1959, when he left for Chicago to work with the legendary Little Walter.

Lay began to work with Howlin' Wolf in 1960 and spent the next six years with that group. He and bassist Jerome Arnold were hired away from Wolf's band by Paul Butterfield in 1966 and became part of the Paul Butterfield Blues Band, recording that classic first album. Lay toured with Butterfield until late in '66 when he accidentally shot himself.

Sam Lay backed Bob Dylan at the historic 1965 Newport Folk Festival, when Dylan first introduced electric-rock to the folk crowd. He went on to record with Dylan on *Highway 61 Revisited.* He can be heard on more than 40 classic Chess blues recordings, and his famous double-shuffle is the envy of every would-be blues drummer. In 1969, Lay played drums for the Muddy Waters *Fathers and Sons* album, now a classic. He also was the original drummer for the James Cotton Blues Band.

Later in 1969, he also worked with the Siegel-Schwall Band. He went on to form the Sam Lay Blues Revival Band, which has involved many players over the years including Jimmy Rogers, George "Wild Child" Butler, Eddie Taylor, and others.

Sam Lay was inducted into the Blues Hall of Fame in 1992 and received a nomination for a W.C. Handy award. He formed the Sam Lay Blues Band and has had recent recordings on Appaloosa Records (*Shuffle Master, Sam Lay Live*) and on Alligator with the Siegel-Schwall Band, with whom he often plays. A 1996 release on Evidence is in the can. — *Michael Erlewine*

In Bluesland / 1968 / Blue Thumb ✦✦

Sam Lay in Bluesland / 1968 / Blue Thumb ✦✦✦

● **Shuffle Master** / 1992 / Appaloosa ✦✦✦✦
Shuffle Master finds Sam Lay in fine form, turning in a propulsive, energetic collection of Chicago blues. There are no revelations here, just Chicago blues played as it should be played, which makes the disc a worthwhile listen. — *Thom Owens*

Stone Blues / 1996 / Evidence ✦✦✦

Live / Jan. 22, 1996 / Appaloosa ✦✦✦

Shuffle Master / 1997 / Appaloosa ✦✦✦

Lazy Lester (Leslie Johnson)

b. Jun. 20, 1933, Torras, LA
Guitar, Harmonica, Percussion, Vocals, Washboard / Electric Louisiana Blues, Electric Swamp Blues, Swamp Blues, Harmonica Blues
His colorful sobriquet (supplied by prolific south Louisiana producer J.D. Miller) to the contrary, harpist Lazy Lester swears he never was all that lethargic. But he seldom was in much of a hurry either, although the relentless pace of his Excello Records swamp blues classics "I'm a Lover Not a Fighter" and "I Hear You Knockin'" might contradict that statement too.

While growing up outside of Baton Rouge, Leslie Johnson was influenced by Jimmy Reed and Little Walter. But his entree into playing professionally arrived quite by accident: while riding on a bus sometime in the mid-'50s, he met guitarist Lightnin' Slim, who was searching fruitlessly for an AWOL harpist. The two's styles meshed seamlessly, and Lester became Slim's harpist of choice.

In 1956, Lester stepped out front at Miller's Crowley, Louisiana studios for the first time. During an extended stint at Excello that stretched into 1965, he waxed such gems as "Sugar Coated Love," "If You Think I've Lost You," and "The Same Thing Could Happen to You." Lester proved invaluable as an imaginative sideman for Miller, utilizing everything from cardboard boxes and claves to whacking on newspapers in order to locate the correct percussive sound for the producer's output.

Lester gave up playing for almost two decades (and didn't particularly miss it, either), settling in Pontiac, MI, in 1975. But Fred Reif (Lester's manager, booking agent, and rubboard player) convinced the harpist that a return to action was in order, inaugurating a comeback that included a nice 1988 album for Alligator, *Harp & Soul*. His swamp blues sound remains as atmospheric (and dare we say it, energetic) as ever. — *Bill Dahl*

☆ **True Blues** / 196 / Excello ✦✦✦✦✦
His original album collects the best of the early Excello sides. Includes "Sugar Coated Love," "I Hear You Knockin'," and "I'm a Lover, Not a Fighter." — *Cub Koda*

Lester's Stomp / 1987 / Flyright ✦✦✦✦
These primitive and rocking '50s sides came from an overlooked harmonica genius who epitomized the ragged-but-right ethic of producer Jay Miller. — *John Floyd*

Lazy Lester Rides Again / Jul. 1987 / King Snake ✦✦✦

Harp & Soul / 1988 / Alligator ✦✦✦✦
After a lengthy hiatus from the music business, Lester was in the midst of his comeback when he waxed this album for Alligator. The overall sound is redolent of those Louisiana swamp blues classics, but with a cannily updated contemporary edge that works well. — *Bill Dahl*

Rides Again / 1988 / Sunjay ✦✦✦✦
His original rediscovery album pairs him with English blues musicians, with surprisingly great results. — *Cub Koda*

Lazy Lester / 1989 / Flyright ✦✦✦✦
Alternate takes and unissued titles from the cache of producer J.D. Miller, whose tiny Crowley, LA studio was the prime site for recording swamp blues during the '50s and '60s. A fine companion to AVI's essential Lester compilation. — *Bill Dahl*

★ **I Hear You Knockin'!!!** / 1995 / Excello/AVI ✦✦✦✦✦
Southern Louisiana swamp blues doesn't get more infectious or atmospheric than in the hands of Lazy Lester, whose late-'50s/early-'60s catalog for Excello Records (produced by the legendary J.D. Miller) is splendidly summarized with the 30 sides here. Lester's insistent harp and laconic vocals shine brightly on the rollicking "I'm a Lover, Not a Fighter," "Sugar Coated Love," "I Hear You Knockin'," and "If You Think I've Lost You," serving to help define the genre's timeless appeal. — *Bill Dahl*

Leadbelly (Huddie William Ledbetter)

b. Jan. 20, 1888, Mooringsport, LA, **d.** Dec. 6, 1949, New York, NY
Guitar, Piano, Accordion, Vocals / Country Blues, Folk-Blues, Folksongs
Leadbelly was the first blues musician to achieve fame among White audiences. For this reason alone, and more for the sheer novelty of his career as an ex-convict-turned-singer than for any recognition of his abilities, he was the first bluesman to be treated as a major media figure in the mainstream press.

Huddie Ledbetter was born on January 20, 1888, not far from the Texas border. He remained in school until he was 12 or 13 and could read and write, and was a precocious child, serious and ambitious beyond his years. Ledbetter was surrounded by a multitude of influences growing out of the post-slavery/post-Reconstruction era of the late 19th century, including blues, spirituals, and minstrel songs. By the time he was 14, he was known for his ability with the guitar and his way with a piano. He played before audiences on most Saturday nights, at parties and square dances in the area around Mooringsport, Louisiana, but before he was far into his teens, he was attracted to the red-light district in Shreveport. Apart from the women, however, the district's main attraction to the teenager was its music. He was married by the first decade of the 20th century, but the relationship and the marriage didn't last. The music, however, did, with an important new wrinkle — Ledbetter switched from the six-string to the 12-string guitar, a pivotal decision in the development of his own career. He was already performing songs of his own and adapting others during the 1890s, and his abilities in this area grew with his experience. He first picked up a song known as "Irene" sometime in the first decade of the 20th century and as "Goodnight, Irene" it became one of Leadbelly's best-known songs.

Sometime around 1915 he made the acquaintance of Blind Lemon Jefferson, from whom he learned slide guitar. Despite some months of working together, Ledbetter was left behind by Jefferson, a result of his inability to stay clear of the law. Finally, in 1917, he was arrested for shooting a man and sentenced by the state of Texas to 30 years in prison. On the Shaw State Prison Farm, Leadbelly's talents served him just as well as they had outside.

His singing and guitar playing made him one of the more popular prisoners. He was ultimately released in 1925 after he played for the visiting Texas governor, Pat Neff, requesting a pardon. The pardon was signed by Neff on virtually his last day in office.

Leadbelly, as he was now known professionally, tried working regular jobs for the remainder of the 1920s, but was never able to stay far from the rambling life that had led him into trouble back in the previous decade. Finally, in 1930, he was arrested and convicted in Louisiana of assault with intent to commit murder, and sentenced to 30 years in the Louisiana State Penitentiary at Angola, a prison farm with a reputation as bad as, or worse, than the Texas prison from which he'd been released. And it was there, in 1933, that he first met John Lomax, an ambitious researcher for the Library of Congress, who was traveling through the South with his son Alan, collecting blues and any other authentic American music that they could find. Leadbelly's reputation within the prison was well-known, and it was inevitable that he would meet the Lomaxes. They found in Leadbelly a talent and a resource beyond anything they could have hoped for — the man was not only a gifted player who exuded a musical charisma that transcended the prison setting, but he was a veritable human jukebox, in the range of songs that he knew. Leadbelly dazzled the Lomaxes with his singing, playing, songwriting, and Lomax recognized in his new discovery a talent that was very different from the makers of the commercial "race" records of the period. Leadbelly's style and repertory were unaffected by the currents running through commercial blues and country music, but a talent that was worth trying to develop commercially, into a valid and successful brand of Black American folk music.

Leadbelly was released in 1934 with help from John Lomax, and began an extended relationship with him and his son, serving as driver and valet while making recordings and preparing plans for concerts. It was Lomax's intention to make Leadbelly and — as his manager and "discoverer" — himself into stars. On the positive side, this resulted in Lomax trying to get Leadbelly to record virtually every song he knew, an impossible task given the sheer range of music to which he'd been exposed since the 1890s, but one that resulted in dozens upon dozens of sides for the Library of Congress, cut on Lomax's relatively crude "portable" recording unit, and later many attempts at commercial recording as well. On the negative side, however, it resulted in a terrible exploitation of Leadbelly, who appeared in photos and on stage in striped prison uniforms, and whose violent past was emphasized along with his musical abilities. The result was a flurry of publicity that brought Leadbelly some exposure in the White community, but also made him give one the impression of a captured savage. It would have been demeaning for any man, but was especially so for Leadbelly, and ultimately not terribly profitable for Lomax. The copyrights that he signed his name to as Leadbelly's songwriting "collaborator" ultimately proved to be worth a small fortune, but at the time, he quickly discovered that sensationalistic press didn't necessarily translate into large paying audiences. Moreover, Leadbelly quickly grew beyond Lomax's ability to control him, and later rebelled at their relationship. And Lomax found out as early as 1935, following Leadbelly's first commercial recording sessions for the American Record Company that Leadbelly's brand of blues was of virtually no interest to Black audiences, who had already moved to more moden sounds. Ironically, the ARC sides contain some of Leadbelly's best music; brought into a real recording studio for the first time, he took to the new environment like a natural, his voice booming larger than life and his guitar captured more crisply than ever before.

Leadbelly moved to New York City, and subsequently split with Lomax, although they remained close. It was in New York that Leadbelly came to find some success, reaching a small, but dedicated, following of White listeners, mostly consisting of folk song enthusiasts and members of the city's uniquely Bohemian intelligentsia. Leadbelly did some sessions for Musicraft, and also for Bluebird label, but his major activities during the early '40s were with Moe Asch, the founder of Folkways Records.

Leadbelly's music at any phase of his career was startling. but his sound also evolved, a process made all the more vivid by the many different versions of his songs that he recorded across his career. By the early '40s, he even began to develop a consciousness that prefigured the topical songwriters of the early '60s. This was all pretty strong stuff to do in the middle of World War II. And, yet, Leadbelly also did whole programs and concerts devoted to songs intended specifically to entertain children and those recordings were among the most successful of the huge body of his work that Moe Asch recorded.

Leadbelly never gave up the hope that he might become a star in the music world, and recognized enough that was special in his life story that he even tried to interest Hollywood in signing him up. That didn't work, although a visit to California did result in a short-lived contract with Capitol Records in 1944, yielding a dozen sides.

Soon after this period, however, he began developing the health problems that would ultimately kill him. Leadbelly continued working into 1949, but it was too early for the folk revival boom that would have embraced him. He played his last concert at the University of Texas on June 15th of that year. The recording of that concert is very poignant—as he leaves the stage, he promises to come back, vowing to get well now that he has a new doctor. Instead, he was hospitalized a month later, and died in New York on December 6, 1949. Two years later, his one-time protégés the Weavers had a million-selling hit with their recording of "Goodnight Irene," starting the whole folk-song revival—and six years later, England's Lonnie Donegan had a hit with a version of "Rock Island Line," a song that Leadbelly adapted and brought to modern audiences.

Leadbelly's place in blues history is a peculiar one; unassailable as a source for much of the country-blues repertory as it has been passed down to us, and a major contributor to the folk music revival of the 1950s, but virtually non-existent in terms of his effect upon the commercial blues market in his own lifetime or since. —*Bruce Eder*

Convict Blues / 1935 / Aldabra ♦♦♦♦
Convict Blues collects a number of recordings he made for the American Record Corporation in 1935, which were, for the most part, never released. These 16 tracks are straight blues songs, delivered with passion. While it's not as essential as his Folkways or Library of Congress recordings, there's a wealth of terrific music here. —*Thom Owens*

Leadbelly [Columbia] / 1935 / Columbia ♦♦♦♦
Columbia's original ARC collection, made up of some of his better 1935 sides. A glorious work that was one of the best collections of its kind until *King of the 12-string Guitar* came out. —*Bruce Eder*

Congress Blues / 194 / Aldabra ♦♦♦♦
Congress Blues collects a batch of folk songs that Leadbelly recorded in the early '40s. There is wonderful music here, to be sure, but it is available on better collections from Folkways and Rounder. —*Thom Owens*

Includes Legendary Performances Never Before Released / Mar. 21, 1952 / Columbia ♦♦♦♦
While one should always be suspicious about how "legendary" material can be that was originally withheld from circulation, there's little that Leadbelly did that isn't worth hearing. That holds true here. —*Ron Wynn*

☆ **Library of Congress Recordings [2 LPs]** / 1966 / Elektra ♦♦♦♦♦
These powerful performances date from 1939-43 when Ledbetter had moved to New York City after his years in prison. He was a fluid performer and his command of his trademark 12-string guitar is evident. Recorded by John and Alan Lomax, these sessions include "BollWeevil," "The Titanic," "Tight like That," and "Henry Ford Blues." —*Richard Meyer*

Good Mornin' Blues (1936-1940) / 1969 / Biograph ♦♦♦♦
Wonderful mid-'30s and early-'40s material from Leadbelly, including some of his finest and most colorful blues tunes and good folk numbers as well. —*Ron Wynn*

Bourgeois Blues: Golden Classics, Pt. 1 / 198 / Collectables ♦♦♦
Thirteen songs, mostly from the early '40s (though there are no credits or sessionography), featuring a wide range of Leadbelly's repertory, from topical to traditional, and with the singer playing accordion in addition to his usual guitar. —*Bruce Eder*

Leadbelly Sings Folk Songs / 1990 / Smithsonian/Folkways ♦♦♦♦
Leadbelly was a consummate song stylist; not necessarily a blues artist, although he certainly could deliver the blues with earnestness and authority. His forte was taking all types of songs, whether they were simple, filled with chilling metaphors, funny stories, or tragic events, and making them unforgettable personal anthems. That's what he does on all 15 cuts on *Leadbelly Sings Folk Songs*, teaming with such fellow greats as Woody Guthrie, Cisco

Houston, and Sonny Terry. Leadbelly made many great albums with Folkways; this was certainly among them. —*Ron Wynn*

Golden Classics: Pt. 2 (Defense Blues) / 1990 / Collectables ♦♦♦
Rather thin at ten songs, of indeterminate origin, but the material is all very strong, including "Defense Blues," "Jim Crow," and a short version of "Midnight Special." —*Bruce Eder*

Sings Folk Songs / 1990 / Smithsonian/Folkways ♦♦♦♦
Included are '40s Folkways recordings with Woody Guthrie, Cisco Houston, and Sonny Terry. —*Mark A. Humphrey*

Alabama Bound / 1990 / RCA ♦♦♦♦
Sixteen of the sides that Leadbelly cut for Victor's Bluebird label in the summer of 1940, many backed by the Golden Gate Singers. The mix of blues with a gospel chorus doesn't always work, although "Pick a Bale of Cotton," "Rock Island Line," and "Midnight Special" are appealing, and there are Leadbelly solo covers of "Roberta," "Easy Rider," "New York City," etc. —*Bruce Eder*

☆ **Gwine Dig a Hole to Put the Devil In** / 1991 / Rounder ♦♦♦♦♦
An excellent sampling of material from Leadbelly's early Library of Congress sessions, including versions of some of the first songs he ever learned, "Green Corn" and "Po' Howard," his song to Governor Neff that helped secure his release from a Texas prison in 1925, his first recorded version of "If It Wasn't for Dickie" (later transformed into "Kisses Sweeter than Wine")—the master of which is, alas, somewhat damaged—and "C. C. Rider." —*Bruce Eder*

Let It Shine on Me / 1991 / Rounder ♦♦♦♦
The third volume of Leadbelly's incredible Library of Congress sessions includes several searing spiritual numbers, among them "Down In The Valley To Pray," "Must I Be Carried To The Sky," "Run Sinners," and "You Must Have That Religion, Hallaloo." The CD begins with an informative interview/performance segment that features Leadbelly answering questions about his life and stylistic influences, then demonstrating techniques and recounting the origins of particular songs. The disc also contains an interesting renditions of "When I Was A Cowboy" and the topical tunes "Mr. Hitler," "The Scottsboro Boys," and "The Roosevelt Song." Leadbelly's mournful, moving, and authoritative vocals, plus his sometimes surging, sometimes reflective guitar playing, were never more moving or appealing than during the Library of Congress sessions. —*Ron Wynn*

☆ **Midnight Special** / 1991 / Rounder ♦♦♦♦♦
The earliest of Leadbelly's surviving Library of Congress recordings, from 1934, in surprisingly good sound. This is where it all started, and the power and sheer kinetic energy of these songs remains undiminished more than 60 years later. Includes "Irene," "Midnight Special," and "Matchbox Blues." —*Bruce Eder*

Leadbelly ("Irene Goodnight") / 1992 / Blues Encore ♦♦♦♦
The best anthology on Leadbelly to date—unfortunately, it's also a bootleg from Italy, where this material is considered fair game. Includes an excellent overview of Leadbelly's work from the 1930s to his final concert in 1949 ("Goodnight Irene"), with recordings from the Victor and ARC sessions as well. Excellent transfer, sketchy notes, decent sessionography. —*Bruce Eder*

Complete Studio Recordings, Vols. 4-5 / 1994 / Document ♦♦♦♦
These two European bootlegs cover a lot of material available elsewhere on legitimate American releases, but between them, they also contain the complete Leadbelly Capitol recording sessions of 1944, which have never surfaced on CD. The quality is superb, and the material is unique as the last commetcial sides that Leadbelly ever cut. —*Bruce Eder*

Kisses Sweeter Than Wine / 1994 / Omega ♦♦♦♦
NOTE: This is actually a Weavers double-CD, and if you buy it for the Leadbelly material, make sure that it has the third bonus disc with his stuff on it inside. A dozen songs cut by Leadbelly for Musicraft in 1947—not mentioned in any discography—and forgotten for the next 46 years, all found on tapes in the label owner's garage when he moved to Florida. The singing is good, the material is unique, and it includes his last recording of "If It Wasn't for Dickie," the Irish folk song Leadbelly taught the Weavers that turned into "Kisses Sweeter than Wine." —*Bruce Eder*

Nobody Knows the Trouble I've Seen, Vol. 5 / Mar. 30, 1994 / Rounder ♦♦♦♦
This is another excellent installment in Rounder's reissue of Leadbelly's Library of Congress recordings. —*AMG*

Pickup on This / Mar. 30, 1994 / Rounder ◆◆◆◆
Like the other volumes that came before it, *Pickup on This* is full of wonderful music and interviews from Leadbelly's Library of Congress recordings. —*AMG*

The Titanic, Vol. 4 / Mar. 30, 1994 / Rounder ◆◆◆◆
Later Leadbelly Library of Congress recordings, from 1939-43, including several children's songs and quasi-biographical and topical material, including "Mister Tom Hughes' Town." —*Bruce Eder*

Leadbelly's Last Sessions / 1995 / Smithsonian/Folkways ◆◆◆
Four CDs containing the best part of Leadbelly's only recordings on magnetic recording tape, which allowed him to stretch his songs to their usual length for the first time on record. The clarity of the recording, the presence of the between-song comments, and the selection of material makes this a seminal part of any serious collection. —*Bruce Eder*

Goodnight Irene [Tradition] / 1996 / Tradition ◆◆◆◆
The date of these recordings is unclear, and the sleeve is not of much help. The liner notes identify them as being taped in 1943 and 1944, while the back cover confidently refers to a 1939 date [though it seems much more likely that they were made in the 1940s]. At any rate, these are very good performances, with Leadbelly in fine voice. Most are performed solo on his 12-string guitar, although Sonny Terry and Josh White make cameos on one track each. "Goodnight Irene," "New Orleans" (essentially the same song as "House of the Rising Sun"), "John Hardy," and "When I Was a Cowboy" are all among the most famous tunes that he helped to popularize. But at a mere 28 minutes, this is pretty short on running time. —*Richie Unterberger*

Leadbelly in Concert / 1996 / Magnum ◆◆◆◆
Leadbelly's final concert from June 15, 1949, reissued on CD at last. The sound is very clean, the fidelity excellent, and the recording indispensable. —*Bruce Eder*

Where Did You Sleep Last Night: Lead Belly Legacy, Vol. 1 / Feb. 20, 1996 / Smithsonian/Folkways ◆◆◆◆
The bulk of the best performances by Leadbelly—whose influence on the folk revival of the 1950s and '60s cannot be overstated—were recorded during the 1940s for Folkways Records founder Moses Asch. Inferior copies and rerecordings of these tunes have appeared over the years, but the original masters have sat in the vaults of Folkways. The three-volume "Leadbelly Legacy" collection shows what we've not been missing: The compilers dug out the best-available versions of Leadbelly's finest songs and carefully transferred them from the original acetate masters. As the liner notes promise, "these recordings can again be heard the way they sounded in the early 1940s, for in the original masters you can still hear the ringing of the guitar and thumping of the bass." This 34-song first volume is a must for anyone interested in the roots of American folk. It opens with "Irene," which (as "Goodnight Irene") became a national hit for the Weavers less than a year after Leadbelly died on welfare; it includes many more of his most-famous tunes, among them "Rock Island Line," "Cotton Fields," and "Good Morning Blues." —*Jeff Burger*

In the Shadow of the Gallows Pole / Apr. 1996 / Rykodisc ◆◆◆
There seems to be some kind of unwritten rule against giving exact session dates on most Tradition CD reissues, although at least one of the tracks comes from 1939. The sleeve does note that the material "is digitally remastered directly from rare, mint condition 78s contained in Leadbelly's first full album, *Negro Sinful Songs,* and from 78s released on the Stinson label." There's some interest in the variety of instrumentation—Leadbelly uses not only his 12-string guitar, but also piano and button accordion (the last of which is used to unusual effect on the version of "John Hardy"). "The Bourgeois Blues" is also a bit unusual in that its lyric derives not from folk traditions, but from an incident in Washington, D.C. in 1935 in which Leadbelly encountered segregation. This couldn't be recommended as one of his more essential releases, however, particularly as the running time is a mere 28 minutes. —*Richie Unterberger*

★ **King of the 12-String Guitar** / 1997 / Columbia/Legacy ◆◆◆◆◆
Although Huddie Ledbetter had recorded for the Library of Congress while still in jail in 1933, this CD contains some of the music from his earliest commercial recording date, only five months after getting out of prison for the second (and final) time. The majority of the material (other than the first four numbers) consists of alternate takes and previously unissued performances, although some of the numbers were formerly out on LPs by Folkways or Biograph. The music (ranging from blues to folk music) is highly recommended both to veteran collectors (who otherwise probably do not have most of these cuts) and to those just discovering the legendary and unique musician. Forty-six at the time, Leadbelly's powerful voice and his work on 12-string guitar are consistently memorable. —*Scott Yanow*

Bourgeois Blues: Lead Belly Legacy, Vol. 2 / Mar. 18, 1997 / Smithsonian/Folkways ◆◆◆◆
Volume two in a three-volume series of the recordings Leadbelly made for Folkways founder Moses Asch is as indispensable as the first. The 28 songs have been beautifully remastered, and the liner notes—including a 1946 tribute by Woody Guthrie—are extensive and revealing. This second CD focuses mostly on best-available versions of songs that first appeared on Folkways' *Easy Rider: Leadbelly's Legacy, Vol. 4* and *Midnight Special.* Among the standout tracks: Leadbelly's own "Bourgeois Blues" and such folk standards as "Careless Love," "John Henry" and "Midnight Special." —*Jeff Burger*

Shout On: Lead Belly Legacy, Vol. 3 / Mar. 17, 1998 / Smithsonian/Folkways ◆◆◆◆
This third and final volume in Smithsonian Folkways' "Leadbelly Legacy" series includes a remastered version of his influential *Shout On* Folkways album, plus more than a dozen other selections taken from various sources. Particularly considering the age of the original masters, the sound quality is remarkable; the liner notes here—including track-by-track commentary and an essay by Pete Seeger—go a long way toward explaining how a poor black prisoner defied all odds to capture the American imagination. This 32-song disc includes excellent readings of "Birmingham Jail," "How Long, How Long," "National Defense Blues," and more, but the highlight is a spirited five-track collaboration with Woody Guthrie and Cisco Houston. —*Jeff Burger*

Led Zeppelin

f. Jul. 1968, London, England, **db.** Dec. 1980
Group / Blues-Rock, Hard Rock, Heavy Metal, Electric British Blues
Led Zeppelin was the definitive heavy metal band. It wasn't just their crushingly loud interpretation of the blues—it was how they incorporated mythology, mysticism, and a variety of other genres (most notably world music and British folk)—into their sound. Led Zeppelin had mystique. They rarely gave interviews, since the music press detested the band. Consequently, the only connection the audience had with the band was through the records and the concerts. More than any other band, Led Zeppelin established the concept of album-oriented rock, refusing to release popular songs from their albums as singles. In doing so, they established the dominant format for heavy metal, as well as the genre's actual sound.

Led Zeppelin formed out of the ashes of the Yardbirds. Jimmy Page had joined the band in its final days, playing a pivotal role on their final album, 1967's *Little Games,* which also featured string arrangements from John Paul Jones. During 1967, the Yardbirds were fairly inactive. While the Yardbirds decided their future, Page returned to session work in 1967. In the spring of 1968, he played on Jones' arrangement of Donovan's "Hurdy Gurdy Man." During the sessions, Jones requested to be part of any future project Page would develop. Page would have to assemble a band sooner than he had planned. In the summer of 1968, the Yardbirds' Keith Relf and James McCarty left the band, leaving Page and bassist Chris Dreja with the rights to the name, as well as the obligation of fulfilling an upcoming fall tour. Page set out to find a replacement vocalist and drummer. Initially, he wanted to enlist Procol Harum's singer Terry Reid and the band's drummer B.J. Wilson, but neither musician was able to join the group. Reid suggested that Page contact Robert Plant, who was singing with a band called Hobbstweedle.

After hearing him sing, Page asked Plant to join the band in August of 1968, the same month Chris Dreja dropped out of the new project. Following Dreja's departure, John Paul Jones joined the group as its bassist. Plant recommended that Page hire John Bonham, the drummer for Plant's old band, the Band of Joy. Bonham had to be persuaded to join the group, as he was being courted by other artists who offered the drummer considerably more money. By September, Bonham agreed to join the band.

Performing under the name the New Yardbirds, the band fulfilled the Yardbirds' previously booked engagements in late September 1968. The following month, they recorded their debut album in just under 30 hours. Also in October, the group switched their name to Led Zeppelin. The band secured a contract with Atlantic Records in the United States before the end of the year. Early in 1969, Led Zeppelin set out on their first American tour, which helped set the stage for the January release of their eponymous debut album. Two months after its release, *Led Zeppelin* had climbed into the US Top Ten. Throughout 1969, the band toured relentlessly, playing dates in America and England. While they were on the road, they recorded their second album, *Led Zeppelin II*, which was released in October of 1969. Like its predecessor, *Led Zeppelin II* was an immediate hit, topping the American charts two months after its release and spending seven weeks at number one. The album helped establish Led Zeppelin as an international concert attraction, and for the next year, the group continued to tour relentlessly.

Led Zeppelin's sound began to deepen with *Led Zeppelin III*. Released in October of 1970, the album featured an overt British folk influence. The group's infatuation with folk and mythology would reach a fruition on the group's untitled fourth album, which was released in November of 1971. *Led Zeppelin IV* was the band's most musically diverse effort to date, featuring everything from the crunching rock of "Black Dog" to the folk of "The Battle of Evermore," as well as "Stairway to Heaven," which found the bridge between the two genres. "Stairway to Heaven" was an immediate radio hit, eventually becoming the most played song in the history of album-oriented radio; the song was never released as a single. Despite the fact that the album never reached number one in America, *Led Zeppelin IV* was their biggest album ever, selling well over 16 million copies over the next two and a half decades.

Led Zeppelin did tour to support both *Led Zeppelin III* and *Led Zeppelin IV*, but they played fewer shows than they did on their previous tours. Instead, they concentrated on only playing larger venues. After completing their 1972 tour, the band retreated from the spotlight and recorded their fifth album. Released in the spring of 1973, *Houses of the Holy* continued the band's musical experimentation, featuring touches of funk and reggae among their trademark rock and folk. *Houses of the Holy* debuted at number one in both America and Britain, setting the stage for a record-breaking American tour. Throughout their 1973 tour, Led Zeppelin broke box-office records—most of which were previously held by the Beatles—across America. The group's concert at Madison Square Garden in July was filmed for use in the feature film *The Song Remains the Same*, which was released three years later. After their 1973 tour, Led Zeppelin spent a quiet year during 1974, releasing no new material and performing no concerts. They did, however, establish their own record label, Swan Song, which released all of Led Zeppelin's subsequent albums, as well as records by Dave Edmunds, Bad Company, the Pretty Things, and several others. *Physical Graffiti*, a double album released in February of 1975, was the band's first release on Swan Song. The album was an immediate success, topping the charts in both America and England. Led Zeppelin was planning to launch a large American tour in the late summer of 1975 when Robert Plant and his wife suffered a serious car crash while vacationing in Greece. Plans for the tour were cancelled and Plant spent the rest of the year recuperating from the accident.

Led Zeppelin returned to action in the spring of 1976 with *Presence*. Although the album debuted at number one in both America and England, the reviews for the album were lukewarm, as was the reception to the live concert film *The Song Remains the Same*, which appeared in the fall of 1976. The band finally returned to tour America in the Spring of 1977. A couple of months into the tour, Plant's six-year-old son Karac died of a stomach infection. Led Zeppelin immediately cancelled the tour and offered no word whether or not it would be rescheduled, causing widespread speculation about the band's future. For a while, it did appear that Led Zeppelin was finished. Robert Plant spent the latter half of 1977 and the better part of 1978 in seclusion. The group didn't begin work on a new album until late in the summer of 1978, when they began recording at ABBA's Polar studios in Sweden. A year later, the band played a short European tour, performing in Switzerland, Germany, Holland, Belgium, and Austria. In August of 1979, Led Zeppelin played two large concerts at Knebworth; the shows would be their last English performances.

In Through the Out Door, the band's much-delayed eighth studio album, was finally released in September of 1979. The album entered the charts at number one in both America and England. In May of 1980, Led Zeppelin embarked on their final European tour. In September, Led Zeppelin began rehearsing at Jimmy Page's house in preparation for an American tour. On September 25, John Bonham was found dead in his bed—following an all-

day drinking binge, he had passed out and choked on his own vomit. In December of 1980, Led Zeppelin announced they were disbanding, since they could not continue without Bonham.

Following the breakup, the remaining members all began solo careers. John Paul Jones never released a solo album. Instead, he returned to producing and arranging. After recording the soundtrack for *Death Wish II*, Jimmy Page compiled the Zeppelin outtakes collection, *Coda*, which was released at the end of 1982. That same year, Robert Plant began a solo career with the *Pictures at Eleven* album. In 1984, Plant and Page briefly reunited in the all-star oldies band the Honeydrippers. After recording one EP with the Honeydrippers, Plant returned to his solo career and Page formed the Firm with former Bad Company singer Paul Rogers. In 1985, Led Zeppelin reunited to play Live Aid, sparking off a flurry of reunion rumors; the reunion never materialized. In 1988, the band re-formed to play Atlantic's 25th Anniversary Concert. During 1989, Page remastered the band's catalog for release on the 1990 box set, *Led Zeppelin*. The four-disc set became the biggest selling multi-disc box set of all time. In 1994, Jimmy Page and Robert Plant reunited to record a segment for *MTV Unplugged*, which was released as *Unledded* in the fall of 1994. Although the album went platinum, the sales were disappointing considering the anticipation of a Zeppelin reunion. The following year, Page and Plant embarked on a successful international tour. — *Stephen Thomas Erlewine*

☆ **Led Zeppelin [I]** / Jan. 12, 1969 / Swan Song ✦✦✦✦✦
Led Zeppelin had a full-formed, distinctive sound from the outset, as their eponymous debut illustrates. Taking the heavy, distorted electric blues of Jimi Hendrix, Jeff Beck, and Cream to an extreme, Zeppelin created a majestic, powerful guitar-rock constructed around simple, memorable riffs and lumbering rhythms. But the key to the group's attack was subtlety—it wasn't just an onslaught of guitar noise, but it was shaded and textured, filled with alternating dynamics and tempos. As *Led Zeppelin* proves, the group was capable of such multi-layered music from the start. Although the extended psychedelic blues of "Dazed and Confused," "You Shook Me," and "I Can't Quit You Baby" often gather the most attention, the remainder of the album is a better indication of what would come later. "Babe I'm Gonna Leave You" shifts from folky verses to pummeling choruses, "Good Times Bad Times" and "How Many More Times" have groovy, bluesy shuffles, "Your Time Is Gonna Come" is an anthemic hard-rocker, "Black Mountain Side" is pure English folk, and "Communication Breakdown" is a frenzied rocker with a nearly punkish attack. Although the album isn't as varied as some of their later efforts, it nevertheless marked a significant turning point in the evolution of hard rock and heavy metal. — *Stephen Thomas Erlewine*

☆ **Led Zeppelin II** / Oct. 22, 1969 / Swan Song ✦✦✦✦✦
Recorded quickly during Led Zeppelin's first American tours, *Led Zeppelin II* provided the blueprint for all the heavy metal bands that followed it. Since the group could only enter the studio for brief amounts of time, the material that comprises *II* is almost entirely re-worked blues and rock 'n' roll standards that the band were performing onstage at the time. Not only did the short amount of time result in a lack of original material, it made the sound more direct. Jimmy Page still provided layers of guitar overdubs, but the overall sound of the album is heavy and hard, brutal and direct. "Whole Lotta Love," "The Lemon Song," and "Bring It on Home" are all based on classic blues songs, only the riffs are simpler and louder, and each song has an extended section for instrumental solos. Out of the remaining six songs, two sport light acoustic touches ("Thank You," "Ramble On"), but the other four are straightahead heavy rock, that follow the formula of the revamped blues songs. While *Led Zeppelin II* doesn't have the eclecticism of their debut, it was arguably more influential. After all, nearly every one of the hundreds of Zeppelin imitators used this record, with its lack of dynamics and its pummeling riffs, as a blueprint. — *Stephen Thomas Erlewine*

☆ **Led Zeppelin III** / Oct. 5, 1970 / Swan Song ✦✦✦✦✦
On their first two albums, Led Zeppelin issued a relentless assault of heavy blues and rockabilly riffs, and *Led Zeppelin III* provided the band with the necessary room to grow musically. While there are still a handful of metallic rockers, *III* is built on a folky, acoustic foundation which gives the music extra depth. And even the rockers aren't as straightforward as before—the galloping "Immigrant Song" is powered by Plant's banshee wail, "Celebration Day" turns blues-rock inside out with a warped slide guitar riff, and "Out on the Tiles" lumbers along with a tricky, multi-part riff. Nevertheless, the heart

of the album lies on the second side, when the band delves deeply into English folk. "Gallows Pole" updates a traditional tune with a menacing flair, and "Bron-Y-Aur Stomp" is an infectious acoustic romp, while "That's the Way" and "Tangerine" are shimmering songs with graceful country flourishes. The band hasn't left the blues behind, but the twisted bottleneck blues of "Hats Off to (Roy) Harper" actually outstrips the epic "Since I've Been Loving You," which is the only time Zeppelin sounds a bit set in their ways. — *Stephen Thomas Erlewine*

★ **Led Zeppelin IV** / Nov. 8, 1971 / Swan Song ♦♦♦♦♦
Encompassing heavy metal, folk, pure rock 'n' roll, and blues, Led Zeppelin's untitled fourth album is a monolithic record, defining not only Led Zeppelin but the sound and style of '70s hard rock. Expanding the breakthroughs of *III*, Zeppelin fuses its majestic hard rock with a mystical, rural English folk that gives the record an epic scope. Even at its most basic—the muscular, traditionalist "Rock & Roll"—the album has a grand sense of drama, which is only deepened by Plant's burgeoning obsession with mythologies, religion and the occult. Plant's mysticism comes to a head in the eerie folk ballad "The Ballad of Evermore," a mandolin-driven song with haunting vocals from Sandy Denny, and on the epic "Stairway to Heaven." Of all of Zeppelin's songs, "Stairway to Heaven" is the most famous, and not unjustly—building from a simple finger-picked acoustic guitar to a storming torrent of guitar riffs and solos, it encapsulates the entire album in one song. Which, of course, isn't discounting the rest of the album. "Going to California" is the group's best folk song, and the rockers are endlessly inventive, whether it's the complex, multi-layered "Black Dog," the pounding hippie satire "Misty Mountain Hop," or the funky riffs of "Four Sticks." But the closer, "When the Levee Breaks," is the one song truly equal to "Stairway," helping give *IV* the feeling of an epic. An apocalyptic slice of urban blues, "When the Levee Breaks" is as forceful and frightening as Zeppelin ever got, and its seismic rhythms and layered dynamics illustrate why none of their imitators could ever equal them. — *Stephen Thomas Erlewine*

☆ **Houses of the Holy** / Mar. 28, 1973 / Swan Song ♦♦♦♦♦
Houses of the Holy follows the same basic pattern as *Led Zeppelin IV*, but the approach is looser and more relaxed. Jimmy Page's riffs rely on ringing, folky hooks as much as thundering blues-rock, giving the album a lighter, more open atmosphere. While the pseudo-reggae of "D'Yer Mak'er" and the affectionate James Brown send-up "The Crunge" suggest that the band was searching for material, they actually contribute to the musical diversity of the album. "The Rain Song" is one of their finest moments, featuring a soaring string arrangement and a gentle, aching melody. "The Ocean" is just as good, starting with a typically heavy, but funky, guitar groove before slamming into an a cappella section and ending with a swinging, doo wop-flavored raveup. With the exception of the rampaging opening number "The Song Remains the Same," the rest of *Houses of the Holy* is fairly straightforward, ranging from the foreboding "No Quarter" and the strutting hard rock of "Dancing Days" to the epic folk/metal fusion "Over the Hills and Far Away." Throughout the record, the band's playing is excellent, making the eclecticism of Page and Plant's songwriting sound coherent and natural. — *Stephen Thomas Erlewine*

☆ **Physical Graffiti** / Feb. 24, 1975 / Swan Song ♦♦♦♦♦
Led Zeppelin returned from a nearly two year hiatus in 1975 with the double-album *Physical Graffiti*, their most sprawling and ambitious work. Where *Led Zeppelin IV* and *Houses of the Holy* integrated the influences on each song, the majority of the songs on *Physical Graffiti* are individual stylistic workouts. The highlights are when Zeppelin incorporate influences together and stretch out into new stylistic territory, most notably on the tense, Eastern-influenced "Kashmir." "Trampled Underfoot," with John Paul Jones' galloping keyboard, is their best funk-metal workout, while "Houses of the Holy" is their best attempt at pop, while "Down By the Seaside" is the closest they've come to country. Even the heavier blues—the 11-minute "In My Time of Dying," the tightly-wound "Custard Pie," and the monstrous epic "The Rover"—are louder, more extended and textured than their previous work. Also, all of the heavy songs are on the first record, leaving the rest of the album to explore more adventurous territory, whether it's acoustic tracks or grandiose but quiet epics like the affecting "Ten Years Gone." The second half of *Physical Graffiti* feels like the group is cleaning the vaults out, issuing every little scrap of music they set to tape in the past few years. That means that the album is filled with songs that aren't quite filler, but they don't quite match the peaks of the album, either. Still, even these songs have their merits—"Sick Again" is the meanest, most decadent rocker they ever recorded and the folky acoustic rock 'n' roll of "Boogie with Stu" and "Black Country Woman" may be tossed off, but they have a relaxed, off-hand charm that Zeppelin never matched. It takes a while to sort out all of the music on the album, but *Physical Graffiti* captures the whole experience of Led Zeppelin at the top of their game better than any of their other albums. — *Stephen Thomas Erlewine*

The Song Remains the Same / 1976 / Swan Song ♦♦
Led Zeppelin's initial popularity was based as much on their concerts as their albums, so it's strange that the group's only official live album is such an uninspired, boring affair. Released in conjunction with the pseudo-documentary film of the same name, *The Song Remains the Same* reproduces the very things that made Zeppelin concerts legendary—lengthy solos, intertwining interplay between Page and Plant, and ridiculously long songs ("Dazed and Confused" is nearly an entire half hour)—but the group's performance is not intoxicating, it's long-winded. As scores of bootlegs prove, Led Zeppelin could produce magic with the same formula, but *The Song Remains the Same* is excrutiatingly dull. — *Stephen Thomas Erlewine*

Presence / 1976 / Swan Song ♦♦♦
Presence scales back the size of *Physical Graffiti* to a single album, but it retains the grandiose scope of the double album. If anything, *Presence* has more majestic epics than its predecessor, opening with the surging ten-minute "Achilles Last Stand" and closing with the meandering, nearly ten-minute "Tea for One." In between, Zeppelin adds the lumbering blues workout "Nobody's Fault but Mine" and the terse, menacing "For Your Life," which is the best song on the album. These four tracks take up the bulk of the album, leaving three lighthearted throwaways to alleviate the foreboding atmosphere of the epics, as well as their pretensions. If all of the throwaways were as focused and funny as those on *Physical Graffiti* or *Houses of the Holy*, Zeppelin would have had another classic on their hands. However, the Crescent City love letter of "Royal Orleans" sags in the middle and the ersatz rockabilly of "Candy Store Rock" doesn't muster up the loose, funky swagger of "Hots on for Nowhere," which it *should* in order to work. The three throwaways are also scattered haphazardly throughout the album, making it seem more ponderous than it actually is, and the result is the weakest album they had yet recorded. — *Stephen Thomas Erlewine*

In Through the Out Door / 1979 / Swan Song ♦♦♦
Between *Presence* and *In Through the Out Door*, disco, punk, and new wave had overtaken rock 'n' roll, and Led Zeppelin chose to tentatively embrace the pop revolutions, adding synthesizers to the mix and emphasizing Bonham's inherent way with a groove. The album's opening number "In the Evening," with its stomping rhythms and heavy, staggered riffs, suggests that the band hasn't strayed from their course, but by the time the rolling shuffle of "South Bound Suarez" kicks into gear, it's apparent that the group have regained their sense of humor. After "South Bound Suarez," the group try a variety of styles, whether it's an overdriven homage to Bakersfield country called "Hot Dog," the layered, Latin-tinged percussion and pianos of "Fool in the Rain," or the slickly seductive ballad "All My Love." "Carouselambra," a lurching, self-consciously ambitious synth-driven number, and the slow blues "I'm Gonna Crawl" aren't quite as impressive as the rest of the album, but the record is a graceful way to close their career, even if it wasn't intended as the final chapter. — *Stephen Thomas Erlewine*

Coda / 1982 / Swan Song ♦♦♦
An odds-n-sods collection assembled after Bonham's death, *Coda* is predictably a hit-or-miss affair. The best material comes from later in their career, including the ringing folk stomp of "Poor Tom," the jacked-up '50s rock 'n' roll of "Ozone Baby," and their response to punk rock, the savage "Wearing and Tearing." The rest of the album, sadly including the Bonham showcase "Bonzo's Montreux," is average, despite the presence of some stellar playing, especially on the early blues-rock blitzkrieg "I Can't Quit You Baby" and "We're Gonna Groove." — *Stephen Thomas Erlewine*

Led Zeppelin [Box Set] / Sep. 1990 / Swan Song ♦♦♦
Led Zeppelin's primary method of artistic expression was their albums. Although they had a handful of hit singles and selected album tracks were played endlessly on the radio, the true range of their music is only evident on the original albums, which were carefully sequenced and assembled. Con-

sequently, the notion of a Led Zeppelin anthology is a bit strange—their records worked as individual pieces. Nevertheless, the four-disc box set *Led Zeppelin* includes most of their best and most famous material. Jimmy Page determined the set's running order, taking the songs out of their familiar contexts and placing them in a new, occasionally jarring, sequence, providing new insights to the band's music that dedicated fans will appreciate. *Led Zeppelin* is the only album in their catalog to include the classic B-side "Hey Hey What Can I Do," as well as their unreleased version of Robert Johnson's "Travelling Riverside Blues" and a live medley of Page's "White Summer/ Black Mountain Side." Most fans will find these three tracks essential, but will balk at the price, especially since all of Zeppelin's albums have been remastered since the original release of the box set. While the box contains a wealth of brilliant music, all of it is better-heard in its original incarnation. — *Stephen Thomas Erlewine*

Led Zeppelin Remasters / Feb. 21, 1992 / Swan Song ✦✦✦
A collection of most of Zeppelin's best-known tracks, this double-disc set only gives a slight idea of what the band accomplished in its career; stick with the original albums instead. — *Stephen Thomas Erlewine*

Led Zeppelin [Box Set 2] / Mar. 19, 1993 / Swan Song ✦✦✦
Rounding up all of the studio tracks that didn't appear on the first box (as well as the pleasant, but unremarkable, "Baby Come on Home"), *Boxed Set 2* is the perfect way to complete a Led Zeppelin library begun with the first box set. — *Stephen Thomas Erlewine*

Complete Studio Recordings / Sep. 24, 1993 / Swan Song ✦✦✦
Collecting all of Led Zeppelin's groundbreaking studio albums (as well as a reworked *Coda*) in one unattractive box, *The Complete Studio Recordings* is only necessary for hardcore fans wishing to replace their old records. Although the artwork inside the package is lavish, the box features no new material or remastering, making it completely irrelevant for those who already own the first two box sets. The music here is brilliant, but it's available in better, more attractive, and less expensive packages. — *Stephen Thomas Erlewine*

BBC Sessions / Nov. 11, 1997 / Atlantic ✦✦✦✦
Led Zeppelin's BBC sessions were among the most popular bootleg items of the rock 'n' roll era, appearing on a myriad of illegal records and CDs. They were all the more popular because of the lack of official Led Zeppelin live albums, especially since *The Song Remains the Same* failed to capture the essence of the band. For anyone that hadn't heard the recordings, the mystique of Zeppelin's BBC Sessions was somewhat mystifying, but the official 1997 release of the double-disc *BBC Sessions* offered revelations for any fan who hadn't yet heard this music. While some collectors will be dismayed by the slight trimming on the "Whole Lotta Love Medley," almost all of the group's sessions are included here, and they prove why live Zeppelin was the stuff of legend. The 1969 sessions, recorded shortly after the release of the first album, are fiery and dynamic, outstripping the studio record for sheer power. Early versions of "You Shook Me," "Communication Breakdown," "What Is & What Should Never Be," and "Whole Lotta Love" hit harder than their recorded counterparts, while covers of Sleepy John Estes' "The Girl I Love She Got Long Black Wavy Hair," Robert Johnson's "Travelling Riverside Blues," and Eddie Cochran's "Something Else" are welcome additions to the Zeppelin catalog, confirming their folk, blues, and rockabilly roots as well as their sense of vision. Zeppelin's grand vision comes into sharper relief on the second disc, which is comprised of their 1971 sessions. They still have their primal energy, but they're more adventurous, branching out into folk, twisted psychedelia, and weird blues-funk. Certainly, *BBC Sessions* is the kind of album that will only appeal to fans, but anyone who's ever doubted Zeppelin's power or vision will be set straight with this record. — *Stephen Thomas Erlewine*

Rosie Ledet

b. Oct. 25, 1971, Louisiana
Vocals / Zydeco
Accordionist, singer and songwriter Mary Roszela Bellard "Rosie" Ledet (pronounced led-dett) was raised on rock 'n' roll music. During her teenage years in southwest Louisiana, she listened to classic rock 'n' roll radio stations in nearby Eunice; her favorite groups included Santana and Z.Z. Top.

Like so many other French kids raised in rural southwest Louisiana, she

paid no particular attention to all the zydeco music that was around her in her formative years; even though her parents had tried to raise her with a healthy respect for zydeco music, the music held little appeal for her as a kid. But one day, after attending a zydeco dance when she was 16, hearing Boozoo Chavis, and meeting Morris—who would later become her husband— she was smitten.

She married Morris, the bassist in her band, when she was 17, and while he was on the road touring regionally with a group he led, she stayed home and took care of her ailing mother-in-law. It was during this period of several years that Ledet worked on her accordion playing, honing her skills. At first, she would play along to the recordings of Boozoo Chavis and John Delafose. She began to learn songs intuitively, by ear, and one day surprised her husband by playing a complete Delafose song. Her husband encouraged young Rosie to continue in her efforts, and within a matter of months, she had recorded a demo of her own songs and secured a record deal with Maison de Soul, a zydeco label in nearby Ville Platte.

In a very short time, the prolific songwriter has released three albums of her own material, and her backing band includes her husband and father-in-law on bass and rub board, respectively. Ledet's albums include *Sweet Brown Sugar* (1994), *Zesty Zydeco* (1995) and *Zydeco Sensation* (1997), all for the Maison de Soul label of the Flat Town Music Co. in Ville Platte. All three of Ledet's albums showcase superb songs, strong vocals and adequate accordion playing.

She and her band began performing in 1994 throughout the Texas-Louisiana triangle, where they continue to concentrate their efforts, and gradually began to spread their touring base to include the rest of the US. In the last two years, Ledet and band have been on several European tours as well. — *Richard J. Skelly*

● **Sweet Brown Sugar** / 1994 / Maison de Soul ✦✦✦✦
Since there aren't many female zydeco singers, the very existence of Rosie Ledet would be noteworthy. Fortunately, her debut album, *Sweet Brown Sugar*, shows that there's a reason to be interested in her outside of sheer novelty. Ledet proves herself to be a strong songwriter and energetic accordionist on *Sweet Brown Sugar*. Her voice may be a little too restrained for some tastes, but she makes up for that with her propulsive, infectious instrumental work. Also, her songs suggest that she could develop into a distinctive lyrical voice in her own right. All in all, it's a fine debut. — *Thom Owens*

Zesty Zydeco / 1995 / Maison de Soul ✦✦
Floyd Soileau's Ville Platte, Louisiana-based Maison de Soul label has been cranking out a lot of fair-to-middling zydeco in recent years, and *Zesty Zydeco* is another effort that fails to rise from the pack. That's too bad, because as one of few female zydeco singers, Rosie Ledet has potential to stand out. There are two terrific songs on this disc: "Casino Nights" (a catchy little tune in which she warns her man that he'll lose her love as well as his money if he keeps going out to play the slot machines instead of staying home with her) and "I'm Gonna Take Care of Your Dog" (a deliciously sexy song about a "pussycat" who threatens to steal another woman's "dog" that keeps coming into her yard). More than any other music in America, zydeco remains a family affair, and her band consists mostly of other Ledets. Zydeco is a simple music form—that's part of its charm—but the same pentatonic ostinatos played over and over on the accordion become monotonous over the length of this CD. — *Steve Hoffman*

Zydeco Sensation / 1997 / Maison de Soul ✦✦✦

Bonnie Lee

b. Jun. 11, 1931, Bunkie, LA
Vocals / Modern Electric Chicago Blues, Chicago Blues
Although she's been singing on the Chicago scene since the 1960s, Bonnie Lee is mostly renowned for one song: the mid-tempo grinder "I'm Good," which has become her trademark (she's cut it several times, including a solid version on bassist Willie Kent's 1992 Delmark set *Ain't It Nice*; and Johnny Winter covered it on his Alligator LP *Third Degree*). — *Bill Dahl*

● **Sweetheart of the Blues** / 1995 / Delmark ✦✦✦✦
Bonnie Lee cut her first full-length album, *Sweetheart of the Blues*, in 1995, nearly 30 years after she established herself as a staple of the Chicago scene. During those years, she sang constantly, and it's clear from the first note that this album is the work of a seasoned pro. Lee pretty much sticks to standards

like "Baby, What You Want Me to Do," "Walking Blues," and "That's All Right," but that's all right, because it gives her the opportunity to wail. And wail she does, proving she's a fine soul-blues vocalist, capable of great things. She doesn't reach greatness here, but *Sweetheart of the Blues* is a classy set of Chicago blues. It's just too bad that it took her so long to cut the record. — *Stephen Thomas Erlewine*

Bryan Lee

b. 1945, WI
Modern Electric Blues
A longtime staple of New Orleans' famed Bourbon Street club circuit, blues guitarist Bryan Lee was born in Wisconsin in 1945. Inspired by B.B. King, Albert King and others, his Midwest upbringing also resulted in a distinctively Chicago-styled sound which his long stay in the South did little to erase. Billed variously as "The Braille Blues Daddy" and "The Blind Blues Daddy," Lee first surfaced in New Orleans in 1983, quickly becoming a favorite of tourists in the city's French Quarter and regularly playing live at least six nights a week; he made his solo debut in 1991 with *The Blues Is...*, followed in 1993 by *Memphis Bound.* After 1995's *Heat Seeking Missile,* Lee issued 1997's *Live at the Old Absinthe House Bar: Friday Night,* an ideal souvenir for the many patrons of his club dates. — *Jason Ankeny*

● **The Blues Is...** / 1991 / Justin Time ◆◆◆◆
Bryan Lee's debut album *Blues Is...* is a solid collection of greasy New Orleans blues. While he may not always have great original songs, Lee can conjure the sound of the swamp with his big, bluesy guitar, and that's enough to make this an entertaining listen, especially for fans of Crescent City blues. — *Thom Owens*

Memphis Bound / 1993 / Justin Time ◆◆◆◆

Braille Blues Daddy / Feb. 21, 1995 / Justin Time ◆◆◆

Heat Seeking Missile / Oct. 1995 / Justin Time ◆◆◆

Live at the Old Absinthe House Bar: Friday Night / Nov. 4, 1997 / Justin Time ◆◆◆

Frankie Lee

b. Apr. 29, 1941, Mart, TX
Vocals / Soul, R&B, Soul Blues, Modern Electric Blues
Vocalist Frankie Lee has always been an engaging and energetic live performer, though his recorded output is still very small, given the number of years he's been around and how legendary his live shows have become. If Denise LaSalle is a modern day Bessie Smith, then Lee is a 1990s Otis Redding. One of Lee's live-show trademarks (like the late Albert Collins' guitar walks) is the point in the show in which he leaves his mic on stage and walks out into his audience, be it a festival of 10,000 people or a small club of 50. Lee's motto is, "whether it's one or 1,000, me and my band are gonna put on a show."

Lee was born April 29, 1941, in rural Mart, TX. His early influences included Sam Cooke, but before that, he sang in church groups. He recalled in several interviews that his grandmother made him sing, never realizing he'd end up singing blues, not gospel. He began recording in 1963 with Don Robey's Duke/Peacock label out of Houston. He recorded three singles that attracted regional attention: "Full Time Lover," "Taxi Blues," and "Hello, Mr. Blues." While he and Sonny Rhodes were living in Austin, Lee was heard by Ike Turner. That night, Turner invited him to join the Ike & Tina Turner road show. He was off with them the next day, gaining invaluable performing experience.

After returning from the road trips with their revue, Lee settled in Houston and had the chance to work with the people he admired, including Big Mama Thornton, Bobby "Blue" Bland, Clarence "Gatemouth" Brown, Ted Taylor, Junior Parker, O.V. Wright, James "Thunderbird" Davis, and Joe Hinton. Don Robey heard Lee in a Houston nightclub and offered him the chance to record. Later, Lee began working with guitarist Albert Collins, and the two became good friends, finally leaving Texas together in 1965 for California. Lee sang with Collins' band for the next six years. By 1971, Lee was in Los Angeles, working with his cousin Johnny "Guitar" Watson. (Watson passed away at age 61 on May 17, 1996.) He recorded for Elka Records, with Watson producing. In 1973, Lee moved north to the San Francisco Bay area, and in the late '70s, he recruited a young guitarist, Robert Cray, to play in his back-

up band. Finally Lee landed a contract with Hightone Records, a then developing label, and recorded his debut album, *The Ladies and the Babies* in 1984.

After successful performances with Sonny Rhodes at the Chicago Blues Festival, Lee moved to New Jersey in 1986, where he quickly established a following at clubs and festivals throughout the northeast. Lee was signed to record for the Flying Fish label in 1992, and *Sooner or Later,* with Doug Newby and the Virginia-based Bluzblasters, was the result. Lee's latest release, *Going Back Home,* is on the San Francisco-based Blind Pig label. The album was actually recorded back in the mid-'80s, but wasn't released until 1994.

Oddly enough, as of the mid-'90s, Lee's live clubs shows were as energetic as ever, and he's lost none of his enthusiasm for performing, despite the fact that he's now in his mid-50s. He's got a whole lot of talent and energy left, so there will be more recordings from this exciting vocalist and showman in the future. Records worth owning include *The Ladies and the Babies* and *Going Back Home.* Any of his singles for the Peacock or Elka labels, such as "Full Time Lover" b/w "Don't Make Me Cry," are collector's items, and should be snatched up without hesitation. — *Richard Skelly*

● **Ladies & the Babies** / Apr. 1986 / Hightone ◆◆◆◆
Frankie Lee's debut album, *The Ladies and the Babies,* was one of the first contemporary blues albums to successfully negotiate the territory between post-Bobby Bland blues and southern soul. As one of the first albums on Hightone Records, the album helped set the stage for the numerous records and artists that teetered between soul and blues. To Lee's immense credit, he achieved this balance quite skillfully, thanks to solid songs, tight arrangements and powerful vocalists. He followed the record with several others quite like it, but none matched the energy or quality of *The Ladies and the Babies.* — *Thom Owens*

Going Back Home / 1994 / Blind Pig ◆◆◆

Lovie Lee

b. Mar. 17, 1909, Chattanooga, TN, **d.** May 23, 1997, Chicago, IL
Piano / Modern Electric Blues, Contemporary Blues
Best known as Muddy Waters' final piano accompanist, the sadly underrecognized Lovie Lee was a longtime staple of the Chicago club circuit. Born Eddie Lee Watson in Chattanooga, Tennessee on March 17, 1909, he worked during the day as a factory woodworker, honing his skills each night in the Chicago blues clubs from the 1950s onward. The adoptive father of harpist Carey Bell, he acquired an impressive local reputation over time, but was little known outside of the Midwest in spite of his association with Waters during the legend's final years. In 1984 and 1989, Lee recorded much of the material which later comprised his 1992 release *Good Candy,* which was rounded out by latter-day efforts cut with Bell; his lone solo release, it too garnered little notice. Lee died May 23, 1997. — *Jason Ankeny*

Good Candy / 1992 / Earwig ◆◆◆

Left Hand Frank

b. Oct. 5, 1935, Greenville, MS, **d.** Jan. 14, 1992, Los Angeles, CA
Guitar, Vocals / Modern Electric Chicago Blues, Electric Chicago Blues
Southpaw guitarist Frank Craig (like many of his peers, he played an axe strung for a right-hander, strapping it on upside down) never really transcended his reputation as a trusty sideman instead of a leader—and that was just fine with him. But he stepped into the spotlight long enough to sing four fine tunes for Alligator's *Living Chicago Blues* anthologies in 1978.

Craig was already conversant with the guitar when he moved to Chicago at age 14. Too young to play inside the Club Zanzibar (where Muddy Waters, Little Walter, and Wolf held forth), Frank and his teenaged pals, guitarist Eddie King and bassist Willie Black, played outside the joint for tips instead. Legit gigs with harpist Willie Cobbs, guitarist James Scott, Jr., Jimmy Dawkins, Junior Wells, Good Rockin' Charles, Jimmy Rogers, and Hound Dog Taylor kept Frank increasingly active on the Chicago circuit from the mid-'50s to the late '70s. He moved to Los Angeles not too long after the Alligator session, eventually hanging up his guitar altogether due to health problems. — *Bill Dahl*

Live at the Knickerbocker Cafe / 1992 / New Rose ◆◆◆◆
Live at the Knickerbocker Cafe was recorded in the late '70s, toward the end

of Left Hand Frank's unheralded career. For much of his life, he worked as a sideman, never officially releasing a studio album as a leader. This album (originally released on the French MCM label) is the only addition to a meager discography, but it demonstrates just how much he had to offer. Left Hand Frank didn't shake up the Chicago blues tradition, choosing to celebrate it instead, and the result is a kinetic, entertaining set of greasy blues. There are a few unexpected flourishes, such as the reverb detour "Surfin' with Frank," that keep things interesting, and the end result is a cool little Chicago blues gem from a guitarist that was sadly underrecorded. — *Thom Owens*

The Legendary Blues Band

f. 1980, Chicago, IL
Group / Electric Chicago Blues, Modern Electric Blues
The Legendary Blues Band includes Calvin Jones (b.1926, Greenwood, MS; bass, violin); Willie Smith (b.1935, Helena, AR; drum); various others on vocals, guitar, harmonica, piano. When the Muddy Waters band quit the master en masse in 1980, most of the sidemen stuck together and formed their own group. The Legendary Blues Band, as they were named, included Pinetop Perkins, Jerry Portnoy, Willie Smith, and Calvin Jones throughout its early years. Short-term member Louis Myers, another Muddy Waters alumnus, appeared as guitarist on the band's first album (Rounder, 1981). The band has since changed personnel with some regularity, and while its lineup has become progressively less "legendary" in name or historic associations, its music has remained solid and true to the mainstream Chicago style. In a later configuration, they even made the *Billboard* Black Music charts. Recent albums have featured guitarist Billy Flynn and harmonicist Madison Slim. The rhythm section of Jones and Smith has anchored the unit throughout the changes, never failing to deliver the Chicago blues with aplomb. — *Jim O'Neal*

Life of Ease / 1981 / Rounder ◆◆◆
Acceptable journeyman classic-style Chicago blues, mixing originals by harmonica player Jerry Portnoy with covers of oldies by Little Richard, Leroy Carr, Jimmy Reed, and the like. — *Richie Unterberger*

● **Red Hot 'n' Blue** / 1983 / Rounder ◆◆◆◆
For their second album, the Legendary Blues Band—featuring members of Muddy Waters' backing band, including Pinetop Perkins, Peter Ward, Calvin Jones, Jerry Portnoy and Willie Smith—nearly captured the big, powerful sound of Muddy at his peak. Perkins and Jones don't have the same presence as Waters, but they're fine vocalists in their own right, and the band itself has the same intoxicating rush that made such latter-day Muddy efforts as *Hard Again* so enjoyable. And that means that *Red Hot 'N' Blue* is as close to Waters as you're going to get without Muddy himself—and that means it's one of the better Chicago blues records of its era.— *Stephen Thomas Erlewine*

Woke up with the Blues / 1989 / Ichiban ◆◆◆

Keepin' the Blues Alive / 1990 / Ichiban ◆◆◆◆
Only bassist Calvin Jones and drummer Willie Smith remain from Muddy Waters' old crew, but guitarist John Duich helps keep the traditional Chicago sound in place. — *Bill Dahl*

U B Da Judge / 1991 / Ichiban ◆◆
When *U B Da Judge* was released in 1991, the Legendary Blues Band's lineup still included former Muddy Waters sidemen Willie Smith (drums, vocals) and Calvin Jones (bass, vocals), as well as harp player Madison Slim, keyboardist Willie O'Shawny and guitarists Billy Flynn and Tony O. *U B Da Judge* isn't a great album by any means, though it has a few decent cuts, including the originals "Watch Your Enemies" and "I Can't Trust You, Man" and a cover of Jimmy Reed's "Don't Say That No More." The CD may have been recorded in Atlanta, but the band's sound is unmistakably Chicago. Completists and diehard collectors may want this so-so CD, but for beginners, the Legendary Blues Band's Rounder albums with Pinetop Perkins would be a much better investment. — *Alex Henderson*

Prime Time Blues / 1992 / Ichiban ◆◆

Money Talks / 1993 / Wild Dog ◆◆◆
All of a sudden, on their 1993's *Money Talks*, drummer Willie Smith has become a very credible singer. — *Bill Dahl*

Keri Leigh

b. Apr. 21, 1969, Birmingham, AL
Bass, Guitar, Harmonica, Drums, Percussion, Vocals / Modern Electric Blues
Vocalist, songwriter, record-producer, journalist and author Keri Leigh is one of these multi-talented, accomplished individuals that the blues music world can't seem to get enough of. And the fact that she's barely 30 years old insures that she'll be around, pursuing her number one passion—singing the blues—for a long time.

Her latest album, *Arrival*, (1995), for the Jackson, MS-based Malaco Records label, isn't with her usual backing band, the Blue Devils, but it was recorded at Muscle Shoals Studios (which Malaco owns), and Leigh and her husband acted as co-producers of the record.

Leigh moved to Austin from her native Oklahoma with her guitarist/husband Mark Lyon, in 1990. Fortunately, they were welcomed for the most part with open arms by the Austin blues community, and certainly by Clifford Antone, owner of Antone's (blues nightclub), who booked them into his place every week for about a year. Within a year or so of her moving to Austin, she began work on her first book, *Stevie Ray: Soul to Soul*, (Taylor Books, Dallas), a passionate account of the ups and downs of the late guitarist's all-too-short life. Leigh first met Vaughan when she interviewed him in 1986, and after several interviews, they became friends. In May 1990, they began work on what was to be his autobiography, but in August of that year, Vaughan was killed in a helicopter accident in Wisconsin.

Leigh's recordings all have a Joplin-esque quality to them, and one way to describe her singing style is as a Janis Joplin for the 1990s. In fact, some critics have described her as the greatest voice to come out of Texas since Joplin.

Leigh has used her background as a radio and newspaper journalist to get publicity for the Blue Devils, and a glance at her overflowing press-clips folder shows what a hustler she is. But Leigh and her band work as hard as any of the other touring blues musicians around the US, and they spend upwards of 150 nights a year on the road. Leigh's husband Lyon is one of the most naturally gifted slide guitarists you'll ever hear, and the ease with which he handles the instrument makes it look deceptively simple. In fact, good blues guitar is very difficult to play, but Lyon has all the moves down pat.

Leigh and her Blue Devils have two releases out on Amazing Records (a now-defunct label), *No Beginner* (1993) and *Blue Devil Blues*, their debut (1991), in addition to their latest Malaco album. *Arrival*, consisting of one-half originals and one-half cover tunes, is certainly the most accessible of her recordings. Leigh and her group have many more good years ahead of them; wherever they go, their affable ways earn them new friends and fans in the blues world. They also have a knack for making new blues converts out of rock 'n' rollers. — *Richard Skelly*

Blue Devil Blues / 1991 / Amazing ◆◆◆
Keri Leigh's debut album isn't much more than standard Texas blues, but her passion for the music shines through every song, and that is what makes it a worthwhile listen. Leigh and guitarist Mark Lyon lead the band through eight covers and three fairly average originals, but they deliver the material with conviction, especially when they attack nuggets like Son House's "Preachin' Blues." Leigh's forceful, raspy voice sounds terrific and Lyon is a good guitarist, but the album is hampered by its predictability. — *Thom Owens*

● **No Beginner** / Jun. 8, 1993 / Amazing ◆◆◆◆
Keri Leigh's second album, *No Beginner*, is a more distinguished effort than her debut. Leigh and her guitarist/husband Lyon stake out a territory between Texas blues and blues-rock, much like their predecessors Stevie Ray Vaughan, Janis Joplin, and ZZ Top. Leigh's music doesn't have as many rock 'n' roll overtones, but she and her band, the Blue Devils, play with a fiery rock energy and that energy comes across more clearly here than on their debut. — *Thom Owens*

Arrival / 1994-1995 / Waldoxy ◆◆◆◆
Keri Leigh is a superior vocalist who is heard at her best during her Waldoxy release singing conventional electric blues where her expressive skills (and her ability to come up with interesting lyrics) can really be heard. She wrote the words to six of the dozen selections but her two strongest performances are actually on the witty and boisterous "Use What You Got" and Koko Taylor's "Voodoo Woman" where she struts her stuff. Also worth hearing are a couple of acoustic country blues numbers although Leigh's occasional depar-

tures into Aretha Franklin-influenced R&B are throwaways. But with Mark Lyon's versatile guitar solos and a fine four-piece horn section offering her strong support, Keri Leigh's release is a well-paced set and an easily recommended release. —*Scott Yanow*

J.B. Lenoir

b. May 5, 1929, Monticello, MS, **d.** Apr. 29, 1967, Urbana, IL
Guitar, Vocals / Electric Chicago Blues, Chicago Blues
Newcomers to his considerable legacy could be forgiven for questioning J.B. Lenoir's gender upon first hearing his rocking waxings. Lenoir's exceptionally high-pitched vocal range is a fooler, but it only adds to the singular appeal of his music. His politically charged "Eisenhower Blues" allegedly caused all sorts of nasty repercussions upon its 1954 emergence on Al Benson's Parrot logo (it was quickly pulled off the shelves and replaced with Lenoir's less controversial titled "Tax Paying Blues").

J.B. (that was his entire legal handle) fell under the spell of Blind Lemon Jefferson as a wee lad, thanks to his guitar-wielding dad. Lightnin' Hopkins and Arthur Crudup were also cited as early influences. Lenoir spent time in New Orleans before arriving in Chicago in the late '40s. Boogie grooves were integral to Lenoir's infectious routine from the get-go, although his first single for Chess in 1951, "Korea Blues," was another slice of topical commentary. From late 1951 to 1953, he waxed several dates for Joe Brown's JOB logo in the company of pianist Sunnyland Slim, drummer Alfred Wallace, and on the romping "The Mojo," saxist J.T. Brown.

Lenoir waxed his most enduring piece, the infectious (and often-covered) "Mama Talk to Your Daughter," in 1954 for Al Benson's Parrot label. Lenoir's 1954-55 Parrot output and 1955-58 Checker catalog contained a raft of terrific performances, including a humorously defiant "Don't Touch My Head" (detailing his brand-new process hairdo) and "Natural Man." Lenoir's sound was unique: saxes (usually Alex Atkins and Ernest Cotton) wailed in unison behind Lenoir's boogie-driven rhythm guitar as drummer Al Galvin pounded out a rudimentary backbeat everywhere but where it customarily lays. Somehow, it all fit together.

Scattered singles for Shad in 1958 and Vee-Jay two years later kept Lenoir's name in the public eye. His music was growing substantially by the time he hooked up with USA Records in 1963 (witness the 45's billing: J.B. Lenoir & his African Hunch Rhythm). Even more unusual were the two acoustic albums he cut for German blues promoter Horst Lippmann in 1965 and 1966. *Alabama Blues* and *Down in Mississippi* were done in Chicago under Willie Dixon's supervision, Lenoir now free to elaborate on whatever troubled his mind ("Alabama March," "Vietnam Blues," "Shot on James Meredith").

Little did Lenoir know his time was quickly running out. By the time of his 1967 death, the guitarist had moved to downstate Champaign—and that's where he died, probably as a delayed result of an auto accident he was involved in three weeks prior to his actual death. —*Bill Dahl*

Natural Man / 1968 / MCA/Chess ✦✦✦✦
This collection of Lenoir's mid-'50s tenure at the label—originally issued in the '70s—duplicates two songs from the Parrot collection (a label which Chess later acquired), but the rest of it is more than worth the effort to seek out. The rocking "Don't Touch My Head," the topical "Eisenhower Blues," and the sexually ambiguous and cool title track are but a few of the magical highlights aboard. Either this or the Parrot sides will do in a pinch, but I can't imagine being without either one. —*Cub Koda*

Crusade / 1970 / Polydor ✦✦✦✦

J.B. Lenoir / 1974 / Polydor ✦✦✦

Chess Blues Master Series / 1976 / Chess ✦✦✦✦
Aside from many fans not being able to properly pronounce his name, J.B. Lenoir also suffered from being severely underrated. He was both a first-rate uptempo vocalist and outstanding interpreter and composer. This double-LP anthology has long since disappeared from general circulation, but should be ardently pursued, as it contains definitive Lenoir cuts from Chess, Parrot, and Checker recorded in the '50s. —*Ron Wynn*

Mojo Boogie / 1980 / Flyright ✦✦✦
J.B. Lenoir made some marvelous recordings for the J.O.B. label in the early '50s, often working with pianist Sunnyland Slim and saxophonist J.T. Brown. They're available on this reissue. —*Ron Wynn*

Chess Masters / 1984 / Chess ✦✦✦

★ **The Parrot Sessions, 1954-55: Vintage Chicago Blues** / 1989 / Relic ✦✦✦✦✦
Lenoir's sound really got locked in during this period, using twin saxes, himself on boogie rhythm guitar (with an occassional minimal solo), revolving piano and bass stools, and Al Gavin—certainly the strangest of all Chicago drummers—constantly turning the beat around. This is Lenoir at his creative and performing best, including his best known songs "Mama Talk To Your Daughter" (with the famous "one note for 12 bars" guitar solo), "Eisenhower Blues," and "Give Me One More Shot," where Gavin starts out the tune on the wrong beat, gets on the right beat by mistake, then 'corrects' himself! Lyrics as metaphorically powerful as any in the blues against grooves alternating between low-down slow ones and Lenoir's patented boogie. —*Cub Koda*

His J.O.B. Recordings 1951-54 / 1991 / Paula/Flyright ✦✦✦✦
These are Lenoir's earliest sides in a very stripped down setting compared to the Parrot and Chess sides. Over half of the 14 sides feature Lenoir on guitar with only Sunnyland Slim on piano and Alfred Wallace on drums in support, with J.T. Brown on tenor sax aboard for the next session. They all suffer from a curiously muffled sound, but early delights like "The Mojo (Boogie)" and "Let's Roll" make all audio points mute. This CD also includes seven tracks fronted by Sunnyland Slim recorded the same day with Lenoir in a supporting role. —*Cub Koda*

Vietnam Blues: The Complete L&R Recordings / 1995 / Evidence ✦✦✦✦
Recorded in September 1966, shortly before his death the following spring, this session was Lenoir's most effective fusion of acoustic blues, African percussion, and contemporary, topical songwriting. "Round And Round," "Voodoo Music," and "Feelin' Good" bring the African influence to the fore, while Lenoir addresses tough issues like Vietnam and discrimination more directly than any other bluesman of the time on cuts like "Down In Mississippi," "Shot On Meredith," and "Vietnam Blues." Supervised by Willie Dixon, this recording also featured top Chicago blues drummer Fred Below. —*Richie Unterberger*

Ron Levy

b. May 29, 1951, Cambridge, MA
Piano, Organ / Modern Electric Blues, Groove
Ron Levy (born Reuvin Zev ben Yehoshua Ha Levi) was born on May 29, 1951, in Cambridge, MA. Although Levy grew up playing clarinet, he switched to piano at age 13 after attending a Ray Charles concert. Then, influenced by Jimmy Smith, Booker T., and Billy Preston, he picked up on the Hammond organ. Within a few years he was working in the Boston area backing up blues acts. Albert King discovered and hired him in 1971 while still in high school. They worked together for 18 months. He then went on to B.B. King's band and worked with King for almost seven years. From 1976 until 1980, Levy worked with the Rhythm Rockers and it was here that he met guitarist Ronnie Earl. Levy joined the Roomful of Blues from 1983 to 1987. Levy's own band, Ron Levy's Wild Kingdom, has recorded a number of fine albums for Black Top, Rounder, and Bullseye, among them 1988's *Safari to New Orleans*, 1993's *B-3 Blues and Grooves* and 1996's *Zim Zam Zoom: Acid Blues on B-3*. —*Michael Erlewine*

Ron Levy's Wild Kingdom / May 1987 / Black Top ✦✦✦
Ten tunes with an all-star cast including Ronnie Earl (guitar), Kim Wilson (harmonica), Greg Piccolo (sax), Wayne Bennett (guitar), and other excellent players. Plenty of fine guitar, keyboards, harmonica, and uptempo blues music. —*Michael Erlewine*

Safari to New Orleans / 1988 / Black Top ✦✦✦
Ron Levy's piano playing shines throughout *Safari to New Orleans*, but he fails to come up with enough strong songs to make the album memorable. —*Thom Owens*

★ **B-3 Blues & Grooves** / Apr. 1, 1993 / Bullseye Blues ✦✦✦✦✦
Ron Levy is one of the finest young masters of the Hammond B-3. Here are 11 soul-satisfying cuts that feature Levy's funky keyboard playing—many written by Levy himself. Those who look for B-3 jams in the soul-jazz vein that are as funky as can be will not be disappointed. This is a great CD to own. —*Michael Erlewine*

Zim Zam Zoom: Acid Blues on B-3 / Mar. 19, 1996 / Bullseye Blues ✦✦✦✦
If you like blues and funky soul-jazz (with just a twist of the future), this is an album to enjoy. Hammond B-3 artist Ron Levy gathers some of the greatest groove players of all time for this steam session, including Melvin Sparks on guitar and the great Idris Muhammad on drums. Call it retro or acid-jazz if you want, but groove lover Levy never stops playing that funky soul-jazz long enough to look back. This album carries the groove tradition on, maintaining that integrity. Produced by Bob Porter. — *Michael Erlewine*

Greaze Is What's Good / Mar. 10, 1998 / Cannonball ✦✦✦
On *Greaze Is What's Good*, Ron Levy is joined by trumpeter Freddie Hubbard, guitarists Melvin Sparks and David T. Walker, drummer Idris Muhammad, and trombonist Steve Turre, plus Memphis blues guitarist Preston Shannon, for a solid set of grooving, bluesy soul-jazz. — *Steve Huey*

Paving the Way / Black Top ✦✦✦

Furry Lewis (Walter Lewis)
b. Mar. 6, 1893, Greenwood, MS, d. Sep. 14, 1981, Memphis, TN
Guitar, Harmonica, Vocals / Acoustic Memphis Blues, Piedmont Blues
Furry Lewis was the only blues singer of the 1920s to achieve major media attention in the '60s and '70s. One of the most recorded of Memphis-based guitarists of the late '20s, Lewis' subsequent fame 40 years later was based largely on the strength of those early sides. One of the very best blues storytellers, and an extremely nimble-fingered guitarist right into his seventies, he was equally adept at blues and ragtime, and made the most out of an understated, rather than an overtly flamboyant style.

Walter Lewis was born in Greenwood, MS, sometime between 1893 and 1900 — the exact year is in dispute, as Lewis altered this more than once. The Lewis family moved to Memphis when he was seven years old, and Lewis made his home there for the remainder of his life. He got the name "Furry" while still a boy, bestowed on him by other children. Lewis built his first guitar when he was still a child from scraps he found around the family's home. Lewis' only admitted mentor was a local guitarist whom he knew as "Blind Joe," who may have come from Arkansas, a denizen of Memphis' Brinkley Street, where the family resided. The middle-aged Blind Joe was Lewis' source for the songs "Casey Jones" and "John Henry," among other traditional numbers. The loss of a leg in a railroad accident in 1917 doesn't seem to have slowed his life or career down — in fact, it hastened his entry into professional music, because he assumed that there was no gainful employment open to crippled, uneducated Blacks in Memphis. Lewis' real musical start took place on Beale Street in the late teens, where he began his career. He picked up bottleneck playing early on, and tried to learn the harmonica but never quite got the hang of it. Lewis started playing traveling medicine shows, and it was in this setting that he began showing off an uncommonly flashy visual style, including playing the guitar behind his head.

Lewis' recording career began in April 1927, with a trip to Chicago with fellow guitarist Landers Walton to record for the Vocalion label, which resulted in five songs, also featuring mandolin player Charles Jackson on three of the numbers. The songs proved that Lewis was a natural in the recording studio, playing to the microphone as easily as he did to audiences in person, but they were not, strictly speaking, representative of Lewis' usual sound, because they featured two backup musicians. In October of 1927 Lewis was back in Chicago to cut six more songs, this time with nothing but his voice and his own guitar. Lewis seldom played with anyone else, partly because of his loose bar structures, which made it very difficult for anyone to follow him. The interplay of his voice and guitar, on record and in person, made him a very effective showman in both venues. Lewis' records, however, did not sell well, and he never developed more than a cult following in and around Memphis. A few of his records, however, lingered in the memory far beyond their relatively modest sales, most notably "John Henry" and "Kassie Jones — Parts 1 and 2," arguably one of the great blues recordings of the '20s.

Lewis gave up music as a profession during the mid-'30s when the Depression reduced the market for country blues. He never made a living from his music — fortunately, he found work as a municipal laborer in Memphis during the '20s, and continued in this capacity right into the 1960s. His brand of acoustic country blues was hopelessly out-of-style in Memphis during the postwar years, and Lewis didn't even try to revive his recording or professional performing career. In the intervening years, he played for friends and

relatives, living in obscurity and reasonably satisfied. At the end of the '50s, however, folksong/blues scholar Sam Charters discovered Lewis and persuaded him to resume his music career. In the interim, all of the blues stars who'd made their careers in Memphis during the '30s had passed on or retired, and Lewis was a living repository of styles and songs that, otherwise, were scarcely within living memory of most Americans.

Lewis returned to the studio under Charters' direction and cut two albums for the Prestige/Bluesville labels in 1961. These showed Lewis in excellent form, his voice as good as ever and his technique on the guitar still dazzling. Audiences — initially hardcore blues and folk enthusiasts, and later more casual listeners — were delighted, fascinated, charmed, and deeply moved by what they heard. Gradually, as the '60s and the ensuing blues boom wore on, Lewis emerged as one of the favorite rediscovered stars of the 1930s, playing festivals, appearing on talk shows, and being interviewed. He proved to be a skilled public figure, regaling audiences with stories of his life that were both funny and poignantly revealing, claiming certain achievements (such as being the inventor of bottleneck guitar) in dubious manner, and delighting the public. After his retirement from working for the city of Memphis, he also taught in an antipoverty program in the city.

Furry Lewis became a blues celebrity during the '70s, following a profile in *Playboy* magazine and appearances on *The Tonight Show*, and managed a few film and television appearances, including one as himself in the Burt Reynolds action/comedy *W.W. and the Dixie Dance Kings*. By this time, he had several new recordings to his credit, and if the material wasn't as vital as the sides he'd cut at the end of the twenties, it was still valid and exceptionally fine blues, and paid him some money for his efforts. Lewis died in 1981 a beloved figure and a recognized giant in the world of blues. His music continues to sell well, and attract new listeners more than 15 years later. — *Bruce Eder*

Furry Lewis Blues / 1959 / Smithsonian/Folkways ✦✦✦

Back on My Feet Again / Apr. 1961 / Prestige/Bluesville ✦✦✦
An April 1961 session of traditional material such as "Shake 'Em on Down," "John Henry," "Roberta," and "St. Louis Blues." The album has been combined with another 1961 LP, *Done Changed My Mind*, for the CD reissue compilation *Shake 'Em on Down*. — *Richie Unterberger*

Done Changed My Mind / May 1961 / Prestige/Bluesville ✦✦✦
A May 1961 session of traditional material along the lines of "Casey Jones" and "Frankie and Johnnie." It's been combined with a similar 1961 LP, *Back on My Feet Again*, onto one disc for the CD reissue compilation *Shake 'em on Down*. — *Richie Unterberger*

On the Road Again / 1970 / Adelphi ✦✦✦

☆ **Shake 'Em on Down** / 1972 / Fantasy ✦✦✦✦✦
A 20-song single CD reissue of Lewis' first modern commercial recordings, done for two Prestige/Bluesville albums (*Back on My Feet Again*, *Done Changed My Mind*) in April and May of 1961 at Sun Studios in Memphis. Lewis is in brilliant form throughout, his fingers nearly as fast and his voice as rich as they were 30-odd years earlier. The disc includes the definitive version of "John Henry" (not just Lewis' definitive version — *the* definitive version), one of the greatest vocal performances ever put on record, and a guitar workout so dazzling that you'd swear there was more than one guy playing. What's more, with the extended running time available on tape (Lewis' sessions in the 1920s having been captured on 78 rpm discs with limited running times), he really stretched out here and obviously loves doing it. The slight reverb in the studio also gives Lewis a larger-than-life stature on this recording. — *Bruce Eder*

Fourth & Beale / 1975 / Lucky Seven ✦✦✦
Recorded in Memphis on March 5, 1969, with Lewis in bed — essentially an impromptu concert for the microphone and whoever happened to be there — these nine tracks show Lewis to fairly good advantage. They're more laidback than his work at the other end of the decade for Prestige/Bluesville, with Lewis playing more slowly and singing more roughly than those earlier sessions. His slide work is still stingingly effective, however, and his voice still highly expressive, and he knows how to put over a song even at this late date, playing with an almost hypnotic intensity — the songs include new renditions of "John Henry" and "Casey Jones," as well as "When the Saints Go Marching In" and W. C. Handy's "St. Louis Blues." — *Bruce Eder*

★ **In His Prime (1927-1928)** / 1988 / Yazoo ✦✦✦✦

The best overview of Lewis' classic late-'20s sides, containing 14 songs from the period (though not "John Henry"), all of which are crisply remastered, showing off both his superb guitar playing and his brilliantly expressive singing (the vocal performance on "Falling Down Blues" alone is worth the price of the disc) to excellent advantage. A seminal part of any blues collection, as well as any collection of Lewis' material. — *Bruce Eder*

☆ **Furry Lewis: Complete Works (1927-1929)** / 1990 / Document ✦✦✦✦✦

This release supplants both the Yazoo *In His Prime* and the Wolf Records 1990 *Complete Works* reviewed in the first edition of this book. This time *everything* that Lewis recorded for Victor and Vocalion during those extraordinary two years of work during the 1920's has been gathered together, including both parts of "Kassie Jones." The sound has been improved as well, and the notes are decent if, as is usual with Document, unexceptional. But this is one instance where Document's release of the complete works of an artist are preferable to Yazoo's picking and choosing. — *Bruce Eder*

Canned Heat Blues: Masters of Memphis Blues / 1992 / BMG ✦✦✦

This 21 song three-artist collection (with Tommy Johnson and Ishmon Bracey) is a good introduction to Lewis' work (or that of the others) for those unwilling to spring for $15 for one of the Yazoo or Wolf releases. The mastering quality is generally excellent, and the eight Lewis songs on hand include both parts of "Kassie Jones," though not "John Henry." It's a beginning, and anyone who likes this sampling can go to the more serious collections. It's apparently out-of-print at this writing, but relatively easy to find. — *Bruce Eder*

Johnie Lewis

b. Oct. 8, 1908, Eufaula, AL

Guitar, Vocals / Acoustic Country Blues, Country Blues, Country Blues

Johnie Lewis was a decent, if unexceptional, singer and guitarist in the Southern rural style, particularly accomplished at playing slide. Though he was born in Alabama and grew into adulthood in Georgia, Lewis spent most of his life in Chicago, moving to the city in the '30s. A painter by profession, Lewis only pursued music as an avocation, but through one of his painting jobs, he came to the notice of a filmmaker doing a documentary about Chicago blues. His appearance in that film lead to recording sessions for Arhoolie in the early '70s. — *Richie Unterberger*

Alabama Slide Guitar / 1970 / Arhoolie ✦✦✦✦

Eighteen songs recorded by Lewis in 1970 and 1971. If Lewis were one of the few practitioners of the Southern country slide blues guitar, this would be an important document. But the fact is that because there are so many similar performers in the style who recorded more prolifically and with greater imagination, it's just a solid journeyman entry in the field. Lewis does have an affable storytelling manner to his songwriting, and gets in some nifty laidback slide licks; a couple of the more ambitious tunes were inspired by Dr. Martin Luther King. — *Richie Unterberger*

Meade "Lux" Lewis (Meade Anderson Lewis)

b. Sep. 4, 1905, Chicago, IL, **d.** Jun. 7, 1964, Minneapolis, MN

Piano / Boogie-Woogie, Piano Blues

One of the three great boogie-woogie pianists (along with Albert Ammons and Pete Johnson) whose appearance at John Hammond's 1938 *Spirituals to Swing* concert helped start the boogie-woogie craze, Meade Lux Lewis was a powerful if somewhat limited player. He played regularly in Chicago in the late '20s and his one solo record of the time "Honky Tonk Train Blues" (1927) was considered a classic. However, other than a few sides backing little-known blues singers, Lewis gained little extra work and slipped into obscurity. John Hammond heard Lewis' record in 1935 and after a search found Lewis washing cars for a living in Chicago. Soon Meade Lux Lewis was back on records, and after the 1938 concert he was able to work steadily, sometimes in duets or trios with Ammons and Johnson. He became the first jazz pianist to double on celeste (starting in 1936) and was featured on that instrument in a Blue Note quartet date with Edmond Hall and Charlie Christian; he also played harpsichord on a few records in 1941. After the boogie-woogie craze ended, Lewis continued working in Chicago and California, recording as late as 1962, although by then he was pretty much forgotten. Meade Lux Lewis led sessions through the years that have come out on MCA,

Victor, Blue Note, Solo Art, Euphonic, Stinson, Atlantic, Storyville, Verve, Tops, ABC-Paramount, Riverside, and Philips. — *Scott Yanow*

☆ **The Complete Blue Note Recordings** / Jan. 6, 1939-Aug. 22, 1944 / Mosaic ✦✦✦✦✦

Mosaic's *Complete Blue Note Recordings* contains all of the recordings Meade Lux Lewis made for the label between 1939 and 1944, making it the definitive statement on the influential boogie-woogie pianist. — *Leo Stanley*

Meade Lux Lewis (1939-1954) / Feb. 1939-Sep. 25, 1954 / Story of Blues ✦✦✦✦

This CD reissue collects together solo, duet, and trio sides by the great boogie-woogie pianist Meade Lux Lewis, many of which do not duplicate other readily available collections. Most of the first nine selections surprisingly feature Lewis playing blues with a light stride rather than a boogie bassline. Two titles from 1944 are more typical of what the public expected, while the final three numbers (from 1953-54) are a bit subpar, sloppy, if spirited honky tonk music played on a poor piano. This CD is a gap filler for completists but otherwise not too essential. — *Scott Yanow*

Meade Lux Lewis [Stinson] / Aug. 18, 1944 / Stinson ✦✦✦

Vintage boogie-woogie and blues from a piano master. Lewis ranked alongside Albert Ammons, Pete Johnson, and Jimmy Yancey as boogie-woogie's finest, and he shows why on this reissued collection featuring Lewis' solos from the mid-'40s. — *Ron Wynn*

● **The Blues Piano Artistry of Meade Lux Lewis** / Nov. 1, 1961 / Original Jazz Classics ✦✦✦✦

Boogie-woogie pianist Meade Lux Lewis' next-to-last record was his first recording in five years and his final opportunity to stretch out unaccompanied. This solo Riverside set (reissued by OJC on CD) as usual finds Lewis generally sticking to the blues (with "You Were Meant for Me" and "Fate" being exceptions), mostly performing originals. On a few of the songs Lewis switches effectively to celeste. It apparently only took Meade Lux Lewis two hours to record the full set and the results are quite spontaneous yet well organized, a fine all-around portrait of the veteran pianist in his later period. — *Scott Yanow*

Noah Lewis

b. Sep. 3, 1895, Henning, TN, **d.** Feb. 7, 1961, Ripley, TN

Acoustic Memphis Blues, Prewar Country Blues

A key figure on the Memphis jug band circuit of the 1920s, singer and harpist Noah Lewis was born September 3, 1895 in Henning, TN. Upon relocating to Memphis, he teamed with Gus Cannon, becoming an essential component of Cannon's Jug Stompers; the group made their debut recordings for the Paramount label in 1927, with several more sessions to follow prior to their final date in late 1930. On a series of sides cut in the first week of October 1929, Lewis made his debut as a name artist, cutting three blistering harmonica solos as well as "Going to Germany," which spotlighted his plaintive vocal style. Later recording with Yank Rachell and John Estes, as the Depression wore on Lewis slipped into obscurity, living a life of extreme poverty; his death on February 7, 1961 was a result of gangrene brought on by frostbite. — *Jason Ankeny*

Smiley Lewis

b. Jul. 5, 1913, DeQuincey, LA, **d.** Oct. 7, 1966, New Orleans, LA

Guitar, Vocals / New Orleans R&B, R&B, New Orleans Blues, Piano Blues

Dave Bartholomew has often been quoted to the effect that Smiley Lewis was a "bad luck singer," because he never sold more than 100,000 copies of his Imperial singles. In retrospect, Lewis was a lucky man in many respects— he enjoyed stellar support from New Orleans' ace sessioneers at Cosimo's, benefited from top-flight material and production (by Bartholomew), and left behind a legacy of marvelous Crescent City R&B. We're lucky he was there, that's for sure.

Born with the unwieldy handle of Overton Lemons, Lewis hit the Big Easy in his mid-teens, armed with a big, booming voice and some guitar skills. He played clubs in the French Quarter, often with pianist Tuts Washington (and sometimes billed as "Smiling" Lewis). By 1947, his following was strong enough to merit a session for DeLuxe Records, which issued his debut 78, "Here Comes Smiley." Nothing happened with that platter, but when Lewis signed with Imperial in 1950 (debuting with "Tee-Nah-Nah") things began to move.

As the New Orleans R&B sound developed rapidly during the early '50s, so did Lewis, as he rocked ever harder on "Lillie Mae," "Ain't Gonna Do It," and "Big Mamou." He scored his first national hit in 1952 with "The Bells Are Ringing," but enjoyed his biggest sales in 1955 with the exultant "I Hear You Knocking" (its immortal piano solo courtesy of Huey Smith). Here's where that alleged bad luck rears its head—pop chanteuse Gale Storm swiped his thunder for any pop crossover possibilities with her ludicrous whitewashed cover of the plaintive ballad.

But Storm wouldn't dare come near its roaring flip, the Joe Turnerish rocker "Bumpity Bump," or some of Smiley Lewis' other classic mid-'50s jumpers ("Down the Road," "Lost Weekend," "Real Gone Lover," "She's Got Me Hook, Line and Sinker," "Rootin' and Tootin'"). In front of the Crescent City's hottest players (saxists Lee Allen, Clarence Hall, and Herb Hardesty usually worked his dates), Lewis roared like a lion.

Strangely, Fats Domino fared better with some of Smiley Lewis' tunes than Lewis did ("Blue Monday" in particular). Similarly, Elvis Presley cleaned up the naughty "One Night" and hit big with it, but Lewis' original had already done well in 1956 (as had his melodic "Please Listen to Me"). His blistering "Shame, Shame, Shame" found its way onto the soundtrack of the steamy Hollywood potboiler *Baby Doll* in 1957 but failed to find entry to the R&B charts.

After a long and at least semi-profitable run at Imperial, Lewis moved over to OKeh in 1961 for one single, stopped at Dot in 1964 just long enough to make a solitary 45 (produced by Nashville deejay Bill "Hoss" Allen), and bowed out with an Allen Toussaint-produced remake of "The Bells Are Ringing" for Loma in 1965. By then, stomach cancer was eating the once-stout singer up. He died in the autumn of 1966, all but forgotten outside his New Orleans homebase.

The ensuing decades have rectified that miscarriage of justice, however. Smiley Lewis' place as one of the greatest New Orleans R&B artists of the 1950s is certainly assured. —*Bill Dahl*

★ **The Best of Smiley Lewis** / Nov. 3, 1992 / Capitol ◆◆◆◆◆
Smiley Lewis made several fabulous singles, had a booming, terrific voice, and received the same great backing and support that defined the city's R&B sound. But Lewis' records seldom made it outside New Orleans, even though they were frequently brilliant. This great 24-track anthology contains the four that did make it to the charts, among them the signature song "I Hear You Knocking." It shows Lewis doing first-rate novelty tracks, ballads, weepers, uptempo wailers and blues, and making wonderful recordings. The set also includes a thorough discography and good notes and is superbly mastered. It's magnificent, exuberant R&B, and deserved a much better national fate than it enjoyed. —*Ron Wynn*

Shame, Shame, Shame / 1993 / Bear Family ◆◆◆◆
Exhaustive, multi-disc set comprising everything recorded on this New Orleans singer. With the songwriting talents of Dave Bartholomew aboard, utilizing the sound of the legendary J&M Studios, and the best Crescent City musicians available, this is truly New Orleans music at its very best. —*Cub Koda*

Jimmy Liggins

b. Oct. 14, 1922, Newby, OK, **d.** Jul. 18, 1983, Durham, NC
Guitar, Vocals / R&B, Jump Blues, Boogie-Woogie
Another of the jump blues specialists whose romping output can be pinpointed as a direct precursor of rock 'n' roll, guitarist Jimmy Liggins was a far more aggressive bandleader than his older brother Joe, right down to the names of their respective combos (Joe led the polished Honeydrippers; Jimmy proudly fronted the Drops of Joy).

Inspired by the success of his brother (Jimmy toiled as Joe's chauffeur for a year), the ex-pugilist jumped into the recording field in 1947 on Art Rupe's Specialty logo. His "Tear Drop Blues" pierced the R&B Top Ten the next year, while "Careful Love" and "Don't Put Me Down" hit for him in 1949. But it's Liggins' rough-and-ready rockers—"Cadillac Boogie," "Saturday Night Boogie Woogie Man," and the loopy one-chord workout "Drunk" (his last smash in 1953)—that mark Liggins as one of rock's forefathers. His roaring sax section at Specialty was populated by first-rate reedmen such as Harold Land, Charlie "Little Jazz" Ferguson, and the omnipresent Maxwell Davis.

Liggins left Specialty in 1954, stopping off at Aladdin long enough to wax the classic-to-be "I Ain't Drunk" (much later covered by Albert Collins) before fading from the scene. —*Bill Dahl*

● **And His Drops of Joy** / 1989 / Specialty ◆◆◆◆
Guitarist Jimmy Liggins swung considerably harder than his brother Joe during his 1947-1953 Specialty stint, presaging rock's rise with his torrid jump blues "Cadillac Boogie," "Saturday Night Boogie Woogie Man," and the marvelously loopy "Drunk." Twenty-five of his best are right here. —*Bill Dahl*

Rough Weather Blues, Vol. 2 / 1992 / Specialty ◆◆◆◆
Twenty-five more Specialty cookers, including an undubbed version of "Drunk," plenty of horn-leavened jump blues outings, and several unissued artifacts (including a rare example of the Drops of Joy getting jazzy on "Now's the Time"). —*Bill Dahl*

Joe Liggins

b. Jul. 9, 1915, Guthrie, OK, **d.** Aug. 1, 1987, Lynwood, CA
Piano, Vocals / R&B, Jump Blues
Pianist Joe Liggins and his band, the Honeydrippers, tore up the R&B charts during the late '40s and early '50s with their polished brand of polite R&B. Liggins scored massive hits with "The Honeydripper" in 1945 and "Pink Champagne" five years later, posting a great many more solid sellers in between.

Born in Oklahoma, Liggins moved to San Diego in 1932. He moved to Los Angeles in 1939 and played with various outfits, including Sammy Franklin's California Rhythm Rascals. When Franklin took an unwise pass on recording Liggins' infectious "The Honeydripper," the bespectacled pianist assembled his own band and waxed the tune for Leon Rene's Exclusive logo. The upshot: an R&B chart-topper. Nine more hits followed on Exclusive over the next three years, including the schmaltzy "Got a Right to Cry," the often-covered "Tanya" (Chicago guitarist Earl Hooker waxed a delicious version), and "Roll 'Em."

In 1950, Joe joined his brother Jimmy at Specialty Records. More hits immediately followed: "Rag Mop," the number one R&B smash "Pink Champagne," "Little Joe's Boogie," and "Frankie Lee." During this period, the Honeydrippers prominently featured saxists Willie Jackson and James Jackson, Jr. Liggins stuck around Specialty into 1954, later turning up with solitary singles on Mercury and Aladdin. But time had passed Liggins by, at least right then; later, his sophisticated approach came back into fashion, and he led a little big band until his death. —*Bill Dahl*

★ **Joe Liggins & the Honeydrippers** / 1989 / Specialty ◆◆◆◆◆
Pianist Joe Liggins presented a fairly sophisticated brand of swinging jump blues to jitterbuggers during the early '50s, when his irresistible "Pink Champagne" scaled the R&B charts. Twenty-five of his very best 1950-1954 Specialty sides grace this collection, including a tasty remake of "The Honeydripper," "Rhythm in the Barnyard," and the syncopated "Going Back to New Orleans" (recently revived by Dr. John). —*Bill Dahl*

Dripper's Boogie, Vol. 2 / 1992 / Specialty ◆◆◆◆
An encore helping of 20 rarities by Joe Liggins from Specialty, dotted with unissued discoveries (including two versions of "Little Joe's Boogie" and "Hey, Betty Martin") from 1950-1954. —*Bill Dahl*

Papa George Lightfoot

b. Mar. 2, 1924, Natchez, MS, **d.** Nov. 28, 1971, Natchez, MS
Harmonica, Vocals / Electric Blues
Thanks to a handful of terrific 1950s sides, the name of Papa Lightfoot was spoken in hushed and reverent tones by 1960s blues aficionados. Then, producer Steve LaVere tracked down the elusive harp master in Natchez, cutting an album for Vault in 1969 that announced to the world that Lightfoot was still wailing like a wildman on the mouth organ. Alas, his comeback was short-lived; he died in 1971 of respiratory failure and cardiac arrest.

Sessions for Peacock in 1949 (unissued), Sultan in 1950, and Aladdin in 1952 preceded an amazing 1954 date for Imperial in New Orleans that produced Lightfoot's "Mean Old Train," "Wine Women Whiskey" (comprising his lone single for the firm), and an astonishing "When the Saints Go Marching In." Lightfoot's habit of singing through his harp microphone further coarsened his already rough-hewn vocals, while his harp playing was simply shot through with endless invention. Singles for Savoy in 1955 and Excello the next year (the latter billed him as "Ole Sonny Boy") closed out Lightfoot's '50s recording activities, setting the stage for his regrettably brief comeback in 1969. — *Bill Dahl*

Rural Blues, Vol. 2 / 1969 / Liberty ♦♦♦

Natchez Trace / 1969 / Vault ♦♦♦♦
Mississippi vocalist and harmonica player "Papa" George Lightfoot made a fine recording in 1969 for Vault, a rare full-length LP. It got limited distribution and disappeared shortly afterward. This is a reissue, and it's vital material. — *Ron Wynn*

● **Goin' Back to the Nachez Trace** / 1995 / Ace ♦♦♦♦
Until producer Steve LaVere rediscovered him in 1969, harp giant Papa Lightfoot was revered for a mere handful of '50s sides. This album for Vault served as his comeback announcement, a gloriously down-in-the-alley affair cut at then-fledgling Malaco studios in Jackson, MS. Six bonus tracks, including three minutes of spoken monologue, have been added to the import CD reissue, enhancing an already fine album. — *Bill Dahl*

Lightnin' Slim

b. Mar. 13, 1913, St. Louis, MO, **d.** Jul. 24, 1974, Detroit, MI
Guitar, Vocals / Electric Louisiana Blues, Electric Swamp Blues, Swamp Blues
The acknowledged kingpin of the Louisiana school of blues, Lightnin' Slim's style was built on his grainy but expressive vocals and rudimentary guitar work, with usually nothing more than a harmonica and a drummer in support. It was down-home country blues edged two steps further into the mainstream; first by virtue of Slim's electric guitar, and secondly by the sound of the local Crowley musicians who backed him being bathed in simmering, pulsating tape echo. As the first great star of producer J.D. Miller's blues talent stable, the formula was a successful one, scoring him regional hits that were issued on the Nashville-based Excello label for over a decade, with one of them, "Rooster Blues," making the national R&B charts in 1959. Combining the country ambience of a Lightnin' Hopkins with the plodding insistence of a Muddy Waters, Slim's music remained uniquely his own, the perfect blues raconteur, even when reshaping other's material to his dark, somber style. He also possessed one of the truly great voices of the blues; unadorned and unaffected, making the world-weariness of a Sonny Boy Williamson sound like the second coming of Good Time Charlie by comparison. His exhortation to "blow your harmonica, son" has become one of the great, mournful catchphrases of the blues, and even on his most rockin' numbers, there's a sense that you are listening less to an uptempo offering than a slow blues just being played faster. Slim always sounded like bad luck just moved into his home approximately an hour after his mother-in-law did.

He was born with the unglamorous handle of Otis Hicks in St. Louis, MO on March 13, 1913. After 13 years of living on a farm outside of the city, the Hicks family moved to Louisiana, first settling in St. Francisville. Young Otis took to the guitar early, first shown the rudiments by his father, then later by his older brother, Layfield. Given his recorded output, it's highly doubtful that either his father or brother knew how to play in any key other than E natural, as Slim used the same patterns over and over on his recordings, only changing keys when he used a capo or had his guitar de-tuned a full step.

But the rudiments were all he needed, and by the late '30s/early '40s he was a mainstay of the local picnic/country supper circuit around St. Francisville. In 1946, he moved to Baton Rouge, playing on weekends in local ghetto bars, and started to make a name for himself on the local circuit, first working as a member of Big Poppa's band, then on his own.

The '50s dawned with harmonica player Schoolboy Cleve in tow, working club dates and broadcasting over the radio together. It was local disc jockey Ray "Diggy Do" Meaders who then persuaded Miller to record him. He recorded for 12 years as an Excello artist, starting out originally on Miller's Feature label. As the late '60s found Lightnin' Slim working and living in Detroit, a second career blossomed as European blues audiences brought him over to tour, and he also started working the American festival and hippie ballroom circuit with Slim Harpo as a double act. When Harpo died unexpectedly in 1970, Slim went on alone, recording sporadically, while performing as part of the American Blues Legends tour until his death in 1974. Lazy, rolling and insistent, Lightnin' Slim is Louisiana blues at its finest. — *Cub Koda*

The Early Years / 1976 / Flyright ♦♦♦♦
There is some duplication here with *Bell Ringer*, although there are also some numbers done even earlier than those. — *Ron Wynn*

Bell Ringer / 1987 / Excello ♦♦♦♦
Superb early Slim Excello material. He never sang with more clarity or conviction, nor did his harmonica or guitar playing ever sound more electrifying than on these songs, many of which were popular singles. Other than Rice Miller's (Sonny Boy Williamson II) definitive anthem, Slim's rendition of "Don't Start Me To Talking" was the finest. — *Ron Wynn*

★ **Rooster Blues** / 1987 / Excello ♦♦♦♦♦
Stark, sparse, swamp blues with the deepest tone in the South Louisiana genre's history. Lightnin' Slim was an Excello mainstay from the mid-'50s to the mid-'60s; 18 of his best J.D. Miller-produced sides reside here. The title track, "Hoo-Doo Blues," "GI Slim," "Tom Cat Blues," and the ribald "It's Mighty Crazy" rate with the guitarist's seminal efforts. — *Bill Dahl*

★ **Rollin' Stone** / 1991 / Flyright ♦♦♦♦♦
With all six sides from Slim's earliest singles for the Feature label, plus excellent alternate takes of his best-known Excello numbers, this album is the perfect place to start. (Import) — *Cub Koda*

☆ **King of the Swamp Blues 1954-61** / 1992 / Flyright ♦♦♦♦♦
Lightnin' Slim true believers who are in it for the long haul will want to take the extra time to search for this one. It's a 20-track collection that brings together a rash of alternate takes, previously unissued sides, studio warmups and the like, all of it recorded by producer Jay Miller between 1954 and 1961. But this is no bottom-of-the-barrel scrapings-slapped-together-for-a-compilation; Slim's outtakes can sometimes be better than some of the later sides that were released on Excello. Running the sequencing on this disc in a somewhat chronological order, we're treated to an unreleased track from what is believed to be Slim's audition for Miller, a bare-bones reading of Jimmy Rogers' "That's All Right." One of the few examples of Slim recording without a harmonica in support, the starkness of his guitar and vocal against the rudimentary drums of disc jockey Ray "Diggy Doo" Meaders makes this the track that fans of the lowdown will enthusiastically embrace. Another unreleased song from the same session is an original, "Love Me for Myself," which again features Slim's guitar front and center doing rare fills in the upper register between vocal lines, a veritable swamp blues version of B.B. King. Several more sides emanate from these first sessions in 1954, including a wobbly tape reel alternate of his first record, "Bad Luck," and Slim in support of harmonica ace Wild Bill Phillips. Phillips' amplified harp tone is huge and distorted on the rocking "Paper In My Shoe" and Slim encores the same supporting role behind Schoolboy Cleve on three tracks, "I'm Him," "She's Gone," and "Strange Letter Blues." Five alternate takes ("I Just Don't Know," "Tom Cat Blues," "G.I. Slim," "I'm Tired of Waiting Baby," and "Hello Mary Lee," with the latter two from 1961) illustrate how Miller and the artists shaped material for release in his Crowley, LA, studio. But mavens of unreleased material will positively revel in the studio warmup of "Don't Mistreat Me," where in mid-song Slim breaks a guitar string and starts cussing out his guitar. Certainly not the place to start with this artist, but an interesting addition to his recorded legacy that hardcore fans will definitely want to pick up. — *Cub Koda*

Hoodoo Blues / 1994 / CSI ♦♦♦
One of many mysterious Classic Sound Inc. blues releases, with no indication of whence the material originated. The sound is decent but nothing special, and some of the balances are haywire (some guitars pushed too far into the mix etc.), but the CD is a mess. The songs include "Rooster Blues" (with an awkward brass section somewhere in the background), "G.I. Blues," "Crazy About You Baby," "My Babe," "Things I Used To Do," "That's All Right," and "Lightning's Bad Luck" (which reappears, in what seems to be the very same cut, as "Bad Luck Blues," seven songs later), all licensed from a British outfit called Prestige Records. The material sounds like it was done much later than Slim's classic Excello sides, leading one to believe that it originated during the British phase of his career, when he was playing to audiences overseas—it could have been a busted "London Sessions"-style collection. For all of its sloppiness, this is a decent budget-priced disc, and a nice appendix to the important part of Slim's career, for all of its mystery—but it's a pity it isn't a live concert, like the Muddy Waters and Howlin' Wolf CSI releases. — *Bruce Eder*

I'm Evil / 1995 / Excello/AVI ◆◆◆◆
A goldmine of 27 1950s and '60s obscurities from one of the lonesomest bayou blues greats ever. Filled with alternate takes and outright unissued efforts, *I'm Evil* reverberates with lowdown treatises that cut to the the heart and soul of the swamp. "Bad Luck," "Mean Ol' Lonesome Train," and "Rock Me Mama" are pure, unadulterated Louisiana blues of the highest order. — *Bill Dahl*

Nothing But the Devil / 1996 / Ace ◆◆◆◆
This 24-song collection undoubtedly overlaps with some of the US-issued Excello material—including the same alternate takes of "Rooster Blues" and "It's Mighty Crazy"—but there's just enough that they don't share to make this worth a look, if not a purchase, by owners of the US material. The sound, as is usual with Ace, is excellent, and the stuff is worthy of inclusion with the best of Slim's work. Among the best tracks here are two outtakes unique to this set at this time, "I'm Leavin' You Baby," on which Slim steps over into Howlin' Wolf territory ("Moanin' at Midnight" etc.), and "Sweet Little Woman," where he crosses swords with Sonny Boy Williamson II. — *Bruce Eder*

Winter Time Blues / May 1998 / Excello ◆◆◆◆

Lil' Ed & the Blues Imperials (Lil' Ed Williams)

f. Apr. 8, 1955, Chicago, IL
Guitar, Vocals / Modern Electric Blues, Modern Electric Chicago Blues
Included are Lil' Ed Williams (vocal, guitar); "Pookie" Young (bass); various others, guitar, drums. Lil' Ed Williams learned his trade as a teenager from his uncle, Chicago slide-guitarist J.B. Hutto, and the resemblance to Hutto, vocally and instrumentally, continues to be no less amazing some 20 years later. If Ed, half-brother Pookie Young, and the latest members of the re-vamped Blues Imperials never do much to modernize their blues or develop a new sound, that will be just fine with the band's growing legion of followers ("Ed Heads," no less), to whom the raucous, rocking slide guitar heritage of Hutto, Hound Dog Taylor, and Elmore James is blues nirvana. — *Jim O'Neal*

Roughhousin' / 1986 / Alligator ◆◆◆
Wild & greasy blues at its best, a two-song session for an anthology turned into an all-night, live-in-the-studio jam. Sounds like it was great fun. — *Niles J. Frantz*

● **Chicken Gravy & Biscuits** / 1989 / Alligator ◆◆◆◆
Wild, raw, rough-edged Chicago slide guitar blues, this is jumpin', partyin' music in the tradition of Hound Dog Taylor and J.B. Hutto (Lil' Ed's uncle). Recorded live in the studio with no overdubs, it includes nine original compositions plus covers of Hutto and Albert Collins tunes. — *Niles J. Frantz*

What You See is What You Get / 1992 / Alligator ◆◆◆
This group fits the bill for listeners who enjoy hard-driving good-time electric blues. Lil' Ed Williams only has an average voice but his slashing guitar works well with rhythm guitarist Mike Garrett and the rest of the quintet (which includes Eddie McKinley on tenor) is well rehearsed and spirited. The result is an above average set of rockish blues that, although not terribly distinctive, is sure to satisfy. — *Scott Yanow*

Charly Lincoln

b. Mar. 11, 1900, Lithonia, GA, **d.** Sep. 28, 1963, Cairo, GA
Guitar, Vocals / Country Blues, Piedmont Blues, Prewar Country Blues
Aliases and psudeoynms aside, Charlie Hicks AKA Charley or Charlie Lincoln was an above-average country blues vocalist. He teamed often with either his brother Robert Hicks AKA Barbecue Bob or with Peg-Leg Howell. His guitar voicings and style were influenced by Curley Weaver, but Hicks was a colorful singer and flashy player. Weaver's mother Savannah taught Lincoln the guitar as a teenager. Lincoln recorded with his brother for Columbia from 1927-1930; he continued playing with him into the '50s, though his performance and playing schedule was highly irregular. A murder conviction ended his career in 1955; he was in prison until his death in 1963. — *Ron Wynn*

Complete Recorded Works (1927-1930) / 1984 / Document ◆◆◆
Document's *Complete Recorded Works (1927-1930)* is an exhaustive overview of Charly Lincoln's career. The exacting chronological sequencing, poor fidelity (all cuts are transferred from original acetates and 78s), and number of performances will appeal more to the serious blues listener, but casual

listeners will find that the collection is of marginal interest for those very reasons. — *Thom Owens*

Hip Linkchain

b. Nov. 10, 1936, Jackson, MS, **d.** Feb. 13, 1989, Chicago, IL
Guitar, Vocals / Electric Chicago Blues
Cancer struck guitarist Hip Linkchain down before he could shed his status as a Chicago blues journeyman. With a fine album on the Dutch Black Magic logo, *Airbusters*, to his credit shortly before he died, Linkchain might have managed to move up a rung or two in the city's blues pecking order had he lived longer.

Born Willie Richard in Mississippi, his odd stage name stemmed from being dubbed "Hipstick" as a lad. (White residents of the area gave his seven-foot-tall dad the name Linkchain because he wore logging chains around his neck). Dad and older brother Jesse both played the blues, and Hip followed in their footsteps. He heard Elmore James, Little Milton, and Sonny Boy Williamson while living in the Delta before relocating to Chicago during the early '50s.

Linkchain made inroads on the competitive Chicago circuit during the '50s and '60s, playing with harpists Dusty Brown, Willie Foster, and Lester Davenport. His own band, the Chicago Twisters, was fronted by a very young Tyrone Davis in 1959. Linkchain cut a handful of very obscure 45s for the tiny Lola and Sanns logos prior to the emergence of his debut domestic album for Teardrop Records, *Change My Blues*, circa 1981. — *Bill Dahl*

I Am on My Way / 197 / MCM ◆◆◆

Change My Blues / Jun. 1983 / Teardrop ◆◆
Anemic album by journeyman Chicago blues guitarist Linkchain that didn't come close to capturing his stinging sound. — *Bill Dahl*

● **Airbusters** / 1993 / Evidence ◆◆◆◆
Linkchain was a solid, no frills bluesman and this album (his last before his death in 1989) showcases him at his best. Loads of great original material, with the added bonus of top notch playing from Chicago's finest blues players. Standout tracks include "Blow Wind Blow," "I'll Overcome," and "Take Out Your False Teeth." — *Cub Koda*

Mance Lipscomb

b. Apr. 9, 1895, Navasota, TX, **d.** Jan. 30, 1976, Navasota, TX
Guitar, Violin, Vocals / Acoustic Texas Blues, Country Blues
Like Leadbelly and Mississippi John Hurt, the designation as strictly a blues singer dwarfs the musical breadth of Mance Lipscomb. A sharecropper/tenant farmer all his life who didn't record until 1960, "songster" fits what Lipscomb did best. A proud, yet unboastful man, Lipscomb would point out that he was an educated musician, his ability to play everything from classic blues, ballads, pop songs to spirituals in a multitude of styles and keys being his particular mark of originality. With a wide-ranging repertoire of over 90 songs, Lipscomb may have gotten a belated start in recording, but left a remarkable legacy (eight albums in fifteen years) to be enjoyed. — *Cub Koda*

★ **Texas Sharecropper & Songster** / 1960 / Arhoolie ◆◆◆◆◆
Arhoolie's *Texas Sharecropper & Songster* is a recording made in 1960, during the blues revival. Prior to the blues revival, Lipscomb was an unknown, and his discovery was one of the positive by-products of the revival. He was a great country-blues man, and this is perhaps his greatest effort, capturing him running through a number of traditional songs. Most of the songs are augmented by his jackknife slide guitar, and all feature his raw, haunted vocals, which make these classic songs sound timeless. — *Thom Owens*

You Got to Reap What You Sow / 1964 / Arhoolie ◆◆◆◆
Mance Lipscomb was a great songster, someone who knew hundreds of songs and could deliver any and all of them in different but effective ways. He sang blues, spirituals, old folk numbers, and his own tunes. Lipscomb had few rivals when it came to telling stories, setting up situations, creating characters, and depicting incidents. This 24-song reissued disc from 1964 puts Lipscomb in a perfect light, ripping through various songs and talking about everything from drugs to domestic conflict and police worries to spiritual concerns. — *Ron Wynn*

Texas Blues Guitar / 1994 / Arhoolie ◆◆◆
A 15-cut disc issued in conjunction with the song transcription book *Mance Lipscomb: Texas Blues Guitar*, this is a fine introduction to the Texas blues-

man's work, and includes acoustic performances of "Ain't It Hard," "Motherless Children," and "You Got to Reap What You Sow." — *Jason Ankeny*

Little Buster and the Soul Brothers

f. Sep. 28, 1942, Hertford, NC
Guitar, Vocals / Electric Blues, Soul, Soul Blues
Anyone lucky enough to stumble across Little Buster's 1995 debut album for Bullseye Blues might well have been asking themselves, "Where's this guy been all this time?" The answer: for the last three decades or so, the blind guitarist has been serving up his soulful brand of blues around his adopted home of Long Island, NY, with his band, the Soul Brothers.

Edward "Little Buster" Forehand left the North Carolina School for the Deaf and Blind when he was 16 years old, moving to New York and breaking into the local R&B scene almost immediately. Buster recorded sparingly during the '60s, waxing the Doc Pomus-penned "Young Boy Blues" for Jubilee in 1967. But the world-at-large remained ignorant of Buster's impressive command of the soul and blues lexicons until 1995, when *Right on Time!* blew onto the contemporary scene like an unexpected breath of fresh air. *Looking for a Home* followed in 1997. — *Bill Dahl*

● **Right on Time** / 1995 / Bullseye Blues ◆◆◆◆
Literally from out of nowhere did this remarkable debut album arise by blind guitarist Little Buster and his combo (he's no stranger to the studio, though, with a handful of late-'60s 45s to his credit). Mixing blues and soul traditions with melismatic passion, Buster was responsible for one of 1995's best albums—debut or otherwise. — *Bill Dahl*

Looking for a Home / Feb. 25, 1997 / Sequel ◆◆◆

Little Charlie & the Nightcats

f. 1976, San Francisco, CA
Group / Modern Electric Blues, Modern Electric Chicago Blues
Little Charlie and the Nightcats have been bringing West Coast clubgoers to their feet with their eclectic, blues-infused repertoire since the mid-'70s. Drawing from styles ranging from Chicago and jazzy West Coast blues to Texas swing to rockabilly to surf music and R&B, the Nightcats sing mostly original songs and are noted for their wry, satirical lyrics; they also perform adaptations of obscure older tunes. Although they primarily perform in California and Oregon, the Nightcats frequently tour across the continent, and have also toured Europe. Their lineup centers upon extraordinary harp player/songwriter/singer Rick Estrin and versatile guitarist Little Charlie Baty; Dobie Strange on drums and bass player Ronnie James Weber, who joined the Nightcats in the mid-'90s, round out the current lineup. — *Sandra Brennan*

All the Way Crazy / 1987 / Alligator ◆◆◆
A very happening debut album, it's funny and danceable. — *Niles J. Frantz*

Disturbing the Peace / 1988 / Alligator ◆◆◆◆
These are jumpin' blues with wild antics, a good sense of humor, tons of fun, often outrageous. Very, very good guitar comes from Charlie Baty and interesting harp from lead vocalist Rick Estrin. — *Niles J. Frantz*

The Big Break / 1989 / Alligator ◆◆◆
Here is another raucous, rollicking release. — *Niles J. Frantz*

Captured Live / 1991 / Alligator ◆◆◆
This enjoyable live set captures the group's manic energy. — *Niles J. Frantz*

Night Vision / 1993 / Alligator ◆◆◆
Unlike their previous efforts (where it sounded like the band pulled the van up to the studio, unloaded their gear, and played a set and split before someone hollered out for last call), this one sounds more like a real album. With Joe Louis Walker producing, the boys explore new twists on their wide-ranging bag of tricks. The band's humor is found in abundance on sleazy blues items like "I'll Never Do That No More" and the soul rocker opener "My Next Ex-Wife," while the boys truly get down to business on the rockabilly-tinged "Backfire" and the smokin' shuffle "Can't Keep It Up." Augmenting their basic lineup are guest appearances by Walker and a host of others in support, making this their most musical sounding album yet. — *Cub Koda*

Straight Up! / 1995 / Alligator ◆◆
Straight Up! is a typically rollicking, humourous collection of updated Chicago blues from Little Charlie & the Nightcats. As with any of the band's

albums, the quality of the material is slightly uneven, but the band's good-natured energy makes those shortcomings somewhat forgiveable, especially if you are already a fan. — *Stephen Thomas Erlewine*

● **Deluxe Edition** / Oct. 28, 1997 / Alligator ◆◆◆◆
Deluxe Edition is a wonderful 15-track collection that compiles all of the highlights from his first six albums for Alligator Records. Although a few of Little Charlie & the Nightcats' albums hold up as individual works, they've all been a little uneven, which means the appearance of this best-of collection is all the more welcome. Not only will it satisfy the needs of the curious, but fans who just want the cream of the crop will be thrilled with this record. — *Thom Owens*

Little Feat

f. 1969, Los Angeles, CA, **db.** 1979
Group / Rock 'n' Roll, Blues-Rock
Though they had all the trappings of a Southern-fried blues band, Little Feat were hardly conventional. Led by songwriter/guitarist Lowell George, Little Feat was a wildly eclectic band, bringing together strains of blues, R&B, country, and rock 'n' roll. The group was exceptionally gifted technically and their polished professionalism sat well with the slick sounds coming out of Southern California during the '70s. However, Little Feat were hardly slick—they had a surreal sensibility, as evidenced by George's idiosyncratic songwriting, which helped the band earn a cult following among critics and musicians. Though the band earned some success on album-oriented radio, the group was derailed after George's death in 1979. Little Feat re-formed in the late '80s, and while they were playing as well as ever, they lacked the skewed sensibility that made them cult favorites. Nevertheless, their albums and tours were successful, especially among American blues-rock fans.

However, Little Feat wasn't conceived as straightahead blues-rock group. Its founding members, Lowell George (vocals, guitar, slide guitar) and Rob Estrada (bass), were veterans of Frank Zappa's Mothers of Invention. George had a long musical career before joining the Mothers. As a child, he and his brother Hampton performed a harmonica duet on television's *Ted Mack's Original Amateur Hour*. During high school, he learned how to play flute, which led to him appearing as an oboist and baritone saxophonist on several Frank Sinatra recording sessions. He formed the folk-rock group the Factory with drummer Richard Hayward in 1965. Before disbanding, the Factory made some recordings for Uni Records, but the tapes sat unreleased until the 1990s. Following the group's demise, George joined the Mothers of Invention where he met Estrada. Zappa convinced George to form his own band after hearing "Willin'," but the guitarist was reluctant to begin a band until he participated in a brief Standells reunion.

George and Estrada formed Little Feat in 1969 with Hayward and keyboardist Billy Payne. Neither its eponymous first album (1971) nor 1972's *Sailin' Shoes* were commercial successes, despite strong reviews. As a result, the group temporarily disbanded, with Estrada leaving music to become a computer programmer. When the group reconvened later in 1972, he was replaced by New Orleans musician Kenny Gradney. In its second incarnation, Little Feat also featured guitarist Paul Barrere and percussionist Sam Clayton, who gave the music a funkier feeling, as demonstrated by 1973's *Dixie Chicken*. The band toured heavily behind the record, building a strong following in the South and on the East Coast. Nevertheless, the group remained centered in Los Angeles, since the members did a lot of session work on the side.

Though the band was earning a cult following, several members of the group were growing frustrated by George's erratic behavior and increasing drug use. Following 1974's *Feats Don't Fail Me Now*, Barrere and Payne became the band's primary songwriters and they were primarily responsible for the jazzy fusions of 1975's *The Last Record Album*. Little Feat continued in that direction on *Time Loves A Hero* (1977), the double-live album *Waiting for Columbus* (1978), and *Down on the Farm* (1979). Frustrated with the band's increasingly improvisational and jazzy nature, George recorded a solo album, *Thanks I'll Eat It Here*, which was released in 1979. Following its release, George announced that Little Feat had broken up, and he embarked on a solo tour. Partway through the tour, he died of an apparent heart attack. *Down on the Farm* was released after his death, as was the rarities collection, *Hoy-Hoy!* (1981).

After spending seven years as sidemen, Payne, Barrere, Hayward, Gradney, and Clayton re-formed Little Feat in 1988, adding vocalist/guitarist Craig Fuller and guitarist Fred Tackett. The heavily-anticipated *Let It Roll* was released in 1988 to mixed reviews, but it went gold. The group's subsequent reunion albums—*Representing the Mambo* (1989), *Shake Me Up* (1991), *Ain't Head Enough Fun* (1995)—each sold progressively less, but the band remained a popular concert attraction, releasing *Under the Radar* in 1998. — *Stephen Thomas Erlewine*

Little Feat / 1971 / Warner Brothers ✦✦✦
Debut album finds Lowell George's songwriting, singing, and playing style in place on his signature song, "Willin'," as well as "Truck Stop Girl" and "Crazy Captain Gunboat Willie." — *William Ruhlmann*

Sailin' Shoes / 1972 / Warner Brothers ✦✦✦✦
A near-peak of songwriting ("Easy to Slip," "Cold, Cold, Cold," "Sailin' Shoes") distinguishes this second album, on which the band finds a perfect second-line groove and Lowell George sings and plays with blues authority. — *William Ruhlmann*

★ **Dixie Chicken** / 1973 / Warner Brothers ✦✦✦✦✦
A reconfigured group adds greater depth to the percussion, along with a rhythm guitarist, who frees Lowell George to slide his way to heaven, and the songs—especially the title track, "Two Trains," and "Fat Man in the Bathtub"—are among George's best. — *William Ruhlmann*

Feats Don't Fail Me Now / 1974 / Warner Brothers ✦✦✦✦
Whereas earlier albums were carried by Lowell George, this one finds the band as a whole at a writing and performing peak, with Bill Payne and Paul Berrere especially standing out on such songs as "Rock and Roll Doctor," "Oh Atlanta," and "Skin It Back." — *William Ruhlmann*

The Last Record Album / 1975 / Warner Brothers ✦✦✦
From this point on, Lowell George's role in Little Feat seems to have diminished, with the group's direction increasingly left in the capable, if less inspired hands, of Bill Payne and Paul Barrere. The album does, however, contain two excellent George originals in "Down Below the Borderline" and "Long Distance Love." — *William Ruhlmann*

Time Loves a Hero / 1977 / Warner Brothers ✦✦✦
Lowell George's gradual disappearance from his own group continued here, with the album containing only one of his solo compositions, "Rocket in My Pocket," which wasn't one of his best. The title track and "Hi Holler," among other tracks, show Paul Barrere and Bill Payne to be talented substitutes, but this album, the original group's final studio effort, does not show them at their best. — *William Ruhlmann*

Waiting for Columbus / 1978 / Warner Brothers ✦✦✦✦
Excellent double-disc live album. — *William Ruhlmann*

Down on the Farm / 1979 / Warner Brothers ✦✦
A scraped-together, post-breakup, contractual obligation album, for charitable fans only. — *William Ruhlmann*

Hoy-Hoy / 1981 / Warner Brothers ✦✦✦✦
Compilation of best songs and odds and ends makes a good wrap-up to the Lowell George years. — *William Ruhlmann*

Let It Roll / Jul. 1988 / Warner Brothers ✦✦✦
Little Feat packed it in after Lowell George's death. It wasn't that the band couldn't survive without him—on their last few albums, he was barely able to carry his weight, only contributing a handful of (admittedly excellent) songs—it just seemed like an appropriate gesture. But in the years following their breakup, none of the members could find a fruitful full-time gig, leading them to get the band back together in 1988 with ex-Pure Prairie League vocalist Craig Fuller as the new frontman. Without George, all of the group's weird, rough edges have been removed, leaving behind a slick, well-oiled groove machine, as *Let it Roll,* the first record by the reunited band, proves. There's no question that these guys have chops, and there's a lot of entertaining music here, along with a handful of solid songs. Still, the breezy title track and the bluesy "Hate to Lose Your Lovin'" don't have the kick of such latter-day cuts as Paul Barrere's funky "All That You Dream," largely because these guys sound like professionals, not a rough and ready working band. That's not necessarily a bad thing, however. Anyone needing a fix of new Little Feat will be pleased with *Let it Roll* to a certain extent, especially since it fails to be embarrassing, but they're unlikely to find this a substitute for *Dixie Chicken.* — *Stephen Thomas Erlewine*

Representing the Mambo / 1989 / Warner Brothers ✦✦
Having demonstrated on *Let It Roll* that they could produce an effective Little Feat soundalike record, the reconstituted band should have stopped while they were ahead. This follow-up shows a decline in songwriting, making the absence of Lowell George unmistakably apparent. — *William Ruhlmann*

Shake Me Up / Sep. 24, 1991 / Morgan Creek ✦✦
With this pedestrian third reunion album, Little Feat should have lost the right to use its noble name. Little of the band's original spark remained. — *William Ruhlmann*

● **Best of Little Feat: As Time Goes By** / Feb. 10, 1994 / Warner Brothers ✦✦✦✦
As Time Goes By: The Best of Little Feat is an extraordinary collection that contains almost every essential Little Feat song from their '70s heyday with Lowell George, plus the two hits ("Let It Roll," "Hate to Lose Your Lovin'") from their late-'80s comeback. Most of the band's albums are worth hearing, but this is a great introduction for the curious and—since it features "Dixie Chicken," "Willin'," "Two Trains," "Fat Man in the Bathtub," "Sailin' Shoes," "Oh Atlanta," and "All That You Dream" in one place—it's a great summation of the group's achievements, and George's songwriting talent in particular. Unfortunately, *As Time Goes By* has only been released by the British division of Warner Brothers, but it's worth tracking down. — *Stephen Thomas Erlewine*

Ain't Had Enough Fun / Apr. 25, 1995 / Zoo ✦✦✦
The members of the group that has the legal right to call itself "Little Feat" perhaps are to be complemented for their realization, after three albums, that having Craig Fuller imitate the voice of the band's deceased founder, Lowell George, was ethically suspect. Or maybe they didn't realize; this album's liner notes say only that "mister fuller decided that the road life was not for him." In any case, the surviving "featsters" have cast against type, recruiting one Shaun Murphy, who can't imitate George, but certainly can imitate longtime Feat booster Bonnie Raitt. The addition of a female voice allows for greater variety in lyric-writing and some entertaining call-and-response singing; however, and more important, it begins to free the group from the ghost of Lowell George. The featsters locate themselves more than ever in the mythology of New Orleans, alternating second-line rhythms with John Lee Hooker boogie. One may still wish they had found another name to distinguish themselves from George's group, but *Ain't Had Enough Fun* is a worthy addition to their catalog on its own terms. — *William Ruhlmann*

Live from Neon Park / Jun. 18, 1996 / Zoo ✦✦✦
Live from Neon Park is an exhaustive double-disc live set recorded on the tour supporting *Ain't Had Enough Fun,* the first Little Feat album that featured vocalist Shaun Murphy. The double-disc features all of the band's best-known material, from "Dixie Chicken" to "Let It Roll." The Feat have always been one of the best live rootsy rock bands, so they naturally give inspired performances, even if they occasionally sound like they've performed these songs one too many times. Still, dedicated Little Feat fans will find this to be an entertaining momento of the latter-day edition of the band. — *Thom Owens*

Little Mike & the Tornadoes

f. New Orleans, NY
Group / Modern Electric Blues
Harmonica player and keyboardist Mike Markowitz, born in Queens, NY, and raised in New York City's burgeoning '80s blues club scene, has made his mark in the blues world through a lot of hard touring and a bit of good old fashioned New York salesmanship, or "chutzpah."

Born November 23, 1955, Markowitz cites his earliest influences as John Lee Hooker, Muddy Waters, and Little Walter Jacobs. In 1978, he formed his first blues band and began playing the blues bars around lower Manhattan, but his reputation began to grow when he began backing up legendary musicians like pianist Pinetop Perkins, Hubert Sumlin, and Jimmy Rogers when they came to New York or New Jersey to perform. Markowitz's passion for blues, as a fan and as a performer, is legendary, and he carried it over into the producer's chair in 1988, when he recorded albums for Perkins and later for Sumlin.

In 1990, Little Mike and the Tornadoes got their own recording contract with Blind Pig, a San Francisco-based label, and his output has been quite prolific since then. The group's first album, *Heart Attack*, includes guest performances by Perkins, Paul Butterfield, and Sumlin. Two years later, he recorded *Payday*, also for Blind Pig, before recording his debut for Flying Fish Records (a label that has since been acquired by Rounder Records), *Flynn's Place*.

Markowitz is an extremely hard working, level-headed blues musician who will no doubt surface again and again on records, whether for Rounder or for some other label. All three of Markowitz's albums are available on compact disc, and worth seeking out. — *Richard Skelly*

● **Heart Attack** / 1990 / Blind Pig ✦✦✦✦
On this competent White-guy bar-band sort-of blues, four cuts feature Paul Butterfield on harp (believed to be his last recordings). Other guests are Ronnie Earl, Pinetop Perkins, Big Daddy Kinsey, and Hubert Sumlin. — *Niles J. Frantz*

Payday / 1992 / Blind Pig ✦✦✦
Little Mike & the Tornadoes don't alter their musical approach on *Payday* at all, but they don't need to—they deliver driving Chicago blues with no frills and lots and lots of passion. The group doesn't just churn out the same old covers, either—they tear through a set of 12 originals that are written in the style of classic '50s and '60s blues. Occasionally their songwriting falters, but never their performances. Every song is delivered with conviction, and Little Mike positively wails on both the piano and harp. — *Thom Owens*

Flynn's Place / 1995 / Flying Fish ✦✦✦
Flynn's Place is another excellent collection of piledriving, good-time blues and boogie from Little Mike & the Tornadoes, featuring a fine selection of originals and smoking solos. — *Thom Owens*

Hot Shot / Jan. 20, 1998 / Wild Dog ✦✦✦
Although not a blues band in the truest sense of the word, consider this their 'roots music' album. Frontman Little Mike Markowitz turns in a batch of original tunes that more than tip their collective and stylistic hat to Willie Dixon, Muddy Waters, Louis Prima, and James Cotton. The band goes through its workmanlike paces and that same blue-collar approach applies to the lyrical themes on these songs, full of tried and true formulaic stories about sex, the road, and bad whiskey and women. It's a shame that the blues can sometimes be reduced down to a pile of cliches, but at least the musical side of the equation works. — *Cub Koda*

Little Milton (Milton Campbell)

b. Sep. 7, 1934, Inverness, MS
Guitar, Vocals / Soul, R&B, Soul Blues, Boogie-Woogie, Modern Electric Blues, Electric Chicago Blues, Electric Blues
One of the great blues guitarists, singers, and composers of all time, Milton began his recording career in Memphis with Sun Records in 1953. Small-label singles followed for Meteor and Bobbin before he landed at Chess records in Chicago in 1961. He became one of the best-selling blues artists of the '60s, with many hit singles, including a No.1 R&B hit "We're Gonna Make It" and items such as "Feel So Bad," "If Walls Could Talk," and "Baby I Love You." There may be soap-opera elements in much of Milton's work, but it is always done with flair and good humor. While the mold was pretty much established during his Checker period, it also worked with his later affiliations at Stax and Glades. His Malaco recordings (dating from 1984) bring the formula of strings, horns, and background vocals up to date, but the blues artistry of Milton still shines through. — *Bob Porter*

We're Gonna Make It / 1965 / Chess ✦✦✦✦

Sings Big Blues / 1968 / Checker ✦✦✦
This is one of the hottest collective blues albums of the '60s. — *Bill Dahl*

If Walls Could Talk / 1970 / MCA/Chess ✦✦✦✦
On *If Walls Could Talk* Little Milton continues to fuse blues with soul—if anything, the album leans toward soul more than blues. Supported by a band with a thick, wailing horn section, Little Milton sings and plays with power. Though there a couple of wonderful solos, the focus of the record is on the songs, which all sound terrific, thanks to Milton's compassionate vocals. — *Thom Owens*

Grits Ain't Groceries / Jan. 1970 / Stax ✦✦✦
Grits Ain't Groceries is another set of soul and R&B songs from the blues

guitarist Little Milton, highlighted by the scorching title track. — *Thom Owens*

Greatest Hits [Chess/MCA] / 1972 / MCA/Chess ✦✦✦
Greatest Hits offers a good sampling of Little Milton's singles for Chess Records in the '60s, including the hits "We're Gonna Make It" and "If Walls Could Talk." It may be a little brief, but there are no bad songs on the record at all and it's an excellent introduction to the guitarist's talents. — *Thom Owens*

Waiting for Little Milton / 1973 / Stax ✦✦✦
Although Little Milton's Stax recordings aren't as blues-oriented as his classic Chess and Checker recordings, there are still plenty of things to recommend about them. Primarily, they're of interest because they focus on his soulful vocals, and those vocals shine on *Waiting for Little Milton*. On the whole, the album is a little uneven—the songs aren't always first-rate and the production is a little too smooth—but the performances make it worthwhile for most dedicated fans. — *Thom Owens*

What It Is / 1973 / Stax ✦✦✦
What It Is captures Little Milton at the 1973 Montreux Blues and Jazz Festival, where the guitarist was in fine form. Throughout the concert, Milton sings and solos with flair, making it more than just another live album from the guitarist and turning it into something special. — *Thom Owens*

Blues 'N Soul / 1974 / Stax ✦✦✦
Blues 'N Soul is one of his best Stax sets. — *Bill Dahl*

Montreux Festival / 1974 / Stax ✦✦✦

Tin Pan Alley / 1975 / Stax ✦✦✦✦
Most of the guitarist's best soul/blues Stax sides of the 1970s with plenty of his crisp guitar. — *Bill Dahl*

Friend of Mine / 1976 / Glades ✦✦✦

☆ **Chess Blues Master Series** / 1976 / Chess ✦✦✦✦✦
Little Milton hit his creative and playing stride at Chess, at least in terms of blues. "Grits Ain't Groceries," "We're Gonna Make It" and many other gems were available on this LP anthology. It's no longer available except in used record stores, but is still worth pursuing. — *Ron Wynn*

Chronicle / 1979 / Stax ✦✦✦✦
This compilation of Little Milton and Albert King material has a leftover feel; the liner notes provide no sources and dates, admitting only that these are "Stax recordings, some never before available on LP." If you're a big fan of one or both of the artists involved, though, it's not bad, with a quality that's generally consistent with their fully-baked Stax-era albums. The Milton half of the program is somewhat inferior to the King tracks, the singer taking a misstep with his version of Charlie Rich's country smash "Behind Closed Doors." — *Richie Unterberger*

Walkin' the Back Streets / 1981 / Stax ✦✦✦✦
Excellent blues-soul set. — *Bill Dahl*

Raise a Little Sand / 1982 / Red Lightnin' ✦✦✦
Raise a Little Sand collects Little Milton's recordings for Sun and Bobbin Records, which rank as his rawest, most exciting work. Although the quality of this package isn't quite as good as it could have been—the sound and the presentation could have been more carefully considered—this is top-notch, essential music that should be heard in any form. — *Thom Owens*

The Blues Is Alright / Dec. 1982 / Evidence ✦✦
The Blues Is Alright leans toward the blues more than his late-'70s and early-'80s collections. However, the quality of Milton's performance isn't quite up to par, making the collection a bit of a disappointment. — *Thom Owens*

Age Ain't Nothin' But a Number / 1983 / Mobile Fidelity ✦✦✦
"Little Milton" Campbell made an excellent modern blues/soul album for MCA in the early '80s that languished due to inadequate promotional efforts. The failure of *Age Ain't Nothin' But a Number* convinced Campbell to move to Malaco. Mobile Fidelity's recent remastered CD reissue of this underrated session provides a perfect sonic framework for Milton's taut, tantalizing, and nicely executed guitar, soulful, often biting vocals, and solid arrangements and songs. The title cut was a mild hit, one of the last times Milton reached the R&B charts, while other numbers such as "Why Are You So Hard To Please," "Don't Leave Me," and "Living On The Dark Side Of Love" were as expertly crafted as any of his best Chess dates. — *Ron Wynn*

Playing for Keeps / 1984 / Malaco ✦✦✦

Playing for Keeps is one of Little Milton's best latter-day albums, featuring a smooth, but not too slick production, impassioned vocals, and a generally strong set of songs, highlighted by "The Blues Is Alright." — *Thom Owens*

Greatest Sides / 1984 / MCA/Chess ✦✦✦✦

Greatest Sides contains a few of Little Milton's best cuts—including "We're Gonna Make It"—but the packaging isn't very good and the songs are presented haphazardly. There might be some good music on *Greatest Sides*, but there are far better compilations to purchase. — *Thom Owens*

Movin' to the Country / 1987 / Malaco ✦✦✦

Annie Mae's Cafe / 1987 / Malaco ✦✦✦

Annie Mae's Cafe is one of the strongest albums Little Milton recorded for Malaco. Milton's solos are crisp and stinging throughout the album and his vocals are impassioned. Because he's in top form, he can save the lesser material and that's what makes the album so consistent. — *Thom Owens*

I Will Survive / 1988 / Malaco ✦✦✦

Back to Back / 1988 / Malaco ✦✦✦

From a soul standpoint, *Back to Back* was the strongest album that Little Milton recorded for Malaco in the 1980s. Though the CD contains a few noteworthy 12-bar numbers (including "Penitentiary Blues" and "It's Hard to Explain"), R&B is dominant. Those who fancy 1970s-type soul shouldn't miss Milton's passionate, confessional storytelling on such treasures as "(I Had) Too Much Heaven Last Night," "Caught in the Act (Of Gettin' It On)," and the heartbreaking "I Was Tryin' Not Break Down." The gruff, big-voiced singer/guitarist even breathes some life into "Wind Beneath My Wings," a corny pop ballad that was unbearably insipid in Bette Midler's hands but is easier to take when Milton gets a hold of it. — *Alex Henderson*

Too Much Pain / 1990 / Malaco ✦✦✦

Though not essential and not as strong as *Back to Back*, *Too Much Pain* was a welcome addition to Milton's catalog. Milton never claimed to be a purist, and the album illustrates his effectiveness as both a bluesman and a soul shouter. Highlights of this likable date range from the smooth 1970s-ish up-town soul of "The Woman I Love" (which wouldn't have been inappropriate on a Harold Melvin & the Bluenotes album), to "So Much Pain," "Count the Days," and Denise LaSalle's amusing "Your Wife Is Cheating On Us." If you're into clever double entendres, get into "Runway," a Stax-ish soul gem that finds Milton equating a cheating lover with an airport runway, in that everyone is landing on her. — *Alex Henderson*

★ **Sun Masters** / 1990 / Rounder ✦✦✦✦✦

While he was at Sun, Little Milton tried a variety of different sounds and styles—sounding like everybody from Elmore James and B.B. King to Fats Domino—which was all tied together by his raw, manic lead guitar. *The Sun Masters* collects many of Milton's absolute finest moments—he never again sounded quite as wild or reckless, either vocally or instrumentally, as he did here. — *Thom Owens*

Strugglin' Lady / 1992 / Malaco ✦✦✦

OK contemporary blues-soul set. — *Bill Dahl*

Welcome to the Club: The Essential Chess Recordings / 1994 / MCA ✦✦✦✦

Greatest Hits [Malaco] / Sep. 5, 1995 / Malaco ✦✦✦

For fans of Little Milton's Chess, Checker, and Sun sides, his '80s records for Malaco aren't particularly attractive, since they are slicker and more polished. Nevertheless, he cut several first-rate songs for the label, songs that showcase his considerable guitar and vocal talents, and the majority of those songs are collected on *Greatest Hits*. It's a solid introduction to the latter part of Milton's career. — *Thom Owens*

Cheatin' Habit / 1996 / Malaco ✦✦✦

Having found a suitable home at Malaco, the leading label of the 1980s and 1990s for Southern soul-blues, Little Milton has settled into a prolific recording schedule; this is his already his tenth CD for the label (eleventh, if you count a greatest hits compilation). It contains ingredients to satisfy his core audience but is not one of his best. The songs are mostly of the cheatin' or leavin' variety (he's cheating or she's cheating, he's leaving or she's leaving). The guitar fills and horn parts are quite formulaic. — *Steve Hoffman*

Reality / 1996 / Malaco ✦✦✦

Some blues enthusiasts would have us believe that Little Milton's heavily arranged Malaco dates have paled in comparison to his Sun, Chess, and Stax output, but in fact, they've been consistent and generally quite enjoyable. The thing is that they have as much to do with soul and R&B as they do with actual 12-bar blues, and if you're a blues purist who isn't comfortable with the idea of Milton recording a lot of songs that would have been appropriate for the O'Jays or the Dramatics in the 1970s, it's best to pass on *Reality*. However, if you hold blues and 1970s soul in equally high regard, you should find the CD appealing. Milton shows how gutsy a bluesman he can be on 12-bar songs like "A Right to Sing the Blues" and "I'm Jealous of Her Husband," but he's equally convincing on the 1970s-type soul of "I Want My Baby Back," "I've Got to Remember," and Bobby Womack's "That's the Way I Feel About It." Milton never claimed to be a purist, and *Reality* points to the fact that he is anything but. — *Alex Henderson*

We're Gonna Make It/Little Milton Sings Big Blues / 1996 / MCA/Chess ✦✦✦✦

Two of Milton's classic mid-'60s Chess albums on one CD makes for a great value. — *Bill Dahl*

★ **Greatest Hits (Chess 50th Anniversary Collection)** / Jun. 17, 1997 / MCA ✦✦✦✦✦

Milton Campbell was a blues chameleon in his early recording career for Sun and Bobbin, changing styles seemingly with every record he made. But he found his groove—a Bobby Bland-style R&B with a bluesy edge to it—when he came to Chess Records in 1963. These 16 tracks collect the highlights of his six-year tenure at the label, featuring the hits "We're Gonna Make It," "Who's Cheating Who?," and "If Walls Could Talk." The majority of the sides feature strong horn charts courtesy of Oliver Sain and Gene Barge, the core of Milton's sound during this period. The stylistic connection of Milton to Bland is no more stronger evidenced than on his cover of "Blind Man," but equal mention in the soulful department must go to the heart-wrenching ballad "Let Me Down Easy" and "Poor Man's Song," one of two songs collected here that Campbell had a hand in writing. Interesting updates of Little Willie John's "All Around the World" ("Grits Ain't Groceries"), Chuck Willis' "I Feel So Bad," and Rosco Gordon's "Just a Little Bit" complete the package. As part of MCA's Chess 50th Anniversary Series, this sweats the two-disc *Welcome to the Club: The Essential Chess Recordings* down to a perfect introductory package to this sometimes misunderstood (is he blues? soul? R&B?) artist. — *Cub Koda*

Count the Days / Sep. 23, 1997 / 601 ✦✦✦✦

I'm a Gambler / Malaco ✦✦✦✦

Malaco releases usually mix straight blues with a slicker variety of R&B aimed at "urban contemporary" radio airplay, but *I'm a Gambler* has a very high blues content. Milton sings with vigor, like he was feeling at the top of his game when he recorded this CD—and no wonder, since the material is quite strong. Highlights include the humorous "Casino Blues," the cocky "Like a Rooster on a Hen," and the bayou swamp rocker "Polk Salad Annie" (which Little Milton really makes his own). — *Steve Hoffman*

Little Richard (Richard Wayne Penniman)

b. Dec. 5, 1935, Macon, GA

Vocals, Piano / R&B, Rock 'n' Roll, New Orleans R&B

One of the original rock 'n' roll greats, Little Richard merged the fire of gospel with New Orleans R&B, pounding the piano and wailing with gleeful abandon. While numerous other R&B greats of the early '50s had been moving in a similar direction, none of them matched the sheer electricity of Richard's vocals. With his bullet-speed deliveries, ecstatic trills, and the overjoyed force of personality in his singing, he was crucial in upping the voltage from high-powered R&B into the similar, yet different, guise of rock 'n' roll. Although he was only a hitmaker for a couple of years or so, his influence upon both the soul and British Invasion stars of the '60s was vast, and his early hits remain core classics of the rock repertoire.

Heavily steeped in gospel music while growing up in Georgia, when Little Richard began recording in the early '50s, he played unexceptional jump blues/R&B that owed a lot to his early inspirations Billy Wright and Roy Brown. In 1955, at Lloyd Price's suggestion, Richard sent a demo tape to Specialty Records, who were impressed enough to sign him and arrange a session for him in New Orleans. That session, however, didn't get off the ground until Richard began fooling around with a slightly obscene ditty during a break. With slightly cleaned-up lyrics, "Tutti Frutti" was the record that gave birth to Little Richard as we know him—the gleeful "woo!"s, the furious piano playing, the sax-driven, pedal-to-the-metal rhythm section. It was also his first hit, although, ridiculous as it now seems, Pat Boone's cover version outdid Richard's on the hit parade.

Pat Boone would also try to cover Richard's next hit, "Long Tall Sally," but by that time it was evident that audiences, Black and White, much preferred the real deal. In 1956 and 1957, Richard reeled off a string of classic hits— "Long Tall Sally," "Slippin' and "Slidin'," "Jenny, Jenny," "Keep a Knockin'," "Good Golly, Miss Molly," "The Girl Can't Help It"—that remain the foundation of his fame. While Richard's inimitable mania was the key to his best records, he also owed a lot of his success to the gutsy playing of ace New Orleans session players like Lee Allen (tenor sax), Alvin Tyler (baritone sax), and especially Earl Palmer (drummer), who usually accompanied the singer in both New Orleans and Los Angeles studios. Richard's unforgettable appearances in early rock 'n' roll movies, especially *The Girl Can't Help It*, also did a lot to spread the rock 'n' roll gospel to the masses.

Little Richard was at the height of his commercial and artistic powers when he suddenly quit the business during an Australian tour in late 1957, enrolling in a bible college in Alabama shortly after returning to the States. Richard had actually been feeling the call of religion for a while before his announcement, but it was nonetheless a shock to both his fans and the industry. Specialty drew on unreleased sessions for a few more hard-rocking singles in the late '50s, but Richard virtually vanished from the public eye for a few years. When he did return to recording, it was as a gospel singer, cutting a few little-heard sacred sides for End, Mercury, and Atlantic in the early '60s.

By 1962, though, Richard had returned to rock 'n' roll, touring Britain to an enthusiastic reception. Among the groups that supported him on those jaunts were the Rolling Stones and the Beatles, whose vocals (Paul McCartney's especially) took a lot of inspiration from Richard's. In 1964, the Beatles cut a knockout version of "Long Tall Sally," with McCartney on lead, that may have even outdone the original. It's been speculated that the success of the Beatles, and other British Invaders who idolized Richard, finally prompted the singer into making a full-scale comeback as an unapologetic rock 'n' roller. Hooking up with Specialty once again, he had a small hit in 1964 with "Bama Lama Bama Loo." These and other sides were respectable efforts in the mold of his classic '50s sides, but tastes had changed too much for Little Richard to climb the charts again. He spent the rest of the '60s in a continual unsuccessful comeback, recording for Vee-Jay (accompanied on some sides by Jimi Hendrix, who was briefly in Richard's band), OKeh, and Modern (for whom he even tried recording in Memphis with Stax session musicians).

It was the rock 'n' roll revival of the late '60s and early '70s, though, that really saved Richard's career, enabling him to play on the nostalgia circuit with great success (though he had one last small hit, "Freedom Blues," in 1970). He had always been a flamboyant performer, brandishing a six-inch pompadour and mascara, and constant entertaining appearances on television talk shows seemed to ensure his continuing success as a living legend. Yet by the late '70s, he'd returned to the church again. Somewhat predictably, he'd eased back into rock and show business by the mid-'80s. Since then, he's maintained his profile with a role in *Down and Out in Beverly Hills*, and guest appearances on soundtracks, compilations, and children's rock records. At this point it's safe to assume that he never will get that much-hungered-for comeback hit, but he remains one of rock 'n' roll's most colorful icons, still capable of turning on the charm and charisma in his infrequent appearances in the limelight. — *Richie Unterberger*

Here's Little Richard / 1957 / Specialty ✦✦✦✦

Little Richard's debut album wasn't released until more than a year after he first broke through nationally with "Tutti Frutti" in early 1956. By the time Specialty Records got around to introducing him to LP buyers, Little Richard had already scored six Top 40 pop hits. This album didn't contain all of them, but it did contain "Tutti Frutti," "Long Tall Sally," "Slippin' and Slidin' (Peepin' and Hidin')," "Rip It Up," "Ready Teddy," "Jenny, Jenny," and "Miss Ann," all of which had made the pop charts and been in the R&B Top Ten. ("True, Fine Mama," also included, would chart as the B-side of "Ooh! My Soul" a year

later.) Thus, *Here's Little Richard* was more of a compilation than just a debut album, a consistent collection containing many of Little Richard's classic recordings. It was also his highest charting and probably best-selling effort. — *William Ruhlmann*

Little Richard [Specialty] / 1958 / Specialty ✦✦✦✦

Like his debut album, *Here's Little Richard*, Little Richard's self-titled second album was, in essence, a compilation record rather than a newly recorded LP. Among its 12 selections were nine songs that had been chart singles between 1956 and 1958, including "Keep A-Knockin'" and "Good Golly, Miss Molly," which had hit the pop Top Ten, and "Lucille," which had topped the R&B charts. Other former singles were "Heeby-Jeebies," "The Girl Can't Help it," "Send Me Some Lovin'" (all three R&B Top Tens), "Ooh! My Soul" (Little Richard's final Top 40 pop hit), "All Around the World," and "Baby Face." Little Richard's spectacular two-year run of hits was over by mid-1958, with the singer having renounced rock 'n' roll as of October 1957, but Little Richard gathers together a generous helping of his most remarkable work. — *William Ruhlmann*

The Fabulous Little Richard / 1959 / Specialty ✦✦✦

With Little Richard having long since given up pop music for religion, Specialty Records released as his third album a collection of tracks recorded mostly at his first session in 1955 (with a few 1956 and 1957 recordings as well). Richard handles these R&B songs well, but, with the exception of the medley "Kansas City/Hey-Hey-Hey-Hey" (later copied note for note by The Beatles), the songs and performances do not match his incendiary hits of the period. — *William Ruhlmann*

Grooviest 17 Original Hits! / 1959 / Specialty ✦✦✦✦

Despite its trendy title, *Grooviest 17 Original Hits!* was the most complete collection of Little Richard's hits yet released. By this point, Little Richard had re-recorded his hits for Vee-Jay, Modern, and OKeh, and Specialty seems to have wanted an album with the word "original" in the title, emphasizing that they possessed the actual hit versions. Taking the 12 tracks from 1963's *His Greatest Hits*, the company added five more tracks, among them "Ready Teddy," "Miss Ann," and "Ooh! My Soul," chart records they had skipped the first time around. "The Girl Can't Help It" still didn't appear on a Little Richard hits collection, but *Grooviest 17 Original Hits!* was the single-disc Little Richard hits collection to own for a long time to come. — *William Ruhlmann*

The Explosive Little Richard / 1967 / OKeh ✦✦✦

In 1966, OKeh Records took its turn at trying to revive the recording career of Little Richard. In the fall of that year, they put him in a studio in Hollywood with his former Specialty Records associate Larry Williams producing, and the two cut this album of rock 'n' roll ravers, which was released in January 1967. Little Richard is as frantic as ever, notably on the lead-off track, "I Don't Want to Discuss It," later a showstopper for Delaney & Bonnie, but rock music trends were far removed from his style of rocking abandon by 1967, and this album went unnoticed. OKeh recorded Little Richard doing his hits that January and released the results several months later as *Little Richard's Greatest Hits Recorded Live*, but that was the end of this comeback. (*The Explosive Little Richard!* originally was released by OKeh Records in January 1967 as OKeh 14117. It has been reissued several times by Epic Records, most recently in 1986 as Epic 40390.) — *William Ruhlmann*

The Rill Thing / 1971 / Reprise ✦✦✦

The Rill Thing represented Little Richard's most serious attempt at a comeback since his 1950s heyday. "Freedom Blues," Richard's debut Reprise single, released in April 1970, was a mid-chart hit, his first in five years. "Greenwood Mississippi," released as a single concurrently with the album, also charted. Richard adopted a cajun/country-rock approach (even covering "Lovesick Blues"), with a heavy beat and twangy guitar backing up his rough, forceful vocals. Despite the indulgence of the rambling ten-minute instrumental title track, the LP was a convincing update on his early work. But it did not propel Little Richard back to the top of the charts. — *William Ruhlmann*

★ 18 Greatest Hits / 1985 / Rhino ✦✦✦✦✦

18 Greatest Hits is the definitive single-disc collection of Little Richard's Specialty singles, especially for listeners who only want the hits. Every one of Richard's biggest hits—"Tutti Frutti," "Long Tall Sally," "Slippin' and Slidin'," "Rip It Up," "Ready Teddy," "The Girl Can't Help It," "Lucille," "Send Me Some Lovin'," "Keep A-Knockin'," "Good Golly Miss Molly"—is here, plus singles like "Heeby-Jeebies," "She's Got It," "Ooh! My Soul," "Miss Ann," "Kansas City/

Hey Hey Hey," and "Bama Lama Bama Loo" that were bigger hits on the R&B charts than the pop charts. All of the singles are presented in chronological order and the disc simply rips it up from beginning to end. It's a definitive collection. — *Stephen Thomas Erlewine*

The Specialty Box Set / 1989 / Specialty ◆◆◆◆
Dig it—a collection of all 73 songs that Little Richard cut for Specialty Records from 1955 through 1959, including early working versions of hits including "Long Tall Sally" and "Slippin' and Slidin'," may seem like overkill to the casual listener, but if you're thinking of buying this three-CD box, chances are you're not a casual listener. And if you're not thinking about it, then you should be. This set covers only four years in Little Richard's career, but manages to sum up virtually everything you need to know about him (his earlier sides, available on Bear Family, are an interesting appendix, but of his later stuff, only the early—and mid-'60s material, with Jimi Hendrix on guitar, hold any significance, mostly as a curiosity). Not only does the music make you want to get up and dance, but the notes—spread out on a lavishly illustrated booklet and the individual jewel boxes—tell the whole story of Specialty Records and the people behind it, including Art Rupe, Bumps Blackwell, Dave Bartholomew, and, of course, Richard Penniman himself. The session information alone could keep owners busy for a week. The sound is nothing less than breathtaking, loud and raunchy but razor sharp, and the price of this set—about $42 retail—makes it competitive with other Little Richard single-disc sets as well as more attractive than the price of boxes devoted to Elvis Presley and Chuck Berry. The only complaint—why couldn't the producers list the songs on the individual jewel boxes? — *Bruce Eder*

The Specialty Box Set [Ace] / 1989 / Ace ◆◆◆◆
For the hardcore Little Richard fan—the kind that has to hear every recording the architect of rock 'n' roll ever made—there's little question that Ace's *Specialty Box Set* is the motherlode. Spanning six discs and over a hundred tracks, this is for serious listeners. Since Specialty's condensed, three-disc version of this set also included numerous working versions, alternate takes and commercials, it was also targeted for dedicated listeners, but this set—which is twice as large—is for fans who love to immerse themselves in minute details and unfinished takes. For those listeners, this set is certainly worth the money, since it is lavishly produced and boasts every single thing Little Richard recorded at the label. But most fans—including most serious listeners—will be satisfied with the more concise, but nevertheless comprehensive, three-disc set on Specialty. — *Stephen Thomas Erlewine*

The Formative Years 1951-53 / Jul. 1989 / Bear Family ◆◆◆◆
Early Richard, pre-"Tutti Frutti." — *Cub Koda*

★ **The Georgia Peach** / Aug. 5, 1991 / Specialty ◆◆◆◆◆
Perhaps the greatest of Little Richard's greatest hits compilations, the 25-track *Georgia Peach* features all of his biggest hits in chronological order, as well as terrific singles that never were as big as "Tutti Frutti" and "Good Golly Miss Molly." On top of the sublime song selection and sound, the liner notes by compiler Billy Vera are splendid and insightful. — *Stephen Thomas Erlewine*

Shag on Down by the Union Hall / Feb. 13, 1996 / Specialty ◆◆◆◆
For those who want more classic Little Richard than a greatest-hits collection but aren't devoted enough to spring for the expensive box sets, this is an excellent anthology of 24 of his best lesser-known tracks. Most of it dates from his classic era at Specialty (1955-57), with alternate takes of a lot of his hits and some decent B-sides; there are also a few songs that he cut for the label during his 1964 comeback, including the minor hit "Bama Lama Bama Loo." — *Richie Unterberger*

Little Sonny (Aaron Willis)

b. Oct. 6, 1932, Greensboro, AL
Harmonica, Vocals / Electric Blues
The Stax empire wasn't exactly renowned for its legion of blues harpists, but Little Sonny found the Memphis firm quite an agreeable home during the early '70s (he even appeared in the label's grandiose concert film, *Wattstax*, albeit very briefly).

Aaron Willis was a product of Detroit's blues scene. He moved to the Motor City in 1953 after growing up on his dad's farm in Alabama (his mom gave him his nickname). When Sonny wasn't working local haunts with John Lee

Hooker, Eddie Burns, Eddie Kirkland, Baby Boy Warren, or Washboard Willie (who gave him his first paying gig), he was snapping photos of the patrons for half a buck a snap.

Sonny Boy Williamson rambled through town in 1955 and gave Willis some valuable pointers. In 1958, Sonny made his blues recording debut, cutting for both Duke ("I Gotta Find My Baby") and local entrepreneur Joe Von Battle, who leased Sonny's "Love Shock" to Nashville's Excello imprint.

The harpist acquired a two-track tape machine and took matters into his own hands during the early '60s, helming his tiny Speedway label. He leased "The Creeper" and "Latin Soul" to Detroit's Revilot Records (his labelmates included Darrell Banks and George Clinton's Parliament) in 1966. That set the stage for his joining Stax's Enterprise label in 1970; his first album was the largely instrumental *New King of the Blues Harmonica*—a rather brash boast for a relative unknown!

Two more Enterprise sets that more effectively featured Sonny's vocal talents soon followed: *Black & Blue* and 1973's *Hard Goin' Up*, the latter distinguished by the Bettye Crutcher-penned "It's Hard Goin' Up (But Twice as Hard Coming Down)" and a variety of other soul-inflected tracks.

Not much was heard of the harpist in recent years until the British Sequel imprint released *Sonny Side Up* in 1995. His backing crew included keyboardist Rudy Robinson and guitarist Aaron Willis, Jr., both of whom graced *Hard Goin' Up* more than two decades before. — *Bill Dahl*

Sonny Side Up / 1995 / Glynn ◆◆◆
It's unequivocally nice to have Little Sonny back in harness after a long recording hiatus, but the harpist's comeback offering suffers from backing that feels too mechanical to really do his supple harp justice. A little more earthiness would have suited the project much better. — *Bill Dahl*

New Orleans R&B Gems / 1995 / Black Top ◆◆◆◆
Little known outside his Crescent City homebase, singer Little Sonny Jones' pipes deserved wider acclaim. Thanks to the efforts of Black Top, who recently reissued this collection on CD, maybe he'll finally receive a little posthumously. Though cut in 1975, the set sounds as though it was done a couple of decades earlier. Pianist Dave "Fat Man" Williams (who handles a few vocals as well), saxists Clarence Ford and David Lastie, and guitarist Justin Adams were all vets of that bygone era, and their love for the genre shines through every infectious track. — *Bill Dahl*

Ann Arbor Blues & Jazz Festival, Vol. 2: Blues with a Feeling / 1995 / Schoolkids ◆◆◆
One of a series of compilations from John Sinclair's stash of tapes from the Ann Arbor fests, this 1972 performance caught Sonny at his funk-tinged finest. He pleased the youthful throng with a few of his own numbers—"The Creeper Returns," "They Want Money"—and harp standards first done by Little Walter and Jimmy Reed. — *Bill Dahl*

● **New King of Blues Harmonica/Hard Goin' Up** / Ace ◆◆◆◆
A import coupling of the harpist's first and third LPs for Stax's Enterprise subsidiary and the best spot to inaugurate a Little Sonny CD collection. 1970's *New King* is mostly instrumental and places Sonny in a funky, contemporary setting; 1973's *Hard Goin' Up* was his best album for the firm, benefitting from excellent material spotlighting his vocal talents in a soul-slanted format. Stax offers *New King* by itself as a domestic CD. — *Bill Dahl*

Little Walter (Marion Walter Jacobs)

b. May 1, 1930, Marksville, LA, **d.** Feb. 15, 1968, Chicago, IL
Harmonica, Vocals, Accordion / R&B, Electric Chicago Blues, Chicago Blues, Electric Harmonica Blues, Electric Blues, Modern Electric Blues, Harmonica Blues
Who's the king of all postwar blues harpists, Chicago division or otherwise? Why, the virtuosic Little Walter, without a solitary doubt. The fiery harmonica wizard took the humble mouth organ in dazzling amplified directions that were unimaginable prior to his ascendancy. His daring instrumental innovations were so fresh, startling, and ahead of their time that they sometimes sported a jazz sensibility, soaring and swooping in front of snarling guitars and swinging rhythms perfectly suited to Walter's pioneering flights of fancy.

Marion Walter Jacobs was by most accounts an unruly but vastly talented youth who abandoned his rural Louisiana home for the bright lights of New Orleans at age 12. Walter gradually journeyed north from there, pausing in Helena (where he hung out with the wizened Sonny Boy Williamson), Memphis, and St. Louis before arriving in Chicago in 1946.

The thriving Maxwell Street strip offered a spot for the still-teenaged phenom to hawk his wares. He fell in with local royalty—Tampa Red and Big Bill Broonzy—and debuted on wax that same year for the tiny Ora-Nelle logo ("I Just Keep Loving Her") in the company of Jimmy Rogers and guitarist Othum Brown. Walter joined forces with Muddy Waters in 1948; the resulting stylistic tremors of that coupling are still being felt today. Along with Rogers and Baby Face Leroy Foster, this super-confident young aggregation became informally known as the Headhunters. They would saunter into South Side clubs, mount the stage, and proceed to calmly "cut the heads" of whomever was booked there that evening.

By 1950, Walter was firmly entrenched as Waters' studio harpist at Chess as well. (Long after Walter had split the Muddy Waters band, Leonard Chess insisted on his participation on waxings—why split up an unbeatable combination?) That's how Walter came to record his breakthrough 1952 R&B chart-topper "Juke"—the romping instrumental was laid down at the tail end of a Waters session. Suddenly Walter was a star on his own, combining his stunning talents with those of the Aces (guitarists Louis and David Myers and drummer Fred Below) and advancing the conception of blues harmonica another few light years with every session he made for Checker Records.

From 1952 to 1958, Walter notched 14 Top Ten R&B hits, including "Sad Hours," "Mean Old World," "Tell Me Mama," "Off the Wall," "Blues with a Feeling," "You're So Fine," a threatening "You Better Watch Yourself," the mournful "Last Night," and a rocking "My Babe" that was Willie Dixon's secularized treatment of the traditional gospel lament "This Train." Throughout his Checker tenure, Walter alternated spine-chilling instrumentals with gritty vocals. (He's always been underrated in that department; he wasn't Muddy Waters or the Wolf, but who was?)

Walter utilized the chromatic harp in ways never before envisioned (check out his 1956 free-form instrumental "Teenage Beat," with Robert Jr. Lockwood and Luther Tucker manning the guitars, for proof positive). 1959's determined "Everything Gonna Be Alright" was Walter's last trip to the hit lists; Chicago blues had faded to a commercial non-entity by then unless your name was Jimmy Reed.

Tragically, the '60s saw the harp genius slide steadily into an alcohol-hastened state of unreliability, his once-handsome face becoming a roadmap of scars. In 1964, he toured Great Britain with the Rolling Stones, who clearly had their priorities in order, but his once-prodigious skills were faltering badly. That sad fact was never more obvious than on 1967's disastrous summit meeting of Waters, Bo Diddley, and Walter for Chess as the Super Blues Band; there was nothing super whatsoever about Walter's lame remakes of "My Babe" and "You Don't Love Me."

Walter's eternally vicious temper led to his violent undoing in 1968. He was involved in a street fight (apparently on the losing end, judging from the outcome) and died from the incident's after-effects at age 37. His influence remains inescapable to this day—it's unlikely that a blues harpist exists on the face of this earth who doesn't worship Little Walter. —*Bill Dahl*

★ **The Best** / 1958 / MCA/Chess ♦♦♦♦♦
If there's a blues harmonica player alive today who *doesn't* have this landmark album in their collection, they're either lying or had their copy stolen by another harmonica player. This 12-song collection is the one that every harmonica player across the board cut their teeth on. All the hits are here; "My Babe," "Blues with a Feeling," "You Better Watch Yourself," "Off the Wall," "Mean Old World" and the instrumental that catapulted him from the sideman chair in Muddy Waters' band to the top of the R&B charts in 1952, "Juke." Walter's influence to this very day is so pervasive over the landscape of the instrument that this collection of singles is truly: 1) one of the all-time greatest blues harmonica albums, 2) one of the all-time greatest Chicago blues albums, and 3) one of the first ten albums you should purchase if you're you're building your blues collection from the ground floor up. —*Cub Koda*

Hate to See You Go / 1969 / MCA/Chess ♦♦♦♦
Another solid collection of tracks recorded between 1952 and 1960 that originally appeared in 1969 as part of the short lived Chess Vintage Blues Masters series. Three of the tracks overlap with the budget compilation *The Best of Little Walter, Volume 2*, but the other 12 are just too good to pass by because of a minor programming gaffe. Standout cuts abound just about anywhere the laser beam falls, but the set closer, the minor-key masterpiece "Blue and Lonesome," just may be the most emotionally terrifying masterpiece of Walter's illustrious career. —*Cub Koda*

Chess Blues Masters Series / May 1977 / Chess ♦♦♦♦
These singles by harmonica magician and vocal ace Marion "Little Walter" Jacobs are among the cornerstones of Chicago blues. They've also been reissued ad infinitum for years, and are now available in a better mastered and annotated two-disc set, *The Essential Little Walter*. —*Ron Wynn*

Boss Blues Harmonica / 1986 / Chess ♦♦♦
For quite a while this double LP (also available for a while, with identical contents, as part of the Chess *Blues Masters* series) was the best Little Walter compilation, but now virtually all of the cuts are available on CD. As for just the music, it's very fine, the 24 selections including much of his most famous and best material. —*Richie Unterberger*

The Blues World of Little Walter / 1988 / Delmark ♦♦♦
If you really want to hear what Little Walter sounded like in his pre-amplified days and early stages of development with the Muddy Waters band, this is the one to get. The title is a bit of a misnomer as Walter is featured more as a sideman to Baby Face Leroy, Muddy Waters and others on early Parkway, Regal and Savoy sides, but it's clear that Walter at this stage of the game should have been paying royalties to both Sonny Boys and Walter Horton in particular. One of the high points features explosive slide work from Waters on a pre-Chess version of "Rollin' & Tumblin'," as crude as a version as you'll ever hear and certainly not to be missed. Although many of these sides have appeared on other compilations (usually taped up off of old scratchy 78s), this one features superior sound taken from the original lacquer masters. —*Cub Koda*

☆ **The Best of Little Walter, Vol. 2** / 1989 / MCA/Chess ♦♦♦♦♦
This ten-song budget compilation continues the overview of Walter's enormous output for the Chess label. For rock fans, the most familiar track on here is the original version of "Boom Boom (Out Go the Lights)." But there's more where that came from, including the smoking uptempo "It Ain't Right," the blistering instrumental "Boogie," and the soulful strut of "I Don't Play." Another bonus is the inclusion of an early Muddy Waters instrumental featuring Walter on acoustic harp, "Evans' Shuffle." A great, cost effective way to add some more Walter to the collection. —*Cub Koda*

☆ **The Chess Years 1952-1963** / 1992 / Charly ♦♦♦♦♦
Damn near everything (*Blues with a Feeling* popped any semblance of absolute completion) that the Chicago harp genius ever waxed for Chess (95 sides in all), spread over four generously programmed discs. Particularly revealing are the lengthy snippets of studio chatter on the final rarities disc—Sonny Boy had nothing on Walter when it came to verbally sparring in the studio with Leonard Chess! —*Bill Dahl*

★ **The Essential** / Jun. 8, 1993 / MCA ♦♦♦♦♦
In many ways, this supplants the original single disc, *Best of Little Walter*, and appends it with 35 more classics of Chicago blues harp genius, although one track from the original 12-song lineup is (perhaps purposely) left off. If you want to start your Walter collection with a nice generous helping of his best, this one runs the entire gamut of his solo career, from the classic 1952 instrumental "Juke" up to the Willie Dixon-penned "Dead Presidents." 46 tracks, one dynamite booklet, nice remastering, a great value for the cash outlay involved, and, best of all, an album title that truly delivers the goods. —*Cub Koda*

Blues Masters / 1994 / Tomato ♦♦
These live performances have been circulating around bootleg channels under a plethora of titles on vinyl and cassette for over a decade and a half. The Otis Rush cuts fare okay, although the sound quality is pretty awful and will generally make any decent stereo playback system sound like there's a pile of blankets draped over the speakers. The Walter cuts are another matter entirely. On one of its earlier vinyl bootleg incarnations, these tracks were purported to be recorded live at Pepper's Lounge in Chicago sometime in the late '60s. If they were, it must have been amateur night. The backing band heard here behind Walter are a bunch of rhythmically challenged ham-fisted hacks who sound like every blues lover's worst nightmare; buzzing obtrusive bass lines, clumsy, lumbering drums that sound like the guy's building a house, and a lead guitar that sounds like he's plugged into a 100-watt kazoo. As for Walter himself, he's in the absolute worst recorded form ever documented. His harp playing is raggedy and short winded (to be fair, by this time he *was* trying to blow with one collapsed lung) and he forgets lyrics

left and right, letting out frustrated yelps as he keeps losing his place mid-song, breaking time constantly. — *Cub Koda*

Blues with a Feeling / Oct. 24, 1995 / MCA/Chess ✦✦✦✦
A 40-song double CD of material that didn't appear on *The Essential Little Walter*. Much of this is pretty rare, having only appeared on long unavailable singles or hard-to-get import LPs; almost a dozen, in fact, had not previously been officially released anywhere. Its appeal isn't limited to collectors, though. Anyone who likes a Little Walter greatest-hits anthology will like this almost as much, including as it does some excellent performances ("Flying Saucer," "Teenage Beat," "Who," "Crazy for My Baby," "Thunderbird") that don't appear on *The Essential Little Walter*. The dozen or so alternate takes get closer to specialist territory, but even so they're worth hearing even if you're not a fanatic, sometimes varying substantially from the official versions. — *Richie Unterberger*

Confessin' the Blues / Nov. 19, 1996 / MCA ✦✦✦✦
This release is a little confusing, coming out as it does more than a year after the release of MCA-Chess' Little Walter rarities collection *Blues With a Feeling*, and two years after the double CD anthology set that contains most of the best parts of this collection. Still, for those who can't afford either of those pricey sets, this disc, coupled with the two best-of-volumes, and the other Walter compilations, fills in some holes that are well worth filling. Made up of songs cut between 1953 and 1959—none of which had ever appeared on LP before the original 1974 release of this collection—the selection features Walter in his prime, playing alongside Robert Lockwood Jr. and Louis Myers or Luther Tucker on guitar (with Muddy Waters present, on slide, on one indispensable track, "Rock Bottom"), mostly Willie Dixon on bass, and Fred Below on the drums, with Lafayette Leake or Otis Spann on piano. His harp work was never less than first rate during the era covered by this collection, and there are some top flight instrumentals featured, but the material (check out "Crazy Legs," with its dazzling interplay between Walter on harp and Louis and Dave Myers on guitars) here also features some of Walter's best singing, including the romantic "One More Chance with You," the quietly raunchy "Temperature," and "Confessin' the Blues." The sound, as is usual on these MCA-Chess reissues, is superb, although certain tracks, such as "I Got to Go," seem slightly compressed. — *Bruce Eder*

★ **His Best (Chess 50th Anniversary Collection)** / Jun. 17, 1997 / MCA ✦✦✦✦✦
As MCA reconfigures their Chess catalog, this 20-track single-disc compilation now takes the place of their original 12-track *Best of Little Walter* collection, a landmark blues album which had remained in print for over three decades. This collection reprises ten of those seminal tracks (leaving off the echoey "Blue Light" and "You Better Watch Yourself," the latter being available on the two-disc anthology *The Essential Little Walter*) and brings ten others cherry-picked from the catalog to the mix. If you've never experienced the innovative instrumental genius of Little Walter, classics like "Juke," "Off the Wall," "Mean Old World," "Sad Hours," "Blues With a Feeling," "My Babe," "Boom Out Goes the Light," "Last Night," "Mellow Down Easy," and "Roller Coaster" (written by Bo Diddley, who also guests on guitar) will come as a major revelation. These are the recordings that changed the sound and style of blues harmonica forever, and everyone who came after him was as influenced by him as jazz saxophonists were by Charlie Parker. Everyone who fancies themselves a blues harmonica player should have this one in their collection as a textbook instructional tool, while the rest of us can just bask in the glow of his genius. Essential first purchase doesn't even begin to describe it. — *Cub Koda*

Blue Midnight / Le Roi du Blues ✦✦✦✦
It's hard to determine the worth of Le Roi du Blues' Little Walter rarity compilations these days. Not only has much of the material been reissued on CD; it's sometimes hard to determine what's been reissued elsewhere and what hasn't, given the minimal differences between some of these alternate takes. It's reasonably certain that *Blue Midnight*, the third and final volume of the series, had the rarest material of the lot, and the most songs that remained unused on Chess' CD compilations. The material is good, but not as impressive as the previous two Le Roi du Blues volumes (*Blue and Lonesome* and *Southern Feeling*), drawing more from his '60s recordings than the other installments. — *Richie Unterberger*

Blue and Lonesome / Le Roi du Blues ✦✦✦✦
Although its legality was dubious, the three-volume Le Roi du Blues series

of rare Little Walter recordings was a model example of rare material being made available to collectors who could simply not locate it otherwise. The first of these, *Blue and Lonesome* is much less desirable than it was pre-1990, though, because most of the songs are now available on domestic Chess CDs. The music is certainly excellent, only a slight notch less impressive than his greatest hits compilation, collecting some rare singles and unissued takes that had been confined to the vaults for decades. — *Richie Unterberger*

Southern Feeling / Le Roi du Blues ✦✦✦✦
Virtually all of this came out on *The Essential Little Walter* and *Blues with a Feeling*, making it unnecessary to hunt this down, despite the high quality of its contents. Diehard collectors, though, might want to do so because of the presence of two very rare tracks by the Coronets, an obscure doo wop group whose 1954 single included harmonica work by Walter. — *Richie Unterberger*

Little Willie Littlefield

b. Sep. 16, 1931, Houston, TX
Piano, Vocals / R&B, Jump Blues, Boogie-Woogie, West Coast Blues, Piano Blues
Before he was 21 years old, Texas-born pianist Little Willie Littlefield had etched an all-time classic into the blues lexicon. Only trouble was, his original 1952 waxing of "Kansas City" (here titled "K.C. Loving") didn't sell sufficiently to show up on the charts (thus leaving the door open for Wilbert Harrison to invade the airwaves with the ubiquitous Jerry Leiber/Mike Stoller composition seven years later).

Influenced by Albert Ammons, Charles Brown, and Amos Milburn, Little Willie was already a veteran of the R&B recording wars by the time he waxed "K.C. Loving," having made his debut 78 in 1948 for Houston-based Eddie's Records while still in his teens. After a few sides for Eddie's and Freedom, he moved over to the Bihari brothers' Los Angeles-headquartered Modern logo in 1949. There he immediately hit paydirt with two major R&B hits, "It's Midnight" and "Farewell" (he added another chart entry, "I've Been Lost," in 1951).

Littlefield proved a sensation upon moving to L.A. during his Modern tenure, playing at area clubs and touring with a band that included saxist Maxwell Davis. At Littlefield's first L.A. session for King's Federal subsidiary in 1952, he cut "K.C. Loving" (with Davis on sax), but neither it nor several fine Federal follow-ups returned the boogie piano specialist to the charts.

Other than a few 1957-58 singles for Oakland's Rhythm logo, little was heard from Little Willie Littlefield until the late '70s, when he began to mount a comeback at various festivals and on the European circuit. While overseas, he met a Dutch woman, married her, and settled in the Netherlands, where he remains active musically. — *Bill Dahl*

Jump with Little Willie Littlefield / 1949-1957 / Ace ✦✦✦✦

● **It's Midnight** / 1979 / Route 66 ✦✦✦✦
Although it may be a little hard to find, *It's Midnight* is a valuable collection that contains the highlights from Little Willie Littlefield's recordings for Modern and Federal between 1949 and 1957. These recordings capture Littlefield at his best, rocking through a number of jump blues, R&B and blues songs, including "K.C. Loving," "It's Midnight," "Farewell," and "I've Been Lost." It's an excellent collection that should be reissued on compact disc. — *Thom Owens*

Johnny Littlejohn (John Funchess)

b. Apr. 16, 1931, Lake, MS, **d.** Feb. 1, 1994, Chicago, IL
Guitar, Vocals / Electric Chicago Blues
Johnny Littlejohn's stunning mastery of the slide guitar somehow never launched him into the major leagues of bluesdom. Only on a handful of occasions was the Chicago veteran's vicious bottleneck attack captured effectively on wax, but anyone who experienced one of his late-night sessions as a special musical guest on the Windy City circuit will never forget the crashing passion in his delivery.

Delta-bred John Funchess first heard the blues just before he reached his teens at a fish fry where a friend of his father's named Henry Martin was playing guitar. He left home in 1946, pausing in Jackson, MS, Arkansas, and Rochester, NY, before winding up in Gary, IN. In 1951, he began inching his way into the Gary blues scene, his Elmore James-influenced slide style making him a favorite around Chicago's south suburbs in addition to steel mill-fired Gary.

Littlejohn waited an unconscionably long time to wax his debut singles for Margaret (his trademark treatment of Brook Benton's "Kiddio"), T-D-S, and Weis in 1968. But before the year was out, Littlejohn had also cut his debut album, *Chicago Blues Stars*, for Chris Strachwitz's Arhoolie logo. It was a magnificent debut, the guitarist blasting out a savage Chicago/Delta hybrid rooted in the early '50s rather than its actual timeframe.

Unfortunately, a four-song 1969 Chess date remained in the can. After that, another long dry spell preceded Littlejohn's 1985 album *So-Called Friends* for Rooster Blues, an ambitious but not altogether convincing collaboration between the guitarist and a humongous horn section that sometimes grew to eight pieces. The guitarist had been in poor health for some time prior to his 1994 passing. — *Bill Dahl*

Johnny Littlejohn & the Chicago Blues All Stars / 1968 / Arhoolie ✦✦✦✦
Tight and intense, this is Littlejohn's finest record to date. Great slide guitar work. — *Cub Koda*

Funky from Chicago / 1973 / Bluesway ✦✦✦

Johnny Little John & Chicago Blues Band / 197 / Arhoolie ✦✦✦✦

So-Called Friends / 1985 / Rooster Blues ✦✦✦
Surrounding Littlejohn with a huge horn section probably wasn't the greatest idea in retrospect; the booming brass detracts at times from his pungent slide work, rather than enhancing it. But hearty renditions of his signature "Chips Flying Everywhere," a sturdy "She's Too Much," and several songs written by bassist Aron Burton recommend the vinyl-only LP nonetheless. — *Bill Dahl*

• **Chicago Blues Stars** / 1991 / Arhoolie ✦✦✦✦
Slide guitar master Littlejohn was already overdue for the full-length album treatment when he waxed this stellar set for Arhoolie in 1969 (enhanced by three bonus cuts on the CD version). A sizzling Chicago combo provides sterling backing as Littlejohn sears the strings on "Dream," "Shake Your Moneymaker," and a rough-edged adaptation of Brook Benton's "Kiddio," his powerhouse vocals consistently stunning. — *Bill Dahl*

Johnny Littlejohn's Blues Party / May 1991 / Wolf ✦✦✦

When Your Best Friends Turn Their Back on You / 1993 / JSP ✦✦✦

Dream / 1995 / Storyville ✦✦✦

Paula Lockheart

Vocals / Modern Acoustic Blues
Talented and interesting vocalist, songwriter, and interpreter of classic blues and jazz. Influences include Bessie Smith, Dinah Washington, Alberta Hunter, and Joe Williams. Paula's recordings generally feature topflight musicians backing her sexy, stylized, understated vocal mannerisms in a variety of settings from solo guitar accompaniment to horn-driven big band in full swing. She continues to perform regularly in and around New York City, along with festival appearances and tours of the US, Canada, and Europe. Paula has performed and recorded with, among others, John Hammond, David Bromberg, and Dr. John. She was nominated for a Handy Blues Award in 1982 and a New York City Music Award in 1986. — *Niles J. Frantz*

• **The Incomplete** / 1980 / Flying Fish ✦✦✦✦
This best-of collection features cuts from her other three Flying Fish releases and is the most effective showcase of her versatility and consistent quality. — *Niles J. Frantz*

It Ain't the End of the World / Flying Fish ✦✦✦
This expressive singer uses a mixture of blues and rock. — *AMG*

Paula Lockheart with Peter Ecklund & Friends / Flying Fish ✦✦✦
This is a strong debut album. — *AMG*

Voo-It / Flying Fish ✦✦✦

Robert Jr. Lockwood

b. Mar. 27, 1915, Marvell, AR
Guitar, Harmonica, Vocals / Chicago Blues, Delta Blues, Electric Delta Blues, Prewar Country Blues
Robert Jr. Lockwood learned his blues first-hand from an unimpeachable source: the immortal Robert Johnson. Lockwood can still conjure up the

bone-chilling Johnson sound whenever he so desires, but he's never been one to linger in the past for long—which accounts for the jazzy swing he often brings to the licks he plays on his 12-string electric guitar.

Now past the age of 80, Lockwood is one of the last living links to the glorious Johnson legacy. When Lockwood's mother became romantically involved with the charismatic rambler in Helena, AR, the quiet teenager suddenly gained a role model and a close friend—so close that Lockwood considered himself Johnson's stepson. Robert Jr. learned how to play guitar very quickly with Johnson's expert help, assimilating Johnson's technique inside and out.

Following Johnson's tragic murder in 1938, Lockwood embarked on his own intriguing musical journey. He was among the first bluesmen to score an electric guitar in 1938 and eventually made his way to Chicago, where he cut four seminal tracks for Bluebird. Jazz elements steadily crept into Lockwood's dazzling fretwork, although his role as Sonny Boy Williamson's musical partner on the fabled KFFA *King Biscuit Time* radio broadcasts during the early '40s out of Helena, AR, probably didn't emphasize that side of his dexterity all that much.

Settling in Chicago in 1950, Lockwood swiftly gained a reputation as a versatile in-demand studio sideman, recording behind harp genius Little Walter, piano masters Sunnyland Slim and Eddie Boyd, and plenty more. Solo recording opportunities were scarce, though Lockwood did cut fine singles for Mercury in 1951 ("I'm Gonna Dig Myself a Hole" and a very early "Dust My Broom") and JOB in 1955 ("Sweet Woman from Maine"/"Aw Aw Baby").

Lockwood's best modern work as a leader was done for Pete Lowry's Trix label, including some startling workouts on the 12-string axe that he daringly added to his arsenal in 1965. He later joined forces with fellow Johnson disciple Johnny Shines for two eclectic early-'80s Rounder albums. Intent on satisfying his own instincts first and foremost, the sometimes taciturn Lockwood is a priceless connection between past and present. — *Bill Dahl*

Steady Rollin' Man / Aug. 12, 1970-Aug. 1970 / Delmark ✦✦✦
Sophisticated, mellow set cut in 1970 that occasionally gets a little too laid-back. Lockwood's complex lead guitar work and aged-in-the-wood vocals are a delight, but guitarist Louis Myers asserts himself as soloist more than he should have in such a situation, making one yearn for more Robert Jr. riffs. — *Bill Dahl*

Contrasts / 1974 / Trix ✦✦✦✦
Robert Jr. Lockwood has never been a conventional musician or blues artist. This was one of a pair of spectacular albums done for Trix in the 1970s. Johnson's version of "Driving Wheel" maintains the spirit of Roosevelt Sykes' familiar rendition, but has his own compelling twists. Otherwise, the session featured Lockwood songs, and he demonstrated the probing, animated qualities that made him a legend and a survivor. — *Ron Wynn*

Blues Live in Japan / 1975 / Advent ✦✦✦
Recorded in concert at Tokyo's Yubin Chokin Hall on November 27th and 28th, 1974, this teams Lockwood with the Aces (Louis Myers on guitar and harmonica, brother Dave on bass, and Fred Below on drums), who backed him so splendidly on Delmark's *Steady Rollin' Man* album. Kicking off with "Sweet Home Chicago," the interplay between Lockwood and Myers is both empathetic and respectful of each other's space. A jazzy "Going Down Slow" and a Robert Johnson-style "Worried Life Blues" are next, setting the stage for Louis Myers' slide work on "Anna Lee" and Mercy Dee's "One Room Country Shack." Lockwood returns center stage on a great version of "Stormy Monday" and his own "Feel All Right Again" before mixing it up with the Aces on "Honky Tonk." The album closes with great versions of "Mean Black Spider" and the encore, "Little and Low," on which Myers blows harp with great passion. The response from the Japanese crowd is so overwhelming that you actually feel the musicians being swept away by it all (the usually taciturn Lockwood even acknowledges this before the encore in his usual phlegmatic way), a sure sign of emotions running rampant and one great live session as a result of it. — *Cub Koda*

Does 12 / 1977 / Trix ✦✦✦✦
Robert Jr. Lockwood made two excellent albums for the Trix label that didn't get the publicity or distribution they merited and quickly disappeared. Muse has recently begun reissuing Trix material, but thus far hasn't gotten to this Lockwood date or its companion. Grab it if you can. — *Ron Wynn*

Hangin' On / 1979 / Rounder ◆◆◆
Two of the principal keepers of the Robert Johnson flame joined forces for a Rounder LP that's stunning in its non-conformity to what purists might like to hear from the two veterans. Jazz and swing influences invest much of the LP, the pair sharing vocal and guitar duties. — *Bill Dahl*

Mr. Blues Is Back to Stay (with Johnny Shines) / 1980 / Rounder ◆◆◆
Another pairing of the venerable Delta blues vets, and it's even less traditional than their previous outing. Utilizing a jazz-steeped two-piece sax section, Lockwood swings with impugnity. Shines had recently suffered a serious stroke that left him unable to play guitar, so his contributions are limited to vocals only. — *Bill Dahl*

● **Plays Robert and Robert** / Nov. 28, 1982 / Black & Blue ◆◆◆◆
Lockwood in a beautifully recorded solo context (cut in France in 1982 for Black & Blue), doing what he does best—his own songs and those of his legendary mentor, Robert Johnson. Purists may quiver at Lockwood's use of the 12-string guitar as his primary axe, but he long ago made the instrument his own blues tool of choice, and he handles its nuances expertly. — *Bill Dahl*

Robert Lockwood / 1991 / Paula ◆◆◆◆
All 20 of these tracks were recorded for JOB in the early '50s, but only half feature Lockwood; the others are Johnny Shines solo sides. The title is a bit misleading; the Lockwood tracks, recorded in 1951 and 1955, mix genuine Lockwood solo performances with sides on which he supported Sunnyland Slim and Alfred Wallace. It's decent sparse, early Chicago blues, though not as good as the preceding Shines tracks on the disc. — *Richie Unterberger*

I Got to Find Me a Woman / Mar. 17, 1998 / Verve ◆◆◆◆
At the age of 82, Robert Lockwood recorded his first album for Verve, a label that developed a reputation for reviving the careers of veteran jazz and blues artists in the '90s. Their touch doesn't fail here—*I Got to Find Me a Woman* is a dynamic contemporary blues album, one that plays to Lockwood's strengths as a singer and guitarist. Divided between acoustic and electric blues, the album is filled with great performances and songs. In addition to classic covers, including "Everyday I Have the Blues" and two selections from Robert Johnson ("Walkin' Blues," "Kindhearted Woman Blues"), there are sturdy originals and contemporary songs that provide an excellent platform for Lockwood to prove that he's still an exceptionally gifted vocalist and guitarist. The album is so strong that the duets with B.B. King and Joe Louis Walker are just the icing on the cake. — *Thom Owens*

Cripple Clarence Lofton (Albert Clemens)

b. Mar. 28, 1887, Kingsport, TN, **d.** Jan. 9, 1957, Chicago, IL
Piano, Vocals / Piano Blues
Cripple Clarence Lofton is one of those colorful names that adorned many an album collection of early boogie-woogie piano 78s in the early days of the '60s folk-blues revival. An early practitioner of the form, along with his fellow contemporaries Cow Cow Davenport, Meade Lux Lewis, Pine Top Smith, and Jimmy Yancey, Lofton was one of the originators who spread the word in Chicago in the early '20s.

The physically challenged nicknamed he used—seen by modern audiences as a tad exploitative, to say the least—was a bit of a ringer. Although he suffered a birth defect in his leg that made him walk with a pronounced limp, it certainly didn't stop him from becoming an excellent tap dancer, his original ticket into show business. He quickly developed a stage act that consisted of pounding out the boogie-woogie on the piano while standing up, dancing, whistling, and vocalizing while—as one old bluesman put it—"carrying on a lotta racket." Lofton's technique—or lack of it—stemmed more from a tent show background and those listening to his earliest and most energetic recordings will quickly attest that hitting every note or making every chord change precisely were not exactly high priorities with him. But this wild, high energy act got the young showman noticed quickly and by the early '30s, he was so much a fixture of Chicago night life firmament that he had his own Windy City nightclub, the oddly named Big Apple. Lofton remained on the scene, cutting sides for the Gennett, Vocalion, Solo Art, Riverside, Session and Pax labels into the '40s. When the boogie-woogie craze cooled off and eventually died down in the late '40s, Lofton went into early retirement, staying around Chicago until his death in 1957 from a blood clot in the brain. — *Cub Koda*

Complete Works, Vol. 1 (1935-1939) / 1935-1939 / Document ◆◆◆◆

Complete Works, Vol. 2 (1939-1943) / 1939-1943 / Document ◆◆◆
Complete Works, Vol. 2 (1939-1943) continues Document's exhaustive overview of Cripple Clarence Lofton's recordings. As with the other installments, the disc features some classic performances, long running time, exacting chronological sequencing, and poor fidelity (all cuts are transferred from original acetates and 78s). The serious blues listener will find all these factors to be positive, but enthusiasts and casual listeners will find that the collection is of marginal interest. — *Thom Owens*

Cripple Clarence Lofton / Jul. 14, 1954 / Riverside ◆◆◆

Cripple Lofton & Walter Davis / Yazoo ◆◆◆◆
Marvelous blues piano and singing from Cripple Clarence Lofton, and nearly as fine an effort from Walter Davis. — *Ron Wynn*

● **Cripple Clarence Lofton, Vol. 1** / RST ◆◆◆◆
Some of Lofton's best, with the selections "Strut That Thing," "Monkey Man Blues," and "Pitchin' Boogie" being particular standouts. (Import) — *Cub Koda*

Lonesome Sundown

b. Dec. 12, 1928, Donaldsville, LA, **d.** Apr. 23, 1995, Gonzales, LA
Guitar, Vocals / Electric Louisiana Blues, New Orleans R&B, Swamp Blues
Unlike many of his swamp blues brethren, the evocatively monickered Lonesome Sundown (the name was an inspired gift from producer J.D. Miller) wasn't a Jimmy Reed disciple. Sundown's somber brand of blues was more in keeping with the gruff sound of Muddy Waters. The guitarist was one of the most powerful members of Miller's south Louisiana stable, responsible for several seminal swamp standards on Excello Records.

The former Cornelius Green first seriously placed his hands on a guitar in 1950, Waters and Hooker providing early inspiration. Zydeco pioneer Clifton Chenier hired the guitarist as one of his two axemen (Phillip Walker being the other) in 1955. A demo tape was enough proof for Miller—he began producing him in 1956, leasing the freshly renamed Sundown's "Leave My Money Alone" to Excello.

There were plenty more where that one came from. Over the next eight years, Sundown's lowdown Excello output included "My Home Is a Prison," "I'm a Mojo Man," "I Stood By," "I'm a Samplin' Man," and a host of memorable swamp classics preceded his 1965 retirement from the blues business to devote his life to the church. It was 1977 before Sundown could be coaxed back into a studio to cut a blues LP; *Been Gone Too Long*, co-produced by Bruce Bromberg and Dennis Walker for the Joliet imprint, was an excellent comeback entry but did disappointing sales (even after being reissued on Alligator). Scattered live performances were about all that was heard of the swamp blues master after that. — *Bill Dahl*

Lonesome Lonely Blues / 1970 / Excello ◆◆◆

Been Gone to Long / 1977 / Hightone ◆◆◆
The Louisiana blues vet's 1977 comeback album was a well-done affair, capturing some of the flavor of his '50s material (but with a modern edge). Producers Bruce Bromberg and Dennis Walker (who doubled on bass) recruited guitarist Phillip Walker, a longtime Sundown cohort, to handle some of the fret load, and the predominantly original songlist was worthy of Sundown's lowdown sound. — *Bill Dahl*

Lonesome Sundown / 1990 / Flyright ◆◆◆◆
Twenty-one sides from producer J.D. Miller's Crowley, LA vaults, dominated by alternate takes of the guitarist's best-known sides and some otherwise unreleased numbers. Backing musicians include keyboardist Katie Webster, harpist Lazy Lester, and drummer Warren Storm. Tough stuff! — *Bill Dahl*

● **I'm a Mojo Man: The Best of the Excello Singles** / 1995 / AVI-Excello ◆◆◆◆
One of the swamp blues stalwarts in south Louisiana producer J.D. Miller's stable receives the deluxe treatment with a 24-song anthology spanning his 1956-1964 Excello tenure. Sundown's sparse, nasty sound was influenced by Muddy Waters as much as the prevailing bayou beat, giving an extra discernible tang to his "Leave My Money Alone," "My Home Is My Prison," and the title cut. — *Bill Dahl*

Big Joe Louis & His Blues Kings

Group / British Blues

Playing and writing electric blues in the mold of the classic '50s Chess Records prototype, Big Joe Louis and his crew suffer the same mixed blessing common to many White (and some British) blues bands. Their command of their instruments and genuine love of the music is offset by mediocre if energetic vocals (from guitarist/singer Louis) and a revivalist mindset that recreates with precision, but lacks original vision. They get credit for writing most of the material on their 1996 CD, *Big Sixteen*, and executing it with assured competence, though they fall into the huge category of bands that could produce a high old time seen live, but aren't anything special on disc. — *Richie Unterberger*

● **Big Sixteen** / 1996 / Ace ♦♦♦♦
Fair modern White blues, distinguished from the bar-band norm by arrangements which consciously echo vintage Chess Records, down to the standup bass and Little George Sueref's able approximations of Little Walter's harmonica style. — *Richie Unterberger*

Joe Hill Louis (Lester Hill)

b. Sep. 23, 1921, Raines, TN, **d.** Aug. 5, 1957, Memphis, TN
Guitar, Harmonica, Drums, Vocals / Electric Memphis Blues, Delta Blues
Joe Hill Louis created quite a racket as a popular one-man blues band around Memphis during the 1950s. If not for his tragic premature demise, his name would surely be more widely revered.

Lester (or Leslie) Hill ran away from home at age 14, living instead with a well-heeled Memphis family. A fight with another youth that was won by young Hill earned him the "Joe Louis" appellation. Harp came first for the multi-instrumentalist; by the late '40s, his one-man musical attack was a popular attraction in Handy Park and on WDIA, the groundbreaking Memphis radio station where he hosted a 15-minute program billed as *The Pepticon Boy*.

Also known as the Be-Bop Boy, Louis made his recording debut in 1949 for Columbia, but the remainder of his output was issued on R&B indies large and small: it's the Phillips (Sam Phillips' first extremely short-lived logo), Modern, Sun, Checker, Meteor, Big Town (where he cut the blistering "Hydramatic Woman," a tune he'd cut previously for Sun in 1953 with Walter Horton on harp, but Phillips never released it), and House of Sound. Louis was only 35 when he died of tetanus, contracted when a deep gash on his thumb became infected. — *Bill Dahl*

The One Man Band / Sep. 1972 / Muskadine ♦♦♦

● **The Be-Bop Boy with Walter Horton and Mose Vinson** / 1992 / Bear Family ♦♦♦♦
Raw, chaotic, one-man band blues of the highest order. Highlights include the original version of "Tiger Man," and Louis' scorching lead guitar work on "She Treats Me Mean and Evil." Compiling virtually all the recordings he made for Sam Phillips in Memphis in the early '50s, this CD also features astonishing harmonica work from Big Walter Horton on several tracks. (Import) — *Cub Koda*

Louisiana Red

b. Mar. 23, 1936, Vicksburg, MS
Guitar, Vocals, Harmonica / Modern Electric Blues, Modern Acoustic Blues
Louisiana Red (born Iverson Minter) is a flamboyant guitarist, harmonica player, and vocalist. He lost his parents early in life through multiple tragedies; his mother died of pneumonia a week after his birth, and his father was lynched by the Klu Klux Klan when he was five. Red began recording for Chess in 1949, then joined the army. After his discharge, he played with John Lee Hooker in Detroit for almost two years in the late '50s. He maintained a busy recording and performing schedule through the 1990s, having done sessions for Chess, Checker, Atlas, Glover, Roulette, L&R, and Tomato among others. — *Ron Wynn*

● **Lowdown Back Porch Blues** / 1963 / Collectables ♦♦♦♦
Recorded in New York with Tommy Tucker, *Lowdown Back Porch Blues* is Louisiana Red's first album and, in many ways, it's his best. Supported by a bare-bones rhythm section, Red plays a number or traditional tunes and originals. His guitar is nearly as powerful and overwhelming as his vocals, making this a truly compelling listen. — *Thom Owens*

Louisiana Red Sings the Blues / 1972 / Atlantic ♦♦♦

Midnight Rambler / 1982 / Tomato ♦♦♦
At times harrowing, this is one of Red's more intense efforts. — *Bill Dahl*

Always Played the Blues / Oct. 31, 1994 / JSP ♦♦♦♦

The Best of Louisiana Red / 1995 / Evidence ♦♦♦♦
Assembled from tapes recorded in New York City with producer Herb Abramson between 1965 and 1973, *The Best of Louisiana Red* is an ideal introduction to one of the blues' most unique and memorable characters. Never a musical innovator, Red's true gift was instead to absorb the lessons of contemporary greats like Muddy Waters and Elmore James, employing their lyrical and instrumental motifs as a means to forge his own evocative style. James' slide guitar, in particular, haunts cuts like "The Story of Louisiana Red," "Where Is My Friend," and "Freight Train to Ride." Red's lyrics, on the other hand, are startlingly original, his surreal narratives unprecedented in the blues canon; the amazing "Red's Dream" details a journey to the U.N. to outline a plan to solve the Cuban missile crisis, while its follow-up, "Red's New Dream," portrays its hero as the first blues singer in outer space. — *Jason Ankeny*

Blues Spectrum of Louisiana Red / Apr. 7, 1998 / JSP ♦♦♦

Love Sculpture

f. 1967, Cardiff, Wales, **db.** 1970
Group / Art-Rock/Progressive-Rock, Blues-Rock
A British blues-rock band of the late '60s that, despite being very good, would normally be relegated to footnote status if it were not for the fact that the lead guitarist of this trio was the soon-to-be-famous Dave Edmunds. Like many similar bands of the times, Love Sculpture was really a showpiece for Edmunds' guitar playing talents (which on the first LP are considerable), and little else. The covers are well chosen, slightly revved-up, but mostly reverent versions of blues classics. They had a fluke hit in 1968 with a cover of the classical piece "Sabre Dance" rearranged for guitar. After two LPs, Love Sculpture split up in 1970. Edmunds went on to solo success ("I Hear You Knockin'") and a long, sometimes contentious relationship with ex-Brinsley Schwarz bassist Nick Lowe, which culminated in the great band Rockpile. Still, Love Sculpture, though slightly dated, is a hoot to listen to today. And Edmunds, full of youthful bravado and dazzling technique, certainly knows his way up and down a fretboard. — *John Dougan*

Blues Helping / 1968 / Rare Earth ♦♦♦♦
As hyperkinetic blues albums by White English kids go, this is a good one. Dave Edmunds, armed only with a 1959 Gibson 335 and a 100-watt Marshall stack, cranks through these recognizable blues covers (with one original instrumental) with reckless abandon and gobs of technique. Backup support is handled by bassist John Williams and drummer Congo Jones, who do their best to keep up and provide a rhythmic foundation for Edmunds to wail over. Edmunds also handled nearly all the vocals, and as blues singers go, he's merely serviceable, but what makes this LP worthwhile is the revved-up guitar playing, especially when Edmunds shreds both Freddy King's "The Stumble" and Willie Dixon's "Wang Dang Doodle." — *John Dougan*

Forms & Feelings / 1969 / Parrot ♦♦♦
Forms & Feelings essentially replicates the high-voltage attack of *Blues Helping*, only with a notable lack of energy and an eye on the charts. It's no coincidence that the group chose to revamp *L'Arlesienne*'s "Farandole," given that "Sabre Dance" was the only thing that distinguished Love Sculpture from the legions of British blues bands. But this time around, "Farandole" and all of *Forms & Feelings* sounded tired and redundant, with only a fraction of the passion that made the debut worthwhile. — *Stephen Thomas Erlewine*

● **Singles A&B's** / 1990 / Harvest ♦♦♦♦
Singles A&B's is a useful overview of Love Sculpture's brief career, containing the majority of their best moments and proving that there was more to this British blues group than their gimmicky cover of "Sabre Dance." — *Stephen Thomas Erlewine*

Billy Love

b. Mississippi
Piano, Vocals / Electric Memphis Blues
There is not a whole lot of tangible information to convey about pianist Billy "Red" Love, who signed to record for fledgling producer Sam Phillips in 1951.

Phillips passed off an early Love performance, "Juiced," to Chess as the latest effort by Jackie Brenston (then red-hot as a result of "Rocket 88").

Love's own debut record, "Drop Top," came out on Chess and reportedly did fairly well regionally, but after a 1952 Chess encore, "My Teddy Bear Baby," Chess dropped him. He stuck around Sun through 1954, working sessions behind Rufus Thomas and Willie Nix and recording a wealth of unissued sides of his own.

Love left plenty of jumping blues behind in the Sun vaults—enough to fill half an LP on Charly that he shared with Little Junior Parker. Love's rocking "Gee I Wish," one of those long-delayed masters, has been revived by guitarist Duke Robillard. Love left Memphis in 1955 for parts unknown. — *Bill Dahl*

Clayton Love

b. Nov. 15, 1927, Mattson, MS
Piano, Vocals / Electric Blues, R&B, Electric Memphis Blues
Pianist Clayton Love was a prominent member of Ike Turner's Kings of Rhythm during the mid-'50s, making some of his finest platters with the legendary band. But Love made his first vinyl appearance on Lillian McMurry's Jackson, MS-based Trumpet Records in 1951 with his own jump band, the Shufflers.

The combo was a fixture around Vicksburg, where Love was attending Alcorn A&M as a pre-med student. Love's cousin, Natchez bandleader Earl Reed, had recorded for Trumpet and recommended his young relative to McMurry. Love's 1951 debut, "Susie"/ "Shufflin' with Love," exhibited infectious enthusiasm if not a great deal of polish. From there, Love moved over to Aladdin in 1952 (with saxist Raymond Hill's band backing him), Modern (with Turner on guitar) in 1954, and in 1957, Love fronted and played the 88s with Turner and the Kings of Rhythm on their Federal platters "Do You Mean It," "She Made My Blood Run Cold," and "The Big Question."

Turner had nothing to do with Love's pair of 1958 singles for St. Louis-based Bobbin Records; bassist Roosevelt Marks led the backing band for the clever coupling "Limited Love"/ "Unlimited Love." Long settled in the Gateway City, Love made an album for Modern Blues Recordings in 1991 with fellow ivories aces Johnnie Johnson and Jimmy Vaughn, *Rockin' Eighty-Eights.* — *Bill Dahl*

● **Blues Come Home** / Oct. 24, 1995 / Monad ◆◆◆

Willie Love

b. Nov. 4, 1906, Duncan, MS, **d.** Aug. 19, 1953, Jackson, MS
Piano, Vocals / Piano Blues, Delta Blues
Harpist Rice Miller, known to his legion of fans across the Delta as Sonny Boy Williamson, first encountered pianist Willie Love in Greenville, MS, in 1942. The talented pair played regularly on Nelson Street, the main drag of the Black section of Greenville, musically intertwining with remarkable empathy. And it was Williamson who brought Love into the fold at Trumpet Records (the label responsible for Love's entire recorded legacy as a leader).

Love was deeply influenced by Leroy Carr and equally conversant on boogies and down-in-the-alley blues. He played piano on several of Sonny Boy Williamson's Trumpet sessions, but Love didn't utilize his pal on any of his own 1951-1953 dates for the Jackson, MS, firm. Love's debut, "Take It Easy, Baby," was a rollicking boogie outing, and he followed it up with the equally sturdy "Everybody's Fishing," "Vanity Dresser Boogie," and "Nelson Street Blues." Love's last session in April of 1953 found him backed by a White bassist and drummer—certainly a rarity for the era. Four months later, Love, who had long suffered from alcoholism, was dead. — *Bill Dahl*

● **Clownin' with the World** / 1993 / Alligator ◆◆◆◆
Instead of assembling a single disc highlighting this Delta piano great, Alligator has spread pianist Willie Love's Trumpet catalog over three marvelous anthologies drawn from the early-'50s archives of Lillian McMurry's Trumpet Records. After eight terrific sides by Sonny Boy, Love pounds out "Take It Easy, Baby," "Little Car Blues," "Feed My Body to the Fishes," and five more, conjuring up a steamy Delta juke joint ambience. — *Bill Dahl*

Delta Blues: 1951 / 1993 / Alligator ◆◆◆
Six more classic 1951 performances by Love from Trumpet's vaults, including the romping "Everybody's Fishing," "My Own Boogie," "Vanity Dresser

Boogie." The pianist shares this disc with country bluesmen Luther Huff and the omnipresent Big Joe Williams; both turned in some inspired work for Lillian McMurry's logo. — *Bill Dahl*

Shout Brother Shout / Oldie Blues ◆◆◆◆
A more varied mix of musical styles than on the first two anthologies (everything from Wally Mercer's rocking R&B to Beverly White's schmaltzy lounge sounds). Love leads three more solid sides from 1953: the title item, "Way Back," and "Willie Mae." — *Bill Dahl*

Trumpet Masters, Vol. 1: Lonesome World Blues / Collectables ◆◆◆◆
Willie Love played exciting, if sometimes unorganized piano and sang in an equally unpredictable and galvanizing fashion. This is how Mississippi juke joints sounded during the early '50s (they're not that different now). — *Ron Wynn*

Robert Lucas

b. Jul. 25, 1962, Long Beach, CA
Harmonica, Vocals, Slide Guitar / Modern Acoustic Blues
West Coast vocalist, guitarist and songwriter Robert Lucas has been forging a path for himself in the blues world since his much-hailed 1990 self-produced debut cassette, *Across the River.* Lucas, based in Long Beach, California, records for the Audioquest label out of San Clemente.

Lucas was born into a middle-class family in Long Beach and was 14 or 15 when he started getting seriously into blues-rock. He had started to play guitar then, inspired by Jimi Hendrix, but gave up on it, concluding his hands were too small. He started playing harmonica instead, listening to recordings by John Mayall and the Bluesbreakers before going back to source material, including the recordings of Little Walter Jacobs, Sonny Boy Williamson, George "Harmonica" Smith, Snooky Pryor, and James Cotton.

Lucas began playing the National steel guitar at 17 when a co-worker at the Long Beach Arena sold him the instrument. Lucas hooked up with guitarist Bernie Pearl and began taking lessons from him. After joining Pearl's band as a harmonica player, he got to play behind the likes of Big Joe Turner, George Smith, Pee Wee Creighton, Lowell Fulson, Eddie "Cleanhead" Vinson, Percy Mayfield, and other West Coast bluesmen. He carefully honed his singing and playing, with Pearl's band and on his own, for several years before forming Luke and the Locomotives in 1986.

Lucas' career as a national touring act was launched when his *Across the River* tape got a rave review in a Los Angeles newspaper. As a result, one of the Audioquest warehouse workers came to see him at a Los Angeles sushi bar. The employee called the company president, who came to hear Lucas that same night.

Lucas is a multi-talented harmonica player, guitarist, singer, and songwriter who can do it all: on one recording for Audioquest, *Usin' Man Blues,* he plays solo, and on another, *Luke and the Locomotives,* he performs with his band. The sound on all of his albums is raw and gritty, with just a few originals on each album. Classic blues fare like Sonny Boy Williamson's "Good Morning Little Schoolgirl" and John Lee Hooker's "Meet Me In the Bottom" are given new life with Lucas' talented hands and vocal chops.

Lucas pays homage to traditional blues but has carefully crafted his own singing and slide guitar style. These talents are on ample display on his albums for Audioquest. His albums include *Luke and the Locomotives, Usin' Man Blues, Built for Comfort, Layaway,* and *Completely Blue,* all recorded since 1990. — *Richard Skelly*

Usin' Man Blues / Jul. 1990 / AudioQuest ◆◆◆◆
Credible acoustic blues with admirable humor. — *Bill Dahl*

Luke & the Locomotives / 1991 / AudioQuest ◆◆◆
Crying out the pains and joys of the blues is not just an act for this band— it genuinely bleeds through. Don't believe it? Look at the back liner note endorsements by Willie Dixon and Robert Jr. Lockwood. Even more brilliant is Lucas' songwriting, poking fun at himself in "Big Man's Mambo," offering the advantages of having a large frame to the ladies. His moaning harmonica effectively plays into the subject of growing old with its aches and pains in "Shed a Tear," and is equally as effective in "I'm So Tired." — *Char Ham*

Built for Comfort / 1992 / AudioQuest ◆◆◆
Another laudable set. — *Bill Dahl*

Layaway / 1994 / AudioQuest ✦✦✦

● **Completely Blue** / May 5, 1997 / AudioQuest ✦✦✦✦
Right from the bongo drum intro on the first number, it's apparent that this album veers in a different direction for Lucas. Add the eerie organ sounds and the jazzy guitar licks, and this album has great musical depth. Even his songwriting expands topic-wise, whether warning his one night stand the consequences of telling all to his wife, or society's lack of common sense while suffering economic woes, even giving a little snippet of commentary on the O.J. Simpson case. There's some magnificent and expansive keyboard work by Fred Kaplan, both on piano and B-3 organ. Along with co-writer/guitarist David Melton, Lucas' "Two for Nothing" is a nice Stax-sounding duet. Joining Melton on guitar duties is former Mighty Flyer Alex Schultz, who can flesh out equally well on rhythm as well as burn on solos. Rounding out and heading for home, Lucas ends with an acoustic interpretation of Hendrix's "Voodoo Chile," which presents how Robert Johnson might have performed it had he lived into the latter half of this century. — *Char Ham*

Willie Mabon

b. Oct. 24, 1925, Hollywood, TN, d. Apr. 19, 1985, Paris, France
Piano, Vocals / R&B, Piano Blues
The sly, insinuating vocals and chunky piano style of Willie Mabon won the heart of many an R&B fan during the early '50s. His salty Chess waxings, "I Don't Know," "I'm Mad," and "Poison Ivy," established the pianist as a genuine Chicago blues force, but he faded as an R&B hitmaker at the dawn of rock 'n' roll.

Mabon was already well-grounded in blues tradition from his Memphis upbringing when he hit Chicago in 1942. Schooled in jazz as well as blues, Mabon found the latter his ticket to stardom. His first sides were a 1949 78 for Apollo as Big Willie and some 1950 outings for Aristocrat and Chess with guitarist Earl Dranes as the Blues-rockers.

But Mabon's asking price for a night's work rose dramatically when his 1952 debut release on powerful Windy City deejay Al Benson's Parrot logo, "I Don't Know," topped the R&B charts for eight weeks after being sold to Chess. From then on, Mabon was a Chess artist, returning to the top R&B slot the next year with the ominous "I'm Mad" and cracking the Top Ten anew with the Mel London-penned "Poison Ivy" in 1954. Throughout his Chess tenure, piano and sax were consistently to the fore rather than guitar and harp, emphasizing Mabon's cool R&B approach. Mabon's original version of Willie Dixon's hoodoo-driven "The Seventh Son" bombed in 1955, as did the remainder of his fine Chess catalog.

Mabon never regained his momentum after leaving Chess. He stopped at Federal in 1957, Mad in 1960, Formal in 1962 (where he stirred up some local sales with his leering "Got to Have Some"), and USA in 1963-64. Mabon sat out much of the late '60s but came back strong after moving to Paris in 1972, recording and touring Europe prolifically until his death. — *Bill Dahl*

Chicago 63 / 1974 / America ♦♦♦♦
Stylish piano and vocals ranging from clever to cranky to anguished. Willie Mabon is seldom powerful, but can convey more shadings and nuances than many blues vocalists or singers in several other genres as well. — *Ron Wynn*

The Seventh Son [LP] / 1981 / Crown Prince ♦♦♦♦
18 sensational Chess sides from 1952-1956 collected on import vinyl, quite a few of which unfortunately don't appear on the Charly CD: "Wow I Feel so Good," "Would You Baby," "Say Man" (not the Bo Diddley routine), "Cruisin'," and "Late Again," for starters. — *Bill Dahl*

Original USA Recordings / 1981 / Flyright ♦♦♦
More Mabon sides, these from 1963-64 and the USA label, that haven't made it to the digital domain yet (at least domestically). The USA stuff wasn't as consistent as his early Chess work, but there are some nice moments—the salacious "Just Got Some," a chunky "I'm the Fixer," and Willie's mouth organ workout "Harmonica Special." — *Bill Dahl*

● Blue Roots, Vol. 16 / 1982 / Chess ♦♦♦♦
While it may be a little difficult to track down, *Willie Mabon: Blue Roots, Vol. 16* is a solid overview of the pianist's greatest sides for Chess Records. Augmented by a couple of pleasant, but ultimately inconsequential, unreleased cuts, the collection is a good way to acquire the original versions of his big Chess hits until Chess gets around to reissuing these on CD. — *Thom Owens*

Seventh Son [CD] / 1993 / Charly ♦♦♦♦
Since MCA hasn't gotten around to this insinuating character's splendid Chess catalog as yet, we'll have to opt for a 16-song import that encompasses his three major hits "I Don't Know," "I'm Mad" (here in alternate take form, for whatever reason), and the Mel London-penned "Poison Ivy." Mabon's ur-ban R&B approach was something of a departure for the Delta-rooted blues prevalent at Chess at the time, but his laconic vocals on "The Seventh Son," "Knock on Wood," and "Got to Have It" made him a star (albeit briefly). — *Bill Dahl*

Chicago Blues Session! / 1995 / Evidence ♦♦♦
Chicago Blues Session! features a session pianist Willie Mabon cut on Independence Day 1979 with guitarist Hubert Sumlin, guitarist Eddie Taylor, bassist Aron Burton and drummer Casey Jones. The album was originally released on the German L&R label, mainly because American labels were shunning the blues. That could be the only reason this album wasn't released at the time, since it's a nice, straightahead Chicago blues record. There are several Mabon originals, all of them strong and memorable, plus several Willie Dixon tracks and a Howlin' Wolf cut. That Howlin' Wolf song is one of a handful of tributes to Chicago blues legends—the others are to Jimmy Reed and Willie Dixon—but the true tribute is the spirit and passion the group puts into their music. That's what makes the album a worthwhile listen for serious fans of Chicago blues. — *Thom Owens*

Lonnie Mack

b. Jul. 18, 1941, Harrison, IN
Guitar, Vocals / R&B, Rock 'n' Roll, Modern Electric Blues, Instrumental Rock
When Lonnie Mack sings the blues, country strains are sure to infiltrate. Conversely, if he digs into a humping rockabilly groove, strong signs of deep-down blues influence are bound to invade. Par for the course for any musician who cites both Bobby Bland and George Jones as pervasive influences.

Fact is, Lonnie Mack's lightning-fast, vibrato-enriched, whammy bar-hammered guitar style has influenced many a picker too—including Stevie Ray Vaughan, who idolized Mack's early singles for Fraternity and later co-produced and played on Mack's 1985 comeback LP for Alligator, *Strike like Lightning.*

Growing up in rural Indiana not far from Cincinnati, Lonnie McIntosh was exposed to a heady combination of R&B and hillbilly. In 1958, he bought the seventh Gibson Flying V guitar ever manufactured and played the roadhouse circuit around Indiana, Ohio, and Kentucky. Mack has steadfastly cited another local legend, guitarist Robert Ward, as the man whose watery-sounding Magnatone amplifier inspired his own use of the same brand.

Session work ensued during the early '60s behind Hank Ballard, Freddy King, and James Brown for Cincy's principal label, Syd Nathan's King Records. At the tail end of a 1963 date for another local diskery, Fraternity Records, Mack stepped out front to cut a searing instrumental treatment of Chuck Berry's "Memphis." Fraternity put the number out, and it leaped all the way up to the Top Five on *Billboard*'s pop charts!

Its hit follow-up, the frantic "Wham!," was even more amazing from a guitaristic perspective with Mack's lickety-split whammy-bar-fired playing driven like a locomotive by a hard-charging horn section. Mack's vocal skills were equally potent; R&B stations began to play his soul ballad "Where There's a Will" until they discovered Mack was of the Caucasian persuasion, then dropped it like a hot potato (its flip, a sizzling vocal remake of Jimmy Reed's "Baby, What's Wrong," was a minor pop hit in late 1963).

Mack waxed a load of killer material for Fraternity during the mid-'60s, much of it not seeing the light of day until later on. A deal with Elektra Records inspired by a 1968 *Rolling Stone* article profiling Mack should have led to major stardom, but his three Elektra albums were less consistent than the Fraternity material. (Elektra also reissued his only Fraternity LP, the seminal *The Wham of That Memphis Man.*) Mack cameoed on the Doors' *Mor-*

rison Hotel album, contributing a guitar solo to "Roadhouse Blues," and worked for a while as a member of Elektra's A&R team.

Disgusted with the record business, Lonnie Mack retreated to Indiana for a while, eventually signing with Capitol and waxing a couple of obscure country-based LPs. Finally, at Vaughan's behest, Mack abandoned his Indiana comfort zone for hipper Austin, TX, and began to reassert himself nationally. Vaughan masterminded the stunning *Strike like Lightning* in 1985; later that year, Mack co-starred with Alligator labelmates Albert Collins and Roy Buchanan at Carnegie Hall (a concert marketed on home video as *Further on down the Road*).

Mack's Alligator encore, *Second Sight*, was a disappointment for those who idolized Mack's playing—it was more of a singer-songwriter project. He temporarily left Alligator in 1988 for major-label prestige at Epic, but *Roadhouses and Dancehalls* was too diverse to easily classify and died a quick death. Mack's most recent album from 1990, *Live! Attack of the Killer V,* was captured on tape at a suburban Chicago venue called FitzGerald's and once again showed why Lonnie Mack is venerated by anyone who's even remotely into savage guitar playing. *— Bill Dahl*

★ **The Wham of that Memphis Man** / 1963 / Alligator ✦✦✦✦✦
This is a vinyl reissue of Lonnie's first album for the Fraternity in 1964, the one thousands of guitarists cut their teeth on. Muddy Waters once sang, "the blues had a baby and they named the baby rock 'n' roll." This is the album that proves it. Instrumental versions of R&B hits ("Memphis," "Susie Q," "The Bounce") rebound against heartfelt soul numbers ("Farther down the Road," "Why?") right next to dazzling fretboard blues romps both slow and fast ("Wham!," "Down and Out"). Lonnie sings his rear end off, the band—with saxes and Hammond organ and pumping soul bass—is right in there and Mack's vibrato-drenched guitar stings, wounds and amazes. It remains his defining moment. *— Cub Koda*

Glad I'm in the Band / 1969 / Elektra ✦✦✦
With the exception of his comeback album for Alligator, *Strike like Lightning,* nothing Mack has done since leaving Fraternity Records has come close to the wham-fisted brilliance of those seminal sides. This LP isn't bad at all, though—besides passable remakes of "Memphis" and "Why," Mack attacks Frankie Ford's "Roberta," Ted Taylor's "Stay Away from My Baby," and Little Willie John's "Let Them Talk," with a slightly rockier edge than his previous stuff. R&B vet Maxwell Davis did the horn charts. *— Bill Dahl*

Whatever's Right / 1969 / Elektra ✦✦✦
With a passel of familiar faces in the cast (ex-James Brown bassist Tim Drummond, pianist Dumpy Rice, harpist Rusty York), the reclusive Mack rocks up some memorable dusties his way—the Falcons' "I Found a Love," Bobby Bland's "Share Your Love with Me," Little Walter's "My Babe," and Jimmy Reed's chestnut "Baby What You Want Me to Do," along with his own "Gotta Be an Answer." *— Bill Dahl*

For Collectors Only / 1970 / Elektra ✦✦✦✦
For Collectors Only is reissue of Mack's sole Fraternity LP. *— Bill Dahl*

Memphis Sounds of Lonnie Mack / 1974 / Trip ✦✦✦✦
Memphis Sounds of Lonnie Mack is a fine collection of rarities recorded for the Fraternity label. *— Bill Dahl*

Home at Last / 1977 / One Way ✦✦
The bearded guitar wonder in a mainstream country setting that largely doesn't do him justice. *— Bill Dahl*

Lonnie Mack with Pismo / 1977 / One Way ✦✦
Country-rock (mostly) from the versatile and unpredictable master picker. Pismo's members included bassist Tim Drummond and keyboardist Stan Szelest (frequent Mack cohorts), while Troy Seals, Graham Nash, and David Lindley contributed to the product as well. The unabashed rockers "Lucy" and "Rock and Roll like We Used To" have some life in them, but some of this stuff is dreary. *— Bill Dahl*

Strike like Lightning / 1985 / Alligator ✦✦✦
Co-produced by Stevie Ray Vaughn, this was Lonnie's ticket back to the show after a few years on the sidelines. To say it was an inspired date would be putting it mildly. With his batteries recharged, Mack was in peak form, playing and singing better than ever. A major highlight is an inspired duet between Stevie and Lonnie on "Wham (Double Whammy)," going toe to toe for several exciting choruses. *— Cub Koda*

Second Sight / 1987 / Alligator ✦✦✦
After the sizzle of *Strike like Lightning,* this mellow set was a major disappointment. Yes, Mack is an exceptional vocalist, but the pop crossover ambience exploited here came at the expense of his unequalled guitar work—not a fair trade at all. *— Bill Dahl*

Attack of the Killer V: Live / 1990 / Alligator ✦✦✦
Cut in front of an appreciative throng at FitzGerald's in suburban Chicago, Mack cuts loose the way he so often does in concert, sticking almost exclusively to his Alligator-era tunes ("Satisfy Suzie," "Cincinnati Jail," the tortured soul ballad "Stop") and never looking too far backwards. *— Bill Dahl*

Lonnie on the Move / 1992 / Ace ✦✦✦✦
Criminally, Mack's seminal LP *Wham of That Memphis Man* remains unavailable on CD. But that doesn't mean Mack's Fraternity era is totally unrepresented in the digital racks. These 19 Flying V-soaked sides pack the same punch and hail from the same mid-'60s timeframe. He unleashes his vibrato-drenched axe on the torrid "Soul Express," "Lonnie on the Move," "Florence of Arabia," and an astonishing instrumental version of "Stand by Me" that'll send aspiring guitarists' jaws crashing to the floor. For a change of pace, "Men at Play" mines a jazzy walking groove to equally satisfying ends. *— Bill Dahl*

Road Houses & Dance Halls / Epic ✦✦
The folks at Columbia had no idea how to market Mack, so this fairly undistinguished album died a quick and practically unnoticed death. *— Bill Dahl*

Doug MacLeod

b. Apr. 21, 1946, New York, NY
Guitar, Vocals / Modern Electric Blues, Acoustic Blues
Unlike some other bluesmen now leading their own bands, guitarist, singer, and songwriter Doug MacLeod spent many years as an apprentice before forming his own band. MacLeod has worked as a sideman for many different artists from the Los Angeles-area blues scene, including Big Joe Turner, Charles Brown, Pee Wee Crayton, Eddie "Cleanhead," Vinson and George "Harmonica" Smith. MacLeod grew up in St. Louis and spent his teen years frequenting the blues clubs there, learning from people like Albert King, Little Milton and Ike and Tina Turner. He took up the bass in his teens and played around St. Louis with local bands before enlisting in the Navy. MacLeod was stationed in Norfolk, VA, and spent his off-duty time playing in blues bars. He eventually settled in Los Angeles, accompanying many other blues performers before forming his own band. His songs have been recorded by Albert King, Albert Collins, and Son Seals. MacLeod's 1984 album, *No Road Back Home,* was nominated for a W.C. Handy Award in 1984 and has since been reissued on compact disc on the Hightone label. MacLeod has three widely available albums—*Come To Find* (1994), which featured Charlie Musselwhite, *You Can't Take My Blues,* Audioquest, 1996, and the aforementioned *No Road Back Home.* The first album features guest appearances by harmonica players Carey Bell and fiddle player Heather Hardy, while the latter features a guest appearance by harp player George Harmonica Smith. MacLeod has also recorded for a variety of independent labels, including such albums as *Woman in the Street, 54th and Vermont* and *Ain't the Blues Evil.* *— Richard Skelly*

No Road Back Home / 1984 / Hightone ✦✦✦✦

Ain't the Blues Evil / 1991 / Volt ✦✦
MacLeod and his band continue in a storytelling, jazz-tinged blues bag, whether in "Just like a Minstrel," where he bemoans the trials and tribulations of road life (eating cold hot dogs and sleeping in dirty hotel rooms), or in "One Fool Lookin' for Another," recalling troubles with women. Hammond B-3 and military drum rolls underlie "Placquemine," telling of a man who trails a lover from place to place, only to find her using him as a stepping stone toward a Hollywood career. Fellow George Smith alumna Rod Piazza accompanies and blows an ultra cool solo on "(I Think You're) Steppin' Out on Me." "SRV (For Stevie Ray)," is an inspirational instrumental which is both a tribute and a thank you to the great Mr. Vaughan. *— Char Ham*

Come to Find / 1994 / AudioQuest ✦✦✦
The sparsity in the arrangements make this album admirable and draw even more attention to the music, both overall and in its subtleties. It showcases brilliantly Bill Stuve's upright bass work, and for Jimi Bott, how unusually placed but effective drumbeats prove him a blues drummer deserving greater recognition. "Since I Left St. Louis" has MacLeod reflecting on his

early adult years of fast life, women, and drinking, and the lessons painfully learned from those experiences. The title track is a realization that making the most out of life is better than a life of abuse, whether it be child abuse, substance abuse, or any other kind. Always a master on the harmonica, Charlie Musselwhite blows on Willie Dixon's "Bring it on Home" and the MacLeod-penned "Lost Something This Morning." A great example of Piedmont-style blues is illustrated in "Old Virginia Stomp," dedicated to mentor Ernest Banks. Backup singers Black Cherry round out the album with the uplifting gospel feel of "Ain't No Grave," which tells of the triumph of the afterlife over death. *— Char Ham*

You Can't Take My Blues / 1996 / AudioQuest ✦✦✦✦
Doug MacLeod displays several sides of his artistry on this AudioQuest CD. His music ranges from solo folk numbers in the idiom of Leadbelly (but covering different subjects) to country blues with a trio, a few romps with the wailing harmonica of Carey Bell and two collaborations with the country fiddle of Heather Hardy. MacLeod's appealing voice is easy to understand, his lyrics are thoughtful and fresh (even when covering universal subjects) and his melodic guitar playing is versatile. MacLeod's well-conceived set should appeal to collectors of acoustic blues and folk music. *— Scott Yanow*

● **Unmarked Road** / Oct. 7, 1997 / AudioQuest ✦✦✦✦
Doug MacLeod's dark singing and sparse guitar playing are a throwback to the country-blues artists of the 1930s, although his lyrics have more modern sensibilities. Much of this superior CD is haunting and mildly disturbing, giving one the feeling that there is a great deal beneath the surface. It is the type of blues/folk recording worth experiencing several times, in contrast to those of recent times that express more obvious sentiments. Bassist Jeff Turmes is on just seven of the dozen songs (five of which also include drummer Stefev Mugalian); three of the remaining tunes are duets by MacLeod with percussionist Oliver Brown, and the two others are unaccompanied solo performances. Although the leader's guitar playing is impressive, it is his distinctive and very sincere voice on his dozen originals that sticks in one's mind. *— Scott Yanow*

Madcat & Kane
f. Ann Arbor, MI
Group / Folk-Blues, Modern Acoustic Blues, Contemporary Folk
Peter "Madcat" Ruth (harmonica) and Shari Kane (guitar, vocals) are a folk-blues duo based in Ann Arbor, MI. Ruth's multi-note style appears on tracks with the Southern rock group Blackfoot among others while Kane's slide work is a descendant of her mentor and leading inspiration, the legendary Johnny Shines. *Key to the Highway* has been released on Schoolkids' Records. *— John Bush*

Key to the Highway / Schoolkids ✦✦✦
Blues-lite, perfect for campfire sing-a-longs (though Madcat Ruth's harp chops are undeniably impressive). *— Bill Dahl*

Magic Sam (Samuel Maghett)
b. Feb. 14, 1937, Grenada, MS, d. Dec. 1, 1969, Chicago, IL
Guitar, Vocals / R&B, Modern Electric Blues, Electric Chicago Blues, Chicago Blues, Blues Revival
No blues guitarist better represented the adventurous modern sound of Chicago's West Side more proudly than Sam Maghett. He died tragically young (at age 32, of a heart attack), right when he was on the brink of climbing the ladder to legitimate stardom—but Magic Sam left behind a thick legacy of bone-cutting blues that remains eminently influential around his old stomping grounds to this day.

Mississippi Delta-born Sam Maghett (one of his childhood pals was towering guitarist Morris Holt, who received his Magic Slim handle from Sam). In 1950, Sam arrived in Chicago, picking up a few blues guitar pointers from his new neighbor, Syl Johnson (whose brother Mack Thompson served as Sam's loyal bassist for much of his professional career). Harpist Shakey Jake Harris, sometimes referred to as the guitarist's uncle, encouraged Sam's blues progress and gigged with him later on, when both were West Side institutions.

Sam's tremolo-rich staccato finger-picking was an entirely fresh phenomenon when he premiered it on Eli Toscano's Cobra label in 1957. Prior to his Cobra date, the guitarist had been gigging as Good Rocking Sam, but Toscano wanted to change his nickname to something old-timey like Sad Sam or Singing Sam. No dice, said the newly christened Magic Sam (apparently Mack Thompson's brainstorm).

His Cobra debut single, "All Your Love," was an immediate local sensation; its unusual structure would be recycled time and again by Sam throughout his tragically truncated career. Sam's Cobra encores "Everything Gonna Be Alright" and "Easy Baby" borrowed much the same melody but were no less powerful; the emerging West Side sound was now officially committed to vinyl. Not everything Sam cut utilized the tune; "21 Days in Jail" was a pseudo-rockabilly smoker with hellacious lead guitar from Sam and thundering slap bass from the ubiquitous Willie Dixon. Sam also backed Shakey Jake Harris on his lone 45 for Cobra's Artistic subsidiary, "Call Me if You Need Me."

After Cobra folded, Sam didn't follow labelmates Otis Rush and Magic Slim over to Chess. Instead, after enduring an unpleasant Army experience that apparently landed him in jail for desertion, Sam opted to go with Mel London's Chief logo in 1960. His raw-boned West Side adaptation of Fats Domino's mournful "Every Night About This Time" was the unalloyed highlight of his stay at Chief; some other Chief offerings were less compelling.

Gigs on the West Side remained plentiful for the charismatic guitarist, but recording opportunities proved sparse until 1966, when Sam made a 45 for Crash Records. "Out of Bad Luck" brought back that trademark melody again, but it remained as shattering as ever. Another notable 1966 side, the plaintive "That's Why I'm Crying," wound up on Delmark's *Sweet Home Chicago* anthology, along with Sam's stunning clippity-clop boogie instrumental "Riding High" (aided by the muscular tenor sax of Eddie Shaw).

Delmark Records was the conduit for Magic Sam's two seminal albums, 1967's *West Side Soul* and the following year's *Black Magic.* Both LPs showcased the entire breadth of Sam's West Side attack: the first ranged from the soul-laced "That's All I Need" and a searing "I Feel So Good" to the blistering instrumental "Lookin' Good" and definitive remakes of "Mama Talk to Your Daughter" and "Sweet Home Chicago," while *Black Magic* benefitted from Shaw's jabbing, raspy sax as Sam blasted through the funky "You Belong to Me," an impassioned "What Have I Done Wrong," and a personalized treatment of Freddy King's "San-Ho-Zay."

Sam's reputation was growing exponentially. He wowed an overflow throng at the 1969 Ann Arbor Blues Festival, and Stax was reportedly primed to sign him when his Delmark commitment was over. However, heart problems were fast taking their toll on Sam's health. On the first morning of December of 1969, he complained of heartburn, collapsed, and died.

Even now, more than a quarter century after his passing, Magic Sam remains the king of West Side blues. That's unlikely to change as long as the sub-genre is alive and kicking. *— Bill Dahl*

Magic Touch / 1966 / Black Top ✦✦✦✦
Another rare glimpse at Magic Sam hard at work, this time at another fabled West Side haunt, Sylvio's, in 1966. No saxes this time, but uncle Shakey Jake was around for a few guest shots, while bassist Mac Thompson and drummer Odie Payne provide supple backing as Sam launches into another terrific set of numbers that for the most part he never recorded in the studio—songs by Freddy King, Albert Collins, James Robins, Junior Parker, and Jimmy McCracklin that briliantly suited his soaring pipes and singular guitar style. *— Bill Dahl*

★ **West Side Soul** / 1967 / Delmark ✦✦✦✦✦
One of the truly essential Chicago blues albums of the 1960s. There's not a weak piece of filler on it—Sam exudes West Side sizzle as he busts loose on "I Don't Want No Woman," "I Need You So Bad," definitive covers of "Sweet Home Chicago" and "Mama Talk to Your Daughter," the clippity-clop finger-twisting instrumental "Lookin' Good," and a soul-slanted "That's All I Need." *— Bill Dahl*

Black Magic / 1968 / Delmark ✦✦✦✦
With the key addition of raspy saxist Eddie Shaw to urge him on, Sam's Delmark encore was another instant classic, containing his R&B-slanted "You Belong to Me" and "What Have I Done Wrong," the bandstand favorites "Just a Little Bit" and "Same Old Blues," and a personalized treatment of Freddy King's "San-Ho-Zay." The album also proved his swan song; he was dead a year later. *— Bill Dahl*

Magic Rocker / 1980 / Flyright ++++

Otis Rush & Magic Sam / 1980 / Flyright ++++

A pair of blues giants, each given ample room. While you can find better Rush and Sam, that's no slam on what's here. What you're getting are excellent songs that didn't make it onto the first reissue of Magic Sam/Shakey Jake material, plus powerhouse Rush that didn't make *Groaning the Blues.* In other words, this isn't exactly fodder. —*Ron Wynn*

Live at Ann Arbor & in Chicago / Jul. 1982 / Delmark +++

Don't let the homemade recording quality put you off for a second, because this is Magic Sam at his whiplash best. —*Cub Koda*

The Late Great Magic Sam / 1984 / Evidence +++

The ten 1963-1964 sides that make up the majority of this set have sort of fallen through the historical cracks over the years. They didn't deserve such shoddy treatment—Sam didn't record "Back Door Friend" or "Hi-Heel Sneakers" anywhere else, and he's in top shape throughout. Two live tracks at the set's close from 1969 don't add much to the overall package. —*Bill Dahl*

The Magic Sam Legacy / 1989 / Delmark ++++

Alternate takes and unissued surprises from the *West Side Soul* and *Black Magic* sessions, along with a couple of welcome 1966 sides ("I Feel So Good" and "Lookin' Good") that didn't see the light of day when they were recorded. Sam's versions of Jimmy Rogers' "Walkin' by Myself" and "That Ain't It" are important additions to his immortal legacy. —*Bill Dahl*

Live at the Alex Club / 1990 / Delmark ++++

For the first half of this frequently amazing disc, Magic Sam plays for his West Side homefolks at the Alex Club. The time is 1963-64, he's backed by saxists A.C. Reed and Eddie Shaw and his longtime bassist, Mac Thompson, and he's blasting the hits of the day with a joyous abandon. A little over six years later, Sam wowed the Ann Arbor Blues Festival with a sensational trio set just as inordinately powerful in its own way. Sound quality is rough on both artifacts, but no matter. —*Bill Dahl*

★ **2 1957-1966** / 1991 / Paula +++++

Never mind Otis Rush and Buddy Guy—this is the bedrock document of Chicago's West Side blues guitar movement. Ten seminal numbers that constitute Sam's complete Cobra stash (notably "All Your Love," "Easy Baby," and the rockabilly-tinged "21 Days in Jail"), another pair by his harp-blowing uncle Shakey Jake, five numbers from 1960 that first appeared on Mel London's Chief logo (a tortured cover of Fats Domino's "Every Night About This Time" is the killer), and a couple of solid 1966 outings that reinforce Sam's standing as the king of the West Side prior to his untimely demise. —*Bill Dahl*

Give Me Time / 1991 / Delmark +++

We now adjourn to Sam's West Side living room, where he's holding court in 1968 with only a few friends and family members on hand. Some of the tunes are familiar—"That's All I Need," "You Belong to Me"—but there are other originals only available here, and the super-intimate atmosphere brings out the intimate side of the late guitarist. —*Bill Dahl*

Magic Slim (Morris Holt)

b. Aug. 7, 1937, Grenada, MS

Guitar, Vocals / Modern Electric Blues, Soul Blues, Electric Chicago Blues

Magic Slim & the Teardrops proudly uphold the tradition of what a Chicago blues *band* should sound like. Their emphasis on ensemble playing and a humongous repertoire that allegedly ranges upwards of a few hundred songs give the towering guitarist's live performances an endearing off-the-cuff quality—you never know what obscurity he'll pull out of his oversized hat next.

Born Morris Holt, the Mississippi native was forced to give up playing the piano when he lost his little finger in a cotton gin mishap. Boyhood pal Magic Sam bestowed his magical moniker on the budding guitarist (times change; Slim's no longer slim). Holt first came to Chicago in 1955, but found that breaking into the competitive local blues circuit was a tough proposition. Although he managed to secure a steady gig for a while with Robert Perkins' band (Mr. Pitiful & the Teardrops), Slim wasn't good enough to progress into the upper ranks of Chicago bluesdom.

So he retreated to Mississippi for a spell to hone his chops. When he returned to Chicago in 1965 (with brothers Nick and Lee Baby as his new

rhythm section), Slim's detractors were quickly forced to change their tune. Utilizing the Teardrops name and holding onto his Magic Slim handle, the big man cut a couple of 45s for Ja-Wes and established himself as a formidable force on the South side—his guitar work dripped vibrato-enriched nastiness, and his roaring vocals were as gruff and uncompromising as anyone's on the scene.

All of a sudden, the recording floodgates opened up for the Teardrops in 1979 after they cut four tunes for Alligator's *Living Chicago Blues* anthology series. Since then, a series of nails-tough albums for Rooster Blues, Alligator, Blind Pig, and a slew for the Austrian Wolf logo have fattened Slim's discography considerably. The Teardrops recently weathered a potentially devastating change when longtime second guitarist John Primer cut his own major-label debut for Code Blue, but with Slim and bass-wielding brother Nick Holt still on board, it's doubtful the quartet's overall sound will change dramatically in Primer's likely absence. —*Bill Dahl*

Highway Is My Home / Nov. 19, 1978 / Evidence +++

Magic Slim's style is a full-speed-ahead, hard-edged, ragged one, with a deep, sometimes sloppy vocal approach and an equally cutting guitar approach. It is not pretty, flashy, pop-oriented, or even particularly appealing, but it is genuine. The stripped-down Slim sound was mostly on target throughout the 10 tracks (one bonus cut) on this late '70s date originally recorded for Black and Blue. This Evidence CD features Slim being assertive, as close to romantic as he can get, and otherwise powering straight ahead. Only on Elmore James' "The Sky Is Crying" does he sound overwhelmed, more by the song's litany (Albert King's equally transcendent version also looms in the background). Otherwise, blues for the non-crossover set. —*Ron Wynn*

Live at the Zoo Bar / 1980 / Candy Apple ++

The towering guitarist and his Teardrops were only hinting at their future greatness when they cut this live set at the Zoo Bar in Nebraska. —*Bill Dahl*

● **Grand Slam** / 1982 / Rooster Blues ++++

Still absent from the CD shelves, this raw-boned LP captures Slim's unpretentious houserocking sound about as well as any studio set possibly could. Among its highlights: the hard-shuffling "Early Every Morning," a surreal "Scuffling," and Slim's tribute to his late pal Magic Sam, "She Belongs to Me." —*Bill Dahl*

Raw Magic / Jun. 1983 / Alligator +++

A more consistent studio collection that first came out over in France and translated well to domestic consumption. Only seven titles, including Slim's lusty "Mama Talk to Your Daughter," a crowd-pleasing "Mustang Sally," and three tunes of the quartet's own making (which is rather rare with this cover-heavy combo). —*Bill Dahl*

TV Dinner Blues / Oct. 1984 / Blue Dog +++

Live at B.L.U.E.S. / 1987 / B.L.U.E.S. R&B ++++

Captured at Chicago's intimate B.L.U.E.S. nightclub, this is surely one of the best live sets the quartet ever committed to tape. The vinyl time constraints limited the program to eight songs, but apart from a marathon "Mother Fuyer," they're not his usual standards—Chuck Willis's grinding "Keep a Drivin'," a resigned "Poor Man but a Good Man," and Slim's own "Help Yourself." —*Bill Dahl*

Gravel Road / 1990 / Blind Pig +++

Another solid Slim set with an additional emphasis on the considerable contributions of second guitarist John Primer, who handles vocals on three cuts (including covers of Otis Redding's "Hard to Handle" and Eugene Church's "Pretty Girls Everywhere"). This was a particularly potent edition of Teardrops, pounding through Slim's own title cut and "Please Don't Waste My Time" and Albert King's shuffling "Cold Women with Warm Hearts" with barroom bravado. —*Bill Dahl*

Taj Mahal (Henry St. Clair Fredericks)

b. May 17, 1942, New York, NY

Banjo, Bass, Guitar, Piano, Vocals, Harmonica / Modern Acoustic Blues, Electric Country Blues

Since the mid-'60s, Taj Mahal has played a vital role in the preservation of traditional blues and African-American roots music. He is a singer, songwriter, composer and noted musicologist who through intensive research creates authentic, rootsy compositions that, while remaining true to tradition, are still relevant to modern audiences and always bear his own unique stamp. Although he frequently ventures into different genres, Mahal's heart and soul belongs to the old-time country blues.

Born Henry Saint Clair Fredericks in New York City (but raised in Springfield, MA) to a gospel-singing South Carolina schoolteacher and a piano-playing West Indian jazz arranger, his passion for the blues began while he was attending the University of Massachusetts in the early '60s. He fell in love with the music of such performers as T-Bone Walker, in which he saw an important African musical tradition that represented for every aspect of life. By keeping the music alive, he would be preserving the African heritage he cherished. In addition to his regular studies, Mahal began to delve into blues history, which led him to explore other forms of Black folk music as well, including West African music, Caribbean, and zydeco, in addition to R&B, rock, and jazz. He already knew how to play the bass, but soon also learned to play the instruments used by old-time musicians, including piano, acoustic guitar, banjo, mandolin, dulcimer, harmonica and assorted flutes. Armed with new knowledge, he began playing the Boston folk circuit.

Following graduation with a BA in Agriculture in 1964, Mahal went to Los Angeles and teamed up with guitarist Ry Cooder to form the Rising Sons, but the band released just one single before breaking up, although more than 20 tracks recorded by the group surfaced on CD in the 1990s. Mahal made his own recording debut for Columbia in 1968 with a self-titled album. He recorded several more albums for the label through the early '70s and at the same time established himself as a popular, charismatic, yet laid-back performer, known for his adventurousness, gentle wit, and intelligence. As the years have passed, Mahal has become known as a musical chameleon, changing and mixing up genres to suit his current interests. He has even recorded children's albums that are anything but childish in their content. Many albums, such as *Like Never Before* (1991) contain an eclectic assortment of styles covering both old songs and his new compositions.

In addition to performing and album work, Mahal has also composed movie soundtracks (*Sounder* and *Sounder II*) and television scores for such shows as *The Man Who Broke a Thousand Chains* and *Brer Rabbit.* In 1991, he composed authentic music for the Broadway production of *Mule Bone,* a Langston Hughes/Zora Neale Hurston play that had been lost since the mid-'30s. As the '90s progress, Mahal continues to contribute and add to his discography. —*Sandra Brennan*

Natch'l Blues / 1968 / Columbia ++++
For some reason, Taj Mahal gets the back of the hand treatment from a lot of blues purists. Sure, his records can get very self-indulgent, but when he turns to blues, you can hear a lot worse than Mahal. This was among his best LPs, with both strong originals and good remakes. —*Ron Wynn*

Taj Mahal [CBS] / 1968 / Columbia ++++
His self-titled debut, with Ry Cooder and Jesse Ed Davis, is first and foremost. —*Mark A. Humphrey*

Giant Step / 1969 / Columbia +++
Giant Step/De Old Folks at Home is a two-record set that features one album of Delta blues that was recorded with a full electric band and one album of solo acoustic blues. The electric record is the better collection, but only by a small margin—the acoustic record suffers from poor production that prevents a listener from completely connecting with Taj Mahal's blues. Nevertheless, there are terrific moments on both records and, on the whole, it is one of his finest albums. —*Thom Owens*

The Blues / 196 / Columbia ++++

Happy Just to Be Like I Am / 1971 / Mobile Fidelity ++++
With *Happy Just to Be Like I Am,* Taj Mahal offers another (possibly his most effective) course in roots music, this time dabbling in Caribbean rhythms in addition to his more-or-less standard take on acoustic country blues. While his good intentions and craftsmanlike execution can't be denied, one hopes the listener will eventually decide to seek out the inspirations for these recordings. —*AMG*

Recycling the Blues & Other Related Stuff / 1972 / Mobile Fidelity +++
The title *Recycling the Blues & Other Related Stuff* certainly sums up the album quite well—that's exactly what Taj Mahal has been doing for several years by this point. The first side features laidback in-the-studio work with

some nice gospel-inflected back-up from the Pointer Sisters. The second (and preferable) side offers a good look at Mahal's stage show. —*AMG*

The Real Thing / 1972 / Columbia ++
The Real Thing is double-live album featuring a new batch of songs as well as some old favorites augmented by, oddly enough, a four-piece tuba section. The change in arrangements may be a point of curiosity, but in the end, the album is bogged down by directionless jamming. —*AMG*

Sounder / 1973 / Columbia ++
On his first film score, *Sounder,* Taj Mahal mixes a handful of originals with fragmented sound effects and incidental passages. Certainly not an easy listen, this is one of his more indulgent studies. —*AMG*

Ooh So Good 'N' Blues / 1973 / Columbia +++
Ooh So Good 'N' Blues takes a more straightahead approach that, with the exception of the the jazzy mis-step titled "Teacup's Jazzy Blues Tune," keeps the experimentation down to a minimum. As a result, this is one of his most consistently enjoyable and even albums. —*AMG*

Mo' Roots / Apr. 1974 / Columbia +++
Mo' Roots finds Mahal stepping away from the blues, choosing instead to focus on reggae. While he can often be faulted for his all-too-academic approach, with *Mo' Roots* he turns in an album that truly expresses his appreciation and connection with the music. —*AMG*

Music Keeps Me Together / 1975 / Columbia ++

Satisfied 'N Tickled Too / 1976 / Columbia ++

Anthology, Vol. 1 (1966-1976) / 1976 / Columbia ++++
Taj Mahal's often-indulgent experimentations have flawed most of his albums to different degrees; *The Taj Mahal Anthology, Vol. 1* rights these self-inflicted wrongs by compiling a coherent look at his early career (1966-1976). Though this collection is currently out-of-print, it provides the best introduction to his easy-going take on the blues. —*AMG*

Music Fuh Ya' / 1977 / Warner Brothers +++

Brothers / 1977 / Warner Brothers ++

Evolution / 1977 / Warner Brothers ++

● **The Best of Taj Mahal, Vol. 1** / 1981 / Columbia ++++
Best of Taj Mahal provides a concise career overview with a broader scope than *Anthology, Vol. 1.* —*AMG*

Live & Direct / 1987 / Laserlight ++
While the disco vibe on some of these tunes is a bit cheesy, there are several outstanding performances by Taj and his International Rhythm Band. Indeed, "Little Brown Dog" catches Taj in one of his transcendental live moments when he gets so down in the groove you never want him to stop. —*Tim Sheridan*

Shake Sugaree / Sep. 1988 / Music For Little People +++
Shake Sugaree is a wonderful children's album. Taj Mahal leads kids through a musical journey, taking them through the Caribbean, Africa, and the Deep South, telling stories and singing songs all the while. Some of the tracks feature a choir composed of his own children, and every song and story is not only entertaining, but educational as well. Simply a delightful record. —*Thom Owens*

Peace Is the World Smiling / 1989 / +++
Peace Is the World Smiling is a sweet, good-natured project by Taj Mahal, Pete Seeger, Holly Near, Sweet Honey in the Rock, and many others that is directed toward world peace. Some of the tracks are bland, but it is hard to criticize the musician's intentions. Besides, there a handful of very nice songs on the album. —*Thom Owens*

Like Never Before / Oct. 1991 / Private Music +++
After a string of children's albums and other side projects, Taj Mahal returns to his roots with *Like Never Before*—an eclectic assortment of styles featuring traditional covers and a new batch of originals. —*AMG*

Mule Bone / Nov. 1, 1991 / Gramavision +++
Taj Mahal won a Grammy nomination with this music from the Broadway production of the Hurston/Hughes play. —*Mark A. Humphrey*

Taj's Blues / Jun. 16, 1992 / Columbia/Legacy ++++
Taj's Blues is an entertainingly diverse record, featuring a variety of blues

and roots-music styles, all fused together into a distinctive sound of its own. Half of the album is played on acoustic, the other with an electric band (which includes guitarists Ry Cooder and Jesse Davis on a handful of tracks), which gives a pretty good impression of the range of Mahal's talents. It's a good collection, featuring many of his best performances for Columbia, including "Statesboro Blues" and "Leaving Trunk," as well as the unreleased "East Bay Woman." — *Thom Owens*

Dancing the Blues / 1993 / Private Music ♦♦♦
Taj Mahal has always been a more inclusive, eclectic musician than even some admirers understand; his work was never simply or totally blues, even though that strain was at the center and seldom far from anything he performed either. That's the case with this newest collection, a 12-song set that includes splendid covers of Muddy Waters and Howlin' Wolf tunes, but also equally respectful, striking renditions of soul standards such as "Mockingbird," with special guest Etta James, and "That's How Strong My Love Is." There are also strong Mahal originals like "Blues Ain't Nothin'" and "Strut," with Mahal singing and playing in his wry, delicate, yet forceful way. — *Ron Wynn*

An Evening of Acoustic Music / 1995 / Traditional&Moderne/Topic ♦♦♦♦
If you've ever caught Taj live solo, this recording, cut during an appearance in Germany, is what you've been waiting for. His sublime performances of "Satisfied and Tickled Too" and "Candy Man" are out of this world. While the inclusion of tuba on a few tracks does prove somewhat annoying, for the most part this is an excellent example of what makes Taj a treasure. — *Tim Sheridan*

Live at Ronnie Scott's, London / Jan. 23, 1996 / DRG ♦♦♦
Recorded in 1988 at the famous Ronnie Scott's Club, Mahal is backed by keyboardist Wayne Henderson, bassist Ward Allen, singer Carey Williams, drummer Ozzie Williams and percussionist Kester Smith. — *Jason Ankeny*

Phantom Blues / Feb. 27, 1996 / Private Music ♦♦♦
An eclectic bluesman would seem to be a contradiction in terms, but Taj Mahal, who has moved through the worlds of folk, rock, and pop to reach his present categorization, fits the description, and here he takes several pop and R&B oldies that came from blues roots—"Ooh Poo Pah Doo," "Lonely Avenue," "What Am I Living For?," "Let the Four Winds Blow"—and returns them to those roots. He also calls in such guest stars as Eric Clapton and Bonnie Raitt, who have more than a nodding acquaintance with the blues, to assist him. The result is progressive blues hybrid that treats the music not as a source, but as a destination. — *William Ruhlmann*

An Evening of Acoustic Music / Oct. 29, 1996 / RFR ♦♦♦
Evening is a live album recorded during Taj Mahal's 1993 European tour, and while it has some good performances—notable "Satisfied N' Tickled Too" and an excellent version of "Stagger Lee"—it's only of interest to dedicated fans of the bluesman. — *Thom Owens*

Señor Blues / Jun. 17, 1997 / Private Music ♦♦♦♦
Señor Blues is one of Taj Mahal's best latter-day albums, a rollicking journey through classic blues styles performed with contemporary energy and flair. There's everything from country-blues to jazzy uptown blues on *Señor Blues*, and Taj hits all of areas in between, including R&B and soul. Stylistically, it's similar to most of his albums, but he's rarely been as effortlessly fun and infectious as he is here. — *Thom Owens*

Shakin' a Tailfeather / Oct. 28, 1997 / Rhino ♦♦♦
This melange of early rock and pop hits like "Rockin' Robin" and traditional songs like "Shortnin' Bread" suffers from an overabundance of sincerity. There's just a bit too much trying to get across a message and too little just having fun. That's a serious problem for a disc aimed at kids. — *Ross Boissoneau*

Sacred Island / Apr. 7, 1998 / Private Music ♦♦♦
Taj Mahal experienced something of a renaissance in the '90s, turning out a series of surprisingly strong records for Private Records. Since the albums were a success, it gave him the opportunity to make *Sacred Island*, a collection of Hawaiian music and Hawaiian-flavored blues. Even though there are a couple of weak moments, it works better than you might think, since Taj Mahal has never been a blues purist. As a result, it's an interesting detour that longtime fans will find fascinating. — *Stephen Thomas Erlewine*

Harvey Mandel

b. Mar. 11, 1945, Detroit, MI
Guitar / Rock 'n' Roll, Psychedelic, Modern Electric Blues, Blues-Rock
In the mold of Jeff Beck, Carlos Santana, and Mike Bloomfield, Mandel is an extremely creative rock guitarist with heavy blues and jazz influences. And like those guitarists, his vocal abilities are basically nonexistent, though Mandel, unlike some similar musicians, has always known this, and concentrated on recordings that are entirely instrumental, or feature other singers. A minor figure most known for auditioning unsuccessfully for the Rolling Stones, he recorded some intriguing (though erratic) work on his own that anticipated some of the better elements of jazz-rock fusion, showcasing his concise chops, his command of a multitude of tone pedal controls, and an eclecticism that found him working with string orchestras and country steel guitar wizards. Mandel got his first toehold in the fertile Chicago White blues-rock scene of the mid-'60s (which cultivated talents like Paul Butterfield, Mike Bloomfield, and Steve Miller), and made his first recordings as the lead guitarist for harmonica virtuoso Charlie Musselwhite. Enticed to go solo by Blue Cheer producer Abe Kesh, Harvey cut a couple of nearly wholly instrumental albums for Phillips in the late '60s that were underground FM radio favorites, establishing him as one of the most versatile young American guitar lions. He gained his most recognition, though, not as a solo artist, but as a lead guitarist for Canned Heat in 1969 and 1970, replacing Henry Vestine and appearing with the band at Woodstock. Shortly afterwards, he signed up for a stint in John Mayall's band, just after the British bluesman had relocated to California. Mandel unwisely decided to use a vocalist for his third and least successful Philips album. After his term with Mayall (on *USA Union* and *Back to the Roots*) had run its course, he resumed his solo career, and also formed Pure Food & Drug Act with violinist Don "Sugarcane" Harris (from the '50s R&B duo Don & Dewey), which made several albums. In the mid-'70s, when the Rolling Stones were looking for a replacement for Mick Taylor, Mandel auditioned for a spot in the group; although he lost to Ron Wood, his guitar does appear on two cuts on the Stones' 1976 album, *Black & Blue*. Recording intermittently since then as a solo artist and a sessionman, his influence on the contemporary scene is felt via the two-handed fretboard tapping technique that he introduced on his 1973 album *Shangrenede*, later employed by Eddie Van Halen, Stanley Jordan, and Steve Vai. — *Richie Unterberger*

Cristo Redentor / 1968 / EG ♦♦♦
Mandel's debut remains his best early work, introducing an accomplished blues-rock guitarist capable of producing smooth, fluid lines and a variety of tasteful distortion and buzzing via an assortment of tone pedals and customized amplifiers. He augmented his flash with an adventurous appetite for orchestrated, quasi-classical strings (especially in the eerie symphonic title cut), jazz-blues-rock fusion in the mold of The Electric Flag (as on "Before Six"), and even a bit of country in the presence of top steel guitarist Pete Drake. Available in its entirety on the reissue compilation *The Mercury Years*. — *Richie Unterberger*

Righteous / 1969 / Philips ♦♦♦
Not as consistent as his debut, due to the presence of a few pedestrian blues-rock numbers. The better tracks, though, show Mandel continuing to expand his horizons with imagination, particularly on the cuts with string and horn arrangements by noted jazz arranger Shorty Rogers. Harvey's workout on Nat Adderley's "Jazz Samba" is probably his best solo performance, and an obvious touchstone for the Latin-rock hybrid of Carlos Santana (whose own debut came out the same year); on the other side of the coin, "Boo-Bee-Doo" is one of his sharpest and snazziest straight blues-rockers. Available in its entirety on the reissue compilation *The Mercury Years*. — *Richie Unterberger*

Games Guitars Play / 1970 / Philips ♦♦
Feeling that he needed a singer to compete commercially, Mandel decided to abandon his instrumental format, taking on multi-instrumentalist Russell Dashiel as lead vocalist for a good share of the tracks. Alas, Dashiel was a mediocre singer who typified some of the lesser White blues-rock stylings of the period, and the material (with a higher percentage of blues and soul covers) was not up to the level of Mandel's first two efforts, although Harvey's playing remained accomplished and imaginative (as is evident on the original instrumental "Ridin' High" and the cover of Horace Silver's

"Senor Blues"). Available in its entirety on the reissue compilation *The Mercury Years*. —*Richie Unterberger*

Baby Batter / 1971 / Janus ◆◆◆◆
Fiery, jazz-influenced, blues-based rock by a former Canned Heat guitarist. —*David Szatmary*

The Snake / 1972 / Janus ◆◆◆
Mandel shares more similarities with Jeff Beck than he's probably willing to admit: both are stunning virtuoso guitarists who can't write consistently first-rate material or sing. Mandel's fifth album, like Beck's best '70s efforts, add bluesy, jazzy shadings to a rock base. But *The Snake* is more firmly entrenched in blues-rock than, say, *Blow by Blow*. Harvey's playing (occasionally augmented by violinist Don "Sugarcane" Harris) is always impressive, but the compositions (all but one instrumental) aren't gripping, and, like much of the genre, meander too much. It's not as good as Mandel's late-'60s recordings for Philips, but it's still one of the better early rock-based fusion recordings. —*Richie Unterberger*

Twist City / 1994 / Western Front ◆◆
Although he took blues guitar to uncharted sonic territory in the late '60s with Charlie Musselwhite and on his own solo discs, this '90s return to 12-bar roots was a bit like forcing Mandel to play handcuffed—he seems constrained by the standard-fare repertoire. Mark Skyer's affected, generic vocals and the title track's trite lyrics don't help. —*Dan Forte*

Snakes & Stripes / 1995 / Clarity ◆◆◆
Back to a more varied approach—encompassing Latin, funk, jazz-rock, and even country ("Country Rose")—with nice results. Nine insturmentals and only two vocals (reprising Canned Heat's "Future Blues" and Pure Food & Drug Act's "My Soul's on Fire"), handled by Lori Davidson, on this live-in-the-studio audiofile set. Mandel's nod to B.B. King on "Mashed Potato Twist" is worth the price of admission. —*Dan Forte*

● **The Mercury Years** / Oct. 24, 1995 / Mercury ◆◆◆◆
Double-CD reissue repackages the entire contents of his first three LPs (1968's *Cristo Redentor*, 1969's *Righteous*, 1970's *Games Guitars Play*) in their original track sequence, with extensive, informative liner notes. It could be that a more selective, single-disc distillation of the best Mercury material that weeded out the more generic blues-rock tunes would have been more effective. Still, it's a good retrospective of the early work of a somewhat overlooked '60s guitar hero, who helped lay the groundwork for the better elements of fusion and Latin-rock cross-fertilization. —*Richie Unterberger*

Baby Batter/Snake / Dec. 12, 1995 / Western Front ◆◆◆◆
Mandel shares more similarities with Jeff Beck than he's probably willing to admit: both are stunning virtuoso guitarists who can't write consistently first-rate material or sing. Mandel's fifth album, *The Snake*, like Beck's best '70s efforts, adds bluesy, jazzy shadings to a rock base, but is more firmly entrenched in blues-rock than, say, *Blow by Blow*. Harvey's playing (occasionally augmented by violinist Don "Sugarcane" Harris) is always impressive, but the compositions (all but one instrumental) aren't gripping, and, like much of the genre, meander too much. It's not as good as Mandel's late-'60s recordings for Philips, but it's still one of the better early rock-based fusion recordings. This two-fer reissue adds his 1971 LP *Baby Batter*. —*Richie Unterberger*

Bob Margolin

b. May 9, 1949, Boston, MA
Guitar / Modern Electric Blues
With each new album, guitarist, singer and songwriter "Steady Rollin'" Bob Margolin continues to expand the boundaries of modern blues. Margolin, a sideman for Muddy Waters from 1973 to 1980 who was part of Waters' legendary performance in the movie *The Last Waltz*, was born and raised in Brookline, Massachusetts, became enamored with the recordings of Chuck Berry while still in high school and began playing out a few years later while attending Boston University in the early 1970s. Working with a variety of Boston area blues bands and one he called the Boston Blues Band, he elected to pursue music full-time. In 1973, he joined Waters on the road and in the studio for seven years, playing festivals and clubs around the US, Canada, and Europe with the legendary bluesman, who died in 1983. Highlights of his career with Waters' band included the taping for *The Last Waltz* on

Thanksgiving Day, 1976, and performing at the White House for Jimmy Carter in August, 1978.

In 1980, two years after getting his nickname from a Boston DJ, Margolin began leading a band under his own name and did so for nine years before recording his first album for Tom Principato's Powerhouse label. He later recorded a second album for Powerhouse, but both are now out of print. He continued touring before getting his second big break in 1993, signing up with Bruce Iglauer's Alligator label, which by then had grown by leaps and bounds and had secured stable worldwide distribution.

Margolin's three albums for Alligator Records are superb recordings that advance the traditional boundaries of the music: *Down in the Alley* (1993), *My Blues and My Guitar* (1995), and *Up and In* (1997). Each one is a delightful mix of familiar blues covers and Margolin's idiosyncratic, insight-filled, and sometimes funny original songs. —*Richard J. Skelly*

The Old School / 1988 / Powerhouse ◆◆◆
The title says it all—*The Old School* adheres to postwar Chicago blues, with a couple of Delta or New Orleans tracks thrown in for good measure. To his credit, Bob Margolin does delve deep into the catalogs of Robert Johnson, Willie Dixon, Muddy Waters, and Percy Mayfield, among others, digging out songs that haven't been covered as frequently as others. His originals—which are in the style of his idols, naturally—can't help but pale next to the classics he's chosen, but they are competent genre exercises. Margolin, on the whole, isn't a particularly remarkable player—he doesn't have a gripping voice or a distinctive slide guitar technique—but he is passionate about this music, and it shows. And that means *The Old School* is entertaining while it's on, but it doesn't leave much of a lasting impression. —*Thom Owens*

● **Chicago Blues** / 1990 / Powerhouse ◆◆◆◆
Best known for his association with Muddy Waters in the 1970s, Steady Rollin' Bob Margolin is reunited with three other former Waters sidemen on this inspired solo effort: pianist Pinetop Perkins, bassist Calvin "Fuzzy" Jones, and drummer Willie "Big Eyes" Smith. The title sums it up—the album may have been recorded in various parts of the South, but the style is pure, unadulterated Chicago blues. A number of gutsy originals are included (most notably, "She and the Devil" and "Born in the Wrong Time") along with such time-honored Muddy Waters classics as "Mean Disposition," "She's So Pretty" and "Rollin' and Tumblin'." As enjoyable as the band recordings are, the most inspired offering is the unaccompanied solo number "Born in the Wrong Time." On this underproduced, demo-quality recording, Margolin rants and raves about life in the early 1990s and says some gut-level things that desperately needed to be said. —*Alex Henderson*

Down in the Alley / 1993 / Alligator ◆◆◆
On *Down in the Alley*, his first album for Alligator Records, Steady Rollin' Bob Margolin doesn't quite follow though on the success of its predecessor *Chicago Blues*, yet that's only a relative scale. Margolin is one of a handful of musicians to keep classic Chicago blues alive in the '90s, both through covers and original material. His association with Muddy Waters is, if anything, overhyped by journalists and Alligator alike, but it has to be said that he does Muddy proud with down-and-dirty recordings like this. Margolin's guitar has true muscle, and there's genuine grit to the recording, unlike many contemporary Chicago blues albums. For some tastes, the album may be a little predictable since he never breaks from the tradition, but anyone looking for a straight-ahead slice of electric blues like Chess used to make them should be pleased with *Down in the Alley*. —*Stephen Thomas Erlewine*

My Blues & My Guitar / Nov. 1995 / Alligator ◆◆◆◆
Steady Rollin' Bob Margolin really comes into his own with *My Blues and My Guitar*, his second album for Alligator Records. He still pays homage to his mentor, Muddy Waters, not only through covers but simply through his driving musical style. He blends the familiar ("Rip It Up," "Going Home," "The Same Thing") with unpredictable ("See Me in the Evening," "Drip Drop," "Peace of Mind") in his choice of covers, and he has written a set of originals that are sturdy and memorable. Furthermore, he has loosened up a little bit, bringing some jazzy flourishes to his solos and nuance to his vocals. The result is one of his strongest albums, one that is exciting upon the first listen and rewarding upon repeated plays. —*Thom Owens*

Up and In / Apr. 29, 1997 / Alligator ◆◆◆◆
Former Muddy Waters sideman and current *Blues Revue* magazine columnist Bob Margolin brings his encyclopedic knowledge of blues and chops

galore with him on this, his third album for Alligator. Ten of the 14 selections are penned by Margolin, with selected covers of material from Bobby Charles, Grady Jackson, Snooky Pryor, and Gladys Knight and the Pips rounding out the mix. This time around Margolin stretches his musical boundaries into new directions, adding to his already wide range of blues subgenres. The title track is a solid homage to Chuck Berry, while Grady Jackson's "Coffee Break" is the kind of atmospheric, sax-driven track that would have fit perfectly on any Aladdin blues-after-hours 10-inch album. "Imagination" gets a true soul workout, as does "The Window," with its funky lead fills. His guitar tone can sometimes get positively trashy and as distorted as any old blues 78 you've ever heard, as on "Alien's Blues" and "Blues for Bartenders" while the cleaner side of his playing comes up for air on "'Bout Out," "Not What You Said Last Night," and the jazzy "Long Ago and Far Away." Margolin turns in a dead-on Muddy Waters slide guitar impression in a duet turn with former Waters piano man Pinetop Perkins on "She and the Devil" while turning in fine slide work on "Goin' Back Out on the Road" and "Why Are People Like That?" As a vocalist, Margolin is still in the passable category; he sings in tune, but seldom displays the kind of passion that earmarks the best of his guitar work. Still, this is his best solo turn to date, with solid playing from guests Kaz Kazanoff, Dave Maxwell, and a host of others. — *Cub Koda*

Johnny Mars

b. Dec. 7, 1942, Laurens, SC

Harmonica, Vocals / Harmonica Blues, Modern Electric Blues

Songwriter, harmonica player, and singer Johnny Mars was raised in a share-cropping family. He was given his first harmonica at age nine. His family lived in various places around the South, including North Carolina, Georgia, and Florida.

When Mars' mother died in 1958, the older family members settled in Florida, while Johnny and his younger brother went to live in New Paltz, N.Y. After he graduated from high school, he played club shows around New York and recorded with his band Burning Bush for Mercury Records.

In the mid-1960s, Mars moved to San Francisco, where he met Dan Kennedy and formed the Johnny Mars Band, playing clubs and festivals in northern California, as well as shows for rock promoter/impresario/producer Bill Graham.

However, Mars could not seem to expand his audience much in San Francisco. After hearing about the greener pastures across the pond from his friend Rick Estrin of Little Charlie and the Nightcats, he toured England in 1972. There he recorded a couple of albums, eventually moving to West London in 1978. Working with producer Ray Fenwick, who also worked with Spencer Davis and Ian Gillan, Mars met with success on the much praised album, *Life on Mars*.

In 1991, Mars became a featured soloist with the British New Wave pop group Bananarama. The group used him on their singles "Preacher Man," "Megalomaniac," and "Long Train Running," and he appeared in the group's video of "Preacher Man." Through the 1990s, Mars retained his strong European fan base, and he enjoys particularly strong followings in Ireland, Scotland, and Scandinavia. Critics there have called him "the Jimi Hendrix of the harmonica." Over the years, Mars has shared bills with Hendrix (before he was well-known) and Magic Sam.

In 1992, after a long absence from the Bay Area blues scene, owing to his new foothold in England and the rest of Europe, Mars was invited to play at the San Francisco Blues Festival. Mars' 1994 US release for MM&K Recordings, *Stateside with Johnny Mars*, features brilliant, original, topical compositions and superb, unique harmonica playing, unfettered by the standard Chicago blues conventions. — *Richard Skelly*

Blues from Mars / 1972 / Polydor ♦♦♦

● **Oakland Boogie** / 1976 / Big Bear ♦♦♦♦
Johnny Mars found his stride on his second album, *Oakland Boogie*. Recorded in London with producer Ray Fenwick, the album is a powerful collection of hard-edged blues-rockers, highlighted by Mars' searing vocals and impassioned, slurred harmonica. — *Thom Owens*

Mighty Mars / 1980 / JSP ♦♦

Life on Mars / 1984 / Lamborghini ♦♦♦

King of the Blues Harp / Oct. 31, 1994 / JSP ♦♦♦♦

Martin, Bogan & Armstrong

f. Virginia

Group / Acoustic Blues

Only violinist, storyteller, and philosopher Howard Armstrong remains to tell of the exploits of this remarkable African American string band. Virginia-born guitar and mandolin blues artist Carl Martin died in 1979, and guitarist Ted Bogan passed away a few years ago. But in their prime, Martin, Bogan, and Armstrong enjoyed multiple incarnations, first (in the '30s) as "The Four Keys," "The Tennessee Chocolate Drops," and the "Wandering Troubadours." They played individually and collectively throughout the mid-South on radio, with medicine shows, and at country jukes before eventually making it to Chicago in the late '30s and '40s, where they made records but mostly supported themselves by what Armstrong calls "pulling doors." This meant going into different cafes and taverns and playing for tips if they weren't thrown out. Playing various ethnic neighborhoods, the group took advantage of Armstrong's gift with languages and learned to sing in a variety of tongues. Best described as an acoustic string band (violin, guitar, mandolin, bass), the group played blues, jazz, pop, country, and various non-English favorites. As skilled musicians eager to earn tips by playing whatever their audiences wanted, they built a necessarily large repertoire.

After years of separation the group reunited as Martin, Bogan, & Armstrong in the early '70s and enjoyed substantial blues revival acclaim. After Carl Martin died, Bogan and Armstrong continued. When I worked with them in 1986, Bogan and Armstrong were still the greatest living exponents of the African American string-band style, equally at home playing blues, swing, jazz, ragtime, or older Black string-band material. Armstrong, who speaks seven languages and is a painter and a sculptor, was a National Heritage Award winner in 1990. What made their music so wonderful, besides its energy and flawless presentation and their personable good humor, was their ability to remind us that good music transcends classifications and a skilled artist can draw from many streams. — *Barry Lee Pearson*

That Old Gang of Mine / 1992 / Flying Fish ♦♦♦
A mixed repertoire for all ethnic audiences. — *Barry Lee Pearson*

Barnyard Dance / 199 / Rounder ♦♦♦

● **Martin Bogan & Armstrong** / Flying Fish ♦♦♦♦
Martin, Bogan & Armstrong is an excellent blues revival recording from Martin, Bogan & Armstrong, who play country-blues, ragtime, jazz and folk with flair on this album. — *Thom Owens*

Roberta Martin

b. Feb. 12, 1907, Helena, AR, **d.** Jan. 18, 1969, Chicago, IL

Piano, Vocals / Black Gospel, Traditional Gospel

This talented pianist started a quartet with Theodore Frye in the '30s. This aggregation gradually evolved into The Roberta Martin Singers by the '50s. It is now known that she copied the piano style of blind pianist Arizona Dranes, who also influenced The Ward Singers. Martin's singers sang loudly and dramatically. She also wasn't concerned about a harmonious sound; when one member of the group was leading a song, whether male or female, you could easily identify the backing voices. This lack of synchronicity made the group's urgent sound a unique and welcome change amid the repetitive quartets of the time. Robert Anderson was one of Martin's principal singers. She herself was referred to as "The Helen Hayes of the Gospel World." She died in 1969. — *Bil Carpenter*

Old Ship of Zion / 1973 / Kenwood ♦♦♦♦
Prime Apollo sides from the late '40s/early '50s with fine leads from Roberta, Bessie Folk, Eugene Smith and Norsalus McKissick. — *Opal Louis Nations*

● **The Best of the Roberta Martin Singers** / 1979 / Savoy ♦♦♦♦
Most of Martin's best early work from the late '40s through the '50s is out of print, but this is a nice introduction to this dynamic singer and group leader. — *Kip Lornell*

Sallie Martin

b. Nov. 20, 1895, Pittfield, GA, **d.** Jun. 18, 1988, Chicago, IL

Vocals / Black Gospel

Proclaimed "The Mother of Gospel" by the National Convention of Gospel Choirs and Choruses, Sallie Martin is widely credited with introducing spiritual music to the masses; while her rough, unmodulated voice lacked the

finesse of many of the singers in her wake, she was an artist who nevertheless commanded absolute respect from both her audiences and peers, and
her innovations forever altered not only the music but also the business
behind it. Martin was born November 20, 1895, in Pittfield, Georgia. After
quitting school during the eighth grade, she moved to Atlanta, where she
began a succession of jobs including babysitting, cleaning houses and washing clothes. In 1916 she joined the Fire Baptized Holiness Church, relishing
the spontaneity and spirit of the Sanctified singing she encountered there.
During the 1920s, Martin, her husband, and their son relocated to Chicago;
following the couple's 1929 divorce, she began working at a nearby hospital,
in her off hours continuing to pursue her interest in gospel.

Through the grapevine, Martin had heard about Thomas A. Dorsey, a one-
time blues pianist whose original gospel songs were electrifying the Chicago
church circuit. Through a mutual friend, she arranged to audition for Dorsey;
despite serious misgivings—her style was thoroughly unrefined, complete
with whooping, groaning and a great deal of physical movement (the latter
a hallmark of the Pentecostal church), and to top it off, she couldn't even read
music—he eventually agreed to let her come aboard, and in early 1932 Martin made her debut with his group at the Ebenezer Baptist Church. A year
passed before she was awarded her first solo, and for all of her lack of polish,
Martin nevertheless instantly connected with audiences; over time Dorsey
became increasingly aware of her value not only as a performer but also as
an entrepreneur, as she took over his music store and within a few months
was turning a tidy profit. Their relationship was often adversarial, but
quickly it was apparent that neither could succeed without the other.

As gospel choruses instructed to sing Dorsey's songs began appearing
throughout the Chicago area, Martin traveled to Cleveland in 1933 to organize a chorus there as well; in the years to follow, she helped set up similar
groups throughout the South and Midwest, and also joined Dorsey in or-
ganzing the annual National Convention of Gospel Choirs and Choruses,
serving as its first vice president until the time of her death. In 1940, however,
relations between Martin and Dorsey reached their breaking point and she
went solo, teaming with a young pianist named Ruth Jones—later to rocket
to fame under the name Dinah Washington—and began touring the country,
traveling a gospel circuit which her earlier journeys had helped establish.
That same year, Martin and gospel composer Kenneth Morris joined forces
with finanical backer Rev. Clarence H. Cobb to found Martin and Morris, Inc.,
a publishing company which in a few years was the biggest of its kind in the
United States.

Martin's touring collaboration with the volatile Jones was short-lived, and
she next began performing with the gifted pianist and arranger Roberta Martin (no relation). Again the partnership did not last, and she next formed her
own ensemble, the Sallie Martin Singers; believed to be the first female
group in gospel history, they existed until the mid-1950s. Despite her national renown, Martin never enjoyed the same kind of success on record
earned by many of her contemporaries; she did score a few hits, however,
among them "Just a Closer Walk with Thee" and "He'll Wash You Whiter
Than Snow," performed with Professor Alex Bradford. An active supporter
of Dr. Martin Luther King, her involvement in the civil rights movement led
to an invitation to attend the 1960 celebration marking the independence of
Nigeria; Martin's visit inspired her to donate to the Nigerian Health Program,
resulting in a state office building named in her honor. An astute business-
woman and tireless supporter of charitable causes, she died in Chicago on
June 18, 1988. —*Jason Ankeny*

★ **Throw Out the Lifeline** / 1950-1952 / Specialty ◆◆◆◆◆
The most instrumentation these tracks ever had was an organ, a piano and
an occasional drum. Originally issued on Specialty Records in the 1950-53
period, these 29 tracks are Black congregational styled numbers, 23 of them
previously unissued. These sides also include six selections where Brother
Joe May joined the singers. Most of the rest finds Sallie and Cora trading
leads. A fine example of Sallie's powers shows up on "Ain't That Good News."
—*Bil Carpenter*

Precious Lord / 1993 / Vee-Jay ◆◆◆◆
Sallie Martin disbanded her famous singing group in the '50s when her
daughter told her she didn't want to do any more tours. She briefly resurrected two new editions in the early '60s and cut two albums for Vee-Jay
before disbanding them again. Although the 23 songs on this single disc
reissue aren't as glorious or memorable as the group's Specialty recordings,

they are still valuable, both to hear Martin's rough but effective leads and
harmonizing with new vocalists, and also because the resignation and
mournful quality in Martin's singing during the 1963 sessions were an indication that she'd had enough of the performance/recording/touring grind.
—*Ron Wynn*

Sara Martin

b. May 18, 1884, Louisville, KY, **d.** May 24, 1955, Louisville, KY
*Vocals, Choir, Chorus / Classic Female Blues, Piedmont Blues, Prewar Coun-
try Blues*
Known in her heyday as "the blues sensation of the West," the big-voiced
Sara Martin was one of the best of the classic female blues singers of the '20s.

Martin began her career as a vaudeville performer, switching to blues
singing in the early '20s. In 1922, she began recording for OKeh Records,
cutting a number of bawdy blues like "Mean Tight Mama." She continued
recording until 1928. During this time, Martin became a popular performer
on the southern Theater Owners' Booking Association circuits, eventually
playing theaters and clubs on the east coast as well.

In the early '30s, Sara Martin retired from blues singing and settled in her
hometown of Louisville, Kentucky. While she was in Louisville, she ran a
nursing home and occasionally sang gospel in church. Sara Martin died after
suffering a stroke in 1955. — *Cub Koda & Stephen Thomas Erlewine*

● **1922-1928** / 1922-1928 / Best of Blues ◆◆◆◆
Best of Blues' *1922-1928* contains 20 tracks Sara Martin recorded during
that six-year span. Martin wasn't one of the greatest of the classic female
blues singers, but she had a strong voice that was enhanced by her supporting musicians. On the earliest cuts here, she's either accompanied by pianists
Fats Waller or Clarence Williams. The remaining tracks find her with small
jazz combos, featuring the likes of Barney Bigard, King Oliver, and Bubber
Miley. Both sections have their share of moments and, overall, the collection does an excellent job of compiling highlights from her peak years.
—*Leo Stanley*

Complete Recorded Works, Vol. 1 (1922-1923) / Feb. 15, 1996 / Document ◆◆◆◆
For completists, specialists and academics, Document's *Complete Recorded
Works, Vol. 1 (1922-1923)* is invaluable, offering an exhaustive overview of
Sara Martin's early recordings. There are some absolutely wonderful, classic
performances on the collection, but the long running time, exacting chronological sequencing, poor fidelity (all cuts are transferred from original acetates and 78s), and sheer number of performances will send casual listeners
in search of something more consistently listenable. — *Thom Owens*

Complete Recorded Works, Vol. 2 (1923-24) / Mar. 5, 1996 / Document
◆◆◆◆

Complete Recorded Works, Vol. 3 (1924-25) / Apr. 9, 1996 / Document
◆◆◆◆

Complete Recorded Works, Vol. 4 (1925-28) / Apr. 9, 1996 / Document
◆◆◆◆

David Maxwell

b. Mar. 10, 1950, Waltham, MA
Piano, Vocals / Modern Electric Blues
Pianist David Maxwell has been a part of the Boston blues scene as a sideman since the late 1960s, but has only in the '90s begun leading his own
band and recording under his own name.

Maxwell took some of his early stylistic cues from the likes of Spann,
Sunnyland Slim, and Pinetop Perkins, also listening to the recordings of Big
Maceo, Ray Charles and Memphis Slim; he became friendly with Muddy
Waters' longtime piano player, Otis Spann, in the late 1960s.

Maxwell went on to back many great players over the years, including
Freddie King, whom he worked with for two years in the early 1970s; Bonnie
Raitt, whom he worked with in 1974 and 1975, while she was still based in
Boston; and James Cotton from 1977 to 1979. He toured Europe and Japan
with Otis Rush in the 1990s, and has performed over the years with dozens
of others, including John Lee Hooker, Jimmy Rogers, Paul Oscher, Hubert
Sumlin, Bob Margolin, John Primer and Ronnie Earl. He has joined many of
these same people on their studio efforts, including Cotton for his 1997
Grammy-winning *Deep in the Blues*. Maxwell also can be heard on the soun-

dtrack to the movie *Fried Green Tomatoes* with longtime Boston musicians Ronnie Earl and Peter Wolf.

Maxwell's debut record for Tone-Cool, *Maximum Blues Piano*, is a collection of instrumental tunes that showcase many of the Boston scene's veteran players: Ronnie Earl and Duke Levine on guitars, Kaz Kazanoff and Gordon Beadle on saxophones, drummer Marty Richards and bassist Marty Ballou. Echoes of all of his influences can be heard throughout the tracks, including Pete Johnson on "Down at A.J.'s Place," and Otis Spann on "Deep into It." —*Richard J. Skelly*

Maximum Blues Piano / 1997 / Tone-Cool ✦✦✦✦
Maxwell's solo debut was a long time in coming, but it was worth the wait, as he neatly sidesteps the curse of the non-vocalist bandleader. Bringing in Darrell Nulisch for one vocal ("Heart Attack") only distracts from this fine instrumental showcase for David's prodigious abilities. Maxwell literally sparkles on the gospel-ish sanctified shout of "Sister Laura Lee," the New Orleans strut of "Breakdown on the Bayou," the boogie woogie classic "Honky Tonk Train," and "Manhattan Max," trading licks throughout with guest stars Ronnie Earl, Duke Levine, and saxman supreme Mark "Kaz" Kazanoff, basically the cream of the New England blues mafia. The fact that Maxwell has learned his slow blues lessons well is exhibited on the Pete Johnson tribute, "Down at P.J.'s Place," "Deep into It" and a seven-minute-plus rendition of Avery Parrish's "After Hours." This is more than just an impressive debut; this is a record of great playing and uncommon musical depth. —*Cub Koda*

Brother Joe May

b. Nov. 9, 1912, Macon, MS, **d.** Jul. 14, 1972
Vocals / Black Gospel
Dubbed "The Thunderbolt of the Middle West" by his mentor, the legendary Willie Mae Ford Smith, Brother Joe May was arguably the greatest male soloist in the history of gospel music; a tenor whose dramatic sense of showmanship was surpassed only by his unparalleled command of vocal dynamics and projection, he possessed a voice of unimaginable range and power, moving from a whisper to a scream without the slightest suggestion of effort. May was born in Macon, Mississippi on November 9, 1912; raised in the Church of God denomination—where all men are called "Brother," hence his stage name—he began singing at the age of nine, later joining the Little Church Out on the Hills' senior choir. His subsequent tenure as a soloist with the Church of God Quartet solidified his strong reputation throughout the Southern gospel circuit.

After graduating high school, May worked as a day laborer in Macon before he and his family relocated to East St. Louis, Illinois in 1941, at which time he hired on at a chemical plant. In the St. Louis area he became a protege of the pioneering Smith, and with her aid honed his sense of phrasing, modeling his own vocal acrobatics on hers; their connection was so strong that May even copied her theatrical performing style. Smith was also the director of the Soloists' Bureau of songwriter Thomas A. Dorsey's National Convention of Gospel Choirs and Choruses, at whose conventions May began to build a name for himself throughout the country; during one such convention in Los Angeles in 1949, he came to the attention of Specialty Records talent scout J.W. Alexander, and upon signing to the label cut his first session later that same year, scoring a major hit with his debut release "Search Me Lord."

May's initial success allowed him to quit his day job by 1950, and he began touring the nation, often performing alongside the likes of the Soul Stirrers and the Pilgrim Travelers. With his titanic voice and commanding stage presence, he was often called "the male Mahalia Jackson," a comparison suggested even by Jackson herself. However, despite his popularity—both "Search Me Lord" and 1950's "Do You Know Him?" were estimated to have sold over one million copies each, making him Specialty's best-selling artist of the period—May never crossed over to white audiences, the ultimate measure of commerical success at that time. Despite acknowledging Bessie Smith as a major early influence, May also refused to pursue a career as a secular blues singer, and his adamant rejection of all musical traditions but gospel likely played a role in his exit from Specialty in 1958.

Now a free agent, May quickly signed with the Nashboro label, where he also began recording many of his own original compositions. As a result of the Nashville-based company's regional focus, the majority of his subsequent

live appearances were scheduled across the Deep South, where his fame continued to grow enormously in the years to follow. An extended stretch of the early 1960s also found May starring in the musical *Black Nativity* in the company of Marion Williams, and after playing Broadway the production toured the US and Europe. After its run was completed, May returned to the South, where his health began to slowly fail; regardless, he maintained his strenuous touring pace, keeping his declining condition a secret even from family members. Finally, while en route to a performance in Thomasville, Georgia, May suffered a massive stroke and died on July 14, 1972 at the age of 60. —*Jason Ankeny*

☆ **Thank You Lord for One More Day** / 1967 / Specialty ✦✦✦✦✦
Thank You Lord for One More Day is a wonderful collection of Brother Joe May's Specialty sides, highlighted by collaborations with Sister Wynona Carr and the Pilgrim Travelers. —*Leo Stanley*

Brother Joe May Story / 1972 / Nashboro ✦✦✦
Here's a 1972 two-record set of 24 gospel songs made popular by Brother Joe May between 1958, when he joined Nashboro after nine years on Specialty, and the time of his demise in 1974. Macon-born May, also known as "the Thunderbolt of the Middle West," was a Pentacostal practioner of the Willie Mae Ford Smithschool of gospel singing. May's powerful tenor impressed and inspired many. It includes some live church recordings and sides made with the Joe May Singers. Notable cuts include the rousing "I've Been Dipped in the Water." This is a fine collection. —*Opal Louis Nations, Roots & Rhythm Newsletter*

★ **In Loving Memory** / 1974 / Specialty ✦✦✦✦✦
In Loving Memory of Brother Joe May is a collection of May's finest shouts and duets on Specialty, supported on some cuts by the Pilgrim Travelers, the Sallie Martin Singers, or a live audience. —*Ron Wynn*

Search Me, Lord / 1974 / Specialty ✦✦✦✦
Authoritative gospel and energized vocals with support from the Pilgrim Travelers and the Sallie Martin Singers. —*Ron Wynn*

Thunderbolt of the Middle West / 1974 / Specialty ✦✦✦
Brother Joe May, the baritone belter from Macon, MS, could, without much effort, move a church through the power of his voice. On these recordings culled from 1952-1955 sessions, May is ably supported by the vocalizing of the Sallie Martin Singers, Sister Wynona Carr, Annette May, and the Pilgrim Travelers. There are 17 lung-splitting solo outings, ten previously unissued. It includes such hits as "Search Me Lord" and "I'm Gonna Live the Life I Sing About in My Song." He was the Caruso of postwar gospel. —*Opal Louis Nations, Roots & Rhythm Newsletter*

Brother Joe May Live, 1952-1955 / 1994 / Specialty ✦✦✦✦
Brother Joe May earned his "Thunderbolt of the Midwest" nickname with incandescent, riveting vocals that could blow a roof off or reduce listeners to tears, often at the same time. The 16 tracks on this CD were done live, usually at services or during church performances, and they frequently paired him with the Sallie Martin Singers. While they and Prof. Earle Hines are fine, May is in another dimension. His flamboyant, dynamic voice shudders, roars, rises, moans and flails, and he fortifies the songs with commentary that's nearly as inspiring. Even devout atheists will be impressed by the power of Brother Joe May. —*Ron Wynn*

The Best of Brother Joe May / Jan. 31, 1995 / Nashboro ✦✦✦✦
The last great recordings by the legendary "Thunderbolt of the Mid-West." Nashboro material. —*Opal Louis Nations*

John Mayall

b. Nov. 29, 1933, Macclesfield, Cheshire, England
Guitar, Harmonica, Keyboards, Vocals, Harmonium, Harpsichord, Organ, Piano, Tambourine, Ukulele / Blues-Rock, British Blues, Electric British Blues, Blues Revival
The elder statesman of British blues, it is Mayall's lot to be more renowned as a bandleader and mentor than as a performer in his own right. Throughout the '60s, his band, the Bluesbreakers, acted as a finishing school for the leading British blues-rock musicians of the era. Guitarists Eric Clapton, Peter Green, and Mick Taylor joined his band in a remarkable succession in the mid-'60s, honing their chops with Mayall before going on to join Cream, Fleetwood Mac, and the Rolling Stones, respectively. John McVie and Mick Fleetwood, Jack Bruce, Aynsley Dunbar, Dick Heckstall-Smith, Andy Fraser

(of Free), John Almond, and Jon Mark also played and recorded with Mayall for varying lengths of times in the '60s.

Mayall's personnel has tended to overshadow his own considerable abilities. Only an adequate singer, the multi-instrumentalist was adept in bringing out the best in his younger charges (Mayall himself was in his thirties by the time the Bluesbreakers began to make a name for themselves). Doing his best to provide a context in which they could play Chicago-style electric blues, Mayall was never complacent, writing most of his own material (which ranged from good to humdrum), revamping his lineup with unnerving regularity, and constantly experimenting within his basic blues format. Some of these experiments (with jazz-rock and an album on which he played all the instruments except drums) were forgettable; others, like his foray into acoustic music in the late '60s, were quite successful. Mayall's output has caught some flak from critics for paling next to the real African-American deal, but much of his vintage work—if weeded out selectively—is quite strong, especially his legendary 1966 LP with Eric Clapton, which both launched Clapton into stardom and kick-started the blues boom into full gear in England.

When Clapton joined the Bluesbreakers in 1965, Mayall had already been recording for a year, and been performing professionally long before that. Originally based in Manchester, Mayall moved to London in 1963 on the advice of British blues godfather Alexis Korner, who thought a living could be made playing the blues in the bigger city. Tracing a path through his various lineups of the '60s is a daunting task. At least 15 different editions of the Bluesbreakers were in existence from January 1963 through mid-1970. Some notable musicians (like guitarist Davy Graham, Mick Fleetwood, and Jack Bruce) passed through for little more than a cup of coffee; Mayall's longest-running employee, bassist John McVie, lasted about four years. The Bluesbreakers, like Fairport Convention or the Fall, was more a concept than an ongoing core. Mayall, too, had the reputation of being a difficult and demanding employer, willing to give musicians their walking papers as his music evolved, although he also imparted invaluable schooling to them while the associations lasted.

Mayall recorded his debut single in early 1964; he made his first album, a live affair, near the end of the year. At this point the Bluesbreakers had a more pronounced R&B influence than would be exhibited on their most famous recordings, somewhat in the mold of younger combos like the Animals and Rolling Stones. Quite respectable it was too, but the Bluesbreakers would take a turn for the purer with the recruitment of Eric Clapton in the spring of 1965. Clapton had left the Yardbirds in order to play straight blues, and the Bluesbreakers allowed him that freedom (or stuck to well-defined restrictions, depending upon your viewpoint). Clapton began to inspire reverent acclaim as one of Britain's top virtuosos, as reflected in the famous "Clapton is God" graffiti that appeared in London in the mid-'60s.

In professional terms, though, 1965 wasn't the best of times for the group, which had been dropped by Decca. Clapton even left the group for a few months for an odd trip to Greece, leaving Mayall to straggle on with various fill-ins, including Peter Green. Clapton did return in late 1965, around the time an excellent blues-rock single, "I'm Your Witchdoctor" (with searing sustain-laden guitar riffs), was issued on Immediate. By early 1966, the band were back on Decca, and recorded their landmark *Bluesbreakers* LP. This was the album that, with its clean, loud, authoritative licks, firmly established Clapton as a guitar hero, on both reverent covers of tunes by the likes of Otis Rush and Freddie King, and decent originals by Mayall himself. The record was also an unexpected commercial success, making the Top Ten in Britain. From that point on, in fact, Mayall became one of the first rock musicians to depend primarily upon the LP market; he recorded plenty of singles throughout the '60s, but none of them came close to becoming a hit.

Clapton left the Bluesbreakers in mid-1966 to form Cream with Jack Bruce, who had played with Mayall briefly in late 1965. Mayall turned quickly to Peter Green, who managed the difficult feat of stepping into Clapton's shoes and gaining respect as a player of roughly equal imagination and virtuosity, although his style was quite distinctly his own. Green recorded one LP with Mayall, *A Hard Road*, and several singles, sometimes writing material and taking some respectable lead vocals. Green's talents, like those of Clapton, were too large to be confined by sideman status, and in mid-1967 he left to form a successful band of his own, Fleetwood Mac.

Mayall then enlisted 19-year-old Mick Taylor; remarkably, despite the consecutive departures of two star guitarists, Mayall maintained a high level of popularity. The late '60s were also a time of considerable experimentation for the Bluesbreakers, which moved into a form of blues-jazz-rock fusion with the addition of a horn section, and then a retreat into mellower, acoustic-oriented music. Mick Taylor, the last of the famous triumvirate of Mayall-bred guitar heroes, left in mid-1969 to join the Rolling Stones. Yet in a way Mayall was thriving more than ever, as the US market, which had been barely aware of him in the Clapton era, was beginning to open up for his music. In fact, at the end of the 1960s, Mayall moved to Los Angeles. 1969's *The Turning Point*, a live, all-acoustic affair, was a commercial and artistic high point.

In America at least, Mayall continued to be pretty popular in the early '70s. His band was no more stable than ever; at various points some American musicians flitted in and out of the Bluesbreakers, including Harvey Mandel, Canned Heat bassist Larry Taylor, and Don "Sugarcane" Harris. Although he's released numerous albums since and remained a prodigiously busy and reasonably popular live act, little of his post-1970 output is worthy of discussion. Following collaborations with an unholy number of guest celebrities, in the early 1980s he reteamed with a couple of his more renowned vets, John McVie and Mick Taylor, for a tour. It's the '60s albums that you want, though there's little doubt that Mayall has over the past decades done a great deal to popularize the blues all over the globe, whether or not the music has meant much on record. *—Richie Unterberger*

John Mayall Plays John Mayall / Mar. 26, 1965 / Decca ✦✦✦
Recorded live at the British club Klooks Kleek in late 1964 before Clapton joined (Roger Dean plays lead guitar), this is a fine set of early British R&B with a more pronounced rock feel (akin to the Rolling Stones) than Mayall's other '60s work. Mayall wrote all but one of the songs on this overlooked but driving, highly enjoyable LP that is recommended to connoisseurs of early British blues-rock. *—Richie Unterberger*

★ **Bluesbreakers with Eric Clapton** / Jul. 1966 / Deram ✦✦✦✦✦
One of the seminal blues albums of the '60s with the Bluesbreakers, capturing Clapton on a series of blues standards, after the pop leanings of the Yardbirds and before the heavy indulgence of Cream. *—William Ruhlmann*

A Hard Road / Feb. 17, 1967 / Deram ✦✦✦
Eric Clapton is usually thought of as Mayall's most important righthand man, but the case could also be made for his successor, Peter Green. The future Fleetwood Mac founder leaves a strong stamp on his only album with the Bluesbreakers, singing a few tracks and writing a couple, including the devastating instrumental "Supernatural." Green's use of thick sustain on this track clearly pointed the way to his use of this feature on Fleetwood Mac's hits "Albatross" and "Black Magic Woman," as well as providing a blueprint for Carlos Santana's style. Mayall acquits himself fairly well on this mostly original set (with occasional guest horns), though some of the material is fairly mundane. Highlights include the uncharacteristically rambunctious "Leaping Christine" and the cover of Freddie King's "Someday After a While (You'll Be Sorry)." *—Richie Unterberger*

John Mayall's Bluesbreakers with Paul Butterfield / Apr. 1967 / Decca ✦✦
A summit meeting of the leading US and UK blues-rock bandleaders of their time resulted in this four-song, seven-inch EP, which, like most such projects, didn't add up to the sum of its parts. By either man's standards, it's routine, if unobjectionable. Mayall takes a much stronger role than Butterfield; "Riding on the L&N" is about the best cut on a disc that also has a version of Junior Wells's "Little By Little" and one Mayall original, "Eagle Eye." Personnel is not listed on this rarity; one could reasonably assume from the date of release that it features the Peter Green version of the Bluesbreakers, but rock reference books are in conflict as to whether Mick Fleetwood and/or Peter Green appear on the disc or not. *—Richie Unterberger*

Crusade / Sep. 1, 1967 / London ✦✦✦✦
The personnel changes in John Mayall's Bluesbreakers continued on his fourth album, and although Mayall had vowed not to, he had added two permanent horn players. Perhaps because he was putting out his second album within a year, Mayall wasn't able to fill up the record with his own compositions and turned to blues standards, which certainly didn't hurt the record overall. Mayall's heroes included Buddy Guy, Otis Rush, Freddie King, and Sonny Boy Williamson, and he did them proud. The album became his third straight UK Top Ten and, following the Bluesbreakers' first US tour in the summer of 1967, his first charting album in America. *—William Ruhlmann*

The Blues Alone / Nov. 1967 / Deram ✦✦✦

The Blues Alone was the first Mayall "solo" album (without the Bluesbreakers). Mayall played and overdubbed all instruments except drums, which were handled by Bluesbreaker Keef Hartley. The album also tried to serve notice that, despite his band being a spawning ground for several British stars by now, the real star of the group was its leader. But it didn't quite prove that since Mayall, while certainly competent on harmonica, keyboards, and guitars, doesn't display the flair of an Eric Clapton or Peter Green, and the overdubbing, as is so often the case, robs the recording of any real sense of interplay. — *William Ruhlmann*

Bare Wires / Jun. 21, 1968 / Deram ✦✦✦

Bare Wires was the first Bluesbreakers album of new studio material since *A Hard Road*, released 16 months before. In that time, the band had turned over entirely, expanding to become a septet. Mayall's musical conception had also expanded — the album began with a 23-minute "Bare Wires Suite," which included more jazz influences than usual and featured introspective lyrics. In retrospect, all of this is a bit indulgent, but at the time it helped Mayall out of what had come to seem a blues straitjacket (although he would eventually return to a strict blues approach). It isn't surprising that he dropped the "Bluesbreakers" name after this release. (The album was Mayall's most successful ever in the UK, hitting No. 3.) — *William Ruhlmann*

Blues from Laurel Canyon / 1968 / Deram ✦✦✦

Blues from Laurel Canyon has a couple of nice passages, but the album suffers from poor songwriting and indulgent solos, both from Mayall and his newly acquired L.A. sidemen. — *Thom Owens*

Looking Back / Aug. 1969 / Deram ✦✦✦

Reasonably interesting collection of non-LP singles from 1964 to 1968, featuring almost all of the notable musicians that passed through the Bluesbreakers throughout the decade. "Sitting in the Rain" (with Peter Green) showcases fine fingerpicking, the haunting "Jenny" is one of Mayall's best originals, and "Stormy Monday" is one of the few cuts from 1966 that briefly featured both Eric Clapton and Jack Bruce. The rest is largely passably pleasant and doesn't rank among Mayall's finest work. — *Richie Unterberger*

The Turning Point / 1969 / Deram ✦✦✦✦

Recorded just after Mick Taylor departed for the Stones, Mayall eliminated drums entirely on this live recording. With mostly acoustic guitars and John Almond on flutes and sax, Mayall and his band, as his typically overblown liner notes state, "explore seldom-used areas within the framework of low volume music." But it does work. The all-original material is flowing and melodic, with long jazzy grooves that don't lose sight of their bluesy underpinnings. Lyrically, Mayall stretches out a bit into social comment on "The Laws Must Change" on this fine, meditative mood album. — *Richie Unterberger*

Empty Rooms / 1969 / Polydor ✦✦✦

This was John Mayall's studio-recorded followup to the live *The Turning Point*, featuring the same drumless quartet of himself, guitarist Jon Mark, reed player Johnny Almond, and bassist Steve Thompson. Mayall was at a commercial and critical peak with this folk-jazz approach; the album's lead-off track, "Don't Waste My Time," had become his sole singles chart entry prior to the LP's release, and although his former label, London, confused matters by releasing the two-year-old *Diary of a Band* [Volume 1] in the US just before this new album appeared in early 1970, the new crop of fans he'd found with *The Turning Point* stuck with him on this gentle, reflective release. *Empty Rooms* hit No. 33 in the US; in the UK it got to No. 9. — *William Ruhlmann*

U.S.A. Union / 1970 / Polydor ✦✦

John Mayall's *Turning Point* band — Jon Mark, Johnny Almond, and Steve Thompson — broke up in June 1970 after a European tour. Mayall then assembled his first all-American band and recorded this album in July. It had more drive than the previous outfit, and Mayall turned to environmentalism on the leadoff track, "Nature's Disappearing." But much of his low-volume, reflective approach remained on an album that was still more of a jazz-pop outing than the blues sessions of his early career. *USA Union* had the highest US chart peak of his career, hitting No. 22. But in the UK, where its title confirmed Mayall's US leanings, the album showed a big dropoff from his usual sales. — *William Ruhlmann*

Back to the Roots / 1971 / Polydor ✦✦✦

For this double-LP, recorded in November 1970, John Mayall gathered together prominent musicians who had played in his bands during the past several years, including Sugarcane Harris, Eric Clapton, Johnny Almond, Harvey Mandel, Keef Hartley, and Mick Taylor. Mayall's compositions aren't all that impressive, but the sidemen frequently shine, especially Clapton. *Back to the Roots* hit No. 52 in the US and No. 31 in the UK, where it was Mayall's final album to reach the charts. It was reissued in altered form under the title *Archives to Eighties* in 1988. (See separate entry.) — *William Ruhlmann*

Thru the Years / 1971 / Deram ✦✦✦✦

A grab bag of rare tracks from the '60s, some of which stand among Mayall's finest. His debut 1964 single "Crawling up a Hill" is one of his best originals; this comp also includes a couple of 1964-65 flipsides that were never otherwise issued in the US. The eight songs featuring Peter Green include some top-notch material that outpaces much of the only album recorded by the Green lineup (*A Hard Road*), particularly the Green originals "Missing You" and "Out of Reach," a great B-side with devastating, icy guitar lines and downbeat lyrics that ranks as one of the great lost blues-rock cuts of the '60s. The set is filled out with a few songs from the Mick Taylor era, the highlight being the vicious instrumental "Knockers Step Forward." Look for the CD reissue and not the early-'70s double US album of the same name, which includes a lot of superfluous material and omits the three 1964-65 songs from British 45s. — *Richie Unterberger*

Memories / Dec. 1971 / Polydor ✦✦✦

Having gone *Back to the Roots*, John Mayall returned to his forward-looking musical explorations with 1971's *Memories*, the true followup to *USA Union*, on which he retained bassist Larry Taylor, replaced Harvey Mandel with guitarist Jerry McGee of the Ventures, and dropped Sugarcane Harris, for an unusually small trio session. Actually, he was still looking back on a set of autobiographical lyrics about growing up, starting with the title track, and including "Grandad" and "Back from Korea." (Forced to compete with the simultaneous release of the London Records compilation *Thru the Years*, *Memories* managed to reach only No. 179 in the US charts.) — *William Ruhlmann*

Ten Years Are Gone / 1973 / Polydor ✦✦✦

Mayall returned to the studio in 1973 for this double album. The ten years Mayall had in mind, of course, were the previous ten, which had seen him start as a local musician in Manchester, England, and emerge a decade, almost two dozen albums, and nearly as many lineups later with an evolved jazz-blues style and an international following. The album allows the ensemble considerable room to solo on Mayall's typically simple, blues-based song structures, and the approach is perhaps excessively casual. The second LP is a live date recorded at the Academy of Music in New York, and here things stretch out even more: "Harmonica Free Form" clocks in at 12 minutes and "Dark of the Night" runs 17:41. — *William Ruhlmann*

Latest Edition / 1974 / Polydor ✦✦✦

The title makes a virtue of necessity, as John Mayall introduces another all-new lineup (actually, bassist Larry Taylor is returning from an older edition). Two guitarists, Hightide Harris and Randy Resnick, lead the band in more of an uptempo R&B style than has been used in much of Mayall's music during the past several years, starting with the timely "Gasoline Blues" (1974 was the year of the gas lines, remember?) and going on to "Troubled Times" (which advises impeaching President Nixon). Still, this was a lackluster set, which is only appropriate since it was Mayall's swan song with Polydor, and the album became his first to miss the charts in the US since 1967. — *William Ruhlmann*

Primal Solos / 1977 / Deram ✦✦

Fuzzy live tapes from 1966 and 1968 of dubious quality, in both sonics and performance. Side One has Clapton on lead and Bruce on bass on familiar Chicago blues standards by the likes of John Lee Hooker, Willie Dixon, and Sonny Boy Williamson. Side Two is from a couple of 1968 gigs with Mick Taylor, with three lengthy tracks that have little to recommend them. For fanatics only. — *Richie Unterberger*

Last of the British Blues / 1978 / One Way ✦✦✦

This was the last of the six albums John Mayall originally made for Blue Thumb/ABC Records between 1975 and 1978, about which he has said, "ABC released six of my albums as a tax write-off. A week after they were released you couldn't find them in any store." It's a live album on which Mayall fronts a quartet consisting of guitarist James Quill Smith (who sings lead on several songs), bassist Steve Thompson, and drummer Soko Richardson. The approach is rock-oriented, and the set list includes such Bluesbreakers favorites as Mose Allison's "Parchman Farm" and Freddie King's "Hideaway" (taken at a frantic tempo), along with the usual complement of generic Mayall originals, among them, a remake of "The Bear" from *Blues From Laurel Canyon*. — *William Ruhlmann*

Behind the Iron Curtain / 1985 / GNP ✦✦
On his first new album in four years (and first new US release in seven years), John Mayall reclaims the "Bluesbreakers" name for the first time in 18 years to highlight a quintet featuring two lead guitarists, Coco Montoya and Walter Trout, along with a rhythm section of Bobby Haynes (bass) and Joe Yuele (drums). The album was recorded in concert in Hungary in June, 1985, and takes a fairly bluesy approach with lots of space for the guitarists to shine, a format similar to that of the Bluesbreakers lineups of 1965-1968. Sound quality is only fair, and this is not an inspired performance, but Mayall has latched onto a cohesive unit here, and the results are encouraging for the future. — *William Ruhlmann*

Chicago Line / Aug. 1988 / Island ✦✦
John Mayall's first new studio album to be released in the US in more than a decade shows that his current crop of Bluesbreakers—Coco Montoya, Walter Trout, Bobby Haynes, and Joe Yuele—who have been together longer than any previous outfit, play like a seasoned blues band, sparking each other (especially guitarists Montoya and Trout), and never falling into complacency. Mayall presides over the music without dominating it, which makes the Bluesbreakers more of a group than they've been since the '60s. — *William Ruhlmann*

Crocodile Walk / 1990 / [bootleg] ✦✦
Pretty fair, if hardly revelatory, compilation of 1965-67 BBC sessions with Mayall's best lineups, variously featuring Roger Dean, Eric Clapton, and Peter Green on guitar. A few of the songs ("Cheating Woman," "Nowhere to Run," "Bye Bye Bird") were never recorded officially by Mayall during this period. Clapton actually doesn't shine particularly brightly on the few tracks that feature his playing, but the fidelity is good and the material pretty strong. The three closing tracks, recorded live with Mick Taylor in 1968, are a waste: lousy sound, tedious jamming. — *Richie Unterberger*

A Sense of Place / Mar. 1990 / Island ✦✦✦
A Sense of Place represents Mayall's full-fledged return to major-label record-making, with all the good and bad things that implies, from a high-profile producer, R.S. Field, to the introduction of such cover material as Wilbert Harrison's "Let's Work Together" and J.J. Cale's "Sensitive Kind." Field uses a spare production style, light on atmosphere and heavy, as is the current fashion, on unusual percussion. This makes for an identifiable sound, to be sure, but you can't help thinking that it isn't what the Bluesbreakers sound like on a good night in a small club. The result, as intended, was Mayall's first chart appearance in 15 years, but as a commercial comeback, the record ultimately failed. — *William Ruhlmann*

● **London Blues (1964-1969)** / Oct. 20, 1992 / Polygram ✦✦✦✦
Featuring forty tracks over two discs, *London Blues* is an excellent collection of most of the best moments from Mayall and the Bluesbreakers' early recordings, a time when Eric Clapton, Peter Green, and Mick Taylor all passed through the band. — *Stephen Thomas Erlewine*

Room to Move (1969-1974) / Oct. 20, 1992 / Polydor ✦✦✦✦
The majority of Mayall and the Bluesbreakers' best material from the early '70s is collected on this 29-track, double-disc set. Although Clapton appears on a couple of songs, the playing on *Room to Move* isn't as universally breathtaking as it is on *London Blues*, but the collection is thoroughly listenable, and it does feature many fine musicians. — *Stephen Thomas Erlewine*

Wake Up Call / Apr. 6, 1993 / Jive/Novus ✦✦✦
Fuelled by Coco Montoya's searing but economical string-slashing, drummer Joe Yuele, and bassist Rick Cortes, John Mayall has managed to keep a stable core of Bluesbreakers together in recent years. Mayall rarely does the same album twice, and *Wake Up Call* finds him returning to a basic, physical sound after 1990's more progressive/highly produced *A Sense of Place*. The

harp whiz has rarely flirted with the pop charts over the decades, a track record that will likely handicap the title track—a potential hit featuring guest vocalist Mavis Staples and some take-charge riffing from former mate Mick Taylor. For pure guitar joy though, Montoya turns the trick all on his own with barnburners "Loaded Dice" and "Nature's Disappearing." — *Roch Parisien*

As it All Began: The Best of John Mayall & the Bluesbreakers 1964-1969 / Jan. 27, 1998 / Polygram ✦✦✦✦
As It All Began: The Best of John Mayall & the Bluesbreakers 1964-1968 is an excellent 20-track retrospective, capturing Mayall's band at their peak. The Bluesbreakers went through several different lineups during those four years, with musicians the caliber of Eric Clapton, Mick Taylor, Paul Butterfield, Mick Fleetwood, John McVie, and Peter Green floating through the group. Hardcore fans of any of those musicians, or of British blues, will naturally want to familiarize themselves with the original albums, but *As It All Began* is a fine sampler for the casual fan, featuring such staples as "Lonely Years," "Bernard Jenkins," "All Your Love," "Parchman Farm," "Double Trouble," "The Death of J.B. Lenoir," and "Miss James." Even at 20 tracks, there are a number of fine moments missing from this collection, but *As it All Began* remains the best available single-disc overview of the Bluesbreakers' prime period. — *Stephen Thomas Erlewine*

Percy Mayfield
....
b. Aug. 12, 1920, Minden, LA, **d.** Aug. 11, 1984, Los Angeles, CA
Piano, Vocals / Soul, R&B, West Coast Blues, Urban Blues, Piano Blues
A masterful songwriter whose touching blues ballad "Please Send Me Someone to Love," a multi-layered universal lament, was a number one R&B hit in 1950, Percy Mayfield had the world by the tail until a horrific 1952 auto wreck left him facially disfigured. That didn't stop the poet laureate of the blues from writing in prolific fashion, though. As Ray Charles' favorite scribe during the '60s, he handed the Genius such gems as "Hit the Road Jack" and "At the Club."

Like so many of his postwar L.A. contemporaries, Mayfield got his musical start in Texas but moved to the coast during the war. Surmising that Jimmy Witherspoon might like to perform a tune he'd penned called "Two Years of Torture," Mayfield targeted Supreme Records as a possible buyer for his song. But the bosses at Supreme liked his own gentle reading so much that they insisted he wax it himself in 1947 with an all-star band that included saxist Maxwell Davis, guitarist Chuck Norris, and pianist Willard McDaniel.

Art Rupe's Specialty logo signed Mayfield in 1950 and scored a solid string of R&B smashes over the next couple of years. "Please Send Me Someone to Love" and its equally potent flip "Strange Things Happening" were followed in the charts by "Lost Love," "What a Fool I Was," "Prayin' for Your Return," "Cry Baby," and "Big Question," cementing Mayfield's reputation as a blues balladeer of the highest caliber. Davis handled sax duties on most of Mayfield's Specialty sides as well. Mayfield's lyrics were usually as insightfully downbeat as his tempos; he was a true master at expressing his innermost feelings, laced with vulnerability and pathos (his "Life Is Suicide" and "The River's Invitation" are two prime examples).

Even though his touring was drastically curtailed after the accident, Mayfield hung in there as a Specialty artist through 1954, switching to Chess in 1955-56 and Imperial in 1959. Charles proved thankful enough for Mayfield's songwriting genius to sign him to his Tangerine logo in 1962; over the next five years, the singer waxed a series of inexorably classy outings, many with Brother Ray's band (notably "My Jug and I" in 1964 and "Give Me Time to Explain" the next year).

It's a rare veteran blues artist indeed who hasn't taken a whack at one or more Mayfield copyrights. Mayfield himself persisted into the '70s, scoring minor chart items for RCA and Atlantic while performing on a limited basis until his 1984 death. — *Bill Dahl*

My Jug and I / 1962 / Tangerine ✦✦✦✦
Mayfield's gentle vocal delivery and the big, brassy sound of Ray Charles' orchestra were a match made in heaven. Mayfield brought some first-class material to this party (which begs for CD reissue): "My Jug and I," "Stranger in My Own Home Town" (later covered by Elvis Presley), the untypically jumping "Give Me Time to Explain," and a handful of Specialty remakes. — *Bill Dahl*

Bought Blues / 1969 / Tangerine ++++
Another elegant, beautifully arranged collection fraught with brilliant, sometimes heartbreaking material: "Ha Ha in the Daytime," "We Both Must Cry," "My Bottle Is My Companion." —*Bill Dahl*

★ **Poet of the Blues** / 1990 / Specialty +++++
The insightful songwriting skills of this West Coaster were matched by his wry, plaintive vocal delivery (Mayfield was usually his own best interpreter). The 25 sides here date from his hit-laden 1950-1954 stay at Art Rupe's Specialty logo and include his univesal lament "Please Send Me Someone to Love," the resolutely downbeat "Strange Things Happening," and "Lost Love," and an ironic "The River's Invitation." Saxman Maxwell Davis led the horn-powered combos providing sympathetic support behind Mayfield. —*Bill Dahl*

Percy Mayfield Live / 1992 / Winner +++
Although the first-ever release of live Mayfield material is culled from performances between 1981 and 1983, the twilight of the singer's blues career, he remains in fine, laidback voice throughout. The selections draw on all periods of his three decades as a songwriter and include "Please Send Me Someone to Love," "The River's Invitation," and "Don't Start Lying to Me." Founding Paul Butterfield Blues Band pianist Mark Naftalin backs Mayfield throughout the collection; he also served as the set's producer. —*Jason Ankeny*

For Collectors Only / Apr. 6, 1992 / Specialty +++
As the title suggests, this gives a deeper look at Mayfield's early career. Alternate takes and unissued material are included. —*Hank Davis*

Memory Pain / Sep. 17, 1992 / Specialty ++++
Ranging from major hits to alternate takes and rarities, this CD (released in 1992) illustrates the prolific nature of Percy Mayfield's Specialty Records output during the 1950s. Though not everything on *Memory Pain* is essential, the collection of early R&B and 12-bar blues is consistently satisfying. The best known song here is the number one hit of 1950, "Please Send Me Someone to Love," and many listeners will also be familiar with such gems as "Strange Things Happening" and the title song. A singer who was flexible as well as charismatic, Mayfield is as convincing on a rare version of the mournful, jazz-tinged "Nightless Lovers" as he is on 12-bar numbers like "My Blues" and "The Big Question." The CD ends on an interesting note with a demo of "Hit the Road Jack" (which became a major hit for Ray Charles). Highly recommended. —*Alex Henderson*

Jerry McCain

b. Jun. 18, 1930, Gadsden, AL
Guitar, Harmonica, Vocals, Drums, Trumpet / R&B, Modern Electric Blues, Harmonica Blues, Swamp Blues
Not only is Alabama-born Jerry McCain a terrific amplified harpist, he's also one of the funniest songwriters working the genre. Has been for more than four decades, as anyone who's dug his out-of-control 1950s Excello rockers "My Next Door Neighbor" and "Trying to Please" will gladly testify.

Little Walter was McCain's main man on harp, an instrument McCain began playing at age five. Walter passed through Gadsden one fateful night in 1953 with his Aces, offering encouragement and a chance to jam at a local nightspot. That same year, "Boogie" McCain made his vinyl debut for Lillian McMurry's Trumpet label in Jackson, MS, with "East of the Sun"/"Wine-O-Wine." His brother Walter played drums on the sides. McCain's 1954 Trumpet encore, "Stay Out of Automobiles"/"Love to Make Up," was solid Southern blues but barely hinted at the galvanic energy of his subsequent output.

Jerry McCain signed with Ernie Young's Nashville-based Excello logo in 1955, cutting "That's What They Want" with his usual sidekick, Christopher Collins, on guitar. "Run, Uncle John! Run," "Trying to Please," the torrid "My Next Door Neighbor" (a prior homemade demo version of the track that surfaced much later was even crazier!), and "The Jig's Up" ranked with McCain's best 1955-57 Excello efforts.

The harpist is probably best-known for his two-sided 1960 gem for Rex Records, "She's Tough"/"Steady." The Fabulous Thunderbirds later appropriated the insinuating mid-tempo A-side, while McCain's harp chops were strikingly showcased on the flip. McCain waxed three 45s for OKeh in Nashville in 1962, utilizing Music Row mainstays Floyd Cramer, Grady Martin, and Boots Randolph as his backup for "Red Top" and "Jet Stream." A series of 1965-68 sides for Stan Lewis' Shreveport-based Jewel Records included a

tailor-made tribute to the company, "728 Texas (Where the Action Is)" (Jewel's address).

After too many years spent in relative obscurity, McCain rejuvenated his fortunes in 1989 by signing with Ichiban Records and waxing a series of outings that displayed both his irreverent wit and a social conscience rare on the contemporary circuit. —*Bill Dahl*

Choo Choo Rock / 1981 / White Label ++++
These demo recordings for Excello (circa 1956) are wild and raucous, featuring overamplified guitars, crashing drums, and bizarre lyrics. What a rock 'n' roll album by Little Walter might have sounded like. —*Cub Koda*

Blues 'n' Stuff / 1989 / Ichiban +++
There's nothing aboard this okay outing that would suggest how amazing McCain's early work for Trumpet, Excello, and Rex was. —*Bill Dahl*

Strange Kind of Feelin' / 1990 / Acoustic Archives +++
These are McCain's earliest sides, cut in 1953 and 1954 for Lillian McMurray's Trumpet label in Jackson, Mississippi. Both sides of his two Trumpet 78s plus the addition of three previously unissued tracks make up his total output for the label, so the collection is filled out with five tracks by Tiny Kennedy plus two by pianist Clayton Love. Although longtime axeman Christopher Collins is well to the fore on these tracks, McCain's harp is somewhat underrecorded, giving a lopsided effect to the music. But minor gems like "Stay Out of Automobiles," "Fall Guy," "Middle of the Night" and "Crazy 'Bout That Mess" are all sign pointers to the Excello material and make this a collection well worth seeking out. —*Cub Koda*

Love Desperado / 1992 / Ichiban +++
The Alabama harpist's contemporary releases for Ichiban are certainly competent, but that insane energy level that marked his Excello output of the '50s is ancient history—and so too, for the most part, is the gleeful irreverence that made his early sides such a delight. —*Bill Dahl*

Struttin' My Stuff / Mar. 29, 1992-Apr. 5, 1992 / Ichiban +++
Alabaman Jerry McCain is a veteran of the blues and in fact recorded for the Trumpet label in Jackson, MS, at the same time as Elmore James and Sonny Boy Williamson. As one would expect, his harp work is both traditional and solid. Although original, his instrumental style bears resemblance to the work of past masters—the Sonny Boys and the Walters—while his original lyrics reflect modern life. This is a fine set of funky, urban blues—a standout from the Ichiban catalogue. —*Larry Hoffman*

I've Got the Blues All over Me / 1993 / Wild Dog +++

● **That's What They Want: The Best of Jerry McCain** / 1995 / AVI-Excello ++++
McCain has always marched to the beat of a different drummer and the proof of it is right here, 23 recordings that define the place where the blues and rock 'n' roll meet at the end of a dark alley. The first 12 tracks are McCain's complete singles output for Excello Records, the sides upon which most of his reputation rests. From the cold hearted bravado of the the title track to the rocking insanity of "Trying to Please," this music is as special as it comes. The following 11 tracks come from homemade demo tapes circa 1955 that were cut in Jerry's living room with a single mike, one track home tape recorder. Featuring grinding, massively distorted guitars, crashing drums, and lyrical texts concerning themselves with going crazy to rock 'n' roll, rock 'n' roll as salvation ("Rock & Roll Ball," "Geronimo's Rock"), or going crazy from outside worldly pressures ("Bell in My Heart," "My Next Door Neighbors"), these masterpieces answer the musical question: what would a rock 'n' roll album by Little Walter have sounded like? —*AMG*

Cash McCall

b. Jan. 28, 1941, New Madrid, MO
Guitar, Vocals / Modern Electric Blues
Guitarist Cash McCall has segued from gospel to soul to blues over a distinguished career spanning more than three decades. Born Morris Dollison, Jr., he found that the best way to exit his rural existence was to enlist in the Army. After completing his hitch, he relocated to Chicago (where his family lived for a time when he was a child). Gospel was Dollison's initial passion—he sang with the Gospel Songbirds (he also played guitar with the group, recording with them for Excello in 1964 with fellow future R&B hitmaker Otis Clay singing lead) and the Pilgrim Jubilee Singers.

He waxed his first secular single, the two-part workout "Earth Worm," for

One-derful Records' M-Pac! subsidiary in 1963 as Maurice Dollison. In 1966, he made a demo of a soul number called "When You Wake Up" that he had penned with producer Monk Higgins. He was doubtless shocked to learn of its subsequent release on the Thomas label, billed to one Cash McCall! The tune proved a national R&B hit, sending the newly christened McCall on the road with Dick Clark's Caravan of Stars (others on the bill: Lou Christie and Mitch Ryder).

Similarly tasty R&B follow-ups for Thomas and Checker failed to hit the same commercial heights. McCall was a valuable session guitarist and composer at Chess, learning the business end of his trade from Chess in-house legend Willie Dixon. McCall's blues leanings grew more prominent during the next decade. He cut an LP for Paula in 1973 called *Omega Man* before relocating to Los Angeles in 1976, his ties to Dixon growing ever stronger. McCall co-produced Dixon's Grammy-winning *Hidden Charms* in 1988 and worked as a sideman with Dixon's band, the All-Stars. McCall currently tours as a solo blues artist. — *Bill Dahl*

No More Doggin' / 1983 / Evidence ◆◆◆
While he rightfully earned his share of renown on the Chicago soul scene of the 1960s as a writer/producer/singer/sideman, guitarist McCall reinvented himself as a bluesman in recent years. This 1983 outing blends both genres on a predominantly original set (the lone cover is an update of Rosco Gordon's "No More Doggin'"). — *Bill Dahl*

● **Cash up Front** / 1987 / Stony Plain ◆◆◆◆
An excellent, varied blues and R&B album, it has ten original compositions. Top-notch session musicians give this the sheen of studio perfection rather than bar-band rawness. Yet McCall can still get down in the alley, as he does on the cheatin' story "Girlfriend, Women, and Wife." — *Niles J. Frantz*

Mighty Sam McClain

b. 1943, Monroe, LA
Vocals / Soul, Modern Electric Blues, Retro-Soul
Vocalist Mighty Sam McClain is a specialist in Southern soul-blues, one of the original masters from the 1960s, when the music enjoyed its peak popularity. He carries on the tradition of vocalists like Bobby Bland, Solomon Burke, Otis Clay, James Carr, and Otis Redding. His excellent 1990s recordings are now widely available, but that wasn't always the case.

Like so many other soul-blues vocalists, McClain began singing gospel in his mother's choir when he was five. At 13, owing to disagreements with his stepfather, he left home and lived with grandparents for a while before hooking up with Little Melvin Underwood. He worked with Underwood first as a valet and later as a featured vocalist in his road show.

His inspirations included Little Willie John, Clyde McPhatter of the Drifters, B.B. King, and Bobby "Blue" Bland. McClain recalled seeing Bland at the city auditorium in Monroe, LA, as a revelatory moment. Years later, McClain would open up for Bland at Tipitina's, a blues club in New Orleans. To this day, he considers Bland's nod of approval a high point of his career.

While working at the 506 Club in Pensacola, FL, in the mid-1960s, he was introduced to producer and DJ Don Schroeder. Working with Schroeder, he recorded Patsy Cline's hit "Sweet Dreams." After this, several other visits to Muscle Shoals Studios in Alabama yielded singles like "Fannie Mae" and "In the Same Old Way." McClain continued to create an ever-broadening audience for his singing via his engagements at the 506 Club and later at the Apollo Theatre in Harlem. He recorded a single for Malaco and two singles for Atlantic in 1971 before falling off the music scene for awhile.

For the next 15 years or so, McClain took menial day jobs, living in Nashville and New Orleans. The Neville Brothers and others from the Crescent City scene have been credited with helping him revive his career as a singer. McClain met Mason Ruffner's drummer Kerry Brown, and the two put a band together. Shortly after, they recorded a single for Carlo Ditta's Orleans label, and McClain's recording and performing career was rejuvenated. After recording with Hubert Sumlin on *Hubert Sumlin's Blues Party* for the Black-Top label in 1987, McClain began to re-establish his former reputation as a great soul-blues singer, touring with Sumlin and his entourage. By the late 1980s, McClain had moved from Houston to Boston. For most of the 1990s, he's lived in Boston and southern New Hampshire.

McClain didn't record his first studio album under his own name until he was 50, through his Boston drummer Lorne Entress, who made a connection with the California-based Audioquest label.

McClain's three Audioquest albums include *Give It up to Love* (1992), *Keep on Moving* (1995), and *Sledgehammer Soul and Down Home Blues* (1996), the last nominated for a W.C. Handy Award. All received rave reviews from the critics, and for the first time in his life, he's in control of his own song publishing rights. Most of the songs on all three albums utilize a full horn section, and on top of this ride McClain's deep, powerful vocals, oftentimes in self-penned songs. (*Give It up to Love* has since been re-released (1997) on the JVC label.)

Since the late 1980s, McClain's career has been on the upswing again, as he's put together some great backing bands and carved a niche for himself in Europe. McClain also continues to tour the US, Europe and Canada. — *Richard Skelly*

Live in Japan / 1988 / Orleans ◆◆◆
A sophisticated bluesman in the tradition of Bobby "Blue" Bland or Joe Williams, Mighty Sam McClain had not recorded in some 13 years when he cut a demo of song called "Pray" in 1984. The demo attracted the attention of a Japanese promoter, who subsequently coordinated the Japanese tour from which this live album, recorded in Tokyo, is culled. Despite the presence of ace session guitarist Wayne Bennett, McClain's backing band is sub-standard and lifeless; few moments generate any heat. — *Jason Ankeny*

● **Give It up to Love** / Nov. 1992 / AudioQuest ◆◆◆◆
McClain sings soul with incredible power—he knows when to pull the punches and when to cool it down. "Give It up to Love," the title track, acknowledges his gospel roots; he performs it as a vocal prayer to God asking for wisdom, love, and strength. Bruce Katz's contributions on B-3 Hammond organ expands McClain's sound, particularly on the "Green Onions"-influenced "What You Want Me to Do." The sparsely effective arrangement on "Here I Go Falling in Love Again" brings McClain up front as he cries of being a soul stripped to the bare bones. Kevin Barry's funky bass blows while McClain declares himself a child of God in "Child of the Mighty Mighty." — *Char Ham*

Keep on Movin' / 1995 / AudioQuest ◆◆◆
McClain pours out his soul, but this album lacks the power evidenced on *Give It up to Love*. The problem lies not with McClain, but with some of his supporting musicians. The closest cohesion exists between McClain and the musician on the title track, while "Who Made You Cry" has McClain sounding sympathetic and helpful to someone's plight, expertly complemented by Kevin Barry on guitar. However, the horn section extenuates the problems by cluttering up the arrangements and detracting from McClain's performance, while the Hammond B-3 lacks a nimble, crisp feel, and at times sounds buried in the mix. — *Char Ham*

Sledgehammer Soul and Down Home Blues / 1996 / AudioQuest ◆◆◆◆
The title of this CD couldn't be more descriptive of its contents, for it illustrates that Mighty Sam McClain is indeed a master of sledgehammer soul and down-home electric blues. Influenced by Bobby "Blue" Bland but nonetheless his own person, the Louisiana native is as charismatic singer who is as convincing on blues gems like "Where You Been So Long," "They Call Me Mighty," and the haunting "When the Hurt Is Over" (the perfect marriage of Bland and John Lee Hooker) as he is on such Southern soul treasures as "Trying to Find Myself" and "Things Ain't What They Used to Be." When it comes to R&B, McClain's approach is essentially Southern and very 1960s-influenced—the sleekness that characterized so much of the soul-pop of Detroit, Philadelphia, and Chicago isn't an influence on this fine album, and he shows no awareness whatsoever of mid-1990s trends in urban contemporary music. But McClain (who is joined by a solid band that includes horns, electric Hammond organ and a rhythm section) does surprise us by embracing reggae on the uplifting "Pray." This is definitely a CD to savor. — *Alex Henderson*

Journey / Mar. 24, 1998 / AudioQuest ◆◆◆
Singing praises to God and sharing his love for others despite having faced tragedy and setbacks in his past, McClain is rather reminiscent of the Biblical character, Job (who despite losing everything, still praised God, and then was blessed with twice as much wealth and a bigger family than before). McClain's life journey has often been rocky; he has faced rejection by his family, survived substance abuse, and been ignored by the music industry despite his hard-working attempts to gain attention. But turning to God, he remained faithful and is now blessed with a critically acclaimed career and

a loving family. This album shares all of this, and his honest, retrospective outlook wins hands down. Take a look at "No More Tears," where he takes the familiar line of "walking the backstreets," translating it to his life experiences—feeling frustrated, moving from place to place without seeing his situation improve. This honesty transcends to the supporting musicians, who give from-the-bottom-of-the-heart solos without sounding mushy, from bassist Tim Ingles' funky jazz feel on "I'm Yours," to Bruce Katz thumping the ivories or the B-3. —*Char Ham*

Tommy McClennan

b. Apr. 8, 1908, Yazoo City, MS, **d.** 1958, Chicago, IL
Guitar, Vocals / Soul Blues, Delta Blues, Prewar Country Blues
A gravel-throated back-country blues growler from the Mississippi Delta, McClennan was part of the last wave of down-home blues guitarists to record for the major labels in Chicago. His rawboned 1939-1942 Bluebird recordings were no-frills excursions into the blues bottoms. He left a powerful legacy that included "Bottle It up and Go," "Cross Cut Saw Blues," "Deep Blue Sea Blues" (aka "Catfish Blues"), and others whose lasting power has been evidenced through the repertoires and re-recordings of other artists. Admirers of McClennan's blues would do well to check out the 1941-1942 Bluebird sessions of Robert Petway, a McClennan associate who performed in a similar but somewhat more lyrical vein. McClennan never recorded again and reportedly died destitute in Chicago; blues researchers have yet to even trace the date or circumstances of his death. —*Jim O'Neal*

★ **Travelin' Highway Man** / 1939-1942 / Travelin' Man ✦✦✦✦✦
Travelin' Highway Man is an excellent, 20-track overview of recordings Tommy McClennan made between 1939 and 1942, offering many of his greatest recordings—"Bottle It Up and Go," "Whiskey Head Woman," "My Baby's Gone," "It's Hard to Be Lonesome," "New Shake 'em on Down"—as well as a thorough biography, making this a cornerstone of any comprehensive Delta blues collection. However, its usefulness has been diminished, since RCA's double-disc set *Bluebird Recordings 1939-1942* offers everything that *Travelin' Highway Man* has in better fidelity; it also has twice the music. —*Thom Owens*

★ **Bluebird Recordings 1939-1942** / 1939-1942 / RCA ✦✦✦✦✦
The *Bluebird Recordings 1939-1942* is a double-disc set that rounds up all of the recordings Tommy McClennan made for Bluebird during those three years. Although the disc may be a little too thorough and academic for some tastes, all of McClennan's seminal recordings are here, making it a key part of any serious blues listener's library. — *Thom Owens*

Guitar King 1939-1942 / 1939-1942 / Epm Musique ✦✦✦✦

Delbert McClinton

b. Nov. 4, 1940, Lubbock, TX
Harmonica, Vocals / Modern Electric Blues, Blues-Rock, Country-Rock
A Texas music institution, McClinton honed his musical chops to razor sharpness as a teenage harmonica man learning firsthand from blues legends traveling through the area. His harp work on Bruce Channel's hit, "Hey Baby," got him on the big time circuit, making it over to tour England and eventually giving harmonica lessons to a young John Lennon. Much behind the scenes work throughout the '60s ensued with McClinton fronting the Rondells, who hit the Hot 100 with "If You Really Want Me to, I'll Go." He hit the charts again in the '70s with Glen Clark as Delbert & Glen. Around this period, McClinton's songs started getting covered by country acts, Waylon Jennings and Emmylou Harris both having hits with his material. The Blues Brothers used his "B-Movie" on their first album and their hit movie. He has released idiosyncratic solo efforts up to the present time and guested on albums with everyone from Roy Buchanan to Bonnie Raitt. A Texas music treasure, we've not heard the last of Delbert McClinton. —*Cub Koda*

Delbert & Glen / 1972 / Clean ✦✦✦

Subject to Change / 1973 / Clean ✦✦✦

Victim of Life's Circumstances / 1975 / ABC ✦✦✦
This album contains a few strong originals and successfully captures McClinton's aggressive blend of country and R&B. — *Rick Clark*

Genuine Cowhide / 1976 / ABC ✦✦✦✦
Genuine Cowhide contains a few strong originals and successfully capture McClinton's aggressive blend of country and R&B. — *Rick Clark*

Love Rustler / 1977 / ABC ✦✦✦

Second Wind / 1978 / Mercury ✦✦✦✦
McClinton lays on the grease with two great originals, "B-Movie" and "Maybe Someday Baby" (featuring a wailing support vocal by Clydie King). Also included is a decent collection of covers ("Spoonful" and "Big River"). —*Rick Clark*

Keeper of the Flame / 1979 / Mercury ✦✦✦

The Jealous Kind / 1980 / Capitol ✦✦✦

Plain from the Heart / 1981 / Capitol ✦✦✦

The Best of Delbert McClinton / 1989 / Curb ✦✦✦✦
It's only 11 tracks, but *The Best of Delbert McClinton* contains nearly everything you need to know about how the eclectic blues/country/soul performer sounds, even if it doesn't have every good song he recorded. Nevertheless, it has the best moments from his early '70s records—including "Two More Bottles of Wine" and "Let Love Come Between Us"—and is a terrific introduction to his work. — *Thom Owens*

Honky Tonkin' [Alligator] / 1989 / Alligator ✦✦✦

Live from Austin / 1989 / Alligator ✦✦✦✦
This rock-solid, gritty roadhouse R&B is performed with a no-nonsense spirit. —*Rick Clark*

I'm with You / 1990 / Curb ✦✦✦

Never Been Rocked Enough / 1992 / Curb ✦✦✦
One of those influential "musician's musician" types, vocalist/harp-player Delbert McClinton was able to call on the likes of Bonnie Raitt, Tom Petty and Melissa Etheridge for support on *Never Been Rocked Enough*. The results cover the whole checkerboard while remaining vintage McClinton: his harp wails on "Everytime I Roll the Dice"; "Can I Change My Mind" flirts with Motown soul; "Blues as Blues Can Get" defines the confessional blues ballad; "I Used to Worry" and the title track chug into Band/Little Feat territory. The disc also includes the performer's Grammy winning duet with Bonnie Raitt, "Good Man, Good Woman." —*Roch Parisien*

Delbert McClinton / Jul. 13, 1993 / Curb ✦✦✦✦

Classics, Vol. 2: Plain from the Heart / Apr. 5, 1994 / Curb ✦✦✦✦
Classics, Vol. 2: Plain from the Heart is a ten-track budget-priced collection that features a good cross-section of highlights from McClinton's Curb and Capitol recordings, including "Be Good to Yourself," "A Fool in Love," "I've Got Dreams to Remember," "In the Midnight Hour," "Sandy Beaches," "Lipstick Traces (On a Cigarette)" and "I Feel So Bad." —*Stephen Thomas Erlewine*

● **Classics, Vol. 1: The Jealous Kind** / Apr. 5, 1994 / Curb ✦✦✦✦
Classics, Vol. 1: The Jealous Kind is a ten-track, budget-priced collection that features a good cross-section of highlights from McClinton's Curb and Capitol recordings, including "Shotgun Rider," "I Can't Quit You," "Going Back to Louisiana," "Take Me to the River" and "My Sweet Baby." — *Stephen Thomas Erlewine*

Great Songs: Come Together / 1995 / Curb ✦✦

One of the Fortunate Few / Oct. 7, 1997 / Rising Tide ✦✦✦
Like the first track says, Delbert McClinton is like an old weakness, comin' on strong. McClinton's music is a hybrid of rock, country and blues, though that's much too analytical for this roadhouse. Sung and played throughout with sass and a knowing grin, this is music that speaks to everyone. And for once the guest artists add just the right amount, neither dominating nor lessening the proceedings. —*Ross Boissoneau*

Charlie McCoy (Papa Charlie)

b. May 26, 1909, Jackson, MS, **d.** Jul. 26, 1950, Chicago, IL
Vocals, Guitar, Mandolin / Delta Blues, Prewar Country Blues
In the company of his older brother Joe, the versatile Charlie McCoy ranked among the great blues accompanists of his era, his nimble, sensitive guitar work enriching recordings from performers including Tommy Johnson and Ishmon Bracey. Born May 26, 1909 in Jackson, Mississippi, the self-taught McCoy was recording regularly by the late 1920s, often alongside Walter

Vincson; he also sat in with the Mississippi Sheiks, Rubin Lacy, Son Spand, and the many other Delta bluesmen who passed through the Jackson area in the years to follow, occasionally appearing on not only guitar but also mandolin (the latter most notably on his mid-1930s sessions backing sister-in-law Memphis Minnie. With his pleasantly high tenor voice, McCoy could well have become a star in his own right, but he seemed to prefer remaining in the background; among his scattered solo sessions is the first known recorded rendition of the song which eventually became "Sweet Home Chicago." Between 1936 and 1939, he also cut a number of sessions with his groups Papa Charlie's Boys and the Harlem Hamfats, the latter also featuring his brother. The war cut short McCoy's career, and he made no more recordings after 1942, dying in Chicago on July 26, 1950. —*Jason Ankeny*

- **Complete Recorded Works (1928-1932)** / 1992 / Document ✦✦✦✦
An excellent 24-track collection, including "Times Ain't What They Used to Be," "Your Valves Need Grinding," and "It's Hot like That." (Import) —*Cub Koda*

Joe McCoy

b. May 11, 1905, Jackson, MS, **d.** Jan. 28, 1950, Chicago, IL
Guitar / Acoustic Chicago Blues, Acoustic Memphis Blues, Prewar Country Blues
Alongside his younger brother Charlie, Joe McCoy is enshrined among the greatest sidemen in blues history, his spartan slide style most notably preserved on the landmark recordings of his wife Memphis Minnie. Born in May 11, 1905 in Jackson, MS, he was primarily known as Kansas Joe McCoy, but his laundry list of aliases includes appearances as the Hillbilly Plowboy, Mud Dauber Joe, Hamfoot Ham, the Georgia Pine Boy, and Hallelujah Joe. A self-taught player, he relocated to Memphis during the mid-1920s, joining Jed Davenport's Beale Street Jug Band and meeting Memphis Minnie. McCoy later became her second husband, and during their six-year marriage accompanied her on such country-blues classics as "Bumble Bee" and "When the Levee Breaks"; the couple migrated to Chicago in 1930, where—in the company of notables like Big Bill Broonzy and Tampa Red—they helped modernize the country-blues sound to fit more comfortably into their new urban surroundings. With his eloquent, inventive guitar work and deep vocals, McCoy could well have risen to stardom in his own right, but he appeared to prefer his sideman role, and after his divorce from Minnie he and sibling Charlie formed the Harlem Hamfats, recording regularly between 1936 and 1939. Upon the group's demise, he founded Big Joe and His Washboard Band, which evolved into Big Joe and His Rhythm during the mid-1940s. McCoy died on January 28, 1950. —*Jason Ankeny*

The Best of Kansas Joe, Vol. 1, 1929-1935 / 1929-1935 / Earl Archives Blues Documents ✦✦✦

Jimmy McCracklin

b. Aug. 13, 1921, St. Louis, MO
Piano, Vocals / R&B, Electric West Coast Blues, Acoustic West Coast Blues, West Coast Blues, Soul Blues, Piano Blues
A full half-century from when he started out in the blues business, Jimmy McCracklin is still touring, recording, and acting like a much younger man. In fact, he vehemently disputes his commonly accepted birthdate—but since he began recording back in 1945, it seems reasonable.
McCracklin grew up in Missouri, his main influence on piano being Walter Davis (little Jimmy's dad introduced him to the veteran pianist). McCracklin was also a promising pugilist, but the blues eventually emerged victorious. After a stint in the Navy during World War II, he bid St. Louis adieu and moved to the West Coast, making his recorded debut for the Globe logo with "Miss Mattie Left Me" in 1945. On that platter, J.D. Nicholson played piano; most of McCracklin's output found him handling his own 88s.
McCracklin recorded for a daunting array of tiny labels in Los Angeles and Oakland prior to touching down with Modern in 1949-50, Swing Time the next year, and Peacock in 1952-54. Early in his recording career, McCracklin had Robert Kelton on guitar, but by 1951, Lafayette "Thing" Thomas was installed as the searing guitarist with McCracklin's Blues Blasters and remained invaluable to the pianist into the early '60s.
By 1954, the pianist was back with the Bihari brothers' Modern logo and really coming into his own with a sax-driven sound. "Couldn't Be a Dream" was hilariously surreal, McCracklin detailing his night out with a woman

sent straight from hell, while a 1955 session found him doubling credibly on harp.
A series of sessions for Bay Area producer Bob Geddins' Irma label in 1956 (many of which later turned up on Imperial) preceded McCracklin's long-awaited first major hit. Seldom had he written a simpler song than "The Walk," a rudimentary dance number with a good groove that Checker Records put on the market in 1958. It went Top Ten on both the R&B and pop charts, and McCracklin was suddenly rubbing elbows with Dick Clark on network TV.
The nomadic pianist left Chess after a few more 45s, pausing at Mercury (where he cut a torrid "Georgia Slop" in 1959, later revived by Big Al Downing) before returning to the hit parade with the tough R&B workout "Just Got to Know" in 1961 for Art-Tone Records. A similar follow-up, "Shame, Shame, Shame," also did well for him the next year. Those sides eventually resurfaced on Imperial, where he hit twice in 1965 with "Every Night, Every Day" (later covered by Magic Sam) and the uncompromising "Think" and with "My Answer" in 1966.
McCracklin's songwriting skills shouldn't be overlooked as an integral factor in his enduring success. He penned the funky "Tramp" for guitarist Lowell Fulson and watched his old pal take it to the rarified end of the R&B lists in 1967, only to be eclipsed by a sassy duet cover by Stax stalwarts Otis Redding and Carla Thomas a scant few months later. Ever the survivor, McCracklin made a string of LPs for Imperial, even covering "These Boots Are Made for Walkin'" in 1966, and segued into the soul era totally painlessly.
Two recent discs for Bullseye Blues prove that McCracklin still packs a knockout punch from behind his piano—no matter what his birth certificate says. —*Bill Dahl*

Twist With / 1961 / Crown ✦✦✦✦
Undoubtedly it was a mite difficult to twist to jump blues records from the mid-'50s, but this budget LP at least gave McCracklin's Modern catalog renewed life in the Crown catalog. Some of his best 1950s rockers: the hilarious "Couldn't Be a Dream," "You Don't Seem to Understand," "Reelin' and Rockin'," "I'm Gonna Tell Your Mother." Overdue for CD reissue!! —*Bill Dahl*

I Just Gotta Know / 1961 / Imperial ✦✦✦✦
It's always a "Shame, Shame, Shame" (to quote one of this LP's best numbers) when a 35-year-old slab of vinyl must be cited as what may be an artist's finest collection—but since no one has yet touched McCracklin's massive '60s Imperial catalog for CD reissue, here you go! Contains his definitive soul-tinged ballad "Just Got to Know," the Amos Milburn-derived jump blues "Club Savoy," and several more late-'50s rockers that Imperial acquired from various small concerns after he began to hit with regularity. —*Bill Dahl*

Jimmy McCracklin Sings / 1961 / Chess ✦✦✦✦
Great late-'50s rocking R&B. —*Bill Dahl*

My Rockin Soul / 1963 / United ✦✦✦

Everynight Everyday / 1965 / Imperial ✦✦✦✦
Another vintage LP by the ex-boxer that's well worth the search. Along with the hit title track, there's a remake of "The Walk," his sturdy "Looking for a Woman," and an energetic "Let's Do It All." —*Bill Dahl*

Think / 1965 / Imperial ✦✦✦✦
There's a ton of great McCracklin material patiently awaiting reissue—this LP boasts the infectious title item, a sinuous "Steppin' Up in Class," and a driving "My Best Friend," for starters. —*Bill Dahl*

New Soul of Jimmy McCracklin / 1966 / Imperial ✦✦✦
On *New Soul of Jimmy McCracklin*, McCracklin has a more modern feel. —*Bill Dahl*

- **My Answer** / 1966 / Imperial ✦✦✦✦
Conveniently enough, Imperial slapped together what amounts to a greatest-hits set here, and it serves as the best available introduction to the pianist's '60s catalog. Contains "Just Got to Know," "Every Night, Every Day," "Think," "Steppin' Up in Class," and the title item—every one of them occupying an intriguing island midway between blues and soul. —*Bill Dahl*

Let's Get Together / 1968 / Minit ✦✦✦
Soul all the way. —*Bill Dahl*

Stinger Man / 1969 / Minit ✦✦✦
All-soul LP. —*Bill Dahl*

High on the Blues / 1971 / Stax ◆◆◆

Given that this was co-produced by Al Jackson (of Booker T. & the MG's) and Willie Mitchell (of Hi Records), and adds embellishment by the Memphis Horns, it's unsurprising that this is very much a soul-blues record. It's a work-manlike effort with an early-'70s Stax period feel, including remakes of two of his past R&B singles, "Think" and "Just Got to Know." The CD reissue adds a couple of previously unreleased bonus tracks. —*Richie Unterberger*

Yesterday Is Gone / 1972 / Stax ◆◆◆

Rockin' Man / 1978 / Route 66 ◆◆◆◆

Early R&B sides from the '50s. —*Bill Dahl*

And His Bluesblasters / 1981 / Ace ◆◆◆◆

My Story / 1991 / Bullseye Blues ◆◆◆◆

Pianist Jimmy McCracklin returned to form with 1991's *My Story,* his first effort for Bullseye Blues. Nine of the 12 songs on the album are brand new originals, all of which prove that McCracklin's talent for turning out well-crafted, memorable blues and R&B songs has not faded. Just as importantly, his chops are fluent, and he's arguably playing better than ever. Much of the album was recorded in New Orleans with a wonderful studio band, featuring drummer Herman Ernest and guitarists John Mooney and Wayne Bennett; among the highlights of these sessions are a pair of duets with Irma Thomas. A handful of cuts were made in Oakland, with Pee Wee Ellis leading a horn section. While the sessions don't quite have the same mood, both are stellar showcases for the revitalized McCracklin and, as *My Story* illustrates, it's just nice to have him back. —*Thom Owens*

Jimmy McCracklin: The Mercury Recordings / 1992 / Bear Family ◆◆◆◆

McCracklin's liaison with Mercury was relatively brief, from late 1958 to the fall of 1960, and Bear Family has only managed to locate 13 songs for this CD. But it's a rewarding chapter in the pianist's endlessly nomadic recording career, featuring his original dance tunes "Georgia Slop" and "Let's Do It (The Chicken Scratch)," a New Orleans-cut cover of Johnny Cash's "Folsom Prison Blues," and some smoothly arranged (by Clyde Otis, Brook Benton's collaborator) pop/R&B outings that suggest Mercury had big plans for McCracklin that never quite panned out. —*Bill Dahl*

Taste of the Blues / 1994 / Bullseye Blues ◆◆◆

Now these are the sort of cameos that make a contemporary blues disc work! Lowell Fulson, Larry Davis, Smokey Wilson, Barbara Lynn, and Johnny Otis all guested on McCracklin's most recent album for Bullseye Blues, making it clear that the pianist is no museum piece with their swinging grooves and sharp solos. —*Bill Dahl*

The Walk: Jimmy at His Best / 1997 / Razor & Tie ◆◆◆◆

McCracklin has always been one of those artists whose currency always ran higher in the black blues community than it has in the subsequent years of white historical revision. But decent career retrospectives of McCracklin—who had sides issued on almost a dozen labels in as many years—on compact disc are somewhere between few and far between and non-existent. But this 20-track single-disc compilation goes a long way toward rectifying that situation. Containing his biggest hits (the title track, the original versions of "The Georgia Slop" and "Get Back"—later hits for Big Al Downing and Roy Head, respectively) along with the best of his Art-Tone and Imperial sides ("Just Got to Know" and "Every Night, Every Day," now both staples of the Chicago blues repertoire after being covered in the early '60s by Magic Sam), this makes a perfect introduction to his style as well as a powerful testament to his superb songwriting skills. —*Cub Koda*

Roots of Rhythm & Blues / Roots ◆◆◆◆

The country of origin of this disc remains murky, but its 18 McCracklin tracks, from his 1957-58 layover at Chess (there was a belated 1962 date as well), are in dire need of domestic reissue—so until that happens, this one (shared with Paul Gayten) will just have to do. McCracklin's smash dance tune "The Walk" is here, along with the amusing playlet "He Knows the Rules" (immaculate axe by Lafayette Thomas), a jumping "Everybody Rock," and another workout that didn't fare as well, "The Wobble." —*Bill Dahl*

Blast 'em Dead! / Ace ◆◆◆◆

McCracklin's vast catalog is perhaps more fully appreciated overseas than in his home. British Ace assembled 18 of the piano-pounder's Duke waxings for this searing LP, which features frequent interjections from guitarist Lafayette Thomas. Jumping stuff! —*Bill Dahl*

Larry McCray

b. Apr. 5, 1960, Magnolia, AR

Guitar, Vocals / R&B, Modern Electric Blues

If contemporary blues has a longterm future as we boldly venture into the 21st century, it's very likely that guitarist Larry McCray will play a recurring role in its ongoing development. His first two albums, *Ambition* and *Delta Hurricane,* signal both a strong commitment to the tradition and the vision to usher the genre in exciting new directions.

McCray's first influence on guitar was none other than his sister, Clara, who toured regionally around Arkansas with her own combo, the Rockets. Clara never got to record her Freddie King-styled blues for posterity—but her little brother has at least partially made up for that omission. Larry followed Clara up to Saginaw, MI, in 1972. She turned him on to the joys of the three Kings (B.B., Freddie, and Albert), Albert Collins, and Magic Sam, and Larry added superheated rock licks (à la Jimi Hendrix and the Allman Brothers) to his arsenal as he began playing the local circuit with his brothers Carl on bass and Steve on drums.

Working on General Motors' assembly line occupied a great deal of Larry McCray's time after he finished high school. But he eventually found enough free hours to put together *Ambition,* his 1991 debut album for Pointblank, in a Detroit friend's basement studio. The stunning set was a convincing hybrid of blues, rock, and soul, McCray combining the interrelated idioms in sizzling fashion. Suddenly, the stocky young guitarist was touring with label-mate Albert Collins. His 1993 Pointblank encore, *Delta Hurricane,* was a slicker affair produced by veteran British blues maven Mike Vernon that McCray much prefers to his homemade debut. He followed *Delta Hurricane* with *Climbin' Up* in 1995 and *Meet Me at the Lake* in 1996. *Born to Play the Blues* appeared in 1998. —*Bill Dahl*

● **Ambition** / 1991 / Charisma ◆◆◆◆

Burly Larry McCray crashed the consciousness of the blues world with his stunning debut album, comprised of equal parts blues, soul, and rock. Guitar fanatics will no doubt wax rhapsodic about McCray's blazing pyrotechnics on "Nobody Never Hurt Nobody with the Blues," but it's the mellower R&B material buried toward the end of the CD—"Secret Lover," "Me and My Baby"—that best displays the warmth of the young bluesman's voice. Tab him for 21st-century blues stardom! —*Bill Dahl*

Delta Hurricane / 1993 / Pointblank ◆◆◆

Blues guitarist and vocalist Larry McCray's second Pointblank CD gets off to a dreary start with the title track, a tune with neither interesting lyrics nor a good arrangement. But after that flop fades, the remaining 10 cuts are almost as powerful as the material on his critically acclaimed debut. McCray has the kind of tough, down-in-the-dirt voice you can neither fake nor acquire. His guitar work is equally authentic; there aren't any flashy phrases or flamboyant riffs, just pile-driving lines, barreling statements, and energetic support for his vocals. There aren't many better contemporary blues albums being made by major labels; McCray is the real deal. —*Ron Wynn*

Meet Me at the Lake / 1996 / ATM ◆◆◆

A good-time workout with the Bluegills backing up McCray. The record grew out of a friendship between McCray and Bluegills leader Charlie Walmsley, and while the result isn't the most stunning blues disc on the market, it's quite enjoyable and good-natured. There's also some nice lead guitar work to recommend it. —*Steven McDonald*

Mississippi Fred McDowell

b. Jan. 12, 1904, Rossville, TN, **d.** Jul. 3, 1972, Memphis, TN

Guitar, Vocals / Delta Blues, Blues Revival

When Mississippi Fred McDowell proclaimed on one of his last albums, "I do not play no rock 'n' roll," it was less a boast by an aging musician swept aside by the big beat than a mere statement of fact. As a stylist and purveyor of the original Delta blues, he was superb; equal parts Charley Patton and Son House coming to the fore through his roughed-up vocals and slashing bottleneck style of guitar playing. McDowell *knew* he was the real deal and while others were diluting and updating their sound to keep pace with the changing times and audiences, Mississippi Fred stood out from the rest of the pack simply by not changing his style one iota. Though he scorned the amplified rock sound with a passion matched by few country bluesmen, he certainly had no qualms about passing any of his musical secrets along to his young, White acolytes, prompting several of them—including a young Bonnie Raitt—to develop slide guitar techniques of their own. Although generally lumped in with other blues "rediscoveries" from the '60s, the most amazing thing about him was that this rich repository of Delta blues had never recorded in the '20s or early '30s, didn't get "discovered" until 1959, and didn't become a full-time professional musician until the mid-'60s.

He was born in 1904 in Rossville, TN, and was playing the guitar by the age of 14 with a slide hollowed out of a steer bone. His parents died when Fred was a youngster and the wandering life of a traveling musician soon took hold. The 1920s saw him playing for tips on the street around Memphis, TN, the hoboing life eventually setting him down in Como, MS, where he lived the rest of his life. There McDowell split his time between farming and keeping up with his music by playing weekends for various fish fries, picnics, and house parties in the immediate area. This pattern stayed largely unchanged for the next 30 years until he was discovered in 1959 by folklorist Alan Lomax. Lomax was the first to record this semi-professional bluesman, the results of which were released as part of an American folk music series on the Atlantic label. McDowell, for his part, was happy to have some sounds on records, but continued on with his farming and playing for tips outside of Stuckey's candy store in Como for spare change. It wasn't until Chris Strachwitz—folk blues enthusiast and owner of the fledgling Arhoolie label—came searching for McDowell to record him that the bluesman's fortunes began to change dramatically.

Two albums, *Fred McDowell, Volume 1 and Volume 2*, were released on Arhoolie in the mid-'60s, and the shock waves were felt throughout the folk-blues community. Here was a bluesman with a repertoire of uncommon depth, putting it over with great emotional force and to top it all off, had seemingly slipped through the cracks of late-'20s/early-'30s field recordings. No scratchy, highly prized 78s on Paramount or Vocalion to use as a yardstick to measure his current worth, no romantic stories about him disappearing into the Delta for decades at a time to become a professional gambler or a preacher. No, Mississippi Fred McDowell had been in his adopted home state, farming and playing all along, and the world coming to his doorstep seemed to ruffle him no more than the little boy down the street delivering the local newspaper.

The success of the Arhoolie recordings suddenly found McDowell very much in demand on the folk and festival circuit, where his quiet good natured performances left many a fan utterly spellbound. Working everything from the Newport Folk Festival to coffeehouse dates to becoming a member of the American Folk Blues Festival in Europe, McDowell suddenly had more listings in his resume in a couple of years than he had in the previous three decades combined. He was also well documented on film, with appearances in *The Blues Maker* (1968), his own documentary *Fred McDowell* (1969) and *Roots of American Music: Country and Urban Music* (1970) being among them. By the end of the decade, he was signed to do a one-off album for Capitol Records (the aforementioned *I Do Not Play No Rock 'n' Roll*) and his tunes were being mainstreamed into the blues-rock firmament by artists like Bonnie Raitt (who recorded several of his tunes, including notable versions of "Write Me a Few Lines" and "Kokomo") and the Rolling Stones, who included a very authentic version of his classic "You Got to Move" on their *Sticky Fingers* album. Unfortunately, this career largess didn't last much longer, as McDowell was diagnosed with cancer while performing dates into 1971. His playing days suddenly behind him, he lingered for a few months into July of 1972, finally succumbing to the disease at age 68. And right to the end, the man remained true to his word; he *didn't* play any rock 'n' roll, just the straight, natural blues. — *Cub Koda*

★ **Mississippi Delta Blues** / Aug. 1964 / Arhoolie ♦♦♦♦♦
Arhoolie's *Mississippi Delta Blues* is one of the definitive Mississippi Fred McDowell albums. Culled from two sessions, recorded in 1964 and 1965 respectively, this blues revival-era recording finds McDowell at his very best, performing powerful versions of traditional Delta blues songs, as well as a handful of originals. McDowell recorded many fine albums, but this is arguably his best. — *Thom Owens*

My Home Is in the Delta / Sep. 1964 / Testament ♦♦♦♦
Mississippi Fred McDowell's home may have been in the Delta, but his music belonged to the world. This is heartfelt, raw, glorious country blues, delivered without an ounce of pretension or nostalgia. — *Ron Wynn*

Mississippi Blues / Dec. 1965 / Black Lion ♦♦♦
Mississippi Fred McDowell played simple, haunting blues with vivid, demonstrative passion and power. He wasn't a great guitarist, but his voicings and backings were always memorable, while his singing never lacked intensity or conviction or failed to hold interest. This 1965 set contains mostly McDowell compositions, with the exception of the set's final number, a nearly seven-minute exposition of Big Bill Broonzy's "Louise." Assisted only at times by his wife Annie, Fred McDowell makes every song entertaining, whether they're humorous, poignant, reflective, or bemused. — *Ron Wynn*

Mississippi Delta Blues 2 / 1966 / Arhoolie ♦♦♦♦

Long Way from Home / 1966 / Original Blues Classics ♦♦♦
Good no-frills set of acoustic solo blues on bottleneck guitar. The accent is on traditional material, including "Milk Cow Blues," "John Henry," "Big Fat Mama," and the title track. — *Richie Unterberger*

Amazing Grace / 1966 / Testament ♦♦♦♦
The connection between rural blues and spiritual music is sometimes overlooked. This 1966 recording, featuring McDowell, his guitar, and the Hunter's Chapel Singers of Como, Mississippi (including his wife Annie Mae), is one of the best illustrations of how closely the styles can be linked. McDowell and company perform what the record subtitle calls "Mississippi Delta spirituals" on this stark and moving set, which includes a version of one of his signature tunes, "You Got to Move." The CD reissue adds three previously unreleased tracks. — *Richie Unterberger*

Fred McDowell / 1966 / Flyright ♦♦♦
This is another well-rounded collection. — *Jas Obrecht*

Mississippi Fred McDowell & His Blues Boys / 1969 / Arhoolie ♦♦♦

I Don't Play No Rock 'n' Roll / 1969 / Capitol ♦♦♦♦
Blues purists were disappointed to hear McDowell pick up an electric guitar for the first time on this LP, as well as work with a young, White rhythm section. To the rest of us, this session sounds pretty good, Fred's vocals, guitar playing, and integrity coming through just as strongly as it had on his acoustic work. The title track, and the rap that opens it up, is a mini-classic in its own right—if McDowell does not play no rock 'n' roll, as he claims, he certainly keeps a beat pretty well. The album, as well as a second one cut at the same sessions (released on the Just Sunshine label) and some previously unreleased tracks, was released as an expanded double CD by Capitol in 1995. — *Richie Unterberger*

Going Down South / 1970 / Polydor ♦♦♦

Mississippi Fred McDowell & Furry Lewis / 1970 / Biograph ♦♦

Mississippi Fred McDowell in London / 1970 / Sire ♦♦♦

Live in New York / 1971 / Oblivion ♦♦♦

Mississippi Fred McDowell and Johnny Woods / 1977 / Rounder ♦♦♦
A nice, laidback set from guitar legend McDowell and his old harmonica sidekick, Johnny Woods. — *Barry Lee Pearson*

☆ **You Gotta Move** / Nov. 30, 1993 / Arhoolie ♦♦♦♦♦
You Gotta Move is an excellent 19-track compilation of McDowell's best-known work, spotlighting his Mississippi Delta slide guitar virtuosity, as well as his superior songwriting skills; perhaps most familiar to many listeners is the title track, which inspired a Rolling Stones cover version on the group's classic *Sticky Fingers* album. — *Jason Ankeny*

Mississippi Fred McDowell / 1995 / Rounder ♦♦♦♦
Tracks drawn from a 1962 recording of McDowell playing in his Como, MS, house. The recordings were initially made purely as a document of a performer and a style, but eventually found their way to record and, finally, to compact disc. Somewhat raw, though the sound is actually very good, the recordings caught McDowell at his best, playing just for his own satisfaction. — *Steven McDonald*

I Do Not Play No Rock 'n' Roll: Complete Sessions / Oct. 24, 1995 / Capitol ♦♦♦♦
A reissue of his popular 1969 electric album, expanded into a double CD with the addition of other material recorded at the same sessions (most of which was issued on an LP on the Just Sunshine label). It makes more sense to pick this up rather than the original vinyl album, as it rounds up all the

material recorded at the *I Do Not Play No Rock 'n' Roll* sessions in November 1969, and adds lengthy liner notes. — *Richie Unterberger*

Steakbone Slide Guitar / Apr. 1996 / Rykodisc ✦✦✦
Ten songs recorded by McDowell when he was appearing in England during the mid-1960s, and originally released on the Transatlantic album *In London, Vol. 2* and the Archive of Folk Music album *Mississippi Fred McDowell*. He performs these numbers, including "You Got to Move," "Levee Camp Blues," "I Heard Somebody Call," "Fred's Worried Life Blues," and "The Train I Ride," with a good deal of forcefulness and tension, although the repertory is hardly unique. The cleaning up of the sources has done a lot of good, although there is some evidence on certain tracks that vinyl sources were used for some of this. — *Bruce Eder*

First Recordings / Sep. 9, 1997 / Rounder ✦✦✦✦
In September, 1959, these 14 seminal tracks were recorded by Alan Lomax. Traversing the South with a bulky reel-to-reel tape recorder, this part of his field trip documents the very first recordings (and subsequent "discovery" in folk circles) of McDowell. The recordings were captured outdoors on a front porch, and even though Lomax was recording him at a semi-professional speed on his tape deck (7 1/2 inches per second as opposed to the then-standard 15 ips), seldom did McDowell's subsequent recordings capture this much ambience. Loose and informal, these sides showcase Fred solo and working in tandem with guitarist Miles Pratcher ("I'm Going down the River," "Shake 'em on Down," "You're Gonna Be Sorry"), the utterly surreal tissue-paper-and-comb work of Fanny Davis and—at various times—his wife Annie Mae ("Keep Your Lamps Trimmed and Burning"), James Shorty ("I Want Jesus to Walk with Me"), Sidney Carter and Rose Hemphill ("When the Train Come Along") on background vocals. As an added bonus for fans and historians alike, ten of the 14 tracks are previously unissued and include some of the best sides Fred ever recorded. — *Cub Koda*

Levee Camp Blues / Feb. 3, 1998 / Testament ✦✦✦
When Mississippi Fred McDowell recorded these sides in March of 1968, producer Pete Welding encouraged McDowell to recall the earliest material he had learned when he first started playing. The result is a selection of tunes that simply don't show up on his other recordings, both stylistically and because of their previously unreleased status. Highlights include "Let Me Lay Down in Your Cool Iron Bed," "My Baby Don't Treat Me like Humankind," "Jim Steam Killed Lula," "Will Me Your Gold Watch and Chain," "Dark Clouds A-Rising" and "Pea Vine Special." Also included are two previously unissued tracks recorded in 1966 before the bulk of this session. — *Cub Koda*

Rev. F.W. McGee

b. Oct. 5, 1890, Winchester, Tennessee, **d.** 1971
Drums / Acoustic Country Blues, Country Gospel
Expertly blending lively congregational singing with powerful preaching, the Reverend F.W. McGee was among the most popular country gospel performers of the pre-Depression era. Born Ford Washington McGee in Winchester, Tennessee on October 5, 1890, he was raised primarily in Hillsboro, Texas; married at the age of 20, within a year he began a career as a teacher, soon after relocating to Oklahoma. Previously a pastor in a Methodist church, McGee converted to Charles H. Mason's Memphis-based Church of God in Christ in 1918, in part attracted to their more energetic singing style. By 1920 he had largely abandoned teaching to pursue preaching full-time, and through his revival meetings became a crucial figure in the GOGIC's encroachment into Kansas and Iowa. He later built a congregation in Oklahoma City with the assistance of the noted sanctified singer/pianist Arizona Dranes; by 1925, McGee had also established the first of two tents in the Chicago area.

When Dranes made her first recordings for OKeh in 1926, she recruited McGee and his Jubilee Singers to back her up; in early 1927, he made his headlining debut—albeit mistakenly labeled "Rev. F.N. McGee"—with "Lion of the Tribe of Judah." He next appeared on Victor a few months later, recording four more titles; among them were "Jonah in the Belly of the Whale" and "With His Stripes We Are Healed," which coupled together on a 78 reportedly sold over 100,000 copies. Another Victor session followed before the end of the year, yielding the hit "Babylon Is Falling Down"; McGee's popularity as a recording artist also greatly increased the size of his congregation, and

by 1928 he had outgrown his tents and built his own Chicago church. His later recording sessions focused primarily on preaching, with musical backing almost incidental; a July 16, 1930, New York City studio date was McGee's last, although he remained active in the GOGIC throughout the decades to follow. He died in 1971. — *Jason Ankeny*

● **Complete Recorded Works, Vol. 1: 1927-1929** / 1992 / Document ✦✦✦✦
Highlighted by "Jonah in the Belly of the Whale" and "With His Stripes We Are Healed," which together combined for one of the biggest "race records" of its time, the first volume in this retrospective of the career of Rev. F.W. McGee assembles some of the finest gospel sides of the pre-war era. Opening with "Lion of the Tribe of Judah," McGee's lone recording for OKeh and a prime example of the sanctified tradition, the disc also includes "The Crooked Made Straight" and "Rock of Ages," both of which are fascinating attempts to combine congregational singing with impassioned preaching. — *Jason Ankeny*

Complete Recorded Works, Vol. 2: 1929-1930 / 1992 / Document ✦✦✦✦
With the second volume in the series, Rev. F.W. McGee's gospel style turns almost exclusively to straightahead preaching, with only minimal musical backing. It's not that much of a stretch to suggest that this kind of gospel is a kind of early precursor to rap—the rhythms and patterns of McGee's preaching are highly musical, and his wordplay on sides like "Women's Clothes (You Can't Hide)" and "Testifyin' Meeting" is lyrical and imaginative. While these sermonizing records are by no means the place for new listeners to begin, for historians they offer fascinating insight into another of the many facets of the pre-war gospel sound. — *Jason Ankeny*

Brownie McGhee (Walter McGhee)

b. Nov. 30, 1915, Knoxville, TN, **d.** Feb. 23, 1996, Oakland, CA
Guitar, Piano, Kazoo, Vocals / Country Blues, Piedmont Blues, Prewar Country Blues, East Coast Blues, Blues Revival
Brownie McGhee's death in 1996 represents an enormous and irreplaceable loss to the blues field. Although he had been semi-retired and suffering from stomach cancer, the guitarist was still the leading Piedmont-style bluesman on the planet, venerated worldwide for his prolific activities both on his own and with his longtime partner, the blind harpist Sonny Terry.

Together, McGhee and Terry worked for decades in an acoustic folk-blues bag, singing ancient ditties like "John Henry" and "Pick a Bale of Cotton" for appreciative audiences worldwide. But McGhee was capable of a great deal more. Throughout the immediate postwar era, he cut electric blues and R&B on the New York scene, even enjoying a huge R&B hit in 1948 with "My Fault" for Savoy (Hal "Cornbread" Singer handled tenor sax duties on the 78).

Walter Brown McGhee grew up in Kingsport, TN. He contracted polio at the age of four, which left him with a serious limp and plenty of time away from school to practice the guitar chords that he'd learned from his father, Duff McGhee. Brownie's younger brother, Granville McGhee, was also a talented guitarist who later hit big with the romping "Drinkin' Wine Spo-Dee-O-Dee"; he earned his nickname, "Stick," by pushing his crippled sibling around in a small cart propelled by a stick.

A 1937 operation sponsored by the March of Dimes restored most of McGhee's mobility. Off he went as soon as he recovered, traveling and playing throughout the Southeast. His jaunts brought him into contact with washboard player George "Oh Red" (or "Bull City Red") Washington in 1940, who in turn introduced McGhee to talent scout J.B. Long. Long got him a recording contract with OKeh/Columbia in 1940; his debut session in Chicago produced a dozen tracks over two days.

Long's principal blues artist, Blind Boy Fuller, died in 1941, precipitating OKeh to issue some of McGhee's early efforts under the sobriquet of Blind Boy Fuller No. 2. McGhee cut a moving tribute song, "Death of Blind Boy Fuller," shortly after the passing. McGhee's third marathon session for OKeh in 1941 paired him for the first time on shellac with whooping harpist Terry for "Workingman's Blues."

The pair resettled in New York in 1942. They quickly got connected with the city's burgeoning folk music circuit, working with Woody Guthrie, Pete Seeger, and Lead Belly. After the end of World War II, McGhee began to record most prolifically, both with and without Terry, for a myriad of R&B labels: Savoy (where he cut "Robbie Doby Boogie" in 1948 and "New Baseball Boogie" the next year), Alert, London, Derby, Sittin' in With and its Jax subsidiary in 1952, Jackson, Bobby Robinson's Red Robin logo (1953), Dot, and Harlem, before crossing over to the folk audience during the late '50s with Terry at his side. One of McGhee's last dates for Savoy in 1958 produced the remarkably contemporary "Living with the Blues," with Roy Gaines and Carl Lynch blasting away on lead guitars and a sound light years removed from the staid folk world.

McGhee and Terry were among the first blues artists to tour Europe during the 1950s, and they ventured overseas often after that. Their plethora of late-'50s/early-'60s albums for Folkways, Choice, World Pacific, Bluesville, and Fantasy presented the duo in acoustic folk trappings only, their Piedmont-style musical interplay a constant (if gradually more predictable) delight.

McGhee didn't limit his talents to concert settings. He appeared on Broadway for three years in a production of playwright Tennessee Williams' *Cat on a Hot Tin Roof* in 1955 and later put in a stint in the Langston Hughes play *Simply Heaven*. Films (*Angel Heart, Buck and the Preacher*) and an episode of the TV sitcom *Family Ties* also benefited from his dignified presence.

The wheels finally came off the partnership of McGhee and Terry during the mid-'70s. Toward the end, they preferred not to share a stage with one another (Terry would play with another guitarist, then McGhee would do a solo), let alone communicate. One of McGhee's final concert appearances came at the 1995 Chicago Blues Festival; his voice was a tad less robust than usual, but no less moving, and his rich, full-bodied acoustic guitar work cut through the cool evening air with alacrity. His like won't pass this way again. —*Bill Dahl*

Brownie McGhee & Sonny Terry Sing / 1958 / Smithsonian/Folkways ✦✦✦✦
One of the duo's best acoustic folk-blues collaborations, originally issued in 1958. They convincingly run through a very enjoyable series of collaborations marked by affectionate interplay, with drummer Gene Moore adding rhythmic power. —*Bill Dahl*

Back Country Blues / Nov. 1958 / Savoy ✦✦✦✦
Brownie McGhee's solo material had a certain charm and compelling quality missing from his collaborations with Terry. For whatever reason, he tended to try more things alone and vary his approach, sound and delivery. This is first-rate country and topical material, delivered without the forced humor that eventually made his dates with Terry more camp than substance. —*Ron Wynn*

The Bluesville Years, Vol. 5: Mr. Brownie & Mr. Sonny / Oct. 6, 1960-Apr. 1962 / Prestige ✦✦✦
The musical partnership of Brownie McGhee and Sonny Terry stood the test of time and quality wise hardly ever wavered below magnificent. This 17-track collection is culled from four excellent Bluesville vinyl albums from the early 1960s and features numerous fine moments. Starting with five selections from Brownie's first solo album for the label, we find the duo augmented with the presence of Bennie Foster on second guitar with Brownie handling all the vocals. Sonny's solo sides emanate from two separate sessions, the first of which features Brownie's famous brother Stick ("Drinkin' Wine Spo-Dee-O-Dee") contributing guitar on three tracks which also include J.C. Burris on second harmonica behind Terry. The second 1960 session features Lightnin' Hopkins as a somewhat chaotic backup guitarist behind Sonny on two cuts. The compilation closes with seven romping, loosely played tracks from a live performance at the Philadelphia folk club, the Second Fret in April of 1962. The oddball instrumentation on several tracks and the guest turns by Stick and Lightnin' makes this a Brownie and Sonny cut above the usual and worth seeking out. —*Cub Koda*

Traditional Blues, Vol. 2 / Feb. 1961 / Smithsonian/Folkways ✦✦✦

Brownie McGhee & Sonny Terry at the 2nd Fret / Mar. 1963 / Bluesville ✦✦✦✦
Brownie McGhee and Sonny Terry were the ultimate blues duo; McGhee's stylized singing and light, flickering guitar was wonderfully contrasted by Terry's sweeping, whirling harmonica solos and intense, country-tinged singing. They were in great form during the 10 tunes featured on this live date, recently reissued on CD. Sometimes, as on "Custard Pie" or "Barking Bull Dog," they're funny; at other times, they were prophetic, chilling or moving. —*Cub Koda*

This is Piedmont blues at its best, and this disc's tremendous remastering provides a strong sonic framework. —*Ron Wynn*

Brownie's Blues / 1971 / Bluesville ✦✦✦
Brownie's Blues was originally released by Bluesville Records in 1962. Supported by his longtime accompanist Sonny Terry, as well as second guitarist Benny Foster, Brownie turns in a nicely understated record that's distinguished by surprisingly harmonically complex and jazzy guitar work. Among the highlights are versions of "Killin' Floor," "Trouble in Mind," and "Every Day I Have the Blues," as well as the boogieing "Jump, Little Children" and "I Don't Know the Reason." —*Thom Owens*

Facts of Life / 1985 / Blue Rock'it ✦✦✦

Hometown Blues / 1990 / Mainstream ✦✦✦✦
Plenty of delightful interplay between McGhee and Terry recommends these 18 1948-1951 sides for producer Bobby Shad for his Sittin' in With label, but they predate the duo's later folk period by a longshot. Back then, they were sitll aiming their output solely at the R&B crowd—meaning "Man Ain't Nothin' but a Fool," "Bad Blood," "The Woman Is Killing Me," and "Dissatisfied Woman" are straightahead, uncompromising New York-style blues. —*Bill Dahl*

● **The Folkways Years (1945-1959)** / 1991 / Smithsonian/Folkways ✦✦✦✦
Folkways Years (1945-1959) is a wonderful 17-track compilation of Brownie McGhee's Folkways recordings. During this time, McGhee became a staple on the blues-folk revival circuit, and accordingly these recordings find the Piedmont bluesman playing in a folk style, which he excelled at. Many of the most powerful tracks are straight from the rural Piedmont tradition, but the folkier material shows what a rich musician he was. It's an excellent sampler, one that demonstrates the depth and breadth of his Folkways recordings. —*Thom Owens*

★ **The Complete Brownie McGhee** / 1994 / Columbia/Legacy ✦✦✦✦✦
Well, complete as far as his pre-war country blues waxings for OKeh sans Sonny Terry (except for one or two where the whooping harpist provided accompaniment). McGhee was working firmly in the Piedmont tradition by 1940, when he signed with OKeh and began cutting the 47 enlightening sides here, which represent some of the purest country blues he ever committed to posterity. —*Bill Dahl*

Climbin' Up / 1995 / Savoy ✦✦✦✦
Nice collection of 1952-1955 sides with an urban blues twist by McGhee, with Terry's contributions limited to harmonica only and guitarists Stick McGhee and Mickey Baker checking in over the course of the dozen entries. McGhee was a world-class electric bluesman, too—a fact that frequently gets lost in the folk-slanted duo material he cut with longtime partner Terry. —*Bill Dahl*

Blues Is Truth / May 21, 1996 / Blues Alliance ✦✦✦✦
Brownie McGhee was 60 when *Blues Is Truth* (reissued on CD by Concord's Blues Alliance label in 1996) was recorded in White Plains, N.Y. in 1976, and the veteran bluesman was still a powerful, authoritative singer. Although not quite in a class with McGhee's magnificent work with Sonny Terry in the 1950s and '60s, *Truth* is a consistently appealing date that unites him with such solid players as guitarist Louisana Red (who's also an excellent singer, though he doesn't sing here), harmonica player Sugar Blue and pianist Sammy Price. McGhee is in fine form on everything from the lonely desperation of "Rainy Day" to the upbeat, party-time atmosphere of "Walk On" and sibling Sticks McGhee's familiar "Wine Sporty Orty." The band is quite cohesive, and McGhee never sounds less than inspired. —*Alex Henderson*

A Long Way from Home / Mar. 24, 1998 / MCA ✦✦✦✦
Music from Brownie and Sonny's latter period, circa March and September of 1969. This combines two albums (*A Long Way from Home* and *I Couldn't Believe My Eyes*, both cut in two days) recorded for ABC-Bluesway, with the inclusion of a stray unreleased track, "Beggin' You," from the second session in September. The personnel stays basically the same for both sessions with excellent rhythm section support from drummer Panama Francis and bassist Jimmy Bond, while the September session also includes Earl Hooker on guitar. Solid, relaxed, rockin' grooves are the hallmarks here with both artists in fine form. —*Cub Koda*

Sticks McGhee

b. Mar. 23, 1917, Kingsport, TN, **d.** Aug. 15, 1961, New York, NY
Guitar, Vocals / Electric Blues, R&B
He may have not been as prolific or celebrated as his brother Brownie, but guitarist Stick McGhee cut some great boozy blues and R&B from 1947 to 1960—including the immortal "Drinkin' Wine Spo-Dee-O-Dee" (a tune that Jerry Lee Lewis, for one, picked up on early in life and has revived often since).

Young Granville McGhee earned his nickname by pushing his polio-stricken older brother Brownie through the streets of Kingsport, TN, on a cart that he propelled with a stick. McGhee was inspired to pen "Drinkin' Wine" while in Army bootcamp during World War II; it was apparently a ribald military chant that the McGhees cleaned up for public consumption later on. Stick McGhee's first recorded version of the tune for J. Mayo Williams' Harlem logo made little impression in 1947, but a rollicking 1949 remake for Atlantic (as Stick McGhee & his Buddies) proved a massive R&B hit (brother Brownie chiming in on guitar and harmony vocal). The tune has attracted countless covers over the years—everyone from Jerry Lee Lewis and Johnny Burnette to Wynonie Harris and Larry Dale has taken a sip from this particular wine flask.

After one more smash for Atlantic, 1951's "Tennessee Waltz Blues," McGhee moved along to Essex, King (where he waxed some more great booze numbers from 1953 to 1955—"Whiskey Women and Loaded Dice," "Head Happy with Wine," "Jungle Juice," "Six to Eight," "Double Crossin' Liquor"), Savoy, and Herald, where he made his last 45 in 1960 before lung cancer cut him down the following year. —*Bill Dahl*

● **Stick McGhee & His Spo-Dee-O-Dee Buddies** / 1953-1955 / Ace ◆◆◆◆
The British Ace label—long a prime source for quality compilations—has done Brownie's little brother proud, collecting his dozen 1953-1955 jump blues sides for the King logo, many of them detailing the effects of booze. Also aboard are four country blues-styled numbers by Ralph Willis, and four more by the pseudonymous Big Tom Collins (two of them feature Brownie McGhee's vocals, the other pair Champion Jack Dupree!). —*Bill Dahl*

Highway of Blues / 1959 / Deluxe ◆◆
Contains some of his fine '50s jump blues tracks for King. —*Bill Dahl*

New York Blues / Feb. 7, 1995 / Ace ◆◆◆◆

Big Jay McNeely

b. Apr. 29, 1927, Watts, CA
Saxophone, Sax (Tenor) / Blues Jazz, R&B, Soul Jazz, Groove, West Coast Blues, Jump Blues
His mighty tenor sax squawking and bleating with wild-eyed abandon, Big Jay McNeely blew up a torrid R&B tornado from every conceivable position—on his knees, on his back, being wheeled down the street on an auto mechanic's "creeper" like a modern-day pied piper. As one of the titans who made tenor sax the solo instrument of choice during rock's primordial era, Big Jay McNeely could peel the paper right off the walls with his sheets of squealing, honking horn riffs.

Cecil McNeely and his older brother Bob (who blew baritone sax lines with Jay in unison precision on some of Jay's hottest instrumentals) grew up in Los Angeles, where jazz reigned on Watts' bustling nightlife strip. Inspired by Illinois Jacquet and tutored by Jack McVea, McNeely struck up a friendship with Johnny Otis, co-owner of the popular Barrelhouse nitery. Ralph Bass, a friend of Otis, produced McNeely's debut date for Savoy Records in 1948 (Savoy boss Herman Lubinsky tagged the saxist Big Jay, in his eyes a more commercial name than Cecil). McNeely's raucous one-note honking on "The Deacon's Hop" gave him and Savoy an R&B chart-topper in 1949, and his follow-up, "Wild Wig," also hit big for the young saxist with the acrobatic stage presence.

From Savoy, McNeely moved to Exclusive in 1949, Imperial in 1950-51, King's Federal subsidiary in 1952-54 (where he cut some of his wildest waxings, including the mind-boggling "3-D"), and Vee-Jay in 1955. McNeely's live shows were the stuff that legends are made of—he electrified a sweaty throng of thousands packing L.A.'s Wrigley Field in 1949 by blowing his sax up through the stands and then from home plate to first base on his back! A fluorescently painted sax that glowed in the dark was another of his show-stopping gambits.

In 1958, McNeely cut his last hit in a considerably less frantic mode with singer Little Sonny Warner. The bluesy "There Is Something on Your Mind" was committed to tape in Seattle but came out on deejay Hunter Hancock's Swingin' imprint the next year. McNeely's original was a huge smash, but it was eclipsed the following year by New Orleans singer Bobby Marchan's dramatic R&B chart-topping version for Fire. Since then, it's been covered countless times, including a fine rendition by Conway Twitty!

Honking saxists had fallen from favor by the dawn of the '60s, so McNeely eventually became a mailman and joined Jehovah's Witnesses (no, that's not the name of a combo). Happily, his horn came back out of the closet during the early '80s. Today, McNeely records for his own little label and tours the country and overseas regularly. This deacon's still hopping! —*Bill Dahl*

Big Jay in 3-D / Aug. 26, 1952-Apr. 8, 1954 / Federal ◆◆◆◆
Honking R&B tenor-sax giant McNeely blows his brains out on these early-'50s stompers for King. Truly astonishing is the torrid "3-D," where Big Jay and his baritone sax-blowing brother Bob play some incredibly complex riffs over one of the fastest tempos imaginable. —*Bill Dahl*

The Deacon Rides Again / 1952-1957 / Marconi ◆◆◆
Hot tenor licks, sweltering vocals from Jesse Belvin, and bluesy inflections courtesy of Mercy Dee. —*Ron Wynn*

Live at Birdland: 1957 / 1957 / Collectables ◆◆◆◆
An amazing artifact from 1957, when live recordings like this one didn't happen very often. A Seattle engineer with a spanking-new stereo tape recorder captured the contents of this disc while McNeely and his swinging combo were working out at a Seattle nightspot called the Birdland. He gets plenty of room to peel the paper from the gin joint's walls as he wails on "Flying Home," "How High the Moon," and "Let It Roll." —*Bill Dahl*

Swingin' / 1958-1960 / Collectables ◆◆◆◆
Gymnastic sax maniac's output for L.A. deejay Hunter Hancock's Swingin' logo during the late '50s and early '60s. Naturally, his smash "There Is Something on Your Mind" is front and center, alongside the oddly titled "Back … Shack … Track," "Psycho Serenade," and "Blue Couch Boogie." Little Sonny Warner is the vocalist on some sides. —*Bill Dahl*

From Harlem to Camden / Aug. 1983-Sep. 1983 / Ace ◆◆◆
An album of lusty, robust honking sax on standard R&B arrangements. —*Ron Wynn*

Meets the Penguins / Oct. 1983 / Ace ◆◆◆
This reissue of raucous, upbeat R&B cuts also includes the doo-wop harmony ensemble The Penguins. —*Ron Wynn*

● **Nervous** / 1995 / Saxophile ◆◆◆◆
A thorough 19-track examination of McNeely's early heyday, incorporating a live 1951 reprise of his signature "Deacon's Hop," the King label classics "3-D," "Nervous Man Nervous," and "Texas Turkey," a handful of live 1957 efforts that include the crazed "Insect Ball," and McNeely's original hit version of the incendiary blues ballad "There Is Something on Your Mind" (with Little Sonny Warner handling the Ray Charles-influenced lead vocal). —*Bill Dahl*

Tony T.S. McPhee

b. Mar. 22, 1944
Guitar, Vocals / Blues-Rock, Psychedelic, Hard Rock
Tony McPhee was part of the first generation of young British blues disciples influenced by Cyril Davies and his band Blues Incorporated. A member of the same generation of young blues buffs as Mick Jagger, Keith Richards and Brian Jones, he never ascended to the heights achieved by the future Rolling Stones, but has recorded a small, highly significant body of blues-rock.

Originally a skiffle enthusiast, he received his first guitar as a Christmas present and formed his first band soon after, while still in school. He gravitated toward the blues during the early '60s, and soon discovered Cyril Davies. After seeing a few performances by Davies with Blues Incorporated at the Marquee Club in London during 1962, he became hopelessly hooked on blues and R&B, and decided to try and make it as a blues singer/guitarist.

McPhee's first group was the Dollarbills, a pop band featuring John Cruickshank on vocals, Pete Cruickshank on bass, and Dave Boorman on drums. He quickly steered toward blues, most notably the sound of John Lee

Hooker, and with the addition of Bob Hall on piano, the group changed its name to the Groundhogs, in recognition of Hooker's "Ground Hog Blues."

The Groundhogs were a very solid blues/R&B outfit, playing soulful American R&B and raw American blues at venues such as Newcastle's Club A-Go-Go, and they subsequently became the backing band to Champion Jack Dupree at a series of gigs at the 100 Club. Finally, in July of 1964, the Groundhogs reached their zenith when they were chosen to back John Lee Hooker himself during his current British tour. Hooker later selected the group to back him on his next tour, and also sent an acetate recording of the group to executives at his label, Vee-Jay Records. That acetate, the hard-rocking, piano-and-harmonica-driven band original "Shake It" backed with a very powerful and persuasive cover of Little Son Jackson's "Rock Me Baby," was released on the Interphon label, a Vee-Jay subsidiary. It failed to reach the charts, but it did mark the group and McPhee's first American release.

Meanwhile, back in England, the group recorded a studio album with Hooker, somewhat misleadingly entitled *Live at the A-Go-Go Club, New York*. The group's fortunes seemed to improve in 1965 when producer Mike Vernon recorded three tracks, "Big Train Blues," "Can't Sit Down," and "Blue Guitar," but none saw any major release or success, and only "Blue Guitar" ever received much US exposure, appearing on the 1970s Sire Records collection *Anthology of British Blues*.

By the end of 1965, the British blues boom had expended itself, and soul was becoming the new sound of choice. McPhee had already shown a predilection for soul music in his writing, especially "Hallelujah," which the group cut with its newly added brass section in 1965. The Groundhogs transformed themselves into a soul band, and were persuaded to record a song called "I'll Never Fall in Love Again." As a first soul outing it was a promising beginning, despite a beat that was too reminiscent of Otis Redding's "Can't Turn You Loose"—the dissonant guitar in the break was a refreshing change that would never have made it out the door at Stax Records. The song failed to get much airplay or achieve a chart position, and its B-side, the upbeat, haunting McPhee original "Over You Baby" disappeared as well.

The Groundhogs split up soon after, and McPhee did session work for a time, as well as recording some blues sides on his own, under the auspices of producer Jimmy Page, that later turned up on various British blues anthologies released by Andrew Loog Oldham's Immediate Records label, backed up by Jo-Ann Kelly and fellow Groundhog Bob Hall. Unlike a lot of other blues enthusiasts from the early '60s, McPhee remained true to his roots, and was good enough to rate a berth as a sessionman on Champion Jack Dupree's 1966 Decca album *From New Orleans to Chicago*.

In August of 1966, McPhee and bassist Pete Cruickshank teamed up with drummer Mike Meekham to form Herbal Mixture, a Yardbirds-like outfit mixing psychedelic and blues sounds at a very high amperage. They were one of the more soulful and muscular psychedelic outfits, reflecting their R&B (as opposed to pop) roots, and even their spaciest material has a bluesy feel. "A Love That's Died" relies on fuzz-tone guitar, and would have made good competition for anything by the Yardbirds had anyone been given a chance to hear it. Their cover of "Over You Baby" is, if anything, superior to the Groundhogs' original, and deserved a better hearing than it got. Herbal Mixture had some success playing the Marquee and Middle Earth clubs in London, and were good enough to get a gig opening for the newly-formed Jeff Beck Group at the London Roundhouse. Their records, however, didn't sell, and at the end of 1967, following Meekham's departure, the band ceased to exist.

McPhee continued playing blues in his spare time, however, and passed through the John Dummer Blues Band during early 1968. His music had left an impression on at least one record company executive—in 1968, Andrew Lauder of United Artists' British operation offered McPhee the chance to record a complete album if he could put together a band. He formed a new Groundhogs, carrying over bassist Pete Cruickshank, and the album *Scratching the Surface* was duly recorded and released that year. Ironically, this incarnation of the Groundhogs, put together for the one album session, ended up lasting far beyond its origins—five additional albums, including his best-known long-player, *Me and the Devil*, were recorded through 1972, and the group has remained a viable unit, continuing to perform in England and the European continent (where there's always work for British blues bands) with McPhee as its leader. *—Bruce Eder*

● **Hooker and the Hogs** / 1965 / Indigo ✦✦✦✦

McPhee and the Groundhogs' most important musical legacy, this 1996 reissue has an unusual history. Tony McPhee and the Groundhogs first played with John Lee Hooker in June of 1964, when John Mayall's Bluesbreakers were unable to fulfill a commitment to back Hooker on the final week of his British tour. The Groundhogs were deputized on the spot and played their first show with him at the Twisted Wheel in Manchester. At the end of the week, Hooker told McPhee how much he liked working with his band and agreed to use the Groundhogs as his backing band on his next visit to England. Hooker was back in May and June of 1965, and not only used them as his band but recorded this album with the Groundhogs. The band was Tony McPhee on guitar, Pete Cruickshank on bass, Dave Boorman on drums, and Tom Parker on keyboards—some of the stuff here may have surfaced elsewhere, on the Interchord label (as *Don't Want Nobody*) with brass dubbed on, but this release consists of the undubbed recordings. The sound is raw, tight, and raunchy, some of the best band-backed recordings of Hooker's career. He's notoriously difficult to play support for because of the spontaneity of his work, but these guys keep up and then some, adding engaging flourishes and grace notes. Hooker is in excellent voice, and his material is as strong as any album in his output, rough, dark, and moody. The ominous, surging "Little Dreamer" is worth the price of admission all but itself. The 11 tracks with the Groundhogs are rounded out with four Hooker solo bonus tracks, which are even louder and more savage than the Groundhogs' stuff, though a little noisy (like that ever mattered with the Hook). *—Bruce Eder*

Dealing with the Devil / 1991 / Sony ✦✦✦

A multi-artist compilation featuring two Tony McPhee numbers, "You Don't Love Me" and the John Lee Hooker-inspired "Ain't Gonna Cry No More," with the singer supported by Jo-Ann Kelly and Bob Hall. Out-of-print. *—Bruce Eder*

Herbal Mixture-Groundhogs / 1996 / Distortion ✦✦✦✦

First-rate blues and R&B-based rock gives way to psychedelic rock, heavy on the fuzz-tones and the soulful lead vocals. This could almost be a lost Yardbirds album, and anyone who digs the group's "Heart Full of Soul" period will love this. Three alternate versions of "A Love That's Died" may seem like overkill, but they're each played in completely different fashion, and they're all fascinating. (Box 1122 Bala-Cynwyd, PA 19004) *—Bruce Eder*

Slide, T.S., Slide / Mar. 19, 1996 / M.I.L. Multimedia ✦✦✦

Now this is more like it—Tony McPhee alone in his home studio with just his Yamaha FG180 on the first six tracks, doing whatever comes to mind. Mostly, as the title suggests, he plays some nimble slide guitar through some appropriately raspy-voiced renditions of "Reformed Man," "Mean Disposition," "Tell Me Baby," and the obviously autobiographical "Hooker & the Hogs." The other nine songs were cut solo by McPhee in concert during 1993, and he comes off even better there, his playing even more nimble and his singing far more expressive on songs like Son House's "Death Letter," Muddy Waters' "I Just Can't Be Satisfied," and Howlin' Wolf's "Down in the Bottom" and "No Place to Go," among others. The fidelity on the live stuff, cut with a Yamaha APX-6 in Vienna, is also excellent. *—Bruce Eder*

Blind Willie McTell (William Samuel McTell)

b. May 5, 1901, Thomson, GA, **d.** Aug. 19, 1959, Milledgeville, GA
Guitar, Harmonica, Accordion, Vocals / Country Blues, East Coast Blues, Piedmont Blues, Prewar Country Blues

Willie Samuel McTell was one of the blues' greatest guitarists, and also one of the finest singers ever to work in blues. A major figure with a local following in Atlanta from the 1920s onward, he recorded dozens of sides throughout the 1930s under a multitude of names—all the better to juggle "exclusive" relationships with many different record labels at once—including Blind Willie, Blind Sammie, Hot Shot Willie, and Georgia Bill, as a backup musician to Ruth Mary Willis. And those may not have been all of his pseudonyms—we don't even know what he chose to call himself, although "Blind Willie" was his preferred choice among friends. Much of what we do know about him was learned only years after his death, from family members and acquaintances. His family name was, so far as we know, McTier or McTear, and the origins of the "McTell" name are unclear. What is clear is that he was born into a family filled with musicians—his mother and his father both played guitar, as did one of his uncles, and he was also related to Georgia Tom Dorsey, who later became the Reverend Thomas Dorsey.

McTell was born in Thomson, GA, near Augusta, and raised near Statesboro. Willie was probably born blind, although early in his life he could perceive light in one eye. His blindness never became a major impediment, however, and it was said that his sense of hearing and touch were extraordinary. His first instruments were the harmonica and the accordion, but as soon as he was big enough he took up the guitar and showed immediate aptitude on the new instrument. He played a standard six-string acoustic until the mid-'20s, and never entirely abandoned the instrument, but from the beginning of his recording career, he used a 12-string acoustic in the studio almost exclusively. Willie's technique on the 12-string instrument was unique. Unlike virtually every other bluesman who used one, he relied not on its resonances as a rhythm instrument, but, instead, displayed a nimble, elegant slide and finger-picking style that made it sound like more than one guitar at any given moment. He studied at a number of schools for the blind, in Georgia, New York, and Michigan, during the early '20s, and probably picked up some formal musical knowledge. He worked medicine shows, carnivals, and other outdoor venues, and was a popular attraction, owing to his sheer dexterity and a nasal singing voice that could sound either pleasant or mournful, and incorporated some of the characteristics normally associated with White hillbilly singers.

Willie's recording career began in late 1927 with two sessions for Victor records, eight sides including "Statesboro Blues." McTell's earliest sides were superb examples of storytelling in music, coupled with dazzling guitar work. All of McTell's music showed extraordinary power, some of it delightfully raucous ragtime, other examples evoking darker, lonelier sides of the blues, all of it displaying astonishingly rich guitar work.

McTell worked under a variety of names, and with a multitude of partners, including his one time wife Ruthy Kate Williams (who recorded with him under the name Ruby Glaze), and also Buddy Moss and Curley Weaver. McTell cut some of his best songs more than once in his career. Like many bluesmen, he recorded under different names simultaneously, and was even signed to Columbia and OKeh Records, two companies that ended up merged at the end of the 1930s, at the same time under two names. His recording career never gave Willie quite as much success as he had hoped, partly due to the fact that some of his best work appeared during the depths of the Depression. He was uniquely popular in Atlanta, where he continued to live and work throughout most of his career, and, in fact, was the only blues guitarist of any note from the city to remain active in the city until well after World War II.

Willie was well known enough that Library of Congress archivist John Lomax felt compelled to record him in 1940, although during the war, like many other acoustic country bluesmen, his recording career came to a halt. Luckily for Willie and generations of listeners after him, however, there was a brief revival of interest in acoustic country blues after World War II that brought him back into the studio. Amazingly enough, the newly founded Atlantic Records—which was more noted for its recordings of jazz and R&B—took an interest in Willie and cut 15 songs with him in Atlanta during 1949. The one single released from these sessions, however, didn't sell, and most of those recordings remained unheard for more than 20 years after they were made. A year later, however, he was back in the studio, this time with his longtime partner Curley Weaver, cutting songs for the Regal label. None of these records sold especially well, however, and while Willie kept playing to anyone who would listen, the bitter realities of life had finally overtaken him, and he began drinking on a regular basis. He was rediscovered in 1956, just in time to get one more historic session down on tape. He left music soon after, to become a pastor of a local church, and he died of a brain hemorrhage in 1959, his passing so unnoticed at the time that certain reissues in the 1970s referred to Willie as still being alive in the 1960s.

Blind Willie McTell was one of the giants of the blues, as a guitarist and as a singer and recording artist. Hardly any of his work as passed down to us on record is less than first rate, and this makes most any collection of his music worthwhile. A studious and highly skilled musician whose skills transcended the blues, he was equally adept at ragtime, spirituals, storysongs, hillbilly numbers, and popular tunes, excelling in all of these genres. He could read and write music in braille, which gave him an edge on many of his sighted contemporaries, and was also a brilliant improvisor on the guitar, as is evident from his records. Willie always gave an excellent account of himself, even in his final years of performing and recording. —*Bruce Eder*

☆ **Atlanta Twelve String** / 1949 / Atlantic ♦♦♦♦♦
In 1949, a brief flurry of interest in old-time country blues resulted in this 15-song session by McTell for the newly formed Atlantic Records. Only two songs, "Kill It Kid" and "Broke Down Engine Blues," were ever issued on a failed single, and the session was forgotten until almost 20 years later. McTell is mostly solo here, vividly captured on acoustic 12-string (his sometime partner Curley Weaver may have been present on some tracks), and in excellent form. The playing and the repertory are representative of McTell as he was at this point in his career, a blues veteran rolling through his paces without skipping a beat and quietly electrifying the listener. Songs include "Dying Crapshooter's Blues," "The Razor Ball," and "Ain't I Grand to Live a Christian." —*Bruce Eder*

Last Session / 1960 / Bluesville ♦♦♦♦
This recording has a less-than-stellar reputation, principally because it was done so late in McTell's career, and it is true that he lacks some of the edge, especially in his singing, that he showed on his other postwar recordings. On the other hand, his 12-string playing is about as nimble as ever and a real treat. McTell cut these sides for record store owner Ed Rhodes, who had begun taping local bluesmen at his shop in Atlanta in the hope of releasing some of it—McTell took to the idea of recording only slowly, then turned up one night and played for the microphone and anyone who happened to be listening, finishing a pint of bourbon in the process—the result was a pricelessly intimate document, some of the words slurred here and there, but brilliantly expressive and stunningly played. No apologies are needed for "The Dyin' Crapshooter's Blues," "Don't Forget It," or "Salty Dog," however. McTell lived a few more years but never recorded again, which is a pity because based on this tape he still had a lot to show people. Rhodes never did anything with the tapes, and might've junked them if he hadn't remembered how important the McTell material was—they turned out to be the only tapes he saved, out of all he'd recorded. —*Bruce Eder*

The Early Years 1927-33 / 1989 / Yazoo ♦♦♦
This is one of the few Yazoo records that cannot be recommended as a potential first choice, because it was done relatively early. The sound is okay, but the song selection—all made up of pre-World War II material, as usual for Yazoo—is rather paltry compared with McTell collections that have come out since. It's not a bad choice, just not as good as some others, and it does include a decent, if limited, cross-section of early material, including "Statesboro Blues." —*Bruce Eder*

Complete Recorded Works, Vol. 2 (1931-1933) / 1990 / Document ♦♦♦♦
The second volume in Document's series opens with the first of two October 1931 sessions pairing Blind Willie McTell with the Atlanta street singer Ruth Willis; although her vocals remain the primary focus, these tracks contain some of McTell's most impressive instrumental work, with his playing deceptively simple and loose. Curley Weaver lends second guitar to a number of other performances, allowing McTell's 12-string to return to its proper position of prominence; also included are his early excursions into gospel, with performances of "Lord Have Mercy If You Please" and "Don't You See How This World Made a Change" distinguished by some devastating slide work. —*Jason Ankeny*

Complete Recorded Works, Vol. 3 (1933-1935) / 1990 / Document ♦♦♦♦
Blind Willie McTell's final pre-war sessions are the subject of the third and last disc in Document's series. The set begins with a September 1933 session covering a wide range of stylistic ground, ranging from the songster staple "Honey Fare Thee Well" (covered here as "East St. Louis Blues") to Bumble Bee Slim's "B and O Blues"; most remarkable is "Bell Street Lightnin'," a gripping and vivid portrait of Depression-era life at its most tragic. The final dates, from April 1935, comprise McTell's material for Decca, recorded with wife Kate and guitarist Curley Weaver; assembled in large part of gospel material, they also include "Hillbilly Willie's Blues," an overt and hugely entertaining attempt to appeal to the Southern white listening audience. —*Jason Ankeny*

☆ **Complete Recorded Works, Vol. 1 (1927-1931)** / 1990 / Document ✦✦✦✦✦
Of all the compilations of McTell's early work, this is probably the most rewarding, because it includes both his Victor songs (including "Statesboro Blues") and his Columbia sides (which have been issued separately by Columbia-Legacy), and RCA-BMG seems to be in no hurry to put any of the Victor material out as a comprehensive collection. The songs all have some noise—there are no "masters" to speak of on acoustic blues of this vintage—but none of it is overly obtrusive, and the orderly chronology is very illuminating. Subsequent volumes from Document are also worthwhile, but Sony-Legacy does have superior workmanship in dealing with much of the same material. —*Bruce Eder*

☆ **Pig 'n Whistle Red** / 1993 / Biograph ✦✦✦✦✦
This collection of 20 songs, cut by McTell with Curley Weaver on second guitar and sharing the vocals, was left out of many McTell biographical accounts until it resurfaced in 1993. Cut for Regal Records in 1950, it's a remarkable document, capturing McTell and Weaver in vivid modern sound, and includes remakes of McTell's 1933 "Talkin' to You Mama" and "Good Little Thing" as well as more recent material that the two had been doing, and even outtakes, showing very different interpretations of the 1920s pop standard "Pal of Mine" and the gospel number "Sending up My Timber." The sheer diversity of material makes this an indispensable (as well as a delightful) recording, and except for some minor tape damage on "A to Z Blues" and one other cut, there are few technical flaws here. The playing is so sharp and crisp, and vocals so delicate in their textures, that this collection has to be considered essential to any serious blues collection. McTell and Weaver were a legendary duo in Atlanta from before World War II, and it is nothing less than a gift to have them still together and in excellent form on this postwar recording. —*Bruce Eder*

★ **The Complete Blind Willie McTell** / 1994 / Columbia ✦✦✦✦✦
All of the recordings Blind Willie McTell made for Columbia, OKeh, and Vocalion between 1929 and 1933 are collected on this essential two-disc set. —*Stephen Thomas Erlewine*

☆ **Definitive** / 1995 / Columbia/Legacy ✦✦✦✦✦
This double-CD set is a little misleading. It is definitive, but only in terms of McTell's Columbia and OKeh sides—you won't find "Statesboro Blues" or his other earliest sides here, because they were done for Victor. But the material that is here is all worthwhile, and this is the best single source for McTell's work for those labels (done under a variety of names) from the mid-'30s, very nicely remastered and thoroughly annotated, although producer Lawrence Cohn concedes that even Sony-Legacy was unable to locate sources on a handful of songs that McTell is known to have recorded. —*Bruce Eder*

The Complete Victor Recordings 1927-1932 / Oct. 1995 / Victor ✦✦✦

Victor Recordings 1927-1934 / Jan. 30, 1996 / BMG ✦✦✦

Medicine Head

f. 1968, Stafford, England, **db.** 1976
Group / British Blues
Formed in Stafford, England in 1968, the British blues duo Medicine Head comprised vocalist/multi-instrumentalist John Fiddler and Peter Hope-Evans, who played the harmonica and jew's harp. Upon their formation at art college, Medicine Head became a staple of the local club circuit, eventually recording a demo which found its way to influential BBC radio personality John Peel, who began championing the track "His Guiding Hand." Other DJs soon followed suit, and quickly the duo was on the brink of stardom.

With Peel's continued assistance, Medicine Head entered the studio to begin recording their 1971 debut LP *New Bottles, Old Medicine*. Their focus shifted from basic blues to a more intricate sound for 1971's *Heavy on the Drum*, produced by former Yardbird Keith Relf; after scoring a surprise hit with the single "(And the) Pictures in the Sky," Hope-Evans left the group, and was replaced by Relf and drummer John Davies for 1972's *The Dark Side of the Moon*. Hope-Evans rejoined prior to 1973's *One and One Is One*, which launched the title track to the Top Three of the UK singles chart.

Now a five-piece also including guitarist Roger Saunders, onetime Family drummer Rob Townsend and bassist George Ford, Medicine Head notched two more hit singles, "Rising Sun" and "Slip and Slide," but 1974's *Thru' a Five* failed to chart, and the group began to disintegrate. Only Fiddler and

Hope-Evans remained by the time of 1976's *Two Man Band*, and after one last single, "Me and Suzy Hit the Floor," Medicine Head officially disbanded. Fiddler later resurfaced in the British Lions, followed by a stint in Box of Frogs and finally a solo career, while Hope-Evans contributed to the Pete Townshend albums *Empty Glass* and *White City*. —*Jason Ankeny*

● **New Bottles & Old Medicine . . . Plus** / 1995 / See For Miles ✦✦✦✦
See for Miles' reissue of Medicine Head's 1971 debut album *New Bottles, Old Medicine* is augmented by a couple of bonus tracks, but the record remains the group's best and bluesiest effort. Medicine Head was never one of the best British blues bands, but there are enough good moments on the record to make it of interest to collectors of that style. —*Thom Owens*

Meditation Singers

f. 1947, Detroit, MI
Group / Traditional Gospel, Black Gospel
While never achieving the national popularity of contemporaries like the Ward Singers or the Caravans, the Meditation Singers were indisputably the premier Detroit-based female gospel group of the 1950s; the first Motor City act to reject a cappella vocal traditions in favor of instrumental backing, their ranks also produced a pair of secular pop stars in Della Reese and Laura Lee. Formed in 1947 as a product of Detroit's New Liberty Baptist Church's renowned Moments of Meditation choir, the Meditation Singers were primarily led by Earnestine Rundless, the wife of onetime Soul Stirrer E.A. Rundless. Created in response to calls from other churches seeking the Moments of Meditation to perform, the group was originally an octet, but their size made crosstown travel prohibitive; upon trimming down to a quartet, the Meditation Singers' original lineup comprised Rundless, Reese (who often assumed lead duties as well), alto Marie Waters (Reese's sister), and soprano Lillian Mitchell.

As the Meditations' notoriety quickly spread, they began performing throughout the Midwest, and in early 1953 cut their first session at a local record store. Reese left the group to pursue pop success soon after, and was replaced by Lee, Rundless' teenage daughter; unbeknownst to the Meditations, their record was then licensed to the Deluxe label, and in short time they were signed to Specialty. By the time of their next session in the spring of 1954, their studio lineup also included co-lead Carrie Williams, tenor Herbert Carson, and pianist Emory Radford; Williams remained with the group only briefly before returning to Detroit to operate a beauty salon, while Carson later enlisted with the Herman Stevens Singers, among others. Poor sales prompted Specialty to drop the Meditations, who then spent the middle years of the 1950s concentrating on the road; by the end of the decade, however, they were working regularly with the legendary James Cleveland, and his involvement led Specialty to offer a new contract.

The Meditations' third Specialty session followed in mid-1959; however, the label soon exited the gospel business altogether, and a fourth session never materialized. Instead, the group signed to the Hob label, recording once more with Cleveland before he left their ranks. Over the course of the 1960s, the Meditations appeared on a series of labels, among them SAR, Chess, Checker, Savoy, and Jewel; they also toured constantly, in 1962 becoming one of the first gospel acts ever to play Las Vegas when they backed Reese during a performance at the Flamingo Casino. Their performance there even caught the attention of Frank Sinatra, who singled out Lee's potential for pop stardom; she remained with the group until 1965, at which time she moved into secular soul music and later scored a hit with "Women's Love Rights." The Meditations carried on in her absence, continuing to tour regularly until the early 1980s. —*Jason Ankeny*

● **Good News** / 1992 / Specialty ✦✦✦✦
This group, centered around the vocal dynamism of founder Ernestine Rundless, often featured the young Della Reese and Laura Lee, who both became popular music luminaries later on. There's piano backing, sporadic lead by the late James Cleveland, and lots of fervent singing. This brings together for the first time the complete, though few in number, 1953-1959 sides by this roof-raising group. —*Opal Louis Nations, Roots & Rhythm Newsletter*

Alright / Jewel ✦✦

Change Is Gonna Come / Jewel ✦✦✦
Ernestine Rundless and the gals shake up the church. —*Opal Louis Nations*

Mellow Fellows

f. Chicago, IL

Group / Modern Electric Chicago Blues, Modern Electric Blues, Contemporary Blues

Now known as the Chicago Rhythm And Blues Kings, the Mellow Fellows held their personnel together after the 1990 death of singer Larry "Big Twist" Nolan. Saxist Terry Ogolini and guitarist Pete Special, co-founders of the group, recruited Twist's pal Martin Allbritton to front the band, and they cut the buoyant *Street Party* for Alligator in 1990 with part-time member Gene "Daddy G" Barge helping out on sax and vocals. When Special split, the band switched-to its current regal billing. —*Bill Dahl*

Street Party / 1990 / Alligator ++++

Martin Allbritton, a melismatic and undeniably more powerful vocalist than the finesse-oriented Twist, proves an eminently worthy successor to the beloved big man on this highly enjoyable effort. Barge also pitches in with a few lead vocals as the group attacks a handful of joyous originals ("We'll Be Friends," "Street Party," "Broad Daylight") and storming R&B classics by Sam & Dave and Harold Burrage. —*Bill Dahl*

Memphis Jug Band

f. Memphis, TN

Group / Acoustic Memphis Blues, Prewar Country Blues

One of the definitive jug bands of the '20s and early '30s, this seminal group was comprised of Will Shade, Will Weldon, Hattie Hart, Charlie Polk, Walter Horton, and others, in various configurations.

Guitarist/harpist Will Shade formed the Memphis Jug Band in the Beale Street section of Memphis in the mid-'20s. A few years after their formation, Shade signed a contract with Victor Records in 1927. Over the next seven years, Shade and the Memphis Jug Band recorded nearly 60 songs for the record label. During this time, a number of musicians passed through the group, including Big Walter Horton, Furry Lewis, and Casey Bill Weldon. Throughout all of the various lineup incarnations, Shade provided direction for the group. The Memphis Jug Band played a freewheeling mixture of blues, ragtime, vaudeville, folk, and jazz, which was all delivered with good-time humor. That loose spirit kept the group and its records popular throughout the early '30s.

Although the group's popularity dipped sharply in the mid-'30s, Will Shade continued to lead the group in various incarnations until his death in 1966. —*Cub Koda & Stephen Thomas Erlewine*

★ **Memphis Jug Band** / 1927-1934 / Yazoo +++++

This definitive 28-song collection by the city's finest jug band spans their output from 1927 to 1934. —*John Floyd*

Complete Recorded Works, Vols. 1-3 / Document ++++

A definitive three-CD set with all the issued material from this groundbreaking jug band. Includes "Cocaine Habit Blues," "Cave Man Blues," the original "He's in the Jailhouse Now," and the always wonderful "I Whipped My Woman with a Single Tree." —*Cub Koda*

Memphis Minnie (Lizzie Douglas)

b. Jun. 3, 1897, Algiers, LA, **d.** Aug. 6, 1973, Memphis, TN

Banjo, Guitar, Vocals / Acoustic Memphis Blues, Acoustic Chicago Blues, Prewar Country Blues

Tracking down the ultimate woman blues guitar hero is problematic because woman blues singers seldom recorded as guitar players and woman guitar players (such as Rosetta Tharpe and Sister O.M. Terrell) were seldom recorded playing blues. Excluding contemporary artists, the most notable exception to this pattern was Memphis Minnie. The most popular and prolific blueswoman outside the vaudeville tradition, she earned the respect of critics, the support of record-buying fans, and the unqualified praise of the blues artists she worked with throughout her long career. Despite her Southern roots and popularity, she was as much a Chicago blues artist as anyone in her day. Big Bill Broonzy recalls her beating both him and Tampa Red in a guitar contest and claims she was the best woman guitarist he had ever heard. Tough enough to endure in a hard business, she earned the respect of her peers with her solid musicianship and recorded good blues over four decades for Columbia, Vocalion, Bluebird, OKeh, Regal, Checker, and JOB.

She also proved to have as good taste in musical husbands as music and sustained working marriages with guitarists Casey Bill Weldon, Joe McCoy, and Ernest Lawlers. Their guitar duets span the spectrum of African American folk and popular music, including spirituals, comic dialogs, and old-time dance pieces, but Memphis Minnie's best work consisted of deep blues like "Moaning the Blues." More than a good woman blues guitarist and singer, Memphis Minnie holds her own against the best blues artists of her time, and her work has special resonance for today's aspiring guitarists. —*Barry Lee Pearson*

★ **Hoodoo Lady (1933-1937)** / 1933-1937 / Columbia +++++

Memphis Minnie is a unique figure in blues history, a female country blues singer who emerged in the late 1920's when the field (at least on record) was exclusively filled by men. But, gender aside, she was one of the most talented blues singer-guitarists of the '30s and '40s. This CD reissue primarily dates from her period between her partnerships with Cousin Joe and Little Son Joe. Minnie is heard mostly playing her variations of goodtime urban blues (a la Bill Broonzy), an even 12 bars to a chorus but with the feeling and emotion of the country blues. Pianist Blind John Davis and Charlie McCoy's mandolin help out on some of the tracks of the accessible set which serves as a fine introduction to Memphis Minnie; five of its 20 selections were previously unreleased. —*Scott Yanow*

1934-1942 / 1934-1942 / Biograph ++++

You can't go wrong with Memphis Minnie at almost any point in her estimable career. During the 1930s and early '40s, she made the adjustment to changing styles, but in the early '30s she *made* the style. The sound quality is pretty good throughout the set, although it's better on the later tunes. —*Ron Wynn*

Blues Classics by Memphis Minnie / Oct. 1965 / Blues Classics ++++

Shaking, volcanic material from the great Memphis Minnie. There weren't many stylists, male or female, who could match Lizzie Douglas when it came to conveying a lyric. She was in peak form on every selection here. —*Ron Wynn*

I Ain't No Bad Gal / 1988 / Portrait +++

Minnie was the toughest guitar-picking femme of bluesdom, with plugged-in 1941 performances that included "Me and My Chauffeur Blues." —*Mark A. Humphrey*

Complete Recorded Works, Vol. 5 (1935-1941) / 1991 / Document ++++

The fifth and final volume in Document's series begins with a mid-1940 studio date, Memphis Minnie's first in over a year; recorded with Little Son Joe on second guitar, these simple, unaffected sides are among her strongest, with tracks like "Ma Rainey" (a tribute to the recently deceased blues great) and "Nothing in Rambling" brimming with confidence and inspiration. Her final pre-war session, recorded late in 1941, closes out the set; performing on amplified guitar, Minnie's music adopts a relatively urbanized sound on tracks like the superb "I Am Sailin'" and "Don't Turn the Card," precipitating the Chicago blues of the postwar era. —*Jason Ankeny*

Complete Recorded Works, Vol. 3 (1931-1932) / 1991 / Document +++

For completists, specialists and academics, Document's *Complete Recorded Works, Vol. 3 (1931-1932)* is invaluable, offering an exhaustive overview of Memphis Minnie's early recordings. For less dedicated listeners, the disc is a mixed blessing. There are some absolutely wonderful, classic performances on the collection, but the long running time, exacting chronological sequencing, poor fidelity (all cuts are transferred from original acetates and 78s), and number of performances are hard to digest. The serious blues listener will find all these factors to be positive, but enthusiasts and casual listeners will find that the collection is of marginal interest for those very reasons. —*Thom Owens*

Complete Recorded Works, Vol. 1 (1935-1941) / 1991 / Document ++++

The first volume in Document's series of Memphis Minnie solo recordings collects the material she cut in Chicago over a period of six sessions between the first weeks of 1935 and Halloween of that same year. Her first sides following her personal and professional breakup with Kansas Joe McCoy, the material suggests a rebirth of sorts, marked by a new sense of experimentation—two tracks, "Let Me Ride" and "When the Saints Go Marching Home," are pure gospel, while "Ball and Chain Blues" is her first step into the band style prevalent at the end of the 1930s. Among the other highlights are the tracks from her final Decca session, a solo date which spotlights her amazing guitar work. —*Jason Ankeny*

Complete Recorded Works, Vol. 2 (1935-1941) / 1991 / Document ✦✦✦
For academics and Memphis Minnie completists, Document's *Complete Recorded Works, Vol. 2 (1935-1941)* is invaluable, but less dedicated listeners will find the disc a mixed blessing. The very things that will appeal to the blues fanatic—the long running time, exacting chronological sequencing, poor fidelity (all cuts are transferred from original acetates and 78s), and large number of performances—are the very reason that casual listeners will want to look elsewhere. —*Thom Owens*

Complete Recorded Works, Vol. 3 (1935-1941) / 1991 / Document ✦✦✦

Complete Recorded Works, Vol. 4 (1938-1939) / 1991 / Document ✦✦✦
The fourth volume in the series opens with Memphis Minnie's lone 1938 studio date; backed by mondolinist (and former brother-in-law) Charlie McCoy, the session possesses elements of the classic string band sound, with sides like "I'd Rather See Him Dead" and "Good Biscuits" among the most sexually explicit in her catalog. The remaining material, all cut in February 1939, is comprised of guitar-duet accompaniments with Little Son Joe, heralding the format consistent throughout the majority of Minnie's pre-war recordings; indeed, as stellar performances of "Keep Your Big Mouth Closed" and "Low Down Man Blues" indicate, perhaps no other arrangement was more ideally suited to her unique style. —*Jason Ankeny*

Complete Recorded Works, Vol. 1 (1929-1930) / 1991 / Document ✦✦✦✦

Complete Recorded Works, Vol. 2 (1930-1931) / 1991 / Document ✦✦✦✦
For academics and Memphis Minnie completists, Document's *Complete Recorded Works, Vol. 2 (1930-1931)* is invaluable, and there are some absolutely wonderful, classic performances on the collection. However, casual listeners will be discouraged by the exacting chronological sequencing, poor fidelity (all cuts are transferred from original acetates and 78s), and sheer number of performances, all of which cut into the collection's casual listenability. —*Thom Owens*

Complete Recorded Works, Vol. 4 (1933-1934) / 1991 / Document ✦✦✦
Although the title credits the material herein to Memphis Minnie and Kansas Joe, very few of the tracks which comprise this volume are actually collaborative efforts between the duo—by 1933 their personal and professional relationships were both on the rocks, with Minnie instead recording solo and Joe working with his guitarist brother Charlie. The Minnie solo sides which open the set are uniformly excellent, with the saucy "My Butcher Man" spotlighting her gifts as a lyricist and the Mississippi-styled "Too Late" underscoring her guitar prowess. By mid-1934, some measure of reconciliation had clearly been reached, as the couple was now performing together again; although their reunion was short-lived—and their subsequent break final—these last sides are also powerful, with the revealing "Moaning the Blues" capping their career in peak form. —*Jason Ankeny*

Complete Recorded Works, Vol. 3 (1931-1932) / 1991 / Document ✦✦✦
The third volume in Document's series picks up in early 1931, with the Depression era in full swing; although Memphis Minnie and Kansas Joe were still actively recording, very little of their material was actually seeing release. Ironically, these were some of the duo's finest sides to date, with Minnie's vocals and guitar work achieving new peaks of poignancy and intensity; with "Shake Mattie" and "My Wash Woman's Gone," she introduces her bottleneck style, while on "Let's Go to Town" she and Joe face off in a fiery instrumental duel. The latter half of the collection, recorded in New York, focuses on more traditional material; their rendition of the minstrel song "Fishin' Blues" is widely assumed to be the inspiration for subsequent versions by Son House, Bumble Bee Slim and many others. —*Jason Ankeny*

☆ **And Kansas Joe: 1929-1934** / 1991 / Document ✦✦✦✦✦
Minnie's earliest recordings with first husband Kansas Joe McCoy. Includes "I Want That," "Bumble Bee," "Squat It," "I Don't Want That Junk Outta You," and the original version of "When the Levee Breaks," later covered by (and re-credited to) Led Zeppelin. —*Cub Koda*

Queen of the Blues / Oct. 7, 1997 / Sony ✦✦✦✦
18 stellar selections recorded between 1929 and 1946 that clearly show what a potent musical force this woman truly was. Working with second and third husbands Kansas Joe McCoy and Ernest "Little Son Joe" Lawlars, this was a prime period for Minnie's creativity, going from the lowdown blues of "Has

Anyone Seen My Man?" to the celebratory novelty of "Joe Louis Strut." Three of the tracks here ("Fashion Plate Daddy," "Killer Diller Blues" and "Please Don't Stop Him") are previously unissued, and the disc transfers are clean and sharp throughout. This perfect little primer set also includes the original version of "When the Levee Breaks," later recorded and partially credited to Led Zeppelin. —*Cub Koda*

Travelling Blues / Aldabra ✦✦✦✦
Travelling Blues collects a number of sessions recorded with Kansas Joe McCoy, Memphis Minnie's second husband. Make no mistake about it—with her impassioned vocals, Memphis Minnie controls these recordings. Although most of these cuts are available on better collections, this album sounds fine and contains a wealth of terrific music. —*Thom Owens*

With Kansas Joe / Blues Classics ✦✦✦✦
When she was married to Kansas Joe McCoy, Memphis Minnie was making wailing blues, memorable laments and brilliant double-entendre tunes. He in turn supplied her with excellent accompaniment and nice complementary vocals. These are simply marvelous songs. —*Ron Wynn*

The Memphis Pilgrims

f. Memphis, TN
Group / Roots-Rock, Blues-Rock
The Memphis Pilgrims, led by guitarist, singer and songwriter Michael Falzarano, have one album out on the Brooklyn-based Relix Records label. Falzarano is a name familiar to followers of Hot Tuna guitarist Jorma Kaukonen; the two frequently perform together at coffeehouses and clubs around the US and Europe. Falzarano's songs appear on the Hot Tuna albums *A Pair a Dice Found* and *Live at Sweetwater*. Falzarano has also written songs for several of Kaukonen's solo albums, including *Land of Heroes* and *Christmas*, both for the American Heritage label.

The group plays heavily blues-based melodic roots-rock. Members of the Memphis Pilgrims include guitarist Jimmy Eppard, bassist Steve Rust, drummer Harvey Sorgen, and keyboardist/accordionist Adam Hurwitz. All have extensive backgrounds as sidemen and studio session musicians. Eppard, based in Woodstock, N.Y., has recorded with members of the Band, the New Bohemians, Pete Seeger and Orleans. Eppard is also an accomplished lap steel and slide guitar player. Bassist Rust has performed with jazz flutist Hubert Laws, Sam and Dave, and jazz saxophonist Nick Brignola. Drummer/percussionist Sorgen has performed and recorded with Ahmad Jamal, Bill Frisell, NRBQ, David Torn and Jack DeJohnette. Keyboardist and accordionist Hurwitz has worked with the Band and Ronnie Hawkins, among others.

Their debut album, *Mecca*, blends elements of rockabilly, blues and soul music with the band's roots-rock base. —*Richard Skelly*

Mecca / 1996 / Relix ✦✦✦

Memphis Slim (John 'Peter' Chatman)

b. Sep. 3, 1915, Memphis, TN, d. Feb. 24, 1988, Paris, France
Piano, Vocals / R&B, Piano Blues
An amazingly prolific artist who brought a brisk air of urban sophistication to his frequently stunning presentation, Memphis Slim assuredly ranks with the greatest blues pianists of all time. He was smart enough to take Big Bill Broonzy's early advice about developing a style to call his own to heart, instead of imitating that of his idol, Roosevelt Sykes. Soon enough, other 88s pounders were copying Slim rather than the other way around—his thundering ivories attack set him apart from most of his contemporaries, while his deeply burnished voice possessed a commanding authority.

As befits his stage name, John 'Peter' Chatman was born and raised in Memphis—a great place to commit to a career as a bluesman. Sometime in the late '30s, he resettled in Chicago and began recording as a leader in 1939 for OKeh, then switched over to Bluebird the next year. Around the same time, Slim joined forces with Broonzy, then the dominant force on the local blues scene. After serving as Broonzy's invaluable accompanist for a few years, Slim emerged as his own man in 1944.

After the close of World War II, Slim joined Hy-Tone Records, cutting eight tracks that were later picked up by King. Lee Egalnick's Miracle label reeled in the pianist in 1947; backed by his jumping band, the House Rockers (its members usually included saxists Alex Atkins and Ernest Cotton), Slim recorded his classic "Lend Me Your Love" and "Rockin' the House." The next year brought the landmark "Nobody Loves Me" (better known via subsequent covers by Lowell Fulson, Joe Williams, and B.B. King as "Everyday I Have the Blues") and the heartbroken "Messin' Around (with the Blues)."

The pianist kept on label-hopping, moving from Miracle to Peacock to Premium (where he waxed the first version of his uncommonly wise downtempo blues "Mother Earth") to Chess to Mercury before staying put at Chicago's United Records from 1952 to 1954. This was a particularly fertile period for the pianist; he recruited his first permanent guitarist, the estimable Matt Murphy, who added some serious fretfire to "The Come Back," "Sassy Mae," and "Memphis Slim USA."

Before the decade was through, the pianist landed at Vee-Jay Records, where he cut definitive versions of his best-known songs with Murphy and a stellar combo in gorgeously sympathetic support (Murphy was nothing short of spectacular throughout).

Slim exhibited his perpetually independent mindset by leaving the country for good in 1962. A tour of Europe in partnership with bassist Willie Dixon a couple of years earlier had so intrigued the pianist that he permanently moved to Paris, where recording and touring possibilities seemed limitless and the veteran pianist was treated with the respect too often denied even African American blues stars at home back then. He remained there until his 1988 death, enjoying his stature as expatriate blues royalty. —*Bill Dahl*

Memphis Slim at the Gate of the Horn / 1959 / Vee-Jay ♦♦♦♦
Only this disc's short length (34 minutes) qualifies as something worthy of complaint; otherwise this is seminal blues piano, performed by a great player and singer, Memphis Slim. This 1959 session had everything: super piano solos, a strong lineup of horn players, clever, well-written and sung lyrics, and a seamless pace that kept things moving briskly from beginning to end. Other than Slim, instrumental honors go to guitarist Matt Murphy, a marvelous accompanist who was able to blend sophistication, technique, and earthiness into one dynamic package. Even at its bargain-basement length, *At the Gate of the Horn* belongs in any blues fan's library. —*Ron Wynn*

Memphis Slim [Chess/MCA] / 1961 / MCA/Chess ♦♦♦♦
A straight CD reissue of a vintage Chess LP, its contents dating back to the early '50s and most tracks originally issued on the Premium logo. Includes an early and very nice reading of "Mother Earth," also sharp as a tack is "Rockin' the Pad." In an unusual move, Slim is joined by a smooth vocal group, the Vagabonds, for "Really Got the Blues." —*Bill Dahl*

Steady Rollin' Blues / 1961 / Bluesville ♦♦♦
Like Slim's other Bluesville work, this is a characteristic and very consistent effort, though not what you would single out as the cream of his recorded work. He varies the program between originals and covers of standards like "Mean Mistreatin' Mama," "Rock Me Baby," and "Goin' Down Slow," providing a touch of unpredictability by switching from the piano to the organ on a few tracks. —*Richie Unterberger*

USA / 1961 / Candid ♦♦♦

Alone with My Friends / Apr. 25, 1961 / Battle ♦♦♦
Memphis Slim devoted all but one of the ten songs on this April 1961 session to covers of some of his favorite songwriters. He's only accompanied by his own piano playing as he provides serviceable, laidback interpretations of numbers by Big Bill Broonzy, Blind Lemon Jefferson, Willie Dixon, Sonny Boy Williamson, and others, as well as his own "Sunnyland Train." Not the first or last place to check out Slim on record. —*Richie Unterberger*

Songs of Memphis Slim and Willie Dixon / May 1961 / Smithsonian/ Folkways ♦♦♦

Memphis Slim: U.S.A. / 1962 / Candid ♦♦♦♦
By 1954, when these 12 tracks were laid down for Chicago's United Records, amazing young guitarist Matt Murphy had joined Slim's House Rockers, taking the band in fascinating modern directions on the title cut, "Sassy Mae," and the astonishing jazz-based instrumental "Backbone Boogie." Now, if Delmark would only reissue this terrific album on CD! —*Bill Dahl*

Memphis Slim & Willie Dixon in Paris / 1962 / Battle ♦♦♦
Recorded live in Paris, this has the two blues legends accompanying each other (Slim on piano, Dixon on bass) and trading lead vocals, backed by drummer Phillipe Combelle. It's not a landmark event in either of the legends' distinguished recording careers, but it's a nice enough outing with a

friendly, low-key tone. Slim recorded a lot of LPs in the early '60s, often as a solo pianist/vocalist, and this is frankly more lively than his norm for the era, if for nothing else than the fact that he's playing in a band. The Dixon-sung tracks are interesting inasmuch as he didn't record much during this period, though he's really adequate at best as a singer. When Slim sings, he sticks mostly to self-penned material; the Dixon-fronted cuts may stir some curiosity among blues fans due to the inclusion of some of Willie's more obscure compositions, like the novelty-tinged "African Hunch with a Boogie Beat." —*Richie Unterberger*

All Kinds of Blues / 1963 / Bluesville ♦♦♦
A good-natured 1961 solo piano session, with Slim's mastery of boogie-woogie styles to the fore on both instrumentals and tunes punctuated by folky monologues. The material's mostly traditional in origin, though Slim wrote the lyrics for the most memorable performance, "Mother Earth." —*Richie Unterberger*

The Real Folk Blues / 1966 / MCA/Chess ♦♦♦♦
Lots of duplication with the other Chess reissue CD here, so take your pick. Or pick 'em both up—you can't go wrong with either one of these early-'50s collections. —*Bill Dahl*

Mother Earth / 1969 / One Way ♦♦♦
Excellent singing and rousing, sparkling barrelhouse, boogie-woogie and straight blues piano playing from a certified legend. Memphis Slim wasn't shy about making records, and they were seldom not worth hearing. This one didn't break the string of quality efforts. —*Ron Wynn*

Messin' Around with the Blues / 1970 / King ♦♦♦♦
He wasn't messing around with either his singing or playing here. Memphis Slim made dozens of albums; most were good, some were very good, and a handful were great. This was among the handful. —*Ron Wynn*

★ **Rockin' the Blues** / 1981 / Charly ♦♦♦♦♦
The most complete gathering of Slim's 1958-1959 Vee-Jay output available on disc (16 songs to the even dozen on the *Gate of Horn* domestic disc) and the best-sounding too. This is the crowning achievement in Memphis Slim's massive legacy—he delivers his classics one right after another, backed by his unparalleled combo that was anchored by Matt "Guitar" Murphy's startlingly fresh solos. Along with the standbys—"Messin' Around," "Mother Earth," "Wish Me Well"—there's the catchy instrumental "Steppin' Out," later covered by Eric Clapton; the romping "What's the Matter," and a blistering "Rockin' the House" where the band nearly sails right out of the studio! —*Bill Dahl*

Memphis Heat / 1981 / IMS ♦♦
The combination of Memphis Slim and Canned Heat didn't generate much in the way of sparks when they were brought together for this set in 1974. And a five-strong edition of the Memphis Horns, brought in at some point to add a little punch to the proceedings, actually seem to get in the way. Safe to skip this one, with so much prime Slim available on CD. —*Bill Dahl*

I Just Keep on Singing the Blues / 1981 / Muse ♦♦♦
He kept singing and playing the blues with gusto and distinction his entire career. This came a bit later in the Memphis Slim legacy, when he was more of an established artist than a maverick performer, but it's still almost as essential as his landmark recordings from the 1950s. —*Ron Wynn*

Life Is Like That / 1990 / Charly ♦♦♦♦
Some of Slim's earliest post-war sides for Miracle and King (1946-1949), and some of his best. He'd already assembled his little combo with saxists Alex Atkins and Ernest Cotton by that time (interchangeable bassists included Willie Dixon and Big Crawford, no drums necessary), and the classics were flowing: "Lend Me Your Love," "Nobody Loves Me" (adapted by Lowell Fulson as "Every Day I Have the Blues"), and the luxurious "Messin' Around with the Blues." —*Bill Dahl*

1960 London Sessions / 1993 / Sequel NEX ♦♦♦
The pianist was quite an attraction when he first ventured overseas, and he received plenty of offers to record while he was there. The uncredited combo on these 15 rare tracks is too timid to give Slim what he needed out of a band, but his irrepressible power saves the show. —*Bill Dahl*

Live at the Hot Club / 1994 / Milan ♦♦
Recorded live in 1980 in Paris, this is not the Memphis Slim that you want

for your collection, unless you're the type that has to have everything in a discography just because it's there. Slim is actually in decent enough form. The problems are that his only accompanist is a clunky drummer, and that the fidelity is fairly funky (although not truly grating). And with so many other Memphis Slim recordings available, this ranks pretty far down the list. — *Richie Unterberger*

Very Best of Memphis Slim: The Blues Is Everywhere / Jan. 5, 1998 / Collectables ♦♦♦
The Very Best of Memphis Slim: The Blues Is Everywhere collects 12 songs Slim recorded in the mid-'60s, probably for King and Scepter Records. While there are some good peroformances on this disc, there are no liner notes explaining the origins of the tracks, and the sound is uneven. It's not a bad collection, especially for collectors searching for a few specific cuts, but novices would be better served by more comprehensive, thorough collections. — *Stephen Thomas Erlewine*

Together Again One More Time/Still Not Ready For . . . / Antone's ♦♦♦
A modern-day reunion of the revered pianist and his favorite guitarist at Austin, TX-based Antone's nightclub, preserved for posterity. They sound mighty happy to see one another. — *Bill Dahl*

Memphis Willie B. (William Borum)

b. Nov. 4, 1911, Shelby County, TN
Vocals, Guitar, Harmonica / Acoustic Memphis Blues, Piedmont Blues
Willie Borum, better known under his recording sobriquet of Memphis Willie B., was a mainstay of the Memphis blues and jug band circuit. Adept at both harmonica and guitar, Borum could add pep to any combination he worked in, as well as leaving a striking impression as a solo artist.

He was born in 1911 in Shelby County, TN. He took to the guitar early in his childhood, being principally taught by his father and Memphis medicine show star Jim Jackson. By his late teens, he was working with Jack Kelly's Jug Busters, working for tips on the street with the occasional house party and country supper rounding out his meager paycheck. This didn't last long, as Borum joined up with the Memphis Jug Band, one of two professional outfits in existence at that time. The group frequently worked what later became W.C. Handy Park in Memphis, their touring stretching all the way down to New Orleans during the Mardi Gras. Sometime in the '30s he learned to play harmonica, being taught by no less a master than Noah Lewis, the best harp blower in Memphis and mainstay of Gus Cannon's Jug Stompers. As his style began to move further away from a strict jug band approach, Willie B. began working on and off with various traveling Delta bluesmen, performing at various functions with Rice Miller, Willie Brown, Garfield Akers, and Robert Johnson. He finally got to make some records in New York under his own name in 1934 for Vocalion, but quickly moved back into playing juke joints and gambling houses with Son Joe, Joe Hill Louis and Will Shade until around 1943, when he became a member of the US Army.

It was a much different world he returned to and after a brief fling at trying to pick up where he left off, Borum soon cashed in his chips and started looking for a day job. That would have been the end of the story, except in 1961 — with the folk and blues revival in full hootenanny steam — Borum was tracked down and recorded an absolutely marvelous session at the Sun studios for Prestige's Bluesville label. It turned into a little bit of a career upswing for the next few years; Willie B. started working the festival and coffeehouse circuit with old Memphis buddies Gus Cannon and Furry Lewis. But then just as quickly, he dropped out of the music scene and eventually out of sight altogether. The reports of his death in the early '70s still remain unconfirmed as of press time. — *Cub Koda*

Introducing Memphis Willie B. / 1961 / Bluesville ♦♦

Hardworking Man Blues / Jun. 30, 1995 / Original Blues Classics ♦♦♦

● **Bluesville Years, Vol. 3** / Prestige ♦♦♦♦
Beale Street Get-Down is the folksiest of the bunch, most of it recorded at the Sun studios in Memphis with country blues guitarists Furry Lewis and Memphis Willie B. (Borum) and pianist Memphis Slim all contributing to the fray. — *Cub Koda*

The Meters

f. 1966, New Orleans, LA, **db.** 1977
Instrumental / R&B, Soul, Funk, New Orleans R&B
The Meters defined New Orleans funk, not only on their own recordings, but also as the backing band for numerous artists, including many produced by Allen Toussaint. Where the funk of Sly Stone and James Brown was wild, careening and determinedly urban, the Meters were down-home and earthy. Nearly all of their own recordings were instrumentals, putting the emphasis on the organic and complex rhythms. The syncopated, layered percussion intertwined with the gritty grooves of the guitar and organ, creating a distinctive sound that earned a small, devoted cult during the '70s, including musicians like Paul McCartney and Robert Palmer, both of whom used the group as a backing band for recording. Despite their reputation as an extraordinary live band, the Meters never broke into the mainstream, but their sound provided the basis for much of the funk and hip-hop of the '80s and '90s.

Throughout their career, the Meters were always led by Art Neville (keyboard, vocals), one of the leading figures of the New Orleans musical community. As a teenager in high school, he recorded the seminal "Mardi Gras Mambo" with his group, the Hawketts, for Chess Records. The exposure with the Hawketts led to solo contracts with Specialty and Instant, where he released a handful of singles that became regional hits in the early '60s. Around 1966, he formed Art Neville and the Sounds with his brothers Aaron and Charles (both vocals), guitarist Leo Nocentelli, drummer Joseph "Zigaboo" Modeliste, and bassist George Porter. The band grew out of informal jam sessions the musicians held in local New Orleans nightclubs. After spending a few months playing under the Sounds name, producer Allen Toussaint and Marshall Sehorn hired the group — without the vocalists — to be the house band for their label Sansu Enterprises.

As the house band for Sansu, the Meters played on records by Earl King, Lee Dorsey, Chris Kenner, and Betty Harris, as well as Toussaint himself. They also performed and recorded on their own, releasing danceable instrumental singles on Josie Records. "Sophisticated Cissy" and "Cissy Strut" became Top Ten R&B hits in the spring of 1969, followed by the number 11 hits "Look-Ka Py Py" and "Chicken Strut" a year later. The Meters stayed at Josie until 1972, and during that entire time they reached the R&B Top 50 consistently, usually placing within the Top 40. In 1972, the group moved to Reprise Records, yet they didn't sever their ties with Sansu, electing to keep Toussaint as their producer and Sehon as their manager. Ironically, the Meters didn't have nearly as many hit singles at Reprise, yet their profile remained remarkably high. If anything, the group became hipper, performing on records by Robert Palmer, Dr. John, Labelle, King Biscuit Boy, and Paul McCartney. By the release of 1975's *Fire on the Bayou*, the Meters had a Top 40 hit with *Rejuvenation*'s "Hey Pocky A-Way" (1974), and they had gained a significant following among rock audience and critics. *Fire on the Bayou* received significant praise, and the group opened for the Rolling Stones on the British band's 1975 and 1976 tours.

During 1975, the Meters embarked on the Wild Tchoupitoulas project with Neville's uncle and cousin George and Amos Landry, two members of the Mardi Gras ceremonial black Indian tribe, the Wild Tchoupitoulas. the Meters, the Landrys and the Neville Brothers — Aaron, Charles, Art and Cyril — were all involved in the recording of the album, which received enthusiastic reviews upon its release in 1976. Cyril joined the Meters after the record's release. Despite all of the acclaim for *The Wild Tchoupitoulas*, its adventurous tendencies indicated that the group was feeling constrained by its signature sound. Such suspicions were confirmed the following year, when they separated from Toussaint and Sehorn, claiming they needed to take control of their artistic direction. Following the split, the Meters released *New Directions* in 1977, but shortly its appearance, Toussaint and Sehorn claimed the rights to the group's name. Instead of fighting, the band broke up, with Art and Cyril forming the Neville Brothers with Aaron and Charles, while the remaining trio became session musicians in New Orleans. Modeliste, in particular, became a well-known professional musician, touring with the New Barbarians in 1979 and moving to LA during the '80s.

The Meters reunited as a touring unit in 1990 with Russell Batiste taking over the drum duties from Modeliste. Four years later, Nocentelli left the band, allegedly because he and Art Neville disagreed whether the band should be paid for samples hip-hop groups took from their old records; he was replaced by Brian Stoltz, who had played with the Neville Brothers. The Meters continued to tour throughout the '90s. — *Stephen Thomas Erlewine*

The Meters / 1969 / Josie ♦♦♦
While this isn't an album in the strictest sense, but a collection of singles, it was certainly welcomed when it was released. This featured some prime cuts from The Meters, the great New Orleans funk ensemble who began doing their own sessions in the late '60s. They only cut two albums for Josie, and both were monsters. Both were later deleted, although the hit singles have since been reissued. — *Ron Wynn*

Look: Ka Py Py / 1970 / Rounder ♦♦♦♦
The Meters' great 1960s singles anticipated the coming of funk. They made short, catchy tunes and scored occasional hits, particularly the single "Look-Ka-Py-Py," one of 12 outstanding tunes on this CD. These were the ultimate party/dance records, and they also showed the link between traditional African rhythms, New Orleans shuffle, second line sounds, soul and funk. Marvelous rhythm music at its hottest. — *Ron Wynn*

Cissy Strut / 1974 / Island ♦♦♦♦
The Meters made their anthemic funk cuts on Josie in the late '60s. The New Orleans crew backed Fats Domino, Lee Dorsey, and Aaron Neville before they started jamming on their own in the late '60s. Island issued this anthology of Josie material in the mid-'70s. It came out in the US too. Rounder has since reissued some of this material. — *Ron Wynn*

Rejuvenation / 1974 / Reprise ♦♦♦
A nice, but not as definitive, mid-'70s Meters session. Their Reprise albums were never as transcendent, energetic, or freewheeling as the Josie tracks, but were better produced and engineered. This was one of the better sessions, and sometimes The Meters seemed to recapture that old New Orleans funk energy. But Reprise's attempts to bring them crossover success inevitably disrupted their chemistry, as they tried to blend a formulaic rock sensibility with the group's close-knit funk. — *Ron Wynn*

The Best of the Meters / 1975 / Virgo ♦♦♦
A good collection of this quintessential New Orleans funk group's best '70s singles for the Reprise label. Of course they did their finest cuts for Josie, but turned in some reasonably good work on Reprise in a more rock/funk direction. "Hey, Pokey-A-Way" was probably the closest Reprise cut to matching the superb Josie singles. But these are the songs that got them gigs with The Rolling Stones and work with Paul McCartney and Robert Palmer, so they did have some value. — *Ron Wynn*

New Directions / 1977 / Warner Brothers ♦♦
This was perhaps the weakest Meters album, with rather mediocre vocals and songs, decent production and arrangements, but little of the fire or zeal that characterized their fine Josie dates and their earlier rock/funk Reprise material. They were nearing the end of the line as a group anyhow, something that this material reflects. — *Ron Wynn*

Good Old Funky Music / 1990 / Rounder ♦♦♦
There are some good moments on this disc, culled from unissued material from the Meters' Josie heyday in the late '60s and early '70s, but there's too much filler. — *Bill Dahl*

The Meters Jam / Mar. 1, 1992 / Rounder ♦♦
The 10 songs on this CD are a mixed bag, mainly because the Meters insisted on singing and simply weren't great vocalists. Their leads and harmonies on "Come Together" and "Bo Diddley," among others, were exuberant, but didn't add much to the proceedings. On the other hand, there haven't been many groups in any style that clicked any more smoothly and soulfully. Their inspired, funky playing almost overshadows the tepid vocals. — *Ron Wynn*

★ **Funkify Your Life** / Feb. 28, 1995 / Rhino ♦♦♦♦♦
Two discs of the Meters is a lot to ask of most casual fans, yet for the devoted few, *Funkify Your Life* is essential. Featuring tracks from both their Josie and Warner years, the double-disc set captures some of the rawest New Orleans funk recorded in the Crescent City. — *Stephen Thomas Erlewine*

★ **Very Best of the Meters** / Jun. 10, 1997 / Rhino ♦♦♦♦♦
In keeping with the drift of Rhino's *Very Best of* volumes, this 16-track disc provides a more concise, budget-minded retrospective for listeners who might not want a set that offers twice as much or more (in this case, Rhino's own two-disc *Funkify Your Life* anthology). That's not necessarily a criti-

cism—funk grooves can get tiring over the course of two hours if you're not a rhythm fiend. Should you want to keep your Meters to the one-sitting level, this smartly chosen, well-annotated set is fine, including all of the cuts ("Cissy Strut," "Sophisticated Cissy," "Look-Ka Py Py," "Hey Pocky A-Way," "Fire on the Bayou") you'd expect to find on a greatest-hits set. — *Richie Unterberger*

The Mighty Clouds of Joy

f. 1959, Los Angeles, CA
Group / Soul, R&B, Black Gospel, Southern Gospel, Traditional Gospel
Contemporary gospel's preeminent group, the Mighty Clouds of Joy carried the torch for the traditional quartet vocal style throughout an era dominated by solo acts and choirs; pioneering a distinctively funky sound which over time gained grudging acceptance even among purists, they pushed spiritual music in new and unexpected directions, even scoring a major disco hit. The Mighty Clouds of Joy were formed in Los Angeles during the mid-1950s by schoolmates Joe Ligon and Johnny Martin; while still in their teens, the original group—which also included brothers Ermant and Elmer Franklin, Leon Polk, and Richard Wallace—made their recorded debut in 1960 with "Steal Away to Jesus," cut for the Peacock label. Their debut LP *Family Circle* arrived a year later. In the years that followed, the Mighty Clouds earned a reputation among gospel's greatest showmen; one of the first groups to incorporate choreographed moves into their act, their nimble footwork and bright, color-coordinated outfits earned them the sobriquet "The Temptations of Gospel." More importantly, they were the first group to add bass, drums, and keyboards to the standard quartet accompaniment of solo guitar, resulting in a sound which horrified traditionalists but appealed to younger listeners—so much so, in fact, that the Mighty Clouds became the first gospel act ever to appear on television's *Soul Train*, where they performed their disco smash "Mighty High." Their crossover success continued with opening slots for secular pop stars including Marvin Gaye, the Rolling Stones, and Paul Simon, whom the group backed during a month-long stint at Madison Square Garden. While lineup changes plagued the Mighty Clouds throughout their career, they remained active through the 1990s; in addition to co-founders Ligon and Wallace, their latter-day incarnation also included Michael McCowin, Wilbert Williams, Johnny Valentine, and Ron Staples. — *Jason Ankeny*

A Bright Side / 1960 / MCA ♦♦♦
The Clouds at their peak. — *Opal Louis Nations*

Family Circle / 1963 / Peacock ♦♦♦♦
Pyrotechnic performances by this sensational group. — *Opal Louis Nations*

The Mighty Clouds Live at the Music Hall / 1966 / Peacock ♦♦♦♦
More church wrecking. — *Opal Louis Nations*

Sing Live Zion Songs / 1968 / Hob ♦♦♦♦
Little Joe Ligon and the group live from Will Rogers Park circa 1958. — *Opal Louis Nations*

The Best of the Mighty Clouds of Joy / 1973 / MCA ♦♦♦♦
Best of the early Peacock material when the quartet was in their prime. — *Opal Louis Nations*

The Best of the Mighty Clouds of Joy, Vol. 2 / 1973 / MCA ♦♦♦
More great singing and shouting from the Peacock vaults. — *Opal Louis Nations*

Live & Direct / 1977 / ABC ♦♦♦♦
Live & Direct is a wonderful, inspiring live recording from the Mighty Clouds of Joy. Although the group was past its peak when they recorded this in the late '70s, they nevertheless retained much of their vocal power, and their interplay is simply breathtaking at times. And, since it features all of their classic material, the album functions as a best-of sampler, and it's certainly not a bad way to become acquainted with this extraordinary group. — *Leo Stanley*

Mighty Clouds of Joy Live / 1990 / MCA ♦♦♦
At the start of their decline in 1971, the Clouds performed and were recorded live at the Apollo Theater in Harlem. Led by the raspy pipes of Little Willie Joe Ligon, the quintet stirred and quelled the audience through a program of gospel standards and personal hits. Boiling points include a devastating version of "Amazing Grace" and testimonial preaching between selections.

Not quite as powerful as the group's 1966 *Live at the Music Hall* album, it's chock full of excitement nevertheless. There's a neglectful lack of pictures and sleeve notes on the otherwise good analog tape transfer. —*Opal Louis Nations, Roots & Rhythm Newsletter*

Memory Lane: The Best of the Mighty Clouds of Joy / 1993 / Word ✦✦✦✦
Word's *Memory Lane: The Best of the Mighty Clouds of Joy* might be a little brief at only ten tracks, but it's a good sampler of the group's latter-day material, including nice performances of such standards as "Wings of Faith," "Walk Around Heaven All Day" and "Will the Circle Be Unbroken." —*Thom Owens*

Glad About It / Oct. 24, 1995 / Hob ✦✦✦✦
Glad About It is a solid effort from the Mighty Clouds of Joy, featuring 12 gospel tracks, both familiar and relatively new. The group has cut better albums, but this is far from bad, and it boasts such fine moments as "There's No Friend Like Jesus," "His Blood for Me," "Have a Little Faith," "Over in Zion," "My Religion" and "Man Can't Get Satisfaction." —*Stephen Thomas Erlewine*

Faith, Mercy, Glory / Jan. 1, 1996 / King ✦✦✦✦
Great collection of recent vintage spiced with previously unissued material. —*Opal Louis Nations*

Glory Hallelujah / Jan. 2, 1996 / MCA Special Products ✦✦✦✦
Ace collection of some of this shouting group's best Peacock sides. —*Opal Louis Nations*

Amos Milburn

b. Apr. 1, 1927, Houston, TX, **d.** Jan. 3, 1980, Houston, TX
Piano, Vocals / Piano Blues, Jump Blues, R&B, West Coast Blues
Boogie piano master Amos Milburn was born in Houston, and he died there a short 52 years later. In between, he pounded out some of the most hellacious boogies of the postwar era, usually recording in Los Angeles for Aladdin Records and specializing in good-natured upbeat romps about booze and its effects (both positive and negative) that proved massive hits during the immediate pre-rock era.

The self-taught 88s ace made a name for himself as the "He-Man Martha Raye" around Houston before joining the Navy and seeing overseas battle action in World War II. When he came out of the service, Milburn played in various Lone Star niteries before meeting the woman whose efforts would catapult him to stardom.

Persistent manager Lola Anne Cullum reportedly barged into Aladdin boss Eddie Mesner's hospital room, toting a portable disc machine with Milburn's demo all cued up. The gambit worked—Amos Milburn signed with Aladdin in 1946. His first date included a thundering "Down the Road Apiece" that presaged the imminent rise of rock 'n' roll. But Milburn was capable of subtler charms too, crooning mellow blues ballads in a Charles Brown-influenced style (the two would later become close friends, playing together frequently).

The first of Milburn's 19 Top Ten R&B smashes came in 1948 with his party classic "Chicken Shack Boogie," which paced the charts and anointed his band with a worthy name (the Aladdin Chickenshackers, natch). A velvet-smooth "Bewildered" displayed the cool after-hours side of Milburn's persona as it streaked up the charts later that year, but it was rollicking horn-driven material such as "Roomin' House Boogie" and "Sax Shack Boogie" that Milburn was renowned for. Milburn's rumbling 88s influenced a variety of famous artists, notably Fats Domino.

With the ascent of "Bad, Bad Whiskey" to the peak of the charts in 1950, Milburn embarked on a string of similarly boozy smashes: "Thinking and Drinking," "Let Me Go Home Whiskey," "One Scotch, One Bourbon, One Beer" (an inebriating round John Lee Hooker apparently enjoyed!), and "Good Good Whiskey" (his last hit in 1954). Alcoholism later brought the pianist down hard, giving these numbers a grimly ironic twist in retrospect. Milburn's national profile rated a series of appearances on the Willie Bryant-hosted mid-'50s TV program *Showtime at the Apollo* (where he gave out with a blistering "Down the Road Apiece").

Aladdin stuck with Milburn long after the hits ceased, dispatching him to New Orleans in 1956 to record with the vaunted studio crew at Cosimo's. There he recut "Chicken Shack Boogie" in a manner so torrid that it's impos-

sible to believe it didn't hit (tenor saxist Lee Allen and drummer Charles "Hungry" Williams blast with atomic power as Milburn happily grunts along with his pounding boogie piano solo). In 1957, he left Aladdin for good.

Amos contributed a fine offering to the R&B Yuletide canon in 1960 with his swinging "Christmas (Comes but Once a Year)" for King. Berry Gordy gave Milburn a comeback forum in 1962, issuing an album on Motown predominated by remakes of his old hits that doesn't deserve its extreme rarity today (even Little Stevie Wonder pitched in on harp for the sessions).

Nothing could jump-start the pianist's fading career by then, though. His health deteriorated to the point where a string of strokes limited his mobility and his left leg was eventually amputated. Not too long after, one of the greatest pioneers in the history of R&B was dead. —*Bill Dahl*

Rockin' the Boogie / 1954 / Aladdin ✦✦✦✦
Just what it promises. —*Bill Dahl*

Let's Have a Party / 1957 / Score ✦✦✦✦
Milburn's Aladdin sides are perfect for any bash. —*Bill Dahl*

The Return of Blues Boss / Apr. 9, 1963 / Motown ✦✦✦
Milburn's sole LP for Motown was an interesting effort that updated his saucy rhythm-and-blues without compromising it. No need to look for the rare original vinyl; it's been reissued in its entirety on *The Motown Sessions, 1962-1964*, which adds several previously unreleased bonus tracks. —*Richie Unterberger*

☆ **The Complete Aladdin Recordings of Amos Milburn** / 1994 / Mosaic ✦✦✦✦✦
Seven discs tracing the entire 1946-1957 Aladdin Records legacy of jump blues pioneer Amos Milburn, whose rippling boogie-based piano talent and predilection of songs about booze made him a postwar R&B superstar. 145 tracks in all (including plenty of unissued goodies) tab this as the ultimate collection for Milburn fans. He boogied like a champ at his first L.A. date for Aladdin with a thundering "Down the Road Apiece" and rocked equally hard a decade later down in New Orleans when he was recutting "Chicken Shack Boogie" with the crew at Cosimo's. Mosaic does their usual elegant presentational job on this R&B legend, not skimping on a thing. Fabulous boxed set. —*Bill Dahl*

★ **Best of Amos Milburn—Down the Road Apiece** / Jan. 11, 1994 / EMI America ✦✦✦✦✦
Pianist Amos Milburn mixed boogie-woogie with vocal energy and intensity to forge a style that was among early R&B's most exciting and appealing. Milburn's 1940s and '50s singles were sometimes fiery and sometimes silly, ranging from drinking songs and celebratory uptempo numbers to stomping instrumentals and an occasional blues or love tune. This excellent 26-track anthology contains such classic Milburn anthems as "Chicken Shack Boogie," "One Scotch, One Bourbon, One Beer," "Let's Have a Party," and "Bad, Bad Whiskey," as well as lesser-known but just as spirited romps. The mastering bolsters the sound, but doesn't deaden it, while Joseph Laredo's liner notes clearly and completely outline Milburn's musical and cultural/historical significance. —*Ron Wynn*

Blues, Barrelhouse & Boogie Woogie: 1946-1955 / 1996 / Capitol ✦✦✦✦
Here's a very reasonable compromise between the pricey Mosaic box and EMI's incomplete single-disc treatment of Milburn's Aladdin legacy: a three-disc, 66-song package that's heavy on boogies and blues and slightly deficient in the ballad department (to that end, his smash "Bewildered" was left off). Everything that is aboard is top-drawer, though—the booze odes, many a party rocker, and a plethora of the double-entendre blues that Milburn reveled in during his early years. The absent 1956 remake of "Chicken Shack Boogie" is a humongous omission, though. —*Bill Dahl*

The Motown Sessions, 1962-1964 / Feb. 1996 / Motown ✦✦✦✦
Signed to Motown years after his peak as an R&B star, Milburn's association with the label turned out to be something of a non-event, producing only an obscure album and flop single. A commercial non-event, that is; Milburn's skills were still intact, resulting in some fine, if somewhat uncharacteristic performances. This compilation reissues that album (*Return of the Blues Boss*) and adds seven unreleased tracks. Milburn may still have been singing blues/R&B, but he was with Motown, which meant that a fair amount of soul-pop flavor inevitably seeped through. You can hear it in the occasional female backup vocals, swinging brass arrangements, and even a brief har-

monica solo by Stevie Wonder on "Chicken Shack Boogie"; the arrangement on "I'll Make It Up to You Somehow" wouldn't have been out of place on an early Mary Wells single. The results are pleasantly surprising, updating Milburn's sound (which would have been quite anachronistic in the early 1960s) into the early soul era. The material is pretty strong, including both bluesy ballads and more uptempo numbers that don't totally smother his boogie-woogie roots. —*Richie Unterberger*

The Best of the Aladdin Recordings / Mar. 19, 1996 / Capitol ◆◆◆◆
Best of the Aladdin Recordings is quite similar to *Best of Amos Milburn—Down the Road Apiece*, which appeared two years before *The Aladdin Recordings*. All the key Milburn tracks are on both collections, and there isn't much difference between the minor cuts, which means either disc is essentially interchangeable and a good addition to a comprehensive R&B collection. —*Thom Owens*

Lizzie Miles (Elizabeth Mary [née Landreaux] Pajaud)

b. Mar. 31, 1895, New Orleans, LA, **d.** Mar. 17, 1963, New Orleans, LA
Vocals / Dixieland, Classic Female Blues
Lizzie Miles was a fine classic blues singer from the 1920s who survived to have a full comeback in the 1950s. She started out singing in New Orleans during 1909-11 with such musicians as King Oliver, Kid Ory, and Bunk Johnson. Miles spent several years touring the South in minstrel shows and playing in theaters. She was in Chicago during 1918-20 and then moved to New York in 1921, making her recording debut the following year. Her recordings from the 1922-30 period mostly used lesser-known players but Louis Metcalf and King Oliver were on two songs apiece and she recorded a pair of duets with Jelly Roll Morton in 1929. Miles sang with A.J. Piron and Sam Wooding, toured Europe during 1924-25 and was active in New York during 1926-31. Illness knocked her out of action for a period but by 1935 she had performed with Paul Barbarin, sang with Fats Waller in 1938, and recorded a session in 1939. Lizzie Miles spent 1943-49 outside of music but in 1950 began a comeback and she often performed with Bob Scobey or George Lewis during her final decade. —*Scott Yanow*

Complete Recorded Works, Vol. 1 (1922-23) / 1922-1923 / Document ◆◆◆◆

Complete Recorded Works, Vol. 2 (1923-28) / 1923-1928 / Document ◆◆◆◆

Complete Recorded Works, Vol. 3 (1928-39) / 1928-1939 / Document ◆◆◆◆

Moans and Blues / 1954 / Cook ◆◆◆◆

With Tony Almerico's Dixieland Band / 1954-1956 / Rondo ◆◆◆
After gaining her initial reputation in the 1920s, Lizzie Miles made a comeback in the 1950s, when she often appeared with Bob Scobey's band. This particular LP is one of several she made for the Cook and Rondo labels late in her career, when her voice was fortunately still in good form. Joined by a spirited New Orleans band, including trumpeter Tony Almerico, trombonist Jack Delaney, and clarinetist Tony Costa, Miles mostly sticks to warhorses, including "Some of These Days," "Bill Bailey," "Waitin' for the Robert E. Lee," and "Darktown Strutters Ball." —*Scott Yanow*

● **Queen Mother of the Rue Royale** / 1955 / Cook ◆◆◆◆
An unjustly forgotten name in classic blues annals. Lizzie Miles was a great entertainer and versatile song stylist who could handle everything from vaudeville to classic blues to traditional New Orleans jazz. She had passed her prime by these recordings, but was still able to retain her grit and intensity while relying on experience rather than power. —*Ron Wynn*

Hot Songs My Mother Taught Me / 1955 / Cook ◆◆◆◆
This is one of the best of Lizzie Miles' 1950s recordings (none of her solo dates have yet been reissued on CD). Eight of the 14 songs find her accompanied by pianist Red Camp; three add the banjo of Albert French; and three are with a Dixieland band headed by trumpeter Tony Almerico. The mostly intimate settings allow the still strong-voiced Miles to put lots of feeling not only into some typical standards, but such numbers as "Take Yo' Finger off It," "A Cottage for Sale," and "Dyin' Rag." —*Scott Yanow*

Steve Miller

b. Oct. 5, 1943, Milwaukee, WI
Vocals, Guitar, Keyboards / Pop-Rock, Blues-Rock, Psychedelic
Steve Miller's career has encompassed two distinct stages: one of the top San Francisco blues-rockers during the late '60s and early '70s, and one of the top-selling pop-rock acts of the mid- to-late '70s and early '80s with hits like "The Joker," "Fly like an Eagle," "Rock'n Me," and "Abracadabra."

Miller was turned on to music by his father, who worked as a pathologist but knew stars like Charles Mingus and Les Paul, whom he brought home as guests; Paul taught the young Miller some guitar chords and let him sit in on a session. Miller formed a blues band, the Marksmen Combo at age 12 with friend Boz Scaggs; the two teamed up again at the University of Wisconsin in a group called the Ardells, later the Fabulous Night Trains. Miller moved to Chicago in 1964 to get involved in the local blues scene, teaming with Barry Goldberg for two years. He then moved to San Francisco and formed the first incarnation of the Steve Miller Blues Band, featuring guitarist James "Curly" Cooke, bassist Lonnie Turner, and drummer Tim Davis. The band built a local following through a series of free concerts and backed Chuck Berry in 1967 at a Fillmore date later released as a live album. Scaggs moved to San Francisco later that year and replaced Cooke in time to play the Monterey Pop Festival; it was the first of many personnel changes. Capitol signed the group as the Steve Miller Band following the festival.

The band flew to London to record *Children of the Future*, which was praised by critics and received some airplay on FM radio. It established Miller's early style as a blues-rocker influenced but not overpowered by psychedelia. The follow-up, *Sailor*, has been hailed as perhaps Miller's best early effort; it reached number 24 on the *Billboard* album charts and consolidated Miller's fan base. A series of high-quality albums with similar chart placements followed; while Miller remained a popular artist, pop radio failed to pick up on any of his material at this time, even though tracks like "Space Cowboy" and "Brave New World" had become FM rock staples. 1971's *Rock Love* broke Miller's streak with a weak band lineup and poor material, and Miller followed it with the spotty *Recall the Beginning ... A Journey from Eden.* Things began to look even worse for Miller when he broke his neck in a car accident and subsequently developed hepatitis, which put him out of commission for most of 1972 and early 1973.

Miller spent his recuperation time reinventing himself as a blues-influenced pop-rocker, writing compact, melodic, catchy songs. This approach was introduced on his 1973 LP *The Joker* and was an instant success, with the album going platinum and the title track hitting number one on the pop charts. Now an established star, Miller elected to take three years off. He purchased a farm and built his own recording studio, at which he crafted the wildly successful albums *Fly like an Eagle* and *Book of Dreams* at approximately the same time. *Fly like an Eagle* was released in 1976 and eclipsed its predecessor in terms of quality and sales (over four million copies) in spite of the long down time in between. It also gave Miller his second number one hit with "Rock'n Me," plus several other singles. *Book of Dreams* was almost as successful, selling over three million copies and producing several hits as well. All of the hits from Miller's first three pop-oriented albums were collected on *Greatest Hits 1974-1978*, which to date has sold over six million copies and remains a popular catalog item.

Miller again took some time off, not returning again until late 1981 with the disappointing *Circle of Love.* Just six months later, Miller rebounded with *Abracadabra*; the title track gave him his third number one single and proved to be his last major commercial success. None of his remaining '80s albums were consistent enough to be critically or commercially successful. A box set covering most of Miller's career was compiled by the artist himself in 1994. —*Steve Huey*

Children of the Future / 1968 / Capitol ◆◆◆◆
Recorded in England with producer Glyn Johns (the Who, the Faces), this debut effort presented Miller as someone who was not only immersed in the blues but also fascinated with sound effects and sequencing, not unlike the Moody Blues or Pink Floyd. As a whole, this album flows nicely. Among the album's many highlights are "Baby's Callin' Me Home" (written by Boz Scaggs), "Stepping Stone," "Roll with It," "Junior Saw It Happen," and the spacey Mellotron-heavy ballad "In My First Mind." —*Rick Clark*

Sailor / 1968 / Capitol ✦✦✦✦
Less than six months after *Children of the Future,* Miller's solid follow-up proved that he wasn't a flash in the pan. Like its predecessor, *Sailor* dabbled in neat segues and effects, but to a lesser degree. Miller shines on the gently acoustic "Quicksilver Girl" and haunting "Dear Mary." *Sailor* has a couple of great rockers with "Living in the USA" (Miller's first hit at number 94) and "Dime a Dance Romance," penned by soon-to-be-departing member Boz Scaggs. — *Rick Clark*

Your Saving Grace / 1969 / Capitol ✦✦✦
This effort is a little more subdued than *Brave New World,* with cuts like "Baby's House" and "Feel So Glad." However, Miller does lay down an authoritative groove on "Don't Let Nobody Turn You Around," while "Little Girl" features some excellent, tasty lead guitar work. Miller also included a spacey reworking of "Motherless Children." Lonnie Turner's daft "Last Wombat in Mecca" is the album's only low point. Considering this was the fourth album Miller released in two years, the weakness is hardly worth mentioning. — *Rick Clark*

Brave New World / 1969 / Capitol ✦✦✦✦
From the anthemic opening title cut, accelerating through to the crash-and-burn closer, "My Dark Hour" (featuring Paul McCartney ghosting on drums, bass, and vocals under the pseudonym of Paul Ramon), *Brave New World* is a tour de force. Other standout tracks include Miller's atmospheric "Seasons," "Kow Kow," and "Space Cowboy," an FM rock classic. — *Rick Clark*

Number Five / 1970 / Capitol ✦✦✦
For this effort Miller went to Nashville, among other places, and recorded a wide range of material that covered everything from waxing poetic about eating hot chili to railing at the industrial military complex. In spite of this album's uneven material, it possesses many strong tunes, including "Going to Mexico," "Good Morning," and "Going to the Country." It also includes "Steve Miller's Midnight Tango." — *Rick Clark*

Rock Love / 1971 / Capitol ✦

● **Anthology** / 1972 / Capitol ✦✦✦✦
This is a smartly assembled best-of collection that provides a good introduction to Miller's work up to this point. Those interested in digging deeper than this should check out *Brave New World, Sailor, Children of the Future,* and *Your Saving Grace,* in that order. — *Rick Clark*

Recall the Beginning: A Journey from Eden / 1972 / Capitol ✦✦✦
After the miserable album *Rock Love,* Miller rebounded somewhat with *Recall the Beginning—A Journey from Eden.* One side is largely throwaway stuff, but the other half features a string of dreamy compositions that culminates with the haunting "Journey from Eden." "Love's Riddle," another track from that grouping, is also fine. — *Rick Clark*

The Joker / 1973 / Capitol ✦✦✦
While not as strong as some of his earlier work, *The Joker*'s title cut (built from a simple guitar riff) was Miller's first huge number one single. "Sugar Babe" and "Something to Believe In" were also highlights. Nevertheless, Miller's focus on basic catchy material laid the groundwork for his incredibly successful late-'70s albums. — *Rick Clark*

Fly like an Eagle / 1976 / Capitol ✦✦✦✦
In his effort to create the ultimate playable album, Miller re-incorporated his interest in spacey sound effects and neat segues and synthesized them with a batch of tightly crafted light pop-rock tunes. The result generated a load of seamless hits like "Take the Money and Run," "Rock'n Me," and the title track. — *Rick Clark*

Book of Dreams / 1977 / Capitol ✦✦✦✦
Recorded at the same time as *Fly like an Eagle,* this album repeated the same formula, with the same big results. Hits included "Jet Airliner" (a slight reworking of an old R&B tune by Paul Pena), "Jungle Love," and "Swingtown." — *Rick Clark*

Greatest Hits 1974-1978 / 1978 / Capitol ✦✦✦✦
Greatest Hits 1974-1978 collects the majority of Steve Miller's biggest hits— "The Joker," "Take the Money and Run," "Rock'n Me," "Fly like an Eagle," "Jet Airliner," "Jungle Love," "Swingtown"—and seven album tracks that received a fair amount of airplay on album rock radio. The collection only covers a total of three albums—*The Joker, Fly like an Eagle, Book of Dreams*—with the latter two providing the bulk of the material. Because of this, "Living in

the USA," one of Miller's biggest hits of the late '60s/early '70s, isn't included but it isn't missed, since all of his other hits of the '70s are included. The thoroughness of *Greatest Hits 1974-1978* makes it an excellent introduction to Miller and for many casual fans, it also means that they can contain their Steve Miller collection to one disc. — *Stephen Thomas Erlewine*

Circle of Love / 1981 / Capitol ✦✦✦
After a four-year layoff, Miller returns with a truly weird album. One half of it is a wandering space-funk jam called "Macho City," the other half featured a couple of decent tunes, which were singles, "Heart like a Wheel" and "Circle of Love." — *Rick Clark*

Abracadabra / 1982 / Capitol ✦✦✦
Even though the catchy title track became a number one hit, returning Miller to the limelight, this album lacked the focus and strong material to provide more staying power. — *Rick Clark*

Steve Miller Band: Live! / 1983 / Capitol ✦✦
This decent live album features a cross-section of hits, including "Living in the USA." — *Rick Clark*

Italian X Rays / 1984 / Capitol ✦✦

Living in the 20th Century / Dec. 15, 1987 / Capitol ✦✦
Miller does a half-assed return to his blues roots with this outing, which was dedicated to Jimmy Reed. Among the more promising numbers was "Nobody but You Baby," but heavily processed rhythm tracks marred what might have been a strong album. — *Rick Clark*

Born 2B Blue / 1988 / Capitol ✦✦✦
After a string of incredibly spotty albums, Miller quits noodling around with synthesizers and gimmicky effects and knuckles down with a smooth collection of jazz standards. Utilizing the formidable talents of vibe player Milt Jackson, Phil Woods (alto sax), and Ben Sidran (keys and coproduction), Miller creates an album that is playful and sophisticated. While his guitar playing is downplayed, Miller shines on "Just a Little Bit," "God Bless the Child," and the swinging "Red Top." — *Rick Clark*

The Best of Steve Miller (1968-1973) / 1990 / Capitol ✦✦✦✦
The Best of 1968-1973 is a solid collection that features many of the highlights from Steve Miller's first five years of recording, including "The Joker," "Living in the USA," "Space Cowboy," and "Gangster of Love." This compilation isn't as consistently thrilling as *Greatest Hits 1974-1978,* which also features "The Joker," and it's not as sharply assembled as 1972's *Anthology,* but it remains an adequate overview of Miller's early records, especially for fans only familiar with *Greatest Hits.* — *Stephen Thomas Erlewine*

Wide River / Jun. 8, 1993 / Polydor ✦✦
Steve Miller returns to the bluesy pop-rock sound that made his career so successful with *Wide River,* a pleasant collection of new songs that will appeal greatly to fans of "The Joker," "Take the Money and Run," and "Rock'n Me." — *AMG*

Steve Miller Band [Box Set] / Jul. 26, 1994 / Capitol ✦✦✦✦
This is one case where the project would have, more than likely, been better served if it was compiled without the help of the artist. This three-disc set is broken down into pre-"Joker" (vol. 1), post-"Joker" (vol. 2), and "Blues" (vol. 3). While Miller aced Vol. 2's song selection, and the third disc is enjoyably playable, it's obvious he holds much of his earlier work in disregard. It's hard to justify why he would perform horrible editing jobs and fade-outs on some of his best early work. Why didn't Miller just include *Anthology,* with a couple of extra cuts, as Disc One? The set does feature great sound and the liner notes and the pictures in the booklet are first-rate. — *Rick Clark*

Roy Milton

b. Jul. 31, 1907, Wynnewood, OK, **d.** Sep. 18, 1983, Los Angeles, CA
Drums, Vocals / R&B, Jump Blues, Blues Jazz, West Coast Blues
As in-the-pocket drummer of his own jump blues combo, the Solid Senders, Roy Milton was in a perfect position to drive his outfit just as hard or soft as he so desired. With his stellar sense of swing, Milton did just that; his steady backbeat on his 1946 single for Art Rupe's fledgling Juke Box imprint, "R.M. Blues," helped steer it to the uppermost reaches of the R&B charts (his assured vocal didn't hurt either).

Milton spent his early years on an Indian reservation in Oklahoma (his maternal grandmother was a native American) before moving to Tulsa. He sang with Ernie Fields' territory band during the late '20s and began doubling on drums when the band's regular trapsman got arrested one fateful evening. In the mood to leave Fields in 1933, Milton wandered west to Los Angeles and formed the Solid Senders. 1945 was a big year for him—along with signing with Juke Box (soon to be renamed Specialty), the band filmed three soundies with singer June Richmond.

"R.M. Blues" was such a huge seller that it established Specialty as a viable concern for the long haul. Rupe knew a good thing when he saw it, recording Milton early and often through 1953. He was rewarded with 19 Top Ten R&B hits by the Solid Senders, including "Milton's Boogie," "True Blues," "Hop, Skip, and Jump," "Information Blues," "Oh Babe" (a torrid cover of Louis Prima's jivey jump), and "Best Wishes." Milton's resident boogie piano specialist, Camille Howard, also sang on several Milton platters, including the 1947 hit "Thrill Me," concurrently building a solo career on Specialty.

After amassing a voluminous catalog as one of Specialty's early bedrocks, Milton moved on to Dootone, King (there he cut the delectable instrumental "Succotash"), and Warwick (where he eked out a minor R&B hit in 1961, "Red Light") with notably less commercial success. Sadly, even though he helped pioneer the postwar R&B medium, rock 'n' roll had rendered Roy Milton an anachronism.

The drummer remained active nonetheless, thrilling the throng at the 1970 Monterey Jazz Festival as part of Johnny Otis' all-star troupe. It's a safe bet he was swinging until the very end. —*Bill Dahl*

The Great Roy Milton / 1963 / Specialty ◆◆◆

Specialty / Feb. 1978 / Specialty ◆◆◆

R.M. Blues / 1985 / Specialty ◆◆◆

Specialty's *R.M. Blues* is a fine collection that features 15 highlights from Roy Milton's jumping Specialty recordings. While his time at Specialty was unquestionably the finest period of his career, and there are some timeless performances here ("R.M. Blues," "Night and Day," "Wakin' Up Baby," "Milton's Boogie," "Information Blues"), these same recordings have appeared on better, more comprehensive CD reissues which are preferable to this LP edition. —*Thom Owens*

★ **Roy Milton & His Solid Senders** / 1990 / Specialty ◆◆◆◆◆

Certainly this is the place to go for Milton's most popular and influential material—a whopping 18 of the 25 cuts made the R&B Top Ten in the late '40s and early '50s. These include such classics as "R.M. Blues," "The Huckebuck," and "Hop, Skip, & Jump" (given a great rockabilly treatment in the 1950s by the Collins Kids). All of the tracks are prime jump blues, Milton occasionally slowing down the boogies into ballads; one number ("Thrill Me") features fellow jump blues star Camille Howard on vocals. —*Richie Unterberger*

Groovy Blues, Vol. 2 / 1992 / Specialty ◆◆◆◆

The rarities and unissued material begin to pop up on *Vol. 2*, making it even more of a feast for collectors. Milton's Solid Senders, featuring pianist/singer Camille Howard, guitarist Johnny Rogers, and a crew of roaring saxmen, were one of the tightest and most respected on the Coast. —*Bill Dahl*

Blowin' with Roy / 1994 / Specialty ◆◆◆◆

The third and presumably final entry in Specialty's exhaustive Milton reissue series is by no means a makeweight affair. Even when the Solid Senders tackled Tin Pan Alley fare like "Along the Navajo Trail," "Coquette," and "When I Grow Too Old to Dream," they swung 'em. More late-'40s/early-'50s rarities and unissued items galore. —*Bill Dahl*

Roy Milton Blues / Speed ◆◆◆

Exciting, stomping, vintage R&B by a great bandleader. —*Ron Wynn*

Mississippi Heat

f. 1992, Chicago, IL
Group / Modern Electric Blues, Contemporary Blues
A contemporary blues combo resurrecting the vintage Chicago sound of the 1950s, Mississippi Heat was formed in the Windy City in 1992 by vocalist/drummer Robert Covington, harpist Pierre Lacocque, guitarists Billy Flynn and James Wheeler, and bassist Bob Stroger. While remaining a fixture on the local club circuit, the band's lineup remained in flux in the years to follow; Covington exited in 1993, and was replaced by vocalist Deitra Farr and drummer Allen Kirk in time to record their debut LP *Straight From the Heart. Learned the Hard Way* followed in 1994, with *Thunder in My Heart*

appearing a year later; both Farr and Kirk exited in 1996, and in 1997 Mississippi Heat welcomed vocalists Mary Lane and Zora Young, pianist Barrelhouse Chuck and drummer Kenny Smith. —*Jason Ankeny*

Straight from the Heart / 1993 / Van der Linden ◆◆◆

Debut by this solid mainstream Chicago outfit, *Straight from the Heart* is harp and guitar dominated. —*Bill Dahl*

● **Learned the Hard Way** / 1994 / Van der Linden ◆◆◆◆

More impressive work by this newcomer group with a classic approach; veteran Deitra Farr is an exceptional vocalist. —*Bill Dahl*

Mississippi Sheiks

f. 1926, Jackson, MS, **db.** 193?
Group / Country Blues, Prewar Country Blues
One of the classic string bands of the late '20s and early '30s, this group featured the talents of Walter Vinson, Bo Carter, and Lonnie Chatmon in various configurations.

Based in Jackson, MS, the group took their name from the Rudolph Valention movie *The Sheik*. Several years after they began performing, the group recorded their first session in 1930. Over the next five years, they cut nearly 70 songs, which ranged from old-timey string songs to racy blues. During this time, the core of the group consisted of fiddler Lonnie Chatmon and guitarist Walter Vinson, with guitarists Bo Carter and Sam Chatmon joining the group frequently; both Carter and Sam also had successful solo careers, which occasionally prevented them from performing with the group.

The Mississippi Sheiks retained their popularity until the end of the '30s, when they slowly faded away from view. —*Cub Koda & Stephen Thomas Erlewine*

☆ **Mississippi Sheiks Complete Recorded Works, Vols. 1-4** / 1991 / Document ◆◆◆◆◆

There's absolutely no way you can go wrong with this superlative four-CD import set of this seminal blues band. Covers everything they ever recorded from 1930 to 1936. —*Cub Koda*

★ **Stop & Listen** / Yazoo ◆◆◆◆◆

Stop and Listen collects 20 tracks the Mississippi Sheiks recorded in the early '30s, gathering together most of their best-known material (including "Sitting on Top of the World"), plus the previously unreleased "Livin' in a Strain." These records are of significant historical importance and this is the definitive compilation of this groundbreaking—and popular—string band. —*Thom Owens*

Mr. B (Mark Lincoln Braun)

b. Michigan
Piano / Piano Blues
Mark Lincoln Braun (aka Mr. B) plays boogie-woogie piano the traditional way, with blues and jazz elements. The Detroit-based artist has released six albums since 1984: *B's Bounce, Detroit Special* (1985), *Shining the Pearls* (1987), *Partners in Time* (1988), *My Sunday Best* (1991) and *Blue Ivory* (1991), a compilation with Roosevelt Sykes, Henry Gray and Boogie-Woogie Red. —*John Bush*

Shining the Pearls / May 1987 / Blind Pig ◆◆◆

Mr. B's *Shining the Pearls* has some fine moments, especially when the pianist sticks to the blues. However, the album suffers from somewhat meandering arrangements and the lack of a rhythm section to keep the whole thing in focus. —*Thom Owens*

Partners in Time / 1988 / Blind Pig ◆◆◆

Partners in Time is a typically tasteful set from Mr. B, featuring a selection of originals peppered with a couple of classic covers. The pianist shows that he's comfortable with the style by dropping allusions to other players, pulling it all together into an enjoyable boogie-woogie romp. —*Thom Owens*

My Sunday Best / 1991 / Schoolkids ◆◆◆◆

Mr. B. (Mark Braun) is an exciting boogie-woogie pianist inspired by Little Brother Montgomery, Boogie Woogie Red, and Sunnyland Slim who also sounds a bit like Ray Bryant in spots. His 1991 live recording (taken from several performances) puts the emphasis on the blues either at romping tempos or as slow drags. Roy Brooks plays drums on half of the dozen numbers (including a spot on musical saw during "Blues for a Carpenter"), Mr. B sings effectively on Blind John Davis' "When I Lost My Baby" and "Roll 'em Pete," and there is enough variety during this spirited set to hold one's interest throughout. The last selection is a bit odd, for when Mark Hynes suddenly starts playing tenor, the performance quickly fades out. But other than that minor (and unexplained) fault, this is a fine set recommended to fans of blues piano. — *Scott Yanow*

● **Hallelujah Train** / Sep. 3, 1994 + Jan. 7, 1995 / Schoolkids ✦✦✦✦
Mr. B (Mark Braun) is a talented boogie-woogie pianist who on this CD teams up successfully with bassist Paul Keller's Bird of Paradise orchestra, a seven-year-old big band from Michigan. The arrangements smoothly integrate Mr. B. into the orchestra and these enthusiastic live performances are often quite memorable. Although largely a "no-name" big band, the many soloists are consistently talented (with the standouts being Mark Hynes on tenor, altoist Scott Peterson and trumpeter Paul Finkbeiner) and the pianist is in consistently inspired form. Highlights include "Hallelujah Train," "Brauny," tributes to Little Brother Montgomery, Horace Silver, and Eddie Palmieri, an exciting rendition of "Down the Road Apiece," "Air Mail Special" and a lengthy "B's Boogie Woogie." Highly recommended. — *Scott Yanow*

McKinley Mitchell

b. Dec. 25, 1934, Jackson, MS, **d**. Jan. 18, 1986, Chicago Heights, IL
Vocals / R&B, Soul, Electric Blues, Soul Blues
Blessed with an extraordinary set of soaring pipes, McKinley Mitchell waxed a series of superb Chicago soul platters during the 1960s, later veering stylistically closer to contemporary blues in his last years of performing.
At age 16, Mitchell was already fronting a gospel group, the Hearts of Harmony, in Jackson. After spending time singing spirituals in Springfield, MS, and Philadelphia, Mitchell hit Chicago in 1958 and went secular. A rocking debut for the tiny Boxer label the next year preceded his signing with George Leaner's fledgling One-derful logo in 1961.
His first single for the firm, the gorgeous soul ballad "The Town I Live In," proved a national R&B hit and launched the imprint in high style. Mitchell's One-derful follow-ups, including the imaginative "A Bit of Soul," failed to equal the heights of his first single; neither did 45s for Chess (produced by Willie Dixon) and a variety of Dixon-owned labels.
Finally, in 1977, Mitchell returned to the R&B charts with "The End of the Rainbow," another beautiful R&B ballad, for Malaco's Chimneyville subsidiary. An eponymous LP for the label the next year stunningly showcased Mitchell's still-potent voice on a program that combined blues and soul material. A 1984 LP for Retta's, *I Won't Be Back for More*, was among the singer's last releases (by then, he was back living in Jackson). — *Bill Dahl*

● **Complete Malaco Collection** / 1992 / Waldoxy ✦✦✦✦
The former Chicago soul singer found new life and a second chance at the brass ring at Malaco during the late '70s. The gent with the soaring pipes wrote the touching ballad "The End of the Rainbow" himself; seldom have singer and song matched any closer. — *Bill Dahl*

Featuring 12 Great Songs / P-Vine ✦✦✦✦
Until someone sorts out precisely who owns the masters originally on Chicago's One-derful label, we'll have to make do (if we can find it, of course) with this Japanese vinyl collection of Mitchell's early-'60s R&B gems. Includes his haunting first hit, "The Town I Live In," and a clever "A Bit of Soul." — *Bill Dahl*

Prince Phillip Mitchell

b. 1945, Louisville, KY
Vocals, Guitar, Piano, Percussion / Disco, Soul, Soul Blues
A veteran composer, vocalist, guitarist, and pianist, Prince Phillip Mitchell's roots are in vintage R&B, although he's better known for soul tunes. Mitchell sang with both The Premiers and The Checkmates in the late '50s and early '60s. He was also a dancer with The Bean Brothers in Los Angeles. Mitchell had hits recorded by Mel & Tim, Millie Jackson, Norman Connors, Joe Simon, and Candi Staton, but hasn't had as much luck on his own as a vocalist. His only moderate hit was "One on One" for Atlantic in 1978, and it only cracked the R&B Top 40. Mitchell has also recorded for Event and Ichiban. — *Ron Wynn*

● **Loner** / 199 / Ichiban ✦✦✦✦
Vocalist/composer Prince Phillip Mitchell sings a mix of bluesy soul and soulful blues on this early '90s date for Ichiban, the Atlanta-based Southern soul and blues label. Mitchell, always a fine, exuberant, earthy vocalist, sounded strong and convincing, but this album did little beyond the South, as has been the case with the bulk of Ichiban material. Fans who preferred the rough songs Mitchell cut in the '60s and early '70s before joining Norman Connors will enjoy hearing him back in that style. — *Ron Wynn*

Top of the Line / Atlantic ✦✦✦
It didn't receive much attention upon its initial release, nor has it gained much of a following in the years since, but *Top of the Line* is a solid soul album. Its production is a little slick, but Prince Phillip Mitchell's vocals are in good form, making the mediocre songs on the record fairly enjoyable. — *Thom Owens*

Little Brother Montgomery

b. Apr. 18, 1906, Kentwood, LA, **d**. Sep. 6, 1985, Champaign, IL
Piano, Vocals / Piano Blues
A notable influence to the likes of Sunnyland Slim and Otis Spann, pianist "Little Brother" Montgomery's lengthy career spanned both the earliest years of blues history and the electrified Chicago scene of the 1950s.
By age 11, Montgomery had given up on attending school to instead play in Louisiana juke joints. He came to Chicago as early as 1926 and made his first 78s in 1930 for Paramount (the booty that day in Grafton, WI, included two of Montgomery's enduring signature items, "Vicksburg Blues" and "No Special Rider"). Bluebird recorded Montgomery more prolifically in 1935-36 in New Orleans.
In 1942, Little Brother Montgomery settled down to a life of steady club gigs in Chicago, his repertoire alternating between blues and traditional jazz (he played Carnegie Hall with Kid Ory's Dixieland band in 1949). Otis Rush benefitted from his sensitive accompaniment on several of his 1957-58 Cobra dates, while Buddy Guy recruited him for similar duties when he nailed Montgomery's "First Time I Met the Blues" in a supercharged revival for Chess in 1960. That same year, Montgomery cut a fine album for Bluesville with guitarist Lafayette "Thing" Thomas that remains one of his most satisfying sets.
With his second wife, Janet Floberg, Montgomery formed his own little record company, FM, in 1969. The first 45 on the logo, fittingly enough, was a reprise of "Vicksburg Blues," with a vocal by Chicago chanteuse Jeanne Carroll (her daughter Karen is following in her footsteps around the Windy City). — *Bill Dahl*

● **Tasty Blues** / 1960 / Original Blues Classics ✦✦✦✦
Unfortunately not available on CD, here's a very attractive example of a pianist with roots dug deep in pre-war tradition updating his style just enough to sound contemporary for 1960. With a little help from bassist Julian Euell and Lafayette Thomas (better-known as Jimmy McCracklin's guitarist), Montgomery swoops through his seminal "Vicksburg Blues" and "No Special Rider" with enthusiasm and élan. — *Bill Dahl*

Little Brother Montgomery / 1961 / Decca ✦✦

Chicago: The Living Legends / 1961 / Original Blues Classics ✦✦✦✦
Chicago: The Living Legends was recorded live at the Birdhouse in Chicago. Much of the record is performed by Montgomery solo, although there's a handful of wonderful cuts that feature him with a small group of traditional jazz musicians. Most of the album is devoted to classic songs from the likes of Duke Ellington and Jelly Roll Morton, yet there are a couple of originals thrown in the mix as well. It's all distinguished by Montgomery's wonderful, laidback performances, which make this a little gem. — *Thom Owens*

Piano, Vocal, and Band Blues / Jul. 1962 / Riverside ✦✦✦

Goodbye Mister Blues / 1973-1976 / Delmark ✦✦✦
While Eurreal "Little Brother" Montgomery was among blues' greatest barrelhouse and boogie pianists, he was also well versed in traditional jazz. This disc's 13 cuts feature him working with The State Street Swingers, an early jazz unit, doing faithful recreations of such chestnuts as "South Rampart St. Parade," "Riverside Blues," and "Panama Rag." Montgomery's vocals were stately, yet exuberant, while his piano solos were loose and firmly in the spirit, showing the link between early jazz and blues. While the emphasis is more on interaction and ensemble playing than individual voices, players expertly maximized their solo time. This is a fine example of a vintage style. — *Ron Wynn*

At Home / 1990 / Earwig ✦✦✦

Very informally recorded for the most part in the latter days of the fabulous pianist's career, these tapes provide a glimpse at what Montgomery played to please himself (and wife Jan, of course). —*Bill Dahl*

Complete Recorded Works (1930-1936) / 1992 / Document ✦✦✦✦

Document's *Complete Recorded Works (1930-1936)* is an invaluable anthology geared towards academics and completists; it offers an exhaustive overview of Little Brother Montgomery's recordings, but one that will be of marginal interest to more casual listeners due to its exacting chronological sequencing, poor fidelity (all cuts are transferred from original acetates and 78s), and overwhelming number of performances. —*Thom Owens*

Complete Recorded Works (1930-1954) / Jun. 2, 1994 / Document ✦✦✦✦

Coco Montoya

b. 1951, Santa Monica, CA
Guitar, Vocals / Modern Electric Blues

Though he grew up as a drummer and was raised on rock 'n' roll, Coco Montoya became an outstanding blues guitarist in the '90s, after stints in the bands of Albert Collins and John Mayall. Montoya debuted as a leader in 1995 with the Blind Pig album *Gotta Mind to Travel*, and garnered an award as Best New Blues Artist at the following year's Handy Awards ceremonies.

Born in Santa Monica, Montoya played drums for a local rock band that toured the region during the mid-'70s, playing in area clubs. Although he had recently been turned on to blues at an Albert King show, he was somewhat unprepared to sit in with another blues legend—the Iceman, Albert Collins—when a bar-owner friend of Montoya invited the bluesman to play at his nightclub. Though his inexperience showed, the young drummer impressed Collins enough to hire him for a Pacific Northwest tour three months later. The tour soon ended, but the pair's affiliation remained for over five years, while Montoya learned much about the handling of blues guitar from the Master of the Telecaster.

By the early '80s, Coco Montoya was back in the small-time nightclub business, playing guitar with several regional bands. At one night's show, he realized that John Mayall was in the audience, so he dedicated a cover of "All Your Love" to the British blues maestro. The song prompted Mayall to hire Montoya as lead guitarist for a new version of the Bluesbreakers he had formed. Despite the enormous pressure of filling a spot once held by Eric Clapton and Peter Green, Montoya jumped at the opportunity.

His first album with the Bluesbreakers came in 1985. John Mayall had not released an album in five years at that point, and the Bluesbreakers had been dead for over 15, but the live album *Behind the Iron Curtain* proved Mayall's viability, thanks mostly to the fiery work of Montoya. The guitarist appeared on three studio albums with Mayall & the Bluesbreakers, but then struck out on his own by the mid-'90s. Signed to Blind Pig, Montoya released-*Gotta Mind to Travel* in 1995, with help from Mayall and another former Bluesbreaker compatriot, rhythm guitarist Debbie Davies. After years of toil under Collins and Mayall, Montoya was finally in the spotlight, and his award as Best New Blues Artist of 1996 proved quite ironic, given his years of experience. His second album, *Ya Think I'd Know Better*, was followed by 1997's *Just Let Go*.—*John Bush*

Gotta Mind to Travel / 1995 / Blind Pig ✦✦✦✦

Years of apprenticeship with Albert Collins and John Mayall paid off handsomely for Montoya on this debut effort. Even with help from some famous friends (Debbie Davies, Al Kooper, Richie Hayward [Little Feat], and both former employers), Montoya asserts himself as the focal point. Sadly, this was one of Collins' last studio appearances before his death, playing on the Lowell Fulson-penned "Talking Woman Blues" (commonly known as "Honey Hush"). Although Montoya showcases his massive guitar muscle, it is merely a fraction of the power of his live performances. —*Char Ham*

● **Ya Think I'd Know Better** / May 1996 / Blind Pig ✦✦✦✦

With his second album *Ya Think I'd Know Better*, Coco Montoya ditches the guest stars and opts for a menu of pure, unadulterated Montoya. The results are quite impressive, to say the least. For the moment, overlook his somewhat pedestrian vocals and just concentrate on his scintillating guitar work. It's no secret that Montoya cultivated a reputation as one of the finest guitarists of the '80s and '90s through his session work, but even those familiar

with his gutsy, electrifying style will be taken aback by the stylistic variety and musical depth on *Ya Think I'd Know Better*. Montoya even pulls skunk-hot solos out of the most predictable blues-rockers, while his smoldering solos on slower numbers like "Dyin' Flu" are passionate and moving. Best of all, Coco puts down his electric for acoustic romps like the earthy "Hiding Place." In short, *Ya Think I'd Know Better* answers the question whether Coco Montoya is a vital bluesman for the '90s, and the answer is an emphatic "yes!" — *Thom Owens*

Just Let Go / Sep. 23, 1997 / Blind Pig ✦✦✦✦

Coco Montoya's often ferocious guitar is the main reason to acquire this 1997 release. His singing is expressive and reasonably effective, but it is the blazing guitar solos that make one wish that he would record a full set of instrumentals; "Cool Like Dat" is a real cooker. Montoya performs some soul, R&B, and even country-tinged music on the set but he is at his best on the blues, particularly the B.B. King-inspired "Do What You Want to Do." Although his backup band is fine, this interesting if not quite essential release is primarily a showcase for the passionate Montoya. Recommended in particular to fans of the rock side of the blues. —*Scott Yanow*

John Mooney

b. Apr. 3, 1955, East Orange, NJ
Guitar, Vocals / Modern Acoustic Blues, Ragtime

John Mooney is a slide guitarist, working primarily in a traditionalist Delta acoustic style. Originally hailing from Rochester, NY, Mooney learned his craft first hand from country blues legend Son House. Later in his career, he moved to New Orleans, switched to electric guitar and began enlivening his music with Second Line rhythms indigenous to the area.

Born in New Jersey but raised in Rochester, New York, John Mooney began playing guitar following a meeting with Son House, who also lived in Rochester. Mooney learned the basics of blues guitar from House and he returned the favor by supporting the guitarist during the mid-'70s. In 1976, Mooney relocated to New Orleans and within a year of his arrival, he landed a contract with Blind Pig. In 1977, he released his debut album, *Comin' Your Way*.

After performing straight acoustic Delta blues for several years, Mooney changed his musical direction in 1983, when he formed Bluesiana, a more eclectic—and electric—outfit. Throughout the '80s, he toured and recorded with Bluesiana, opening for the likes of Albert King, Bonnie Raitt, and Clarence "Gatemouth" Brown. After a few years of touring, Mooney was able to sign another record contract, releasing *Telephone King* on the Powerhouse label. Throughout the late '80s and early '90s, Mooney toured consistently and released albums on a variety of different record labels. —*Cub Koda & Stephen Thomas Erlewine*

Comin' Your Way / 1979 / Blind Pig ✦✦✦

This album features acoustic guitar and arresting vocals on high-energy blues. —*AMG*

Late Last Night / 1980 / Bullseye Blues ✦✦✦✦

Bluesman John Mooney has a very appealing tone in his slide guitar work, a relatively strong voice and, by varying moods, subject matter and grooves, he put together a particularly strong program for his Bullseye Blues debut. Influenced by both the country blues and country music, Mooney's guitar acts as both a contrasting and a complementary voice to his vocals, sometimes functioning in unison and other times as an equal partner in a musical "conversation." Enjoyable music. — *Scott Yanow*

Telephone Blues / Mar. 1984 / Powerhouse ✦✦✦

● **Telephone King** / 1991 / Blind Pig ✦✦✦✦

Contemporary blues musicians tend to sound more reverential than stirring, but not John Mooney. He's not doing tributes, he's having a party, and that's the spirit that makes this session both intriguing and enjoyable. —*Ron Wynn*

Testimony / 1992 / Domino ✦✦✦✦

Testimony captures the driving intensity of John Mooney's live shows. Recorded with a stellar supporting band—featuring drummer Johnny Vidcovich and the Meters' bassist George Porter, Jr.—*Testimony* featuring seven covers (including cuts by Robert Johnson and Son House) and seven originals, which are easily among the best that Mooney has ever written. But the key to the record is the sound—not only is Mooney's guitar playing hot and greasy, but there's a tense fury to his vocals that brings the whole thing to a boil. *Testimony* is a gripping listen and one of the best albums Mooney ever recorded. — *Thom Owens*

☆ **Against the Wall** / Apr. 1996 / House of Blues ♦♦♦♦♦
Mooney is one of a handful of younger blues players who has forged his own style, a jarring juxtaposition of angular Delta guitar and funky New Orleans backbeats. He explores the dark sides of those traditions in *Against the Wall*, a harrowing and stark work. Mooney's voice and guitar, both quivering, conjure up the image of a lost soul at a Delta crossroads at midnight; his shadowy bass—and-drum rhythm section evokes the ominous powers of voodoo. Standouts include "Sacred Ground," which opens the set, and "Somebody Been Missing Somebody (2 Long)," which closes it. On "Late on in the Evening," a mournful blues about a marital breakup, if the verse about his little boy begging him not to go doesn't get you, the stinging, Muddy Waters-style slide guitar break surely will. Very minimalist production throughout illustrates the principle that, in roots music, less equals more. — *Steve Hoffman*

Dealing with the Devil / Apr. 15, 1997 / RFR ♦♦♦
Known for his extreme energy and passionate playing, this disc features him playing acoustically by himself in a live setting, and he is every bit as alive and dynamic here as with a full band. But he can also be refined—listen to his subtle playing and impeccable timing on "U Told Me," or the quiet control of "It Don't Mean a Doggone Thing." He never seems to put his slide down, and that is to his benefit, as his is some of the most inventive slide playing there is. Evidently he studied with and had as his mentor Son House. This disc should not be missed. — *Bob Gottlieb*

Aaron Moore

Vocals / Piano Blues, Contemporary Blues
Chicago-based blues pianist, singer and songwriter Aaron Moore is locally famous, but still rather obscure on the national blues scene. Moore spent most of the last 40 years in Chicago, backing up a long list of musicians including Little Walter, Lonnie Brooks, Hound Dog Taylor, Howlin' Wolf, Muddy Waters, and B.B. King. Born and raised in Greenwood, Mississippi, Moore was encouraged in his piano playing by his mother, who was a music teacher and church piano player; early on, he was influenced by Curtis Jones, and later Memphis Slim. Later on, after moving to Chicago, he learned from boogie-woogie paragon Roosevelt Sykes, and the two would often team up in blues clubs around Chicago. Moore worked for the city of Chicago for 36 years and played blues strictly on a freelance basis on weekends, backing up local bluesmen in club shows. After retiring from the Chicago Sanitation Department, Moore relocated to Milwaukee in 1990 and has been poised to make blues his full-time vocation in his retirement years. On *Hello World*, his 1996 Delmark release, Moore is accompanied by James Wheeler, guitar; Willie Black, bass; and Huckleberry Hound, drums. — *Richard Skelly*

Hello World / Nov. 26, 1996 / Delmark ♦♦♦

Alex Moore

b. Nov. 22, 1899, Dallas, TX, **d.** Jan. 20, 1989, Dallas, TX
Piano, Vocals / Piano Blues
One of the last of the old-time Texas barrelhouse pianists, Alex Moore was an institution in Dallas, his lifelong home. A colorful entertainer with a poetic gift for rambling improvisations, Moore had one of the longest recording careers in blues history (his first sides for Columbia were made in 1929; his final session was in 1988). Yet it was hardly one of the most prolific, as there were usually lengthy gaps between sessions. The spontaneous, autobiographical nature of his latter-day recordings imbue his albums with a special charm.

Moore began performing in the early '20s, playing clubs and parties around his hometown of Dallas; he usually performed under the name Whistlin' Alex. In 1929, he recorded his first sessions, which were for Columbia Records. The sides didn't gain much attention and Moore didn't record again until 1937, when he made a few records for Decca. Between his first and second sessions, he continued to play clubs in Dallas. The time span between his second session in 1937 and his third was even longer than the time between his first and second—Moore didn't record again until 1951, when RPM/Kent had him cut several songs. Throughout the '40s and '50s, Moore

performed in clubs throughout Dallas, occasionally venturing to other parts of Texas.

Alex Moore's national break coincided with the blues revival of the early '60s. Arhoolie Records signed the pianist in 1960, and those records helped make him a national name. For the rest of the '60s, he played clubs and festivals in America, as well as a handful of festival dates in Europe. Although he didn't make many records in the '70s and '80s, Moore continued to perform until his death in 1989. The year before his death, he recorded a final session for Rounder Records, which was released as the *Wiggle Tail* album. — *Jim O'Neal & Stephen Thomas Erlewine*

Wiggle Tail / 1988 / Rounder ♦♦♦
Wiggle Tail turned out to be Alex Moore's final recording, and while that makes it a little bittersweet, it's nice that he was able to sign out with such a lovely album. There's nothing new here, to be sure, just Texas blues, but the years have been kind to Moore—he's still able to play with grace and passion. These performances might not have the spark and excitement of his classic '50s recordings, but hearing an old master play the blues is always a welcome, revealing experience. — *Thom Owens*

● **From North Dallas to the East Side** / 1994 / Arhoolie ♦♦♦♦
Recorded over three separate dates spanning 1947 to 1969, *From North Dallas to the East Side* is an excellent overview of Moore's singular combination of boogie and barrelhouse; his wildly improvised lyrics are sometimes hilarious, sometimes grim, and always singular. — *Jason Ankeny*

● **Complete Recorded Works (1929-1951)** / Jun. 2, 1994 / Document ♦♦♦♦
Complete Recorded Works (1929-1951) rounds up all of Whistlin' Alex Moore's early recordings for Columbia, Decca and RPM/Kent. The sound quality is a little rough, and since it spans several decades, the collection doesn't quite gel into a cohesive listening experience, but there's no denying that these rowdy barrelhouse blues are powerful and entertaining—they're worth the time of any serious piano blues fan. — *Stephen Thomas Erlewine*

Ice Pick Blues / Oct. 20, 1995 / Collectables ♦♦♦

Gary Moore

b. Apr. 4, 1952, Belfast, Northern Ireland
Guitar, Vocals / Hard Rock, Blues-Rock
Belfast native Gary Moore first achieved renown as the lead guitarist of hard rockers Thin Lizzy. After playing with a band called the Boys, Moore formed a new band—Skid Row—featuring bassist Brendan Shields, drummer Noel Bridgeman, and singer Phil Lynott, who left to form Thin Lizzy while Moore remained to pursue a record deal with the help of Fleetwood Mac guitarist Peter Green. Skid Row recorded three albums before Moore left for a solo career, releasing his first album, *Grinding Stone*, in 1973. Lynott then invited Moore to join Thin Lizzy as a replacement for guitarist Eric Bell; Moore stayed for a short time before leaving to pursue session work, which he has continued off and on throughout his career. Moore joined the fusion outfit Colosseum II in 1975 and rejoined Thin Lizzy in 1977 as a full-time member, appearing on their 1979 album *Black Rose*. In the middle of a 1979 American tour, Moore left Thin Lizzy again to form the unsuccessful G-Force; his single "Parisienne Walkways," from the solo LP *Back on the Streets*, became a UK hit that May.

Moore recorded a series of moderately successful albums during the 1980s and had popular UK numbers with "Empty Rooms" in 1985 and a collaboration with Lynott, "Out in the Fields." 1989's *After the War* showed the influence of Celtic music, but Moore's breakthrough came with the following year's *Still Got the Blues*. Toning down the hard rock feel of many of his previous recordings, Moore mixed traditional blues standards with a sprinkling of originals and delivered a superb performance vocally and instrumentally, and the album became a critical and commercial success. Moore followed his surprise success with *After Hours*, which featured guest spots from B.B. King and Albert Collins and solidified Moore's reputation as a blues-rocker of note. Moore recorded a side project called BBM in 1994 with former Cream rhythm section Jack Bruce and Ginger Baker, and in 1995, he released a tribute album to his idol, Peter Green, composed entirely of Green originals played on a guitar Green had given him years ago. — *Steve Huey*

Back on the Streets / 1979 / Grand Slamm ♦♦

Corridors of Power / 1982 / Mirage ♦♦♦

Corridors of Time offers several distinct musical styles by New Age music pioneer Steven Halpern. His two "Fantasy" pieces for spatially expanded piano (lots of pedal and echo) create a drone effect with undulating waves of octaves and embellishments. Spacy synthesizer effects add other drones and mind-bending sounds and dimensions. The effect is very relaxing, like floating. Halpern's synthesizer pieces use percolating and unfolding electronic sequences with deep "aum" drones to keep the mind anchored. These pieces differ from Halpern's typical relaxation sound (i.e., the gentle clarion), but they are meditative in their own way. "Diana's Dream Theme" features Diana Allen's enchantingly echoed voice, which seems to lasso across the heavens. Even more variety from Halpern as the title cut features even sharper synthesized sequences; "Round Midnight in Marrakesh" features Middle Eastern rhythms. As Halpern points out in the tape's liner notes, this album is not one of his "Anti-Frantic Alternative" series. It is meant for meditation and visual mind tripping, and an enjoyable excursion it is, too. — *Carol Wright*

After the War / 1989 / Virgin ♦♦♦

• Still Got the Blues / May 1990 / Charisma ♦♦♦♦

Relieved from the pressures of having to record a hit single, he cuts loose on some blues standards as well as some newer material. Moore plays better than ever, spitting out an endless stream of fiery licks that are both technically impressive and soulful. It's no wonder *Still Got the Blues* was his biggest hit. — *David Jehnzen*

After Hours / Mar. 10, 1992 / Charisma ♦♦♦♦

Not wanting to leave a good thing behind, Moore reprises *Still Got the Blues* on its follow-up, *After Hours*. While his playing is just as impressive, the album feels a little calculated. Nevertheless, Moore's gutsy, impassioned playing makes the similarity easy to ignore. — *David Jehnzen*

Blues Alive / Jul. 1, 1992 / Virgin ♦♦♦

Live at the Marquee Club / Jul. 1, 1992 / Castle ♦♦

Blues for Greeny / 1995 / Charisma ♦♦♦

Gary Moore's tribute to Fleetwood Mac guitarist Peter Green, *Blues for Greeny*, is more of a showcase for Moore's skills than Green's songwriting. After all, Green was more famous for his technique than his writing. Consequently, Moore uses Green's songs as a starting point, taking them into new territory with his own style. And Moore positively burns throughout *Blues for Greeny*, tearing off licks with ferocious intensity. If anything, the album proves that Moore is at his best when interpreting other people's material — it easily ranks as one of his finest albums. — *Stephen Thomas Erlewine*

Ballads & Blues 1982-1994 / Mar. 21, 1995 / Charisma ♦♦♦♦

Rev. James Moore

b. Detroit, MI
Vocals / Black Gospel
Accorded entry into the gospel field thanks to a scholarship received at the 1974 Gospel Music Workshop of America, Rev. James Moore earned a record contract with Savoy that same year and began releasing albums. Born in Detroit, he made his first appearance at the front of church at the age of seven and was introduced to gospel matriarch Mattie Moss Clark by a friend. With the help of Clark — and the tremendous influence of the Revs. James Cleveland and Richard White — Moore entered gospel music with 1974's *I Thank You Master*. He was also invited by Rev. Gerald Thompson to appear on his LP *I Can't Stop Now* that same year.

Rev. James Moore recorded infrequently during the 1980s (for a variety of labels), but returned to Malaco/Savoy in 1988 for *Live: Rev. James Moore*. The album hit the Top Ten on the gospel charts, and earned Moore a Stellar Award for Best Male Solo Performance. He appeared on the debut album by the Mississippi Mass Choir in 1987, and enjoyed the LP's enormous success (over half a year at the top of the gospel charts, almost a dozen awards from GMWA and Dove; the choir returned the favor by appearing on one of his albums, 1991's *Live with the Mississippi Mass Choir*. It also went to number one, prompting live albums recorded in Moore's hometown of Detroit and Jackson State University during the mid-'90s. His 1994 album *I Will Trust in the Lord* earned Rev. Moore his first Grammy nomination. — *John Bush*

Live: Rev. James Moore / 1988 / Malaco ♦♦♦

Live with the Mississippi Mass Choir / 1991 / Malaco ♦♦♦

• Live in Detroit / 1993 / Malaco ♦♦♦♦

Live in Detroit is a ten-track album that captures the Rev. James Moore live in concert in the early '90s. Moore is in great form, adding life to the music when the going gets predictable, even on the overly familiar "He Was There All the Time." Occasionally, Moore gets carried away with preaching and testifying, letting the songs run on a little too long — "He's All I Need" clocks in at nearly 13 minutes — but it's easy to hear that this was captivating live, even if the kineticism is lessened on record. There are better Moore albums and better live Moore albums available, but once you get to listening to *Live in Detroit*, you're likely to get caught up in the infectious spirit of this usually rousing music. — *Thom Owens*

I Will Trust in the Lord / 1994 / Malaco ♦♦♦♦

Brothers & Sisters I Will Be Praying for You / Oct. 4, 1994 / A&M ♦♦♦♦

Live at Jackson State University / 1995 / Malaco ♦♦♦♦

It Ain't Over (Till God Says It's Over) / Aug. 5, 1997 / Malaco ♦♦♦

Johnny B. Moore

b. Jan. 24, 1950, Clarksdale, MS
Guitar, Vocals / Electric Chicago Blues
Very few young Chicago bluesmen bring the depth and knowledge of tradition to the table that Johnny B. Moore does. His sound is a slightly contemporized version of what's been going down on the West Side for decades, emblazoned with Moore's sparkling rhythmic lead guitar lines and growling vocals.

Moore first met the legendary Jimmy Reed in Clarksdale, when he was only eight years old. By the time he was 13 or so, Moore was sharing a bandstand or two with Reed up in Chicago. Letha Jones, widow of piano great Johnny Jones, took an interest in Moore's musical development, spinning stacks of blues wax for the budding guitarist.

Moore joined Koko Taylor's Blues Machine in 1975, touring and recording with the Chicago blues queen (on her 1978 LP for Alligator, *The Earthshaker*). He went out on his own around the turn of the '80s, waxing a fine 1987 album for B.L.U.E.S. R&B, *Hard Times*, that impressively spotlighted his versatility.

After some rough spots, Moore is now more visible than ever on the Chicago circuit, with two new albums (one for Austrian Wolf, *Live at Blue Chicago*, for Delmark). In addition to playing as a leader, Moore is likely to turn up on local stages as a sideman behind everyone from Mary Lane and Karen Carroll to rock-solid bassist Willie Kent. If Johnny B. Moore isn't a star in the making, there's no justice in the blues world. — *Bill Dahl*

Lonesome Blues Chicago Blues Session, Vol. 5 / Jun. 15, 1993 / Wolf ♦♦♦

Live at Blue Chicago / 1996 / Delmark ♦♦♦♦

• Johnny B. Moore / Feb. 6, 1996 / Delmark ♦♦♦♦

Johnny B. Moore's eponymous effort for Delmark record is arguably his best record yet. There's nothing that different on the surface — it's still the same overdriven Chicago blues that is his trademark — but there's more passion and fire to his performances here, and that's enough to make the album worth a listen by hardcore Chicago blues fans. — *Thom Owens*

Troubled World / Apr. 29, 1997 / Delmark ♦♦♦

911 Blues / Jul. 1, 1997 / Wolf ♦♦♦

Ace Moreland

b. Oklahoma
Guitar, Harmonica / Blues-Rock
Oklahoma-born blues/rock singer, guitarist, and harmonica player. Part Cherokee Indian, Ace Moreland has cut two rocking discs at Bob Greenlee's Florida studios. *Sizzlin' Hot*, issued on King Snake in 1990, featured Edgar Winter on alto sax, while *I'm a Damn Good Time*, Moreland's 1992 follow-up, was released on Ichiban. — *Bill Dahl*

• Sizzlin' Hot / 1990 / Ichiban ♦♦♦♦

Ace Moreland isn't a particularly distinctive guitarist or singer. He's content to turn out Southern-fried hard rock and heavy boogie without attempting to update the sound whatsoever. That's not necessarily a bad thing, since Moreland does this stuff fairly well. There isn't much spark or originality to his playing, but his debut *Sizzlin' Hot* is a reasonably appealing record that should satisfy fans of Southern blues-rock, at least initially. It may not leave many lasting impressions, but it sounds good while it's playing and suggests that, with a little effort, Moreland could develop into a strong journeyman guitarist. — *Thom Owens*

I'm a Damn Good Time / 1992 / Ichiban ✦✦✦

I'm a Jealous Man / 1993 / Wild Dog ✦✦✦
By the time Ace Moreland recorded his third album, *I'm a Jealous Man*, his Southern blues-rock had become a little bit staid and predictable. There still were good moments on the record, but there were no new twists on his horn-spiked contemporary blues. Moreland's problem is that he doesn't break tradition enough, preferring to stick with tried and tested. That can be good when he's digging out forgotten classics like B.B. King's "Sell My Monkey," but most of the original songs on the album are simply perfunctory and performed in a similar fashion. That may be enough for his cult, but they also may find it a little frustrating that he's stuck in a rut. — *Thom Owens*

Keepin' a Secret / Feb. 20, 1996 / King Snake ✦✦✦✦

Jimmy Morello

Vocals / Modern Electric Blues
A powerful vocalist and super-quick drummer, Jimmy Morello began playing drums at age 11 and formed his first band at 13. His vocal style has been influenced by great blues shouters like Roy Brown, Big Joe Turner, and Jimmy Rushing. His mother's record collection had an impact on him in his early years, vocal groups like the Platters, the Drifters, the Coasters, and others. He fell in love with blues music after attending a revue concert in 1971 with Ray Charles, T-Bone Walker, and Jimmy Reed. Shortly after this, he befriended a Pittsburgh DJ who introduced him to Louisiana Red. Red took a shine to Morello's band, Cold Steel, and the two began working together regularly in Pittsburgh blues venues. After becoming a tight working unit, they hit the road, playing Washington, DC, Philadelphia, Boston and other cities around the Northeast.

After Red left for Europe in 1980, Morello moved to Sacramento, CA, to join the Blue Flames. By 1989, Morello moved to Phoenix, AZ, where he hooked up with the Rocket 88s, playing drums and singing with that band for four years. After leaving the Rocket 88s, Morello toured with former Muddy Waters guitarist "Steady Rollin'" Bob Margolin. Returning to Phoenix, he put together his own band, the Stingrayz, which featured his drum kit front and center, so he could sing and play drums simultaneously, much the same way Doyle Bramhall does.

Morello recorded two albums with Dallas-based guitarist Pat Boyack (with whom he had worked in the Rocket 88s) for Rounder's Bullseye Blues label. More road work followed those two mid-1990s releases, and finally in 1997, Morello got his own album, showcasing his own songs and singing, on the London-based JSP Records. Titled *Can't Be Denied*, it features Morello's kinetic drumming and powerful blues shouter-styled vocals. He dedicated the album to some of his mentors: Big Al Smith, Roy Brown, Big Joe Turner, and William Clarke. — *Richard Skelly*

Can't Be Denied / Feb. 25, 1997 / JSP ✦✦✦

Mike Morgan

b. Nov. 30, 1959, Dallas, TX
Guitar, Harmonica / Electric Texas Blues, Modern Electric Blues, Contemporary Blues, Harmonica Blues
A Texas blues band, with twangy guitarist Mike Morgan and vocalist/harpist Lee McBee prominently spotlighted, this Dallas quartet is set squarely in The Lone Star blues tradition. Their 1990 debut for Black Top, *Raw & Ready*, was followed by the more polished *Mighty Fine Dancin'* the next year. — *Bill Dahl*

Raw and Ready / 1990 / Black Top ✦✦✦
Atmospheric but somewhat derivative contemporary Texas guitar blues. — *Bill Dahl*

● **Mighty Fine Dancin'** / 1991 / Black Top ✦✦✦✦
The production may be a little bit cleaner than on *Raw and Ready*, but the Mike Morgan Crawl have turned out a better record the second time around with *Mighty Fine Dancin'*. The key is in the musicianship, which is skilled and accomplished, making the record a classy blues showcase. Some tastes might prefer a looser, rawer atmosphere, but the strong playing and solid song selection make *Mighty Fine Dancin'* a mighty fine time. — *Thom Owens*

Full Moon over Dallas / 1992 / Black Top ✦✦✦✦
Full Moon over Dallas is a fun set of driving roadhouse blues and R&B, highlighted by Mike Morgan's piercing guitar and Lee McBee's hard-edged vocals. The set may be a little to predictable for some tastes—they rarely deviate from the standard Texas blues formula—but their songwriting is good and their sound is tight, even if it is a bit too polished. — *Thom Owens*

Ain't Worried No More / Mar. 30, 1994 / Black Top ✦✦✦

Let the Dogs Run / Aug. 2, 1994 / Black Top ✦✦✦

Looky Here! / Jun. 1996 / Black Top ✦✦✦✦
Longtime frontman and vocalist Lee McBee left Mike Morgan's the Crawl after the recording of *Let the Dogs Run*. Morgan chose to replace him not with another harpist but with Chris Whynaught, a powerful vocalist and saxophonist. His presence gives the band a stronger R&B edge, which revitalizes the group's Texas blues and makes *Looky Here* into their most enjoyable record in years. — *Thom Owens*

The Road / Mar. 10, 1998 / Black Top ✦✦✦✦
The savage combination of Lee McBee's harp attack and Mike Morgan's smoking guitar makes for some full-tilt Texas roadhouse blues. Standouts include McBee's countrified "I'm Blue" and Morgan's chilly "You Did Me a Favor," a song that doubles as an excellent argument for stalking laws. — *Tim Sheridan*

Teddy Morgan

b. Jul. 8, 1971, Minneapolis, MN
Guitar, Vocals / Modern Electric Blues
Minneapolis native Teddy Morgan began playing guitar in his early teen years. As a singer and songwriter, Morgan was first influenced by Bob Dylan, but after hearing an album by Lightnin' Hopkins, he decided to pursue a straightahead blues track instead. Although he paid attention to Dylan's blues as well as the Allman Brothers and Jimi Hendrix, Morgan wanted to play blues full-time; but, like so many other younger players, he is influenced almost as much by blues-rock as he is by classic blues players like Hopkins. Morgan quit high school at 17 and the next year joined the Lamont Cranston Band, which led to the chance to record and tour with James Harman and R.J. Mischo. The Fabulous Thunderbirds' Kim Wilson heard Morgan playing guitar in a club and took Morgan under his wing, encouraging him to come to Austin to check out the blues club scene there. Clifford Antone, the owner of Austin's longest-running blues club, Antone's, flew Morgan down to Austin to perform, and Morgan soon became part of the talent roster at the Antone's label. When the Antone's label formed a partnership with Discovery Records, Morgan's recording career got a boost, as much of the Antone's back catalog was reissued. Morgan has two albums out on the Antone's/Discovery label: 1994's *Ridin' in Style*, with his band the Sevilles, and 1996's *Louisiana Rain*, which features Kim Wilson on harp, Derek O'Brien and Gurf Morlix on guitars, and "Blue" Gene Taylor on piano. — *Richard Skelly*

Ridin' in Style / 1994 / Discovery ✦✦✦✦

Teddy Morgan & the Sevilles / 1995 / Antone's ✦✦✦

● **Lousiana Rain** / Sep. 9, 1996 / Discovery ✦✦✦✦
Louisiana Rain is a delightfully eclectic romp that effectively showcases the full range of Teddy Morgan's talents. Although he is fluent in a number of different styles, Morgan is no mere blues encyclopedist—he has absorbed classic blues traditions and spiked them with a modern spirit and a sense of swing. Most of the album is devoted to country-blues and jump blues, all of which are given a nice, laidback sense of swing which is utterly charming. — *Thom Owens*

Buddy Moss (Eugene Moss)

b. Jan. 16, 1914, Jewel, GA, **d.** Oct. 19, 1984, Atlanta, GA
Vocals, Guitar, Harmonica / Country Blues, Piedmont Blues, Prewar Country Blues, East Coast Blues

Eugene "Buddy" Moss was, in the estimation of many blues scholars, the most influential East Coast blues guitarist to record in the period between Blind Blake's final sessions in 1932 and Blind Boy Fuller's debut in 1935. A younger contemporary of Blind Willie McTell and Curley Weaver, Eugene Buddy Moss was part of a near-legendary coterie of Atlanta bluesmen, and one of the few of his era lucky enough to work into the blues revival of the 1960s and '70s. A guitarist of uncommon skill and dexterity, he was a musical disciple of Blind Blake, and may well have served as an influence on Piedmont-style guitarist Blind Boy Fuller. Although his career was halted in 1935 by a six-year jail term, and then by the Second World War, Moss lived long enough to be rediscovered in the 1960s, when he revealed a talent undamaged by time or adversity.

Moss was one of 12 children born to a sharecropper in Jewel, a town in Warren County, GA, midway between Atlanta and Augusta. There is some disagreement about his date of birth, some sources indicating 1906 and many others of more recent vintage claiming 1914. He began teaching himself the harmonica at a very early age, and he played at local parties around Augusta, where the family moved when he was four and remained for the next 10 years. By 1928, he was busking around the streets of Atlanta. "Nobody was my influence," he told Robert Springer of his harmonica playing, in a 1975 interview. "I just kept hearing people, so I listen and I listen, and listen, and it finally come to me."

By the time he arrived in Atlanta, he was good enough to be noticed by Curley Weaver and Robert "Barbecue Bob" Hicks, who began working with the younger Moss. It was Weaver and Bob that got him his first recording date, at the age of 16, as a member of their group the Georgia Cotton Pickers, on December 7, 1930 at the Campbell Hotel in Atlanta, doing four songs for Columbia: "I'm on My Way Down Home," "Diddle-Da-Diddle," "She Looks So Good," and "She's Comin' Back Some Cold Rainy Day." The group that day consisted of Barbecue Bob and Curley Weaver on guitars and Moss on harmonica. Nothing more was heard from Buddy Moss on record until three years later. In January of 1933, however, he made his debut as a recording artist in his own right for the American Record Company in New York, accompanied by Fred McMullen and Curley Weaver, cutting three songs cut that first day, "Bye Bye Mama," "Daddy Don't Care," and "Red River Blues."

In the three years leading up to that date, he'd taught himself the guitar, at which he became so proficient that he was a genuine peer and rival to Weaver. He frequently played with Barbecue Bob, and after Bob died of pneumonia on October 21, 1931, he found a new partner and associate in Blind Willie McTell, performing with the Atlanta blues legend as local parties in the Atlanta area. By the time he started recording in 1933, Moss was so good as a player and singer, that all 11 songs that he cut during the four days of sessions were released, far more than saw the light of day from McMullen or Weaver at those same sessions.

In later years, Moss credited Barbecue Bob with being a major influence on his playing, which would be understandable given the time they spent together. Scholars also attribute Blind (Arthur) Blake as a major force in his development, with mannerisms and inflections that both share. It is also suggested by Alan Balfour and others that Moss may have been an influence on no less a figure than Blind Boy Fuller, although who influenced whom is anyone's guess—it is clear that Moss' first recordings display some inflections and nuances that Fuller didn't put down on record until some years later.

The January 1933 sessions also featured Moss returning to the mouth harp, as a member of the Georgia Browns—Moss, Weaver, McMullen, and singer Ruth Willis—for six songs done at the same sessions. But it was on the guitar that Moss would make his name over the next five years.

Moss' records were released simultaneously on various budget labels associated with ARC, and were so successful that in mid-September of 1933, he was back in New York along with Weaver and Blind Willie McTell. Moss cut another dozen songs for the company, this time accompanied by Curley Weaver, while he accompanied Weaver and McTell on their numbers.

These songs sold well enough, that he was back in New York in the summer of 1934, this time as a solo guitarist/singer, to do more than a dozen tracks. At this point, Moss' records were outselling those of big name colleagues Weaver and McTell, and were widely heard through the southern and border states. This body of recordings also best represents the bridge that Moss provided between Blind Blake and Blind Boy Fuller—his solo version of "Some Lonesome Day," and also "Dough Rollin' Papa," from 1934 advanced ideas in playing and singing that Blind Boy Fuller picked up and adapted to his own style, while one could listen to "Insane Blues" and pick up the lingering influence of Blind Blake.

By August of 1935, Moss saw his per-song fee doubled from $5 to $10 (in a period when many men were surviving on less than that per week), and when he wasn't recording, he was constantly playing around Atlanta alongside McTell and Weaver. When Moss returned to the studio in the summer of 1935, it was with a new partner, Josh White, working under his alias as "The Singing Christian." The two recorded a group of 15 songs in August of 1935, and it seemed like Moss was destined to outshine his one-time mentors Weaver and McTell, when personal and legal disaster struck.

In an incident that has never been fully recounted or explained, Moss was arrested, tried, and convicted in the murder of his wife and sentenced to a long prison term. The truth behind the crime and validity of the subsequent conviction were further called into doubt by the efforts that began almost immediately to secure Moss' release, all to no avail until 1941, when a combination of his own good behavior as a prisoner, coupled with the entreaties of two outside sponsors willing to assure his compliance with parole helped get him out of jail. It was while working at Elon College under the parole agreement that he met a group of blues musicians that included Sonny Terry and Brownie McGhee.

In October of 1941, Moss, Terry, and McGhee went to New York to cut a group of sides for OKeh/Columbia, including 13 numbers by Moss featuring his two new colleagues. Only three of the songs were ever released, and then events conspired to cut short Moss' recording comeback. The entry of the United States into World War II in December of the same year forced the government to place a wartime priority on the shellac used in the making of 78-rpm discs—there was barely enough allocated to the recording industry to keep functioning, and record companies were forced to curtail recordings by all but the most commercially viable artists; a ban on recording work by the Musicians' Union declared soon after further restricted any chance for Moss to record; and the interest in acoustic country blues, even of the caliber that he played, seemed to be waning, further cutting back on record company interest.

Moss continued performing in the area around Richmond, VA, and Durham, NC, during the mid-'40s and with Curley Weaver in Atlanta during the early 1950s, but music was no longer his profession or his living. He went to work on a tobacco farm, drove trucks, and worked as an elevator operator, among other jobs, over the next 20-odd years.

Although he still occasionally played in the area around Atlanta, Moss was largely forgotten. Despite the fact that reference sources even then referred to him as one of the most influential bluesmen of the 1930s, he was overlooked by the blues revival. In a sense, he was cheated by the fact that his recording career had been so short—1933 to 1935—and had never recovered from the interruption in his work caused by his stretch in prison.

Fate stepped in, in the form of some unexpected coincidences. In 1964, he chanced to hear that his old partner Josh White was giving a concert at Emory University in Atlanta. Moss visited White backstage at the concert, and the white acolytes hanging around established legend White suddenly discovered a blues legend in their midst. He was persuaded to resume performing in a series of concerts before college audiences, most notably under the auspices of the Atlanta Folk Music Society and the Folklore Society of Greater Washington. He also had new recording sessions for the Columbia label in Nashville, but none of the material was ever issued.

A June 10, 1966 concert in Washington, DC, was recorded and portions of it were later released on the Biograph label. Moss played the Newport Folk Festival in 1969, and appeared at such unusual venues as New York's Electric Circus during that same year. During the 1970s, he played the John Henry Memorial Concert in West Virginia for two consecutive years, and the Atlanta Blues Festival and the Atlanta Grass Roots Music Festival in 1976.

Buddy Moss died in Atlanta in October of 1984, once again largely forgotten by the public. In the years since, his music was once again being heard courtesy of the Biograph label's reissue of the 1966 performance and the

Austrian Document label, which has released virtually every side that he released between 1930 and 1941. As a result, his reputation has once again grown, although he is still not nearly as well known among blues enthusiasts as Blind Willie McTell or Blind Boy Fuller. — *Bruce Eder*

● **Buddy Moss 1933-1935** / 1933-1935 / Document ✦✦✦✦
Document's *Buddy Moss 1933-1935* does a nice job of collecting the highlights from the Piedmont bluesman's peak years, making it a solid single-disc introduction to the influential guitarist. — *Thom Owens*

Atlanta Blues Legend / 1967 / Biograph ✦✦✦✦
Recorded live on June 10, 1966 at a Washington, DC, concert, this 11-song album (fleshed out to 18 numbers on CD with additional live tracks from elsewhere) was considered miraculous in its own time, and remains so. Moss' fingering was slowed only slightly from the ravages of time, and his voice had aged beautifully. He gets sympathetic harmonica accompaniment (some of it most impressive, especially on "Pushin' It") from Jeff Espina and occasional help (seemingly unneeded) from a second guitarist billed only as "J.J." Moss, who was then either 52 or 60 years old, rises to the occasion, turning in some dazzling acoustic guitar work (check out "Comin' Back"), very moving and expressive singing, and overall a performance that one can only guess is uncannily like the kind he would've done 30 years earlier. Included are fresh renditions of "Oh Lawdy Mama" and Moss' own, unique renditions of "I'm Sitting on Top of the World" and "Key to the Highway" (done as a guitar showcase that would put Eric Clapton and Duane Allman to shame, and referred to here as "I've Got to Keep to the Highway"). One of the most impressive, and maybe the best, of all 1960s rediscovery records by any '30s blues star—64 minutes of pure golden blues. — *Bruce Eder*

Complete Recorded Works, Vols. 1-3 / 1992 / Document ✦✦✦✦
These three CDs contain all of Moss' recordings made between January 1933 and October 1941. The sound is generally good to excellent, and as for the material, it is just about the most sophisticated and beautifully played Atlanta blues of its period. From his very earliest sessions in January of 1933, Buddy Moss made his guitar sing almost like a human voice even *without* a slide, just strumming, and his own voice was one of the most expressive in the blues. And when he played slide . . . well, Atlanta blues didn't get any better than this, especially with Curley Weaver ("Prowling Woman" and "T.B.'s Killing Me," for the guitar duet, are worth the price of *Vol. I*) or Fred McMullen providing the second guitar part (and Blind Willie McTell's voice turning up every so often), or, a little later, Josh White playing with him. Among the more fascinating anomalies is "Daddy Don't Care" from *Volume I*, which anticipates Blind Boy Fuller's "You've Got Something There." But the real reason for getting these three discs—and all three are necessary—is to take in one of the genuine, deserving blues giants in history on 67 of the greatest sides ever laid down. — *Bruce Eder*

Rediscovery / Biograph ✦✦✦
Piedmont blues master Buddy Moss featured in a good blues revival session. — *Barry Lee Pearson*

Matt Murphy

b. Dec. 29, 1927, Sunflower, MS
Guitar, Vocals / Electric Chicago Blues, Modern Electric Blues
Probably best-known for playing behind the Blues Brothers (and appearing prominently in their 1980 hit movie), Matt "Guitar" Murphy deserves enshrinement in the blues-guitar hall of fame anyway. His jazz-tinged, stunningly advanced riffing behind Memphis Slim elevated the towering pianist's 1950s output for United and Vee-Jay Records to new heights.

Guitar playing ran in the Murphy household (which moved from Mississippi to Memphis when Matt was a toddler). Matt and his brother Floyd both made a name for themselves on the early-'50s Memphis scene (that's Floyd on Little Junior Parker & the Blue Flames' 1953 Sun waxings of "Feelin' Good" and "Mystery Train"). Matt played with Howlin' Wolf as early as 1948 (harpist Little Junior Parker was also in the band at the time). Murphy added hot licks to early sides by Parker and Bobby Bland for Modern before latching on with Memphis Slim's House Rockers in 1952. Normally, the veteran pianist eschewed guitarists altogether, but Murphy's talent was so prodigious that he made an exception.

Murphy's consistently exciting guitar work graced Slim's United waxings from 1952-54 and his 1958-59 platters for Vee-Jay. Another solid Memphis

Slim LP for Strand in 1961 and dates with Chuck Berry, Otis Rush, Sonny Boy Williamson, Etta James, and the Vibrations at Chess preceded Murphy's memorable appearance on the 1963 American Folk Blues Festival tour of Europe (along with Slim, Sonny Boy Williamson, Muddy Waters, Lonnie Johnson, Big Joe Williams, Victoria Spivey, and Willie Dixon). On that pioneering tour (promoted by Lippmann and Rau), Murphy commanded the spotlight with a thrilling "Matt's Guitar Boogie" that showcased his ultra-clean rapid-fire picking.

Harpist James Cotton was the sweaty beneficiary of Murphy's prowess during much of the 1970s. Murphy's crisp picking matched Cotton's high-energy blowing on the harpist's 1974 Buddah album *100% Cotton* (the guitarist penned a non-stop "Boogie Thing" for the set). From there, it was on to aiding and abetting John Belushi and Dan Aykroyd's antic mugging, both on stage and in *The Blues Brothers* flick (where he played Aretha Franklin's guitarist hubby, convinced to come out of retirement by the boys in black).

Murphy has toured as a bandleader in recent years, having recorded an album of his own in 1990, *Way Down South,* for Antone's (with brother Floyd on rhythm guitar). His repertoire encompasses blues, funk, jazz, R&B, and even a few of those Blues Brothers chestnuts (he usually carries someone in the entourage to sing 'em, Belushi-style). Murphy's latest disc, *The Blues Don't Bother Me!,* recently emerged on Roesch Records. — *Bill Dahl*

● **Way Down South** / 1990 / Discovery ✦✦✦✦
The dazzling guitarist has recorded very sparingly as a leader over the course of his long career, preferring the relative anonymity of sideman duties behind Memphis Slim, James Cotton, and the Blues Brothers. But he acquits himself most competently here, mixing blues, funk, R&B, and a little jazz into his sparkling fretwork. His brother Floyd Murphy, a Memphis blues guitar legend himself, is on hand for a family reunion. — *Bill Dahl*

Blues Don't Bother Me / Mar. 26, 1996 / Roesch ✦✦✦

Bobby Murray

b. Jun. 9, 1953, Nagoya, Japan
Guitar / Modern Electric Blues
Longtime Etta James band guitarist Bobby Murray spent many years carefully honing his guitar-playing skills around the blues clubs of San Francisco and Oakland. In the 1970s and '80s, he played backup for musicians like Sonny Rhodes and Frankie Lee before getting a big break in 1988 and joining up with James' Roots Band. Murray was born in 1953 in Nagoya, Japan, grew up in Tacoma, WA, and cites Albert Collins as one of his most important guitar influences. Murray and Robert Cray went to high school together, and upon their graduation, they booked Collins for the school's graduation party; the three became friends and later went on to appear in concert together often. Murray, who spent many years in apprenticeship, learned from some of the best the Bay Area had to offer, sharing stages with Charlie Musselwhite, Otis Rush, Jimmy Witherspoon, Taj Mahal, and John Lee Hooker, among others. He can be heard on B.B. King's Grammy Award-winning album, *Blues Summit*, and he duets with former classmate Cray on King's "Playing With My Friends." Murray's style is fluid and rhythmic, and, freely admitting he's not one of the world's greatest singers, often has a singing guitarist with him. There's plenty of guitar wizardry from Murray on his debut album, *The Blues Is Now,* released in 1996 on the New York-based Viceroots label, with guests including vocalist Frankie Lee and organist Jimmy Pugh. — *Richard Skelly*

● **The Blues Is Now** / Feb. 13, 1996 / Viceroy ✦✦✦
Longtime sideman Bobby Murray shines on his solo debut album, *The Blues Is Now.* Murray wisely hired Freddie Hughes and Frankie Lee as vocalists, freeing him to concentrate on his guitar. And he's a fine guitarist, as he proves here, turning out jazzy, classy solos that separate him from the rest of the crowd. That's the key to *The Blues Is Now*—Murray plays it cool where others play it hot, and that turns out to be rather refreshing. — *Thom Owens*

Charlie Musselwhite

b. Jan. 31, 1944, Kosciusko, MS
Guitar, Harmonica, Vocals / Electric Chicago Blues, Modern Electric Blues, Harmonica Blues
Harmonica wizard Norton Buffalo can recollect a leaner time when his record collection had been whittled down to only the bare essentials: *The Paul*

Butterfield Blues Band and *Stand Back! Here Comes Charley Musselwhite's South Side Band*. Butterfield and Musselwhite will probably be forever linked as the two most interesting, arguably most important, products of the "White blues movement" of the mid-to-late '60s—not only because they were near the forefront chronologically, but because they each stand out as being especially faithful to the style. Each certainly earned the respect of his legendary mentors. No less than the late Big Joe Williams said, "Charlie Musselwhite is one of the greatest living harp players of country blues. He is right up there with Sonny Boy Williams [I], and he's been my harp player ever since Sonny Boy got killed."

It's interesting that Big Joe specifies "country" blues, because, even though he made his mark leading electric bands in Chicago and San Francisco, Musselwhite began playing blues with people he'd read about in Sam Charters' *Country Blues*—Memphis greats like Furry Lewis, Will Shade and Gus Cannon. It was these rural roots that set him apart from Butterfield, and decades later Charlie began incorporating his first instrument, guitar.

Born in Kosciusko, MS, in 1944, Charlie's family moved north to Memphis, where he went to high school. Musselwhite migrated north in search of the near mythical $3.00-an-hour job (the same lure that set innumerable Blacks on the same route), and became a familiar face at blues haunts like Pepper's, Turner's, and Theresa's, sitting in with and sometimes playing alongside harmonica lords such as Little Walter, Shakey Horton, Good Rockin' Charles, Carey Bell, Big John Wrencher, and even Sonny Boy Williamson. Before recording his first album, Musselwhite appeared on LPs by Tracy Nelson and John Hammond and dueted (as "Memphis Charlie") with Shakey Horton on Vanguard's *Chicago/The Blues/Today* series.

When his aforementioned debut LP became a standard on San Francisco's underground radio, Musselwhite played the Fillmore Auditorium and never returned to the Windy City. Leading bands that featured greats like guitarists Harvey Mandel, Freddie Roulette, Luther Tucker, Louis Myers, Robben Ford, Fenton Robinson, and Junior Watson, Charlie played steadily around Bay Area bars and mounted somewhat low-profile national tours. It wasn't until the late '80s, when he conquered a career-long drinking problem, that Musselwhite began touring worldwide to rave notices. Today he is busier than ever. —*Dan Forte*

★ **Stand Back! Here Comes Charlie Musselwhite's Southside Band** / 1967 / Vanguard ◆◆◆◆◆
Charlie Musselwhite's earliest recording (reissued on CD) features the fine blues harmonica player when he was 22. His repertoire on this set has a few unusual selections including an instrumental version of "Christo Redemptor" (a jazz hit of the period interpreted here similar to a funeral march) and the effective one-chord vamp "Strange Land." Barry Goldberg's organ sounds very dated throughout the set and the musicians are sometimes out-of-tune but Harvey Mandel's guitar playing is consistently creative and Musselwhite (whose gruff and untrained voice was already recognizable) already showed real maturity in his playing. —*Scott Yanow*

Stone Blues / 1968 / Vanguard ◆◆◆

Charlie Musselwhite / 1968 / Vanguard ◆◆◆

Louisiana Fog / 1968 / Cherry Red ◆◆◆
The first disappointment in the Musselwhite catalog, this hodgepodge of material and sidemen still has some standouts, especially Little Richard's R&B ballad "Directly from My Heart"—which features the Ford brothers and Tim Kaihatsu and Clay Cotton (back in the lineup from the *Stone Blues* days). "Big Legged Woman" and "Takin' Care of Business" are respectable, but overall the album ranges from uneven to subpar. —*Dan Forte*

Blues from Chicago / 1968 / Cherry Red ◆◆◆

☆ **Tennessee Woman** / 1969 / Vanguard ◆◆◆◆◆
The addition of jazz pianist Skip Rose gave a new dimension to the ensemble sound, and provided a perfect foil to Charlie's own soloing—especially on the re-take of "Cristo Redentor," extended to 11 minutes, shifting to double-time in spots. Rose's instrumental, "A Nice Day for Something," is a welcome change of pace, and Musselwhite's "Blue Feeling Today" compares favorably to fine covers of Little Walter and Fenton Robinson tunes. —*Dan Forte*

Memphis Charlie / 1969 / Arhoolie ◆◆◆◆
The 14 performances on *Memphis Charlie* include some loose live sides and even a taste of slide guitar from Musselwhite. They're the work of a more mature artist than the brash kid on *Stand Back*. —*AMG*

Chicago Bues Star / 1969 / Blue Thumb ◆◆◆

Mylon / 1971 / Cotillion ◆◆◆

Takin' My Time / 1974 / Arhoolie ◆◆◆◆
Another highly talented and original ensemble—Rose still on piano, with the Ford brothers (Pat and Robben), on drums and guitar, respectively. Again, Rose contributes an original departure, the solo piano ballad "Two Little Girls"—and, as usual, it is to Charlie's credit that he welcomed such far-from-blues mood swings. Otherwise, the band's (especially Robben's) jazzier leanings were checked at the studio door, and Robben's guitar is mixed too low throughout. At this stage, Charlie was changing personnel too quickly to give any unit a second chance in the studio, which would have been especially interesting with this outfit. —*Dan Forte*

Goin' Back down South / 1975 / Arhoolie ◆◆◆
Combining two leftovers from *Takin' My Time* with a much later session featuring Chicago pianist Lafayette Leake didn't do much for this LP's continuity, but it was nice to see the tracks see the light of day (especially Robben Ford's jazz intro "Blue Stu," a rare recorded example of him on alto sax). Ussel and Leake together proves a natural, especially on "On the Spot Boogie," with Musselwhite quoting Charlie Parker's "Now's the Time." Musselwhite's guitar playing makes its first appearance on vinyl here: the primitive country blues of "Taylor, Arkansas" and a nod to Earl Hooker's slide playing, "Blue Steel." —*Dan Forte*

Leave the Blues to Us / 1975 / Capitol ◆◆
Musselwhite's major-label debut was unfortunately a lackluster run-through. This isn't a bad album; it's just that there's nothing very special about it. His working band centered around Kaihatsu and Sevareid (again, from *Stone Blues*), with the addition of saxophonist Ray Arvizu, a honking tenor as opposed to Robben Ford's jazzy alto. Cameos by Barry Goldberg and Mike Bloomfield only add to an inexplicably cacophonous mix; Goldberg's organ on "Keys to the Highway" is especially obnoxious. Charlie's singing and harp playing are well and good, but this sounds surprisingly *low*-budget compared to his previous independent releases. —*Dan Forte*

Light of Your Shadow / 1977 / Sussex ◆◆◆

Times Gettin' Tougher Than Tough / 1978 / Crystal Clear ◆◆◆
Cutting an audiofile session direct-to-disc (meaning that each entire side of the LP is recording live in the studio, with the band literally pausing between tunes, then forging ahead), someone came up with the bright idea of teaming Charlie with a band that he (mostly) had never played with, including a three-piece horn section. Under normal circumstances (retakes, overdubs, mixing—Charlie's vocals should be louder) this could have been a killer; as it is, it's yet another interesting side of this complex bluesman. Horns and piano (Skip Rose returns) give "Help Me" a whole new wrinkle, and Mose Allison's "Nightclub" is channeled through "Got My Mojo Working." Interesting, yes; definitive, no. —*Dan Forte*

Harmonica According to Charlie / 1979 / Kicking Mule ◆◆◆
Ostensibly an instructional blues harp album (with an exhaustive accompanying book penned by Charlie), this is emotional and listenable rather than academic. Charlie covers a wide range of blues styles (and harp positions), and ventures to the outer fringes of the genre for the instrumentals "Hard Times" (from Ray Charles' sax man David "Fathead" Newman) and his Latin original "Azul Para Amparo" (backed only by guitarist Sam Mitchell). The English studio band is sympathetic, especially pianist Bob Hall. —*Dan Forte*

Dynatones Live—Featuring Charlie Musselwhite / 1982 / War Bride ◆◆
After several years without a new record, this confusing item appeared—in hindsight, looking like a scam to launch Charlie's backup band into a career of its own. Musselwhite gets second billing, even though he sings five of the seven vocal tunes—the lone instrumental being a so-so version of his by-now signature piece "Cristo Redentor"—and the crowd that came to this live gig no doubt didn't see "Dynatones" on the marquee. Confusing. But around this itme that had become the norm in Charlie's recording career. —*Dan Forte*

Tell Me Where Have All the Good Times Gone / 1984 / Blue Rock'it ◆◆◆◆
Drummer/label head Pat Ford reunited with Charlie and brought along brother Robben on guitar, producing this return to form. Charlie is up to the task in all departments—singing, playing (great tone), and especially songwriting (the title tune and "Seemed Like the Whole World Was Crying," in-

spired by Muddy Waters' death)—but it had been a while since Robben had played lowdown blues (touring with Joni Mitchell, putting in countless hours in L.A. studios). Pianist Clay Cotten is in fine form, and it may have been wiser to give the guitar chair to Tim Kaihatsu, who by this time had seniority (in terms of hours on the bandstand with Musselwhite) over any of Charlie's alumni. The to-be-expected-by-now deviations this time out: Don & Dewey's "Stretchin' Out," an impressive chromatic harp rendering of "Exodus," and Charlie's solo guitar outing, "Baby-O." Easily Charlie's best-engineered album (nice job, Greg Goodwin). — *Dan Forte*

Memphis Tennessee / 1984 / Mobile Fidelity ◆◆◆◆
Though steel guitarist Freddie Roulette was pictured on *Tennessee Woman*, he did not play on the album; luckily he is given ample space here, and the combination of his eerie vocal-like sound, Jack Myers' solid but adventurous bass playing, and Skip Rose's jazz piano voicings made this edition of the Musselwhite band one of the most original blues outfits ever. Charlie is in fine form as well, on a rock-solid cover of Muddy's "Trouble No More," a lyrical reading of "Willow Weep for Me," and his harp tour de force "Arkansas Boogie." — *Dan Forte*

Mellow-Dee / 1986 / Crosscut ◆◆
By this time Charlie was confident enough to include four acoustic guitar vehicles—one ("Baby Please Don't Go") with overdubbed harp, one ("I'll Get a Break") from his old pal Will Shade of the Memphis Jug Band. The ensemble numbers feature a German backup band with expatriate Jim Kahr on guitar. A more expansive workout (than the Chicago BlueStars' version) on "Coming Home Baby" is nice, and "Cristo Redentor" (Charlie's fourth recording of the song, this time subtitled "Slight Return") gets a beautiful piano-harp duet treatment. Unfortunately the proceedings are sabotaged by completely inappropriate engineering—mechanical-sounding drums, tons o' reverb, way too much high-end. Ouch! — *Dan Forte*

Ace of Harps / 1990 / Alligator ◆◆◆
"This is the best band I've ever had," Musselwhite proclaims on the back of this LP; longtime fans would find that debatable. Rather than schooled on the Chess sounds that provided Charlie with his foundation, these guys play a Malaco strain of blues, and Tommy Hill is simply one of the busiest (read: obnoxious) drummers anywhere. A "Boogie Chillen" takeoff ("River Hip Mama") is surprisingly *not* just same-old, same-old, but for the most part the funkified blues contrasts sharply with the album's two most poignant numbers, the jazz standard "Yesterdays" (with Charlie on chromatic, borrowing from trumpeter Clifford Brown's "strings" album) and "My Road Lies in Darkness"—just Charlie and his acoustic guitar. — *Dan Forte*

Signature / Oct. 1991 / Alligator ◆◆◆
Signature is a typically engaging release from Charlie Musselwhite. The harpist runs through a set of modern blues, complete with jazz and funk overtones—indeed, there are two straight jazz instrumentals, "Catwalk" and "What's New?," which showcase his astonishing technique. Not only is Musselwhite in fine form, his band is tight, soulful, and sympathetic, making *Signature* a worthwhile listen for most blues fans. — *Thom Owens*

In My Time / 1993 / Alligator ◆◆◆◆
Charlie Musselwhite takes four different approaches on this Alligator release. On two tracks, he turns to guitar, proving a competent instrumentalist and convincing singer in a vintage Delta style. He also does two gospel numbers backed by the legendary Blind Boys of Alabama, which are heartfelt, but not exactly triumphs. Musselwhite reveals his jazz influence on three tracks, making them entertaining harmonica workouts. But for blues fans, Musselwhite's biting licks and spiraling riffs are best featured on such numbers as "If I Should Have Bad Luck" and "Leaving Blues." Despite the diverse strains, Musselwhite retains credibility throughout while displaying the wide range of sources from which he's forged his distinctive style. — *Ron Wynn*

Rough News / Apr. 8, 1997 / Virgin ◆◆◆
With much of the backing personnel returning from his outstanding 1993 Alligator release *In My Time*, a mediocre follow-up album would be unexpected. Yet something is missing from this Pointblank release, aside from the extensive liner notes. Charlie's voice is not as casual, his band not as loose, and the end result is an album that at times seems too formulaic. Undoubtedly Charlie still has a set of the best harp chops in the business, but the moments that rise to the top from this CD (such as the instrumental

title track) are much less frequent than listeners spoiled by *In My Time* may care for. — *Jeff Crooke*

Cambridge Blues / Big Beat ◆◆◆
Yet another intriguing setting: Musselwhite in an essentially acoustic trio format, backed by pianist Bob Hall and acoustic guitarist Dave Peabody, both from England, live at that country's Cambridge Folk Festival. The crowd's thunderous response says it all—a rare and satisfying night by three great blues players, each skilled in the art of supportive interplay. — *Dan Forte*

Blues Never Die / Vanguard ◆◆◆◆
This may be an overview of Musselwhite's career (from the late '60s to the present—with some previously unreleased tracks, including the title cut), but it is not the best introduction to the artist. For that, his Vanguard '60s output is still recommended, along with the 1984 session on Blue Rock'it and Alligator's *In My Time*. — *Dan Forte*

Louis Myers

b. Sep. 18, 1929, Byhalia, MS, **d.** Sep. 5, 1994, Chicago, IL
Guitar, Harmonica, Vocals / Electric Chicago Blues, Modern Electric Chicago Blues
Though he was certainly capable of brilliantly fronting a band, remarkably versatile guitarist/harpist Louis Myers will forever be recognized first and foremost as a top-drawer sideman and founding member of the Aces—the band that backed harmonica wizard Little Walter on his immortal early Checker waxings.

Along with his older brother David—another charter member of the Aces—Louis left Mississippi for Chicago with his family in 1941. Fate saw the family move next door to blues great Lonnie Johnson, whose complex riffs caught young Louis' ear. Another Myers brother, harp-blowing Bob, hooked Louis up with guitarist Othum Brown for house party gigs. Myers also played with guitarist Arthur "Big Boy" Spires before teaming with his brother David on guitar and young harpist Junior Wells to form the first incarnation of the Aces (who were initially known as the Three Deuces). In 1950, drummer Fred Below came on board.

In effect, the Aces and Muddy Waters traded harpists in 1952, Wells leaving to play with Waters while Little Walter, just breaking nationally with his classic "Juke," moved into the front man role with the Aces. Myers and the Aces backed Walter on his seminal "Mean Old World," "Sad Hours," "Off the Wall," and "Tell Me Mama" and at New York's famous Apollo Theater before Louis left in 1954 (he and the Aces moonlighted on Wells' indispensable 1953-54 output for States).

Plenty of sideman work awaited Myers—he played with Otis Rush, Earl Hooker, and many more. But his own recording career was practically non-existent; after a solitary 1956 single for Abco, "Just Whaling"/"Bluesy," that found Myers blowing harp in Walter-like style, it wasn't until 1968 that two Myers tracks turned up on Delmark.

The Aces reformed during the 1970s and visited Europe often as a trusty rhythm section for touring acts. Myers cut a fine set for Advent in 1978, *I'm a Southern Man*, that showed just how effective he could be as a leader (in front of an L.A. band, no less). Myers was hampered by the effects of a stroke while recording his last album for Earwig, 1991's *Tell My Story Movin'.* He courageously completed the disc but was limited to playing harp only. His health soon took a turn for the worse, ending his distinguished musical career. — *Bill Dahl*

● **I'm a Southern Man** / 1978 / Advent ◆◆◆◆
Despite his vaunted reputation as a versatile standout on the Windy City circuit, Louis Myers seldom recorded as a leader. This is the best set he did as a front man; cut in 1978, it was ironically recorded in Hollywood. Fellow ex-Little Walter sideman Freddy Robinson shared guitar duties with Myers (who also played harp) on a well-produced set strong on tradition but with one eye cocked toward contemporary developments (witness Myers' stylish diatribe on "Women's Lib"). — *Bill Dahl*

Walking the Blues / 1983 / JSP ◆◆◆

Tell My Story Movin' / 1992 / Earwig ◆◆◆
Since a serious stroke had largely robbed Myers of his revered ability to play guitar, this effort really isn't indicative of his vast talent. But you've got to give him points for courage—Myers summoned up the strength to play harp

and sing on what would be his final release. A nice Chicago combo that included guitarists Steve Freund and John Primer undoubtedly put Myers' mind at ease. — *Bill Dahl*

Sam Myers (Sammy Myers)

b. Mar. 19, 1936, Laurel, MS

Harmonica, Drums, Vocals / Electric Harmonica Blues, Soul Blues

Sam Myers got a second chance at the brass ring, and he's happily made the most of it. As frontman for Anson Funderburgh & the Rockets, the legally blind Myers' booming voice and succinct harp work have enjoyed a higher profile recently than ever before.

Although he was born and mostly raised in Mississippi, Myers got into the habit of coming up to visit Chicago as early as 1949 (where he learned from hearing Little Walter and James Cotton). Myers joined a band, King Mose & the Royal Rockers, after settling in Jackson, MS, in 1956. Myers' 1957 debut 45 for Johnny Vincent's Ace logo, "Sleeping in the Ground"/"My Love Is Here to Stay," featured backing by the Royal Rockers.

Myers played both drums and harp behind slide guitar great Elmore James at a 1961 session for Bobby Robinson's Fire label in New Orleans. Myers cut a standout single of his own for Robinson's other logo, Fury Rec-

ords, the year before that coupled his appealing remake of Jimmy Reed's "You Don't Have to Go" with "Sad, Sad Lonesome Day."

Myers made some albums with a loosely-knit group called the Mississippi Delta Blues Band for TJ during the early '80s before teaming up with young Texas guitar slinger Funderburgh, whose insistence on swinging grooves presents the perfect backdrop for Myers. Their first collaboration for New Orleans-based Black Top Records, 1985's *My Love is Here to Stay,* was followed by several more albums — *Sins, Rack 'em Up, Tell Me What I Want to Hear,* 1995's *Live at the Grand Emporium* — each one confirming that this is one of the most enduring blues partnerships of the 1990s. — *Bill Dahl*

● **My Love Is Here to Stay** / 1985 / Black Top ✦✦✦✦
Young Texas guitarist Anson Funderburgh and veteran harpist Sam Myers got along so well during the making of this fine set that they got their act together and took it on the road. Happily, it remains there, with Myers deftly fronting Funderburgh's Rockets. Myers' booming voice and rocking harp and Funderburgh's crisp, tradition-laden lead guitar mesh beautifully here — the disc features brash remakes of Myers' past triumphs "My Love Is Here to Stay" and "Poor Little Angel Child" and a host of fresh titles. — *Bill Dahl*

Down Home in Mississippi / TJ ✦✦✦

Mark Naftalin

b. Aug. 2, 1944, Minneapolis, MN
Piano, Organ, Guitar, Accordion, Vibes, Keyboards / Modern Electric Blues
Blues musician, composer, and producer Mark Naftalin played keyboards with the original Paul Butterfield Blues Band from 1965 to 1968. Since then he has recorded with top blues players like John Lee Hooker, Otis Rush, Percy Mayfield, James Cotton, Michael Bloomfield, Lowell Fulson, Big Joe Turner, and dozens of others—a sideman on over 100 albums.

Naftalin is sought after for his elegant, understated keyboard accompaniment and tasty solos. Although first known as an organist, he has also recorded on piano, guitar, accordion, vibes, and various electric keyboards. In his solo concerts he plays mostly acoustic piano.

Born in Minneapolis, MN, in 1944, Naftalin moved to Chicago in 1961 and enrolled at the University of Chicago, where he jammed along on piano at many of the campus "twist parties," the rage at the time. It was at these parties that Naftalin had his first opportunity to play with harmonica player Paul Butterfield and guitarist Elvin Bishop, the nucleus of what was to become the Paul Butterfield Blues Band.

In 1964, Naftalin moved to New York City, where he spent a year at the Mannes College of Music, and it was there that he sat in with the Butterfield band during a recording session warmup song, playing the Hammond organ (for the first time!). Michael Bloomfield had recently joined the band. The group liked the organ sound (and his playing) and Naftalin went on to record eight of the 11 songs on the first Butterfield album that very day. Butterfield asked Naftalin to join the group during that first session.

In the late '60s, after the first four Butterfield albums, Naftalin went out on his own, settling in the San Francisco Bay Area. There he put together the Mark Naftalin Rhythm & Blues Revue and has been active in blues and rock recording sessions, solo gigs, and revue shows, and as a producer of concerts, festivals, and radio shows. He also played with Michael Bloomfield as a duo and in a band (most often called Mike Bloomfield & Friends) from the late '60s through the mid-'70s, and hosted *Mark Naftalin's Blue Monday Party,* a weekly blues show (1979-1983) that featured over 60 blues artists and groups and was the scene of 86 live radio broadcasts and three TV specials.

More recently, Naftalin has produced the Marin County Blues Festival (1981 to the present) and has been the associate producer of the Monterey Jazz Festival's Blues Afternoon (1982-1991). His weekly radio show, *Mark Naftalin's Blues Power Hour* has been on the air almost continuously since 1979 on San Francisco's KALW-FM.

Currently Naftalin heads up the Blue Monday Foundation and produces recordings for his label, Winner Records, whose most recent releases are the Paul Butterfield Blues Band's *Strawberry Jam*—live nightclub recordings of the Butterfield band in their heyday—and the classic *Percy Mayfield Live.* He performs, both solo and ensemble, in the Bay Area and elsewhere, often with slide guitar virtuoso Ron Thompson, a longtime associate.

Upcoming for Mark Naftalin as we go to press is the Winner album *East-West Live,* which documents the Butterfield band performing that historic composition in three venues. (See: The Paul Butterfield Blues Band)
—Michael Erlewine

Steve Nardella

b. Jun. 26, 1948, Providence, RI
Guitar, Harmonica, Vocals / Blues-Rock, Rock 'n' Roll, Modern Blues
Strong, American roots-music performer, equally adept at rockabilly and low-down blues. His first known recording behind Detroit bluesman Bobo Jenkins on "Shake 'Em on Down" also featured the debut work of Austin,

Texas mainstay Sarah Brown and Fran Christina of the Fabulous Thunderbirds. Formed local Boogie Brothers band with Brown, Christina, and John Nicholas (Asleep at the Wheel, Guitar Johnny & the Guitar Rockers), backing every blues legend who came into their native Ann Arbor, appearing on Atlantic's 1972 Ann Arbor Blues & Jazz Festival behind Johnny Shines and doing their own solo turn. After nucleus of band moved to Boston with Nicholas, Nardella formed the Silvertones with local guitar hot-shot George Bedard, recording one fine album for the Blind Pig label. Has continued on his own since then, expanding his musical genres beyond just straight blues forms and turning out some interesting music along the way.
—Cub Koda

It's All Rock & Roll / 1979 / Blind Pig ♦♦♦
Extraordinary rock, R&B, and rockabilly influences all come out of Nardella's love for blues. As well as possessing a strong voice, Nardella is also an electrifying guitarist in the Chuck Berry mold. Nardella's a rare bird, with more talent than he can harvest. *—Michael G. Nastos*

● **Daddy Rollin' Stone** / 1993 / Schoolkids ♦♦♦♦
Well over a decade after he released his first album, the Detroit roots-rocker Steve Nardella recorded his second album, *Daddy Rollin' Stone,* for the fledgling Ann Arbor label Schoolkids Records. During that decade, Nardella kept busy, supporting a number of visiting bluesmen and playing many gigs on his own. That hard work paid off big time on *Daddy Rollin' Stone.* While the record doesn't quite capture the energy of Nardella's live shows, it nevertheless functions as a good showcase for his talents, proving that he's a consummate roots-rocker, capable of playing rockabilly and blues with equal flair. His voice isn't distinctive, but his guitar and passion are, and that's why *Daddy Rollin' Stone* is a modest triumph. *—Thom Owens*

Nathan & the Zydeco Cha-Chas

f. 1963, St. Martinville, Louisiana
Group / Zydeco
One of the few contemporary zydeco bandleaders to adopt the piano accordion in favor of the button model, Nathan Williams fully exploited the instrument's versatility to forge a sound which—while remaining steeped in tradition—also harnessed elements of pop, R&B, and blues. Born in St. Martinville, Louisiana, in 1963, his earliest influences included his uncle Harry Hypolite, the longtime guitarist with Clifton Chenier. Williamson left home at the age of 15 to work with his older brother Sidney in Lafayette, there acquiring his first accordion; he honed his skills at Sidney's club El Sid O's, where patrons were allowed free admission until the teen had sufficiently mastered the instrument. (His primary tutor was Stanley "Buckwheat" Dural.) In 1987 he and backing band the Zydeco Cha-Chas cut their first single "Everybody Calls Me Crazy" for Sidney's El Sid O label; a major regional hit, the disc soon made it way to Rounder Records, which quickly signed Williams to record 1988's *Zydeco Live!* with Boozoo Chavis. His solo debut *Steady Rock* appeared the following year, revealing not only an electrifying player, but also a gifted songwriter; in 1990 the group resurfaced with *Your Mama Don't Know,* and in the wake of an extended tour delivered *Follow Me Chicken* in 1993. *Creole Crossroads* appeared in 1995.
—Jason Ankeny

Steady Rock / 1989 / Rounder ♦♦♦
Nathan Williams has emerged near the head of the class among contemporary zydeco artists. This release featured mostly zydeco-tinged versions of blues and R&B tracks, although the cuts "Zydeco Joe" and "Everything on the Floor" were closer in structure and arrangements to straight zydeco. But Williams' voice, flair and, energy, coupled with his band's ability to keep the

beat moving, helped him retain a sizable following among Louisiana music purists, yet also branch out and do material that could gain attention from less knowledgeable fans. It was fiery, enjoyable music, produced with a modern sensibility and performed in vintage fashion. — *Ron Wynn*

Your Mama Don't Know / Oct. 1990 / Rounder ✦✦✦
Nathan Williams continued his string of solid releases with this 1991 date. It included good pop and R&B tracks like "Outside People" and "Don't Burn No Bridges," plus vibrant traditional material such as "El Sid O's Zydeco Boogaloo" and "Mardi Gras Zydeco." Williams again sang with zest, drive, and non-stop intensity, while the band showed once more why they're considered the tightest unit working in the genre. There weren't any surprises nor low points, just a consistently fine set spotlighting the best group in 1990s zydeco. — *Ron Wynn*

● **Follow Me Chicken** / 1993 / Rounder ✦✦✦✦
A rich product of the Creole-American culture in Louisiana, singer/accordion player Nathan Williams and his band the Zydeco Cha Chas became one of the most popular zydeco dance bands of the late '80s and early to late '90s. *Follow Me Chicken* points to the fact that while Williams is very much an admirer of the great Clifton Chenier, he's also a fine artist in his own right. This CD is full of surprises — in addition to providing sweaty originals like "Hey Maman" and "Tout Partout Mon Passe," *Chicken* finds Williams interpreting bluesman Z.Z. Hill's "I Need Someone to Love Me" and translating Stevie Wonder's 1977 hit "Isn't She Lovely" into French Creole. Another high point of the risk-taking album is "Mama's Tired," which combines zydeco with both ska and 1960s-type soul. And African influences are incorporated on "Zydeco Road" and "Zydeco Is Alright," both of which employ guest Kenyatta Simon on the djembe (a West African instrument). *Follow Me Chicken* is a disc that zydeco enthusiasts should make a point of obtaining. — *Alex Henderson*

Creole Crossroads / Oct. 3, 1995 / Rounder ✦✦✦

I'm a Zydeco Hog / Aug. 5, 1997 / Rounder ✦✦✦

Kenny Neal

b. Oct. 14, 1957, Los Angeles, CA
Guitar, Harmonica, Vocals / Modern Electric Blues
The future of Baton Rouge swamp blues lies squarely in multi-instrumentalist Kenny Neal's capable hands. Along with a select few others (Larry Garner, for one), the second-generation southern Louisiana bluesman is entirely cognizant of the region's venerable blues tradition and imaginative enough to steer it in fresh directions — as his five albums for Alligator confirm.

Neal was exposed to the swamp blues sound from day one. His dad, harpist Raful Neal, was a Baton Rouge blues mainstay whose pals included Buddy Guy and Slim Harpo (the latter handed three-year-old Kenny an old harp one day as a toy, and that was it). At age 13, Neal was playing in his father's band, and he picked up a bass at 17 for Buddy Guy.

The guitarist recruited some of his talented siblings to form the Neal Brothers Blues Band up in Toronto (brother Noel later played bass behind James Cotton; five other Neal brothers also play in various bands!) before returning stateside. In 1987, Kenny Neal cut his debut LP for Florida producer Bob Greenlee — a stunningly updated swamp feast initially marketed on King Snake Records as *Bio on the Bayou*. Alligator picked it up the following year, retitled it *Big News from Baton Rouge!!*, and young Neal was on his way.

Neal's sizzling guitar work, sturdy harp, and gravelly, aged-beyond-his-years vocals have served him well ever since. An acclaimed 1991 stint on Broadway in a production of *Mule Bone* found him performing acoustic versions of Langston Hughes' poetry set to music by Taj Mahal. His last Alligator set, 1994's *Hoodoo Moon*, rates as one of his most satisfying outings to date. — *Bill Dahl*

Bio on the Bayou / 1987 / King Snake ✦✦✦✦
The debut release for the second-generation bayou blues guitarist/harpist, whose gruff-before-their-time vocals retain their swamp sensibility while assuming a bright contemporary feel that tabs him as a leading contender for future blues stardom. [*Big News from Baton Rouge* was originally released in 1987 as *Bio on the Bayou* on King Snake Records.] — *Bill Dahl*

Big News from Baton Rouge!! / 1987 / Alligator ✦✦✦✦
The debut release for the second-generation bayou blues guitarist/harpist, whose gruff-before-their-time vocals retain their swamp sensibility while as-

suming a bright contemporary feel that tabs him as a leading contender for future blues stardom. [*Big News from Baton Rouge* was originally released in 1987 as *Bio on the Bayou* on King Snake Records.] — *Bill Dahl*

Devil Child / 1989 / Alligator ✦✦✦✦
Backed by a punchy horn section and sizzling rhythms, Neal didn't suffer from any sophomore jinx. Between Neal, his bass-playing co-producer Bob Greenlee, and drummer Jim Payne, there's some very crafty songwriting going on here — "Any Fool Will Do," "Bad Check," and "Can't Have Your Cake (And Eat It Too)" are among the standouts. — *Bill Dahl*

Walking on Fire / 1991 / Alligator ✦✦✦✦
Another in the remarkably consistent Alligator catalog of Kenny Neal that strikingly captures his contemporary Baton Rouge blues sound. He gets a little hot help from the Horny Horns — alto saxist Maceo Parker and trombonist Fred Wesley — who once filled a smiliar role behind the Godfather of Soul himself, James Brown. Two songs find Neal going the unplugged route, just as he had performed them in the Broadway musical *Mule Bone*. — *Bill Dahl*

Bayou Blood / 1992 / Alligator ✦✦✦✦
You really can't go wrong with any of the guitarist's fine Alligator albums, but this one sparkles as brightly as any, with memorable outings like "Right Train, Wrong Track," "That Knife Don't Cut No More," and the steamy title track. Neal's albums are invariably dominated by well-chosen originals — no small feat these days. — *Bill Dahl*

Hoodoo Moon / 1994 / Alligator ✦✦✦✦
Neal is one of the most impressive young blues artists on the scene today — a fact borne out by the contents of this collection. Ably backed by a band that includes his brother Noel on bass and keyboardist Lucky Peterson, Neal indulges in a couple of covers this time, but the majority of the disc is original and incendiary. — *Bill Dahl*

● **Deluxe Edition** / Oct. 28, 1997 / Alligator ✦✦✦✦
Deluxe Edition is a great compilation of 15 highlights from Kenny Neal's first five albums for Alligator Records. Neal's records were more consistent than those from some of his Alligator peers, but this best-of-collection is welcome since it provides a nice introduction for the neophyte. And, since it isolates the cream of the crop on one record, it's also not a bad bet for serious fans who want all the good stuff in one place. — *Thom Owens*

Raful Neal

b. Jun. 6, 1936, Baton Rouge, LA
Harmonica, Vocals / Modern Electric Blues, Electric Louisiana Blues, Electric Swamp Blues
When he wasn't busy siring progeny (the Neal household produced ten kids, most of them seemingly now playing the blues), Raful Neal was staking his claim as one of the top harpists on the Baton Rouge blues front. Unfortunately, until recently, his discography didn't reflect that status — but albums for Alligator and Ichiban have righted that injustice.

Neal took up the harp at age 14, tutored by a local player named Ike Brown and influenced by Chicago mainstay Little Walter. Neal's first band, the Clouds, also included guitarist Buddy Guy. The harpist debuted on vinyl in 1958 with a 45 for Don Robey's Houston-headquartered Peacock Records. But "Sunny Side of Love," fine though it was, didn't lead to an encore for Peacock or anywhere else until much later, when Neal turned up with 45s on Whit, La Louisiane, and Fantastic.

Neal's debut album, the aptly titled *Louisiana Legend,* first emerged on Bob Greenlee's King Snake Records and was picked up by Alligator in 1990. *I Been Mistreated,* Neal's equally swampy follow-up, was released on Ichiban the following year; sons Noel (on bass) and Raful Jr. (on guitar) pitched in to help their old man out. — *Bill Dahl*

● **Louisiana Legend** / 1990 / Alligator ✦✦✦✦
Kenny Neal's dad Raful is a longtime Baton Rouge swamp blues stalwart whose own discography is way sparser than it should be. This album, first out on Bob Greenlee's King Snake logo, is an atmospheric indication of what the elder Neal can do with a harmonica, mixing covers ("Steal Away," "Honest I Do," "No Cuttin' Loose") with spicy originals. — *Bill Dahl*

I Been Mistreated / 1991 / Ichiban ✦✦✦✦
Neal wrote the majority of the sides on this satisfying disc himself. His supple band includes two sons, Raful, Jr. on guitar and Noel on bass, and Lucky Peterson on keys. — *Bill Dahl*

Jimmy Nelson

b. Apr. 17, 1928, Philadelphia, PA
Vocals / R&B, Texas Blues

Heavy-voiced Jimmy Nelson was very briefly a star in 1951, when his downbeat "T-99 Blues" topped the R&B charts for Modern Records' RPM subsidiary. Strangely, he was unable to ever return back to hitdom, despite some very worthy follow-ups.

Though he was based out of Houston, Nelson did most of his early recording in California. After debuting on wax in 1948 with a single for Olliet, he cut his only smash, the aforementioned "T-99 Blues," at the Clef Club in Richmond, TX, in 1951, with backup from pianist Peter Rabbit's trio. (The exultant slow blues was covered by bandleader Tiny Bradshaw for King.)

From then on, Nelson did his studio work for RPM in L.A. with a cadre of the city's top session men: saxist Maxwell Davis, pianist Willard McDaniel, guitarist Chuck Norris, bassists Red Callender and Ted Brinson, and drummer Lee Young. For unknown reasons, the ominous "Meet Me with Your Black Dress On," "Second Hand Fool," "Sweetest Little Girl," and the rest failed to repeat for the singer.

Nelson made a single for Chess in Houston in 1955 (the typically laidback "Free and Easy Mind"), ventured next to Ray Dobard's Bay Area-based Music City diskery in 1957 to wax "The Wheel," and tried his luck with a variety of tiny Texas labels during the mid-'60s with no further success. At last report, Nelson was still active vocally. —*Bill Dahl*

- **Jimmy Mr T99 Nelson** / 1981 / Ace ◆◆◆◆
No CD exists containing Texas shouter Nelson's early-'50s output for Modern, but Ace did assemble a nice vinyl collection of his best material that'll have to suffice (if you can find it) until they get around to issuing it digitally. —*Bill Dahl*

Tracy Nelson

b. Dec. 27, 1947, Madison, WI
Vocals, Keyboards / Soul, Modern Blues

A very versatile and talented vocalist, Tracy Nelson is better known for her role as lead singer of Mother Earth. The Nashville sextet had three albums in a country-rock vein make the charts in the late '60s and early '70s. But Nelson is just as capable in soul, R&B, and blues, though she hasn't released many records in that style. Her albums for Flying Fish were more indicative of her eclecticism, but her R&B and blues roots are really evident on her 1993 release, *In the Here and Now,* and 1995's *I Feel So Good*—both on Rounder Records.

Born in California but raised in Madison, Wisconsin, Nelson began playing music when she was a student at the University of Wisconsin. Nelson began singing folk and blues at coffeehouses and R&B and rock 'n' roll at parties with a covers band called the Fabulous Imitators. In 1964, she recorded an album for Prestige, *Deep Are the Roots,* which was produced by Sam Charters.

Two years after recording *Deep Are the Roots,* Nelson headed out to the West Coast, spending some time in Los Angeles before settling in San Francisco. After arriving in San Francisco, she formed Mother Earth in 1968, moving the group to Nashville the following year. The band stayed together for five years, recording several albums for Mercury Records, among a handful of other labels. Nelson left the band in the mid-'70s, embarking on a solo career that saw her release albums for a variety of labels, including Columbia, Atlantic, and Flying Fish.

Tracy Nelson continued to record and perform into the '90s. In 1993, she released *In the Here and Now,* her first album for Rounder Records and, not coincidentally, her first straight blues record since she began recording in the '60s. Nelson followed *In the Here and Now* with several acclaimed records of gritty blues-rock for Rounder. —*Ron Wynn & Stephen Thomas Erlewine*

Deep Are the Roots / 1965 / Prestige ◆◆◆

Mother Earth / 1972 / Reprise ◆◆◆◆

Poor Man's Paradise / 1973 / CBS ◆◆◆◆

Tracy Nelson / 1974 / Atlantic ◆◆◆

Sweet Soul Music / 1975 / One Way ◆◆◆◆

Time Is on My Side / 1976 / One Way ◆◆◆

Homemade Songs / 1978 / Flying Fish ◆◆◆
This album features gospel-tinged blues from this big-voiced, intense singer. —*AMG*

Come See About Me / 1980 / Flying Fish ◆◆
Her second Flying Fish album features R&B music. —*AMG*

In the Here & Now / Jun. 1, 1993 / Rounder ◆◆◆◆
Tracy Nelson's lack of commercial success has always been baffling, even though her voice and style are too eclectic to be pigeonholed into any trend. This Rounder release features her in a suitable forum—singing blues and R&B with strength, depth and passion. Nelson doesn't just cover such songs as Elmore James' "It Hurts Me Too" or Willie Dixon's "Whatever I Am (You Made Me)"; she probes, tears, stretches and extends them, making the lyrics and sentiments her own through intense, animated singing and phrasing. The final number, a first-rate cover of Percy Mayfield's "Please Send Me Someone to Love," matches her with the great Irma Thomas, another blues and R&B survivor. It's a fitting conclusion to an album that comes quite close to displaying Tracy Nelson's complete skills and persona. —*Ron Wynn*

I Feel So Good / 1995 / Rounder ◆◆◆

Homemade Songs/Come See About Me / 1996 / Flying Fish ◆◆◆◆

Move On / Jul. 29, 1996 / Rounder ◆◆◆
The third album in Tracy Nelson's '90s comeback, *Move On* finds her sharing the microphone with the likes of Delbert McClinton, Phoebe Snow, Bonnie Raitt, and Maria Muldaur (the last three on "Ladies' Man"), singers with whom she shares a taste in bluesy rock with a country tinge. She is in typically fine voice on a set of songs more notable for the tasty playing on them than for their distinctiveness. The best among them is Nelson's own "Playin' It Safe" (one of her four compositions) which has a gospel feel to support the lyric's sage advice. Blues fans who caught up with Nelson on 1993's *In the Here and Now* or 1995's *I Feel So Good* may find this album, with its pop, rock, and R&B elements, a bit eclectic for their taste, but fans of Bonnie Raitt who long for her earlier, grittier music may find a new heroine. —*William Ruhlmann*

- **The Best of Tracy Nelson/Mother Earth** / Sep. 9, 1996 / Reprise Archives ◆◆◆◆
Janis Joplin may have gotten all of the fame and glory, but she was far from the only White female blues shouter to emerge from the San Francisco music scene of the mid-'60s; *The Best of Tracy Nelson/Mother Earth* is proof positive of that, providing an excellent introduction to one of the more sadly overlooked talents of her time and place. Despite any number of passing similarites to Joplin, Nelson sings with greater finesse; her style is more adaptable as well, capable of fitting comfortably into R&B, psychedelia, and pop ballads, all the while remaining grounded in classic roots music traditions. Highlighted by her perennial "Down So Low"—subsequently recorded by everyone from Linda Ronstadt to Etta James—this 17-track compilation also spotlights performances spanning from a wrenching cover of Little Willie John's "Need Your Love So Bad" to contemporary material like Steve Young's "Seven Bridges Road" and John Hiatt's "Thinking of You," offering a comprehensive overview of her earliest and most enduring work. —*Jason Ankeny*

Tracy Nelson Country / Sep. 9, 1996 / Warner Brothers ◆◆◆◆
Unfortunately for the general public, Tracy Nelson has never achieved the celebrity and general acclaim of, say, Bonnie Raitt, her most similar compatriot in the blue-eyed blues field; but it sure ain't for lack of talent or pipes. Technically, Nelson is a far superior vocalist than Raitt, possessing a full-throttle voice that can spar with Etta James or Aretha Franklin without breaking a sweat. Raitt is laidback and subtle; Nelson is upfront and in your face. When you pull Toni Tennille away from the mushy Captain & Tennille ditties and her over-orchestrated pop standards of late, you can hear some of that same gutsy backwoods emotion that Nelson radiates. Save any number of Black soul singers, Nelson is essentially without a peer of equal recognition. As the lead singer for Mother Earth, a pioneering White blues band, Nelson was asked to record a solo country album by steel guitarist Pete Drake who had previously worked with country star Melba Montgomery and produced Mother Earth's country album. Originally released in 1969

with some of Music City's most royal musicians holding court, the ten original album tunes and three other remnants of that week-long session are included here. On Tammy Wynette's "Stand By Your Man," Tracy picks up the ballad's pace a beat, but not as rapidly as Candi Staton's ferocious 1971 version. Still, Nelson wraps her tonsils around the lyrics and finishes it with a rousing bending of notes. On Elvis Presley's rocker "That's All Right, Mama," Nelson sizzles, and on Boz Scaggs' almost vaudevillian "Now, You're Gone" blues she gives a Broadway-bound performance. On Chuck "The Sheik of the Blues" Willis' soft shuffle "You're Still My Baby," the harmonica and handclaps are so spirited it sounds as if the listener is in the midst of the session. With the Jordanaires' deliciously baritone call-and-response background vocals, Nelson pleads with assurance on the bluesy "I Wanna Be Your Mama Again." Although Nelson covered traditional country material such as Dolly Parton's "Why, Why, Why," Hank Williams' "I'm So Lonesome I Could Cry," Don Gibson's "Blue Blue Day" and Patsy Cline's "I Fall To Pieces" and the then-original "Sad Situation," those are not the highlights. The album's very best selections were the least known. The self-penned "Stay As Sweet As You Are" had a mellow Southern rock feeling with a distinctive country string refrain in the background. "Can't Go On Loving You" is sweetly plaintive, while the desperate "Wait, Wait, Wait" reveals a woman begging her man for one more chance. The manner in which she modulates her plea on the fade is captivating and inventive phrasing. A woman trusting a man whom she's found to have cheated on her yet again provides the backdrop for Hank Williams' "You Win Again." With that in mind, Nelson becomes the victim as she makes this a midtempo fifties-style R&B ballad with a keyboard workout that would make Fats Domino proud. To then say that Nelson wails her betrayal on the song would be putting it lightly. She lives it for four minutes and fifteen seconds. In fact, she lives all of these songs. That's how life must be in Tracy Nelson country. — Bill Carpenter

The Neville Brothers

f. 1977, New Orleans, LA
Group / R&B, Soul, Funk, New Orleans R&B
Throughout their long careers as both solo performers and as members of the group which bore their family name, the Neville Brothers proudly carried the torch of their native New Orleans' rich R&B legacy. Although the four siblings—Arthur, Charles, Aaron, and Cyril—did not officially unite under the Neville Brothers aegis until 1977, all had crossed musical paths in the past, while also enjoying success with other unrelated projects: eldest brother Art was the first to tackle a recording career, when in 1954 his high school band the Hawketts cut "Mardi Gras Mambo," a song which later became the annual carnival's unofficial anthem. Both Aaron and Charles later joined the Hawketts as well, and when Art joined the Navy in 1958, he handed Aaron the group's vocal reins.

Two years later, Aaron scored his first solo hit, "Over You"; in 1966, he notched a pop smash with the classic "Tell It Like It Is," a lush ballad showcasing his gossamer vocals. Art, meanwhile, returned from the service to begin his own solo career, and recorded a series of regional hits like "Cha Dooky Doo," "Zing Zing," and "Oo-Whee Baby." In 1967, he formed Art Neville and the Sounds, which included both Aaron and Charles as featured vocalists and quickly became a sensation on the local club circuit.

In 1968 producer Allen Toussaint hired the group as the house band for his Sansu Enterprises; minus Aaron and Charles, the Sounds evolved into a highly-regarded rhythm section which backed artists as diverse as Lee Dorsey, Robert Palmer, and Labelle before eventually finding fame on their own as the Meters. Consequently, Aaron resumed his solo career, although with only sporadic success; as a result, he also worked as a dock hand. Charles, meanwhile, relocated to New York City, where his skills as a saxophonist led to tenures with a variety of jazz bands; after returning to New Orleans, he was arrested for possession of marijuana and served a three-year sentence at the Angola Prison Farm.

In 1975, the Meters backed the Wild Tchoupitoulas, a group led by the Nevilles' uncle, George "Big Chief Jolly" Landry. Both Aaron and Charles were enlisted for the session, as was youngest brother Cyril; when the Meters disbanded the following year, the four brothers backed the Tchoupitoulas on tour, and in 1977 they offically banded together as the Neville Brothers. Despite their gift for intricate four-part harmonies, their self-titled 1978 debut

unsuccessfully cast the vocal quartet as a disco band, and following a dismal response they were dropped by their label, Capitol.

The Nevilles spent the following three years without a contract, but after signing with A&M, fan Bette Midler helped secure the services of producer Joel Dorn for 1981's superior *Fiyo on the Bayou*, which spotlighted Aaron's angelic tenor on standards like "Mona Lisa" and "The Ten Commandments of Love" along with renditions of "Iko Iko" and "Brother John." Despite widespread critical acclaim, the album sold poorly, and again the Nevilles were cut loose from their contract. After signing to the tiny Black Top label, they issued 1984's *Neville-ization*, an incendiary live set recorded at the Crescent City landmark Tipitina's which featured Duke Ellington's "Caravan" and Aaron's perennial "Tell It Like It Is" alongside the brothers' own "Africa" and "Fear, Hate, Envy, Jealousy."

After another concert album, 1987's *Live at Tipitina's*, the Nevilles signed with EMI and returned to the studio in 1987 with *Uptown*, which again met with commercial failure despite cameo appearances from Keith Richards, Jerry Garcia and Carlos Santana. In 1989, they re-signed to A&M and recruited the services of famed New Orleans producer Daniel Lanois; the atmospheric *Yellow Moon*, the group's finest hour, finally earned them success on the charts, thanks in part to the anthemic single "Sister Rosa." 1990's *Brother's Keeper* fared even better, no doubt spurred by Aaron's concurrent success with Linda Ronstadt on the smash duet "Don't Know Much."

In subsequent years, Aaron reignited his solo career while also remaining with his brothers; while the Nevilles retained their cult following with LPs like 1992's *Family Groove*, 1994's *Live on Planet Earth*, and 1996's *Mitakuye Oyasin Oyasin/All My Relations*, Aaron scored a Top Ten hit in 1991 with the single "Everybody Plays the Fool," taken from the Ronstadt-produced *Warm Your Heart*. In 1993, he notched a minor hit with "Don't Take Away My Heaven" from the LP *The Grand Tour;* a year later, he found success with "I Fall to Pieces," a duet with country star Trisha Yearwood. In 1990, Charles issued the jazz collection *Charles Neville and Diversity*. In addition, a second generation of Nevilles also began making their mark on music; in 1988, Aaron's son Ivan, a member of Keith Richards' backing band the X-Pensive Winos, released his solo debut, *If My Ancestors Could See Me Now. —Jason Ankeny*

Fiyo on the Bayou / Apr. 1981 / A&M ++++
A brilliant updating of the New Orleans R&B sound to include strains of Cajun, rock, and reggae on standards ranging from "Hey Pocky Way" to "The Ten Commandments of Love" and "Sitting in Limbo." — William Ruhlmann

Neville-Ization / Jun. 1984 / Black Top +++
It took Black Top Records two years to put this record out after the Neville Brothers recorded it live at Tipitina's in New Orleans in September, 1982, and one reason may be that it presents a mediocre, going-through-the-motions set. At their best, the Nevilles achieve a transcendent musical mixture, and even at the level of mere professionalism they're an impressive unit, but this just isn't the live album of which they are capable. — William Ruhlmann

★ Treacherous: A History of the Neville Brothers / 1986 / Rhino +++++
The music of the Neville Brothers was more a matter of rumor than documentation to most record buyers outside the New Orleans area until 1986, when Rhino Records finally gathered together their various solo and group records dating back 30 years and presented their story coherently on this two-disc set. Suddenly, it all makes sense, and the Nevilles' mixture of styles emerges as a singular American genre unto itself. This record is a revelation. — William Ruhlmann

Uptown / Mar. 1987 / EMI America ++
The Neville Brothers displayed their eclecticism on this lone EMI album. They played with some high class guest stars, including Branford Marsalis, Jerry Garcia, Ronnie Montrose, Carlos Santana, and Keith Richards. But despite these excellent musicians and The Nevilles' usual tight playing and exuberant collective vocals, once more, the album failed to either get them a huge hit or faithfully recreate the quality of their live shows. —Ron Wynn

Yellow Moon / 1989 / A&M ++++
The Neville Brothers made a bid for pop-rock stardom with this well-produced album for A&M, their first under a new pact with the label inked in the late '80s. It was certainly as solid as any they cut for A&M; the vocals were both nicely arranged and expertly performed, the arrangements were

basically solid, and the selections were intelligently picked and sequenced. The album charted and remained there for many weeks, while the Nevilles toured and generated lots of interest. It didn't become a hit, but it did respectably and represents perhaps their finest overall pop LP. — *Ron Wynn*

Brother's Keeper / Jul. 1990 / A&M ✦✦✦
All of the Neville Brothers' recent albums for A&M have been frustrating, uneven propositions, with great performances followed by disjointed numbers, and the studio productions seldom conveying the excitement and fire this group routinely generates in concert. The same holds true for this release, even though it got more pop exposure and chart penetration than any previous Neville Brothers album. But despite their energetic vocals and often superb instrumental interaction, this release still didn't come close to presenting the Neville Brothers on a good night, much less a great one. — *Ron Wynn*

Treacherous Too: A History of the Neville Brothers, Vol. 2 (1955-1987) / Feb. 1, 1991 / Rhino ✦✦✦✦
Okay, there's no such thing as secondhand revelation, but the Neville Brothers had more than enough stray tracks from their decades of local music-making around New Orleans to justify this second, single-disc follow-up to Rhino's first Nevilles history. There's more of an emphasis on novelty material here, but once again you can hear the roots of the Nevilles' cross-genre appeal in pop, R&B, and soul music dating back to the 1950s. Since most of these songs were recorded as singles, they have an immediate surface appeal, but repeated listenings also bring out the sounds of the tight session bands (including members of the Meters) who backed the Nevilles up. Actually, it's only the five 1980s tracks from just-okay albums like *Neville-ization* and *Uptown* that keep this collection from classic status, not the older stuff. — *William Ruhlmann*

Live on Planet Earth / Apr. 19, 1994 / A&M ✦✦✦
Clearly, this is intended to be the definitive live document of a band that has always been defined by its live work. Clocking in at 71 minutes, the album was culled from a world tour. The rhythm section of drummer Willie Green and bassist Tony Hall keeps up a steady groove from song to song, and The Nevilles trade off lead and harmony vocals on original songs that range across their career and add everything from Bob Marley compositions to "Love the One You're With" and "Amazing Grace." They Neville-ize all comers, throwing them into the pot and coming out with a tasty gumbo. If there's anything missing, it's the small club atmosphere from which The Nevilles emerged: this is a wide-screen treatment of a music that gained impact from its intimacy but now seeks to form a global conga line. — *William Ruhlmann*

Mitakuye Oyasin Oyasin/All My Relations / May 14, 1996 / A&M ✦✦✦
The Neville Brothers have made a family affair of their first studio album in four years, writing much of the material themselves and co-producing the record with James Stroud. As a result, they are making less of an effort to secure a pop hit this time, even though they do throw in a little rap and a funky cover of Bill Withers' "Ain't No Sunshine." But part of the reason they tend to be more interesting live than on record is that, beyond being well-meaning, they haven't got much to say. Most of the songs here are homilies to brotherhood, responsibility, and environmentalism, set against tracks that evoke Brazilian music, mbaqanga, reggae, R&B, and soul and are heavy on percussion and horns. Occasionally, as on the respectable cover of the Grateful Dead's "Fire of the Mountain," with guest guitarist Bob Weir, or on Aaron Neville's typically ethereal "Saved By the Grace of Your Love," the music transcends both the message and the groove. But this is an album of small pleasures rather than the larger statement it seems intended to be. — *William Ruhlmann*

The Very Best of the Neville Brothers / Jan. 14, 1997 / Rhino ✦✦✦✦
Sixteen-track compilation focusing almost exclusively on the period spanning the late '70s to the late '80s. A couple of Aaron Neville's big '60s hits ("Tell It like It Is" and "Over You") are thrown in as well, as are a couple of cuts from the Wild Tchoupitoulas' 1976 album. Some may argue that the Nevilles' sprawling output is too difficult to condense into a single disc. On the other hand, given how often they're criticized for underachieving on record, this is a pretty suitable purchase for someone whose interest only runs deep enough for one anthology. — *Richie Unterberger*

Hambone Willie Newbern

b. 1899, **d.** 1947
Guitar, Vocals / Acoustic Memphis Blues, Prewar Country Blues
Little is known about blues songster Hambone Willie Newborn; a mere half-dozen sides comprise the sum of his recorded legacy, but among those six is the first-ever rendition of the immortal Delta classic "Roll and Tumble Blues." Reportedly born in 1899, he first began to make a name for himself in the Brownsville, Tennessee area, where he played country dances and fish fries in the company of Yank Rachell; later, on the Mississippi medicine show circuit, he mentored Sleepy John Estes (from whom most of the known information about Newbern originated). While in Atlanta in 1929, Newbern cut his lone session; in addition to "Roll and Tumble," which became an oft-covered standard, he recorded songs like "She Could Toodle-Oo" and "Hambone Willie's Dreamy-Eyed Woman's Blues," which suggest an old-fashioned rag influence. By all reports an extremely ill-tempered man, Newbern's behavior eventually led him to prison, where a brutal beating is said to have brought his life to an end around 1947. — *Jason Ankeny*

The Greatest Songsters: Complete Works (1927-1929) / 1990 / Document ✦✦✦✦

Robert Nighthawk (Robert McCollum)

b. Nov. 30, 1909, Helena, AR, **d.** Nov. 5, 1967, Helena, AR
Guitar, Harmonica, Vocals / Acoustic Chicago Blues, Electric Chicago Blues, Chicago Blues
Of all the pivotal figures in blues history, certainly one of the most important was Robert Nighthawk. He bridged the gap between Delta and Chicago blues effortlessly, taking his slide cues from Tampa Red and stamping them with a Mississippi edge learned first hand from his cousin, Houston Stackhouse. Though he recorded from the '30s into the early '40s under a variety of names—Robert Lee McCoy, Rambling Bob, Peetie's Boy—he finally took his lasting sobriquet of Robert Nighthawk from the title of his first record, "Prowling Night Hawk." It should be noted that the huge lapses in the man's discography are direct results of his rambling nature, taciturnity, and seeming disinterest in making records. Once you got him into a studio, the results were almost always of a uniform excellence. But it might be two years or more between sessions!

Nighthawk never achieved the success of his more celebrated pupils, Muddy Waters and Earl Hooker, finding himself to be much happier to be working one nighters in taverns and the Maxwell Street open market on Sundays. He eventually left Chicago for his hometown of Helena, AR, where he briefly took over the King Biscuit Radio Show after Sonny Boy Williamson died while seemingly working every small juke joint that dotted the landscape until his death from congestive heart failure in 1967. Robert Nighthawk is not a name that regularly gets bandied about when discussing the all-time greats of the blues. But well it should, because his legacy was all pervasive; his resonant voice and creamy smooth slide guitar playing (played in standard tuning, unusual for a bluesman) would influence players for generations to come and many of his songs would later become blues standards. — *Cub Koda*

Bricks in My Pillow / 1977 / Pearl Flapper ✦✦✦
A very nice compilation of at least one extant take of Nighthawk's complete output for the Chicago-based United label, recorded in 1951 and 1952. Similar in feel to the Chess sides with the addition of Jump Jackson's rock-sock drumming, these 12 sides find Nighthawk exploring familiar turf on the slow ones ("Crying Won't Help You" and "The Moon Is Rising" are two of his best) while kicking up his heels on the fast boogies like Jim Jackson's "(Gonna Move To) Kansas City" and "Take It Easy Baby." Of particular interest is the adaptation of an old Delta solo piece "Maggie Campbell," here treated to a full band rhumba beat arrangement that actually works. — *Cub Koda*

Complete Recorded Works (1937-1940) / 1985 / Wolf ✦✦✦✦
For a glimpse into Nighthawk's earliest sides for the Victor label, this is the place to go. The sound—all of it taken off old 78s with little regard for modern noise reduction—is less than stellar, but the performances are nothing but. This includes the tune that gave his permanent non de plume, "Prowling Night Hawk." — *Cub Koda*

★ **Live on Maxwell Street** / 1988 / Rounder ✦✦✦✦✦
Recorded by Norman Dayron live on the street (one can actually hear cars

driving by!) in 1964 with just Robert Whitehead on drums and John Lee Granderson on rhythm guitar in support, Nighthawk's slide playing (and single string soloing, for that matter) are nothing short of elegant and explosive. Highlights include "The Maxwell Street Medley" which combines his two big hits "Anna Lee" and "Sweet Black Angel," a mind altering 12 bar solo on "The Time Have Come" which proves that Nighthawk's lead playing was just as well developed as his slide work, and a couple of wild instrumentals with Carey Bell sitting in on harmonica. Nighthawk sounds cool as a cucumber, presiding over everything with an almost genial charm while laying the toughest sounds imaginable. One of the top three greatest live blues albums of all time. — *Cub Koda*

Black Angel Blues / 1991 / Charly ♦♦♦

Robert Nighthawk and Houston Stackhouse / 1994 / Testament ♦♦♦♦

Masters of the Modern Blues / 1995 / Testament ♦♦♦♦

Toasting the Blues / Nov. 21, 1995 / Inside Sounds ♦♦♦

The Nighthawks

f. 1972, Washington, D.C.
Group / R&B, Rock 'n' Roll, Hard Rock, Modern Blues
A hard-driving DC-based bar band with strong Chicago blues roots. Formed in 1972 by harpist and vocalist Mark Wenner and guitarist Jimmy Thackery, the band earned a reputation as a solid outfit through more than a decade of touring and recording projects with John Hammond and former members of Muddy Waters' band. Thackery left in 1986, but Wenner regrouped around longtime members Jan Zukowski on bass and Pete Ragusa on drums. *Trouble*, their recent release on Powerhouse, is a blend of blues, R&B, and rock influences, with a typically energetic sound born in thousands of one-night stands across the country. — *Bill Dahl*

Rock and Roll / 1972 / Aladdin ♦♦♦

● **Open All Nite** / 1976 / Mobile Fidelity ♦♦♦♦
This longtime Washington D.C. blues-rock aggregation made one of its more complete and satisfying albums with this date. Everything, from the vocals to the good mix of bar-band arrangements and explosive solos, clicked. — *Ron Wynn*

Jacks & Kings / 1977 / Genes ♦♦♦♦
Classic material and stirring playing. A must-find. — *Michael G. Nastos*

Side Pocket Shot / 1977 / Adelphi ♦♦♦
A studio album with The Rhythm King's Horns. Another solid album. — *Michael G. Nastos*

Live at the Psychedelly / Jan. 1977 / Adelphi ♦♦♦
The Nighthawks, at their heart, are a bar band in the best sense of the term—they're at their best in a live setting. *Live at the Psychedelly* captures them at their mid-'70s peak, running through standards ("Jail House Rock," "Hound Dog") and contemporary rockers ("Can't Get Next to You," "Whammer Jammer," "Tripe Face Boogie"), with fire and energy. The CD reissue includes four bonus tracks recorded at the El Mocambo. — *Thom Owens*

The Nighthawks / 1980 / Mercury ♦♦♦

10 Years Live / 1982 / Varrick ♦♦♦♦
A highly recommended two-fer that celebrates their decade together. — *Michael G. Nastos*

Best of the Nighthawks / 1982 / Genes ♦♦♦

Rock-N-Roll / 1983 / Varrick ♦♦♦

Jacks & Kings 'full House / 1983 / Adelphi ♦♦♦

Backtrack / 1988 / Varrick ♦♦♦

Live in Europe / 1990 / Varrick ♦♦♦

Hard Living / 1991 / Varrick ♦♦♦♦

Trouble / Jan. 1991 / Powerhouse ♦♦♦♦
Trouble is one of the Nighthawks' better latter-day records. The group doesn't do anything different—they still plow through blues, rock 'n' roll, and R&B with gusto—but the difference is the group has a great set of songs and energetic performances which propel the album to the status of a first-rate, good-time party record. — *Thom Owens*

Rock This House / 1993 / Big Mo ♦♦♦
A live set of dependably accomplished bar-band contemporary blues with a slight rock edge. The set list won't win any prizes for originality, with covers of moldies by Muddy Waters, Jimmy Reed, Merle Travis, James Brown, Carl Perkins, and Otis Rush, and just one original tune. Yet it's executed quite compentently, and the fidelity is good. — *Richie Unterberger*

Pain & Paradise / 1996 / Big Mo ♦♦♦
With harmonica player/singer Mark Wenner, bassist Jan Zukowski, and drummer/singer Pete Ragusa now well into their third decade together, the Nighthawks are a veteran blue-collar band that gets the job done, and *Pain & Paradise* is one of their better studio efforts. Guitar chores are now handled by relative newcomer Pete Kanaras, who replaced Danny Morris. The Nighthawks' reach never exceeds their grasp, and this album displays their excellent grasp of the Muddy Waters/Little Walter-style Chicago blues and bar-band rock 'n' roll that lie at the core of their sound. They kick butt enough that you know you've been kicked, but not so much that it hurts, and they're even confident enough to ease up every now and then. — *Steve Hoffman*

Ollie Nightingale

b. Batesville, TN
Vocals / Soul, Electric Blues, Soul Blues
Call him a blues singer if you prefer, but Ollie Nightingale will likely always be recalled most readily for the emotionally charged Memphis soul he cut from 1968 to 1970 as front man for the Nightingales.

Like most great soul singers, Ollie Hoskins came straight out of church musically. He was the lead singer of the Dixie Nightingales, a Memphis spiritual aggregation, by 1958, when they made their vinyl debut on tiny Pepper Records. Influenced by gospel greats Kylo Turner and Ira Tucker, Hoskins hung in with the group as they moved to Nashboro in 1962 before signing with Stax's short-lived Chalice gospel logo.

Stax exec Al Bell convinced the group to go pop in 1968, though that sanctified spirit rings through melismatically on their R&B hits "I Got a Sure Thing," "You're Leaving Me," and "I've Got a Feeling." Hoskins went solo at the turn of the decade, billing himself as Ollie Nightingale and scoring a couple of R&B chart items ("It's a Sad Thing" and "May the Best Man Win") in 1971-72. The Nightingales soldiered on, recruiting singer Tommy Tate to replace him in the studio.

Nightingale remains a popular blues and soul singer around Memphis. He recently did a performing cameo in *The Firm*, a movie thriller starring Tom Cruise. — *Bill Dahl*

● **I'll Drink Your Bathwater, Baby** / 1995 / Ecko ♦♦♦♦
After spending several years performing in local Memphis clubs, Ollie Nightingale was given the opportunity to return the recording studio to cut his first full-length solo album. The resulting record, *I'll Drink Your Bathwater, Baby,* may have had an ugly title, but the record itself was an excellent slice of contemporary soul-blues. Nightingale tears through the selection of originals and covers with true passion, elevating the average songs to something quite passionate and inspired. It's an excellent way to revive his recording career. — *Thom Owens*

Tell Me What You Want Me to Do / Jul. 30, 1996 / Ecko ♦♦♦

Make It Sweet / Sep. 23, 1997 / Ecko ♦♦♦

Hammie Nixon (Hammie Nickerson)

b. Jan. 22, 1908, Brownsville, TN, d. Aug. 17, 1984, Jackson, TN
Harmonica, Guitar / Harmonica Blues
Harmonica player Hammie Nixon was born on January 22, 1908, in Brownsville, TN. An orphan at a young age, he was raised by foster parents. He began his career as a professional harmonical player in the 1920s, but also played the kazoo, guitar, and jug. He performed with Sleepy John Estes for more than 50 years, first recording with Estes in 1929 for the Victor label. He also recorded with Little Buddy Doyle, Lee Green, Charlie Pickett, and Son Bonds.

Nixon helped to pioneer the use of the harmonica as an accompaniment instrument with a band in the 1920s. Previous to that time, it had been mostly a solo instrument. He played with many jug bands. After Estes died,

Nixon played with the Beale Street Jug Band (also called the Memphis Beale Street Jug Band) from 1979 onward. Hammie Nixon died August 17, 1984. — *Michael Erlewine*

● **Tappin' That Thing** / 1984 / High Water ✦✦✦✦

Former Sleepy John Estes musical partner moves out on his own with this collection of solo recordings from the early '80s. Produced by David Evans for a small record company run out of the University of Memphis (High Water), these recordings find Nixon laying down vocals and working his magic on jug, kazoo, and harmonica in more of a jug band setting. This compilation brings together both sides of a High Water single, an entire vinyl abum on the same label and the inclusion of three previously unissued tracks, all recorded between 1982 and 1984. That Nixon still had a lot of gas left in the tank is very evident from the energetic versions of "Sugar Mama," "It's a Good Place to Go," "Viola Lee Blues," "Bottle Up and Go," "Kansas City Blues," and the title track. The inclusion of drums on three tracks blasts the music further into the realm of an amplified session, but Nixon retains his country edges regardless of setting. — *Cub Koda*

Darrell Nulisch

b. Sep. 14, 1952, Dallas, TX

Vocals, Harmonica / Electric Blues, Modern Electric Blues, Contemporary Blues

Best known for his work as a vocalist and harpist in blues combos including Ronnie Earl's Broadcasters and Anson Funderburgh's Rockets, Darrell Nulisch also pursued a solo career. Born in Dallas in 1953, he made his solo debut in 1991 with *Business as Usual; Bluesoul* followed in 1996. — *Jason Ankeny*

● **Business as Usual** / 1991 / Black Top ✦✦✦✦

Darrell Nulisch burns throughout *Business as Usual*, but his band fails to give him the needed rhythmic support that would have made this album great. As it is, it's merely a good set of contemporary blues, made worthwhile by Nulisch's dynamic harp. — *Thom Owens*

Bluesoul / 1996 / Higher Plane ✦✦✦

St. Louis Jimmy Oden (James Burke Oden)

b. Jun. 26, 1903, Nashville, TN, **d.** Dec. 30, 1977, Chicago, IL
Piano, Vocals / Electric Chicago Blues, Piano Blues
Few blues songs have stood the test of Father Time as enduringly as "Goin'
Down Slow." Its composer, St. Louis Jimmy Oden, endured rather impressively himself—he recorded during the early '30s and was still at it more
than three decades later.

If not for a fortuitous move to St. Louis circa 1917, James Oden might
have been known as Nashville Jimmy. He fell in with pianist Roosevelt Sykes
on the 1920s Gateway City blues circuit (the two remained frequent musical
partners through the ensuing decades). Oden enjoyed a fairly prolific recording career during the 1930s and '40s, appearing on Champion, Bluebird
(where he hit with "Goin' Down Slow" in 1941), Columbia, Bullet in 1947,
Miracle, Aristocrat (there he cut "Florida Hurricane" in 1948 accompanied
by pianist Sunnyland Slim and a young guitarist named Muddy Waters),
Mercury, Savoy, and Apollo.

Scattered singles for Duke (with Sykes on piano) and Parrot (a 1955 remake of "Goin' Down Slow") set the stage for Oden's 1960 album debut for
Prestige's Bluesville subsidiary (naturally, it included yet another reprise of
"Goin' Down Slow"). Oden was backed by guitarist Jimmie Lee Robinson
and a swinging New York rhythm section. As much a composer as a performer, Oden wrote "Soon Forgotten" and "Take the Bitter with the Sweet" for
Muddy Waters. —*Bill Dahl*

1932-1948 / Sep. 22, 1932-Dec. 14, 1944 / Story of Blues ◆◆◆◆
A solid sixteen-track import collection of Oden's earliest and best sides.
—*Cub Koda*

Goin' Down Slow / Nov. 19, 1960 / Original Blues Classics ◆◆◆◆
Oden offers ten of his own compositions on his first full-length album session, with low-key backing from a full band (Robert Banks' piano is especially prominent). He's a serviceable though not outstanding vocalist, and
offers his tales with a sort of good-natured fatalism, the most celebrated
number being the title track. While he was an outstanding songwriter, it may
have been best that Oden's compositions are primarily known through the
interpretations of others. On this recording at least, the arrangements could
really benefit from less uniformity, the tempo rarely escaping a pace somewhere between slow and medium. —*Richie Unterberger*

● **Back on My Feet Again** / 1995 / Collectables ◆◆◆◆
Although little discographical info is offered in its liner notes, this collection
presumably dates from the 1930s and '40s. Oden's dignified, slightly dry
vocal delivery rings true on these sides, which include a fine vintage rendition of his signature tune, "Going Down Slow." —*Bill Dahl*

Complete Works, Vol. 1 / May 1, 1995 / Document ◆◆◆

Complete Works, Vol. 2 / May 1, 1995 / Document ◆◆◆

Andrew Odom

b. Dec. 15, 1936, Denham Springs, LA, **d.** Dec. 23, 1991, Chicago, IL
Vocals / Modern Electric Chicago Blues
Eminently capable of serving up spot-on imitations of both Bobby "Blue"
Bland and B.B. King, Andrew Odom was also a man of many interrelated
nicknames: Big Voice, B.B., Little B.B., B.B. Junior. Perhaps his chameleonic
talents held him back; Odom was a journeyman Chicago singer who recorded relatively sparingly.

Like the majority of his peers, Odom started out singing spirituals but fell
in with Albert King and Johnny O'Neal on the St. Louis blues scene of the
mid-'50s and began plying his trade there. He made an unobtrusive re-

cording debut in 1961, singing "East St. Louis" with the band of one Little
Aaron for the highly obscure Marlo imprint. He arrived in Chicago around
1960, hooking up with Earl Hooker as the slide guitar wizard's vocalist. A
single for Nation Records in 1967 (as Andre Odom) preceded his debut album for ABC-BluesWay (cut in 1969, it remained in the can for quite a while
before the label finally issued it).

A guest spot on Jimmy Dawkins' encore Delmark LP, *All for Business*,
was a highlight of the '70s for the singer. He cut his own album for the French
Isabel label in 1982 in the company of Magic Slim & the Teardrops (reissued
by Evidence in 1993), but it was a 1992 set for Flying Fish, *Goin' to California*
(co-produced by guitarist Steve Freund), that probably captured his considerable vocal charms the best.

Odom was a popular attraction on the Windy City circuit right up until
the fateful night when he suffered a heart attack while driving from Buddy
Guy's Legends to another local blues mecca, the Checkerboard Lounge. He's
been missed ever since. —*Bill Dahl*

Farther on the Road / 1969 / Bluesway ◆◆
Disappointing debut album by the Chicago singer with the mellifluous pipes.
Even with Earl Hooker on lead guitar, the spark just wasn't here. —*Bill Dahl*

● **Going to California** / 1992 / Flying Fish ◆◆◆◆
Not long before he died, Odom made the album of his life with a combo
called the Gold Tops, who provided precisely the right backing to properly
spotlight his booming voice. A few overdone standards—"Rock Me Baby,"
"Woke Up This Morning," "Next Time You See Me"—intrude a bit, but Odom's
own "Bad Feelin'," "Why Did You Leave Me," and "Come to Me" make impassioned amends. Steve Freund, best-known for his long stint with Sunnyland
Slim, contributes stellar lead guitar. —*Bill Dahl*

Omar & the Howlers

f. Austin, TX
Group / Rock 'n' Roll, Blues-Rock, Electric Texas Blues
The European blues fans all adore Austin, TX-based guitarist, singer and
songwriter Omar Kent Dykes. That's because he fits the stereotypical image
many of them have of the American musician: he's tall, wears cowboy boots
and has a deep voice with a Southern accent. However, Dykes does not carry
a gun, and though he looks rough and tough, he's actually an incredibly
peaceful and intelligent musician, and a veteran at working a crowd in a
blues club or a festival. While Dykes still has a sizeable American audience
owing to his albums for Columbia Records, he still spends a good portion of
his touring year at festivals and clubs around Europe.

Among White blues musicians, Dykes is truly one of a kind, a fact that
Columbia Records recognized in the 1980s, when he recorded for them.
These days, Dykes and his band, the Howlers, record for the Austin, TX-based
Watermelon Records label. Since being dropped by Columbia Records after
the company was bought by Sony, Dykes' independent-label output since
1990 has been nothing short of extraordinary. His albums since 1990 include
Monkey Land (1990, Antone's) *Live at Paradiso, Blues Bag* and *Courts of
Lulu* (all for Rounder), as well as *Muddy Springs Road* (1995) and *World
Wide Open* (1996). Dykes' 1987 debut for Columbia, *Hard Times in the Land
of Plenty*, sold upwards of 500,000 copies, excellent numbers for a blues
album.

Omar Kent Dykes was born in 1950, in McComb, MS, the same town from
which Bo Diddley hails. He first set foot into neighborhood juke joints at age
12, he recalled. After he'd been playing guitar for awhile, he went back into
the juke joint. After graduating from high school, Dykes lived in Hattiesburg
and Jackson, MS, for a few years before relocating to Austin in 1976. He'd

heard the blues scene in Texas was heating up. At that time, Stevie Ray Vaughan was still playing with Paul Ray and the Cobras.

"I know Stevie Ray had a big impact on me, 'cause he was such a great guy. But I think everybody in the blues scene around here influenced everyone else," he said in a 1994 interview. "The blues scene is tight and loose at the same time, everybody is rooting for everybody else, because it helps everybody else out when one artist is on the radio," he added.

To hear how Dykes has developed as a songwriter in the 1990s, check out *Muddy Springs Road* or *World Wide Open,* his two recent releases for Watermelon Records. To hear the finesse, fury and excitement of one of his live shows, pick up *Live at Paradiso* (Rounder) recorded at the club by the same name in Amsterdam. — *Richard Skelly*

Big Leg Beat / 1980 / Amazing ♦♦♦
Omar & the Howler's debut *Big Leg Beat* is an impressive piece of work. Omar Kent Dykes was an imposing, forceful vocalist from the start and the Howlers are a tough, exciting band, slamming through gritty Chicago blues with passion. Although they made better albums later in their career, *Big Leg Beat* remains an invigorating listen. — *Thom Owens*

● **I Told You So** / 1984 / Austin ♦♦♦♦
I Told You So is one of the finest records Omar & the Howlers ever released, filled with roaring, impassioned performances and a sharp set of material. — *Thom Owens*

Hard Times in the Land of Plenty / 1987 / Columbia ♦♦♦♦
For their major-label debut, Omar & the Howlers were trimmed down to a trio, but that didn't decrease their power. If anything, the group sounds leaner and meaner. *Hard Times in the Land of Plenty* is one of their finest releases for this reason — it's a rough and tumble collection that is driven as much by fine original songwriting as it is by the band's edgy sound. — *Thom Owens*

Live at Paradiso / Sep. 1991 / Bullseye Blues ♦♦
For a band that usually sounds alive and vibrant on record, *Live at Paradiso* is a disappointingly sedate live album from Omar & the Howlers. Although there are a couple of fine moments scattered throughout the album, there's not enough to make the album a captivating listen. — *Thom Owens*

Courts of Lulu / 1992 / Bullseye Blues ♦♦♦
Omar & The Howlers' misadventures at the majors began when they trimmed the blues and padded the rock. Since returning to Rounder/ Bullseye, they have smartly managed to keep the balance, and that's the case on their latest. The 13 tracks alternate between boogie shuffles, swaggering wailers, and heartache testimonies, with Omar's flailing guitar and spiraling harmonica nicely backed by his trio and such assistants as organist Reese Wynans, vocalist Kris McKay and saxophonist John Mills. Plenty of blues and more than enough rock fervor. — *Ron Wynn*

Blues Bag / 1992 / Bullseye Blues ♦♦
This CD was the solo debut of vocalist-guitar Omar, the leader of Omar and the Howlers. Although his musicianship is strong (as is the harmonica playing of Fingers Taylor), it may take listeners a little while to get used to Omar's voice which is a mixture of Howlin' Wolf and disc jockey Wolfman Jack! The first nine songs on the CD are essentially duets between Omar and Taylor with the final six tracks adding electric bassist Bruce Jones and drummer Gene Brandon. Many of the songs are light-hearted and, despite a certain lack of variety, blues fans will find the set difficult to resist. — *Scott Yanow*

World Wide Open / 1996 / Watermelon ♦♦♦
Supported by a new batch of Howlers, Omar Dykes doesn't show any signs of wear and tear on *World Wide Open.* The band continues to turn out a gut-busting mixture of blues and dirty rock 'n' roll, occasionally sounding like Howlin' Wolf, other times like the Stones or Creedence Clearwater Revival. As always, the quality of songs is slightly inconsistent but the band never sounds tired — they perform with as much energy, if not more, than they ever have. — *Thom Owens*

Southern Style / Feb. 4, 1997 / Watermelon ♦♦♦
Omar shakes up the Howlers' lineup yet again for *Southern Style,* yet the changes don't affect his sound much at all. Working with guitarist Stephen Bruton, bassist Paul Junior, drummer Steve Kilmer, percussionist Mark Hallman and organist Nick Connolly, Omar Dykes kicks out a set of swampy blues-rock that alternates between New Orleans grunge and tight Memphis grooves. Though the band sounds great, the lack of compelling material

means *Southern Style* isn't appealing to anyone but specialists. — *Thom Owens*

Monkey Land / Feb. 11, 1997 / Antone's ♦♦♦
A solid effort, it benefits from its excellent label. — *David Szatmary*

Paul Oscher
b. Apr. 5, 1950, Brooklyn, NY
Harmonica / Chicago Blues
Guitarist, singer, songwriter, pianist and harp player Paul Oscher has paid his dues, and then some. Those who have been following blues for a long time will remember Oscher from the late 1960s as the white kid who played harmonica in the Muddy Waters Band.

Blues caught the Brooklyn-raised Oscher's ears at age 12 and he began playing professionally at age 15, frequenting clubs like the Baby Grand, the 521 Club and the Seville Lounge. Oscher also made frequent trips to the Apollo Theater in the mid-1960s. On one trip, he met guitarist Muddy Waters, and a friendship between the two developed. Several years later, Waters' band was in New York and they needed a harmonica player; Oscher got the nod. Oscher joined Waters on stage for two numbers, "Baby Please Don't Go" and "Blow Wind Blow." Waters hired him. As a full member of Waters' band, he had the chance to rub shoulders with greats like Otis Spann, Sammy Lawhorn and S.P. Leary. Oscher, the only white member of the band, performed with Waters through tours of the US, Europe and Canada. He also recorded with Waters' band at the Chess Studios in Chicago.

As one who was there at the height of the late 1960s blues renaissance, Oscher's harmonica playing influenced lots of other players who came to prominence after him. His sessionography is extensive, including albums with Johnny Copeland, Muddy Waters, Otis Spann, Luther Johnson and Johnny Young.

Oscher's veteran skills on guitar and harmonica are showcased on his debut for the New York-based Vice Roots Records, a division of Viceroy Music. Oscher's *Knockin' On the Devil's Door,* a 1996 release, brought his music before a bigger audience. Provided he can back it up with the kind of touring required to support independent records, Oscher should find himself in demand again on the festival/club circuit around the US and Europe. Oscher's debut for Viceroots was produced by a longtime admirer, Dave Peverett, from the blues-rock quartet Foghat. — *Richard Skelly*

● **Knockin' on the Devil's Door** / Mar. 19, 1996 / Vice Roots ♦♦♦♦
After years of being a sideman and gigging without recorded, Paul Oscher — a former harpist for Muddy Waters — made his first album, *Knockin' on the Devil's Door,* in 1996. Oscher stays true to his Chicago blues roots, but he wisely doesn't run through the same old standards again. Instead, he's written a set of impassioned originals, augmented by a couple of appropriate covers. Working with a talented supporting group — featuring harpist Steve Guyger, bassist Mudcat Ward, pianist David Maxwell and drummer Big Eyes Smith — Oscher devotes himself to guitar, showing a flair for gritty riffs and solos. But the key to the record's success are his fully realized originals, which make the album an impressive, if much belated, debut. — *Thom Owens*

New York Really Has the Blues / Spivey ♦♦♦
The Oscher Chicago Breakdown Blues Band's *New York Really Has the Blues* was a bit of an all-star session organized by Paul Oscher, the former harpist for Muddy Waters. Assembling a great cast of musicians — including Victoria Spivey, Sugar Blue, Smokey Hogg, Ben Jackson, Robert Ross and Sonny Boy Parker — Oscher leads the group through a number of Chicago standards. At times, there are a few too many cooks in the kitchen, but the record remains quite enjoyable. — *Thom Owens*

Johnny Otis (John Veliotes)
b. Dec. 28, 1921, Vallejo, CA
Piano, Drums, Vocals, Vibes / R&B, Electric West Coast Blues, West Coast Blues, Jump Blues
Johnny Otis has modeled an amazing number of contrasting musical hats over a career spanning more than half a century. Bandleader, record producer, talent scout, label owner, nightclub impresario, disc jockey, TV variety show host, author, R&B pioneer, rock 'n' roll star — Otis has answered to all those descriptions and quite a few more. Not bad for a Greek-American who

loved jazz and R&B so fervently that he adopted the African-American culture as his own.

California-born John Veliotes changed his name to the blacker-sounding Otis when he was in his teens. Drums were his first passion—he spent time behind the traps with the Oakland-based orchestra of Count Otis Matthews and kept time for various Midwestern swing outfits before settling in Los Angeles during the mid-'40s and joining Harlan Leonard's Rockets, then resident at the Club Alabam.

It wasn't long before the Alabam's owner entreated Otis to assemble his own orchestra for house-band duties. The group's 1945 debut sides for Excelsior were solidly in the big-band jazz vein and included an arrangement of the moody "Harlem Nocturne" that sold well. Shouter Jimmy Rushing fronted the band for two tracks at the same date. Otis' rep as a drummer was growing; he backed both Wynonie Harris and Charles Brown (with Johnny Moore's Three Blazers) that same year.

The Otis outfit continued to record for Excelsior through 1947 (one date featured Big Jay McNeely on sax), but his influence on L.A.'s R&B scene soared exponentially when he and partner Bardu Ali opened the Barrelhouse Club in Watts. R&B replaced jazz in Otis' heart; he pared the big band down and discovered young talent such as the Robins, vocalists Mel Walker and Little Esther Phillips, and guitarist Pete Lewis that would serve him well in years to come.

Otis signed with Newark, NJ-based Savoy Records in 1949, and the R&B hits came in droves: "Double Crossing Blues," "Mistrustin' Blues," and "Cupid's Boogie" all hit number one that year (in all, Otis scored ten Top Ten smashes that year alone!); "Gee Baby," "Mambo Boogie," and "All Nite Long" lit the lamp in 1951, and "Sunset to Dawn" capped his amazing run in 1952 (vocals were shared by Esther, Walker, and other members of the group). By then, Otis had branched out to play vibes on many waxings.

In late 1951, Otis moved to Mercury, but apart from a Walker-led version of Floyd Dixon's "Call Operator 210," nothing found pronounced success with the public. A 1953-55 contract with Don Robey's Peacock logo produced some nice jump blues sides but no hits (though the Otis orchestra backed one of his many discoveries, Big Mama Thornton, on her chart-topping "Hound Dog," as well as a young Little Richard while at Peacock). Otis was a masterful talent scout; among his platinum-edged discoveries were Jackie Wilson, Little Willie John, Hank Ballard, and Etta James (he produced her debut smash "Roll with Me Henry").

In 1955, Otis took studio matters into his own hands, starting up his own label, Dig Records, to showcase his own work as well as his latest discoveries (including Arthur Lee Maye & the Crowns, Tony Allen, and Mel Williams). Rock 'n' roll was at its zenith in 1957, when the multi-instrumentalist signed on with Capitol Records; billed as the Johnny Otis Show, he set the R&B and pop charts ablaze in 1958 with his shave-and-a-haircut beat, "Willie and the Hand Jive," taking the vocal himself (other singers then with the Otis Show included Mel Williams and the gargantuan Marie Adams & the Three Tons of Joy). During the late '50s, Otis hosted his own variety program on Los Angeles television, starring his entire troupe (and on one episode, Lionel Hampton), and did a guest shot in a 1958 movie, *Juke Box Rhythm.*

After cutting some great rock 'n' roll for Capitol from 1957 to 1959 with only one hit to show for it, Otis dropped anchor at King Records in 1961-62 (in addition to his own output, Otis' band also backed Johnny "Guitar" Watson on several sides). Later in the decade, Otis recorded some ribald material for Kent and watched as his young son Shuggie built an enviable reputation as a blues guitarist while recording for Columbia. Father and son cut an album together for Alligator in 1982, accurately entitled *The New Johnny Otis Show.*

In recent years, the multi-talented Otis added operating a California health-food emporium to his endless list of wide-ranging accomplishments. If blues boasts a renaissance man amongst its ranks, Johnny Otis surely fills that bill. —*Bill Dahl*

Rock and Roll Hit Parade, Vol. 1 / 1957 / Dig ♦♦♦

Enjoyable sound-alike covers of popular mid-'50s R&B hits by Otis, singers Mel Williams and Arthur Lee Maye, and the Jayos. —*Bill Dahl*

The Johnny Otis Show / 1958 / Savoy ♦♦♦♦

Some of the R&B bandleader's earliest and best work (1945-51) for Savoy. The cast includes singers Little Esther and Mel Walker, The Robins, and guitarist Pete Lewis. —*Bill Dahl*

Live at Monterey / 1971 / Epic ♦♦♦♦

An R&B oldies show with a difference, the artists represented the cream of the crop of jump blues, and in 1970, they were still in fine form. The disc stars Otis, Esther Phillips, Eddie Vinson, Joe Turner, Ivory Joe Hunter, Roy Milton, Roy Brown, Pee Wee Crayton, and Johnny's guitar wielding son, Shuggie. —*Bill Dahl*

New Johnny Otis Show / 1982 / Alligator ♦♦♦

This features recent recordings with Shuggie Otis. Nice, but non-essential. —*Mark A. Humphrey*

The Capitol Years / 1989 / Capitol ♦♦♦♦

Unfortunately now out-of-print, this set anthologizes Otis' late-'50s rise to rock 'n' roll fame, thanks to his shave-and-a-haircut special "Willie and the Hand Jive." Like every other style of R&B Otis drifted into, he excelled at it—"Castin' My Spell," "Crazy Country Hop," "Willie Did the Cha Cha," and "Three Girls Named Molly" are catchy rockers. Otis had a terrific band—guitarist Jimmy Nolen (later James Brown's main axeman), pianist Ernie Freeman, drummer Earl Palmer, and a tight horn section (along with singers Marie Adams and Mel Williams) gave him all the help he could possibly need. —*Bill Dahl*

Let's Live It Up / 1991 / Charly ♦♦♦

Otis stopped off at King Records for a while during the early '60s, making clever 45s that no one paid much attention to. Twenty-two of them are here, including five by the late Johnny "Guitar" Watson (whose "In the Evenin'" is chillingly direct). It's a mixed bag—vocal group stuff, twist workouts, and the inevitable sequel "Hand Jive One More Time" (alas, nobody did). —*Bill Dahl*

Be Bop Baby Blues / 1991 / Night Train ♦♦♦

A bit skimpy at 14 songs, this disc casts Otis mostly in a bandleader role on late-'40s sides culled from the Excelsior, Supreme, and Swing Time labels. Vocalists fronting the Otis outfit include the extremely obscure Joe Swift, Earl Jackson, Clifford "Fat Man" Blivens, and Johnny Crawford. Swinging, horn-leavened jump blues all the way. —*Bill Dahl*

Creepin' with the Cats: The Legendary Dig Masters / 1991 / Ace ♦♦♦

Twenty-two tracks, almost half previously unreleased, from circa 1956-57 that Otis recorded for his own short-lived Dig label. Not as vivacious as the sides he recorded for Capitol in the late '50s, this is spirited but generic jump blues/R&B, divided evenly between vocals and instrumentals. Occasional cuts like the silly novelty instrumental "Ali Baba's Boogie" stand out from the pack. The one commanding greatest interest is "Hey! Hey! Hey!," which served as the model for Little Richard's version, which in turned was covered by the Beatles in the mid-'60s (as "Kansas City"). —*Richie Unterberger*

★ Original Johnny Otis Show / 1994 / Savoy ♦♦♦♦♦

Twenty-seven of the Otis aggregation's best early sides for Savoy and Excelsior, including a slew of the group's early-'50s Little Esther and/or Mel Walker-fronted R&B smashes ("Mistrustin' Blues," "Cry Baby," "Sunset to Dawn"). Jimmy Rushing and the Robins also share vocal duties, as does Otis himself on a jumping "All Nite Long." This is one time when the bonus cuts are on the vinyl version—it contained 32 cuts appearing on a *Completer Disc* that Savoy Jazz reissued at the same time as this CD. The original artwork and liner notes have been reduced so much for the CD that they're unreadable (Pete Welding's essay deserves more respect). —*Bill Dahl*

Too Late to Holler / 1994 / Night Train ♦♦♦♦

A more generous selection of late-'40s Swing Time and Excelsior sides, again featuring Swift (who dominates the compilation), Jackson, and Blivens in front of the powerful Otis orchestra. Very little duplication exists between the two discs. —*Bill Dahl*

Jack Owens

b. Nov. 17, 1904, Bentonia, MS, d. Feb. 9, 1997, Yazoo City, MS
Guitar, Vocals / Country Blues, Delta Blues
Like Skip James, Owens hails from Bentonia, MS. Owens is much less famous than James, but he's often compared to Skip due to his high, rich vocals and intricate guitar styles, which finds him using several tunings and occasional minor keys. His material, it must be noted, is not nearly as strong or tightly constructed as James', although it draws from some of the same sources. Noted folklorist and blues scholar David Evans made several recordings with Owens in the late '60s and early '70s. —*Richie Unterberger*

It Must Have Been the Devil / 1971 / Testament ♦♦♦
Although this album is credited to Owens and Bud Spires, it's really Owens'
show; Spires adds some harmonica accompaniment to Jack's playing and
singing. Although David Evans (who produced these recordings) intimates
that Owens is better than Skip James in his liner notes, it's really not that
hard to figure out why James is better known; James' songs are simply better
written, more gripping, and more memorable, and Owens tends to ramble
pleasantly. If you're looking for the Bentonia sound, though, this is certainly a
down-home, well-recorded representation, and has an advantage over those
vintage James (or any vintage blues) sides in that the fidelity is much, much
clearer. Recorded in 1970, the 1995 CD reissue adds five previously unreleased tracks. — *Richie Unterberger*

Jay Owens

b. Sep. 6, 1947, Lake City, FL
Vocals / Modern Electric Blues, Soul Blues
A top-notch sideman and songwriter, Jay Owens also enjoyed acclaim as a
solo artist. Born Isaac Jerome Owens in Lake City, Florida on September 6,
1947, he learned to sing in the church where his mother presided as minister;
at the age of 11, he received his first guitar, and began performing professionally while in high school. With his friend Johnny Kay, Owens went on to lead
many of the most notable Tampa Bay/St. Petersburg-area backing bands
of the 1970s and 1980s, among them the Barons, the Funk Bunch and the
Dynamites; artists he supported included Stevie Wonder, Al Green, O.V.
Wright, and Donny Hathaway. With more than 100 songs to his credit as
well, Owens formed his own band during the late 1980s; he made his solo
debut in 1993 with *The Blues Soul of Jay Owens*, followed in 1995 by *Movin'
On. — Jason Ankeny*

The Blues Soul of Jay Owens / 1993 / Indigo ♦♦♦♦

● **Moving On** / 1995 / Code Blue ♦♦♦♦
The production may be a little too clean and the playing may be a little too
pat, but there's no denying that *Moving On* is the work of a fine blues craftsman. Jay Owens has written a set of strong songs in the soul-blues tradition,
spiking his straightahead foundation with flourishes of funk and Chicago
blues. Owens delivers his songs with passion, which make the weaker moments sound convincing, thereby elevating *Moving On* to the status of his
best latter-day effort. — *Thom Owens*

Earl Palmer (Earl C. Palmer)

b. Oct. 25, 1924, New Orleans, LA
Drums / R&B, Rock 'n' Roll
Earl Palmer was first-call drummer on the New Orleans R&B recording scene from 1950 to 1957. Talk about a supreme recommendation—in a city renowned for its second-line rhythms and syncopated grooves, Palmer was the man, playing on countless sessions by all the immortals: Little Richard, Fats Domino, Smiley Lewis, Dave Bartholomew, and too many more to list here.

Born to a mother who was a vaudevillian, little Earl Palmer was learning rhythmic patterns as a tap dancer at age four. Such contacts led him to be around drum kits on a regular basis, and it didn't take him long to master them. Be-bop jazz was his first love, but R&B and blues paid the bills starting in 1947, when Palmer joined Bartholomew's band.

Palmer remained the king of the traps at Cosimo's fabled recording studio until 1957, when a Shirley & Lee session led to an A&R offer from Aladdin Records boss Eddie Mesner. Palmer found studio work just as plentiful in Los Angeles, making major inroads into the rock, jazz, and soundtrack fields as well as playing on countless R&B dates with his frequent compadres Rene Hall on guitar and saxist Plas Johnson. Occasionally, Palmer would record as a leader—the instrumental "Johnny's House Party" for Aladdin, a couple of early-'60s albums for Liberty.

But even the best session men grapple with a certain sense of anonymity. So the next time you pull out Little Richard's "Tutti Frutti," Smiley Lewis' "I Hear You Knockin'," Lloyd Price's "Lawdy Miss Clawdy," or Fats Domino's "The Fat Man," please keep in mind that it's Earl Palmer feverishly stoking that beat—with a saucy second-line sensibility that drove those songs in fresh, utterly innovative directions. —*Bill Dahl*

Drumsville / 1961 / Liberty ✦✦✦

● **Percolator Twist** / 1962 / Liberty ✦✦✦
Strictly-by-the-book album of formulaic twist instrumentals that exhibits precious little of the imaginative rhythmic flair that had previously made Palmer such an in-demand New Orleans session drummer. —*Bill Dahl*

The Paramount Singers

f. 1936, Austin, TX
Group / Traditional Gospel, Black Gospel
Although eclipsed in popularity by contemporaries including the Soul Stirrers and the Dixie Hummingbirds, the Paramount Singers were among the longest-lived gospel groups of the modern era, upholding the tradition of classic a cappella harmonizing for well over half a century. Assembled in Austin, TX, in 1936, the Paramounts initially consisted of two pairs of brothers, Geno & Kermit Terrell and Ermant & A.C. Franklin, in addition to Herbert Sneed and Ben Williams. Sneed had been replaced by James Medlock—later of the Soul Stirrers—by the time they recorded for the Library of Congress in 1941; months later, however, the group's original incarnation came to an end when the Terrell brothers were drafted to fight in World War II, and upon receiving their respective discharges both siblings settled in the San Francisco area. There they reunited with Williams to form a new Paramounts lineup, also enlisting two other Austin natives, Sam Reece and Victor L. Medearis.

This new incarnation of the Paramount Singers' roster was in a seemingly constant state of flux, and in time Geno Terrell and Williams were the lone remaining original members; they were soon joined by new recruits Vance "Tiny" Powell, Archie Reynolds, E. Morris Kelley, and, albeit briefly, Paul Foster, who also later rose to fame as a member of the Soul Stirrers. Foster's

replacement was Joseph Dean, who signed on in 1948; three years later, Powell exited to join the Five Blind Boys of Mississippi, but soon returned to the Paramounts' fold. Despite recording for nationally distributed companies like Coral and Duke between the late 1940s and mid-1950s, the Paramounts never earned the notoriety of many of their peers, largely because their day jobs and family ties kept their touring activity confined almost exclusively to the West Coast; Dean once even rejected an offer to join the famed Spirit of Memphis simply because of their hectic traveling schedule.

A 1955 session for Duke was the Paramounts' last commercial recording for close to four decades, but the group continued regularly performing throughout the years to follow. The lineup shifts continued—Powell again exited in 1963 to pursue a career singing the blues, although he continued to rehearse with the Paramounts until his 1973 death, while the 1979 death of co-founder Williams cost the group not only their bass singer but also their guitar accompaniment. Unable to find a compatible bass vocalist, Reynolds took over the bottom himself; when no suitable guitarist arose, the Paramounts, who had long included a number of a cappella numbers in their repertoire, simply began performing without any instrumental backing at all, and found that many audiences seemed to prefer their new style. In 1992, the Paramounts—now consisting of Reynolds and Dean in addition to relative newcomers Clyde Price, J.B. Williams, William Johnson, and the Rev. Odis Brown—issued *Work and Pray On*, their first new record in 37 years. —*Jason Ankeny*

Work & Pray On / 1992 / Arhoolie ✦✦✦✦
Work & Pray On is recorded by a latter-day incarnation of the Paramount Singers. Only two of the members of the sextet were part of the group in the '40s, yet the group still carried on with their classic sound, updated slightly with fresh arrangements. The album suffers from having a few too many undistinguished songs and running a little too long, but it remains an excellent example of how good classic gospel can be. —*Leo Stanley*

● **Paramount Singers** / ✦✦✦✦
The Paramounts of San Francisco hail back to the early '40s, when the Library of Congress field unit recorded them. During the '50s they cut sides for Trilon, Olliet, Coral and Duke, and it is this style of close harmony a cappella which, in all its richness and simplicity, is faithfully reproduced here on this excellent recently etched ten-song set. It's great old-time jubilee singing from Doe Dean—first lead (who has a voice like Rev. Claude Jeter), Odie Brown—second lead, Archie Reynolds, Gene Terrell, Clyde Price, and J.W. Williams (cassette only). —*Opal Louis Nations, Roots & Rhythm Newsletter*

Bobby Parker

b. Aug. 31, 1937, Lafayette, LA
Guitar, Vocals / Modern Blues
Guitarist, singer and songwriter Bobby Parker is one of the most exciting performers in modern blues, and it's quite apparent he'll inherit the top blues spots left open by the unfortunate, early passings of people like Albert King, Johnny "Guitar" Watson and others. That's because Parker can do it all: he writes brilliant songs, he sings well, and he backs it all up with powerful, stinging guitar. But things weren't always so good for Parker, and much of his newfound success is the result of years of hard work and struggling around the bars in Washington, D.C. and Virginia.

Parker has two brilliant albums out on the Black Top label out of New Orleans (distributed by Rounder), *Shine Me Up* (1995) and *Bent Out of Shape* (1993).

He was born August 31, 1937 in Lafayette, Louisiana, but raised in southern California after his family moved to Los Angeles when he was six. Going to school in Hollywood, the young Parker was bitten by the scenery, and decided he wanted to be in show business. At the Million Dollar Theatre, he saw big stage shows by Count Basie, Duke Ellington, Billy Eckstine, and Lionel Hampton. Although he had an early interest in jazz, the blues bit him when artists like T-Bone Walker, Lowell Fulson, Johnny "Guitar" Watson, and Pee Wee Crayton came to town.

He began playing in the late '50s as a guitarist with Otis Williams and the Charms after winning a talent contest sponsored by West Coast blues and R&B legend Johnny Otis. Later, he backed Bo Diddley, which included an appearance on *The Ed Sullivan Show* before joining the touring big band of Paul "Hucklebuck" Williams. He settled in Washington, D.C. in the 1960s, dropping out of Williams' band and making a go of it on his own.

He is perhaps best-known for his 1961 song, "Watch Your Step," a single for the V-Tone label that became a hit on British and US R&B charts. Parker's song was later covered by several British blues groups, most prominent among them the Spencer Davis Group. And though Parker may not yet be a name as familiar to blues fans as say, Eric Clapton or B.B. King, he's been cited as a major musical influence by Davis, John Mayall, Robin Trower, Clapton, Jimmy Page, drummer Mick Fleetwood, John Lennon, and, most importantly, Carlos Santana. Parker's style has been described by his protege Bobby Radcliff as Guitar Slim meets James Brown, and that's not that far off the mark. In the summer of 1994, Santana was so happy about Parker's comeback on the BlackTop/Rounder label that he took him on the road for some arena shows on the East and West Coasts.

"Carlos likes to tell people that he saw me playing in Mexico City when he was a kid, and that inspired him to pick up the guitar," Parker explained in a recent interview. Santana pays homage to Parker on his *Havana Moon* album, on which he covers "Watch Your Step." Dr. Feelgood also covered the tune in the 1970s.

For the rest of the 1990s, Parker is destined to be one of the major players on the blues circuit, provided his stellar output and rigorous touring schedules continue. Unlike so many other blues musicians, Parker's live shows are almost entirely his own songs. He does very few covers.

"Unless the music of the day has some kind of substance to it, the blues always comes back," Parker says, adding, "I think Stevie Ray Vaughan had a lot to do with bringing the blues to White audiences, and Z.Z. Hill helped bring the Black audience back to the blues." —*Richard Skelly*

● **Bent Out of Shape** / 1993 / Black Top ✦✦✦
The production on *Bent Out of Shape* may be a little too clean, but that can't distract from the fact that Bobby Parker's belated first album is a storming statement of purpose. His songwriting is sturdy and memorable, his singing impassioned and his guitar simply stings. He could have carried the album with just a little combo, but he's assembled a large, soulful backing band that gives the album soulful finesse. It would have been nice if the production was a little grittier, since Parker's performances are, but there's no denying his playing and songs elevate *Bent Out of Shape* to the status of one of the best blues records of the early '90s. —*Thom Owens*

Shine Me Up / 1995 / Black Top ✦✦✦
Guitarist Bobby Parker continued his '90s comeback with *Shine Me Up*, an album filled with fiery leads and gritty, soulful R&B-based material. —*Thom Owens*

Junior Parker (Herman Parker)

b. May 27, 1932, Clarksdale, MS, d. Nov. 18, 1971, Chicago, IL
Harmonica, Vocals / Soul, R&B, Soul Blues, Electric Memphis Blues
His velvet-smooth vocal delivery to the contrary, Junior Parker was a product of the fertile postwar Memphis blues circuit whose wonderfully understated harp style was personally mentored by none other than regional icon Sonny Boy Williamson.

Herman Parker, Jr. only traveled in the best blues circles from the outset. He learned his initial licks from Williamson and gigged with the mighty Howlin' Wolf while still in his teens. Like so many young blues artists, Little Junior (as he was known then) got his first recording opportunity from talent scout Ike Turner, who brought him to Modern Records for his debut session as a leader in 1952. It produced the lone single "You're My Angel," with Turner pounding the 88s and Matt Murphy deftly handling guitar duties.

Parker and his band, the Blue Flames (including Floyd Murphy, Matt's

brother, on guitar), landed at Sun Records in 1953 and promptly scored a hit with their rollicking "Feelin' Good" (something of a Memphis response to John Lee Hooker's primitive boogies). Later that year, Little Junior cut a fiery "Love My Baby" and a laidback "Mystery Train" for Sun, thus contributing a pair of future rockabilly standards to the Sun publishing coffers (Hayden Thompson revived the former, Elvis Presley the latter).

Before 1953 was through, the polished Junior Parker had moved on to Don Robey's Duke imprint in Houston. It took a while for the harpist to regain his hitmaking momentum, but he scored big in 1957 with the smooth "Next Time You See Me," an accessible enough number to even garner some pop spins.

Criss-crossing the country as headliner with the Blues Consolidated package (his support act was labelmate Bobby Bland), Parker developed a breathtaking brass-powered sound (usually the work of trumpeter/Duke-housebandleader Joe Scott) that pushed his honeyed vocals and intermittent harp solos with exceptional power. Parker's updated remake of Roosevelt Sykes' "Driving Wheel" was a huge R&B hit in 1961, as was the surging "In the Dark" (the R&B dance workout "Annie Get Your Yo-Yo" followed suit the next year).

Parker was exceptionally versatile—whether delivering "Mother-In-Law Blues" and "Sweet Home Chicago" in faithful downhome fashion, courting the teenage market with "Barefoot Rock," or tastefully howling Harold Burrage's "Crying for My Baby" (another hit for him in 1965) in front of a punchy horn section, Parker was the consummate modern blues artist, with one foot planted in Southern blues and the other in uptown R&B.

Once Parker split from Robey's employ in 1966, though, his hitmaking fortunes declined. His 1966-68 output for Mercury and its Blue Rock subsidiary deserved a better reception than it got, but toward the end, he was covering the Beatles ("Taxman" and "Lady Madonna," for God's sake!) for Capitol. A brain tumor tragically silenced Junior Parker's magic-carpet voice in late 1971 before he reached his 40th birthday. —*Bill Dahl*

Blues Consolidated (Barefoot Rock & You Got Me) / May 1958 / Duke ✦✦✦✦
Half Parker, half Bland, all great '50s Texas blues and R&B. —*Bill Dahl*

Driving Wheel / 1962 / Duke ✦✦✦✦
Junior's emerging from his fin-tailed Cadillac on the front of this vintage LP, which contains all kinds of gems not on MCA's CD. For example: an irresistibly upbeat "How Long Can This Go On," the richly arranged blues ballads "I Need Love So Bad" and "Someone Somewhere," Junior's dance hit "Annie Get Your Yo Yo" (all done with Duke's brassy house band), and the New Orleans-cuts "The Tables Have Turned" and "Foxy Devil." —*Bill Dahl*

The Best of Junior Parker / 1967 / Duke ✦✦✦✦
Solid hits package. —*Bill Dahl*

Like It Is / 1967 / Mercury ✦✦✦
Blues with a smooth R&B tinge. —*Bill Dahl*

Baby Please / 1967 / Mercury ✦✦✦
Parker traveled back to his old Memphis stomping grounds to cut this quality set for Mercury under Bobby Robinson's supervision with a coterie of the city's hotter young R&B-oriented studio hands: guitarists Reggie Young and Tommy Cogbill, organist Bobby Emmons, and Willie Mitchell's horn section. "Just like a Fish," "Cracked Up over You," and "Sometimes I Wonder" are among its smooth highlights. —*Bill Dahl*

Blues Man / 1969 / Minit ✦✦✦
Soulful blues hybrid. —*Bill Dahl*

Honey-Drippin' Blues / 1969 / Blue Rock ✦✦✦✦
Junior Parker a Chicago soul singer? Yeah, on at least four cuts of this fine LP for Mercury's Blue Rock R&B subsidiary. "I'm So Satisfied" (penned by Cash McCall), "Ain't Gon' Be No Cutting Aloose" (later covered by James Cotton for Alligator), "You Can't Keep a Good Woman Down," and "Easy Lovin'" stem from a soulful 1969 date in the Windy City. Also aboard: considerably bluesier remakes of Lowell Fulson's "Reconsider Baby" and Percy Mayfield's "What a Fool I Was." —*Bill Dahl*

Sometime Tomorrow / 1973 / Bluesway ✦✦✦
Cobbled together from mostly unissued performances out of the Duke vaults, we have here a nice Parker LP anthology emphasizing his early-to-mid-'60s soul-inflected sound. He whoops it up like Little Richard on the

torrid "If You Can't Take It (You Sure Can't Make It)" (sensible, since Richard wrote it), and gives a warm reading to "Today I Sing the Blues" (generally associated with female singers, primarily Helen Humes amd Aretha Franklin). —*Bill Dahl*

The ABC Collection / 1976 / ABC ✦✦✦✦
Housed in something that looks vaguely like a square gray envelope that's guaranteed to wear out if you're not careful, this album is still one of the only places to locate many of Parker's best 1958-1966 Duke sides (unless you've got the 45s salted away somewhere). "Man or Mouse," "Dangerous Woman," the two-part "These Kind of Blues," and "I'll Forget About You" are prime vehicles for Parker's uncommonly smooth vocals and occasional harp blasts. —*Bill Dahl*

Mystery Train / 1990 / Rounder ✦✦✦✦
This excellent little compilation features at least one extant take of everything Junior and his original band, the Blue Flames, recorded at Sun Records between 1952 to 1954. His debut single for the label and his first hit, the classic "Feelin' Good" is aboard as well as the equally fine (but originally unissued) "Feelin' Bad." His leanings toward smoother Roy Brown stylings are evident with tracks like "Fussing and Fighting Blues" and "Sitting and Thinking," but the follow-up to his first Sun single, the original version of "Mystery Train" and two takes of the flip side, "Love My Baby," are the must-hears on this collection. Fleshing out Parker's meager output for Sun are essential early tracks from James Cotton. Cotton doesn't blow harp on any of these, but the sax-dominated "My Baby," and especially "Cotton Crop Blues" and "Hold Me in Your Arms" with Pat Hare on super distorted blistering guitar is Memphis-'50s blues at its apex. Hare himself also rounds out the compilation with two tracks, the prophetic "I'm Gonna Murder My Baby" (Hare did exactly that and spent the rest of his life behind bars as a result) and the previously unissued "Bonus Pay." Don't let the short running time of this CD stop you from picking this one up; the music is beyond excellent. —*Cub Koda*

★ **Junior's Blues/The Duke Recordings, Vol. 1** / 1992 / MCA ✦✦✦✦✦
After the non-success of "Mystery Train" on the R&B charts, Parker jumped contract and signed with Don Robey's Houston-based Duke Records. With his smooth vocal approach, Parker clearly envisioned himself as the next Roy or Charles Brown. But from the evidence of these early sides, it's clear that Robey wanted to piggyback off the success of the Sun sound. Tracks like "I Wanna Ramble" were virtual carbon copies of the "Feelin' Good" riff and Parker's recasting of old favorites like Robert Johnson's "Sweet Home Chicago," Roosevelt Sykes' "Driving Wheel," "Yonder's Wall," and "Mother-In-Law Blues," were all clearly in the down-home vein that Parker felt was too "old timey" for an up-to-date musician/vocalist of his caliber. His first big hit for the label, the horn-driven "Next Time You See Me" is here with others in the same vein, but this otherwise excellent collection is curiously missing "Pretty Baby," Parker's version of Howlin' Wolf's "Riding in the Moonlight," certainly one of his best. —*Cub Koda*

Love Ain't Nothin But a Business Goin' On / Feb. 18, 1997 / Simitar ✦✦✦

Kenny Parker

Guitar, Vocals / Modern Electric Blues
In the mid-'90s, Detroit blues guitarist and songwriter Kenny Parker released his debut album for the London-based JSP Records, *Raise the Dead*. Parker's blues education began with the Beatles in the early 1960s, but it wasn't long before he discovered the roots of their music. Parker grew up in Albion, Michigan and began playing in his first band, the Esquires, at 14. He begin listening to Albert King and B.B. King in high school via the local record store, and he took his inspiration from them. He graduated from Eastern Michigan University in 1976 and took a job in a Cadillac factory while looking around for the right opportunities to play blues at night. He began working with a paragon of the Detroit scene, Mr. Bo (Louis Bo Collins), and later joined the Butler Twins.

While Parker toured Europe with the Butler Twins, JSP founder John Stedman heard him and decided to sign him up for his own recording. The Butler Twins accompany Parker on his debut recording, and he's also backed by harp master Darrell Nulisch, best known for his work with Anson Funderburgh and the Rockets. The Butler Twins and Nulisch contribute vocals on Parker's *Raise the Dead*, and since Parker doesn't consider himself a singer, his guitar playing takes center stage. —*Richard Skelly*

Raise the Dead / Nov. 12, 1996 / JSP ✦✦✦

Michael Parrish

Guitar, Keyboards, Vocals / American Trad Rock, Country Blues
The country-blues unit the Michael Parrish Band comprised singer/guitarist/keyboardist Parrish, guitarists Chris Hansen and Jonny Sheehan, bassist Joe Engravalle, and drummer Tommy Kaelin. A Bay Area native, Parrish travelled to Chicago to tenure as the pianist for blues vocalist B.B. Odum before, at the urging of producer and folklorist Tim Duffy, moving to North Carolina to contribute to a series of blues field recordings later released as Music Maker label's audiophile blues series. After touring with the likes of Guitar Gabriel and Big Boy Henry, Parrish also appeared on seven tracks on the 1995 LP *A Living Past: The Music Maker Patron Sampler,* followed later that year by *Came So Far* and *Guitar Gabriel Volume 1.* He and Duffy also teamed as a folk duo, the Puritans. After touring in support of *Automobility,* his 1995 debut solo effort (self-released on his Geographic Records label), Parrish returned to New York City, where he formed a band comprising former Other Half members Hansen and Engravalle, onetime Hatters drummer Kaelin, and occasional songwriter Sheehan; after issuing their 1997 disc *Beautiful Rocks,* the Michael Parrish Band played several dates on the H.O.R.D.E. tour. —*Jason Ankeny*

Beautiful Rocks / 1997 / Geographic ✦✦✦
The Michael Parrish Band's debut *Beautiful Rocks* minimizes the traditional blues flavor of Parrish's earlier work to adopt a rootsier, more rough-edged sensibility closer in spirit to the alternative country movement; tracks like "Bird Brain Daddy" and "Listen to This Jive" should also appeal to fans of Blues Traveller and other American Trad Rock acts. —*Jason Ankeny*

Charley Patton

b. 1887, Edwards, MS, d. Apr. 28, 1934, Indianola, MS
Guitar, Vocals / Delta Blues, Prewar Country Blues
If the Delta country blues has a convenient source point, it would probably be Charley Patton, its first great star. His hoarse, impassioned singing style, fluid guitar playing and unrelenting beat made him the original king of the Delta blues. Much more than your average itinerant musician, Patton was an acknowledged celebrity and a seminal influence on musicians throughout the Delta. Rather than bumming his way from town to town, Patton would be called up to play at plantation dances, juke joints, and the like. He'd pack them in like sardines everywhere he went, and the emotional sway he held over his audiences caused him to be tossed off of more than one plantation by the ownership, simply because workers would leave crops unattended to listen to him play any time he picked up a guitar. He epitomized the image of a '20s "sport" blues singer; rakish, raffish, easy to provoke, capable of downing massive quantities of food and liquor, a woman on each arm with a flashy, expensive looking guitar fitted with a strap and kept in a traveling case by his side, only to be opened up when there was money or good times involved. His records—especially his first and biggest hit, "Pony Blues"—could be heard on phonographs throughout the South. Although he was certainly not the first Delta bluesman to record, he quickly became one of the genre's most popular. By late-'20s Mississippi plantation standards, Charley Patton was a star, a genuine celebrity.

Although Patton was roughly five-foot-five and only weighed a spartan 135 pounds, his gravelly, high-energy singing style (even on ballads and gospel tunes it sounded this way) made him sound like a man twice his weight and half again his size. Sleepy John Estes claimed he was the loudest blues singer he ever heard and it was rumored that his voice was loud enough to carry outdoors at a dance up to 500 yards away without amplification. His vaudeville-style vocal asides—which on record give the effect of two people talking to each other—along with the sound of his whiskey- and cigarette-scarred voice would become major elements of the vocal style of one of his students, a young Howlin' Wolf. His guitar playing was no less impressive, fueled with a propulsive beat and a keen rhythmic sense that would later plant seeds in the boogie style of John Lee Hooker. Patton is generally regarded as one of the original architects of putting blues into a strong, syncopated rhythm and the strident tone he achieves on record was achieved by tuning his guitar a step to a step and a half above standard pitch instead of using a capo. His compositional skills on the instrument are illustrated by his penchant for finding and utilizing several different themes as background accompaniment in a single song. His slide work—either played in his lap like a Hawaiian guitar and fretted with a pocket knife or in the more conventional manner with a brass pipe for a bottleneck—was no less inspiring, finishing vocal phrases for him and influencing contemporaries like Son House and up and coming youngsters like Robert Johnson. He also popped his bass strings (a technique he developed some 40 years before funk bass players started doing the same thing), beat his guitar like a drum and stomped his feet to reinforce certain beats or to create counter rhythms, all of which can be heard on various recordings. Rhythm and excitement were the bywords of his style.

The second, and equally important, part of Patton's legacy handed down to succeeding blues generations was his propensity for entertaining. One of the reasons for Charley Patton's enormous popularity in the South stems from him being a consummate barrelhouse entertainer. Most of the now-common guitar gymnastics modern audiences have come to associate with the likes of a Jimi Hendrix, in fact, originated with Patton. His ability to "entertain the peoples" and rock the house with a hell-raising ferociousness left an indelible impression on audiences and fellow bluesmen alike. His music embraced everything from blues, ballads, and ragtime to gospel. And so keen were Patton's abilities in setting mood and ambience, that he could bring a barrelhouse frolic to a complete stop by launching into an impromptu performance of nothing but religious-themed selections and still manage to hold his audience spellbound. Because he possessed the heart of a bluesman with the mindset of a vaudeville performer, hearing Patton for the first time can be a bit overwhelming; it's a lot to take in as the music and performances can career from emotionally intense to buffoonishly comic, sometimes within a single selection. It is all strongly rooted in '20s Black dance music and even on the religious tunes in his repertoire, Patton fuels it all with a strong rhythmic pulse.

He first recorded in 1929 for the Paramount label and within a year's time, he was not only the largest-selling blues artist but—in a whirlwind of recording activity—also the music's most prolific. Patton was also responsible for hooking up fellow players Willie Brown and Son House with their first chances to record. It is probably best to issue a blanket audio disclaimer of some kind when listening to Patton's total recorded legacy, some 60 odd tracks total, his final session done only a couple of months before his death in 1934. We will never know what Patton's Paramount masters really sounded like. When the company went out of business, the metal masters were sold off as scrap, some of it used to line chicken coops! All that's left are the original 78s—rumored to have been made out of inferior pressing material commonly used to make bowling balls (!)—and all of them are scratched and heavily played, making all attempts at sound retrieval by current noise-reduction processing a tall order indeed. That said, it is still music well worth seeking out and not just for its place in history. Patton's music gives us the first flowering of the Delta blues form, before it became homogenized with turnarounds and 12-bar restrictions, and few humans went at it so agressively. —*Cub Koda*

★ **Founder of the Delta Blues** / 1969 / Yazoo ♦♦♦♦♦
A cornerstone of any blues collection, this is where you start. As compilations go, this originally started life as a double record set featuring all of Patton's best known titles and sound wise was miles above all previous versions. Its compact disc incarnation here trims the tune list to 24 tracks, but all the seminal tracks are here: "Pony Blues," "High Water Everywhere," "Screamin' and Hollerin' the Blues," "A Spoonful Blues," "Shake It and Break It" and the wistful "Poor Me," recorded at his final session in 1934, a scant two months before he died. —*Cub Koda*

☆ **King of the Delta Blues** / 1991 / Yazoo ♦♦♦♦♦
This excellent companion volume to the above pulls together 23 more Patton tracks (including some alternate takes that were for years thought to be lost) to give a much more complete look at this amazing artist. It's interesting here to compare the tracks from his final session to his halcyon output from 1929. Highlights include "Mean Black Cat Blues," Patton's adaption of "Sitting on Top of the World" ("Some Summer Day") and both parts of "Prayer of Death," originally issued under the non de plume of "Elder J.J. Hadley." The sound on this collection is vastly superior from a noise reduction standpoint to its companion volume. —*Cub Koda*

Complete Recorded Works, Vols. 1-3 / Document ♦♦♦♦
This is a 61-track, three-CD set that encompasses a complete chronological run of Patton's recorded output. All of his solo sides are here, his duets with Bertha Lee and Henry Sims and his backup work behind both of them. All previous incarnations of this material don't sound near as good as they do on these three volumes, all of them given the full deluxe Cedarization noise reduction treatment from the Document folks. This is as nice as this stuff's probably ever gonna sound, thus justifying the usual hefty import price. —*Cub Koda*

Odie Payne

b. Aug. 27, 1926, Chicago, IL, **d.** Mar. 1, 1989, Chicago, IL
Drums / Chicago Blues
Drummer Odie Payne was born in Chicago on August 27, 1926. Fascinated by music as a child, Payne listened to everything he could get his hands on—classical, pop, musicals, big band. Even as a teen he would sneak into clubs to watch and listen to what the drummers were doing. He studied music through high school and was drafted into the Army when his schoolwork fell off. After release from the military, Payne studied drums and graduated with high honors from the Roy C. Knapp School of Percussion. While playing with pianist Johnny Jones in 1949, Payne met Tampa Red and soon joined Red's band. They played and recorded together for several years. Payne states that he apprenticed himself to Red.

In 1952 Payne and pianist Johnny Jones became part of Elmore James' dance band the Broomdusters. Payne stayed with the band for three years, but recorded with James until 1959—recording some 31 singles. He became a highly sought after studio musician and, in the later 1950s, recorded on many essential recordings for the Cobra label, including artists like Otis Rush, Magic Sam, and Buddy Guy. Odie Payne developed the famous double-shuffle, later used by Fred Below and Sam Lay to great effect. Payne recorded for Chess including a number of classic Chuck Berry tunes like "Nadine" and "No Particular Place to Go." He recorded with most of the great Chicago blues artists: Otis Rush, Sonny Boy Williamson II, Muddy Waters, Jimmy Rogers, Eddie Taylor, Magic Sam, Yank Rachell, Sleepy John Estes, Little Brother Montgomery, Memphis Minnie, and many others.

Much watched and admired by other Chicago drummers, Payne was perhaps most famous for his trademark use of the cowbell, lightning-fast bass drum pedal, and extended cymbal and drum rolls. Odie Payne died March 1, 1989, in Chicago. Loved and respected by those who knew him, Payne served as a role model for many working musicians. —*Michael Erlewine*

Peg Leg Sam

b. Dec. 18, 1911, Jonesville, SC, **d.** Nov. 27, 1977, Jonesville, SC
Harmonica, Vocals / Country Blues, Prewar Country Blues
Peg Leg Sam was a performer to be treasured, a member of what may have been the last authentic traveling medicine show, a harmonica virtuoso, and an extraordinary entertainer. Born Arthur Jackson, he acquired his nickname after a hoboing accident in 1930. His medicine show career began in 1938, and his repertoire—finally recorded only in the early '70s—reflected the rustic nature of the traveling show. "Peg" delivered comedy routines, bawdy toasts, and monologs; performed tricks with his harps (often playing two at once); and served up some juicy Piedmont blues (sometimes with a guitar accompanist, but most often by himself). Peg Leg Sam gave his last medicine-show performance in 1972 in North Carolina and was still in fine fettle when he started making the rounds of folk and blues festivals in his last years. —*Jim O'Neal*

● **Joshua** / 1975 / Tomato ♦♦♦♦
Originally released on the indie label Blue Labor in 1975, *Joshua* is the first record Peg Leg Sam ever recorded, and it certainly shows his roots as a medicine show performer. The music falls halfway between medicine show burlesque and straight country-blues. Peg Leg Sam was a fine harmonica player and guitarist who captured the essence of the medicine show, even after that tradition had died. Louisiana Red, who accompanies Peg Leg on several tracks, doesn't quite get into the spirit and sounds uncomfortable with the material, which only shows that Sam was a master of a forgotten art. Nevertheless, to many blues fans, this music may sound more like a historical curiosity than a lost treasure. —*Thom Owens*

Early in the Morning / May 21, 1996 / Blues Alliance ✦✦✦

Peg Leg Sam with Louisiana Red / Tomato ✦✦✦✦

Recorded shortly before his death, this album features Peg Leg Sam with Louisiana Red performing a set of old-timey, traditional blues—the kind of that was frequently heard at travelling medicine shows. Although it was recorded late in his career, the album captures the essence of Peg Leg Sam. —*Thom Owens*

Pinetop Perkins

b. Jul. 13, 1913, Belzoni, MS
Guitar, Piano, Vocals / Piano Blues

He admittedly wasn't the originator of the seminal piano piece "Pinetop's Boogie Woogie," but it's a safe bet that more people associate it nowadays with Pinetop Perkins than with the man who devised it in the first place, Clarence "Pinetop" Smith.

Although it seems as though he's been around Chicago forever, the Mississippi native actually got a relatively late start on his path to Windy City immortality. It was only when Muddy Waters took him on to replace Otis Spann in 1969 that Perkins' rolling mastery of the ivories began to assume outsized proportions.

Perkins began his blues existence primarily as a guitarist, but a mid-'40s encounter with an outraged chorus girl toting a knife at a Helena, AR, nightspot left him with severed tendons in his left arm. That dashed his guitar aspirations, but Joe Willie Perkins came back strong from the injury, concentrating solely on piano from that point on.

Perkins had traveled to Helena with Robert Nighthawk in 1943, playing with the elegant slide guitarist on Nighthawk's KFFA radio program. Perkins soon switched over to rival Sonny Boy Williamson's beloved *King Biscuit Time* radio show in Helena, where he remained for an extended period. Perkins accompanied Nighthawk on a 1950 session for the Chess brothers that produced "Jackson Town Gal," but Chicago couldn't hold him at the time.

Nighthawk disciple Earl Hooker recruited Perkins during the early '50s. They hit the road, pausing at Sam Phillips' studios in Memphis long enough for Perkins to wax his first version of "Pinetop's Boogie Woogie" in 1953. He settled in downstate Illinois for a spell, then relocated to Chicago. Music gradually was relegated to the back burner until Hooker coaxed him into working on an LP for Arhoolie in 1968. When Spann split from Muddy Waters, the stage was set for Pinetop Perkins' re-emergence.

After more than a decade with the Man, Perkins and his bandmates left en masse to form the Legendary Blues Band. Their early Rounder albums (*Life of Ease, Red Hot 'n' Blue*) prominently spotlighted Perkins' rippling 88s and rich vocals. He had previously waxed an album for the French Black & Blue logo in 1976 and four fine cuts for Alligator's *Living Chicago Blues* anthologies in 1978. Finally, in 1988, he cut his first domestic album for Blind Pig, *After Hours*.

Ever since then, Pinetop Perkins has made up for precious lost time in the studio. Discs for Antone's, Omega (*Portrait of a Delta Bluesman*, a solo outing that includes fascinating interview segments), Deluge, Earwig, and several other firms ensure that his boogie legacy won't be forgotten in the decades to come. —*Bill Dahl*

Boogie Woogie King / Nov. 1, 1976 / Evidence ✦✦✦

Although he did not have an album issued under his name as a leader until 1988, pianist Pinetop Perkins actually should have had one released in 1976, when he cut tracks on this recently reissued Evidence CD for the Black and Blue label. They did not appear until 1992, which is a shame. Perkins' trademark boogie-woogie riffs, rumbling rhythms, left-hand lines, and spinning phrases were in fine form. His accompaniment and supporting phrases behind guitarist/vocalist Luther Johnson Jr. are equally tasty and inviting. Johnson, as erratic a performer as any in contemporary blues, came ready to play and sing on this date. His vocals had plenty of grit, conviction, and energy, while his playing had no excesses and was delivered with zip and flair. —*Ron Wynn*

● **After Hours** / 1988 / Blind Pig ✦✦✦✦

Easy-grooving blues and boogie is backed by the competent New York City-based blues band Little Mike and the Tornadoes. Though Perkins followed Otis Spann as the piano player in the Muddy Waters band, these are the first domestically available recordings under his own name. —*Niles J. Frantz*

Pinetop's Boogie Woogie / 1992 / Discovery ✦✦✦✦

The maze of new and recent discs by this veteran Chicago piano man can be daunting, but rest assured that this is one of his best to date. Many of the songs are Perkins standbys—"Kidney Stew," "Caldonia," and of course, "Pinetop's Boogie Woogie"—but the backing here is so stellar (sidemen include harpists James Cotton and Kim Wilson, guitarists Matt Murphy, Jimmy Rogers, Hubert Sumlin, and Duke Robillard, and several driving rhythm sections)—that the project rises above most of Perkins' output. —*Bill Dahl*

On Top / Jan. 1992 / Deluge ✦✦✦

Solid entry in Perkins' ever-growing discography of contemporary CDs. —*Bill Dahl*

Portrait of a Delta Bluesman / 1993 / Vanguard ✦✦✦✦

Considerably more ambitious than just another Perkins set, this solo disc intersperses key songs from his storied history with interview segments that reveal much about the man himself, from his Delta beginnings to when he replaced Otis Spann in Muddy Waters' vaunted band. —*Bill Dahl*

Live Top / 1995 / Deluge ✦✦✦

A very competent combo offers incendiary support behind the veteran Chicago pianist throughout the album, recorded live before an appreciative gathering. —*Bill Dahl*

With the Blue Ice Band / 1995 / Earwig ✦✦

The pianist is as charming and effervescent as ever on this live/studio outing—but he's often undermined by the presence of mediocre harpist Chicago Beau and an Icelandic band that doesn't know the meaning of the words subtlety or taste. Rock-drenched guitar solos fly with abandon, destroying any semblance of Chicago-style ambience. —*Bill Dahl*

Born in the Delta / May 27, 1997 / Telarc ✦✦✦

Pinetop Perkins was 83 when he recorded *Born in the Delta* in 1996. As a singer, Perkins still had plenty of soul and spirit and got his points across convincingly. And as a pianist, he still had sizable chops. In terms of material, Perkins tends to favor blues standards that have been done to death, including Jimmy Reed's "Baby, What You Want Me to Do?," Peter Chatman's "Everyday I Have the Blues," Leroy Carr's "How Long, How Long Blues," and Paul Gayton's "For You My Love." One could nitpick about the onetime Muddy Waters sideman so often choosing the obvious, but given how much fun he's clearly having at this session, it's hard to complain. Thankfully, Perkins gives himself sufficient solo space, and he has competent support in harmonica player Jerry Portnoy and electric guitarist Tony O. —*Alex Henderson*

Down in Mississippi / Jan. 13, 1998 / HMG ✦✦✦

Despite the romantic title, these are private recordings done in Pinetop's home in Chicago in 1996 and 1997. This album finds him in an unaccompanied solo setting, with the first six selections featuring him manning an electric piano while the other seven tracks put him behind a conventional acoustic model. Lots of boogies and shuffles here for Perkins to stretch out on, and he pays tribute to many of his early inspirations, like Sunnyland Slim, Leroy Carr, Eddie Boyd, and others. Highlights include "Kidney Stew," "Pinetop's Boogie Woogie," "Song for Sunnyland Slim," "Five Long Years," and the title track. If you want to hear a boogie-woogie master unencumbered by surrounding instruments in the band and laying it down with élan and pizzazz, this disc fills the bill nicely. —*Cub Koda*

Bill Perry

Guitar, Vocals / Modern Blues, Modern Electric Blues

Although guitarist, songwriter and singer Bill Perry may seem like a newcomer to the blues scene to some, he's actually put in a long apprenticeship with folk-rock singer Richie Havens. Perry was Havens' main guitarist for shows he performed with a band through the 1980s.

Signed in 1995 to an unprecedented five-album deal with the Pointblank/ Virgin label, Perry's future looks bright because he's a sharp songwriter, an adequate singer and a fiery guitar player. Perry's style could best be characterized as hard-driving blues for the 1990s. Perry's song, "Fade to Blue" is covered by Havens on his recent album, *Cuts to the Chase*.

Perry was born in the upstate town of Chester, New York and grew up in a music-filled household. His grandmother played organ in the church, but a young Perry was attracted to his father's Jimmy Smith albums, which featured guitarist Kenny Burrell. Perry began playing guitar at age six and played in his first talent show at 13. By high school, he led bands as vocalist and lead guitarist before graduation. After graduating, he lived in California and Colorado, all the while honing his distinctive guitar playing. He moved back to upstate New York and accompanied Havens on most of his shows with a band through the 1980s. Perry toured with the Band's Garth Hudson and Levon Helm at the same time he was working with Havens, and all that traveling spurred him on to form his own band, and he did in the early '90s.

Look for more brilliant albums and a whole lot of live shows from this guitarist for the rest of the 1990s. He loves playing live, and he knows how to pace his sets to get maximum audience response. —*Richard Skelly*

● **Love Scars** / Feb. 6, 1996 / Pointblank ✦✦✦✦
Love Scars is an impressive debut from Bill Perry, a singer-songwriter that fuses '70s folk with blues. Perry occasionally can sound too earnest—which could be expected from a former supporting musician for Richie Havens—but there's genuine skill and craft in his songs. His lyrics are strong and melodies are sturdy, and they're delivered with conviction, which makes up for the occasional awkward moments that should be expected from a debut record. Still, those little missteps are nowhere near enough to prevent *Love Scars* from being a promising debut. —*Thom Owens*

Greycourtlightning / Mar. 31, 1998 / Pointblank ✦✦✦✦
On his second album, *Greycourtlightning,* Bill Perry stakes out new territory by delivering a tight, focused effort where the songs are fleshed out by other instruments as much as his guitar. Perry's songs follow blues conventions, but twist them slightly, making them sound fresh and exciting. Furthermore, his playing is filled with unexpected turns, as he throws in jazz, folk and rock flourishes to his blistering solos. With its selection of great songs and great playing, *Greycourtlightning* proves that Perry's debut, *Love Scars,* was no fluke. —*Thom Owens*

James Peterson

b. Nov. 4, 1937, Russell County, AL
Guitar, Vocals / Modern Electric Blues
Florida-based guitarist, singer and songwriter James Peterson plays a gritty style of southern-fried blues that is at times reminiscent of Howlin' Wolf and other times more along the lines of Freddie King. He formed his first band while he was living in Buffalo, NY and running Governor's Inn, House of Blues in the 1960s. He and his band would back up the traveling musicians who came through, including blues legends like Muddy Waters, Howlin' Wolf, Big Joe Turner, Freddie King, Lowell Fulson, and Koko Taylor.

Peterson was born November 4, 1937, in Russel County, AL. Peterson was strongly influenced by gospel music in the rural area he grew up in, and he began singing in church as a child. Thanks to his father's jukejoint, he was exposed to blues at an early age, and later followed in his footsteps in upstate New York. After leaving home at age 14, he headed to Gary, Indiana, where he sang with his friend John Scott. While still a teen, he began playing guitar, entirely self-taught. Peterson cites musicians like Muddy Waters, Howlin' Wolf (Chester Burnett), Jimmy Reed, and B.B. King as his early role models. After moving to Buffalo, NY, in 1955, he continued playing with various area blues bands, and ten years later, he opened his own blues club.

In 1970, Peterson recorded his first album, *The Father, Son and the Blues* on the Perception/Today label. While he ran his blues club at night, he supplemented his income by running a used-car lot during the day. Peterson's debut album was produced and co-written with Willie Dixon, and it featured a then-five-year-old Lucky Peterson on keyboards. Peterson followed it up with *Tryin' to Keep the Blues Alive* a few years later. Peterson's other albums include *Rough and Ready* and *Too Many Knots* for the Kingsnake and Ichiban labels in 1990 and 1991, respectively.

The album that's put Peterson back on the road as a national touring act is his 1995 release, *Don't Let the Devil Ride* for the Jackson, Mississippi-based Waldoxy Records. A master showman who has learned from the best and knows how to work an audience, he's also a crafty songwriter endowed with a deep, gospel-drenched singing style. —*Richard Skelly*

● **Rough and Ready** / 1990 / Kingsnake ✦✦✦✦
A pleasant album of original compositions by this Alabama-born bluesman, it features James' son Lucky Peterson (Alligator recording artist) on guitar and keyboards. —*Niles J. Frantz*

Too Many Knots / 1991 / Ichiban ✦✦✦

Don't Let the Devil Ride / Mar. 21, 1995 / Waldoxy ✦✦✦

Preachin' the Blues / 1996 / Waldoxy ✦✦✦

Lucky Peterson

b. Dec. 13, 1964, Buffalo, NY
Organ, Bass, Guitar, Piano, Drums, Vocals / Modern Electric Blues
Child-prodigy status is sometimes difficult to overcome upon reaching maturity. Not so for Lucky Peterson—he's far bigger (in more ways than one) on the contemporary blues circuit than he was at the precocious age of six, when he scored a national R&B hit with the Willie Dixon-produced "1-2-3-4."

Little Lucky Peterson was lucky to be born into a musical family. His dad, James Peterson, owned the Governor's Inn, a popular Buffalo, NY, blues nightclub that booked the biggies: Jimmy Reed, Muddy Waters, Bill Doggett. The latter's mighty Hammond B-3 organ fascinated the four-and-a-half-year-old lad, and soon Peterson was on his way under Dixon's tutelage. "1-2-3-4" got Peterson on *The Tonight Show* and *The Ed Sullivan Show,* but he didn't rest on his laurels—he was doubling on guitar at age eight, and at 17, he signed on as Little Milton's keyboardist for three years.

A three-year stint with Bobby Bland preceded Peterson's solo career launch, which took off when he struck up a musical relationship with Florida-based producer Bob Greenlee. Two Greenlee-produced albums for Alligator, 1989's *Lucky Strikes!* and the following year's *Triple Play,* remain his finest recorded offerings. Extensive session work behind everyone from Etta James and Kenny Neal to Otis Rush also commenced during this period.

In 1992, Peterson's first Verve label album, *I'm Ready,* found him boldly mixing contemporary rock and soul into his simmering blues stew. Two more high-energy Verve sets have followed, making it clear that Peterson's luck remains high (as does his father's, who's fashioned his own career as a bluesman in recent years with albums for Ichiban and Waldoxy). —*Bill Dahl*

Ridin' / Mar. 1984 / Evidence ✦✦✦✦
As a child prodigy, keyboardist and organist Lucky Peterson's exploits were legendary. The stories grew even more widespread as he became a teen and stints with Little Milton and Bobby "Blue" Bland only added to his fame. But Peterson's records have not always justified or reaffirmed his reputation. That is not the case with the cuts on this 1984 set, recently reissued by Evidence. The spiraling solos, excellent bridges, turnbacks, pedal maneuvers, and soulful accompaniment are executed with a relaxed edge and confident precision. If you have wondered whether Lucky Peterson deserves the hype and major label bonanza, these songs are the real deal. —*Ron Wynn*

Lucky Strikes / 1989 / Alligator ✦✦✦✦
Peterson's real coming-out party as a mature blues triple threat: his guitar and keyboard skills are prodigious (though he's no longer a child prodigy), and his vocals on "Pounding of My Heart," "Can't Get No Loving on the Telephone," and "Heart Attack" (all written by producer/bassist Bob Greenlee) served notice that more than luck was involved in Peterson's adult rise to fame. —*Bill Dahl*

● **Triple Play** / 1990 / Alligator ✦✦✦✦
Even more impressive than his previous Alligator set, thanks to top-flight material like "Don't Cloud up on Me," "Let the Chips Fall Where They May," and "Locked Out of Love," the fine house band at Greenlee's King Snake studios, and Peterson's own rapidly developing attack on two instruments. —*Bill Dahl*

I'm Ready / Aug. 1992 / Verve ✦✦✦
Lucky Peterson is a smooth operator, cool and always in control with a guitar tone reminiscent of the more restrained sides of Roy Buchanan or Carlos Santana. He's capable of lashing out, though, as the livewire showstopper "Don't Cloud up on Me" ably proves. But this versatile musician is most distinctive with his Hammond organ and Wurlitzer electric piano sound, instruments that he's been playing professionally since the age of five. Check out the heady swirl of instrumental workout "Junk Yard" on this front although comparisons to Billy Preston will be inevitable. —*Roch Parisien*

Beyond Cool / 1994 / Verve ✦✦
Once Peterson arrived at Verve, his taste in material seemed to sail right out the window. This disc is confusingly unfocused (rock influences are as prominent as blues) and a far cry indeed from his fine Alligator sets of a precious few years before. —*Bill Dahl*

Lifetime / Mar. 5, 1996 / Verve ✦✦✦

Move / Feb. 10, 1998 / Polygram ✦✦✦
Call this Peterson's 'back to my roots' blues album, but it finds him in more retro territory than his previous outings. There's a distinctive Albert King–Freddie King–Albert Collins almost-'70s feel to all the music here and the support of roots players like Johnny B. Gayden, Dennis Chambers and Butch Bonner makes this much more of a ensemble effort. Highlights include the storming "You're the One for Me," a great King-like solo on "Tin Pan Alley," an instrumental tribute to Albert Collins on "Pickin'," and oddball covers of the Isley Brothers' "It's Your Thing" and Prince's "Purple Rain." Peterson is stylistically all over the road on this disc but his versatility on both guitar and keyboards ultimately pays off in the end. — *Cub Koda*

Kelly Joe Phelps

b. Oct. 5, 1959, Sumner, WA
Vocals / Modern Electric Blues
Portland, Oregon-based acoustic/slide guitar player and singer-songwriter Kelly Joe Phelps has been carving a growing niche for his music throughout the 1990s through two well-received albums, *Lead Me On* (Burnside Records, 1995), and *Roll Away The Stone* (Rykodisc, 1997).

Phelps was raised in Washington and learned country and folk songs from his father, as well as drums and piano. At first, he concentrated on free jazz and took his cues from musicians like Ornette Coleman, Miles Davis and John Coltrane before finding his true calling as a blues musician in the late '80s, when he began listening to acoustic blues masters like Fred McDowell and Robert Pete Williams. He began singing and recorded his critically praised debut in 1994. Six original songs showcase Phelps' ability in the blues idiom, but he also tackles, and does justice to, traditional numbers like "Motherless Children" and "Fare Thee Well."

Phelps, as deft and creative an acoustic slide guitarist as you'll hear anywhere in the US, can be heard on Greg Brown's album *Further In*, Tony Furtado's album *Roll My Blues Away*, and Townes Van Zandt's *The Highway Kind*. In recent years, he's opened shows for B.B. King, Leo Kottke, Keb' Mo', Robben Ford, and Little Feat. — *Richard Skelly*

Lead Me On / 1995 / Burnside ✦✦✦✦
This is the real deal—Phelps performs with the full authority and authenticity of the Delta bluest tradition without ever once sounding like a Folkways museum piece. There's nothing more to it than the 34-year-old's raspy, swamp-infused vocals, lapstyle acoustic guitar played using fingerpicking and slide, and self-accompanied stomp-box percussion. For the six originals and seven gospel and prewar blues selections on offer here, it's more than enough. File alongside the likes of Ben Harper and Keb' Mo'. — *Roch Parisien*

● **Roll Away the Stone** / Aug. 26, 1997 / Rykodisc ✦✦✦✦
If anything, *Roll Away the Stone* is an even better record than Kelly Joe Phelps' debut, *Lead Me On*. Phelps continues to grow as both a musician and songwriter, and his interpretations of classic blues songs show increased imagination. Although it's based in classic blues, this music doesn't sound ancient—it sounds vital and alive, like any great music should. — *Thom Owens*

Brewer Phillips

b. Nov. 16, 1924, Coila, MS
Guitar, Vocals / Chicago Blues
Brewer Phillips is one of the more unique sidemen in Chicago blues history. His guitar playing combines the rhythmic sense of an Eddie Taylor (an early childhood friend and fishing buddy) with the stinging lead work of a Pat Hare. Born on a plantation in Coila, MS, he came under the early tutelage of Memphis Minnie and grew up with the legends of the blues all around him, seeing many of them perform first hand. After leaving Mississippi, he moved to Memphis, becoming a professional musician and making his first recordings as a member of Bill Harvey's band, along with a session behind pianist Roosevelt Sykes that has yet to surface. Best-known for his work as a member of the Houserockers (see Hound Dog Taylor entry), his backup work behind Taylor—a trio with no bass player—finds him alternating between the icepick-in-your-ear sheet-metal lead tones produced from his battered Telecaster to comping bass lines while simultaneously combining chords, all of it executed with a thumbpick and bare fingers. It's a sound

totally rooted in the juke joint sounds of Phillips' Mississippi upbringing and there's simply no equal to it in the blues today. Since Taylor's death in 1976, he has recorded on his own and worked sporadically with J.B. Hutto, Lil Ed, Cub Koda, and others while remaining a largely shadowy figure in Chicago blues circles. — *AMG*

● **Good Houserockin'** / 1995 / Wolf ✦✦✦✦
This combines various late-'70s and early-'80s recordings into one package. The first 11 tracks are from Phillips' 1982 solo album for the label, *Ingleside Blues*. The next six tracks were recorded live in 1977 in Vienna and Boston, featuring Brewer fronting J.B. Hutto and the Houserockers. The last two sides are unissued leftovers from the 1980 Cub Koda and the Houserockers' *It's the Blues!* album. Phillips' longtime playing partner, drummer Ted Harvey, is present on all 19 tracks and shares billing with him on this disc. Some of the recording quality (especially on the live Hutto tracks) is unbelievably crude and harsh sounding, making the overall sound of this disc very spotty and uneven. This collection is probably the most complete—though not necessarily the best—collection of Phillips' solo work. — *AMG*

Homebrew / Feb. 6, 1996 / Delmark ✦✦✦
It's amazing to think that Brewer Phillips would be 70-plus years old before releasing his US debut album, but after a couple of years in virtual seclusion, Delmark coaxed him back into the studio for this fine set. Phillips' regular working band is aboard with pianist Aaron Moore handling the bulk of the vocals, Magic Sam's drummer, Robert "Huckleberry Hound" Wright, and Willie Black on bass providing simple but effective support. Phillips sings on the Jimmy Reed classic "You Don't Have to Go," "Looking for a Woman" and "Lunch Bucket Blues" and his single string work is highlighted on the instrumental title track. A simple, laidback album with some surprising fireworks in all the unexpected places. — *Cub Koda*

Gene Phillips

b. Jul. 25, 1915, St. Louis, MO
Guitar, Vocals / R&B, West Coast Blues, Jump Blues
A West Coast session stalwart who appeared on a myriad of jump blues waxings during the late '40s and early '50s, guitarist Gene Phillips faded from view even before the dawn of rock 'n' roll. Any serious collector of the Bihari brothers' budget-priced Crown albums (you know, the ones with those ubiquitous cheesy cover illustrations by artist "Fazzio") should be intimately familiar with Phillips' LP—it's one of the best Crown acquisitions you can possibly make (especially since there's no CD equivalent yet).

The T-Bone Walker-influenced Phillips recorded extensively for the Biharis' Modern Imprint from 1947 through 1950. His often-ribald jump blues gems for the firm included "Big Legs," "Fatso," "Rock Bottom," "Hey Now," and a version of Big Bill Broonzy's witty standard "Just a Dream." Phillips' bandmates were among the royalty of the L.A. scene: trumpeter Jake Porter, saxists Marshall Royal Maxwell Davis, and Jack McVea, and pianist Lloyd Glenn were frequently on hand. Phillips returned the favor in Porter's case, singing and playing on the trumpeter's 1947 dates for Imperial.

After a 78 of his own for Imperial in 1951 ("She's Fit 'n Fat 'n Fine"), Phillips bowed out of the recording wars as a leader with a solitary 1954 effort for Combo, "Fish Man," backed by McVea's band. — *Bill Dahl*

Gene Phillips and the Rockers / 1963 / Crown ✦✦✦

● **Gene Phillips** / Ace ✦✦✦✦
No CD presence for late-'40s/early-'50s Los Angeles guitar stalwart Phillips yet, but Ace was kind enough to assemble a nice cross-section of his jumping R&B sides a while back. — *Bill Dahl*

Piano Red (William Lee Perryman)

b. Oct. 19, 1911, Hampton, GA, **d.** Jul. 25, 1985, Decatur, GA
Piano, Vocals / Piano Blues
Willie Perryman went by two nicknames during his lengthy career, both of them thoroughly apt. He was known as Piano Red because of his albino skin pigmentation for most of his performing life. But they called him Doctor Feelgood during the '60s, and that's precisely what his raucous, barrelhouse-styled vocals and piano were guaranteed to do: cure anyone's ills and make them feel good.

Like his older brother, Rufus Perryman, who performed and recorded as Speckled Red, Willie Perryman showed an aptitude for the 88s early in life.

At age 12, he was banging on the ivories, influenced by Fats Waller but largely his own man. He rambled some with blues greats Barbecue Bob, Curley Weaver, and Blind Willie McTell during the 1930s (and recording with the latter in 1936), but mostly worked as a solo artist.

In 1950, Red's big break arrived when he signed with RCA Victor. His debut Victor offering, the typically rowdy "Rockin' with Red," was a huge R&B hit, peaking at number five on *Billboard*'s charts. It's surfaced under a variety of guises later: Little Richard revived it as "She Knows How to Rock" in 1957 for Specialty, Jerry Lee Lewis aced it for Sun (unissued at the time), and pint-sized hillbilly dynamo Little Jimmy Dickens beat 'em both to the punch for Columbia.

"Red's Boogie," another pounding rocker from the pianist's first RCA date, also proved a huge smash, as did the rag-tinged "The Wrong Yo Yo" (later covered masterfully by Carl Perkins at Sun), "Just Right Bounce," and "Laying the Boogie" in 1951. Red became an Atlanta mainstay in the clubs and over the radio, recording prolifically for RCA through 1958 both there and in New York. There weren't any more hits, but that didn't stop the firm from producing a live LP by the pianist in 1956 at Atlanta's Magnolia Ballroom that throbbed with molten energy. Chet Atkins produced Red's final RCA date in Nashville in 1958, using Red's touring band for backup.

A 1959 single for Checker called "Get Up Mare" and eight tracks for the tiny Jax label preceded the rise of Red's new guise, Dr. Feelgood & the Interns, who debuted on Columbia's OKeh subsidiary in 1961 with a self-named rocker, "Doctor Feel-Good," that propelled the aging piano pounder into the pop charts for the first time. Its flipside, "Mister Moonlight" (penned and ostensibly sung by bandmember Roy Lee Johnson), found its way into the repertoire of the Beatles. A subsequent remake of "Right String but the Wrong Yo-Yo" also hit for the good doctor in 1962. The Doc remained with OKeh through 1966, recording with veteran Nashville saxist Boots Randolph in his band on five occasions.

Red remained ensconced at Muhlenbrink's Saloon in Atlanta from 1969 through 1979, sandwiching in extensive European tours along the way. He was diagnosed with cancer in 1984 and died the following year. *—Bill Dahl*

Piano Red in Concert / 1956 / Groove ✦✦✦
On this pioneering live set cut at Atlanta's Magnolia Ballroom, the sound is surprisingly clean and Red rocks the house! *—Bill Dahl*

Jump Man, Jump / 1956 / Groove ✦✦✦✦
Raucous barrelhouse blues and boogies with a hot R&B combo on these swinging sides. *—Bill Dahl*

Doctor Feelgood / 1962 / OKeh ✦✦

Dr. Feelgood All Alone with His Piano / 1975 / Arhoolie ✦✦✦

Atlanta Bounce / 1992 / Arhoolie ✦✦✦
Two distinct timeframes are represented on this slightly schizophrenic disc. Much of it is comprised of latter-day barrelhouse and blues waxed by Arhoolie, but there's also a thrilling handful of raucous live items from a 1956 concert at Atlanta's Magnolia Ballroom that capture the albino 88s ace at his most enthralling. *—Bill Dahl*

The Doctor Is In! / 1993 / Bear Family ✦✦✦✦
This four-CD set, containing 122 songs (23 of them previously unreleased) cut between July 1950 and March 1966 for RCA, Groove, OKeh, and Columbia, is, literally, the best of Piano Red, and may be the best box in the entire Bear Family catalog. This is about as good as piano blues and R&B got, and also some of the best piano-based rock 'n' roll you'll ever hear—rivaling *anything* that Jerry Lee Lewis or Little Richard ever cut—with barely a second-rate track; even the 23 previously unissued songs, three of them live, are comparable to anything on Red that RCA or Groove ever released. Even the multiple versions of his signature tune, "Right String But the Wrong Yo-Yo," are welcomed, from its lean, mean piano-bass-drums original 1950 version, to the live 1955 rendition and the broader 1961 remake (at the "Mr. Moonlight" session), because they're each different enough to justify their presence. And, yet, the most amazing thing about the 16 years covered on these four discs is the consistency of the music and performances—Red hardly changed at all until the early 1960s, always giving his audience a good show whether he was making records or playing live. Even in his later incarnation as "Dr. Feelgood," there isn't a sharp line of demarcation in his sound; the piano is little less prominent, and there are backup singers, but he's still the same man making pretty much the same music. From "Jumpin' the Boogie" and

"Rockin' with Red" from 1950 at the opening of Disc One, recorded with nothing but piano, bass, and drums, he adds saxes and guitars, but there isn't a lot that's too different—it's all high-octane, good-time keyboard blues. Discs Two and Three are arguably the best parts of the set, with Red at the peak of his prowess as a pianist and singer, going through the best parts of his studio history and the uncut tape of his legendary live 1955 Atlanta show—the bonus tracks unique to this set are concert versions of "Pay It No Mind," "Teen-Age Bounce," and Hank Williams's "Hey Good Lookin'." Red made the jump into rock 'n' roll more easily than most bluesmen of his age, with the result that his music from this period is as solid as anything else he ever did. Still later, on Disc Four, once he moves into a more produced, pop-oriented R&B sound, he holds up almost as well—the pity is that OKeh never capitalized on the Beatles' cover of "Mr. Moonlight," but this disc also proves that the song wasn't a fluke in his career, either. The sound is excellent (RCA and Columbia/OKeh apparently took good care of the masters), the notes are thorough, and the $100 list price of this 122-song set makes it proportionately *more* attractive than any $15/15-song best-of on Red that might ever show up (and there *isn't* one). *—Bruce Eder*

● **Wildfire** / Matchbox ✦✦✦✦
Although it's hardly comprehensive, Matchbox's *Wildfire* is the best available single-volume sampler of Piano Red's music, containing 12 of his greatest numbers, including "Red's Boogie" and "Diggin' the Boogie." *—Thom Owens*

Rod Piazza

b. Dec. 18, 1947, Riverside, CA
Harmonica, Vocals / Modern Electric Blues, West Coast Blues
A California-based blues bandleader, harmonica and singer, Rod Piazza's stratospheric harmonica wailings owe a heavy debt to both Little Walter and George "Harmonica" Smith.

Piazza began his professional career as a member of the Dirty Blues Band in the mid-'60s. The Dirty Blues Band recorded two albums for ABC/Bluesway—an eponymous debut in 1967 and 1968's *Stone Dirty*. Rod left the band after the release of *Stone Dirty,* choosing to hit the road with his idol, George "Harmonica" Smith instead. Over the next decade and a half, Piazza and Smith performed together frequently under the name Bacon Fat; they also recorded the occasional album. In 1969, Bacon Fat released their eponymous debut album on Blue Horizon.

While he was performing with Smith, Piazza released his own solo albums, the first of which—*Rod Piazza Blues Man*—appeared on LMI in 1973. The second, *Chicago Flying Saucer Band,* was released in 1979 on Gangster Records.

As Smith's health began to decline in the early '80s, Piazza assembled the Mighty Flyers—which featured his wife Honey Alexander on keyboards—which began playing clubs in 1980. Between 1981 and 1985, the Mighty Flyers released three albums—*Radioactive Material* (1981), *File Under Rock* (1984), and *From the Start to the Finish* (1985). During the early '80s, Piazza became a session musician, working with artists as diverse as Pee Wee Crayton and Michelle Shocked. In the mid-'80s, he began a full-fledged solo career, releasing *Harpburn* on Murray Brothers in 1986 and *So Glad to Have the Blues* in 1988.

Piazza and the Mighty Flyers signed a contract with Black Top Records in 1991; the label later re-released the group's albums on CD. Throughout the '90s, Piazza continued to record and perform with the Mighty Flyers, releasing the occasional solo album. *—Cub Koda & Stephen Thomas Erlewine*

Bluesman / 1973 / LMI ✦✦✦

Harpburn / 1986 / Black Top ✦✦✦

So Glad to Have the Blues / 1988 / Murray Bros ✦✦✦

Blues in the Dark / 1991 / Black Top ✦✦✦✦
A contemporary band, led by harmonica player/vocalist Piazza, has nice piano from Honey Alexander. *—Niles J. Frantz*

Alphabet Blues / 1992 / Black Top ✦✦✦✦
Another fine effort from Rod Piazza and the Mighty Flyers, *Alphabet Blues* alternates between first-rate slow blues and cooking uptempo boogies and shuffles, both of which showcase their versatile, many-sided talents. There are a few weak songs, but the album on the whole is quite entertaining. *—Thom Owens*

• **The Essential Collection** / 1992 / Hightone ✦✦✦✦
Compilation of fairly recent sides by the powerhouse West Coast harpist; like most of his work, it smokes! — *Bill Dahl*

Live at B.B. King's Blues Club / 1994 / Big Mo ✦✦✦
This harp master really turns out the discs; boogies and blues. — *Bill Dahl*

California Blues / Feb. 4, 1997 / Black Top ✦✦✦

Tough and Tender / Jul. 8, 1997 / Tone-Cool ✦✦✦
Tough and Tender was the first new studio for Piazza and the Mighty Flyers since 1992's *Alphabet Blues*. The kickoff track, "Power of the Blues," announces their triumphant return with a clarion call from Rod that "we've got the power of the blues." Piazza's harmonica is locked in sync with guitarist Rick "L.A. Holmes" Holmstrom's on the intro before Holmstrom whips off a slashing solo in the middle that recalls the phrasing of both T-Bone Walker and Pee Wee Crayton. Rod's solo on this opener is also textbook playing, full of taste, control and the deepest of tones. The title track is a new Piazza classic that illustrates the empathy between every player in the band with Honey Piazza's boogie-woogie piano soloing making an apt foil for Rod's chromatic harp work. "She Can't Say No" and "Sea of Fools" brings Jonny Viau's and Allen Ortiz's horn to the party for New Orleans style R&B and a blues rhumba. Piazza's harp is highlighted again on the instrumental "The Teaser." Other highlights include the loping West Coast swing of "Blues and Trouble," the jazzy instrumental "Under the Big Top," Honey's showcase on "Hang Ten Boogie," and the set-closing "Searching for a Fortune." This album clearly shows why Piazza and his band have been favorites on the blues circuit for quite some time and why that fan base shows no signs of getting smaller. — *Cub Koda*

Greg Piccolo

b. May 10, 1951, Westerly, RI
Sax (Tenor), Vocals / Jump Blues, R&B
Former Roomful of Blues vocalist and sax man Greg Piccolo was born May 10, 1951, in Westerly, RI. At the age of 13 he was playing sax with a six-piece rock band, the *Rejects.* Two years later he joined Duke Robillard as a vocalist for the *Variations,* a British Invasion cover band. Piccolo rejoined Robillard in 1970 to create that first Roomful of Blues, inspired by the R&B band, the Buddy Johnson Orchestra. The group was further modified in 1971 and Piccolo began playing sax. The band worked up and down the Northeast gradually building up a national following. Robillard left the group in 1979 and was replaced by blues guitarist Ronnie Earl. By this time, Piccolo was the *de facto* leader. *Dressed Up to Get Messed Up* features a number of his compositions. The group stayed together until the early '90s when Piccolo went out on his own.
Piccolo has released two solo albums in the acid-jazz vein, *Heavy Juice* on Black Top Records (1990) and *Acid Blue* (1995) on Fantasy. Greg Piccolo lives in Rhode Island and records for Fantasy. (See: Roomful of Blues) — *Michael Erlewine*

• **Heavy Juice** / May 9, 1990-May 13, 1990 / Black Top ✦✦✦✦
These stomping tenor sax instrumentals come from the jazz and R&B repertoire of the '40s and '50s. Many Roomful of Blues alumni, such as Duke Robillard (g) and Al Copley (p), contribute. It doesn't rock any harder than this. — *Bob Porter*

Acid Blue / Jun. 1995 / Fantasy ✦✦✦✦

Red Lights / Jun. 3, 1997 / Fantasy ✦✦✦✦
Former Roomful of Blues saxophonist Greg Piccolo stretches his musical wings even further on this, his third solo outing since leaving the group in 1990. In addition to his brawny tenor sax wailings, Piccolo also plays lead guitar (in a crude, but effective style somewhat reminiscent of Roy Buchanan and Carlos Santana) and alto sax this time around, coaxing acid-jazz sounds out of the latter instrument. With his regular working combo Heavy Juice providing stellar support in a multiplicity of styles (Piccolo jumps from swing to bop to acid jazz to soul ballads and even a taste of rock'n'roll on this one) and 14 Karat Soul providing backup vocals on "Money" and the title track, *Red Lights* is Greg Piccolo's most musically ambitious album to date. — *Cub Koda*

Dan Pickett

b. Aug. 31, 1907, Pike County, AL, **d.** Aug. 16, 1967, Boaz, AL
Guitar, Vocals / Country Blues, Piedmont Blues
Reissuers have unearthed little information about Dan Pickett: He may have come from Alabama, he played a nice slide guitar in a Southeastern blues style, and he did one recording session for the Philadelphia-based Gotham label in 1949. That session produced five singles, all of which have now been compiled along with four previously unreleased sides on a reissue album that purports to contain Pickett's entire recorded output—unless, of course, as some reviewers have speculated, Dan Pickett happens also to be Charlie Pickett, the Tennessee guitarist who recorded for Decca in 1937. As Tony Russell observed in *Juke Blues,* both Picketts recorded blues about lemon-squeezing, and Dan uses the name Charlie twice in the lyrics to "Decoration Day." 'Tis from such mystery and speculation that the minds of blues collectors do dissolve. — *Jim O'Neal*

• **1949 Country Blues** / 1990 / Collectables ✦✦✦✦
1949 Country Blues is an invaluable reissue of ten sides originally released on 78s during 1949, plus four previously unreleased songs. During the '60s, these sides were highly collectable, and earned the reputation of being among the finest country-blues. That reputation wasn't misguided—he was truly unique among country bluesmen. Pickett had a distinctive rhythmic style and unique phrasing that makes his records compelling decades after his release. He made songs from the likes of Blind Boy Fuller ("Lemon Man," also known as "Let Me Squeeze Your Lemons") and Leroy Carr ("How Long") sound like his own. At times, the music on *1949 Country Blues* is simply astonishing. No serious blues collector should be without this disc. — *Thom Owens*

Pilgrim Jubilee Singers

f. Chicago, IL
Group / Black Gospel
Since the early '50s, the Pilgrim Jubilee Singers have used their hard, rockin' gospel music as a powerful means of testifying their faith, love, and charitable hope that humanity will find a way to bring itself closer to the kingdom of heaven. Over its long history, the group has undergone numerous personnel changes. The first incarnation originated in the 1940s on the Mississippi Delta by Elgie and Theopholis Graham, but the most famous version of the Pilgrim Jubilees began in Chicago, 1952, when younger Graham brothers Clay and Cleve resurrected the group. Since then, these two have remained the group's spiritual and musical core. While growing up in Mississippi, all four Graham brothers were trained to sing. It was Theopholis who left the first group to live in Chicago; the rest of his brothers followed in 1951, and all four briefly sang in that group. The Pilgrim Jubilees toured quite a bit (when not working their day jobs, which for the Graham brothers meant working in their separate barber shops), and this proved too much for the older brothers, who gradually dropped out. Shortly thereafter, Clay and Cleve invited baritone Major Roberson and lead singer Percy Clark (both from Mississippi) to join. They also took on guitarist Richard Crume and bassist Roosevelt English, and began recording; through the 1950s, they released sides and albums for assorted labels, including Peacock, Chance, and Nashboro. Soon after signing to Peacock in 1960, the band gained national exposure with their label debut, "Stretch Out." Its success allowed the Pilgrim Jubilees to finally go professional. Crume eventually left the group to join the Soul Stirrers, but the other three have remained together and carried on into the '90s. — *Sandra Brennan*

Walk On / 1963 / Peacock ✦✦✦✦
Fine close harmony quartet with both talent and conviction. — *Opal Louis Nations*

★ **Walk On/The Old Ship of Zion** / 1964 / Mobile Fidelity ✦✦✦✦✦
Mobile Fidelity's *Walk On/The Old Ship of Zion* combines two Peacock albums—1962's *Walk On* and 1964's *The Old Ship of Zion*—on one compact disc. Both albums capture the Pilgrim Jubilee Singers at their peak, demonstrating that they were one of the greatest hard gospel quartets of their time. — *Leo Stanley*

☆ **Back to Basics** / 1990 / Malaco ✦✦✦✦✦
Another solid effort recorded by this label, which helped to bring good Southern gospel music into the '90s. — *Kip Lornell*

Gospel Roots / 1990 / Malaco ✦✦✦
This dynamic album shows why The Pilgrim Jubilees have remained one of the most respected "hard" gospel groups for so many years. — *Kip Lornell*

Homecoming / May 23, 1995 / Nashboro ✦✦✦
Possibly the last significant sides by this major post-war quartet. Nashboro source. — *Opal Louis Nations*

Pilgrim Travelers

f. Houston, TX
Group / Black Gospel, Traditional Gospel
The Specialty label's most prolific gospel act, the Pilgrim Travelers were among the most successful and influential groups of gospel's golden era; famed for their distinctive "walking rhythm" sound, they also earned renown for their riotous live perfomances and breathless showmanship. The Pilgrim Travelers were formed in Houston during the early 1930s by Joe Johnson and Willie Davis; the latter relocated the group to Los Angeles in 1942, taking with him cousins Kylo Turner and Keith Barber. By mid-1945, their ranks included bass Raphael Taylor as well as J.W. Alexander, a light tenor and onetime semi-pro baseball player with Negro league teams including the Ethiopian Clowns and the New Orleans Crescent Stars; he soon assumed managerial control of the group as well.

Like other groups of the period, the Pilgrim Travelers consciously modeled their sound after the Soul Stirrers and the Golden Gates; although Turner was naturally a baritone, he sang in a note-bending falsetto style not far removed from pop crooning, while his co-lead Barber possessed a pure, sweet voice and a flamboyant stage presence. To give the Travelers an edge on the competition, Alexander pushed his partners to hone a tightly choreographed live show which over the years became increasingly frenetic, much to the delight of the many women attending their performances. In early 1947, the group made their first recordings, issuing singles on a handful of tiny L.A. labels; by the end of the year they signed to Specialty, at which time they brought on board a new baritone, Jesse Whitaker, to replace Davis.

After a handful of a cappella songs, the Travelers began recording their material with a microphone picking up the sound of their percussive foot-tapping; Specialty's early press for the group proclaimed "Something New — Walking Rhythm Spirituals," and the unique sound quickly caught on with consumers. In 1948, the group issued six singles; after just three the following year, in 1950 Specialty released no less than ten Pilgrim Travelers sides, all of them to strong sales (particularly "Jesus Met the Woman at the Well" and "Mother Bowed"). However, at the peak of their success, Barber was involved in a 1950 auto accident which left his voice ravaged; at the same time, the emergence of the Soul Stirrers' Sam Cooke made Turner's vocal style appear increasingly outdated, and seemingly overnight the group's fortunes began to wane.

In the years to follow, lineup changes plagued the Pilgrim Travelers as well — in 1954 Taylor was replaced by bass George McCurn, and by the middle of the decade both Turner and Barber had exited; by the time of their 1956 demise, the ensemble had recorded over 100 songs. A later incarnation of the group, dubbed simply the Travelers, included Lou Rawls, but was otherwise unremarkable. In 1959, Alexander teamed with Sam Cooke to found SAR Records; the new company attempted to relaunch Turner's career, but in the passing years the singer had succumbed to alcoholism, and he arrived in Los Angeles too drunk to enter the studio. He eventually returned to Texas, where he died a few years after his cousin Barber; Whitaker retired to his family farm in New Jersey, while Alexander remained a sought-after producer and manager. — *Jason Ankeny*

Lou Rawls & the Pilgrim Travelers [Andex] / 1957 / Andex ✦✦✦✦
Lou's finest moments with the group at its best. — *Opal Louis Nations*

Lou Rawls & the Pilgrim Travelers [Capitol] / 1962 / Capitol ✦✦✦
Lou and the group singing Soul Stirrers songs and arrangements. — *Opal Louis Nations*

The Best of the Pilgrim Travelers, Vol. 1 / 1970 / Specialty ✦✦✦✦
Classic Travelers material, 1950-54. — *Opal Louis Nations*

The Best of the Pilgrim Travelers, Vol. 2 / 1971 / Specialty ✦✦✦✦
More toe-tapping with leads Keith Barber and Kylo Turner. — *Opal Louis Nations*

Shake My Mother's Hand / 1972 / Specialty ✦✦✦
Close a cappella singing to that unmistakable walking-in-rhythm. — *Opal Louis Nations*

● **The Best of the Pilgrim Travelers, Vol. 1-2** / 1990 / Specialty ✦✦✦✦
Reissue of the quartet's two fine albums of the early 1970s filled with great toe-tapping gospel. — *Opal Louis Nations*

Walking Rhythm / 1992 / Specialty ✦✦✦✦
This is the first of two CD collections of prime a cappella close harmony gospel in walking rhythm by The Pilgrim Travelers. Contained are unissued, alternate, and previously issued-on-wax sides from the stunnning lead chops of Kylo Turner and Keith Barber, who fronted L.A.'s Travelers during the 1947-1956 Specialty sojourn. The quintet cut over 100 sides during this time. The selection here is drawn from the 1947 through 1951 time frame. They're taken from original 16-inch metal masters and filtered through a non-noise system to produce fine presence and sound clarity. — *Opal Louis Nations, Roots and Rhythm Newsletter*

Everytime I Feel the Spirit / Chameleon ✦✦✦
This is a tepid collection of traditional gospel sung in The Pilgrims' inimitable style without the bite of earlier work for Specialty, Andex, and Capitol. The album, first issued on Kent in 1971, contains the voices of lead singer Kylo Turner, who joined the group in 1945, and J.W. Alexander, also a member of long standing who managed the group and produced many of the outfit's later post-Specialty recordings. The songs cut at these sessions should have proven more exciting, as Harold Battiste handled the musical arrangements, but somehow the group lacked enthusiasm. — *Opal Louis Nations, Roots & Rhythm Newsletter*

Better Than That / Specialty ✦✦✦
The Pilgrim Travelers were Specialty's most prolific group, recording more than any their other ensemble in any style. They were versatile enough to be sensational as an a cappella unit, and almost as magnificent with instrumental accompaniment. The 28 cuts from this most recent anthology shows them adjusting to instrumental support, as lead vocalists Kylo Turner and Keith Barber effectively duel and contrast against organs, keyboards, bass and drums. The collection also contains 13 previously unissued songs, most of them incredible unaccampied performances. They may not have been Specialty's greatest gospel group, but The Pilgrim Travelers weren't far behind The Soul Stirrers. — *Ron Wynn*

Lonnie Pitchford

b. Oct. 8, 1955, Lexington, MS
Delta Blues
Diddley bow player Lonnie Pitchford was an obscure Delta blues player until he was "discovered" by ethnomusicologist Worth Long. He began to attract crowds playing the music of Robert Johnson, songs like "Come On in My Kitchen" and "Terraplane Blues," on his one-stringed didley bow. Pitchford began playing Johnson's tunes after meeting guitarist Robert Jr. Lockwood at the World's Fair in Knoxville, Tennessee. Lockwood showed Pitchford some basic Johnson chord changes and arrangements, and for several years after that, Pitchford was accompanied by the late Alabama bluesman Johnny Shines, as well as Lockwood.

Pitchford began making his one-stringed diddley bows as a five-year-old, fashioning them mostly out of parts from old electric guitars. Also an accomplished six-string guitarist and piano player, Pitchford has forged his reputation as a skilled diddley bow player. His fascination with blues began as a child, when he heard blues and gospel on the radio. Raised in a musical family, Pitchford got his start playing house parties and learned a lot from his father and brothers, who also played blues guitar and piano.

Pitchford's festival resume includes the Smithsonian Festival of American Folklife in Washington, D.C., and several major blues gatherings around the South. He was one of the youngest performers at the 1984 Downhome Blues Festival in Atlanta.

Pitchford's albums include *All Around Man* for Rooster Blues, a 1994 release, as well as several compilations, including *Mississippi Moan*, a 1988 release on the German L&R Records; *Roots of Rhythm and Blues: A Tribute to the Robert Johnson Era*, a 1992 Columbia Records release, and *Deep Blues* (1992), for Anxious Records.

Although he's put in dynamic, spirited performances at the Smithsonian

Festivals, Pitchford unfortunately doesn't tour much because of his lack of recordings. There aren't a great many clubs for him to play around Lexington, so he makes occasional road trips to Memphis and other cities where his music is appreciated. He divides his time between road trips to play blues and working as a carpenter. Voted as one of *Living Blues* magazine's "top 40 under 40" new blues players to watch, with any luck, Pitchford's authentic, acoustic Delta blues will find a larger following in years to come. —*Richard Skelly*

All Around Man / Oct. 11, 1994 / Rooster Blues ✦✦✦

Cousin Joe Pleasant

b. Dec. 20, 1907, Wallace, LA, **d.** Oct. 2, 1989, New Orleans, LA
Vocals, Guitar, Piano / New Orleans R&B, Blues, New Orleans Blues
Few blues legends have the presence of mind to write autobiographies. Fortunately, Pleasant Joseph did, spinning fascinating tales of a career in his 1987 tome *Cousin Joe: Blues from New Orleans* that spanned more than half a century.

Growing up in New Orleans, Pleasant began singing in church before crossing over to the blues. Guitar and ukulele were his first axes. He eventually prioritized the piano instead, playing Crescent City clubs and riverboats. He moved to New York in 1942, gaining entry into the city's thriving jazz scene (where he played with Dizzy Gillespie, Sidney Bechet, Charlie Parker, Billie Holiday, and a host of other luminaries).

He recorded for King, Gotham, Philo (in 1945), Savoy, and Decca along the way, doing well on the latter logo with "Box Car Shorty and Peter Blue" in 1947. After returning to New Orleans in 1948, he recorded for DeLuxe and cut a two-part "ABCs" for Imperial in 1954 as Smilin' Joe under Dave Bartholomew's supervision. But by then, his recording career had faded.

The pianist was booked on a 1964 *Blues and Gospel Train* tour of England, sharing stages with Muddy Waters, Otis Spann, Brownie McGhee and Sonny Terry, and Sister Rosetta Tharpe and appearing on BBC-TV with the all-star troupe. He cut a 1971 album for the French Black & Blue label, *Bad Luck Blues*, that paired him with guitarists Gatemouth Brown and Jimmy Dawkins and a Chicago rhythm section—hardly the ideal situation, but still a reasonably effective showcase for the ebullient entertainer (it was reissued in 1994 by Evidence). —*Bill Dahl*

● **Bad Luck Blues** / Nov. 1971 / Evidence ✦✦✦✦
The New Orleans pianist ventured overseas in 1971 and waxed this CD along the way with a mighty unlikely band: guitarists Gatemouth Brown and Jimmy Dawkins and a Chicago rhythm section (bassist Mac Thompson and drummer Ted Harvey). A lesser musician might have wilted with players so unfamiliar with his basic approach, but Pleasant's bubbly ebullience and the strength of his "Box Car Shorty," "Life Is a One Way Ticket," and "Railroad Porter Blues" saved the day. —*Bill Dahl*

Bluesman from New Orleans / 1974 / Big Bear ✦✦✦✦

Gospel Wailing / 1982 / Big Bear ✦✦✦

Jerry Portnoy

b. Nov. 25, 1943, Evanston, IL
Harmonica, Vocals / Modern Electric Harmonica Blues
Another ex-Muddy Waters employee, Jerry Portnoy's biting, flailing harmonica style rivals any within contemporary blues circles for fluency, range, or emotional range. His vocals are effective enough, especially when punctuated by his harp accompaniment and solos.

Portnoy began his professional musical career as part of Muddy Waters' backing band in the early '70s. Jerry replaced Mojo Buford in 1974 and he stayed with the band for six years. During his tenure with Waters, he appeared on the albums *I'm Ready, Muddy "Mississippi" Waters Live*, and *King Bee*. In 1980, Portnoy, bassist Calvin Jones, pianist Pinetop Perkins, and drummer Willie Smith all left Muddy to form the Legendary Blues Band.

Throughout the early '80s, Portnoy stayed with the Legendary Blues Band, recording the albums *Life of Ease* and *Red Hot & Blue*. In 1986, he left the band and he briefly retired. By the end of 1987, he had returned to the scene, founding the Broadcasters with Ronnie Earl. Two years later, he and Earl had a falling out, causing Jerry to leave the group. Portnoy formed his own band, the Streamliners in 1989. Two years later, the band released their debut, *Poison Kisses*, on Modern Blues Recordings. Between 1991 and 1993,

Portnoy was part of Eric Clapton's All-Star Blues Band. After leaving Clapton's band in 1993, he played a number of concerts, releasing his second album, *Home Run Hitter*, in 1995. —*Ron Wynn & Stephen Thomas Erlewine*

● **Poison Kisses** / 1991 / Modern Blues ✦✦✦✦
Jerry Portnoy's debut album, *Poison Kisses*, is a fine set of rollicking Chicago blues. Portnoy is at his best when he is blowing away on the harp, and there's no exception to the rule here—the whole album can fall apart when he's simply singing, but when he's playing the harp, the music catches fire. Worthwhile for harmonica fans. —*Thom Owens*

Home Run Hitter / 1995 / Indigo ✦✦✦

Powder Blues Band

f. 1978
Group / Modern Blues
Guitarist Tom Lavin, bassist Jack Lavin and a keyboard player formed Powder Blues Band in 1978, later adding trumpeter Mark Hasselbach, drummer Duris Maxwell and saxophonists Wayne Kozak, Gordie Bertram, and David Woodward. The group signed with Capitol, which released *Uncut* and *Powder Blues* in 1980. Other albums include *Thirsty Ears* (1981), *Party Line* (1982), *Red Hot/True Blue* (1983), *First Decade-Greatest Hits* (1990), and *Let's Get Loose* (1993). —*John Bush*

Uncut / 1980 / RCA ✦✦✦

● **Powder Blues** / 1980 / Liberty ✦✦✦✦

Red Hot/True Blue / 1983 / Flying Fish ✦✦✦

Duffy Power

b. Sep. 9, 1941
Vocals, Harmonica / British Invasion, Blues-Rock
Power is a lost figure of the '60s who drifted into the inner circle of British blues after a middling career as a teen idol in the early '60s. He recorded one of the first Beatle covers (on an early 1963 single of "I Saw Her Standing There"), and never experienced acclaim as a commercial pop singer or blues vocalist. But he recorded some fine, little-known blues-cum-R&B/rock sides in the '60s, some of which featured present and future members of the Graham Bond Organisation, Cream, and Pentangle. The pleasures of Power are subtle and not easily captured in print. He doesn't have the best voice, and will never be mistaken for a Steve Winwood or Eric Burdon. But his original material is strong, his arrangements imaginative, and his performance sincere; he's grounded in the blues, but doesn't fall into shopworn clichés, bringing a lot of himself and the innovations of British '60s rock into the picture. —*Richie Unterberger*

Mary Open the Door / 1986 / Rock Machine ✦✦✦✦
His best recordings, as noteworthy for the players on the album as Power himself. Laid down sometime in the mid-'60s, Power (who sings and plays occasional guitar and harp) is backed by a rotating ensemble including, at various points, John McLaughlin and Jack Bruce (before they gained fame), as well as future Pentangle members Danny Thompson and Terry Cox. Neither as rock-oriented as the Stones nor as strictly revivalist as Alexis Korner (with whom Power played for a time), this is one of the best British blues recordings, cutting straight down the middle between gutbucket blues and soulful R&B. Divided equally between Power originals and R&B blues covers, the material and performances are spare, powerful, and as consistent as any '60s British blues album. Unfortunately, these sessions were unissued for several years, surfacing briefly under the title *Innovations* in 1970 on the British Transatlantic label. This reissue on another tiny British label is equally obscure, but should not be missed by fans of '60s British R&B. —*Richie Unterberger*

Blues Power / 1992 / See for Miles ✦✦✦✦
Most of the recordings on *Blues Power* were originally released on Power's self-titled album on the tiny UK Spark label in 1969. Duffy says in the liner notes of this reissue that the album was never intended for release, and that these sessions were acoustic demos for an LP that never got produced with the arrangements he had envisioned. That may be so, but it's still a worthy document of this underrated British bluesman at his most bare-boned and haunting. With just his guitar and harmonica, Power runs through both moody originals and covers of R&B/blues standards (with The Beatles' "Fix-

ing a Hole" thrown in) that are rearranged and drastically stripped down. This reissue includes the 15 tracks from the 1969 release, a couple more from the same sessions that were issued on the extremely obscure *Firepoint* compilation album, and three from the mid-'60s (also included on the *Little Boy Blue* reissue) that also explore acoustic moods, forming a picture of Power's most intimate work. —*Richie Unterberger*

● **Little Boy Blue** / 1992 / Edsel ◆◆◆◆
His best recordings, as noteworthy for the players on the album as Power himself. Laid down sometime in the mid-'60s, Power (who sings and plays occasional guitar and harp) is backed by a rotating ensemble including, at various points, John McLaughlin and Jack Bruce (before they gained fame), as well as future Pentangle members Danny Thompson and Terry Cox. Neither as rock-oriented as the Stones nor as strictly revivalist as Alexis Korner (with whom Power played for a time), this is one of the best British blues recordings, cutting straight down the middle between gutbucket blues and soulful R&B. Divided equally between Power originals and R&B blues covers, the material and performances are spare, powerful, and as consistent as any '60s British blues album. Unfortunately, these sessions were unissued for several years, surfacing briefly under the title *Innovations* in 1970 on the British Transatlantic label. This reissue on another tiny British label is equally obscure, but should not be missed by fans of '60s British R&B. —*Richie Unterberger*

Just Say Blue / 1995 / Retro ◆◆◆◆
While not up to the level of the other vintage Power compilations available (*Little Boy Blue* and *Blues Power*), this is a worthwhile supplement to those CDs, featuring 21 tracks of rare and unreleased material cut by the singer from 1965 to 1971. The first half, focusing on his 1965-67 output, is the more interesting portion by a considerable margin, as much for the jazz-blues-R&B fusion of the arrangements (featuring contributions from Jack Bruce, John McLaughlin, Ginger Baker, and Pentangle's Danny Thompson and Terry Cox) as Power's singing. The early-'70s songs that make up the remainder of the disc have a more pedestrian blues-rock feel, but there are some good, inspired moments, with cameos by Rod Argent, Thompson, Cox, and Alexis Korner. —*Richie Unterberger*

Elvis Presley (Elvis Aron Presley)

b. Jan. 8, 1935, Tupelo, MS, **d.** Aug. 16, 1977, Memphis, TN
Guitar, Vocals / Rock & Roll, Pop-Rock, Rockabilly, Pop
Elvis Presley listed in a book on the blues? Why not, he's listed and/or mentioned in any development of the music that mentions White people playing it and doing it with enough success that the *world* just happened to take notice. His is the one story in this book that doesn't really need to be embellished or listed in even the most cursory detail; there's tons of books, movies for television, videotapes and magazines totally devoted to exploring that subject in beyond-finite detail. He has become an American icon, having been transformed from a White hillbilly musician who sang the blues to a cultural concept, from a human being to a wine decanter. If you *don't* know who Elvis was, we can only assume that your spaceship landed from Mars just a few hours ago. His emotional link to the blues and its basis to the development of his style, therefore, will be supported by two salient quotes that nicely and emphatically validate his presence between these covers. One comes from ace writer (and Elvis biographer) Peter Guralnick's liner notes to an all-blues Elvis compilation, *Reconsider Baby:* "I remember the first time I met the great bluesman, Howlin' Wolf, in 1966. He started talking about White blues singers, a new concept at the time. He liked Paul Butterfield, he said, also "that other boy—what's his name? Somewhere out in California, that 'Hound Dog' number." He was talking about Elvis Presley. But surely Elvis couldn't be considered strictly a *blues* singer, somebody pointed out. Maybe not, conceded Wolf in that great hoarse growl of his, but "he *started* from the blues. If he stopped, he stopped. It's nothing to laugh at. *He made his pull from the blues."*

The second quote comes from the man himself in June of 1956, one of the few interviews where he ever discussed his musical roots, seemingly amazed by all the fuss his version was causing at the time: "The colored folks been singing it and playing it just like I'm doin' it now, man, for more years than I know. They played it like that in their shanties and their juke joints, and nobody paid it no mind 'til I goosed it up. I got it from them. Down in Tupelo, Mississippi, I used to hear old Arthur Crudup bang his box the way I do now,

and I said if I ever got to the place where I could feel all old Arthur felt, I'd be a music man like nobody ever saw." Needless to say that at a very real level, he connected big time and that the world saw and heard his message. On the strength of the two above quotes, the defense rests. The rest is not only history, but the history of rock 'n' roll as well. —*Cub Koda*

☆ **Reconsider Baby** / 1985 / RCA ◆◆◆◆◆
A 12-song, budget-priced compilation of Elvis' most notable blues sides for the label. A good place to start digging Elvis' commitment to the music—always returning to it right up through the '70s like an old friend, whenever he needed a quick fix of the *real* thing—as he takes on everything from R&B slices like Tommy Tucker's "High Heel Sneakers" to Percy Mayfield's "Stranger in My Own Home Town." Major highlights on this collection are Elvis playing acoustic rhythm guitar and driving the band through a take of the Lowell Fulson title track, blistering versions of two Arthur Crudup songs, an unreleased Sun recording of Lonnie Johnson's "Tomorrow Night," and the R-rated take of Smiley Lewis' "One Night (of Sin)." —*Cub Koda*

☆ **The Memphis Record** / 1987 / RCA ◆◆◆◆◆
Coming hot off the heels of his breakthrough NBC special in 1968, Presley returned to Memphis to record for the first time in 12 years and laid down 20 tracks in the space of four days. He was hot, he was inspired, and it's all here. —*Cub Koda*

★ **The Complete Sun Sessions** / 1987 / RCA ◆◆◆◆◆
This is it, your perfect starting point to understanding how Elvis—as Howlin' Wolf so aptly put it—"made his *pull* from the blues." All the source points are there for the hearing; Arthur Crudup's "That's All Right (Mama)," Roy Brown's "Good Rockin' Tonight," Kokomo Arnold's "Milkcow Blues Boogie," Arthur Gunter's "Baby, Let's Play House," and Junior Parker's "Mystery Train." Modern day listeners coming to these recordings for the first time will want to reclassify this music into a million subgenres, with all the hyphens firmly in place. But what we ultimately have here is a young Elvis Presley, mixing elements of blues, gospel and hillbilly music together and getting ready to unleash its end result—rock 'n' roll—on an unsuspecting world. —*Cub Koda*

☆ **The King of Rock 'n' Roll: The Complete 50's Masters** / Jun. 23, 1992 / RCA ◆◆◆◆◆
A casual Elvis fan wanting to assemble a decent overview of the King's '50s sides could probably sweat it down to the *Sun Sessions* CD and Volume 1 of the *Top Ten Hits* compilation. But for those of you who take your '50s Presley seriously, *The King of Rock 'n' Roll—The Complete 50's Masters* is absolutely essential. For the hardcore Elvis fan, the booklet and CD graphics for this five-disc set provide incentive enough to justify its purchase. The liner notes by Presley expert Peter Guralnick are passionate, contagious in their enthusiasm, and filled with a real sense of history, time, and place. The treasure-trove of unpublished photos, session information and Elvis memorabilia accompanying the booklet text are no less inspiring. But it's the music (140 tracks in all) that's the real meat and potatoes of this set. Every studio track cut during the '50s—the seminal Sun sides, the early RCA hits, movie soundtracks, alternates, live performances, rarities (including both sides of the long-lost acetate he cut for his mother back in 1953)—it's all here in one gorgeous package. Soundwise, this box makes any of the previous issues of this material pale by comparison, the proper (non-reverbed) inclusion of the Sun masters being a particular treat. This is no mere rehash of what's been around a dozen times before—there's a lot of thought and care behind this package, and no serious fan of American rock 'n' roll should consider a collection complete without it. —*Cub Koda*

☆ **From Nashville to Memphis: The Essential 60's Masters** / Sep. 28, 1993 / RCA ◆◆◆◆◆
Continues the tradition of first-quality sound remastering and packaging. Much of Elvis' '60s work is arguably not as essential as the '50s stuff, but this meticulous five-disc/130-track set makes an impressive case for the defense. A thick booklet contains riveting liner notes, full-color photos, complete discography and session listings; a sheet of RCA album cover stamps tops off the set. —*Roch Parisien*

Amazing Grace: His Greatest Sacred Songs / Oct. 25, 1994 / RCA ◆◆◆
Elvis recorded quite a bit of gospel over the course of his career, and this two-CD, 55-song set has the bulk of it. Most of this is drawn from his three gospel LPs (*His Hand in Mine*, 1960; *How Great Thou Art*, 1967; *He Touched Me*, 1972), as well as a 1957 EP. Presley was undoubtedly heavily influenced

by gospel (at times he indicated regret at not having chosen to become a gospel singer), and this material has played pretty well with critics. Elvis sings with skill and reasonable commitment, and the backing musicians include such Elvis/Nashville standbys as Scotty Moore, Hank Garland, Floyd Cramer, Charlie McCoy, Pete Drake, the Jordanaires, and James Burton. At the same time, let's have a reality check here. Rock- and pop-oriented fans are going to find this two-and-a-half hour set tough going, unless they have a taste for spirituals as well. Things get a little more accessible when the tempos brighten, but often it's on the sedate side. For both collectors and listeners, highlights of the collection are five previously unreleased tracks from 1972. Recorded with only Charlie Hodges on piano and J.D. Sumner & the Stamps on backing vocals, they present Presley's gospel at its sparsest and most spontaneous. —*Richie Unterberger*

☆ **Walk a Mile in My Shoes: The Essential 70's Masters** / Oct. 10, 1995 / RCA ✦✦✦✦✦

In most conventional rock criticism, Elvis Presley's '70s records are considered his weakest, as they were recorded while he was falling deeper into drug addiction. However, as Dave Marsh argues in the liner notes of *Walk a Mile in My Shoes—The Essential 70's Masters*, the music on the five-CD box set is among the most personal and adventurous of Elvis' career, even if the individual albums don't always reflect that diversity. By cutting away all of the dross that accumulated over the decade and sequencing the songs in a logical, entertaining manner, *Walk a Mile in My Shoes* supports the argument. On the first two discs, all of the singles Presley released during the '70s are presented, and while there are a couple of weak numbers, the music stands as an impressive continuation of his artistic rebirth of the late '60s. —*Stephen Thomas Erlewine*

Elvis Presley '56 / Mar. 5, 1996 / RCA ✦✦✦✦

Sure, the music on here's great. How could it not be? It has 22 of his hottest tracks from his first year at RCA, including not only the hits "Heartbreak Hotel," "Hound Dog," "Don't Be Cruel," and "Too Much," but such noted early rockers as "My Baby Left Me," "Blue Suede Shoes," "Money Honey," and "So Glad You're Mine." From a collector's viewpoint, though, you have to wonder whether it was really necessary. The only previously unreleased item is a sparser early take of "Heartbreak Hotel." Everything else has been widely available (even on CD) for years, and it's a good bet that many of the Elvis fans who buy this already have virtually all of the contents on the *King of Rock 'n' Roll* box set. —*Richie Unterberger*

Jimmy Preston

b. Aug. 18, 1913, Chester, PA
Saxophone, Drums, Keyboards / R&B, Jump Blues

Alto sax blower Jimmy Preston is another one of the legion of postwar R&B figures that can accurately be cited as a genuine forefather of rock 'n' roll. His chief claim to fame: the blistering 1949 smash "Rock the Joint," which inspired a groundbreaking cover by Bill Haley & the Comets in 1952.

"Rock the Joint" wasn't Preston's first trip to the R&B Top Ten. Earlier in 1949, he'd hit with "Hucklebuck Daddy." Both were cut for Ivin Ballen's Philadelphia-based Gotham logo. The scorching sax breaks on "Rock the Joint" weren't Preston's doing, but tenor saxist Danny Turner's. Preston cut rather prolifically for Gotham through much of 1950 (including a session with jazzman Benny Golson on tenor sax) before switching to Derby Records and scoring his last hit, "Oh Babe" (with a vocal by Burnetta Evans). The 1950 date for the New York label was apparently his last. —*Bill Dahl*

Jimmy Preston / 1990 / Collectables ✦✦✦✦

Jump blues pioneer Preston, a solid alto saxist, with some of his 1949-1950 outings for Philadelphia's Gotham imprint. The titles tell it all: "Swingin' in the Groove," "Hang Out Tonight," "Estellina Bim Bam." —*Bill Dahl*

● **Rock the Joint, Vol. 2** / 1990 / Collectables ✦✦✦✦

Saxman Preston waxed one of the first legitimately traceable rock 'n' roll singles with his scorching jumper "Rock the Joint" for Philadelphia-based Gotham Records in 1949. It's here, along with his inexorably swinging "Hucklebuck Daddy," "Messin' with Preston," and "They Call Me the Champ." —*Bill Dahl*

1948-50 / Nov. 28, 1995 / Flyright ✦✦✦✦

Lloyd Price

b. Mar. 9, 1933, Kenner, LA
Vocals / Rock & Roll, New Orleans R&B, R&B

Not entirely content with being a 1950s R&B star on the strength of his immortal New Orleans classic "Lawdy Miss Clawdy," singer Lloyd Price yearned for massive pop acceptance. He found it, too, with a storming rock 'n' roll reading of the ancient blues "Stagger Lee" and the unabashedly pop-slanted "Personality" and "I'm Gonna Get Married," (the latter pair sounding far removed indeed from his Crescent City beginnings).

Growing up in Kenner, a suburb of New Orleans, Price was exposed to seminal sides by Louis Jordan, the Liggins brothers, Roy Milton, and Amos Milburn through the jukebox in his mother's little fish-fry joint. Lloyd and his younger brother Leo (who later co-wrote Little Richard's "Send Me Some Lovin'") put together a band for local consumption while in their teens. Bandleader Dave Bartholomew was impressed enough to invite Specialty Records boss Art Rupe to see the young singer (this was apparently when Bartholomew was momentarily at odds with his longtime employers at rival Imperial).

At his very first Specialty date in 1952, Price sang his classic eight-bar blues "Lawdy Miss Clawdy" (its rolling piano intro courtesy of a moonlighting Fats Domino). It topped the R&B charts for an extended period, making Lloyd Price a legitimate star before he was old enough to vote. Four more Specialty smashes followed: "Oooh, Oooh, Oooh," "Restless Heart," "Tell Me Pretty Baby," "Ain't It a Shame"—before Price was drafted into the Army and deposited most unhappily in Korea.

When he finally managed to break free of the military, Lloyd Price formed his own label, KRC Records, with partners Harold Logan and Bill Boskent and got back down to business. "Just Because," a plaintive ballad Price first cut for KRC, held enough promise to merit national release on ABC-Paramount in 1957 (his ex-valet, Larry Williams, covered it on Price's former label, Specialty).

"Stagger Lee," Price's adaptation of the old Crescent City lament "Stack-A-Lee," topped both the R&B and pop lists in 1958. By now, his sound was taking on more of a cosmopolitan bent, with massive horn sections and prominent pop background singers. Dick Clark insisted on toning down the violence inherent to the song's storyline for the squeaky-clean *American Bandstand* audience, accounting for the two different versions of the song you're likely to encounter on various reissues.

After Lloyd Price hit with another solid rocker, "Where Were You (On Our Wedding Day)?," in 1959, the heavy brass-and-choir sound became his trademark at ABC-Paramount. "Personality," "I'm Gonna Get Married," and "Come Into My Heart" all shot up the pop and R&B lists in 1959, and "Lady Luck" and "Question" followed suit in 1960.

Always a canny businessman, Price left ABC-Paramount in 1962 to form another firm of his own with Logan. Double L Records debuted Wilson Pickett as a solo artist and broke Price's Vegas lounge-like reading of "Misty" in 1963. Later, he ran yet another diskery, Turntable Records (its 45s bore his photo, whether on his own sizable 1969 hit "Bad Conditions" or when the single was by Howard Tate!), and operated a glitzy New York nightspot by the same name.

But the music business turned sour for Price when his partner, Logan, was murdered in 1969. He got as far away from it all as he possibly could, moving to Africa and investing in nonmusical pursuits. Perfect example: he linked up with electric-haired Don King to promote Muhammad Ali bouts in Zaire (against George Foreman) and Manila (against Joe Frazier). He indulged in a few select oldies gigs (including an appearance on NBC-TV's *Midnight Special*), but overall, little was seen of Lloyd Price during the 1970s.

Returning to America in the early '80s, he largely resisted performing until a 1993 European tour with Jerry Lee Lewis, Little Richard, and Gary US Bonds convinced him there was still a market for his bouncy, upbeat oldies. Price's profile has been on the upswing ever since—he recently guested on a PBS-TV special with Huey Lewis & the News, and regularly turns up to headline the Jazz & Heritage Festival in his old hometown. —*Bill Dahl*

Mr. Personality / 1959 / ABC ✦✦✦

Recorded in absolutely breathtaking stereo that greatly enhances the brass-heavy arrangements, this LP is worth grabbing any time you run across it. Sure, Lloyd Price sounds offkey on the Tin Pan Alley chestnuts "I Only Have

Eyes for You" and "Time After Time," but a forceful "I Want You to Know," the torchy "Dinner for One," and a rocking "Is It Really Love?" make up for the intrusions. —*Bill Dahl*

Mr. Personality Sings the Blues / 1960 / ABC ✦✦✦✦
Blues was no big stretch for the vocalist—his Crescent City output was solidly rooted in the idiom. On this LP, he does a fine job on Eddie Vinson's "Kidney Stew," Paul Perryman's "Just to Hold My Hand," and his own blasting "I've Got the Blues and the Blues Got Me." —*Bill Dahl*

Sings the Million Sellers / 1961 / ABC ✦✦✦
Lloyd Price sang the hits of the immediate timeframe on this long out-of-print album, doing particular justice to "Ain't That Just like a Woman" (then a minor seller for Fats Domino), the Miracles' "Shop Around," the Midnighters' "The Hoochie Coochie Coo," and the Drifters' "I Count the Tears." Uptown soul arrangements by future Motown staffer Gil Askey give Price full-bodied support. —*Bill Dahl*

● **Greatest Hits [MCA]** / 1982 / MCA ✦✦✦✦
Price wasn't content with R&B fame; he yearned for pop acceptance too. He got plenty at ABC-Paramount from 1957 to 1960 (the timeframe this 18-song retro addresses). Creating a brassy, accessible sound, Price hit huge with his rock 'n' roll rendition of "Stagger Lee" (here in two versions—original and *American Bandstand*-sanitized) and went all the way pop with the undeniably catchy "Personality." Innovative arrangements and Price's earnest vocals greatly distinguish "Have You Ever Had the Blues?," "Lady Luck," "Three Little Pigs," and "Where Were You (On Our Wedding Day)," and there's a previously unissued "That's Love" to further up the ante. —*Bill Dahl*

★ **Lawdy!** / Aug. 5, 1991 / Specialty ✦✦✦✦✦
Twenty-five stellar 1952-1956 examples of why Lloyd Price ranks with the greatest R&B performers ever to emerge from the Crescent City. Beginning with his debut smash "Lawdy Miss Clawdy," Price wails the rocking "Mailman Blues," "Where You At?," "Rock 'N' Roll Dance," and "Baby Please Come Home" in front of fat sax cushions, rolling pianos, and steamy rhythm sections. —*Bill Dahl*

Heavy Dreams, Vol. 2 / 1993 / Specialty ✦✦✦✦
No discernible artistic dropoff on Specialty's encore Price retrospective, distinguished by his classics "Oooh-Oooh-Oooh," "Tell Me Pretty Baby," "Ain't It a Shame?" (not Fats Domino's hit), "Country Boy Rock," and "Why" (he's later recut the latter for ABC-Paramount). —*Bill Dahl*

● **Lloyd Price Sings His Big Ten** / Feb. 8, 1994 / Capitol/Curb ✦✦✦✦
Like all standard Curb anthologies, this is too skimpy, numbering ten tracks. It does, however, include all of Price's major hits—"Stagger Lee," "Personality," "I'm Gonna Get Married," "Where Were You on Our Wedding Day," "Lady Luck." And in its favor, it also includes the most famous of his pre-ABC hits, "Lawdy Miss Clawdy." —*Richie Unterberger*

Sammy Price (Samuel Blythe Price)

b. Oct. 6, 1908, Honey Grove, TX, d. Apr. 14, 1992, New York, NY
Piano / Boogie-Woogie, Swing, Early R&B Jazz, Piano Blues, Jump Blues
Sammy Price had a long and productive career as a flexible blues and boogie-woogie-based pianist. He studied piano in Dallas and was a singer and dancer with Alphonso Trent's band during 1927-30. In 1929 he recorded one solitary side under the title of "Sammy Price and his Four Quarters." After a few years in Kansas City he spent time in Chicago and Detroit. In 1938 Price became the house pianist for Decca in New York and appeared on many blues sides with such singers as Trixie Smith and Sister Rosetta Tharpe. He led his own band on records in the early '40s which included (on one memorable session) Lester Young. Price worked steadily on 52nd Street, in 1948 played at the Nice Festival with Mezz Mezzrow, spent time back in Texas and then a decade with Red Allen; he was also heard on many rock 'n' roll-type sessions in the 1950s. In later years he recorded with Doc Cheatham and Sammy Price was active until near his death, 63 years after his recording debut. —*Scott Yanow*

1929-1941 / Sep. 29, 1929-Dec. 10, 1941 / Classics ✦✦✦✦
This single CD from the European Classics label collects all of pianist Sammy Price's postwar recordings as a leader. Despite its title, only two titles preceded the 1940-41 period: "Blue Rhythm Stomp" by Price's Four Quarters in 1929, and "Nasty But Nice," which finds Price on the same day accompanying trombonist Bert Johnson. Otherwise, the music features Price's Texas

Blusicians, New York-based septets and octets put together especially for recordings. The emphasis is on blues, with Price taking several vocals, but such notable guests as altoist Don Stovall, trumpeters Shad Collins and Emmett Berry and (on four songs) tenor great Lester Young uplift the music. Recommended to small-group swing collectors. —*Scott Yanow*

Singin' with Sammy, Vol. 1 / May 18, 1938-Apr. 6, 1944 / Contact ✦✦✦
As a house pianist for the Decca label, Sammy Price recorded with quite a few vocalists during the period covered by this European LP. Many of the 14 selections on this LP are a bit rare. They find Price swinging with small groups behind such blues-oriented singers as Ollie Shepard (on a date including tenor saxophonist Chu Berry), Jimmie Gordon, Yack Taylor, Perline Ellison, Bea Booze, Christine Chatman and Lem Johnson. In addition, Price has the chance to be in the spotlight and sing "Queen Street Blues." An interesting, if not essential collection. —*Scott Yanow*

Sammy Price and His Bluisicians—1944 / Mar. 1, 1944 / Circle ✦✦✦✦
This LP has all of the music that pianist Sammy Price and his sextet (which includes trumpeter Bill Coleman, tenor saxophonist Ike Quebec, altoist Joe Eldridge, the young bassist Oscar Pettiford and drummer Hal "Doc" West) recorded at a radio transcription session in 1944. As was often true of many of the Circle LPs from the mid-'80s, the set is programmed somewhat eccentrically, with some (but not all) of the incomplete and alternate takes issued on a different side of the LP than the other versions, making it difficult to trace the evolution of a performance. There are eight songs in all (mostly basic originals, plus "Sweet Lorraine" and "Honeysuckle Rose"); the eight master takes are joined by four full-length alternate versions, four incomplete takes and five false starts. But due to the very interesting players—Coleman and Quebec were in prime form during this era—swing collectors will want this release. —*Scott Yanow*

In Paris / 1956 / Brunswick ✦✦✦✦
With Sidney Bechet (sop sax), Price's "Bluesicians" hit on old-time and good time standards—Bechet, as always, in fine tune. —*Michael G. Nastos*

Rib Joint—Roots of Rock & Roll / Oct. 17, 1956-Mar. 24, 1959 / Savoy ✦✦✦✦
Here's a two-LP set that truly deserves immediate CD reissue. Price led a mighty New York R&B combo through three Savoy Records sessions in 1956-57 that elicited some sizzling instrumentals: "Rib Joint" (here in two takes), "Back Room Rock," "Juke Joint," "Chicken Out," and "Ain't No Strain" (sidemen included guitarist Mickey Baker and saxman King Curtis). A slightly more restrained 1959 date sans sax that comprises the second LP is no less joyful. —*Bill Dahl*

Blues and Boogies / Nov. 14, 1969 / Black & Blue ✦✦✦✦
Price is heard here on solo piano and vocal, playing eight Price originals and "See See Rider." It is good to hear him alone on this rare solo album, recorded in France. —*Michael G. Nastos*

Barrelhouse and Blues / Dec. 4, 1969 / Black Lion ✦✦✦✦
After being largely off records (at least as a leader) since 1961, pianist Sammy Price recorded four sets in Europe for Black & Blue and Black Lion before disappearing from records again until 1975. This CD reissues a surprisingly Dixieland-ish outing with a British sextet that includes trumpeter Keith Smith, trombonist Roy Williams, and clarinetist Sandy Brown. Since Price loved to play boogie-woogie and blues, there is a fair sampling of that music on the date (including "West End Boogie" and "Boogie Woogie Minuet"), and such Dixieland favorites as "Rosetta," "Keeping Out of Mischief Now," and "Royal Garden Blues." An exuberant, spirited set with all of the musicians playing in fine form. —*Scott Yanow*

Fire / May 1, 1975 / Black & Blue ✦✦✦
This LP by pianist Sammy Price (put out domestically by Classic Jazz) can easily be split into two parts. Seven songs pay tribute in their titles to France and showcase Price mostly playing blues in a trio with bassist Carl Pruitt and drummer J.C. Heard. The remaining four songs add a trio of veteran swing-era horn players (trumpeter Doc Cheatham, trombonist Gene "Mighty Flea" Conners, and altoist Ted Buckner) on three blues and the one non-Price standard "Tain't Nobody's Business If I Do." Although the inclusion of the horns gives added interest to the date, there is a certain sameness to much of the material and a predictability to the enjoyable but unsurprising outcome. —*Scott Yanow*

Boogie & Jazz Classics / May 25, 1975 / Black & Blue ✦✦✦✦
Price, a delightful, romping pianist in the vintage barrelhouse and boogie-

woogie genres, interpreted, reworked, and remade a series of traditional blues and jazz tunes on this fine 1975 release. Everything, from song selection to solos, is wonderful. — *Ron Wynn*

Copenhagen Boogie / Sep. 1, 1975 / Storyville ✦✦✦✦
Pianist Sammy Price's solo and trio work tended to emphasize the blues and boogie-woogie, so it was always fun to hear him playing jazz standards with a larger group. Although this LP has five blues-oriented pieces (including "St. Louis Blues"), it also finds Price taking an unaccompanied solo on "Begin the Beguine" and jamming "Honeysuckle Rose" and "Please Don't Talk About Me When You're Gone." On most of the songs, Price is joined by a four-horn sextet from Scandinavia that includes trombonist/leader Ole "Fessor" Lindgreen, trumpeter Finn Otto Hansen, and two fine reed players. The ensembles are consistently joyous; Price is still in prime form at this late date (he was 67), and the results are quite enjoyable. — *Scott Yanow*

Just Right / Nov. 2, 1977 / Black & Blue ✦✦✦
A sextet with George Kelly (sax) and Freddie Lonzo (tb) plays two of Price's tunes, five standards (two by W.C. Handy), and one by trumpeter Johnny Lettman. — *Michael G. Nastos*

Sweet Substitute / Nov. 1, 1979 / Sackville ✦✦✦✦
71 years old at the time, pianist Sammy Price had been a working jazz, blues and boogie-woogie musician for over 50 years when he recorded this set of unaccompanied solos. Typecast as a blues musician (partly because that was his favorite music), Price here also performs a variety of swing standards including "It Don't Mean a Thing," "A Hundred Years From Today," "Don't Blame Me" and "Stormy Weather." He shows throughout the melodic, relaxed and bluesy date that he was a superior swing player. This LP is worth searching for. — *Scott Yanow*

Paradise Valley Duets / Feb. 26, 1988-Feb. 28, 1988 / Parkwood ✦✦✦✦
Veteran pianist Sammy Price, who was 79 at the time of this project (which might be his last recording), is heard performing a set of duets with three different Detroit-based musicians. There are three songs apiece with either the modern but flexible trumpeter Marcus Belgrave or George Benson (no relation to the guitarist) on alto or tenor; in both cases, Price performs two swing standards and an original blues. The second side of the small-label LP has five duets by Price with drummer J.C. Heard, including "Honeysuckle Rose," "After Hours," and a romping "Little Rock Getaway." Delightful music. — *Scott Yanow*

King of Boogie Woogie / 1995 / Storyville ✦✦✦
On this odd CD reissue, pianist Sammy Price seems intent on becoming the Muhammad Ali of jazz. He brags throughout the liner notes about how he is the king of boogie-woogie and might very well (based on his five vocals on the date) also be the king of the crooners. In reality, Price's piano playing on the basic material (lots of blues and a few standards) is fine, while his vocals are a novelty at best. With backup work from bassist Arvell Shaw and drummer Panama Francis, this is a decent but not particularly riveting set. — *Scott Yanow*

● **And the Blues Singers** / Wolf ✦✦✦✦
When the Austrian Wolf logo decided to pay tribute to pianist Sammy Price's prolific legacy as both leader and sideman, they really did it up right. Ninety-four sides on four discs dating from 1929 to 1950 spotlight Price's rippling ivories behind a plethora of vocalists—Peetie Wheatstraw, Harmon Ray, Bea Booze, Johnny Temple, Monette Moore, Scat Man Bailey, and a great many more—as well as some very tasty instrumentals of his own. — *Bill Dahl*

Louis Prima

b. Dec. 7, 1911, New Orleans, LA, d. Aug. 24, 1978, New Orleans, LA
Trumpet, Vocals / Dixieland, Swing, Early R&B Jazz, Traditional Pop, Jump Blues
Louis Prima became very famous in the 1950s with an infectious Las Vegas act co-starring his wife (singer Keely Smith) that mixed together R&B (particularly the honking tenor of Sam Butera), early rock 'n' roll, comedy and Dixieland. Always a colorful personality, Prima was leading a band in New Orleans when he was just 11. In 1934 he began recording as a leader with a Dixieland-oriented unit and soon he was a major attraction on 52nd Street. His early records often featured George Brunies and Eddie Miller, and Pee Wee Russell was a regular member of his groups during 1935-36. Prima, who composed "Sing, Sing, Sing" (which for a period was his theme song),

recorded steadily through the swing era, had a big band in the 1940s and achieved hits in "Angelina" and "Robin Hood." In 1954 he began having great success in his latter-day group (their recordings on Capitol were big sellers and still sound joyous today), emphasizing vocals and Butera's tenor, but he still took spirited trumpet solos. Although he eventually broke up with Keely Smith, Louis Prima (who voiced a character in Walt Disney's animated film *The Jungle Book* in 1966) remained a popular attraction into the 1970s. — *Scott Yanow*

1934-1935, Vol. 1 / Sep. 27, 1934-Apr. 8, 1935 / TOM ✦✦✦✦
On the first of four Louis Prima LPs released by the collector's label titled The Old Masters (TOM), the popular musician is heard on his first 16 recordings. At the time Prima and fellow trumpeter-vocalist Wingy Manone were major entertainers on New York's 52nd Street. Unfortunately none of the records in this series give exact personnel and dates (discographies have to be consulted) but Prima's sidemen for the freewheeling performances (which are halfway between dixieland and swing) are quite impressive including trombonist George Brunies, clarinetist Sidney Arodin, tenor-saxophonist Eddie Miller, and pianist Claude Thornhill. Highlights of the good-time performances include "Jamaica Shout," "Long About Midnight," "Breakin' the Ice," and "Let's Have a Jubilee." — *Scott Yanow*

1935-1936, Vol. 2 / Apr. 3, 1935-Nov. 30, 1935 / TOM ✦✦✦✦
The second of four Louis Prima LPs put out by the TOM (The Old Masters) label continues the chronological reissuance of the trumpeter-vocalist's earliest recordings. Personnel and exact dates are not given on the record (which looks like a bootleg) but it is worth noting that on all but the first two songs (which have Eddie Miller), Pee Wee Russell is the clarinetist. Prima, who is the main star, fortunately gave Russell plenty of solo space (the other players are lesser-known). Highlights include "Chinatown, My Chinatown," "Basin Street Blues," "I'm Shooting High," and "I've Got My Fingers Crossed," but in general all 16 selections are quite enjoyable and show that Louis Prima was an appealing entertainer from the start. — *Scott Yanow*

1936, Vol. 3 / Feb. 28, 1936-Nov. 16, 1936 / TOM ✦✦✦✦
On the third of four Louis Prima albums on this obscure label (which has reissued all of the trumpeter-vocalist's earliest recordings but unfortunately does not provide recording dates or personnel), Louis Prima is heard with a septet on six numbers and his short-lived big band on ten others. A constant force during the performances (and functioning as a co-star) is the unique clarinetist Pee Wee Russell, the only "name" player among the sidemen. Among the highpoints are "Dinah," "Alice Blue Gown," "Cross Patch," "Mr. Ghost Goes to Town," and the earliest version of Prima's famous composition, "Sing, Sing, Sing" (from Feb. 28, 1936). All of these albums are highly recommended to swing collectors but will probably be difficult to find. — *Scott Yanow*

1937-1938, Vol. 4 / May 20, 1937-May 16, 1938 / TOM ✦✦✦✦
The fourth and final LP in the TOM label's Louis Prima series has 16 titles cut during a one-year period. With the departure of clarinetist Pee Wee Russell, Prima's sidemen (which include altoist George Moore, tenor-saxophonist Joe Catalyne, clarinetist Meyer Weinberg, and pianist Frank Pinero) lack any recognizable names but the swing/dixieland music is quite consistent. Prima alternated ballads with stomps and his personable vocals and New Orleans-oriented trumpet keep the performances interesting. Best are "Fifty-Second Street," "Tin Roof Blues" (the lone instrumental), "Now They Call It Swing," and "Rosalie." — *Scott Yanow*

Plays Pretty for the People [Savoy] / Feb. 1944-Jan. 1947 / Savoy ✦✦✦✦
This CD contains a cross-section of Louis Prima's big band recordings of the mid-'40s. While Prima had a fine orchestra (which featured some vocals from Lily Ann Carol), the leader was essentially the whole show. A masterful entertainer who became popular during the swing era, Prima sang well and also played fine New Orleans trumpet. Not all of his humor has dated well but most of the 20 selections on this CD still can communicate to today's listeners. Highpoints include "Robin Hood," "Angelina," "Brooklyn Boogie," and "Chinatown, My Chinatown." This is one of the few Louis Prima swing-era CDs currently available. — *Scott Yanow*

Angelina / Jun. 1950 / Viper's Nest ✦✦✦✦
Swing may have been dead by 1950 but one cannot tell that from this excellent CD which has three radio broadcasts from the Louis Prima big band. Prima, an exciting performer, shows his versatility on a diverse program and

takes quite a few hot trumpet solos while his wife Keely Smith (just 22 at the time) is heard on some ballads. However it is the sound of Prima's excellent and hard-swinging orchestra that is the biggest revelation; it is a pity that the personnel is unknown. The repertoire ranges from swing (the driving "Boogie in the Bronx" is most notable) and a few dixieland numbers to versions of Prima's hits (such as "Robin Hood" and "Angelina") and some standards. Taken from Prima's second of three periods (after he broke up his regular dixieland band of the 1930's and a few years before he hit it big in Las Vegas), this set is quite definitive of his music of the time. — *Scott Yanow*

★ **Capitol Collectors Series** / Apr. 19, 1956-Feb. 23, 1962 / Capitol ◆◆◆◆◆
What Louis Prima accomplished musically in the company of Sam Butera and the Witnesses and vocalist Keely Smith is in hard evidence on this excellent 26-track compilation. All the classics are aboard ("Angelina-Zooma Zooma," "That Old Black Magic," "I've Got You Under My Skin," "Buona Sera"—which includes a great snippet of studio chatter kicking it off—"Oh Marie," and the obligatory "Just A Gigolo-I Ain't Got Nobody") with excellent liner notes from Scott Shea and crisp transfers of the original masters. Although this duplicates several tracks with Rhino's *Zooma! Zooma!* compilation (now long out of print), with the addition of several singles and unissued tracks, this stands as the best single-disc collection available of Prima's tenure with Capitol Records. The perfect place to start your Louis Prima collection. — *Cub Koda*

☆ **The Wildest!** / Jan. 1957 / Capitol ◆◆◆◆◆
Although Louis Prima had been popular for 20 years before recording this LP, this set was his biggest breakthrough to mass appeal. The trumpeter-vocalist, his wife-singer Keely Smith and the group (the Witnesses) headed by the R&Bish tenor Sam Butera made for explosive music that was perfectly captured on this classic disc. The mixture of Prima's humor, dixieland, early rhythm and blues, Keely Smith's fine voice and the honking tenor made this unit a big hit in Las Vegas. The two medleys ("Just a Gigolo/I Ain't Got Nobody" and "Basin Street Blues/When It's Sleepy Time Down South") are often jubilant and the individual features are at the same level. Memorable music. — *Scott Yanow*

Zooma Zooma: The Best of Louis Prima / Jan. 1957-Feb. 1959 / Rhino ◆◆◆◆
This excellent sampler LP gives listeners some of the highpoints of Louis Prima's popular Capitol recordings. Although largely superceded by his CD in the Capitol Collectors series, this is an excellent all-round collection. The trumpeter-vocalist and singer Keely Smith are heard at their best on several medleys (particularly "I'm in the Mood for Love/Basin Street Blues," "Just a Gigolo/I Ain't Got Nobody," and "When You're Smiling/The Sheik of Araby") and their rendition of "That Old Black Magic" is classic. An ideal Las Vegas party band, Prima, Keely, tenor saxophonist Sam Butera, and the Witnesses were a perfect combination. — *Scott Yanow*

The Call of the Wildest / Jul. 1957 / Capitol ◆◆◆◆
Louis Prima's second Capitol LP with Keely Smith, Sam Butera, and the Witnesses is just as exciting as his first. The trumpeter-vocalist was a natural entertainer and comedian, and all of his skills are on evidence during this spirited program. The honking tenor of Sam Butera, Keely Smith's appealing voice, and the mixture of dixieland and R&B results in some remarkable and very accessible music. Highlights include the medley of "When You're Smiling" and "The Sheik of Araby," trombonist Red Blount's feature on "Blow, Red, Blow," "Pennies from Heaven," "The Birth of the Blues," and "When the Saints Go Marching In." What a band. — *Scott Yanow*

The Wildest Show at Tahoe / Jan. 1958 / Capitol ◆◆◆◆
This was the third straight classic album by trumpeter-singer Louis Prima with his wife-singer Keely Smith and the spirited R&B tenor-saxophonist Sam Butera; it is as exciting as the first two. Recorded live in Lake Tahoe, the band romps through four medleys (including "On the Sunny Side of the Street/Exactly Like You"), and "Don't Worry 'Bout Me/I'm in the Mood for Love"), Keely's feature on "A Foggy Day," Butera's showcase on "Come Back to Sorrento," and trombonist Red Blount's extroverted rendition of "How High the Moon." Toss in a few vocal duets and the results are quite memorable. All three of these Capitol records (which have thus far only been reissued on CD in samplers) are highly recommended for they document a unique group at the height of its power. — *Scott Yanow*

Plays Pretty for the People [Jazz Band] / 1963-1964 / Jazz Band ◆◆◆
Although Louis Prima and Keely Smith had split up by the time of the two live performances that comprise this collector's LP, Prima (on vocals and occasional trumpet) was still in fine form. Teamed with a future wife (singer Gia Maione) and still using R&B tenor Sam Butera and the Witnesses (which featured the extroverted trombonist Little Red Blount), Prima mixes together his older hits (including "Buona Sera," "Robin Hood," and "Sing, Sing, Sing") with some Dixieland standards and more recent material. The recording quality is decent and, even with Smith's absence, Prima sounds quite happy to be performing. — *Scott Yanow*

The Capitol Recordings / 1994 / Bear Family ◆◆◆◆
Louis Prima was a musical genius and part of the unsung hero squad who was doing rock 'n' roll before they had a name for it. He was a jazz trumpeter with a blasting, fervent style, a songwriter of no little import (the big-band evergreen "Sing, Sing, Sing," the jump-band classic "Oh Babe!," and the doo wop smoothie "A Sunday Kind of Love"), a crazed rhythmic singer, an engaging entertainer who could crack up the joint while simultaneously rockin' it and a bandleader without compare. He recorded for almost 40 years, from his debut 1933 Bluebird 78 as head of the Hotcha Trio to his final recordings issued on his own Prima label in the early '70s. In between time, he went through record companies as if nothing could hold him back with Decca, Vocalion, Majestic, Hit, Robin Hood, Jubilee, RCA Victor, Capitol, and Dot being counted up as stops along the way. He also went through five wives in the process, the last two—Keely Smith and Gia Maione, both of whose work is represented in this box—being pressed into service as the female vocalist/comedic foil in the act. Which brings us to the celebratory goods of this excellent as always Bear Family box, crammed to the bursting point with eight CDs. Since Keely Smith, Sam Butera, and the Witnesses (Prima's ace backing unit) all recorded as solo acts during this period, they're exhaustively represented by this box as well. The first three discs cover all of Prima's studio sides and starts up the live recordings with the 1962 Harrah's Club in Tahoe sides, while disc four covers all of the seminal live tracks from 1957 and 1958. Discs five and six are the complete Keely Smith solo recordings, while the last two round up all the sides by Sam Butera and the Witnesses. The truly amazing thing about the 199 (!!!) tracks collected here is how little of it is unissued material. Even if Prima cut some duds now and then, it's pretty wild that Capitol used up damn near every last thing the man ever committed to magnetic tape, all of it the high quality of rockin' mayhem he was laying down. And rock it does, all of it infested with much good humor along with Prima's and Butera's other contribution to big-beat mania, the invention of the Vegas shuffle, a loping beat that could be sped up to almost double tempo on any given number. This effect—the solid core of Prima's rockin' groove—is best heard on tracks like "When You're Smiling/The Sheik of Araby," the later version from the *Hey Boy! Hey Girl!* movie soundtrack of "Oh Marie" (stupendous in the scattin' and honkin' exchange between Prima and Butera), "Basin Street Blues/When It's Sleepy Time Down South," and of course "Just a Gigolo/I Ain't Got Nobody," the track that David Lee Roth brought to the charts in the '80s. The duets with Keely Smith ("I've Got You Under My Skin," "That Old Black Magic") and Sam Butera (Richard Berry's "Next Time," here in both studio and extended live versions) are here to savor as well and it's all very fine, indeed. After four discs of Prima's wild-ass genius, the next two of Keely Smith with big-band backings from Nelson Riddle and Billy May will seem sedate by comparison, but they're '50s-style Capitol tracks with their own definable charm. Great tunes and arrangements, plus the inclusion of her duets with Frank Sinatra makes a nice bonus highlight. The final two discs of Sam Butera come much closer to Prima's rockin' slant on things, with rocked-up jazz classics and R&B tunes galore keeping the party goin' all night long. Needless to say, if you're a Louis Prima fan bordering on fanatic, this is the one to have. — *Cub Koda*

John Primer

b. Mar. 3, 1945, Camden, MS
Guitar, Vocals / Modern Electric Chicago Blues, Modern Electric Blues, Chicago Blues, Electric Blues
By any yardstick, Chicago guitarist John Primer has paid his dues. Prior to making what he's hoping will be his breakthrough for Mike Vernon's Atlan-

tic-distributed Code Blue label, *The Real Deal,* Primer spent 13 years as the ever-reliable rhythm guitarist with Magic Slim & the Teardrops. Before that, he filled the same role behind Chicago immortals Muddy Waters and Willie Dixon.

All that grounding has paid off handsomely for Primer. His sound is rooted in the classic Windy City blues sound of decades past: rough-edged and uncompromising and satisfying in the extreme. He's one of the last real traditionalists in town.

By the time he came to Chicago in 1963, Primer was thoroughly familiar with the lowdown sounds of Waters, Wolf, Jimmy Reed, B.B. and Albert King, and Elmore James. He fronted a West Side outfit for a while called the Maintainers, dishing out a mix of soul and blues, before joining the house band at the South side blues mecca Theresa's Lounge for what ended up a nine-year run. Elegant guitarist Sammy Lawhorn proved quite influential on Primer's maturing guitar approach during this period.

Always on the lookout for aspiring talent, Willie Dixon spirited him away for a 1979 gig in Mexico City. After a year or so as one of Dixon's All-Stars, Primer was recruited to join the last band of Muddy Waters, playing with the Chicago blues king until his 1983 death. Right after that, Primer joined forces with Magic Slim; their styles interlocked so seamlessly that their partnership seemed like an eternal bond.

But Primer deserved his own share of the spotlight. In 1993, Michael Frank's Chicago-based Earwig logo issued Primer's debut domestic disc, *Stuff You Got to Watch.* It was a glorious return to the classic '50s Chicago sound, powered by Primer's uncommonly concise guitar work and gruff, no-nonsense vocals. With the 1995 emergence of *The Real Deal*—produced by Vernon and featuring all-star backing by harpist Billy Branch, pianist David Maxwell, and bassist Johnny B. Gayden, Primer's star appears ready to ascend at last. *—Bill Dahl*

Poor Man Blues: Chicago Blues Session, Vol. 6 / 1991 / Wolf ♦♦♦♦
Poor Man Blues: Chicago Blues Session, Vol. 6 showcases the exceptional guitar skills of John Primer, who long served as a guitarist for Muddy Waters and Magic Slim. Primer falls somewhere between the two, turning out tough Chicago blues fueled by his biting slide guitar. His original songs aren't particularly interesting, but they function as good vehicles for exciting jams. In the end, Primer might not add anything new to Chicago blues, but he has a great time playing, and it sure is fun to listen to him play. *—Thom Owens*

Stuff You Got to Watch / 1993 / Earwig ♦♦♦♦
Chicago guitarist Primer's domestic debut album was doubtless an eye-opener for anyone not familiar with his searing slide work and sturdy vocal abilities. Apart from a very ill-advised cover of Glen Campbell's "Rhinestone Cowboy" (yuck!), the album resonates with mean, lowdown guitar work and fine ensemble backing. *—Bill Dahl*

● **The Real Deal** / 1995 / Atlantic ♦♦♦♦
Thought they didn't make traditional Chicago blues albums worthy of the name anymore? Guess again: Primer's major-label bow is an entirely satisfying affair produced by Mike Vernon that's long on intensity and devoid of pretension. Lots of originals; a handful of well-chosen covers, and a vicious band (pianist David Maxwell and harpist Billy Branch solo stunningly) help make the set go, while Primer grabs hold of the opportunity with a vise-like grip and makes believe it's the 1950s all over again. *—Bill Dahl*

Cold Blooded Blues Man / Apr. 23, 1997 / Wolf ♦♦♦

Gary Primich

b. Apr. 20, 1958, Chicago, IL
Harmonica, Vocals / Modern Electric Harmonica Blues
Don't let his intelligence, charm and self-effacing manner fool you: Gary Primich is one bad-ass harmonica player. And he's more than competent guitar player, too.

Primich was born April 20, 1958 in Chicago and raised in nearby Gary, Indiana. He learned harmonica from the masters at the Maxwell Street Market in nearby Chicago as a teen. By the early '80s, however, Primich became dissatisfied with the blues scene in Chicago, and in 1984, shortly after he earned his degree in radio and television from Indiana University, he moved to Austin, Texas.

After landing a job at the University of Texas doing electrical work, he

began to work as a sideman at Austin area clubs. In 1987, he ran into former Frank Zappa/Mothers of Invention drummer Jimmy Carl Black, who had also relocated to Austin, and the two formed a band, the Mannish Boys. Their debut album on the now-defunct Amazing Records label was called *A L'il Dab'll Do Ya.* Though Black left the band, Primich led the Mannish Boys through another album for Amazing, *Satellite Rock.* Both albums attracted sufficient attention to Primich that he was able to record under his own name for the Amazing label, and in 1991 he cut his self-titled debut for the label. He followed it up with *My Pleasure* in 1992. After Amazing Records folded, he was picked up by the Chicago-based Flying Fish label. Primich recorded two equally brilliant albums for Fish, and they include *Travelin' Mood* (1994) and *Mr. Freeze* (1995).

On his last two albums for Flying Fish (a label that has since been acquired by Rounder Records), Primich's talents as a songwriter really start to come through, and as of this writing, he was without a label, but still nurturing his fan base through almost constant touring. *—Richard Skelly*

Gary Primich / 1991 / Amazing ♦♦♦
Gary Primich's eponymous album is an uneven collection, hampered by a handful of rote, by-the-book tracks but its best moments are vibrant, eclectic and quite exciting. Unfortunately, the album gets off to a weak start, running through a bunch of uptempo blues-rockers. After those are through, Primich begins to open up his sound, diving deep into New Orleans R&B, as well as some jump blues and Latin-tinged rhythms. It's on these numbers that Primich reveals his talents as a vocalist and harpist, not on the conventional numbers. *—Thom Owens*

● **My Pleasure** / 1992 / Amazing ♦♦♦♦
My Pleasure is pretty much straight-up Chicago blues, delivered with authority by Gary Primich. Fellow harpist James Harman produced the record, and he tames Primich's more adventurous qualities. However, he does bring out the grease and grit of Primich's straightforward blues that was lacking on the previous record, which makes this a very enjoyable, if predictable, album. *—Thom Owens*

Hot Harp Blues / 1993 / Amazing ♦♦♦♦

Travelin' Mood / 1994 / Flying Fish ♦♦

Mr. Freeze / 1995 / Flying Fish ♦♦♦♦
Although he had made solid, workmanlike albums in the past, *Mr. Freeze* is where all the cherries came up at once on Gary Primich's musical slot machine. While his harp playing was never in dispute, his vocals on this outing finally find their own style, sounding for the first time comfortable, assured, and totally in the pocket. Kicking off with the high-octane shuffle "Bad Poker Hand" featuring Mark Korpi's stylistic nod to Brewer Phillips, Primich contributes four of his own compositions to this 13-tracker while jumping on such stylistically diverse material as Gene Ammons' "Red Top" and Washboard Sam's "Easy Ridin' Mama," vaulting between subgenres with consummate ease. Other highlight tracks include a harp showcase on "You Came A Long Way From St. Louis" and the rumbling boogie of Mark Korpi's "Slap You Silly." Featuring guest turns from the aforementioned Korpi, bassist supreme Sarah Brown, Mark Rubin, Gene Taylor, and acoustic slide man Steve James along with Gary's regular working band, there's a wide variety of real good stuff to enjoy here. If you were to pick just one album to start absorbing this harp blower's eclectic genius, this one would make a perfect calling card. *—Cub Koda*

Company Man / 1997 / Black Top ♦♦♦♦
Primich's recording career has been indeed a work in progress, with his earliest efforts showing much promise with a workmanlike aura to them, with each new release heading into some mighty cool terrain, taking—as always—the path less traveled. And *Company Man* is certainly the most adventurous of his releases to date, taking his fine songwriting craft and huge harp tone in a multitude of directions. Needless to say, the highlights abound throughout, but most notable in passing are a pair of Smiley Lewis numbers, "Jail Bird" and "Hook, Line, and Sinker," with the former getting the jug-band romp of its life, the Big Walter-borrows-Little Walter's-band instrumental "Varmint," or the jazzy-as-hell "Ain't You Trouble." Or that eerie minor-key voodoo piece, "What's It Gonna Be," or the lowdown "Dry County Blues," which is probably the dirtiest *sounding* vocal Primich has ever laid down, pure gravel all the way. *—AMG*

Professor Longhair (Henry Roeland Byrd)

b. Dec. 19, 1918, Bogalusa, LA, **d.** Jan. 30, 1980, New Orleans, LA
Piano, Vocals / Rock & Roll, New Orleans R&B, New Orleans Blues, Piano Blues

Justly worshipped a decade-and-a-half after his death as a founding father of New Orleans R&B, Roy "Professor Longhair" Byrd was nevertheless so down-and-out at one point in his long career that he was reduced to sweeping the floors in a record shop that once could have moved his platters by the boxful.

That Fess made such a marvelous comeback testifies to the resiliency of this late legend, whose Latin-tinged rhumba-rocking piano style and croaking, yodeling vocals were as singular and spicy as the second-line beats that power his hometown's musical heartbeat. Byrd brought an irresistible Caribbean feel to his playing, full of rolling flourishes that every Crescent City ivories man had to learn inside out (Fats Domino, Huey Smith, and Allen Toussaint all paid homage early and often).

Roy Byrd grew up on the streets of the Big Easy, tap dancing for tips on Bourbon Street with his running partners. Local 88s aces Sullivan Rock, Kid Stormy Weather, and Tuts Washington all left their marks on the youngster, but Byrd brought his own conception to the stool. A natural-born card shark and gambler, Longhair began to take his playing seriously in 1948, earning a gig at the Caldonia Club. Owner Mike Tessitore bestowed Byrd with his professorial nickname (due to Byrd's shaggy coiffure).

Longhair debuted on wax in 1949, laying down four tracks (including the first version of his signature "Mardi Gras in New Orleans," complete with whistled intro) for the Dallas-based Star Talent label. His band was called the Shuffling Hungarians, for reasons lost to time! Union problems forced those sides off the market, but Longhair's next date for Mercury the same year was strictly on the up-and-up. It produced his first and only national R&B hit in 1950, the hilarious "Bald Head" (credited to Roy Byrd & his Blues Jumpers).

The pianist made great records for Atlantic in 1949, Federal in 1951, Wasco in 1952, and Atlantic again in 1953 (producing the immortal "Tipitina," a romping "In the Night," and the lyrically impenetrable boogie "Ball the Wall"). After recuperating from a minor stroke, Longhair came back on Lee Rupe's Ebb logo in 1957 with a storming "No Buts—No Maybes." He revived his "Go to the Mardi Gras" for Joe Ruffino's Ron imprint in 1959; this is the version that surfaces every year at Mardi Gras in New Orleans.

Other than the ambitiously arranged "Big Chief" in 1964 for Watch Records, the '60s held little charm for Longhair. He hit the skids, abandoning his piano playing until a booking at the fledgling 1971 Jazz & Heritage Festival put him on the comeback trail. He made a slew of albums in the last decade of his life, topped off by a terrific set for Alligator, *Crawfish Fiesta.*

Longhair triumphantly appeared on the PBS-TV concert series *Soundstage* (with Dr. John, Earl King, and the Meters), co-starred in the documentary *Piano Players Rarely Ever Play Together* (which became a memorial tribute when Longhair died in the middle of its filming; funeral footage was included), and saw a group of his admirers buy a local watering hole in 1977 and rechristen it Tipitina's after his famous song. He played there regularly when he wasn't on the road; it remains a thriving operation.

Longhair went to bed on January 30, 1980, and never woke up. A heart attack in the night stilled one of New Orleans' seminal R&B stars, but his music is played in his hometown so often and so reverently, you'd swear he was still around. —*Bill Dahl*

New Orleans Piano / 1972 / Atlantic ♦♦♦♦
All 16 of the Atlantic sides from 1949 and 1953 (including a handful of alternate takes) on one glorious disc. Longhair's work for the label was notoriously marvelous—this version of "Mardi Gras in New Orleans" reeks of revelry in the streets of the French Quarter; "She Walks Right In" and "Walk Your Blues Away" ride a bedrock boogie, and "In the Night" bounces atop a parade-beat shuffle groove and hard-charging saxes. —*Bill Dahl*

Rock 'n Roll Gumbo / 1977 / Dancing Cat ♦♦♦♦
It features great renditions of New Orleans standards such as "Junco Partner" and "Rockin' Pneumonia" with an all-star band that features Clarence "Gatemouth" Brown on guitar and violin. —*Bruce Boyd Raeburn*

Live on the Queen Mary / 1978 / One Way ♦♦
Okay live set taped at a Paul McCartney shindig. —*Bill Dahl*

Crawfish Fiesta / 1980 / Alligator ♦♦♦♦
Probably the best of all the many albums Longhair waxed during his comeback (and likely the last). A tremendously tight combo featuring three horns and Dr. John on guitar delightfully back the Professor every step of the way as he recasts Solomon Burke's "Cry to Me" and Fats Domino's "Whole Lotta Loving" in his own indelible image and roars, yodels, and whistles out wonderful remakes of his own oldies "Big Chief" and "Bald Head." —*Bill Dahl*

Mardi Gras in New Orleans / 1981 / Nighthawk ♦♦♦♦
Plenty of rarities are featured on this valuable cross-section of the Professor's early releases. Both sides of the pianist's first two 78s for Star Talent Records are aboard, as well as sides he cut for Mercury, Federal ("Curly Haired Baby," "Gone So Long"), Wasco ("East St. Louis Baby"), Atlantic, and Ebb. —*Bill Dahl*

House Party / 1987 / Rounder ♦♦♦
A classic pairing, Professor Longhair meets New Orleans guitar-legend Snooks Eaglin and drummer "Zig" Modeliste of The Meters. —*Bruce Boyd Raeburn*

Mardi Gras in Baton / 1991 / Rhino ♦♦♦♦
Some of the earliest sides from Longhair's rediscovery period (1971-72), featuring a lot of tunes inexorably associated with him through previous versions and a few ("Jambalaya," "Sick and Tired") that weren't. An added bonus is the magical presence of guitarist Snooks Eaglin, whose approach is every bit as singular as the Professor's was. —*Bill Dahl*

★ **Fess: Professor Longhair Anthology** / Nov. 16, 1993 / Rhino ♦♦♦♦♦
The rhumba-rocking rhythms of Roy "Professor Longhair" Byrd live on throughout Rhino's 40-track retrospective of the New Orleans icon's amazing legacy. Most of the seminal stuff arrives early on: "Bald Head," the rollicking ode Byrd cut for Mercury in 1950, is followed by a raft of classics from his 1949 and 1953 Atlantic dates ("Tipitina," "Ball the Wall," "Who's Been Fooling You"), the storming 1957 "No Buts—No Maybes" and "Baby Let Me Hold Your Hand" for Ebb, and his beloved "Go to the Mardi Gras" as waxed for Ron in 1959. The second disc is a hodge-podge of material from his 1970s comeback, all of it wonderful in its own way but not as essential as the early work. —*Bill Dahl*

Houseparty New Orleans Style / 1994 / Rounder ♦♦♦♦
Boiling blues and trademark Afro-Latin and boogie-woogie riffs were the menu when Professor Longhair brought his Crescent City music show to Baton Rouge and Memphis in 1971 and 1972, respectively. The 15 numbers on this set matched the great pianist with an esteemed array of musicians that included outstanding guitarist Snooks Eaglin on both sessions, and fine rhythm sections as well. Eaglin's flashy, inventive solos were excellent contrasts to Longhair's rippling keyboard flurries and distinctive mix of yodels, yells, cries and shouts. —*Ron Wynn*

Professor's Blues Revue

db. 1992
Group / Modern Electric Blues, Modern Electric Chicago Blues

"Professor" Eddie Lusk worked frequently as a session keyboardist during the 1970s and '80s on the Chicago blues scene. His own revue showcased several singers over the years, notably Gloria Hardiman (featured on their "Meet Me With Your Black Drawers On" on Alligator's 1987 anthology, *The New Bluebloods*) and Karen Carroll, principal singer on the band's 1989 Delmark album, *Professor Strut.* Tragically, Lusk took his own life by plunging into the Chicago River. —*Bill Dahl*

Professor Strut / 1989 / Delmark ♦♦♦
Eddie Lusk's only solo album is a blues revue, as he leads a variety of singers through several classic blues songs from all of the blues's subgenres. The concept is good one, but the performance is decidedly uneven—several of the singers are mediocre and the fidelity on the release is poor. For those that want to sit through the rough spots, they'll find a handful of good solos, but not much more. —*Thom Owens*

Snooky Pryor (James Edward Pryor)

b. Sep. 15, 1921, Lambert, MS

Harmonica, Drums, Vocals / Electric Chicago Blues, Modern Electric Blues, Chicago Blues, Electric Blues, Harmonica Blues

Only in the last few years has Snooky Pryor finally begun to receive full credit for the mammoth role he played in shaping the amplified Chicago blues harp sound during the postwar era. He's long claimed he was the first harpist to run his sound through a public-address system around the Windy City—and since nobody's around to refute the claim at this point, we'll have to accept it! He's still quite active musically, having cut two potent discs for Austin, TX-based Antone's Records in recent years.

James Edward Pryor was playing harmonica at the age of eight in Mississippi. The two Sonny Boys were influential to Pryor's emerging style, as he played around the Delta. He hit Chicago for the first time in 1940, later serving in the Army at nearby Fort Sheridan. Playing his harp through powerful Army PA systems gave Pryor the idea to acquire his own portable rig once he left the service. Armed with a primitive amp, he dazzled the folks on Maxwell Street in late 1945 with his massively amplified harp.

Pryor made some groundbreaking 78s during the immediate postwar Chicago blues era. Teaming with guitarist Moody Jones, he waxed "Telephone Blues" and "Boogie" for Planet Records in 1948, encoring the next year with "Boogy Fool"/"Raisin' Sand" for JOB with Jones on bass and guitarist Baby Face Leroy Foster in support. Pryor made more more classic sides for JOB (1952-53), Parrot (1953), and Vee-Jay ("Someone to Love Me"/"Judgment Day") in 1956, but commercial success never materialized. He wound down his blues-playing in the early '60s, finally chucking it all and moving to downstate Ullin, IL, in 1967.

For a long while, Pryor's whereabouts were unknown. But the 1987 Blind Pig album, *Snooky,* produced by guitarist Steve Freund, announced to the world that the veteran harpist was alive and well, his chops still honed. A pair of solid discs for Antone's, *Too Cool to Move* and *In This Mess up to My Chest,* followed. Pryor stays just as busy as he cares to nowadays, still ensconced in Ullin (where life is good and the fishing is easy). —*Bill Dahl*

★ **Snooky Pryor [Flyright]** / 1969 / Flyright ✦✦✦✦✦
These tracks from the JOB label, recorded from the early '50s to early '60s, include the classics "Boogie" and "Stockyard Blues" and the raucous, echo-laden stomp of "Boogie Twist." These are Pryor's finest moments on wax. —*Cub Koda*

Do It If You Want / 1973 / Bluesway ✦✦
Homesick James & Snooky Pryor / 1974 / Caroline ✦✦✦
Snooky & Moody / 1980 / Flyright ✦✦✦✦
The team of Snooky Pryor and Moody Jones doesn't have the same reputation as other tandems like Leroy Carr and Scrapper Blackwell or Tampa Red

and Big Maceo Merriweather, but they certainly created several fine numbers themselves. This collection highlights several of them, showing that each musician was a capable performer and interpreter. —*Ron Wynn*

Snooky / 1987 / Blind Pig ✦✦✦✦
An outstanding comeback effort by Chicago harp pioneer Snooky Pryor, whose timeless sound meshed well with a Windy City trio led by producer/guitarist Steve Freund for this set. Mostly Pryor's own stuff—"Why You Want to Do Me Like That," "That's the Way to Do It," "Cheatin' and Lyin'"—with his fat-toned harp weathering the decades quite nicely. —*Bill Dahl*

Snooky Pryor [Paula] / 1991 / Paula/Flyright ✦✦✦✦
If anyone doubts the longevity and journeyman greatness of Snooky Pryor, this collection of sides should do much to quiet them. Starting with the 1947 Floyd Jones (the classic "Stockyard Blues") and Johnny Young sessions for Old Swingmaster with Snooky in support and running right from the early '50s into the early-'60s sides for the JOB label with "Boogie Twist" (his Vee-Jay and Parrot sides are not here), this is ground floor Chicago blues one step removed from Maxwell Street. Lots of unissued sides-all of them great-plus the inclusion of the instrumental "Boogie," which became the blueprint for Little Walter's hit "Juke." Pryor's finest moments on wax. —*Cub Koda*

Too Cool to Move / 1992 / Antone's ✦✦✦✦
Another excellent recent set from the veteran harpist, cut down in Austin with a mixture of Texans and Chicagoans in support: pianist Pinetop Perkins, guitarists Duke Robiilard and Luther Tucker, and drummer Willie "Big Eyes" Smith. Pryor's made quite a substantial to his long-dormant discography in the last few years. —*Bill Dahl*

In This Mess Up to My Chest / 1994 / Antone's ✦✦✦✦
Pryor reaffirms his mastery of postwar blues harp over the course of this sturdy set, again done with the help of some fine Texas and Chicago players. Pryor's downhome vocals shine on the distinctive "Bury You in a Paper Sack" and "Stick Way Out Behind." —*Bill Dahl*

Mind Your Own Business / Jan. 14, 1997 / Discovery ✦✦✦
Good chunky barroom blues on this outing from a grand old harmonica player. Pryor saves the serious energy for his harp blowing, but he does just fine as a vocalist too, with a nicely aged and lived-in voice. Everybody on the record has a set place and knows their moves, and that's okay too. This is a good-times kind of album. —*Steven McDonald*

Hand Me Down Blues / Relic ✦✦✦✦
A nice 16 track compilation of rare blues material from the Parrot label, this features both sides of Snooky's lone single for the label, "Crosstown Blues" and "I Want You For Myself." Also features obscure and unissued tracks by Little Willie Foster ("Four Day Jump"), Dusty Brown ("Yes She's Gone"), John Brim ("Gary Stomp"), Sunnyland Slim ("Devil Is a Busy Man"), early Albert King ("Little Boy Blue" and the title track), plus Henry Gray with four previously unissued sides, all of them sloppy and great. —*Cub Koda*

R

Yank Rachell (James Rachell)

b. Mar. 16, 1910, Brownsville, TN, **d.** Apr. 9, 1997, Indianapolis, IN
Guitar, Harmonica, Mandolin, Vocals / Country Blues, Piedmont Blues, Prewar Country Blues

Best known for his down-home mandolin playing, guitarist, vocalist, and songwriter Yank Rachell played a central role in several of the most exciting chapters in blues history. Born in either Mississippi or Tennessee, he took up mandolin as a youngster and was soon making the rounds with the Brownsville, TN, blues crowd: John Estes, John Lee "Sonny Boy" Williamson, Jab Jones, and Homesick James Williamson. During the '30s he was part of the vibrant St. Louis blues community, working with Henry Townsend and Big Joe Williams before moving on to Chicago. For the past thirty years he has resided in Indianapolis, presiding over still another blues community, which once included Shirley Griffith, J.T. Adams, and guitarist Pete Franklin. When I met Rachell in the early '70s, he had put an electric band together with his son-in-law and some local R&B players. Although much of his recording career with Victor, ARC, Bluebird, and Delmark was spent accompanying others, he composed and sang powerful songs such as "Lake Michigan Blues" and "Gravel Road Woman." When he visited my classroom in 1976, he told the students he co-authored the classic "Schoolgirl" with his one-time partner Sonny Boy Williamson. Explaining his music, he said: "I learned it the hard way, out in the country all by myself—so far back in the woods my breath smelled like cord wood." Throughout his lengthy career, his music changed little, holding a country dance flavor. At the same time, he demonstrated a remarkable ability to play with other musicians—the mark of a seasoned string-band veteran. For 60 years Rachell worked in various ensemble formats, but his heart remained with his string-band roots. *—Barry Lee Pearson*

Complete Recorded Works, Vol. 1 (1934-38) / 1934-1938 / Wolf ✦✦✦

Complete Recorded Works, Vol. 2 (1938-1941) / 1938-1941 / Wolf ✦✦✦✦

Mandolin Blues / 1986 / Delmark ✦✦✦

● **Chicago Style** / 1987 / Delmark ✦✦✦✦
While Yank Rachell was past his prime when he began recording for Delmark in the 1960s, he was still an effective, often exciting vocalist and mandolin player. He seldom sounded more striking and enjoyable than on the nine cuts that comprised *Chicago Style*, recently reissued on CD. Rachell sang with a spirited mix of irony, anguish, dismay, and bemusement on such numbers as "Depression Blues," "Diving Duck," and "Going to St. Louis." *—Ron Wynn*

Blues Mandolin Man / Blind Pig ✦✦✦
This contains fine material by one of the few great mandolin bluesmen. *—Barry Lee Pearson*

Bobby Radcliff

b. Sep. 22, 1951, Washington, D.C.
Guitar, Vocals / R&B, Modern Electric Blues, Chicago Blues

Although Bobby Radcliff has spent the last 25 years honing his craft in bars around his native Washington, D.C., and in New York City and Chicago, the 45-year-old guitarist, singer, and songwriter is just now coming into his prime.

Born September 22, 1951, Radcliff grew up in Bethesda, MD and had easy access to Washington, D.C. blues clubs, where he learned from people like Bobby Parker. Before graduating from high school, he'd already made several trips to Chicago to meet his idol, Magic Sam Maghett, owing to a small but growing blues club scene in Washington. Radcliff began playing when he was 12, and he started off taking classical guitar lessons. After his guitar

teacher showed him some blues, he began buying every blues guitar album he could get his hands on.

In 1977, Radcliff moved to New York City and worked in a bookstore by day until 1987, when he realized he was making enough money playing in clubs to give up his day job. Since he hooked up his recording deal with BlackTop Records, Radcliff has toured the US, Canada, and Europe more than a dozen times, and his fiery guitar playing is always a festival crowd-pleaser.

Parker has three excellent albums out on the Black Top label that showcase his songwriting, guitar playing, and soulful singing. They include his debut, *Dresses Too Short* (1989), *Universal Blues* (1991), and *There's a Cold Grave in Your Way* (1994). Collectors will seek out his 1985 vinyl release, *Early in the Morning*, on the A-Okay label. *—Richard Skelly*

● **Dresses Too Short** / Oct. 1989 / Black Top ✦✦✦✦
Bobby Radcliff turns in a tight, tough update of Magic Sam-style Chicago blues with *Dresses Too Short*. The songs are either too familiar or a weak approximation of the genre, but the playing throughout is terrific—his guitar playing is alternately subtle and ferocious. Best of all is the handful of tracks cut with Ronnie Earl & the Broadcasters who spur Radcliff on to his best performances. *—Thom Owens*

Universal Blues / 1991 / Black Top ✦✦✦
Universal Blues is another successful reworking of Chicago blues from Bobby Radcliff. It's less flashy than the previous *Dresses Too Short*, but that's a plus—without all the pyrotechnics, Radcliff's guitar actually sounds more powerful and versatile, which makes the album quite entertaining. *—Thom Owens*

There's a Cold Grave in My Way / 1994 / Black Top ✦✦✦✦

Live at the Rynborn / Apr. 15, 1997 / Black Top ✦✦✦

The Radio Kings

b. 1991, Boston, MA
Group / Modern Electric Blues

A Boston-based traditional blues duo almost eerily reminiscent of the like-minded Fabulous Thunderbirds, the Radio Kings primarily comprised vocalist/harpist Brian Templeton and guitarist Michael Dinallo. Formed in 1991, the group debuted in 1994 with the Icehouse label release *It Ain't Easy,* a showcase for their clear affection for the gritty sound of giants including Howlin' Wolf, Little Walter, and Slim Harpo; *Live at B.B. King's* followed a year later, and in 1998, the Radio Kings returned with *Money Road. —Jason Ankeny*

Live at B.B. King's / Oct. 10, 1995 / Priority ✦✦✦

It Ain't Easy / Jan. 23, 1996 / Priority ✦✦✦

● **Money Road** / Feb. 10, 1998 / Bullseye Blues ✦✦✦✦
If the Radio Kings sound more than a little bit like the Fabulous Thunderbirds, it's more than just the similar instrumentation. T-Bird drummer Fran Christina's brother Bob is the drummer in this band, and singer/harmonica man Brian Templeton sounds so much like Kim Wilson, both vocally and instrumentally, that you have to keep checking the personnel credits in the CD booklet. The final nail in the coffin is Michael Dinallo's expert Jimmie Vaughan imitations on guitar, however unintentional. That said, they nonetheless turn in a disc full of original material that would probably be more impressive if there was an equally original approach applied in presenting it. High spots of the material include "Money in My Pocket," "Virginia," the Lazy Lester soundalike "Disturb Me Baby," "Song of Love," and the title track. *—Cub Koda*

Ma Rainey (Gertrude Rainey)

b. Apr. 26, 1886, Columbus, GA, **d.** Dec. 22, 1939, Columbus, GA
Vocals / Classic Female Blues, Blues

Ma Rainey wasn't the first blues singer to make records, but by all rights she probably should have been. In an era when women were the marquee names in blues, Ma Rainey was once the most celebrated of all—the "Mother of the Blues" had been singing the music for more than 20 years before she made her recording debut (Paramount, 1923). With the advent of blues records, she became even more influential, immortalizing such songs as "C.C. Rider," "Bo-Weavil Blues," and "Ma Rainey's Black Bottom." Like the other classic blues divas, she had a repertoire of pop and minstrel songs as well as blues, but she maintained a heavier, tougher vocal delivery than the cabaret blues singers who followed. Ma Rainey's records featured her with jug bands, guitar duos, and bluesmen such as Tampa Red and Blind Blake, in addition to the more customary horns-and-piano jazz-band accompaniment (occasionally including such luminaries as Louis Armstrong, Kid Ory, and Fletcher Henderson).

Born and raised in Columbus, GA, Ma Rainey (born Gertrude Pridgett) began singing professionally when she was a teenager, performing with a number of minstrel and medicine shows. In 1904, she married William "Pa" Rainey and she changed her name to "Ma" Rainey. The couple performed as "Rainey and Rainey, Assassinators of the Blues" and toured throughout the south, performing with several minstrel shows, circuses, and tent shows. According to legend, she gave a young Bessie Smith vocal lessons during this time. By the early '20s, Ma Rainey had become a featured performer on the Theater Owners' Booking Association circuit.

In 1923, Ma Rainey signed a contract with Paramount Records. Although her recording career lasted only a mere six years—her final sessions were in 1928—she recorded over one hundred songs and many of them, including "C.C. Rider" and "Bo Weavil Blues," became genuine blues classics. During these sessions, she was supported by some of the most talented blues and jazz musicians of her era, including Louis Armstrong, Fletcher Henderson, Coleman Hawkins, Buster Bailey, and Lovie Austin.

Rainey's recordings and performances were extremely popular among Black audiences, particularly in the south. After reaching the height of her popularity in the late '20s, Rainey's career faded away in the early '30s as female blues singing became less popular with the blues audience. She retired from performing in 1933, settling down in her hometown of Columbus. In 1939, Ma Rainey died of a heart attack. She left behind an immense recorded legacy, which continued to move and influence successive generations of blues, country, and rock 'n' roll musicians. In 1983, Rainey was inducted into the Blues Foundation's Hall of Fame; seven years later, she was inducted to the Rock & Roll Hall of Fame. —*Jim O'Neal & Stephen Thomas Erlewine*

★ **Ma Rainey's Black Bottom** / Jun. 1975 / Milestone ✦✦✦✦✦
The archetypal "classic" blues femme belter on 1924-1928 recordings, with Fletcher Henderson on piano and Coleman Hawkins bass sax on two tracks. —*Mark A. Humphrey*

Black Bottom / 1990 / Yazoo ✦✦✦✦

Complete Recorded Works: 1928 Sessions / Jun. 2, 1994 / Document ✦✦✦✦

Bonnie Raitt

b. Nov. 8, 1949, Burbank, CA
Guitar, Vocals / Blues-Rock, Singer-Songwriter, Pop-Rock, Adult Contemporary

Long a critic's darling, singer/guitarist Bonnie Raitt did not begin to win the comparable commercial success due her until the release of the aptly titled 1989 blockbuster *Nick of Time;* her tenth album, it rocketed her into the mainstream consciousness nearly two decades after she first committed her unique blend of blues, rock, and R&B to vinyl. Born in Burbank, California on November 8, 1949, she was the daughter of Broadway star John Raitt, best known for his starring performances in such smashes as *Carousel* and *Pajama Game*. After picking up the guitar at the age of 12, Raitt felt an immediate affinity for the blues, and although she went off to attend Radcliffe in 1967, within two years she had dropped out to begin playing the Boston folk and blues club circuit. Signing with noted blues manager Dick

Waterman, she was soon performing alongside the likes of idols including Howlin' Wolf, Sippie Wallace, and Mississippi Fred McDowell, and in time earned such a strong reputation that she was signed to Warner Bros.

Debuting in 1971 with an eponymously titled effort, Raitt immediately emerged as a critical favorite, applauded not only for her soulful vocals and thoughtful song selection but also for her guitar prowess, turning heads as one of the few women to play bottleneck. Her 1972 follow-up, *Give It Up*, made better use of her eclectic tastes, featuring material by contemporaries like Jackson Browne and Eric Kaz, in addition to a number of R&B chestnuts and even three Raitt originals. 1973's *Takin' My Time* was much acclaimed, and throughout the middle of the decade she released an LP annually, returning with *Streetlights* in 1974 and *Home Plate* a year later. With 1977's *Sweet Forgiveness*, Raitt scored her first significant pop airplay with her hit cover of the Del Shannon classic "Runaway"; its follow-up, 1979's *The Glow*, appeared around the same time as a massive all-star anti-nuclear concert at Madison Square Garden mounted by MUSE (Musicians United for Safe Energy), an organization she'd cofounded earlier.

Throughout her career, Raitt remained a committed activist, playing hundreds of benefit concerts and working tirelessly on behalf of the Rhythm and Blues Foundation. By the early '80s, however, her own career was in trouble—1982's *Green Light*, while greeted with the usual good reviews, again failed to break her to a wide audience, and while beginning work on the follow-up, Warners unceremoniously dropped her. By this time, Raitt was also battling drug and alcohol problems as well; she worked on a few tracks with Prince, but their schedules never aligned and the material went unreleased. Instead, she finally released the patchwork *Nine Lives* in 1986, her worst-selling effort since her debut. Many had written Raitt off when she teamed with producer Don Was and recorded *Nick of Time;* seemingly out of the blue, the LP won a handful of Grammys, including Album of the Year, and overnight she was a superstar. 1991's *Luck of the Draw* was also a smash, yielding the hits "Something to Talk About" and "I Can't Make You Love Me." After 1994's *Longing in Their Hearts*, Raitt resurfaced in 1998 with *Fundamental*. —*Jason Ankeny*

Bonnie Raitt / 1971 / Warner Brothers ✦✦✦
By the time Raitt recorded this impressive self-titled debut, she had developed quite a set of blues chops playing with artists like Mississippi Fred McDowell, Howlin' Wolf, and other blues greats. In fact, she enlisted Chicago-bluesmen Junior Wells and A.C. Reed to aid in the proceedings, which are relaxed and earthy. —*Rick Clark*

Give It Up / Sep. 1972 / Warner Brothers ✦✦✦✦
Raitt's sophomore release is a classic. Of all the albums from her days with Warner, this is the one that put together her folky singer-songwriter sensitivities with her love for country-blues. *Give It Up*, which took 13 years to go gold, showcased an intelligent song selection, with tracks by Jackson Browne ("Under the Falling Sky"), Eric Kaz ("Love Has No Pride"), and Joel Zoss ("Been Too Long at the Fair"). Her self-penned "Love Me like a Man" highlighted her impressive guitar technique. —*Rick Clark*

Takin' My Time / 1973 / Warner Brothers ✦✦✦✦
Raitt continued her streak of quality albums with *Takin' My Time*. Like her previous efforts, Raitt drew from the cream of the songwriting crop. Randy Newman's "Guilty" and Jackson Browne's "I Thought I Was a Child" are highlights. —*Rick Clark*

Streetlights / 1974 / Warner Brothers ✦✦✦
This album was undermined by slick production and unnecessary orchestration. At the time, Raitt seemed to be fighting the production by Jerry Ragovoy. Versions of Joni Mitchell's "That Song About the Midway" and Allen Toussaint's "What Is Success?" are the main highlights of the album. —*Rick Clark*

Homeplate / 1975 / Warner Brothers ✦✦✦
On this return to form, Raitt shines with some great songs, particularly "Good Enough," "Your Sweet and Shiny Eyes," and "Run Like a Thief." —*Rick Clark*

Sweet Forgiveness / Apr. 1977 / Warner Brothers ✦✦
One of Raitt's lesser efforts, it includes her version of Del Shannon's "Runaway," a minor hit despite being pretty lifeless-sounding. Even though the production isn't quite as slick as *Streetlights*, the relatively weak selection of material is this album's failing. —*Rick Clark*

The Glow / 1979 / Warner Brothers ✦✦✦
With the success of "Runaway," Warner felt it was time to take Raitt all the way by pairing her up with hit-producer Peter Asher (Linda Ronstadt, James Taylor). Gone is the natural earthiness Raitt possessed on her first albums. In its place was an airbrushed slickness—from the cover photo all the way down to the grooves. A rendition of Isaac Hayes and David Porter's "Your Good Thing" and an original, "Standing by the Same Old Love" are among *The Glow*'s few highlights. The single from this album was a Robert Palmer song, "You're Gonna Get What's Coming." — *Rick Clark*

Green Light / 1982 / Warner Brothers ✦✦✦✦
Raitt dumps the slick stuff and goes for the grit with this energetic set, featuring her band, which included keyboardist Ian MacLagan (whose credits included the Stones and Faces). Raitt's sensitive electric slide-guitar work was finally up front in the mix. It's one of her very best albums. Raitt does spirited versions of NRBQ's "Green Light" and "Me and the Boys." Other standouts include the reckless rockers "Willya Wontcha" and "I Can't Help Myself." "River of Tears" is a powerful track that Raitt has dedicated to the memory of Little Feat's Lowell George in shows over the years. — *Rick Clark*

Nine Lives / 1986 / Warner Brothers ✦✦✦
Bonnie Raitt's ninth and final album for Warner Bros. Records was a star-crossed affair that began in 1983 in a session with producer Rob Fraboni, which was a typical Raitt mixture of different genres and songwriters, from Jerry Williams ("Excited") and Eric Kaz ("Angel") to reggae star Toots Hibbert ("True Love Is Hard to Find") in a style similar to her 1982 LP *Green Light*. This record seems to have been rejected by Warner, but three years later Raitt returned to the studio with Bill Payne (Little Feat) and George Massenburgh and cut a group of commercial-sounding songs by the likes of Bryan Adams and Tom Snow. *Nine Lives* splits the difference between the two sessions, with four tracks rescued from 1983, and five added from 1986, plus the theme from a forgotten Farrah Fawcett movie ("Stand Up to the Night" from *Extremities*). The result is predictably scattered and strained, and it was Raitt's lowest-charting album since her debut. Not surprisingly, it was also the last straw in her relationship with Warner. — *William Ruhlmann*

● **Nick of Time** / Mar. 1989 / Capitol ✦✦✦✦
Few comebacks have been as celebrated as Raitt's multi-platinum hit *Nick of Time*, an album that included some of her strongest performances as a musician and singer. The determined "I Will Not Be Denied" seemed to say it all. Her poignant self-penned title cut revealed Raitt as a mature songwriter, on the level of the best writers whose work she had covered. She dug deep with some solid roadhouse R&B in "Love Letter," "Road's My Middle Name," and "Real Man." Her playful version of John Hiatt's "Thing Called Love" was another highlight. All in all, this is a very seamless album. Highly recommended. — *Rick Clark*

The Bonnie Raitt Collection / Jun. 28, 1990 / Warner Brothers ✦✦✦✦
A good (not great) sampler of Raitt's years at Warner, it's also a good starting place. — *Rick Clark*

Luck of the Draw / Jun. 1991 / Capitol ✦✦✦✦
Raitt followed *Nick of Time* with *Luck of the Draw*, another great album. Among the album's many highlights are "I Can't Make You Love Me" and a duet with Delbert McClinton on "Good Man, Good Woman." — *Rick Clark*

Longing in Their Hearts / Mar. 14, 1994 / Capitol ✦✦✦✦
On the follow-up to the follow-up (and another million-selling No. 1 hit), Bonnie Raitt contributes more than her usual share of original songs, writing four songs herself and setting a lyric of her husband's to music for a fifth. Elsewhere, she draws on such strong writers as Richard Thompson and Paul Brady, all for a collection devoted to devotion. Song after song expresses passion, usually with happy results—this is not the album of a woman with the blues. Even when she's dressing down a parent in her own "Circle Dance," Raitt offers forgiveness and understanding. There, and in other songs, the object of her emotions rarely seems to be perfect, but she takes that in and loves him, anyway. Co-producer Don Was provides a detailed production in which single elements—an accordion, a harmony vocal by Levon Helm or David Crosby—effectively color arrangements and complement Raitt's always soulful singing. — *William Ruhlmann*

Road Tested / Nov. 7, 1995 / Capitol ✦✦✦✦
In a 24-year recording career, Bonnie Raitt had not previously released a live album, so this concert set was overdue. Coming off three multi-platinum studio albums, Raitt and Capitol pulled out all the stops, compiling a 22-track, double-disc package from dates recorded in July 1995 in Portland and Oakland. Raitt ranged over her career, reaching back to her early folk-blues days and forward to the pop-rock songs that finally made her a big star in the late '80s and early '90s. She also shared the spotlight with such guests as Bruce Hornsby, Ruth Brown, Charles Brown, Kim Wilson of the Fabulous Thunderbirds, Bryan Adams, and Jackson Browne. But that didn't keep an artist who has spent the bulk of her career pleasing live audiences rather than cutting hits from displaying her personal warmth along with her singing and playing skills. She also introduced half a dozen songs new to her repertoire, including a surprising cover of Talking Heads' "Burning Down the House" and a few that had potential to help promote the album as singles, including "Never Make Your Move Too Soon" and "Shake a Little." Inexplicably, Capitol (which probably wished the album had been a more reasonably priced single-disc) failed to bring the record home to consumers. The company's choice for a single was the anonymous Adams rocker "Rock Steady," done as a duet with him—apparently, they were confusing Raitt with Tina Turner. As a result, the album stopped at gold, spending less than six months in the charts. Despite that commercial disappointment, it will be for many Bonnie Raitt fans an example of her at her best that effectively bridges the two parts of her career, and also a good sampler for first-time listeners. — *William Ruhlmann*

Fundamental / Apr. 7, 1998 / Capitol ✦✦✦
Apparently in an attempt to find new sounds that would appeal to a new audience, Bonnie Raitt severed her ties with her comeback producer Don Was for *Fundamental*, hiring those masterminds of experimental adult pop, Mitchell Froom and Tchad Blake. Although Froom and Blake have worked with a number of singer-songwriters and roots musicians—including Elvis Costello, Suzanne Vega, Richard Thompson, Los Lobos, and Crowded House—they often emphasize the production over the song, pouring on layers of effects and novelty instruments that tend to obscure the songs and performances. While they don't go overboard on *Fundamental*, like they did on Los Lobos' *Colossal Head*, they have pushed too much of their own style on Raitt. There are good songs scattered throughout the record, but it's hard to pick them out underneath the gauzy, murky production. Eventually, the album becomes a bit of a chore, since the sounds wear on the ears. That's too bad, because Raitt remains a vital artist—it's just that Froom and Blake haven't allowed her to rely on her talents here. — *Stephen Thomas Erlewine*

David "Kid" Ramos

b. Orange County, California
Guitar / Contemporary Blues
Guitarist Kid Ramos should be familiar to most fans of blues-rock through his work with Kim Wilson's Fabulous Thunderbirds.

Ramos was raised in Orange County, California, the son of an opera singer. He got his first guitar at 14, but it was the nylon-string variety, so he quickly exchanged it for a steel-string guitar. Ramos' father decided to enroll him in lessons at the local music store, and Ramos proved to be a diligent student. He read *Guitar Player* magazine on his lunch hour at school and practiced every night. He wore out his copies of B.B. King's classic album *Live at the Regal*, and also listened to T-Bone Walker records. After graduating from high school in 1980, Ramos met harmonica player James Harman, who immediately recognized Ramos had potential to be one of the great blues guitarists of the next generation. After sitting in with Harman's band on three occasions, Ramos was tapped to be the group's new guitarist at age 21. Ramos listened to Harman's old recordings and immersed himself in practice and live shows until 1989, when the road life got to be too much for a man about to be married.

Ramos joined Roomful of Blues, filling in for their guitarist after he broke his shoulder, and then began playing with the Blue Shadows as they evolved into the Red Devils, an L.A.-area band. In the early '90s, after Kim Wilson saw him perform, he was asked to join the Fabulous Thunderbirds.

Ramos has an exquisitely good, tone-filled album on the BlackTop label out of New Orleans, *Two Hands One Heart*, a 1995 release. He injects new life into Elmore James' "I Was a Fool," and Don Robey's "Win with Me." His originals also demonstrate that Ramos will be a force to be reckoned with in the blues world for a long time to come. After all, he hasn't yet hit 40. On his debut for Black Top, Ramos is accompanied by Lynnwood Slim on harmonica and vocals, Fred Kaplan on keyboards, and Richard Innes on drums.

Ramos' stellar command of the guitar can also be heard on the Fabulous Thunderbirds' 1995 release for Private Music, *Roll of the Dice.* — *Richard Skelly*

Two Hands One Heart / Oct. 1995 / Black Top ◆◆◆

Al Rapone

b. 1936, Lake Charles, Louisiana
Accordion, Vocals / Zydeco, Contemporary Blues
The brother of zydeco's renowned Queen Ida, accordionist and guitarist Al Rapone was not only a driving force behind the success of his sister but also a noted solo performer. Born Al Lewis in Lake Charles, Louisiana in 1936, he first picked up the accordion at age 13, and following the family's relocation to California he was regularly performing live throughout the West Coast by the early '50s. Within a few years, Rapone also began playing guitar, quickly becoming a noted sideman on the San Francisco blues circuit, where he backed the likes of Big Mama Thornton, Clarence Gatemouth Brown, and Jimmy Reed; while in college, he studied composing, producing, and arranging, and after graduation formed a group with his sister. However, as Queen Ida soon settled down to raise a family, Rapone assembled a new unit, the Bon Ton Zydeco Band, and over time forged a unique sound combing his distinctive guitar leads with zydeco accordion and country music rhythms. Ida began sitting in with the group during the mid-'70s, and as her career blossomed, the Bon Ton Zydeco Band mutated to become her permanent backing band; Rapone served not only as his sister's ace sideman but also as her producer and arranger, helming her 1982 Grammy-winner *Queen Ida and the Bon Ton Zydeco Band on Tour,* as well as composing one of her best-loved songs, "Frisco Zydeco." Soon afterwards, Rapone left the group to again pursue a solo career, enjoying his greatest success in Germany, where he recorded efforts including 1982's *Cajun Creole Music* and 1984's *C'est La Vie;* upon returning stateside, he settled in New Orleans, issuing *Zydeco to Go* in 1990. — *Jason Ankeny*

C'est La Vie! / 1984 / L & R Music ◆◆◆

Zydeco to Go / Oct. 1990 / Blind Pig ◆◆◆◆
On his second album, *Zydeco to Go,* Al Rapone turns out an infectious, joyful record, filled with good spirits and great music. The album is firmly in the classic zydeco tradition, spiked with some blues, R&B, and Cajun country, and Rapone shines on each of the tracks, as does his supple, sympathetic supporting band. His cousin, Roy L. Chantier, drops in to sing a couple of tracks, turning "Our Hearts Will Dance in Love Again" into a beautiful thing and making sure that "Good Ole Cajun Music" and "Yvette U.B. Dancin'" catch fire. Still, this is Rapone's show, and he keeps things cooking with his robust accordion and gleeful vocals. All in all, *Zydeco to Go* is a good-time record that delivers. — *Thom Owens*

● **Plays Tribute: A Tribute to Clifton Chenier** / May 6, 1997 / Atomic Theory ◆◆◆◆
It may be a salute to the master of zydeco, but Al Rapone's *A Tribute to Clifton Chenier* is a terrific testimonial to his own talents as well. Part of the reason the album works so well is that there isn't a weak song on the record—in fact, almost all of the 15 songs are acknowledged zydeco classics. These songs give Rapone a platform for his rambunctious, infectious accordion style. He plays these songs a little bluesier than Chenier, but it's great to hear them played in a different way, and the record itself is just a blast. — *Thom Owens*

Moses Rascoe

b. Jul. 27, 1917, Windsor, NC, **d.** Mar. 6, 1994, Lebanon, PA
Guitar, Vocals / Modern Acoustic Blues
Moses Rascoe got his first guitar in North Carolina at the age of 13 and turned professional in Pennsylvania some 50-odd years later. In between, he traveled the roads as a day laborer and truck driver, playing guitar only for "a dollar or a drink," as he told Jack Roberts in *Living Blues.* But he'd picked up plenty of songs over the years, from old Brownie McGhee Piedmont blues

to Jimmy Reed's '50s jukebox hits, and when he retired from trucking at the age of 65, he gave his music a shot. The local folk-music community took notice, as did blues and folk festivals from Chicago to Europe. Rascoe recorded his first album live at Godfrey Daniels, a Pennsylvania coffeehouse, in 1987. — *Jim O'Neal*

Blues / 1987 / Flying Fish ◆◆◆◆
A former truck driver turned touring bluesman, Rascoe primarily covers other people's tunes and classic blues themes. There is much Jimmy Reed and "traditional" material. — *Niles J. Frantz*

Johnny Rawls

Vocals / Soul Blues, Contemporary Blues
Singer, songwriter, guitarist, arranger, and producer Johnny Rawls draws on the 1950s' and '60s' deep soul-blues tradition in his guitar playing, yet his lyrics and singing are completely 1990s.

Rawls got his early musical education from his grandfather, John Paul Newson, a blind guitarist who played around the Hattiesburg area. Rawls began playing clarinet and saxophone in third grade, and by the time he was in his teens, the band instructor hired Rawls to play in his band. As a teen, Rawls had the opportunity to back singers like Joe Tex and Z.Z. Hill. He began playing guitar at age 12, learning as much as he could from players in other area blues bands. After leaving Mississippi for a year when he was 17, he returned, determined to form his own blues/soul ensemble. They found work backing up touring musicians and by the mid-'70s, Rawls joined O.V. Wright's band, working with Wright until his death in 1980. After Wright's death, the band continued to perform his music for 13 years as the O.V. Wright Band, opening shows for people like B.B. King, Little Milton Campbell, and Bobby Bland. In the mid-'80s, the O.V. Wright Band also toured with Little Johnny Taylor, Latimore, B.B. Coleman, Blues Boy Willie, and others, including Lynn White.

Working with guitarist L.C. Luckett, Rawls recorded 45 rpm singles for his own label, Touch Records, and continued working around the South, touring regionally with soul-blues singers. In 1994, Rawls and Luckett recorded their first album, *Can't Sleep at Night,* for the Rooster Blues label. In 1995, Rawls parted with Luckett to lead a new group and found a record company that was interested, the London-based JSP label. *Here We Go,* his debut for JSP Records, was recorded in 1996, and since then, he's followed it up with *Louisiana Woman,* a 1997 release.

Rawls carries on the soul-blues tradition of people like O.V. Wright, Otis Redding, and Z.Z. Hill in his singing style and guitar playing, but his arrangement, production and lyrics are steeped in the 1990s techniques and subject matter. Rawls is a true soul-blues renaissance man and with any luck. — *Richard Skelly*

● **Here We Go** / Aug. 27, 1996 / JSP ◆◆◆◆
Johnny Rawls turns in an impressive debut with *Here We Go.* Although he doesn't do anything new to the soul-blues genre, the record is entertaining in the vein of Z.Z. Hill and latter-day Bobby Bland. Rawls has a powerful, soulful voice which can make mediocre material sound convincing. Unfortunately, there are a few too many half-hearted cuts here, but that doesn't prevent the album from being a promising debut. — *Thom Owens*

Louisiana Woman / Sep. 9, 1997 / JSP ◆◆◆

Dave Ray & Tony Glover

Vocals, Guitar, Harmonica / Modern Acoustic Blues
Minnesota based singer/guitarist Dave "Snaker" Ray and harmonica player Tony "Little Sun" Glover recorded both solo, duet, and trio efforts with guitarist/singer-songwriter "Spider" John Koerner throughout the early '60s. Among the first to successfully tackle the Delta Blues form and do it well. — *AMG*

Ashes in My Whiskey / 1990 / Rough Trade ◆◆◆
Ashes in My Whiskey is the first studio record Ray & Glover made since 1965 and it proves that even with the extended layoff, the duo remained vital. They play a set of 15 acoustic, traditional blues numbers that include a couple of startlingly successful originals, particularly the haunting "HIV Blues." But the key to the record's success is the sympathetic, natural interplay the guitar-

ist and harpist have—their performances offer definitive proof that many bluesmen get better with age. — *Thom Owens*

Kenny "Blue" Ray

b. Jan. 11, 1950, Lodi, CA
Guitar / Modern Electric Blues

Guitarist Kenny "Blue" Ray has the kind of fat guitar overtones, complex chord changes, and lightning-fast chops that tend to draw rock fans into the blues fold. Not unlike Stevie Ray Vaughan, Ray's playing owes almost as much to his rock influences as to his blues mentors.

Ray's resume includes performances and recording sessions with William Clarke, Little Charlie and the Nightcats, Charlie Musselwhite, Smokey Wilson, and a bevy of other West Coast blues stylists.

Ray first became interested in music via his father, who played guitars, harmonica, fiddle, and piano. Seeing Elvis Presley perform on the *Ed Sullivan Show* was a turning point for him, and later that year, his father bought him a guitar. As a youngster, Ray would listen to disc jockey Wolfman Jack at night, listening to music by Jimmy Reed, Howlin' Wolf, and others. Ray often skipped school to play guitar with his friends. He made his amateur debut at a high school dance in the mid-'60s.

While in the Air Force, Ray was stationed in London from 1969 to 1972. There, he met Ferdnand Jones and began playing '60s-style soul and blues. After coming back to the US, Ray toured with the Paul Hermann Band until 1975, when he took a job as lead guitarist with Little Charlie and the Nightcats, then a regional northern California band.

In 1976, Ray left the Nightcats to head back to Los Angeles. There, he became part of the house band at a club run by guitarist and singer Smokey Wilson. Onstage at Wilson's Pioneer Club, Ray had the chance to back up legendary artists like Big Joe Turner, Pee Wee Crayton, Lowell Fulson, and Big Mama Thornton. A few years later, Ray made his recording session debut with the likes of harmonica player William Clarke and vocalist Finis Tasby.

After moving to Austin, Texas in 1980, Ray joined the Marcia Ball Band, touring with her for four years around the Texas Triangle. Ray can be heard on Ball's 1985 album for Rounder, *Soulful Dress*. He befriended guitarist Stevie Ray Vaughan and continued his career as a session man, recording with Ball, Mitch Woods, Charlie Musselwhite, Greg "Fingers" Taylor, Ron Thompson, and Tommy Castro, among dozens of others.

By 1990, Ray decided it was time to start leading his own band, and in 1994, he recorded *Fired Up!*, the first album for his own Blue Ray/Tone King label. Ray's releases helped broaden his touring base beyond central Texas and northern California. His other mid-'90s recordings include *Cadillac Tone* (1995), *Pull the Strings* (1996), and *Git It!* (1997), all for his own Blue Ray/Tone King label. Most recently, Ray recorded *In All of My Life* (1997) for the London-based JSP Records. He was accompanied by John Firmin (tenor sax), of the Johnny Nocturne Band, as well as Rob Sudduth of Huey Lewis and the News on baritone and tenor saxes.

On record and on stages around the US, Ray's guitar playing reflects his smorgasbord of influences: Albert King, Stevie Ray Vaughan, Albert Collins, and Aaron "T-Bone" Walker. His vocals are powerful and soul-filled. Ray continues to tour around the US, Canada, and Europe. — *Richard Skelly*

Fired Up / 1995 / Blue Ray ♦♦♦

● **In All of My Life** / May 6, 1997 / JSP ♦♦♦♦
Kenny Ray delivered on his promise with 1997's *In All of My Life*. Working with vocalist Jimmy Morello and a horn section, Ray has created an album that hits as hard as blues but swings like soul. He keeps things from becoming predictable by contributing some gutsy, idiosyncratic guitar work. Morello's vocals follow the same path, and the result is a wonderful blues record that honors traditions by not being beholden to them. — *Thom Owens*

A.C. Reed

b. May 9, 1926, Wardell, MO, **d.** 1976
Saxophone, Vocals / Electric Chicago Blues, Soul Blues, Modern Electric Chicago Blues

To hear tenor saxist A.C. Reed bemoan his fate onstage, one might glean the impression that he truly detests his job. But it's a tongue-in-cheek complaint—Reed's raspy, gutbucket blowing and laidback vocals bely any sense of boredom.

Sax-blowing blues bandleaders are scarce as hen's teeth in Chicago; other than Eddie Shaw, Reed's about all there is. Born in Missouri, young Aaron Corthen (whether he's related to blues legend Jimmy Reed remains hazy, but his laconic vocal drawl certainly mirrors his namesake) grew up in downstate Illinois. A big-band fan, he loved the sound of Paul Bascomb's horn on an obscure Erskine Hawkins 78 he heard tracking on a tavern jukebox so much that he was inspired to pick up a sax himself.

Arriving in Chicago during the war years, he picked up steady gigs with Earl Hooker and Willie Mabon before the '40s were over. In 1956, he joined forces with ex-Ike Turner cohort Dennis "Long Man" Binder, gigging across the southwest for an extended period. Reed became a valuable session player for producer Mel London's Age and Chief labels during the early '60s; in addition to playing on sides by Lillian Offitt, Ricky Allen, and Hooker, he cut a locally popular 1961 single of his own for Age, "This Little Voice."

More gems for Age—"Come on Home," "Mean Cop," "I Stay Mad" —followed. He cut 45s for USA in 1963 ("I'd Rather Fight than Switch"), Cool ("My Baby Is Fine," a tune he's recut countless times since), and Nike ("Talkin' 'bout My Friends") in 1966, and "Things I Want You to Do" in 1969 for T.D.S.

Reed joined Buddy Guy's band in 1967, visiting Africa with the mercurial guitarist in 1969 and, after harpist Junior Wells teamed with Guy, touring as opening act for the Rolling Stones in 1970. He left the employ of Guy and Wells for good in 1977, only to hook up with Alligator acts Son Seals and then the Master of the Telecaster, Albert Collins. Reed appeared on Collins' first five icy Alligator LPs, including the seminal *Ice Pickin'.*

During his tenure with Collins, Reed's solo career began to reignite, with four cuts on the second batch of Alligator's *Living Chicago Blues* anthologies in 1980 and two subsequent LPs of his own, 1982's *Take These Blues and Shove 'em!* (on Ice Cube Records, a logo co-owned by Reed and drummer Casey Jones) and *I'm in the Wrong Business!* five years later for Alligator (with cameos by Bonnie Raitt and Stevie Ray Vaughan). Reed remains an active force on the Chicago circuit with his band, the Spark Plugs (get it? AC sparkplugs? Sure you do!). — *Bill Dahl*

Take These Blues and Shove 'em / 1982 / Rooster Blues ♦♦♦
The first of the saxist's humorous diatribes detailing his tongue-in-cheek hatred of his life's calling. His argument doesn't hold water, though, since the LP is so refreshingly funky ("I Am Fed Up with This Music" remains a bandstand staple for him) and enjoyable. Drummer Casey Jones, Reed's longtime bandmate behind Albert Collins, co-produced with the sardonic horn man. — *Bill Dahl*

● **I'm in the Wrong Business** / 1987 / Alligator ♦♦♦♦
Solid, soulful blues, often with humorous, self-deprecating lyrics, comes from the well-respected vocalist, tenor player, composer, and veteran of the bands of Albert Collins, Buddy Guy, Magic Sam, and Son Seals. Reed has been called "the definitive Chicago blues sax player." This album features Reed's band, with guests Bonnie Raitt and Stevie Ray Vaughan. — *Niles J. Frantz*

Dalton Reed

b. Aug. 23, 1952, Cade, LA, **d.** Sep. 24, 1994, Minneapolis, MN
Vocals / Modern Louisiana Blues

Dalton Reed attempted to keep the sweet sound of deep soul alive in the '90s. The Lafayette, LA, singer comes from a gospel background—a prerequisite for success in the genre—and cut his first single for his own little label in 1986.

When he was child, Dalton Reed sang gospel in church and played trumpet in his high school marching band. Reed fell in love with R&B and soul as a teenager, prompting him to join a few local bands. Soon, he formed his own group, Dalton Reed and the Musical Journey Band. In a short while, the band was playing bars and clubs throughout Louisiana, Alabama, and Texas.

Reed founded his own record label, Sweet Daddy Records, in 1986, releasing his debut single, "Givin' on in to Love," that same year. Within a few years after the formation of Sweet Daddy, Dalton and his brother Johnny Reed formed another independent label, Reed Brothers Records.

In 1990, Bullseye Blues signed Dalton Reed and the label released his debut album, *Louisiana Soul Man*, the following year. Three years later, his second album, *Willing & Able*, appeared. When he wasn't recording, Reed toured, playing concerts throughout America. — *Bill Dahl*

Louisiana Soul Man / Dec. 1991 / Bullseye Blues ♦♦♦
Dalton Reed's *Louisiana Soul Man* establishes the singer as an heir to the deep Southern soul of such artists as Otis Redding, Arthur Conley, and Percy

Sledge. Despite the title, there's no hint of cajun music or zydeco on the record—it's pure testifying from start to finish. The new material is usually quite good, and it should be with songwriters like Doc Pomus, Dr. John, Dan Penn, and Delbert McClinton involved. *Louisiana Soul Man* is for anyone who believed that pure Southern soul died with Otis Redding. *—Thom Owens*

● **Willing & Able** / Mar. 30, 1994 / Bullseye Blues ✦✦✦✦
Dalton Reed is a classic gospel-based soul vocalist. There's nothing sophisticated in his approach, staid in his delivery, or polite and detached in his sound. He explodes, attacks, and rips through the 10 tracks on his second Bullseye blues LP, his voice full of animation and expressiveness. These songs are done in the vivid, overwrought manner considered too intense by the urban contemporary tastemakers; you won't hear trendy backgrounds or drum machines on these numbers. This is unapologetic soul from a vocalist who will never appeal to the crossover audience, but is making some of the better R&B in today's market. *— Ron Wynn*

Francine Reed

b. Jul. 11, 1947, Kankakee, IL
Vocals / Modern Electric Blues
Vocalist Francine Reed can't remember a time when she didn't sing. In her youth, the Chicago-born, Phoenix-raised song stylist sang in church and in grammar school. She began singing professionally with her family when she was five and continued into her teens. She got married young and had four children, whom she ended up raising alone. She worked a variety of day jobs and kept her singing career an avocation until 1985, when some friends introduced her to Lyle Lovett. Lovett was interested in finding a female vocalist for his new band and found his singer in Reed. She toured with Lovett for ten years as a member of Lovett's Large Band, and did several TV performances with the Texas singer-songwriter. While her association with Lovett continues, she has embarked on the kind of solo career she always wanted when working the day jobs to support her family.

To date, Reed has recorded two albums for the Atlanta-based Ichiban label in 1995 and 1996. Her amphitheater performances with Lovett must have surely had an effect on sales of both of her records. Reed also got a few other nice breaks, including the chance to do some singing for TV commercials. Tom Cruise cranks her album up in a scene from the 1993 movie *The Firm.*

Reed's two albums for Ichiban include *I Want You to Love Me* (1995) and *Can't Make It on My Own* (1996). The former features a duet with bandleader Lovett, while the latter includes a duet with Delbert McClinton. On both albums, Reed continues the tradition already set down by great women soul-blues vocalists like Carla Thomas, Irma Thomas, and Etta James. *—Richard Skelly*

● **I Want You to Love Me** / Apr. 25, 1995 / Ichiban ✦✦✦✦
By the time she released her debut album, Francine Reed had established herself as a fine blues singer through her work with Lyle Lovett. *I Want You to Love Me* proves that she can do it on her own. Lovett drops in for the opening cut, "Why I Don't Know," but this remains Reed's show, and she shows she knows what she's doing. She can sing sultry slow blues, belt out soul, and get down and dirty—in short, she can do it all. Furthermore, she has the songs to prove her talents, relying on classics from Jerry Butler and Muddy Waters, among others. The result is a thoroughly entertaining record from an accomplished artist. *— Thom Owens*

Can't Make It on My Own / 1996 / Ichiban International ✦✦✦

Jimmy Reed (Mathis James Reed)

b. Sep. 6, 1925, Dunleith, MS, **d.** Aug. 29, 1976, Oakland, CA
Guitar, Harmonica, Vocals / R&B, Electric Chicago Blues, Chicago Blues, Harmonica Blues, Blues Revival
There's simply no sound in the blues as easily digestible, accessible, instantly recognizable and as easy to play and sing as the music of Jimmy Reed. His best-known songs—"Baby, What You Want Me to Do," "Bright Lights, Big City," "Honest I Do," "You Don't Have to Go," "Going to New York," "Ain't That Lovin' You Baby," and "Big Boss Man"—have become such an integral part of the standard blues repertoire, it's almost as if they have existed forever. Because his style was simple and easily imitated, his songs were accessible to just about everyone from high school garage bands having a go at it to

Elvis Presley, Charlie Rich, Lou Rawls, Hank Williams, Jr., and the Rolling Stones, making him—in the long run—perhaps the most influential bluesman of all. His bottom string boogie rhythm guitar patterns (all furnished by boyhood friend and longtime musical partner Eddie Taylor), simple two-string turnarounds, countryish harmonica solos (all played in a neck rack attachment hung around his neck), and mush mouthed vocals were probably the first exposure most White folks had to the blues. And his music—lazy, loping, and insistent and constantly built and reconstructed single after single on the same sturdy frame—was a formula that proved to be enormously successful and influential, both with middle-aged Blacks and young White audiences for a good dozen years. Jimmy Reed records hit the R&B charts with amazing frequency and crossed over onto the pop charts on many occasions, a rare feat for an unreconstructed bluesman. This is all the more amazing simply because Reed's music was nothing special on the surface; he possessed absolutely no technical expertise on either of his chosen instruments and his vocals certainly lacked the fierce declamatory intensity of a Howlin' Wolf or a Muddy Waters. But it was *exactly* that lack of in-your-face musical confrontation that made Jimmy Reed a welcome addition to everybody's record collection back in the '50s and '60s. And for those aspiring musicians who wanted to give the blues a try, either vocally or instrumentally (no matter what skin color you were born with), perhaps Billy Vera said it best in his liner notes to a Reed greatest hits anthology: "Yes, anybody with a range of more than six notes could sing Jimmy's tunes and play them the first day Mom and Dad brought home that first guitar from Sears & Roebuck. I guess Jimmy could be termed the '50s punk bluesman."

Reed was born on September 6, 1925, on a plantation in or around the small burg of Dunleith, MS. He stayed around the area until he was 15, learning the basic rudiments of harmonica and guitar from his buddy Eddie Taylor, who was then making a name for himself as a semi-pro musician, working country suppers and juke joints. Reed moved up to Chicago in 1943, but was quickly drafted into the Navy, where he served for two years. After a quick trip back to Mississippi and marriage to his beloved wife Mary (known to blues fans as "Mama Reed"), he relocated to Gary, IN, and found work at an Armour Foods meat packing plant while simultaneously breaking into the burgeoning blues scene around Gary and neighboring Chicago. The early '50s found him working as a sideman with John Brim's Gary Kings (that's Reed blowing harp on Brim's classic "Tough Times" and its instrumental flipside, "Gary Stomp") and playing on the street for tips with Willie Joe Duncan, a shadowy figure who played an amplified, homemade one-string instrument called a Unitar. After failing an audition with Chess Records (his later chart success would be a constant thorn in the side of the firm), Brim's drummer at the time—improbably enough, future blues guitar legend Albert King—brought him over to the newly formed Vee-Jay Records where his first recordings were made. It was during this time that he was reunited and started playing again with Eddie Taylor, a musical partnership that would last off and on until Reed's death. Success was slow in coming, but when his third single, "You Don't Have to Go" backed with "Boogie in the Dark," made the No. 5 slot on *Billboard*'s R&B charts, the hits pretty much kept on coming for the next decade.

But if selling more records than Muddy Waters, Howlin' Wolf, Elmore James, or Little Walter brought the rewards of fame to his doorstep, no one was more ill-equipped to handle it than Jimmy Reed. With signing his name for fans being the total sum of his literacy, combined with a back-breaking road schedule once he became a name attraction and his self-description as a "liquor glutter," Reed started to fall apart like a cheap suit almost immediately. His devious schemes to tend to his alcoholism—and the just plain aberrant behavior that came as a result of it—quickly made him the laughing stock of his show business contemporaries. Those who shared the bill with him in top-of-the-line R&B venues like the Apollo Theater—where the story of him urinating on a star performer's dress in the wings has been repeated verbatim by more than one old-timer—still shake their heads and wonder how Jimmy could actually stand up straight and perform, much less hold the audience in the palm of his hand. Other stories of Jimmy being "arrested" and thrown into a Chicago drunk tank the night before a recording session also reverberate throughout the blues community to this day. Little wonder then that when he was stricken with epilepsy in 1957, it went undiagnosed for an extended period of time, simply because he had experienced so many attacks of delirium tremens, better known as the "DTs." Eddie Taylor would relate how he sat directly in front of Reed in the studio, instructing him while the tune was being recorded, exactly when to start to start singing, when to blow his harp, and when to do the turnarounds on his guitar. He also appears, by all accounts, to have been unable to remember the lyrics to new songs—even ones he had composed himself—and Mama Reed would sit on a piano bench and whisper them into his ear, literally one line at a time. Blues fans who doubt this can clearly hear the proof on several of Jimmy's biggest hits, most notably "Big Boss Man" and "Bright Lights, Big City," where she steps into the fore and starts singing along with him in order to keep him on the beat.

But seemingly none of this mattered. While revisionist blues historians like to make a big deal about either the lack of variety of his work or how later recordings turned him into a mere parody of himself, the public just couldn't get enough of it. Jimmy Reed placed 11 songs on the *Billboard* Hot 100 pop charts and a total of 14 on the R&B charts, a figure that even a much more sophisticated artist like B.B. King couldn't top. To paraphrase the old saying, nobody liked Jimmy Reed but the people.

Reed's slow descent into the ravages of alcoholism and epilepsy roughly paralleled the decline of Vee-Jay Records, which went out of business at approximately the same time that his final 45 was released, "Don't Think I'm Through." His manager, Al Smith, quickly arranged a contract with the newly formed ABC-Bluesway label and a handful of albums were released into the '70s, all of them lacking the old charm, sounding as if they were cut on a musical assembly line. Jimmy did one last album, a horrible attempt to update his sound with funk beats and wah-wah pedals, before becoming a virtual recluse in his final years. He finally received proper medical attention for his epilepsy and quit drinking, but it was too late and he died trying to make a comeback on the blues festival circuit on August 29, 1976.

All of this is sad beyond belief, simply because there's so much joy in Jimmy Reed's music. And it's that joy that becomes self evident every time you give one of his classic sides a spin. Although his bare bones style influenced everyone from British Invasion combos to the entire school of Louisiana swamp blues artists (Slim Harpo and Jimmy Anderson in particular), the simple indisputable fact remains that—like so many of the other originators in the genre—there was only one Jimmy Reed. —*Cub Koda*

I'm Jimmy Reed / 1959 / Vee-Jay ✦✦✦✦
This debut album, loaded with classic hits, is the perfect place to begin any Reed collection. —*Bill Dahl*

The Best of Jimmy Reed [Vee-Jay] / 1961 / Vee-Jay ✦✦✦✦
Another tough-to-beat old album full of Reed's finest and most influential work. —*Bill Dahl*

★ **Live at Carnegie Hall: The Best of Jimmy Reed** / Aug. 1961 / Mobile Fidelity ✦✦✦✦✦
This was originally issued as a vinyl double album by Vee-Jay in the early '60s. The first 12 tracks are not "live" at all (the disclaimer is in the liners) but instead are some nice middle-period studio tracks while the following dozen constitutes a "reissue" of the label's *Best of Jimmy Reed* album. Stereophiles will love this as the sound is Mobile Fidelity impeccable, even on the mono masters, while stereo masters of such classics as "Baby What You Want Me to Do" and "Big Boss Man" sound almost revelatory. Not the place to start (even with most of the hits aboard), but if you have to have some classic Jimmy Reed in clean stereo, this is the place to go. —*Cub Koda*

Just Jimmy Reed / 1962 / Vee-Jay ✦✦✦
Strong Vee-Jay collection. —*Bill Dahl*

The Best of the Blues / 1963 / Vee-Jay ✦✦✦✦

The Blues Is My Business / May 1976 / Vee-Jay ✦✦✦
Decent LP with several rarities. —*Bill Dahl*

High & Lonesome / 1981 / Charly ✦✦✦✦
A great collection of Reed's earliest and rarest sides. —*Cub Koda*

Upside Your Head / 1985 / Charly ✦✦✦✦
The loping, laconic Jimmy Reed sound was never better than during his Vee-Jay years. This is a tremendous collection gathering 16 tunes from the mid-'50s to the mid-'60s. Since Vee-Jay is now issuing Reed titles themselves, you might want to save the import difference and get them, but if you ever see this, don't hesitate to get it either on disc or in vinyl. —*Ron Wynn*

Big Boss Blues / 1986 / Charly ✦✦✦✦
Although many "best of Jimmy Reed" compilations exist on the market

(most with variable sound quality and maddening duplication), this import features all the influential hits and is the perfect place to start. —*Cub Koda*

Bright Lights, Big City / 1988 / Chameleon ✦✦✦
One of the many "best of Jimmy Reed" albums released over the years, *Bright Lights, Big City* is a 16-song CD that the independent Chameleon put out in 1988 for its Vee-Jay Hall of Fame series. The liner notes are poor; exact recording dates and personnel are missing, and a brief summary only scratches the surface in describing Reed's accomplishments. But the sound quality isn't bad, and the material itself is nothing to complain about. Laidback hits like "Baby, What You Want Me to Do," "Big Boss Man," "Honest I Do," and "Shame, Shame, Shame" are included along with some enjoyable rarities, including the playful "Sugar, Sugar," the infectious "Don't Say Nothin'" and "Honey, Where You Goin'." These 16 songs certainly wouldn't be a bad introduction to Reed's legacy, but a bluesman of his magnitude deserves better than Chameleon's skimpy, inadequate liner notes. —*Alex Henderson*

Ride 'em on Down / 1989 / Charly ✦✦✦✦
Reed shares this compilation with Eddie Taylor (with Reed in support on four tracks) and features a dozen tracks from Reed's early days. Good sound throughout (this has the most listenable disc transfer of Reed's first single "High & Lonesome") and the perfect companion piece to the above. —*Cub Koda*

Best of Jimmy Reed [JCI] / 1990 / JCI ✦✦
More than a few best-of-compilations by Jimmy Reed by have been released over the years. This particular release came out in 1990 as part of JCI's poorly assembled Masters of the Blues series, for which the small, L.A.-based label dug into the Chess or Vee-Jay vaults and released CDs by John Lee Hooker, Howlin' Wolf, Muddy Waters, Etta James, and others. The packaging and liner notes on *The Best of Jimmy Reed* are embarassing—neither exact recording dates nor personnel are listed—although the selections are first rate. From "Bright Lights, Big City" and "Big Boss Man" to "Pretty Thing," "Honest I Do," and "Baby, What You Want Me To Do," most of Reed's essential Vee-Jay hits are here. Everything on this 18-song CD illustrates just how charismatic and distinctive a bluesman Reed was, but sadly, the sound quality is far from ideal—digital remastering was never JCI's strong point. Between the sound and the packaging, JCI should have been ashamed. —*Alex Henderson*

Jimmy Reed / 1991 / Paula/Flyright ✦✦✦
With so much attention paid to Jimmy's seminal Vee-Jay sides, it's hard to realize that he had a recording career that extended past the label's demise in the mid-'60s. But with manager Al Smith producing, Reed turned out a bushel basket of albums for the ABC-Bluesway and Exodus labels, the best of which are collected here. These 21 tracks—recorded between 1966 and 1971—vary quite a bit from the original vinyl issues, which were edited and sometimes retitled for release. Not Reed at his best, but for a complete picture of the man and his music, you'll definitely want to add this one to the pile. —*Cub Koda*

★ **Speak the Lyrics to Me, Mama Reed** / Jan. 1993 / Vee-Jay ✦✦✦✦✦
Although many *Best of Jimmy Reed* compilations exist on the market (most with variable sound quality and maddening duplication), this 25-tracker is currently the one to beat. Including all the influential hits and a few of the best rare ones ("You Upset My Mind" and the single version of "Little Rain," different than the take on his debut album), this features impeccable sound (except on the disc transfer of Reed's first single, "High & Lonesome") and is the perfect place to start. —*Cub Koda*

Classic Recordings / 1995 / Tomato ✦✦✦✦
This three-CD, 55-song box is the most comprehensive domestic retrospective of Reed's career (a six-CD box is available on import). The material is fine and consistent, but this isn't the best deal for either the average fan or the completist. Reed is one of the most homogenous blues greats, and unless your interest is deep, three CDs at once will become monotonous; you're better off with one of the several fine single-disc compilations available. Also, this has no information whatsoever on release dates or session info, and inexplicably omits one of his two Top 40 hits, "Honest I Do" (covered by the Rolling Stones on their first album). —*Richie Unterberger*

Lula Reed

Vocals / R&B, Electric R&B
A longtime cohort of pianist/producer Sonny Thompson, singer Lula Reed recorded steadily for Cincinnati-based King Records during the mid-'50s after

debuting on wax in 1951 to sing Thompson's original version of the moving ballad "I'll Drown in My Tears" (a 1956 smash for Ray Charles as "Drown in My Own Tears").

After serving as Thompson's vocalist at first, the attractive chanteuse was sufficiently established by 1952 to rate her own King releases. She was versatile, singing urban blues most of the time but switching to gospel for a 1954 session. Reed's strident 1954 waxing "Rock Love" was later revived by labelmate Little Willie John. She briefly moved to the Chess subsidiary Argo in 1958-59 but returned to the fold in 1961 (as always, under Thompson's direction) on King's Federal imprint. While at Federal, she waxed a series of sassy duets with guitarist Freddy King in March of 1962. Another move—to Ray Charles' Tangerine logo in 1962-63—soon followed. After that, her whereabouts are unknown. —Bill Dahl

● **Blue and Moody** / 1959 / King ◆◆◆◆
The longtime protegé of King Records house pianist/arranger/producer Sonny Thompson possessed a sultry style well-suited to blues ballads in the urban vein and lighthearted upbeat fare—both of which reside on this reissue of her vintage King album. —Bill Dahl

Johnny Reno

b. AR
Sax (Baritone), Sax (Tenor) / R&B, Retro-Soul
Best known as the frontman of the jump-blues revival unit the Sax Maniacs, tenor saxophonist Johnny Reno was also among the most prominent sidemen on the contemporary Texas blues circuit. A native of Arkansas, Reno first emerged during the late '70s as a member of Stevie Ray Vaughan's Triple Threat Revue; from 1980 to 1983, he also played with the Fort Worth-based Juke Jumpers. He led the Sax Maniacs for much of the decade, and alongside such like-minded groups as Roomful of Blues helped keep the horn-powered sound of traditional jump-blues alive during the modern era. At the tail end of the '80s, he formed the Johnny Reno Band, a more rock-influenced concern than his previous projects; after spending the early '90s touring with Chris Isaak, Reno then moved on to his next retro-styled band, the self-expanatory Lounge Kings. —Jason Ankeny

Born to Blow / 1983 / Black Top ◆◆◆◆
Johnny Reno & the Sax Maniacs is arguably the best release the saxophonist and his band have ever cut, a jumping, swinging set of blues and R&B in the style of classic '50s swing. — Thom Owens

Full Blown / 1985 / Rounder ◆◆◆

● **Johnny Reno & the Sax Maniacs** / 198 / Black Top ◆◆◆◆

Sonny Rhodes

b. Nov. 3, 1940, Smithville, TX
Bass, Guitar, Guitar (Steel), Vocals / Modern Electric Blues, Texas Blues
Blues guitarist, singer and songwriter Sonny Rhodes is such a talented songwriter, so full of musical ideas, that he's destined to inherit the seats left open by the untimely passing of blues greats like Albert King and Albert Collins.

Born November 3, 1940 in Smithville, TX, he was the sixth and last child of Le Roy and Julia Smith, who were sharecroppers. Rhodes began playing seriously when he was 12, although he got his first guitar when he was eight as a Christmas present. Rhodes began performing around Smithville and nearby Austin in the late '50s, while still in his teens. Rhodes listened to a lot of T-Bone Walker when he was young, and it shows in his playing today. Other guitarists he credits as being influences include Pee Wee Crayton and B.B. King. Rhodes' first band, Clarence Smith and the Daylighters, played the Austin area blues clubs before Rhodes decided to join the Navy after graduating from high school.

In the Navy, he moved west to California, where he worked for awhile as a radio man and closed-circuit Navy ship disc-jockey, telling off-color jokes in between the country and blues records he would spin for the entertainment of the sailors.

Rhodes recorded a single for Domino Records in Austin, "I'll Never Let You Go When Something Is Wrong," in 1958, and also learned to play bass. He played bass behind Freddie King and his friend Albert Collins. After his stint in the Navy, Rhodes returned to California while in his mid-20s, and lived in Fresno for a few years before hooking up a deal with Galaxy Records in Oakland. In 1966, he recorded a single, "I Don't Love You No More" b/w

"All Night Long I Play the Blues." He recorded another single for Galaxy in 1967 and then in 1978, out of total frustration with the San Francisco Bay Area record companies, he recorded "Cigarette Blues" b/w "Bloodstone Beat" on his own label. Rhodes toured Europe in 1976, and that opened a whole new European market to him, and he was recorded by several European labels, but without much success. His European recordings include *I Don't Want My Blues Colored Bright* and a live album, *In Europe*. In desperation again, Rhodes went into the studio again to record an album in 1985, *Just Blues*, on his own Rhodesway label.

Fortunately, things have been on track for Rhodes since the late '80s, when he began recording first for the Ichiban label and later for Kingsnake. His albums for Ichiban include *Disciple of the Blues* (1991) and *Living Too Close to the Edge* (1992).

More recently, Rhodes has gotten better distribution of his albums with the Sanford, Florida-based Kingsnake label. Aside from his self-produced 1985 release *Just Blues* (now available on compact disc through Evidence Music), his best albums include the ones he's recorded for Kingsnake, for these are the records that have gotten Rhodes and his various backup bands out on the road together throughout the US, Canada, and Europe. They include *The Blues Is My Best Friend* and his 1995 release, *Out of Control*. On these albums we hear Rhodes, the fully developed songwriter, and not surprisingly, both releases drew high marks from blues critics. —Richard Skelly

Disciple of the Blues / 1991 / Ichiban ◆◆◆◆
This be-turbaned bluesman plays lap steel guitar. This is a good one, but he's got an even better one in him. —Niles J. Frantz

● **Livin' Too Close to the Edge** / 1992 / Ichiban ◆◆◆◆
Livin' Too Close to the Edge is an exciting, blistering set of contemporary blues, drivin by Sonny Rhodes' innovative lap steel playing. — Thom Owens

The Blues Is My Best Friend / 1994 / King Snake ◆◆◆

Won't Rain in California / Feb. 22, 1996 / Epm Musique ◆◆◆

Out of Control / Mar. 19, 1996 / King Snake ◆◆◆◆

I Don't Want My Blues Colored Bright / May 27, 1997 / Black Magic ◆◆◆

Born to Be Blue / Sep. 23, 1997 / Kingpin ◆◆◆

Rev. D.C. Rice

b. 1888, Barbour County, Alabama, **d.** Mar. 1973
Vocals / Black Gospel
The sound of Reverend D.C. Rice is one part fiery preaching and two parts scratchy-but-sanctified singing. It is also heavily influenced by the 78s of Reverend J.M. Gates and most especially by those of Rev. F.W. McGee. Born and raised a Baptist's son in Barbour County, Alabama, Rice left his rural home in the late teens and moved to Chicago. There he joined Bishop Hill's Pentecostal congregation at the Church of the Living God. Around 1920, following the death of Bishop Hill, Rice became the leader of a tiny Church of the Living God congregation; he was a strong preacher and soon found himself attracting a following. After hearing the recordings of the aforementioned preachers, he was inspired to make his own records and so went to Vocalion to meet with Jack Knapp. Knapp sent some folks to Rice's next Sunday gathering, but was unimpressed and refused to record Rice. But a few days later, Knapp had a sudden, inexplicable change of heart and called Rice in to record in exchange for $75 a side, but no royalties. On these sung sermons, Rice was typically accompanied by percussion, a trombone, piano, and bass. The ensuing discs, of which "I'm on the Battlefield of the Lord" (1929) is his best known, were distributed liberally throughout Chicago; by August 1928, he had ten singles out and was giving Sunday services on the radio. He continued recording for Vocalion through 1930. He then twice tried to sign to Paramount, but got no contract and so moved to lead a church in Jackson, Alabama, for two years. He then began preaching at the Oak Street Holiness Church in Montgomery. Rice was appointed Bishop of the Apostolistic [sic] Overcoming Holy Church of God, for Alabama, Florida, and Georgia in 1941. Although he made other recordings after Vocalion, they have been lost. —Sandra Brennan

● **Complete Recorded Works (1928-1930)** / 1928-1930 / Document ◆◆◆◆
Complete Recorded Works (1928-1930) is an excellent disc that contains all 20 known preformances from the Rev. D.C. Rice, an impassioned country-

blues gospel singer. These are some of the finest blues-gospel recordings of their era, and this is likely the best presentation they'll ever receive. — *Thom Owens*

Tommy Ridgley

b. Oct. 30, 1925, New Orleans, LA
Piano, Vocals / R&B, Electric New Orleans Blues, Dixieland, Modern Electric Blues, New Orleans Blues

Tommy Ridgley was on the Crescent City R&B scene when it first caught fire, and he remains a proud part of that same scene today. That's a lot of years behind a microphone, but Ridgley doesn't sound the slightest bit tired; his 1995 Black Top album *Since the Blues Began* rates with his liveliest outings to date.

Ridgley cut his debut sides back in 1949 for Imperial under Dave Bartholomew's direction. His "Shrewsbury Blues" and "Boogie Woogie Mama" failed to break outside of his hometown, though. Sessions for Decca in 1950 and Imperial in 1952 (where he waxed the wild "Looped") preceded four 1953-55 sessions for Atlantic that included a blistering instrumental, "Jam Up," that sported no actual Ridgley involvement but sold relatively well under his name (incomparable tenor saxist Lee Allen was prominent).

New York's Herald Records was Ridgley's home during the late '50s. The consistently solid singer waxed "When I Meet My Girl" for the firm in 1957, encoring with a catchy "Baby Do-Liddle." From there, it was on to his hometown-based Ric logo, where he laid down the stunning stroll-tempoed "Let's Try and Talk It Over" and a bluesy "Should I Ever Love Again" in 1960. He recorded intermittently after leaving Ric in 1963, waxing a soulful "I'm Not the Same Person" in 1969 for Ronn.

Ridgley always remained a hometown favorite even when recording opportunities proved scarce. Happily, *Since the Blues Began* ranked with 1995's best albums, Ridgley sounding entirely contemporary but retaining his defining Crescent City R&B edge. — *Bill Dahl*

● **The New Orleans King of the Stroll** / 1988 / Rounder ✦✦✦✦
Tommy Ridgley was a solid R&B vocalist who was quite successful with novelty tunes and silly songs, but was also a good romantic balladeer. This 15-track collection mostly covers Ridgley material from 1960 to 1964 for the Ric label, and ranges from laments like "Please Hurry Home" and "I Love You Yes I Do" to such comic material and dance-based numbers as "Double Eyed Whammy" and "The Girl from Kooka Monga." Ridgley wasn't as booming or dynamic as some other Crescent City vocalists, but made several nice period pieces and soul tunes, several of which are included on this set. — *Ron Wynn*

She Turns Me On / 1992 / Modern Blues ✦✦✦
Competent contemporary effort that proved Ridgley's voice was still in excellent shape, albeit a less engaging outing overall than his subsequent Black Top release. — *Bill Dahl*

The Herald Recordings / 1992 / Collectables ✦✦✦✦
There's some very nice late-'50s New Orleans R&B recommending this 17-track collection, along with a few superfluous instrumental backing tracks that could have safely been jettisoned altogether. Ridgley's stint at Herald included the sizzling "When I Meet My Girl," "Baby Do Little," and several more impressive rocking efforts, backed by the esteemed crew at Cosimo's Crescent City studio—saxist Lee Allen, etc. — *Bill Dahl*

Since the Blues Began / 1995 / Black Top ✦✦✦✦
The veteran New Orleans singer remains a contemporary force to be reckoned with. Guitarist Snooks Eaglin, bassist George Porter, Jr., and saxist Kaz Kazanoff help Ridgley out on what's easily his finest contemporary release. There are a handful of remakes of his earlier triumphs, but for the most part, he is commendably living in the present, incorporating funk-tinged rhythms into his delectable musical gumbo. — *Bill Dahl*

Bob Riedy

Piano / Piano Blues

Blues fans on Chicago's North Side couldn't avoid pianist Bob Riedy during the 1970s. Tirelessly gigging with his own band and booking various clubs at the same time, Riedy helped pioneer the area's now-thriving blues circuit. Ironically, he's not around to enjoy it—he hasn't been sighted around the Windy City in years. — *Bill Dahl*

Just off Halsted / Mar. 1975 / Flying Fish ✦✦✦✦
As you might guess from the title, here are blues played by a band from the Windy City. — *AMG*

● **Bob Riedy Blues Band** / 1977 / Rounder ✦✦✦✦
The Bob Riedy Blues Band is a reissue of the group's 1977 album *Lake Michigan Ain't No River*, a storming set featuring a cameo from famed harpist Carey Bell. While the album doesn't really offer any surprises, it's a fine collection of straight-ahead Chicago blues that may please fans of the genre. — *Thom Owens*

Paul Rishell

b. Jan. 17, 1950, Brooklyn, NY
Guitar, Vocals / Modern Acoustic Blues

Boston-area blues guitarist and singer Paul Rishell specializes in the country blues, but in recent years, he's been proving his mettle on occasional gigs with an electric band as well. Rishell has been riding the wave of renewed interest in acoustic music in general, and he's taken his style of acoustic country blues to festivals and clubs around the US, often accompanied by his harmonica playing partner, Little Annie Raines. Before he ever entered the recording studio, Rishell spent many years studying his craft, and he's shared stages with great people: Son House, Johnny Shines, Howlin' Wolf, Sonny Terry and Brownie McGhee, Buddy Guy and Junior Wells, John Lee Hooker and Bonnie Raitt. Rishell has three albums out on the Tone-Cool label, *Blues on Holiday* (1990), *Swear to Tell the Truth* (1993), and *I Want You to Know* (1996). — *Richard Skelly*

Blues on a Holiday / 1990 / Tone-Cool ✦✦✦✦
Blues on a Holiday is divided between full-band numbers and songs guitarist Paul Rishell performed on a solo guitar. Both sides are exciting, offering invigorating updates of Delta and Chicago blues. Although the solo numbers—which were all performed on a National Steel—are raw and exciting, the songs recorded with a full band give a good idea of the depths of Rishell's talent. It is on these songs that he really tears loose, demonstrating what a versatile guitarist he is. — *Thom Owens*

Swear to Tell the Truth / 1993 / Tone-Cool ✦✦✦
The tendency to be snide and cynical whenever encountering contemporary versions of vintage country blues is great, mainly because there is no way anyone singing Skip James or Son House tunes in the 1990s could possibly best the originals. Paul Rishell's versions of their songs are neither faceless covers nor spectacular reworkings; they are merely Rishell's earnest attempt to communicate the music he loves. Sometimes it works and other times it doesn't, but it is never pretentious or solemn. The better tracks are the jumping version of Earl Hooker's "Do You Swear to Tell the Truth," with guitar by Ronnie Earl, and Rishell's own "I'm Gonna Jump and Shout." This is not Hall of Fame stuff, but it also should not be curtly dismissed or unfairly ridiculed. — *Ron Wynn*

● **I Want You to Know** / 1996 / Tone-Cool ✦✦✦✦
The team of guitarist Paul Rishell and Annie Raines on harmonica (both sing) is so appealing that their acoustic duets make the occasional guests (and electrification of the music) seem unnecessary although Ronnie Earl gets in a few good guitar solos. Five originals by the Rishell/Raines team fit right in with songs by the likes of Blind Boy Fuller, Bo Carter, Babecue Bob, J.B. Lenoir, Otis Spann, Peg Leg Howell, and Big Bill Broonzy. A touching version of "I Shall Not Be Moved" is the set's highpoint but all of the 16 selections (which range from country blues and early folk music to later electric blues) are well worth hearing. Highly recommended roots music. — *Scott Yanow*

Duke Robillard

b. Oct. 4, 1948, Woonsocket, RI
Guitar, Vocals / Modern Blues

Duke Robillard is one of the founding members of Roomful of Blues, as well as one of the guitarists that replaced Jimmie Vaughan in the Fabulous Thunderbirds in 1990. Between that time, Robillard pursued a solo career that found him exploring more musically adventurous territory than either Roomful of Blues or the T-Birds. On his solo recordings, the guitarist dips into blues, rockabilly, jazz, and rock 'n' roll, creating a unique fusion of American roots musics.

In 1967, Duke Robillard formed Roomful of Blues in Westerly, Rhode Island. For the next decade, he led the band through numerous lineup changes before he decided that he had grown tired of the group. Robillard left the band in 1979, initially signing on as rockabilly singer Robert Gordon's lead guitarist. After his stint with Gordon, Robillard joined the Legendary Blues Band.

In 1981, the guitarist formed a new group, the Duke Robillard Band, which soon evolved into Duke Robillard & the Pleasure Kings. After a few years of touring the group landed a contract with Rounder Records, releasing their eponymous debut album in 1984. For the rest of the decade, Robillard and the Pleasure Kings toured America and released a series of albums on Rounder Records. Occasionally, the guitarist would release a jazz-oriented solo album.

In 1990, Robillard joined the Fabulous Thunderbirds. Even though he had become a member of the Austin group, the guitarist continued to record and tour as a solo artist, signing with the major label Point Blank/Virgin in 1994. *— Stephen Thomas Erlewine*

Too Hot to Handle / 1985 / Rounder ♦♦♦

Rockin' Blues / 1988 / Rounder ♦♦♦
Robillard, both a good blues guitarist and knowledgeable swing player, displays his rocking side on this '88 date. There are flashier solos, more uptempo cuts, and an aggressive, frenetic quality that's missing on Robillard's jazz-oriented releases. *— Ron Wynn*

You Got Me / 1988 / Rounder ♦♦♦♦
Duke Robillard's sessions have alternated between jazzy, sophisticated, low-key ventures, and bluesy, more energetic, rousing dates. This was on the robust side, matching Robillard's guitar and good-natured, celebratory vocals with the talents of a great guest corps that included Dr. John and Ron Levy on keyboards, guitarist Jimmie Vaughan, bassist Thomas Enright and drummer Tommy DeQuattro (The Pleasure Kings). These weren't always musical triumphs, but even the songs that didn't quite work were entertaining, while the more inspirational offerings like "You're the One I Adore" and "Don't Treat Me Like That" nicely balance tremendous instrumental support with energetic vocal performances. *— Ron Wynn*

Swing / Oct. 1988 / Rounder ♦♦♦
While he makes his fame and fortune cutting blues-rock, guitarist Duke Robillard periodically issues albums of stylish, restrained, subtly swinging jazzy material. This date included guest appearances from swing-influenced contemporary instrumentalists, such as tenor saxophonist Scott Hamilton and guitarist Chris Flory, who teams with Robillard on "Glide On" for some excellent twin guitar fireworks. Otherwise, it's Jim Kelly who matches licks with Robillard on "Jim Jam" and "What's Your Story, Morning Glory." It's relaxed, elegant music, with just enough grit to keep things interesting. *— Ron Wynn*

Duke Robillard & the Pleasure Kings / 1989 / Rounder ♦♦♦
Featuring fine T-Bone Walker-influenced guitar and vocals from the leader, these trio recordings mostly contain original compositions. This is good for what it is, but it seems to lack the punch that larger instrumentation might provide. *— Bob Porter*

Turn It Around / 1990 / Rounder ♦♦♦
Guitarist Duke Robillard emphasized the rocking blues and barrelhouse side of his musical personality on this '91 session that highlighted what was then his band. Vocalist Susan Forrest provided a lusty, sensual quality while bassist Scott Appelrough and drummer Doug Hinman laid down sparse rhythmic backgrounds. Robillard provided the lead guitar presence and energy, adding more flashy chords, riffs, licks and driving solos than on his more restrained jazz-based material. It was an effective session, though Forrest's vocals weren't always as hard-hitting as the material demanded. But Robillard and his mates provided instrumental cover when Forrest didn't quite hit the mark, and were even more on target when she did. *— Ron Wynn*

● **After Hours Swing Session** / May 1990 / Rounder ♦♦♦♦
While guitarist Duke Robillard has won widespread popularity for his facility with rocking blues and barrelhouse numbers, he also loves understated, quietly swinging jazz fare. He got a chance to demonstrate his proficiency in this style on this intimate combo session. The eight songs featured on the CD include brisk workouts as well as light-hearted numbers that showcase Robillard's decent, if not great, voice, along with his fluid, tasty fills and crisp,

clean acoustic and electric guitar solos. Here's another side of Duke Robillard, one that deserves equal billing with the flashy, burning one. *— Ron Wynn*

Minor Swing / 1992 / North Star ♦♦♦

Temptation / 1994 / Pointblank ♦♦♦♦
It may not offer anything new, but *Temptation* is a solid album from Duke Robillard. Supported by drummer Jeffery McAllister and bassist Marty Ballou, he runs through a set of nine originals and two covers, playing with typical taste and class. Robillard's blues doesn't really burn with intensity; rather, it simmers with style. That means this *Temptation* is slyly seductive, and while there are a few missteps along the way, it's still a successful seduction. *— Thom Owens*

Duke's Blues / Jan. 23, 1996 / Pointblank ♦♦♦
With *Duke's Blues*, guitarist Duke Robillard pays tribute to his blues idols, such as Albert Collins, T-Bone Walker, Guitar Slim, and Lowell Fulsom. As expected, it's an affectionate and professional tribute. Robillard works with an augmented blues combo, featuring a second guitarist, piano, and a small horn section. The band runs through the material precisely and efficiently. Although there's plenty of fine musicianship throughout *Duke's Blues*, it's the kind of record to admire, not love—it's expertly executed, but it never catches fire. *— Thom Owens*

Dangerous Place / Jun. 3, 1997 / Virgin ♦♦♦♦
Duke Robillard's place in blues history seems secure—the founder of Roomful of Blues, a stint in the Fabulous Thunderbirds, and a veteran of sessions with such venerable bluesmen as Snooky Pryor, Jimmy Witherspoon, John Hammond, and Pinetop Perkins, R&B queen Ruth Brown, the king of Kansas City swing Jay McShann, and rock legend Bob Dylan—and in this *Dangerous Place*, the writer, arranger, producer, singer, guitarist and leader of the Duke Robillard Band presents a total tour de force of all the different dimensions of that deceptively simple music known as "the blues": the brass-stoked swing of "Had to Be Your Man"; the straight-from-the-gut Chicago harp-and-guitar moan of "No Time"; the heartbreak of "All Over but the Paying"; the wry joviality of "I May Be Ugly (But I Sure Know How to Cook)"; the ruminative "Can't Remember to Forget" (courtesy of the pen of former Eric Clapton and Muddy Waters harpmeister Jerry Portnoy); and the slinky and silky set-ending instrumental "Black Negligee." The Duke's electric guitar solo in the sexy, sassy "Ain't Nothing Like You (Where I Come From)," typical of this entire album, is an absolute model of sheer style and sly wit. *— Chris Slawecki*

Plays Jazz: The Rounder Years / Oct. 21, 1997 / Bullseye Blues ♦♦♦
This disc is the companion to *Duke Robillard Plays Blues*, another anthology of tracks recorded for Rounder's Bullseye Blues subsidiary. Of the two discs, this one is definitely the most fun. That's mainly because when Duke Robillard says "jazz" he means it more in the Louis Jordan sense than the Duke Jordan sense. The uptempo numbers are that sort of jump blues, proto-R&B-type thing that Joe Jackson went for on his *Jumpin' Jive* album—you keep expecting to hear Cab Calloway chime in on the choruses. "Shivers," "Sweet Georgia Brown," and "Shufflin' with Some Barbeque" are the best examples of Duke's affectionate retroactivity; he throws off elegant and speedy guitar runs with giddy abandon, and his band positively cooks. The cool urbanity of a song like "I'll Never Be the Same" calls for a bit more voice than Duke has to offer, but to his credit, he doesn't try to gussy it up; but that makes him honest, not fun to listen to. *— Rick Anderson*

Plays Blues: The Rounder Years / Oct. 21, 1997 / Bullseye Blues ♦♦♦
You cannot deny that Duke Robillard knows his way around the fretboard. Unfortunately, as a bandleader, his touch is more deft when handling jazz rather than blues. While striving for a fat, gritty aesthetic, he comes off sounding more like second-rate Eric Clapton instead of his hero, T-Bone Walker. What is perhaps most aggravating about this compilation is how consistently Robillard fails while at the same time displaying such talent. On every track he seems to strain to express something he is simply not able to deliver. *— Tim Sheridan*

Rev. Cleophus Robinson

b. Mar. 18, 1932, Canton, MS
Vocals / Ragtime, Classic Jazz
While never achieving the commercial success of many of his contemporaries, the Rev. Cleophus Robinson was a prominent figure on the gospel circuit

throughout the better part of the postwar era, perhaps best known for hosting a coast-to-coast gospel television series which ran for a quarter century. Born March 18, 1932 in Canton, Mississippi, according to family legend Robinson suddenly sang his first gospel song, "Who Will Be Able to Stand?," at the age of three; from that point on, he sang regularly while working in the cotton fields, influenced in great measure by his mother Lillie, a gospel shouter in the tradition of Mahalia Jackson whose own vocal prowess was renowned throughout the region. As a teen, Robinson gave his first solo recitals at St. John's Church of Canton; in 1948 he moved to Chicago, where he performed in a variety of area churches and appeared with the Roberta Martin Singers alongside Jackson herself.

Through Evelyn Gay of the Gay Sisters, Robinson was introduced to Miracle Records chief Lee Egalnick, and in September 1949 he went into the studio to make his debut recordings. Credited as Bro Cleophus Robinson, he issued the single "Now Lord"; sales were unimpressive, and he soon relocated to Memphis, where he moved in with his uncle, the Reverend L.A. Hamblin (who in 1968 recorded the sermon "When God Walks out of the Field" for the Jewel label). After finishing high school, Robinson began his own weekly radio show, *The Voice of the Soul,* and began regularly appearing with famous gospel artists as they passed through town, among them Brother Joe May, who became something of a mentor to the young singer. During the same period he began collaborating with pianist Napoleon Brown, who played with Robinson both on record and at live dates for the next several decades.

In 1953, Robinson signed to the Houston-based Peacock Records, soon issuing the single "In the Sweet By and By"; he released several more efforts for the label, none of them hugely successful, before deciding to pursue a career as an actor. After enrolling as a drama major at Leymole College, he frequently found himself called away from his studies to promote his records; his grades suffered, and after a year he returned to music full-time. By 1956, Robinson's gospel career was in a rut, and he had yet to score a hit record; that all changed upon the release of "Pray for Me," a duet recorded with his sister Josephine James. A year later, he moved to St. Louis to accept a position with the Bethelem Missionary Baptist Church, resulting in an erratic recording schedule which ended with the 1962 release of the LP *Pray for Me.* Throughout the decade, Robinson also hosted his *Hour of Faith* weekly radio program; beginning in 1964, he also starred in his own gospel TV program.

In 1962, Robinson signed to Battle Records, a subsidiary of Riverside, and there recorded a number of tracks backed by the Gospel Chimes before returning to Peacock in 1964. His first release after going back to the label, "Solemn Prayer," was that rare sermon record which became a major seller. Later that same year, he moved to Savoy, scoring another hit a year later with "How Sweet It Is to Be Loved by God"; by the end of 1965, he had again returned to Peacock, where his music adopted a bluesier flavor. After touring Europe, Robinson made yet another label change in 1969, this time jumping to Nashboro; there he scored his biggest hit ever with "Wrapped Up, Tied Up, Tangled Up," a crossover hit with white audiences as well. It led to a return engagement with Savoy in the 1970s, and in 1975 he appeared at the Montreux Jazz Festival in Switzerland. Robinson's pace slowed in the years to follow, although in 1980 he sang at the White House and in 1986 notched another hit with "Save a Seat for Me." —*Jason Ankeny*

Rev. Cleophus Robinson with Jessy Dixon & the Gospel Chimes / 1962 / Battle ✦✦✦✦
Robinson fronting a gospel quartet—some rare and great moments. —*Opal Louis Nations*

God's Sons and Daughters / 1965 / Peacock ✦✦✦✦
Striking renditions with great organ and guitar accompaniment. —*Opal Louis Nations*

Wrapped Up, Tied Up, Tangled Up / Jun. 20, 1995 / Nashboro ✦✦✦✦
All his best-selling and best-sounding sides from his stay on the Nashboro label during the 1970s. —*Opal Louis Nations*

What You Need / Nov. 14, 1995 / Malaco ✦✦✦

Live in St. Louis / Sep. 30, 1997 / Malaco ✦✦✦✦

● **Someone to Care (The Battle Sessions)** / Specialty ✦✦✦✦
If anything could be considered a sleeper among the most recent Fantasy

Legends of Gospel line, that might be the CD featuring Rev. Cleophus Robinson. The Reverend cut several songs for Riverside's subsidiary Battle label, which didn't last very long. After more than 30 years, these songs are again available, and its fire and fury might surprise those looking for sedate, reverential praise tracks. Rev. Robinson was a shouter and wailer, although he could also do mournful, moving ballads. But the uptempo stompers are the cuts to savor among the 28, with Rev. Robinson's rippling voice getting more and more hypnotic as it goes up the ladder. —*Ron Wynn*

Fenton Robinson

b. Sep. 23, 1935, Minter City, MS, **d.** Nov. 25, 1997
Guitar, Vocals / Modern Electric Blues, Chicago Blues, Modern Electric Chicago Blues, Texas Blues
His Japanese fans reverently dubbed Fenton Robinson "the mellow blues genius" because of his ultra-smooth vocals and jazz-inflected guitar work. But beneath the obvious subtlety resides a spark of constant regeneration—Robinson tirelessly strives to invent something fresh and vital whenever he's near a bandstand.

The soft-spoken Mississippi native got his career going in Memphis, where he'd moved at age 16. First, Rosco Gordon used him on a 1956 session for Duke that produced "Keep on Doggin'." The next year, Fenton made his own debut as a leader for the Bihari brothers' Meteor label with his first reading of "Tennessee Woman." His band, the Dukes, included mentor Charles McGowan on guitar; T-Bone Walker and B.B. King were Robinson's idols.

1957 also saw Fenton team up with bassist Larry Davis at the Flamingo Club in Little Rock. Bobby Bland caught the pair there and recommended them to his boss, Duke Records prexy Don Robey. Both men made waxings for Duke in 1958, Robinson playing on Davis' classic "Texas Flood" and making his own statement with "Mississippi Steamboat." Robinson cut the original version of the often-covered Peppermint Harris-penned slow blues "As the Years Go Passing By" for Duke in 1959 with New Orleans prodigy James Booker on piano. The same date also produced a terrific "Tennessee Woman" and a marvelous blues ballad, "You've Got to Pass This Way Again."

Fenton moved to Chicago in 1962, playing South side clubs with Junior Wells, Sonny Boy Williamson, and Otis Rush and laying down the swinging "Say You're Leavin'" for USA in 1966. But it was his stunning slow blues "Somebody (Loan Me a Dime)," cut in 1967 for Palos, that insured his blues immortality. Boz Scaggs liked it so much that he covered it for his 1969 debut LP. Unfortunately, he initially also claimed he wrote the tune; much litigation followed.

John Richbourg's Sound Stage 77 labels, it's safe to say, didn't really have a clue as to what Fenton Robinson's music was all about. The guitarist's 1970 Nashville waxings for the firm were mostly horrific—Robinson wasn't even invited to play his own guitar on the majority of the horribly unsubtle rock-slanted sides. His musical mindset was growing steadily jazzier by then, not rockier.

Robinson fared a great deal better at his next substantial stop: Chicago's Alligator Records. His 1974 album *Somebody Loan Me a Dime* remains the absolute benchmark of his career, spotlighting his rich, satisfying vocals and free-spirited, understated guitar work in front of a rock-solid horn-driven band. By comparison, 1977's *I Hear Some Blues Downstairs* was a trifle disappointing despite its playful title track and a driving T-Bone tribute, "Tell Me What's the Reason."

Alligator issued *Nightflight,* another challenging set, in 1984, then backed off the guitarist. His most recent disc, 1989's *Special Road,* first came out on the Dutch Black Magic logo and was reissued by Evidence Music not long ago. Robinson now resides in downstate Illinois, visiting his old stomping grounds only sporadically. —*Bill Dahl*

Monday Morning Boogie & Blues / 1972 / 77 ✦✦
Too rock oriented. —*Bill Dahl*

★ **Somebody Loan Me a Dime** / 1974 / Alligator ✦✦✦✦✦
One of the most subtly satisfying electric blues albums of the 1970s. Robinson never did quite fit the "Genuine Houserocking Music" image of Alligator Records—his deep, rich baritone sounds more like a magic carpet than a piece of barbed wire, and he speaks in jazz-inflected tongues, full of complex surprises. The title track hits with amazing power, as do the chugging "The Getaway," a hard-swinging "You Say You're Leaving," and the minor-key "You

Don't Know What Love Is." In every case, Robinson had recorded them before, but thanks to Bruce Iglauer's superb production, a terrific band, and Robinson's musicianship, these versions reign supreme. — *Bill Dahl*

I Hear Some Blues Downstairs / 1977 / Alligator ✦✦✦
A disappointment in its inconsistency following such a mammoth triumph as his previous set, yet not without its mellow delights. The title track is untypically playful; Robinson's revisiting of the mournful "As the Years Go Passing By" is a moving journey, and his T-Bone Walker tribute "Tell Me What's the Reason" swings deftly. On the other hand, a superfluous remake of Rosco Gordon's "Just a Little Bit" goes nowhere, and nobody really needed another "Killing Floor." — *Bill Dahl*

Getaway / 197 / 77 ✦✦✦
More rock-slanted '70s stuff. — *Bill Dahl*

Blues in Progress / 1984 / Black Magic ✦✦✦
Smooth and jazzy. — *Bill Dahl*

Nightflight / 1984 / Alligator ✦✦✦
For the most part, another easy-going trip to the mellower side of contemporary blues, Robinson's jazzy tone and buttery vocals applied to a couple of his '50s-era numbers ("Crazy Crazy Lovin'" and "Schoolboy") along with some intriguing new items and Lowell Fulson's mournful "Sinner's Prayer." Tasty backing helps too. — *Bill Dahl*

Special Road / Apr. 1989 / Evidence ✦✦✦
Fenton Robinson is among the second-line blues musicians who have come close but never made it over the hump. He has certainly got the guitar goods, and his vocals are often memorable and anguished. Unfortunately, the 13 songs he did on this 1989 date were mostly good but nowhere as intense as he has delivered on other occasions. Neither is the instrumental work on this Evidence CD; his solos are firmly articulated, often elaborately constructed and paced, but they lack impact. Too many times Robinson falls just short of turning in a triumphant or exciting number, either through a less than emphatic vocal or a mundane solo. This is not necessarily a bad session, just a disappointing one. — *Ron Wynn*

Mellow Fellow / 1993 / Charly ✦✦
Clearly, the folks at Sound Stage 77 Records had no idea what Fenton Robinson was all about during his 1970-1971 stay there. Hell, they even took the guitar out of his hands altogether at one dreadful session reproduced on this 19-track retrospective in its entirety, entrusting the lead work instead to some pitiful rock players better left anonymous. The last few sides are much better—"Little Turch" actually sounds like Robinson, his elegant guitar work back up front where it belongs. — *Bill Dahl*

Freddy Robinson

b. Feb. 24, 1939, Memphis, TN
Guitar / Blues Jazz, Modern Blues, Northern Soul
Blues fans know him as one of harp genius Little Walter's studio accompanists during the latter portion of his tenure at Chess. Jazz aficionados are aware of him for the albums he did for World Pacific. Freddy Robinson has been one versatile guitarist across the decades.

Robinson played both bass and guitar behind Walter at Chess circa 1959-60. His own recording career commenced in 1962 with a jazz-laced instrumental pairing, "The Buzzard"/"The Hawk," for King's short-lived Queen subsidiary. He gave singing a try in 1966, cutting "Go-Go Girl" for Checker (with Barbara Acklin and Mamie Galore helping out as background vocalists). By 1968, he was recording with pianist Monk Higgins and the Blossoms (Darlene Love's vocal group) in Los Angeles for Cobblestone.

Blues fans may find the material Robinson cut for a Stax LP in 1972 noteworthy; "At the Drive-In" and "Bluesology" are in-the-alley blues efforts that hark back to the guitarist's early days in Chicago. Robinson later recorded for Al Bell's ICA logo. — *Bill Dahl*

The Coming Atlantis / Apr. 1970 / World Pacific ✦✦✦
Freddie Robinson's debut album *Coming Atlantis* is plagued by some late-'60s cliches—hippie lyrics, spacy instrumental interludes and some blues-rock flourishes—but there are some strong blues songs and soloing from Robinson that make it worth a listen. — *Thom Owens*

● **At the Drive In** / 1972 / Enterprise ✦✦✦✦
It's rather hard to get a handle on this phase of Robinson's career—there's some reasonably lowdown blues with the guitarist speaking the lyrics as much as singing them here, but he was mainly a jazz musician by then. — *Bill Dahl*

Off the Cuff / Mar. 1974 / Enterprise ✦✦

Ikey Robinson

b. Jul. 28, 1904, Dublin, VA, **d.** Oct. 25, 1990, Chicago, IL
Banjo, Guitar, Vocals / Classic Jazz
Ikey Robinson was an excellent banjoist and singer who was versatile enough to record both jazz and blues from the late '20s into the late '30s. Unfortunately he spent long periods off records after the swing era, leading to him being less known than he should be. After working locally, Robinson moved to Chicago in 1926, playing and recording with Jelly Roll Morton, Clarence Williams, and (most importantly) Jabbo Smith during 1928-29. He led his own recording sessions in 1929, 1931, 1933, and 1935 (all have been reissued on a CD from the Austrian label RST). Robinson played with Wilbur Sweatman, Noble Sissle, Carroll Dickerson, and Erskine Tate in the '30s, recorded with Clarence Williams and led small groups from the '40s on. In the early '60s he was with Franz Jackson and in the '70s (when he was rediscovered) he had an opportunity to tour Europe and be reunited with Jabbo Smith. — *Scott Yanow*

● **"Banjo" Ikey Robinson** / Jan. 4, 1929-May 19, 1937 / RST ✦✦✦✦
It would not be an understatement to call this CD definitive of Ikey Robinson's work since it includes every selection (except for two songs that have Half Pint Jaxon vocals) ever led by the banjoist/vocalist. The diversity is impressive, for Robinson is heard (on "Got Butter on It" and "Ready Hokum") with a hot group featuring cornetist Jabbo Smith, singing the blues, performing with The Hokum Trio and The Pods of Pepper (both good-time bands), backing singer Charlie Slocum and heading his own Windy City Five (a fine swing group) in 1935; he even plays clarinet on one song. This consistently enjoyable Austrian import is well worth searching for. — *Scott Yanow*

Jimmy Lee Robinson

b. Apr. 30, 1931, Chicago, IL
Guitar / Chicago Blues
Unlike many of his Chicago blues contemporaries, Jimmie Lee Robinson wasn't a Mississippi Delta emigre. The guitarist was born and raised right in the Windy City—not far from Maxwell Street, the fabled open-air market on the near West side where the blues veritably teemed during the 1940s and '50s.

Robinson learned his lessons well. He formed a partnership with guitarist Freddy King in 1952 for four years (they met outside the local welfare office), later doing sideman work with Elmore James and Little Walter and cutting sessions on guitar and bass behind Little Walter, Eddie Taylor, Shakey Jake, and St. Louis Jimmy Oden. Robinson cut three singles for the tiny Bandera label circa 1959-60; the haunting "All My Life" packed enough power to be heard over in England, where John Mayall faithfully covered it. Another Bandera standout, "Lonely Traveller," was revived as the title track for Robinson's 1994 Delmark comeback album.

Europe enjoyed a glimpse of Robinson when he hit the continent as part of Horst Lippmann and Fritz Rau's 1965 American Folk Blues Festival alongside John Lee Hooker, Buddy Guy, and Big Mama Thornton. After that, his mother died, and times grew tough. Robinson worked as a cabbie and security guard for the Board of Education for a quarter century or so until the members of the Ice Cream Men—a young local band with an overriding passion for 1950s blues—convinced Robinson that he was much too young to be retired. They've been proven right ever since. — *Bill Dahl*

Lonely Traveller / 1994 / Delmark ✦✦✦✦
Jimmie Lee Robinson doesn't do everything in the standard 12-bar blues form; sometimes he half-sings, half-talks through songs, or varies the tempo, breaks up the rhythms and paces the performances in an unusual manner. His solos also aren't the usual piercing or flashy phrases and riffs, but sometimes more decorative or sparse underneath the words. His diverse style and

unpredictable vocal manner make this one of the more striking modern blues outings in quite some time, despite the fact that he's neither a great vocalist nor a spectacular instrumentalist. But he's written much of the material, and those songs that he covers, such as Lightnin' Hopkins' "Can't Be Successful" or Big Bill Broonzy's "Ken to the Highway," are certainly not reflective of their original creators. — *Ron Wynn*

Tad Robinson

b. Jun. 24, 1956, New York, NY
Vocals, Harmonica / Electric Blues, Soul, Soul Blues
Tad Robinson would have fit in snugly with the blue-eyed soul singers of the 1960s. His vocals virtually reeking of soul, he's capable of delving into a straightahead Little Walter shuffle or delivering a vintage O.V. Wright R&B ballad. Add his songwriting skills and exceptional harp technique and you have quite the total package.

Robinson grew up in New York City on a nutritious diet of Stax, Motown, and Top 40, digging everyone from Otis Redding and Arthur Alexander to Eric Burdon and Joe Cocker. He matriculated at Indiana University's school of music in 1980, fronting a solid little combo on the side called the Hesitation Blues Band that made it up to Chicago now and then (where he soon relocated).

Long respected locally, his reputation outside the city limits soared when he took over as vocalist with Dave Specter & the Bluebirds. Their 1994 Delmark disc, *Blueplicity,* was an inspiring marriage of Robinson's soaring vocals and Specter's tasty, jazz-laced guitar and featured the striking Robinson-penned originals "What's Your Angle," "Dose of Reality," and "On the Outside Looking In."

Delmark granted Tad Robinson his own album later that year. *Ode to Infinity* escorted him even further into soul territory (guests on the set included Mighty Flyers guitarist Alex Schultz, the mystical Robert Ward, and Specter). Now living once more in Indiana, Robinson still makes it into Chicago on a regular basis (but never frequently enough for his followers). — *Bill Dahl*

● **One to Infinity** / 1994 / Delmark ✦✦✦✦
Harpist Robinson displays his multi-faceted talents, exploring a multitude of shades of blues and soul. The backing on each song neatly fits the piece — guitarist Robert Ward briefly turns up as a sideman as Robinson proves he's one of the top young vocalists on the contemporary circuit. — *Bill Dahl*

Rockin' Sidney

b. Apr. 9, 1938, Lebeau, LA, **d.** Feb. 25, 1998
Guitar, Organ, Harmonica, Accordion, Vocals / Soul, Zydeco, Electric Louisiana Blues, Electric Swamp Blues
With his 1985 novelty smash "My Toot Toot," Rockin' Sidney scored zydeco's first true international hit. Born Sidney Semien on April 9, 1938 in Lebeau, Louisiana, he began playing harmonica and guitar professionally while in his teens, and made his first R&B-styled recordings on the Fame and Jin imprints during the late '50s; his first regional hit, "No Good Woman," appeared in 1962. Between the mid-'60s and the late '70s, Sidney cut well over 50 singles for the Louisiana-based Goldband label, working in a variety of contemporary blues, soul, and R&B modes; none proved successful, however, and upon learning the accordion he began playing zydeco. He issued his first true zydeco record, *Give Me a Good Time Woman,* on the Maison de Soul label in 1982; two years later he cut *My Zydeco Shoes Got the Zydeco Blues,* which included the track "My Toot Toot." Although Sidney himself was reportedly unhappy with the song, it became a local jukebox hit, and soon regional radio stations began playing it regularly; in time, the single became a grass-roots smash, selling well over a million copies on its way to charting in the US and the UK and even winning a Grammy Award. While Sidney never again reached the same commercial peaks, he remained one of zydeco's most notable artists, setting up his own label, Bally Hoo, and touring regularly until his death on February 25, 1998. — *Jason Ankeny*

● **My Toot Toot [Maison de Soul]** / 1986 / Maison de Soul ✦✦✦✦
Rockin' Sidney had the biggest zydeco release of all time—"My Toot Toot"—and it has enjoyed many subsequent covers. Some of this release is unfortunately unacceptable, as it includes updated covers, but he rises above it most of the time. — *Jeff Hannusch*

Rogers & Buffalo

Guitar, Harmonica / Acoustic Blues
Slide guitarist/producer Roy Rogers and harmonica maestro Norton Buffalo teamed up for a one-off side project with surprisingly down-home results. — *Cub Koda*

● **R & B** / 1991 / Blind Pig ✦✦✦✦
R&B is straight out of the Sonny Terry and Brownie McGee book—a set of stripped-down acoustic blues. Roy Rogers and Norton Buffalo both play with surprising grit and unsurprising affection, making it a very pleasurable tribute. — *Thom Owens*

Travellin' Tracks / 1992 / Blind Pig ✦✦✦

Jimmy Rogers (James A. Lane)

b. Jun. 3, 1924, Ruleville, MS, **d.** 1997
Guitar, Harmonica, Piano, Vocals / R&B, Electric Chicago Blues, Chicago Blues
Guitarist Jimmy Rogers is the last living connection to the groundbreaking first Chicago band of Muddy Waters (informally dubbed the Headhunters for their penchant of dropping by other musicians' gigs and "cutting their heads" with a superior onstage performance). Instead of basking in worldwide veneration, he's merely a well-respected Chicago elder boasting a seminal 1950s Chess Records catalog, both behind Waters and on his own.

Born James A. Lane (Rogers was his stepdad's surname), the guitarist grew up all over: Mississippi, Atlanta, West Memphis, Memphis, and St. Louis. Actually, Rogers started out on harp as a teenager. Big Bill Broonzy, Joe Willie Wilkins, and Robert Jr. Lockwood all influenced Rogers, the latter two when he passed through Helena. Rogers settled in Chicago during the early '40s and began playing professionally around 1946, gigging with Sonny Boy Williamson, Sunnyland Slim, and Broonzy.

Rogers was playing harp with guitarist Blue Smitty when Muddy Waters joined them. When Smitty split, Little Walter was welcomed into the configuration, Rogers switched over to second guitar, and the entire postwar Chicago blues genre felt the stylistic earthquake that directly followed. Rogers made his recorded debut as a leader in 1947 for the tiny Ora-Nelle logo, then saw his efforts for Regal and Apollo lay unissued.

Those labels' monumental errors in judgment were the gain of Leonard Chess, who recognized the comparatively smooth-voiced Rogers' potential as a blues star in his own right. (He first played with Muddy Waters on an Aristocrat 78 in 1949 and remained his indispensable rhythm guitarist on wax into 1955.) With Walter and bassist Big Crawford laying down support, Rogers' debut Chess single in 1950, "That's All Right," has earned standard status after countless covers, but his version still reigns supreme.

Rogers' artistic quality was remarkably high while at Chess. "The World Is in a Tangle," "Money, Marbles and Chalk," "Back Door Friend," "Left Me with a Broken Heart," "Act like You Love Me," and the 1954 rockers "Sloppy Drunk" and "Chicago Bound" are essential early-'50s Chicago blues.

In 1955, Rogers left Muddy Waters to venture out as a bandleader, cutting another gem, "You're the One," for Chess. He made his only appearance on *Billboard's* R&B charts in early 1957 with the driving "Walking by Myself," which boasted a stunning harp solo from Big Walter Horton (a last-second stand-in for no-show Good Rockin' Charles). The tune itself was an adaptation of a T-Bone Walker tune, "Why Not," that Rogers had played rhythm guitar on when Walker cut it for Atlantic.

By 1957, blues was losing favor at Chess, the label reaping the rewards of rock via Chuck Berry and Bo Diddley. Rogers' platters slowed to a trickle, though his 1959 Chess farewell, "Rock This House," ranked with his most exciting outings (Reggie Boyd's light-fingered guitar wasn't the least of its charms).

Rogers virtually retired from music for a time during the '60s, operating a West Side clothing shop that burned down in the aftermath of Dr. Martin Luther King's tragic assassination. He returned to the studio in 1972 for Leon Russell's Shelter logo, cutting his first LP, *Gold-Tailed Bird* (with help from the Aces and Freddie King). There have been a few more fine albums since then, notably *Ludella,* a 1990 set for Antone's—but Rogers hasn't fattened his discography nearly as much as some of his contemporaries have. Jimmy's son, Jimmy D. Lane, plays rhythm guitar in his dad's band and fronts a combo of his own on the side. — *Bill Dahl*

Gold-Tailed Bird / 1972 / Shelter ✦✦✦

Roger's attempt to break through to a new, younger audience was less exciting than his Chess years but plausible nonetheless. —*Bill Dahl*

Sloppy Drunk / Dec. 8, 1973-Dec. 15, 1973 / Black & Blue ✦✦✦

Blues legend Jimmy Rogers had not worked steadily prior to cutting these early '70s tracks since 1960. His return on this session's 16 tracks, originally recorded for Black and Blue and now reissued on CD by Evidence, was not a heralded one because there was not much mainstream attention paid to blues at the time. But Rogers' voice was in above-average shape; his sound, range, and tone were anguished and expressed with vigor and clarity. While Willie Mabon's tinkling piano chords and figures moved in and out of loping arrangements, Rogers played easy, penetrating fills, never trying for spectacular effects but nicely punctuating his leads. —*Ron Wynn*

That's All Right / 1974 / Black & Blue ✦✦

Bluemasters / 1976 / Chess ✦✦✦✦

This fine two-LP compilation of his early Chess sides deserves CD reissue soon. —*Bill Dahl*

★ **Chicago Bound** / 1976 / MCA/Chess ✦✦✦✦✦

The logical place to inaugurate any Rogers collection is this perennially acclaimed 14-song retrospective of the guitarist's 1950s Chess years. Most of the big ones are here for your perusal: "That's All Right," "Sloppy Drunk," "You're the One," "Walking by Myself," and the thundering title track. Peerless band support from the likes of Muddy Waters, Little Walter, Otis Spann, and Walter Horton. This is a cornerstone of Chicago blues history. —*Bill Dahl*

Living the Blues / 1976 / Vogue ✦✦

Live / 1982 / JSP ✦✦

Feelin' Good / 1985 / Murray Bros ✦✦✦✦

This Blind Pig CD reissues material from 1983-84. The legendary veteran Jimmy Rogers (taking most of the vocals and occasional guitar solos) is heard teamed up with the talented harmonica player Rod Piazza and his jumping group. The results are consistently exciting. Piazza's harmonica serves as a perfect foil to Rogers' voice, and the impressive backup band (which also features Honey Piazza on piano) clearly enjoys jamming on the basic blues changes. The many strong solos and the superior material make this an easily recommended set. —*Scott Yanow*

☆ **That's All Right** / 1989 / Charly ✦✦✦✦✦

Quite a few important items from Rogers' classic Chess catalog that aren't on *Chicago Bound* turn up on this 24-track British import (along with the prerequisite hits, natch), notably a torrid "Rock This House" (Reggie Boyd's mercurial guitar solos are stunning), the downcast "The World's in a Tangle," a rhumba-beat "My Baby Don't Love Me No More" with a tremendous Walter Horton harp solo, and the bizarre "My Last Meal." —*Bill Dahl*

Ludella / 1990 / Antone's ✦✦✦✦

One of the most enriching contemporary items in Rogers' growing album catalog. Combining studio tracks with live performances, the set trods heavily on the past with loving renditions of "Rock This House," "Ludella," "Sloppy Drunk," and "Chicago Bound." Kim Wilson proves a worthy harp disciple of Little Walter, while bassist Bob Stroger and drummer Ted Harvey lay down supple grooves behind the blues great. —*Bill Dahl*

Chicago's Jimmy Rogers Sings the Blues / 1990 / DCC ✦✦✦

With Ronnie Earl and the Broadcasters / 1994 / Bullseye Blues ✦✦✦

Despite Earl's love and mastery of the '50s Chicago sound and Rogers' still-sharp talents, there's something about this live set that never really takes flight. Maybe it was just a matter of the two factions not being totally familiar with one another, but something's missing in the sparks department. —*Bill Dahl*

Blue Bird / 1994 / JVC ✦✦

Complete Shelter Recordings: Chicago Blues Masters, Vol. 2 / Oct. 24, 1995 / Capitol ✦✦✦✦

Rogers re-emerged after a long layoff with a 1972 album for Leon Russell's Shelter label called *Gold-Tailed Bird*. It wasn't the equivalent of his immortal Chess stuff, but the Shelter sides, here in their entirety, are pretty decent themselves (and no wonder, with the Aces, Freddy King, and reliable Chicago pianist Bob Riedy all involved). A few extra numbers not on the original Shelter LP make this 18-song set even more solid. —*Bill Dahl*

● **Complete Chess Recordings (Chess 50th Anniversary)** / Apr. 8, 1997 / MCA ✦✦✦✦

While the 1976 issue of *Chicago Bound*, the first collection of Jimmy Rogers' Chess material has been rightly hailed as a definitive cornerstone in absorbing the history of early Chicago blues; sadly, that vinyl album has been out of print for a number of years with virtually nothing in the catalog to take its place. Until now. This two-CD (in a single-disc package) anthology collects up everything that appeared on *Chicago Bound*, a number of notable cuts from a two-vinyl-disc anthology that was barely released in the late-70s, and no less than ten unreleased alternate takes from a variety of sessions with one of them, "Luedella," emanating from his first solo session in 1950. The singing, playing, and songwriting is virtually a textbook for the early Chicago style, as the players involved include Muddy Waters, Little Walter, Otis Spann, Willie Dixon, and Big Walter Horton, with all but Horton and Dixon regular mainstays of Muddy's original band, the blueprint of the early electric band sound. While some novices will find a two-disc set perhaps more than they want to pop for, this is as good as '50s Chicago blues gets, and no collection should really be without this one. —*Cub Koda*

Jimmy Rogers / Chess ✦✦✦

The ultimate in cheap packaging, and with barely acceptable sound quality to boot, this set nevertheless contains absolutely essential music. There are several Rogers gems from the early and mid-'50s, and also some other cuts culled from various reissues. —*Ron Wynn*

Roy Rogers

b. Jul. 28, 1950, Redding, CA
Guitar, Vocals / Modern Acoustic Blues

A northern California-based blues guitarist, Roy Rogers works firmly out of a Delta blues acoustic style and is particularly good with a slide. A member of John Lee Hooker's '80s Coast to Coast band, Rogers produced and played on Hooker's Grammy-winning album, *The Healer* and its follow-up, *Mr. Lucky*.

During the early '70s, Rogers played with a variety of Bay Area bar bands. In 1976, he and harpist David Burgin recorded *A Foot in the Door*, which was released on Waterhouse Records. For the next few years, he played in various bands before he formed his own, the Delta Rhythm Kings, in 1980. Two years later, John Lee Hooker asked Rogers to join his Coast to Coast Band and the guitarist accepted.

Rogers stayed with Hooker for four years, leaving in 1986. That same year, he released his debut album, *Chops Not Chaps*, on Blind Pig Records. The record was successful with blues audiences and was nominated for a WC Handy Award. In 1987, he released his second solo album, *Slidewinder*, which was followed two years later by *Blues on the Range*. In 1990, Rogers produced John Lee Hooker's Grammy-winning comeback album, *The Healer*. The following year, he produced Hooker's *Mr. Lucky*, which also won a Grammy.

In 1991, Roy Rogers recorded a duet album, *R&B*, with harmonica player Norton Buffalo. The following year, the duo released another record, *Travellin' Tracks*. Rogers continued to pursue a solo career, performing concerts across America and recording the occasional album like 1998's *Pleasure + Pain*. —*Stephen Thomas Erlewine*

Chops Not Chaps / Sep. 1986 / Blind Pig ✦✦✦

Roy Rogers' debut album *Chops Not Chaps* is a fine blues-rock album, driven by his dynamite slide guitar. The album alternates between covers of blues classics and originals that are effective, but not particularly remarkable. Nevertheless, the quality of Rogers' performance makes this an impressive and memorable debut. —*Thom Owens*

● **Slidewinder** / 1988 / Blind Pig ✦✦✦✦

Slidewinder is one of Roy Rogers' best albums, a collection of smoking hot contemporary blues, ranging from jacked-up rocking boogie numbers and dirty Chicago blues to stripped-down acoustic numbers. It all works equally well, especially the two stellar duets with pianist Allen Toussaint. —*Thom Owens*

Blues on the Range / 1989 / Blind Pig ✦✦✦

Blues on the Range is a nice, but not particularly noteworthy, set of traditional blues. What makes the album worth a listen is Rogers' facility as a slide player—he can make his guitar sing. However, the quality of the songs and performances are slightly uneven, making it only of interest to diehard fans. — *Thom Owens*

R&B / 1991 / Blind Pig ✦✦

Slide of Hand / Jul. 27, 1993 / Liberty ✦✦✦

Slide Zone / 1994 / Capitol ✦✦

Rhythm and Groove / Apr. 1996 / Pointblank ✦✦✦

Pleasure & Pain / Jun. 2, 1998 / Virgin ✦✦✦
Caught between the blues and rock, *Pleasure & Pain* is an odd and appropriately-titled effort from Roy Rogers. He's at his best when he's turning out modernized Delta blues, either acoustically or on electric, but this album moves a little too close to blues-rock, as on the awkward "You Can't Stop Now," which features Sammy Hagar on vocals. The tendency toward overdriven blues-rock and funky workouts hampers the album, but there's also some fine straight blues playing that makes the record worth a listen for longtime Rogers fans. — *Thom Owens*

The Rolling Stones

f. Jan. 1963, London, England
Group / Rock 'n' Roll, British Invasion, British Blues, Hard Rock, Pop-Rock, Electric British Blues
By the time the Rolling Stones began calling themselves the World's Greatest Rock & Roll Band in the late '60s, they had already staked out an impressive claim on the title. As the self-consciously dangerous alternative to the bouncy Merseybeat of the Beatles in the British Invasion, the Stones had pioneered the gritty, hard-driving blues-based rock 'n' roll that came to define hard rock. With his preening machismo and latent maliciousness, Mick Jagger became the prototypical rock frontman, tempering his macho showmanship with a detached, campy irony, while Keith Richards and Brian Jones wrote the blueprint for sinewy, interlocking rhythm guitars. Backed by the strong, yet subtly swinging rhythm section of bassist Bill Wyman and drummer Charlie Watts, the Stones became the breakout band of the British blues scene, eclipsing such contemporaries as the Animals and Them. Over the course of their career, the Stones never really abandoned blues, but as soon as they reached popularity in the UK, they began experimenting musically, incorporating the British pop of contemporaries like the Beatles, Kinks, and Who into their sound. After a brief dalliance with psychedelia, the Stones re-emerged in the late '60s as a jaded, blues-soaked hard rock quintet. The Stones always flirted with the seedy side of rock 'n' roll, but as the hippie dream began to break apart, they exposed and reveled in the new rock culture. It wasn't without difficulty, of course. Shortly after he was fired from the group, Jones was found dead in a swimming pool, while at a 1969 free concert at Altamont, a concertgoer was brutally murdered during the Stones' show. But the Stones never stopped going. For the next thirty years, they continued to record and perform, and while their records weren't always blockbusters, they were never less than the most visible band of their era—certainly, none of their British peers continued to be as popular or productive as the Stones. And no band since has proven to have such a broad fan base or far-reaching popularity, and it is impossible to hear any of the groups that followed them without detecting some sort of influence, whether it was musical or aesthetic.

Throughout their career, Mick Jagger (vocals) and Keith Richards (guitar, vocals) remained at the core of the Rolling Stones. The pair initially met as children at Dartford Maypole County Primary School. They drifted apart over the next ten years, eventually making each other's acquaintance again in 1960, when they met through a mutual friend, Dick Taylor, who was attending Sidcup Art School with Richards. At the time, Jagger was studying at the London School of Economics and playing with Taylor in the blues band Little Boy Blue and the Blue Boys. Shortly afterward, Richards joined the band. Within a year, they had met Brian Jones (guitar, vocals), a Cheltenham native who had dropped out of school to play saxophone and clarinet. By the time he became a fixture on the British blues scene, Jones had already had a wild life. He ran away to Scandinavia when he was 16; by that time, he had already fathered two illegitimate children. He returned to Cheltenham after a few months, where he began playing with the Ramrods. Shortly afterward, he moved to London. where he played in Alexis Korner's group, Blues Inc. Jones quickly decided he wanted to form his own group and adver-

tised for members; among those he recruited was the heavyset blues pianist Ian Stewart.

As he played with his group, Jones also moonlighted under the name Elmo Jones at the Ealing Blues Club. At the pub, he became reacquainted with Blues, Inc., which now featured drummer Charlie Watts, and, on occasion, cameos by Jagger and Richards. Jones became friends with Jagger and Richards, and they soon began playing together with Dick Taylor and Ian Stewart; during this time, Mick was elevated to the status of Blues Inc's lead singer. With the assistance of drummer Tony Chapman, the fledgling band recorded a demo tape. After the tape was rejected by EMI, Taylor left the band to attend the Royal College of Art; he would later form the Pretty Things. Before Taylor's departure, the group named themselves the Rolling Stones, borrowing the moniker from a Muddy Waters song.

The Rolling Stones gave their first performance at the Marquee Club in London on July 12, 1962. At the time, the group consisted of Jagger, Richards, Jones, pianist Ian Stewart, drummer Mick Avory, and Dick Taylor, who had briefly returned to the fold. Weeks after the concert, Taylor left again and was replaced by Bill Wyman, formerly of the Cliftons. Avory also left the group—he would later join the Kinks—and the Stones hired Tony Chapman, who proved to be unsatisfactory. After a few months of persuasion, the band recruited Charlie Watts, who had quit Blues Inc. to work at an advertising agency once the group's schedule became too hectic. By 1963, the band's lineup had been set, and the Stones began an eight-month residency at the Crawdaddy Club, which proved to substantially increase their fan base. It also attracted the attention of Andrew Loog Oldham, who became the Stones' manager, signing them from underneath Crawdaddy's Giorgio Gomelsky. Although Oldham didn't know much about music, he was gifted at promotion, and he latched upon the idea of fashioning the Stones as the bad-boy opposition to the clean-cut Beatles. At his insistence, the large yet meek Stewart was forced out of the group, since his appearance contrasted with the rest of the group. Stewart didn't disappear from the Stones; he became one of their key roadies and played on their albums and tours until his death in 1985.

With Oldham's help, the Rolling Stones signed with Decca Records, and that June, they released their debut single, a cover of Chuck Berry's "Come On." The single became a minor hit, reaching No. 21, and the group supported it with appearances on festivals and package tours. At the end of the year, they released a version of Lennon-McCartney's "I Wanna Be Your Man" which soared into the Top 15. Early in 1964, they released a cover of Buddy Holly's "Not Fade Away," which shot to No. 3. "Not Fade Away" became their first American hit, reaching No. 48 that spring. By that time, the Stones were notorious in their homeland. Considerably rougher and sexier than the Beatles, the Stones were the subject of numerous sensationalistic articles in the British press, culminating in a story about the band urinating in public. All of these stories cemented the Stones as a dangerous, rebellious band in the minds of the public, and had the effect of beginning a manufactured rivalry between them and the Beatles, which helped the group rocket to popularity in the US. In the spring of 1964, the Stones released their eponymous debut album, which was followed by "It's All Over Now," their first UK No. 1. That summer, they toured America to riotous crowds, recording the *Five by Five* EP at Chess Records in Chicago in the midst of the tour. By the time it was over, they had another No. 1 UK single with Howlin' Wolf's "Little Red Rooster." Although the Stones had achieved massive popularity, Oldham decided to push Jagger and Richards into composing their own songs, since they—and his publishing company—would receive more money that away. In June of 1964, the group released their first original single "Tell Me (You're Coming Back)," which became their first American Top 40 hit. Shortly afterward, a version of Irma Thomas' "Time Is on My Side" became their first US Top Ten. It was followed by "The Last Time" in early 1965, a No. 1 UK and Top Ten US hit that began a virtually uninterrupted string of Jagger-Richards hit singles. Still, it wasn't until the group released "(I Can't Get No) Satisfaction" in the summer of 1965 that they were elevated to superstars. Driven by a fuzz-guitar riff designed to replicate the sound of a horn section, "Satisfaction" signaled that Jagger and Richards had come into their own as songwriters, breaking away from their blues roots and developing a signature style of big, bluesy riffs and wry, sardonic lyrics. It stayed at No. 1 for four weeks and began a string of Top Ten singles that ran for the next two years, including such classics as "Get off My Cloud," "19th Nervous Breakdown,"

"As Tears Go By," and "Have You Seen Your Mother, Baby, Standing in the Shadow?"

By 1966, the Stones had decided to respond to the Beatles' increasingly complex albums with their first album of all-original material, *Aftermath*. Due to Brian Jones' increasingly exotic musical tastes, the record boasted a wide range of influences, from the sitar-drenched "Paint It, Black" to the Eastern drones of "I'm Going Home." These eclectic influences continued to blossom on *Between the Buttons*, (1967) the most pop-oriented album the group ever made. Ironically, the album's release was bookended by two of the most notorious incidents in the band's history. Before the record was released, the Stones performed the suggestive "Let's Spend the Night Together," the B-side to the medieval ballad "Ruby Tuesday," on *The Ed Sullivan Show*, which forced Jagger to alter the song's title to an incomprehensible mumble, or else face being banned. In February of 1967, Jagger and Richards were arrested for drug possession, and within three months, Jones was arrested on the same charge. All three were given suspended jail sentences, and the group backed away from the spotlight as the summer of love kicked into gear in 1967. Jagger, along with his then-girlfriend Marianne Faithfull, went with the Beatles to meet the Maharishi Mahesh Yogi; they were also prominent in the international broadcast of the Beatles' "All You Need Is Love." Appropriately, the Stones' next single, "Dandelion"/"We Love You," was a psychedelic pop effort, and it was followed by their response to *Sgt. Pepper*, *Their Satanic Majesties Request*, which was greeted with lukewarm reviews.

The Stones' infatuation with psychedelia was brief. By early 1968, they had fired Andrew Loog Oldham and hired Allen Klein as their manager. The move coincided with their return to driving rock 'n' roll, which happened to coincide with Richards' discovery of open tunings, a move that gave the Stones their distinctively fat, powerful sound. The revitalized Stones were showcased on the malevolent single "Jumpin' Jack Flash," which climbed to No. 3 in May 1968. Their next album, *Beggar's Banquet*, was finally released in the fall, after being delayed for five months due its controversial cover art of a dirty, graffiti-laden restroom. An edgy record filled with detours into straight blues and campy country, *Beggar's Banquet* was hailed as a masterpiece among the fledgling rock press. Although it was seen as a return to form, few realized that while it opened a new chapter of the Stones' history, it also was the closing of their time with Brian Jones. Throughout the recording of *Beggar's Banquet*, Jones was on the sidelines due to his deepening drug addiction and his resentment of the dominance of Jagger and Richards. Jones left the band on June 9, 1969, claiming to be suffering from artistic differences between himself and the rest of the band. On July 3, 1969—less than a month after his departure—Brian Jones was found dead in his swimming pool. The coroner ruled that it was "death by misadventure," yet his passing was the subject of countless rumors over the next two years.

By the time of his death, the Stones had already replaced Brian Jones with Mick Taylor, a former guitarist for John Mayall's Bluesbreakers. He wasn't featured on "Honky Tonk Women," a No. 1 single released days after Jones' funeral, and he contributed only a handful of leads on their next album, *Let It Bleed*. Released in the fall of 1969, *Let It Bleed* was comprised of sessions with Jones and Taylor, yet it continued the direction of *Beggar's Banquet*, signaling that a new era in the Stones' career had begun, one marked by ragged music and an increasingly wasted sensibility. Following Jagger's filming of *Ned Kelly* in Australia during the first part of 1969, the group launched their first American tour in three years. Throughout the tour—the first where they were billed as the World's Greatest Rock & Roll Band—the group broke attendance records, but it was given a sour note when the group staged a free concert at Altamont Speedway. On the advice of the Grateful Dead, the Stones hired Hell's Angels as security, but that plan backfired tragically. The entire show was unorganized and in shambles, yet it turned tragic when the Angels murdered a young Black man, Meredith Hunter, during the Stones' performance. In the wake of the public outcry, the Stones again retreated from the spotlight and dropped "Sympathy for the Devil," which some critics ignorantly claimed incited the violence, from their set.

As the group entered hiatus, they released the live *Get Yer Ya-Ya's Out* in the fall of 1970. It was their last album for Decca/London, and they formed Rolling Stones Records, which became a subsidiary of Atlantic Records. During 1970, Jagger starred in Nicolas Roeg's cult film *Performance* and married Nicaraguan model Bianca Perez Morena de Macias, and the couple quickly entered high society. As Jagger was jet-setting, Richards was slumming, hang-

ing out with country-rock pioneer Gram Parsons. Keith wound up having more musical influence on 1971's *Sticky Fingers*, the first album the Stones released though their new label. Following its release, the band retreated to France on tax exile, where they shared a house and recorded a double album, *Exile on Main St.* Upon its May 1972 release, *Exile on Main St.* was widely panned, but over time it came to be considered one of the group's defining moments.

Following *Exile*, the Stones began to splinter in two, as Jagger concentrated on being a celebrity and Richards sank into drug addiction. The band remained popular throughout the '70s, but their critical support waned. *Goats Head Soup*, released in 1973, reached No. 1, as did 1974's *It's Only Rock 'n' Roll*, but neither record was particularly well received. Taylor left the band after *It's Only Rock 'n' Roll*, and the group recorded their next album as they auditioned new lead guitarists, including Jeff Beck. They finally settled on Ron Wood, former lead guitarist for the Faces and Rod Stewart, in 1976, the same year they released *Black N' Blue*, which only featured Wood on a handful of cuts. During the mid- and late '70s, all the Stones pursued side projects, with both Wyman and Wood releasing solo albums with regularity. Richards was arrested in Canada in 1977 with his common-law wife Anita Pallenberg for heroin possession. After his arrest, he cleaned up and was given a suspended sentence the following year. The band reconvened in 1978 to record *Some Girls*, an energetic response to punk, new wave, and disco. The record and its first single, the thumping disco-rocker "Miss You," both reached No. 1, and the album restored the group's image. However, the group squandered that goodwill with the follow-up *Emotional Rescue*, a number one record that nevertheless received lukewarm reviews upon its 1980 release. *Tattoo You*, released the following year, fared better both critically and commercially, as the singles "Start Me Up" and "Waiting on a Friend" helped the album spend nine weeks at No. 1. The Stones supported *Tattoo You* with an extensive stadium tour captured in Hal Ashby's movie *Let's Spend the Night Together* and the 1982 live album *Still Life*.

Tattoo You proved to be the last time the Stones completely dominated the charts and the stadiums. Although the group continued to sell out concerts in the '80s and '90s, their records didn't sell as well as previous efforts, partially because the albums suffered due to Jagger and Richards' notorious mid-'80s feud. Starting with 1983's *Undercover*, the duo conflicted about which way the band should go, with Jagger wanting the Stones to follow contemporary trends and Richards wanting them to stay true to their rock roots. As a result, *Undercover* was a mean-spirited, unfocused record that received relatively weak sales and mixed reviews. Released in 1986, *Dirty Work* suffered a worse fate, since Jagger was preoccupied with his fledgling solo career. Once Jagger decided that the Stones would not support *Dirty Work* with a tour, Richards decided to make his own solo record with 1988's *Talk Is Cheap*. Appearing a year after Jagger's failed second solo album, *Talk is Cheap* received good reviews and went gold, prompting Jagger and Richards to reunite late in 1988. The following year, the Stones released *Steel Wheels*, which was received with good reviews, but the record was overshadowed by its supporting tour, which grossed over $140 million and broke many box office records. In 1991, the live album *Flashback*, which was culled from the *Steel Wheels* shows, was released.

Following the release of *Flashback*, Bill Wyman left the band; he published a memoir, *Stone Alone*, within a few years of leaving. The Stones didn't immediately replace Wyman, since they were all working on solo projects; this time, there was none of the animosity surrounding their mid-'80s projects. The group reconvened in 1994 with bassist Darryl Jones, who had previously played with Miles Davis and Sting, to record and release the Don Was-produced *Voodoo Lounge*. The album received the band's strongest reviews in years, and its accompanying tour was even more successful than the *Steel Wheels* tour. On top of being more successful than its predecessor, *Voodoo Lounge* also won the Stones their first Grammy for Best Rock Album. Upon the completion of the *Voodoo Lounge* tour, the Stones released the live, "unplugged" album *Stripped* in the fall of 1995. — *Stephen Thomas Erlewine*

The Rolling Stones (England's Newest Hitmakers) / May 30, 1964 / ABKCO ✦✦✦✦

The group's debut album was the most uncompromisingly blues/R&B-oriented full-length recording they would ever release. Mostly occupied with covers, this was as hard-core as British R&B ever got; it's raw and ready. But the Stones succeeded in establishing themselves as creative interpreters, putting '50s and early '60s blues, rock, and soul classics (some quite obscure to White audiences) through a younger, more guitar-oriented filter. The record's highlighted by blistering versions of "Route 66," "Carol," the hyper-tempoed "I Just Want to Make Love to You," "I'm a King Bee," and "Walking the Dog." Their Bo Diddleyized version of Buddy Holly's "Not Fade Away" gave them their first British Top Ten hit (and their first small American one). The acoustic ballad "Tell Me" was Jagger-Richards' first good original tune, but the other group-penned originals were little more than rehashed jams of blues cliches, keeping this album from reaching truly classic status. *— Richie Unterberger*

12 X 5 / Oct. 17, 1964 / ABKCO ✦✦✦✦

The evolution from blues to rock accelerated with the Stones' second American LP. They turned soul into guitar rock for the hits "It's All Over Now" and "Time Is on My Side" (the latter of which was their first American Top Ten single). "2120 South Michigan Avenue" is a great instrumental blues-rock jam; "Around and Around" is one of their best Chuck Berry covers; and "If You Need Me" reflects an increasing contemporary soul influence. On the other hand, the group originals (except for the propulsive "Empty Heart") are weak and derivative, indicating that the band still had a way to go before they could truly challenge the Beatles' throne. *— Richie Unterberger*

☆ **The Rolling Stones Now!** / Apr. 1965 / ABKCO ✦✦✦✦✦

Although their third American LP was patched together (in the usual British Invasion tradition) from a variety of sources, it's their best early R&B-oriented effort. Most of the Stones' early albums suffer from three or four very weak cuts; *Now!* is almost uniformly strong start-to-finish, the emphasis on some of their Blackest material. The covers of "Down Home Girl," Bo Diddley's vibrating "Mona," Otis Redding's "Pain in My Heart," and Barbara Lynn's "Oh Baby" are all among the group's best R&B interpretations. The best gem is "Little Red Rooster," a pure blues with wonderful slide guitar from Brian Jones (and a No. 1 single in Britain, although it was only an album track in the US). As songwriters, Jagger and Richards are still struggling, but they come up with one of their first winners (and an American Top 20 hit) with the yearning, soulful "Heart of Stone." *— Richie Unterberger*

Out of Our Heads / Aug. 1965 / ABKCO ✦✦✦✦

In 1965, the Stones finally proved themselves capable of writing classic rock singles that mined their R&B/blues roots, but updated them into a more guitar-based, thoroughly contemporary context. The first enduring Jagger-Richards classics are here—"The Last Time," its menacing, folky B-side "Play with Fire," and the riff-driven "Satisfaction," which made them superstars in the States and defined their sound and rebellious attitude better than any other single song. On the rest of the album, they largely opted for mid-'60s soul covers, Marvin Gaye's "Hitch Hike," Otis Redding's "Cry to Me," and Sam Cooke's "Good Times" being particular standouts. "I'm All Right" (based on a Bo Diddley sound) showed their '65 sound at its rawest, and there are a couple of fun, though derivative, bluesy originals in "The Spider and the Fly" and "The Under Assistant West Coast Promotion Man." *— Richie Unterberger*

December's Children / Dec. 1965 / ABKCO ✦✦✦✦

The last Stones album in which cover material accounted for 50% of the content was thrown together from a variety of singles, British LP tracks, outtakes, and a cut from an early '64 UK EP. Haphazard assembly aside, much of it's great, including the huge hit "Get Off of My Cloud" and the controversial, string-laden acoustic ballad "As Tears Go By" (a Top Ten item in America). Raiding the R&B closet for the last time, they also offered a breathless run-through of Larry Williams' "She Said Yeah," a sultry Chuck Berry cover ("Talkin' About You"), and exciting live versions of "Route 66" and Hank Snow's "I'm Moving On." More importantly, Jagger-Richards' songwriting partnership had now developed to the extent that several LP-only tracks were reasonably strong in their own right, such as "I'm Free" and "The Singer Not the Song." And the version of "You Better Move On" (which had featured on a British EP at the beginning of 1964) was one of their best and most tender soul covers. *— Richie Unterberger*

Big Hits High Tide and Green Grass / Mar. 1966 / ABKCO ✦✦✦✦

All of their American hits from "Not Fade Away" through "19th Nervous Breakdown," as well as a couple of B-sides. The music's great, of course, although several decades later, there are more wide-ranging compilations of their '60s classics available. *— Richie Unterberger*

☆ **Aftermath** / Jun. 1966 / ABKCO ✦✦✦✦✦

The Rolling Stones finally delivered a set of all-original material with this LP, which also did much to define the group as the bad boys of rock 'n' roll with their sneering attitude toward the world in general and the female sex in particular. The borderline misogyny could get a bit juvenile in tunes like "Stupid Girl." But on the other hand the group began incorporating the influences of psychedelia and Dylan into their material with classics like "Paint It Black," an eerily insistent No. 1 hit graced by some of the best use of sitar (played by Brian Jones) on a rock record. Other classics included "Mother's Little Helper" (whose lyrics had extremely blatant and controversial drug references); Jones also added exotic accents with his vibes (on the jazzy "Under My Thumb") and dulcimer (the delicate Elizabethan ballad "Lady Jane"). Some of the material is fairly ho-hum, to be honest, as Jagger and Richards were still prone to inconsistent songwriting; "Goin' Home," a 11-minute blues jam, was remarkable more for its barrier-crashing length than its content. Look out for an obscure gem, however, in the brooding, meditative "I Am Waiting." *— Richie Unterberger*

Got Live If You Want It / Nov. 4, 1966 / ABKCO ✦✦

A live document of the Brian Jones-era Stones sounds enticing, but the actual product is a letdown. The sound is lousy, and for that matter not all of it's live; a couple of old studio R&B covers were augmented by screaming fans that had obviously been overdubbed. Partially recorded at a 1966 Royal Albert Hall performance (where the audience rioted at the opening of the concert), the performances and singing are on the sloppy side (and sometimes alarmingly out of tune), the sound balance is atrocious, and several of the songs are taken at a let's-get-this-over-with-and-off-the-stage-before-we-get-torn-apart pace. It's a fun souvenir in its own way; just don't expect top-notch value, even factoring in the primitive state of live rock recording technology in 1966. *— Richie Unterberger*

☆ **Between the Buttons** / Jan. 1967 / ABKCO ✦✦✦✦✦

The Rolling Stones' 1967 recordings are a matter of some controversy; many critics felt that they were compromising their raw, rootsy power with trendy emulations of the Beatles, Kinks, Dylan, and psychedelic music. Approach this album with an open mind, though, and you'll find it to be one of their strongest, most eclectic LPs, with many fine songs that remain unknown to all but Stones devotees. The lyrics are getting better (if more savage), and the arrangements more creative, on brooding near-classics like "All Sold Out," "My Obsession," and "Yesterday's Papers." "She Smiled Sweetly" shows their hidden romantic side at its best, while "Connection" is one of the record's few slabs of conventionally driving rock. But the best tracks were the two songs that gave the group a double-sided No. 1 in early 1967: the lustful "Let's Spend the Night Together" and the beautiful, melancholy "Ruby Tuesday," which is as melodic as anything Jagger and Richards would ever write. *— Richie Unterberger*

Flowers / Jun. 1967 / ABKCO ✦✦✦✦

Dismissed as a ripoff of sorts by some critics, as it took the patchwork bastardization of British releases for the American audience to extremes, gathering stray tracks from the UK versions of *Aftermath* and *Between the Buttons*, 1966-67 singles (some of which had already been used on the US editions of *Aftermath* and *Between the Buttons*), and a few outtakes. Judged solely by the music, though, it's rather great. "Mother's Little Helper," "Lady Jane," "Ruby Tuesday," and "Let's Spend the Night Together" are all classics (although they had all been on LP before); the 1966 single "Have You Seen Your Mother, Baby, Standing in the Shadow" makes its first album appearance, and is the early Stones at their most surrealistic and angst-ridden. A lot of the rest of the cuts rate among their most outstanding 1966-67 work. "Out of Time" is hit-worthy in its own right (and in fact topped the British charts in an inferior cover by Chris Farlowe); "Back Street Girl," with its European waltz flavor, is one of *the* great underrated Stones songs. The same goes for the psychedelic Bo Diddley of "Please Go Home," and the acoustic, pensively sardonic "Sittin' on a Fence," with its strong Appalachian flavor. Almost every track is strong, so if you're serious about your Stones, don't pass this by just because a bunch of people slag it as an exploitative marketing trick (which it is). There's some outstanding material you can't get anywhere else, and the album as a whole plays very well from end-to-end. *— Richie Unterberger*

Their Satanic Majesties Request / Nov. 1967 / ABKCO ✦✦✦

Without a doubt, no Rolling Stones album—and, indeed, very few rock albums from any era—split critical opinion as much as the Rolling Stones' psychedelic outing. Many dismiss the record as sub-*Sgt. Pepper* posturing; others confess, if only in private, to a fascination with the album's inventive arrangements, which incorporated some African rhythms, mellotrons, and full orchestration. Never before or since did the Stones take so many chances in the studio. This writer, at least, feels that the record has been unfairly undervalued, partly because purists expect the Stones to constantly champion a blues 'n' raunch worldview. About half the material is very strong, particularly the glorious "She's a Rainbow," with its beautiful harmonies, piano, and strings; the riff-driven "Citadel"; the hazy, dream-like "In Another Land," Bill Wyman's debut writing (and singing) credit on a Stones release; and the majestically dark and doomy cosmic rocker "2000 Light Years from Home," with some of the creepiest synthesizer effects (devised by Brian Jones) ever to grace a rock record. The downfall of the album was caused by some weak songwriting on the lesser tracks, particularly the interminable psychedelic jam "Sing This All Together (See What Happens)." It's a much better record than most people give it credit for being, though, with a strong current of creeping uneasiness that undercuts the gaudy psychedelic flourishes. In 1968, the Stones would go back to the basics, and never wander down these paths again, making this all the more of a fascinating anomaly in the group's discography. —*Richie Unterberger*

☆ **Beggars Banquet** / Nov. 1968 / ABKCO ◆◆◆◆◆
The Stones forsook psychedelic experimentation to return to their blues roots on this celebrated album, which was immediately acclaimed as one of their landmark achievements. A strong acoustic Delta blues flavor colors much of the material, particularly "Salt of the Earth" and "No Expectations," which features some beautiful slide guitar work. Basic rock and roll was not forgotten, however: "Street Fighting Man," a reflection of the political turbulence of 1968, was one of their most innovative singles, and "Sympathy for the Devil," with its fire-dancing guitar licks, leering Jagger vocal, African rhythms, and explicitly satanic lyrics, was an image-defining epic. On "Stray Cat Blues," Jagger and buddies begin to explore the kind of decadent sexual sleaze that the group would take to the point of self-parody by the mid-'70s. At the time, though, the approach was still fresh, and the lyrical bite of most of the material ensured its place as one of the top blues-based rock records of all time. —*Richie Unterberger*

Through the Past Darkly (Big Hits, Vol. 2) / Sep. 1969 / ABKCO ◆◆◆◆
Their biggest '60s hits, from "Paint It Black" onward. Like *High Tide and Green Grass*, it's somewhat redundant these days, as all of the tracks appear on the more extensive *Hot Rocks* anthologies. What's in the grooves, though, is wall-to-wall classic, including "Ruby Tuesday," "Let's Spend the Night Together," "Jumpin' Jack Flash," "Honky Tonk Woman," "Have You Seen Your Mother, Baby, Standing in the Shadow," "She's a Rainbow," "Street Fighting Man," and more. —*Richie Unterberger*

☆ **Let It Bleed** / Nov. 28, 1969 / ABKCO ◆◆◆◆◆
Mostly recorded without Brian Jones, who died several months before its release (although he does play on two tracks), and was replaced by Mick Taylor (who also plays on just two songs). This extends the rock 'n' blues feel of *Beggar's Banquet* into slightly harder-rocking, more demonically sexual territory. The Stones were never as consistent on album as their main rivals, the Beatles, and *Let It Bleed* suffers from some rather half-assed tracks, like "Monkey Man" and a countrified remake of the classic "Honky Tonk Woman" single (here titled "Country Honk"). Yet some of the songs are among their very best, especially "Gimme Shelter," with its shimmering guitar lines and apocalyptic lyrics; the harmonica-driven "Midnight Rambler"; the druggy party ambience of the title track; and the stunning "You Can't Always Get What You Want," which was the Stones' "Hey Jude" of sorts, with its epic structure, horns, philosophical lyrics, and swelling choral vocals. "You Got the Silver" (Keith Richards' first lead vocal) and Robert Johnson's "Love in Vain," by contrast, were as close to the roots of acoustic down-home blues as the Stones ever got. —*Richie Unterberger*

Get Yer Ya-Ya's Out / Sep. 4, 1970 / ABKCO ◆◆◆◆
Recorded during their American tour in late 1969, and centered around live versions of material from the *Beggars Banquet*-*Let It Bleed* era. Often acclaimed as one of the top live rock albums of all time, its appeal has dimmed a little today. The live versions are reasonably different from the studio ones, but ultimately not as good, a notable exception being the long workout of

"Midnight Rambler," with extended harmonica solos and the unforgettable section where the pace slows to a bump-and-grind crawl. Some Stones aficionados, in fact, prefer a bootleg from the same tour (*Liver Than You'll Ever Be*, to which this LP was unleashed in response), or their amazing the-show-must-go-on performance in the jaws of hell at Altamont (preserved in the *Gimme Shelter* film). Fans that are unconcerned with picky comparisons such as these will still find *Ya Ya's...*an outstanding album, and it's certainly the Stones' best official live recording. —*Richie Unterberger*

☆ **Sticky Fingers** / Apr. 23, 1971 / Virgin ◆◆◆◆◆
Pieced together from outtakes and much-labored-over songs, *Sticky Fingers* manages to have a loose, ramshackle ambience that belies both its origins and the dark undercurrents of the songs. It's a weary, drug-laden album—well over half of the songs explicitly mention drug use, while the others merely allude to it either in subject matter or their tone—that never fades away, but it barely keeps afloat. Apart from the classic opener "Brown Sugar" (a gleeful tune about slavery, interracial sex, lost virginity and not in that order), the long workout "Can't You Hear Me Knocking" and the mean-spirited "Bitch," *Sticky Fingers* is a slow, bluesy affair, with a few country touches thrown in for good measure. The laidback tone of the album gives ample room for new lead guitarist Mick Taylor to stretch out, particularly on the extended coda of "Can't You Hear Me Knocking." But the key to the album isn't the instrumental interplay, although that is terrific, it's the utter weariness of the songs. "Wild Horses" is their first non-ironic stab at country song and it is a beautiful, heart-tugging masterpiece. Similarly, "I Got the Blues" is a ravished, late-night classic that ranks among their very best blues. "Sister Morphine" is a horrific overdose tale and "Moonlight Mile," with Paul Buckmaster's grandiose strings, is a perfect closure—sad, yearning, drug-addled and beautiful. With its off-handed mixture of decadence, roots-music, and outright malevolence, *Sticky Fingers* set the tone for the rest of the decade for the Stones. —*Stephen Thomas Erlewine*

Hot Rocks 1964-1971 / Jan. 1972 / ABKCO ◆◆◆◆
This important double-disc anthology contains their biggest hits on London, as well as many of their most popular album tracks. A stereo version of "Satisfaction" is the highlight, and worth the price, even though the US mono version is also pretty cool. —*Bruce Eder*

☆ **Exile on Main Street** / May 12, 1972 / Virgin ◆◆◆◆◆
Greeted with decidedly mixed reviews upon its original release, *Exile on Main Street* has become generally regarded as the Rolling Stones' finest album. Part of the reason why the record was initially greeted with hesitant reviews is that it takes a while to assimilate. A sprawling, weary double album encompassing rock 'n' roll, blues, soul and country, *Exile* doesn't try anything new on the surface, but the substance is new. Taking the bleakness that underpinned *Let It Bleed* and *Sticky Fingers* to an extreme, *Exile* is a weary record, and not just lyrically. Jagger's vocals are buried in the mix, and the music is a series of dark, dense jams, with Keith Richards and Mick Taylor spinning off incredible riffs and solos. And the songs continue the breakthroughs of their three previous albums. No longer does their country sound forced or kitschy—it's lived-in and complex, just like the group's forays into soul and gospel. While the songs, including the masterpieces "Rocks Off," "Tumbling Dice," "Torn and Frayed," "Happy," "Let It Loose," and "Shine a Light," are all terrific, they blend together, with only certain lyrics and guitar lines emerging from the murk. It's the kind of record which is gripping upon the first listen, but each listen reveals something new—few other albums, let alone double albums, have been so rich and masterful as *Exile on Main Street*, and it stands as not only one of the Stones' best records, but sets a remarkably high standard for all of hard rock. —*Stephen Thomas Erlewine*

● **More Hot Rocks (Big Hits and Fazed Cookies)** / Nov. 1972 / ABKCO ◆◆◆◆
Hot Rocks covers most of the monster hits from the Stones' first decade that remain in radio rotation in the '90s. *More Hot Rocks* goes for the somewhat smaller hits, some of the better album tracks, and a whole LP side worth of rarities that hadn't yet been available in the United States when this compilation was released in 1972. The material isn't as famous as what's on *Hot Rocks*, but the music is almost as excellent, including such vital cuts as "Not Fade Away," "It's All Over Now," "The Last Time," "Lady Jane," the psychedelic "Dandelion," "She's a Rainbow," "Have You Seen Your Mother, Baby, Standing in the Shadow?," "Out of Time," "Tell Me," and "We Love You." The eight

rarities are pretty good as well, including their 1963 debut single "Come On," early R&B covers of "Fortune Teller" and "Bye Bye Johnnie," great slide guitar on Muddy Waters' "I Can't Be Satisfied," and the soulful 1966 UK B-side, "Long Long While." — *Richie Unterberger*

Goats Head Soup / Aug. 31, 1973 / Virgin ◆◆◆

Compared to the monumental *Exile on Main Street*, *Goats Head Soup* is bound to sound inferior, and it does. Nevertheless, the album doesn't deserve its bad reputation. It might be careless and decadent, but that excess is quite intoxicating, as the nasty rocker "Star Star" and the finely crafted ballad "Angie" prove. — *Stephen Thomas Erlewine*

It's Only Rock and Roll / Oct. 18, 1974 / Virgin ◆◆◆

It's uneven, but at times *It's Only Rock and Roll* catches fire. The songs and performances are stronger than those on *Goats Head Soup;* the tossed-off numbers sound effortless, not careless. Throughout, the Stones wear their title as the "World's Greatest Rock & Roll Band" with a defiant smirk, which makes the bitter cynicism of "If You Can't Rock Me" and the title track all the more striking, and the reggae experimentation of "Luxury," the aching beauty of "Time Waits for No One," and the agreeable filler of "Dance Little Sister" and "Short and Curlies" all the more enjoyable. — *Stephen Thomas Erlewine*

Metamorphosis / Jun. 1975 / ABKCO ◆◆

A motley assortment of '60s outtakes, apparently compiled by the Stones' former managers to squeeze every last drop from the group's songwriting backlog. Most of the cuts are demos of weak Jagger-Richards songs that became flop singles for other artists; it's likely that some of the Stones don't even play on much of the album. The versions of "Out of Time" and "Heart of Stone" are abominable when compared to the more widely known original renditions. The late-'60s outtakes that make up most of side two (including a rare Bill Wyman original, "Downtown Suzie") probably do feature the actual group, but quite simply don't cut it. And did we mention the atrocious cover design? A couple exceptions make the LP worth picking up for Stones fanatics: a decent mid-'60s cover of Chuck Berry's "Don't Lie to Me," and "If You Let Me," a nice folk-rock outtake from *Between the Buttons*. Note: The British version contains two additional tracks. — *Richie Unterberger*

Black & Blue / Apr. 20, 1976 / Virgin ◆◆◆

Ron Wood's first album with the Stones finds the band working through a number of reggae—and funk-tinged numbers, trying to expand their sound. Consequently, songs are sacrificed for grooves; only the ballads "Memory Motel" and "Fool to Cry" are fully developed, but the grooves that dominate the album are strong enough to make the record successful. — *Stephen Thomas Erlewine*

Love You Live / Sep. 23, 1977 / Rolling Stones ◆◆

Recorded on the supporting tour for 1976's *Black & Blue*, the double-album set *Love You Live* is an adequate live album, capturing the Stones' transition from a lean, lethal rock 'n' roll band to accomplished show men. As show men, they aren't as compelling as they are when they're rockers, but the show-biz glitz of Mick Jagger's arena-rock schitck remains thoroughly entertaining, even when it robs the music of its power. — *Stephen Thomas Erlewine*

☆ Some Girls / Jun. 9, 1978 / Virgin ◆◆◆◆◆

During the mid-'70s, the Rolling Stones remained massively popular, but their records suffered from Jagger's fascination with celebrity and Keith's worsening drug addictions. By 1978, both punk and disco had swept the group off the front pages, and *Some Girls* are their fiery response to the younger generation. Opening with the disco-blues thump of "Miss You," *Some Girls* is a tough, focused, and exciting record, full of more hooks and energy than any record since *Exile on Main Street*. Even though the Stones make disco into their own, they never quite take punk on their own ground. Instead, their rockers sound harder and nastier than they have in years. Taking "Star Star" as a starting point, the Stones run through the seedy homosexual imagery of "When the Whip Comes Down" before landing on the bizarre, borderline misogynist vitriol of the title track, Keith's ultimate outlaw anthem "Before They Make Me Run," and the decadent closer, "Shattered." In between, they deconstruct the Temptations' "(Just My) Imagination," offer a devastating, snide country parody ("Far Away Eyes") and contribute "Beast of Burden," one of their very best ballads. *Some Girls* may not have the backstreet aggression of their '60s records, or the majestic, drugged-out murk

of their early-'70s work, but in its glitzy, decadent hard rock, it offers a definitive Stones album. — *Stephen Thomas Erlewine*

Emotional Rescue / Jun. 23, 1980 / Virgin ◆◆◆

Coasting on the success of *Some Girls*, the Stones offered more of the same on *Emotional Rescue*. Comprised of leftovers from the previous album's sessions and hastily written new numbers, *Emotional Rescue* may consist mainly of filler, but it's expertly written and performed filler. The Stones toss off throwaways like the reggae-fueled, mail-order bride anthem "Send It to Me" or rockers like "Summer Romance" and "Where the Boys Go" with an authority that makes the record a guilty pleasure, even if it's clear that only two songs—the icy but sexy disco-rock of "Emotional Rescue" and the revamped Chuck Berry rocker "She's So Cold"—come close to being classic Stones. — *Stephen Thomas Erlewine*

Tattoo You / Aug. 30, 1981 / Virgin ◆◆◆◆

Like *Emotional Rescue* before it, *Tattoo You* was comprised primarily of leftovers, but unlike its predecessor, it never sounds that way. Instead, *Tattoo You* captures the Stones at their best as a professional stadium-rock band. Divided into a rock 'n' roll side and a ballad side, the album delivers its share of thrills on the tight, dynamic first side. "Start Me Up" became the record's definitive Stonesy rocker, but the frenzied doo wop of "Hang Fire," the reggae jam of "Slave," the sleazy Chuck Berry rockers "Little T&A" and "Neighbours," and the hard blues of "Black Limousine" are all terrific. The ballad side suffers in comparison, especially since "Heaven" and "No Use in Crying" are faceless. But "Worried About You" and "Tops" are effortless, excellent ballads, and "Waiting on a Friend," with its Sonny Rollins sax solo, is an absolute masterpiece, with a moving lyric that captures Jagger in a shockingly reflective and affecting state of mind. "Waiting on a Friend" and the vigorous rock 'n' roll of the first side make *Tattoo You* an essential latter-day Stones album, ranking just a few notches below *Some Girls*. — *Stephen Thomas Erlewine*

Still Life / Jun. 1, 1982 / Rolling Stones ◆

Like *Love You Live* before it, *Still Life* showcases the Stones as pure entertainers, although the band adds enough rhythmic grit to keep the record from sinking into pure show-biz formula. Nevertheless, it isn't nearly enough grit to make it rock as hard as *Get Yer Ya-Ya's Out*. Or even *Love You Live*, depressingly enough. — *Stephen Thomas Erlewine*

Undercover / Nov. 7, 1983 / Virgin ◆◆◆

As their most ambitious album since *Some Girls*, *Undercover* is a weird, wild mix of hard rock, new wave pop, reggae, dub, and soul. Even with all the careening musical eclecticism, what distinguishes *Undercover* is its bleak, nihilistic attitude—it's teeming with sickness, with violence, kinky sex, and loathing dripping from almost every song. "Undercover of the Night" slams with echoing guitars and rubbery bass lines, as Jagger gives a feverish litany of sex, corruption, and suicide. It set the tone for the rest of the album, whether it's the runaway nymphomaniac of "She Was Hot" or the ridiculous slasher imagery of "Too Much Blood." Only Keith's "Wanna Hold You" offers a reprieve from the carnage, and its relentless bloodletting makes the album a singularly fascinating listen. For some observers, that mixture was nearly too difficult to stomach, but for others, it's a fascinating record, particularly since much of its nastiness feels as if the Stones, and Jagger and Richards in particular, are running out of patience with each other. — *Stephen Thomas Erlewine*

Dirty Work / 1986 / Virgin ◆◆◆

Reuniting after three years and one solo album from Mick Jagger, the Rolling Stones attempted to settle their differences and craft a comeback with *Dirty Work*, but the tensions remained too great for the group. Designed as a return to their rock 'n' roll roots after several years of vague dance experiments, *Dirty Work* is hampered by uneven songs and undistinguished performances, as well as a slick, lightly synthesized production that instantly dates the album to the mid-'80s. Jagger often sounds like he's saving his best work for his solo records, but a handful of songs have a spry, vigorous attack— "One Hit (To the Body)" is a classic, and "Winning Ugly" and "Had It With You" have a similar aggression. Still, most of *Dirty Work* sounds as forced as the cover of Bob & Earl's uptown soul obscurity "Harlem Shuffle," leaving the album as one of the group's most undistinguished efforts. — *Stephen Thomas Erlewine*

☆ **Singles Collection: The London Years** / 1989 / ABKCO ✦✦✦✦✦
The three-disc box set *Singles Collection: The London Years* contains every single the Rolling Stones released during the '60s, including both the A and B-sides. It is the first Stones compilation that tries to be comprehensive and logical—for all their attributes, the two *Hot Rocks* sets and the two *Big Hits* collections didn't present the singles in chronological order. In essence, the previous compilations were excellent samplers, where *Singles Collection* tells most of the story (certain albums, like *Aftermath, Beggars Banquet* and *Let It Bleed*, fill in the gaps left by the singles). The Rolling Stones made genuine albums—even their early R&B/blues albums were impeccably paced—but their singles had a power all their own, which is quite clearly illustrated by the *Singles Collection*. By presenting the singles in chronological order, the set takes on a relentless, exhilerating pace with each hit and neglected B-side piling on top of each other, adding a new dimension to the group; it has a power it wouldn't have had if it tried to sample from the albums. Although it cheats near the end, adding singles from the *Metamorphosis* outtakes collection and two singles from *Sticky Fingers*, this captures the essence of the '60s Stones as well as any compilation could. Casual fans might want to stick with the *Hot Rocks* sets, since they just have the hits, but for those that want a little bit more, the *Singles Collection* is absolutely essential. —*Stephen Thomas Erlewine*

Steel Wheels / Aug. 1989 / Virgin ✦✦✦
The band's best album of the '80s, embracing blues, classic rock, and even psychedelia ("Continental Drift"). —*Bruce Eder*

Flashpoint / Apr. 1991 / Rolling Stones ✦✦
The live follow-ups and a fond look back on 25 years of decadence. —*Bruce Eder*

Jump Back: The Best of the Rolling Stones 1971-1993 / Nov. 19, 1993 / Virgin ✦✦✦✦

Voodoo Lounge / Jul. 19, 1994 / Capitol ✦✦✦
While *Voodoo Lounge* sounds amazingly like the Stones' classic records from the early '70s, it's rather inconsistent and too long to make it one of their major works. Instead, it's simply another solid Stones record, with some fine tracks and typically strong playing. —*Stephen Thomas Erlewine*

Stripped / Nov. 14, 1995 / Virgin ✦✦✦
Despite the odds, the Rolling Stones' *Stripped* held out great promise. *Voodoo Lounge* was an energized return to studio form for the Borg of rock 'n' roll road shows. From that platform, the idea of taking it back to small clubs, live, lean, and pared down without succumbing to the worn "unplugged" treadmill, seemed an inspired move. Patched together from an embroidery of tour rehearsals and live club dates in Paris and Amsterdam, the project was an extension of acoustic sets the group introduced on the North American leg of the *Voodoo Lounge* tour. The concept offered an invigorating opportunity to dust off some rough gems from the past that no longer felt at home on scoping stadium stages. Unfortunately, the cover photo depicting a lean, determined, leather-clad combo in spartan black and white proves to be misleading advertising. Within the brave packaging lies a listless, lethargic Dorian Gray bluff. Spongy keyboards gunk many of the tracks. The much-touted cover of Dylan's "Like a Rolling Stone" remains pointlessly devoted to the original. There are lazy, somnambulant versions of "I'm Free" and "Let It Bleed"; Keith Richards' painfully intoned "Slipping Away"; the dozens of lost songs that any fan would chose to have renovated before "Angie." —*Roch Parisien*

R.S.V.P. [bootleg] / 1996 / Cool Blokes Production ✦✦✦
A 78-minute disc of alternate mixes and outtakes from the *Beggars Banquet* session, in superb sound. This effectively acts as an alternate version of *Beggars Banquet* itself. There are different versions/mixes of every track from that album except "Street Fighting Man," along with five songs (some instrumental) never released by the Stones. It might read more exciting than it plays. Some of the alternates differ in such subtle ways that they sound all but identical to the official versions, although trainspotters will appreciate differences like the prominent organ at the tag of "No Expectations." The otherwise unreleased tunes, which are loose, bluesy thangs with considerable funky charm, have already been found on various late-'60s Stones boots, although the sound quality here is unbeatable. Hardcore Stones scholars, though, will find the disc worth getting. —*Richie Unterberger*

Rolling Stones Rock & Roll Circus / Oct. 15, 1996 / ABKCO ✦✦✦
The most interesting archival release of the Rolling Stones since *More Hot Rocks*, 20 years ago, and the first issue of truly unreleased material by the Stones from this period. And the Stones have some competition from the Who, Taj Mahal, and John Lennon on the same release. Filmed and recorded on December 10-11, 1968 at a North London studio, *Rock & Roll Circus* has been, as much as the Beach Boys' *Smile*, "the one that got away" for most '60s music enthusiasts. The Jethro Tull sequence is the standard studio track, but the rest—except for the Stones' "Salt of the Earth"—is really live. The Who's portion has been out before, courtesy of various documentaries, but Taj Mahal playing some loud electric blues is new and great, the live Lennon rendition of "Yer Blues" is indispensable, and the Stones' set fills in lots of blanks in their history—"Jumpin' Jack Flash" in one of two live renditions it ever got with Brian Jones in the lineup, "Sympathy for the Devil" in an intense run-through, "Parachute Woman" as a lost live vehicle for the band, "You Can't Always Get What You Want" as a show-stopping rocker even without its extended ending (no Paul Buckmaster choir), and "No Expectations" as their first piece of great live blues since "Little Red Rooster." It's a must-own, period. —*Bruce Eder*

Bridges to Babylon / Sep. 23, 1997 / Virgin ✦✦✦
Voodoo Lounge confirmed that the Stones could age gracefully, but it never sounded modern; it sounded classicist. With its successor, *Bridges to Babylon*, Mick Jagger was determined to bring the Rolling Stones into the '90s, albeit tentatively, and hired hip collaborators like the Dust Brothers (Beck, Beastie Boys) and Danny Saber (Black Grape) to give the veteran group an edge on their explorations of drum loops and samples. Of course, the Stones are the Stones, and no production is going to erase that, but the group is smart enough—or Keith Richards is stubborn enough—to work within their limitations and to have producer Don Was act as executive producer. As a result, *Bridges to Babylon* sounds like the Stones without sounding tired. The band is tight and energetic, and there's just enough flair to the sultry "Anybody Seen My Baby?," the menacing "Gunface," and the low-key, sleazy "Might as Well Get Juiced" to make them sound contemporary. But the real key to the success of *Bridges to Babylon* is the solid, craftsmanlike songwriting. While there aren't any stunners on the album, nothing is bad, with rockers like "Flip the Switch" and "Low Down" sounding as convincing as ballads like "Already Over Me." And, as always, Keith contributes three winners—including the reggae workout "You Don't Have to Mean It" and the slow-burning "How Can I Stop"—that cap off another fine latter-day Stones record. —*Stephen Thomas Erlewine*

Bright Lights, Big City / [bootleg] ✦✦✦✦
As you'd expect, there are a ton of Rolling Stones bootlegs, but there isn't a great deal of essential material from the '60s to be found on them. The exceptions are these outtakes from 1963 and 1964, which have popped up under quite a few guises, but most frequently under the *Bright Lights, Big City* title. The five early-1963 demos were cut shortly before they signed with Decca, and capture the band at their bluesiest and blackest; when Brian Jones was being frozen out of The Stones in the late '60s, it's said that he would play these for listeners as examples of the purity of the group's original vision. With clear fidelity, the standards of these performances are well up to official release; "Baby What's Wrong," "Road Runner," and "I Want to Be Loved" are downright electrifying. The four 1964 cuts were recorded at Chess Studios, and again (with the possible exception of the jam "Stewed and Keefed") are well up to release quality, with fine, spare readings of "Hi-Heel Sneakers," Howlin' Wolf's "Down in the Bottom," and Big Bill Broonzy's "Tell Me Baby." Essential for serious fans. —*Richie Unterberger*

BBC Sessions / [bootleg] ✦✦✦
The Rolling Stones' BBC sessions haven't been accorded the same deluxe bootleg treatment as those of the Beatles, for two big reasons: they didn't record nearly as much for the Beeb as the Fab Four, and (unlike the Beatles) didn't record many tracks that they didn't release on record. Good fidelity tapes exist of a few dozen of their mid-'60s BBC airshots, and fans will find them worth picking up. Heavy on R&B covers (the Stones, like the Beatles, didn't record for the BBC after 1965), the tracks, as is par for the course on radio sessions, don't better or usually even equal the studio renditions, but have an interesting rougher live feel. They did manage to let rip on a half-dozen or so unreleased covers, and these items are naturally the most interesting, especially their takes on "Memphis, Tennessee" and their incendiary

"Roll Over Beethoven," which is perhaps even better than the well-known Beatle version. —*Richie Unterberger*

Out of Time / Monroe ✦✦✦✦
A great concept for an album that, no matter what Allen Klein might say, helps more people than it hurts: 16 songs assembled from the '60s B-sides, import-only singles, compilations, and soundtracks that have proven extremely hard to find in America. A few of the songs did finally show up on ABKCO's *Singles Collection.* but many remain unavailable. And some of these items are very good: a longer version of the smoking "2120 South Michigan Avenue" instrumental (only issued in Germany), the long, very different take of "Everybody Needs Somebody to Love" that was issued on their second British LP, "I've Been Loving You Too Long" minus the overdubbed screams on *Got Live If You Want It*, the Italian version of "As Tears Go By," Jagger's "Memo from Turner" (from the *Performance* soundtrack), and two early songs that only showed up on the British version of *Metamorphosis.* "I Want to Be Loved" and "I Wanna Be Your Man" (which were officially reissued on *Singles Collection*) are among their best early tracks. Good sound, topped off with a superb picture sleeve of the Stones in drag in 1966, add up to an LP that is essential for serious Stones fans, and indeed better than many of their "official" albums. —*Richie Unterberger*

Tricky Fingers & Sticky Ringers / Luna ✦✦✦
"Alternate versions" of entire albums are somewhat in vogue by rock bootleggers, who compile entire CDs of alternate/live takes of songs from one specific full-length recording. This is one attempt at an alternate version of *Sticky Fingers*, and not bad, though not as successful as it may appear from a glance at the sleeve. There are indeed alternate studio takes of "Brown Sugar," "Wild Horses," "Sister Morphine," "You Gotta Move," and "Bitch." In fact, there are four different versions of "Brown Sugar" alone, including the famous one with a prominent slide guitar. The thing is, they really aren't *that* different; at a casual listen, they sound almost exactly like the album versions, sometimes amounting to nothing more drastic than different mixes. And it's uncertain whether the live versions of "Dead Flowers" and "Can't You Hear Me Knocking" actually come from 1969-1971, as the sleeve claims. A 14-minute performance of "Can't You Hear Me Knocking" sounds particularly enticing, but this fair-quality live recording (no source given) doesn't sound like it's from the *Sticky Fingers* period; indeed, it sounds suspiciously like it might be from a Jagger-less side project of Keith Richards or somebody. These reservations aside, hard-core Stones fans may find this worthwhile, with a 66-minute running time and the addition of a cover of Chuck Berry's "Let It Rock" (which was not included on *Sticky Fingers*). —*Richie Unterberger*

Roomful of Blues

f. 1967, Providence, RI
Group / Jump Blues, Modern Electric Blues
Nine-piece blues/jump band from Providence, Rhode Island, formed in 1967. Has recorded and toured tirelessly for over two decades, while eschewing the standard Chicago blues band/Muddy Waters approach for a horn-dominated style that owes more to jazz leanings and late-'40s blues masters like Wynonie Harris, Roy Brown, and Big Joe Turner. More than capable of backing artists like Turner, Eddie "Cleanhead" Vinson (both of whom had Roomful back them for complete albums) as well as delivering the goods on their own, major players who have come through the ranks over the years have included guitarists Duke Robillard and Ronnie Earl, bassist Preston Hubbard and drummer Fran Christina (Fabulous Thunderbirds). They continued performing into the 1990s, issuing LPs including 1994's *Dance All Night* and 1995's *Turn It on, Turn It Up.* —*AMG*

Roomful of Blues / 1979 / Island ✦✦✦

• **Let's Have a Party** / Nov. 1979 / Antilles ✦✦✦✦
Decent to good R&B-influenced jump and party blues. This group has always been great live; their albums have always been mixed affairs, and this was no different. —*Ron Wynn*

Hot Little Mama / 1981 / Varrick ✦✦✦

Dressed Up to Get Messed Up / 1984 / Varrick ✦✦

Live at Lupo's Heartbreak Hotel / Nov. 1987 / Varrick ✦✦✦
Live at Lupo's Heartbreak Hotel is a fine, but unremarkable, set Roomful of Blues recorded in the late '80s. The source material—Fats Domino, Howlin'

Wolf, etc.—is fine and there are good solos scattered throughout the album, but the entire record never quite catches fire. —*Thom Owens*

Dance All Night / May 28, 1994 / Bullseye Blues ✦✦✦✦
This incarnation of Roomful of Blues includes vocalist and harmonica player Sugar Ray Norcia taking the singing spotlight, Matt McCabe now their pianist and Chris Vachon principal guitarist. This CD blends blues and R&B classics with a couple of originals; highlights include a fine reading of Smiley Lewis' "Lillie Mae," a remake of "Hey Now" originally done by Ray Charles and Norcia's fiery vocal and torrid harmonica solo on Little Walter Jacobs' "Up the Line." This is faithful to the classic tradition, but contains enough contemporary qualities to have a fresh and inviting sound. —*Ron Wynn*

Turn It on! Turn It Up! / Oct. 3, 1995 / Bullseye Blues ✦✦✦
Roomful of Blues' *Turn It on, Turn It Up* is a typically infectious set of barroom burners from the popular blues-rockers. Not all of the songs are particularly memorable, but they play with a joyous energy that makes the shortcomings easy to accept. —*Sara Sytsma*

Under One Roof / Dec. 2, 1995-Dec. 7, 1995 / Bullseye Blues ✦✦✦
At its best, Roomful of Blues is a throwback to the heated jump bands of the early '50s, which blended hard-driving swing with the extroverted emotions of early R&B. However, this particular release is different than expected. Listeners who hope to hear extended solos and riotous ensembles are sure to be disappointed, for much of the time Roomful of Blues sounds like an anonymous backup group put together specifically to accompany singer Sugar Ray Norcia. Sugar Ray is a versatile and talented singer, and his repertoire ranges from a Basie blues to tunes that are closer to rock, soul and even country. If one comes to this CD without false expectations, the music is enjoyable on its own level, but from the jazz standpoint, the release is rather routine and not very significant. —*Scott Yanow*

First Album / 1996 / Varrick ✦✦✦

Two Classic Albums / May 5, 1997 / 32 Jazz ✦✦✦✦

Bobby Rush (Emmit Ellis, Jr.)

b. Nov. 10, 1940, Homer, LA
Vocals / Modern Electric Blues, Retro-Soul
The creator of a singular sound which he dubbed "folk-funk," multi-instrumentalist Bobby Rush was among the most colorful characters on the contemporary chitlin circuit, honing a unique style which brought together a cracked lyrical bent with elements of blues, soul and funk. Born Emmit Ellis, Jr. in Homer, Louisiana on November 10, 1940, he and his family relocated to Chicago in 1953, where he emerged on the West Side blues circuit of the 1960s, fronting bands which included such notable alumni as Luther Allison and Freddie King. However, as Rush began to develop his own individual sound, he opted to forgo the blues market in favor of targeting the chitlin circuit, which offered a more receptive audience for his increasingly bawdy material; he notched his first hit in 1971 with his Galaxy label single "Chicken Heads," and later scored with "Bow-Legged Woman" for Jewel. He appeared on a wide variety of labels as the decade progressed, culminating in the 1979 LP *Rush Hour*, produced by Kenny Gamble and Leon Huff for their Philadelphia International imprint. During the early '80s, Rush signed with the LaJam label, where he remained for a number of years; there his work became increasingly funky and deranged, with records like 1984's *Gotta Have Money* and 1985's *What's Good for the Goose Is Good for the Gander*, often featuring material so suggestive he refused to re-create it live. During the mid-'90s, Rush moved to Waldoxy, heralding a return to a soul-blues sound on LPs including 1995's *One Monkey Don't Stop No Show* and 1997's *Lovin' a Big Fat Woman.* —*Jason Ankeny*

Rush Hour / 1979 / Philadelphia International ✦✦✦✦
Kenny Gamble and Leon Huff produced *Rush Hour*, Bobby Rush's belated full-length debut album, for the Philadelphia International label. By that time, their patented Philly soul sound was out of favor, and they wisely chose not to impose it on Rush. Nevertheless, the album is considerably slicker than any of his Ichiban albums. Oddly, this is hardly a problem, since Rush always favored soul more than blues and had a fondness for funk. The only real flaw with the record is that the material is a bit uneven, but the quality of the performances carries it over rough spots and helps make the record one of the best in his catalog. —*Thom Owens*

Handy Man / 1992 / Urgent! ◆◆◆

Like any of Bobby Rush's '90s recordings for Urgent! and Ichiban, *Handy Man* is a pretty good album that draws from Chicago blues and Southern soul equally. Rush gives some good performances which carry the album through some lame original songs and flat, synth-laden production, complete with robotic drum machines. Of course, this holds true for almost any of Rush's albums, which means you've got to take what you can get, and here you get a couple of good songs balanced by a lot of filler. And Rush fans should be used to that by now. — *Thom Owens*

● **Instant Replays: The Hits** / 1992 / Ichiban ◆◆◆◆

Instant Replays: The Hits is a good overview of Bobby Rush's '80s recordings for Urgent! and Ichiban, capturing all of the highlights from such funky, greasy blues albums as *Gotta Have Money* and *What's Good for the Goose is Good for the Gander*. — *Thom Owens*

One Monkey Don't Stop No Show / 1995 / Waldoxy ◆◆

Bobby Rush is a no-holds-barred showman, and his R-rated live shows are an unforgettable (if politically incorrect) experience. That makes it a pity that this recording (like many of his others) is so forgettable. He takes blues standards, adds a few lyric snippets of his own, and transforms their melodies into virtually identical funky vamps. This quickly gets uninteresting. The extensive use of synthesizers doesn't help. And claiming authorship of songs that are so obviously mere adaptations of others' is a dubious practice. — *Steve Hoffman*

She's a Good Un (It's Alright) / Dec. 5, 1995 / Ronn ◆◆◆

Sue / May 28, 1996 / La Jam ◆◆◆

It's Alright, Vol. 2 / May 7, 1997 / Ronn ◆◆◆

Lovin' a Big Fat Woman / May 27, 1997 / Waldoxy ◆◆◆

What's Good for the Goose Is Good for the Gander / Aug. 26, 1997 / La Jam ◆◆◆

Otis Rush

b. Apr. 29, 1934, Philadelphia, MS
Guitar, Vocals / Soul, R&B, Electric Chicago Blues, Chicago Blues, Electric Blues

Breaking into the R&B Top Ten his very first time out in 1956 with the startlingly intense slow blues "I Can't Quit You Baby," southpaw guitarist Otis Rush subsequently established himself as one of the premier bluesmen on the Chicago circuit. He remains so today.

Rush is often credited with being one of the architects of the West Side guitar style, along with Magic Sam and Buddy Guy. It's a nebulous honor, since Otis Rush played clubs on Chicago's South Side just as frequently during the sound's late-'50s incubation period. Nevertheless, his esteemed status as a prime Chicago innovator is eternally assured by the ringing, vibrato-enhanced guitar work that remains his stock-in-trade and a tortured, super-intense vocal delivery that can force the hairs on the back of your neck upwards in silent salute.

If talent alone were the formula for widespread success, Rush would currently be Chicago's leading blues artist. But fate, luck, and the guitarist's own idiosyncrasies have conspired to hold him back on several occasions when opportunity was virtually begging to be accepted.

Rush came to Chicago in 1948, met Muddy Waters, and knew instantly what he wanted to do with the rest of his life. The omnipresent Willie Dixon caught Rush's act and signed him to Eli Toscano's Cobra Records in 1956. The frighteningly intense "I Can't Quit You Baby" was the maiden effort for both artist and label, streaking to No. 6 on *Billboard*'s R&B chart.

His 1956-58 Cobra legacy is a magnificent one, distinguished by the Dixon-produced minor-key masterpieces "Double Trouble" and "My Love Will Never Die," the nails-tough "Three Times a Fool" and "Keep on Loving Me Baby," and the rhumba-rocking classic "All Your Love (I Miss Loving)." Rush apparently dashed off the latter tune in the car en route to Cobra's West Roosevelt Road studios, where he would cut it with the nucleus of Ike Turner's combo.

After Cobra closed up shop, Rush's recording fortunes mostly floundered. He followed Dixon over to Chess in 1960, cutting another classic (the stunning "So Many Roads, So Many Trains") before moving on to Duke (one solitary single, 1962's "Homework"), Vanguard, and Cotillion (there he cut the underrated Mike Bloomfield-Nick Gravenites-produced 1969 album

Mourning in the Morning, with yeoman help from the house rhythm section in Muscle Shoals).

Typical of Rush's horrendous luck was the unnerving saga of his *Right Place, Wrong Time* album. Laid down in 1971 for Capitol Records, the giant label inexplicably took a pass on the project despite its obvious excellence. It took another five years for the set to emerge on the tiny Bullfrog label, blunting Rush's momentum once again (the album is now available on Hightone).

An uneven but worthwhile 1975 set for Delmark, *Cold Day in Hell*, and a host of solid live albums that mostly sound very similar kept Rush's gilt-edged name in the marketplace to some extent during the 1970s and '80s, a troubling period for the legendary southpaw.

In 1986, he walked out on an expensive session for Rooster Blues (Louis Myers, Lucky Peterson, and Casey Jones were among the assembled sidemen), complaining that his amplifier didn't sound right and thereby scuttling the entire project. Alligator picked up the rights to an album he had done overseas for Sonet originally called *Troubles, Troubles*. It turned out to be a prophetic title: much to Rush's chagrin, the firm overdubbed keyboardist Lucky Peterson and chopped out some masterful guitar work when it reissued the set as *Lost in the Blues* in 1991.

Finally, in 1994, the career of this Chicago blues legend began traveling in the right direction. *Ain't Enough Comin' In*, his first studio album in 16 years, was released on Mercury and ended up topping many blues critics' year-end lists. Produced spotlessly by John Porter with a skin-tight band, Rush roared a set of nothing but covers—but did them all his way, his blistering guitar consistently to the fore.

Once again, a series of personal problems threatened to end Rush's long-overdue return to national prominence before it got off the ground. But he's been in top-notch form the last year-and-a-half, fronting a tight band that's entirely sympathetic to the guitarist's sizzling approach. Rush recently signed with the House of Blues' fledgling record label, instantly granting that company a large dose of credibility and setting himself up for another large-scale career push when the album is completed.

It still may not be too late for Otis Rush to assume his rightful throne as Chicago's blues king. — *Bill Dahl*

This One's a Good Un / 1968 / Blue Horizon ◆◆◆◆

Mourning in the Morning / Aug. 1969 / Atlantic ◆◆◆

Panned by many a critic upon its 1969 release, Otis Rush's trip to Muscle Shoals sounds pretty fine now (with the obvious exceptions of "My Old Lady" and "Me," which no amount of time will ever save). The house band (including Duane Allman and drummer Roger Hawkins) picks up on Rush's harrowing vibe and runs with it on the stunning "Gambler's Blues," a chomping "Feel So Bad," and a shimmering instrumental treatment of Aretha Franklin's "Baby I Love You." — *Bill Dahl*

Door to Door (With Albert King) / Jun. 1970 / MCA/Chess ◆◆◆◆

Although Albert King was pictured on the front cover and has the lion's share of tracks on this excellent compilation, six of the fourteen tracks come from Rush's shortlived tenure with the label and are some of his very best. Chronologically, these are his next recordings after the Cobra sides and they carry a lot of the emotional wallop of those tracks, albeit with much loftier production values with much of it recorded in early stereo. Oddly enough, some of the material ("All Your Love," "I'm Satisfied [Keep on Loving Me Baby]") were remakes—albeit great ones—of tunes that Cobra had already released as singles! But Rush's performance of "So Many Roads" (featuring one of the greatest slow blues guitar solos of all time) should not be missed at any cost. — *Cub Koda*

Otis Rush / 1972 / Blue Horizon ◆◆◆◆
1956-58 Cobra classics. — *Bill Dahl*

Screamin' & Cryin' / Nov. 26, 1974 / Evidence ◆◆◆

Otis Rush's crunching guitar and vocals were never more emphatic than during the '70s when it seemed that he would actually find the pop attention and mass stardom he deserved. These mid-'70s tracks were originally cut for the Black and Blue label, with Rush playing grinding, relentless riffs and creating waves of sonic brilliance through creatively repeated motifs, jagged notes, and sustained lines and licks, while hollering, screaming, moaning, and wailing. Jimmy Dawkins, an outstanding lead artist in his own right, has also long been one of Chicago's great rhythm artists and shows it by adding plenty of tinkling, crackling figures and lines in the backgrounds. While not as consistently riveting as his live Evidence date, this one is also a valuable Rush document. — *Ron Wynn*

Cold Day in Hell / 1976 / Delmark ✦✦✦
Inconsistent but sometimes riveting 1975 studio set that hits some high highs (a crunchy "Cut You a Loose," the lickety-split jazzy instrumental "Motoring Along") right alongside some incredibly indulgent moments. But that's Otis—the transcendent instants are worth the hassle. — *Bill Dahl*

Right Place, Wrong Time / Feb. 1976 / Hightone ✦✦✦✦
Among the undisputed high points in Rush's checkered career is this 1971 studio set, originally done for Capitol (who astonishingly took a pass on the finished product). Rush has seldom sounded more convincing vocally than on the downtrodden title track, and his surging reading of Ike Turner's "I'm Tore Up" rates with his best up-tempo vehicles. — *Bill Dahl*

Lost in the Blues / Oct. 1977 / Alligator ✦✦✦
The powers-that-be at Alligator were subjected to a fair amount of criticism for taking a 1977 album of standards that Rush had cut in Sweden and over-dubbing Lucky Peterson's keyboards to make the thing sound fuller and more contemporary. History, after all, should not be messed with. But it's still a reasonably successful enterprise, Rush imparting his own intense twist to "I Miss You So," "You Don't Have to Go," and "Little Red Rooster." — *Bill Dahl*

Live in Europe / Oct. 1977 / Evidence ✦✦✦✦
Recorded in France back in 1987, this ten-song set finds Otis backed by strong trio support throughout in a delightfully engaged performance. Though several live albums exist on him, seldom has his declamatory vocals and stinging left-handed upside down guitar style been so well documented. Rush puts forth solo after solo, each with its own unique set of twists and turns, making this a veritable textbook of what he does best. Inspired listening and highly recommended. — *Cub Koda*

So Many Roads / 1978 / Delmark ✦✦✦
This concert LP was recorded live in Japan. — *Bill Dahl*

Troubles Troubles / 1978 / Sonet ✦✦✦
Low-key collection of standards. — *Bill Dahl*

Groaning the Blues / 1980 / Flyright ✦✦✦✦
This mixes gems and alternate takes previously issued on a limited edition Blue Horizon LP. The Rush Cobra material has been issued and reissued so much that you can get burned with the various titles and editions floating around. This is aimed more at the completists and Rush freaks than the general consumer. — *Ron Wynn*

Tops / 1985 / Blind Pig ✦✦✦
There are simply too many live albums by Rush on the market to keep track of anymore. This was one of the earlier entries, cut in 1985 with a West Coast combo following Rush pretty well. Since the same basic set list turns up on most every one of these things, there's not really a whole lot of difference between any of 'em (but go with Delmark's *So Many Roads* first). — *Bill Dahl*

★ **Cobra Recordings, 1956-1958** / 1989 / Paula/Flyright ✦✦✦✦✦
Otis Rush's debut recordings for the Cobra label are defining moments of Chicago blues. Seldom had a young Windy City artist recorded with this much harrowing emotion in both his singing and playing, simultaneously connecting with the best that Delta blues had to offer while plunging head-long into the electric future. These are the songs that continue to be the building blocks of his legend; "All Your Love", "Double Trouble", "I Can't Quit You, Baby," "Groaning The Blues," "It Takes Time," and "Checking on My Baby" are all singular masterpieces. This single disc collection features all 16 Cobra sides issued as singles plus the bonus of four alternate takes, all presented here with the best sound to date. These are milestone recordings in the history of the blues and an essential part of anyone's collection. — *Cub Koda*

Ain't Enough Comin' In / 1994 / This Way Up ✦✦✦✦
With sympathetic production from John Porter, a great lineup of players who follow him every bluesy turn of the way and a dozen well chosen pieces of material, Rush wipes the uninspired album slate clean with this one. Everything that makes Otis a unique master of his form is here to savor, from his passionate vocals to the shimmering finger vibrato he applies to the liquid tones of his Fender Stratocaster. While Rush has tackled some of this mate-

rial on other outings, never has it been served up so passionately as it is here. Even the re-cut of his famous Duke 45 "Homework" burns with a new intensity that makes you believe that this is one opportunity that Rush—at least this time—refused to let go by the boards. — *Cub Koda*

This Way / 1994 / Mercury ✦✦✦✦
Otis Rush has never recorded or performed consistently. That's what makes this recent session so welcome; Rush gets first-rate production, engineering, and material. There's only one original out of 12 cuts, but when he's putting his stamp on classics by Albert and B.B. King, Sam Cooke, Ray Charles, and Percy Mayfield, it's hard to complain. Rush emphasizes uptempo, surging numbers rather than slow tunes, and there aren't many examples of his jagged, cutting solos, but Rush's vocals are among his most dynamic and arresting in many years. This is certainly his finest work since the 1970s Bullfrog sessions. — *Ron Wynn*

So Many Roads: Live / Aug. 1, 1995 / Delmark ✦✦✦✦
There's a pile of Otis Rush live albums in the bins now, but this was the one that made everybody sit up and take notice and it's still his best. Recorded live outdoors in a Tokyo park in the Summer of 1975 with thousands of fans hanging on every note and word, Otis digs deep and delivers some of the most inspired singing and playing he's ever comitted to magnetic tape. All the performances are of a nice, comfortable lenth with none of the interminable soloing that mars other Rush live sets. This is the one to have. — *Cub Koda*

Live at the Chicago Blues Festival / Intermedia ✦✦✦✦
Who knows where these live tracks were done, or when? If the sound wasn't so bad, they'd rate with his better concert efforts. It also includes latter-day Little Walter sides which are less inspired. — *Bill Dahl*

Jimmy Rushing (James Andrew Rushing)

b. Aug. 26, 1903, Oklahoma City, OK, **d.** Jun. 8, 1972, New York, NY
Vocals / Swing, Blues Jazz, East Coast Blues, Jump Blues
He was known as "Mr. Five-by-Five"—an affectionate reference to his height and girth—as a blues shouter who defined and then transcended the form. The owner of a booming voice that radiated sheer joy in whatever material he sang, Jimmy Rushing could swing with anyone and dominate even the loudest of big bands. Rushing achieved his greatest fame in front of the Count Basie band from 1935 to 1950, yet unlike many band singers closely associated with one organization, he was able to carry on afterwards with a series of solo recordings that further enhanced his reputation as a first-class jazz singer.

Raised in a musical family, learning violin, piano, and music theory in his youth, Rushing began performing in nightspots after a move to California in the mid-'20s. He joined Walter Page's Blue Devils in 1927, then toured with Bennie Moten from 1929 until the leader's death in 1935, going over to Basie when the latter picked up the pieces of the Moten band. The unquenchably swinging Basie rhythm section was a perfect match for Rushing, making their earliest showing together on a 1936 recording of "Boogie Woogie" that stamped not only Rushing's presence onto the national scene but also that of Lester Young. Rushing's recordings with Basie are scattered liberally throughout several reissues on Decca, Columbia and RCA. While with Basie, he also appeared in several film shorts and features.

After the Basie ensemble broke up in 1950, a victim of hard times for big bands, Rushing briefly retired, then formed his own septet. He started a series of solo albums for Vanguard in the mid-'50s, then turned in several distinguished recordings for Columbia in league with such luminaries as Dave Brubeck, Coleman Hawkins, and Benny Goodman, the latter of whom he appeared with at the Brussels World's Fair in 1958 as immortalized in "Brussels Blues." He also recorded with Basie alumni such as Buck Clayton and Jo Jones, as well as with the Duke Ellington band on *Jazz Party*. He appeared on TV in *The Sound of Jazz* in 1957, was featured in Jon Hendricks' *The Evolution of the Blues*, and also had a singing and acting role in the 1969 film *The Learning Tree*. — *Richard S. Ginell*

● **The Essential Jimmy Rushing** / Dec. 1, 1954-Mar. 5, 1957 / Vanguard ✦✦✦✦
This single CD reissues an earlier Jimmy Rushing two-LP set, leaving off two cuts due to lack of space. Jimmy Rushing, who may very well have been the definitive male big-band singer, sticks mostly to blues and Kansas City swing on the release and is backed by a variety of top swing all-stars including

most notably tenor-saxophonist Buddy Tate, trumpeter Emmett Berry and trombonists Lawrence Brown and Vic Dickenson. The sidemen receive plenty of space for concise solos, particularly pianists Pete Johnson and Sammy Price. The performances (plus the 11 other songs that are awaiting reissue someday) are among the most rewarding of Jimmy Rushing's post-Basie career and are full of joy and timeless swing. — *Scott Yanow*

Mr. Five by Five / Nov. 7, 1956-Jul. 13, 1960 / Topaz ✦✦✦
From 1956-60, veteran swing/blues singer Jimmy Rushing recorded six albums for Columbia. Most of the sets have not yet been reissued on CD, so this two-LP sampler from 1980 (which inexcusably does not give the recording dates) is still worth picking up by listeners lucky enough to run across it. Rushing is featured in eight different settings on 30 selections, including with all-star groups featuring trumpeter Buck Clayton, tenors Coleman Hawkins and Buddy Tate, trombonist Dickie Wells, and pianist Ray Bryant. In addition, there are numbers with the Dave Brubeck Quartet, the Benny Goodman big band, and (on four previously unreleased songs) fellow singer Helen Humes and tenor saxophonist Ben Webster. Throughout the high-quality program, Rushing is heard in prime form, making one wonder why so much of this swinging material has not been brought back yet. — *Scott Yanow*

Rushing Lullabies / Mar. 1960 / Columbia Special Products ✦✦✦
Although named after a former LP, this CD actually contains the complete contents of two albums (the other one was called *Little Jimmy Rushing and the Big Brass*) plus a brief previously unreleased number. Known for his renditions of swing-oriented blues, but also quite effective on ballads and jumping standards, the great singer is featured with a big band (which has solo space for many musicians, including tenors Buddy Tate and Coleman Hawkins, trumpeter Buck Clayton, and trombonist Dicky Wells) and a sextet with Tate, organist Sir Charles Thompson, and pianist Ray Bryant. These were two of Rushing's better sets from the 1950s, and he is heard throughout the mostly veteran tunes in top form. Highlights include "I'm Coming Virginia," "Mister Five by Five," "When You're Smiling," "Good Rockin' Tonight," and "Russian Lullaby." — *Scott Yanow*

Everyday I Have the Blues / 1967 / Bluesway ✦✦✦✦
A CD reissue of the great blues shouter Jimmy Rushing singing recreated versions of his classics with the Basie band. This originally came out in the mid-'50s, when Rushing had left Basie and was heading his own band. While these versions aren't the definitive ones, they're far from bad. — *Ron Wynn*

Bluesway Sessions / Feb. 9, 1967-Feb. 10, 1967 / Charly ✦✦✦✦
Singer Jimmy Rushing's two albums for Bluesway have been reissued in full on this British double-LP from 1986. Although recorded near the end of Rushing's life, he still sounds strong on the set of blues, ballads, and swinging material. The first album finds Rushing joined by the Oliver Nelson Orchestra (which includes fluegelhornist Clark Terry and trombonist Dicky Wells), while the other has a septet that includes Wells, tenor saxophonist Buddy Tate, and pianist Dave Frishberg, plus a slightly funky studio rhythm section. Both combinations work well, and Rushing shows plenty of spirit throughout the performances (most of which have not yet been reissued on CD). — *Scott Yanow*

Gee, Baby, Ain't I Good to You / Oct. 30, 1967 / Master Jazz ✦✦
This is a decent session that, considering the lineup, does not live up to its potential. At what was essentially a jazz party held in a recording studio, the musicians (trumpeter Buck Clayton, trombonist Dickie Wells, tenor-saxophonist Julian Dash, pianist Sir Charles Thompson, bassist Gene Ramey, and drummer Jo Jones) are all veterans of the famous series of Buck Clayton jam sessions held in the 1950s and, along with singer Jimmy Rushing, the majority are alumni of the Count Basie Orchestra. The problem is that their rendition of the blues and swing standards are often quite loose, there are a generous amount of missteps and, although Clayton is heroic under the circumstances (this was one of his final recordings before ill health caused his retirement), most of the musicians would have benefited from running through the songs an additional time. It's recommended only to completists. — *Scott Yanow*

Who Was It Sang That Song / Oct. 30, 1967 / Master Jazz ✦✦✦
Recorded the same day as the music released on the Master Jazz album *Gee Baby, Ain't I Good to You*, this is the superior of the two recordings. This CD reissue not only has the original five songs from the LP, but also previously unreleased versions of "Deed I Do," Sir Charles Thompson's "Almost Home," and "Moten Stomp." The classic swing singer Jimmy Rushing is joined by six veterans, including three fellow Basieites: trumpeter Buck Clayton (near the end of his playing career), trombonist Dickie Wells, and drummer Jo Jones, plus Julian Dash on tenor, bassist Gene Ramey and pianist Thompson. They jam enthusiastically, if predictably on loose versions of jazz standards including "Baby Won't You Please Come Home," a blues medley, and "All of Me." — *Scott Yanow*

The You and Me That Used to Be / Oct. 1971 / Bluebird ✦✦✦✦
On this straight CD reissue of Jimmy Rushing's final recording sessions, the singer is in spirited form despite being little more than a year from his death. On the ten swing standards and a lone blues ("Fine and Mellow"), Rushing is joined by pianist Dave Frishberg (also responsible for the arrangements), bassist Milt Hinton, and drummer Mel Lewis, plus either Ray Nance on cornet and violin and tenor saxophonist Zoot Sims, or Budd Johnson (on soprano), and Al Cohn (on tenor). Touching renditions of "I Surrender Dear" and "More Than You Know" find Rushing backed only by Frishberg's very able piano. This recommended CD is proof that "Mr. Five by Five" (whose career spanned more than 40 years) went out on top. — *Scott Yanow*

Rushing Lullabies/Little Jimmy Rushing & the Big Brass / Apr. 29, 1997 / Sony ✦✦✦✦
Although named after a former LP, this CD actually contains the complete contents of two albums (the other one was called *Little Jimmy Rushing and the Big Brass*), plus a brief previously unreleased number. Known for his renditions of swing-oriented blues, but also quite effective on ballads and jumping standards, the great singer is featured with a big band (which has solo space for many musicians, including tenors Buddy Tate and Coleman Hawkins, trumpeter Buck Clayton, and trombonist Dicky Wells) and a sextet with Tate, organist Sir Charles Thompson, and pianist Ray Bryant. These were two of Rushing's better sets from the 1950s, and he is heard throughout the mostly veteran tunes in top form. Highlights include "I'm Coming Virginia," "Mister Five by Five," "When You're Smiling," "Good Rockin' Tonight," and "Russian Lullaby." — *Scott Yanow*

Saffire the Uppity Blues Women

f. Virginia
Group / Modern Acoustic Blues

The ladies from Saffire, at one point in the early '90s, just considered themselves blues historians, but since their performing career has gotten launched on the festival circuit, they've become much more than that. All three have developed into talented songwriters. Since blues fans are always looking for fresh themes or new twists on old themes, this trio is a sought-after club and festival act. The core members of this Virginia-based group include pianist Ann Rabson (b. April 12, 1945) and Gaye Adegbalola (b. March 21, 1944), and while the trio was accompanied for a while by bassist Earlene Lewis, she has since left the group. Lewis was replaced by mandolinist Andra Faye McIntosh, also from the Washington, D.C./Virginia area. Rabson worked as a computer programmer and Adegbalola was an award-winning teacher before they gave up their day jobs to play blues full-time for a living.

Saffire has no shortage of fresh ideas. The group has recorded five albums for the Chicago-based Alligator Records label since 1990. Their two more recent albums, *Cleaning House* (1996) and *Old, New, Borrowed and Blue* (1994), showcase the trio's songwriting skills, although there are also a few covers, reinterpreted in their own distinctive way. These acoustic musicians inject a sense of humor into their songs and take it with them on stage. The group's other albums for Alligator include their 1990 debut, *Saffire the Uppity Blues Women* (1990), *Hot Flash* (1991), and *Broadcasting* (1992). Their prolific output as songwriters is matched only by their desire to tour, as they perform everywhere and anywhere, having already made several US, Canadian and European tours.

The group's fundamental appeal—to growing numbers of music fans who don't know much about blues—is their original songs and their ability to dig up and reinterpret old blues gems from the 1920s and '30s. They specialize in songs made by the sassy original blues divas including Bessie Smith, Ma Rainey, Memphis Minnie, and Ida Cox. — *Richard Skelly*

Saffire the Uppity Blues Women / 1990 / Alligator ♦♦♦

In 1984 three middle-aged women (guitarist Gaye Adegbalola, bassist Earlene Lewis and pianist Ann Rabson) came together to play blues as Saffire. Their 1990 Alligator CD is still Saffire's best all-around recording. Even overlooking the novelty of three women giving a female and middle-aged slant to the blues, this is a highly enjoyable and musical set. Assisted on three numbers by Mark Wenner's harmonica, Saffire plays spirited versions of such tunes as "Middle Aged Blues Boogie," "Even Yuppies Get The Blues," "Fess Up When You Mess Up," "I Almost Lost My Mind," and their theme "Wild Women Don't Have the Blues." Recommended. — *Scott Yanow*

● Hot Flash / 1991 / Alligator ♦♦♦♦

In many ways, *Hot Flash* is the definitive Saffire album. Racy and sassy—and to some tastes cutesy—the album is a fun, free-thinking update of classic female blues, performed with gusto and verve. The instrumentation is sparse—a piano, guitar, bass, harmonica, and kazoo provide the foundation of the music—but the focus of these songs is solely on the vocals, which are vigorous and humorous and if you share Saffire's sense of humor, it's a rollicking good time. — *Thom Owens*

Broadcasting / 1992 / Alligator ♦♦♦

Between *Hot Flash* and *Broadcasting,* Saffire lost a bassist, but added a mandolin, fiddler, an organist, and an electric guitarist, which gives *Broadcasting* a fuller, richer sound. Fortunately, that hasn't distracted attention from the bawdy, sassy vocals of Ann Rabson and Gaye Adegbalola, who still exhibit a raw, natural charisma. And the material—which ranges from fresh interpretations of warhorses from Louis Jordan and Hank Williams to clever originals—is all first-rate, helping make the album one of the group's best efforts. — *Thom Owens*

Old, New, Borrowed, & Blue / 1994 / Alligator ♦♦

Old, New, Borrowed, & Blue finds Saffire's sound bordering on the formulaic—songs like "Bitch with a Bad Attitude" and "There's Lighting in These Thunder Thighs" are simply too cutesy and too predictable—but there is still plenty for their fans to treasure on the record. — *Thom Owens*

Cleaning House / May 21, 1996 / Alligator ♦♦♦

Another generally likable album from Saffire, *Cleaning House* contains plenty of the bold, sassy material (e.g., "Hungry Woman's Blues," "If Love Hurts, You're Not Doing It Right," "Tomorrow Ain't Promised") listeners have come to expect from the band that half seriously, half tongue-in-cheek, bills itself as the Uppity Blues Women. All three women take turns on lead vocals; Andra Faye McIntosh's singing is particularly enjoyable. The 17-song acoustic set includes five originals from band member Gaye Adegbalola, three originals from bandmate Ann Rabson, and a spirited variety of songs written by old-timers like Memphis Minnie and contemporary songsmiths like Rick Estrin. — *Steve Hoffman*

Live and Uppity / Mar. 10, 1998 / Alligator ♦♦♦♦

Saffire has been bringing their "uppity" brand of blues to stages from quite some time, and it was inevitable that a live album would rear its head sooner or later. But recording this one over a three-night stand at the Brans of Wolf Trap is a class-A affair all the way. With the ladies in top form, playing to an adoring audience cheering them on with every line, there's a symbiosis happening on this recording between audience and performers that seldom gets captured on a live album. There's no point in listing highlights simply because every track is a winner, and while the group's strong feminist stance is off-putting to some blues fans, none of them were in the audience on the nights these recordings were made, that's for sure. — *Cub Koda*

The Middle Aged Blues / Saffire ♦♦♦

Middle Aged Blues is Saffire's debut tape and the vocal trio has already developed a distinctive style. Although some listeners might find their material a bit too jokey, it's clear that the group is having fun with their material. They have respect for blues traditions, particularly classic female blues, but they don't merely regurgitate the same songs in the same fashion—Saffire makes them loose and fun, like you were eavesdropping on a party. *Middle Aged Blues* isn't as fully formed as their later albums for Alligator, but it still has plenty of good times. — *Thom Owens*

Doug Sahm

b. Nov. 6, 1941, San Antonio, TX
Guitar, Vocals, Violin / Rock 'n' Roll, Tex-Mex, Blues-Rock, Roots-Rock, Americana, Country-Rock, Progressive Country

Guitarist, composer, arranger and songwriter Doug Sahm hasn't exactly carved a niche for himself as a straight-ahead blues player over the years. But one of his recent albums, *The Last Real Texas Blues Band* (1994) Antone's, was nominated for a Grammy award. It's a firecracker of an album, perhaps the best thing he's ever recorded.

Sahm, born November 6, 1941 in San Antonio, Texas, is a knowledgeable music historian and veteran performer who's equally comfortable in a range of styles, including Texas blues, country, rock 'n' roll, Western swing, and cajun. He began his performing career at age nine when he was featured on a San Antonio area radio station, playing steel guitar. Sahm began recording for a procession of small labels (Harlem, Warrior, Renner and Personality), in 1955 with "A Real American Joe" under the name Little Doug Sahm. Three years later he was leading a group called the Pharoahs. Sahm recorded a series of singles for Texas-based record companies including "Crazy Daisy" (1959), "Sapphire" (1961), and "If You Ever Need Me" (1964). After being prompted in 1965 to assemble a group by producer Huey Meaux, Sahm asked his friends Augie Meyers (keyboards), Frank Morin (saxophone), Harvey Kagan (bass) and Johnny Perez (drums), if they would join him. Meaux gave the group the name the Sir Douglas Quintet. The group had some success on the radio with "The Rains Came," but Sahm later moved to California after the group broke up, where he formed the Honkey Blues Band. He reformed his Quintet in California and recorded a now-classic single, "Mendocino." The resulting album was a ground-breaking record in the then emerging country-rock scene. The Sir Douglas Quintet followed *Mendocino* with *Together After Five*, another album that led them to a larger fan base.

But it was Atlantic Records producer Jerry Wexler who realized that country-rock sounds were coming into vogue (and there was no place in Nashville for people like Sahm), so he signed both Sahm and Willie Nelson. One of his greatest albums, *Doug Sahm and Band*, (1973, Atlantic) was recorded in New York City with Bob Dylan, Dr. John and accordionist Flaco Jiminez, and a resulting single, "Is Anybody Going To San Antone?" had some radio success. The Sir Douglas Quintet got back together again to record two more albums, *Wanted Very Much Alive* and *Back To The 'Dillo*.

Among Sahm's most essential blues records are *Hell of a Spell* (1980, Takoma), a blues album dedicated to Guitar Slim, and his Grammy-nominated studio album for Antone's, *The Last Real Texas Blues Band*.

For his other material, there are several good compilations, including *The Best of Doug Sahm* (Rhino). — *Richard Skelly*

Honky Blues (Sir Douglas) / 1968 / Smash ✦✦✦

Mendocino / Apr. 1969 / Smash ✦✦✦✦

Together After Five / 1970 / Smash ✦✦✦✦

Rough Edges / 1973 / Mercury ✦✦

Doug Sahm & the Band / Jan. 1973 / Atlantic ✦✦✦
Since major label Atlantic signed Doug Sahm as a solo artist and put him in a New York studio with top-flight producers Jerry Wexler and Arif Mardin and star sidemen like Bob Dylan, Dr. John, and David Bromberg (not to mention old stalwarts like Augie Meyers, Flaco Jimenez, and Martin Fierro), you might expect that the resulting album would be Sahm's big career move, a swing toward professionalism and the mainstream, and that's how it was perceived when it was released. Maybe that's why it also was dismissed when it didn't become a big hit. Trouble is, the record isn't slick at all—it sounds as loose as any of the Sir Douglas Quintet albums, if a little more country-oriented. But the album remains a Bob Dylan curio; Dylan's otherwise unavailable composition "Wallflower" is included, and he sings it and "Blues Stay Away From Me" with Sahm. — *William Ruhlmann*

Return of the Formerly Bros. / 1988 / Rykodisc ✦✦✦✦
Texan folk hero Sir Doug Sahm meets underrated guitarist Amos Garrett and ex-Blasters keyboardist Gene Taylor and they cook like an Austin barbecue. (Originally released on Stony Plain Records in Canada in 1988, *The Return Of The Formerly Brothers* was released in the US by Rykodisc in 1989.) — *Jeff Tamarkin*

Juke Box Music / 1989 / Antone's ✦✦✦✦
Supported by the Antone's house band, Doug Sahm runs through 15 R&B and doo-wop classics for *Juke Box Music*. Oddly there's no Tex-Mex here, considering that Sahm is one of the defining figures of the genre, but that's just a minor complaint, since the music here is just terrific. There's a wonderful relaxed quality to the performances, and the song selection boasts a number of forgotten gems, resulting in a little treasure for fans of R&B and American roots music. — *Thom Owens*

● **The Best of Doug Sahm (1968-1975)** / 1991 / Rhino ✦✦✦✦
This is not as thorough as *Sir Doug's Recording Trip*, but it's easier to find and gives you 22 essential tracks in sterling digital fidelity. — *John Floyd*

Last Real Texas Blues Band Feat. Doug Sahm / 1994 / Discovery ✦✦✦
The Last Real Texas Blues Band is a typically eclectic and enjoyable record from Doug Sahm, but what makes it different than the rest of his catalog is focus. Where most of Sahm's albums are equally divided between the pedestrian and the genius, *The Last Real Texas Blues Band* is a nearly perfect

roots record, boasting both a stellar set of songs and exciting, unpredictable performances that make it arguably his best record ever. — *Thom Owens*

The Best of Doug's Sahm's Atlantic Sessions / 1995 / Rhino ✦✦✦✦

Curtis Salgado & the Stilettos

f. Feb. 4, 1954, Everett, WA
Harmonica, Vocals / Modern Electric Blues
While a longtime fixture of the Pacific Northwest blues community, singer/harpist Curtis Salgado ironically earned his greatest notoriety as the reputed inspiration behind John Belushi's character in *The Blues Brothers*. Born in Everett, Washington on February 4, 1954, he first emerged during the mid-1970s as the lead vocalist of the Robert Cray Band, making his recorded debut on the group's 1979 effort *Who's Been Talkin;* after leaving Cray in 1982, Salgado also fronted Roomful of Blues between 1984 and 1986. Upon forming his own band the Stilettos, he signed to the JRS label to issue his 1991 solo debut *Curtis Salgado and the Stilettos; More Than You Can Chew* followed in 1995, and two years later he resurfaced with *Hit It 'n' Quit It*, recorded with guitarist Terry Robb. — *Jason Ankeny*

● **Curtis Salgado & the Stilettos** / 1991 / JRS ✦✦✦✦
Curtis Salgado's first album, *Curtis Salgado & the Stilettos*, captures the vocalist at his very best, storming through a set of originals and covers that fall halfway between gritty Chicago blues and sweaty Stax soul. Salgado had long ago proven that he was a fine singer, but this proves he can do it on his own, without Robert Cray or Roomful of Blues—not only can he lead a band, but he can write fine songs in his own right. — *Thom Owens*

More Than You Can Chew / May 16, 1995 / Priority ✦✦✦✦

Hit It & Quit It / Jun. 10, 1997 / Lucky ✦✦✦

Sam Brothers

f. Louisiana
Group / Zydeco
The Sam Brothers—vocalist and bandleader Leon, lead guitarist Carl, bassist Glen, washboard player Calvin and drummer Rodney—were among zydeco's most prominent family acts, making their initial splash while still in their teens and later becoming one of the most electrifying bands on the contemporary zydeco circuit. The Houston-based siblings took their earliest inspiration from their father Herbert Sam, himself a part-time accordionist who led his own five-piece zydeco band; as each of the brothers learned his respective instrument he then joined the group, and when Herbert retired from active duty the Sam Brothers—a.k.a. the Sam Brothers Five—were officially born. In 1979, the teens were discovered by Arhoolie Records producer Chris Strachwitz at the New Orleans Jazz and Heritage Festival; not only did Strachwitz organize a West Coast tour, but he also recorded their debut LP, the live *Sam Brothers Five. Cruisin' On* followed in 1981, after which the brothers spent the rest of the decade focusing on performing live; finally, in 1989 they returned to the studio to record *Zydeco Brotherhood*. — *Jason Ankeny*

● **Zydeco Brotherhood** / 1989 / Maison de Soul ✦✦✦✦
Not the most original of zydeco groups, The Sam Brothers still manage to jam a lot of energy into the covers they interpret. — *Jeff Hannusch*

Lafayette Zydeco / 1992 / Arhoolie ✦✦✦✦

Les Sampou

Vocals / Folk-Blues, Singer-Songwriter
The young, up-and-coming Les Sampou may be a relative newcomer to the international folk/blues festival circuit, but she writes songs like she's been around forever. Her record deal came about relatively easily compared to the way a lot of blues and folk singers struggle in obscurity for years before being discovered.

The Boston-based Sampou released an album herself, *Sweet Perfume* (1994), before being signed to Flying Fish/Rounder Records in 1995. Although by that point she'd already made the rounds of coffeehouses and folk festivals around the Northeast, it wasn't until after the release of her debut, *Fall From Grace*, that she began to take on a national and international profile. Although it's easy to call her a contemporary blues singer, and she does play blues exceedingly well, there's a singer-songwriter side of her that comes out on her debut album in songs like "The Things I Should've Said" and "Home Again." Other tracks, like "Weather Vane" and "Fall From Grace," show her bluesier side.

The Boston-raised Sampou did not get the music bug until she was in her early 20s, after seeing Ellen McIlwaine at a coffeehouse in Cambridge, Mass. Shortly after that revelatory experience, Sampou began taking lessons, learning acoustic blues from Boston-based acoustic blues master Paul Rishell. After she began getting steady work in coffeehouses around the ultra-competitive Boston scene in the late 1980s and early 1990s, she made the break and quit her day job as a part-time editor to pursue her musical dreams. The initial result was a superb album, *Sweet Perfume*, her self-released 1994 debut. The follow-up, *Fall From Grace* (1996), is even better, and shows that Sampou is equally at home playing traditional blues, self-penned blues or self-penned ballads. Harmonica player Jerry Portnoy, a great songwriter himself, can be heard as well. — *Richard Skelly*

Fall from Grace / 1996 / Rounderq ◆◆◆

Jumpin' Johnny Sansone

b. West Orange, New Jersey
Harmonica / Modern Electric Blues
Like his friend Sonny Landreth, harmonica player/accordionist Jumpin' Johnny Sansone takes his songwriting cues from the things he sees in his New Orleans home. Many of the songs on *Crescent City Moon*, his debut for Rounder's Bullseye Blues label, are inspired by the sights, sounds and smells of the Crescent City.

Sansone left his native West Orange, New Jersey at 17 in 1975 to attend college in Colorado on a swimming scholarship. He began playing harmonica at age 13, also accompanying himself on guitar. "I was trying to be Jimmy Reed in our basement," he recalled in a 1997 interview. Sansone's father was a professional saxophonist who played with various jazz groups on the Newark, N.J. club scene.

Sansone lived in Colorado, Austin, Boston, and Chapel Hill, N.C. before moving to New Orleans in 1990. The whole time, he led regional touring bands, most notably Jumpin' Johnny and the Blues Party. Even though he's not yet 40, Sansone is no spring chicken when it comes to getting out on the road and supporting his independently released records. In 1987, Sansone and his former band, known as Jumpin' Johnny and the Blues Party, recorded an album *Where Yat?* for the Kingsnake label of Sanford, Florida. Jumpin' Johnny and the Blues Party also recorded and released *Mister Good Thing* for the Atlanta-based Ichiban label in 1991.

Sansone began playing accordion after attending Clifton Chenier's funeral, and Sansone said that some people assume they're zydeco musicians when they see him carrying it into a club.

Crescent City Moon (1997, Bullseye Blues) received rave reviews from around the country. The album fuses Chicago blues, swamp boogie and lyrical images of New Orleans and the bayou country of southwest Louisiana. All of the songs on his debut album are his own, except his cover of Ted Hawkins' "Sweet Baby."

Sansone has won numerous awards in the Crescent City, including *Offbeat* magazine's annual "Best of the Beat" competition, where he won four awards after he released *Crescent City Moon* on his own label in 1996. Sansone won Song of the Year, Best Harmonica Player, Best Blues Band, and Best Blues Album of the Year.

Over the years, to get money together for various recording projects, Sansone has worked construction jobs. But with his new deal with Rounder's Bullseye Blues subsidiary, he should be able to take his artistry to the next level, touring nationally and internationally. — *Richard Skelly*

Mr. Good Thing / Mar. 1991 / King Snake ◆◆◆

● **Crescent City Moon** / 1997 / Bullseye Blues ◆◆◆◆
Sansone's second full-length album finds him stretching his creative wings, as a singer, multi-instrumentalist, and most importantly, as a songwriter. The Louisiana bred Sansone has a much different spin on his music, embracing Cajun, New Orleans, Southern soul, Chicago and Mississippi blues, with his nothing special but real solid accordion playing sharing equal space with his inventive harmonica work. Aside from a swamp style cover of Ted Hawkins' "Sweet Baby" featuring Sonny Landreth on slide guitar, everything on this disc emanates from Sansone's pen and there's not a track aboard that's nothing less than interesting here. As Sansone changes gears from the soul classic of the future "Your Kind of Love" to the Slim Harpo-ish "Crawfish Walk" to

the 'kordeen boogie romp of "Destination Unknown" to the eerie minor key blues of the title track, this is an album with a lot of music to savour from an artist with a different slant to all things rootsy. Proof positive that it doesn't all have to be rehashes of Clifton Chenier or Little Walter. — *Cub Koda*

Santana (Devadip Carlos Santana)

f. 1966, San Francisco, CA
Guitar / Rock 'n' Roll, Blues-Rock, Fusion, Psychedelic, Pop-Rock
Santana is the name of a band that has successfully married elements of blues, rock, and Latin music and enjoyed international acclaim for more than two decades. It is also the name of the guitarist, Carlos Santana, who has led that band and made other recordings over the same period of time. In its original manifestation, the Santana Blues Band was a group of equals, with Carlos named as leader only because of a musicians-union requirement that such a designation be made. The group was formed in San Francisco in the mid-'60s and first gained recognition in the same dance halls that hosted the psychedelic rock groups of the era, although, with its Latin and African roots, Santana never quite fit in with the psychedelic sound. The group came under the direction of promoter Bill Graham and had already scored a contract with Columbia when it appeared at the Woodstock Festival in August 1969. Personnel at that time, in addition to Carlos, included Gregg Rolie (vocals and keyboards), Dave Brown (bass), Mike Shrieve (drums), Armando Peraza (percussion and vocals), and Mike Carabello and Jose Areas (percussion).

Santana, the debut album, was a massive success, including the No. 4 hit "Evil Ways." *Abraxas* (1970) did even better, topping the charts for six weeks and featuring the hits "Black Magic Woman" and "Oye Como Va." For *Santana III* (1971), the group expanded to a septet with the addition of guitarist Neal Schon, though an additional six sidemen were listed in the album credits. This album was No. 1 for five weeks.

Guitarist Santana released a live duet album with drummer and vocalist Buddy Miles (later a member of Santana) in 1972; then came the fourth Santana Band album, *Caravanserai*, on which different musician credits were listed for each track, none of them including bassist Dave Brown or percussionist Mike Carabello. The album was a Top Ten hit. Carlos released another duet album in 1973 with guitarist John McLaughlin (the two shared a guru), followed by *Welcome*, credited to "The New Santana Band," its only remaining original members being Santana, Mike Shrieve, Armando Peraza, and Jose Areas (Rolie and Schon had decamped to found Journey).

In subsequent years, "Santana" for the most part referred to Carlos and a band of hired musicians playing in the established Santana style, while the leader also made occasional solo albums that varied the style somewhat. In 1992, Santana ended his long association with Columbia and signed to Polydor, which set up a custom label for him, calling for him to sign his own new acts. — *William Ruhlmann*

Santana / Aug. 1969 / Columbia ◆◆◆◆
This first release from this powerhouse band, on the heels of their appearance at the Woodstock Festival, was a revelation for many rock fans. The blend of Latin rhythms with rock beats was made more remarkable by Carlos Santana's searing guitar work. While the sound on the initial CD release was flat, this remastered edition boasts crisp sound and a bonus of three songs from the Woodstock performance, including the riveting "Soul Sacrifice." Worth the price, even if you've got the earlier version. — *Tim Sheridan*

★ **Abraxas** / Sep. 1970 / Columbia ◆◆◆◆◆
The San Francisco Bay Area rock scene of the late '60s was one that encouraged radical experimentation and discouraged the type of mindless conformity that's often plagued corporate rock. When one considers just how different Santana, Jefferson Airplane, Moby Grape and the Grateful Dead sounded, it becomes obvious just how much it was encouraged. In the mid-'90s, an album as eclectic as *Abraxas* would be considered a marketing exec's worst nightmare. But at the dawn of the 1970s, this unorthodox mix of rock, jazz, salsa and blues proved quite successful. Whether adding rock elements to salsa king Tito Puente's "Oye Como Va," embracing instrumental jazz-rock on "Incident at Neshabur" and "Samba Pa Ti" or tackling moody blues-rock on Fleetwood Mac's "Black Magic Woman," the band keeps things unpredictable yet cohesive. Many of the Santana albums that came out in the '70s are worth acquiring, but for novices, *Abraxas* is an excellent place to start. [Columbia/Legacy's 1998 reissue of *Abraxas* featured three previously unre-

leased tracks—"Se A Cabo," "Toussaint L'Overture," "Black Magic Woman/ Gypsy Queen" —which were all recorded live at the Royal Albert Hall on April 18, 1970.] —*Alex Henderson*

Santana III / Sep. 1971 / Columbia ✦✦✦✦
This studio effort is the last by the lineup that many consider to be Santana's best. The improvisational feel on this disc is freer than on earlier efforts, but it does lead to a bit of meandering. On the whole, this was another terrific effort by the masters of Latin rock. This reissue clears up a muddy original CD release with 24-bit remastering, adding three bonus live tracks from their performance at the close of the Fillmore West in 1971. —*Tim Sheridan*

Carlos Santana & Buddy Miles! Live! / Jun. 1972 / Columbia ✦✦
From December 1971 to April 1972, Carlos Santana and several other members of Santana toured with drummer/vocalist Buddy Miles, a former member of the Electric Flag and Jimi Hendrix's Band of Gypsys. The resulting live album contained both Santana hits ("Evil Ways") and Buddy Miles hits ("Changes"), plus a 25-minute, side-long jam. It was not, perhaps, the live album Santana fans had been waiting for, but at this point in its career, the band could do no wrong. The album went into the Top Ten and sold a million copies. (Reissued on CD on September 6, 1994.) —*William Ruhlmann*

Caravanserai / Oct. 1972 / Columbia ✦✦✦✦
Drawing on rock, salsa and jazz, Santana recorded one imaginative, unpredictable gem after another in the 1970s. But *Caravanserai* is daring even by Santana's high standards. Carlos Santana was obviously very hip to jazz-fusion—something the innovative guitarist provides a generous dose of on the largely instrumental *Caravanserai*. Whether its approach is jazz-rock or simply rock, this album is consistently inspired and quite adventurous. Full of heartfelt, introspective guitar solos, it lacks the immediacy of *Santana* or *Abraxas*. Like the type of jazz that influenced it, this pearl (which marked the beginning of keyboardist/composer Tom Coster's highly beneficial membership in the band) requires a number of listenings in order to be absorbed and fully appreciated. But make no mistake: this is one of Santana's finest accomplishments. —*Alex Henderson*

Love Devotion Surrender / 1973 / Columbia ✦✦✦
A duo album by John McLaughlin and Carlos Santana, this recording presents the two guitarists attempting jazz-fusion versions of the work of John Coltrane and McLaughlin compositions. Santana's fire is dampened somewhat by the solemn proceedings, but his commercial power held: this was the sixth straight Santana-related album to go gold, but the first to miss the Top Ten. —*William Ruhlmann*

Welcome / Nov. 1973 / Columbia ✦✦✦
On the group's fifth album, "The New Santana Band," as it was called, was an octet. Musically, the album was something of a companion piece to Carlos Santana's duet album with John McLaughlin, *Love Devotion Surrender,* even including a song by that title and, like the earlier record, containing compositions by McLaughlin and John Coltrane. In addition to the jazz influences, there was also a new blues sound courtesy of Leon Thomas, a smooth-voiced singer in the Joe Williams tradition. The record was musically adventurous, but as Santana continued to diverge from its Latin rock roots, its popularity eroded. —*William Ruhlmann*

Lotus / May 1974 / Columbia ✦✦✦✦
Recorded in Japan in July 1973, this massive live album, originally on three LPs and now on two compact discs, was available outside the United States in 1974, but held back from domestic release until long into the CD age. It features the same "New Santana Band" that recorded *Welcome* and combines that group's jazz and spiritual influences with performances of earlier Latin rock favorites like "Oye Como Va." —*William Ruhlmann*

● **Greatest Hits** / Jul. 1974 / Columbia ✦✦✦✦
This ten-song sampler presents the best of Santana, 1969-71, the period of its greatest popularity. The hits include "Black Magic Woman," "Evil Ways," "Everybody's Everything," and "Oye Como Va." But note that this is a bare minimum of prime Santana. Not only does the sampler choose from only Santana's first three albums, but it leaves out such seminal numbers as "Nobody to Depend On" and "Soul Sacrifice." Those looking for a more extensive overview should consider *Viva Santana!* —*William Ruhlmann*

Illuminations / Sep. 1974 / Columbia ✦✦
For his third duet album, Carlos Santana, who had been performing the

works of John Coltrane, paired with Coltrane's widow, harpist/keyboardist Alice Coltrane, on this instrumental album. Side one includes several contemplative, string-filled numbers, while side two presents Santana's re-creation of John Coltrane's late free-jazz style in "Angel of Sunlight." Columbia Records can't have been pleased at Santana's determined drift into esoteric jazz: *Illuminations* was the first of the nine Santana-related albums so far released in the US not to go gold. —*William Ruhlmann*

Borboletta / Oct. 1974 / Columbia ✦✦✦
Borboletta was the first new Santana band studio album in 11 months and the group's sixth overall. Once again, individual credits were listed for each song. The main problem was that the band seemed to be coasting; Carlos turned in the usual complement of high-pitched lead guitar work, and the percussionists pounded away, but the Santana sound had long since taken over from any individual composition, and the records were starting to sound alike. That, in turn, started to make them inessential; *Borboletta* spent less time in the charts than any previous Santana album. —*William Ruhlmann*

Amigos / Mar. 1976 / Columbia ✦✦✦✦
By the release of *Amigos*, the Santana band's seventh album, only Carlos Santana and David Brown remained from the band that conquered Woodstock, and only Carlos had been in the band continuously since. Meanwhile, the group had made some effort to arrest its commercial slide, hiring an outside producer, David Rubinson, and taking a tighter, more uptempo, and more vocal approach to its music. The overt jazz influences were replaced by strains of R&B/funk and Mexican folk music. The result was an album more dynamic than any since *Santana III* in 1971. "Let It Shine" (No. 77), an R&B-tinged tune, became the group's first chart single in four years, and the album returned Santana to Top Ten status. —*William Ruhlmann*

Festival / Jan. 1977 / Columbia ✦✦✦
Santana's follow-up to its comeback album, *Amigos,* was another David Rubinson-produced effort that moved back toward more of a Latin-rock feel, although it retained an essentially pop focus—"The River" was the first real vocal ballad on a Santana album. If any doubt still existed that the group was no longer a band of equals but a platform for its lead guitarist, the current lineup dispelled that; Carlos Santana was now the only original member of the band left. Although the album went gold, the lack of a hit single hurt the album's commercial standing; its No. 27 peak was the lowest yet for a Santana Band album. —*William Ruhlmann*

Moonflower / Oct. 1977 / Columbia ✦✦✦
Santana, which was renowned for its concert work dating back to Woodstock, did not release a live album in the US until this one, and it's only partially live, with studio tracks added, notably a cover of the Zombies' "She's Not There" (No. 27) that became Santana's first Top 40 hit in five years. The usual comings and goings in band membership had taken place since last time; the track listing was a good mixture of the old—"Black Magic Woman," "Soul Sacrifice"—and the recent. With the added radio play of a hit single, *Moonflower* went Top Ten and sold a million copies, the first new Santana album to do that since 1972, and also the last. —*William Ruhlmann*

Inner Secrets / Oct. 1978 / Columbia ✦✦
Since he had joined Santana in 1972, keyboard player Tom Coster had been Carlos Santana's right-hand man, playing, co-writing, co-producing, and generally taking the place of founding member Greg Rolie. But Coster left the band in the spring of 1978, to be replaced by keyboardist/guitarist Chris Solberg and keyboardist Chris Ryne. Despite the change, the band soldiered on, and with *Inner Secrets* they scored three chart singles: the discoish "One Chain (Don't Make No Prison)" (No. 59), "Stormy" (No. 32), and a cover of Buddy Holly's "Well All Right" (No. 69), done in the Blind Faith arrangement. (There seems to be a Steve Winwood fixation here. The album also featured a cover of Traffic's "Dealer.") The singles kept the album on the charts longer than any Santana LP since 1971, but it was still a minor disappointment after *Moonflower*, and in retrospect seems like one of the band's more compromised efforts. —*William Ruhlmann*

Oneness: Silver Dreams Golden Realities / Mar. 1979 / Columbia ✦✦✦
This is the first Carlos Santana solo album. It features members of the Santana band as backup, however, so the difference between a group effort and a solo work seems to be primarily in the musical approach, which is more esoteric and more varied than on a regular band album. The record is mostly instrumental and given over largely to contemplative ballads, although there

is also, for example, in the song "Silver Dreams Golden Smiles," a traditional pop ballad sung by Saunders King. — *William Ruhlmann*

Marathon / Sep. 1979 / Columbia ♦♦

Marathon marked the addition of keyboard player Alan Pasqua and singer Greg Walker's replacement by singer/guitarist Alex Ligertwood in the Santana lineup. Otherwise, the album was notable for consisting entirely of band-written material, although those songs were in the established R&B/rock style evolved on albums like *Amigos, Festival,* and *Inner Secrets.* The formula seemed to be wearing thin by now, however, as, even with a Top 40 hit in "You Know That I Love You" (No. 35), *Marathon* became the first Santana album to fall below the 500,000-sales mark necessary for gold record certification. (It has since made the mark.) — *William Ruhlmann*

The Swing of Delight / Aug. 1980 / Columbia ♦♦

For his second "solo" album, Carlos Santana used Miles Davis' famed '60s group—Herbie Hancock, Wayne Shorter, Ron Carter, and Tony Williams—plus members of the current Santana band, for a varied, jazz-oriented session that was one of his more pleasant excursions from the standard Santana sound. (Originally released as a double-LP, *The Swing of Delight* was reissued on a single CD.) — *William Ruhlmann*

Zebop! / Apr. 1981 / Columbia ♦♦

On *Zebop!,* a Santana band featuring newcomer Richard Baker on keyboards tried to preserve the better elements of the first and third trilogies of Santana albums—there was a heavy component of Latin-flavored percussion topped by Carlos' biting lead guitar work, and there were also three pop cover songs in Cat Stevens' "Changes," J.J. Cale's "The Sensitive Kind," and Russ Ballard's "Winning." The double strategy worked. "Winning" (No. 17) became Santana's first Top 20 single in a decade, "The Sensitive Kind" (No. 56) also charted, and the album was Santana's first Top Ten, gold-selling hit in four years. — *William Ruhlmann*

Shango / Aug. 1982 / Columbia ♦♦

Shango is notable for featuring the return, in the role of co-producer and cosongwriter, of original Santana keyboardist Greg Rolie. The main producer, however, was Bill Szymczyk (James Gang, Eagles), who gave Santana an unusually sharp rock sound resulting in two more hit singles, "Hold On" (No. 15) and "Nowhere to Run" (No. 66), although the band once again slipped below Top Ten, gold-selling status, with the album peaking at only No. 22, and even this was the highest Santana would get from here on out. — *William Ruhlmann*

Havana Moon / Apr. 1983 / Columbia ♦♦♦

The third Carlos Santana solo album marks a surprising turn toward 1950s rock 'n' roll and Tex-Mex, with covers such as Bo Diddley's "Who Do You Love" and Chuck Berry's title song. Produced by veteran R&B producers Jerry Wexler and Barry Beckett, the album features an eclectic mix of sidemen, including Booker T. Jones of Booker T & the MG's, Willie Nelson, and the Fabulous Thunderbirds. *Havana Moon* is a light effort, but it's one of Santana's most enjoyable albums, which may explain why it was also the best-selling Santana album outside the group releases in ten years. — *William Ruhlmann*

Beyond Appearances / Feb. 1985 / Columbia ♦♦

Seven months in the making, and appearing two and a half years after Santana's last album, *Beyond Appearances* was produced by Val ("Bette Davis Eyes") Garay in a hot 1980s style replete with prominent synthesizers and drum machines. In the interim, the band had undergone changes, with Alphonso Johnson replacing David Margen on bass, Chester D. Thompson and David Sancious replacing Richard Baker on keyboards, Chester Cortez Thompson replacing Graham Lear on drums, and singer Greg Walker rejoining. Garay co-wrote "Say It Again" (No. 46), Santana's final Hot 100 entry (a remake of Curtis Mayfield's "I'm The One Who Loves You" hit No. 102), but this latest pop interpretation of the Santana sound did not endear it to fans, and, at a peak of No. 50, *Beyond Appearances* was the lowest charting Santana album yet. — *William Ruhlmann*

Freedom / Feb. 1987 / Columbia ♦♦♦

Freedom marked several reunions in the Santana band, which was now a nonet. In addition to Carlos, the band consisted of percussionists Armando Pereza, Orestes Vilato, and Raul Rekow, returning drummer Graham Lear, bassist Alphonso Johnson, returning keyboardist Tom Coster, keyboardist Chester Thompson and, on lead vocals, Buddy Miles, who had made a duet

album with Santana 15 years before. Credited as an "additional musician" was keyboard player Greg Rolie, an original member. The music also marked a return from the hyper-pop sound of Val Garay on *Beyond Appearances* to a more traditional Santana Latin rock style. Thus, *Freedom* was a literal return to form, but, unfortunately, not to the quality of early Santana albums. And the group's commercial decline continued, with the LP getting to only No. 95. — *William Ruhlmann*

Blues for Salvador / Oct. 1987 / Columbia ♦♦♦♦

On previous "solo" albums, Carlos Santana had made noticeable stylistic changes and worked with jazz, pop, and even country musicians. On this, his fourth Carlos Santana release, the line between a "solo" and a "group" project is blurred; this record is really a catchall of Santana band outtakes and stray tracks. For example, included are an instrumental version of "Deeper, Dig Deeper" from *Freedom* and an alternate take of "Hannibal" from *Zebop!,* as well as "Now That You Know" from the group's 1985 tour. Given the variety of material, the album is somewhat less focused than most Santana band albums, but there are individual tracks that are impressive, notably "Trane," which features Tony Williams on drums. (*Blues for Salvador* won the Grammy Award for Best Rock Instrumental Performance.) — *William Ruhlmann*

Viva Santana! / Aug. 1988 / Columbia ♦♦♦♦

A lovingly assembled two-disc retrospective set that collects the best of the Santana band, along with many interesting rarities. — *William Ruhlmann*

Spirits Dancing in the Flesh / Jun. 1990 / Columbia ♦♦♦

Following a 1989 20th-anniversary reunion tour to promote *Viva Santana!,* Carlos Santana reorganized the band as a sextet and recorded *Spirits Dancing in the Flesh,* Santana's 15th and final studio album for Columbia Records. It was an unusually eclectic collection, featuring songs by Curtis Mayfield ("Gypsy Woman"), the Isley Brothers ("Who's That Lady"), and Babatunde Olatunji ("Jin-Go-Lo-Ba"). For all those influences, it was more of a straightforward, guitar-heavy rock album than usual. Coming more than three years after Santana's last new album, *Freedom,* it sold to the band's core audience only, reaching No. 85. — *William Ruhlmann*

Milagro / May 5, 1992 / Polydor ♦♦♦

Santana signed to Polydor in 1991 after 22 years with Columbia Records. Their label debut has a somewhat elegiac tone, beginning with a stage introduction by the late promoter Bill Graham and featuring an excerpt from a speech by Dr. Martin Luther King, Jr., solos taken from Miles Davis and John Coltrane, and music written by Bob Marley, Coltrane, and Gil Evans. Despite the presence of all these heroic ghosts, however, *Milagro* is only an average Santana release, familiar-sounding but undistinguished, and it failed to arrest the band's commercial slide, becoming the first new Santana studio album not to crack the Top 100. — *William Ruhlmann*

Sacred Fire: Santana Live in South America / Oct. 19, 1993 / Polydor ♦♦

For its third live album, Santana introduced a new bass player, Myron Dove, and added guitarist Jorge Santana (Carlos Santana's brother) and singer Vorriece Cooper to bring the band up to nine members. Adopting the mantle of Bob Marley, the band played "Esperando," which borrowed Marley's characteristic audience chant. Much of the album, however, is given over to repeating Santana's earliest hits—"No One to Depend On," "Black Magic Woman," "Soul Sacrifice," etc.—which should please the band's new record label (it's always good to have versions of the hits in your catalog), but which make the album inessential for fans. *Sacred Fire* spent one week at No. 181 in the charts, the worst performance ever for a Santana album. — *William Ruhlmann*

Dance of the Rainbow Serpent / Aug. 8, 1995 / Columbia ♦♦♦

Guitarist Carlos Santana continues to record music but, when contemplating his body of work, it's difficult not to telescope to the "vintage" 1969-1975 period, from first albums *Santana* and *Abraxas* through to *Lotus.* *Dance of the Rainbow Serpent* offers a well-rounded, three-disc overview of his career, but it remains the sultry Latin rhythms and stinging guitar of the early years—captured on disc one, subtitled *Heart*—that prove most invigorating. The obvious hits like "Evil Ways" and "Black Magic Woman" are all included of course, although these are scorched by the speedy pyrotechnics of the likes of "Toussaint Overture" from *Lotus.* The second disc, mistitled *Soul,* covers material that is, to be kind, bland and overproduced. Without the Latin edge, there's nothing to distinguish the contents from a hundred other MOR performers. Third disc *Spirit* is more diverse and satisfying; delving into the funkier examples of his later work, plus sessions with John Lee Hooker (including hit "The Healer") and previously unreleased material (including a workout with Living Color's Vernon Reid). In all, plenty here to chew on for fans of Santana's fluid, spiritual style—with one of three discs left to gather. —*Roch Parisien*

Live at the Fillmore 1968 / Mar. 11, 1997 / Sony ♦♦♦
Two-CD package drawn from performances at the Fillmore West in December 1968, with an early lineup including Bob Livingston on drums and Marcus Malone on congas (both of whom would be gone by the time the group recorded their official debut in 1969). The band sound only a bit more tentative here than they would in their Woodstock-era incarnation, running through several of the highlights of their first album ("Jingo," "Persuasion," "Soul Sacrifice," and "Treat"). More interesting to collectors will be the five songs that have not previously appeared on any Santana recording, including covers of songs by jazzmen Chico Hamilton and Willie Bobo, and a half-hour original jam that concludes the set, "Freeway." The sound is excellent, and the arrangements a bit more improv-oriented than what ended up on the early studio records. Its appeal isn't solely limited to committed fans; on its own terms it's a fine release, highlighted by some burning organ-guitar interplay in particular. —*Richie Unterberger*

● **The Best of Santana** / Mar. 31, 1998 / Sony ♦♦♦♦
The Best of Santana is a 16-track collection that greatly expands the scope of Santana's previous hits compilation, *Greatest Hits*. Drawing from the band's entire 30-year career, the disc contains such familiar items as "Evil Ways," "Jingo," "Black Magic Woman/Gypsy Queen" and "Oye Como Va," but it also has a number of longtime favorites of the band and fans. Furthermore, all the songs have been subjected to Super Bit remastering, resulting in the best sound ever. For some casual fans, *Greatest Hits* remains definitive, since it's a portrait of the band at its peak, but anyone wanting a career-spanning single-disc compilation will find that *The Best of Santana* suits their needs. —*Stephen Thomas Erlewine*

Satan & Adam

f. 1986, Harlem, NY
Group / Modern Acoustic Blues
The blues duo of guitarist, singer and songwriter Sterling Magee and harmonica player Adam Gussow have paid their dues. They began their career on the street. On the corner of Seventh Avenue and 125th Street, to be exact, and within a matter of weeks, they were drawing crowds to their corner, people pausing on their way home from work to stop and listen. For five years, nearly every afternoon that weather permitted, the pair would meet on the corner and Magee would set up his simple stool, drum kit, guitar and amplifier. Using a combination of foot stomps, tambourines, hi-hat cymbals and his guitar, Magee gives the duo a full sound.

Magee and Gussow specialize in funky, gritty, electric urban blues, and there are few groups or artists anywhere who sound anything remotely like them. Gussow's exquisite harmonica solos complement the driving, open-toned guitar playing of Magee, who prefers to be called Mr. Satan, and who frequently refers to Gussow in live performances as Mr. Gussow.

The pair have such a unique sound, it seems they're destined for a major label, given their knowledge and experience with blues. Magee, born May 20, 1936 in Mississippi and raised in Florida, began his career playing piano in churches in both states. Since the early '80s, he's played on Harlem streets, but in the 1960s he was a key session guitarist, playing on recordings by James Brown, King Curtis, George Benson and others. Adam Gussow, born April 3, 1958 and raised in Rockland County, N.Y., was a Princeton-educated harmonica player who had a little uptown apartment, and in passing Magee one day on the street in 1985, he asked if he could sit in on harmonica. That was the start of a musical and social relationship between the two that continues to this day.

The pair have recorded several critically acclaimed albums for the now-defunct Flying Fish label, and they include *Harlem Blues* (1991) and *Mother Mojo* (1993). Satan and Adam also performed in U2's *Rattle and Hum* movie. On their *Mother Mojo*, the group reinterprets and funkifies well-known songs like Herbie Hancock's "Watermelon Man" and Joe Turner's "Crawdad Hole." Their most recent recording *Living on the River* (1996) is on the New York State-based Rave On Records label.

Satan and Adam have redefined and shaped the sound of modern blues so much that their track, "I Want You" from their *Harlem Blues* debut was included on a Rhino Records release, *Modern Blues of the 1990s*. Look for more great albums from this duo for years to come. —*Richard Skelly*

● **Harlem Blues** / 1991 / Flying Fish ♦♦♦♦
Harlem Blues sounds exactly like how Satan & Adam would sound playing on a street corner—it's raw and tough, with a surprisingly adventurous streak. Satan and Adam stick to a basic acoustic blues duo, but their rhythms and techniques occasionally stray into funkier, jazzier territory. And that sense of careening unpredictability is what makes *Harlem Blues* so entertaining—they might be playing blues in a traditional style, but the end result is anything but traditional. —*Thom Owens*

Mother Mojo / Jan. 1993 / Flying Fish ♦♦♦
Mother Mojo was an excellent follow-up to Satan & Adam's first-rate debut, *Harlem Blues*. The duo hasn't abandoned their minimalist guitar and harp blues, but there is a loose energy that keeps the music fresh and consistently engaging. —*Thom Owens*

Living on the River / Jun. 5, 1996 / Rave On ♦♦♦
Satan & Adam continue to mine the same two-man streetcorner busker groove that has served them so well on this, their third album. The music is kept raw and alive in pursuing this, but on several tracks their sound is fleshed out with guest appearances from Ernie Colon on percussion, the Uptown Horns and background singers appearing on their version of "Proud Mary." But despite the additions, their basic sound is every bit as unfettered as one would expect from these two blues anomalies. —*Cub Koda*

Savoy Brown

f. 1966, United Kingdom
Group / Blues-Rock
Part of the late-'60s blues-rock movement, Britain's Savoy Brown never achieved as much success in their homeland as they did in America, where they promoted their albums with non-stop touring. The band was formed and led by guitarist Kim Simmonds, whose dominating personality has led to myriad personnel changes; the original lineup included singer Bruce Portius, keyboardist Bob Hall, guitarist Martin Stone, bassist Ray Chappell, and drummer Leo Manning. This lineup appeared on the band's 1967 debut *Shake Down*, a collection of blues covers. Seeking a different approach, Simmonds dissolved the group and brought in guitarist Dave Peverett, bassist Rivers Jobe, drummer Roger Earl, and singer Chris Youlden, who gave them a distinctive frontman with his vocal abilities, bowler hat, and monocle. With perhaps its strongest lineup, Savoy Brown quickly made a name for itself, now recording originals like "Train to Nowhere" as well. However, Youlden left the band in 1970 following *Raw Sienna*, and shortly thereafter, Peverett, Earl, and new bassist Tony Stevens departed to form Foghat, continuing the pattern of consistent membership turnover. Simmonds collected yet another lineup and began a hectic tour of America, showcasing the group's now-refined bluesy boogie-rock style, which dominated the rest of their albums. The group briefly broke up in 1973, but re-formed the following year and has continued to tour and record ever since. Simmonds has remained undeterred by a revolving-door membership and declining interest (no Savoy Brown album has charted in the US since 1981's *Rock & Roll Warriors*). —*Steve Huey*

Blue Matter / 1969 / Deram ♦♦♦♦
A great album, a classic which includes "Louisiana Blues" and "Train to Nowhere." —*Michael G. Nastos*

Raw Sienna / 1970 / Deram ♦♦♦♦
A blues-rock standard. —*Michael G. Nastos*

Street Corner Talking / 1971 / Deram ♦♦♦♦
Rockin' blues, English style, exemplified by the cover of Willie Dixon's "Wang Dang Doodle" and original material ranging from the pulsating "Let It Rock" to the almost Top 40-sounding "Tell Mama." Savoy Brown delivers another solid, if rather predictable, set typical of the British blues of the era. —*James Chrispell*

Hellbound Train / 1972 / Deram ♦♦♦
The title track, a nine-minute slice of swamp boogie, is the show stopper on this Savoy Brown outing. Nothing else here shines as brightly, perhaps be-

cause of the numerous personnel changes over the previous years, which had begun to take their toll on the vitality of the boogie-rock Savoy Brown had become so famous for. —*James Chrispell*

● **The Savoy Brown Collection (Chronicles Series)** / Jul. 20, 1993 / Polygram ✦✦✦✦
This double-disc set is all you may ever need of Savoy Brown. It includes their biggest hit, "Tell Mama." Like all Polygram *Chronicles* sets, this features great sound, smart track selections, thoughtful liner notes, and good photos. What more could you ask for? —*Rick Clark*

Charlie Sayles

b. Jan. 4, 1948, Woburn, MA
Harmonica / Modern Electric Blues
Harmonica player Charlie Sayles is starting to carve out a hard-fought niche for himself in US blues circles, thanks to some help from the London-based JSP Records. Sayles has two excellent albums out on the JSP label, *Night Ain't Right* (1990) and *I Got Something to Say*, a 1995 release.

Although life hasn't been easy for Sayles, he seems to have come through the traumas okay. They started in his childhood, when he was shifted from his broken home to a long procession of foster homes. He ended up joining the Army in the late 1960s and was promptly shipped to South Vietnam. His tour of duty ended in 1971, and he came back to Massachusetts for a time. Sayles picked up the blues harp while he was in Vietnam and made a slow adjustment back to civilized society upon his return from three years in the infantry. He discovered Sonny Boy Williamson (Rice Miller's) music after he returned home and learned all he could from those recordings. Sayles began to make trips to New York City, Atlanta, St. Louis and other cities, playing on the streets for tips from passersby in 1974 and for several years thereafter. He worked when he needed money as a day laborer. He hasn't had a real day job since then, patiently plying his craft in clubs, on street corners and more recently, at blues festivals.

What shows in Sayles' playing are the long periods of time he spent honing his craft on the streets and in subway stations. His approach as a solo artist was to get as full and bandlike a sound as he could with his harp. It appears to have paid off, because Sayles is unlike other harp players; his playing is full of extended phrasing and super-quick changes in register. Sayles uses the harmonica as a melodic device while coaxing sharp, almost percussive sounds from it as well.

Sayles began to develop his songwriting voice in the mid-1970s as well, and his debut for the JSP label is far from a straightahead blues album. On his second JSP release, Sayles artfully blends funky, gritty urban blues sounds with original, down-to-earth lyrics, successfully avoiding a lot of blues cliches.

Perhaps his first big break was being "discovered" by Ralph Rinzler, an organizer for the Smithsonian Festival of American Folklife. Rinzler paired Sayles up with Pete Seeger, and after a variety of festival appearances, Sayles ended up moving to Washington, D.C. By the early 1980s, while living in Washington, Sayles had begun to form his first bands.

Sayles' first record, *Raw Harmonica Blues*, was issued in 1976, long before blues became fashionable, on the Dusty Road label. Sayles didn't record again for 15 years, when he got picked up by JSP Records. *I Got Something to Say* has some prominent guests on it, including Washington's most celebrated blues guitar player, Bobby Parker. Also performing on the record is guitarist Deborah Coleman. Both of Sayles' JSP recordings are well worth seeking out, even at import prices, because of his original take on blues music. Sayles would be the first to tell you that he's not a straightahead Chicago blues player. He takes a much more mongrelized approach to the music, mixing in elements of New Orleans funk, Chicago blues and rock 'n' roll in his playing. —*Richard Skelly*

● **Night Ain't Right** / 1990 / JSP ✦✦✦✦
Charlie Sayles' *Night Ain't Right* is an impressive comeback, finding the harpist in prime form. The key to the record's success is the way Sayles twists conventions around, finding tastes of flourishes funk and jazz within the genre's boundaries. His willingness to play with the music is the reason why *Night Ain't Right* is a modern-day Chicago blues record worth exploring. —*Thom Owens*

I Got Something to Say / Oct. 3, 1995 / JSP ✦✦✦

Buddy Scott

b. Jan. 9, 1935, Jackson, MS, d. Feb. 5, 1994, Chicago, IL
Guitar, Vocals / Electric Chicago Blues
Chicago guitarist Kenneth "Buddy" Scott hailed from an extended musical brood, to put it mildly. His brothers, singer Howard and guitarist Walter, are mainstays on the local scene; his son, guitarist Thomas "Hollywood" Scott, leads Tyrone Davis' Platinum Band, and even his grandmother Ida knew her way around a guitar—she played on the South Side with the likes of Little Walter and Sonny Boy Williamson back in the 1950s.

Buddy Scott left Mississippi for Chicago at age seven. Both his mom and local legend Reggie Boyd tutored him as a guitarist. Like several of his brothers, Buddy was a member of a local doo wop vocal group, the Masqueraders, during the early '60s, and recorded a few singles with his siblings as the Scott Brothers later in the decade. He was best known as leader of Scotty & the Rib Tips, who were staples of the South and West Side blues circuit; they were featured on Alligator's second batch of *Living Chicago Blues* anthologies in 1980.

By the time Scott caught his big major-label break with Verve in 1993 with his debut domestic album, *Bad Avenue*, it was too late for him to capitalize on his belated good fortune. The stomach cancer that had been gaining on him did him in shortly after its release. —*Bill Dahl*

● **Bad Avenue** / Oct. 19, 1993 / Verve ✦✦✦✦
Not the perfect vehicle for the late Chicago blues guitarist—it's a tad too slick, and some of the song choices fall into the realm of overworked cliche—but Scott's major-label debut album was a credible swan song, his enthusiastic vocals and clean guitar work ringing through well. —*Bill Dahl*

E.C. Scott

Vocals / Contemporary Blues
Modern blues singer E.C. Scott brings a funky '90s sensibility to her classic soul and gospel influences. Raised in Oakland, California, Scott grew up listening to gospel singers like Shirley Caesar and Inez Andrews; as she grew older, she began to ignore her mother's restrictions on secular music and sampled the sounds of the rich soul music on her sisters' radio. Scott was singing in nightclubs by the time she was 16, but her marriage soon put her career on hiatus. When her two children were old enough, Scott decided to resume her singing career with her family's blessing; she initially worked as a jazz stylist, but soon returned to the blues and R&B she knew well. Scott put together a backing band called Smoke and played the San Francisco club scene, becoming the house band at Slim's for a year and self-releasing the single "Just Dance" b/w "Let's Make It Real" in 1991. Scott built up her local fan base and performed at several blues festivals around the US before signing to Blind Pig in 1994. Her debut album, *Come Get Your Love*, was released the following year; it was followed in 1998 by *Hard Act to Follow*. —*Steve Huey*

Come Get Your Love / 1995 / Blind Pig ✦✦✦

● **Hard Act to Follow** / Jan. 2, 1998 / Blind Pig ✦✦✦✦
Soul singer extraordinaire E.C. Scott comes back from her 1995 debut with perhaps even a stronger album the second time at bat. Ten of the 11 tunes on here emanate from her prolific pen (the only cover is her interpretation of the Eurythmics' "Missionary Man"), and her earthy, engaging style is heard to great effect on the opener, "Steppin' Out on a Saturday Night," the bouncy shuffle "Don't Touch Me," the slow blues "Lyin' and Cheatin'" and the title track. Her time is impeccable, her phrasing straight and true, and every vocal on here is chock full of deep feeling; as a modern-day example of a soul-blues album, this one's about as good as the form gets. —*Cub Koda*

Son Seals

b. Aug. 13, 1942, Osceola, AR
Guitar, Drums, Vocals / Electric Chicago Blues, Modern Electric Chicago Blues
It all started with a phone call from Wesley Race, who was at the Flamingo Club on Chicago's South Side, to Alligator Records owner Bruce Iglauer. Race was raving about a new find, a young guitarist named Son Seals. He held the phone in the direction of the bandstand, so Iglauer could get an on-site report. It didn't take long for Iglauer to scramble into action. Alligator issued Seals' 1973 eponymous debut album, which was followed by six more.

Son Seals, born Frank Seals, was born into the blues. His dad operated a juke joint called the Dipsy Doodle Club in Osceola, AR, where Sonny Boy Williamson, Robert Nighthawk, and Albert King cavorted up front while little Frank listened intently in back. Drums were the youth's first instrument; he played them behind Nighthawk at age 13. But by the time he was 18, Son Seals turned his talents to guitar, fronting his own band in Little Rock.

While visiting his sister in Chicago, he hooked up with Earl Hooker's Roadmasters in 1963 for a few months, and there was a 1966 stint with Albert King that sent him behind the drumkit once more. But with the death of his father in 1971, Seals returned to Chicago, this time for good. When Alligator signed him up, his days fronting a band at the Flamingo Club and the Expressway Lounge were numbered.

Seals' jagged, uncompromising guitar riffs and gruff vocals were showcased very effectively on that 1973 debut set, which contained his "Your Love Is like a Cancer" and a raging instrumental called "Hot Sauce." *Midnight Son*, his 1976 encore, was by comparison a much slicker affair, with tight horns, funkier grooves, and a set list that included "Telephone Angel" and "On My Knees." Seals cut a live LP in 1978 at Wise Fools Pub, another studio concoction, *Chicago Fire*, in 1980, and a solid set in 1984, *Bad Axe*, before having a disagreement with Iglauer that that was patched up in 1991 with the release of his sixth Alligator set, *Living in the Danger Zone. Nothing but the Truth* followed in 1994, sporting some of the worst cover art in CD history but a stinging lineup of songs inside. Another live recording was planned for June of 1996 at Buddy Guy's Legends.

Seals prefers to remain close to his Chicago home these days, holding his touring itinerary to an absolute minimum. That means that virtually every weekend he can be found somewhere on the North Side blues circuit, dishing up his raw-edged brand of bad blues axe to local followers. — *Bill Dahl*

The Son Seals Blues Band / 1973 / Alligator ✦✦✦✦
The Chicago mainstay's debut album was a rough, gruff, no-nonsense affair typified by the decidedly unsentimental track "Your Love Is like a Cancer." Seals wasn't all that far removed from his southern roots at this point, and his slashing guitar work sports a strikingly raw feel on his originals "Look Now, Baby," "Cotton Picking Blues," and "Hot Sauce" (the latter a blistering instrumental that sounds a bit like the theme from *Batman* played sideways). — *Bill Dahl*

● **Midnight Son** / 1976 / Alligator ✦✦✦✦
A much more polished set than its predecessor, *Midnight Son* is a particularly effective effort with several numbers that remain in Seals' onstage repertoire to this day—"Telephone Angel," "On My Knees," the jumping "Four Full Seasons of Love." The addition of a brisk horn section enhanced his staccato guitar attack and uncompromising vocals, rendering this his best set to date. — *Bill Dahl*

Live & Burning / 1978 / Alligator ✦✦✦✦
Lives up to its billing. Seals' smoking set, caught live at Chicago's long-gone (and definitely lamented) Wise Fools Pub, finds him attacking a sharp cross-section of material—Detroit Junior's deliberate "Call My Job," Elmore James' "I Can't Hold Out," his own "Help Me, Somebody"—with an outstanding band in tow—saxist A.C. Reed, guitarist Lacy Gibson, pianist Alberto Gianquinto, bassist Snapper Mitchum, and drummer Tony Gooden. — *Bill Dahl*

Chicago Fire / 1980 / Alligator ✦✦✦
Son Seals in an experimental mood, utilizing chord progressions that occasionally don't quite fit together seamlessly (but give him an A for trying to expand the idiom's boundaries). Less innovative but perhaps more accessible are his smoking covers of Albert King's "Nobody Wants a Loser" and Junior Parker's "Goodbye Little Girl." — *Bill Dahl*

Bad Axe / 1984 / Alligator ✦✦✦✦
One of Son Seals' finest collections, studded with vicious performances ranging from covers of Eddie Vinson's "Person to Person" and Little Sonny's "Going Home (Where Women Got Meat on Their Bones)" to his own "Can't Stand to See Her Cry" and swaggering "Cold Blood." Top-drawer Windy City studio musicians lay down skin-tight grooves throughout. — *Bill Dahl*

Living in the Danger Zone / 1991 / Alligator ✦✦✦
The guitarist keeps his string of consecutive fine releases alive with a studio-cut disc that sizzles with bandstand-level velocity (until its last cut, anyway). "Frigidaire Woman," "Woman in Black," and "Bad Axe" rate with the high-

lights; the self-pitying ballad closer "My Life" is the worst thing Seals has ever put on tape for Alligator. — *Bill Dahl*

Nothing But the Truth / 1994 / Alligator ✦✦✦✦
The grotesque cover illustration is an abomination, but the contents are right in the growling grizzly bear style that we've come to expect. Only four Seals-penned originals, but the R&B-laced "Life Is Hard" and "I'm Gonna Take It All Back" are quality efforts. So is his heartfelt tribute to Hound Dog Taylor, "Sadie." — *Bill Dahl*

Spontaneous Combustion / 1996 / Alligator ✦✦✦
Son Seals is a very powerful performer. While his vocals are full of passion, it is Seals' explosive guitar solos (egged on by two fine horn players who have some solo spots and a driving rhythm section) that are most notable. Recorded live at Buddy Guy's Legends in Chicago, Seals' interpretations of these spirited blues would certainly please the club owner. This enthusiastic set serves as a perfect introduction to the accessible and memorable blues of Son Seals. — *Scott Yanow*

Marvin Sease

b. Feb. 16, 1946, South Carolina
Vocals / Retro-Soul, Soul, Modern Electric Blues
Despite a lack of attention from most print sources and other common avenues of publicity in the blues world, Marvin Sease has turned his smooth, X-rated ladies' man persona into a cottage industry complete with merchandising in the Deep South. Sease straddles the line between blues and gospel-drenched soul, much like fellow Southern singers Johnnie Taylor and Tyrone Davis. But his often racy lyrics and concert performances, coupled with the advantages of major-label distribution, have ensured Sease a strong following, particularly among female fans enamored of his signature song and breakthrough jukebox hit—the provocative, innuendo-laced "Candy Licker." Born in Blackville, S.C., Sease got his start by joining a gospel group in nearby Charleston called the Five Gospel Singers, and moved to New York at age 20, where he joined another gospel group called the Gospel Crowns. Preferring rhythm & blues, though, Sease put together a backing band (called Sease) featuring his three brothers. When this venture failed, Sease began singing to pre-recorded backing tracks at local dances and clubs, self-released several 45s, and eventually scored a regular gig at a Brooklyn nightspot called the Casablanca. Gunning for greater success, Sease recorded a self-titled LP in 1986 featuring one of his most popular songs, "Ghetto Man," and began working the South's so-called chitlin circuit of ghetto bars, rural juke joints, and blues festivals. While shopping the LP, released on his own Early label, to record stores, Sease stumbled upon a contact who eventually got him a deal with Polygram, which re-released the LP on London/Mercury in 1987 with the addition of the newly recorded, ten-minute track "Candy Licker." "Candy Licker" became an underground success on jukeboxes across the South; it was too explicit for radio airplay, but audiences—especially female ones—flocked to see Sease in concert. Over the next ten years, Sease recorded a string of albums for London/Mercury (*Breakfast*, 1987; *The Real Deal*, 1989; *Show Me What You Got*, 1991) and the New York-based Jive (*The Housekeeper*, 1993; *Do You Need a Licker?*, 1994; *Please Take Me*, 1996) that sold consistently well, although none have yet matched the performance of *Marvin Sease*, which hit number 14 on *Billboard*'s R&B chart and number 114 on the pop chart. — *Steve Huey*

Marvin Sease / 1986 / London ✦✦✦✦
Marvin Sease hadn't quite perfected his vulgar soul on his eponymous debut album, but he certainly hinted at his new direction with the epic "Candy Licker." That final number pointed the way to the sex-drenched future, but the remainder of the album was relatively tame, as Sease just concentrated on sweaty Southern soul. He may not have found his gimmick, but he was nevertheless a good singer, and since it shies away from carnality, the album may actually be preferable to his later work for more conservative soul fans. — *Thom Owens*

Breakfast / Dec. 1987 / London ✦✦✦✦
For anyone who loves soul, listening to a Marvin Sease record is likely to be a frustrating experience. There's little questioning that he has a rich, soulful voice and can replicate the sweat-soaked, gritty sound of Stax soul or the bedroom crooning of Al Green at the drop of a hat. It's his subject matter, however, that may make blues and soul fans balk: Sease likes it dirty. Scratch

that—he likes it *vulgar*, if "Condom on Your Tongue" and "I Ate You for My Breakfast" are any indication. That can be a problem for anyone with queasy stomachs, since Sease likes to belt out his dirty words, unless it's on the slow songs, where he murmurs his sweet, filthy nothings, presumably to get you in the mood. Musically, there's no way to fault *Breakfast*—it's first-rate retro-soul—but if you don't like nasty pillow talk, chances are the music isn't going to make this *Breakfast* digestible. —*Stephen Thomas Erlewine*

Tell Me Why / Jul. 31, 1989 / London ♦♦

The Real Deal / Sep. 15, 1989 / London ♦♦♦
The formula shows signs of strain. —*Ron Wynn*

Show Me What You Got / Oct. 8, 1991 / Mercury ♦♦
Marvin Sease generated a lot of noise on the Southern soul circuit in the late '80s with his albums, which combined a lowdown blues sensibility with some very adult (at times vulgar) sexual commentary. But things had pretty much run their creative course by the time this early-'90s LP was issued. Even fans on the dirtfloor circuit had heard Sease do this kind of material one time too many; he hadn't evolved, nor had the ballads and slower blues/soul cuts gotten any better. —*Ron Wynn*

The Housekeeper / Apr. 27, 1993 / Jive/Novus ♦♦♦

Do You Need a Licker / Oct. 25, 1994 / Jive ♦♦

Please Take Me / Apr. 16, 1996 / Jive ♦♦♦

The Best of Marvin Sease / May 20, 1997 / Polygram ♦♦♦♦
The Best of Marvin Sease is the first comprehensive collection of Sease's best bawdy, funky '70s soul, culled from his four albums for Polygram. Among the 15 tracks are the notorious "Candy Licker" and a single that had never been available on an album prior to this collection. —*Stephen Thomas Erlewine*

The Bitch Git It All / Oct. 28, 1997 / Jive ♦♦♦
Another year, another Marvin Sease record. Throughout the years, Sease has stayed the same, turning out Southern soul in the classic sense, but spiking it with vulgar, raunchy lyircs. Despite its title, *The Bitch Git It All* isn't among his rudest work—there's still a bit of profanity, to be sure, but not on the level of his early albums, and that makes the record a bit more palatable for the timid. He still has a problem coming up with consistently compelling material, but *The Bitch Git It All* remains one of his stronger records. —*Thom Owens*

Brother John Sellers

b. May 27, 1924, Clarksdale, MS
Vocals / Folk-Blues
Somewhat in the mold of Josh White and (to a lesser degree) Leadbelly, Brother John Sellers was an African-American all-around folk entertainer, singing blues, folk, gospel, and bits of jazz. Born in Clarksdale, MS, he joined the mass migration to Chicago at the age of 11. In the mid-'50s, he recorded one of the earlier long-playing albums aimed at the folk audience, which included accompaniment by Sonny Terry and the original Count Basie rhythm section. —*Richie Unterberger*

● **Sings Blues & Folk Songs** / 1954 / Vanguard ♦♦♦♦
A bit tame even by the standards of the folk revival, this showcased Sellers as a smooth and accomplished presenter of folk, blues, and a bit of jazz. The singer mixed original compositions with standards like "John Henry," "Down By the Riverside," and "Nobody Knows the Trouble I Have Seen" on a set that seemed conscientiously programmed to demonstrate his versatility. The blues and folk numbers were graced by harmonica from Sonny Terry; the less successful jazzy efforts had accompaniment from a combo featuring the original Count Basie rhythm section. —*Richie Unterberger*

Brother John Sellers / Sep. 8, 1954 / Vanguard ♦♦♦

The Sensational Nightingales

f. 194?
Group / Black Gospel, Southern Gospel, Traditional Gospel
The Sensational Nightingales were assembled in the '40s. In 1957 they appeared on the Gospel Train tour with The Clara Ward Singers and five other big-name gospel acts. Members included Julius Cheeks (lead), Carl Coates (bass), JoJo Wallace (tenor), Howard Carroll (baritone), and Paul Gwens (tenor). Their noted hit was "See How They Done My Lord." One of the earli-

est gospel quintets, they recorded and toured throughout the 1990s. Many of their '50s and '60s sides (found on MCA reissues) feature the stunning vocals of Rev. Julius Cheeks. As with Archie Brownlee, Cheeks reaches an intensity that distorts the actual recordings, and his style has been heavily "borrowed" by Bobby Bland, Wilson Pickett, and others. The later recordings by Charles Johnson are smoother and slicker, but still top-notch. —*Bil Carpenter & Billy C. Wirtz*

Songs of Praise / 1959 / Peacock ♦♦♦♦
The hardest-singing lead in gospel. Beautiful harmonies. —*Opal Louis Nations*

Glory, Glory / 1963 / Peacock ♦♦♦♦
More fine singing with soul and conviction at the helm. —*Opal Louis Nations*

It's Gonna Rain Again / 1975 / MCA ♦♦♦
Reissue of one of the quartet's best 1970s Peacock albums. Featuring Charles Johnson. —*Opal Louis Nations*

Jesus Is Coming / 1976 / MCA ♦♦♦
Beautiful songs done up in country-hymn fashion by lead soloist Charles Johnson. ABC Paramount material. —*Opal Louis Nations*

The Best of the Sensational Nightingales / 1978 / MCA ♦♦♦♦
Some of Rev. Julius Cheeks and the group's finest efforts on Peacock from the 1950s. —*Opal Louis Nations*

Victory Is Mine / 1980 / Malaco ♦♦♦
This release has soaring unison vocals on such songs as "He'll Answer Prayer," "He May Not Knock No More," and "Occupy Till He Comes." They also put a nice contemporary touch on "Power In The Blood," and "Open Up My Eyes" has a moving, personalized approach. This isn't earthshaking Sensational Nightingales material, but it's well done and faithful to the genre in mood and approach. —*Ron Wynn, Rejoice*

God Is Not Pleased / Mar. 24, 1998 / Malaco ♦♦♦♦
God Is Not Pleased is a fine latter-day effort from the Sensational Nightingales, who by this point feature a lineup of Jo Jo Wallace, Horace Thompson, and Richard Luster; this triumvirate also handled production duties. —*Steve Huey*

● **Heart & Soul/You Know Not . . .** / Mobile Fidelity ♦♦♦♦
The CD remastering of these two early-'70s albums by this fine harmony quintet is well worth owning. *Heart and Soul* is taken from the better pre-Paramount days (1970-1971), and *You Know Not the Hour* presents the group in a later, more hymnal song setting, both with Charles Johnson on lead. —*Kip Lornell*

Charlie Sexton

b. Aug. 11, 1968, Austin, TX
Vocals, Guitar / Pop-Rock, Blues-Rock, Singer-Songwriter
Although only in his early 30s, guitarist, singer and songwriter Charlie Sexton has already had several phases to his career. Sexton, raised in Austin, Texas, made his debut with *Pictures For Pleasure* in 1985 at age 16. He followed that up with a self-titled second album when he was 20. Because word of his reputation as a prodigy guitar player spread far and wide, he found himself an in-demand session player while still in his late teens, and he had the opportunity to record with Ron Wood, Keith Richards and Bob Dylan.

Born to a mother who was just 16 when she gave birth to Charlie, he and his mother moved to Austin when he was just four. His mother would get him out to clubs like the Armadillo World Headquarters and the Soap Creek Saloon. Places like the Split Rail and Antone's blues club became his classrooms. After living outside of Austin for a while with his mother, he moved back to Austin when he was 12, and the musicians around Austin, his heroes, people like Jimmie Vaughan and Stevie Ray Vaughan, Joe Ely, and others, took him in and put him up where he could learn more of a living on his own.

From 1992 until 1994, he was a member of Austin's Arc Angels, along with Doyle Bramhall II, Tommy Shannon, and Chris "Whipper" Layton. That group recorded one self-titled album, released in 1992 on Geffen Records. By the time the Arc Angels decided to disband, Sexton was 24 years old and already pegged as a blues musician. But in fact, Sexton plays gutsy, fluid blues guitar, but also spirited rock 'n' roll guitar.

In 1994 and 1995, he formed and recorded with his new group, the Charlie

Sexton Sextet, and his debut for MCA Records, *Under The Wishing Tree*, was released in 1995. Sexton's album was well-received by the critics. *Under The Wishing Tree* presents Sexton in an array of musical genres, touching on Celtic flavored rock, folk-rock and blues. There is a lot of interplay between guitars, violins, cellos, Dobros and mandolins on the recording, and Sexton's vocals ride high on top of the melodies. On his 1995 tour to support the album, he was accompanied by Susan Boelz, violin, Michael Ramos, organ, and George Reiff, bass, and Rafael Gayol, drums.

As a songwriter, Sexton writes about what he knows, so Texas themes permeate his songs. He considers Bob Dylan his strongest songwriting influence, while he counts Austin legends Jimmie Vaughan and the late Stevie Ray Vaughan among his prime influences for guitar playing. His lyrics mix autobiographical experiences with images that are open to interpretation. More great things are in the offing for this young guitarist, singer and songwriter. — *Richard Skelly*

● **Pictures for Pleasure** / 1985 / MCA ✦✦✦✦
Like many teenagers, Charlie Sexton lusted after rock stardom — the only difference was, he had a chance to pursue his dream. Sexton certainly looked like the part, with his high cheek bones and pompadour, but since he was living in the '80s instead of the '50s he worshipped, his producers decided to push him toward new wave for his debut album, *Pictures for Pleasure*. The teenaged guitarist had been bashing out blues and roots-rock around his native Austin, Texas, but the market for that music was limited — hence the decision to layer the record with drum machines and synthesizers. Through sheer dumb luck, they came up with a classic MTV hit with the moody "Beat's So Lonely," where Sexton comes on like James Dean in Duran Duran clothing, crooning with Bryan Ferry's voice. There's nothing nearly as good on the remainder of *Pictures for Pleasure*, not only because the material is uneven, but because none of the other material benefits with the new wave treatment. That said, it's still a more interesting and entertaining record than many of Sexton's straitlaced latter-day blues efforts, where he often sounds just a bit too respectful. — *Stephen Thomas Erlewine*

Charlie Sexton / 1989 / MCA ✦✦✦✦
An about-face, with more emphasis on Sexton's guitar playing and Texas roots. — *Cub Koda*

Under the Wishing Tree / 1995 / MCA ✦✦✦

Mem Shannon

b. Dec. 21, 1959, New Orleans, LA
Vocals / R&B, Retro-Soul, Modern Electric Blues
Guitarist, singer and songwriter Mem Shannon is one of young lions of blues who believes in expanding the parameters of the music. His two albums for Rykodisc, *A Cab Driver's Blues* (his 1995 debut) and *Mem Shannon's 2nd Blues Album* (1997), are both worth seeking out in record stores. Shannon brilliantly combines elements of funk, jazz and rock 'n' roll into his guitar playing, and his soulful vocals are not your run-of-the-mill stylings. In fact, most things about Shannon are exceptional: the way he write songs, the way he sings them, and the way he presents them. He's a rock 'n' roll kid who played in a variety of cover bands in high school in his native New Orleans, but he always had a healthy appreciation for blues and gospel music.

Shannon was born in New Orleans and began playing clarinet at age 9. By the time he was 15, he was playing guitar, inspired by his father's blues record collection, but it wasn't until he saw B.B. King that he got serious about it and began practicing in earnest. He began playing in Top 40 and wedding bands around the Crescent City. His first band after high school, the Ebony Brothers Hot Band, played dances, parties and neighborhood bars. His second group, Free Enterprize, found work doing covers. However, his father passed away unexpectedly in 1981, and as the oldest son in a close-knit family, he began driving a cab to help the family pay bills. He also played guitar in the Dedicators, a gospel group, but there was no money whatsoever in that.

He put his music aside for awhile, but began playing again in 1990 after being encouraged to do so by Peter Carter, his old bassist from Free Enterprize. Shannon began working out lyrics and song ideas and working with Carter again. His songs were inspired partly by his life and experiences driving a cab. Regular club gigs followed at a few clubs in the French Quarter. In 1991, he spotted an ad in the local newspaper advertising a talent contest. Shannon and the Membership won the contest, ensuring them a spot at

the New Orleans Jazz and Heritage Festival, plus $1,000 and a television commercial. Later in 1991, Shannon and the Membership went to the Long Beach Blues Festival's talent contest, but lost out in the finals and didn't get to play the festival.

After making a demo tape of his material, he got some interest from JSP, a London-based blues label, but an area producer offered his services to re-record some of the songs on Shannon's demo. The producer, Mark Bingham, brought Shannon's music to the attention of Joe Boyd of Hannibal Records in 1994. Boyd was impressed, and on Oct. 15, 1995, Shannon's debut, *A Cab Driver's Blues*, was released.

The album drew critical praise from far and wide, but it also got him an extraordinary amount of publicity. Because of the interesting nature of the recording, which includes snippets of conversation with passengers from his cab interspersed with the music, Shannon's story attracted the attention of producers at PBS-TV, CBS-TV's *Sunday Morning* and editors at the *New York Times*.

By April of 1996, at the annual New Orleans Jazz and Heritage Festival, Shannon announced from the stage that he was giving up his job as a cab driver to play blues full-time. He hasn't looked back and thanks to good booking agents and his own work ethic, he's already toured extensively around the US, Europe and Canada. Shannon is the first major new talent to come out of New Orleans in some time, and since thousands of foreigners visit New Orleans every spring for JazzFest, Shannon forged his reputation as an international touring musician easily.

Shannon's music isn't stuck in a jump-shuffle mode. He takes a broader view, incorporating elements of funk, jazz, swamp-rock, and classic rock into the Membership's blues-based sound. The band funks it up with varying shuffle drum backbeats, throbbing bass lines, a wailing saxophone and feathery keyboard treatments. And there is room in Shannon's view of himself as a bluesman for political and social commentary in songs like "Wrong People In Charge," "Charity," and "Down Broke." — *Richard Skelly*

● **A Cab Driver's Blues** / Oct. 1995 / Hannibal ✦✦✦✦
Mem Shannon's first album, *A Cab Driver's Blues*, became a minor media sensation upon its 1995 release due to circumstance more than music. Shannon's story is fascinating — he's a New Orleans taxi driver who wanted to get out of the business and become a bluesman. That's basically what all the songs on the album are about, whether they're about the job ("5th Ward Horseman," "$17.00 Brunette"), domestic problems ("My Baby's Been Watching TV") or just life in general ("Food Drink and Music," "Ode to Benny Hill"). Shannon's songs have so much specificity and detail that they wind up being much more interesting than the average contemporary blues album. Also, his warm, laidback musical style is idiosyncratic and unpredictable. His delivery is friendly and conversational — he often sounds as if he's singing directly to the listener. And it's that special, intimate quality that makes *A Cab Driver's Blues* a truly unique and special contemporary blues record. — *Thom Owens*

Second Blues Album / Apr. 29, 1997 / Hannibal ✦✦✦

Preston Shannon Band

Guitar, Vocals / Modern Electric Blues
Memphis-based guitarist, singer and songwriter Preston Shannon delivers soul-filled vocals atop his burning, venom-tipped guitar chords. His voice is deep and guttural, and he's a veteran of hundreds of live club shows and recording sessions as a sideman. Shannon's specialty is a blend of Southern-fried soul and blues, and his albums and live shows — always with a horn section — are an eclectic mix of danceable, grooving tunes and slow, soulful ballads.

Born in Olive Branch, Mississippi, Shannon's family moved to Memphis when he was eight. Although his Pentecostal parents didn't initially accept his fascination with blues music, they eventually did when they saw how serious he was about pursuing the music for his livelihood. Shannon served as a member of a popular 1970s bar band, Amnesty, and played in a succession of other Memphis-area bands while working by day for a hardware company. Finally, he decided to play music full time when he landed a spot in soul-blues belter Shirley Brown's band. It wasn't until 1991 that he put together his own band and began playing the clubs on Beale Street and other places. In the early 1990s, he was discovered playing in a Beale Street blues club by producer/keyboardist Ron Levy, who brought Shannon's talents to the attention of executives at Rounder Records. Shortly afterwards, in 1994, his first widely distributed recording was issued on the label.

Shannon has recorded two albums for the Rounder Bullseye Blues subsidiary, *Break the Ice* (1994) and *Midnight In Memphis* (1996). Both albums more than adequately showcase his talents as a singer who can alternate between uptempo, gospel-inspired numbers and slower, soulful love songs and ballads. Shannon's guitar playing contains echoes of the Kings, Albert and B.B., T-Bone Walker, and some of the rhythmic sensibilities of Little Milton Campbell. Of the two albums, *Midnight In Mempis* is just a bit more eclectic; the mix of styles made it a radio-ready record for blues and soul stations in the South. For many years a homebody who couldn't be heard much outside the Memphis city limits, Shannon has done some road work in recent years, traveling to blues festivals around the US — *Richard Skelly*

Break the Ice / 1994 / Bullseye Blues ♦♦♦

● **Midnight in Memphis** / Apr. 1996 / Bullseye Blues ♦♦♦♦
King Curtis once recorded a groovy tune on which he described and demonstrated the recipe for "Memphis Soul Stew" ("a pound of fatback drums," "a half pint of horns," "a pinch of organ," etc.). *Midnight in Memphis* is like a Memphis *Blues* Stew seasoned with chunks of soul; it combines every tasty ingredient to be found in both the blues and soul cookbooks. Co-producers Ron Levy (an aficionado of the Memphis sound) and Willie Mitchell (one of the creators of that sound) work with guitarist/vocalist Shannon (a regular on the current Memphis scene) to create one of the strongest contemporary soul-blues albums of the decade. On cuts like the slow-burner "The Feeling Is Gone," the sexual epic "The Clock," and the knockout "Size 12 Shoes," Shannon's gritty vocals convey so much commitment and authority as to enthrall the listener, especially when the CD is played loud as it obviously was meant to be. Shannon hit the ground running on his debut album *Break the Ice*. On *Midnight in Memphis* he soars. — *Steve Hoffman*

Eddie Shaw

b. Mar. 20, 1937, Stringtown, MS
Saxophone, Vocals / Electric Chicago Blues
When it comes to blues, Chicago's strictly a guitar and harmonica town. Saxophonists who make a living leading a blues band in the Windy City are scarce as hen's teeth. But Eddie Shaw has done precisely that ever since his longtime boss, Howlin' Wolf, died in 1976.

The powerfully constructed tenor saxist has rubbed elbows with an amazing array of luminaries over his 40-plus years in the business. By the time he was age 14, Shaw was jamming with Ike Turner's combo around Greenville, MS. At a gig in Itta Bena where Shaw sat in, Muddy Waters extended the young saxman an invitation he couldn't refuse: a steady job with Waters' unparalleled band in Chicago. After a few years, Shaw switched his onstage allegiance to Waters' chief rival, the ferocious Howlin' Wolf, staying with him until the very end and eventually graduating to a featured role as Wolf's bandleader.

Eddie Shaw also shared a West side bandstand or two along the way with Freddy King, Otis Rush, and Magic Sam. The saxist did a 1966 session with Sam that produced his first single, the down-in-the-alley instrumental "Blues for the West Side" (available on Delmark's *Sweet Home Chicago* anthology). Shaw also blew his heart out on Sam's 1968 Delmark encore LP, *Black Magic*.

Shaw's own recording career finally took off during the late '70s, with a standout appearance on Alligator's *Living Chicago Blues* anthologies in 1978, his own LPs for Simmons and Rooster Blues, and fine recent discs for Rooster Blues (*In the Land of the Crossroads*) and Austrian Wolf (*Home Alone*). Eddie Shaw, who once operated the hallowed 1815 Club on West Roosevelt Road (one of Wolf's favorite haunts), has sired a couple of high-profile sons: diminutive Eddie Jr., known as Vaan, plays lead guitar with Eddie's Wolf Gang and has cut a pair of his own albums for Wolf, while husky Stan Shaw is a prolific character actor in Hollywood. — *Bill Dahl*

Movin' and Groovin' Man / May 14, 1982 / Evidence ♦♦♦
Tenor saxophonist Eddie Shaw is a rarity in blues circles—a first-class instrumentalist who is not a guitarist or pianist. Shaw is a soulful, exuberant player whose lusty licks make a solid counterpoint to his rough-hewn vocals and narratives. While Shaw carries the majority of the load on this 10-cut date from 1982 previously recorded for Isabel (reissued on CD by Evidence) it is guitarist Melvin Taylor who is the revelation as second soloist. Between his

work with Lucky Peterson, his own CD, and his brisk, sizzling solos and accompaniment here, Taylor merits high praise as a workmanlike, flexible contributor. The others, with the exception of the great Eddie "Cleanhead" Vinson, are heady pros capably handling limited support duties. — *Ron Wynn*

King of the Road / Sep. 1986 / Rooster Blues ♦♦♦♦
A revealing compilation of the ballsy Chicago saxist's earlier work (1966-1984) that certainly deserves to be on CD but isn't yet. "Blues for the West Side" and "Lookin' Good," both with Magic Sam, are highlights of Shaw's entire career, while his vocal talents are well-served on "It's All Right," an amusing "I Don't Trust Nobody," and his touching tribute "Blues Men of Yesterday." — *Bill Dahl*

● **In the Land of the Crossroads** / 1992 / Rooster Blues ♦♦♦♦
The best contemporary Shaw offering, cut in his old Mississippi stomping grounds with his trusty combo, the Wolf Gang. Lots of lyrically unusual originals—"Dunkin' Donut Woman," "Wine Head Hole," and "She Didn't Tell Me Everything," for starters—and Shaw's usual diamond-hard horn lines and commanding vocals make this a standout selection. — *Bill Dahl*

Trail of Tears / 1994 / Wolf ♦♦♦♦

Home Alone / 1995 / Wolf ♦♦♦♦
Although it's pressed on an Austrian logo, Eddie Shaw's rollicking recent disc was waxed in his Chicago hometown with the Wolf Gang (son Vaan on guitar, longtime bassist Shorty Gilbert, and drummer Tim Taylor) summoning up solid support. Once again, Shaw tackles some interesting subjects—he fantasizes about "Blues in Paris," decried being "Home Alone," and searches out an endorsement deal with "Motel Six" via his sprightly musical tribute to the budget chain. — *Bill Dahl*

The Blues Is Nothing But Good News! / 1996 / Wolf ♦♦♦

Can't Stop Now / Apr. 29, 1997 / Delmark ♦♦♦

Robert Shaw

b. Aug. 9, 1908, Stafford, TX, **d.** May 18, 1985, Austin, TX
Piano, Vocals / Texas Blues, Piano Blues
He didn't record much at all—a marvelous 1963 album for Almanac, reissued on Chris Strachwitz's Arhoolie label, remains his principal recorded legacy—but barrelhouse pianist Robert Shaw helped greatly to establish a distinctive regional style of pounding the 88s around Houston, Fort Worth, and Galveston during the 1920s and '30s.

Those decades represented Shaw's playing heyday, when he forged a stunning barrelhouse style of his own in the bars, dance halls, and whorehouses along the route of the Santa Fe railroad. Shaw got around—in 1933, he had a radio program in Oklahoma City. But by the mid-'30s, Shaw relegated his playing to the back burner to open a grocery store. Mack McCormick coaxed him back into action in 1963 and the results as collected on Arhoolie were magnificent; "The Cows" was a piece of incredible complexity that would wilt anything less than a legitimate ivories master. Shaw continued to perform stateside and in Europe intermittently during the 1970s, turning up unexpectedly in California in 1981 to help Strachwitz celebrate Arhoolie's 20th anniversary. — *Bill Dahl*

● **The Ma Grinder** / 1963 / Arhoolie ♦♦♦♦
Stunning solo Texas blues and barrelhouse piano by the late pianist. The most amazing material, produced by Mack McCormick in Austin, dates from 1963—the rhythmically and technically complex "The Cows" is a tour de force, and "The Ma Grinder" and "The Clinton" aren't far behind. Later numbers from 1973 and 1977 prove that Shaw's skills didn't degenerate with time. — *Bill Dahl*

Texas Barrelhouse Piano / Dec. 1980 / Arhoolie ♦♦♦♦

Kenny Wayne Shepherd

b. Jun. 12, 1977, Shreveport, LA
Guitar, Vocals / Modern Electric Blues, Contemporary Blues
Kenny Wayne Shepherd and his group have exploded on the scene in the mid-'90s and garnered huge amounts of radio airplay on commercial radio, which historically has not been a solid home for blues and blues-rock music, with the exception of Stevie Ray Vaughan in the mid-'80s.

Shepherd was born June 12, 1977 in Shreveport, Louisiana. The Shreveport native began playing at age 7, figuring out Muddy Waters licks from his father's record collection (he has never taken a formal lesson). At age 13, he was invited onstage by New Orleans bluesman Brian Lee and held his own for several hours; thus proving himself, he decided on music as a career. He formed his own band, which featured lead vocalist Corey Sterling, gaining early exposure through club dates and, later, radio conventions. Shepherd's father/manager used his own contacts and pizazz in the record business to help land his son a major label record deal with Irving Azoff's Giant Records. *Ledbetter Heights*, his first album, was released two years later in 1995. *Ledbetter Heights* was an immediate hit, selling over 500,000 by early 1996. Most blues records never achieve that level of commerical success, much less ones released by artists that are still in their teens.

Although Shepherd—who has been influenced by (and has sometimes played with) guitarists Stevie Ray Vaughan, Albert King, Slash, Robert Cray, and Duane Allman—is definitely a performer who thrives in front of an audience, *Ledbetter Heights* is impressive for it's range of styles: acoustic blues, rockin' blues, Texas blues, Louisiana blues. The only style that he doesn't tackle is Chicago blues, owing to Shepherd's home base smack dab in the middle of the Texas triangle. —*Steve Huey & Richard Skelly*

● **Ledbetter Heights** / Oct. 1995 / Giant ✦✦✦✦
You would never guess from Kenny Wayne Shepherd's fiery playing that the guitarist is still only in his teens. On his debut, *Ledbetter Heights,* Shepherd burns through a set of rather generic blues-rock ravers that are made special by his exceptional technique. It may still be a while before he says something original, but he plays with style, energy, and dedication, which is more than enough for a debut album. —*Thom Owens*

Trouble Is / Oct. 7, 1997 / Revolution/Warner Brothers ✦✦✦
Instead of breaking from his high-energy, high-voltage blues-rock, Kenny Wayne Shepherd offers more of the same on his second album, *Trouble Is.* While the record lacks the surprise and impact of *Ledbetter Heights,* it's clear that Shepherd is growing as a guitarist, developing a cleaner, more nuanced technique. He still suffers from a lack of an original voice, plus a lack of strong material, but his growth as a guitarist compensates for what's missing. —*Thom Owens*

Lonnie Shields

b. Apr. 17, 1956, West Helena, AR
Guitar, Vocals / Modern Acoustic Blues
Guitarist, singer and songwriter Lonnie Shields' *Portrait* (Rooster Blues) was praised by critics as one of the best debut albums of the year when it was released in 1992. Since then, the high praise from all corners of the world has continued for Shields' simple yet complex style of soulful, rhythmic blues.

Shields was brought up in a family where the church played a central role in daily life, and his gospel roots show through in everything he sings. He began playing soul and funk before discovering the Delta blues through his friend Sam Carr. Shields worked with Carr in the Unforgettable Blues Band and took as his other mentors local musicians like Frank Frost and Big Jack Johnson. Later, he discovered B.B. King, whom he considers his primary influence.

Shields formed his first group when he was 15. Called the Checkmates, they took their musical cues from the sounds of Earth, Wind and Fire and the Isley Brothers. After the band broke up, Shields gave up playing guitar for some time until he met drummer Sam Carr in Lula, Mississippi. Carr was insistent that Shields learn to play authentic blues, and a short time later, he was out on the road with Carr, Frank Frost and Big Jack Johnson.

After Shields played the King Biscuit Blues Festival in Helena, Arkansas in 1986, he was asked to record a single for the Rooster Blues label. This in turn led to his first album for Rooster Blues, released in 1993. The album got him noticed in the blues world and let to a broader touring base that included festival stops around the Northeast.

More recently, Shields has recorded and released *Tired of Waiting* (1996) and *Blues Is On Fire* (1997) for the London-based JSP Record label. A second Rooster Blues album, *Midnight Delight,* was scheduled for release in 1998.

In 1996, Shields moved from his Arkansas base to eastern Pennsylvania, outside of Philadelphia. He continues to perform around the US, Europe and Canada. —*Richard Skelly*

● **Portrait** / 1992 / Rooster Blues ✦✦✦✦
Lonnie Shields' debut album *Portrait* introduced an accomplished, talented

bluesman, one that was equally capable of playing guitar with abandon and delivering a song with soul. Unlike many of his peers, he doesn't oversell a song, he caresses it with his voice, knowing when to bring it all back home. Supported by guitarist Jack Johnson, keyboardist Frank Frost and drummer Sam Carr, he's able to pull off contemporary blues, laidback soul and funky grooves, resulting in a truly impressive and detailed *Portrait.* —*Thom Owens*

Tired of Waiting / Jun. 18, 1996 / JSP ✦✦✦✦

Blues Is on Fire / Sep. 23, 1997 / JSP ✦✦✦✦

Johnny Shines (John Ned Shines)

b. Apr. 26, 1915, Frayser, TN, **d.** Apr. 20, 1992, Chicago, IL
Guitar, Vocals / Delta Blues, Electric Delta Blues, Electric Chicago Blues
Johnny Shines' best material crackles with energy. In his prime, his slashing slide guitar carried more of the spirit of his onetime running mate Robert Johnson than any other traditional blues artist. Shines, however, was never a Johnson imitator. He had his own sound, his own guitar style, and a voice that can still take you on a roller coaster ride. (However, he did learn from Johnson and his classic recordings. "Ramblin'" and "Dynaflow Blues" feel like Johnson's best work.) Shines has too much personal magnetism to be confused with anyone else. Like many artists of his generation, he is also master of the spoken word, a gifted storyteller, a social critic, and a historian dedicated to telling the truth. On stage or off, he pulls no punches, and his independent spirit and readiness to fight for what he perceives to be fair have no doubt ruffled the feathers of the movers and shakers in Chicago's blues business.

Shines' distinctive style and songwriting skills should have brought him fame and fortune in music, but such was not the case. During the '40s and '50s, when he was at his peak, he only issued a handful of records. Although critically acclaimed today, these were not sufficient to keep him in the business at the time. Working outside of music in the '50s and over much of his career, he returned to the studio with Pete Welding in the '60s. These Chicago sessions showed his musical power had not diminished. Subsequent recordings, including his collaboration with Robert Jr. Lockwood, have generally maintained a high quality. His later guitar work was hampered by a stroke, but he remained a powerful artist sustained by one of the all-time great blues voices. —*Barry Lee Pearson*

Master of the Modern Blues, Vol. 1 / 1966 / Testament ✦✦✦✦

Last Night's Dream / 1968 / Warner Brothers ✦✦✦✦
It's no wonder that this album, cut in 1968 with British blues maven Mike Vernon at the helm, works so well. When you team a rejuvenated Shines with his longtime compadres Horton, Spann, bassist Willie Dixon, and drummer Clifton James, a little blues history was bound to be made. —*Bill Dahl*

Johnny Shines with Big Walter Horton / Nov. 1969 / Testament ✦✦✦✦
Outstanding late-'60s Shines material matching him with a sterling lineup. Big Walter Horton is awesome on harmonica, a young Luther Allison doesn't dissipate his brilliance on haphazard soul and funk, and pianist Otis Spann and drummer Fred Below are super on their cuts. The date combines 1966 and 1969 sessions; there's another LP with a full collection culled from 1966. —*Ron Wynn*

Sittin' on Top of the World / 1972 / Biograph ✦✦✦

Johnny Shines / 1972 / Blue Horizon ✦✦✦
On this eclectic and largely electric 1970 set, Shines is joined by an all-star West Coast band comprised of guitarist Phillip Walker, pianist Nat Dove, bassist Charles Jones, drummer Murl Downy and sax player David II. The music dips into soul balladry ("Just a Little Tenderness") and Chicago boogie ("Give My Heart a Break"), and on a handful of tracks, including "Too Lazy," "Skull and Crossbones Blues," "Vallie Lee," and "Ramblin'," the band steps aside to allow Shines to go it alone. —*Jason Ankeny*

Johnny Shines [Advent] / 1974 / Advent ✦✦✦
Johnny Shines made this good, if not great, LP for Advent during a period when he was going ignored despite still being in solid form. There are strong vocals, fine arrangements, and guitar support, but the production and the songs are too inconsistent to label this a significant session. —*Ron Wynn*

Too Wet to Plow / 1975 / Blue Labor ✦✦✦
Johnny Shines was far from predictable. Though he recorded his share of inspired electric dates, he had no problem turning around and delivering a

stripped-down, all-acoustic Delta blues session like *Too Wet To Plow*. Recorded in Edmonton, Canada in 1975 and reissued on CD by Concord Jazz's Blues Alliance label in 1996, *Too Wet to Plow* finds Shines in excellent form. His solid accompaniment includes harmonica player Sugar Blue and bassist Ron Rault, as well as guitarist/singer Louisiana Red (a superb bluesman who isn't nearly as well known as he should be), and Shines clearly has a strong rapport with them on "Red Sun," "Traveling Back Home" and other highly personal originals. Although Shines' own songs are dominant, one of the album's high points is an interpretation of Robert Johnson's "Hot Tamale." Highly recommended. — *Alex Henderson*

Johnny Shines [Hightone] / 1976 / Hightone ✦✦✦

Hey Ba-Ba-Re-Bop / 1978 / Rounder ✦✦✦✦
Delta blues vocalist, guitarist and composer Johnny Shines hadn't yet encountered the physical difficulties that made his final years so troubling when he recorded the 13 selections on this CD. He could still sing and moan with intensity and passion, hold a crowd hypnotized with his remembrances and asides, and play with a mix of fury and charm. While the menu includes oft-performed chestnuts "Sweet Home Chicago," "Terraplane Blues" and "Milk Cow Blues," there wasn't anything staid or predictable about the way Shines ripped through the lyrics and presented the music. If you missed it the first time around, grab this one immediately. — *Ron Wynn*

Dust My Broom / 1980 / Flyright ✦✦✦✦

Traditional Delta Blues / 1991 / Biograph ✦✦✦✦
Robert Johnson's pal pays homage on acoustic recordings from 1972-1974. — *Jas Obrecht*

★ **Johnny Shines & Robert Lockwood** / 1991 / Paula/Flyright ✦✦✦✦✦
Shines has half of this 20-track disc, the remainder being devoted to sides from the same era featuring Robert Lockwood. Recorded in 1952 and 1953 for the JOB label, this is Shines at his most primal, working with a drumless trio; Big Walter Horton plays harmonica on the 1953 sides. These tracks decidedly outshine the Lockwood efforts (also recorded for JOB in the early '50s), some of which only feature Robert as a sideman. — *Richie Unterberger*

Mr. Cover Shaker / 1992 / Biograph ✦✦✦

Masters of Modern Blues / 1994 / Testament ✦✦✦✦
After stepping away from the music business altogether for a while, Shines came back strong during the mid-'60s, recording far more prolifically than his first time around. This 1966 date is one of his best, spotlighting his booming pipes and sturdy guitar in front of an all-star Chicago crew: Walter Horton on harp, pianist Otis Spann, and drummer Fred Below. — *Bill Dahl*

Worried Blues Ain't Bad / May 21, 1996 / Blues Alliance ✦✦✦
It wasn't until 1996 (four years after Johnny Shines' death) that this rare 1974 session finally saw the light of day. The 1960s had found the singer/guitarist successfully embracing electric blues some of the time and working with such Chicagoans as Otis Spann, Luther Allison, and Big Walter Horton, but when he recorded what would become the CD *Worried Blues Ain't Bad*, it was back to an entirely acoustic Delta-blues approach. Though Shines had his own style, it's hard to miss Robert Johnson's influence on such heartfelt originals as "Went to the River to Drown," "Devil's Daughter," and "Down In Spirit." Minimalism is the rule here, and Shines' sidemen (Don Audet on harmonica, Richard Baker on second acoustic guitar, and Bob Derkach on upright bass) do their part to keep things personal and intimate. It's just unfortunate that this solid date went unreleased for 22 years. — *Alex Henderson*

Back to the Country / Blind Pig ✦✦✦
Back to the Country finds Johnny Shines, accompanied by Snooky Pryor, running through a selection of standards, many of which they had played in their prime. At the time they made *Back to the Country,* they were well into old age, and had suffered some losses. Shines, in particular, was hit hard by the ravages of old age, suffering a stroke in the late '80s. As a result, Shines couldn't play guitar for this session, so producer John Nicholas and Kent Du Chane pick up the slack. This doesn't really hurt the music, but it's disheartening and awkward to listen to the album knowing that Shines isn't able to perform. That said, there are some nice moments on the record — Shines and Pryor have a nice rapport which shines through despite difficulties — but overall, it's hard not to view this as a nostalgia exercise. — *Thom Owens*

J.D. Short

b. Feb. 26, 1902, Port Gibson, MS, **d.** Oct. 21, 1962, St. Louis, MO
Harmonica, Vocals / Acoustic Blues, Acoustic Memphis Blues, Prewar Country Blues
Gifted with a striking and almost immediately identifiable vocal style characterized by an amazing vibrato, J.D. Short was also a very versatile musician. He played piano, saxophone, guitar, harmonica, clarinet and drums. Growing up in the Mississippi Delta, Short learned guitar and piano. He was a frequent performer at house parties before he moved to St. Louis in the '20s. Short played with the Neckbones, Henry Spaulding, Honeyboy Edwards, Douglas Williams, and Big Joe Williams from the '30s until the early '60s. He recorded for Vocalion, Delmark, Folkways, and Sonet. Short was in the 1963 documentary *The Blues*, but died before it was released. — *Ron Wynn*

Legacy of the Blues, Vol. 8 / 1962 / GNP ✦✦✦

● **Stavin' Chain Blues** / Jul. 1965 / Delmark ✦✦✦✦
He could sing, wail, holler or moan traditional Delta blues with a lot of names that were much bigger. J.D. Short didn't make a lot of records, but the few he cut during the 1930s should be heard over and over to truly appreciate their quality. — *Ron Wynn*

Siegel-Schwall Band

f. Chicago, IL
Group / Electric Chicago Blues, Modern Electric Blues, Modern Electric Chicago Blues
Paul Butterfield and Elvin Bishop were not the only White dudes that formed a blues band in Chicago in the early '60s. Corky Siegel and Jim Schwall formed the Siegel-Schwall Band in the mid-'60s in Chicago and worked as a duo playing blues clubs like Pepper's Lounge, where they were the house band. All of the great blues players would sit in — all the time. Corky Siegel played harp and electric Wurlitzer piano, with an abbreviated drum set stashed under the piano; Jim Schwall played guitar and mandolin. Both sang.

Corky Siegel was born in Chicago on October 24, 1943; Jim Schwall was born on November 11, 1942, also in Chicago. Corky Siegel met Jim Schwall in 1964, when they were both music students at Roosevelt University — Schwall studying guitar, Siegel studying classical saxophone and playing in the University Jazz Big Band. Corky Siegel first became interested in the blues that same year. Schwall's background ran more to country and bluegrass. The Siegel-Schwall Band approach to music (and blues) was lighter than groups like Butterfield or Musselwhite, representing somewhat more of a fusion of blues and more country-oriented material. They seldom played at high volume, stressed group cooperation, and shared the solo spotlight.

When the Butterfield band left their in gig at Big John's on Chicago's North Side, it was the Siegel-Schwall Band that took their place. Signed by Vanguard scout Sam Charters in 1965, they released their first album in 1966, the first of five they would do with that label. Bass player Jack Dawson, formerly of the Prime Movers Blues Band, joined the band in 1967.

In 1969 the band toured playing the Fillmore West, blues/folk festivals, and many club dates — one of several White blues bands that introduced the blues genre to millions of Americans during that era. They were, however, the first blues band to record with a full orchestra, performing *Three Pieces for Blues Band and Symphony Orchestra* in 1971 with the San Francisco Orchestra. Later that year, the band signed with RCA (Wooden Nickel) and produced five albums in the next four years. The band broke up in 1974.

In 1987, the band reformed and produced a live album on Alligator, *The Siegel-Schwall Reunion Concert*. Jim Schwall is a university professor of music in Kalamazoo, MI. Corky Siegel has been involved in many projects over the years that fuse classical music with blues, including his current group Chamber Blues — a string quartet, with a percussionist (tabla), and Siegel on piano and harmonica. And on rare occasions, the old band still gets together and performs. — *Michael Erlewine*

Siegel Schwall Band / 1966 / Vanguard ✦✦✦
Their debut album is played a little too timidly to stand up to repeated listenings in today's noisy world, but their takes on Jimmy Reed's "Going to New York" and others are fascinating nonetheless. A different way of approaching any color blues, period. — *Cub Koda*

Say Siegel Schwall / 1967 / Vanguard ✦✦✦✦
For all parties concerned, this was the group's breakthrough album. Corky Siegel's emotional harp work and foxy, sly (almost cutesy) vocals, coupled with a hot rhythm section and Jim Schwall's cardboard sounding acoustic with a pickup guitar work made this the one that connected big with White audiences. Some of it rocks, some of it boogies, some of it's downright creepy and eerie. Worth seeking out. — *Cub Koda*

Shake / 1968 / Vanguard ✦✦✦
Shake! was probably the group's second best album and certainly the one that came the closest to representing their live act. The major highlight is their take on Howlin' Wolf's "Shake for Me." Lots of fun and fireworks on this one, the sound of a band at the top of their game. — *Cub Koda*

Siegel Schwall 70 / 1970 / Vanguard ✦✦✦

Sleepy Hollow / 1972 / Wooden Nickel ✦✦✦

953 West / 1973 / Teldec ✦✦✦

Live Last Summer / 1974 / Wooden Nickel ✦✦✦

R I P Siegel Schwall / 1974 / Wooden Nickel ✦✦✦

Three Pieces for Blues & Orchestra / 1974 / Polydor ✦✦
This is *not* an album—or a piece of music—to be neutral about. Collaborations between the high brow and the low down have always been dicey (anyone ever heard Albert King playing with a symphony orchestra?), but this one will definitely leave on one side of the debate or the other; either you'll hail it as the blues brought "uptown" or as an experiment gone terrible awry. — *Cub Koda*

The Best of Siegel Schwall / Dec. 1974 / Vanguard ✦✦✦✦
Vinyl best-of compilation that hits a few (but not all) of the high notes of their tenure with Vanguard Records. — *Cub Koda*

Reunion Concert / 1988 / Alligator ✦✦
The coziness the band always had on their good nights seems totally lost on this live radio broadcast. Proof positive that you can't go home again. File under "guess you had to be there." — *Cub Koda*

● **Where We Walked (1966-1970)** / 1991 / Vanguard ✦✦✦✦
A very nice, fairly thorough, compilation that supersedes the old vinyl collection on several levels; nice mastering, better notes, and nicer selection. For a basic introduction to their sound, this one's hard to beat. — *Cub Koda*

Corky Siegel

b. Oct. 24, 1943, Chicago, IL
Harmonica, Keyboards, Vocals / Modern Electric Blues
The Siegel-Schwall Blues Band, with Corky Siegel, gained popularity when his band and Seiji Ozawa's Chicago Symphony Orchestra collaborated on William Russo's *Three Pieces for Blues Band and Symphony Orchestra* in 1968. The next year, he recorded with the New York Philharmonic. These projects led to Siegel's work for Alligator Records, *Corky Siegel's Chamber Blues.* It has been performed throughout America, at the Aspen Music Festival, Chicago's Orchestra Hall and UCLA's Fine Arts Series. — *John Bush*

Corky Siegel / 1974 / Dharma ✦✦

● **Chamber Blues** / 1994 / Alligator ✦✦✦
Corky Siegel decided to return to solo recording in the early '90s, prompted by a few reunion concerts with his old partner, Jim Schwall. Instead of taking the easy way out and running through a few standards predictably, Siegel came up with the *Chamber Blues* project. As the title suggests, *Chamber Blues* fuses blues with classical music and blues. Specifically, it features a string quartet, Siegel on piano and harmonica, and a tabla player. It certainly sounds intriguing on paper, but it never quite gels, since it's always possible to visualize the scaffolding that supports the music. Still, Siegel proves himself to be more ambitious than the average blues musician, and more adventurous blues listeners may find this worth exploring at least once. — *Thom Owens*

Terrance Simien

b. Sep. 3, 1965, Eunice, LA
Accordion, Vocals / Zydeco
One of zydeco's most soulful vocalists and fieriest accordionists, Terrance Simien was also among the music's most pop-oriented artists, infusing his sound with elements of R&B, funk, gospel and reggae. Born September 3, 1965 in Eunice, Louisiana, he first heard zydeco at local dances as a boy, but did not show any real interest in the music until it began growing in popularity during the early 1980s. After learning the accordion and writing a handful of songs in collaboration with his brother Greg, Simien formed his first band; in the years to follow, he honed his chops in area zydeco clubs each weekend, working as a bricklayer during the day. His big break arrived in 1984, when an appearance at the New Orleans World's Fair launched him to the attention of Paul Simon, with whom Simien recorded a cover of Clifton Chenier's "You Used to Call Me." He also was tapped to appear in the feature film *The Big Easy,* writing and performing a song with star Dennis Quaid. With his band the Mallet Playboys, Simien made his full-length debut in 1990 with *Zydeco on the Bayou; There's Room for Us All* followed in 1993. — *Jason Ankeny*

● **Zydeco on the Bayou** / 1990 / Restless ✦✦✦✦
A modern zydeco artist whose songs aren't yet in an essential category. More rock than zydeco, but lots of energy nonetheless. — *Ron Wynn & Jeff Hannusch*

There's Room for Us / Sep. 17, 1993 / Black Top ✦✦✦

Jam the Jazzfest [EP] / Apr. 7, 1998 / Tone-Cool ✦✦✦
Before the release of his third full-length album, Simien released this five-song EP. A tribute to his regular appearances at the New Orleans Jazz Fest, Terrance cooks up a potent groove on the title track. A medley of "Iko Iko/Brother John/Jambalaya" stretches out to almost seven minutes, followed by a great version of Dylan's "Baby Stop Crying." A great little zydeco instrumental, "Macque Choux," sets the stage for the closer, "May Your Music Live On," a tribute to John Delafose, one of Terrance's early influences. As always, the Mallet Playboys keep the groove steady and rocking throughout. As a stopping-off point between full length projects, this makes a wonderful appetizer. — *Cub Koda*

Frankie Lee Sims

b. Apr. 30, 1917, New Orleans, LA, **d.** May 10, 1970, Dallas, TX
Guitar, Vocals / Electric Texas Blues, Country Blues, Texas Blues, Acoustic Texas Blues, Piedmont Blues
A traditionalist who was a staunch member of the Texas country blues movement of the late '40s and early '50s (along with the likes of his cousin Lightnin' Hopkins, Lil' Son Jackson, and Smokey Hogg), guitarist Frankie Lee Sims developed a twangy, ringing electric guitar style that was irresistible on fast numbers and stung hard on the downbeat stuff.

Sims picked up a guitar when he was 12 years old. By then, he had left his native New Orleans for Marshall, TX. After World War II ended, he played local dances and clubs around Dallas and crossed paths with T-Bone Walker. Sims cut his first 78s for Herb Rippa's Blue Bonnet Records in 1948 in Dallas, but didn't taste anything resembling regional success until 1953, when his bouncy "Lucy Mae Blues" did well down south.

The guitarist recorded fairly prolifically for Los Angeles-based Specialty into 1954, then switched to Johnny Vincent's Ace label (and its Vin subsidiary) in 1957 to cut the mighty rockers "Walking with Frankie" and "She Likes to Boogie Real Low," both of which pounded harder than a ballpeen hammer.

Sims claimed to play guitar on King Curtis' 1962 instrumental hit "Soul Twist" for Bobby Robinson's Enjoy label, but that seems unlikely. It is assumed that he recorded for Robinson in late 1960 (the battered contents of three long-lost acetates emerged in 1985 on the British Krazy Kat label).

Sims mostly missed out on the folk-blues revival of the early '60s that his cousin Lightnin' Hopkins cashed in on handily. When he died at age 53 in Dallas of pneumonia, Sims was reportedly in trouble with the law due to a shooting incident and had been dogged by drinking problems. — *Bill Dahl*

● **Lucy Mae Blues** / 1970 / Specialty ✦✦✦✦
This collection of Sims' Specialty sides, primarily in a drums and electric guitar format, is pretty hard to beat. It combines all of the original singles, the extra tracks from his lone album plus unissued material and until further alternate takes come to light, the best overview of his tenure with the label. Some tracks are augmented with harmonica and/or string bass, but it's Frankie Lee's guitar and sly vocals that drive things along. Until his early Bluebonnet and later Ace material is cobbled together to complete the picture, this compilation is all you'll need. — *Cub Koda*

Hal "Cornbread" Singer (Harold Singer)

b. Oct. 8, 1919, Tulsa, OK

Sax (Tenor) / Swing, Early R&B Jazz, Groove, Jazz Blues

Equally at home blowing scorching R&B or tasty jazz, Hal "Cornbread" Singer has played and recorded both over a career spanning more than half a century. Singer picked up his early experience as a hornman with various Southwestern territory bands, including the outfits of Ernie Fields, Lloyd Hunter, and Nat Towles. He made it to Kansas City in 1939, working with pianist Jay McShann (whose sax section also included Charlie Parker) before venturing to New York in 1941 and playing with Hot Lips Page, Earl Bostic, Don Byas, and Roy Eldridge (with whom he first recorded in 1944). After the close of the war, Singer signed on with Lucky Millinder's orchestra.

Singer had just fulfilled his life's ambition—a chair in Duke Ellington's prestigious reed section—in 1948 when a honking R&B instrumental called "Cornbread" that he'd recently waxed for Savoy as a leader began to take off. That presented a wrenching dilemma for the young saxist, but in the end, his decision to go out on his own paid off—"Cornbread" paced the R&B charts for four weeks and gave him his enduring nickname. Another of his Savoy instrumentals, "Beef Stew," also cracked the R&B lists.

Singer recorded rocking R&B workouts for Savoy into 1956 (the cuisine motif resulting in helpings of "Neck Bones," "Rice and Red Beans," and "Hot Bread"), working with sidemen including pianists Wynton Kelly and George Rhodes, guitarist Mickey Baker, bassist Walter Page, and drummer Panama Francis. One of his last dates for the firm produced the torrid "Rock 'n' Roll," which may have featured Singer as singer as well as saxist!

By the late '50s, Singer had abandoned rock 'n' roll for a life as a jazz saxist. He recorded for Prestige in a more restrained manner in 1959 and stayed in that general groove. Singer relocated to Paris in 1965, winning over European audiences with his hearty blowing and engaging in quite a bit of session work with visiting blues and jazz luminaries. The old R&B fire flared up temporarily in 1990, when he cut *Royal Blue* for Black Top with boogie piano specialist Al Copley. — *Bill Dahl*

● **Rent Party** / Jun. 1948-May 3, 1956 / Savoy ✦✦✦✦

Tenor saxophonist Hal Singer, who had a surprise hit with "Cornbread" which led to him leaving Duke Ellington's Orchestra shortly after joining it (he had temporarily become more popular than Ellington), was a honker if not a screamer. His 16 R&B-ish sides that are reissued on this CD are full of spirited and joyfully repetitious tenor. Most of the chord changes are related to "Flying Home" or the blues although Singer did sneak in a couple of ballads ("Indian Love Call" and "Easy Living"). Singer did not have any future hits that would quite equal "Cornbread" (a one-note blues that is the leadoff cut) but he remained a popular attraction on the R&B circuit for a decade. These jump sides (which also include such memorable numbers as "Hot Rod" and "Rock 'N' Roll") might be a bit lightweight compared to the bop music of the time but they are quite fun. This is Hal Singer's definitive set. — *Scott Yanow*

Blue Stompin' / Feb. 20, 1959 / Prestige ✦✦✦✦

This is a fun set of heated swing with early R&B overtones. The title cut is a real romp, with tenor saxophonist Hal Singer and trumpeter Charlie Shavers not only constructing exciting solos but riffing behind each other. With the exception of the standard "With a Song in My Heart," Singer and Shavers wrote the remainder of the repertoire, and with the assistance of a particularly strong rhythm section (pianist Ray Bryant, bassist Wendell Marshall, and drummer Osie Johnson), there are many fine moments on this enjoyable set. Recommended. — *Scott Yanow*

Royal Blue / 1990 / Black Top ✦✦✦

There's no way that this collaboration between the veteran saxist and boogie piano specialist Al Copley could equal the searing power of Singer's late-'40s/early-'50s sides for Savoy; a few too many years had passed for Singer to play in the same searing fashion. But his jazzy riffs and Copley's keyboard antics are enjoyable enough in their own right. — *Bill Dahl*

T-Bone Singleton

b. New Orleans, LA

Guitar, Vocals / Modern Electric Blues

Guitarist, singer and songwriter T-Bone Singleton was born in New Orleans and grew up in Baton Rouge, where he still lives. JSP Records of London recently released his debut recording, *Walkin' the Floor,* which represents some of his best songs over a ten-year period.

As a youth, T-Bone recalls seeing and hearing the old-style Southern swamp bluesmen like Silas Hogan and Guitar Kelley playing in local cafes, and musicians like Slim Harpo and Lightning Slim were also frequent performers in Baton Rouge juke joints. Singleton was raised on gospel and soul music and became interested in guitar after hearing his neighbor play, and he began playing a nylon-stringed acoustic guitar at 14. In high school, he worked nights with his father building cabinets, and it was on a job with his father that he got his first electric guitar and amplifier. Within months, he was playing guitar and bass in a gospel group and playing soul music with high school friends. Later, he began playing in clubs in north Baton Rouge until he was approached in the mid-1970s by Buddy Powell, who asked him to become the guitarist for his band, the Condors. The regional band toured the Gulf Coast for several years, playing blues, soul and Top 20 hits until Powell quit to become musical director at Gloryland Baptist Church.

Singleton went on to become an ordained minister and has delivered numerous sermons since then, but he still has no full-time position as a pastor. Like many other bluesmen from the South, Singleton's style of blues guitar playing and singing is heavily gospel-oriented, and these days, he still plays local clubs in and around Baton Rouge and has made several appearances at the annual River City Blues Festival.

His 1996 JSP Records release, *Walkin' the Floor,* is a small fraction of his output from the last ten years, and the ever-inventive songwriter and guitarist probably has another three albums worth of material ready to be recorded. Well-respected in Baton Rouge, Singleton's debut album was produced by blues guitarist and singer Larry Garner. — *Richard Skelly*

Walkin' the Floor / Jun. 4, 1996 / JSP ✦✦✦

TV Slim (Oscar Wills)

b. Feb. 10, 1916, Houston, TX, **d.** Oct. 21, 1969, Klingman, AZ

Guitar, Vocals / Electric Blues, R&B, Country Blues

Oscar "TV Slim" Wills' hilarious tale of a sad sack named "Flat Foot Sam" briefly made him a bankable name in 1957. Sam's ongoing saga lasted longer than Slim's minute or two in the spotlight, but that didn't stop him from recording throughout the 1960s.

Influenced by DeFord Bailey and both Sonny Boy Williamsons on harp and Guitar Slim on axe while living in Houston, Wills sold one of his early compositions, "Dolly Bee," to Don Robey for Junior Parker's use on Duke Records before getting the itch to record himself. To that end, he set up Speed Records, his own label and source for the great majority of his output over the next dozen years.

The first version of "Flat Foot Sam" came out on a tiny Shreveport logo, Cliff Records, in 1957. Local record man Stan Lewis, later the owner of Jewel/Paula Records, reportedly bestowed the colorful nickname of TV Slim on Wills; he was a skinny television repairman, so the handle fit perfectly.

"Flat Foot Sam" generated sufficient regional sales to merit reissue on Checker, but its ragged edges must have rankled someone at the Chicago label enough to convince Slim to recut it in much tighter form in New Orleans with the vaunted studio band at Cosimo's. This time, Robert "Barefootin'" Parker blew a strong sax solo, Chess A&R man Paul Gayten handled piano duties, and Charles "Hungry" Williams laid down a brisk second-line beat. It became Slim's biggest seller when unleashed on another Chess subsidiary, Argo Records.

Slim cut a torrent of 45s for Speed, Checker, Pzazz, USA, Timbre, Excell, and Ideel after that, chronicling the further adventures of his prime meal-ticket with "Flat Foot Sam Made a Bet," "Flat Foot Sam Met Jim Dandy," and "Flat Foot Sam No. 2." Albert Collins later covered Slim's Speed waxing of the surreal "Don't Reach Cross My Plate." Wills died in a car wreck outside Klingman, AZ, in 1969 en route home to Los Angeles after playing a date in Chicago. — *Bill Dahl*

Slo Leak

Group / Blues-Rock

Producer Danny Kortchmar (Billy Joel, Spin Doctors, Fabulous Thunderbirds), also a guitarist, decided to form his own blues band in the mid-1990s. Called Slo-Leak, the band is composed of Kortchmar on guitar, ex-Paul Butterfield bassist Harvey Brooks and vocalist/guitarist Charlie Karp.

For the purposes of their first album, *Slo Leak*, on Pure Records, out of Georgetown, CT, the trio used two drummers, Leroy Clouden and James Wormworth. Other musicians, most from the New York City area, include Steve Russell on harmonica, Rob Paparozzi on harmonica, Fred McFarlane on piano and Chris Eminizer on tenor and baritone saxophones.

Aside from working with Butterfield for many years, bassist Brooks also forged a reputation for his work with Bob Dylan and the Doors. Guitarist and vocalist Karp has recorded and toured with Buddy Miles, Aerosmith, Buster Poindexter, and Meatloaf.

The members of Slo-Leak show some taste and knowledge of the idiom in the songs they cover, obscure gems like Willie Dixon's "I Cry For You," Lightnin' Hopkins' "Katie Mae," Bo Diddley's "You Don't Love Me," and Jimmy Liggins' "Drunk," but they do so in a 1990s blues-rock fashion. The group's founders, Karp, Kortchmar, and Brooks, also throw in a few self-penned songs on their debut album. Unless this group is ready to tour, however, chances are their renown won't spread much beyond New York City and Westport, Connecticut, where Kortchmar and much of the rest of the band are based. —*Richard Skelly*

Slo Leak / Aug. 27, 1996 / Pure ◆◆◆

Drink Small

b. Jan. 28, 1933, Bishopville, SC
Guitar, Vocals / Acoustic Blues
The breadth of Drink Small's repertoire is fascinating in itself, but what's even more impressive is his depth as a performer in any of his chosen genres. His records may suddenly shift from a solo acoustic blues-guitar track to a smooth soul ballad with horns to who-knows-what, yet Small never seems to be caught out of place. He can be gruff and rough, clean and modern, or light and bouncy, altering his voice and guitar to suit the mood. Rated one of America's top gospel guitarists before he turned to blues in the late '50s, the South Carolina "Blues Doctor" for years had only one 45 on the market (Sharp, 1959). His discography has recently begun to grow considerably, finally revealing the extent of his songwriting and performing talents. —*Jim O'Neal*

I Know My Blues Are Different / 1976 / Southland ◆◆

● **The Blues Doctor** / 1990 / Ichiban ◆◆◆◆
Drink's own special blend of Delta, Chicago, and Carolina blues, it includes some band stuff, some solo stuff. Particularly wonderful is Drink's rich, gospel-influenced bass voice. A truly unique artist sharing his unique point of view, Drink includes a couple of saucy items ("Tittie Man" and "Baby, Leave Your Panties Home") along with covers of "Little Red Rooster" and "Stormy Monday Blues." —*Niles J. Frantz*

Round Two / 1991 / Ichiban ◆◆◆
With more good stuff, it's much like the first. Highlights: the cautionary "D.U.I." and the funky "Don't Let Nobody Else." —*Niles J. Frantz*

Bessie Smith

b. Apr. 15, 1894, Chattanooga, TN, d. Sep. 26, 1937, Clarksdale, MS
Vocals / Classic Jazz, Classic Female Blues, Traditional Jazz
The first major blues and jazz singer on record and one of the most powerful of all time, Bessie Smith rightly earned the title of "The Empress of the Blues." Even on her first records in 1923, her passionate voice overcame the primitive recording quality of the day and still communicates easily to today's listeners (which is not true of any other singer from that early period). At a time when the blues were in and most vocalists (particularly vaudevillians) were being dubbed "blues singers," Bessie Smith simply had no competition.

Back in 1912, Bessie Smith sang in the same show as Ma Rainey, who took her under her wing and coached her. Although Rainey would achieve a measure of fame throughout her career, she was soon surpassed by her protégé. In 1920 Bessie had her own show in Atlantic City and in 1923 she moved to New York. She was soon signed by Columbia and her first recording (Alberta Hunter's "Downhearted Blues") made her famous. Bessie worked and recorded steadily throughout the decade, using many top musicians as sidemen on sessions including Louis Armstrong, Joe Smith (her favorite cornetist), James P. Johnson, and Charlie Green. Her summer tent show

Harlem Frolics was a big success durinq 1925-27 and Mississippi Days in 1928 kept the momentum going.

However by 1929 the blues were out-of-fashion and Bessie Smith's career was declining despite being at the peak of her powers (and still only 35!). She appeared in *St. Louis Blues* that year (a low-budget movie short that contains the only footage of her) but her hit recording of "Nobody Knows You When You're Down and Out" predicted her leaner Depression years. Although she was dropped by Columbia in 1931 and made her final recordings on a four-song session in 1933, Bessie Smith kept on working. She played the Apollo in 1935 and substituted for Billie Holiday in the show *Stars over Broadway*. The chances are very good that she would have made a comeback, starting with a Carnegie Hall appearance at John Hammond's upcoming "From Spirituals to Swing" concert, but she was killed in a car crash in Mississippi. Columbia has reissued all of her recordings, first in five two-LP sets and more recently on five two-CD boxes that also contain her five alternate takes, the soundtrack of *St. Louis Blues* and an interview with her niece Ruby Smith. "The Empress of the Blues," based on her recordings, will never have to abdicate her throne! —*Scott Yanow*

☆ **The Complete Recordings, Vol. 1** / Feb. 16, 1923-Apr. 8, 1924 / Columbia/ Legacy ◆◆◆◆◆
In the 1970s Bessie Smith's recordings were reissued on five double LPs. Her CD reissue series also has five volumes (the first four are double-CD sets) with the main difference being that the final volume includes all of her rare alternate takes (which were bypassed on LP). The first set (which, as with all of the CD volumes, is housed in an oversize box that includes an informative booklet) contains her first 38 recordings. During this early era, Bessie Smith had no competitors on record and she was one of the few vocalists who could overcome the primitive recording techniques; her power really comes through. Her very first recording (Alberta Hunter's "Down Hearted Blues") was a big hit and is one of the highlights of this set along with "'Tain't Nobody's Bizness If I Do" (two decades before Billie Holiday), "Jail-House Blues" and "Ticket Agent, Ease Your Window Down." Smith's accompaniment is nothing that special (usually just a pianist and maybe a weak horn or two) but she dominates the music anyway, even on two vocal duets with her rival Clara Smith. All of these volumes reward close listenings and are full of timeless recordings. —*Scott Yanow*

★ **The Essential Bessie Smith** / Apr. 11, 1923-Nov. 24, 1933 / Columbia/ Legacy ◆◆◆◆◆
Although there are a multitude of box sets chronicling Bessie's entire recorded career, this two-disc, 36-song set sweats it down to the bare essentials in quite an effective manner. Bessie could sing it all, from the lowdown moan of "St. Louis Blues" and "Nobody Knows You When You're Down and Out" to her torch treatment of the jazz standard "After You've Gone" to the downright salaciousness of "Need a Little Sugar in My Bowl." Covering a time span from her first recordings in 1923 to her final session in 1933, this is the perfect entry-level set to go with. Utilizing the latest in remastering technology, these recordings have never sounded quite this clear and full, and the selection—collecting her best-known sides and collaborations with jazz giants like Louis Armstrong, Coleman Hawkins and Benny Goodman—is first rate. If you've never experienced the genius of Bessie Smith, pick this one up and prepare yourself to be devastated. —*Cub Koda*

★ **The Collection** / 1923-1933 / Columbia ◆◆◆◆◆
While there's no denying the importance and quality of Columbia/Legacy's *Complete Recordings* series, nine discs may seem a bit intimidating to the newcomer. *Collection*, a mid-priced, 16-track collection which spans most of Smith's career, ultimately does a better service to the casual listener with a limited budget. This is probably the best introduction—undoubtedy many will seek out the more comprehensive packages afterwards. —*Chris Woodstra*

☆ **The Complete Recordings, Vol. 2 (1924-1925)** / Apr. 8, 1924-Nov. 18, 1925 / Columbia/Legacy ◆◆◆◆◆
Bessie Smith, even on the evidence of her earliest recordings, well deserved the title "Empress of the Blues" for in the 1920s there was no one in her league for emotional intensity, honest blues feeling and power. The second of five volumes (the first four are two-CD sets) finds her accompaniment improving rapidly with such sympathetic sidemen as trombonist Charlie Green, cornetist Joe Smith, and clarinetist Buster Bailey often helping her

out. However they are overshadowed by Louis Armstrong, whose two sessions with Smith (nine songs in all) fall into the time period of this second set; particularly classic are their versions of "St. Louis Blues," "Careless Love Blues" and "I Ain't Goin' to Play Second Fiddle." Other gems on this essential set include "Cake Walkin' Babies from Home," "The Yellow Dog Blues," and "At the Christmas Ball." — *Scott Yanow*

The Complete Recordings, Vol. 5: The Final Chapter / May 6, 1925-Nov. 24, 1933 / Sony/Legacy ◆◆◆◆

Bessie Smith cut 160 sides for the Columbia and OKeh labels between 1923 and 1933, and the four previous two-CD/cassette boxed sets of her complete recordings released in the 1990s covered 154 of them, which introduces the question, what can a fifth two-CD/cassette boxed set contain in addition to the remaining six cuts? First, there are five previously unreleased alternate takes; second, there is the 15-minute low-fi soundtrack to the two-reel short *St. Louis Blues*, which constitutes the only film of Smith; and third, taking up all of the second CD/cassette, there are 72 minutes of interview tapes of Ruby Smith, Bessie Smith's niece, who traveled as part of her show. The box contains a "Parental Advisory—Explicit Lyrics" warning because of the nature of Ruby Smith's reminiscences. You won't learn much about Bessie Smith's music from her niece's remarks, but you will learn a lot about her sexual preferences. — *William Ruhlmann*

The Complete Recordings, Vol. 3 / Nov. 20, 1925-Feb. 16, 1928 / Columbia/ Legacy ◆◆◆◆

On the third of five volumes (the first four are double-CD box sets) that reissue all of her recordings, the great Bessie Smith is greatly assisted on some of the 39 selections by a few of her favorite sidemen: cornetist Joe Smith, trombonist Charlie Green, and clarinetist Buster Bailey. But the most important of her occasional musicians was pianist James P. Johnson, who makes his first appearance in 1927 and can be heard on four duets with Bessie including the monumental "Back Water Blues." Other highlights of this highly recommended set (all five volumes are essential) include "After You've Gone," "Muddy Water," "There'll Be a Hot Time in the Old Town Tonight," "Trombone Cholly," "Send Me to the 'Lectric Chair," and "Mean Old Bedbug Blues." The power and intensity of Bessie Smith's recordings should be considered required listening; even 70 years later they still communicate. — *Scott Yanow*

The Complete Recordings, Vol. 4 / Feb. 21, 1928-Jun. 11, 1931 / Columbia/ Legacy ◆◆◆◆

The fourth of five volumes (the first four are two-CD sets) that reissue all of Bessie Smith's recordings traces her career from a period when her popularity was at its height down to just six songs away from the halt of her recording career. But although her commercial fortunes might have slipped, Bessie Smith never declined and these later recordings are consistently powerful. The two-part "Empty Bed Blues" and "Nobody Knows You When You're Down and Out" (hers is the original version) are true classics and none of the other 40 songs (including the double-entendre "Kitchen Man") are throwaways. With strong accompaniment during some performances by trombonist Charlie Green, guitarist Eddie Lang, Clarence Williams' band, and on ten songs (eight of which are duets) the masterful pianist James P. Johnson, this volume (as with the others) is quite essential. — *Scott Yanow*

American Legends #14 / Laserlight ◆◆◆

Like other volumes in LaserLight's 20-album *American Legends* series, the Bessie Smith disc presents a miscellaneous collection of tracks with next-to-nothing in the way of annotation. Smith's catalog is controlled by Columbia Records, which seems to be the source for the 12 performances here, but they have been licensed from Rod McKuen's Stanyan Records and are attributed to "the collection of T. Richard Williams." In any case, such tracks as "'Tain't Nobody's Business" and "St. Louis Blues" are among Smith's classics, and at a $9.98 list price, it should be possible to obtain this album for much less than any of the Columbia/Legacy box sets. But for that you're only getting a taste of what is best experienced as a sumptuous meal. — *William Ruhlmann*

Byther Smith

b. Apr. 17, 1933, Monticello, MS

Bass, Guitar, Vocals / Chicago Blues, Modern Electric Blues, Electric Blues

Strictly judging from the lyrical sentiment of his recordings to this point, it might be wise not to make Chicago guitarist Byther Smith angry. Smitty's

uncompromising songs are filled with threats of violence and ominous menace (the way blues used to be before the age of political correctness), sometimes to the point where his words don't even rhyme. They don't have to, either—you're transfixed by the sheer intensity of his music.

Smitty came to Chicago during the mid-'50s after spending time toiling on an Arizona cattle ranch. He picked up guitar tips from J.B. Lenoir (his first cousin), Robert Jr. Lockwood, and Hubert Sumlin, then began playing in the clubs during the early '60s. Theresa's Lounge was his main haunt for five years as he backed Junior Wells; he also played with the likes of Big Mama Thornton, George "Harmonica" Smith, and Otis Rush.

A couple of acclaimed singles for C.J. (the two-part "Give Me My White Robe") and BeBe ("Money Tree"/"So Unhappy") spread his name among aficionados, as did a 1983 album for Grits, *Tell Me How You Like It*. But it's only since during the last few years that the rest of the country has begun to appreciate Smitty, thanks to a pair of extremely solid albums on Bullseye Blues: 1991's *Housefire* (first out on Grits back in 1985) and *I'm a Mad Man* two years later. With a new set on Delmark and a stepped-up touring itinerary on the horizon, Smitty's just hitting his stride. — *Bill Dahl*

Tell Me How Do You Like It / 1983 / Grits ◆◆◆◆

Fine guitar from this longtime Chicago bluesman, including four originals. — *Barry Lee Pearson*

Big Shot Smitty / Apr. 1986 / Mina ◆◆◆

Addressing the Nation with the Blues / 1989 / JSP ◆◆◆

Smith was so far outside the domestic blues loop that this Chicago-cut set only found release on a British logo, JSP. It was our loss—Smith is typically brusque and ominous, threatening to "Play the Blues on the Moon" and "Addressing the Nation with the Blues" as only he can. Nothing derivative about his lyrical muse—he's intense to the point of allowing his words not to rhyme to make his points, while his lead guitar work is inevitably to the point. — *Bill Dahl*

Housefire / 1991 / Bullseye Blues ◆◆◆

An unheralded gem that fell through the cracks during its initial issue in 1985 and definitely deserved its higher Bullseye Blues profile six years later. Except for a stinging cover of Detroit Junior's "Money Tree" that leads off, Smitty wrote the entire disc, and it's typically singular stuff: a paranoid "The Man Wants Me Dead," a promise to "Live On and Sing the Blues," all solidly backed by a sympathetic combo. — *Bill Dahl*

● ### I'm a Mad Man / 1993 / Bullseye Blues ◆◆◆◆

Smitty's unequivocally not mellowing with age. This set finds him physically threatening some poor slob in "Get Outta My Way" and generally living up to the boast of the title track. As his profile finally rises, Smith is receiving a little high-profile assistance—Ron Levy produced the set and handles keyboards, while the Memphis Horns add their punchy interjections wherever appropriate. — *Bill Dahl*

Blues Knights (With Larry Davis) / 1994 / Evidence ◆◆◆

Davis and Smith both acquit themselves well and are backed by the same band. — *Bill Dahl*

Mississippi Kid / 1996 / Delmark ◆◆◆

All Night Long / 1997 / Delmark ◆◆◆

Sporting a dozen Smith originals, *All Night Long* is also a showcase for his incendiary guitar skills. — *Jason Ankeny*

Carrie Smith

b. Aug. 25, 1941, Fort Gaines, GA

Vocals / Blues, Swing

A blues belter in the classic tradition, Carrie Smith was born August 25, 1941 in Fort Gaines, Georgia. Despite making her debut at the 1957 Newport Jazz Festival while a member of a New Jersey church choir, she did not truly emerge on the jazz circuit until the early 1970s, in the company of Big "Tiny" Little. In November of 1974, Smith's riveting performance as Bessie Smith (no relation) in Dick Hyman's Carnegie Hall production of *Satchmo Remembered* brought her fame throughout the international musical community. Soon she began touring as a solo act, and in a short time began recording as well; still, despite subsequent performances in conjunction with the New York Jazz Repertory Orchestra, Tyree Glenn and the World's Greatest Jazz Band, Smith remained little more than a cult figure in the US, proving better received in Europe. While rooted firmly in the blues and gospel, she was a singer of considerable range and depth, as recordings like 1976's *Do Your Duty* and the following year's *When You're Down and Out* prove; despite never earning significant success, she remained an active figure both on stage and in the studio through the 1990s. — *Jason Ankeny*

Do Your Duty / Jul. 26, 1976 / Classic Jazz ✦✦✦
Nice updated set of classic blues done in a strutting, assertive fashion by Carrie Smith. Smith, also a good singer in a jazzy vein, was among the few surviving female vocalists capable of doing authentic bawdy blues, and she shows how it's done throughout this date. — *Ron Wynn*

● **Confessin' the Blues** / Jul. 26, 1976-Jul. 19, 1977 / Evidence ✦✦✦✦
This CD reissues not only Carrie Smith's original hard-to-find *Black & Blue* LP but six selections from two other sessions including three previously unissued alternate takes. Smith, who was coming into her own during this period, is in top form on a variety of vintage material ranging from Bessie Smith songs in the 1920s to the '50s Ruth Brown hit "Mama He Treats Your Daughter Mean" and Big Bill Broonzy's "When I've Been Drinkin'." It is interesting to hear some of the altered lyrics which have been changed to reflect a female rather than a male singing; "I Want a Little Boy" is the most obvious example. Most selections find Smith backed by a quartet that includes tenor saxophonist George Kelly and pianist Ram Ramirez while a few of the added tracks have short spots for trumpeter Doc Cheatham and trombonist Vic Dickenson. This is one of the best Carrie Smith CDs currently available. — *Scott Yanow*

Nobody Wants You / Apr. 23, 1977 / Black & Blue ✦✦✦
Smith, among the last surviving classic blues greats, shows how it's done on this set. She can sing bawdy, rocking tunes or turn slow and sentimental, and her voice hasn't lost its richness or impact over the years. — *Ron Wynn*

Carrie Smith / Nov. 15, 1978-Nov. 16, 1978 / West ✦✦✦

Every Now and Then / Nov. 1993 / Silver Shadow ✦✦✦✦

Fine and Mellow / 1995 / Audiophile ✦✦✦

Funny Papa Smith (John T. Smith)

b. 1890, Texas, **d.** 1940
Guitar, Vocals / Acoustic Texas Blues
J.T. "Funny Paper" Smith was a pioneering force behind the development of the Texas blues guitar style of the pre-war era; in addition to honing a signature sound distinguished by intricate melody lines and simple, repetitive bass riffs, he was also a gifted composer, authoring songs of surprising narrative complexity. A contemporary of such legends as Blind Lemon Jefferson and Dennis "Little Hat" Jones, next to nothing concrete is known of John T. Smith's life; assumed to have been born in East Texas during the latter half of the 1880s, he was a minstrel who wandered about the panhandle region, performing at fairs, fish fries, dances, and other community events (often in the company of figures including Tom Shaw, Texas Alexander, and Bernice Edwards). Smith settled down long enough to record some 22 songs between 1930 and 1931, among them his trademark number "Howling Wolf Blues, Parts One and Two"; indeed, he claimed the alternate nickname "Howling Wolf" some two decades before it was appropriated by his more famous successor, Chester Burnett. (The true story behind Smith's more common nickname remains a matter of some debate—some blues archivists claim he was instead dubbed "Funny Papa," with the "Funny Paper" alias resulting only from record company error.) His career came to an abrupt end during the mid-'30s, when he was arrested for murdering a man over a gambling dispute; Smith was found guilty and imprisoned, and is believed to have died in his cell circa 1940. — *Jason Ankeny*

● **The Howling Wolf (1930-1931)** / 1971 / Yazoo ✦✦✦✦
This is fine guitar-based Texas country blues by an artist completely unlike the later Howlin' Wolf. — *Mark A. Humphrey*

Complete Recorded Works (1930-1931) / 1991 / Document ✦✦✦✦
For completists, specialists and academics, Document's *Complete Recorded Works (1930-1931)* is invaluable, offering an exhaustive overview of Funny Paper Smith's recordings. For less dedicated listeners, in spite of some of the wonderful, classic performances present, the disc will probably prove more of a chore to get through. The features that make it appealing to academics—long running time, exacting chronological sequencing, poor fidelity (all cuts

are transferred from original acetates and 78s), and exhaustive number of performances—will likely impair its overall listenability for more casual audiences. — *Thom Owens*

True Texas Blues / 1995 / Collectables ✦✦✦

George Harmonica Smith

b. Apr. 22, 1924, Helena, AR, **d.** Oct. 2, 1983, Los Angeles, CA
Harmonica, Vocals / Electric Harmonica Blues, West Coast Blues, Harmonica Blues
George Smith was born on April 22, 1924 in Helena, AR, but was raised in Cairo, IL. At age four, Smith was already taking harp lessons from his mother, a guitar player and a somewhat stern taskmaster—it was a case of get-it-right-or-else. In his early teens, he started hoboing around the towns in the South and later joined Early Woods, a country band with Early Woods on fiddle and Curtis Gould on spoons. He also worked with a gospel group in Mississippi called the Jackson Jubilee Singers.

Smith moved to Rock Island, IL, in 1941 and played with a group that included Francis Clay on drums. There is evidence that he was one of the first to amplify his harp. While working at the Dixie Theater, he took an old 16mm cinema projector, extracted the amplifier/speaker, and began using this on the streets.

His influences include Larry Adler and later Little Walter. Smith would sometimes bill himself as Little Walter Jr. or Big Walter. He played in a number of bands including one with a young guitarist named Otis Rush and later went on the road with the Muddy Waters Band, after replacing Henry Strong.

In 1954, he was offered a permanent job at the Orchid Room in Kansas City where, early in 1955, Joe Bihari of Modern Records (on a scouting trip), heard Smith, and signed him to Modern. These recording sessions were released under the name Little George Smith, and included "Telephone Blues" and "Blues in the Dark." The records were a success.

Smith traveled with Little Willie John and Champion Jack Dupree on one of the Universal Attractions tours. While on the tour, he recorded with Champion Jack Dupree in November of 1955 in Cincinnati, producing "Sharp Harp" and "Overhead Blues." The tour ended in Los Angeles and Smith settled down—spending the rest of his life in that city.

In the late '50s he recorded for J&M, Lapel, Melker, and Caddy under the names Harmonica King or Little Walter Junior. He also worked with Big Mama Thornton on many shows.

In 1960, Smith met producer Nat McCoy who owned Soloplay and Carolyn labels, with whom he recorded ten singles under the name of George Allen. In 1966, while Muddy Waters was on West Coast, he asked Smith to join him and they worked together for a while, recording for Spivey Records.

Smith's first album on World Pacific *A Tribute to Little Walter* was released in 1968. In 1969 Bob Thiele produced an excellent solo album of Smith on Bluesway, and later made use of Smith as a sideman for his Blues Times label, including sets with T-Bone Walker, and Harmonica Slim. Smith met Rod Piazza, a young White harp player and they formed the Southside Blues Band, later known as Bacon Fat.

In 1969, Smith signed with UK producer Mike Vernon and did the *No Time for Jive* album. Smith was less active in the 1970s, appearing with Eddie Taylor and Big Mama Thornton. Around 1977, Smith became friends with William Clarke and they began working together. Their working relationship and friendship continued until Smith died on October 2, 1983.

William Clarke, Smith's protégé, writes, "He had a technique on the chromatic harp where he would play two notes at once, but one octave apart. He would get an organ-type sound by doing this. George really knew how to make his notes count by not playing too much and taking his time by letting the music unfold easily. He could also swing like crazy and was a first-class entertainer. I have heard from a friend that they had seen George Smith in the 1950s playing a club in Chicago, tap dancing around everybody's drinks on top of the bar while playing his harp.

"I have been with him in church and seen him play amplified harmonica by himself. This was very soulful. I have never heard George play a song the same way twice. He was very creative and played directly from his heart. He admired all great musicians but had his own sound and style. He was a true original. Mr. Smith would always give 100% on stage whether or not there were 1 or 1,000 people listening. This was his performing style, *always*.

"George Smith greatly admired harmonica player Larry Adler, and although Adler used the octave technique on the harp also, George really was the one that developed this to its full potential. Before Mr. Smith, nobody in blues had used this octave technique. An extremely kind and gentle man, George always went all out to help other harmonica players. Everybody liked George Smith. He played a huge role in advancing blues harmonica and should never be forgotten. You can hear the influence of George Smith in most everyone playing blues harmonica today, whether directly or indirectly. He also was a great blues singer. He had a huge baritone voice that conveyed great emotion and soulfulness."

Recommended Smith recordings include *Blowin' the Blues* (1960) on Pea Vine, *Tribute to Little Walter* (1968) on Liberty, *No Time for Jive* (1970) on Blue Horizon, *Of the Blues* (1973) re-issued on Crosscut Records, and *Little George Smith* (1991) on Ace Records. — *Michael Erlewine*

● **Tribute to Little Walter** / 1968 / World Pacific ◆◆◆◆
The L.A. harp ace pays tribute to one of his peers and influences with a well-conceived set of Little Walter covers. — *Bill Dahl*

No Time to Jive / 1970 / Blue Horizon ◆◆◆
Laidback L.A. session from 1969 produced by Mike Vernon for his Blue Horizon label that's dominated by a mellow feel. There are a few upbeat items — "Before You Do Your Thing (You'd Better Think)" and "Soul Feet" — but mostly George sits back and blows with a relaxed ease. His sidemen include guitarists Pee Wee Crayton and Marshall Hooks, pianist J.D. Nicholson, and drummer Richard Innes. — *Bill Dahl*

Arkansas Trap / 1971 / Deram ◆◆

George Smith of the Blues / 1973 / Bluesway ◆◆◆

Harmonica Ace: The Modern Masters / 1993 / Capitol ◆◆◆◆
Smith cut these sides for Joe Bihari of Modern Records shortly after he left the Muddy Waters Band in the early '50s. He is featured here with a rhythm section framed by horns arranged by the legendary and prolific Maxwell Davis. Smith's innate sense of drive and swing, coupled with his rich and diverse palette of texture and tone, truly place him in the very first rank of modern harp masters. This disc is aptly described by note-writer Ray Topping as "a lasting memorial to one of the last great harp players of the postwar blues scene." — *Larry Hoffman*

Oopin' Doopin' Doopin' / 199 / Ace ◆◆◆

Huey "Piano" Smith

b. Jan. 26, 1934, New Orleans, LA
Piano / New Orleans R&B, R&B
At one time a madcap vocalist and underrated pianist, Huey "Piano" Smith was a star in New Orleans during the '50s. He sang with Earl King in the early '50s, then recorded with Guitar Slim from 1951 to 1954. He did several sessions and also led The Clowns, whose roster at one point included Bobby Marchan. Smith's biggest hit wasn't the song he's best known for, "Rocking Pneumonia and the Boogie Woogie Flu," but "Don't You Just Know It," which was his only Top Ten pop and R&B hit. It reached No. 4 R&B and No. 9 pop in 1958, a year after "Rocking Pneumonia" peaked at No. 5 R&B. Smith kept going until he became a Jehovah's Witness and left the music business. — *Ron Wynn*

● **Rock & Roll Revival** / Jan. 1991 / Ace ◆◆◆◆
A terrific sixteen-track collection of Huey "Piano" Smith & the Clowns' biggest hits and best material, including "Rocking Pneumonia" and "Don't You Just Know It," plus a couple of fine previously unreleased tracks. — *Stephen Thomas Erlewine*

This Is Huey Piano Smith / Apr. 21, 1998 / Music Club ◆◆◆◆
For years, Huey "Piano" Smith lacked a comprehensive overview of his recording career, and no compilation ever appeared on CD in the United States. The budget-line label Music Club rectified that situation in 1998 with the release of *This is Huey Piano Smith*, an 18-track collection that features all of his hit singles for Ace plus several failed singles and New Orleans staples. Smith's hits and standards — "Rockin' Pneumonia and the Boogie-Woogie Flu," "Don't You Just Know It," "High Blood Pressure," "Pop-Eye," the original version of "Sea Cruise," with his vocals instead of Frankie Ford's — are so good that it's an inevitable disappointment to find many of the songs here are blatant attempts to get back on the charts ("Tu-Ber-Cu-Lucas and the Sinus Blues," "Would You Believe It (I Have a Cold)"). These fall flat, as do a

couple of the other cuts, but unfortunately, that's an accurate portrait of Smith's career — he had a handful of wonderful, essential songs and was a hell of a performer, but he wasn't a consistent hitmaker. Nevertheless, the strong stuff is so good — even essential — that this is still highly recommended for New Orleans R&B fans and R&B fans in general. — *Stephen Thomas Erlewine*

Having A Good Time With Huey "Piano" Smith & His Clowns / Westside ◆◆◆◆
Next to Professor Longhair and Fats Domino, no one better typified the New Orleans piano style than the work of Huey "Piano" Smith. This 24-track, single-disc compilation is the first proposed installment of Huey and the Clowns' tenure with the Jackson, Mississippi-based Ace label, home to his biggest hits. Kicking off with parts one and two of his first hit, "Rockin' Pneumonia and the Boogie Woogie Flu" (although the second part used here seems one overdub away from the single version issued), more obscure but equally worthwhile items like "Little Liza Jane," "Just a Lonely Clown," "Would You Believe It (I Have a Cold)," and "She Got Low Down" sit comfortably next to the hits ("High Blood Pressure," "Don't You Just Know It," "Tu-Ber-Cu-Lucas and the Sinus Blues," "Don't You Know Yockomo," and "Pop-Eye"), making this volume a perfect introduction to the music of this Crescent City genius. Transfers are as crisp as you could ask for, and the packaging and liner notes are equally fine. — *Cub Koda*

Mamie Smith

b. May 26, 1883, Cincinnati, OH, d. Aug. 16, 1946, New York, NY
Vocals / Classic Female Blues
Though technically not a blues performer, Mamie Smith notched her place in American music as the first black female singer to record a vocal blues. That record was "Crazy Blues" (rec. Aug. 10, 1920), which sold a million copies in its first six months and made record labels aware of the huge potential market for "race records," thus paving the way for Bessie Smith (no relation) and other blues and jazz performers. An entertainer who sported a powerful, penetrating, feminine voice with belting vaudeville qualities, as opposed to blues inflections, Smith toured as a dancer with Tutt-Whitney's Smart Set Company in her early teens and sang in Harlem clubs before World War I. Apparently, Smith's pioneering recording session was an accident, since she was filling in for Sophie Tucker, but the success of the record made her wealthy.

Soon thereafter, Smith began touring and recording with a band called the Jazz Hounds, which featured such jazz notables as Coleman Hawkins, Bubber Miley, Johnny Dunn, etc., and she toured with the bands of Andy Kirk and Fats Pichon in the 1930s. She also appeared in several films, including *Paradise in Harlem* late in her life (1939). She recorded several sides for OKeh during her heyday; one unissued take of "My Sportin' Man" is included on Columbia's *Roots N' Blues Retrospective 1925-1950* box set. In the 1980s, all of her recordings were reissued on LP by the imported Document label. — *Richard S. Ginell*

● **Complete Recorded Works, Vol. 1** / 1920-1921 / Document ◆◆◆◆
This first volume of a five-volume import set of her complete recordings features her earliest and best sides, including the classic "Crazy Blues." — *Cub Koda*

Complete Recorded Works, Vol. 2 (1921-1922) / 1921-1922 / Document ◆◆◆◆

Complete Recorded Works, Vol. 3 / -192 / Document ◆◆◆◆

Complete Recorded Works, Vol. 4 / -193 / Document ◆◆◆◆

Pinetop Smith (Clarence Smith)

b. Jun. 11, 1904, Troy, AL, d. Mar. 15, 1929, Chicago, IL
Piano, Vocals / Boogie-Woogie, Piano Blues
One of the driving forces behind the advent of boogie-woogie piano, Clarence "Pine Top" Smith ranks among the most influential blues figures of the 1920s. Born January 11, 1904 in Troy, Alabama, he was raised in nearby Birmingham; a self-taught player, he began performing at area house parties while in his mid-teens, and after relocating to Pittsburgh accompanied Ma Rainey and Butterbeans & Susie. On the advice of fellow pianist Cow Cow Davenport — himself a seminal figure in boogie-woogie's development — Smith relocated to Chicago in 1928, where he lived in the same apartment

house as Meade "Lux" Lewis and Albert Ammons, conditions that resulted in frequent all-night jam sessions; there, he also made a name for himself on the city's house-rent party and club circuits. While boogie-woogie's exact origins are a mystery, Smith's energetic "Pine Top's Boogie Woogie" (cut during his first Vocalion label sessions in 1928) marked the first known use of the phrase on record, and its lyrics—a cry of "Hold it now ... Stop ... Boogie Woogie!"—became the template for any number of subsequent piano tunes. Another recording session followed in early 1929, but just weeks later, on March 15, Smith's bright career came to an abrupt halt when he was shot and killed by a stray bullet during a dancehall fracas; he was just 25 at the time of his death, leaving behind a legacy of only 11 recorded tracks. —*Jason Ankeny*

Pine Top Smith (With Jelly Roll Morton) / 1950 / Brunswick ◆◆◆

Tab Smith (Talmadge Smith)

b. Jan. 11, 1909, Kingston, NC, **d.** Aug. 17, 1971, St. Louis, MO
Sax (Alto) / Swing, Early R&B Jazz, Jump Blues
Tab Smith's career can easily be divided into two. One of the finest altoists to emerge during the swing era, Smith became a popular attraction in the R&B world of the 1950s due to his record "Because of You." After early experience playing in territory bands during the 1930s, Tab Smith played and recorded with Lucky Millinder's Orchestra (1936-38) and then freelanced with various swing all-stars in New York. He had opportunities to solo with Count Basie's band (1940-42) before returning to Millinder (1942-44) and took honors on a recording of "On the Sunny Side of the Street" with a stunning cadenza that followed statements by Coleman Hawkins, Don Byas and Harry Carney. After leaving Millinder, Smith led his own sessions which became increasingly R&B-oriented (he never became involved with bop). His string of recordings for United in the 1950s (which are being reissued by Delmark on CD) made him a fairly major name for a time even though he had a relatively mellow sound and avoided honking. In the early '60s Tab Smith retired to St. Louis and later became involved in selling real estate. —*Scott Yanow*

Joy at the Savoy / May 10, 1944-May 18, 1954 / Saxophonograph ◆◆◆
Stalwart 40s and 50s swing and honking sax cuts. —*Ron Wynn*

★ **I Don't Want to Play in the Kitchen** / May 10, 1944-1956 / Saxophonograph ◆◆◆◆◆
Tab Smith made his first solo recordings shortly after leaving Lucky Millinder's band, and they're collected on the fine *I Don't Want to Play in the Kitchen*. The material on the album features Smith running through a number of different bands and vocalists—including Trevor Bacon, Robbie Kirk, and Betty Mays—but throughout it all, the distinguishing factor is his lovely saxophone, which sounds warm and appealing even on these swinging jump blues numbers. —*Leo Stanley*

Jump Time / Aug. 28, 1951-Feb. 26, 1952 / Delmark ◆◆◆◆
Altoist Tab Smith, who first gained recognition with Count Basie's Orchestra in the mid-'40s, became an unexpected R&B star in the early '50s, thanks in large part to his hit version of "Because of You." Between 1951-57, Smith recorded 90 songs for the United Record Company of which only 48 were issued. Delmark, in their CD reissue series, plans to come out with all of the music in chronological order. This first release has the initial 20 (including the hit) and Tab Smith sounds fine on the sweet ballads, blues and concise jump tunes; the backup crew includes trumpeter Sonny Cohn, tenor Leon Washington and either Lavern Dillon or Teddy Brannon on piano. —*Scott Yanow*

Because of You / Aug. 28, 1951-1955 / Delmark ◆◆◆
This LP, which had a dozen of altoist Tab Smith's better recordings for the United label, has been superceded by Delmark's CD reissue series which will eventually include all 90 of Smith's sides. This best-of set does have more than its share of enjoyable ballads, blues, novelties, and jump tunes from Smith, who had a big commercial hit in 1951 with "Because of You." Commercial but enjoyable music. —*Scott Yanow*

Ace High / Feb. 26, 1952-Apr. 23, 1953 / Delmark ◆◆◆◆
During 1951-57, Tab Smith recorded extensively for the United label, and although he was initially popular (due to the hit record "Because of You"), nearly half of the 90 titles he cut went unissued. Delmark in their Tab Smith CD series plans to eventually come out with all of the performances. Their

second Tab Smith release has 20 selections, including five songs being released for the first time. Smith, a former swing stylist who was best known in the R&B market during the 1950s, was not a honker like many others in the genre, and his mixture of relatively gentle stomps and ballads is appealing. The distinctive altoist (who takes four vocals) is often joined by Sonny Cohn (mistakenly listed as "Sammy Cohn") or Irving Woods on trumpet and Leon Washington or Charlie Wright on tenor, along with a rocking rhythm section, on four complete sessions from 1952-53. Fun if not essential music. —*Scott Yanow*

Red, Hot and Cool Blues / 195? / United ◆◆◆
Alto saxophonist Tab Smith, along with many other instrumentalists who got their starts in the swing era, decided against playing bop and instead helped forge a new style, one that merged swing arrangements with explosive, gospel-tinged vocals; the results were R&B. This album is a collection featuring vintage R&B and blues material, supported by Smith's surging saxophone. —*Ron Wynn*

Top 'n' Bottom / Feb. 10, 1998 / Delmark ◆◆◆
The third CD volume of altoist Tab Smith's United recordings features 21 selections, 14 of which had never been released before. The music ranges from Johnny Hodges-type small-group stomping swing and R&B-ish jump sides to sentimental ballads and a few vocal numbers (featuring unidentified singers). Among the personnel are trumpeter Irving Woods, pianist Teddy Brannon, and drummer Walter Johnson. Accessible and fairly creative jazz, conservative for the early '50s but still quite enjoyable. —*Scott Yanow*

Willie "The Lion" Smith
(William Henry Joseph Bonaparte Bertholoff Smith)

b. Nov. 25, 1897, Goshen, NY, **d.** Apr. 18, 1973, New York, NY
Piano / Stride, Classic Jazz, Piano Blues
Willie "The Lion" Smith in the 1920s was considered one of the big three of stride piano (along with James P. Johnson and Fats Waller) even though he made almost no recordings until the mid-'30s. His mother was an organist and pianist and Smith started playing piano when he was six. He earned a living playing piano as a teenager, gained his nickname "the Lion" for his heroism in World War I and after his discharge he became one of the star attractions at Harlem's nightly rent parties. Although he toured with Mamie Smith (and played piano on her pioneering 1920 blues record "Crazy Blues"), Smith mostly freelanced throughout his life. He was an influence on the young Duke Ellington (who would later write "Portrait of the Lion") and most younger New York-based pianists of the 1920s and '30s. Although he was a braggart and (with his cigar and trademark derby hat) appeared to be a rough character, Smith was actually more colorful than menacing and a very sophisticated pianist with a light touch. His recordings with his Cubs (starting in 1935) and particularly his 1939 piano solos for Commodore (highlighted by "Echoes of Spring") cemented his place in history. Because he remained very active into the early '70s (writing his memoirs *Music on My Mind* in 1965), for quite a few decades Willie "the Lion" Smith was considered a living link to the glory days of early jazz. —*Scott Yanow*

● **Willie "The Lion" Smith 1925-1937** / Nov. 5, 1925-Sep. 15, 1937 / Classics ◆◆◆◆
Willie "The Lion" Smith, one of stride piano's Big Three of the 1920s (along with James P. Johnson and Fats Waller), recorded a lot less than his two friends. In fact, with the exception of two selections apiece with the Gulf Coast Seven in 1925 (which features trombonist Jimmy Harrison and clarinetist Buster Bailey) and 1927's Georgia Strutters (starring singer Perry Bradford, Harrison, and cornetist Jabbo Smith), along with the rare and originally unreleased 1934 solo piano showcase "Finger Buster," this CD does not get started until 1935. Smith's Decca recordings of 1935 and 1937 were formerly quite obscure, showcasing his piano with three different versions of "His Cubs." The Lion is heard with a Clarence Williams-type quartet which includes cornetist Ed Allen and clarinetist Cecil Scott; matched up with trumpeter Dave Nelson and clarinetist Buster Bailey in a septet; and temporarily heading an early version of the John Kirby Sextet on a session dominated by drummer O'Neil Spencer's vocals. Highlights of this historic and enjoyable CD include "Santa Claus Blues," "Keep Your Temper," "Blues, Why Don't You Let Me Alone," and the earliest recording of the Lion's most famous composition, "Echo of Spring." —*Scott Yanow*

Willie "The Lion" Smith 1937-1938 / Sep. 15, 1937-Nov. 30, 1938 / Classics ✦✦

The second Classics CD in their Willie "The Lion" Smith series is surprisingly weak. Of the 25 selections, 21 actually feature the dated organ of Milt Herth. Smith's presence in the trio (with drummer-vocalist O'Neil Spencer) fails to uplift the music (Herth's wheezing organ mostly drowns him out) although guitarist Teddy Bunn helps a bit on the last seven numbers. Easily the best selections on the CD are two songs performed by Willie "The Lion" Smith and His Cubs (a septet with trumpeter Frankie Newton and clarinetist Buster Bailey) and a pair of duets with drummer Spencer on Smith's own "Passionette" and "Morning Air." But the preceding and following volumes in this program are much more valuable. — *Scott Yanow*

The Original 14 Plus Two / Nov. 30, 1938 + Jan. 10, 1939 / Commodore ✦✦✦✦

This 1981 LP, released through Columbia, has the highpoints of Willie "The Lion" Smith's career. On Jan. 10, 1939 he recorded 14 piano solos including eight of his own impressionistic compositions. These include such classics as "Echoes of Spring," "Passionette," "Morning Air," and the rambunctious "Finger Buster" and find the pianist at the top of his form. Also on this LP are his versions of six standards along with two numbers ("Three Keyboards" and "The Lion and the Lamb") from a slightly earlier session in which he plays with drummer George Wettling and fellow pianists Joe Bushkin and Jess Stacy. This is essential music which has fortunately been reissued on CD by the European Classics series. — *Scott Yanow*

★ **Willie "The Lion" Smith 1938-1940** / Nov. 30, 1938-Feb. 17, 1940 / Classics ✦✦✦✦✦

This is the one Willie "The Lion" Smith CD to get. The bulk of the release features Smith on 14 piano solos from Jan. 10, 1939 performing six standards and eight of his finest compositions. Although Smith (with his derby hat and cigar) could look quite tough, he was actually a sensitive player whose chord structures were very original and impressionistic. On such numbers as "Echoes of Spring" (his most famous work), "Passionette," "Rippling Waters," and "Morning Air," Smith was at his most expressive. In addition, this CD has a couple of collaborations with fellow pianists Joe Bushkin and Jess Stacy and a four-song swing/dixieland 1940 session with an octet featuring trumpeter Sidney DeParis. Because of the classic piano solos, this memorable set is quite essential. — *Scott Yanow*

Willie "The Lion" Smith / Dec. 1, 1949-Dec. 24, 1949 / GNP ✦✦✦

On this album, Willie "The Lion" Smith is featured either as a piano soloist, in duets with drummer Wallace Bishop or in a quartet with Bishop, trumpeter Buck Clayton, and clarinetist Claude Luter. Eight of the 12 selections were also included on a similarly titled Inner City LP although four were not. While the Inner City set is preferable (it has 16 cuts), the GNP LP will probably be a little easier to find. The Lion is in particularly fine form on "Relaxin'," "Contrary Motions," "Portrait of the Duke," and "La Madelon." — *Scott Yanow*

Willie the Lion Smith / Dec. 1, 1949-Jan. 29, 1950 / Inner City ✦✦✦✦

This out-of-print LP has some of the highlights of pianist Willie "The Lion" Smith's four recording sessions recorded in Paris for the Vogue label during 1949-50. For the fine all-round showcase, the Lion is heard performing six originals in duet with drummer Wallace Bishop (including "Echoes of Spring," "Portrait of the Duke," and "Contrary Motion"), playing six romping piano solos (including his rendition of James P. Johnson's "Carolina Shout") and jamming three standards and a blues in a dixieland quartet with trumpeter Buck Clayton, clarinetist Cladue Luter and drummer Bishop. The performances overlap with a similar GNP/Crescendo LP but this is the better buy although both sets will be difficult to find. — *Scott Yanow*

The Lion of the Piano / 1951 / Commodore ✦✦✦

Echoes of Spring / 1965 / Milan ✦✦✦

On this CD pianist Willie "The Lion" Smith is featured during a solo concert from France. The recording quality is just ok and Smith's performance (which combines his piano with a few unfortunate vocals and a little reminiscing) was typical for the period but his piano playing is generally pretty strong. He performs four of his originals (including "Echoes of Spring" and "Zig Zag"), a few standards, a James P. Johnson medley, a medley of songs associated with some of his favorite pianists, Chopin's "Polonaise" and even "La Marseillaise." Although not quite essential, there are enough colorful mo-

ments on this set to make the date recommended to Willie "The Lion" Smith collectors. — *Scott Yanow*

Pork and Beans / Nov. 8, 1966 / Black Lion ✦✦✦✦

One of the last of the major stride pianists, Willie "The Lion" Smith pays tribute to some of his contemporaries during this solo studio set. Smith performs four numbers by Luckey Roberts, three by Eubie Blake, two apiece from Fats Waller and George Gershwin, and four veteran standards. Smith was in the last part of his musical prime and is still quite strong on this spirited and definitive late-period program, infusing his hot stride with impressionistic ideas. — *Scott Yanow*

Duets / Feb. 20, 1967 / Sackville ✦✦✦

To relieve the workload late in his career, Willie "The Lion" Smith often hired fellow pianist Don Ewell to join him for duets. On this Sackville session, Smith and Ewell romp on a variety of superior swing standards including "I've Found a New Baby," "I Would Do Anything for You," "Everybody Loves My Baby," and "You Took Advantage of Me." Although not as significant as other individual sets of Smith and Ewell, the combination works well, making this date easily recommended to fans of stride piano. — *Scott Yanow*

Memoirs of Willie the Lion Smith / Apr. 25, 1968-Apr. 28, 1968 / RCA ✦✦✦✦

This double LP is the equivalent of Jelly Roll Morton's *Library of Congress* recordings. The legendary Willie "The Lion" Smith reminisces about his colorful life, plays some piano and warbles out some vocals. Particularly interesting are his stories of the early days, his medleys of songs associated with Eubie Blake, James P. Johnson, Fats Waller, and Duke Ellington, and his performances of eight of his own compositions, some of which are quite obscure. Not everything works and some of the talking rambles on a bit, but overall this is a fascinating historical document that has many interesting moments. — *Scott Yanow*

Relaxin' / 1970-1971 / Chiaroscuro ✦✦✦✦

For this Chiaroscuro LP (not yet reissued on CD), veteran stride pianist Willie "The Lion" Smith is heard in the studio in 1970 and live at a club in 1971, in both cases usually accompanied by drummer Dude Brown. The well-rounded program mostly sticks to veteran standards (including "I've Found a New Baby," "Nagasaki," and "Keeping Out of Mischief Now") plus "Chopin Variations" and three versions of "Relaxing" which Smith was using as a theme song. This fine outing (one of the Lion's last) is worth searching for. — *Scott Yanow*

Willie the Lion and His Washington Cubs / Feb. 20, 1971 / Fat Cat Jazz ✦✦✦✦

Willie "The Lion" Smith passed away in 1973 but this live jam session set shows that two years before his death he still retained most of his power. Teamed with Australian trumpeter Tony Newstead, clarinetist Tommy Gwaltney, bassist Van Perry, and drummer Skip Tomlinson, Smith runs through ten veteran warhorses and brings a great deal of joy to such songs as "Ain't She Sweet," "Louisiana," "Darktown Strutters' Ball" (which has one of Fat Cat McRee's two vocals), and "Love Is Just Around the Corner." This hard-to-find Fat Cat LP can easily be enjoyed by Dixieland and Willie "The Lion" Smith collectors. — *Scott Yanow*

Willie Mae Ford Smith

b. 1906, Rolling Fort, MS, d. Feb. 2, 1994, St. Louis, MO
Vocals / Black Gospel

Considered the greatest of the "anointed singers"—artists who live according to the spirit, and who perform with the ultimate aim of saving souls—Willie Mae Ford Smith was among the most legendary gospel vocalists of her era; rarely recorded, her enormous reputation instead rested almost entirely on her incendiary live performances, where her dramatic, physical style inspired many of the finest soloists to follow in her wake. She was also the first to introduce the "song and sermonette," the act of delivering a lengthy sermon before, during or after a performance. Smith was born in 1906 in Rolling Fork, Mississippi and raised in Memphis; one of 14 children, she was the daughter of a railroad brakeman who relocated the family to St. Louis in 1918. There her mother opened a restaurant, where Smith soon began working full-time, leaving school during the eighth grade; though raised as a devout Baptist, she sang everything from blues to reels as a child, but upon forming her family quartet the Ford Sisters, she turned solely to gospel.

Debuting at the National Baptist Convention in 1922, the Fords created a sensation with their performances of "Ezekiel Saw the Wheel" and "I'm in His Care." After her sisters married and quit the group, Smith mounted a solo career; a high soprano, she briefly flirted with pursuing classical music, but was so profoundly moved by Detroit's Madame Artelia Hutchins' performance at the 1926 Baptist Convention that she returned to gospel once and for all. Upon marrying a man who operated a general hauling business, Smith began touring to supplement their household income; with the exception of the legendary Sallie Martin, she was arguably the first gospel performer to tour relentlessly, conducting musical revivals in many of the cities she visited. In her travels Smith crossed paths with Thomas A. Dorsey, who in 1932 invited her to Chicago to help organize the National Convention of Gospel Choirs and Choruses. She later formed a St. Louis chapter, and was the longtime head of the soloists' bureau.

Smith's rendition of her own composition "If You Just Keep Still," delivered at the 1937 National Baptist Convention, set a new standard for solo singing; just as influential was her skill as an arranger, with her radical reinterpretations of chestnuts like "Jesus Loves Me," "Throw Out the Lifeline," and "What a Friend We Have in Jesus" galvanizing a new generation of singers to include the songs in their repertoires. As a teacher, Smith also mentored Brother Joe May, Myrtle Scott, Edna Gallmon Cooke, and Martha Bass. She joined the Church of God Apostolic in 1939, and immediately her music reflected the rhythm and energy of the sanctified church; still, she did not finally begin recording until the end of the following decade—with her protegé May enjoying massive success with her style, she saw no point in entering the studio. Only a handful of Smith recordings were issued in her own lifetime, and by the early 1950s she had turned to evangelical work; still, she continued to remain a great inspiration, dying on February 2, 1994. —*Jason Ankeny*

● **Mother Willie Mae Ford Smith** / Spirit Feel ✦✦✦✦
Mother Willie Mae Ford Smith & Her Children is a compilation that highlights some of the best performances by Ms. Smith and her musical progeny. —*Kip Lornell*

Willie Mae Ford Smith / Savoy ✦✦✦✦
Includes "I Must Tell Jesus" and "He Never Left Me Alone." —*Bil Carpenter*

Going on with the Spirit / Nashboro ✦✦✦
Of special note: "Give Me Wings" and "I've Got a Secret." —*Bil Carpenter*

Chris Smither

b. Nov. 11, 1944, New Orleans, LA
Guitar, Vocals / Blues-Rock, Modern Acoustic Blues
Like John Hammond and a handful of other musicians whose careers began in the 1960s blues revival, guitarist, singer, and songwriter Chris Smither can take pride in the fact that he's been there since the beginning. Except for a few years when he was away from performing in the 1970s, Smither has been a mainstay of the festival, coffee house and club circuits around the US, Canada, and Europe since his performing career began in earnest in the coffeehouses in Boston in the spring of 1966.

Smither is best known for his great songs, items like "Love You like a Man" and "I Feel the Same," both of which have been recorded by guitarist Bonnie Raitt. Raitt and Smither got started at about the same time in the coffeehouse scene around Boston, though Smither was born and raised in New Orleans, the son of university professors.

Smither's earliest awareness of blues and folk music came from his parents' record collection. In a 1992 interview, he recalled it included albums by Josh White, Susan Reed and Burl Ives. After a short stint taking piano lessons, Smither switched to ukulele after discovering his mother's old instrument in a closet. The young Smither was passionately attached to the ukulele, and now, years later, it helps to explain the emotion and expertise behind his unique finger-picking guitar style. Smither discovered blues music when he was 17 and heard a Lightnin' Hopkins album, *Blues in the Bottle*. The album was a major revelation to him and he subsequently spent weeks trying to figure out the intricate guitar parts he'd heard on that record. Smither moved to Boston after realizing he was a big fish in a small pond in the New Orleans folk/coffeehouse circuit of the mid-'60s. Also, acoustic blues pioneer Ric Von Schmidt had recommended Smither check out the Boston folk/blues scene.

Smither recorded his first couple of albums for the Poppy label in 1970 and 1971, *I'm a Stranger Too* and *Don't It Drag On*. In 1972, Smither recorded a third album, *Honeysuckle Dog*, for United Artists, that was never released.

On the sessions for that album, he was joined in the studio by his old friends Bonnie Raitt and Mac Rebennack, aka Dr. John. After a long bout with alcohol, Smither launched his recording career again in the late '80s, although he was performing through the whole time he wasn't sober.

His return to a proper recording career, due to a deal with Flying Fish Records, didn't happen again until 1991, when the label released *Another Way to Find You*, a folk-blues album. Smither did record for Adelphi label in 1984, *It Ain't Easy*, which has since been re-released on compact disc. Since then, he's more than proved his mettle as an enormously gifted songwriter, releasing albums of mostly his own compositions for the Flying Fish and Hightone labels. Smither's other albums include *Happier Blue* (1993, Flying Fish) and *Up on the Lowdown* (1995, HighTone Records).

Any of Smither's Flying Fish releases or his HighTone release are worthy of careful examination by guitarists and students of all schools of blues music. Smither is still to some extent an unheralded master of modern acoustic blues. Fortunately, his festival bookings through the 1990s have elevated his profile to a higher level than he's ever enjoyed previously. —*Richard Skelly*

Don't It Drag on / 1972 / Poppy ✦✦✦

It Ain't Easy / 1984 / Adelphi ✦✦✦

Another Way to Find You / 1991 / Flying Fish ✦✦✦✦
This captures folk-blues guitarist-singer-songwriter Smither playing live in the studio for a hand-picked audience over the Christmas holidays in 1989. Smither presents 17 songs of his own derivation and others, blasting it all out in a couple of sharp sets in the time-honored folk music club tradition. His guitar work is clean and well played, and his vocals attain a sense of engagement throughout. While his interpretations of tunes by Chuck Berry, Randy Newman, Elizabeth Cotton, Willie McTell, Jimmy Reed, and others are fine, the true highlights come with the originals "Lonely Time," "Don't Drag It On," "A Song for Susan," "Lonesome Georgia Brown," "I Feel the Same," and the title track. —*Cub Koda*

● **Happier Blue** / 1993 / Flying Fish ✦✦✦✦
All the elements of Chris Smither's distinctive style are here: passionate vocals, his cool songs, and some covers. This is a NAIRD award winning album. —*Richard Meyer*

Small Revelations / Jan. 14, 1997 / Hightone ✦✦✦

I'm a Stranger Too/Don't Drag It On / Mar. 25, 1997 / Collectables ✦✦✦
Chris Smither's first two albums, *I'm a Stranger Too* and *Don't Drag It On*, were combined on this single-CD reissue by Collectables. Although the sound and the packaging could be a little better, this still is a fine way for collectors to pick up these two records on disc. —*Stephen Thomas Erlewine*

Little Smokey Smothers

b. Jan. 2, 1939, Tchula, MS
Guitar, Vocals / Electric Chicago Blues
Not to be confused with his late older brother Big Smokey, Albert "Little Smokey" Smothers began to transcend his journeyman status in 1993 with a superlative Dick Shurman-produced album for the Dutch Black Magic label, *Bossman: The Chicago Blues of Little Smokey Smothers*. The set happily reunited him with his ex-guitar pupil Elvin Bishop and his cousin, singer Lee Shot Williams.

Little Smokey rolled into Chicago during the mid-'50s, landing gigs with guitarist Arthur "Big Boy" Spires and pianist Lazy Bill Lucas and playing with Howlin' Wolf on the 1959 Chess session that produced "I've Been Abused" and "Mr. Airplane Man." Smothers fell in with young White harpist Paul Butterfield when the latter was just starting out in the early '60s and is still fondly recalled as a major influence by his buddy Bishop, who would go on to make history as Butterfield's slashing axeman after Smothers left the harpist's employ.

There was a time during the '70s when Little Smokey pretty much gave up music, but he slid back into playing gradually during the next decade with the Legendary Blues Band. Heart problems temporarily shelved Smothers for a spell not too long ago, but he's back in action now. —*Bill Dahl*

● **Bossman—Chicago Blues of 1993** / 1993 / Black Magic ✦✦✦✦
Sizzling and long-overdue debut album by the veteran Chicago bluesman, whose approach is considerably more contemporary than that of his late older brother. Producer Dick Shurman recruited vocalist Lee Shot Williams (Smokey's cousin) and Elvin Bishop (who Smokey tutored during the early

'60s) for this project, a fine showcase for Smothers' hearty vocals and expressive guitar. — *Bill Dahl*

Otis Smokey Smothers

b. Mar. 21, 1929, Lexington, MS, **d.** Jul. 23, 1993, Chicago, IL
Guitar, Vocals / Electric Chicago Blues
The Chicago blues scene boasted its own pair of Smothers Brothers, but there was nothing particularly amusing about their tough brand of blues music. The older of the two by a decade, Otis "Big Smokey" Smothers was first to arrive in the Windy City from Mississippi in the mid-'40s. Howlin' Wolf liked the way he played enough to invite him into the Chess studios as his rhythm guitarist on several 1956-57 sessions (songs included "Who's Been Talking," "Tell Me," "Going Back Home," and "I Asked for Water").

Federal Records found Smothers' simple shuffle sound immensely appealing in 1960, recording 12 tracks by the good-natured bluesman with labelmate Freddy King handling lead guitar duties (King, Federal's parent logo, even issued a Smothers LP that's worth a pretty penny today). A four-song 1962 session that included "Way Up in the Mountains of Kentucky" and an updated version of the Hank Ballard & the Midnighters classic "Work with Me Annie" ("Twist with Me Annie") completed his Federal tenure.

Apart from a 1968 single for Gamma ("I Got My Eyes on You"), Smothers didn't make it back onto wax until 1986, when Red Beans Records, a small Chicago outfit run by pianist Erwin Helfer and guitarist Pete Crawford, brought him back to the record racks with an LP called *Got My Eyes on You* that showed his style hadn't changed a whit with the decades. Smokey Smothers was a beloved Chicago traditionalist until the very end. — *Bill Dahl*

● **Sings the Backporch Blues** / 1961 / King ♦♦♦♦
Lowdown Chicago blues album that's exceedingly rare on vinyl but well worth the search. Smothers was a master of the slow-grinding shuffle, and some tracks sport the presence of Freddy King on lead guitar. — *Bill Dahl*

Drivin Blues / 196? / King ♦♦♦♦
Uncompromising Chicago blues. — *Bill Dahl*

Got My Eyes on You / May 1987 / Red Beans ♦♦♦
The guitarist's only other album was a decent representation of his gutbucket sound, backing him with a crew of sympathetic young traditionalists that didn't update his basic shuffles a bit. — *Bill Dahl*

Second Time Around / Sep. 3, 1996 / Crosscut ♦♦♦

Jim Solberg

Guitar / Modern Electric Blues
Whenever Luther Allison toured the US in the '90s, he was backed by the Jim Solberg Band. Solberg and Allison had a long, friendly working relationship that dates back to the early 1970s, when Allison was living in Milwaukee.

Solberg, a talented guitarist, singer and songwriter, frequently co-wrote with Allison, but since Luther spent a good portion of each year in Europe, touring out of his home in Paris, Solberg toured with his band under his own name when Allison was not around. In the late '90s, Solberg released several albums under his own name for the Atomic Theory label. The records drew high praise from critics, and well they should — Solberg was no spring chicken when it comes to playing blues and touring. He has broken many a guitar string and logged thousands of miles in his van since he started to get serious about the music in the late 1960s.

Solberg was raised in Eau Claire and Milwaukee, Wisconsin, and worked in various psychedelic blues cover bands (fashionable in the late 1960s) before moving to Vancouver, B.C. as a conscientious objector in 1968. After returning to the US after the war, Solberg formed a band called Whirlhouse. That group didn't last very long, and in 1970, he toured with the Sam Lays Blues Band, which included Big Walter "Shakey" Horton, Eddie Taylor and Johnnie Young. In 1972, working with bassist Jon Paris, he formed a band called Dynamite Duck. Paris would later go on to accompany Johnny Winter as bassist for the next 14 years. Beginning in 1975, Solberg toured with Jimmy Reed and began his full time association with Allison. Solberg and his bands backed Allison from 1975 to 1979, pausing only to tour with John Lee Hooker, whom Solberg would rejoin for another tour in 1981. After Alli-

son relocated permanently to Paris, Solberg worked with the Milwaukee group Short Stuff, a group led by harp player Jim Liban.

In the 1980s, Solberg toured with Hooker, the Legendary Blues Band, the Nighthawks, and Elvin Bishop, among others. In 1987 Solberg opened his own club, the Stone's Throw, in Eau Claire, Wisconsin.

After Allison signed to the Chicago-based Alligator Records in 1993, the Jim Solberg Band, in its then-incarnation, renewed its relationship with Allison, acting as his touring band on domestic dates and select overseas shows. Much of Allison's debut for Alligator, *Soul Fixin' Man,* (1993) was co-written and arranged by Solberg. Solberg, a true blues veteran, was also heavily involved in the songwriting and arranging for Allison's two final albums for Alligator, *Blue Streak* (1996) and *Reckless* (1997).

By the very nature of his job as a sideman, it may take a while for the blues-buying public to realize that Solberg is a phenomenally talented songwriter, guitarist, and singer in his own right. Both *See That My Grave Is Kept Clean* or *One of These Days* are superb, highly recommended albums. — *Richard Skelly*

● **See That My Grave Is Kept Clean** / Aug. 1, 1995 / MP ♦♦♦♦
Jim Solberg's debut album *See That My Grave Is Kept Clean* is a storming collection of hard-driving electric blues. Before he had the chance to make this record, Solberg perfected his trade by working as a sideman. Those years slinging a guitar paid off in spades, as this record demonstrates. There's a maturity to his style, but there's also unbridled energy — the combination is, at times, irresistible. The songs may be a little uneven, but there's no denying that Solberg and his crack supporting band have made *See That My Grave Is Kept Clean* into something to remember. — *Thom Owens*

One of These Days / 1996 / Atomic Theory ♦♦♦

L.A. Blues / May 5, 1998 / Atomic Theory ♦♦♦
An album from Luther Allison's long-standing bandleader of the last several years. Released a few months after Allison's death, the album can be taken as a tribute album by Solberg of sorts to his old boss. Utilizing a strong, distorted tone throughout, Solberg keeps Luther's high-energy approach alive on a batch of shuffles ("Bubba's Boogie," "Must Be a Reason"), slow blues ("L.A. Blues," "Ballad of a Thin Man"), and uptempo rockers ("Wally World USA," "Rhumba Juice"). Midtempo shuffles abound in tracks like "A Closer Walk with Thee," "Robb's Souffle," and the closing "Happy Snails." The music on this record is heartfelt and inspired, a moving tribute. Fans of Allison's final work will say his memory is well served here. — *Cub Koda*

The Soul Stirrers

f. 1927, Trinity, Texas
Group / Soul, Black Gospel, R&B, Traditional Gospel
Indisputably among the premier gospel groups of the modern era, the Soul Stirrers pioneered the contemporary quartet sound. Pushing the music away from the traditional repertoire of jubilees and spirituals towards the visceral, deeply emotional hard gospel style so popular among postwar listeners, the group's innovative arrangements — they were the first quartet to add a second lead — and sexually-charged presence irrevocably blurred the lines between religious and secular music while becoming a seminal influence on the development of rock 'n' roll and soul, most notably by virtue of their connection to the legendary Sam Cooke. The Soul Stirrers' origins date back to 1926, where in the town of Trinity, Texas, baritone Senior Roy Crain formed a quartet with a number of other teens with whom he attended church. After one of the group's early appearances, a member of the audience approached Crain to tell him how their performance had "stirred his soul," and from this chance compliment the Soul Stirrers were officially born.

The original group fell apart soon after, but Crain continued to pursue a singing career; upon relocating to Houston during the early 1930s, he joined a group called the New Pleasant Green Singers on the condition that they change their name to the Soul Stirrers. So rechristened, this incarnation of the quartet made a 1936 field recording for Alan Lomax; as other members dropped out, Crain brought in replacements, finally arriving at the classic early lineup which also included bass Jesse Farley, baritone T.L. Bruster, second lead James Medlock, and, most notably, lead R.H. Harris, whose high, crystalline voice remains the inspiration for virtually all great male quartet leads to follow since. After moving to Chicago, the Soul Stirrers began shifting away from the signature tight harmonies and compact songs of traditional gospel towards a harder style distinguished by shifting leads and performances elongated to increase their emotional potency; they also began performing new material from the pens of Thomas A. Dorsey, Kenneth Morris, and others.

Throughout the 1940s, the Soul Stirrers' reputation grew; not only were they constantly on tour, but they booked most of the major gospel programs in the Chicago area—in their spare hours, they even operated their own cleaning business. When the grind got to be too much for Medlock, he retired from the road, and was replaced by onetime Golden Echo Paul Foster. In early 1950, the Soul Stirrers signed to the Specialty label, debuting with the single "By and By"; it was quickly followed by "I'm Still Living on Mother's Prayer" and "In That Awful Hour," both originals composed by Detroit's Reuben L.C. Henry. In total, the Soul Stirrers recorded over two dozen tracks for Specialty in 1950 before Harris quit the group that same year; many predicted a dire future, especially when it was announced that his replacement was a relatively unknown 20-year-old named Sam Cooke. When Cooke made his recording debut with the Soul Stirrers in 1951, however, any reservations were quickly dispelled—blessed with a gossamer voice even sweeter and more graceful than Harris', he would take the group to even greater heights than before.

The first Soul Stirrers 78 to feature Cooke, "Jesus Gave Me Water," was a major hit, and with his good looks the young singer made an instant impact with female audiences, in the process becoming the gospel circuit's first sex symbol. The group's popularity continued to soar, but as the Soul Stirrers entered their third decade, the daily grind began to wear on its members, and soon Bruster retired; he was replaced by baritone Bob King, who also doubled as a guitarist, becoming their first-ever steady instrumentalist. In 1954, the Soul Stirrers briefly added Julius Cheeks to their roster; after lending his raspy vocals to a recording of "All Right Now," however, contractual obligations forced him to exit almost as quickly as he arrived. In 1956, Cooke finally crossed over to the pop market, and was replaced by ex-Highway QC Johnnie Taylor; while Taylor himself would also enjoy pop success in the years to follow, he failed to command the same devotion as his predecessor. Lineup changes continued regularly in the years to follow, but the Soul Stirrers forged on with new, younger members keeping the group afloat into the 1990s. —*Jason Ankeny*

☆ **Shine on Me** / 1950 / Specialty ♦♦♦♦♦
This contains 26 previously released tracks, alternate takes, and unissued tracks (ca. 1950) by the legendary quintet and features postwar gospel's finest and most influential soloist, R.H. Harris. —*Opal Louis Nations*

Heaven Is My Home / 1953-1959 / Specialty ♦♦♦♦
The Soul Stirrers have been gospel's most honored and recognized vocal group since the '40s, when R.H. Harris made musical history by shifting the genre's focus from unison singing to improvisational theatrics and inter-group dynamics. The selections on their most recent reissue cover a significant and too-often ignored aspect of the ensemble's history; the music of its other premier lead singers besides Harris and Sam Cooke. Paul Foster and Johnnie Taylor, the set's featured vocalists, weren't virtuosos like Harris or Cooke; they relied on timing, delivery, and fervor. —*Ron Wynn*

Jesus Be a Fence Around Me / 1961 / Sar ♦♦♦♦
Sweet soul in Cooke-ing tradition. —*Opal Louis Nations*

Gospel Pearls / 1962 / Sar ♦♦♦♦
Strong lead work from Cooke, Outler, Harris and Leroy Crume. Also features the Gospel Paraders. —*Opal Louis Nations*

★ **The Soul Stirrers** / 1964 / Specialty ♦♦♦♦♦
Specialty's *Soul Stirrers* is a wonderful, definitive collection that contains the best moments from the seminal gospel group, including material recorded with all four lead vocalists—Sam Cooke, Johnnie Taylor, R.H. Harris, and Paul Foster. —*Leo Stanley*

The Original Soul Stirrers Featuring Sam Cooke / 1964 / Specialty ♦♦♦♦
Strong collection of most of Sam's best-loved gospel songs with the group. —*Opal Louis Nations*

The Best of the Soul Stirrers / 1966 / Checker ♦♦♦♦
Willie wails in the Cooke tradition. Fine singing by all. —*Opal Louis Nations*

The Golden Gospel / 1967 / Checker ♦♦♦♦
Great moments. Successful pairing of choir with quartet. —*Opal Louis Nations*

The Thrilling Soul Stirrers in Concert (Live) / 1968 / Checker ♦♦♦♦
Vocal pyrotechnics by Rogers and Martin Jacox in live setting. —*Opal Louis Nations*

Gospel Music / 1969 / ♦♦♦♦
The most impressive and influential gospel quartet of the pre—and post-war era. Strong leads and perfect soul-inspired harmonies. 1940s recordings. —*Opal Louis Nations*

Sam Cooke & the Original Soul Stirrers / 1971 / Specialty ♦♦♦♦
A mixture of gems highlighting the lead vocals of Sam, Johnnie Taylor, Paul Foster, and R.H. Harris. —*Opal Louis Nations*

Going Back to the Lord Again / 1972 / Specialty ♦♦♦♦
The best of the Crume Bros. set of S.S. featuring Miles and Jacox. —*Opal Louis Nations*

Resting Easy / 1984 / Chess ♦♦♦
Fine 1960s gospel singing and soulful lead work by Little Willie Rogers. —*Opal Louis Nations*

A Tribute to Sam Cooke / 1984 / MCA ♦♦♦
Little Willie Rogers personalizes some of Cooke's finest songs on this 1960s Chess reissue. —*Opal Louis Nations*

In the Beginning / 1991 / Ace ♦♦♦♦
Ace's *In the Beginning* is an excellent collection of recordings the Soul Stirrers made in the early '50s. The disc is augmented by several solo cuts from Sam Cooke, making it an excellent distillation of the essence of the group's stirring, extraordinary music. —*Leo Stanley*

Sam Cooke with the Soul Stirrers / 1992 / Specialty ♦♦♦
This 1992 reissue features previously unreleased material. Sam Cooke incorporated the styles of Archie Brownlee, R. H. Harris, and Julius Cheeks (along with his own natural abilities) to become, as many say, the best all-around gospel and R&B singer ever. This recording gives 25 reasons why people might say that. —*Billy C. Wirtz*

Jesus Gave Me Water / 1992 / Specialty ♦♦♦♦
Sam Cooke was one of the most original and influential vocal stylists of all time. You can hear him in all his glory (1951-1955) without edits or overdubs; his peerless soaring melismas are a joy. Catch also the anguished spiritual tones of the great Paul Foster, Sr., as he alternates sparingly with Cooke. The first eight cuts are pure unadulterated a cappella. It includes the "long" version (one of three different unissued renderings) of "All Right Now," sung blazingly by gospel's hardest lead, Rev. "June" Julius Cheeks. This is a once-in-a-lifetime treat. —*Opal Louis Nations, Roots & Rhythm Newsletter*

Swing Time Gospel, Vol. 1 / Jul. 25, 1995 / Night Train ♦♦♦♦
Important release of 1940s-1950s jubilee quartet material. Includes the Soul Stirrers. —*Opal Louis Nations*

● **The Gospel Soul of Sam Cooke, Vol. 2** / Specialty ♦♦♦♦
The Gospel Soul of Sam Cooke & the Soul Stirrers, Vol. 2 is being promoted under Sam Cooke's name, but it's really the Stirrers' show with first-class titles like "Farther Along" and "I'm So Glad." Some of Cooke's greatest moments, ca. 1951-1955, with great second-lead support from Paul Foster Sr. Includes three previously unreleased cuts. —*Kip Lornell*

The Last Mile of the Way / Specialty ♦♦♦
While the Soul Stirrers' catalog has been thoroughly documented on past Specialty reissues, the 28 tracks presented on this most recent set shows that even their secondary and/or alternate cuts were outstanding. They pioneered the use of a double lead, with Sam Cooke's wondrous tenor contrasted by several other superb vocalists from Paul Foster to Julius Cheeks. There's even one cut where guitarist Bob King takes a turn at the microphone and doesn't disgrace himself. Although many of these songs have been previously released, it's instructive to hear the discussions, fragments and partial pieces that show The Soul Stirrers experimenting and perfecting the formula that made gospel history. —*Ron Wynn*

Heritage / Jewel ♦♦♦
This, by the Crume Brother set of The Soul Stirrers, first surfaced as a single-volume collection on Jewel entitled *Heritage Vols. 1 & 2* in 1974. The personnel consists of the late veteran founder J.J. Farley (bass), Arthur Crume (lead and rhythm guitar), Rufus Crume (bass), Eddie Huffman (tenor), and Dillard Crume (lead guitar and the group's arranger/producer). This is fine high-

spirited gospel with grit and conviction sung in the old-time way. The booklet gives a handy list of the group's most important albums. —*Opal Louis Nations, Roots & Rhythm Newsletter*

Strength, Power and Love / Jewel ✦✦✦
Strong singing, sweet and sanctified with plenty of melodic harmony. —*Opal Louis Nations*

Heritage, Vol. 2 / Jewel ✦✦✦
Reworking of some of the group's earlier charts on Checker and Specialty. —*Opal Louis Nations*

Clarence Spady

b. Jul. 1, 1961, Paterson, NJ
Vocals / Modern Electric Blues
Guitarist, singer and songwriter Clarence Spady, a 30-something blues musician, has a bright future. Spady, born and raised in Paterson, N.J., but now living in Scranton, PA, has been credited with taking the music in new and exciting directions, writing at times introspective, autobiographical blues lyrics for the 1990s.

His debut for the Philadelphia-based Evidence Music, *Nature of the Beast*, received critical praise from all corners of the blues world, and he's signed to a multi-album deal with the label. (Spady recorded the album independently before executives at Evidence signed him.) Like diddley bow player Lonnie Pitchford, Spady was cited by Living Blues magazine as one of the "Top 40 under 40" blues players to watch in the future.

Spady learned blues from his father, and played his first professional show as a five-year-old in kindergarten, where he performed B.B. King and James Brown tunes for his classmates.

Raised in Scranton, Pa., where he's still based, Spady would sit on his dad's lap and watch him play guitar until bedtime. Spady got his first guitar at age four; blues fever caught him early on, and he's never let it go. His first show came later that year, when he was six, playing with his father, older brother, aunt, and uncle at the Paterson Elks Club in New Jersey. Like any good bluesman, Spady was raised singing in church, which he attended every Sunday with his mother. Unlike other Southern bluesmen who were raised just a generation earlier, the blues were not forbidden in the Spady household; quite the contrary, they were encouraged, since his father and other relatives played the music. Spady sang gospel music in church and took his cue from the secular music of the day played on the radio around New York City, including James Brown, the Isley Brothers, and Jimi Hendrix. He counts B.B. King and Albert Collins among his main blues mentors, and throughout his formative years, Spady played with various rock and gospel groups, honing his chops in the hope that one day he would lead his own blues band.

After he graduated from high school in 1979, Spady hit the road with regional groups and spent most of the 1980s with the Greg Palmer Band, which opened for major touring acts like the Temptations, the Four Tops, and the Spinners. After getting off the road in 1987, Spady played lead guitar in several Scranton-area blues bands and also directed the Shiloh Baptist Church Choir. By the early 1990s, Spady decided to lead his own band.

Much of the material on *Nature of the Beast* is drawn from his personal experience with drugs and his former relationships with women. Although he's long since dropped the drug habit he picked up in his years after high school, the experiences provided him with fodder for some of the songs on his debut.

Spady's multi-album deal with Evidence Music was formalized in February, 1996, after the company agreed to remaster and repackage *Nature of The Beast*, the independently released album which got him radio airplay and allowed him to tour clubs and festivals up and down the East Coast.

Spady will be a force in the blues world for a long time to come, as he backs up great singing with stellar guitar playing and a creative muse for blues lyric writing that the world will find refreshing. —*Richard Skelly*

Nature of the Beast / 1996 / Evidence ✦✦✦

Charlie Spand

Piano, Vocals / Piano Blues
Next to nothing is known about barrelhouse pianist Charlie Spand—the 33 scattered tracks which comprise his recorded legacy are virtually the only concrete proof that he ever existed. Although his exact origins are unclear,

his 1940 recording "Alabama Blues" contains references to his birth there; academics also offer his earlier performances of "Mississippi Blues" and "Levee Camp Man" as strong evidence of a connection to the Delta. However, Spand first made a name for himself as a product of the fecund Detroit boogie-woogie scene of the 1920s; between 1929 and 1931, he cut at least 25 tracks for the Paramount label, duetting with Blind Blake on a rendition of "Moanin' the Blues." His trail is next picked up in 1940, when he recorded eight final tracks in Chicago backed by Little Son Joe and Big Bill Broonzy; at that point, however, Spand seemingly vanished into thin air, and his subsequent activities both in and out of music remain a mystery. —*Jason Ankeny*

● **Complete Paramounts Works (1929-1931)** / 1992 / Document ✦✦✦✦
Document's *Complete Paramounts Works (1929-1931)* is an invaluable Charlie Spand anthology for completists and academic types. Less dedicated listeners will find some absolutely wonderful, classic performances, but not an exhilarating, start-to-finish listen—the long running time, exacting chronological sequencing, and poor fidelity (all cuts are transferred from original acetates and 78s), make it hard to digest. The more serious, intellectual blues listener will find all these factors to be positive, but enthusiasts and casual listeners will find that the collection is of marginal interest for those very reasons. —*Thom Owens*

Otis Spann

b. Mar. 21, 1930, Jackson, MS, **d.** Apr. 24, 1970, Chicago, IL
Piano, Vocals / R&B, Electric Chicago Blues, Piano Blues, Blues Revival
An integral member of the non-pareil Muddy Waters band of the 1950s and 1960s, pianist Otis Spann took his sweet time in launching a full-fledged solo career. But his own discography is a satisfying one nonetheless, offering ample proof as to why so many aficionados considered him then and now as Chicago's leading postwar blues pianist.

Spann played on most of Waters' classic Chess waxings between 1953 and 1969, his rippling 88s providing the drive on Waters' seminal 1960 live version of "Got My Mojo Working" (cut at the prestigious Newport Jazz Festival, where Spann dazzled the assembled throng with some sensational storming boogies).

The Mississippi native began playing piano by age eight, influenced by local ivories stalwart Friday Ford. At 14, he was playing in bands around Jackson, finding more inspiration in the 78s of Big Maceo, who took the young pianist under his wing once Spann migrated to Chicago in 1946 or 1947.

Spann gigged on his own and with guitarist Morris Pejoe before hooking up with Waters in 1952. His first Chess date behind the Chicago icon the next year produced "Blow Wind Blow." Subsequent Waters classics sporting Spann's ivories include "Hoochie Coochie Man," "I'm Ready," and "Just Make Love to Me."

Strangely, Chess somehow failed to recognize Spann's vocal abilities. His own Chess output was limited to a 1954 single, "It Must Have Been the Devil," that featured B.B. King on guitar, and sessions in 1956 and 1963 that remained in the can for decades. So Spann looked elsewhere, waxing a stunning album for Candid with guitarist Robert Jr. Lockwood in 1960, a largely solo outing for Storyville in 1963 that was cut in Copenhagen, a set for British Decca the following year that found him in the company of Waters and Eric Clapton, and a 1964 LP for Prestige where Spann shared vocal duties with bandmate James Cotton. Testament and Vanguard both recorded Spann as a leader in 1965.

The Blues Is Where It's At, Spann's enduring 1966 album for ABC-Bluesway, sounded like a live recording but was actually a studio date enlivened by a gaggle of enthusiastic onlookers that applauded every song (Waters, guitarist Sammy Lawhorn, and George "Harmonica" Smith were among the support crew on the date). A Bluesway encore, *The Bottom of the Blues* followed in 1967 and featured Otis' wife, Lucille Spann, helping out on vocals.

Spann's last few years with Muddy Waters were memorable for their collaboration on the Chess set *Fathers and Sons*, but the pianist was clearly ready to launch a solo career, recording a set for Blue Horizon with British blues-rockers Fleetwood Mac that produced Spann's laidback "Hungry Country Girl." He finally turned the piano chair in the Waters band over to Pinetop Perkins in 1969, but fate didn't grant Spann long to achieve solo stardom. He was stricken with cancer and died in April of 1970. —*Bill Dahl*

Is the Blues / 1960 / Candid ✦✦✦✦

Otis Spann Is the Blues / Aug. 1960 / Candid ✦✦✦✦
He may not have been *the* blues, but he was sure close to being *the blues pianist*. Spann provided wonderful, imaginative, tasty piano solos and better-than-average vocals, and was arguably the best player whose style was more restrained than animated. Not that he couldn't rock the house, but Spann's forte was making you think as well as making you dance. — *Ron Wynn*

★ **Complete Candid Recordings—Otis Spann/Lightnin' Hopkins Sessions** /
Aug. 23, 1960 / Mosaic ✦✦✦✦✦
With Robert Lockwood, Jr. Two classic Spann albums: *Otis Spann Is the Blues* and *Walkin' the Blues*. Early, potent Spann with flawless liner notes and a complete discography. Also included are the Candid sessions of Lightnin' Hopkins. — *Michael Erlewine*

Blues Are Where It's At / Aug. 1967 / HMV ✦✦✦✦

Cracked Spanner Head / 1969 / Deram ✦✦✦

The Blues Never Die! / Oct. 1969 / Original Blues Classics ✦✦✦✦
Boasting fellow Chicago blues dynamo James Cotton on both harmonica and lead vocals, *The Blues Never Die!* is one of Otis Spann's most inspired albums. When this session was recorded for Prestige's Bluesville subsidiary in 1964, Spann was still best known for playing acoustic piano in Muddy Waters' band. But *The Blues Never Die!* (which Fantasy reissued on CD in 1990 for its Original Blues Classics series) shows that he was as great a leader as he was a sideman. From Willie Dixon's "I'm Ready" (a Chess gem Spann had played numerous times with Waters) and Elmore James' "Dust My Broom" to Cotton's spirited "Feelin' Good" and Spann's dark-humored "Must Have Been the Devil," Spann and Cotton enjoy a very strong rapport on this consistently rewarding date. — *Alex Henderson*

Sweet Giant of the Blues / 1970 / Blues Time ✦✦✦

★ **Walking the Blues** / 1972 / Candid ✦✦✦✦✦
Walking the Blues is arguably the finest record Otis Spann ever cut, boasting 11 cuts of astounding blues piano. On several numbers, Spann is supported by guitarist Robert Jr. Lockwood and their interaction is sympathetic, warm and utterly inviting. Spann relies on originals here, from "Half Ain't Been Told" to "Walking the Blues," but he also throws in a few standards ("Goin' Down Slow," "My Home Is in the Delta") that help draw a fuller portrait of his musicianship. Most importantly, however, is the fact that *Walking the Blues* simply sounds great—it's some of the finest blues piano you'll ever hear. — *Thom Owens*

Blues of Otis Spann . . . Plus / 1993 / See for Miles ✦✦✦
A Mike Vernon-produced British album from 1964 that was one of Spann's first full-length dates as a leader. Nice band, too: Muddy Waters on guitar, bassist Ransom Knowling, and drummer Willie "Big Eyes" Smith, along with a young Eric Clapton playing on a couple of cuts. Spann plays a harpsichord on a few items; needless to say, they aren't the album's shining moments! — *Bill Dahl*

Otis Spann's Chicago Blues / 1994 / Testament ✦✦
Recorded in 1965 and 1966, these 15 tracks are divided between solo piano performances and pieces with a full band, with support from guitarist Johnny Young and members of the Muddy Waters Band. The variation in approach means that this isn't the most consistent Spann album, and the material and performances don't rank among his best either, although they're reasonably solid. Includes some of the rare tracks on which Spann played organ rather than piano. — *Richie Unterberger*

Down to Earth / 1995 / MCA ✦✦✦✦
Both of the great Chicago pianist's albums for ABC-Bluesway, characterized with rippling piano and ruminative vocals. Backed in style by his mates in the Muddy Waters band (including the man himself), Spann responds to a studio full of people on "Popcorn Man," "Steel Mill Blues," and "Nobody Knows Chicago like I Do." Spann's 1967 encore LP united him in the studio with wife Lucille for several vocals. — *Bill Dahl*

Live the Life / Jun. 10, 1997 / Testament ✦✦✦✦
This release brings together 16 tracks of rare and previously unissued Otis Spann to compact disc, recorded between 1964 and 1969. Featuring the blues piano genius in both solo context and playing behind a bevy of Chicago artists in a variety of settings, this plows through the old Testament Pete Welding tape vaults to uncover new treasures by the carload. Muddy

Waters is listed on the front cover, and indeed, 12 of the 16 songs here are played in his company, most of it in the unusual role of backup musician to Otis. The compilation begins with five songs from a Martin Luther King tribute concert in 1968 featuring Otis and Muddy Waters on acoustic guitar performing as an "unplugged" duo, including a heartfelt "Tribute to Martin Luther King" standing next to his own tribute to Big Maceo Merriweather, "Worried Life Blues." Next up are seven tracks from a late-1960s (unknown date and point of origin) Muddy Waters concert, kicking off with Otis doing a rip roaring "Kansas City" and a somber take of "Tin Pan Alley" and dueting later with Muddy on a gospel tinged "I Wanna Go Home." Spann's piano work in both of these live settings is nothing short of elegant and extraordinary, whether he's soloing, comping perfectly behind Muddy's vocals or directing the band with an all-knowing lick. Two solo tracks from 1965 ("Everything's Gonna Be Alright" and "What's On Your Worried Mind") are followed by two compilation closers showcasing Otis as a session player behind Johnny Young ("Mean Old Train") and harmonica man Slim Willis ("My Baby Left Me"). Perhaps not the most essential Otis Spann collection you'll ever hear (and certainly not the place to start), but one that nonetheless showcases his wide range of talents, both as a frontman and sideman par excellence. — *Cub Koda*

Speckled Red (Rufus Perryman)

b. Oct. 23, 1892, Monroe, LA, **d.** Jan. 2, 1973, St. Louis, MO
Piano, Organ / Blues Jazz, Piano Blues
Pianist Speckled Red (born Rufus Perryman) was born in Monroe, LA, but he made his reputation as part of the St. Louis and Memphis blues scenes of the '20s and '30s. Red was equally proficient in early jazz and boogie woogie—his style is similar to Roosevelt Sykes and Little Brother Montgomery.

Speckled Red was born in Louisiana, but he was raised in Hampton, Georgia, where he learned how to play his church's organ. In his early teens, his family—including his brother Willie Perryman, who is better-known as Piano Red—moved to Atlanta, Georgia. Throughout his childhood and adolescence he played piano and organ and by the time he was a teenager, he was playing house parties and juke joints. Red moved to Detroit in the mid-'20s and while he was there, he played various night clubs and parties. After a few years in Detroit, he moved back south to Memphis. In 1929, he cut his first recording sessions. One song from these sessions, "The Dirty Dozens," was released on Brunswick and became a hit in late 1929. He recorded a sequel, "The Dirty Dozens, No. 2," the following year, but it failed to become a hit.

After Red's second set of sessions failed to sell, the pianist spent the next few years without a contract—he simply played local Memphis clubs. In 1938, he cut a few sides for Bluebird, but they were largely ignored.

In the early '40s, Speckled Red moved to St. Louis, where he played local clubs and bars for the next decade and a half. In 1954, he was rediscovered by a number of blues aficionados and record label owners. By 1956, he had recorded several songs for the Tone record label and began a tour of America and Europe. In 1960, he made some recordings for Folkways. By this time, Red's increasing age was causing him to cut back the number of concerts he gave. For the rest of the '60s, he only performed occasionally. Speckled Red died in 1973. — *Stephen Thomas Erlewine & Michael G. Nastos*

● **Dirty Dozens** / 196 / Delmark ✦✦✦✦
If you have trouble keeping track of the "reds," Rufus G. Perryman was "Speckled Red," while William Lee Perryman was either "Piano Red" or "Doctor Feelgood." In addition, Speckled Red's style contained more rag and folk elements than "Piano Red"'s, as this set reveals. But both reds talked a lot trash, and Speckled Red had a lighter barrelhouse approach than his younger brother. — *Ron Wynn*

Piano Blues / 197 / Storyville ✦✦✦✦

Speckled Red / 1991 / Storyville ✦✦✦

Blues Masters, Vol. 11 / 1991 / Storyville ✦✦✦✦

Complete Recorded Works 1929-1938 / Jun. 2, 1994 / Document ✦✦✦

Dave Specter

b. May 21, 1963, Chicago, IL
Guitar, Vocals / Modern Electric Blues
In a relatively short timeframe, Chicago guitarist Dave Specter has found his way onto the blues equivalent of the fast track. Just over a decade ago, the

towering guitarist with the carefully coiffed hair first made his presence felt as a good-natured bouncer at B.L.U.E.S., a Windy City blues mecca. Now, he's got four acclaimed albums in the Delmark catalog, every one a satisfying, challenging mix of blues (Specter lists influences including T-Bone Walker, Pee Wee Crayton, Magic Sam, and Otis Rush) and jazz (Kenny Burrell's another of his main men).

The native of Chicago's Northwest Side didn't even grab a guitar until he was 18 years old, inspired by his harp-blowing older brother Howard. In 1985, he hired on at B.L.U.E.S., making valuable contacts on the job that led to sideman gigs with Johnny Littlejohn, Son Seals, and the Legendary Blues Band before he assembled his own outfit, the Bluebirds, in 1989.

Since Specter doesn't sing, he recruited deep-voiced crooner Barkin' Bill Smith as his first vocalist. The two shared the spotlight on Specter's alluring 1991 Delmark debut, *Bluebird Blues*. After Smith departed, Specter latched on to another West side veteran, Jesse Fortune, backing the singer on his 1993 Delmark set *Fortune Tellin' Man*. Dazzling harpist Tad Robinson took over front-man duties for the Bluebirds' 1994 disc *Blueplicity* and *Live in Europe* the next year. Currently, California harpman Lynwood Slim is the band's resident singer.

Jazz is growing increasingly prominent in Specter's evolving guitar attack. He imported legendary organist Brother Jack McDuff to provide a Hammond B-3 cushion for his latest Delmark project. Squeezing frequent European tours in between a myriad of local gigs, Specter wears his love for swinging blues tradition on his sleeve—and it fits him well. — *Bill Dahl*

Bluebird Blues with Ronnie Earl / 1991 / Delmark ++++
There wasn't any musical generation gap between young Chicago guitarist Specter and his much older front man Barkin' Bill Smith. Specter's love for the electrified 1950s styles of Magic Sam, T-Bone Walker, and B.B. King blended well with Smith's deep, almost crooning baritone pipes on what was the debut album for both men. Lots of breezy swing informs the retro-styled set. — *Bill Dahl*

● **Blueplicity** / 1994 / Delmark ++++
Sometimes conviction, charm and humor can be as important as performing proficiency. While there's little in the playing or singing of guitarist Dave Specter or vocalist/harmonica player Tad Robinson that you haven't heard before, they so obviously enjoy what they're doing and communicate it so well that you eventually overlook their familiar material and become engrossed in their performances. This disc has a gritty, rough-edged sound often missing from modern blues dates. The menu ranges from jazzy tunes to lowdown wailers, soul-tinged pieces, and uptempo instrumentals. — *Ron Wynn*

Live in Europe / 1995 / Delmark ++++
Specter, his ultra-soulful singer/harpist of the time Tad Robinson, and his swinging Bluebirds ventured over to Germany on tour in 1994, cutting this fine set over two memorable nights. Robinson, now on his own, was an exceptional match for Specter's concise, crisp guitar style; equally conversant in blues and soul, Robinson is also an exceptional songscribe who penned three of the disc's highlights ("On the Outside Looking In," "Sweet Serenity," "Dose of Reality"). More straight blues than on *Blueplicity:* "Little by Little," "Bad Boy," "Kidney Stew," Little Walter's "It's Too Late Brother." — *Bill Dahl*

Left Turn on Blue / 1996 / Delmark +++

Blues Spoken Here / Mar. 24, 1998 / Delmark +++

Victoria Spivey (Victoria Regina Spivey)

b. Oct. 15, 1906, Houston, TX, d. Oct. 3, 1976, New York, NY
Vocals, Piano / Classic Female Blues, Acoustic Chicago Blues
Victoria Spivey was one of the more influential blues women simply because she was around long enough to influence legions of younger women and men who rediscovered blues music during the mid-'60s US blues revival brought about by British blues bands as well as their American counterparts, like Paul Butterfield and Elvin Bishop. Spivey could do it all: she wrote songs, sang them well, and accompanied herself on piano and organ, and occasionally ukulele.

Spivey began her recording career at age 19 and came from the same rough-and-tumble clubs in Houston and Dallas that produced Sippie Wallace. In 1918, she left home to work as a pianist at the Lincoln Theater in Dallas. In the early 1920s, she played in gambling parlors, gay hangouts and

whorehouses in Galveston and Houston with Blind Lemon Jefferson. Among Spivey's many influences was Ida Cox, herself a sassy blues woman, and taking her cue from Cox, Spivey wrote and recorded tunes like "TB Blues," "Dope Head Blues," and "Organ Grinder Blues" in the 1920s. Spivey's other influences included Robert Calvin, Sara Martin, and Bessie Smith. Like so many other women blues singers who had their heyday in the 1920s and '30s, Spivey wasn't afraid to sing sexually suggestive lyrics, and this turned out to be a blessing nearly 40 years later in the sexual revolution of the 1960s and early '70s.

She recorded her first song, "Black Snake Blues," for the OKeh label in 1926, and then worked as a songwriter at a music publishing company in St. Louis in the late 1920s. In the 1930s, Spivey recorded for the Victor, Vocalion, Decca and OKeh labels, and moved to New York City, working as a featured performer in a number of African-American musical revues, including the "Hellzapoppin' Revue." In the 1930s, she recorded and spent time on the road with Louis Armstrong's various bands. By the 1950s, Spivey had left show business and sang only in church. But in forming her own Spivey Records label in 1962, she found new life in her old career. Her first release on her own label featured Bob Dylan as an accompanist. As the folk revival began to take hold in the early 1960s, Spivey found herself an in-demand performer on the folk-blues festival circuit. She also performed frequently in nightclubs around New York City. Unlike others from her generation, Spivey continued her recording career until well into the 1970s, performing at the Ann Arbor Blues and Jazz Festival in 1973 with Roosevelt Sykes. Throughout the 1960s and 1970s, she had an influence on musicians as varied as Dylan, Sparky Rucker, Ralph Rush, Carrie Smith, Edith Johnson, and Bonnie Raitt.

Spivey's many albums for Spivey and other labels include the excellent *Songs We Taught Your Mother* (1962), which also includes contributions from Alberta Hunter and Lucille Hegamin, *Idle Hours* (1961), *The Queen and Her Knights* (1965) and *The Victoria Spivey Recorded Legacy of the Blues* (1970).

In 1970, Spivey was awarded a "BMI Commendation of Excellence" from the music publishing organization for her long and outstanding contributions to many worlds of music. After entering Beekman Downtown Hospital with an internal hemorrhage, she died a short while later in 1976. Spivey is buried in Hempstead, N.Y. — *Richard Skelly*

● **1926-1931** / 1926-1931 / Document ++++
Spivey is in marvelous form throughout. This album features the classics "Steady Grind," "Black Snake Blues," and "Blood Thirsty Blues." — *Cub Koda*

Recorded Legacy of the Blues / Apr. 27, 1927-Mar. 12, 1937 / Spivey ++++
Victoria Spivey started her own Spivey label in 1961, and ran it successfully for 15 years. This album is the only Spivey release to reissue some of her earlier vintage material. The 14 selections (which give discographical details, although they are not programmed in chronological order) feature the classic blues singer on sessions from 1927-29, 1931 and 1936-37 using such sidemen as guitarists Lonnie Johnson and Tampa Red and trumpeters Louis Armstrong (on "How Do You Do It That Way"), King Oliver, Red Allen, and Lee Collins; some of the versions are rare alternate takes. Although it is a pity that all of Spivey's early recordings were not put out by her label, this is a valuable collection. — *Scott Yanow*

And Her Blues, Vol. 2 / Jun. 10, 1961-Jun. 4, 1972 / Spivey +++
Victoria Spivey, a classic blues singer of the 1920s, started her own label Spivey in 1961 and kept it going for 15 years. This LP, released posthumously, has three solo performances from 1961 (on which the singer plays either piano or ukulele), a trio rendition of "The Rising Sun" from 1962 with clarinetist Eddie Barefield, four numbers from 1972 in small combos and a loose three-song live performance from 1963 with a guitarist and a kazoo player. Although not essential, the music on this set is enjoyable and should be of interest to jazz historians. — *Scott Yanow*

Woman Blues! / Sep. 1961 / Bluesville ++++
Shortly before she formed her own Spivey label, veteran classic blues singer Victoria Spivey made a fine duo album (reissued on CD in the Original Blues Classic series) with guitarist/vocalist Lonnie Johnson whom she had last recorded with back in 1929. Spivey, 55 at the time, is also heard playing piano, and she takes four of the ten selections as solo performances. All of the compositions are hers, including "Christmas Without Santa Claus," "I'm a Red Hot Mama," "Grow Old Together," and "I Got Men All Over This Town."

Recommended as a strong example of Victoria Spivey's later work. —*Scott Yanow*

And Her Blues / Feb. 12, 1962 / Spivey ✦✦✦✦
Victoria Spivey's first full-length set for her Spivey label is one of her best. Joined by Eddie Barefield (on alto and clarinet) and drummer Pat Wilson, Spivey mostly plays piano, but also has two songs apiece on organ and ukelele. Her singing voice was still in fine form, and she performs a dozen of her own blues (most recently written at the time), including "Grant Spivey," "From Broadway to 7th Avenue," "Cool Papa" and "Buddy Tate." —*Scott Yanow*

A Basket of Blues / Feb. 21, 1962-Aug. 16, 1962 / Spivey ✦✦✦✦
This LP, the first release from the Spivey label, has quite a grab bag of performers. Victoria Spivey and Hannah Sylvester (her only recordings after 1923) take four vocals apiece, while Lucille Hegamin has three (the trio were all classic blues veterans of the 1920s); the backup band includes tenor saxophonist Buddy Tate (who is featured on the lone instrumental "Swingin' Away"), Eddie Barefield on alto and clarinet, pianist Sadik Hakim and (on one song) trumpeter Dick Vance. With the exception of the instrumental and the standard "He May Be Your Man," all of the music was composed by Victoria Spivey. An interesting if increasingly difficult-to-find blues set. —*Scott Yanow*

Three Kings and the Queen / Mar. 14, 1962-1963 / Spivey ✦✦✦
This sampler features pianist Roosevelt Sykes, guitarists Lonnie Johnson and Big Joe Williams, and pianist Victoria Spivey on four vocal selections apiece. With the exception of the closing "Thirteen Hours" (which has Spivey joining Sykes for a piano duet) and a pair of Joe Williams tracks (which utilize the then-unknown harmonica player Bob Dylan), all of the performances are unaccompanied. Although each of the blues greats have recorded more classic performances elsewhere, this obscure LP from the Spivey label has its colorful moments. —*Scott Yanow*

Spivey's Blues Parade / 1963-1965 / Spivey ✦✦✦
This LP is a grab bag of previously unreleased numbers recorded for the Spivey label and put together as a blues revue. There are many all-stars involved, plus fine supporting players including Sippie Wallace (heard on a remake of her hit "I'm a Mighty Tight Woman"), Sonny Boy Williamson, Lonnie Johnson, guitarists John Hammond, Benny Jefferson and Johnny Shines, pianists Sunnyland Slim and Little Brother Montgomery, altoist Eddie Barefield, trumpeter Dick Vance, singers Pat Blackman, Carolina Rose, Nita Washington, Little Sonny Parker and Delsey McKay, harmonica players Bill Dicey, Sugar Blue, and Walter "Shakey" Horton, comedian Billy Mitchell, and Victoria Spivey herself. Nothing essential occurs, but taken as a whole, it makes for an entertaining show. —*Scott Yanow*

The Queen and Her Knights / Apr. 12, 1965 / Spivey ✦✦✦
Victoria Spivey had an unlikely comeback in the 1960s, emerging from a long period off the blues scene to record frequently and run her own successful Spivey label. Although known as a classic blues singer, she was flexible enough to record country-blues too, and to hold her own in collaborations with other famous performers. This little-known LP features such immortal bluesmen as guitarist Lonnie Johnson, pianist Little Brother Montgomery, and pianist Memphis Slim, along with guest drummer Sonny Greer. Spivey takes most of the vocals, Montgomery has two, Johnson and Slim are featured on one selection apiece, and Spivey also has vocal duets with Slim ("I'm a Tigress") and Johnson ("Somebody's Got to Go"). Spirited if not quite essential music. —*Scott Yanow*

Houston Stackhouse

b. Sep. 28, 1910, Wesson, MS, **d.** Sep. 23, 1980, Houston, TX
Guitar, Vocals / Delta Blues
The mentor of Delta slide virtuoso Robert Nighthawk, Houston Stackhouse never achieved the same commercial or artistic success as his famed pupil, and remained little known outside of his native Mississippi. Born in the small town of Wesson on September 28, 1910, he was a devotee of Tommy Johnson, whose songs he frequently covered; neither an especially gifted singer nor guitarist, he was quickly surpassed by the young Nighthawk, although the student repaid his debts by backing Stackhouse on a series of sessions cut during the mid- to late 1960s. Outside of the rare European tour, Stackhouse

was primarily confined to playing Delta border towns throughout the majority of his career; he died in Houston, Texas in 1980. —*Jason Ankeny*

Cryin Won't Help You / Nov. 4, 1994 / Genes ✦✦✦

The Staple Singers

f. 1951, Chicago, IL
Group / Soul, Country-Soul
The Staples story goes all the way back to Winona, MS, in 1915. It was then and there that patriarch Roebuck Staples entered the world. A contemporary and familiar of Charley Patton, Roebuck quickly became adept as a solo blues guitarist, entertaining at local dances and picnics. Gradually drawn to the church, by 1937 he was singing and playing guitar with a spiritual group based out of Drew, MS., the Golden Trumpets. Moving to Chicago four years later, he continued playing gospel music with the Windy City's Trumpet Jubilees. A decade later Pops Staples (as he had become known) presented two of his daughters, Cleotha and Mavis, and his one son, Pervis, in front of a church audience, and the Staple Singers were born.

The Staples recorded in an older, slightly archaic, deeply Southern spiritual style first for United and then for Vee-Jay. Pops and Mavis Staples shared lead vocal chores, with most records underpinned by Pops' heavily reverbed Mississippi cottonpatch guitar. In 1960 the Staples signed with Riverside, a label that specialized in jazz and folk. With Riverside and later Epic, the Staples attempted to move into the then-burgeoning White folk boom. Two Epic releases, "Why (Am I Treated So Bad)" and a cover of Stephen Stills' "For What It's Worth," briefly graced the pop charts in 1967.

In 1968 the Staples signed with Memphis-based Stax. The first two albums, *Soul Folk in Action* and *We'll Get Over*, were produced by Steve Cropper and backed by Booker T and the MG's. The Staples were now singing entirely contemporary "message" songs such as "Long Walk to D.C." and "When Will We Be Paid." In 1970 Pervis Staples left, and was replaced by sister Yvonne Staples. Even more significantly, Al Bell took over production chores. Bell took them down the road to Muscle Shoals, and things got decidedly funky.

Starting with "Heavy Makes You Happy (Sha-Na-Boom Boom)" and "I'll Take You There," the Staples counted 12 chart hits at Stax. When Stax encountered financial problems, Curtis Mayfield signed the Staples to his Curtom label and produced a number one hit in "Let's Do It Again." The Staples went on to continued chart success, albeit less spectacularly, with Warner, through 1979. One more album followed on 20th Century-Fox in 1981. After a three-year hiatus, they signed a two-album deal with Private I and hit the R&B charts five more times, once with an unlikely cover of Talking Heads' "Slippery People."

The Staple Singers found a new audience in 1994 when they teamed with Marty Stuart to perform "The Weight" on the *Rhythm, Country and Blues* LP for MCA. —*Rob Bowman*

Uncloudy Day/Will the Circle Be Unbroken / 1955-1960 / Vee-Jay ✦✦✦✦
The Staple Singers brilliantly fused gospel, folk, blues, and soul into a cohesive, commercially potent sound in the '50s and '60s. They perfected this approach during their tenure at Vee-Jay, the first label that allowed the twangy, expert guitar licks of Roebuck "Pop" Staples to be heard in the group's mix and fully presented their harmonies. This single disc contains two pivotal Staples albums; *Uncloudy Day* includes such gospel favorites as "I Know I Got Religion" and "Let Me Ride," while *Will the Circle Be Unbroken* offers the splendid title track, plus masterpieces like "Pray On" and "Come Up in Glory." —*Ron Wynn*

Uncloudy Day [1959] / 1959 / Vee-Jay ✦✦✦✦
Classic folk-rooted gospel from this mixed group. Stinging Delta guitar. Stunning harmonies. —*Opal Louis Nations*

The 25th Day of December / 1962 / Riverside ✦✦✦✦
The group's finest 1960s collection. —*Opal Louis Nations*

Hammer and Nails / Oct. 1962 / Riverside ✦✦✦
Fine material, beautifully recorded and produced. —*Opal Louis Nations*

Great Day / 1963 / Milestone ✦✦✦
This two-album Fantasy reissue is an anthology of the material the Staples recorded for Riverside between 1960 and 1963. For Riverside, the Staples recorded mostly gospel but the shouting was toned down a bit. A few modern-day "message" songs make their way into their repertoire as well, includ-

ing Bob Dylan's "Masters of War." Not quite as cataclysmic as their Vee-Jay material but still essential. — *Rob Bowman*

Make You Happy / 1964 / Epic ✦✦✦
From Riverside, the Staples moved on to Columbia subsidiary Epic in 1964. With Epic, they delved further into the secular realm, hitting the pop charts twice with Pops Staples' plaintive "Why Am (I Treated So Bad)?" and a cover of Stephen Stills' "For What It's Worth." Both are included on this two-disc anthology, as is a stunning side of live performance. Great stuff. — *Rob Bowman*

Freedom Highway / 1965 / Columbia ✦✦✦
Classic live in-church Epic recordings from the height of the civil rights movement of 1965. — *Opal Louis Nations*

Soul Folk in Action / 1968 / Stax ✦✦✦
The Staples' debut Stax release included covers of Otis Redding's "(Sittin' on) The Dock of the Bay" and the Band's "The Weight." Steve Cropper produced and the Stax songwriting staff concocted a number of socially concious lyrics, the most notable being "Long Walk to D.C." — *Rob Bowman*

Pray On / 1968 / Hob ✦✦✦✦
The Staple Singers recorded ten 78s over a four-year period for Chicago's Vee-Jay. These have been reissued countless times in various forms. The Charly CD is simply the most recent. For Vee-Jay the Staples recorded a number of Pops Staples originals as well as radical rearrangements of standards. Pops Staples and Mavis Staples shared the lead singing chores, with Pervis and Cleotha Staples moaning in the background. Superb gospel shouting. — *Rob Bowman*

Will the Circle Be Unbroken / 1969 / Buddah ✦✦✦
More fine singing plus live recordings. — *Opal Louis Nations*

We'll Get Over / 1970 / Stax ✦✦✦
Their second Stax release was similar to *Soul Folk in Action*. The album's highlight is Randall Stewart's "When Will We Be Paid?" — *Rob Bowman*

The Staple Swingers / 1971 / Stax ✦✦✦
The Staples' first album produced by Al Bell and recorded in Muscle Shoals hit the winning formula. Other changes saw Pervis Staples departing just before the album was recorded and being replaced by sister Yvonne Staples. Everything was now in place for the Staples' golden years. Three songs, "Heavy Makes You Happy," "Love Is Plentiful," and "You've Got to Earn It," all charted. — *Rob Bowman*

Be Altitude: Respect Yourself / 1972 / Stax ✦✦✦
The Staples' finest single album, containing three Top Ten R&B hits, "Respect Yourself," "I'll Take You There," and "This World." The first two also were pop Top 20s, "I'll Take You There" going all the way to No. 1. — *Rob Bowman*

Be What You Are / 1973 / Stax ✦✦✦
Continuing in the same vein, *Be What You Are* contained three chart hits, the title song, "If You're Ready (Come Go with Me)," and "Touch a Hand, Make a Friend." The Stax songwriters, combined with Mavis Staples' unbelievably seductive vocals, were on a roll. — *Rob Bowman*

City in the Sky / 1974 / Stax ✦✦✦
Stax was teetering on its last legs, but the label still managed to squeeze two final chart hits out of the Staple Singers in the title cut and "My Main Man." A cut below the previous three albums. — *Rob Bowman*

The Best of the Staple Singers [Stax] / 1975 / Buddah ✦✦✦
Exactly what the title implies — seven monster soul hits plus three judiciously chosen album cuts. One chart hit, "Oh La De Dah," makes its only album appearance here. This disc is nearly too rich for one sitting. Early-'70s soul simply does not get better. — *Rob Bowman*

Let's Do It Again / 1975 / Curtom ✦✦✦
As Stax neared bankruptcy, the Staples signed with Curtis Mayfield's Curtom label for this soundtrack album. The title track was a No. 1 hit and "New Orleans" reached No. 70, returning the Staples to the upper echelons of the charts for the last time. — *Rob Bowman*

Chronicle / 1979 / Stax ✦✦✦✦
Released in 1979, *Chronicle* remains a near-definitive overview of the Staple Singers' time at Stax Records, containing 12 tracks including such classic soul singles as "Heavy Makes You Happy (Sha-Na-Boom-Boom)," "You've Got to Earn It," "Touch a Hand (Make a Friend)," "If You're Ready (Come Go

with Me)," "Be What You Are," "Respect Yourself," and "I'll Take You There." — *Stephen Thomas Erlewine*

Turning Point / 1984 / Epic/Legacy ✦✦✦✦
The last of the truly great gospel sides by this seminal family folk-gospel outfit. — *Opal Louis Nations*

★ **The Best of the Staple Singers** / Oct. 17, 1990 / Stax ✦✦✦✦✦
The best and most famous cuts from their glory years at Stax. Includes their massive hits "Respect Yourself" and "I'll Take You There," less famous but similar gospel-funk fusions like "Touch a Hand (Make a Friend)" and "Heavy Makes You Happy (Sha-Na-Boom Boom)," and less expected items like a cover of "(Sittin' On) The Dock of the Bay." It does not, however, have their 1975 nunber one single "Let's Do It Again," which they recorded just after cutting their ties to Stax. — *Richie Unterberger*

Uncloudy Day [1995] / May 30, 1995 / Charly ✦✦✦✦
Classic Vee-Jay 1950s sides with previously unreleased alternates. The very best Staples recordings with Pops and Mavis on lead mike. — *Opal Louis Nations*

The Very Best of the Staple Singers, Vol. 1: Live / Mar. 3, 1998 / Collectables ✦✦✦
1950s Vee-Jay classics with Pops' Delta guitar and Mavis' deep, compelling vocals. — *Opal Louis Nations*

The Very Best of the Staple Singers, Vol. 2: On My Way to Heaven / Mar. 3, 1998 / Collectables ✦✦✦
The cream of the cream. Their choice Vee-Jay sides. — *Opal Louis Nations*

Greatest Hits / Fantasy ✦✦✦✦
A reissue of some of the fine Riverside sides (ca. 1962-1964) produced by Orrin Keepnews. This package actually does contain many of their best-known selections (like "Hammer and Nails") and is a good value for the money. — *Kip Lornell*

Pop Staples

b. Dec. 2, 1915, Winoma, MS
Guitar, Vocals / Soul, Country-Soul
The patriarch of one of music's most successful families, Pop Staples worked with everyone from Robert Johnson to Curtis Mayfield. Roebuck Staples was born December 2, 1915 in Winona, Mississippi; a close friend of Charley Patton, he also played not only with Johnson but also such legends as Son House and Robert Jr. Lockwood, becoming a top-notch blues guitarist in the process. Increasingly drawn to the church, he joined the gospel group the Golden Trumpets in 1937, and upon relocating to Chicago in 1941, he signed on with the Windy City's Trumpet Jubilees; by the following decade, Staples was regularly performing at services in the company of his daughters Mavis and Cleotha and son Pervis, and soon they began appearing professionally as the Staple Singers. While originally a gospel group, the family achieved their first commercial success with a more contemporary soul sound honed during the late 1960s while signed to the Stax label; by the early 1970s, the Staples even moved into funk, scoring a major pop hit with "I'll Take You There." After signing with Mayfield's Curtom label, they also found success with "Let's Do It Again." Pop Staples did not pursue a solo career prior to releasing 1992's *Peace to the Neighborhood*, which returned him to his blues and gospel roots. Its follow-up, 1994's *Father Father*, earned a Grammy for Best Contemporary Blues Album. — *Jason Ankeny*

● **Peace to the Neighbourhood** / 1992 / Pointblank ✦✦✦✦
78-year-old Pop Staples puts a lot of younger performers to shame with his integrity-laden solo release *Peace to the Neighbourhood*. The founder of The Staples Singers combines joyous soul and gospel with swampy funk and blues. Of course, it doesn't hurt to have the rest of The Staples, and admirers Bonnie Raitt, Jackson Browne, and Ry Cooder along for the ride. Includes the street-wise, anti-drug-culture "Miss Cocaine." — *Roch Parisien*

Father Father / 1994 / Pointblank ✦✦✦

Steampacket

f. 1965, **db.** 1965
Group / British Invasion, British Blues
Because their ranks included a future superstar, the Steampacket have received more attention than they really deserve. Featuring vocalists Rod Stew-

art, Long John Baldry, and Julie Driscoll, as well as organist Brian Auger, misleading reissues of the group's demos bill the act as "the first supergroup." That's simply not the case. They were an interesting conglomeration, and innovative in the respect of featuring several singers. But their true status is as a short-lived footnote, and not one that rates as a highlight of any of the principals' careers.

The Steampacket were formed in mid-1965, after the demise of Baldry's backing outfit, the Hoochie Coochie Men. Baldry envisioned a soul-type revue, each singer taking the material for which he or she was most suited. Management by Giorgio Gomelsky (who also handled the Yardbirds and several other interesting British groups) and a supporting slot on the Rolling Stones' summer 1965 British tour seemed to promise a bright future.

Their professional activities were complicated by the fact that Baldry and Stewart retained separate managers for their individual careers. Additionally, Baldry was already signed to United Artists as a solo act, thwarting Gomelsky's plans to record the band. This led to disputes between the different managers, and the Steampacket broke up before they managed to enter the studio.

Officially enter the studio, that is. Gomelsky did record some tapes with the band at a rehearsal at the famous Marquee club in London. These have been reissued numerous times since the 1970s, and show the band to be a competent but hardly thrilling soul-rock outfit, anchored instrumentally by Auger's jazz-blues organ. Stewart moved on to the Jeff Beck Group, the Faces, and solo stardom; Baldry moved into middle-of-the-road pop, landing some British hit singles in the late '60s. Auger had recorded as a backup musician on Baldry's mid-'60s solo records, and his Brian Auger Trinity group continued working with Julie Driscoll, reaching the UK Top Five in 1968 with "This Wheel's on Fire." —*Richie Unterberger*

● **The Steampacket Featuring Rod Stewart** / 1992 / Charly ◆◆◆◆
Also packaged (with equal exploitation) as *The First Supergroup*, it's unfair to judge the Steampacket on the basis of these demos, which were never intended for release. Still, what exists is a fair but unremarkable vestige of a typical mid-'60s British club band, perhaps more soul-oriented than most, heavily reliant upon American covers. Their most distinguishing feature was Brian Auger's bubbly organ, whose style was indebted to American soul-jazz keyboardists like Ramsey Lewis and Jimmy Smith. Despite the title, Stewart only sings lead on one track, "Can I Get a Witness," which is available on Rod's *Storyteller* boxed set. The much inferior Baldry is heard much more often, and the program also includes some instrumental showcases for Auger. —*Richie Unterberger*

Corey Stevens

b. Illinois
Guitar, Vocals / Country-Rock, Singer-Songwriter
Born and raised in Illinois, Corey Stevens was 11 years old when he first picked up a guitar. By 15 he was playing rhythm guitar and writing songs in bands. During college he studied music and eventually earned a degree. Upon graduation, a move to Los Angeles solidified the dreams Stevens had held in his heart since childhood. Paying his dues was like doing hard time, but a job teaching third grade made life a little easier and allowed Stevens to keep a band together and begin his first recording project. Spending ten years teaching was a positive experience that helped build character. Along the way, Corey met and married Linda, a voice and piano teacher. They had one child, a daughter who truly is the apple of her father's eye. An early comparison to the late Stevie Ray Vaughan was a mixed blessing that forced Stevens to push himself in order to make his own statement. In 1995, with the expertise of producer/gunslinger Edward Tree, the first project was released. *Blue Drops of Rain*, originally released on Eureka Records, brought attention and opportunity to a man who had worked 14 years to get a break. The project also brought Corey to the attention of Discovery Records, which licensed *Blue Drops of Rain* and funded a second project. 1996 saw chart action that lasted into 1997 and the release of *Road to Zen*, also produced by Tree. A road warrior who continues to tour alone and with the likes of Lynyrd Skynyrd, Corey Stevens has distinguished himself as an artist of integrity and vision. —*Jana Pendragon*

Blue Drops of Rain / 1995 / Eureka ◆◆◆◆
This first project by Corey Stevens is an energetic, witty combination of country, rock and blues. Stevens exhibits a talent for writing the kind of songs

that appeal to a wide variety of listeners. Always poignant, Stevens can cover a tune and make it his own, as he does here with the R.G. Ford song "Crosscut Saw." He can also hold his own when tackling a Stevie Ray Vaughan number—his version of "Lenny" is graphic in its approach and delivery. As for his own tunes, "Gone Too Long," "Goin' Crazy" and the title cut all come across with panache. A most impressive first round for a man with the promise of a long career. —*Jana Pendragon*

● **The Road to Zen** / May 5, 1997 / Discovery ◆◆◆◆
Making a name for himself from live performances and a successful first release, being proclaimed the heir to Stevie Ray Vaughan, Stevens shows himself to be a more mature, evolved guitarist, writer and performer. While not as raw as his freshman effort, *Blue Drops of Rain*, Stevens continues to build a rock-solid career. *Road to Zen* features more of Stevens' guitar style as well as a tighter production spearheaded by Edward Tree. A passionate performer, this comes through clearly. Especially effective is the Linda and Corey Stevens effort, "Only One for You," a tribute to their partnership; also good are "Lessons of Love," "Take It Back," and "Charles Bronson Vibe." With all cuts written by Stevens this time, he establishes himself as a talent to be reckoned with in several different arenas. —*Jana Pendragon*

Frank Stokes

b. Jan. 1, 1888, Whitehaven, TN, **d.** Sep. 12, 1955, Memphis, TN
Guitar, Vocals / Acoustic Memphis Blues, Prewar Country Blues
Frank Stokes and partner Dan Sain recorded as The Beale Street Shieks, a Memphis answer to the musical Chatmon family string band, the Mississippi Shieks. According to local tradition, Stokes was already playing the streets of Memphis by the turn of the century, about the same time the blues began to flourish. As a street artist, he needed a broad repertoire of songs and patter palatable to Blacks and Whites. A medicine show and houseparty favorite, Stokes was remembered as a consummate entertainer who drew on songs from the 19th and 20th centuries with equal facility. Solo or with Sain and sometimes fiddler Will Batts, Stokes recorded 38 sides for Paramount and Victor. These treasures include blues as well as older pieces: "Chicken You Can't Roost Too High for Me," "Mr. Crump Don't Like It," an outstanding version of "You Shall" (commonly known as "You Shall Be Free"), and "Hey Mourner," a traditional comic anticlerical piece. Stokes possessed a remarkable declamatory voice and was an adroit guitarist. His duets with Sain merit special attention because of their subtle interplay and propulsive rhythm. —*Barry Lee Pearson*

★ **The Frank Stokes Victor Recordings (1928-1929)** / 1928-1929 / Document ◆◆◆◆◆
Document's *Frank Stokes Victor Recordings (1928-1929)* is a companion piece to their previous *Beale Street Shieks*, containing some great early Memphis blues recorded with fiddler Will Batts. —*Thom Owens*

The Beale Street Sheiks / 1990 / Document ◆◆◆◆
Forget the shaky sound and noise on some of the tracks, and the slightly sketchy notes, and the fact that some tracks on this supposedly "complete" collection are missing—these are Paramount recordings, and we're lucky to have what we do, as good as it does sound. What's here are 19 songs cut by Frank Stokes and Dan Sane between August of 1927 and March of 1929. Included are lyrics on numbers like "You Shall" (in two different versions, either one worth the price of the disc) that constitute historical artifacts, going back to the era of slavery; topical songs like "Mr. Crump Don't Like It," that tell of Memphis' life and death as a blues Mecca; and infectiously catchy pieces like the sly, witty, supposedly anti-prostitution pieces like "It's a Good Thing" (also in two different versions). At their best, which is most of this CD, they had an appeal that transcended the decades—the interweaving of the two guitars is about as tight as anything in blues, the rhythms are catchy, and the vocal phrasing by Stokes is delicious. —*Bruce Eder*

The Memphis Blues / Yazoo ◆◆◆◆
No one in the Memphis minstrel/traveling show or early blues tradition had a more distinguished career than Frank Stokes. This is marvelous, inspiring guitar, done in such a spry and captivating manner that you forget Stokes got his start working alongside a blackface comedian in the early '20s, or that much of this material by even 1950s standards was borderline offensive at best. —*Ron Wynn*

Storyville

f. 1994, Texas

Group / Alternative Pop-Rock

Veterans from dozens of blues jam-sessions and all-star backing bands, the members of Storyville—all native Texans—gelled at just such a jam, in 1994 at the Austin club known as Antone's. Bassist Tommy Shannon and drummer Chris Layton had played in Stevie Ray Vaughan's Double Trouble for ten years before the bluesman's death in 1990, and both moved on to the Arc Angels before meeting the other members of Storyville. Lead guitarist David Holt played on the Mavericks' debut album, and appeared with rhythm guitarist David Grissom in Joe Ely's backing band. Grissom had gained his early experience touring with John Mellencamp and the Allman Brothers. The only member of the band with less than ten sideman credits, vocalist Malford Milligan, sang with the Austin band Stick People before the formation of Storyville—named, of course, in honor of New Orleans' historic red-light district.

After several sessions to work out their bluesy soul/R&B, Storyville hopped into the recording studio and produced an album for November Records. Released the same year of the band's foundation, *The Bluest Eyes* won the band six awards at the 1995 Austin Music Awards, including Best Band and Best Single. The LP was rated highly in mainstream publications, and earned Storyville a major-label contract, with the Atlantic subsidiary Code Blue. Though the band released no new material during 1995, three more trophies at that year's Austin Music Awards were forthcoming. Second album *A Piece of Your Soul* was released in 1996, followed in 1998 by *Dog Years*. —*John Bush*

Bluest Eyes / 1994 / November ♦♦♦

● **Piece of Your Soul** / 1996 / Code Blue ♦♦♦♦
Storyville's second album, *Piece of Your Soul*, is a gritty Texas blues record, but it's delivered with enough rock 'n' roll savvy to crossover into the mainstream. That's not to say that the group has watered-down the greasy roadhouse R&B that is their stock and trade—they simply inject it with a shot of feverish rock 'n' roll energy, and that's what makes *Piece of Your Soul* a successful follow-up to the award-winning debut, *The Bluest Eyes*. —*Thom Owens*

Dog Years / Jun. 16, 1998 / Atlantic ♦♦♦
Storyville doesn't change their tune much on *Dog Years*, their first major label effort and third album overall. Granted, the album has a slicker sound than its predecessors, but at its core it remains a hard-rocking blend of Texas blues-rock and Southern rock. The primary pleasure of *Dog Years* is hearing the band play. David Grissom and Dave Holt may not be distinctive guitarists, but they're solid musicians, pushing the record in the right direction. The songs themselves aren't particularly memorable, but there's enough energy in the hard rockers—the ballads fall a little flat—to make it an enjoyable contemporary Southern blues-rock record. —*Stephen Thomas Erlewine*

Angela Strehli

b. Nov. 22, 1945, Lubbock, TX

Vocals / Modern Electric Blues

Don't let her lack of albums fool you: vocalist Angela Strehli is an immensely gifted singer and songwriter, a Texas blues historian, impresario and fan. Born November 22, 1945 in Lubbock, Texas, Strehli comes out of the same school of hippie folksingers that gave rise to some of Americana music's most gifted writers, people like Jimmie Dale Gilmore and her brother Al Strehli.

Raised in Lubbock and inspired by the mix of blues, country and rock 'n' roll she heard on West Texas early-'60s radio, she learned harmonica and played bass before becoming a full-time vocalist. Despite the fact that her recordings are scant, Strehli spends a good portion of each year performing live shows in Europe and around the US and Canada.

You can hear Strehli, who's now based in San Francisco, in all her glory on *Soul Shake* (1987, Antone's Records), *Dreams Come True*, with Lou Ann Barton and Marcia Ball (Antone's, 1990), and *Blonde and Blue* (1993, Rounder Records). Of these, *Blonde and Blue* seems to best showcase her talents as a vocalist and writer of quality songs. Strehli, an avid student of the blues and a sharp blues historian who helped build the Austin blues scene with club-owner Clifford Antone and musicians like Kim Wilson and the Vaughan brothers, knows enough about the state of the art to know there's an awful lot of albums out there. As a result, she takes her time writing and weeding out less than top-notch songs and records albums of lasting significance.

"My thinking has always been that volume is not so great, what's more important is the quality of the material," she explained in a 1995 interview in Austin. —*Richard Skelly*

● **Soul Shake** / Nov. 1987 / Antone's ♦♦♦♦
Soul Shake is an excellent album that effectively captures Angela Strehli's gritting, hard-edged roadhouse blues. Not only is her singing gutsy and powerful, the band is tough and the songs are first-rate, making *Soul Shake* a welcome reminder of the power of straightahead Texas blues-rock. —*Thom Owens*

Blonde and Blue / 1993 / Rounder ♦♦♦♦
The danger for modern blues performers is turning into a parody of what you're allegedly celebrating or honoring. Vocalist Angela Strehli avoids that trap by simply being herself; her honesty and individuality makes her cover of Major Lance's "Um, Um, Um, Um, Um" a legitimate treatment. Strehli's tough-talking personna was tailor-made for such songs as "Two Bit Texas Town" and "Go On," while she managed to register pain without pathos on "Can't Stop These Teardrops" and "I'm Just Your Fool." Only on Elmore James' "The Sun Is Shining" did she falter, more because Albert King has established a credible alternate vision of that number. But she makes up for that with the remarkable closing tune "Going To That City." While she doesn't eclipse Sister O.M. Terrell's transcendent original, she comes as close as anyone possibly could to providing a treatment that's just as valid. —*Ron Wynn*

Percy Strother

b. Jul. 23, 1946, Vicksburg, MS

Guitar, Vocals / Modern Electric Blues

For a sense of the blues at its most tangible, one needs to look no further than singer/guitarist Percy Strother, who triumphed over incredible tragedy to create music of genuine pain and sorrow. Born July 23, 1946 in Vicksburg, Mississippi, he was still a child when his father died violently; his mother passed away shortly afterward, and rather than submitting to life in an orphanage, Strother simply took to the road. He drifted from job to job for a number of years, all the while fighting a battle with alcoholism; discovering the blues turned his life around, however, and after sobering up he began teaching himself guitar, honing his chops in virtual anonymity before recording his debut LP *A Good Woman Is Hard to Find* in 1992. *The Highway Is My Home* followed in 1995, and in 1997 Strother returned with *It's My Time*. —*Jason Ankeny*

Highway Is My Home / May 30, 1995 / Black Magic ♦♦♦♦

A Good Woman is Hard to Find / Apr. 16, 1996 / Blue Loon ♦♦♦

● **It's My Time** / Nov. 18, 1997 / JSP ♦♦♦♦
It's My Time may be Percy Strother's best record yet, capturing his explosive soul-blues in all of its raging intensity. Truth be told, Strother hasn't really ever given a bad performance on record, but the key to the album's success is that he has a set of terrific original songs which effectively showcase his raging, soulful roar and his blistering guitar. This is raw soul, with little of the slickness that distinguishes latter-day retro-soul—and that's why it's worth hearing. —*Thom Owens*

Studebaker John

b. Nov. 5, 1952, Chicago, IL

Vocals, Harmonica / Modern Electric Chicago Blues

Taking his stage name from an automobile he once owned, Studebaker John Grimaldi was a product of the vibrant blues scene of Chicago's West Side. Born November 5, 1952, his father was himself an amateur musician, and as a youngster Grimaldi began playing the many instruments lying about the house. Becoming a fixture at the open-air flea markets in the Maxwell Street area—a venue for countless blues buskers—he began focusing on harmonica after catching performances from the likes of Little Walter and Sonny Boy Williamson; after taking in a Hound Dog Taylor club date, Grimaldi also turned to guitar. He formed the blues-rock band the Hawks during the early 1970s as a showcase for his reedy vocals, primal harp sound and blistering slide guitar skills, and in the years to follow also developed into a fine songwriter; while keeping his day job as a construction worker, Grimaldi began recording during the mid-1980s, issuing a live Netherlands set later re-released domestically as *Rockin' the Blues '85*. His next major release was 1994's *Too Tough*, followed in 1995 by *Outside Lookin' In*. He maintained a prolific recording schedule in the years to come, issuing *Tremoluxe* in 1996 and *Time Will Tell* in 1997. —*Jason Ankeny*

Too Tough / 1994 / Blind Pig ♦♦♦♦

Rockin' the Blues '85 / 1994 / Double Trouble ♦♦♦

● **Outside Lookin' In** / 1995 / Blind Pig ♦♦♦♦
Outside Lookin' In finds Studebaker John perfecting his overdriven, propulsive Chicago blues. His originals may not always be memorable, but they're sturdy vehicles for his hard-driving harmonica and gutsy guitar. Studebaker hasn't changed his style at all—essentially, this is the same album he's delivered before, and he made several others like it afterward—but this is the one that features his best playing. —*Thom Owens*

Studebaker John & the Hawks / Mar. 26, 1996 / Blind Pig ♦♦♦

Tremoluxe / Apr. 1996 / Blind Pig ♦♦♦

Time Will Tell / Sep. 23, 1997 / Blind Pig ♦♦♦♦
Studebaker John, who dominates this release, has diverse talents in four areas: as a guitarist, harmonica soloist, singer and songwriter. His abilities on both guitar and harmonica are quite impressive, playing the very different instruments with equal intensity and passion. In contrast, John's singing is serviceable, and none of his dozen originals on his fourth Blind Pig release are destined to become standards. Overall, this bluesy, often high-powered set is a good showcase for his playing, although one would love to hear Studebaker John perform blues standards sometime. —*Scott Yanow*

Born to Win / 199 / Double Trouble ♦♦♦

Sugar Ray & the Bluetones

f. 1992, Orange County, CA
Harmonica, Vocals / Modern Electric Blues, Heavy Metal, Ska-Punk
East Coast based blues band fronted by singer/harmonica man Ray Norcia and featuring guitar work over the years by Ronnie Earl (Roomful of Blues, Ronnie Earl & the Broadcasters) and Kid Bangham (The Fabulous Thunderbirds). —*AMG*

Sugar Ray and the Bluetones / 1980 / Baron ♦♦♦

● **Knockout** / 1989 / Varrick ♦♦♦♦
A surprisingly tasteful and solidly swinging album, Sugar Ray is a powerhouse vocalist and a more-than-respectable harp player. There are some good songs, too, especially the slow blues "I'm Tortured." —*Niles J. Frantz*

Don't Stand in My Way / 1990 / Bullseye Blues ♦♦♦
There's more swagger and less swing; it's still quite good. —*Niles J. Frantz*

Hubert Sumlin

b. Nov. 16, 1931, Greenwood, MS
Guitar, Vocals / Electric Chicago Blues, Modern Electric Blues
Quiet and extremely unassuming off the bandstand, Hubert Sumlin played a style of guitar incendiary enough to stand tall beside the immortal Howlin' Wolf. The Wolf was Sumlin's imposing mentor for more than two decades, and it proved a mutually beneficial relationship; Sumlin's twisting, darting, unpredictable lead guitar constantly energized the Wolf's 1960s Chess sides, even when the songs themselves (check out "Do the Do" or "Mama's Baby" for conclusive proof) were less than stellar.

Sumlin started out twanging the proverbial broom wire nailed to the wall before he got his mitts on a real guitar. He grew up near West Memphis, AR, briefly hooking up with another young lion with a rosy future, harpist James Cotton, before receiving a summons from the mighty Wolf to join him in Chicago in 1954.

Sumlin learned his craft nightly on the bandstand behind Wolf, his confidence growing as he graduated from rhythm guitar duties to lead. By the dawn of the '60s, Sumlin's slashing axe was a prominent component on the great majority of Wolf's waxings, including "Wang Dang Doodle," "Shake for Me," "Hidden Charms" (boasting perhaps Sumlin's greatest recorded solo), "Three Hundred Pounds of Joy," and "Killing Floor."

Although they had a somewhat tempestuous relationship, Sumlin remained loyal to Wolf until the big man's 1976 death. But there were a handful

of solo sessions for Sumlin before that, beginning with a most unusual 1964 date in East Berlin that was produced by Horst Lippmann during a European tour under the auspices of the American Folk Blues Festival (the behind-the-Iron Curtain session also featured pianist Sunnyland Slim and bassist Willie Dixon).

Only in the last few years has Sumlin allowed his vocal talents to shine. He's recorded solo sets for Black Top and Blind Pig that show him to be an understated but effective singer—and his guitar continues to communicate most forcefully. —*Bill Dahl*

My Guitar & Me / Dec. 1975 / Evidence ♦♦
Sumlin's exceptionally low-key vocals and unexceptional backing by two-thirds of the Aces, pianist Willie Mabon, and rhythm guitarist Lonnie Brooks render this 1975 session pretty disposable overall. Sumlin cops plenty of solo space, but there's too little of the unredictable fire that greatly distinguished his work with Howlin' Wolf. —*Bill Dahl*

Groove / 1976 / Black & Blue ♦♦♦

Kings of Chicago Blues, Vol. 2 / 197? / Vogue ♦♦♦

Blues Party / 1987 / Black Top ♦♦♦
Sumlin still wasn't totally prepared for solo stardom by the time of this disc, relying on the hearty contributions of guitarist Ronnie Earl and soul-searing singer Mighty Sam McClain to get over. —*Bill Dahl*

● **Heart & Soul** / 1989 / Blind Pig ♦♦♦♦
The veteran guitarist sounds more confident and expressive vocally here than on any other of his contemporary recordings. Backing by harpist James Cotton, along with Little Mike & the Tornadoes, is nicely understated, affording Sumlin just enough drive without drowning his easygoing vocals out (no small feat). —*Bill Dahl*

Healing Feeling / 1990 / Black Top ♦♦♦
An improvement over his previous Black Top disc, especially on Sumlin's two vocal showcases, "Come Back Little Girl" and "Honey Dumplins." James "Thunderbird" Davis is also on board in a guest role, though he has to share his mike time with the considerably less remarkable Darrell Nulisch, who dominates the vocals. —*Bill Dahl*

Blues Anytime! / 1994 / Evidence ♦♦♦♦
A remarkable 1964 session produced by Horst Lippmann behind the Iron Curtain in East Germany that found Sumlin trying for the first time on record to sing. He played both electric and acoustic axe on the historic date, sharing the singing with more experienced hands Willie Dixon and Sunnyland Slim (Clifton James is on drums). All three Chicago legends acquit themselves well. —*Bill Dahl*

Sunnyland Slim (Albert Luandrew)

b. Sep. 5, 1907, Vance, MS, **d.** Mar. 17, 1995, Chicago, IL
Piano, Vocals / Piano Blues, Electric Chicago Blues, Delta Blues
Exhibiting truly amazing longevity that was commensurate with his powerful, imposing physical build, Sunnyland Slim's status as a beloved Chicago piano patriarch endured long after most of his peers had perished. For more than 50 years, the towering Sunnyland had rumbled the ivories around the Windy City, playing with virtually every local luminary imaginable and backing the great majority in the studio at one time or another.

He was born Albert Luandrew in Mississippi and received his early training on a pump organ. After entertaining at juke joints and movie houses in the Delta, Luandrew made Memphis his homebase during the late '20s, playing along Beale Street and hanging out with the likes of Little Brother Montgomery and Ma Rainey.

He adopted his colorful stage name from the title of one of his best-known songs, the mournful "Sunnyland Train." The downbeat piece immortalized the speed and deadly power of a St. Louis-to-Memphis locomotive that mowed down numerous people unfortunate enough to cross its tracks at the wrong instant.

Slim moved to Chicago in 1939 and set up shop as an in-demand piano man, playing for a spell with John Lee "Sonny Boy" Williamson before waxing eight sides for RCA Victor in 1947 under the somewhat misleading handle of "Doctor Clayton's Buddy." If it hadn't been for the helpful Sunnyland, Muddy Waters may not have found his way onto Chess; it was at the pianist's 1947 session for Aristocrat that the Chess brothers made Waters' acquaintance.

Aristocrat (which issued his harrowing "Johnson Machine Gun") was but one of a myriad of labels that Sunnyland recorded for between 1948 and 1956: Hytone, Opera, Chance, Tempo-Tone, Mercury, Apollo, JOB, Regal, Vee-Jay (unissued), Blue Lake, Club 51, and Cobra all cut dates on Slim, whose vocals thundered with the same resonant authority as his 88s. In addition, his distinctive playing enlivened hundreds of sessions by other artists during the same timeframe.

In 1960, Sunnyland Slim traveled to Englewood Cliffs, NJ, to cut his debut LP for Prestige's Bluesville subsidiary with King Curtis supplying diamond-hard tenor sax breaks on many cuts. The album, *Slim's Shout*, ranks as one of his finest, with definitive renditions of the pianist's "The Devil Is a Busy Man," "Shake It," "Brownskin Woman," and "It's You Baby."

Like a deep-rooted tree, Sunnyland Slim persevered despite the passing decades. For a time, he helmed his own label, Airway Records. As late as 1985, he made a fine set for the Red Beans logo, *Chicago Jump*, backed by the same crack combo that shared the stage with him every Sunday evening at a popular North Side club called B.L.U.E.S. for some 12 years.

There were times when the pianist fell seriously ill, but he always defied the odds and returned to action, warbling his trademark Woody Woodpecker chortle and kicking off one more exultant slow blues as he had done for the previous half century. Finally, after a calamitous fall on the ice coming home from a gig led to numerous complications, Sunnyland Slim finally died of kidney failure in 1995. He's sorely missed. *—Bill Dahl*

House Rent Party / 1949 / Delmark ++++
From deep in the vaults of Apollo Records comes this sensational collection of 1949 artifacts by the veteran pianist, along with sides by singer St. Louis Jimmy, young pianist Willie Mabon, and two unissued sides by guitarist Jimmy Rogers (including a pre-Chess rendition of his seminal "That's All Right"). Slim's mighty roar shines on "Brown Skin Woman," "I'm Just a Lonesome Man," and "Bad Times (Cost of Living)," all from the emerging heyday of the genre. *—Bill Dahl*

Sunnyland Slim [Flyright] / 1951-1955 / Flyright ++++
This vinyl compendium of the pianist's work as leader and sideman for the JOB label from 1951 to 1955 contains some of his hardiest sides. His vocal roar on the jumping "When I Was Young" and a lowdown "Worried About My Baby" and "Down Home Child" is exemplary, while the swinging instrumental "Bassology" verges on a Count Basie motif. Slim's 88s anchor sides by J.B. Lenoir, Johnny Shines, and drummer Alfred Wallace to complete the LP. *—Bill Dahl*

Midnight Jump / 1969 / Blue Horizon ++++

● Slim's Shout / 1969 / Prestige ++++
You wouldn't think that transporting one of Chicago's reigning piano patriarchs to Englewood Cliffs, NJ would produce such a fine album, but this 1960 set cooks from beginning to end. His swinging New York rhythm section has no trouble following Slim's bedrock piano, and the estimable King Curtis peels off diamond-hard tenor sax solos in the great Texas tradition that also mesh seamlessly. Slim runs through his standards—"The Devil Is a Busy Man," "Shake It," "It's You Baby"—in gorgeous stereo, and two unissued bonus cuts (including another of his best-known tunes, "Everytime I Get to Drinking") make the CD reissue even more appealing. *—Bill Dahl*

Slim's Got His Thing Goin' On / 1969 / World Pacific +++

Legacy of the Blues / 1975 / Storyville +++

Chicago Jump / Apr. 1986 / Evidence ++++
The last of Slim's great band-backed albums, cut with yeoman help from his longtime combo (guitarist Steve Freund and drummer Robert Covington share the vocals). At the heart of the matter are Slim's rolling 88s and still-commanding vocals, invested with experience beyond all comprehension. *—Bill Dahl*

Be Careful How You Vote / 1989 / Earwig ++++
This CD reissues a variety of recordings cut by the veteran blues pianist/vocalist Sunnyland Slim during 1981-83 for his private label Airway Records. In his mid-70s at the time, Slim's energetic vocals and powerful piano playing belie his age. As is typical of the pioneer Chicago bluesman, he allocated plenty of solo space to his sidemen (which include Hubert Sumlin, Eddie Taylor, Lurrie Bell, or Magic Slim on guitar) although there was never any doubt about who was in control. The intelligent lyrics, high musician-

ship, mood variation (including two excellent instrumentals) and spirited playing make this a highly enjoyable and recommeded date despite the LP-length playing time. *—Scott Yanow*

Live in Europe / 1991 / Airway +++
A labor of love project by Slim's longtime saxman Sam Burckhardt, who assembled this collection of informally taped performances from the pianist's Germany stopover on April 23, 1975. Burckhardt wasn't playing his horn that day; instead, he laid down a simple backbeat on drums and let Sunnyland do the rest. Sturdy versions of many of the pianist's signature numbers grace the disc. *—Bill Dahl*

Live at the D.C. Blues Society / 1994 / Mapleshade +++
Sunnyland Slim's brand of weary blues, punctuated by rolling piano accents and boogie riffs, predates both the rise and fall of Delta blues and the emergence of its urban successor. Slim toured the South in the '20s, '30s, and early '40s, then left for Chicago and has been there ever since. This blend of Delta and urban sensibilities has been infused in his songs since he began recording and permeates the 14 selections on the 1987 CD *Live At The D.C. Blues Society*. Although long since past his vocal peak, Slim still spins a nifty yarn and mournful lament. *—Ron Wynn*

Sunnyland Train / 1995 / Evidence +++
There are definite signs of Slim's increasing frailty on this solo outing from the 1980s, but the majestic power of his aging frame comes through frequently nevertheless. *—Bill Dahl*

Swamp Dogg (Jerry Williams)

b. Jul. 1942, Portsmouth, VA
Vocals, Piano, Keyboards / R&B, Soul, Blues-Rock
One of the great characters in rock and soul music is Jerry Williams, better known as the eccentric, idiosyncratic, and always entertaining Swamp Dogg (no relation to Snoop Doggy Dogg). A Virginia native, Williams invented his own legend by claiming that he had little proper schooling, only to wake up one day and find himself a musical genius (his words). Actually, Williams is very talented, and an early association with Jerry Wexler and Phil Walden led to him working for a number of years as a producer, engineer and occasional songwriter with Atlantic in the '60s. At decade's end, however, he decided that the time was right to unleash Swamp Dogg's singular view of the world on an unsuspecting public. The initial result was one of the most gloriously gonzo soul recordings of all time, *Total Destruction to Your Mind*. Along with living up to its title, it was a renegade chunk of not-quite-commercial music, with an unforgettable (though fuzzy) cover shot of the portly Dogg in his underwear. Although undeniably great, *Total Destruction to Your Mind* is one of the most obscure soul records ever made. That, however, has nothing to do with the music, which rocks in a way reminiscent of Solomon Burke or Wilson Pickett. It may have to do with Dogg's worldview, part libertarian politics, part Zappa-style critiques of commerciality and capitalism, and part horny male, the latter defining for better and worse his view of women. Although he spent years working in the industry, Dogg was simply not the standard-issue soul type. And that was good. Dogg has continued to make records, albeit infrequently, since 1969, some good, a few great, and most all extremely difficult to find. With contemporary soul (Boyz II Men, En Vogue, Mary J. Blige) sounding increasingly mannered and sterile, Dogg's yelling, screaming and general craziness is missed. Thankfully, he hasn't disappeared for good, although he only makes records when he feels like it. His last release, *Surfin' In Harlem*, came out in 1991. And as is often the case with quirky "legends," what he's up to at any given time is the source of wild speculation. It would be wise to not count him out; just when you think this Dogg is down and out, he sneaks up and bites you. *—John Dougan*

Total Destruction to Your Mind / 1970 / Canyon ++++
Easily on my Top Ten list of long-out-of-print records that deserve a CD reissue. The title track is a slam-bangin' chunk of rock and funk that's pushed by a great session band including guitarist Jesse Carr and drummer Johnny Sandlin, and is easily Dogg's finest moment on record. But the rest of this is great too, ranging from the consumer nightmare "Synthetic World" to the paternity blues of "Mama's Baby, Daddy's Maybe." Plus, Dogg is a great singer, and his dizzying range gets a workout on these songs. Good luck finding a copy. *—John Dougan*

Rat On / 1971 / Elektra ++++
The cover of this LP—Swamp Dogg riding a white rat, hands raised and fists

clenched in triumph—lets you know that you're not in for any ol' R&B record, even before the needle hits the grooves. It's a satisfying continuation of the eclectic soul-singer-songwriter mix of his debut. Vocally, Swamp Dogg sounds like a cross between General Johnson (of Chairmen of the Board) and Van Morrison; as a songwriter, he's his own man. With the exception of Sly Stone, no other soul men of the period were investigating controversial topics with such infectious musicality and good humor. He takes on promiscuity with unbridled frankness in cuts like "Predicament No. 2," bemoans the eternal delay of American justice for minorities in "Remember I Said Tomorrow," and twists Irving Berlin's "God Bless America" into a protest song (and also, bizarrely, covers the Bee Gees' "Got to Get a Message to You"). None of this endeared him to industry insiders, and Swamp Dogg was dropped by Elektra after the album's release. It's long been out of print, but in the UK Charly has reissued it on CD on a two-fer with *Total Destruction of Your Mind*. — *Richie Unterberger*

Cuffed, Collared and Tagged / 1972 / Cream ◆◆◆◆
This UK import, part of a two-fer, features a great band with dynamite lyrics. — *Richard Pack*

Gag a Maggot / 1973 / Stonedogg ◆◆◆◆
Another great album title, another tiny label, another great record long forgotten. Not as consistently manic as *Destruction*, *Maggot* is as ferocious sounding and does have a good cover of Wilson Pickett's "In The Midnight Hour." Never one to let a love lyric go by without a sarcastic twist, Dogg's love song here is called "I Couldn't Pay For What I Got Last Night." — *John Dougan*

I'm Not Selling Out, I'm Buying In / 1981 / Takoma ◆◆◆◆
After years of keeping a low profile, Dogg emerged from out of nowhere with this fine record. Instead of streamlined hard soul, this record carries a rock 'n' roll clout that keeps even its most banal moments ("Wine, Women and Rock 'n' Roll") from terminal tedium. Song title highlight: Dogg's duet with Esther Phillips, "The Love We Got Ain't Worth Two Dead Flies." Kind of says it all, doesn't it. — *John Dougan*

Total Destruction of Your Mind/Rat on / 1991 / Charly ◆◆◆◆
These two early Swamp Dogg albums were unheralded landmarks of early '70s soul; Charly has now combined both of them onto a single-disc CD reissue. The liner notes seem to have been written by someone who speaks English as a third language, but that minor gripe aside, this probably contains the singer's most significant work. — *Richie Unterberger*

Surfin' in Harlem / Oct. 31, 1991 / Volt ◆◆
Come the 1990s, Swamp Dogg's voice still sounds fine, and he's still singing about racism and promiscuity with some wit. He's still a soul inconoclast, and for some longtime fans, that in itself might be enough to recommend this album. It couldn't be classified among his better releases, though, chiefly because the updated soul backing is sort of leaden. "I've Never Been to Africa (And It's Your Fault)," however, was a strong contender for Song Title of the Month award. — *Richie Unterberger*

● **The Best of 25 Years of Swamp Dogg** / Mar. 5, 1996 / Pointblank ◆◆◆◆
The 18-track retrospective *Best of 25 Years of Swamp Dogg* collects many of the highlights from his scattershot career. Concentrating on his '80s output, the compilation doesn't provide a definitive portrait of the warped blues and soul man, but it does offer enough of his best material to make it an excellent introduction. — *Stephen Thomas Erlewine*

Swan Silvertones (Four Harmony Kings)

f. 1938, Coalwood, West Virginia
Group / Black Gospel, R&B, Traditional Gospel
The Swan Silvertones are a premiere gospel group and one of the great music experiences awaiting anyone who has never heard them. If you are not a fan of gospel music or "religious" music of any kind, don't let that fact deter you from having this unique listening experience. This is pure music at the highest level.

The a cappella quartet Four Harmony Kings was created by tenor Claude Jeter in 1938 in Coalwood, West Virginia, but the name was changed to the Swan Silvertones when they began a 15-minute radio show sponsored by the Swan Bakery Company on the Knoxville station WBIR in 1942. They developed a national reputation during their contract with King Records from 1946 to 1951, recording some 21 recordings (mostly in the jubilee gospel style) including "I Cried Holy" and "Go Ahead." They joined Specialty

Records from 1951 to 1953, but issued only four singles (in a more contemporary, harder style) before they were dropped by that label. The early group had lead singers Jeter and Solomon Womack, tenors Robert Crenshaw and John Manson, baritone John H. Myles, and bass Henry K. Bossard.

They really came into their own when they signed and recorded with Vee-Jay and recorded with that label from 1956 through 1964. The smoother Vee-Jay sound is probably due to arranger Paul Owens, who joined the group in 1952. Influenced by jazz-vocal groups like the Four Freshmen and the Hi-Los, Owens smoothed out the sound and made it more contemporary, even progressive. Starting in 1956, the group began adding instruments to what had been up until then a purely vocal or a capella sound. The excellent guitarist Linwood Hargrove added greatly to the emerging Vee-Jay sound and the additions (on recordings) of jazz sidemen Bob Cranshaw on bass and Walter Perkins —founding members of MJT (3)—on drums completed the sound.

Perhaps their greatest hit was "Oh Mary Don't You Weep," released in 1959—an incredible listening experience. It is in this song that Claude Jeter intones the phrase "I'll be a bridge over deep water, if you trust in my name" that inspired Paul Simon to compose "Bridge Over Troubled Water" some years later. The Swan Silvertones had a great effect on many rock (Al Kooper) and country (Gary Stewart) artists. During their nine years at Vee-Jay, the main members of the group were tenor (and falsetto) Claude Jeter, baritone John H. Myles, tenor Paul Owens, and bass William Conner. Other singers who were in the group during that time were tenors Dewey Young, Robert Crutcher, and Louis Johnson. When Vee-Jay closed in 1965, the group moved to Hob records, where they did one last album before Claude Jeter left to record on his own and focus on his ministry. — *Michael Erlewine*

Heavenly Light / 1952 / Specialty ◆◆◆◆
The Swan Silvertones only recorded for Specialty Records from 1952 until 1955, and it's generally not considered a prime period in their tenure. But this set of newly released performances from the early '50s, most of which even the label lacks information about, show that they did turn in some top-flight outings during that period. Ten of the tracks were done live before hollering, celebrating audiences that weren't attending a concert, but participating in a spiritual renewal. The other eight are studio numbers, but they contain the same intensity and spark that make this a memorable Swan Silvertones document. — *Ron Wynn*

Pray for Me / 1956-1961 / Vee-Jay ◆◆◆
This is early Swan Silvertones on Vee-Jay, recorded in sessions in 1956, 1957, and 1961 but not compiled and released as an album until 1974. It is available on the Vee-Jay two-fer *The Swan Silvertones* along with another great album, *Let's Go to Church Together*. — *Michael Erlewine*

The Swan Silvertones [1959] / 1959 / Vee-Jay ◆◆◆◆
The classic collection with all of Jeter's most memorable moments. — *Opal Louis Nations*

Singing in My Soul [Vee-Jay] / 1960 / Vee-Jay ◆◆◆◆
Here is one of the classic Vee-Jay albums (12 tracks) of vintage Swan Silvertones. These tracks came from six sessions for Vee-Jay when the group was at its creative peak. The album includes "End of My Journey," "Jesus is Alright with Me," and their version of "Rock My Soul." — *Michael Erlewine*

The Swan Silvertones [1962] / 1962 / Vee-Jay ◆◆◆◆
The Swans at the peak of perfection. — *Opal Louis Nations*

Blessed Assurance / 1963 / Vee-Jay ◆◆◆◆
Great singing. Well produced. Fine arrangements. — *Opal Louis Nations*

☆ **Let's Go to Church Together** / 1964 / Vee-Jay ◆◆◆◆◆
This is quintessential Swan Silvertones at their peak. Songs like "Love Lifted Me," and "I'll Be Satisfied"—12 songs from a single session in 1964 have captured some of the finest work of this legendary group. This makes for deep satisfying listening. — *Michael Erlewine*

Glory Gospel / 1967 / Hob ◆◆◆◆
The last truly great Swans collection with Jeter at the helm. — *Opal Louis Nations*

Love Lifted Me / 1970 / Specialty ◆◆◆◆
Tight harmonies, soaring high tenor lead set against hard-sung preaching to create heightened effect. Circa 1951-56. — *Opal Louis Nations*

My Rock / 1972 / Specialty ✦✦✦✦
More gospel in the spirit, circa 1952-57. — *Opal Louis Nations*

Get Right with the Swan Silvertones / 1982 / Rhino ✦✦✦✦
A reissue of various '50s and '60s singles and album sides plus two unissued cuts. Lead vocal dynamics from Rev. Claude Jeter, Paul Owens, and Louis Johnson. This well-rounded and amply annotated cross-section deserves serious consideration. — *Kip Lornell*

★ **Swan Silvertones** / 1993 / Specialty ✦✦✦✦✦
Here is perhaps the best of the Vee-Jay albums (12 tracks) of vintage Swan Silvertones. These tracks came from six sessions for VeeJay when the group was at its creative peak—perhaps the single best album they ever put out. It contains their hit "Oh Mary Don't You Weep," "How I Got Over," "My Rock," "The Lord's Prayer," "When Jesus Comes," and "Great Day in December"— all incredible music experiences. — *Michael Erlewine*

★ **Swan Silvertones/Singin' in My Soul** / Oct. 1993 / Vee-Jay ✦✦✦✦✦
Here is one CD with two classic VeeJay albums (24 tracks) of vintage Swan Silvertones. These tracks (both albums) came from six sessions for Vee-Jay when the group was at its creative peak. The album *Swan Silvertones* is perhaps the single best album they ever put out, containing 12 tunes including their hit "Oh Mary Don't You Weep," "How I Got Over," "My Rock," "The Lord's Prayer," "When Jesus Comes," and "Great Day in December"—all incredible music experiences. The music continues with the album *Singin' in My Soul*, 12 more prime Vee-Jay cuts including "End of My Journey," "Jesus is Alright with Me," and their version of "Rock My Soul." — *Michael Erlewine*

Do You Believe: The Very Best of the Swan Silvertones / Mar. 3, 1998 / Collectables ✦✦✦✦
All you want to hear of the Vee-Jay sides by Rev. Claude Jeter and the boys. — *Opal Louis Nations*

☆ **The Best of Swan Silvertones** / Chameleon ✦✦✦✦✦
This is a reissue of a Vee-Jay LP principally drawn from other Vee-Jay albums issued in 1960 and 1963. Rev. Claude Jeter's swooping falsetto is heard in all its magnificence. So is the preaching style of Louis Johnson and the soft, soulful tones of the great Paul Owens. It contains definitive quintet versions of "The Lord's Prayer," "Blessed Quietness," "Jesus Remembers," and "Great Day in December." These cuts are postwar gospel milestones and memories of how dramatic and spiritually uplifting gospel music had become. It's a must for all serious collectors of postwar gospel music if you don't already have the reissue of these tracks on Rhino or New Cross. — *Opal Louis Nations, Roots & Rhythm Newsletter*

☆ **Pray For Me/Let's Go To Church Together** / Vee-Jay ✦✦✦✦✦
The Swan Silvertones perfected their shimmering, explosive vocals while on Vee-Jay Records from 1956-1964. The elastic, dazzling falsetto of Claude Jeter, which was later adapted and reworked by Al Green, was contrasted by any number of powerful second lead singers within the group: Paul Owens, Louis Johnson, or Azell Monk. The songs on this disc, with one exception, cover the Silvertones' last great period and offer resounding harmonies, soaring leads, and remarkable music. The lead selection, "Sinners Crossroad," is actually the Silver Quintette, an Indiana group probably most famous for having on its roster two future soul stars in Roscoe Robinson and Joe Henderson. — *Ron Wynn*

☆ **Love Lifted Me/My Rock** / Specialty ✦✦✦✦✦
Some of the best hard-gospel harmonizing from the mid-'50s, most notably "How I Got Over" and "My Rock." The group's toughest sides, with firm conviction from lead soloists Solomon Womack, Rev. Bob Crenshaw, Dewey Young, and Paul Owens. — *Kip Lornell*

Singing in My Soul [Up Front] / Up Front ✦✦✦✦
Great sessions of 1956-57. — *Opal Louis Nations*

Roosevelt Sykes

b. Jan. 31, 1906, Elmar, AR, **d.** Jul. 17, 1983, New Orleans, LA
Piano, Vocals / Piano Blues, Acoustic Chicago Blues
Next time someone voices the goofball opinion that blues is simply too depressing to embrace, sit 'em down and expose 'em to a heady dose of Roosevelt Sykes. If he doesn't change their minds, nothing will.

There was absolutely nothing downbeat about this roly-poly, effervescent pianist (nicknamed "Honeydripper" for his youthful prowess around the

girls), whose lengthy career spanned the pre-war and postwar eras with no interruption whatsoever. Sykes' romping boogies and hilariously risqué lyrics (his double-entendre gems included "Dirty Mother for You," "Ice Cream Freezer," and "Peeping Tom") characterize his monumental contributions to the blues idiom—he was a pioneering piano-pounder responsible for the seminal pieces "44 Blues," "Driving Wheel," and "Night Time Is the Right Time."

Sykes began playing while growing up in Helena. At age 15, he hit the road, developing his rowdy barrelhouse style around the blues-fertile St. Louis area. Sykes began recording in 1929 for OKeh and was signed to four different labels the next year under four different names (he was variously billed as Dobby Bragg, Willie Kelly, and Easy Papa Johnson)! Sykes joined Decca Records in 1935, where his popularity blossomed.

After relocating to Chicago, Sykes inked a pact with Bluebird in 1943 and recorded prolifically for the RCA subsidiary with his combo, the Honeydrippers, scoring a pair of R&B hits in 1945 (covers of Cecil Gant's "I Wonder" and Joe Liggins' "The Honeydripper"). The following year, he scored one more national chart item for the parent Victor logo, the lowdown blues "Sunny Road." He also often toured and recorded with singer St. Louis Jimmy Oden, the originator of the classic "Going Down Slow."

In 1951, Sykes joined Chicago's United Records, cutting more fine sides over the next couple of years. A pair of Dave Bartholomew-produced 1955 dates for Imperial in New Orleans included a rollicking version of "Sweet Home Chicago" that presaged all the covers that would surface later on. A slew of albums for Bluesville, Folkways, Crown, and Delmark kept Sykes on the shelves during the 1960s (a time when European tours began to take up quite a bit of the pianist's itinerary). He settled in New Orleans during the late '60s, where he remained a local treasure until his death.

Precious few pianists could boast the thundering boogie prowess of Roosevelt Sykes—and even fewer could chase away the blues with his blues as the rotund cigar-chomping 88s ace did. — *Bill Dahl*

Complete Recorded Works, Vol. 1 (1929-1930) / 1929-1930 / Document ✦✦✦✦
All of Roosevelt Sykes' recordings between 1929 and 1942 are collected on this seven-volume series; it is essential for hardcore fans of blues piano. — *AMG*

The Return of Roosevelt Sykes / 1960 / Bluesville ✦✦✦✦
Sykes' lyrical images are as vivid and amusing as ever on this 1960 set, with titles like "Set the Meat Outdoors" and "Hangover" among its standouts. Other than drummer Jump Jackson, the quartet behind the pianist is pretty obscure, but they rock his boogies with a vengeance. Contains a nice remake of his classic "Drivin' Wheel." — *Bill Dahl*

The Honeydripper / 1961 / Prestige ✦✦✦✦
Roosevelt Sykes expertly fit his classic downhome piano riffs and style into a fabric that also contained elements of soul, funk and R&B. The nine-cut date, recently reissued by Original Blues Classics, included such laments as "I Hate To Be Alone," "Lonely Day" and "She Ain't For Nobody," as well as the poignant "Yes Lawd" and less weighty "Satellite Baby" and "Jailbait." Besides Sykes' alternately bemused, ironic and inviting vocals, there's superb tenor sax support from King Curtis, Robert Banks' tasty organ and steady, nimble bass and drum assistance by Leonard Gaskins and drummer Belton Evans. — *Ron Wynn*

Roosevelt Sykes Sings the Blues / 1962 / Crown ✦✦✦
Long out-of-print LP on the cheaply pressed Crown logo that nevertheless impressively captured Sykes' rough-and-tumble boogie and blues prowess in a band setting. — *Bill Dahl*

Gold Mine: Live in Europe / 1969 / Delmark ✦✦✦
This 1966 solo set was recently reissued on CD as *Gold Mine*. — *Bill Dahl*

The Country Blues Piano (1929-1932) / 1972 / Yazoo ✦✦✦✦
Featured is this Arkansas-born pianist/songster in some of his best early outings. — *Mark A. Humphrey*

Raining in My Heart / 1987 / Delmark ✦✦✦✦
Amazingly, this fine collection of Sykes' early-'50s sides for Chicago's United Records still awaits its reincarnation. That's a shame, since it contains some of the pianist's finest work with his jumping combo, the Honeydrippers (with unusual augmentation from violinist Remo Biondi on one 1952 date). "Toy Piano Blues" finds Sykes switching over to celeste, but "Too Hot to Handle,"

"Walking the Boogie," and "Fine and Brown" are in the customary Sykes mode. — *Bill Dahl*

★ **Roosevelt Sykes (1929-1941)** / 1988 / Story of Blues ✦✦✦✦
A good sampling of some of Sykes' best tracks, it offers a perfect introduction to this seminal pianist. — *AMG*

Blues by Roosevelt "The Honey-Dripper" Sykes / 1995 / Smithsonian/ Folkways ✦✦✦✦
Other than a cameo piano appearance by his producer (and peer) Memphis Slim on the appropriately titled "Memphis Slim Rock," this is a stellar solo outing by the prolific pianist from 1961. He belts out a booming "Sweet Old Chicago," takes a trip to Chicago's South side on "47th Street Jive," and indulges in a little ribald imagery for "The Sweet Root Man." — *Bill Dahl*

● **Boogie Honky Tonk** / Oldie Blues ✦✦✦✦
Vinyl compilation of the pianist's 1944-1947 output for RCA with his jumping little combo, the Honeydrippers, all of it cut in Chicago. Backed by a myriad of swinging Windy City sidemen (saxists Leon Washington, J.T. Brown, and Bill Casimir; bassist Ransom Knowling, drummers Jump Jackson and Judge Riley), Sykes rips through "Peeping Tom," the wonderfully titled "Flames of Jive," and his often-covered "Sunny Road" with ebullient charm. — *Bill Dahl*

T-Lou

f. Grand Coteau, LA
Group / Zydeco
A leading light of the Los Angeles zydeco scene, singer and accordionist T-Lou was born Louis Joseph Eaglin in Grand Coteau, Louisiana; the son of sharecroppers, he taught himself guitar at the age of 15 and later played bass in a high school R&B combo. Upon graduating high school, he relocated to Houston before settling in California; there T-Lou attended a Clifton Chenier concert and fell under zydeco's sway, soon learning accordion and forming the Los Angeles Zydeco Band. After issuing 1985's *T-Lou and His Los Angeles Zydeco Band*, he continued playing regularly along the West Coast in the years leading up to the release of 1993's *Super Hot. —Jason Ankeny*

T-Lou and His L.A. Zydeco Band / 1985 / Maison de Soul ◆◆◆◆
T-Lou and His Los Angeles Zydeco Band is a solid zydeco album and a very impressive debut from the accordionist. His L.A.-based band sound like they're natural-born Louisianans (granted, many of them are transplants), and the record rocks with true energy and spirit, even when the recording is a little too clean. *— Thom Owens*

● **Super Hot** / 1993 / Maison de Soul ◆◆◆◆
It took T-Lou a few years to follow-up his debut, but *Super Hot* makes it clear that the wait was worthwhile. It's nothing but straight-up, traditional zydeco, but the music is performed with so much energy, the result is simply intoxicating. T-Lou's nine original songs prove that he's a solid songwriter, and they give the record a solid foundation upon which he contributes a series of truly intoxicating performances that confirm his place as one of the best zydeco performers of the '90s. *— Thom Owens*

Tampa Red (Hudson Whittaker)

b. Jan. 8, 1904, Smithville, GA, d. Mar. 19, 1981, Chicago, IL
Guitar, Piano, Kazoo, Vocals / Acoustic Chicago Blues, Electric Chicago Blues, Piano Blues
Out of the dozens of fine slide guitarists who recorded blues, only a handful—Elmore James, Muddy Waters, and Robert Johnson, for example—left a clear imprint on tradition by creating a recognizable and widely imitated instrumental style. Tampa Red was another influential musical model. During his heyday in the '20s and '30s, he was billed as "The Guitar Wizard," and his stunning slide work on steel National or electric guitar shows why he earned the title. His 30-year recording career produced hundreds of sides: hokum, pop, and jive, but mostly blues (including classic compositions "Anna Lou Blues," "Black Angel Blues," "Crying Won't Help You," "It Hurts Me Too," and "Love Her with a Feeling"). Early in Red's career, he teamed up with pianist, songwriter, and latter-day gospel composer Georgia Tom Dorsey, collaborating on double entendre classics like "Tight Like That."

Listeners who only know Tampa Red's hokum material are missing the deeper side of one of the mainstays of Chicago blues. His peers included Big Bill Broonzy, with whom he shared a special friendship. Members of Lester Melrose's musical mafia and drinking buddies, they once managed to sleep through both games of a Chicago White Sox doubleheader. Eventually alcohol caught up with Red, and he blamed his latter-day health problems on an inability to refuse a drink.

During Red's prime, his musical venues ran the gamut of blues institutions: down-home jukes, the streets, the vaudeville theater circuit, and the Chicago club scene. Due to his polish and theater experience, he is often described as a city musician or urban artist in contrast to many of his more limited musical contemporaries. Furthermore, his house served as the blues community's rehearsal hall and an informal booking agency. According to the testimony of Broonzy and Big Joe Williams, Red cared for other musicians by offering them a meal and a place to stay and generally easing their transition from country to city life.

Today's listener will enjoy Tampa Red's expressive vocals and perhaps be taken aback by his kazoo solos. His songwriting has stood the test of time, and any serious slide guitar student had better be familiar with Red's guitar wizardry. *— Barry Lee Pearson*

Tampa Red (1928-1942) / Dec. 11, 1928-Feb. 6, 1942 / Story of Blues ◆◆◆◆
Tampa Red sang and played the guitar and kazoo with a joy and flair that made almost every tune he did instantly unforgettable. His early work has been reissued and repackaged so often that it's easy to get caught in the mire. These are marvelous cuts, matching him with various accompanists, including Georgia Tom (later Dr. Thomas A. Dorsey), and offering the best in double-entendre, rags, topical and novelty material. *— Ron Wynn*

The Complete Bluebird Recordings, Vol. 1: 1934-1936 / Mar. 22, 1934-Apr. 1, 1936 / RCA ◆◆◆◆
The Complete Bluebird Recordings, Vol. 1: 1934-1936 is a double-disc set containing 46 songs Tampa Red recorded for Bluebird in the mid-'30s, when he was one of the most popular and influential bluesmen in America. The length of the collection means that it's only of interest to serious blues fans and scholars, which is a shame, because there are many wonderful performances scattered throughout the set that demonstrate Tampa Red's mastery of the guitar and the blues song. *— Thom Owens*

The Complete Bluebird Recordings, Vol. 2: 1936-1938 / 1936-1938 / RCA ◆◆◆◆
Bluebird Recordings 1936-1938 is a comprehensive, double-disc set covering the final two years Tampa Red spent at the label. Many classic songs, including "Someday I'm Bound to Win" and "Seminole Blues," are here, but the compilation is primarily of value to blues historians, since its very comprehensiveness makes it a little intimidating for casual fans. Nevertheless, the set is impeccably produced, and any serious fan of Tampa Red or the blues would do well to add it to their collection. *— Thom Owens*

Don't Tampa with the Blues / Nov. 1961 / Prestige ◆◆◆◆

☆ **Bottleneck Guitar (1928-1937)** / 1974 / Yazoo ◆◆◆◆◆
Yazoo's *Bottleneck Guitar (1928-1937)* is a great collection of early recordings from slide guitarist Tampa Red. The 14-track collection has a number of classic solo cuts from Tampa—including "You Gotta Reap What You Sow" and "Seminole Blues"—plus duets with the likes of Georgia Tom and Ma Rainey, making it an excellent overview of his earliest sides. *— Thom Owens*

The Guitar Wizard (1935-1953) / 1975 / Blues Classics ◆◆◆◆
This is later-period Tampa Red, and some of the older songs in particular lack the pep he injected into his classic cuts. The sound quality is decent and the vocals mostly good. But don't listen to this stuff before you hear the anthemic material, or you won't understand what made Tampa Red a special player. *— Ron Wynn*

☆ **Tampa Red: Guitar Wizard** / Oct. 1975 / RCA ◆◆◆◆◆
Thirty-two of Red's premier tracks from his RCA Bluebird days dating from 1934-1953 (talk about longevity!) on two slabs of vinyl (with exhaustive liner notes by Jim O'Neal). Red's rousing kazoo blasts power many of these essential sides, which feature legends like pianists Black Bob, Blind John Davis, and Johnny Jones in support roles. Red's last few Victor sides were right in the stylistic heart of the later Chicago sound; the remarkable Latin-tinged

"Rambler's Blues" boasts a spine-tingling amplified harp solo from Big Walter Horton. — *Bill Dahl*

It's Tight like That / 1976 / Blues Document ◆◆◆◆
Superb slide and suggestive hokum from 1928-1942. — *Jas Obrecht*

Bawdy Blues / 1977 / Bluesville ◆◆◆
Latter-day Tampa, from the late '50s to early '60s, with Memphis Slim and Lonnie Johnson. — *Jas Obrecht*

Don't Tampa with the Blues / 1982 / Bluesville ◆◆◆
The kazoo-toting bluesman wasn't as powerful a presence when he came back in 1960 to record this set in a solo setting as he was in his Bluebird heyday, but it's hard to resist these agreeable versions of "Let Me Play with Your Poodle," "Love Her with a Feeling," and "It's Tight like That" nonetheless. — *Bill Dahl*

Complete Recorded Works, Vol. 1 (1928-1929) / 1991 / Document ◆◆◆◆
Tampa Red's complete recordings from 1928 to 1934 are collected on this five-disc series. — *AMG*

★ **It Hurts Me Too: The Essential Recordings** / 1994 / Indigo ◆◆◆◆◆
A magnificent primer on the catalog of this prolific guitar/kazoo ace that spans 1928-1942. Opening with his immortal hokum duet with "Georgia Tom" Dorsey, the bawdy "It's Tight like That," the disc makes clear just how seminal Red's Chicago-cut output was—here are the original versions of "It Hurts Me Too," "Love with a Feeling," "Don't You Lie to Me," and the double-entendre hoots "She Wants to Sell My Monkey" and "Let Me Play with Your Poodle." — *Bill Dahl*

The Guitar Wizard [CD] / 1994 / Columbia/Legacy ◆◆◆◆
Some of the earliest work (1928-1934) by the slide guitar great, ranging from the irresistible hokum he served up with piano-playing partner "Georgia Tom" Dorsey ("Dead Cats on the Line," "No Matter How She Done It") to the gorgeous "Black Angel Blues" (eventually known as "Sweet Little Angel") and the solo guitar masterpieces "Things 'Bout Comin' My Way" and "Denver Blues." — *Bill Dahl*

Tarheel Slim (Alden Bunn)

f. Sep. 24, 1924, Wilson, NC, **db.** Aug. 21, 1977, The Bronx, NY
Guitar, Vocals / R&B, Electric Blues, East Coast Blues, Piedmont Blues
Talk about a versatile musician: Alden Bunn recorded in virtually every postwar musical genre imaginable. Lowdown blues, gospel, vocal group R&B, poppish duets, even rockabilly weren't outside the sphere of his musicianship.

Spirituals were Bunn's first love. While still in North Carolina during the early '40s, the guitarist worked with the Gospel Four and then the Selah Jubilee Singers, who recorded for Continental and Decca. Bunn and Thurman Ruth broke away in 1949 to form their own group, the Jubilators. During a single day in New York in 1950, they recorded for four different labels!

One of those labels was Apollo, who convinced them to go secular. That's basically how the Larks, one of the seminal early R&B vocal groups whose mellifluous early-'50s Apollo platters rank with the era's best, came to be. Bunn sang lead on a few of their bluesier items ("Eyesight to the Blind," for one), as well as doing two sessions of his own for the firm in 1952 under the name of Allen Bunn. As Alden Bunn, he encored on Bobby Robinson's Red Robin logo the next year.

Bunn also sang with another R&B vocal group, the Wheels. And coupled with his future wife, Anna Sanford, Bunn recorded as the Lovers; "Darling It's Wonderful," their 1957 duet for Aladdin's Lamp subsidiary, was a substantial pop seller. (Ray Ellis did the arranging.)

Tarheel Slim made his official entrance in 1958 with his wife, now dubbed Little Ann, in a duet format for Robinson's Fire imprint ("It's Too Late," "Much Too Late"). Then old Tarheel came out of the gate like his pants were on fire with a pair of rockabilly raveups of his own, "Wilcat Tamer" and "Number 9 Train," with Jimmy Spruill on blazing lead guitar.

After a few years off the scene, Tarheel Slim made a bit of a comeback during the early '70s, with an album for Pete Lowry's Trix logo that harked back to Bunn's Carolina blues heritage. It would prove his last. — *Bill Dahl*

No Time at All / Jun. 1977 / Trix ◆◆◆◆

Number 9 Train / 1980 / Charly ◆◆◆

● **The Red Robin & Fire Years** / Collectables ◆◆◆◆
Slim was quite an eclectic soul during his 1950s tenure with Bobby Robinson's Red Robin and Fire imprints (as this set conclusively shows). New York blues, pop/R&B duets with Little Ann, even blistering rockabilly-tinged outings ("Number 9 Train," and "Wildcat Tamer") were all well within the versatile guitarist's stylistic scope. — *Bill Dahl*

Finis Tasby

b. 1940, Dallas, TX
Bass, Vocals / Modern Electric Blues
Although he only recently recorded his first nationally distributed full-length album, Los Angeles-based singer and songwriter Finis Tasby is no spring chicken in the blues world. Tasby has been singing in the Los Angeles area for years, and for years before that in Dallas.

Tasby was born in Dallas, TX, in 1940. He formed a band called the Thunderbirds in Dallas in 1962. While working with the Thunderbirds, Tasby played bass and sang backup vocals behind legendary blues singer-songwriter Z.Z. Hill. Hill eventually secured a recording contract, as did Hill's replacement, Joe Simon. From the mid-'60s, Tasby led the band, delivering lead vocals and playing bass. When not touring under their own name, the Thunderbirds backed up the likes of Clarence Carter, Lowell Fulson, and Freddie King, touring regionally throughout Texas and Oklahoma.

In 1973, Tasby moved to Los Angeles and found a home in that city's blues clubs. He formed a new group in Los Angeles and had the chance to open for B.B. King, Percy Mayfield, and Big Mama Thornton.

Tasby recorded several singles in the '70s and '80s: "Get Drunk and Be Somebody," in 1978, and "Blues Mechanic," a 1985 release for Ace Records. Tasby also landed an acting role in the film *Sharkey's Machine* with Burt Reynolds, all the while playing regularly around L.A. blues clubs with his own Finis Tasby Band. Most recently, three of Tasby's songs from his Shanachie Records debut, *People Don't Care* (1995), were featured in the mid-'90s film *The Babysitter*. While his singles are surely collectors' items, his 1995 Shanachie release is still readily available. Accompanying Tasby on *People Don't Care* are some world class talents: Lowell Fulson, Elvin Bishop, Mick Taylor, and Vernon Reid, formerly of the rock group Living Colour. While some tracks on the album are less appealing, urban contemporary pop-blues, other tracks reveal Tasby's authentic Texas blues roots.

Tasby, a prolific songwriter, has many more good albums in his notebooks. Let's hope circumstances allow him to record and tour a lot more outside of Los Angeles. — *Richard Skelly*

People Don't Care / 1995 / Shanachie ◆◆◆

Taste

f. 1966, Ireland, **db.** 1971
Group / Blues-Rock
Before becoming a solo star, Rory Gallagher fronted the blues-rock trio Taste, which experienced reasonable success in the UK in the late '60s and early '70s. Taste were molded very much on the model of Cream, adding some folk, pop, and jazz elements to a blues-rock base, and featuring a virtuosic guitarist. They weren't in the same league as Cream, particularly in the songwriting department, and were (like Cream) prone to occasional blues-rock bombast. But they weren't a bad band in their own right, exhibiting a lighter touch than most British Blues boom outfits.

The focus of Taste was always upon Gallagher. In addition to playing accomplished and versatile lead guitar, he sang in a gentle but convincing fashion, and wrote the band's original material. Much of Taste's repertoire was more restrained and balanced than the territory Gallagher would explore on his '70s outings, which placed more emphasis upon Rory as guitar hero. Gallagher also played occasional saxophone and harmonica with the group.

Gallagher formed the first version of Taste in his native Ireland in 1966, with bassist Eric Kittringham and drummer Norman Damery. In May of 1968, he relocated to London and, still months shy of his 20th birthday, formed a new version of Taste with bassist Charlie McCracken (who had played bass with Spencer Davis, though not at the peak of Davis' hitmaking days) and drummer John Wilson (who had been a drummer with Them, likewise not during one of their well-known incarnations). Two studio albums followed in 1969 and 1970, the second of which made the British Top

20. Taste were still virtually unknown in the States when they broke up shortly afterwards, although a couple of live albums were released in the early '70s to keep some product on the shelves. — *Richie Unterberger*

● **The Best of Taste** / 1994 / Polydor ◆◆◆◆
A well-chosen 16-track retrospective, mostly drawn from the band's two studio albums. Not in the upper echelon of British blues, but not far from that level either, showing Rory Gallagher capable of a wider compositional and interpretive range than some listeners may recall. — *Richie Unterberger*

Baby Tate

b. Jan. 28, 1916, Elberton, GA, **d.** Aug. 17, 1972, Columbia, SC
Guitar, Vocals / Piedmont Blues, Prewar Country Blues
In the course of his nearly 50-year career, guitarist Baby Tate recorded only a handful of sessions. The bulk of his life was spent as a sideman, playing with musicians like Blind Boy Fuller, Pink Anderson, and Peg Leg Sam.

Born Charles Henry Tate, he was born in Elberton, GA, but raised in Greenville, SC. When he was 14 years old, Tate taught himself how to play guitar. Shortly afterward, he began playing with Blind Boy Fuller, who taught Tate the fundamentals of blues guitar. When he was in his late teens, Baby began playing with Joe Walker and Roosevelt Brooks; the trio played clubs throughout the Greenville area.

In 1932, Tate stopped working with Walker and Brooks, hooking up with Carolina Blackbirds. The duo played a number of shows for the radio station WFBC. For most of the '30s, Baby played music as a hobby, performing at local parties, celebrations, and medicine shows.

Tate served in the US Army in the late '30s and early '40s. While he was stationed in Europe, he played local taverns and dances. In 1942, he returned to Greenville, SC, where he earned a living doing odd jobs around the town. Tate picked up music again in 1946, setting out on the local blues club circuit. In 1950, he cut several sessions for the Atlanta-based Kapp label.

In the early '50s, Baby moved to Spartanburg, SC, where he performed both as a solo act and as a duo with Pink Anderson. Tate and Anderson performed as duo into the '70s.

In 1962, Tate recorded his first album, *See What You Done*. The following year, he was featured in the documentary film, *The Blues*. For the rest of the decade, Baby Tate played various gigs, concerts, and festivals across America. With the assistance of harmonica player Peg Leg Sam, Baby Tate recorded another set of sessions in 1972. Later that year, Tate suffered a fatal heart attack. He died on August 17, 1972. — *Stephen Thomas Erlewine*

● **Blues of Baby Tate: See What You Done Done** / 1962 / Original Blues Classics ◆◆◆◆
Recorded during the blues revival of the early '60s, *The Blues of Baby Tate: See What You Done Done* is a wonderful collection of country blues. Tate's teacher was Blind Boy Fuller, and his influence shines through on the album. That doesn't mean that *See What You Done Done* is simply a Fuller record, however—Tate has absorbed his influence and developed his own warm, rambling style that suits these traditional numbers perfectly. — *Thom Owens*

Tommy Tate

b. Sep. 29, 1944, Homestead, FL
Vocals / R&B, Soul
Florida vocalist Tommy Tate is a consistent, if unspectacular, Southern soul wailer. He debuted on Rise in 1964, and continued recording for OKeh, Verve, and Big Ten before joining the Nightingales at Stax in 1970. He returned to the solo scene a couple of years later, recording for Koko. He had a Top 30 R&B single with "School of Love" in 1972, and it has been his only substantial hit. But Tate has kept plugging, working in Mississippi clubs and recording for Juana, Sundance, and other independents. His most recent release was *Love Me Now* for Ichiban's subsidiary label Urgent in 1992. — *Ron Wynn*

Love Me Now / Sep. 9, 1992 / Urgent! ◆◆◆
Tommy Tate tried his luck with the Urgent label, an Atlanta-based company distributed by Ichiban. He had some nice, but dated material done in vintage 1960s and '70s soul style. They attempted at times to update the framework with drum machines and other trappings, but wound up with another strictly regional item, although it's not that bad for fans of the genre. — *Ron Wynn*

Eddie Taylor

b. Jan. 29, 1923, Benoit, MS, **d.** Dec. 25, 1985, Chicago, IL
Guitar, Vocals / R&B, Electric Chicago Blues, Modern Electric Blues
When you're talking about the patented Jimmy Reed laconic shuffle sound, you're talking about Eddie Taylor just as much as Reed himself. Taylor was the glue that kept Reed's lowdown grooves from falling into serious disrepair. His rock-steady rhythm guitar powered the great majority of Reed's Vee-Jay sides during the 1950s and early '60s, and he even found time to wax a few classic sides of his own for Vee-Jay during the mid-'50s.

Eddie Taylor was as versatile a blues guitarist as anyone could ever hope to encounter. His style was deeply rooted in Delta tradition, but he could snap off a modern funk-tinged groove just as convincingly as a straight shuffle. Taylor viewed Delta immortals Robert Johnson and Charley Patton as a lad, taking up the guitar himself in 1936 and teaching the basics of the instrument to his childhood pal Reed. After a stop in Memphis, he hit Chicago in 1949, falling in with harpist Snooky Pryor, guitarist Floyd Jones, and—you guessed it—his old homey Reed.

From Jimmy Reed's second Vee-Jay date in 1953 on, Eddie Taylor was right there to help Reed through the rough spots. Taylor's own Vee-Jay debut came in 1955 with the immortal "Bad Boy" (Reed returning the favor on harp). Taylor's second Vee-Jay single coupled two more classics, "Ride 'em on Down" and "Big Town Playboy," and his last two platters for the firm, "You'll Always Have a Home" and "I'm Gonna Love You," were similarly inspired. But Taylor's records didn't sell in the quantities that Reed's did, so he was largely relegated to the role of sideman (he recorded behind John Lee Hooker, John Brim, Elmore James, Snooky Pryor, and many more during the '50s) until his 1972 set for Advent, *I Feel So Bad*, made it abundantly clear that this quiet, unassuming guitarist didn't have to play second fiddle to anyone. When he died in 1985, he left a void on the Chicago circuit that remains apparent even now. They just don't make 'em like Eddie Taylor anymore. — *Bill Dahl*

I Feel So Bad / 1972 / Hightone ◆◆◆◆
One of the Chicago guitarist's most satisfying contemporary albums, this 1972 set (first issued on Advent) was cut not in the Windy City, but in Los Angeles in 1972 with a combo featuring Phillip Walker on second guitar and George Smith on harp. Taylor was no strict traditionalist; he was as conversant with funk-tinged modern rhythms as with Delta-based styles—and he exhibits both sides of his musical personality on this one. — *Bill Dahl*

Ready for Eddie / 1972 / Big Bear ◆◆

Bad Boy a Long Way from Chicago / 1978 / P-Vine ◆◆◆

Big Town Playboy / 1981 / Charly ◆◆◆◆
Nice cuts from the sorely underrated Eddie Taylor, who found in death the respect and widespread praise he'd earned while alive. This contains some of his best songs and hottest playing. — *Ron Wynn*

Still Not Ready for Eddie / Jul. 1988 / Antone's ◆◆◆
Shows signs of the brilliance that we've long come to expect from the uncommonly versatile Taylor, but clearly not the equal of some of the other Taylor sets on the market. — *Bill Dahl*

☆ **Bad Boy** / 1993 / Charly ◆◆◆◆◆
The Delta-rooted mid-'50s Vee-Jay label classics by perennially underrated Chicago guitarist Eddie Taylor, who stepped out of Jimmy Reed's shadow long enough to leave behind "Bad Boy," "Big Town Playboy," "Ride 'Em on Down," the bouncy "I'm Gonna Love You," and several more brilliant sides. Fifteen songs in all, including five from 1964 that are scarcely less impressive than his previous stuff. — *Bill Dahl*

My Heart is Bleeding / 1994 / Evidence ◆◆◆
Credible set from 1980 mostly cut in Chicago but first out on the German L+R logo. Taylor's in typically solid form, and his tough backing includes the marvelous Sunnyland Slim on piano and harpist Carey Bell. Taylor pays homage to his pal Jimmy Reed with a loping "Going to Virginia" and Muddy Waters on "Blow Wind Blow," but "Soul Brother" rides a chunky R&B groove that's a long way from Reed's rudimentary rhythms. The last five sides stem from a 1980 European tour (with Hubert Sumlin and Bell handling some of the vocals) and don't add much to the package. — *Bill Dahl*

Long Way from Home / Nov. 1995 / Blind Pig ◆◆◆
Okay effort from the venerable Chicago guitarist's later days that's not as essential as Taylor's prior recording activities. — *Bill Dahl*

★ **Ride 'Em on Down** / Charly ✦✦✦✦✦

An absolutely essential 24-track collection which alternates 12 of Eddie's classic Vee-Jay sides (including "Bad Boy," "Big Town Playboy," "Find My Baby," "Looking for Trouble" and the title track) with a dozen more early Jimmy Reed sides with Taylor in support. As a collection of Taylor's best solo sides, it's as complete as any on the market. As a sample of Taylor's impeccable backup work behind Reed—while containing no hits—it stands by itself as a very nice collection of rarities that shows both artists off to good advantage. As a document of early-'50s Chicago blues, it's a major brick in the wall. As seamless blues groove listening, consider it a must-have. — *Cub Koda*

Hound Dog Taylor (Theodore Roosevelt Taylor)

b. Apr. 12, 1915, Natchez, MS, **d.** Dec. 17, 1975, Chicago, IL
Guitar, Vocals / Electric Chicago Blues, Modern Electric Blues, Chicago Blues

Alligator Records, Chicago's leading contemporary blues label, might never have been launched at all if not for the crashing, slashing slide guitar antics of Hound Dog Taylor. Bruce Iglauer, then an employee of Delmark Records, couldn't convince his boss, Bob Koester, of Taylor's potential, so Iglauer took matters into his own hands. In 1971, Alligator was born for the express purpose of releasing Hound Dog's debut album. We all know what transpired after that.

Named after President Theodore Roosevelt, Mississippi-native Taylor took up the guitar when he was 20 years old. He made a few appearances on Sonny Boy Williamson's fabled KFFA *King Biscuit Time* radio broadcasts out of Helena, AR, before coming to Chicago in 1942. It was another 15 years before Taylor made blues his full-time vocation, though. Taylor was a favorite on the South and West sides during the late '50s and early '60s. It's generally accepted that Freddy King copped a good portion of his classic "Hide Away" from an instrumental he heard Taylor cranking out on the bandstand.

Taylor's pre-Alligator credits were light—only a 1960 single for Cadillac baby's Bea & Baby imprint ("Baby Is Coming Home"/"Take Five"), a 1962 45 for Carl Jones' Firma Records ("Christine"/"Alley Music"), and a 1967 effort for Checker ("Watch Out"/"Down Home") predated his output for Iglauer.

Taylor's relentlessly raucous band, the HouseRockers, consisted of only two men, though their combined racket sounded like quite a few more. Second guitarist Brewer Phillips, who often supplied buzzing pseudo-bass lines on his guitar, had developed such an empathy with Taylor that their guitars intertwined with ESP-like force, while drummer Ted Harvey kept everything moving along at a brisk pace.

Their eponymous 1971 debut LP contained the typically rowdy "Give Me Back My Wig," while Taylor's first Alligator encore in 1973, *Natural Boogie*, boasted the hypnotic "Sadie" and a stomping "Roll Your Moneymaker." *Beware of the Dog*, a live set, vividly captured the good-time vibe that the perpetually beaming guitarist emanated, but Taylor didn't live to see its release—he died of cancer shortly before it hit the shelves.

Hound Dog Taylor was the obvious inspiration for Alligator's "Genuine Houserocking Music" motto, a credo Iglauer's firm still tries to live up to today. He wasn't the most accomplished of slide guitarists, but Hound Dog Taylor could definitely rock any house he played at. — *Bill Dahl*

★ **Hound Dog Taylor & the Houserockers** / 1971 / Alligator ✦✦✦✦✦

The first album and the perfect place to start. Wild, raucous, crazy music straight out of the South Side clubs. The incessant drive of Hound Dog's playing is best heard on "Give Me Back My Wig," "55th Street Boogie" and "Taylor's Rock," while the sound of Brewer Phillips' Telecaster on "Phillips' Theme" gives new meaning to the phrase "sheet metal tone." One of the greatest slide guitar albums of all time. — *Cub Koda*

Natural Boogie / 1973 / Alligator ✦✦✦✦

Hound Dog's second album was every bit as wild as the first, bringing with it a fatter sound and a wider range of emotions and music. A recut here of Hound Dog's first single, "Take Five," totally burns the original while the smoldering intensity of "See Me In the Evening" and "Sadie" take this album to places the first one never reached. — *Cub Koda*

Beware of the Dog / 1975 / Alligator ✦✦✦✦

This was Hound Dog's posthumous live album containing performances that are even steamier than the first two studio albums, if such a notion is possible. For lowdown slow blues, it's hard to beat the heartfelt closer "Freddie's Blues" and for surreal moments on wax, it's equally hard to beat the funk-

house turned looney bin dementia of "Let's Get Funky" or the hopped up hillbilly fever rendition of "Comin' Around The Mountain." — *Cub Koda*

Genuine Houserocking Music / 1982 / Alligator ✦✦✦

With Alligator label prexy Bruce Iglauer recording some 20 or 30 tracks over two nights everytime the band went into the studio, there were bound to be some really great tracks lurking in the vaults and these are it. Noteworthy for the great performance of Robert Johnson's "Crossroads," (previously only available as a Japanese 45) but also for the "rock 'n' roll" inclusion of "What'd I Say" and Brewer Phillips' take on "Kansas City." No bottom of the barrel scrapings here. — *Cub Koda*

Live at Joe's Place / 1992 / New Rose ✦✦✦✦

1972 live recordings in Boston. They're drunk, they're out of tune, but the crowd goes nuts and the overall vibe cancels out any musical inconsistencies. Doesn't really add anything to the Alligator legacy, as it's extremely loose and chaotic, but it's great fun anyway. — *Cub Koda*

Have Some Fun / 1992 / Wolf ✦✦✦

More 1972 live recordings from Joe's Place. Different song selection, somewhat better fidelity. Confusingly for people who'll want to order this as an import, it's issued under the name "The Houserockers" with only Hound Dog's photo on the front! — *Cub Koda*

Freddie's Blues / 1993 / Wolf ✦✦✦

This is the third volume of live recordings from Joe's Place in Cambridge, MA in 1972. Six of the 11 tunes here are instrumentals (four of them featuring the lead guitar of Brewer Phillips), and while Taylor and the Houserockers are generally in rare form here, some chaotic moments ("Let's Get Funky") do abound, but that's half the fun and charm of it all. — *Cub Koda*

Live at Florence's / 1997 / JSP ✦✦✦

This is the first Hound Dog Taylor material to be released without the approval of Alligator or the Taylor estate and the first whose origins are totally suspect; in short, one step away from being a bootleg, making its non-appearance on compact disc no small mystery. The fidelity is strictly cheap tape recorder on a table by the bandstand quality; one can hear people walking in front of the single microphone, the signal is full of extra distortion and occasional dropouts, and the editing on this album is nothing short of truly annoying. But if—as the old adage goes—the play is the thing, then *this* is the Hound Dog Taylor and the Houserockers album to avidly track down, as the band is absolutely in their home turf element, rocking the house down to the bricks and then some. There are only two vocals among the ten selections here and that actually aids the listenability of the record, as Hound Dog's vocals on "Rock Me" and Elmore James' "I Held My Baby Last Night" are completely reduced to audio mush between the low grade microphone he's singing into and the lo-fi recording itself. But the instrumentals cover a wide area, indeed. Some, like "Comin' Round The Mountain," "Let's Get Funky," and "Goodnight Boogie" are simply superior in their original Alligator versions. But storming takes on "You Can't Sit Down," the mistitled (to grab publishing credit) "Stompin'"—actually "Howlin' For My Darling"—and "Juke Joint Boogie" tip the scales into making this a tough-to-find piece that's well worth any effort it takes to acquire a copy. Not the place to start, and certainly for completists only, but some of the best and nastiest Hound Dog you'll ever hear. — *Cub Koda*

Houserockin' Boogie / 1997 / JSP ✦✦✦

This second album of recordings from Florence's (Taylor and the Houserockers' regular Sunday afternoon everybody-can-sit-in gig) is just as crude and low fidelity as the first one. It also features the maddening (and disreputable) practice of retitling tunes so the record company can cop the publishing rights, a most odious business move. Future Houserocker Lefty Dizz is featured sitting in with the band (minus Taylor) on "Ships on the Ocean," although the credits do not list him at all. Probably the toughest to locate of all the semi-legal Hound Dog Taylor and although the perfect bookend companion to *Live At Florence's*, for diehard completists only who are willing to hunt it down. — *Cub Koda*

Jude Taylor

b. 1949, Grand Coteau, Louisiana
Vocals, Accordion / Zydeco

A zydeco performer in the blues-based tradition of Clifton Chenier, Creole singer and accordionist Jude Taylor was born in Grand Coteau, Louisiana in

1949. After growing up singing in church and school choirs, he later fronted a number of blues combos before turning to zydeco after receiving an accordion as a gift from his brother-in-law; assembling a backing band dubbed the Burning Flames which included his sons "Curly" on drums and Errol on rubboard, Taylor debuted in 1994 with the LP *The Best of Zydeco. Zydeco Bayou!* followed in 1997. — *Jason Ankeny*

- **The Best of Zydeco** / Dec. 14, 1994 / Mardis Gras ✦✦✦✦
The title of *The Best of Zydeco* makes it sound like a greatest-hits collection, but the record is actually Jude Taylor's debut effort. The accordionist has assembled a great band—including his sons Curly (drums) and Errol (rubboard)—and leads them through rollicking zydeco and steamy slow blues. Occasionally, he flirts with soul and blues, such as on a cover of Clarence Carter's "Strokin'," but Taylor is at his best when he sticks to classic zydeco sounds. The inclusion of these storming, party-oriented tracks is how *The Best of Zydeco* nearly lives up to its name. — *Thom Owens*

Zydeco Bayou / Jun. 3, 1997 / Mardis Gras ✦✦✦

Koko Taylor

b. Sep. 28, 1935, Memphis, TN
Vocals / R&B, Electric Chicago Blues, Modern Electric Chicago Blues, Classic Female Blues

She's the undisputed queen of Chicago blues. Has been for decades. And truthfully, no one has even mounted a serious challenge to Koko Taylor's magnificent reign in recent memory.

Born and raised on a Memphis farm, young Cora Walton was urged to sing gospel by her folks but found the blues she heard on B.B. King's local radio show too powerful to resist. Big Mama Thornton and Bessie Smith were influential to her developing singing style, but so were Muddy Waters and Howlin' Wolf.

Along with her future husband, Robert "Pops" Taylor, she moved to the Windy City at age 18 and found work cleaning houses in the suburbs. Meanwhile, she and Pops would make the South side scene, checking out her idols in person. Naturally, Taylor grabbed any chance to sit in that came her way.

In 1962, Willie Dixon caught Taylor's act and took over as her mentor. He produced her 1963 debut 45 for USA, "Honky Tonky," then got her signed to Chess. There she enjoyed one of the last legitimate Chicago blues hits with her rousing rendition of the Dixon-penned party classic "Wang Dang Doodle." It went all the way to number four on *Billboard*'s R&B charts in 1966. Dixon's role as writer/producer was a prominent one on Taylor's eponymous Chess debut LP, but none of her encores enjoyed the same success level as "Wang Dang Doodle" (still her enduring signature song).

After a dry spell, Taylor joined Bruce Iglauer's Alligator Records in 1975 (she was the fledgling firm's first female artist). Her Grammy-nominated Alligator album debut, *I Got What It Takes*, catapulted Koko Taylor back into the blues limelight, and six more sets for the label have kept her there. She's got a skin-tight band called the Blues Machine, a closet full of Handy Awards, a 1984 Grammy, and made a memorable singing cameo in director David Lynch's bizarre film *Wild at Heart*.

Koko Taylor's raspy growl is a beloved Chicago fixture, just like deep-dish pizza and Michael Jordan. A recent attempt to market a nightclub under her name didn't pan out for long, but that setback was momentary; the queen's regal reign continues. — *Bill Dahl*

Koko Taylor / 1969 / Chess ✦✦✦✦
Straight digital reissue of Taylor's debut Chess album from 1969. Produced by Willie Dixon (who can intermittently be heard as a duet partner), the set is one of the strongest representations of the belter's Chess days available, with her immortal smash "Wang Dang Doodle," the chunky "Twenty-Nine Ways," "I'm a Little Mixed Up," and "Don't Mess with the Messer." Top-flight session musicians on Taylor's 1965-1969 output included guitarists Buddy Guy, Matt Murphy, and Johnny Shines, and saxman Gene "Daddy G" Barge. — *Bill Dahl*

Basic Soul / 1972 / Chess ✦✦✦

South Side Lady / Dec. 1, 1973 / Evidence ✦✦✦
Cut during the period when she was between Chess and Alligator, this 15-song selection, cut in a French studio and live in the Netherlands in 1973, is a potent set that finds her ably backed by the Aces, guitarist Jimmy Rogers, and pianist Willie Mabon. Lots of familiar titles—a live "Wang Dang Doodle,"

studio remakes of "I'm a Little Mixed Up" and "Twenty-Nine Ways"—and a few numbers that aren't usually associated with Chicago's undisputed blues queen. — *Bill Dahl*

Southside Baby / 1975 / Black & Blue ✦✦✦
Taylor's first Alligator album is as tough and uncompromising as any she's done for the the the firm. — *Bill Dahl*

I Got What It Takes / 1975 / Alligator ✦✦✦✦
The queen's first album for Alligator, and still one of her very best to date. A tasty combo sparked by guitarists Mighty Joe Young and Sammy Lawhorn and saxist Abb Locke provide sharp support as the clear-voiced Taylor belts Bobby Saxton's "Trying to Make a Living," Magic Sam's "That's Why I'm Crying," her own "Honkey Tonkey" and "Voodoo Woman," and Ruth Brown's swinging "Mama, He Treats Your Daughter Mean." — *Bill Dahl*

Queen of the Blues / 1975 / Alligator ✦✦✦✦
Co-producer Bruce Iglauer anticipated a future trend by making this a set filled with cameos—but the presence of Lonnie Brooks, James Cotton, Albert Collins, and Son Seals is entirely warranted and the contributions of each work quite well in the context of the whole. Taylor's gritty "I Cried like a Baby" and a snazzy remake of Ann Peebles' "Come to Mama" are among the many highlights. — *Bill Dahl*

★ **What It Takes: The Chess Years** / 1977 / MCA/Chess ✦✦✦✦✦
With 18 tracks spanning 1964-1971, this compilation receives the nod over the shorter *Koko Taylor* (eight cuts double off anyway). Opening with her nails-tough "I Got What It Takes," the disc boasts "Wang Dang Doodle," several sides never before on album, and the strange previously unissued "Blue Prelude." Four 1971 tracks from Taylor's tough-to-find second Chess album, *Basic Soul*, are also aboard (including "Bills, Bills and More Bills" and her queenly version of "Let Me Love You Baby"). Producer Willie Dixon's guiding hand is apparent everywhere. — *Bill Dahl*

The Earthshaker / 1978 / Alligator ✦✦✦✦
Koko Taylor's Alligator encore harbored a number of tunes that still pepper her set list to this day—the grinding "I'm a Woman" and the party-down specials "Let the Good Times Roll" and "Hey Bartender." Her uncompromising slow blues "Please Don't Dog Me" and a sassy remake of Irma Thomas' "You Can Have My Husband" also stand out, as does the fine backing by guitarists Sammy Lawhorn and Johnny B. Moore, pianist Pinetop Perkins, and saxman Abb Locke. — *Bill Dahl*

From the Heart of a Woman / Jan. 1981 / Alligator ✦✦✦
Another very credible outing, though Taylor's not quite convincing on the jazzily swinging "Sure Had a Wonderful Time Last Night." Far more suited to her raspy growl are her own "It Took a Long Time," a funky "Something Strange Is Going On," and Etta James' moving soul ballad "I'd Rather Go Blind" (beautifully complemented by Criss Johnson's liquidic guitar). — *Bill Dahl*

An Audience with Koko Taylor / 1987 / Alligator ✦✦✦
Growling and lightly lacking in dynamics. — *Bill Dahl*

Live from Chicago / 1987 / Alligator ✦✦✦
Unfortunately, Koko Taylor's only domestic live album to date was cut with one of the lesser incarnations of her band, the Blues Machine, whose work could have displayed considerably more subtlety and swing than it does. Still, the set offers a vivid portrait of Chicago's blues queen in action, with faithful recitals of "Wang Dang Doodle," "I'm a Woman," and "Let the Good Times Roll." — *Bill Dahl*

Jump for Joy / 1990 / Alligator ✦✦✦
A slightly slicker Koko Taylor than we've generally been accustomed to, with nice horn arrangements by Gene Barge that farme the blues queen's growl effectively. A Taylor duet with Lonnie Brooks would normally be something to savor, but they're saddled here with an extremely corny "It's a Dirty Job" that's beneath both their statures. Taylor wrote four of that disc's best numbers herself, including "Can't Let Go" and the title cut. — *Bill Dahl*

Wang Dang Doodle / Jul. 1, 1991 / Huub ✦✦✦

Force of Nature / 1993 / Alligator ✦✦✦✦
A solid contemporary blues album that ranges from Taylor's own "Spellbound" and "Put the Pot On," a rendition of Toussaint McCall's tender soul lament "Nothing Takes the Place of You," and a saucy revival of the old Ike & Tina Turner R&B gem "If I Can't Be First." Gene Barge once again penned

the horn charts, Carey Bell contributes his usual harp mastery to Taylor's remake of Little Milton's "Mother Nature," and only Buddy Guy's over-the-top guitar histrionics on "Born Under a Bad Sign" grate. Long may the queen reign! — *Bill Dahl*

Little Johnny Taylor (Johnny Lamar Taylor)

b. Feb. 11, 1943, Memphis, TN
Vocals / Soul, Soul Blues, R&B, Modern Electric Blues, Chicago Blues, Jump Blues, Jazz Blues, Northern Soul
Some folks still get them mixed up, so let's get it straight from the outset. Little Johnny Taylor is best-known for his scorching slow blues smashes "Part Time Love" (for Bay Area-based Galaxy Records in 1963) and 1971's "Everybody Knows About My Good Thing" for Ronn Records in Shreveport, LA. He's definitely not the suave Sam Cooke protégé that blitzed the charts with "Who's Making Love" for Stax in 1968; that's Johnnie Taylor, who added to the confusion by covering "Part Time Love" for Stax.

Another similarity between the two Taylors: both hailed from strong gospel backgrounds. Little Johnny came to Los Angeles in 1950 and did a stint with the Mighty Clouds of Joy before going secular. Influenced by Little Willie John, he debuted as an R&B artist with a pair of 45s for Hunter Hancock's Swingin' logo, but his career didn't soar until he inked a pact with Fantasy's Galaxy subsidiary in 1963 (where he benefited from crisp production by Cliff Goldsmith and Ray Shanklin's arrangements).

The gliding mid-tempo blues "You'll Need Another Favor," firmly in a Bobby Bland mode, was Taylor's first chart item. He followed it up with the tortured R&B chart-topper "Part Time Love," which found him testifying in gospel-fired style over Arthur Wright's biting guitar and a grinding, horn-leavened downbeat groove. The singer also did fairly well with "Since I Found a New Love" in 1964 and "Zig Zag Lightning" in 1966.

Taylor's tenure at Stan Lewis' Ronn imprint elicited the slow blues smash "Everybody Knows About My Good Thing" in 1971 and a similar witty hit follow-up, "Open House at My House," the next year (both were covered later by Z.Z. Hill for Malaco). While at Ronn, Little Johnny cut some duets with yet another Taylor, this one named Ted (no, they weren't related either). He hasn't recorded much of late, but Little Johnny Taylor remains an active performer. — *Bill Dahl*

Part Time Love / 1962 / Galaxy ✦✦✦✦

Little Johnny Taylor [Galaxy] / 1963 / Galaxy ✦✦✦✦
Terrific brass, heavy charts by Roy Shanklin push Taylor's soulful pipes heavenward on this great LP that includes hit "Part Time Love." — *Bill Dahl*

Everybody Knows About My Good Thing / 1970 / Ronn ✦✦✦✦
A great simmering soul-blues album crying out for digital reincarnation. Two R&B hits— "It's My Fault Darling" and the ironic two-part title cut, later revived by Z.Z. Hill—share microgroove space with eight more solid efforts, supervised by Miles Grayson (who co-wrote a good deal of the album). — *Bill Dahl*

Open House / 1973 / Ronn ✦✦✦
Another hot mixture of blues and soul. — *Bill Dahl*

Super Taylors / 1974 / Ronn ✦✦✦
Now here'a a relic from Taylor's prolific early '70s Ronn tenure that is available on CD. Although they weren't related (except by label), the "Super Taylors" shared this album like long-lost brothers. Four duets find the two complementing one another most soulfully; otherwise, the album is comprised of solo sides by both (including Taylor's "Everybody Knows About My Good Thing"). — *Bill Dahl*

Little Johnny Taylor [Ronn] / 1979 / Ronn ✦✦✦

I Shoulda Been a Preacher / 1981 / Red Lightnin' ✦✦✦✦
Only his pastor knows that for sure, but this is one wailing collection. It contains the hottest gospel-tinged singles Little Johnny Taylor cut for Galaxy, and anyone turned off by the tepid material coming out for Ichiban should consult these before hopping off the bandwagon. — *Ron Wynn*

Stuck in the Mud / 1988 / Ichiban ✦✦✦

Ugly Man / 1989 / Ichiban ✦✦✦
Frankly, Taylor's voice isn't what it used to be, but this contemporary effort isn't without its merits. — *Bill Dahl*

● **Greatest Hits** / Fantasy ✦✦✦✦
The gospel-tinged and decidedly soul-inflected 1963-1968 blues sides of Little Johnny Taylor on Galaxy Records benefitted from marvelous horn-powered arrangements by Ray Shanklin that brilliantly pushed Taylor's melismatic vocals. Naturally, the impassioned "Part Time Love" is included, along with the Bobby Bland-tinged mid-tempo groover "You'll Need Another Favor," a delicious "Since I Found a New Love," and the blistering "You Win, I Lose." Seventeen tracks in all, many of them bolstered by Arthur Wright's stinging guitar. — *Bill Dahl*

Melvin Taylor

b. Mar. 13, 1959, Jackson, MS
Guitar / Modern Electric Blues, Modern Electric Chicago Blues
Taylor grew up hearing the songs of Muddy Waters and other bluesmen being played around the house. When he grew older, but was still too young to go to the clubs, he would hang around outside local blues bars, just listening and learning. As a teen, he joined the Transitors, an R&B-oriented teen quartet managed by the man who was to become his father-in-law. This band ended in the early '80s.

He was then invited by blues piano great Pinetop Perkins to join the Legendary Blues Band, which had been Muddy Waters' backup band. He was flattered, said yes, and they toured the West Coast and then Europe. His guitar playing so impressed the European audiences that Taylor has been invited back, year after year. He grew to love the European audiences and recorded two albums for the French label Isabel, *Blues on the Run* and *Plays the Blues for You*. These are now available on Evidence. He has also backed Lucky Peterson and Eddie Shaw in the recording studio.

When he wasn't in Europe, he played in the many remaining Chicago blues clubs (backing a variety of acts) and finally settled in Rosa's lounge in Chicago as his main venue. In recent years he has been influenced by jazz guitarists Kenny Burrell, Wes Montgomery, and George Benson and has integrated some of that great tradition into his playing. A fusion of blues and jazz guitar styles with some rock (Jimi Hendricks) thrown in, Taylor plays some funky direct blues with a lot of the wah-wah pedal and effects thrown in. — *Michael Erlewine*

● **Blues on the Run** / Apr. 1982 / Evidence ✦✦✦✦
Melvin Taylor may run a little long at times on his *Blues on the Run*, but that gives him the opportunity to dazzle with the full scope of his chops. He can play Chicago blues as gritty as anyone, but he can also rock hard and has enough sensitivity for jazz. Hearing him run through all these styles is a little dizzying, however, especially since he doesn't know when to let a little space into the music. Nevertheless, the record functions as an effective showcase for his talents. — *Thom Owens*

Melvin Taylor Plays the Blues for You / Mar. 21, 1984 / Isabel ✦✦✦✦
Guitarist Melvin Taylor's fluid, smartly constructed solos and understated yet winning vocals are surprises on this 1984 nine-track set recorded for Isabel and recently reissued by Evidence on CD. Taylor is not a fancy or arresting singer but succeeds through his simple, effective delivery of lyrics, slight inflections, and vocal nuances. His guitar work is impressive, with skittering riffs, shifting runs, and dashing solos. Organist/pianist Lucky Peterson is an excellent second soloist, adding cute background phrases at times, then stepping forward and challenging or buttressing Taylor's playing with his own dazzling lines. — *Ron Wynn*

Melvin Taylor & the Slack Band / Oct. 17, 1995 / Evidence ✦✦✦

Dirty Pool / Aug. 12, 1997 / Evidence ✦✦✦✦

Sam Taylor

Vocals, Guitar / New York Blues
Vocalist, guitarist, and songwriter Sam Taylor is the son of the late saxophonist Sam "the Man" Taylor. The younger Taylor didn't really grow up with his father, though, as Sam Sr. left the family to find a better career in New York. Taylor's family eventually moved to Brooklyn, and the young Sam was influenced by his mother, who also came from a performing background in vaudeville shows. He began singing in church at age five and later trained to become a boxer. He eventually fought as a pro boxer for 86 bouts and then found a more peaceful pursuit with his guitar. But through it all, he kept up his gospel singing and songwriting efforts.

Taylor has been recording since 1959. His discography and sessionography credits include Atlantic, Colpix, Capitol, Roulette, Stax, and Road Show Records. As a songwriter, he's written songs recorded by Sam and Dave, Elvis Presley, Freddie King, Jackie Wilson, Jimmy Witherspoon, Esther Phillips, Brook Benton, the Beach Boys, Maxine Brown, and Joey Dee and the Starlighters. As a guitarist and singer, he's accompanied the likes of Otis Redding, the Isley Brothers, Albert Collins, T-Bone Walker, Tracy Nelson and Mother Earth, Big Joe Turner and the Drifters.

Taylor recorded two albums for the Tucson-based Trope Records in 1995, *Desert Soul* and *Bluz Man*. On both his records for Trope, Taylor is accompanied by Heather "Lil Mama" Hardy on violin, Ed DeLucia on guitar, Mike Nordberg on bass, and Jerome Kimsey on drums. Taylor continues to tour regionally around the Southwest. Trope Records had plans to release two more recordings of Taylor's in 1996 or 1997. In the meantime, Taylor is a regular at B.B. King's in Los Angeles and remains active on the southern California and Southwest festival circuit. — *Richard Skelly*

Susan Tedeschi

b. Nov. 9, 1970
Guitar, Vocal / Modern Electric Blues
Guitarist, singer and songwriter Susan Tedeschi is part of the new generation of blues musicians looking for ways to keep the form exciting, vital, vital, evolving. Tedeschi's live shows are by no means straight-ahead urban blues. Instead, she freely mixes classic R&B, blues, and her own gospel and blues-flavored original songs into her sets. She's a young, sexy, sassy blues belter with musical sensibilities that belie her years.

Tedeschi began singing when she was four and was active in local choir and theater in Norwell, a southern suburb of Boston. She began singing at 13 with local bands and continued her music studies at Berklee, honing her guitar skills and also joining the Reverence Gospel Ensemble. She started the first incarnation of her blues band upon graduating in 1991, with vocalist/guitarist Adrienne Hayes, a fellow blues enthusiast whom she met at the House of Blues in Cambridge, MA. Bonnie Raitt, Janis Joplin, and Boston-area singer Toni Lynn Washington were Tedeschi's most important influences; in starting her band, in fact, she used Washington's backing band and hustled up gigs on nights when Washington and her band were not already booked. Since they began performing around Boston's fertile blues scene, Tedeschi and her band developed into a tightly knit, road-ready group, and have played several major blues festivals. Guitarist Sean Costello has since replaced original guitarist and co-vocalist Hayes, who left the group to pursue her own musical interests.

The Susan Tedeschi Band's first album, *Just Won't Burn*, was released on the Boston-based Tone-Cool Records in early 1998. The band for her debut on Tone-Cool includes guitarist Costello, bassist Jim Lamond and drummer Tom Hambridge; guitarist Hayes also contributes. *Just Won't Burn* is a powerful collection of originals, plus a sparkling cover of John Prine's "Angel From Montgomery," a tune often covered by vocalist Phoebe Snow. But Tedeschi and band also do justice to a tune Ruth Brown popularized, "Mama, He Treats Your Daughter Mean," and Junior Wells' "Little By Little." — *Richard J. Skelly*

Just Won't Burn / Feb. 10, 1998 / Tone-Cool ♦♦♦♦
Boston-area favorite Tedeschi makes a favorable impression with this, her debut disc. Susan plays a wicked, simplistic style of guitar and, coupled with a vocal style that embraces both Bonnie Raitt and Janis Joplin textures, writes some great little songs that frame both skills in sharp focus. Producer/drummer Tom Hambridge supplies songwriting retro ready-mades in the opener "Rock Me Right," the soul ballad "It Hurt So Bad" and co-writing with Tedeschi on the closing "Friar's Point," a down and dirty shuffle. Guest turns from Annie Raines on harmonica, Adrienne Hayes on guitar, Ian Kennedy on fiddle and Buck & Bird Taylor's backup vocals on Junior Wells' "Little By Little" keep the mix interesting. But the real star of the show here is Tedeschi, her vocals, her guitar and her songs, an impressive debut indeed. — *Cub Koda*

Johnny "Geechie" Temple

b. Oct. 18, 1906, Canton, MS, **d**. Nov. 22, 1968, Jackson, MS
Guitar, Vocals, Bass / Urban Blues, Delta Blues
Johnnie Temple is one of the great unsung heroes of the blues. A contemporary of Skip James, Son House, and other Delta legends, Temple was one of

the very first to develop the now-standard bottom-string boogie bass figure, generally credited to Robert Johnson.

Born and raised in Mississippi, Temple learned to play guitar and mandolin as a child. By the time he was a teenager, he was playing house parties and various other local events. Temple moved to Chicago in the early '30s, where he quickly became part of the town's blues scene. Often, he performed with Charlie and Joe McCoy. In 1935, Temple began his recording, releasing "Louise Louise Blues" the following year on Decca Records.

Although he never achieved stardom, Temple's records—which were released on a variety of record labels—sold consistently throughout the late '30s and '40s. In the '50s, his recording career stopped, but he continued to perform, frequently with Big Walter Horton and Billy Boy Arnold. Once electrified post-war blues overtook acoustic blues in the mid-'50s, Temple left Chicago and moved to Mississippi. After he returned to his home-state, he played clubs and juke joints around the Jackson area for a few years before he disappeared from the scene. Johnny Temple died in 1968. — *Cub Koda & Stephen Thomas Erlewine*

1935-1939 / 1935-1939 / Document ♦♦♦♦
A solid collection of Temple's earliest sides, including the killer "Lead Pencil Blues." — *Cub Koda*

● **Complete Recorded Works, Vol. 1** / 1994 / Document ♦♦♦♦
Temple's first recordings, beginning with the classic "Lead Pencil Blues" and three other songs (best of all, "Pig Boat Whistle") from his May 14, 1935 sessions for Vocalion. "Lead Pencil Blues" was the first known use on record of the "walking bass" (Temple called it "running bass") figure on the bottom string, which would become a blues commonplace in just a few years, popularized by Robert Johnson. Alas, these were also the most country-sounding records that Temple ever recorded—their lack of success convinced producers that Temple needed a more sophisticated sound, and all of his subsequent sessions, beginning 18 months later with "New Vicksburg Blues," feature a prominent piano sharing the spotlight with the guitar, and the latter instrument played by Charlie McCoy. It's all solid Chicago blues, "Louise Louise Blues," "Snapping Cat," and "So Lonely and So Blue" all being worth the price of the disc by themselves. Much of the later material, especially from the 1938 sessions backed by the Harlem Hamfats, is very smooth, commercial Chicago blues. Most of the sources are in better than decent condition, except for a very noisy "Beale Street Sheik," which can be forgiven as a previously unissued Vocalion side. — *Bruce Eder*

Complete Recorded Works, Vol. 2 / 1994 / Document ♦♦♦♦
Another 23 sides, covering the years 1938 through 1940. The sound on these records is much more jazz than blues, especially in the guitar and clarinet playing, and it sold, "Big Leg Woman" being a major hit and "Mississippi Woman's Blues" repeating the same melody. By the end of the decade, Temple would be working with Lonnie Johnson, one of the jazziest of blues guitarists, and jazz legend clarinetist Buster Bailey, and doing his most mainstream popular music, in terms of sound. The raunchiness of his material was still pronounced and delightful, however, from "Big Leg Woman" and "Grinding Mill" (another musical metaphor for impotence) to "Jelly Roll Bert" (featuring some delightful guitar/voice call-and-response work between Temple and axman Teddy Bunn), "Mississippi Woman's Blues," and "Better Not Let My Good Gal Catch You Here"—it's all surprisingly sophisticated, however, especially with the echo-y piano back-up, and more evocative of a Chicago club than any roadhouse. Temple's guitar playing may have lacked the jazz inflections that his recording manager was looking for, but his voice was one of the best in blues, alternately mournful and leering, with a surprising amount of power and expressiveness. — *Bruce Eder*

Complete Recorded Works, Vol. 3 / May 1, 1995 / Document ♦♦♦

Ten Years After

f. 1967, Nottingham, England, **db.** 1975
Group / Blues-Rock, Electric British Blues
Ten Years After is a British blues-rock quartet consisting of Alvin Lee (born Dec 19, 1944), guitar and vocals; Chick Churchill (born Jan 2, 1949), keyboards; Leo Lyons (born Nov 30, 1944) bass; and Ric Lee (born Oct 20, 1945), drums. The group was formed in 1967 and signed to Decca in England. Its first album was not a success, but its second, the live *Undead* (1968) containing "I'm Going Home," a six-minute blues workout by the fleet-fingered

Alvin hit the charts on both sides of the Atlantic. *Stonedhenge* (1969) hit the UK Top Ten in early 1969. Ten Years After's US breakthrough came as a result of its appearance at Woodstock, at which it played a nine-minute version of "I'm Going Home." Its next album, *Ssssh*, reached the US Top 20, and *Cricklewood Green*, containing the hit single "Love Like a Man," reached No. 14. *Watt* completed the group's Decca contract, after which it signed with Columbia and moved in a more mainstream pop direction, typified by the gold-selling 1971 album *A Space in Time* and its Top 40 single "I'd Love to Change the World." Subsequent efforts in that direction were less successful, however, and Ten Years After split up after the release of *Positive Vibrations* in 1974. They reunited in 1988 for concerts in Europe and recorded their first new album in 15 years, *About Time*, in 1989. — *William Ruhlmann*

Undead / 1968 / Deram ✦✦✦✦
Recorded live in a small London club, *Undead* contains the original "I'm Going Home," the song which brought Ten Years After its first blush of popularity following the Woodstock festival and film in which it was featured. However, the real strength of this album is side one, which contains two extended jazz jams, "I May Be Wrong but I Won't Be Wrong Always" and Woody Herman's "Woodchopper's Ball," both of which spotlight guitarist Alvin Lee's amazing speed and technique. Side two is less interesting, with an extended slow blues typical of the time, a drum solo feature, and the rock 'n' roll rave-up of "I'm Going Home." — *Jim Newsom*

Ssssh / 1969 / Beat Goes On ✦✦✦✦
This was Ten Years After's new release at the time of their incendiary performance at the Woodstock Festival in August, 1969. As a result, it was their first hit album in the US, peaking at No. 20 in September of that year. This recording is a primer of British blues-rock of the era, showcasing Alvin Lee's guitar pyrotechnics and the band's propulsive rhythm section. As with most of TYA's work, the lyrics were throwaways, but the music was hot. Featured is a lengthy cover of Sonny Boy Williamson's "Good Morning Little Schoolgirl," with reworked lyrics leaving little doubt what the singer had in mind for the title character. Also included was a twelve-bar blues song with the ultimate generic blues title, "I Woke Up This Morning." *Ssssh* marked the beginning of the band's two-year run of popularity on the US album charts and in the "underground" FM-radio scene. — *Jim Newsom*

● **Cricklewood Green** / Apr. 1970 / Chrysalis ✦✦✦✦
Cricklewood Green provides the best example of Ten Years After's recorded sound. On this album, the band and engineer Andy Johns mix studio tricks and sound effects, blues-based song structures, a driving rhythm section, and Alvin Lee's signature lightning-fast guitar licks into a unified album that flows nicely from start to finish. *Cricklewood Green* opens with a pair of bluesy rockers, with "Working on the Road" propelled by a guitar and organ riff that holds the listener's attention through the use of tape manipulation as the song develops. "50,000 Miles Beneath My Brain" and "Love Like a Man" are classics of TYA's jam genre, with lyrically meaningless verses setting up extended guitar workouts that build in intensity, rhythmically and sonically. The latter was an FM-radio staple in the early '70s. "Year 3000 Blues" is a country romp sprinkled with Lee's silly sci-fi lyrics, while "Me and My Baby" concisely showcases the band's jazz licks better than any other TYA studio track, and features a tasty piano solo by Chick Churchill. It has a feel similar to the extended pieces on side one of the live album, *Undead*. "Circles" is a hippie-ish acoustic guitar piece, while "As the Sun Still Burns Away" closes the album by building on another classic guitar-organ riff and more sci-fi sound effects. — *Jim Newsom*

Watt / Dec. 1970 / Chrysalis ✦✦✦✦
Watt had many of the same ingredients as its predecessor, *Cricklewood Green*, but wasn't nearly as well thought out. The band had obviously spent much time on the road, leaving little time for developing new material. Consequently, a cover of Chuck Berry's "Sweet Little Sixteen," recorded live at the Isle of Wight Festival, is included here, as is a short instrumental with the uninspired title "The Band With No Name." Other song titles like "I Say Yeah" and "My Baby Left Me" betray the lack of spark in Alvin Lee's songwriting. Nonetheless, his guitar work is fast and clean (though the licks are beginning to sound repetitive from album to album), and the band continues to cook in the manner exemplified best on *Cricklewood Green*. — *Jim Newsom*

A Space in Time / 1971 / Chrysalis ✦✦✦✦
A Space in Time was Ten Years After's best-selling album. This was due primarily to the strength of "I'd Love to Change the World," the band's only hit single, and one of the most ubiquitous AM and FM radio cuts of the summer of 1971. TYA's first album for Columbia, *A Space in Time* has more of a pop-oriented feel than any of their previous releases had. The individual cuts are shorter, and Alvin Lee displays a broader instrumental palette than before. In fact, six of the disc's ten songs are built around acoustic guitar riffs. However, there are still a couple of barn-burning jams. The leadoff track, "One of These Days," is a particularly scorching workout, featuring extended harmonica and guitar solos. After the opener, however, the album settles back into a more relaxed mood than one would have expected from Ten Years After. Many of the cuts make effective use of dynamic shifts, and the guitar solos are generally more understated than on previous outings. The production on *A Space in Time* is crisp and clean, a sound quite different from the denseness of its predecessors. Though not as consistent as *Cricklewood Green*, *A Space in Time* has its share of sparkling moments. — *Jim Newsom*

Alvin Lee & Company / 1972 / Deram ✦✦
After Ten Years After found commercial success with a new record label, Columbia, and the hit single "I'd Love to Change the World," the band's former label released this collection of outtakes from earlier recording sessions. One listen shows why these tracks were not included on album releases at the time of their recording. — *Jim Newsom*

Rock & Roll Music to the World / 1972 / Chrysalis ✦✦✦

Recorded Live / 1973 / Chrysalis ✦✦✦

Positive Vibrations / 1974 / Chrysalis ✦
There's not much happening here. By the time *Positive Vibrations* was released, Ten Years After had run out of gas. Leader Alvin Lee had already released two solo albums, "On the Road to Freedom" and "In Flight," and the band was simply going through the motions on this album. The band broke up following its release. — *Jim Newsom*

Greatest Hits / 1977 / Deram ✦✦✦✦
The group's 1968-1970 best, including the hit "Love like a Man" and the Woodstock version of "I'm Going Home." — *William Ruhlmann*

● **Essential** / 1991 / Chrysalis ✦✦✦✦
While it doesn't include all of their prime material, *Essential* features enough of their best songs to make it a fine introduction. — *AMG*

Ssssh/Cricklewood Green / Feb. 25, 1997 / Mobile Fidelity ✦✦✦✦
Mobile Fidelity reissued two of Ten Years After's best albums, 1969's *Ssssh* and 1970's *Cricklewood Green*, on one gold disc in 1997. These records are among the group's best and this is a good way to acquire them, but fans should know that this disc costs more than buying the two records separately. For audiophiles, this won't be a problem, since the remastered tapes will be worth the extra money, but less dedicated fans should be aware of the steep retail price of this disc. — *Stephen Thomas Erlewine*

Sonny Terry & Brownie McGhee

b. Oct. 24, 1911, Greensboro, GA, **d.** Mar. 11, 1986, Mineola, NY
Harmonica, Vocals / Country Blues, Piedmont Blues, Acoustic Blues, Electric Blues, Folk-Blues
The joyous whoop that Sonny Terry naturally emitted between raucous harp blasts was as distinctive a signature sound as can possibly be imagined. Only a handful of blues harmonicists wielded as much of a lasting influence on the genre as did the sightless Terry (Buster Brown, for one, copied the whoop and all), who recorded some fine urban blues as a bandleader in addition to serving as guitarist Brownie McGhee's longtime duet partner.

Saunders Terrell's father was a folk-styled harmonica player who performed locally at dances, but blues wasn't part of his repertoire (he blew reels and jigs). Terry wasn't born blind—he lost sight in one eye when he was five, the other at age 18. That left him with extremely limited options for making any sort of feasible living, so he took to the streets armed with his trusty harmonicas. Terry soon joined forces with Piedmont blues pioneer Blind Boy Fuller, first recording with the guitarist in 1937 for Vocalion.

Terry's unique talents were given an extremely classy airing in 1938 when he was invited to perform at New York's Carnegie Hall at the fabled From Spirituals to Swing concert. He recorded for the Library of Congress that same year and cut his first commercial sides in 1940. Terry had met McGhee in 1939, and upon the death of Fuller, they joined forces, playing together on a 1941 McGhee date for OKeh and settling in New York as a duo in 1942. There they broke into the folk scene, working alongside Lead Belly, Josh White, and Woody Guthrie.

While Brownie McGhee was incredibly prolific in the studio during the mid-'40s, Terry was somewhat less so as a leader (perhaps most of his time was occupied by his prominent role in *Finian's Rainbow* on Broadway for approximately two years beginning in 1946). There were sides for Asch and Savoy in 1944 before three fine sessions for Capitol in 1947 (the first two featuring Stick McGhee rather than Brownie on guitar) and another in 1950.

Terry made some nice sides in an R&B mode for Jax, Jackson, Red Robin, RCA Victor, Groove, Harlem, Old Town, and Ember during the '50s, usually with Brownie close by on guitar. But it was the folk boom of the late '50s and early '60s that made Brownie and Sonny household names (at least among folk aficionados). They toured long and hard as a duo, cutting a horde of endearing acoustic duet LPs along the way, before scuttling their decades-long partnership amidst a fair amount of reported acrimony during the mid-'70s. — *Bill Dahl*

★ **The Folkways Years, 1944-1963** / 1944-1963 / Smithsonian/Folkways ✦✦✦✦✦

Terry embodied country-blues harmonica whoops and train/hound imitations. The best of his Folkways performances are truly stunning. — *Mark A. Humphrey*

Sing / 1958 / Smithsonian/Folkways ✦✦✦✦

Sonny's Story / 1960 / Original Blues Classics ✦✦✦

Sonny's Story is an excellent showcase for Sonny Terry's talents, which sometimes went unheralded because they largely were showcased in the shadow of Brownie McGhee. Here, Terry is largely playing solo acoustic, with J.C. Burris joining in for harmonica duets every so often; Sticks McGhee and drummer Belton Evans also play on a few cuts. Unlike some solo acoustic blues albums, *Sonny's Story* is positively infectious. It's hard not to get caught up in Terry's shouts and boogies, and that's one major reason why this is among his best solo recordings. — *Thom Owens*

Just a Closer Walk with Thee / Nov. 1960 / Fantasy ✦✦✦

Just a Closer Walk with Thee is a live album Sonny Terry and Brownie McGhee recorded in 1957. What distinguishes this from their other live records is that it contains nothing but religious songs. In actuality, it isn't that different from their other recordings, since all the music is performed in a country-blues style, similar to the work of Rev. Gary Davis (whose "Get Right Church" is covered here). Nevertheless, it's nice to hear Sonny & Terry tackle this material, and it makes for a small, forgotten gem in their catalog. — *Thom Owens*

Sonny & Brownie at Sugar Hill / Dec. 1961 / Original Blues Classics ✦✦✦

Sonny & Brownie at Sugar Hill is a live album recorded at the famous San Franciscan nightclub. Both musicans were in fine form, with each getting a chance to sing some of their standards, including "Sweet Woman Blues," "Born to Live the Blues," "Baby, I Knocked on Your Door," and "I Got a Little Girl." Their interplay is always a joy to hear, and while there are some better live shows available, this is thoroughly entertaining and worth the time of any of their fans. — *Thom Owens*

Sonny Is King / 1963 / Bluesville ✦✦✦

Half of *Sonny Is King* is devoted to a rare session between Sonny Terry and Lightnin' Hopkins. The two guitarists are supported by bassist Leonard Gaskin and drummer Belton Evans, but the rhythm section fails to kick the pair into overdrive, and much of the music disappointingly meanders. Sometimes change is not a good thing. That's proven by the second side of the album, where Terry falls into the comfortable setting of duetting with Brownie McGhee. While these aren't among the duo's very best recordings, they are nonetheless enjoyable, suggesting that there's something to be said for the familiar. — *Thom Owens*

Live at the 2nd Fret / 1963 / Prestige ✦✦✦✦

Guitar Highway / 1963 / Verve ✦✦✦

Hometown Blues / 1969 / Ace ✦✦✦✦

Early-'50s sides catch this prolific duo at their best. — *Bill Dahl*

Whoopin' / 1984 / Alligator ✦✦✦

The textbook charge usually levelled against Alligator sessions are that they're sanitized. You couldn't lodge that one against this set with a straight face; if anything, somebody turned Sonny Terry loose. It didn't hurt that Johnny Winter was around on guitar and piano, playing gritty blues with a passion. It didn't help that Terry didn't put any amplified muscle behind his harmonica, however. Otherwise, this is a strong session. — *Ron Wynn*

Sonny Terry [Collectables] / 1987 / Collectables ✦✦✦✦

Harmonica player and vocalist Sonny Terry cut some stunning material for Gotham in the early '50s. Some of it was issued, and much of it wasn't. This is a healthy chunk of things that were and weren't released, with good remastering embellishing Terry's cutting vocals and splintering harmonica. — *Ron Wynn*

California Blues / 1990 / Fantasy ✦✦✦

Po' Boys / 1994 / Drive Archive ✦✦✦

McGhee and Terry in their folkie mode again, most of the ten selections stemming from a 1960 LP for Vee-Jay. One of their anthems, "Walk On," receives a spirited reading, as do "Down by the Riverside" and "Trouble in Mind." — *Bill Dahl*

Sonny Terry [Capitol] / 1995 / Capitol ✦✦✦✦

Some of the whooping harmonicist's finest stuff as a bandleader, dating from his 1947-1950 Capitol Records tenure. Brownie McGhee handles the guitar on two sessions, his brother Stick on the other two, but Terry is front and center on all. Contains all 16 numbers Terry did for the major label, notably "Whoopin' the Blues," "Custard Pie Blues," and "Beer Garden Blues." — *Bill Dahl*

Whoopin' the Blues: the Capitol Recordings, 1947-1950 / Oct. 1995 / Capitol ✦✦✦

Complete Recorded Works, Vol. 1 / Jan. 10, 1996 / Document ✦✦✦✦

Blowin' the Fuses / Apr. 1996 / Rykodisc ✦✦✦

Jimmy Thackery

b. May 19, 1953, Pittsburgh, PA
Guitar, Vocals / Modern Electric Blues

Singer, songwriter and guitar virtuoso Jimmy Thackery has carved an enviable niche for himself in the world of electric blues. Known for his gritty, blue-collar approach and marathon live shows, Thackery was for many years part of the Nighthawks, one of the hardest-working blues bar bands in North America; since the late '80s, he has been touring and recording under his own name, and has found widespread acceptance on the festival circuit. His hard-edged, tough-as-nails approach to guitar playing and his trio's driving rhythm section holds appeal for fans of both the straight-ahead blues of Muddy Waters and the roots-rock of Bruce Springsteen and Joe Grushecky. Like the Nighthawks and Grushecky's Houserockers, much of the material Thackery performs can safely be called blues or blues-rock. Hardcore blues like "It's My Own Fault" and popular blues-rock chestnuts like "Red House" from Jimi Hendrix are fair game for Thackery and his Drivers, who include Michael Patrick on bass and Mark Stutso on drums and vocals.

Born in Pittsburgh, Thackery was raised in Washington, D.C. In high school, he played in a band with Bonnie Raitt's brother, David, who exposed him to the music of Buddy Guy; Thackery saw both Guy and Jimi Hendrix perform in Washington, D.C. Thackery joined the Nighthawks in 1974, after being introduced to harmonica man Mark Wenner by fellow guitarist Bobby Radcliff, who was then based in D.C. Thackery recorded more than 20 albums with the Nighthawks and toured the U.S., Canada, Europe and Japan. He left the band in 1987 and struck out on his own, needing a break from the Nighthawks' 300-nights-a-year tour schedule.

He formed a new band, Jimmy Thackery and the Assassins, and toured the East Coast heavily with that band until they split up in 1991. Since then Thackery has been leading a trio, Jimmy Thackery and the Drivers, and quickly forged a name for himself on the blues festival and club circuit through a prolific recording pace and a lot of roadwork. His albums for the San Francisco-based Blind Pig label include *Empty Arms Motel* (1992), *Sideways In Paradise, Jimmy Thackery* and *John Mooney* (all 1993), *Trouble Man* (1994), *Wild Night Out* (1995), *Drive to Survive* (1996), and *Switching Gears* (1998). His 1998 album includes guest performances by Joe Louis Walker, Lonnie Brooks, Chubby Carrier and Francine Reed, but any of Thackery's albums will delight fans of tough, heavy, driving guitar playing. For a taste of his thorough mastery of several styles, *Drive to Survive* touches on rockabilly, jazz, bebop, and surf music. Most of Thackery's albums include at least a few covers mixed in with his batch of self-penned songs. —*Richard J. Skelly*

● **Empty Arms Motel** / 1992 / Blind Pig ✦✦✦✦
Not a prolific composer, Thackery's strength lies in strong arrangements that make other people's material his own. He covers Stevie Ray Vaghan's "Rude Mood," and one suspects there will be comparisons made in this direction. His solos burn the motel down on Luther Johnson's "Lickin' Gravy," and he manages a more than credible job on Hendrix's "Red House."Of the two self-penned numbers, the title track is a convincing boogie driven by an ultra-cool, echoed, chicken-scratch guitar riff, while "Getting Tired of Waiting" offers a more traditional blues shuffle. —*Roch Parisien*

Sideways in Paradise / 1993 / Blind Pig ✦✦✦
A collection of acoustic delights recorded by Jimmy Thackery and John Mooney in 1985. Vintage blues and ragtime played by a pool in Jamaica. Guitars, mandocello, mandolins and guttural vocals are backed by native tree frogs (which sound a lot like crickets). —*Roch Parisien*

Trouble Man / 1994 / Blind Pig ✦✦✦✦

Wild Night Out! / 1995 / Blind Pig ✦✦✦

Drive to Survive / 1996 / Blind Pig ✦✦✦

Switching Gears / Jan. 2, 1998 / Blind Pig ✦✦✦
Thackery's sixth album for Blind Pig (counting his acoustic duo album with John Mooney, *Sideways In Paradise*) finds him bringing high-profile guests to the party this time around. Lonnie Brooks guests on a stretched-out version of B.B. King's "It's My Own Fault," while Chubby Carrier brings his accordion and much Louisiana swamp feel to "Take Me With You When You Go." Joe Louis Walker guests on one of his tunes, "If This Is Love," and vocalist Reba Russell, keyboardist Al Gamble, and saxophonist Joe McGlohon all contribute to other tracks, taking the sound away from Thackery's usual blues-rock power trio format. —*Cub Koda*

Sister Rosetta Tharpe

b. Mar. 20, 1921, Cotton Plant, AR, **d.** Oct. 9, 1973, Philadelphia, PA
Vocals, Guitar / Black Gospel, Jump Blues, Classic Female Blues
Alongside Willie Mae Ford Smith, Sister Rosetta Tharpe is widely acclaimed among the greatest Sanctified gospel singers of her generation; a flamboyant performer whose music often flirted with the blues and swing, she was also one of the most controversial talents of her day, shocking purists with her leap into the secular market—by playing nightclubs and theatres, she not only pushed spiritual music into the mainstream, but in the process also helped pioneer the rise of pop-gospel. Tharpe was born March 20, 1921 in Cotton Plant, Arkansas; the daughter of Katie Bell Nubin, a traveling missionary and shouter in the classic gospel tradition known throughout the circuit as "Mother Bell," she was a prodigy, mastering the guitar by the age of six. At the same time she attended Holiness conventions alongside her mother, performing renditions of songs including "The Day Is Past and Gone" and "I Looked Down the Line."

In time the family relocated to Chicago, where Tharpe began honing her unique style; blessed with a resonant vibrato, both her vocal phrasing and guitar style drew heavy inspiration from the blues, and she further aligned herself with the secular world with a sense of showmanship and glamour unique among the gospel performers of her era. Signing to Decca in 1938, Tharpe became a virtual overnight sensation; her first records, among them Thomas A. Dorsey's "Rock Me" and "This Train," were smash hits, and quickly she was performing in the company of mainstream superstars including Cab Calloway and Benny Goodman. She led an almost schizophrenic existence, remaining in the good graces of her core audience by recording material like "Precious Lord," "Beams of Heaven" and "End of My Journey" while also appealing to her growing white audience by performing rearranged, up-tempo spirituals including "Didn't It Rain" and "Down by the Riverside."

During World War II, Tharpe was so popular that she was one of only two black gospel acts—the Golden Gate Quartet being the other—to record V-Discs for American soldiers overseas; she also toured the nation in the company of the Dixie Hummingbirds, among others. In 1944, she began recording with boogie-woogie pianist Sammy Price; their first collaboration, "Strange Things Happening Every Day," even cracked *Billboard*'s race records Top Ten, a rare feat for a gospel act and one which she repeated several more times during the course of her career. In 1946 she teamed with the

Newark-based Sanctified shouter Madame Marie Knight, whose simple, un-affected vocals made her the perfect counterpoint for Tharpe's theatrics; the duo's first single, "Up Above My Head," was a huge hit, and over the next few years they played to tremendous crowds across the church circuit.

However, in the early '50s Tharpe and Knight cut a handful of straight blues sides; their fans were outraged, and although Knight soon made a permanent leap into secular music—to little success—Tharpe remained first and foremost a gospel artist, although her credibility and popularity were seriously damaged. Not only did her record sales drop off and her live engagements become fewer and farther between, but many purists took Tharpe's foray into the mainstream as a personal affront; the situation did not improve, and she spent over a year touring clubs in Europe, waiting for the controversy to die down. Tharpe's comeback was slow but steady, and by 1960 she had returned far enough into the audience's good graces to appear at the Apollo Theatre alongside the Caravans and James Clevleland. While not a household name like before, she continued touring even after suffering a major stroke in 1970, dying in Philadelphia on October 9, 1973. —*Jason Ankeny*

Gospel 1938-1943 / 1938-1943 / Frémeaux & Associés ✦✦✦✦
Ironically, singer/guitarist Sister Rosetta Tharpe's twin gospel and blues career stunted both, and the fact that she was a woman singing solo in an era of male quartets didn't help. But she was one of the finest of all solo gospel singers and a highly individual one. These stunning, mostly acoustic, performances are pinnacles of the African-American religious tradition. —*John Storm Roberts, Original Music*

● **Sacred & Secular** / 1941-1969 / Rosetta ✦✦✦✦
Sacred & Secular is a wonderful collection of 16 tracks Sister Rosetta Tharpe recorded between 1941 and 1969. Although Tharpe recorded both sacred and secular material, as this title indicates, this collection favors religious music. All of the music here features her supported by a band, ranging from by an orchestra conducted by Leroy Kirkland to small combos led by Lucky Millinder and Sam Price. While many critics and fans prefer Tharpe's solo performances (only one solo performance, a live cut from 1969, is present), these group sessions offer ample proof that Tharpe is compelling in nearly any setting. —*Thom Owens*

Sister Rosetta Tharpe/The Sam Price Trio / 1958 / Decca ✦✦✦✦
Fine singing and excellent blues-laden guitar playing; circa 1944-49. —*Opal Louis Nations*

Live in 1960 / 1960 / Southland ✦✦✦
Sister Rosetta Tharpe was a talented jazz guitarist and vocalist who, although she spent most of her later years finding fame as a gospel singer, never turned her back on her jazz roots. On this 1991 CD taken from a previously unreleased European concert, Tharpe is heard solo, entertaining and uplifting the audience. Although there are a few more ballads than usual, the set has plenty of variety, lots of sincere feeling, and high levels of musicianship from the unique performer. Highlights include "He's Got the Whole World In His Hands," "Didn't It Rain," "The Gospel Train," and "Down By the Riverside." —*Scott Yanow*

Gospel Train, Vol. 2 / 1960 / Lection ✦✦✦
This was recorded later than the material on *Volume 1*, some of Sister Rosetta's worst, most-overproduced recordings. —*Opal Louis Nations*

Live in Paris: 1964 / 1964 / French Concerts ✦✦✦
A nice, rather folk-like concert performance in front of an enthusiastic audience. —*Kip Lornell*

Live at the Hot Club de France / 1966 / Milan ✦✦✦
Live at the Hot Club de France was recorded in 1966. At first, Sister Rosetta Tharpe seems a little uneasy in front of the French audience, but she soon loosens up, tearing through a set of spiritual standards (plus a handful of originals). There isn't much guitar on the record, but Tharpe's impassioned voice makes this a concert worth hearing. —*Thom Owens*

Gospel Train / 1989 / Polygram ✦✦✦✦
Super collection of the gal's best Mercury sides; circa 1956. —*Opal Louis Nations*

Sincerely, Sister Rosetta Tharpe / 1992 / Rosetta ✦✦✦
Boasting such classic numbers as "Down by the Riverside," "Swing Low Sweet Chariot," and "Sometimes I Feel Like a Motherless Child," *Sincerely,*

Sister Rosetta Tharpe is a collection of material the seminal gospel singer recorded in the '40s. Although it's not comprehensive, it's one of the best samplings of its kind in existence. — *Thom Owens*

Complete Recorded Works, Vol. 1 (1938-41) / Feb. 20, 1996 / Document ✦✦✦
Her first sides, sacred and secular, with and without Lucky Millinder. Some soundtracks. — *Opal Louis Nations*

Complete Recorded Works, Vol. 2 (1942-1944) / Feb. 20, 1996 / Document ✦✦✦
For completists, specialists and academics, Document's *Complete Recorded Works, Vol. 2 (1942-1944)* is an invaluable overview of Sister Rosetta Tharpe's early recordings. For less dedicated listeners, the disc is a mixed blessing. The disc features a long running time, exacting chronological sequencing, and poor fidelity (all cuts are transferred from original acetates and 78s). While the serious blues listener will find all these factors to be positive, enthusiasts and casual listeners will find that the collection is of marginal interest for those very reasons. — *Thom Owens*

Hans Theessink

b. Apr. 5, 1948, Enschede, Netherlands
Guitar, Harmonica, Jew's-Harp, Mandolin, Violin / Modern Electric Blues
Dutch blues guitarist, singer, and songwriter Hans Theessink has been carving a niche for himself in the US market through the late '80s and early '90s. It's no easy task growing up in the Netherlands and teaching oneself the blues, but perhaps that's the reason Theessink's guitar stylings are so unique. Theessink became hooked on blues as a teenager listening to the radio, playing mandolin and guitar. His favorites became Big Bill Broonzy, Sonny Terry, and Brownie McGhee, but later on he was exposed to a wider variety of influences. Theessink was 12 or 13 when he began playing guitar in earnest, and by his late teens he was playing in clubs and coffeehouses around Germany and the Netherlands.

Theessink began his recording career in 1970 for a variety of small labels in Netherlands and Germany, and continued perfecting his craft and honing his skills at clubs and festivals across Europe. Through the 1970s, his eventual goal was to come to America to learn firsthand from the masters in the Mississippi Delta. It would be 1979 before Theessink would make it to America, and not surprisingly, his first stop was the Mississippi Delta. The trip proved fruitful, as he met and jammed with many Delta musicians, absorbing all he could from them and eventually incorporating their knowledge into his own style.

Theessink's US albums include two albums for Flying Fish/Rounder Records, *Baby Wants to Boogie* (1987) and *Johnny and the Devil* (1989). More recently, his other domestically available albums for a variety of labels include *Call Me* (1992), *Hans Theessink and Blue Groove: Live* (1993), *Hard Road Blues* (1995), and *Crazy Moon* (1997). — *Richard Skelly*

Next Morning at Sunrise / 1970 / Autogram ✦✦✦✦

Klasselotteriet / 1976 / Rillerod ✦✦✦

Slow and Easy / 1978 / Blue Bird ✦✦✦

Late Last Night / 1980 / Kettle ✦✦✦

Antoon Met 'N Bok / 1981 / Jama ✦✦✦

Cushioned for a Soft Ride Inside / 1982 / Autogram ✦✦✦

Titanic / 1983 / Extraplatte ✦✦✦

All Night Long / 1986 / Extraplatte ✦✦✦

● **Baby Wants to Boogie** / 1987 / Flying Fish ✦✦✦✦
Hans Theessink often gets the short end of the stick because he's a Dutch bluesman, which means he couldn't possibly be "legitimate" in the eyes of some critics. That's not really fair, since he's actually an imaginative, unpredictable guitarist. Granted, his albums can sound a little sterile, but that criticism can be applied to most contemporary blues albums. The main problem with his records is that they're interchangeable—all of them sound similar and all of them are about as strong as their predecessor. *Baby Wants to Boogie* isn't particularly different from his other albums, but it does have some good songs and solos, making it as good a place to learn about Theessink as any. — *Thom Owens*

Johnny and the Devil / 1989 / Blue Groove ✦✦✦

Johnny & the Devil / 1989 / Flying Fish ✦✦

Call Me / 1992 / Deluge ✦✦✦

Live / 1993 / Minor Music ✦✦✦✦

Hard Road Blues / May 23, 1995 / Minor Music ✦✦✦✦

Crazy Moon / May 27, 1997 / RFR ✦✦✦

Them

f. 1964, Belfast, Northern Ireland, **db.** 1971
Group / British Invasion, Rock 'n' Roll, British Blues
Not strictly a British group, but packaged as part of the British Invasion, Them forged their hard-nosed R&B sound in Belfast, Ireland, moving to England in 1964 after landing a deal with Decca Records. The band's simmering sound was dominated by boiling organ riffs, lean guitars, and the tough vocals of lead singer Van Morrison, whose recordings with Them rank among the very best performances of the British Invasion. Morrison also wrote top-notch original material for the outfit, whose lineup changed numerous times over the course of their brief existence. As a hit-making act, their résumé was brief—"Here Comes the Night" and "Baby Please Don't Go" were Top Ten hits in England, "Mystic Eyes" and "Here Comes the Night" made the Top 40 in the US—but their influence was considerable, reaching bands like the Doors, who Them played with during a residency in Los Angeles just before Van Morrison quit the band in 1966. Their most influential song of all, the classic three-chord stormer "Gloria," was actually a B-side, although the Shadows of Knight had a hit in the US with a faithful, tamer cover version.

Morrison has recalled his days with Them with some bitterness, noting that the heart of the original group was torn out by image-conscious record company politics, and that session men (including Jimmy Page, who played a scorching solo on "Baby Please Don't Go") often replaced members on recordings. That may be, but whether the records are faithful to the original Them sound or not, they were usually great—in addition to hits, Them released a couple fine albums and several flop singles that mixed fine Morrison compositions with hot R&B and soul covers, as well as a few songs written for them by producers like Bert Berns (who penned "Here Comes the Night"). After Morrison left the group, Them splintered into the Belfast Gypsies, who released a decent album that (except for the vocals) approximated Them's early records, and a psychedelic outfit that kept the name Them, releasing four fairly weak LPs with little resemblance to the tough sounds of their mid-'60s heyday. — *Richie Unterberger*

Them [CD] / 1965 / Decca ✦✦✦✦
The debut album by the group, also known as *The Angry Young Them*, and half its tracks make it a dead-on rival to the Stones' debut album. This reissue features the album's original British configuration ("Just a Little Bit," "I Gave My Love a Diamond," "Bright Lights, Big City," and "My Little Baby" are here, "One Two Brown Eyes" and "Here Comes the Night" are absent); "My Little Baby" was no huge loss, being a pale imitation of "Here Comes the Night," but the omitted "Just a Little Bit" features a Howlin' Wolf/"Spoonful"-style performance by Van Morrison that would have incinerated a lot of American teens. On the other hand, Morrison's soul-shouting performance on the deleted "I Gave My Love a Diamond," appropriated by Bert Berns from the public domain "Cherry Song," would have shocked any folkie familiar with the original. Morrison's "You Just Can't Win" isn't nearly as impressive, but even as a time-filler it isn't half bad. And then there's "Gloria," rock's ultimate '60s sex anthem, and one of the handful of white-authored songs that can just about hold its own against any blues standard you'd care to name. — *Bruce Eder*

Them Again [Decca] / Apr. 1966 / Decca ✦✦✦
The group's second and, for all intents and purposes, last full album was recorded while Them was in a state of imminent collapse. To this day, nobody knows who played on the album, other than Van Morrison and bassist Alan Henderson, though it is probable that Jimmy Page was seldom very far away when Them was recording. The 16 songs here are a little less focused than the first LP. The material was cut under siege conditions, with a constantly shifting lineup and a grueling tour schedule; essentially, there was no "group" to provide focus to the sound, only Morrison's voice, so the material bounces from a surprisingly restrained "I Put a Spell on You" to the garage-punkoid

"I Can Only Give You Everything." Folk-rock rears its head not only on the moody cover of Dylan's "It's All Over Now, Baby Blue" but also the Morrison-authored "My Lonely Sad Eyes," but the main thrust is soul, which Morrison oozes everywhere—while there's some filler, his is a voice that could easily have knocked Mick Jagger or Eric Burdon off their respective perches. — *Bruce Eder*

Backtrackin' / 1974 / London ◆◆◆
This collection of ten tracks from all phases of their career is haphazard, but the material is mostly excellent. Highlights include their blistering raveup of "Baby Please Don't Go" with Jimmy Page on guitar, a Top Ten hit in Britain; the angry cover of Paul Simon's "Richard Cory," their breakneck version of Slim Harpo's "Don't Start Crying Now," which was their first single in 1964; the great obscure, bluesy Morrison-penned B-side, "All for Myself," and the vicious cover of the R&B standard "Just a Little Bit." — *Richie Unterberger*

Story of Them / 1977 / London ◆◆◆
Another ragtag compilation of material that somehow hadn't found its way to an American album, this uneven but worthy collection is divided between R&B covers (Jimmy Reed's "Bright Lights, Big City" and Jimmy Witherspoon's "Times Gettin' Tougher Than Tough" are the best) and some good Morrison originals. Of those, the folk-tinged "Philosphy" and "Friday's Child" point to his more expressive solo work, and "The Story of Them" is a rambling, seven-and-a-half-minute autobiographical talking blues about the group's early days. — *Richie Unterberger*

● **Them Featuring Van Morrison [CD]** / 1987 / London ◆◆◆◆
Not to be confused with the identically titled Parrot Records release, which is an out-of-print 20-track double-LP set, this is a 13-track single CD set and a US reissue of the Decca UK LP from 1982. It would have been less confusing if they had called it *Them's Greatest Hits*, since it is primarily a singles compilation. But then, only four of Them's singles were hits, either in the UK or the US—"Baby, Please Don't Go," "Gloria," "Here Comes the Night," and "Mystic Eyes," all included here. Also featured are such non-charting singles as "Don't Start Crying Now," "One More Time," "(It Won't Hurt) Half As Much," and "Richard Cory." This is not the ideal Them compilation, but this is the one that contains Them's most familiar material. — *William Ruhlmann*

The Story of Them Featuring Van Morrison / 1997 / Deram ◆◆◆◆
Long-overdue double CD, collecting all but one of the 50 songs (only "Mighty Like a Rose" is missing) the legendary British blues band left behind in the English Decca and American London vaults. The sound is a significant improvement over prior reissues—really loud, the way it was meant to be heard—with little touches like "The Story of Them Parts 1 and 2" linked together. It doesn't follow chronological order of release, but the order is entertaining, with alternate takes (stereo single mixes, American single edits, etc.) broken up between the two discs. It would have been nice to have had recording dates and personnel, but considering the fact that the band's lineup, apart from Morrison and bassist Alan Henderson, seemed to change every month, it's conceivable that any session information would be suspect. And one wishes for a coherent essay on the history of the band to go with the spread of photographs of the different lineups that are reprinted here. — *Bruce Eder*

Earl Thomas

b. 1960
Bass / Modern Electric Blues, Piano Blues
22-year-old dental student Earl Thomas had never picked up a microphone in his life until he was nearly killed after losing his footing at the edge of a 50-foot ravine and slid all the way down, landing unconscious on a pile of broken glass and debris. Luckily, Thomas was only bruised, but not knowing the extent of the damage upon regaining consciousness, he reflected on his disappointment at not having pursued his dream of becoming a singer, and resolved to do just that if he survived. Nine years later, he recorded 1991's *Blue ... Not Blues*, a record strongly influenced by his parents' love of blues and gospel music and his own affinity for '60s and '70s soul. His "I Sing the Blues" became a hit for Etta James, and he played European music festivals with such artists as Elvis Costello and B.B. King. His second album, *Extra Soul*, was released in 1994. — *Steve Huey*

● **Blue ... Not Blues** / 1991 / Bizarre ◆◆◆
Earl Thomas' debut album *Blue ... Not Blues* blends the sensuality of Stax soul with the grittiness of modern electric blues. Given that Thomas didn't make this album until he had a particularly gruesome brush with death, it may seem a little churlish to point out that some of the songs are underdeveloped, but that's just a sign that it is indeed his debut. The real indication of his talent is the power of his voice and the way his best songs, such as "Nothing Left to Lose" and "The Way She Shakes That Thang," show that he has a knack for crafting memorable contemporary blues songs. That is what makes *Blue ... Not Blues* a successful debut. — *Thom Owens*

Extra Soul / 1994 / Bizarre Planet ◆◆◆

Henry Thomas

b. 1874, Big Sandy, TX, **d.** 1930
Vocals, Guitar / Country Blues, Prewar Country Blues
Texas songster Henry Thomas remains a relative stranger who made some great recordings, then returned to obscurity. Evidence suggests he was an itinerant street musician, a musical hobo who rode the rails across Texas and possibly to the World Fairs in St. Louis and Chicago just before and after the turn of the century. Most agree he was the oldest African-American folk artist to produce a significant body of recordings. His projected 1874 birthdate would predate Charley Patton by a good 17 years. Like Patton and a handful of other musicians generally termed songsters (including John Hurt, Jim Jackson, Mance Lipscomb, Furry Lewis, and Leadbelly), Thomas' repertoire bridged the 19th and 20th centuries, providing a compelling glimpse into a wide range of African-American musical genres. The 23 songs he cut for Vocalion between 1927 and 1929 include a spiritual, ballads, reels, dance songs, and eight selections titled blues. Obviously dance music, his songs were geared to older dance styles shared by Black and White audiences.

Thomas' sound, like his repertoire, is unique. He capoed his guitar high up the neck and strummed it in the manner of a banjo, favoring dance rhythm over complex fingerwork. On many of his pieces, he simultaneously played the quills or panpipes, a common but seldom-recorded African-American folk instrument indigenous to Mississippi, Louisiana, and Texas. Combining the quills, a limited-range melody instrument, with his banjo-like strummed guitar produced one of the most memorable sounds in American folk music. For example, his lead-in on "Bull Doze Blues" still worked as a hook when recycled 40 years later by blues/rockers Canned Heat in their version of "Going Up the Country." "Ragtime Texas," as Thomas was known, provides a welcome inroad to 19th-century dance music, but his music is neither obscure nor merely educational: it has a timeless quality—and while it may be an acquired taste, once you catch on to it, you're hooked. — *Barry Lee Pearson*

★ **Texas Worried Blues: Complete Recordings** / 1989 / Yazoo ◆◆◆◆◆
Songster Thomas plays a cross-section of blues and pre-blues with a unique guitar-and-panpipes instrumentation. Although it may sound archaic to the beginner, given time it will get your toes tapping and quickly become a favorite. — *Barry Lee Pearson*

Sings the Texas Blues / 1991 / Origin ◆◆◆◆

Irma Thomas

b. Feb. 18, 1941, Ponchatoula, LA
Vocals / Soul, New Orleans R&B, Classic Female Blues
Radiating an outgoing joy that's inevitably at the heart of her infectious vocal delivery, Irma Thomas has no rivals as the Soul Queen of New Orleans. Working at a Crescent City nightery as a waitress in 1959, Thomas sat in one night with Tommy Ridgley's band and made such a favorable impression that the veteran bandleader hustled her into the studio shortly thereafter to wax her first hit for the Ron label, the driving "Don't Mess with My Man." She joined forces with producer Allen Toussaint to make some of her most moving outings for Minit Records during the early '60s, notably "It's Raining," "Ruler of My Heart," and "Cry On," before venturing to the West Coast, where she cut both her biggest seller, the lushly produced "Wish Someone Would Care," and her best-known song, the original "Time Is on My Side"—and she's still bitter enough about the Rolling Stones' cover stealing her thunder to discourage requests for the tune.

The highly adaptable chanteuse also made some sizzling soul at Rich Hall's Muscle Shoals studio for Chess in the summer of 1967 before cooling off for a while during the '70s. But she's back now, as radiant as ever—and for convincing proof, listen to her buoyant 1990 concert performance on Rounder, *Live! Simply the Best*. Now that's truth in packaging!

Irma Thomas finally fulfilled a lifelong ambition in 1993 by recording her first gospel release. *Walk Around Heaven* was as magnificently sung and emotionally convincing as any of her classic New Orleans soul cuts. Thomas followed the album in 1997 with *The Story of My Life*, which featured several songs written by Dan Penn. — *Bill Dahl*

Wish Someone Would Care / 1964 / Imperial ✦✦✦✦

Irma Thomas has been New Orleans' reigning soul queen since the early '60s, and this landmark album was her most stunning and complete session. It didn't make her a national star, but it showed vulnerability as captivating as lust, anger or pain. Thomas' voice seemed deliberately frail at times, but she made "Time Is On My Side" and "I Wish Someone Would Care" remarkable triumphs. There were many other fine songs, such as "I Need Your Love So Bad," "Please Send Me Someone To Love" and "Break-A-Way." It remains one of the greatest soul albums ever recorded. — *Ron Wynn*

Take a Look / 1968 / Imperial ✦✦✦

The songs from Irma Thomas' Imperial sessions are timeless and magnificent; they've also been constantly reissued and are available all over the place. That reduces the value of this anthology, one of two that were issued featuring her Imperial cuts. Every significant song from both of these releases has subsequently been compiled and issued on the EMI domestic CD package. — *Ron Wynn*

Time is on My Side [Kent] / 1983 / Kent ✦✦✦✦

Solid 16-song compilation of material from the mid-'60s. Most of this is duplicated by the more extensive CD compilations of the same era on EMI and Razor & Tie. But it's not entirely superfluous; five of the songs don't appear on either of the other collections. Those tracks are worth hearing, particularly the gutsy soul-pop concoction "Baby Don't Look Down," one of Randy Newman's earliest compositions. — *Richie Unterberger*

The New Rules / 1986 / Rounder ✦✦✦

Irma Thomas balanced classic and contemporary sensibilities on this 1986 album. She did such songs as "Gonna Cry 'Til My Tears Run Dry" and "I Gave You Everything" from the 1960s, and also did more recent tunes, such as the title track and a good remake of "The Wind Beneath My Wings (Hero)." In the 1980s, there was little interest at urban contemporary stations in older, more soulful artists, and thus this worthy session got almost no attention outside New Orleans and the South. However, Irma Thomas can still sing with authority and quality. — *Ron Wynn*

The Way I Feel / 1988 / Rounder ✦✦✦✦

Irma Thomas deserves hits and wider exposure more than almost any other R&B vocalist you could name. While the material on this album was uneven, she retained her credibility regardless. It took real guts to cover "Dancing In The Street" and "Baby I Love You," and even more talent not to be subsumed by their history. She's vibrant on "Old Records," hard-hitting on "You Don't Know Nothin' About Love," and poignant on "Sorry Wrong Number," "Sit Down and Cry" and "I'll Take Care Of You." — *Ron Wynn*

Ruler of Hearts / 1989 / Charly ✦✦✦

Sides from her early-'60s Minit sessions. The most New Orleans R&B-influenced of Thomas' early work, it includes "Cry On," "It's Raining," and "Ruler Of My Heart," as well as lesser-known but equally moving cuts like "Two Winters Long" and "It's Too Soon To Know." — *Richie Unterberger*

Something Good: Muscle Shoals / 1990 / Chess ✦✦✦✦

Thomas' brief liaison with Chess in 1967 saw her, like labelmates Laura Lee and Etta James, record in Muscle Shoals' Fame studios to tap into the southern/deep soul grooves that were one of the hottest tickets in soul music at the time. Commercially, these sessions (all recorded in June and July of '67) weren't a success. It's also fair to say that they don't rate as her finest work of the '60s; her early New Orleans sessions, along with her pop-rock sides of the mid-'60s, featured both stronger material and more suitable accompaniment. That's hardly a knock, though; these were solid soul performances paced by Thomas' habitual excellent, committed vocals. But there's a bit of a generic Stax/Volt feel, and not much of the material (which features several compositions by Otis Redding and the Spooner Oldham-Dan Penn team) leaps out and grabs you. It's still worth finding if you're an Irma fan, with 14 tracks that include several Chess singles and nine songs recorded for

an unreleased LP that were previously unavailable in the United States. — *Richie Unterberger*

Live: Simply the Best / 1991 / Rounder ✦✦✦✦

Irma Thomas has long been an institution in New Orleans-based R&B. This live CD is both a strong introduction to her powerful voice and a summation of her career up to 1990, mixing together remakes of some of her mid-'60s recordings with more current material. Cheered on by an enthusiastic crowd, Irma Thomas sounds inspired and in her prime for the consistently passionate set. Of the highlights, "Hip Shakin' Mama" is a humorous blues," "I Needed Somebody" is especially soulful (if overly repetitive near its conclusion), "It's Raining" is memorable and the "Second Line Medley" effectively mixes in a touch of dixieland with R&B. An excellent introduction to the talented Irma Thomas. — *Scott Yanow*

★ Time Is on My Side: The Best of Irma Thomas, Vol. 1 / Apr. 21, 1992 / EMI America ✦✦✦✦✦

Twenty-three sides representing the cream of Irma Thomas' brilliant Minit/Liberty years (1961-1966), when her reputation as "The Soul Queen of New Orleans" was built. Virtually all her best-known tunes are here—"Wish Someone Would Care," "Ruler of My Heart," "It's Raining," and "Time Is on My Side" (covered note-for-note by the Stones). Beautiful singing from one of the first ladies of soul music. Essential. — *Christine Ohlman*

True Believer / Jun. 1992 / Rounder ✦✦✦✦

Like her first two efforts for Rounder, *True Believer* is a stellar collection of contemporary soul performed in the classic '50s New Orleans tradition. The difference is in conception. *True Believer* focuses on heartbreak songs, and there is genuine anguish in Irma Thomas' voice, making new songs by the likes of Dan Penn, Dr. John, Tony Joe White, Allen Toussaint, and Doc Pomus sound like instant classics. Another excellent effort from a woman who has plenty to her credit. — *Thom Owens*

Walk Around Heaven: New Orleans Gospel Soul / Oct. 1993 / Rounder ✦✦✦

During R&B's glory years—the 1950s, '60s and '70s—the African-American church provided one great singer after another. Church choirs served as a magnificent training ground for so many of the great soul shouters, and it clearly had a positive effect on Irma Thomas (arguably the greatest female soul singer to come out of New Orleans). At 52, Thomas celebrated her gospel heritage with this solid, heartfelt CD. Thomas' voice had held up quite well since the '60s, and she brings an impressive range and a seemingly endless supply of emotion to songs like "Where We'll Never Grow Old," "Ask What You Will," and "Careful Hands." *Walk Around Heaven* reminds us that as impressive as her contributions to secular soul have been, Thomas hasn't forgotten the church. — *Alex Henderson*

Sweet Soul Queen of New Orleans: The Irma Thomas Collection / Feb. 20, 1996 / Razor & Tie ✦✦✦✦

23-track collection of early and mid-'60s sides largely duplicates the material on EMI's *Time Is on My Side* collection, with some additions and subtractions. The EMI set has a very slight edge, though for most listeners either compilation will do the job. It's too bad somebody doesn't take the plunge and issue an 80-minute CD documenting this era; as it is, serious Irma fans will need to get each best-of, as each contains tracks not on the other. — *Richie Unterberger*

Story of My Life / Feb. 11, 1997 / Rounder ✦✦✦✦

The Story of My Life stands out among latter-day Irma Thomas albums not only because she gives a consistently excellent performance, but because the record boasts three new songs from Dan Penn, who wrote some of the greatest soul songs of the '60s. While his new songs ("Hold Me While I Cry," "I Count the Teardrops," "I Won't Cry for You") aren't quite as strong as his best, they are nevertheless wonderful contemporary soul numbers, and they help make the record, the remainder of which is comprised of covers and slightly weaker new numbers, one of Thomas' best latter-day albums. — *Stephen Thomas Erlewine*

James "Son" Thomas

b. Oct. 14, 1926, Eden, MS, **d.** Jun. 26, 1993
Guitar, Vocals / Delta Blues
One of the last great traditional Delta blues musicians, James "Son" Thomas' style conveyed the power, earnesty and integrity of masterful country artists

like Arthur "Big Boy" Crudup. Thomas grew up on a farm in Mississippi and played in juke joints and barrelhouses before he began recording in the late '60s. He appeared in the films *Delta Blues Singer: James "Sonny Ford" Thomas* in 1970 and *Give My Poor Heart Ease: Mississippi Delta Bluesmen* in 1975, plus the short *Mississippi Delta Blues* in 1974. Thomas also made festival appearances in the '70s and '80s. He recorded for Transatlantic, Matchbox, Southern Folklore and regional labels in the '60s, '70s and '80s. — *Ron Wynn*

• **Son Thomas: Son Down on the Delta** / 1981 / Flying High ++++
Son Thomas: Son Down on the Delta is a very good live album recorded in Fort Worth, TX in 1981. Thomas largely sticks to standards here, but the reason to listen to him is the subtle textures of his guitar and voice, which make these well-known songs come alive. — *Thom Owens*

Jesse Thomas

b. Feb. 3, 1911, Logansport, LA., **d.** 1995
Guitar / Texas Blues, Acoustic Texas Blues, Jump Blues, Piedmont Blues
The brother of Texas bluesman Willard "Ramblin'" Thomas, Jesse "Babyface" Thomas never had the success of his more famous sibling. He moved to Dallas in 1929, when Blind Lemon Jefferson and Lonnie Johnson were in their heyday, and tried to establish himself but found little success in recording work for numerous labels right up through the 1940s. His early acoustic playing was heavily influenced by Lonnie Johnson and Blind Blake, but he later developed a style of his own. Unlike his older brother, Babyface Thomas was not a slide player. He also tended to write and sing about more upbeat and romantic subjects than Ramblin Thomas. He favored a highly rhythmic and animated style on his instrument—he also lasted into the electric blues era, and he could make some brilliant amplified dance music—"Double Do Love You" could recall T-Bone Walker at his best, and anticipates the work of Chuck Berry by several years. During the 1960s, after moving back to Shreveport, LA, he did some soul-styled recordings for his own label, which failed to find an audience. — *Bruce Eder*

Complete Recorded Works 1948-1958 / Jun. 2, 1994 / Document +++

• **Dallas Blues Before 1950** / 1995 / Collectables ++++
Ramblin' Thomas is the better known artist on this 16 song collection, but Babyface Thomas has eight songs featured, recorded for the Houston-based Freedom label in 1949. His music is more upbeat and playful than that of Ramblin' Thomas, with no slide playing, but a very nimble technique. The strangest cut here is "Good Night," a distinctly non-blues romantic number that features a whistled, bird-like accompaniment on the break and a harmony accompaniment. "Same Old Stuff" boasts a rippling guitar part, and is clearly in a more modern Texas blues style, evoking images of T-Bone Walker, while "Double Do Love You" anticipates images of Chuck Berry (especially his "Guitar Boogie"), and two more tracks are in a big-band blues idiom, complete with saxes. There's lots more Babyface Thomas out there, making these eight songs a decent if unambitious introduction to his music. — *Bruce Eder*

Lookin' for That Woman / Feb. 1996 / Black Top +++

Ramblin' Thomas

Guitar, Vocals / Texas Blues, Acoustic Texas Blues
A fine Texas blues guitarist who was also an effective singer, "Ramblin'" Thomas made some tremendous recordings for Paramount and Victor in the '20s and '30s. He was a brilliant slide technician though he didn't use it all that often, and his singing was riveting and distinctive. — *Ron Wynn*

• **1928-1932** / 1928-1932 / Document ++++
Solid but thematically unvarying country blues from a fine practitioner. "Ramblin'" Thomas told great stories and backed himself just as nicely. — *Ron Wynn*

Ramblin' Mind Blues / Biograph ++++
His name probably came more from his life than his playing style, but Ramblin' Thomas also roamed within his songs. Still, there are plenty of fine vocals and old-time guitar work on this session. — *Ron Wynn*

Rockin' Tabby Thomas

b. Louisiana
Vocals, Piano, Guitar / Electric Louisiana Blues
A solid Louisiana vocalist who plays both guitar and piano, "Rockin'" Tabby Thomas has been cutting stirring recordings since the mid-'50s. He's teamed often with harmonica players Whispering Smith and Lazy Lester, and has done several sessions for Maison De Soul and various labels owned by Jay Miller.

Thomas was born in Baton Rouge, LA, but he began his musical career in San Francisco, which is where he was stationed while in the army. After he completed his time in the service, Thomas stayed in San Francisco, playing shows and talent contests. He happened to win a talent contest, which led to a record contract with Hollywood Records. Hollywood issued "Midnight Is Calling," which gained no attention, and the label dropped Thomas.

After the failure of "Midnight Is Calling," Tabby Thomas returned to Baton Rouge. He began playing local clubs with his supporting band the Mellow, Mellow Men. In 1953, the group recorded two songs—"Thinking Blues" and "Church Members Ball"—for the Delta label. After those songs didn't gain much attention, Thomas went through a number of record labels—including Feature, Rocko, and Zynn—before having a hit on Excello Records in 1962 with "Voodoo Party."

Thomas wasn't able to record a hit follow-up to "Voodoo Party" and by the end of the '60s, he retired from performing music. His retirement was short-lived—in 1970, he founded his own record label, Blue Beat. In addition to releasing Thomas' own recordings, Blue Beat spotlighted emerging Baton Rouge talent. Within a few years, the label was very successful and Thomas began his own blues club, Tabby's Blues Box and Heritage Hall. By the mid-'80s, the club was the most popular blues joint in Baton Rouge.

Although he had become a successful businessman in the late '70s, Thomas continued to perform and record. All of his efforts—from his recordings and concerts, to his label and nightclub—made Tabby Thomas the leading figure of Baton Rouge's blues scene for nearly three decades. Thomas was still active in the '90s, although he wasn't performing as frequently as he had in the past. — *Ron Wynn & Stephen Thomas Erlewine*

Rockin' with the Blues / 1985 / Maison de Soul +++

• **King of Swamp Blues** / 1988 / Maison de Soul ++++
Good, hard-rocking Louisiana blues with just a tinge of swamp from Rockin' Tabby Thomas. What he lacks in vocal range, he compensates for with exuberance. The backing band is no all-star unit, but they provide some solid grooves behind Thomas' surging leads. — *Ron Wynn*

Swamp Blues Man / Nov. 28, 1995 / Dejan ++++

Rufus Thomas

b. Mar. 26, 1917, Cayce, MS
Vocals / Soul, R&B, Electric Memphis Blues
Few of rock 'n' roll's founding figures are as likable as Rufus Thomas. From the 1940s onward, he has personified Memphis music; his small but witty cameo role in Jim Jarmusch's *Mystery Train*, a film which satirizes and enshrines the city's role in popular culture, was entirely appropriate. As a recording artist, he wasn't a major innovator, but he could always be depended upon for some good, silly, and/or outrageous fun with his soul dance tunes. He was one of the few rock or soul stars to reach his commercial and artistic peak in middle age, and was a crucial mentor to many important Memphis blues, rock, and soul musicians.

Thomas was already a professional entertainer in the mid-'30s, when he was a comedian with the Rabbit Foot Minstrels. He recorded music as early as 1941, but really made his mark on the Memphis music scene as a deejay on WDIA, one of the few Black-owned stations of the era. He also ran talent shows on Memphis' famous Beale Street that helped showcase the emerging skills of such influential figures as B.B. King, Bobby Bland, Junior Parker, Ike Turner, and Roscoe Gordon.

Thomas had his first success as a recording artist in 1953 with "Bear Cat," a funny answer record to Big Mama Thornton's "Hound Dog." It made number three on the R&B charts, giving Sun Records its first national hit, though some of the sweetness went out of the triumph after Sun owner Sam Phillips lost a lawsuit for plagiarizing the original Jerry Leiber/Mike Stoller tune.

Thomas, strangely, would make only one other record for Sun, and recorded only sporadically throughout the rest of the 1950s.

Thomas and his daughter Carla would become the first stars for the Stax label, for whom they recorded a duet in 1959, "'Cause I Love You" (when the company was still known as Satellite). In the '60s, Carla would become one of Stax's biggest stars. On his own, Rufus wasn't as successful as his daughter, but issued a steady stream of decent dance/novelty singles.

These were not deep or emotional statements, or meant to be. Vaguely prefiguring elements of funk, the accent was on the stripped-down groove and Rufus' good-time vocals, which didn't take himself or anything seriously. The biggest by far was "Walking the Dog," which made the Top Ten in 1963, and was covered by the Rolling Stones on their first album.

Thomas hit his commercial peak in the early '70s, when "Do the Funky Chicken," "(Do the) Push and Pull," and "The Breakdown" all made the R&B Top Five. As the song titles themselves make clear, funk was now driving his sound rather than blues or soul. Thomas drew upon his vaudeville background to put them over onstage with fancy footwork that displayed remarkable agility for a man well into his 50s. The collapse of the Stax label in the mid-'70s meant the end of his career, basically, as it did for many other artists with the company. *— Richie Unterberger*

Walking the Dog / 1964 / Stax ✦✦✦✦
One of the artists who defined Memphis soul and put Stax Records on the map, Rufus Thomas is known for liking his R&B hard-edged, gritty and earthy. That approach served him impressively well on his debut album *Walking the Dog*. In contrast to the sleeker, more elaborate production style favored by the Northern soulsters of Motown, Thomas rejects pop elements altogether and thrives on rawness on his hits "Walking the Dog" (a song covered by Aerosmith in the '70s) and "The Dog," as well as inspired versions of "Land of 1000 Dances" (which became a major hit for Wilson Pickett), Lee Dorsey's "Ya Ya," and John Lee Hooker's "Boom Boom." Thomas was in his mid-40s when these fun, infectious recordings were made, and he definitely lives up to his title "The World's Oldest Teenager" (a title later given to Dick Clark as well). Reissued on CD in the early 1990s, *Walking the Dog* is an album Memphis soul aficionados shouldn't overlook. *— Alex Henderson*

Funky Chicken / Jun. 1969 / Stax ✦✦✦
Thomas' first album following Stax's break from Atlantic (and in fact his first since 1963) had "Do the Funky Chicken" at its centerpiece, so the emphasis upon good-humored dance tunes was unsurprising. There were some weird moments, particularly the down-and-bestial seven-minute update of "Sixty Minute Man" (on which Rufus sounds like he's singing in tongues), a remake of "Bear Cat," and a two-part version of "Old McDonald Had a Farm." Still, the slightly goofy uptempo arrangements can get a little tiresome, and as his best hits from the period are better than the album-only tracks, almost everyone should just stick with a compilation. The CD adds seven bonus tracks from 1968-74 singles, which are OK but not essential; Eddie Floyd's "Funky Mississippi" (from 1968) is about the best. *— Richie Unterberger*

May I Have Your Ticket Please / 1969 / Stax ✦✦✦
Rufus Thomas played it halfway between inspired lunacy and straight soul sanity, and was only partly successful here. Thomas hadn't yet found the formula for dance/novelty success, and didn't really have any strong singles on this release. His bluesy vocals were well done, but not enough to generate any action for the record. *— Ron Wynn*

The Crown Prince of Dance / 1973 / Stax ✦✦✦✦
The "world's oldest teenager" was springy, sassy, and jubilant when he cut this date in the mid-'70s. Thomas, whose career goes back to the days of the Rabbit Foot Minstrels, made some brilliant novelty cuts for Stax in the 1970s. He simply went into the studio and clowned, backed by the great Stax session pros. The results are comic gems, numbers that are purposefully lightweight and succeed without sounding sappy. *— Ron Wynn*

If There Were No Music / 1977 / Avid ✦✦✦
Rufus Thomas was on Avid when he issued this 1977 album, and the difference between this label and Stax was evident in the colorless backing, routine production, and general blandness of the tracks featured on the LP. Thomas tried to whip up some enthusiasm, and his rendition of the title cut came close to generating some attention for the album. But it was weighted down with too much disposable fodder, and not a single definitive dance or novelty classic to boot. *— Ron Wynn*

I Ain't Gettin' Older, I'm Gettin' Better / 1977 / Avid ✦✦
Rufus Thomas was right vocally, but otherwise this album didn't live up to the title. After years of inspired productions, arrangements, and compositions, Thomas didn't get similar treatment for his debut on the Avid label. They did a respectable job, but didn't get him any hits or inventive novelty tunes. Thomas eventually went from being a hit act to a nostalgia/oldies performer. *— Ron Wynn*

Chronicle / 1986 / Stax ✦✦✦✦
Half of *Chronicle* features the greatest hits of Rufus Thomas' daughter, Carla, while the other half features the best of the man himself; it's a good introduction to the music of both artists. *— AMG*

That Woman Is Poison! / 1988 / Alligator ✦✦
A masterful comeback album from a blues and soul veteran who was assumed to be ready for the retirement home. Rufus Thomas went back to the comic blues that had been his forte in the 1950s, and the edge in his voice and defiance in his tone proclaimed that he wasn't finished yet. After years of taking heat from purists for not issuing enough "real" blues albums, Alligator didn't get nearly enough credit for being the only label to give Rufus Thomas a fair shot in the 1980s. *— Ron Wynn*

Can't Get Away from This Dog / 1992 / Stax ✦✦✦
Can't Get Away from This Dog gathers 20 previously unreleased Rufus Thomas recordings from the Stax vaults. Stylistically, fans won't find any surprises — this is still hard-hitting, hard-driving Memphis soul — but they'll find a couple of hidden treasures, such as versions of "Wang Dang Doodle," "Reconsider Baby," and "Barefootin'," as well as alternates of "Walking the Dog," "Jump Back," and "Can Your Monkey Do the Dog?" Some of Thomas' original material is a little thin — there's only so many times you can work the word "dog" into a song title, after all — but this is a surprisingly successful collection of rarities that will not only satiate diehards, but will entertain casual fans as well. *— Stephen Thomas Erlewine*

● **Do the Funky Somethin': The Best of Rufus Thomas** / Apr. 1996 / Rhino ✦✦✦✦
Overdue career-spanning collection of his best material, centering around his Stax hits from the '60s and early '70s. The whole "dog" series of novelty dance songs from 1963-64 is here, as well as the hit "Jump Back" and a clutch of Stax singles that weren't hits, but became pretty well-known anyway, like "Sister's Got a Boyfriend" and "Sophisticated Sissy." There are also the early-'70s funk dance hits "Do the Funky Chicken," "(Do the) Push and Pull," "The Breakdown," and "Do the Funky Penguin," a couple of '60s duets with his daughter Carla, and his 1953 blues single "Bear Cat (The Answer to Hound Dog)," the first hit on Sun Records. A few other compilations have gone into specific phases of his career in greater depth, but this is certainly the best overview of a man who offered some of the funkiest and funniest Memphis soul around. *— Richie Unterberger*

Dave Thompson

b. 1971, Jackson, MS
Guitar, Vocals / Contemporary Blues
Blues guitarist, singer, and songwriter Dave Thompson combines the blues-rock edge of Stevie Ray Vaughan with the Delta sounds that surrounded him while growing up. Thompson still makes his home in Mississippi, and his playing displays the raw juke joint tones of his mentors, people like Roosevelt "Booba" Barnes and Junior Kimbrough. Thompson has one album out on the Fat Possum/Capricorn label, *Little Dave and Big Love*, a 1995 release.

Thompson began playing guitar when he was nine, when his father purchased a Teisco Del Ray model from Sears and began teaching his son the rudiments of blues. Thompson's father died four years later. By the time he was 16, his talent and drive caught the attention of Roosevelt "Booba" Barnes, who drafted Thompson as a rhythm guitarist. Barnes moved to Chicago in 1988, but Thompson continued playing with other members of Barne's group, called the F.M. Stereo Band. While working with Barnes' band, Thompson lost his mother to cancer and was incarcerated several times on drug-related charges.

Now in his mid-20s, Thompson plays a style of contemporary blues that's accessible to younger fans of the music, because of his thoroughly modern approach to the idiom. On his debut album, his influences shine through: Barnes, Otis Rush, Albert King and even a bit of Stevie Ray Vaughan. His technique is awesome, combining quick note runs with crisp, clear chord changes and powerful vocals. Using a quarter for a pick and WD-40 on his fretboard, Thompson plays inspired blues guitar that grabs you by the throat and doesn't let go.

Most recently, Thompson, who lives in Leland, MS, was working in a trio format with bass and drum accompaniment. Thompson's raw, straight-up guitar technique and backing bands are fantastic, and while he's not one of the great blues lyric writers of all time, he could develop into one, as he only recently began writing his own songs. His years of experience, building his chops accompanying Barnes and others, more than makes up for his relative lack of an individualized songwriting voice. —*Richard Skelly*

Little Dave and Big Love / 1995 / Fat Possum ✦✦✦

Ron Thompson

b. Jul. 5, 1953, Oakland, CA
Guitar, Vocals / Modern Electric Blues, Boogie-Woogie
After honing his chops behind Little Joe Blue and John Lee Hooker, guitarist Ron Thompson went solo in 1980, forming his own blues/roots-rock trio, the Resisters. *Just Like a Devil*, a 1990 release on pianist Mark Naftalin's Winner label, was culled from Thompson's appearances on Naftalin's *Blue Monday Party* radio program.

Born and raised in Oakland, CA, Thompson began playing guitar when he was 11, picking up slide guitar shortly afterward. When he was in his late teens, he was playing slide guitar with Little Joe Blue. For about five years, he worked in local Bay Area clubs, both as a solo artist and a supporting musician. In 1975, John Lee Hooker asked Thompson to join his backing band and the guitarist accepted. For the next three years, he played with Hooker, developing a national reputation.

Thompson left Hooker in 1978. Two years later, he formed his own band, the Resistors, and landed a contract with Takoma Records. Thompson's debut album, *Treat Her Like Gold*, appeared in 1983. Although he launched a solo career, Thompson continued to play with a number of other musicians, including Lowell Fulson, Etta James, and Big Mama Thornton. In 1987, his second album, *Resister Twister*, was released; it was followed shortly afterward by *Just Like a Devil*. Thompson continued to perform throughout the late '80s and '90s, although he didn't record quite as frequently. —*Bill Dahl & Stephen Thomas Erlewine*

Treat Her Like Gold/No Bad Days / 1983 / Takoma ✦✦✦

● **Resister Twister** / 1987 / Blind Pig ✦✦✦✦
Resister Twister, the second album from Ron Thompson, is an enjoyable soul-blues collection that finds the slide guitarist at the peak of his form. There's not much original on the record, but Thompson plays very, very well, and the result is a fun contemporary blues recording. —*Thom Owens*

Just Like a Devil / 1990 / Winner ✦✦✦

Big Mama Thornton (Willie Mae Thornton)

b. Dec. 11, 1926, Montgomery, AL, **d.** Jul. 25, 1984, Los Angeles, CA
Harmonica, Drums, Vocals / Electric West Coast Blues, Texas Blues
Willie Mae "Big Mama" Thornton only notched one national hit in her lifetime, but it was a true monster. "Hound Dog" held down the top slot on *Billboard*'s R&B charts for seven long weeks in 1953. Alas, Elvis Presley's rocking 1956 cover was even bigger, effectively obscuring Thornton's chief claim to immortality.

That's a damned shame, because Thornton's menacing growl was indeed something special. The hefty belter first opened her pipes in church but soon embraced the blues. She toured with Sammy Green's Hot Harlem Revue during the 1940s. Thornton was ensconced on the Houston circuit when Peacock Records boss Don Robey signed her in 1951. She debuted on Peacock with "Partnership Blues" that year, backed by trumpeter Joe Scott's band.

But it was her third Peacock date with Johnny Otis' band that proved the winner. With Pete Lewis laying down some truly nasty guitar behind her, Big Mama shouted "Hound Dog," a tune whose authorship remains a bone of contention to this day (both Otis and the team of Jerry Leiber and Mike Stoller claim responsibility) and soon hit the road a star.

But it was an isolated incident. Though Thornton cut some fine Peacock follow-ups—"I Smell a Rat," "Stop Hoppin' on Me," "The Fish," "Just like a

Dog"—through 1957, she never again reached the hit parade. Even Elvis was apparently unaware of her; he was handed "Hound Dog" by Freddie Bell, a Vegas lounge rocker. Early-'60s 45s for Irma, Bay-Tone, Kent, and Sotoplay did little to revive her sagging fortunes, but a series of dates for Arhoolie that included her first vinyl rendition of "Ball and Chain" in 1968 and two albums for Mercury in 1969-70 put her back in circulation (Janis Joplin's overwrought but well-intentioned cover of "Ball and Chain" didn't hurt either). Along with her imposing vocals, Thornton began to emphasize her harmonica skills during the 1960s.

Thornton was a tough cookie. She dressed like a man and took no guff from anyone, even as the pounds fell off her once-ample frame and she became downright scrawny during the last years of her life. Medical personnel found her lifeless body in an L.A. rooming house in 1984. —*Bill Dahl*

In Europe: Big Mama Thornton with Muddy Waters' Blues Band / 1965 / Arhoolie ✦✦✦✦
Live sessions with the Muddy Waters Blues Band. —*Barry Lee Pearson*

Big Mama Thorton in Europe / Sep. 1966 / Arhoolie ✦✦✦✦

Big Mama the Queen at Monterey / Dec. 1967 / MCA ✦✦✦✦

She's Back / 1968 / Back Beat ✦✦✦✦
Growling Texas blues; includes "Hound Dog." —*Bill Dahl*

Ball N' Chain / 1968 / Arhoolie ✦✦✦
Arhoolie's *Ball N' Chain* is a terrific collection of late-'60s recordings from Big Mama Thornton. Supported on various tracks by Lightnin' Hopkins and Larry Williams, Big Mama runs through such familiar items as "Hound Dog," "Sometimes I Have a Heartache," "Sweet Little Angel," "Little Red Rooster," "Wade in the Water" and "Ball and Chain," turning in generally powerful performances. By and large, these don't necessarily rival her classic '50s recordings, but they are worth investigating if you're looking for something more. —*Thom Owens*

Stronger Than Dirt / 1969 / Mercury ✦✦✦

The Way It Is / 1970 / Mercury ✦✦✦

Jail / 1975 / Vanguard ✦✦✦

Sassy Mama / 1975 / Vanguard ✦✦✦

The Original Hound Dog / 1990 / Ace ✦✦✦✦
This British import compilation of Peacock sides is a bit more comprehensive than the domestic *Hound Dog* anthology, including a few more tracks (22 in all, some previously unreleased). The MCA collection, more readily available for most North American consumers, should suffice for most listeners. If you come across this one first, though, it's certainly an equal or greater value, highlighted by "Hound Dog" and "I Smell a Rat" (both written by the Leiber-Stoller songwriting team in their early days). —*Richie Unterberger*

● **Hound Dog: The Peacock Recordings** / 1992 / MCA ✦✦✦✦
Let's face it, Big Mama Thornton will always be chiefly recalled for her growling 1952 reading of the Jerry Leiber-Mike Stoller classic "Hound Dog." But the other 17 sides on this collection of her 1952-1957 output for Don Robey's Peacock Records aren't exactly makeweight. Thornton's mighty roar was backed by the jumping combos of Johnny Otis and saxist Bill Harvey, producing additional gems in "My Man Called Me," "They Call Me Big Mama," "The Fish," and a duet with the ill-fated Johnny Ace, "Yes Baby." —*Bill Dahl*

George Thorogood

f. Dec. 31, 1952, Wilmington, DE
Guitar, Vocals / Blues-Rock, Rock 'n' Roll, Boogie Rock
A blues-rock guitarist who draws his inspiration from Elmore James, Hound Dog Taylor, and Chuck Berry, George Thorogood never earned much respect from blues purists, but he became a popular favorite in the early '80s through repeated exposure on FM radio and the arena rock circuit. Thorogood's music was always loud, simple, and direct—his riffs and licks were taken straight out of '50s Chicago blues and rock 'n' roll—but his formulaic approach helped him gain a rather large audience in the '80s, when his albums regularly went gold.

Originally, Thorogood was a minor-league baseball player, but decided to become a musician in 1970 after seeing John Paul Hammond in concert. Three years later, he assembled the Destroyers in his home state of Delaware; in addition to Thorogood, the band featured bassist Michael Lenn, second guitarist Ron Smith, and drummer Jeff Simon. Shortly after the group was formed, he moved them to Boston, where they became regulars on the blues club circuit. In 1974, they cut a batch of demos which were later released in 1979 as the *Better than the Rest* album.

Within a year of recording the demos, the Destroyers were discovered by John Forward, who helped them secure a contract with Rounder Records. Before they made their first album, Lenn was replaced by Billy Blough. Thorogood and the Destroyers' eponymous debut was released in early 1977. The group's second album, *Move It on Over*, was released in 1978. The title track, a cover of Hank Williams' classic, was pulled as a single and it received heavy FM airplay, helping the album enter the American Top 40 and go gold. Its success led to MCA's release of *Better than the Rest*, which the band disdained. In 1980, Ron Smith left the band and the group added a saxophonist, Hank Carter and released their third album, *More George Thorogood & the Destroyers*.

Following the release of *More George Thorogood*, the guitarist signed with EMI Records, releasing his major-label debut *Bad to the Bone* in 1982. The title track of the album became his first major crossover hit, thanks to MTV's saturation airplay of the song's video. The album went gold and spent nearly a full year on the charts. Thorogood's next three albums after *Bad to the Bone* all went gold. Between *Bad to the Bone* and Thorogood's next album, 1985's *Maverick*, the Destroyers added a second guitarist, Steve Chrismar.

By the beginning of the '90s, Thorogood's audience began to decrease. None of the albums he released went gold, even though the title track from 1993's *Haircut* was a number-two album rock hit. Despite his declining record sales, Thorogood continued to tour blues and rock clubs and he usually drew large crowds. — *Stephen Thomas Erlewine*

George Thorogood & the Destroyers / 1977 / Rounder ✦✦✦✦
Contains Thorogood's crowd-pleasing rendition of John Lee Hooker's "One Bourbon, One Scotch, One Beer." Its basic approach—heavy on Thorogood's bluesy guitar playing—serves as the prototype for every Destroyers record that followed. — *William Ruhlmann*

Move It on Over / 1978 / Rounder ✦✦✦
In 1978, George Thorogood was just beginning to make some noise on the blues-rock circuit. This was his second album, and what's now almost a cliche then sounded fresh and vital. Thorogood's energy, rousing vocals and driving guitar playing came roaring through on inspired covers of Elmore James' "The Sky Is Crying," Bo Diddley's "Who Do You Love," and Chuck Berry's "It Wasn't Me." He even did a credible Piedmont blues on Brownie McGhee's "So Much Trouble." While Thorogood went on to make more commercially succesful albums, the spirit and innocence in his early releases has seldom been duplicated. This Rounder CD reissue returns him to a simpler, and in some ways superior, period. — *Ron Wynn*

More George Thorogood & the Destroyers / 1980 / Rounder ✦✦
George Thorogood was honing his focus and getting the Destroyers concept down pat on this 1980 album. He hadn't yet become so established and comfortable that his rocking blues licks and vocals were more show business than intensity and energy. Thorogood's playing and singing on such tracks as "House of Blue Lights," "Night Time" and "I'm Wanted" were earnest enough to make the treatments convincing, and retain interest. While this wasn't quite as memorable as his earlier dates, George Thorogood still had the hunger that fueled his breakout sessions. — *Ron Wynn*

Bad to the Bone / 1982 / EMI America ✦✦✦✦
Though songs such as "Back to Wentzville" are credited to Thorogood, he'd be the first to admit that they are proudly derivative of Chuck Berry and his other mentors. The title track, another Thorogood copyright, has become ubiquitous in *Terminator 2* and the *Problem Child* movies and elsewhere, but it's still terrific. — *William Ruhlmann*

Maverick / Dec. 1984 / Rounder ✦✦✦

Live / 1986 / EMI America ✦✦

Born to Be Bad / 1988 / EMI America ✦

Boogie People / Jan. 1991 / EMI America ✦✦✦✦
George Thorogood can usually be counted on to deliver infectious, rowdy blues-rock, and *Boogie People* is no exception. Though not quite on a par with *Bad to the Bone*, this is an unpretentious party album with more than a

few assets. The splendor of Chess Records had long been one of Thorogood's primary inspirations, so it shouldn't come as a major surprise that his versions of John Lee Hooker's "Mad Man Blues," Howlin' Wolf's "No Place To Go," and Muddy Waters' "Can't Be Satisfied" are as appealing as they are. The Delaware singer managed to offend the "Political Correctness Police" with "If You Don't Start Drinkin' (I'm Gonna Leave)," which finds a drunken man chastising his companion for choosing to remain sober. But they missed a key point: this song is an example of pure humor that, like so many blues songs before it, isn't meant to be taken all that seriously. — *Alex Henderson*

● **The Baddest of George Thorogood & the Destroyers** / Jul. 28, 1992 / EMI America ✦✦✦✦
The aptly-titled *The Baddest of George Thorogood & the Destroyers* offers a dozen tracks that cleanse the church of rock'n'roll of all but its most basic elements: guitar, bass, drums, and a pile of Chuck Berry, Bo Diddley, and Rolling Stone licks. Delaware's George Thorogood has never quite captured his wildman live presence in the studio, but having all his best material gathered on one disc—including "Bad to the Bone," "Move It on Over," and "One Bourbon, One Scotch, One Beer"—makes for a great party. Steve Morse's liner notes are brief but, like the songs, get right to the point... cut to the bone, you might say. — *Roch Parisien*

Haircut / Jul. 27, 1993 / EMI America ✦✦
You wouldn't expect any changes from George Thorogood, whose pile-driving rocking-blues and boogie have maintained their appeal despite the emergence of numerous similar-sounding ensembles. Thorogood's rough-hewn singing and always tantalizing playing are on target through the usual mix of originals and covers (this time including Bo Diddley and Willie Dixon). Besides the bonus of major label engineering and production, Thorogood's work has never lost its edge because he avoids becoming indulgent or a parody, and continues to sound genuinely interested in and a fan of the tunes he's doing. — *Ron Wynn*

Let's Work Together Live / 1995 / EMI America ✦✦
George Thorogood hasn't changed his sound at all since his first live album, the aptly-titled *Live*. That's not necessarily a bad thing—his beer-stained bare-bones boogie has always satisfied his fans and it is never lacking in energy, particularly when he is stoked by the enthusiasm of a live crowd. But that doesn't guarantee that *Let's Work Together Live* will be a successful, enjoyable record. Quite simply, that energy does not translate to tape very well, leaving *Let's Work Together* curiously unengaging and somewhat distant. There are good moments scattered throughout the record, but it never pulls together into a cohesive album. — *Stephen Thomas Erlewine*

Rockin' My Life Away / Mar. 25, 1997 / Capitol ✦✦
As the title says, George Thorogood has been rockin' his life away, churning out a series of heavy blues-rock records, all of them stylistically identical to each other. *Rockin' My Life Away* is no exception to the rule, and while it is marginally better than the tepid *Haircut*, it sounds so damned similar to all of his other records that even fans have to wonder what the point is anymore. There are some differences, most notably that the selection of material is more interesting than before—out of the ten covers, there are songs by John Hiatt ("The Usual"), Jerry Lee Lewis, Frank Zappa, and Chuck Willis—and while he's losing energy as he ages, it actually adds some subtlety to his music. Still, if *Rockin' My Life Away* is anything, it's bloozy boogie and it's predictable, and for longtime fans, the lack of spark may cancel out the strength of the material. — *Stephen Thomas Erlewine*

Allen Toussaint

b. Jan. 14, 1938, New Orleans, LA
Vocals, Piano, Keyboards / New Orleans R&B, R&B, Electric Louisiana Blues
His inherently funky piano work heavily influenced by his Crescent City forefathers—Professor Longhair, Huey "Piano" Smith, and Fats Domino—and with a heavy dose of Ray Charles, a young visionary named Allen Toussaint almost singlehandedly fashioned a fresh, vital New Orleans R&B sound for the early '60s. Earning a vaunted reputation as a session pianist, Toussaint debuted on vinyl in 1958 with an obscure RCA album whimsically billed as "A. Tousan." When Joe Banashak inaugurated his Minit label in 1960, Tous-

saint joined the firm as A&R man and quickly proved himself the ultimate behind-the-scenes wizard on the New Orleans scene. During the early to mid-'60s, Toussaint tirelessly wrote, arranged, produced, and played on hits by Ernie K-Doe, Irma Thomas, Jessie Hill, Chris Kenner, Barbara George, Lee Dorsey, Benny Spellman, the Showmen, and many more, his rolling keyboards vital to the charm of virtually all of them.

After unleashing the Meters on the world, Toussaint finally began to step out as a front man in 1970, although his low-key vocals have never achieved quite the same level of success as his previous productions for others. His brilliant compositions have been covered by everyone from Herb Alpert & the Tijuana Brass to Robert Palmer and Bonnie Raitt. Allen Toussaint's stature as a New Orleans musical giant endures.

Allen Toussaint found a new audience in 1994 when he joined country legend Chet Atkins for an updated rendition of "Southern Nights" on the CD *Rhythm, Country and Blues. —Bill Dahl*

The Wild Sound of New Orleans / 1958 / RCA Victor ◆◆◆◆
His debut album, featuring a killer band, storming second-line instrumentals, and Toussaint's rolling 88s. —*Bill Dahl*

Toussaint / 1971 / Scepter ◆◆◆
New Orleans production and performing wizard Allen Toussaint launched his solo career with this early-'70s release. But for some strange reason, the same performer who's written and produced marvelous material for Irma Thomas, Lee Dorsey, Chocolate Milk, and General Johnson among others, was never able to score the same success working as a lead act. There was nothing on this album even in the same arena as his classic R&B tunes, and throughout Toussaint's run of solo releases, only the song "Southern Nights," which Glen Campbell made a hit, could be even mentioned in the same sentence with Toussaint classics like "Ride Your Pony" or "It Will Stand." —*Ron Wynn*

Motion / Aug. 1978 / Reprise ◆◆◆
A nicely produced, competently performed, but disappointing album by New Orleans giant Allen Toussaint. He seemed unable to find a groove or a sound, dabbling in pop, light R&B, rock, and mild funk, but never coming close to duplicating prior magical productions or compositions. This was perhaps Toussaint's least impressive material, and was especially surprising in light of the artistic success of his prior Warner Bros. album *Homage.* —*Ron Wynn*

● **Allen Tousaint Collection** / Apr. 30, 1991 / Reprise ◆◆◆◆
R&B with some meat on its bones from New Orleans songwriter/producer Toussaint. This retrospective collection covers four albums since 1970, including his one album for Scepter, *From a Whisper to a Scream.* The music is often dark, without being depressing, horn driven and loosely propelled along by the rhythm section. It's the sort of music that may not be immediate, but given a few chances it'll work its way right under the skin and stay there. What's sad is that they rarely make music like this anymore—this is music out of blood and bone. —*Steven McDonald*

The Complete "Tousan" Sessions / 1992 / Bear Family ◆◆◆◆
A compilation of instrumentals from 1958 and 1959 featuring Toussaint at the top of his form, *The Complete "Tousan" Sessions* is a wonderful portrait of the seminal New Orleans pianist; it's also the first time this material has ever been available on CD. —*Stephen Thomas Erlewine*

Connected / May 7, 1996 / NYNO ◆◆◆◆
Allen Toussaint's name became synonymous with New Orleans music, even though he didn't seem to "do" the records, his name was on as producer, arranger, or writer on records by artists such as Ernie K-Doe or Irma Thomas. This is his first studio album in at least a decade, and it is a very worthy effort of all self-penned songs that seem to be a mix of old and new (if not in age, at least in feel). He is supported by an extremely worthy cast of the finest New Orleans musicians. Funky material like "Funky Bars," "Ahya," and the rolling gait of "Oh My" stands next to much softer pieces that require a more versatile voice. There are times when his voice doesn't have that reaching pain, for instance, that Aaron Neville gave to "Wrong Number." On most cuts, his easy delivery is just what is called for, and his rollicking piano is always perfectly matched to the song. This is not a disc of memories, though it may bring up a few, it is fresh new funk and roll from the city where American music has always stretched to new levels. —*Bob Gottlieb*

Henry Townsend (Too Tight Henry)
b. Oct. 27, 1909, Shelby, MS
Guitar, Piano, Vocals / Country Blues, Piano Blues, Acoustic Memphis Blues, Prewar Country Blues
Influenced by Roosevelt Sykes and Lonnie Johnson, Henry Townsend was a commanding musician, adept on both piano and guitar. During the '20s and '30s, Townsend was one of the musicians that helped make St. Louis one of the blues centers of America.

Townsend arrived in St. Louis when he was around 10 years old, just before the '20s began. By the end of the '20s, he had landed a record contract with Columbia, cutting several sides of open-tuning slide guitar for the label. Two years later, he made some simliar recordings for Paramount. During this time, Townsend began playing the piano, learning the instrument by playing along with Roosevelt Sykes records. Within a few years, he was able to perform concerts with pianists like Walter Davis and Henry Brown.

During the '30s, Townsend was a popular session musician, performing with many of the era's most popular artists. By the late '30s, he had cut several tracks for Bluebird. Those were among the last recordings he ever made as a leader. During the '40s and '50s, Townsend continued to perform and record as a session musician, but he never made any solo records.

In 1960, he led a few sessions, but they didn't receive much attention. Toward the end of the '60s, Townsend became a staple on the blues and folk festivals in America, which led to a comeback. He cut a number of albums for Adelphi and he played shows throughout America. By the end of the '70s, he had switched from Adelphi to Nighthawk Records.

Townsend had become an elder statesmen of St. Louis blues by the early '80s, recording albums for Wolf and Swingmaster and playing a handful of shows every year. *That's the Way I Do It,* a documentary about Townsend, appeared on public television in 1984. During the late '80s, Townsend was nearly retired, but he continued to play the occasional concert. —*Cub Koda & Stephen Thomas Erlewine*

Tired of Bein' Mistreated / 1962 / Bluesville ◆◆◆

Music Man / Dec. 1975 / Adelphi ◆◆◆

Mule / 1980 / Nighthawk ◆◆◆◆
Venerable St. Louis guitarist and pianist Henry Townsend mostly stuck to the keyboard on this outstanding session. It was forceful, wonderfully sung and alternately moving, impressive and inspiring. —*Ron Wynn*

● **Henry Townsend & Henry Spaulding** / 1986 / Wolf ◆◆◆◆
Wolf's *Henry Townsend & Henry Spaulding* isn't a collaboration—it's a collection that features the 13 known songs Townsend recorded between 1929 and 1937, plus the two songs Spaulding recorded in 1929. Spaulding's pair are fine country-blues, but the true value in this disc is that it features the majority of Townsend's early work. He recorded four other songs during this era, but those are currently missing, which means this is the closest thing to a "complete" document of his earliest recordings. Most of his recordings find him alone with a guitar and these are wonderful, haunting country-blues. A couple of other cuts are duets between Townsend and pianist Roosevelt Sykes, while the remainder feature him with a small group featuring piano, harmonica and guitar. These are great performances, and rank among the most underrated sides of their era. —*Thom Owens*

Tre
b. Grenada, MS
Guitar, Vocals / Modern Electric Blues
The son of bluesman L.V. Banks, the singer/guitarist known simply as Tre carried on the traditions of his father's music, recapturing the sound and feeling of '50s-era Chicago blues with accuracy and real affection. Born Tre Hardiman in Grenada, MS, he was raised on Chicago's South Side, initially playing rock and R&B; his musical allegiance moved to the blues while backing Banks between 1981 and 1987, during which time he honed a fluid, shimmering guitar style. Tre's solo debut, *Delivered for Glory—Reclaiming the Blues,* appeared in 1996; the follow-up, *Blues Knock'n Baby—* recorded with backing band the Blueknights—was released a year later. —*Jason Ankeny*

● **Delivered for Glory: Reclaiming the Blues** / Mar. 19, 1996 / JSP ◆◆◆◆
Delivered for Glory: Reclaiming the Blues is a promising debut from Tre, the

son of L.V. Banks. There are some Banks influences on the record, particularly in his guitar phrasing, but the record remains grounded in Chicago blues, with the occasional uptown flourish that distinguishes it from the pack of modern electric blues. He needs to grow as a songwriter, but he shows enough potential as a vocalist and guitarist to have *Delivered for Glory* be a strong debut. — *Thom Owens*

Blues Knock'n Baby / Jul. 1, 1997 / Wolf ✦✦✦

Robin Trower

b. Mar. 9, 1945, London, England
Guitar / Blues-Rock, Hard Rock
Guitarist Robin Trower began his career in a British R&B group called the Paramounts in 1963, which evolved into Procol Harum following a breakup. Trower left for a solo career in 1971 owing to a divergence of musical direction; while his former group was exploring its classical-rock leanings, Trower wanted to continue playing the Clapton- and Hendrix-influenced power-trio blues-rock that had inspired him. Trower's first project, the quartet Jude, went nowhere, and he took a year off to form a power trio with bassist Jimmy Dewar and drummer Reg Isadore. Trower's early work strongly recalled that of Jimi Hendrix, almost to the point of imitation, but constant touring established him as a new guitar hero and landed two gold Top Ten albums in 1974's *Bridge of Sighs* and 1975's *For Earth Below*. The latter LP featured ex-Sly and the Family Stone drummer Bill Lordan. Trower returned to his R&B roots for *In City Dreams* and *Caravan to Midnight;* in danger of losing his audience, Trower returned to rock on *Victims of the Fury.*

In 1981, Trower and Lordan formed BLT with ex-Cream bassist Jack Bruce, recording one album as a group and another credited to Bruce and Trower. The Robin Trower Band was re-formed in 1983, and has continued to record for several labels in spite of declining success and varying personnel. During the '90s, Trower continued to tour and record, as well as produce records for other musicians. — *Steve Huey*

Twice Removed from Yesterday / 1973 / Chrysalis ✦✦✦✦
The classic solo debut by this former Procol Harum guitarist has moody Hendrix-inspired guitar, plus James Dewar's magnificent whiskey-throated vocals. — *Michael P. Dawson*

Bridge of Sighs / 1974 / Chrysalis ✦✦✦✦
Trower's second album is another solid effort. — *Michael P. Dawson*

For Earth Below / 1975 / Chrysalis ✦✦✦
His third album is less consistent than the previous two but still contains much excellent material. — *Michael P. Dawson*

Live / 1976 / Chrysalis ✦✦✦✦
A truly fine live set, it was recorded in Sweden. — *Michael P. Dawson*

Long Misty Days / 1976 / Chrysalis ✦✦✦
A good mix of down-and-dirty blues, it also features Trower's ethereal ballads. — *Michael P. Dawson*

In City Dreams / 1977 / Chrysalis ✦✦✦
Slightly funkier than the previous albums, it's still highlighted by a delicate ballad, "Bluebird," and the majestic title track. — *Michael P. Dawson*

Caravan to Midnight / 1978 / Chrysalis ✦✦✦
It continues the funkier direction of *In City Dreams.* — *Michael P. Dawson*

Victims of the Fury / 1980 / Chrysalis ✦✦✦

B.L.T. / 1981 / Chrysalis ✦✦✦
Trower is joined by Cream bassist/vocalist Jack Bruce, and drummer Bill Lordan. — *Michael P. Dawson*

Truce / 1982 / Chrysalis ✦✦

Back It Up / 1983 / Chrysalis ✦✦✦

Beyond the Mist / 1985 / Passport ✦✦

Passion / 1987 / GNP ✦✦

Take What You Need / 1988 / Atlantic ✦✦✦

No Stopping Anytime / 1989 / Chrysalis ✦✦✦✦
This is a compilation from Trower's two collaborations with Cream bassist Jack Bruce. — *Michael P. Dawson*

In the Line of Fire / 1990 / Atlantic ✦✦

● **Essential** / 1991 / Chrysalis ✦✦✦✦
Essential is a strong single-disc collection that features 16 highlights from Robin Trower's long career at Chrysalis, including such staples as "Too Rolling Stoned," plus several key album tracks. While such albums as *Bridge of Sighs* work as individual albums, this does a nice job of rounding up highlights from uneven records, making it a nice sampler both for casual fans and the curious. — *Stephen Thomas Erlewine*

Collection / Jun. 30, 1992 / Castle ✦✦✦✦

Twice Removed from Yesterday/Bridge of Sighs / 1997 / Beat Goes On ✦✦✦✦
Robin Trower's two best albums, *Twice Removed from Yesterday* and *Bridge of Sighs*, were combined on this single disc from Beat Goes On. — *Stephen Thomas Erlewine*

Live/For Earth Below / Apr. 8, 1997 / Beat Goes On ✦✦✦
Robin Trower's third album, 1975's *For Earth Below* is less consistent than the previous two but still contains much excellent material; the Beat Goes On label's reissue teams it with 1976's *Live*, a truly fine set recorded in Sweden. — *Michael P. Dawson*

Long Misty Days/In City Dreams / May 20, 1997 / Beat Goes On ✦✦✦
A good mix of down-and-dirty blues, 1976's *Long Misty Days* also features Trower's ethereal ballads. Its 1977 follow-up *In City Dreams*—also included on this two-fer—is slightly funkier than the previous albums, but still highlighted by a delicate ballad, "Bluebird" and the majestic title track. — *Michael P. Dawson*

Caravan to Midnight/Victims of the Fury / Jun. 24, 1997 / Beat Goes On ✦✦✦✦
Caravan to Midnight, first released in 1978, continues the funkier direction of the previous *In City Dreams;* the Beat Goes On label's reissue pairs the album with its 1980 follow-up, *Victims of the Fury.* — *Michael P. Dawson*

Derek Trucks

Guitar / Blues-Rock
Blues/blues-rock guitarist Derek Trucks is the nephew of longtime Allman Brothers drummer Butch Trucks. He displays a command of slide guitar styles that run the gamut from blues to classic R&B and early rock 'n' roll to classic jazz. Although blues players like Buddy Guy, Elmore James, and Duane Allman have been a strong influence on Trucks' slide guitar playing, so have pre-1970s jazz players like Coltrane, Charlie Parker, and Sun Ra.

Trucks began playing guitar when he was nine, and shared stages and sat in with the likes of Buddy Guy and the Allman Brothers Band by the time he was 12. Trucks began his professional career playing with blues bands around his native Jacksonville, FL, and formed his own group in high school. Before the age of 20, Trucks shared stages and jammed with Bob Dylan, Joe Walsh and Stephen Stills.

The Butch Trucks Band, which has members ranging in age from their 20s to their 40s, released their self-titled debut album in 1997 on Landslide Records. — *Richard J. Skelly*

Derek Trucks / Oct. 7, 1997 / Landslide ✦✦✦

The Trumpeteers

db. 1948
Group / Black Gospel, Traditional Gospel
Influenced by the Golden Gate Quartet and led by the spectacular singing of Joe Johnson, this quartet hit the public's consciousness in the late '40s with "Milky White Way," which they recorded for Score Records. Other members included Raleigh Tunrage (tenor), Joseph Armstrong (baritone), and James Keels (bass). There were numerous personnel changes, and they disbanded upon Johnson's death in 1948. — *Bil Carpenter & Kip Lornell*

1948-1959 / 1948-1959 / ✦✦✦✦
Joe Johnson & the Trumpeteers Quartet were extremely popular during the late '40s and early '50s, due in part to "Milky White Way." The tape mostly covers the Score/Aladdin years 1947-1949 before their appearance on King, OKeh, Gotham, Grand & Jubilee labels. Their style is close harmony jubilee with sparse guitar chordings. Three Nashboro cuts from the late '50s are also included. There's some duplication with a Gospel Jubilee LP. There's good

overall sound quality (cassette only). *—Opal Louis Nations, Roots & Rhythm Newsletter*

★ **Milky White Way** / 1956 / Score ♦♦♦♦♦
One of the last great jubilee singing quartets. Score and Grant material. 1947-54. *—Opal Louis Nations*

In Memory of Laura / 1970 / Jewel ♦♦♦♦
Very talented mixed family group. *—Opal Louis Nations*

The Mighty Number / HSF ♦♦♦♦
The group's impressive comeback album. *—Opal Louis Nations*

Bessie Tucker

b. Texas
Vocals / Classic Female Blues, Acoustic Texas Blues, Prewar Country Blues
Very little is known of the classic blues belter Bessie Tucker, a product of the folk and field holler vocal traditions of her native East Texas region. A woman whose petite frame belied the earthy power of her voice, her legend is largely founded on a bawdy 1928 Memphis session for the Victor label on which she was accompanied by pianist K.D. Johnson; the date yielded her best-known track, "Penitentiary" (sung in honor of an institution to which she was reportedly no stranger). A 1929 date followed, at which time Tucker disappeared from performing, apparently for good; no data exists on the later events of her life. *—Jason Ankeny*

★ **Complete Works (1928-1929)** / 1991 / Document ♦♦♦♦♦
Document's *Complete Works (1928-1929)* is an exhaustive overview of Bessie Tucker's recordings from that period. Completists and academics will find the exacting chronological sequencing, poor fidelity (all cuts are transferred from original acetates and 78s), and number of performances to be positive factors, but enthusiasts and casual listeners will find that the collection is of marginal interest for those very reasons. *—Thom Owens*

Luther Tucker

b. Jan. 20, 1936, Memphis, TN, **d.** Jun. 18, 1993, San Rafael, CA
Guitar / Chicago Blues
Guitarist Luther Tucker was born on January 20, 1936, in Memphis, TN, but relocated to Chicago's South side when Tucker was around seven years of age. His father, a carpenter, built Tucker his first guitar and his mother, who played boogie-woogio piano, introduced him to Big Bill Broonzy around that time. He went on to study guitar with Robert Jr. Lockwood, for whom he had the greatest admiration and respect. Tucker worked with Little Walter Jacobs for seven years and played on many of Walter's classic sides. He also recorded with Otis Rush, Robben Ford, Sonny Boy Williamson II, Jimmy Rogers, Snooky Pryor, Muddy Waters, John Lee Hooker, Elvin Bishop, and James Cotton.

In the mid-'60s, Tucker was featured in the James Cotton Blues Band and traveled with that band extensively. He relocated to Marin County, CA, in 1973 and formed the Luther Tucker Band. He played in clubs in the San Francisco Bay area until his death on June 18, 1993, in Greenbrae, CA. Luther Tucker, who was soft-spoken and even shy, was one of a handful of backup artists (the Four Aces/Jukes were others) who helped to create and shape the small combo sound of Chicago blues. Unfortunately, they seldom get much credit. Yet, as the history of Chicago blues gets written, there will be more and more time to discover the wonderful understated rhythmic guitar mastery of Luther Tucker. *—Michael Erlewine*

● **Sad Hours** / 1990 / Antone's ♦♦♦♦
This album is more of a memorial to late guitarist Tucker (who died in June 1993) than a solo debut (the tracks were recorded three years before his death). Still, it's a very nice, soulful slice of the funkier edge of blues, a good tribute, and showcases some nice guitar work. *—Steven McDonald*

Tommy Tucker (Robert Higginbotham)

b. Mar. 5, 1933, Springfield, OH, **d.** Jan. 17, 1982, Newark, NJ
Piano, Vocals / R&B, Electric R&B
When Tommy Tucker ordered his lady to "put on her hi-heel sneakers" in 1964, the whole world was listening, judging from the myriad of covers and sequels that followed in its wake.

Robert Higginbotham (Tucker's legal handle) grew up in Springfield, getting his little fingers accustomed to the ivories by age seven. Tucker joined

saxist Bobby Wood's band in the late '40s as its piano player. When vocal groups became the rage, the band switched gears and became the Cavaliers, a doo wop outfit that remained intact into the late '50s. Tucker put together his own combo after that to play bars in Dayton, his personnel including guitarist Weldon Young and bassist Brenda Jones.

The trio eventually relocated to Newark, NJ, setting Tucker up for his debut solo session in 1961 for Atco. "Rock and Roll Machine" was issued as by Tee Tucker and already exhibited the gritty, Ray Charles-inflected vocal delivery that Tucker later used to great advantage. His traveling companions did pretty well for themselves, too: renamed Dean & Jean, they hit big in 1963-64 with the lighthearted duets "Tra La La La Suzy" and "Hey Jean, Hey Dean" for Rust Records.

Tommy Tucker fortuitously hooked up with Atlantic Records co-founder Herb Abramson, who was working as an independent R&B producer during the early '60s. Among their early collaborations was the lowdown Jimmy Reed-style shuffle "Hi-Heel Sneakers" (Dean Young was the nasty lead guitarist). Abramson leased it to Checker Records and watched it sail to the upper reaches of the pop charts in early 1964. A terrific Checker LP and a trip to Great Britain were among the immediate upshot for the organist.

R&B star Don Covay co-wrote Tucker's follow-up, "Long Tall Shorty," an amusing tune in a similar groove. It barely scraped the lower end of the charts, and Tucker never scored another hit. That didn't stop Abramson from trying, though—he produced Tucker singing a soulful "That's Life" in 1966 for his own Festival label, while "Alimony," another standout Checker 45, certainly deserved a better reception than it got in 1965.

Although the majority of his waxings were under Abramson's supervision, Tucker did travel to Chicago in 1966 to record with producer Willie Dixon in an effort to jump-start his fading career. "I'm Shorty" had Dixon contributing harmony vocals and Big Walter Horton on harp, but it didn't do the trick.

Abramson admirably stuck by his protégé, recording him anew for at least another decade, but most of the mixed results just gathered dust in his vaults. Tucker was still musically active when he died, a relatively young man, in 1982. *—Bill Dahl*

● **Hi Heel Sneakers** / 1964 / Checker ♦♦♦♦
Until some enterprising CD reissue label assembles a decent Tucker package, this ancient slab of vinyl will remain a prime collecto's item. A dozen of his best blues and soul outings for producer Herb Abramson, including the two hits, the grinding soul rockers "Just for a Day," "I Don't Want 'Cha," and "I Warned You About Him" (oodles of Ray Charles influence on all of 'em), and an absolutely stunning "Come Rain or Come Shine." *—Bill Dahl*

Mother Tucker / 1974 / Red Lightnin' ♦♦♦
Leftovers from deep in the Abramson archives. A precious few tracks—"Lean Greens," "Drunk"—possess the same gritty charm that invested Tucker's greatest hit, "Hi-Heel Sneakers" (here in longer, unedited form with Tucker's faltering organ solo intact). Most of the 16-song LP is comprised of demo tapes and other flotsam that doesn't present the keyboardist in the best light. *—Bill Dahl*

Big Joe Turner (Joseph Vernon Turner)

b. May 18, 1911, Kansas City, MO, **d.** Nov. 24, 1985, Inglewood, CA
Vocals / Swing, Jump Blues, R&B, Jazz, Rock 'n' Roll
The premier blues shouter of the postwar era, Big Joe Turner's roar could rattle the very foundation of any gin joint he sang within—and that's without a microphone. Turner was a resilient figure in the history of blues—he effortlessly spanned boogie-woogie, jump blues, even the first wave of rock 'n' roll, enjoying great success in each genre.

Turner, whose powerful physique certainly matched his vocal might, was a product of the swinging, wide-open Kansas City scene. Even in his teens, the big-boned Turner looked entirely mature enough to gain entry to various K.C. niteries. He ended up simultaneously tending bar and singing the blues before hooking up with boogie piano master Pete Johnson during the early '30s. Theirs was a partnership that would endure for 13 years.

The pair initially traveled to New York at John Hammond's behest in 1936. On December 23, 1938, they appeared on the fabled Spirituals to Swing concert at Carnegie Hall on a bill with Big Bill Broonzy, Sonny Terry, the Golden Gate Quartet, and Count Basie. Big Joe and Johnson performed "Low Down Dog" and "It's All Right, Baby" on the historic show, kicking off a boogie-woogie craze that landed them a long-running slot at the Cafe Society (along with piano giants Meade Lux Lewis and Albert Ammons).

As 1938 came to a close, Turner and Johnson waxed the thundering "Roll 'Em Pete" for Vocalion. It was a thrilling uptempo number anchored by Johnson's crashing 88s, and Turner would re-record it many times over the decades. Turner and Johnson waxed their seminal blues "Cherry Red" the next year for Vocalion with trumpeter Hot Lips Page and a full combo in support. In 1940, the massive shouter moved over to Decca and cut "Piney Brown Blues" with Johnson rippling the ivories. But not all of Turner's Decca sides teamed him with Johnson; Willie "The Lion" Smith accompanied him on the mournful "Careless Love," while Freddie Slack's Trio provided backing for "Rocks in My Bed" in 1941.

Turner ventured out to the West Coast during the war years, building quite a following while ensconced on the L.A. circuit. In 1945, he signed on with National Records and cut some fine small combo platters under Herb Abramson's supervision. Turner remained with National through 1947, belting an exuberant "My Gal's a Jockey" that became his first national R&B smash. Contracts didn't stop him from waxing an incredibly risqué two-part "Around the Clock" for the aptly named Stag imprint (as Big Vernon!) in 1947. There were also solid sessions for Aladdin that year that included a wild vocal duel with one of Turner's principal rivals, Wynonie Harris, on the ribald two-part "Battle of the Blues."

Few West Coast indie labels of the late '40s didn't boast at least one or two Turner titles in their catalogs. The shouter bounced from RPM to Down Beat/Swing Time to MGM (all those dates were anchored by Johnson's piano) to Texas-based Freedom (which moved some of their masters to Specialty) to Imperial in 1950 (his New Orleans backing crew there included a young Fats Domino on piano). But apart from the 1950 Freedom 78, "Still in the Dark," none of Big Joe's records were selling particularly well. When Atlantic Records bosses Abramson and Ahmet Ertegun fortuitously dropped by the Apollo Theater to check out Count Basie's band one day, they discovered that Turner had temporarily replaced Jimmy Rushing as the Basie band's front man, and he was having a tough go of it. Atlantic picked up his spirits by picking up his recording contract, and Big Joe Turner's heyday was about to commence.

At Turner's first Atlantic date in April of 1951, he imparted a gorgeously world-weary reading to the moving blues ballad "Chains of Love" (co-penned by Ertegun and pianist Harry Van Walls) that restored him to the uppermost reaches of the R&B charts. From there, the hits came in droves: "Chill Is On," "Sweet Sixteen" (yeah, the same downbeat blues B.B. King's usually associated with; Turner did it first), and "Don't You Cry" were all done in New York, and all hit big.

Big Joe Turner had no problem whatsoever adapting his prodigious pipes to whatever regional setting he was in. In 1953, he cut his first R&B chart-topper, the storming rocker "Honey Hush" (later covered by Johnny Burnette and Jerry Lee Lewis), in New Orleans, with trombonist Pluma Davis and tenor saxman Lee Allen in rip-roaring support. Before the year was through, he stopped off in Chicago to record with slide guitarist Elmore James' considerably rougher-edged combo and hit again with the salacious "T.V. Mama."

Prolific Atlantic house writer Jesse Stone was the source of Turner's biggest smash of all, "Shake, Rattle and Roll," which proved his second chart-topper in 1954. With the Atlantic braintrust reportedly chiming in on the chorus behind Turner's rumbling lead, the song sported enough pop possibilities to merit a considerably cleaned-up cover by Bill Haley & the Comets (and a subsequent version by Elvis Presley that came a lot closer to the original leering intent).

Suddenly, at the age of 43, Big Joe Turner was a rock star. His jumping follow-ups—"Well All Right," "Flip Flop and Fly," "Hide and Seek," "Morning, Noon and Night," "The Chicken and the Hawk"—all mined the same good-time groove as "Shake, Rattle and Roll," with crisp backing from New York's top session aces and typically superb production by Ertegun and Jerry Wexler.

Turner turned up on a couple episodes of the groundbreaking TV program *Showtime at the Apollo* during the mid-'50s, commanding center stage with a joyous rendition of "Shake, Rattle and Roll" in front of saxman Paul "Hucklebuck" Williams' band. Nor was the silver screen immune to his considerable charms: Turner mimed a couple of numbers in the 1957 film *Shake Rattle & Rock* (Fats Domino and Mike "Mannix" Connors also starred in the flick).

Updating the pre-war number "Corrine Corrina" was an inspired notion that provided Turner with another massive seller in 1956. But after the two-sided hit "Rock a While"/"Lipstick Powder and Paint" later that year, his Atlantic output swiftly faded from commercial acceptance. Atlantic's recording strategy wisely involved recording Turner in a jazzier setting for the adult-oriented album market; to that end, a Kansas City-styled set (with his former partner Johnson at the piano stool) was laid down in 1956 and remains a linchpin of his legacy.

Turner stayed on at Atlantic into 1959, but nobody bought his violin-enriched remake of "Chains of Love" (on the other hand, a revival of "Honey Hush" with King Curtis blowing a scorching sax break from the same session was a gem in its own right). The '60s didn't produce too much of lasting substance for the shouter—he actually cut an album with longtime admirer Haley and his latest batch of Comets in Mexico City in 1966!

But by the tail end of the decade, Big Joe Turner's essential contributions to blues history were beginning to receive proper recognition; he cut LPs for BluesWay and Blues Time. During the '70s and '80s, Turner recorded prolifically for Norman Granz's jazz-oriented Pablo label. These were super-relaxed impromptu sessions that often paired the allegedly illiterate shouter with various jazz luminaries in what amounted to loosely-run jam sessions. Turner contentedly roared the familiar lyrics of one or another of his hits, then sat back while somebody took a lengthy solo. Other notable album projects included a 1983 collaboration with Roomful of Blues, *Blues Train*, for Muse. Although health problems and the size of his humongous frame forced him to sit down during his latter-day performances, Turner continued to tour until shortly before his death in 1985. They called him the Boss of the Blues, and the appellation was truly a fitting one: when Big Joe Turner shouted a lyric, you were definitely at his beck and call. —*Bill Dahl*

☆ **Big, Bad & Blue: The Big Joe Turner Anthology** / Dec. 30, 1938-Jan. 26, 1983 / Rhino ✦✦✦✦✦
Rhino has done a stellar job of cross-licensing to present an exhaustive three-disc, 62-track compilation that traces the booming jump blues belter's recording career from its Kansas City-bred beginnings with pianist Pete Johnson in 1938 through the postwar years with the National, Aladdin, Down Beat, and Freedom labels and on into his R&B heyday on Atlantic from 1951 to 1959. Of course, all the great prototypical rockers are aboard—"Honey Hush," "Shake, Rattle and Roll," "Flip Flop and Fly," Corrine Corrina"—and the set closes with three far more recent entries that are the weakest tracks on the entire anthology. The sheer power of Big Joe's pipes was overwhelming, his combos cooked mercilessly, and this set is one to get. —*Bill Dahl*

I've Been to Kansas City / Nov. 11, 1940-Jul. 17, 1941 / Decca ✦✦✦✦
This excellent 1990 CD reissues singer Big Joe Turner's first eight recordings for Decca and the six songs (plus two alternate takes) that he made with the remarkable pianist Art Tatum. Turner is joined by trumpeter Hot Lips Page and a top Kansas City group (including pianist Pete Johnson) for "Piney Brown Blues," has four surprisingly effective duets with the sophisticated pianist Willie "The Lion" Smith and is backed by pianist Sammy Price's trio for three of the four numbers that he recorded on July 17, 1941. The Tatum sides (highlighted by the classic "Wee Baby Blues" and "Corrine, Corrina") also feature trumpeter Joe Thomas and (on two songs) clarinetist Edmond Hall prominent in the backup group. Just 29 and 30 during this time, Turner already sounded quite mature and powerful. —*Scott Yanow*

☆ **Complete 1940-1944** / Nov. 11, 1940-Nov. 13, 1944 / Official ✦✦✦✦✦
Big Joe Turner's 25 Decca recordings are all included on this excellent set. The music is consistently exciting and finds the blues singer in prime form. His accompaniment is quite varied and always colorful with such pianists as Art Tatum, Pete Johnson, Willie "the Lion" Smith (a perfect match), Sam Price, and the surprisingly effective Freddie Slack all getting their spots. Turner had a remarkably long and commercially successful career considering that he never changed his basic approach; he just never went out of style. —*Scott Yanow*

Every Day in the Week / Sep. 8, 1941-Apr. 13, 1967 / GRP/Decca ✦✦✦
Most of the material on this grab bag dates from early- and mid-'40s sessions for Decca. Rather muted and jazzy in feel, they're made more interesting or tedious, depending on your perspective, by the inclusion of many alternate takes (some previously unissued). As these are grouped together one after another, it can make tough listening for the general fan, although Turner

completists will appreciate the attention to detail. Rounding out the collection are four 1963-64 tracks which awkwardly update Turner's R&B with modern soul and pop touches, and a track from a 1967 Bluesway LP. — *Richie Unterberger*

Have No Fear, Big Joe Turner Is Here / Feb. 2, 1945-Nov. 29, 1947 / Savoy ✦✦✦✦
Producer Herb Abramson's first encounters with Big Joe Turner weren't at Atlantic, but for the National logo, where Turner paused from 1945 to 1947 and cut the 26 swinging numbers on this collection. For once, the CD format limits the amount of selections rather than enlarging it; the original two-LP version of this package boasted a few more cuts. Pete Johnson returns to run the 88s on the first seven numbers (including a two-part cover of Saunders King's "S.K. Blues"), and familiar names like saxman Wild Bill Moore and drummer Red Saunders also turn up. "Sally Zu-Zazz," "I Got Love for Sale," and "My Gal's a Jockey" capture the peerless shouter at his ribald best. — *Bill Dahl*

Tell Me Pretty Baby / Nov. 1947-1949 / Arhoolie ✦✦✦✦
Lusty, romping jump blues and boogies from 1947-1949 that team Big Joe Turner with his longtime piano partner Pete Johnson and a coterie of solid L.A. sessioneers. The two dozen entries include party rockers like "Wine-O-Baby Boogie," "Christmas Date Boogie," "I Don't Dig It," and an incredibly raunchy two-part "Around the Clock Blues" (where Turner spends his time in a by-the-hour sexual tryst). — *Bill Dahl*

Rhythm & Blues Years / Apr. 17, 1951-Sep. 29, 1959 / Atlantic ✦✦✦✦
Picks up the rest of the 1950s Atlantic Records motherlode. The Chicago-cut double-entendre gem "TV Mama" (with Elmore James on guitar), the lighthearted rockers "Rock a While," "Morning Noon & Night," and "Lipstick, Powder & Paint," and a rip-snorting remake of Turner's classic "Roll 'Em Pete," here titled "(We're Gonna) Jump for Joy," that in its own way rivals the original (King Curtis' blistering sax solo doesn't hurt), are among the many highlights on the 28-song collection. — *Bill Dahl*

★ **Big Joe Turner's Greatest Hits** / Apr. 19, 1951-Jan. 22, 1958 / Atlantic ✦✦✦✦✦
The best single-disc collection available of Turner's seminal 1950s Atlantic sides (21 sides in all). Most of the essential stuff is here—the world-weary blues ballads "Chains of Love" and "Sweet Sixteen," the rockers "Shake, Rattle and Roll," "Flip Flop and Fly," and "Boogie Woogie Country Girl," and a lusty "Well All Right" that rates with Turner's best jump blues outings ever. — *Bill Dahl*

☆ **Boss of the Blues** / Mar. 6, 1956-Mar. 7, 1956 / Atlantic ✦✦✦✦✦
During an era when Big Joe Turner recordings were often surprise hits with rock 'n' roll fans (particularly "Shake, Rattle and Roll"), he occasionally recorded no-nonsense blues-oriented jazz dates too. This reissue album matched Turner for one of the last times with the veteran boogie-woogie pianist Pete Johnson and also includes a variety of top swing players: trumpeter Joe Newman, trombonist Lawrence Brown, altoist Pete Brown, tenor saxophonist Frank Wess, guitarist Freddie Green, bassist Walter Page, and drummer Cliff Leeman. It is not surprising, considering the number of Basieites on the date, that the band often sounds like a Count Basie combo. Turner is in top form on remakes of some of his early tunes (including "Cherry Red," "Roll 'Em Pete" and "Wee Baby Blues"), a few traditional blues and a couple of swing standards. This music should appeal to many listeners. — *Scott Yanow*

Big Joe Rides Again / Mar. 7, 1956-Sep. 10, 1959 / Atlantic ✦✦✦✦
With the exception of one selection ("Pennies from Heaven") left over from his 1956 record *The Boss of the Blue*, the music on this album was all recorded in September 1959. Veteran blues singer Big Joe Turner returns to his roots, belting out blues and early standards while accompanied by an octet arranged by Ernie Wilkins. Among the key sidemen are the great tenor Coleman Hawkins, trombonist Vic Dickenson, trumpeter Paul Ricard and altoist Jerome Richardson; and the highlights include "Nobody in Mind," "Rebecca," and "Don't You Make Me High." An excellent outing for Turner, whose boisterous style would be largely unchanged over his half-century career. — *Scott Yanow*

Singing the Blues / Dec. 1967 / Mobile Fidelity ✦✦✦
Big Joe Turner made relatively few recordings during 1960-66 but things started to look up in 1967 when he began recording for Bluesway. His initial Bluesway set has been reissued as a Mobile Fidelity audiophile CD. Backed

by some top studio players of the era (Buddy Lucas on tenor and harmonica along with a four-piece rhythm setion), the 56-year old classic blues singer shows that he was still in prime form. Nothing too surprising occurs other than the fact that the ten songs are all Turner's originals. Best-known are the two vintage hits "Roll 'Em Pete" and "Cherry Red" while some of the newer tunes are more forgettable although still delivered with spirit. — *Scott Yanow*

Bosses of the Blues, Vol. 1 / Aug. 18, 1969-Aug. 19, 1969 / RCA/Bluebird ✦✦✦✦
Two Bluesway albums recorded on consecutive days are reissued in full on this single CD. Big Joe Turner sings eight numbers while T-Bone Walker stretches out on seven; both mix together remakes of earlier hits with some newer material. While Turner is accompanied by an orchestra, Walker is joined by a crack studio group with some space allocated to the young tenor Tom Scott. Although not essential, this CD finds the two bluesmen in excellent form; pity that they did not record together. — *Scott Yanow*

Texas Style / Apr. 26, 1971 / Evidence ✦✦✦
This somewhat obscure Black & Blue session (reissued by Evidence on CD) features the great blues singer Big Joe Turner a year before he hooked up with the Pablo label. Turner is backed by a particularly colorful and supportive trio comprised of pianist Milt Buckner (the master of block chords), bassist Slam Stewart (who takes a few of his trademark solos in which he sings along with his bowed bass), and veteran swing drummer Jo Jones. Turner was still in his prime at the time and, even if his material was not too adventurous, the music (which includes a few newer bluish originals plus such standbys as "Cherry Red" and "'Tain't Nobody's Bizness If I Do") is performed with enthusiasm and solid swing. — *Scott Yanow*

Flip, Flop & Fly / Apr. 17, 1972 + Apr. 24, 1972 / Pablo ✦✦✦✦
Big Joe Turner's first of many recordings for Pablo was not initially released until 1989. In the spring of 1972 the 60-year-old blues singer toured Europe with the Count Basie Orchestra and this CD has music from two concerts. Turner's repertoire offered few surprises at that late date (he mostly performs remakes of earlier hits) but his interplay with the Basie big band makes this set somewhat special. Among the soloists heard from are tenors Eddie "Lockjaw" Davis and Jimmy Forrest, trumpeter Pete Minger, altoist Curtis Peagler, and trombonist Al Grey along with Basie himself. Easily recommended to Big Joe Turner fans and a rare opportunity for him to be heard fronting a solid big band. — *Scott Yanow*

Life Ain't Easy / Jun. 3, 1974 / Pablo ✦✦✦
Big Joe Turner's Pablo recordings of 1974-84 tended to be loose and sometimes a bit sloppy (with some overlong performances) but they were always full of spirit. On this particular CD, Turner's classic singing is matched with a mostly all-star crew including trumpeter Roy Eldridge, trombonist Al Grey, tenor saxophonist Lee Allen, bassist Ray Brown, and drummer Earl Palmer (along with guitarist Thomas Gadson and Jimmy Robins on piano and organ). Turner performs Woody Guthrie's "So Long" and five of his recent originals; Eldridge and Grey's occasional competitive solos uplift the music. — *Scott Yanow*

The Trumpet Kings Meet Joe Turner / Sep. 19, 1974 / Original Jazz Classics ✦✦✦✦
This album has a most unusual session. Veteran blues singer Joe Turner and his usual rhythm section of the mid-'70s (which includes guitarist Pee Wee Crayton) are joined by four notable trumpeters: Dizzy Gillespie, Roy Eldridge, Harry "Sweets" Edison, and Clark Terry. On three blues (including the 15-minute "I Know You Love Me Baby") and "'Tain't Nobody's Bizness If I Do," the group stretches out with each of the trumpeters getting ample solo space. It is not a classic outing (a little more planning and better material might have helped) but it is colorful and unique enough to be easily recommended to straightahead jazz and blues fans. — *Scott Yanow*

Stormy Monday / Sep. 19, 1974-Jun. 22, 1978 / Pablo ✦✦✦
This 1991 CD contains six selections taken from Big Joe Turner's 1974-78 Pablo sessions but never previously released. The veteran blues singer is joined by a variety of famous and obscure musicians with guitarist Pee Wee Crayton and pianist Lloyd Glenn appearing on the majority of the tracks. The most interesting selection, "Stormy Monday," is taken from a 1974 encounter with trumpeters Roy Eldridge, Dizzy Gillespie, Clark Terry, and Harry "Sweets" Edison. The first half of the ten-minute performance works well, with each of the trumpeters getting a solo, but then it rambles on aim-

lessly, demonstrating why the performance went unreleased. The other five numbers (which include one appearance by altoist Eddie "Cleanhead" Vinson) are more coherent and Turner sounds consistently strong. Overall this is a worthwhile set for Big Joe Turner fans. — *Scott Yanow*

Everyday I Have the Blues / Mar. 3, 1975 / Original Jazz Classics ◆◆◆◆
This CD reissues one of Big Joe Turner's better Pablo releases. In 1975 Turner's voice was still strong and he had a compatible four-piece group that featured veteran guitarist Pee Wee Crayton. With guest Sonny Stitt contributing typically boppish solos on tenor and alto, Turner sings mostly familiar material (including "Stormy Monday," "Piney Brown" and "Shake, Rattle and Roll") plus his recent "Martin Luther King Southside." Recommended. — *Scott Yanow*

The Midnight Special / Mar. 27, 1976 / Pablo ◆◆◆◆
Big Joe Turner had the ability to turn every song into the blues. He displays that skill on this loose Pablo session (reissued on CD) during such nonblues songs as "I Left My Heart in San Francisco," "I'm Gonna Sit Right Down and Write Myself a Letter," "I Can't Give You Anything but Love," and "You're Driving Me Crazy." In addition to a four-piece rhythm section of obscure but compatible players, Turner is joined by trumpeter Jake Porter, Roy Brewster on baritone horn, and Curtis Kirk on harmonica. A slightly off-the-wall set that stands apart from most of Turner's Pablo dates. — *Scott Yanow*

Things That I Used to Do / Feb. 8, 1977 / Original Jazz Classics ◆◆◆◆
This is one of Big Joe Turner's best albums of his last period. Turner is in fine form and joined by some superb blues and jazz musicians. Altoist Eddie "Cleanhead" Vinson (pity that he didn't have a vocal duet with Turner) and trumpeter Blue Mitchell get some solo space as does the veteran R&B tenor Wild Bill Moore, pianist Lloyd Glenn, and guitarist Gary Bell. Mitchell can be heard on many of the tunes setting hot ensemble riffs. There are some loose spots but the spirit is definitely there and Turner's voice can be heard still in its prime on such tunes as "Jelly Jelly Blues," "Shake It and Break It," and "St. Louis Blues." Fun music. — *Scott Yanow*

In the Evening / Oct. 1977 / Pablo ◆◆◆
Many of Big Joe Turner's Pablo recordings matched him with big names, but this workout finds him jubilant and in top form singing with some lesser-known musicians (altoist Bob Smith, Herman Bennett on second guitar, pianist J.D. Nicholson, bassist Winston McGregor, drummer Charles Randall, and the only "name" of the date, guitarist Pee Wee Crayton). The solos of Smith (who sounds like a mixture of Tab Smith and Johnny Hodges) and Crayton are consistently excellent, and Big Joe turns everything into blues, including such unlikely material as "Sweet Lorraine" and "Pennies from Heaven." This CD reissue gives listeners a good example of what it was like to catch the great blues singer during a club date with a pickup band. — *Scott Yanow*

Nobody in Mind / 1982 / Original Jazz Classics ◆◆◆◆
Blues singer Big Joe Turner is in good form on this late-period session. In addition to his usual rhythm section (featuring guitarist Pee Wee Crayton), Turner is joined by two notable soloists: trumpeter Roy Eldridge (whose determination makes up for his occasional misses) and vibraphonist Milt Jackson. Other than "Red Sails in the Sunset" (which is largely turned into a blues), the music is fairly typical for Turner but the spirit and sincerity of the singer and his sidemen make this CD reissue worth picking up. — *Scott Yanow*

Blues Train / Jan. 26, 1983 / Muse ◆◆◆
Big Joe Turner was a bit past his prime at age 72, when he recorded this set, but he was clearly inspired by the opportunity to sing with Roomful of Blues. Turner stars on seven numbers (including "I Want a Little Girl," which has a piano solo by guest Dr. John), and there are also two instrumentals that let the impressive band stretch out. With the group featuring guitarist Ronnie Earl, Greg Piccolo on tenor, trumpeter Bob Enos, and trombonist Porky Cohen, among others, Turner was ably supported, and his high spirits made the music well worth hearing. — *Scott Yanow*

Kansas City Here I Come / Feb. 1984 / Original Jazz Classics ◆◆◆
Big Joe Turner's next-to-last recording is certainly listenable but not prime material. Turner's elocution became quite blurry in his later years with a lot of slurring of words and rather loose singing and yet his ability to express blues feeling and his sense of swing were unimpaired. Among the mostly obscure backup crew are tenor saxophonist Lee Allen, Jerry Jumonville on

baritone and alto, and guitarist Terry Evans but in general the playing is pretty anonymous. This CD, one of many Big Joe Turner releases currently available, is mostly for completists. — *Scott Yanow*

Patcha, Patcha All Night Long / Apr. 11, 1985 / Original Jazz Classics ◆◆◆
This CD reissue, which is subtitled "Joe Turner Meets Jimmy Witherspoon," does not quite deliver on its promise. Turner (who would pass away within a year) and Witherspoon only actually meet up on the first two numbers and, other than some interplay on "Patcha, Patcha," the matchup generates few sparks. However the individual features (two songs apiece) are excellent, particularly Witherspoon's "You Got Me Runnin'" and Turner's "The Chicken and the Hawk." In addition there are many fine solos from altoist Red Holloway, Lee Allen on tenor, and guitarist Gary Bell. This is a worthwhile and obviously historic set, recommended as much to blues as jazz collectors. — *Scott Yanow*

Jumpin' with Joe: The Complete Aladdin & Imperial Recordings / Jan. 11, 1994 / EMI America ◆◆◆◆
Big Joe Turner's remarkable recordings for Atlantic and Decca have been frequently reissued and evaluated. But his singles for other labels haven't gotten similar treatment, which makes this 18-cut single-disc anthology of Aladdin and Imperial material so welcome. These were recorded in the late '40s and early '50s and were closer to the Kansas City swing Turner had done earlier in his career; there was more emphasis on lyric interpretation, swing, and timing than sheer volume and volcanic, non-stop hollering. Although these songs aren't remembered as fondly as the landmark Atlantic numbers, they're just as important a part of Turner's legacy. — *Ron Wynn*

Have No Fear, Joe Turner Is Here / 1996 / Pablo ◆◆◆
Big Joe Turner really stretches out during this Pablo date (reissued on CD), singing only five songs: an 11-minute version of Woody Guthrie's "How Come My Dog Don't Bark," three basic originals and "Rocks In My Bed." Sticking to the blues, Turner is joined by four horns (including altoist Bobby Smith), pianist Lloyd Glenn, and a rhythm section that includes guitarist Pee Wee Crayton (the most prominent soloist). The very spontaneous music has plenty of riffing from the horns and fine late-period shouting from Big Joe. — *Scott Yanow*

★ **Very Best of Big Joe Turner** / Feb. 3, 1998 / Rhino ◆◆◆◆◆
The Very Best of Big Joe Turner is an excellent 16-track collection that features his biggest hits from 1951-1959, including "Chains of Love," "Sweet Sixteen," "Honey Hush," "TV Mama," "Shake, Rattle and Roll," "Well All Right," "Flip Flop and Fly," "Hide and Seek," "The Chicken and the Hawk (Up, Up and Away)," "Boogie Woogie Country Girl," "Corrine Corrina," and "Midnight Special Train." All of his best-known songs in their hit versions are available on this concise, affordable disc, which makes for an ideal introduction to this legendary R&B vocalist. — *Stephen Thomas Erlewine*

Ike Turner

b. Nov. 5, 1931, Clarksdale, MS
Guitar, Piano, Vocals / R&B, Soul, Soul Blues, Electric Memphis Blues
It is arguably true that Ike Turner would have never amounted to more than a footnote of rock history if he hadn't joined forces with Tina Turner in 1960. But as a solo artist, he's an important footnote. In 1951, he made a lasting contribution to the music by playing piano on Jackie Brenston's "Rocket 88," which is often cited as one of the very first rock 'n' roll records. That session was one of the first blues/R&B/rock 'n' roll dates produced in Sun Studios in Memphis; Turner learned guitar shortly afterwards, and backed up other R&B artists at Sun in the early '50s. Throughout the decade, the guitarist and piano player was a prolific session player, contributing to records by blues legends Elmore James, Howlin' Wolf, and Otis Rush.

Ike also backed a host of obscure R&B artists in his early years, occasionally issuing discs under his name. Not much of a singer, both his own records and the ones he contributed to and/or produced often showcased his stinging, bluesy licks, and the best of his solo outings tended to be his instrumentals. He continued to put out the occasional solo session and work with other artists after he hooked up with Tina, sometimes under the name Ike Turner's Kings of Rhythm. His career has lurched along in obscurity since he broke up with Tina in the mid-'70s, though he remains active. — *Richie Unterberger*

Trailblazer / 1957 / Charly ◆◆◆◆
During 1956 and early 1957, Ike Turner's Kings of Rhythm recorded for the

Cincinnati-based Federal label—the group's personnel included Raymond Hill and Eddie Jones on tenor sax, Jackie Brenston on baritone sax, Annie Mae Wilson and Fred Sample on piano, Jessie Knight, Jr. on bass, Eugene Washington on drums, and Turner on guitar, with vocalists including Brenston and Billy Gayles. This is some of the most solid material in Turner's output, with a rich, soulful sound, more polished than most of the group's output on Cobra. Some of the music is derivative—in seeking chart success, the group at various times sought to emulate the Coasters, Bill Justis et al, but they almost always put their own spin on these numbers. Billy Gayles' impassioned vocals on "No Coming Back," Jackie Brenston's boisterous rendition of "The Mistreater," and the rest are all worth the price of admission, which is fairly low on this mid-priced import—but, surprisingly, some of the best stuff on here is by the Kings of Rhythm backing the vocal group the Gardenias ("Miserable," one of the best tracks among these 20, remained unreleased until 1991). And the real treat here is Turner's guitar pyrotechnics. He could strum along like most band guitarists, and occasionally did this, but he preferred to step out front and, having discovered the use of the tremelo arm on his guitar, he fairly tortures the instrument on several of these sides (check out the break on "No Comin' Back," and his accompaniment on "She Made My Blood Run Cold," itself an R&B track deserving of legendary status), and even gets a Hawaiian sound out of his instrument on "Trail Blazer." Fans of rock 'n' roll guitar must own this record. —*Bruce Eder*

Ike Turner Rocks the Blues / 1963 / Crown ++++
Ike Turner's Kings of Rhythm, rocking the blues in 1954, with a 23-year-old Turner performing some astonishing guitar acrobatics only a couple of years after taking up the instrument, including the legendary "All the Blues, All the Time." The only pity is that this 1950s material only exists on this incredibly expensive import from Japan, when it ought to be out at an affordable price over here. The late Lester Bangs called it "one of the greatest albums ever made, if not the absolute certifiable Greatest Guitar Album of All Time," and understandably so. —*Bruce Eder*

1958-1959 / May 13, 1993 / Paula ++++
Ever the hustler, Ike Turner found himself picking up some extra money on a road trip through Chicago recording for Cobra Records both as a bandleader and sideman. After contributing the sparkle to several Otis Rush classics (an alternate of one of them, "Keep On Loving Me Baby" is found here) and some early Buddy Guy sides, Turner also recorded a handful of sides, scant few of them seeing release until now. This CD collects them all up, including surviving alternate versions and is a delightful fly on the wall invite to a 1950s Chicago blues session. —*Cub Koda*

● **I Like Ike! The Best of Ike Turner** / Nov. 15, 1994 / Rhino ++++
18 songs spotlighting Turner's work as a bandleader, guitarist, and solo artist from 1951 to 1972, concentrating heavily on his work in the 1950s and early '60s. Leading off with Jackie Brenston's classic "Rocket 88," it includes rare singles featuring Turner by Dennis Binder, the Sly Fox, Willie King, and others, along with rare Turner solo recordings, some under the pseudonym Icky Renrut, and a 1958 45 with Tina, then known as Annie Mae Bullock, on backing vocals. These singers are usually journeymen, frankly, and the material is rather standard-issue R&B; better are the instrumentals, which give Ike a chance to really strut his distinctive tone. —*Richie Unterberger*

Rhythm Rockin' Blues / Nov. 1995 / Ace +++
While Ike Turner's prodigious talents as a musician, producer, and hustler have been dealt the short end of the stick, his music and vibe should be enshrined as some of the best of early rock 'n' roll. Recording for one company after another, Turner produced a body of pre-Tina work utterly overwhelming in its scope. The major highlight here is "All the Blues, All the Time" from *Ike Turner Rocks the Blues* (one of the great unsung budget albums of all time), where Turner's wild-ass guitar playing takes on B.B. King, Elmore James, Little Son Jackson, John Lee Hooker, and Floyd Murphy. Turner was also a great boogie-woogie/rock 'n' roll piano man, too, and the ghost of Fats Domino and Guitar Slim's hit "The Things You Used to Do" looms large on a lot of tracks here as Turner was chasing after the hit sounds of the day. Johnny Wright's "The World Is Yours" and Turner's own "The Way You Used to Treat Me" come close to Guitar Slim, while tracks like Dennis "Long Man" Binder's "I Miss You So" plow Fats' sax romp territory. Bottom line is here's a collection of 1954 Ike Turner tracks that gives a much bigger picture of a man with prodigious talents and a short bank roll playing his way out of Clarksdale, MS. —*Cub Koda*

Vaughan Brothers

f. 1990
Group / Modern Electric Blues
Brothers Jimmie and Stevie Ray Vaughan got together for what would tragically be their first and last studio collaboration in the spring of 1990. That August, just before the release of the album, Stevie was killed in a helicopter crash. The public heard "Tick Tock" for the first time at Stevie's funeral in Dallas. —*Dan Forte*

Family Style / Jan. 1990 / Epic ♦♦♦
With slick production from Nile Rodgers and employing neither guitarist's band (Double Trouble nor the Fabulous Thunderbirds), this is bluesy, but far from purist. Jimmie makes his vocal debut on "White Boots" and "Good Texan," and the brothers blur the lines between their expected guitar styles— Stevie sometimes going for a less sustainy twang, Jimmie moving into Albert King territory. When standard blues is the order of the day (the slow instro "Brothers"), the key word is "standard"—bordering on run-of-the-mill. Instrumentals "D/FW" and "Hillbillies from Outer Space" fare better—offering ZZ Top crunch and Santo & Johnny steel, respectively. —*Dan Forte*

Jimmie Vaughan

b. Mar. 20, 1951, Dallas, TX
Guitar, Vocals / Roots-Rock, Modern Electric Blues, Modern Electric Texas Blues
As a founding member of the Fabulous Thunderbirds, Jimmie Vaughan was one of the leading Austin, TX guitarists of the late '70s and '80s, responsible for opening the national market up for gritty roadhouse blues and R&B. Influenced by guitarists like Freddie King, B.B. King, and Albert King, Vaughan developed a tough, lean sound that became one of the most recognizable sounds of '70s and '80s blues and blues-rock. For most of his career, Vaughan co-led the Fabulous Thunderbirds with vocalist Kim Wilson. It wasn't until 1994 that he launched a full-fledged solo career.

Born and raised in Dallas, TX, Jimmie Vaughan began playing guitar as a child. Initially, Vaughan was influenced by both blues and rock 'n' roll. While he was in his teens, he played in a number of garage rock bands, none of which attained any success. At the age of 19, he left Dallas and moved to Austin. For his first few years in Austin, Vaughan played in a variety of blues bar bands. In 1972, he formed his own group, the Storm, which supported many touring blues musicians.

In 1974, Vaughan met a vocalist and harmonica player named Kim Wilson. Within a year, the pair had formed the Fabulous Thunderbirds along with bassist Keith Ferguson and drummer Mike Buck. For four years, the T-Birds played local Texas clubs, gaining a strong fan base. By the end of the decade, the group had signed a major label contract with Chrysalis Records and seemed bound for national stardom. However, none of their albums became hits and they were dropped by Chrysalis at the end of 1982.

At the same time the T-Birds were left without a recording contract, Jimmie's younger brother, Stevie Ray Vaughan, came storming upon the national scene with his debut album, *Texas Flood.* For the next few years, Stevie Ray dominated not only the Texan blues scene, but the entire American scene, while Jimmie and the Thunderbirds were struggling to survive. The T-Birds finally received a new major label contract in 1986 with Epic/Associated and their first album for the label, *Tuff Enuff,* was a surprise hit, selling over a million copies and spawning the Top Ten hit title track.

The Fabulous Thunderbirds spent the rest of the '80s trying to replicate the success of *Tuff Enuff,* often pursuing slicker, more commercially-oriented directions. By 1989, Jimmie Vaughan was frustrated by the group's musical

direction and he left the band. Before launching a solo career, he recorded a duet album with his brother, Stevie Ray, *Family Style.* Following the completion of the record, Stevie Ray Vaughan died in a tragic helicopter crash in August of 1990. *Family Style* appeared just a few months later, in the fall of 1990.

After Stevie Ray's death, Jimmie took a couple of years off, in order to grieve and recoup. After a couple of years, he began playing the occasional concert. In 1994, he returned with his first solo album, *Strange Pleasures,* which received good reviews and sold respectably. Vaughan supported *Strange Pleasures* with a national tour. *Out There* followed in 1998. —*Stephen Thomas Erlewine*

● **Strange Pleasure** / 1995 / Epic ♦♦♦♦
Vaughan's solid solo debut is loaded with good-time Austin roadhouse blues-influenced rock. Guest artists include Lou Ann Barton, Dr. John and Nile Rodgers. Lovers of a good earthy groove and fine economical guitar work should pick up on this. —*Rick Clark*

Out There / Jun. 9, 1998 / Sony ♦♦♦
Jimmie Vaughan's second solo album, *Out There,* is quite similar to its predecessor, *Strange Pleasure,* delivering a familiar blend of Texas blues and roadhouse blues-rock. Of course, that isn't a problem. Ever since the Fabulous Thunderbirds, Vaughan has been at the forefront of Texas blues-rock, and while he's calmed down some with age, he remains a vital, classy guitarist— even on the weaker material, his tasteful solos are utterly engaging. It's too bad that his material doesn't always match his skills, but there's enough straight-ahead, enjoyable music here to make it worth a listen. —*Stephen Thomas Erlewine*

Stevie Ray Vaughan

b. Oct. 3, 1954, Dallas, TX, **d.** Aug. 27, 1990, East Troy, WI
Guitar, Vocals / Blues-Rock, Modern Electric Blues, Modern Electric Texas Blues
With his astonishingly accomplished guitar playing, Stevie Ray Vaughan ignited the blues revival of the '80s. Vaughan drew equally from bluesmen like Albert King, Otis Rush, and Muddy Waters, and rock 'n' roll players like Jimi Hendrix and Lonnie Mack, as well as the stray jazz guitarist like Kenny Burrell, developing a uniquely eclectic and fiery style that sounded like no other guitarist, regardless of genre. Vaughan bridged the gap between blues and rock like no other artist had since the late '60s. For the next seven years, Stevie Ray was the leading light in American blues, consistently selling out concerts while his albums regularly went gold. His tragic death in 1990 only emphasized his influence in blues and American rock 'n' roll.

Born and raised in Dallas, Stevie Ray Vaughan began playing guitar as a child, inspired by older brother Jimmie. When he was in junior high school, he began playing in a number of garage bands, which occasionally landed gigs in local nightclubs. By the time he was 17, he had dropped out of high school to concentrate on playing music. Vaughan's first real band was the Cobras, who played clubs and bars in Austin during the mid-'70s. Following that group's demise, he formed Triple Threat in 1975. Triple Threat also featured bassist Jackie Newhouse, drummer Chris Layton, and vocalist Lou Ann Barton. After a few years of playing Texas bars and clubs, Barton left the band in 1978. The group decided to continue performing under the name Double Trouble, which was inspired by the Otis Rush song of the same name; Stevie Ray became the band's lead singer.

For the next few years, Stevie Ray Vaughan and Double Trouble played the Austin area, becoming one of the most popular bands in Texas. In 1982, the band played the Montreux Festival and their performance caught the attention of David Bowie and Jackson Browne. After Double Trouble's performance, Bowie asked Vaughan to play on his forthcoming album, while Browne offered the group free recording time at his Los Angeles studio, Downtown; both offers were accepted. Stevie Ray laid down the lead guitar tracks for what became Bowie's *Let's Dance* album in late 1982. Shortly afterward, John Hammond, Sr. landed Vaughan and Double Trouble a record contract with Epic and the band recorded their debut album in less than a week at Downtown.

Vaughan's debut album, *Texas Flood*, was released in the summer of 1983, a few months after Bowie's *Let's Dance* appeared. On its own, *Let's Dance* earned Vaughan quite a bit of attention, but *Texas Flood* was a blockbuster blues success, receiving positive reviews in both blues and rock publications, reaching number 38 on the charts, and crossing over to album rock radio stations. Bowie offered Vaughan the lead guitarist role for his 1983 stadium tour, but Stevie Ray turned him down, preferring to play with Double Trouble. Stevie Ray and Double Trouble set off on a successful tour and quickly recorded their second album, *Couldn't Stand the Weather*, which was released in May of 1984. The album was more successful than its predecessor, reaching number 31 on the charts; by the end of 1985, the album went gold. Double Trouble added keyboardist Reese Wynans in 1985, before they recorded their third album, *Soul To Soul*. The record was released in August, 1985 and was also quite successful, reaching number 34 on the charts.

Although his professional career was soaring, Vaughan was sinking deep into alcoholism and drug addiction. Despite his declining health, Stevie Ray continued to push himself, releasing the double live album *Live Alive* in October of 1986 and launching an extensive American tour in early 1987. Following the tour, Vaughan checked into a rehabilitation clinic. The guitarist's time in rehab was kept fairly quiet and for the next year, Stevie Ray and Double Trouble were fairly inactive. Vaughan performed a number of concerts in 1988, including a headlining gig at the New Orleans Jazz & Heritage Festival, and wrote his fourth album. The resulting record, *In Step*, appeared in June of 1989 and became his most successful album, peaking at number 33 on the charts, earning a Grammy for Best Contemporary Blues Recording, and going gold just over six months after its release.

In the spring of 1990, Stevie Ray recorded an album with his brother Jimmie, which was scheduled for release in the fall of the year. In the late summer of 1990, Vaughan and Double Trouble set out on an American headlining tour. On August 26, 1990, their East Troy, WI gig concluded with an encore jam featuring guitaritsts Eric Clapton, Buddy Guy, Jimmie Vaughan, and Robert Cray. After the concert, Stevie Ray Vaughan boarded a helicopter bound for Chicago. Minutes after its 12:30 AM takeoff, the helicopter crashed, killing Vaughan and the other four passengers. Vaughan was only 35 years old.

Family Style, Stevie Ray's duet album with Jimmie Vaughan, appeared in October and entered the charts at number seven;. *Family Style* began a series of posthumous releases that were as popular as the albums Stevie Ray released during his lifetime. *The Sky is Crying*, a collection of studio outtakes compiled by Jimmie Vaughan, was released in October of 1991; it entered the charts at number ten and went platinum three months after its release. *In the Beginning*, a recording of a Double Trouble concert in 1980, was released in the fall of 1992 and the compilation *Greatest Hits* was released in 1995. — *Stephen Thomas Erlewine*

Texas Flood / 1983 / Epic ✦✦✦✦
A late-arriving star, Vaughan did not make his first album until the age of 28. By that time he had become a seasoned player, so this doesn't really sound like a debut album; rather, it sounds like a blues guitar master at the top of his form. Highlights include "Pride & Joy," "Love Struck Baby," "Lenny," and the hard blues title cut. — *William Ruhlmann*

Couldn't Stand the Weather / 1984 / Epic ✦✦✦✦
Vaughan does not ease up on this second set, even taking on Jimi Hendrix in a rendition of "Voodoo Chile (Slight Return)," and handling it beautifully. — *William Ruhlmann*

Soul to Soul / 1985 / Epic ✦✦✦✦
Soul to Soul shows that Vaughan is a great guitarist, but everybody already knew that. What makes this album different from his two previous efforts is the inspired backing of Double Trouble—who finally sound like they aren't intimdated by their leader—and Vaughan's considerably more soulful and assertive vocals. — *Stephen Thomas Erlewine*

Live Alive / Jul. 1986 / Epic ✦✦✦
Live Alive is a magnificent double-length showcase for Stevie Ray Vaughan's guitar playing, featuring a number of extended jams on a selection of most of the best material from Vaughan's first three albums, plus covers of "Willie the Wimp," "I'm Leaving You (Commit a Crime)," and Stevie Wonder's "Superstition." The album may not be exceptionally tight or concise, but then again, that's not the point. The renditions here sound less polished than the studio versions, with Vaughan's guitar tone bitingly down and dirty. Not only does *Live Alive* provide an excellent overview of Vaughan's inconsistent early output, but it also makes a fine complement to the rather skimpy *Greatest Hits*, as only four songs overlap. — *Steve Huey*

In Step / Jun. 1989 / Epic ✦✦✦✦
Vaughan sounds just as fierce sober as he did before, and he is beginning to bloom as a songwriter, a fact most notable on the driving "The House Is Rockin'" and the confessional "Wall of Denial." — *William Ruhlmann*

The Sky Is Crying / Nov. 5, 1991 / Epic ✦✦✦✦
The posthumously assembled ten-track outtakes collection *The Sky Is Crying* actually proves to be one of Vaughan's most consistent albums, rivaling *In Step* as the best outside of the *Greatest Hits* collection. These songs were recorded in sessions spanning from 1984's *Couldn't Stand the Weather* to 1989's *In Step* and were left off of the LPs for whatever reason (or, in the case of *Soul to Soul*'s "Empty Arms," a different version was used). What makes the record work is its eclectic diversity—Vaughan plays slide guitar on "Boot Hill" and acoustic on "Life By the Drop"; he smokes on the slow blues of "May I Have a Talk With You" and the title track just as much as on the uptempo Lonnie Mack cover "Wham"; and he shows the jazzy side of his playing on Hendrix's "Little Wing" and Kenny Burrell's "Chitlins Con Carne." But it's not just musical diversity that makes the record work, it's also Vaughan's emotional range. From the morbidly dark "Boot Hill" to the lilting "Little Wing" to the exuberant tributes to his influences—Lonnie Mack on "Wham" and Albert King on "The Sky Is Crying"—Vaughan makes the material resonate, and in light of his death, "The Sky Is Crying" and the touching survivor-story ballad "Life By the Drop" are two of the most moving moments in Vaughan's oeuvre. — *Steve Huey*

In the Beginning / Oct. 6, 1992 / Epic ✦✦
Although this is a very rough early concert from 1980, this album captures an energetic Stevie Ray Vaughan still developing his signature style, which makes it essential for fans. — *Stephen Thomas Erlewine*

★ **Greatest Hits** / Nov. 21, 1995 / Epic ✦✦✦✦✦
Stevie Ray Vaughan was a great guitarist, but he had trouble making consistent albums. *Greatest Hits* rectifies that problem by collecting all of his best-known tracks, from "Pride and Joy" to "Crossfire." Not only is it a terrific introduction, it's his most consistent album, demonstrating exactly why he was one of the most important guitarists of the '80s. — *Stephen Thomas Erlewine*

Live at Carnegie Hall / Jul. 29, 1997 / Sony ✦✦✦✦
Live at Carnegie Hall captures Stevie Ray Vaughan on the supporting tour for his second album, 1984's *Couldn't Stand the Weather*. The Carnegie Hall concert was a special show, since it was the only time Vaughan and Double Trouble added a brass section to augment their sound; in addition, the concert featured guest appearances from Stevie's brother Jimmie and Dr. John. There might have been more musicians than usual onstage, but Stevie Ray remains the center of attention, and he is prime form here, tearing through a selection of his best-known songs which generally sound tougher in concert than they do in the studio. It's the best live Stevie Ray record yet released. — *Thom Owens*

Maurice John Vaughn

b. Nov. 6, 1952, Chicago, IL
Guitar, Saxophone, Vocals / Modern Electric Blues, Modern Electric Chicago Blues

Maurice John Vaughn's 1984 debut set, *Generic Blues Album*, came packaged in a plain white jacket, its title unceremoniously stamped on its front like a package of no-brand rice on a grocer's shelf. It looked like the cleverest of publicity ploys, but in reality, it was a simple economic necessity—Vaughn's own Reecy label was operating on a shoestring.

Vaughn is no longer a blues unknown. With a challenging 1993 album on

Alligator (*In the Shadow of the City*) melding blues, soul, funk, and other contemporary influences, he's grown into one of Chicago's most interesting and versatile younger blues artists. Fluent on both guitar and sax, Vaughn played both in sideman roles prior to stepping out on his own.

Sax came first. Vaughn grew up on Chicago's South side, blowing his horn with various R&B groups and recording with the Chosen Few for Chi-Sound Records in 1976. When sax gigs grew scarce, Vaughn began to emphasize his guitar skills. Blues guitarist Phil Guy recruited him and his band for a 1979 Canadian tour, and the genre appealed to him. Vaughn later held down sideman spots with Luther Allison, Son Seals, Valerie Wellington, and A.C. Reed.

Alligator Records retained the no-frills packaging when it reissued *Generic Blues Album* after Vaughn sang "Nothing Left to Believe In" on the label's 1987 anthology *The New Bluebloods*. *In the Shadow of the City* came in 1993. And despite the cover art on his first LP, there's nothing generic at all about Maurice Vaughn's brand of soulful blues. — *Bill Dahl*

● **Generic Blues Album** / 1984 / Alligator ✦✦✦✦
Anything but generic, this is actually powerful, contemporary, funky Chicago blues. With excellent musicianship, Vaughn performs interesting songs focusing on the trials of modern urban life and work. Vaughn, a top session player, sings and plays guitar and sax. — *Niles J. Frantz*

In the Shadow of the City / 1993 / Alligator ✦✦✦✦
The Chicago guitarist/saxist spreads his stylistic wings considerably further than he did on his debut, embracing funk more fully than his first time around but offering enough tasty contemporary blues to keep everyone happy. The prolific triple threat (he's also an engaging singer) wrote all but three tracks himself (one of the covers is the shuffling "Small Town Baby"; its composer, veteran pianist Jimmy Walker, plays on the cut). — *Bill Dahl*

Eddie "Cleanhead" Vinson

b. Dec. 18, 1917, Houston, TX, **d.** Jul. 2, 1988, Los Angeles, CA
Sax (Alto), Vocals / Bop, Early R&B Jazz, Jump Blues, R&B, Jazz, Groove, West Coast Blues, New York Blues
An advanced stylist on alto saxophone who vacillated throughout his career between jump blues and jazz, bald-pated Eddie "Cleanhead" Vinson (he lost his hair early on after a botched bout with a lye-based hair-straightener) also possessed a playfully distinctive vocal delivery that stood him in good stead with blues fans.

Vinson first picked up a horn while attending high school in Houston. During the late '30s, he was a member of an incredible horn section in Milton Larkin's orchestra, sitting next to Arnett Cobb and Illinois Jacquet. After exiting Larkin's employ in 1941, Vinson picked up a few vocal tricks while on tour with bluesman Big Bill Broonzy. Vinson joined the Cootie Williams Orchestra from 1942 to 1945. His vocals on trumpeter Williams' renditions of "Cherry Red" and "Somebody's Got to Go" were in large part responsible for their wartime hit status.

Vinson struck out on his own in 1945, forming his own large band, signing with Mercury, and enjoying a double-sided smash in 1947 with his romping R&B chart-topper "Old Maid Boogie" and the song that would prove his signature number, "Kidney Stew Blues" (both songs featured Vinson's instantly identifiable vocals). A 1949-52 stint at King Records produced only one hit, the amusing sequel "Somebody Done Stole My Cherry Red," along with the classic blues "Person to Person" (later revived by another King artist, Little Willie John).

Vinson's jazz leanings were probably heightened during 1952-53, when his band included a young John Coltrane. Somewhere along about here, Vinson wrote two Miles Davis classics, "Tune Up" and "Four." Vinson steadfastly kept one foot in the blues camp and the other in jazz, waxing jumping R&B for Mercury (in 1954) and Bethlehem (1957), jazz for Riverside in 1961 (with Cannonball Adderly), and blues for Blues Time and ABC-BluesWay. A 1969 set for Black & Blue, cut in France with pianist Jay McShann and tenor saxophonist Hal Singer, beautifully recounted Vinson's blues shouting heyday (it's available on Delmark as *Kidney Stew Is Fine*). A much later set for Muse teamed him with the sympathetic little big band approach of Rhode Island-based Roomful of Blues. Vinson toured the States and Europe frequently prior to his 1988 death of a heart attack. — *Bill Dahl*

Eddie Cleanhead Vinson Sings / Sep. 1957 / Bethlehem ✦✦✦✦
One of only two albums that altoist/singer Eddie "Cleanhead" Vinson led during 1956-66, this infectious set finds him performing some of his best-

known tunes. With assistance by a medium-size group that plays in a Count Basie groove (including such Basie-ites as trumpeter Joe Newman, trombonist Henry Coker, either Frank Foster or Paul Quinichette on tenor, and pianist Nat Pierce), Cleanhead makes such songs as "Kidney Stew," "Caldonia," "Cherry Red," "Is You Is or Is You Ain't My Baby" and "Hold It Right There" sound full of joy. This CD reissue adds three alternate takes that were originally recorded in stereo. A good sampling of the great Cleanhead. — *Scott Yanow*

Back in Town / Sep. 1957 / Bethlehem ✦✦✦
Although he had achieved a certain amount of popularity in the late '40s with his blues vocals and boppish alto, Eddie "Cleanhead" Vinson's Bethlehem album was one of only two recordings he made as a leader between 1956-66. With arrangements by Ernie Wilkins, Manny Albam, and Harry Tubbs, and his sidemen including several members (past and present) of the Count Basie Orchestra, the blues-oriented music (which gives Vinson a chance to sing such material as "It Ain't Necessarily So," "Is You Is or Is You Ain't My Baby" and "Caledonia") is quite enjoyable and really rocks; pity that this record did not catch on. — *Scott Yanow*

Cleanhead & Cannonball / Sep. 19, 1961 + Feb. 14, 1962 / Landmark ✦✦✦✦
During these two sessions, Eddie "Cleanhead" Vinson was joined by the Cannonball Adderley Quintet. Five of the ten selections were previously unissued altogether until this album came out in 1988. On Vinson's vocal numbers he is backed by altoist Cannonball Adderley, cornetist Nat Adderley, pianist Joe Zawinul, bassist Sam Jones and drummer Louis Hayes. Unfortunately on the instrumentals and the one vocal tune ("Kidney Stew") in which he plays, Vinson is the only altoist as Cannonball sits out; it's a pity that the two very different stylists did not have a chance to trade off. Despite that missed opportunity, the music on this release is quite worthy with Cleanhead in top form on such numbers as "Person to Person," "Just a Dream" and the three instrumentals. — *Scott Yanow*

Old Kidney Stew Is Fine / Mar. 26, 1969 + Mar. 28, 1969 / Delmark ✦✦✦✦
Eminently swinging disc cut in Europe with T-Bone Walker on guitar. — *Bill Dahl*

Kidney Stew Is Fine / Mar. 28, 1969 / Delmark ✦✦✦✦
Although its programming has been juggled a bit and the CD has been given liner notes, this Delmark release is a straight reissue of the original LP. Clocking in at around 38 minutes, the relatively brief set is the only recording that exists of Vinson, pianist Jay McShann, and guitarist T-Bone Walker playing together; the sextet is rounded out by the fine tenor Hal Singer, bassist Jackie Sampson, and drummer Paul Gunther. Vinson, whether singing "Plese Send Me Somebody to Love," "Just a Dream," and "Juice Head Baby" or taking boppish alto solos, is the main star throughout this album (originally on Black & Blue), a date that helped launch Vinson's commercial comeback. — *Scott Yanow*

You Can't Make Love Alone / Jun. 18, 1971 / Mega ✦✦✦
Eddie "Cleanhead" Vinson was in inspired form at the 1971 Montreux Jazz Festival. He stole the show when he sat in with Oliver Nelson's big band during their "Swiss Suite" and played a brilliant blues alto solo. The same day he recorded this Mega album but, due to its extreme brevity (under 24 minutes), perhaps this label should have changed its name to "Mini." Despite the low quantity, the quality of his performance (on which Vinson is joined by the guitars of Larry Coryell and Cornell Dupree, pianist Neal Creque, bassist Chuck Rainey and drummer Pretty Purdie) makes this album still worth acquiring, although preferably at a budget price. Vinson takes "Straight No Chaser" as an instrumental and does a fine job of singing "Cleanhead Blues," "You Can't Make Love Alone," "I Had a Dream" and "Person to Person." — *Scott Yanow*

Jamming the Blues / Jul. 2, 1974 / Black Lion ✦✦✦✦
For this lesser-known outing (reissued on CD), the great altoist and blues singer Eddie "Cleanhead" Vinson is heard in fine form at the 1974 Montreux Jazz Festival. With fine support from a four-piece rhythm section that includes pianist Peter Wingfield and some solo space for tenor-saxophonist Hal Singer, Vinson plays a few of his familiar but always welcome numbers ("Just A Dream," "Person To Person" and "Hold It Right There") plus "Laura" and some basic instrumental blues. An excellent outing from a performer who was claimed by both the jazz and blues worlds. — *Scott Yanow*

Cherry Red Blues / 1976 / King/Gusto ++++

Somehow, amidst all the CD reissues from the King Records unleashed by Charly, Ace, Rhino, and King's current ownership, this versatile alto saxist has fallen through the cracks. Thus, this two-LP collection, boasting all but a handful of his jumping 1949-1952 outings for King, remains your best introduction to the Cleanheaded one's R&B output (along with the 1945-1947 sides he waxed for Mercury, which grace the seven-disc anthology *Blues, Boogie, & Bop: The 1940s Mercury Sessions*). —*Bill Dahl*

The Clean Machine / Feb. 22, 1978 / Muse ++++

What makes this album different from many of Eddie "Cleanhead" Vinson's is that four of the seven selections are taken as instrumentals. Vinson's alto playing has long been underrated due to his popularity as a blues singer, so this release gives one the opportunity to hear his bop-influenced solos at greater length. With the assistance of a strong rhythm section led by pianist Lloyd Glenn and some contributions from trumpeter Jerry Rusch and Rashid Ali on tenor, Vinson is in excellent form throughout this enjoyable set. —*Scott Yanow*

● **Hold It Right There!** / Aug. 25, 1978-Aug. 26, 1978 / Muse ++++

After years of neglect, Eddie "Cleanhead" Vinson was finally receiving long overdue recognition at the time of this live session—one of six albums recorded during a week at Sandy's Revival. Two of these albums featured tenors Arnett Cobb and Buddy Tate in lead roles. While Vinson has fine blues vocals on "Cherry Red" and "Hold It," it is his boppish alto solos on "Cherokee," "Now's the Time," and "Take the 'A' Train" (the latter also having spots for Cobb and Tate) that make this set recommended to blues and bop fans alike. —*Scott Yanow*

Live at Sandy's / Aug. 25, 1978-Aug. 26, 1978 / Muse ++++

Muse recorded six albums during one week at Sandy's Jazz Revival, a club in Beverly, MA; two of them (this one and *Hold It Right There*) feature the blues vocals and alto solos of Eddie "Cleanhead" Vinson. Some of the songs also have the tenors of Arnett Cobb and Buddy Tate in a supporting role but this album is largely Vinson's show. Backed by a superb rhythm section (pianist Ray Bryant, bassist George Duvivier, and drummer Alan Dawson), Vinson takes four fine vocals and plays many swinging alto solos including one on "Tune Up," a song he wrote that has been mistakenly credited to Miles Davis for decades. —*Scott Yanow*

I Want a Little Girl / Feb. 10, 1981 / Pablo ++++

Eddie "Cleanhead" Vinson, 64 at the time of this Pablo recording, is in superior form on the blues-oriented material. With Art Hillery (on piano and organ) and guitarist Cal Green leading the rhythm section, and trumpeter Martin Banks and the tenor of Rashid Ali offering contrasting solo voices, this is a particularly strong release. It is true that Vinson had sung such songs as "I Want a Little Girl," "Somebody's Got to Go," and "Stormy Monday" a countless number of times previously but he still infuses these versions with enthusiasm and spirit, making this set a good example of Cleanhead's talents in his later years. —*Scott Yanow*

☆ **And Roomful of Blues** / Jan. 27, 1982 / Muse +++++

If there were justice in the world, Eddie "Cleanhead" Vinson would have been able to tour with this type of group throughout much of his career. Roomful of Blues, a popular five-horn nonet, has rarely sounded more exciting than on this musical meeting with the legendary singer/altoist. Vinson himself is exuberant on some of the selections, particularly "House of Joy," one of five instrumentals among the eight selections. Whether one calls it blues, bebop or early rhythm & blues, this accessible music is very enjoyable and deserves to be more widely heard. Among the supporting players, tenorman Greg Piccolo, trumpeter Bob Enos, and guitarist Ronnie Earl (in one of his earliest recordings) win honors. —*Scott Yanow*

Mose Vinson

b. Aug. 7, 1917, Holly Springs, MS
Piano, Vocals / Piano Blues

A Memphis piano institution for more than half a century, Mose Vinson recorded a handful of unreleased sides for Sun in 1953 (recently liberated by Bear Family) and did scattered session work for Sam Phillips as well. He remains an active performer.

Vinson began playing piano as a child in the Mississippi Delta, initially playing in his local church. By his teens, he had begun playing jazz and blues.

In 1932, he moved to Memphis, TN, where he played local juke joints and parties throughout the '30s and '40s. In the early '50s, Sam Phillips had Vinson accompany a number of Sun Records blues artists, most notably James Cotton in 1954. During that time, Phillips also had Vinson cut some tracks, but they remained unreleased until the '80s.

For the next three decades, Vinson continued to perform at local Memphis clubs. However, he didn't play as frequently as he did in the previous two decades. In the early '80s, the Center for Southern Folklore hired Vinson to perform at special cultural festivals, as well as local schools. For the next two decades, he played concerts, eductational and cultural festivals associated with the Center for Southern Folklore. —*Bill Dahl & Stephen Thomas Erlewine*

● **Memphis Piano Blues Today** / 1990 / Wolf ++++

Memphis Piano Blues Today collects a number of latter-day recordings from Mose Vinson. Although he's past his prime, the pianist is still in good form and, since he recorded so infrequently as a leader, this is a valuable addition to any serious fan of piano blues and Memphis blues. —*Thom Owens*

Walter Vinson

b. Feb. 2, 1901, Bolton, MS, **d.** Apr. 22, 1975, Chicago, IL
Guitar, Violin, Vocals / Memphis Blues

One half of the legendary Mississippi Sheiks, singer/guitarist Walter Vinson was also among the most noteworthy blues accompanists of his era. Born February 2, 1901 in Bolton, MS, Vinson (also known variously as Vincson and Vincent) began performing as a child, and during his teen years was a fixture at area parties and picnics. Even from the outset, however, he rarely if ever appeared as a solo act, seemingly much more at home in duets and trios; towards that end, during the 1920s he worked with Charlie McCoy, Rubin Lacy, and Son Spand before forging his most pivotal and long-lasting union, with Lonnie Chatmon, in 1928. In addition to teaming with Chatmon in the Mississippi Sheiks, Vinson also recorded with him in the Mississippi Hot Footers, and even worked with Chatmon's brothers Bo and Harry. Upon the Sheiks' 1933 dissolution, Vinson recorded with various players in areas ranging from Jackson, MS, to New Orleans, to finally Chicago; while an active club performer during the early 1940s, by the middle of the decade he had begun a lengthy hiatus from music which continued through 1960, at which point he returned to both recording and festival appearances. Hardening of the arteries forced Vinson into retirement during the early '70s; he died in Chicago in 1975. —*Jason Ankeny*

● **Complete Recorded Works in Chronological Order** / Document ++++

Complete Recorded Works in Chronological Order collects all of Mississippi Sheiks leader Walter Vinson's solo recordings from the '30s. While his recordings with the Sheiks are better and more influential, these are nevertheless excellent country-blues recordings that should be sought out by fans of the genre. —*Thom Owens*

Jimmy Vivino

b. Jan. 10, 1955
Guitar / Modern Electric Blues

Guitarist, singer and songwriter Jimmy Vivino has enjoyed a high-visibility gig in recent years as part of the Max Weinberg Seven on TV's *Late Night with Conan O'Brien*. Vivino began his musical education on trumpet, an instrument his father Jerome also played; his earliest musical memories are of his father spinning Louis Armstrong and Roy Eldridge records at their home in Glen Rock, NJ. By the time he was in high school, he was playing lead trumpet and arranging for big bands.

After hearing producer/impresario Al Kooper play organ with Blood, Sweat & Tears, Vivino was inspired to begin teaching himself organ. He didn't begin playing guitar until 1978, studying with Joe Cinderella and jazz guitarist Jack Wilkins. Given his love for Louis Armstrong, he was naturally drawn to blues—in particular, the music of the Paul Butterfield Blues Band with guitarist Michael Bloomfield. In the late '70s and early '80s, he was able to meet Muddy Waters on several occasions through his friend Brian Bisesi, who was an auxiliary guitarist when Waters was passing through the New Jersey/New York area.

Allan Pepper, the owner of New York's Bottom Line nightclub, took an active interest in Vivino's career as a guitarist and arranger, and soon Vivino found himself working with musicians as varied as Phoebe Snow, Laura

Nyro, Felix Cavaliere and Dion. Vivino also played with Jules Shear and Steve Holly in a New York group called the Reckless Sleepers.

After Al Kooper asked Vivino to assemble a band for his New York performances, mostly at the Bottom Line, Vivino began accompanying him there, later recording with him on the MusicMasters/BMG albums *Soul of a Man* and *Rekooperator*. Vivino later began playing with Chuck Berry pianist Johnnie Johnson in 1990, all the while honing his finger-picking chops with John Sebastian's J-Band.

Since *Late Night With Conan O'Brien* began in 1992, Vivino has been an integral part of the Max Weinberg Seven. He'd known Weinberg from a regional R&B group, Killer Joe, which both were a part of. Although he has the benefit of a glamorous day job as part of the house band for O'Brien's show, he remains a humble student of the blues.

When Vivino finally had the chance to record his own album, it was not a moment too soon. Unlike a lot of more seasoned musicians, Vivino has al-ways been ambitious, involving himself in a multitude of bands and projects, learning as much as could about various musical genres from the best available sources. Not surprisingly, Vivino decided to record his debut album the old-fashioned way. He and his band cut it in the space of two days, without rehearsing the material backwards and forwards. This contributes an air of spontaneity and a live feeling to *Do What Now?* (MusicMasters/BMG, 1997). He's joined by his musical heroes, Al Kooper (who produced the album) and bassist Harvey Brooks; guests on *Do What, Now?* include former Stevie Ray Vaughan keyboardist Reese Wynans, John Sebastian on harmonica, and Sam Bush on mandolin.

When he's not taping shows with O'Brien, Vivino can be found hanging out in New York's blues clubs at night, sometimes to sit in, other times to just sit and listen. *—Richard J. Skelly*

Do What, Now? / Mar. 11, 1997 / Music Master ✦✦✦

Albertina Walker

b. Aug. 1930, Chicago, IL
Vocals / Black Gospel, Traditional Gospel
Born in Chicago, Walker sang with the Pete Williams Singers and the Robert Anderson Singers before forming the Caravans in 1951. Among the Caravans' classics were "Mary Don't You Weep," "Soldiers in the Army," "The Solid Rock," and "The Blood Will Never Lose Its Power." Since 1960 Walker has been a solo singer, maintaining her ties to traditional gospel. *—Bil Carpenter*

Tell the Angels / 1960 / Savoy ♦♦♦
Her 1960 debut, after the Caravans. *—Bil Carpenter*

● **God Is Love** / 1975 / Lection ♦♦♦♦
God Is Love ranks among Albertina Walker's best recordings, capturing the gospel vocalist at her most moving and simply best. It may be a latter-day album from Walker, but her power and influence is readily apparent. *—Thom Owens*

You Believed in Me / 1991 / Benson ♦♦♦
This recent album includes "Working on a Building." *—Bil Carpenter*

Live / 1992 / Benson ♦♦♦
Albertina Walker's second album for Benson Records finds the former lead singer of the Caravans running through nine of her most popular songs—including "You've Been So Good," "That's the Way Heaven Will Be," "Watch Tower," "He Knows (Just How Much You Can Bear)," "My Best Friend," "I've Got a Feeling," "Day by Day," and "I Can Go to God in Prayer"—in concert. Supported by the Trinity All Nations Choir, Walker turns in a wonderful performance. Even cameos from Ralph Lofton, Derrick Lee, and Darius Brooks can't take the spotlight away from Walker, who once again proves why she is considered one of the greatest singers in contemporary gospel. *—Thom Owens*

Albertina Walker Live / 1992 / A&M ♦♦♦
Good singing in the grand tradition. *—Opal Louis Nations*

Gospel Greats / Sep. 13, 1994 / Benson ♦♦♦

The Best Is Yet to Come / Savoy ♦♦♦
Albertina Walker has a deeper, sometimes huskier voice than Inez Andrews or Shirley Caesar, but is no less a vocal magician. She stretches out the lines and lets the mood build on such songs from this LP as "Thank You For One More Day," "He's My Everything," and "Let Jesus Come Into My Heart..." There's a grandiose, smashing feeling that Walker puts into every verse on this album, allowing her to lift up the occasional flat tune or spice up the overdone references. She also holds her own when the Allegro Triboro Mass Choirs come in....*—Ron Wynn, Rejoice*

My Time Is Not Over / Word ♦♦♦♦
We have here a collection of mainly traditionally based gospel songs sung by the legendary ex-Caravan lead Albertina Walker, recorded in Franklin and Nashville, TN, with the soloist's own choir. It's the "Nashville" of the West Point Missionary Baptist Church, supported and overdubbed by a full rhythm section plus horns on occasions. Walker can still belt it out with the best of them and does an impressive job on "He Answered Me" (with her own overdubs) and "Give Your Life to Jesus." Her rich, soulful voice is set against modern choir arrangements and percussive effects. *—Opal Louis Nations, Roots & Rhythm Newsletter*

Freedom / Jewel ♦♦♦♦
Good rousing material by this important aggregation. *—Opal Louis Nations*

Joe Louis Walker

b. Dec. 25, 1949, San Francisco, CA
Guitar, Vocals / R&B, Modern Electric Blues, Texas Blues
Without a doubt one of the most exciting and innovative artists gracing contemporary blues, guitarist Joe Louis Walker has glowed like a shining blue beacon over the last decade. His 1986 debut album for HighTone, *Cold Is the Night*, announced his arrival in stunning fashion; his subsequent output on HighTone and Verve has only served to further establish Walker as one of the leading younger bluesmen on the scene.

Walker traveled a circuitous route to get to where he is today. At age 14, he took up the guitar, playing blues (with an occasional foray into psychedelic rock) on the mushrooming San Francisco circuit. For a while, Walker roomed with Mike Bloomfield, who introduced him to Jimi Hendrix and the Grateful Dead and taught him some very useful licks. Walker even made a brief pilgrimage to Chicago to check out the blues scene there.

But by 1975, Walker was burned out on blues and turned to God, singing for the next decade with a gospel group, the Spiritual Corinthians. When the Corinthians played the 1985 New Orleans Jazz & Heritage Festival, Walker was inspired to embrace his blues roots again. He assembled a band, the Boss Talkers, and wrote some stunning originals that ended up on *Cold Is the Night* (co-produced by Bruce Bromberg and Dennis Walker).

More acclaimed albums for HighTone—1988's *The Gift, Blue Soul* the next year, and two riveting sets cut live at Slim's in 1990—preceded a switch to the major Verve imprint and three more discs that were considerably more polished than their grittier HighTone counterparts.

Joe Louis Walker is quite the total package, as tremendously assured on a down-in-the-alley acoustic solo outing as he is performing a thoroughly modern R&B-laced number with his latest crew of Boss Talkers. Expect more great things from him in years to come. *—Bill Dahl*

Cold Is the Night / 1986 / Hightone ♦♦♦♦
The Bay Area blues guitarist's debut album sounds underproduced compared to what would soon follow—and that's no knock. Walker's gritty, expressive vocals and ringing, concise guitar work shine through loud and clear in front of his band, the Boss Talkers. Walker and his producers Dennis Walker and Bruce Bromberg wrote virtually the entire set, including the slashing "Cold Is the Night," "Don't Play Games," and "One Woman." *—Bill Dahl*

● **The Gift** / 1988 / Hightone ♦♦♦♦
Although it didn't enjoy the major label hype that his current output does, Walker's HighTone encore just may be his finest album of all, filled with soulful vocal performances, bone-cutting guitar work, and tight backing from the Boss Talkers and the Memphis Horns. Honestly, you can't go wrong with any of Walker's remarkably consistent HighTone discs—but give this one the slightest of edges over the rest. *—Bill Dahl*

Blue Soul / 1989 / Hightone ♦♦♦♦
Another winner sporting memorable songs ("T.L.C.," "Personal Baby," "City of Angels," "Prove Your Love"), sinuous grooves, and a whole lot of vicious guitar from one of the hottest relatively young bluesmen on the circuit. He goes it alone on the finale, "I'll Get to Heaven on My Own," sounding as conversant with the country blues tradition as he does with the contemporary stuff. *—Bill Dahl*

Live at Slim's, Vol. 1 / 1991 / Hightone ♦♦♦♦
Walker was hot enough over the course of a two-day stand at Slim's in San Francisco to warrant the issue of two full albums from the dates. The first is a sizzling combination of past triumphs, new items, and covers of Clifton

Chenier's "Hot Tamale Baby," Junior Wells' "Little By Little" (with Huey Lewis, no less, on harp), and a saucy duet with Angela Strehli on the old Fontella Bass/Bobby McClure rocker "Don't Mess Up a Good Thing." — *Bill Dahl*

Live at Slim's / May 1991 / Hightone ✦✦✦✦
Joe Louis Walker has always been a more probing and exciting blues musician than Robert Cray, although I wouldn't pick him in a singing contest. This live set features Walker at his hottest, and it clicks despite some occasional engineering difficulties. — *Ron Wynn*

Live at Slim's, Vol. 2 / Nov. 1992 / Hightone ✦✦✦✦
More from that searing Slim's engagement, including Joe Louis ripping through Ray Charles' "Don't You Know," Little Milton's "Love at First Sight," and Rosco Gordon's overworked "Just a Little Bit," along with his own gems. Huey Lewis turns up again as the harpist on Walker's version of Haskell Sadler's "747." — *Bill Dahl*

Blues Survivor / Oct. 19, 1993 / Verve ✦✦✦
By no means a bad album, Walker's major-label debut just wasn't quite as terrific as what directly preceded it. The studio atmosphere seems a bit slicker than before, and the songs are in several cases considerably longer than they need to be (generally in the five-to-seven-minute range). A reworking of Howlin' Wolf's "Shake for Me" is the only familiar entry. — *Bill Dahl*

Jlw / 1994 / Polygram ✦✦✦
Another overly polished effort that nevertheless packs a punch on many selections. Walker's songwriting is considerably less prominent, with only three self-penned tunes on the disc this time. Otis Blackwell's pulsating "On That Power Line" and the Don Gardner & Dee Dee Ford dustie "I Need Your Lovin'" receive spirited revivals, and there's an acoustic duet with James Cotton, "Going to Canada." — *Bill Dahl*

Blues of the Month Club / Sep. 12, 1995 / Verve ✦✦✦
Walker's latest is, alas, also his weakest to date—strange, since he shares production credit this time with the legendary Steve Cropper. Once again, some songs drag on far after their logical conclusions; also, Walker doesn't quite possess the pipes to effectively belt the old Jackie Brenston rouser "You've Got to Lose." The title track, with Cropper co-featured on guitar, is a clever piece of material, but overall, the slick production values strip some of the grit from Walker's incendiary attack. — *Bill Dahl*

Hello Everybody / Oct. 1995 / Verve ✦✦✦

Great Guitars / Apr. 8, 1997 / Polygram ✦✦✦
Joe Louis Walker is a powerful blues guitarist and singer whose versatility and musical courage are showcased throughout this frequently rousing set. Walker collaborates (and sometimes battles it out) with Bonnie Raitt, Ike Turner, Otis Rush, Buddy Guy, Matt "Guitar" Murphy, Taj Mahal, Robert Lockwood Jr. and the Johnny Nocturne Horns on one song apiece, in addition to having three features of his own. Of the many highlights, "Low Down Dirty Blues" (which features Walker and Raitt jamming on slide guitars), the 1940s jump band feel of "Mile-Hi Club," the Walker-Guy guitar explosions on "Every Girl I See," the joyful encounter with Matt Murphy on "Nighttime" and Lockwood's appearance on "High Blood Pressure" are all quite memorable. This all-star gathering works quite well and is consistently memorable; all 11 selections are well worth hearing. — *Scott Yanow*

Joe Walker

b. Dec. 13, 1944, Lafayette, LA
Vocals / Zydeco
With a signature sound bridging the gap between zydeco and Southern soul music, singer and multi-instumentalist Joe Walker was best known as an ace sideman prior to his rediscovery during the early 1990s. Born December 13, 1944 in Lafayette, LA, he played guitar in Rockin' Dopsie's band while still in his teens, later backing Rockin' Sidney on a number of singles cut for the Goldband label during the 1960s. Upon relocating to the Lake Charles area in 1967, Walker formed a band to back soul and blues artists like Tyrone Davis and Barbara Lynn as they passed through town; after a decade of regional success, however, the rise of disco brought an end to the combo's career. With a keyboard and drum machine in tow, Walker then turned to performing as a solo lounge act; during the blues revival of the mid-1980s he returned to the studio as a respected session man, leading to his discovery

in 1991 by Cajun producer Lee Lavergne. His solo debut LP, *The Soulful Side of Zydeco*, appeared later that year, and was followed in quick succession by 1992's *Zydeco Fever* and 1993's *In the Dog House.* — *Jason Ankeny*

Zydeco Fever / 1992 / Zane ✦✦✦

● **In the Dog House** / 1993 / Zane ✦✦✦✦
In the Dog House illustrates that Joe Walker is a zydeco musician with true ambition and range. There are a number of rollicking zydeco cuts here, but he also injects soul into his style, plays a few straight blues cuts and contributes a lovely, lilting waltz. It's a diverse array of sounds, but it all holds together because of his stellar musicianship. *In the Dog House* isn't your average party zydeco record, but it's worth the attention of any serious fan of the style who wants to hear a musician with a little imagination. — *Thom Owens*

Phillip Walker

b. Feb. 11, 1937, Welsh, LA
Guitar, Vocals / Modern Electric Blues, Texas Blues
Despite recording somewhat sparingly since debuting as a leader in 1959 on Elko Records with the storming rocker "Hello My Darling," Louisiana-born guitarist Phillip Walker enjoys a sterling reputation as a contemporary blues guitarist with a distinctive sound honed along the Gulf Coast during the 1950s.

A teenaged Walker picked up his early licks around Port Arthur, TX, from the likes of Gatemouth Brown, Long John Hunter, Lightnin' Hopkins, and Lonnie "Guitar Junior" Brooks. Zydeco king Clifton Chenier hired Walker in 1953 as his guitarist, a post he held for three-and-a-half years.

In 1959, Walker moved to Los Angeles, waxing "Hello My Darling" for producer J.R. Fulbright (a song he's revived several times since, most effectively for the short-lived Playboy logo). Scattered 45s emerged during the '60s, but it wasn't until he joined forces with young producer Bruce Bromberg in 1969 that Walker began to get a studio foothold. Their impressive work together resulted in a 1973 album for Playboy, *Bottom of the Top*, that remains Walker's finest to date.

Walker cut a fine follow-up set for Bromberg's Joliet label, *Someday You'll Have These Blues*, that showcased his tough Texas guitar style (it was later reissued by Alligator). Sets for Rounder and HighTone were high points of the 1980s for the guitarist. His 1995 set for Black Top, *Working Girl Blues*, shows that Walker remains at peak operating power, combining attractively contrasting tracks waxed in New Orleans and Los Angeles. — *Bill Dahl*

● **Bottom of the Top** / 1973 / Hightone ✦✦✦✦
There weren't many blues albums issued during the early '70s that hit harder than this one. First out on the short-lived Playboy logo, the set firmly established Walker as a blistering axeman sporting enduring Gulf Coast roots despite his adopted L.A. homebase. Of all the times he's cut the rocking "Hello My Darling," this is indeed the hottest, while his funky, horn-driven revival of Lester Williams' "I Can't Lose (With the Stuff I Lose)" and his own R&B-drenched "It's All in Your Mind" are irresistible. After-hours renditions of Sam Cooke's "Laughing & Clowning" and Long John Hunter's "Crazy Girl" are striking vehicles for Walker's twisting, turning guitar riffs and impassioned vocal delivery. — *Bill Dahl*

Someday You'll Have These Blues / 1977 / Hightone ✦✦✦
Recorded in 1975-76 and initially out on the short-lived Joliet logo (later Alligator picked it up; it's now out on HighTone), this collection wasn't quite the masterpiece that its predecessor was ("Breakin' Up Somebody's Home" and "Part Time Love" were hardly inspired cover choices), the set does have its moments—the uncompromising title track and "Beaumont Blues," to cite a couple. — *Bill Dahl*

Blues Show Live at Pit Inn / 1980 / Ypuiteru ✦✦

From L.A. to L.A. / 1982 / Rounder ✦✦✦
Walker's tunes from 1969, 1970, and 1976 sessions, were produced by Bruce Bromberg and recorded with Lonesome Sundown. They're very nice. — *Niles J. Frantz*

Tough As I Want to Be / 1984 / Rounder ✦✦✦✦
Hotter and fiercer than other recordings, these originals and covers come from Lowell Fulson and Jimmy McCracklin. — *Niles J. Frantz*

Blues / 1988 / Hightone ◆◆◆

Contains a rich, reassuring reading of "Don't Be Afraid of the Dark," a tune generally associated with HighTone stablemate Robert Cray (Walker's version was reportedly waxed the day before Cray's), with the Memphis Horns adding extra punch. — *Bill Dahl*

Big Blues from Texas / 1994 / JSP ◆◆◆

Nice comeback set after a lengthy absence from the recording scene that was cut in London under the direction of guitarist Otis Grand (who shares axe duties throughout). Why this Louisiana-born guitarist hasn't been recorded more heavily is a mystery; he seldom fails to connect, and this import is no exception to the rule. — *Bill Dahl*

Working Girl Blues / 1995 / Black Top ◆◆◆◆

Walker remains in fine form on this recent set, a mix of remakes of past triumphs ("Hello, My Darling," "Hey, Hey Baby's Gone") and fresh explorations. Two distinct bands were utilized — a New Orleans crew populated by bassist George Porter, Jr., and his funky cohorts, and an L.A. posse with more of a straight-up swinging feel. — *Bill Dahl*

T-Bone Walker (Aaron Thibeaux Walker)

b. May 28, 1910, Linden, TX, **d.** Mar. 16, 1975, Los Angeles, CA

Guitar, Vocals / Electric Texas Blues, Texas Blues

Modern electric blues guitar can be traced directly back to this Texas-born pioneer, who began amplifying his sumptuous lead lines for public consumption circa 1940 and thus initiated a revolution so total that its tremors are still being felt today.

Few major postwar blues guitarists come to mind that don't owe T-Bone Walker an unpayable debt of gratitude. B.B. King has long cited him as a primary influence, marveling at Walker's penchant for holding the body of his guitar outward while he played it. Gatemouth Brown, Pee Wee Crayton, Goree Carter, Pete Mayes, and a wealth of other prominent Texas-bred axemen came stylistically right out of Walker during the late '40s and early '50s. Walker's nephew, guitarist R.S. Rankin, went so far as to bill himself as T-Bone Walker, Jr. for a 1962 single on Dot, "Midnight Bells Are Ringing" (with his uncle's complete blessing, of course; the two had worked up a father-and-son-type act long before that).

Aaron Thibeault Walker was a product of the primordial Dallas blues scene. His stepfather, Marco Washington, stroked the bass fiddle with the Dallas String Band, and T-Bone followed his stepdad's example by learning the rudiments of every stringed instrument he could lay his talented hands on. One notable visitor to the band's jam sessions was the legendary Blind Lemon Jefferson. During the early '20s, Walker led the sightless guitarist from bar to bar as the older man played for tips.

In 1929, Walker made his recording debut with a single 78 for Columbia, "Wichita Falls Blues"/"Trinity River Blues," billed as Oak Cliff T-Bone. Pianist Douglas Fernell was his musical partner for the disc. Walker was exposed to some pretty outstanding guitar talent during his formative years; besides Jefferson, Charlie Christian — who would totally transform the role of the guitar in jazz with his electrified riffs much as Walker would with blues, was one of his playing partners circa 1933.

T-Bone Walker split the Southwest for Los Angeles during the mid-'30s, earning his keep with saxist Big Jim Wynn's band with his feet rather than his hands as a dancer. Popular bandleader Les Hite hired Walker as his vocalist in 1939. Walker sang "T-Bone Blues" with the Hite aggregation for Varsity Records in 1940, but didn't play guitar on the outing. It was about then, though, that his fascination with electrifying his axe bore fruit; he played L.A. clubs with his daring new toy after assembling his own combo, engaging in acrobatic stage moves — splits, playing behind his back — to further enliven his show.

Capitol Records was a fledgling Hollywood concern in 1942, when Walker signed on and cut "Mean Old World" and "I Got a Break Baby" with boogie master Freddie Slack hammering the 88s. This was the first sign of the T-Bone Walker that blues guitar aficionados know and love, his fluid, elegant riffs and mellow, burnished vocals setting a standard that all future blues guitarists would measure themselves by.

Chicago's Rhumboogie Club served as Walker's home away from home during a good portion of the war years. He even cut a few sides for the joint's house label in 1945 under the direction of pianist Marl Young. But after a

solitary session that same year for Old Swingmaster that soon made its way onto another newly established logo, Mercury, Walker signed with Los Angeles-based Black & White Records in 1946 and proceeded to amass a stunning legacy.

The immortal "Call It Stormy Monday (But Tuesday Is Just as Bad)" was the product of a 1947 Black & White date with Teddy Buckner on trumpet and invaluable pianist Lloyd Glenn in the backing quintet. Many of Walker's best sides were smoky after-hours blues, though an occasional up-tempo entry — "T-Bone Jumps Again," a storming instrumental from the same date, for example — illustrated his nimble dexterity at faster speeds.

Walker recorded prolifically for Black & White until the close of 1947, waxing classics like the often-covered "T-Bone Shuffle" and "West Side Baby," though many of the sides came out on Capitol after the demise of Black & White. In 1950, Walker turned up on Imperial. His first date for the Los Angeles indie elicited the after-hours gem "Glamour Girl" and perhaps the penultimate jumping instrumental in his repertoire, "Strollin' with Bones" (Snake Sims' drum kit cracks like a whip behind Walker's impeccable licks).

Walker's 1950-54 Imperial stint was studded with more classics: "The Hustle Is On," "Cold Cold Feeling," "Blue Mood," "Vida Lee" (named for his wife), "Party Girl," and, from a 1952 New Orleans jaunt, "Railroad Station Blues," which was produced by Dave Bartholomew. Atlantic was T-Bone Walker's next stop in 1955; his first date for them was an unlikely but successful collaboration with a crew of Chicago mainstays (harpist Junior Wells, guitarist Jimmy Rogers, and bassist Ransom Knowling among them). Rogers found the experience especially useful; he later adapted Walker's "Why Not" as his own Chess hit "Walking by Myself."

With a slightly more sympathetic L.A. band in staunch support, Walker cut two follow-up sessions for Atlantic in 1956-57. The latter date produced some amazing instrumentals ("Two Bones and a Pick," "Blues-rock," "Shufflin' the Blues") that saw him duelling it out with his nephew and jazzman Barney Kessel (Walker emerged victorious in every case).

Unfortunately, the remainder of Walker's discography isn't of the same sterling quality for the most part. As it had with so many of his peers from the postwar R&B era, rock's rise had made Walker's classy style an anachronism (at least during much of the 1960s). He journeyed overseas on the first American Folk Blues Festival in 1962, starring on the Lippmann & Rau-promoted bill across Europe with Memphis Slim, Willie Dixon, and a host of other American luminaries. A 1964 45 for Modern and an obscure LP on Brunswick preceded a pair of BluesWay albums in 1967-68 that restored this seminal pioneer to American record shelves.

European tours often beckoned. A 1968 visit to Paris resulted in one of his best latter-day albums, *I Want a Little Girl,* for Black & Blue (and later issued stateside on Delmark). With expatriate tenor saxophonist Hal "Cornbread" Singer and Chicago drummer S.P. Leary picking up Walker's jazz-tinged style brilliantly, the guitarist glided through a stellar set list.

Good Feelin', a 1970 release on Polydor, won a Grammy for the guitarist, though it doesn't rank with his best efforts. A five-song appearance on a 1973 set for Reprise, *Very Rare,* was also a disappointment. Persistent stomach woes and a 1974 stroke slowed Walker's career to a crawl, and he died in 1975.

No amount of written accolades can fully convey the monumental importance of what T-Bone Walker gave to the blues. He was the idiom's first true lead guitarist, and undeniably one of its very best. — *Bill Dahl*

☆ **T-Bone Blues** / 1959 / Atlantic ◆◆◆◆◆

The last truly indispensable disc of the great guitar hero's career, and perhaps the most innately satisfying of all — these mid-'50s recordings boast magnificent presence, with Walker's axe so crisp and clear it seems as though he's sitting right next to you as he delivers a luxurious remake of "Call It Stormy Monday." Atlantic took some chances with Bone, dispatching him to Chicago for a 1955 date with Junior Wells and Jimmy Rogers that produced "Why Not" and "Papa Ain't Salty." Even better were the 1956-57 Los Angeles dates that produced the scalding instrumental "Two Bones and a Pick" (finding Walker duelling it out with nephew R.S. Rankin and jazzman Barney Kessel). — *Bill Dahl*

Sings the Blues / 1959 / Imperial ◆◆◆◆

These early-'50s Imperial sides find the Texas guitar pioneer in top form. — *Bill Dahl*

Singing the Blues / 1960 / Imperial ✦✦✦✦
More early-'50s gems. — *Bill Dahl*

I Get So Weary / 1961 / Imperial ✦✦✦✦
Still another LP of Walker's elegant guitar and smooth vocals. — *Bill Dahl*

Great Blues Vocals and Guitar / 1963 / Capitol ✦✦✦✦

I Want a Little Girl / 1967 / Delmark ✦✦✦✦
This pioneering artist had more influence in the shaping of modern blues guitar styles than anyone on the planet. His was a cross-genre genius that skirted the boundaries of blues, R&B, jump, jazz, and pop. He appears on nearly 50 labels in a studio career that spanned over 30 years, and very little of this output falters even slightly. This tasty set made originally for the Black and Blue label in 1968 features him with a like-minded unit of tenor sax, piano, bass, and drums that provides a solid and excellent groove throughout. Musically, this is truly the genius at home, calling the shots. — *Larry Hoffman*

Funky Town / 1969 / Beat Goes On ✦✦✦

Dirty Mistreater / 1973 / Bluesway ✦✦✦
A reissue of a 1973 Bluesway album, it shows T-Bone near the end. — *Hank Davis*

Classics of Modern Blues / Aug. 1975 / Blue Note ✦✦✦✦
This two-LP set contains most of Walker's seminal sides for Imperial (cut in 1952-53). — *Bill Dahl*

T-Bone Walker / 197 / Blue Note ✦✦✦
A scholarly 17-track compilation, it has great photos and notes, and features selections from 1929 to 1953. For the serious collector. — *Hank Davis*

Original 1945-50 Performances / 197 / EMI ✦✦✦✦
A deep look into T-Bone's roots, it features 12 classic performances, including the original "Stormy Monday Blues." — *Hank Davis*

Inventor of the Electric Guitar Blues / 1983 / Blues Boy ✦✦✦✦
Some formative and masterful recordings by Aaron T-Bone Walker, among the greatest pure vocalists in modern blues history. The find is a side with Walker playing 1929 country blues and sounding just as comfortable and exciting as he does on the 16 other 1940s and '50s numbers. — *Ron Wynn*

The Hustle Is On / 1990 / Sequel ✦✦✦✦
Nice CD compilation of Imperial material. — *Bill Dahl*

☆ **The Complete Recordings of T-Bone Walker 1940-1954** / Oct. 1990 / Mosaic ✦✦✦✦✦
A six-CD boxed set—an education in the lineage of urban blues. It appears that T-Bone Walker had a greater influence on urban blues players than any other single talent. His guitar, vocals, song selection, and sheer style live on today in nearly every blues performer. He is the master. — *Michael Erlewine*

Rare T-Bone / 1991 / Off-Beat ✦✦✦
A compilation of ten tracks, recorded late in Walker's career on albums for the Bluesway label. His vocal and instrumental power is undiminished on these solid sides, which are somewhat overlooked in comparison to his work in the '40s and '50s. Soul and funk touches update his sound without sounding contrived. As an overview of the Bluesway period, though, it's too skimpy, with sub-standard liner notes and track documentation. — *Richie Unterberger*

★ **The Complete Imperial Recordings** / 1991 / EMI America ✦✦✦✦✦
Another essential T-Bone Walker stake, this time a two-disc dish with 52 sensational tracks from his stint at Lew Chudd's Imperial Records. Whether waxing with his own jump blues unit in L.A. or Dave Bartholomew's hard-drivers in New Orleans, Walker always stayed true to his vision, and the proof was in the grooves: "Glamour Girl," "The Hustle Is On," "Tell Me What's the Reason," "High Society," "Cold, Cold Feeling," and the immaculate jumping instrumental "Strollin' with Bones" all date from this historic period of Walker's legacy. — *Bill Dahl*

☆ **Complete Capitol/Black & White Recordings** / 1995 / Capitol ✦✦✦✦✦
Three-CD, 75-track box of T-Bone Walker's recordings for the Capitol and Black & White labels in the 1940s. From a historical perspective, this is perhaps the most important phase of Walker's evolution. It was here where he perfected his electric guitar style, becoming an important influence on everyone from B.B. King down. It was also here where he acted as one of the key players in small combo West Coast bands' transition from jazz to a more jump blues/R&B-oriented sound (though most of these sides retain a pretty

strong jazz flavor). These sessions, which include the original version of his most famous tune ("Call It Stormy Monday"), have previously been chopped up into small morsels for reissue, or incorporated into the mammoth limited-edition Mosaic box set; this isolates them more conveniently. At the same time, it may be too extensive for some listeners, especially with the abundance of alternate takes (which are placed right after the official versions). Excellent liner notes, although the discographical information is surprisingly inconsistent. — *Richie Unterberger*

Sippie Wallace (Beulah Thomas)

b. Nov. 1, 1898, Houston, TX, **d.** Nov. 1, 1986, Detroit, MI
Vocals / Blues, Classic Female Blues
A classic female blues singer from the '20s, Wallace kept performing and recording until her death. She was a major influence on a young Bonnie Raitt, who recorded several of Wallace's songs and performed live with her.

The daughter of a Baptist deacon, Sippie Wallace (born Beulah Thomas) was born and raised in Houston. As a child, she sang and played piano in church. Before she was in her teens, she began performing with her pianist brother Hersal Thomas. By the time she was in her mid-teens, she had left Houston to pursue a musical career, singing in a number of tent shows and earning a dedicated fan base. In 1915, she moved to New Orleans with Hersal. Two years later, she married Matt Wallace.

In 1923, Sippie, Hersal, and their older brother George moved to Chicago, where Sippie became part of the city's jazz scene. By the end of the year, she had earned a contract with OKeh Records. Her first two songs for the label, "Shorty George" and "Up the Country Blues," were hits and Sippie soon became a star. Throughout the '20s, she produced a series of singles that were nearly all hits. Wallace's OKeh recordings featured a number of celebrated jazz musicians, including Louis Armstrong, Eddie Heywood, King Oliver, and Clarence Williams; both Hersal and George Thomas performed on Sippie's records as well, in addition to supporting her at concerts. Between 1923 and 1927, she recorded over 40 songs for the OKeh. Many of the songs that were Wallace originals or co-written by Sippie and her brothers.

In 1926, Hersal Thomas died of food poisoning, but Sippie Wallace continued to perform and record. Within a few years, however, she stopped performing regularly. After her contract with OKeh was finished in the late '20s, she moved to Detroit in 1929. In the early '30s, Wallace stopped recording, only performing the occasional gig. In 1936, both George Thomas and her husband Matt died. Following their deaths, Sippie joined the Leland Baptist Church in Detroit, where she was an organist and vocalist; she stayed with the church for the next 40 years.

Between 1936 and 1966, Sippie Wallace was inactive on the blues scene—she only performed a handful of concerts and cut a few records. In 1966, she was lured out of retirement by her friend Victoria Spivey, who convinced Sippie to join the thriving blues and folk festival circuit. Wallace not only joined the circuit, she began recording again. Her first new album was a collection of duets with Spivey, appropriately titled *Sippie Wallace and Victoria Spivey*, which was recorded in 1966; the album wasn't released until 1970. Also in 1966, Wallace recorded *Sippie Wallace Sings the Blues* for Storyville, which featured support from musicians like Little Brother Montgomery and Roosevelt Sykes. The album was quite popular, as were Sippie's festival performances.

In 1970, Sippie Wallace suffered a stroke, but she was able to continue recording and performing, although not as frequently as she had before. In 1982, Bonnie Raitt—who had longed claimed Sippie as a major influence—helped Wallace land a contract with Atlantic Records. Raitt produced the resulting album, *Sippie*, which was released in 1983. *Sippie* won the W.C. Handy Award for best blues album of the year and was nominated for a Grammy. The album turned out to be Sippie Wallace's last recording—she died in 1986, when she was 88 years old. — *Stephen Thomas Erlewine & Cub Koda*

Complete Recorded Works, Vol. 1 (1923-25) / 1923-1925 / Document ✦✦✦

● **1923-1929** / 1923-1929 / Document ✦✦✦✦
Document's *1923-1929* is an excellent 18-track collection of Sippie Wallace's first recordings. Many of her very best (and most notorious) songs, such as "I'm a Mighty Tight Woman," are included among these performances, most of which feature Wallace supported by a solitary piano; a few of the cuts have Sippie supported by a small jazz combo. Since Sippie Wallace's classic work

has not been widely distributed, this is the best collection simply by default, but even if there were more discs available, *1923-1929* would still rank among the best compilations, since it has many of her best songs presented in the best fidelity possible. — *Thom Owens*

Complete Recorded Works, Vol. 2 (1925-45) / 1925-1945 / Document ◆◆◆

Women Be Wise / Oct. 31, 1966 / Alligator ◆◆◆
Recorded on Halloween night, 1966, in Copenhagen, Denmark, this one of the few great "blues rediscovery" albums that comes by its reputation honestly. With Roosevelt Sykes and Little Brother Montgomery sharing the piano stool, Sippie clearly shows that the intervening years had, indeed, been kind to her, belting out one great tune after another. Listing highlights is superfluous, simply because every track's a gem. The no-frills production is warm and cozy enough to make you feel like you're hearing the world's greatest one-woman concert right in your living room. And you're glad you bought a ticket. — *Cub Koda*

Mercy Dee Walton

b. Aug. 3, 1915, Waco, TX, **d.** Dec. 2, 1962, Stockton, CA
Piano, Vocals / Piano Blues, West Coast Blues
Mose Allison certainly recognized the uncommon brilliance of pianist Mercy Dee Walton. The young jazz-based Allison faithfully covered Walton's downtrodden "One Room Country Shack" in 1957, four years after Walton had waxed the original for Los Angeles-based Specialty Records (his original was a huge R&B smash).

Walton was a Texas émigré, like so many other postwar California R&B pioneers, who had played piano around Waco from the age of 13 before hitting the coast in 1938. Once there, the pianist gigged up and down the length of the Golden State before debuting on record in 1949 with "Lonesome Cabin Blues" for the tiny Spire logo, which became a national R&B hit. Those sides were cut in Fresno, but Los Angeles hosted some of the pianist's best sessions for Imperial in 1950 and Specialty in 1952-53.

Walton, who usually recorded under the handle of Mercy Dee, was a talented songsmith whose compositions ran the gamut from lowdown blues to jumping R&B items. A half dozen tracks for the Bihari brothers' Flair imprint in 1955 included "Come Back Maybellene," a rocking sequel to Chuck Berry's then-current hit.

After a lengthy layoff, Walton returned to the studio in a big way in 1961, recording prolifically for Chris Strachwitz's Arhoolie label with his northern California compatriots: K.C. Douglas on guitar, harpist Sidney Maiden, and drummer Otis Cherry (some of this material ended up on Prestige's Bluesville subsidiary). It's very fortunate that Strachwitz took an interest in documenting Walton's versatility, for in December of 1962, the pianist died. — *Bill Dahl*

One Room Country Shack / 1952-1953 / Specialty ◆◆◆
Unlike many other blues performers who migrated to California, Mercy Dee Walton didn't change or rework his style to fit the new environment. Rather than becoming a more sophisticated singer or a more jazz-oriented instrumentalist, Walton kept making the same countrified, intimate, simple songs, replete with down-home imagery and sung in a weary, cautionary tone, backed by sparse piano accompaniment. The material on *One Room Country Shack*, a 24-song collection of Walton originals, could have been cut in Texas or Mississippi for that matter. It includes a remake of his landmark 1949 number "Lonesome Cabin Blues" and the marvelous title cut, which was later covered by Mose Allison. — *Ron Wynn*

Troublesome Mind / 1961 / Arhoolie ◆◆◆◆
Fine 16-song selection from the California-based pianist's 1961 sessions for Chris Strachwitz's Arhoolie logo. A trio of sympathetic cohorts (harpist Sidney Maiden, guitarist K.C. Douglas, and drummer Otis Cherry) give the music a rough-edged barroom feel as Dee pounds out "After the Fight," "Call the Asylum," and a nice remake of his dour "One Room Country Shack." — *Bill Dahl*

Mercy Dee Walton & His Piano / 1961 / Arhoolie ◆◆◆
● **Mercy Dee** / Aug. 1962 / Original Blues Classics ◆◆◆◆
Whether you know him as Mercy Dee Walton, Mercy Dee or just plain Mercy, there was no doubt that he could write some incredible songs and spin some wonderful yarns. The playing wasn't bad either, and these early-'60s recordings are among his finest. — *Ron Wynn*

Pity and a Shame / 196 / Original Blues Classics ◆◆◆

Danger Zone (1949-55) / Feb. 20, 1996 / RST ◆◆◆◆

Clara Ward

f. Aug. 21, 1924, Philadelphia, PA, **db.** Jan. 16, 1973, Los Angeles, CA
Group / Black Gospel, Traditional Gospel
Widely acclaimed among the greatest soloists in gospel history, Clara Ward was also the subject of much criticism from purists—with her backing group the Ward Singers, she pushed gospel out of the church and into the nightclubs, infusing the music with a shot of glitz and glamour the likes of which had never before been seen. Decked out in colorful gowns, towering wigs and dazzling jewelry, the Wards sang only the biggest pop-gospel hits, flamboyantly delivered for maximum commercial appeal; while many observers decried their clownish onstage behavior as demeaning not only to the music but also to their African-American heritage, at their creative peak the group was a true phenomenon, combining superb soloists, exceptional material and innovative arrangements to leave an indelible mark on the generations of spiritual performers who followed.

Born in Philadelphia on August 21, 1924, Ward was unquestionably the driving creative force behind her group's success, but the business smarts belonged to her mother, Gertrude Mae Murphy Ward. The textbook stage mother, Gertude and her husband relocated to the Philadelphia area from a life of abject poverty in rural South Carolina; the family struggled throughout the Depression, but in 1931 she was struck by a vision which commanded her to begin a singing career. Forming a family group which included Clara and her sister Willa on piano, Gertrude quickly emerged among the most forceful promoters in all of gospel—a gifted vocalist in her own right, her truest talents were nonetheless of an entrepreneurial nature, and after a transcendent performance at the 1943 National Baptist Convention, the Ward Singers were one of the top attractions on the church circuit.

The Wards' success, however, did not come without a price—Clara, the star of the group, later admitted to constant frustrations with her life as a teen phenomenon, and although she loved gospel, it appears unlikely that she would have pursued a singing career if not for the constant pressure applied by her mother. By the late 1940s, the group had grown so successful that they added a pair of new members, Henrietta Waddy and Marion Williams, a Miami teen whose powerhouse voice became the Wards' trademark. With Williams installed as soloist, the Wards hit their creative peak, issuing such masterful hits as "Surely God Is Able" and "Packin' Up." For her part, Clara remained content to remain somewhat in the background, accompanying the group on piano while Williams stole the spotlight.

While her gorgeous alto was the centerpiece of hits like "How I Got Over," arguably Ward's greatest strength was as an arranger; "Surely," the group's biggest hit, even introduced a new waltz rhythm into the gospel lexicon. The Wards—who by now also included Frances Steadman and Kitty Parham—were also the first gospel group to employ the switch-lead style of the shouting quartets, always keeping at least four vocalists in their ranks at all times. The consenus pick as the best hymn singers in the business, the Wards also rejected the homespun choir robes of the past in favor of elaborate costumes—according to legend, on one occasion their infamous wigs grew so tall that they actually touched the ceiling. Throughout the 1950s, they were among gospel's elite, scoring more hits and making more money than any group before them.

During the early '50s, the Wards began regularly touring with the Reverend C.L. Franklin of Detroit; the father of Aretha Franklin—herself an admitted disciple of Clara Ward—he was a gifted singer and preacher in his own right, and as his star rose the group's fame continued to grow. However, in 1958, Williams quit, and the bottom fell out—Parham and Steadman exited as well, all over their notoriously low salaries, and although new recruits including Thelma Jackson, Carrie Williams and Jessie Tucker were quickly brought in, the Wards' popularity nosedived. By 1961, amid considerable hoopla, they moved to the club circuit, playing Las Vegas and even Disneyland all to the shock of gospel traditionalists; white audiences were intrigued, and the group continued touring throughout the 1960s, until Ward's declining health forced her into retirement. She died January 16, 1973. — *Jason Ankeny*

Surely God Is Able / 1955 / Savoy ◆◆◆
The Pilgrim Jubilees were among the greatest of Mississippi quartets: subtle

swing, fine guitar, and a terrific time-sense. A treasure trove, it was deleted a while back. The Ward Singers brought free quartet singing to a pinnacle in the 1950s, and this album has some of their most moving songs, among them "Surely God Is Able" and "He Knows How Much I Can Bear." (The cover's claim of mid-price status became history when the label changed hands.) —*John Storm Roberts, Original Music*

Lord Touch Me / 1956 / Savoy ✦✦✦✦
More passion and drive, circa 1953-55. —*Opal Louis Nations*

That Old Landmark / 1958 / Savoy ✦✦✦✦
Some of the group's most memorable compositions. —*Opal Louis Nations*

Down by the Riverside (Live at the Town Hall, NY) / 1958 / Dot ✦✦✦✦
Gospel excitement with the group in full throttle, backed by lap-steel guitar whiz Sammy Fein. —*Opal Louis Nations*

Memorial Album / 1988 / Savoy ✦✦✦
Fine performances by the "core" group from the early 1950s. —*Opal Louis Nations*

The Very Greatest / 1995 / Nashboro ✦✦✦✦
Surprisingly fine material from this leading diva's later repertoire. Nashboro sides. —*Opal Louis Nations*

The Clara Ward Singers / Roulette ✦✦✦
Includes pleasant but not essential selections by this popular group. —*Kip Lornell*

The Best of the Ward Singers / Savoy ✦✦✦✦
The Clara Ward Singers have been called the greatest group, together with the Roberta Martin Singers, produced by gospel. She herself was a magnificent singer—the inspiration for Aretha Franklin—and among those who came out of the group was the superb Marion Williams. Stylistically, the Ward Singers represented an early stage in the move to a deliberate and dramatic use of a fervor that had once been purely religious. —*John Storm Roberts, Original Music*

Gospel Soul of Clara Ward / ✦✦✦✦
Here's a surprising set of joyful-sounding gospel songs recorded some time in the early '70s that gives us an idea of how magnificent the Ward Singers sounded in their heyday during the '50s. All the songs are carefully arranged to evoke the feel of a live church performance, with high-spirited renditions of "What Jesus Is to Me" and "It May Be the Best for Me." There's lots of jubilant singing and tambourine banging. —*Opal Louis Nations, Roots & Rhythm Newsletter*

★ **Clara Ward Singers** / ✦✦✦✦✦
Clara Ward Singers contains 22 tracks the group recorded for Roulette Records in 1963. Although Ward had been a well-known vocalist for nearly 20 years at the time these songs were recorded, she had lost none of her power, and these are as energetic and represenative as any she has ever recorded. The presence of a jumping slide guitarist is slightly surprising, but he gets into the spirit of things, helping propel these sessions to joyful new heights. Highly recommended. —*Leo Stanley*

Robert Ward

b. Oct. 15, 1938, Luthersville, GA
Guitar, Vocals / Soul Blues, R&B, Modern Electric Blues
Comeback tales don't come any more heartwarming (or unlikely) than Robert Ward's. Totally off the scene and thought by many aficionados to be dead, Ward's chance encounter with guitar-shop owner Dave Hussong in Dayton, OH, set off a rapid chain of events that culminated in Ward's 1990 debut album for Black Top, *Fear No Evil*, and a second chance at the brass ring.

Ward's first taste of stardom came as leader of the Ohio Untouchables (who later mutated into the Ohio Players long after Ward's departure) during the early '60s. Born into impoverished circumstances in rural Georgia, Ward had picked up his first guitar at age ten. Singles by Sister Rosetta Tharpe, B.B. King, and Muddy Waters left their mark on the youth. After a stint in the Army, Ward came home in 1959 and joined his first band, the Brassettes (who also included Roy Lee Johnson, soon to join Piano Red's band and croon "Mister Moonlight").

Tired of seeing little monetary reward for opening for the likes of James Brown and Piano Red with the Brassettes, Ward moved to Dayton, OH, in

1960. Inspired by hard-bitten FBI man Eliott Ness on TV's *The Untouchables*, Ward recruited bassist Levoy Fredrick and drummer Cornelius Johnson to form the first edition of the Ohio Untouchables. Ward's trademark vibrato-soaked guitar sound was the direct result of acquiring a Magnatone amplifier at a Dayton music store. Lonnie Mack was so entranced by the watery sound of Ward's amp that he bought a Magnatone as well; both still utilize the same trademark sound to this day.

Detroit producer Robert West signed the Untouchables to his LuPine logo in 1962. Ward's quirky touch was beautifully exhibited on the hard-bitten "I'm Tired," a chilling doo wop-tinged "Forgive Me Darling," and the exotic "Your Love Is Amazing" for LuPine. In addition, the Untouchables backed Wilson Pickett and the Falcons on their gospel-charged 1962 smash "I Found a Love."

Ward and his band also briefly recorded for Detroit's Thelma Records, waxing the driving blues "Your Love Is Real" and a soul-sending "I'm Gonna Cry a River." Ward left the Untouchables in 1965 (to be replaced by Leroy "Sugarfoot" Bonner), stopping at Don Davis' Groove City label long enough to cut a super Detroit soul pairing, "Fear No Evil" (the original version) and "My Love Is Strictly Reserved for You," circa 1966-67.

During the early '70s, Ward worked as a session guitarist at Motown, playing behind the Temptations and the Undisputed Truth (he was an old pal of Joe Harris, lead singer of the latter group). But when his wife died in 1977, Ward hit the skids. He moved back to Georgia, and served a year in jail at one point (ironically, one of his prison mates was singer Major Lance, whose career was at similarly low ebb).

In 1990, that auspicious encounter with Hussong started the ball rolling for Ward's return to action. Black Top boss Hammond Scott signed the guitarist and produced the amazing *Fear No Evil* and a credible 1993 follow-up, *Rhythm of the People*. The label recently issued a third set, *Black Bottom*, that once again captured Ward's curiously mystical appeal. Today, Ward lives in tiny Dry Branch, GA, with his second wife Roberta, who contributed background vocals to his encore album. —*Bill Dahl*

★ **Fear No Evil** / 1990 / Black Top ✦✦✦✦✦
One of the most amazing comeback stories of the modern blues era was ignited by this astonishing album. Robert Ward hadn't recorded as a leader in close to a quarter century, but his melismatic, almost mystical vocal quality and quirky, vibrato-enriched guitar sound utterly vital and electrifying as he revives some of his own obscure oldies ("Your Love Is Amazing," "Forgive Me Darling," "Strictly Reserved for You") and debuts a few new compositions for good measure. One of the classic blues/soul albums of the '90s. —*Bill Dahl*

Rhythm of the People / 1993 / Black Top ✦✦✦
Disappointing sequel to Ward's magnificent first Black Top disc—his vocals don't sound nearly as hearty this time around, and a some of the songs just aren't up to par ("All Proud Races" is downright stupid). There's a taste of gospel in "What a Friend We Have in Jesus," Ward's own take on "I Found a Love," and a steamy remake of James Brown's "And I Do Just What I Want." —*Bill Dahl*

Robert Ward / Apr. 1, 1993 / Black Top ✦✦✦

Hot Stuff / 1995 / Relic ✦✦✦✦
These are the first magnificent 1960s waxings of guitarist Robert Ward & the Ohio Untouchables for the tiny LuPine, Thelma, and Groove City logos; full of fiery soul, watery, vibrato-enhanced axe, and sinuous rhythms. Ward's piercing vocals on "I'm Tired," "Your Love Is Amazing," and "Fear No Evil" are mesmerizing. Also aboard are four classic cuts by the Wilson Pickett-led Falcons from 1962 with the Untouchables in support (the gospel-soaked "I Found a Love" was a legit smash, while Ward sears the strings on their "Let's Kiss and Make Up"). —*Bill Dahl*

Black Bottom / Oct. 17, 1995 / Black Top ✦✦✦✦
Now this is more like it. Ward is back in top form for his third Black Top outing, with better songs (most of them originals), skin-tight support from the Black Top house band, and plenty of that singularly gurgly guitar that inspired Lonnie Mack to follow Ward's lead and buy a Magnatone amp when he was starting out. —*Bill Dahl*

Twiggs County Soul Man / Feb. 4, 1997 / Black Top ✦✦✦

Baby Boy Warren (Robert Warren)

b. Aug. 13, 1919, Lake Providence, LA, d. Jul. 1, 1977, Detroit, MI
Guitar, Vocals / Electric Blues
The denizens of Detroit's postwar blues scene never really received their due (except for John Lee Hooker, of course). Robert "Baby Boy" Warren compiled a sterling discography from 1949 to 1954 for a variety of Motor City firms without ever managing to transcend his local status along Hastings Street.

After honing his blues guitar approach in Memphis (where he was raised), Warren came to Detroit in 1942 to work for General Motors and gig on the side. The fruits of his first recording session in 1949 with pianist Charley Mills supporting him came out on several different logos: Prize, Staff, Gotham, even King's Federal subsidiary. A second date in 1950 that found him backed by pianist Boogie Woogie Red was split between Staff and Sampson; Swing Time snagged "I Got Lucky"/"Let's Renew Our Love" and pressed it for West Coast consumption.

One of his most memorable sessions took place in 1954, when wizened harpist Sonny Boy Williamson came to Detroit and backed Warren on "Sanafee" and "Chuc-A-Luck," which found their way to Nashville's Excello label. Joe Von Battle's JVB imprint unleashed Warren's "Hello Stranger" and "Baby Boy Blues" from the same date. That same year, a single for powerful Chicago deejay Al Benson's Blue Lake Records coupled "Mattie Mae" and "Santa Fe."

The 1970s brought Baby Boy Warren a taste of European touring, though nothing substantial, before he passed away in 1977. —*Bill Dahl*

● **Baby Boy Warren** / BBW ✦✦✦✦
This may be a bootleg vinyl album (issued at various times with different covers ranging from a mocked up newspaper headline to a grotesque, sloppy cartoon impressionistic rendering of the bluesman) taped off of old scratchy 78s, but it's the only place you're going to hear the recorded output of this marvelous Detroit bluesman. Recording for JVB, Excello, Drummond, Staff and Gotham, Warren's sense of song structure owes a strong debt to Robert Johnson and his lyrics are full of wry humor and mordant wit. As the leader of the first great band to emerge from the Detroit blues scene, the lineup of players on these sides include Boogie Woogie Red on piano, Calvin Frazier (another running buddy of Robert Johnson) on lead guitar, the self describable Washboard Willie and on four tracks, Sonny Boy Williamson, moonlighting away from the King Biscuit Boys. Highlights include "Not Welcome Anymore," "Baby Boy Blues," the stomping instrumental "Chuck-a-Luck," "Mattie Mae," "Hello Stranger" (a different version of "Mattie Mae" from a later session) and a driving take on Robert Johnson's "Stop Breaking Down." Next to the early work of John Lee Hooker and a stray anthology, this is Detroit blues at its finest. —*Cub Koda*

Washboard Sam (Robert Brown)

b. Jul. 15, 1910, Walnut Ridge, AR, d. Nov. 13, 1966, Chicago, IL
Vocals, Washboard / Acoustic Chicago Blues, Prewar Country Blues
A popular hokum blues artist, Washboard Sam recorded hundreds of records in the late '30s and '40s, usually with singer/guitarist Big Bill Broonzy. Out of all the washboard players of the era, Sam was the most popular, which was due not only to his to his washboard talent, but also his skills as a songwriter, as well as his strong voice. As an accompanist, Washboard Sam not only played with Broonzy, but also with bluesmen like Bukka White, Memphis Slim, Willie Lacey, and Jazz Gillum.

Washboard Sam (born Robert Brown) is the illegitimate son of Frank Broonzy, who also fathered Big Bill Broonzy. Sam was raised in Arkansas, working on a farm. He moved to Memphis in the early '20s to play the blues. While in Memphis, he met Sleepy John Estes and Hammie Nixon and the trio played street corners, collecting tips from passer-bys. In 1932, Washboard Sam moved to Chicago. Initially he played for tips, but soon he began performing regularly with Big Bill Broonzy. Within a few years, Sam was supporting Broonzy on the guitarist's Bluebird recordings. Soon, he was supporting a number of different musicians on their recording sessions, including pianist Memphis Slim, bassist Ransom Knowlin, and a handful of saxophone players, who all recorded for Bluebird.

In 1935, Washboard Sam began recording for both Bluebird and Vocalion Records, often supported by Big Bill Broonzy. Throughout the rest of the '30s and the '40s, Sam was one of the most popular Chicago bluesmen, selling numerous records and playing to packed audiences. After World War II, his audience began to shrink, largely because he had difficulty adapting to the new electric blues. In 1953, Washboard Sam recorded a session for Chess Records and then retired. In the early '60s, Willie Dixon and Memphis Slim tried to persuade Sam to return to the stage to capitalize on the blues revival. Initially, he refused, but in 1963 began performing concerts in clubs and coffeehouses in Chicago; he even played a handful of dates in Europe in early 1964.

Washboard Sam made his final recordings for the small Chicago-based label Spivey in 1964. The following year, his health quickly declined and he stopped recording and playing shows. In November of 1966, he died of heart disease. —*Stephen Thomas Erlewine & Cub Koda*

● **Blues Classics by Washboard Sam 1935-1941** / 1935-1941 / Blues Classics ✦✦✦✦
Blues Classics by Washboard Sam 1935-1941 is an excellent collection of 14 songs Sam recorded during those six years. Almost of his classic numbers—"Mama Don't Allow," "Back Door," "Low Down Woman," and "Digging My Potatoes" among them—are here in pretty good fidelity, making this a good single-disc overview for listeners who don't want to invest in Document's exhaustive multi-volume series of Washboard Sam's *Complete Recorded Works*. —*Thom Owens*

Washboard Sam (1935-1947) / Jan. 1991 / Story of Blues ✦✦✦
Forget the washboard, which was almost more a prop than an instrument. Robert Brown was a captivating vocalist and an expert at working off his sidemen, and he coaxed creditable riffs out of that washboard, even if they all sounded the same. This is peak material, done when he was in excellent voice and hadn't yet gotten stagnant in his material or approach. —*Ron Wynn*

Rockin' My Blues Away / Feb. 1992 / RCA ✦✦✦✦
Washboard Sam recorded many selections as both a leader and as a sideman for Bluebird from 1936-49. His citified country blues were a transition music between the Delta blues and early R&B while being quite likable in their own right. On this fine CD sampler, Sam's strong voice is greatly assisted by his half-brother Big Bill Broonzy's guitar. A certain sameness creeps in by the fifth song, but the party music (all from 1941-42 except for one session from 1947) is quite accessible and enjoyable. —*Scott Yanow*

Complete Recorded Works, Vol. 1 (1935-1949) / Jun. 2, 1994 / Document ✦✦✦

Complete Recorded Works, Vol. 2 (1935-1949) / Jun. 2, 1994 / Document ✦✦✦

Complete Recorded Works, Vol. 3 / Jun. 2, 1994 / Document ✦✦✦

Complete Recorded Works, Vol. 4 / Jun. 2, 1994 / Document ✦✦✦

Complete Recorded Works, Vol. 5 / Jun. 2, 1994 / Document ✦✦✦

Complete Recorded Works, Vol. 6 / Jun. 2, 1994 / Document ✦✦✦

Complete Recorded Works, Vol. 7 / Jun. 2, 1994 / Document ✦✦✦

Washboard Blues 1935-1941 / Feb. 18, 1997 / Epm Musique ✦✦✦✦
Washboard Blues 1935-1941 is an excellent overview of Washboard Sam's great tracks, containing all the highlights from his peak years. It's ideal for the curious, or listeners who don't want to dig as deep as Document's multi-volume *Complete Recorded Works* series. —*Thom Owens*

Washboard Sam, Vol. 1 / Document ✦✦✦✦
Eighteen sides from the classic Bluebird period, with solid support from Big Bill Broonzy, Black Bob, and Blind John Davis. Includes "Who Pumped the Wind in My Doughnut" and "He's a Creepin' Man." —*Cub Koda*

Albert Washington

b. Aug. 17, 1935, Rome, GA
Clarinet, Sax (Tenor) / Soul, Juke Joint Blues
Singer and songwriter Albert Washington has spent most of his career singing in the blues clubs around Cincinnati, OH, and his home in Long Island, NY. Washington, who is blind, released two recordings for Iris Records in the 1990s, *Step It Up & Go* in 1993 and *A Brighter Day* in 1994.

One of four children of Jerry and Helen Washington, Albert's love of blues and gospel made itself known at a very early age. Washington remembers wanting to play his uncle's guitar at age five. At seven, he made his own guitar out of a gasoline can using rubber bands as strings. After losing his father at age nine, Washington got a job washing dishes after school to help his mother with the bills. After moving to Newport, KY, with his family while in his teens, Washington was encouraged by his mother to continue his gospel singing, but not his blues singing. At 16, he joined the Gospelaires, then recording for Don Robey's Duke and Peacock labels out of Houston. A few years later, he formed his own gospel group, the Washington Singers. In his late teens, Washington would sneak into blues clubs in nearby Cincinnati every chance he had, and there he was first exposed to the music of artists like Sam Cooke, Big Maybelle, Charles Brown, and Amos Milburn.

Washington cites B.B. King as most influential on his style of singing and guitar playing, which is heavily sprinkled with his gospel singing roots. Shortly after his mother died, he began singing blues as often as he could at the Vet's Inn in Cincinnati, where he worked with a house band for 16 years. In 1962, he recorded his first single for the Finch label in Cincinnati, and it was later released on the Bluestown label. His 1964 singles for the VLM label, including a song he wrote called "Haven't Got a Friend," got him noticed in England, and this in turn led to a deal with Fraternity Records in 1966. Lonnie Mack joined Washington on several singles for Fraternity recorded in 1969. In 1970, he recorded two singles for the Jewel label before finally recording his first LP for the Detroit-based Eastbound Records in 1972.

Because of complications from diabetes, Washington lost his sight, and his career fell into a trough from the mid-'70s to the early '90s.

But despite the crippling effects of diabetes and the tragedies that befell him over the course of his life, Washington remains an upbeat, positive figure.

In January, 1993, Long Island-based Iris Records released his first recording in two decades, *Step It Up & Go*. He began touring regionally again, but he still frequents clubs in Long Island. His 1994 follow up album, *A Brighter Day,* was named one of the top three blues recordings of 1994 by France's Academie Du Jazz. Washington continues to perform in blues clubs around Long Island. — *Richard Skelly*

● **Step It Up & Go** / 1993 / Iris ✦✦✦✦
Albert Washington's debut album *Step It Up & Go* is an impressive, soul-tinged collection of contemporary blues highlighted by Washington's powerful voice and knack for writing sturdy, memorable songs. Unlike some modern blues albums, *Step It Up & Go* has true grit to it, which brings true heart and soul to these songs and makes it a record well worth exploring. — *Thom Owens*

Brighter Day / 1994 / Iris ✦✦✦

Dinah Washington (Ruth Lee Jones)

b. Aug. 29, 1924, Tuscaloosa, AL, **d.** Dec. 14, 1963, Detroit, MI
Vocals / Standards, Traditional Pop, Jump Blues, Classic Female Blues, Ballads

Dinah Washington was at once one of the most beloved and controversial singers of the mid-20th century—beloved to her fans, devotees and fellow singers; controversial to critics who still accuse her of selling out her art to commerce and bad taste. Her principal sin, apparently, was to cultivate a distinctive vocal style that was as much at home in all kinds of music, be it R&B, blues, jazz, middle-of-the-road pop—and she probably would have made a fine gospel or country singer had she the time. Hers was a gritty, salty, high-pitched voice, marked by absolute clarity of diction and clipped, bluesy phrasing. Dinah's personal life was turbulent, with seven marriages behind her, and her interpretations showed it, for she displayed a tough, totally unsentimental, yet still gripping hold on the universal subject of lost love. She has had a huge influence on R&B and jazz singers who have followed in her wake, notably Nancy Wilson, Esther Phillips, and Diane Schuur, and her music is abundantly available nowadays via the huge seven-volume series *The Complete Dinah Washington on Mercury.*

Born Ruth Lee Jones, she moved to Chicago at age three and was raised in a world of gospel, playing the piano and directing her church choir. At 15, after winning an amateur contest at the Regal Theatre, she began performing in nightclubs as a pianist and singer, opening at the Garrick Bar in 1942. Talent manager Joe Glaser heard her there and recommended her to Lionel Hampton, who asked her to join his band. Hampton says that it was he who

gave Ruth Jones the name Dinah Washington, although other sources claim it was Glaser or the manager of the Garrick Bar. In any case, she stayed with Hampton from 1943 to 1946 and made her recording debut for Keynote at the end of 1943 in a blues session organized by Leonard Feather with a sextet drawn from the Hampton band. With Feather's "Evil Gal Blues" as her first hit, the records took off, and by the time she left Hampton to go solo, Washington was already an R&B headliner. Signing with the young Mercury label, Washington produced an enviable string of Top Ten hits on the R&B charts from 1948 to 1955, singing blues, standards, novelties, pop covers, even Hank Williams' "Cold, Cold Heart." She also recorded many straight jazz sessions with big bands and small combos, most memorably with Clifford Brown on *Dinah Jams* but also with Cannonball Adderley, Clark Terry, Ben Webster, Wynton Kelly, and the young Joe Zawinul (who was her regular accompanist for a couple of years).

In 1959, Washington made a sudden breakthrough into the mainstream pop market with "What a Diff'rence a Day Makes," a revival of a Dorsey Brothers hit set to a Latin American bolero tune. For the rest of her career, she would concentrate on singing ballads backed by lush orchestrations for Mercury and Roulette, a formula similar to that of another R&B-based singer at that time, Ray Charles, and one that drew plenty of fire from critics even though her basic vocal approach had not changed one iota. Although her later records could be as banal as any easy-listening dross of the period, there are gems to be found, like Billie Holiday's "Don't Explain," which has a beautiful, bluesy Ernie Wilkins chart conducted by Quincy Jones. Struggling with a weight problem, Washington died of an accidental overdose of diet pills mixed with alcohol at the tragically early age of 39, still in peak voice, still singing the blues in an L.A. club only two weeks before the end. — *Richard S. Ginell*

The Best in Blues / Dec. 29, 1943-Jun. 10, 1953 / Mercury ✦✦✦
This 1997 CD is an expanded reissue of a reissue. The original 1957 record featured the great singer Dinah Washington on a variety of "greatest hits" dating back to 1943. The blues-oriented material included "Evil Gal Blues," "Trouble In Mind," "TV Is the Thing This Year," and "New Blowtop Blues," and was taken from five different sessions spanning a decade. The CD adds three songs and four alternate takes from the same dates; despite what it says on the liners, all of these tracks have been released previously. Despite a few multiple versions, this accessible music serves as a fine introduction to the spirited early style of Dinah Washington. — *Scott Yanow*

Slick Chick: R&B Years / Dec. 29, 1943-Nov. 17, 1954 / EmArcy ✦✦✦✦
This double LP has the cream of Dinah Washington's early recordings. She recorded extensively for Mercury and EmArcy and all of the performances are available on multi-disc sets but, for those listeners who want just a sampling of Dinah Washington at her best, this two-fer is the one to get. All 16 of her R&B hits from 1949-54 are here plus her very first recording session (which is highlighted by the original version of "Evil Gal Blues") and seven other selections. Whether backed by the Gerald Wilson Orchestra, Tab Smith, Cootie Williams, an all-star unit headed by drummer Jimmy Cobb, or studio orchestras, she is in superb form. — *Scott Yanow*

Wise Woman Blues / 1943-Aug. 26, 1963 / Rosetta ✦✦✦✦
This Rosetta LP draws its material from three sources. Eight of the 15 recordings are from Dinah Washington's Apollo sessions of December 1945 (all of which are included on Delmark's CD). Six songs are taken from live performances with Lionel Hampton's orchestra during 1943-1945 and "Do Nothing Till You Hear from Me" is a real rarity with Washington backed by Duke Ellington's Orchestra in 1963. The extensive liner notes (which have ten pictures of the singer from various stages of her career) are a major plus. — *Scott Yanow*

Mellow Mama / Dec. 10, 1945-Dec. 13, 1945 / Delmark ✦✦✦✦
Dinah Washington's first solo recordings (with the exception of a session supervised by Lionel Hampton in 1943) are included on this Delmark repackaging of her Apollo sides. Recorded in Los Angeles during a three-day period, the 12 selections feature the singer with a swinging jazz combo that has tenor-saxophonist Lucky Thompson, trumpeter Karl George, vibraphonist Milt Jackson, and bassist Charles Mingus among its eight members. The 21-year-old Washington was already quite distinctive at this early stage and easily handles the blues and jive material with color and humor. Recommended despite the brevity (34 minutes) of the CD. — *Scott Yanow*

★ **The Complete Dinah Washington on Mercury, Vol. 1 (1946-1949)** / Jan. 14, 1946-Sep. 27, 1949 / Mercury ✦✦✦✦✦

All of Dinah Washington's studio recordings from 1946-61 have been re-issued in definitive fashion by Polygram on seven three CD sets. *Volume 1* finds the youthful singer (who was 21 on the earliest sessions) evolving from a little-known but already talented singer to a best-selling R&B artist. Ranging from jazz and spirited blues to middle-of-the-road ballads, this set (as with the others in the *Complete* series) includes both gems and duds but fortunately the great majority fall into the former category. The backup groups include orchestras led by Gerald Wilson, Tab Smith, Cootie Williams, Chubby Jackson, and Teddy Stewart, and there are a dozen strong numbers with just a rhythm section. The first five volumes in this series are highly recommended. — *Scott Yanow*

Verve Jazz Masters, Vol. 19: Dinah Washington / Oct. 3, 1946-Oct. 6, 1959 / Verve ✦✦✦✦

Dinah Washington's *Verve Jazz Masters, Vol. 19* may not be a definitive overview of her time at the label, but it's nevertheless a good 16-track sampler, containing excellent versions of such songs as "What a Difference a Day Makes," "Please Send Me Someone to Love," "Cold, Cold Heart," "This Can't Be Love," "A Foggy Day," "Pennies from Heaven," "Our Love is Here to Stay," and "Unforgettable." — *Stephen Thomas Erlewine*

☆ **The Complete Dinah Washington on Mercury, Vol. 2 (1950-1952)** / Feb. 7, 1950-May 6, 1952 / Mercury ✦✦✦✦✦

Dinah Washington was a best-selling artist on the R&B charts during this period but she was also a very versatile singer who could easily handle swinging jazz, schmaltzy ballads, blues, and novelties with equal skill. The second of these seven three-CD sets in Mercury's *Complete* program mostly finds Washington being accompanied by studio orchestras although the Ravens join her on two numbers and drummer Jimmy Cobb heads a couple of jazz groups (including one with both Ben Webster and Wardell Gray on tenors). Not every selection is a classic but the quality level is quite high and the packaging is impeccable. Recommended. — *Scott Yanow*

☆ **Complete Dinah Washington on Mercury, Vol. 3 (1952-1954)** / 1952-Aug. 14, 1954 / Mercury ✦✦✦✦✦

Of the seven three-CD sets in Mercury's *Complete* series of Dinah Washington recordings, this is the most jazz-oriented one. The versatile singer participates in a very memorable jam session with an all-star group (featuring Clifford Brown, Maynard Ferguson, and Clark Terry on trumpets!), meets up with Terry and tenor-saxophonist Eddie Lockjaw Davis on another spontaneous date (highlighted by uptempo rops on "Bye Bye Blues" and "Blue Skies") and has several classic collaborations with the warm Lester Youngish tenor of Paul Quinichette. There are a few commercial sides with studio orchestras that are included (since they took place during the same period) but those are in the great minority on this essential volume. — *Scott Yanow*

Jazz Sides / Jun. 15, 1954-Jul. 6, 1958 / Emarcy ✦✦✦✦

This two-LP set has many of singer Dinah Washington's most exciting jazz performances. For the first album Washington is joined by such masterful players as trumpeter Clark Terry, trombonist Jimmy Cleveland, and tenorman Paul Quinichette on a variety of Quincy Jones arrangements. Four other selections are from a particularly heated session with an explosive nonet propelled by Terry and tenor-saxophonist Eddie "Lockjaw" Davis; "Bye Bye Blues" is really taken uptempo but somehow Washington still sounds under control. The final four numbers are from the 1958 Newport Jazz Festival (with solos from pianist Wynton Kelly and vibraphonist Terry Gibbs) and can be considered her final jazz sides before going strictly commercial. All of this valuable music has since been reissued on Mercury's *Complete* series. — *Scott Yanow*

☆ **Complete Dinah Washington on Mercury, Vol. 4 (1954-1956)** / Nov. 2, 1954-Apr. 25, 1956 / Mercury ✦✦✦✦✦

The fourth of seven three-CD sets in Mercury's *Complete* series alternates between strong swinging jazz with the likes of trumpeter Clark Terry, tenor-saxophonist Paul Quinichette, pianist Wynton Kelly, and altoist Cannonball Adderley, and middle-of-the-road pop performances with studio orchestras. The third volume is the strongest in this series but the first five sets all contain more than enough jazz to justify their purchase. *Vol. 4* really attests to Dinah Washington's versatility. — *Scott Yanow*

☆ **Complete Dinah Washington on Mercury, Vol. 5 (1956-1958)** / Jun. 25, 1956-Jul. 6, 1958 / Mercury ✦✦✦✦✦

Mercury has given the great singer Dinah Washington the complete treatment with seven three-CD sets that contain all of her recordings during the 1946-61 period, practically her entire career. *Vol. 5* is the final volume to be highly recommended, since it has her final jazz sessions. On many of these performances she is backed by orchestras led by Quincy Jones, Ernie Wilkins (including a tribute to Fats Waller) or Eddie Chamblee in arrangements that often leave room for short statements from some of the sidemen; one of the albums with Chamblee has a full set of songs associated with Bessie Smith. *Vol. 5* (which contains only a few commercial sides) concludes with her strong performance at the 1958 Newport Jazz Festival. — *Scott Yanow*

The Bessie Smith Songbook / Dec. 30, 1957-Jan. 20, 1958 / EmArcy ✦✦✦

It was only natural that the "Queen of the Blues" should record songs associated with the "Empress of the Blues." The performances by the septet/octet do not sound like the 1920s and the purposely ricky-tick drumming is insulting, but Dinah Washington sounds quite at home on this music. "Trombone Butter" (featuring trombonist Quentin Jackson in Charlie Green's role), "You've Been a Good Ole Wagon," "After You've Gone," and "Back Water Blues" are highpoints as she overcomes the cornball arrangements. — *Scott Yanow*

What a Diff'rence a Day Makes! / Feb. 19, 1959-Aug. ??, 1959 / Mercury ✦✦✦✦

Dinah Washington's career reached a turning point with this album. A very talented singer who could interpret jazz, blues, pop, novelties, and religious songs with equal skill, Washington had an unexpected pop hit with her straightforward version of "What a Diff'rence a Day Makes." From then on she would only record with commercial studio orchestras and stick to middle-of-the-road pop music. This 1959 set is not as bad as what would follow, with such songs as "I Remember You," "I Thought About You," "Manhattan," and "A Sunday Kind of Love" all receiving tasteful melodic treatment (although no chances are taken) by Washington and an orchestra conducted and arranged by Belford Hendricks. — *Scott Yanow*

Complete Dinah Washington on Mercury, Vol. 6 (1958-1960) / Feb. 19, 1959-Nov. 12, 1960 / Mercury ✦✦

Up until 1959, Dinah Washington was able to excel in every musical setting that she found herself. A strong jazz/blues vocalist who had many R&B hits, Washington always sounded confident and soulful even when backed by insipid studio orchestras. However after her Feb. 19, 1959 recording of "What a Diff'rence a Day Makes" became a major hit and she gained fame, Dinah Washington stuck to safely commercial pop music. Even when she was singing superior songs during the 1959-63 period, Washington was always backed by large orchestras outfitted with extremely commercial charts better suited to country-pop stars. The sixth in Mercury's series of three-CD sets starts with the Feb. 19 session and covers 21 months in Dinah Washington's career. Most of the 73 performances are difficult to sit through. — *Scott Yanow*

Unforgettable / Aug. 1959-Jan. 15, 1961 / Mercury ✦✦

After her hit of "What a Diff'rence a Day Makes" in 1959, Dinah Washington largely discarded her blues and jazz roots (at least on recordings) and played the role of a pop star. This CD (which has the original LP program of 12 songs joined by six others) finds Washington singing brief (mostly under three-minute) versions of standards in hopes of gaining another hit. The backing is strictly commercial and, although some may enjoy "This Bitter Earth," "The Song Is Ended," and "A Bad Case of the Blues," the music is consistently predictable and disappointingly forgettable. — *Scott Yanow*

Complete Dinah Washington on Mercury, Vol. 7 (1961) / 1961 / Mercury ✦✦

The seventh and final volume in Mercury's *Complete* series of Dinah Washington's recordings has impeccable packaging and largely inferior music, at least from the jazz standpoint. After recording a surprising hit version of "What a Diff'rence a Day Makes" in 1959, the singer stuck exclusively to middle-of-the-road pop music with large string orchestras on her recordings. This three-CD set (which contains Washington's final 67 recordings for Mercury plus a recently discovered alternate take from 1947) is often difficult to sit through for it totally lacks surprises, suspense, or spontaneity. For completists only, but get the first five volumes. — *Scott Yanow*

In Love / May 1962-Aug. 1962 / Roulette ♦♦
Dinah Washington's final four years of recordings (1959-63) were purely commercial. Even her mannerisms and phrasing leaned closer to middle-of-the-road pop than to her roots in jazz and blues. For this so-so Roulette CD, Washington interprets standards and current pop tunes in very predictable fashion. Everything has the impression of being planned in advance and the accompanying orchestra (arranged by Don Costa) is quite anonymous. Pass on this and get Dinah Washington's earlier jazz sides instead. — *Scott Yanow*

Back to the Blues / Jul. 5, 1962-Nov. 29, 1962 / Roulette ♦♦♦♦
Prior to her 1959 hit "What a Difference a Day Makes," nearly every Dinah Washington recording (no matter what the style) was of interest to jazz listeners. However, after her unexpected success on the pop charts, most of Washington's sessions for Mercury and Roulette during the last four years of her life were quite commercial, with string arrangements better suited to country singers and Dinah nearly parodying herself with exaggerated gestures. Fortunately, this 1997 CD reissue brings back an exception, a blues-oriented collection that features Washington returning to her roots, backed by a jazz-oriented big band (although with occasional strings and background voices); in addition to the original program, there are previously unreleased versions of "No One Man" and "Me and My Gin." Eddie Chamblee and Illinois Jacquet have some tenor solos, guitarist Billy Butler is heard from and the trumpet soloist is probably Joe Newman. In general, this is a more successful date than Dinah Washington's earlier investigation of Bessie Smith material, since the backup band is more sympathetic and the talented singer is heard in prime form. Dinah Washington clearly had a real feeling for this bluesy material. — *Scott Yanow*

Jazz Profile, Vol. 5 / 1962-1963 / Blue Note ♦♦♦
This set is a bit out of place in this collector's series, for it is really a gap-filler, mostly comprised of Dinah Washington recordings from her last two years that have not (with a few exceptions) been included in other CD reissues. Washington was at her best prior to 1959, but her later recordings are not without interest. Backed by an unidentified big band with occasional strings (why is no personnel given?), the music is superior to Dinah's later Mercury records and shows that she was still very much in her prime. Also obvious is how much of an influence she became on many black female singers that followed her. An excellent overview of her last period, recorded just prior to Washington's premature death, the 14 selections (highlighted by "The Blues Ain't Nothin'" and "I Wanna Be Around") are taken from six of her seven Roulette albums. — *Scott Yanow*

Dinah '63 / 1963 / Roulette ♦♦
It is fairly easy to evaluate Dinah Washington's recordings. Before 1959 virtually everything she recorded (even when in a commercial setting) is worth acquiring but the opposite is true of the records from her final period (1959-63). As a pop artist, Washington was better than many but only a shadow of what she had been. Her pre-planned emotions and exaggerated mannerisms on her Roulette recordings (of which *Dinah '63* was one of her last) get tiring very fast. — *Scott Yanow*

The Ultimate Dinah Washington / Polygram ♦♦♦
Abbey Lincoln compiled *The Ultimate Dinah Washington*, a 16-track selection of her best-known songs that offers an excellent introduction to her Verve recordings. Although purists and collectors will have little use for this set, it suits the purposes of neophytes and curious listeners quite well. Among the highlights are "What a Diff'rence a Day Made," "Back Water Blues," "Cry Me a River," "I Wanna Be Loved," "Cold, Cold Heart," "Harbor Lights," "You Don't Know What Love Is," "I Won't Cry Anymore," "Unforgettable," and "The Bitter Earth." — *Stephen Thomas Erlewine*

Ernestine Washington

b. Arkansas, **d.** Jul. 5, 1983, Brooklyn, NY
Vocals / Black Gospel
Born in Arkansas, Madame Ernestine B. Washington grew up on the sanctified gospel of the '20s, singing primarily for her husband's church and denomination, Washington Temple C.O.G.I.C. Though inspired by the controlled Baptist style of the Roberta Martin Singers, she had a strident voice and was known to be a singing shouter in the mode of Mahalia Jackson. Her rare and most important recordings were executed from the late '40s through the '50s. — *Bil Carpenter*

● **In Washington Temple** / 1958 / Collectors Issue ♦♦♦♦
Sensational solos are supported rousingly by Brooklyn's Congregation of the Washington Temple C.O.G.I.C. Reissue of material recorded in 1958. — *Opal Louis Nations*

Complete Recorded Works (1943-48) / Sep. 10, 1996 / Document ♦♦♦♦
One of gospel's premier female soloists who recorded with both Bunk Johnson and the Dixie Hummingbirds. — *Opal Louis Nations*

Toni Lynn Washington

b. Boston, MA
Vocals / Modern Electric Blues
Boston-based blues singer Toni Lynn Washington recorded and released *Blues at Midnight* for the Tone-Cool subsidiary of Rounder Records in 1995. Washington is considered Boston's "queen of the blues," where she has a long and storied history on the club scene.

Raised in a procession of gospel choirs in Southern Pines, NC, Washington performed with classic R&B artists like Sam and Dave and Jackie Wilson throughout the South in her youth. Washington also made USO tours of the US and Asia in the 1960s and recorded the Top 50 single "Dear Diary" for the New Orleans-based Conti label, then a subsidiary of Atlantic Records.

After two decades off the road and out of the recording studio, Washington returned to performing in 1992 with a ten-piece band. On her debut for Tone-Cool, *Blues at Midnight*, Washington comes across best as an interpreter: she tackles B.B. King's "Ask Me No Questions," Jimmy Reed's "Ain't That Loving You Baby," and a tune popularized by Jimmy Rushing and the Basie Orchestra and T-Bone Walker, "Evening."

It's My Turn Now followed in 1997. — *Richard Skelly*

Blue at Midnight / 1995 / Tone-Cool ♦♦♦

● **It's My Turn Now** / Oct. 7, 1997 / Tone-Cool ♦♦♦♦
This disc is a professional R&B exercise by a seasoned pro, but it lacks the punch to really hit home. While Toni Lynn Washington's voice is full of confidence, it's a bit thin, which robs the songs of forceful delivery. Ultimately, this effort ends up sounding like the work of a wedding party band instead of a time-tested R&B outfit. The predominance of originals in the playlist is to be commended, however. Standouts include "Just Around the Corner" and the title track. — *Tim Sheridan*

Tuts Washington

b. Jan. 24, 1907, New Orleans, LA, **d.** Aug. 5, 1984, New Orleans, LA
Piano / Boogie-Woogie, Dixieland, Modern Electric Blues, New Orleans Blues
Isidore "Tuts" Washington (also widely known as "Papa Yellow") was 76 years old at the time of the release of his first solo recording. He began playing piano at age ten and worked with a number of famed New Orleans bandsmen—Kid Rena, Papa Celestin, Kid Punch Miller—over the course of his long career. In the late '30s he made trips to California and in 1950 joined the Tab Smith Orchestra in St. Louis for a time. During the better part of the '40s he worked in a trio backing up blues singer Smiley Lewis, which took him to various locations from Oklahoma to Florida. In 1958 he was with the Clyde Kerr Orchestra in New Orleans, and a decade later made several excursions up the Mississippi River on the Delta Queen. From 1968 to 1973 Tuts held forth at the Court of Two Sisters Restaurant in the French Quarter, then moving on to the piano bar at the Caribbean Room of the Pontchartrain Hotel in the early 80s. He died while performing on stage at the 1984 New Orleans World's Fair.

Tuts Washington identified Joseph Louis "Red" Cayou, an itinerant New Orleans pianist, as a prime influence on his early playing. He developed his repertoire by following the brass bands on the streets of New Orleans, memorizing the tunes and working out his own versions at home. He was self-taught at first but eventually took lessons at age 18; apparently his "professor" felt that Tuts was already too advanced to benefit from basic instruction, and at that point he turned to "Red" Caillou, whose hands he described as "like lightning." Washington specialized in instrumental pieces, but he also maintained a number of bawdy blues songs which he delivered with an impish relish. As the recognized "dean" of New Orleans piano players by the mid-century, he is credited frequently as a major influence on Fats Domino, Professor Longhair, James Booker, Dr. John, and Allen Toussaint. —*Bruce Boyd Raeburn*

● **New Orleans Piano Professor** / Apr. 1984 / Rounder ✦✦✦✦
Venerable New Orleans pianist Tuts Washington didn't get many chances to record during his lifetime. This 1983 session, now available on CD, was his most extensive project, with 23 songs covering everything from spirituals to traditional jazz numbers, pop pieces, novelty tunes, blues and country. Washington played them all in a seamless manner, displaying the mix of boogie-woogie and barrelhouse riffs, R&B, blues and gospel elements, Afro-Latin and Caribbean rhythmic accents, and jazz phrasing and licks mastered through many decades of playing in bars and clubs. This was his chance in the spotlight, and Washington didn't waste it. —*Ron Wynn*

Walter Washington

b. Dec. 21, 1943, New Orleans, LA
Guitar, Vocals / Soul, R&B, Soul Blues, Acoustic Texas Blues
Walter Washington became a local legend in the Black clubs of New Orleans in the '70s and '80s and worked his way up to national status with a series of well-received albums and appearances. His recording affiliations have likewise moved from local to national independent to major label. An innovative guitarist and fine singer who has also done some excellent work with vocalist Johnny Adams, Washington does not perform in the classic New Orleans R&B mold but incorporates soul, funk, jazz, and blues with fluency and power.

Washington was born and raised in New Orleans, where he performed in his mother's church choir as a child. As he grew older, he fell in love with blues and R&B and he learned how to play guitar. His first big break came in the form of a supporting role for vocalist Johnny Adams, working with the singer in the late '50s. In the early '60s, Washington became a member of Lee Dorsey's touring band; after that engagment was through, he worked with Irma Thomas.

In the mid-'60s, Washington formed his own band, the All Fools Band, and began headlining at local New Orleans clubs. By the early '70s, his popularity had grown enough to earn him a slot on a European package tour of New Orleans R&B acts. In the late '70s, he toured Europe on his own with his new band, the Roadmasters.

Washington began his recording career relatively late, cutting his first album in 1981. The record, *Rainin' In My Heart,* appeared on a small independent label called Hep Me; it was later re-released on Maison de Soul. Four years after his debut, Washington landed a contract with Rounder Records, releasing *Wolf Tracks* in 1986. The guitarist recorded two more albums for Rounder—*Out of the Dark* (1988) and *Wolf at the Door*—before moving the major-label, Point Blank/Charisma in 1991. Throughout the '90s, Washington continued to perform regularly, particularly in New Orleans clubs, and he recorded occasionally. —*Jim O'Neal & Stephen Thomas Erlewine*

Wolf Tracks / 1986 / Rounder ✦✦✦
Guitarist/vocalist Walter "Wolfman" Washington didn't get his shot on a national label until his 1986 debut for Rounder. While the album wasn't flawless, he possessed a strong, often compelling voice and was a skilled guitarist who could play effectively in a blues, R&B or jazz mode. Washington turned in a competent cover of the Tyrone Davis hit "Can I Change My Mind," spun a good yarn on "You Got Me Worried" and sounded weary, forlorn, and anguished on various cuts. Although his songs weren't exactly lyrical triumphs, they were earnestly performed, and Washington displayed more than enough talent to justify subsequent followups. —*Ron Wynn*

Out of the Dark / 1988 / Rounder ✦✦✦
Truly soulful blues and R&B, it's funky and inspired. —*Niles J. Frantz*

● **Out of the House** / 1988 / Rounder ✦✦✦✦
Walter "Wolfman" Washington's second Rounder session mixed Crescent City R&B and jazz licks with contemporary and vintage songs and production. Washington's cover of "Ain't That Loving You," while not quite as dramatic as Bobby "Blue" Bland's, was still outstanding, while he was appropriately ironic and bemused on "You Can Stay but the Noise Must Go" and vividly soulful on "Save Your Love for Me" and "Steal Away." Only on "Feel So Bad," a questionable song at best, did he sound strained and unfocused. Washington's guitar playing was sharp, creative and tasty without being self-indulgent. It wasn't the kind of glossy, trendy work that garners the pop spotlight, but Washington showed progress and fine skills. —*Ron Wynn*

Heatin' It Up / 1991 / Rounder ✦✦✦

Sada / 1991 / Pointblank ✦✦✦
Walter Washington's *Sada* is a blues album only in the loosest sense of the term—Washington draws from Southern soul and funk as much as Chicago blues. Even so, he and his band are accomplished professionals, capable of negotiating every twist and turn in the music. The uptempo numbers are fun, but the best part about the record are the ballads—Washington is a smooth, seductive singer and he makes all of his slow ones sound heartfelt and genuine. —*Thom Owens*

Wolf at the Door / 1991 / Rounder ✦✦✦✦
Most of this CD from Walter "Wolfman" Washington puts the focus on his voice, which is reminiscent of a young Ray Charles. The horn arrangements look back towards 1960s Motown, and five of the six tracks fall squarely into the idiom of pre-disco R&B, with touches of funk and gospel. "Peepin'" is a bit of a surprise, a minor-toned instrumental with Tom Fitzpatrick's soprano in the lead and some nice George Benson-ish guitar by Washignton. Even better are the last three tracks: the joyful blues "Tailspin," a minor blues ("At Night In the City"), and a bluesy ballad ("Don't Say Goodbye"). Wolfman Washington's versatility is quite impressive, making this a fairly memorable recording. —*Scott Yanow*

Funk Is in the House / Apr. 7, 1998 / Bullseye Blues ✦✦✦✦
The bass-popping funk of this veteran outfit is well showcased on this effort. While they don't break new ground with standard workouts like "Funkyard," there is an honesty to this music that adds real appeal. The live sound of this studio recording is another plus. —*Tim Sheridan*

Ethel Waters (Ethel [Née Howard] Waters)

b. Oct. 31, 1896, Chester, PA, **d.** Sep. 1, 1977, Chatsworth, CA
Vocals / Classic Jazz, Swing, Traditional Pop, Classic Female Blues
Ethel Waters had a long and varied career and was one of the first true jazz singers to record. Defying racism with her talent and bravery, Waters became a stage and movie star in the '30s and '40s without leaving the US. She grew up near Philadelphia and, unlike many of her contemporaries, developed a clear and easily understandable diction. Originally classified as a blues singer (and she could sing the blues almost on the level of a Bessie Smith), Waters' jazz-oriented recordings of 1921-28 swung before that term was even coined. A star early on at theatres and nightclubs, Waters introduced such songs as "Dinah," "Am I Blue" (in a 1929 movie) and "Stormy Weather." She made a smooth transition from jazz singer of the '20s to a pop music star of the '30s and she was a strong influence on many vocalists including Mildred Bailey, Lee Wiley and Connee Boswell. Waters spent the latter half of the '30s touring with a group headed by her husband-trumpeter Eddie Mallory and appeared on Broadway (*Mamba's Daughter* in 1939) and in the 1943 film *Cabin in the Sky;* in the latter she introduced "Taking a Chance on Love," "Good for Nothing Joe," and the title cut. In later years Waters was seen in nonmusical dramatic roles and after 1960 she mostly confined her performances to religious work for the evangelist Billy Graham. The European Classics label has reissued all of Ethel Waters' prime recordings and they still sound fresh and lively today. —*Scott Yanow*

Ethel Waters 1921-1923 / Mar. 21, 1921-Mar. 1923 / Classics ✦✦✦✦
Ethel Waters was one of the few singers from the early '20s whose early recordings are still quite listenable. This CD from the Classics label has her first 22 sides (many previously rare including five interesting instrumentals by Waters' band) and, although not on the same level as her performances from a few years later, the music is quite good for the time period. The sidemen are mostly obscure but include pianist Fletcher Henderson and cornetists Gus Aiken and Joe Smith with the highlights being "The New York Glide," "Down Home Blues," "There'll Be Some Changes Made," and "Midnight Blues." —*Scott Yanow*

Jazzin' Babies Blues, Vol. 2 (1921-1927) / Mar. 21, 1921-Oct. 14, 1927 / Biograph ✦✦✦
From the start of her career, Ethel Waters was one of the most accomplished jazz singers on record. This Biograph LP (the second of two) offers proof for it contains her very first session and, with one exception (a previously unissued version of "One Sweet Letter from You" from 1927), sticks to the 1921-24 period. The recording quality is a bit primitive and the backup work (except for brief appearances by cornetists Joe Smith and Tommy Ladnier) is forget-

table but Waters' smooth and appealing voice cuts through the years.
— *Scott Yanow*

Oh Daddy, Vol. 1 (1921-1924) / May 1921-Apr. 1924 / Biograph ◆◆◆
Ethel Waters had a fairly long and very productive career as a singer and actress. This Biograph LP (the first of two) reissued for the first time many of her earliest recordings, 14 selections (all but one from 1921-23). The backup work and recording quality are a bit primitive but Ethel Waters was already near the top of the field, one of the first jazz (as opposed to blues) singers to record. "Oh Daddy," "There'll Be Some Changes Made," "You Can't Do What My Last Man Did," and "Sweet Man" are highlights of this enjoyable set. — *Scott Yanow*

1923-1925 / Mar. 1923-Jul. 28, 1925 / Classics ◆◆◆◆
The European Classics label's Ethel Waters program completely wipes out all of the other Waters reissues for it reissues all of her recordings from her prime years in chronological order. Since the singer was very consistent, there are very few duds and many gems in these sets. This particular CD traces Ethel Waters during a two-year period; both the recording quality and her accompaniment greatly improve during this time; cornetist Joe Smith is a standout and pianist Fats Waller is present on "Pleasure Mad" and "Back-Bitin' Mamma." Highlights includes "You Can't Do What My Last Man Did," "Sweet Georgia Brown," "Go Back Where You Stayed Last Night," and "Sympathetic Dan." — *Scott Yanow*

Ethel Waters (1924-1928) / Mar. 1924-Aug. 23, 1928 / Wolf ◆◆◆◆
This LP from the Austrian Wolf label reissues 20 of Ethel Waters' rarer recordings from the 1924-28 period. Although it has been succeeded by the Classics *Complete* series, this album filled a lot of gaps when it was released and was quite generous with 20 selections and nearly an hour of music. "Sympathetic Dan," "Home," "Take Your Black Bottom Outside," and "Do What You Did Last Night" are highpoints of the fine release. — *Scott Yanow*

Ethel Waters' Greatest Years / Apr. 29, 1925-Mar. 30, 1934 / Columbia ◆◆◆◆
When this two-LP set was originally released, it was the definitive Ethel Waters reissue although now it has been succeeded by Classics' more complete CD program. However this two-fer is still the best single package ever released of the singer. The first album (covering 1925-28) focuses on her jazz years and has particularly strong contributions from cornetist Joe Smith and pianist James P. Johnson among others; "Sweet Georgia Brown," "Go Back Where You Stayed Last Night," "You Can't Do What My Last Man Did," "Sweet Man," "I've Found a New Baby," "Sugar," "Guess Who's in Town," and "My Handy Man" all qualify as classics. The second album mostly dates from 1929-34 and finds Waters joined by studio orchestras on most tracks. The emphasis is on ballads and sweet melodies but Waters still excels, particularly on "Waiting at the End of the Road," "Porgy," and "A Hundred Years from Today." This set is highly recommended to listeners who do not have the Classics CDs. — *Scott Yanow*

★ **1925-1926** / Aug. 25, 1925-Jul. 29, 1926 / Classics ◆◆◆◆◆
This CD in the Classics *Complete* Ethel Waters series contains plenty of gems including "You Can't Do What My Last Man Did," the original version of "Dinah," "Shake That Thing," "I've Found a New Baby" (which has some memorable cornet playing from Joe Smith), "Sugar," and "Heebies Jeebies." On "Maybe Not at All" Ethel Waters does eerie imitations of both Bessie Smith and Clara Smith. She had few competitors as a jazz singer during this era and the mostly intimate recordings (12 of the 23 tracks find her backed by just a pianist) feature Waters at her best. — *Scott Yanow*

Ethel Waters on Stage/Screen (1925-1940) / Oct. 20, 1925-Nov. 7, 1940 / Columbia ◆◆◆◆
The Columbia LP features Ethel Waters performing 16 songs that debuted in shows or movies. With the exception of "Dinah" (this 1925 version is the original one) and "I'm Coming Virginia," all of the music dates from the 1929-40 era when Waters was better known as a musical comedy star than as a jazz singer. However, although the backing is generally a bit commercial, her performances of such numbers as "You're Lucky to Me," "Stormy Weather," "Taking a Chance on Love," and "Cabin in the Sky" are consistently memorable and definitive. — *Scott Yanow*

☆ **1926-1929** / Sep. 14, 1926-May 14, 1929 / Classics ◆◆◆◆◆
Few female jazz singers were on Ethel Waters' level during this period, just Bessie Smith and Annette Hanshaw, and all three were quite different from each other. Waters has rarely sounded better than on the four numbers in

which she is backed rather forcefully by pianist James P. Johnson (particularly "Guess Who's in Town" and "Do What You Did Last Night") but she is also in fine form on the other small-group sides. "I'm Coming Virginia," "Home," "Take Your Black Bottom Outside," "Someday Sweetheart," and "Am I Blue" (which she introduced) are among the many gems on this highly recommended entry in Classics' complete series. — *Scott Yanow*

1929-1931 / Jun. 6, 1929-Jun. 16, 1931 / Classics ◆◆◆◆
During the period covered in this CD from Classics' *Complete* Ethel Waters series, the singer was quickly developing into a top musical comedy and Broadway star. Although her backup was not as jazz-oriented as previously (despite the presence of such players as clarinetist Benny Goodman, trombonist Tommy Dorsey, Jimmy Dorsey on clarinet and alto and trumpeter Manny Klein), Waters' renditions of many of these future standards are definitive, particularly "True Blue Lou," "Waiting at the End of the Road," "Porgy," "You're Lucky to Me," and "When Your Lover Has Gone." Superior jazz-oriented singing from one of the very best. — *Scott Yanow*

1931-1934 / Aug. 10, 1931-Sep. 5, 1934 / Classics ◆◆◆◆
Ethel Waters was one of the very few Black performers who was able to keep working in music during the early years of the Depression; in fact her fame grew during the period covered by this excellent CD from Classics' *Complete* series. Among her backup musicians on these consistently excellent sides are violinist Joe Venuti, the Dorsey Brothers, trumpeter Bunny Berigan, trombonist Jack Teagarden, clarinetist Benny Goodman, members of the Chick Webb big band, and the entire Duke Ellington orchestra (the latter on "I Can't Give You Anything but Love" and "Porgy"). Highpoints include the Ellington tracks, "St. Louis Blues" (with The Cecil Mack Choir), the original version of "Stormy Weather," "A Hundred Years from Today," and a remake of "Dinah." Highly recommended as are all of the Ethel Waters Classics discs. — *Scott Yanow*

Foremothers, Vol. 6 / Nov. 9, 1938-Aug. 15, 1939 / Rosetta ◆◆◆◆
This very attractive Rosetta LP (which has definitive liner notes and numerous pictures) includes all of singer Ethel Waters' 16 Bluebird recordings of 1938-39. She is accompanied by two different bands led by her husband (trumpeter Eddie Mallory) with Benny Carter on alto and clarinet and trombonist Tyree Glenn (doubling on vibes) among the sidemen. Waters was not a major part of the swing era but her own career (on stage and in films) was booming around this period. Her voice is heard in its prime on a variety of period pieces which are highlighted by "Old Man Harlem," "Georgia on My Mind," "Jeepers Creepers," and "They Say." — *Scott Yanow*

Performing in Person: Highlights from Her Illustrious Career / 195? / Monmouth Evergreen ◆◆◆
Ethel Waters is heard at the twilight of her career during this live performance. Recorded a decade after her last studio recordings, this was the singer's final nonreligious album. Accompanied by pianist Reginald Beane, Waters revisits most of her hits ("Am I Blue," "Dinah," "Porgy," "Supper Time," "Stormy Weather," and a medley from "Cabin in the Sky") and shows that, even at this late stage, her voice was still quite expressive. This is an LP that her many fans will want to search for. — *Scott Yanow*

Muddy Waters (McKinley Morganfield)

b. Apr. 4, 1915, Rolling Fort, MS, **d.** Apr. 30, 1983, Westmont, IL
Guitar, Vocals / R&B, Electric Chicago Blues, Chicago Blues, Delta Blues, Electric Blues, Blues Revival
A postwar Chicago blues scene without the magnificent contributions of Muddy Waters is absolutely unimaginable. From the late '40s on, he eloquently defined the city's aggressive, swaggering, Delta-rooted sound with his declamatory vocals and piercing slide guitar attack. When he passed away in 1983, the Windy City would never quite recover.

Like many of his contemporaries on the Chicago circuit, Waters was a product of the fertile Mississippi Delta. Born McKinley Morganfield in Rolling Fork, he grew up in nearby Clarksdale on Stovall's Plantation. His idol was the powerful Son House, a Delta patriarch whose flailing slide work and intimidating intensity Waters would emulate in his own fashion.

Musicologist Alan Lomax traveled through Stovall's in August of 1941 under the auspices of the Library of Congress, in search of new talent for purposes of field recording. With the discovery of Morganfield, Lomax must have immediately known he'd stumbled across someone very special.

Setting up his portable recording rig in the Delta bluesman's house, Lomax captured for Library of Congress posterity Waters' mesmerizing rendition of "I Be's Troubled," which became his first big seller when he recut it a few years later for the Chess brothers' Aristocrat logo as "I Can't Be Satisfied." Lomax returned the next summer to record his bottleneck-wielding find more extensively, also cutting sides by the Son Simms Four (a string band that Waters belonged to).

Waters was renowned for his blues-playing prowess across the Delta, but that was about it until 1943, when he left for the bright lights of Chicago. A tiff with "the bossman" apparently also had a little something to do with his relocation plans. By the mid-'40s, Waters' slide skills were becoming a recognized entity on Chicago's South side, where he shared a stage or two with pianists Sunnyland Slim and Eddie Boyd, and guitarist Blue Smitty. Producer Lester Melrose, who still had the local recording scene pretty much sewn up in 1946, accompanied Waters into the studio to wax a date for Columbia, but the urban nature of the sides didn't electrify anyone in the label's hierarchy and remained unissued for decades.

Sunnyland Slim played a large role in launching the career of Muddy Waters. The pianist invited him to provide accompaniment for his 1947 Aristocrat session that would produce "Johnson Machine Gun." One obstacle remained beforehand: Waters had a day gig delivering venetian blinds. But he wasn't about to let such a golden opportunity slip through his talented fingers. He informed his boss that a fictitious cousin had been murdered in an alley, so he needed a little time off to take care of business.

When Sunnyland was finished that auspicious day, Waters sang a pair of numbers, "Little Anna Mae" and "Gypsy Woman," that would become his own Aristocrat debut 78. They were rawer than the Columbia stuff, but not as inexorably down-home as "I Can't Be Satisfied" and its flip, "I Feel like Going Home" (the latter was his first national R&B hit in 1948). With Big Crawford slapping the bass behind Waters' gruff growl and slashing slide, "I Can't Be Satisfied" was such a local sensation that even Muddy Waters himself had a hard time buying a copy down on Maxwell Street.

He assembled a band that was so tight and vicious on stage that they were informally known as the Headhunters; they'd come into a bar where a band was playing, ask to sit in, and then "cut the heads" of their competitors with their superior musicianship. Little Walter, of course, would single-handedly revolutionize the role of the harmonica within the Chicago blues hierarchy; Jimmy Rogers was an utterly dependable second guitarist, and Baby Face Leroy Foster could play both drums and guitar. On top of their instrumental skills, all four men could sing powerfully.

1951 found Waters climbing the R&B charts no less than four times, beginning with "Louisiana Blues," and continuing through "Long Distance Call," "Honey Bee," and "Still a Fool." Although it didn't chart, his 1950 classic "Rollin' Stone" provided a certain young British combo with a rather enduring name. Leonard Chess himself provided the incredibly unsubtle bass-drum bombs on Waters' 1952 smash "She Moves Me."

"Mad Love," his only chart bow in 1953, is noteworthy as the first hit to feature the rolling piano of Otis Spann, who would anchor the Waters aggregation for the next 16 years. By this time, Foster was long gone from the band, but Rogers remained, and Chess insisted that Walter—by then a popular act in his own right—make nearly every Waters session into 1958 (why break up a winning combination?). There was one downside to having such a peerless band; as the ensemble work got tighter and more urbanized, Waters' trademark slide guitar was largely absent on many of his Chess waxings.

Willie Dixon was playing an increasingly important role in Muddy Waters' success. In addition to slapping his upright bass on Waters' platters, the burly Dixon was writing one future bedrock standard after another for him: "I'm Your Hoochie Coochie Man," "Just Make Love to Me," and "I'm Ready"; seminal performances all, and each blasted into the uppermost reaches of the R&B lists in 1954.

When labelmate Bo Diddley borrowed Waters' swaggering beat for his strutting "I'm a Man" in 1955, Muddy turned around and did him tit for tat by reworking the tune ever so slightly as "Mannish Boy" and enjoying his own hit. "Sugar Sweet," a piledriving rocker with Spann's 88s anchoring the proceedings, also did well that year. 1956 brought three more R&B smashes: "Trouble No More," "Forty Days & Forty Nights," and "Don't Go No Farther."

But rock 'n' roll was quickly blunting the momentum of veteran blues aces like Waters; Chess was growing more attuned to the modern sounds of

Chuck Berry, Bo Diddley, the Moonglows, and the Flamingos. Ironically, it was Muddy Waters that had sent Berry to Chess in the first place.

After that, there was only one more chart item, 1958's typically uncompromising (and metaphorically loaded) "Close to You." But Waters' Chess output was still of uniformly stellar quality, boasting gems like "Walking Thru the Park" (as close as he was likely to come to mining a rock 'n' roll groove) and "She's Nineteen Years Old," among the first sides to feature James Cotton's harp instead of Walter's, in 1958. That was also the year that Muddy Waters and Spann made their first sojourn to England, where his electrified guitar horrified sedate Britishers accustomed to the folksy homilies of Big Bill Broonzy. Perhaps chagrined by the response, Waters paid tribute to Broonzy with a solid LP of his material in 1959.

Cotton was apparently the bandmember that first turned Muddy on to "Got My Mojo Working," originally cut by Ann Cole in New York. Waters' 1956 cover was pleasing enough but went nowhere on the charts. But when the band launched into a supercharged version of the same tune at the 1960 Newport Jazz Festival, Cotton and Spann put an entirely new groove to it, making it an instant classic (fortuitously, Chess was on hand to capture the festivities on tape).

As the 1960s dawned, Muddy Waters' Chess sides were sounding a trifle tired. Oh, the novelty thumper "Tiger in Your Tank" packed a reasonably high-octane wallop, but his adaptation of Junior Wells' "Messin' with the Kid" (as "Messin' with the Man") and a less-than-timely "Muddy Waters Twist" were a long way removed indeed from the mesmerizing Delta sizzle that Waters had purveyed a decade earlier.

Overdubbing his vocal over an instrumental track by guitarist Earl Hooker, Waters laid down an uncompromising "You Shook Me" in 1962 that was a step in the right direction. Drummer Casey Jones supplied some intriguing percussive effects on another 1962 workout, "You Need Love," which Led Zeppelin liked so much that they purloined it as their own creation later on.

In the wake of the folk-blues boom, Waters reverted to an acoustic format for a fine 1964 LP, *Folk Singer*, that found him receiving superb backing from guitarist Buddy Guy, Dixon on bass, and drummer Clifton James. In October, he ventured overseas again as part of the Lippmann & Rau-promoted American Folk Blues Festival, sharing the bill with Sonny Boy Williamson, Memphis Slim, Big Joe Williams, and Lonnie Johnson.

The personnel of the Waters band was much more fluid during the 1960s, but he always whipped them into first-rate shape. Guitarists Pee Wee Madison, Luther "Snake Boy" Johnson, and Sammy Lawhorn, harpists Mojo Buford and George Smith, bassists Jimmy Lee Morris and Calvin "Fuzz" Jones, and drummers Francis Clay and Willie "Big Eyes" Smith (along with Spann, of course) all passed through the ranks.

In 1964, Waters cut a two-sided gem for Chess, "The Same Thing"/"You Can't Lose What You Never Had," that boasted a distinct 1950s feel in its sparse, reflexive approach. Most of his subsequent Chess catalog, though, is fairly forgettable. Worst of all were two horrific attempts to make him a psychedelic icon. 1968's *Electric Mud* forced Waters to ape his pupils via an unintentionally hilarious cover of the Stones' "Let's Spend the Night Together" (session guitarist Phil Upchurch still cringes at the mere mention of this album). *After the Rain* was no improvement the following year.

Partially salvaging this barren period in his discography was the *Fathers and Sons* project, also done in 1969 for Chess, which paired Muddy Waters and Spann with local youngbloods Paul Butterfield and Mike Bloomfield in a multi-generational celebration of legitimate Chicago blues.

After a period of steady touring worldwide but little standout recording activity, Waters' studio fortunes were resuscitated by another of his legion of disciples, guitarist Johnny Winter. Signed to Blue Sky, a Columbia subsidiary, Waters found himself during the making of the first LP, *Hard Again*—backed by pianist Pinetop Perkins, drummer Willie Smith, and guitarist Bob Margolin from his touring band, Cotton on harp, and Winter's slam-bang guitar, Waters roared like a lion who had just awoken from a long nap.

Three subsequent Blue Sky albums continued the heartwarming back-to-the basics campaign. In 1980, his entire combo split to form the Legendary Blues Band; needless to note, he didn't have much trouble assembling another one (new members included pianist Lovie Lee, guitarist John Primer, and harpist Mojo Buford).

By the time of his death in 1983, Muddy Waters' exalted place in the history of blues (and 20th-century popular music, for that matter) was eternally assured. The Chicago blues genre that he turned upside down during the years following World War II would never recover—and that's a debt we'll never be able to repay. —*Bill Dahl*

First Recording Sessions 1941-1946 / 1941-1946 / Document ✦✦✦✦

The landmark sides which comprise Muddy Waters' *First Recording Sessions* trace the early evolution of one of the blues' most enduring greats, offering invaluable insight into the primal influences which helped shape his musical identity. The profound influence of Waters' idol Son House is most indelibly etched into these early sides, with the bottleneck guitar sound on the first cuts "Country Blues" and "I Be's Troubled"—both recorded by Alan Lomax in 1941—a prime example of the Mississippi blues style of the period. When Lomax returned a year later, he recorded Waters in a string band also including violinist Son Simms, guitarist Percy Thomas and mandolinist Louis Ford; among the tracks they cut is "Take a Walk with Me," in all likelihood inspired by Robert Lockwood. By the final group of songs, dating from 1946, Waters was in Chicago, and here his guitar style began to move towards his future trademark sound, which is most in evidence on the classic closer, the two-part "Rollin' and Tumblin'." —*Jason Ankeny*

★ The Best of Muddy Waters [Chess] / 1957 / MCA/Chess ✦✦✦✦✦

If you're building your Muddy Waters collection from the ground up, you can do no better than this compact disc reissue of his first album featuring 12 tightly compacted gems of seminal Chicago blues. This release features the original versions of "I'm Your Hoochie-Coochie Man," "Long Distance Call," "I'm Ready," "Honey Bee," "I Just Wanna Make Love to You," "Still a Fool," and a song called "Rollin' Stone," which provided the name inspiration for a hippie rock magazine and a group of British musicians. 30 plus years after its original release, it still stands as the perfect introduction to his music and one of the top five greatest Chicago blues albums of all time. —*Cub Koda*

☆ At Newport / 1960 / MCA/Chess ✦✦✦✦✦

For many back in the early '60s, this was their first exposure to live recorded blues and it's still pretty damn impressive some 30 plus years down the line. Muddy, with a band featuring Otis Spann, James Cotton, and guitarist Pat Hare, lays it down tough and cool with a set that literally had 'em dancing in the aisles by the set closer, a ripping version of "Got My Mojo Working," reprised again in a shorter encore version. Kicking off with a version of "I've Got My Brand on You" that positively burns the relatively tame, in comparison, studio take, Muddy heads full bore through impressive versions of "Hoochie Coochie Man," Big Bill Broonzy's "Feel So Good," and "Tiger in Your Tank." A great breakthrough moment in blues history, preserved for posterity. —*Cub Koda*

Folk Festival of the Blues / 1963 / MCA ✦✦✦

This is undoubtedly one of the more problematic listings in this book. It's a compilation album that isn't, a live album that isn't (at least in a couple of spots), and a Muddy Waters album that isn't, if one counts the appearances by four other artists on it. But for all things it isn't, it is also just happens to be one of the greatest and certainly most underrated live blues album of all time, unbelievably crude, raw, and as real as it gets. Originally issued on Chess' Argo label during the height of the folk music blues revival (hence the goofy title), this was a record that was aimed at a White market who responded in kind, with this album making its way into a number of record collections, the majority of them owned by guitar players on both American and foreign shores. But anybody purchasing it thinking they were getting some nice acoustic coffeehouse type blues were in for the reality check shock of their lives. Recorded on July 26, 1963 at a WPOA live radio broadcast emceed by local Chicago disc jockey Big Bill Hill emanating from the Copacabana Club (hence when this was reissued in 1967, it was retitled *Blues From Big Bill's Copacabana*, a vinyl incarnation worth tracking down as that version is the only issuance of the true stereo master), this features Buddy Guy's band with Muddy's right hand man Otis Spann ensconsed at the piano stool as the backup band for everybody. You can literally hear the sweat on the tape, it's that real. Although Big Bill announces the presence of Little Walter and Sonny Boy Williamson on the album's intro, Walter and Sonny Boy are no-shows, with the studio version of Williamson's "Bring It On Home" appearing here with dubbed on applause, this along with the studio version of Buddy Guy's "Worried Blues" being the two bits of audio chicanery presented here. Everything else, however, is just amazingly raw, crude, blistering peformances with some of the most electrifying Buddy Guy guitar

ever comitted to magnetic tape, droning saxes, thundering drums, and Otis Spann anchoring everything with consummate elegance as nobody's bothered to check their tuning in the last half dozen drinks or more. The audience ambience on this disc is worth the price of admission alone; when Big Bill stumbles over his introductory salutations at the front of the record, a drunk starts laughing right in his face. The combination of performances of Buddy Guy, Howlin' Wolf, Willie Dixon, and Sonny Boy Williamson in tandem with Waters would certainly checklist this one into 'various artists' category, but with half of the 10 tracks being fronted by Waters, it's clearly Muddy's show all the way. His performances of "I Got My Mojo Working," "She's 19 Years Old," "Clouds In My Heart," "Sitting And Thinking," and the vocal trio effort with Guy and Dixon on the show opening "Wee Wee Baby" are nothing less than exemplary, the man is simply singing his ass off on here. Guy plays some scarifying guitar licks behind Waters in answer and that framed against Spann's sparkling piano work makes this almost the great lost live Muddy Waters album. But no matter how you slice it or end up filing it, one would be very hard pressed indeed to find a live blues album that captures the spirit and a moment in time the way this one does. Unavailable on compact disc as of press time, but worth tracking down in its vinyl incarnations at any cost. —*Cub Koda*

Muddy Waters Sings Big Bill Broonzy / 1964 / MCA/Chess ✦✦✦✦

Waters' tribute album to the man who gave him his start on the Chicago circuit, this stuff doesn't sound much like Broonzy so much as a virtual recasting of his songs into Muddy's electric blues style. Evidently the first time Waters and his band were recorded in stereo, the highlights include high voltage takes on "When I Get to Drinkin'" and "The Mopper's Blues," with some really great harp from James Cotton as an added bonus. —*Cub Koda*

Folk Singer / Apr. 1964 / Chess ✦✦✦✦

Muddy Waters obliterates the folk/blues distinction with this fine set. It's been reissued on cassette but not CD, so look hard and long for the vinyl, as it boasts superior sound quality. —*Ron Wynn*

The Real Folk Blues / 1965 / MCA/Chess ✦✦✦✦

Once Chess discovered a White folk-blues audience ripe and ready to hear the real thing, they released a series of albums under the *Real Folk Blues* banner. This is one of the best entries in the series, a mixed bag of early Chess sides from 1949-1954, some of it hearkening back to Muddy's first recordings for Aristocrat with only Big Crawford on string in support with some wonderful full band sides rounding out the package to give everyone the big picture. A couple of highlights to pay special attention to are the cha cha/shuffle strut of the band charging through "Walkin' Through the Park" and the "I'm a Man"-derived nastiness of "Mannish Boy." —*Cub Koda*

Live Recordings 1965-1973 / 1965-1973 / Wolf ✦✦✦

These are ten tracks of Waters pretty much on top of his game, with the bulk of them coming from 1965-68 and featuring Pinetop Perkins, Carey Bell, and Sammy Lawhorn in support. Three tracks from 1973 may sport better fidelity than the scratchier-sounding mid-'60s stuff, but every track's a gem no matter how you slice it. — *Cub Koda*

Muddy Brass & the Blues / 1967 / Chess ✦✦

Mid-'60s action from the Chicago blues king, who was apparently due for an updated sound in the eyes of the Chess braintrust. So they overdubbed a brass section on Waters' competent renderings of a variety of old standards that intrudes as often as it enhances. —*Bill Dahl*

More Real Folk Blues / 1967 / MCA/Chess ✦✦✦✦

The companion volume to the first Waters entry in the series is even more down home than the first. Featuring another brace of early Chess sides from 1948-1952, this release features some essential tracks not found on *The Chess Box*. With the bludgeoning stomp of "She's Alright" featuring Elgin Evans' kickass drumming and the moody introspection of "My Life Is Ruined" to be counted up among the numerous highlights, this is a fine budget package that Muddy (and lovers of early Chicago blues) fans certainly shouldn't overlook. —*Cub Koda*

Super Super Blues Band / 1968 / Chess ✦✦

Featuring Bo Diddley stubbing his toe on a wah-wah pedal, Wolf and Muddy clearly ill at ease trying to sing songs they don't know and a super annoying female chorus giving out banshee shrieks approximately every 45 seconds, this is one very chaotic, untogether super session to try and wade through. — *Cub Koda*

Electric Mud / 1968 / Chess ✦✦
In an attempt to make Muddy more sellable to his newly-found White audience, Chess lumbered him with Hendrix-influenced psychedelic blues arrangements for *Electric Mud*. Commercially, actually, the results weren't bad; Marshall Chess claims it sold between 150,000 and 200,000 copies. Musically, it was as ill-advised as putting Dustin Hoffman into a *Star Wars* epic. Guitarists Pete Cosey and Phil Upchurch are very talented players, but Muddy's brand of downhome electric blues suffered greatly at the hands of extended fuzzy solos. Muddy and band overhaul classics like "I Just Want to Make Love to You" and "Hoochie Coochie Man," and do a ludicrous cover of "Let's Spend the Night Together"; wah-wah guitars and occasional wailing soprano sax bounce around like loose basketballs. It's a classically wrongheaded, crass update of the blues for a modern audience. The 1996 CD reissue adds interesting historical liner notes. — *Richie Unterberger*

Super Blues / Nov. 1968 / Chess ✦✦
This is the first of two super session albums that Chess produced in the late '60s. Time has been a bit kinder to this one, featuring Muddy, Bo Diddley and Little Walter, than the one cut a year later with Howlin' Wolf standing in for Walter. It's loose and *extremely* sloppy, the time gets pushed around here and there and Little Walter's obviously in bad shape, his voice rusted to a croak and trying to blow with a collapsed lung. But there are moments where Bo's heavily tremoloed guitar sounds just fine and the band kicks it in a few spots and Muddy seems to be genuinely enjoying himself. Granted, these moments are few and way too far between, but at least nobody's playing a wah-wah pedal on here. — *Cub Koda*

Fathers and Sons / 1969 / Vogue ✦✦✦
This is a 1969 "super session" that actually works, teaming up Muddy with Paul Butterfield, Michael Bloomfield, Duck Dunn, Otis Spann, Buddy Miles, and Sam Lay sharing the drum stool. Originally issued as a double album, one disc featured studio remakes while the other disc featured the whole gang live in concert in front of a super enthusiastic audience. No new material to speak of, but some really great performances and the "youngsters" give the old man the backing he deserves. — *Cub Koda*

After the Rain / 1969 / Chess ✦
Another psychedelic mess. — *Bill Dahl*

They Call Me Muddy Waters [I] / 1970 / MCA/Chess ✦✦✦
Upon its original 1970 release, this was a Grammy winner for Best Ethnic/Traditional Recording. A quarter of a century later, it seems like an interesting, but diffuse, collection of Muddy Waters tracks, running chronologically from 1951 up to 1967. Excepting the title track and a couple others, there's nothing really indispensable here. A good one to add to the collection after you've picked up on a half dozen others. — *Cub Koda*

Goin' Home: Live in Paris 1970 / 1970 / New Rose ✦✦✦
Goin' Home: Live in Paris 1970 finds Muddy supported by his longtime backing band — guitarists Pee-Wee Madison and Sam Lawhorn, pianist Pinetop Perkins, bassist Calvin Jones, and drummer Willie Smith — as well as harpist Carey Bell on several tracks. Waters performed many of his familiar numbers — "Honey Bee," "Trouble No More," "Hoochie Coochie Man," "Mojo Workin'" — in front of a small French crowd, and while the performances aren't crackling with energy, they have a nice, relaxed and friendly vibe that makes the album worth checking out. — *Thom Owens*

A.K.A. McKinley Morganfield / 1971 / Chess ✦✦✦✦

The London Muddy Waters Sessions / 1971 / Chess ✦✦
If you like hearing '70s British rock stars attempting to jam with one of the originators of the form, then you'll probably like the results from this tepid 1971 session. Only the late Irish guitarist Rory Gallagher seems to be interacting with the old master here (and guitarist Sammy Lawhorn) while Stevie Winwood, Georgie Fame, and Mitch Mitchell seem to be totally lost. — *Cub Koda*

Live at Mister Kelly's / Jun. 1971 / MCA/Chess ✦✦✦
Pretty decent live set, taped at a legendary and now-defunct Chicago nightspot not exactly known for presenting blues. Muddy Waters had one of his finer bands for the 1971 sessions — harpists James Cotton and Paul Oscher, guitarists Pee Wee Madison and Sammy Lawhorn, bassist Calvin Jones, and

drummer Willie Smith push the Chi-town blues king as he tries his hand at "Boom Boom," "You Don't Have to Go," and "Nine Below Zero" (along with a few of his own classics). — *Bill Dahl*

Can't Get No Grindin' / 1973 / Chess ✦✦✦
After eight or nine years of pleasing reissues offset with idiotic experiments (the *Super Blues* sessions and the two psychedelic albums *Electric Mud* and *After the Rain*), Muddy returned to form with a new band on this 1973 outing. Sounding positively encumbered and armed with a pretty great batch of tunes, this was his finest album in a quite a few years. — *Cub Koda*

London Revisited / 1974 / Chess ✦✦
As mediocre as its predecessor. — *Bill Dahl*

Muddy & the Wolf / 1974 / Chess ✦✦✦
The title is a bit of a ringer, since this isn't a collaborative effort in any way, shape or form. This contains a half dozen live Waters tracks with Mike Bloomfield, Paul Butterfield, and Otis Spann culled from the *Father & Sons* sessions and also features tracks by Howlin' Wolf from his London sessions with Eric Clapton and Ringo Starr. File under "just okay." — *Cub Koda*

Woodstock Album / 1975 / Chess ✦✦✦✦
Of all the post-*Fathers & Sons* attempts at updating Muddy's sound in collaboration with younger white musicians, this album worked best because they let Muddy be himself, producing music that compared favorably to his concerts of the period, which were wonderful. His final album for Chess (recorded at Levon Helm's Woodstock studio, not in Chicago), with Helm and fellow Band-member Garth Hudson teaming up with Muddy's touring band, it was a rocking (in the bluesy sense) soulful swansong to the label where he got his start. Muddy covers some songs he knew back when (including Louis Jordan's "Caldonia" and "Let The Good Times Roll"), plays some slide, and generally has a great time on this Grammy-winning album. This record got lost in the shuffle between the collapse of Chess Records and the revival of Muddy's career under the auspices of Johnny Winter, and was forgotten until 1995. The CD contains one previously unreleased number, "Fox Squirrel." — *Bruce Eder*

Live at Jazz Jamboree '76 / 1976 / Poljazz ✦✦✦
Released on the small Poljazz label, *Live at Jazz Jamboree '76* is a minor but valuable addition to the live Muddy Waters catalog. Recorded at the Palace of Culture and Sciences in Warsaw, Poland, the 14-track album finds Muddy in good form. Part of the reason the concert works is that his supporting band is excellent, boasting such musicians as pianist Pinetop Perkins, harpist Jerry Portnoy, and guitarists Luther Johnson and Bob Margolin. They give Waters enthusiastic support, bringing the music alive. Even better, the set list isn't entirely predictable, so you can hear Muddy and the band work out on such numbers as "Screamin' and Cryin'," "Blow Wind Blow," "Howlin' Wolf," and "Caledonia," which makes this an interesting disc for hardcore fans. — *Thom Owens*

Hard Again / May 1977 / Blue Sky ✦✦✦✦
By the mid-'70s Muddy Waters was all but forgotten as a viable recording entity. But one person who hadn't forgotten — and was willing to put his rock stardom on the line for it — was Johnny Winter. He assembled a crack backing unit with himself, Pinetop Perkins, and James Cotton blowing their brains out and fueled the fire even further with top notch material Like "The Blues Had a Baby and They Named It Rock 'n' Roll." The end result was the finest latter day album of Muddy's long career and the only one that can sit comfortably on the shelf next to his Chess classics. — *Cub Koda*

I'm Ready / Jun. 1978 / Blue Sky ✦✦✦
Another fine latter-day effort. — *Bill Dahl*

Muddy "Mississippi" Waters: Live / 1979 / Blue Sky ✦✦✦✦
Featuring fierce, declamatory vocals and an otherworldly slide, this documents a bluesman at the height of his powers. — *Jas Obrecht*

King Bee / 1981 / Blue Sky ✦✦✦
Waters' 1981 swan song was recorded with Johnny Winter. — *Jas Obrecht*

Hoochie Coochie Man / 1983 / LRC ✦✦✦✦
The source for this 1964 live performance appears to be Lippmann and Rau, the sponsors of Europe's American Folk-Blues Festival. The legitimacy of the release, despite the presence of an address for the company, is called into question by the misspelling of Muddy's real last name, Morgenfield, in the writing credit. But considering that Chess Records never recorded Muddy's

live set during this era, this disc is priceless. Otis Spann is at the piano, George Smith plays sax, Sammy Lawhorn is the second guitarist, and Francis Clay and Luther Johnson are the rhythm section. The dozen songs include "Country Boy," "Baby Please Don't Go," "Sweet Little Angel," and "Rock Me Baby." The show is loose and lively, the band incredibly tight (especially Johnson and Clay on bass and drums), including a delightfully sly, teasing performance on "Hoochie Coochie Man," a rip-roaring "Sittin' and Thinkin'," and surging, volcanic renditions of "Long Distance Call," "She's Nineteen Years Old," and "County Jail." The sound is generally excellent as well, making this an indispensable part of any serious blues collection, and doubly so for Muddy's fans. — *Bruce Eder*

Rare & Unissued / 1984 / MCA/Chess ◆◆◆◆
Compiler Dick Shurman rummaged around in the voluminous Chess vaults long enough to emerge with this sterling 14-song collection of unissued and rare sides, most of them dating from Waters' 1947-1954 heyday. "Little Anna Mae," "Feel like Going Home," and "You're Gonna Miss Me" spotlight his stark Delta roots; "Stuff You Gotta Watch," "Smokestack Lightnin'," and "Born Lover" boast fuller Waters bands of immense power and drive. — *Bill Dahl*

Trouble No More/Singles (1955-1959) / 1989 / MCA/Chess ◆◆◆◆
This is an excellent compilation of some of Muddy Waters' lesser-anthologized singles, all of them dating from the late '50s. Some of these were surprisingly hard to acquire in *any* form until this appeared; the original version of "Got My Mojo Working," for instance, as well as some of his higher-profile tracks, like "Rock Me," "Trouble No More," "Close to You," and "Don't Go No Further." All of these tracks appear on the *Chess Box*, so if you have that one, you don't need this one. But if you don't, you do. — *Richie Unterberger & Cub Koda*

★ **The Chess Box** / Mar. 1990 / MCA/Chess ◆◆◆◆◆
Multi-disc box sets are a nettlesome proposition for the casual blues fan and even some hardliners. Most folks just don't have the time or the attention span to stay with one artist over the course of three to four hours of material and because the very best sides are usually spread out over the various discs, just popping one in might not give you the artistic quick fix you're seeking. But if you've decided that Muddy's your main man and you want to build a Chicago blues collection that's comprehensive and expansive, this three-disc box just might be your first stop. While there's a European box that's far more exhaustive (and expensive, sporting both dodgy sound quality and dubious legality), this one is far easier to digest. If you want to go for the big one, this is it. — *Cub Koda*

The Complete Muddy Waters 1947-1967 / 1992 / Charly ◆◆◆◆
No, this mammoth nine-disc compilation—205 tracks in all—isn't actually complete, since alternate takes have since turned up on a couple of items. Further, the sound quality is decidedly spotty, and Charly's legal right to put Chess material on the market at all has long been in question. But this is the only place CD enthusiasts are currently going to find more than a few indispensable 1950s sides that MCA hasn't gotten around to releasing quite yet. And the final disc holds some enlightening alternate takes (including a whopping eight run-throughs of "Woman Wanted" and nine versions of "Read Way Back") that may never see domestic light of day. For aficionados only, make no mistake! — *Bill Dahl*

Blue Sky / Jun. 16, 1992 / Columbia/Legacy ◆◆◆◆
This is a nice collection paring down the best of the material Waters recorded for the Blue Sky label between 1976 to 1980. With Johnny Winter in the producer's chair, the backings are sympathetic and the songs are great (some of them remakes of earlier Chess material): these are the tracks that garnered three consecutive Grammy Awards (for Best Ethnic or Traditional Recording) for Waters. And that can't be *all* bad. Not the place to start by any means, but definitely worth a listen or two. — *Cub Koda*

Live in 1958 / 1993 / MW ◆◆◆
In the fall of 1958, Muddy Waters came to England to perform for the first time. With his regular pianist Otis Spann along for the ride and backed by the jazzy, horn-dominated Chris Barber band, Muddy's declamatory vocals and electric slide guitar (set at Chicago blues tavern levels) proved to be too much reality for purist British audiences to handle. He immediately toned down his approach to appease the straight-laced Brits, and what survives

here is the complete concert from the following night at the Manchester Free Trade Hall, dubbed from the only existing acetate. — *Cub Koda*

☆ **The Complete Plantation Recordings** / Jun. 8, 1993 / MCA ◆◆◆◆◆
At long last, Muddy's historic 1941-1942 Library of Congress field recordings are all collected in one place, with the best fidelity that's been heard thus far. Waters performs solo pieces (you can hear his slide rattling against the fretboard in spots) and band pieces with the Son Sims Four, "Rosalie" being a virtual blueprint for his later Chicago style. Of particular note are the inclusion of several interview segments with Muddy from that embryonic period and a photo of Muddy playing on the porch of his cabin, dressed up and looking sharper than any Mississippi sharecropper on Stovall's plantation you could possibly imagine. This much more than just an important historical document; this is some really fine music imbued with a sense of place, time, and loads of ambience. Beyond essential. — *Cub Koda*

One More Mile / 1994 / MCA/Chess ◆◆◆◆
A double CD of 41 tracks, none of which are found on *The Chess Box*. With only three exceptions, none of them have ever been available on an American album before, and quite a few were never previously released anywhere. During most of his stay at Chess, Muddy's output was remarkably prolific and consistent. If you are interested enough in him to own more than one of his albums, you'll like what you hear on this collection, which matches or nearly matches the standards of his best work. Lots of rarities spanning the late '40s to the early '70s, with some special points of interest: the original 1955 version of "I Want To Be Loved," covered by the Rolling Stones on the B-side of their very first single, finally makes its first appearance on an American album, and the final 11 songs are from a previously unreleased 1972 Swiss radio broadcast, showcasing Muddy in a drummer-less trio. — *Richie Unterberger*

Muddy Waters in Concert / 1996 / One Way ◆◆◆◆
This is a later concert performance by Muddy, from sometime in the mid-'70s to judge by the repertory ("Garbage Man," "Corrina, Corrina," "Caldonia," and "Screamin' and Cryin'," in addition to "Hoochie Coochie Man," "Got My Mojo Working," "Howlin' Wolf" etc.). There are no credits or dates mentioned, but that's not really important. The performance and recording are both excellent—the sound is bigger and busier, as well as somewhat more elegant, than Muddy's mid-'60s work, and the repertory is different from both his official Chess and Columbia live albums, so it's a must-own. This same performance previously appeared in a fairly widely distributed CD from Classic Sound Inc., and either is acceptable. — *Bruce Eder*

★ **His Best: 1947-1955** / 1997 / Chess ◆◆◆◆◆
This entry into MCA's Chess 50th Anniversary Collection now officially takes the place of *The Best of Muddy Waters* as an essential first purchase in building a Muddy Waters collection, as the original 12-song collection has been forced out of print with the issuance of this 20-tracker. All 12 songs that comprise the budget priced *The Best of Muddy Waters* are aboard, with eight more essential goodies from his first great period of creativity, including great early ones like "Rollin' and Tumblin'," "Train Fare Blues," and "I Feel like Going Home." The one ringer that keeps this collection from being *The Best of Muddy-plus* is an alternate take of "Hoochie Coochie Man" in place of the original issued master, a production error of the highest order. It's a radically different-sounding one, too, with some surprisingly sloppy unthought-out harp work from Little Walter (at one point he simply stops playing), but with a far more intense vocal from Muddy than the issued version. But it is the issued version which by rights *should* have been the one heard here, as this *is* supposed to be a true best-of compilation. That niggling point aside, this collection (part of a two-volume best-of retrospective, the second covering the years 1956 to 1964) sports far superior sound and excellent liner notes, and will now take pride of place as the essential first purchase toward building the perfect Muddy Waters collection. — *Cub Koda*

Muddy Waters & Friends / 1997 / Just a Memory ◆◆◆
Eleven songs cut by Muddy at an informal session in a Montreal hotel room on Oct. 18. 1967, recorded by Michael Nerenberg. The tape is sort of the companion to the *Folk Singer* album that he'd cut a few years earlier—Muddy is joined on acoustic guitar and vocals by Otis Spann, Sam Langhorn, John "Mojo" Buford, and Luther Johnson. The sound is rough, and there's a certain amount of talk and ambient noise, especially on "Little Anna Mae."

Other songs include "My Home Is In the Delta," "Take a Little Walk," "Crazy About You Baby," and "Mean Disposition," all done with Muddy in good form—this was when he was in his fifties, and before the car accident and subsequent health problems that slowed him down, and given the fact that Chess didn't record Muddy for an official live album until a few years after this, *Muddy Waters & Friends* partly fills a gap in his history. Still, this isn't a definitive recording, because Muddy and company were winging the sound, and had no inkling that what they were taping would ever be heard publicly. *—Bruce Eder*

Paris 1972 / Mar. 4, 1997 / Pablo ✦✦✦
Not released until 1997, this is an expectedly professional set from Muddy with a solid band, the most notable sidemen being pianist Pinetop Perkins, harmonica player George "Mojo" Buford, and guitarist Louis Myers. There aren't many surprises in the set, including such standards as "Hoochie Coochie Man," "Honey Bee," "Walking Thru the Park," "Rollin' n' Tumblin'," "Walkin' Blues," and "Got My Mojo Workin'," as well as a few obscure items like "Clouds in My Heart." The sound is good, but it's hard to recommend this to anyone but hardcore fans, as Muddy did more exciting renditions of the best tunes on the original Chess recordings and, in some cases, other live albums. This has a comfortable, easygoing feel that's conservative, if only in relation to Waters' own best work. It's kind of redundant for those with big Muddy collections, and not a recommended starting point for others. *—Richie Unterberger*

☆ **His Best: 1956-1964** / May 20, 1997 / MCA ✦✦✦✦✦
The second volume in MCA's Chess Anniversary Series chronicling the best of Muddy Waters picks up in 1956, a prolific year for the bluesman. The first eight tracks of this 20-track collection were recorded that year: "All Aboard," featuring both James Cotton and Little Walter on twin harmonicas, "Forty Days and Forty Nights," "Just to Be With You," "Don't Go No Farther," "Diamonds at Your Feet," "I Love the Life I Live," "Rock Me," and the studio version of "I Got My Mojo Working." By now Waters was a rhythm & blues star, as far removed from the Clarksdale plantation he grew up on as you could get. He also had developed the modern-day blues band lineup and by this time had his running like a well-oiled machine. Little Walter (by now a star in his own right) was still on call for studio dates and if not, Walter Horton, Otis Spann and Jimmy Rogers were still in the lineup. By 1958's "She's Nineteen Years Old," Muddy had built up his second great band with James Cotton, Pat Hare and Luther Tucker on guitars, and Francis Clay on drums, the unit he would take to Newport in 1960. It's this unit that contributes so mightily to "Walkin' Thru the Park," "She's Into Something," and Big Bill Broonzy's "I Feel So Good." Two of Muddy's most influential tracks, "You Shook Me" and "You Need Love" (the blueprint for Led Zepplin's "Whole Lotta Love") curiously feature Earl Hooker on slide guitar, along with A.C. Reed and John "Big Moose" Walker, the core of the Age-Profile label's house band. A pair of tracks from his now-celebrated *Folk Singer* album with Buddy Guy and Willie Dixon ("My Home Is In the Delta" and "Good Morning Little Schoolgirl") offset the collection's final selections, Willie Dixon's "The Same Thing" and Muddy's classic "You Can't Lose What You Ain't Never Had," a perfect closer for this essential collection. Again, the audiophile concerns that brought us to compact discs makes this an excellent upgrade even if this material already resides in your collection. *—Cub Koda*

King of the Electric Blues / Oct. 7, 1997 / Sony ✦✦✦
The first 20-bit remastering of any of Muddy's late career work for Johnny Winter's Blue Sky label is of considerable interest. The fact that, in the wake of the earlier *Blues Sky* best-of disc, there's enough material to do another 60-minute-plus collection, also speaks well for this catalog. The clarity of the Super Bit Mapping audio brings out a sharpness in these recordings that the original vinyl and CD issues barely hinted at. The stuff is finally mastered at the volume it always should have been (this is a potential lease-breaker) and more than justifies the purchase. The music isn't as viscerally exciting as Muddy's work for Chess—he's slower, starts at a lower energy level, and takes his time building up intensity, but the climaxes are majestic. The playing is also as solid as ever, and Muddy still had a considerable amount to say musically. *Blues Sky* still has the edge for songs, although the producers here have wisely included Muddy's covers of songs that he liked by John Lee (Sonny Boy) Williamson, Arthur Crudup, and Big Joe Williams, in addition to some of his own tunes. *—Bruce Eder*

Johnny "Guitar" Watson

b. Feb. 3, 1935, Houston, TX, **d.** May 17, 1996, Chicago, IL
Guitar, Vocals / Soul, R&B, Urban, Texas Blues
"Reinvention" could just as easily have been Johnny "Guitar" Watson's middle name. The multi-talented performer parlayed his stunning guitar skills into a vaunted reputation as one of the hottest blues axemen on the West Coast during the 1950s. But that admirable trait wasn't paying the bills as the 1970s rolled in. So he totally changed his image to that of a pimp-styled funkster, enjoying more popularity than ever before for his down-and-dirty R&B smashes "A Real Mother for Ya" and "Superman Lover."

Watson's roots resided within the fertile blues scene of Houston. As a teen, he played with fellow Texas future greats Albert Collins and Johnny Copeland. But he left Houston for Los Angeles when he was only 15 years old. Back then, Watson's main instrument was piano; that's what he played with Chuck Higgins' band when the saxist cut "Motorhead Baby" for Combo in 1952 (Watson also handled vocal duties).

He was listed as Young John Watson when he signed with Federal in 1953. His first sides for the King subsidiary found him still tinkling the ivories, but by 1954, when he dreamed up the absolutely astonishing instrumental "Space Guitar," the youth (he was two days short of his 17th birthday!) had switched over to guitar. "Space Guitar" ranks with the greatest achievements of its era—Watson's blistering rapid-fire attack, done without the aid of a pick, presages futuristic effects that rock guitarists still hadn't mastered another 15 years down the line.

Watson moved over to the Bihari brothers' RPM label in 1955 and waxed some of the toughest upbeat blues of their timeframe (usually under saxist Maxwell Davis' supervision). "Hot Little Mama," "Too Tired," and "Oh Baby" scorched the strings with their blazing attack; "Someone Cares for Me" was a churchy Ray Charles-styled slow-dragger, and "Three Hours Past Midnight" cut bone-deep with its outrageous guitar work and laidback vocal (Watson's cool phrasing as a singer was scarcely less distinctive than his playing). He scored his first hit in 1955 for RPM with a note-perfect cover of New Orleanian Earl King's two-chord swamp ballad "Those Lonely Lonely Nights."

Though he cut a demo version of the tune while at RPM, Watson's first released version of "Gangster of Love" emerged in 1957 on Keen. Singles for Class ("One Kiss"), Goth, Arvee (the rocking introduction "Johnny Guitar"), and Escort preceded a hookup with Johnny Otis at King during the early '60s. He recut "Gangster" for King, reaching a few more listeners this time, and dented the R&B charts again in 1962 with his impassioned, violin-enriched blues ballad "Cuttin' In."

Never content to remain in one stylistic bag for long, Watson landed at Chess just long enough to cut a jazz album in 1964 that placed him back behind the 88s. Along with longtime pal Larry Williams, Watson rocked England in 1965 (their dynamic repartee was captured for posterity by British Decca). Their partnership lasted stateside through several singles and an LP for OKeh; among their achievements as a duo was the first vocal hit on "Mercy, Mercy, Mercy" in 1967 (predating the Buckinghams by a few months).

Little had been heard of this musical chameleon before he returned decked out in funk threads during the mid-'70s. He hit with "I Don't Want to Be a Lone Ranger" for Fantasy before putting together an incredible run at DJM Records paced by "A Real Mother for Ya" in 1977 and an updated "Gangster of Love" the next year.

After a typically clever "Strike on Computers" nicked the R&B lists in 1984, Watson again seemed to fall off the planet. But counting this remarkable performer out was always a mistake. *Bow Wow*, his 1994 album for Al Bell's Bellmark logo, returned him to prominence and earned a Grammy nomination for best contemporary blues album, even though its contents were pure old-school funk. Sadly, in the midst of a truly heartwarming comeback campaign, Watson passed away while touring Japan in 1996. *—Bill Dahl*

★ **Gangster of Love** / 1958 / Charly ✦✦✦✦✦
The innovative guitar wizard when he was young and wearing his Texas blues roots prominently on his sleeve. Watson spent two stints at King/Federal, both of them sampled here: his 1953-54 output includes the incomparable "Space Guitar," a sizzling "Half Pint of Whiskey," and a woozy "Gettin' Drunk." The 1961-63 King stuff is headed by the definitive version of "Gang-

ster of Love," the searing soul-tinged "Cuttin' In," and a chunky "Broke and Lonely." —*Bill Dahl*

Johnny Guitar Watson / 1963 / King ✦✦✦✦
Fine collection of guitarist's innovative '50s and '60s stuff. —*Bill Dahl*

I Cried for You / 1963 / Cadet ✦✦
Watson was highly versatile on this jazz piano set, but *I Cried for You* is no big thrill. —*Bill Dahl*

Larry Williams Show with JG Watson / 1965 / Decca ✦✦✦
Exciting pairing tears up Britain. —*Bill Dahl*

Blues Soul / 1965 / MCA/Chess ✦✦✦
This 1965 album, later reissued under the title of *I Cried for You*, displays an entirely different facet of the multitalented R&B star's musical personality. Here he's an accomplished jazz pianist in a trio setting, giving old standards like "Witchcraft" and "Misty" his own vocal twist. Lowell Fulson's "Reconsider Baby" is the only blues number on the LP. —*Bill Dahl*

Two for the Price of One / 1967 / OKeh ✦✦✦
Watson and Williams sing rockin' soul. —*Bill Dahl*

Listen / 1973 / Fantasy ✦✦✦

Gangster Is Back / 1975 / Red Lightnin' ✦✦
Digital reissue of an old Red Lightnin' bootleg covering Watson's 1950s output that was revered back in the pre-CD era but sounds very rough now. One thing in its favor: the disc sports Watson's otherwise digitally unavailable 1957 version of "Gangster of Love" for Keen. —*Bill Dahl*

I Don't Want to Be Alone Stranger / 1975 / Fantasy ✦✦✦

Ain't That a Bitch / 1976 / Collectables ✦✦✦✦
The first of Watson's monstrously popular funk-based albums for DJM, and in all likelihood, the best of the lot. The title cut of the 1976 album is a sardonic gem, Watson's sinuous guitar licks a far cry from his brash '50s sound. The intimate "I Want to Ta-Ta You Baby," "Superman Lover," and "I Need It" also rate with Watson's most alluring old school R&B output. —*Bill Dahl*

Real Mother for Ya / 1977 / Collectables ✦✦✦
Obviously, the storming funk workout that gives this 1977 gold album its title is the album's principal draw (it's been covered countless times, but never duplicated). As was his wont by this time, the multitalented Watson plays everything except drums and horns. —*Bill Dahl*

Funk Beyond the Call of Duty / Feb. 1977 / Collectables ✦✦✦
Less consistent than its immediate predecessors but still a reasonably good funky time, as Johnny Guitar once again displays his streetwise humor on "It's About the Dollar Bill" and "Barn Door" on the 1977 set. —*Bill Dahl*

Hot Little Mama / 1978 / Big Town ✦
Avoid these '50s RPM sides with overdubbed modern instrumentation. —*Bill Dahl*

Love Jones / 1980 / Collectables ✦✦
Watson's once-innovative funk formula was showing major signs of wear and tear by the time this 1980 album hit the charts. Weird and spacy in spots, and seldom any too interesting. —*Bill Dahl*

I Heard That / 1985 / Charly ✦✦✦✦
King-Federal sides from the '50s and '60s includes the amazing "Space Guitar." —*Bill Dahl*

Three Hours Past Midnight / 1991 / Flair ✦✦✦✦
Watson's mid-'50s catalog for the Bihari brothers' Flair logo is unassailable with searing rockers like "Oh Baby," "Hot Little Mama," and "Ruben" and the blistering slow blues title cut. Unfortunately, this 16-song collection utilizes inferior alternate takes on several of the most important titles. On the positive side, it contains both sides of his rare 1959 single for Class, "One Kiss"/"The Bear." —*Bill Dahl*

● **Gonna Hit That Highway: The Complete RPM Recordings** / 1992 / P-Vine ✦✦✦✦
No such omissions with this two-disc Japanese set—not only are the official versions of all of Watson's vicious RPM sides here, so are a plethora of alternate takes and extreme rarities (including a demo version of "Gangster of Love" as "Love Bandit"). Could be tough to locate, but for anyone seri-

ously into this brilliant guitarist's early blues output, absolutely essential! —*Bill Dahl*

Listen/I Don't Want to Be Alone, Stranger / 1992 / Ace ✦✦✦✦
Watson's first two funk-slanted albums, combined conveniently on one disc. *Listen* dates from 1973, *I Don't Want to Be Alone* from two years later, and both are very together funk outings with a heady dose of modern blues at their core. —*Bill Dahl*

Giant / 1994 / Collectables ✦✦✦
Disco rhythms rear their repetitive head on much of this 1978 set, making it a whole lot less likable than Watson's earlier DJM albums. But his updated "Gangster of Love" packs a killer groove and sports some nice, very concise blues guitar work by the man. —*Bill Dahl*

The Best of Johnny "Guitar" Watson / Nov. 5, 1996 / Renaissance ✦✦✦

Junior Watson

Guitar, Vocals / West Coast Blues
Despite playing the role of perrenial sideman, often in fine bands that left much to be desired in the visibility department, Mike "Junior" Watson was, and is, one of the most influential blues guitarists of his generation. In fact, following Robben Ford's defection into fusion, Watson was rivaled only by Hollywood Fats as king of the hill in California and only by Jimmie Vaughan anywhere else. While he and Vaughan have radically different approaches, Watson's arch-top-cheapo-through-reverb-tank sound has much in common with Hollywood Fats', as does his ability to nail seemingly every traditional electric blues style. But whereas Fats was a master of mimckry, Watson has a spontaneous, original bent laced with his oddball sense of humor. After starting out with harpist Gary Smith in Northern California in the early '70s, he teamed with Rod Piazza's Mighty Flyers (née Flying Sauce Band) for 11 years, where he was instrumental in injecting the Chicago-styled blues band (and countless others in its wake) with ample doses of swing, culling licks from guitarists Bill Jennings, Tiny Grimes, and Billy Butler. Along the way he gigged with Charlie Musselwhite, Jimmy Rogers, Luther Tucker, and others, eventually joining the '80s edition of Canned Heat, with whom he continues to tour. —*Dan Forte*

● **Long Overdue** / Jan. 24, 1994 / Black Top ✦✦✦✦
Giving jump blues and early R&B a kick in its baggy pants, Watson's aptly-titled solo debut revealed what only guitarists (the more conscientious of them) had known for more than a decade: Here is a 6-stringer of rare talent, with the unique ability to play authentically *and* spontaneously—all-too-often contradictory paths in the late '70s blues revival. The best and most fitting compliment one could give a Watson solo is that it makes you laugh; this is blues of the rent party variety and Watson never lapses into the maudlin. Along with singers Brenda Burns and Lynwood Slim (on harp as well), Watson favors us with half a dozen surprisingly confident vocals. In fact, the only criticism is that his voice is sometimes too low in the mix. —*Dan Forte*

Noble Watts

b. Feb. 17, 1926, DeLand, FL
Saxophone, Sax (Tenor) / Electric Blues, East Coast Blues
The 1950s R&B scene was rife with fire-breathing tenor sax honkers. Noble "Thin Man" Watts was one of the most incendiary. Watts enrolled at Florida A&M University in 1942 (his mates in the school marching band included future jazz luminaries Nat and Cannonball Adderly). The Griffin Brothers, one of Dot Records' top R&B acts (obviously, this was before the days when Randy Wood's label provided safe haven for the hopelessly pale likes of Pat Boone and Gale Storm) hired young Noble Watts after he got out of college. Watts joined baritone saxist Paul "Hucklebuck" Williams in 1952, recording with him for Jax and taking sax solos behind Dinah Washington, Amos Milburn, and Ruth Brown on the groundbreaking mid-'50s TV program *Showtime at the Apollo* (Williams led the house band for the Willie Bryant-hosted extravaganza). Later, there was a stint with Lionel Hampton.

Watts' own discography commenced in 1954 with a tasty coupling for DeLuxe ("Mashing Potatoes"/"Pig Ears and Rice"). A 1956 single for Vee-Jay with Williams' band ("South Shore Drive") came just prior to Watts' salad days on the New York-based Baton label. With his band, the Rhythm Sparks, in support, Watts wailed "Easy Going," "Blast Off," "Shakin'," "Flap Jack," and quite a few more searing instrumentals for Baton from 1957 to 1959, the biggest of all being "Hard Times (The Slop)," which propelled the saxist onto the pop charts in December of 1957. Guitar twanger Duane Eddy must have dug what he heard—he covered the grinding shuffle for Jamie a few years later. That wasn't Noble Watts' only connection to rock 'n' roll—he played behind Jerry Lee Lewis, Buddy Holly, Chuck Berry, the Everly Brothers, and many more on various late-'50s package tours.

Boxer Sugar Ray Robinson managed Watts during the late '50s and early '60s, recruiting the saxist to lead the house band at the pugilist's Harlem lounge. Things got thin for the Thin Man during the '60s (45s for Sir, Cub, Enjoy, Peanut, Jell, Clamike, and Brunswick came and went without much notice) and '70s, but he mounted a comeback bid in 1987 with a fresh album, *Return of the Thin Man*, for Bob Greenlee's King Snake logo (later picked up by Alligator). *King of the Boogie Sax* followed in 1993 for Ichiban's Wild Dog imprint. Watts continues to work as a session saxist for Greenlee when he's not pursuing his own interests. — *Bill Dahl*

● **Return of the Thin Man** / 1987 / Alligator ♦♦♦♦
After taking several years off, Noble Watts returned in 1987 with *Return of the Thin Man*. Instead of following through on his storming, honking '50s and '60s R&B, Watts decided to take things in a different direction, toning things down a bit and concentrating on mellow grooves. There are a couple of uptempo workouts, of course, but the songs that make a lasting impression on *Return of the Thin Man* are the slower, conversational pieces that are warm, relaxed and friendly. It's the sound of an aging master who has found strength in maturity and isn't afraid to celebrate that fact. — *Thom Owens*

Noble & Nat / 1990 / Kingsnake ♦♦♦♦

King of the Boogie Sax / 1993 / Wild Dog ♦♦♦
A less inspired follow-up to Watts' previous outings for King Snake. — *Bill Dahl*

Carl Weathersby

b. Feb. 24, 1953, Jackson, MS
Guitar / Electric Chicago Blues
Vocalist, songwriter, and guitarist Carl Weathersby is a soul-blues crooner in the classic Chicago tradition. Best known for his work with Billy Branch and Sons of the Blues, Weathersby's first album, 1996's *Don't Lay Your Blues on Me*, was hailed as genuine, state-of-the-art Chicago blues for the '90s. Weathersby released his second album, *Looking Out My Window*, in 1997, and the raves continued; the song "The Blues Follow Me Around," which Weathersby first recorded with Branch, was nominated for a Handy Award.

Born in Jackson, MS, Weathersby was eight when his family moved to East Chicago, Indiana. He spent his summers back home with relatives in Mississippi. Weathersby grew up immersed in blues music and has many family links to the blues, R&B, and Motown legacies: he's related to the late Leonard "Baby Doo" Caston, Willie Dixon's pianist in the Big Three Trio, a popular Chicago group in the early 1950s; Weathersby's cousin is Leonard Caston, Jr., a member of the Chicago soul group the Radiants, who had a 1965 Chess Records hit with "Voice Your Choice"; singer G.C. Cameron from the Motown group the Spinners is another cousin. Additionally, a neighbor was a cousin of Hound Dog Taylor, and Weathersby's father was friendly with Albert King. One day while Weathersby was practicing King's licks from a 45 rpm recording of "Crosscut Saw," his father and King overheard him. King encouraged the boy, who hadn't realized his identity until then, and eventually hired him as a rhythm guitarist for short road trips in 1979, 1980, and 1982.

Before becoming a full-time musician with Branch's Sons of the Blues, Weathersby worked in a steel mill, as a police officer, and as a prison guard. He also spent time in Vietnam serving in the Army from 1971 to 1977. His life experiences in all four occupations are rich fodder for his songwriting, which is as fresh, original and life-affirming as one is likely to find from any other contemporary blues player.

Weathersby spent 14 years, from 1982 to 1996, with harmonica player Branch's Sons of the Blues before he decided to have a go at leading a band under his own name. For both of his Evidence albums, Weathersby is accompanied by two great New Orleans musicians, who add just the right touches of funk to the band's sound: David Torkanowsky on piano and keyboards and Herman Ernest III on drums, the latter a key element in Dr. John's quartet, the Lower 911. Weathersby's first album, *Don't Lay Your Blues On Me*,

won nominations in the 1996 *Living Blues* Critics' Awards for Best New Blues Album, Best Blues Album, and Best Debut Album. Weathersby was also nominated for a 1997 W.C. Handy Blues Award for Best New Blues Artist. — *Richard J. Skelly*

● **Don't Lay Your Blues on Me** / 1996 / Evidence ♦♦♦♦
Weathersby's debut CD as a session leader is a satisfactory set of contemporary guitar-driven blues. Since 1982, he's been guitarist with Chicago harp player Billy Branch's Sons of the Blues. Weathersby plays in an Albert King style, typically bending and sustaining each note for all it's worth. Although his career is not associated with New Orleans, he recorded this album there with ace Crescent City sidemen Lee Zeno on bass, Herman Ernest on drums, and Dave Torkanowsky on keyboards. They lay down a solid foundation that really cooks. — *Steve Hoffman*

Looking Out My Window / Aug. 26, 1997 / Evidence ♦♦♦♦
Although *Looking Out My Window* doesn't quite reach the same heights as Carl Weathersby's debut, *Don't Lay Your Blues on Me*, that's merely a relative judgment—the album remains an engaging piece of modern blues. Weathersby draws from both the Delta and Chicago traditions, creating a nice fusion. Occasionally, his playing is a little too flashy—if he reigned himself in, he would wind up saying more—but there's enough excitement in the band's interaction to make this a satisfying second effort. — *Thom Owens*

Curley Weaver

b. Mar. 26, 1906, Covington, GA, **d.** Sep. 20, 1962, Almon, GA
Guitar, Vocals / Country Blues, Piedmont Blues, Prewar Country Blues
Curley Weaver, who was known for much of his life as "the Georgia Guitar Wizard," is only just beginning to be appreciated as one of the best players ever to pick up a six-string instrument. Although he recorded a fair number of sides on his own during the '20s and '30s, Weaver was most commonly heard in performances and recordings in association with his better known colleagues Blind Willie McTell (with whom he worked from the '30s until the early '50s), Barbecue Bob, and Buddy Moss. Weaver was born in Newton County, GA, in Covington, and was raised on a cotton farm. His mother, Savanah Shepard, encouraged him to sing from a very early age and also taught him to play the guitar, beginning when he was ten years old. Savanah Shepard was a renowned guitarist in her own right around Newton County, and also taught guitar legends Barbecue Bob and his brother, Charlie Lincoln, to play the instrument when they were children. Her musical interests lay in gospel but, as in the case of Hicks and Lincoln, her son gravitated in the opposite direction, toward the blues. Curley Weaver learned to play slide guitar from two legendary (and, alas, never recorded) local bluesmen, Nehemiah Smith and Blind Buddy Keith. He showed extraordinary aptitude and, at age 19, teamed up with harmonica player Eddie Mapp, and moved to Atlanta. There he hooked up with Barbecue Bob and Charlie Lincoln, who quickly showed their younger friend the ins-and-outs of life, busking on Decatur Street, the heart of Atlanta's Black entertainment district, with its bars, restaurants, clubs, and theaters.

The association between the three guitarists was to prove providential. Barbecue Bob emerged as a local star first and, as a consequence, was also the first to go into the recording studio for the Columbia Records label in 1927—his first releases sold well, and he, in turn, arranged for his brother and Curley Weaver to make their debuts in the studio the following year. Weaver paid his first visit to the recording studio in Atlanta on October 26, 1928, laying down two tracks, "Sweet Petunia" and "No No Blues." Weaver's debut led to more recording work, both as a solo act and in the company of Eddie Mapp, as well as Barbecue Bob. It was also through the recording studio, appearing as the Georgia Cotton Pickers in association with Barbecue Bob, that Weaver first made the acquaintance of Buddy Moss, a 16-year-old harmonica player who learned guitar from Weaver and Bob and later emerged as a major star on the instrument himself. The two were to work together throughout the decade.

Although many of Weaver's recording sessions in the 1930s were in New York, he kept his home base in Atlanta for his entire life, and it was while playing at clubs, parties, dances, picnics, and even on street corners in the early part of the decade that he struck up the most important professional relationship of his life, with Blind Willie McTell. A renowned 12-string guitarist, McTell had begun his recording career in 1927, and was a local legend around Atlanta. The two played and recorded together for 20 years or more, and comprised one of the most important and celebrated East Coast blues teams in history. Weaver's most renowned recordings were done in association either with McTell or Moss, the latter under the guise of the Georgia Browns, during the mid-'30s. His playing, either on its own or in association with either McTell or Moss, was nothing less than dazzling. It wasn't possible for Weaver to sustain his brilliance, though not for lack of his ability or trying. The mid-'30s were a trying time for most blues players. The boom years of the late teens and very early '30s had seen lots of opportunities to perform and record. The Great Depression destroyed much of the marketplace that had led to these successes, and sales by the mid-'30s had, for most bluesmen, dried up considerably from their former levels, and most labels cut back on the chances they were offering to record.

For Weaver, the decade was an even more bitter period. Barbecue Bob had died of pneumonia at the beginning of the 1930s. Eddie Mapp was killed, and Buddy Moss ended up in prison at age 21 on a five-year stretch that halted his career, essentially permanently. Weaver continued playing with McTell across the South, but the onset of the Second World War saw even a lot of this activity dry up. He continued to play around Atlanta, and in 1950 cut an album's worth of material with McTell for the Regal label. He continued playing whenever he could, and was reunited with Moss in a trio that performed in northern Georgia but never recorded. Weaver's performing career was brought to a halt only by the failure of his eyesight. He passed away three years later, in 1962, remembered around Atlanta and by serious blues enthusiasts elsewhere, but largely unheralded during the blues revival that he'd just missed being a part of.

Curley Weaver was, by virtue of his virtuosity and the associations that he kept throughout his life and career, a guitarist's guitarist, a virtuoso among a small coterie of Atlanta-based guitar wizards. He never had the renown of Blind Willie McTell, but he was Willie's equal and match in just about every conceivable respect as a player and singer, his six-string being perfectly mated to Willie's 12-string. When he was playing or recording with McTell, Moss, or Barbecue Bob, the results were the blues equivalent of what rock people later would've called a "super-session" except that, as a listen to the surviving records reveals, the results were more natural and overpowering— these guys genuinely liked each other, and loved playing together, and it shows beyond the virtuosity of the music, in the warmth and elegance of the playing and the sound. — *Bruce Eder*

★ **Georgia Guitar Wizard (1928-1935)** / 1987 / Story of Blues ✦✦✦✦✦
These are 16 of the greatest blues sides ever to come out of Atlanta, and a match for the best work of Blind Willie McTell, Barbecue Bob, and Buddy Moss (whose harmonica playing on the Georgia Browns' "Decatur Street 81" reveals him to be an equally formidable talent on that instrument), who are all over these sides as well. The sound is a little rough at times, and even more than a little, and there are some major gaps between 1929 and 1933— including his renowned "Guitar Rag"—but none of the flaws do violence to the music, and all that is here is worth the price of admission. One important bonus—the presence of "Oh Lawdy Mama," the song that later, in Willie Dixon's hands, evolved into the blues standard "Down in the Bottom" (which was even cut by the Rolling Stones, in what might be their best early blues side); it was also cut by Buddy Moss a year earlier as a solo number. — *Bruce Eder*

☆ **Complete Studio Recordings** / 1990 / Document ✦✦✦✦✦
Weaver's complete recordings, taking into account all of the sessions for Moss, McTell et al. where he played guitar, would comprise a lot more than the 19 tracks here, but that's no reason not to spring for this slightly more expensive collection, which doesn't entirely overlap with the Story of Blues disc. — *Bruce Eder*

Sylvester Weaver

b. Jul. 25, 1897, Louisville, KY, **d.** Apr. 4, 1960, Louisville, KY
Guitar, Vocals / Country Blues, Piedmont Blues, Prewar Country Blues
The pioneering guitarist from the early days of the blues, Weaver created the enduring classic "Guitar Rag," later popularized as "Steel Guitar Rag." He was adept at everything from ragtime to slide guitar stylings, all performed with great technical skill and a marvelous sense of time. — *Cub Koda*

● **Smoketown Strut** / 1923 / Agram ✦✦✦✦
Weaver's earliest and best sides, including "Guitar Rag." The sound is horrible in spots, but every note of the music is great. — *Cub Koda*

Complete Recorded Works, Vol. 1 (1923-1927) / 1923-1927 / Document ✦✦✦✦

Complete Recorded Works, Vol. 2 (1927) / 1927 / Document ✦✦✦✦

"Boogie" Bill Webb

b. 1926, Jackson, MS, **d.** Aug. 23, 1990, New Orleans, LA
Guitar, Vocals / Electric Country Blues, Delta Blues
Although he lived in New Orleans most of his life, and none other than Fats Domino brought him to Imperial Records for his recording debut in 1953, Boogie Bill Webb was never much a part of the New Orleans R&B scene. Webb's music grew out of the Jackson area country-blues tradition of Tommy Johnson and others, and he retained a down-home, idiosyncratic approach to a wide range of material from C&W to R&B and traditional jazz. Beginning in 1966, Webb recorded occasionally for folklorists and field researchers, finally recording his first full album in 1989 with funding from the Louisiana Endowment for the Humanities. Album producer Ben Sandmel, who also played drums with Webb for five years, described Boogie Bill's approach as "quirky, often anarchic," but it is appealing in its very unpredictability, humor, and warmth. — *Jim O'Neal*

● **Drinkin' & Stinkin'** / 1989 / Flying Fish ✦✦✦✦
Boogie Bill had cut a few stray sides for Imperial back in the early '50s that surfaced on vinyl in the '70s on a couple of blues compilations, but this is his only full-length album. Produced by journalist and Hackberry Rambler drummer Ben Sandmel (who thumps the tubs and scrubs the washboard on this), Webb was in fine and totally idiosyncratic form on this. The tunes range from recreations of his early sides ("Bill's Boogie Woogie"), tunes learned from Leadbelly ("Red Cross Store"), Lowell Fulson ("Black Night"), and Tommy Johnson (a heartfelt tribute version of "Canned Heat"), originals that have deep roots in vaudeville ("You Can't Tell My Business After Dark") and the slow blues title track), Black oral tradition "toasts" ("Paul Jones and Little Virginia Dare"), and a ballad, "Love Me Cause I Love My Baby So," that is so structurally odd in its meter that it almost qualifies as abstract art. As if this wasn't wide-ranging enough, Webb closes the album with his version of King Curtis' "Soul Serenade," showing that his singular disregard for time isn't just restricted to older blues forms. Few blues albums are as much fun as this, or stamped with the full force of an artist's personality. — *Cub Koda*

Katie Webster

b. Jan. 9, 1939, Houston, TX, **d.** Houston, TX
Organ, Piano, Vocals, Harmonica / R&B, Electric New Orleans Blues, Electric Louisiana Blues, Electric Swamp Blues, Modern Electric Chicago Blues
A piano-pounding institution on the southern Louisiana swamp blues scene during the late '50s and early '60s, Katie Webster later grabbed a long-deserved share of national recognition with three recent Alligator albums before a 1993 stroke temporarily shelved her.

Poor Kathryn Thorne had to deal with deeply religious parents that did everything in their power to stop their daughter from playing R&B. But the rocking sounds of Fats Domino and Little Richard were simply too persuasive. Local guitarist Ashton Savoy took her under his wing, sharing her 1958 debut 45 for the Kry logo ("Baby Baby").

Webster rapidly became an invaluable studio sessioneer for Louisiana producers J.D. Miller in Crowley and Eddie Shuler in Lake Charles. She played on sides by Guitar Junior (Lonnie Brooks), Clarence Garlow, Jimmy Wilson, Lazy Lester, and Phil Phillips (her gently rolling 88s powered his hit "Sea of Love").

The young pianist also waxed some terrific sides of her own for Miller from 1959 to 1961 for his Rocko, Action, and Spot labels (where she introduced a dance called "The Katie Lee"). Webster led her own band, the Uptighters, at the same time she was spending her days in the studio. In 1964, she guested with Otis Redding's band at the Bamboo Club in Lake Charles and so impressed the charismatic Redding that he absconded with her. For the next three years, Webster served as his opening act!

The 1970s were pretty much a lost decade for Katie Webster as she took care of her ailing parents in Oakland, CA. But in 1982 a European tour beckoned, and she journeyed overseas for the first of many such jaunts. The Alligator connection commenced in 1988 with some high-profile help: Bonnie Raitt, Robert Cray, and Kim Wilson all made guest appearances on *The*

Swamp Boogie Queen. The lovably extroverted boogie pianist encored with *Two-Fisted Mama!* and *No Foolin'!* before suffering the stroke. — *Bill Dahl*

You Know That's Right / Apr. 1985 / Arhoolie ◆◆◆

I Know That's Right (CD) / 1987 / Arhoolie ◆◆◆

I Know That's Right is an okay step in the venerable boogie pianist's come-back bid, but the mediocre band backing she receives on most cuts doesn't add much to the swampy brew. — *Bill Dahl*

Swamp Boogie Queen / 1988 / Alligator ◆◆◆◆

Lovable Katie Webster had some high-profile help for this impressive come-back album—Bonnie Raitt shares the vocal on "Somebody's on Your Case" and plays guitar on "On the Run," Kim Wilson duets with Webster for a cover of Johnnie Taylor's "Who's Making Love" (a track that Robert Cray contributes crisp guitar to). Throughout, Webster's vocals are throatier than they used to be (she soulfully covers one-time mentor Otis Redding's "Fa-Fa-Fa-Fa-Fa [Sad Song]" and "Try a Little Tenderness"), while her driving left hand still lays down some powerhouse boogie rhythms. — *Bill Dahl*

Two-Fisted Mama! / 1990 / Alligator ◆◆◆◆

Another impressive showcase for Katie Webster's rollicking 88s and earthy vocals. Other than the Memphis Horns, no special guests this time—just Webster and her tight trio (anchored by guitarist Vasti Jackson). — *Bill Dahl*

● **Katie Webster** / 1991 / Paula/Flyright ◆◆◆◆

Webster is at her full bayou-bred boogie-blues best here, when she was the queen of south Louisiana's swamp sessioneers. Webster's own late-'50s/early-'60s output for producer J.D. Miller was no less captivating; her self-named dance number "The Katie Lee" and "Mama Don't Allow" that uproots the Gary US Bonds party vibe to New Orleans are two of the best items on the 20-track disc. There's also her blues-drenched "No Bread, No Meat" and a nice version of "Sea of Love" (Webster added the gently rolling piano to Phil Phillips' original hit). — *Bill Dahl*

No Foolin'! / 1991 / Alligator ◆◆◆

Katie Webster is a powerful singer who can really belt out the blues, but perhaps her greatest skill is her two-handed piano solos. On this CD she is featured on a fairly wide range of material within the idiom including a zydeco-flavored blues, a sincere blues ballad ("It's Mighty Hard"), a couple of Motownish soul numbers, a rock and rollish "Those Lonely Lonely Nights" (on which she shares vocals with Lonnie Brooks) and, best of all, a variety of basic blues. Although she also contributes some atmospheric chordal organ, it is Katie Webster's piano playing that gives her music its most distinctive personality. A fun set. — *Scott Yanow*

Monster Mike Welch

b. Boston, MA

Vocals, Guitar / Modern Electric Blues

Monster Mike Welch is a Boston-area blues guitarist, vocalist, and songwriter who has released two albums on the Rounder Tone-Cool subsidiary. The fact that he's so good and hasn't yet hit 20 is part of the reason why they call him "Monster." Welch got his moniker from actor/comedian/Blues Brother Dan Aykroyd.

Welch's two releases for Tone-Cool, which essentially launched his career as an international touring act, include a 1996 release, *These Blues Are Mine*, and his 1997 album *Axe to Grind.*

He began his blues education with his father's record collection, and he picked up the guitar at age eight and tried to emulate the sounds he heard from recordings by Magic Sam, Earl Hooker, and B.B. King. Welch also studied the rock 'n' roll and blues-rock records of the Beatles and the Rolling Stones, but after hearing more of Albert King and other blues guitarists, he found his calling in life.

When he was 11, his parents began driving him to blues jams around Boston. In the clubs, Welch learned from some of the greats of that scene, including Ronnie Earl and Luther "Guitar Jr." Johnson. Welch was invited to play at the opening of the first House of Blues club in Cambridge, Mass. in 1992. After co-owner Aykroyd heard him, his nickname changed from "Little Mikey" to "Monster Mike."

A few months later, Welch began working with George Lewis, who ran the blues jams at House of Blues, to put together the Monster Mike Welch Band. Welch is accompanied on his records by Lewis on guitar, Jon Ross on bass, and Warren Grant on drums. Welch's biting, stinging Albert King-style

guitar playing has better-than-average backing from these three on his two Tone-Cool releases.

The crop of original songs he wrote on his first two albums for Tone-Cool demonstrate his prowess as a crafty blues songwriter. Whether he decides to go on to college or not, Welch has a bright future. All indications are that Welch, who got a flood of publicity because of his age, and was even quoted in *People* magazine—"being an adolescent is more than enough blues for anyone to handle"—should go on to a lengthy and varied career as a blues-man. — *Richard Skelly*

● **These Blues Are Mine** / 1996 / Tone-Cool ◆◆◆◆

He was only 16 years old at the time of release, but you wouldn't know it from the way he plays guitar—this kid has the chops some seasoned professionals dream of, and has gained a lot of respect for them. The big problem comes when he opens his mouth to sing—he does a creditable job of trying to nail down that rough blues vocal tone, but he more often than not sounds just like a kid trying to get to a grown-up voice. Meanwhile, his band is well-worn and the songwriting is definitely up to par. — *Steven McDonald*

Axe to Grind / Feb. 11, 1997 / Tone-Cool ◆◆◆

Casey Bill Weldon

b. Jul. 10, 1909, Alaska, **d.** 196?

Vocals, Guitar (Steel) / Acoustic Blues, Prewar Country Blues, Country Blues, Acoustic Chicago Blues

Among the premier "Hawaiian" guitarists, Will "Casey Bill" Weldon's voicings, fluidity, and tunings were creative and imaginative, as were his arrangements. He was married to Memphis Minnie in the '20s, and they made some superb recordings together in the late '20s. Weldon played in medicine shows before beginning his recording career in 1927 for Victor. There were later dates for Champion, Vocalion and Bluebird. Weldon recorded and played with the Memphis Jug Band, Charlie Burse and the Picaninny Jug Band, and the Brown Bombers of Swing. He moved to the West Coast in the '40s and purportedly recorded for several soundtracks. Weldon moved to Detroit and left the music world in the '60s. — *Ron Wynn*

Complete Recorded Works, Vol. 1 / Jun. 2, 1994 / Document ◆◆◆

Complete Recorded Works, Vol. 2 / Jun. 2, 1994 / Document ◆◆◆

Complete Recorded Works, Vol. 3 / Jun. 2, 1994 / Document ◆◆◆

● **Bottleneck Guitar Trendsetters of the 1930's** / Yazoo ◆◆◆◆

Outstanding bottleneck guitar and above-average singing from Casey Bill Weldon, one of the least publicized but tremendous prewar stylists. — *Ron Wynn*

Valerie Wellington

b. Nov. 14, 1959, Chicago, IL, **d.** Jan. 3, 1991, Maywood, IL

Vocals / Modern Electric Blues, Modern Electric Chicago Blues

Valerie Wellington took the Chicago blues scene by surprise in 1982, perhaps not forgoing her classical training as an opera singer as much as using it to enhance her work in the blues. As a blueswoman she fit right in, not only becoming a regular in the blues clubs but also compiling an impressive the-atrical resume for her portrayals of Ma Rainey and Bessie Smith—women who, like opera singers, learned to project their voices without microphones. The influence of Koko Taylor has also been evident in Wellington's blues approach, which combines classic vaudeville-era blues with hard-driving Chicago sounds. Her power-packed voice has been heard on only a few re-cord releases but has been featured frequently in TV and radio commercials. — *Jim O'Neal*

● **Million Dollar $ecret** / Oct. 1984 / Flying Fish ◆◆◆◆

Wellington is a powerful yet subtle vocalist, backed by some of the best Chicago blues players, including Sunnyland Slim, Billy Branch, Casey Jones, and Magic Slim & the Teardrops. The CD reissue contains two bonus tracks. — *Niles J. Frantz*

Life in the Big City / 1991 / GBW ◆◆

Want to hear the late Chicago belter warble "Trouble in Mind" in Japanese? That's the strongest track on her last disc, but much of the set is pretty mun-dane. — *Bill Dahl*

Junior Wells (Amos Blackmore)

b. Dec. 9, 1934, Memphis, TN, d. Jan. 15, 1998, Chicago, IL
Harmonica, Vocals / R&B, Electric Chicago Blues, Modern Electric Chicago Blues, Modern Electric Blues, Blues Revival, Harmonica Blues

He was one bad dude, strutting across the stage like a harp-toting gangster, mesmerizing the crowd with his tough-guy antics and rib-sticking Chicago blues attack. Amazingly, Junior Wells kept at precisely this sort of thing for over 40 years—he was an active performer from the dawn of the 1950s to his death in the late '90s.

Born in Memphis, Wells learned his earliest harp licks from another future legend, Little Junior Parker, before he came to Chicago at age 12. In 1950, the teenager passed an impromptu audition for guitarists Louis and David Myers at a house party on the South side, and the Deuces were born. When drummer Fred Below came aboard, they changed their name to the Aces.

Little Walter left Muddy Waters in 1952 (in the wake of his hit instrumental, "Juke"), and Wells jumped ship to take his place with Waters. That didn't stop the Aces (who joined forces with Little Walter) from backing Wells on his initial sessions for States Records, though—his debut date produced some seminal Chicago blues efforts, including his first reading of "Hoodoo Man," a rollicking "Cut That Out," and the blazing instrumentals "Eagle Rock" and "Junior's Wail."

More fireworks ensued the next year when he encored for States with a mournful "So All Alone" and the jumping "Lawdy! Lawdy!" (Muddy Waters moonlighted on guitar for the session). Already Wells was exhibiting his tempestuous side—he was allegedly AWOL from the Army at the time.

In 1957, Wells hooked up with producer Mel London, who owned the Chief and Profile logos. The association resulted in many of Wells' most enduring sides, including "I Could Cry" and the rock 'n' rolling "Lovey Dovey Lovely One" in 1957; the grinding national R&B hit "Little by Little" (with Willie Dixon providing vocal harmony) in 1959, and the R&B-laced classic "Messin' with the Kid" in 1960 (sporting Earl Hooker's immaculate guitar work). Wells' harp was de-emphasized during this period on record in favor of his animated vocals.

With Bob Koester producing, the harpist cut an all-time classic LP for Delmark in 1965. *Hoodoo Man Blues* vividly captured the feel of a typical Wells set at Theresa's Lounge, even though it was cut in a studio. With Buddy Guy (initially billed as "Friendly Chap" due to his contract with Chess) providing concise lead guitar, Wells laid down definitive versions of "Snatch It Back and Hold It," "You Don't Love Me," and "Chittlin' Con Carne."

The harpist made his second appearance on the national R&B lists in 1968 with a James Brown-tinged piece, "You're Tuff Enough," for Mercury's feisty Blue Rock logo. Wells had been working in this bag for some time, alarming the purists but delighting R&B fans; his brass-powered 1966 single for Bright Star, "Up in Heah," had previously made a lot of local noise.

After a fine mid-'70s set for Delmark (*On Tap*), little was heard from Wells on vinyl for an extended spell, though he continued to enjoy massive appeal at home (Theresa's was his principal haunt for many a moon) and abroad (whether on his own or in partnership with Guy; they opened for the Rolling Stones on one memorable tour and cut an inconsistent but interesting album for Atco in the early '70s).

Toward the end of his career, Wells just didn't seem to be into recording anymore; a pair of sets for Telarc in the early '90s were major disappointments, but his last studio session, 1997's *Come on in This House*, found him on the rebound and the critics noticed—the album won the W.C. Handy Blues Award for Traditional Blues Album in 1997. Even when he came up short in the studio, Wells remained a potent live attraction, cutting a familiar swaggering figure, commanding the attention of everyone in the room with one menacing yelp or a punctuating blast from his amplified harmonica. He continued performing until he was diagnosed with lymphatic cancer in the summer of 1997. That fall, he suffered a heart attack while undergoing treatment, sending him into a coma. Wells stayed in the coma until he passed away on January 15, 1998. A handful of compilations were released shortly after his death, as was the film *Blues Brothers 2000*, which featured a cameo by Wells. —*Bill Dahl*

★ **Hoodoo Man Blues** / 1965 / Delmark ✦✦✦✦✦
One of the truly classic blues albums of the 1960s, and one of the first to fully document the smoky ambience of a night at a West side nightspot in the superior acoustics of a recording studio. Wells just set up with his usual

cohorts—guitarist Buddy Guy (billed as "Friendly Chap" on first vinyl pressings), bassist Jack Myers, and drummer Billy Warren—and proceeded to blow up a storm, bringing an immediacy to "Snatch It Back and Hold It," "You Don't Love Me," "Chitlin Con Carne," and the rest that is absolutely mesmerizing. —*Bill Dahl*

It's My Life, Baby / 1966 / Vanguard ✦✦✦
Partly live from Pepper's Lounge in Chicago, with Buddy Guy and Freddy Below. Junior's first Vanguard album. —*Barry Lee Pearson*

You're Tuff Enough / 1968 / Blue Rock ✦✦✦✦
Another period of the veteran Chicago harp man's career that awaits CD documentation—and one of the most exciting. Wells' late-'60s output for Bright Star and Mercury's Blue Rock subsidiary frequently found him mining funky James Brown grooves (with a bluesy base, of course) to great effect—"Up in Heah" and his national smash "You're Tuff Enough" are marvelous examples of his refusal to bend to purists' wishes (though there's a glorious version of Bobby Bland's blues-soaked "You're the One" that benefits handily from Sammy Lawhorn's delicate guitar work). —*Bill Dahl*

Comin' at You / 1968 / Vanguard ✦✦✦
Another eminently solid outing by the legendary harpist that captures his trademark persona in a studio setting. The band is quite tight—Buddy Guy and Lefty Dizz are the guitarists, Douglas Fagan plays sax, and Clark Terry, believe it or not, occupies a third of the trumpet section—and the set list is dominated by oldies from both Sonny Boys, Willie Dixon, and John D. Loudermilk (Junior invests his "Tobacco Road" with a lights-out toughness that Nashville Teens could never even imagine). —*Bill Dahl*

Live at the Golden Bear / Dec. 1969 / Blue Rock ✦✦✦
The swaggering harpman took his act on the road to Huntington Beach, CA to do this live set with his touring quartet of the moment. Virtually nothing but blues and soul standards that show his wide stylistic range—alongside tunes by Muddy Waters, both Sonny Boys and the Wolf resides an impassioned reading of James Brown's "Please, Please, Please." —*Bill Dahl*

South Side Blues Jam / 1970 / Delmark ✦✦✦
Enjoyable but less electrifying follow-up to *Hoodoo Man Blues*, cut in 1969-1970—looser, with longer songs that afford more room to stretch out instrumentally but don't quite equal the stunning precision of what came before. Buddy Guy returns on guitar; Otis Spann is the pianist, and Fred Below keeps superb time. —*Bill Dahl*

In My Younger Days / 1972 / Red Lightnin' ✦✦
Good collection of 16 early sides from 1953-62. The earliest tracks are straight blues, and Wells at his most conventional. Starting with the late-'50s performances, he began to broaden his influences into his trademark blend of blues, R&B, rock, and even some Latin music. Earl Hooker lends his guitar to the early-'60s tracks, which are highlighted by the original version of his signature tune, "Messin' with the Kid." —*Richie Unterberger*

Play the Blues / 1972 / Atlantic ✦✦✦
Buddy Guy and Junior Wells seldom made more effective records than this celebrated album (reissued on CD in 1992). There were none of the erratic vocals, questionable song selection or rambling solos that sometimes plagued their live shows. Wells was sizzling and aggressive as lead vocalist, Guy's solos were controlled and disciplined, yet strikingly effective in uptempo and ballad situations, while saxophonist A.C. Reed provided soulful and shattering fills and solos behind the vocalists and during the interludes. They were helped by assorted rock luminaries from Eric Clapton, J. Geils and Magic Dick to Dr. John. This deserves a place among the other tremendous items in the Rhino/Atlantic R&B Masters series. —*Ron Wynn*

On Tap / Mar. 1975 / Delmark ✦✦✦
Underrated mid-'70s collection boasting a contemporary, funky edge driven by guitarists Phil Guy and Sammy Lawhorn, keyboardist Big Moose Walker, and saxman A.C. Reed. Especially potent is the crackling "The Train I Ride," a kissin' cousin to Little Junior Parker's "Mystery Train." —*Bill Dahl*

Blues Hit Big Town / 1977 / Delmark ✦✦✦✦
Why isn't this seminal collection of the harpist's earliest 1953-1954 sides for States Records available on CD? Its Chicago blues treasures include Wells' first waxing of "Hoodoo Man," a jumping "Cut That Out" and "Tomorrow Night," and slashing showcases for the young bluesman's amplified harp: "Eagle Rock," "Junior's Wail." Junior's sidemen are the absolute cream of

the crop—Muddy Waters, the Aces, Elmore James, pianists Otis Spann and Johnny Jones—making these 12 sides all the more indispensable. —*Bill Dahl*

Pleading the Blues / Oct. 31, 1979 / Isabel ✦✦✦
Recorded on Halloween night in 1979, this pairs up Wells and Guy in a fashion that hasn't been heard since *Hoodoo Man Blues*, their first, and best collaboration. Solid backing by the Philip Guy band (Buddy's brother) makes this album a rare treat. —*Cub Koda*

Drinkin' TNT 'n Smokin' Dynamite / Jun. 1982 / Blind Pig ✦✦✦
Live at Montreux, featuring Jr. and Buddy. —*Bill Dahl*

Harp Attack! / 1990 / Alligator ✦✦✦✦
Along with his Windy City peers James Cotton, Carey Bell, and Billy Branch, Wells trades harp solos and vocals on this raucous meeting of the minds. Junior's front and center on a fine rendition of Sonny Boy II's "Keep Your Hands Out of My Pockets" and the tailor-made "Somebody Changed the Lock" and "Broke and Hungry," obviously relishing the camaraderie between himself and his fellow harmonica giants. —*Bill Dahl*

● **1957-1966** / 1991 / Paula ✦✦✦✦
The indispensable sides for Mel London's Profile, Chief, and Age labels (and a few for USA Records that directly followed). Backed by a modern-sounding crew that included immaculate guitarist Earl Hooker, saxist A.C. Reed, and keyboardist Johnny "Big Moose" Walker. Wells enjoyed a considerable R&B hit with the grinding "Little by Little," glides atop a churning rhythm groove on the original "Messin' with the Kid," rocks "Lovey Dovey Lovely One," and the hokey-but-fun "I Need Me a Car," and blows some husky amplified harmonica on "Cha Cha Cha in Blue" and "Calling All Blues." —*Bill Dahl*

Alone & Acoustic / 1991 / Alligator ✦✦✦

Undisputed Godfather of the Blues / Dec. 1992 / GBW ✦✦✦
About half is a decent Junior Wells album. The other half's mired in hopelessly overdone standards that we've heard a few too many times before—but every once in a while, he exhibits signs of the old fire. —*Bill Dahl*

Better Off with the Blues / Jun. 1993 / Telarc ✦✦
Remarkably mundane effort that leaves one with the impression that Wells didn't care a whole lot about making this disc. Even the presence of Buddy Guy, Lucky Peterson, and bassist Johnny B. Gayden can't save the overly slick set, where Wells waxes one more "Messin' with the Kid," a dire reading of the country/soul standby "Today I Started Loving You Again," and a way-too-long title track. —*Bill Dahl*

Come on in This House / Feb. 1997 / Telarc ✦✦✦✦
Junior Wells' penchant for clowning around sometimes conflicts with his craftsmanship, but he's all business on *Come On In This House*, his most unadulterated blues record since his highly acclaimed *Hoodoo Man Blues* of more than 30 years vintage. This is what has come to be known as an "unplugged" session—that is, predominately, although not exclusively, acoustic instrumentation. Producer John Snyder's concept was threefold: (1) to team Wells with some of the era's top younger traditional blues guitarists—Corey Harris, Alvin Youngblood Hart, Sonny Landreth, Bob Margolin, and John Mooney, (2) to have those musicians, in various combinations, accompany Wells on a variety of slide guitars, and (3) to concentrate on vintage Chicago and Delta blues from the repertoires of Rice Miller, Little Walter, Tampa Red, Arthur Crudup, and Wells himself. The result is a virtual slide-guitar mini-fest and a demonstration of the timeless appeal of classic blues done well. Wells' vocals are deep and manly; his harp playing is high-pitched, like a child's pleading. A surprising highlight is the only contemporary tune on the disc, Tracy Chapman's "Give Me One Reason." New Orleans drummer Herman Ernest III, who appears on 11 of the 14 cuts, does a masterful job laying down understated rhythmic grooves. —*Steve Hoffman*

Live at Buddy Guy's Legends / Jun. 24, 1997 / Telarc ✦✦✦
Backed by a funk-minded, James Brown-influenced band, Junior Wells is in good form on these live recordings from Buddy Guy's Legends in Chicago. Wells (who was 61 when this CD was recorded) really comes alive in front of a live audience, and he's certainly in a very extroverted mood on such familiar material as "Hoodoo Man," "Little By Little," and his signature tune, "Messin' With the Kid." Wells has been one of Brown's most ardent admirers for a long time, and he frequently shows his love of the Godfather's soul/funk innovations without letting us forget that he's a bluesman first and

foremost. Although this CD doesn't offer a lot of surprises, it's an invigorating documentation of the energy and passion Wells brings to the stage. —*Alex Henderson*

Keep on Steppin': The Best of Junior Wells / Feb. 24, 1998 / Telarc ✦✦✦
The title's a bit of a ringer here; this is actually what Telarc considers the best tracks Wells recorded for their label between 1993 and 1997. Taken from his last four albums before his untimely death in early 1998, Wells won a fair amount of trophies with this quartet of albums, and while the material isn't anything that's going to make a hardline fan want to toss out their copies of *Hoodoo Man Blues*, the music and production are exemplary on every track. Guest appearances proliferate on every number and the work from Sonny Landreth, John Mooney, Derek Trucks, Lucky Peterson, Corey Harris, Bob Margolin, and Carlos Santana keep these tunes on firmly contemporary footing. —*Cub Koda*

Best of the Vanguard Years / Mar. 10, 1998 / Vanguard ✦✦✦✦
Best of the Vanguard Years collects Junior Wells' material from the *Chicago! The Blues! Today!* various-artists series, live and studio tracks from the albums *It's My Life, Baby!* and *Comin' at You*, and a smattering of rare and/or unreleased cuts. As a Wells retrospective, it's irredeemably incomplete, covering as it does his output for only one label, but the fine-quality material does make it an engaging listen, and it may be a good way for some collectors to plug holes in their Wells discographies. —*Steve Huey*

Everybody's Gettin' Some / Telarc ✦✦
Makes his prior Telarc offering look like a masterpiece by comparison. A passel of superfluous guest stars—Bonnie Raitt, Carlos Santana, Sonny Landreth—unite to produce the most worthless Wells album ever down in Louisiana rather than in Wells' Chicago stomping grounds. Why he wanted to remake songs from the songbooks of WAR and Bill Withers is a mystery better left for future generations to ponder. —*Bill Dahl*

Peetie "The Devil's Son-In-Law" Wheatstraw
(William Bunch)

b. Dec. 21, 1902, Ripley, TN, **d.** Dec. 21, 1941, East St. Louis, IL
Piano, Vocals / Piano Blues, Acoustic Memphis Blues, Prewar Country Blues
A very popular bluesman in the '30s and early '40s, pianist Peetie Wheatstraw's signature vocal phrase, "Oh well well," was adapted by several bluesmen, Muddy Waters among them.

Born William Bunch, Peetie Wheatstraw arrived in East St. Louis around 1929, when he was about 27 years old; not much is known about his life before that date, although it is speculated that he was raised in Cotton Plant, AR. When he arrived in East St. Louis, the pianist adopted the Peetie Wheatstraw name, which derives from an old folk story.

Inspired by the success of the guitar/piano duets of Scrapper Blackwell and Leroy Carr, Wheatstraw set out to find a guitarists to collaborate with. He wound up playing with a number of different musicians—including Kokomo Arnold, Charlie McCoy, Bumble Bee Slim, Casey Bill Weldon, and Charley Jordan—but his primary collaborator was Lonnie Johnson. Wheatstraw recorded with all of these guitarists, releasing records on Decca, Vocalion, and Bluebird throughout the '30s. His records were quite popular, largely due to his unique, laidback singing and his provocative lyrics.

At the height of his popularity in 1941, Peetie Wheatstraw was killed when his car was hit by an oncoming train at a railroad crossing. After his death, his distinctive vocal phrasing lived on in the music of everyone from Big Bill Broonzy and Champion Jack Dupree to Muddy Waters and Johnny Shines. —*Cub Koda & Stephen Thomas Erlewine*

Complete Works, Vol. 1 / May 1, 1995 / Document ✦✦✦

Complete Works, Vol. 2 / May 1, 1995 / Document ✦✦✦

Complete Works, Vol. 3 / May 1, 1995 / Document ✦✦✦

Complete Works, Vol. 4 / May 1, 1995 / Document ✦✦✦

Complete Works, Vol. 5 / May 1, 1995 / Document ✦✦✦

Complete Works, Vol. 6 / May 1, 1995 / Document ✦✦✦

Complete Works, Vol. 7 / May 1, 1995 / Document ✦✦✦

The Blues / 1997 / Fremeaux ✦✦✦✦
This 36-song double-CD collection from France is the most comprehensive collection of Wheatstraw's music available, covering a significant spread of his music from 1931 until 1941 and his moves from St. Louis to Chicago

and New York. The self-proclaimed "Devil's Son In Law" is represented by the song of that name and its B-side, "Peetie Wheatstraw," on the opening two tracks—the mastering is very clean, sufficient to give Charlie McCoy's guitar a hearing. Wheatstraw's own guitar—seldom recorded—is heard as a rhythm instrument surrounded by trumpet and violin on the jazzy "Throw Me in the Alley," from 1934. Some of the later recordings on disc two, dating from 1939 on, also feature blues/jazz crossover legend Lonnie Johnson on guitar and jazz trumpet man Jonah Jones. The sound is surprisingly good throughout, the notes are, alas, only partly in English, but the $20 price is just right. (French import) —*Bruce Eder*

● **The Devil's Son-in-Law** / Blues Document ◆◆◆◆
Blues Document's *The Devil's Son-In-Law* (not to be confused with Best of Blues' similarly titled effort) is a strong overview of Peetie Wheatstraw's recordings between 1930 and 1941, containing a total of 20 tracks. The collection does a nice job of balancing his piano, guitar and vocal efforts, containing such signature tracks as "Ooh Well, Well," "Meat Cutter Blues," "Beggar Man Blues," and "I Want Some Sea Food." —*Stephen Thomas Erlewine*

Whispering Smith

b. Jan. 25, 1932, Brookhaven, MS, **d.** Apr. 28, 1984, Baton Rouge, LA
Harmonica, Vocals / Electric Swamp Blues, Electric Louisiana Blues
Harpist Whispering Smith made it in on the tail end of the swamp blues movement that swept the Baton Rouge region, working with Lightnin' Slim and Silas Hogan before making his own fine singles for Crowley, LA, producer J.D. Miller.

Alternating down-in-the-bayou entries such as "Mean Woman Blues" (not the Elvis Presley/Roy Orbison rocker), "I Tried So Hard," and "Don't Leave Me Baby" with the storming instrumentals "Live Jive" (also featuring the fleet guitar of Ulysses Williams) and "Hound Dog Twist," Smith was an excellent performer who arrived in Crowley just a trifle late, after the heyday of the swamp blues sound.

Excello decided to give swamp music another try in 1970 without Miller's expert supervision, inviting Smith back to cut an LP in Baton Rouge that just didn't live up to his former glory. —*Bill Dahl*

Over Easy / 1971 / Blue Horizon ◆◆◆◆

Artie White

b. Apr. 16, 1937, Vicksburg, MS
Vocals / Soul, R&B, Soul Blues, Electric Blues
Very few Chicago blues artists were able to pierce the R&B charts during the 1970s, when interest in the genre was at rock-bottom. But smooth-voiced Artie "Blues Boy" White managed the rare feat with his 1977 single for Altee, "Leanin' Tree."

Gospel was White's initial musical pursuit. He sang with a spiritual aggregation, the Harps of David, at the age of 11 prior to coming to Chicago in 1956. More church singing was in store for White with the Full Gospel Wonders. The singer claims that he was lured into singing the devil's music by a well-heeled gent who drove up to an unsuspecting White in a flashy Cadillac and promised him $10,000 to record some blues songs!

White's '70s singles for PM and Gamma stiffed, but with the advent of "Leanin' Tree," White was able to command a nice asking price on the Chicago circuit (and still does). For a while, White tried his hand at running a blues club, Bootsy's Lounge. But performing and recording won out; White waxed a terrific debut LP in 1985 for Shreveport-based Ronn Records called *Blues Boy.*

White signed with Ichiban in 1987 and waxed six fine sets in the soul-blues vein (enough to merit a *Best Of* CD in 1991, which made seven), utilizing Chicago songwriter Bob Jones (the composer of "Leanin' Tree") and labelmate Travis Haddix as chief sources of material. On 1989's *Thangs Got to Change*, White enjoyed the presence of Little Milton Campbell, one of his prime influences, on lead guitar. —*Bill Dahl*

Blues Boy / 1985 / Ronn ◆◆◆◆
Blues Boy's first album, dating back to the mid-'80s, also ranks as one of his most soulfully satisfying, thanks to the contemporary grooves of a Chicago outfit called Amuzement Park and White's smoky, Little Milton-influenced vocal delivery. He delivers a fine remake of his own modern blues "Leaning

Tree" and Little Beaver's "Jimmie" and adapts Aretha Franklin's "Chain of Fools" to his own rich vocal range. —*Bill Dahl*

Nothing Takes the Place of You / 1987 / Ichiban ◆◆◆
Artie White's Ichiban debut is typically confident and soulful. Along with standards by Toussaint McCall and Willie Nelson, White does a solid job on a sheaf of original material and Z.Z. Hill's anguished "I Need Someone." —*Bill Dahl*

Where It's at / 1989 / Ichiban ◆◆◆
Sam Cooke, Clarence Carter, and Al Green receive the cover treatment this time, but White and his usual cohorts (writers Bob Jones and Travis Haddix, in addition to the singer himself) penned the majority of the fine blues-soul set. A fine band helps, too: guitarists Criss Johnson and Pete Allen and a six-piece horn section led by Willie Henderson frame White's husky vocals beautifully. —*Bill Dahl*

Thangs Got to Change / 1989 / Ichiban ◆◆◆
Little Milton Campbell—one of Artie White's principal influences and advisors—wrote a good portion of this typically solid soul-blues collection, and White covers numbers by Lowell Fulson, Brook Benton, and B.B. King for flavor. —*Bill Dahl*

Tired of Sneaking Around / 1990 / Ichiban ◆◆◆◆
White is a B.B. King-sounding singer, with an original overall sound, who makes great records with big-band feel. There's lots of horns and stuff. —*Niles J. Frantz*

● **The Best of Artie White** / 1991 / Ichiban ◆◆◆◆
A well-selected 12-song overview of White's prolific tenure at Ichiban. His delivery, pitched somewhere between blues and soul, is equally effective on the contemporary blues-based items "Hattie Mae" and "Jodie," the soul-slanted "Dark End of the Street" (though he can't give James Carr a run for his money in the intensity department) and Toussaint McCall's tender "Nothing Takes the Place of You." —*Bill Dahl*

Dark End of the Street / 1991 / Ichiban ◆◆◆◆
Whether it's blues, soul, or something midway between the two, White does a fine job throughout this disc. Travis Haddix, once White's Ichiban labelmate, contributes three nice tunes, Bob Jones a couple more, and White dips into past triumphs by B.B. King, Ike Turner, James Carr, and Little Milton for the rest. —*Bill Dahl*

Hit & Run / 1992 / Ichiban ◆◆◆◆
Without a great deal of fanfare, Artie White released a steady stream of quality contemporary releases on Ichiban, each straddling the sometimes imperceptible fence between blues and deep soul. This one's no exception—backed by a Chicago combo called Masheen Co., White delivers originals penned by Travis Haddix, Bob Jones (the title cut), and himself in assured, smooth style. —*Bill Dahl*

Different Shades of Blue / 1994 / Waldoxy ◆◆◆

Back Home to Clarksdale, A Tribute to Muddy Walters / Feb. 25, 1997 / Waldoxy ◆◆◆◆

Bukka White (Booket T. Washington White)

b. Nov. 12, 1906, Houston, MS, **d.** Feb. 26, 1977, Memphis, TN
Guitar, Harmonica, Piano, Vocals / Delta Blues, Prewar Country Blues
Achieving a distinctive musical voice is a highly prized blues value, yet few artists develop an easily recognizable vocal and instrumental style that is uniquely theirs. Bukka White was one of those remarkable artists with an overall approach and composition style that were unusual, yet he was a popular houseparty musician and a successful recording artist. Although he had a second career during the blues revival and remained a powerful performer, his best work was on his 1937 and 1940 Vocalion sides, reissued by Columbia. They feature down-home country-blues at its best, personal, moving, and instrumentally compelling. White's percussive approach to his open G-tuned steel National can be imitated but not duplicated. Like other Delta artists, White's sound was melodically simple but rhythmically complex. Sporting an attack vaguely reminiscent of Big Joe Williams, White worked his guitar like a drum, adding rhythmic nuances with his chording hand on the guitar neck. On his '40s session, he added further percussive rhythm. Many of White's pieces employ spoken or chanted passages, especially his train songs, which combined talking blues and train effects. His compositions generally

either fall outside mainstream blues or bridge sacred and secular traditions, as in his classic "Fixing to Die." Moody and introspective, his songs let you into his life, detailing his experiences as a prisoner at Mississippi's notorious Parchman Farm or as a hobo riding the rails. His dance songs, such as "Bukka's Jitterbug Swing," aptly demonstrate his skills as a houseparty performer and bear out his reputation as a breakdown artist, which means people danced so hard to his beat that they literally broke the floors down at the jukes and plantation balls over which he reigned. —*Barry Lee Pearson*

Sky Songs, Vol. 1 / Nov. 1963 / Arhoolie ✦✦✦
White's material on *Sky Songs* is almost wholly improvised, resulting in seven epic tracks—powerful stuff. —*Jason Ankeny*

☆ **Legacy of the Blues** / 1969 / Sonet ✦✦✦✦✦
A CD reissue of the recordings that led to Bukka White's rediscovery, made by Ed Denson and John Fahey at a Memphis rooming house in 1963, nearly a quarter century after his last recordings. White is in astonishingly good form, as both a singer and guitarist—his rendition of "Baby Please Don't Go" is closer to what one by Howlin' Wolf might have sounded like, with an almost palpable fury and desperation, and none of the cultured smoothness of the familiar versions by Big Joe Williams or Muddy Waters. "Aberdeen Mississippi Blues," "New Orleans Streamline," "Parchman Farm Blues," and "Shake 'em on Down" have an almost preternatural power, and White gets his one acoustic guitar to make sounds one would expect should require two or three. Of almost equal importance, he reminisces about Charley Patton for several minutes. Denson and Fahey caught this blues master at the right time, just the right moment, rising to the sudden occasion to make a new record, spontaneous and unplanned, and got something about as valuable as any of Alan Lomax's field recordings of the 1940s. [Note: These recordings may be available at some point on domestic labels as well as this Sonet import from England]. —*Bruce Eder*

☆ **Parchman Farm** / 1970 / Columbia ✦✦✦✦✦
Brilliant country blues from Bukka White, whose churning, rousing vocal approach was complemented by a crackling guitar style. —*Ron Wynn*

☆ **The Complete Sessions 1930-1940** / 1976 / Travelin' Man ✦✦✦✦✦
Travelin' Man's *Complete Sessions 1930-1940* is a strong, 20-track collection of Bukka White's earliest recordings. Although the sound is a little raw, the music itself has lost none of its power over the years. Many of his greatest songs—"Shake 'em on Down," "Pinebluff, Arkansas," "Parchman Farm Blues," "Fixin' to Die," "New Frisco Train," and "I Am in the Heavenly Way"—are here in arguably their best versions. This is a valuable disc, but it may be difficult to find. In that case, Columbia/Legacy's *Complete Bukka White* may be a good substitute, since it contains 14 of this disc's 20 tracks. —*Thom Owens*

Three Shades of Blues / 1989 / Biograph ✦✦✦
Three Shades of Blues comprises a selection of tracks cut by Bukka White, Skip James, and Blind Willie McTell, all recorded during different eras. James' tracks were made in 1964, the first he cut since 1931. James fares the worst—he sounds unsure of himself and several of the songs are painful to listen to. The five White tracks were recorded in 1974, after he was released from prison; while his voice does sound worn, they're fascinating historical items. McTell's recordings are taken from the last commerical sessions he made in 1949, and they're more than historical curiosities—he sounds as haunted and powerful as he ever has. —*Thom Owens*

Legacy of the Blues, Vol. 1 / 1991 / GNP ✦✦✦

Shake 'Em on Down / 1993 / ROIR ✦✦✦✦
This fine collection supplants *Parchman Farm* as the definitive set spotlighting Bukka White's Vocalion country blues recordings. —*Ron Wynn*

★ **The Complete Bukka White** / 1994 / Columbia ✦✦✦✦✦
All of Bukka White's landmark recordings for Vocalion and OKeh Records are collected on this brilliant single disc. —*AMG*

1963 Isn't 1962 / 1994 / Genes ✦✦✦
Bukka White was "rediscovered"—alive and well, despite rumors that he'd died a violent death sometime after his last official recording session in 1940—by blues enthusiasts John Fahey and Ed Denson. These live tapes, made late that year by Fahey and Denson, were among the first tangible results of that rediscovery. This older cousin to B.B. King still had all of his stuff—he was only in his mid-50s, and unlike a lot of older bluesmen who

were well past their primes for the '60s blues revival, he could still play and sing up a storm. Indeed, he was playing faster and more precise in 1963 than he was in 1940, and his slide work shimmers and glistens throughout this CD, and the voice is superb as well. Opening with "Streamline Special," he goes through a dazzling display of repertory, sounding like two or three players at once as he works the strings, playing lead and rhythm simultaneously on his acoustic guitar, in pieces running anywhere from a minute and a half to eight minutes or more. King has admitted trying to recreate White's sound with an electric playing, but these tapes show just how much of a losing battle that was, against this acoustic guitar virtuoso. —*Bruce Eder*

Aberdeen Mississippi Blues / Travelin' Man ✦✦✦
Aberdeen Mississippi Blues collects some of the sessions he cut in 1937 for Vocalion. Although the music is superb, it is available in better collections. —*Thom Owens*

Josh White

b. Feb. 11, 1908, Greenville, MS, **d.** Sep. 5, 1969, Manhasset, NY
Guitar, Vocals / Folk-Blues, Piedmont Blues
Most blues enthusiasts think of Josh White as a folk revival artist. It's true that the second half of his music career found him based in New York playing to the coffeehouse and cabaret set and hanging out with Burl Ives, Woody Guthrie, and fellow transplanted blues artists Sonny Terry and Brownie McGhee. When I saw him in Chicago in the 1960s his shirt was unbuttoned to his waist à la Harry Belafonte and his repertoire consisted of folk revival standards such as "Scarlet Ribbons." He was a show business personality—a star renowned for his sexual magnetism and his dramatic vocal presentations. What many people don't know is that Josh White was a major figure in the Piedmont blues tradition. The first part of his career saw him as apprentice and lead boy to some of the greatest blues and religious artists ever, including Willie Walker, Blind Blake, Blind Joe Taggart (with whom he recorded), and allegedly even Blind Lemon Jefferson. On his own, he recorded both blues and religious songs, including a classic version of "Blood Red River." A fine guitar technician with an appealing voice, he became progressively more sophisticated in his presentation. Like many other Carolinians and Virginians who moved north to urban areas, he took up city ways, remaining a fine musician if no longer a down-home artist. Like several other canny blues players, he used his roots music to broaden and enhance his life experience, and his talent was such that he could choose the musical idiom that was most lucrative at the time. —*Barry Lee Pearson*

Complete Recorded Works, Vol. 1 (1929-1933) / Jun. 2, 1994 / Document ✦✦✦

Complete Recorded Works, Vol. 2 (1933-1935) / Jun. 2, 1994 / Document ✦✦✦

Complete Recorded Works, Vol. 3 (1935-1940) / Jun. 2, 1994 / Document ✦✦✦

Roots of the Blues / Sep. 27, 1994 / Legacy ✦✦✦✦

Complete Recorded Works, Vol. 4 (1940-41) / Nov. 30, 1995 / Document ✦✦✦✦

★ **The Legendary Josh White** / 1996 / MCA ✦✦✦✦✦
This is a two-record set that has a good sampling of White's major songs. —*Michael Erlewine*

Blues Singer 1932-1936 / Feb. 6, 1996 / Sony/Legacy ✦✦✦✦
The suave and debonair blues sex symbol in his earliest and purest period, when the Piedmont influence was at its peak in his playing. This is strong stuff, eons away from the collegiate crowd-pleasing folkie stuff he engaged in during the '60s: "Milk Cow Blues," "Lazy Black Snake Blues," and "Silicosis Is Killin' Me" are acoustic solo blues of a consistently high quality, and there are a few religious tunes thrown in to spotlight the other side of White's early recording activities. —*Bill Dahl*

Complete Recorded Works, Vol. 5 (1944) / Jan. 2, 1998 / Document ✦✦✦

Complete Recorded Works, Vol. 6 (1944-1945) / Jan. 2, 1998 / Document ✦✦✦

Free & Equal Blues / Mar. 17, 1998 / Smithsonian/Folkways ✦✦✦✦
Josh White's smooth delivery stands out in the folk-blues canon. It deftly straddles the more accessible pop sound of the Ink Spots and the roots edge of Leadbelly. This collection gathers his Folkways recordings from the '40s,

which are often remarkable in their stylistic range. Of particular note is the jazzy "Minute Man," with a combo featuring Mary Lou Williams on piano. — *Tim Sheridan*

Lavelle White

b. Jul. 3, 1929, Amite, LA
Vocals / Chicago Blues
Texas-based vocalist and songwriter "Miss" Lavelle White has a significant discography of singles, most dating back to the 1950s and '60s, but she only released her first full length album, *Miss Lavelle*, on the Austin, Texas-based Antone's label in 1994. To say the album has been a long time coming would be the understatement of the year, for White's talents as a songwriter and singer were well-known in 1950s Houston, where she recorded several singles for the Duke/Peacock labels. In the late '50s, her labelmates included Bobby "Blue" Bland, B.B. King, and Junior Parker. *Miss Lavelle* was White's first recording of any kind, in fact, in 30 years. The fact that it's a gorgeous album helped White play some large blues festivals in the last couple of years across the US, Canada, and Europe, but for a number of years when she had no record deal, White continued to enterain club crowds with her singing in Chicago, Texas, Louisiana, and Florida.

White's first big break as a vocalist came about with something she wrote for herself, "If I Could Be with You," and a procession of other singles followed for the Duke/Peacock label, including "Just Look at You Fool," "Stop These Teardrops," and "The Tide of Love." Unlike many other blues singers, White didn't get started recording until she was 25, thanks to fellow Houstonian Johnny "Clyde" Copeland, who brought White to Duke/Peacock owner Don Robey's attention.

White, now in her 50s, began writing poems and songs when she was 12, she said in a 1994 interview.

"Hardships in life made me start to write," she explained, "and the first record I cut was with a gospel group, 'Precious Lord, Lead Me On.'" When she was 16, White moved to Houston and fell into the city's burgeoning blues club scene with Clarence Hollimon, who now records with his wife Carol Fran for the Rounder label.

She released her first album, *Miss Lavelle*, in 1994. It was followed three years later by *It Haven't Been Easy*. — *Richard Skelly*

● **Miss Lavelle** / May 28, 1994 / Antone's ✦✦✦✦
Today, more than 30 years after she got her humble start in the blues clubs in Houston, Lavelle White sings as well as she ever did, and though she's had time off from the road over the years, she's never stopped singing or writing songs. All of this is apparent with one listen to *Miss Lavelle*. The dignified manner in which White conducts herself on stage, dressed in flashy outfits and walking about confidently, is something that was instilled in her from an early age. This respect for the stage, or stage presence, that is apparent when Miss Lavelle White performs is something the younger generation of blues players (and many rock 'n' rollers) seem to lack. — *Richard Skelly*

It Haven't Been Easy / Jan. 14, 1997 / Discovery ✦✦✦

Chris Whitley

b. Aug. 31, 1960, Houston, TX
Vocals, Guitar / Singer-Songwriter, Blues-Rock, Roots-Rock, Americana
Chris Whitley is a Texas-based singer-songwriter who initially began his career as a bluesy roots-rocker, but as his career progressed, he moved deeper into rock 'n' roll and alternative rock. Though Whitley's albums usually received postiive reviews, they rarely sold, and his tendency to rework his sound prevented him from developing a sizable cult following among singer-songwriter fans.

As a child, Whitley moved frequently through the Southeast, eventually moving with his mother to Mexico when his parents divorced when he was 11; they later settled in a log cabin in Vermont. At the age of 15, he began playing guitar, inspired by Creedence Clearwater Revival, Johnny Winter, and Jimi Hendrix, eventually learning how to play slide guitar. He quit high school a year before graduation, moving to New York City, where he busked on the streets. One of his performances was witnessed by a listener who ran a travel agency, and decided that Whitley would be a success in Belgium and offered to send him to Europe. With nothing to lose, Whitley accepted the offer.

Once in Belgium, Whitley recorded a series of albums that flip-flopped

between blues, rock, and funk. The records made him a minor success in Belgium, but he decided to return to New York anyway in 1990. He happened to meet producer Daniel Lanois later that year. Impressed by Whitley's songs, Lanois helped set up a deal with Columbia Records for the songwriter, and produced his first album. Released in the spring of 1991, Whitley's US debut *Living with the Law* was an atmospheric set of blues and folk-rock that received glowing reviews and earned him a slot opening for Tom Petty & the Heartbreakers.

Though *Living with the Law* seemed to position Chris Whitley for a breakthrough into a cult audience, he waited four years to deliver his second record, *Din of Ecstasy*. An attempt to connect with the hard-edged mainstream alternative-rock audience that developed in the years following the release of *Living with the Law*, the grunge-flavored *Din of Ecstasy*—which was released on Columbia's recently-developed "alternative" subsidiary, WORK—received mixed reviews and alienated his roots-rock audience without winning him new fans. Two years later, Whitley released *Terra Incognita*, which combined elements of his first two records. *Dirt Floor* followed in 1998. — *Stephen Thomas Erlewine*

● **Living with the Law** / Dec. 5, 1991 / Columbia ✦✦✦✦
A stirring and classy debut of well-crafted blues, which was released to a flurry of critical praise. Whitley combines dreamy storytelling with commanding electric guitar work—all with the touch of a journeyman's blues. — *Donna DiChario*

Din of Ecstasy / 1995 / Work ✦✦
On his second album, Whitley abandons the atmospheric acoustic blues-rock of his debut for a hard-hitting, grungy guitar attack. Appropriately, the songs are all about losers and hard times—it's a dark, bleak album, twisting through its songs with a grim determination. The problem is, it doesn't always work. Whitley's lyrics are still rooted in the folk-blues storytelling tradition, while his music follows the rules of contemporary hard rock, complete with start-stop dynamics and thick layers of distortion. However, he can't write riffs that equal the best of Nirvana, Pearl Jam, and Soundgarden, nor does he have melodies to rival theirs. His music works best at a lyrical level and the musical approach on *Din of Ecstasy* obscures his lyrics, making the record a muddled affair. — *Stephen Thomas Erlewine*

Terra Incognita / Feb. 18, 1997 / Sony ✦✦✦
On *Terra Incognita*, Chris Whitley incorporates the grunge flourishes of *Din of Ecstasy* into the roots-rock foundations of his debut, *Living with the Law*. Instead of relying on processed distorted guitars, Whitley uses noise as texture, which helps his songs breathe. While the musical direction of *Terra Incognita* is considerably more focused than its confused predecessor, Whitley's songwriting remains uneven. Though he has written a better, more diverse record than before, he has yet to produce a set of songs that demonstrate the depth and variety of *Living with the Law*. Too often, he relies on cliches or simplistic ideas, like the single "Automatic," but when he digs a little deeper, his songs still resonate deeply, which means *Terra Incognita* is a partial, not a full, comeback. — *Stephen Thomas Erlewine*

Dirt Floor / Mar. 17, 1998 / ✦✦✦

Wild Tchoupitoulas

f. Louisiana
Group / Zydeco, New Orleans R&B
The Wild Tchoupitoulas—Spy Boy (Amos Landry), Trail Chief (Booker Washington), Big Chief Jolly (George Landry), Flag Boy (Carl Christmas), The Third Chief (Thomas Jackson), and Second Chief (Norman Bell)—are a Mardi Gras ceremonial parade group and "Black Indian tribe" based in New Orleans. George Landry is an uncle to the Neville brothers. *The Wild Tchoupitoulas* is their only album. — *William Ruhlmann*

★ **Wild Tchoupitoulas** / 1976 / Mango ✦✦✦✦✦
The Wild Tchoupitoulas—a group of Mardi Gras Indians headed by George "Big Chief Jolly" Landry—only released one album, but that one record caused a sensation upon its initial 1976 release. It was one of the first records of the album-rock generation that captured the heady gumbo of New Orleans R&B and funk. Landry may have fronted the Wild Tchoupitoulas, but the key to the record's success was his nephews, Charles and Cyril Neville, who headed the rhythm section. They drafted in their brothers, Art and Aaron, to harmonize, and thereby unwittingly gave birth to the band that became the

Neville Brothers. Still, the fact that *The Wild Tchoupitoulas* ranks among the great New Orleans albums isn't because of the Nevilles themselves, but the way the Tchoupitoulas lock into an extraordinary hybrid that marries several indigenous New Orleans musics, with swampy, dirty funk taking its place in the forefront. There are only eight songs, and they are all strung together, as if they're variations on the same themes and rhythms. That's a compliment, by the way, since the organic, flowing groove is the key to the album's success. — *Stephen Thomas Erlewine*

Robert Wilkins (Rev. Robert Timothy Wilkins)

b. Jan. 16, 1896, Hernando, MS, **d.** May 26, 1987, Memphis, TN
Guitar, Vocals / Country Blues, Acoustic Memphis Blues, Prewar Country Blues

A superior guitarist, Robert Wilkins projected a relaxed ease on his exquisite country-blues 78s. He was working as a Pullman porter in Memphis when he was hired by Victor to record in 1928. He was soon back in the studio for Brunswick and Vocalion. The 1929 "That's No Way to Get Along," the most famous of his pre-war 78s, was covered by the Rolling Stones as "Prodigal Son."

Wilkins' great Mississippi vibrato was similar to that of Frank Stokes and Joe Callicott, and his records show considerable finesse with rag and blues guitar. Ungoverned by standard 12-bar conventions, Wilkins created his own structures and was especially strong in open E, as heard in "That's No Way to Get Along" and the spooky one-chord "Rollin' Stone." He crafted lyrics into coherent narratives, carefully avoiding any hint of the risqué. He showed up at the Chicago World's Fair but did most of his playing in Memphis and Hernando. Unnerving violence at a houseparty prompted him to quit the blues in 1936 and find Jesus. In 1964 a rediscovered Rev. Robert Wilkins, spiritual singer and minister of the Church of God in Christ, hit the folk circuit and made some deeply moving records. He refused to play blues but did recycle some old riffs. Near the end of his life, Rev. Wilkins was seen working as a root doctor on a Memphis side street. He lived to be 91. — *Jas Obrecht*

Memphis Blues 1928-1935 / 1928-1935 / Document ✦✦✦✦
Document's *Memphis Blues 1928-1935* contains the 14 Robert Wilkins sides that are currently in circulation, augmented with cuts by a pair of country bluesmen, Tom Dickinson and Allen Shaw. Since Wilkins' recordings are also available on Yazoo's *Original Rolling Stone*, which is easier to find than this disc, *Memphis Blues 1928-1935* isn't a necessary purchase for Wilkins fans, unless they're serious country-blues fans who want the cuts by Dickinson and Shaw, as well. — *Thom Owens*

☆ **Memphis Gospel Singer** / Jul. 1964 / Piedmont ✦✦✦✦✦
Recorded in 1964 during the blues revival, *Memphis Gospel Singer* is a stunning rediscovery album from Robert Wilkins. The country bluesman largely plays original material, and his new versions of such songs as "That's No Way to Get Along" rival his first recorded versions. Throughout the album he turns equally impressive performances, elevating *Memphis Gospel Singer* to the status of one of the key blues revival and country-blues gospel records. — *Thom Owens*

Remember Me / 1971 / Genes ✦✦✦
Although he left the world of blues for gospel, Rev. Robert Wilkins never abandoned his guitar or toned down his brilliant instrumental tendencies; he simply took his rampaging playing style and used it in the service of the Lord. While he wasn't in peak form for this newly discovered and released 1971 concert, he was far from second-rate. He performed 13 cuts and sang with passion, power and conviction. Robert Palmer's liner notes outline Wilkins' contributions and style. — *Ron Wynn*

★ **The Original Rolling Stone** / 1980 / Yazoo ✦✦✦✦✦
Yazoo's *Original Rolling Stone* is a wonderful disc containing 14 of the 17 sides Robert Wilkins recorded before the war. Wilkins was one of the great country-blues artists, and these songs—including "Rollin' Stone," "That's No Way to Get Along," "Jailhouse Blues," and "I'll Go with Her"—became legendary, not only because the songs were terrific (which they are) but also because the performances are intense and haunting. *Original Rolling Stone* features these songs in the best fidelity possible, along with some fairly good liner notes, making this the best package of his most influential recordings. — *Thom Owens*

Alanda Williams

Vocals / Modern Electric Blues
Alanda Williams is one of the young lions on the Dallas/Fort Worth Texas blues scene. The vocalist continues the tradition of beer joint blues set down by people like Robert Ealey and U.P. Wilson.

Williams began playing drums at age five, inspired by James Brown's drummer. When he was 16, Williams met Brown's drummer in Memphis and had the chance to play with him on stage, and that made a lasting impression on the young Williams, who had already begun singing at age 12 at the Baptist church in Pace. Williams' grandfather was the choir director, and he encouraged the young man to sing, even though he was already obsessed with playing drums and a little guitar.

Williams credits his influences as people like Brown, the Temptations, Marvin Gaye, and Curtis Mayfield. After joining a gospel group, the Sons of the South, at age 14, he sang gospel for another six years, recording one album with the group. At 20, he got a music scholarship to Coahoma Junior College and Jackson State College and received formal training there. In 1968, Williams moved to Philadelphia, where he started a soul group, For Love, which opened for the Platters, the Drifters, and other touring vocal groups. After meeting Charlie Brown from the Coasters, who liked Williams' singing, he joined the group and toured extensively.

Between 1970 and 1991, Williams toured the world with the Coasters, eventually settling in Fort Worth in 1991. He formed his own group, the Soul Kings, and began performing around Fort Worth and Dallas clubs. The Soul Kings can be heard backing up guitarist U.P. Wilson on his first recording for JSP Records, and it was his relationship with Wilson that led Williams to his own contract with the label. In 1997, JSP Records released *Kid Dynamite*, Williams' debut album under his own name. On *Kid Dynamite*, Williams is accompanied by some of the Dallas/Fort Worth scene's brightest stars: Tone Sommer, Andrew Junior Boy Jones, Ty Grimes, and Joe Rios. — *Richard Skelly*

Kid Dynamite / Apr. 8, 1997 / JSP ✦✦✦

Big Joe Williams

b. Oct. 16, 1903, Crawford, MS, **d.** Dec. 17, 1982, Macon, MS
Guitar, Vocals / Delta Blues, Electric Delta Blues, Prewar Country Blues, Blues Revival

Big Joe Williams may have been the most cantankerous human being who ever walked the earth with guitar in hand. At the same time, he was an incredible blues musician: a gifted songwriter, a powerhouse vocalist, and an exceptional idiosyncratic guitarist. Despite his deserved reputation as a fighter (documented in Michael Bloomfield's bizarre booklet *Me and Big Joe*), artists who knew him well treated him as a respected elder statesman. Even so, they may not have chosen to play with him, because—as with other older Delta artists if you played with him you played by his rules.

As protégé David "Honeyboy" Edwards described him, Williams in his early Delta days was a walking musician who played work camps, jukes, store porches, streets, and alleys from New Orleans to Chicago. He recorded through five decades for Vocalion, OKeh, Paramount, Bluebird, Prestige, Delmark, and many others. As a youngster, I met him in Delmark owner Bob Koester's store, the Jazz Record Mart. At the time, Big Joe was living there when not on his constant travels. According to Charlie Musselwhite, he and Big Joe kicked off the blues revival in Chicago in the '60s.

When I saw him playing at Mike Bloomfield's "blues night" at the Fickle Pickle, Williams was playing an electric nine-string guitar through a small ramshackle amp with a pie plate nailed to it and a beer can dangling against that. When he played, everything rattled but Big Joe himself. The total effect of this incredible apparatus produced the most buzzing, sizzling, African-sounding music I have ever heard.

Anyone who wants to learn Delta blues must one day come to grips with the idea that the guitar is a drum as well as a melody-producing instrument. A continuous, African-derived musical tradition emphasizing percussive techniques on stringed instruments from the banjo to the guitar can be heard in the music of Delta stalwarts Charley Patton, Fred McDowell, and Bukka White. Each employed decidedly percussive techniques, beating on his box, knocking on the neck, snapping the strings, or adding buzzing or sizzling effects to augment the instrument's percussive potential. However, Big Joe Williams, more than any other major recording artist, embodied the concept of guitar-as-drum, bashing out an incredible series of riffs on his G-tuned nine-string for over 60 years. — *Barry Lee Pearson*

Piney Woods Blues / 1958 / Delmark ✦✦✦
Fine Delmark cuts from the late-'50s rediscovery phase of Big Joe's career. — *Barry Lee Pearson*

Nine String Guitar Blues / 1961 / Delmark ✦✦✦✦
The title says it all — Big Joe Williams plays a custom-made nine-string guitar, which sounds like no other instrument in existence. That alone would give his stripped-down acoustic Delta blues a new spin, but he brings so much grit and passion to his performances, they would have sounded fresh and vital anyway. — *Thom Owens*

Blues on Highway 49 / 1961 / Delmark ✦✦✦
One of Big Joe Williams' better releases, *Blues on Highway 49* is a tense, gritty set of roadhouse blues. Williams' stinging playing and singing brings out the best in such songs as "Tiajuna Blues" and "45 Blues" — he shows exactly how Delta blues could be updated. — *Thom Owens*

Walking Blues / Oct. 1961 / Fantasy ✦✦✦

Blues for 9 Strings / Mar. 1963 / Bluesville ✦✦✦

Back to the Country / 1964 / Testament ✦✦✦✦
Fellow Mississippians Jimmy Brown on fiddle and Willie Lee Harris on harmonica augment Big Joe's down-home Delta blues from the blues revival of the 70s. — *Barry Lee Pearson*

Big Joe Williams at Folk City / 1964 / Prestige-Bluesville ✦✦✦
Cut at Gerdes Folk City in New York on February 26, 1962, this record shows Big Joe Williams in top late-era form, enjoying himself before an audience of mostly white college kids and beats. He plays his signature nine-string guitar, accompanying himself on kazoo, which basically works (even subbing for what would have been a fuzz-tone guitar on "Bugle Blues"), although the kazoo was never meant to be captured in digital sound. The material includes Tommy McClennan's "Bottle Up and Go" and 11 traditional songs, including the intense "Trouble Take Me to My Grave" (his version of a song more familiar in Muddy Waters' version as "I Can't Be Satisfied"), "Mink Coat Blues," and "Burned Child Is Scared of Fire," all done in lively fashion with daunting finger-picking. Williams left behind several folk club recordings from the early '60s, and they make a good contrast to the vast body of studio recordings from the same era. He was evidently at his best playing directly to an audience. — *Bruce Eder*

● **Early Recordings 1935-41** / 1965 / Mamlish ✦✦✦✦
This blues legend and guitar wizard's best initial Bluebird recordings, including the best versions of "49 Highway" and "Baby Please Don't Go" from 1935. — *Barry Lee Pearson*

Classic Delta Blues / 1966 / Milestone ✦✦✦
Classic Delta Blues collects 12 cuts Big Joe Williams cut in 1964. For these recordings, he played a standard six-string guitars instead of hauling out his custom nine-string and the effects are pleasant, but not revelatory. — *Thom Owens*

Stavin' Chain Blues / 1966 / Delmark ✦✦✦✦
A CD reissue of 1958 recordings, it includes four previously unreleased tracks. This is raw but beautiful country-blues, featuring the otherworldly sound of Big Joe's nine-string guitar. — *Niles J. Frantz*

Live at Folk City / 1968 / Bluesville ✦✦

Hand Me Down My Old Walking Stick / Oct. 1969 / World Pacific ✦✦✦✦
This disc is drawn from tapes made solo by Big Joe Williams in October of 1968, in London for Liberty Records, using his usual jerry-rigged nine-string guitar with a pickup. The resulting session, a mix of numbers improvised on the spot and established part of his repertory (including the obligatory "Baby Please Don't Go"), was one of the recordings that Williams was most pleased with, among the many records that he cut during this era. The material mostly shows him creating spontaneously (including a distinctly bluesy "She'll Be Comin' Round The Mountain"), and recreating old songs in a new mode. "Baby Please Don't Go" resembles none of his many other renditions of the piece, or any of the various covers done by white rock and blues performers, with far more animated and intricate playing throughout, Williams making bold, slashing attacks on his instrument. "Everybody's Gonna Miss Me When I'm Gone" is more mellow and brooding, and closer in spirit

to some of his more reflective acoustic blues performances — but the amplification adds a piercing level of intensity to his slide playing. The balances are a little haywire at times (the engineers don't seem to have found their way properly until "Buffalo," a track on which his rhythm playing is most prominent), thanks to the radical changes in timbre and volume in Williams' playing, but the record is still mesmerizing. — *Bruce Eder*

Big Joe Williams [Storyville] / 1975 / Storyville ✦✦✦

Malvina My Sweet Woman (M) / 1988 / Oldie Blues ✦✦✦✦

Shake Your Boogie / 1990 / Arhoolie ✦✦✦✦
Arhoolie reissued two of Big Joe Williams' seminal rediscovery albums on one disc in 1990. The first, 1960's *Tough Times*, ranks among his best; the second, 1969's *Thinking of What They Did*, isn't as strong, but the two albums provide an excellent introduction to this Delta bluesman. — *Stephen Thomas Erlewine*

Delta Blues: 1951 / 1991 / Trumpet ✦✦✦✦
Although the early '50s were not a great time for delta blues musicians, there remained some proficient players performing in this vein throughout the South. The three presented on this new collection of classic Trumpet recordings include Big Joe Williams, known for his nine-string guitar and robust singing, Luther Huff, a good, if derivative vocalist/guitarist, and the spry pianist and vocalist Willie Love, an exuberant performer whose Three Aces band at various times contained Elmore James and Little Milton. This anthology includes 18 selections that show the link between older, traditional blues and the urban, electric sounds that emerged as the idiom's dominant form later in the decade. — *Ron Wynn*

Complete Works, Vol. 1 (1935-1941) / 1991 / Document ✦✦✦
For completists, specialists and academics, Document's *Complete Works, Vol. 1 (1935-1941)* is an invaluable, exhaustive overview of Big Joe Williams' early recordings. There are some absolutely wonderful, classic performances on the collection, but the long running time, exacting chronological sequencing, poor fidelity (all cuts are transferred from original acetates and 78s), and number of performances are hard to digest. The serious blues listener will find all these factors to be positive, but enthusiasts and casual listeners will find that the collection is of marginal interest for those very reasons. — *Thom Owens*

Complete Works, Vol. 2 (1945-1949) / 1991 / Document ✦✦✦
For completists, specialists and academics, Document's *Complete Works, Vol. 2 (1945-1949)* is invaluable, offering an exhaustive overview of Big Joe Williams' later recordings. As with the first volume, the chronological sequencing, poor fidelity, and long running time will render the collection of interest more to serious blues fanatics than to casual listeners. — *Thom Owens*

Have Mercy! / Apr. 1996 / Rykodisc ✦✦✦

Baby Please Don't Go / Wolf ✦✦✦✦
Seventy minutes of Big Joe Williams' recordings in the prime of his life, from 1935 thru 1947, and in surprisingly good sound. Along with the *original* recording of "Baby Please Don't Go," other highlights include "Little Leg Woman" and "49 Highway Blues" (with Henry "Too Tight Henry" Townsend on second guitar), his 1941 recordings of "Crawling King Snake," and "Throw A Boogie Woogie." The notes are sketchy but the session information is fair. Some of the material here was available paired off with John Lee "Sonny Boy" Williamson material on RCA's *Throw a Boogie Woogie*, but that disc seems to be out-of-print, and the majority of this disc is unique. — *Bruce Eder*

Brooks Williams

b. Statesboro, GA
Guitar, Vocals / Singer-Songwriter, Contemporary Folk
Folk-blues guitarist and singer Brooks Williams is as adept playing traditional blues as he is singing his own contemporary folk songs. His voice has been endlessly compared to James Taylor's, and yet his unique renderings of self-penned and blues classics on guitar make him an original.

Based in western Massachusetts for most of the 1990s, Williams was born in Statesboro, GA, and lived in other small towns in Georgia, Alabama, and Mississippi while growing up. In his youth, he heard a lot of gospel and roadhouse blues, but after he discovered rock 'n' roll, he forgot about blues until one day in 1987, when he opened for blues/folk diva Rory Block at a club in upstate New York. Block inspired Williams to rediscover the acoustic blues he knew in his youth, and he began teaching himself songs by Robert Johnson, Muddy Waters, and Little Walter Jacobs.

Williams began to draw more of his performing persona from classic blues, and while working the folk circuit, opening up for crafty songwriters like Cheryl Wheeler, Bill Morrissey, and John Hiatt, he also began to develop his own skills as a songwriter. Since then, Williams' live shows have become an artful mix of classic acoustic blues, original blues songs, and self-penned contemporary folk songs. His development as a songwriter has been speedy, and he's got a slew of albums to prove it—*Seven Sisters* (1997), *Knife Edge* (1996), *Inland Sailor* (1994), *Back to Mercy* (1992), all for the Green Linnet Redbird label—as well as 1991's *How the Night-Time Sings*, 1990's *North from Statesboro*, and 1989's *Red Guitar Plays Blue* on his own Red Guitar Blue Music label. —*Richard Skelly*

● **North from Statesboro** / 1990 / Red Guitar ✦✦✦✦
Brooks Williams' debut album, *North from Statesboro*, falls halfway between the mellow folk-pop of James Taylor and the relaxed, respectful folk-blues of such contemporaries as Rory Block. Williams devotes his album to original songs, including instrumentals and musical adaptations of Robert Frost poems ("Acquainted with the Night"). Occasionally, he gets a little too wordy for his own good, but that doesn't prevent *North from Statesboro* from being an engaging collection of quietly lovely folk-blues. — *Thom Owens*

How the Night-Time Sings / 1991 / Red Guitar ✦✦✦✦
"Jubilee" is a joyous lush song, and "Hard Love" is also excellent. —*Richard Meyer*

Back to Mercy / 1992 / Green Linnet ✦✦✦
William's third album has more ambitious production but it always serves to support his strong singing. Here are songs of hope and human renewal. —*Richard Meyer*

Inland Sailor / 1994 / Green Linnet ✦✦✦
Brooks Williams has delivered another collection of expressive original songs about romance and the underlying spiritual nature of life. As we have come to expect, it is distinguished by exceptional guitar work and his carefully articulated vocals. For the sake of guitarists among his audience, Williams has noted the tuning and capo positions he uses for each song. —*Richard Meyer*

Knife Edge / 1995 / Green Linnet ✦✦✦

Seven Sisters / Aug. 12, 1997 / Green Linnet ✦✦✦✦

Jody Williams

b. Feb. 3, 1935, Mobile, AL
Guitar, Vocals / Electric Chicago Blues
Retired from the Chicago blues business for decades, Jody Williams' stinging lead guitar work is still stirringly felt every time someone punches up Billy Boy Arnold's "I Was Fooled," Bo Diddley's "Who Do You Love," Otis Spann's "Five Spot," or Williams' eerie minor-key instrumental masterpiece, "Lucky Lou."

Born in Alabama, Joseph Leon Williams moved to Chicago at age six. He grew up alongside Bo Diddley, the two trading licks as kids and playing for real by 1951. By the mid-'50s, Williams was ensconced as a Chicago session guitarist of high stature, but he began to grow disenchanted when the signature lick he created for newcomer Billy Stewart's Argo waxing of "Billy's Blues" was appropriated by Mickey Baker for the Mickey & Sylvia smash "Love Is Strange." Baker apparently caught Williams playing the riff in Washington, D.C., at the Howard Theatre. When the legal smoke had cleared, Bo Diddley's wife owned the writing credit for "Love Is Strange" and Jody Williams had zipola for monetary compensation.

Williams made his recording debut (singing as well as playing) as a leader for powerhouse deejay Al Benson's Blue Lake imprint in 1955: "Looking for My Baby" was credited to Little Papa Joe. That alias pattern held in 1957, when Argo unleashed "Lucky Lou" and its sumptuous slow blues vocal flip "You May" as by Little Joe Lee (quite a band here—saxists Harold Ashby and Red Holloway, keyboardist Lafayette Leake, and bassist Willie Dixon). In 1960, Herald Records labeled him Sugar Boy Williams on "Little Girl." 1960s outings for Nike, Jive, Smash, and Yulando round out Williams' slim discography.

At last report, Jody Williams was working as a computer maintenance

technician and burglar alarm installer, his salad days as one of Chicago's hottest young guitar slingers in the regrettably distant past. —*Bill Dahl*

● **Leading Brand [6 Track]** / 1977 / Red Lightnin' ✦✦✦✦
A bootleg LP, very welcome nevertheless in its day, spotlighting two of Chicago's most advanced blues pickers of the '50s and early '60s. Earl Hooker's brilliant stuff for producer Mel London dominates, but the last six sides showcase Jody Williams' taut, ringing guitar lines (especially on 1957's West Side-styled minor-key "Lucky Lou") and smooth vocals on "You May" and "Looking for My Baby." —*Bill Dahl*

Joe Williams (Joseph Goreed)

b. Dec. 12, 1918, Cordele, GA
Vocals / Blues, Swing, Standards, Traditional Pop
Joe Williams was possibly the last great big band singer, following in the tradition of Jimmy Rushing but carving out his own unique identity. Equally skilled on blues (including double entendre ad-libs), ballads, and standards, Williams has always been a charming and consistently swinging performer. In the late '30s Williams performed regularly with Jimmie Noone; he gigged with Coleman Hawkins and Lionel Hampton in the early '40s and toured with Andy Kirk during 1946-47. After stints with Red Saunders and Hot Lips Page and recordings with King Kolax (including a 1951 version of "Every Day I Have the Blues"), Williams joined Count Basie's Orchestra in 1954. During the next seven years he and Basie had a mutually satisfying relationship, both making each other more famous! His version of "Every Day" with Count became his theme song while many other pieces (such as "Goin' to Chicago" and "Smack Dab in the Middle") became permanent parts of Williams' repertoire. After leaving Basie in 1961, the singer worked with the Harry Edison quintet for a couple of years and has freelanced as a leader ever since, having occasional reunions with the Basie band. His collaborations with Cannonball Adderley and George Shearing were successful as was an album with the Thad Jones/Mel Lewis Orchestra. Joe Williams has remained one of the most popular and talented singers in jazz. —*Scott Yanow*

Everyday I Have the Blues / 1951-Sep. 28, 1953 / Savoy ✦✦✦✦
From the Roulette catalog, this superior Joe Williams/Count Basie collaboration finds the singer concentrating on the blues with consistently excellent results. In addition to a remake of the title cut, Williams is heard at his best on the classic "Going to Chicago" and such numbers as "Just a Dream," "Cherry Red," and "Good Mornin' Blues." This LP is well worth searching for. —*Scott Yanow*

★ **Count Basie Swings / Joe Williams Sings** / Jul. 17, 1955-Jul. 26, 1955 / Verve ✦✦✦✦✦
This is the definitive Joe Williams record, cut shortly after joining Count Basie's orchestra. Included are his classic versions of "Every Day I Have the Blues," "The Comeback," "Alright, Okay, You Win," "In the Evening," and "Teach Me Tonight." Williams' popularity was a major asset to Basie and getting to sing with that swinging big band on a nightly basis certainly did not harm the singer. This gem belongs in everyone's jazz collection. —*Scott Yanow*

A Swingin' Night at Birdland / Jun. 1962 / Capitol ✦✦✦✦
In 1961, after six years as one of the main attractions of Count Basie's orchestra, Williams (with Basie's blessing) went out on his own. One of his first sessions was this live recording cut at Birdland with a strong quintet that featured trumpeter Harry "Sweets" Edison and Jimmy Forrest on tenor. Williams mostly sings standards and ballads but also tosses in a few of his popular blues (including "Well Alright, OK, You Win" and "Goin' to Chicago") during a well-rounded and thoroughly enjoyable set. —*Scott Yanow*

Me and the Blues / Jan. 2, 1963-Dec. 5, 1963 / RCA ✦✦✦✦
This CD is a straight reissue of the original LP and features singer Joe Williams backed by a studio orchestra headed and arranged by Jimmy Jones. Williams mostly sticks to blues-oriented material but there is a surprising amount of mood variation on the dozen selections along with short solos by trumpeters Thad Jones and Clark Terry, altoist Phil Woods and Seldon Powell on tenor; Ben Webster has a guest spot on "Rocks in My Bed." Williams, heard at the peak of his powers, is at his best on "Me and the Blues," "Rocks in My Bed," "Work Song," and "Kansas City." —*Scott Yanow*

Jump for Joy / Feb. 1, 1963-Mar. 13, 1963 / RCA ✦✦✦✦
Surprisingly, this excellent set by singer Joe Williams has mostly not been reissued yet on CD; only a couple tracks appeared on a Bluebird sampler. The classic singer is backed by a big band (and in some cases a smaller group from the orchestra) arranged by Oliver Nelson and Jimmy Jones. Doing his best to escape from the stereotype of being strictly a blues singer, Williams performs both superior standards and obscurities on the spirited LP. Highlights include "Wrap Your Troubles in Dreams," "It's a Wonderful World," "Just A-Sittin' and A-Rockin'," and "Jump for Joy." Worth searching for. — *Scott Yanow*

● **The Overwhelmin'** / Feb. 6, 1963-Jun. 18, 1965 / Bluebird ✦✦✦✦
A CD sampler taken from five former LPs, this fine CD features Joe Williams doing three songs from Duke Ellington's play *Jump for Joy*, five numbers at the 1963 Newport Jazz Festival (during which he is joined by trumpeters Clark Terry and Howard McGhee) and tenor greats Coleman Hawkins, Zoot Sims and Ben Webster), four blues backed by an all-star jazz group and five ballads in front of an orchestra. Although it would be preferable to have each of the five original albums intact, this superb collection features Joe Williams on a wide variety of material, and he is heard close to his peak throughout. — *Scott Yanow*

☆ **Presenting Joe Williams and Thad Jones-Mel Lewis** / Sep. 30, 1966 / Solid State ✦✦✦✦✦
This was a logical matchup. The Thad Jones-Mel Lewis orchestra, heard during its first year in existence when it was really an all-star ensemble, does an excellent job of accompanying Joe Williams on a few of his standards (including "Gee Baby, Ain't I Good to You," "Come Sunday," and "Smack Dab in the Middle") and a few more obscure tunes. Even though Thad Jones' charts allocate little solo space to the many great sidemen, Williams is in such fine form on this out-of-print LP that one barely notices. — *Scott Yanow*

☆ **And the Thad Jones/Mel Lewis Orchestra** / Sep. 1966 / Blue Note ✦✦✦✦✦
This CD reissues one of Joe Williams' finest recordings. Accompanied by the Thad Jones/Mel Lewis Orchestra, the singer is heard at the peak of his powers. The big band primarily functions as an ensemble (Snooky Young gets off some good blasts on "Nobody Knows the Way I Feel This Morning") but the inventive Thad Jones arrangements insure that his illustrious sidemen have plenty to play. Many of the selections (half of which have been in the singer's repertoire ever since) are given definitive treatment on this set (particularly a humorous "Evil Man Blues," "Gee Baby Ain't I Good to You?," and "Smack Dab in the Middle") and Williams scats at his best on "It Don't Mean a Thing." Get this one. — *Scott Yanow*

Live in Vegas / 1971 / Monad ✦✦✦✦
This previously unreleased set features Joe Williams at a late-night performance in Las Vegas. Very well-recorded, the music offers few surprises but finds the singer in prime form. Although the Count Basie Orchestra backs him on most selections, the personnel is not listed, there are no significant solos and Basie himself is probably not on most of the tracks. The breezy liner notes say that "John Young, pianist extraordinaire" sat in during "Midnight Medley" (four ballads and "Thou Swell") and "Going to Chicago"; is this the Chicago-based player of the early '60s? Highlights include an animated "Nobody Loves You When You're Down & Out" (during which Williams really tells a story with the words), "Going to Chicago" (on this version he sings all of the famous big-band riffs along with his regular vocal) and the joyous "Smack Dab in the Middle." This is an excellent recording, easily recommended to Joe Williams fans. — *Scott Yanow*

Joe Williams Live / Aug. 7, 1973 / Fantasy ✦✦✦✦
Williams meets the Cannonball Adderley Septet on this rather interesting session. The expanded rhythm section (which includes keyboardist George Duke and both acoustic bassist Walter Booker and the electric bass of Carol Kaye) gives funky accompaniment to Williams while altoist Cannonball and cornetist Nat have some solo space. Actualy the singer easily steals the show on a rather searing version of "Goin' to Chicago Blues," his own "Who She Do" and a few unusual songs, including Duke Ellington's "Heritage." — *Scott Yanow*

Prez Conference / 1979 / GNP ✦✦✦✦
Dave Pell's Prez Conference was to Lester Young what Supersax is to Charlie Parker. Pell's short-lived group featured harmonized Lester Young solos recreated by three tenors and a baritone; their matchup with singer Joe Williams

is quite enjoyable. Since Young was in Count Basie's orchestra when Jimmy Rushing was the vocalist, Joe Williams has a rare opportunity to give his own interpretation to Rushing and Billie Holiday classics like "I May Be Wrong," "You Can Depend on Me," "If Dreams Come True," and "Easy Living." A delightful and swinging date. — *Scott Yanow*

Nothin' but the Blues / Nov. 16, 1983-Nov. 17, 1983 / Delos ✦✦✦✦
Sticking to blues, Joe Williams is in prime form on this special session. His backup crew includes such all-stars as tenor-saxophonist Red Holloway, organist Brother Jack McDuff and (on alto and one lone vocal) the great Eddie "Cleanhead" Vinson. The many blues standards are familiar but these versions are lively and fresh. — *Scott Yanow*

I Just Wanna Sing / Jun. 29, 1985-Jun. 30, 1985 / Delos ✦✦✦✦
For this session, Joe Williams is backed by such master jazzmen as trumpeter Thad Jones, the contrasting tenors of Eddie "Lockjaw" Davis and Benny Golson, and guitarist John Collins. The material varies from the dated humor of "It's Not Easy Being White" to classic versions of "Until I Met You" and "I Got It Bad." Joe Williams is in prime form and this is one of his better sessions from his later years. — *Scott Yanow*

Every Night: Live at Vine St. / May 7, 1987-May 8, 1987 / Verve ✦✦✦✦
The focus is entirely on Joe Williams (who is backed by a standard four-piece rhythm section) during this live session from Vine Street. Then 69, Williams had not lost a thing and his voice has rarely sounded stronger. This version of "Every Day I Have the Blues" is transformed into Miles Davis' "All Blues," Williams revives Eubie Blake's "A Dollar for a Dime" and sounds wonderful on such songs as "Too Marvelous for Words," "I Want a Little Girl," and "Roll 'em Pete." This is the best of Joe Williams' records from the '80s. — *Scott Yanow*

Ballad and Blues Master / May 7, 1987-May 8, 1987 / Verve ✦✦✦✦
Taken from the same sessions that had previously resulted in *Every Night*, the identical adjectives apply. Joe Williams is in superior form for this live date, putting a lot of feeling into such songs as "You Can Depend on Me," "When Sunny Gets Blue," and "Dinner for One Please, James." A closing blues medley is particularly enjoyable and the backup by a quartet that includes pianist Morman Simmons and guitarist Henry Johnson is tasteful and swinging. — *Scott Yanow*

In Good Company / Jan. 19, 1989-Jan. 21, 1989 / Verve ✦✦✦✦
A bit of a grab-bag, this CD finds Joe Williams joined by Supersax on two numbers, doing a pair of vocal duets with Marlena Shaw ("Is You Is or Is You Ain't My Baby" is excellent), teaming up with vocalist/pianist Shirley Horn for two ballads and being joined by the Norman Simmons Quartet for the remainder. Sticking mostly to standards, Joe Williams shows that at 70 he still had the magic. — *Scott Yanow*

Live at Orchestra . . . / Nov. 20, 1992 / Telarc ✦✦✦✦
Joe Williams is so closely associated with the Count Basie Orchestra that it is difficult to believe that this Telarc CD was his first recording with jazz's great institution in over 30 years. Williams (in generally fine form despite an occasionally raspy voice) performs a well-rounded set of blues, ballads, and standards with the Frank Foster-led Basie orchestra, combining some of his older hits with a few newer songs such as Grady Tate's "A Little at a Time" and "My Baby Upsets Me." Foster's sidemen are mostly heard in an ensemble role with all of the instrumental solos being rather brief; there is little interaction with the vocalist. That fault aside, this is one of Joe Williams' better recordings of the past decade. — *Scott Yanow*

Here's to Life / Aug. 16, 1993-Aug. 18, 1993 / Telarc ✦✦
Joe Williams loves the string arrangements of Robert Farnon and the sappy ballad "Here's to Life" but in truth the charts border on muzak and the slow tempos on this Telarc CD have little variety. Reminiscent a bit of Nat King Cole's string sessions of the 1950s with Gordon Jenkins, there is little jazz content to this set. Williams is in particularly strong form, interpreting the ballads in dramatic and sensitive fashion, but, despite his charm, this is one of his lesser recordings. — *Scott Yanow*

Feel the Spirit / Sep. 20, 1994-Sep. 23, 1994 / Telarc ✦✦✦
Joe Williams had been wanting to record an album of spirituals since 1957 and this is it. The veteran singer gives a blues feeling and swing to the traditional pieces which range from the rollicking title cut to "Go Down Moses," "I Couldn't Hear Nobody Pray," and "The Lord's Prayer." He is assisted by

Marlena Shaw (a particularly effective partner on three of the numbers) and a five-piece chorus on four other songs. The backing usually features Patrice Rushen getting organ sounds out of her synthesizer. Despite the one-message content, the music has more variety than one might expect and Joe Williams acquits himself very well on this sincere and heartfelt effort. — *Scott Yanow*

The Best of Joe Williams: The Roulette, Solid State & Blue Note Years / Blue Note ◆◆◆◆

The Best of Joe Williams: The Roulette, Solid State & Blue Note Years is an excellent sampler of Williams' work for Roulette and Solid State, providing a terrific overview of Williams' early records. Most of these 18 tracks feature Williams with the Count Basie Orchestra; there are also several cuts with Jimmy Jones, Harry "Sweets" Edison, Horace Ott, Jimmy Mundy, the Thad Jones-Mel Lewis Orchestra and Lambert, Hendricks, and Ross. For anyone wondering why Williams is considered one of the great blues and big band vocalists, this offers a reason why. — *Stephen Thomas Erlewine*

Juanita Williams

Vocals / Modern Blues

Although Juanita Williams may seem like a new face on the blues scene, one listen to her brilliant debut album on the Big Mo label, *Introducing Juanita Williams*, and you realize this woman is a pro. In fact, she's spent the last 20 years as lead vocalist for the Airmen of Note, a prestigious Air Force Big Band originally founded by Glenn Miller. Williams began singing in the church, but her secular influences eventually stole her heart, and they included singers like Etta James and Aretha Franklin. However, Williams' voice, passion, and energy are completely unique. — *Richard Skelly*

● **Introducing Juanita Williams** / 1994 / Big Mo ◆◆◆◆

The comparisons to Aretha Franklin are inevitable, but Juanita Williams' voice and passion are her own. Her debut, *Introducing Juanita Williams*, features a wide-ranging sample of modern and classic blues tunes, everything from Ike and Tina Turner's "Crazy About You Baby" to Freddie King's "That Will Never Do" and Bobby Bland's "Two Steps from the Blues." Anybody who has doubts about the future of women blues vocalists should pick up Williams' impressive debut. — *Richard Skelly*

Lee "Shot" Williams

b. May 21, 1938, Lexington, MS

Vocals / Soul Blues

Vocalist Lee "Shot" Williams sings a style of Southern soul-blues in keeping with the tradition of vocalists like Bobby "Blue" Bland, Johnnie Taylor, and Albert King. He got the nickname "Shot" from his mother at a young age, owing to his fondness for wearing suits and dressing up as a "big shot."

Williams grew up with guitar player Little Smokey Smothers and knew his older brother, Big Smokey Smothers. Williams' stepsister, Arlean Brown, was surrounded by a family of musicians, and the Brown brothers gave Williams his first introduction to blues performing via the juke joints of the Delta.

Williams moved to Detroit in 1954 and to Chicago in 1958. He rejoined Little Smokey Smothers there and got to know other paragons of Chicago blues, including Magic Sam (McGhee) and Howlin' Wolf. Williams began singing with Smokey's band in 1960 and a few years later joined Magic Sam's band as a vocalist.

In 1962, Williams recorded his first singles for Chicago's Foxy label, "Hello Baby" and "I'm Trying." He recorded a series of singles for other labels, including King/Federal, Palos, Gamma, Shama and Tchula. His 1964 recording "Welcome to the Club" was a hit in Chicago, so much so that it was later covered by guitarist/singer Little Milton Campbell for Checker Records in 1965. Another regional hit, "I Like Your Style," came out in 1969 and was later covered by Junior Parker. (Williams remade the single in 1993.)

After joining up with guitarist Earl Hooker, he had his first experience on the road as part of a touring band in the mid-'60s, playing around the South. Williams also served tenures with Little Milton and Bobby "Blue" Bland.

His first album under his own name, *Country Disco*, was released on the Roots label in 1977. In the 1980s, Williams moved back to Memphis, where he had spent many of his earlier years, knowing there would still be an audience for his brand of soul-blues. He released an album on cassette and recorded for a Japanese label in 1992. Later that year, his guest vocals on his cousin's album prompted the Black Magic label to look into recording Williams with his own band. The result, *Cold Shot*, was released in 1995, demonstrating Williams' gospel-inflected, powerful vocals in the proper setting. Williams is accompanied by a seasoned team of studio musicians, including former Albert Collins bassist Johnny Gayden, Ronnie Earl organist Tony Zamagni, saxist Charles Kimble, and trumpeter Mike Barber of the Chicago Playboy Horns. The album was voted best blues album of 1995 in a poll conducted by the magazine *Living Blues*. On *Cold Shot*, Williams interprets familiar covers by Gladys Knight, "Neither One of Us," and Wilson Pickett's "Don't Let the Green Grass Fool You."

His debut for the Memphis-based Ecko Records, *Hot Shot*, was released in 1996. Williams made an appearance at the 1994 Chicago Blues Festival, and while it boosted his visibility, he continues to perform mostly in clubs around the US. — *Richard Skelly*

Lee Williams & Cymbals & Friends / Jun. 25, 1994 / Collectables ◆◆◆

Cold Shot / 1995 / Black Magic ◆◆◆

Competent modern soul-blues with a friendly, non-threatening tone, augmented by a three-man brass section, the Chicago Playboy Horns. — *Richie Unterberger*

● **Hot Shot** / Oct. 15, 1996 / Ecko ◆◆◆◆

Hot Shot may be the best record Lee "Shot" Williams has yet released, due both to the quality of the performances and songwriting. He has re-recorded many of his older singles for the album, giving them appropriately greasy, energetic performances. Unfortunately, the production is a little too polished to make *Hot Shot* really sound like a rockin' juke joint, but there's no discounting the passion in Williams' performances. — *Thom Owens*

Lester Williams

b. Jun. 24, 1920, Groveton, TX, **d.** Nov. 13, 1990, Houston, TX

Bass, Guitar, Vocals / R&B, Texas Blues

Though little known outside of the Houston blues circuit where he made his home for several decades, vocalist/guitarist Lester Williams was a local phenomenon during the early 1950s whose success even led to an appearance at Carnegie Hall. Born in Groveton, Texas on June 24, 1920, he grew up infatuated with the sound of T-Bone Walker, whose style Williams consciously emulated; after serving in World War II, he formed his own combo, and in 1949 signed on with the Houston-based Macy's Records. The label's then-stockboy, Steve Poncio, produced Williams' debut single "Winter Time Blues"; it became a regional hit, although subsequent efforts were less successful. However, by 1951 Poncio owned and operated his own distributorship, United Distributors, and through various channels struck up a business relationship with Specialty Records owner Art Rupe; as a result, Williams joined the Specialty stable, and with Poncio again behind the boards scored his biggest hit in 1952 with "I Can't Lose with the Stuff I Use," a track later covered by B.B. King. The song was another regional smash, and was sufficiently popular on a national basis to land the singer on a February 1953 Carnegie Hall bill which also included Dinah Washington, Billy Eckstine, and Nat King Cole. Williams' follow-ups failed to catch on, however, and by 1954 he was regularly performing on Houston station KLVL and touring throughout the South. He later recorded on Duke before one final date for Imperial in 1956; in the years to follow he remained a staple of the Houston club circuit, touring Europe four years prior to his death on November 13, 1990. — *Jason Ankeny*

The Godfather of Blues / Apr. 1949-Apr. 1953 / Collectables ◆◆◆

● **I Can't Lose with the Stuff I Use** / 1952-1953 / Specialty ◆◆◆◆

Singer/guitarist Lester Williams wasn't an innovative player or a top-flight vocalist; still, he made good, occasionally great music that was enjoyable and reflective of a prime blues/R&B period. Williams' one moment in the spotlight came via the hit "I Can't Lose with The Stuff I Use," a great single that had wit, stinging guitar licks, stomping rhythms, and his finest vocal. It was later covered by B.B. King, and the song helped Williams get a Carnegie Hall gig. That song leads off a new 25-track disc covering Lester Williams' tunes from 1952 and 1953. There's little here that's new, but plenty that's worth hearing. — *Ron Wynn*

Texas Troubadour / 1995 / Ace ◆◆◆◆

Marion Williams

b. Aug. 29, 1927, Miami, FL, d. Jul. 2, 1994, Philadelphia, PA
Vocals, Keyboards / Black Gospel, Traditional Gospel

With an amazing grace, a powerful, yet lyrical voice and unmatched improvisation skills, Marion Williams punctuated her sanctified shouting with gut-wrenching growls, low moans, joyful whoops and soaring, angelic falsettos that made her one of the most influential singers in gospel music. In her heyday she was hailed by some critics as one the greatest singers in the US.

Williams was born in a Miami ghetto, the daughter of a West Indian butcher and a South Carolina laundry woman. When not working, her father would give music lessons, while her devout mother introduced to her to religion. Williams' own love of gospel music began in childhood, and she would sing and listen to it at every opportunity. One of her older brothers frequently played blues and jazz on the family jukebox; although gospel was Williams' main interest, her music is infused with elements of those jukebox tunes, as well as the calypso music played throughout her neighborhood. When she was nine, her father died, and at age 14, Williams quit school to work all day in the laundry beside her mother. Later the responsibility for supporting the family fell totally on Williams' young shoulders when her mother lost both legs due to diabetes. Still her interest in sanctified gospel continued, and on weekends she sang in church programs and on street corners. She was particularly inspired by the Smith Jubilee Singers (her favorites) and the Kings of Harmony; influential soloists included such women as Mary Johnson Davis and particularly Sister Rosetta Tharpe. Williams' extraordinary singing attracted considerable attention, but though attempts were made to steer her into everything from opera to the blues, she was determined to spread the gospel and by 1946 was known as the best gospel soloist in Miami.

While at a Clara Ward and the Ward Singers program, Williams was called up to sing. Impressed, Clara and Gertrude Ward invited the young singer to join their nationally known group. The following year, she joined the Wards and remained with them for the next eleven years as their star attraction. Her natural sparkle and enthusiasm in performance earned her the nickname "Miss Personality." She made her recording debut singing "How Far Am I from Canaan" with the Ward Singers in 1948 for Savoy; it was the Rev. W. Herbert Brewster-penned "Surely God Is Able" that made Williams and the Ward Singers stars. During their dynamic performances, it was not uncommon for audience members to fall out in frenzied ecstasy, something Williams encouraged by getting right down into the audience, sashaying about and shouting at the top of her lungs, occasionally sitting demurely upon listeners' laps, and even literally trying to pack up the earthly goods of audience members during her renditions of her second big hit, "Packin' Up." She put so much into her performances with the Ward Singers that in time she began suffering "nervous spells" in which she would yell just to express the remaining energy generated by singing those high notes. Williams and a few others from the group left in 1958 to form Stars of Faith.

The Stars of Faith got off to a rocky start as they lacked many of the things that made the Wards great, including Gertrude's ability to manage, Clara's driving vision, and Brewster's exquisite songs. It did not help that Williams was not putting the energy into singing she did with the Wards. She frequently allowed other group members to do the shouting and avoided the vocal extremes that characterized her earlier work. The lull continued until 1961, when she again found Jesus and approached music with renewed vigor. She and the Stars got major exposure when they appeared in the off-Broadway production *Black Nativity* and began touring North America and Europe. Williams left the group in 1965 to launch a solo career. Returning to Europe, she appeared in an unsuccessful show until her mother's death caused her to go back to Miami. It was at her mother's funeral that she became committed, bringing back her old fire to her new career. Starting at Yale, Williams began a long series of college campus tours that gave her the opportunity to thrill audiences in North America, Europe (where she also appeared at jazz festivals), Africa and the Caribbean with stirring renditions of such great songs as "Jesus Is All" and her biggest solo hit, the reflective "Standing Here Wondering Which Way to Go."

Though she died in 1994, Marion Williams' influence upon contemporary music continues to be felt. Back in the '50s, her unique singing style, that inimitable hollering and whooping, inspired artists such as Little Richard and the Isley Brothers to emulate her. — *Sandra Brennan*

Standing Here Wondering Which Way to Go / 1971 / Atlantic ✦✦✦✦

The New Message / Jan. 1971 / Atlantic ✦✦✦✦
Some of the late gospel diva's finest moments. — *Opal Louis Nations*

Surely God Is Able / 1989 / Spirit Feel ✦✦✦✦
A very strong soloist who reworked classic gospel material from the '30s and '40s into a wonderful 1989 album. — *Kip Lornell*

Back to the Cross / Oct. 25, 1990 / Light ✦✦✦✦

★ **Strong Again** / 1991 / Spirit Feel ✦✦✦✦✦
Eclectic though satisfying 20-cut album by this major singer, her most impressive solo set in recent years. Sparse accompaniment; mainly traditional material. Excellent. — *Kip Lornell*

If You Ever Needed the Lord Before / Jul. 28, 1992 / Columbia/Legacy ✦✦✦✦
Stunning sides by this glorious gospel diva and ex-Ward singer. — *Opal Louis Nations*

Can't Keep It to Myself / 1993 / Shanachie ✦✦✦✦
Marion Williams has a majesty in her voice, a power in her delivery and a compelling, dynamic quality that underscores her vocals. This new disc features 22 awesome performances recorded with minimal, sympathetic accompaniment and little production support; just mostly Williams' smashing, note-bending, soaring vocals. She flies on slow, bluesy numbers, testifies and shouts on originals like "Ride in the Clouds" and "I'll Never Return No More" and turns old standards such as Roberta Martin's "God's Amazing Grace" and Rev. Thomas A. Dorsey's "Live the Life I Sing About in My Song" into gripping, fresh reaffirmations of her own faith. — *Ron Wynn*

☆ **My Soul Looks Back: The Genius of Marion Williams 1962-1992** / 1994 / Shanachie ✦✦✦✦✦
A retrospective look at some of this great singer's solo work with emphasis on traditional material. — *Opal Louis Nations*

God & Me / Jan. 27, 1994 / Vee-Jay ✦✦✦✦

Born to Sing the Gospel / 1995 / Shanachie ✦✦✦✦
Born to Sing the Gospel returns Marion Williams to her home church, Philadelphia's B.M. Oakley Memorial Church of God in Christ; the material is engagingly varied, spanning from the bluesy original "Sometimes I Ring Up Heaven" to the traditional title track to the medley of the classics "Christ Is All" and "Jesus Is All." Though in fine form throughout, Williams hits her peak on "Death in the Morning," her delivery charged with all of the raw power of a field recording. [Shanachie's CD reissue appends five tracks not included on the original LP.] — *Jason Ankeny*

This Too Shall Pass / Sep. 12, 1995 / Nashboro ✦✦✦✦
Ten-song celebrations by one of the world's greatest gospel singers. Nashboro sides. — *Opal Louis Nations*

Through Many Dangers / Sep. 24, 1996 / Shanachie ✦✦✦✦

Somebody Bigger than You and I / Relic ✦✦✦
Her first album after leaving The Ward Singers. Recorded in 1958, it includes "I Can't Forget." — *Bil Carpenter*

Robert Pete Williams

b. Mar. 14, 1914, Zachary, LA, d. Dec. 31, 1980, Rosedale, LA
Guitar, Vocals / Acoustic Louisiana Blues, Acoustic Blues, Electric Blues, Country Blues, Blues Revival

Discovered in the Louisiana State Penitentiary, Robert Pete Williams became one of the great blues discoveries during the folk boom of the early '60s. His disregard for conventional patterns, tunings, and structures kept him from a wider audience, but his music remains one of the great, intense treats of the blues.

Williams was born in Zachary, LA, the son of sharecropping parents. While he was a child, he worked the fields with his family; he never attended school. Williams didn't begin playing blues until his late teens, when he made himself a guitar out of a cigar box. Playing his homemade guitar, Williams began performing at local parties, dances, and fish fries at night while he worked during the day. Even though he was constantly working, he never made quite enough money to support his family, which caused considerable tension between him and his wife—according to legend, she burned his guitar one night in a fit of anger.

Despite all of the domestic tension, Williams continued to play throughout the Baton Rouge area, performing at dances and juke joints. In 1956, he shot and killed a man in a local club. Williams claimed the act was in self-defense, but he was convicted of murder and sentenced to life in prison. He was sent to Angola prison, where he served for two years before being discovered by ethnomusicologists Dr. Harry Oster and Richard Allen. The pair recorded Williams performing several of his own songs, which were all about life in prison. Impressed with the guitarist's talents, Oster and Allen pleaded for a pardon for Williams. The pardon was granted in 1959, after he had served a total of three and a half years. For the first five years after he left prison, Williams could only perform in Lousiana, but his recordings—which appeared on Folk-Lyric, Arhoolie, and Prestige, among other labels—were popular and he received positive word of mouth reviews.

In 1964, Williams played his first concert outside of Louisiana—it was a set at the legendary Newport Folk Festival. Williams' performance was enthusiastically received and he began touring the United States, often playing shows with Mississippi Fred McDowell. For the remainder of the '60s and most of the '70s, Robert Pete Williams constantly played concerts and festivals across America, as well a handful of dates in Europe. Along the way, he recorded for a handful of small independent labels, including Fontana and Storyville. Williams slowed down his work schedule in the late '70s, largely due to his old age and declining health. The guitarist died on December 31, 1980, at the age of 66. —*Cub Koda & Stephen Thomas Erlewine*

Robert Pete Williams, Vol. 2 / 1959 / Arhoolie ✦✦✦
This second volume of newly released (on CD) Robert Pete Williams material was mostly recorded in Louisiana in 1959, shortly after Williams was paroled from Angola by Governor Earl Long. The cuts recorded during this time reflect both his appreciation for being out of jail and his understanding that he was still not completely free. The searing "All Night Long," "I Got the Blues So Bad," and "This Train Is Heaven Bound" are punctuated by equally gripping guitar accompaniment on either 6- or 12-string. There's also material recorded later in his career in Berkeley. The three cuts from 1970 show Williams in a more reflective mode, though no less powerful. These are two of nine previously unissued cuts comprising the majority of the disc. —*Ron Wynn*

★ **Angola Prisoner's Blues** / Mar. 1961 / Arhoolie ✦✦✦✦✦
Not enough great things to say about this one, one of the finest field recordings ever done anywhere. If Robert Pete's "Prisoner's Talking Blues" doesn't move you, check your heart into your refrigerator's freezer section. —*Cub Koda*

Free Again / Nov. 1961 / Original Blues Classics ✦✦✦✦

Legacy of the Blues, Vol. 9 / 1973 / GNP ✦✦✦✦

Rural Blues (With Snooks Eaglin) / 197 / Storyville ✦✦✦✦
Not only does Snooks Eaglin prove a fine partner for Robert Pete Williams, but his vocals and playing have seldom been more disciplined and exciting. —*Ron Wynn*

Blues Masters / 1991 / Storyville ✦✦✦

Robert Pete Williams, Vol. 1 / 1994 / Arhoolie ✦✦✦
Robert Pete Williams' music had the striking lyricism and highly individualized sound of the great Delta blues masters, but it was made well after the heyday of that style. Williams improvised considerably in his performances, using blues' language but varying his approach. These songs were mostly recorded at the Angola State Penitentiary. While Williams sings mournful, anguished blues with spectacular impact, he also can turn around and do more joyous fare effectively. His vigorous accompaniment, especially on six-string guitar, is just as creative and stunning as his vocals. This 15-cut disc, which has five bonus cuts, is most welcome. —*Ron Wynn*

When a Man Takes the Blues / 1994 / Arhoolie ✦✦✦✦
Important collection of Williams' best early work. —*Bill Dahl*

I'm as Blue as a Man Can be / 1994 / Arhoolie ✦✦✦✦
More classic early sides. —*Bill Dahl*

Homesick James Williamson

b. Apr. 3, 1910, Somerville, TN
Guitar, Vocals / Electric Chicago Blues
His correct age may remain in doubt (he's claimed he was born as early as 1905), but the slashing slide guitar skills of Homesick James Williamson have never been in question. Many of his most satisfying recordings have placed him in a solo setting, where his timing eccentricities don't disrupt the proceedings (though he's made some fine band-backed waxings as well).

Williamson was playing guitar at age ten and soon ran away from his Tennessee home to play at fish-fries and dances. His travels took the guitarist through Mississippi and North Carolina during the 1920s, where he crossed paths with Yank Rachell, Sleepy John Estes, Blind Boy Fuller, and Big Joe Williams.

Settling in Chicago during the 1930s, Williamson played local clubs and recorded for RCA Victor in 1937. The miles and gigs had added up before Williamson made some of his finest sides in 1952-53 for Art Sheridan's Chance Records (including the classic "Homesick" that gave him his enduring stage name).

James also worked extensively as a sideman, backing harp great Sonny Boy Williamson in 1945 at a Chicago gin joint called the Purple Cat and during the 1950s with his cousin, slide master Elmore James (to whom Homesick is stylistically indebted). He also recorded with James during the 1950s. Homesick's own output included crashing 45s for Colt and USA in 1962, a fine 1964 album for Prestige, and four tracks on a Vanguard anthology in 1965.

Williamson has never stopped recording and touring; he's done recent albums for Appaloosa and Earwig. No matter what his current chronological age, there's nothing over-the-hill about the blues of Homesick James Williamson. —*Bill Dahl*

● **Blues on the South Side** / 1964 / Prestige ✦✦✦✦
Probably the best album the slide guitarist ever laid down (originally for Prestige in 1964). His stylistic similarities to his cousin, the great Elmore James, are obvious, but Homesick deviates repeatedly from the form. Tough as nails with a bottleneck, he goes for the jugular on "Goin' Down Swingin'," "Johnny Mae," and "Gotta Move," supported by pianist Lafayette Leake, guitarist Eddie Taylor, and drummer Clifton James. —*Bill Dahl*

Homesick James Williamson & Snooky Pryor / 1973 / Caroline ✦✦✦

Ain't Sick No More / 1973 / Bluesway ✦✦✦

Chicago Blues Festival, Vol. 1 / 197 / Black & Blue ✦✦✦

Goin Back in the Times / 1994 / Earwig ✦✦✦
A credible, reflective return to the slide guitar veteran's country blues days. —*Bill Dahl*

Juanita / Mar. 18, 1997 / Evidence ✦✦✦

Chicago Slide Guitar Legend / 1998 / Official ✦✦✦✦
This (apparently) quasi-legal 26-song collection, the first on CD for Homesick James Williamson, is some of the best electric Chicago blues you can buy, covering his 1950s and early-'60s career; to judge from the sound and the appearent personnel, it's drawn from releases on Chance, Colt, Bluesville, and USA, among other labels, including two different takes (the second, slower one is better) of his Chance Records debut "Lonesome Old Train," an alternate take of "Johnny Mae" (a song he later cut for Prestige), and his signature tune, "Homesick Blues." The sound is raw but clean—it sounds like the makers got a good tape source, rather than using vinyl. Or, rather, it's as clean as James' amplified bottleneck (which is recorded very close) could ever get—he uses layers of distortion in a manner that distantly prefigures Jimi Hendrix, although his playing is much crunchier than Hendrix's, maybe a little closer in texture to Hubert Sumlin or Willie Johnson. The backing band, which rocks real hard (check out "Williamson's Boogie") includes Chicago stalwarts like Baby Face Leroy Foster, Snooky Pryor, *et al*, making this collection of a piece with any Chess stuff of the era. And the stuff itself is mostly good, occasionally priceless, most notably James' unabashed rewrite of "Got Love If You Want It" entitled "The Woman I Love"; Williamson and Sunnyland Slim also get a really cool featured spot together, a boogie number called "Sunnyland/Homesick Special" that really rocks. Williamson's

singing is also secure and occasionally even inspired, as on "My Kind of Woman," where he almost overshadows his guitar. The influence of Elmore James obviously shows through everywhere (especially on "Farmers Blues" and "Homesick Blues"), and anyone who can't get enough of the latter's sides will probably want to get hold of this disc. — *Bruce Eder*

Sonny Boy Williamson [II] (Aleck Ford "Rice" Miller)

b. Dec. 5, 1899, Glendora, MS, **d.** May 25, 1965, Helena, AR
Harmonica, Vocals / R&B, Electric Delta Blues, Electric Chicago Blues, Delta Blues, Chicago Blues, Electric Blues, Harmonica Blues, Blues Revival

Sonny Boy Williamson was, in many ways, the ultimate blues legend. By the time of his death in 1965, he had been around long enough to have played with Robert Johnson at the start of his career and Eric Clapton, Jimmy Page, and Robbie Robertson at the end of it. In between, he drank a lot of whiskey, hoboed around the country, had a successful radio show for 15 years, toured Europe to great acclaim and simply wrote, played, and sang some of the greatest blues ever etched into black phonograph records. His delivery was sly, evil, and world-weary, while his harp-playing was full of short, rhythmic bursts one minute and powerful, impassioned blowing the next. His songs were chock full of mordant wit, with largely autobiographical lyrics that hold up to the scrutiny of the printed page. Though he took his namesake from another well-known harmonica player, no one really sounded like him.

A moody, bitter, and suspicious man, no one wove such a confusing web of misinformation as Sonny Boy Williamson II. Even his birth date (stated as December 5, 1899 in most reference books, but some sources claim his birth may have been in either 1897 or 1909) and real name (Aleck or Alex or Willie "Rice"—which may or may not be a nickname—Miller or Ford) cannot be verified with absolute certainty. Of his childhood days in Mississippi, absolutely nothing is known. What *is* known is that by the mid-'30s, he was traveling the Delta working under the alias of Little Boy Blue. With blues legends like Robert Johnson, Robert Nighthawk, Robert Jr. Lockwood, and Elmore James as interchangeable playing partners, he worked the juke joints, fish fries, country suppers, and ballgames of the era. By the early '40s, he was the star of KFFA's *King Biscuit Time*, the first live blues radio show to hit the American airwaves. As one of the major ruses to occur in blues history, his sponsor—the Interstate Grocery Company—felt they could push more sacks of their King Biscuit Flour with Miller posing as Chicago harmonica star John Lee "Sonny Boy" Williamson. In today's everybody-knows-everything video age, it's hard to think that such an idea would work, much less prosper. After all, the real Sonny Boy was a national recording star, and Miller's vocal and harmonica style was in no way derivative of him. But Williamson had no desire to tour in the South, so prosper it did, and when John Lee was murdered in Chicago, Miller became—in his own words—"the original Sonny Boy." Among his fellow musicians, he was usually still referred to as Rice Miller, but to the rest of the world he did, indeed, become *the* Sonny Boy Williamson.

The show was an immediate hit, prompting IGC to introduce Sonny Boy Corn Meal, complete with a likeness of Williamson on the front of the package. With all this local success, however, Sonny Boy was not particularly anxious to record. Though he often claimed in his twilight years that he had recorded in the '30s, no evidence of that appears to have existed. Lillian McMurray, the owner of Trumpet Records in Jackson, MS, had literally tracked him down to a boarding house in nearby Belzoni and enticed him to record for her. The music Sonny Boy made for her between 1951 to 1954 show him in peak form, his vocal, instrumental, and songwriting skills honed to perfection. Williamson struck paydirt on his first Trumpet release, "Eyesight to the Blind" and though the later production on his Chess records would make the Trumpet sides seem woefully under-recorded by comparison, they nonetheless stand today as classic performances, capturing juke-joint music in one of its finest hours.

Another major contribution to the history of the blues occurred when Sonny Boy brought *King Biscuit Time* guest star Elmore James into the studio for a session. With Williamson blowing harp, a drummer keeping time, and the tape machine running surreptitiously, Elmore recorded the first version of what would become his signature tune, Robert Johnson's "Dust My Broom." By this time Sonny Boy had divorced his first wife (who also happened to be the Howlin' Wolf's sister) and married Mattie Gordon. This would prove to be the longest and most enduring relationship of his life

outside of music, with Mattie putting up with the man's rambling ways, and living a life of general rootlessness in the bargain. On two different occasions Sonny Boy moved to Detroit, taking up residence in the Baby Boy Warren band for brief periods, and contributed earth-shattering solos on Warren sides for Blue Lake and Excello in 1954.

By early 1955, after leasing a single to Johnny Vincent's Ace label, McMurray had sold Williamson's contract to Buster Williams in Memphis, who in turn sold it to Leonard Chess in Chicago. All the pieces were finally tumbling into place, and Sonny Boy finally had a reason to take up permanent residence north of the Mason-Dixon line; he now was officially a Chess recording artist. His first session for Chess took place on August 12, 1955, and the single pulled from it, "Don't Start Me to Talkin'," started doing brisk business on the R&B charts. By his second session for the label, he was reunited with longtime musical partner Robert Jr. Lockwood. Lockwood—who had become one of the original King Biscuit Boys—had become *de facto* house guitarist for Chess, as well as moonlighting for other Chicago labels. With Lockwood's combination of Robert Johnson rhythms and jazz chord embellishments, Williamson's harp and parched vocals sounded fresher than ever and Lockwood's contributions to the success of Sonny Boy's Chess recordings cannot be overestimated.

For a national recording artist, Williamson had a remarkable penchant for pulling a disappearing act for months at a time. Sometimes, when Chicago bookings got too lean, he would head back to Arkansas, fronting the *King Biscuit* radio show for brief periods. But in 1963 he was headed to Europe for the first time, as part of the American Folk Blues Festival. The folk music boom was in full swing and Europeans were bringing over blues artists, both in and past their prime, to face wildly appreciative White audiences for the first time. Sonny Boy unleashed his bag of tricks and stole the show every night. He loved Europe and stayed behind in Britain when the tour headed home. He started working the teenage beat club circuit, touring and recording with the Yardbirds and Eric Burdon's band, whom he always referred to as "de Mammimals." On the folk blues tours, Sonny Boy would be very dignified and laidback. But in the beat club setting, with young, White bands playing on eleven behind him, he'd pull out every juke-joint trick he used with the King Biscuit Entertainers and drive the kids nuts. "Help Me" became a surprise hit in Britain and across Europe. Now in his mid-60s (or possibly older), Williamson was truly appreciative of all the attention, and contemplated moving to Europe permanently. But after getting a harlequin, two-tone, city gentleman's suit (complete with bowler hat, rolled umbrella and attaché case full of harmonicas) made up for himself, he headed back to the States—and the Chess studios—for some final sessions. When he returned to England in 1964, it was as a conquering hero. One of his final recordings, with Jimmy Page on guitar, was entitled "I'm Trying to Make London My Home."

In 1965, he headed home, back to Mississippi one last time, and took over the *King Biscuit* show again. Still wearing his custom-made suit, he regaled the locals with stories of his travels across Europe. Some were impressed, others who had known him for years felt he could have just as well substituted the name "Mars" for Europe in explaining his exploits, so used were they to Sonny Boy's tall tales. But after hoboing his way around the United States for thirty-odd years, and playing to appreciative audiences throughout Europe, Sonny Boy had a perfectly good reason for returning to the Delta; he had come home to die. He would enlist the help of old friends like Houston Stackhouse and Peck Curtis to take him around to all the back-road spots he had seen as a boy, sometimes paying his respects to old friends, other days just whiling away an afternoon on the banks of a river fishing.

When Ronnie Hawkins' ex-bandmates, the Hawks, were playing in the area, they made a special point of seeking out Sonny Boy and spent an entire evening backing him up in a juke joint. All through the night, Williamson kept spitting into a coffee can beside him. When Robbie Robertson got up to leave the bandstand during a break, he noticed the can was filled with blood. On May 25, 1965, Curtis and Stackhouse were waiting at the KFFA studios for Sonny Boy to do the daily *King Biscuit* broadcast. When Williamson didn't show, Curtis left the station and headed to the rooming house where Sonny Boy was staying, only to find him lying in bed, dead of an apparent heart attack. He was buried in the Whitfield Cemetery in Tutwiler, MS, and his funeral was well-attended. As Houston Stackhouse said, "He was well thought of through that country." He was elected to the Blues Foundation Hall of Fame in 1980. — *Cub Koda*

Down & Out Blues / 1959 / MCA/Chess ◆◆◆◆
Retaining photographer Don Bronstein's cover shot of a disheveled bum lying on the sidewalk (some former Chess artist, perhaps?) Sonny Boy Williamson's original 1959 album made it to digital reissue but has now been supplanted by MCA's exhaustive *The Essential Sonny Boy Williamson.* Still, for a budget price, there's a dozen unforgettable tracks: "Don't Start Me to Talkin'," his Checker debut; "All My Love in Vain," "Wake Up Baby," "99," "Cross My Heart," "Let Me Explain," and "The Key (To Your Door)." *— Bill Dahl*

Help Me / 1964 / Chess ◆◆◆◆

In Memorium / 1965 / Chess ◆◆

The Real Folk Blues / 1965 / MCA/Chess ◆◆◆◆
With the exception of "Dissatisfied," cut in 1957, everything on this dozen-track comp dates from 1960-63 and holds "One Way Out," "Checkin' Up on My Baby," "Trust My Baby," and the catchy, country-tinged "Peach Tree," which drives along with a pronounced bounce. *— Bill Dahl*

More Folk Blues / 1966 / Chess ◆◆◆◆

Sonny Boy Williamson & the Yardbirds / 1966 / Mercury ◆◆

More Real Folk Blues / Sep. 1967 / MCA/Chess ◆◆◆◆
More good early-'60s Chess Recordings from Sonny Boy Williamson. "Help Me," "Bye Bye Bird," and "Nine Below Zero" have been covered by numerous blues and rock acts. Most of the songs, however, show up on the *Essential* best-of collection. *— Richie Unterberger*

One Way Out / 1968 / MCA/Chess ◆◆◆◆
Sly son-of-a-gun that he was, old Sonny Boy Williamson found a way to weld the twist to the blues with his rousing 1961 title track, with guitarists Robert Jr. Lockwood and Luther Tucker positively blazing in supple support. Fourteen more gems make this one a must: 1955's "Good Evening Everybody," "Work with Me" and "You Killing Me," all with Muddy Waters and Jimmy Rogers in support; the sturdy "Keep It to Yourself" from the next year, and a forceful "This Is My Apartment." *— Bill Dahl*

Bummer Road / 1969 / MCA/Chess ◆◆◆◆
Yes, this is the album where Williamson and Leonard Chess get down to some serious cussing during their hilariously heated exchange while recording "Little Village." But there are plenty more reasons to pick up this CD than that one: his lascivious Yuletide ditty "Santa Claus"; the stirring "Unseen Eye" and "Keep Your Hand Out of My Pocket," the leering "She Got Next to Me." Everything here was done between 1957 and 1960—prime years for the wily harpist at Chess. *— Bill Dahl*

☆ **Sonny Boy Williamson** / 1976 / Chess ◆◆◆◆◆
Good two-LP, 28-song anthology of Williamson's best Chess material. All but a half dozen of these cuts appear on the more extensive *Essential* CD. *— Richie Unterberger*

Chess Masters / 1981 / Chess ◆◆◆◆

☆ **King Biscuit Time** / 1989 / Arhoolie ◆◆◆◆◆
Sonny Boy's early Trumpet sides, 1951. The original "Eyesight To The Blind", "Nine Below Zero" and "Mighty Long Time" are Sonny Boy at his very best. Added bonuses include Williamson backing Elmore James on his original recording of "Dust My Broom" and a live KFFA broadcast from 1965. *— Cub Koda*

Clownin' With the World / 1989 / Trumpet ◆◆◆◆
This batch of mostly unreleased Trumpet blues cuts from the early '50s offers some sizzling, if sometimes uneven, material by Sonny Boy Williamson II (Rice Miller) and Willie Love. Each gets eight numbers, with Williamson's being recorded both in Houston and Jackson, MS, while Love did all of his in Jackson. Williamson's ripping, searing harmonica and craggy vocals were then becoming popular, while Love's equally decisive singing and wild, carefree tunes were also attracting big audiences. This is undiluted, frequently chaotic, and always enjoyable music. *— Ron Wynn*

Keep It to Ourselves / 1990 / Analogue ◆◆◆◆
An intimate 1963 collection of Sonny Boy Williamson in solo and duet (with guitarist Matt Murphy) formats; on three tracks, pianist Memphis Slim hops aboard. This delightful addendum to Williamson's electric output of the same era was cut in Denmark and first issued on Storyville. *— Bill Dahl*

The Chess Years / 1991 / Charly ◆◆◆◆
This import multi-disc boxed set of Williamson's Chess sides (1955-1964) is a definitive overview. *— Cub Koda*

★ **The Essential Sonny Boy Williamson** / Jun. 8, 1993 / MCA ◆◆◆◆◆
Two-disc compilation offering 45 of the wizened harmonica genius' best efforts for the Chess brothers, this is the best domestic Williamson package you'll find. Not everything you might want, but pretty close to it: "Don't Start Me to Talkin'," "Let Me Explain," "The Key (To Your Door)" (an alternate take), "Bring It on Home," "Help Me," "One Way Out," "Your Funeral and My Trial," and plenty more. With Robert Jr. Lockwood and Luther Tucker peeling off sizzling guitar riffs behind him, Williamson always had a trick or two up his sleeve until the end. *— Bill Dahl*

Goin' in Your Direction / 1994 / Trumpet ◆◆◆◆
Alligator continues its Trumpet reissue series with an excellent 15-cut anthology covering early Rice Miller (Sonny Boy Williamson II) material, some of it also including guitarist Arthur "Big Boy" Crudup and guitarist Bobo "Slim" Thomas. Miller was honing the uncanny technique that made him a harmonica legend, playing long overtones, spitting lines, droning and angular phrases that are now part of blues lore. His voice was gaining strength and stature, and he repeatedly demonstrated the kind of vocal character and instrumental acumen later immortalized on his Chess sessions. Alligator has found a genuine treasure chest with this series. *— Ron Wynn*

Trumpet Masters, Vol. 5: From the Bottom / 1994 / Collectables ◆◆◆◆
As you would expect, Sonny Boy Williamson II's Trumpet sides were rough, raspy and combative, punctuated by biting harmonica and accented by his piercing vocals. This CD cleans up the sound a bit, but not enough to rob it of its energy or grit. *— Ron Wynn*

In Europe with Clapton, Dixon and Spann / 1995 / Evidence ◆◆◆
More highlights from Sonny Boy Williamson's overseas travels, in a wide variety of settings—during the 1963 and 1964 American Folk Blues Festivals with old friends like Willie Dixon, Sunnyland Slim, Hubert Sumlin and Matt Murphy behind him, and for nine tracks, with the Yardbirds in support. The latter combination works pretty well—Clapton and company offer reverent, laidback rhythms that seldom intrude and often mesh nicely. *— Bill Dahl*

★ **His Best** / May 20, 1997 / MCA ◆◆◆◆◆
While some hardliners will point to his early 1950s Trumpet recordings as his most undiluted work, Sonny Boy's tenure at Chess Records was his longest and most successful and therefore deserves first look for the novice coming to this remarkable bluesman at ground level. This 20-track collection takes 17 tracks from the excellent two-disc *Essential Sonny Boy Williamson* collection and adds "Sad To Be Alone," "My Younger Days" and an alternate session-second version of "One Way Out" with Buddy Guy on guitar (yes, *this* is the version that the Allman Brothers used as the blueprint for their cover version) to the final mix. This is another entry into MCA's Chess 50th Anniversary Series and the digital transfers here are exemplary, making this an automatic audio upgrade for those who already have this material in their collection. Because his output for the label was of such a uniformly high quality, virtually everything Williamson put down on tape at the Chess studios could make a final cut on any best of package you'd want to put together on the man. So bemoaning the absence of any track here would be minor critical carping, especially in light of no less than five other Sonny Boy Chess packages still being in print at press time. But if you're only going to own *one* of them and your wallet tends to shy away from two-disc anthologies, this makes an excellent first purchase. *— Cub Koda*

Sonny Boy Williamson [I] (John Lee Williamson)

b. Mar. 30, 1914, Jackson, TN, d. Jun. 1, 1948, Chicago, IL
Harmonica, Vocals / Acoustic Chicago Blues, Chicago Blues
Easily the most important harmonica player of the pre-war era, John Lee Williamson almost single-handedly made the humble mouth organ a worthy lead instrument for blues bands—leading the way for the amazing innovations of Little Walter and a platoon of others to follow. If not for his tragic murder in 1948 while on his way home from a Chicago gin mill, Williamson would doubtless have been right there alongside them, exploring new and exciting directions.

It can safely be noted that Williamson made the most of his limited time on the planet. Already a harp virtuoso in his teens, the first Sonny Boy (Rice

Miller would adopt the same monicker down in the Delta) learned from Hammie Nixon and Noah Lewis and rambled with Sleepy John Estes and Yank Rachell before settling in Chicago in 1934.

Williamson's extreme versatility and consistent ingenuity won him a Bluebird recording contract in 1937. Under the direction of the ubiquitous Lester Melrose, Sonny Boy Williamson recorded prolifically for Victor both as a leader and behind others in the vast Melrose stable (including Robert Lee McCoy and Big Joe Williams, who in turn played on some of Williamson's sides).

Williamson commenced his sensational recording career with a resounding bang. His first vocal offering on Bluebird was the seminal "Good Morning School Girl," covered countless times across the decades. That same auspicious date also produced "Sugar Mama Blues" and "Blue Bird Blues," both of them every bit as classic in their own right.

The next year brought more gems, including "Decoration Blues" and "Whiskey Headed Woman Blues." The output of 1939 included "T.B. Blues" and "Tell Me Baby," while Williamson cut "My Little Machine" and "Jivin' the Blues" in 1940. Jimmy Rogers apparently took note of Williamson's "Sloppy Drunk Blues," cut with pianist Blind John Davis and bassist Ransom Knowling in 1941; Rogers adapted the tune in storming fashion for Chess in 1954. 1941's motherlode also included "Ground Hog Blues" and "My Black Name," while the popular "Stop Breaking Down" (1945) found the harpist backed by guitarist Tampa Red and pianist Big Maceo.

Sonny Boy cut more than 120 sides in all for RCA from 1937 to 1947, many of them turning up in the postwar repertoires of various Chicago blues giants. His call-and-response style of alternating vocal passages with pungent harmonica blasts was a development of mammoth proportions that would be adopted across-the-board by virtually every blues harpist to follow in his wake.

But Sonny Boy Williamson wouldn't live to reap any appreciable rewards from his inventions. He died at the age of 34, while at the zenith of his popularity (his romping "Shake That Boogie" was a national R&B hit in 1947 on Victor), from a violent bludgeoning about the head that occurred during a strong-arm robbery on the South side. "Better Cut That Out," another storming rocker later appropriated by Junior Wells, became a posthumous hit for Williamson in late 1948. It was the very last song he had committed to posterity. Wells was only one young harpist to display his enduring allegiance; a teenaged Billy Boy Arnold had recently summoned up the nerve to knock on his idol's door to ask for lessons. The accommodating Sonny Boy Williamson was only too happy to oblige, a kindness Arnold has never forgotten (nor does he fail to pay tribute to his eternal main man every chance he gets). Such is the lasting legacy of the blues' first great harmonicist. — *Bill Dahl*

Complete Recorded Works, Vols. 1-5 / 1937-1947 / Document ◆◆◆◆
His complete works 1937-1947 in chronological order. Sonny Boy was a major influence (both harmonica and vocals) on many of the younger Chicago bluesmen, in particular: Junior Wells. — *Michael Erlewine*

Sonny Boy Williamson, Vol. 1 (1937-1939) / 1937-1939 / Qualiton ◆◆◆◆
This artist was perhaps the most significant pioneer of the city-styled, horn-oriented blues harp—a style brought to perfection by Little Walter. Williamson adapted the country-styled, chordal-rhythmic technique that he learned from Noah Lewis and Hammie Nixon to suit the demands of the evolving urban blues styles. These 24 tracks include Sonny Boy's first six records cut in 1937 and sport an imposing list of sidemen: Robert Nighthawk, Big Joe Williams, Henry Townsend, Walter Davis, Yank Rachell, Big Bill Broonzy, and Speckled Red. This is a definitive collection. — *Larry Hoffman*

Throw a Boogie Woogie (With Big Joe Williams) / Apr. 1990 / RCA ◆◆◆◆
Eight indispensable Bluebird sides dating from 1937-38—right at the very beginning of his reign as king of blues harpists—that display precisely why Williamson was such a revered innovator (and continues to be even now). Highlights include his classic "Good Morning School Girl" and "Sugar Mama Blues." He shares the disc with itinerant rambler Big Joe Williams, whose eight 1937-41 selections include six featuring Sonny Boy playing harp behind the nine-string guitarist. — *Bill Dahl*

★ **Sugar Mama** / 1995 / Indigo ◆◆◆◆◆
A well-researched 24-track compendium of the first Sonny Boy Williamson's massively influential Bluebird catalog that spans 1937-1942. Besides being

such an innovator on the mouth organ, Williamson's songs themselves have stood the test of time strikingly—"Good Morning School Girl," "Blue Bird Blues," "Decoration Blues," "Sloppy Drunk Blues," and many more on the collection are recognized classics. — *Bill Dahl*

Complete Bluebird Recordings, Vol. 1: 1937-1938 / Feb. 27, 1996 / BMG ◆◆◆◆

The Bluebird Recordings 1937-1938 / Jan. 28, 1997 / RCA ◆◆◆◆
This 24-track overview of the blues harp master's brief tenure with the Bluebird label includes "Good Morning School Girl," probably Williamson's best known work thanks to subsequent covers by Howlin' Wolf and the Grateful Dead. — *Jason Ankeny*

The Bluebird Recordings 1938 / Apr. 29, 1997 / RCA ◆◆◆◆
Picking up where *Bluebird Recordings 1937-1938* left off, *Bluebird Recordings 1938* features the remaining 18 tracks that Sonny Boy Williamson recorded for the label in '38. These are the recordings that established Williamson's career, and several of his classics, including "Deep Down in the Ground," as well as several duets with Speckled Red are included here. — *Thom Owens*

Chick Willis (Robert Willis)

b. Sep. 29, 1934, Cabiness, GA
Vocals, Guitar / Modern Electric Blues, R&B
Cousin to the late blues ballad singer Chuck Willis, Robert "Chick" Willis is primarily beloved for his ribald, dozens-based rocker "Stoop Down Baby." The guitarist cut his original version in 1972 for tiny La Val Records of Kalamazoo, MI, selling a ton of 45s for the jukebox market only (the tune's lyrics were way too raunchy for airplay).

The Atlanta-born Willis left the military in 1954, hiring on as valet and chauffeur to cousin Chuck, then riding high with his many R&B hits for OKeh Records. At that point, Chick's primary role on the show was as a singer (he made his own vinyl debut in 1956 with a single, "You're Mine," for Lee Rupe's Ebb Records after winning a talent contest at Atlanta's Magnolia Ballroom), but he picked up the guitar while on the road with his cousin (Chick cites Guitar Slim as his main man in that department).

When Chuck died of stomach problems in 1958, Willis soldiered on, pausing in Chicago to work as a sideman with slide guitar great Elmore James. A few obscure 45s ("Twistin' in the Hospital Ward," cut for Alto in 1962, sounds promising) preceded the advent of "Stoop Down Baby," which Willis has freshened up for countless sequels ever since (he developed the song by teasing passersby with his ribald rhymes while working in a carnival variety show).

Risqué material has remained a staple of Willis' output in recent years. He cut several albums for Ichiban, notably 1988's *Now!*, *Footprints in My Bed* in 1990, and *Back to the Blues* in 1991. — *Bill Dahl*

● **Stoop Down Baby. . . Let Your Daddy See** / 1972 / Collectables ◆◆◆◆
Here's the signifyin' original "Stoop Down Baby" in its long, unexpurgated version as issued on the tiny La Val label in 1972. "Mother Fuyer" travels the same salacious route, but Chick Willis has a serious side too—a pair of Guitar Slim covers spotlight Willis' stinging guitar and sturdy singing. — *Bill Dahl*

Now / 1988 / Ichiban ◆◆
Willis updates his biggest seller with a "Stoop Down '88," and there's a leering "I Want to Play with Your Poodle," and "I Want a Big Fat Woman" for those who like their blues blue. — *Bill Dahl*

Footprints in My Bed / 1990 / Ichiban ◆◆◆◆
One of the few real blues LPs to post a warning about explicit lyrics, though it seems pretty tame in these rap-hardened times. Nevertheless, "Jack You Up," "Nuts for Sale," and "Big Red Caboose" are firmly in the best risque Willis tradition—and very well produced and played to boot. — *Bill Dahl*

Back to the Blues / 1991 / Ichiban ◆◆◆
Willis takes things a little more seriously than usual, concentrating largely on covers of material by Percy Mayfield, Howlin' Wolf, Clarence Carter, and Guitar Slim. His own contributions include "I Ain't Jivin' Baby" and "Bow-Legged Woman" (he couldn't resist the raunchy stuff entirely!). — *Bill Dahl*

Holdin' Hands with the Blues / 1992 / Ichiban ◆◆
Thanks to a weak selection of songs and an indifferent production, *Holdin' Hands with the Blues* is one of Chick Willis' lesser efforts. Occasionally, he

works up a nice lascivious snarl and spits out a couple of good solos, but for the most part, the record falls into predictable, uninspiring, dirty-minded shuffles and boogies. — *Thom Owens*

Nasty Chick / 1992 / Ichiban ✦✦✦

I Got a Big Fat Woman / 1994 / Ichiban ✦✦

Chuck Willis (Harold Willis)

b. Jan. 31, 1928, Atlanta, GA, **d.** Apr. 10, 1958, Atlanta, GA
Vocals / R&B

There were two distinct sides to Chuck Willis. In addition to being a convincing blues shouter, the Atlanta-born Willis harbored a vulnerable blues balladeer side. In addition, he was a masterful songwriter who penned some of the most distinctive R&B numbers of the 1950s. We can't grant him principal credit for his 1957 smash adaptation of "C.C. Rider," an irresistible update of a classic folk-blues, but Willis did write such gems as "I Feel So Bad" (later covered by Elvis Presley, Little Milton, and Otis Rush), the anguished ballads "Don't Deceive Me (Please Don't Go)" and "It's Too Late" (the latter attracting covers by Buddy Holly, Charlie Rich, and Otis Redding) and his swan song, "Hang Up My Rock and Roll Shoes."

Harold Willis (he adopted Chuck as a stage handle) received his early training singing at YMCA-sponsored "Teenage Canteens" in Atlanta and fronting the combos of local bandleaders Roy Mays and Red McAllister. Powerful deejay Zenas "Daddy" Sears took an interest in the young vocalist's career, hooking him up with Columbia Records in 1951. After a solitary single for the major firm, Willis was shuttled over to its recently reactivated OKeh R&B subsidiary.

In 1952, he crashed the national R&B lists for OKeh with a typically plaintive ballad, "My Story," swiftly encoring on the hit parade with a gentle cover of Fats Domino's "Goin' to the River" and his own "Don't Deceive Me" the next year and "You're Still My Baby" and the surging Latin-beat "I Feel So Bad" in 1954. Willis also penned a heart-tugging chart-topper for Ruth Brown that year, "Oh What a Dream."

Willis moved over to Atlantic Records in 1956 and immediately enjoyed another round of hits with "It's Too Late" and "Juanita." Atlantic strove mightily to cross Willis over into pop territory, inserting an exotic steel guitar at one session and chirpy choirs on several more. The strategy eventually worked when his 1957 revival of the ancient "C.C. Rider" proved the perfect number to do the "Stroll" to; *American Bandstand* gave the track a big push, and Willis had his first R&B number one hit as well as a huge pop seller (Gene "Daddy G" Barge's magnificent sax solo likely aided its ascent).

Barge returned for Willis' similar follow-up, "Betty and Dupree," which also did well for him. But the turban-wearing crooner's time was growing short — he had long suffered from ulcers prior to his 1958 death from peritonitis. Much has been made of the ironic title of his last hit, the touching "What Am I Living For," but it was no more a clue to his impending demise than its flip, the joyous "Hang Up My Rock and Roll Shoes." Both tracks became massive hits upon the singer's death, and his posthumous roll continued with "My Life" and a powerful "Keep A-Driving" later that year.

Willis' cousin, Robert "Chick" Willis, who began his career as a backup singer for Chuck, remains active nationally. — *Bill Dahl*

My Story / 1980 / Columbia ✦✦✦✦

Not as exhaustive as Legacy's subsequent look at Willis' early-to-mid-'50s hitmaking stint at OKeh, but this 14-tracker still gets the job done with the smooth ballads "Going to the River," "Don't Deceive Me," and "My Story" and Willis' surging, Latin-tempoed original "I Feel So Bad." — *Bill Dahl*

Let's Jump Tonight! The Best of Chuck Willis: 1951-1956 / 1994 / Epic/Legacy ✦✦✦✦

Before his brief turn as a rock 'n' roll star with Atlantic, Willis cut a lot of material for OKeh in much more of an R&B/jump blues vein. This 26-cut collection includes all of his early and mid-'50s R&B hits — "My Story," "Goin' To The River," "Don't Deceive Me," "You're Still My Baby," and his most famous number from this period, "I Feel So Bad" (revived by Elvis Presley, among others). The influence of Joe Turner, Charles Brown, early Lloyd Price, and similar performers is strongly felt; Willis could shout competently, but was much better on the emotional R&B ballads. Not as strong or distinctive as his Atlantic material, this includes several cuts that were previously unreleased or previously unavailable in the US — *Richie Unterberger*

★ **Stroll On: The Chuck Willis Collection** / Oct. 19, 1994 / Razor & Tie ✦✦✦✦✦

All 25 of the versatile Atlanta-bred singer's Atlantic Records sides, presented beautifully (every R&B reissue on CD should be packaged so well, with plenty of brilliant stereo). Willis really hit his stride at Atlantic, doing the Stroll with his easy-going "C.C. Rider" and "Betty and Dupree" (both boasting darting sax breaks from Gene Barge), baring his tender soul on a devotional "What Am I Living For," and taking R&B into fresh directions with a jumping "Kansas City Woman," the relentless "Keep A-Drivin'," and a buoyant "Hang Up My Rock and Roll Shoes." — *Bill Dahl*

Little Sonny Willis (Aaron Willis)

b. Oct. 6, 1932, Greensboro, AL
Harmonica, Guitar / Electric Harmonica Blues, Piano Blues

A product of the Detroit blues circuit, Little Sonny Willis was a superior vocalist and harpist whose work bridged the gap between the R&B sound of the 1950s and the southern soul flavor of the following decade. Born Aaron Willis on October 6, 1932 in Greensboro, AL, he cut his earliest singles for Duke and Excello, scoring his first hit, "Love Shock," in 1958; he enjoyed little success in the years to come, however, but after recording for the tiny Revilot imprint in 1966, he landed on the influential Stax label. Beginning with 1970's *New King of Harmonica*, Willis reached his artistic peak while at Stax, skillfully refining his soulful style; however, none of his work for the label — which also included 1971's *Black and Blue* and 1974's *Hard Goin' Up* — found an audience, and over time he receded from view, last appearing on Parliament's 1980 LP *Trombipulation*. — *Jason Ankeny*

● **New King of Blues Harmonica** / 1970 / Stax ✦✦✦✦

New King of Blues Harmonica, the first album recorded by Little Sonny, finds the harpist living up to his name, turning out a hard-driving collection of Chicago blues. At times, he's a little too hung up on sounding like Sonny Boy Williamson, but for the most part, this is thoroughly enjoyable, high-octane Chicago blues. However, the presence of an organ on most of the record may be a little distracting for purists. — *Thom Owens*

Hard Goin' Up / Mar. 1974 / Enterprise ✦✦✦

Because he hasn't promoted himself aggressively enough, Little Sonny isn't nearly as well known in either blues or R&B circles as he should be. But make no mistake, Sonny is a first-class electric bluesman who's also a pearl of a soul singer. And he excels in both areas on *Hard Goin' Up*, which Fantasy reissued on CD in the US in 1997. "You Made Me Strong," "It's Hard Going Up (But Twice as Hard Coming Down)," and "You Can Be Replaced" illustrate his mastery of the 12-bar form, while "You're Spreading Yourself a Little Too Thin" and "Do It Right Now" are invigorating examples of the type of horn-driven, sock-it-to-'em soul music Sonny embraced with such conviction. The punchy "My Woman Is Good to Me" was a minor hit, and *Hard* made it to No. 42 on Billboard's R&B albums chart. It's possible that had it not been for the problems Stax was having with CBS at the time, the album would have enjoyed a lot more exposure. At any rate, *Hard Goin' Up* is one of Sonny's finest accomplishments. — *Alex Henderson*

Black & Blue / 1992 / Stax ✦✦✦✦

Sonny's second Enterprise LP was an impressive affair showcasing both his sinuous harp and rich vocals. Includes the Al Bell-produced "Where Women Got Meat on Their Bones" (later covered by Son Seals) and a fine rendition of "Wade in the Water." — *Bill Dahl*

Hop Wilson (Harding Wilson)

b. Apr. 27, 1927, Grapeland, TX, **d.** Aug. 27, 1975, Houston, TX
Guitar, Vocals / Electric Texas Blues, Acoustic Texas Blues

Slide guitar blues with an Elmore James flavor played on an eight-string table (non-pedal) steel guitar was the trademarked sound of Houston blues legend Hop Wilson. Strictly a local phenomenon, Wilson recorded fitfully and hated touring. Though he also played fine down-home blues on conventional electric guitar and was a powerful singer as well, it is Wilson's unique slide stylings that remain a signature influence on Johnny Winter and Jimmie Vaughan, to name a few.

Wilson learned how to play guitar and harmonica as a child. By the time he was 18, he received his first steel guitar and began playing it at local Houston juke joints and clubs. His musical career was interrupted when he served in World War II. After his discharge from the Army, he decided to pursue a serious career as a blues musician, performing with Ivory Semien's group in the late '50s. Wilson and Semien recorded a number of sides for Goldband Records in 1957.

Hop Wilson didn't lead his own sessions until 1960, when he signed with the Ivory record label. Wilson only recorded for the label for two years—his final sessions were in 1961. After 1961, Wilson concentrated on playing local Houston clubs and bars. He continued to perform in Houston until his death in 1975. — *Cub Koda & Stephen Thomas Erlewine*

Blues with Friends at Goldband / 1986 / Goldband ✦✦✦
These are the original trio sides with King Ivory Lee Semiens on drums and Ice Water Jones on string bass. Again, a bout a side of Hop on this vinyl issue, but unfortunately some of the tracks have electric bass and/or piano overdubbed to make them stereo recordings. — *Cub Koda*

● **Steel Guitar Flash!** / 1988 / Ace ✦✦✦✦
Although the majority of the recordings collected here already show up on Bullseye Blues' 1991 reissue, *Houston Ghetto Blues*, this is the one to get. The main reason for this is the inclusion of all the known extant tracks cut in the '50s for the Lake Charles, LA Goldband label, where Hop's versions of "Chicken Stuff" and "Rockin' in the Coconut Top" became tri-state biggies, giving him his 15 seconds of fame and influencing the likes of a young Johnny Winter and other young Texan slideslingers in the process. With his drummer/sometimes-vocalist King Ivory Lee Semien banging the daylights out of a set that sounds like Salvation Army rejects (check out the floor-tom intro on the Goldband version of "Rockin' in the Coconut Top" and you'll see what I mean), a string bass played by the ubiquitous "Ice Water" Jones and a crackling, wires sticking out of it steel guitar going to places Elmore James could only think of after watching a bad sci-fi movie, Hop Wilson's dour singing delivery combined with his wild-ass playing becomes a whole genre of blues in and of itself and one well worth investigating. With a full generous 29 tracks aboard (including Hop and the boys backing up Fenton Robinson and Larry Davis on newly discovered cuts) covering all the Goldband, Trey and Ivory takes known to exist, this is now *the* definitive Hop Wilson collection and reason enough to start haunting the blues import bins to track it down. Programming tip; for full frontal assault, program up tracks 13 and 25-29 first and prepare yourself for something real special. There was only one Hop Wilson and here's where you check in to get his message. — *Cub Koda*

Rockin' Blues Party / 1989 / Charly ✦✦✦✦
A vinyl abum with a full side of Hop Wilson, featuring alternate (and superior) takes of all the classic Goldband sides. Import. — *Cub Koda*

Houston Ghetto Blues / Nov. 1993 / Bullseye Blues ✦✦✦✦
This collects up 18 later early-'60s sides for the Houston based Ivory label, owned by fellow bandmate, drummer King Ivory Lee Semien. Not really the place to start, as the Goldband sides are vastly superior. — *Cub Koda*

Kim Wilson

b. Jan. 6, 1951, Detroit, MI
Harmonica, Vocals / Electric Texas Blues, Modern Electric Texas Blues, Harmonica Blues
Harmonica player, songwriter, and singer Kim Wilson is as much a student and historian of classic blues as he is one of the US's top harmonica players. Simply put, Wilson has taste; when he enters the recording studio, he has a clear vision of what he wants his next record to sound like. Aside from all this, he's also an extremely hard worker and a major road hog, spending upwards of 200 nights a year on the road, playing festivals and clubs throughout the US, Canada, and Europe with his own Kim Wilson band and leading the Fabulous Thunderbirds.

Although he's long been known as the charismatic frontman for the Fabulous Thunderbirds, Wilson's solo albums—which feature bands of his own choosing for different tracks—is where the genius in his work shows through most clearly. Born January 6, 1951 in Detroit, Wilson grew up in California. His parents were singers who would sing popular standards on the radio, and while Wilson took trombone and guitar lessons, he didn't discover blues until he was a senior in high school. Wilson's father later worked for General Motors and raised his family in Goleta, CA, he recalled in a 1994 interview in his adopted hometown of Austin.

"We weren't rich, but we were alright," he recalled. Wilson dropped out of

college and began playing blues full time in 1970. Wilson had a rented room and lived the hippie existence, getting his harmonica chops together by playing with traveling blues musicians like Eddie Taylor. Even though Wilson had only switched to harmonica in his senior year in high school, his progress on the instrument was rapid and every bit as all-consuming as his blues record-buying habit. Charlie Musselwhite, John Lee Hooker, and Sonny Rhodes were among the other Bay Area musicians Wilson befriended and worked with in clubs. But Wilson didn't meet his biggest mentor until after he moved to Austin in the mid-'70s.

"Muddy Waters was my biggest mentor. He really made my reputation for me, and that was a fantastic time of my life, being associated with that man," he recalled of his early days with the Fabulous Thunderbirds in Austin. There, at the Antone's blues nightclub, Wilson and his Thunderbirds would back up whoever came into town, and it didn't take long for the band to realize they had Waters' blessing.

As a songwriter, Wilson takes his cue from the long-forgotten names like Tampa Red, Roosevelt Sykes, and Lonnie Johnson. His 1993 solo album, *Tigerman*, for the Austin-based Antone's label, features just three of his own tunes. Being the student of the blues that he is, Wilson was understandably hesitant to record too many of his own tunes when he'd already had a vision in his head of how he was going to rework classics like Joe Hill Louis' "Tiger Man," the album's title track. He followed up his debut with the equally brilliant *That's Life* (1994), also for Antone's, and again this recording contains just three self-penned songs.

Both of Wilson's solo albums are solid productions, highly recommended for harmonica students and fans of classic Texas blues and rhythm & blues. Meanwhile, in recent years, Wilson's career has taken a boost with a major-label deal with Private Music/BMG for the Fabulous Thunderbirds and with his frequent concert appearances with Bonnie Raitt. — *Richard Skelly*

Tigerman / 1993 / Antone's ✦✦
Tigerman, the first solo effort from the Fabulous Thunderbirds' frontman, Kim Wilson, is an uneven album, hampered by the uncertainness of Wilson and his band. They run through a standard set of blues-rock, plus Texas- and Chicago-style shuffles and boogies, but they never really let loose. Consequently, there are pleasant, enjoyable spots on the album, but never anything truly memorable. — *Thom Owens*

● **That's Life** / 1994 / Discovery ✦✦✦✦
On *That's Life*, Kim Wilson's second solo album, the vocalist/harpist hits on the right formula of Texas roadhouse blues and gritty blues-rock, turning out a uniformly satisfying album. Some of the original songs are a little weak, but the performances are convincing and enjoyable, even if they don't offer a new spin on Texas blues-rock. — *Thom Owens*

My Blues / Nov. 4, 1997 / Blue Collar ✦✦✦
Since the last Fabulous Thunderbirds album didn't feature any of the current band members except founder Kim Wilson, one may fairly ask what the difference is these days between a T-Birds record and a Wilson solo disc. The answer, at least on the basis of this one, seems to be that, while the T-Birds sessions find Wilson coming up with mostly original material in a blues-rock mode, his solo work consists mostly of covers in a straight electric blues mode. Here Wilson evokes such heroes as Muddy Waters, Sonny Boy Williamson, and, especially, Little Walter in three live-to-tape sessions cut in the fall of 1996 with a band led by pianist Fred Kaplan and bassist Larry Taylor. Junior Watson and Rusty Zinn alternate on guitar, while some tracks instead feature a two-man horn section of Scott Steen on trumpet and Tom Fabre on tenor saxophone. They acquit themselves well, though as with all such ventures, the obvious question for the record buyer is, why not listen to the originals instead? — *William Ruhlmann*

Smokey Wilson (Robert Lee Wilson)

b. Jul. 11, 1936, Glen Allen, MS
Guitar, Vocals / Electric Blues, Electric West Coast Blues
When Los Angeles-based guitarist Smokey Wilson really got serious about setting a full-fledged career as a bluesman in motion, it didn't take him long to astound the aficionados with an incendiary 1993 set for Bullseye Blues, *Smoke n' Fire*, that conjured up echoes of the Mississippi Delta of his youth.

Robert Lee Wilson lived and played the blues with Roosevelt "Booba" Barnes, Big Jack Johnson, Frank Frost, and other Mississippi stalwarts before relocating to L.A. in 1970 when he was 35 years old. But instead of grabbing for the gold as a touring entity, he opened the Pioneer Club in Watts, leading the house band and nobly booking the very best in blues talent (all-star attractions at the fabled joint included Joe Turner, Percy Mayfield, Pee Wee Crayton, Albert Collins, and plenty more).

Wilson recorded sparingly at first, his LPs for Big Town not doing the man justice. A 1983 set for Murray Brothers (recently reissued on Blind Pig) with harpist Rod Piazza and Hollywood Fats on rhythm guitar may have been the turning point; clearly, he was gearing up to leave his Mississippi mark on Southern California blues.

Smoke n' Fire and its 1995 encore, *The Real Deal* (a title now used for three contemporary blues albums in a year's time: John Primer and Buddy Guy have also claimed it), nominate Smokey Wilson as one of the hottest late-bloomers in the blues business. — *Bill Dahl*

● **Smoke n' Fire** / 1993 / Bullseye Blues ✦✦✦✦
Transplanted Mississippian Smokey Wilson has made plenty of records, but usually for poorly distributed regional labels. So although he is far from a newcomer, he might as well be a fledgling rookie to the average listener. The songs, aside from the lyrically commendable but awkward *Don't Burn Down L.A.*, are primarily his own urgent expositions on love, life's unfairness, and pain. His playing blends slamming fills, chunky riffs, and sonic barrages mixed with expert uses of distortion, bent notes, and flashy chords. This is the kind of no-nonsense set that has earned Rounder/Bullseye its exemplary reputation. — *Ron Wynn*

The Real Deal / 1995 / Bullseye Blues ✦✦✦✦
More steady-burning blues sparked by Wilson's unyielding guitar work and mean vocals. One difference — he goes the unplugged route on solo versions of Muddy Waters' "Feel like Going Home" and his own "Son of a... Blues Player." Elsewhere, it's electric juke-joint nirvana, Wilson cutting close to the bone on "Rat Takin' Your Cheese," "I Wanna Do It to You Baby," and "House in Hollywood." — *Bill Dahl*

88th Street Blues / Nov. 1995 / Blind Pig ✦✦✦
The barbed-wire vocals and slashing guitar of Mississippi-bred Smokey Wilson blend well with harpist Rod Piazza and company on this 1983 set first out on Murray Bros. Records. Not quite as stunning as his more recent work for Bullseye Blues, but definitely has some incendiary moments. — *Bill Dahl*

The Man from Mars / 1997 / Bullseye Blues ✦✦✦
This West Coast-based guitarist shines brilliantly on his third album for Bullseye Blues. While some of his earlier locally produced efforts have been uneven affairs, here kudos must go forth to producer and keyboard sideman Ron Levy. Levy keeps Wilson's guitar tone at sting and bite level 10 and his vocals right up front and toasty, surrounding him with a solid rhythm section and spare horn stabs. Eight of the 12 songs here are from Smokey's prolific pen, including "You Don't Drink What I Drink," the title track, "Too Drunk to Drive," "Don't Tangle with Me," and "Black Widow," winners all. A quartet of covers (Magic Sam's "Easy Baby," Elmore James' "Something Inside of Me" and a pair of Howlin' Wolf tunes, "Louise" and "44 Blues," with the latter featuring a guest turn from James Harman) rounds out this excellent session. Those who can't get enough of nasty, stinging lead guitar lines would do well to investigate this album. — *Cub Koda*

With the William Clark Band / May 27, 1997 / Black Magic ✦✦✦✦
This is a reissue, originally released 1990, issued posthumously in the memory of harmonica virtuoso William Clarke, who plays prominently along with his band. Both frequently performed together at Wilson's Pioneer Club and their close friendship is reflected in the musical interaction of Wilson's Mississippi roots mixed with Clarke's hard-blowin' harp attack. Wilson described his life best in "Tell Me What Do You See" with the words, "I've been all around the world/And blues is all I know to play." Other greats hop along for the ride, including keyboardist Fred Kaplan, and Mighty Flyers alumni Junior Watson and Alex Schultz. It's no accident that Wilson has some of Howlin' Wolf's vocal mannerisms on the song named after the Wolf himself. The story is that Wolf "willed" his voice to Wilson during one of Wolf's shows. — *Char Ham*

U.P. Wilson

b. Sep. 4, 1935, Shreveport, LA
Guitar, Vocals / Electric Texas Blues, Modern Electric Blues
Fort Worth-based guitarist, singer and songwriter U.P. Wilson plays a startlingly refreshing style of deep Southern soul-blues that is gospel inflected

and rural, yet urban. His very rhythmic guitar playing is showcased on three albums for JSP Records, and it appears that after years of being known as a regional performer around Texas, Wilson is ready to take his show on the road. Wilson has recorded three albums for the London-based JSP Records— *Boogie Boy: Return of the Texas Tornado* in 1994, *This Is U.P. Wilson* (1995), and *Whirlwind*, a 1996 release. Wilson also has two early 1990s recordings for the small Texas labels Red Lightnin' and Double Trouble.

Raised in West Dallas, Wilson learned his craft in the rough and tumble beer joints around the South and West Sides of the city, taking his cues from the likes of ZuZu Bollin, Cat Man Fleming, Frankie Lee Sims, Mercy Baby, and Nappy "Chin" Evans. Wilson moved from Dallas to Fort Worth and formed a band called the Boogie Chillun with drummer and vocalist Robert Ealey. Later, he worked with Cornell Dupree before Dupree left to become a favorite session guitarist.

By the late 1970s, Wilson and Ealey were frequenting a Fort Worth club called the New Bluebird, where they were attracting ever-growing legions of true Texas blues fans. Wilson began recording locally in 1987 and touring again around Texas. Since the mid-'90s release of his JSP albums, Wilson and his band have toured regionally around the South, pleasing audiences with his inventiveness, clever songwriting, great arrangements, and sheer originality. — *Richard Skelly*

Wild Texas Guitar / 1989 / Double Trouble ✦✦✦✦

This Is U.P. Wilson / 1995 / JSP ✦✦✦

Boogie Boy: Texas Guitar Returns / Jan. 31, 1995 / JSP ✦✦✦✦

Whirlwind / 1996 / JSP ✦✦✦

Good Bad Blues / May 19, 1998 / JSP ✦✦✦✦

U.P. Wilson with Paul Orta & the Kingpins / Red Lightnin' ✦✦✦

● **Attack of the Atomic Guitar** / Red Lightnin' ✦✦✦✦
This slashing live CD by the underrecorded veteran Texas guitarist includes harpist Paul Orta and the Kingpins providing support. — *Bill Dahl*

Johnny Winter

b. Feb. 23, 1944, Leland, MS
Guitar, Vocals, Harmonica / Blues-Rock, Modern Electric Texas Blues
Blues guitarist Winter became a major star in the late '60s and early '70s. Since that time he's confirmed his reputation in the blues by working with Muddy Waters and continuing to play in the style, despite musical fashion. Born in Leland, MS, Winter formed his first band at 14 with his brother Edgar in Beaumont, TX, and spent his youth in recording studios cutting regional singles and in bars playing the blues. His discovery on a national level came via an article in *Rolling Stone* in 1968, which led to a management contract with New York club owner Steve Paul and a record deal with Columbia. His debut album (there are numerous albums of juvenilia), *Johnny Winter,* reached the charts in 1969. Starting out with a trio, Winter later formed a band with former members of the McCoys, including second guitarist Rick Derringer. It was called Johnny Winter And. He achieved a sales peak in 1971 with the gold-selling *Live/Johnny Winter And.* He returned in 1973 with *Still Alive and Well,* his highest-charting album. His albums became more overtly blues-oriented in the late '70s and he also produced several albums for Muddy Waters. In the '80s he switched to the blues label Alligator for three albums, and has since recorded for the labels MCA and Pointblank/Virgin. — *William Ruhlmann*

Johnny Winter [Columbia] / 1969 / Columbia ✦✦✦✦
Winter's stunning debut features his fiery blues playing in both electric and acoustic settings, with backup that includes Willie Dixon. — *William Ruhlmann*

● **Second Winter** / 1969 / Columbia ✦✦✦✦
Winter leans more toward mainstream rock 'n' roll, though the guitar playing remains fierce. Originally a three-sided LP, this now makes a long CD. — *William Ruhlmann*

Johnny Winter And... / 1970 / Columbia ✦✦✦✦
Winter puts together a new band and takes on the assistance of Rick Derringer, who coproduces and provides such great songs as "Rock and Roll, Hoochie Koo." — *William Ruhlmann*

Johnny Winter And... Live / 1971 / Columbia ◆◆◆
Winter and his new band turn out hard-rock versions of "Jumpin' Jack Flash," "Johnny B. Goode," and other rock 'n' roll favorites. — *William Ruhlmann*

Still Alive and Well / 1973 / Columbia ◆◆
Still Alive and Well proved to the record buying public that Johnny Winter was both. This is a truly enjoyable album, chock full of great tunes played well. Johnny's version of the Rolling Stones' "Silver Train" shows us the potential this song has and what the Stones failed to capture. Everything here is good, so get it and dig in. — *James Chrispell*

Saints & Sinners / 1974 / Columbia ◆◆◆
Johnny Winter's sixth Columbia album was also his second since his comeback from drug addiction. Its predecessor, *Still Alive and Well,* had been his highest charting effort. *Saints & Sinners* was just as energetically played, but its mixture of material, including 1950s rock 'n' roll oldies like Chuck Berry's "Thirty Days," Larry Williams' "Bony Moronie," and Leiber and Stoller's "Riot in Cell Block No. 9," recent covers like the Rolling Stones' "Stray Cat Blues," and a couple of originals, was more eclectic than inspired. (Van Morrison completists should note that the album also contains Winter's cover of Morrison's "Feedback on Highway 101," a typical bluesy groove song that Morrison recorded for his 1973 *Hardnose the Highway* album but dropped. Winter's is the only released recording of the song.) Abetted by the members of the old Johnny Winter And band, Rick Derringer, Randy Hobbs, and Richard Hughes, plus his brother Edgar and Dan Hartman, Winter produced forceful hard rock focused on his searing lead guitar runs and rough-edged voice. It was the less-impressive choice of material that kept this collection from matching its predecessor. (Originally released in February 1974, *Saints & Sinners* was reissued on February 27, 1996 with the previously unreleased song "Dirty," a Winter original, added. The slide guitar-and-flute track is not consistent with the rest of the album, but it is interesting to hear. Wonder who played the flute?) — *William Ruhlmann*

John Dawson Winter III / 1974 / Blue Sky ◆◆

Captured Live! / 1976 / Blue Sky ◆◆◆

Nothin' but the Blues / 1977 / Blue Sky ◆◆◆◆
After a long period making rock records, Winter fronts the Muddy Waters band (with Waters singing) on this Chicago blues workout. He sounds happier than ever before. — *William Ruhlmann*

White Hot & Blue / 1978 / Blue Sky ◆◆◆◆

Raisin' Cain / 1980 / Blue Sky ◆◆◆

Guitar Slinger / 1984 / Alligator ◆◆◆◆
The first of three blues albums recorded after a four-year studio hiatus finds Winter as fleet-fingered as before and sounding more vocally involved than in some of the later Columbia material. — *William Ruhlmann*

Serious Business / 1985 / Alligator ◆◆

Third Degree / 1986 / Alligator ◆◆◆

The Winter of '88 / 1988 / Voyager ◆◆

Birds Can't Row Boats / 1988 / Relix ◆◆◆◆
Aside from "Ice Cube" (a 1959 instrumental), these tracks date from 1965-68. Many are previously unissued or only available on rare 45s. Those accustomed to his more famous recordings are in for a jolt, as this shows Johnny in several unexpected settings: grinding Texas psych-punk, the British Invasion-cum-folk-rock garage single "Gone for Bad," blue-eyed R&B/soul, an Everly Brothers cover, a *Highway 61*-era Dylan imitation, and even a shit-kickin' C&W tune. There are also some straight, predominantly acoustic blues numbers. — *Richie Unterberger*

A Lone Star Kind of Day / 1990 / Relix ◆◆◆

Let Me In / Aug. 1991 / Pointblank ◆◆◆◆
Let Me In is a star-studded all-blues set from Johnny Winter, featuring cameos from Dr. John, Albert Collins, and several others. Though the set focuses on blues material, Winters can never leave his rock roots behind—the sheer volume and pile-driving energy of his performances ensures that. For most of the record, his enthusiasm is contagious, but there are a couple of bland, generic exercises that fail to work up a head of steam. But there is a lovely acoustic number called "Blue Mood," which shows Winter trying to stretch a bit by playing jazzy licks. It's a refreshing change of pace. — *Thom Owens*

Scorchin' Blues / Jun. 16, 1992 / Epic ◆◆
Scorchin' Blues marries tracks from Johnny Winter's early Columbia albums—including the classic National steel-driven "Dallas" from his 1969 debut—with material from his return-to-roots Blue Sky-period in the late '70s. The aggressive playing and raunchy vocals will appeal to both blues and rock fans, and Ben Sandmel crams an authoritative biography into seven pages, complete with interesting Winter quotes. The one downside: a miserly ten tracks spread over only 45 minutes of playing time. — *Roch Parisien*

Collection / Jun. 30, 1992 / Castle ◆◆◆

Hey, Where's Your Brother? / Jul. 1992 / Pointblank ◆◆◆
On the classic, 1972 live album *Roadwork,* Edgar Winter immortalized the words, when introducing brother Johnny: "Everybody asks me... where's your brother?" It's a question that fans have besieged both Winters with for over two decades, and now Johnny gets a chance to return the tribute with his latest. Edgar does in fact guest on the sessions, blowing sax and tinkling keys on a few tracks, and dueting with big bro on a superb, seasonal rendition of "Please Come Home for Christmas." — *Roch Parisien*

A Johnny Winter: A Rock n' Roll Collection / 1994 / Columbia/Legacy ◆◆◆◆
A two-CD survey of Winter's recordings for Columbia between 1969 and 1979, the era of his greatest commercial success. This collects many of his most popular tracks, though it doesn't do much to argue a case for artistic diversity. Includes two otherwise unavailable songs: an alternate take of "30 Days," and a previously unreleased 1973 cover of Robert Johnson's "Come on in My Kitchen." — *Richie Unterberger*

Livin' in the Blues / Mar. 12, 1996 / Sundazed ◆◆◆

Ease My Pain / Mar. 12, 1996 / Sundazed ◆◆◆

Relix Records Best of Blues, Vol. 2 / Apr. 15, 1997 / Relix ◆◆◆

White Hot Blues / Oct. 7, 1997 / Sony ◆◆◆
Slowly over the years, perhaps through sheer survival, if nothing else, Johnny Winter has finally forged a reputation as a real bluesman rather than a flashy guitar player with a built-in genetic gimmick to sell himself with. That his blues has always been rock 'n' roll and his rock 'n' roll has always been blues is no better highlighted than on this 16-track collection. The raw rock of "Highway 61 Revisited" and the live version of "Johnny B. Goode" sit just fine next to the burner "Be Careful with a Fool," perhaps Winter's finest slow blues performance. The performances span his tenure with Columbia from 1969 to 1980, with the other highlights including "Too Much Seconal," "New York, New York," "Leland Mississippi Blues," and "The Crawl." This may just very well be some of the best blues-rock guitar your money can buy. — *Cub Koda*

Live in NYC '97 / Mar. 10, 1998 / Virgin ◆◆◆◆
Johnny Winter assembled *Live in NYC '97* with assistance of his fan club, drawing all of the recordings from an April 1997 performance at the Bottom Line. Produced by Winter's longtime colleague Dick Shurman, the record doesn't follow the predictable pattern of a live album—instead of hits, it offers fan favorites and covers, which makes for a much more interesting listen. Throughout the album, Winter simply rips, tearing through all five songs with blistering energy. This is the live album hardcore fans have been wanting for years, and it doesn't fail to deliver on its promise. — *Stephen Thomas Erlewine*

Jimmy Witherspoon (James Witherspoon)

b. Aug. 8, 1923, Gurdon, AR, **d.** Sep. 18, 1997, Los Angeles, CA
Vocals / Swing, Jazz-Blues, Urban Blues, Texas Blues, Jump Blues
One of the great blues singers of the post-World War II period, Jimmy Witherspoon was also versatile enough to fit comfortably into the jazz world. As a child he sang in a church choir, and made his debut recordings with Jay McShann for Philo and Mercury in 1945 and 1946. His own first recordings, using McShann's band, resulted in a No. 1 R&B hit in 1949 with "Ain't Nobody's Business Parts 1 & 2" on Supreme Records. Live performances of "No Rollin' Blues" and "Big Fine Girl" provided 'Spoon with two more hits in 1950.

The mid-'50s were a lean time, with his style of shouting blues temporarily out of fashion; singles were tried for Federal, Chess, Atco, Vee-Jay, and others, with little success. Witherspoon's album *Live at the Monterey Jazz Festival*

(HiFi Jazz) from 1959 lifted him back into the limelight. Partnerships with Ben Webster or Groove Holmes were recorded, and he toured Europe in 1961 with Buck Clayton, perfoming overseas many more times in the decades to follow; some memorable music resulted, but Witherspoon's best '60s album is *Evening Blues* (Prestige), which features T-Bone Walker on guitar and Clifford Scott on saxophone. Despite contracting throat cancer in the early '80s, Witherspoon remained active, a popular attraction until his death in 1997. — *Bob Porter & Scott Yanow*

Jimmy Witherspoon & Jay McShann / 1947-1949 / Black Lion ✦✦✦✦
Although Jimmy Witherspoon gets first billing on this CD reissue, he actually only has vocals on 11 of the 24 selections and is just present on three of the seven sessions; highpoints include two versions of his signature song "Ain't Nobody's Business." Pianist Jay McShann is the real leader of these Los Angeles recordings and the brand of music he performs mixes together swing, blues, slight touches of bebop and early R&B. Most of the songs are basic originals and there are spirited solos from many lesser-known horn players; only the young trumpeter Art Farmer, his brother bassist Addison Farmer, and the popular studio tenor saxophonist Maxwell Davis are still remembered. In addition to Witherspoon (who is in excellent early form), Lois Booker, Maxine Reed, and Crown Prince Waterford also take vocals. An easily recommended set of rarities from the later period of Kansas City jazz. — *Scott Yanow*

Ain't Nobody's Business [Polydor] / May 9, 1949-1950 / Polydor ✦✦✦✦
It is unfortunate that the recording dates and personnel are not given on this budget CD, for the performances (although not always that well-recorded) are excellent. Singer Jimmy Witherspoon is heard near the beginning of his career. Five songs (the third through the seventh) are taken from a Pasadena concert on May 9, 1949. Backed by pianist Gene Gilbeaux's quartet (with Donald Hill featured on alto), Witherspoon is in extroverted form entertaining the enthusiastic crowd; on "New Orleans Woman," a few unidentified horns honk away to the audience's enjoyment. Of the other five songs, two are from 1950 ("I Done Found Out" and "Fickle Woman") and have Witherspoon backed by a nonet including pianist Jay McShann and tenor saxophonist Maxwell Davis. "Good Jumpin'" is with the Buddy Floyd sextet in 1948, and two others are not listed in discographies. But details aside, the enjoyable music straddles the boundary between blues, early R&B and jazz. — *Scott Yanow*

Goin' to Kansas City Blues / Dec. 4, 1957-Dec. 5, 1957 / RCA ✦✦✦✦
A reunion of sorts with McShann, with whom Witherspoon had sung for four years in the late '40s. A relaxed, swinging set that bisects jazz and blues, it holds no great surprises, but 'Spoon fans will find this an enjoyable and accomplished record. About half of the material was penned by McShann or Witherspoon, including a remake of "Confessin' the Blues," and "Blue Monday Blues," 'Spoon's adaptation of "Kansas City Blues." — *Richie Unterberger*

Olympia Concert / Apr. 22, 1961 / Inner City ✦✦✦✦
Recorded in Paris when he was touring with a group dominated by Count Basie alumni, this concert features singer Jimmy Witherspoon in prime form. His repertoire was fairly typical (highlighted by "See See Rider," "Roll 'em Pete," and his biggest hit "'T Ain't Nobody's Business") but Witherspoon pours so much enthusiasm and soul into the music that he sounds as if he had recently discovered the songs. This sadly out-of-print LP also features some short solos and excellent support from 'Spoon's sidemen: trumpeters Buck Clayton and Emmett Berry, trombonist Dicky Wells, altoist Earl Warren, tenor saxophonist Buddy Tate, pianist Sir Charles Thompson, bassist Gene Ramey, and drummer Oliver Jackson. Fortunately the band appeared on television in Europe and a Shanachie video (readily available) has been released of the Buck Clayton All-Stars. — *Scott Yanow*

Roots (Jazzlore, Vol. 34) / May 23, 1962 / Atlantic ✦✦✦✦
This album features singer Jimmy Witherspoon in a perfect setting, interpreting older blues and Kansas City swing standards while accompanied by a fine two-horn sextet. Witherspoon's friend tenor saxophonist Ben Webster has plenty of solos as does trumpeter Gerald Wilson (in one of his last recordings as an active player). Witherspoon sounds quite inspired on such songs as "I'd Rather Drink Muddy Water," "Confessin' the Blues," "Nobody Knows You When You're Down and Out," and "Cherry Red." — *Scott Yanow*

Evenin' Blues / 1963 / Original Blues Classics ✦✦✦✦
A good relaxed (but not laidback) session, and one of his bluesier ones, with

organ, Clifford Scott (who played on Bill Doggett's "Honky Tonk") on sax, and T-Bone Walker on guitar. Nothing too adventurous about the song selection, including well-traveled items like "Good Rockin' Tonight" and "Kansas City," but Witherspoon sings them with ingratiating soul, reaching his peaks on his cover of "Don't Let Go" (perhaps better than the hit version by Roy Hamilton) and the late-night ambience of the title track. The CD reissue adds previously unissued alternate takes of four of the songs. — *Richie Unterberger*

Baby Baby Baby / 1963 / Original Blues Classics ✦✦✦
Veteran singer Jimmy Witherspoon is in good voice on this CD reissue, performing a dozen two- to four-minute songs that include such blues standards as Duke Ellington's "Rocks in My Bed," "Bad Bad Whiskey," "One Scotch, One Bourbon, One Beer," and "It's a Lonesome Old World." He is joined by a quintet featuring altoist Leo Wright and guitarist Kenny Burrell on the first eight numbers and a background septet (with trumpeter Bobby Bryant and Arthur Wright on harmonica) for the remainder of the set. The music is enjoyable if not classic and should please Witherspoon's many fans. — *Scott Yanow*

Blues Around the Clock / Nov. 5, 1963 / Original Blues Classics ✦✦✦
Veteran singer Jimmy Witherspoon (who bridges the gap between jazz and blues) mostly sticks to the latter on this spirited set. His backup group (organist Paul Griffin, guitarist Lord Westbrook, bassist Leonard Gaskin, and drummer Herbie Lovelle) is fine in support, but the spotlight is almost entirely on Witherspoon throughout these ten concise performances, only one of which exceeds four minutes. Highlights include "No Rollin' Blues," "S.K. Blues," and "Around the Clock." Witherspoon is in fine voice and, even if nothing all that memorable occurs, the music is enjoyable. — *Scott Yanow*

Some of My Best Friends Are the Blues / 1964 / Prestige ✦✦✦
Jimmy Witherspoon is accompanied by a large orchestra arranged by Benny Golson for a set emphasizing slow tempos (even on "And the Angels Sing" and "Who's Sorry Now"), ballads, and blues. Nothing all that memorable occurs but the singer is in strong voice and his fans will want to pick up this interesting CD reissue. — *Scott Yanow*

Blues for Easy Livers / 1965-1966 / Prestige ✦✦✦
Despite the title, this actually leans considerably further to the jazz side of Witherspoon's muse than the blues one, with backing by Pepper Adams on baritone sax, Roger Kellaway on piano, Bill Watrous on trombone, Richard Davis on bass, and Mel Lewis on drums. The songs, too, are much more in the jazz/pop vein than the blues/jazz one, heavy on standards by the likes of Johnny Mercer, the Gershwins, and Ellington. Witherspoon's one of the masters of closing-time bluesy jazz, and he doesn't let anyone down on this relaxed (but not sleepy) session. — *Richie Unterberger*

★ **The Spoon Concerts** / 1972 / Fantasy ✦✦✦✦✦
This single-CD (which reissues all of the music from an earlier two-LP set) includes the highpoint of singer Jimmy Witherspoon's career. On October 2, 1959 he appeared at the Monterey Jazz Festival and created such a sensation that it caused his career to go through a renaissance. Heard at the peak of his powers, Witherspoon holds his own with a mighty group of veterans (trumpeter Roy Eldridge, both Ben Webster and Coleman Hawkins on tenors, clarinetist Woody Herman, pianist Earl Hines, bassist Vernon Alley, and drummer Mel Lewis). Although the five-song set only lasted 25 minutes, Witherspoon's performance was the hit of the festival. The other half of this CD features Witherspoon romping through ten mostly-traditional blues songs two months later with Webster, baritonist Gerry Mulligan, pianist Jimmy Rowles, bassist Leroy Vinnegar, and drummer Mel Lewis; the performance is equally exciting. Highly recommended, this CD is the one truly essential Jimmy Witherspoon release. — *Scott Yanow*

Love Is a Five Letter Word / 1975 / LAX ✦✦
Jimmy Witherspoon travelled to London to record *Love is a Five Letter Word* with producer Mike Vernon in 1974, and the pair came up with a surprise — a glossy album that owed as much to pop and contemporary soul as it did to the blues. In fact, there's not much on *Love is a Five Letter Word* that sounds like true, gutbucket blues — it all sounds processed and stylized, as if he was reaching for a hit. Some of the results work, but Witherspoon's true essence is buried by the slick groove, steel guitars, and electric sitars. For anyone but completists, *Love is a Five Letter Word* isn't particularly worth exploring. — *Stephen Thomas Erlewine*

Live / 1979 / MCA ✦✦✦
Jimmy Witherspoon sticks exclusively to the blues during this Los Angeles club date from 1976. Guitarist Robben Ford's fiery Chicago blues playing is consistently exciting and imaginative, often stealing the show from 'Spoon. This CD can easily be enjoyed by fans of both blues and swinging jazz. — *Scott Yanow*

Sings the Blues / 1980 / Muse ✦✦✦✦
The Savoy Sultans, as revived by drummer Panama Francis, was one of the hottest small-group swing bands of the late '70s/early '80s. Singer Jimmy Witherspoon fits right in with the group, emphasizing the Kansas City swing and blues side of his repertoire. With the Sultans (a nonet also including trumpeters Francis Williams and Irv Stokes, tenorman George Kelly, and pianist Red Richards) inspiring him, Witherspoon revives some of the most memorable songs associated with Jimmy Rushing including "Sent for You Yesterday," "I Want a Little Girl," and "Boogie Woogie." This highly recommended set is one of Jimmy Witherspoon's best from his later years. — *Scott Yanow*

Jimmy's Blues / 1983 / MCA ✦✦✦
This out-of-print MCA album from 1983 reissued a fairly obscure session from singer Jimmy Witherspoon. Backed by a Los Angeles rhythm section that includes pianist Charles Brown (who unfortunately does not sing on this date) along with tenor saxophonist Red Holloway (who is not included in the personnel listing), Witherspoon sticks mostly to blues with tunes by Brownie McGhee, Art Hillery (who plays organ on one song), Buddy Scott and four of his own originals (including "You Can't Do a Thing When You're Drunk" and "Pillar to Post"). This set (originally titled *Huhh*) was cut for the Bluesway label. — *Scott Yanow*

Patcha, Patcha, All Night Long / Apr. 11, 1985 / Pablo ✦✦✦
This wouldn't find a place in the cutting edge of either Turner or Witherspoon's catalog, but it's a decent enough 1985 session of Kansas City-type blues/jazz. Saxophonists Red Holloway and Lee Allen are the featured players in a band which bisects the swing and jump blues idioms, Witherspoon acquitting himself better than Turner (the latter of whom died later that year). — *Richie Unterberger*

Midnight Lady Called the Blues / 1986 / Muse ✦✦✦✦
Singer Jimmy Witherspoon was starting to show his age by 1986 but he is in pretty strong form on these seven selections co-composed by Dr. John and Doc Pomus. With altoist Hank Crawford (who also wrote some of the arrangements) and tenor saxophonist David "Fathead" Newman contributing plenty of solos while pianist Dr. John leads the rhythm section, the spirited set has more than its share of interesting and exciting moments despite the obscurity of the material. — *Scott Yanow*

Rockin' L.A. / 1988 / Fantasy ✦✦✦✦
This CD finds Jimmy Witherspoon at age 65 on one of his last fairly strong records before his voice began to really shrink and fade. 'Spoon, assisted on this live set by tenor saxophonist Teddy Edwards, pianist Gerald Wiggins, bassist John Clayton and drummer Paul Humphrey, revives some of his hits, performs a pair of medleys and emphasizes swinging blues and ballads. Highlights include "Sweet Lotus Blossom" (a standard whose authorship should not have been credited to Witherspoon), "Stormy Monday," and "I Want a Little Girl." Easily recommended to Jimmy Witherspoon fans. — *Scott Yanow*

Spoon So Easy: The Chess Years / 1990 / MCA/Chess ✦✦✦
By the mid-'50s it seemed that Jimmy Witherspoon's brand of Kansas City blues was going permanently out of style; Big Joe Turner was starting to turn towards rock 'n' roll and many of the older singers were no longer recording. Witherspoon, who was only in his early 30s, was flexible enough to fit into different situations so the Chess label (best-known for its intense Chicago blues) took a chance on him. This CD contains most of Witherspoon's records for the Chess and Checker labels: five that were issued and nine that remained in the vaults until the release of this CD in 1990. Unfortunately Witherspoon did not have any hits during this era (his comeback would not really get going until his appearance at the 1959 Monterey Jazz Festival) but fortunately these records did survive. 'Spoon is actually heard in good form and, even if the personnel is mostly unidentified, he received suitable backup. Since all but three of Witherspoon's Chess re-

cordings are on this CD (which clocks in around 39 minutes), one does wonder why it was not decided to make this a "complete" set. — *Scott Yanow*

★ **Blowin' in from Kansas City** / 1993 / Capitol ✦✦✦✦✦
These 20 tunes pair the great Mr. Witherspoon with the finest jazz, jump, and blues talent around. Jay McShann, Maxwell Davis, Tiny Webb, and Chuck Norris are only a few of the first-rate session-men and arrangers who grace the tracks of this essential CD. A special mention must be made of tenor sax legend Ben Webster, whose solo on "I'm Going Around in Circles" is simply magnificent. This is quintessential Kansas City blues. Of all the shouters, Witherspoon is perhaps the greatest singer. — *Larry Hoffman*

Jay's Blues / 1996 / Charly ✦✦✦✦
Jay's Blues is a fine collection of early-'50s jump blues sides that Jimmy Weatherspoon cut for Federal Records. This 23-track collection offers a good retrospective of one of Weatherspoon's most neglected—and admittedly, uneven—periods. — *Thom Owens*

☆ **'Spoon & Groove** / Apr. 1996 / Rykodisc ✦✦✦✦
This was originally released as *Groovin' & Spoonin'* on Olympic 7107. It's a decent if unremarkable set of blues-jazz, heavier on the blues, with organist Groove Holmes being Witherspoon's most important sideman on this date (which also features tenor saxophonist Teddy Edwards). Several of the numbers are shopworn standards like "Take This Hammer," "Key to the Highway," "Please Send Me Someone to Love," and "Since I Fell for You," though everything's performed with taste. If you're looking for Witherspoon blues-jazz with an organ groove, the 1963 album *Evenin' Blues* (1963) is more highly recommended, though *'Spoon & Groove* has no serious flaws. — *Richie Unterberger*

Mitch Woods

b. Apr. 3, 1951, Brooklyn, NY
Piano, Vocals / Boogie-Woogie, Jump Blues, Modern Electric Blues, Chicago Blues, Electric Blues
Dubbing his swinging approach "rock-a-boogie," pianist Mitch Woods and His Rocket 88s have revived the jump-blues approach of the '40s and '50s on three Blind Pig albums.

Originally from Brooklyn, NY, Mitch Woods moved to San Francisco in 1970. While he was growing up in Brooklyn, he studied both jazz and classical music, but when he relocated to the Bay Area, he primarily played jump blues and R&B. San Franciscan guitarist HiTide Harris introduced Woods to the joyous jive of Louis Jordan, and the pianist's musical tastes were transformed. Between 1970 and 1980, Woods performed as a solo artist, gigging at a number of local clubs. In 1980, he formed the Rocket 88s—which featured Harris on guitar—and four years later, the band released their debut album, *Steady Date*, on Blind Pig. The album led to concerts at national blues clubs and festivals, as well as several European dates in 1987.

In 1988, Woods and the Rocket 88s released their second album, *Mr. Boogie's Back in Town*, and embarked on another round of shows in America, Canada, and Europe. Three years later, their third album, *Solid Gold Cadillac*, appeared. Woods and the Rocket 88s continued to tour and perform in the '90s, releasing their fourth album, *Shakin' the Shack*, in 1993. — *Bill Dahl & Stephen Thomas Erlewine*

Steady Date with Mitch Woods & His Rocket 88's / 1984 / Blind Pig ✦✦

Mr. Boogie's Back in Town / 1988 / Blind Pig ✦✦✦
Jump-blues and boogie with a rockabilly edge. — *Niles J. Frantz*

● **Solid Gold Cadillac** / 1991 / Blind Pig ✦✦✦✦
With West Coast jump blues and boogie-woogie piano. this is tasty, if not particularly original. Charlie Musselwhite guests on harp. — *Niles J. Frantz*

Shakin' the Shack / 1993 / Blind Pig ✦✦
Woods—a boogie-woogie pianist of first order—is rooted in good-timey rock, with interesting tangents into the Louisiana bayou ("Zydeco Boogie") and New Orleans Mardi Gras ("Hattie Queen"). "Boogie" is the operative word here, with the lead track, "Honkin', Shoutin', Pumpin', Poundin'," accurately setting the tone. — *Roch Parisien*

Keeper of the Flame / Oct. 29, 1996 / Viceroy ✦✦✦

Big John Wrencher

b. Feb. 12, 1924, Sunflower, MS, **d.** Jul. 15, 1977
Harmonica, Vocals / Electric Chicago Blues, Harmonica Blues
The Maxwell Street open air market was a seven- to ten-block area in Chicago that from the 1920s to the mid-'60s played host to various blues musicians—both professional and amateur—who performed right on the street for tips from passersby. Most of them who started their careers there (like Little Walter, Earl Hooker, Hound Dog Taylor and others) moved up to the more comfortable confines of club work. But one who stayed and became a most recognizable fixture of the area was a marvelous harmonica player and singer named One-Arm or Big John Wrencher.

Wrencher was born in Sunflower County, MS, in 1924 on a plantation. His youthful interest in music—particularly the harmonica—kept him on the move as a traveling musician, playing throughout Tennessee and neighboring Arkansas from the late '40s to the early '50s. In 1958, Big John lost his left arm in a car crash in Memphis. By the early '60s, he had moved North to Chicago and quickly became a regular fixture on Maxwell Street, always working on Sundays from 10:00 A.M. to nearly 3:00 in the afternoon virtually non-stop, as Sundays were the big payday for most busking musicians working the area.

Although cupping both harmonica and bulky microphone in one hand (which he also sang through), Wrencher's physical challenge seemingly did little to alter the hugeness of his sound or the slurring attack he brought to the instrument. Usually backed by nothing more than an electric guitar and a drummer, Big John's sound and style was country juke joint blues brought to the city and amplified to the maximum. A flamboyant showman, he'd put on quite a show for the people on the street, moving and dancing constantly while the cigar box was passed around for tips. By all accounts, no one was ever disappointed by the show or the music.

But despite his enormous playing and performing talents, the discography on Wrencher, unfortunately, remains woefully thin. He appears to have played on a session with Detroit bluesman Baby Boy Warren in the '50s, but this tape appears to be lost to the ravages of time. His first official recordings surfaced on a pair of Testament albums from the '60s, featuring Big John in a sideman role behind slide legend Robert Nighthawk. His only full album of material surfaced in the early '70s on the Barrelhouse label. Producer George Paulus also used him as a backing musician behind slide guitarist but these sides laid unissued until recently, showing up piecemeal on various compilations.

After years of vacillating between his regular Maxwell Street gig and a few appearances on European blues festivals, Wrencher decided to go back to Mississippi to visit family and old friends in July of 1977. While swapping stories of his travels with some buddies at bluesman Wade Walton's barber shop in Clarksdale, he suddenly dropped dead from a heart attack at the age of 54. As a heartfelt (and somewhat surreal) memorial to his old pal, Big John's final bottle of whiskey is permanently ensconced on a shelf at Walton's barbershop. —*Cub Koda*

Big Johns Boogie / 1974 / Big Bear ✦✦✦
● **Maxwell Street Alley Blues** / 1978 / Barrelhouse ✦✦✦✦
While most blues albums bear romantic-sounding titles like the one used here, this is the real deal. Wrencher's one-armed amplified harp playing is perfectly supported by the lone guitar of Little Buddy Scott and the bar-bones basic drumming of Playboy Vinson. Listing titles is superfluous, since the feel and the ambience is the important thing. But blues albums seldom capture that elusive quality the way it is here, and that's the secret of its charm. Superlative in every regard, this is a great album by a very under-recorded artist. —*Cub Koda*

Billy Wright

b. May 21, 1932, Atlanta, GA, **d.** Oct. 27, 1991, Atlanta, GA
Vocals, Fiddle / R&B, Jump Blues
A prime influence on Little Richard during his formative years, "Prince of the Blues" Billy Wright's hearty shouting delivery was an Atlanta staple during the postwar years.

Wright was a regular at Atlanta's 81 Theatre as a youth, soaking up the vaudevillians before graduating to singing and dancing status there himself. Saxist Paul "Hucklebuck" Williams caught Wright's act when they shared a bill with Charles Brown and Wynonie Harris at Atlanta's Auditorium, recommending the teenaged singer to Savoy Records boss Herman Lubinsky.

Wright's 1949 Savoy debut, "Blues for My Baby," shot up to number three on *Billboard*'s R&B charts, and its flip, "You Satisfy," did almost as well. Two more of Wright's Savoy 78s, "Stacked Deck" and "Hey Little Girl," were also Top Ten R&B entries in 1951. The flamboyant Wright set his pal Little Richard up with powerful WGST deejay Zenas Sears, who scored the newcomer his first contract with RCA in 1951. It's no knock on Richard to note that his early sides sound very much like Billy Wright.

Wright recorded steadily for Savoy through 1954, the great majority of his sessions held in his hometown with hot local players (saxist Fred Jackson and guitarist Wesley Jackson were often recruited). After he left Savoy, Wright's recording fortunes plummeted—a 1955 date for Don Robey's Peacock diskery in Houston and sessions for Fire (unissued) and Carrollton in 1959 ended his discography. Wright later emceed shows in Atlanta, remaining active until a stroke in the mid-'70s slowed him down. —*Bill Dahl*

Stacked Deck / 1980 / Route 66 ✦✦✦✦
The title track was a major R&B hit for Wright in 1951, and there are 13 more gems by the animated blues shouter on this import piece of vinyl. Everything's from the Savoy vaults except for an ultra-rare Wright cover of Billy Ward & the Dominoes' "Do Something for Me" that was cut live at Atlanta's Harlem Theatre in 1952. —*Bill Dahl*

Goin' Down Slow (Blues, Soul & Early R 'n' R, Vol. 1) / 1984 / Savoy ✦✦✦✦
Crying and pleading the blues, Wright's early-'50s Savoy output was very influential. —*Bill Dahl*

● **Billy Wright** / 1994 / Savoy Jazz ✦✦✦✦
15 of the Atlanta jump blues shouter's very best outings for Savoy, spanning 1949-1954. Wright's pleading style, a large influence indeed on a developing Little Richard, is irresistibly spotlighted on "After Awhile," "I Remember," and the romping "Billy's Boogie Blues." —*Bill Dahl*

Hey Baby, Don't You Want a Man Like Me? / 1995 / Ace ✦✦✦

Jimmy Yancey (James Edward Yancey)

b. 1894, Chicago, IL, **d.** Sep. 17, 1951, Chicago, IL
Piano / Boogie-Woogie, Piano Blues

One of the pioneers of boogie-woogie piano, Jimmy Yancey was generally more subtle than the more famous Albert Ammons, Pete Johnson, and Meade Lux Lewis, falling as much into the blues genre as in jazz. Yancey, who could romp as well as anyone, made many of his most memorable recordings at slower tempos. No matter what key he played in, Yancey ended every song in E flat, leading to some hilarious conclusions to some recordings. He worked in vaudeville as a singer and tap dancer starting at age six and in 1915 settled in Chicago as a pianist. But Yancey spent his last 26 years (from 1925 on) earning his living as a groundskeeper at Comiskey Park for the Chicago White Sox. He played part-time in local clubs and began recording in 1939, on a few occasions backing his wife, singer Mama Yancey. Jimmy Yancey never achieved the fame of his contemporaries but he remained a major influence on all practioners in the genre. *— Scott Yanow*

In the Beginning / May 4, 1939 / Solo Art ◆◆◆◆
This LP has 12 of the 17 selections that pianist Jimmy Yancey cut during his first recording session. All of the music (plus the missing titles) have been reissued in full on CD by Document but this album has the advantage of also having Rudi Blesh's extensive and informative liner notes. Yancey's subtle boogie-woogie style is heard in prime form on solo performances originally cut for Solo Art. *— Scott Yanow*

☆ **Complete Recorded Works, Vol. 1 (1939-1940)** / May 4, 1939 + Oct. 25, 1939 / Document ◆◆◆◆◆
The first of three Document CDs that reissue all of pianist Jimmy Yancey's recordings (other than his final Atlantic session) is filled with classic performances. Yancey, a subtle boogie-woogie/blues pianist who was a major influence and inspiration on the better-known players of the 1930s, is featured on his first two solo sessions including "The Fives," "La Salle Street Breakdown," "South Side Stuff," "Yancey's Getaway," "Yancey Stomp," and "State Street Special." Highly recommended as are the two following volumes in this valuable Document series. *— Scott Yanow*

☆ **Complete Recorded Works, Vol. 2 (1940-1943)** / Feb. 23, 1940-Dec. 1943 / Document ◆◆◆◆◆
On the second of three CDs that trace virtually his entire recording career, pianist Jimmy Yancey is showcased on a variety of solo tracks. Two number from February 1940 are highlighted by the classic "Bear Trap Blues." There are a couple of numbers made for the tiny Art Center Jazz Gems label, a four-song (plus two alternate takes) definitive set cut for Bluebird (which includes "Death Letter Blues" and "Yancey's Bugle Call") and nine songs (five previously unissued) from 1943; on one version of "How Long Blues," Mama Yancey sings while Jimmy switches to the spooky sounding harmonium. This set also has Jimmy Yancey's only four recorded vocals, which are quite effective even though his voice is limited. All three volumes in this series are highly recommended for the subtle pianist, who made expert use of space and ended every tune in E flat. *— Scott Yanow*

The Yancey-Lofton Sessions, Vol. 1 / Dec. 1943 / Storyville ◆◆◆◆
The music on this LP (which has been reissued on CD by Document) is timeless. The first of two volumes is comprised of three of the only four piano solos made by the obscure ragtime-oriented Alonzo Yancey (Jimmy's older brother), seven by the lyrical Jimmy Yancey (including "Death Letter Blues" which has a rare vocal) and six from the erratic but exciting Cripple Clarence Lofton. All three pianists are heard in prime form and contrast

each other very well. Easily recommended to jazz, blues, and boogie-woogie collectors who do not already have the Document CDs. *— Scott Yanow*

The Yancey-Lofton Sessions, Vol. 2 / Dec. 1943 / Storyville ◆◆◆◆
This is the second of two LPs reissuing the 1943 recordings of pianists Jimmy and Alonzo Yancey and Cripple Clarence Lofton. Alonzo Yancey (Jimmy's older brother) only recorded four numbers in his life; three are on *Vol. 1* while his "Ecstatic Rag" is a highlight on this album. In addition there are nine numbers from Jimmy Yancey (including two that have vocals by Mama Yancey) and four from Lofton. Overall the music is quite enjoyable and unique in its own way; all of it has since been reissued on CD. *— Scott Yanow*

★ **Complete Recorded Works, Vol. 3 (1943-1950)** / Dec. 1943-Dec. 23, 1950 / Document ◆◆◆◆◆
The third of three CDs tracing the recording career of the unique boogie-woogie pianist Jimmy Yancey, whose subtlety could often result in some dramatic music, completes his December 1943 session and also has his December 23, 1950 solo set; his final recordings from July 1951 are available on an Atlantic release. The 1943 titles, three of which were previously unreleased, include two with Mama Yancey vocals (on one Jimmy switches to harmonium) and is highlighted by "White Sox Stomp," "Yancey Special," and two versions of "Pallet on the Floor." After the six fine titles from 1950, this CD finishes off with the only four numbers that Jimmy's older brother, the more ragtime-oriented Alonzo Yancey, ever recorded. Although his style was different, on "Ecstatic Rag" Alonzo does sound a bit like Jimmy. All three of these Document CDs, plus the Atlantic set, are highly recommended and preferable to the piecemeal domestic Bluebird reissues. *— Scott Yanow*

Chicago Piano, Vol. 1 / Jul. 18, 1951 / Atlantic ◆◆◆◆
Jimmy Yancey was one of the pioneer boogie-woogie pianists but, unlike many of the other pacesetters, he had a gentle and thoughtful style that also crossed over into the blues. This Atlantic CD, a straight reissue of the 1972 LP, contains Yancey's final recordings, cut just eight weeks before his death from diabetes. The pianist is in fine form on these introspective and often emotional performances which, with the exception of Meade Lux Lewis' "Yancey Special" and the traditional "Make Me a Pallet on the Floor," are comprised entirely of Yancey's originals. His wife Mama Yancey takes five memorable vocals on this memorable set of classic blues. *— Scott Yanow*

Mama Yancey

b. Jan. 1, 1896, Cairo, IL, **d.** Apr. 19, 1986, Chicago, IL
Vocals / Classic Female Blues

The other half of the blues team led by pioneering boogie-woogie pianist Jimmy Yancey, Estelle "Mama" Yancey was a talented vocalist known for her warm sense of humor and great command of the stage. In her childhood, Estelle Harris sang in church choirs and learned guitar. Jimmy Yancey, who had traveled the US and Europe as a vaudeville dancer, married Estelle in 1917, when she was 21. Yancey often sang with her husband at informal gatherings, house rent parties and clubs in the 1930s and '40s in Chicago. Because Jimmy Yancey was not that good a blues singer, but was a great boogie-woogie/blues piano player, Estelle recorded frequently with her husband.

Yancey sang with her husband in 1948 at Carnegie Hall, and this performance in turn led to Jimmy Yancey's last recording with Mama, *Pure Blues*, in 1951 for a fledgling Atlantic Records. Jimmy Yancey died a few months later from a stroke brought on by complications from diabetes, but Estelle continued to perform and record. One of the best examples of her soulful, expressive vocals can be found on an album for Atlantic, *Jimmy and Mama Yancey: Chicago Piano, Vol. 1.*

Mama Yancey's recordings with other pianists include *South Side Blues* for the Riverside label (1961), some records with Art Hodes for Verve in 1965, and *Maybe I'll Cry* with Erwin Helfer for the Red Beans label in 1983, at age 87. Yancey died in 1986. — *Richard Skelly*

Mama Yancey Sings / 1965 / Smithsonian/Folkways ✦✦✦

● **Blues** / Jan. 1966 / Verve ✦✦✦✦

Blues, Mama Yancey's 1966 effort for Verve Records, finds the esteemed pianist maturing quite gracefully, turning a nicely understated collection of standards and originals. Throughout it all, her boogie-woogie piano sounds rich and friendly, offering a nice introduction to her groundbreaking wrok. — *Thom Owens*

Maybe I'll Cry / 1983 / Evidence ✦✦✦✦

The Yardbirds

f. 1963, Surrey, England, **db.** Jul. 1968
Group / British Invasion, Blues-Rock, Psychedelic, British Blues, Rock 'n' Roll, Electric British Blues

The Yardbirds are mostly known to the casual rock fan as the starting point for three of the greatest British rock guitarists—Eric Clapton, Jeff Beck, and Jimmy Page. Undoubtedly these three figures did much to shape the group's sound, but throughout their career, the Yardbirds were very much a unit, albeit a rather unstable one. And they were truly one of the great rock bands—one whose contributions went far beyond the scope of their half dozen or so mid-'60s hits ("For Your Love," "Heart Full of Soul," "Shapes of Things," "I'm a Man," "Over Under Sideways Down," "Happenings Ten Years Time Ago"). Not content to limit themselves to the R&B and blues covers they concentrated upon initially, they quickly branched out into moody, increasingly experimental pop-rock. The innnovations of Clapton, Beck, and Page redefined the role of the guitar in rock music, breaking immense ground in the use of feedback, distortion, and amplification with finesse and breathtaking virtuosity. With the arguable exception of the Byrds, they did more than any other outfit to pioneer psychedelia, with an eclectic, risk-taking approach that laid the groundwork for much of the hard rock and progressive rock from the late '60s to the present.

No one could have predicted the band's metamorphosis from their humble beginnings in the early '60s in the London suburbs as the Metropolis Blues Quartet. By 1963, they were calling themselves the Yardbirds, with a lineup featuring Keith Relf (vocals), Paul Samwell-Smith (bass), Chris Dreja (rhythm guitar), Jim McCarty (drums), and Anthony "Top" Topham (lead guitar). The 16-year-old Topham was only to last for a very short time, pressured to leave by his family. His replacement was an art-college classmate of Relf's, Eric Clapton, nicknamed "Slowhand."

The Yardbirds quickly made a name for themselves in London's rapidly exploding R&B circuit, taking over the Rolling Stones' residency at the famed Crawdaddy club. The band took a similar guitar-based, frenetic approach to classic blues/R&B as the Stones, and for their first few years they were managed by Giorgio Gomelsky, a colorful figure who had acted as a mentor and infomal manager for the Rolling Stones in that band's early days.

The Yardbirds made their first recordings as a backup band for Chicago blues great Sonny Boy Williamson, and little of their future greatness is evident in these sides, in which they were still developing their basic chops. (Some tapes of these live shows were issued after the group had become international stars; the material has been reissued ad infinitum since then.) But they really didn't find their footing until 1964, when they stretched out from straight R&B rehash into extended, frantic guitar-harmonica instrumental passages. Calling these ad hoc jams "rave ups," the Yardbirds were basically making the blues their own by applying a fiercer, heavily amplified electric base. Taking some cues from improvisational jazz by inserting their own impassioned solos, they would turn their source material inside out and sideways, heightening the restless tension by building the tempo and heated exchange of instrumental riffs to a feverish climax, adroitly cooling off and switching to a lower gear just at the point where the energy seemed uncontrollable. The live 1964 album *Five Live Yardbirds* is the best document of their early years, consisting entirely of reckless interpretations of US R&B/blues numbers, and displaying the increasing confidence and imagination of Clapton's guitar work.

As much they might have preferred to stay close to the American blues and R&B that had inspired them (at least at first), the Yardbirds made efforts to crack the pop market from the beginning. A couple of fine studio singles of R&B covers were recorded with Clapton that gave the band's sound a slight polish without sacrificing its power. The commercial impact was modest in the UK and non-existent in the States, however, and the group decided to change direction radically on their third single. Turning away from their blues roots entirely, "For Your Love" was penned by British pop-rock songwriter Graham Gouldman, and introduced many of the traits that would characterize the Yardbirds' work over the next two years. The melodies were strange (by pop standards) combinations of minor chords; the tempos slowed, speeded up, or ground to a halt unpredictably; the harmonies were droning, almost Gregorian; the arrangements were, by the standards of the time, downright weird, though retaining enough pop appeal to generate chart action. "For Your Love" featured a harpsichord, bongos, and a menacing Keith Relf vocal; it would reach No. 2 in Britain, and No. 6 in the States.

For all its brilliance, "For Your Love" precipitated a major crisis in the band. Eric Clapton wanted to stick close to the blues, and for that matter didn't like "For Your Love," barely playing on the record. Shortly afterwards, around the beginning of 1965, he left the band, opting to join John Mayall's Bluesbreakers a bit later in order to keep playing blues guitar. Clapton's spot was first offered to Jimmy Page, then one of the hottest session players in Britain; Page turned it down, figuring he could make a lot more money by staying where he was. He did, however, recommend another guitarist, Jeff Beck, then playing with an obscure band called the Tridents, as well as having worked a few sessions himself.

While Beck's stint with the band lasted only about 18 months, in this period he did more to influence the sound of '60s rock guitar than anyone except Jimi Hendrix. Clapton saw the group's decision to record adventurous pop like "For Your Love" as a sellout of their purist blues ethic. Beck, on the other hand, saw such material as a challenge that offered room for unprecedented experimentation. Not that he wasn't a capable R&B player as well—on tracks like "The Train Kept A-Rollin'" and "I'm Not Talking," he coaxed a sinister sustain from his instrument by bending the notes and using fuzz and other types of distorted amplification.The Middle Eastern influence extended to his work on all of their material, including his first single with the band, "Heart Full of Soul," which (like "For Your Love") was written by Gouldman. After initial attempts to record the song with a sitar had failed, Beck saved the day by emulating the instrument's exotic twang with fuzz riffs of his own. It became their second Transatlantic Top Ten hit; the similar "Evil-Hearted You," again penned by Gouldman, gave them another big British hit later in 1965.

The chief criticism that could be levied against the band at this point was their shortage of quality original material, a gap addressed by "Still I'm Sad," a haunting group composition based around a Gregorian chant and Beck's sinewy, wicked guitar riffs. In the United States, it was coupled with "I'm a Man," a rehaul of the Bo Diddley classic that built to an almost avant-garde climax, Beck scraping the strings of the guitar for a purely percussive effect; it became a Top 20 hit in the United States in early 1966. Beck's guitar pyrotechnics came to fruition with "Shapes of Things," which (along with the Byrds' "Eight Miles High") can justifiably be classified as the first psychedelic rock classic. The band had already moved into social comment with a superb album track, "Mr. You're a Better Man than I"; on "Shapes of Things" they did so more succinctly, with Beck's explosively warped solo and feedback propelling the single near the US Top Ten. At this point the group were as innovative as any in rock 'n' roll, building their résumé with the similar hit follow-up to "Shapes of Things," "Over Under Sideways Down."

But the Yardbirds could not claim to be nearly as consistent as peers like the Beatles, Rolling Stones, and Kinks. 1966's *Roger the Engineer* was their first (and, in fact, only) studio album comprised entirely of original material, and highlighted the group's erratic quality, bouncing between derivative blues-rockers and numbers incorporating monks-of-doom chants, Oriental dance rhythms, and good old guitar raveups, sometimes in the same track. Its highlights, however, were truly thrilling; even when the experiments weren't wholly successful, they served as proof that the band were second to none in their appetite for taking risks previously unheard of within rock.

Yet at the same time, the group's cohesiveness began to unravel when bassist Samwell-Smith—who had shouldered most of the production responsibilities as well—left the band in mid-1966. Jimmy Page, by this time fed up with session work, eagerly joined on bass. It quickly became apparent that Page had more to offer, and the group unexpectedly reorganized, Dreja switching from rhythm guitar to bass, and Page assuming dual lead guitar duties with Beck.

It was a dream lineup that was, like the best dreams, too good to be true, or at least to last long. Only one single was recorded with the Beck/Page lineup, "Happenings Ten Years Time Ago," which—with its astral guitar leads, muffled explosions, eerie harmonies, and enigmatic lyrics—was psychedelia at its pinnacle. But not at its most commercial—in comparison with previous Yardbirds singles, it fared poorly on the charts, reaching only No. 30 in the States. Around this time, the group (Page and Beck in tow) made a memorable appearance in Michaelangelo Antonioni's film classic *Blow Up*, playing a reworked version of "The Train Kept-A-Rollin'" (retitled "Stroll On"). But in late 1966, Beck—who had become increasingly unreliable, not turning up for some shows and suffering from nervous exhaustion—left the band, emerging the following year as the leader of the Jeff Beck Group.

The remaining Yardbirds were determined to continue as a quartet, but in hindsight it was Beck's departure that began to burn out a band that had already survived the loss of a couple important original members. Also to blame was their mysterious failure to summon original material on the order of their classic 1965-66 tracks. More to blame than anyone, however, was Mickey Most (Donovan, Herman's Hermits, Lulu, the Animals), who assumed the producer's chair in 1967, and matched the group with inappropriately lightweight pop tunes. The band's unbridled experimentalism would simmer in isolated moments on some B-sides and album tracks, like "Puzzles," the psychedelic U.F.O. instrumental "Glimpses," and the acoustic "White Summer," which would serve as a blueprint for Page's acoustic excursions with Led Zeppelin. "Little Games," "Ha Ha Said the Clown," and "Ten Little Indians" were all low-charting singles for the group in 1967, but were travesties compared to the magnificence of their previous hits, trading in fury and invention for sappy singalong pop. The 1967 *Little Games* album (issued in the US only) was little better, suffering from both hasty, anemic production and weak material.

The Yardbirds continued to be an exciting concert act, concentrating most of their energies upon the United States, having been virtually left for dead in their native Britain. The B-side of their final single, the Page-penned "Think About It," was the best track of the entire Jimmy Page era, showing they were still capable of delivering intriguing, energic psychedelia. It was too little too late—the group were truly on the wane by 1968, as an artistic rift developed within the ranks. To overgeneralize somewhat, Relf and McCarty wanted to pursue more acoustic, melodic music; Page especially wanted to rock hard and loud. A live album was recorded in New York in early 1968, but scrapped; overdubbed with unbelievably cheesy crowd noises, it was briefly released in 1971 after Page had become a superstar in Led Zeppelin, but was withdrawn in a matter of days (it has since been heavily bootlegged). By this time the group was going through the motions, leaving Page holding the bag after a final show in mid-1968. Relf and McCarty formed the first incarnation of Renaissance. Page fulfilled existing contracts by assembling a "New Yardbirds" that, as many know, would soon change their name to Led Zeppelin.

It took years for the rock community to truly comprehend the Yardbirds' significance; younger listeners were led to the recordings in search of the roots of Clapton, Beck, and Page, each of whom had become a superstar by the end of the 1960s. Their wonderful catalog, however, has been subject to more exploitation than any other group of the '60s; dozens, if not hundreds, of cheesy packages of early material are generated throughout the world on a seemingly monthly basis. Fortunately, the best of the reissues cited below (on Rhino, Sony, Edsel, and EMI) are packaged with great intelligence, enabling both collectors and new listeners to acquire all of their classic output with a minimum of fuss and repetition. — *Richie Unterberger*

Five Live Yardbirds / Dec. 1964 / Rhino ✦✦✦✦
Recorded live at London's Marquee Club, *Five Live Yardbirds* is the best document of Eric Clapton's work with the band. Tracks like "Too Much Monkey Business," "Got Love If You Want It," and "Smokestack Lightning" were good representations of The Yardbirds' "rave-ups," which were open-ended improvisations that helped lay the groundwork for groups like Cream and the Jimi Hendrix Experience. — *Rick Clark*

Roger the Engineer / 1966 / Edsel ✦✦✦✦
Once Jeff Beck joined the Yardbirds, the group began to explore uncharted territory, expanding their blues-rock into wild sonic permutations of psyche-

delia, Indian music, and avant-garde white noise. Each subsequent single displayed a new direction, one that expanded on the ideas of the previous single, so it would seem that *Roger the Engineer*—Beck's first full album with the group and the band's first album of all original material—would have offered them the opportunity to fully explore their adventurous inclinations. Despite a handful of brilliant moments, *Roger the Engineer* falls short of expectations, partially because the band is reluctant to leave their blues roots behind and partially because they simply can't write a consistent set of songs. At their best on *Roger*, the Yardbirds strike a kinetic balance of blues-rock form and explosive psychedelia ("Lost Woman," "Over, Under Sideways, Down," "The Nazz Are Blue," "He's Always There," "Psycho Daisies") but they can also bog down in silly eastern drones (although "Happenings Ten Years Time Ago" is a classic piece of menacing psychedelia) or blues tradition ("Jeff's Boogie" is a pointless guitar workout that doesn't even showcase Beck at his most imaginative. The result is an unfocused record that careens between the great and the merely adequate but the Yardbirds always had a problem with consistency—none of their early albums had the impact of the singles, and *Roger the Engineer* suffers from the same problem. Nevertheless, is the Yardbirds' best individual studio album, offering some of their very best psychedelia, even if it doesn't rank among the great albums of its era. — *Stephen Thomas Erlewine*

Sonny Boy Williamson & the Yardbirds / 1966 / Mercury ✦✦
An exploitative album, released in 1966 shortly after the Yardbirds had their first American hits. This is a live show from late 1963, on which Chicago blues great Sonny Boy Williamson is backed by an extremely green Yardbirds. Yes, Eric Clapton is on here; no, he doesn't play well, managing some thin, extremely tentative solos that find him stumbling occasionally. It's really not that bad, though, as Sonny Boy himself sings well. But it should really be treated as a Sonny Boy Williamson release that happens to have a soon-to-be-famous-but-still-embryonic band in the background, in the manner of the sides the Beatles cut in Hamburg supporting Tony Sheridan. All of the material, and even some unreleased/alternate takes from the same dates, has since shown up on anthologies that are much easier to find than this instant collector's item. — *Richie Unterberger*

Live Yardbirds Featuring Jimmy Page / 1971 / Epic ✦✦
Recorded at New York's Anderson Theatre on March 30, 1968, this was released super-briefly in 1971, and almost immediately withdrawn when Jimmy Page took legal action against the record on grounds of "lack of quality performance." It immediately became a highly valued collector's item, and naturally became heavily bootlegged as well, showing up under a number of titles. As enticing as it sounds, the content itself is pretty disappointing, primarily because Epic took the idiotic step of overdubbing over-the-top crowd noises (once described by Page as "bullfight roars"). That's not the only problem—the sound quality isn't very good, and Keith Relf isn't in very good voice, sounding as if he's a few shows away from giving out. It's too bad, because there is some interesting stuff here, mostly focused around Page's playing, which is very good. Of special note is "White Summer," an 11-minute "I'm a Man," a massive guitar solo on "Mr. You're a Better Man than I," and a version of "Dazed and Confused," which became one of Led Zeppelin's showpieces (although the Yardbirds never recorded it in the studio). The concert is now available in a more-or-less over-the-counter fashion as part of the Dutch live compilation *Rare Concerts 1965-1968*. — *Richie Unterberger*

More Golden Eggs / 1974 / Trademark Of Quality ✦✦✦
20 years later, this sequel to *Golden Eggs* actually offers much more of value to the collector than the original installment. Although some of this (like the '66 B-side "Psycho Daisies") finally became easily available on reissues, most of this has not. And this includes some pretty interesting stuff—live TV broadcasts with Jeff Beck from the mid-'60s, the super-rare and super-moody second Keith Relf solo single "Shapes in My Mind" (two versions!), a pre-Yardbirds Jimmy Page solo single, and downright weird Europop bubblegum numbers that the group (actually Relf with sessionmen) recorded for an Italian single. There's also an actual lengthy interview with Keith Relf on a printed insert; if you're lucky, the copy you hunt down will have this intact. Pricey and hard to find, but worth the search for Yardbird fanatics. — *Richie Unterberger*

Last Rave-Up in L.A. / 1979 / Glimpses ✦✦
A three-record set of the Yardbirds with Jimmy Page, recorded live in May

and June of 1968, may sound real enticing, especially given the general scarcity of material that Page recorded with the band. But you should think real hard before forking over for it (in the unlikely event you can find a copy). The sound quality is abysmal, obviously recorded by a single mike somewhere not too close to the stage; you can barely hear the vocals and the instruments. Nor are the performances that great; the band sounds ragged though not quite dispirited. If the fidelity on these performances had been acceptable, there would have been some interesting, extremely extended versions of standbys like "I'm a Man," "I Wish You Would," and "White Summer" to be heard, along with the pre-Led Zep incarnation of "Dazed and Confused," finding the band improvising and jamming to a degree not allowable in the studio. —*Richie Unterberger*

★ **Greatest Hits, Vol. 1: 1964-1966** / 1986 / Rhino ♦♦♦♦♦
Sonically, these tracks fail to match the brilliance and warmth of the original vinyl pressings, but *Greatest Hits* has more punch. "For Your Love" is an exception, with the record version sounding extremely compressed. Of the various Yardbird collections that exist, this is still the most intelligently chosen, even though it lacks key tracks from *Roger the Engineer*. —*Rick Clark*

On Air / 1991 / Band of Joy ♦♦♦
Like most of the major British Invasion bands, the Yardbirds recorded many sessions for the BBC during their heyday. *On Air* contains 27 of these, recorded between 1965 and 1968; 21 of them feature Jeff Beck, the rest Jimmy Page (Eric Clapton is not featured on any). The BBC sessions offered listeners the opportunity to hear groups in a relatively live setting with relatively good sound quality, and that's basically what you get here. Most of their major hits—"For Your Love," "Heart Full of Soul," "Shapes of Things," "Over Under Sideways Down," "Still I'm Sad"—are included. By and large, these versions don't differ enormously from the studio cuts, with slightly different arrangements and guitar solos. One could argue, of course, that with a band so responsible for pushing rock guitar to the stratosphere, different guitar solos are a tasty discovery. And they are interesting, but they don't outdo the stellar studio renditions. Of most interest, if not highest quality, are a few covers never waxed by the group on their official releases: "Dust My Blues," "The Sun Is Shining," Garnett Mimms' "My Baby," and Dylan's "Most Likely You'll Go Your Way." On cuts like "I'm Not Talking" and "Too Much Monkey Business," Beck's pyrotechnics are truly breathtaking. But generally this release is more for Yardbirds fans than novices. —*Richie Unterberger*

Vol. 2: Blues, Backtrack's, and Shapes of Things / Oct. 1, 1991 / Sony ♦♦♦♦
Another double-disc set, this covers some later hits (including the classic future-rock of "Shapes of Things"), *Roger the Engineer* outtakes, and various other oddities. The sound on some of the outtakes is pretty respectable, considering some of them were taken from the original acetates. —*Rick Clark*

Vol. 1: Smokestack Lightning / Oct. 1, 1991 / Sony ♦♦♦♦
This double-disc set focuses on tracks from *For Your Love* and *Having a Rave-Up with the Yardbirds*. Included are live tracks recorded at the Crawdaddy Club while touring with Sonny Boy Williamson. Most of these tracks on *Smokestack Lightning* (as well as *Blues, Backtracks*) were mastered off of safety tapes, as opposed to the original masters, since EMI England has possession of them. Considering that EMI won't release the masters to anyone, this is a respectable sound—though not as good as the first vinyl pressings. —*Rick Clark*

The Yardbirds Little Games Sessions & More / Aug. 25, 1992 / EMI America ♦♦♦
This digitally remastered 32-track, double-disc set covers Jimmy Page's tenure with the Yardbirds. This period didn't contain the band's best work, mainly because Mickie Most's poppish production reined in the band's experimental strengths. Nevertheless, tracks like "Little Games," "Puzzles," "Smile on Me," "Drinking Muddy Water," and a wonderful acoustic version of Jimmy Page's "White Summer" make this a good overview of the Yardbird's final stretch as a band. This set includes extensive liner notes and discography— a real treat for fans. —*Rick Clark*

BBC Radio Sessions / Jun. 30, 1993 / Dutch East ♦♦♦
A cut-down single-CD, 26-song version of the British *Where the Action Is* double set, with duplicate Jeff Beck/Jimmy Page tracks eliminated and notes by *Trouser Press's* Ira Robbins aimed specifically at an American audience, with few recollections about early/mid-'60s musical and cultural life in En-

gland and more analysis. Otherwise identical, but about $10 cheaper for nine fewer songs, although the Dylan cover is included here. —*Bruce Eder*

Live Saga 63-67 / 1994 / Import ♦♦♦
An import compilation of borderline legality, combining some oft-rehashed live releases with some much rarer live '60s performances. The most important tracks by far are the first eight, taken from a Swedish show in 1967, with Jimmy Page on guitar. These cuts, more than almost anything the Page lineup recorded in the studio, comprise the best evidence of how well Jimmy and the group could play at their best, when they were unencumbered by unsympathetic producers and material. The sound quality is very good, and the performances are good to excellent, including reprises of several of their biggest hits, the otherwise unavailable Dylan cover "Most Likely You Go Your Way and I'll Go Mine," and an extended psychedelic version of "I'm a Man" with violin-guitar bowing by Page. Other rarities on the disc—four songs from Germany in 1967 (w/Page), one from France in 1965 (w/Beck)— are okay, but more in the hardcore collector category. The CD is filled out by six songs from *Five Live Yardbirds* (which has been reissued zillions of times) and a live '63 version of "Honey in Your Hips." —*Richie Unterberger*

Little Games [1996 Expanded] / Nov. 12, 1996 / EMI ♦♦♦
A curious release that basically condenses 1992's *Little Games Sessions & More* 32-track double CD into a 26-song, single-disc package. Six of the less essential cuts from the expanded version were dropped, with all of the group's principal 1967-68 material (from the *Little Games* LP and a few non-LP singles) remaining, along with a few alternates and outtakes. You don't lose that much in the transition, but it's annoying because anybody who bothers to track down this stuff in the first place is probably a collector who would prefer the double CD with everything, rather than a slightly abridged version. —*Richie Unterberger*

Where the Action Is / Oct. 7, 1997 / Cleopatra ♦♦♦
An astonishingly fine, generally high-quality live-in-the-studio anthology, covering the Jeff Beck and Jimmy Page periods in the band's history. Buying it should be a no-brainer for any real Yardbirds fan, as it matches any of the hours of Beatles outtakes and BBC sessions issued in the 1990s in both importance and vitality. The double-CD set consists of 35 live BBC and Stockholm radio performances that are more than sufficiently different from the group's studio sides to justify the purchase, all in superb sound with a healthy, robust volume and presence, except for the typical anemic bass of the period. Disc one is the BBC material, 27 songs performed with Jeff Beck and Jimmy Page on guitars, covering "I Ain't Got You" through to "Little Games," "Goodnight Sweet Josephine," "My Baby," and "Think About It"— no Eric Clapton-era tapes have survived. These raw, single-take renditions showcase the sheer dexterity and power of this band better than any studio sides. The Jimmy Page material shows the fissures in the band, with less sense of a tightly knit group and more of four guys who just happen to be together, rather like the Beatles' *White Album* sessions. The Stockholm tracks on Disc two have more hiss but also better-recorded bass and drums, and feature a nicely raw cover of Dylan's "Most Likely You'll Go Your Way," one of many outside songs (Velvet Underground tracks included) that the group did in concert but never put on their records. The notes feature an in-depth interview with Jim McCarty and Chris Dreja in which they recall the early and mid-'60s, the recording procedure at the BBC, the stresses within the group, and, curiously, the virtues of the bootleg *Last Rave-Up in L.A.* —*Bruce Eder*

Live at the BBC / Oct. 7, 1997 / Warner Archives ♦♦♦
The Yardbirds recorded several live sessions for the BBC between 1965 and 1968, following Eric Clapton's departure from the band. These recordings have previously been released on bootlegs and small independent labels but Warner Archives' *The Yardbirds BBC Sessions* marks the first big-budget, official release of the material. The disc contains 26 tracks—20 featuring Jeff Beck, six featuring Jimmy Page—which is slightly less than some editions of this same material, but that won't matter to anyone but completists since the gist is the same: the Yardbirds were a tough live band that essentially recreated its studio recordings on the BBC stage. There are slight differences in the guitar solos but the songs are so short, neither Beck or Page have the opportunity to completely tear loose. Nevertheless, hardcore Yardbirds fans will relish the few rarities here, which mainly are covers the band never recorded in the studio: "Dust My Broom," "Most Likely You Go Your Way

(And I'll Go Mine)," "My Baby" and "The Sun Is Shining." Then again, hardcore fans are the ones that will buy *BBC Sessions* in the first place, since the differences between the live and studio are so minute, only the dedicated will care. Casual fans, on the other hand, will find this disc entertaining but ultimately unnecessary. — *Stephen Thomas Erlewine*

Golden Eggs / Berkeley ◆◆◆
One of the first widely circulated bootlegs of a non-superstar (but hugely important) act, this did collectors quite a service at the time, assembling 17 of the Yardbirds' rarest tracks—from non-LP singles, soundtracks, and rare LPs—onto one disc. The passage of time and the digital age, though, has made this virtually useless: most of the tracks show up on the Sony and EMI CD reissues. The only true rarities to be found here now are the two songs that comprised the rare '66 solo single by Keith Relf, "Mr. Zero"/"Knowing," which are odd bits of baroquely produced folk-pop not at all like the Yardbirds' own records. Beware of cheap-quality reproductions of the original (always fair game in the bootleg business), on which some tracks lack a stereo channel from the original recordings. — *Richie Unterberger*

Johnny Young (John O. Young)

b. Jan. 1, 1918, Mississippi, **d.** Apr. 18, 1974, Chicago, IL
Guitar, Mandolin, Vocals / Acoustic Chicago Blues, Chicago Blues, Electric Chicago Blues, Electric Blues, Electric Memphis Blues
Although the mandolin is not an instrument commonly associated with Chicago blues, it has been used by Chicago-based string bands or on Chicago-made recordings by artists such as Carl Martin, Charles and Joe McCoy, and Yank Rachell. However, the only artist to use it successfully in the later electric blues format was Mississippi-born bluesman Johnny Young. An important figure in blues history, Young loved the rough-and-tumble string-band tradition of the Delta, a style that readily coexisted with blues.

Young's initial 1947 Chicago classic, "Money Taking Women," exhibits the same exuberant down-home sound, fusing blues with the older country breakdown traditions. The string-band ensemble sound suited street performance as well, whether in Memphis or in Chicago's open-air Maxwell Street Market, where Young and his cronies were brought in off the streets to record. Over the years, Young's mandolin activity declined as Chicago's African-American blues audience demanded a more modern and urban sound. Since Young was also a skilled guitarist and a fine vocalist, he easily weathered the transition.

During the late '60s, an emerging White blues-revival audience proved eager for Young's mandolin styling. Unlike Yank Rachell, whose mandolin playing retained an older string-band feel, Young's style was firmly grounded in a more contemporary postwar blues idiom, and he interacted well with other electric blues artists. Through his life, he had worked with the major figures of blues history, including Sonny Boy Williamson, Muddy Waters, Walter Horton, and Otis Spann. He was, he insisted, born to be a musician. When I interviewed him shortly before he died, he told me how he had struggled all his life trying to make it in the music business. An emotional man, he hoped he would live long enough to make enough money to buy a house. He never made it. — *Barry Lee Pearson*

Chicago Blues Band / 1966 / Arhoolie ◆◆◆◆
James Cotton nearly blew the roof off on harmonica, and Otis Spann added some wonderful rumbling piano. Johnny Young's spirited guitar, vocals, and occasional mandolin provided the final elements for a superb mid-'60s date. — *Ron Wynn*

Chicago/The Blues/ Today! Vol. 3 / 1967 / Vanguard ◆◆◆◆

● **Chicago Blues** / 1968 / Arhoolie ◆◆◆◆
This is an excellent '60s recording by the down-home urban singer, guitarist, and mandolinist, accompanied by Otis Spann on piano and James Cotton and Big Walter Horton on harmonicas. — *Mark A. Humphrey*

Fat Mandolin / 1970 / Blue Horizon ◆◆◆

I Can't Keep My Foot from Jumping / 1973 / Bluesway ◆◆

Johnny Young and His Friends / 1994 / Testament ◆◆◆
Recorded in informal settings between 1962 and 1966, this presents Young with various configurations, with major Chicago blues talents like Otis Spann, Robert Nighthawk, Little Walter, and Walter Horton lending a hand at different points (Young also plays solo on a couple of numbers). Only three

cuts feature drums, so this is usually at the midpoint between Delta blues and the electric Chicago sound; Young usually plays guitar, but also brings out his mandolin for a couple of songs. Warm performances, though not especially noteworthy. The CD reissue adds four previously unreleased bonus cuts. — *Richie Unterberger*

Mighty Joe Young

b. Sep. 23, 1927, Shreveport, LA
Guitar, Vocals / Electric Chicago Blues, Chicago Blues, Electric Blues
Although physical problems have curtailed his guitar playing in recent years, there was a time during the late '70s and early '80s when Mighty Joe Young was one of the leading blues guitarists on Chicago's budding North Side blues circuit.

The Louisiana native got his start not in the Windy City, but in Milwaukee, where he was raised. He earned a reputation as a reliable guitarist on Chicago's West Side with Joe Little & His Heart Breakers during the mid-'50s, later changing his onstage allegiance to harpist Billy Boy Arnold. Young recorded with Arnold for Prestige and Testament during the '60s and backed Jimmy Rogers for Chess in 1958.

After abortive attempts to inaugurate a solo career with Jiffy Records in Louisiana in 1955 and Chicago's Atomic-H label three years later, Young hit his stride in 1961 with the sizzling "Why Baby"/"Empty Arms" for Bobby Robinson's Fire label. Young gigged as Otis Rush's rhythm guitarist from 1960 to 1963 and cut a series of excellent Chicago blues 45s for a variety of firms: "I Want a Love," "Voo Doo Dust," and "Something's Wrong" for Webcor during the mid-'60s; "Something's Wrong" for Webcor in 1966; "Sweet Kisses" and "Henpecked" on Celtex and "Hard Times (Follow Me)" for USA (all 1967); and "Guitar Star" for Jacklyn in 1969. Young even guested on Bill "Hoss" Allen's groundbreaking 1966 syndicated R&B TV program *The Beat* in Dallas. Late-'60s session work included dates with Tyrone Davis and Jimmy Dawkins.

Delmark issued Young's solo album debut, *Blues with a Touch of Soul*, in 1971, but a pair of mid-'70s LPs for Ovation (1974's *Chicken Heads* and an eponymous set in 1976) showcased the guitarist's blues-soul synthesis far more effectively. Young's main local haunt during the '70s and early '80s was Wise Fools Pub, where he packed 'em in nightly (with Freddy King's brother, Benny Turner, on bass). — *Bill Dahl*

Blues with a Touch of Soul / 1971 / Delmark ◆◆
Soporific album debut for the Chicago guitarist—only seven songs, many of them way too long (10:40 of "Somebody Loan Me a Dime" being the worst offender), that sport little of the excitement of Young's '60s 45s for a variety of local firms. Young doesn't sound like he was prepared for the opportunity, and the stiff two-piece horn section doesn't help either. — *Bill Dahl*

Legacy of the Blues, Vol. 4 / 1972 / GNP ◆◆◆

Chicken Heads / 1974 / Ovation ◆◆◆◆
One of Mighty Joe Young's best efforts (and one that's not out on CD), an up-to-the-minute effort that combines soul and blues most effectively. Predominantly original material that suits his booming vocals and stinging guitar well. Nice band, too: bassist Louis Satterfield, drummer Ira Gates, and keyboardist Floyd Morris were all veterans of the '60s soul session scene. — *Bill Dahl*

● **Mighty Joe Young** / 1976 / Ovation ◆◆◆◆
Another out-of-print collection that's the crown jewel in Young's album discography. Many of Young's finest originals—"Need a Friend," "Takes Money," "Take My Advice (She Likes the Blues and Barbecue)"—reside in their most memorable recorded forms on this worthwhile LP. — *Bill Dahl*

Bluesy Josephine / Nov. 28, 1976 / Evidence ◆◆◆
Not exactly the most incendiary outing that Chicago guitarist Mighty Joe Young has ever cut. This 1976 album was cut in France for Black & Blue with a handful of Chicago stalwarts, but the excitement that Young routinely summoned up back home is in short supply as he walks through "Sweet Home Chicago" and "Five Long Years." Young's own "Takes Money" and "Need a Friend" are a definite improvement on those shopworn standards, but with only seven selections ("Teasing the Blues" runs 10:27), there isn't a lot to choose from. — *Bill Dahl*

Live at the Wise Fools / 1990 / Quicksilver ◆◆
For much of the 1970s and '80s, guitarist Mighty Joe Young "owned" Chica-

go's cozy Wise Fools Pub—at least musically speaking. He was the club's top draw, but this live disc, caught at the late and still-lamented Wise Fools, finds him sticking to the tiredest of warhorses. "Stormy Monday," "Turning Point," "That's All Right," and "I Can't Quit You Baby" may have wowed the home-folks, but they don't hold up all that well when transferred to the digital format. Young's quartet features Freddie King's brother, Benny Turner, on bass, and Lafayette Leake on piano. —*Bill Dahl*

Mighty Man / May 5, 1997 / Blind Pig ✦✦✦✦
Young embarked on this album in early 1986, financing it himself, determined to finally complete a project his way. But surgery and the subsequent rehabilitation time needed to repair a pinched nerve in his neck (making him unable to play guitar) shelved the project for many years. Young continued writing and recording, however and with the help of musicians, friends, family, and Blind Pig's Jerry Del Giudice, the project reached completion a decade later. Guitarist Will Crosby handles all the solo work here (Young plays on the three tracks that were completed before his accident), and the majority of tracks feature his son on rhythm guitar. With co-producer Willie Henderson and Gene "Daddy G" Barge doing the horn charts, Leo Davis on keyboards, and the rhythm section of veterans Bernard Reed and B.J. Jones, the resulting mixture is, in Young's words, "a different sound." Those familiar with his spate of 45s for Webcor, Atomic H, USA, and Celtex from the mid-'60s will recognize the direct link these sides have to classic period Chicago-style soul-blues. Tracks like "Turning Point," "Got My Mind on My Woman," "Got a Hold on Me," and the ballad "Bring It On" are soul music deluxe with strong blues roots, and if his fiery guitar work has been silenced, the 70-year-old bluesman continues to look forward with this release. Billy Branch makes a guest appearance on "Wishy Washy Woman," perhaps the most straightahead thing on here. While comeback albums are usually imbued with nostalgia, this one is as present-time as you could ask for, and in this case, that's a very good thing. —*Cub Koda*

Tony Z

b. Boston, MA

Organ / Modern Electric Blues, Soul Blues, Blues Jazz

Hammond B-3 blues organist Tony Z. was long a fixture on the New England blues club circuit, and for two years as part of Boston-area guitarist Ronnie Earl's touring band, the Broadcasters.

Born and raised in Boston, Tony Zamagni began playing organ at St. Patrick's School in Roxbury. He cut his musical teeth with the Boston band Combat Zone and then went on to play with the Platters for the next ten years. He spent most of the latter part of the 1980s trying to organize his own touring band (no small feat) and working as a session player in Miami for TK Records, where he recorded an LP with the group Miami. After meeting Ronnie Earl through a mutual friend, trumpeter Bob Enos, Zamagni teamed up with the guitarist and joined his road band, the Broadcasters, from 1989 to 1991.

In 1991, Zamagni moved to Chicago, where he worked for three years with guitarist Larry McCray and found work as a session musician on albums by Son Seals, Saffire, Little Smokey Smothers, and Lee "Shot" Williams.

Zamagni's debut album, *Get Down with the Blues*, was released on Rounder's Tone-Cool subsidiary in 1995. The outing is first-class, self-produced in Chicago's Streeterville Studios with some stellar backing musicians: former Roomful of Blues guitarist Duke Robillard, drummer Bernard "Pretty" Purdie, saxophonist Houston Person, harmonica master Sugar Blue, and former Albert Collins band bassist Johnny B. Gayden.

Zamagni carries on the jazz/blues organ tradition forged by organists like Jimmy McGriff and Jimmy Smith, and continues to record as a sideman and tour as a bandleader. —*Richard Skelly*

Get Down with the Blues / 1995 / Tone-Cool ✦✦✦

● **Kiss My Blues** / Jan. 13, 1998 / Tone-Cool ✦✦✦✦
Keyboardist Tony Z uses the Hammond B-3 organ blues sound and style to paint a new tapestry of music on this disc. The groove on this album is immensely fortified by the formidable presence of Cornell Dupree on guitar, Bernard Purdie on drums and Chuck Rainey on bass as the rhythm section. But instead of aping the tunes and styles of B-3 masters like Jimmy Smith, Jimmy McGriff, or Groove Holmes, Tony comes to the plate with a batch of his own songs for this album. With Lenny Pickett emoting soulfully on saxophone and a two-song guest turn from Kim Wilson on harmonica, this session goes into realms previously uncharted by your Hammond B-3 practitioner, retro or otherwise. Highlights include "Voodootize Me Baby," "All Alone," "You Ain't Who You Think You Are," and "Communicate." —*Cub Koda*

Rusty Zinn

b. Apr. 3, 1970, Long Beach, CA

Guitar / Contemporary Blues

A young, red-haired guitarist with a monster tone and technique that belies his 20-something years, Rusty Zinn grew up in the Santa Cruz mountains in northern California. He was introduced to classic R&B through his mother's collection of 45 singles, which included rare discs from Fats Domino and Elvis Presley. While in his teens, his brother brought home recordings by Muddy Waters and Howlin' Wolf, and these proved to be a revelation for the young blues aficionado. He would empty his pockets regularly to purchase blues recordings and became fascinated by the guitar stylings of Robert Jr. Lockwood, Eddie Taylor, Luther Tucker, and Jimmy Rogers. These records

prompted him to begin playing guitar at 17. He had some background in music, having played drums when he was younger, but he enjoyed another crystallizing moment when he saw Luther Tucker perform with Jimmy Rogers at a local club. He credits the nightclub showcase with changing his life, and he sought out all the recordings he could find with Luther Tucker as a sideman, which included records by Little Walter Jacobs, Muddy Waters, Sonny Boy Williamson, and James Cotton. A year later, when Zinn again went to see his idol, Tucker invited him on stage. Tucker took the young Zinn under his wing and shared guitar techniques with him. Meanwhile, Zinn was working with several northern California blues bands in the late '80s, and he was often tapped to back touring musicians like Snooky Pryor and Rogers.

After joining Mark Hummel's band, Zinn honed his craft through hundreds of shows and thousands of miles. One of the shows with Hummel's band was at the San Francisco Blues Festival, where Zinn was introduced to harp player Kim Wilson. Wilson invited Zinn to come to Austin's Arlyn Studios to play on his 1993 album *Tigerman*, for the Antone's label. Wilson soon put together a band that included Zinn on guitar, ex-Canned Heat bass player Larry Taylor, and former Blaster "Blue" Gene Taylor on keyboards. Zinn toured around with Wilson and his band, surprising Wilson with the dexterity of his playing at such a young age (he was then in his early 20s).

In early 1996, Wilson approached BlackTop Records executives about recording Zinn, and fortunately, they agreed with him.

To date, Zinn has released one album for the Crescent City-based BlackTop Records, *Sittin' and Waitin'* (1996). Naturally, he's accompanied by his friend and mentor Kim Wilson throughout his first album, who also served as producer. —*Richard Skelly*

Sittin' & Waitin' / Jun. 18, 1996 / Black Top ✦✦✦

Zydeco Force

f. Opelousas, Louisiana

Group / Zydeco

Originally formed in the spirit of the rural, old-time zydeco style, over time the Opelousas, Louisiana-based group Zydeco Force began moving towards a funkier, more bass-driven sound reflecting a wide range of influences. Upon debuting in 1988, Zydeco Force comprised bandleader Bobby "Mann" Robinson, vocalist/accordionist Jeffery Broussard (the son of Lawtell Playboys frontman Delton Broussard), his brothers Hebert on rubboard and Shelton on guitar, and drummer Raymond Thomas. Quickly their propulsive sound caught on with dancehall audiences throughout Louisiana and East Texas, and in 1990 they released their self-titled debut LP, followed a year later by *The Sun's Going Down*. After issuing 1992's *Shaggy Dog Two-Step*, Zydeco Force returned in 1994 with *The Zydeco Push*, with the title track spawning a lambada-like dance craze among fans. *It's La-La Time* followed in 1995. —*Jason Ankeny*

Zydeco Push / 1994 / Maison de Soul ✦✦✦
Zydeco Force are caught between trying to extend their popularity with pop covers and then verifying their credentials doing Clifton Chenier's "I'm on the Wonder" and Lightnin' Hopkins' "12-String Boogie." As a result, an air of confusion reigns, and they seldom sound either comfortable or creditable. —*Ron Wynn*

● **It's La La Time** / Apr. 11, 1995 / Flat Town ✦✦✦✦

Zydeco Hurricanes

Group / Zydeco

The Zydeco Hurricanes were led by guitarist Selwyn Cooper, a noted sideman who toured with such renowned figures as Clifton Chenier, Buckwheat

Zydeco, Rockin' Dopsie, and Fernest Arceneaux. Additionally including bassist Alonzo Johnson, Jr., (himself a Chenier alum as well) and former Buckwheat Zydeco drummer Nathaniel Jolivette, as well as two newcomers—vocalist/accordionist John Wilson and washboard player Adam Robinson—the Zydeco Hurricanes made their debut in 1994 with *Louisiana Zydeco!* —*Jason Ankeny*

Louisiana Zydeco / Mar. 28, 1995 / Mardis Gras ♦♦♦♦

ZZ Top

f. 1970, El Paso, TX
Group / Blues-Rock, Rock 'n' Roll, Boogie Rock, Hard Rock
This sturdy American blues-rock trio from Texas consists of Billy Gibbons (guitar), Dusty Hill (bass), and Frank Beard (drums). They were formed in 1970 in and around Houston from rival bands the Moving Sidewalks (Gibbons) and the American Blues (Hill and Beard). Their first two albums reflected the strong blues roots and Texas humor of the band. Their third album (*Tres Hombres*) gained them national attention with the hit "La Grange," a signature riff tune to this day, based on John Lee Hooker's "Boogie Chillen." Their success continued unabated throughout the '70s, culminating with the year-and-a-half-long Worldwide Texas Tour.

Exhausted from the overwhelming work load, they took a three-year break, then switched labels and returned to form with *Deguello* and *El Loco*, both harbingers of what was to come. By their next album, *Eliminator,* and its worldwide smash follow-up, *Afterburner,* they had successfully harnessed the potential of synthesizers to their patented grungy blues-groove, giving their material a more contemporary edge while retaining their patented Texas style. Now sporting long beards, golf hats, and boiler suits, they met the emerging video age head-on, reducing their "message" to simple iconography. Becoming even more popular in the long run, they moved with the times while simultaneously bucking every trend that crossed their path. As genuine roots musicians, they have few peers; Gibbons is one of America's finest blues guitarists working in the arena of rock idiom—both influenced by the originators of the form and British blues-rock guitarists like Peter Green—while Hill and Beard provide the ultimate rhythm section support. The only rock 'n' roll group that's out there with its original members still aboard after 20-plus years, ZZ Top's music is always instantly recognizable, eminently powerful, profoundly soulful, and 100% American in derivation. They have continued to support the blues through various means, perhaps the most visible when they were given a piece of wood from Muddy Waters' shack in Clarksdale, MS. The group members had it made into a guitar, dubbed the "Muddywood," then sent it out on tour to raise money for the Delta Blues Museum. ZZ Top's support and link to the blues remains as rock solid as the music they play. —*Cub Koda*

ZZ Top's First Album / 1970 / Warner Brothers ♦♦♦
This Texas trio's debut was a gritty exercise in bare-boned blues boogie. Tracks like "Brown Sugar," "Neighbor Neighbor," and "Shakin' Your Tree" helped establish them as a regionally successful act in the South. —*Rick Clark*

Rio Grande Mud / 1972 / Warner Brothers ♦♦♦
Rio Grande Mud possessed a beefier sound than its predecessor. The "Brown Sugar"-style "Francine" became their first hit at No. 69. Other highlights included "Chevrolet" and "Just Got Paid." —*Rick Clark*

Tres Hombres / 1973 / Warner Brothers ♦♦♦♦
Constant touring and favorable radio exposure made *Tres Hombres* ZZ's first hit album, thanks in no small part to "La Grange," an ode to a whorehouse. By this album, Billy Gibbons had practically perfected his distinctively dirty electric-guitar sound. His riffs and chordal voicings were also more memorable. Highlights included "Beer Drinkers & Hell Raisers," "Precious & Grace," and the two-some "Waitin' for the Bus," and "Jesus Just Left Chicago." —*Rick Clark*

Fandango / 1975 / Warner Brothers ♦♦♦
Fandango is a half-studio/half-live effort. The concert side is a fairly straightahead, no-nonsense affair, which includes a version of "Jailhouse Rock." The studio side featured their first Top 40 hit, "Tush" (No. 20). The hyper-boogie of "Heard It on the X" was another popular track off of this release. —*Rick Clark*

The Best of ZZ Top / 1977 / Warner Brothers ♦♦♦♦
The sound may be a little muddy, but this anthology is still the best representation of ZZ's early work. It contains classic rude, riff-heavy blues-rockers like "Just Got Paid," "Jesus Just Left Chicago," "Heard It on the X," "Tush," and "La Grange." —*Rick Clark*

Deguello / 1979 / Warner Brothers ♦♦♦♦
Deguello was ZZ's best album from their pre-robotic blues-rock period—the last reminder of what a tough ensemble this trio could be. It was the first time they infused their lunkhead approach to fast cars, kinky girls, and partying with some bizarre humor. Their version of Sam & Dave's "I Thank You" (No. 34) became their first Top 40 hit in five years. Other highlights included the oddball "Manic Mechanic," a rip-roaring version of Elmore James' "Dust My Broom," the funky boogie of "Cheap Sunglasses," and "Fool for Your Stockings," a down-and-dirty fetish blues. —*Rick Clark*

El Loco / 1981 / Warner Brothers ♦♦♦
Not as strong as *Deguello*, *El Loco* vacillates between half-baked ballads ("Leila") and novelty rockers ("Party on the Patio," "Groovy Little Hippie Pad," "Heaven, Hell, or Houston"). "Pearl Necklace," with its not-too-subtle sexual double-entendre and Police-inspired groove, was a big AOR hit. —*Rick Clark*

Eliminator / 1983 / Warner Brothers ♦♦♦♦
Hardcore fans might have cried "sellout," but ZZ's introduction of a streamlined synth-heavy sound (and three slickly produced T&A videos) turned this trio from potential blues-rock has-beens to multi-platinum purveyors of space boogie. Most of this album became a staple on album rock radio, with "Gimme All Your Lovin'," "Sharp Dressed Man," and "Legs" becoming the primary hits. —*Rick Clark*

Afterburner / 1985 / Warner Brothers ♦♦♦
Basically a carbon-copy of *Eliminator, Afterburner* continued ZZ's winning streak, which includes four hit singles: "Sleeping Bag," "Stages," "Rough Boy," and "Velcro Fly." —*Rick Clark*

Recycler / 1990 / Warner Brothers ♦♦♦
ZZ seemed to be running low on good material as they cranked up the Fairlights for a third go-round. "My Head's in Mississippi," however, is a fine rocker, which synthesized the gritty virtues of their earlier sound with the hi-tech gloss of their later work. *Recycler* also includes "Doubleback," their hit from the movie *Back to the Future—Part III.* —*Rick Clark*

Greatest Hits / Apr. 14, 1992 / Warner Brothers ♦♦♦♦
An 18-song compilation, it features the greatest hits of ZZ Top's MTV era, including "Gimme All Your Lovin'," "Sharp Dressed Man," "Tush," "Pearl Necklace," "Cheap Sunglasses," "Sleeping Bag," "Rough Boy," and a remixed version of "Legs." It's a good, fun collection that should have been sequenced better and, unfortunately, omits a few good songs. —*AMG*

Antenna / Jan. 18, 1994 / RCA ♦♦♦
Like precious few bands from the '70s whose best work is mummified daily thanks to classic rock radio, ZZ Top just keeps rolling on into the next decade. There"s much to love here, from the downright nasty stomp of "Fuzzbox Voodoo," the powerhouse slow blues of "Cover Your Rig," the bass pumping looniness of "Girl in a T-Shirt," to the slow grind of "Breakaway." While Billy Gibbon's guitar tones on this album are highly reminiscent of *Tres Hombres* (an early high-water mark for the band), the high production sheen from their '80s albums remains intact. But Gibbons hasn't played with this much over-the-top abandon since their pre-beard 'n' babes days, and that's what separates this album from the three that came before it. —*Cub Koda*

One Foot in the Blues / Nov. 22, 1994 / Warner ♦♦
Before they sweated their image down to beards, babes, and hot rods, ZZ Top were a down 'n' dirty blues-rock trio with a bonafide hot guitar player in Billy Gibbons. On this 14-track offering Warners goes back through the back ZZ catalog and cobbles together an interesting collection of the Texas trio's bluesier sides that originally appeared on their earliest albums. Highlights include "Brown Sugar," "A Fool for Your Stockings," "My Head's in Mississippi," "Apologies to Pearly" and Gibbons' storming stringwork on "Bar-B-Q." —*Cub Koda*

Rhythmeen / Sep. 17, 1996 / RCA ♦♦♦
ZZ Top's long-awaited return to the blues finally arrived in 1996, well over a decade after they abandoned their simple three-chord boogie for a synth and drum machine-driven three-chord boogie. Like *Antenna* before it,

Rhythmeen is stripped of all the synthizers that characterized the group's albums since *Eliminator* but the key difference between the two albums is how *Rhythmeen* goes for the gut, not the gloss. It's a record that is steeped in the blues and garage rock, one that pounds out its riffs with sweat and feeling. Though ZZ Top sounds reinvigorated, playing with a salacious aban- don they haven't displayed since the '70s, they simply haven't come up with enough interesting songs and riffs to make it a true return to form. For dedi- cated fans, it's a welcome return to their classic "La Grange" sound, but any- one with a just a passing interest in the band will wonder where the hooks went. — *Stephen Thomas Erlewine*

15 Down Home Country Blues Classics / 1996 / Arhoolie ✦✦✦
The origins of the blues can be found in the grooves of this fine budget-priced sampler, which includes performances from Mississippi Fred McDowell ("Frisco Line"), the Black Ace ("Drink On, Little Girl"), Bukka White ("Columbus Mississippi Blues"), and Big Joe Williams ("Brother James"). — *Jason Ankeny*

15 Down Home Gospel Classics / Jan. 20, 1998 / Arhoolie ✦✦✦
Arhoolie, as is made plain in this 15-song sampler of their gospel catalog, does not favor slick modern spiritual music. (Or, as they say straight-up in the brief liner note, "The selections on this disc are not by trendy, popular massed choirs.") Much of this is in fact gospel-blues: spiritually oriented numbers by major bluesmen Big Joe Williams, Mance Lipscomb, Robert Pete Williams, Jesse Fuller (a nice slide guitar treatment of "Amazing Grace"), and Fred McDowell, as well as more contemporary steel guitar-flavored gospel by Aubrey Ghent. The arrangements are sparse (sometimes acoustic) and the vocals are soulful, not just by the aforementioned acts, but also by such relative unknowns as the Campbell Brothers, who work more in a contemporary electric vein. It's not being heretical to say that there's more passion and musical quality on this compilation than there is on innumerable glossily produced gospel recordings by feel-good ensembles with higher profiles. By the way, the track by steel guitarist Black Ace, "Farther Along," was previously unissued on CD. — *Richie Unterberger*

15 Down Home Urban Blues Classics / 1996 / Arhoolie ✦✦✦
A fine introduction to the form, *15 Down Home Urban Blues Classics* features recordings from Sonny Boy Williamson ("Pontiac Blues"), Big Mama Thornton ("Big Mama's Bumble Bee"), Charlie Musselwhite ("Up and Down the Avenue"), and Katie Webster ("I Know That's Right"). — *Jason Ankeny*

40th Anniversary Blues / 1993 / Delmark ✦✦✦
Delmark's jazz anthology deserves praise despite the fundamental problems inherent within the sampler concept; the same holds true for its blues collection. This is a good 19-cut retrospective item containing exceptional cuts by Robert Jr. Lockwood, Otis Rush, J.B. Hutto, Roosevelt Sykes, and Magic Sam, plus nice ones from Jimmy Johnson, Arthur Crudup, Yank Rachell, and Big Joe Williams. But no Eddie "Cleanhead" Vinson? — *Ron Wynn*

Ace Blues Masters, Vol. 2: 4th and Beale and Further South / Westside ✦✦✦✦
This second volume of blues recordings from the vaults of the Jackson, MS, based Ace label yields several tracks to make this a compilation well worth revisiting again and again. It kicks off with six songs from a 1954 unissued session on Memphis musician Joe Hill Louis with Joe Hill trimming his one man band approach down to singing and playing guitar while a three piece combo beefs up the ensemble sound. Also on board are four songs from Arthur "Big Boy" Crudup's 1952 session for the label. Two of these tracks ("My Baby Boogies All The Time" and "I Wonder") saw issuance as a single on Ace while an atmospheric "Mean Old World" later came out on a Japanese album. The real motherlode on this compilation, however, is the nine tracks that comprise Texas guitarist's Frankie Lee Sims entire output for the label, including a spirited "What Will Lucy Do?," his big hit "Walkin' With Frankie," and the previously unissued "How Long." Closing out the collection on a very high note are the two singles—one on Ace, the other on Ric—by drummer/vocalist Julius "Mercy Baby" Mullins. His steaming shuffle "Marked Deck" features one of the longest verses in 12 bar blues history, a whopping 28 bar count that leaves the musicians lunging for the second change in two different spots. Obscure, wonderful music that deserves a place on compact disc and in most anyone's blues collection. — *Cub Koda*

Alive Down South / Jul. 29, 1997 / White Clay ✦✦✦
The musical history of Macon, Georgia is undeniably rooted in the R&B, Southern rock, and blues that exploded from the region in the late '60s and early '70s. *Alive Down South* features previously unreleased live recordings from some of Southern rock's most influential and popular artists—the Allman Brothers Band, Wet Willie, Stillwater, the Dixie Dregs, Sea Level, and Elvin Bishop. The cuts on this disc were remastered and sequenced to sound like one continuous concert, making the music showcased here bold, robust and definitely alive, like its title implies. Stillwater is captured live at the "Rebel Jam" in Atlanta in 1978 doing "Out On a Limb" and "Mind-Bender," followed by the Dixie Dregs from the same venue contributing "Take It Off the Top" and their musical tribute to the home of their label (Capricorn), "Macon Bacon." Elvin Bishop is featured on two of his good-natured tunes from an unspecified date, "Stealin' Watermelons" and "Goin' Fishin'." One of the earliest acts to sign with Capricorn, Wet Willie, is represented by a pair of tunes (Little Willie John's and Little Milton's "Grits Ain't Groceries" and "Everything That'Cha Do") recorded at the Roxy in Los Angeles in 1976. Sea Level, the offshoot project consisting of the rhythm section from the Allman Brothers Band is also captured live at the Roxy with "Take Out Some Insurance" and "Tidal Wave," a song from their first album. Following this is the Allman Brothers Band at the Nassau Coliseum in 1976 with "Statesboro Blues" (featuring a rough-as-a-cob vocal from Gregg Allman) and an uptempo version of "One Way Out" that the crowd responds quite audibly to. The disc closes out with a jam between Sea Level and the Dixie Dregs ("Hot 'Lanta Jam") that really shines as Chuck Leavell tags it with a beautiful coda, incorporating "Little Martha," the Duane Allman and Dickey Betts acoustic tune that closes the *Eat a Peach* album. For lovers of classic Southern rock, this disc provides a treasure trove of performances. — *Cub Koda*

All Night Long They Play the Blues / 1992 / Specialty ✦✦✦✦
This excellent soul-blues '60s anthology comes from the Galaxy label vaults. — *Bill Dahl*

Alley Special / 1990 / Collectables ✦✦✦✦
These are blues of various styles and consistently high quality, released on the Gotham and 20th Century labels, with three previously unreleased cuts. Raw, early electric blues from the late '40s and early '50s. Includes Muddy Waters' first commercial recording. — *Niles J. Frantz*

Alligator Records—25th Anniversary Collection / Mar. 1996 / Alligator ✦✦✦✦
This is a specially priced, two-CDs-for-the-price-of-one photocube set, loaded with great stuff from Charlie Musselwhite, Koko Taylor, Lonnie Brooks, Johnny Winter, Billy Boy Arnold, Lonnie Mack, and a host of others who've trotted their wares on the label over the years. Besides giving the novice one great introduction to the label (as the music runs from traditional to modern), the big bonus here is a treasure trove of previously unissued tracks from Roy Buchanan (a chaotic version of Link Wray's "Jack the Ripper"), Floyd Dixon (a recut of his Blues Brothers-approved hit "Hey Bartender"), Albert Collins and Johnny Copeland in a marvelous out-take from the *Showdown!* album ("Something to Remember You By") and the band that started it all, Hound Dog Taylor & the HouseRockers, with a crazed version of Elmore James' "Look on Yonder's Wall," as sloppy as it is cool. Very good stuff and at these prices, a bargain and then some. — *Cub Koda*

The Alligator Records Christmas Collection / 1992 / Alligator ✦✦✦
This entertaining CD serves a dual purpose, introducing listeners to many of the blues artists who have recorded for Alligator and giving consumers a rare Christmas blues record. The performers include Koko Taylor, Kenny

Neal, Lil' Ed & the Blues Imperials, Katie Webster (on a rollicking "Deck the Halls With Boogie Woogie"), William Clarke, Tinsley Ellis, Charles Brown ("Boogie Woogie Santa Claus"), Son Seals, Lonnie Brooks, Little Charlie & the Nightcats, Elvin Bishop, Saffire, Clarence "Gatemouth" Brown and Charlie Musselwhite. With the exception of Bishop's "The Little Drummer Boy" and Musselwhite's "Silent Night," all of the selections are originals by the artists. Although the musicians all play in the same general genre, this set has enough variety (and good feelings) to hold one's interest throughout. — *Scott Yanow*

The Alligator Records 20th Anniversary Tour / 1993 / Alligator ✦✦✦
Recorded on live on Alligator Records' 20th Anniversary Tour, this double disc set is a showcase for the label's artists. Featuring an array of their most popular acts — Koko Taylor, Lonnie Brooks, Lil' Ed and the Blues Imperials, Elvin Bishop — the record doesn't deliver any surprises, yet these performances are frequently more exciting than the studio versions. — *Stephen Thomas Erlewine*

American Folk Blues Festival: 1962-1965 / Dec. 1995 / Evidence ✦✦✦✦
This expanded reissue of the first four years of the American Folk Blues Festival (previously out from Optimism) is well worth a look. The American Folk Blues Festival was Europe's first major blues package tour, organized by German blues enthusiast Horst Lippmann, with Chicago blues giant Willie Dixon putting many of the early lineups and bands together. From 1962 until 1971, it was responsible for bringing over dozens of the most celebrated American blues artists, from Muddy Waters and Howlin' Wolf on down, and presenting them to audiences across Europe, from England to Poland. For many of the musicians, these were the largest audiences they'd ever played to, and the first (and often only) decent money they ever made, collecting $1000 or more a show — $100 would have been considered good at most clubs in the States. A few, like Sonny Boy (Rice Miller) Williamson, liked Europe so much that they stayed as long as possible, some (like Eddie Boyd) permanently. Rock fans also owe Lippmann a debt — along with Giorgio Gomelsky, he was responsible for teaming up the Yardbirds with Sonny Boy Williamson, and for the taping of the resulting 1963-vintage live and studio recordings, capturing two sets of legends. This five-CD set captures the vital early years of the festival more fully than any prior issues, with previously unreleased bonus tracks by Muddy Waters, John Lee Hooker, Buddy Guy, Willie Dixon, Memphis Slim, Big Joe Williams, Big Mama Thornton, J.B. Lenoir, Roosevelt Sykes, Sleepy John Estes, and Sugar Pie DeSanto. Some of the bonus repertory overlaps, as there were many songs that the participants on different programs in different years shared. The 1962 volume was recorded live in Hamburg on October 18, and has no extra tracks, but the material is so vital and robust that this volume, featuring Memphis Slim, John Lee Hooker, T-Bone Walker, Sonny Terry, and Brownie McGhee, never needed it. The 1963 disc, recorded live in Bremen on October 13, however, opens with three previously unreleased live Memphis Slim cuts that are worth the price of the disc by themselves, and follows these with a previously unissued Muddy Waters solo acoustic guitar piece (Willie Dixon's "My Captain") and three more never-reissued numbers featuring Muddy backed by Dixon, Otis Spann, and Matt "Guitar" Murphy. The three Sonny Boy Williamson bonus tracks, "That's All I Want, Baby," "Don't Misuse Me," and "I'm Gettin' Tired," were very late in the day and constitute some of the very last songs left behind by the increasingly ailing harp legend. The second volume of 1963 material offers an outtake of "Goin' Down Slow" by Otis Spann, Victoria Spivey ("T.B. Blues"), Big Joe Williams doing "Baby Please Don't Go," "Big Roll Blues," and "Back In the Bottom Blues," and Lonnie Johnson performing "Careless Love" and "C.C. Rider." The 1964 volume is a little less enhanced — unfortunately, there are no extra tracks by Howlin' Wolf — with two songs by Willie Dixon ("Weak Brain and Narrow Mind," "Big Legged Woman") and one song each by Sonny Boy Williamson, Sleepy John Estes and Hammie Nixon ("Your Best Friend's Gone"), and Sugar Pie DeSanto ("Baby What You Want Me To Do"). The 1965 volume was always the odd one in this series; as a studio recording rather than a concert document, it lacks the vibrancy of the earlier volumes, but its eight bonus tracks do include some interesting moments by Buddy Guy ("South Side Jump"), Big Mama Thornton ("Hound Dog"), John Lee Hooker ("Della Mae"), and Big Walter Horton ("Blues Harp Shuffle"). The sound quality is good, but a full set of notes might have been nice, as more than 30 years have passed since the musical events captured here actually took place. — *Bruce Eder*

Angels in Houston / Oct. 17, 1990 / Rounder ✦✦✦✦
Great Duke recordings from the late '50s and '60s of Bobby Bland, James Davis, Larry Davis, and Fenton Robinson. Includes Bland's classic "Yield Not to Temptation." — *Barry Lee Pearson*

Antone's — Bringing You the Best in Blues / 1989 / Antone's ✦✦✦✦
A sampler of artists on this Austin, TX, label, it includes a variety of Texas blues and R&B, originally released 1987-1990. Featured are Otis Rush, Angela Strehli, Doug Sahm, Matt "Guitar" Murphy, and several others. — *Niles J. Frantz*

Antone's 10th Anniversary Anthology, Vol. 1 / 1986 / Antone's ✦✦✦✦
Chicago blues living legends were recorded live at a popular Austin, TX, club in July 1985. Included is Buddy Guy, Jimmy Rogers, Eddie Taylor, James Cotton, Snooky Pryor, Otis Rush, Albert Collins, and more. The CD has three bonus cuts. Good sound and very good performances. — *Niles J. Frantz*

Antone's 10th Anniversary Anthology, Vol. 2 / 1991 / Antone's ✦✦✦✦
This very consistent live package was cut at the Austin club. It includes incendiary tracks by Buddy Guy and Matt "Guitar" Murphy. — *Bill Dahl*

Antone's 20th Anniversary / Jul. 29, 1996 / Discovery ✦✦✦
Antone's 20th Anniversary is a double-disc set that celebrates the legendary Texas club and its rich musical legacy. Over the course of the set, some of the biggest and best names of not only Texas blues, but American blues contribute positively ripping live tracks — it's always a joy to hear the likes of Buddy Guy, James Cotton, Kim Wilson, and Doug Sahm, and each of these artists, among many others, turn in first-rate contributions on this set. For a strong encapsulation of the American blues/blues-rock scene of the '70s, '80s, and '90s, *Antone's 20th Anniversary* delivers the goods. — *Thom Owens*

Aristocrat of the Blues (Chess 50th Anniversary Collection) / Aug. 26, 1997 / MCA ✦✦✦✦
The 51 songs here represent some of the highlights from the vaults of Aristocrat, the precursor to the Chess label — but to get the rarities by St. Louis Jimmy, Forest City Joe, Little Johnny Jones, and Robert Nighthawk, listeners should be prepared to buy 25 Muddy Waters songs they likely already own. Actually, despite that drawback, this collection is fascinating for the perspective it gives to the history of Chess Records and the development of Chicago blues between 1947 and 1950. The earliest tracks are '40s big-band-influenced R&B: The Five Blazes, featuring pianist/singer-songwriter Ernie Harper; the ominous "Ice Man Blues" and the raunchy "Fishin' Pole" by Tom Archia, fronting a sax-dominated outfit with Jo Jo Adams and Sheba Griffin on vocals, respectively; "Boogie Woogie Blues" by Clarence Samuels; and "Bilbo Is Dead" by Andrew Tibbs. The Chess sound as we've come to know it arrives with Sunnyland Slim, and the guitar blues that Chess became famous for doesn't show up until the Muddy Waters tracks "Gypsy Woman," "Little Anna Mae," etc. Muddy is nearly omnipresent, represented by 25 songs of his own here, and playing on many of the others. Of the rest, Robert Nighthawk, a one-time mentor to Muddy, has six songs represented here, while Forest City Joe has one ("Memory of Sonny Boy"). Forrest Sykes has one song, a rip-roaring piano instrumental, and St. Louis Jimmy Oden gets two. The quality throughout is crisp, sharp, finely detailed, and loud, with each song remastered in 20-bit high-definition sound, making them superior to any other CD package of this material. Given the familiarity of the Muddy songs, however, it might have been wiser to just do a three-CD Aristocrat box with a broader cross-section of the label's output. — *Bruce Eder*

☆ **The Atlantic Blues Box** / 1986 / Atlantic ✦✦✦✦✦
The Atlantic Blues Box includes four discs, with each focusing on a different style — vocalists, Chicago, guitar, and piano (each available seperately as well). If you've got the money, this is a worthwhile addition to any blues collection. — *Bill Dahl*

The Back Against the Wall: Texas Country / 1992 / Collectables ✦✦
Very uneven; a few vintage gems alternate with truly mediocre contemporary sides. — *Bill Dahl*

Backwood Blues 1926-1935 / Jan. 10, 1996 / Document ✦✦✦
Backwood Blues 1926-1935 contains a selection of material from the early country-blues singers. The best-known name is Bo Weavel Jackson, who has the best cuts on this 18-track collection; Bobby Grant, King Solomon Hill and Lane Hardin are the other singers here. While the Jackson cuts are uniformly interesting, much of the music here is only appealing to specialists and aca-

demics. For anyone else, the exacting chronological sequencing, poor fidelity (everything was transferred from acetates and 78s), and uneven performances make this collection of marginal interest. — *Thom Owens*

Bad, Bad Whiskey (The Galaxy Masters) / 1994 / Specialty ✦✦✦✦
A subsidiary of Fantasy, the Galaxy label recorded a diverse assortment of soul and R&B in the '60s and early '70s. This is a 26-track compilation of highlights from the company's output, covering 1962 to 1972. Landing the occasional minor R&B chart hit, Galaxy couldn't be said to have an especially distinctive label sound, though their efforts were on the whole bluesier than much soul of the era. But this is still a decent grab bag of odds and ends from soul's vintage period, with obscure sides by well-known performers like Betty Everett, Little Johnny Taylor, Lenny Williams, Charles Brown, Johnny "Guitar" Watson, Merl Saunders, and a host of unknowns. Especially good are the three sides by Rodger Collins, whose 1966 single "She's Looking Good" (which leads off the CD) was one of the better regional soul hits of the '60s, and was covered by Wilson Pickett for a Top 20 smash a couple of years later. — *Richie Unterberger*

Barrelhouse Women, Vol. 2 (1924-1928) / Mar. 18, 1997 / Document ✦✦✦✦
Barrelhouse Women, Vol. 2 (1924-1928) contains an abundance of cuts from the obscure female blues singers Sodarisa Miller, Alice Pearson, Mattie Dorsey and Star Page. Miller has 15 tracks, Pearson has five, Dorsey has four and Page has two. For specialists, this is interesting material, but for anyone else, the approach of the collection is too academic to be of interest. — *Stephen Thomas Erlewine*

The Beauty of the Blues / 1991 / Columbia/Legacy ✦✦✦✦
This is a beautiful 18-track collection from a sampling of Columbia/Legacy's *Roots 'N' Blues* series. The recordings, from 1929-1947, include a wide variety of traditional blues and blues-related styles. Excellent sound, with music from Robert Johnson, Big Bill Broonzy, and others. — *Niles J. Frantz*

The Best of Chess Blues / Oct. 17, 1990 / MCA ✦✦✦
This continuing series, six volumes to date, features rare and obscure '50s tracks by Chess blues stalwarts, including Howlin' Wolf, Little Walter, Sonny Boy Williamson, and many more. — *Hank Davis*

The Best of Chicago Blues [LP] / 1973 / Vanguard ✦✦✦✦
These mostly '60s recordings of tough Chicago blues were produced by Samuel Charters and feature James Cotton, Junior Wells, Otis Spann, Buddy Guy, J.B. Hutto, Homesick James, Big Walter Horton, and Junior Young. They're very successful snapshots of what was happening in the Chicago blues bars at that time. — *Niles J. Frantz*

The Best of Duke-Peacock Blues / 1992 / MCA ✦✦✦
Interesting collection of sides from this seminal Texas label. Highlights include sides by Bobby Bland ("Stormy Monday," "Turn On Your Lovelight"), Otis Rush ("Homework"), Junior Parker ("Driving Wheel"), and Larry Davis' original version of "Texas Flood," made popular to a new audience by Stevie Ray Vaughan. — *Cub Koda*

The Best of Excello Records / 1995 / AVI/Excello ✦✦✦✦
Although several overviews of the Excello label exist (including Rhino's two-volume set), this single-disc thumbnail collection may be the most digestible and therefore the best of the bunch. With a generous 30 tracks on a single disc to recommend it for openers, this collection tries to hit virtually all popular strains that the label dabbled in, from big city blues to doo wop to rockabilly to rhythm & blues to its best known swamp blues offerings. With hits aboard like Slim Harpo's "Raining in My Heart" and "Baby, Scratch My Back," the Gladiolas' original version of "Little Darlin'," Lillian Offitt's "Miss You So," the Marigolds' "Rollin' Stone," and Guitar Gable's "Congo Mombo," this collection delves far further into collectors' favorites, including "Hey! Baby" by rockabilly Al Ferrier, "Wild Cherry" by Leroy Washington, "Now That She's Gone" by the King Crooners, and the original version of "This Should Go on Forever" by Guitar Gable. The blues quotient inherent in the label's output is also well represented with the inclusion of "Rooster Blues" by Lightnin' Slim, "Baby Let's Play House" by Arthur Gunter, "My Next Door Neighbor" by Jerry McCain, "My Home Is a Prison" by Lonesome Sundown, and "I Hear You Knockin'" by Lazy Lester. All in all, a collection that's hard to beat, especially if your budget doesn't extend to multi-disc retrospectives. — *Cub Koda*

The Best of the Blues [K-Tel] / 1993 / K-Tel ✦✦✦
Budget 10 track compilation of classic tracks from the genre's biggest stars.

Hard core fans will already have these, but this makes a perfect primer for those beginning to investigate the roots of rock. — *Cub Koda*

The Best of the Blues [Pair] / 1988 / Pair ✦✦✦
This disc (subtitled "A Summit Meeting") isn't exactly the "best of the blues" by any means, but it is a fine—though edited—live concert, from Lincoln Center's Philharmonic (now Avery Fisher) Hall in June of 1973. Big Mama Thornton is in excellent form, doing "Little Red Rooster" and "Ball and Chain," Eddie "Cleanhead" Vinson is represented by "Back Door Blues," "Hold It Right There," "Kidney Stew," and "They Call Me Mr. Cleanhead," and Arthur "Big Boy" Crudup sings "That's All Right." But the big treat is Muddy Waters, in one of his first appearances after the car crash that nearly took his life, doing "Long Distance Call," "Where's My Woman Been," and "Got My Mojo Workin'." The sound is excellent, and the performances are all very strong. Serious fans, however, should be aware that a European double-CD set exists, which includes four more songs off the original double album. But as a mid-priced release that is easily available, this isn't bad. — *Bruce Eder*

Big Road Blues: The Real Thing from Mississippi / 1992 / Collectables ✦✦✦
Another uneven collectables collection, it has some rough but atmospheric (and totally obscure) early-'50s material mixed with later efforts by Houston Stackhouse. — *Bill Dahl*

Black Top Blues Cocktail Party / 1991 / Black Top ✦✦✦✦
This features non-album tracks from the label's roster. — *Robert Gordon*

Black Top Blues-A-Rama, Vol. 1 / 1988 / Black Top ✦✦✦
1988 live sides by Anson Funderburgh, Sam Myers, organist Ron Levy and sax wailer Grady Gaines. Typically hot and sweaty. — *Bill Dahl*

Black Top Blues-A-Rama, Vol. 2 / 1988 / Black Top ✦✦✦
Three R&B vets (Nappy Brown, Earl King, James Davis) and relative newcomer Ronnie Earl live in '88. — *Bill Dahl*

Black Top Blues-A-Rama, Vol. 3 / Jul. 1, 1991 / Black Top ✦✦✦
One of the weaker entries in the series; James Davis is top notch, Ron Levy and Bobby Radcliff somewhat less so. — *Bill Dahl*

Black Top Blues-A-Rama, Vol. 4: Down & Dirty / 1990 / Black Top ✦✦✦
All Houston saxman Grady Gaines and hit Texas Upsetters. Cut live in '89 at Tipitina's. — *Bill Dahl*

Black Top Blues-A-Rama, Vol. 5 / 1991 / Black Top ✦✦✦

Black Top Blues-A-Rama, Vol. 6: Live at Tipitina's / 1992 / Black Top ✦✦✦
Very strong lineup; stunning Snooks Eaglin sides, four wild efforts by guitarist Hubert Sumlin and reliably rocking Anson Funderburgh and Sam Myers. — *Bill Dahl*

Black Top Blues-A-Rama, Vol. 7: Live at Tipitinas / 1993 / Black Top ✦✦✦
Robert Ward makes his live recording debut on this simmering 1992 *Blues-a-Rama* set. Also aboard is bluesy zydeco-expert Lynn August and three numbers by Carol Fran and Clarence Holliman. — *Bill Dahl*

Black Top Blues-A-Rama: A Budget Sampler / 1990 / Black Top ✦✦✦✦
This 21-track sampler of Black Top Records music is a very good example of contemporary blues, with a focus on Texas and Louisiana. — *Niles J. Frantz*

Blind Pig Artists: 20th Anniversary Collection / Apr. 22, 1997 / Blind Pig ✦✦✦
San Francisco's Blind Pig Records celebrates their 20th anniversary with this two-disc, 36-track collection featuring over two hours' worth of highlights from their many releases with a few unreleased bonus tracks to spice up the mix. Originally started as a sideline to a blues club in Ann Arbor, MI, with an ear toward documenting the local scene and blues artists that played there regularly, Blind Pig has grown to record new artists like Debbie Davies, Joanna Connor, Tommy Castro, Jimmy Thackery, and Sarah Brown while more traditional bluesmen like Otis Rush, Snooky Pryor, Walter Horton, James Cotton and Jimmy Rogers have all stopped in at various points and recorded an album or two for the label. Although the label already has one retrospective available (*The Blind Pig Sampler*), this one brings matters more up to date, including tracks from Coco Montoya ("Monkey See, Monkey Do"), Chubby Carrier ("Wastin' Time"), Sarah Brown ("Bad Thing"), Studebaker John & the Hawks ("Two Time Boogie"), and sides from the aforementioned Thackery, Connor, Davies, and Castro. The traditional side of things is shored up by tracks from James Cotton ("Take Me Back"), Johnny Shines

("Blues Come From Texas"), Snooky Pryor ("Crazy 'Bout My Baby"), Otis Rush ("Right Place, Wrong Time"), and John Lee Hooker's version of "Terraplane Blues," taken from his guest appearance on a Roy Rogers album. Four previously unissued bonus tracks courtesy of Big Walter Horton ("If I Get Lucky"), Roosevelt Sykes ("I Wonder"), Pinetop Perkins ("Worried Life Blues"), and Henry Gray ("Cold Chills") make this collection another must-have. With sides from artists as diverse as soul singers Otis Clay and E.C. Scott to Preacher Boy and the Gospel Hummingbirds aboard, this double-disc set reaffirms the label's commitment to releasing brand-name blues and roots music. Blind Pig has released a multitude of great music in their 20 years as a label, and here's where you can pick up on some of the best of it. — *Cub Koda*

Blow It Til You Like It / Charly ◆◆◆◆
More blues and R&B harmonica are included on this generous 24-track import sampler. — *Hank Davis*

☆ **Blue Flames: Sun Blues Collection** / 1990 / Rhino ◆◆◆◆◆
A skimpy (18 songs) but tremendous set of Sam Phillips' gutbucket blues recordings, all are of early-'50s vintage and exquisitely remastered. Most of the big names are here. — *John Floyd*

Blue Ladies [Memphis Archives] / Mar. 7, 1921-Oct. 28, 1925 / Memphis Archives ◆◆◆◆
This collector's CD has 18 selections from early classic blues singers. In addition to Bessie Smith, Mamie Smith, Clara Smith, Ida Cox, Trixie Smith, Ma Rainey, and Ethel Waters, a variety of lesser-known vocalists are represented: Edith Wilson, Clementine Smith, Sara Martin, Maggie Jones, Margaret Johnson, Rosa Henderson, Lucille Hegamin, Dora Carr, Mary Stafford, Viola McCoy, and Ethel Ridley. The majority of the selections were formerly rare (including Mary Stafford's "I'm Gonna Jazz My Way Straight Through Paradise") and the sidemen include Johnny Dunn, Coleman Hawkins, Charlie Green, Louis Metcalf, Tommy Ladnier, Cow Cow Davenport, Joe Smith, and even Louis Armstrong, making this a CD worth picking up by '20s collectors. — *Scott Yanow*

Blues Across America: The Chicago Scene / Jan. 20, 1998 / Cannonball ◆◆◆
Blues Across America—The Chicago Scene assembles tracks from performers including Robert Plunkett, Emery Williams Jr. and Little Arthur Duncan. While the material ranges from superb to mediocre, the collection is nevertheless a good introduction to the contemporary Windy City blues community. — *Jason Ankeny*

Blues Across America: The Dallas Scene / Oct. 14, 1997 / Cannonball ◆◆◆
New recordings produced by former Rounder/Bullseye Blues session whiz Ron Levy. Part of a projected series highlighting regional blues scenes, this volume features three of Dallas, TX's, more unsung, but interesting, bluesmen. Kicking off with the sheet-metal tone of Henry Qualls' guitar work ("Squirrel Sandwich," "Elmo Boogie") to the citified sound of pianist Big Al Dupree ("Waitin' On My Rider") to the B.B. King-inspired style of Charles Young and "Jr. Boy" Jones (featuring a six minute B.B./Little Joe Blue medley), this collection gives an idea of the marvelous cross-section of blues still alive in the Dallas area. — *Cub Koda*

Blues As Big As Texas, Vol. 1 / 1991 / Collectables ◆◆◆◆
Previously unreleased Texas blues were digitally remastered from the original tapes. Various artists recorded between 1958 and 1971 in Houston (one cut in Beaumont, TX) include Johnny Copeland, Gatemouth Brown, Percy Mayfield, and more. It's a good and varied set. — *Niles J. Frantz*

The Blues Came Down from Memphis [CD] / 1988 / Charly ◆◆◆◆
Nice overview of Sun Records' early-'50s blues recordings on a single disc CD, primarily sticking to an issued singles format. Perfect place to start. — *Cub Koda*

Blues Deluxe / 1989 / Alligator ◆◆◆◆
A 1989 reissue, this budget CD (only 39 minutes long) was recorded live at the 1980 Chicagofest. Included are Muddy Waters, Koko Taylor, Willie Dixon, and three others. — *Niles J. Frantz*

Blues Hangover / 1995 / AVI/Excello ◆◆◆◆
This two disc, 43 track collection collects up a treasure trove of rare and unissued performances from the vaults of Excello Records. All but one of the 17 tracks collected on the first disc were produced by Jay Miller in his Crow-

ley, LA, studio, home of Excello's unmistakable "swamp blues" sound. The first 10 tracks are by Jimmy Anderson, who impersonates the vocal and harmonica style of Jimmy Reed so pervasively, it's downright eerie. Three tracks from Whispering Smith, a stray Lightnin' Slim cut, and both sides of the mysterious Blue Charlie single are aboard, as well as rare singles from the equally mysterious Ole Sonny Boy, Little Al (Gunter) and Little Sonny. But the true find here is the first time release of 15 tracks from a 1966 audition tape by one Early Drane. For all intents and purposes, this appears to be the same "Earl Draines" that recorded for the label as part of The Bluesrockers ("Calling All Cows") in the mid '50s. But these remarkable tapes are the man alone in his living room, singing and playing a quirky collection of original material, blues and gospel covers that careen from brilliant to downright loony. Add to this lineup four tracks by Detroit bluesman Baby Boy Warren (featuring Sonny Boy Williamson on harmonica) and two early-'60s stereo swingers by the little known James Stewart and you've got an Excello rarities packages that's pretty hard to beat. — *AMG*

Blues Harmonica Spotlight / Nov. 10, 1992 / Black Top ◆◆◆◆
Blues Harmonica Spotlight focuses on New Orleans label's generous array of blues-harp talent. — *Bill Dahl*

Blues Is Killin' Me / 1991 / Paula/Flyright ◆◆◆◆
Twenty track, rock solid collection of classic blues sides from Chicago's JOB label, primarily focusing on both sides of original issue 78s by Floyd Jones, Memphis Minnie, Baby Face Leroy and Little Hudson's Red Devil Trio with a few unissued surprises rounding out the already excellent package. — *Cub Koda*

Blues Masters, Vol. 10: Blues Roots / 1993 / Rhino ◆◆◆
Expertly compiled, annotated, and in most cases recorded, by pioneering blues researcher Samuel Charters, this volume explores all areas of the blues' origins. Featuring devastating recordings of prison work hands, native African music to Texas prison songs, this is as hard core a collection as you're likely to find, yet still very accessible to the average fan. — *Cub Koda*

☆ **Blues Masters, Vol. 11: Classic Blues Women** / 1993 / Rhino ◆◆◆◆
Although it is now a male dominated field, the earliest to record and have success in the blues field were women. This volume not only collects many of the great recordings by these women (Mamie, Trixie and Bessie Smith, Billie Holiday, Sippie Wallace, Ma Rainey), but also holds the distinction in the series of being one of the few that offers multiple selections by some of these artists. Highly recommended. — *Cub Koda*

☆ **Blues Masters, Vol. 12: Memphis Blues** / 1993 / Rhino ◆◆◆◆
Running the blues history of America's craziest city from early offerings by Cannon's Jug Stompers and the Memphis Jug Band to early Sun recordings from the '50s by Junior Parker, Rufus Thomas, and Joe Hill Louis, this is undoubtedly one of the best compiled volumes in the series. — *Cub Koda*

Blues Masters, Vol. 13: New York City Blues / 1993 / Rhino ◆◆◆◆
While other volumes in the series showcase the down home aspects of the music, this one highlights the big band sound. Great sides by Lionel Hampton ("Hamp's Boogie Woogie"), Duke Ellington, Buddy Johnson, Count Basie, Sam "The Man" Taylor ("Oo-Wee"), and Lucky Millinder showcase a side to the music that is seldom heard. — *Cub Koda*

★ **Blues Masters, Vol. 14: More Jump Blues** / 1993 / Rhino ◆◆◆◆◆
Just as essential as the previous Rhino jump blues collection (volume five of the *Blues Masters* series), this has classics by Floyd Dixon ("Hey Bartender"), Joe Liggins ("Pink Champagne"), Joe Turner, Wynonie Harris, Ruth Brown, Big Maybelle, and Louis Jordan. It also takes some chances by presenting cuts by performers not strictly identified with the style, like Louis Prima, Bobby Charles (the original version of Bill Haley's "See You Later Alligator"), Little Richard, and Faye Adams, whose rousing "I'll Be True" is a touchstone of early R&B. — *Richie Unterberger*

Blues Masters, Vol. 15: Slide Guitar Classics / 1993 / Rhino ◆◆◆◆
The final volume in the series (at least for now) features seminal and classic tracks from Elmore James ("Dust My Broom"), Muddy Waters ("Honey Bee"), and Hound Dog Taylor to modern day disciples like Johnny Winter and Ry Cooder. Blind Willie Johnson's "Dark Was The Night, Cold Was The Ground" is worth the price of admission alone. — *Cub Koda*

☆ **Blues Masters, Vol. 1: Urban Blues** / 1992 / Rhino ◆◆◆◆◆
While more horn-driven and less guitar reliant than other forms of blues,

the urban style nonetheless provides its own spectacular highlights, some of the best of which are right here. The first volume in this 15 volume series features classic performances by Eddie "Cleanhead" Vinson, Dinah Washington, T-Bone Walker, Charles Brown, Joe Turner, and Jimmy Witherspoon. Where the blues meets the jazz and heads uptown for a party. —*Cub Koda*

☆ **Blues Masters, Vol. 2: Post-War Chicago Blues** / 1992 / Rhino ◆◆◆◆◆
Excellent 18-track compendium of all the major movers and shakers who helped shape the Chicago blues scene in the '50s. Everyone is well represented here, and major stars like Muddy Waters and Howlin' Wolf stand next to behind-the-scenes geniuses like Earl Hooker and Jody Williams for an interesting and accurate blend. —*Cub Koda*

☆ **Blues Masters, Vol. 3: Texas Blues** / 1992 / Rhino ◆◆◆◆◆
The best that the Lone Star state has had to offer over a 60 year period is right here, from Blind Lemon Jefferson's "Match Box Blues" (1927) to Stevie Ray Vaughn's live version of "Flood Down In Texas (Texas Flood)" from 1986. This compilation also features great sides by The Fabulous Thunderbirds, Lightnin' Hopkins, T-Bone Walker, and Albert Collins. As an introduction to the Texas blues style, this is a pretty darn good one. —*Cub Koda*

★ **Blues Masters, Vol. 4: Harmonica Classics** / 1992 / Rhino ◆◆◆◆◆
This typically ace installment of the *Blues Masters* series has examples *par excellence* from most of the major electric blues harmonica geniuses, including Little Walter, Junior Wells, Sonny Boy Williamson, James Cotton, Paul Butterfield, Billy Boy Arnold, Lazy Lester, and Jimmy Reed. And while there are a few expected classics here (Little Walter's "Juke," Sonny Boy Williamson's "Help Me," Junior Wells' "Messin' with the Kid," Slim Harpo's "I Got Love If You Want It"), there are numerous delightful obscurities, like Jerry McCain's "Steady," Walter Horton's "Easy" (credited to "Jimmy & Walter"), and Snooky Pryor's "Boogie Twist." Charlie Musselwhite's 11-minute adaptation of the jazz tune "Christo Redemptor" is superb and challenges conventional ideas of what should and shouldn't be done with a blues harmonica. —*Richie Unterberger*

☆ **Blues Masters, Vol. 5: Jump Blues Classics** / 1992 / Rhino ◆◆◆◆◆
Jump blues, of course, was crucial to the birth of R&B and rock 'n' roll. More importantly, the infectious swing, grit, and humor were great in themselves. *Jump Blues Classics* collects 18 tracks from the golden days of the genre in the late '40s and '50s. Most of the pioneers of the style are here—Joe Turner, Wynonie Harris, Roy Brown, Ruth Brown, Roy Milton, Big Jay McNeely, and others, even Louis Prima. The collection includes several cuts that were revived to become rock 'n' roll classics, including "The Train Kept A-Rollin'" (Tiny Bradshaw), "Shake, Rattle, And Roll" (Joe Turner), "Good Rockin' Tonight" (Wynonie Harris), "Hound Dog" (Big Mama Thornton), and the little-known original, pre-Muddy Waters version of "Got My Mojo Working" (Ann Cole). This is, of course, just the surface of a genre that was hugely successful in its time, producing hundreds of memorable recordings. This well-annotated anthology is a good starting point and a good representative sampling for those who only want the cream of the crop in their collection. —*Richie Unterberger*

★ **Blues Masters, Vol. 6: Blues Originals** / 1993 / Rhino ◆◆◆◆◆
It's unfortunate, but it's true: the original versions of many blues classics aren't nearly as well known as their hit covers by (usually white) rock groups. That's not to say that some of these covers aren't great as well, but it's both educational and enjoyable to hear them from the source's mouth. *Blues Originals* contains 18 original versions of classics that went on to reach a wide audience via covers by the Stones, Yardbirds, Elvis, Led Zeppelin, the Doors, and others. The Chess stable of Howlin' Wolf, Muddy Waters, Bo Diddley, Little Walter, and Sonny Boy Williamson is represented here, of course, along with standards by Elmore James, Otis Rush, Robert Johnson, Slim Harpo, and Jimmy Reed. Mixed in with great and fairly available performances like Bo Diddley's "I'm A Man" and Howlin' Wolf's "Back Door Man" are some quite obscure and collectable delights. Arthur Crudup's original version of "That's All Right," covered by Elvis Presley for his first single, has been surprisingly hard to find over the years; ditto for Muddy Waters' "You Need Love," which formed the blueprint for Led Zeppelin's "Whole Lotta Love." Even most Yardbirds fanatics are unaware that the prototype for "Lost Woman" was taken from (and retitled from) an obscure Snooky Pryor single, "Someone To Love Me." And even many Chicago blues fanatics will be surprised to find the original version of "Got My Mojo Working," which was not

recorded by Muddy Waters, but little-known jump blues singer Ann Cole. A fine collection, mixing together famous standards and obscure gems with thorough liner notes. —*Richie Unterberger*

Blues Masters, Vol. 7: Blues Revival / 1993 / Rhino ◆◆◆◆
It's hard to believe from the vantage point of a period when blues songs are used for network television commercials, but it wasn't so long ago that the blues was, though hardly in danger of extinction, certainly limited to a pretty specialized audience. The blues revival of the early '60s brought the music back into the spotlight through its prominence at major folk festivals and college concerts, the rediscovery of several legends like Skip James and Mississippi John Hurt, and the efforts of several musicians and record labels to popularize the work of the form's originators. *Blues Revival* covers a lot of these bases. This 17-track collection includes some of the biggest hit blues singles of the '60s (by Jimmy Reed, John Lee Hooker, Slim Harpo, and B.B. King), '60s recordings by acoustic Delta blues giants like Mississippi Fred McDowell and Son House, hot electric Chicago blues by Junior Wells and Muddy Waters, and white, rock-oriented revivalists like Paul Butterfield, John Mayall, and Canned Heat. Seasoned collectors won't find anything too obscure here, but it's a handy primer to some of the best blues recorded during an era in which the idiom reestablished itself as a vital and living form. —*Richie Unterberger*

Blues Masters, Vol. 8: Mississippi Delta Blues / 1993 / Rhino ◆◆◆
The title for this volume is a bit of a misnomer. While there is easily half a compilation's worth of authentic acoustic material here (including classics by Tommy Johnson, Charlie Patton, Willie Brown, and Robert Johnson), the inclusion of tracks by B.B. and Albert King and recorded in Chicago sides by Howlin' Wolf, Elmore James, and Robert Nighthawk do much to blur the distinctiveness of this package. —*Cub Koda*

Blues Masters, Vol. 9: Postmodern Blues / 1993 / Rhino ◆◆◆◆
A wonderful compendium of artists and styles illustrating the coming of blues into the mainstream. This volume features representative tracks by B.B. King, Albert Collins, Albert King, George Thorogood, Stevie Ray Vaughn, Johnny Winter, and The Fabulous Thunderbirds. The modern sound at its best, and most diverse. —*Cub Koda*

☆ **Rhino Blues Masters Collection** / Rhino ◆◆◆◆◆
Spanning 15 volumes while covering pretty much the entire history of the genre, the Rhino *Blues Masters* series is the one blues collection that both neophytes and long-time fans can heartily embrace. Subtitled 'the essential blues collection,' it is all of that and more. With each volume devoted to the diverse styles the music entails, the series boasts both thoughtful selection and excellent sound and annotation, utilizing some of the best authorities on the subject. While the compilation form has existed as long as the microgroove long playing record, this is the first time that a comprehensive series has been launched, licensing from a myriad of other labels. While other record companies tend to keep the best material for their own anthologies, Rhino went all out in this endeavor, and many of the important tracks in this series are seeing their first issuance in the compilation format (Robert Johnson, for example), while others are being reissued for the first time since the advent of the 78-rpm phonograph record. All in all, a series that will stand for decades to come as an essential building block for anyone's blues collection. —*Cub Koda*

☆ **Blues Masters, Vol. 16: More Harmonica Classics** / 1998 / Rhino ◆◆◆◆◆
With such a wealth of great harmonica blues out there, and with such an outstanding track record on Rhino's part in general when it comes to historical compilations, it's no surprise that their second anthology of harmonica blues is just as good as the first. There are fine cuts by many big guns here, including Little Walter, both Sonny Boy Williamsons, James Cotton, Jimmy Reed, Junior Wells, Paul Butterfield, Slim Harpo, and Sonny Terry (whose hard-rocking, electric "Hootin' Blues No. 2," from a 1956 RCA single, is a highlight). The less obvious choices make this a pleasure for mid-level blues fans looking for something they haven't heard before as well as more familiar material: Papa Lightfoot's "Jump the Boogie" is great early raw electric blues with vocals that sound as if the mike was covered with sandpaper, and Doctor Ross' "Come Back Baby" is one of the most primordial blues recorded at Sun. —*Richie Unterberger*

Blues Masters, Vol.17: More Postmodern Blues / 1998 / Rhino ◆◆◆◆
Putting together a compilation of "postmodern" (post-1970) blues is a chal-

lenge because the classics of the era are not as commonly agreed upon as they are for previous decades, and because the form has been more static than it was in the earlier days of the blues' evolution. It's not as good as Rhino's previous *Postmodern Blues* compilation (issued as Vol. 9 of the *Blues Masters* series), but it still has a good alternation of good cuts by major figures (the Allman Brothers, Albert King, B.B. King, James Cotton, Little Milton, Robert Cray, Koko Taylor, Albert Collins), solid journeyman types (Johnny Copeland, Joe Louis Walker, Luther Allison, Johnny Adams), and the occasional name that still isn't widely known to the general audience (W.C. Clark, Larry Garner). Soul-blues-funk-rock fusion is often characteristic of the selections, but there is is a nod to acoustic traditions by Keb' Mo'. — *Richie Unterberger*

☆ **Blues Masters, Vol.18: More Slide Guitar Classics** / 1998 / Rhino ✦✦✦✦✦
Rhino's second slide guitar anthology leads off with a couple of dyed-in-the-wool classics with Muddy Waters' "I Can't Be Satisfied" and Elmore James' "The Sky Is Crying." But the emphasis on this 18-track disc is much more on little-heard delights that might come as surprises even to knowledgeable blues fans. Earl Hooker's "Wah Wah Blues" shows him playing around with the wah-wah pedal to great effect in late 1968; Boyd Gilmore's 1952 single "All My Dreams" has great raw soloing from Elmore James (spliced in from James' "Please Find My Baby" single); Chuck Berry's "Blues for Hawaiians" reveals a little-noted aspect of his playing; and Eddie "One String" Jones' "John Henry" is a primitive one-string blues that takes the slide back to its diddley bow origins. There's also the strange rockabilly-blues hybrid "Rocking in the Coconut Top" by Hop Wilson, with weird background noises that sound like balloons being rubbed. There are also plenty of quality selections by bigger names like Blind Willie Johnson, J.B. Hutto, Robert Junior Lockwood, Son House, Tampa Red, and Johnny Winter, with the expected expert liner notes by Cub Koda. — *Richie Unterberger*

Blues Next: The New Generation / Feb. 24, 1998 / Similar ✦✦✦
This budget priced 11-track compilation highlights selections from contemporary blues artists and blues-rockers in a wide range of styles that holds together nicely. Pulling together selections all recorded in the '90s, this features modern day blues-rockers like Monster Mike Welch ("Axe To Grind"), Tinsley Ellis ("To The Devil For A Dime"), Chris Duarte ("My Way Down"), Corey Stevens, and Tommy Castro ("This Soul Is Mine") pitted against more traditionally minded or rootsier players like Bernard Allison, Lucky Peterson, Coco Montoya ("Same Dog"), and Smokin' Joe Kubek ("Can't See For Lovin'"). Transfers are clear and crisp and fans of modern day blues who like a lot of guitar solos to go with it will love this one. — *Cub Koda*

Blues Piano Orgy / 1972 / Delmark ✦✦✦✦
A sensational keyboard anthology with great cuts by Speckled Red, Roosevelt Sykes, and Little Brother Montgomery. — *Ron Wynn*

Blues at Newport: Recorded Live at the Newport Folk Festival 1959-1964 / Vanguard ✦✦✦
Blues at Newport—Newport Folk Festival 1959-64 offers fine performances by John Hurt, Skip James, Rev. Gary Davis, Robert Wilkins, and others. — *Mark A. Humphrey*

Blues from "Big Bill's Copacabana" Live / Oct. 17, 1990 / Chess ✦✦✦✦
Classic 1963 Chicago blues. — *Bill Dahl*

Blues from the Montreux Jazz Fest. / 1991 / Malaco ✦✦✦✦
Recorded at the Montreux Jazz Festival in Switzerland, during the Malaco Records European Tour in 1989, it features Bobby Bland, Denise LaSalle, Johnnie Taylor, and Mosley & Johnson. Anything LaSalle has done lately is worth listening to, and it's nice to have a snapshot of her in-concert style. — *Niles J. Frantz*

Blues in D Natural / 1979 / Red Lightnin' ✦✦✦
Bootleg-quality sound, but no quarrel with selections by Earl Hooker, Robert Nighthawk, Frankie Lee Sims, and Sly Williams. — *Bill Dahl*

Blues in the Mississippi Night / Jul. 13, 1991 / Rykodisc ✦✦✦✦
This pioneering, documentary-style recording was produced by Alan Lomax and laid unissued for decades after its 1946 recording due to its frank discussion of racism by Big Bill Broonzy, Sonny Boy Williamson, and Memphis Slim. — *Bill Dahl*

Blues in the Night [Laserlight] / May 26, 1992 / Laserlight ✦✦✦
More of a live jazz set than blues, with organists Jimmy McGriff and Groove Holmes. Only harpist Jr. Parker really qualifies as straight blues. — *Bill Dahl*

The Blues, Vol. 4 [Chess/MCA] / Jul. 6, 1989 / Chess ✦✦✦✦
More classic Chess blues. — *Bill Dahl*

The Blues, Vol. 5 [Chess/MCA] / Aug. 27, 1990 / Chess ✦✦✦✦
Classic Chess hits and a few obscurities (Jimmy Nelson, Percy Mayfield). — *Bill Dahl*

Bluesiana Hot Sauce / 1993 / Shanachie ✦✦✦
Joe Ferry brought Art Blakey, David Newman and Dr. John together for the concept album *Bluesiana Triangle* in 1989. This latest project, conceived as a tribute to the prior Bluesiana records, again links jazz, R&B and rock players doing both pop and improvisational material, with the funds again going to the homeless. The assembled cast included trombonist Ray Anderson, harmonica ace Toots Thielemans at his bluesiest on "Brickyard Blues," and soulful tenor from Mike Brecker. Living Colour drummer Will Calhoun was once more funky and in the groove, contributing a solid vocal on "Ruby's Flowers," his own composition. This group does an admirable job of saluting the original cast while also making its own effective statement. — *Ron Wynn*

The Bluesville Years, Vol. 1: Big Blues Honks and Wails / 1995 / Prestige ✦✦✦✦
For almost a decade Bluesville operated as a subsidiary label to the indie jazz pioneer Prestige Records. With a chaotic catalog, they issued everything from barrelhouse piano players working with hipster jazz combos to semi-pro street singers to tons of Lightnin' Hopkins albums. What we have here are the beginnings of the modern blues album as we know it. The Bluesville label captured that awkward moment in time where the blues first lost its commercial restraints and started making music of a different power, and a nice cross section of it is here on all four of these volumes. There's a decidedly acoustic air to everything here, even the wilder Chicago sides. If you've been brought up on a steady blues album diet of electric guitars and heavy drumming, some of this will sound almost quaint by comparison, but it's well worth a listen. The first entry in the series, *Big Blues, Honks and Wails* features tracks by piano giants Sunnyland Slim and Roosevelt Sykes and uptown blues belters Mildred Anderson, Jimmy Witherspoon and Al Smith paired with small, jazz oriented combos with sax legends King Curtis, Eddie "Lockjaw" Davis and Clifford Scott honkin' away. — *Cub Koda*

The Bluesville Years, Vol. 2: Feelin' Down on the South Side / 1995 / Prestige ✦✦✦✦
Feelin' Down on the South Side culls the best of the albums that were cut in Chicago with top flight selections by Billy Boy Arnold, Homesick James, Otis Spann, and James Cotton. Cotton's "One More Mile To Go" with its voodoo backup chorus from the Muddy Waters band is downright bone chilling and eerie. — *Cub Koda*

The Bluesville Years, Vol. 3: Beale Street Get-Down / 1995 / Prestige ✦✦✦✦
Beale Street Get-Down is the folksiest of the bunch, most of it recorded at the Sun studios in Memphis with country-blues guitarists Furry Lewis and Memphis Willie B. (Borum) and pianist Memphis Slim all contributing to the fray. — *Cub Koda*

The Bluesville Years, Vol. 4: In the Key of Blues / 1995 / Prestige ✦✦✦✦
The final volume, *In the Key of Blues*, features an all-piano fest with boogies and blues from Mercy Dee Walton, Little Brother Montgomery, Curtis Jones, and still more from Sykes and Memphis Slim. — *Cub Koda*

Boogie Blues: Women Sing & Play / Mar. 1930-Oct. 31, 1961 / Rosetta ✦✦✦
All 16 performances on this LP are boogie-blues and put the spotlight on female singers and/or pianists. There is a wide variety of material ranging from a Lil Armstrong piano solo from the soundtrack of the TV movie *Chicago & That Jazz* in 1961 to Memphis Minnie, Ella Fitzgerald ("Cow Cow Boogie"), and Dorothy Donegan in 1942. Other performers include Georgia White, Helen Humes, Lucille Bogan, Hazel Scott, Merline Johnson, Sweet Georgia Brown, Gladys Bentley, Christine Chatman, Hadda Brooks, Myrtle Jenkins, Sister Rosetta Tharpe, and Mary Lou Williams. As usual with Rosetta's albums, this obvious labor of love has informative liner notes, colorful pictures, and many rare recordings that have not yet been reissued on CD. — *Scott Yanow*

Boogie Woogie Blues / Sep. 1922-Apr. 1927 / Biograph ✦✦✦
Biograph has come out with many releases of piano rolls through the years. This CD has some by Cow Cow Davenport, James P. Johnson, Clarence Williams, Jimmy Blythe, Hersal Thomas, Lemuel Fowler, and two totally forgot-

ten names: Everett Robbins and Clarence Johnson. As is usual with piano rolls, the rhythms are inflexible and the touch a bit unnatural so it may take listeners a while to get used to these performances. The emphasis is more on blues than on boogie-woogie, but in general the music is fine for this idiom although not as lively as real piano solos. — *Scott Yanow*

Booze & The Blues / Feb. 6, 1996 / Sony Legacy ✦✦✦
Booze & the Blues is a thoroughly entertaining collection of 22 pre-war blues songs about wine, drinking, whiskey, and blues. It's a gimmicky excuse for a collection, but it works, not only because the songs and performances are good, but because the tracks all have a similar spirit. Among the highlights are tracks by Memphis Minnie, Mississippi Sheiks, Robert Hicks, the Memphis Jug Band, Amos Easton, Lucille Bogan, Peetie Wheatstraw, and Joshua White. — *Stephen Thomas Erlewine*

Bullseye Blues Christmas / Nov. 1995 / Bullseye Blues ✦✦✦
A slightly low-key, funky brand of blues is served up on *Bullseye Blues Christmas*, combining new and previously released flavorful seasonings from the likes of Champion Jack Dupree, Luther Guitar Junior Johnson, and the Persuasions. — *Roch Parisien*

Can't Keep from Crying: Topical Blues on the Death of President Kennedy / 1994 / Testament ✦✦✦✦
In the wake of John Kennedy's assassination, Pete Welding recorded over a dozen acoustic blues tributes to the late president for this compilation in late 1963 and early 1964. Big Joe Williams, Otis Spann, and Johnny Young are the only widely recognized names on the disc, which also features performers like Mary Ross, Fannie Brewer, and Jimmy Brown. It's hard to be critical about a project devoted to such an emotional and devastating event, but this doesn't hold up too well as more than a slice of history. However heartfelt these pieces may have been, the compositions are not outstanding, and it's wearying to hear more than a dozen topical blues on *any* subject all in a row. The CD reissue adds previously unreleased tracks by Johnny Young and Avery Brady. — *Richie Unterberger*

☆ Chess Blues / 1992 / MCA ✦✦✦✦✦
Superlative four-CD box set, featuring important tracks by all the main stars of the label (Muddy Waters, Howlin' Wolf, Little Walter, Sonny Boy Williamson), as well as much previously unreleased material. A well-done retrospective of Chicago blues in its heyday, as recorded by America's greatest blues label, Chess. — *Cub Koda*

Chess Blues Classics: 1947-1956 / 1997 / Chess-MCA ✦✦✦✦
Part of a two-volume set as part of MCA's Chess 50th Anniversary collection, this offers a 16-track thumbnail sketch of the sounds that made the label the tops in the blues field. Beginning with two Aristocrat sides (the label's original moniker) from 1948 and 1949 featuring Muddy Waters ("I Can't Be Satisfied") and Little Johnny Jones ("Big Town Playboy" with Muddy on backup guitar), the collection rolls through its treasures chronologically, virtually cherry-picking the hits from the innumerable classics stored in the Chess vaults. With Jimmy Rogers' "That's All Right," Eddie Boyd's "Twenty-Four Hours," John Lee Hooker's "Sugar Mama," Lowell Fulson's "Reconsider Baby," and J.B. Lenoir's "Eisenhower Blues" providing nice changes of pace from the big hits of Muddy, Howlin' Wolf, Sonny Boy Williamson, and Little Walter aboard, this is by no means a lightweight collection. As a greatest-hits package, perhaps one could easily nitpick over what *isn't* on here, while also just as easily dismissing their inclusion as another repackaging of the same old stuff. But as a simple-to-digest primer of some of the best the label had to offer during its first landmark decade in business, this compilation hits the bullseye in a big way. A perfect one to stick in a multi-disc CD player, hit shuffle play, and prepare to be continually pleased. — *Cub Koda*

Chess Blues Classics: 1957-1967 / 1997 / Chess-MCA ✦✦✦✦
This second volume of a two-volume entry in MCA's Chess 50th Anniversary reissue series chronicles the second decade of blues classics produced by the landmark company. Although Chess' big four (Muddy Waters, Howlin' Wolf, Little Walter, and Sonny Boy Williamson) are all finely represented, influential sides by Elmore James ("Madison Blues"), Otis Rush ("So Many Roads, So Many Trains"), and John Lee Hooker (his monochord boogie treatment of Amos Milburn's "One Bourbon, One Scotch, One Beer") pepper the mix as well. As Chess moved into the soul market, so it was that latter-day blues sides by Little Milton, Koko Taylor, and Etta James took on a more pronounced R&B edge, and it is these sides that close this compilation in a near

perfect bookend fashion. Extra special highlight: Etta James' nitro reading of Jimmy Reed's "Baby, What You Want Me to Do," recorded live in 1964. — *Cub Koda*

Chess Blues Guitar: Two Decades of Killer Fretwork, 1949-1969 / Jan. 13, 1998 / MCA ✦✦✦✦
This 45-song, two-disc collection is subtitled "two decades of killer fretwork," and never was a set so aptly described. Chess Records was the home to seemingly every hot guitar player in the Chicago area, and many of them make their appearance here. Besides the usual label guitar hotshots (Muddy Waters, Jimmy Rogers, Chuck Berry, Bo Diddley, Buddy Guy, Lowell Fulson, Earl Hooker, Otis Rush, Robert Nighthawk, Little Milton), space is given to sideman work from legends like Hubert Sumlin and Robert Jr. Lockwood and great one-offs by lesser-known artists like Jody Williams, Danny Overbea, Eddie Burns, Joe Hill Louis, Morris Pejoe, Lafayette Thomas and others. It seems as if everyone recorded for Chess at one time or another, also explaining the inclusion of tracks by John Lee Hooker, Albert King, Clarence "Gatemouth" Brown, Lonnie Brooks, Hound Dog Taylor, and Elmore James. If electric blues guitar's your thing, then look no further than this fine two-disc compilation. — *Cub Koda*

Chess Blues Piano Greats (Chess 50th Anniversary Collection) / Jun. 17, 1997 / MCA ✦✦✦✦
Back before the electric guitar became the primary focal instrument of the blues, two-fisted piano players dominated the genre, and record companies flocked to record them. Chess Records was no exception, and this two-disc, 45-track anthology shines the spotlight on four of the best who ever sat on the piano stool at the Chess studios. The first disc begins with 20 tracks from Eddie Boyd (eight of them previously unissued in the US), full of introspective reflection and the darkest of moods. Kicking off with one of his big hits, "24 Hours," the dourness of Boyd's work reaches epic proportions on tunes like "I Began to Sing the Blues," "Third Degree," and "Blues for Baby," the latter featuring stellar jazz guitar runs and chordal work from Robert Jr. Lockwood. Even on uptempo numbers like "Hard Time Getting Started," "Nothing But Trouble," and "Just a Fool," the somber nature of Boyd's delivery cuts through everything, underscoring the bouncier lilt of these tracks with a much darker cast. Finishing out the disc are four tracks from Otis Spann, comprising the A- and B-sides of his lone 1954 single for the label ("It Must Have Been The Devil" and the instrumental "Five Spot," both sides featuring a rare maverick uncredited appearance by B.B. King on a Chess record) and two sides from a 1956 session that stayed unreleased for several decades, both featuring shattering harp work from Walter Horton. The second disc collects 18 sides from Willie Mabon (three sides previously unreleased), including his big hits "I Don't Know," "I'm Mad," "Poison Ivy" and Willie Dixon's "The Seventh Son." Mabon was much more an R&B novelty entertainer than a hard bluesman (think Cripple Clarence Lofton as opposed to Big Maceo Merriweather), but his more down-home side comes up for air on "Willie's Blues," pitting solid piano work against Dixieland trumpet growls. The anthology finishes out with three tracks from Chess session stalwart Lafayette Leake, who backed everyone from Chuck Berry to Howlin' Wolf and yet remains Chess Records' true mystery man. Lafayette was most elusive when it came time to record under his own name, but a stray instrumental from 1957 ("Slow Leake") stands alongside two live tracks recorded in Montreux, Switzerland in 1972 as his meager frontman legacy for the label. Although there's no Sunnyland or Memphis Slim aboard (two other Chess piano greats equally worthy of a separate anthology), this is a fine collection that is most deserving of an encore. — *Cub Koda*

Chicago Ain't Nothin' But a Blues Band / 1972 / Delmark ✦✦✦✦
Solid collection of sides from Chicago's Atomic H label with JoJo Williams, J.T. Brown and Eddie Clearwater's earliest recordings being among the highlights. — *AMG*

Chicago Blues Anthology [Chess] / 1984 / Chess ✦✦✦✦
A wonderful 24-cut set of raw, early Chicago blues from the Chess label, Delta blues influences are evident in the work of Johnny Shines, Robert Nighthawk, and Floyd Jones. A more modern, urban style is shown by Buddy Guy and Otis Rush on this worthwhile collection. — *Niles J. Frantz*

Chicago Blues Harmonicas / 1990 / Paula/Flyright ✦✦✦✦
The four remaining JOB sides by Pryor ("Boogy Fool," "Raisin' Sand," "Cryin' Shame," and "Eighty Nine Ten") are to be found here on this compilation,

with Snooky also found in support on two tracks from a 1949 Baby Face Leroy session. With the other 13 tracks including John Lee Henley's "Rhythm Rockin' Boogie," Walter Horton's "Have A Good Time," and rare but notable sides by Sonny Boy Williamson, Little Willie Foster, and Louis Myers And The Aces, this is a harmonica rarities package that's pretty tough to beat. — *Cub Koda*

Chicago Blues Masters, Vol. 3 / Jun. 3, 1997 / Capitol ◆◆◆
Chicago Blues Masters, Vol. 3 is an odd collection, featuring 14 tracks from Shakey Jake, ten cuts from James Cotton (including his inexplicable cover of Todd Rundgren's "Kiddy Boy"), and 14 cuts from George "Harmonica" Smith. There's enough from each artist to constitute a full collection, but these songs are all thrown together without much rhyme or reason. Furthermore, the recordings are latter-day efforts, all of which are interesting, but not necessarily among their best work. Consequently, it's primarily of interest to hardcore fans and collectors—the kind of listener who will sift through the mediocre recordings to find the good stuff. — *Stephen Thomas Erlewine*

Chicago Blues of the 1950's / May 20, 1997 / Paula ◆◆◆
This compilation gathers some of the seldom-anthologized blues rarities of the era as originally issued on the Cobra, JOB, ABCO and Chief labels in Chicago. Kicking off with both sides of Guitar Shorty's Cobra single ("Irma Lee" and "You Don't Treat Me Right"), the first half delves into the Cobra catalog to bring tracks by Lee Jackson, Clarence Jolly, Sunnyland Slim, and an alternate take of Magic Sam's "Easy Baby" to the mix. Following this is a major dip into the JOB vaults, bringing an unreleased Moody Jones ("Why Should I Worry") and ten tracks from John and Grace Brim, including five previously unissued sides. Completing this treasure trove of rarities is the inclusion of both sides of Morris Pejoe's single for Cobra's ABCO subsidiary, "Screaming and Crying" and "Maybe Blues," and Lillian Offitt's "Will My Man Be Home Tonight," featuring excellent slide guitar work from Earl Hooker. — *Cub Koda*

Chicago Boogie: 1947 / 1983 / St. George ◆◆◆◆
All the earliest Maxwell Street acetate recordings from the short-lived Ora Nelle label, featuring the earliest sides of Little Walter, Jimmy Rogers, Johnny Young and Othum Brown. Delta bluesman Johnny Temple's "Olds 98 Blues", done Robert Johnson style with an electric guitar, is a particular standout. — *Cub Koda*

Chicago Boss Guitars / 1991 / Paula ◆◆◆◆
Otis Rush shares this compilation with Buddy Guy's early Artistic sides and five alternate takes from Magic Sam. The nine Cobra alternates by Rush are raw and even awkward in spots when compared to the issued versions, but chock full of emotional intensity. If you're a Cobra Records alternate take freak, here's the motherlode. — *Cub Koda*

Chicago South Side, 1927-31 / May 1926-Mar. 1932 / Historical ◆◆◆◆
Although the music on this sampler does not contain complete sessions, this LP is well worth searching for. The performances are quite spirited, featuring music from J.C. Cobb's Grains of Corn, Roy Palmer's Alabama Rascals, Jimmy Wade's Dixielanders, Jimmy Bertrand's Washboard Wizards, Harry Dial's Blusicians, and Jimmie Noone. Among the star soloists are cornetists Punch Miller, Junie Cobb on reeds, clarinetists Darnell Howard and Johnny Dodds, the great trombonists Roy Palmer, Louis Armstrong (two of the Bertrand performances), and pianists Jimmy Blythe and Earl Hines. These performances are consistently joyful and essential to '20s collectors in one form or another. — *Scott Yanow*

Chicago South Side, Vol. 2: 1927-29 / Jul. 20, 1927-Jul. 27, 1931 / Historical ◆◆◆◆
This consistently enjoyable LP has a variety of performances recorded in Chicago during 1927-31. The songs in this collection are not reissued as complete sessions but what is here is often quite memorable: three numbers from Jimmy Noone, two apiece by Tiny Parham, the Dixie Rhythm Kings, the Chicago Footwarmers, the State Street Ramblers, and Jimmny Blythe's Washboard Wizards, and one song from Willie Hightower. With the sidemen including pianists Earl Hines and Jimmy Blythe, cornetists Punch Miller and Natty Dominique and the great clarinetist Johnny Dodds, the music is often quite special and always spirited. — *Scott Yanow*

☆ **Chicago: The Blues Today!, Vol. 1** / Oct. 1966 / Vanguard ◆◆◆◆◆
Junior Wells, J.B. Hutto, and Otis Spann are all superlative on this groundbreaking 1966 anthology. — *Bill Dahl*

● **Chicago: The Blues Today!, Vol. 2** / 1966 / Vanguard ◆◆◆◆
After his tenure at Chess, Otis Rush signed with Duke Records in Houston, who released only one 45 during his entire five-year stay at the label. This Vanguard session from 1966 was his first in several years and finds him in exemplary form. Backed by a tough little club band, Otis' guitar tone is crystal clear and well focused, while his singing is simply superb. With two excellent instrumentals aboard ("Rock" is Otis' version of Earl Hooker's "Universal Rock"), the other big ticket highlight is the version of "I Can't Quit You, Baby" that Led Zepplin would later copy note for note on their first album. This is part of a three volume series and also features excellent tracks by James Cotton ("Cotton Crop Blues" and a wild version of "Rocket 88") and Homesick James. — *Cub Koda*

☆ **Chicago: The Blues Today!, Vol. 3** / 1966 / Vanguard ◆◆◆◆◆
This is one of the all-time great blues series ever recorded. Aside from the classic Chess albums (Muddy Waters, Little Walter, Howlin' Wolf, etc.), there is no better introduction to Chicago-style blues than this three-volume set. Each one is incredible. This third album contains the Johnny Shines Blues Band, Johnny Young's South Side Blues Band, and Big Walter Horton's Blues Harp Band with Memphis Charlie Musselwhite. Here are the original Chicago artists who have grown up and played together for most of their lives, so the musical time is spacious—wide open. This is South Side Chicago blues with a trace of country at its best. Big Walter Horton plays some of the best harmonica of his career on this album. Listening to Horton on backup and solo harp is an education. This album is definitive. — *Michael Erlewine*

Clownin' with the World / 1989 / Acoustic Archives ◆◆◆◆
Wonderful CD from the vaults of Trumpet Records. Features unissued Sonny Boy Williamson sides and great tracks by his piano playin' buddy, Willie Love. — *AMG*

The Cobra Records Story / Apr. 26, 1993 / Capricorn ◆◆◆◆
This double-disc set featuring over 50 tracks from the vaults of Eli Toscano's Cobra Records also includes the half dozen or so most important tracks recorded by Ike Turner's Kings of Rhythm between 1958 and 1959, plus other artists' sides that they played on. — *Bruce Eder*

The Copulatin' Blues Compact Disc / Apr. 29, 1929-Feb. 5, 1940 / Stash ◆◆◆
The Stash label began in 1976 with a dozen or so LPs that featured subject matter from the '30s that was considered risque for the period. In the case of this album, the 16 selections all have to do with sex; several cuts were previously unreleased and few had very wide circulation. Such top jazz and blues artists as Sidney Bechet, Lil Johnson, Bessie Smith ("Do Your Duty" and "I Need a Little Sugar in My Bowl"), the Harlem Hamfats, Merline Johnson, Tampa Red, Grant & Wilson, Jelly Roll Morton ("Winin' Boy"), and Lucille Bogan (an absolutely filthy "Shave 'em Dry") are heard from. Some of this music has been reissued by Stash through its subsidiary Jass on CD but not in the same format. — *Scott Yanow*

Copulatin' Blues, Vol. 2 / Jan. 26, 1929-1955 / Stash ◆◆◆
This collection contains a truthful warning and description: "A Party Record for Adults—Screen Before Airplay." It is doubtful if more than a couple of these 15 selections could be played on the radio, even now. Mostly dating from the '30s, the risque performances include several (including a very profane "parody" by the Clovers in the '50s) that were previously unissued. Best is "The Duck's Yas Yas" by Eddie Johnson and his Crackerjacks, "It Feels So Good" by the Hokum Boys, and the classic "Pussy" by Harry Roy's Bat Club Boys. — *Scott Yanow*

☆ **Country Blues Bottleneck Guitar Classics** / 1972 / Yazoo ◆◆◆◆◆
The first and possibly best anthology of pre-war bottleneck guitar (1926-1937), this includes the singing slides of Robert Johnson, Bukka White, Memphis Minnie, and—although scarcely country blues—a stunning "St. Louis Blues" by Jim and Bob, the Genial Hawaiians! — *Mark A. Humphrey*

Dark Muddy Bottom Blues / 1972 / Specialty ◆◆◆◆
Most of the 12 tracks on this 1972 blues compilation were previously unissued. Artists include John Lee Hooker, Lightnin' Hopkins, Mercy Dee, Big Joe Williams, and others. — *AMG*

Dealing with the Devil: The Immediate Blues Story, Vol. 2 / 1980 / Immediate ◆◆◆
Dealing with the Devil: The Immediate Blues Story—Vol. 2 is early British

blues, featuring Eric Clapton, Jeff Beck, Jon Lord, Ron Wood, and other not-yet superstars in some rough, raw performances. — *Bruce Eder*

Deep Blue: 25 Years of Blues on Rounder Records / Sep. 12, 1995 / Rounder ◆◆◆
Over the course of two CDs, *Deep Blue—25 Years of Blues on Rounder Records* rounds up the highlights of Rounder's blues catalog, including tracks from Professor Longhair, Clarence "Gatemouth" Brown, Lowell Fulson, Robert Nighthawk, Champion Jack Dupree, Luther "Guitar Junior" Johnson, Ronnie Earl, and Smokin' Joe Kubek, among many others. It's a fairly consistent collection, giving a good representation of the record label's catalog. — *Stephen Thomas Erlewine*

Deep in the Soul of Texas / 1991 / Collectables ◆◆◆◆
Texas soul from the '60s and '70s includes some previously unissued material. — *Niles J. Frantz*

Deep in the Soul of Texas, Vol. 2 / Nov. 30, 1992 / Collectables ◆◆◆◆
More lone-star obscurities. — *Bill Dahl*

Delta Blues: 1951 / 1990 / Acoustic Archives ◆◆◆◆
Great compilation from Jackson, MS's Trumpet Records. Features early '50s sides by Big Joe Williams, wonderful acoustic duets by the Huff Brothers, and the last recordings of original King Biscuit Boy Willie Love. A wonderful document. — *AMG*

Dig These Blues: The Legendary Dig Masters / 1992 / Ace ◆◆◆◆
Johnny Otis produced these hot R&B sides for his Dig label during the mid-'50s. — *Bill Dahl*

Don't Leave Me Here: The Blues of Texas, Arkansas & Louisiana, 1927-1932 / Aug. 12, 1991 / Yazoo ◆◆◆◆
Don't Leave Me Here: The Blues of Texas, Arkansas & Louisiana is a 14-track country-blues collection of recordings from 1927-1932. This contains a variety of traditional acoustic blues styles from the Gulf Coast area. Highlights include King Solomon Hill and Little Hat Jones. — *Niles J. Frantz*

Drop Down Mama / 1970 / Chess ◆◆◆◆
Nighthawk's early sides for Chess back when they were still called Aristocrat. Includes the original "Sweet Black Angel," which later became a hit for B.B. King as "Sweet Little Angel," and "Anna Lee," two of his very best. Even with minimal band support on these sides, Nighthawk's voice and slide guitar resonates like an orchestra. This wonderful compilation also features seminal tracks by Johnny Shines ("So Glad I Found You"), Floyd Jones ("Dark Road"), Big Boy Spires ("One of These Days"), and Honeyboy Edwards doing the title track with a full band. Truly a compilation that should be residing in everyone's collection. — *Cub Koda*

Drove from Home Blues / 1988 / Flyright ◆◆◆◆
This is an interesting collection of tunes recorded by artists who are virtually unknown. The music is excellent, finding its niche in the stylish, pre-rockabilly/R&B world—a reflection of the work being done in the late '40s and early '50s by artists such as Arthur Crudup, Lightnin' Hopkins, Tommy McClennan, and Blind Boy Fuller. The music of Wright Holmes, for example, is cast in a Lightnin' Hopkins' mold, but his imaginative guitar style is very wild and unconventional. In addition, harpist Sonny Boy Johnson emerges from the John Lee "Sonny Boy" Williamson school. Also present is Muddy Waters' very first commercial recording. — *Larry Hoffman*

☆ **Duke-Peacock's Greatest Hits** / 1992 / MCA ◆◆◆◆◆
Don Robey, something of an infamous figure even in the rough-and-tumble world of '50s R&B labels, owned one of the first successful black-owned labels in the country. His output was rich and varied. *Duke-Peacock's Greatest Hits* offers a revealing overview of his operation, beginning with small hits by two of the company's humongous female belters—Big Mama Thornton's "Hound Dog" and Marie Adams' "I'm Gonna Play the Honky Tonks." Johnny Ace, Bobby Bland, and Junior Parker are represented by a few of their biggest hits, but it's the relatively unknown "Pack Fair and Square" by San Antonio pianist Big Walter Price that wields a knockout punch. Vocal groups aren't forgotten, with sides by Norman Fox and the Rob Roys and the El Torros, and a foray into "rockabilly" is recalled by the Original Casuals' "So Tough." — *Bill Dahl*

☆ **The Earliest Negro Vocal Quartets (1894-1928)** / 1894 / Document ◆◆◆◆◆
A treasure trove for archivists, *Earliest Negro Vocal Quartets (1894-1928)*

compiles 23 impossibly rare recordings spotlighting the African American four-part harmony singing style which predated both jazz and the blues. The real treat here is the lone surviving recording by the Standard Quintette, 1894's "Keep Movin'"; a cylinder cut for Columbia, it is in fact the only black music recording of its time to survive into the 20th century, and as a piece of history alone it's invaluable. The first-ever commercial recordings by a black group, cut in 1902 by the Dinwiddie Colored Quartet, are included, as well as are tracks by the Apollo Male Quartette and Polk Miller & His Old South Quartette. Understandably, the music here is buried under considerable surface noise; casual listeners may wish to pass. But for historians the release of *Earliest Negro Vocal Quartets (1894-1928)* is a major event. — *Jason Ankeny*

East Coast Blues: 1926-1935 / Sep. 30, 1991 / Yazoo ◆◆◆◆
A fine assortment from Carl Martin, Willie Walker, William Moore, Blind Blake, Bayless Rose, and other East Coast guitarists. There are several very traditional blues like "Black Dog Blues" and "Crow Jane," plus lots of good ragtime guitar. For serious guitar players and Piedmont blues fans. — *Barry Lee Pearson*

The Essential Blues / 1995 / House of Blues ◆◆◆
Essential Blues is an attempt to trace the evolution of the music from the Mississippi Delta to Chicago and other modern, urban cities. It does a fairly good job in providing a brief history, but the main strength of the collection simply comes from the music. Featuring cuts from Lightnin' Hopkins, Howlin' Wolf, B.B. King, Slim Harpo, Junior Parker, Elmore James, Albert Collins, and many, many others, it's a quick and effective way to sample a variety of different blues styles. For neophytes, *Essential Blues* does offer a splendid introduction to the genre. — *Stephen Thomas Erlewine*

Evidence Blues Sampler / Oct. 1, 1992 / Evidence ◆◆◆
Evidence's blues reissue campaign has been exhaustive and diverse in its artistic and stylistic range, something that is reflected in this 15-cut sampler culled from various sessions. There is vintage material from John Lee Hooker, J.B. Hutto, and the tandem of Junior Wells and Buddy Guy, plus classic R&B by Louis Jordan and Big Joe Turner, and contemporary blues by Magic Slim, Lonnie Brooks, and Luther Johnson, Jr. You can also hear Otis Rush and Luther Allison at their best or Pinetop Perkins offering prototypical boogie-woogie and rumbling piano licks. — *Ron Wynn*

Excello Blues: House Rockin' & Hip Shakin' / Nov. 4, 1997 / Hip-O ◆◆◆
This 16-track collection rounds up the usual favorites (Slim Harpo's "I'm A King Bee," Arthur Gunter's "Baby Let's Play House," Lazy Lester's "Sugar Coated Love," Lightnin' Slim's "Rooster Blues") along with others less often anthologized like Jerry McCain's "My Next Door Neighbor" and "That's What They Want," Leroy Washington's "Wild Cherry," Jimmy Anderson's "Naggin'," Whispering Smith's "I Tried So Hard," and the alternate take of Lazy Lester's "I'm a Lover, Not a Fighter." A solid mid-line collection that makes a perfect introduction into the blues side of this legendary label. — *Cub Koda*

Excello Harmonica Blues Variety / 1994 / AVI/Excello ◆◆◆◆
This is a 39-track, double-CD package collecting up various stray cuts in the Excello vaults by artists who didn't leave enough tracks behind to justify having compilations under their own names. The highlights include nine tracks by Jimmy Reed sound-alike Jimmy Anderson, Lightnin' Slim sideman Lazy Lester, and 10 tracks by Jerry McCain and His Upstarts. Add to this stray singles by Baby Boy Warren (with Sonny Boy Williamson), Little Sonny, Whispering Smith, and the obscure Ole Sonny Boy and you have a package that fills up the holes in your Excello collection quite nicely. Over half of the tracks are dubbed from disc, but the music's fine just the same. — *Cub Koda*

The Fifties: Juke Joint Blues / 1987 / Capitol ◆◆◆◆
This is a valuable look at some of the toughest Delta and West Coast blues sides issued by Modern Records in the '50s. — *Bill Dahl*

Free at Last: Gospel Quartets from Chalice / May 5, 1997 / Specialty ◆◆◆◆
Stax Records launched a gospel subsidiary called Chalice during the mid-'60s that, although short-lived, recorded some remarkable quartets from Memphis and surrounding areas. This 24-track compilation gathers up some ultra-rare selections from that label's archives, including such then-topical songs as the Dixie Nightingales' "The Assasination" (a harrowing lament for President John F. Kennedy) and the Jubilee Hummingbirds' "Our Freedom Song," all about Dr. Martin Luther King's receipt of the Nobel Peace Prize. What is especially appealing is the crack instrumental support behind these

various quartets being provided by Steve Cropper, Al Jackson, Jr., Isaac Hayes, and other Stax R&B session stalwarts. Selections from the Stars of Virginia and the Pattersonaires complete the package. Note: this compilation was previously released by Ace Records (UK) as *Disturb My Soul: Gospel from Stax Records' Chalice Label. — Cub Koda*

Genuine Houserockin' Music, Vol. 1 / 1986 / Alligator ✦✦✦✦
These virtually interchangeable samplers of good-time, high-energy, modern R&B were produced by Chicago's Alligator label. Lonnie Brooks, Lonnie Mack, Koko Taylor, Fenton Robinson, Albert Collins, and others are included. Slick and well-produced. — *Hank Davis*

Genuine Houserockin' Music, Vol. 2 / 1987 / Alligator ✦✦✦

Genuine Houserockin' Music, Vol. 3 / 1988 / Alligator ✦✦✦

Genuine Houserockin' Music, Vol. 4 / Aug. 30, 1990 / Alligator ✦✦✦

Georgia Blues (1928-1933) / Jun. 2, 1994 / Document ✦✦✦✦
The Atlanta blues scene of the '20s was among the most fertile in all the South, with a steady stream of rural musicians converging on the city hoping to gain exposure playing the local club circuit, with any luck rising to perform at Decatur Street's famed 81 Theatre; *Georgia Blues 1928-1933* assembles sides from some of the era's most prominent artists, among them Curley Weaver, Fred McMullen, and harpist Eddie Mapp. Far and away the best-known of the featured artists, Weaver is captured at the dawn of his career; on his first sides, among them "No No Blues," he sounds remarkably like fellow Atlanta bluesmen the Hicks brothers. The little-known McMullen is the wild card here, a slide guitarist also noted for his picking finesse; of his seven tracks, the best is "DeKalb Chain Gang," a cut so vividly harrowing it seems undoubtedly autobiographical. — *Jason Ankeny*

Golden Age Gospel Choirs / Dec. 24, 1997 / Specialty ✦✦✦✦
This entry into Specialty's *Legends of Gospel* series brings together 23 selections from four groundbreaking gospel choirs. The Back Home Choir of Newark, NJ, clocks in with ten performances from 1962, with "Climbing High Mountains," "He Knows How Much We Can Bear," and "Without God I Can Do Nothing" being particular standouts. Next up is the Pentecostal Choir of Detroit with two rousing selections, "Prayer Wheel Turning Over" and "How Glad I Am." The Helen Robinson Youth Choir from Chicago contributes three tracks from a previously unreleased 1959 session for Specialty, including "Sit Down Children," "Working on the Building," and "Run & Help Us All." Closing out the set is a 1954 Choir album session from the Voices of Victory. Intended to simulate an actual church service, their set starts with an invocation and ends with a benediction, with the strong musical highlights "I'm So Glad Jesus Lifted Me," "Lord, Lord, Lord," "The Angels Keep Watching," and "Blessed Assurance" sandwiched in between. Once again compiling material from the Specialty and Tru-Sound labels, this brings together some great gospel performances culled from two different decades. — *Cub Koda*

Golden Age Gospel Quartets, Vol. 1 (1947-1954) / Dec. 24, 1997 / Specialty ✦✦✦✦
The accent is on harmony in this collection of 26 tracks from the gospel side of the Specialty Records vaults. The bulk of the selections here are previously unissued and in the main feature a cappella performances. Besides worthy entries from the Pilgrim Travelers ("The Old Rugged Cross"), the Soul Stirrers ("By and By"), the Swan Silvertones ("I'm Coming Home"), and the Five Blind Boys of Alabama ("Marching Up to Zion"), this disc also boasts equally fine performances from lesser-known groups like the Paramount Singers ("He Means So Much to Me"), the Southern Harmonizers ("What Are They Doing in Heaven Today?"), Golden Echoes ("Since I Laid My Burden Down"), Detroiters ("Let Jesus Lead You"), Chosen Gospel Singers ("Leaning on the Lord"), and the West Coast Jubilees ("Since Jesus Came into My Heart"). Recorded between 1947 and 1954, the set runs in roughly chronological order to better spotlight the change in gospel singing from a cappella to full rhythm section backing during this time period. A remarkable set of recordings. — *Cub Koda*

Golden Age Gospel Quartets, Vol. 2 (1954-1963) / Dec. 24, 1997 / Specialty ✦✦✦✦
The second volume in Specialty's *Legends of Gospel* series is best seen as a companion volume to its predecessor, picking up right where the first volume left off. Starting with sides from 1954, it furthers chronicles important performances from the Specialty Records vaults of the Soul Stirrers ("He'll

Make a Way," "Be With Me Jesus"), the Chosen Gospel Singers ("The Lifeboat Is Coming," "What a Wonderful Sight"), the Pilgrim Travelers ("Straight Street," "Did You Stop to Pray This Morning?"), and the Original Five Blind Boys of Alabama ("Broken Heart of Mine," "Goodbye Mother"). But also aboard are early-'60s sides recorded for the New York-based Tru-Sound and Battle labels by the Gate City Singers ("Peace in the Valley"), the Capitol City Stars ("Friends Talk About Me"), the Clefs of Calvary ("Troubles of This World"), and the Gable-Airs ("Travelin' Shoes"). An important chunk of gospel history to savor. — *Cub Koda*

Good Time Blues: Harmonicas, Kazoos, Washboards & Cow-Bells / 1991 / Columbia/Legacy ✦✦✦✦
This CD sampler largely lives up to its name. Subtitled "Harmonicas, Kazoos, Washboards & Cow-Bells," the collection consists of goodtime blues performed by an assortment of artists. Many of the bands feature washboards, but a kazoo only pops up on one song. Actually, it is the harmonica players (particularly Will Shade, Buddy Moss, Robert Lee McCoy, and Sonny Terry) who generally take solo honors. A certain sameness emerges by the fifth or sixth song, but taken in small doses, this often exuberant music is enjoyable. There are selections by the Mississippi Jook Band, the Memphis Jug Band, Son Becky, Charlie Burse's Memphis Mudcats, the Georgia Browns, the Georgia Cotton Pickers, Big Joe and his Washboard Band, Buddy Moss, Memphis Slim, Sonny Terry/Jordan Webb, and Bernice Edwards. Four of the selections were previously unreleased. — *Scott Yanow*

☆ **Gospel Warriors** / 1990 / Spirit Feel ✦✦✦✦✦
Spanning a half century of classic performances, *Gospel Warriors* assembles 16 tracks from some of the church circuit's most renowned female soloists, among them Marion Williams, Bessie Griffin, and Sister Rosetta Tharpe. While each vocalist is clearly a singular talent, listening to their music side by side offers real insight into their common gifts for improvisation; all are in total command of melody, tone, and lyric, transcending their material to enjoy an unparalleled sense of creative freedom. An ideal introduction for new gospel listeners, the collection's highlights include Tharpe's "Just a Closer Walk with Thee," Williams' "It's Getting Late in the Evening," and Clara Ward's "Precious Lord." — *Jason Ankeny*

Got Harp, If You Want It! / Nov. 10, 1993 / Blue Rock-It ✦✦✦✦
A decent overview of postwar blues harmonica, but hardly comprehensive. — *Ron Wynn*

Got My Mojo Working / 1991 / Flyright ✦✦✦✦
Collection of blues sides recorded for New York's Baton label in the mid-to-late '50s, featuring Chris Kenner's first recording and Ann Cole's original, pre-Muddy Waters version performance of the title track. — *Cub Koda*

The Great 1955 Shrine Concert / 1993 / Specialty ✦✦✦✦
The power and splendor that was gospel in the '50s radiates throughout the performances on *The Great 1955 Shrine Concert.* The Pilgrim Travelers, with twin powerhouse leads Kylo Turner and Keith Barber, get things started in fiery fashion, followed by the dynamic Caravans, whose roster at that time included Albertina Walker and Rev. James Cleveland, who doubled as a pianist. Also on the bill are Brother Joe May, justifying his "Thunderbolt of the Midwest" nickname, the Soul Stirrers with Sam Cooke still in the fold, and the Original Gospel Harmonettes, concluding the proceedings with a flourish. Anyone who attended certainly felt the spirit, as will anyone who listens to this magnificent 14-song set. — *Ron Wynn*

Great Blues Guitarists: String Dazzlers / Aug. 1991 / Columbia/Legacy ✦✦✦✦
Ten excellent blues guitarists are heard on 20 selections dating from 1924-40 on this enjoyable CD reissue from the Columbia/Legacy series. Included are Sylvester Weaver (the first blues guitarist to record an unaccompanied solo), the team of Lonnie Johnson & Eddie Lang (who are heard on a pair of duets and with singer Texas Alexander), the influential Big Bill Broonzy (superb on "How You Want It Done?"), the always passionate Blind Willie Johnson, Blind Willie McTell, Casey Bill Weldon, Blind Lemon Jefferson ("Black Snake Moan"), Joshua White, and Tampa Red. Three previously unheard selections are included on this fine overview but completists will probably prefer to skip over the set in favor of the more comprehensive Document CD's. — *Scott Yanow*

☆ **The Great Bluesmen at Newport** / 1976 / Vanguard ✦✦✦✦✦
These performances come from 1959-1965 by rediscovery legends Son

House, Mississippi John Hurt, Skip James, Sleepy John Estes, and other compelling singers and guitarists such as Robert Pete Williams, John Lee Hooker, and Mississippi Fred McDowell. — *Mark A. Humphrey*

☆ **The Great Gospel Men** / 1995 / Shanachie ◆◆◆◆◆
A wide range of magnificent vocals are displayed on *The Great Gospel Men*, a 27-song anthology. Some names such as Brother Joe May, Rev. James Cleveland, and Professor Alex Bradford are familiar even to non-gospel fans; others, like the intense Robert Anderson, Professor J. Earle Hines, Norsalus McKissick, Robert Bradley, and R.L. Knowles, are known only to the hardcore, and even they probably haven't heard many songs by any one artist. This collection alternates nicely between slow and fast pieces, giving each artist a chance to demonstrate their skills. — *Ron Wynn*

☆ **The Great Gospel Women** / 1993 / Shanachie ◆◆◆◆◆
Like its male counterpoint, this anthology spotlights contributions from both famous stars (Mahalia Jackson, Marion Williams, Dorothy Love Coates, Sister Rosetta Tharpe) and obscure figures (Mary Johnson Davis, Jessie Mae Renfro, Lucy Smith, and Goldia Haynes, among others), presenting a hefty 31 selections. While some might quibble that celebated stars Jackson and Williams get six tracks apiece, it's hard to argue with the greatness of what's presented by them. Others who give head-turning performances include Frances Steadman, Roberta Martin, and Clara Ward. — *Ron Wynn*

Great Gospel Women, Vol. 2 / 1995 / Shanachie ◆◆◆◆
The Great Gospel Women, Vol. 2 is a worthy follow-up to the first edition of the series; wisely refusing to mess with a good thing, producer Anthony Heilbut holds over most of the same artists from before, dipping into the well for more classic material from soloists including Mahalia Jackson, Marion Williams, Clara Ward, and Sister Rosetta Tharpe. While the overall quality is somewhat diluted this time out, in its favor the disc offers two more tracks than its predecessor, as well as choice cuts from performers making their series debut, among them Bessie Griffin, Ernestine B. Washington, Edna Gallmon Cooke, Imogene Green and Myrtle Scott. An excellent companion piece. — *Jason Ankeny*

Greatest Gospel Gems / 1991 / Specialty ◆◆◆◆
An excellent 24-song sampling of '50s and '60s sacred testifying from the vaults of Specialty Records, it includes essential cuts from Dorothy Love Coates, the Swan Silvertones, and Sam Cooke and the Soul Stirrers. — *John Floyd*

Greatest Gospel Gems, Vol. 1 / Oct. 17, 1990 / Specialty ◆◆◆◆
Heart-stopping gospel by the Soul Stirrers, Robert Anderson, Gospel Harmonettes, etc. — *Opal Louis Nations*

Greatest Gospel Gems, Vol. 2 / Oct. 17, 1990 / Specialty ◆◆◆◆
More gospel greats by Prof. Alex Bradford, Brother Joe May, Rev. James Cleveland, and more. — *Opal Louis Nations*

● **The Greatest in Country Blues (1929-1956), Vol. 1** / Jan. 1, 1992 / Story of Blues ◆◆◆◆
Story of the Blues has provided one of the best introductions to acoustic country blues with its three-volume *Greatest in Country Blues* series. While it collects most of the major figures as well as the obscure and their finest performances, there are a certain number of odd ommissions such as Reverend Gary Davis and Robert Nighthawk that prevent it from being the definitive country blues set. Nevertheless, each of the three volumes are an invaluable reference as well as an interesting listen for both the specialist and the novice. — *Chris Woodstra*

● **The Greatest in Country Blues (1929-1956), Vol. 3** / Sep. 1, 1992 / Story of Blues ◆◆◆◆
Anyone interested in a survey of early blues will be thrilled with having any of these three historical volumes, suited to both novice and connoisseur alike. Each provides a dazzling, panoramic survey of artists both famous and obscure and covers every region known to have nurtured the music. *Volume 2* features Skip James' "Devil Got My Woman," Robert Johnson's "Preaching' Blues," and Kokomo Arnold's "Paddlin' Madeline Blues." From Texas Alexander there is a version of "Levee Camp Moan Blues," which is made timeless by the incomparable guitar of Lonnie Johnson. Great instrumentals like Palmer McAbee's "Railroad Piece" and the Dallas String Band's "Dallas Rag" add spice, and there are also first-rate entries by more obscure giants like

King Solomon Hill, George "Bullet" Williams, "Hi" Henry Brown, and Blind Joe Taggart. — *Larry Hoffman*

Grinder Man Blues: Masters of Blues Piano / 1990 / RCA ◆◆◆◆
Six tracks each come from Little Brother Montgomery (1935-1936), Memphis Slim (1940-1941), and Big Maceo Merriweather (1941-1945). With piano blues and boogie-woogie, it's wonderful listening from beginning to end. — *Niles J. Frantz*

Guitar Player Presents Electric Blues, Vol. 1 / 1991 / Rhino ◆◆◆
Excellent 18-track CD compilation featuring definitive sides by Muddy Waters, Otis Rush, Hound Dog Taylor, Albert King, Eddie Taylor, and many more. — *Cub Koda*

Guitar Player Presents Electric Blues, Vol. 2 / 1991 / Rhino ◆◆◆
Companion volume to the above with excellent selections from B.B. King, Albert Collins, Eric Clapton, Michael Bloomfield, Magic Sam, Buddy Guy, and a dozen others. — *Cub Koda*

Guitar Wizards: 1926-1935 / Feb. 19, 1992 / Yazoo ◆◆◆◆
This is an excellent collection of great pre-war blues guitarists. — *Mark A. Humphrey*

Gulf Coast Blues, Vol. 1 / 1990 / Black Top ◆◆◆◆
Contemporary Texas and Louisiana blues come from four artists deserving wider attention. Carol Fran, Joe "Guitar" Hughes, and Grady Gaines each contribute two cuts, with four from Teddy Reynolds. Fran and Reynolds are the highlights, and each deserve their own full releases. — *Niles J. Frantz*

Hand Me Down Blues Chicago Style / 1990 / Relic ◆◆◆◆
One of the finest '50s Chicago Blues compilations in existence, taken from the vaults of Parrot-Blue Lake Records. Unissued sides and rare singles create an incredible ambience here. Essential listening. — *Cub Koda*

Harlem Rock 'n' Blues, Vol. 3 / 1995 / Collectables ◆◆◆
This continues the theme. Material that either influenced or reflected evolutionary trends in blues and R&B. — *Ron Wynn*

Harmonica Blues / 1991 / Yazoo ◆◆◆◆
This is a fine collection of pre-war harp performances. — *Mark A. Humphrey*

Harmonica Blues Kings / 1986 / Delmark ◆◆◆◆
Featuring a side each of Big Walter Horton and Alfred "Blues King" Harris in primarily supporting roles behind various vocalists from the vaults of United/States Records, 1954. Raw, lively harmonica and another missing piece of the early Chicago blues puzzle. — *AMG*

Harp Attack! / 1991 / Alligator ◆◆◆◆
This 11-track CD spotlights four Chicago harmonica players—Carey Bell, Billy Branch, James Cotton, and Junior Wells—in new recordings. All have played with Muddy Waters or Willie Dixon's Chicago Blues All-Stars (or both). This is solid, electric-band-style Chicago blues. — *Niles J. Frantz*

Harps, Jugs, Washboards & Kazoos / Jun. 1926-Oct. 10, 1940 / RST ◆◆◆◆
Included on this fun CD from the Austrian RST label are all of the recordings done by the Five Harmaniacs (which date from 1926-27), the Salty Dog Four (from 1930-31 and also known as the Red Devils), the Scorpion Washboard Band (1933), and Rhythm Willie and his Gang (1940). While Rhythm Willie's group is an acoustic blues quartet led by a harmonica player, Scorpion has a kazoo and washboard (along with more conventional instruments), the Salty Dog Four uses kazoo, violin, and sometimes mandolin, and the Harmaniacs have harmonica, kazoo, and washboard. The goodtime music overall falls between jazz and blues and is difficult to resist, particularly tunes such as "Sadie Green, The Vamp of New Orleans," "Coney Island Washboard," "What Did Romie-O Juliet (When He Climbed Her Balcony)," and "Bedroom Stomp." — *Scott Yanow*

Hound Dog Taylor: A Tribute / 1998 / Alligator ◆◆◆
In many respects, you could call Hound Dog Taylor a cult artist. Respected by bluesmen and critics alike, he built a small devoted following across America simply by touring constantly. There were no hits and very few covers of his songs, but his rowdy concerts and his incendiary records on Alligator convinced any who heard him. In the process, he put Alligator Records on the blues map, so it only makes sense that the label return the favor with *Hound Dog Taylor: A Tribute*, one of the few blues tributes that really works. Taylor's wild, careening slide guitar became one of the more influential sounds in contemporary blues, as evidenced by this quality-packed record.

Out of the 14 tracks, only George Thorogood's thuggish "I Just Can't Make It" falls flat, but the quality of the remaining cuts is so high that is forgiveable. Luther Allison's "Give Me Back My Wig" rocks; Gov't Mule's "Gonna Send You Back to Georgia" is tough; Vernon Reid & Alvin Youngblood Hart do a nice acoustic reading of "It's Alright"; Steady Rollin' Bob Margolin turns "See Me in the Evening" into an appealing straightforward blues-rocker; and Cub Koda tears through "Take Five" with the help of Hound Dog's backing band, the Houserockers. Moments like these are what elevates this tribute album above the average. — *Stephen Thomas Erlewine*

House Rockin' Blues / 1995 / Ace ✦✦✦✦
Compilations of vintage Chess material seem to be plentiful these days, but this excellent collection of strictly uptempo material should not be passed by at any cost. With a healthy 27 tracks aboard, the highlights are numerous with the label's stars and second stringers like Howlin' Wolf, J.B. Lenoir, John Brim, Billy Boy Arnold, Bo Diddley, Willie Mabon, Elmore James, and Otis Rush all present and accounted for. But rather than opt for the same tracks that have been around the block time and again, true obscurities like the anonymous Little Luther's "The Twirl," G.L. Crockett's "Look out Mabel," the previously unissued Robert Nighthawk with Buddy Guy shuffle, "Someday," "Tired of Crying over You" by Morris Pejoe, and "He Knows the Rules" by Jimmy McCracklin pepper the mix to keep the collectors happy as well. If the boogie side of the Chess canonade is your particular cup of coffee, this collection is the one you'll keep going back to time and again. Great! — *Cub Koda*

How Blue Can You Get?: Great Blues Vocals in the Jazz Tradition / Jun. 29, 1938-Nov. 20, 1963 / Bluebird ✦✦✦
Most of the 19 vocals on this interesting but not essential sampler feature jazz singers performing blues including Louis Armstrong, Jack Teagarden, Mildred Bailey, Wingy Manone, Fats Waller, Billy Eckstine, Jimmy Rushing, Joe Williams, Helen Humes, and Hot Lips Page. There are a couple of ringers tossed in, particularly Leadbelly doing his classic version of "Good Morning Blues" and Little Richard starting his recording career with a Leonard Feather blues. The music mostly falls into the swing tradition; only two selections are more recent than 1951. — *Scott Yanow*

If It Ain't a Hit ... / Zu-Zazz ✦✦✦✦
X-rated Blues is the theme here with selections ranging from totally raunchy to mildly titillating, with great listening and a full dollop of humor throughout. Features under-the-counter performances by Jackie Wilson, LaVern Baker, Chick Willis, the Clovers, and the Fred Wolff Combo. Blues with a nudge and a wink to it. — *Cub Koda*

The Immediate Blues, Vol. 1: Stroll On / 1991 / Sony ✦✦✦✦
The Yardbirds, Eric Clapton, and a brace of early British bluesmen playing on what were intended as demos. Not profound, but entertaining. — *Bruce Eder*

Ind. Women's Blues 2: Big Mamas / Apr. 1925-1953 / Rosetta ✦✦✦
Despite the title of this LP, many of the 16 blues and jazz singers heard here were not necessarily "big" physically but women in control of their situations, at least on these records. There is one song apiece from Ethel Waters, Edith Johnson, Viola McCoy, Hattie McDaniel (the same person as the actress), Issie Ringgold, Gussie Williams, Clara Smith, Ida Cox, Julia Lee, Susie Edwards, Martha Copeland, Ora Alexander, Rosa Henderson, Bea Foote, Billie Holiday, and Ella Johnson, and the majority are still quite rare. All of the Rosetta releases are worth searching for and this attractive album is no exception. — *Scott Yanow*

Ind. Women's Blues 3: Super Sisters / Apr. 9, 1927-May 3, 1955 / Rosetta ✦✦✦
The third of four LPs issued by Rosetta in its *Independent Women's Blues* series has 16 blues and jazz recordings, one apiece from Ida Cox, Bertha Idaho, Helen Humes (in 1927), Sara Martin, Mildred Bailey, Sweet Peas Spivey, Lil Johnson, Trixie Smith, Susie Edwards, Lucille Bogan, Cleo Gibson, Martha Copeland, Edith Johnson, Albennie Jones, Lizzie Miles, and Ella Fitzgerald. Many of these valuable performances are still quite rare and have not yet been reissued on CD. — *Scott Yanow*

Ind. Women's Blues 4: Sweet Petunias / Jun. 20, 1929-Jun. 5, 1956 / Rosetta ✦✦✦
There is a wide variety of vocals on this Rosetta LP which, with one exception (O'Neil Spencer's "Sweet Patootie" with Sidney Bechet), features female singers. Such fine vocalists as June Richmond, Annisteen Allen, Mary Dixon, Etta

Jones ("The Richest Guy in the Graveyard"), Monette Moore, Mae West, Stella Johnson, Ella Johnson, Bea Foote, Chippie Hill, Victoria Spivey, the Bandanna Girls, Betty Hall Jones, Helen Humes, and Big Mama Thornton perform one song apiece. Most of the recordings are rare and this appealing set, *Vol. 4* of Rosetta's *Independent Women's Blues* series, is easily recommended. — *Scott Yanow*

Jackson Blues: 1928-1938 / Jul. 1, 1991 / Yazoo ✦✦✦✦
Featured are Tommy Johnson and the school of Delta blues he inspired in Jackson, MS. — *Mark A. Humphrey*

☆ **Jubilation: Great Gospel Performances, Vol. 1 (Black Gospel)** / Jan. 1992 / Rhino ✦✦✦✦✦
Jubilation: Great Gospel Performances, Vol. 1 offers a first-rate introduction and overview of the key players in Black gospel, including stellar performances by Mahalia Jackson, the Soul Stirrers, the Swan Silvertones, Shirley Caesar, Aretha Franklin, and James Cleveland, and many other wonderful artists. — *Thom Owens*

☆ **Jubilation: Great Gospel Performances, Vol. 2 (More Black Gospel)** / Feb. 1992 / Rhino ✦✦✦✦✦
Like the title says, there's more of the same as the first volume, including the Staple Singers, the Original Gospel Harmonettes, Prof. Alex Bradford, the Harmonizing Four, Sam Cooke with the Soul Stirrers, and more. — *AMG*

Jubilee Jezebels, Vol. 2 / Jul. 8, 1997 / Sequel ✦✦✦
The second volume in this fine series brings together some of the fine female R&B and pop performers who recorded for Jerry Blaine's Jubilee, Josie, or Port labels between 1952 and 1964. The bulk of the material comes from the early to mid-'50s, prime years for Blaine's labels, with only five of the 25 tracks emanating from 1964. The transfers sound bright and sharp, even on the tunes that were dubbed from disc. Several of the performers reappear from the initial volume, with Edna McGriff represented by three tracks, six tracks by Little Sylvia (who would later become Sylvia of Mickey & Sylvia, of "Love Is Strange" fame), and two tracks each from Gloria Mann, Gloria Alleyne, Patti Jerome, Faye Simmons, Carol Fran, and Big Maybelle, plus single track entries from Fay Simmons ("I Can See Through You"), Ann Marie ("Runaround"), Viola Watkins ("Paint a Sky for Me," which features the Crows on backup vocals), the Enchanters ("Today Is Your Birthday"), and a 1957 cut by Della Reese, a bluesy reading of the old standard "I Cried for You." As the booklet states, this compilation makes a really great all-female R&B review. — *Cub Koda*

● **Juke Joint Jump: Boogie Woogie Celebration** / Nov. 2, 1931-Jul. 7, 1961 / Columbia/Legacy ✦✦✦✦
While some purists would like to compartmentalize boogie woogie into a nice, neat box as strictly a form of piano blues, this 18-track collection clearly demonstrates that the form lends itself to a wide variety of treatments. Tracks like "Baby Boogie Woogie" by country picker Curley Weaver, "Boogie Woogie" by Delta Cum. Detroit bluesman Calvin Frazier, and jazz visionary Art Tatum's "Tatum Pole Boogie," do much to support that claim, as does the inclusion of tracks from Red Saunders, Adrian Rollini, and Harry James. Much of the material reprised here comes from one of the very first Columbia 78 RPM "albums," a collection of boogie woogie classics produced by John Hammond, the man who brought the music into national vogue in the late '30s by simply letting giants like Albert Ammons, Meade Lux Lewis, Pete Johnson, and Big Joe Turner do their thing. As a musical flavor of the month, boogie woogie lasted long enough into the '40s to have its rhythms incorporated into Tin Pan Alley fodder, but its influence lasted much longer than that. And here are 18 perfect examples of its timeless appeal, minus the commercial affectations. — *Cub Koda*

Jump 'n Shout! (New Orleans Blues) / Apr. 16, 1995 / Pearl Flapper ✦✦✦
Solid New Orleans anthology. — *Bill Dahl*

Jumpin' Like Mad: Cool Cats & Hip Chicks / Jun. 3, 1997 / Capitol ✦✦✦
This highly enjoyable two-CD set is comprised of 51 selections by over 40 different groups. Very much a sampler of the Capitol and Aladdin catalogs, the music emphasizes medium-tempo and rollicking blues, with an occasional slower piece tossed in for variety. In addition to such hits as "Cow Cow Boogie," "Jumpin' with Symphony Sid," and "He's a Real Gone Guy," there are also previously unreleased selections from Ella Mae Morse, Johnny Mercer, Harry "The Hipster" Gibson, and Gene Ammons. The performers range from jazz players to those more closely associated with blues and early R&B;

among the participants are Jesse Price, Kay Starr, T-Bone Walker, the King Cole Trio, the Cootie Williams Orchestra, Big Jay McNeely, and Louis Jordan, plus many others. Fun party music. — *Scott Yanow*

● **Kansas City Blues 1944-1949** / Jun. 3, 1997 / Capitol ✦✦✦✦
This wonderful three-CD set, released in 1997, has 73 consistently exciting— and mostly formerly rare—performances from Kansas City-based players, released complete and in chronological order. Pianist Jay McShann, vocalist/ pianist Julia Lee, pianist/singer Buster Moten, blues singer Walter Brown, saxophonist Tommy Douglas, and vocalist Tiny Kennedy are the leaders of the overlapping groups, and although the sidemen are mostly obscure (other than tenorman Ben Webster, who is on two dates), they show plenty of talent and color. The styles range from urban blues and Julia Lee's sly double-entendre songs to heated instrumentals that hint strongly at early R&B. Very enjoyable and accessible music quite suitable both for parties and for close listening. — *Scott Yanow*

Keys to the Crescent City / 1991 / Rounder ✦✦✦
The revelation on this CD anthology spotlighting three New Orleans greats and one West Coast blues legend (Charles Brown) was the late Willie Tee. Tee, who died in 1993, was known for his soulful vocals and skillful writing, but was undervalued as a pianist. He demonstrated with his voicings and solos on "Can It Be Done" and "In the Beginning" that he also merited attention as a keyboard stylist. Charles Brown turned in his customary polished, first-rate vocal and instrumental job on his three tunes, while Eddie Bo's singing exceeded his piano playing, and Art Neville demonstrated again why he should do more recording outside the arenas of the Neville Brothers and the Meters. — *Ron Wynn*

Legends of Guitar: Electric Blues, Vol. 1 / 1990 / Rhino ✦✦✦✦
This very consistent post-war blues-guitar collection includes Muddy Waters, T-Bone Walker, B.B. King, Guitar Slim, Earl Hooker, and Otis Rush contributing their vintage classics. — *Bill Dahl*

Legends of Guitar: Electric Blues, Vol. 2 / 1991 / Rhino ✦✦✦
Slightly less consistent than its predecessor, it's still loaded with gems—18 tracks including Clarence Gatemouth Brown, Albert Collins, Lowell Fulson, Magic Sam, etc. — *Bill Dahl*

Legends of the Blues, Vol. 1 / Feb. 1991 / Columbia/Legacy ✦✦✦✦
This CD serves as a perfect introduction to pre-war blues for the novice since it contains fine examples of the music of 20 blues artists: Bessie Smith, Blind Lemon Jefferson, Mississippi John Hurt, Blind Willie Johnson, Bo Carter, Blind Willie McTell, Lonnie Johnson, Charley Patton, Leroy Carr, Josh White, Leadbelly, Peetie Wheatstraw, Robert Johnson, Blind Boy Fuller, Big Bill Broonzy, Memphis Minnie, Bukka White, Muddy Waters, Big Joe Williams, and Son House. Four selections are from the '20s, Son House's "Death Letter" is from 1965, and otherwise the music dates from 1931-47. The who's who roster includes practically every early great (Tampa Red is missing but Washboard Sam and the first Sonny Boy Williamson appear as sidemen) and, with nine previously unreleased selections (both alternate takes and "new" performances), this CD is an essential purchase for both beginners and veteran collectors alike. — *Scott Yanow*

Legends of the Blues, Vol. 2 / Sep. 10, 1991 / Columbia/Legacy ✦✦✦✦
As with the first volume in the series Columbia/Legacy blues series, this CD has one selection apiece from 20 important blues artists, including many previously unissued (at least on Columbia) songs and alternate takes. The fact that 13 of the tracks are at best quite unfamiliar should make the set (in the absence of more "complete" collections) of interest to even veteran fans and well worth acquiring as an introduction for beginners. The music ranges from intimate country-blues to hokum, from early efforts by T-Bone Walker, Roosevelt Sykes, and Champion Jack Dupree to prime Tampa Red, Lucille Bogan, and Charlie Spand; there are also selections from Texas Alexander, Robert Hicks, Curly Weaver, Bessie Jackson, Walter Roland, Bumble Bee Slim, Buddy Moss, Robert Wilkins, Lil Johnson, Casey Bill Weldon, Victoria Spivey, Curtis Jones, Merline Johnson, Bill "Jazz Gillum," and Brownie McGhee. — *Scott Yanow*

Living Chicago Blues, Vol. 1 / 1978 / Alligator ✦✦✦✦
Arguably the best entry in this pioneering anthology series, this features excellent sides by guitarist Jimmy Johnson and saxophonist Eddie Shaw. — *Bill Dahl*

Living Chicago Blues, Vol. 2 / 1978 / Alligator ✦✦✦
This set is almost as incendiary as Vol. 1, thanks to four sides each from Magic Slim, Lonnie Brooks, and Pinetop Perkins. — *Bill Dahl*

Living Chicago Blues, Vol. 3 / 1980 / Alligator ✦✦✦
Laconic saxman A.C. Reed and crisp guitarist Lacy Gibson are standouts. — *Bill Dahl*

Living Chicago Blues, Vol. 4 / 1980 / Alligator ✦✦✦
Not quite as strong, although witty pianist Detroit Jr and guitarist Andrew Brown contribute strong tracks. — *Bill Dahl*

Living Chicago Blues, Vol. 5 / Oct. 17, 1990 / Alligator ✦✦✦✦

Living Chicago Blues, Vol. 6 / Oct. 17, 1990 / Alligator ✦✦✦

Lonesome Road Blues: 15 Years in the Mississippi Delta, 1926-1941 / Yazoo ✦✦✦✦
Tommy Johnson's influence is again here on *Lonesome Road Blues—15 Years in the Mississippi Delta,* which includes other fine pre-war Delta blues. — *Mark A. Humphrey*

Long Man Blues / Apr. 16, 1995 / Pearl Flapper ✦✦✦✦
Chicago blues obscurities from the '50s United/States vaults, including highlights Dennis Binder, Harold Burrage, Arbee Stidham, Jack Cooley, and Cliff Butler. — *Bill Dahl*

Louisiana Blues / 1970 / Arhoolie ✦✦✦✦
This is distinctive swamp blues by Henry Gray, Silas Hogan, Whispering Smith, and Guitar Kelley. — *Hank Davis*

Louisiana Scrapbook / 1987 / Rykodisc ✦✦✦
Contemporary Louisiana sounds were presented on this 18-track compilation, culled from various albums. While veteran stylists like Irma Thomas, Tuts Washington, and Johnny Adams were included, the disc contained cuts by other acts not so readily identified with the state (Marcia Ball) and sorely neglected artists (Phillip Walker, James Booker, Lonesome Sundown), as well as then-emerging stars (the Dirty Dozen Brass Band, Beausoleil) and both Zydeco (Buckwheat Zydeco) and Cajun performers (D.L. Menard, Jo-El Sonnier). — *Ron Wynn*

Low Blows: An Anthology of Chicago Harmonica Blues / 1994 / Rooster Blues ✦✦✦✦
Low Blows: An Anthology of Chicago Blues is a scatter-shot compilation of great early-'70s recordings by Chicago's better-known (Walter Horton, Carey Bell) and lesser-known (Big John Wrencher, Good Rockin' Charles Edwards) harmonica men. A missing chapter in blues history. — *Cub Koda*

☆ **Mama Let Me Lay It on You (1926-1936)** / Apr. 8, 1991 / Yazoo ✦✦✦✦✦
A fine collection of East Coast blues, including vintage Josh White, Pink Anderson, and guitarists Blind Blake and Willie Walker. — *Barry Lee Pearson*

Masters of Modern Blues / Testament ✦✦✦
This compilation of sides culled from three different sessions featuring Robert Nighthawk, Johnny Young, and Houston Stackhouse mark the first official recordings of Big John Wrencher. Although he's relegated to a sideman role here behind Nighthawk and Young, he appears on nine of the 18 tracks on this excellent collection. While the addition of a drummer would have placed the Nighthawk-Young-Wrencher trio in a less deliberate folk-blues setting, the music (which also includes Nighthawk's last session from 1967, playing bass behind Delta blues legend Houston Stackhouse with King Biscuit Boy drummer Peck Curtis) is just about as superb as one can expect from mid-'60s collector-oriented recordings, and helps to flesh out Wrencher's meager discography. — *Cub Koda*

Masters of the Delta Blues: The Friends of Charlie Patton / 1991 / Yazoo ✦✦✦✦
Subtitled "The Friends of Charlie Patton," this CD perfectly anthologizes some of the best and rarest tracks by early Delta Blues legends like Son House, Tommy Johnson, and Bukka White. Rough sounds in spots, but indispensable nonetheless. — *Cub Koda*

Matchbox Days / Mar. 25, 1997 / Big Beat ✦✦✦
The late-'60s British blues boom was dominated by electric blues-rock blues bands. Yet there was also an active acoustic blues scene, though it made considerably less commercial impact. Record-wise, much of the activity centered around the Matchbox label, on which the bulk of the music on this 22-track compilation was originally released. Jo-Ann Kelly and Dave Kelly are

the only names that might be remotely familiar to American listeners. There are also cuts by Wizz Jones, the Panama Limited Jug Band, Mike Cooper, and Ian Anderson (the Ian Anderson who now runs *Folk Roots* magazine, not the Ian Anderson from Jethro Tull), and others. White British blues sometimes takes quite a critical beating, but despite the fact that the guitar playing here is considerably more impressive than the singing, this is a perfectly respectable, very listenable compilation of an underappreciated facet of the British blues boom. The performances are sharp and committed, and there's a reasonable amount of variety, from the straight Delta blues derivations through the imaginative jug band revivalism of the Panama Limited Jug Band. Maybe you don't need many British '60s acoustic blues albums in your collection, but if you only want one, this would be a good choice. —*Richie Unterberger*

Mean Mothers, Vol. 1 / May 17, 1926-Aug. 17, 1949 / Rosetta ✦✦✦
The Rosetta label specializes in prebop recordings from jazz women. This LP, Rosetta's initial release, features 16 different singers interpreting lyrics that in one way or another claim their independence from unreliable men: Martha Copeland, Bessie Brown, Maggie Jones ("You Ain't Gonna Feed in My Pasture Now"), Susie Edwards, Bernice Edwards, Gladys Bentley, Mary Dixon, Bertha Idaho, Rosa Henderson, Harlem Hannah, Lil Armstrong, Blue Lou Barker ("I Don't Dig You Jack"), Rosetta Howard, Ida Cox, Lil Green (the original version of "Why Don't You Do Right"), and Billie Holiday ("Baby Get Lost"). The album is a good introduction to the classic blues singers of the '20s and '30s. —*Scott Yanow*

☆ **Mean Old World: The Blues from 1940 to 1994** / 1996 / Smithsonian Institution Press ✦✦✦✦
This four-disc set is just what you might expect from Smithsonian—comprehensive and well-conceived. It contains representative major blues figures for each time period for the years 1940 through 1994—everyone from Ma Rainey to Taj Mahal. For most periods, the selection is excellent. The only downside to this approach is that for time periods with great blues activity, some major artists have been dropped from the collection, while for other time periods with low blues activity, minor artists are included. This approach results in biographies and selections for artists like Earl Hooker, Big Walter Horton, and J.B. Hutto missing from the collection. Aside from the above complaint, this is the best collection for its size (four discs) that has been produced to date. The artists selected and the selections for each of the artists are in most cases excellent—the best of the best, so to speak. This is a veritable tour of the best in recorded blues. The 90-page liner notes by Larry Hoffman contain copious notes on the various selections, including artist biographies (and photos!), comments on the takes, etc.—perhaps the most thorough liner notes of their kind. The introductory essay focuses more on race relations than on the blues music. —*Michael Erlewine*

Memphis Masters: Early American Blues Classics / 1994 / Yazoo ✦✦✦
A companion to Yazoo's excellent *Mississippi Masters* collection, this time focusing on Memphis artists recorded between 1927 to 1934. The tracks collected here offer up a musical ambience that accurately depicts time and place with classic selections from acknowledged area kingpins Frank Stokes, Furry Lewis, Gus Cannon's Jug Stompers, Memphis Minnie, Joe McCoy, and Jack Kelly. Like its companion volume, this 20-track compilation is mastered direct from extremely rare old 78s—in some cases, the only copies known to exist—and the sound varies wildly from track to track. But the music is so great and of such major historical significance, the 78 surface noise that remains only seems to add to the charm and romance of it all. —*Cub Koda*

Mississippi Burnin' Blues, Vol. 2 / 1995 / Mardi Gras ✦✦
A collection of urban Delta blues from artists like Eddie Raspberry and Melvin "Smokehouse" Moore, *Mississippi Burnin' Blues, Vol. 2* is a fitfully entertaining disc, but it doesn't provide any true highlights. —*Thom Owens*

Mississippi Delta Blues Jam in Memphis, Vol. 1 / 1993 / Arhoolie ✦✦✦
Field recording from 1967-68 is best known for Robert Nighthawk. —*Bill Dahl*

Mississippi Delta Blues, Vol. 1: Blow My Blues Away / 1994 / Arhoolie ✦✦✦✦
George Mitchell still recorded several vibrant, distinctive Delta blues performances here. The artists he chronicled ranged from such legendary greats as Robert Nighthawk, Johnny Woods, and Fred McDowell to obscure but exciting performers such as Napoleon Strickland, Peck Curtis, and Do-Boy Dia-

mond. Their songs were quite simple; many were reworked tunes they had heard and/or played all their lives. They performed with no fanfare, sophisticated support to cover flaws, or pretension. The songs were about heartbreak, anguish, disappointment, and indignation, and sometimes about getting drunk, sexual potency, or whatever else came to mind. There are 12 unreleased cuts among these 23 numbers, and the mastering and notes provide an added bonus to this nice set. —*Ron Wynn*

☆ **Mississippi Girls** / Sep. 1991 / Story Of Blues ✦✦✦✦
This is an important collection, because it helps fill the gap in the recorded history of blueswomen who played and sang outside of the well-known sphere of the "classic singers" such as Ma Rainey and Bessie Smith. The highlights here are the two recordings of Mattie Delaney, a wonderful singer/guitarist about whom almost nothing is known. Fine also are the more rough-hewn offerings of Rosie Mae Moore who is accompanied by talented veterans Charlie McCoy and Ishmon Bracey. Although the Geechie Wiley/Elvie Thomas duets are marred by a scratchy background, they also are well worth hearing. —*Larry Hoffman*

Mister Charlie's Blues: 1926-1938 / Oct. 9, 1992 / Yazoo ✦✦✦
A fascinating exploration of blues-drenched, pre-war hillbilly recordings includes the great fingerpicked guitar of Sam McGee. —*Mark A. Humphrey*

Modern Blues Legends / Jan. 16, 1996 / ORC ✦✦✦
Modern Blues Legends is a solid collection of some of the most popular blues-rock artists of the late '80s and '90s. Featuring favorites like Johnny Winter, Robben Ford, Buddy Guy, Danny Gatton, and the Fabulous Thunderbirds, the album might lean to heavily on rock influences—Big Head Todd & the Monsters and Paul Rodgers contribute tracks, after all—but the music is fine and the disc does give a good feeling of the era. —*Stephen Thomas Erlewine*

● **Modern Chicago Blues** / Testament ✦✦✦✦
Producer Pete Welding made many recordings for Testament in the early- and mid-'60s at the start of the blues revival, and this is a grab bag of 21 tracks he recorded in Chicago between 1962 and 1966. This isn't post-war Chicago blues as many listeners picture the form. Only four of the cuts have drums, and not all of them are electric; it's more like a document of country blues getting citified, rather than the full electric Chicago band sound. The actual music—mixing performances by well-known figures like Robert Nighthawk and Big Walter Horton with unknowns like Wilbert Jenkins and John Lee Granderson—is respectable, but won't excite many listeners other than hardcore devotees. There are some nice moments on the way, though, like Maxwell Street Jimmy's fine variation of John Lee Hooker's "Dimples," and the roll and tumble sound of Johnny Young (the only musician here to use a drummer). The CD reissue adds five previously unreleased tracks. —*Richie Unterberger*

Mojo Workin': Blues for Next Generation / Oct. 7, 1997 / Sony ✦✦✦
This is a 16-track sampler from various entries in Columbia's *Mojo Workin'* series, which gets pared down to a one-big-hit-per-artist format, starting with Robert Johnson's "Cross Road Blues" and Memphis Minnie's "When the Levee Breaks" and finishing up with Stevie Ray Vaughan's "Texas Flood" and Keb' Mo's "Am I Wrong." The stopping-off points in between include entries from Muddy Waters ("The Blues Had a Baby and They Named It Rock'n' Roll"), Blind Boy Fuller ("Rag Mama Rag"), Blind Willie McTell ("Southern Can Is Mine"), Blind Willie Johnson ("Motherless Children"), and Bessie Smith ("It Makes My Love Come Down"), along with more modern tracks from Taj Mahal ("Last Fair Deal Gone Down"), the Electric Flag ("Killing Floor") and Johnny Winter ("Johnny B. Goode"). Perhaps not so surprisingly, this mixing of time frames, styles and divergent approaches to the blues makes for some fine listening, as well as making this a nice entry-level disc. —*Cub Koda*

Mojo Workin': The Best of Ace Blues / 1995 / Ace ✦✦✦✦
This 20-track collection puts together essential tracks by some of the biggest names in the genre. Elmore James, John Lee Hooker, Smokey Hogg, B.B. King, Slim Harpo, Albert King, Lowell Fulson, Lonesome Sundown, Howlin' Wolf, Johnny "Guitar" Watson, Arthur Gunter, Lazy Lester, Pee Wee Crayton, Ike Turner, and Lazy Lester are all represented by at least one track apiece and, in most cases, some of their representative work. A pretty great primer that serves not only as something of a greatest-hits package for the novice, but as just plain great listening for the hardliners as well. —*Cub Koda*

New Bluebloods / 1987 / Alligator ✦✦✦✦
An attempt to document "the next generation of Chicago blues," this is generally a very exciting and successful collection, including the Kinsey Report, Lil' Ed and the Blues Imperials, Valerie Wellington, and several more. — *Niles J. Frantz*

New Orleans Blues: Troubles Troubles / Feb. 14, 1992 / Rounder ✦✦✦✦
This is a sampler of late-'50s and early-'60s Ric and Ron label music by Edgar Blanchard, Mercy Baby, and Eddie Lang. — *Hank Davis*

New Orleans Jazz & Heritage Festival: 1976 / 1976 / Rhino ✦✦✦
This features Hopkins live on three tracks, playing a Stratocaster, raw and distorted, dragging a rhythm section by the scruff of the neck. Worth it for these three tracks alone. — *Cub Koda*

News & the Blues: Telling It Like It Is / Feb. 1991 / Columbia ✦✦✦✦
Like any form of popular music, the blues has reflected the social conditions of the times, sometimes quite explicitly. *News & the Blues* offers 20 songs from the Columbia vaults from between 1927 and 1947. The Depression is reflected often, as expected, but there are also songs about natural disasters, public figures like Joe Louis, World War II, and even the atomic bomb. Memphis Minnie and Bill Gaither even take the step of recording specific tributes to other blues singers (Ma Rainey and Leroy Carr respectively). Many of the performers are well-known—Bessie Smith, Mississippi John Hurt, Big Bill Broonzy, Charlie Patton, Memphis Minnie, Bukka White—and several others are unknown to any but blues scholars (Jack Kelly, Homer Harris, Alfred Fields). Like several of Columbia's anthologies that are loosely grouped under a theme, you don't necessarily have to have a keen interest in the album concept to appreciate the music, which is an above-average gathering of early blues tracks of various styles. — *Richie Unterberger*

Old Town Blues, Vol. 1: Downtown Sides / 1993 / Ace ✦✦✦
Twenty-two blues tracks recorded in the '50s for New York's Old Town label, most of which were unissued at the time. The core of this anthology is the 11 songs by Sonny Terry & Brownie McGhee, who do electrified city blues with an audible influence from Chicago performers like Bo Diddley and Jimmy Reed. It's not the style they're most renowned for, perhaps, but the results are pretty good. The rest of the CD is a hodgepodge of miscellany, including decent raw electric blues from James Wayne, fairly anonymous sides by Little Willie and Bob Gaddy, and a couple of rare Willie Dixon items from an unissued acetate of demos. — *Richie Unterberger*

Orig. American Folk Blues Festival / 1962 / PolyGram ✦✦✦✦
Recorded live in a studio in Hamburg, Germany, in October 1962. Includes artists involved with that year's American Folk Blues Festival tour, with generally relaxed and reflective performances. The artists include T-Bone Walker, Sonny Terry, and John Lee Hooker. — *Cub Koda*

Original Blues Classics / Apr. 16, 1995 / Original Blues Classics ✦✦✦
This 15-track compilation serves as a fine sampler of the OBC label. Included are "Trouble in Mind" (King Curtis), "I've Got Mine" (Pink Anderson), "The Dyin' Crapshooter's Blues" (Blind Willie McTell), and "Say No to the Devil" (Rev. Gary Davis). — *Roundup Newsletter*

Out of the Blue [Rykodisc] / 1985 / Rykodisc ✦✦✦✦
A 17-cut sampler of some of Rounder's blues and blues-related releases of the period, it features "straight" blues from J.B. Hutto, Phillip Walker, and Johnny Copeland; blues-rock from the Nighthawks and George Thorogood; soulful blues from Johnny Adams and Ted Hawkins; plus cuts from Buckwheat Zydeco, piano-great James Booker, John Hammond, Solomon Burke, and several more. The Adams, Walker, and Copeland cuts are particularly nice, as is one entry from Marcia Ball and the Legendary Blues Band. — *Niles J. Frantz*

Paint It Blue: Songs of the Rolling Stones / Oct. 14, 1997 / A&M ✦✦✦
The idea behind *Paint It Blue: Songs of the Rolling Stones* is such a simple, appealing one that it's a wonder that the record wasn't made before 1997. The Stones never made any secret of their debt to the blues, so it makes sense that their songs would sound good when performed by blues and R&B artists. That's the idea behind *Paint It Blue*—contemporary blues and R&B artists sing some of the band's bluesiest songs. While some may quibble that the idea is a little too cute, the performances by Luther Allison ("You Can't Always Get What You Want"), Junior Wells ("(I Can't Get No) Satisfaction"), Taj Mahal ("Honky Tonk Women"), Clarence "Gatemouth" Brown ("Ventila-

tor Blues"), the Holmes Bros. ("Beast of Burden"), and Bobby Womack ("It's All Over Now"), among many others, are hard to argue with. It's a rock-solid record that confirms what great songwriters Mick Jagger and Keith Richards are. — *Stephen Thomas Erlewine*

Planet Blues: the World of Blues-Rock / 1993 / Rhythm Safari ✦✦✦
There are so many blues anthologies and samplers currently available that most, if not all, of the music contained here can be found elsewhere. The disc succeeds in its objective—to show the links between urban blues and modern rock. Indeed, songs like Eric Clapton's "Tribute To Elmore" or Canned Heat's "Dimple" are literally electric blues done by rockers. Likewise, the Bo Diddley, Howlin' Wolf, and Muddy Waters numbers were blueprints fully studied and absorbed by the entire first wave of British invaders. These are fun tracks and worth having, whether you get them here or somewhere else. — *Ron Wynn*

☆ **Play My Juke Box: East Coast Blues (1943-1954)** / Nov. 28, 1995 / Flyright ✦✦✦✦✦
Bruce Bastin's English Flyright label—only one of the magnificent tributaries of his Interstate Music Company—has consistently demonstrated a union of fine scholarship and great music. This collection of mostly little-known East Coast blues artists is no exception. There are seven tracks of singer/guitarists, four harp/guitar duets, four piano/guitar pairings, two guitar duos, and one arresting cut featuring three harps plus vocals. Artists such as Skoodle-Dum-Doo & Sheffield, Boy Green, Robert Lee Westmoreland, Marilyn Scott, and Sonny Jones serve up a startling reminder of all the amazing talent that has gone unrecognized over the years. — *Larry Hoffman*

Pot, Spoon, Pipe and Jug / May 19, 1924-Dec. 1975 / Stash ✦✦✦
The Stash label made its original reputation by releasing around a dozen LPs filled with mostly little-known vintage recordings of jazz and blues artists discussing (often in veiled ways) drugs and sex. This album sticks to the former and is (with two exceptions) from the 1927-41 period. Highlights include a test-pressing version of Cab Calloway's classic "Kickin' the Gong Around," Cab's famous "Reefer Man," Stuff Smith's humorous "You'se a Viper," Lil Green's "Knockin' Myself Out" and Blue Lu Barker's "Don't You Make Me High." — *Scott Yanow*

Prime Chops: Blind Pig Sampler / 1990 / Blind Pig ✦✦✦✦
A 14-track sampler, it has a variety of contemporary blues sounds. — *Niles J. Frantz*

Prime Chops: Blind Pig Sampler, Vol. 2 / 1993 / Blind Pig ✦✦✦
Plenty of choice blues, roots rock, gospel, and zydeco. You can sample 19 tracks from the Blind Pig catalogue at a budget price here, including Jimmy Thackery and the Drivers, Joanna Connor, Roy Rogers, Little Mike and the Tornadoes, and more…— *Roch Parisien*

RCA Victor Blues & Rhythm Revue / Dec. 1987 / RCA ✦✦✦✦
A great 25-cut cross-section of Nipper's R&B activities 1940-59, the set includes everyone from Count Basie to Little Richard to the Dew Droppers to the Isley Brothers. — *Bill Dahl*

Rare Chicago Blues / May 1, 1993 / Bullseye Blues ✦✦✦
Recorded between 1962 and 1968 by Norman Dayron, *Rare Chicago Blues* is an enthralling collection of rare blues from artists like Otis Spann, Little Brother Montgomery, Big Joe Williams, and Robert Pete Williams, as well as several others. Captured live in clubs and on the street, these tracks give a good taste of what real, gritty urban blues sounded like in the '60s and is worthwhile for true blues aficionados. — *Stephen Thomas Erlewine*

Rare Country Blues / Jun. 2, 1994 / Document ✦✦✦
This is an enjoyable trip into the lesser-known recesses of pre-World War II blues, covering artists who didn't record enough to justify separate CDs of their own. Opening with a pair of tracks by Virginia-born Seth Richard, including his kazoo-highlighted signature tune "Skoodeldum-Doo," it leads us to four extraordinarily dexterous solo guitar, songster-type numbers by Memphis-based, Texas-born Charlie Kyle, to the sole known song by the mystery-shrouded guitarist/singer "Freezone." Most of this material is fairly primitive, having been recorded in the late '20s, but the sound is anything but—Document has given us a pretty clean account of most of the early stuff, a match for any company's reissues of material from this era; only Freezone's side (from Paramount, of course) is somewhat substandard. Willie Harris' four numbers may have been done in Chicago, and feature a prominent

piano (likely played by Charles Avery), but his style shows off his Mississippi roots, especially the slide playing. Leola Manning's six songs present religious lyrics in a blues setting, sung in a style resembling Memphis Minnie's, and anticipating the kind of hybrid performing that bluesmen-turned-ministers Gary Davis and others turned toward in the '60s. Jazzbo Tommy Settlers' eight songs, dating from 1937, are the most acquired taste here—the first four are Paramount titles and suffer from abysmal sound, coupled with the fact that they are dominated by the kazoo, while the second four, issued by ARC, are of significantly better quality and feature a full band, with piano and guitar. The latter are the choice parts of Settlers' output. — *Bruce Eder*

Raunchy Business: Hot Nuts & Lollypops / Aug. 1991 / Columbia ♦♦♦♦
This sex-based set of early blues-oriented recordings has 19 double entendre songs and a humorous (and quite profane) "alternate" version of Lucille Bogan's "Shave 'em Dry" that still could not be played on the radio. Among the performers are Lil Johnson, Lonnie Johnson, Barrel House Annie, Bo Carter, and Buddy Moss. With titles such as "Sam the Hot Dog Man," "The Best Jockey in Town," "If It Don't Fit, Don't Force It," "Banana In Your Fruit Basket" and "You Got to Give Me Some of It," the subject matter is easy to figure out. — *Scott Yanow*

The Real Blues Brothers / 1987 / DCC ♦♦♦♦
This is a nice Vee-Jay collection with representative cuts from Pee Wee Crayton, John Lee Hooker, Jimmy Reed, Lightnin' Hopkins, Billy Boy Arnold, Memphis Slim, and a stray track from Brownie McGhee and Sonny Terry. The big ticket for collectors on this one, however, is the inexplicable bonus of a previously unissued Eddie Taylor number, "Leave This Neighborhood," reason enough for hardcore fans to want to add this one to the collection. — *Cub Koda*

Reefer Madness / Feb. 8, 1924-1944 / Stash ♦♦♦
By the time Stash came out with this LP, its 20th release, one would think that the label had run out of vintage drug and sex songs to reissue. However the quality of these performances is still pretty high and, although some of the musicians were quite obscure, there are also selections from Cow Cow Davenport, Buck Washington, Louis Armstrong (1928's "Muggles"), Mills Blue Rhythm Band, Mezz Mezzrow, Fats Waller, and Django Reinhardt. This collection is not essential but remains quite fun. — *Scott Yanow*

Reefer Songs: Original Jazz & Blues Vocals / Jun. 17, 1932-Nov. 2, 1945 / Stash ♦♦♦♦
This LP was the very first release by the Stash label and, as with its first dozen or so collections, it features vintage material that deals with illicit subject matter. Many of the marijuana and drug-based recordings here are on this set including Stuff Smith's "Here Comes the Man with the Jive" (which features some hot Jonah Jones trumpet), Trixie Smith's "Jack I'm Mellow," Barney Bigard's "Sweet Marijuana Brown" (which has Art Tatum on piano), Andy Kirk's "All the Jive Is Gone," and Harry "The Hipster" Gibson's classic "Who Put the Benzedrine in Mrs. Murphy's Ovaltine?" Other performers include Cab Calloway, Benny Goodman, Buster Bailey, Sidney Bechet, the Harlem Hamfats, Chick Webb, and Clarence Williams. Some of this material has since been reissued on CD but the original set is still the best. — *Scott Yanow*

☆ **Riot in Blues** / Oct. 25, 1990 / Mobile Fidelity ♦♦♦♦♦
Excellent Lightnin' Hopkins, Sonny Terry, Brownie McGhee, James Wayne, and early Ray Charles scat singing. Partially field-recorded by Bob Shad in the early '50s. The best cuts include "Wayne's Junco Partner" and "Hopkins' Buck Dance Boogie." — *Barry Lee Pearson*

Risky Blues (R&B) / 1971 / King ♦♦♦♦
Old King LP boasting ribald early-'50s jump blues by Wynonie Harris, Bull Moose Jackson, etc. — *Bill Dahl*

Roots 'N' Blues: The Retrospective 1925-1950 / Jun. 30, 1992 / Columbia/ Legacy ♦♦♦♦
Roots 'n' Blues: the Retrospective presents five hours of music over four discs, covering the traditional recordings made by Columbia Records and its associated labels from 1925 to 1950. As an all-inclusive survey of American roots music, this set is an invaluable library piece and a good reference, but where this collection really stands out is in its presentation. The collection does a better service than the more academic studies by including a variety of styles—including early string band recordings, spirituals, jugbands, blues, cajun, and country music, mixing the better known artists with the more

obscure—in the end, the diversity makes for good listening as well as a good learning experience. — *Chris Woodstra*

Roots of Rhythm & Blues: A Tribute to the Robert Johnson Era / Sep. 1, 1992 / Columbia/Legacy ♦♦♦♦
This live program featured some of the late legend's old partners—Honeyboy Edwards, Johnny Shines, Robert Jr. Lockwood—and some of his contemporary successors, such as Lionel Pitchford and Cephas & Wiggins paying heartfelt tribute. — *Bill Dahl*

☆ **Roots of Robert Johnson** / 1990 / Yazoo ♦♦♦♦♦
Robert Johnson's small body of recordings have become almost larger than life. Many novice listeners probably think the Delta blues began and ended with him. This 14-song collection traces the origins of Johnson's music, uncovering the roots of his tormented, anguished lyrics, and the origins of his wildly influential guitar style. Some of the finest songs by luminaries like Skip James, Charlie Patton, Son House, Kokomo Arnold, and Lonnie Johnson are included. It's not only of use for Johnson archivists but for anyone interested in the greatest pre-war Delta blues. — *Bruce Boyd Raeburn*

Roots of the Blues / 1977 / New World ♦♦♦
This fine concept recording by Alan Lomax compares an American and a Senegalese (Africa) holler. It also includes elements of work songs, Black string bands, church music, and other styles that fed into the blues before moving on to early blues styles themselves. The rarity of most of the cuts would make this a gem, even without Lomax's analysis. — *David L. Mayers*

Sacred Steel Guitar / Jan. 21, 1997 / Arhoolie ♦♦♦♦
This is one amazing collection. Subtitled "Traditional Sacred African-American Steel Guitar Music in Florida," this multi-artist chronicling of this seldom-heard genre is a musical and emotional delight. The electric lap steel guitar has been the instrument of choice in both the Jewel Dominion and Keith Dominions (both African American Holiness-Pentecostal churches) since the late '30s, replacing the traditional church organist. This collection showcases the pioneering work of five of its best known and most influential sacred steel practitioners: Willie Eason, Sonny Treadway, Glenn Lee, Henry Nelson, and his son, Aubrey Ghent. Their individual approaches to this style range from crude blues-based slides and slurs (blues table steel master Hop Wilson is called to mind more than once here) to highly technical flourishes bordering on country pedal steel sounds, with all of it played with a sincerity and spirit indigenous to the music, which is nothing short of heartfelt and energetic. Split evenly between instrumentals and the instrument interfacing with the congregation and choir at live religious services, the music runs the gamut from still and beautiful (Sonny Treadway's instrumentals) to the wild and abandoned playing of Aubrey Ghent. This is 75 minutes of music that will appeal to blues and gospel and even retro-minded rock 'n' roll fans willing to take the time to explore this fascinating genre. — *Cub Koda*

St. Louis Blues (1929-1935) / Sep. 30, 1991 / Yazoo ♦♦♦
More fine pre-war blues. — *Mark A. Humphrey*

The Shouters / Savoy ♦♦♦
'40s and '50s jump blues from Gatemouth Moore, H-Bomb Ferguson, Eddie Mack, and Nappy Brown, whose scorching rockers are among the highlights of this two-LP set. — *Bill Dahl*

Shoutin' Swingin' & Makin' Love / Apr. 9, 1991 / MCA ♦♦♦♦
Included are Jimmy Witherspoon, Al Hibbler, and other urbane blues-jazz belters in full cry on Chess. — *Mark A. Humphrey*

Sissy Man Blues: Str't & Gay Blues / 1989 / Vintage Jazz ♦♦♦
Twenty-five straight and gay blues from 1924-1941 are featured by various artists. — *Jas Obrecht*

The Slide Guitar: Bottles, Knives, & Steel, Vol. 1 / Feb. 1991 / Columbia/ Legacy ♦♦♦♦
This CD is a hodgepodge sampling of blues records featuring mostly prewar slide guitarists ranging from the simplicity of Barbecue Bob (who was much better-known as a pianist) and Sylvester Weaver to the sophistication of Blind Willie McTell (backing Ruth Willis on "Experience Blues") and Tampa Red. Among the highlights are Blind Willie Johnson's wordless "Dark Was the Night" and Tampa Red's goodtime "You Can't Get That Stuff No More," and also featured are Charley Patton, Blind Boy Fuller, Leadbelly, Casey Bill Weldon, Buddy Woods, Robert Johnson, Bukka White, Sister O.M. Terrell, and Son House. With the exception of two later cuts, all of the music

(which includes a pair of previously unreleased selections) dates from 1927-40. An interesting if not quite essential sampler. — *Scott Yanow*

Slide Guitar: Bottles, Knives, & Steel, Vol. 2 / Feb. 1991 / Columbia/Legacy ✦✦✦
This is another excellent volume of various styles of blues slide guitar from Columbia's *Roots & Blues* series. — *AMG*

Slidin' . . . Some Slide / 1948-1993 / Rounder ✦✦✦
Rounder's recent anthology of vintage and modern slide guitar playing is neither a disposable batch of recent hits nor merely a showcase for guitar freaks; it is a wonderful collection documenting the way bottleneck and slide styles have evolved. The sampler contains classics from Muddy Waters, Elmore James, Earl Hooker, J.B. Hutto, Hop Wilson, and Hound Dog Taylor that are either transcendent or delightful. They have also chosen songs from contemporary acts that demonstrate real craft and appreciation for the style; George Thorogood's nearly eight-minute workout on "Delaware Slide" and Sonny Landreth's "Zydeco Shuffle" are grinding, stunning treatments. This is one sampler with real musical and historical value. — *Ron Wynn*

Smackin' That Wax: the Kangaroo Records Story . . . / Nov. 30, 1992 / Collectables ✦✦✦✦
Obscure but solid '50s and '60s Texas blues and R&B, it includes a very early Albert Collins single. — *Bill Dahl*

Sorry But: Women's RR Blues / Dec. 4, 1923-Feb. 9, 1942 / Rosetta ✦✦✦
Subtitled "Women's Railroad Blues," this LP consists of 15 songs that feature female vocalists singing about trains. Often the subject matter has to do with boyfriends who were able to escape the South while the females were stuck home. Although there is a certain amount of repetition, there are many rarities on this album with generally fine performances from Trixie Smith, Clara Smith, Bessie Smith, Ada Brown, Sippie Wallace, Martha Copeland, Bessie Jackson, Lucille Bogan, Blue Lou Barker, Sister Rosetta Tharpe, and Nora Lee King. An interesting set with colorful liner notes. — *Scott Yanow*

The Soul of Chicago / 1993 / Shanachie ✦✦✦✦
Distinguished gospel music critic, author, producer, and label executive Anthony Heilbut has provided many wonderful anthologies. For this one, he has taken 11 surviving artists from the golden age and recorded them in a traditional setting with their familiar spare backings (mostly piano, guitar, and organ). The results are both impressive and memorable; Robert Anderson, Delois Barrett Campbell, Rev. Samuel Patterson, Gladys Beamon Gregory and the Gay Family, among others, don't just sound good, but almost as fabulous as they did in their heyday. They have the spirit just as if they were performing and recording all the time, yet many of them have not sung regularly in decades. The quality of this masterful session blows most contemporary gospel out of the water. — *Ron Wynn*

The Soul of R&B Revue: Live at the Lonestar Roadhouse / Dec. 1992 / Shanachie ✦✦✦
OK recreation of '60s soul sound. — *Bill Dahl*

The Soul of Texas Blues Women: Good 'Ol Texas 60s Soul and Blues / 1991 / Collectables ✦✦✦
This very interesting, although uneven collection includes female blues and soul vocalists recorded between 1961 and 1970. — *Niles J. Frantz*

● **The Sound of the Delta** / Jun. 1966 / Testament ✦✦✦✦
Blues scholar Pete Welding assembled these 19 recordings—most solo, all acoustic, most prominently featuring guitar and vocal—between 1963 and 1965, just as the blues revival was gathering steam. This isn't the best Delta blues compilation, as an introduction or a general sampler. If you can't get enough of the stuff, though, it certainly stands up well. Big Joe Williams and Fred McDowell are the only well-known performers, but the others—obscure names like Arthur Weston and the delightfully raw-voiced Ruby McCoy—are generally in the same league. It's well-recorded, and contains a reasonable variety of styles. The CD reissue adds bonus tracks by Williams and Avery Brady that were not included on the original version. — *Richie Unterberger*

☆ **Sounds of the South** / Jul. 20, 1993 / Atlantic ✦✦✦✦✦
This compilation gathers some of the finest of musicologist Alan Lomax's field recordings together on four CDs. What is preserved are examples of American music not broadly documented: field hollers and folk tales, prison

work songs and hardcore banjo breakdowns. This is an important collection that offers rewards for every kind of music lover. — *Tim Sheridan*

Southern Blues / Savoy ✦✦✦✦
A wide-ranging '50s blues/R&B two-LP set, including Billy Wright, John Lee Hooker, Huey Smith, and Earl King. — *Bill Dahl*

Southern Rhythm & Rock / Rhino ✦✦✦
Southern Rhythm & Rock (The Best of Excello Records—Vol. 2) is the second volume of the Excello Records collection, with its companion *Sound of the Swamp*. This volume rounds up some wild and woolly R&B obscurities. — *John Floyd*

1929-1937 / 1989 / Story Of Blues ✦✦✦
St. Louis' red-light district became a magnet for many of the greatest blues pianists and singers of the era. This 19-track CD features many of the best of them. Well-known and accomplished ticklers such as Roosevelt Sykes, Henry Brown, Aaron "Pinetop" Sparks, and the High Sheriff himself, Peetie Wheatstraw, play host to singers such as Mary Johnson, Elizabeth Johnson, Dorotha Trowbridge, and Alice Moore—who, despite their relative obscurity, are quite talented and turn in more than a few minor classics. Spicing the instrumental mix are trombonist Ike Rodgers and guitarist Lonnie Johnson. Despite the poor sound quality of the first four tracks, this music is well-chosen and highly recommended. — *Larry Hoffman*

The Stax Blues Brothers / 1970 / Stax ✦✦✦✦
A decent collection of Stax blues artists of the '70s, it includes Albert King, Johnnie Taylor, and others. — *Dan Heilman*

Stax Blues Mast / Jul. 1, 1991 / Stax ✦✦✦
A decent overview of Stax blues artists; inferior to individual records by Albert King and Little Milton. — *Ron Wynn*

Stone Rock Blues / 1994 / Chess ✦✦✦
"The original recordings of songs covered by the Rolling Stones" is understandably heavy on the blues, R&B, and early rock 'n' roll chestnuts they gleaned from Chess Records. Chuck Berry and Muddy Waters are, unsurprisingly, the most heavily represented artists here; seven Chuck tunes, five by Muddy (one of which, "Rollin' Stone," wasn't actually recorded by the Stones, but is included because it inspired their name). This 18-song collection is filled out by a couple of Bo Diddley tracks, Howlin' Wolf's "Little Red Rooster," and three songs outside of Chess' black music axis: Dale Hawkins' rockabilly classic "Suzie Q," Buddy Holly's "Not Fade Away" (which of course relied heavily on the Bo Diddley beat), and Arthur Alexander's early soul ballad "You Better Move On." What this collection doesn't have are the early soul classics by Otis Redding, Sam Cooke, Wilson Pickett, Marvin Gaye, and more obscure singers like Barbara Lynn and Gene Allison that formed another vital component of their early cover material. It's missing a few stray tracks by Slim Harpo, Rufus Thomas, Hank Snow, Larry Williams, and others that were covered by the Stones on their early albums. And it doesn't have Berry's "Let It Rock," which was available (albeit briefly) on a British maxi-single in the early '70s. But Chuck, Muddy, and Bo were their greatest influences, when you get down to it, and this is a handy basic primer of the blueprints for the Stones' early repertoire, with decent liner notes. — *Richie Unterberger*

★ **Storefront & Streetcorner Gospel (1927-1929)** / Jun. 2, 1994 / Document ✦✦✦✦✦
Assembling the complete recorded works of A.C. & Blind Mamie Forehand, Washington Phillips and Luther Magby, *Storefront and Streetcorner Gospel (1927-1929)* offers a fascinating glimpse into the kind of spiritual music commonly heard throughout the urban areas of the south during the last years of the pre-Depression era. The common thread among these performers is their choice of unusual accompaniment—the Dallas-based Phillips is backed by the dolceola, an ethereal variant of the dulcimer, while the Forehands employ antique cymbals and Magby uses a harmonium; little or nothing is known about the various artists, yet their music still packs a punch all these decades later. — *Jason Ankeny*

☆ **The Story of the Blues** / Jan. 1, 1995 / Columbia ✦✦✦✦✦
An excellent blues sampler, it ranges from pre-war to the '60s, offering a broader palette of "shades of blue" than most. — *Mark A. Humphrey*

Straight and Gay / Dec. 10, 1924-Jun. 30, 1941 / Stash ✦✦✦
The Stash label had, by the release of this LP in 1979, almost totally ex-

hausted its collection of vintage recordings dealing with the subject matters of drug and sex. However with titles such as "Anybody Here Want to Try My Cabbage" (featuring singer Maggie Jones accompanied by Louis Armstrong), "Take Your Hand Off It," "Sissy Man," and "Two Old Maids in a Folding Bed," there were obviously still a few fiery titles left to be reissued. Highlights include Sippie Wallace's famous "I'm a Mighty Tight Woman" and Victoria Spivey's initial recording "Black Snake Blues"; the other important performers are Lonnie Johnson, Lil Johnson, Washboard Sam, Mae Glover, Blanche Calloway, the Hokum Boys, Papa Charlie Jackson, Josh White, Ma Rainey (with Doc Cheatham on soprano in 1926), Monette Moore, Blind Willie McTell, and Lucille Bogan. — *Scott Yanow*

Streetwalking Blues / Dec. 9, 1924-1956 / Stash ♦♦♦
One of many Stash LPs that reissued vintage recordings dealing with sexual topics, this album has performances by many fine blues and jazz singers including Memphis Minnie, Maggie Jones ("Good Time Flat Blues" with Louis Armstrong), Virginia Liston, Lil Johnson, Sam Theard, Billie Pierce (from 1956), Clarence Williams, Lonnie Johnson (1941's "Crowin' Rooster Blues"), Georgia White, Ma Rainey, Clara Smith, Irene Scruggs, Bertha "Chippie" Hill, and Lucille Bogan. With titles such as "I've Got What It Takes," "I'm in the Racket," "Kitchen Mechanic Blues," and "Shave 'Em Dry," one gets the idea what this album is about pretty quickly. Most of these formerly rare performances (some of which have been reissued by Stash on their Jass subsidiary) are quite enjoyable. — *Scott Yanow*

Sun Records Harmonica Classics / 1990 / Rounder ♦♦♦♦
Brilliant compilation of Blues sides cut at the Sun studios in the early '50s, featuring indispensable tracks by Walter Horton ("Easy" being one of the greatest harmonica instrumentals of all time), Joe Hill Louis, and Doctor Ross. — *Cub Koda*

Sun Records: The Blues Years / Charly ♦♦♦♦
Gigantic nine record box with a 44 page booklet, this comes the closest to documenting the wide breadth of blues recordings done by Sam Phillips at the Sun studios in Memphis during the early '50s. A landmark achievement. — *Cub Koda*

Superblues: All-Time Classic Blues Hits, Vol.1 / 1990 / Stax ♦♦♦♦♦
The three-volume *Superblues* series may not have enough rare/unusual items for the collector, or enough of a solid connecting thread for the more general listener. For those who just want a varied assortment of top-notch blues (mostly from the '50s and '60s) in their collection, though, they're good deals. They cover a pretty wide territory of both top blues stars and lesser-known singers, and draw more from urban R&B—and jump blues-influenced cuts than most similar compilations. They also have generous playing times, and offer enough liner notes to provide a context for non-experts. Vol.1 has classics by B.B. King, Ike & Tina Turner, Jimmy Reed, Koko Taylor, Bobby "Blue" Bland, Albert King, Little Milton, Howlin' Wolf, and others. — *Richie Unterberger*

Superblues: All-Time Classic Blues Hits, Vol.2 / 1991 / Stax ♦♦♦♦
More soul and R&B influences are heard on this volume than the first, though it's not a detriment. The 18 tracks include prize items by Guitar Slim, Lloyd Price, Lowell Fulson, Elmore James, and Sonny Boy Williamson, with some bluesy Southern soul by O.V. Wright and Johnnie Taylor. Also has some little-anthologized gems, most notably Gene Allison's "You Can Make It If You Try" (covered by the Rolling Stones on their first album) and Jimmy Hughes' magnificent bluesy soul ballad, "Steal Away." — *Richie Unterberger*

Superblues: All-Time Classic Blues Hits, Vol. 3 / 1995 / Stax ♦♦♦♦
Another solid outing in the *Superblues* series. The 19 cuts include classics by Little Walter, Elmore James, Jimmy Reed, and Billy Boy Arnold ("I Wish You Would"); vintage jump blues by Jimmy Liggins, Joe Liggins, and Camille Howard; and soul blues by Little Johnny Taylor and Little Milton. This has a significantly higher percentage of obscure names than the previous two volumes, with worthy items (some of which were one-shot R&B hits) by Mercy Dee Walton, Larry Dale, Eddie Taylor, Larry Birdsong, Larry Davis, Ted Taylor, Frankie Lee Sims, and others. — *Richie Unterberger*

Sweet Home Chicago / Nov. 1988 / Delmark ♦♦♦♦
Solid '60s sides by Magic Sam, Eddie Shaw, Luther Allison, and Louis Myers. — *Bill Dahl*

Talkin' Trash / 1990 / Greasy ♦♦♦
A very obscure R&B compilation with great irreverent jump and jivey blues from 1954-1963. The title cut is worth the price, but check out "Your Wire's Been Tapped" and "Roll Dem Bones." — *Richard Meyer*

A Taste of the Blues, Vol. 1 / 1993 / Vee-Jay ♦♦♦♦
At 25 tracks, 69-minutes of running time, and musician-historian Billy Vera doing the compilation, there's little to quibble about here, as all the selections are first-rate. Kicking off with the one-two punch of Jimmy Reed's "Boogie in the Dark" and Eddie Taylor's "Bad Boy," other highlights include J.B. Lenoir's thinly veiled rewrite of Ray Charles' classic ("Do What I Say"), the hopelessly obscure Morris Pejoe's "Hurt My Feelings," while Billy (The Kid) Emerson's "Every Woman I Know (Is Crazy About an Automobile)" just may be one of the finest car songs of all time. Add to the mix Snooky Pryor's "Judgement Day," a pair of Elmore James classics (the original versions of "It Hurts Me Too" and "The 12 Year Old Boy"), Billy Boy Arnold's "Rockinitis," John Lee Hooker's Live at Newport performance of "Tupelo," and Pee Wee Crayton's scorching guitar solo on "The Telephone Is Ringing," and you have a compilation that's mighty hard to beat. Sound quality on all this is first-rate, thanks to the digital-remastering work of Bob Fisher. — *Cub Koda*

A Taste of the Blues, Vol. 2 / Oct. 1993 / Vee-Jay ♦♦♦♦
A 26 track comp of more obscure and rare Vee-Jay sides, this time featuring a previously unissued Snooky Pryor track, "You Tried To Ruin Me." Also includes tracks from Elmore James, Eddie Taylor, and Pee Wee Crayton, plus the added bonus of the first time CD issue of Jimmy Reed's "I'm Gonna Ruin You." — *Cub Koda*

Testament Records Sampler / 1995 / Testament ♦♦♦
This covers the story of Pete Welding's Testament blues label (now being brought to compact disc via Hightone Records), inspired by Delmark Records and driven by a desire just to get great blues recordings onto the market. This story is told both in this 23-track CD sampler and in the liner notes by Welding, who explains that he didn't care, when he started the label, whether or not it was commercially successful—his job paid well enough. Testament proceeded to release a stream of amazing blues and R&B albums over the years, ranging from an anthology of Southern black fife and drum bands all the way to roaring electric blues that'll set fire to the hair in your ears. This sampler is 72 minutes of amazing selections from 23 different albums, and if you're a blues fan unfamiliar with Testament's CD releases, it may very well present a danger to your bank account. The sampler itself is priced cheaply enough to present a temptation, and you should let yourself be tempted. — *Steven McDonald*

Texas Blues [Arhoolie] / 1992 / Arhoolie ♦♦♦♦
This excellent collection features eight little-known blues artists who recorded for Bill Quinn's Gold Star label in Houston. There are 27 tracks in all—split unequally between acoustic guitar/vocal (16) and piano/vocal (11). Lil' Son Jackson is perhaps the best-known, and his ten tracks are all good, rocking acoustic blues. There are also tunes by L.C. Williams, a polished and imaginative guitarist, and one magnificent track by the obscure Buddy Chiles. — *Larry Hoffman*

Texas Country Blues 1948-1951 / 1994 / Flyright ♦♦♦♦
Another entry in Flyright's ongoing quest to present the rare and the wonderful, this collects up some impossibly hard to find Texas 78s originally released on short-lived, dime-sized labels like Talent, Freedom, Nucraft, ARC, Bluebonnet, and the colorfully named Oklahoma Tornado! Honeyboy Edwards and Frankie Lee Sims are the only "big names" aboard, but the remainder of the tracks featuring Rattlesnake Cooper, James Tisdom, Andrew Thomas, Willie Lane, Monister Parker, Leroy "Country" Johnson, and others clearly illustrate how big the looming presence (both commercially and artistically) of Lightnin' Hopkins already was at this early stage of the game. — *Cub Koda*

Texas Guitar Greats / 1991 / Collectables ♦♦♦
Texas blues, boogie, and blues-rock recorded from 1962-1988, it includes several previously unreleased cuts, with Johnny Winter, Freddie King, Gatemouth Brown, and Johnny Copeland, among others. — *Niles J. Frantz*

Texas Guitar Killers / Oct. 24, 1995 / Capitol ♦♦♦
Part of Capitol's ongoing development of its vaults, this two-disc set was produced by the late Pete Welding (whose function is being taken over by

Billy Vera for future projects.) The 39 cuts feature T-Bone Walker, Gatemouth Brown, Lowell Fulson, Lightnin' Hopkins, Smokey Hogg, and Pee-Wee Crayton, with sides drawn from their stints with Imperial and Aladdin. While the intent is to represent Texas blues artists from those labels (with recordings from 1945 to 1953), the result is a fascinating conglomeration of styles that have a bit less to do with guitar than the album title would lead one to believe. Still, it's a fine compilation, wonderfully produced, marvelously annotated and a lot of fun to listen to—T-Bone Walker, particularly, was a fine jazz vocalist, as well as a brilliant guitar player whose onstage antics provided the model for Chuck Berry. —*Steven McDonald*

☆ **Texas Music: Postwar Blues Combos** / 1994 / Rhino ✦✦✦✦✦
Texas blues is harder to define and pigeonhole than, say, Chicago electric blues, or Mississippi Delta country blues. In general terms, the Texas blues of the immediate post-war era often featured hard-driving, jazzy guitar lines, a jump blues influence, occasional brass, and a generally lighter, sunnier attitude than its more famous Chicago cousin. This is a fine 18-song survey of Texas blues from the late '40s to the early '70s, including both giants (T-Bone Walker, Bobby Bland, Freddie King, Albert Collins) and names that are known only to blues collectors (Frankie Lee Sims, Goree Carter, Zuzu Bollin). Some of the selections, even by some of the more well-known names, are damned rare; there are mighty hard-to-find '50s singles by Collins, Gatemouth Brown, and Johnny Copeland (as well as one very well-known single, Ivory Joe Hunter's "Since I Met You Baby"). There are a good variety of styles here, encompassing both bluesy ballads and boogies; the thrilling instrumental string-benders by Clarence Green, Albert Collins, and T-Bone Walker may be the highlights. Whatever your preference, it's a fine survey/introduction to vintage Texas electric blues, and it's a good bet that even listeners with big blues collections won't have a lot of the rarities here. —*Richie Unterberger*

★ **Texas Piano Blues 1929-48** / May 1, 1991 / Story Of Blues ✦✦✦✦✦
This is a good collection of piano-accompanied vocals sporting bluesmen who worked the lumber camps and oil fields of rural Texas, as well as the red-light districts of cities like Galveston and Houston. Big Boy Knox shows a strong city influence in his decorative right-hand work, as does Robert Cooper, whose playing points to the influence of Fats Waller. Joe Pullem is on board with his hit, "Black Gal," which is perhaps overstated by three takes and a variation. The vocals are good, however, and the piano playing is uniformly excellent. Stylistically, this music falls somewhere between ragtime, blues, and vaudeville. —*Larry Hoffman*

Texas Sax Greats / Nov. 30, 1992 / Collectables ✦✦✦✦
Slightly inconsistent but rewarding R&B sax compilation; Big Sambo, Link Davis, and Henry Hayes provide best moments. —*Bill Dahl*

Them Dirty Blues / 1989 / Jass ✦✦✦✦
The thin line between provocative and obscene, suggestive and disgusting, gets examined and stretched throughout the 50 tracks presented on the 1989 two-disc set *Them Dirty Blues*. Many of these songs could be deemed sexist using a '90s measuring stick; on the other hand, many are also quite funny, language notwithstanding. They are reflective of a time when audiences were willing to accept songs with either overt carnal themes or with an implicit, yet rather pronounced sexuality. —*Ron Wynn*

Tomato Delta Blues Package / 1994 / Tomato/Rhino ✦✦✦✦
While there's no denying the greatness of the performers spotlighted on this 16-track anthology, Tomato/Rhino played a bit loose with its definition of "Delta blues." Leadbelly, for example, was more of a classic folk singer with blues ties, while Sonny Terry And Brownie McGhee were Piedmont blues performers, and the songs by Howlin' (not Howling) Wolf and the Little Walter/Otis Rush duo aren't Delta blues either. Licensing problems probably reared their heads here; witness the absence of Charlie Patton, Robert Johnson, Son House, Tommy Johnson, or Sonny Boy Williamson (John Lee). There's still some good material, notably Arthur "Big Boy" Crudup, Mississippi Fred McDowell, Johnny Shines, Mississippi John Hurt, and decent (though hardly sensational) Lightnin' Hopkins and John Lee Hooker. —*Ron Wynn*

Tribute to Stevie Ray Vaughan / Aug. 7, 1996 / Epic ✦✦✦✦
Unlike most tribute albums from the '90s, *A Tribute to Stevie Ray Vaughan* isn't a lifeless collection of piecemeal studio performances—it's a fiery, living tribute, which is only fitting for a guitarist that shone intensely and brightly during his brief life. Recorded live in Stevie Ray's hometown of Austin, Texas, the album features many of Vaughan's idols, friends, and admirers ripping through his most famous numbers. Many of these musicians—including his brother Jimmie, Eric Clapton, Robert Cray, and Buddy Guy—played with Stevie the night he died, which makes the record all the more poignant; also on hand are superstars like B.B. King, Bonnie Raitt, Dr. John, and Art Neville. Although the memory and occasion remain bittersweet, the music on the album is simply teeming with life—everybody plays their heart out. Best of all are the collective jams at the end and the two new songs, "Six Strings Down" and "SRV Blues," which were written in Vaughan's memory. In short, it's what a tribute should be—a celebration of life, not death. —*Thom Owens*

Tuesday's Just As Bad / Nov. 17, 1994 / K-Tel ✦✦✦
Companion volume to K-Tel's *Best of the Blues*, this one features 10 more indispensable cuts from Muddy Waters, Howlin' Wolf, Elmore James, B.B. King, and others. Great listening even if you already have the songs on other compilations. —*Cub Koda*

Up Jumped the Blues / 1996 / Music Club ✦✦✦
This 18-track budget-priced compilation features an uptempo collection of tracks from the vaults of the British JSP firm, who long have recorded visiting American blues artists with varying results. The highlights this time are numerous and the quality stays high—as all compilations should be—but several are worthy of special mention. Phillip Walker with Otis Grand do a nice opening turn with "Don't Leave Me Baby," Carey Bell checks in with a live rendition of Little Walter's "Leaving in the Morning (I Got to Go)," as well as a nice duet with son Lurrie on "The Gladys Shuffle," and Buddy Guy is rockin' with "Girl You're Nice and Clean." Little Willie Littlefield checks in with some two-fisted piano boogie on "(Sit Right Down And) Cry over You"; U.P. Wilson contributes a nice instrumental in "Half Step" and a scorching shuffle with "Need the Need"; Johnny "Big Moose" Walker takes it back home with "Rambling Woman"; Guitar Shorty contributes two tracks with Otis Grand; and Hubert Sumlin's vocal on "Look Don't Touch" is both mellow and affecting. This compilation also includes tracks by Charlie Sayles, Phil Guy, Johnny Mars, Larry Garner, Byther Smith, Tre', and Tutu Jones. With a 77-minute running time and excellent liner notes from Bill Dahl, this is one blues compilation that's a solid value for the money. —*Cub Koda*

★ **Wade in the Water, Vol. 1: Concert Tradition** / May 1, 1994 / Smithsonian/Folkways ✦✦✦✦✦
This four-disc set, drawn from the musical examples to Bernice Johnson Reagon's outstanding National Public Radio series on African American gospel music, deals respectively with the concert tradition in spiritual singing, the 19th-century roots of African American congregational singing, the pioneering composers, and community gospel. As ballet music lacks a dimension without the dance, the CDs lack a dimension without the powerful mind tying the whole thing together. And to have included some of the non-African-American roots Professor Reagon illustrated in the programs would also have made this more than just another fine gospel set. But "just another fine gospel set" is pretty fine in its own right. —*John Storm Roberts, Original Music*

☆ **Wade in the Water, Vol. 2: 19th Century Roots** / May 1, 1994 / Smithsonian/Folkways ✦✦✦✦✦
Wade in the Water, Vol. 2: African American Congregational Singing offers a glimpse into the long history of black congregational vocals and worshiping practices, a tradition dating back centuries which once accounted for much of the oral transmission passed from generation to generation. Fascinatingly, the songs are never rehearsed—singers learn while they perform; and while organized gospel choirs have since become more widely recognized, the congregational style still thrives, with six of the modern era's most stirring representatives—among them the McIntosh County Shouters, the Seniorlites, and the Rev. C.J. Johnson & Family—featured on this disc. —*Jason Ankeny*

☆ **Wade in the Water, Vol. 3: African American Gospel: the Pioneering Composers** / 1995 / Smithsonian/Folkways ✦✦✦✦✦
Wade in the Water, Vol. 3: African American Gospel focuses on six of the pioneering composers of the genre—Rev. Charles Albert Tindley, Lucie Eddie (Elizabeth) Campbell, Rev. William Herbert Brewster, Roberta Martin, Kenneth Morris, and the incomparable Thomas A. Dorsey. Recorded between

1992 and 1993, the disc features new renditions of such perennials as "Just a Closer Walk with Thee," "Precious Lord," "How I Got Over," and "We'll Understand It Better By and By." — *Jason Ankeny*

Wade in the Water, Vol. 4: African American Community Gospel / 1994 / Smithsonian/Folkways ✦✦✦✦

The final release in the series, *Wade in the Water, Vol. 4: African American Community Gospel* focuses on the sacred music of two vastly different areas of the US — Washington D.C. and rural Alabama — to illustrate the differences brought about by local perspective. The eight Alabama tracks run the gamut from newly arranged renditions of traditional favorites to popular hits to original compositions; all are in the quartet style, which remains the primary gospel vehicle throughout the state — group anniversary celebrations are even regularly held, with other quartets traveling from miles around to perform in their peers' honor. In D.C., the trend is towards performances connected with the worship services of the urban church community; again, however, the scope is vast, including traditional styles, processional praise songs, and a contemporary reading of "Peace in the Valley." — *Jason Ankeny*

Wake up Dead Man: Black Convict Worksongs from Texas / 1994 / Rounder ✦✦✦✦

African-American worksongs were more than a functional tool or a root of the blues. They were a monument to the indomitability of the human spirit, and a major African survival into the 20th century. They're long gone now, but not forgotten by anybody who's heard these superb examples from the '60s, or Alan Lomax's earlier recordings from Parchman Farm in Mississippi. Fine notes are included, too. — *John Storm Roberts, Original Music*

Warrior on the Battlefield: A Capella Trail Blazers — '20s-'40s / Oct. 21, 1997 / Rounder ✦✦✦✦

Twenty-five performances by African-American gospel quartets of the South, recorded between 1927 and 1942. The Silver Leaf Quartette of Norfolk and the Golden Gate Quartet get the most airtime (six and five tracks respectively), though there's also space for less familiar names like the Davis Bible Singers and the T.C.I. Womens Four. This documents Black gospel music in its transition from barbershop quartets to more polished forms, and while the sound quality isn't as dynamic as what you'll find on contemporary releases, the performances are generally much less showy. — *Richie Unterberger*

We Love You Bobby: A Tribute To Bobby Bland / 1992 / Collectables ✦✦✦

There's not much Bland influence on many of them, but these mostly '60s Texas R&B sides are soulful nonetheless. — *Bill Dahl*

Weed: A Rare Batch / Oct. 1928-Nov. 1947 / Stash ✦✦✦

As is usual with most of Stash's earliest releases, much of the music on this LP refers in one way or another to drugs in its lyrics, but these jazz and blues performances from the swing era are most notable for the fine playing by a wide variety of artists. There is one selection apiece from Chick Webb (Ella Fitzgerald singing "When I Get Low I Get High"), Tampa Red, Oscar's Chicago Swingers, Carl Martin, the Harlem Hamfats, Julia Lee, Sammy Price, Cootie Williams (a hot version of "Ol' Man River"), Adrian Rollini, Lorraine Walton, Yack Taylor ("Knockin' Myself Out"), Blue Steele, and Lucille Bogan ("Pot Hound Blues"). Many of these selections have yet to be reissued on CD. — *Scott Yanow*

White Country Blues, 1926-1938 ... / Apr. 27, 1993 / Columbia/Legacy ✦✦✦✦

Country artists sing pre-war blues-influenced songs. — *Bill Dahl*

Wild About My Lovin': Beale Street Blues 1928-30 / Aug. 13, 1991 / RCA ✦✦✦✦

Superb, eclectic music from Depression-era Memphis, remastered from the original source recordings. The material on *Wild About My Lovin'* is drawn from singers Frank Stokes and Jim Jackson and from a pair of the era's most popular jug bands, (Gus) Cannon's Jug Stompers and the Memphis Jug Band, whose "Stealin'" (included here) was later recorded by Bob Dylan. — *Jason Ankeny*

Windy City Blues / Jul. 10, 1992 / Nighthawk ✦✦✦✦

Subtitled, "The Transition: 1935 to 1953," this 12 track collection documents primarily the work of Southern born blues artists who immigrated to Chicago before World War II, but whose careers endured into the postwar era. Starting with Aaron "Pinetop" Sparks' 1935 recording of the blues classic "Everyday I Have The Blues," the collection runs in chronological order, featuring several selections from the "Bluebird beat" period of Chicago blues. The State Street Boys' "Sweet To Mama" is an all-star aggregation featuring Big Bill Broonzy, violinist Carl Martin, pianist Black Bob, and Jazz Gillum on harmonica. Another Bluebird alumni, Washboard Sam, is aboard with "Easy Ridin' Mama," recorded in 1937. John Lee "Sonny Boy" Williamson is aboard with two tracks, "Sunnyland" and "My Little Cornelius," both from 1938. Robert Lee McCoy is featured on the 1937 recording that gave him his signature piece, "Prowlin' Nighthawk." Robert Jr. Lockwood is documented with two of his earliest sides from 1941 ("Black Spider Blues" and "I'm Gonna Train My Baby") and a pair from a decade later, "Dust My Broom" and "Gonna Dig Myself A Hole." A late 1951 Tampa Red side, "Green and Lucky Blues," is also a standout, along with a 1953 Johnny Shines track ("Please Don't"), finding him in an unusual band setting with Elmore James' saxman J.T. Brown and Sunnyland Slim on piano. Two tracks each from Guitar Pete Franklin and Tony Hollins round out this excellent collection. — *Cub Koda*

Wizards from the Southside / Oct. 17, 1990 / Chess ✦✦✦✦

This is a great sampler of the finest in classic Chicago blues — perfect for those listeners who are looking for a taste of the best of the genre. Included are "Evil" by Howlin' Wolf (two wolf-tracks in all); "Rollin' and Tumblin'" by Muddy Waters (five); "Walkin' the Boogie" by John Lee Hooker (one); "Bring It on Home" by Sonny Boy Williamson (one), "I'm a Man" by Bo Diddley (two); and "Mellow Down Easy" by Little Walter (two). All of these fabulous sides were cut between 1950-61 — the Golden Era of Southside Chicago blues. — *Larry Hoffman*

Women of Gospel's Golden Age, Vol. 1 / 1994 / Specialty ✦✦✦✦

Although women have been at the forefront of gospel innovation since the beginning, the domination of male quartets may have fooled some into thinking they weren't that important. Anyone holding that mistaken impression will surely know better after hearing the 28 remarkable cuts on this valuable anthology. New Orleans' wondrous Bessie Griffin, whose vibrant, dazzling voice was overlooked due to Mahalia Jackson, gets the spotlight with six amazing numbers. She's not alone there, however; everyone from the famous Clara Ward Singers and Dorothy Love Coates to the lesser-known Sallie Martin Singers sounds fantastic. — *Ron Wynn*

Wrapped in My Baby / 1989 / Pearl Flapper ✦✦✦✦

Basement rehearsal recordings from the early '50s for the United/States labels, featuring Morris Pejoe's raw'n'rockin' "Let's Get High" from a full unissued session, plus four amazing sides from Arthur "Big Boy" Spires. Another missing chapter of Chicago blues history brought to light, simply incredible. — *Cub Koda*

Music is food for the soul. It is one of the best medicines that I know of and the better the music, the better I feel. Hearing the good stuff makes all the difference. And that is what this book is all about–how to locate the best blues music. Blues is so radical–such a root music–that it fuses with and gives rise to other music genres with ease. Jazz critics point out that the roots of jazz can be found in the blues. This article is about where in jazz blues lovers can hear and feel those roots–the blues in jazz.

A little background on where I am coming from: I have been a blues and jazz lover for over 37 years. In the late '50s and very early '60s there was a strong jazz scene in Ann Arbor, MI, where I grew up. This was before liquor by the glass became legal in 1963, after which a lot of the jazz scene moved into the clubs. Most any night of the week, but in particular on weekends, there was live jazz played in houses and apartments. Teenagers like myself were tolerated and we hung out. Players like Bob James, Ron Brooks, Bob Pozar, and Bob Detwiler were playing straight-up bop and exploring some cool jazz. The music and the parties often went on all night. On occasion, I heard Cannonball Adderley and others play in one of the many Detroit clubs like the Minor Key. Jazz records were big, too. I can remember staying up all night listening to John Coltrane's *My Favorite Things* album over and over when it first came out. This was about 1960.

I fell in with the folk scene in the early '60s and managed to hitch-hike all over the country several times. A fantastic guitarist by the name of Perry Lederman, a young singer/songwriter by the name of Bob Dylan, and I hitched together for a stretch. Later I helped to put on the first Bob Dylan concert in Ann Arbor. During that time, I hung out with the New Lost City Ramblers, Ramblin' Jack Elliot, the Country Gentlemen, Joan Baez, and some other great folk artists that you may never have heard of.

It was in those years that I got introduced to blues and gospel music. The Swan Silvertones, an a cappella gospel group of infinite beauty, had an enormous effect on me in 1964 when I first heard their records. I had also been listening to classical music for a number of years, but had no real guidance. I spent all of 1964 listening to and learning in depth about classical music from a real expert. Then in 1965 I helped to form a band called the Prime Movers. Although we never recorded, we were no slouch. Iggy Pop was our drummer, avant-garde composer "Blue" Gene Tyranny our keyboardist, music columnist Dan Erlewine played lead guitar, Jack Dawson (later in the Siegel-Schwall Blues Band) was on bass, and I sang and played amplified harmonica.

Sometime in 1965 we heard the Paul Butterfield Blues Band live. That changed my life. We got to know those guys and they introduced us to all of the blues we had not yet found out for ourselves. We became, in an instant, the Prime Movers Blues Band. That was a time.

The net effect of all of this was that, during the 1960s, I listened to blues records day and night trying to learn to play the licks. And I just loved the music. In the mid-'60s, thanks to Bob Koester of Delmark Records, I heard players like Little Walter, Magic Sam, Junior Wells, and many others live in the Chicago clubs. Later, working with various blues and jazz festivals, I had the good fortune to interview (audio and video) just about any blues player you could name that was around back then, and most of them still were.

This article is about blues in jazz, and I am getting to that. My main love is the blues and it took me some time to get much into jazz. In the beginning about the only way I could hear jazz was through a blues filter, so any jazz I got into had to have those blues elements. Now that I know my way around the jazz catalog, I know that it contains some real treasures for blues lovers. But don't expect the standard 12-bar blues progression. Blue notes are found in jazz, but seldom in the form we are used to in blues recordings. It is the blues as a feeling, the soulful experience of the blues and gospel elements that can be found in jazz. So, I am writing this for blues lovers who may want to explore jazz through the same blues doorway I went through.

The jazz I love is the blues in jazz, whether that means bluesy jazz, funky jazz, original funk, or soul jazz–terms which I will explain in due course. I tend not to like (very much) jazz that does not have some kind of blues or modal element in it. Swing and bop, to the degree that they lack the roots sound of blues and gospel, fail to hold my attention. I like my jazz with blues, please.

Something I realized some time ago is that jazz (and most kinds of music) are either energizing or calming in their overall effect. If you are the kind of person who needs something to get you moving (to energize you), then you will be attracted to music that is agitating and energizing, like marches, Dixieland, bop, free jazz, and other forms of progressive jazz. It appeals to those who need that cup of coffee in life–get a move on! It stirs you up.

However, if you are a person (like me) who tends to be very active and sometimes even hyper, then you need music to relax and calm you, like blues, original funk, soul jazz–groove music. It helps to get you in a soothing groove that dissipates energy–relief! Regardless of the fact that as a person we may (in general) be drawn to music that either stimulates or calms us, at times all of us may need some pick-me-up music and at other times some slow-me-down stuff.

You will find that the above (admittedly simplistic) concept works very well. Blues and the blues that is in jazz (for the most part) has to do with the release and expression of feelings. The effect is calming to the system. It is "get down" and relaxin' music. Here is a brief tour of the bluesy stuff in jazz.

An Abbreviated History of Blues in Jazz

This is an abbreviated history because I want to just skip over the standard playing-the-blues-progression in jazz stuff. There is not much of it anyway. If you like blues, you already know that by now. For now, we will also pass on all of the old-time blues found in traditional jazz–the early New Orleans jazz. There is plenty of great old blues and blues-like music to hear there, and you will want to hear it someday. But it is just too much like the blues that you already know. The same goes for what few blues tunes came out of the swing and big-band era. You don't need a guide to check swing blues tunes out because there are not that many of them. When you can find them, they are pretty much straight-ahead blues songs or tunes played with a big band. Further, the arranged feeling of the big band is not up to the impromptu kind of blues feeling you may be used to, so let's pass on that too.

When I speak of blues in jazz, I mean some get-down funky blues sounds in jazz that you have not heard before, so let's just get to that. If this history stuff bores you, skip over it and just read the recommended albums list. Start finding and listening to some of the picks. As mentioned, we will pass over the earlier forms of jazz including the New Orleans varieties, Dixieland, and swing. However, since a lot of the bluesier jazz that may interest you grew out of bop (bebop), you will need to know what bop is and how that musical style came to be. We will start there.

Bop (bebop)–Bop distinguished itself from the popular big-band swing music out of which it emerged by the fact that it is most often played in small groups. You can hear each of the players as separate sounds. And while swing can have a groove that soothes you, bop is wake-me-up music. Its faster tempos, more elaborate melodies, and complex harmonies do not tend to establish a groove. It is more frenetic, even frantic, than swing. In other words, this is not relaxin' music. Bop has an attitude.

Unlike the large swing bands where there were a few featured soloists, most members of the small combo could and did solo–democratic. In addition to an increase in improvisation and solo virtuosity, there was little dependence on arrangements. And fast tempos too. Bop is more energetic (read agitating) than swing, with the rhythm section keeping the time on the ride cymbal. Bop tunes can be very fast, often with elaborate harmonies and complex chord changes that take an expert player to negotiate. In fact, fluency in bop became the benchmark of the young jazz musician. Bop is sophisticated music that can be, for many, somewhat of an acquired taste. In this respect it resembles classical music. Here are some bop artists and sample albums of them at their best:

Bop originators:

Charlie Parker (just about any album; the box sets are the best)
Dizzy Gillespie, *Dizziest*/Bluebird
Thelonious Monk, *Thelonious with John Coltrane*/OJC
Bud Powell, *Genius of Powell Vol. 1*/Polygram
Dexter Gordon, *Our Man in Paris*/Blue Note
Miles Davis, *First Miles*/Savoy
Fats Navarro, *The Fabulous Fats Navarro, Vol 1–2*/Blue Note
Sonny Stitt, *Constellation*/Muse
J.J. Johnson, *The Eminent Jay Jay Johnson Vol. 1*/Blue Note
Max Roach, *Freedom Now Suite*/Columbia
Lucky Thompson, *Lucky Strikes!*/Prestige
Tad Dameron, *Mating Call*/Prestige

1950s Bop Players:

Sonny Rollins, *Newk's Time*/Blue Note
Jackie McLean, *Let Freedom Ring*/Blue Note
Oscar Peterson, *The Trio*/Pablo
Clifford Brown, *Brownie*/Emarcy
Phil Woods, *Pairing Off*/Prestige
Kenny Dorham, *Una Mas*/Blue Note
Barry Harris, *Live in Tokyo*/Xanadu
Tommy Flanagan, *Thelonica*/Enja

1970-1980s Bop Revival:

Richie Cole, *New York Afternoon-Alto Madness*/Muse
Chris Hollyday, *Ho, Brother*/Jazzbeat

Blues in Bop:

Thelonious Monk, *The Thelonious Monk Trio*/Prestige
Miles Davis & Milt Jackson, *Bag's Groove*/Prestige
Miles Davis, *Walkin'*/Prestige
Horace Silver, *Senor Blues*/Blue Note

Hard Bop–Hard bop was a reaction to the somewhat brittle and intellectual nature of straight bop. Hard bop distinguished itself from bop by its simple melodies, slower tempos, and avoidance of the (by then) clichéd bop chord changes. The constant uptempo frenetic quality of bop pieces is absent. Tunes are often in the minor mode, much slower paced, and often moody–more feeling and thoughtful. Hard bop reaches into the blues and gospel tradition for substance to slow the up-tempo bop music down, stretch the time out, and imbue the music

with more feeling. It was as if jazz had once again found its roots and been nourished. The public thought so too, because it was more approachable than bop. Hard bop is one big step toward establishing a groove, but it lacks what has come to be known as a groove, as in "groove" music. Blues lovers will appreciate the more bluesy nature of hard bop, but probably still yearn for more blues yet.

Hard Bop Pioneers:

Horace Silver, *Pieces of Silver*/Blue Note
Art Blakey and the Jazz Messengers, *Moanin'*/Blue Note
Cannonball Adderley Quintet, *Quintet at the Light-house*/Landmark
Nat Adderley, *Work Song*/Riverside
Art Farmer, *Meet the Jazztet*/Chess
Crusaders, *Freedom Sounds*/Atlantic
Lou Donaldson, *Blues Walk*/Blue Note
Kenny Dorham, *Trumpet Toccata*/Blue Note
Donald Byrd, *House of Byrd*/Prestige

Coltrane-Influenced Hard Bop:

Wayne Shorter, *Native Dancer*/Columbia
Freddie Hubbard, *Hub-Tones*/Blue Note
McCoy Tyner, *Sahara*/Milestone
Herbie Hancock, *Maiden Voyage*/Blue Note
Joe Henderson, *Page One*/Blue Note
Weather Report (Joe Zawinul), *Mysterious Traveler*/Columbia

Mainstream Hard Bop:

Sonny Rollins, *Saxophone Colossus and More*/OJC
John Coltrane, *Blue Trane*/Blue Note
Wynton Kelly, *Kelly Blue*/Riverside
Clifford Jordan, *Glass Bead Game*/Strata-East
Booker Ervin, *The Book Cooks*/Affinity
George Coleman, *Amsterdam After Dark*/Timeless
Charlie Rouse, *Two Is One*/Strata-East
Harold Land, *The Fox*/Contemporary
Blue Mitchell, *The Thing to Do*/Blue Note
Kenny Dorham, *Afro-Cuban*/Blue Note
Oliver Nelson, *Soul Battle*/Prestige
Hank Mobley, *Soul Station*/Blue Note
Wes Montgomery, *Incredible Jazz Guitar of Wes Mont-gomery*/Riverside

Funky Jazz–Some hard-bop players, like pianist Horace Silver, began to include even more feeling in their playing by adding blues riffs and various elements from gospel music to their playing. Silver, considered by many to be the father of funk, describes funk: "Funky means earthy, blues-based. It may not be blues itself, but it has that down-home feel to it. Playing funky has nothing to do with style; it's an approach to playing ... 'Soul' is the same basically, but there's an added dimension of feeling and spirit to soul–an in-depth-ness. A soulful player might be funky or he might not be."

The hard bop jazz that they were playing became, in Silver's hands, still more earthy, bluesy or, as it was called, "funky". This was jazz, but with a funky flavor. It is quite easy to distinguish this funky jazz from the all-out jazz funk described below. I really like funky jazz because it sometimes has a groove, but I love jazz funk better because in that music there is a total groove.

Horace Silver, *Song for My Father*/Blue Note
Cannonball Adderley, *Somethin' Else*/Blue Note
Nat Adderley, *Work Song*/Riverside
Bobby Timmons, *Moanin'*/Milestone

The Blues Groove—Groove Music

The whole thing about groove music is that everything exists to establish and maintain the groove. Solos, egos, instruments–what have you–only exist to lay down the groove and to get in it. There is a steady constant beat that can become drone-like or trance-like. You get in a groove and you stay in the groove and that feels good. There are no absolute rules about what makes groove music. Anything can happen as long as the effect is to put you in and keep you in the groove. It often has a Hammond organ in the sound, but not always. It can have any number of instruments doing all kinds of solos and what-not as long as these things don't break the groove. Everything exists to create and maintain the groove. Blues lovers tend to like groove music because the blues is nothing but a groove.

Groove music can be uptempo or slow, bright or dark, but the net effect of getting in a groove is always to satisfy and relax. There is always a constant rhythm section driving the groove, invariably danceable. Grooves have a funky, earthy flavor and blues and gospel elements are essential. All grooves are bluesy, by definition. It can be as funky and nasty as you want to be, but groove is not stir-it-up music. It is always cool-you-down music. If it is not relaxing, then it is not groove. Which is not to say that groove is not energetic or fast paced. It may sound wild, but the final effect is a groove. Although I hesitate to characterize it this way, groove music is almost a little trance-like. The result of the funkiest, baddest piece of groove music is a bit of clear sailing–relaxation. Get in the groove! That's the place to BE.

Original Funk/Soul Jazz–The transformation of bop did not always stop with hard bop or even funkified jazz. Some players dove rather than dipped into the roots music and an even more bluesy music was born that came to be called funk or soul jazz. For the first time, we are talking real groove music.

Funkified jazz, also called soul jazz, jazz funk, original funk, or just plain funk, is a form of jazz that originated in the mid-'50s–a type of hard bop. It is often played by small groups–trios led by a tenor or alto sax, pianist, guitar and the Hammond organ. Funk music is very physical, usually "down and dirty."

Funk or soul jazz emerged as a reaction to the bop/cool jazz (cool, intellectualized) prevalent at the time. Funky music is everything that bop/cool jazz is not. It is hot, sweaty and never strays far from its blues roots. The term "soul" is a link to gospel roots; "funk" links to blues roots. This fusion of jazz with blues and gospel elements became known as "soul jazz" during the 1950s, partly through the promotion of the Cannonball Adderley Quintet as a "soul-jazz" group.

Fast-paced funk pieces have a bright melodic phrasing set against a hard, percussive dance rhythm. Funk ballads are never more than a few steps from the blues. Above all, this is dynamic relaxin' music that is easy to listen to–the groove. Those of you who like blues and R&B (and gospel), but find some jazz just a touch remote, may well like original funk. There is no better music to kick back to than this.

Jazz funk is sometimes called "original funk" to distinguish it from the contemporary funk music of the James Brown/George Clinton variety. Along with blues and gospel, original funk or soul jazz had some R&B (soul music) elements thrown into the mix and the resulting fusion was even more to the public's taste. Soul jazz has remained one of the most popular and successful forms of jazz to this very day. Bop is stir-it-up music while funk or soul jazz (no matter how uptempo or percussive) is at heart calm-you-down or groove music. Here are some classic funk albums:

Eddie Lockjaw Davis, *Cookbook, Vol. 1–3*/OJC
Gene Ammons, *Gene Ammons Story: Organ Combos*/Prestige
Arnett Cobb, *Smooth Sailing*/OJC
Red Holloway, *Cookin' Together*/OJC
Willis Jackson, *Bar Wars*/Muse
Ike Quebec, *Blue and Sentimental*/Blue Note
Bobby Timmons, *Soul Man*/Prestige

Johnny Hammond Smith, *Breakout*/Kudu
Harold Vick, *Steppin' Out*/Blue Note
Harold Mabern, *Rakin' & Scrapin'*/Prestige
Stanley Turrentine, *Comin' Your Way*/Blue Note
Houston Person, *Soul Dance*/Prestige
Grover Washington, *Mister Magic*/Motown
Harold Mabern, *Rakin' and Scrapin'*/OJC
Cornell Dupree, *Coast to Coast*/Antilles
Les McCann, *Swiss Movement*/Atlantic (soul jazz)

Organ Combos–At the heart of original funk and soul jazz sits the Hammond organ, 400 pounds of musical joy. This unwieldy piece of equipment can do it all–work by itself, as a duo, trio, quartet, or with a full band. It is a full band. More important is the fact that the Hammond organ sound pretty much defines real funk. There is something about the percussive sound and the adjustable attack/decay effects that, coupled with the famed (rotating horns) Leslie speakers, epitomizes that music called funk.

Whatever the reason, you will find a Hammond organ at the center (or as backup) of the majority of soul jazz recordings, not to mention contemporary funk and R&B recordings. Jimmy Smith is the man who tamed the great beast and turned the Hammond from a roller-rink calliope into a serious jazz instrument. The story is that Smith locked himself in a warehouse with a Hammond for almost a year and came out playing that sound we all love.

And Smith is just the tip of the iceberg. There are many fine Hammond players that are every bit as great in their own way, names like Richard Groove Holmes, Jimmy McGriff, Shirley Scott, Charles Earland, John Patton, Larry Young, and others. Put a Hammond organ and some drums together with a tenor sax or guitar and you have all you need for some real funky music. This is groove music par excellence.

Jimmy Smith, *Back at the Chicken Shack*/Blue Note
Jimmy McGriff, *At the Apollo*/Collectables
Jack McDuff, *Live!*/Prestige
Richard Groove Holmes, *After Hours*/Pacific Jazz
Don Patterson, *Genius of the B-3*/Music
John Patton, *Let em' Roll*/Blue Note
Shirley Scott, *Blue Flames*/OJC
Charles Earland, *Black Talk*/Prestige
Charles Kynard, *Reelin' with the Feeling*/Prestige
Larry Young, *The Complete Blue Note Larry Young*/Mosaic
Joey DeFrancesco, *All of Me*/Columbia

The Commercialization of Soul Jazz–Soul jazz sometimes gets a not-so-great rap. Anything so potent and popular lends itself to misuse and a great many so-called soul jazz albums were recorded that had no "soul"–bad commercial funk. On the theory that you never know what is enough until you have more than enough, artists sought to increase their popularity by making their music more and more commercial until, in the end, they lost touch with the roots of the music–the soul.

To make matters worse, the advent of bop and the various forms of progressive jazz that grew out of bop, gave birth to a somewhat elitist, conservative, and overly intellectualized attitude–the jazz purist. This purist looks down on jazz that partakes too much of its blues and gospel roots, and any R&B influences are really frowned upon. These mainstream jazz purists used the overt commercialism aspect of soul jazz as grounds to dismiss the entire music offhand. Funk and soul jazz was somehow (in their opinion) not as worthy of respect as the bop or progressive jazz they admired. The fact that soul jazz is the most successful and popular form of jazz was cited as further proof of its commonness. This elitist attitude is now on the decline and soul jazz is beginning to take its place in the history of jazz as a legitimate form. Soul jazz reissues are a hot item. It is a fact that most great jazz performers also have a funky or soul side and albums to prove it. Often very little is written about the soul jazz side of these artists.

Well, there you have a quick tour of the funkier side of jazz–groove music. It is important to point out that soul jazz, although always popular with the people, has received short shrift from the jazz elite. The attitude is that groove music is something, like the blues, which should be kept in the closet. That time has passed.

Groove Masters

We are coming out of a time when jazz has been measured by how outstanding the soloist is–how high can they fly? Critics only seem to know how to rate what stands out. This won't work for groove music. In groove, the idea is to lay down a groove, get in it, and deepen it. Groove masters always take us deeper into the groove. These artists are our windows into the groove, and their hearts become the highway over which the groove can run. They reinvest. And we ride the groove.

This is why jazz critics have either passed (never got it) over groove masters like Grant Green and Stanley Turrentine or heard something without knowing what to make of what they heard (and felt). If music is not viewed as such an intellectual thing (something to see) but rather more of a feeling kind of thing, then groove masters can be appreciated. You may not see the groove masters, but you sure can feel them. In groove, the solo (and all else) only exists if it adds to the groove. Witness Grant Green's incredible single-note repetitions. Who would ever think to do that? You wouldn't dare think of that. It is done by pure feeling. It feels good and you keep doing it. Nothing to think about.

Stanley Turrentine has been laying down grooves for many a year for all to hear. I am surprised at how many books don't even mention him. Grant Green has received even shorter shrift. There have been a few voices crying in the wilderness of soul jazz criticism. Producer Bob Porter of Atlantic Records and Bob Rusch of *Cadence* magazine have always known and told us about the groove. Recording engineer Rudy Van Gelder is another pre-eminent groove expert. More than half of all great soul jazz sessions were recorded by Van Gelder. The next time you hear some real groove music, particularly if there is a Hammond organ on it, just check the album for this engineer's name.

Grant Green: THE Groove Master–All that I can say about Grant Green is that he is *the* groove master. Numero uno. He is so deep in the groove that most people have no idea what's up with him. Players like Stanley Turrentine, Jimmy Smith, Kenny Burrell, and many other really great soul jazz artists are also groove masters. But the main man is Grant Green. He is so far in the groove that it will take decades for us to bring him out in full. He is just starting to be discovered.

To get your attention and make clear that I am saying something here, consider the singing voice of Bob Dylan. A lot of people say the guy can't sing. But it's not that simple. He is singing. The problem is that he is singing so far in the future that we can't yet hear the music. Other artists can sing his tunes and we can hear that all right. Given enough time, enough years, that gravel-like voice will sound as sweet to our ears as any velvet-toned singer. Dylan's voice is all about microtones and inflection. For now that voice is hidden from our ears in time so tight that there is no room (no time) yet to hear it. Some folks can hear it now. I, for one, can hear the music in his voice. I know many of you can too. Someday everyone will be able to hear it, because the mind will unfold itself until even Dylan's voice is exposed for just what it is–a pure music. But by then our idea of music will also have changed. Rap is changing it even now.

Billie Holiday is another voice that is filled with microtones that emerge through time like an ever-blooming flower. You (or I) can't hear the end or root of her singing, not yet anyway. As we try to listen to Holiday (as we try to grasp that voice), we are knocked out by the deep information there. We try to absorb it, and before we can get a handle on her voice (if we dare listen!) she entrances us in a delightful dream-like groove and we are lost to criticism. Instead we groove on and reflect about this other dream that we have called life. All great musicians do this to us.

Grant Green's playing at its best is like this too. It is so recursive that instead of taking the obvious outs we are used to hearing, Green in-

stead chooses to reinvest–to go in farther and deepen the groove. He opens up a groove and then opens up a groove and then opens a groove, and so on. He never stops. He opens a groove and then works to widen that groove until we can see into the music, see through the music into ourselves. He puts everything back into the groove that he might otherwise get out of it. He knows that the groove is the thing and that time will see him out and his music will live long. That is what grooves are about and why Grant Green is *the* groove master.

Blues in Jazz and R&B

There are forms of blues in jazz other than the groove music presented above. Here are a few notes on some of the major styles:

Blues Shouters and Singers–There are blues singers who tend toward jazz, and almost all jazz singers sing some blues. This is not the place to point these out since they are more-or-less straight-ahead blues singers when they sing blues. The one exception, of course, is Billie Holiday. Holiday is probably the most seminal singer ever recorded. But is her music the blues? Everything she sings is way beyond blues and blues is supposed to be the root music. Holiday is the equivalent of Delta blues singer Robert Johnson in that she is seminal–pure source. Period.

If you have not listened to Billie Holiday and gotten into her music to the point of real distraction (being moved!), then you have missed one of the premiere music experiences of a lifetime. Enough said.

Bluesy Jazz–There is also a style of blues-laden jazz that is not so much funky as downright bluesy. Kenny Burrell is perhaps the chief exponent of this style of jazz. Bluesy jazz has a slow or mid-tempo and is easy to listen to–relaxing. It makes great background or dinner music and yet is integral and stands on its own merits as a music. A lot of artists play bluesy jazz; some play it often. Much bluesy jazz can establish a groove.

Kenny Burrell, *Midnight Blue*/Blue Note
The Three Sounds (Gene Harris), *Introducing the Three Sounds*/
　Blue Note
Ron Carter, *Jazz: My Romance*/Blue Note
Grant Green, *Born to be Blue*/Blue Note
Ray Bryant, *All Blues*/Pablo
Red Garland, *Soul Junction*/Prestige
Wynton Kelly, *Kelly Blue*/Riverside

Blues/Funk Sax: Honkers, Screamers & Bar Walkers–Although the emergence of blues sax can be traced all the way back to the great Ben Webster, the honkin', screaming tenor sax of the bar-walking variety originated with Illinois Jacquet and was carried to its logical conclusion with the R&B sax of King Curtis. The term "bar walkin'" came from the habit of emotionally driven sax players walking on the top of a bar among the customers playing at a frenzied pitch–often in contests with another sax player walking from the other end of the bar. This honkin' blues-drenched sax style was as much performance bravado as sheer music. As Cannonball Adderley said about the funky big-toned sax, "It's the moan inside the tone." Since many of the main players in this style hailed from the Southwest, players in this style are often referred to as "Texas tenors." Some of the main artists in this style include Al Sears, Big Jay McNeely, Willis Jackson, Sil Austin, Lee Allen, Rusty Bryant, Hal Singer, and Sam "The Man" Taylor. Most of these players came out of the large swing bands and either formed their own groups or found work in various R&B settings. This raunchy honkin' music scratches that blues itch and satisfies. This is often groove material.

Since many of these sax players can (and often had to) play it all–blues, R&B, honkin' sax, soul jazz, straight jazz, etc.–they are listed here together. I have made some notes to guide you as to their main directions. If you can find the three-CD collection called *Giants of the*

Blues and Funk Tenor Sax (Prestige 3PCD-2302-2), you will get a superb 23-cut collection with many extended solos and liner notes by Bob Porter. Worth ordering or searching for.

Sax: Blues, R&B, Funk: Honkers and Bar Walkers

Lee Allen (R&B) *Walkin' with Mr. Lee*/Collectables
Gene Ammons (R&B, bop, soul jazz) *Boss Tenors–Straight Ahead from Chicago 1961*/Verve
Sil Austin (blues) *Slow Rock Rock*/Wing
Earl Bostic (R&B) *Best of Earl Bostic*/Deluxe
Rusty Bryant (R&B, soul jazz) *Rusty Bryant Returns*/OJC
Arnett Cobb (blues, soul jazz) *Smooth Sailing*/OJC
King Curtis (R&B, soul jazz) *Soul Meeting*/Prestige
Hank Crawford (soul jazz) *Soul Survivors*/Milestone
Eddie Lockjaw Davis (blues, soul jazz) *Cookbook, Vol. 1–3*/OJC
Jimmy Forrest (blues, bop, soul jazz) *Out of the Forest*/Prestige
Frank Foster (blues) *Soul Outing*/Prestige
Johnny Griffin (bop, hard bop, blues) *Big Soul Band*/OJC
Eddie Harris (soul jazz) *Best of*/Atlantic
Coleman Hawkins (blues, hard bop)
Red Holloway (soul jazz) *Cookin' Together*/Prestige
Joe Houston (R&B Honker, blues)
Willis Jackson (R&B, funk) *Bar Wars*/Muse
Illinois Jacquet (Honker, blues, R&B) *Blues: That's Me!*/OJC
Big Jay McNeely (R&B, Honker, blues)
Wild Bill Moore (blues) (Look for him as a sideman)
Oliver Nelson (blues, out) *Soul Battle*/OJC
David Fathead Newman (R&B, soul jazz) *Lonely Avenue*/Atlantic
Harold Ousley (blues, soul jazz) *Sweet Double Hipness*/Muse
Houston Person (soul jazz) *Goodness*/OJC
Ike Quebec (blues, soul jazz) *Blue and Sentimental*/Blue Note
Al Sears (blues) *The Swingville All-Stars*/Swingville
Hal Singer (blues) *Blue Stompin'*/Prestige
Sonny Stitt (bop, soul jazz) *Soul Summit*/Prestige
Buddy Tate (blues) *Tate's Date*/Swingville
Sam "The Man" Taylor (blues, R&B)
Eddie Cleanhead Vinson (blues) *Kidney Stew*/Black & Blue
Ernie Watts (blues, bop, soul jazz) *Ernie Watts Quartet*/JVC

Blues in Free Jazz–Blues in free jazz are present; the notes are there. The problem is that the constant beat is missing and thus the groove never gets laid down. More important, most free jazz is stir-it-up music rather than cool out. While this is great music, it is not groove music. Here are some outstanding examples of some blues in free jazz.

Archie Shepp, *Attica Blues*/Impulse
Oliver Nelson, *Screamin' the Blues*/New Jazz
Charles Mingus, *Charles Mingus Presents Charles Mingus*/Candid
John Coltrane, *Love Supreme*/Impulse
Sun Ra, *The Heliocentric Worlds of Sun Ra*/ESP
Ornette Coleman, *Tomorrow is the Question*/Contemporary

Blues in Jazz Rock & Fusion–The same is true for most jazz rock as for free jazz. The notes occur but the energy is more agitating than not and the groove is seldom established.

Crusaders, *Crusaders 1*/Blue Thumb
David Sanborn, *Backstreet*/Warner Brothers
Mahavishnu Orchestra, *The Inner Mounting Flame*/Columbia
Miles Davis, *Star People*/Columbia

I hope that some of what I have written here will help blues lovers push off from the island of blues out into the sea of jazz. You can always head back to the solid ground of blues if you can't get into the jazz. Blues and jazz are not mutually exclusive. Blues in jazz has been a thrilling ride (groove) for me and I have found a whole new music that satisfies much like the blues satisfy. I listen to groove music all the time. If you find some great groove styles that I have not mentioned here, drop me a line. I want to hear them.

Thanks.

Michael Erlewine
c/o All-Music Guide
315 Marion Avenue
Big Rapids, MI 49307
Phone: (616) 796-3437
e-mail: Michael@TheNewAge.com

Here is something that I wished I had when I first started to get into groove and blues jazz—a quick guide to the best recordings. It can save you both time and money. These are some of the main jazz (and R&B) artists with a strong blues content. You will want to hear them out. In each case I have tried to point out key albums that are worth a listen from a blues or groove perspective. The albums are rated and reviewed (where possible) to give you insight into why these might or might not interest you. A short biography is also included and sometimes additional notes on how to approach the artist from a blues perspective. We would need a whole book to do this right, and the *All Music Guide to Jazz* (2nd edition) is available when you are. I am sorry to say that many of the albums listed below are not available on CD. Some probably never will be. Although I love CDs, I have had to get back into vinyl to hear a lot of this music. Many of you will also—back to the old record bins. It's worth it if the music is there. And it is. I hope you enjoy this short guide to groove music. — *Michael Erlewine*

Cannonball Adderley (Julian Edwin Adderley)

b. Sep. 15, 1928, Tampa, FL, d. Aug. 8, 1975, Gary, IN
Alto Saxophone / Hard Bop, Soul-Jazz, Groove
One of the great alto saxophonists, Cannonball Adderley had an exuberant and happy sound (as opposed to many of the more serious stylists of his generation) that communicated immediately to listeners. His intelligent presentation of his music (often explaining what he and his musicians were going to play) helped make him one of the most popular of all jazzmen.

Adderley already had an established career as a high school band director in Florida when during a 1955 visit to New York he was persuaded to sit in with Oscar Pettiford's group at the Cafe Bohemia. His playing created such a sensation that he was soon signed to Savoy and persuaded to play jazz full-time in New York. With his younger brother cornetist Nat, Adderley formed a quintet that struggled until its breakup in 1957. Adderley then joined Miles Davis, forming part of his super sextet with John Coltrane and participating on such classic recordings as *Milestones* and *Kind of Blue*. Adderley's second attempt to form a quintet with his brother was much more successful and in 1959 with pianist Bobby Timmons he had a hit recording of "This Here." From then on, Adderley always was able to work steadily with his band.

During its Riverside years (1959-63), the Adderley Quintet primarily played soulful renditions of hard bop, and Adderley really excelled in the straightahead settings. During 1962-63 Yusef Lateef made the group a sextet, and pianist Joe Zawinul was an important new member. The collapse of Riverside resulted in Adderley signing with Capitol and his recordings became gradually more commercial. Charles Lloyd was in Lateef's place for a year (with less success) and then with his departure the group went back to being a quintet. Zawinul's 1966 composition "Mercy, Mercy, Mercy" was a huge hit for the group, Adderley started doubling on soprano and the Quintet's later recordings emphasized long melody statements, funky rhythms, and electronics. However during his last year, Adderley was revisiting the past a bit and on *Phenix* he recorded new versions of many of his earlier numbers. But before he could evolve his music any further, Adderley died suddenly from a stroke. — *Scott Yanow*
Groove: Adderley is one of the pioneers of soul jazz, in the sense of jazz played with a funky soul flavor, so don't look for your standard organ-combo groove music. It was the Cannonball Adderley Quintet that was first refered to by critcs as a "soul-jazz" group. Cannonball jazz is sunny, not dark. It is bright and clear. The album *Somethin' Else* is a good place to start. — *Michael Erlewine*

☆ **Somethin' Else** / Mar. 9, 1958 / Blue Note ◆◆◆◆◆
Shortly after Adderley broke up his original quintet and joined Miles Davis' sextet, he recorded this LP with Davis in the rare role of a sideman. Actually Davis dominates several of the selections (including "Autumn Leaves," "Love for Sale," and "One for Daddy-o") but both hornmen (backed by pianist Hank Jones, bassist Sam Jones and drummer Art Blakey) sound quite inspired by each other's presence. — *Scott Yanow*

★ **Things Are Getting Better** / Oct. 28, 1958 / Original Jazz Classics ◆◆◆◆◆
Adderley teams up with vibraphonist Milt Jackson, pianist Wynton Kelly, bassist Percy Heath, and drummer Art Blakey for a jubilant and often-explosive session on this CD reissue. On tunes such as "Things Are Getting Better," "Just One Of Those Things," and a memorable "Sidewalks Of New York," the altoist-leader is quite joyful in his solos, really ripping into the material. This set is a very good example of early Adderley, recorded a year before his quintet caught on. — *Scott Yanow*

● **Cannonball and Coltrane** / Feb. 3, 1959 / EmArcy ◆◆◆◆
This LP (whose contents have been reissued many times) features the Miles Davis Sextet of 1959 without the leader. Altoist Cannonball Adderley and tenor-saxophonist John Coltrane really push each other on these six selections with this version of "Limehouse Blues" really burning. Coltrane's very serious sound is a striking contrast to the jubilant Adderley alto; the latter is showcased on "Stars Fell on Alabama." With pianist Wynton Kelly, bassist Paul Chambers, and drummer Jimmy Cobb playing up to their usual level, this gem is highly recommended. — *Scott Yanow*

● **Cannonball Adderley Quintet in San Francisco** / Oct. 18, 1959 + Oct. 20, 1959 / Original Jazz Classics ◆◆◆◆
Cannonball Adderley had struggled unsuccessfully with a quintet during 1955-57, giving up for a time to play with Miles Davis' group. In 1959 his new quintet suddenly caught on with the release of this very exciting live album, which has been reissued on CD in the Original Jazz Classics series. With cornetist Nat Adderley, pianist Bobby Timmons, bassist Sam Jones, and drummer Louis Hayes, Cannonball had the top new jazz group of 1959. Their version of Timmons' "This Here" was a major hit and the other numbers on this famous date (which include "Spontaneous Combustion," "Hi-Fly," "You Got It," "Bohemia After Dark" and "Straight No Chaser") are also quite enjoyable, showing why Adderley's group was a pacesetter in funky soul jazz and proving that they could outswing most of their competition. This gem is essential for all jazz collections. — *Scott Yanow*

Cannonball Adderley Collection, Vol. 1: Them Dirty Blues / Feb. 1, 1960 / Landmark ◆◆◆◆
The first of seven LPs that reissue recordings from his period with Riverside contains several notable selections. The first side (which has pianist Bobby Timmons well-featured with bassist Sam Jones, drummer Louis Hayes, cornetist Nat Adderley and the leader/altoist) includes the original versions of Timmons' "Dat Dere" (his follow-up to "This Here" which is heard here in two takes), Sam Jones' "Del Sasser" and Nat's "Work Song"; the latter was previously unissued. On the flip side (with Barry Harris in Timmons' place), the quintet performs the initial "official" version of "Work Song," a heated "Jeannine," "Easy Living," and "Them Dirty Blues." Lots of classic music comes from this influential soul-jazz band. — *Scott Yanow*

Cannonball Adderley Collection, Vol. 5: The Quintet at the Lighthouse / Oct. 16, 1960 / Landmark ◆◆◆◆
This is a fine all-around set from the Cannonball Adderley Quintet of 1960 with the altoist/leader, cornetist Nat Adderley, pianist Victor Feldman, bassist

Sam Jones, and drummer Louis Hayes. The fifth of seven LPs reissued by Orrin Keepnews and taken from Adderley's Riverside years finds his band in top form on the original version of "Sack O' Woe," a previously unissued "Our Delight," Jimmy Heath's "Big 'P,'" and "Blue Daniel" among others. It's a strong introduction to the music of this classic hard bop group. *— Scott Yanow*

What Is This Thing Called Soul? / Nov. 22, 1960-Nov. 23, 1960 / Original Jazz Classics ✦✦✦✦

Cannonball Adderley's 1960 Quintet (with cornetist Nat Adderley and pianist Victor Feldman) was in top form during their tour of Europe. Norman Granz did not release the music heard on this CD until almost 25 years after the fact but the strong solos and enthusiastic ensembles had not dated nor faded with time. These versions of "The Chant," "What Is This Thing Called Love?," and "Big 'P'" make for interesting comparisons with the better-known renditions. Adderley fans will want this set. *— Scott Yanow*

The Quintet Plus / May 11, 1961 / Original Jazz Classics ✦✦✦✦

For this CD reissue of a Riverside date, altoist Cannonball Adderley's 1961 Quintet (which includes cornetist Nat Adderley, pianist Victor Feldman, bassist Sam Jones, and drummer Louis Hayes) is joined by guest pianist Wynton Kelly on five of the eight selections, during which Feldman switches quite effectively to vibes. The music falls between funky soul-jazz and hard bop, and each of the performances (particularly "Star Eyes" and "Well You Needn't") is enjoyable. The CD adds a new alternate take of "Lisa" and the previously unissued "O.P." to the original program. *— Scott Yanow*

Cannonball Adderley Collection, Vol. 2: Bossa Nova / Dec. 7, 1962-Dec. 11, 1962 / Landmark ✦✦✦

Recorded when the bossa nova craze was generating steam, this was one of the better albums of the genre. Adderley wisely cut his lone bossa nova record with South American musicians, a group called the Bossa Rio Sextet that included pianist Sergio Mendes and future Weather Report member Dom Um Romao on drums. Adderley's sound on alto was well attuned to this music (as was his upbeat musical personality, as can be heard on "Once I Loved" and two versions of "Corcovado." *— Scott Yanow*

Mercy, Mercy, Mercy / Oct. 20, 1966 / Capitol ✦✦✦✦

This set (reissued on CD) is one of Adderley's finest albums of his last decade. "Mercy, Mercy, Mercy," a soulful Joe Zawinul melody that is repeated several times without any real improvisation, became a surprise hit, but the other selections on this live date ("Fun," "Games," "Sticks," "Hippodelphia," and "Sack O'Woe") all have plenty of fiery solos from the quintet (which is comprised of the leader on alto, cornetist Nat Adderley, pianist Joe Zawinul, bassist Victor Gaskin, and drummer Roy McCurdy). Adderley sounds quite inspired (his expressive powers had expanded due to the unacknowledged influence of the avant-garde), and Nat Adderley shows just how exciting a player he was back in his prime. "Sack O'Woe" is particularly memorable. This CD, which is far superior to most of Adderley's later Capitol recordings, is highly recommended. *— Scott Yanow*

74 Miles Away/Walk Tall / Jun. 12, 1967-Jun. 24, 1967 / Capitol ✦✦✦✦

With the hit "Mercy, Mercy, Mercy" still reverberating on the sales charts, Capitol simply had the Quintet crank out one live club date after another at this point, hoping for another smash. They never really got one, but Cannonball and Nat Adderley, in league with pianist Joe Zawinul, bassist Victor Gaskin, and drummer Roy McCurdy, left a strong legacy like this vigorous live Hollywood gig. One of Nat's best gospel-styled hip-shakers, "Do Do Do," opens the record, and Joe Zawinul comes up with another bluesy, catchy self-help tune in the vein of "Mercy" called "Walk Tall," prefaced by another of Adderley's wryly inspirational talks. Indeed Adderley was such an ingratiating speaker that he could even deliver a gracious ode to a critic, in this case Leonard Feather prior to his eloquent performance of Feather's "I Remember Bird." Yet the Adderleys and Zawinul could also take off and offer exploratory, nearly avant-garde solos on Zawinul's Middle-Eastern-flavored montuna in 7/4 time, "74 Miles Away" (which presages some of Joe's experiments with Weather Report). This was a rare thing, a group that could grab the public's attention and gently lead them into more difficult idioms without pandering or condescension. *— Richard S. Ginell*

Accent on Africa / Jun. 13, 1968-Jun. 14, 1968 / Capitol ✦✦✦

Though labeled as a Cannonball Adderley Quintet session, this is actually a

workout with a percussion section loaded with African drums, a big band, and in spots, voices—all unidentified. Nevertheless, this is one of the best and most overlooked of the Cannonball Adderley Capitols, a rumbling session that bursts with the joy of working in an unfamiliar yet vital rhythmic context. Cannonball turns in one of his swinging-est solos through a Varitone electronic attachment on Caiphus Semenya's "Gumba Gumba" and "Marabi" is a real hip-jiggler; you can't sit still through it. Other highlights include Cannon preaching blue smoke in his own Afro-Cuban-blues-flavored "Hamba Nami," a dignified trip through Wes Montgomery's "Up and At It," and Nat Adderley's commanding work on cornet at all times. *— Richard S. Ginell*

Greatest Hits / Jan. 20, 1998 / Milestone ✦✦✦✦

"Greatest Hits" in this case means some of Cannonball Adderley's best-known numbers for the Riverside label—all delivered at their glorious, uncut original length, complete with several of Cannonball's ingratiating spoken intros. Since a few of the obvious choices ("Work Song," "Jive Samba," "Sack O' Woe") were sold by Riverside to Cannonball, who then gave them to Capitol in the '60s and were otherwise unavailable in the Fantasy catalogue, their inclusion here gives the set a boost. There are some glaring omissions from the Riverside years—where's "Hi Fly?," where's "Dat Dere?"—but at least eight different albums with seven different instrumental lineups are represented, including the Quintet, Sextet, sessions with Milt Jackson and Bill Evans, and a big band led by Ernie Wilkins. The highly-partial, always vainglorious original producer Orrin Keepnews made the choices and also contributed the liner notes, which make for a good read. This, combined with Capitol's own Best Of CD, will give you a decent launching pad for exploring the Adderley brothers' soul-jazz celebrations of the 1960s. *— Richard S. Ginell*

Nat Adderley

b. Nov. 25, 1931, Tampa, FL
Cornet / Hard Bop, Soul-Jazz, Groove

Nat Adderley's cornet (which in its early days was strongly influenced by Miles Davis) was always a complementary voice to his brother Cannonball Adderley in their popular quintet. His career ran parallel to his older brother for quite some time. Nat Adderley took up trumpet in 1946, switched to cornet in 1950 and spent time in the military, playing in an Army band during 1951-53. After a period with Lionel Hampton (1954-55), Adderley made his recording debut in 1955, joined Cannonball Adderley's unsuccessful quintet of 1956-57 and then spent periods with the groups of J.J. Johnson and Woody Herman before hooking up with Cannonball again in Oct. 1959. This time the group became a major success and Nat Adderley remained in the quintet until Cannonball Adderley's death in 1975, contributing such originals as "Work Song," "Jive Samba," and "The Old Country" along with many exciting hard bop solos. Nat Adderley, who was at the peak of his powers in the early to mid-'60s and became adept at playing solos that dipped into the subtone register of his horn, has led his own quintets since Cannonball Adderley's death; his most notable sidemen were altoists Sonny Fortune (in the early '80s) and Vincent Herring. Although his own playing has declined somewhat (Adderley's chops no longer have the endurance of his earlier days), Adderley has continued recording worthwhile sessions. Many but not all of his recordings through the years (for such labels as Savoy, EmArcy, Riverside, Jazzland, Atlantic, Milestone, A&M, Capitol, Prestige, Steeple Chase, Galaxy, Theresa, In & Out, Landmark, Evidence, Enja, Timeless, Jazz Challenge, and Chiaroscuro) are currently available. *— Scott Yanow*

Introducing Nat Adderley / Sep. 6, 1955 / EmArcy ✦✦✦

Branching Out / Sep. 1958 / Original Jazz Classics ✦✦✦✦

Cornetist Nat Adderley's debut for Riverside (reissued on CD in the OJC series) was recorded about a year before he permanently rejoined his brother Cannonball Adderley's Quintet. Teamed with tenor-saxophonist Johnny Griffin and the Three Sounds (the popular soul jazz rhythm section comprised of pianist Gene Harris, bassist Andy Simpkins, and drummer Bill Dowdy), Adderley is in excellent form on such tunes as "Well You Needn't," "Don't Get Around Much Anymore," and "I Never Knew" in addition to two of his lesser-known originals. Adderley and Griffin made for an exciting frontline. *— Scott Yanow*

● **Work Song** / Jan. 25, 1960-Jan. 27, 1960 / Original Jazz Classics ◆◆◆◆
This CD reissue brings back a near-classic by cornetist Nat Adderley. Utilizing a cornet-cello-guitar frontline (with Sam Jones and Wes Montgomery) along with a top-notch rhythm section (pianist Bobby Timmons, Percy Heath or Keter Betts on bass, and drummer Louis Hayes), Adderley performs a fine early version of his greatest hit ("Work Song") and helps introduce Cannonball Adderley's "Sack O' Woe." Four songs use a smaller group with Timmons absent on "My Heart Stood Still" (which finds Keter Betts on cello and Jones on bass), "Mean To Me" featuring Adderley backed by Montgomery, Betts, and Hayes, and two ballads ("I've Got a Crush on You" and "Violets For Your Furs") interpreted by the Adderley-Montgomery-Jones trio. No matter the setting, Nat Adderley is heard throughout in peak form, playing quite lyrically. Highly recommended. — *Scott Yanow*

That's Right!: Nat Adderley & The Big Sax Section / Aug. 9, 1960 + Sep. 15, 1960 / Original Jazz Classics ◆◆◆◆
Nat Adderley has seldom played with more fire, verve, and distinction than he did on *That's Right!* It placed him in the company of an expanded sax section that included his brother Cannonball Adderley on alto, Yusef Lateef on tenor, flute, and oboe, Jimmy Heath and Charlie Rouse on tenor, and baritone saxophonist Tate Houston. Solos crackled, the backing was tasty and stimulating, and the eight songs ranged from brisk standards to delightful originals. This CD reissue, despite lacking any new or alternate material, is most welcome due to the full, striking sound that the big reed section provided. — *Ron Wynn*

Natural Soul / Sep. 23, 1963 / Milestone ◆◆◆
With Kenny Burrell (g) and Junior Mance (p). — *Michael Erlewine*

You Baby / Mar. 26, 1968-Apr. 4, 1968 / A&M ◆◆◆◆
As Cannonball Adderley moved with the times in the late '60s, so did brother Nat Adderley on his own. While Adderley generally buys into Creed Taylor's A&M mixture of top-flight jazz talent, pop tunes and originals, and orchestrations packaged in bite-sized tracks, this album has its own pleasingly veiled yet soulful sound quite apart from its neighbors in the A&M/CTI series. Give credit to Adderley's successful use of a Varitone electronic attachment on his cornet, giving the horn an "electric blue" sound which he handles with marvelous rhythmic dexterity. Add Joe Zawinul's lively, funky electric piano from Cannonball Adderley's quintet, as well as the brooding, genuinely classically-inspired orchestrations of Bill Fischer that only use violas, cellos, and flutes. While not always technically perfect, Adderley's solos have soul and substance; his brief, catchy bop licks on "Halftime" are some of the best he ever played and on Zawinul's "Early Minor," he evokes a sense of loneliness that Miles would have admired. A lovely, intensely musical album, well worth seeking out. — *Richard S. Ginell*

Calling out Loud / Nov. 19, 1968-Dec. 4, 1968 / A&M ◆◆◆◆
For his second and alas, last album for A&M, Nat Adderley reunites with Joe Zawinul and the greatly underrated arranger Bill Fischer, this time with a tight, often surprisingly progressive concept in mind. All the tunes are by the above three, all are linked by classical arrangements for winds to form a suite, yet both Adderley and Zawinul are given plenty of room to burn. Adderley's "Biafra," clearly written with the then-raging Nigerian civil war in mind, sets the thoughtful mood, contrasting a moving dirge with buoyant extended solos by Adderley and Zawinul. Adderley plays on both acoustic and electric Varitone cornet; it's amazing how the latter alters his boppish personality into something more sensitive and soulful. Fischer's charts are always intriguing, brooding even when the music is joyous, and already Zawinul is displaying some of the freedom on electric piano that would soon emerge with Miles Davis and Weather Report. Indeed, Zawinul's "Grey Moss" and Fischer's "Nobody Knows" sound like cautious prototypes for portions of Miles' *Bitches Brew*. A fascinating album, beautifully produced, with mordant cover art (firecrackers). — *Richard S. Ginell*

Gene Ammons

b. Apr. 14, 1925, Chicago, IL, **d.** Aug. 6, 1974, Chicago, IL
Tenor Saxophone / Bop, Hard Bop, Soul-Jazz, Groove
Gene Ammons, who had a huge and immediately recognizable tone on tenor, was a very flexible player who could play bebop with the best (always battling his friend Sonny Stitt to a tie) yet was an influence on the R&B world. Some of his ballad renditions became hits and, despite two unfortu-

nate interruptions in his career, Ammons remained a popular attraction for 25 years.

Son of the great boogie-woogie pianist Albert Ammons, Gene Ammons (who was nicknamed "Jug") left Chicago at age 18 to work with King Kolax's band. He originally came to fame as a key soloist with Billy Eckstine's orchestra during 1944-47, trading off with Dexter Gordon on the famous Eckstine record *Blowing the Blues Away*. Other than a notable stint with Woody Herman's Third Herd in 1949 and an attempt at co-leading a two tenor group in the early '50s with Sonny Stitt, Ammons worked as a single throughout his career, recording frequently (most notably for Prestige) in settings ranging from quartets and organ combos to all-star jam sessions. Drug problems kept him in prison during much of 1958-60 and, due to a particularly stiff sentence, 1962-69. When Ammons returned to the scene in 1969 he opened up his style a bit, including some of the emotional cries of the avant-garde while utilizing funky rhythm sections, but he was still able to battle Sonny Stitt on his own terms. Ironically the last song that he ever recorded (just a short time before he was diagnosed with terminal cancer) was "Goodbye." — *Scott Yanow*

Groove: Ammons' big tone and bluesy sound was a huge influence on the jazz scene. The fact that he could play in many jazz styles made him even more seminal. I have tried to list some of his more soul-jazz (organ combo) albums, but he recorded a lot and you may find you like a wide variety of his bluesy, soulful sessions. — *Michael Erlewine*

☆ **The Happy Blues** / Apr. 23, 1956 / Original Jazz Classics ◆◆◆◆
This is one of the great studio jam sessions. Tenor saxophonist Gene Ammons is teamed up with trumpeter Art Farmer, altoist Jackie McLean, pianist Duke Jordan, bassist Addison Farmer, drummer Art Taylor, and the congas of Candido for four lengthy selections. Best is "The Happy Blues," which has memorable solos and spontaneous but perfectly fitting riffing by the horns behind each others' solos. The other numbers ("The Great Lie," "Can't We Be Friends," and "Madhouse") are also quite enjoyable, making this a highly recommended set. — *Scott Yanow*

Funky / Jan. 11, 1957 / Original Jazz Classics ◆◆◆◆
The Gene Ammons all-star jam session recordings of the 1950s are all quite enjoyable and this one is no exception. The great tenor is matched with trumpeter Art Farmer, altoist Jackie McLean, guitarist Kenny Burrell, pianist Mal Waldron, bassist Doug Watkins, and drummer Art Taylor for lengthy versions of "Stella By Starlight," the Burrell blues "Funky," and a pair of numbers by arranger Jimmy Mundy. All of the horns plus Burrell and Waldron get ample solo space and Ammons seems to really inspire his sidemen on these soulful bop jams. — *Scott Yanow*

Groove Blues / Jan. 3, 1958 / Original Jazz Classics ◆◆◆◆
On Jan. 3, 1958, Gene Ammons led one of his last all-star jam sessions for Prestige. The most notable aspect to this date (which resulted in two albums of material) is that it featured among its soloists John Coltrane, on alto. This CD, a straight reissue of one of the original LPs, includes baritonist Pepper Adams, the tenor of Paul Quinichette and Coltrane on two of the four selections, and Jerome Richardson's flute during three of the songs in addition to a fine rhythm section (pianist Mal Waldron, bassist George Joyner, and drummer Art Taylor). This set consists of three of Waldron's originals in addition to the standard ballad "It Might as Well Be Spring," and it (along with the CD *The Big Sound*) fully documents the productive day. — *Scott Yanow*

The Gene Ammons Story: Organ Combos / Jun. 17, 1960 + Nov. 28, 1961 / Prestige ◆◆◆◆
Gene Ammons recorded frequently for Prestige during the 1950s and early 1960s, and virtually all of the tenor's dates were quite rewarding. This two-LP set reissues *Twistin' the Jug* plus part of *Angel Eyes* and *Velvet Soul*. Ammons, a bop-based but very versatile soloist, sounds quite comfortable playing a variety of standards and lesser-known material in groups featuring Jack McDuff or Johnny "Hammond" Smith on organ and either trumpeter Joe Newman or Frank Wess on tenor and flute. This version of "Angel Eyes" became a surprise hit. — *Scott Yanow*

Soul Summit / Jun. 13, 1961-Apr. 13, 1962 / Prestige ◆◆◆◆
This single CD reissues all of the music from two LPs titled *Soul Summit* and *Soul Summit, Vol. 2*. The latter session is one of the lesser known of the many collaborations of tenors Gene Ammons and Sonny Stitt, who are joined by organist Jack McDuff and drummer Charlie Persip. Their six perfor-

mances are primarily riff tunes with "When You Wish upon a Star" taken at a medium pace and "Out in the Cold Again" the lone ballad. The second half of this CD features Ammons on two songs ("Love I've Found You" and a swinging "Too Marvelous for Words") with a big band arranged by Oliver Nelson, jamming "Ballad for Baby" with a quintet, sitting out of "Scram" (which stars McDuff and the tenor of Harold Vick) and backing singer Etta Jones on three numbers, of which, "Cool, Cool Daddy" is the most memorable. Overall, this is an interesting and consistently swinging set that adds to the large quantity of recordings that the great Ammons did during the early '60s. — *Scott Yanow*

★ **Boss Tenors: Straight Ahead from Chicago 1961** / Aug. 27, 1961 / Verve ♦♦♦♦♦

There are perhaps no better tenors, no better jazz. This is definitive. With Sonny Stitt. — *Michael G. Nastos*

Sil Austin

b. Sep. 17, 1929, Dunnellon, FL
Tenor Saxophone / Groove, East Coast Blues, Jump Blues
R&B tenor saxman and band leader Sil (Silvester) Austin was born September 17, 1929 in Dunnellon, FL. In 1946, Austin won a talent show at the Apollo theater in New York City for a version of "Danny Boy." In 1949, he worked with Roy Eldridge and then with Cootie Williams from 1949 to 1952. From 1953 to 1954 he was with Tiny Bradshaw. Ella Fitzgerald recorded Austin's composition "Ping Pong" and then gave him the title as a nickname. He later signed with Mercury and recorded with his own band. His R&B hits include "Slow Walk." — *Michael Erlewine*

Slow Rock Rock / Oct. 15, 1956-Oct. 19, 1956 / Wing ♦♦♦♦

● **Sil Austin Plays Pretty for the People** / Mercury ♦♦♦♦

George Benson

b. Mar. 22, 1943, Pittsburgh, PA
Guitar, Vocals / Hard Bop, Crossover Jazz, Pop, R&B
George Benson is simply one of the greatest guitarists in jazz history, but he is also an amazingly versatile musician—and that frustrates critics to no end who would paint him into a narrow bop box. He can play in just about any style—from swing to bop to R&B to pop—with supreme taste, a beautiful rounded tone, terrific speed, a marvelous sense of logic in building solos, and always, an unquenchable urge to swing. His inspirations may have been Charlie Christian and Wes Montgomery—and he can do dead-on impressions of both—but his style is completely his own. Not only can he play lead brilliantly, he is also one of the best rhythm guitarists around, supportive to soloists and a dangerous swinger, particularly in a soul-jazz format. Yet Benson can also sing in a lush soulful tenor with mannerisms similar to those of Stevie Wonder and Donny Hathaway—and it is his voice that has proved to be more marketable to the public than his guitar. Benson is the guitar-playing equivalent of Nat Cole—a fantastic pianist whose smooth way with a pop vocal eventually eclipsed his instrumental prowess in the marketplace—but unlike Cole, Benson has been granted enough time after his fling with the pop charts to reaffirm his jazz guitar credentials, which he still does at his concerts.

Benson actually started out professionally as a singer, performing in nightclubs at eight, recording four sides for RCA's "X" label in 1954, forming a rock band at 17 while using a guitar that his stepfather made for him. Exposure to records by Christian, Montgomery, and Charlie Parker got him interested in jazz, and by 1962, the teenaged Benson was playing in Brother Jack McDuff's band. After forming his own group in 1965, Benson became another of talent scout John Hammond's major discoveries, recording two highly-regarded albums of soul jazz and hard bop for Columbia and turning up on several records by others, including Miles Davis' *Miles In The Sky*. He switched to Verve in 1967, and shortly after the death of Montgomery in June 1968, producer Creed Taylor began recording Benson with larger ensembles on A&M (1968-69) and big groups and all-star combos on CTI (1971-1976).

While the A&M and CTI albums certainly earned their keep and made Benson a guitar star in the jazz world, the mass market didn't catch on until he began to emphasize vocals after signing with Warner Bros. in 1976. His first album for WB, *Breezin'*, became a Top 10 hit on the strength of its sole vocal track "This Masquerade," and this led to a string of hit albums in an

R&B-flavored pop mode, culminating with the Quincy Jones-produced *Give Me The Night*. As the '80s wore on, though, Benson's albums became riddled with commercial formulas and inferior material, with his guitar almost entirely relegated to the background. Perhaps aware of the futility of chasing the charts (after all, "This Masquerade" was a lucky accident), Benson reversed his field late in the '80s to record a fine album of standards, *Tenderly*, and another with the Basie band, his guitar now featured more prominently. His pop-flavored work also improved noticeably in the '90s. Benson retains the ability to spring surprises on his fans and critics, like his dazzlingly idiomatic TV appearance and subsequent record date with Benny Goodman in 1975 in honor of John Hammond, and his awesome command of the moment at several Playboy Jazz Festivals in the '80s. — *Richard S. Ginell*

The New Boss Guitar / May 1, 1964 / Original Jazz Classics ♦♦♦♦
A definitive early album, it features Brother Jack McDuff (organ). — *Michael G. Nastos*

George Benson/Jack McDuff / May 1, 1964 + Oct. 19, 1965 / Prestige ♦♦♦♦
Guitarist George Benson spent an important period early in his career as a sideman with organist Jack McDuff. This two-LP set brings back two albums that they recorded together; one was originally under Benson's name while the other was led by McDuff. With tenor saxophonist Red Holloway adding his distinctive solo voice, this quartet/quintet (depending on whether they use a bassist) was an exciting blues-oriented unit that was rightfully popular in the mid-'60s. The two-fer gives one a valuable look at George Benson in his early years. — *Scott Yanow*

It's Uptown / 1965 / Columbia ♦♦♦
While George Benson's solid jazz reputation supposedly rests on his early John Hammond-produced Columbia albums, one listen to this disc will reveal that his interests roamed widely from the beginning. Yes, there is plenty of straight-forward bop playing here, with Benson stretching his technical chops on "Hello Birdie" and "Myna Bird Blues" and ruminating thoughtfully on "Willow Weep For Me." But Benson also had an interest in quasi-rock 'n' roll, producing Wes-like octaves on "Young Jaguar," and some Bo Diddley-in-Spain rhythm chording on "Bullfight." The young George sounds pure and mellifluous on three vocal numbers, the basic elements of his later successes mostly in place. Yet Benson's backing combo doesn't click on all cylinders; Lonnie Smith is reliable on organ but Ronnie Cuber's blunt baritone sax is rather cumbersome here. — *Richard S. Ginell*

Benson Burner / 1965-1966 / Columbia ♦♦♦
Some but not all of guitarist George Benson's Columbia records (plus some unreleased songs and other tunes that he recorded under organist Lonnie Smith's name) are included on this out-of-print double-LP. Fitting into the soul-jazz/hard bop idiom, Benson (who at the time was heavily influenced by Wes Montgomery and Charlie Christian, but already had his own approach) is mostly heard in a quartet with organist Smith, baritonist Ronnie Cuber, and drummer Jimmy Lovelace, although some selections add horns (including trumpeter Blue Mitchell) and more players in the rhythm section. The majority of the songs are basic originals by Benson or Smith, and the emphasis is on soulful swinging. Fine music. — *Scott Yanow*

The George Benson Cookbook / Aug. 1, 1966-Oct. 19, 1966 / Columbia ♦♦♦♦
The second of Benson's John Hammond-produced albums is far and away the superior of the pair, mixing down-to-basics, straight-ahead jazz with soul-drenched grooving. Suddenly Benson's backup group—same as that of *Uptown*, with Benny Green added on trombone now and then—has found its bearings and apropos to the title, they can cook, even sizzle. The effect upon Benson's own playing is striking; with something to react against, his sheer ability to swing advances into the realm of awesome. The rapid-fire work on "The Cooker" and "Ready And Able" will make you gasp. Only one vocal here, an exuberant "All Of Me." — *Richard S. Ginell*

Giblet Gravy / Feb. 1967 / Verve ♦♦♦♦
No, we're not in Creed Taylor country yet but we might as well be, for many of the ingredients that would garnish Benson's albums with Taylor are already present in this often enjoyable prototype. The immediate goal was to groom Benson as the next Wes Montgomery (who was about to leave Verve)—and so he covers hit tunes of the day ("Sunny," "Along Comes Mary," "Groovin'"), playing either with a big band-plus-voices or a neat quintet anchored by Herbie Hancock, and the sound is contoured to give his guitar a

warm mellow ambience. But the eclectic Benson is his own man, as his infectious repeated-interval rhythm trademark tells us on his self-composed title track, and despite Tom McIntosh's mostly lame arrangements, George's work is always tasty and irresistibly melodic. —*Richard S. Ginell*

The Silver Collection / Feb. 1967-Nov. 1968 / Verve ✦✦✦
Most of the tracks from Benson's two Verve albums, *Giblet Gravy* and *Goodies*, were deposited here in one of the label's earliest CDs. As such, it exists to plug a small hole in the collections of Benson fans, for it is hardly a prime choice if you want a representative Benson sampler. —*Richard S. Ginell*

☆ **Shape of Things to Come** / Aug. 27, 1968-Oct. 22, 1968 / A&M ✦✦✦✦
Upon Wes Montgomery's sudden death June 15, 1968, Creed Taylor signed Benson up and immediately thrust him onto the master's pedestal—or so the line has it. While this smashing debut for A&M has some of the Wes trappings—Don Sebesky's charts, Herbie Hancock and Ron Carter in the rhythm team—Benson triumphantly stamps his own image on the sessions with his infectious riffing, R&B slant, and solid jazz licks, propelled by Wes Covington's soulful organ and Leo Morris' driving drums. Just once, Benson tries a Varitone hookup with multi-speed overdubbings a la Les Paul on the title track; he would never use it again on discs but it is a great, futuristic electronic guitar trip, driven hard by a sizzling rhythm section and decorated sparingly by Sebesky. This superbly-produced record made Benson a formidable pop/jazz guitar star, not a mere Montgomery clone. —*Richard S. Ginell*

Verve Jazz Masters 21 / 1968-1969 / Polygram ✦✦✦
This is a more satisfactory summary of George Benson's late-'60s recordings than the early CD era's *Silver Collection* because it includes a pair of the later A&M recordings and a couple of guest spots on a Jimmy Smith album from that period. At this time, Benson, still in his mid-20s, was solidifying his reputation as a tremendously fluent and powerful guitar soloist, with plenty of hard bop facility and a genuine taste for R&B riffing and swinging. The eloquent slow blues of "Low Down and Dirty," the wild, weird use of a Varitone octave multiplier on "The Shape of Things to Come," and the gutsy if occasionally scattered bop licks as a foil for the smoldering Smith (with drummer Donald Bailey) on "The Boss" go a long way toward illustrating Benson's range here. —*Richard S. Ginell*

The Other Side of Abbey Road / Oct. 22, 1969-Nov. 9, 1969 / A&M ✦✦✦✦
Just three weeks after the US release of the Beatles' swan song *Abbey Road*, Creed Taylor ushered Benson into the studio to begin a remarkably successful pop/jazz translation of the record (complete with a parody of the famous cover, showing George with guitar crossing an Eastern urban street). It is a lyrical album, with a hint of the mystery and a lot of the cohesive concept of the Beatles' original despite the scrambled order of the tunes. Benson is given some room to stretch out on guitar, sometimes in a bluesy groove, and there are more samples of his honeyed vocals than ever before (oddly, his voice would not be heard again by record-buyers until he signed with Warner Bros.). Don Sebesky's arrangements roam freely from Baroque strings to a full-throated big band, and Freddie Hubbard, Sonny Fortune, and Hubert Laws get some worthy solo space. Yet for all its diversity, the record fits together as a whole more tightly than any other George Benson project, thanks to his versatile talents and the miraculous overarching unity of the Beatles' songs. One wonders if the Fab Four liked it, too. —*Richard S. Ginell*

☆ **Beyond the Blue Horizon** / Feb. 2, 1971-Feb. 3, 1971 / Columbia ✦✦✦✦✦
Having taken Benson along with him when he founded CTI, Creed Taylor merely leaves the guitarist alone with a small group on his first release. The payoff is a superb jazz session where Benson rises to the challenge of the turbulent rhythm section of Jack DeJohnette and Ron Carter, with Clarence Palmer ably manning the organ. Benson is clearly as much at home with DeJohnette's advanced playing as he was in soul/jazz (after all, he did play on some Miles Davis sessions a few years before), and his tone is edgier, with more bite, than it had been for awhile. The lyrical Benson is also on eloquent display in "Ode To A Kudu" (heard twice on the CD, as is "All Clear"), and there is even a somewhat experimental tilt toward Afro-Cuban-Indian rhythms in "Somewhere To The East." A must-hear for all aficionados of Benson's guitar. —*Richard S. Ginell*

White Rabbit / Nov. 23, 1971-Nov. 30, 1971 / Columbia ✦✦✦✦
For Benson's second CTI project, producer Creed Taylor and arranger Don Sebesky successfully place the guitarist in a Spanish-flavored setting full of flamenco flourishes, brass fanfares, moody woodwinds, and such. The idea

works best on "California Dreamin'" (whose chords are based on Andalusian harmonies), where, driven by Jay Berliner's exciting Spanish rhythm guitar, Benson comes through with some terrifically inspired playing. On "El Mar," Berliner is replaced by Benson's protege Earl Klugh (then only 17) in an inauspicious—though at the time, widely-heralded—recorded debut. The title track is another winner, marred only by the out-of-tune brasses at the close, and in a good example of the CTI classical/jazz formula at work, Heitor Villa-Lobos' "Little Train of the Caipira" is given an attractive early-'70s facelift. Herbie Hancock gets plenty of nimble solo space on Rhodes electric piano, Airto Moreira contributes percussion and atmospheric wordless vocals, and Ron Carter and Billy Cobham complete the high-energy rhythm section. In this prime sample of the CTI idiom, everyone wins. —*Richard S. Ginell*

Earl Bostic

b. Apr. 25, 1913, Tulsa, OK, **d.** Oct. 28, 1965, Rochester, NY
Alto Saxophone / R&B, Swing, Groove
Earl Bostic's roots and foundation were steeped in jazz and swing, but he later became one of the most prolific R&B bandleaders. His searing, sometimes bluesy, sometimes soft and moving, alto-sax style influenced many players, including John Coltrane. His many King releases, which featured limited soloing and basic melodic and rhythmic movements, might have fooled novices into thinking Bostic possessed minimal skills; but Art Blakey once said, "Nobody knew more about the saxophone than Bostic, I mean technically, and that includes Bird." Bostic worked in several Midwest bands during the early '30s, then studied at Xavier University. He left school to tour with various groups, among them a band co-led by Charlie Creath and Fate Marable. He moved to New York in the late '30s, where he was a soloist in the bands of Don Redman, Edgar Hayes, and Lionel Hampton. Bostic also led his own combos, whose members included Jimmy Cobb, Al Casey, Blue Mitchell, Stanley Turrentine, Benny Golson, and Coltrane. Bostic toured extensively through the '50s, while cutting numerous sessions for King. His recording of "Flamingo" in 1951 was a huge hit, as were the songs "Sleep," "You Go to My Head," "Cherokee," and "Temptation." Bostic recorded for Allegro, Gotham, and King from the late '40s to the mid-'60s. He made more than 400 selections for King; the label would use stereo remakes of songs with different personnel, then use the same album numbers. After a heart attack, Bostic became a part-time player. His mid-'60s albums were more soul-jazz than R&B. Several of his King LPs are available on CD. —*Ron Wynn and Michael Erlewine*
Groove: There are a ton of Bostic albums out there, at least in vinyl. Don't be put off by their hokey album titles, cover art, arrangements, and/or song lists. This guy rocks and was on just about all the time. Remember that Stanley Turrentine and John Coltrane (and many other sax players) learned directly from Bostic. The great jazz drummer Art Blakey says, "Nobody knew more about the saxophone than Bostic. I mean technically, and that includes Bird." This is hard-rockin', raunchy R&B saxophone at its best. —*Michael Erlewine*

● **The Best of Earl Bostic** / 1956 / Deluxe ✦✦✦✦
A nice cross-section of this fiery alto-saxist's '50s output, it includes his hits "Sleep" and "Flamingo." —*Bill Dahl*

Showcase of Swinging Dance Hits / 1958 / King ✦✦✦
Perhaps his best rocking and uptempo instrumental pop and R&B material. This album was aimed at the jukebox market and weighted toward the hottest, most furiously played cuts in the Bostic repertoire. Bostic was as technically accomplished as any alto saxophonist in his era, but he wasn't able to show that while on King. This album was one of the few times that he was able to really show his skills on uptempo material. —*Ron Wynn*

Ray Bryant (Raphael Bryant)

b. Dec. 24, 1931, Philadelphia, PA
Piano / Bop, Swing, Soul-Jazz, Groove
Although he could always play bop, Ray Bryant's playing combines together older elements (including blues, boogie-woogie, gospel, and even stride) into a distinctive, soulful and swinging style; no one plays "After Hours" quite like him.

The younger brother of bassist Tommy Bryant and the uncle of Kevin and Robin Eubanks (his sister is their mother), Bryant started his career playing with Tiny Grimes in the late '40s. He became the house pianist at the Blue

Note in Philadelphia in 1953 where he backed classic jazz greats (including Charlie Parker, Miles Davis, and Lester Young) and made important contacts. He accompanied Carmen McRae (1956-57), recorded with Coleman Hawkins and Roy Eldridge at the 1957 Newport Jazz Festival (taking a brilliant solo on an exciting version of "I Can't Believe That You're in Love with Me") and played with Jo Jones' trio (1958). Bryant settled in New York in 1959, played with Sonny Rollins, Charlie Shavers and Curtis Fuller and soon had his own trio. He had a few funky commercial hits (including "Little Susie" and Cubano Chant") which kept him working for decades. Bryant has recorded often throughout his career (most notably for Epic, Prestige, Columbia, Sue, Cadet, Atlantic, Pablo, and EmArcy) and even his dates on electric piano in the '70s are generally rewarding. However, Bryant is heard at his best when playing the blues on unaccompanied acoustic piano. — *Scott Yanow*

Groove: Ray Bryant puts out great blues piano for up-front evaluation or just easy, kick-back listening. This is bluesy jazz. — *Michael Erlewine*

Alone with the Blues / Dec. 19, 1958 / Original Jazz Classics ✦✦✦
Ray Bryant's first solo piano album is rightfully considered a classic. Bryant, at the time thought of as a young modern traditionalist, has always felt perfectly at home playing the blues. He performs five original and diverse blues on this set along with "Lover Man" and "Rockin' Chair," showing that he really never needed a bassist or a drummer to sound like a complete band. This Prestige album was reissued in the Original Jazz Classics but thus far only as an LP; highly recommended in any case. — *Scott Yanow*

● **Montreux '77** / Jul. 13, 1977 / Original Jazz Classics ✦✦✦✦
Ray Bryant's fourth recorded solo piano recital (and second in less than a year) was performed at the 1977 Montreux Jazz Festival and is a particularly well-rounded set. Bryant plays spirituals, blues, swing standards, John Lewis' "Django," and the obscure "Jungle Town Jubilee." His distinctive and soulful style fits well into every setting, making this an easily recommended set that will satisfy most musical tastes. — *Scott Yanow*

All Blues / Apr. 10, 1978 / Original Jazz Classics ✦✦✦
Ray Bryant (piano), Sam Jones (bass), and Grady Tate (drums)—a classic trio of jazz greats playing bluesy jazz. Mostly at slower tempos, this is very listenable. Most important, the groove is maintained throughout, so you know what you are getting. — *Michael Erlewine*

Blue Moods / Feb. 15, 1987 / EmArcy ✦✦✦✦
Outstanding trio date with Bryant offering teeming phrases, sweeping statements, and some wonderful ballads, backed by bassist Rufus Reid and drummer Freddie Waits. Not only great playing all around, but an excellent recording as well. — *Ron Wynn*

Rusty Bryant

b. Nov. 25, 1929, Huntington, WV, **d.** Mar. 25, 1991, Columbus, OH
Tenor Saxophone / Post-Bop, Soul-Jazz, Groove, Hard Bop
Among the finest funky and soul-jazz tenors of the '70s, Bryant is noted for his thick tone, robust sound, and jam-session-style albums. Bryant is one of the original bar-walking sax players.

Royal G. "Rusty" Bryant was born on November 25, 1929 in Huntington, West Virginia, but was raised in Columbus, OH. He credits Gene Ammons and Sonny Stitt as his main influences. He played with and learned from Tiny Grimes and Stomp Gordon, and was leading his own groups by 1951. Bryant toured with Hammond organist Mike Marr during the '60s. He settled in Columbus, OH. — *Michael Erlewine & Ron Wynn*

Night Train Now! / 1969 / Prestige ✦✦✦
An effort very much consistent with producer Bob Porter's Prestige "house" soul-jazz sound, utilizing players who would contribute to many other similar efforts in the late '60s and early '70s, particularly guitarist Boogaloo Joe Jones and drummer Bernard Purdie. These beefy, straightforward grooves include a remake of Bryant's arrangement of "Night Train" (one of his most popular recordings in the version he cut for Dot). The writing credit for "Funky Rabbits" is given as "unknown," but it sure sounds a lot to these ears like a retitled version of Ray Charles' "Hallelujah, I Love Her So." The *Legends of Acid Jazz* CD reissue combines this and the 1970 session *Soul Liberation* onto one disc. — *Richie Unterberger*

Rusty Bryant Returns / Feb. 17, 1969 / Original Jazz Classics ✦✦✦✦
Recorded in Englewood Cliffs, NJ. This is great funk music! Rusty Bryant on amplified alto sax (Conn Multi-Vider)—his only LP on alto! This is his take-

off album for Prestige, after which he went on to make a lot of great music from 1968-1974. On this session is Grant Green, playing some great funk guitar. Sonny Phillips on Hammond organ fills out that classic small-group sound. — *Michael Erlewine*

● **Legends of Acid Jazz** / Oct. 6, 1969 + Jun. 15, 1970 / Prestige ✦✦✦✦
Presenting both the 1969 album *Night Train Now!* and the 1970 follow-up *Soul Liberation* in their entirety, this 73-minute disc is the best document of Bryant at his soul-jazz peak. — *Richie Unterberger*

Soul Liberation / Jun. 15, 1970 / Prestige ✦✦✦✦
This has a bluesier, harder R&B feel than his previous effort (*Night Train Now*), courtesy of a revamped lineup featuring Charles Earland on organ, Melvin Sparks on guitar, and Idris Muhammad on drums. The title track is Bryant's most famous composition. The *Legends of Acid Jazz* CD reissue combines this and the 1970 session *Soul Liberation* onto one disc. — *Richie Unterberger*

Milt Buckner

b. Jul. 10, 1915, St. Louis, MO, **d.** Jul. 27, 1977, Chicago, IL
Organ, Piano / Swing, Groove
Milt Buckner had a dual career. As a pianist he largely invented the "locked hands" style (parallel chords) that was adopted by many other players including George Shearing and Oscar Peterson. And as an organist he was one of the top pre-Jimmy Smith stylists, helping to popularize the instrument.

The younger brother of altoist Ted Buckner (who played with Jimmie Lunceford), Milt Buckner grew up in Detroit and gigged locally in addition to arranging for McKinney's Cotton Pickers in 1934. He came to fame as pianist and arranger with Lionel Hampton (1941-48, 1950-52 and occasionally in later years) where he was a crowd pleaser. During 1948-50 Buckner led his own bands and after 1952 he generally played organ with trios or quartets. In later years he sometimes teamed up with Illinois Jacquet or Jo Jones. Buckner recorded many dates as a leader, particularly for Black & Blue in the '70s. — *Scott Yanow*

Groove: There are some good Buckner solo albums and a few are listed here, but you will tend to find him as a sideman on albums by Illinois Jacquet, Arnet Cobb, and Clarence Gatemouth Brown. — *Michael Erlewine*

● **Rockin' Hammond** / Feb. 22, 1956-Mar. 15, 1956 / Capitol ✦✦✦✦
Classic organ combo with a master. From blues to ballads. A fine representation of Buckner's brilliance. — *Michael G. Nastos*

Green Onions / Feb. 21, 1975 / Inner City ✦✦✦✦
From 1966-77, organist Milt Buckner recorded often for European labels. This particular set (originally cut for the Black & Blue label) was one of the very few to be made available domestically. It came out on Inner City's Classic Jazz subsidiary, and it is a bit of an oddity. Buckner, through overdubbing, performs on organ, piano, and vibes (which he rarely played), and even takes an eccentric vocal on "Green Onions." To confuse matters, pianist Andre Persiany is also heard on some numbers, along with blues guitarist Roy Gaines, bassist Roland Lobligeois, and drummer Panama Francis. The music itself is much less complicated, swing standards plus Buckner's "Pour Toutes Mes Soeurs" and "Milt's Boogie." Fun good-time music that will be difficult to find. — *Scott Yanow*

Kenny Burrell (Kenneth Earl Burrell)

b. Jul. 31, 1931, Detroit, MI
Guitar / Bop, Groove
Kenny Burrell has been a very consistent guitarist throughout his career. Cool-toned and playing in an unchanging style based in bop, Burrell has always been the epitome of good taste and solid swing. Duke Ellington's favorite guitarist (though he never actually recorded with him), Burrell started playing guitar when he was 12 and he debuted on records with Dizzy Gillespie in 1951. Part of the fertile Detroit jazz scene of the early '50s, Burrell moved to New York in 1956. Highly in-demand from the start, Burrell has appeared on a countless number of records during the past 40 years as a leader and as a sideman. Among his more notable associations have been dates with Stan Getz, Billie Holiday, Milt Jackson, John Coltrane, Gil Evans, Sonny Rollins, Quincy Jones, Stanley Turrentine, and Jimmy Smith. Starting in the early '70s Burrell began leading seminars and teaching, often focusing on Duke Ellington's music. He toured with the Phillip Morris Superband

during 1985-86 and has led three-guitar quintets but generally Kenny Burrell plays at the head of a trio/quartet. — *Scott Yanow*

Groove: Burrell never stoops to playing needless riffs and other technical "noise" — virtuosity for its own sake. His melodic sense is strong and his playing elegant. Here is bluesy jazz that is easy to listen to, yet never boring or trite. As a sideman, Burrell has graced over 200 albums — J. Coltrane, Stan Getz, Billie Holiday, Milt Jackson, Hubert Laws, Sonny Rollins, Jimmy Smith, Stanley Turrentine, and more. You can always count on him for tasteful solos, and superb backup. The fact that his albums make great background music is no put down. — *Michael Erlewine*

Blue Moods / Feb. 1, 1957 / Prestige ◆◆◆◆
Smooth, cool, yet musically impressive late '50s date that has both blowing session fervor and soulful undergirding. Burrell's fluid guitar voicings and Cecil Payne's robust baritone make nice partners, while Tommy Flanagan adds his usual sparkling piano riffs and solos, and bassist Doug Watkins teams with Elvin Jones, who shows he can drive a date without dominating things on drums. — *Ron Wynn*

Kenny Burrell / Feb. 1, 1957 / Prestige ◆◆◆
His first Prestige recording (in NYC) with an all-Detroit crew (plus baritone sax) in New York. Burrell as we love him — clear, bluesy, with a touch of funk. — *Michael Erlewine*

K.B. Blues / Feb. 10, 1957 / Blue Note ◆◆◆
Worth searching for. Burrell with funky pianist Horace Silver and Hank Mobley on tenor sax. As you might guess, the tunes are mostly blues. — *Michael Erlewine*

Two Guitars / Mar. 5, 1957 / Original Jazz Classics ◆◆◆
For this 1957 studio session (which has been reissued on CD in the OJC series), the two distinctive but complementary guitarists Kenny Burrell and Jimmy Raney are teamed together in a septet with trumpeter Donald Byrd, altoist Jackie McLean, pianist Mal Waldron, bassist Doug Watkins, and drummer Art Taylor. The full group gets to stretch out on originals by Watkins, McLean ("Little Melonae"), and three from Waldron, while the two standards ("Close Your Eyes" and "Out of Nowhere") are individual features for Burrell and Raney. This is a well-rounded set that may not contain any real surprises but will be enjoyed by collectors of hard bop. — *Scott Yanow*

● **Blue Lights, Vols. 1-2** / May 14, 1958 / Blue Note ◆◆◆◆
The music on this 1997 two-CD set was originally on two LPs and already previously reissued as a pair of CDs. Guitarist Kenny Burrell leads a very coherent jam session in the studio with a particularly strong cast that also includes trumpeter Louis Smith, both Junior Cook and Tina Brooks on tenors, either Duke Jordan or Bobby Timmons on piano, bassist Sam Jones, and drummer Art Blakey. The material consists of basic originals and standards and has excellent playing all around; six of the nine tunes are over nine minutes long. At that point in time, Cook and Brooks had similar sounds, but fortunately, the soloists are identified in the liner notes for each song. The solo star is often trumpeter Louis Smith, who fell into obscurity after a few notable appearances on Blue Note during the period (including his own brilliant date, *Here Comes Louis Smith*). He was one of the finest of the Clifford Brown-influenced players of the period and deserves much greater recognition. This is a recommended reissue for hard bop collectors who do not already have the two individual CDs. — *Scott Yanow*

On View at the Five Spot Cafe / Aug. 25, 1959-Aug. 26, 1959 / Blue Note ◆◆◆◆
This likable live set from guitarist Kenny Burrell has a strong supporting cast (Tina Brooks on tenor, either Bobby Timmons or Roland Hanna on piano, bassist Ben Tucker, and drummer Art Blakey) and the original five-song program has been expanded on this CD to eight tunes. The swinging music, highlighted by "Lady Be Good," "Birks Works," the blues "36-23-36," and Burrell's feature on "Lover Man," is quite mainstream for the period and predictably excellent. — *Scott Yanow*

Bluesin' Around / Nov. 21, 1961-Apr. 30, 1962 / Columbia ◆◆◆
Released for the first time on this 1983 LP, the music on the set features guitarist Kenny Burrell in quartet/quintets with either tenor great Illinois Jacquet, trombonist Eddie Bert or altoist Leo Wright, and either pianist Hank Jones or organist Jack McDuff. It is odd that Columbia did not issue any of the straightahead music at the time, considering McDuff's popularity, for the results, even with a few dated numbers such as "Mambo Twist," are excellent.

After a short while, this LP went out of print and the music has yet to resurface on CD. — *Scott Yanow*

☆ **Midnight Blue** / Jan. 6, 1963 / Blue Note ◆◆◆◆◆
This album was one of guitarist Kenny Burrell's best-known sessions for the Blue Note label, although it has yet to be reissued on CD. Burrell is matched with tenor saxophonist Stanley Turrentine, bassist Major Holley, drummer Bill English, and Ray Barretto on conga for a blues-oriented date highlighted by "Chitlins Con Carne," "Midnight Blue," "Saturday Night Blues," and the lone standard "Gee Baby Ain't I Good to You." — *Scott Yanow*

Crash! / Feb. 26, 1963 / Prestige ◆◆◆
Burrell with Jack McDuff on the Hammond organ and Harold Vick on tenor sax. Includes the tune "Grease Monkey." — *Michael Erlewine*

Freedom / Mar. 27, 1963 / Blue Note ◆◆◆◆
A date with the Kenny Burrell Sextet that includes Stanley Turrentine (sax), Herbie Hancock (p), Ben Tucker (b), Bill English (d), and Ray Barrett (cga). A funky blues set. — *Michael Erlewine*

Blue Bash / Jul. 16, 1963 / Verve ◆◆◆
Groove great Kenny Burrell and Jimmy Smith (Hammond organ) together on the same album. Includes a rendition of "Fever." — *Michael Erlewine*

Soul Call / Apr. 7, 1964 / Original Jazz Classics ◆◆◆
Guitarist Kenny Burrell alternates blues and ballads on this swinging quintet set with pianist Will Davis, bassist Martin Rivera, drummer Bill English, and Ray Barretto on congas. The music is melodic and boppish, although no real surprises occur. By this time, Burrell was a very respectful player, upholding the tradition rather than offering any real innovations. This CD reissue will still be enjoyed by his fans. — *Scott Yanow*

Arnett Cobb

b. Aug. 10, 1918, Houston, TX, **d.** Mar. 24, 1989, Houston, TX
Tenor Saxophone / Swing, Early R&B Jazz, Groove, Soul-Jazz, New York Blues

A stomping Texas tenor player in the tradition of Illinois Jacquet, Arnett Cobb's accessible playing was between swing and early rhythm & blues. After playing in Texas with Chester Boone (1934-36) and Milt Larkin (1936-42), Cobb emerged in the big leagues by succeeding Illinois Jacquet with Lionel Hampton's Orchestra (1942-47). His version of "Flying Home No. 2" became a hit and he was a very popular soloist with Hampton. After leaving the band, Cobb formed his own group but his initial success was interrupted in 1948 when he had to undergo an operation on his spine. After recovering he resumed touring. But a major car accident in 1956 crushed Cobb's legs, and he was reduced to using crutches for the rest of his life. However by 1959 he returned to active playing and recording. Cobb spent most of the '60s leading bands back in Texas but starting in 1973 he toured and recorded more extensively including a tenor summit with Jimmy Heath and Joe Henderson in Europe as late as 1988. Arnett Cobb made many fine records through the years for such labels as Apollo, Columbia/OKeh, Prestige (many of the latter are available on the OJC series), Black & Blue, Progressive, Muse, and Bee Hive. — *Scott Yanow*

Groove: It is unfortunate that there is not a lot of Arnett Cobb available yet on CD. Your best bet may be to search the old vinyl bins for the odd survivor from another era. Worth finding. — *Michael Erlewine*

● **Blows for 1300** / May 1947-Aug. 1947 / Delmark ◆◆◆◆
This Delmark CD reissues all 15 of Arnett Cobb's recordings for Apollo. The spirited tenor (who straddled the boundaries between swing and early R&B) is in prime early form with his sextet on a variety of basic material, much of it blues-oriented. Milt Larkin takes vocals on three of the tracks and there are short solos by either Booty Wood or Al King on trombone, but otherwise the main focus is on Cobb's tough tenor. This very accessible music is both danceable and full of exciting performances that were formerly rare. — *Scott Yanow*

Blow, Arnett, Blow / Jan. 9, 1959 / Original Jazz Classics ◆◆◆◆
Arnett Cobb's debut for Prestige and his first recording as a leader in three years (due to a serious car accident in 1956) is an explosive affair. Cobb is matched up with fellow tough tenor Eddie "Lockjaw" Davis and there are plenty of sparks set off by their encounter. With organist Wild Bill Davis, bassist George Duvivier, and drummer Arthur Edgehill keeping the proceedings heated, Cobb and Davis tangle on a variety of basic material, alternating

uptempo romps such as "Go Power" and "Go Red Go" with slightly more sober pieces highlighted by "When I Grow Too Old to Dream." This is a great matchup (reissued on CD in the OJC series) that lives up to its potential. — *Scott Yanow*

Go Power! / Jan. 9, 1959 / Prestige ++++
Madcap exchanges with Eddie "Lockjaw" Davis (ts). If you find it, savor the purchase. — *Ron Wynn*

Smooth Sailing / Feb. 27, 1959 / Original Jazz Classics +++
This CD reissue brings back a typically swinging date by tenor saxophonist Arnett Cobb. The colorful trombonist Buster Cooper (who was not featured in enough small group sessions through the years) seems to inspire Cobb; the rhythm section (organist Austin Mitchell, bassist George Duvivier, and drummer Osie Johnson) is also a strong asset for this music. Four standards (three from the swing era plus Cobb's "Smooth Sailing") alternate with a blues and a couple of uptempo riff numbers. Arnett Cobb's solos are typically emotional and generally exciting during the fine set. — *Scott Yanow*

Party Time / May 14, 1959 / Prestige ++++
Tenor saxophonist Arnett Cobb, who was inactive between 1957 and 1958 due to a serious auto accident, recorded three strong albums for Prestige during the first half of 1959. This CD reissue is the only one of the trio that features Cobb as the only horn and backed by a pianist (Ray Bryant) instead of an organ player. With bassist Wendell Marshall, drummer Art Taylor, and Ray Barretto on conga completing the group, most of the focus is on Cobb's tough yet flexible tenor. Such songs as "When My Dreamboat Comes Home," "Blues in the Closet," and a remake of "Flying Home" make this the definitive Arnett Cobb album from the era. Highly recommended. — *Scott Yanow*

Blue and Sentimental / Oct. 31, 1960-Nov. 13, 1960 / Prestige +++
This CD reissue combines together tenor saxophonist Arnett Cobb's two LPs, *Sizzlin'* and *Ballads by Cobb*. The former session has a good mixture of stomps and ballads with highlights including "Black Velvet," "Georgia on My Mind," and "The Way You Look Tonight." The latter date (originally cut for the Moodsville label) is all slow ballads and, despite the warmth in Cobb's tone, a certain sameness pervades the performances. Pianist Red Garland and drummer J.C. Heard are on both sessions with either George Tucker or George Duvivier on bass. Good music but not quite essential. — *Scott Yanow*

Wild Man from Texas / May 6, 1976-May 30, 1976 / Collectables +++
This Black & Blue session, made available domestically on a Classic Jazz LP in the late '70s, has some typically rambunctious playing by tenor saxophonist Arnett Cobb. The tough tenor is featured in a larger group than usual (a nonet also including trumpeter Wallace Davenport, trombonist Buster Cooper, fellow tenor Eddie Chamblee, and organist Milt Buckner) with side one consisting of three romps (including "Smooth Sailing" and "Flying Home") and the second half made up of three ballads (highlighted by "The Nearness of You"). Cobb, who had emerged a couple years earlier after a decade spent sticking close to Texas, was still in prime form, making this hard-to-find set worth the search. — *Scott Yanow*

Funky Butt / Jan. 22, 1980 / Progressive +++
Arnett Cobb, a tenor from the '40s who (like Illinois Jacquet) fused together some of the most exciting aspects of swing and early R&B, is in typically exuberant form on this quartet set with pianist Derek Smith, bassist Ray Drummond, and drummer Ronnie Bedford. Cobb is warm on the ballads but the stomps (particularly "Jumpin' at the Woodside" and "I Got Rhythm") are what make this record most memorable. — *Scott Yanow*

John Coltrane

b. Sep. 23, 1926, Hamlet, NC, **d.** Jul. 17, 1967, New York, NY
Soprano Saxophone, Tenor Saxophone / Hard Bop, Avant-Garde, Free Jazz, Groove
The most influential jazz musician of the past 40 years (only Miles Davis comes close), one of the greatest saxophonists of all time and a remarkable innovator, John Coltrane certainly made his impact on jazz!

Unlike most musicians, Coltrane's style changed gradually but steadily over time. His career can be divided into at least five periods: Early days (1947-54), searching stylist (1955-56), sheets of sound (1957-59), the classic quartet (1960-64), and avant-garde (1965-67). Originally an altoist, he played in a Navy band during his period in the military, recording four privately issued songs in 1946. He settled in Philadelphia and then toured with King

Kolax (1946-47), switched to tenor when he played with Eddie "Cleanhead" Vinson (1947-48), joined the Dizzy Gillespie big band (1948-49), and was with Dizzy Gillespie's sextet (1950-51). Radio broadcasts from the latter association find Coltrane sounding heavily influenced by Dexter Gordon and hinting slightly at his future sound. He followed that gig with periods spent with the groups of Gay Crosse (1952), Earl Bostic (1952), Johnny Hodges (1953-54), and in Philadelphia for a few weeks with Jimmy Smith (1955).

The John Coltrane story really starts with his joining the Miles Davis Quintet in 1955. At first some observers wondered what Miles saw in the 28-year old tenor who had an unusual sound and whose ideas sometimes stretched beyond his technique. However Davis was a masterful talent scout who could always hear potential greatness. Coltrane improved month-by-month and by 1956 was competing with Sonny Rollins as the top young tenor; he even battled him to a draw on their recording of "Tenor Madness." Coltrane (along with Red Garland, Paul Chambers and Philly Joe Jones) formed an important part of the classic Miles Davis Quintet, recording with Miles for Prestige and Columbia during 1955-56. In addition Trane was starting to be featured on many of Prestige's jam-session-oriented albums.

1957 was the key year in John Coltrane's career. Fired by Miles Davis due to his heroin addiction, Coltrane permanently kicked the habit. He spent several months playing with Thelonious Monk's Quartet, a mutually beneficial association that gave Monk long-overdue acclaim and greatly accelerated the tenor's growth. His playing became even more adventurous than it had been, he recorded *Blue Train* (his first great album as a leader) and, when he rejoined Miles Davis in early 1958, Coltrane was unquestionably the most important tenor in jazz. During his next two years with Davis, Trane (whose style had been accurately dubbed "sheets of sound" by critic Ira Gitler) really took the chordal improvisation of bop to the breaking point, playing groups of notes with extreme speed and really tearing into the music. In addition to being one of the stars of Davis' recordings (including *Milestones* and *Kind of Blue*), Coltrane signed a contract with Atlantic and began to record classics of his own; "Giant Steps" (with its very complex chord structure) and "Naima" were among the many highlights.

By 1960 John Coltrane was long overdue to be a leader and Miles Davis reluctantly let him go. 'Trane's direction was changing from utilizing as many chords as possible (it would be difficult to get any more extreme in that direction) to playing passionately over one or two-chord vamps. He hired pianist McCoy Tyner, drummer Elvin Jones, and went through several bassists (Steve Davis, Art Davis, Reggie Workman) before settling on Jimmy Garrison in late 1961. The first artist signed to the new Impulse label, Coltrane was given complete freedom to record what he wanted. He had recently begun doubling on soprano, bringing an entirely new sound and approach to an instrument previously associated with the Dixieland of Sidney Bechet (although Steve Lacy had already started specializing on it) and Coltrane's 1960 Atlantic recording of "My Favorite Things" became a sort of theme song that he revisited on a nightly basis.

John Coltrane continued to evolve during 1961-64. He added Eric Dolphy as part of his group for a period and recorded extensively at the Village Vanguard in late 1961; the lengthy explorations were branded by conservative critics as "anti-jazz." Partly to counter their stereotyping (and short memories), 'Trane recorded with Duke Ellington in a quartet, a ballad program, and a collaboration with singer Johnny Hartman; his playing throughout was quite beautiful. But live in concert his solos (which could be 45 minutes in length) were always intense and continually searching. He utilized such songs as "Impressions" (which used the same two-chord framework as Miles Davis' "So What") and "Afro Blue" for long workouts and took stunning cadenzas on the ballad "I Want to Talk About You." In addition to the Impulse! recordings, European radio broadcasts have since been released that show Coltrane's progress and consistency. And in December 1964 he displayed his vast interest in Eastern religion by recording the very popular *A Love Supreme*.

In 1965 it all began to change. Influenced and inspired by the intense and atonal flights of Albert Ayler, Archie Shepp and Pharoah Sanders, Coltrane's music dropped most of the melodies and essentially became passionate sound explorations. *Ascension* from mid-year featured six additional horns (plus a second bassist) added to the quartet for almost totally free improvisations. Fast themes (such as "One Down, One Up" and "Sun Ship") were quickly disposed of on the way to waves of sound. Coltrane began to use Pharoah Sanders in his group to raise the intensity level even more and when he hired Rashied Ali as second drummer, it eventually caused McCoy Tyner (who said he could no longer hear himself) and Elvin Jones to depart.

In 1966 Coltrane had a quintet consisting of his wife Alice on piano, Sanders, Ali, and the lone holdover Jimmy Garrison. After a triumphant visit to Japan, Coltrane's health began to fail. Although the cause of his death on July 17, 1967 was listed as liver cancer, in reality it was probably overwork. Coltrane used to practice ten to twelve hours a day and when he had a job (which featured marathon solos), he would often spend his breaks practicing in his dressing room! It was only through such singlemindedness that he could reach such a phenomenal technical level, but the net result was his premature death.

Virtually every recording that John Coltrane made throughout his career is currently available on CD, quite a few books about him have been written and a video (*The Coltrane Legacy*) gives today's jazz followers an opportunity to see him performing on a pair of half-hour television shows. Since Coltrane's passing no other giant has dominated jazz on the same level. In fact many other saxophonists have built their entire careers on exploring music from just one of John Coltrane's periods! — *Scott Yanow*

Groove: Here is another jazz giant that is so seminal that he affected everyone who heard him. No, Coltrane is not a soul-jazz groove artist. However, in tunes like "My Favorite Things," the groove is way deep and long. Blues and groove lovers will tend to go for earlier Coltrane, and some of them are listed below. If you have the bucks, the eight-disc set on Atlantic, *Heavyweight Champion: The Complete Atlantic Recordings of John Coltrane* is perhaps the most incredible music in one box I know of. — *Michael Erlewine*

John Coltrane with Kenny Burrell / Apr. 18, 1957-Mar. 7, 1958 / Prestige ◆◆◆
Tenor-saxophonist John Coltrane and guitarist Kenny Burrell are the alleged co-leaders of the two sessions included on this two-LP set but actually the second date (originally titled *The Cats*) was really under pianist Tommy Flanagan's direction; in fact Flanagan contributed four of the five compositions. Throughout, though, Coltrane is really the most significant soloist, whether on a brief duet with Burrell ("Why Was I Born"), in a quintet, or (with the addition of trumpeter Idrees Sulieman) a sextet. — *Scott Yanow*

Lush Life / May 31, 1957-Jan. 10, 1958 / DCC ◆◆◆◆
The music on this CD reissue is taken from three separate sessions led by John Coltrane. Most rewarding are memorable versions of "Like Someone in Love," "I Love You," and "'Trane's Slo Blues" that feature the masterful tenor accompanied by just bassist Earl May and drummer Art Taylor; "Like Someone in Love" in particular is given definitive treatment. Of the two other songs, "I Hear a Rhapsody" finds Coltrane accompanied by pianist Red Garland, bassist Paul Chambers, and drummer Al "Tootie" Heath while "Lush Life" is played with a quintet also featuring trumpeter Donald Byrd, Garland, Chambers, and drummer Louis Hayes. — *Scott Yanow*

★ **Blue Train** / Sep. 15, 1957 / Blue Note ◆◆◆◆◆
A landmark album—stunning. This is Coltrane's only Blue Note recording as a leader, and he never made a better album in this particular hard-bop style. A must-hear for all jazz fans, *Blue Train* includes Coltrane's most impressive early composition, "Moment's Notice." With outstanding performances from sidemen Lee Morgan (tpt), Curtis Fuller (tb), and Kenny Drew (p). [*Blue Train* was reissued in 1997 with early takes of "Blue Train" and "Lazy Bird" added.] — *Michael Erlewine*

Soultrane / Feb. 7, 1958 / Original Jazz Classics ◆◆◆◆
Tenor saxophonist John Coltrane, who had recently rejoined Miles Davis' group, teams up with pianist Red Garland, bassist Paul Chambers and drummer Art Taylor for a fine set which has been reissued on CD. Coltrane performs his earliest rendition of "I Want to Talk About You" (although without a closing cadenza), "Good Bait," "You Say You Care," "Theme for Ernie," and "Russian Lullaby." This is excellent music that falls short of being classic but Coltrane and Garland always made for a complementary team. — *Scott Yanow*

☆ **Heavyweight Champion: The Complete Atlantic Recordings** / Jan. 15, 1959-May 25, 1961 / Rhino/Atlantic ◆◆◆◆◆
John Coltrane's two years with Atlantic can be thought of as his "middle period" during which he evolved from his sheets of sound approach to intense explorations over two-chord vamps. It is difficult to see how Rhino

could have done a better job with this reissue for they have come out with every scrap that could be found from Coltrane's Atlantic period. On the seven-CD box set is reissued the complete contents of the albums *Bags & Trane*, *Giant Steps*, *Coltrane Jazz*, *My Favorite Things*, *Coltrane Plays the Blues*, *Olé Coltrane*, *The Avant-Garde*, and *Coltrane's Sound*, the selections originally issued on *Alternate Takes* and three "new" alternate takes, plus (for the final CD) many previously unheard versions of five numbers including nine takes of "Giant Steps!" With such supporting players as vibraphonist Milt Jackson (who was actually the co-leader of *Bags and Trane*), pianists Hank Jones, Cedar Walton, Tommy Flanagan, Wynton Kelly, and McCoy Tyner, bassists Paul Chambers, Charlie Haden, Percy Heath, Steve Davis, Art Davis, and Reggie Workman, drummers Connie Kay, Lex Humphries, Art Taylor, Jimmy Cobb, Ed Blackwell, and Elvin Jones, trumpeters Don Cherry and Freddie Hubbard, and Eric Dolphy on alto and flute, it is not too surprising that the music is both innovative and classic. This perfectly-done box (which also has a fine booklet) is essential for all serious jazz collections. — *Scott Yanow*

★ **Giant Steps** / Apr. 1, 1959 / Atlantic ◆◆◆◆◆
This is one of John Coltrane's classic sets; in fact this CD reissue (which adds alternate takes to five of the seven original recordings) almost doubles one's pleasure. In "Giant Steps" Coltrane built a tongue-twister of chord changes (stretching bop to its logical breaking point) which he would soon abandon in favor of long drones on simpler patterns. Not only does this CD give one the two earliest versions of "Giant Steps" but also "Naima," "Cousin Mary," "Spiral," "Syeeda's Song Flute," the underrated but remarkable "Countdown," and "Mr. P.C." Recorded while Coltrane was still with Miles Davis' group, this CD (which mostly features pianist Tommy Flanagan, bassist Paul Chambers, and drummer Art Taylor) made it obvious that Coltrane had something very important of his own to say and that he would need his own band in the future to fully express himself. — *Scott Yanow*

Coltrane Plays the Blues / Oct. 24, 1960 / Atlantic ◆◆◆◆
Recorded during the same week as his original version of "My Favorite Things," this LP by John Coltrane features six blues-oriented originals (five by 'Trane) including "Blues to Bechet" and "Mr. Syms." The music is more melodic than usual with Coltrane playing soprano on two of the six tracks; "Blues to You" is the best showcase for his intense tenor. — *Scott Yanow*

Coltrane's Sound / Oct. 24, 1960 / Atlantic ◆◆◆◆
Although one may not think of *Coltrane's Sound* as being one of John Coltrane's most famous recordings, when one looks at its contents it quickly becomes obvious that this set ranks near the top. This CD reissue contains such classic material as "Central Park West," "Equinox," a reharmonized (and influential) version of "Body and Soul," the underrated "Satellite," "Liberia," and an intense rendition of "The Night Has a Thousand Eyes." Also included on this reissue is an alternate version of "Body and Soul" and the lesser-known "262." Co-starring pianist McCoy Tyner, bassist Steve Davis, and drummer Elvin Jones, this set is highly recommended. — *Scott Yanow*

☆ **My Favorite Things** / Oct. 24, 1960-Oct. 26, 1960 / Atlantic ◆◆◆◆◆
This LP was very influential when it came out and remains a classic. The first full album by the classic John Coltrane Quartet (with pianist McCoy Tyner, drummer Elvin Jones, and their bassist of the time Steve Davis) consists of a fiery "Summertime," the lyrical "But Not for Me," a nice ballad for 'Trane's soprano on "Everytime We Say Goodbye," and most importantly, the lengthy "My Favorite Things." On the latter Coltrane, who had used a seemingly endless number of chords on the prior year's "Giant Steps," reduces the chords to a minimum and plays passionately over a repetitious vamp, creating startlingly new music. This set has since been reissued on CD and in one form or another is essential. — *Scott Yanow*

Afro Blue Impressions / Oct. 22, 1963 / Pablo ◆◆◆◆
Taken from several European concerts (producer Norman Granz is vague about the exact dates but those listed are educated guesses), this double CD finds John Coltrane and his classic Quartet playing their standard repertoire of the period. The nine songs include "Chasin' the Trane," "My Favorite Things," "Afro Blue," "I Want to Talk About You," "Impressions," and "Naima." No new revelations occur but this is a strong all-around set of 'Trane near his peak. — *Scott Yanow*

Hank Crawford (Bennie Ross Crawford, Jr.)

b. Dec. 21, 1934, Memphis, TN

Alto Saxophone / R&B, Soul-Jazz, Hard Bop, Groove

Hank Crawford's greatest contribution to music has been his soulful sound, one that is immediately idenitifiable and flexible enough to fit into several types of settings. Early on he played with B.B. King, Bobby Bland, and Ike Turner in Memphis before moving to Nashville to study at Tennessee State College. He gained fame with Ray Charles (1958-63), at first playing baritone before switching to alto and becoming the music director. During 1959-69 Crawford recorded a popular series of soul-jazz albums for Atlantic that made his reputation. His '70s sets for Kudu were more commercial and streakier but in 1982 Crawford started recording regularly for Milestone, often matched up with organist Jimmy McGriff or pianist Dr. John. An influence on David Sanborn, Crawford's very appealing sound can still be heard in prime form in the mid-'90s. — *Scott Yanow*

Groove: Hank Crawford has recorded a lot. He is another artist who can play it all. You may want to search for albums with a small group format or where he is working with known funky players like Jimmy McGriff, David Fathead Newman, Jimmy Ponder, or Dr. John. — *Michael Erlewine*

Heart and Soul: The Hank Crawford Anthology / Jul. 5, 1958-Sep. 9, 1992 / Rhino/Atlantic ◆◆◆

This is one of the better of Rhino's two-CD samplers of Atlantic jazz artists. Altoist Hank Crawford, one of the most soulful stylists to emerge during the '60s, is heard on 31 of his best recordings, 27 as a leader plus sideman appearances with Ray Charles, David "Fathead" Newman, B.B. King, and Etta James. Crawford's sound and style were virtually the same in the '90s as they were in the '60s although the settings changed a bit. Highlights of this well-conceived introduction include "Please Send Me Someone to Love," "Two Years of Torture," "Don't Get Around Much Anymore," "The Very Thought of You," "Trouble in Mind," and "Hank's Groove." Recommended to listeners not familiar with the beauty of Hank Crawford's playing. — *Scott Yanow*

Memphis, Ray and a Touch of Moody / Oct. 7, 1960-Feb. 11, 1965 / 32 Jazz ◆◆◆

Altoist Hank Crawford is not quite at peak form on the LPs which comprise this two-fer reissue, but it contains enough moments of excitement to ensure that serious fans will want to add *Memphis Ray/Touch of Moody* to their collections anyway. — *Jason Ankeny*

After Hours / Oct. 19, 1965-Jan. 19, 1966 / Atlantic ◆◆◆

The most unusual aspect to this straight CD reissue of a Hank Crawford Atlantic LP is that the altoist plays some very effective piano on two numbers including a lengthy feature on "After Hours." Fortunately his alto playing is not neglected and he really shows off his appealing tone on "Who Can I Turn To," "Makin' Whoopee," and "When Did You Leave Heaven." A fine soulful crossover set that is quite accessible and melodic. — *Scott Yanow*

Soul Survivors / Jan. 29, 1986-Jan. 30, 1986 / Milestone ◆◆◆◆

Can't beat the lineup: McGriff with Hank Crawford on alto sax, George Benson (or Jim Pittsburgh) on guitar, and Bernard Purdie (or Mel Lewis) on drums. This is another of the fine Milestone recordings of McGriff produced by Bob Porter. No disappointments here. Includes version of "One Mint Julep," "Because of You," and the Crawford original "The Peeper." Very nice. — *Michael Erlewine*

Mr. Chips / Nov. 1986 / Milestone ◆◆◆

A decent but not overly memorable outing by Hank Crawford, this CD (other than "Robbins' Nest") features the distinctive altoist mostly playing R&Bish material while accompanied by a funky rhythm section that includes guitarist Cornell Dupree and keyboardist Richard Tee plus a four-horn rhythm section; Leon Thomas takes a vocal on "You Send Me." — *Scott Yanow*

Soul Brothers / Jun. 15, 1987+Jun. 16, 1987 / Milestone ◆◆◆

Hank Crawford with Jimmy McGriff on the Hammond B-3 and George Benson (or Jimmy Ponder) on guitar. Worth seeking out. — *Michael Erlewine*

Steppin' Up / Jun. 15, 1987-Jun. 16, 1987 / Milestone ◆◆◆◆

Jimmy McGriff with Hank Crawford on alto sax, Jimmy Ponder on guitar, Billy Preston on piano, and Vance James on drums—an excellent group. Produced by Bob Porter, this has tunes like "Something for Bubba," and Percy

Mayfield's "River's Invitation" that are standouts. This combination of players is all that you need for some funky jazz. — *Michael Erlewine*

● **On the Blue Side** / Apr. 4, 1989+Aug. 9, 1989 / Milestone ◆◆◆◆

With Jimmy McGriff on Hammond organ and Jimmy Ponder on guitar. Funky, mellow, and gritty. — *Ron Wynn*

Portrait / Mar. 19, 1991-Mar. 20, 1991 / Milestone ◆◆◆

With David Fathead Newman on tenor sax, Jimmy Ponder on guitar, and Johnny Hammond on the organ. Here is Crawford's latest collection of funky cuts and mellow ballads. — *Ron Wynn*

Road Tested / Jun. 30, 1997-Jul. 1, 1997 / Milestone ◆◆◆◆

Jimmy McGriff continued on a high roll on his second tour with Milestone, taping another dual-billed soul-jazz album with the redoubtable Hank Crawford. You know what to expect by now—hardass, down-home, blues-drenched organ trio-plus-sax grooving—but this is a really potent gusher of that genre, rising to the level of McGriff's idiom-defining *The Dream Team* from 1996. Throughout, Crawford produces some sterling roadhouse tenor work and guitarist Wayne Boyd stays resolutely in the pocket. Drummer Bernard Purdie stokes the engines from the opening crack of the funky "Peanuts," contributes to a refreshingly kicking transformation of "I Only Have Eyes for You," and lays on a devastating backbeat whenever asked. John Coltrane's minor blues "Mr. P.C." also responds well to the soul-jazz treatment. Recorded the old-fashioned Prestige way—in two sessions, with Bob Porter producing in Rudy Van Gelder's studio—it's amazing and gratifying that bluesicians are still allowed to make records this way. — *Richard S. Ginell*

Eddie "Lockjaw" Davis

b. Mar. 2, 1922, New York, NY, **d.** Nov. 3, 1986, Culver City, CA

Tenor Saxophone / Bop, Hard Bop, Swing, Groove, Soul-Jazz, Latin Jazz

Possessor of a cutting and immediately identifiable tough tenor tone, Eddie "Lockjaw" Davis could hold his own in a saxophone battle with anyone. Early on he picked up experience playing with the bands of Cootie Williams (1942-44), Lucky Millinder, Andy Kirk (1945-46) and Louis Armstrong. He began heading his own groups from 1946 and Davis' earliest recordings as a leader tended to be explosive R&B affairs with plenty of screaming from his horn; he matched wits successfully with Fats Navarro on one session. Davis was with Count Basie's Orchestra on several occasional (including 1952-53, 1957 and 1964-73) and teamed up with Shirley Scott's trio during 1955-60. During 1960-62 he collaborated in some exciting performances and recordings with Johnny Griffin, a fellow tenor who was just as combative as Davis. After temporarily retiring to become a booking agent (1963-64), Davis rejoined Basie. In his later years Lockjaw often recorded with Harry "Sweets" Edison, and he remained a busy soloist up until his death. Through the decades he recorded as a leader for many labels including Savoy, Apollo, Roost, King, Roulette, Prestige/Jazzland/Moodsville, RCA, Storyville, MPS, Black & Blue, Spotlite, Steeple Chase, Pablo, Muse, and Enja. — *Scott Yanow*

Groove: Davis recorded a lot, so I have picked out a few albums where he is working with one of the B-3 masters. His work with Shirley Scott is consistent and probably gives you the best entry point into this great bluesy tenor. — *Michael Erlewine*

The Eddie Lockjaw Davis Cookbook / Jun. 20, 1958 / Prestige ◆◆◆◆

This CD reissue adds a slightly later version of "Avalon" to the original LP program. Tenor saxophonist Eddie "Lockjaw" Davis and his regular organist of the period Shirley Scott are joined by bassist George Duvivier, drummmer Arthur Edgehill, and flutist Jerome Richardson for the first of three entries in their *Cookbook* series; two of the originals on the set are "The Chef" and "In the Kitchen." In addition to three blues at various tempos, Davis is quite warm on the ballad "But Beautiful" while the boppish "Three Deuces" finds Richardson switching to tenor and holding his own with Lockjaw. — *Scott Yanow*

Jaws / Sep. 12, 1958 / Prestige ◆◆◆

Tenorman Eddie "Lockjaw" Davis and organist Shirley Scott co-led a popular combo during 1956-60, recording many albums and helping to popularize the idiom. This particular CD reissue of an LP (which at 37 minutes is a bit brief) finds the quartet (with bassist George Duvivier and drummer Arthur Edgehill) interpreting eight swing standards, alternating ballads with romps. It's a fine all-around showcase for the accessible group. — *Scott Yanow*

Smokin' / Sep. 12, 1958 + Dec. 5, 1958 / Original Jazz Classics ✦✦✦✦
Tenor-saxophonist Eddie "Lockjaw" Davis cut enough material during these two sessions to fill up four records. The seven selections included on this brief 36-minute CD (a straight reissue of an LP recorded during the same period as Davis' better-known *Cookbook* albums) also include Jerome Richardson (switching between flute, tenor and baritone) on three of the numbers, bassist George Duvivier, and drummer Arthur Edgehill. Together the group swings hard on basic originals, blues, and an occasional ballad, showing why this type of accessible band was so popular during the era. — *Scott Yanow*

The Eddie Lockjaw Davis Cookbook, Vol. 3 / Dec. 15, 1958 / Prestige ✦✦✦✦
Tenorman Eddie "Lockjaw" Davis made quite a few records with organist Shirley Scott during the late '50s. The basic originals in their *Cookbook* series tended to have titles that dealt with cooking; in this case "Heat 'N' Serve," "The Goose Hangs High," and "Simmerin'" apply as does the standard "My Old Flame." Jerome Richardson's flute, baritone, and tenor gives this CD reissue some variety, bassist George Duvivier and drummer Arthur Edgehill are fine in support and Shirley Scott shows that she was one of the top organists to emerge after the rise of Jimmy Smith. But Davis is the main star and his instantly recognizable sound is the most memorable aspect to this swinging session. — *Scott Yanow*

The Eddie Lockjaw Davis Cookbook, Vol. 2 / Dec. 1958 / Original Jazz Classics ✦✦✦✦
Eddie "Lockjaw" Davis' "cookbook" series helped make the group that the tenorman had in the late '50s with organist Shirley Scott famous. The quintet (which also includes flutist Jerome Richardson, bassist George Duvivier, and drummer Arthur Edgehill) is heard on this CD reissue performing three Davis-Scott originals, "Stardust," "I Surrender Dear," and a version of "Willow Weep for Me" that was originally part of a sampler. The straightahead music is interpreted quite colorfully by Davis and his group, one of the first popular organ combos. — *Scott Yanow*

Very Saxy / Apr. 29, 1959 / Prestige ✦✦✦
Tenor saxophonist Eddie "Lockjaw" Davis and his quartet (which includes organist Shirley Scott, bassist George Duvivier, and drummer Arthur Edgehill) welcome three immortal tenors (Coleman Hawkins, Arnett Cobb, and Buddy Tate) to what became a historic and hard-swinging jam session. On three blues, an original based on the chord changes of "Sweet Georgia Brown" and "Lester Leaps In," the four tenors battle it out and the results are quite exciting. The spirited music on this memorable LP will hopefully be reissued on CD eventually for the performances live up to their great potential. — *Scott Yanow*

Jaws in Orbit / May 1, 1959 / Original Jazz Classics ✦✦✦
The group that Eddie "Lockjaw" Davis led with organist Shirley Scott during the latter half of the '50s was quite accessible and did a great deal to popularize the organ band in jazz. This CD reissue features the duo joined by bassist George Duvivier, drummer Arthur Edgehill, and the obscure trombonist Steve Pulliam for a typically swinging set of basic originals and standards. Highlights include a hard-swinging "Intermission Riff" and "Our Delight." — *Scott Yanow*

Gentle Jaws / Dec. 11, 1959 + Jan. 31, 1960 / Prestige ✦✦✦
The Moodsville label was a subsidiary of Prestige in the late '50s/early '60s that sought to document jazz artists exclusively playing ballads so as to win over the mood music audience of the time. This 75-minute reissue CD combines together two sessions featuring the warm tenor of Eddie "Lockjaw" Davis. On the first half he "sits in" with the Red Garland Trio (that date was originally issued under Garland's name) while on the latter half he is backed by the Shirley Scott Trio with organist Scott switching to piano. The standard-dominated program is tasteful but uneventful and the similarity of the tempos succeeds in making the results more successful as background music than as creative jazz. — *Scott Yanow*

Trane Whistle / Sep. 20, 1960 / Original Jazz Classics ✦✦✦✦
This CD reissue brings back an Eddie "Lockjaw" Davis session in which the distinctive tenor saxophonist is joined by a 13-piece big band arranged by Oliver Nelson. Most significant is the inclusion of the original version of "Stolen Moments" (here called "The Stolen Moment" and predating the more

famous Oliver Nelson recording by several months). Eric Dolphy is in the backup group but is not heard in a solo capacity. There are some spots for trumpeters Richard Williams, Clark Terry, and Bobby Bryant along with Nelson on alto but this is primarily Davis' showcase. On a set comprised of four Oliver Nelson originals, the ballad "You Are Too Beautiful" and the leader's "Jaws," Lockjaw as usual shows plenty of emotion during his driving solos. — *Scott Yanow*

★ **Live at Minton's** / Jan. 6, 1961 / Prestige ✦✦✦✦✦
This duo (tenor saxophonists Eddie "Lockjaw" Davis and Johnny Griffin) made about a dozen LPs together, most for Jazzland and Prestige, and they are all worth investigating. They had a special affinity for pianist Thelonious Monk's music, and while there were other sets which emphasize that better, the Monk pieces ("Straight No Chaser"/"In Walked Bud") included in the program on this live set were among the highlights. — *Bob Rusch, Cadence*

Streetlights / Nov. 15, 1962 / Prestige ✦✦✦✦
This CD combines together the music from two complete LPs (*I Only Have Eyes for You* and *Trackin'*) that were recorded the same day with the identical personnel. Eddie "Lockjaw" Davis' tough tenor is well featured with his regular group of the time, a combo consisting of the powerful organist Don Patterson (who dominates many of the ensembles), guitarist Paul Weeden (talented but quite obscure), drummer Billy James, and guest bassist George Duvivier. The emphasis is on standards and intense blowing (even on the ballads) with the set being a good example of a strong tenor organ band. — *Scott Yanow*

Save Your Love for Me / Jun. 20, 1966-Aug. 3, 1967 / Bluebird ✦✦✦
This "best of" collection draws its 14 selections from three Victor albums by tenor saxophonist Eddie "Lockjaw" Davis: *Lock the Fox, The Fox and the Hounds*, and *Love Calls*. Although it would be preferable to acquire all three out-of-print albums (which represent the bulk of Davis' 1963-69 recordings), there are some strong performances included on this sampler. Davis is heard as the only horn in a sextet with pianist Ross Tompkins and percussionist Ray Barretto, accompanied by a 17-piece big band arranged by Bobby Plater and on a combo date highlighted by two numbers ("The Man with the Horn" and "A Weaver of Dreams") in which he interacts with fellow tenor Paul Gonsalves. — *Scott Yanow*

Jackie Davis

b. Dec. 13, 1920, Jacksonville, FL
Organ / Groove, Soul Jazz
Organist Jackie Davis was born December 13, 1920 in Jacksonville, FL. He was playing around town since he was nine years old and became part of an orchestra at ten. At the age of eleven Davis had saved and bought his own piano for $45. He played for dances, one nighters, and wherever he could find a gig. He studied with Earl Hines.

Davis graduated from Florida A&M in 1942 with a degree in music. He was listening to players like Milt Herth and George Wright, but it was "Wild" Bill Davis who opened his eyes to the power of the organ.

He was a student of Louis Jordan and spent some 14 months in his band. He recorded with Capitol Records for sixteen years.

Davis made several albums in the '50s and '60s for Pacific Jazz, Vic, Trend, Capitol, and Warner Bros. in the '50s and '60s, most of them done in a soul jazz vein, though he switched to gospel for his last recordings. These were mostly small trio or combo dates, though there was also one with a trombone group, another with a vocal choir. — *Michael Erlewine & Ron Wynn*

● **Easy Does It** / Jan. 15, 1963 / Warner Brothers ✦✦✦✦
Jumpin' Jackie / 1983 / Capitol ✦✦✦

Miles Davis

b. May 25, 1926, Alton, IL, d. Sep. 28, 1991, Santa Monica, CA
Trumpet / Bop, Cool, Hard Bop, Avant-Garde, Fusion, Groove, Jazz-Fusion
Miles Davis had quite a career, one with so many innovations that his name is one of the few that can be spoken in the same sentence with Duke Ellington. As a trumpeter, Davis was never a virtuoso on the level of his idol Dizzy Gillespie but by 1947 he possessed a distinctive cool-toned sound of his own. His ballad renditions (utilizing a Harmon mute) were exquisite yet never predictable, he mastered and then stripped down the bebop vocabulary to

its essentials, and he generally made every note count; as with Thelonious Monk, less was more in Davis' music.

But Davis was much more than just a trumpeter. As a bandleader he was a brilliant talent scout, able to recognize potential in its formative stage and bring out the best in his sidemen. Among the musicians who greatly benefitted from their association with Davis were Gerry Mulligan (virtually unknown when he played with Miles' Birth of the Cool Nonet), Gil Evans, John Coltrane, Red Garland, Paul Chambers, Philly Joe Jones, Cannonball Adderley, Bill Evans, Jimmy Cobb, Wynton Kelly, George Coleman, Wayne Shorter, Herbie Hancock, Ron Carter, Tony Williams, Chick Corea, Jack De-Johnette, Dave Holland, John McLaughlin, Joe Zawinul, Keith Jarrett, Steve Grossman, Gary Bartz, Dave Liebman, Al Foster, Sonny Fortune, Bill Evans (the saxophonist), Kenny Garrett, Marcus Miller, Mike Stern and John Scofield. This partial list forms a who's who of modern jazz.

In addition to his playing and nurturing of young talent, Miles Davis was quite remarkable in his rare ability to continually evolve. Most jazz musicians (with the exceptions of John Coltrane and Duke Ellington) generally form their style early on and spend the rest of their careers refining their sound. In contrast Miles Davis every five years or so would forge ahead, and due to his restless nature he not only played bop but helped found cool jazz, hard bop, modal music, his own unusual brand of the avant-garde, and fusion. Jazz history would be much different if Davis had not existed.

Born in Alton, IL, Miles Davis grew up in a middle-class family in East St. Louis. He started on trumpet when he was nine or ten, played in his high-school band, and picked up early experience gigging with Eddie Randall's Blue Devils. Miles Davis has said that the greatest musical experience of his life was hearing the Billy Eckstine Orchestra (with Dizzy Gillespie and Charlie Parker) when it passed through St. Louis.

In September 1944 Davis went to New York to study at Juilliard but spent much more time hanging out on 52nd Street and eventually dropped out of school. He played with Coleman Hawkins, made his recording debut in early 1945 (a rather nervous session with singer Rubberlegs Williams) and by late 1945 was playing regularly with Charlie Parker. Davis made an impression with his playing on Bird's recordings of "Now's the Time" and "Billie's Bounce." Although influenced by Dizzy Gillespie, even at this early stage the 19-year old had something of his own to contribute.

When Charlie Parker went with Gillespie out to California, Miles followed him a few months later by travelling cross-country with Benny Carter's Orchestra. He recorded with Parker in California, and when Bird formed a quintet in New York the following year, Davis was a key member. By late 1948 when he went out on his own, Miles Davis had formed a nonet that with arrangements by Gerry Mulligan, Gil Evans, and John Lewis, helped usher in "cool jazz." Although the group only had one paying job (two weeks in September 1948 as an intermission band for Count Basie at the Royal Roost), its dozen recordings for Capitol were highly influential in the West Coast jazz movement.

Typically, by the time his nonet dates were renamed "Birth of the Cool," Davis had moved on. He played at the Paris Jazz Festival in 1949 with Tadd Dameron and during 1951-54 was recording music with such sidemen as J.J. Johnson, Jimmy Heath, Horace Silver, Art Blakey and Sonny Rollins that directly led to hard bop. However this was very much an off period for Davis because he was a heroin addict who was only working on an irregular basis. In 1954 he used all of his will power to permanently kick heroin and his recording that year of "Walkin'," although overlooked at the time, is a classic.

1955 was Davis' breakthrough year. His performance of "'Round Midnight" at the Newport Jazz Festival alerted the critics that he was "back." Davis formed his classic quintet with John Coltrane, Red Garland, Paul Chambers, and Philly Joe Jones and during 1955-56 they recorded four well-received albums for Prestige and 'Round Midnight for Columbia. Davis' muted ballads were very popular and he became a celebrity. Even the breakup of the quintet in early 1957 did not slow up the momentum. Davis recorded the first of his full-length collaborations with arranger Gil Evans (Miles Ahead) which would be followed by Porgy and Bess (1958) and Sketches of Spain (1960); on these recordings Davis became one of the first trumpeters to stretch out on fluegelhorn. In 1957 he went to France to record the soundtrack for Lift to the Scaffold and then in 1958 he formed his greatest band, a super sextet with Coltrane, Cannonball Adderley, Bill Evans, Paul Chambers, and Philly Joe Jones. Although Evans and Jones were eventually

succeeded by Wynton Kelly and Jimmy Cobb, all of the recordings by this remarkable group somehow live up to their potential with Milestones and Kind of Blue being all-time classics that helped to introduce modal (or scalar) improvising to jazz.

If Miles Davis had retired in 1960, he would still be famous in jazz history, but he had many accomplishments still to come. The sextet gradually changed with Adderley departing and Coltrane's spot being taken first by Sonny Stitt then Hank Mobley. Although 1960-63 is thought of as a sort-of resting period for Davis, his trumpet chops were in prime form and he was playing at the peak of his powers. With the departure of the rhythm section in 1963, it was time for Miles to form another group. By 1964 he had a brilliant young rhythm section (Herbie Hancock, Ron Carter, and Tony Williams) who were open to the innovations of Ornette Coleman in addition to funky soul-jazz. With George Coleman on tenor, the sidemen really inspired Davis and, although he was sticking to his standard repertoire, the renditions were full of surprises and adventurous playing. By late 1964 Coleman had departed and, after Sam Rivers filled in for a European tour, Wayne Shorter was the new tenor. During 1965-68 Miles Davis' second classic quintet bridged the gap between hard bop and free jazz, playing inside/outside music that was quite unique. Although at the time the quintet was overshadowed by the avant-garde players, in the '80s the music of this group would finally become very influential, particularly on Wynton and Branford Marsalis.

During 1968-69 Miles Davis' music continued to change. He persuaded Hancock to use electric keyboards, Shorter started doubling on soprano, the influence of rock began to be felt and, after the rhythm section changed (to Chick Corea, Dave Holland, and Jack DeJohnette), Davis headed one of the earliest fusion bands. Rock and funk rhythms combined with jazz improvisations to form a new hybrid music and Davis' recordings of In a Silent Way and Bitches Brew (both of which used additional instruments) essentially launched the fusion era.

Many of Davis' fans essentially write off his post-1968 music, not realizing that not all of the recordings sound the same and that some were more successful than others. If Davis had sold out so as to gain a larger audience, then why did he record so many 20-minute jams that could not possibly be played on the radio? During 1970-75 the ensembles of his group (which sometimes utilized two or three guitars and a couple of keyboardists) became quite dense, the rhythms were often intense, and Davis unfortunately often used electronics that distorted the sound of his horn. Actually the only album from this era that is a complete failure is On the Corner (Davis is largely absent from that fiasco) and Live/Evil, Jack Johnson, and 1975's Panagea all have memorable sections.

And then suddenly in 1975 Davis retired. He was in bad health and, as he frankly discusses in his autobiography Miles, very much into recreational drugs. The jazz world speculated about what would happen if and when he returned. In 1981 Davis came back with a new band that was similar to his '70s group except that the ensembles were quite a bit sparser. The rock influence was soon replaced by funk and pop elements and, as he became stronger, Davis' trumpet playing proved to still be in excellent form. He toured constantly during his last decade and his personality seemed to have mellowed a bit. Where once he had been quite forbidding and reluctant to be friendly to nonmusicians, Davis was at times eager to grant interviews and talk about his past. Although he had never looked back musically, in the summer of 1991 he shocked everyone by letting Quincy Jones talk him into performing Gil Evans arrangements from the past at the Montreux Jazz Festival. Even if he had Wallace Roney and Kenny Garrett take some of the solos, Davis was in stronger-than-expected form playing the old classics. And then two months later he passed away at the age of 65.

There are currently over 120 valuable Miles Davis recordings in print including many live sets issued on European labels. Taken as a whole, these form quite a legacy. — Scott Yanow

Groove: Miles Davis is another great artist who helped to create and excel in so many different jazz styles that it can be confusing where to start listening. Kind of Blue is on every top-100 jazz-album list I have ever seen, and for good reason. Another fine place to begin is the Blue Note release called Ballads & Blues. I have listed some good albums below. Earlier Davis may be better. From the time of Bitches Brew on, blues lovers may have trouble getting into the sounds. But be sure to pay your respect to Miles Davis. He is the very heart of the blues and (like John Coltrane) has shaped the very core of jazz itself. — *Michael Erlewine*

Ballads and Blues / Apr. 20, 1953-Mar. 9, 1958 / Blue Note ✦✦✦✦
What a treat! An incredible compilation for those Davis fans who love his cooler bluesy/modal material. The brilliant producer Michael Cuscuna has combed through the early Davis "Birth of the Cool" sessions (1950), several Blue Note sessions in 1952 and 1954, plus one cut from the classic Adderley/Davis album *Somethin' Else* to create a cool blues compilation of Davis' stuff stripped of all the bop up-tempo elements. The result is a precursor to *Kind of Blue*, an album that shows all of the bluesy cool Miles Davis that many of us are so very fond of. Don't miss it. — *Michael Erlewine*

☆ **Bags Groove** / 1954 / Original Jazz Classics ✦✦✦✦✦
Sterling sessions with Miles and Monk (p), Milt Jackson (vib), Sonny Rollins (ts), and Horace Silver (p). — *Ron Wynn*

★ **Round About Midnight** / Oct. 27, 1955-Sep. 10, 1956 / Columbia ✦✦✦✦✦
Davis' first Columbia album is a classic. His quintet (with tenor-saxophonist John Coltrane, pianist Red Garland, bassist Paul Chambers, and drummer Philly Joe Jones) was quickly becoming one of the pacesetters in jazz and each of these six performances are memorable. In addition to the definitive non-Monk rendition of "'Round Midnight," one hears the quintet making such diverse songs as "Ah-Leu-Cha," Cole Porter's "All of You," "Tadd's Delight" and "Dear Old Stockholm" sound as if they were all written for the group. Their version of "Bye Bye Blackbird" is the ultimate in cool sophistication. — *Scott Yanow*

☆ **Cookin'** / Nov. 16, 1955-Oct. 26, 1956 / Original Jazz Classics ✦✦✦✦✦
Trumpeter Miles Davis (along with tenor-saxophonist John Coltrane, pianist Red Garland, bassist Paul Chambers, and drummer Philly Joe Jones) are heard on this CD reissue performing such tunes as "My Funny Valentine" (Davis' earliest version of this standard), "Blues by Five," "Airegin" and a medley of "Tune Up" and "When Lights Are Low." Both the quintet and the music qualify as classic; all four of their Prestige albums are easily recommended. — *Scott Yanow*

☆ **Workin'** / 1956 / Original Jazz Classics ✦✦✦✦✦
Miles Davis' 1956 Quintet was one of his classic groups, featuring tenor-saxophonist John Coltrane, pianist Red Garland, bassist Paul Chambers, and drummer Philly Joe Jones. They recorded four albums for Prestige in two marathon sessions. Among the highlights are "It Never Entered My Mind," "Four," "In Your Own Sweet Way," and two versions of "The Theme." The music is essential in one form or another. — *Scott Yanow*

☆ **Steamin'** / May 11, 1956-Oct. 26, 1956 / Original Jazz Classics ✦✦✦✦✦
This classic Prestige session (one of four cut for the label by Davis' first permanent group) has been reissued many times. Davis is heard with his classic quintet of 1956 (which featured tenor-saxophonist John Coltrane, pianist Red Garland, bassist Paul Chambers, and drummer Philly Joe Jones) performing six numbers, all of which are somewhat memorable. Highpoints are "Surrey with the Fringe on Top," "Diane," and "When I Fall in Love"; Davis' muted tone rarely sounded more beautiful. — *Scott Yanow*

☆ **Milestones** / Feb. 4, 1958-Mar. 4, 1958 / Columbia ✦✦✦✦✦
Kind of Blue might have received most of the acclaim but *Milestones*, the recorded debut of the Miles Davis Sextet, is in the same league. This remarkable super group (featuring Davis' trumpet, tenor-saxophonist John Coltrane, altoist Cannonball Adderley, pianist Red Garland, bassist Paul Chambers, and drummer Philly Joe Jones) was arguably the greatest one Davis ever led. "Two Bass Hit" features the two saxes trading off with fire and "Billy Boy" showcases the Red Garland trio (showing what they learned from Ahmad Jamal), but "Straight No Chaser" really demonstrates what a powerhouse band this was. — *Scott Yanow*

☆ **Kind of Blue** / Mar. 2, 1959-Apr. 22, 1959 / Columbia ✦✦✦✦✦
Miles Davis' most famous recording remains his most influential. It is not just that this album helped popularize modal jazz (improvising based on modes or scales rather than running chord changes) or that it introduced two future standards ("So What" and "All Blues") and three other gems ("Freddie Freeloader," "Blue in Green" and "Flamenco Sketches"). Most impressive is how the solos of Miles Davis, John Coltrane, and Cannonball Adderley (what a lineup), despite their differing styles, fit the songs perfectly. Bill Evans returned to the sextet for this date (Wynton Kelly plays piano on "Freddie Free-

loader") while bassist Paul Chambers and drummer Jimmy Cobb are superb in support. The 1997 reissue has the music at last at the correct pitch and added an alternate take of "Flamenco Sketches" to the classic program. — *Scott Yanow*

Live in Stockholm 1960 / Mar. 22, 1960 / Royal Jazz ✦✦✦✦
This remarkable two-CD set features John Coltrane with the Miles Davis Quintet just a short time before 'Trane went out on his own. Davis sounds inspired by his star tenor and although Coltrane was reportedly bored with the repertoire ("On Green Dolphin Street," "All Blues," "Fran-Dance," "Walkin'" and two versions of "So What"), he is at his most explorative throughout this often-stunning music. In addition, the rhythm section (pianist Wynton Kelly, bassist Paul Chambers, and drummer Jimmy Cobb) had been together for two years and is really tight. This highly recommended set also includes a brief interview with Coltrane from this period. — *Scott Yanow*

Wild Bill Davis

b. Nov. 24, 1918, Glasgow, MO, **d.** Aug. 17, 1995, Moorestown, NJ
Organ / Swing, Groove
Prior to the rise of Jimmy Smith in 1956, Wild Bill Davis was the pacesetter among organists. He actually played guitar and wrote arrangements for Milt Larkin's legendary band during 1939-42. Davis played piano with Louis Jordan's Tympany Five (1945-49) before switching to organ in 1950 and heading his own influential organ/guitar/drums trios. Davis was originally supposed to record "April in Paris" with Count Basie's Orchestra in 1955 but when he could not make the session, Basie used his arrangement for the full band and had a major hit. In addition to working with his own groups in the '60s, Davis made several albums with his friend Johnny Hodges, leading to tours during 1969-71 with Duke Ellington. In the '70s he recorded for *Black & Blue* with a variety of swing all-stars and played with Lionel Hampton, appearing at festivals through the early '90s. — *Scott Yanow*
Groove: An early jazz-organ pioneer, Davis tends to be found in a large-group format. You can find him as a sideman if you look for him. He played behind Illinois Jacquet, Lionel Hampton, Frank Foster, and Sonny Stitt on occasion. — *Michael Erlewine*

The Music from Milk and Honey / Feb. 1962 / Prestige ✦✦
W/ Charlie Shavers. — *AMG*

Con Soul and Sax / Jan. 7, 1965 / RCA ✦✦✦✦
W/ Johnny Hodges. — *AMG*

● **In Atlantic City** / Aug. 10, 1966+Aug. 11, 1966 / RCA ✦✦✦✦
W/ Johnny Hodges. — *AMG*

Impulsions / May 9, 1972+May 10, 1972 / Black & Blue ✦✦✦

Joey De Francesco

b. 1971, Philadelphia, PA
Organ, Trumpet / Bop, Soul-Jazz, Hard Bop, Groove
The comeback of the organ in jazz during the late '80s was partly due to the rise of Joey DeFrancesco, a brilliant and energetic player whose style is heavily influenced by Jimmy Smith.

Joey DeFrancisco was born April 10, 1971 in Springfield, PA and was raised in the Philadelphia area. The son of Papa John DeFrancisco, a fierce Hammond organ player himself, Joey got an early start on piano when he was five and within a year had switched to his father's instrument, the organ.

He won all kinds of major awards in high school including the Philadelphia Jazz Society's McCoy Tyner Scholarship. In the first Thelonious Monk International Jazz Piano Competition in 1987 he was a finalist at the age of 16. He is a decent player too.

He had a record contract with Columbia, was playing with Miles Davis (1988) by the time he left high school and has led his own groups ever since. DeFrancesco is the most important new organist to emerge during the past decade. He has recorded for Columbia, Muse, and Big Mo. — *Scott Yanow & Michael Erlewine*

● **Where Were You?** / Jun. 1990 / Columbia ✦✦✦✦
On his second recording, organist Joey DeFrancesco is heard in settings ranging from a quartet to a large orchestra. Although he is generally the main star, DeFrancesco welcomes such guests as tenors Illinois Jacquet and Kirk Whalum (heard on two songs apiece including both jamming on "Red Top") and guitarist John Scofield. DeFrancesco holds his own and is in top form

on such selections as "Teach Me Tonight," "Where Were You," "But Not for Me," and "Love Attack." — *Scott Yanow*

Reboppin' / 1992 / Columbia ✦✦✦✦

Organist Joey DeFrancesco had an opportunity on his fourth Columbia project to mostly perform with his own group, a trio consisting of guitarist Paul Bollenback and drummer Byron Landham. Among the guests on a few selections are trumpeter Jim Henry, tenor saxophonist Tony Malaby and, on "Family Jam," guitarist Johnny DeFrancesco (Joey's brother) and organist John DeFrancesco (their father). Special treats are Joey DeFrancesco's effective trumpet solos on four of the 14 selections; highlights overall include "Sister Sadie," "Big Bad Jim," "Evidence" and "Bye Bye Blackbird." — *Scott Yanow*

Live at the 5 Spot / 1993 / Columbia ✦✦✦

Organist Joey DeFrancesco clearly had a good time during this jam session. His fine quintet (which has strong soloists in altoist Robert Landham, trumpeter Jim Henry, and especially guitarist Paul Bollenback) starts things off with a runthrough of "rhythm changes" during "The Eternal One" and the hornless trio cuts loose on a swinging "I'll Remember April," but otherwise all of the other selections feature guests. Tenors Illinois Jacquet, Grover Washington, Jr., Houston Person, and Kirk Whalum all fare well on separate numbers (Jacquet steals the show on "All of Me") and on the closing blues DeFrancesco interacts with fellow organist Captain Jack McDuff. Few surprises occur overall (the tenors should have all played together) but the music is quite pleasing and easily recommended to DeFrancesco's fans. — *Scott Yanow*

Cornell Dupree

b. Dec. ??, 1942, Fort Worth, TX
Guitar / Soul-Jazz, Groove

Long a top R&B session player, Cornell Dupree led excellent jazz-oriented sets for Amazing and Kokopelli in the early '90s, showing that he was capable of also playing swinging jazz. Dupree was with King Curtis in 1962 before becoming a studio musician.

He has recorded with artists like Harry Belafonte, Joe Cocker, Michael Bolton, Lou Rawls, Roberta Flack, Robert Palmer, Lena Horne, and Mariah Carey—over 2500 albums as a sideman!

He toured with Aretha Franklin (1967-76) and a variety of top pop and R&B acts and in the early '70s worked with the group Stuff. His 1988 solo album *Coast to Coast* won a Grammy. Dupree's blues-oriented guitar style continues to be in demand. — *Michael Erlewine & Scott Yanow*

Shadow Dancing / May 1979 / MSG ✦✦✦

Dupree on guitar with Hank Crawford on alto sax and organist Jimmy Smith playing the electric piano. Includes a rendition of "The Creeper." — *Michael Erlewine*

Coast to Coast / 1988 / Antilles ✦✦✦✦

Some excellent session players sound hot on the R&B, tepid on the fusion. — *Ron Wynn*

● Bop 'n' Blues / Nov. 15, 1994-Feb. 13, 1995 / Kokopelli ✦✦✦✦

Guitarist Cornell Dupree has long been famous for his blues and R&B solos, so even he was surprised (and a bit apprehensive) when label-head Herbie Mann suggested he record a variety of bop-oriented standards. As it turned out, several of the tunes were blues anyway (such as "Bags' Groove," "Now's the Time," and "Walkin'") and Dupree was free to adapt the other songs to his own style. "Freedom Jazz Dance" became a funky vamp while "My Little Suede Shoes" was drastically slowed down and stretched out. With backing from a versatile rhythm section and occasional contributions from altoist Bobby Watson, trumpeter Terell Stafford, and baritonist Ronnie Cuber, Dupree sounds perfectly at home throughout this fine CD, even on "Manteca" and "'Round Midnight." — *Scott Yanow*

Charles Earland

b. May 24, 1941, Philadelphia, PA, d. 1997
Organ, Synthesizer / Soul-Jazz, Hard Bop, Groove

Charles Earland came into his own at the tail end of the great '60s wave of soul-jazz organists, gaining a large following and much airplay with a series of albums for the the Prestige label. While heavily indebted to Jimmy Smith and Jimmy McGriff, Earland comes armed with his own swinging, technically agile, light-textured sound on the keyboard and one of the best walk-

ing-bass pedal techniques in the business. Though not an innovative player in his field, Earland can burn with the best of them when he is on.

Earland actually started his musical experiences surreptitiously on his father's alto sax as a kid, and when he was in high school, he played baritone in a band that also featured fellow Philadelphians Pat Martino on guitar, Lew Tabackin on tenor, and yes, Frankie Avalon on trumpet. After playing in the Temple University band, he toured as a tenor player with McGriff for three years, became infatuated with McGriff's organ playing, and started learning the Hammond B-3 at intermission breaks. When McGriff let him go, Earland switched to the organ permanently, forming a trio with Martino and drummer Bobby Durham. He made his first recordings for Choice in 1966, then joined Lou Donaldson for two years (1968-69) and two albums before being signed as a solo artist to Prestige. Earland's first album for Prestige, *Black Talk!*, became a best-selling classic of the soul-jazz genre; a surprisingly effective cover of the Spiral Starecase's pop-rock hit "More Today Than Yesterday" from that LP received saturation airplay on jazz radio in 1969. He recorded eight more albums for Prestige, one of which featured a young unknown Philadelphian named Grover Washington, Jr., then switched to Muse before landing contracts with Mercury and Columbia. By this time, the organ trio genre had gone into eclipse, and in the spirit of the times, Earland acquired some synthesizers and converted to pop/disco in collaboration with his wife, singer-songwriter Sheryl Kendrick. Kendrick's death from sickle-cell anemia in 1985 left Earland desolate, and he stopped playing for awhile, but a gig at the Chickrick House on Chicago's South Side in the late '80s brought him out of his grief and back to the Hammond B-3. Two excellent albums in the old soul-jazz groove for Milestone followed, and the '90s found him returning to the Muse label. — *Richard S. Ginell*

★ Black Talk! / Dec. 15, 1969 / Original Jazz Classics ✦✦✦✦✦

This CD reissue of a Prestige date is one of the few successful examples of jazz musicians from the late '60s taking a few rock and pop songs and turning them into creative jazz. Organist Charles Earland and his sextet, which includes trumpeter Virgil Jones, Houston Person on tenor, and guitarist Melvin Sparks, perform a variation of "Eleanor Rigby" titled "Black Talk," two originals, a surprisingly effective rendition of "Aquarius" and a classic rendition of "More Today than Yesterday." Fans of organ combos are advised to pick up this interesting set. — *Scott Yanow*

Soul Crib / 1969 / Choice ✦✦✦

Earland with George Coleman on tenor sax, Jimmy Ponder on guitar, and Walter Perkins on drums. — *Michael Erlewine*

Black Drops / Jun. 1, 1970 / Prestige ✦✦✦

Early soul-jazz, occasional R&B and pop cuts from organist Charles Earland, just cutting his third album as a leader at that time. His organ solos were sometimes churning and impressive, but at other times bogged down in cliches and repetitive phrases. But the potential Earland showed on most cuts has since materialized. — *Ron Wynn*

Living Black! / Sep. 17, 1970 / Prestige ✦✦✦✦

One of the best Charles Earland albums ever released, *Living Black!* is noteworthy not only for his inspired organ playing, but also for the dynamic tenor sax of Grover Washington, Jr. When *Living Black!* was recorded live at the Key Club in Newark, N.J. in 1970, Washington was only 26, and he wouldn't record for the first time as a leader until *Inner City Blues* the following year. But Earland, who knew Washington from his native Philadelphia, realized that the saxman showed enormous promise, and it's evident that Earland's faith in him was completely justified when they dig into Miles Davis' "Milestones" and Benny Golson's "Killer Joe," as well as the funky "Westbound No.9." After being out of print for many years, *Living Black!* was finally reissued on CD in 1997 with two previously unreleased bonus tracks: "More Today Than Yesterday" (which was first a hit for the soul-flavored pop group the Spiral Starecase in 1969, but soon became Earland's theme song) and a passionate version of the Motown tune "Message From a Black Man." Rounding out the lineup are guitarist Maynard Parker, trumpeter Gary Chandler, drummer Jesse Kilpatrick, and percussionist Buddy Caldwell—all of them competent and hard-swinging, though little known. *Living Black!'s* debut on CD was long overdue. — *Alex Henderson*

Leaving This Planet / Dec. 11, 1973-Dec. 13, 1973 / Prestige ✦✦✦✦

A definite departure from the type of earthy, groove-oriented soul-jazz he usually embraced, *Leaving This Planet* is perhaps Charles Earland's most ambitous album—not necessarily his best, but certainly his most surprising. Responding to the fusion revolution, Earland plays keyboards and various synthesizers in addition to his usual Hammond B-3 organ and thrives in a very electric setting. The album (reissued on a 79-minute CD in 1993) isn't fusion in the same sense as Miles Davis, Larry Coryell, or Weather Report—rather, he incorporates funk and rock elements in a manner not unlike the early-'70s experiments of tenor saxophonist Joe Henderson and trumpeter Freddie Hubbard. And in fact, those greats (as well as trumpeter Eddie Henderson) are among the superb soloists featured. Whether the Philadelphian is embracing Hub's "Red Clay" or Henderson's "Recorda-Me" or fine compositions of his own (which range from the congenial, pleasant "Brown Eyes" to the abstract "Warp Factor 8"), he leaves no doubt just how much he's enjoying this surprising change of pace. —*Alex Henderson*

Smokin' / 1977 / Muse ♦♦♦
Fine mid-'70s sextet set featuring Earland's customary soul-jazz, blues, and funk, with uptempo and ballad originals. Tenor saxophonists David Schnitter and George Coleman excel, as does guitarist Jimmy Ponder. —*Ron Wynn*

Front Burner / Jun. 27, 1988-Jun. 28, 1988 / Milestone ♦♦♦
Charles Earland is among the most consistent of organists, with nearly every one of his recordings on that instrument (as opposed to his interlude on synthesizers) being easily recommended to soul-jazz and hard bop collectors. For this CD, Earland heads a sextet also including trumpeter Virgil Jones (long an underrated player), Bill Easley on tenor, guitarist Bobby Broom, drummer Buddy Williams and occasionally Frank Colon on conga. Other than a throwaway version of the theme from *Moonlighting,* the mostly basic music on this set is rewarding, with Earland infusing the tunes with plenty of grease and funk. —*Scott Yanow*

Third Degree Burn / May 15, 1989-May 16, 1989 / Milestone ♦♦♦♦
This excellent CD features organist Charles Earland, guitarist Bobby Broom, drummer Buddy Williams, and percussionist Ralph Dorsey being joined by trumpeter Lew Soloff and either Grover Washington (on two songs) or David Newman (appearing on the other four) on tenor or soprano. The material may be unfamiliar (other than a Michael Jackson song), but the music is prime soul-jazz, with Earland's cooking organ keeping the proceedings quite heated. One of Charles Earland's best recordings of the '80s. —*Scott Yanow*

Whip Appeal / May 23, 1990 / Muse ♦♦♦♦
A jazz version of Babyface's "Whip Appeal"? It's hard to believe, but then, Charles Earland has always had an impressive ability to recontextualize pop and R&B songs that seem most unlikely vehicles for jazz improvisation. On this fine CD, which marked the beginning of his association with Muse Records, Earland transforms that "urban contemporary" number into hard-swingin' soul-jazz, successfully revisits the Spiral Staircase's "More Today than Yesterday" and adds a lot of grit and spice to something not exactly known for those things: Kenny G's "Songbird." The latter does have a pretty melody, and it becomes quite soulful in the imaginative hands of Earland—whose excellent support includes fellow Philadelphian Johnny Coles (fluegelhorn) and long-time ally Houston Person (tenor sax). —*Alex Henderson*

Unforgettable / Dec. 1991 / Muse ♦♦♦♦
Charles Earland is definitely a survivor. The Hammond hero had lost his first wife to cancer when he made a triumphant return to soul-jazz in the late '80s, and he had recovered from a major heart attack when he recorded the appropriately titled *Unforgettable.* Earland was in the Intensive Care Unit in August 1991, and by December 1991, was back in the studio to record this superb and varied CD. The Philadelphian stressed that he was lucky to be alive, and he celebrates his survival with imaginative interpretations of everything from Joe Henderson's "The Kicker" to Nat King Cole's "Unforgettable" (which he takes a medium speed instead of its usual ballad tempo) to Santana's "Europa." Earland has consistently demonstrated that commercial appeal and accessibility can go hand-in-hand with musical integrity, and *Unforgettable* is one of many fine examples. —*Alex Henderson*

I Ain't Jivin' I'm Jammin' / Dec. 11, 1992 / Muse ♦♦♦
The easy-going and the laid-back dominate *I Ain't Jivin', I'm Jammin',* an album that isn't quite in a class with *Black Talk!, Whip Appeal,* or *Unforgettable,* but is nonetheless a welcome addition to Charles Earland's catalogue. The improviser swings hard and passionately on Wayne Shorter's "Tell It Like It Is," but his mellow side wins out on such congenial, groove-oriented

jazz/R&B fare as pianist Neal Creque's "Cease the Bombing" and the originals "Sweety Pie," "World of Competition" and "Thinking of You." Even at his most relaxed, though, Earland's music is undeniably gritty. Among the noteworthy soloists employed this time are trombonist Clifford Adams, guitarist Oliver Nevels and the promising young tenor & soprano saxman Eric Alexander. —*Alex Henderson*

Jazz Organ Summit / 1998 / Cannonball ♦♦♦♦
One night in Chicago in 1997, four masters of the Hammond B-3 got together for a one-time-only showcase. The results are captured here on a must-buy album for jazz organ fans. While Earland, Dr. Lonnie Smith, and Jimmy McGriff all make nice contributions, it was Johnny "Hammond" Smith who delivered the evening's most poignant performance. Seriously ill with cancer, he made a special trip from his home in California to take part in this concert, which would turn out to be his last. He died just 11 days later. Listen closely to his emotional reading of the ballads "This Masquerade Is Over" and "Summertime" for an example of dignity and artistry in jazz. —*Joel Roberts*

Jimmy Forrest

b. Jan. 24, 1920, St. Louis, MO, d. Aug. 26, 1980, Grand Rapids, MI
Tenor Saxophone / Swing, Early R&B Jazz, Groove
A fine all-round tenor player, Jimmy Forrest is best-known for recording "Night Train," a song that he "borrowed" from the last part of Duke Ellington's "Happy Go Lucky Local." While in high school in St. Louis, Forrest worked with pianist Eddie Johnson, the legendary Fate Marable, and the Jeter-Pillars Orchestra. In 1938 he went on the road with Don Albert and then was with Jay McShann's Orchestra (1940-42). In New York Forrest played with Andy Kirk (1942-48) and Duke Ellington (1949) before returning to St. Louis. After recording "Night Train," Forrest became a popular attraction and recorded a series of jazz-oriented R&B singles. Among his most important later associations were with Harry "Sweets" Edison (1958-63), Count Basie's Orchestra (1972-77), and Al Grey with whom he co-led a quintet until his death. Forrest recorded for United (reissued by Delmark), Prestige/New Jazz (1960-62) and Palo Alto (1978). —*Scott Yanow*

★ **Night Train** / Nov. 27, 1951-Sep. 7, 1953 / Delmark ♦♦♦♦♦
Jimmy Forrest had a tremendous hit in 1951 with "Night Train," a simple blues riff he lifted from Duke Ellington's "Happy Go Lucky Local." Although the tenorman was not able to duplicate that song's appeal with any other recording, he was a popular performer on the R&B circuit throughout the '50s. Virtually all of his records from the era (originally made for the United label) are on this CD reissue, including five selections not previously released. The tough-toned Forrest was not really a screamer or a honker, and the 17 numbers on the set should be of interest both to early R&B and jazz collectors. Recorded in Chicago, Forrest fronts a rhythm section that includes either Charles Fox or Bunky Parker on piano, and sometimes trumpeter Chauncey Locke or trombonist Bert Dabney. The music is very enjoyable and highly recommended. —*Scott Yanow*

All the Gin Is Gone / Dec. 10, 1959-Dec. 12, 1959 / Delmark ♦♦♦♦
This was the first album that tenor saxophonist Jimmy Forrest made after his R&B phase ended. Particularly notable is that the set served as the recording debut of guitarist Grant Green; completing the band are pianist Harold Mabern, bassist Gene Ramey, and drummer Elvin Jones. The top-notch group performs two ballads, "Caravan" and three basic Forrest originals, including the title cut. The music is essentially melodic and blues-based hard bop that looks toward soul-jazz. Everyone sounds in fine form. —*Scott Yanow*

Black Forrest / Dec. 10, 1959-Dec. 12, 1959 / Delmark ♦♦♦
This 1972 LP, a complement to *All the Gin Is Gone,* released the remainder of tenor saxophonist Jimmy Forrest's two Delmark sessions, including four alternate takes and five other songs. Forrest sounds fine, guitarist Grant Green was making his debut on record, and the rhythm section (pianist Harold Mabern, bassist Gene Ramey, and drummer Elvin Jones) plays up to par. Get *All the Gin Is Gone* first, and then, if one wants to hear the rest of the story, this set. —*Scott Yanow*

Forrest Fire / Aug. 9, 1960 / Original Jazz Classics ♦♦♦♦
During 1961, Jimmy Forrest recorded four albums for Prestige and its subsidiary New Jazz, all of which have been reissued on CD in the Original Jazz

Classics series. The appealing tenor is matched up with 20-year-old organist Larry Young, guitarist Thornel Schwartz, and drummer Jimmie Smith. They perform two jump tunes ("Dexter's Deck" and Doug Watkins' "Help"), a pair of blues, a swinging version of Irving Berlin's "Remember," and a lone ballad ("When Your Lover Has Gone"). Excellent music that is also quite accessible. — *Scott Yanow*

Out of the Forrest / Apr. 18, 1961 / Original Jazz Classics ✦✦✦✦
This CD reissue is an excellent example of tenor saxophonist Jimmy Forrest in a soulful but fairly straight-ahead setting. Accompanied by pianist Joe Zawinul, bassist Tommy Potter, and drummer Clarence Johnston, Forrest revives his "Bolo Blues," plays his basic "Crash Program," and otherwise sticks to melodic standards. His highly expressive powers and ability to say a lot with a few notes is very much in evidence on this excellent set. — *Scott Yanow*

Sit Down and Relax with Jimmy Forrest / Sep. 1, 1961 / Original Jazz Classics ✦✦✦✦
The large warm tone of Jimmy Forrest is well featured on this CD reissue of a Prestige LP. Joined by guitarist Calvin Newborn (pianist Phineas' brother has rarely had such a good opportunity to stretch out), pianist Hugh Lawson, bassist Tommy Potter, and drummer Clarence Johnston, Forrest plays melodically but with his own brand of soul. The group performs three swing-era standards, "Tin Tin Deo," Duke Ellington's "Rocks In My Bed," "The Moon Was Yellow," and a version of "That's All" that was recorded on the same date but originally issued on a different album. This CD gives one a good example of Forrest's playing and fortunately his solos are not as relaxed and laidback as the album's title might imply. — *Scott Yanow*

Most Much / Oct. 19, 1961 / Original Jazz Classics ✦✦✦✦
Jimmy Forrest was a very consistent tenor, able to infuse bop and swing standards with soul and his distinctive tone. With the assistance of pianist Hugh Lawson, bassist Tommy Potter, drummer Clarendon Johnson, and Ray Barretto on congas, Forrest explores mostly veteran tunes, such as a jumping "Annie Laurie," the calypso "Matilda," a sentimental "My Buddy," "Robbins Nest," and even "Sonny Boy." Enjoyable music from the warm tenor. — *Scott Yanow*

Heart of the Forrest / Dec. 28, 1978 / Palo Alto ✦✦✦
Despite his general popularity, tenor saxophonist Jimmy Forrest only led this one session after 1962. Recorded less than two years before his death, Forrest was at the time co-leading a group with trombonist Al Grey. This live club date (released on a 1982 Palo Alto LP and not reissued yet on CD) features Forrest in a trio with organist Shirley Scott and drummer Randy Marsh. Although nothing too unexpected occurs on the five veteran standards (which include "Annie Laurie," "Take the 'A' Train," and Forrest's big hit, "Night Train"), the swinging and soulful music is quite infectious. — *Scott Yanow*

Frank Foster

b. Sep. 23, 1928, Cincinnati, OH
Tenor Saxophone / Swing, Hard Bop, Groove
A very talented tenor saxophonist and arranger, Frank Foster has been associated with the Count Basie Orchestra off and on since 1953. Early on he played in Detroit with the many talented local players and, after a period in the Army (1951-53), he joined Basie's big band. Well-featured on tenor during his Basie years (1953-64), Foster also contributed plenty of arrangements and such originals as "Down for the Count," "Blues Backstage" and the standard "Shiny Stockings." In the latter half of the '60s Foster was a freelance writer. In addition to playing with Elvin Jones (1970-72) and occasionally with the Thad Jones/Mel Lewis Orchestra, he led his Loud Minority big band. In 1983 Foster co-led a quintet with Frank Wess and he toured Europe with Jimmy Smith in 1985. Although influenced by John Coltrane in his playing, Foster was able to modify his style when he took over the Count Basie ghost band in 1986, revitalizing it and staying at the helm until 1995. Outside of his Basie dates, Foster has led sessions for Vogue, Blue Note (1954 and 1968), Savoy, Argo, Prestige, Mainstream, Denon, Catalyst, Bee Hive, Steeple Chase, Pablo, and Concord. — *Scott Yanow*

The House That Love Built / Sep. 1982 / Steeple Chase ✦✦✦✦

Two for the Blues / Oct. 11, 1983 + Oct. 12, 1983 / Pablo ✦✦✦✦
This CD reissue of a Pablo date features Frank Foster (on tenor and soprano)

and Frank Wess (tenor, flute, and alto) at their best. They perform three Wess originals, one by Foster, and a variety of mostly underplayed standards (including Neal Hefti's "Two for the Blues," plus "Spring Can Really Hang You Up the Most") and a surprisingly uptempo "Send In the Clowns." With pianist Kenny Barron, bassist Rufus Reid, and drummer Marvin "Smitty" Smith offering stimulating support, this is an excellent showcase for the two Franks. A follow-up Concord set (*Frankly Speaking*) used the same personnel. — *Scott Yanow*

Frankly Speaking / Dec. 1984 / Concord Jazz ✦✦✦✦
Using the same personnel as the previous year's *Two for the Blues* (Frank Foster on tenor and soprano, Frank Wess on tenor and flute, pianist Kenny Barron, bassist Rufus Reid, and drummer Marvin "Smitty" Smith), this set gets the slight edge and is an excellent introduction to the playing of the two Count Basie saxophonists. Foster contributes two originals (including the classic "Blues Backstage"), Wess brought in "Up and Coming," and the quintet also performs five jazz standards including "When Did You Leave Heaven," Hoagy Carmichael's "One Morning In May," and Neal Hefti's "Two Franks." Recommended. — *Scott Yanow*

● **Leo Rising** / Aug. 23, 1996-Aug. 24, 1996 / Arabesque ✦✦✦✦
Frank Foster, who in 1995 willingly gave up leadership of the Count Basie Orchestra after nine years of traveling the world (and playing "Jumpin' at the Woodside" and his own "Shiny Stockings" on a nightly basis), is heard here at the top of his form. Whether swinging on his blues "You're Only as Old as You Look," showing off the influence of John Coltrane during some modal material, playing some intense soprano on the title track, or jamming on rhythm changes with guest trumpeter Derrick Gardner during "Derricksterity," Foster (67 at the time) makes every note count. The all-star rhythm section sounds quite inspired by the veteran tenor's ideas and enthusiasm (Scott and McBride have many excellent short solos), while trumpeter Gardner contributes a pair of fiery statements. This is one of Foster's finest small-group dates and is highly recommended. — *Scott Yanow*

Ronnie Foster

b. May 13, 1950, Buffalo, NY
Organ, Synthesizer, Piano, Keyboards / Contemporary Funk, Soul-Jazz, Groove, Instrumental Pop
Since his initial solo style favored funky vamps instead of risky improvisation, organist Ronnie Foster was frequently dismissed by jazz purists during the peak of his career in the first half of the '70s. However, he was a talented mainstream funk and soul-jazz keyboardist who managed to cultivate a successful career as a sideman (working frequently with George Benson, in particular) and producer during the late '70s, '80s, and '90s. Furthermore, his '70s records for Blue Note became cult items among a new generation of listeners raised on acid-jazz. Even if he rarely led a session after 1979, Foster wound up playing a some sort of a role in mainstream and funk-jazz during the '80s and '90s.

A native of Buffalo New York, Foster learned to play piano as a child, being taught in the traditional classical style. However, jazz intrigued him more, and when he was a teenager he began to pursue that direction. Eventually, he attended a jam session where there was an organ in addition to a piano. After playing the organ, he decided to concentrate on the instrument. He listened to Jimmy Smith, gradually making his way to more adventurous players like Larry Young. A local Buffalo organist, Joe Madison, gave him advice, and Foster practiced regularly at a studio where he would rent a room with an organ for 60 cents an hour.

Eventually, Foster began playing local and New York clubs. He slowly built a following, playing with such musicians as Stanley Turrentine, Grant Green, and George Benson. By the early '70s, he had formed a group called Energy II. Grant Green had Foster play on his *Alive* album, and the organist's performance impressed the label's Dr. George Butler, who offered Foster a contract.

Ronnie Foster recorded *Two Headed Freap*, his first album for Blue Note, in January of 1972. A funky set of soul-jazz, the album didn't receive much attention or critical praise, and neither did its follow-up, *Sweet Revival*, which was recorded in December of that year. He cut *Live at Montreux* in July of 1973, which was followed in 1974 by *On the Avenue* and in 1975 by *Cheshire*, his final album for Blue Note. He then moved to Columbia, where he released *Love Satellite* in 1978 and *Delight* in 1979.

A session for ProJazz, entitled *Racer*, followed a few years later, but Foster effectively retired from leading groups in the early '80s in order to concentrate on session work. During the '70s, he had played on numerous George Benson records, as well as records by Stevie Wonder, Roberta Flack, Earl Klugh, Jimmy Ponder, Stanley Clarke, and Lalo Schifrin. Throughout the '80s, Foster continued to play on a wide variety of sessions and eventually moved into production. Among the musicians he worked with in the '80s were Jimmy Smith, Klugh, Flack, Harvey Mason, Stanley Turrentine, David Sanborn, Djavan, and Grover Washington Jr. Foster continued the same path in the '90s, playing with many of the same musicians, as well as Lee Ritenour, Roland Vazquez, and the Temptations, among others. His own records were rediscovered by a new generation of listeners in the '90s, as well, with several of his records used as source material for sample-heavy acid-jazz and hip-hop records. — *Stephen Thomas Erlewine*

The Two Headed Freap / Jan. 20, 1972-Jan. 21, 1972 / Blue Note ♦♦♦♦
Ronnie Foster's debut album *Two Headed Freap* is a set of contemporary funky soul-jazz from the early '70s, which means it sounds closer to the soundtrack of a lost blaxploitation flick than *Back at the Chicken Shack, Pt. 2.* Foster certainly does display a debt to Jimmy Smith, but his playing is busier than Smith's and a bit wilder. Ironic, then, that his playing is in service to the groove and blends into the mix of wah-wah guitars, funk rhythms, electric bass, harps, and percolating percussion. Everything on *Two Headed Freap* is about glitzy groove—it sounds cinematic, colorful, and funky. It's true that there is little real improvisation here and the songs all have a similar groove, but it's worked well, and the music is ultimately appealing to fans of this genre. Jazz purists—even soul-jazz purists—will likely find this music a little monotonous and commercial, but fans of early-'70s funk from Sly Stone to Herbie Hancock will find something of interest here. — *Stephen Thomas Erlewine*

Sweet Revival / Dec. 14, 1972-Dec. 15, 1972 / Blue Note ♦♦♦♦
"Let me begin by saying that this is not the greatest Jazz album you've ever heard." So states critic/DJ Harry Abraham in the liner notes on the back of *Sweet Revival,* Ronnie Foster's second album as a leader. Abraham was obviously trying to deflect criticism that this record is, in his words, "a commercial album that could have just as easily been titled "Ronnie Foster plays the Top 40 hits of the Seventies with Horns, Strings, and Voices," but nothing he could write would make this album acceptable to jazz purists. Foster's fondness for funky soul-jazz would be enough to earn the disdain of some critics, but he compounds his problems by piling on contemporary funk, soul and pop influences. Sweet, sweeping strings straight out of Philadelphia are all over *Sweet Revival,* as are wah-wah and fuzz guitars, slap bass, electric pianos, vocal choruses and electric sitars. Half of the album is devoted to pop covers ("Back Stabbers," "Me and Mrs. Jones," "Alone Again (Naturally)"), with a couple of fusion numbers and originals thrown in for good measure. Certainly, this is the stuff that enrages jazzbos, and the album does sound like the soundtrack for a cut-rate blaxploitation flick, but that's part of its appeal. Fans of that sound will find much of the album appealing, even if the vocals can sound eerie (check out the heavily echoed intro to "Where Is the Love?") and the sitars sound silly. Although the album sounds dated, the grooves are funky, and *Sweet Revival* remains one of the most engaging records of groovy, jazzy funk-soul of its era. — *Stephen Thomas Erlewine*

● **On the Avenue** / Apr. 30, 1974 + May 1, 1974 / Blue Note ♦♦♦♦
His most interesting jazz-influenced release. — *Ron Wynn*

Grant Green

b. Jun. 6, 1931, St. Louis, MO, **d.** Jan. 31, 1979, New York, NY
Guitar / Hard Bop, Soul-Jazz, Groove
Grant Green was born in St. Louis on June 6, 1931, learned his instrument in grade school from his guitar-playing father and was playing professionally by the age of thirteen with a gospel group. He worked gigs in his home town and in East St. Louis, Illinois until he moved to New York in 1960 at the suggestion of Lou Donaldson. Green told Dan Morgenstern in a *Down Beat* interview "The first thing I learned to play was boogie woogie. Then I had to do a lot of rock and roll. It's all blues, anyhow."

His extensive foundation in R&B combined with a mastery of bebop and simplicity that put expressiveness ahead of technical expertise. Green was a superb blues interpreter, and his later material was predominantly blues and R&B, though he was also a wondrous ballad and standards soloist. He was a particular admirer of Charlie Parker, and his phrasing often reflected it.

Green played in the '50s with Jimmy Forrest, Harry Edison, and Lou Donaldson.

He also collaborated with many organists, among them Brother Jack McDuff, Sam Lazar, Baby Face Willette, Gloria Coleman, Big John Patton, and Larry Young. During the early '60s, both his fluid, tasteful playing in organ/guitar/drum combos and his other dates for Blue Note established Green as a star, though he seldom got the critical respect given other players. He was off the scene for a bit in the mid-'60s, but came back strong in the late '60s and '70s. Green played with Stanley Turrentine, Dave Bailey, Yusef Lateef, Joe Henderson, Hank Mobley, Herbie Hancock, McCoy Tyner, and Elvin Jones.

Sadly, drug problems interrupted his career in the '60s, and undoubtedly contributed to the illness he suffered in the late '70s. Green was hospitalized in 1978 and died a year later. Despite some rather uneven LPs near the end of his career, the great body of his work represents marvelous soul-jazz, bebop, and blues.

A severely underrated player during his lifetime, Green is one of the great unsung heroes of jazz guitar. Like Stanley Turrentine, he tends to be left out of the books. Although he mentions Charlie Christian and Jimmy Raney as influences, Green always claimed he listened to horn players (Charlie Parker and Miles Davis) and not other guitar players, and it shows. No other player has this kind of single-note linearity (he avoids chordal playing). There is very little of the intellectual element in Green's playing, and his technique is always at the service of his music. And it is music, plain and simple, that makes Green unique.

Green's playing is immediately recognizable—perhaps more than any other guitarist. Green has been almost systematically ignored by jazz buffs with a bent for the cool side, and he has only recently begun to be appreciated for his incredible musicality. Perhaps no guitarist has ever handled standards and ballads with the brilliance of Grant Green. Mosaic, the nation's premier jazz reissue label, issued a wonderful collection *The Complete Blue Note Recordings with Sonny Clark,* featuring prime early '60s Green albums plus unissued tracks. Some of the finest examples of Green's work can be found there. — *Michael Erlewine and Ron Wynn*

Grant's First Stand / Jan. 28, 1961 / Blue Note ♦♦♦
His first album, with Baby Face Willette on Hammond organ and Ben Dixon on drums. Hard to find. Some of this material was released in Japan. — *Michael Erlewine*

Jazz Profile / Jan. 28, 1961-May 20, 1965 / Blue Note ♦♦♦♦
Jazz Profile compiles highlights from Grant Green's recordings for Blue Note, drawing a rough portrait of his career. The compilation features both soul-jazz and hard-bop cuts, giving a good sense of Green's depth and range. While there isn't anything here that will appeal to collectors, *Jazz Profile* does offer a nice introduction for curious listeners. — *Leo Stanley*

Green Blues / Mar. 15, 1961 / Muse ♦♦♦
With Frank Haynes on tenor sax, Billy Gardner on piano, Ben Tucker on bass, and Dave Bailer on drums. Originally issued on *Jazztime* under Dave Bailey's name, and now reissued in this format. This is early Green, his second session, and the music is straight-ahead mainstream jazz with a bluesy flavor. This material is available on *Reaching Out,* a release on the Black Lion label. — *Michael Erlewine*

Reaching Out / Mar. 15, 1961 / Black Lion ♦♦♦
Green is in fine form as is pianist Gardner (better known as an organist), but the album is perhaps most valuable for the contributions of the obscure tenorman Frank Haynes who died in 1965; his sound will remind some a little of Stanley Turrentine. — *Scott Yanow, Cadence*

Green Street / Apr. 1, 1961 / Blue Note ♦♦♦♦
Most of guitarist Grant Green's recordings of the '60s feature him in larger groups, making this trio outing with bassist Ben Tucker and drummer Dave Bailey (a CD reissue of the original LP plus two added alternate takes) a strong showcase for his playing. Green, whose main competitor on guitar at the time was Wes Montgomery, already had his own singing sound and a highly individual hornlike approach. He stretches out on a full set of attractive originals plus "'Round Midnight" and "Alone Together," so this reissue is an excellent introduction to his appealing and hard-swinging style. — *Scott Yanow*

Sunday Mornin' / Jun. 4, 1961 / Blue Note ✦✦✦
Sunday Mornin' is Green's fourth album with Blue Note and his first quartet with a piano rather than a Hammond organ. Sidemen includes Kenny Drew (piano), Ben Dixon (drums), and Ben Tucker (bass). The result is a sound that is spacious and crisp—a solid setting for Green's single-note leads. This early Grant Green is straight-ahead jazz with a bluesy tone, similar to what you will find on his album *Matador*. Tunes include the blues "Freedom March," the gospel-influenced "Sunday Mornin'," the lovely theme from "Exodus," a delicate rendition of Billie Holiday's "God Bless the Child," and a great version of the Miles Davis classic "So What." —*Michael Erlewine*

Grantstand / Aug. 1, 1961 / Blue Note ✦✦✦✦
A quartet session with Yusef Lateef (ts, fl) and vintage Jack McDuff on the Hammond organ. Al Harewood is on drums, the organ taking up the bass chores. The 15-minute "Blues in Maude's Flat" is very nice indeed, and "My Funny Valentine" (with Lateef on flute) is just plain lovely. No one does standards like Green. —*Michael Erlewine*

Remembering / Aug. 29, 1961 / Blue Note ✦✦✦✦
Available perhaps in Japan, this early Green date includes Horace Parlan on piano, Wilber Ware on bass, and Al Harewood on drums. Mostly standards. —*Michael Erlewine*

Standards / Aug. 29, 1961 / Blue Note ✦✦✦✦
Standards contains the bulk of a trio session Grant Green recorded with bassist Wilbur Ware and drummer Al Harewood on August 29, 1961 (part of this material had been previously issued on the *Remembering* album). The trio ran through seven standards, including "You Stepped Out of a Dream," "Love Walked In," "I'll Remember April," "All the Things You Are," and "If I Had You," which is also present in an alternate take. All three musicians give remarkably sensitive performances—this context brings out the best in Green, who plays with grace, style and passion, breathing life into these familiar songs. —*Stephen Thomas Erlewine*

Born to Be Blue / Dec. 11, 1961 + Mar. 1, 1962 / Blue Note ✦✦✦✦
This is the one to get, a taste of what is in the (now out-of-print) Mosaic box set *The Complete Blue Note Recordings of Grant Green with Sonny Clark*. This is vintage Green with Sonny Clark on piano and Ike Quebec on tenor sax. The combination is mesmerizing. This is the stuff groove addicts dream of—a desert island classic pick. Green is the master of standards and the set includes "Someday My Prince Will Come," "Count Every Star," and "Back in Your Own Back Yard." Aside from being just the best jazz, it makes for great easy-listening music. Grandma will love it too. —*Michael Erlewine*

Gooden's Corner / Dec. 23, 1961 / Blue Note ✦✦✦✦
This is an album of real beauty and synergy between Green and pianist Sonny Clark, who along with Sam Jones on bass and Louis Hayes on drums rounds out the quartet. Green, an expert with standards, offers "Moon River," "On Green Dolphin Street," and "Count Every Star." This album was also released on *The Complete Blue Note Recordings of Grant Green and Sonny Clark*. —*Michael Erlewine*

★ **The Complete Blue Note with Sonny Clark** / Dec. 23, 1961-Sep. 7, 1962 / Mosaic ✦✦✦✦✦
Guitarist Grant Green and pianist Sonny Clark recorded together on five separate occasions during the 1961-62 period, but virtually none of the music was released domestically until decades later. These performances were clearly lost in the shuffle, for the solos are of a consistently high quality, and the programs were well-paced and swinging. Now, the long-lost music (much of which had been previously available only in Japan) is saved for posterity on this Mosaic limited-edition four-CD box set. Green and Clark blend together well; tenor saxophonist Ike Quebec joins their quartet for one session; and the final two numbers add Latin percussion. All of this music should be enjoyed by hard bop fans. Includes the Blue Note albums *Gooden's Corner*, *Nigeria*, *Oleo*, *Born to Be Blue* (w/ Ike Quebec), and unissued tracks. —*Scott Yanow*

☆ **The Complete Quartets with Sonny Clark** / Dec. 23, 1961-Sep. 7, 1962 / Blue Note ✦✦✦✦✦
Mosaic released a four-disc box set titled *The Complete Blue Note with Sonny Clark* in 1991, rounding up everything that the guitarist and pianist recorded together between 1961 and 1962. Blue Note's 1997 version of the set, *The Complete Quartets with Sonny Clark*, trims Mosaic's collection by two discs, offering only the quartet sessions (the Ike Quebec sessions, *Born*

to Be Blue and *Blue and Sentimental*, are available on individual discs). In some ways, this actually results in a more unified set, since it puts Green and Clark directly in the spotlight, with no saxophone to compete for solos, but it doesn't really matter if the music is presented as this double-disc set, the four-disc box or the individual albums—this is superb music, showcasing the guitarist and pianist at their very best. All of the sessions are straightahead bop but the music has a gentle, relaxed vibe that makes it warm, intimate and accessible. Grant and Clark's mastery is subtle—the music is so enjoyable, you may not notice the deftness of their improvisation and technique—but that invests the music with the grace, style and emotion that distinguishes *The Complete Quartets*. Small group hard-bop rarely comes any better than this. —*Stephen Thomas Erlewine*

Nigeria / Jan. 13, 1962 / Blue Note ✦✦✦✦
This is a great album with the classic synergy of Green and pianist Sonny Clark, who along with Sam Jones on bass and Art Blakey complete the quartet. This album was also released on *The Complete Blue Note Recordings of Grant Green and Sonny Clark*. Just classic Green. —*Michael Erlewine*

Oleo / Jan. 31, 1962 / Blue Note ✦✦✦✦
This is an another excellent album with Green and pianist Sonny Clark, who along with Sam Jones on bass and Louis Hayes on drums make the foursome. The entire album is fine with "My Favorite Things," an old favorite of Green. This album was also released on *The Complete Blue Note Recordings of Grant Green and Sonny Clark*. If you can find this album, or the Mosaic set anywhere, you will be very satisfied. The best. —*Michael Erlewine*

The Latin Bit / Apr. 26, 1962 / Blue Note ✦✦✦
A good title, these are Latin standards with Grant Green in Latin mode and performing standards like "Tico Tico," "Brazil," "Grenada," "Besame Mucho," and "Hey There." The group includes Johnny Acea (p), Wendell Marshall (b), Willie Bobo (d), and added percussion from Carlos "Potato" Valdez on conga and Garvin Masseaux on chekere. As an added bonus, Ike Quebec plays on two of the standards. One wonders whether these standards were often played by Green. The brightness of the Latin tunes replaces the more substantial soul-jazz feel Grant fans expect. Still, Green in his prime. —*Michael Erlewine*

Goin' West / Nov. 30, 1962 / Blue Note ✦✦✦
Another Blue Note album yet to be reissued, this one (like *Feelin' the Spirit*) includes Herbie Hancock on piano, Reggie Workman on bass, and Billy Higgins on drums. Includes tunes like (can you believe?) "On Top of Old Smokey," and "Tumbling Tumbleweeds." Only Green could carry this off, but he is "the man" when it comes to standards. —*Michael Erlewine*

Feelin' the Spirit / Dec. 21, 1962 / Blue Note ✦✦✦✦
An entire album of spirituals—all jazz instrumentals. Green, already a bluesy guitarist, lets himself out in the gospel format. The result is an album that remains true to both the soul-jazz and gospel genres. With Green on this date is Herbie Hancock on piano. Every Grant Green fan loves this unique gospel-toned album. It includes standards like "Just a Closer Walk with Thee," "Nobody Knows the Trouble I've Seen," and "Sometimes I Feel Like a Motherless Child." A Grant Green classic. —*Michael Erlewine*

Am I Blue? / May 16, 1963 / Blue Note ✦✦✦✦
A date for Blue Note with Joe Henderson (tenor sax), John Patton (Hammond organ), Johnny Coles (tpt), and Ben Dixon (d). —*Michael Erlewine*

★ **Idle Moments** / Nov. 4, 1963 / Blue Note ✦✦✦✦✦
Excellent mid-sized group album, with Green in good form. Bobby Hutcherson (vibes) in the group produces a somewhat different sound than the usual Green album, so make a note of that. Duke Pearson is there on piano along with Joe Henderson (ts), who is hot. All things considered, the groove is there and this is worth having. —*Michael Erlewine*

Solid / Jun. 12, 1964 / Blue Note ✦✦✦✦
Not released until 1979, this set contains more challenging material than many of guitarist Grant Green's other Blue Note sessions. In a state-of-the-art sextet with tenor saxophonist Joe Henderson, altoist James Spaulding, pianist McCoy Tyner, bassist Bob Cranshaw, and drummer Elvin Jones, Green performs tunes by Duke Pearson, George Russell ("Ezz-thetic"), Sonny Rollins, Henderson ("The Kicker"), and his own "Grant's Tune." Perhaps this music was considered too uncommercial initially or maybe it was simply

lost in the shuffle. In any case, this is one of Grant Green's finer recordings. — *Scott Yanow*

Talkin' About! / Sep. 11, 1964 / Blue Note ◆◆◆
A rare trio date for Grant Green with Larry Young (organ), and Elvin Jones (d). Although Green was the leader for this date, it is now available on the Mosaic label as part of *The Complete Blue Note Recordings of Larry Young*. One of the first albums by Larry Young. This is classic Green. — *Michael Erlewine*

Street of Dreams / Nov. 16, 1964 / Blue Note ◆◆◆
Vibist Bobby Hutcherson joins Green, Larry Young (organ), and Elvin Jones (d) for this fine release, which is now available on the Mosaic label as part of *The Complete Blue Note Recordings of Larry Young*. This is great soul-jazz Larry Young and Green is, as usual, just excellent. Contains "Somewhere in the Night" and "Street of Dreams." — *Michael Erlewine*

I Want to Hold Your Hand / Mar. 31, 1965 / Blue Note ◆◆◆◆
Tenor saxophonist Hank Mobley joins Green, Larry Young (organ), and Elvin Jones (d) for this very excellent album, which is now available on the Mosaic label as part of *The Complete Blue Note Recordings of Larry Young* (worth getting while it is still available!) Unlike some of Young's later work, this music is in the soul-jazz vein and under Green's lead. It has groove and great playing from Green and Young. — *Michael Erlewine*

☆ **Matador** / May 20, 1965 / Blue Note ◆◆◆◆◆
This is an exceptional Grant Green album for several reasons. For one, it (along with *Solid*) is one of very few Green outings that are straight-ahead jazz, rather than out-and-out soul-jazz. Second, this is one of Coltrane's finest bands with Green as the featured soloist rather than Coltrane — McCoy Tyner (p), Bob Cranshaw (b), and Elvin Jones (d). Coltrane had just finished recording his classic album *Crescent* and the band is hot. Green shows a lot of guts to lead this band, not to mention tackling the Coltrane hit "My Favorite Things" and pulls it off. Green's soul-jazz fans need not fear that this is too dry. This is a great album and classic Grant Green. — *Michael Erlewine*

His Majesty, King Funk / May 26, 1965 / Verve ◆◆◆
Don't be scared off by the title of this album; this is not Green's later commercial stuff. This is excellent Grant Green with Larry Young on organ, Harold Vick on sax, Ben Dixon on drums, and Candido Camero on conga — essentially a classic funk piece. And this is soul-jazz with a deep groove. This is the last of five albums Green recorded with Larry Young. Produced by Creed Taylor, this is the only album Green did for Verve and perhaps his last real jazz album before several years of inactivity, after which he became somewhat more commercial in his approach. Includes the standard "That Lucky Old Sun." — *Michael Erlewine*

His Majesty King Funk / Up With Donald Byrd / May 26, 1965 / Verve ◆◆◆
This single Verve CD reissues the complete contents of two unrelated LPs: Grant Green's *His Majesty King Funk* (great title) and *Up with Donald Byrd*. Unfortunately the music overall is not as rewarding as Green and Byrd's work of the period for Blue Note. Green is okay with a quintet that includes tenor-saxophonist Harold Vick and organist Larry Young but the material (mainly fairly simple funk riffs) is disappointing. Trumpeter Donald Byrd has a potentially strong group with both Jimmy Heath and Stanley Turrentine on tenors along with pianist Herbie Hancock and guitarist Kenny Burrell. However, the three — or four-voice "Donald Byrd Singers" and the arrangements by Claus Ogerman weigh down the date. Each album watered down its music to an extent in hopes of gaining commercial success but neither really caught on. The results are interesting but somewhat forgettable. — *Scott Yanow*

Iron City / 1967 / Muse ◆◆◆
Recorded for Muse Records in 1967, as Grant Green was on an extended recording hiatus — it was his only record between 1965's *His Majesty, King Funk*, his only album for Verve, and 1969's *Carryin' On*, his return to Blue Note — *Iron City* actually captures the guitarist in fine form, jamming on six blues and R&B numbers with his longtime cohorts, organist Big John Patton and drummer Ben Dixon. The trio had long ago perfected their interplay, and they just cook on *Iron City*, working a hot groove on each song. Even the slow blues "Motherless Child" has a distinct swing in its backbeat, but most of the album finds the trio tearing through uptempo grooves with a vengeance. Green's playing is a bit busier than normal and he solos far more often than Patton, who lays back through most of the album, providing infec-

tious vamps and lead lines. The two styles intermesh perfectly with Dixon's deft drumming, resulting in a fine, overlooked date that showcases some of Green's hottest, bluesiest playing. — *Stephen Thomas Erlewine*

Carryin' On / Oct. 3, 1969 / Blue Note ◆◆
Grant Green's recording career was just starting to slip at the time of this release although the talented guitarist always played as well as he could under the circumstances. He manages to uplift the dated R&Bish and pop material a bit but his backup band (which includes tenor-saxophonist Claude Bartee and either Clarence Palmer or Earl Neal Creque on electric piano) seems content to repeat the same grooves endlessly and play it safe, making this CD reissue of rather limited interest. — *Scott Yanow*

Green Is Beautiful / 1970 / Blue Note ◆◆◆
Of the five songs included on this CD reissue, the first three are one-chord vamps; none of these renditions were destined to be remembered as classics. "Ain't It Funky Now" makes the set worthwhile for it has tenor-saxophonist Claude Bartee doing a close imitation of Eddie Harris and trumpeter Blue Mitchell taking an exciting solo. But the unimaginative material in general does not really inspire guitarist Grant Green and keeps this CD from being too essential. — *Scott Yanow*

Alive! / Aug. 15, 1970 / Blue Note ◆◆
Grant Green was one of the most consistent and versatile guitarists of the '60s but once 1970 came around his recording career became quite erratic. This CD reissue brings back a rather weak effort with Green's sextet (which at the time included Claude Bartee on tenor, vibraphonist William Bivens, and either Ronnie Foster or Earl Neal Creque on organ) playing R&B cliches while laying forever on one chord. There are many more rewarding Grant Green sets than this one. — *Scott Yanow*

Visions / May 21, 1971 / Blue Note ◆◆◆
Grant Green's early-'70s recordings for Blue Note are continually attacked by jazz critics for being slick, overly commercial sessions that leaned closer to contemporary pop and R&B than hard bop or soul-jazz. There's no denying that Green, like many of his Blue Note contemporaries, did choose a commercial path in the early '70s, but there were some virtues to these records, and *Visions* in particular. Often, these albums were distinguished by hot, funky workouts in the vein of Sly Stone or James Brown, but that's not the case here. On *Visions*, the guitarist crafted a set of appealingly melodic, lightly funky pop-jazz, concentrating on pop hits like "Does Anybody Really Know What Time It Is," "Love On a Two Way Street," "We've Only Just Begun," and "Never Can Say Goodbye." Supported by minor-league players, Green nevertheless turns in an elegant and dignified performance — after stating the melody on each song, he contributes typically graceful, memorable solos. Simply put, he sounds fresh, and his playing here is the best it has been since 1965's *His Majesty, King Funk*. Ultimately, *Visions* is a bit laidback, and the electric piano-heavy arrangements are a little dated, but Grant Green never made a commercial pop-jazz album as appealing and satisfying as *Visions*. — *Stephen Thomas Erlewine*

Shades of Green / Nov. 23, 1971 / Blue Note ◆◆
A Blue Note date with a large group including about horns, reeds, woodwinds, vibes, et al. Consists of standards and even a medley. This is not the old Grant Green. — *Michael Erlewine*

Live at the Lighthouse / Apr. 21, 1972 / Blue Note ◆◆◆
There is lot of fat to the live jams heard on this out-of-print Blue Note double-LP. With the many dated verbal introductions and overly lengthy one-chord funk vamps, this session should have been edited down to one album. Guitarist Grant Green's group (which includes Claude Bartee on tenor and soprano, vibraphonist Gary Coleman, organist Shelton Lester, electric bassist Wilton Felder, drummer Greg Williams, and percussionist Bobbye Hall) is actually quite good and Bartee was an underrated saxophonist. But none of the six selections (which include "Betcha By Golly Wow" and Donald Byrd's "Fancy Free") are all that memorable even if there are lots of good feelings. The overall results in this stretched-out format are far from essential. — *Scott Yanow*

The Main Attraction / Mar. 1976 / Kudu ◆◆◆
Guitarist Grant Green's first album in four years and next-to-last recording as a leader looks attractive from the LP jacket but is actually a distinct disappointment. Joined by studio musicians (including flutist Hubert Laws and tenor-saxophonist Michael Brecker), Green plays three rather forgettable and

lengthy pieces. Arranger David Matthews tries his best but the material is too weak to be made interesting and the musicians sound as if they were counting off the minutes to lunch. This LP does give one a chance to hear Grant Green near the end of his career (his attractive tone and swinging style were still intact) but the out-of-print album is hardly worth looking for. — *Scott Yanow*

The Best of Grant Green, Vol. 1 / Blue Note ◆◆◆

While the "best-of" format often leaves quite a bit to be desired in a jazz setting, this set contains good Green material from his most productive period, the early and mid-'60s. There's a nice mix between uptempo and slower numbers, standards and his own compositions, as well as soul-jazz and straight mainstream and bop material. Although this isn't as far-reaching or comprehensive as Green's Mosaic set, this set will satisfy the needs of those unfamiliar with his work or listeners who just want a good cross-section of his cuts. — *Ron Wynn*

The Best of Grant Green, Vol. 2 / Blue Note ◆◆◆◆

Grant Green signed to Blue Note for a second time in 1969. Where his first stint with the label was nearly all hard bop, the recordings from his second stay were almost all funky soul-jazz. Predictably, these are sessions that jazz purists have dismissed throughout the years, even though—when judged strictly on the level of funky, groove-oriented dance music—the music is quite strong. During the '80s and '90s, dance and hip-hop fans rediscovered Green's records from the late '70s and sampled his playing and grooves on their own records. Blue Note assembled *The Best of Grant Green, Vol. 2* to capitalize on the popularity of this acid-jazz movement. All of the material on this disc is drawn from albums— *The Final Countdown, Live At the Lighthouse, Visions*—that never received much attention in jazz circles. Nevertheless, fans of this sound find *The Best of Grant Green, Vol. 2* to be a delight—there's a lot of wonderfully funky, dense grooves on here, and many of the songs have been out of print since their original issue. Hard bop fans will not reconsider their negative opinion of this music based on this compilation, but acid-jazz, groove and hip-hop fans will find this disc to be an excellent addition to their Grant Green collection. — *Stephen Thomas Erlewine*

Johnny Griffin

b. Apr. 24, 1928, Chicago, IL
Tenor Saxophone / Bop, Hard Bop, Groove
Once accurately billed as "the world's fastest saxophonist," Johnny Griffin (an influence tonewise on Rahsaan Roland Kirk) has been one of the top bop-oriented tenors since the mid-'50s. He gained early experience playing with the bands of Lionel Hampton (1945-47) and Joe Morris (1947-50) and also jammed regularly with Thelonious Monk and Bud Powell. After serving in the Army (1951-53), Griffin spent a few years in Chicago (recording his first full album for Argo) and then moved to New York in 1956. He held his own against fellow tenors John Coltrane and Hank Mobley in a classic Blue Note album, was with Art Blakey's Jazz Messengers in 1957, and proved to be perfect with the Thelonious Monk Quartet in 1958 where he really ripped through the complex chord changes with ease. During 1960-62 Griffin co-led a "tough tenor" group with Eddie "Lockjaw" Davis. He emigrated to Europe in 1963 and became a fixture on the Paris jazz scene both as a bandleader and a major soloist with the Kenny Clarke-Francy Boland Big Band. In 1973 Johnny Griffin moved to the Netherlands but has remained a constant world traveller, visiting the US often and recording for many labels including Blue Note, Riverside, Atlantic, Steeple Chase, Black Lion, Antilles, Verve, and some European companies. — *Scott Yanow*
Groove: Griffin plays a lot of bop and hard bop and that may not be exactly what groove lovers are seeking. However, he is so good that you want at least to find one of those dates when he battles with Eddie "Lockjaw" Davis or some other tough tenor to take the measure of him. He plays a hard horn. — *Michael Erlewine*

Introducing Johnny Griffin / Apr. 17, 1956 / Blue Note ◆◆◆◆

This CD reissue does not have tenor saxophonist Johnny Griffin's first recording as a leader (he made a few sides for OKeh in 1953 and a full album for Argo a few months earlier in 1956), but it gained Griffin a great deal of attention. Soon billed as "the world's fastest saxophonist," Griffin was also a superior ballad interpreter with a fairly distinctive tone of his own. With strong support given by pianist Wynton Kelly, bassist Curly Russell, and

drummer Max Roach, Griffin romps on three of his originals, barn-busting versions of "The Way You Look Tonight" and "Cherokee" (the latter two were released for the first time domestically on this CD), and a couple of ballads. Superior music. — *Scott Yanow*

☆ A Blowing Session / Apr. 6, 1957 / Blue Note ◆◆◆◆◆

More than just a mere "blowing session," these four jams (on a pair of standards and two Johnny Griffin compositions) match together three very different tenor stylists: Griffin, Hank Mobley, and John Coltrane. Although the solos and trade-offs are often quite combative, the result is a three-way deadheat, for each of these tenor greats has a different approach and a distinctive sound. Of all of the '50s jam sessions, this is one of the most successful and exciting. — *Scott Yanow*

★ The Congregation / Oct. 13, 1957 / Blue Note ◆◆◆◆◆

The great tenor-saxophonist Johnny Griffin is heard in top form on this near-classic quartet set. Assisted by pianist Sonny Clark, bassist Paul Chambers, and drummer Kenny Dennis, Griffin is exuberant on "The Congregation" (which is reminiscent of Horace Silver's "The Preacher"), thoughtful on the ballads and swinging throughout. It's recommended for bop collectors. — *Scott Yanow*

The Big Soul Band / May 24, 1960-Jun. 3, 1960 / Original Jazz Classics ◆◆◆

Tenor-saxophonist Johnny Griffin is showcased with a ten-piece group on this CD reissue of a Riverside LP which is augmented by a previously unreleased version of "Wade in the Water." The repertoire is a bit unusual with some spirituals (including "Nobody Knows the Trouble I've Seen" and "Deep River"), a tune apiece by Bobby Timmons ("So Tired") and Junior Mance, and three originals from Norman Simmons who arranged all of the selections. Trumpeter Clark Terry and trombonists Matthew Gee and Julian Priester have some short solos but the emphasis is on the leader who is in typically spirited and passionate form. — *Scott Yanow*

Griff and Lock / Nov. 4, 1960 + Nov. 10, 1960 / Original Jazz Classics ◆◆◆◆

Eddie "Lockjaw" Davis and Johnny Griffin co-led a combo during 1960-62, a perfect outlet for the two very competitive and distinctive tenors. This reissue set (which also features pianist Junior Mance, bassist Larry Gales, and drummer Ben Riley) is highlighted by heated versions of James Moody's "The Last Train from Overbrook," "Second Balcony Jump," "I'll Remember April," and "Good Bait." Easily recommended to straightahead jazz fans. — *Scott Yanow*

Toughest Tenors / Nov. 4, 1960-Feb. 5, 1962 / Milestone ◆◆◆

During the early '60s, Johnny Griffin and Eddie "Lockjaw" Davis matched forces and put together a consistently exciting quintet. The two tenors (both of whom had very distinctive sounds) brought out the best in each other in these frequently combative encounters. This two-LP set has 13 selections taken from five separate albums and gives one a well-rounded portrait of the legendary group. The music ranges from bop standards to a trio of Thelonious Monk tunes. — *Scott Yanow*

Live at Minton's / Jul. 6, 1961 / Prestige ◆◆◆◆

During the night of July 6, 1961, the two-tenor quintet co-led by Johnny Griffin and Eddie "Lockjaw" Davis recorded enough material to fill up four LPs; surprisingly, Fantasy has not yet reissued any of the sets in their Original Jazz Classics series. Two of the albums (*The Tenor Scene* and *The Midnight Show*) were last available as this two-LP set. Griffin and Davis, competitive tenors with different sounds, battle each other on ten selections with the assistance of pianist Junior Mance, bassist Larry Gales, and drummer Ben Riley. Highlights of the frequently hard-charging date include "Straight No Chaser," "Woodyn' You," "I'll Remember April," "In Walked Bud," and "Our Delight." Exciting music that deserves to be made more widely available. — *Scott Yanow*

Tough Tenor Favorites / Feb. 5, 1962 / Jazzland ◆◆◆◆

Johnny Griffin and Eddie "Lockjaw" Davis, the two "tough tenors" in question, always made for an exciting team. With pianist Horace Parlan, bassist Buddy Catlett, and drummer Ben Riley completing the quintet for this CD reissue of a Jazzland date from 1962, Griff and Lockjaw are in top form and quite competitive on a variety of standards. Highlights include "Blue Lou," "Ow," "I Wished on the Moon," and "From This Moment On." The main winner in these fiery tenor "battles" is the listener. — *Scott Yanow*

Soul Groove / May 14, 1963 + May 16, 1963 / Atlantic ✦✦✦
A soul session with John Patton (or Hank Jones) on the Hammond organ and Matthew Gee on trombone. — *Michael Erlewine*

Eddie Harris

b. Oct. 20, 1934, Chicago, IL, **d.** Nov. 5, 1996, Los Angeles, CA
Tenor Saxophone / Soul Jazz, Hard Bop, Groove
Eddie Harris had a diverse and erratic recording career, leading to many observers greatly underrating his jazz talents. Harris has had his own sound on tenor since at least 1960, his improvisations range from bop to free, he was a pioneer with utilizing the electric sax (and was much more creative on it than most who followed), he introduced the reed trumpet, is a fine pianist (one of his first professional jobs was playing piano with Gene Ammons), composed the standard "Freedom Jazz Dance" and, although his vocals are definitely an acquired taste, he is a skilled comedian.

After getting out of the military, Harris' very first recording resulted in a hit version of "Exodus." His high-note tenor playing (which managed to sound comfortable in the range of an alto or even soprano) was well-featured on a series of strong selling Vee-Jay releases (1961-63). After two outings for Columbia (1964), he switched to Atlantic for a decade. In 1966 Harris started utilizing an electric sax and he debuted the popular "Listen Here" (although the 1967 recording is better-known). At the 1969 Montreux Jazz Festival Harris and Les McCann made for a very appealing combination, recording such songs as "Compared to What" and "Cold Duck Time." Harris' later output for Atlantic was streaky, sometimes rock-oriented, and occasionally pure comedy. Later in life he recorded generally recorded strong jazz sets for such labels as Impulse, Enja, and Steeple Chase while remaining a unique musical personality. — *Scott Yanow*

★ **Exodus to Jazz** / Jan. 17, 1961 / Vee-Jay ✦✦✦✦✦
This reissue of tenor saxophonist Eddie Harris' debut as a leader brings back his hit recording of "Exodus" (here heard in both the single and the full-length versions) and a variety of appealing originals. Harris, whose impressive range often puts him in the alto (and even soprano) register, was distinctive from the start. Joined by a fine Chicago-based quintet that also features pianist Willie Pickens and guitarist Joe Diorio, Harris is in top form on this classic session. — *Scott Yanow*

The Artist's Choice: The Eddie Harris Anthology / Jan. 1961-Feb. 20, 1977 / Rhino ✦✦✦
This two-CD sampler from Rhino Records jumps all over the place. Most of tenor-saxophonist Eddie Harris' classics are here (including "Exodus," "Listen Here," and "Freedom Jazz Dance") but it is strange that the music was not programmed in strict chronological order since Harris (the master of the electronic sax) did evolve and go through different periods. Actually the recordings from the '60s tend to be far superior to Harris' later output and it is odd that none of his more successful comedy numbers from later years (or anything after 1977) were included. Although reasonable as an introduction to Eddie Harris' career, many aspects of this wide-ranging artist are missing and nearly all of this music is currently available on other CDs, making this twofer more of a frivolity than a necessity. — *Scott Yanow*

Bossa Nova / 1963 / Vee-Jay ✦✦✦✦
When the bossa nova wave came crashing through America, naturally the folks at VeeJay thought that their star saxophonist should give it a shot—and this LP came and went with the tide. But far from being a casual response to a fad, this is a great record, one where Harris came to his own comfortable accommodation with the Brazilian idiom without the aid of a single Luiz Bonfa or A.C. Jobim standard. Harris not only retains his own sound, he leans pleasingly into the bossa groove with a lightness of tone and swing that rivals pack leader Stan Getz, and he even stretches out into feverish Coltrane territory in his solo on the ten-minute "Cev Y Mar." Credit a young neighborly Argentinian, the endlessly versatile Lalo Schifrin, for the solid piano work, half of the tunes, and the gritty group arrangements, but it is Eddie who comes up with the most beguiling composition, "Lolita Marie." Also guitarist Jimmy Raney checks in on a few tracks with some relaxed bop licks. — *Richard S. Ginell*

The In Sound/Mean Greens / Aug. 9, 1965-Jun. 7, 1966 / Rhino ✦✦✦✦
This CD from Rhino's valuable Atlantic reissue program combines together two former LPs from the 1965-67 period. *The In Sound* is among tenor-

saxophonist Eddie Harris' most significant recordings, highlighted by the original version of his "Freedom Jazz Dance," and including a memorable rendition of "The Shadow of Your Smile," three standards and a blues. Harris is assisted by an all-star rhythm section (pianist Cedar Walton, bassist Ron Carter, and drummer Billy Higgins) and, on three selections, trumpeter Roy Codrington. The lesser-known *Mean Greens* set (comprised entirely of originals except for Harris' high-note treatment of "It Was a Very Good Year") utilizes the same personnel on the first four numbers and is just as exciting with the calypso "Yeah Yeah Yeah" being a highpoint. The final three performances are more unusual for Harris switches to electric piano and jams with a Latin rhythm section; included is the original (and somewhat obscure) recording of "Listen Here" which predates his hit version by over a year. Overall this CD is a well-rounded and highly recommended set. — *Scott Yanow*

The Best of Eddie Harris / Aug. 9, 1965-Apr. 19, 1969 / Atlantic ✦✦✦
Part of a massive Atlantic *Jazz Anthology* series in 1970, this LP-turned-CD was skimpy in its day, and now serves as the sketchiest of introductions to this bewilderingly eclectic saxophonist/inventor/pianist/bopper/balladeer/funkmeister, etc. etc. Even assuming the limited time frame, why were three of Harris' seven Atlantic albums up to that point (*Mean Greens, The Tender Storm, Silver Cycles*) not even represented, and where is that galvanic swinger "Sham Time"? That said, there is still an awful lot of great '60s jazz on this record anyway: the funky-funky hit version of "Listen Here," two of its soulful successors, "Live Right Now" and "Movin' on Out"; the enduring pretzel-like "Freedom Jazz Dance;" a nice cover of "The Shadow of Your Smile;" and the lush, perhaps even tongue-in-cheek "Theme in Search of a Movie." Buy this only if you cannot afford the far-more-comprehensive two-CD box, *Artist's Choice.* — *Richard S. Ginell*

☆ **Electrifying Eddie Harris** / Apr. 20, 1967 / Atlantic ✦✦✦✦✦
This is one of tenor-saxophonist Eddie Harris' most famous and significant LPs. He displays his mastery of the electronic varitone saxophone (virtually the only player before John Klemmer to get his own sound on the electric sax) during the memorable "Theme in Search of a Movie" and particularly on his hit version of "Listen Here." A couple of tunes add a pair of percussionists and "Sham Time" features a horn section in back of Harris; the basic quartet is comprised of the leader, pianist Jodie Christian, bassist Melvin Jackson, and drummer Richard Smith. A classic date. — *Scott Yanow*

The Electrifying Eddie Harris/Plug Me In / Apr. 20, 1967-Mar. 15, 1968 / Rhino ✦✦✦✦
This CD combines two fine Harris dates from 1967 and 1968. *The Electrifying Eddie Harris* had bluesy, soulful examples of Harris on baritone sax. "Listen Here" ranked second only to "Freedom Jazz Dance" among his most popular compositions, while he stretched out on "Spanish Bull." "Theme In Search Of A Movie," "Sham Time," and "Judie's Theme" were goodtime concessions to pop and jazz-soul audiences, yet still retained some fiber and spark. Once more, Harris found a good compromise between artistic and commercial concerns, although this date was more weighted toward funk and pop. — *Ron Wynn*

☆ **Swiss Movement** / Jun. 1969 / Atlantic ✦✦✦✦✦
With Les McCann. Contains the monster hit "Compared to What." A must-buy. — *Michael G. Nastos*

Come on Down! / 1970 / Atlantic ✦✦✦✦
The album title and the weird cover portrait of Eddie with an orange substituting for his head refer to the recording locale—Miami. The rationale might have been to give Miami the same down-home soul appeal that Muscle Shoals and Memphis were enjoying at the time. Certainly Harris got a romping soul/jazz/rock session out of the trip, a bit overloaded on the electric guitar side, but invigorating. Ira Sullivan joins the fracas now and then with some uninhibited trumpet, Donald "Duck" Dunn (from Booker T. & the MG's) is the anchor on bass and supersessionman Cornell Dupree dominates the guitars. The centerpiece is a long, frantic, rowdy, R&B remake of "Live Right Now" where Harris seems to be jooglin' around on electric sax as part of the rhythm section, and "Fooltish" has a loose swaggering appeal. "Really" finds him soulfully crooning through his electric horn for the first time, and "Why Don't You Quit" builds inexorably to a majestic Echoplex extravaganza. Worth hunting for in the LP bins. — *Richard S. Ginell*

Live at Newport / 1970 / Atlantic ✦✦✦

Eddie Harris hit the 1970 Newport Jazz Festival head on with his satchel of electronic sax gear, funky soul/jazz track record, and a quartet with Jodie Christian now anchored on electric piano. Naturally there would be some funk on display ("Carry on Brother") and guest vocalist Eugene McDaniels, composer of "Compared to What," comes up with a lame, hectoring sequel, "Silent Majority." Yet a good deal of this truncated edition of Harris' Newport set is pitched at a more abstract level. "Don't You Know the Future's in Space," with its tumbling drums and outbreaks of near freeform reed trumpet (a Harris invention), is already in progress when we fade into the track, and "South Side" is a rough-and-tumble jazz sprint, with Harris delivering a complex cerebral solo. These advanced tracks didn't win him any points with the critics of the time but hindsight reveals that harmonically as well as electronically, Harris was ahead of most of the pack. As a bonus, the LP includes a short post-set speech in which Harris prophesizes that his reed trumpet will be a godsend for brass players (who, alas, completely ignored it). —*Richard S. Ginell*

Gene Harris

b. Sep. 1, 1933, Benton Harbor, MI

Piano / Soul Jazz, Hard Bop, Groove

One of the most accessible of all jazz pianists, Gene Harris' soulful style (influenced by Oscar Peterson and containing the bluesiness of a Junior Mance) is immediately likable and predictably excellent. After playing in an Army band (1951-54) he formed a trio with bassist Andy Simpkins and drummer Bill Dowdy which was by 1956 known as the Three Sounds. The group was quite popular and recorded regularly during 1956-70 for Blue Note and Verve. Although the personnel changed and the music became more R&B-oriented in the early '70s, Harris retained the Three Sounds name for his later Blue Note sets. He retired to Boise, ID, in 1977 and was largely forgotten when Ray Brown persuaded him to return to the spotlight in the early '80s. Harris worked for a time with the Ray Brown Trio and has led his own quartets ever since, recording regularly for Concord and heading the Phillip Morris Superband on a few tours. —*Scott Yanow*

Groove: Gene Harris (The Three Sounds), along with Kenny Burrell, helped to write the book on bluesy jazz. The Stanley Turrentine album *Blue Hour* has Harris and the Three Sounds on it. Worth looking for. Gene Harris is always very listenable either from a jazz perspective or as integral background music. —*Michael Erlewine*

Live at the It Club / Mar. 6, 1970 / Blue Note ✦✦✦

A later version of pianist Gene Harris' Three Sounds is featured on this live session which was released for the first time on a 1996 CD. Harris, bassist Henry Franklin, and drummer Carl Burnette play well enough but the material is uninspired and no real surprises occur. The Three Sounds were a bit funkier during this period than it had been earlier but the results are more routine than soulful. —*Scott Yanow*

Black and Blue / Jun. 29, 1991 / Concord Jazz ✦✦✦✦

Although there are few actual blues on this CD, pianist Gene Harris gives all of the songs (whether complex standards, ballads, or near-blues) a bluesy feel, adding soul and a church feeling to each of the melodies. With the assistance of guitarist Ron Eschete, bassist Luther Hughes, and drummer Harold Jones, Harris is in typically fine form. —*Scott Yanow*

Red Holloway

b. May 31, 1927, Helena, AR

Alto Saxophone, Tenor Saxophone / Bop, Swing, Soul-Jazz, Groove

An exuberant player with attractive tones on both tenor and alto, Red Holloway is also a humorous blues singer. Whether it be bop, blues or R&B, Holloway can hold his own with anyone. Holloway played in Chicago with Gene Wright's big band (1943-46), served in the Army and then played with Roosevelt Sykes (1948) and Nat Towles (1949-50) before leading his own quartet (1952-61) during an era when he also recorded with many blues and R&B acts. Holloway came to fame in 1963 while touring with Jack McDuff, making his first dates as a leader for Prestige (1963-65). Although he has cut many records in R&B settings, Red Holloway is a strong bop soloist at heart as he proved in the '70s when he battled Sonny Stitt to a tie on their recorded collaboration. He has mostly worked as a leader since then but has also guested with Juggernaut and the Cheathams and played with Clark Terry on an occasional basis. —*Scott Yanow*

Burner / Oct. 10, 1963 / Prestige ✦✦✦

Early date with Holloway and John Patton (or George Butcher) on Hammond organ. —*Michael Erlewine*

Cookin' Together / Feb. 2, 1964 / Original Jazz Classics ✦✦✦✦

For this set, tenor saxophonist Red Holloway, who was a regular member of organist Jack McDuff's group, used McDuff's sidemen (who included guitarist George Benson) and the organist himself. This Prestige date has thus far only been reissued by the OJC series on LP. The material is comprised of Burt Bacharach's "Wives and Lovers," "This Can't Be Love," and five Holloway originals, which have more diversity than one might expect. An interesting aspect to the soulful and swinging set is that McDuff made his debut on piano for two songs. —*Scott Yanow*

Brother Red / Feb. 6, 1964-Feb. 7, 1964 / Prestige ✦✦✦✦

The 11 selections included on this CD reissue include seven songs from a session headed by tenor-saxophonist Red Holloway that used the members of the Jack McDuff Quintet (with the organist, guitarist George Benson, bassist Wilfred Middlebrooks, and drummer Joe Dukes), three pieces from a McDuff date in which the lead voices are backed by an orchestra arranged by Benny Golson, and a selection from a sampler. The material varies a bit ("Wives and Lovers" and Holloway's soul ballad "No Tears" are forgettable) but the blues and the uptempo pieces (highlighted by "This Can't Be Love") are quite enjoyable and the underrated saxophonist is in excellent form. —*Scott Yanow*

Red Soul / Dec. 1965 / Prestige ✦✦✦

Good to get, if you can find it. Holloway with Lonnie Smith on organ and George Benson on guitar. Tunes like "Big Fat Lady" and "Good and Groovy." —*Michael Erlewine*

The Late Show, Vol. 2: Live at Maria's Memory Lane Supper Club / May 1986 / Fantasy ✦✦✦

● **Locksmith Blues** / Jun. ??, 1989 / Concord Jazz ✦✦✦✦

This is a fun set, which is not surprising when one considers that two of jazz's most good-humored players (saxophonist Red Holloway and fluegelhornist Clark Terry) are the co-leaders. The sextet (which also includes pianist Gerald Wiggins, guitarist Phil Upchurch, bassist Richard Reid, and drummer Paul Humphrey) plays a colorful set of jazz standards, including "Red Top," "Come Sunday," and "Cotton Tail," and three basic Holloway originals, one of which ("Locksmith Blues") finds Holloway and C.T. clearly enjoying themselves while sharing the vocals. Everyone is heard in top form, making this straightahead CD an excellent example of the co-leaders' talents. —*Scott Yanow*

Legends of Acid Jazz / Prestige ✦✦✦✦

Red Holloway recorded four albums for Prestige during 1963-65 but did not have another opportunity to lead his own record date until 1982. This 1998 CD reissues his first (The Burner) and fourth (Red Soul) sets for Prestige. The earlier session is the most interesting of the two for, in addition to Holloway (who is heard throughout on tenor), there are fine solos from the bluesy guitarist Eric Gale and organist John Patton; two of the numbers ("Crib Theme" and "The Burner") are extended (over ten-minutes) workouts. The later album matches Holloway with guitarist George Benson (his associate at the time with Jack McDuff's combo) and either organist Dr. Lonnie Smith or pianist Norman Simmons. Although Red Holloway would continue to grow as a highly expressive blues-based soloist through the years, these performances (soul-jazz that occasionally becomes hard bop) show that he was already a fairly distinctive and powerful soloist as early as 1963. —*Scott Yanow*

Richard "Groove" Holmes (Richard Arnold Holmes)

b. May 2, 1931, Camden, NJ, **d.** Jun. 29, 1991, St. Louis, MO

Organ / Hard Bop, Soul-Jazz, Groove

Revered in soul-jazz circles, Richard "Groove" Holmes was an unapologetically swinging Jimmy Smith admirer who could effortlessly move from the grittiest of blues to the most sentimental of ballads. Holmes, a very accessible, straight-forward and warm player who was especially popular in the Black community, had been well respected on the Philadelphia/Southern New Jersey circuit by the time he signed with Pacific Jazz in the early '60s and started receiving national attention by recording with such greats as Ben

Webster and Gene Ammons. Holmes, best known for his hit 1965 version of "Misty," engaged in some inspired organ battles with Jimmy McGriff in the early '70s before turning to electric keyboards and fusion-ish material a few years later. The organ was Holmes' priority in the mid-to-late '80s, when he recorded for Muse. Holmes was still delivering high-quality soul-jazz for that label (often featuring tenor titan Houston Person) when a heart attack claimed his life at the age of 60 in 1991. — *Alex Henderson*

Groove: There are not a lot of bad Richard Groove Holmes recordings and his vinyl stuff turns up here and there. Worth snapping up. Many soul-jazz listeners feel that Holmes is the definitive organist when it comes to laying down a strong groove. The recently reissued Holmes album *After Hours* on Pacific Jazz might be a good place to start. — *Michael Erlewine*

Groove / Mar. 1961 / Pacific Jazz ✦✦✦✦
When the participants on this CD reissue gathered together in March 1961, it was with the objective of recording a Les McCann vocal album. However, the band had such a good time during their warmup that McCann and the others agreed that it would be a crime to waste the opportunity. Organist Richard "Groove" Holmes, whom McCann had recently discovered, was made the leader; a few jump tunes and originals were agreed upon, and the result is a loose, enjoyable jam session. In addition to Holmes' appealing organ and McCann's typically funky piano, a major bonus is the brilliant playing of tenor saxophonist Ben Webster, whose tone was at its most gorgeous during this period. The five songs on the original LP are joined by a number that was last on a sampler, a McCann vocal track ("Next Spring"), and a previously unreleased version of "Just Friends." The spontaneous and soulfully swinging music, which also features trombonist Tricky Lofton, guitarist George Freeman, and drummer Ron Jefferson, is easily recommended. — *Scott Yanow*

Groovin' with Jug / Aug. 15, 1961 / Pacific Jazz ✦✦✦✦
Recorded live at The Black Orchid and at The Pacific Jazz Studio earlier that afternoon. Ammons at his peak of popularity, Holmes just about to become well-known — the only date they ever played together. Both players are on. Holmes, also a bassist and famous for his organ bass lines, can be heard to good advantage on "Morris the Minor." — *Michael Erlewine*

After Hours / 1961 / Pacific Jazz ✦✦✦✦
The original *After Hours* album had Joe Pass on guitar, and Lawrence Marable on drums. This combines most of another album (*Tell It Like It Is*) with Gene Edwards on guitar. This is early Groove Holmes, 13 tracks in all. This is fine soul-jazz and it is clear why many feel that Holmes is the man of the groove, when it comes to the Hammond B-3. — *Michael Erlewine*

Somethin' Special / Apr. 1962 / Pacific Jazz ✦✦✦
Somethin' Special is a laidback, funky classic which features Richard "Groove" Holmes trading licks with pianist Les McCann, saxophonist Clifford Scott and guitarist Joe Pass, who makes one of his first recorded appearances on this album. It's a fine, infectious album, highlighted by Holmes and McCann's stylish solo. Blue Note's 1997 CD reissue features two bonus cuts, including one that features saxophonist Ben Webster. — *Leo Stanley*

Soul Message / Aug. 3, 1965 / Original Jazz Classics ✦✦✦✦
Organist Richard "Groove" Holmes hit upon a successful formula on this Prestige session (reissued on CD in the OJC series), mixing together boogaloo rhythms with emotional solos. His doubletime version of "Misty" became a big hit, and the other selections, including Horace Silver's "Song for My Father" and a pair of soulful originals, are in a similar vein. The lone ballad of the set ("The Things We Did Last Summer") is a fine change of pace. With the assistance of guitarist Gene Edwards and drummer Jimmie Smith, Groove Holmes shows that it is possible to create music that is both worthwhile and commercially successful. — *Scott Yanow*

Misty / Aug. 3, 1965-Aug. 12, 1966 / Original Jazz Classics ✦✦✦✦
Organist Richard "Groove" Holmes in the mid-'60s had a hit with his medium-tempo rendition of "Misty." This CD reissue has the original short version (which was cut as a 45) plus other medium-tempo ballads performed in similar fashion. Holmes and his trio (featuring guitarist Gene Edwards and drummer George Randall) play enjoyable if not overly substantial versions of such songs as "The More I See You," "The Shadow of Your Smile," "What Now My Love," and "Strangers in the Night," trying unsuccessfully for an-

other pop hit; the organist's sound is more appealing than some of the tunes. — *Scott Yanow*

★ **Blue Groove** / Mar. 15, 1966-May 29, 1967 / Prestige ✦✦✦✦✦
This CD, which reissues two former LPs by Richard "Groove" Holmes (*Get Up & Get It* and *Soul Mist*), showcases the organist in a quintet featuring the tenor of Teddy Edwards and guitarist Pat Martino, with his trio, and (on two standards) with trumpeter Blue Mitchell and tenor-saxophonist Harold Vick. Overall, this 73-minute set has many fine solos, spirited ensembles, and two well-rounded programs. — *Scott Yanow*

The Groover! / Feb. 14, 1968 / Prestige ✦✦✦
Holmes acquits himself well, if with few surprises, on this trio session with Billy Jackson on drums and either George Freeman or Earl Maddox on guitar. The organist shows his hundred-miles-per-hour capabilities on the frantic opener "Speak Low," but hits a more sensitive groove for "Blue Moon," and gets close to an R&B mood on the longest cut, the eight-minute "The Walrus." This has been reissued with another 1968 session, *That Healin' Feelin',* on the single-disc Prestige CD *Legends of Acid Jazz.* — *Richie Unterberger*

Legends of Acid Jazz / Feb. 14, 1968-Aug. 26, 1968 / Prestige ✦✦✦✦
Other than the fact that it features Richard "Groove" Holmes' groovin' organ, the music on this 1997 CD reissue (which contains all of the selections from the LPs *The Groover* and *That Healin' Feelin*) has little to do with acid-jazz, but certainly qualifies as superior soul-jazz. The last in a long string of Prestige recordings that Holmes had initiated in 1965 is a consistently hard-swinging set. The earlier date matches the organist with either George Freeman or Earl Maddox on guitar and drummer Billy Jackson, while the later date has notable playing by Rusty Bryant (on tenor and alto), the highly expressive guitar of Billy Butler, and drummer Herbie Lovelle. More bop-oriented than normal, the reissue includes such numbers as "Speak Low," "Blue Moon," "Just Friends," "On a Clear Day," and the Johnny Hodges/Al Sears hit "Castle Rock." Recommended. — *Scott Yanow*

☆ **That Healin' Feelin'** / Aug. 26, 1968 / Prestige ✦✦✦✦✦
Holmes at the helm of a strong quartet, with especially notable contributions from Rusty Bryant (himself a soul-jazz artist of note) on sax and Billy Butler on guitar. The title track and "Irene Court" have especially nimble touches, and "Laura" slows the tempo down for some sensuous soloing by Bryant; the honky-tonk treatment of "See See Rider" gets closest to straight R&B territory. This has been reissued with another 1968 session, *The Groover!,* on the single-disc Prestige CD *Legends of Acid Jazz.* — *Richie Unterberger*

Double Exposure / 1973 / LRC ✦✦
This album contains two albums, one by Groove Holmes and the other by Jimmy McGriff. They do not play together here. Holmes is with Kwasi Jay Ourba on bongo/congas, Garald Hubbard on guitar, Jerry Jemmott on bass, Larry Willis on piano and drums. Six cuts are by McGriff and five are by Groove Holmes. The tunes "Catherine" and "Rainy Day" are very nice. — *Michael Erlewine*

Comin' on Home / 1974 / Blue Note ✦✦✦
Funky and nice. — *Ron Wynn*

Shippin' Out / Jun. 1977 / Muse ✦✦✦✦
After cutting a few albums for Groove Merchant in 1972-73, organist Groove Holmes was largely away from records (other than an odd date for Flying Dutchman) until this set, his Muse debut. Back in a comfortable setting, heading a soul-jazz quintet that also includes tenor saxophonist Dave Schnitter (best known for his association with Art Blakey's Jazz Messengers), guitarist Steve Giordano, drummer Idris Muhammad, and Buddy Caldwell on conga, Holmes explores a wider range of songs than usual. In addition to his basic blues "Shippin' Out," the organist swings "Where or When," a faster-than-usual version of "Stella By Starlight," Chick Corea's "Windows," and even a credible interpretation of "Feelings." This fine Muse LP, which would be followed by several other rewarding efforts, has yet to be reissued on CD. — *Scott Yanow*

Blues All Day Long / Feb. 24, 1988 / Muse ✦✦✦✦
Blues All Day Long is an example of an artist excelling by sticking with what he does best. Richard "Groove" Holmes was a master of the grittiest of blues and the most romantic of ballads — two of the things that make the album the soul-jazz triumph it is. Whether savoring the richness of the blues on "Groove's Groove" (not to be confused with the gem he recorded on 1965's

Soul Message) and "Slo Blooze," displaying his mastery of ballads on "These Foolish Things," or getting unapologetically funky on Benny Golson's "Killer Joe," the spirited Jimmy Smith disciple makes *Blues* a most welcome addition to his catalogue. Holmes has highly enthusiastic support in big-toned tenor titan Houston Person, trumpeter Cecil Bridgewater, guitarist Jimmy Ponder, drummer Cecil Brooks III, and percussionist Ralph Dorsey, all of whom seem quite inspired by the South Jersey native's down-home soulfulness. — *Alex Henderson*

Hot Tat / Sep. 5, 1989 / Muse ✦✦✦✦
Richard "Groove" Holmes had less than two years to live when he recorded *Hot Tat*, but the Hammond B-3 great gives little or no indication that his health was in decline on this enjoyable, though not essential, soul-jazz date. Much of the time, Holmes is in a relaxed mood and generally favors what is essentially mood music — but mood music with integrity. Most of the players heard on 1988's *Blues All Day Long* are employed on this album, including tenor saxophonist Houston Person, trumpeter Cecil Bridgewater, guitarist Jimmy Ponder, and percussionist Ralph Dorsey. But this time, Holmes works with bassist Wilbur Bascomb instead of handling all of the bass work himself, and employs Greg Bandy in place of Cecil Brooks III. *Hot Tat* will be of interest primarily to "Groove" Holmes' diehard fans; for more casual listeners, *Blues All Day Long* would be a better introduction to his Muse output. — *Alex Henderson*

Groove's Groove / Feb. 28, 1991 / 32 Jazz ✦✦✦
There's no rhyme or reason to *Groove's Groove*. The ten songs on the album were recorded at various dates during 1977, 1980 and 1988, all with different lineups. There is one thing holding them together — it's all hot soul-jazz, with exceptionally funky playing from Groove Holmes. Spinning out busy, overloaded lines and chords from his organ, Holmes gets deep into the groove, turning everything into a speedy, bluesy soul-jazz workout — even the standard "Stella By Starlight" is taken at a breakneck pace. His bandmates, for the most part, follow his lead, turning in funky performances that keep the music in the groove. The playing may be a little too busy for some tastes — Holmes and guitarist Gerald Smith trading skittering, frenzied solos on "Broadway" could make heads spin — but the resulting record burns with energy, and that alone is enough to recommend it. — *Stephen Thomas Erlewine*

Joe Houston

Tenor Sax / Groove, Soul-Jazz, Fusion
Joe Houston is a honking R&B saxman of wallpaper-peeling potency who recorded for virtually every major independent R&B label in Los Angeles during the '50s. When the jump blues tradition faded, he segued right into rock 'n' roll, even cutting budget "twist" and "surf" albums for Crown that didn't sound very different from what he was doing a decade before.

Houston played around Houston (Texas, that is) with the bands of Amos Milburn and Joe Turner during the late '40s. It was Turner who got the young saxist his first deal with Freedom Records in 1949. Houston found his way to the West Coast in 1952 and commenced recording for labels big and small: Modern, RPM, Lucky, Imperial, Dootone, Recorded in Hollywood, Cash, and Money (as well as the considerably better-financed Mercury, where he scored his only national R&B hit, "Worry, Worry, Worry," in 1952).

Houston's formula was simple and savagely direct — he'd honk and wail as hard as he could, from any conceivable position: on his knees, lying on his back, walking the bar, etc. His output for the Bihari brothers' Crown label (where he was billed "Wild Man of the Tenor Sax") is positively exhilarating: "All Nite Long," "Blow Joe Blow," and "Joe's Gone" are herculean examples of single-minded sax blasting.

Houston remains active musically, emphasizing his blues vocal talent more than he used to. — *Bill Dahl*

● **Cornbread and Cabbage Greens** / 1952 / Specialty ✦✦✦✦
Los Angeles was a mecca for honking, wailing R&B tenor saxmen during the '50s, and Joe Houston was one of the wildest in town. Twenty-six blasting workouts from the early-to-mid-'50s mark this CD as the best digital indication of Houston's sax-sational wailing now available (pretty much the only vintage one on the shelves, in fact). "All Night Long," "Celebrity Club Drag," —and "Rockin' and Boppin'" are among the highlights, taken from the archives of John Dolphin's Recorded in Hollywood and Cash labels. — *Bill Dahl*

Rockin' at the Drive in / 1984 / Ace ✦✦✦✦
Fourteen characteristic sax-driven R&B tunes, most instrumental, from the '50s. There's no duplication with the Specialty *Cornbread and Cabbage Greens* CD, except for the well-known "All Night Long," so it's worth finding if you want more than one Houston collection. — *Richie Unterberger*

The Blues & Nothin' Else / Shattered ✦✦✦✦
Of all the honkers who worked the table tops out on the West Coast, one of the very best was "Big" Joe Houston. Able to jump from big band to small combo blues and R&B with consummate ease, Houston was one of the first to test the waters of the newly emerging style that would become known as rock 'n' roll. Cutting one brilliant single after another for a variety of labels — and seeing his early work among the first to be anthologized on a myriad of budget label albums — Houston was the California version of the tenor men who honked and walked the bars in the Big Apple, often outdoing his New York contemporaries with sides of fervent blasting that could not be denied. Fortunately for us, that fervent blasting is alive and well and beating right alongside Houston's big heart on this, his first new album in a good number of years. The most notable fact is that Joe is singing on everything, relegating his tenor work to no more than a couple of choruses on each tune, framing it in proper perspective as another soloist in the very rockin' band that backs him here. The really good news is that Houston's voice is every bit as rough hewn as his sax playing, making you wonder why it took this long to get it properly documented on record. The final track lets you know that the man still has it and really isn't rationing *anything*; the set closer, "Full Of Misery," is eight minutes and 25 seconds of Joe making a rarely heard appearance on alto sax, playing the blues all by his lonesome, and making it sound oh so sweet. — *Cub Koda*

Willis "Gator" Jackson

b. Apr. 25, 1932, Miami, FL, **d.** Oct. 25, 1987, New York, NY
Tenor Saxophone / Early R&B Jazz, Hard Bop, Soul-Jazz, Groove
An exciting tenor saxophonist whose honking and squeals (although influenced by Illinois Jacquet) were quite distinctive, Willis Jackson was also a strong improviser who sounded perfectly at home with organ groups. He played locally in Florida early on until joining Cootie Williams (on and off during 1948-55). His two-sided honking feature "Gator Tail" with "Cootie" (which earned him a lifelong nickname) was a hit in 1948, and he started recording as a leader in 1950. Jackson was married to singer Ruth Brown for eight years and often appeared on her recordings during this era. His extensive series of Prestige recordings (1959-64) made him a big attraction on the organ circuit. Although generally overlooked by critics, Willis Jackson continued working steadily in the '70s and '80s. In 1977 he recorded one of the finest albums of his career for Muse, *Bar Wars*. — *Scott Yanow*
Groove: Willis Jackson recorded a lot of soul jazz albums, many with Hammond B-3 masters like Charles Earland or Jack McDuff. It is unfortunate that not much of this material has been released on CD, so you may have to work over the vinyl bins. Whatever tthe case, you don't want to miss Willis "Gator" Jackson. — *Michael Erlewine*

● **Call of the Gators** / Dec. 21, 1949-May 2, 1949 / Delmark ✦✦✦✦

Please Mr. Jackson / May 25, 1959 / Original Jazz Classics ✦✦✦✦
Willis "Gator" Jackson originally made a strong impression as a honking R&B player, first with the Cootie Williams Orchestra, then with his own popular bands. In 1959, starting with this Prestige set (which has been reissued on CD), Jackson made his mark on soul-jazz. Teamed with the up-and-coming organist Jack McDuff, guitarist Bill Jennings, bassist Tommy Potter, and drummer Alvin Johnson, Gator is heard modifying his style a little (gone are most of the screams) in favor of swinging. He performs four group originals, "Come Back to Sorrento," and "Memories of You" with soulful feeling. — *Scott Yanow*

Cool Gator / May 25, 1959-Aug. 16, 1960 / Original Jazz Classics ✦✦✦✦
This late 1980s reissue (which has not yet come out on CD) features Willis "Gator" Jackson in one of his earlier jazz sets. Having made his initial reputation as a honking and screaming R&B star, Jackson by 1959 had formed a soul-jazz group that included guitarist Bill Jennings and the young organist Jack McDuff. On this program, the tenor plays a typical set from the era: three standards, the jump tune "A Smooth One," and a couple of his basic originals. Enjoyable and accessible music that swings and contains its share of soul. — *Scott Yanow*

★ **Together Again** / May 25, 1959-Aug. 16, 1960 / Prestige ✦✦✦✦✦
Jackson with Jack McDuff on the Hammond B-3 and Bill Jennings on guitar.
— *Michael Erlewine*

Together Again, Again / May 25, 1959-Dec. 31, 1961 / Prestige ✦✦✦
Jackson with Jack McDuff on the Hammond B-3 and Bill Jennings on guitar.
Tunes like "Snake Crawl" and "Backtrack" should give you a clue as to the
music on this album. — *Michael Erlewine*

Gentle Gator / Jan. 10, 1961-Oct. 30, 1962 / Prestige ✦✦
Tenor-saxophonist Willis Jackson is best-known as a passionate and screaming tenorman who puts a lot of emotion in his playing. This CD reissue is a
change of pace for it consists of ballads taken from four of "Gator's" Prestige
and Moodsville albums of 1961-62. Jackson plays tastefully and sticks close
to the melodies, sounding in good form on such songs as "Estrellita," "Girl
of My Dreams," "Home," and "They Didn't Believe Me." However due to the
sampler nature of the collection, the sameness of mood and the overly restrained solos, this CD is of lesser interest. — *Scott Yanow*

Thunderbird / Mar. 31, 1962 / Prestige ✦✦✦✦
Great Jackson, robust Freddy Roach organ. — *Ron Wynn*

Loose / Mar. 26, 1963 / Prestige ✦✦✦
Willis with Carl Wilson on Hammond organ. — *Michael Erlewine*

More Gravy / Oct. 24, 1963 / Prestige ✦✦✦
Still more. Jackson with Carl Wilson on Hammond organ. — *Michael
Erlewine*

With Pat Martino / Mar. 21, 1964 / Prestige ✦✦✦✦
Although guitarist Pat Martino (19 at the time) gets second billing on this
CD reissue, tenor-saxophonist Willis Jackson is the main star throughout.
Recorded live at the Allegro in New York on March 21, 1964, this CD releases
the complete contents of two Jackson LPs (*Action* and *Live Action*). "Gator
Tail" puts on his usual exuberant show with screams and honks being a
logical part of his colorful style. The music, fairly basic material with a few
standards and blues tossed in, gives listeners a good example of Jackson's
music of the '60s; the quintet also includes trumpeter Frank Robinson, organist Carl Wilson, and drummer Joe Hadrick. An enjoyable crowd-pleasing set.
— *Scott Yanow*

Star Bag / Mar. 22, 1968 / Prestige ✦✦✦
Willis Jackson with Trudy Pitts on the Hammond B-3. — *Michael Erlewine*

Gatorade / Aug. 1971 / Prestige ✦✦✦
The music on this obscure LP was not released until 1982 and quickly disappeared. Tenor saxophonist Willis Jackson plays funky jazz that is very much
of the period with organist Carl Wilson, guitarist Boogaloo Joe Jones, drummer Jerry Potter, and Buddy Caldwell on conga. Jackson performs the current
pop tunes "Hey Jude" and "The Long and Winding Road," plus a pair of blues
(including his "Pow"), and a couple of originals. Fun but not overly substantial music. — *Scott Yanow*

Headed and Gutted / May 16, 1974 / Muse ✦✦✦✦
Willis "Gator" Jackson's series of albums for Muse during the '70s helped
keep alive the soulful, tough tenor tradition of Illinois Jacquet, Gene Am-
mons and (later on) Houston Person. On this particular set, the participation
of guitarist Pat Martino made the date more notable than it might have been.
With Mickey Tucker on keyboards, electric bassist Bob Cranshaw, drummer
Freddie Waits, and Richard Landrum and Sonny Morgan on percussion, Jackson still sounds very much in his prime, particularly on the exciting "Gator
Whale." The other selections tend to emphasize ballads ("My One and Only
Love" is fairly memorable) and funky jazz, although "The Way We Were" did
not really need to be recorded again. — *Scott Yanow*

In the Alley / 1976 / Muse ✦✦✦
"In the Alley" and "Niamani" are the highlights of this typical but often exciting outing for veteran tenor Willis Jackson. The music includes blues, romps,
a ballad, and funky vamps. Jackson is assisted by pianist Sonny Phillips,
organist Carl Wilson, guitarist Jimmy Ponder, bassist Jimmy Lewis, drummer
Yusef Ali, and percussionist Buddy Caldwell. This worthy set has not yet been
reissued on CD. — *Scott Yanow*

Bar Wars / Dec. 21, 1977 / Muse ✦✦✦✦
Willis Jackson, a veteran of the jazz-oriented R&B music of the late '40s, was
a powerful tenor in the tradition of Gene Ammons. This is a particularly
exciting release with Charles Earland pumping away at the organ, guitarist

Pat Martino offering a contrasting solo voice, and Jackson in top form, wailing away on the uptempo pieces. The CD reissue of the original LP adds
two alternate takes to the program. The chord changes might be fairly basic
but Willis Jackson plays with such enthusiasm and exuberance that it almost
sounds as if he had discovered the joy of playing music. — *Scott Yanow*

Nothing Butt / Jun. 1980 / Muse ✦✦✦
Tenor saxophonist Willis Jackson got into a routine on his Muse albums, but
never lost his enthusiasm and creativity within the genre. This album features Jackson on a current hit ("Just the Way You Are"), a couple of ballads,
and three romps ("Nothing Butt," "Hittin' and Missin'," and "Move"). Guitarist
Pat Martino is heard in excellent form just before a serious illness; organist
Charles Earland is up to his usual groovin' form, and drummer Grady Tate
and percussionist Buddy Caldwell keep the music moving. An excellent
effort full of enjoyable and fairly accessible music. — *Scott Yanow*

Legends of Acid Jazz / Prestige ✦✦✦✦
Willis "Gator" Jackson's initial reputation was made as a honking and
screaming tenor-saxophonist with Cootie Williams' late 1940s orchestra and
on his own R&B-ish recordings. By 1959, Jackson had de-emphasized some
of his more extroverted sounds (although they occasionally popped up) and
had reemerged as a solid swinger influenced by Gene Ammons and (on ballads) Ben Webster. This CD reissue from 1998 brings back in full two of
Jackson's 1959-60 LPs: Blue Gator and Cookin' Sherry. Some of the music
(which often falls into the soul-jazz idiom) is reminiscent of the funky groove
music that would become popular in the late 1960s. Jackson sounds fine and
is joined throughout by guitarist Bill Jennings, organist Jack McDuff, one of
three bassists, one of two drummers, and sometimes Buck Clarke on conga.
The accessible music alternates between warm ballads and jump tunes.
— *Scott Yanow*

Illinois Jacquet (Jean Baptiste Illinois Jacquet)

b. Oct. 31, 1922, Boussard, LA
*Tenor Saxophone, Alto Saxophone, Bassoon / Bop, Swing, Early R&B Jazz,
Groove*

One of the great tenors, Illinois Jacquet's 1942 "Flying Home" solo is considered the first R&B sax solo and spawned a full generation of younger tenors
(including Joe Houston and Big Jay McNeely) who built their careers from
his style and practically from that one song!

Jacquet, whose older brother Russell (1917-1990) was a trumpeter who
sometimes played in his bands, grew up in Houston. His tough tone and
emotional sound defined the Texas tenor school. After playing locally, he
moved to Los Angeles where in 1941 he played with Floyd Ray. He was the
star of Lionel Hampton's 1942 big band ("Flying Home" became a signature
song for Jacquet, Hampton, and even Jacquet's successor Arnett Cobb), and
also was with Cab Calloway (1943-44) and well-featured with Count Basie
(1945-46). Jacquet's playing at the first Jazz at the Philharmonic concert
(1944) included a screaming solo on "Blues" that found him biting on his
reed to achieve high register effects; the crowd went wild. He repeated the
idea during his appearance in the 1944 film short *Jammin' the Blues*. In
1945 Jacquet put together his own band and both his recordings and live
performances were quite exciting. He appeared with JATP on several tours
in the 1950s, recorded steadily and never really lost his popularity. In the
'60s he sometimes doubled on bassoon (usually for a slow number such as
"'Round Midnight"), and it was an effective contrast to his stomping tenor. In
the late '80s Jacquet started leading an exciting part-time big band that thus
far has only recorded one album, an Atlantic date from 1988. Through the
years Jacquet (whose occasional features on alto are quite influenced by
Charlie Parker) has recorded as a leader for such labels as Apollo, Savoy,
Aladdin, RCA, Verve, Mercury, Roulette, Epic, Argo, Prestige, Black Lion,
Black & Blue, JRC, and Atlantic. — *Scott Yanow*

Groove: This is where all that honkin', bar-walkin' sax came from — Mr. Illinois Jacquet. However, a lot of the more soul-jazz flavored Jacquet is not
available on CD. His work with organist Milt Buckner is worth seeking out.
Jacquet wrote the book on the tough-tenor sound. — *Michael Erlewine*

Go Power / Mar. 15, 1966-Mar. 17, 1966 / Cadet ✦✦✦
Tenor-saxophonist Illinois Jacquet teams up with organist Milt Buckner and
drummer Alan Dawson for this live LP that has not yet been reissued on
CD. The distinctive tenor roars through "Illinois Jacquet Flies Again" and
"On A Clear Day," sounds warm on "Robbin's Nest" and "I Want A Little Girl"

and is heard throughout in prime form. Buckner's heavy organ sound takes a bit of getting used to (this set would have been much better if he had been on piano) but he does push Jacquet to some fiery playing. — *Scott Yanow*

The Soul Explosion / Mar. 25, 1969 / Original Jazz Classics ✦✦✦✦
The great tenor Illinois Jacquet is joined by a ten-piece group that includes trumpeter Joe Newman and Milt Buckner on piano and organ for this 1969 Prestige studio session which has been reissued on CD by the OJC series. Jacquet is in prime form, particularly on "The Soul Explosion" (which benefits from a Jimmy Mundy arrangement), a definitive "After Hours," and a previously unissued version of "Still King." This blues-based set is full of soul but often swings quite hard with the focus on Jacquet's exciting tenor throughout. — *Scott Yanow*

★ **The Blues: That's Me!** / Sep. 16, 1969 / Original Jazz Classics ✦✦✦✦✦
Tenor-saxophonist Illinois Jacquet is heard in top form throughout this quintet set with pianist Wynton Kelly, guitarist Tiny Grimes, bassist Buster Williams, and drummer Oliver Jackson. The music, which falls between swing, bop, and early rhythm & blues, is generally quite exciting, especially "Still King," "Everyday I Have the Blues," and the lengthy title cut. A particular surprise is a moody version of "'Round Midnight" which features some surprisingly effective Illinois Jacquet, on bassoon. This CD reissue is highly recommended. — *Scott Yanow*

Genius at Work / Apr. 13, 1971-Apr. 14, 1971 / Jzm ✦✦✦
This live set with organist Milt Buckner and drummer Tony Crombie is quite fun. Tenor great Illinois Jacquet roars throughout "The King," "C Jam Blues" and "Take The 'A' Train," makes a warm ballad statement on "Easy Living," and on "I Wanna Blow Now" he takes an enthusiastic vocal that is highlighted by a surprisingly effective imitation of Ella Fitzgerald. The LP has been long out-of-print but it is worth picking up even if Buckner's organ playing lacks much subtlety. — *Scott Yanow*

Blues from Louisiana / Jul. 7, 1973 / Classic Jazz ✦✦✦✦
This was an odd record, taken either from different live sessions or as part of a bigger all star bash...."On A Clear Day" was open, loose, and swingingly pushed by Jacquet's big throaty vibrato on tenor; "Marlow's La. Blues" was a slow d-r-a-w-n out funky teaser climactic and worried to death by organist Milt Buckner and Jacquet. — *Bob Rusch, Cadence*

Loot to Boot / 197 / LRC ✦✦
Has duos with Jacquet and Wild Bill Davis on the Hammond B-3. — *Michael Erlewine*

The Cool Rage / Verve ✦✦✦✦
Tenor-saxophonist Illinois Jacquet recorded steadily for Verve during 1951-57 but unfortunately his recordings have yet to be coherently reissued. This attractive two-LP set from 1982 gives listeners a good sampling of Jacquet's Verve sides (particularly during 1951-54), although it does skip around chronologically. Jacquet is heard in a variety of settings ranging from a quartet with organist Wild Bill Davis to a big band; among his sidemen are pianist Hank Jones, trumpeter Russell Jacquet, baritonists Cecil Payne and Leo Parker, and even Count Basie (who sits in on organ for a few numbers). A special highpoint are two songs that match Jacquet with fellow tenor Ben Webster. — *Scott Yanow*

Boogaloo Joe Jones

Guitar / Soul-Jazz, Hard Bop
Ivan Jones learned the guitar himself on a three-string instrument that he received as a gift from his father in 1956. He was influenced most by Tal Farlow and Billy Butler, but gravitated toward the R&B juke-joint jazz Butler was popularizing with Bill Doggett. Jones lived in South New Jersey most of his life and worked in and around the Atlantic City area with chitlin-circuit heroes like Wild Bill Davis, Willis Jackson, and Charlie Ventura. He made his solo debut on Prestige in 1967, but earned the name "Boogaloo Joe" following a 1969 record of that title. Perhaps the demeaning name distinguished him from the other Jo(e) Jones of jazz, but it suited his style well. While jazz went through some drastic changes during his recording career (1967-76), Jones' sound and style stayed remarkably consistent. His distinctive and likable sound coupled catchy chordal vamps with astonishing rapid-fire single-note playing. He could handle familiar pop covers ("Light My Fire," "Have You Never Been Mellow") and ballads. But he really excelled in the jazz-funk groove and proved himself a first-rate blues player. He recorded with Groove

Holmes, Houston Person, Rusty Bryant, Harold Mabern, and, most notably, Willis Jackson. Jones, whose distinctive and likable sound never got its due over the course of eight solid Prestige records (and one on his own Joka label in 1975), is finding new life on CD thanks to the apt and rapt attention of the acid-jazz crowd. — *Douglas Payne*

● **Legends of Acid Jazz** / Aug. 4, 1969+Feb. 16, 1970 / Prestige ✦✦✦✦
Jones isn't at the top of the heap as far as late '60s soul-jazz hybrids go; if you want guitar in particular, you're better off starting with Grant Green (to name one). But if guitar-organ-sax groove jazz is one of the bumps on your backbone, you'll be reasonably pleased with the consistent, slightly laidback mood funk of this set, which combines *Right On Brother* (1969) and *Boogaloo Joe* (1970) onto one CD. — *Richie Unterberger*

King Curtis (Curtis Ousley)

b. Feb. 7, 1934, Fort Worth, TX, **d.** Aug. 14, 1971, New York, NY
Tenor Saxophone / R&B, Groove, East Coast Blues, Southern Soul, Hard Bop
King Curtis was the last of the great R&B tenor sax giants. He came to prominence in the mid-'50s as a session musician in New York, recording, at one time or another, for most East Coast R&B labels. A long association with Atlantic/Atco began in 1958, especially on recordings by the Coasters. He recorded singles for many small labels in the '50s—his own Atco sessions (1958-1959), then Prestige/New Jazz and Prestige/TruSound for jazz and R&B albums (1960-1961). Curtis also had a No. 1 R&B single with "Soul Twist" on Enjoy Records (1962). He was signed by Capitol (1963-1964), where he cut mostly singles, including "Soul Serenade." Returning to Atlantic in 1965, he remained there for the rest of his life. He had solid R&B single success with "Memphis Soul Stew" and "Ode to Billie Joe" (1967). Beginning in 1967, Curtis started to take a more active studio role at Atlantic—leading and contracting sessions for other artists, producing with Jerry Wexler and later on his own. He also became the leader of Aretha Franklin's backing unit, the Kingpins. He compiled several albums of singles during this period. All aspects of his career were in full swing at the time he was murdered in 1971. — *Bob Porter*

The New Scene of King Curtis / 1960 / Original Jazz Classics ✦✦✦✦
At first glance, this would appear to be a CD reissue well worth picking up. R&B tenor saxophonist King Curtis is heard in a rare jazz outing, holding his own with cornetist Nat Adderley (in prime form), pianist Wynton Kelly, bassist Paul Chambers and drummer Oliver Jackson on four originals and "Willow Weep for Me." But the single-CD *Soul Meeting* not only contains this entire session, but another related six-song set as well. Only get this particular release if it is found at a budget price. — *Scott Yanow*

● **Soul Meeting** / Sep. 18, 1960 / Prestige ✦✦✦✦
King Curtis, an influential and greatly in-demand R&B tenorman, made relatively few jazz dates in his career. This CD has two of the best, complete albums originally called *The New Scene of King Curtis* and *Soul Meeting;* the former is also available as a separate CD but should be skipped in favor of this one. Curtis teams up with the passionate cornetist Nat Adderley, pianist Wynton Kelly, either Paul Chambers or Sam Jones on bass, and Oliver Jackson or Belton Evans on drums. The music is blues-based bop, with seven basic Curtis originals and four standards. Highly recommended, this set serves as proof that King Curtis could have been a viable jazz player. — *Scott Yanow*

Old Gold / Sep. 19, 1961 / Tru ✦✦✦
King Curtis with Jack McDuff on the Hammond organ, Billy Butler and Eric Gale on guitar. Funky renditions of standards like "Honky Tonk" and "Fever." — *Michael Erlewine*

Country Soul / 1962 / Capitol ✦✦
This album of country standards was intended to be King Curtis' answer to Ray Charles' *Modern Sounds in Country and Western Music*. It never sold remotely as well as Charles' album, primarily because of Curtis' more perfunctory singing and some unwise choices of music to cover—"Night Train To Memphis," "Raunchy" (which *is* an instrumental), and "I'm Movin' On" work as R&B instrumentals, with the latter benefiting from some sizzling interplay between the guitars, the trumpets, and Curtis' sax. But "High Noon" and "Home On the Range" are a lot less convincing, conceptually as well as in execution. There are a few surprises, however, such as a version of "Your

Cheatin' Heart" that tries desperately to transform itself into "Stand By Me." (out of print) — *Bruce Eder*

Blow Man, Blow! / May 22, 1962-Mar. 12, 1965 / Bear Family ✦✦✦✦
71 songs spread among three CDs, covering King Curtis' tenure at Capitol from 1962 until 1965. This wasn't the most productive period in Curtis' career, but it was his first chance to make records on more than a piecemeal basis under his own name; the result is a dazzling array of sounds and songs. Hidden among the country covers and abortive early sides on Disc One is a lot of gold, most notably "Slow Drag" and the previously unreleased "New Dance," which features some killer guitar; the early unissued material is superb, including the Curtis original "Frisky," a slow version of "Alexander's Ragtime Band," the beguiling "Sukiyaki," and a gorgeous bossa nova called "Amorosa." (Many of these tracks feature guitarist Cornell Dupree, who was to figure in Curtis' most successful records for Capitol.) Disc Two is where things start to cook: from "More Soul" on through to the previously unreleased "Hung Over," there's not a note of filler on the disc, which encompasses all of the *Soul Serenade* album as well as a brace of unreleased songs and some very fine singles, including a dazzling cover of the Acker Bilk standard "Stranger on the Shore," and a soulful recomposition of Jackie Gleason's "Melancholy Serenade." Disc Three comprises material ranging from reinterpretations of pop standards like "Moon River" and "The Girl From Ipanema" through a dozen covers of Sam Cooke songs, all worthwhile. — *Bruce Eder*

The Best of King Curtis / Aug. 23, 1962-Mar. 11, 1965 / Capitol ✦✦✦✦
Best of King Curtis collects the bulk of King Curtis' singles for Capitol, plus selected album tracks. Although he didn't have many hits while on Capitol — only "Soul Serenade" hit the charts — this collection demonstrates the depths of Curtis' talents, showcasing his stabs at jazz and blues in addition to his trademark R&B. *Instant Soul* remains a stronger introduction, but for fans that want to dig a little deeper, *The Best of King Curtis* is an excellent purchase. — *Stephen Thomas Erlewine*

Soul Serenade / 1964 / Capitol ✦✦✦✦
Curtis' second Capitol album is a triumph on every level. The tragedy is that, apart from the hit title track, almost nothing off of this superb album was heard by the public — most of the singles he was doing were very different from this material. The album featured Curtis' covers of songs like the Bill Doggett co-authored "Honky Tonk," Chuck Berry's "Memphis," the hottest, most soulful version of the Champs' old hit "Tequila" ever recorded, and Herbie Hancock's "Watermelon Man," as well as a re-recording of his hit "Soul Twist," and a version of his "Night Train," a big hit for Jimmy Forrest. Maybe the biggest surprise here is the cover of the blues standard "Hide Away," written by Curtis' old friend Freddie King. Sharing the spotlight with Curtis' sax throughout this record is Cornell Dupree on lead guitar, adding just the right accompaniment variously as a lead and rhythm instrument — the two make the oft-heard cover of "Hide Away" by John Mayall and Eric Clapton sound like a poor demo. There's not a wrong or wasted note. — *Bruce Eder*

Plays Hits Made by Sam Cooke / Mar. 9, 1965+Mar. 11, 1965 / Capitol ✦✦✦✦
This is about the only Sam Cooke tribute record — other than individual songs cut by Otis Redding — that one could imagine Cooke himself not only would have approved of fully, but might have enjoyed himself, had it been recorded under other circumstances. One could even visualize him dancing to the versions of "Shake," which does have a few echoes of "Night Train" in it, or "Twistin' The Night Away" or "Good Times." Curtis had known and worked with Cooke, and the singer's shooting death late in 1964 affected the saxophonist deeply, as it did millions of people. This album was the result, a dozen covers that blow away most any other Sam Cooke tribute album (including the still highly collectible Supremes' *We Remember Sam Cooke*). (out of print) — *Bruce Eder*

Blues at Montreux / 1971 / Atlantic ✦✦✦
This live set from the 1971 Montreux Jazz Festival was co-led by tenor saxophonist King Curtis (who tragically would be killed three months later) and veteran blues pianist/vocalist Champion Jack Dupree. With guitarist Cornell Dupree (in excellent form), bassist Jerry Jemmott, and drummer Oliver Jackson laying down the foundation, Curtis and Dupree find a great deal of common musical ground. Dupree has quite a few witty vocals (particularly the near-classic "Junker's Blues") while taking choruses of irregular length that

keep his sidemen continually guessing. Curtis' distinctive tenor is also heard from, making one truly regret both that this was his final recording and that this LP's music has yet to be reissued on CD. — *Scott Yanow*

● **Instant Soul: The Legendary King Curtis** / Oct. 19, 1994 / Razor & Tie ✦✦✦✦
King Curtis has never been served with a comprehensive collection until *Instant Soul*, which features the best instrumental singles the distinctive, soulful, and influential tenor saxophonist ever recorded. — *Stephen Thomas Erlewine*

The Complete Enjoy Sessions / 1995 / Relic ✦✦✦✦
King Curtis never officially "joined" Bobby Robinson's Enjoy label. Rather, he came aboard only provisionally, willing to cut a couple of sides and see if they hit, and once they did, he would sign. Robinson ran the session for "Soul Twist" and got Curtis to feature the guitar, the organ, and the piano alternating with his sax — the record became Curtis' first hit, and an album followed, but Curtis never signed to Enjoy, choosing to go with Capitol Records instead in May 1962. The 15 songs here were all that came of his early 1962 association with Robinson, bold numbers mostly featuring very prominent guitar (played by Billy Butler and Joe Richardson) and organ (by Ernie Hayes) — check out "What'd I Say Pts. 1 and 2" — and even a harmonica solo by the King himself on "Harmonica Twist," along with the expected sax breaks. Robinson's big discovery was that Curtis blew all the way through his previous records, rather than using his band for contrast. The sound is excellent, and the notes, though a little sketchy, tell us a lot about how these records, among Curtis' best (certainly superior to the country & western venture Capitol threw him into) were made. — *Bruce Eder*

Charles Kynard

b. Feb. 20, 1933, St. Louis, MO, **d.** Jul. 8, 1979, Los Angeles, CA
Organ / Soul-Jazz, Groove
Organ, electric bass. Kynard is an organist whose jazz-funk leanings rival his predecessors and peers, though not eclipsing them. Solid, though never flashy. He also plays electric bass. Kynard's album *Reelin' with the Feelin'* has been sampled and appears on several acid-jazz releases. — *Michael G. Nastos & Michael Erlewine*

Charles Kynard / 1962-1963 / World Pacific ✦✦✦✦
Kynard's best combo effort. Shows him in a more favorable light as a soul-jazz proprietor. — *Michael G. Nastos*

Where It's at / 1962-1963 / Pacific Jazz ✦✦✦
Kynard with funky guitarist Howard Roberts, Clifford Scott (sax), and Milt Turner (d). This is Kynard's first album and it has not been reissued. — *Michael Erlewine*

Professor Soul / Aug. 6, 1968 / Prestige ✦✦✦✦
Charles Kynard with Cal Green on guitar and Johnny Kirkwood on drums. This 1968 gem, which has not been reissued, has a rendition of "Christo Redentor." — *Michael Erlewine*

The Soul Brotherhood / Mar. 10, 1969 / Prestige ✦✦✦✦
They have got to reissue this one! Here is Kynard with Grant Green on guitar, Blue Mitchell on trumpet, and David "Fathead" Newman on sax. — *Michael Erlewine*

● **Reelin' with the Feelin'** / Aug. 11, 1969 / Prestige ✦✦✦✦
Although Charles Kynard led a date for Pacific Jazz in the early '60s and five albums for Prestige from 1968-70, he never really became famous. A fine organist in the style of Jimmy Smith, Kynard could always groove and chug along with the best of them. This Prestige date (reissued on an LP in the Original Jazz Classics series but not yet on CD) matches Kynard with an interesting cast of players: tenor saxophonist Wilton Felder (of the Jazz Crusaders), guitarist Joe Pass (a few years before he became famous for his Pablo recordings), electric bassist Carol Kaye, and drummer Paul Humphrey. The music is quite groove-oriented and chiefly of interest for the contrasting solos of Kynard, Felder, and Pass. — *Scott Yanow*

Afro-Disiac / Apr. 6, 1970 / Prestige ✦✦✦✦
Another Kynard gem that we are waiting for a reissue of. This album features Kynard with Grant Green on guitar and Houston Person on sax. I have not been able to find a copy, but those who know it say that this is the one to hear. I can't wait. — *Michael Erlewine*

Wa-Tu-Wa-Zui / Dec. 14, 1970 / Prestige ◆◆◆
Kynard with Rusty Bryant on sax, Virgil Jones on trumpet, and Melvin Sparks on guitar. — *Michael Erlewine*

Yusef Lateef (William Evans)

b. Oct. 9, 1920, Chatanooga, TN
Tenor Saxophone, Flute, Oboe / Hard Bop, Post-Bop
Yusef Lateef has long had an inquisitive spirit and he was never just a bop or hard bop soloist. Lateef, who does not care much for the name "jazz," has consistently created music that has stretched (and even broke through) boundaries. A superior tenor-saxophonist with a soulful sound and impressive technique, Lateef by the '50s was one of the top flutists around. He also developed into the best jazz soloist to date on oboe, an occasional bassoonist, and introduced such instruments as the argol (a double clarinet that resembles a bassoon), shanai (a type of oboe) and different types of flutes. Lateef played "world music" before it had a name and his output was much more creative than much of the pop and folk music that passes under that label in the 1990s.

Lateef grew up in Detroit and began on tenor when he was 17. He played with Lucky Millinder (1946), Hot Lips Page, Roy Eldridge, and Dizzy Gillespie's big band (1949-50). He was a fixture on the Detroit jazz scene of the '50s where he studied flute at Wayne State University. Lateef began recording as a leader in 1955 for Savoy (and later Riverside and Prestige) although he did not move to New York until 1959. By then he already had a strong reputation for his versatility and for his willingness to utilize "miscellaneous instruments." Lateef played with Charles Mingus in 1960, gigged with Donald Byrd, and was well-featured with the Cannonball Adderley Sextet (1962-64). As a leader his string of Impulse recordings (1963-66) were among the finest of his career although Lateef's varied Atlantic sessions (1967-76) usually also had some strong moments. He spent some time in the '80s teaching in Nigeria. His Atlantic records of the late '80s were closer to mood music (or new age) than jazz but in the '90s (for his own YAL label) Yusef Lateef has recorded a wide variety of music (all originals) including some strong improvised music with the likes of Ricky Ford, Archie Shepp, and Von Freeman. — *Scott Yanow*

Groove: Yusef Lateef is not a groove master. Lateef's fusion of blues and Eastern sounds was a pioneer effort and the sound he gets is unique—very lovely indeed. Blues lovers will know just where he is coming from. The Rhino/Atlantic two-disc anthology *Every Village Has a Song* lays it all out for you. — *Michael Erlewine*

● **Every Village Has a Song: The Yusef Lateef Anthology** / May 6, 1949-Mar. 1976 / Rhino/Atlantic ◆◆◆◆
This good two-disc set covers Lateef's tenure at Atlantic as well as featuring formative material from early sessions for Transition, Prestige/Moodsville, Riverside, Impulse, Blue Note, and Savoy. The discs show Lateef honing a thick, bluesy, expressive tenor tone in the beginning, evolving into a superior straight jazz player, then expanding his repertoire and choice of instruments and contexts. His flute playing became arguably superior to his tenor, while his solos on oboe, shenai, and other previously little-known instruments enabled Lateef to create arresting, fresh, and ultimately significant music. While the sampler approach can't fully document his contributions, it's a solid introduction for those unfamiliar with his output. — *Ron Wynn*

Other Sounds / Oct. 11, 1957 / Original Jazz Classics ◆◆◆◆
These recordings are among his early African/Middle Eastern fusion efforts, with many exotic instruments. — *Myles Boisen*

Cry!/Tender / Oct. 11, 1957+Oct. 16, 1959 / Original Jazz Classics ◆◆◆◆
This well-rounded program, reissued on CD in the OJC program, features Yusef Lateef (tripling on tenor, flute and oboe) heading a quintet also including trumpeter Lonnie Hillyer, pianist Hugh Lawson, bassist Herman Wright, and drummer Frank Gant. The music alternates between straightahead pieces and more atmospheric and exotic works. An earlier track ("Ecaps") features Lateef with a different quintet that also includes fluegelhornist Wilbur Harden. — *Scott Yanow*

Blues for the Orient / Oct. 11, 1957+Sep. 5, 1961 / Prestige ◆◆◆◆
This double-LP from 1974 has the complete contents of two Yusef Lateef Prestige albums: *Eastern Sounds* and *The Sounds of Yusef*. The latter date

(which has not yet been reissued on CD) is from 1957 and features Lateef, fluegelhornist Wilbur Harden, pianist Hugh Lawson, bassist Ernie Farrow, and drummer Oliver Jackson all doubling on unusual instruments such as the argol, Turkish finger cymbals, a 7-Up bottle, balloons, a rabat, and an earthboard. They perform a romping version of "Take the 'A' Train," Harden's "Playful Flute," and three diverse Lateef originals. The later session, which has Lateef (on tenor, oboe, and flute) playing with the Barry Harris trio, ranges from his famous version of "Love Theme from *Spartacus*," and "Blues for the Orient" to "The Plum Blossom" and several obscure but enjoyable originals. This music is highly recommended in one form or another. — *Scott Yanow*

Yusef Lateef / Oct. 11, 1957-Dec. 29, 1961 / Prestige ◆◆◆◆
This excellent two-LP set combines together material taken from three Yusef Lateef LPs; all of Lateef's Prestige and New Jazz recordings were very effectively reissued in Prestige's admirable two-fer series. Lateef, one of the first jazz musicians to integrate aspects of Middle Eastern music into his playing, not only performs on tenor and flute during these sessions but also oboe (he was probably jazz music's greatest oboeist ever) and the argol. These performances (with such sidemen as fluegelhornist Wilbur Hardin, trumpeter Lonnie Hillyer, and pianists Hugh Lawson and Barry Harris) range from atmospheric modal ballads to straightahead stomping. This two-fer is a fine example of Yusef Lateef at his best. — *Scott Yanow*

The Three Faces of Yusef Lateef / May 9, 1960 / Original Jazz Classics ◆◆◆◆
Lateef's first album as a multi-instrumental player after his move from Detroit to New York City. With Ron Carter (b, cello), Hugh Lawson (p), Herman Wright (b), and Lex Humphries (d). This is an early attempt at fusion—mixing jazz with Eastern motifs and classical flavors. — *Michael Erlewine*

The Centaur and the Phoenix / Oct. 4, 1960+Oct. 6, 1960 / Original Jazz Classics ◆◆◆◆
For this CD reissue of a Riverside date, the great multi-reedist Yusef Lateef (who switches between tenor, flute, oboe, and the argol) is joined on most selections by five other horns (including a bassoonist) and a rhythm section headed by pianist Joe Zawinul. The music has a lot of diversity, from stomps and ballads to Eastern-influenced explorations; two "bonus cuts" from the same date match Lateef with a four-piece rhythm section that includes pianist Barry Harris and two percussionists. Highlights include "Everyday I Fall in Love," "Summer Song," "Jungle Fantasy," and "The Centaur and the Phoenix." Virtually everything that Yusef Lateef recorded during this era is well worth acquiring. — *Scott Yanow*

☆ **Eastern Sounds** / Sep. 5, 1961 / Original Jazz Classics ◆◆◆◆◆
Although originally issued on the Moodsville label (a subsidiary of Prestige), this classic Yusef Lateef date is not all ballads. Accompanied by pianist Barry Harris, bassist Ernie Farrow, and drummer Lex Humphries, Lateef (switching between tenor, oboe, and flute) is quite memorable on such pieces as the "Love Theme from *Spartacus*," "Blues for the Orient," "Don't Blame Me," and "The Plum Blossom." He has long been a true original with an active musical curiosity and this set gives listeners a strong example of his work. — *Scott Yanow*

Jazz Around the World / Dec. 19, 1963-Dec. 20, 1963 / Impulse! ◆◆◆◆
Yusef Lateef's Impulse recordings of 1963-66 were among the finest of his career. This out-of-print LP, his first effort for Impulse, features Lateef not only on tenor, flute, and oboe but bassoon and shanas. Performing with a quintet that also includes trumpeter Richard Williams, pianist Hugh Lawson, bassist Ernie Farrow, and drummer Lex Humphries, Lateef plays a variety of folk melodies from other countries along with a few originals and a memorable version (on oboe) of "Trouble in Mind." — *Scott Yanow*

Re-Evaluations: The Impulse Years / Dec. 19, 1963-Jun. 16, 1966 / Impulse! ◆◆◆◆
Multi-instrumentalist Yusef Lateef recorded eight albums for the Impulse label during the 1963-66 period. All are worth acquiring, but as a sampler this two-LP set (which draws its 18 selections from six of the albums) gives one a fine all-around picture of Lateef's many talents. He is heard on his highly appealing tenor, playing flute, jamming "Exactly like You" and an emotional "Trouble in Mind" on oboe, utlizing the exotic shannas and theremin (the latter being an early electronic instrument), and even having a few rare outings on alto. The music ranges from bop and ballads to some avant-garde explorations and mood pieces. — *Scott Yanow*

★ **Live at Pep's** / Jun. 29, 1964 / Impulse! ♦♦♦♦♦
This mid-'60s concert was one of Lateef's finest, as it perfectly displayed his multiple influences and interests. There were hard bop originals, covers of jazz classics like Oscar Pettiford's "Oscarlypso" (a CD bonus track) and Leonard Feather's "Twelve Tone Blues," as well as an unorthodox but effective version of Ma Rainey's "See See Rider." On "Sister Mamie," "Number 7," and drummer James Black's "The Magnolia Triangle," Lateef moved away from strict jazz, although he retained his improvisational flair. Lateef played meaty tenor sax solos, entrancing flute and bamboo flute offerings, and also had impressive stints on oboe, shenai, and argol. This was a pivotal date in his career, and those unaware of it will get a treat with this disc. — *Ron Wynn*

A Flat, G Flat and C / May 8, 1966-May 9, 1966 / Impulse! ♦♦♦♦
Yusef Lateef (heard on tenor, alto, flute, oboe, and the mysterious-sounding theremin) is in explorative and consistently colorful form on this out-of-print LP, one of many Impulse! sessions that are long overdue to be reissued on CD. With the assistance of pianist Hugh Lawson, bassist Reggie Workman, and drummer Roy Brooks, Lateef performs ten songs (eight are his originals) that are all at least in abstract form related to the blues. Well worth several listens. — *Scott Yanow*

The Complete Yusef Lateef / May 31, 1967 / Atlantic ♦♦♦♦
Yusef Lateef's first Atlantic album was one of his better ones for the label. Performing on flute, tenor, alto, and oboe ("In the Evening"), Lateef is assisted by pianist Hugh Lawson, bassist Cecil McBee, and drummer Roy Brooks on a wide-ranging program that ranges from the feel of New Orleans and blues to boogaloo rhythms and the soulful spiritual "Rosalie." This LP is long overdue to be reissued on CD. — *Scott Yanow*

The Diverse Yusef Lateef/Suite 16 / Jan. 15, 1970-Nov. 2, 1970 / Rhino ♦♦♦♦
For this single CD Rhino combined together two complete LPs from Yusef Lateef's period on Atlantic. Although there are some period trappings and the use of a vocal group on a few selections, the music sounds fairly fresh and its diversity (ranging from exotic vamps to the adventurous seven-movement "Symphonic Blues Suite") is a major strength. Earl Klugh's solo guitar rendition of "Michelle" is pleasant if out-of-place and there are some forgettable tracks but Lateef's willingness to take chances, his highly individual sound on his instruments (tenor, flute, oboe, and a rare outing on soprano), and the impressive amount of variety make this a recommended set. — *Scott Yanow*

Ron Levy

b. May 29, 1951, Cambridge, MA
Piano, Organ / Modern Electric Blues, Groove
Ron Levy (born Reuvin Zev ben Yehoshua Ha Levi) was born on May 29, 1951, in Cambridge, MA. Although Levy grew up playing clarinet, he switched to piano at age 13 after attending a Ray Charles concert. Then, influenced by Jimmy Smith, Booker T., and Billy Preston, he picked up on the Hammond organ. Within a few years he was working in the Boston area backing up blues acts. Albert King discovered and hired him in 1971 while still in high school. They worked together for 18 months. He then went on to B.B. King's band and worked with King for almost seven years. From 1976 until 1980, Levy worked with the Rhythm Rockers and it was here that he met guitarist Ronnie Earl. Levy joined the Roomful of Blues from 1983 to 1987. Levy's own band, Ron Levy's Wild Kingdom, has recorded a number of fine albums for Black Top, Rounder, and Bullseye, among them 1988's *Safari to New Orleans*, 1993's *B-3 Blues and Grooves*, and 1996's *Zim Zam Zoom: Acid Blues on B-3*. — *Michael Erlewine*

Ron Levy's Wild Kingdom / May 1987 / Black Top ♦♦♦
Ten tunes with an all-star cast including Ronnie Earl (guitar), Kim Wilson (harmonica), Greg Piccolo (sax), Wayne Bennett (guitar), and other excellent players. Plenty of fine guitar, keyboards, harmonica, and up-tempo blues music. — *Michael Erlewine*

★ **B-3 Blues & Grooves** / Apr. 1, 1993 / Bullseye Blues ♦♦♦♦♦
Ron Levy is one of the finest young masters of the Hammond B-3. Here are 11 soul-satisfying cuts that feature Levy's funky keyboard playing—many written by Levy himself. Those who look for B-3 jams in the soul-jazz vein that are as funky as can be will not be disappointed. This is a great CD to own. — *Michael Erlewine*

Zim Zam Zoom: Acid Blues on B-3 / Mar. 19, 1996 / Bullseye Blues ♦♦♦♦
If you like blues and funky soul-jazz (with just a twist of the future), this is

an album to enjoy. Hammond B-3 artist Ron Levy gathers some of the greatest groove players of all time for this steam session, including Melvin Sparks on guitar and the great Idris Muhammad on drums. Call it retro or acid-jazz if you want, but groove lover Levy never stops playing that funky soul-jazz long enough to look back. This album carries the groove tradition on, maintaining that integrity. Produced by Bob Porter. — *Michael Erlewine*

Greaze Is What's Good / 1998 / Cannonball ♦♦♦
On *Greaze Is What's Good*, Ron Levy is joined by trumpeter Freddie Hubbard, guitarists Melvin Sparks and David T. Walker, drummer Idris Muhammad, and trombonist Steve Turre, plus Memphis blues guitarist Preston Shannon, for a solid set of groovin', bluesy soul-jazz. — *Steve Huey*

Harold Mabern

b. Mar. 20, 1936, Memphis, TN
Piano / Hard Bop, Groove, Soul-Jazz
One of several excellent hard bop pianists from the Memphis area, Harold Mabern has led relatively few dates through the years but he has always been respected by his contemporaries. He played in Chicago with MJT + 3 in the late '50s and then moved to New York in 1959. Mabern worked with Jimmy Forrest, Lionel Hampton, the Jazztet (1961-62), Donald Byrd, Miles Davis (1963), J.J. Johnson (1963-65), Sonny Rollins, Freddie Hubbard, Wes Montgomery, Joe Williams (1966-67), and Sarah Vaughan. During 1968-70 Mabern led four albums for Prestige, he was with Lee Morgan in the early '70s, and in 1972 he recorded with Stanley Cowell's Piano Choir. In more recent times Harold Mabern recorded as a a leader for DIW/Columbia and Sackville and toured with the Contemporary Piano Ensemble (1993-95). — *Scott Yanow*

Rakin' and Scrapin' / Dec. 23, 1968 / Prestige ♦♦♦♦
Reissued on LP but not yet CD, this Prestige set features the excellent hard bop pianist Harold Mabern heading a quintet also including trumpeter Blue Mitchell, tenor saxophonist George Coleman, bassist Bill Lee, and drummer Hugh Walker. Other than a brief throwaway version of "I Heard It Through the Grapevine" (which finds Mabern switching to electric piano), the music is essentially boppish, with some ballads and blues included. Nothing too substantial occurs, but it is a good modern mainstream effort for the era. — *Scott Yanow*

Workin' and Wailin' / Jun. 30, 1969 / Prestige ♦♦♦
The date utilizes trumpeter Virgil Jones, tenor saxophonist George Coleman, bassist Buster Williams, and drummer Idris Muhammad on four challenging Mabern originals and Johnny Mandel's "A Time for Love." — *Scott Yanow*

Wailin' / Jun. 30, 1969 + Jan. 26, 1970 / Prestige ♦♦♦♦
This CD reissue combines together two sessions ('Workin' & Wailin' and Greasy Kid Stuff) led by pianist Harold Mabern during 1969-70. The first date utilizes trumpeter Virgil Jones, tenor-saxophonist George Coleman, bassist Buster Williams, and drummer Idris Muhammad on four challenging Mabern originals and Johnny Mandel's "A Time for Love." However it is the second session that is most memorable for, in addition to Mabern, Williams, and Muhammad, it features trumpeter Lee Morgan and flutist Hubert Laws; the latter mostly plays some surprisingly passionate tenor that makes one wish he had performed on tenor more through the years. Excellent advanced hard bop music that hints at fusion. — *Scott Yanow*

Greasy Kid Stuff! / Jan. 26, 1970 / Prestige ♦♦♦
This session is most memorable for, in addition to Mabern, Williams, and Muhammad, it features trumpeter Lee Morgan and flutist Hubert Laws; the latter mostly plays some surprisingly passionate tenor that makes one wish he had performed on tenor more through the years. Excellent advanced hard bop music that hints at fusion. — *Scott Yanow*

★ **The Leading Man** / Nov. 9, 1992-Apr. 12, 1993 / Columbia ♦♦♦♦♦
A brilliant pianist who continues to develop and has found his own voice in the modern mainstream, Harold Mabern chose consistently superior tunes for his Columbia CD, ranging from Wes Montgomery's "Full House" (featuring guitarist Kevin Eubanks in a duet with the leader) and songs by Wayne Shorter, Coltrane, and Bird, to his own "B&B" (a ballad dedicated to Clifford Brown and Booker Little) and the pop tune "Save the Best for Last." Although one can hear aspects of McCoy Tyner's chord voicings in some of Mabern's solos, he has plenty of very individual ideas; check out his near-miraculous playing on "Moment's Notice." With strong support from drummer Jack De-

Johnette and either Christian McBride or Ron Carter on bass (in addition to two appearances by trumpeter Bill Mobley), this is one of Mabern's most impressive outings to date and it is highly recommended. — *Scott Yanow*

Les McCann

b. Sep. 23, 1935, Lexington, KY
Piano, Vocals, Keyboards / Soul-Jazz, Hard Bop, Groove
Les McCann reached the peak of his career at the 1968 Montreux Jazz Festival, recording "Compared to What" and "Cold Duck Time" for Atlantic (*Swiss Movement*) with Eddie Harris and Benny Bailey. Although he has done some worthwhile work since then, much of it has been anti-climactic.

Les McCann first gained some fame in 1956 when he won a talent contest in the Navy as a singer that resulted in an appearance on television on *The Ed Sullivan Show*. After being discharged, he formed a trio in Los Angeles. McCann turned down an invitation to join the Cannonball Adderley Quintet so he could work on his own music. He signed a contract with Pacific Jazz and in 1960 gained some fame with his albums *Les McCann Plays the Truth* and *The Shout*. His soulful funk style on piano was influential and McCann's singing was largely secondary until the mid-'60s. He recorded many albums for Pacific Jazz during 1960-64, mostly with his trio but also featuring Ben Webster, Richard "Groove" Holmes, Blue Mitchell, Stanley Turrentine, Joe Pass, the Jazz Crusaders, and the Gerald Wilson Orchestra. McCann switched to Limelight during 1965-67 and then signed with Atlantic in 1968. After the success of *Swiss Movement*, McCann emphasized his singing at the expense of his playing, and he began to utilize electric keyboards. His recordings became less interesting from that point on and, after his Atlantic contract ran out in 1976, McCann appeared on records much less often. However he stayed popular and a 1994 reunion tour with Eddie Harris was quite successful. A mid-'90s stroke put him out of action for a time and weakened his keyboard playing (his band began carrying an additional keyboardist) but McCann returned to a more active schedule during 1996 and was still a powerful singer. — *Scott Yanow*

● **Les McCann Anthology: Relationships** / Feb. 1960-Nov. 1972 / Rhino ◆◆◆◆
One of the many two-CD samplers of Atlantic jazz artists put together by Rhino Records, this retrospective has some the highpoints of pianist-vocalist Les McCann's career but is far from perfect. The first CD is purely instrumental, showcasing McCann with several of his trios and in collaborations with organist Richard "Groove" Holmes, the tenors of Ben Webster and Stanley Turrentine, the Jazz Crusaders, and Gerald Wilson's Orchestra. The second half of the two-fer has three selections on which McCann backs singer Lou Rawls (why were these included?) and just two vocals from the pianist. "Compared to What" and "Cold Duck Time" (from his famous meeting with Eddie Harris at the 1968 Montreux Jazz Festival) have been reissued several times, there are no selections from the 1973-95 period, and the music is not programmed in strictly chronological order. Taken as a whole, there is plenty of rewarding music on the collection (including "The Truth," "The Shampoo," "A Little 3/4 for God & Co.," and "With These Hands"), but McCann's vocalizing and his post-1972 music should not have been neglected. — *Scott Yanow*

Les McCann in New York / Dec. 28, 1960 / Pacific Jazz ◆◆◆◆
The original Les McCann LP of the same name featured the soulful pianist heading a group consisting of Stanley Turrentine and Frank Haynes on tenors, trumpeter Blue Mitchell, bassist Herbie Lewis, and drummer Ron Jefferson on five of his originals, including "A Little 3/4 for God & Co." The CD reissue adds a previously unissued sixth song from the session ("Someone Stole My Chitlins"), plus two formerly unknown numbers from a truncated 1960 date in which McCann, Lewis, and Jefferson are joined by vibraphonist Bobby Hutcherson (at the beginning of his career) and Curtis Amy on tenor. The music overall is fairly definitive soul-jazz and finds McCann in prime form throughout a spirited instrumental program. — *Scott Yanow*

Les McCann Sings / Aug. 1961 / Pacific Jazz ◆◆◆◆
A super set with Ben Webster (ts) and Groove Holmes on organ. Soul-jazz and blues at their best. — *Ron Wynn*

Les is More / 1967 / Night ◆◆
Joel Dorn's short-lived Night Music label featured private tapes of some of his favorite jazz artists. Pianist/vocalist Les McCann had collected 500 mostly undated private tapes through the years (the dates listed above are estimates) and this CD is drawn from that archive. McCann and his 1967 trio

perform the groove tune "Maleah" and "With These Hands" (the latter has McCann's vocal) while "Samia" reunites the pianist with Eddie Harris. There are also a few numbers without McCann. One features singer Roberta Flack (a few months before cutting her first record for Atlantic) and there is an odd collage of L.A. appearances by such artists as Cannonball Adderley, Stanley Turrentine, and Carmen McRae but unfortunately those are just excerpts. "Clapformation" features an excellent R&B alto solo by Gerald Albright from very early in his career and there is also a later version of McCann's hit "Compared to What." Very much a mixed bag, this CD (which is far from essential) is a historical curiosity at best. — *Scott Yanow*

★ **Much Les** / Jul. 22, 1968-Jul. 24, 1968 / Rhino ◆◆◆◆◆
This straight CD reissue of an Atlantic LP offers one a pretty definitive look at Les McCann in his prime. The pianist/singer develops long funky vamps that swing, sings "With These Hands" and, even with a string section added to four of the six numbers and three also having two percussionists, the emphasis is on McCann's trio with bassist Leroy Vinnegar and drummer Donald Dean. This is high-quality and intelligent groove music. — *Scott Yanow*

☆ **Swiss Movement: Montreux 30th Anniversary Edition** / Jun. 1969 / Rhino ◆◆◆◆◆
One of the most popular soul-jazz albums of all time, and one of the best, although Harris (and trumpeter Benny Bailey) had never played or rehearsed with the Les McCann Trio before, and indeed weren't even given the music. Perhaps that sparked the spontaneous funk that comes through clearly on the tape of this show, recorded at the Montreux Festival in 1969. It's actually much more of a showcase for McCann than Harris, although the tenor saxist's contributions are significant. The sole vocal, a version of Gene McDaniels' "Compared to What," remains McCann's signature tune. It's worth picking up Rhino's "Montreux 30th Anniversary Edition," as it adds a nine-minute bonus track ("Kaftan") and historical liner notes. — *Richie Unterberger*

Talk to the People / May 1972 / Atlantic ◆◆◆◆
While *Invitation to Openness* was Les McCann's progressive statement of 1972, this was his populist sermon, with a title to match. With four vocals among the seven tracks, *Talk to the People* preaches earthily in the funky soul/jazz and R&B languages of the time, with some social comment besides. Having gone completely over to the Rhodes electric piano and Hohner clavinet, McCann became a fervent convert—indeed, he and Stevie Wonder were the funky-butt champs of the clavinet in the '70s—and he could beat on them with the rhythmic snap of a conga drummer. "Shamading" may be the funkiest, hip-shaking thing Les has ever recorded; the cool, swaggering funkathon "North Carolina" runs a close second; and the best of the vocals is a very gritty and convincing treatment of Marvin Gaye's "What's Going On." Although there are some weak links in this chain of tunes, the highs are sky-high, and they represent some of Les' peak studio performances. — *Richard S. Ginell*

Live at Montreux / Jun. 24, 1972 / Atlantic ◆◆◆◆
Having rocketed the Montreux Jazz Festival to prominence in 1968 with *Swiss Movement*, Atlantic naturally thought they could score again four years later with the superfunky electric edition of Les McCann Ltd. While there were no major hits this time, Atlantic got enough from Les' set to put out a hot double album loaded with gritty vocals, gospel-drenched electric piano, cooking instrumentals, plenty of his popular protest songs, and a few new numbers such as the driving "Cochise." Backed with stone-tough grooves by Jimmy Rowser (bass), Buck Clarke (congas, percussion) and Donald Dean (drums), most of Les' performances are at least the equal of his studio recordings, though the inevitable return of "Compared to What" falls short of the pacesetting version of 1968. Eddie Harris didn't turn up this time at Montreux, but Rahsaan Roland Kirk did, wandering in on the middle of "Get Yourself Together," doing a wailing thing like an air raid siren and a funky impromptu encore. For a vivid snapshot of Les McCann at the high noon of his career, this double-LP set is worth scouring the used racks for. — *Richard S. Ginell*

Jack McDuff (Eugene McDuffy)

b. Sep. 17, 1926, Champaign, IL
Organ / Soul-Jazz, Hard Bop, Groove
A marvelous bandleader and organist as well as capable arranger, "Brother" Jack McDuff has one of the funkiest, most soulful styles of all time on the

Hammond B-3. His rock-solid bass lines and blues-drenched solos are balanced by clever, almost pianistic melodies and interesting progressions and phrases. McDuff began as a bassist playing with Denny Zeitlin and Joe Farrell. He studied privately in Cinncinnati and worked with Johnny Griffin in Chicago. He taught himself organ and piano in the mid-'50s, and began gaining attention working with Willis Jackson in the late '50s and early '60s, cutting high caliber soul-jazz dates for Prestige. McDuff made his recording debut as a leader for Prestige in 1960, playing in a studio pickup band with Jimmy Forrest. They made a pair of outstanding albums, *Tough Duff* and *The Honeydripper*. McDuff organized his own band the next year, featuring Harold Vick and drummer Joe Dukes. Things took off when McDuff hired a young guitarist named George Benson. They were among the most popular combos of the mid-'60s, and made several excellent albums. McDuff's later groups at Atlantic and Cadet didn't equal the level of the Benson band, while later dates for Verve and Cadet were uneven, though generally good. McDuff experimented with electronic keyboards and fusion during the '70s, then in the '80s got back in the groove with the Muse session *Cap'n Jack*. Other musicians McDuff played with in the '60s and '70s include Joe Henderson, Pat Martino, Jimmy Witherspoon, David "Fathead" Newman, Rahsaan Roland Kirk, Sonny Stitt, and Gene Ammons. There are only a few McDuff sessions available on CD, though they include the fine sessions with Forrest. His work with Benson has also been reissued on CD. — *Ron Wynn and Bob Porter*

Tough 'Duff / Jul. 12, 1960 / Original Jazz Classics ✦✦✦✦
McDuff's second lead session for Prestige. Good small-group Hammond organ funk—provided you like vibes, which is not a usual funk instrument. The title cut is excellent. Jimmy Forrest (ts) is in top form here. With Lem Winchester (vib). — *Michael Erlewine*

The Honeydripper / Feb. 3, 1961 / Original Jazz Classics ✦✦✦✦
This CD reissue is possibly most significant for being guitarist Grant Green's recording debut. Organist Jack McDuff, the tough-toned tenor Jimmy Forrest, Green, and drummer Ben Dixon make for a potent and swinging combination. The repertoire (which has three standards and three originals, including "Whap") is comprised of blues, blues-oriented tunes (including "I Want a Little Girl"), and Henry Mancini's "Mr. Lucky." Due to the high-quality solos, which are full of personality, this reissue is highly recommended to fans of the genre. — *Scott Yanow*

Goodnight, It's Time to Go / Jul. 14, 1961 / Prestige ✦✦✦
McDuff on the Hammond B-3 along with Grant Green on guitar and Harold Vick on tenor sax. What more could you ask for? — *Michael Erlewine*

On with It / Dec. 1, 1961 / Prestige ✦✦✦
This forgotten session (organist Jack McDuff's fifth for Prestige as a leader) was not released initially until 1971 and has yet to be reissued on CD. With the exception of "Hey Lawdy Mama" and Ray Charles' "Drown In My Own Tears," the six selections are originals by the leader. In general, with the exception of the ballad "Dink's Dream," the music is essentially bluesy funk with fine tenor solos by Harold Vick (who switches to flute for the ballad), and good backup playing by guitarist Eddie Diehl and drummer Joe Dukes. The results are danceable, yet full of honest feeling and some chancetaking within the boundaries of soul-jazz. Pity that the date is so obscure. — *Scott Yanow*

Brother Jack Meets the Boss / Jan. 23, 1962 / Original Jazz Classics ✦✦✦✦
It is not too surprising that this is a very successful soul-jazz/hard bop outing for it teams organist Brother Jack McDuff with the great tenor Gene Ammons. The quintet (which also includes the notable Harold Vick on second tenor, guitarist Eddie Diehl, and drummer Joe Dukes) performs three basic McDuff tunes, Eddie "Cleanhead" Vinson's "Mr. Clean," Horace Silver's "Strollin'," and the still-viable swing standard "Christopher Columbus." Ammons, whose every note was always full of passion, fits in perfectly with McDuff's group; this accessible set has been reissued on CD. — *Scott Yanow*

Mellow Gravy / Jan. 23, 1962 / Prestige ✦✦✦
Smoking Gene Ammons (ts) and the great Hammond B-3 from McDuff. — *Ron Wynn*

The Best of Sonny Stitt with Jack McDuff / Feb. 16, 1962 + Sep. 17, 1963 / Prestige ✦✦✦✦
Jack McDuff and Sonny Stitt? You bet. I'll buy that anytime. Some nasty stuff. — *Michael Erlewine*

Screamin' / Oct. 23, 1962 / Original Jazz Classics ✦✦✦✦
Organist Jack McDuff teams up with his regular drummer Joe Dukes, altoist Leo Wright and guitarist Kenny Burrell for a spirited blues-oriented set which has been reissued on CD in the OJC series. "Soulful Drums," featuring Dukes' drum breaks, was a minor hit. Other selections on this generally fine organ date include spirited versions of "He's a Real Gone Guy," "After Hours" and "One O'Clock Jump" even if the title cut does not quite live up to its name. — *Scott Yanow*

Somethin' Slick / Jan. 8, 1963 / Prestige ✦✦✦
McDuff with Kenny Burrell on guitar and Harold Vick on tenor sax. — *Michael Erlewine*

Crash! / Jan. 8, 1963 + Feb. 26, 1963 / Prestige ✦✦✦✦
Organist Jack McDuff has long had a powerful style and the two former LPs that are combined on this single CD offer some strong examples of his accessible playing. In both cases McDuff is joined by guitarist Kenny Burrell (in fact one of the two sets was originally under Burrell's name), drummer Joe Dukes and occasionally Ray Barretto on congas. In addition Harold Vick is on tenor for most selections and Eric Dixon guests on tenor and flute during three songs. Highlights include a driving "How High the Moon," "Love Walked In," and a pair of original blues: "Smut" and "Our Miss Brooks." McDuff and Burrell work together quite well. This 76-minute CD is easily recommended to fans of the jazz organ. — *Scott Yanow*

★ **Brother Jack McDuff Live!** / Jun. 5, 1963 / Prestige ✦✦✦✦✦
Good as organist Jack McDuff's studio recordings are from the early '60s, it is his live sets that are truly exciting. This single CD combines together two former in-concert LPs and find McDuff leading a very strong group that features the young guitarist George Benson, tenorman Red Holloway, drummer Joe Dukes, and on a few numbers the second tenor of Harold Vick. The material (cooking blues, standards, Latin numbers and originals) has plenty of variety and drive. McDuff really pushes Benson and Holloway, and the music is both accessible and creative. — *Scott Yanow*

The Best of Brother Jack McDuff Live! / Jun. 5, 1963-Jul. 4 1964 / Prestige ✦✦✦
Textbook soul jazz from a founding father. Organist Brother Jack McDuff didn't invent the bluesy, riff- and backbeat-laden instrumental style called soul-jazz, but he sure helped make it popular. This anthology contains some early '60s McDuff material, including some tracks with guitarist George Benson. You can get all this somewhere else, but as a sampler or introductory package, it's a good collection. — *Ron Wynn*

Brother Jack Live! at the Jazz Workshop / Oct. 3, 1963 / Prestige ✦✦✦
Organist Jack McDuff enjoyed some pop recognition in 1963, when his combo recorded at The Jazz Workshop featured a young, blazing guitarist influenced by Wes Montgomery. George Benson's torrid licks and blues fills make this among his hottest albums, along with McDuff's always-smoking, relentless organ accompaniment, transitional lines, and solos. — *Ron Wynn*

Dynamic! / Feb. 6, 1964-Feb. 7, 1964 / Prestige ✦✦✦
With George Benson on guitar. — *AMG*

Legends of Acid Jazz / Jul. 1964 / Prestige ✦✦✦✦
While these 12 selections were originally released on six different albums between 1965 and 1969, all of them were cut during July 1964: nine at a New York studio session, and three (embellished by Benny Golson big-band arrangements) live at Stockholm. Thus it makes for a thematically coherent compilation, every track featuring a young George Benson on guitar and Joe Dukes on drums; Red Holloway plays tenor sax on all but two songs. It's top-drawer soul-jazz, recommended to those who might find some of McDuff's other releases too homogenous, as his B-3 travels through diverse moods here: the uptempo blues of "Scufflin'," the slow-burning funk of "Our Miss Brooks," and R&B/soul in the cover of "I Got a Woman." The closing "Lexington Avenue Line" is the oddest track, though quite a good one, sounding like a movie soundtrack theme with its dramatic strings. — *Richie Unterberger*

Do It Now! / Dec. 15, 1966 / Atlantic ✦✦✦
After a long string of Prestige recordings, organist Jack McDuff recorded a few LPs for Atlantic (all of which are currently out of print) in a similar soul-jazz style. The only change was that the length of the tunes tended to fall into the potential radio airplay range of four to six minutes. McDuff and his regular group of the period (Leo Johnson and Danny Turner on reeds,

underrated guitarist Melvin Sparks, and drummer Ray Appleton) swing their way through five of McDuff's originals and two obscurities with plenty of spirit, if not a great deal of originality. — *Scott Yanow*

Live It Up / 1967 / Sugar Hill ◆◆◆
Steaming soul-jazz, funk, blues, and ballads keyed by the whirling, soulful solos, bass pedal work, and direction of organist Jack McDuff. This was one of four fine albums he did for Atlantic in 1966 and 1967. — *Ron Wynn*

Down Home Style / 1969 / Blue Note ◆◆◆◆
A set of gritty electric funk and soulful blues, *Down Home Style* is an excellent showcase for Brother Jack McDuff's gripping, funky style. Inspired more by the tight grooves of Stax Records than be-bop, *Down Home Style* features McDuff leading a small group through a number of R&B grooves, ranging from the stuttering "The Vibrator" and dirty funk of "Butter (For Yo Popcorn)" to the slow blues of "Memphis in June." Occasionally, the group is augmented by a punchy horn section, but the record is designed as a showcase for McDuff's wild, intoxicating Hammond organ, and he runs with it, demonstrating every one of his tricks. — *Stephen Thomas Erlewine*

The Re-Entry / Mar. 1988 / 32 Jazz ◆◆◆◆
After a busy recording career in the '60s, organist Jack McDuff was erratically documented in commercial settings in the '70s and was in danger of being forgotten when he launched his successful comeback with this Muse album in 1988. At the age of 61, McDuff proved to still be in his prime as he burned on three originals, two obscurities, and "Laura" with both Houston Person and Ron Bridgewater on tenors, trumpeter Cecil Bridgewater, guitarist John Hart, and drummer Grady Tate. The music falls between hard bop and soul-jazz and should satisfy fans of those styles. — *Scott Yanow*

Color Me Blue / May 1991+Mar. 1992 / Concord Jazz ◆◆◆◆
Recent cuts showing that organist Jack McDuff can still stomp through bluesy wailers, pound the bass pedals, and lead a hot combo through funky, exuberant numbers. He's heading a group with former band members like guitarist George Benson and drummer Joe Dukes, plus saxophonist Red Holloway, guitarist Ron Eschete, and Phil Upchurch, among others. — *Ron Wynn*

The Heatin' System / Oct. 24, 1994-Oct. 25, 1994 / Cadet ◆◆◆
Plenty of funk, sax-wallop, and organ soul. — *Ron Wynn*

That's the Way I Feel About It / Dec. 16, 1996-Jan. 23, 1997 / Concord Jazz ◆◆◆
At times, McDuff demonstrates how soul-jazz organ stars used to make albums back in their '60s heyday, playing then-current pop hits like "The Age of Aquarius" and the theme from "Mission: Impossible" (which, thanks to cinema, was a hit all over again in 1996 when this CD was made). We also hear McDuff trying out his vocal cords for the first time on Louis Jordan's "Saturday Night Fish Fry"; actually, he merely talks the lyrics over the rhythm section—and at 70, he's entitled to this charming lark. Otherwise, this is another fine, home-cookin' soul-jazz session, with McDuff's Hammond B-3 burning at its usual low-intensity, high-blues-content level. Chris Potter dances around the organ on flutes, Andrew Beals and Jerry Weldon offer solid solos on alto and tenor respectively, and the rest of the Heatin' System runs the gamut from Latin to soul-deep grooves. Fans of the genre can buy with peace of mind. — *Richard S. Ginell*

Jimmy McGriff

b. Apr. 3, 1936, Philadelphia, PA
Organ / Soul-Jazz, Hard Bop, Groove
Jimmy McGriff calls himself a blues organ player—and that's the feeling he delivers in his best soul-jazz albums, with plenty of deep, in-the-pocket swing punctuated by grunting chords in the bass. Though both his parents were pianists, McGriff started on bass and sax, picking up drums, vibraphone, and ultimately piano as a teenager. After studying at Combe College of Music in Philadelphia and Juilliard, McGriff became an MP in Korea and worked on the Philadelphia police force for two years. After deciding upon music as a career, he studied organ with Jimmy Smith, Richard "Groove" Holmes, and Milt Buckner and scored a hit record "I Got a Woman" in 1962 (No. 20 on the pop charts). This led to a string of R&B hit singles for Sue Records, followed by a prolific series of organ sessions for Solid State (where another substantial hit, "The Worm," emerged in 1969), Blue Note, Capitol, Groove Merchant, and LRC. In the '70s, following the trends of the time, McGriff began to turn toward pop and fusion, adopting electronic keyboards with

mixed results. But when he signed with Milestone in 1983, McGriff returned to the Hammond B-3 organ and soul-jazz, anticipating the organ jazz revival with a series of strong, gritty albums, some of which feature Hank Crawford as co-leader. After bouncing around on a number of labels and idioms in the '90s, McGriff returned to Milestone in late 1996 with the soulfully sophisticated *The Dream Team*. — *Richard S. Ginell*

Groove: McGriff has several distinct periods and the quality of his recordings can depend upon which period you are listening in. For my money, his early stuff on the Sue label is his best and unique in organ jazz in that it typifies what every soul-jazz listener hopes to hear from early sixties Hammond organ. Albums like *Got a Woman, One of Mine, At the Apollo, Jimmy McGriff at the Organ*, and *Blues for Mr. Jimmy*—all originally released on the Sue and now available on Collectables label. The Collectables reissues have terrible sound quality; probably pulled from vinyl—who knows? In spite of the sound quality, the music is great and should be heard. These albums all have great cuts mixed in with mediocre or bad tracks. Even so, this is hi-impact driven McGriff that has little relation to much of his later work.

McGriff's work for Solid State and Groove Merchant under the production of Sonny Lester is for the most part well worth hearing. You can almost go by looking at how many players are on the session—the less the better. In particular, in the late '70s, McGriff's larger band material should be avoided since this is pop-oriented and has little jazz content.

Then comes McGriff's excellent work for Milestone, albums like *Countdown, Skywalk, State of the Art, The Starting Five, Blue to the Bone, Steppin Up*, and his collaboration with Hank Crawford, *Soul Survivors*. Produced by blues-funk expert Bob Porter, this series finds McGriff playing jazz and soul jazz and catering less to the pop market. Although never reaching the searing intensity of his early work on Sue, this is all very listenable.

In the early 1990s, McGriff on Headstart is more synthesizer-drenched pop pap. His Telarc material in the mid-'90s with alto-saxist Hank Crawford is once again worth picking up. — *Michael Erlewine*

☆ **I've Got a Woman** / 1963 / Collectables ◆◆◆◆◆
McGriff's first album is great. The title cut was in the top 20 in 1962. Also on the same album is "M.G. Blues" and "All About My Girl." This session features McGriff, Richard Easley on drums, and Walter Miller on guitar. Hi-impact early McGriff is the still the best, and this is the album that started it all, on the Sue label. Three cuts available on the Collectables CD *A Toast to Jimmy McGriff's Golden Classics*. — *Michael Erlewine*

★ **At the Apollo** / 1963 / Collectables ◆◆◆◆◆
The third album from McGriff on the Sue label was recorded live at New York's Apollo Theater in 1963. It features McGriff with Rudolph Johnson on tenor sax, Larry Frazier on guitar, and Willie Jenkins on drums. Contains a great versin of "Red Sails in the Sunset" and "A Thing for Jug." — *Michael Erlewine*

Jimmy McGriff at the Organ / 1963 / Sue ◆◆◆
McGriff with Rudolph Johnson on soprano and tenor sax, Larry Frazier on guitar, and Jimmie Smith on drums. This album contains the classic McGriff cut "Kiko," "That's All," and "Hello Betty." This is drum/sax driven McGriff at his best. — *Michael Erlewine*

Topkapi / 1964-1965 / Sue ◆◆◆
This finds McGriff with pre-recorded tracks with a horn section, guitar, bass, drums, and a string section. The material was arranged and directed by Fred Norman. The album consists of 12 movie and TV themes with McGriff and "orchestra." The orchestra sounds like Muzak, but McGriff sounds like McGriff. How the two got together beats me. — *Michael Erlewine*

Blues for Mister Jimmy / 1965 / Collectables ◆◆◆
His last date for the Sue label is a trio, McGriff with Larry Frazier on guitar and Jimmie Smith on drums. Nine bluesy tunes including "Turn Blue," a classic McGriff instrumental. — *Michael Erlewine*

A Bag Full of Soul / 1966 / Solid State ◆◆◆
McGriff with funk guitarist Thornell Schwartz. — *Michael Erlewine*

The Worm / Sep. 1968 / Solid State ◆◆◆
A high point of soul-jazz and funk. Both commercial and substantial. — *Ron Wynn*

The Funkiest Little Band in the Land / 1969 / LRC ◆◆◆
This is a collection of McGriff with small bands during the years from 1968

to 1974, before he went to the large orchestra format. Produced by Sonny Lester, many of these appeared on the Groove Merchant label. Includes a lot of funky stuff with titles like "Super Funk," "Fat Cakes," "Groove Fly," and "Dig On it." There are 13 cuts and plenty of vintage McGriff. —*Michael Erlewine*

Electric Funk / Sep. 1969 / Blue Note ◆◆◆
The title of *Electric Funk* may lead you to believe that it's a set of unrepentant, rampaging hard funk, but that's not quite the case. The record is laid-back but undeniably funky, with Jimmy McGriff and electric pianist Horace Ott leading an unnamed group through a set of soul workouts. It's not jazz, it's jazzy soul, and it's among the funkiest of any soul-jazz records from the late '60s, filled with stuttering drum breaks, lite fuzz guitars, elastic bass, smoldering organ, and punchy, slightly incongruous horn charts. —*Stephen Thomas Erlewine*

Let's Stay Together / 1972 / Simitar ◆◆◆
McGriff with funk guitarist Thornell Schwartz. —*Michael Erlewine*

Come Together / 1973 / Groove Merchant ◆◆
McGriff and Richard Groove Holmes on the same ticket. —*Michael Erlewine*

Main Squeeze / 1976 / Groove Merchant ◆◆◆
McGriff with the funky guitar of Jimmy Ponder and Connie Lester on alto sax. —*Michael Erlewine*

City Lights / Dec. 19, 1980+Feb. 4, 1981 / Jazz America ◆◆◆◆
To a large extent, organist Jimmy McGriff made his mark recording with large bands in the mid- to late 1960s, often for the Solid State label. His career became a bit more aimless in the late '70s, when the organ was out of fashion, but he returned to prime form on this album. In reality, McGriff's playing was always fairly similar to Jimmy Smith's, and although not that distinctive, he found his own sound within the Smith tradition of groovin' organists. This LP for the short-lived Jazz America label matches McGriff with four horns (including tenor saxophonist Harold Vick and trumpeter Danny Moore) and a four-piece rhythm section which includes guitarist Jimmy Ponder and drummer Idris Muhammad. The repertoire is fairly typical for soul-jazz, including "Teach Me Tonight" and some funky blues, and the music is pleasing. —*Scott Yanow*

Movin' Upside the Blues / Dec. 19, 1980-Jan. 24, 1981 / Jazz America ◆◆◆◆
For his second Jazz America LP, organist Jimmy McGriff is heard on one selection (Kenny Burrell's "All Day Long") left over from the first session (which features a septet including Harold Vick on tenor and trumpeter Danny Moore), plus four numbers from 1981 with altoist Arnold Sterling, guitarist Jimmy Ponder, trumpeter Bill Hardman, and Vick. As usual, most of the music is blues-based, although the inclusion of "Moonlight Serenade" in this soul-jazz setting is a pleasant surprise. —*Scott Yanow*

Countdown / Apr. 27, 1983-Apr. 28, 1983 / Milestone ◆◆◆◆
His first for Milestone. Produced by Bob Porter, McGriff with two saxes, trombone, guitar, and drums for what the liner notes call a "big band sound" combo. Plenty of good funky organ. Some of the numbers are a little too smooth (too many horns) for my taste. —*Michael Erlewine*

Skywalk / Mar. 19, 1984-Mar. 20, 1984 / Milestone ◆◆◆
Organist Jimmy McGriff's second Milestone recording is his only one for the label that has not yet been reissued on CD. Heard with a nonet on three numbers, a quintet on two songs, and an 11-piece outfit during his "Skywalk," McGriff is in his usual fine form on such tunes as "Jersey Bounce" and "Let's Stay Together." Outside of altoist Bill Easley and guitarist Jimmy Ponder, the sidemen are pretty obscure, although quite capable in this setting. —*Scott Yanow*

The Starting Five / Oct. 14, 1986-Oct. 15, 1986 / Milestone ◆◆◆◆
Here is McGriff with two terrific blues honkin' sax masters—Rusty Bryant and David "Fathead" Newman. Add Mel Brown and Wayne Boyd on guitar plus Bernard Purdie on drums and you have a recipe for funk. Produced by Bob Porter, this is perhaps the best of McGriff's Milestone output. —*Michael Erlewine*

Blue to the Bone / Jul. 19, 1988-Jul. 20, 1988 / Milestone ◆◆◆◆
McGriff with Bill Easley on sax, Melvin Sparks on guitar, Bernard Purdie on drums, and Al Grey on trombone. The trombone is not that often found in the small-organ combo format and may not appeal to everyone. Smooth, yet funky. —*Michael Erlewine & Ron Wynn*

You Ought to Think About Me / 1990 / Headfirst ◆◆◆
Although Jimmy McGriff temporarily switched labels from Milestone to Headfirst in 1990, his brand of swinging funk and blues-oriented jazz was virtually unchanged. Utilizing a quintet that includes the reeds of Bill Easley, trumpeter Stanton Wilson, and guitarist Rodney Jones, McGriff explores a wide-ranging set filled with originals and such tunes as "The Way You Look Tonight," "America the Beautiful," "Ain't No Mountain High Enough," and a medley of "One O'Clock Jump" and "C Jam Blues." The results are predictably excellent. —*Scott Yanow*

On the Blue Side / May 1990 / Milestone ◆◆◆◆
An updated version of the vintage McGriff formula: bluesy, soulful organ fare with a balance struck between jazz sensibility and a funk/R&B groove. —*Ron Wynn*

In a Blue Mood / 1991 / K-Tel ◆◆
One of his albums on Headfirst, after leaving Milestone and the great production work of Bob Porter. McGriff on organ and keyboards plus a group with synthesizers, sax, guitar, drums, vocals, and what-not make this more pop-oriented fare than organ funk. Where's Bob Porter when you need him. —*Michael Erlewine*

Right Turn on Blues / Jan. 22, 1994-Jan. 23, 1994 / Telarc ◆◆◆◆
There was virtually no prior planning for this meeting between organist Jimmy McGriff and altoist Hank Crawford, but none was needed. The veterans had already recorded four prior albums together, so they simply jammed through blues, ballads, and a few basic originals without any difficulty; Crawford could play this material blindfolded. McGriff sets the grooves expertly with his foot-pedal basswork, with assistance from guitarist Rodney Jones and drummer Jesse Hameen. The overall result is an enthusiastic session of foot-tapping music. No real surprises occur, but lovers of hard-swinging organ combos have nothing to complain about. —*Scott Yanow*

Blues Groove / Jul. 21, 1995-Jul. 22, 1995 / Telarc ◆◆◆◆
Organist Jimmy McGriff and altoist Hank Crawford always make for a potent team. With guitarist Wayne Boyd and drummer Vance James completing the quartet, McGriff and Crawford explore an appealing mixture of blues, soulful ballads, and riff tunes. Few surprises occur but many of the songs (particularly "Movie' Upside the Blues," "The Sermon," "When I Fall in Love," and "Mercy, Mercy, Mercy") are fairly memorable. The fans of these fine players will not be disappointed. —*Scott Yanow*

The Dream Team / Aug. 19, 1996 / Milestone ◆◆◆◆
Jimmy McGriff moves back to the Milestone label in style with a great soul-jazz quintet, with whom he recorded one of his best Milestone albums, *The Starting Five*. This time, with no apologies to the notorious O.J. Simpson legal staff, he calls his quintet "the Dream Team"—and for this kind of music, indeed they are. McGriff strokes his Hammond XB-3 keys and pedals with a relaxed in-the-pocket feeling; with this group, he doesn't have to push, nor should he. David "Fathead" Newman holds down the tenor chair, Red Holloway (replacing the late Rusty Bryant) is on alto and tenor, Mel Brown plays really tasty guitar, and Bernard Purdie powers the drums. Check out the effortlessly sauntering, hip-swinging boogaloo of "Fleetwood Stroll" or the slow, deeply soulful treatment of Willie Nelson's country standard "Funny How Time Slips Away" or the oooh-ain't-that-funky "McGriffin." Everybody swings, everybody listens intuitively to each other and feels the down-home churchy grooves, and they recorded it all in one day at Rudy Van Gelder's studio. This has the ingredients for ranking as an instant classic in this idiom. —*Richard S. Ginell*

Toast to Golden Classics / Collectables ◆◆◆◆
This is a compilation of ten cuts taken from the six early Sue albums, one or two from each. The sound is bad, but it will give you a taste of the Sue material—all the best cuts. These early Sue albums are now all available on Collectables and worth hearing, despite the sound. —*Michael Erlewine*

Jazz Collector Edition / LaserLight ◆◆◆
This is a reissue of two 1970s McGriff albums, *Groove Grease* (1971) and *Main Squeeze* (1974) originally released on the Groove Merchant label. The first has McGriff with Jimmy Ponder (g) and Eddie Gladden (d). The second album has mixed personnel including Everett Barksdale (g), Cliff Davis (sax), Murray Wilson (tpt), and Johnny Board (baritone sax). In general, nice, laid-back playing. —*Michael Erlewine*

One of Mine / Sue-Collectables ✦✦✦
His second album, again on Sue. This has been reissued on Collectables. This session has McGriff with Morris Dow on lead guitar and harmonic, Larry Frazier on rhythm guitar, and Willie "Saint" Jenkins on drums. It features the title cut and "The Last Minute"—ten hi-energy cuts. —*Michael Erlewine*

Jimmy McGriff/Groove Holmes: Double Exposure / LRC ✦✦✦
This album contains two albums, one by Groove Holmes and the other by Jimmy McGriff. They do not play together here. McGriff is with George Freeman on guitar, Eddie Gladden on drums, and James Peacock on conga. Six cuts by McGriff and five by Groove Holmes. —*Michael Erlewine*

Greatest Hits / Blue Note ✦✦✦✦
Blue Note's *Greatest Hits* doesn't limit itself to the recordings Jimmy McGriff made for the label during the late '60s and early '70s. Instead, it culls from his Sue, Veep, and Solid State recordings as well, making it a definitive overview of his career as a gritty, funky singles artist. And, as *Greatest Hits* demonstrates, McGriff could create a monster groove, making his singles intoxicating slices of funky jazz. All of his R&B hits—"I've Got a Woman," "All About My Girl," "Kiko," "The Worm"—are here, as are lesser-known singles and terrific album tracks, resulting in a compilation that isn't just a terrific introduction for neophytes, but also a useful retrospective for collectors. —*Stephen Thomas Erlewine*

Oliver Nelson

b. Jun. 4, 1932, St. Louis, MO, **d.** Oct. 27, 1975, Los Angeles, CA
Alto Saxophone, Tenor Saxophone / Post-Bop, Hard Bop, Groove
Oliver Nelson was a distinctive soloist on alto, tenor, and even soprano but his writing eventually overshadowed his playing skills. He became a professional early on in 1947, playing with the Jeter-Pillars Orchestra and with St. Louis big bands headed by George Hudson and Nat Towles. In 1951 he arranged and played second alto for Louis Jordan's big band and followed with a period in the Navy and four years at a university. After moving to New York, Nelson worked briefly with Erskine Hawkins, Wild Bill Davis, and Louie Bellson (the latter on the West Coast). In addition to playing with Quincy Jones' Orchestra (1960-61), between 1959-61 Nelson recorded six small-group albums and a big-band date; those gave him a lot of recognition and respect in the jazz world. *Blues and the Abstract Truth* (from 1961) is considered a classic and helped to popularize a song that Nelson had included on a slightly earlier Eddie "Lockjaw" Davis session, "Stolen Moments." He also fearlessly matched wits effectively with the explosive Eric Dolphy on a pair of quintet sessions. But good as his playing was, Nelson was in greater demand as an arranger, writing for big-band dates of Jimmy Smith, Wes Montgomery, and Billy Taylor among others. By 1967 when he moved to Los Angeles, Nelson was working hard in the studios, writing for television and movies. He occasionally appeared with a big band, wrote a few ambitious works, and recorded jazz on an infrequent basis, but Oliver Nelson was largely lost to jazz a few years before his unexpected death at age 43 from a heart attack. —*Scott Yanow*

Meet Oliver Nelson / Oct. 30, 1959 / Original Jazz Classics ✦✦✦✦
Oliver Nelson's debut as a leader found him at the age of 27 already a distinctive and skilled tenor-saxophonist. For this quintet set (reissued on CD in the OJC series), Nelson teams up with the veteran trumpeter Kenny Dorham, pianist Ray Bryant, bassist Wendell Marshall, and drummer Art Taylor for four of his originals plus the ballads "Passion Flower" and "What's New." Although none of these Nelson tunes caught on, this was an impressive beginning to a short but productive career and gives one a strong example of the multi-talented Nelson's tenor playing. —*Scott Yanow*

Takin' Care of Business / Mar. 22, 1960 / Original Jazz Classics ✦✦✦✦
Oliver Nelson would gain his greatest fame later in his short life as an arranger/composer but this superior session puts the emphasis on his distinctive tenor and alto playing. In a slightly unusual group (with vibraphonist Lem Winchester, organist Johnny "Hammond" Smith, bassist George Tucker, and drummer Roy Haynes), Nelson improvises a variety of well-constructed but spontaneous solos; his unaccompanied spots on "All the Way" and his hard-charging playing on the medium-tempo blues "Groove" are two of the many highpoints. Nelson remains a vastly underrated saxophonist and all six performances on this recommended CD reissue (four of them his originals) are excellent. —*Scott Yanow*

Nocturne / Aug. 23, 1960 / Original Jazz Classics ✦✦✦
This relaxed set (originally on the Prestige subsidiary Moodsville) puts the emphasis on ballads and slower material. Nelson (switching between alto and tenor) is joined by vibraphonist Lem Winchester, pianist Richard Wyands, bassist George Duvivier and drummer Roy Haynes for four standards and three of his originals (including the swinging "Bob's Blues"). Everyone plays well but the intentional lack of mood variation keeps this release from being all that essential. —*Scott Yanow*

Soul Battle / Sep. 9, 1960 / Original Jazz Classics ✦✦✦✦
This intriguing session matches together three powerful tenor players: Oliver Nelson, King Curtis (in a rare jazz outing), and Jimmy Forrest. With fine backup work by pianist Gene Casey, bassist George Duvivier, and drummer Roy Haynes, the tenors battle to a draw on a set of blues and basic material (including a fine version of "Perdido"). This CD reissue adds one selection ("Soul Street") from the same date to the original LP program and is easily recommended to fans of big-toned tenors and straightahead swinging. —*Scott Yanow*

★ **The Blues and the Abstract Truth** / 1961 / Impulse! ✦✦✦✦✦
This was Oliver Nelson's finest recording and one of the top jazz albums of 1961, a true classic. The lineup is an inspired one: Nelson on tenor and alto, Eric Dolphy doubling on alto and flute, a young trumpeter named Freddie Hubbard, baritonist George Barrow for section parts, pianist Bill Evans, bassist Paul Chambers, and drummer Roy Haynes. The contrasting voices of the soloists really uplift these superior compositions which are highlighted by "Stolen Moments" (a future standard), the fun "Hoe-Down," and "Yearnin." Dolphy cuts everyone but Nelson and Hubbard are also in top form. —*Scott Yanow*

Main Stem / Aug. 25, 1961 / Original Jazz Classics ✦✦✦✦
Unlike most of Oliver Nelson's recordings, this one has the feel of a jam session. A CD reissue of a Prestige set, Nelson (on tenor and alto) teams up with trumpeter Joe Newman (in exciting form), pianist Hank Jones, bassist George Duvivier, drummer Charlie Persip, and Ray Barretto on congas for two superior standards ("Mainstem" and "Tangerine") and four of Nelson's more basic originals. The spirited solos of Nelson and Newman are strong reasons to get this colorful session. —*Scott Yanow*

David "Fathead" Newman

b. Feb. 24, 1933, Dallas, TX
Flute, Tenor Saxophone, Alto Saxophone / Soul-Jazz, Hard Bop, Groove
As a teenager, David Newman played professionally around Dallas and Fort Worth with Charlie Parker's mentor, Buster Smith, and also with Ornette Coleman in a band led by tenor saxophonist Red Connors. In the early '50s, Newman worked locally with such R&B musicians as Lowell Fulson and T-Bone Walker. In 1952, Newman formed his longest-lasting and most important musical association with Ray Charles, who had played piano in Fulson's group. Newman stayed with Charles' band from 1954-64, while concurrently recording as a leader and a sideman with, among others, his hometown associate, tenor saxophonist James Clay. Upon leaving Charles, Newman stayed in Dallas for two years. He then moved to New York, where he recorded under King Curtis and Eddie Harris; he also played many commercial and soul dates. Newman returned to Charles for a brief time in 1970-71; from 1972-4 he played with Red Garland and Herbie Mann. Newman parlayed the renown he gained from his experience with Charles into a fairly successful recording career. In the '60s and '70s, he recorded a series of heavily orchestrated, pop-oriented sides for Atlantic, and in the '80s he led the occasional hard bop session, but Newman's metier was as an ace accompanist. Throughout his career he recorded with a variety of non-jazz artists; Newman's brawny, arrogant tenor sound graced the albums of Aretha Franklin, Dr. John, and many others. It is, in fact, Newman's terse, earthy improvisations with Charles that remain his most characteristic work. —*Chris Kelsey*

★ **House of David: The David "Fathead" Anthology** / 1952-1989 / Rhino ✦✦✦✦✦
There have not been many saxophonists and flutists more naturally soulful than David "Fathead" Newman. This two-disc set captures Newman at his best. He never really was an album artist; each LP has had its nuggets, and that's what this captures. It has Newman wailing the blues, then stretching out in the Ray Charles band. He covers a Beatles tune, then an Aaron Neville

number. He backs Aretha Franklin and pays homage to the great Buster Cooper. This is one anthology that can be recommended without hesitation, because there aren't going to be many complete Newman albums coming down the reissue pike. — *Ron Wynn*

Fathead: Ray Charles Presents David Newman / Nov. 5, 1958 / Atlantic ✦✦✦✦
The talented David Newman, who alternates on this album between tenor and alto, made his debut as a leader at this session. Since he was in Ray Charles' band at the time, Newman was able to use Charles on piano along with Hank Crawford (here called Bennie Crawford) on baritone, trumpeter Marcus Belgrave, bassist Edgar Willis, and drummer Milton Turner. The music is essentially soulful bebop with the highlights including "Hard Times," "Fathead," "Mean To Me," and "Tin Tin Deo." Everyone plays well and this was a fine start to David "Fathead" Newman's career. — *Scott Yanow*

It's Mister Fathead / Nov. 5, 1958-Mar. 4, 1964 / 32 Jazz ✦✦✦
Although best-known as a tenor saxophonist, David "Fathead" Newman is an equally talented altoist and flutist. This 1998 double-CD brings back Fathead's first four sets as a leader (originally made for the Atlantic label) and the dates give one a definitive portrait of Newman in a variety of jazz settings. *Ray Charles Presents David Newman* (which is highlighted by "Hard Times," "Weird Beard," "Sweet Eyes," and "Mean To Me") teams the leader with trumpeter Marcus Belgrave, Hank Crawford (who sticks to baritone), and pianist Ray Charles in a sextet. *Straight Ahead* has Newman joined by pianist Wynton Kelly, bassist Paul Chambers, and drummer Charlie Persip. The 1960 date starts off with "Batista's Groove" (which borrows some of its ideas from "Giant Steps") and sometimes has Newman showing off the influence of John Coltrane on tenor. However his flute playing on "Night of Nisan" is quite original and Newman holds his own with the rather illustrious rhythm section. *Fathead Comes On*, performed by a quintet, is most notable for trumpeter Belgrave's consistently inventive playing while *House of David* (from 1967) finds the leader recalling Stanley Turrentine a bit with a quartet also featuring organist Kossie Gardner and guitarist Ted Dunbar. Even with a few lightweight tracks on the latter session, the music overall is rewarding with "The Holy Land" being a highlight. Highly recommended. — *Scott Yanow*

Straight Ahead / Dec. 21, 1960 / Atlantic ✦✦✦✦
Newman with Wynton Kelly on piano, Paul Chambers on bass, and Charlie Persip on drums. — *AMG*

Heads Up / 1961 / Atlantic ✦✦✦
For this superior showcase, tenorman David Newman (who also plays some alto and flute) jams on four jazz standards and his own "Heads Up" and "For Buster" while joined by a top-notch rhythm section consisting of vibraphonist Steve Nelson, pianist Kirk Lightsey, bassist David Williams, and drummer Eddie Gladden. Although often placed in more tightly arranged settings throughout his career, Newman really excels in a small-group format, where his soulful tones and expertise at jamming over common chord changes are best displayed. This was one of his better sets, even though the album is not very well known. — *Scott Yanow*

Lonely Avenue / Nov. 2, 1971-Nov. 4, 1971 / Atlantic ✦✦✦
An OK but not too essential LP, this effort by David Newman (heard on tenor and flute) leans more to the R&B side, featuring Newman with an oversized rhythm section that includes vibraphonist Roy Ayers (who also plays keyboards), Bags Costello on organ and piano, and guitarist Cornell Dupree. The tunes, mostly recent originals (also the traditional "Precious Lord") are interpreted soulfully by Newman, but little memorable occurs. — *Scott Yanow*

Back to Basics / May 1977-Nov. 1977 / Milestone ✦✦
A '91 CD reissue of a late '70s session by tenor saxophonist and flutist David Newman, which emphasized his patented soul-jazz and blues while matching Newman with different players on various tracks, rather than having a fixed rhythm section. The top guest stars included keyboardists Hilton Ruiz and George Cables and guitarist Lee Ritenour. — *Ron Wynn*

Still Hard Times / Apr. 1982 / Muse ✦✦✦✦
Saxophonist in his prime. Tuneful and exuberant. — *Michael G. Nastos*

Fire! Live at the Village Vanguard / Dec. 22, 1988-Dec. 23, 1988 / Atlantic ✦✦✦✦
For this excellent all-around date, David Newman and a fine rhythm section

(pianist Kirk Lightsey, vibraphonist Steve Nelson, bassist David Williams, and drummer Marvin "Smitty" Smith) are joined by tenor saxophonist Stanley Turrentine on "Wide Open Spaces" (a tune that years earlier Newman had recorded with fellow tenor James Clay), altoist Hank Crawford on "Lonely Avenue," and both Mr. T. and Crawford on two other songs. In addition, Newman takes "Filthy McNasty" as a flute feature and is showcased on the opening "Old Devil Moon." An enjoyable set of soulful, straight-ahead jazz. — *Scott Yanow*

Harold Ousley (Harold Lomax Ousley)

b. Jan. 33, 1929, Chicago, IL
Tenor Saxophone, Flute / Blues Jazz, Groove, Swing, Soul-Jazz
A competent funk and soul jazz saxophonist and flutist, Harold Ousley's bluesy playing on organ combo dates, rock 'n' roll tunes and backing vocalists was stronger than much of what he did when leading groups. His albums were often uneven, both in terms of compositional quality and playing. Ousley began his professional career in the '40s, and at one point backed Billie Holiday. During the '50s, he played with King Kolax and Gene Ammons and worked in circus bands. Ousley backed Dinah Washington at the 1958 Newport Jazz Festival, an engagement that led to him winning a recording deal. He traveled to Paris the next year with a song revue, then worked with Clark Terry, Howard McGhee, Machito, and Joe Newman in the '60s. Ousley began leading his own groups and recording with organ combos, notably Brother Jack McDuff, in the mid-'60s. He worked with Lionel Hampton and Count Basie in the '70s. Ousley currently has no releases available on CD. — *Ron Wynn*

Tenor Sax / 1961 / Bethlehem ✦✦✦✦

● **The People's Groove** / 1972 / Muse ✦✦✦✦
Saxophonist who worked with Dinah Washington. The all-star cast includes Ray McKinney (b), Bobby Rose (g), and Norman Simmons (p). — *Michael G. Nastos*

Don Patterson (Donald B. Patterson)

b. Jul. 22, 1936, Columbus, OH, d. Feb. 10, 1988, Philadelphia, PA
Organ / Soul-Jazz, Hard Bop, Groove
Columbus Ohio born Don Patterson began his musical career as a pianist, inspired by Erroll Garner. A solid soul-jazz, blues and hard bop organist with a pianistic background, Patterson didn't utilize the pedals or play with as much rhythmic drive as some other stylists, but developed a satisfactory alternative approach. Patterson's organ solos were smartly played, and more melodic than explosive. He switched from piano in 1956 after hearing Jimmy Smith. Patterson made his organ debut in 1959, and worked with Sonny Stitt, Eddie "Lockjaw" Davis, Gene Ammons and Wes Montgomery in the early '60s. He recorded with Ammons, Stitt, and Eric Kloss in the early and mid-'60s. Patterson worked often in a duo with Billy James and made several recordings in the '60s and '70s as a leader. He and Al Grey worked together extensively in the '80s. Patterson recorded as a leader for Prestige and Muse. He has one session available on CD. — *Ron Wynn and Michael G. Nastos*
Groove: Unfortunately, like many of the great soul-jazz players, not much Don Patterson has been released on CD. You will find him backing up any number of other players however like Sonny Stitt and Eddie "Lockjaw" Davis. — *Michael Erlewine*

Goin' Down Home / Jan. 22, 1963 / Cadet ✦✦✦✦
Trio with Patterson on the Hammond B-3, Paul Weeden on guitar, and Billy James on drums. Includes the Nat Adderley tune "Worksong." — *Michael Erlewine*

The Exciting New Organ of Don Patterson / May 12, 1964 / Prestige ✦✦✦✦
Great album with Booker Ervin on tenor sax. — *Michael Erlewine*

Legends of Acid Jazz / May 12, 1964 / Prestige ✦✦✦✦
Among all the practitioners of soul-jazz during the genre heyday of the late '60s into the '70s, Hammond B-3 organ groovemeister Don Patterson and modern Texas tenor Booker Ervin (also a veteran of jazz ensembles led by Randy Weston and Charles Mingus) are among those usually overlooked. Yet the pair teamed up to release several albums during that time that were, if not standards of the genre precisely, full of vitality and fever—Ervin's playing, especially, often sounded so emotional and combustible that it seemed like he was suffering a nervous breakdown through his horn, perhaps a resi-

due of his time with Mingus. *Legends of Acid Jazz: Don Patterson / Booker Ervin* surfs the cream of three mid-'60s recording sessions: in a trio setting with drummer Billy James, all five selections from *The Exciting New Organ of Don Patterson*, including one of Miles Davis' early signature tunes, "Oleo" (actually a Sonny Rollins composition); the title track from *Hip Cake Walk*, a 17-minute monument to the soulful power of organ that endured as Patterson's most-beloved hip-swiveler (featuring Leonard Houston on alto sax); and "Love Me With All Your Heart" from *Patterson's People*. *Legends of Acid Jazz: Don Patterson / Booker Ervin* suffers only slightly from a program that leans heavily toward the mainstream—"Love Me With …" goes more than six minutes, and "When Johnny Comes Marching Home" nearly eleven. — *Chris Slawecki*

The Boss Men / Dec. 1965 / Prestige ◆◆◆
Don Patterson with Sonny Stitt on alto sax and Billy James on drums. —*AMG*

Mellow Soul / May 10, 1967 / Prestige ◆◆◆
A trio date with David Fathead Newman on sax and flute plus Billy James on drums. —*AMG*

Four Dimensions / Aug. 25, 1967 / Prestige ◆◆◆
Patterson with Houston Person (sax), Pat Martino (g), and Billy James (d). —*AMG*

● **Dem New York Blues** / Jun. 5, 1968 + Jun. 2, 1969 / Prestige ◆◆◆◆
Despite claims to the contrary, organist Don Patterson was very much of the Jimmy Smith school, a hard-driving player with fine improvising skills but lacking a distinctive sound of his own. This CD (which reissues two complete LPs) features Patterson in prime form in a quintet with trumpeter Blue Mitchell, Junior Cook on tenor, and guitarist Pat Martino, and with a separate group that features trumpeter Virgil Jones and both George Coleman and Houston Person on tenors. Although "Oh Happy Day" is a throwaway, Patterson's spirited renditions of the blues and standards make this a fairly definitive example of his talents. —*Scott Yanow*

Funk You / Sep. 24, 1968 / Prestige ◆◆◆
With Charles McPherson on alto sax, Sonny Stitt on alto/tenor, Pat Martino on guitar, and Billy James on drums. —*AMG*

The Return Of … / Oct. 30, 1972 / Muse ◆◆◆◆
Quartet with Eddie Daniels (ts), Ted Dunbar (g), and Freddie Waits (d). Any Don Patterson album is worthwhile. —*Michael G. Nastos*

The Genius of the B-3 / Oct. 30, 1972 / Muse ◆◆◆◆
A fine album (fast and slow) with Patterson in excellent form. There is some very nice soul-jazz here. CD clocks out at 43 minutes. —*Michael Erlewine*

These Are Soulful Days / Sep. 17, 1973 / Muse ◆◆◆◆
Quartet with this great Hammond B-3 organist, Jimmy Heath (sax), Pat Martino (g) and A. Heath (d). —*Michael G. Nastos*

Movin' Up / Jan. 31, 1976 / Muse ◆◆◆◆
At the time that Don Patterson recorded this album (his next-to-last as a leader), organ records had become fairly rare. The organ was in danger of being replaced altogether by synthesizers, and even Patterson utilizes an Arp String Ensemble in places. However, his playing on the six numbers is very much in the Jimmy Smith tradition. Altoist Richie Cole co-stars, and Vic Juris (Cole's guitarist), and drummer Billy James are both major assets. Cole contributed three of the six numbers, including "Trenton Makes the World Takes" and the "Cherokee"-based "Harold's House of Jazz," so this is very much a bop-oriented set. "The Good Life" is a feature for Patterson without Cole; also on the LP (not yet reissued on CD) are Horace Silver's "Room 608" and the theme song from the movie *The World of Susie Wong*. A fine effort that should please hard bop and soul-jazz collectors. —*Scott Yanow*

Big John Patton

b. Jul. 12, 1935, Kansas City, MO
Organ / Hard Bop, Soul-Jazz, Groove
Big John Patton was not nearly as well-known as other warriors in the organ jazz field of the '60s, yet he could be counted upon for a reliable, even fervent collection of blues and bop-saturated licks and steady bass lines on the Hammond B-3. Mostly self-taught with some rudimentary instruction from his mother, Patton started playing piano in 1948, eventually landing a gig with the Lloyd Price touring band from 1954 to 1959 before moving to New York. Once there, he began to make the transition from piano to organ, learning a

lot from future two recording mates, drummer Ben Dixon and guitarist Grant Green. He recorded with Lou Donaldson for Blue Note from 1962 to 1964 and, after impressing Blue Note founder Alfred Lion, made the first of a string of albums as a leader for the label in 1963. Interestingly, many of his albums, though scheduled for release, never saw the light of day until after Blue Note's resurrection in 1985. When the Hammond B-3 and soul-jazz went out of fashion in the '70s, Patton's career went into eclipse as well, and he settled in East Orange, NJ. But shortly after he started recording again in 1983, Patton was rediscovered by a younger generation, particularly the avant-garde figure John Zorn, who began using his sound out of its usual context on recordings like *The Big Gundown* and *Spillane*'s "Two-Lane Highway." —*Richard S. Ginell*

Along Came John / Apr. 5, 1963 / Blue Note ◆◆◆◆
By the time John Patton recorded *Along Came John*, his debut as a leader, he had already become a familiar name around the Blue Note studios. He, guitarist Grant Green, and drummer Ben Dixon had become the label's regular soul-jazz rhythm section, playing on sessions by Lou Donaldson, Don Wilkerson, and Harold Vick, among others. They had developed an intuitive, empathetic interplay that elevated many of their sessions to near-greatness, at least in the realm of soul-jazz. That's one of the reasons why *Along Came John* is so successful—the three know each other so well that their grooves are totally natural, which makes them quite appealing. These original compositions may not all be memorable, but the band's interaction, improvisation, and solos are. Tenor saxophonists Fred Jackson and Harold Vick provide good support, as well, but the show belongs to Patton, Green, and Dixon, who once again prove they are one of the finest soul-jazz combos of their era. —*Stephen Thomas Erlewine*

Blue John / Jul. 11, 1963-Aug. 2, 1963 / Blue Note ◆◆◆◆
This is a fairly bright bit of soul-jazz, not quite as heavy as your normal soul-jazz session. There is nice guitar by Grant Green. The trumpet of Tommy Turrentine and the stritch (two saxophones braced together) of George Braith are not your usual soul-jazz instruments. The dual-horn sound of the stritch ends up sounding too much like honking car horns for my taste. It is hard to stay in the groove in the middle of the freeway. But any John Patton is worth having. —*Michael Erlewine*

The Way I Feel / Jun. 19, 1964 / Blue Note ◆◆◆
For his third album, Big John Patton decided to expand his band to quintet. Retaining the services of his longtime colleagues, guitarist Grant Green and drummer Ben Dixon, he hired tenor saxophonist Fred Jackson (who also played on *Along Came John*) and trumpeter Richard Williams. The combination of two horns can occasionally overshadow the groove Patton, Green, and Dixon lay down, but for the most part, the musicians augment the music instead of detracting from it. Nevertheless, the combo never manages to match the peaks of *Along Came John* and *Blue John*. There are several fine moments on the record, and Green and Patton are typically enjoyable, but the record overall is a slight disappointment after its two predecessors. —*Stephen Thomas Erlewine*

Oh Baby / Mar. 8, 1965 / Blue Note ◆◆◆◆
Patton's fourth album for Blue Note. Big John Patton with Grant Green on guitar and Harold Vick on tenor sax. With tunes like "Fat Judy" and "Good Juice," there is no worry about there being a groove. The addition of a trumpet (Blue Mitchell) means you have a horn section, and this tends to be a little much now and again. Although a little on the light side, thanks to Patton and Green, the groove does go down. —*Michael Erlewine*

★ **Let 'em Roll** / Dec. 11, 1965 / Blue Note ◆◆◆◆◆
Patton with Grant Green (guitar), Otis Finch (drums), and Bobby Hutcherson (vibes). Grant Green provides just superb musings. While vibes is not a usual instrument for soul-jazz sessions, this album works anyway and the groove is established. Grant Green and Patton are just a great combination. —*Michael Erlewine*

Got a Good Thing Goin' / Apr. 29, 1966 / Blue Note ◆◆◆◆
Grant Green always brought out the best in Big John Patton. Almost any record that featured the guitarist and organist was dominated by their scintillating interplay, and it always sounded like they were trying to top each other's blistering, funky solos. Patton and Green rarely sounded better than they did on *Got a Good Thing Goin',* a 1966 session that functioned as a showcase for the pair's dynamic interaction and exciting, invigorating solos.

In particular, the duo's mastery is evident because there are no horns to stand in the way—only drummer Hugh Walker and conga player Richard Landrum provide support, leaving plenty of room for Green and Patton to run wild. All five numbers—two originals by Patton and Green, two pop covers ("Ain't That Peculiar," "Shake") and Duke Pearson's "Amanda"—are simple blues and soul-jazz songs that provide ample space for the guitarist and organist to stretch out. And they do stretch out—as a pair, they have never sounded so fiery or intoxicating. Fans of hard bop may find the songs a little too simple, but hot, uptempo soul-jazz rarely comes any better than it does on *Got a Good Thing Goin'. — Stephen Thomas Erlewine*

That Certain Feeling / Mar. 8, 1968 / Blue Note ◆◆◆

It took Big John Patton nearly two years to return to the studio as a leader following the sessions that produced the exceptional *Got a Good Thing Goin'.* When he finally cut its sequel, *That Certain Feeling,* the musical climate had changed just enough to make a difference in his music. Where *Got a Good Thing Goin'* was down and dirty, *That Certain Feeling* was smooth. That's not to say that it didn't groove—it was just cleaner, which means that the groove wasn't as infectious or hot as before. Still, Patton and his band—guitarist Jimmy Ponder, tenor saxophonist Junior Cook, and drummer Clifford Jarvis—play very well, and there are moments when everything comes together and it just cooks. And those are the moments that make *That Certain Feeling* worth a search. — *Stephen Thomas Erlewine*

Boogaloo / Aug. 9, 1968 / Blue Note ◆◆◆

Big John Patton with a trumpet and sax, drums, and conga. Harold Alexander (sax) plays a little out for a standard soul-jazz session and the combination of the horns amounts to what it should be—a horn section. For me, this never gets down to the business of being soul music. The groove is weak or not there. — *Michael Erlewine*

Understanding / Oct. 25, 1968 / Blue Note ◆◆

Patton with saxman Harold Alexander and drums. Alexander is playing sax that is just a tad too "out" for an organ combo that is standard for soul-jazz, thus turning the sound toward something other than a real groove. If you like progressive sax, you might be able to stay in the groove. Not me, the sound keeps popping me out. I like to get in the groove and ride. — *Michael Erlewine*

Accent on the Blues / Jun. 9, 1969 + Aug. 15, 1969 / Blue Note ◆◆◆

Most John Patton albums are hard-driving, edgy soul-jazz and funk, and the title of *Accent on the Blues* makes the record seem like it would be no different than his other sessions. Of course, that isn't the case. *Accent on the Blues* is among the most atmospheric music Patton has ever made. While it stops short of being free, it's hardly funky soul-jazz, and that may disappoint some fans of his rip-roaring style. Nevertheless, the album is a rewarding listen, primarily because it displays a more reflective side of his talent, demonstrating that he can hold his own among the likes of guitarist James "Blood" Ulmer and saxophonist Marvin Cabell. — *Stephen Thomas Erlewine*

Memphis to New York Spirit / Jun. 9, 1969 + Oct. 2, 1970 / Blue Note ◆◆◆

Although it was scheduled for release two times, *Memphis to New York Spirit* didn't appear until 1996, over 25 years after it was recorded. The album comprises the contents of two separate sessions—one recorded in 1970 with guitarist James "Blood" Ulmer, drummer Leroy Williams, and saxophonist/flutist Marvin Cabell; the other recorded in 1969 with Cabell, Williams, and saxophonist George Coleman—that were very similiar in concept and execution. Patton leads his combo through a selection of originals and covers that range from Wayne Shorter and McCoy Tyner to the Meters. Though the group is rooted in soul-jazz, they stretch the limits of the genre on these sessions, showing a willingness to experiment, while still dipping into the more traditional blues and funk reserves. Consequently, *Memphis to New York Spirit* doesn't have a consistent groove like some other Patton records, but when it does click, the results are remarkable; it's a non-essential but worthy addition to a funky soul-jazz collection. — *Stephen Thomas Erlewine*

Soul Connection / Jun. 7, 1983 / Nilva ◆◆◆

Quintet — *AMG*

This One's for J.A. / 1998 / Diw ◆◆◆

On the third album of his '90s comeback, Big John Patton chooses to create a relaxed vibe, smoothly grooving through a surprising choice of material. Most of the record consists of challenging songs like Coltrane's "Syeeda's Song Flute" and Grachan Moncur III's "Sonny's Back," which gives Patton—

as well as his supporting band, featuring guitarist Ed Cherry and tenor saxophonist Dave Hubbard—the chance to create intricate yet accessible music. This is music that can be heard as simply a good groove yet it rewards careful listening. *This One's for J.A.* again confirms that Patton has made one of the rare comebacks in jazz—one that does justice to his earlier work. — *Stephen Thomas Erlewine*

Houston Person

b. Nov. 10, 1934, Florence, SC
Tenor Saxophone / Soul-Jazz, Hard Bop, Groove
In the '90s Houston Person has kept the soulful thick-toned tenor tradition of Gene Ammons alive, particularly in his work with organists. After learning piano as a youth, Person switched to tenor. While stationed in Germany with the army, he played in groups that also included Eddie Harris, Lanny Morgan, Leo Wright, and Cedar Walton. Person picked up valuable experience as a member of Johnny Hammond's group (1963-66) and has been a bandleader ever since, often working with his wife, singer Etta Jones. A duo recording with Ran Blake was a nice change of pace but most of Houston Person's playing has been done in blues-oriented organ groups. He has recorded a consistently excellent series of albums for Muse. — *Scott Yanow*

Goodness! / Aug. 25, 1969 / Original Jazz Classics ◆◆◆◆

Tenor saxophonist Houston Person was still a relatively new name at the time he recorded this set, his sixth session for Prestige. The funky music (which includes the hit title song) emphasizes boogaloos, danceable rhythms and repetitive vamps set down by the rhythm section (organist Sonny Phillips, guitarist Billy Butler, electric bassist Bob Bushnell, drummer Frankie Jones, and Buddy Caldwell on congas), but it is primarily Person's passionate tenor solos that will come the closest to holding on to the attention of jazz listeners. The music is generally quite commercial and is certainly not recommended to bebop purists, although it has some strong moments. But overall these performances succeed more as background music than as creative jazz. — *Scott Yanow*

The Truth! / Feb. 23, 1970 / Prestige ◆◆◆

One of a steady string of Houston Person Prestige albums (the seventh of 11), this particular effort has not yet been reissued on CD. The thick-toned tenor saxophonist plays soulful boogaloos, ballads, and blues with a fine group also including organist Sonny Phillips, guitarist Billy Butler, electric bassist Bob Bushnell, drummer Frankie Jones and Buddy Caldwell on conga. Although not essential, the soul-jazz date finds all of the musicians in fine form. — *Scott Yanow*

Person to Person / Oct. 12, 1970 / Prestige ◆◆◆

Soul-jazz that inclines more to the "soul" part of the compound than many such Prestige efforts of the time. The material gets a little close to pop at times (Bacharach-David's "Close to You," Stevie Wonder's "Yester-Me, Yester-You, Yesterday"), but Person's tone is always earthy (never more so than on Ray Charles' "Drown in My Own Tears"). Grant Green is the most notable member of the band on this session, which was teamed with the 1971 LP *Houston Express* on the 1996 CD reissue *Legends of Acid Jazz. — Richie Unterberger*

Legends of Acid Jazz / Oct. 12, 1970-Apr. 9, 1971 / Prestige ◆◆◆◆

Houston Person was among the guttiest of the gutbucket saxophonists of the soul-jazz golden age—for proof, look no further than *Legends of Acid Jazz: Houston Person,* which compiles two of the saxman's most popular releases, *Person to Person!* and *Houston Express* (both originally released in 1970). *Express* featured the "funkmaster general" of the tenor saxophone with a tight, pocket-sized ensemble (including guitarist Grant Green and drummer Idris Muhammad), while, on *Person!,* his supporting ensemble expanded to include trumpet players Cecil Bridgewater and Thad Jones, guitarist Billy Butler and another kindred spirit and prince of funk on his instrument, Motown bassist Gerry Jemmott. *Legends of Acid Jazz: Houston Person* provides a high-voltage cover version extravaganza, including "(For God's Sake) Give More Power to the People" (the Chi-Lites), "Close to You" (the Carpenters), "Yester-Me, Yester-You, Yester-Day" (Stevie Wonder), "Young, Gifted and Black" (Aretha Franklin), "Just My Imagination" (the Temptations), and "Lift Every Voice and Sing," which Person describes in his liner notes as the "black national anthem." Person and friends turn every one of these, and others such as his own "Up at Joe's, Down at Jim's" and his trademark "The Houston

Express" into stinging, swinging, original-sounding opuses of funk. — *Chris Slawecki*

Houston Express / Apr. 8, 1971 / Prestige ++++

As period soul-jazz goes, this is considerably above the average. It's funky, but not in the bland crossover sense; there's a sense of jazz ensemble discipline to the arrangements, but it's still R&B-based enough to groove to. Cecil Bridgewater (trumpet), Billy Butler (guitar), Bernard Purdie (drums), and Motown bassist Gerry Jemmott are among the more notable contributors to this 1971 session. This and another 1971 LP, *Houston Express*, were combined onto one CD reissue in 1996, *Legends of Acid Jazz*. — *Richie Unterberger*

Stolen Sweets / Apr. 29, 1976 / Muse ++++

First-rate soul-jazz, funk, blues, and ballads by tenor saxophonist Houston Person. Vocalist Etta Jones wasn't on this session, so things were mostly uptempo and cooking, with plenty of robust tenor from Person, tasty guitar by Jimmy Ponder, swirling organ riffs, and support from Sonny Phillips, and percussion and rhythmic assistance from Frankie Jones and Buddy Caldwell. — *Ron Wynn*

The Nearness of You / Nov. 1977 / Muse +++

The soulful and always-swinging tenor Houston Person is in typically fine form on this enjoyable LP (not yet reissued on CD). Joined by trumpeter Virgil Jones, guitarist Melvin Sparks, organist Charles Earland, Sonny Phillips on electric piano, bassist Mervyn Bronson, drummer Grady Tate, and percussionist Lawrence Killian, Person explores such numbers as "Freddie the Freeloader" and "Mean to Me." Singer Etta Jones pops by for one song, the blues "Please Mr. Person" (based on "Please Mr. Johnson" by the Buddy Johnson band of the '40s). A fun date. — *Scott Yanow*

Suspicions / Apr. 24, 1980 / Muse +++

Some robust funk and fine soul licks, plus solid mainstream fare. — *Ron Wynn*

• **Basics** / Oct. 12, 1987 / Muse ++++

Tenor saxophonist Houston Person has stuck to his singular musical path throughout his career, playing uncomplicated but soulful and swinging renditions of blues, ballads, and jazz standards for a couple decades, ignoring current (and usually short-lived) musical trends. For this set, he is joined by pianist Stan Hope, bassist Peter Martin Weiss, drummer Cecil Brooks III, and Ralph Dorsey on congas for six superior vintage tunes. When Person adds his soul to "What a Difference a Day Made," "Stormy Weather," or "Some Other Spring," the songs sound brand new and almost as if they were written for him. Recommended. — *Scott Yanow*

Something in Common / Feb. 23, 1989 / Muse ++++

Houston Person is one of the last in a long line of thick-toned tenors who display soul in every note they play while bassist Ron Carter's versatility is legendary (it seems as if he has spent half of his life in recording studios). Their duet CD, although not inevitable, works out quite well. Carter not only sets the rhythms behind Person but sometimes plays chords (a la Count Basie guitarist Freddie Green) or the melody in unison with the tenor, continually keeping the music flowing in an unhurried and relaxed fashion. None of the selections (seven standards plus "Blues for Two") are taken faster than medium tempo and Person has been chewing up these chord changes for years, so the main attractions of this date are the instrumentation and the strong interplay between Person and Carter. The results are both relaxed and successful. — *Scott Yanow*

The Party / Nov. 14, 1989 / Muse ++++

Good soul-jazz and blues session, with young lion organist Joey DeFrancesco providing the funky undercurrent to tenor saxophonist Houston Person's thick, authoritative solos and Randy Johnston and Bertell Knox filling the spaces on bass and drums, plus Sammy Figueroa adding some Afro-Latin fiber for additional support. — *Ron Wynn*

Why Not! / Oct. 5, 1990 / Muse ++++

Houston Person's warm tenor tone, effortless swing, and skill at playing with organists have been taken for granted through the years, since he breaks no new boundaries and is very consistent. On this CD, he forged a new partnership with the young organist Joey DeFrancesco, and they work together perfectly on a set of blues, ballads and standards. Randy Johnston adds some nice George Benson-ish guitar solos; Sammy Figueroa's congas are an added

plus, and trumpeter Phillip Harper (despite his entrance in the wrong key on "Namely You") tries his best to fill in for Lee Morgan. — *Scott Yanow*

Island Episode / May 5, 1997 / Prestige +++

All of the music on this 1997 CD was previously unreleased. Eight of the nine selections date from 1973 and match the great soul-jazz tenor Houston Person with a Latin-oriented band that also includes trumpeter Victor Paz, Hank Jones (on electric piano), guitarist Jimmy Ponder, bassist Andy Gonzalez, an unidentified drummer, percussionist Jerry Gonzalez and Nicky Marrero on timbales. Although there are dated aspects to the music, Person fares well. The other selection is from 1971, a funky number with a medium-size group that includes organist Ernie Hayes. Overall, a worthwhile set, if not essential. — *Scott Yanow*

Ike Quebec

b. Aug. 17, 1918, Newark, NJ, **d.** Jan. 16, 1963, New York, NY

Tenor Saxophone / Swing, Early R&B Jazz, Groove, Hard Bop, Soul-Jazz

Influenced by Coleman Hawkins and Ben Webster but definitely his own person, Ike Quebec was one of the finest swing-oriented tenor saxmen of the '40s and '50s. Though he was never an innovator, Quebec had a big, breathy sound that was distinctive and easily recognizable, and he was quite consistent when it came to down-home blues, sexy ballads and uptempo aggression. Originally a pianist, Quebec switched to tenor in the early '40s and showed that he had made the right decision on excellent 78s for Blue Note and Savoy (including his hit "Blue Harlem"). As a sideman, he worked with Benny Carter, Kenny Clarke, Roy Eldridge, and Cab Calloway. In the late '40s, the saxman did a bit of freelancing behind the scenes as a Blue Note A&R man and brought Thelonious Monk and Bud Powell to the label. Drug problems kept Quebec from recording for most of the '50s, but he made a triumphant comeback in the early '60s and was once again recording for Blue Note and doing freelance A&R for the company. Quebec was playing as authoritatively as ever well into 1962, giving no indication that he was suffering from lung cancer, which claimed his life at the age of 44 in 1963. — *Alex Henderson*

Groove: Ike Quebec is a direct hit with most blues fans. This guy plays from the heart in an understated yet warm manner that is endearing from the first listen. If you can obtain one of the albums with Quebec and Grant Green, then the magic gets even better. The Mosaic boxed set *The Complete Blue Note 45 Sessions* is worth an explanation. It was common practice to take the best cut from a popular album, put it on a 45, and release it to juke boxes all over the country. It meant extra income. A certain kind of soulful romantic bluesy sound was what did well on the jukes—beer drinkin' music. Ike Quebec was asked to create such 45s just for juke-box release. There were no albums. People loved them and so will you. This is great bluesy music. You can order these by mail only from Mosaic Records, 35 Melrose Place, Stamford, CT 06904. Ask for their catalog—the best jazz reissues label on the planet. — *Michael Erlewine*

☆ **Complete Blue Note Recordings** / Jul. 18, 1944-Sep. 23, 1946 / Mosaic +++++

This limited-edition four-LP box set from Mosaic has all of the early Blue Note recordings of tenors John Hardee and Ike Quebec. The little-known Hardee's three sessions are all from 1946 (one is under the leadership of guitarist Tiny Grimes) and find him in top form on a variety of swing-based originals, along with a few standards. In addition to Grimes, the sidemen include trombonist Trummy Young, guitarist Jimmy Shirley, and pianists Marlowe Morris and Sammy Benskin. Hardee would eventually settle in Texas as a full-time educator. In contrast, Ike Quebec, who is showcased on five dates (including 11 previously unissued performances), would achieve a bit of fame (his recordings of "Blue Harlem" and "If I Had You" gained some attention) before drugs forced him off the scene in the '50s; he would make a brief comeback in the early '60s prior to his premature death. Quebec's early Blue Note dates are superior examples of small-group swing and have solo space for some notable stars: guitarist Tiny Grimes, pianist Ram Ramirez, trumpeters Jonah Jones, Buck Clayton and Shad Collins, and trombonists Tyree Glenn and Keg Johnson. This 1984 box is certainly definitive but promises to be difficult to find. — *Scott Yanow*

☆ **Complete Blue Note 45 Sessions** / Jul. 1, 1959-Feb. 13, 1962 / Mosaic +++++

During his comeback years (1959-62) after a decade mostly off the scene, tenor saxophonist Ike Quebec recorded frequently for Blue Note. He started off with a session aimed at the 45 jukebox market and, although he eventually made a few full-length albums for the label, Quebec cut four 45 dates over a two-year period. This limited-edition (and now out-of-print) three-LP Mosaic box set has all of the jukebox sessions. Most of the 26 selections clock in between four and seven minutes in addition to concise and soulful solos. Quebec, who was in consistently prime form during his last period, is joined by groups featuring either Skeeter Best or Willie Jones on guitar and Edwin Swanston, Sir Charles Thompson, or Earl Van Dyke on organ. Fun and generally danceable music. — *Scott Yanow*

Ballads / Sep. 25, 1960–Mar. 21, 1962 / Blue Note ✦✦✦
Tenor saxophonist Ike Quebec always had a big, warm sound, and he was particularly expert on ballads. This 1997 sampler CD surprisingly does not have any examples of his early work on Blue Note in the mid—to late '40s, instead concentrating on selections from four of Quebec's seven late-period Blue Note albums, a few songs originally issued as 45s, and "Born to Be Blue," which is taken from an album by guitarist Grant Green. The eight ballads are all standards and put the focus very much on Quebec, making for a fine mood album even if acquiring the full sessions (all but "It Might As Well Be Spring" are currently available on CD) is preferable. — *Scott Yanow*

Heavy Soul / Nov. 26, 1961 / Blue Note ✦✦✦✦
The thick-toned tenor Ike Quebec is in excellent form on this CD reissue of a 1961 Blue Note date. His ballad statements are quite warm and he swings nicely on a variety of medium-tempo material. Unfortunately, organist Freddie Roach has a rather dated sound which weakens this session a bit; bassist Milt Hinton and drummer Al Harewood are typically fine in support. Originals alternate with standards with "Just One More Chance," "The Man I Love," and "Nature Boy" (the latter an emotional tenor-bass duet) being among the highlights. — *Scott Yanow*

It Might As Well Be Spring / Dec. 9, 1961 / Blue Note ✦✦✦
Working with the same quartet that cut *Heavy Soul*—organist Freddie Roach, bassist Milt Hinton, and drummer Al Harewood—Ike Quebec recorded another winning hard bop album with *It Might As Well Be Spring*. In many ways, the record is a companion piece to *Heavy Soul*. Since the two albums were recorded so close together, it's not surprising that there are a number of stylistic similarities, but there are subtle differences to savor. The main distinction between the two dates is that *It Might As Well Be Spring* is a relaxed, romantic date comprised of standards. It provides Quebec with ample opportunity to showcase his rich, lyrical ballad style, and he shines throughout the album. Similarly, Roach has a tasteful, understated technique, whether he's soloing or providing support for Quebec. The pair have a terrific, sympathetic interplay that makes *It Might As Well Be Spring* a joyous listen. — *Stephen Thomas Erlewine*

● **Blue and Sentimental** / Dec. 16, 1961 + Dec. 23, 1961 / Blue Note ✦✦✦✦
Of tenor saxophonist Ike Quebec's six Blue Note albums from the 1961-62 period, this is the definitive one. The CD reissue (which adds "new" versions of "That Old Black Magic" and "It's All Right With Me" to the original LP program) mostly features Quebec in a quartet with guitarist Grant Green, bassist Paul Chambers, and drummer Philly Joe Jones; "Count Every Star" has Quebec joined by Green, pianist Sonny Clark, bassist Sam Jones, and drummer Louis Hayes. Although some of the renditions are medium-tempo swingers, it is the soulful ballad versions of "Blue and Sentimental" and "Don't Take Your Love from Me" that are most memorable. Recommended. — *Scott Yanow*

Congo Lament / Jan. 20, 1962 / Blue Note ✦✦✦
Africa meets Harlem with soul in a rousing Quebec date. — *Ron Wynn*

Easy Living / Jan. 20, 1962 / Blue Note ✦✦✦✦
This CD reissue (which adds three songs to the original LP) is really two sets in one. The first five selections are a blues-oriented jam session that matches together the contrasting tenors of Ike Quebec and Stanley Turrentine with trombonist Bennie Green, pianist Sonny Clark, bassist Milt Hinton, and drummer Art Blakey. However it is the last three numbers ("I've Got a Crush on You," "Nancy with the Laughing Face," and "Easy Living") that are most memorable; ballad features for Quebec's warm tenor. All in all this set gives one a definitive look at late-period Ike Quebec. — *Scott Yanow*

Bossa Nova Soul Samba / Oct. 5, 1962 / Blue Note ✦✦✦
This CD reissues veteran tenor saxophonist Ike Quebec's final recording as a leader, cut a little more than three months before his death. Recorded during a period when seemingly everyone was making a bossa-nova record, Quebec's effort is a bit unusual in that none of the musicians (guitarist Kenny Burrell, bassist Wendell Marshall, drummer Willie Bobo, and percussionist Garvin Masseaux) were associated with Brazilian (as opposed to Afro-Cuban) jazz. While Quebec emphasizes warm long tones (reminiscent of Coleman Hawkins) in a romantic fashion, his sidemen play light and appealing bossa rhythms. The result is high-quality melodic Brazilian dance music (despite the lack of any Jobim songs) with Burrell in particular being quite effective; the pleasing program concludes with three previously unissued alternate takes. — *Scott Yanow*

The Art of Ike Quebec / Nov. 13, 1962–Oct. 5, 1962 / Blue Note ✦✦✦
Tenor-saxophonist Ike Quebec recorded six albums for Blue Note during his last period before passing away in Jan. 1963. This single CD has at least one selection from each of the records (11 in all) that, when taken as a whole, gives one a good idea as to how strong Quebec was still sounding. Although his fans will want to get the individual records (four of the six are currently available on CDs), this is an excellent sampler. Among the other players are organist Freddie Roach, guitarists Grant Green and Kenny Burrell, pianist Sonny Clark, drummers Art Blakey and Billy Higgins, trombonist Bennie Green, and tenor great Stanley Turrentine. — *Scott Yanow*

Mel Rhyne

b. Oct. 12, 1936, Indianapolis, IN
Organ / Hard Bop, Groove
Organist Melvin Rhyne's greatest fame is his participation on four Wes Montgomery Riverside sessions (including Wes' first and last album for the label). Fortunately, Rhyne survived long enough after some lean years to return to the major-league jazz scene and record some CDs of his own. Born in Indianapolis, Rhyne (a largely self-taught pianist) was an important part of the city's jazz scene. He played with the then-unknown Roland Kirk during 1955-56 and soon switched to organ. He also had opportunities to back a series of blues (including T-Bone Walker and B.B. King) and R&B artists. Rhyne was part of Montgomery's group for most of 1959-64. In 1969, he moved to Madison, Wisconsin, and four years later he relocated to Milwaukee, where he remained active if obscure for the next two decades. In 1990 he emerged, recording with Herb Ellis and Brian Lynch. Mel Rhyne has since recorded two excellent sets for Criss Cross, including a quartet session that has Joshua Redman as his sideman, and shown that he is an excellent soul-jazz and hard bop soloist in his own right. — *Scott Yanow*

Organ-izing / Mar. 31, 1960 / Jazzland ✦✦✦✦
With Johnny Griffin on tenor sax and Blue Mitchell on trumpet. —*Michael G. Nastos*

The Legend / Dec. 30, 1991 / Criss Cross ✦✦✦✦
Other than an obscure date for Jazzland in 1960, this CD was organist Melvin Rhyne's debut as a leader. Famous for his association with Wes Montgomery but in obscurity ever since in Milwaukee, Rhyne gradually emerged during the late '80s and was found to still be in prime form. Joined by guitarist Peter Bernstein and drummer Kenny Washington, Rhyne had the rare opportunity of being the center of attention on this set, which includes a variety of standards (such as "Groovin' High," "Old Folks," and "Stompin' at the Savoy") plus Eddie "Lockjaw" Davis' "Licks A-Plenty" and Montgomery's "The Trick Bag." The easily recommended CD concludes with a lengthy "Blues for Wes," which finds trumpeter Brian Lynch and tenor saxophonist Don Braden making the group a quintet. — *Scott Yanow*

● **Boss Organ** / Jan. 6, 1993 / Criss Cross ✦✦✦✦
Mel Rhyne, best known for his association in the '60s with Wes Montgomery, re-emerged with this Criss Cross CD as one of the finest jazz organists around. He is matched with guitarist Peter Bernstein, drummer Kenny Washington, and the young tenor great Joshua Redman for a set of good-natured and often hard-swinging performances. In addition to superior versions of "All God's Chillun Got Rhythm" and "Jeannine," the quartet explores lesser-known songs such as Hubert Laws' "Shades of Light," Stevie Wonder's "You and I," and Mel Torme's "Born to Be Blue." The music is consistently stimulating and swinging. — *Scott Yanow*

Howard Roberts (Howard Mancel Roberts)

b. Oct. 2, 1929, Phoenix, AZ, **d.** Jun. 28, 1992, Seattle, WA
Guitar / Cool

Howard Roberts was a talented guitarist on the level of a Barney Kessel or Herb Ellis who spent most of his career playing commercial music in the studios. Shortly after he moved to Los Angeles in 1950, Roberts was firmly entrenched in the studios although on occasion he recorded jazz (most notably twice for Verve during 1956-59, a Concord session from 1977 and one for Discovery in 1979); however most of his other output (particularly for Capitol in the '60s) is of lesser interest. The co-founder of the Guitar Institute of Technology in Hollywood, Roberts was an enthusiastic and talented educator and wrote a regular instructional column for *Guitar Player*. — *Scott Yanow*

Mr. Roberts Plays Guitar / 1956 / Norgran ++++

Guitarist Howard Roberts' first record as a leader (which unfortunately has not yet been reissued on CD) was one of his very best. Roberts, who would spend most of his career as a studio musician, is featured on this album in several settings: with tenor saxophonist Bob Cooper in a pianoless quartet, and with a rhythm section that includes either a quartet of strings or woodwinds. Some tunes have tight arrangements (by Bill Holman, Jack Montrose, Al Cohn, Marty Paich, or Bob Enevoldsen) and others are more freewheeling, including a jammed version of "Indiana." Throughout, Roberts is heard in excellent form, whether on "Serenata Burlesca," Cohn's "Al Moore," or "My Shining Hour." Recommended. — *Scott Yanow*

Velvet Groove / Oct. 16, 1956 + 1959 / Verve ++++

The Movin' Man / 1957 / Verve +++

More mainstream than later organ/funky efforts, the sidemen are not at his level. It is still a very listenable set, a fine glimpse of his early bop-style playing. — *David Nelson McCarthy*

Color Him Funky / Feb. 12, 1963-Feb. 13, 1963 / Capitol +++

Recorded with organ trio, Howard is slick and soulful. Find this one on vinyl and you'll smile and tap your foot. The organ sounds a bit dated, but it's part of the charm. — *David Nelson McCarthy*

H.R. Is a Dirty Guitar Player / Jun. 3, 1963-Jun. 16, 1963 / Capitol ++++

This is classic Roberts. A very nice album to have around. — *Michael Erlewine*

● **The Real Howard Roberts** / Aug. 26, 1977 / Concord Jazz ++++

Most of guitarist Howard Roberts' recordings through the years (particularly a long string for Capitol in the '60s) were quite commercial, featuring brief versions of current pop tunes. A versatile studio player, Roberts finally had an opportunity in 1977 to record some no-nonsense, straight-ahead jazz. This set (reissued on CD) matches Roberts in a quartet with pianist Ross Tompkins, bassist Ray Brown, and drummer Jimmie Smith, playing some standards (including Herbie Hancock's "Dolphin Dance," "Gone With the Wind," and "Angel Eyes"), Michael Franks' "Lady Wants to Know" and Brown's "Parking Lot Blues." This is one of the few examples of Howard Roberts showing what a strong jazz player he could be. — *Scott Yanow*

Shirley Scott

b. Mar. 14, 1934, Philadelphia, PA

Organ / Hard Bop, Soul-Jazz, Groove

An admirer of the seminal Jimmy Smith, Shirley Scott has been one of the organ's most appealing representatives since the late '50s. Scott, a very melodic and accessible player, started out on piano and played trumpet in high school before taking up the Hammond B-3 and enjoying national recognition in the late '50s with her superb Prestige dates with tenor sax great Eddie "Lockjaw" Davis. Especially popular was their 1958 hit "In the Kitchen." Her reputation was cemented during the '60s on several superb, soulful organ/soul-jazz dates where she demonstrated an aggressive, highly rhythmic attack blending intricate bebop harmonies with bluesy melodies and a gospel influence, punctuating everything with great use of the bass pedals. Scott married soul-jazz tenor man Stanley Turrentine, with whom she often recorded in the '60s. The Scott/Turrentine union lasted until the early '70s, and their musical collaborations in the '60s were among the finest in the field. Scott wasn't as visible the following decade, when the popularity of organ

combos decreased and labels were more interested in fusion and pop-jazz (though she did record some albums for Chess/Cadet and Strata East). But organists regained their popularity in the late '80s, which found her recording for Muse. Though known primarily for her organ playing, Scott is also a superb pianist—in the '90s, she has played piano exclusively on some trio recordings for Candid, and embraced the instrument consistently in Philly jazz venues. — *Alex Henderson and Ron Wynn*

Great Scott! / May 27, 1958 / Prestige +++

Workin' / May 27, 1958-Mar. 24, 1960 / Prestige +++

One of several trio and/or combo works that organist Shirley Scott recorded for Prestige in the late '50s and early '60s. Her swirling, driving lines, intense bass pedal support, and bluesy fervor were ideal for the soul-jazz format, and this is a typical example. — *Ron Wynn*

Shirley Scott Trio / May 27, 1958-Apr. 8, 1960 / Moodsville +++

A trio recording with Scott, George Tucker on bass, and Earl Coleman (vcl). Originally released on Moodsville. — *Michael Erlewine*

Now's the Time / May 27, 1958-Mar. 31, 1964 / Prestige +++

This is early Scott, several takes from different session for this Prestige release. — *Michael Erlewine*

Soul Searching / Dec. 4, 1959 / Prestige +++

Shirley Scott with Wendell Marshall on bass and Arthur Edgehill on drums. Includes title tune and "Boss." — *AMG*

Stompin' / Apr. 8, 1960-Mar. 24, 1961 / Prestige +++

Here is Scott with Ronnell Bring (p), Wally Richardson (g), Peck Morrison (b), and Roy Haynes (d). Includes a rendition of Nat Adderley's "Work Song." — *Michael Erlewine*

Soul Sisters / Jun. 23, 1960 / Prestige +++

With Lem Winchester on vibes, George Duvivier on bass, and Arthur Edgehill on drums. A dauntless, swinging affair. — *Ron Wynn*

Like Cozy / Sep. 27, 1960 / Moodsville ++

Her standard trio with George Duvivier on bass and Arthur Edgehill on drums. — *AMG*

Satin Doll / Mar. 7, 1961 / Prestige +++

With George Tucker on bass and Jack Simplkins on drums. A bit more prim, though Scott still burns. — *Ron Wynn*

Hip Soul / Jun. 2, 1961 / Prestige ++++

Here is Stanley Turrentine recording under the name Stan Turner. Slashing, aptly titled. — *Ron Wynn*

Legends of Acid Jazz / Jun. 2, 1961 + Nov. 17, 1961 / Prestige ++++

A smart combination of two 1961 albums, *Hip Soul* and *Hip Twist*, both of which featured Stanley Turrentine on sax. *Hip Soul* is the smokier and livelier of the pair, especially on "Stanley's Time" and the Turrentine-composed title track; the material is delivered with a taut intelligence. *Hip Twist* doesn't suffer much in comparison, though, and gives Scott a bit more presence, as she introduces several themes with impassioned swirls; unlike *Hip Soul*, it has a couple of tunes from her own pen. — *Richie Unterberger*

Blue Seven / Aug. 22, 1961 / Prestige +++

A quintet with Roy Brooks (d), Oliver Nelson (ts), and Joe Newman (tpt) plays one Scott original, the title song by Sonny Rollins, and an excellent "Wagon Wheels." — *Michael G. Nastos*

Hip Twist / Nov. 17, 1961 / Prestige +++

Scott with Stanley Turrentine (sax), George Tucker (b), and Otis Finch (d). Any Turrentine/Scott albums are worth hearing, even with a title like this one. — *Michael Erlewine*

Shirley Scott Plays Horace Silver / Nov. 17, 1961 / Prestige ++++

Just what it says. The queen of the Hammond organ (along with Henry Grimes (b) and Otis Finch (d)) plays compositions by the funk-master himself, Horace Silver. Included are "Senor Blues" and "The Preacher." — *Michael Erlewine*

Happy Talk / Dec. 5, 1962 / Prestige +++

Trio with Scott with Earl May (b) and Roy Brooks (d). — *AMG*

☆ **Sweet Soul** / Dec. 5, 1962 / Prestige +++++

Reissued from the "Happy Talk" session this features Earl May on bass and

Roy Brooks on drums. It includes a nice "Jitterbug Waltz." All are standards. — *Michael G. Nastos*

Soul Is Willing / Jan. 10, 1963 / Prestige ◆◆◆◆
This is a good album that shows the husband and wife team of Shirley Scott and Stanley Turrentine in their usual, excellent form— a fine example of organ combo soul-jazz. Now part of the Prestige two-fer called *Soul Shoutin'.* — *Michael Erlewine*

☆ **Soul Shoutin'** / Jan. 10, 1963+Oct. 15, 1963 / Prestige ◆◆◆◆◆
Organist Shirley Scott and her then-husband tenor great Stanley Turrentine always made potent music together. This CD, which combines together the former Prestige LPs *The Soul Is Willing* and *Soul Shoutin',* finds "Mr. T." at his early peak, playing some intense yet always soulful solos on such pieces as Sy Oliver's "Yes Indeed," "Secret Love" and his memorable originals "The Soul Is Willing" and "Deep Down Soul." Scott, who found her own niche within the dominant Jimmy Smith style, swings hard throughout the set and (together with drummer Crassella Oliphant and either Major Holley or Earl May on bass) the lead voices play with such consistent enthusiasm that one would think these were club performances. Highly recommended. — *Scott Yanow*

☆ **For Members Only/Great Scott!** / Aug. 22, 1963-May 20, 1964 / Impulse! ◆◆◆◆◆
During the '60s, Shirley Scott's Impulse albums were often split between big band selections (with orchestras arranged by Oliver Nelson) and trio features. This CD reissue from 1989 includes all of the contents from two of Scott's better Impulse albums, *Great Scott* and *For Members Only.* In general the eight trio numbers are the most rewarding performances on the disc since the material is fairly superior while the big band tracks emphasize then-current show and movie tunes. Overall this generous CD gives one a good overview of Shirley Scott's playing talents. — *Scott Yanow*

Blue Flames / Mar. 31, 1964 / Original Jazz Classics ◆◆◆◆
All of the many collaborations between organist Shirley Scott and tenor saxophonist Stanley Turrentine in the '60s resulted in high-quality soul-jazz, groovin' music that was boppish enough to interest jazz listeners and basic enough for a wider audience. This CD reissue has the duo (joined by bassist Bob Cranshaw and drummer Otis "Candy" Finch) performing a pair of Scott originals, Benny Golson's "Five Spot After Dark," Sonny Rollins' obscure "Grand Street" and the veteran standard "Flamingo." The only fault of this CD reissue is its brief length, just 32 minutes. — *Scott Yanow*

The Great Live Sessions / Sep. 23, 1964 / ABC/Impulse ◆◆◆
Recorded live at the Front Room in Newark, NJ, the album includes ten tracks with a quartet including Stanley Turrentine (ts). On a rare night for music, the band delivered on all counts. You can't go wrong here. — *Michael G. Nastos*

● **Queen of the Organ** / Sep. 23, 1964 / Impulse! ◆◆◆◆
This CD reissue brings back all of the music previously put out on the two-LP set *The Great Live Sessions* with the exception of one number ("Shirley's Shuffle") left out due to lack of space; with over 70 minutes of music, one cannot complain too much about the omission. Overall, this is a pretty definitive live set featuring organist Shirley Scott, tenor saxophonist Stanley Turrentine, bassist Bob Cranshaw, and drummer Otis "Candy" Finch, one of the great soul-jazz combos of the '60s. In addition to a swinging "Just In Time" and Duke Ellington's "Squeeze Me, But Please Don't Tease Me," the set mostly features obscurities and originals, plus a surprisingly effective version of the Beatles' "Can't Buy Me Love." The musicians sound quite heated and consistently inspired. Highly recommended. — *Scott Yanow*

Soul Duo / Aug. 19, 1966+Aug. 22, 1966 / Impulse! ◆◆◆◆
This is one of organist Shirley Scott's lesser-known Impulse LPs (not yet reissued on CD), a quartet outing with fluegelhornist Clark Terry, drummer Mickey Roker, and either George Duvivier or Bob Cranshaw on bass. Together they perform four Scott originals, a pair of C.T.'s compositions, the swinging "Until I Met You" and the standard "Heat Wave." Although not playing with the force that Stanley Turrentine exhibited when jamming with the organist, Clark Terry adds humor and a wistfulness to the date that easily compensates. — *Scott Yanow*

Girl Talk / Jan. 12, 1967-Jan. 13, 1967 / Impulse! ◆◆◆
Trio. Album includes one Scott original. The rest, including the classic title track, are standards. A bit sweet. — *Michael G. Nastos*

Soul Song / Sep. 9, 1968 / Atlantic ◆◆
Organist Shirley Scott's first of three Atlantic LPs (all are very difficult to find these days) was her last recording with her husband, tenor saxophonist Stanley Turrentine, who would soon gain great fame along with a divorce. Although Scott plays well enough and the supporting cast (which includes guitarist Eric Gale) is funky, the material is quite erratic, including Ray Stevens' "Mr. Businessman," "Like A Lover" (which has a rare vocal by the organist), and "Blowin' In The Wind." This collector's item has its interesting moments, but it is one of Shirley Scott's less significant dates. — *Scott Yanow*

Shirley Scott and the Soul Saxes / Jul. 9, 1969 / Atlantic ◆◆◆
Steamy workout with Scott, Hank Crawford (as), King Curtis (ts), and David Newman (ts). — *Ron Wynn*

One for Me / Nov. 1974 / Strata East ◆◆◆◆
The record is a beauty with Harold Vick, perhaps the most suited and sensitive horn player Ms. Scott has worked with … (a) thoroughly enjoyable album of bop stream music, and while it is nothing overly heavy or deep, it's thoughtfully and sensitively produced and of its kind an almost perfect album. — *Bob Rusch, Cadence*

Blues Everywhere / Nov. 1991 / Candid ◆◆◆◆
Recent trio session with Scott and Arthur Harper (b) and Mickey Roker (d). The twist is that Scott is playing acoustic piano throughout. It's not the usual sound, but she can play that thing. — *Michael Erlewine*

Al Sears

b. Feb. 21, 1910, Macomb, IL, d. Mar. 23, 1990, New York, NY
Tenor Saxophone / Early R&B Jazz, Swing, Groove
It is ironic that tenor saxophonist Al Sears' one hit, "Castle Rock," was recorded under Johnny Hodges' name (the altoist is virtually absent on the record!), denying Sears his one chance at fame. Sears had actually had his first important job in 1928 replacing Hodges with the Chick Webb band. However despite associations with Elmer Snowden (1931-2), Andy Kirk (1941-42), Lionel Hampton (1943-4), and with his own groups (most of 1933-41), it was not until Sears joined Duke Ellington's Orchestra in 1944 that he began to get much attention. His distinctive tone, R&Bish phrasing and ability to build up exciting solos made him one of Ellington's most colorful soloists during the next five years although his period was overshadowed by both his predecessor (Ben Webster) and his successor (Paul Gonsalves). Among Sears' many recordings with Ellington are notable versions of "I Ain't Got Nothing but the Blues" and a 1945 remake of "It Don't Mean a Thing." Sears worked with Johnny Hodges' group during 1951-52, recorded a variety of R&B-oriented material in the '50s and cut two excellent albums for Swingville in 1960 before going into semi-retirement. — *Scott Yanow*

● **Swing's the Thing** / Nov. 29, 1960 / Swingville ◆◆◆◆
Al Sears had the misfortune of having his one hit "Castle Rock" released under the leadership of Johnny Hodges, cheating him of his one chance at fame. A fine swing-based tenor who could stomp and honk with the best of them (although he rarely screamed), Sears had relatively few opportunities to record as a leader and this CD (which reissues a 1960 LP) was one of his last. Sears (along with pianist Don Abney, guitarist Wally Richardson, bassist Wendell Marshall, and drummer Joe Marshall) sticks to basic originals, blues, and standards and is in top form on these swinging and generally accessible performances. — *Scott Yanow*

Horace Silver

b. Sep. 2, 1928, Norwalk, CT
Piano / Hard Bop, Soul-Jazz, Groove
From the perspective of the late '90s, it is clear that few jazz musicians have had a greater impact on the contemporary mainstream than Horace Silver. The hard bop style that Silver pioneered in the '50s is now dominant, played not only by holdovers from an earlier generation, but also by fuzzy-cheeked musicians who had yet to be born when the music fell out of critical favor in the '60s and '70s.

Silver's earliest musical influence was the Cape Verdean folk music he heard from his Portugese-born father. Later, after he had begun playing piano and saxophone as a high schooler, Silver came under the spell of blues singers and boogie-woogie pianists, as well as boppers like Thelonious Monk and Bud Powell. In 1950, Stan Getz played a concert in Hartford, Connecticut, with a pickup rhythm section that included Silver, drummer Walter Bolden, and bassist Joe Calloway. So impressed was Getz, he hired the whole trio. Silver had been saving his money to move to New York anyway; his hiring by Getz sealed the deal. Silver worked with Getz for a year, then began to freelance around the city with such big-time players as Coleman Hawkins, Lester Young, and Oscar Pettiford. In 1952, he recorded with Lou Donaldson for the Blue Note label; this date led him to his first recordings as a leader. In 1953, he joined forces with Art Blakey to form a cooperative under their joint leadership. The band's first album, *Horace Silver and the Jazz Messengers*, was a milestone in the development of the genre that came to be known as hard bop. Many of the tunes penned by Silver for that record—"The Preacher," "Doodlin'," "Room 608"—became jazz classics. By 1956, Silver had left the Messengers to record on his own. The series of Blue Note albums that followed established Silver for all time as one of jazz's major composer/pianists. LPs like *Blowin' the Blues Away* and *Song for My Father* (both recorded by an ensemble which included Silver's longtime sidemen Blue Mitchell and Junior Cook) featured Silver's harmonically sophisticated and formally distinctive compositions for small jazz ensemble.

Silver's piano style—terse, imaginative, and utterly funky—became a model for subsequent mainstream pianists to emulate. Some of the most influential horn players of the '50s, '60s, and '70s first attained a measure of prominence with Silver—musicians like Donald Byrd, Woody Shaw, Joe Henderson, Benny Golson, and the Brecker brothers all played in Silver's band at a point early in their careers. Silver has even affected members of the avant-garde; Cecil Taylor confesses a Silver influence, and trumpeter Dave Douglas played briefly in a Silver combo.

Silver recorded exclusively for Blue Note until that label's eclipse in the late '70s, whereupon he started his own label, Silveto. Silver's '80s work was poorly distributed. During that time he began writing lyrics to his compositions; his work began to display a concern with music's metaphysical powers, as exemplified by album titles like *Music to Ease Your Disease* and *Spitualizing Your Senses*. In the '90s, Silver abandoned his label venture and began recording for Columbia. With his re-emergence on a major label, Silver is once again receiving a measure of the attention his contribution deserves. Certainly, no one has ever contributed a larger and more vital body of original compositions to the jazz canon. —*Chris Kelsey*

Groove: Horace Silver is another great jazz master and the pioneer of what we call funky jazz. Don't look for deep soul grooves here, because that's not Silver's bag. We can thank him for reaching into blues and soul roots and showing jazz artists how to give the music a little more substance at a time when bop was just about played out. He wrote some lovely songs and has a very special funky-jazz sound. —*Michael Erlewine*

Jimmy Smith

b. Dec. 8, 1925, Norristown, PA

Organ / Soul-Jazz, Hard Bop, Groove

Though he never received any exaggerated title like the king of soul-jazz, Jimmy Smith certainly ruled the Hammond organ in the '50s and '60s. He revolutionized the instrument, showing it could be creatively used in a jazz context and popularized in the process. His Blue Note sessions from 1956 to 1963 were extremely influential and are highly recommended. Smith turned the organ into almost an ensemble itself. He provided walking bass lines with his feet, left hand chordal accompaniment, solo lines in the right and a booming, funky presence that punctuated every song, particularly the uptempo cuts. Smith turned the fusion of R&B, blues and gospel influences with bebop references and devices into a jubilant, attractive sound that many others immediately absorbed before following in his footsteps. Smith initially learned piano, both from his parents and on his own. He attended the Hamilton School of Music in 1948, and Ornstein School of Music in 1949 and 1950 in Philadelphia. Smith began playing the Hammond in 1951, and soon earned a great reputation that followed him to New York, where he debuted at the Cafe Bohemia. A Birdland date and 1957 Newport Jazz Festival appearance launched Smith's career. He toured extensively through the '60s and '70s. His Blue Note recordings included superb collaborations with Kenny Burrell, Lee Morgan, Lou Donaldson, Tina Brooks, Jackie McLean, Ike Quebec, and Stanley Turrentine among others. He also did several trio recordings, some which were a little bogged down by the excess length of some selections. Smith scored more hit albums on Verve from 1963 to 1972, many of them featuring big bands and using fine arrangements from Oliver

Nelson. These included the excellent *Walk On The Wild Side.* But Verve went to the well once too often seeking crossover dollars, loading down Smith's late '60s album with hack rock covers. His '70s output was quite spotty, though Smith didn't stop touring, visiting Israel and Europe in 1974 and 1975. He and his wife opened a club in Los Angeles in the mid-'70s. Smith resumed touring in the early '80s, returning to New York in 1982 and 1983. He resigned with Blue Note in 1985, and has done more representative dates for them and Milestone in the '90s. —*Ron Wynn and Bob Porter*

Groove: Jimmy Smith is THE man on Hammond organ. At his best, he is the best there is. Which does not mean that all of his stuff is the best. It's not. He made a lot of albums and some of them are just average sounding. As a blues lover, I can't recommend his big band recordings, no matter how many awards they win. The fact to my ears is that the Hammond organ IS a big band—all by itself. Sticking Smith in the middle of a large group is just not helpful. You can't salt the salt, as they say. And you lose all of those crystal clear sax and guitar solos that come out in a trio or quartet. Stick with Smith's small combo stuff and that means, until lately, his early stuff. —*Michael Erlewine*

A New Sound, A New Star: Jimmy Smith at the Organ, Vols. 1-2 / Feb. 13, 1956 + Feb. 18, 1956 / Blue Note ✦✦✦✦
The emergence of Jimmy Smith in 1956 was quite noteworthy—here was an organist who could play his instrument with the facility of a Charlie Parker and yet could also dig into a lowdown blues. Smith's first three LPs (*At the Organ, Vols. 1-3*) are reissued in full on this double CD, along with four previously unreleased cuts and one selection ("I Can't Give You Anything But Love") only out earlier as a single. Although Smith's basic sound was slightly different than it would become (in fact, on the opening "The Way You Look Tonight," he often sounds like his main predecessor, Wild Bill Davis), he clearly had something new and fresh to offer. It is on the uptempo burners (such as "Lady Be Good" and "The Champ") that Jimmy Smith immediately showed the jazz world that he had no competitors. Even four decades later, he remains the dominant force on virtually all organists. Teamed with guitarist Thornel Schwartz and either Ray Perry (for the first nine numbers) or Donald Bailey on drums, Smith (who had only taken up the organ three years earlier) is well featured on 28 spirited selections. A historic set. —*Scott Yanow*

The Champ / Mar. 11, 1956 / Blue Note ✦✦✦✦
Recorded in NYC. When first issued, many thought there were two players here, or overdubs. Just early Smith cookin'. —*Michael Erlewine*

Greatest Hits, Vol. 1 / Mar. 27, 1956-Feb. 8, 1963 / Blue Note ✦✦✦✦
This double LP, even with its clichéd title, is a real gem. It contains eight of the greatest performances recorded by organist Jimmy Smith during his important period with Blue Note. "The Champ" from his second recording features Smith taking around 50 choruses on a blazing blues, and it set a standard that has still not been surpassed. Also included on this valuable two-fer (some of the material has since been reissued on CD) are "All Day Long," a 20-minute "The Sermon," "Midnight Special," "When Johnny Comes Marching Home," "Can Heat," "Flamingo," and "Prayer Meetin'." In the supporting cast are trumpeter Lee Morgan, altoist Lou Donaldson, Tina Brooks and Stanley Turrentine on tenors, guitarists Kenny Burrell, Thornel Schwartz, and Quentin Warren, and drummers Art Blakey and Donald Bailey. This set serves as a perfect introduction to Jimmy Smith's early years and has lots of hard-swinging and soulful jams. —*Scott Yanow*

The Sounds of Jimmy Smith / Feb. 11, 1957 / Blue Note ✦✦✦
This LP, which has been included as part of a Mosaic Jimmy Smith three-CD box set, features the organist playing a pair of rare unaccompanied solos on "All the Things You Are" and a fairly free "The Fight" and jamming several songs ("Zing Went the Strings of My Heart," "Somebody Loves Me," and "Blue Moon") with his trio. Art Blakey fills in for drummer Donald Bailey on "Zing" while guitarist Eddie McFadden is heard throughout the three selections. Excellent straightahead jazz from the innovative organist. —*Scott Yanow*

A Date with Jimmy Smith, Vol. 2 / Feb. 11, 1957-Feb. 12, 1957 / Blue Note ✦✦✦
This LP is one of five that has been reissued by Mosaic in a three-CD box set. For the jam session date altoist Lou Donaldson has a duet with organist Jimmy Smith on "I'm Getting Sentimental over You," and together they match up forces in a sextet with trumpeter Donald Byrd, Hank Mobley on

tenor, guitarist Eddie McFadden, and drummer Art Blakey, playing lengthy versions of Mobley's "Groovy Date" and Duke Ellington's "I Let a Song Go out of My Heart." All of the Jimmy Smith jam sessions are easily recommended to fans of straightahead jazz; get the Mosaic box. — *Scott Yanow*

A Date with Jimmy Smith, Vol. 1 / Feb. 11, 1957-Feb. 12, 1957 / Blue Note ✦✦✦

After cutting five albums with his trio, organist Jimmy Smith on Feb. 11, 1957, recorded with trumpeter Donald Byrd, altoist Lou Donaldson, and tenor saxophonist Hank Mobley in a sextet that also included guitarist Eddie McFadden, and drummer Art Blakey. Among the five songs recorded that day, two (lengthy versions of "Falling in Love with Love" and "Funk's Oats") are included on this LP along with a shorter trio rendition of "How High the Moon" from two days later with McFadden and drummer Donald Bailey in a trio. All of this music has been reissued by Mosaic on a definitive CD box set. — *Scott Yanow*

☆ **The Complete February 1957 Jimmy Smith Blue Note Sessions** / Feb. 11, 1957-Feb. 13, 1957 / Mosaic ✦✦✦✦

It would not be an overstatement to say that organist Jimmy Smith was busy during Feb. 11-13, 1957, for he recorded enough material for these three CDs, 21 often-lengthy performances that originally appeared on five LPs plus three others that had been previously unissued. Smith is not only heard early in his career with his regular trio but in a sextet with trumpeter Donald Byrd, altoist Lou Donaldson, tenor-saxophonist Hank Mobley, and drummer Art Blakey, in duets with Donaldson and with a quartet that also stars guitarist Kenny Burrell. These jam sessions feature plenty of exciting solos over fairly common chord changes and, despite the heavy competition, Jimmy Smith (who is still the king of the jazz organ) is the dominant force. Recommended. — *Scott Yanow*

The Best of Jimmy Smith / Feb. 12, 1957-Jan. 3, 1986 / Blue Note ✦✦✦✦

Small-group setting. Selections from some of Smith's best Blue Note albums, such as: *The Sermon, Go for Whatcha Know, Midnight Special, Back at the Chicken Shack, A New Sound,* and *At the Organ.* — *Michael Erlewine*

Jimmy Smith Trio + LD / Jul. 4, 1957 / Blue Note ✦✦✦

Theoretically, the pairing of Jimmy Smith and Lou Donaldson is a smart idea. Both musicians were instrumental in the development of soul-jazz and were recognized as among the leaders of their genre. Instead of catching fire, however, *Jimmy Smith Trio + LD,* falls flat. There are a few moments that fulfill the duo's potential—both Smith and Donaldson trade hot lines on "Star Eyes"—but in general, the session is a bland but pleasant offering nothing truly memorable. — *Stephen Thomas Erlewine*

House Party / Aug. 25, 1957 / Blue Note ✦✦✦✦

Music from two different sessions are included on this enjoyable LP. All of organist Jimmy Smith's jam sessions are worth acquiring although several (such as this one) have been long out of print. Lengthy versions of "Au Privave" and "Just Friends" and more concise renditions of "Lover Man" and "Blues After All" match Smith with quite a variety of all-stars: trumpeter Lee Morgan, trombonist Curtis Fuller, Lou Donaldson or George Coleman on altos, Tina Brooks on tenor, guitarists Kenny Burrell or Eddie McFadden, and Art Blakey or Donald Bailey on drums. Everyone plays up to par and the passionate solos (and Smith's heated background riffing) keep the proceedings continually exciting. — *Scott Yanow*

Confirmation / Aug. 25, 1957+Feb. 25, 1958 / Blue Note ✦✦✦✦

Organist Jimmy Smith led a series of exciting jam sessions for Blue Note from 1957-60, including the three selections heard on this LP. These performances were not released for the first time until 1979, but their quality is as strong as Smith's other output from the era. "Confirmation" matches Smith with altoist Lou Donaldson, tenor Tina Brooks, trumpeter Lee Morgan, guitarist Kenny Burrell, and drummer Art Blakey, while a 15-minute rendition of "What Is This Thing Called Love" and a 20-minute "Cherokee" have Morgan, Burrell, Blakey, trombonist Curtis Fuller and George Coleman on alto. The heated solos are quite enjoyable, and the organist keeps the momentum constantly flowing throughout this infectious set. — *Scott Yanow*

Lonesome Road / Nov. 20, 1957 / Blue Note ✦✦✦✦

Jimmy Smith recorded for Blue Note so frequently during the late '50s that many of his sessions remained unreleased for years. The music that com-

prises *Lonesome Road* sat in the vaults for years, until the Japanese division of Blue Note released the album in the '80s. Since Smith had so many albums on the market, it's understandable that Blue Note wanted to limit the number of records they released from him, but the music on *Lonesome Road* is almost as fine as that on *The Sermon* or *Groovin' at Small's Paradise.* Smith, guitarist Eddie McFadden, and drummer Donald Bailey play a selection of eight standards, but the songs don't sound stale; they sound fresh and alive. A few of the ballads are a little slow and treacly, but many of the numbers cook, with a couple of the songs featuring Smith at his hottest. It doesn't have the mastery he would later demonstrate on *Back at the Chicken Shack,* nor is it quite as consistent as *The Sermon,* but *Lonesome Road* is worthwhile for any fan of Smith. — *Stephen Thomas Erlewine*

☆ **The Sermon** / Feb. 25, 1958 / Blue Note ✦✦✦✦✦

This CD reissue has two of the three selections (the 20-minute "The Sermon" and "Flamingo") from the original LP, adding five additional selections that are related. With such soloists as trumpeter Lee Morgan, trombonist Curtis Fuller, altoist Lou Donaldson, Tina Brooks on tenor, either Eddie McFadden or Kenny Burrell on guitar, and Art Blakey or Donald Bailey on drums. The straightahead music is as good as one would expect (with the lengthy title cut being the obvious highpoint), and the CD overall offers listeners a strong dose of Jimmy Smith's Blue Note period. — *Scott Yanow*

☆ **Cool Blues** / Apr. 7, 1958 / Blue Note ✦✦✦✦✦

This CD should greatly interest all Jimmy Smith collectors, including those who already have the original LP. In addition to four excellent selections (quintets with altoist Lou Donaldson, Tina Brooks on tenor, guitarist Eddie McFadden, either Art Blakey or Donald Bailey on drums, and the organist/leader), there are three previously unissued numbers from the same gig, featuring the quartet of Donaldson, Smith, McFadden, and Bailey. The repertoire is filled with blues and bop standards and the soloing is at a consistently high and hard-swinging level. Jimmy Smith fans will be pleased. — *Scott Yanow*

On the Sunny Side / Jul. 15, 1958 / Blue Note ✦✦✦✦

Organist Jimmy Smith recorded quite a bit of material for Blue Note during 1956-63. This 1981 LP released for the first time eight selections cut during four sessions in the late '50s. In all cases, Smith is joined by guitarist Kenny Burrell and drummer Donald Bailey; Stanley Turrentine makes the group a quartet on "The Sunny Side of the Street" while his fellow tenor Percy France does the same on his original "Apostrophe." All of the songs (other than the latter) are standards and the tunes generally clock in around a concise five minutes. The results are predictably swinging and highlights include "On the Sunny Side," "Since I Fell for You," "Bye Bye Blackbird," and "I'm Just a Lucky So and So." Excellent music. — *Scott Yanow*

Home Cookin' / Jul. 15, 1958-Jun. 16, 1959 / Blue Note ✦✦✦✦

Organist Jimmy Smith and guitarist Kenny Burrell always had a close musical relationship, making each of their joint recordings quite special. This LP features the pair along with drummer Donald Bailey and (on four of the seven songs) the obscure but talented tenor saxophonist Percy France. The emphasis is on blues and basic material including versions of "See See Rider," Ray Charles' "I Got a Woman," and several group originals, and as usual, the performances are swinging and soulful. The CD reissue adds five "new" performances to the original seven. — *Scott Yanow*

☆ **Crazy! Baby** / Jan. 4, 1960 / Blue Note ✦✦✦✦✦

Unlike most of the Jimmy Smith recordings from the era, this CD reissue (which adds "If I Should Lose You" and "When Lights Are Low" to the original LP program) features organist Jimmy Smith's regular group (rather than an all-star band). With guitarist Quentin Warren and drummer Donald Bailey completing the trio, Smith is heard in peak form on swinging and soulful versions of such tunes as "When Johnny Comes Marching Home," "Makin' Whoopee," "Sonnymoon for Two," and "Mack the Knife." Despite claims and some strong challenges by others, there has never been a jazz organist on the level of Jimmy Smith. — *Scott Yanow*

Open House/Plain Talk / Mar. 22, 1960 / Blue Note ✦✦✦✦

A two-fer with two classic Smith albums, *Open House* and *Plain Talk* on one CD. Recorded in Hackensack, NJ. Studio session featuring Blue Mitchell (tpt), Ike Quebec (ts), and Jackie McClean (as). This is essentially a jam session without Smith's regular sidemen. More mainstream than most, but very nice tracks—fast and slow. This is an excellent album. —*Michael Erlewine*

★ **Back at the Chicken Shack** / Apr. 25, 1960 / Blue Note ✦✦✦✦✦
This may be the quintessential funky soul-jazz album. Period. I know of no better single recording and this is the one I would have to take to that desert island when I go. The term "all star" was coined for this group. Jimmy Smith is as hot as he gets and so is Stanley Turrentine on tenor sax. Just hot! Kenny Burrell is in top form too and Donald Bailey keeps the beat tight. Every jazz fan should hear it and every groove fan must own it. Also see the Smith album *Midnight Special*, which was recorded at the same session. —*Michael Erlewine*

☆ **Midnight Special** / Apr. 25, 1960 / Blue Note ✦✦✦✦✦
Recorded in Englewood Cliffs, NJ. Small Group. This was recorded at the same session as *Back at the Chicken Shack*, and it is also as fine—that is: magical! This is a must-have for jazz organ fans. With Stanley Turrentine (ts) and Kenny Burrell (g). Every collector of groove music should have a copy. —*Michael Erlewine*

Prayer Meetin' / Jun. 13, 1960+Feb. 8, 1963 / Blue Note ✦✦✦✦
With Stanley Turrentine. Fine Album. Small group. Smith's last Blue Note album until 1986 (*Go for Whatcha Know*). Also, last two cuts from Jun. 13, 1960, were released in Japan on an album: *Special Guests*. —*Michael Erlewine*

I'm Movin' On / Jan. 31, 1963 / Blue Note ✦✦✦
This CD reissue of a formerly rare date has a perfectly suitable title for it is the first of four albums that organist Jimmy Smith made within an eight-day period for Blue Note before permanently leaving the label for Verve. Although notable for matching Smith with guitarist Grant Green in what would be their only joint recording (drummer Donald Bailey completes the trio), the music is fairly typical of a Jimmy Smith session with the repertoire including blues, a couple of standards and ballads. The solos are well-played but nothing too surprising occurs (except perhaps for the sappiness of "What Kind of Fool Am I"); the original LP program is expanded by the inclusion of two other selections from the same date. —*Scott Yanow*

Bucket! / Feb. 1, 1963 / Blue Note ✦✦✦
Recorded at Englewood Cliffs, NJ. Trio session. Typically resolute Smith cuts. —*Ron Wynn*

Rockin' the Boat / Feb. 2, 1963 / Blue Note ✦✦✦✦
Organist Jimmy Smith's next-to-last LP for Blue Note after a very extensive seven-year period is up to his usual level. With altoist Lou Donaldson joining Smith's regular group (which included guitarist Quentin Warren and drummer Donald Bailey), the quartet swings with soul on such fine numbers as "When My Dream Boat Comes Home," "Can Heat," "Please Send Me Someone to Love," and "Just a Closer Walk with Thee." With the exception of the closing ballad, "Trust in Me," all seven of the selections are closely related to the blues. This is fine music well deserving of being reissued on CD someday. —*Scott Yanow*

Talkin' Verve: Roots of Acid Jazz / Mar. 20, 1963-Sep. 11, 1972 / Verve ✦✦✦✦
Designed to appeal to hip-hop and acid jazz fans, not jazz purists, *Talkin' Verve: The Roots of Acid Jazz* collects 14 tracks Jimmy Smith cut for Verve during the late '60s. Comprised of pop covers and funky workouts, the music is "jazzy," not jazz—there's little improvisation on the record, but there is a lot of hot vamping, with Smith creating dense, funky chord clusters, and bluesy leads. It's music that is devoted to the groove, and while a few of these cuts fall flat—"Ode to Billlie Joe" has no funk in it, no matter how hard you try—for the most part *Talkin' Verve* is soulful fun. Not much of this sounds like acid jazz, especially since the rhythms are a little stiff, but it's enjoyable lite-funk, and it's more palatable in the compilation than it is on their original albums. —*Stephen Thomas Erlewine*

Live at the Village Gate / May 31, 1963 / Metro ✦✦✦✦
Recorded at the Village Gate, NYC. Smith in a trio setting. Plenty of fine playing. —*Ron Wynn*

Blue Bash / Jul. 25, 1963-Jul. 26, 1963 / Verve ✦✦✦
Recorded in NYC. Good '60s sessions. —*Ron Wynn*

Organ Grinder Swing / Jun. 14, 1965-Jun. 15, 1965 / Verve ✦✦✦✦
Most of organist Jimmy Smith's recordings for Verve during the mid-to-late

'60s were with big bands, making this trio outing with guitarist Kenny Burrell and drummer Grady Tate a special treat. This CD reissue is a throwback to Smith's Blue Note sets (which had concluded two years earlier) and gives the organists the opportunity to stretch out on three blues and three standards. This release shows that, even with all of his commercial success during the period, Jimmy Smith was always a masterful jazz player. —*Scott Yanow*

☆ **The Dynamic Duo** / Sep. 21, 1966+Sep. 28, 1966 / Verve ✦✦✦✦✦
This CD—a straight reissue of the original LP—is a classic. Organist Jimmy Smith and guitarist Wes Montgomery, both the main pacesetters on their instruments at the time, make for a perfect team on quartet renditions (with drummer Grady Tate and percussionist Ray Barretto) of "James and Wes" and "Baby, It's Cold Outside." However, it is the three numbers with a big band arranged by Oliver Nelson (particularly "Night Train" and a very memorable version of "Down by the Riverside") that really stick in one's mind. Although it is unfortunate that the Smith-Wes collaboration was short-lived (just one other album), it is miraculous that they did find each other and created this brilliant music. —*Scott Yanow*

Further Adventures of Jimmy and Wes / Sep. 21, 1966-Sep. 28, 1966 / Verve ✦✦✦✦
Organist Wes Montgomery and guitarist Wes Montgomery did all of their recordings together during several sessions in September 1966, but despite the relatively low quantity, the results were consistently memorable. This CD, a follow-up to *The Dynamic Duo*, has one selection ("Milestones") in which the two lead voices are joined by Oliver Nelson's big band and several numbers (including the pop hits "King of the Road" and "Call Me") with a quartet that also includes drummer Grady Tate and percussionist Ray Barretto. Although not reaching the heights of the other set, this CD has more than its share of exciting solos from the immortal co-leaders. —*Scott Yanow*

Respect / Jun. 2, 1967+Jun. 14, 1967 / Verve ✦✦
Organist Jimmy Smith, joined by one of two guitar/bass/drums rhythm sections, mostly sticks to then-current R&B hits on this out-of-print LP. He does what he can with "Mercy, Mercy, Mercy," a brief "Respect" and "Funky Broadway" while contributing his own blues "T-Bone Steak." The 31-minute set has its moments but no real surprises, swinging funkily throughout. —*Scott Yanow*

The Boss / Nov. 20, 1968 / Verve ✦✦✦
Recorded at Paschal's La Carousel, Atlanta, GA. Lots of fine solos. George Benson (g) does best soul-jazz work since McDuff days. —*Ron Wynn*

Root Down / Feb. 8, 1972 / Verve ✦✦
Recorded in Los Angeles. Typical soul-jazz date. —*Ron Wynn*

Bluesmith / Sep. 11, 1972 / Verve ✦✦✦✦
It is ironic that one of Jimmy Smith's best Verve releases would be his next-to-last for the label. This surprisingly freewheeling but relaxed jam session also features Teddy Edwards on tenor, guitarist Ray Crawford, bassist Leroy Vinnegar, drummer Donald Dean, and the congas of Victor Pantoja. Together they perform five of Smith's fairly basic originals and Harvey Siders' "Mournin' Wes," a tribute for Wes Montgomery. Fine straightahead music that deserves to be reissued again. —*Scott Yanow*

Off the Top / Jun. 7, 1982 / Elektra ✦✦✦✦
It had been nine years since organist Jimmy Smith recorded for a major label when Bruce Lundvall approached him to make an album for Elektra Musician. Smith plays some unusual material (including Lionel Richie's "Endless Love" and the "Theme from *M.A.S.H.*") on this LP but swings everything and has a particularly strong supporting cast—guitarist George Benson, Stanley Turrentine on tenor, bassist Ron Carter, and drummer Grady Tate. A fine comeback date. —*Scott Yanow*

Fourmost / Nov. 16, 1990-Nov. 17, 1990 / Milestone ✦✦✦✦
Organist Jimmy Smith has a reunion on this CD with his 30 plus-year associates tenor saxophonist Stanley Turrentine and guitarist Kenny Burrell along with drummer Grady Tate. Together they play spirited and creative versions of standards and blues. The highpoints include "Midnight Special," a swinging "Main Stem," Tate's warm vocal on "My Funny Valentine," and a lengthy rendition of "Quiet Nights." Suffice it to say that this all-star date reaches its

potential and is easily recommended to fans of straightahead jazz. —*Scott Yanow*

Johnny "Hammond" Smith

b. Dec. 16, 1933, Louisville, KY, **d.** Jun. 4, 1997, Chicago, IL
Organ / Soul-Jazz, Hard Bop, Groove
Johnny (Robert) "Hammond" Smith was born on December 16, 1933 in Louisville, KY. From a musical family, he learned piano early on. Bud Powell and Art Tatum were his idols. Originally a pianist based in Cleveland, after hearing Wild Bill Davis he switched to the organ. Also known as Johnny Hammond, Smith worked for a period in the late '50s as Nancy Wilson's accompanist but had spent most of his career as a leader, recording a series of enjoyable soul-jazz albums for Prestige during 1959-1970. Although he also utilized synthesizers in the 1970s, Smith in the 1980s and '90s (before being struck down by cancer) stuck exclusively to the organ in a timeless style unchanged from three decades before. Johnny "Hammond" Smith was one of the many organists to come to prominence in the 1960s who was greatly influenced by Jimmy Smith. —*Michael Erlewine & Scott Yanow*

All Soul / Sep. 11, 1959 / New Jazz ✦✦✦
Smith with Thornell Schwart on guitar. —*AMG*

That Good Feelin' / Nov. 4, 1959 / Prestige ✦✦✦✦

Black Coffee / Nov. 8, 1962 / Riverside ✦✦✦✦
Two of organist Johnny "Hammond" Smith's earliest gems (*Black Coffee* and *Mr. Wonderful*) are reissued in full on this single CD. Although influenced by Jimmy Smith, this particular organist was also a strong grooving player, able to play both blues and more complicated chord changes. He is showcased with a quartet that includes tenor saxophonist Seldon Powell and guitarist Eddie McFadden, and in a quintet with McFadden, tenorman Houston Person, and trumpeter Sonny Williams; in both cases Leo Stevens is on drums. The material (which includes eight colorful originals," "I Remember Clifford," "Body and Soul," and "He's a Real Gone Guy" among the 15 numbers) has a fair amount of variety, and Johnny "Hammond" Smith is heard at his best throughout this reissue. —*Scott Yanow*

Mr. Wonderful / 1963 / Riverside ✦✦✦
A fine set that holds some appeal for the straight jazz crowd as well as the organ soul-jazz clique, with the presence of Houston Person on tenor saxophone. Smith penned most of the eight tracks, getting into some compulsive grooves on "Blues for De-De" and "Mr. Wonderful" in particular. The LP was combined with the rougher-edged 1962 live record *Black Coffee* on the 78-minute CD version of *Black Coffee* issued by Milestone in 1997. —*Richie Unterberger*

The Stinger / May 7, 1965 / Prestige ✦✦✦✦
Organist Johnny "Hammond" Smith is a decent soul-jazz player. He plays in short, swirling bursts and uses the bass pedals in a pounding, aggressive manner. These are primarily uptempo and funky jam numbers, particularly the title track. —*Ron Wynn*

Soul Talk / May 19, 1969 / Prestige ✦✦✦✦
With Rusty Bryant on saxes, Wally Richardson on guitar, Bob Bushnell on bass, and Bernard Purdie on drums. —*Michael Erlewine*

● **Legends of Acid Jazz** / May 19, 1969 + Dec. 22, 1969 / Prestige ✦✦✦✦
Out of all the soul-jazz organ players, only one was so thoroughly funked out that he personally adopted the name of his favorite keyboard, the B-3: Johnny "Hammond" Smith. While not as important in the development of jazz styles as other keyboard players such as Jimmy Smith, "Hammond" Smith displayed an earthy, swinging talent worth listening to. *Legends of Acid Jazz: Johnny "Hammond" Smith* compiles under a single cover two albums Smith recorded in 1969, *Soul Talk* and *Black Feeling!* (complete with the liner notes from both original issues). On *Legends,* Smith gets down in the heady company of, among others, tenor saxophonist Rusty Bryant, funky drummer Bernard Purdie, and guitarist Wally Richardson; Richardson here pays tribute to his bandmates with his compositions "Purdie Dirty" and "Johnny Hammond Boogaloo." *Legends* includes the pop covers "When Sunny Gets Blue" and "This Guy's In Love With You," opens with the original version of Smith's hit "Soul Talk," and concludes with the updated version he later recorded for *Black Feeling.* Not groundbreaking, but solid and a funky good time. —*Chris Slawecki*

Dr. Lonnie Smith (Lonnie Smith)

Organ / Hard Bop, Soul-Jazz, Groove
Organist Lonnie Smith has often been confused with keyboardist/pianist Lonnie Liston Smith—and, in fact, more than a few retailers have wrongly assumed that they're one and the same. In the mid-'60s, the Hammond hero earned recognition for his membership in George Benson's classic quartet before going on to play with Lou Donaldson (contributing some memorable solos to the alto saxman's hit 1967 album *Alligator Boogaloo*) and recording enjoyable dates of his own for Blue Note. For all their accessibility and commercial appeal, funk-influenced Smith sessions like 1968's *Think* and 1970's *Drives* showed that he could be quite imaginative. Smith, who later entered academia and became Dr. Lonnie Smith, remained an inspired representative of soul-jazz and did some solid work with Donaldson in the '90s. —*Alex Henderson*

Finger Lickin' Good / Nov. 1967 / Columbia ✦✦✦

● **Think** / Jul. 23, 1968 / Blue Note ✦✦✦✦
Organist Lonnie Smith's second recording as a leader and first of two for Blue Note is one of his strongest dates. Teamed up with trumpeter Lee Morgan, tenor saxophonist David Newman, guitarist Melvin Sparks, drummer Marion Booker, Jr., and three percussionists, Smith performs R&B-ish material in a soul-jazz vein. With Morgan and Newman playing stimulating solos and the leader keeping the performances grooving, the music is both accessible and challenging. This CD reissue is well worth picking up. —*Scott Yanow*

Turning Point / Jan. 3, 1969 / Blue Note ✦✦✦
Most Blue Note soul-jazz albums from the late '60s went one of three ways: it either was a straightahead commercial session, a slightly psychedelic outing or a funky workout with a vague Black-power theme. Lonnie Smith had followed the latter path with *Think*, the predecessor to *Turning Point*, and there are still remenants of that style on this session, particularly in the opening cover of Don Covay's "See Saw." Nevertheless, *Turning Point* is a more adventurous affair than *Think*, finding Smith—as well as trumpeter Lee Morgan, trombonist Julian Priester, guitarist Melvin Sparks, tenor saxophonist Bennie Maupin, and drummer Leo Morris—exploring territory that isn't quite free, but certainly more "out there" than the average soul-jazz session. In particular, Smith's originals "Slow High" and "Turning Point" reach the outer edges of the style, playing with dissonance, complex melodies, and expansive sound structures. Despite all these free flourishes, *Turning Point* remains a soul-jazz record and it has all the trappings of its era—the take on "Eleanor Rigby" finds the group approximating psychedelia. While the more adventurous elements of *Turning Point* make for an intriguing listen, the album isn't quite as enjoyable as the harder grooving sessions or the spacier soul-jazz records from the same era. Nevertheless, it's a worthwhile listen. —*Stephen Thomas Erlewine*

Move Your Hand / Aug. 9, 1969 / Blue Note ✦✦✦✦
Move Your Hand was recorded live at Club Harlem in Atlantic City on August 9, 1969. Organist Lonnie Smith led a small combo—featuring guitarist Larry McGee, tenor saxist Rudy Jones, bari saxist Ronnie Cuber, and drummer Sylvester Goshay—through a set that alternated originals with two pop covers, the Coasters' "Charlie Brown" and Donovan's "Sunshine Superman." Throughout, the band works a relaxed, bluesy, and, above all, funky rhythm; they abandon improvisation and melody for a steady groove, so much that the hooks of the two pop hits aren't recognizable until a few minutes into the track. No one player stands out, but *Move Your Hand* is thoroughly enjoyable, primarily because the group never lets their momentum sag throughout the session. Though the sound of the record might be somewhat dated, the essential funk of the album remains vital. —*Stephen Thomas Erlewine*

Drives / Jan. 2, 1970 / Blue Note ✦✦✦
The declining days of Blue Note brought out many blatant attempts to make hit records at the sacrifice of the music. Organist Lonnie Smith has always been a fine player and his quintet on this date includes baritonist Ronnie Cuber but the material is quite crummy. An unsuccessful search for humor on "Seven Steps to Heaven," the odd vocal sounds heard on "Psychedelic Pi," Smith's vocal on "Twenty Five Miles," and an attempt to uplift "Spinning Wheel" are strong reasons to skip this CD reissue altogether. —*Scott Yanow*

Live at Club Mozambique / May 1970 / Blue Note ✦✦✦✦
Recorded on May 21, 1970, at Detroit's Club Mozambique, this was shelved and remained unreleased until it was retrieved for CD issue in 1995. It's odd

that Blue Note decided to sit on it for so long, because it ranks as one of Lonnie's better sets. The band, featuring George Benson on guitar, is relaxed and funky without being in your face about it, and unlike much soul-jazz of the time, most of the material is original, Smith having penned six of the eight numbers. Although the riffs often owe a lot to James Brown, this is definitely at least as much jazz as soul, with Lonnie taking a rare vocal turn on "Peace of Mind." —*Richie Unterberger*

Melvin Sparks

b. Mar. 22, 1946
Guitar / Groove, Soul-Jazz, Fusion
Although not a huge name in jazz, Melvin Sparks brought his Grant Green-influenced guitar to quite a few soul-jazz and organ-combo recordings of the late '60s and early '70s. A lover of jazz as well as R&B and blues, the Houston native took up the guitar at 11 and was only 13 when he sat in with B.B. King. In 1963, he joined the Upsetters, an R&B show band that backed Little Richard, Sam Cooke, and other big names. After leaving the Upsetters, Sparks played with Jack McDuff in 1966-67. The improviser was very much in demand in the late '60s and early '70s, and he was featured on sessions by Charles Earland, Sonny Stitt, Lou Donaldson, Rusty Bryant, Sonny Phillips, Reuben Wilson, and Johnny "Hammond" Smith, among others. Sparks delivered his first album as leader, *Sparks!*, for Prestige in 1970, and recorded a few more Prestige dates before providing *Melvin Sparks* for Westbound in 1975. When soul-jazz's fortunes declined in the mid-'70s, the guitarist wasn't working as much. The only album Sparks recorded as a leader in the '80s was 1981's *Sparkling* on Muse, although he was featured as a sideman on sessions by Houston Person, Hank Crawford, and Jimmy McGriff during that decade. The '90s saw a lot of renewed interest in soul-jazz, and in 1997, he returned to the studio for his Cannonball date *I'm a Gittar Player*. —*Alex Henderson*

Sparks! / Sep. 14, 1970 / Prestige ◆◆◆
A solid soul-jazz outing that looks to commercial material for the bulk of the set, but doesn't unduly compromise itself in a pop direction. Sparks was one of the bluesiest soul-jazz guitarists, and his tart tone shares space here with deep grooves from Leon Spencer on organ. The brass, handled by Virgil Jones (trumpet) Houston Person (tenor sax), and John Manning (tenor sax), is usually secondary to the guitar-organ riffs. Sparks remakes Sly Stone's "Thank You," the Coasters' "Charlie Brown," and Eric Burdon & War's "Spill the Wine" as lengthy instrumentals—commercial choices, to be sure, but executed with relaxed grit. Rounding out the program is a Rodgers-Hart cover and a Leon Spencer original. The entire album is available on the *Legends of Acid Jazz* CD reissue, which also includes his 1971 follow-up, *Spark Plug*. —*Richie Unterberger*

● **Legends of Acid Jazz** / Sep. 14, 1970-Mar. 8, 1971 / Prestige ◆◆◆◆
Combines his *Sparks!* (1970) and *Spark Plug* (1971) albums onto one CD, serving as the best compilation of his soul-jazz sessions for Prestige. —*Richie Unterberger*

Spark Plug / Mar. 8, 1971 / Prestige ◆◆◆
Sparks used a similar soul-jazz approach as he had on his previous Prestige session (*Sparks!*), revamping the lineup to put Reggie Roberts on organ and a young Grover Washington, Jr. on tenor sax (Idris Muhammad remained behind the drums). He also introduced some compositions of his own this time around; three of the five numbers are Sparks originals. It's more relaxed, funky, occasionally bluesy jazz with guitar and organ to the fore, very much of a piece with the Prestige soul-jazz "house" sound circa 1970. Pleasant fare, although it does tend to fade into suitable background music instead of attracting attention or intense scrutiny. The entire album is available on the *Legends of Acid Jazz* CD reissue, which also includes everything from *Sparks!* —*Richie Unterberger*

Texas Twister/75 / Oct. 1995 / ACE ◆◆
I'm a 'Gittar' Player / Sep. 30, 1997 / Cannonball ◆◆◆◆
Although he appeared on countless R&B and soul-jazz sessions in the '60s and early '70s, Melvin Sparks has recorded only sporadically as a leader over the years. The late '90s found the swinging, Grant Green-influenced guitarist recording for the Minneapolis-based Cannonball label and playing much the same type of groove-oriented organ-combo music he'd been embracing 25 and 30 years earlier. Recalling his work with Charles Earland, *I'm a 'Gittar'*

Player employs Ron Levy on the Hammond B-3 and offers a very accessible fusion of jazz, R&B, blues, and pop that often sounds like it could have been recorded in 1970. The only thing letting you know that this decent, enjoyable CD wasn't recorded back then is some Salt-N-Pepa-ish rapping that Sparks' daughters Ayisha and Idrissa provide on a remake of KC & the Sunshine Band's "Get Down Tonight." Otherwise, a retro outlook prevails. From the Latin-influenced "Jiggy" (which bears a definite resemblance to War's 1970 hit "Spill the Wine") to congenial numbers like "Sparkling," "Taste the Flavor," and "Mr. Texas," *I'm a 'Gittar' Player* demonstrates that jazz can have commercial appeal and pop leanings without sacrificing the type of spontaneity and blues feeling that make it jazz in the first place. —*Alex Henderson*

Sparks!/Akilah / BGP ◆◆◆◆
Sparks! is a solid soul-jazz outing that looks to commercial material for the bulk of the set, but doesn't unduly compromise itself in a pop direction. Sparks was one of the bluesiest soul-jazz guitarists, and his tart tone shares space here with deep grooves from Leon Spencer on organ. The brass, handled by Virgil Jones (trumpet), Houston Person (tenor sax), and John Manning (tenor sax), is usually secondary to the guitar-organ riffs. Sparks remakes Sly Stone's "Thank You," the Coasters' "Charlie Brown," and Eric Burdon & War's "Spill the Wine" as lengthy instrumentals—commercial choices, to be sure, but executed with relaxed grit. Rounding out the program is a Rodgers-Hart cover and a Leon Spencer original. BGP's reissue also includes Sparks' 1973 effort *Akilah*. —*Richie Unterberger*

Sonny Stitt (Edward Stitt)

b. Feb. 2, 1924, Boston, MA, **d.** Jul. 22, 1982, Washington, DC
Tenor Saxophone, Alto Saxophone / Bop, Groove
Charlie Parker has had many admirers and his influence can be detected in numerous styles, but few have been as avid a disciple as Sonny Sitt. There was almost note-for-note imitation in several early Stitt solos, and the closeness remained until Stitt began de-emphasizing the alto in favor of the tenor, on which he artfully combined the influences of Parker and Lester Young. Stitt gradually developed his own sound and style, though he was never far from Parker on any alto solo. A wonderful blues and ballad player whose approach was one of the influences on John Coltrane, Stitt could rip through an uptempo bebop stanza, then turn around and play a shivering, captivating ballad. He was an alto saxophonist in Tiny Bradshaw's band during the early '40s, then joined Billy Eckstine's seminal big band in 1945, playing alongside other emerging bebop stars like Gene Ammons and Dexter Gordon. Stitt later played in Dizzy Gillespie's big band and sextet. He began on tenor and baritone in 1949, and at times was in a two-tenor unit with Ammons. He recorded with Bud Powell and J.J. Johnson for Prestige in 1949, then did several albums on Prestige, Argo, and Verve in the '50s and '60s. Stitt led many combos in the '50s, and rejoined Gillespie for a short period in the late '50s. After a brief stint with Miles Davis in 1960, he reunited with Ammons and for a while was in a three tenor lineup with James Moody. During the '60s, Stitt also recorded for Atlantic, cutting the transcendent *Stitt Plays Bird* that finally addressed the Parker question in epic fashion. He continued heading bands, though he joined the Giants of Jazz in the early '70s. This group included Gillespie, Art Blakey, Kai Winding, Thelonious Monk, and Al McKibbon. Stitt did more sessions in the '70s for Cobblestone, Muse, and others, among them another definitive date, *Tune Up*. He continued playing and recording in the early '80s, recording for Muse, Sonet, and Who's Who In Jazz. He suffered a heart attack and died in 1982. —*Ron Wynn and Bob Porter*

Groove: Here is another very prolific player that did all kinds of gigs, played all kinds of music. There are so many Sonny Stitt albums that it is hard to know where to begin. Take a look at some of the selections listed below, not all of which are available without a search. You will like Stitt because he really kicks butt on the saxophone—one tough horn player. —*Michael Erlewine*

Stitt Meets Brother Jack / Feb. 16, 1962 / Original Jazz Classics ◆◆◆◆
Sonny Stitt (who sticks on this CD reissue to tenor) meets up with organist Brother Jack McDuff (along with guitarist Eddie Diehl, drummer Art Taylor, and Ray Barretto on congas) for a spirited outing. Two standards ("All of Me" and "Time After Time") are performed with a variety of blues-based originals and the music always swings in a soulful boppish way. Worth picking up although not essential. —*Scott Yanow*

Soul Classics / Feb. 16, 1962-Feb. 15, 1972 / Original Jazz Classics ♦♦
This CD is a sampler of Sonny Stitt's Prestige recordings. Stitt (mostly heard here on tenor) is accompanied by organists (Brother Jack McDuff, Don Patterson, or Gene Ludwig) on all but one selection but unfortunately half of the performances find him utilizing an electrified varitone sax that watered down his sound and buried his individuality. This set can be safely passed by. — *Scott Yanow*

Nuther Fu'ther / Feb. 19, 1962 / Prestige ♦♦♦
Fine soul jazz with Jack McDuff (organ). — *Ron Wynn*

Soul Summit / Feb. 19, 1962 / Prestige ♦♦♦♦
With Jack McDuff. — *AMG*

Low Flame / Apr. 4, 1962 / Jazzland ♦♦♦
Stitt with Don Patterson on the Hammond B-3 and Paul Weedon on guitar. — *AMG*

Soul Shack / Sep. 17, 1963 / Prestige ♦♦♦
With Brother Jack McDuff on the Hammond B-3. — *AMG*

Primitivo Soul / Dec. 31, 1963 / Prestige ♦♦♦
Excellent soul jazz and blues numbers by alto and tenor saxophonist Sonny Stitt, who plays with almost unrelenting energy and drive throughout this session. This was a typical date, but Stitt's earthy playing moved it beyond cliche and convention. — *Ron Wynn*

Soul People / Aug. 25, 1964 / Prestige ♦♦♦♦
There are dozens of Sonny Stitt records available at any particular time; this CD reissue is one of the better ones. Mostly sticking to tenor, Stitt battles fellow tenor Booker Ervin with assistance from the fine organist Don Patterson and drummer Billy James on five selections and a ballad medley from 1964. Because both Stitt and Ervin always had very individual sounds, their tradeoffs are quite exciting and end up a draw. Among the "bonus" cuts of this CD are a feature for Patterson with a trio in 1966 ("There Will Never Be Another You") and a collaboration between Stitt, Patterson, James, and guitarist Grant Green on a 1966 version of "Tune Up." Enjoyable and generally hard-swinging music. — *Scott Yanow*

Made for Each Other / Jul. 13, 1968 / Delmark ♦♦
Sonny Stitt's regular group of the period (which included organist Don Patterson and drummer Billy James) plays a wide variety of material on this LP, ranging from "The Very Thought of You" and two versions of "Funny" to "Blues for J.J." and some then-current pop tunes. Unfortunately the set is from the period when Stitt often used a Varitone electronic attachment on his alto and tenor which gave him a much more generic sound, lowering the quality of this music despite some strong improvisations. It is an okay set that could have been better. — *Scott Yanow*

The Bubba's Sessions with Eddie "Lockjaw" Davis & Harry "Sweets" Edison / Nov. 11, 1981 / Who's Who In Jazz ♦♦♦♦
The second of two Who's Who LPs recorded during a club appearance by Sonny Stitt (who doubles here on alto and tenor) has guest appearances by tenor-saxophonist Eddie "Lockjaw" Davis and trumpeter Harry "Sweets" Edison in addition to fine backup work from pianist Eddie Higgins, bassist Donn Mast, and drummer Duffy Jackson. This may look like a budget album but the playing (particularly by Stitt) on the blues, standards, and ballads is top notch. Until the music is reissued on CD, this LP and the complementary set *Sonny, Sweets & Jaws* are collector's items. — *Scott Yanow*

Buddy Tate (George Holmes Tate)

b. Feb. 22, 1913, Sherman, TX
Tenor Saxophone, Clarinet / Swing, Groove
One of the more individual tenors to emerge from the swing era, the distinctive Buddy Tate came to fame as Herschel Evans's replacement with Count Basie's Orchestra. Earlier he had picked up valuable experience playing with Terrence Holder (1930-33), Count Basie's original Kansas City band (1934), Andy Kirk (1934-35), and Nat Towles (1935-39). With Basie a second time during 1939-48, Tate held his own with such major tenors as Lester Young, Don Byas, Illinois Jacquet, Lucky Thompson, and Paul Gonsalves. After a period freelancing with the likes of Hot Lips Page, Lucky Millinder, and Jimmy Rushing (1950-52), Tate led his own crowd-pleasing group for 21 years (1953-74) at Harlem's Celebrity Club. During this period Tate also took time out to record in a variety of settings (including with Buck Clayton and

Milt Buckner) and he was one of the stars of John Hammond's Spirituals to Swing concert of 1967. Tate has kept busy since the Celebrity Club association ended, recording frequently, co-leading a band with Paul Quinichette in 1975, playing and recording in Canada with Jay McShann and Jim Galloway, visiting Europe many times and performing at jazz parties; he was also a favorite sideman of Benny Goodman's in the late '70s. Although age had taken its toll, in the mid-'90s Buddy Tate played and recorded with both Lionel Hampton and the Statesmen of Jazz. — *Scott Yanow*

Swinging Like Tate / Feb. 12, 1958 + Feb. 26, 1958 / London ♦♦♦
For this CD reissue, which brings back material originally recorded by Stanley Dance for the Felsted label, veteran swing tenor Buddy Tate is heard at the head of two different groups for three obscure songs apiece. The first half has Tate leading his Celebrity Club Orchestra, a four-horn octet that lacked any big names but worked regularly throughout the era. For the second half, Tate is teamed with some of the Count Basie alumni including trumpeter Buck Clayton, trombonist Dicky Wells, altoist Earle Warren, and drummer Jo Jones. The music overall is fine mainstream jazz of the 1950s that is easily recommended to straightahead jazz fans although little unexpected or all that memorable occurs. — *Scott Yanow*

Swinging Scorpio / 1974 / Black Lion ♦♦♦♦
Although Buck Clayton was no longer playing trumpet by 1974 due to health problems, he was still writing swinging compositions. On this CD reissue, tenor saxophonist Buddy Tate and trumpeter Humphrey Lyttelton (both of whom double on clarinet) perform eight of Buck's tunes in an English septet also including altoist Bruce Turner, Kathleen Stobart (on tenor and baritone), pianist Mick Pyne, bassist Dave Green, and drummer Tony Mann. The material (and many of the sidemen) may be obscure, but the music is fairly enjoyable; Clayton's arranged ensembles are an added plus. — *Scott Yanow*

The Texas Twister / Feb. 21, 1975 / New World ♦♦♦♦
The music on this New World release (originally put out by Master Jazz) is very much in the vein of Count Basie. Buddy Tate (playing tenor and clarinet in addition to taking a few of Jimmy Rushing-style vocals) is joined by fellow tenor Paul Quinichette (making one of his few recordings of the 1970s), pianist Cliff Smalls (an underrated swing player), bassist Major Holley, and drummer Jackie Williams. Other than the opening original "The Texas Twister" and Tate's ballad feature on "Talk Of The Town," all of the music is from the Basie book including "Chicago," "Boogie Woogie," and "Topsy." All of the musicians (most of whom were not making too many recordings in the mid-'70s) sound somewhat inspired and are in fine form. — *Scott Yanow*

Jive at Five / Jul. 23, 1975 / Storyville ♦♦♦♦
During an era when mainstream jam sessions were fairly rare and fusion reigned, Storyville documented an all-star group mostly comprised of swing era veterans. Tenor-saxophonist Buddy Tate, trombonist Vic Dickenson, and trumpeter Doc Cheatham (who was 70 at the time and just beginning to emerge as a soloist) make for a potent frontline, pianist Johnny Guarnieri is heard in prime form, and bassist George Duvivier and drummer Oliver Jackson are typically tasteful in support. Two alternate takes were added to the original seven-song program for this CD reissue and there are features for Dickenson (who sings and plays his own "Constantly"), Cheatham ("I've Got A Right To Sing The Blues") and Tate ("There Goes My Heart"). However it is the four group jams that are most exciting. Easily recommended to mainstream jazz fans. — *Scott Yanow*

★ **Hard Blowin'** / Aug. 25, 1978-Aug. 26, 1978 / Muse ♦♦♦♦♦
Muse has released at least six albums of material recorded at Sandy's Jazz Revival in Massachusetts during a week in 1978. This is veteran tenor Buddy Tate's most rewarding album from the engagement and a fine all-around showcase. Accompanied by pianist Ray Bryant, bassist George Duvivier, and drummer Alan Dawson, Tate stretches out on four familiar standards and shows listeners that he really had one of the more distinctive tenor sounds of the swing era. Recommended. — *Scott Yanow*

Live at Sandy's / Aug. 25, 1978-Aug. 26, 1978 / Muse ♦♦♦♦
One of the six Muse albums recorded at Sandy's Jazz Revival in Massachusetts during an engagement in 1978, this is essentially tenor veteran Buddy Tate's set although altoist Eddie "Cleanhead" Vinson and tenor Arnett Cobb join in on the closing blues "She's Got It." Tate is in fine form on the other four songs which includes an outing on clarinet for "Blue Creek," a warm version of the ballad "Candy," and two lengthy jams with pianist Ray Bryant,

bassist George Duvivier, and drummer Alan Dawson. Consistently swinging music and one of the better Buddy Tate recordings currently available. — *Scott Yanow*

Sam "The Man" Taylor (Samuel L. Taylor)

b. Jul. 12, 1916, Lexington, TN

Tenor Saxophone / Blues Jazz, Groove, Jump Blues, R&B, Soul-Jazz

A certified honking sax legend, Sam "The Man" Taylor's non-stop drive and power worked perfectly in swing, blues, and R&B sessions. He had a huge tone, perfect timing, and sense of drama, as well as relentless energy and spirit. Taylor began working with Scat Man Crothers and the Sunset Royal Orchestra in the late '30s. He played with Cootie Williams and Lucky Millinder in the early '40s, then worked six years with Cab Calloway. Taylor toured South America and the Caribbean during his tenure with Calloway. Then Taylor became the saxophonist of choice for many R&B dates through the '50s, recording with Ray Charles, Buddy Johnson, Louis Jordan, and Big Joe Turner among others. He also did sessions with Ella Fitzgerald and Sy Oliver. During the '60s, Taylor led his own bands and recorded in a quintet called the Blues Chasers. He currently has one session available on CD recorded in the late '50s with Charlie Shavers and Urbie Green. — *Ron Wynn*

● **The Bad and the Beautiful** / Sep. 2, 1962 / Prestige ♦♦♦♦

The Three Sounds (Three Sounds)

f. 1957

Group / Soul-Jazz, Groove, Hard Bop, Post-Bop, Ballads

The Three Sounds were one of the most popular artists on Blue Note Records during the late '50s and '60s, thanks to their nimble, swinging, blues-inflected mainstream jazz. Since their records sounded interchangeable and their warm, friendly jazz was instantly accessible, many critics dismissed the group at the time as lounge-jazz, but in the '90s, critical consensus agreed that the group's leader, pianist Gene Harris, was an accomplished, unique stylist whose very ease of playing disguised his technical skill. Similarly, his colleagues, bassist Andrew Simpkins and drummer Bill Dowdy, were a deft, capable rhythm section that kept the group in an appealing, bluesy groove. That groove was so appealing that the Three Sounds maintained a large fan following into the late '60s. During the group's prime period—from their 1958 debut for Blue Note to the departure of Dowdy in 1967—the Three Sounds cut an enormous number of records. Many records hit the shelves, while others stayed in the vaults, to be issued at a later date. Throughout it all, the trio's sound remained essentially the same, with no real dip in quality until the group began to splinter in the late '60s.

Gene Harris was at the center of the Three Sounds throughout its entire existence. A native of Benton Harbor, Michigan, he began playing piano as a child, performing in public at the age of six. He soon became distracted by boxing and sports, but he continued to perform music, occasionally in a trio with drummer Bill Dowdy. After they graduated from high school in 1951, both Harris and Dowdy joined the Army and were assigned to different units. However, both men were discharged in 1954, and after they left the Army, they began pursuing different musical careers. Harris played with a variety of bands throughout the South and Midwest, while Dowdy moved to Chicago and played with a number of blues and jazz bands. Two years later, both musicians happened to settle in South Bend, Indiana and decided to form a band called the Four Sounds with bassist Andrew Simpkins and a tenor saxophonist. After running through a number of tenor saxophonists unsuccessfully, the three musicians decided to jettison the horn from their group and become the Three Sounds. For the next two years, the group played regularly at Midwest venues, particularly in Ohio. They played as a trio, and they also supported such soloists as Lester Young and Sonny Stitt. During this time, Horace Silver became a fan of the group and recommended them to Alfred Lion, the head of Blue Note. Despite the good word, the group remained unsigned. They toured with Stitt and relocated to Washington, D.C., where they worked as a trio and as a rhythm section for touring soloists; during this time, they played with such musicians as Miles Davis and Kenny Burrell. In the fall of 1958, they moved to New York to work with Stitt. Shortly after they moved to the city, they signed to Blue Note, in addition to supporting Nat Adderley on a Riverside session.

The Three Sounds cut their first album for Blue Note in September of 1958. That record, *Introducing the Three Sounds*, became an unexpected

success among record buyers, and the group's live performances earned fans like Horace Silver, Sonny Stitt, Miles Davis, and Cannonball Adderley, even if critics tended to dismiss the group. In particular, a *Down Beat* reviewer panned the album, but that didn't stop the public from buying the record, which soon became one of the most popular jazz records of its years. Blue Note had the band re-enter the studio in February of 1959 to cut their second album, *Bottoms Up*. It was the third of a total of 17 sessions at Rudy Van Gelder's studio (*Introducing* had taken two sessions to complete). At one point, Harris estimated that the group has released 35 albums worth of material, with many left in the vaults. During their first stint at Blue Note, they released the following, in addition to *Introducing* and *Bottoms Up*: *Good Deal, Feelin' Good, Moods, Here We Come, It Just Got to Be, Hey There!, Out of This World*, and *Black Orchid*. The Three Sounds also supported such Blue Note artists as Stanley Turrentine and Lou Donaldson on several recording dates.

The Three Sounds continued successfully on Blue Note until 1962, when they switched labels shortly after recording *Black Orchid*. They cut one album, *Blue Genes*, for Verve, then moved to Mercury, where they made three records between December 1962 and 1964. Later in 1964, the trio signed to Limelight, where they made three records. In October of 1966, the group returned to Blue Note and recorded *Vibrations*. Shortly after the sessions, drummer Bill Dowdy left the group and was replaced by Donald Bailey, who made his first recorded appearance with the group on 1967's *Live at the Lighthouse*. That album was followed in 1968 by *Coldwater Flat*, an album that found the trio augmenting their sound with a string section. By the time the group returned to the studio in September 1968 to cut *Elegant Soul*, Bailey was replaced by Carl Burnett. *Elegant Soul* continued the pattern of smooth, string-heavy productions, as did 1969's *Soul Symphony*. By the time the group made *Soul Symphony*, bassist Andrew Simpkins had left the trio and was replaced by Henry Franklin.

Soul Symphony, for most intents and purposes, was the last record the Three Sounds made. They continued to perform live, and one of those concerts is documented on *Live at the It Club*, a 1970 date which was released in 1995. Later in 1970, Monk Montgomery replaced Franklin, but this version of the Three Sounds never recorded. Instead, Harris embarked on a solo career in 1971, releasing *Gene Harris & the Three Sounds*, which also featured Burnett and electric bassist Luther Hughes, along with a number of session men. From that point on, Harris concentrated on his solo career, recording for Blue Note over the next six years. Once his contract expired, Harris retired to Boise, Idaho, where he worked as a musical director at a hotel. Eventually, he returned to music after bassist Ray Brown convinced the pianist to play on an album for Pablo. Harris resumed his solo career in 1985, signing with Concord Jazz. His new albums, combined with CD reissues of classic Three Sounds dates, prompted a positive critical re-evluation of his music, and he maintained a strong reputation into the late '90s. — *Stephen Thomas Erlewine*

Groove: Here is bluesy jazz at its best. That some jazz purists think it should be discounted because it makes as good background (read dinner) music as foreground listening is just silly. The fact that you can play this music for your Grandma is not a fault. It's a virtue. There is that great Three Sounds album under Stanley Turrentine's name, *Blue Hour*. — *Michael Erlewine*

☆ **Introducing the Three Sounds** / Sep. 16, 1958 + Sep. 18, 1958 / Blue Note ♦♦♦♦♦

What's remarkable about *Introducing the Three Sounds* is how the trio's lightly swinging sound arrived fully intact. From the basis of this album, it sounds as if pianist Gene Harris, bassist Andrew Simpkins, and drummer William Dowdy have been playing together for years. There's empathetic, nearly intuitive interplay between the three musicians, and Harris' deft style already sounds mature and entirely distinctive. There's no question that this music is easy to listen to, but dismissing it because of that would be wrong—there's genuine style in their light touch and in Harris' bluesy compositions. The Three Sounds never really deviated from the sound they established on *Introducing*, but that's one of the things that is so remarkable—they were fully formed on their very first album. Even if it was a peak, it wasn't the only peak in their career. They would often match the heights of this album, but this debut remains a shining jewel in their catalog, and the way to become acquainted with their sound. [The CD reissue of *Introducing the Three Sounds* contains the five outtakes plus the alternate take of "Goin' Home" that originally comprised the Japanese album, *Introducing the Three Sounds, Vol. 2.*] — *Stephen Thomas Erlewine*

Introducing the Three Sounds, Vol. 2 / Sep. 16, 1958 + Sep. 18, 1958 / Blue Note ✦✦✦✦

During the '70s, the Japanese division of Blue Note began issuing previously unreleased sessions that had sat in the vaults for decades. Most of these records were comprised of entirely unheard sessions. Others, like *Introducing the Three Sounds, Vol. 2*, were comprised of outtakes and alternate takes from beloved Blue Note albums. *Vol. 2* contains five songs that were recorded during the *Introducing* sessions but remained unreleased, as well as an alternate take of "Goin' Home." Stylistically, this music is identical to the initial release (or any other Three Sounds album, for that matter), and it should please any fan of the trio, but there's little reason to seek this record out, since all of the material was released as bonus tracks on the CD reissue of *Introducing the Three Sounds.* — *Stephen Thomas Erlewine*

● **The Best of the Three Sounds** / 1958 / Blue Note ✦✦✦✦
The Best of the Three Sounds is a good overview of the trio's original stint at Blue Note. A handful of songs on this 13-song collection date from their late-'60s return to the label, when they played everything a little funkier than they did in their earlier days, but the bulk of the disc is comprised of their classic late-'50s and early-'60s records. Since all of the Three Sounds' albums sound quite similar and are of a consistently high quality, a novice could pick up any album and have a satisfactory introduction, but this nevertheless does a good job of picking up highlights like "Bobby," "Willow Weep for Me," "On Green Dolphin Street," "Poinciana," "Stompin' at the Savoy," and "At Last." It's a nice introduction to one of the most consistently entertaining and accessible artists on Blue Note's roster. — *Stephen Thomas Erlewine*

Bottoms Up! / Feb. 11, 1959 / Blue Note ✦✦✦
The second record by the Three Sounds (which, like too many of their recordings, has yet to be reissued on CD in the US) features the increasingly popular group in prime form. Pianist Gene Harris, bassist Andy Simpkins, and drummer Bill Dowdy are in top form performing their brand of funky jazz, which left plenty of room for inventive solos along with the percolating grooves. On this set, the trio plays seven standards (including "Besame Mucho," "Love Walked In," and "I Could Write a Book"), plus the original "Jinne Lou." Well worth searching for. — *Scott Yanow*

Good Deal / May 20, 1959 / Blue Note ✦✦✦
Good Deal is a typically fine record from the Three Sounds, who were beginning to hit their stride when this session was recorded in May of 1959. Like most of their records, it's laidback—even when the group works a swinging tempo, there's a sense of ease that keeps the mood friendly, relaxed, and mellow. Balancing standards like "Satin Doll," "Soft Winds," and "That's All" with bop ("Robbin's Nest"), calypso ("St. Thomas") and originals, the Three Sounds cover a lot of stylistic territory, putting their distinctive stamp on each song. It's very accessible, pleasant soul-jazz, and mainstream hard bop, but Gene Harris' masterful technique means that *Good Deal* rewards close listening as well. — *Stephen Thomas Erlewine*

Standards / Oct. 10, 1959-Jun. 28, 1962 / Blue Note ✦✦✦✦
Released in 1998, *Standards* is comprised of 12 previously unreleased recordings the Three Sounds made on several different sessions in 1959 and 1962. All of the songs are familiar—"Makin' Whoopee," "Cry Me a River," "Witchcraft," "Stay as Sweet As You Are," "The Best Things In Life Are Free," "Red Sails in the Sunset," "Good Night Ladies"—and are given the familiar Three Sounds treatment, and the results are typically tasteful and delightful. — *Stephen Thomas Erlewine*

Feelin' Good / Jun. 28, 1960 / Blue Note ✦✦✦✦
An appropriate title for an utterly charming set from the Three Sounds. The trio works familiar territory on *Feelin' Good*, playing a set of swinging hard bop and classy soul-jazz, but there's a definite spark in the air. Working from a diverse set of standards, originals, contemporary jazz, and blues, the Three Sounds created a cheerful, uptempo record. Its very ease is deceptive—the music is so accessible and entertaining, it's easy to overlook the sheer musical mastery of the group, which performs at something of a peak on this record. Gene Harris sounds better than ever, turning in an elegant interpretation of "It Could Happen to You," but he's just as able to inject "When I Fall In Love" with unexpectedly vigorous swing and make Monk's "Straight No Chaser" a foot-tapping, danceable delight. Bassist Andrew Simpkins and

drummer Bill Dowdy follow Harris with graceful, imperceptible ease. It captures the Three Sounds at a peak, which means *Feelin' Good* is an excellent example of early soul-jazz. — *Stephen Thomas Erlewine*

Moods / Jun. 28, 1960 / Blue Note ✦✦✦✦
The Three Sounds open their signature sound a bit on the romantic *Moods*. They retain the same light touch that made their early albums so enjoyable, but they add more textures to the mix. Light Latin rhythms permeate *Moods*, from the inventive reworking of Cole Porter's "Love for Sale" to Harris' original "Tammy's Breeze." Like its predecessor, *Feelin' Good*, this record has a bluesy, soulful streak to its personality, as evidenced by the mellow take on "On Green Dolphin Street," the hep swing of "Loose Walk," and the infectious cover of Ellington's "I'm Beginning to See the Light." Occasionally, the Three Sounds play it a little too cool—while the slow, relaxed "Things Ain't What They Used to Be" manages to be engaging, "Li'l Darlin'" slows down to a crawl—but on the whole, *Moods* is an endearing collection of appealing mainstream jazz. — *Stephen Thomas Erlewine*

Here We Come / Dec. 13, 1960-Dec. 14, 1960 / Blue Note ✦✦✦
Here We Come is a typically classy and entertaining collection from the Three Sounds. The group stretches out on these pop standards and Gene Harris originals a little more than normal, which gives the pianist an opportunity to flaunt his underrated chops. Stylistically, nothing has changed—this is still light, deftly swinging mainstream jazz—but with songs like "Summertime" and "Our Love is Here to Stay," *Here We Come* has a bit of a romantic feeling, which is certainly welcome. Of course, that's balanced by the jumping title track and "Poinciana," among others, but overall the album has a warm, relaxed vibe that makes the romanticism particularly welcoming. — *Stephen Thomas Erlewine*

It Just Got to Be / Dec. 13, 1960-Dec. 14, 1960 / Blue Note ✦✦✦
The material that comprises *It Just Got to Be* was recorded during the same sessions as *Here We Come*, and like that album, this record has its share of romantic standards, including "Stella By Starlight" and "The Nearness of You." *It Just Got to Be* also captures the Three Sounds in the mood to stretch out and improvise a little (ironically, two of the three original compositions are the shortest songs on the album). The performances throughout the record are predictably swinging and enjoyable, even if they find the trio taking no stylistic chances. That lack of adventure doesn't matter, though—the Three Sounds excel at making unpretentious, unabashedly enjoyable mainstream jazz, and there's something endearing about their ability to produce a body of work of consistently high quality. — *Stephen Thomas Erlewine*

Hey There! / Aug. 13, 1961 / Blue Note ✦✦✦
Hey There! finds the Three Sounds keeping themselves slightly in check, turning in snappy, concise versions of jazz and pop standards, as well as jumping originals from Gene Harris. The shorter song lengths mean that the trio emphasizes melody even more than usual, but that's hardly a bad thing. Each Three Sounds record thrives on laidback swing and deft melodic flourishes. By bringing these elements to the forefront, they highlight their accessibility, but that results in a thoroughly enjoyable record. Their technical prowess is better heard on records where they stretch out a bit more, but *Hey There!* is another artist record from the most consistently entertaining artist on Blue Note's roster. — *Stephen Thomas Erlewine*

Babe's Blues / Aug. 31, 1961-Mar. 8, 1962 / Blue Note ✦✦✦✦
The accessible and enjoyable material on this Blue Note album was not released for the first time until 1986. The popular Three Sounds (pianist Gene Harris, bassist Andy Simpkins, and drummer Bill Dowdy) perform mostly standards on the album, infusing their swinging music with funk, soul, and sincere feeling. Highlights include Randy Weston's "Babe's Blues," "Work Song," and "Shiny Stockings." — *Scott Yanow*

Out of This World / Feb. 4, 1962-Feb. 8, 1962 / Blue Note ✦✦✦✦
Out of This World relies less on originals than before, concentrating on standards which sound startlingly fresh. It's the loose, flexible groove that's the key. Simpkins and Dowdy keep things on track, while Gene Harris plays—he can be nimble, he can pound, but he keeps the music flowing at a nice, easy pace. He has a good sense of the groove, and he stays within the groove even as he plays a lot of notes; it's truly an indivdual style. Despite the R&B-flavored arrangements on "Girl of My Dreams" and the swinging, gospel-inflected "Sanctified Sue," *Out of This World* is a particularly light and breezy record from the Three Sounds. They're just as comfortable stretching out

with the groove as they are with keeping things short, simple, and concise—either way, it's thoroughly enjoyable music. But no matter how easy the group is to enjoy, they have true style, as Harris' bluesy flourishes and the rhythm section's supple support illustrate. It's hard to sound this light and easy, and the Three Sounds pull it off with grace. —*Stephen Thomas Erlewine*

Black Orchid / Mar. 7, 1962-Mar. 8, 1962 / Blue Note ✦✦✦✦
Between 1958 and 1962, the Three Sounds were one of the most prolific artists on Blue Note, recording over ten albums worth of material during those four years. During all that time, the group never changed their style much, concentrating on lightly swinging, lightly soulful mainstream jazz that balanced jazz and pop standards with bluesy originals. As time progressed, they veered closer to soul-jazz, but each of their records sounded quite similiar and were equally satisfying. *Black Orchid*, their last album for Blue Note in the early '60s (they would rejoin the label in another four years), was no exception to the rule. It displays their knack for deftly swinging uptempo numbers, light blues, and sensitive standards. If anything, it swings a little harder and is a little more soulful than some of its predecessors. Again, the very fact that the music is instantly enjoyable and accessible makes some jazz critics write the Three Sounds off, but Gene Harris, Andrew Simpkins, and Bill Dowdy are genuine stylists with prodigious technique. It's difficult to make music this consistently enjoyable, and the Three Sounds illustrate that they have the knack once again on *Black Orchid*. —*Stephen Thomas Erlewine*

Blue Genes / Oct. 13, 1962 / Verve ✦✦✦

Live at the Living Room / 1964 / Mercury ✦✦✦
The Three Sounds (pianist Gene Harris, bassist Andy Simpkins, and drummer Bill Dowdy) were quite popular in the early to mid-'60s and recorded many albums, but surprisingly few have been reissued on CD yet. This Mercury LP finds the trio mostly sticking to bluesy material, plus a couple of Oscar Peterson tunes ("Blues for Big Scotia" and the joyous "Hymn to Freedom"). Whether it be "Glory of Love," "Willow Weep for Me," or even "Mississippi Mud," every song sounds a bit like the blues on this hard-to-find set. —*Scott Yanow*

Vibrations / 1966 / Blue Note ✦✦✦
The Three Sounds' return to Blue Note wasn't a celebrated event—no exact date even exists for these sessions, although in all likelihood it was recorded somewhere in October 1966. Even if the event was poorly documented, it was fairly important for the label, because it signaled that they were backing away from the adventurous hard bop and free jazz they had been recording, and were considering concentrating on the commercially oriented, mainstream soul-jazz the Three Sounds pioneered. Since *Vibrations* was recorded in 1965, not 1959, there were differences in the trio's approach. Pianist Gene Harris tried organ on a few tracks, and the group tackled contemporary R&B hits ("Let's Go Get Stoned," "Fever," "Yeh Yeh") as well as MOR pop ("It Was a Very Good Year"). The subtle tweaking makes no real difference in the group's sound, since on previous records they took the same approach (only without an organ), but *Vibrations* doesn't make the first rank of Three Sounds records because the performances are a little stiff, and the infrequent organ sounds a little awkward. There are certainly plenty of good things here—and there are more good than bad things—but *Vibrations* primarily offers the kind of pleasures that are only meaningful to dedicated fans. —*Stephen Thomas Erlewine*

Live at the Lighthouse / Jul. 1967 / Blue Note ✦✦✦✦
Shortly after the *Vibrations* sessions, the Three Sounds had their first major personnel shakeup when William Dowdy left the group. Donald Bailey replaced the drummer, and the group played a number of live dates over the course of 1967. During that summer, their concerts at the famed Los Angeles venue the Lighthouse were recorded and released as *Live at the Lighthouse*. The selection of nine Three Sounds staples gives the group a chance to stretch out and prove that they could survive without Dowdy. Not only do they prove that they can carry on without him, they flourish. The music on *Live at the Lighthouse* is hotter than some of their studio recordings, pulsating with energy and good feelings, demonstrating that they had worked out any of the problems that hampered *Vibrations*. It's their finest set since *Black Orchid*. —*Stephen Thomas Erlewine*

Live at the It Club / 1970 / Blue Note ✦✦✦
Recorded in 1970 but not released until 1996, *Live At the "It Club"* shows the Three Sounds pulling out funky, gritty rhythms out of their basic bluesy hard-bop sound. The group's funky influences are most noticeable in the rhythm section of drummer Carl Burnette and bassist Henry Franklin, who had been playing with Harris for only a short time when this set was recorded. The rhythm section pushes Harris, making the music loose and swinging—the groove matters more than anything on the album. Occasionally, the energy of the Three Sounds lags, but *Live at the "It Club"* is an enjoyable piece of grooving soul-jazz. —*Stephen Thomas Erlewine*

Bobby Timmons

b. Dec. 19, 1935, Philadelphia, PA, **d.** Mar. 1, 1974, New York, NY
Piano / Hard Bop, Soul-Jazz, Groove
Bobby Timmons became so famous for the gospel and funky blues cliches in his solos and compositions that his skills as a Bud Powell-inspired bebop player have been long forgotten. After emerging from the Philadelphia jazz scene, Timmons worked with Kenny Dorham (1956), Chet Baker, Sonny Stitt, and the Maynard Ferguson Big Band. He was partly responsible for the commercial success of both Art Blakey's Jazz Messengers and Cannonball Adderley's Quintet. For Blakey (who he was with during 1958-59), Timmons wrote the classic "Moanin'" and, after joining Adderley in 1959, his song "This Here" (followed later by "Dat Dere") became a big hit; it is little wonder that Adderley was distressed when Timmons in 1960 decided to return to the Jazz Messengers. "Dat Dere" particularly caught on when Oscar Brown, Jr. wrote and recorded lyrics that colorfully depicted his curious son. Timmons, who was already recording as a leader for Riverside, soon formed his own trio but was never able to gain the commercial success that his former bosses enjoyed. Stereotyped as a funky pianist (although an influence on many players including Les McCann, Ramsey Lewis, and much later on Benny Green), Timmons' career gradually declined. He continued working until his death at age 38 from cirrhosis of the liver. —*Scott Yanow*

☆ **This Here Is Bobby Timmons** / Jan. 13, 1960-Jan. 14, 1960 / Original Jazz Classics ✦✦✦✦✦
This is a classic Riverside set that has been reissued on CD in the Original Jazz Classics series. Pianist Bobby Timmons by early 1960 had already had successful stints with Art Blakey (where he contributed "Moanin'") and Cannonball Adderley (writing "This Here" and "Date Dere"). For his first recording as a leader, Timmons (whose "funky" style was beginning to become very influential) performs those three hits along with his own "Joy Ride" and five standards in a trio with bassist Sam Jones and drummer Jimmy Cobb. Always more than just a soul jazz pianist, Timmons (who effectively takes "Lush Life" unaccompanied) became a bit stereotyped later in his career but at this early stage was at the peak of his creativity. Essential music. —*Scott Yanow*

Soul Time / Aug. 12, 1960+Aug. 17, 1960 / Riverside ✦✦✦✦
Pianist Bobby Timmons, best known for his sanctified and funky playing and composing, is mostly heard in a straightahead vein on this CD reissue of a Riverside session. Timmons' four originals ("So Tired" is most memorable) alternate with three standards and are interpreted by a quartet with trumpeter Blue Mitchell, bassist Sam Jones, and drummer Art Blakey. The swinging music is well-played, making this a good example of Bobby Timmons playing in a boppish (as opposed to funky) setting. —*Scott Yanow*

● **Moanin'** / Aug. 12, 1960-Sep. 10, 1963 / Milestone ✦✦✦✦
Compilation of five different albums 1960-1963. Great collection and collectable. —*Michael G. Nastos*

Easy Does It / Mar. 13, 1961 / Original Jazz Classics ✦✦✦✦
Pianist Bobby Timmons, who became famous for his funky originals and soulful playing, mostly sticks to more bop-oriented jazz on this trio set with bassist Sam Jones and drummer Jimmy Cobb. He provides three originals (none of which really caught on) and is in excellent form on the five standards with highlights including "Old Devil Moon," "I Thought About You," and "Groovin' High." The Riverside CD reissue shows that Timmons was a bit more versatile than his stereotype; in any case the music is excellent. —*Scott Yanow*

In Person / Oct. 1, 1961 / Original Jazz Classics ✦✦✦✦
For this excellent live set (recorded at the Village Vanguard), pianist Bobby

Timmons, bassist Ron Carter, and drummer Albert "Tootie" Heath perform a couple of the pianist's originals ("So Tired" and "Popsy") along with some standards. The funky bop-oriented music is quite enjoyable and was very popular during the early '60s. The CD reissue adds previously unreleased versions of "They Didn't Believe Me" and "Dat Dere" to the original program. Easily recommended. — *Scott Yanow*

Born to Be Blue / Sep. 1963 / Original Jazz Classics ✦✦✦✦
Throughout his career, Bobby Timmons was typecast as a soulful and blues-oriented pianist due to his hits ("Moanin'," "This Here," and "Dis Dat"). But as he shows on this 1963 trio date (with either Sam Jones or Ron Carter on bass and drummer Connie Kay), Timmons was actually a well-rounded player when inspired. The repertoire on his CD ranges from bop to spirituals, from three diverse originals to "Born to Be Blue." This is excellent music but unfortunately Timmons would not grow much musically after this period. His CD is worth picking up. — *Scott Yanow*

Workin' Out / Oct. 21, 1964 + Jan. 20, 1966 / Prestige ✦✦✦✦
This CD reissues the contents of two of pianist Bobby Timmons' most advanced recordings of the '60s. For an example of how the popular pianist had continued to evolve after his early funk hits, listen to his often-bitonal solo on "Bags' Groove" from 1964. That session features Timmons in a quartet with vibraphonist Johnny Lytle, bassist Keter Betts, and drummer William "Peppy" Hinnant and is filled with subtle surprises. The second recording is even more interesting for Timmons as he is teamed with tenor-saxophonist Wayne Shorter, bassist Ron Carter and drummer Jimmy Cobb in 1966. The immediately recognizable Shorter in particular plays very well (this version of his "Tom Thumb" is its earliest recording) and the very modern playing of Carter pushes Timmons to really stretch himself. Both of these generally overlooked sessions (even Shorter's best fans may not know about his collaboration with Timmons) were formerly rare and are quite adventurous, making this a highly recommended acquisition that falls somewhere between hard bop and the early avant-garde. — *Scott Yanow*

The Soul Man / Jan. 20, 1966 / Prestige ✦✦✦
With Wayne Shorter on tenor sax. Plenty of funk, blues, and soul-jazz, plus great piano. — *Ron Wynn*

Soul Food / Sep. 30, 1966 + Oct. 14, 1966 / Prestige ✦✦✦
Ron Carter on bass and Wayne Shorter on sax. — *Michael Erlewine*

Stanley Turrentine

b. Apr. 5, 1934, Pittsburgh, PA
Tenor Saxophone / Soul-Jazz, Hard Bop, Groove
While highly regarded in soul-jazz circles, Stanley Turrentine is one of the finest tenor saxophonists in any style in modern times. He excels at uptempo compositions, in jam sessions, interpreting standards, playing the blues or on ballads. His rich, booming and huge tone, with its strong swing influence, is one of the most striking of any tenor stylist, and during the '70s and '80s made otherwise horrendous mood music worth enduring.

To give you an idea where Turrentine is coming from: Early on, he toured with the R&B band of Lowell Fulson (1950-1951) whose featured pianist at the time was a young Ray Charles. From 1953-1954 he worked with Earl Bostic (perhaps the greatest R&B sax player of all time), where he replaced John Coltrane. He also worked and cut his first albums with Max Roach (1959-1960). Turrentine started recording as a leader on Blue Note in 1959 and 1960, while also participating in some landmark Jimmy Smith sessions such as *Midnight Special, Back at the Chicken Shack,* and *Prayer Meeting.*

His decade plus association with Shirley Scott was both professional and personal, as they were married most of the time they were also playing together. They frequently recorded, with the featured leader's name often depending on the session's label affiliation. When they divorced and split musically in the early '70s, Turrentine became a crossover star on CTI. Several of his CTI, Fantasy, Elektra and Blue Note albums in the '70s and '80s made the charts. Though their jazz content became proportionally lower, Turrentine's playing remained consistently superb. He returned to straight ahead and soul-jazz in the '80s, cutting more albums for Fantasy and Elektra, then returning to Blue Note. He's currently on the Musicmasters label. Almost anything Turrentine's recorded, even albums with Stevie Wonder cover songs, are worth hearing for his solos. Many of his classic dates, as well as recent material, is available on CD.

Turrentine is an original, a one-of-a-kind. He does not fit neatly into ordinary jazz categories. What makes Turrentine great is his deep love of the roots of jazz—blues and groove music. He never abandoned these roots to join the more cerebral set of jazz soloists. His recording partnership with Jimmy Smith has given us some of the finest funk groove music of all time, a high-water mark for both artists. This man likes to groove and play funky music! He won't be tamed!

"The Turrentine tenor displays none of the weak-kneed and frazzle-but-tocked bleatings of many tenor sax deviates, but relies on the truly large tone of the big tenor sounds of the old masters." —Dudley Williams, reviewer for Bluenote — *Bob Porter, Michael Erlewine, and Ron Wynn*

Look Out / Jun. 18, 1960 / Blue Note ✦✦✦✦
With Horace Parlan (p), George Tucker (b), and Al Harewood (d). Recorded at Englewood Cliffs, NJ. Small group. 1987 reissue of excellent soul-jazz. — *Ron Wynn*

Blue Hour / Dec. 16, 1960 / Blue Note ✦✦✦✦
With the Three Sounds —Gene Harris (p), Andrew Simpkinds (b), and William Dowdy (d). Recorded in Englewood Cliffs, NJ. A small group setting. This is a beautiful album of relaxed, bluesy sound. — *Michael Erlewine*

Comin' Your Way / Jan. 20, 1961 / Blue Note ✦✦✦✦
With Tommy Turrentine (tp), Horace Parlan (p) George Tucker (b), and Al Harewood (d). Recorded at Englewood Cliffs, NJ. Small group. 1988 reissue of a sumptuous '60s soul-jazz date. Horace Parlan at his bluesy best. — *Ron Wynn*

Up at Minton's, Vol. 1 / Feb. 23, 1961 / Blue Note ✦✦✦✦
Here is Turrentine with the groove master Grant Green on guitar together at New York's Minton's Playhouse for a live recording. This is very early Green, not long after he relocated to New York from St. Louis. The rhythm section is the trio known as Us Three—Horace Parlan (p), George Tucker (b), and Al Harewood (d). This is available as a two-CD set from Blue Note and should grace every Turrentine or Green fan's shelves. Although not as funky as he would get, this is wonderful easy-paced listening. Plenty of bluesy soulful music. — *Michael Erlewine*

Up at Minton's, Vol. 2 / Feb. 23, 1961 / Blue Note ✦✦✦✦
Here is Turrentine with the groove master Grant Green on guitar together at New York's Minton's Playhouse for a live recording. This is very early Green, not long after he relocated to New York from St. Louis. The rhythm section is the trio known as Us Three—Horace Parlan (p), George Tucker (b), and Al Harewood (d). This is available as a 2-CD set from Blue Note and should grace every Turrentine or Green fan's shelves. Although not as funky as he would get, this is wonderful easy-paced listening. Plenty of bluesy soulful music. — *Michael Erlewine*

Up at Minton's / Feb. 23, 1961 / Blue Note ✦✦✦✦
This is a particularly solid double CD featuring tenor-saxophonist Stanley Turrentine, guitarist Grant Green, pianist Horace Parlan, bassist George Tucker, and drummer Al Harewood during a frequently exciting live set. Although recorded early in the careers of Turrentine and Green, both lead voices are easily recognizable with Green actually taking solo honors on several of the pieces. Standards and a couple of blues make up the repertoire, giving listeners a definitive look at the soulful Mr. T. near the beginning of his productive musical life. — *Scott Yanow*

Dearly Beloved / Jun. 8, 1961 / Blue Note ✦✦✦✦
A trio recording from Blue Note has Turrentine with Shirley Scott on Hammond organ and Roy Brooks on drums. This is the first recording with Turrentine and Scott, who would work together for ten years, later becoming married. — *Michael Erlewine*

Z.T.'s Blues / Sep. 13, 1961 / Blue Note ✦✦✦✦
An all-star lineup has Turrentine with Grant Green on guitar and Tommy Flanagan on piano. The rhythm section has Paul Chambers on bass and Art Taylor on drums. Green and Turrentine made few albums together, but the combination is a natural—the two greatest groove masters, bar none. Flanagan seldom appears in this type of setting and his playing is very tasteful. A studio recording by Rudy Van Gelder at Englewood Cliffs, NJ. If you can find a copy of this, it is a keeper. — *Michael Erlewine*

★ **That's Where It's At** / Jan. 2, 1962 / Blue Note ✦✦✦✦✦
A Blue Note release with Les McCann on piano, Herbie Lewis on bass, and

Otis Finch on drums. Small group format. Excellent (and exciting) soul-jazz session with Turrentine blowing hot. — *Ron Wynn & Michael Erlewine*

Jubilee Shout / Oct. 18, 1962 / Blue Note ✦✦✦✦
Featuring Turrentine with Sonny Clark on piano and Kenny Burrell on guitar. Also including Tommy Turrentine (tp), Butch Warren (b), and Al Harewood (d). Recorded at Englewood Cliffs, NJ, by Rudy Van Gelder. Here is classic funky soul-jazz groove, three up-tempo, three slow. Sonny Clark (p) soars, Turrentine red-hot. — *Ron Wynn & Michael Erlewine*

Never Let Me Go / Jan. 18, 1963 + Feb. 13, 1963 / Blue Note ✦✦✦
An early Blue Note album with the Stanley Turrentine Quintet: Turrentine, Shirley Scott (organ), Major Bolley (b), Al Harewood (d), and Ray Barretto (cga). — *Michael Erlewine*

A Chip off the Old Block / Oct. 21, 1963 / Blue Note ✦✦✦✦
On Blue Note with Turrentine, Blue Mitchell (tp), Shirley Scott (organ), Earl May (b), and Al Harewood (d). This is a studio recording by Van Gelder. Bluesy with tunes like "Midnight Blue" and "Blues in Hoss' Flat." — *Michael Erlewine*

Hustlin' / Jan. 24, 1964 / Blue Note ✦✦✦
A classic small group with Turrentine on tenor sax, Shirley Scott on the Hammond organ, and Kenny Burrell on guitar. The rhythm section has Bob Cranshaw on bass and Otis Finch on drums. Includes a version of "Goin' Home." — *Michael Erlewine*

☆ **Let It Go** / Sep. 21, 1964 + Apr. 15, 1966 / Impulse! ✦✦✦✦✦
This is vital Turrentine with Shirley Scott on Hammond organ, Ron Carter on bass, and Mack Simpkins on drums. This album includes some additional tracks that were originally released on the Shirley Scott album *Everybody Loves a Lover*. Recorded in Englewood Cliffs, NJ. Husband and wife team Turrentine and Scott (organ) produce one classic soul-jazz groove album. — *Michael Erlewine*

Rough 'n Tumble / Jul. 1, 1966 / Blue Note ✦✦✦✦
A somewhat larger group (eight pieces) with Grant Green (g), Blue Mitchell (tp), James Spaulding (as), Pepper Adams (bar), and McCoy Tyner on piano. Recorded at NYC. One of his most popular, tightest soul-jazz releases. — *Ron Wynn*

Easy Walker / Jul. 8, 1966-May 23, 1969 / Blue Note ✦✦✦✦
Easy Walker is a fairly standard but highly enjoyable small-group soul-jazz session from Stanley Turrentine. Backed by a rhythm section of pianist McCoy Tyner, drummer Mickey Roker, and bassist Bob Cranshaw, Turrentine turns in a number of rich, round, and full-bodied leads which are perfectly complemented by Tyner's strutting, sympathetic piano. Largely divided between mid-tempo grooves and slow blues, with a couple of pop covers like "What the World Needs Now Is Love" thrown in, *Easy Walker* doesn't offer much challenging material, but it does let the musicians work a good groove, and occasionally showcase their improvisational skills, making it a good, relaxing soul-jazz session. The 1997 CD reissue features four bonus tracks which were recorded with drummer Billy Cobham and bassist Gene Taylor, along with Tyner; the highlight of these is a breezy version of Antonio Carlos Jobim's "Wave." — *Stephen Thomas Erlewine*

The Spoiler / Sep. 22, 1966 / Blue Note ✦✦✦✦
Other than a few short spots, Stanley Turrentine is the only significant soloist on this CD reissue which features a diverse program including "When the Sun Comes Out," "Maybe September," "You're Gonna Hear from Me," and a previously unreleased rendition of Max Roach's jazz waltz "Lonesome Lover." Although he is accompanied by an all-star group that includes trumpeter Blue Mitchell, altoist James Spaulding, baritonist Pepper Adams and pianist McCoy Tyner, Turrentine's sidemen could almost have been anonymous studio players for the tenor is the dominant voice throughout. It is surprising that Pearson did not make more extensive use of the other musicians' unique talents, particularly Tyner. However, despite some potentially indifferent material, Turrentine is in fine form throughout the date, even finding something to say on "Sunny." "La Fiesta" (no relation to the later Chick Corea tune) is the highpoint of a largely enjoyable set. — *Scott Yanow*

Ain't No Way / May 10, 1968 / Blue Note ✦✦✦
Turrentine in small-group format. The cast includes Shirley Scott on the Hammond organ, McCoy Tyner on piano, Jimmy Ponder on guitar, Bob Cran-

shaw on bass, and Ray Lucas on drums. Substitute Gene Taylor (b) and Billy Cobham (d) for some cuts. — *Michael Erlewine*

Common Touch! / Aug. 30, 1968 / Blue Note ✦✦✦
This CD reissue brings back an easy-listening set in which tenor saxophonist Stanley Turrentine teams up with his then-wife, organist Shirley Scott, in what was probably their last joint recording. The original LP program is joined by "Ain't No Way" from a slightly earlier date with similar personnel. Even on "Blowin' In the Wind," Turrentine's soulful solos uplift the material, while Scott offers light accompaniment and some gospellish ideas of her own; guitarist Jimmy Ponder also has some spots on the quintet set. Although not essential (no one seems to sweat much and none of the tempos are above a slow-medium pace), this lazy date has its pleasurable moments. — *Scott Yanow*

Look of Love / Sep. 29, 1968-Oct. 6, 1968 / Blue Note ✦✦✦✦
Larger group setting that was recorded at Englewood Cliffs, NJ. Both romantic and lusty, nice sessions. — *Ron Wynn*

Straight Ahead / Nov. 24, 1984 / Blue Note ✦✦✦
Recorded at Power Play Studios, Long Island City, NY. Smaller group. Turrentine with George Benson (g), Jimmy Smith (organ), Ron Carter (b), and Jimmy Madison (d). On two cuts, also Jimmy Ponder (g), and Les McCann (p). Great combination of musicians as on earlier cookers, but time has passed—it does not come off. Pleasant enough though, but lacks high spots. — *Michael Erlewine*

Ballads / Nov. 16, 1993 / Blue Note ✦✦✦
Although he's a monster tenor soloist on funky, exuberant, bluesy soul-jazz, Stanley Turrentine is even more awesome on ballads. His rich, steamy sound, full tone, and ability to pace and develop moods is ideal for show tunes and sentimental love songs. This nine-track set begins with Turrentine nicely caressing the melody and turning in a standout treatment on "Willow Weep For Me," continuing through tearjerkers ("Since I Fell For You") and blues anthems ("God Bless The Child"), and closing with Thad Jones' beautiful "A Child Is Born." Turrentine is matched with numerous premier players, and pianist McCoy Tyner, guitarist Jimmy Smith, and even Turrentine's brother Tommy (trumpet) gently support and complement the main soloist. One of the best Blue Note special discs, featuring moving, frequently hypnotic playing from a true tenor great. — *Ron Wynn*

Rudy Van Gelder

Engineer / Hard Bop, Soul-Jazz, Groove
Van Gelder, who is as "with it" today as in the beginning, made this fascinating response to a question about digital recorders in a 1986 radio interview by Ben Sidran of National Public radio:

Van Gelder: If I'm going to do a session and I can choose what I want to choose, I will choose a digital recorder. There's just no question about it.

Sidran: What about the technical criticism of digital recording that I've read about, the problems of it feeling is some ways unnatural?

Van Gelder: Digital recording has been totally reliable for me. It finally does what a tape machine should do—really, just store what you're putting into it. No analog machine ever made could do that correctly. None. Not even the best, the most expensive, could ever do what a properly designed two-track digital machine will do. We're talking about clarity of sound, clean sound, wide range, beautiful, no noise problem. To me, it's made working a pleasure. It's like starting all over again and being excited about things, like being able to play back a great sound to the group right after they've played it, and they can hear it right then. Everybody knows it's good. Before they go home. (Quoted with permission from Mosaic Records staff.)

Note: Rudy Van Gelder has recorded more hard bop and funk than any man or woman alive. And no one has recorded Hammond organ jazz like Van Gelder. If it's a Blue Note or Prestige album that has been recorded in Hackensack or Englewood Cliffs, NJ, then chances are it's a Van Gelder recording. — *Michael Erlewine*

Harold Vick

b. Apr. 3, 1936, Rocky Mount, NC, **d.** Nov. 13, 1987, New York, NY
Tenor Saxophone, Flute, Soprano Saxophone / Soul-Jazz, Hard Bop, Groove
An excellent thick-toned tenor, Harold Vick sounded quite at home in hard bop and soul-jazz settings. His uncle Prince Robinson (a reed player from

the '20s) gave him a clarinet when he was 13 and three years later Vick switched to tenor. He rose to prominence playing with organ combos in the mid-'60s, recording and performing with Jack McDuff, Jimmy McGriff, and Big John Patton among others. He started recording as a leader in 1966 and among his other associations were Jack DeJohnette's unusual group Compost (1972), Shirley Scott in the mid-'70s and Abbey Lincoln with whom he recorded two Billie Holiday tributes for Enja just a short time before his death. — *Scott Yanow*

● **Steppin' Out** / May 27, 1963 / Blue Note ✦✦✦✦
This soul-jazz outing by tenor-saxophonist Harold Vick (his recording debut as a leader) casts him in a role that was often occupied by Stanley Turrentine. Vick, with a quintet that also includes trumpeter Blue Mitchell, guitarist Grant Green, organist John Patton, and drummer Ben Dixon, performs four blues, a slightly trickier original (five of the six songs are his) plus the ballad "Laura" on this CD reissue. There are no real surprises but no disappointments either on what would be Harold Vick's only chance to lead a Blue Note date; at 27 he was already a fine player. — *Scott Yanow*

Winston Walls

Organ, Vocals / Soul-Jazz, Hard Bop, Groove
Winston Walls was born in Charleston, West Virginia, the son of well-known R&B pianist Harry Van Walls (with Joe Turner). At 15 Walls already knew some piano and had been playing in church and school for several years. He then learned drums from Frank Thompson and got a job playing drums for Bill "Honky Tonk" Doggett's band. He soon switched to organ and filled in on breaks for Doggett.

He acknowledges Jimmy Smith and Jack McDuff as major influences and has toured the country, playing with the Pointer Sisters, Sonny Stitt, Dionne Warwick, Al Green, Charlie Pride, Ike & Tina Turner, and Lou Donaldson.

His jazz organ also includes elements of R&B, rock, country, and gospel. He once toured with Jimmy Smith, Groove Holmes, and Jack McDuff, but had never recorded a solo album. Then in 1993 he recorded a live session with fellow organist (and friend) Brother Jack McDuff which has been released on Schoolkids' Records. — *Michael Erlewine*

Boss of the B-3 / Oct. 25, 1993-Oct. 26, 1993 / Schoolkids ✦✦✦✦
Long overdue (like about 30 years!) debut album for Walls who is, as one reviewer put it, "the best organ player you never heard of." You can hear him now in live concert with long-time friend and rival Jack McDuff. You guessed it. McDuff and Walls battle it out as in days of yore, note for note and screeching chord against chord. This is a classic jam battle with a few vocals thrown in for diversion. McDuff is bound to let Walls (after all these years) be heard, so he does not struggle too hard. Good funk fun. Live set means balance a little off, but who cares. — *Michael Erlewine*

Grover Washington, Jr.

b. Dec. 12, 1943, Buffalo, NY
Tenor Saxophone, Alto Saxophone, Soprano Saxophone / Soul-Jazz, Crossover Jazz, Groove
One of the most popular saxophonists of all time (even his off records have impressive sales), Grover Washington, Jr. has long been the pacesetter in his field. His roots are in R&B and soul-jazz organ combos, but he also fares very well on the infrequent occasions when he plays straight-ahead jazz. A highly influential player, Washington has sometimes been blamed for the faults of his followers; Kenny G. largely based his soprano sound on Grover's tone. However, most of the time (except when relying on long hit medleys), Washington pushes himself with the spontaneity and chance-taking of a masterful jazz musician.

Grover Washington, Jr., whose father also played saxophone, started playing music when he was ten and within two years was working in clubs. He picked up experience touring with the Four Clefs from 1959-63 and freelancing during the next two years, before spending a couple years in the Army. He moved to Philadelphia in 1967, becoming closely identified with the city ever since, and worked with several organists including Charles Earland and Johnny Hammond Smith, recording as a sideman for the Prestige label. His biggest break occurred in 1971, when Hank Crawford could not make it to a recording date; Washington was picked as his replacement, and the result was *Inner City Blues*, a big seller. From then on he became a major name,

particularly after recording 1975's *Mister Magic* and 1980s *Winelight;* the latter included the Bill Withers hit "Just the Two of Us."

Although some of his recordings since then find him coasting a bit, Washington usually stretches himself in concert, being almost overqualified for the R&B-ish music that he performs. He has developed his own personal voices on soprano, tenor, alto, and even his infrequently used baritone. Grover Washington Jr. has recorded as a leader for Kudu, Motown, Elektra and Columbia and has made notable guest appearances on dozens of records ranging from pop to straightforward jazz. — *Scott Yanow*

Inner City Blues / Sep. 1971 / Kudu ✦✦✦✦
Grover Washington Jr's debut as a leader is a classic of its kind. Straddling the boundary between soul-jazz and R&Bish crossover, Washington on alto and tenor (under the direction of Creed Taylor and utilizing the arrangements of Bob James) puts plenty of feeling into his soulful versions of "Mercy Mercy Me," "Ain't No Sunshine," "Georgia On My Mind," and "I Loves You Porgy." It is obvious from listening to this music alone that he was destined to be a star. — *Scott Yanow*

● **Mister Magic** / Nov. 1974 / MoJazz ✦✦✦✦
This is one of Grover Washington Jr's best-loved recordings and considered a classic of R&Bish jazz. All four songs (which includes Billy Strayhorn's "Passion Flower") are quite enjoyable but it is "Mister Magic" that really caught on as a major hit. Bob James provided the colorful if somewhat commercial arrangements, there are spots for guitarist Eric Gale, and Washington (mostly on tenor and soprano) is heard in particularly creative form. Highly recommended. — *Scott Yanow*

☆ **Winelight** / Jun. 1980 / Elektra ✦✦✦✦✦
Grover Washington, Jr., has long been one of the leaders in what could be called rhythm & jazz, essentially R&B-influenced jazz. *Winelight* is one of his finest albums, and not primarily because of the Bill Withers hit "Just the Two of Us." It is the five instrumentals that find Washington (on soprano, alto, and tenor) really stretching out. If he had been only interested in sales, Washington's solos could have been half as long and he would have stuck closely to the melody. Instead he really pushes himself on some of these selections, particularly the title cut. A memorable set of high-quality and danceable soul-jazz. — *Scott Yanow*

Anthology [Elektra] / 1980-1984 / Elektra ✦✦✦
Anyone who's seen Grover Washington, Jr. live can attest to the fact that whether he's playing electric jazz/funk or going acoustic on Billy Strayhorn's music, the Philly resident is a masterful saxman who has as much technique as he does soul and charisma. However, the distinctive saxman's studio recordings (which range from outstanding to watered down) haven't always demonstrated just how commanding and improvisor he can be. *Anthology,* a 1985 CD focusing on his work for Elektra, contains more hits than misses. Well worth hearing are jazz/R&B/pop instrumentals like the congenial "East River Drive" and the seductive "Let It Flow" and the R&B numbers "The Best Is Yet to Come" (which boasts a heartfelt vocal by Patti LaBelle) and Washington's major hit with Bill Withers "Just the Two of Us." Unfortunately, Elektra made the mistake of including Washington's pointless version of reggae king Bob Marley's "Jammin'" (which is more of a pop cover than a genuine jazz interpretation), the insipid "Jet Stream" and the pleasant but not very memorable "In the Name of Love." — *Alex Henderson*

Ernie Watts

b. Oct. 23, 1945, Norfolk, VA
Tenor Saxophone, Flute, Alto Saxophone / Post-Bop, Crossover Jazz, Instrumental Pop, Bossa Nova
Because he was involved in many commercial recording projects from the mid-'70s through the early '80s and on an occasional basis ever since, some observers wrote Ernie Watts off prematurely as a pop/R&B tenorman. Actually Watts' main hero has always been John Coltrane and his more recent work reveals him to be an intense and masterful jazz improviser who has developed his own sheets of sound approach along with a distinctive and soulful sound. After attending Berklee, he had an important stint with Buddy Rich's big band (1966-68) before moving to Los Angeles. Watts worked in the big bands of Oliver Nelson and Gerald Wilson, recorded with Jean-Luc Ponty in 1969 and became a staff musician for NBC, performing with the Tonight Show Band on a regular basis. His own records of the '70s and early

'80s were generally poppish (1982's *Chariots of Fire* was a big seller) and Watts played frequently with Lee Ritenour and Stanley Clarke in addition to recording with Cannonball Adderley (one of his idols) in 1972. However, Watts' work became much more interesting from a jazz standpoint starting in the mid-'80s when he joined Charlie Haden's Quartet West and started recording no-nonsense quartet dates for JVC. Watts has developed into one of the most powerful of tenormen with complete control over his horn and the ability to bring intensity and passion (plus taste) to any musical situation. — *Scott Yanow*

Ernie Watts Quartet / Dec. 1987 / JVC ✦✦✦✦
After years of being heard primarily in commercial settings, Ernie Watts finally had an opportunity to record exactly what he wanted as a leader on this JVC CD. Watts, in a quartet with pianist Pat Coil, bassist Joel DiBartolo, and drummer Bob Leatherbarrow, features his Coltrane-influenced tenor and a bit of alto and soprano on some group originals and standards (including "My One and Only Love," "Skylark," and "Body and Soul"). One of his finest recordings to date. — *Scott Yanow*

● **Reaching Up** / Oct. 7, 1993-Oct. 8, 1993 / JVC ✦✦✦✦
For this quartet set with pianist Mulgrew Miller, bassist Charles Fambrough and drummer Jack DeJohnette, Ernie Watts definitely came to play. Virtually all of his solos are high-powered and even his ballad statements are filled with clusters of passionate notes. Trumpeter Arturo Sandval has two appearances and makes the music even more hyper. In addition, the rhythm section keeps the proceedings consistently stimulating. The main focus on these standards and originals is generally on Watts' tenor and, even though there isn't all that much variety, this CD is a strong example of his jazz talents. — *Scott Yanow*

Unity / Dec. 13, 1994-Dec. 14, 1994 / JVC ✦✦✦✦
The most unusual aspect to Ernie Watts' latest recording is that the great tenor is joined by a two-bass quartet. Eddie Gomez on acoustic and Steve Swallow on electric blend together quite well, are featured in a delightful version of Oscar Pettiford's "Tricotism," and (with pianist Geri Allen and drummer Jack Dejohnette) keep the accompaniment consistently stimulating. Watts is in top form throughout this fine modern mainstream date, playing with both passion and lyricism on a variety of standards and originals (which, in addition to four songs from the leader, include one apiece from DeJohnette and Swallow). There is just enough variety to keep the proceedings from ever getting predictable, making this one of Watts' finest sessions. — *Scott Yanow*

Baby Face Willette

b. Sep. 11, 1933
Organ / Soul-Jazz, Hard Bop, Groove
"Baby Face" Willette was born on September 11, 1933 in New Orleans. The nickname "Baby Face" was due to his youthful appearance. He started playing piano at the age of four, mostly due to the influence of his uncle Fred Freeman, a pianist of some popularity in the '20s. He is largely self-taught and never learned to read music. His father, a minister, and his mother, a missionary, had Willette playing church organ fairly early on. But his main instrument was to remain, for many years, the piano.

He started out professionally working with gospel and rhythm & blues groups in his late teens, and was soon touring extensively in the US, Canada, and Cuba. He traveled almost non-stop for some 15 years, working with R&B groups like Big Jay McNeely, Johnny Otis, Joe Houston, Roy Brown, Guitar Slim, King Colax, and the Caravan Gospel singers.

While visiting Chicago, he became intrigued by the sounds the organ could produce after hearing several outstanding gospel organists (Herman Stevens and Mayfield Wood) demonstrate the range and power of the instrument. He was turned on to jazz around that time after listening to Charlie Parker records. Jazz became his main passion from that time forward. As for influences, he credits Jimmy Smith and Shirley Scott on the Hammond B-3, and jazz greats Thelonious Monk, Bud Powell, Erroll Garner, and Oscar Peterson. There is not a lot of recorded Willette material available, with *Stop and Listen* being the album to hear. — *Michael Erlewine*

Face to Face / Jan. 30, 1961 / Blue Note ✦✦✦✦
His first album, this is straight-ahead bluesy jazz rather than real groove music (even with Grant Green on the date), mostly due to the hard, bright

sax of tenor player Fred Jackson, whose playing is in the style of Gene Ammons. All but one of the tunes ("Whatever Lola Wants") are by Willette. — *Michael Erlewine*

● **Stop and Listen** / May 22, 1961 / Blue Note ✦✦✦✦
This is an excellent bluesy groove album, a trio with guitarist Grant Green and Ben Dixon on drums. There are some Willette originals ("Jumpin' Jupiter" stands out), plus a very nice rendition of "Worksong," and the standards "Willow Weep for Me" and "At Last," which give Green a chance to stretch out and show his stuff. This is a very enjoyable album and worth seeking out. — *Michael Erlewine*

Larry Young (Khalid Yasin Abdul Aziz)

b. Oct. 7, 1940, Newark, NJ, **d.** Mar. 30, 1978, New York, NY
Organ / Hard Bop, Post-Bop, Fusion, Groove, Soul-Jazz
If Jimmy Smith was "the Charlie Parker of the organ," Larry Young was its John Coltrane. One of the great innovators of the mid- to late '60s, Young fashioned a distinctive modal approach to the Hammond B-3 at a time when Smith's earthy, blues-drenched soul-jazz style was the instrument's dominant voice. Initially, Young was very much a Smith admirer himself. After playing with various R&B bands in the '50s and being featured as a sideman with tenor saxman Jimmy Forrest in 1960, Young debuted as a leader that year with *Testifying*, which, like his subsequent soul-jazz efforts for Prestige, *Young Blues* (1960) and *Groove Street* (1962), left no doubt that Smith was his primary inspiration. But when Young went to Blue Note in 1964, he was well on his way to becoming a major innovator. Coltrane's post-bop influence asserted itself more and more in Young's playing and composing, and his work grew much more cerebral and exploratory. *Unity,* recorded in 1965, remains his best-known album. Quick to embrace fusion, Young played with Miles Davis in 1969, John McLaughlin in 1970, and Tony Williams' groundbreaking Lifetime in the early '70s. Unfortunately, his work turned uneven and erratic as the '70s progressed. Young was only 37 when, in 1978, he checked into the hospital suffering from stomach pains, and died from untreated pneumonia. The Hammond hero's work for Blue Note (as both a leader and a sideman) was united for Mosaic's limited-edition six-CD box set *The Complete Blue Note Recordings.* — *Alex Henderson*
Groove: Larry Young has been called the jazz organist's "jazz organist." His first album *Testifying* sounds a little like Jimmy Smith when he's cookin', and the next few (with Grant Green on guitar) are just plain great soul-jazz. From there on Larry Young takes the Hammond B-3 through soul-jazz, beyond, and "out." Young's playing is different from other Hammond B-3 masters, quite unique, but very definitely worth hearing. Young manages to find a soft spot in every jazz organist's heart. — *Michael Erlewine*

Testifying / Aug. 2, 1960 / Original Jazz Classics ✦✦✦
Organist Larry Young was 19 when he made this, his debut recording. Although he would become innovative later on, Young at this early stage was still influenced by Jimmy Smith even if he had a lighter tone; the fact that he used Smith's former guitarist, Thornel Schwartz, and a drummer whose name was coincidentally Jimmie Smith kept the connection strong. R&Bish tenor Joe Holiday helps out on two songs and the music (standards, blues, and ballads) always swings. Easily recommended to fans of the jazz organ. — *Scott Yanow*

Young Blues / Sep. 30, 1960 / Original Jazz Classics ✦✦✦✦
Organist Larry Young's second recording (cut shortly before he turned 20) is the best from his early period before he completely shook off the influence of Jimmy Smith. With guitarist Thornel Schwartz in top form, and bassist Wendell Marshall and drummer Jimmie Smith excellent in support, Young swings hard on a few recent jazz originals, some blues and two standards ("Little White Lies" and "Nica's Dream"). Recommended as a good example of his pre-Blue Note work. — *Scott Yanow*

Groove Street / Feb. 27, 1962 / Prestige ✦✦✦
Larry Young's third and final Prestige recording (reissued in the *OJC* series on CD) concludes his early period; he would next record as a leader two and a half years later on Blue Note, by which time his style would be much more original. For his 1962 outing, Young is joined by the obscure tenor Bill Leslie, guitarist Thornel Schwartz and drummer Jimmie Smith for some original blues and two standards ("I Found a New Baby" and "Sweet Lorraine"). Nothing all that substantial occurs, but fans of Jimmy Smith will enjoy the similar style that Larry Young had at the time. — *Scott Yanow*

☆ **Complete Blue Note Recordings** / Sep. 11, 1964-Feb. 7, 1969 / Mosaic ✦✦✦✦✦

Larry Young, one of the most significant jazz organists to emerge after the rise of Jimmy Smith, is heard on this limited-edition six-CD set at the peak of his creativity [The set comprises the following original albums: Grant Green *Talkin' About*, Larry Young *Into Somethin'*, Green *Street of Dreams*, Green *I Want to Hold Your Hand*, Young *Unity*, Young *Of Love and Peace*, Young *Contrasts*, Young *Heaven on Earth*, Young *Mother Ship*, Young *40 Years of Jazz*, *The History of Blue Note* (box 4 Dutch), Young *The World of Jazz Organ* (Japanese), Young *The Blue Note 50th Anniversary Collection Volume Two: The Jazz Message*]. Formerly available as nine LPs (three of which were actually under guitarist Green's leadership), Young was still very much under Smith's influence on the first four sessions (which features a trio with Green and drummer Elvin Jones, plus guests Sam Rivers or Hank Mobley on tenor and vibraphonist Bobby Hutcherson). However, starting with the monumental *Unity* session (a quartet outing with Joe Henderson on tenor, trumpeter Woody Shaw, and Elvin Jones), Young emerged as a very advanced and original stylist in his own right. The final four dates are generally pretty explorative and feature such notable sidemen as altoist James Spaulding and Byard Lancaster, guitarist George Benson, and trumpeter Lee Morgan, along with some forgotten local players. This definitive Larry Young set is highly recommended. — *Scott Yanow*

Into Somethin' / Nov. 12, 1964 / Blue Note ✦✦✦✦

Larry Young, who like most organists originally sounded close to Jimmy Smith, took a big step away from the organ's dominant influence on this adventurous and colorful set, which was his debut as a leader for Blue Note. Performing with a quartet also including tenor saxophonist Sam Rivers, guitarist Grant Green, and drummer Elvin Jones, Young performs four of his originals plus Green's "Plaza De Toros." Other than the blues "Backup," the music is fairly complex, grooving in its own fashion and showing that Young was quite aware of John Coltrane's modal excursions. — *Scott Yanow*

★ **Unity** / Nov. 10, 1965 / Blue Note ✦✦✦✦✦

This is a classic album, the finest of organist Larry Young's career. On this date (a quartet outing with trumpeter Woody Shaw, tenor saxophonist Joe Henderson and drummer Elvin Jones), Young emerged as the first original voice on the organ since Jimmy Smith. Young keeps up with his illustrious sidemen on three Shaw originals (best known is "The Moontrane"), Henderson's "If," "Monk's Dream," and the standard "Softly as In a Morning Sunrise." The performances grow in interest with each listen and find all of the musicians inspired by each other and by the high-quality material. A gem. — *Scott Yanow*

Of Love and Peace / Jul. 28, 1966 / Blue Note ✦✦✦✦

By 1966, Larry Young was playing music that fell between advanced hard bop/soul-jazz and the avant-garde. For this stimulating Blue Note date

(which has been reissued as part of Young's Mosaic box set), the organist meets up with trumpeter Eddie Gale (who was playing with Cecil Taylor during this era), altoist/flutist James Spaulding, and three obscure but fine sidemen: tenor saxophonist Herbert Morgan and both Wilson Moorman III and Jerry Thomas on drums. Two of the selections ("Of Love and Peace" and "Falaq") are essentially free improvisations that have a momentum and purpose of their own, moving forward coherently. In addition, Young and his group perform adventurous versions of "Pavanne" and "Seven Steps To Heaven." Very stimulating and intriguing music, this was one of Young's best recordings. — *Scott Yanow*

Contrasts / Sep. 18, 1967 / Blue Note ✦✦✦

Larger-group format with Tyrone Washington, Herbert Morgan (ts), Hank White (flg), Eddie Wright (g), Eddie Gladden (d), Stacey Edwards (cga), and Althea Young (vcl). This is more "out" than the earlier material and does not fit into the standard soul-jazz groove style. This album is available as part of the Mosaic box set *The Complete Blue Note Recordings of Larry Young*. — *Michael Erlewine*

Heaven on Earth / Feb. 9, 1968 / Blue Note ✦✦✦

Organist Larry Young, who really found his own sound back in 1965 with the classic *Unity* album, is deep in the funk on this later Blue Note album (which has been included in the Mosaic box set *The Complete Blue Note Recordings of Larry Young*). With altoist Byard Lancaster, tenor-saxophonist Herbert Morgan, guitarist George Benson, and drummer Eddie Gladden completing the quintet, there are some explorative solos but the less imaginative funk rhythms lower the content of the music somewhat. Young's wife Althea Young has an effective vocal on "My Funny Valentine," but overall this is a lesser effort. — *Scott Yanow*

Mother Ship / Feb. 7, 1969 / Blue Note ✦✦✦✦

Organist Larry Young's final Blue Note album was not released until 1980. Teamed up with tenor saxophonist Herbert Morgan, the great trumpeter Lee Morgan, and drummer Eddie Gladden, Young performs five of his originals which range from the funky "Street Scene" and the samba "Love Drops" to a spacy "Trip Merchant," and the complex "Visions." This highly original set does not deserve to be so obscure. — *Scott Yanow*

The Art of Larry Young / 1992 / Blue Note ✦✦✦✦

The Art of Larry Young is a seven-track collection that draws highlights from the organist's five years at Blue Note during the mid- to late '60s. During that time, Young established himself as one of the most adventurous organists in jazz, unafraid to break free from the confines of soul-jazz and tackle free jazz. While missing many fine tracks, this isn't a bad summary of his accomplishments, and since many of his Blue Note albums are hard to find — they've either been reissued in the expensive, limited-edition Mosaic box or limited-edition CDs — this compilation is even more valuable. — *Stephen Thomas Erlewine*

The Roots of the Blues

The origins of the blues–a form which really didn't have a name until the early 20th century, although it had surely been around for some time before then–are impossible to pin down with any degree of certainty. There's the convenient thesis that the blues were imported to North America when African slaves were shipped to the continent in the centuries preceding the Civil War. Much of the blues is undeniably African in origin, but in fact there were many other influences that shaped the music as well. It's also reasonably certain that the blues did not take a recognizable shape until African-Americans were a large, established part of the population of the American South.

Formulating the origins of the blues is a much more difficult task than, say, describing the birth of rock 'n' roll. For one thing, there are no tapes or recordings available to trace and document the sounds as they coalesced prior to 1900. The standard historical record of written and oral accounts, too, is much sketchier than it is for comparitively recent genres. Offering postulations and generalizations in a short overview such as this, really, is just asking for trouble–there are plenty of blues and folklore scholars that will challenge whatever point of view is espoused, often armed with considerable evidence. This piece will simply identify some of the likely sources. Readers interested in investigating the topic in greater depth will find many book-length studies of the subject in libraries and bookstores with a large selection.

The African roots of the blues are undeniable, particularly in the griots of western Africa. The griots functioned as sorts of musical storytellers for their communities, no doubt singing about subjects like romance, family, famine, ruling governments, and struggle that are commonplace in blues music–and, indeed, folk/popular music as a whole. They often used stringed instruments that bore some resemblance to ones that became prevalent in blues. When Ali Farka Toure of Senegal reached an international audience in the 1980s and 1990s, he was frequently described as "the African John Lee Hooker"; it's possible that his work is also an illustration of the close ties between the blues and some strains of African music.

Blues music, however, most likely didn't approach anything resembling its 20th-century form until slavery was instituted in the American South. The mere fact that the slaves came from many different regions and spoke many different languages, for one thing, would have worked against the retention of the music of their homeland as they began working together. Subsequent generations lost the tongues of their mothers and fathers, by necessity adopting English, the language of their overlords.

The brutal and inhumane conditions of slavery, from some viewpoints, may have seemed to make it unlikely that any forms of artistic expression could develop and thrive. In some respects, however, slavery fostered such musical communication, simply as a means of making life bearable. Work songs and field hollers, some of the most oft-discussed precursors to the blues, were chanted and sung as the slaves worked or endured their punishment. They were also a means of telling stories, passing the endless hours of toil, or simply venting emotion that was impossible to express in more confined or closely supervised circumstances. The call-and-response quality of some blues music (and much gospel) may have derived in part from such singing; the blues' concentration upon earthy, day-to-day realities and struggles may have some of its roots in these styles as well.

The history of American popular music is often one of Black and White styles meeting and mixing. As wide as the racial divide was in slavery days, the music of American Blacks inevitably absorbed a lot of White flavor, from European, Southern folk, and Appalachian influences. In their limited contact with Whites, Blacks were also exposed to piano and string instruments that would figure strongly in their own music. By the time blues began to be recorded in the early 1920s, guitars and pianos were the most frequent instruments of choice among blues artists.

There was also the considerable influence of the church. Gospel music afforded the African-American community opportunities to sing with committed fervor. The harmonies and solo vocal styles associated with vocal music have left a strong imprint on Black music to this day, including the blues. Relatively recent releases like Mississippi Fred McDowell's recordings of spirituals in the 1960s demonstrate how strong the ties can be between down-home blues and gospel; Reverend Gary Davis was another acoustic bluesman known for performing a lot of gospel material.

The extraordinary power of the rural blues recorded in the 1920s and 1930s have sometimes left the impression that deep blues dominated the music of Southern Black communities. The repertoire of Black musicians from the Deep South was much more diverse than many people realize. Blues music was often only one element of their repertoire; some singers who only recorded blues music were likely able to play pop, country, and ragtime tunes as well in live performance, as the circumstances of the occasion demanded. Some of these musicians performed as part of traveling minstrel, vaudeville, and medicine shows; occasionally ones who toured with such concerns in the early 20th century would survive to make recordings in the early days of the LP, such as Pink Anderson. Ragtime styles also made their way onto blues records, not only via pianists but guitarists such as Reverend Gary Davis.

Jug bands and the all-around entertainers that have been dubbed "songsters" are sometimes also thought of as precursors to the blues, although many such musicians were actually contemporaries of the early blues artists, and recorded often in the 1920s and 1930s. Jug bands like the Mississippi Sheiks and those of Gus Cannon used instruments not associated with the blues these days, such as the washboard, kazoo, and fiddle. They also frequently espoused a good-time air, in contrast to the more melancholic tone of deep rural guitar blues. They were still a vital part of the African-American popular music of the South in the 1930s, although afterwards their styles were deemed hokey and passé, a relic of the minstrel tradition.

The wide repertoire of Southern Black music lived on in blues performers that have come to be called the "songsters," who are examined in greater depth in a separate piece. They could play blues, certainly, but also folk tunes, country songs, pop, ragtime, and spirituals. Some of the oldest bluesmen who made it onto record, such as pan quill pipe player Henry Thomas (famous for "Bull Doze Blues," which Canned Heat turned into "Going Up the Country'), were songsters. The eclecticism of the songsters lived on in some performers who became popular during the 1960s blues revival, such as Mance Lipscomb and Mississippi John Hurt. Leadbelly and Josh White could be called "songsters" of sort, although they were more commonly categorized as folk singers, or blues/folk singers.

The blues, or forms closely tied to the blues, had likely existed for some time, and in various blends of the previously described styles, before its famous "discovery," at least in terms of verified historical accounts, by W.C. Handy, who recalled hearing something resembling the blues as early as 1892. The incident that has been enshrined in popular legend, however, occurred in Tutwiler, Mississippi, in 1903, as Handy, a black bandleader of a minstrel orchestra, was waiting for a train. In his autobiography, *Father of the Blues*, he recalls listening to the guitarist that began to play:

"The singer repeated the line three times, accompanying himself on the guitar with the weirdest music I had ever heard. The tune stayed in my mind. When the singer paused, I leaned over and asked him what the words meant. He rolled his eyes, showing a trace of mild amusement. Perhaps I should have known, but he didn't mind explaining. At Morehead, the eastbound and westbound met and crossed the north and southbound trains four times a day…

"He was simply singing…as he waited. This was not unusual. Southern Negroes sang about everything. Trains, steamboats, steam whistles, sledge hammers, fast women, mean bosses, stubborn mules–all became subjects for their songs. They accompany themselves on anything from which they can extract a musical sound or rhythmical effect, anything from a harmonica to a washboard."

Despite his title "Father of the Blues," Handy did not invent the blues. He was responsible for popularizing them by copyrighting and publishing blues compositions. "Memphis Blues," published in 1912, was the first one; "St. Louis Blues," which followed in 1914, was his most successful, and indeed one of the most popular tunes of any kind in the 20th century, performed and recorded

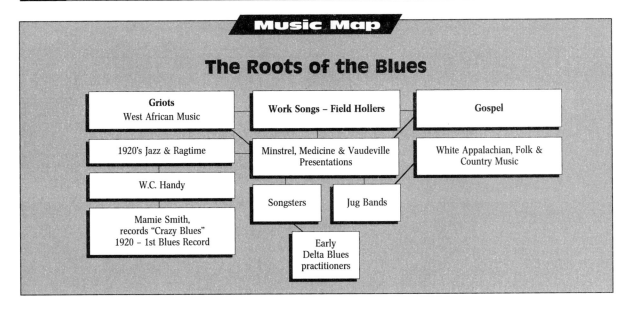

Music Map

The Roots of the Blues

Griots
West African Music

Work Songs – Field Hollers

Gospel

1920's Jazz & Ragtime

Minstrel, Medicine & Vaudeville Presentations

White Appalachian, Folk & Country Music

W.C. Handy

Songsters

Jug Bands

Mamie Smith, records "Crazy Blues" 1920 – 1st Blues Record

Early Delta Blues practitioners

---

by numerous jazz, blues, and pop artists. Handy published/wrote other numbers in the same vein, such as "Yellow Dog Blues" and "Beale Street Blues" (named after the main thoroughfare of the Black community in Memphis).

"St. Louis Blues" can sound more like jazz than blues to contemporary listeners, perhaps reflecting the fact that Handy was steeped not the blues but in brass bands, which may have shaped his arrangements. The same can be said of the first popular blues recordings of the 1920s, mostly performed by women with jazz accompanists, who sang such pop- and jazz-influenced "blues" compositions as those devised by Handy. Arguably, these records reflected a more urban and pop-oriented sensibility than what you would have heard from the mouths of the proto-blues and early blues performers of the South.

Those early blues songs and singles, however, were responsible to some degree for codifying certain blues trademarks. The blues is too volatile a form to ever be standardized, but much of it is typified by a 12-bar structure and three-line verses that follow what is called an AAB rhyming scheme. These are the traits, more than any other, that have endured in much (perhaps most) acoustic and modern electric blues, live or recorded, to this day.

Modern mass communications–the phonograph record and radio–began to unify the blues stylistically, exposing listeners and musicians to sounds, similar and different, from other regions. The inherent demands of a two- or three-minute 78 RPM single also necessitated a brevity and conciseness, forcing musicians to cut down the length of their songs, and perhaps to adopt certain standard methods (like the 12-bar structure and AAB scheme) to present their music commercially. The similar structure of many blues songs may have even been matters of convenience or imitation in many cases.

What's certain is that after the phenomenal success of Mamie Smith's "Crazy Blues" (the first blues record) in 1920, and many other women singers performing in a similar vein over the next few years, the record industry–then in its infancy–was eager to record blues artists of all kinds, with a particular eye toward what was then called the "race" (i.e. African-American) market. This led to labels scouring several regions for talent, particularly the South, where most blues performers were based. Here they encountered the guitarists who sang deep country blues, as well as songsters and jug bands. Blues was off and running as an established part of the music industry, with an ever-widening repertoire of songs and styles that has endured to this day as one of the most popular and important forms of American music.

–Richie Unterberger

6 Recommended Albums:

Various Artists, *Blues Masters, Vol. 10: Blues Roots* (Rhino)
Various Artists, *Afro-American Spirituals, Work Songs and Ballads* (Library of Congress)
Various Artists, *Negro Work Songs and Calls* (Library of Congress)
Various Artists, *The Sounds of the South* (Atlantic)

Eddie "One-String" Jones, *One String Blues* (Gazell)
Ali Farka Toure, *The Source* (Hannibal)

Jug Bands

Jug bands may be only a footnote in the birth of the blues. Some may dispute whether they belong in the mainstream of blues history at all, finding it more convenient to categorize them as old-time folk music. The relatively few recordings that blues-influenced jug bands made in the 1920s and 1930s, at the very least, give us valuable insight into the roots of the blues, at a time when it had not solidified into guitar-based music that usually adhered to 12-bar structures. It also yields its share of high-spirited tunes in the bargain.

Some historians have speculated that at the turn of the century, jug band-type outfits were more common in the Southern African-American community than performers playing what we would now call the blues. The instrumentation and arrangements of the jug bands were often an outgrowth of the minstrel/vaudeville/traveling medicine shows that toured the South. String bands were a feature of many of these outfits, and the emphasis was on good-time entertainment, not the hard times and weighty expression that many associate with the blues.

A great deal of the charm of the jug bands was due to the homemade, almost improvised nature of the instruments. There were kazoos, washboards, washtubs, spoons, and all manner of percussion produced by items more commonly associated with work tools or playthings; like jugs, but also pipes, pans, and more. Even the relatively conventional instruments, like fiddles and guitars, were sometimes made from scrap materials, like cigar boxes.

Elaborates Francis Davis in *The History of the Blues*, "Jug bands differed in size and instrumentation, though they invariably included either a harmonica or a kazoo as a lead melodic voice, a variety of string instruments, and at least one band member providing a bass line by blowing rhythmically across the top of a jug–a poor man's tuba, as it were. Like the rural fife-and-drum bands of which we have regrettably few recorded examples, jug bands can be heard as a missing link between the blues and the music of West Africa …

"Along with the washboard bands in which a simple laundry device was transformed into a percussion instrument, the jug bands were a tribute to the ingenuity shown by impoverished rural Blacks in expressing themselves musically on whatever they found at hand. For that matter, [early jug band leader Gus] Cannon fashioned his first banjo out of a bread pan and a broom handle. And there are obvious parallels to be drawn between the use of such homemade or 'nonmusical' instruments then and similar practices in hip-hop, most notably 'scratching.'"

Many of the jug bands that were active in the early 1900s didn't have professional aspirations; the ones that did were doubtless undiscovered by record companies. Like the barrelhouse blues pianists of the early 1900s, their representation on record is fairly scant, and certainly not fully documented for lis-

Music Map

Jug Bands

Early Jazz Combos
Circa 1900–1920: Buddy Bolden, Kid Oliver,
Louis Armstrong, Original Dixieland Jazz Band

Noah Lewis
*Harmonica and
Songwriter*
Walter Horton worked
Memphis jazz band
circuit

Gus Cannon
*Jug and Banjo,
Leader of Gus Cannon's
Jug Stompers*
Generally credited as
originator or popularizer
of the genre

Will Shade
Guitar and Harmonica
Principal and star of
Memphis Jug Band

Memphis Jug Band
Cannon's biggest
competition in Memphis

teners of future decades who wish to get a relatively complete picture of the style. And many of the ones that did get to record only issued a single or two before vanishing into oblivion, only accessible today via obscure compilations aimed at a very small and specialized collector market.

Of the jug bands that managed to record in the 1920s and 1930s, more noteworthy ones emerged from Memphis than anywhere else. The most influential were the ones led by Gus Cannon, much of whose repertoire was grounded in a definite blues base. The most celebrated of Cannon's local rivals were the Memphis Jug Band; unlike many of the jug bands, they recorded prolifically, helping ensure that their reputation would outlive them. Individual stars within these bands were harmonica player Noah Lewis (an associate of Cannon's) and guitarist-harmonica player Will Shade, the most prominent member of the Memphis Jug Band.

Even at the time that Cannon and the Memphis Jug Band were recording, the jug band style was being threatened on several fronts. Country blues was evolving into a far more guitar-oriented form that put the emphasis on solo vocals; African-American bands were turning increasingly to swing and big band jazz. The jug bands may have reminded some African-Americans of a minstrel and blackface tradition that they were eager to evolve from, or even forget. The Depression meant a severe cutback on commercial blues recordings of all kinds, and the jug bands were hit especially hard; very few commercial jug band recordings were made after the 1930s, and by the subsequent decade, the genre had pretty much vanished as a commercial consideration anyway.

Long after the prime of the Memphis jug bands, however, the influence of the music would linger. The Rooftop Singers, one of the more commercial ensembles of the early '60s folk revival, took Gus Cannon's "Walk Right In" to the top of the pop charts in 1963. The folk revival also spun off a small jug band revival of its own, the most successful act being Jim Kweskin & His Jug Band, featuring Maria and Geoff Muldaur (although the group's repertoire was not limited to the blues). And the Grateful Dead, who dug very deep into the blues backlog for some of their covers, included Cannon's "Viola Lee Blues" on their first album.

—Richie Unterberger

5 Recommended Albums:

Gus Cannon's Jug Stompers, *The Complete Recordings* (Yazoo)
The Memphis Jug Band, *Memphis Jug Band* (Yazoo)
Various Artists, *The Jug & Washboard Bands, Vol. 1 (1924–31)* (RST Blues Documents)
Various Artists, *The Jug, Jook & Washboard Bands* (Blues Classics)
Jim Kweskin & His Jug Band, *Greatest Hits* (Vanguard)

Delta Blues

No other style of the blues has exerted such a grip on the popular imagination as the one associated with the Mississippi Delta. The image of the wracked bluesman hunched over his acoustic guitar, exorcising the demons from the depths of his soul, his rhythmic force often accentuated by thrilling slide guitar–this is a caricature that originated from Delta blues. Like any caricature, it's prone to over-generalizations that tend to obscure the considerable stylistic range of the form, and the eccentricities to be found in the repertoire of its major exponents. But there's no doubt that Delta blues epitomizes the music at its most emotional and expressive.

The history of Delta blues is inseparable from the African-American culture of the region itself. The Delta refers to the northwestern part of the state, where the fertile soil gave rise to many plantations. These were owned by Whites and worked mostly by Blacks, who often harvested the land as sharecroppers. The conditions for sharecroppers may have been better than those they endured in slavery, but not by a great deal. Backbreaking labor and low wages were the norm, as well as racial intolerance and segregation.

No amount of romanticization can obscure the grinding poverty of the everyday lives of the plantation workers. But the conditions of the Delta were conducive to the development of a sort of indigenous music. Huge numbers of African-Americans were working and living together in close promixity, exchanging the music and folk traditions they had developed and experienced over generations. In many instances, they were too poor to travel even moderate distances (and in any case didn't have the spare time to do so), intensifying the ferment of musical elements that gave birth to a distinctive style.

As hard as the plantation work was, there was still time for entertainment, in both informal settings and weekend parties. Musicians were in demand for these events, and often they would circulate between different plantations. The solo guitarist was a natural fit for these situations; full bands would have found spontaneous ensemble traveling more difficult, both logistically and economically. In comparison to many other instruments, the guitar was relatively inexpensive and more portable. These factors may have accounted for the predominance of the solo guitarist in Mississippi Delta blues (not to mention country blues as a whole). Delta blues was certainly one of the first forms of the music, if not the first, to emphasize the guitar, an association that characterizes much blues music to the present day.

Robert Palmer, a Delta blues authority as both a critic and a record producer (and author of a book-length study of the subject, *Deep Blues*), explains in his liner notes to *Blues Masters Vol. 8: Mississippi Delta Blues* that "Delta blues is a dialogue between the overt and the hidden. The music's apparent simplicity–basic verse forms, little or no harmonic content, melodies with as few as three principal pitches–is superficial. Apparently straightforward rhythmic drive often proves, on careful listening, to be the by-product of a mercurial interplay between polyrhythms, layered in complex relationships. The music's supreme rhythmic masters–Charley Patton, Robert Johnson–kept several rhythms going simultaneously, like a juggler with balls in the air or like the most gifted modern jazz drummers. Sometimes the music seems to lie behind the beat and rush just ahead of it at the same time....

"The simplest way to characterize the music's origin is as a turn-of-the-century innovation, accommodating the vocal traditions of work songs and field hollers to the expressive capabilities of a newly popular stringed instrument, the guitar. Older black ballads and dance songs, preaching and church singing, the rhythms of folk drumming, and the ring shout of 'holy dance' fed into the new music as well. But the richly ornamented, powerfully projected singing style associated with the field holler was dominant, which is hardly surprising; the Delta is more or less one big cotton field."

The man usually recognized as the first exponent of the Delta blues is Charlie Patton. Most blues scholars, and indeed many general fans, are now well aware that Patton didn't invent the Delta blues; he was simply one of the first to record it, and was adept at absorbing many of the regional elements that were in the air. As David Evans writes in *The Blackwell Guide to the Blues*, "In Patton's blues, and indeed in his spirituals, ballads, and ragtime tunes, may be found fully formed all the essential characteristics of the Deep South blues style–the gruff impassioned voice suggesting the influence of country preaching and gospel singing style (which he displayed on his religious recordings), the percussive guitar technique, the bending of strings and use of slide style, the driving rhythms and repeated riffs, the traditional lyric formulas, and the simple harmonic structures.

"Patton, however, also displays one highly individual characteristic: he sings about his own experiences and events he observed–frequently ones outside the realm of the usual man-woman relationships in the blues–always shaping his lyrics from a highly personal point of view." Indeed, the Delta blues as a whole were often more personal, earthy, and downcast than much popular music,

Music Map

Delta Blues

Charlie Patton 1st great star of the Delta Blues

Son House, Willie Brown, Tommy Johnson, Tommy McClennan, Ishmon Bracey, Robert Johnson, Skip James, Bukka White, Mississippi John Hurt	Johnny Shines, Eddie Taylor, Muddy Waters, Robert Nighthawk, John Lee Hooker, Howlin' Wolf, Elmore James, Mississippi Fred McDowell

reflecting the struggles and bitter realities of Southern Blacks in the early 1920s, as well as the basic details of rural life.

Other Mississippi bluesmen were already recording in the late 1920s. The most important of these was probably Tommy Johnson, a contemporary of Patton's who knew and learned much from the guitarist; Ishman Bracey, who was an associate of Johnson's for a long time, also did a good deal of recording in the era. Much of the activity in this scene centered around the plantation of Will Dockery, where Patton and Johnson would often play, influencing such Dockery residents as the young Howlin' Wolf. The success of Patton's recordings in the race market led labels to issue 78s by other Delta bluesmen, the most notable of which was Son House, another musician who knew Patton well.

The most individual and eccentric of the Delta bluesmen, Skip James, was in a sense not a Delta bluesman at all. James was based in the tiny Mississippi hill town of Bentonia, whose isolation may have contributed to the development of his musical idiosyncrasies. His minor guitar tunings and strange, often falsetto vocals are very unusual for the country blues genre. It's the dark, anguished power of his compositions, though, that may hold the most enduring appeal for listeners throughout the ages.

The devastating effects of the Depression on the music industry meant that Delta bluesmen were rarely afforded the opportunity to record after the 1930s. Hence the abrupt end of the recording careers of singers like James, House, and others in the early 1930s, not to be resumed until their rediscovery several decades later (if they were still alive, or could still be found). Many others, doubtlessly, never had the chance to record at all, due either to the lack of opportunity within the record business, or the simple luck of the draw when companies scouted for talent.

But the most legendary Delta bluesman of all, Robert Johnson, didn't do any of his recording until 1936. Several books and film productions have been based around his life, much of which is based on legend, as the basic facts of his life (many of which were garnered from acquaintances and traveling companions, such as guitarist Johnny Shines) are surrounded by considerable mystery and confusion. The apocryphal story of how he sold his soul to the devil at the crossroads (a prominent image in Southern Black music and culture) provided the basis for one of his most famous songs, and indeed for an entire Hollywood movie.

What we have for real, however, are the 29 songs he recorded in two sessions in 1936 and 1937. In addition to synthesizing much of what was best about the Delta blues, Johnson's songwriting, vocals, and instrumental skill also brought the music closer to a more modern sensibility, particularly in the haunted, agonized individuality of his songs. Famed talent scout and record producer John Hammond was trying to get in touch with Johnson to participate in the pivotal Spirituals To Swing concert at New York's Carnegie Hall in 1938, but the guitarist was impossible to locate. Shortly afterwards, it was discovered that he had died in August 1938, another incident that is shrouded in mystery, though many believe that he was poisoned.

Another Delta great who didn't make his best recordings until well after the early '30s was Bukka White. White, yet another guitarist who had met and been influenced by Charley Patton, actually made his recording debut in 1930 as a religious singer. His best music, however, dates from a 1940 session in Chicago. White's rhythmic guitar approach, tough lyrical attitude (he was fresh from a stint in Mississippi's notorious Parchman Farm), and accompaniment from Washboard Sam gave his music a hard-driving force. Combined with the

fact that the fidelity on these sides is somewhat better than the more primitive recordings of the late '20s and '30s, this makes White's brand of Delta blues more accessible to many contemporary listeners than much of what was recorded a decade or so earlier.

The Delta blues, of course, didn't die just because it wasn't being recorded often. In the early 1940s, Muddy Waters was recorded for the Library of Congress by folklorist Alan Lomax, playing in an acoustic Delta style. Just a few years later, Waters would be bringing Delta blues into the electric age after moving to Chicago, using some of the same sources for songs, and playing guitar in a similar (but amplified) style. He was merely the most famous of the musicians who did so; others included Johnny Shines, Robert Nighthawk, John Lee Hooker, Howlin' Wolf, and Elmore James.

The Delta bluesmen that had never electrified, and never recorded after the 1930s, had seemingly vanished into the corridors of time. Until the early 1960s, that is, when young enthusiasts, fired by a revival of interest in the blues, determined to trace and track down survivors from the era. They found a lot more than they could have hoped for, both in the way of living embodiments of old blues traditions, and actual blues singers from the Delta who were known only as names on rare 78s.

Skip James, Son House, and Bukka White were all rediscovered in this fashion, and launched new recording and performing careers based around the folk circuit and the LP market. There were also discoveries of elderly guitarists who had never recorded in the first place, some of whom also began professional careers, Mississippi Fred McDowell being the most successful. All of them played to far greater audiences in their old age than they had in their prime, often touring internationally, providing one of the music industry's too-rare tales of cosmic justice.

Many listeners who have never heard bona fide Delta blues have been exposed to it indirectly via rock covers, particularly Cream's versions of Robert Johnson's "Cross Road Blues" (retitled "Crossroads") and Skip James' "I'm So Glad." The Rolling Stones did Robert Johnson's "Love In Vain" and Mississippi Fred McDowell's "I've Got to Move," and explored the Delta blues style with considerable success on albums like *Beggar's Banquet* and *Let It Bleed* in the late '60s. Bonnie Raitt toured with McDowell in his final years, and openly credited him as a major influence. Canned Heat and Captain Beefheart were two of the most prominent rock acts of the late '60s that delved into the Delta for much of their inspiration.

The surprise success of Robert Johnson's box set, which sold several hundred thousand copies in the early 1990s, supplied proof that the original article will continue to enthrall audiences. This in turn greased the wheels for the reissue of many other compilations of early Delta blues, helping to ensure that the sound–which can still be heard as a living music in pockets of the actual Delta–will not be forgotten by subsequent generations.

—Richie Unterberger

10 Recommended Albums:

Various Artists, *Blues Masters Vol. 8: Mississippi Delta Blues* (Rhino)
Robert Johnson, *The Complete Recordings* (CBS)
Skip James, *The Complete Early Recordings* (Yazoo)
Various Artists, *Roots of Robert Johnson* (Yazoo)
Charley Patton, *Founder of the Delta Blues* (Yazoo)
Tommy Johnson, *Complete Recorded Works* (Document)
Bukka White, *The Complete Bukka White* (Columbia)
Muddy Waters, *The Complete Plantation Recordings* (MCA)
Son House, *Delta Blues: The Original Library of Congress Sessions from Field Recordings 1941–42* (Biograph)
Mississippi Fred McDowell, *Mississippi Delta Blues* (Arhoolie)

Piedmont Blues

Although Mississippi Delta blues may be the most renowned style of early acoustic blues, guitar-based forms of acoustic blues also thrived elsewhere. One of the most fertile regions was the Piedmont, the southeastern area of the United States stretching from Richmond, VA, to Atlanta, GA. It encompasses music made both in the Appalachian foothills and big cities. Atlanta, base of Blind Willie McTell, Barbecue Bob, and others, was the most active urban center of southeastern blues (early Atlanta blues, it should be noted, is sometimes associated by authorities with the Piedmont style, but sometimes not specifically affiliated with it, or simply grouped in with southeastern regional sounds as a whole).

Styles could vary considerably within this region, but they were often distinguished from other blues recorded in the 1920s and 1930s by a more rhythmic base, and an emphasis on fingerpicking style of guitar playing. As Barry Lee Pearson explained in a previous edition of *The All Music Guide*, "The Piedmont guitar style employs a complex fingerpicking style in which a regu-

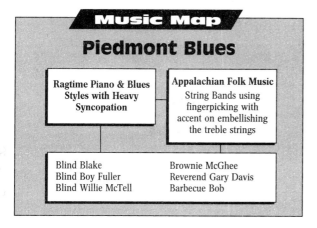

Music Map

Piedmont Blues

Ragtime Piano & Blues Styles with Heavy Syncopation	Appalachian Folk Music String Bands using fingerpicking with accent on embellishing the treble strings

Blind Blake	Brownie McGhee
Blind Boy Fuller	Reverend Gary Davis
Blind Willie McTell	Barbecue Bob

lar, alternating-thumb bass pattern supports a melody on treble strings. The guitar style is highly syncopated and connnects closely with an earlier string-band tradition integrating ragtime, blues, and country dance songs. It's excellent party music with a full, rock-solid sound."

The relatively large numbers of blind guitarists from this region that recorded–Blind Blake, Blind Boy Fuller, and Blind Willie McTell being the most famous–is less surprising when considering the daunting career prospects facing blind African-Americans of the era. Certainly they wouldn't be able to work at most of the jobs available to Southern Blacks at the time, most of which involved skilled and unskilled manual labor. The limited social services available to Blacks made the prospect of useful education unlikely. Playing for money in urban neighborhoods, if one had the skills to entertain and the wherewithal to survive on the streets, was actually one of the better options.

Several of the Piedmont bluesmen were instrumental virtuosos whose versatility could encompass other styles as well; Blind Willie McTell proved himself a master of the 12-string guitar, a relatively uncommon instrument in country blues. Ragtime styles were a particularly significant influence, much more so than they were in the Delta. The tone tended to be lighter than Delta blues as well, though as songwriters the Piedmont players were certainly capable of serious reflection.

Ruminating further on the distinction between Delta and southeastern styles in *The History of the Blues*, Francis Davis speculates that the region's economy was "more diverse than that of Mississippi, and this contributed to a greater diversity of musical styles … there were fewer restrictions on black mobility than in either Mississippi or Texas, and consequently, a greater degree of interplay between Black and White musicians. The songs of such Atlantic Seaboard fingerpickers as Blind Blake, Blind Willie McTell, and Blind Boy Fuller were more geniunely songlike than their contemporaries in the Delta and the Southwest. These guitarists were relative sophisticates, with an intuitive grasp of passing chords offsetting a rhythmic conception anchored in older ragtime and minstrel songs."

Plenty of Piedmont blues was recorded in the late 1920s and early 1930s. But as in other pockets of the blues market, the Depression–and then the onset of World War II–meant that recording activity of blues singers from the area came to a virtual halt. The style didn't die, but it was rarely documented on record from the mid-1930s onwards. Blind Boy Fuller died in 1941, and Blind Blake vanished; Willie McTell did some more recording for both the Library of Congress and commercial labels, though by the end of World War II, his style was appreciated more widely by folklorists than the commercial audience.

The blues revival of the '60s paid much more attention to Delta blues than southeastern styles, but the Piedmont influence was felt in the successful, lengthy careers of Reverend Gary Davis and the duo of Brownie McGhee and Sonny Terry, all of whom were extremely popular with folk audiences. Performers of subsequent eras have also continued to dip into the repertoire of the Piedmont school, the most prominent example being the Allman Brothers' blues-rock adaptation of McTell's "Statesboro Blues."

—*Richie Unterberger*

8 Recommended Albums:

Blind Willie McTell, *The Definitive Blind Willie McTell* (Columbia)
Blind Blake, *Ragtime Guitar's Foremost Fingerpicker* (Yazoo)
Blind Boy Fuller, *Blind Boy Fuller* (Document)

Barbecue Bob, *Chocolate to the Bone* (Yazoo)
Brownie McGhee, *Complete Brownie McGhee* (Columbia/Legacy)
Reverend Gary Davis, *1935–49* (Yazoo)
Various Artists, *East Coast Blues, 1926–1935* (Yazoo)
Various Artists, *The Georgia Blues, 1927–33* (Yazoo)

Lester Melrose
& Early Chicago Blues

Downhome Delta blues didn't mutate into Chicago electric blues overnight when Muddy Waters arrived on his train from Clarksdale, Mississippi in 1943. Even before Muddy had set foot in the city, Chicago had a thriving urban blues scene that did much to link country and urban styles. Much of the best blues to come out of the region in the 1930s and 1940s was recorded by one man, producer and A&R director Lester Melrose.

In the 1990s, with a record industry overstuffed with artists, producers, and corporate decision-makers from top to bottom, it's hard to imagine one person wielding as much influence as Melrose did at his peak. Two of the biggest labels in the world–Columbia and Victor–relied upon Melrose to develop much of the blues talent on its roster. (Victor placed these blues artists on a subsidiary, Bluebird.) The musicians that Melrose assembled read like a who's who of early blues, including Big Bill Broonzy, Tampa Red, Memphis Minnie, John Lee "Sonny Boy" Williamson, Big Joe Williams, Bukka White, Washboard Sam, and Arthur "Big Boy" Crudup.

Many of Melrose's artists came from rural backgrounds; you couldn't get much deeper into the Delta than Bukka White, whom Melrose recorded shortly after his release from a sentence at the notorious Parchman Farm. Melrose's chief contribution to modernizing the blues was to establish a sound with full band arrangements. With ensemble playing, a rhythm section, and even some electricity, these clearly prefigured the Chicago electric blues sound that would begin to explode in the late 1940s.

Comments Robert Palmer in *Deep Blues*, "Melrose's artists had downhome backgrounds: Tampa Red, a top-selling blues star since the late '20s, was from Georgia; John Lee 'Sonny Boy' Williamson, who was largely responsible for transforming the harmonica from an accompanying instrument into a major solo voice, was from Jackson, TN, just north of Memphis; Washboard Sam was from Arkansas; Big Bill Broonzy was a Mississippian by birth. But in the interests of holding onto their increasingly urbanized audience and pleasing Melrose, who was interested both in record sales and in lucrative publishing royalties, they recorded several kinds of material, including jazz and novelty numbers, and began to favor band backing.

"During the mid-'30s the bands tended to be small–guitar and piano, sometimes a clarinet, a washboard, a string bass. But by the time Muddy arrived in Chicago, the 'Bluebird Beat,' as it has been called, was frequently carried by bass and drums. The music was a mixture of older black blues and vaudeville styles and material with the newer swing rhythms. Some of the records even featured popular Black jazzmen."

Melrose was the sort of all-around enterpreneur that was much more common in the early days of the music business. He was not just a producer in the sense of overseeing sessions, but also a talent scout and a song publisher. His involvement in the actual music, however, was substantial. He established a consistent sound for his productions by often using his artists to play on each other's records (often they would rehearse at Tampa Red's house). Washboard Sam, for instance, was often used to supply a percussive beat, even if (as on Bukka White's material) he was the sole accompanist. In this sense, too, Melrose helped establish prototypes for "house bands" that gave important labels like Chess an identifiable sound and led listeners to expect a certain artistic quality from a company's roster, rather than just a bunch of artists that all happened to play blues.

It didn't hurt, of course, that the musicians themselves were about as talented as any group that consistently worked for the same operation. For starters, there was the greatest early blues harmonica player in Sonny Boy Williamson I (not to be confused with the other great Sonny Boy Williamson, Rice Miller, who would later record for Chess); the best early woman blues singer/guitarist, Memphis Minnie; and Big Bill Broonzy, one of the most prolific songwriters of the pre-World War II era. He also did his part to push country blues into something approaching rock 'n' roll by recording Arthur "Big Boy" Crudup, whose "That's All Right Mama" was covered by Elvis Presley in 1954 for his first single.

Elvis would also turn in covers of Crudup's "My Baby Left Me" and "So Glad You're Mine" for two of his most exciting mid-'50s recordings. By that time, Melrose had been left in the dust by the rawer, louder, and far more electric Chicago blues sound that had been developed at Chess Records and elsewhere in the late 1940s and early 1950s. Ironically, Melrose had been the first to

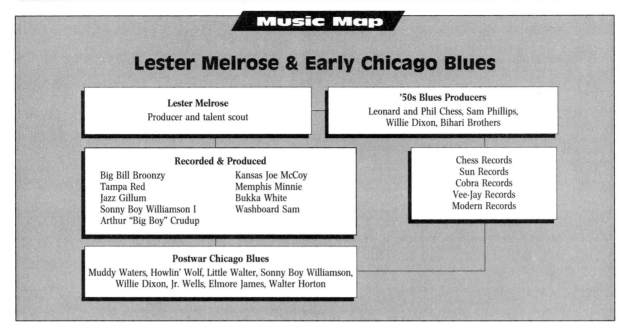

Music Map

Lester Melrose & Early Chicago Blues

Lester Melrose		'50s Blues Producers
Producer and talent scout		Leonard and Phil Chess, Sam Phillips, Willie Dixon, Bihari Brothers

Recorded & Produced		Chess Records
Big Bill Broonzy — Kansas Joe McCoy		Sun Records
Tampa Red — Memphis Minnie		Cobra Records
Jazz Gillum — Bukka White		Vee-Jay Records
Sonny Boy Williamson I — Washboard Sam		Modern Records
Arthur "Big Boy" Crudup		

Postwar Chicago Blues

Muddy Waters, Howlin' Wolf, Little Walter, Sonny Boy Williamson, Willie Dixon, Jr. Wells, Elmore James, Walter Horton

record Muddy Waters, at a 1946 session, but Muddy really didn't find his voice in the studio until a couple of years later with Chess.

Melrose's assocation with Columbia and Victor had far-reaching consequences that ensured the preservation of his work for future generations, in ways that no one could have foreseen back in the 1930s and 1940s, when blues was recorded strictly for the "race" market. These powerful labels were still powerful players in the record industry 50 years later, when the compact disc began to take over from vinyl, and when the blues audience had expanded to include many Black and White collectors and enthusiasts. In the 1990s, much of the classic work that Melrose recorded has been reissued on CD. As a consequence it's far more widely available–and widely respected–than it's ever been before.

—Richie Unterberger

7 Recommended Albums:

Big Bill Broonzy, *Good Time Tonight* (CBS)
Memphis Minnie, *Hoodoo Lady (1933–37)* (CBS)
Tampa Red, *Guitar Wizard* (RCA)
Washboard Sam, *Rockin' My Blues Away* (RCA)
Bukka White, *The Complete Bukka White* (Columbia)
Sonny Boy Williamson I, *Throw a Boogie-Woogie (With Big Joe Williams)* (RCA)
Arthur "Big Boy" Crudup, *That's All Right Mama* (RCA)

Classic Women Blues Singers

The image of the blues as a man hunched over his acoustic guitar in the Mississippi Delta–or, alternately, hunched over his electric axe or harmonica as he moans into a microphone at a sweaty club–is so ingrained in the collective consciousness that it comes as a shock to many to learn that the first blues stars were women. Indeed, women dominated the recorded blues field in the 1920s, the first decade in which a market for blues records existed. Except for the very most famous of these singers, these pioneers are largely forgotten today, having been retroactively surpassed in popularity by some Southern bluesmen who only recorded a precious handful of sides in the '20s and '30s. But these women were the performers who first took blues to a national audience.

The popularity of the early blueswomen was intimately tied to the birth of the recording industry itself. There were many kinds of nascent blues on the rise in the early 20th century–Delta guitarists, yes, but also songsters, jug bands, and dance bands that employed elements of jazz, blues, and pop. And there was the

vaudeville stage circuit, which frequently featured women singers. Presenting productions that toured widely, the musicians involved couldn't help but be exposed to blues forms, if they hadn't been already.

It so happened that female-sung blues, with a prominent vaudeville-jazz-pop flavor, was the first kind of blues to be recorded for the popular audience. There are many possible reasons for this. Perhaps the record companies felt that other styles of blues were too raw to market. Or they may have been largely unaware of more rural and Southern blues styles. The female vaudevillian blues singers had a jazzier and more urban sound that commercial companies may have been more likely to encounter and stamp with approval.

What's far more certain is that "Crazy Blues," recorded by Mamie Smith in 1920, was the first commercial recording of what came to be recognized as the blues. By the standards of the day, the record was a phenomenal success, selling 75,000 copies within the first month–in an era, it must be remembered, when much of the U.S. population, and an even higher percentage of the U.S. African-American population, didn't own a record player. It set off an immediate storm of records in the same vein, by Smith and numerous other women.

But to today's listener, "Crazy Blues" hardly sounds like a blues at all. It sounds more like vaudeville, with a bit of the blues creeping into the edges of the vocal delivery and the song structure. The more judgmental might find that it resembles the music found in contemporary Broadway productions that offer a nostalgic facsimile of pre-Depression Black theater. The song has to be taken in the context of its era, however. It was the first time anything with some allegiance to the blues form had been recorded–and the industry quickly found that such productions were being bought not just by Blacks, but by all Americans.

Mamie Smith's success opened the floodgates for numerous blueswomen to record in the 1920s, often on the Okeh and Paramount labels. Ida Cox, Sippie Wallace, Victoria Spivey, Lucille Bogan, Ethel Waters, and Alberta Hunter are some of the most famous; there were many others. The best of them were Ma Rainey and Bessie Smith, both of whom had rawer, more emotional qualities that give their recordings a feel more akin to what later listeners expect of the blues.

Today, the early recordings by the "classic" female blues singers, as they have sometimes been labeled, sound as much or more like jazz as blues. The vocalists were usually accompanied by small jazz combos, often featuring piano, cornet, and other horn instruments. The guitar, the instrument associated with the blues more than any other, was frequently absent, and usually secondary when it was used. Lots of early jazz stars, in fact, can be heard on the early blueswomen's records, including Louis Armstrong, King Oliver, Duke Ellington, and Coleman Hawkins.

Yet the music *is* identifiable as blues, primarily via the vocal phrasing and the widespread use of the 12-bar song structures that are among the blues'

Music Map

Classic Women Blues Singers

Mamie Smith
"Crazy Blues" 1st Blues Record – 1920

| Ida Cox, Sippie Wallace, Victoria Spivey, Lucille Bogan, Alberta Hunter | **The Queens** Bessie Smith Ma Rainey | Ethel Waters, Dinah Washington, Billie Holiday |

Bonnie Raitt, Tracy Nelson, Janis Joplin

most immediate trademarks. And it was not a form that thrived in isolation from the other styles of blues that were emerging throughout America. As top blues scholar Samuel Charters writes in his liner notes to *Blues Masters Volume 11: Classic Blues Women*, "Even the men living in the South and playing the blues for themselves and their neighbors learned many of their songs from the records that made their way down to local music stores or came through the post office from the mail-order blues companies in Chicago. If they didn't learn the songs themselves, they learned the form and the style of what the record companies thought of as the blues.

"So when the companies sent scouts to find new artists in the South, what they found were the same three or four ways of putting blues verses together. After the sweeping success of the first recordings by women blues artists, the 12-bar harmonic form on the records had become so ubiquitous that even the Delta players who only fingered a single chord on their guitars managed to suggest all the usual chord changes with their singing."

The blues could also be heard in the singers' frank discussions of topics like sex, infidelity, and money and drink problems, often with a palpable hurt. These were offered with a female perspective that has never been as widespread in the blues since, as the music came to be dominated by male performers after the Depression. Listeners from all eras can cut through the often scratchy recordings to find the seeds of the blues, and much modern pop music, in their depiction of hard times, and the struggle and endurance necessary to survive them. It's not all bleakness—the celebratory tunes could have a frank bawdiness, particularly when dealing with sexual double entendres, that would probably generate warning stickers if they were being purchased by today's teenagers.

The onset of the Depression meant hard times for the record business, as it did for every other industry. The craze for female blues singers, which may have already peaked in the mid-'20s, was over, and not just because of artistic trends. Record labels in general were recording less sides. And they weren't eager to devote a lot of resources to the "race" market, populated as it was by the poorest Americans. These African-American listeners would have even less purchasing power in the 1930s, as the Depression lowered their already low standard of living.

But it wasn't just economic factors that heralded the demise of the classic women blues singers. Urban African-American music was becoming more uptempo and elaborate. The swing and big band sound came to fruition in the 1930s, making the staider accompaniment common to many '20s female blues recordings sound tame in comparison. And the vaudeville/theatrical circuit that supported the singers was crumbling, threatening their livelihood just years after they enjoyed positively unimaginable wealth (by the standards of African-Americans of the '20s). Many were unable to make records or, after a few years, even perform; the tale of Mamie Smith, who died penniless in 1946, is unfortunately not unique. Bessie Smith and Ma Rainey would themselves be dead by 1940.

It may be that many of the women who would have been blues singers had they started in the 1920s ended up as jazz ones. Jazz as a whole proved much more fruitful for women singers fronting a band than blues would in the ensuing decades. Billie Holiday, acclaimed by many as one of the finest singers of any kind in the 20th century, certainly owed a great deal to the female blues vocalists of the '20s. Several of her earlier sides in particular could just as well

be classified as blues as jazz. The blues feel remained prominent in many if not most of the major female jazz singers, from Dinah Washington to Cassandra Wilson.

The original female blues stars of the '20s didn't always disappear entirely. Alberta Hunter, for instance, if anything became more popular after the 1920s, and made an unexpectedly successful comeback as a senior citizen in the 1970s and 1980s, after about 25 years of retirement. Ethel Waters expanded into jazz, and then into movies, getting an Academy Award nominiation for Best Supporting Actress for a 1949 film. Victoria Spivey, returning to active recording in the 1960s, started her own label; Bob Dylan made his first appearance on an official recording for the company, playing harmonica on a Big Joe Williams session.

The blues revival of the 1960s, however, largely passed the classic female blues singers by, though Sippie Wallace did record an album with the Jim Kweskin Jug Band. The vocalists were a considerable influence on pioneering '60s rock singers Janis Joplin and Tracy Nelson (who recorded an entire album of Ma Rainey and Bessie Smith songs in her folkie days), thereby influencing rock performers who had never heard the originals. In any case, the styles that the early women blues singers brought to record had by then infiltrated all of blues, rock, soul, and pop, to be heard in almost everyone from Aretha Franklin on down.

—Richie Unterberger

10 Recommended Albums:

Various Artists, *Blues Masters, Vol. 11: Classic Blues Women* (Rhino)
Bessie Smith, *The Collection* (CBS)
Ma Rainey, *Ma Rainey* (Milestone)
Sippie Wallace, *1923–29* (Alligator)
Victoria Spivey, *1926–31* (Document)
Mamie Smith, *In Chronological Order, Vol. 1* (Document)
Lucille Bogan, *1923–35* (Story of Blues)
Alberta Hunter, *Young Alberta Hunter* (Vintage Jazz)
Ethel Waters, *Jazzin' Babies' Blues, 1921–1927* (Biograph)
Various Artists, *Women's Railroad Blues: Sorry But I Can't Take You* (Rosetta)

Jump Blues

The currents of jazz and blues may have run closer together in the 1940s than they did in any other decade. One of the biggest offshoots of this cross-breeding was jump blues, a form that thrived in the late 1940s and early 1950s in particular. With its rhythmic swing, boisterous vocalists, and often light-hearted songs about partying, drinking, and jiving, it hasn't lent itself to as extensively to critical analysis as styles like rural Delta guitarists or electric Chicago blues. During the decade or so when it thrived, however, it laid much of the groundwork for what became known as rhythm and blues, and thus by extension rock 'n' roll.

The roots of jump blues, like many popular styles that became widespread in the middle of the 20th century, can be traced to larger trends of social modernization. In the 1940s, the large big bands of the 1930s scaled back into smaller combos, partially because of economic considerations (particularly during World War II) that made supporting a large ensemble difficult. There were still plenty of African-American patrons for dance halls, however, who wanted a sound that was both danceable and loud. This led many swing bands to place a greater emphasis on honking saxophones and hard-driving vocalists who could be heard over the din, often categorized after the event as "honkers and shouters."

There were many notable forerunners of the jump blues sound to be heard in the jazz community of the 1930s. Pianists like Meade Lux Lewis, Albert Ammons, and Jimmy Yancey devised boogie-woogie patterns; singers like Slim Gaillard and Cab Calloway sang hipster lyrics (sometimes dubbed "jive") with links to both blues and pop traditions. The midwestern cities of Kansas City and St. Louis acted as incubators for the jump blues scene, with their heritage of hot swing bands with vocalists that were open to the influence of the blues.

As Peter Grendysa writes in his liner notes to Rhino's *Blues Masters, Vol. 5: Jump Blues Classics*, "The antiphonal (call-and-response) characteristic of African music so evident in country blues and gospel was adapted by jump blues, often with the voice of the saxophone played against the vocalist, who shouted rather than sang the lyrics. The saxophone was played wth athletic power and exuberance; the saxman squeezing out honks, bleats, and squeals to the delight of the crowds and the dismay of traditional jazz fans. Strong backbeats were provided by the drummer's snares and rim shots on the second and fourth beats of every bar and reinforced by the bass player marking every beat."

Some of the first performers to sing in a readily identifiable jump blues

Jump Blues

Small Jazz Combos '30s & '40s
Louis Armstrong Hot Five/Hot Seven, Benny Goodman Trio/Quartet/Sextet, Count Basie's Kansas City Six

Big Bands with a Beat
Count Basie, Chick Webb, Benny Goodman, Lionel Hampton, Cab Calloway, Louis Prima

Boogie-Woogie Piano
Meade Lux Lewis, Cow Cow Davenport, Cripple Clarence Loston, Albert Ammons, Jimmy Yancey

The Piano Players
Nat "King" Cole Trio, Charles Brown, Amos Milburn, Sammy Price

Louis Jordan & His Tympani Five
Most innovative and successful jump blues combo of all time

Jump Blues as Rock 'n' Roll
Louis Prima w/ Sam Butera, Chuck Berry, Bill Haley & the Comets

The Ladies
Wynona Carr, Camille Howard, Big Mama Thornton, Ruth Brown, Faye Adams, Lavern Baker, Ann Cole, Big Maybelle

Honkers & Shouters
Big Jay McNeely, Big Joe Turner, Joe Houston, Sam "the Man" Taylor, Wynonie Harris, Roy Brown, Red Prysock, Bullmoose Jackson, Nappy Brown, Billy Wright

The Bands
Tiny Bradshaw, Roy Milton, Joe Liggins, Jimmy Liggins, Johnny Otis

style were very grounded in the jazz world. Big Joe Turner, one of the few performers to bridge the jazz, R&B, and rock 'n' roll eras, had been singing jazz since the late 1930s, even appearing at the famed Spirituals to Swing concert in 1938 at New York's Carnegie Hall. Turner may be more responsible than anyone else for founding the "shouting" school of R&B singing, emphasizing smooth but commanding vocal presence. Based (like Turner) in Kansas City, bandleader Jay McShann may be most famous for cultivating the talents of the young Charlie Parker, but he also did his part to create jump blues by employing Walter Brown, another of the earliest shouters.

The most influential architect of jump blues, however–indeed, one of the more significant figures in 20th century American music–was alto saxophonist and singer Louis Jordan. After serving in Chick Webb's band in the 1930s, he formed his own outfit, the Tympany Five. In the mid- and late-1940s, he ran off an astonishing series of R&B hits that set much of the tone for the jump blues genre, especially the fast, danceable rhythms and the joking, novelty-tinged lyrics–traits that did not pass unnoticed by Chuck Berry. Jordan was also a rock 'n' roll forefather in that he was one of the first R&B performers to make significant inroads into the pop and White audiences.

Jump blues really began exploding commercially after World War II, as America got set to relax and party after years of contributing to the war effort, as jazz headed off in directions less conducive to dancing, and as large numbers of African-Americans moved from the country to the city, taking some of the country blues tradition with them. The West Coast, particularly Los Angeles, was a hotbed of jump blues/proto-R&B. There was a large Black community (many recent arrivals), and large numbers of small combo bands looking to survive the transition from big bands to earthier small ones. And there were new independent labels cropping up–Specialty, Modern, Aladdin, Swingtime–that saw a niche for Black popular music that was being ignored by the majors.

Los Angeles in particular was a breeding ground for the saxophonists that would become known as the honkers–musicians who got a grainy, squealing tone and summon frenetic bursts of notes on the uptempo tunes. They were often great showmen in concert as well, playing on their backs sometimes to whip the crowds into more frenzy. Illinois Jacquet had set a model of sorts for the style on his classic soloing on Lionel Hampton's huge hit "Flying Home" and his work on the live Norman Granz Jazz At The Philharmonic recordings, which introduced a few elements that would become widespread in R&B and rock 'n' roll. Big Jay McNeely, Joe Houston, and Chuck Higgins were some of the most noteworthy saxophonists of the style, sometimes doing without vocals

entirely, the sheer bravado of their solos being enough to build their studio tracks around.

The West Coast favored an urbane brand of jump blues that owed much to jazz. Electric guitar pioneer T-Bone Walker is usually thought of as a bluesman, but certainly his 1940s recordings–which are usually pegged as his best and most influential–incorporated a lot from jazz and jump blues. Though not a bluesman per se, Nat King Cole in his early days would approach a jump blues mood, and traces of his suave charm can be found in many 1940s jump blues sides.

Several West Coast bandleaders had a lot of success in the late 1940s with a sort of polished grit. On Specialty Records alone, there was Joe Liggins, his brother Jimmy, and Roy Milton. Milton, though only a hazily remembered figure, was a huge star in his day, landing well over a dozen singles in the R&B Top Ten in the late 1940s and early 1950s. His pianist, Camille Howard, was a notable recording artist in her own right, and a premier example of a jazz-boogie performer who seemed to have gotten dragged into the R&B world more by happenstance and the forces of historical change than anything else. Johnny Otis would organize a lot of L.A. talent as a bandleader, vocalist, talent scout, promoter, label owner, and general all-around champion of the scene.

The boogie-woogie-derived structure of much jump blues lent itself well to pianists, and several of the best jump blues singers also excelled at the keyboards. Prominent among them were Amos Milburn, who could handle both Charles Brown-ish ballads and rowdy songs about drinking, and Floyd Dixon, famous as the originator of "Hey Bartender," served to the masses decades later via the Blues Brothers. For those who liked their jump blues a bit rougher, there were the pre-eminent shouters, Roy Brown and Wynonie Harris. Both of them had big R&B hits with "Good Rockin' Tonight," and both were influences upon Elvis Presley, who would make the tune his second Sun single. Jump blues also had more room for female participation than many other blues subgenres, with Camille Howard and Wynona Carr both scoring substantial successes for Specialty, and R&B-based singers like Big Maybelle and Big Mama Thornton recording singles heavily indebted to the style.

There was an enormous number of jump blues records cut between 1945 and 1955, and a brief survey of some of the most famous pianists, bandleaders, saxophonists, shouters, and women singers still leaves out a great many names that are treasured by blues and R&B fans. Just to scratch the surface, you could mention shouter Nappy Brown, Tiny Bradshaw (who did the original version of "The Train Kept A-Rollin'"), Red Prysock, Bullmoose Jackson, the pre-Atlantic recordings of Ray Charles, and Billy Wright (the last of whom was

Little Richard's chief early inspiration). The Savoy label alone recorded enough singers, briefly and extensively, to generate numerous various artist compilations.

Yet by the mid-'50s, the jump blues style was definitely on the wane. It was a story that has repeated itself numerous times throughout the history of pop–a whole school of stylists, seemingly at its peak, was swept aside by a horde of younger and rawer upstarts. It wasn't just a few Elvis Presleys and Little Richards, though–it was the whole tidal wave of rock 'n' roll.

Certainly the dividing line between jump blues and R&B is a very fine one. A transitional figure like Jackie Brenston, for instance, could fall into either camp. Early sides by Atlantic R&B artists like Ruth Brown and LaVerne Baker sometimes owed a lot to jump blues and the same could be said of early rock instrumentalists like Bill Doggett. And many early doo-wop sides have a lot of jump blues in them–listen to Drifters tracks like "Fools Fall In Love" or "Such a Night" for the evidence. But the hard fact was that R&B, and its close relation rock 'n' roll, had dropped much of the jazz and boogie-woogie so prominent in jump blues. The most raucous sounds of its saxophones were retained, but there was progressively more emphasis on electric guitars, group vocals, and younger performers with a greater appeal to teenagers.

By 1956, most of the jump blues stars were scuffling for survival. Some adapted to the rock 'n' roll era with some success, most notably Joe Turner and Johnny Otis; others tried to adapt to rock 'n' roll trends unsuccessfully, like Roy Brown and even Louis Jordan. There were a few, like Turner and Jimmy Witherspoon, who could slide back into the jazz world if they wished, having never strayed far from it in the first place. Sometimes an old star would surface unexpectedly like Amos Milburn, who had a surprise tenure with Motown in the early 1960s.

Unless you're a devoted collector or scholar, it can seem as though most jump blues greats have vanished into a black hole of history. Perhaps that's because the form bridged blues, jazz, R&B, and pop, without quite fitting into any of the forms comfortably. Another factor is the general absence of hot guitar solos, a general touchstone for most modern fans connecting with older forms of blues.

Jump blues, however, is blues at its most fun–a call to arms not to bewail tribulations or reflect upon the abyss, but to let loose, wail, and party. In the bargain, it was probably *the* most important foundation for what became known in the 1950s as R&B, and gave us much of the rhythm and humor that we take for granted in contemporary rock, blues, and soul.

—*Richie Unterberger & Cub Koda*

12 Recommended Albums:

Various Artists, *Blues Masters Vol. 5: Jump Blues Classics* (Rhino)
Various Artists, *Blues Masters Vol. 14: More Jump Blues* (Rhino)
Big Joe Turner, *Big, Bad & Blue: The Joe Turner Anthology* (Rhino)
Louis Jordan, *The Best of Louis Jordan* (MCA)
Roy Milton, *Roy Milton & His Solid Senders* (Specialty)
T-Bone Walker, *The Complete Capitol Black & White Recordings* (Capitol)
Amos Milburn, *Down the Road Apiece: The Best of Amos Milburn* (EMI)
Joe Houston, *Cornbread and Cabbage Greens* (Specialty)
Floyd Dixon, *Marshall Texas is My Home* (Specialty)
Roy Brown, *Good Rocking Tonight: The Best of Roy Brown* (Rhino)
Wynonie Harris, *Bloodshot Eyes: The Best of Wynonie Harris* (Rhino)
Various Artists, *The Original Johnny Otis Show* (Savoy)

Louisiana Blues

Long hailed as the birthplace of jazz, and a crucible of all kinds of roots sounds, New Orleans has influenced the course of American music as much as any other city. It does not, however, loom as large in the history of the blues as one might expect. Certainly regions like Chicago, Memphis, and the Mississippi Delta have produced many more performers of note; each of those areas also has a far more distinctive blues style. New Orleans is much more the champion of old-school jazz and funky rhythm and blues. But the city, and the state of Louisiana, have made some estimable contributions to the history of blues, even if these are somewhat harder to finger and pigeonhole than many others.

As Robert Palmer muses in *Deep Blues,* "It seems strange that New Orleans, the metropolis at the mouth of the Mississippi River, didn't attract more Delta bluesmen. Rice Miller and Elmore James performed there frequently during the '40s, playing in the streets before they graduated to club engagements, and other Mississippi bluesmen paid occasional visits. But New Orleans had its own indigenous brand of blues, a jazz-oriented style that had more to do with Texas and Kansas City music than with the Delta and often made use of the Afro-Caribbean rhythm patterns that have survived in the city's folklore since the celebrated slave gatherings that took place in Congo Square."

Not that deep blues was totally unknown in the region. Whatever vestiges of country blues may have remained in the area after World War II can be heard, at least in part, on *Bloodstains on the Wall: Country Blues From Specialty,* a compilation of performances recorded by the L.A.-based label in New Orleans. And some of the most traditional styles of Louisiana blues may have been preserved on sessions by Robert Pete Williams, who was recorded by folklorist Harry Oster in the Louisiana State Penitentiary in the late 1950s (Williams went on to make other records as well after his release from prison).

The most significant urban blues to originate from the city, however, was recorded in 1953 by Guitar Slim, who originally hailed from the Delta. "The Things That I Used To Do," one of the biggest R&B hits of 1954, was Slim's definitive statement, as much gospel/R&B as blues, with the spiritual, funky feel that characterizes much New Orleans music. It's been speculated that the bandleader on the session, a young Ray Charles, was inspired to try a similar fusion of the gospel and secular on his own records as a result of the record's enormous success. The blues factor of Guitar Slim's equation, though, was unmistakable in his electric guitar work, which by the standards of the time was unimaginably hard and fuzzy.

Most New Orleans R&B of the '50s could not be comfortably classified as blues, as Guitar Slim was. With its funky rhythms and pop/jazz influences, it looked forward to rock 'n' roll (or indeed *was* rock 'n' roll) and soul music much more than it looked to blues roots. The line between blues and R&B can get thin, of course, as it does with jump blues; many if not most of the great New Orleans R&B/rock performers had a bluesy feel. None of this should obscure the fact that whatever it's called, it's a mammoth body of great music, available on numerous reissues.

Some Crescent City artists were bluesier than others, though, one of the most famous being pianist Professor Longhair, a beloved figure who symbolizes New Orleans music to many listeners. A similar but more obscure figure is James Booker who, like Longhair, had a career renaissance in the '70s and '80s. For guitarists, you could check out Snooks Eaglin, who, in the songster tradition, led simultaneous careers as a commercial New Orleans R&B artist (for Imperial) and an acoustic blues/folk singer (for Prestige, Arhoolie, and other labels). Imperial was also responsible for recording some West Coast blues artists in New Orleans with hopes of reviving their flagging careers, including Roy Brown and Pee Wee Crayton. New Orleans guitar blues was kept alive through the '60s by Earl King, who flavored his touch with rock and soul, a combination appreciated by Jimi Hendrix, who covered King's "Come On."

A more distinctive Louisiana blues sound, that of "swamp" blues, was produced elsewhere in the state by Baton Rouge artists Slim Harpo, Lightnin' Slim, Silas Hogan, Lonesome Sundown, and Lazy Lester. All of them recorded under the direction of Crowley, Louisiana producer Jay Miller, producing a unique blues sound and style characterized by lazy beats, relaxed vocals, doomladen reverberant production, trebly guitar work, odd percussion effects, and wailing harmonica. Slim Harpo was the greatest of these figures, and his compelling combinations of snaky guitar riffs and raw harmonica blasts were a huge influence on several British Invasion bands. Indeed, he spun a virtual catalog of material that would be covered by U.K. groups, including "I'm a King Bee" and "Shake Your Hips" (the Rolling Stones), "Got Love If You Want It" (the Kinks and Yardbirds), "Don't Start Crying Now" (Them), and "Raining in My Heart" (the Pretty Things); Slim himself made a well-deserved entry into the Top Twenty in 1966 with "Baby Scratch My Back." Although not from Louisiana originally, pianist Katie Webster also made her mark on swamp blues, as a session musician for Jay Miller and a sporadic recording artist on her own.

New Orleans is a famed melting pot of sounds and cultures, and one of its most distinctive regional musics, zydeco, certainly owes a visible debt to the blues. Performers such as Clifton Chenier, Boozoo Chavis, and Rockin' Dopsie are in the main beyond the scope of this book, as they draw from cajun, pop, R&B, and folk sources more than blues to devise their rhythmic brew. The best of them are certainly worth checking out, however, as an interesting branch of the roots music tree with definite ties to the blues in the phrasing and some of the rhythms and songs.

Although blues does not have as extensive a tradition in New Orleans as it does in some other cities, it's better positioned to thrive in the area these days than in most other parts of the country, simply because the region has an extensive support system for locally performed roots music. That's true at both the club/jukejoint level and internationally renowned festivals; the annual New Orleans Jazz & Blues Festival features carloads of blues performers from all over (in addition to numerous other jazz, R&B, and rock acts). Family connections to the music seemed to have endured better in Louisiana than some other regions, and performers like Guitar Slim Jr., Kenny Neal (son of Raful), and Chris Thomas (son of Tabby) have all kept the blues flame burning with recent recordings. —*Richie Unterberger*

14 Recommended Albums:

Various Artists, *Bloodstains on the Wall: Country Blues From Specialty* (Specialty)
Robert Pete Williams, *Those Prison Blues* (Arhoolie)
Guitar Slim, *Sufferin' Mind* (Specialty)
Professor Longhair, *Fess: Professor Longhair Anthology* (Rhino)
Slim Harpo, *Hip Shakin': The Excello Collection* (Rhino)
Snooks Eaglin, *The Complete Imperial Recordings* (Capitol)
Lightnin' Slim, *Rooster Blues* (Excello)
Lazy Lester, *I Hear You Knockin'* (Excello)
Lonesome Sundown, *I'm A Mojo Man* (Excello)
Silas Hogan, *Trouble* (Excello)
Katie Webster, *Katie Webster* (Paula)
Clifton Chenier, *Zydeco Dynamite: The Clifton Chenier Anthology* (Rhino)
Various Artists, *Alligator Stomp Vol. 1-3* (Rhino)
Various Artists, *Crescent City Soul: The Sound of New Orleans 1947-1974* (EMI)

Harmonica Blues

Perhaps there is something special about free reeds (harmonica, accordion, concertina) that appeals to the human ear and soul–the sounds made when air rushes over a metal reed. The blues harp can have an intensity that reaches right past any personality barriers and grabs at the feelings like few instruments can. The plaintive wail of an acoustic harp (harmonica) and the powerful intensity of amplified harmonica are important sounds that are featured in the blues tradition.

Since the blues became amplified and electrified, the harmonica has been a staple for many bands–not as ubiquitous as the guitar, perhaps, but more the rule than the exception. The instrument has often served a horn-like function in the blues combo (giving rise to its nickname as the "Mississippi saxophone"), producing the sorts of full-bodied, grainy sounds that are nigh impossible to manufacture from string instruments.

Prior to World War II, the harmonica was not as prominent an instrument in live or recorded blues, and certainly very secondary in comparison to guitars and pianos. To get a facsimile of horn-like fullness, early blues recordings were apt to use other instruments; the kazoo was often employed on the records of jug bands (although Noah Lewis' work with Cannon's Jug Stompers are some of the earliest–and finest–recorded examples of blues harmonica on disc), and pan quill pipes were sometimes used, a famous example being Henry Thomas' "Bull Doze Blues" (which was remade into a pop hit by Canned Heat in the late '60s as "Going Up the Country"). The mysterious George "Bullet" Williams appears to be one of the first harmonica players to be recorded in the '20s before disappearing into the mists of time. DeFord Bailey was an extremely popular harmonica virtuoso in the 1920s and 1930s via his frequent appearances on the Grand Old Opry, though he was not solely a blues player, per-

forming country and folk tunes as well. Sonny Terry may have been the most notable country blues harmonica man, later finding favor with the blues/folk crossover audience, both in his long-standing partnership with guitarist Brownie McGhee and his work as accompanist to artists like Leadbelly.

The man who did the most to popularize the instrument as well as linking country and urban blues together was undoubtedly John Lee "Sonny Boy" Williamson, now forever listed in the history books as Sonny Boy Williamson I. His use of "choked" notes and wah-wah hand effects, coupled with great songwriting and swinging vocals, made him the first great star of the instrument. His influence spread through the blues community like wildfire, spawning a raft of acolytes and making him literally one of the godfathers of the postwar Chicago scene. His recordings from the 1930s and 1940s popularized songs that would resurface in the repertoires of major Chicago blues stars like Junior Wells and Muddy Waters. His stabbing death in 1948 robbed the blues of one of its true original voices.

The reason for the numerical appendage to John Lee's name can be directly traced to a bit of chicanery involving a Mississippi blues harp genius named Rice Miller. Traversing the South in the '30s and '40s as Little Boy Blue, Miller worked with Robert Johnson, a young Howlin' Wolf and myriad others, living the hard life of an itinerant bluesman. When the Interstate Grocers Association decided to broadcast him live on the King Biscuit Time radio show on KFFA from Helena, Arkansas, they decided to change his name into something more recognizable to blues listeners. After the senseless death of Williamson (who never toured the South, but whose records were nonetheless enormously popular), Miller became "the original" Sonny Boy Williamson; blues reference works now differentiate between the two men by referring to Miller as Sonny Boy Williamson II. Sonny Boy II (actually older than John Lee by about 15 years) did a lot to popularize harmonica blues with his broadcasts in the 1940s, and with his first recordings for the Trumpet label in the early '50s, the popularity of both eventually luring him north to Chicago where he became one of the shining jewels in the Chess Records blues crown.

But with the rise of the electric sound on the Chicago blues scene, the man who really changed it all was Little Walter, who is still acknowledged as the top virtuoso of blues harmonica. Walter Jacobs occupies a position in the history of the blues harmonica comparable to Charlie Parker's in the history of the jazz saxophone, or Jimi Hendrix's in the history of rock guitar. It was Walter, more than anyone else, who was responsible for establishing the basic vocabulary of the instrument, especially as it's used in electric blues bands.

A professional musician from about the time he entered his teenage years, Walter's arrival in Chicago in the late '40s found him playing for tips on Maxwell Street in the then-popular style of Sonny Boy I. By the early '50s however, all of that changed, with Walter being one of the first to start amplifying his harp. Armed with a cheap microphone, cupping his hands over it to create incredible amounts of distortion through his amplifier, and taking rhythmic cues from jump blues and jazz, Little Walter popularized the sound most people associate with amplified blues harp. The volume and power increased

Music Map

Blues Harp (Harmonica): A Short History

Acoustic Beginnings (Chordal Harp)
Early acoustic harp included training whistle, vaudeville, ragtime, jazz

Jug Memphis Bands
Will Shade, Gus Cannon, Jug Stompers, with Noah Lewis

Grand Old Opry Radio with DeFord Bailey
Sonny Terry, foremost folk/blues acoustic players

John Lee Sonny Boy Williamson I
Major influence in the transition from chordal harp to its use as a melodic-line-oriented, lead instrument

Down-Home Electric
Jimmy Reed, Dr. Isiah Ross

Sonny Boy Williamson II
(Rice Miller) An original blues giant with a unique sound, and a touch of country never far away

Rhythm & Blues
Slim Harpo, Raful Neal, Lazy Lester

Urban Harps
Buster Brown, Mofo Buford, Frank Frost, George Harmonica Smith.

Muddy Waters Blues Band
Muddy Waters was the Miles Davis of the blues. Almost every major harp player worked in his band– even Junior Wells and Walter Horton. Yet is was Little Walter who set the tone for what became the high-powered Chicago blues sound.

Big Walter Horton
Perhaps the most beautiful of all harp players

Little Walter
High-intensity Chicago harp at its best

Junior Wells
Outstanding funky blues

Great Younger Harp Players

James Cotton
The last of Muddy's great players

Paul Butterfield
The finest early White player

Phil Wiggins
Modern acoustic country harp

Charlie Musselwhite
Fine early White player

William Clarke
One of the best White players today

Carey Bell
Good modern player

Jerry Portnoy
with Muddy Waters

Billy Branch
Aggressive young modern player

James Harman, Gary Primich, Rod Piazza, King Biscuit Boy, Paul deLay

when he began to record in the studio, first as a part of Muddy Waters' band on a brace of influential sides, and then (after his 1952 hit "Juke") as a solo artist. Walter also used several different kinds of harmonica to increase his sonic range, often alternating between a standard harp and a more complex chromatic one (sometimes in mid-song) that gave him a greater variety of tones and note choices.

In the original edition of *The Rolling Stone Record Guide*, John Swenson summed up Walter's mammoth significance well: "Every harmonica player after Little Walter has in some way been influenced by his style, especially rock players, from John Mayall to Magic Dick of the J. Geils Band. Jacobs was able to take hard bop melodic ideas from contemporary saxophonists and match them to a simpler but more forceful blues rhythm with heavily emphasized guitar parts, suggesting a further link between bop-era jazz players and rock 'n' roll. The Little Walter harmonica style thus transposed saxophone ideas into terms compatible with and influential on guitars." Not to be overlooked are his considerable talents as a songwriter, singer, and sideman, all of which helped make him one of the true greats of early electric Chicago blues.

Not as well-known as Little Walter was, no overview of blues harmonica greats could be considered complete without an equal nod to the "other Walter," the magnificent Big Walter Horton. Playing from the time he was a mere child, Horton was a fixture on the Memphis music scene, playing with everyone from semi-pro jug bands to the earliest electric combos. Several reports have Horton actually blowing amplified harp in the late '40s and the younger Jacobs learned much from the older musician when the two met up in Chicago in the early '50s. Capable of blowing with a sweet lyricism one moment and astonishing power the next, his style owed no stylistic debt to anyone and he could play both unamplified and electric styles with ease. The effect of Big Walter's harp is always soothing, slowing and opening up the time and the mind.

Most of the great Chicago electric blues harmonica players served at one time or another in the band of Muddy Waters. Little Walter, James Cotton, Junior Wells, the wonderful George "Harmonica" Smith, and Walter Horton all played and recorded with him in the '50s and early '60s. Cotton and Wells especially were successful in establishing careers as bandleaders in the 1960s, playing in styles which effectively drew from contemporary rock and soul influences. Each of them were only a little younger than Little Walter, but the king of the blues harmonica went into a sad decline in the 1960s that saw increasingly sporadic and unimpressive recordings before his death, at the age of 37, in 1968 in a street fight.

The harmonica was a more established presence in the blues of Chicago than anywhere else, and the city was home to several other notable players. Billy Boy Arnold cut some great singles for Vee-Jay records in the 1950s, and also made important contributions to rock 'n' roll as a sideman on some of Bo Diddley's early records. Some Chicago blues greats who were not really identified primarily as harmonica players could use the instrument effectively, like Jimmy Reed and Howlin' Wolf. Compilations like *Sun Records Harmonica Classics*, which features '50s blues recorded in Memphis, serve notice that not all harmonica blues of note originated from Chicago, and the country blues sounds of Joe Hill Louis and the one-man band of Doctor Ross offer a decided change of pace from the more pervasive Windy City sounds. Another stylistic strain also worth investigating is the swamp blues sound from Louisiana, with Slim Harpo and Lazy Lester being its two best-known exponents.

As Chicago blues was an enormous influence upon R&B-oriented British Invasion bands, it's no surprise that many U.K. rock groups of the '60s featured members (usually the lead vocalists) who were reasonably proficient on the instrument. It's not often noted, but singers like Mick Jagger, Keith Relf (of the Yardbirds), John Mayall, Van Morrison, and Paul Jones (of Manfred Mann) could blow with bluesy soul when appropriate. As the British Invasion turned into blues-rock and progressive rock, the instrument was used with less frequency, but could still be whipped out with impressive effect, as Mick Jagger demonstrated on "Midnight Rambler."

As further proof that good blues has no color, some of the best American harmonica blues players of recent years have been White. Paul Butterfield and Charlie Musselwhite–both of whom rose through the Chicago club scene in the 1960s and came by their blues honestly, learning first hand from their idols–certainly had technique and feeling to match the best of them, whether playing straight Chicago blues or (in Butterfield's case) blues rock. Notable White virtuosos of more recent years include Kim Wilson of the Fabulous Thunderbirds, Rod Piazza, Magic Dick, Paul deLay, and William Clarke–possibly the most inventive and original harmonica player currently out there.

Harmonica-playing bandleaders may not be as prominent as they were in the Chicago of the '50s and '60s, but harmonica is still very much part of the standard contemporary blues scene. Many of the masters, like James Cotton, are still around and very active, for one thing; with his recent national album deals, Billy Boy Arnold may be more well known now (at least outside of Chicago) than he was when he was recording in the '50s. A recent blowout supersession of sorts (between Junior Wells, James Cotton, Carey Bell, and Billy Branch) demonstrated the enduring appeal of harmonica showcases. And two of the most noted modern acoustic blues acts, Satan & Adam and Cephas & Wiggins, prominently feature the instrument. And for every person who is inspired to take the instrument up to their lips and try and make a sound with it, there's always the chance that another blues master is a-borning. The history of blues harmonica is still being written.

—*Richie Unterberger, Cub Koda and Michael Erlewine*

16 Recommended Albums:

Various Artists, *Blues Masters Vol. 4: Harmonica Classics* (Rhino)
Sonny Terry, *The Folkways Years, 1944–63* (Smithsonian/Rounder)
Sonny Boy Williamson I, *Throw a Boogie-Woogie* (RCA)
Little Walter, *Essential* (Chess)
Little Walter, *Blues with a Feeling* (Chess)

Sonny Boy Williamson II, *King Bisuit Time* (Arhoolie)
Sonny Boy Williamson II, *Essential* (Chess)
Big Walter Horton, *Chicago–The Blues–Today! Volume 3* (Vanguard)
Big Walter Horton, *The Soul of Blues Harmonica* (Chess)
Junior Wells, *Hoodoo Man Blues* (Delmark)
William Clarke, *Blowin' Like Hell* (Alligator)
Various Artists, *Sun Records Harmonica Classics* (Rounder)
James Cotton, *Best of the Verve Years* (Verve)
The Paul Butterfield Blues Band, *Paul Butterfield Blues Band* (Elektra)
Charlie Musselwhite, *Ace of Harps* (Alligator)
Junior Wells, James Cotton, Carey Bell, and Billy Branch, *Harp Attack!* (Alligator)

Memphis Blues

A visit to Memphis' Beale Street these days is like walking through a museum or movie set. Clubs, stores, and even museums still do business, but more as an homage to the past than as a part of a vibrant present. For decades, however, Beale Street was known as "the Main Street of Negro America," a drag where Black business thrived during the day, and entertainment/nightlife during the night.

Music, naturally, was a big part of that scene, and although the blues weren't the only game in that part of town, it played a big part for several decades. As early as 1912, the community had an anthem, "Memphis Blues," penned by W.C. Handy. In the years prior to World War II, there was a diverse mixture of blues performers, from jugbands to Delta guitarists. In the early 1950s, it was the most important crucible of the electric blues bar Chicago. Memphis blues has also played a huge role in the evolution of American popular music via its influence on the early rockabilly music and '60s soul empire for which Memphis is also renowned.

As one of the major urban centers of the South, Memphis attracted a large African-American population for a long time before the blues became widely known. Though it wasn't far North enough for many Blacks, who went on to Northern cities (especially Chicago) for more racial tolerance and economic opportunity, Memphis was as far as many newcomers to the urban experience got. Even those who eventually went on to Chicago and other cities would frequently stop in Memphis on the way, whether to live for a few years or for only a bit.

W.C. Handy, one of the key forefathers of the blues, based himself and his band in Memphis in 1909. Handy's form of dance music was more blues-influenced than actual blues, and in the 20th century, Memphis was as well known or more for its jazz musicians (Jimmie Lunceford being one of the most famous) than its blues. To this day, Memphis harbors so many different types of roots music that its regional styles are difficult to categorize, and such was the case with Memphis blues prior to World War II. It was always around, but not nearly as identifiable as, for example, the Delta blues so abundant in Mississippi. The city was noted as the home of several blues jug bands (the Memphis Jug Band and Gus Cannon's group being some of the most famous), as well as a few fine blues guitarists, such as Furry Lewis and Robert Wilkins. Blues was often available at the park off Beale Street that now bears Handy's name, as local and itinerant musicians would often play for tips for anyone who was interested.

It was with the post-war amplification of the blues, however, that Memphis really began to leave its mark. Society itself was becoming more urban, higher-paced, and electrified, and two of the important figures in Memphis blues made much of their initial impact not as musicians, but as radio announcers on WDIA (the first radio station in the U.S. to employ an all-Black format, although it was White-owned). One was guitarist B.B. King, who used his experience at WDIA to perfect his diction and absorb the influence of gospel and early R&B music. With his 1951 #1 R&B hit "Three O'Clock Blues," King launched a hugely successful and influential career that was vital to the urbanization of the blues, and by extension blues' eventual entry into mainstream American culture.

The other important WDIA disc jockey was Rufus Thomas, all-around entertainment personality who, more than just about any other living legend, epitomizes Memphis music. Before working for WDIA, Thomas met King when he emceed amateur night shows at the Palace Theater on Beale Street. At that time Thomas may have been more of a general R&B scenester than a professional musician. But it was as a singer that he would play a vital role in Sun Records, the label that would do more to spread the influence of Memphis blues than any other.

Sun was run by Sam Phillips, a young man with a genuine feel and appreciation for the forms of Black popular music in the region. The company is most famous, of course, for launching the career of Elvis Presley, as well as several other rockabilly stars (Carl Perkins, Johnny Cash, Jerry Lee Lewis). When it began operations in the early '50s, however, it recorded mostly Black artists

Music Map

Memphis Blues

W.C. Handy
Wrote "Memphis Blues" in 1912

Jug Bands & Street Musicians	Memphis in the Late '40s/Early '50s	Sun Rockabilly/Memphis R&B 1954-1968
Furry Lewis, Frank Stokes, Gus Cannon, Robert Wilkins, Memphis Willie Borum, Noah Lewis, Will Shade, Joe McCoy, Memphis Minnie, Jack Kelly, Walter Horton	Joe Hill Louis, B.B. King, Rufus Thomas, Walter Horton, Hot Shot Love, Jimmy De Berry, Howlin' Wolf, Bobby Blue Bland, Junior Parker, Pat Hare, Johnny Ace, Willie Johnson, Sammy Lewis, Little Milton	Elvis Presley, Carl Perkins, Jerry Lee Lewis, Albert King, Stax Records
		Memphis Soul Scene Booker T. & the MGs, Willie Mitchell, Bill Black Combo

and the sounds were those of blues/R&B, rockabilly not having been invented yet. (The history of Sun is examined more fully in a separate essay.)

The Memphis Recording Service, as Sun was originally named, at first leased sides to other labels. Early records by B.B. King, Howlin' Wolf, Rosco Gordon, and others were handled by labels like Chess and RPM. Jackie Brenston's "Rocket 88" (actually Ike Turner's Kings Of Rhythm), from 1951, is often cited as one of the first rock 'n' roll records. With the Howlin' Wolf sides in particular, Phillips developed the harshly amplified, spare sound that would be characteristic of the Memphis blues he recorded during this period, which was somewhat rawer and more countrified than its Chicago cousin.

Phillips began putting his blues sides out on his label, Sun, rather than leasing them. Sun's first national R&B hit was Rufus Thomas' "Bear Cat," an answer record to Big Mama Thornton's "Hound Dog." Thomas himself, ironically, only recorded one more single for the label (though he would become a soul star in the '60s and '70s at Stax). There was plenty of other talent around, and during the first half of the '50s Sun recorded seminal sides by Junior Parker, Walter Horton, James Cotton, Little Milton, and Rosco Gordon, as well as obscurities by the likes of Pat Hare, Joe Hill Louis, D.A. Hunt, and Doctor Ross that would attain legendary status among collectors and scholars decades later.

The rise and fall of Memphis electric blues in this period is heavily intertwined with developments at Sun Records. In 1954, Phillips began recording Elvis Presley, a 19-year-old who had done his share of hanging out on Beale Street, checking out the blues singers and buying his clothes at Lansky's, a Beale Street store that catered to many local Blacks. It's almost redundant to point this out now, but Elvis was the single most important figure in the birth of rockabilly, which blended country and western with blues, R&B, and elements of gospel and pop. Memphis blues singers had done much to foster this combination, especially given that Phillips developed much of his studio acumen by overseeing their sessions. Indeed, Elvis covered Junior Parker's biggest hit, "Mystery Train," for his last Sun single, and one of his greatest performances on record.

Phillips turned his focus to the White country and rockabilly artists on his roster, especially after selling Presley's contract to RCA in late 1955, which gave him the capital to properly promote Perkins, Cash, Lewis, et al.

The truth, of course, is more complicated than that. If he had made blues/R&B his only priority, Phillips would have been an admirable idealist, perhaps. He also would have been waging a futile fight against inevitable historical forces. The biggest of these was rock 'n' roll, of course, Black and White, which in 1956 overran the recording industry. Even within blues, though, there was the magnet of Chicago, with its monolithic blues scene and its most powerful label, Chess.

Even if rockabilly had not intervened, the Memphis community had already begun to lose its most promising musicians to other cities. Howlin' Wolf, perhaps the greatest of the blues talents to enter the Memphis Recording Service, was signed by Chess and moved to Chicago, well before Presley's advent. James Cotton (who joined Muddy Waters' band before becoming a star on his own) and guitarist Pat Hare (who also played with Waters for a while) also relocat-

ed to Chicago. Even Sonny Boy Williamson, a musician just across the Mississippi River (in Helena, AR) with some ties to the Memphis scene, would not truly make his mark until after recording for Chess in Chicago. The city guaranteed blues performers more work, more musicians to choose from, and, should they be picked up by local labels, more effective national promotion.

It may also be that some of the blues artists in Memphis were in embryonic states of artistic development that could not be fully nurtured by the metropolis. Junior Parker and Little Milton, for instance, really hit their commercial stride as soul/blues artists in the '60s (and Little Milton would record for the Memphis-based Stax label, among others). B.B. King, another bluesman with prominent R&B and soul influences, became in the 1960s a national figure who recorded in various distant cities, cultivating a sound that was too broad in scope to be pigeonholed as part of a regional movement. Ike Turner (never really identified with the Memphis scene) would move his base of operations to St. Louis, and move into rock and soul with his wife Tina.

Memphis blues didn't die, of course; it was too deeply embedded in the city's music scene to do so. But the focus of the city's African-American popular music production in the '60s and '70s was very much soul, specifically at Stax and Hi Records. Stax usually had some blues/soul hybrids on its roster, achieving a good deal of success with Albert King, who worked with Booker T. & the MG's on many of his records. The demise of Stax in the mid-'70s, however, meant lean times for Black music as a whole in the city.

Blues is still heard and recorded in Memphis these days, even if it has a somewhat folkloric bent. Renowned blues scholar and author David Evans has marshalled some fine down-home blues for the High Water label in recent years, most notably by guitarist Jessie Mae Hemphill. B.B. King owns a club on Beale Street, although he hasn't lived in Memphis for ages. And though it's more of a tourist attraction than a happening area, Beale Street and vicinity offers several places of homage for the serious blues fan, including the Center for Southern Folklore; a good, if seriously undervisited, blues museum; the famous Schwab's variety store (serving the community since 1876); The Memphis Music Museum; Handy Park; and, a mile or two away, Sun Studios, which remains open for tours.

—*Richie Unterberger & Cub Koda*

10 Recommended Albums:

Memphis Jug Band, *Memphis Jug Band* (Yazoo)
Various Artists, *Ten Years in Memphis, 1927–1937* (Yazoo)
Various Artists, *A Sun Blues Collection* (Rhino)
Various Artists, *Blues Masters Vol. 12: Memphis Blues* (Rhino)
B.B. King, *The Best of B.B. King, Vol. 1* (Flair)
Howlin' Wolf, *Rides Again* (Flair)
Junior Parker, James Cotton, & Pat Hare, *Mystery Train* (Rounder)
Albert King, *Born under a Bad Sign* (Mobile Fidelity)
Various Artists, *Memphis Masters* (Yazoo)
Various Artists, *The Blues Came Down From Memphis* (Charly)

Music Map

Piano Blues Stylists by Region

St. Louis Lee Green, Roosevelt Sykes, Peetie Wheatstraw, Henry Townsend, Walter Roland, Walter Davis	**Indianapolis** Leroy Carr	**Memphis & The Delta** Little Brother Montgomery, Sunnyland Slim, Booker T. Laury, Memphis Slim, Jab Jones, Piano Red, Mose Vinson
Chicago Willie Mabon, Otis Spann, Detroit Jr., Henry Gray, Eddie Boyd, Art Hodes	**Kansas City** Jay McShann, Count Basie, Pete Johnson	**California** Charles Brown, Amos Milburn, Percy Mayfield
Texas Alex Moore, Dr. Hepcat, Rob Cooper, Dave Alexander, Sammy Price	**New Orleans** Cousin Joe, Archibald, Smiley Lewis, Jack Dupree, Professor Longhair, Fats Domino	**Other Major Players** Speckled Red, Ray Charles

Piano Blues

The piano hasn't occupied as prominent a place in the blues as the guitar; in terms of blues virtuosos of recent decades, there may even be more harmonica players than keyboard specialists. The piano will certainly always have a place in the blues combo for both its rhythmic and melodic qualities, despite the hysterical predictions of some observers that the synthesizer will soon make it obsolete. Many of blues' finest singers and songwriters have been piano players; blues piano has also played a big part in influencing the directions of jazz, rock, and soul music.

Blues piano styles have much of their origins in the rough-and-tumble barrelhouses and railroad/lumber camps of the late 1800s and early 1900s. Here pianists had to develop a rhythmic, aggressive sound to be heard above the crowd, and to keep pace with the rowdy atmosphere. It's no accident that some of the early blues piano greats are noted for a "barrelhouse" style.

In some respects, early piano players may have been at a disadvantage when competing with guitarists and other instrumentalists. The acoustic guitar (or, say, the harmonica) is extremely portable, a big plus for musicians working the road in the days when private automobile travel was a lot less common. It might not have been as much as a drawback as one may think, though. Most settlements had entertainment establishments with house pianos; if residents or travelers could prove their skills, they were often welcome to have at it.

There's little question that considerably more blues guitarists were recorded than blues pianists in the early days of the phonograph. Blues scholars justifiably bewail the loss of important chapters in blues history because of the preferences of the companies responsible for recording blues in the 1920s and 1930s. Many pianists hardly recorded at all, and are now only represented on obscure import blues compilations. Many, no doubt, never had the opportunity to record at all.

Blues pianists, however, began to be recorded shortly after the first appearance of the blues itself on record. Some of the most significant early ones were Cow Cow Davenport, Roosevelt Sykes, and Clarence "Pine Top" Smith. Smith's "Pine Top's Boogie-Woogie," from 1929, is generally credited with introducing the term "boogie-woogie" into widespread use.

The boogie-woogie piano style is characterized by a 12-bar blues structure and constantly repeating rhythmic patterns of the left hand, while the right hand plays the melodies and improvisations. It quickly caught on, not just in blues, but in popular music as a whole; millions of people who couldn't tell you diddley squat about Robert Johnson know exactly what a boogie-woogie is. Boogie-woogie patterns would become a foundation of jazz in the 1930s and 1940s, jump blues in the 1940s and 1950s, and early R&B/rock 'n' roll in the 1950s.

Records by blues pianists in the 1930s, however, didn't necessarily showcase their instrumental skills. As Mike Rowe notes in *The Blackwell Guide to the Blues*, "There had been a subtle change in the market for piano blues. Those pianists, such as Leroy Carr, Walter Davis, and even Roosevelt Sykes, who had lasted out the Depression were popular for their songs and singing; that they played piano was incidental. While the sawmill pianists played for dancers and had to survive on pianistic prowess, the blues pianist of the urban 1930s had to achieve success as a singer or songwriter. Piano blues had been taken out of the lumber camps and whorehouses and into the homes of an increasingly sophisticated urban audience.

"This accent on the content of the song meant that pianists had little encouragement to stretch themselves, and Davis or Peetie Wheatstraw, for example, could make recording after recording using the same introduction and tempo, which tended to mask their abilities as pianists. Boogie-woogie had become integrated into blues accompaniments, and ragtime was all but eliminated. There was a smoother, more regular sound to the 1930s piano blues, and although a few field trips by Bluebird, Decca, and ARC preserved some regional styles, and the iconoclastic Texas piano in particular, it was the cities such as Chicago and St. Louis that provided the bulk of the artists."

Key figures in the urbanization of blues piano–really, in the urbanization of the blues as a whole–would include Big Maceo Merriweather, Champion Jack Dupree, Sunnyland Slim, and Jimmy Yancey. Boogie-woogie was certainly a big element in swing and big band jazz, and several blues-based boogie-woogie pianists, such as Meade Lux Lewis, Albert Ammons, and Pete Johnson, fed into the jazz tributary with work that straddled the line between the two genres. A Carnegie Hall appearance in 1938 featuring all three of the aforementioned boogie-woogie specialists did much to popularize and legitimize the style.

When the blues started to electrify in Chicago and elsewhere during the 1940s and 1950s, the guitar and harmonica assumed more prominence than the piano. This wasn't true on the West Coast, however, were jump blues reigned supreme between the mid-'40s and mid-'50s. Jump blues' blend of blues and jazz ingredients made it a natural for pianists, and some of jump blues' greatest performers were keyboardist/singers. Amos Milburn, Floyd Dixon, and Camille Howard were some of the best; their achievements are described in greater depth in the jump blues essay. Several other West Coast blues pianists made their mark with a more ballad-inclined, gospel-influenced R&B style, including Charles Brown, Percy Mayfield, Cecil Gant (a great boogie-woogie player as well), and–on his earliest sides–Ray Charles. The blues/jazz piano connection would be kept alive, to a much subtler degree, via the work of blues-and boogie-influenced soul/jazz organists/pianists of the '60s and '70s, such as Jimmy Smith, Big John Patton, and Jimmy McGriff.

There was still room for a piano in the classic-style Chicago electric blues

Music Map

Songsters

Repertoire from the 19th and 20th Centuries including blues, ballads, spirituals, and popular tunes

Texas/Louisiana	Memphis	Mississippi	East Coast
Henry Thomas, Mance Lipscomb Leadbelly, Rabbit Brown	Furry Lewis, Jim Jackson, Frank Stokes, Will Shade, Robert Wilkins	John Hurt, Charley Patton "Hambone," Willie Newburn	William Moore, Luke Jordan, Bill Williams, John Jackson, Honny "Rufe"

lineup, as Otis Spann proved during his lengthy stint with Muddy Waters. It took a while for Spann to emerge from Waters' shadow, but recordings on his own established him as a worthy artist in his own right, and perhaps the finest of the post-World War II piano players. Other players of note on the Chicago blues scene were Memphis Slim, Little Johnny Jones (whose two-fisted work as a member of Elmore James' Broomdusters made the absence of a rhythm guitar in that band totally unnoticeable), Roosevelt Sykes, Eddie Boyd, Willie Mabon, and Johnnie Johnson, who's probably more famous for his contributions to rock 'n' roll, as the pianist featured on many of Chuck Berry's classic sides.

Piano players as stars or singers, rather than side musicians, have been much thinner on the ground in the last few decades than they were 50–60 years ago. Louisiana was something of a pocket of blues and blues-influenced pianists; Professor Longhair, James Booker, and Katie Webster (all of whom have ties of varying strength to the region) developed some of the funkiest and most idiosyncratic styles to be found in the whole blues piano idiom. Memphis Slim and Pinetop Perkins, among others, kept old-school blues piano styles alive with frequent touring well past the 1960s. Keyboards are still a staple of many a blues band, and will probably remain so. But the day may have passed when piano players exerted as fundamental an influence on the direction of the blues as they did in the heyday of boogie-woogie and barrelhouse.

—Richie Unterberger

16 Recommended Albums:

Cow Cow Davenport, *Alabama Strut* (Magpie)
Roosevelt Sykes, *Roosevelt Sykes (1929–41)* (Story of Blues)
Leroy Carr, *Naptown Blues* (Yazoo)
Albert Ammons, *King of Boogie-Woogie (1939–1949)* (Blues Classics)
Meade Lux Lewis, *Complete Blue Note Recordings* (Mosaic)
Jimmy Yancey, *Vol. 1 (1939–40)* (Document)
Big Maceo, *King of Chicago Blues Piano, Vol. 1 & 2* (Arhoolie)
Amos Milburn, *Down the Road Apiece: The Best of Amos Milburn* (EMI)
Floyd Dixon, *Marshall Texas Is My Home* (Specialty)
Camille Howard, *Vol. 1: Rock Me Daddy* (Specialty)
Cecil Gant, *Rock the Boogie* (Krazy Kat)
Sunnyland Slim, *Sunnyland Slim* (Flyright)
Otis Spann, *Otis Spann Is the Blues* (Candid)
Professor Longhair, *Fess: Professor Longhair Anthology* (Rhino)
James Booker, *New Orleans Piano Wizard: Live!* (Rounder)
Memphis Slim, *Rockin' the Blues* (Charly)

Songsters

The blues was such a young form when it first started to be recorded that not all of its early stars would have identified themselves as blues artists. Nor, indeed, were all of them blues artists all of the time. For many African-American singers and musicians, blues was just part of their repertoire. They were also able and willing to play country tunes, spirituals, popular standards, ragtime, jug band, folk songs, and more.

These are the artists labeled by researchers as "songsters." The songsters haven't fared nearly as well as, say, the acoustic guitarists of the Mississippi Delta in the annals of blues history. They often espouse a homey, sunny, good-

timey air that is at odds with the serious, forceful image of the blues that many expect. To listeners accustomed to contemporary blues, rock, and pop, their arrangements and delivery can sound quaintly old-fashioned. Yet the best of the songsters made important contributions to blues history, worth recognizing even by those who much prefer their blues deep and down-home.

It's no accident that some of the most notable songsters were the very oldest blues singers to record; their material would naturally tend to be older in origin, and less shaped by the blues trends of the early 20th century. One of the most famous, and probably the oldest, was Henry Thomas (b. 1874). Only about a third of his two dozen sides were titled as blues; he also cut ballads, reels, and dance songs, often using the pan quill pipes, an unconventional instrument rarely heard today. He achieved a good deal of posthumous fame when his "Bull Doze Blues" was adapted by Canned Heat for their hit "Going Up the Country" in the late '60s. Bob Dylan included a song that Thomas had recorded, "Honey, Just Allow Me One More Chance," on his second LP (*Freewheelin' Bob Dylan*, 1963); the original liner notes explain that the tune "was first heard by Dylan from a recording by a now-dead Texas blues singer. Dylan can only remember that his first name was Henry."

One of the most frequently discussed songsters, Frank Stokes, betrayed the considerable influence of traveling medicine shows in which he participated. As a member of a cast that had to entertain lots of people in different regions, Stokes and similar songsters could have been expected to develop a wide range of material. Pink Anderson, another veteran of medicine shows, survived into the era of the long-playing record, and his '50s and '60s recordings offer better fidelity for those that find the primitive audio of the '20s too hard to handle.

Mississippi John Hurt was another guitarist with songster leanings who survived into the folk revival. Hurt recorded some stellar material in the late 1920s, and then a number of LPs after his rediscovery in the early '60s. His early 78s are more esteemed by blues collectors than his latter efforts, but again you get the choice between better fidelity and performances that are closer to the source of the songster milieu, whatever your preference may be. Quite a few will want to hear Hurt in both contexts; his good-natured, gospel-influenced singing and accomplished fingerpicking makes his work more accessible to contemporary listeners than any of the original songsters.

The songster tradition lived on to a large degree in the work of subsequent singers who held strong appeal for both the blues and folk audiences. They've been usually classified as folk or folk/blues singers rather than songsters for this reason, and also because their work has less of an air of all-around entertainment than Stokes, Thomas, harmonica player DeFord Bailey (who was a regular on the Grand Ole Opry in the '20s and '30s), or '20s songsters like Peg Leg Howell.

The most famous of these blues/folk crossover artists was Leadbelly, discovered by John Lomax in a Louisiana prison in 1933. With his huge repertoire, stellar vocal and instrumental skills, and extremely colorful life, Leadbelly qualifies as one of the giants of 20th-century American music, worth learning about even by music fans who've never heard any of his records. The eclectic approach of Leadbelly enabled him to circulate easily in a New York-based community of folkies that also included Woody Guthrie and the duo of Brownie McGhee and Sonny Terry, two other performers who were also comfortable with both blues and folk.

Also treading the line between blues and folk was Josh White, who in his youth had recorded spirituals under his own name and blues under a pseudo-

Music Map

West Coast Blues

T-Bone Walker

Texas Bluesman moves to California, popularized jazz style that becomes the West Coast Sound

Pee Wee Crayton, Charles Brown, Lowell Fulson, Amos Milburn, Johnny Guitar Watson, Jimmy McCracklin	Roy Milton, Percy Mayfield, Nat "King" Cole, Johnny Otis, Ray Charles, Roy Brown, Big Jay McNeely, Joe Houston, Jimmy Liggins	Shuggie Otis, William Clarke, Johnny Heartsman, Canned Heat, Rod Piazza, Joe Louis Walker, Ted Hawkins

nym, along with the virtually forgotten Brother John Sellers. There was always a home for White on the folk circuit, and after the rediscovery of Hurt, Furry Lewis, and Mance Lipscomb (the latter of whom had never previously recorded) around 1960, acoustic blues legends also tapped into the folk constituency to get a second wind on their professional careers. Hurt, Lipscomb, and White were certainly not songsters in the classic sense, but their versatility owed quite a bit to the songster tradition, enabling them to bring the blues sensibility to many listeners who may have never been introduced to it otherwise.

—*Richie Unterberger*

11 Recommended Albums:

Henry Thomas, *Texas Worried Blues* (Yazoo)
Frank Stokes, *The Memphis Blues* (Yazoo)
Mississippi John Hurt, *1928 Sessions* (Yazoo)
Mississippi John Hurt, *The Immortal* (Vanguard)
Peg Leg Howell, *1928–29* (Matchbox)
Peg Leg Howell, *The Legendary Peg Leg Howell* (Testament)
Leadbelly, *King of the 12-String Guitar* (CBS)
Leadbelly, *Midnight Special* (Rounder)
Pink Anderson, *Ballad & Folksinger, Vol. 3* (Prestige/ Bluesville)
Josh White, *Legendary Josh White* (MCA)
Mance Lipscomb, *Texas Sharecropper & Songster* (Arhoolie)

West Coast Blues

West Coast blues–it's undeniably a phrase with less instant hipster credibility than, say, Chicago blues or Delta blues. The cities of Los Angeles and San Francisco simply don't embody the hard times associated with the blues' origins in the South, or the hothouse conditions that gave rise to much classic electric blues in the North. As the stereotype would have it, life is mellower, the pace slower, the living easier, and the weather sunnier on the West Coast– not the kinds of conditions which have, in the minds of many listeners, been conducive to breeding the best kinds of blues music. The West Coast, however, has been home to many leading blues performers, although it may not have developed as identifiable a sound as some other regions.

When we talk about West Coast blues, we're really talking about California blues, most of which was centered around the Los Angeles and the San Francisco Bay areas. There's not much of a prewar Californian blues tradition, which must be at least partially attributable to the fact that the African-American communities there weren't nearly as large in the beginning of the 20th century. The Black population of the state, however, would swell in the 1940s, the westward migration enhanced by the need for immense manpower to work in the U.S. defense industry during World War II. These new arrivals needed entertainment, and the local jazz and blues club scene heated up quickly.

The towering figure of West Coast blues may be guitarist T-Bone Walker, a relocated Texan who had made his first recordings in the late 1920s. Walker was a crucial figure in the electrification and urbanization of the blues, proba-

bly doing more to popularize the use of electric guitar in the form than anyone else. Much of his material had a distinct jazzy jump blues feel, an influence that would characterize much of the most influential blues to emerge from California in the 1940s and 1950s.

Many of the most popular blues performers to base themselves in California during the 1940s and 1950s were originally from Texas, perhaps accounting from some of the earthiest qualities of West Coast blues. Besides Walker, there was Pee Wee Crayton (a guitarist who modeled his style after T-Bone's), Charles Brown, Lowell Fulson, Joe Houston, Amos Milburn, Johnny "Guitar" Watson, and (after the mid-'50s) Big Mama Thornton. At times it seemed as though Texas was the true breeding ground of West Coast blues–Los Angeles just happened to be where it was refined and recorded.

There was an obvious reason, however, why so much blues was recorded in Los Angeles, as it was the city where many of the independent labels specializing in blues and R&B originated in the 1940s. Specialty, Imperial, Aladdin, and the umbrella of labels run by the Bihari brothers (RPM, Modern, Kent, Flair, and Crown) were the most famous of these. Their importance cannot be overestimated, for the simple reason that they were determined to record and distribute blues music that the big major companies were uninterested in, or not even aware of in the first place.

The history of early West Coast blues is heavily intertwined with that of jump blues, the snappy, rhythmic hybrid of jazz and blues that reigned supreme over much of the R&B world in the late 1940s and early 1950s. That history is covered in greater depth in a separate essay. For now, it should be noted that many of the greatest jump blues musicians were based in California, be they acrobatic saxophonists (Big Jay McNeely, Joe Houston), pianist/vocalists (Amos Milburn, Floyd Dixon, Camille Howard, Little Willie Littlefield), guitarists (Walker, Crayton), or bandleaders like Roy Milton.

A flipside of the uptempo jump bluesters were the singers who specialized in piano ballads that also drew from gospel and the pop-jazz of Nat King Cole. Charles Brown and Percy Mayfield were the most prominent of these vocalists; Ray Charles, based in Seattle at the outset of his career but recording for the Los Angeles-based Swingtime label, also did quite a bit of recording in this vein before devising a more personal style. Today, these figures are all recognized as forefathers of soul music, making it a matter of good-natured debate as to whether they should be classified as blues or just plain R&B.

The R&B/blues line also gets thin when discussing the career of Johnny Otis, the bandleader who did as much as anyone to build the Los Angeles R&B community. Otis made plenty of blues/R&B hybrid recordings on his own, but he arguably made greater contributions as a promoter and organizer of live shows, DJ, producer, and general champion of talent. He did much to further the careers of Little Esther and Etta James, two singers who, again, are better classified as R&B singers than blues ones, though their allegiance to blues styles is certainly visible.

Urbane forms of blues may have dominated the early post-war Californian scene, but there was room for grittier performers as well, such as the aforementioned Pee Wee Crayton, and Johnny "Guitar" Watson, whose futuristic style has been rightly cited as an influence on Jimi Hendrix. Nor was it confined solely to Los Angeles. San Francisco and Oakland were home to a small but notable blues scene, the most prominent spokesman being Jimmy McCracklin, who had a crossover rock 'n' roll Top Ten hit in 1958 with "The Walk." Pee Wee Crayton was also based in San Francisco when he emerged, although he made his most important recordings in Los Angeles.

Blues, as it did throughout the rest of the country, fell on leaner times in California in the 1960s, as rock, surf, and soul dominated the industry. Los Angeles' increasingly central position within the recording industry may have, if anything, decreased the presence of the blues within the city itself. Rock and pop musicians of all kinds were flocking to L.A. studios, and the big and small companies–more of whom were based in L.A. now than anywhere else–wanted to come up with successes in these fields, not the blues, which were considered passé by many, and had certainly long passed its commercial peak.

Tireless keepers of the flame such as Johnny Otis and his son Shuggie, however, ensured that the blues community continued to function, even if at a somewhat subterranean level. As there has been everywhere since the 1960s, interest in the blues among the White audience on the West Coast has become much more commonplace. San Francisco and Los Angeles are each home to some of the biggest and most successful blues festivals in the world, and each have a decent number of venues for both local and visiting blues artists.

Some of the most notable blues performers of recent times have come from California, even if there's not much that can be pigeonholed as especially "regional" about their sound. Johnny Heartsman, who's been active since the 1950s, really made his true impact with nationwide audiences in the 1980s and 1990s. From San Francisco, Joe Louis Walker is one of the most successful bluesmen of recent times, noted for his effective incorporation of rock and gospel influences into his material. Walker established himself as a recording artist on the San Francisco Bay Area-based Hightone label, one of the top contemporary roots music companies in the United States.

Southern California has been home to many White blues bands as well, producing two noted harmonica virtuosos in William Clarke and Rod Piazza (and, way back in the 1960s, one of the most successful American blues-rock groups, Canned Heat). And throughout the 1980s, you could walk down the tourist-congested boardwalk of Venice Beach in Los Angeles and find Ted Hawkins playing for change for passerby. A repository of acoustic folk/blues in the urban madness that now suffuses the L.A., Hawkins achieved recognition as one of the top practitioners of contemporary acoustic blues before his premature death in the mid-1990s–giving California, perhaps, the acoustic blues roots it never really had.

—*Richie Unterberger*

15 Recommended Albums:

T-Bone Walker, *The Complete Capitol/Black & White Recordings* (Capitol)
T-Bone Walker, *The Complete Imperial Recordings* (EMI)
Pee Wee Crayton, *Rocking Down on Central Avenue* (Ace)
Amos Milburn, *Down the Road Apiece: The Best of Amos Milburn* (EMI)
Floyd Dixon, *Marshall Texas Is My Home* (Specialty)
Roy Milton, *Roy Milton and His Solid Senders* (Specialty)
Percy Mayfield, *Poet of the Blues* (Specialty)
Charles Brown, *Driftin' Blues: The Best of Charles Brown* (EMI)
Johnny "Guitar" Watson, *Three Hours Past Midnight* (Flair)
Lowell Fulson, *San Francisco Blues* (Black Lion)
Johnny Otis, *The Johnny Otis Show* (Savoy)
Jimmy McCracklin, *Everybody Rock: Let's Do It! The Best of Jimmy McCracklin* (Domino)
Johnny Heartsman, *The Touch* (Alligator)
Joe Louis Walker, *The Gift* (Hightone)
Ted Hawkins, *Happy Hour* (Rounder)

Chicago Blues

Probably no strain of blues has a more universally recognized form, feel, and sound than Chicago blues. Chicago is where the music became amplified and had the big beat put to it and like Muddy Waters said, the blues had a baby and they named it rock 'n' roll. As a simple point of reference, it's the music that most sounds like '50s rhythm and blues/rock 'n' roll, its first notable offspring; when you hear a TV commercial with blues in it, it's usually the Chicago style they're playing. It's the sound of amplified harmonicas, electric slide guitars, big boogie piano, and a rhythm section that just won't quit, with fierce, declamatory vocals booming over the top of it. It's the genius of Muddy Waters, Howlin' Wolf, Elmore James, and Little Walter knocking an urban audience on their collective ears at some smoky, noisy South side tavern, then transmitting that signal to the world. It's the infectious boogie of Hound Dog Taylor, John Brim, Jimmy Reed, and Joe Carter mining similar turf while Robert Nighthawk and Big John Wrencher lay it down with rough and tumble combos Sunday mornings on the Maxwell Street open-air market. And it's the up-to-date, gospel-inspired vocals and B.B. King single-note style of Otis Rush, Magic Sam, and Buddy Guy meshing with it all. Though there's much primitive beauty to be found in this strain of the music, there's nothing subtle about it; its rough edge ambience is the sound of the Delta, coming to terms with the various elements of city life and plugging in and going electric to keep pace with a changing world. Chicago blues was the first style to reach a mass audience and, with the passage of time, the first to reach a worldwide audience as well. When average Joes think of the blues, one of two musical sounds pop into their brain pan; one is the sound of Delta blues–usually slide-played on an acoustic guitar. The other–if it's played through an amplifier–is almost always Chicago blues.

Although the Windy City had a burgeoning blues scene before World War II (see separate essay on Lester Melrose and Early Chicago Blues), a number of elements combined after the war to put the modern Chicago scene into motion.

First, there was the societal aftermath of World War II to deal with. Blacks–after serving their country and seeing how the rest of the world was–came back home, packed up their few belongings and headed north to greener pastures, better paying jobs and the promise of a better life. It was a simple case of "how ya keep 'em down on the farm"; once Blacks had left the oppression of Southern plantation life behind and "had seen the world," the prospect of toiling in a meat packing plant in Chicago looked a whole lot more upscale than standing behind a mule somewhere in Mississippi.

And so they headed north. This influx of new migrants all finding new jobs and housing also infused Chicago with a lot of capital to be had and spent in these flush post-War times. The rise of the independent recording label after shellac rationing (and the development of space-age plastics) also had a lot to do with the development of the sound as well. New record labels that dealt exclusively with blues for a Black market started to proliferate after 1950. Chess and its myriad subsidiaries and Vee-Jay had the lion's share of the market, but medium-to-tiny imprints like Ora-Nelle (an offshoot of the Maxwell Street Radio Repair Shop), JOB, Tempo Tone, Parkway, Cool, Atomic H, Cobra, Chance, Opera, United, States, Blue Lake, Parrot, C.J., and others all helped to bring the music to a wider audience.

Up to this point, John Lee "Sonny Boy" Williamson, Big Bill Broonzy, and Tampa Red were the three acknowledged kingpins of the local scene, but their hegemony was soon to be challenged and eventually relinquished to the new breed. The new migrants wanted to be citified and upscale, but still had strong down-home roots that needed to be tended to. The jazzier jump blues offerings in the city were fine, but newly arrived Southerners wanted something a little more gritty, packed with a little more realism and a lot more emotional wallop. One day a train dropped a young slide guitarist from Mississippi into the city and soon the new audience had the sound and the style that suited their needs, urban, rural, and emotional. Muddy Waters had come to Chicago and the sound of Chicago blues as we know it was about to be born.

Waters worked the house party circuit at first, driving a truck by day and playing his music wherever he had the chance. He fell in with a loose group of players which included guitarists Baby Face Leroy Foster, Blue Smitty, and Jimmy Rogers. Muddy tried to plug into the Melrose style recording scene three years after arriving, but a one-off recording session issued on Columbia under an assumed name did the singer little good. The sound was urban, but it wasn't *his* style, the sound that captivated his listeners at house rent parties along the South side.

Muddy noticed two things about playing in Chicago. One, he needed amplification if he was going to be heard over the noisy din in a neighborhood tavern. He needed an electric guitar and an amplifier to go with it and he needed to turn both of them full blast if he was going to make an impression. Secondly, he needed a band; not a band with trumpets and saxophones in it, but a modern version of the kind of string band he worked in around Clarksdale, MS. It stands as a testament to Muddy Waters' genius that he created the blueprint for the first modern electric blues band and honed that design into a modern, lustrous musical sheen. There had certainly been blues combos in the city previous to Waters' arrival, but none sounded like this.

Muddy's first band was called the Headhunters because of their habit of blowing any band they came in contact with off the stage, and usually taking their gig from them in the bargain. Although Muddy was having hits on Chess with just his guitar and a string bass in support, in a live situation it was a different matter entirely. Baby Face Leroy Foster was soon replaced by Elgar Edmonds (aka Elgin Evans) on drums, Jimmy Rogers wove complex second guitar patterns into the mix, and due time, Otis Spann would bring his beautiful piano stylings to the combo, following Muddy's every move. But it was with the addition of harmonica genius Little Walter that the face of the Chicago blues sound began to change. If Muddy and Jimmy's guitars were amplified and cranked up, Walter got his own microphone and amplifier and responded in kind. Though others played electric before him (Walter Horton among them), it was Little Walter who virtually defined the role and sound of amplified harmonica as it sat in this new band context. His honking, defiant tone–full of distortion, hand-controlled compression wedded to swooping saxophone-styled licks–became *the* sound for every aspiring combo and harmonica player to go after. By the time Walter left Muddy to form his own band, the Jukes (named after his hit instrumental), his sound was so pervasive that club owners would only hire combos that had a harmonica player working in that style. Bands would do without a drummer if need be, but the message was clear; one had to have that harp in order to work.

Soon there were newly amplified bands springing up everywhere and coming from everywhere, as the word was soon out that Chicago was quickly becoming the new promised land of the blues. The competition was fierce and tough, with lesser bands like Bo Diddley's Langley Avenue Jivecats or Earl Hooker working for tips on Maxwell Street, while others squeezed onto postage stamp-sized stages just trying to establish their reputations. Among these were future blues legends in the making Big Walter Horton, Johnny Shines, J.B. Lenoir, Snooky Pryor, Jimmy Reed, John Brim, Billy Boy Arnold, and J.B. Hutto. Muddy Waters' first challenge to his newly acquired crown as king of the circuit came from Memphis bluesman Howlin' Wolf. Wolf had just signed a contract with Chess Records and had a hit on the R&B charts to go with it. He came into town, looking for work and by all accounts, Muddy was most helpful in getting him started. But what started as professional courtesy soon blossomed into a bitter, intense rivalry between the two bandleaders that lasted until Wolf's death in 1976. They'd steal sidemen from each other, compete with each other over who would record Willie Dixon's best material and

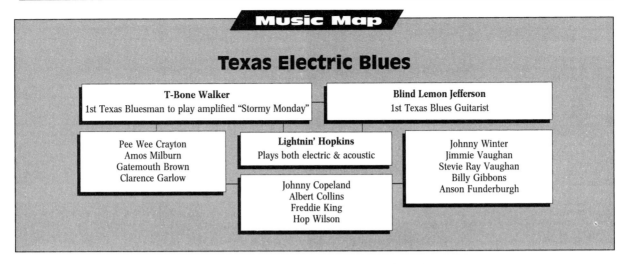

Music Map

Texas Electric Blues

T-Bone Walker
1st Texas Bluesman to play amplified "Stormy Monday"

Blind Lemon Jefferson
1st Texas Blues Guitarist

Pee Wee Crayton
Amos Milburn
Gatemouth Brown
Clarence Garlow

Lightnin' Hopkins
Plays both electric & acoustic

Johnny Winter
Jimmie Vaughan
Stevie Ray Vaughan
Billy Gibbons
Anson Funderburgh

Johnny Copeland
Albert Collins
Freddie King
Hop Wilson

when booked on the same bill together, would pull every trick possible to try and outdo each other onstage.

The preponderance here on the club scene in Chicago is pivotal in understanding how the music developed. For all their business acumen and commercial expertise, Chess and every other Chicago label that was recording this music was doing it because it was *popular* music in the Black community. This was an untapped market that was tired of being spoon fed Billy Eckstine and Nat King Cole records and wanted to be sent back home, and a three-minute 78 of it just might hit the spot. Just like every other honest trend or development in American music, it simply happened; the people responded, and somebody was smart enough to record it and sell it.

But by the mid-'50s–as one bluesman put it–"the beat had changed." The blues *did* have a baby and they *did* name it rock 'n' roll. Suddenly everyone from Big Joe Turner to Bo Diddley were being lumped in with Elvis and Bill Haley and a hundred vocal groups named after birds or automobiles. The Black audience started to turn away from blues to the new music and suddenly the local scene needed a fresh transfusion of new blood. Over on the West side, younger musicians were totally enamored of the B.B. King style of playing and singing and began to incorporate both into a new Chicago blues hybrid. Working with a pair of saxes, a bass player and a drummer, most West Side combos were scaled down approximations of B.B.'s big band. When the group couldn't afford the sax section, the guitarists started throwing in heavy jazz chord-like fills to flesh out the sound. Suddenly Otis Rush, Buddy Guy, and Magic Sam were on equal footing with the established heavies, and even Howlin' Wolf and Elmore James started regularly recording and playing with saxophones. As rhythm and blues started getting a harder-edged sound as it moved into soul music territory by the mid-'60s, the blues started keeping its ear to the ground and its beat focused on the dance floor. While the three primary grooves up til now had been a slow blues, a boogie shuffle and a "cut shuffle" (like Muddy's "Got My Mojo Working"), suddenly it was okay to put a blues to a rock groove, sometimes with quite satisfying results.

One of the first to mine this turf was harmonica ace Junior Wells. Wells' first hit, "Messing With The Kid," was blues with a driving beat and a great guitar riff, signaling that once again, the blues had reinvented itself to keep with the crowd. Working in tandem with Buddy Guy at Pepper's Lounge, the duo worked like a downscale miniature blues'n'soul show, combining funky beats with the most down in the alley blues imaginable. By the middle '60s, Chicago produced its first racially mixed combo with the birth of the highly influential Paul Butterfield Blues Band, featuring the high-voltage guitar work of Michael Bloomfield and members from Howlin' Wolf's rhythm section. And the permutations that have come since then and flourish in the current Chicago club scene echo those last two developments of the Chicago style. The beats and bass lines may get funkier in approach, the guitars might be playing in a more modern style, sometimes even approaching rock pyrotechnics, in some cases. But every time a harmonica player cups his instrument around a cheap microphone or a crowd calls out for a slow one, the structure may change, and every musician and patron doffs their symbolic hats in appreciation to Muddy Waters and the beginnings of the Chicago blues, still very much alive and well today.

—*Cub Koda*

14 Recommended Albums:

Muddy Waters, *The Best Of Muddy Waters* (MCA-Chess)
Little Walter, *The Best Of Little Walter* (MCA-Chess)
Jimmy Reed, *Speak The Lyrics To Me, Mama Reed* (Vee-Jay)
Howlin' Wolf, *Howlin' Wolf/Moanin' In The Moonlight* (MCA-Chess)
Various Artists, *Chicago/The Blues/Today!, Volumes 1–3* (Vanguard)
Junior Wells, *Hoodoo Man Blues* (Delmark)
Otis Rush, *1956–1958* (Paula)
Elmore James, *The Best Of Elmore James–The Early Years* (Ace)
Hound Dog Taylor, *Hound Dog Taylor & The HouseRockers* (Alligator)
Various Artists, *Blues Masters, Volume 2: Postwar Chicago* (Rhino)
Paul Butterfield, *Paul Butterfield Blues Band* (Elektra)
Magic Sam, *West Side Soul* (Delmark)

Texas Electric Blues

The sound of Texas electric blues is difficult to define in general terms, not least because the sheer size of the state has given rise to several diverse sub-branches. Almost all blues fans can agree that they like the Texas sound; very few can actually agree on what it *is*. What's more, it's a matter of some debate whether some major performers should be considered as Texas blues artists at all, since musicians like Freddie King, Bobby "Blue" Bland, T-Bone Walker, and Amos Milburn were only based there during part of their careers, often making their most influential recordings elsewhere. Saying that Texas blues has a distinctively earthy quotient won't do, either: What kind of blues worthy of the name *isn't* earthy?

In general terms, however, it can be said that Texas blues is a somewhat more variable animal than, say, Chicago blues or Memphis blues. A country feel is often detectable, and it's more open to outside R&B influences. Bold touches of brass are frequent, and the guitar, usually played with dazzling single-string virtuosity, is king; the harmonica, in comparison to Chicago, is much more secondary. There's also a sense of joyous showmanship that often comes across on the records, which frequently have a small-club feel, even if they've been recorded in state-of-the-art studios.

Texas does have an estimable history of acoustic country blues talent. Blind Lemon Jefferson may be the most famous of the early Texas blues singers; Lightnin' Hopkins (who played in both acoustic and electric styles), aside from John Lee Hooker, may have made more records than any blues artist; Mance Lipscomb was a notable footnote to the early '60s blues revival, as one of the relatively few elderly bluesmen that emerged during that era who hadn't actually made any records before being "rediscovered." For the purposes of this piece, however, we'll focus on Texas blues after the advent of the electric guitar.

One Texan is the figure more responsible for electrifying the blues than any other. T-Bone Walker, born in 1910 in Texas, had in fact relocated to Los Angeles by the time he made his most influential sides in 1940s. Owing much to jazz as well as urban R&B, these were some of the first, if not the very first, blues sides that employed clean, horn-like single-string soloing in a style that came to be identified with much modern electric blues, from B.B. King on down. As John Morthland explains in the liner notes to *Texas Music Vol. 1:*

Postwar Blues Combos, "After feeling out the possibilities created by electricity, he began phrasing saxlike lines that exploited the guitar's new tonal capabilities and hanged it from a rhythm to a lead instrument. Adapting rhythmic and harmonic ideas from jazz, T-Bone would hold his guitar sideways against his chest … and drag his pick across the strings for a fat, clean sound that he'd break up with grinding downstrokes."

The Texas-L.A. connection was so well-traveled in the 1940s that it bore some resemblance to the railroad that shuttled seemingly nonstop between the Mississippi Delta and Chicago. Besides Walker, native Texans Amos Milburn, Pee Wee Crayton (a T-Bone Walker disciple), Charles Brown, Percy Mayfield, and Lowell Fulson all launched their careers after moving to California and hooking up with the independent R&B labels sprouting in Los Angeles.

Texas itself wasn't entirely bereft of recording opportunities. The most prominent R&B label, Duke/Peacock, was based in Houston. Duke/Peacock owner Don Robey was legendary for his iron hand, running his operation with a parsimonious, intimidating attitude that would result in hosts of anecdotes surfacing several decades later. Even today, some musicians are reluctant to discuss his rumored gangster-like tactics, and somewhat less so to note his practice of assigning songwriting credits and royalties to himself with reckless abandon.

Nevertheless, Duke/Peacock recorded some excellent blues in the '50s by artists like Big Mama Thornton, Junior Parker, and Bobby Bland. The latter two singers are not from Texas, but Bland in particular has come to represent the sort of blues/R&B/soul hybrids that are important facets of Texas blues, even if they were developed primarily in Texas studios, rather than within the Texas blues scene itself. Bland's extensive association with Duke/Peacock, which lasted throughout the '60s as well as the '50s, is usually rated as the finest blues/soul of all time, notable for its gospel vocal influence and blaring horn charts as well as its blues elements.

Bland's brassy soul blues may have been Texas' most successful blues export on record, but in practice, the guitar remained king. Clarence "Gatemouth" Brown, Johnny Copeland, and Albert Collins all began recording guitar-heavy material on Texas labels in the '50s, although Collins and Copeland wouldn't really achieve top-level national blues stardom for another two or three decades. Like most noted Texas electric blues guitarists, they were top showmen as well, the late Collins often using a guitar lead of 100 feet or so to enable him to wander around the audience while he played.

Freddie King is the most famous Texas blues guitarist to emerge during this era, though again it's almost arbitrary as to whether he should be classified as a Texas bluesman or not. He was born in Texas, but moved to Chicago as a teenager, and recorded his prime work for the Cincinnati-based King label. However you might classify his statehood, he was certainly one of the most important electric blues guitarists of his time, producing an authoritative, distorted tone that was a big influence on Eric Clapton in particular. He was also eager to incorporate R&B and soul influences into his repertoire, and was comfortable as both a vocal and instrumental artist, scoring his biggest hit with the instrumental "Hide Away" in 1961. Fans of Texas blues–indeed, blues fans of all kinds–should look for a video compilation of his mid-'60s performances on the Dallas-based R&B/soul television show, *The Beat*, which includes some guitar sparring with Clarence "Gatemouth" Brown (who led the house band). Although slide guitar wasn't heard much in Texas blues, Hop Wilson's idiosyncratic work on a non-pedal steel guitar in the '50s is a sound no lover of blues can afford to miss.

With its constant interchange between Black and White styles, it's not surprising that Texas developed a healthy White blues-rock scene in the late '60s and 1970s. Johnny Winter was the most well known of its early practitioners, playing in both traditional styles and more southern rock-influenced ones; his brother Edgar also had some national success, though with a far more rock-oriented sound. The late Texan Stevie Ray Vaughan is probably the most famous blues-rocker of recent times, and was the primary torch-bearer for the whole modern day blues-rock genre prior to his unexpected death in 1990.

Texas will likely continue to supply a stream of blues talent due to its oft-thriving club scene, particularly in Austin, Texas. The world is now well aware of the many talented White blues bands to emerge from the area, the best and most recognizable of those being the Fabulous Thunderbirds, which were founded by Stevie Ray Vaughan's brother Jimmie. The presence of one of the world's leading blues clubs, Antone's, in the city bodes well for ongoing development of regional blues talent.

—*Richie Unterberger*

10 Recommended Albums:

Various Artists, *Blues Masters Series, Vol. 3: Texas Blues* (Rhino)
Various Artist, *Texas Music, Vol. 1: Postwar Blues Combos* (Rhino)
T-Bone Walker, *The Complete Black & White Recordings* (Capitol)

Bobby "Blue" Bland, *I Pity the Fool* (MCA)
Clarence "Gatemouth" Brown, *The Original Peacock Recordings* (MCA)
Albert Collins, *Ice Pickin'* (Alligator)
Hop Wilson, *Steel Guitar Flash!* (Ace)
Freddie King, *Hide Away: The Best of Freddie King* (Rhino)
Johnny Winter, *Johnny Winter* (Columbia)
Stevie Ray Vaughan, *Greatest Hits* (Epic)

Blues Slide Guitar

The swooping, stinging sound of the slide guitar is one of the most striking and popular characteristics of the blues. It's also one of the sounds that most audibly links rural traditions with urban ones, and acoustic styles with the electric age. Some guitarists, like Elmore James and his acolytes Hound Dog Taylor and J.B. Hutto, have more or less built their entire style around it; many others brandish their command of the slide at least occasionally.

The origins of the use of the slide guitar in the blues–like many topics concerning the origins of the blues as a whole–are subject to varying historical interpretations. Some assert that the style didn't become widespread until it became popular in Hawaii in the 1890s, spreading to the mainland by the turn of the century. Joseph Kekuku has been credited with popularizing the concept of fretting guitar strings with objects rather than fingers, and the influence of the slide guitar as it was played in Hawaii became influential in pop music as a whole, not just within the blues.

On the other hand, in *Deep Blues*, Robert Palmer writes that "the slide technique was originally associated with an African instrument that has been reported from time to time in the American South, the single-stringed musical bow. One-stringed instruments played with sliders seem to have survived principally among Black children, who would nail a length of broom wire to a wall and play it with a rock or pill bottle slider.

"The appearance of Black slide guitarists in the early 1900s has often been linked to the popularization of a similar technique by Hawaiian guitarists, but slide guitar wasn't native to Hawaii; it was introduced there between 1893 and 1895, reputedly by a schoolboy, Joseph Kekuku. It did not spread from Hawaii to the mainland until 1900, when it was popularized by Frank Fererra, and by that time Black guitarists in Mississippi were already fretting their instruments with knives or the broken-off necks of bottles."

The instrument that Palmer refers to is sometimes called the diddley bow, and is perhaps more common than he infers in this passage. A lot of the children who played with the diddley bow as a household toy became guitar players who adapted the technique to a proper instrument. And some of those musicians became professional, taking the rudiments of the technique with them even when they moved from the barn to the city. One of the most fascinating blues albums of all time was recorded by Eddie "One-String" Jones in 1960, then a homeless man on Los Angeles' Skid Row, who played a piece of wire on a 2 x 4 board with a whiskey flask. His album, *One String Blues*, may be the closest modern listeners can get to hearing the square root of the blues. Another interesting variation to this homemade instrument can be heard on a handful of mid-'50s recordings on the Specialty label by Willie Joe Duncan playing a larger electric version of the diddley bow called the Unitar. Whatever the case, there can be no doubt that the slide guitar caught on quickly with blues musicians. Its keening wail emulated in some respects the moans and cries of the human voice, and was a great medium for conveying the intense emotions of the songs, whether joyful or sorrowful. It also did not demand a lot in the way of high-tech equipment: pocket knives and a thimble-shaped piece of metal were adaptable for the purpose. One of the most popular vehicles for playing slide was a bottleneck that was shaped over flame; hence the term for "bottleneck" guitar, which is slide guitar as produced by such a device.

In his liner notes to *Blues Masters, Vol. 15: Slide Guitar Classics*, Cub Koda further distinguishes the style from its possible Hawaiian origins: "The major difference came largely in how the instrument was held. Hawaiian guitar was played with the instrument lying flat on the player's lap; this style was adapted by Whites to form the steel-guitar sound in country music.

"But by and large…black blues musicians replaced the steel bar with a bottleneck or metal tube fitted to one finger and simply continued to play the guitar in the standard Spanish position. Although the slide produced the same whiny effects that the bar did for Hawaiian guitarists, it was used more for lead fills, an extension of the singer's voice, allowing the instrument to be fretted for somewhat conventional chording when not in use. By the time examples of this type of playing started appearing on phonograph records in the late '20s, the banjo's days as a popular blues instrument were numbered; slide guitar was in."

The slide guitar is often associated with Delta blues, although its use was, in fact, widespread throughout the music. Delta bluesmen, however, may have been more responsible than any others for midwifing the style's transition

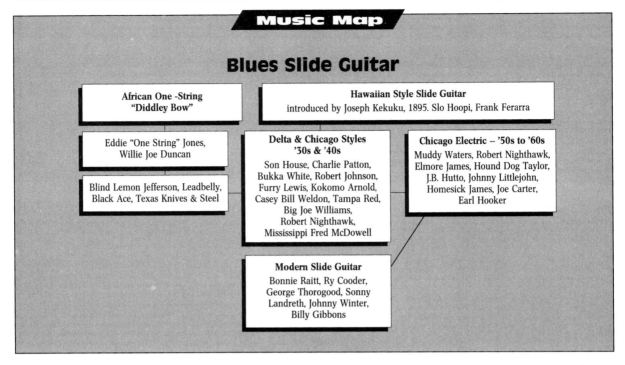

Music Map

Blues Slide Guitar

African One-String "Diddley Bow"

Hawaiian Style Slide Guitar
introduced by Joseph Kekuku, 1895. Slo Hoopi, Frank Ferarra

Eddie "One String" Jones, Willie Joe Duncan

Delta & Chicago Styles '30s & '40s
Son House, Charlie Patton, Bukka White, Robert Johnson, Furry Lewis, Kokomo Arnold, Casey Bill Weldon, Tampa Red, Big Joe Williams, Robert Nighthawk, Mississippi Fred McDowell

Chicago Electric – '50s to '60s
Muddy Waters, Robert Nighthawk, Elmore James, Hound Dog Taylor, J.B. Hutto, Johnny Littlejohn, Homesick James, Joe Carter, Earl Hooker

Blind Lemon Jefferson, Leadbelly, Black Ace, Texas Knives & Steel

Modern Slide Guitar
Bonnie Raitt, Ry Cooder, George Thorogood, Sonny Landreth, Johnny Winter, Billy Gibbons

from acoustic to electric music. Charlie Patton, the first great star of Mississippi blues, left several excellent recorded examples behind, utilizing the slide to answer his own vocal lines. His contemporaries Son House and Bukka White took the style and sound content one step further with their allegiance to the metal bodied National guitar, which produced a loud, astringent sound built more on sheer volume than subtlety. The Nationals and Dobro models were the true link between acoustic and electric guitars. They were called "ampliphonic" guitars in early catalogs and Delta players quickly adapted to them for two basic reasons: 1) they were loud enough to be heard over the din in a juke joint, and 2) they could be used to bash an adversary senseless with seemingly little damage to the instrument itself. Certainly Robert Johnson–an artist who had an absolute mastery of *all* guitar styles–is probably the best known Delta slide practioner, with his work on classics like "Crossroads Blues" and "Come On In My Kitchen" standing tall as the epitome of taste, tone and feeling that modern-day artists working in the genre still aspire to. There was Muddy Waters, influenced by both Son House and Robert Nighthawk, who electrified the blues in Chicago. His 1948 "I Can't Be Satified"/"Feel Like Going Home" single, repeatedly referred to as a defining moment of early electric blues, utilized prominent slide guitar. Robert Nighthawk, who started recording in the '30s on acoustic and later went electric, was also a prime mover and shaker on the instrument. Playing in standard guitar tuning (most slide players tune their instrument to an open chord, usually pitched to E or G), Nighthawk's touch and tone were the smoothest and creamiest. Though largely a forgotten figure today, Nighthawk taught his style to Waters and Chicago's most versatile blues guitarist, Earl Hooker, and his influence extended all the way to Southern rocker Duane Allman.

One guitarist went as far as to make the electric slide guitar his defining trademark. Even listeners who aren't blues fans can identify the classic riff that Elmore James used on "Dust My Broom," the song that probably embodies the electric slide guitar sound more than any other. James' strongest suit, his unsurpassed mastery of the electric slide idiom fused with extreme volume and a unrelenting attack which he put to use on numerous recordings in the 1950s and early 1960s, is still the most prevalent style of slide guitar playing being heard today. He spawned a raft of Chicago acolytes who adapted his raw sound and style to their own needs, among them Hound Dog Taylor, Joe Carter, and J.B. Hutto. Elmore James had a particularly strong influence on British guitarists of the 1960s. Brian Jones, whose slide work graced a handful of early Rolling Stones sides, worked on the British beat club circuit as Elmo(re) Lewis and Jeremy Spencer of Fleetwood Mac–the biggest band of the late-'60s British blues boom besides John Mayall's Bluesbreakers–worshiped James' approach,

and his immersion in Elmore's style approached the level of recreated art. To the larger record-buying public, James was immortalized in a spoken aside on the Beatles' "For You Blue," a George Harrison composition that prominently featured slide in the Elmore style.

Many blues-rock guitarists picked up the slide style, like Jeff Beck and Mike Bloomfield; though it didn't dominate their playing, they could summon the technique when called for. The best American blues-rock slide guitarist was certainly Duane Allman, who put the sound in the spotlight on Allman Brothers staples like their update of Blind Willie McTell's "Statesboro Blues." Duane's style evolved from the combination of Elmore's distorted tone and Earl Hooker's elegant standard tuning flourishes wedded to the extreme volume from Marshall stack amplification. Another modern master of the slide idiom was Ry Cooder, who did not limit its application to the blues or blues-rock, using it for his diverse explorations of many kinds of roots music, as well as in his voluminous soundtrack work. And certainly no dissertation of modern slide styles could leave out George Thorogood and Bonnie Raitt, both of whom have gone on to great success in the rock field. Raitt, who toiled for years on the blues circuit before her breakthrough, is one of the finest slide players going, being prominently influenced (and personally instructed) by her mentors, Mississippi Fred McDowell and Son House. Thorogood's hamfisted approach took Hound Dog Taylor's bare-bones raucous style and reduced it even further, if such a notion was possible.

Today, the slide guitar continues to have a standard place in the repertoire of many blues performers, whether as an integral component or an occasional spotlight. Like the blues itself, its frequent use in mainstream settings like film soundtracks (by Cooder and others) means that blues slide guitar is no longer thought of as something exotic, but as part of the vernacular of American music.
—*Richie Unterberger & Cub Koda*

8 Recommended Albums:

Various Artists, *Blues Masters, Vol. 15: Slide Guitar Classics* (Rhino)
Various Artists, *Slide Guitar–Bottle Knives & Steel, Vol. 1 & 2* (CBS)
Various Artists, *Bottleneck Guitar Masterpieces* (Yazoo)
Robert Johnson, *King of the Delta Blues Singers* (CBS)
Elmore James, *The Sky is Crying* (Rhino)
Hound Dog Taylor, *Hound Dog Taylor & The HouseRockers* (Alligator)
Eddie "One-String" Jones, *One-String Blues* (Gazell)
Robert Nighthawk, *Live on Maxwell Street* (Rounder)

Music Map

Jazz-Blues Crossover

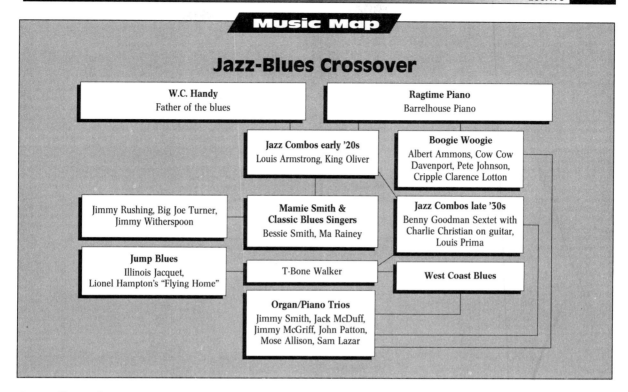

Jazz-Blues Crossover

Blues and jazz draw from a wellspring of similar roots in African-American popular music and culture. The paths of each genre have diverged widely since the beginning of the 1900s, but before 1950, the styles were often deeply intertwined with each other. It's a marriage that will endure to some degree as long as blues and jazz are around; even today, contemporary jazz acts throw in plenty of bluesy quotes, and many musicians boast service in both jazz bands and R&B/blues outfits. Many festivals spotlight both blues and jazz artists, the most famous of them being the annual New Orleans Jazz & Blues festival. Not many current artists, however, could be said to straddle the blues/jazz fence to such an extent that they could be classified as members of either camp.

The distinctions were much blurrier in the early 1900s, when both blues and jazz had yet to fully form their identities. The influence of ragtime music and barrelhouse piano styles were strong formative elements of each. W.C. Handy, the Father of the Blues, led brass bands whose instrumentation and arrangements were likely more akin to jazz. The first artists to record the blues were women singers, but these were the blues more in song structure and vocal phrasing than in the jazz/pop arrangements, which employed jazz greats such as Louis Armstrong and Coleman Hawkins. (The significance of the classic female blues singers is detailed in a separate essay.) Much later, in the 1950s, traditional jazz bandleader Chris Barber would play a key role in exposing the blues in his native Britain by featuring bluesmen as part of his shows, often imported from the States.

The most active period of cross-fertilization between blues and jazz may have been the 1930s and 1940s, when swing and big band styles were at their peak, and when the blues was moving toward a fuller and more citified sound. Jazz was still often played in dance halls, and needed some singers and song structures to help maintain its accessibility. Blues was moving toward a more sophisticated sound that would soon encompass full bands and electricity. Each form had much to learn from the other.

Several of the early big bands featured vocalists that not only borrowed from the blues in their songs and phrasing, but in turn influenced the evolution of other bluesmen. Jimmy Rushing, in his work with Count Basie, may have been the first notable blues-based singer to front a big band with a precursor to the "shouting" style. This was developed to its fullest shortly afterwards by singers with Kansas City-based swing bands, including Big Joe Turner, Jimmy Witherspoon, and Walter Brown.

Brown and Witherspoon both sang with the band of pianist Jay McShann, the bandleader with whom Charlie Parker first recorded. McShann is one of the artists most likely to be found in either the blues or jazz section of fine record stores; Turner and Witherspoon, throughout their career, moved with ease between the jazz and R&B worlds, sometimes changing their focus to fit the requirements of the gig or the record date. Eddie "Cleanhead" Vinson, who doubled on vocals and saxophone, was another performer who would be hard to tie to either style; he could not only sing the blues, but could play bop jazz as well, and led a band including John Coltrane in the late '40s, long before Coltrane made his mark on the jazz world.

Besides the "shouters," the main tributary of blues feeding into jazz was found in the boogie-woogie pianists of the late '30s and early '40s. Taking some cues from blues styles that had been developed in barrelhouses, Albert Ammons, Pete Johnson, and Meade Lux Lewis were the most instrumental figures in introducing boogie-woogie to jazz. The famed Spirituals To Swing concerts in New York City's Carnegie Hall in the late 1930s found the marriage between the idioms at their peak, featuring pioneers like Ammons, Johnson, Lewis, and Turner on the same stage; Robert Johnson, interestingly, was also planned to be included in the events, but died before he could be contacted.

Jazz greats would often use bluesy riffs and signatures in their work; the Rhino collection *Blues Masters, Vol. 13: New York City Blues* contains some good illustrations. The wild sax solo of Illinois Jacquet in Lionel Hampton's "Flying Home" rates as a leading forerunner of R&B, particularly the "honking" style of sax associated with the form. The shouters, honkers, and boogie-woogie would coalesce in the 1940s into jump blues, which in some senses was the ultimate jazz-blues fusion. As pioneered by Louis Jordan, Roy Milton, and many others starting in the mid-'40s (again, detailed in a separate essay), jump blues took the above factors and added a raw power and playful pop elements (particularly in the vocals) to the equation, while maintaining a rhythmic base and instrumentation quite close to swing jazz in some ways.

Jump blues wasn't composed solely of the above elements. The introduction of the electric guitar had far-reaching effects on pop music that nobody could have guessed in 1940, when a jazzman, Charlie Christian, established himself as the first virtuoso of the instrument. Christian can't be considered a blues/jazz artist (though examples of bluesy playing can be heard in his scant body of recorded work), but there's no question that he was a huge influence on the jump blues guitarists, particularly T-Bone Walker, one of the key figures of both jump blues and West Coast blues. Walker's single-string solos owed so much to jazz, as played by Christian on guitar and other jazzers on other instruments, that a case can be made for classifying Walker as a blues/jazzman as well, though his songs and roots were very much in the blues camp.

On the whole, the end of the jump blues phenomenon spelled an end to the intense interchange between blues and jazz. Jazz was evolving into be-bop and beyond; jump blues fed into R&B and rock 'n' roll. Chuck Berry's "Maybellene" may owe a little to jazz, for example, but the distance between Chuck Berry and, say, a mid-'50s jazz artist like Clifford Brown is a lot further than the distance between Louis Jordan and Lionel Hampton. Jazz bands were less oriented toward the dance halls now, and less apt to employ singers for that purpose, although some (such as Joe Williams, not to be confused with Big Joe Williams the country blues singer) kept the flame of old-school Jimmy Rushing-type vocals alive.

It's interesting to note, though, that quite a few major jazzmen were schooled in blues/R&B bands, or recorded sessions with them to help pay the rent, from Coltrane and Coleman on down. There was some movement in the other direction as well; guitarist Mickey Baker originally had his heart set on being a jazz musician, but instead became one of the best blues influenced rock 'n' roll guitarists of all time–partly, again, as a result of being repeatedly called upon to play R&B sessions. Earl Bostic, who played in Lionel Hampton's band in the 1940s, found his true calling as an R&B saxophonist. Two respected jazz players, saxophonists David "Fathead" Newman and Hank Crawford, had bluesy leanings that would come in handy when they worked as sidemen on some of Ray Charles' bluesiest recordings. But even here, the relationship between blues and jazz grows increasingly tangential.

The blues-jazz link had another fling in the '60s, albeit in a somewhat distant form, in the work of several keyboardists. Organists Jack McDuff, Jimmy McGriff, Jimmy Smith, and John Patton, nowadays recognized as pioneers of "soul-jazz," often drew upon blues styles and material; one of Smith's biggest set pieces, for instance, was a cover of "I've Got My Mojo Working." Jazz pianist/vocalist Mose Allison (who began recording in the late 1950s) had a distinctive bluesy hipster style, both on originals like "Young Man's Blues" and "Parchman Farm," and covers of songs by Willie Dixon and Sonny Boy Williamson; he'd prove to be an unexpected influence on British groups like the Who, Yardbirds, and John Mayall, all of whom covered Allison songs. In Britain itself, Georgie Fame took up a blues/jazz style similar to Allison's, though with much more of a pop/R&B base.

—*Richie Unterberger*

15 Recommended Albums:

Various Artists, *Blues Masters, Vol. 11: Classic Blues Women* (Rhino)
Various Artists, *Blues Masters, Vol. 13: New York City Blues* (Rhino)
Jimmy Rushing, *The Essential Jimmy Rushing* (Vanguard)
Big Joe Turner, *Complete 1940–1944* (Official)
Jimmy Witherspoon & Jay McShann, *Jimmy Witherspoon & Jay McShann* (DA)
Albert Ammons, *King of Boogie (1939–1949)* (Blues Classics)
Meade Lux Lewis, *1939–1954* (Story of Blues)
Various Artists, *Blues Masters, Vol. 5: Jump Blues Classics* (Rhino)
Various Artists, *Blues Masters, Vol. 14: More Jump Blues* (Rhino)
Louis Jordan, *The Best of Louis Jordan* (MCA)
T-Bone Walker, *The Complete Capitol/Black & White Recordings* (Capitol)
Mose Allison, *Greatest Hits* (Prestige)
Ray Charles, *Blues & Jazz* (Rhino)
Various Artists, *Blue Funk: The History of the Hammond Organ* (Blue Note)
Eddie "Cleanhead" Vinson, *And Roomful of Blues* (Muse)

Soul Blues

The blues is sometimes stereotyped as a purist sort of music that strays little from its conventions. While it's true that it's more static than some other styles, it's never been immune from outside trends. The classic female blues singers of the '20s drew heavily from vaudevillian pop; blues electric guitar pioneer T-Bone Walker had a lot of jazz on his mind; the jump blues greats took from jazz and R&B in almost equal measures. And soul music has exerted a substantial influence upon the blues since the 1960s.

Some more skeptical blues fans may assert that many blues artists put some soul in their music as a matter of professional survival. The broader, more likely truth is that blues performers of the late 20th century cannot help but reflect some of the musical and social climate of their time. Soul music was one of the primary voices of African-American culture in the 1960s and 1970s. Much more often than not, performers schooled in the blues added soul flavor not just to adapt, but because they genuinely loved and were inspired by soul music.

Soul blues has been with us since soul music itself began to form as a distinct entity in the early '60s; precursors of soul music like Percy Mayfield and Charles Brown had already mixed R&B, gospel, and blues a good decade or more prior to that. The first, and maybe the best, of the soul/blues singers is Bobby "Blue" Bland. Bobby actually began recording in the early '50s, and always had a strong R&B flavor from the git-go. He truly reached his stride, however, in the 1960s, when he recorded an extraordinarily lengthy series of fine singles that incorporated horn charts and the sort of gospel-inflected vocals common to most great soul singers. Many of these weren't confined to the specialist blues markets, but were genuine big R&B hits, occasionally making the pop charts as well. Line up a few listeners against a wall, play them Bland's greatest hits, and ask them whether to classify the results as blues or soul; you'll probably end up with something close to a 50-50 split, or at least with a lot of people who can't make up their minds.

Bland is an unusual textbook example of a virtually equal blues/soul hybrid. One of his chief inspirations, B.B. King, has never been thought of as a soul man, but has often had a prominent gospel and soul feel to his work. This was particularly true in the late '60s, when he frequently employed a large horn section, and for a while enlisted the services of arranger Johnny Pate, who had contributed to classic Chicago soul records by the likes of Major Lance and the Impressions. Two other Kings, Freddie and (especially) Albert, maintained some presence on the R&B charts with their blends of fierce blues guitar and contemporary soul-leaning material.

Horns were key ingredients in updating '50s blues, or '50s R&B/blues, for the '60s audiences. By extension, they also enabled some performers to maintain a foothold on the R&B charts, while the more guitar-harmonica-oriented "classic" combos were confined to more specialized audiences and a lower level of the club circuit. Junior Parker, Little Milton, and Lowell Fulson (famous for "Tramp")–all of whom had roots in pre-1960s blues and R&B–were some of the most successful of them. Some of the more purist-minded blues collectors much prefer these singers' earlier work, finding their later soul/blues too smooth and urbane, although in all cases these artists found their greatest popular success with their soul-conscious tunes.

Not all veterans in the '50s were as successful with this strategy. Amos Milburn, for instance, recorded an odd album for Motown in the early '60s that rounded off his jump blues with typical early '60s Motown production values. Although the results actually weren't that bad, it was an instant collector's item (and, predictably enough, reissued on CD with bonus cuts in the mid-1990s). It's not too well known that Motown occasionally tried to do similar things with a few other blues artists in the early '60s, as can be heard on the *Motown's Blue Evolution* compilation.

There were also a number of hard-core blues acts who simply added a dollop of soul to the proceedings without diminishing their basic power or substantially altering the focus of their guitar-bass-drums lineup. Major Chicago blues stars Junior Wells, Buddy Guy, and Magic Sam all made some of their best recordings in the 1960s; all of them added a bit of inventive soul sophistication in their songwriting and arrangements without sounding forced. Check out Wells' vocal mannerisms on much of his 1965 classic, *Hoodoo Man Blues* (also featuring Buddy Guy), which betrays a definite James Brown influence.

Speaking of JB, it wasn't unknown (although not very common either) for established soul singers to delve into the blues occasionally. Brown did this more often than most, though mostly limiting his blues excursions to album tracks. Nothing could hide the fact that he was far more talented and innovative as an R&B/soul/funk pioneer than a straight blues singer, but the double CD *Messin' with the Blues* compiles his most blues-oriented material; it's not so bad, and there's a lot more of it than you would guess.

In *The Blackwell Guide to Blues*, Jeff Hannusch defines soul blues as "singers that have a gospel background and who bring an urgent 'churchy' approach to their music." Such performers usually fall on the soul side of the soul/blues hybrid. Artists such as Otis Clay, Little Johnny Taylor, and O.V. Wright are apt to strike many listeners not so much as blues singers, but as soul singers with a bluesy feel. Whether you classify them within the rubric of the blues or not, there's no doubt that the aforementioned vocalists enjoy a lot of appeal among both blues and soul fans (who, of course, are often one and the same).

Soul/blues as an artistic force diminished, naturally, when soul music itself began to be superseded by disco in the mid-'70s, and then by rap and urban contemporary in the '80s and '90s, among the Black audience. The Malaco label was sort of a stronghold for "old-school" soul/blues, releasing efforts in the style by Z.Z. Hill, Denise LaSalle, and Latimore, as well as recording veterans who had fallen out of favor with mainstream audiences, such as Johnnie Taylor, Bobby "Blue" Bland, and Little Milton. Some of the Malaco titles proved surprisingly popular with a Black audience supposedly only concerned with less traditional styles. Hill's *Down Home* in particular was a popular success that exceeded all expectations.

Music Map

Blues Rediscoveries

Folklorists who searched and rediscovered or discovered the remaining greats and collected important information on the rest	The Greats that were found...
Alan Lomax, Mack McCormick, David Evans, Chris Strachwitz, Ed Denson, John Fahey, Al Wilson, Samuel Charters	Son House, Skip James, Mississippi John Hurt, Bukka White, Robert Pete Williams, Smoky Babe, Furry Lewis, Memphis Willie B., Drifting Slim, Mississippi Fred McDowell, Mance Lipscomb, Peg Leg Howell

More often than not, though, Malaco product was much more soul than blues. Many listeners who aren't concerned with critical distinctions would even be unlikely to classify it as soul/blues at all, but merely as rootsy soul. Popular blues and soul were so thin on the ground in the early half of the 1980s that one sometimes got the feeling that critics were championing the Malaco sound not on its merit, but because it was utilizing some of the proper approved ingredients, and there were so few other releases of the sort attracting any attention outside of the specialized/collector audiences.

Soul/blues as a label is applied to few current releases, but that may be because soul itself has been permanently absorbed into the fabric of contemporary blues. Many if not most of today's top electric blues performers–Robert Cray, Joe Louis Walker, Koko Taylor, and Jimmy Johnson (brother of soul singer Syl Johnson), to name a few–put a lot of soul flourishes into their songwriting, arrangements, and vocal delivery. The recently deceased Ted Hawkins also showed how soul could figure in contemporary acoustic blues. A rap-hip-hop/blues fusion, however, doesn't seem imminent, although White alternative rockers like Beck, G. Love, and Bobby Sichran have given it a try.

—*Richie Unterberger*

20 Recommended Recordings:

Bobby "Blue" Bland, *I Pity the Fool* (MCA)
Bobby "Blue" Bland, *Turn On Your Love Light* (MCA)
Various Artists, *Soul Shots, Vol. 7: Urban Blues* (Rhino)
B.B. King, *Blues on Top of Blues* (BGO)
Junior Parker, *Junior's Blues: The Duke Recordings, Vol. 1* (MCA)
Little Milton, *Chess Blues Master Series* (Chess)
Lowell Fulson, *Blue Days, Black Nights* (Ace)
Amos Milburn, *The Motown Sessions, 1962–1964* (Motown)
Various Artists, *Motown's Blue Evolution* (Motown)
James Brown, *Messing with the Blues* (Polydor)
Albert King, *Born under a Bad Sign* (Mobile Fidelity)
Various Artists, *The Stax Blues Brothers* (Stax)
Z.Z. Hill, *Down Home* (Malaco)
Junior Wells, *Hoodoo Man Blues* (Delmark)
Magic Sam, *West Side Soul* (Delmark)
Otis Clay, *Soul Man: Live in Japan* (Rooster Blues)
Johnnie Taylor, *Raw Blues* (Stax)
Robert Cray, *Strong Persuader* (Mercury)
Ted Hawkins, *Happy Hour* (Rounder)
Joe Louis Walker, *Blue Soul* (Hightone)

Blues Rediscoveries

When blues enthusiasts pawed through their collection of rare 78s in the 1950s, performers like Robert Johnson, Bukka White, and Skip James were little more than names on a label. There was little, if any, historical information that documented how these singers lived, where they came from, how they came to be recorded (however briefly), or how they felt about their life and art. Looking at the records and imagining who the performers may have been seemed as futile as trying to touch a ghost; in many cases, it was uncertain whether these singers, few of whom had recorded after the early 1940s, were still alive or not.

A few of these collectors and enthusiasts became determined to tackle the challenge of chasing down these ghosts, dead or alive. Sam Charters' *The Country Blues* (published in 1959), and other scholarly studies that treated the

blues as an art form worthy of serious respect, ignited a hunger for more information about its originators. Listening to the records (which, in the late 1950s, were themselves hard to come by) wasn't enough; surely these men and women had stories to tell, and, if they were still alive and healthy, more songs to sing. Folklorists and general enthusiasts such as Mack McCormick, David Evans, Chris Strachwitz, Alan Lomax, John Fahey, and Ed Denson, were dedicated enough to start to comb the American South for living embodiments of the blues tradition. What they found was more than they could have possibly hoped existed.

By the mid-'60s, Bukka White, Skip James, Son House, Mississippi John Hurt, and Furry Lewis had all been relocated. They had not willfully vanished into obscurity, or deliberately retired from music. Their recording careers had come to an end, often under premature circumstances. In most instances they continued to play music for live audiences, for their families, or simply for themselves. However, in the absence of opportunities to record in the studio, or to play for large audiences in an African-American community that was increasingly less interested in rural blues, they had turned to other sources of livelihood, unaware of the increasing appeal of their music to White audiences.

Finding these legends of the past often required efforts bordering on private detective work. Skip James and Son House, it has been reported, were rediscovered on the exact same day in 1964, though in widely differing circumstances; James was ill in Tunica County Hospital in Mississippi, while House wasn't in the South at all, having relocated to upstate New York about 20 years previously. John Fahey found Bukka White by writing a letter to "Bukka White, Old Blues Singer, c/o General Delivery, Aberdeen, MS" (a town that happened to be mentioned in one of White's songs); a relative of White's who worked for the post office chanced upon the correspondence, and helped direct Fahey to Memphis, where White had been living since the early 1940s.

No doubt a good film lies in the haphazard and semi-comic circumstances of these searches. In his novel *Nighthawk Blues*, Peter Guralnick tells of three obsessive blues collectors who, after years of passionate correspondence, decide to meet face-to-face and embark upon a search of the South for one of their heroes, only to find that they can't stand each other. Guralnick also tells the true story, in his essay collection *Feel Like Going Home*, of the extreme difficulty in finding a bluesman who had already been rediscovered (Robert Pete Williams), as he navigates the Louisiana backroads with few clues or landmarks to guide him. Then there were the adjustments that some of the performers had to make as they readied themselves for new audiences. Dick Waterman, who located House in Buffalo and managed the guitarist, told the following story in Francis Davis' *History of the Blues*:

"A month or so later, we brought Son to Cambridge, Massachusetts, to get him ready for the Newport Folk Festival [and introduced him to] Al Wilson, who later moved to Los Angeles and was a founding member of the group Canned Heat. Al played open-tuning bottleneck and could play all the styles. He could play Bukka White, Son House, Charley Patton, and Blind Lemon Jefferson–he could really play. And he sat down with Son, knee to knee, guitar to guitar, and said, 'Okay, this is the figure that in 1930, you called "My Black Mama,"' and played it for him. And Son said, 'Yeah, *yeah*, that's me, that's me. I played that.'

"And then Al said, 'Now about a dozen years later, when Mr. Lomax came around, you changed the name to "My Black Woman," and you did it this way.' He showed him. And Son would say, 'Yeah, yeah. I got my recollection now, I got my recollection now.' And he would start to play, and the two of them played together. Then, Al reminded him of how he changed tunings, and played his own "Pony Blues" for him. There would not have been a rediscov-

British Blues

Big Bill Broonzy Plays successful concert tour of England, early '50s	**Muddy Waters** Brings Chicago blues to U.K. folkies, 1958

Alexis Korner & Cyril Davies,
special unit in Chris Barber Band,
go electric from Blues
Incorporated, 1958

| The Rolling Stones,
John Mayall's Bluesbreakers,
Fleetwood Mac, Cream,
Duster Bennett | **Blues Inc. Alumni**
Mick Jagger, Jack Bruce,
Charlie Watts, Ginger Baker,
Graham Bond, Long John Baldry,
Jack Bruce, Brian Jones | The Animals, The Yardbirds,
Santa Barbara Machine Head,
Savoy Brown, Ten Years After,
Jo Ann Kelly, Chicken Shack,
Gary Moore, Jimi Hendrix |

ery of Son House in the 1960s without Al Wilson. Really. Al Wilson taught Son House how to play Son House."

In many (but not all) cases, the actual skills of the performers were barely diminished, or undiminished. Since their "retirements," an LP market had developed for country blues, as well as a college/festival-oriented folk circuit that was eager to hear the music performed live. James, White, House, Hurt, and others resumed their careers with considerable success, with assistance from committed managers like Dick Waterman and sympathetic record labels like Vanguard.

Some purists held that the best work of these resuscitated legends were their original 78s, recorded in the artists' relative youth, in the 1920s and 1930s. Contemporary albums, they contended, were pale shadows of the glory of the vintage singles. For the most part, though, those who bought the LPs disagreed, finding them powerful statements on their own terms. There were also the considerations that in the '60s, before vintage blues reissue compilations were common, many listeners didn't have the patience to relocate the rare original singles; and even if they could hear the originals, non-fanatics often much preferred the clear sound of modern studios to the scratchy and hissy original 78s. Certainly James, Hurt, and White made some good records in the 1960s, and proved to be engaging and passionate live acts.

Another welcome result of the search for old blues legends was the discovery (as opposed to rediscovery) of elderly talents that had never recorded before. Folklorist Alan Lomax included Mississippi Fred McDowell on his landmark box set of the late 1950s, *The Sounds of the South*, which documented all sorts of American folk styles. McDowell went on to a lengthy and successful career that found him recording several albums, touring with Bonnie Raitt, and having one of songs, "You Got To Move," covered by the Rolling Stones on *Sticky Fingers*. Mance Lipscomb, a songster-type guitarist from Texas, released several well-received albums on Arhoolie. Robert Pete Williams was, like Leadbelly 25 years before him, discovered in the late '50s behind bars at a Louisiana penitentiary. Folklorist Harry Oster recorded him and helped arranged for his pardon, and Williams, one of the most idiosyncratic country bluesmen, went on to record more material and tour.

The 1960s, and in some cases the 1970s, found many of the rediscovered blues singers touring internationally, where they were sometimes filmed by organizations such as the BBC. Sometimes their compositions were covered by major rock groups, such as James' "I'm So Glad," giving those performers some measure of comfortable financial compensation for their work. In addition to generating some fine music, the blues revival enabled these originators to live out their later years with dignity, giving them the widespread acclaim they had often been denied in their younger years–an appropriate closure that any fan of the blues could appreciate.

—*Richie Unterberger*

9 Recommended Albums:

Various Artists, *Great Bluesmen at Newport* (Vanguard)
Skip James, *Skip James Today!* (Vanguard)
Mississippi John Hurt, *The Immortal* (Vanguard)
Son House, *Father of the Delta Blues: The Complete 1965 Sessions* (CBS)
Bukka White, *Big Daddy* (Biograph)
Robert Pete Williams, *Angola Prisoner's Blues* (Arhoolie)
Mississippi Fred McDowell, *Mississippi Delta Blues* (Arhoolie)
Mance Lipscomb, *Texas Sharecropper & Songster* (Arhoolie)
Peg Leg Howell, *The Legendary Peg Leg Howell* (Testament)

British Blues

The term British blues is an anomaly. By rights, it shouldn't even exist. After all, Great Britain coming into the 20th century had no blues tradition, or any basis for it. Blues in Britain was an American import, much the same as rock 'n' roll, but predating it by a few years.

During the early 1950's, the first American blues artists had made brief sojourns to England and found the environment fertile. The bookings were good, the money better than they could get in America, and there was enthusiasm from a small but dedicated audience.

Big Bill Broonzy was the first American bluesman of any note to appear in England. He got to make his first of many recordings for France's Vogue label on that first visit to Europe, and was back a year later for another tour and more recording for Vogue.

Ironically, Broonzy did not play the material that he was most closely associated with in America on these tours. He was, of course, one of Chicago's top bluesmen, but the British weren't looking for authentic Chicago blues, but for something much more rudimentary. They perceived American blues as a brand of folk music, and for these appearances in England Broonzy adopted a deliberately archaic country blues persona, doing material that he had never really played before. He played acoustic guitar, and performed folk songs on these tours, interspersing country blues with protest material that were perceived by British audiences as merely another strain of topical blues.

Broonzy returned again in 1955 and cut several sides for Pye Records; the producer for these sessions was future British pop recording impresario Joe Meek. Among those recordings, available on CD under the title *Big Bill Broonzy: The 1955 London Sessions*, are a handful of those topical songs, most notably the poignant "When Do I Get To Be Called A Man."

The man responsible for bringing Broonzy to England was Chris Barber, leader of a jazz band that included a small group dedicated to American blues. Guitarist Alexis Korner and blues harpist Cyril Davies formed the core of

Barber's blues unit, performing a set during the band's shows that proved especially popular with a small but vocal part of Barber's audience.

Meanwhile, Barber continued to book American performers, who kept coming over and finding the atmosphere and the money very much to their liking. But it was Muddy Waters' visit to England in 1958 that provided the real flashpoint for British blues, as well as showing how far the English audiences had to go in their understanding of the genre.

Muddy went on stage in England for the first time backed by Otis Spann and members of Barber's band, playing an electric solid body Fender guitar. This was a shock to British audiences, especially the folk purists and jazz aficionados who made up most of the crowd that night–authentic American blues as the British understood it had nothing to do with electric guitar. More striking still, Muddy had his instrument turned up to his usual Chicago-scale decibel level. If the sight of the amplified guitar startled the audience, the slashing tone that it generated caused outrage and a near panic among the purists. Muddy's performances on the 1958 tour were greeted with ecstatic press coverage and unbridled enthusiasm by concertgoers, after the initial "shock" of his first performance wore off. His concerts had attracted thousands of fans from all over England who had only heard of him, including many younger blues enthusiasts who were only just beginning to discover the music that Korner and Davies had been playing all along.

By this time, Korner and Davies had split with Barber and after Muddy's tour, they chose to plug in themselves. From 1958 on, they began playing electric blues with a new, inspired urgency. The band was called Blues Incorporated, and featured, at various times, Art Wood (elder brother of Ron Wood) on vocals, Graham Bond, Long John Baldry, Charlie Watts, Jack Bruce and Ginger Baker. Basically anyone with talent and the right instrument could sit in, and those that did in the early period of the band's existence included Mick Jagger and Brian Jones.

By 1962, Blues Incorporated had been given a residency at the Marquee Club in London, and it was here that the band recorded their first album–and the first blues long-player ever made in England–for Britain's Decca Records. *R&B From the Marquee* was recorded live by producer/impresario Jack Good (best remembered for creating the American television series *Shindig*) after hours at the club.

But by the time it was released, Korner and Davies had split up over Korner's desire to add horns–which Davies abhorred–to the group's lineup. Davies formed the Cyril Davies All-Stars, a very promising group. The band got to record a handful of singles before Davies was stricken with leukemia and died early in 1964. Korner kept Blues Incorporated going in different incarnations through 1966, but by that time the main thrust of British blues had passed him by.

From the days of its residency at the Marquee, the original Blues Incorporated served as a catalyst for the formation of numerous bands that would lay claim to dominance of British blues. John Mayall's Bluesbreakers featuring Eric Clapton, the original Fleetwood Mac with Peter Green, and Cream could all trace their roots back to Blues Incorporated.

But it was the Rolling Stones that dominated the pack. From 1963 onward the Rolling Stones were the definitive British blues band, although after their chart-topping success with a cover of Willie Dixon's "Little Red Rooster," the blues would serve more as a source of inspiration than songs for the group's most visible work.

Meanwhile, American blues had become big business in England and throughout Europe. Beginning in 1962, with the first American Folk-Blues Festival organized by German blues enthusiast Horst Lippmann, dozens of American blues stars–including Muddy Waters, Howlin' Wolf, and Sonny Boy Williamson II–had begun making annual or semi-annual treks to Europe, appearing throughout Europe. These tours were extremely lucrative for the performers, and the fees were many times what these men and women could have expected to make in a week of working in American blues clubs. Some of the players, such as Eddie Boyd and Champion Jack Dupree, ultimately made their homes in Europe in the wake of their performing experience. The American and younger British enthusiasts also got to work together on occasion; Sonny Boy Williamson recorded with both the Yardbirds and the Animals, and also toured backed by both of those bands and the original R&B-based Moody Blues.

The Rolling Stones manifested their love of American blues in a slightly different fashion, covering songs by Willie Dixon and Muddy Waters on their singles and albums, and insisting that Howlin' Wolf be their featured guest for their debut appearance on *Shindig* in America. The sight of the Stones genuflecting before the 6' 4", 250-pound Howlin' Wolf (making his first appearance on American network television) revealed as much about the groups' origins and tastes as their own records of the era did, and more about the roots of British rock than any routinely vacuous interviews of the period.

Although there were a handful of British blues pianists and harpists, the dominant instrument was the guitar. Muddy Waters marveled at the array of axemen he encountered in England, many of whom impressed him with their technical skills, although he doubted that England could produce a truly effective blues singer. Eric Burdon and Mick Jagger came the closest in the vocal department, but among guitarists, the list was virtually endless, beginning with Eric Clapton, Keith Richards, Jeff Beck, and Brian Jones, and ending later in the decade with Jimmy Page, Mick Taylor, and Peter Green.

The Rolling Stones' success made it possible for their manager, Andrew "Loog" Oldham, to form his own independent label, Immediate Records, which became a vehicle for many blues-based outfits and performers, including Fleetwood Mac, Santa Barbara Machine Head (whose members later formed the core of the original Deep Purple), Savoy Brown, T.S. McPhee, Jo-Ann Kelly, and Dave Kelly. Jimmy Page, Jeff Beck, and Eric Clapton also recorded a large handful of instrumental tracks that later turned up on Immediate, to the distress and embarrassment of all concerned.

By 1966, the British blues boom had become an explosion as electric British blues began to dominate the entire field. Cream, Fleetwood Mac, the Yardbirds, Ten Years After, and, later on, Led Zeppelin–dominated by the sounds of guitarists Eric Clapton, Peter Green, Jeremy Spencer, Jeff Beck, Alvin Lee, and Jimmy Page–came to define British blues, and by the end of the 1960's, British blues had become a part of mainstream rock on both sides of the Atlantic. Absorbed by the British in the 1950s and very early 1960s, the blues as they played it was carried back across to America by bands like the Stones and the Animals, and re-absorbed by the Americans, in the guise of the Allman Brothers and other Southern rock bands of the era like ZZ Top.

—*Bruce Eder*

15 Recommended Albums:

Animals, *The Complete Animals* (EMI)
Blues Incorporated, *R&B From the Marquee* (Mobile Fidelity)
Duster Bennett, *Justa Duster* (Blue Horizon)
Cream, *Fresh Cream* (Polydor)
John Mayall's Bluesbreakers, *Featuring Eric Clapton* (Polygram)
John Mayall, *London Blues (1964–1969)* (Polygram)
Rolling Stones, *Rolling Stones (England's Newest Hitmakers)* (ABKCO)
Rolling Stones, *Rolling Stones Now!* (ABKCO)
Rolling Stones, *12 x 5* (ABKCO)
Yardbirds, *Five Live Yardbirds* (Rhino)
Yardbirds, *Smokestack Lightning* (Sony Music)
Fleetwood Mac, *Black Magic Woman* (Epic)
Various Artists, *Anthology of British Blues, Vols. 1 and 2* (Immediate)
Various Artists, *Dealing With the Devil* (Sony Music)
Various Artists, *Stroll On* (Sony Music)

Blues Rock

The blues and rock 'n' roll are often divided by the thinnest of margins. Blues, more than any other musical style, influenced the birth of rock 'n' roll, and the amplified electric blues of Chicago, Memphis, and other cities during the 1950s was separated from the new music only by its more traditional chord patterns, cruder production values, and narrower market. The term "blues rock" came into being only around the mid-'60s, when White musicians infused electric blues with somewhat louder guitars and flashy images that helped the music make inroads into the White rock audience.

Many of the early blues rockers were British musicians who had been schooled by Alexis Korner. Helping to organize the first overseas tours by many major American bluesmen, Korner–as well as his former boss Chris Barber, and his early collaborator Cyril Davies–was more responsible than any other musician for introducing the blues to Britain. More important, he acted as a mentor to many younger musicians who would form the R&B-oriented wing of the British Invasion, including Jack Bruce, members of Manfred Mann, Eric Clapton, and, most significantly, the Rolling Stones, whose lead vocalist, Mick Jagger, sang with Korner before the Stones were firmly established. (The evolution of British blues is discussed in more depth in a separate piece.)

The Rolling Stones featured a wealth of blues in their early repertoire. They and other British groups like the Yardbirds and Animals brought a faster and brasher flavor to traditional numbers. They would quickly branch out from 12-bar blues to R&B, soul, and finally, original material of a much more rock-oriented nature, without ever losing sight of their blues roots. Several British acts, however, were more steadfast in their devotion to traditional blues, sacrificing commercial success for purism. These included the Graham Bond Organization (featuring future Cream members Jack Bruce and Ginger Baker) and, most significantly, John Mayall's Bluesbreakers. In early 1965, Mayall's group provided a refuge for Eric Clapton, who left the Yardbirds on the eve of international success in protest to their forays into pop-rock. His sole album

Music Map

Blues Rock

Originators

Muddy Waters, Howlin' Wolf, Chuck Berry, Sonny Boy Williamson, Bo Diddley, Little Walter, Elmore James, Jimmy Reed, Robert Johnson, Willie Dixon, B.B. King, Albert King/Freddie King

The U.S.A.

Paul Butterfield Blues Band, Blues Project, Bob Dylan, John Hammond, Jr., Johnny Winter, Canned Heat, Steve Miller, Roy Buchanan

The Present

Stevie Ray Vaughan, The Fabulous Thunderbirds, Kenny Wayne Sheppard, Gary Moore, Chris Duarte, ZZ Top, George Thorogood, Robert Cray

The U.K.

Alexis Korner, Cyril Davies, Blues Incorporated, The Rolling Stones, John Mayall's Bluesbreakers, Cream, Ten Years After, Foghat, Savoy Brown, Rory Gallagher, Juicy Lucy, Chicken Shack, Climax Blues Band, Fleetwood Mac, The Yardbirds, The Animals

---

with Mayall, *Bluesbreakers With Eric Clapton* (1966), was an unexpected Top Ten hit in the U.K. Clapton's lightning fast and fluid leads were vastly influential, both on fellow musicians and in introducing tough electric blues to a wider audience.

While Clapton would rapidly depart the Bluesbreakers to form Cream (who took blues rock to more amplified and psychedelic levels), Mayall continued to be Britain's foremost exponent of blues rock, as a bandleader of innumerable Bluesbreakers lineups. Many musicians of note were schooled by Mayall, the most prominent being Clapton's successors, Peter Green and future Rolling Stone Mick Taylor. Like Clapton, Green left Mayall after just one album, forming the first incarnation of Fleetwood Mac with a couple members of Mayall's rhythm section, John McVie and Mick Fleetwood.

Under Green's helm, Fleetwood Mac were the finest British blues-rock act of the late '60s. They invested electric Chicago blues with zest and humor, but their own material–featuring Green's icy guitar tone (praised by no less a master than B.B. King), rich vocals, and personal, often somber lyrics–was more impressive, and extremely successful in Britain,where they racked up several hit albums and singles. As a bandleader of rotating lineups featuring budding guitar geniuses, Chicago harmonica player Paul Butterfield was Mayall's American counterpart; the two even recorded a rare EP together in the late '60s. The Paul Butterfield Blues Band's first pair of albums featured the sterling guitar duo of Michael Bloomfield and Elvin Bishop, as well as members of Howlin' Wolf's band in the rhythm section. Willing to tackle soul, jazz, and even psychedelic jams in addition to Chicago blues, they were the first American blues-rock band, and the best.

While blues rock was less of a commercial or artistic force in the U.S. than the U.K., several other American blues rockers of note emerged in the '60s. Canned Heat were probably the most successful, reaching the Top 20 with "On The Road Again" and an electric update of an obscure rural blues number, "Going Up The Country." Steve Miller played mostly blues, with Barry Goldberg and as the leader of his own band, in his early days before tuning into the psychedelic ethos of his adopted base of San Francisco. The Electric Flag, featuring Michael Bloomfield, mixed blues-rock with psychedelic music and tentative outings into an early version of jazz-rock. Captain Beefheart was briefly a White counterpart to Howlin' Wolf before heading off on a furious avant-garde tangent, though his growling vocals always seemed to maintain an unfathomable link to the Delta.

In New York, Bob Dylan used Bloomfield on much of his *Highway 61 Revisited* album, and teamed with the Butterfield Band for his enormously controversial electric appearance at the 1965 Newport Folk Festival. John Hammond, Jr. recorded blues rock in the mid-'60s with future members of the Band, and Dion cut some overlooked blues-rock sides after being exposed to classic blues by the legendary Columbia A&R man John Hammond, Sr. The Blues Project–led by Al Kooper–often reworked blues songs with rock arrangements, although their musical vision was too eclectic to be pigeonholed as blues rock.

The influence of the first generation of blues rockers is evident in the early recordings of Jimi Hendrix, and indeed Jimi would always feature a strong element of the blues in his material. Albert King and B.B. King couldn't be called blues rockers by any stretch of the imagination, but their late '60s material betrays contemporary influences from the worlds of rock and soul that found them leaning more in that direction. Early hard rock bands like Led Zeppelin, Free, and the Jeff Beck Group played a great deal of blues, though not enough for purists to consider them actual blues acts.

The blues rock form became more pedestrian and boogie-oriented as the '60s came to a close. From Britain, Ten Years After, Savoy Brown, the Climax Blues Band, Rory Gallagher, Chicken Shack, Juicy Lucy, the Groundhogs, and Foghat all achieved some success. In the U.S., blues rock was the cornerstone of the Allman Brothers' innovative early '70s recordings (which in turned spawned the blues-influenced school of Southern rock), and Johnny Winter had success with a much more traditional approach.

Roy Buchanan, once billed (for a public television special) as "the best unknown guitarist in the world," had turned down an opportunity to join the Rolling Stones before concentrating on a solo career. Buchanan's vocals weren't strong enough to front a band, and thus his records were primarily instrumental showcases, although he did hire singers for his group. The same approach had been used by a couple of other brilliant guitarists with similar vocal liabilities, Jeff Beck and Harvey Mandel. Mandel, like Beck, was too eclectic to be categorized as a blues-rocker, but was often grounded in blues forms, and was a member of Canned Heat for a time.

Another guitarist who was more of an instrumentalist/ composer than a singer, and who was associated with Captain Beefheart and the Rolling Stones, was Ry Cooder, whose palette is really way too diverse to fall within blues-rock. Some would classify another associate of Cooder's, Taj Mahal, as a blues-rocker, but an equal or greater number would simply see Mahal as a modern-day bluesman, albeit one with rock influences (especially in the mid-'60s, when he played with Cooder in an L.A. folk-rock-blues group, the Rising Sons).

While blues rock hasn't been a major commercial force since the late '60s, the style has spawned some hugely successful acts, like ZZ Top and Foghat, as well as influencing all hard rock since the late '60s to some degree. Those that kept the faith tended to concentrate on the more limited market of independent labels and small clubs, with the demand for party and boogie bands in small venues being a constant. Hence the appellation "bar band," one that serves as both a badge of honor and a putdown, depending upon the context and the tastes of the listener.

In general terms, second- and third-generation blues-rock bands have tended to prioritize instrumental virtuosity (unkinder souls would say instrumental flash) over vocal prowess. Guitarists Pat Travers and George Thorogood (noted for his crude, but effective, slide work) would fall in this

Music Map

Modern Acoustic Blues

Originators	The '60s and '70s	Today
Leadbelly, Blind Lemon Jefferson, Charlie Patton, Son House, Robert Johnson, Robert Pete Williams, John Lee Hooker, Jesse Fuller, Doctor Ross, Lightnin' Hopkins, J.B. Lenoir, Brownie McGhee, Sonny Terry, Mississippi Fred McDowell	Koerner, Ray & Glover, Dave Van Ronk, John Hammond, Jr., Taj Mahal, Ry Cooder, John Mayall, Duster Bennett, Jo Ann Kelly	Bonnie Raitt, John Cephas & Phil Wiggins, Ted Hawkins, Lonnie Pitchford, Rory Block, Corey Harris

category, as would Stevie Ray Vaughan in the '80s, although his more tasteful excursions would find favor with both critics and popular audiences. Vaughan was based in Austin, Texas, a constant hotbed of blues-rock acts, due to its thriving roots music scene and small club circuit. The Fabulous Thunderbirds were easily the best–and most influential–of the blues-influenced outfits to emerge from that community. The success of '90s artists like Kenny Wayne Sheppard, Chris Duarte, and British guitarist Gary Moore shows that the audience for blues-rock is far from dead. Many guitarists, like Jeff Healey, Sonny Landreth, and Tinsley Ellis, enjoy a large and steady live following belied by their relatively modest record sales, as do original blues-rock vets like Johnny Winter. And, of course, some blues-influenced singer/guitarists are huge superstars, the biggest being Eric Clapton (who returned to pure blues on 1994's *From the Cradle*) and Bonnie Raitt (an accomplished slide blues guitarist who was more rooted in traditional blues styles when she began recording in the early '70s). Some Black blues bands have absorbed large influences from the rock world; the Robert Cray Band are the most well known of these, and there are others, such as Michael Hill's Blues Mob. And it is a cliche, but it is often true, that many white listeners would be unaware of black blues performers if they hadn't been led to them through the work of White blues-rock bands.

—Richie Unterberger

20 Recommended Albums:

John Mayall, *Bluesbreakers with Eric Clapton* (Deram)
John Mayall, *London Blues (1964–1969)* (PolyGram)
The Paul Butterfield Blues Band, *The Paul Butterfield Blues Band* (Elektra)
The Paul Butterfield Blues Band, *East-West* (Elektra)
Fleetwood Mac, *Black Magic Woman* (Epic)
Jimi Hendrix, *Blues* (MCA)
The Graham Bond Organization, *The Sound of '65* (Edsel)
Captain Beefheart, *Legendary A&M Sessions* (A&M)
Canned Heat, *Best of Canned Heat* (EMI)
Cream, *Fresh Cream* (Polydor)
John Hammond Jr., *So Many Roads* (Vanguard)
The Allman Brothers, *At Fillmore East* (Polydor)
Duffy Power, *Mary Open the Door* (Demon/Edsel)
Johnny Winter, *A Rock N' Roll Collection* (Columbia/ Legacy)
Roy Buchanan, *Sweet Dreams: The Anthology* (Polydor)
Bonnie Raitt, *Bonnie Raitt* (Warner Bros.)
George Thorogood, *The Baddest of George Thorogood & the Destroyers* (EMI)
Stevie Ray Vaughan, *Greatest Hits* (Epic)
The Fabulous Thunderbirds, *The Essential* (Chrysalis)
Eric Clapton, *From the Cradle* (Reprise)

Modern Acoustic Blues

Modern acoustic blues isn't exactly a dying art, but it's certainly one that's bound to take a back seat to modern electric blues, perhaps forever. Electricity has been a staple of blues music for about 50 years. Emerging blues performers (and, for that matter, most middle-aged ones) have never known a world

in which electric modern conveniences and electric instruments were not commonplace items. Being men and women of their time, most blues musicians are eager to make their mark with an electric sound, not an acoustic one. But there will always be a room for the intimate and stark qualities associated with acoustic instruments, and modern blues has had its share of interesting unplugged moments.

Electric bluesmen made conscious decisions to go unplugged for suitable occasions, especially when the folk circuit opened up to blues artists. John Lee Hooker, in particular, had simultaneous careers going for the electric R&B market and for the LP-oriented acoustic audience. To this day, he has an equal command of the electric and acoustic idioms. Snooks Eaglin and Lightnin' Hopkins were other important bluesmen who could alternate between the two worlds with grace. Labels like Arhoolie, Prestige, and Testament recorded plenty of acoustic blues in the 1960s, though these in the main reached back to a pre-World War II sensibility; one-man-band Dr. Isiah Ross' *Call the Doctor* outing on Testament is certainly worth hearing as an example of how full band arrangements can be emulated by one multi-instrumentalist.

One of the most overlooked and important pioneers of modern acoustic blues was J.B. Lenoir, who made his original mark as a second-tier electric Chicago blues guitarist in the 1950s. In the '60s, Lenoir found his greatest appreciation via European tours, and deliberately turned toward solo acoustic guitar arrangements. Lenoir recorded two acoustic albums, issued in Europe only, in the mid-'60s (with some minimal percussion from Fred Below and occasional backup vocal by Willie Dixon) that are notable not just for his full, rich guitar and vocals, but for their groundbreaking subject matter.

Lenoir had already revealed an unusually political bent in the 1950s on "Eisenhower Blues" and "Korea Blues." On the *Alabama Blues* and *Down in Mississippi* albums, he tackled the issues of civil rights, segregation, and Vietnam directly, as well as recording more celebratory songs that suggested African rhythmic and melodic roots. (The *Rolling Stone Record Guide* once called him the "Samuel Fuller of the blues," in acknowledgement of his social realism.) Lenoir, who died in 1967, is still an obscure figure, although he deeply impressed John Mayall, who recorded a song in his honor, and arranged for a posthumous compilation of some of his acoustic work.

Some of the most effective modern acoustic blues stylists had their roots in the blues/folk revival of the 1960s. Dave Van Ronk and Koerner, Ray, and Glover were among the earliest ones, but the best blues guitarists to emerge from this scene were John Hammond and Rory Block. Hammond, inspired by the work of early bluesmen like Son House and Robert Johnson, has sometimes offered capable electric work as well; Block is a more acoustic-oriented performer, and also covers a great deal of material by the likes of Tommy Johnson and Charley Patton. It may that their principal contributions are as instrumentalists rather than singers/composers, but they've done a lot to preserve the traditions of deep acoustic blues.

The British blues boom of the late '60s gave rise to a few acoustic interpreters, most of whom are known, like Jo Ann Kelly, only as names on obscure import compilations. The most entertaining of the lot was probably Duster Bennett, who was once described as "England's answer to Jesse Fuller" for his remarkable one-man band performances. In the late 1960s John Mayall, never one to be satisfied with his personnel for too long, determined to explore an acoustic format while retaining a full band; *The Turning Point* (1969) was a very successful effort in this vein, both commercially and artistically.

For audiences with a rock orientation, the most accessible of the modern

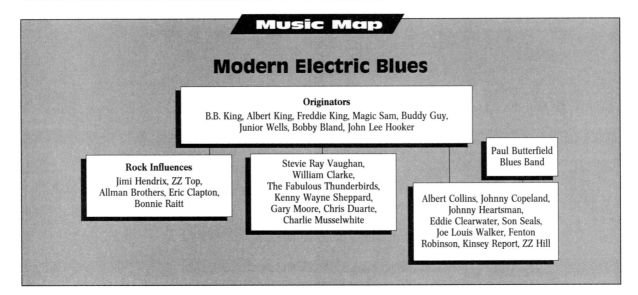

Music Map

Modern Electric Blues

Originators
B.B. King, Albert King, Freddie King, Magic Sam, Buddy Guy,
Junior Wells, Bobby Bland, John Lee Hooker

Rock Influences
Jimi Hendrix, ZZ Top,
Allman Brothers, Eric Clapton,
Bonnie Raitt

Stevie Ray Vaughan,
William Clarke,
The Fabulous Thunderbirds,
Kenny Wayne Sheppard,
Gary Moore, Chris Duarte,
Charlie Musselwhite

Paul Butterfield
Blues Band

Albert Collins, Johnny Copeland,
Johnny Heartsman,
Eddie Clearwater, Son Seals,
Joe Louis Walker, Fenton
Robinson, Kinsey Report, ZZ Hill

acoustic blues performers may be Taj Mahal, who's been making albums since the late '60s. Mahal is a master of Delta-ish acoustic blues, but is also eclectic, blending the blues sensibility with some rock and roots music influences, including calypso and reggae. That may make him too eclectic to be classified as a blues performer, at least in the eyes of some listeners, but it also ensures that his work holds greater interest for listeners who want something a little more ambitious than modern interpretations/updates of classic styles. An occasional associate of Taj's, Ry Cooder, could also be placed into this category. Cooder's plate is more diverse than Mahal's, and actually may be as diverse as anybody's, but often has a blues base. It's his soundtrack work, to the surprise of some, that often holds his bluesiest efforts.

Modern acoustic blues acts don't necessarily have to be solo performers. The duo act of John Cephas and Phil Wiggins have updated the Piedmont guitar-harmonica stylings of Brownie McGhee and Sonny Terry, occasionally nodding to gospel and R&B influences. Satan and Adam have had some success with a similar lineup, and Saffire, an all-woman trio, put a spin on things by mixing original material with covers of songs by classic women blues singers like Bessie Smith and Ma Rainey.

Some of the press championed Ted Hawkins as the great acoustic blues hope of the 1990s. Hawkins was "discovered" playing for tourists on the Venice Beach boardwalk in Los Angeles, and got much of his initial acclaim in England, rather than the United States. The acoustic guitarist owed a lot to soul music as well, his sweet vocals sometimes generating comparisons to Sam Cooke. After some albums for independent labels, Hawkins was discovered (again) by the major Geffen label, and may have been poised for a breakthrough to a wider audience before his unexpected death in the mid-1990s. His death, however, didn't mean the death of acoustic blues; younger performers are waiting in the wings, most notably Corey Harris, whose well-received acoustic debut was noted for its African influence and its committed interpretation of Delta blues styles.

—Richie Unterberger

12 Recommended Albums:

John Lee Hooker, *The Country Blues of John Lee Hooker* (Riverside)
Lightnin' Hopkins, *Lightnin' Hopkins* (Smithsonian/
    Rounder)
Dr. Isiah Ross, *Call the Doctor* (Testament)
J.B. Lenoir, *Down in Mississippi* (L&R)
John Hammond, *Live* (Vanguard)
Rory Block, *High Heeled Blues* (Rounder)
Taj Mahal, *Taj Mahal* (CBS)
Ry Cooder, *Music By Ry Cooder* (Reprise)
John Mayall, *The Turning Point* (Deram)
John Cephas & Phil Wiggins, *Dog Days of August* (Flying Fish)
Ted Hawkins, *The Next Hundred Years* (DGC)
Corey Harris, *Between Night and Day* (Alligator)

Modern Electric Blues

Ask a room full of blues fans to appraise the state of contemporary electric blues, and you'll end up with almost as many opinions as there are people. In some senses, the blues has never been in better shape. Lots of major cities have clubs that feature the blues regularly, and the specialized market that attends to blues recordings is fairly healthy, though rarely cracking the pop charts. The blues has effectively penetrated the American mainstream via television specials, omnipresent use in films and commercials, and frequent representation at major music festivals.

Many blues fans, however, fret that the music isn't as good as it used to be, or at least isn't evolving in satisfactory directions. Every form of music will have its share of naysayers that bewail the passing of the good old days; it's human nature to find the grass greener on the other side of the fence. It's also hard to gain perspective on an era when you're right in the middle of it. But the blues, like everything else at the end of the 20th century, is in a state of post-modernism that can make it difficult to identify trends or major developments.

The period that "contemporary electric blues" refers to varies from analyst to analyst; more out of convenience than anything else, it can be defined as the decades following the "blues revival" of the 1960s. The survival of the blues itself, though often shaky, would never again be questioned. The challenge facing new and old artists alike would be to build upon the enormous body of classic work produced between 1920 and 1970 without sounding repetitious or abandoning the fundamental structures of the music. Looking back over the last couple of decades, we can at least zero in on a few widespread developments: the absorption of rock and soul influences, the proliferation of White blues or blues/rock bands, and the longevity/endurance of living legends who made their first recordings before the 1970s.

Rock and soul had already started to infiltrate hard-core electric blues in the 1960s, in the work of Junior Wells, Buddy Guy, Magic Sam, Albert King, Freddie King, Bobby Bland, and B.B. King, to name just a few. There was also the frequent blues influence to be found in the work of Jimi Hendrix, who could at some points have been considered something of an avant-garde bluesman. Electric blues combos of recent decades have continued to reflect the rock and soul scene, as heard in the fierce, lengthy guitar solos, the occasional funk-influenced rhythms, and the brass sections that are often used to punch things up on stage and in the studio. Some old-school Chicago electric blues players emerged into the spotlight in the 1970s, such as Fenton Robinson, Luther Allison, and Son Seals (who themselves were not ignorant of soul music). But much new talent boasted an increasing appetite for music that was somewhat less grounded in electric blues conventions, though retaining an urban polish.

Purists who dismiss the rock and soul-inflected blues artists of recent years as sell-outs are overlooking the fact that in order for the blues to survive as a living tradition, it cannot exist in a vacuum. From its inception, the blues has always responded to developments in popular music as a whole: the use of the guitar and piano in American folk and gospel, the percussive rhythms of jazz, the lyrics of Tin Pan Alley, and the widespread use of amplification and electric instruments all helped shape the evolution of the blues in the first half of the 20th century.

The blues artists that began to record in the 1970s and 1980s were also men and women of their time, listening not only to blues, but also to rock, pop, soul, and psychedelia. The result has been mixtures of the above elements, found in the funky, guitar-based sound of the Kinsey family, the soulish electric blues of Jimmy Johnson (brother of soul singer Syl Johnson), the African-leaning beats of some of Johnny Copeland's material, the soul-rock-blues fusion of Joe Louis Walker (who drew upon his extensive tenure on the gospel circuit), the horns that pepper some of Koko Taylor's records, or even the classical operatic training of the late Valerie Wellington. The most successful "crossover" efforts in these veins, by far, have been waxed by Robert Cray, whose modernized sound appeals to rock and pop audiences. His *Strong Persuader*, from 1986, became an unexpected pop hit, and he is one of the few blues performers of any era to dent the Top 40 of the pop album charts.

Those who like their soul-blues more downhome, and less oriented toward guitar showmanship, could look to offerings from the Malaco label, which gave a second lease on life to veterans like Z.Z. Hill, Bobby Bland, Denise LaSalle, and Johnnie Taylor. These records generally enjoyed a more predominantly Black audience than those by electric guitar-oriented bands, finding a niche among soul fans who felt disenfranchised by the move towards disco and rap music in R&B. For these listeners, Z.Z. Hill's *Down Home* album of the early '80s was just as pivotal a release as Robert Cray's *Strong Persuader*, demonstrating that earthy contemporary blues could achieve a measure of commercial success.

In recent years the torch for the limited contemporary soul-blues market has been picked up by the Atlanta-based Ichiban label. And zydeco, a whole strain of music with strong ties to the blues, whose exposure had primarily been limited to Louisiana, reached an all-time high of popularity in the 1980s and 1990s. Also providing a rawer alternative to slicker electric guitar sounds was the Fat Possum label, which gave deep South jukejoint veterans like Junior Kimbrough and R.L. Burnside their first national exposure.

The role of White musicians in the blues is a minefield of controversy in some quarters, as anyone who has read the letters section of *Living Blues* magazine over the last few years could tell you. The blues-rock explosion of the late '60s may have peaked with acts like Cream, Jimi Hendrix, and the Allman Brothers, but the number of bands performing and recording in the style has remained pretty high. They rarely scale the pop charts anymore (acts like Stevie Ray Vaughan and the Fabulous Thunderbirds being the exception), but work frequently in urban clubs, and record often for independent labels. And some rock stars, like Bonnie Raitt and Eric Clapton, keep elements of the blues at the top of the charts and throughout the airwaves, although they don't limit themselves to blues material exclusively.

By and large, the White blues bands of recent times place a greater emphasis on instrumental virtuosity than other factors. Many of them have also been called "bar bands," a designation that can carry positive or negative connotations, depending upon your taste. The most frequent criticism leveled at the performers is a lack of soul in the vocals, a lack of songwriting imagination, and a certain generic, shallow flashiness that sometimes gives way to overlong solos that play much better in a sweaty club than a compact disc.

The market is overcrowded with generic White blues band records (as it is with many other kinds of music, Black and White), but that shouldn't disguise the emergence of some genuine blues talents in recent decades. Texan Stevie Ray Vaughan was hailed as the Great White Hope in the blues field until his premature, accidental death in 1990, although he will most likely be remembered primarily as a guitarist rather than a singer. California was a breeding ground for modern harmonica virtuosos, including William Clarke, Rod Piazza, and Charlie Musselwhite (the last of whom had moved to the state after starting in Chicago in the 1960s). John Hammond, since the '60s, has been a living repository of sorts for most acoustic and electric blues guitar styles. The Fabulous Thunderbirds, featuring Jimmy Vaughan (brother of Stevie Ray) and Kim Wilson, were the best exponent of blues as you might experience it in a Texas club.

Blues, like jazz and folk, gives its performers a much longer lease on life than rock, rap, or pop. Blues acts do not so much reach a several-year peak and burn out, as they do reach that peak and maintain it, decade after decade. One of the pleasures of seeing B.B. King, Junior Wells, or Buddy Guy, is the knowledge that they'll sound about every bit as good now as they did 20 or 30 years ago. Such veterans have formed sturdy pillars of the modern electric blues scene simply by continuing to be themselves; Buddy Guy, for instance, seems to just get more and more popular, making inroads into the mainstream with his recent albums. And there's the case of John Lee Hooker, who reached his commercial peak as a senior citizen with his CD *The Healer*, and started to show up on the list of Grammy nominations after only about 40 years as a top bluesman.

In some cases the recent records of the blues vets don't match the best of their classic work, often due to a lack of good new material, or ill-conceived production, but the performers can usually be counted upon to deliver the goods live. To enhance the appeal of middle-aged and elderly blues artists, labels sometimes flavor their new releases with high-profile appearances by rock and pop stars. Hooker's '90s albums are prime examples of studio recordings that are jammed with celebrity cameos. It's an approach that doesn't wash well with many blues fans, but it does have the effect (as the Blues Brothers did in the late '70s) of leading lots of listeners with no blues schooling to the source, which can't be a bad thing.

The general ever-widening acceptance of the blues has also helped some performers break into a national audience after years or even decades of regional concentration and sporadic recording. Albert Collins, Johnny Copeland, and Johnny Heartsman are prominent examples of major bluesmen who began making records in the '50s and '60s, but are thought of as modern electric bluesmen that didn't make their true impact until the 1970s and 1980s. All of them proved extremely adaptable to the rock and soul influences that had infiltrated the music; fortunately the blues is willing to embrace artists who come into their musical prime in middle age, rather than dismiss them as non-contenders after a certain point in their youth.

If much contemporary blues has an easygoing, cheery air, that could be indicative of the whole form's emergence from the collector underground and African-American neighborhoods into the everyday fabric of life. Black America has changed a great deal since the early 1900s, as well, and this too is reflected in the lyrical and musical values of today's electric blues stars. For those who find the music's use at sporting events and television commercials gratuitously exploitative, there's plenty of the authentic thing to be found with just a little effort.

—Richie Unterberger

20 Recommended Albums:

Various Artists, *Blues Masters, Vol. 9: Postmodern Blues* (Rhino)
Various Artists, *Blues Fest: Modern Blues of the '70s* (Rhino)
Various Artists, *Blues Fest: Modern Blues of the '80s* (Rhino)
Various Artists, *Blues Fest: Modern Blues of the '90s* (Rhino)
Son Seals, *The Son Seals Blues Band* (Alligator)
Robert Cray, *Strong Persuader* (Mercury)
Z.Z. Hill, *Down Home* (Malaco)
The Kinsey Report, *Edge of the City* (Alligator)
Valerie Wellington, *Million Dollar Secret* (Flying Fish)
Joe Louis Walker, *The Gift* (Hightone)
Eric Clapton, *From the Cradle* (Reprise)
John Lee Hooker, *The Healer* (Chameleon)
Stevie Ray Vaughan, *Greatest Hits* (Epic)
The Fabulous Thunderbirds, *The Essential Fabulous Thunderbirds Collection* (Epic)
Albert Collins, *Ice Pickin'* (Alligator)
Johnny Copeland, *Bringin' It All Back Home* (Rounder)
Junior Kimbrough, *All Night Long* (Fat Possum)
R.L. Burnside, *Too Bad Jim* (Fat Possum)
Fenton Robinson, *I Hear Some Blues Downstairs* (Alligator)
Buddy Guy, *Damn Right, I've Got the Blues* (Silvertone)

Independent Blues Labels:
The 1940s and 1950s

In many respects, 1945 was an incredibly scary time to be in America. World War II was finally over, and the country prepared to adjust from a wartime economy to a peacetime one that would need to reintegrate millions of returning veterans. The atomic bomb cast a cloud over the future of the planet; the rise of communism in the Soviet Union and Eastern Europe was sowing seeds of fear and paranoia. Many wanted to do nothing more than resume life as normal, but the fact was that changing geopolitics, new technology, and developing mass media meant that life could never be the same.

But at the same time, life had never been more exciting. The United States had finally recovered from the effects of the Depression, and those who had survived the war with their families and health intact were ready to relax and, to a degree, party. Music was needed, and with the end of wartime rationing of certain materials, the record industry could resume full-scale operations after years of manufacturing restrictions. It was in this uncertain, yet intoxicating, climate that a boomlet of independent labels helped lay the foundation for the recording and distribution of post-war blues music.

Historically, the music business has always been dominated by about a half-dozen "major" labels. Their names and initials change according to corporate transactions and mergers, but in the middle of the 1940s they were Columbia, Victor, Decca, Capitol, Mercury, and MGM. Ever since the blues began to be recorded, the major labels had paid some attention to the music, often placing the artists on subsidiary companies that were geared toward the "race" (i.e. Black) audience. Hence the appearance of so many CD reissues of ancient blues on huge labels like Sony and BMG.

An independent label formed in the 1940s faced enormous obstacles in competing against the majors, but also had enormous opportunities. Blues, R&B, and hillbilly artists were still recording for big companies in the 1940s, but not in great numbers; the labels focused their energies on pop music that was oriented towards White Americans. This, naturally, left a vacuum in the marketplace, and several million disenfranchised listeners. Blues, R&B, and country were exploding as live, regional phenomenons, but weren't adequately represented on record. Demand necessitates supply, and numerous independent labels emerged to fill the gap.

There were no rule books for the new upstarts to adhere to, and one imagines that day-to-day life for these fledgling operations was both nerve-wracking and tremendously exciting. They didn't have the funds, state-of-the-art studios, or massive distribution networks that gave the Columbias of the world such huge advantages. All of them had to do things the hard way, driving from town to town to push their latest singles from the trunks of their cars, collect payments from shaky distributors and retailers, and chat up the local DJs in hopes of getting their releases on the air. What they usually had, above all, were ears to the ground: a real feel for what the communities of minority audiences–Blacks, Southern Whites, and teenagers–were listening to, on the regional radio stations (itself an exploding phenomenon of the time), the jukeboxes, and in the dance halls. This was true whether the label owners were Black or, as they were in many cases, White, sometimes being minorities of sorts themselves with Jewish and/or immigrant backgrounds.

Out of this crazy-quilt milieu came the labels so near and dear to the hearts of millions of blues, rock, and R&B fans: Chess, Sun, Specialty, Aladdin, Modern, King, Atlantic, Imperial, Vee-Jay, Duke/Peacock, and others. None of them focused on the blues exclusively: indeed, few of them even focused on Black music exclusively. All of them, however, wanted in on the R&B market, to varying degrees. And thus it was that most of the best blues artists of the 1940s and 1950s recorded for these labels.

As far as establishing a label or "house" sound, **Chess** and **Sun** were probably the most distinctive of these operations, and their histories are outlined in separate essays. While other prominent indies of the period may not have developed a production style as immediately distinctive, several made especially noteworthy contributions to blues and R&B history, and usually made a mark on rock 'n' roll as well. In the mid-1940s, several companies sprouted up in Los Angeles, where the record and entertainment industry (which was then centered in New York) was truly beginning to establish roots. These labels also did a great deal to develop styles of blues/R&B that became identified with the West Coast, particularly jump blues.

One of the most important L.A. operations was **Specialty**, founded in 1945 by Art Rupe; that same year, it had one of the first truly monster independent R&B hits, Roy Milton's "R.M. Blues." Milton was one of the label's biggest stars, scoring nearly 20 R&B hits in a jump blues style; Camille Howard (Milton's pianist), Jimmy Liggins, Joe Liggins, and Floyd Dixon also had hits for the label, employing the boogie-woogie pianos and honking saxes that were early R&B staples. Specialty was also one of the first companies to scout the burgeoning New Orleans R&B scene, recording hugely influential hits in the early half of the 1950s by Lloyd Price and Guitar Slim.

Specialty was not solely devoted to R&B; it had an extensive gospel line as well, the jewel in the crown being the Soul Stirrers, who featured the young Sam Cooke. They landed one of the biggest original rock 'n' roll stars, Little Richard, and also had some success in the rock field with Larry Williams and Don and Dewey. Yet by the late '50s, Specialty was winding down its activities; Art Rupe was finding lucrative economic opportunities outside of the record business. It's also been suggested that he was discouraged by the success of Sam Cooke, who became a huge pop star after Rupe, frightened of tampering with the gospel singer's track record, refused to release secular material by Cooke on Specialty, giving both Cooke and producer Bumps Blackwell their walking papers in the bargain. Numerous well-packaged Specialty reissues have appeared on the market since the label sold its catalog to Fantasy in 1990.

Aladdin, also formed in L.A. in 1945, was a virtual storehouse of West Coast jump blues/R&B pianists, recording Amos Milburn, Floyd Dixon, and Charles Brown. The "honking" element of West Coast jump blues was provided by saxophonist Big Jay McNeely. In the mid-'50s, like some other labels, they got a cut of the New Orleans R&B/rock scene with the vocal duo of Shirley & Lee.

Modern, yet another L.A. company formed in 1945 (by the Bihari brothers), also had some tentacles into the West Coast blues/R&B scene, with a roster including Floyd Dixon (who recorded for several labels during his prime), Etta James, and saxophonist Joe Houston. In comparison with Aladdin and Specialty, however, they had a greater taste for guitar-focused, grittier blues, releasing sides by Jimmy McCracklin, Johnny "Guitar" Watson, and Pee Wee Crayton. They were also aggressive in scouting talent outside of their region, distributing some of the first nationally popular recordings by blues legends John Lee Hooker, B.B. King, and Elmore James, all of whom were based east of the Mississippi. In the '50s, they formed active subsidiary labels, RPM and Flair; when times became leaner, however, they focused on budget LP compilations for another of their subsidiaries, the Crown label.

A final L.A. giant was **Imperial**, founded in the late 1940s. Although it made significant contributions to West Coast blues by recording guitarists T-Bone Walker and Jimmy McCracklin, it will be mainly remembered for its forays into New Orleans R&B. No other label based outside of New Orleans (and maybe none within New Orleans) had as much success with Crescent City music, principally with Fats Domino, who spun out a series of hits for about a decade. Dave Bartholomew was an instrumental factor in many of Imperial's New Orleans hits as a producer and arranger, for Domino and others; the label also recorded some blues-oriented singers in New Orleans, like Roy Brown, Pee Wee Crayton, and Snooks Eaglin, in attempts to give them a commercial direction more in line with rock 'n' roll's burgeoning popularity. The label's days as a major power came to an end with its sale to Liberty in 1963, when Domino's chart success finally ceased, and the company's biggest star, Rick Nelson, had been lured away to a major label.

Chicago blues was considerably rawer and more guitar-based than the kind usually issued by the West Coast labels, and Chess, though the giant in the field, wasn't the only game in town. **Vee-Jay**, also based in the Windy City, had two of the most commercially successful bluesmen of the era, Jimmy Reed and

Music Map

Independent Blues Labels: The 1940s and 1950s

The Majors
Columbia, Victor, Decca, Capitol, Mercury and MGM
Little to no outlets for black music, especially blues

West Coast
Specialty, Aladdin, Modern, RPM, Flair, Crown, Imperial, Swing Time

Midwest and South
Chess, Checker, Vee-Jay, JOB, Fortune, King, Sun, Ace, Duke, Peacock, Cobra, Trumpet, Jewel, Excello

East Coast
Atlantic, Herald, Fire, Fury, Enjoy, Savoy

John Lee Hooker (it should be noted that Hooker recorded for quite a few labels in his early career, often for several simultaneously, and occasionally under pseudonyms). Lesser-known but great sides were also recorded for Vee-Jay by harmonica player/singer Billy Boy Arnold and Eddie Taylor, who was Jimmy Reed's guitarist. In the early '60s, it had huge successes in the pop market with early recordings by the Four Seasons and the Beatles, but went belly-up in the mid-'60s.

A Chicago R&B label that flamed briefly and brightly was **Cobra**, who lured Chess bassist/arranger/songwriter Willie Dixon away for a brief time in the late '50s. If for nothing else, the label gained a niche in blues history for waxing classic early sides by Otis Rush that rate among the best and most chilling electric blues ever recorded. Magic Sam also recorded notable early sides for the label, although he wouldn't truly reach his peak until the '60s.

King, based in Cincinnati, was one of the most versatile independent labels of the time: R&B may have been its bread and butter, but it also made a great deal of key hillbilly records. But it certainly had an impressive roster of both blues shouters (Wynonie Harris, Bullmoose Jackson, Eddie "Cleanhead" Vinson) and instrumental-oriented honkers (Big Jay McNeely, organist Bill Doggett, Tiny Bradshaw, Earl Bostic, and others). In the 1960s it also had claim to one of the decade's most commercially successful blues guitarists, Freddie King. By that time, though, it was heavily reliant upon the empire of soul brother #1, James Brown. King was sold to Polydor in the early 1970s; in recent years compilations of important King R&B/blues artists have appeared on Rhino.

A major outpost of Southern blues was **Duke/Peacock**, founded by legendary micro-manager Don Robey in Houston. In addition to recording Big Mama Thornton and Texan guitarists like Clarence "Gatemouth" Brown, Duke did its part to point the way for soul by recording two of the leading soul-bluesmen, Bobby "Blue" Bland and Junior Parker. The label seemed comfortable with both guitar-focused material and sophisticated horn arrangements that played off the gospel-influenced vocals of Bland in particular.

Excello, though founded in Nashville, really made its mark on blues history through its Louisiana-based artists, including Slim Harpo, Lightnin' Slim, and Lazy Lester. These were the singers who, aided by producer Jay Miller, were the key exponents of "swamp blues." By lending the musicians sympathetic production and the freedom to be more or less themselves, Miller was one of several producers who cultivated a characteristic sound, Sam Phillips (at Sun) and Leonard Chess (at Chess) being two of the most notable others.

New York is not noted as a groundswell of down-home blues, and it may be that the key contribution of **Atlantic** was in tilling the field for R&B, rock 'n' roll, and soul, rather than developing straight blues. The company can't be overlooked, however, due to its crucial role in midwifing blues-derived R&B into more urbanized forms with a greater appeal to a younger audience. Joe Turner, Ray Charles, Sticks McGhee, Chuck Willis, Ruth Brown, and LaVern Baker were just some of the most prominent players with Atlantic contracts. And the label did record some straight-up blues, even if much of it tended to be with artists that made their most significant music for other operations.

A smaller notable independent based in New York City was Bobby Robinson's **Fire** label, with the active Fury and Enjoy subsidiaries. Robinson recorded some of the rawest guitar blues of the era, including some of Elmore James's best work. Buster Brown's "Fannie Mae" was one of the most undiluted blues records ever to make the Top Forty. And Fire was also responsible for Wilbert Harrison's #1 hit "Kansas City," which may be the ultimate example of shuffle blues transposed into rock 'n' roll, one of the key ingredients being Jimmy Spruill's scintillating guitar solo.

This roundup, it should be noted, has only encompassed some of the most active independent companies that recorded blues music between 1945 and 1960. Others made significant contributions, such as Savoy, which recorded a good deal of jump blues by Johnny Otis and others, and Trumpet, which released some primeval Southern blues in the early '50s by Sonny Boy Williamson and others. In the 1990s, Capricorn Records dedicated a series of box sets to such labels, including ones for Cobra, Fire/Fury, Jewel/Paula, and Swingtime. Charlie Gillett's *The Sound of the City*, a history of rock 'n' roll's first two decades, does an excellent job of detailing the many influential independent early rock and R&B labels, and is recommended further reading.

There were many tiny companies that released regional singles in small quantities; some lasted for only one or two 45s. Most of these can now only be enjoyed on small-run import reissues (if they even made it that far). But their deep obscurity, and the relatively raw production values employed on some of them, doesn't mean that they can't be just as enjoyable as sides produced on the "big" indies.

Independent rock and R&B labels, by and large, were reducing their blues rosters by the dawn of the 1960s. This was not necessarily, as some might charge, a reflection of lack of interest in the blues by the label owners, or ingratitude towards the artists that had helped put them on the map in the first place. The independents, it must be remembered, were not PBS; they were commercial enterprises that needed chart hits and cash flow. In focusing their energies elsewhere, they were usually responding to trends in the overall marketplace, most notably the increasing success of rock 'n' roll. And a lot of the biggest independents didn't even survive the competition of the era, going under or selling their catalog to other companies; Atlantic, which is still thriving today, is more the exception than the rule.

R&B itself was loosening its ties to the blues, and looking forward to soul music. Some artists, like Bobby Bland, Little Milton, Albert King, and Freddie King, were well-suited for adapting to the new era; unfortunately, most of the blues stars of the '40s and '50s were left out in the cold. It should be noted that a lot of indies didn't give up on the blues completely; Motown, the most successful of the whole lot, made little-noticed recordings with Amos Milburn and Earl King in the 1960s. But the commercial momentum of American pop had shifted away from blues and hardcore R&B, leaving the blues in the hands of a devoted but more specialized audience.

And the needs of that audience would be addressed from the 1960s onwards by independent companies. These, however, were independent companies that were not as concerned with commercial chart success as satisfying the tastes of a niche market that included increasingly younger, more affluent, and White listeners. The prime medium would not be the 45 single, but the long-playing record and, much later, the compact disc. The stories of those independents–Arhoolie, Delmark, Alligator, Fat Possum, and others–is told in a separate sidebar. The legacy of the earlier generation of independents is readily available for today's audience, however, on a plethora of CD reissues, several of which provide thematically linked (and sometimes, truth to tell, haphazard) overviews of the labels' valuable contributions to American music.—*Richie Unterberger*

5 Recommended Albums:
Various Artists, *Chess Blues* (Chess)
Various Artists, *A Sun Blues Collection* (Rhino)
Various Artists, *The Specialty Story* (Specialty)
Various Artists, *Atlantic Blues Box* (Atlantic)
Various Artists, *The Cobra Records Story* (Capricorn)

Music Map

Sun Records—The Blues Years

Sam Phillips
forms Memphis Recording Service, 1950, forms Sun Records, 1952

1950 – 1952 Records & Leases to Chess, 4 Star & Modern:	1952 – 1954/Sun Records Begins	1954 – 1959/Sun, Rockabilly, Country
Howlin' Wolf	Walter Horton	Elvis Presley
B.B. King	Jimmy De Berry	Johnny Cash
Joe Hill Louis	Little Milton	Jerry Lee Lewis
Walter Horton	Doctor Ross	Roy Orbison
Dr. Ross	Joe Hill Louis	Billy Riley
Jackie Brenston	James Cotton	Warren Smith
Rosco Gordon	Pat Hare	Sonny Burgess
Rufus Thomas	Frank Frost	Ray Harris
Harmonica Frank Floyd	Earl Hooker	Jack Earls
Ike Turner & The Kings of Rhythm	Charlie Booker	Charlie Feathers
	Billy the Kid Emerson	Carl Perkins
	Rosco Gordon	The Miller Sisters
	D.A. Hunt	Charlie Rich
	Mose Vinson	Ernie Chaffin
	Big Memphis Marainey	Barbara Pittman
	Rufus Thomas	

Sun Records—The Blues Years

In the late 1940s, Memphis, TN, was still very much a segregated city. The many boundaries that separated Black and White social life also separated the musical communities, despite the cracks starting to force open via radio stations like WDIA and WHBQ, which broadcast blues and R&B to young listeners in the region like Elvis Presley. Recognizing the genius of several blues performers in the Memphis area, there was one man, Sam Phillips, who became determined to record the music and bring it wider recognition.

As a radio engineer, Phillips had already gained technical expertise and appreciation for a wide variety of Black and White popular music. Recording and distributing it was a huge challenge, as it was for many other independent regional labels of the time that handled R&B or hillbilly records for minority audiences. Explained Phillips to Robert Palmer in *Deep Blues*, "I thought it was vital music ... and although my first love was radio, my second was the freedom we tried to give the people, Black and White, to express their very complex personalities, personalities these people didn't know existed in the '50s. I just hope I was a part of giving the influence to the people to be free in their expression."

How much of Phillips' operation was artistic altruism, and how much the hopes of a businessman seeing a gap in the existing market, continues to be a matter of some historical debate. There's no question, though, that Phillips was *the* man for recording blues in Memphis as the '50s dawned. Initially he focused not on pressing discs on his own label, but recording local sides at his Memphis Recording Service studio that would be leased to labels that were not in Memphis itself. Phillips was fortunate to be situated in a city that was a hotbed of blues talent, and he quickly arranged for recordings by B.B. King, Howlin' Wolf, Jackie Brenston, Rosco Gordon, and others to be leased to the Modern and Chess labels.

"I opened the Memphis Recording Service," elaborated Phillips in *Good Rockin' Tonight* (by Colin Escott with Martin Hawkins), "with the intention of recording singers and musicians from Memphis and the locality who I felt had something that people should be able to hear. I'm talking about blues–both the country style and the rhythm style–and also about gospel or spiritual music and about White country music. I always felt that the people who played this type of music had not been given the opportunity to reach an audience. I feel strongly that a lot of the blues was a real true story. Unadulterated life as it was.

"My aim was to try and record the blues and other music I liked and to prove whether I was right or wrong about this music. I knew or I *felt* I knew, that there was a bigger audience for blues than just the Black man of the mid-South. There were city markets to be reached, and I knew that Whites listened to blues surreptitiously."

Any characteristic sound that could be attached to Phillips' blues productions resulted not so much from what he brought to the sessions, but what he *didn't* do. He was astute enough to realize that the singers and musicians had a power that would have been diminished by extraneous production or a conscious softening of rough edges. Thus, he concentrated on getting the best performances from his artists without coaxing them into changing their styles, and obtaining takes that were sufficiently commercial for release without losing their spontaneity.

He was also clever enough to capitalize upon accidents that could have been categorized as mistakes, as when Ike Turner's band (featuring vocalist-saxophonist Jackie Brenston) arrived at the studio with a damaged guitar speaker. Other producers might have cancelled the session until the speaker could be fixed, but Phillips and the musicians found they liked the distorted guitar sound it produced. It would end up featuring prominently on Brenston's big hit, "Rocket 88," which is repeatedly referred to by historians as one of the first rock 'n' roll records.

By 1952 Phillips, realizing that companies were going to start beating him to the punch by recording regional artists directly instead of leasing his masters, started the Sun label. (He had released a record by Joe Hill Louis in 1950 on the Phillips imprint.) The next few years found Sun releasing a few dozen blues/R&B sides that, although not nearly as great in quantity as those of Chess to the North, were nearly on the same level in terms of quality and historical influence. "Bear Cat," Rufus Thomas' answer record to Big Mama Thornton's "Hound Dog," was Sun's first big national R&B hit, although some of the sweetness went out of that triumph when a lawsuit from the "Hound Dog" publishers wiped out its profits.

Never releasing too much material by any one blues artist (although the vaults and subsequent reissues have yielded tons of unissued sides), Sun did have some further success in the R&B market with items like Junior Parker's "Feelin' Good." Parker's follow-up, "Mystery Train," didn't do as well, although it became one of the core classics of Memphis music, particularly after it was covered a couple of years later on the fifth and final single of a fellow Sun artist, Elvis Presley.

By that time, the focus of Sun Records had tilted almost entirely towards the White artists on its roster. Phillips had never stuck to recording Black musicians exclusively (although he issued almost nothing but blues records in the early days of the label), and the fortuitous discovery of Elvis in 1954 had resulted in the birth of rockabilly with Presley's first single, "That's All Right Mama." Elvis, of course, took much of his inspiration from the blues, both in vocal delivery and his choice of early cover material. By 1955, it became apparent that Elvis was Sun's ticket to much greater commercial success than anything they could achieve in blues/R&B, although the singles with Parker, Little Milton, James Cotton, and obscure artists like Doctor Ross, Frank Frost, Billy "The Kid" Emerson, and future Muddy Waters band guitarist Pat Hare seemed to bode well for continued success in the blues field.

Sun's subsequent move into rock 'n' roll has been criticized by some, including Rufus Thomas, but a quick look at the release schedule shows that Phillips was issuing blues singles alongside hillbilly records and the emerging rockabilly sound. Indeed, Phillips was recording Frank Frost for his Phillips International label in the '60s, after most of his big stars had left for greener pastures.

In *Good Rockin' Tonight*, Phillips himself rejoins, "Keep in mind that there were a number of very good R&B labels. The base wasn't broad enough because of racial prejudice. It wasn't broad enough to get the amount of commercial play and general acceptance overall–not just in the South. So I knew what I had to do to broaden the base of acceptance."

Phillips achieved that by focusing on White country and–later–rockabilly artists, especially after he sold Presley's contract to RCA in late 1955 for $35,000, the bulk of which went back into his desperately cash-starved label. In retrospect, it seems he had little choice in the matter. Distributors were paying him on the sales of Presley singles with blues returns by the carload, and labels like Duke, RPM, and Chess were swiftly decimating his blues artist roster. The Bihari brothers (who owned the Crown, RPM, Modern, and Flair labels) actually started their Meteor label in Memphis with the express purpose of putting Phillips out of business. With the capital from the Presley sale, he was able to promote and distribute his remaining roster much more effectively. Carl Perkins, Johnny Cash, Jerry Lee Lewis, and Charlie Rich all became stars in the late '50s as Sun artists.

Whether Phillips could have done this with Black blues artists is doubtful. The sheer rawness of the Sun blues sides–both in the performances and the spartan production–still make them difficult to listen to today and made them even tougher to program on radio back then. As a businessman with a tiny two-person operation, Phillips was torn between the music he loved and what would sell and reach a wider audience. Also, by the time of the twin national breakthrough of Presley and Carl Perkins' "Blue Suede Shoes," blues was by and large a spent commercial force in the Black community, with doo-wop groups and R&B singers now dominating the charts. Thus it was that many of Phillips' blues artists had their greatest commercial success on other labels. One could reasonably argue that Presley, Perkins, Cash, and Lewis reached their artistic peak at Sun. But one could not say the same for B.B. King, Howlin' Wolf, Junior Parker, Little Milton, Walter Horton, and Rufus Thomas, all of whom truly found their calling with other concerns, often in much more of a blues/soul vein in the 1960s, or even (in Thomas' case) as a straight soul singer with few overt ties to the blues at all.

As such, the relatively slim oeuvre of Sun blues recordings is more of a vault for the embryonic talents of major blues performers than their very best work. Which is not to suggest that what was preserved wasn't very good, far from it. The Chess brothers, for all their business acumen and "feel" for the music, could never have produced sides with the stark, lonesome feel of Big Walter Horton's "Easy" or the violent agression contained in James Cotton's "Cotton Crop Blues." And in the broader sense, few labels have done as much to weave the blues into mainstream American culture as Sun, both by giving major bluesmen their first opportunity to record and reach audiences beyond the region, and by exposing it (albeit indirectly) to the American masses via its incorporation into the rockabilly of Presley, Perkins, et al.

—*Richie Unterberger & Cub Koda*

7 Recommended Sun Albums:

Various Artists, *A Sun Blues Collection* (Rhino)
Various Artists, *Sun Records: The Blues Years, 1950–1956* (Charly)
Junior Parker, James Cotton, & Pat Hare, *Mystery Train* (Rhino)
Howlin' Wolf, *Rides Again* (Flair/Virgin)
B.B. King, *The Memphis Masters* (Ace)
Various Artists, *Sun Records Harmonica Classics* (Rounder)
Joe Hill Louis, *The Be-Bop Boy* (Bear Family)

Chess Records

Some may argue that the history of blues is one of musicians, regions, and movements rather than something so business-oriented as a record label. Chess Records, however, is not just some record label. It's a sound in itself–a

sound which, for many, epitomizes the best of Chicago blues, and maybe even the best electric blues has to offer. Through the recordings of Muddy Waters, Little Walter, Howlin' Wolf, and many other talents great and small, the Chicago-based label and its subsidiaries (Checker and Argo, later renamed Cadet) did an enormous amount to amplify the blues, record some of its greatest talents, and bring the form into the modern era.

These are achievements that few could have foreseen when the label was founded by Leonard and Phil Chess in the 1940s. The brothers had come to the United States from Poland in the late 1920s. In 1947 Leonard Chess was a nightclub owner in Chicago, entering the record business by buying into the local Aristocrat label. Aristocrat was not a blues label at its outset, recording pop and jazz. Its Chicago base, however, was in close proximity to more blues talent than any other Northern city, with more musicians relocating from the South all the time.

In the late '40s, Chicago blues–in its raw, amplified state–had yet to be captured on record in all its primal immediacy. Aristocrat had skirted around the blues with jazz-blues sorts of outings by the likes of Andrew Tibbs, and employed guitarist Muddy Waters as a sideman on a 1947 single by pianist Sunnyland Slim. But it would be Muddy's own efforts, starting with 1948's "I Can't Be Satisfied"/"I Feel Like Going Home," that truly began to urbanize and electrify the sound of the Delta. The Chess brothers became progressively more active in the blues field, and by 1950 they had taken over the Aristocrat label entirely, changing its name to Chess.

Although Waters was already starting to use a full band in his club appearances, Chess at first went easy on all-out amplification in the recording studio, preferring not to tamper with the stripped accompaniment that had proved so succesful on Muddy's first big hit. Early classics were recorded with Waters accompanied by no one except Big Crawford on bass ("I Can't Be Satisfied") and sometimes just with Muddy and his electric guitar ("Rollin' Stone"). Other musicians like Little Walter (harmonica) and Jimmy Rogers (guitar) started to come in as well, not only on Muddy's singles, but on those of some other Chess artists. By the early '50s, the addition of drums made the switch to electric blues complete, providing in the process the prototype for the guitars-bass-drums-harmonica lineup that would serve as the "classic" model for both electric blues and rock 'n' roll.

Chess blues singles quickly developed an identifiable sound. A haunting and spacious echo was created by, according to Peter Guralnick's *Feel Like Going Home*, "rigging a loudspeaker and a microphone at both ends of a sewer pipe" and "a primitive system of tape delay." The voices and instruments often sounded slightly overamplified and recorded at levels that frequently intruded into the red zone. This resulted in recordings that preserved the focused punch of the small blues combo while maximizing its sonic power. Particularly in the early days, consistency was assured by using many of the same musicians (who often released records of their own as well) to play on Chess sessions, forming a sort of floating house band. "Session men" like Little Walter, Willie Dixon, and Jimmy Rogers are well known, of course; more obscure are performers like drummer Fred Below, whose swinging backbeat did much to establish the bedrock of both electric blues and rock 'n' roll.

While Phil Chess focused on the business end of the label, his brother Leonard concentrated on the studio. Historians have sometimes hinted that he was capturing magic more by accident than design. It's true that a Jewish Polish immigrant may not have been as attuned to the nuances of Delta-cum-Chicago blues as the musicians, but Chess deserves considerable credit for crafting the sound that appeared on the grooves. Leonard Chess apparently had a genuine knack for getting the best out of his performers in the studio and refining their material into a product that was both commercial and artistic. On more than one memorable occasion, dissatisfied with the drum sound he was getting, he played the bass drum himself.

Leonard Chess' principal aide de camp was house bassist Willie Dixon. Dixon worked countless sessions in the '50s and '60s, though he briefly left Chess in the late '50s to work for the Chicago-based rival Cobra label. It's as a songwriter, however, that Dixon will be most remembered, penning numerous classics for Waters, Little Walter, Howlin' Wolf, and many other artists in the Chess stable. Chess expanded its roster rapidly in the early half of the 1950s, as electric Chicago blues became a major presence on the R&B charts. On swings through other regions to distribute and promote their records, the Chess brothers would check out and sometimes sign talent. They would also lease material cut elsewhere, the most famous example being their distribution of several crucial sides cut by Sam Phillips in Sun Studios in Memphis. After a bitter rivalry with the Bihari brothers (to whom Phillips was also leasing material) Chess would place the most promising of the Sun recorded artists, Howlin' Wolf, on its own label.

There was plenty of home-grown talent in Chicago, of course. From within Muddy Waters' own band, Little Walter became a solo star, and Jimmy Rogers and pianist Otis Spann also had solid recording careers without nearly as much

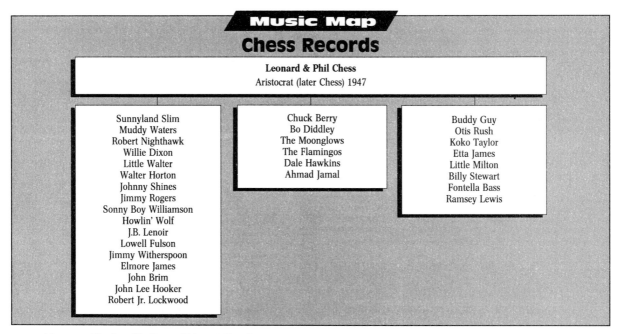

Music Map

Chess Records

Leonard & Phil Chess
Aristocrat (later Chess) 1947

Sunnyland Slim	Chuck Berry	Buddy Guy
Muddy Waters	Bo Diddley	Otis Rush
Robert Nighthawk	The Moonglows	Koko Taylor
Willie Dixon	The Flamingos	Etta James
Little Walter	Dale Hawkins	Little Milton
Walter Horton	Ahmad Jamal	Billy Stewart
Johnny Shines		Fontella Bass
Jimmy Rogers		Ramsey Lewis
Sonny Boy Williamson		
Howlin' Wolf		
J.B. Lenoir		
Lowell Fulson		
Jimmy Witherspoon		
Elmore James		
John Brim		
John Lee Hooker		
Robert Jr. Lockwood		

commercial success. The four W's–Waters, Walter, Wolf, and Sonny Boy Williamson–would become Chess' most durable blues artists. J.B. Lenoir, Lowell Fulson, and Willie Mabon, although not as iconic, also recorded a good deal of material for the label.

Chess' lengthy associations with Waters, Walter, Wolf, and Williamson were in fact more the exception than the rule. Throughout the '50s, it seemed like the label gave most major electric blues performers a trial at one time or another, although it wouldn't stick with them for very long. Thus it was that a who's who of modern blues passed through the Chess pipeline at one point or another. Elmore James, Otis Rush, John Lee Hooker, Johnny Shines, Robert Nighthawk, Billy Boy Arnold, Buddy Guy, and Memphis Minnie are not principally known for their Chess recordings, but all of them recorded or released products for the company, often in enough quantity to generate their own reissue LPs years later.

The wealth of Chess reissue LPs can give the understandable impression that the label was recording a bottomless well of classic blues throughout the '50s. However, Chess was never exclusively a blues concern, and in fact experienced its greatest commercial success with the rock 'n' roll artists Chuck Berry and Bo Diddley. The success of Berry in particular, and the diminished presence of electric blues on the R&B charts in the second half of the 1950s, meant that Chess began to put more effort into its non-blues product. That didn't just mean guitar rockers like Berry–Chess also recorded a good deal of R&B, doo-wop (Flamingos, Moonglows) and jazz (Ahmad Jamal), and even handled Dale Hawkins' great rockabilly recordings.

In the 1960s, blues occupied a less central position within the company. Blues was not the music of choice for many African-American listeners anymore, having been overtaken by rock 'n' roll, R&B, and then modern soul music. Little Walter was in a artistic decline, exacerbated by health and personal problems; Sonny Boy Williamson died in the mid-'60s; Muddy Waters, who had begun to tour England and Europe, was now broadening into the LP market, with albums such as *Muddy Waters: Folk Singer* being packaged for the White folk music crowd.

Chess' greatest commercial successes in the 1960s were not in the blues field, but in soul (with Etta James, Billy Stewart, and Fontella Bass) and soul-jazz (Ramsey Lewis). At this time the old guard rock 'n' rollers, Berry and Diddley, were finding their share of the marketplace shrinking. This sales decline, ironically, coincided with a period in which Chess Records were beginning to retroactively attain legendary status among some young White enthusiasts, particularly musicians in British Invasion bands. The Rolling Stones, who put a ton of Chess recordings into their early repertoire, paid homage to the label by recording at Chess Studios in 1964, in the midst of their first American tour.

Chess did not give up on their original stars, or the blues–Howlin' Wolf, for instance, recorded some of his greatest material in the '60s, and Koko Taylor established herself as one of the premier blueswomen. At times, however, it

seemed to be making desperate attempts to make their blues artists sound more contemporary by adding rock and soul influences. Misbegotten albums–such as Waters' *Muddy, Brass & the Blues* (with overdubbed horns on some tracks), "supersession" albums pairing different bandleaders, psychedelic-influenced records with Waters (*Electric Mud*) and Howlin' Wolf (*This is Howlin' Wolf's New Album–He Doesn't Like It*)–all backfired artistically and commercially. Most of them have stayed mercifully unreissued in the digital age.

After Leonard Chess died in 1969, the company was sold to GRT, and control of the label passed to his son, Marshall. Chess in the '70s was a sad echo of its glory days, and Marshall and Phil Chess would soon leave the company (Marshall to head up the Rolling Stones' new label), which wound down its activities as an ongoing concern. That left a huge back catalog, coveted by collectors (and just plain fans) the world over.

Despite the almost inexhaustible supply of great blues material, the Chess reissue program of the past two decades has been erratic until quite recently. A couple of domestic series, ranging from thorough double-LP retrospectives to interesting packages of obscure performers like John Brim, were halted or went out of print as the Chess catalog changed ownership. For a time, it was owned by the Sugar Hill label (most famous for its early rap productions); the Sugar Hill series, too, soon came to a stop. For a while, Chess reissues were easier to acquire as imports than they were in their land of origin, the United States. What's more, serious collectors, to their frustration, found many rare and unreleased tracks appearing on various European and Japanese compilations while remaining unavailable in the U.S.

Ownership of the catalog passed to MCA, with plans for comprehensive reissue programs remaining vague. Happily, this situation was remedied in the CD age, with Chess/MCA embarking upon a series of comprehensive reissues that restored almost all of the catalog to availability, including much of the rare and out-of-print material that had only surfaced on imports or bootlegs as well as material that had never surfaced. The intentions and achievements of the Chess brothers have remained the subject of mixed scrutiny. They do, however, deserve an enormous amount of credit for recognizing the best in electric blues talent, distributing it, and translating it into recorded music that will endure for ages. —*Richie Unterberger & Cub Koda*

15 Recommended Chess Albums

Various Artists, *Chess Blues Box*
Muddy Waters, *The Chess Box*
Howlin' Wolf, *The Chess Box*
Little Walter, *The Essential*
Sonny Boy Williamson, *The Essential*
Muddy Waters, *One More Mile*
Howlin' Wolf, *Ain't Gonna Be Your Dog*

Little Walter, *Blues with a Feeling*
Jimmy Rogers, *Chicago Bound*
J.B. Lenoir, *Natural Man*
Buddy Guy, *The Complete Chess Studio Sessions*
Koko Taylor, *What It Takes: The Chess Years*
Willie Dixon, *The Chess Box*
Otis Rush/Albert King, *Door to Door*
Elmore James, *Whose Muddy Shoes*

Independent Blues Labels:
The 1960s to the Present

While major labels continue to record a few major performers, such as Robert Cray and Buddy Guy, the overwhelming majority of contemporary blues music is to be found on independent companies–that is, labels that are not owned or distributed by the large corporations of Sony, BMG, CEMA, PGD, UNI, or WEA. Outfits such as Arhoolie, Delmark, Vanguard, Testament, Alligator, Hightone, and Fat Possum have played a huge role in both recording the best blues of the past few decades, and of preserving the best of past and living blues traditions. The relatively small commercial market for blues in recent times has virtually ensured that these operations are run by proprietors who are enthusiasts first, and their priorities are usually reflected in the music they release.

In the 1940s and 1950s, the blues enjoyed a much higher profile in the charts, carving out a sizable chunk of the R&B market. Independent labels like Chess, Sun, Vee-Jay, and Specialty were responsible for recording the greatest blues music of the era, often fostering production techniques that helped shape and advance the music itself. (The histories of these independents are detailed in other essays in this book.) But by the end of the 1950s, blues had lost much of its audience share to the onslaught of R&B and rock and roll; it would lose more in the '60s with the British Invasion, Motown, folk-rock, psychedelia, soul, and other tremors revolutionizing the world of popular music. Those independents that had recorded blues, if they survived into the 1960s, usually cut back or eliminated their blues rosters.

The decline of the blues as a commercial force, however, coincided with a couple of developments that would create an opening for entirely different kinds of independents. The late 1940s saw the introduction of the long-playing record, which in turn harvested more diverse sorts of productions than had been available on singles. The 1950s brought the stirrings of a folk/blues "revival" that widened the audience for blues music from its African-American base into an increasingly White and young listenership, often to be found in colleges and coffeehouses. Some of these fans were dedicated enough to write books on the subject, track down surviving blues legends, and make recordings of their own.

Some of the first modern blues independents took a folkloric approach to their releases, especially in the beginning. The **Prestige/Riverside/Bluesville** family, in addition to recording first-generation country bluesmen like Pink Anderson, arranged for John Lee Hooker and Snooks Eaglin to record acoustic (or at least solo) material for albums, although Hooker and Eaglin maintained simultaneous electric, full-band recording careers for the R&B market. Once the blues revival was in gear in the 1960s, **Testament** produced recordings of obscure country blues singers like Jack Owens, and also arranged for overlooked electric Chicago bluesmen like Johnny Shines to get some quality studio time. It even released an album of topical songs about John Kennedy shortly after he was assassinated.

Arhoolie, founded by German immigrant Chris Strachwitz, took a sort of field recording approach to some of its best releases. Driving around Texas and the South, as several blues scholars of the time did in hopes of encountering legends past and present, Strachwitz also took time to record some of the more interesting musicians with whom he crossed paths. His first release, Mance Lipscomb's *Texas Songster* (1960), initially pressed in a quantity of only 250 copies, is still in print. Lipscomb, like some of Arhoolie's other finds–Robert Pete Williams (actually recorded by Harry Oster in 1959 and 1960) was the most famous–had never recorded before. But the label also cut sessions, under pretty basic conditions, with performers who already had something of a reputation, such as Lightnin' Hopkins.

Arhoolie didn't limit itself to newly recorded sessions, arranging (to this day) for reissues of vintage material by Hopkins, Sonny Boy Williamson, and far more obscure performers such as Black Ace. They also don't limit themselves to blues, covering roots folk styles of all kinds–there are more cajun albums than blues ones in their catalog, which also includes quite a bit of world, country, and Tejano music. As we go to press in 1996, Arhoolie maintains a busy release schedule and large back catalog; they also founded the leading roots music mail-order service Down Home Music, which was sold to different ownership a few years ago.

By traveling to the source and recording their artists without adornment, Arhoolie was in some senses following the path of folklorists like the Lomaxes, who had recorded legends like Leadbelly, Muddy Waters, and Son House for the Library of Congress. Arhoolie releases, as well as similar ones by some other labels, differed from the Library of Congress and Folkways catalogs, however, in crucial respects. Sure, they aimed to preserve important elements of the blues tradition that were overlooked, or maybe even in danger of extinction. However, their albums were not primarily produced for academic archives, but for general listening pleasure. Commercial considerations were not paramount, but if the releases could help the musicians make a living, and generate enough profit to keep the label owners above water (and able to record more blues/roots music), so much the better.

At the outset of the blues revival, the new blues independents usually focused on acoustic recordings. This might have reflected the influence of the folk crowd buying many of the records, and the precedents set by folkloric field recordings of previous times. The electric blues was somehow felt by some to be more authentic, less sullied by the dirty waters of mass production. Electric blues continued to thrive, though, and by the mid-'60s it was obvious that the same people buying Rolling Stones and Paul Butterfield albums would also be willing to take a crack at LPs by living Chicago blues legends.

The Chicago-based **Delmark** label was instrumental in translating the energy of contemporary electric blues onto LP for the '60s market. Delmark owner Bob Koester had been recording acoustic blues since the 1950s, when he worked with musicians like Sleepy John Estes and Big Joe Williams. In the late 1950s, he moved to Chicago, where he operated the Jazz Record Mart retail store. The store was a meeting ground for many key musicians and supporters of the blues scene; employees who worked at the Jazz Record Mart at one time include guitarist Mike Bloomfield, harmonica player Charlie Musselwhite, the founders of *Living Blues* magazine, and some future label owners, including Bruce Iglauer (who now runs Alligator Records).

"The Jazz Record Mart was like a bridge between the blues world on the South and West Sides and the growing world of White international blues fans who hung out at the Jazz Record Mart, who came here to find out about gigs, musicians," Iglauer told the *Chicago Tribune* in 1993. "There were little signs, pieces of paper taped to the walls about various gigs at ghetto taverns.

"It was an incredible flow of musicians through there because it was one of the few ways that they could get a break. There weren't a lot of companies recording Chicago blues at that time, so musicians came to hang out at the Jazz Record Mart in hopes of attracting Bob's attention."

That's because Koester ran Delmark Records, which, like Arhoolie, did not limit itself to the blues, also releasing many fine and influential jazz albums by the likes of Sun Ra and the Art Ensemble of Chicago. He caught the lightning of Chicago electric club blues on record with his 1965 release by Junior Wells, *Hoodoo Man Blues*. As Koester claimed in the sleeve notes, "It is damn near the first LP by a Chicago blues band. Chess and a few other labels had reissued 45s by Muddy Waters, Sonny Boy Williamson, Howling Wolf, Jimmy Reed, Elmore James, etc. but virtually no one had tried to capture the Chicago blues sound free of the limitations of jukebox/airplay promotion."

Like some of the best blues producers, Koester realized that a less-is-more approach emphasizing spontaneity would make his artists comfortable and yield the best results in the studio. As Wells recalled in the same *Chicago Tribune* article, "When I did 'Hoodoo Man' for a guy a long time ago on a 78, he took it over to the radio station and asked them to play it. They threw it on the floor and broke it, stomped on it. When I started recording for Bob, he wanted me to do the 'Hoodoo Man' and I really wasn't interested in doing it because of the disappointment from what happened to me when I was much younger. He kept talking to me about it, so I tried it and I'm proud of the record now … Bob was the type of person, he just made everything so easy, you couldn't help but to get something good from it. He just let you go with it."

Hoodoo Man Blues also featured Buddy Guy on guitar (early pressings of the album credited the guitar work to the transparent pseudonym of "Friendly Chap"). *Hoodoo Man Blues* eventually passed the 50,000 mark in sales, an astronomical number for an independent blues album. It remains the best seller in the Delmark catalog, but the label would also record quite a few other important titles, most notably by Magic Sam, J.B. Hutto, Jimmy Dawkins, and Luther Allison. Koester's label and store are still going strong today, though Koester himself is semi-retired.

Other labels made some important recordings of '60s electric blues for the LP market. **Vanguard**, which had already recorded significant acoustic '60s blues in the studio and at the Newport Folk Festivals, produced the excellent three-volume *The Blues Today!* series, featuring tracks by Wells, J.B. Hutto, Otis Spann, Otis Rush, Johnny Shines, James Cotton, and others. **Verve** (which was distributed by MGM) recorded LPs with Cotton that also crossed over to the rock audience to some extent. The label that would truly take electric Chicago blues to the end of the century, however, was the one founded by Bruce Iglauer, Alligator.

Iglauer was inspired to found Alligator, as he writes in the liner notes to the label's 25th anniversary collection, "by the music that I heard in the little clubs on the South and West Sides in the Black neighborhoods, where the city's (and the world's) greatest blues bands made music for their local fans. The blues clubs had been the heart of Chicago's Black music scene for over 30 years before I arrived there as a 'blues pilgrim' back in 1970. These weren't show lounges or theaters, but corner bars and taverns, often in grimly depressed neighborhoods, that put a chain across the doorway on weekends and charged 50 cents or a dollar to hear some of the most intense, fiery, and deeply emotional music you can imagine."

For a long time, Alligator was a one-man show, run by Iglauer out of his apartment. Releases by artists like Son Seals, Fenton Robinson, and Hound Dog Taylor put Alligator on the map, but the label didn't become a force until its *Living Chicago Blues* series of the late 1970s and early 1980s, exposing major overlooked talents such as Jimmy Johnson. Over five years later, the similar *New Bluebloods* anthology did the same for another generation of Chicago blues, including tracks by the Kinsey Report, Lil' Ed & the Blues Imperials, and Valerie Wellington.

Today Alligator's staff has swelled to over 20, and there are more than 150 albums in the catalog. Plenty of Chicago artists continue to record for the label, but Alligator has made a determined effort to seek talent from outside the region in recent years, including some Louisiana swamp blues performers. Uptempo Chicago-style blues is Alligator's most distinguishing trademark, but the roster has become fairly diverse, including White blues-rockers like Johnny Winter and Elvin Bishop, roots music gadfly Delbert McClinton, and acoustic artists Cephas & Wiggins, Saffire, and Corey Harris. It's also given several old-school veterans who were unable to pick up a contract for years a new lease on life, such as harmonica player Billy Boy Arnold. It also reissued long-unavailable recordings of primeval blues from the '50s from the Trumpet label.

Despite selling only about 10,000-25,000 copies of the average title, Alligator dominates the contemporary indie blues market; sometimes it seems that every other blues Grammy goes to the Alligator label. There are several other companies dedicated to the work of contemporary electric blues bands, Black and White, including Blind Pig, Black Top, and Antone's. There also continue to be roots/folk labels that issue occasional blues albums, such as Ichiban, Hightone, and Flying Fish.

Not every post-1960 blues label limited its aims to the collector audience. The most successful of these may have been **Malaco**, which in the minds of some fans is as much a soul/R&B label as a blues label. Its roster included soul stars fallen on leaner times, such as Johnnie Taylor and Bobby "Blue" Bland, as well as some younger acts. While much of their catalog appealed to the blues audience, it undoubtedly aimed for, and got, many listeners who hungered for some contemporary Southern soul-styled music in the absence of such recordings in the disco/dance/rap-dominated R&B charts. Z.Z. Hill's *Down Home Blues* (1982) was an unexpected commercial success, proving that not all independent blues albums had to be confined to a ghettoized listenership.

For those who found Malaco's brand of Southern blues/soul too slick, alternatives arose in the early 1990s that were rawer and more down-home than they probably could have imagined. The Mississippi-based **Fat Possum** label was founded in the early 1990s by two *Living Blues* contributors in their twenties, Matthew Johnson and Peter Lee. Dissatisfied with what they perceived as the unwarranted slickness of many contemporary blues recordings, they headed out to their own back yard for something different, cruising the juke joints and country stores of rural Mississippi, where a fierce and untamed brand of electric blues was played for the locals. The result was recordings by artists like R.L. Burnside and Junior Kimbrough that got some of the most positive critical attention of any 1990s blues releases.

Johnson told the *Boston Phoenix* that he and Lee decided to form Fat Possum "after hearing so many slick albums that sound nothing like what you hear on a Saturday night in Mississippi. We're trying to get a quality that's different from most of the other blues records you hear today. I find most of the blues records coming out just unlistenable. What is primitive to most people, we would consider slick. We prefer what [music critic and producer] Bob Palmer calls 'guerrilla recording,' just going out into the bars and juke joints and letting the tape roll."

It's tempting to think of Fat Possum's proprietors as updated variations of the blues revivalists of the 1960s, who searched the Southern back roads for living exponents of deep acoustic blues, overlooked and forgotten by the modern world. A difference, of course, is that these are electric musicians, playing not on their porches, but in centers of day-to-day community life. Their relative isolation from the urban world has resulted in a certain primitive quality–replete with odd tunings and unsteady time meters–that seems unaffected by the slicker qualities of contemporary music. Artists like CeDell Davis, who plays an irregularly tuned guitar with a table knife, are, if not representative of a dying breed, at the very least unique. The earthy quality of the Fat Possum releases is

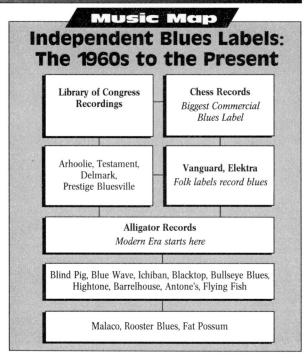

Independent Blues Labels: The 1960s to the Present

Library of Congress Recordings	**Chess Records** *Biggest Commercial Blues Label*
Arhoolie, Testament, Delmark, Prestige Bluesville	**Vanguard, Elektra** *Folk labels record blues*

Alligator Records
Modern Era starts here

Blind Pig, Blue Wave, Ichiban, Blacktop, Bullseye Blues, Hightone, Barrelhouse, Antone's, Flying Fish

Malaco, Rooster Blues, Fat Possum

maintained by a pared-to-the-bone recording budget. Most albums are recorded in a day or two, in facilities like Jimmy's Auto Care in Oxford, Mississippi; the total budget for a full-length recording has never exceeded $4,000.

Despite the acclaim that's rung through higher echelons like the *New York Times*, Fat Possum's sales haven't torn the roof off the juke joint. After their first release (R.L. Burnside's *Bad Luck City*) moved 713 units, it considered folding. But the partners found an investor in John Herrmann, who plays keyboards for the Southern rock group Widespread Panic. Widespread Panic's label, Capricorn, is now distributing Fat Possum. The involvement of rock/blues scholar Robert Palmer in several releases as producer has also helped raise the label's profile.

Living Blues magazine founder Jim O'Neal's Mississippi-based **Rooster Blues** label makes similar albums. His activities led him to a bona fide modern-day blues rediscovery of harmonica player Willie Cobb, who wrote the standard "You Don't Love Me." He refutes the notion that Rooster Blues and Fat Possum are comparable to archivists, bringing independent blues labels full circle to the folkloric activities of the late '50s and early '60s.

"The very little [recording] that was done over the past three decades or so was mostly folklorists or Europeans doing some kind of field recording," he told *Billboard*. "The contemporary blues here–the blues you were hearing in the juke joints–wasn't getting recorded. There's a void to be filled. There's still a lot of great talent. It's the birthplace of the blues, and it's still giving birth to a lot of great artists."

Concurred Fat Possum's Matthew Johnson in the *Boston Phoenix*, "We're not some kind of purists making field recordings. This is rockin' stuff; this music gets people moving. The stuff that purists go for is just garbage to me. Especially the acoustic records. Nobody plays acoustic guitar anymore except rich white people. Down here, a musician's got the juke box to compete with. The guys in Mississippi are the first to chuck their acoustic guitars when they bring back some good festival money." *–Richie Unterberger*

10 Recommended Albums:
Mance Lipscomb, *Texas Songster* (Arhoolie)
Dr. Isiah Ross, *Call The Doctor* (Testament)
Various Artists, *Great Bluesmen at Newport* (Vanguard)
Junior Wells, *Hoodoo Man Blues* (Delmark)
Magic Sam, *West Side Soul* (Delmark)
Various Artists, *Chicago: The Blues Today! Vol. 1-3* (Vanguard)
Various Artists, *Living Chicago Blues, Vol. 1-4* (Alligator)
Various Artists, *New Bluebloods* (Alligator)
Various Artists, *25th Anniversary Collection* (Alligator)
R.L. Burnside, *Bad Luck City* (Fat Possum)

The Blues as Folklore

The onslaught of the Depression in the 1930s spelled the end of the recording careers for many blues artists, as well as nipping many others in the bud before they had even had a chance to begin. Between the mid-1930s and mid-1950s, country blues was documented on record sporadically. The commercial record companies of the time had turned their attention elsewhere; wide interest in the blues' roots, from national and/or White audiences, wouldn't gain momentum until the seeds of the blues/folk revival were planted in the late 1950s.

Our archive of country blues style from this era–and indeed, our knowledge of traditional blues as a whole–would be much poorer if not for the pioneering efforts of a few dedicated folklorists. The institution most responsible for preserving this work was the Library of Congress, who arranged for important field recordings for use in their collection. While the tone and packaging of these performances could tend toward the scholarly and museum-like, more often they resulted in music that, unfettered by commercial considerations of sales and image, gave us a glimpse of authentic blues and folk.

By far the most important of these archivists were John A. Lomax and his son Alan. The senior Lomax, a colorful figure worthy of a book of his own, had been collecting songs since his teenage years in the Southwest. After education at Harvard, he continued his field work on a more formal basis. As early as 1907, he made cylinder recordings of cowboy songs, which are the first folk songs in English to be recorded by an American. In 1910 he published a collection, *Cowboy Songs and Other Frontier Ballads*, one of the most famous works of its sort.

In the early 1930s, however, Lomax was struggling to make a living at his chosen profession. It was with great enthusiasm that he became curator of the Library of Congress' Archive of Folk Song. The Archive had been established in 1928, but under Lomax's efforts it would truly fulfill its mission of recording and preserving important American folk music. In these endeavors, he was greatly aided by his son, Alan, who was still a teenager when the Lomaxes set out to collect songs for John's *American Folk Songs and Ballads* project in 1933. The work would also involve a lot of recording, with what was then considered state-of-the-art portable equipment (which weighed a good 315 pounds).

The Lomaxes had only been on the road for a little over a month when they hit more paydirt than they could have ever expected. They did some of their recording in prison, figuring that long-time inmates were more apt to preserve traditional styles in the absence of contact from the outside world. July 1933 found them at Louisiana's Angola Penitentiary, where they discovered 12-string guitarist and singer Leadbelly, one of the major figures in 20th-century American music. In addition to being a galvanizing performer, Leadbelly was also a walking encyclopedia of American folk song, his repertoire encompassing blues, folk, spirituals, and more.

As Charles Wolfe & Kip Lornell observe in *The Life & Legend of Leadbelly*, "The recordings by Leadbelly made by the Lomaxes had historical significance beyond the fact that they were the first ones of a man who would become a major figure in American music. The whole idea of using a phonograph to preserve authentic folk music was still fairly new. Most of John Lomax's peers were involved in collecting songs the classic way: taking both words and melody down by hand, asking the singer to perform the song over and over until the collector had 'caught' it on paper…

"John Lomax sensed at once the limitations of this kind of method, especially when getting songs from African-American singers, whose quarter tones, blue notes, and complex timing often frustrated White musicians trying to transcribe them with European notation systems. The whole concept of field recording was, in 1933 and still today, radically different from the popular notion of recording. Field recordings are not intended as commercial products, but as attempts at cultural preservation. There is no profit motive, nor any desire to make the singer a 'star.' As have hundreds of folk song collectors after him, John Lomax had to persuade his singers to perform, to explain to them why their songs were important, and to convince the various authorities–the wardens, the trusties, the bureaucrats–that this was serious, worthwhile work. He faced the moral problem of how to safeguard the records and the rights of the singers–a problem he solved in this instance by donating the discs to the Library of Congress.

"He had to overcome the technical problems involved in recording outside a studio; one always hoped for quiet, with no doors slamming or alarms going off, but it was always a risk. His new state-of-the-art recording machine sported a new microphone designed by NBC, but there were no wind baffles to help reduce the noise when recording outside. Lomax learned how to balance sound, where to place microphones, how to work echoes and walls, and soon was a skilled recordist."

Leadbelly was released from prison shortly afterwards, becoming an assistant/chauffeur of sorts to Lomax. Their stormy relationship would dissolve with some acrimony within a few years, but not before Leadbelly had started a successful professional career, introducing many folk and blues classics to the public before his death in 1949. His Library of Congress recordings, eventually numbering over 200 songs, constitute much of his most important recorded work.

John and Alan Lomax didn't record only blues, or even focus on the blues. They recorded all sorts of folk music, from many different regions, including Cajun music, narratives of ex-slaves, and songs from California labor camps. By the late 1930s, John Lomax, already into his sixties, was less active in the field than Alan, who also recorded jazz, preserving a dozen albums' worth of Jelly Roll Morton singing and talking. Alan also recorded pianists Albert Ammons, Meade Lux Lewis, and Pete Johnson for the Library of Congress around the time of the famous Spirituals to Swing concert (which took place in New York City's Carnegie Hall in 1938). All three of those pianists, though really part of jazz, made their imprint on blues history by helping to popularize the boogie-woogie style. The elder Lomax was not retired, and in 1940 made a significant contribution to the blues library by recording Blind Willie McTell.

Alan undertook his most important blues sessions on behalf of the Library of Congress in the early 1940s, as part of a project documenting Black music in Coahoma County, Mississippi. On these trips he found Muddy Waters and Son House, whose recordings were summaries of Delta blues styles past and present. House (who, apparently unbeknownst to Lomax, had already recorded a few commercial sides) would soon move to New York State, not to be rediscovered until the 1960s blues revival. Waters, who recorded for Lomax as an acoustic guitarist, would take Delta blues into the future after moving to Chicago in 1943. Lomax also made interesting deep blues recordings in 1946 with Big Bill Broonzy, Sonny Boy Williamson, and Memphis Slim that also included, as many of the Library of Congress recordings do, conversation with the participants; this was issued by Rykodisc in the 1990s as *Blues in the Mississippi Night*.

Alan Lomax, as stated previously, was not a blues specialist. He devoted the next five decades to championing folk music of all sorts. His late '50s recordings of styles associated with the American South, available on Atlantic's *The Songs of the South* box set, resulted in the discovery of Mississippi Fred McDowell (who had never previously recorded), who became one of the most popular acoustic performers of the '60s blues revival. He was a director of the Newport Folk Festival, and his staunch love of traditional styles led to some notoriety when he expressed resistance to the introduction of electric instruments into festival events in the mid-'60s. Much of his life is recounted in his 1993 book, *The Land Where the Blues Began*.

The Library of Congress was not the sole organization dedicated to preserving traditional blues on record. Moe Asch's Folkways label, which began operations in the 1940s, recorded a mammoth body of folk music of all sorts, which naturally included some blues. Leadbelly, Brownie McGhee, and Sonny Terry were some of the most prominent blues artists who did some recordings for the Folkways label. Before his death, Asch sold the Folkways catalog to the Smithsonian, which is engaged in an ongoing series of CD reissues of important Folkways sessions.

Some of the early albums arising from the 1960s blues revival were folk-

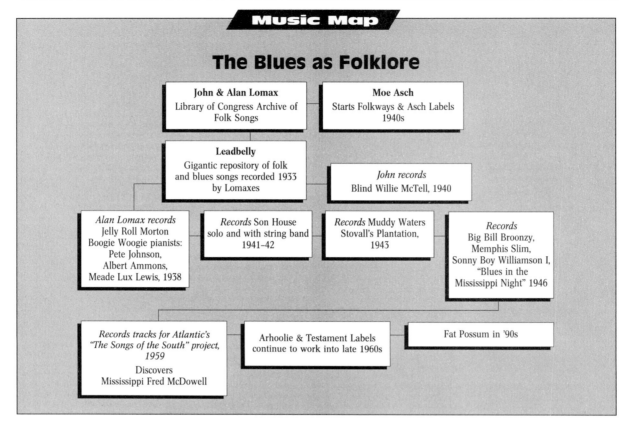

Music Map

The Blues as Folklore

John & Alan Lomax
Library of Congress Archive of Folk Songs

Moe Asch
Starts Folkways & Asch Labels
1940s

Leadbelly
Gigantic repository of folk and blues songs recorded 1933 by Lomaxes

John records
Blind Willie McTell, 1940

Alan Lomax records
Jelly Roll Morton
Boogie Woogie pianists:
Pete Johnson,
Albert Ammons,
Meade Lux Lewis, 1938

Records Son House
solo and with string band
1941–42

Records Muddy Waters
Stovall's Plantation,
1943

Records
Big Bill Broonzy,
Memphis Slim,
Sonny Boy Williamson I,
"Blues in the
Mississippi Night" 1946

*Records tracks for Atlantic's
"The Songs of the South" project,
1959*
Discovers
Mississippi Fred McDowell

Arhoolie & Testament Labels
continue to work into late 1960s

Fat Possum in '90s

loric in bent, inasmuch as they documented living exponents of rural traditions. There was Robert Pete Williams, for instance, discovered (like Leadbelly) at Angola Penitentiary in the late 1950s. The Arhoolie label presented many blues and folk artists *au naturel*, coming up with a major find in Texas songster Mance Lipscomb. Testament Records issued titles by Jack Owens, Mississippi Fred McDowell, and others. Yet these recordings differed from the Library of Congress and Folkways sessions in that they were less geared toward, well, the library, and more for the general listener. They were not just concerned with documenting obscure and threatened styles, but in presenting material that could be enjoyed on its own terms, and prove modestly profitable in a small commercial niche market.

That doesn't mean that the Library of Congress recordings need to remain stored in the library. The performers the Lomaxes and others recorded may not have been playing for the general consumer, but they often gave their all. To an extent that the folklorists may not have realized, their work can serve purposes that are entertaining and inspirational, as well as educational.

—Richie Unterberger

11 Recommended Albums:

Leadbelly, *Midnight Special* (Rounder)
Leadbelly, *Leadbelly Sings Folk Songs* (Smithsonian/ Folkways)
Various Artists, *Afro-American Blues and Game Songs* (Library of Congress)
Various Artists, *Negro Blues and Hollers* (Library of Congress)
Various Artists, *Negro Work Songs and Calls* (Library of Congress)
Muddy Waters, *The Complete Plantation Recordings* (MCA)
Son House, *Delta Blues: The Original Library of Congress Sessions from Field Recordings 1941–42* (Biograph)
Blind Willie McTell, *Complete Library of Congress Recordings (1940)* (Document)
Various Artists, *Brownie McGhee & Sonny Terry Sing* (Smithsonian/Folkways)
Various Artists, *Blues in the Mississippi Night* (Rykodisc)

Robert Pete Williams, *Angola Prisoner's Blues* (Arhoolie)

The Blues Revival

Any retrospective of the 1960s blues revival begs a rhetorical question: How could the blues be revived when it wasn't dead? Yes, in some respects, the blues scene was struggling in the late 1950s. The blues' presence on the R&B charts had been diminished by rock 'n' roll, doo-wop, and pure R&B recordings that were pointing the way for soul music. Country blues was rarely recorded; many of its greatest heroes had vanished into obscurity or died.

Yet the blues had never come close to dying. In urban centers, especially Chicago, electric blues legends continued to perform and record regularly, though they may have peaked in terms of vinyl sales. Hit blues singles on the R&B and even pop charts were not unknown; Jimmy Reed and John Lee Hooker had some of their biggest hits around 1960. Although the commercial market for acoustic blues was virtually nonexistent, many performers continued to play the music in Mississippi, Memphis, Texas, and elsewhere, either professionally, for their family or friends, or (in relatively rare cases) behind prison bars.

The "blues revival" really does not refer to the rebirth of the music, but an awakening of wider interest in the blues, particularly among younger White listeners. During its first few decades, blues recordings had been primarily marketed to Black consumers, and primarily played live to Black audiences. Blues performers that made a big impression with White listeners often had a good measure of crossover folk appeal, such as Leadbelly and Josh White. Names like Robert Johnson, Bukka White, and Charley Patton were virtually unknown; electric blues stars like Muddy Waters and Elmore James were not as totally obscure, but still little recognized within the White audience.

But in the late 1950s and early 1960s, young Whites were starting to trace American roots music backwards from rock 'n' roll, through to its sources in blues and folk. Often they were college-educated and relatively affluent, with affiliations in both the countercultural and academic communities. Some have taken a sociological perspective and mused that these listeners were rebelling

Music Map

Blues Revival

Oldtime	Electric Originators	White guys plug in
Bluesmen play for White audiences as part of Folk Music Revival, 1960s.	*(Who reach white audiences)*	*early-to-mid-'60s*
Son House, Skip James, Mississippi John Hurt, Lightnin' Hopkins, John Lee Hooker	Muddy Waters, Howlin' Wolf, Sonny Boy Williamson, Albert King, B.B. King, Freddie King, Slim Harpo, Lightnin' Slim, Buddy Guy	Paul Butterfield Blues Band, John Mayall's Bluesbreakers, The Rolling Stones, The Animals, The Yardbirds

against their comfortable, conformist upbringings, or hungering for an authenticity that they had been denied. The simpler explanation is that the blues was too good a thing to be kept a secret: larger and larger groups of Americans were responding to the power and magic of the music, especially after the blues revival made it easier to discover, hear, and see.

A small band of enthusiasts–their curiosity piqued by the great recordings they had been able to locate, and the little information that was available to them–began to undertake serious record collecting, documentation, and recording of the blues. Writers like Samuel Charters and Paul Oliver did a lot to get the ball rolling by publishing studies of the evolution of the blues that were both serious and accessible. Folklorists like Alan Lomax (who had been recording blues and folk for many years), and just plain fans like Chris Strachwitz and guitar virtuoso John Fahey, tracked down or discovered downhome blues singers for recording purposes. Often these champions of the blues would double as writers, record producers, promoters, and managers, fueled by their consuming love of the music.

Initially, the blues revival was acoustic in tone. This may have been the result of purists who felt that the authenticity of the music was smothered by electric amplification that pulled it from its populist roots (a theory that doesn't hold up well in light of the fact that millions of working-class African-Americans were listening to electric blues regularly). It could have also been a side effect of the coffeehouse/college circuit that promoted most blues shows for the White college audience in the early '60s, which emphasized acoustic performers, not electric ones. Many of the White singers on the early '60s folk scene would include blues material in their sets, most notably Dave Van Ronk, Bob Dylan, and the trio of Koerner, Ray, & Glover.

The blues revival was aided and abetted by the development of the LP market. In 1960, those blues artists who recorded for an almost exclusively Black/R&B audience concentrated almost solely upon 45 RPM singles. To address the Whiter and more affluent market, they would focus upon long-playing records. In some cases, blues singers would maintain separate careers for the different markets, such as Snooks Eaglin, who recorded New Orleans R&B for Imperial, and as the blues/folk streetsinger Blind Snooks Eaglin for Prestige. John Lee Hooker had R&B hits with a full electric band, like "Boom Boom," at the same time he was recording acoustic LPs; the liner notes to some of his early albums seem almost apologetic about his electric recordings, as if to infer that his acoustic albums were more authentic.

Several labels addressed the widening White audience for blues, including Arhoolie, Testament, and the Prestige/Riverside/ Bluesville family. Often they brought original bluesmen of the '20s and '30s back to the studio after several decades of professional retirement, or even found some elderly acoustic blues singers who had never received the opportunities to record in the first place (phenomenons which are examined in more depth in a separate essay). Large festivals booked these artists and made live recordings of the events, the most notable of which was the Newport Folk Festival. And blues performers began to cross the Atlantic in large numbers for European tours, which both exposed the music on a whole new international scale, and gave the performers themselves a sense of just how much they were treasured, by an audience they hadn't quite expected to reach.

The initial impetus of the blues revival largely ignored contemporary electric performers, but the purist ethic couldn't survive for long. In England at least, the die had been cast back in 1958, when Muddy Waters first toured Britain. American bluesmen had already been touring the country earlier in the 1950s, with assistance from British jazz and blues musicians like Chris Barber and Alexis Korner. Apparently British audiences conceived of the blues as a primarily acoustic medium as well, and were astounded when Waters showed up with an electric guitar. That proved too loud and brash for some British listeners and critics, who might have saved themselves the shock if they had just listened to a few of Muddy's records, virtually all of which were Chicago electric blues.

Recalled Waters in James Rooney's *Bossmen*, "When I first went to England in '58 I didn't have no idea what was going on. I was touring with Chris Barber–a Dixieland band. They thought I was a Big Bill Broonzy–which I wasn't. I had my amplifier and [pianist Otis] Spann and I was going to do a Chicago thing; we opened up in Leeds, England. I was definitely too loud for them then. The next morning we were in the headlines of the paper– 'Screaming Guitar and Howling Piano.' That was when they were into the folk thing before the Rolling Stones."

When he made his next British tour in 1962, the tide had shifted. "I went back–took my acoustic with me–and everybody's hollering, 'Where's your amplifier?' I said, 'When I was here before they didn't like my stuff.' But those English groups had picked up on my stuff and went wild with it. I said, 'I never know what's going on.' A bunch of those young kids came around. They could play. They'd pick up my guitar and fool with it. Then the Rolling Stones came out named after my song, you know, and recorded 'Just Make Love to Me' and the next I knew they were out there. And that's how people in the States really got to know who Muddy Waters was."

Young musicians like the Rolling Stones were making their own brand of rhythm and blues, inspired by artists like Muddy Waters; Mick Jagger and Keith Richard had discovered their mutual interest in the music, in fact, when Keith spotted Mick carrying a Chess Records album in a train. They and other early British Invasion bands like the Yardbirds, Animals, Them, and the Kinks covered many blues and R&B songs on their early records, inventing a form of rock 'n' roll with heavy roots in the sources. Young British and American listeners were bound to be curious about the songs' original performers and writers, leading them back to the bluesmen and blueswomen themselves, many of whom were still in their prime.

Some purists have accused such bands of exploiting the music for their own ends, watering it down for a White teenage audience to achieve a commercial success that wouldn't have been possible with the real deal. It's an argument that doesn't wash for a lot of people. These groups were genuinely exciting and original, and quickly evolved from covering import records into writing their own material. Bands like the Beatles, Stones, and John Mayall's Bluesbreakers never made a secret of their influences, often taking time to publicly praise and acknowledge their inspirations, and refusing to pretend that they were the first to be playing such music; Jagger once commented in an interview, "What's the point in listening to us doing 'I'm a King Bee' when you can hear Slim Harpo do it?" The Rolling Stones went as far as to record at Chess Studios during their first tour, and to have Howlin' Wolf perform with them on television in the mid-'60s.

By the mid-'60s, America was beginning to develop its own White blues rockers, particularly in Chicago. Paul Butterfield led the best of these bands, which also included guitarists Michael Bloomfield and Elvin Bishop, as well as a Black rhythm section of veterans from the Chicago blues/R&B scene. Also gigging in Chicago were harmonica player Charlie Musselwhite and, (for a time) Steve Miller. In Southern California, one of the leading collectors of rare blues records, Bob Hite, helped form one of the most successful blues-rock bands of the late '60s, Canned Heat.

The blues-rock acts are discussed in a separate essay; their importance to the blues revival was helping to focus attention not just on acoustic bluesmen, but on Black electric blues bands and guitarists, many of whom had only been active for a decade or less, hardly qualifying for "revival." This also meant that such electric performers could now take a crack at the LP market, particularly if their 45 chart action wasn't so hot. Chess had already tried to sell Muddy Waters to the blues revival crowd with an album entitled *Muddy Waters, Folk Singer,* which actually wasn't much different from his prime electric material.

The Delmark label was one of the first to take the plunge into electric blues albums, with Junior Wells and Magic Sam. Wells' *Hoodoo Man Blues* (1965) is sometimes referred to as the first electric blues session conceived of as an *album* rather than a collection of tracks, and made no attempt to dilute the power or lower the volume for White listeners. Verve did the same with James Cotton, and Vanguard's excellent *The Blues Today!* series did much to present the blues as a living, thriving, often electric medium, not one that had to be presented as a sort of living museum piece in order to qualify for approval.

The albums in turn helped performers like Wells, Albert King, B.B. King, and Buddy Guy break into a whole new circuit that could find them sharing the bill with White rock bands, and playing to larger audiences that could include as many or more Whites as Blacks. Nor did their festival appearances have to be at folk events, which sometimes weren't eager to book electric acts; festivals devoted to blues, or giving equal weight to blues and jazz, began to appear, such as the Ann Arbor Blues Festival. Both enterprising small independents and large major labels belatedly became aware of the thousands of classic blues sides that were unavailable, leading to blues reissues programs that continue to expand to this day.

By the end of the 1960s, blues was not a dominant force on the commercial market, but nobody was checking for vital signs either–many of its greatest musicians were performing to bigger audiences, and making better livelihoods, than they ever had. Since then, there's more or less constant talk of the blues making a comeback, or surging in popularity–but never talk of the blues dying. The blues, it seems, will never die–and never need to be "revived" again.

—*Richie Unterberger*

10 Recommended Albums:

Various Artists, *Blues Masters, Vol. 7: Blues Revival* (Rhino)
Various Artists, *Blues at Newport: Newport Folk Festival 1959–64*
   (Vanguard)
Various Artists, *Chicago: The Blues Today! Vol. 1–3* (Vanguard)
Robert Pete Williams, *Angola Prisoner's Blues* (Arhoolie)
John Lee Hooker, *The Country Blues of John Lee Hooker* (Prestige)
Mance Lipscomb, *Texas Sharecropper & Songster* (Arhoolie)
Muddy Waters, *Folk Singer* (Chess)
The Rolling Stones, *The Rolling Stones (England's Newest Hitmakers)*
   (ABKCO)
The Paul Butterfield Blues Band, *The Paul Butterfield Blues Again* (Elektra)
John Mayall, *Bluesbreakers with Eric Clapton* (PolyGram)

The Blues Box Set

Some would say that the blues was never meant to be an elite kind of thing, displayed on the mantelpiece like some kind of trophy. With the widespread popularity of the box set in the 1990s, though, that's what it sometimes becomes. The proliferation of box sets could be taken as an indication of the respect that classic rock, pop, and blues now generates in our culture (and marketplace). Not everyone, however, is certain that box sets are fulfilling their mission of offering the biggest bang for the buck.

Box sets have been a part of the music business for decades, although they were initially much more apt to be employed for classical recordings or special projects, like scholarly ethnomusicology documentaries. For the pop and rock audience, occasional box sets were produced (often in limited press runs) for artists with unusually devoted followings, like the Beatles, Elvis, and Brian Eno. This started to change in the mid-'80s, when a five-record live Bruce Springsteen box became a best seller. Around the same time, a Bob Dylan box set, *Biograph,* entered the Top Forty, which probably helped convince labels that there was a viable market for multi-disc archival retrospectives.

Biograph also set a model of sorts for box set packages: some classic hits, some key album cuts, some rarities, and some previously unreleased material, as well as a lavish booklet. It took a while for this new strategy to trickle down to the blues world. After all, a very small percentage of record owners of any kind ever buy box sets; an even smaller number buy them on anything approaching a regular basis. And, as we all know too well, the blues represents a very small share of the overall demographic that consumes music.

On the other hand, blues fans, at the risk of generalizing, take their music more seriously than the average Joe. Import companies such as Charly and

Bear Family had realized this even before the mid-'80s, producing occasional box sets aimed squarely at the collector. And when they decided to go the box set route, they really went to town, often tracking down every item available, and raiding the vault for unreleased treasures and alternate takes.

When American companies began to issue blues boxes, they were considerably more selective, which is a mixed blessing. Many listeners, to be honest, lack the interest or patience to wade through every last B-side, or to hear successive alternate takes of the same song in a row. Box sets could be regarded as a selective weeding of an artist's oeuvre, in which only the very cream of the crop is bundled into a nifty package.

The Chess label, in particular, tapped into the market with enthusiasm, giving Muddy Waters, Howlin' Wolf, Willie Dixon, Chuck Berry, and Bo Diddley the box set treatment. There were also various artist box sets covering Chess material as a whole, an approach also employed by Specialty (which is now owned by Fantasy). Capricorn dug into the vaults of some somewhat obscure labels, such as Fire/Fury, Swingtime, Jewel/Paula, and Cobra. And the Robert Johnson box set (which was actually only two discs) was the surprise success story of the decade, selling several hundred thousand copies.

Not a great many blues heroes command a large enough following to make domestic box sets a viable proposition. Accordingly, plenty of two-disc packages are produced, sometimes in slip-cases, that fall just shy of bona fide "box" status. With the CD affording room for as much as 80 minutes a disc, however, such anthologies actually cram in as much music as would have fit on three or four average-length vinyl LPs. Chess, Legacy, and Rhino have been particularly active in establishing lines of double CDs; the recently established Capitol Blues series sometimes does this as well, and occasionally fits in *three* CDs to a standard-sized package, as they did with T-Bone Walker and John Lee Hooker.

Are there box sets out there that serve as introductions to the blues as a whole, or important blues styles? Not as many as you might think. Licensing hurdles, for one thing, are formidable obstacles to assembling material from many different labels in one place; even if they can be overcome, labels may find that complicated process not worth the bother or the expense. Thus it is that most various artist boxes tend to be material from the same label. The Smithsonian has put together a couple of all-purpose-type introductions to the blues, although listeners with a reasonably sizable blues collection may find little there that they don't already own. The 15-volume *Blues Masters* series on Rhino is really the best project of that sort ever attempted, but it isn't available in the box form, except for a package containing the first five volumes. A box that had all 15 might be a desirable thing, but would certainly cost in the neighborhood of $200 or more.

In any event, however, a lot of boxes don't exactly turn out to be the last word. Labels often can't resist adding some hard-to-find tracks: B-sides, unreleased outtakes, live cuts, and the like. The presence of such material is usually quite welcome. The problem is that the collectors who covet such morsels almost inevitably own the bulk of the famous material on the box set already, sometimes several times over. And the more general fan, who's buying the box mostly for the "hits," doesn't really care about the unreleased material, or finds it something of a distraction from the main menu.

All of which leads the collector to pose some pretty tough, but merited, questions. Who is the typical box set–with its mixture of hits, rarities, and album cuts–really satisfying? The casual fan will be more likely to pick up a greatest hits collection, or one or two albums, and leave it at that. The completist isn't satisfied either; it's rare that a box will doggedly cover everything that an artist has released during a certain time period, or for a certain label. For that, the big league collector will still favor those obscure import companies that do the job right.

Listeners who are serious fans of an artist, but not unduly concerned with fancy packaging or remastering, find themselves caught in the middle. Enticed by rare and unreleased cuts that appear on almost every one of these sets–but rarely make up the majority of the content–they often find themselves paying quite a few dollars for the five to 15 cuts from a multi-disc box that they really want, and repurchasing quite a bit of music that they already have in their collections, and had no intention of buying again. And it's rare that a record company will accomodate these discerning listeners by issuing a separate collection that only contains the sought-after rarities. You could say that box sets give you access to more blues music than ever before–but at a higher price.

—*Richie Unterberger*

Blues Reissues

Taxes, global warming, geopolitical strife, overpopulation, pollution, invasion of privacy by super-sophisticated technologies ... ah, but living in the 1990s does have its small pleasures. One advantage that won't make as many headlines as the above calamities is the increasing ease of collecting vintage blues music. It is no exaggeration to say that, on the whole, it's much easier to collect blues recordings of the 1920s, or blues recordings of the 1950s, now than it was when the music was first released. Not everything's been reissued, of course, but today's blues collector is offered (some would say confronted) with a dazzling variety of options that would have been unimaginable even 20 years ago. Dozens of companies in the U.S. and abroad offer an extensive line of blues reissues of all styles; some labels specialize in nothing but the blues.

Part of the reason the blues needed to be "revived" in the 1960s was that the music itself was so hard to come by on record. There's a bit of romance attached to the old days, when being a blues collector was akin to being a member of a secret society. Finding original blues 78s by the likes of Son House and Blind Lemon Jefferson involved searching through thrift stores, garage sales, warehouses, old radio station libraries, or canvassing neighborhoods in which the residents were likely to own the singles (and part with them for a monetary sum). Finding old singles of just a few years back by electric Chicago bluesmen was no easy task either. Some of the most active blues collectors became celebrities themselves, such as Bob Hite (who helped form Canned Heat), acoustic guitarist John Fahey, and Barry Hansen, who gained fame as syndicated radio personality Dr. Demento.

Getting there is sometimes half the fun in record collecting, and no doubt there was an element of excitement involved in diving into a dumpster on the edge of town that's missing these days when we drive down to the local mini-mall. Most blues fans, though, cannot spare the time for such pursuits, chained to more mundane realities like jobs and families. Nor, frankly, do most of us want to spend weekends (or weeks) on end in search of the original recordings. For the most part, you can't beat blues reissues for convenience, in terms of both time and money saved.

Ever since the LP was introduced, there have been various artist and single artist blues compilations. Many (if not most) Chess Records albums of the 1950s and 1960s were essentially compilations of singles, offering handy primers for those born too late to get the original 45s, or those who simply wanted the best of them in one place. But overall, the reissue programs of big and small labels in the 1950s and 1960s were sporadic, perhaps because they didn't always have an idea of how large the potential audience was, or to whom it should be marketed. Robert Johnson's vastly influential *King of the Delta Blues Singers* LP, for instance, appeared in the early '60s on Columbia as a roots-of-jazz sort of title.

The true impetus for comprehensive blues reissues programs came from unexpected sources. British and European blues fans had long been remarkably enthusiastic collectors, dating back to the early '60s, when English kids like Mick Jagger would actually mail-order Chess albums direct from the company itself in Chicago. In the 1970s, British and European labels began to license and reissue vintage rock and blues in quantities that had been considered, for whatever reason, unrealistic in the land of the blues' origin, the United States.

Charly was the initial leader of the field, given a leg up on the competition with its pipeline to the vast Sun catalog. They were soon joined by companies like Ace, Bear Family, Beat Goes On, Flyright, Document, and others. Often the releases were packaged and thoroughly annotated with love and scholarship that had been conspicuously absent from many American productions of the type. There were even box sets, as well as previously unissued material that had never seen the light of day in the U.S.

This led to a frustrating situation for the many American consumers who wanted such albums. Most of the imports could be found with a little effort, in large stores or, failing that, specialty mail-order houses. The irony of needing to buy imports of such fundamentally American records was not lost on consumers or retailers, who shook their heads in half-disbelief at the necessity of needing to buy records from Europe or even Japan, usually at high prices, because U.S. labels wouldn't release the music. Due to some cumbersome legalities, at times American consumers found themselves unable to purchase material that was easily available to Japanese or European consumers, but could not be legally imported into the States.

The U.S., it should be noted, was not totally inactive in the blues reissue arena. Rhino, the leading American reissue company, produced occasional classy packages for artists like Slim Harpo; Arhoolie arranged for the re-release of some very obscure blues of all kinds. Yazoo was (and remains) incredibly active in the field of pre–World War II music, to the point where if any country or old-time blues packages were produced in the States, it seemed like a better-than-even bet that it would bear the Yazoo imprint.

Labels like Yazoo, Document, and Matchbox deserve a Red Badge of Courage of sorts for diving so deep into a field that will never yield big commercial returns. The companies are catering to the *very* specialized collector to offer music that is both out of fashion, and unable to compete with other reissues in terms of sound quality. Much of the material on their albums is remastered from existing copies of old 78s in dedicated archivists' collections, the

source tapes (if there were any to begin with) having long vanished. This means that many modern-day listeners are simply unable to put up with the relatively primitive audio and the remaining scratches and hisses, although modern CD technology has paved the way for some surprisingly clear transfers.

Beginning in the late 1980s, the explosion of compact disc technology (which has rendered new vinyl releases all but obsolete) has led to a corresponding explosion in the reissue market. The logic behind this is quirky, but basically it seems as though many labels realized that many listeners were interesting in 'upgrading' their scratchy vinyl records with CDs of the same material. American labels in particular also realized that many consumers were interested in buying albums and compilations of artists whose work had lingered out of print for quite some time.

Thus they began reissuing their own back catalog in addition to licensing it, eventually creating entire subsidiaries like Legacy and Capitol Blues for that purpose. Relative to new artists, the production, royalty, and promotion costs on reissues were minimal. Many of these reissues added the further enticements of additional bonus tracks (sometimes unreleased, sometimes from rare non-LP singles), remastering and remixing, and scholarly liner notes. For artists with wide appeal, these factors were often combined into box sets (see separate essay).

The watershed event that led to the windfall of blues reissues is easy to pinpoint. In 1990, Columbia/Legacy released a double-CD box set of Robert Johnson recordings that, to the shock of everyone, sold over half a million copies. Here was undeniable proof that blues fans would support quality reissues in force, even old ones with relatively raunchy fidelity. Very few blues reissues could approach such sales figures–Robert Johnson, after all, has been mythologized to death, and praised to the heavens by numerous rock stars like Eric Clapton and Keith Richard. But it probably did serve as evidence that old blues reissues stood a very good chance of accumulating a modest profit, or at least breaking even. Columbia/Legacy itself embarked on a lengthy series of reissues that continues to the present, including some names that remain pretty obscure to pop audiences (Bukka White, Blind Willie Johnson, Blind Boy Fuller), and thematic anthologies devoted to the slide guitar and topical blues. The label also released no less than five Bessie Smith compilations as the kind of series that had historically only been undertaken by small foreign companies.

Another welcome development of the CD age has been the reactivation of most of the Chess catalog. MCA, indeed, produced several box sets for the greatest blues stars, as well as entire boxes showcasing the output of what was probably the greatest blues label of all time. Capricorn, which had experienced its greatest success as the home of the Allman Brothers, arranged for box sets spotlighting the contributions of smaller but significant labels to the blues, such as Fire/Fury, Jewel/Paula, Cobra, and Swingtime.

There's no question that CD technology has done much to increase the availability of vintage blues music. Whether it's the best format to hear the music, however, remains a hot matter of debate among fans and critics, despite the clarity of sound that can be achieved with state-of-the-art transfers from tape and vinyl.

Rock and R&B historian Charlie Gilliett, for instance, writes in *The Sound of the City* that "although compilations on CD provide a convenient way for the armchair listener to hear music from another ear, it's important to bear in mind that not all of them manage to recapture the true experience of how the music sounded at the time. The deep and wide grooves of 78 RPM singles generated a big, warm sound which progressively disappeared with each successive format–45 RPM singles, 33 RPM albums, and digitally-mastered CDs all tended to favor higher frequencies, at the expense of the 'bottom end.' Played through the huge speakers of jukeboxes, 78s delivered a massive sound which can only be vaguely approximated by CDs on a domestic hi-fi or portable system. Owners of Elvis' 78 RPM singles on Sun justifiably believe that no other format has come close to reproducing their impact. It may help to turn up the bass on your amp, but you'll never quite get there.

"When 45 RPM singles became the standard format for pop music, and the focus of mastering engineers shifted from jukeboxes to radio, it became common practice to vari-speed tapes to raise the tempo, add compression to make records seem louder, and boost treble frequencies to enable them to cut through on poor quality transistor radios. Sometimes records which sounded terrific on the radio could be hard to bear on a good home system, where their harsh, brittle power seemed inappropriate. So now, when mastering compilations of these old records, engineers have to strike a balance between acknowledging their original function while seeking to meet a new generation's expectations of a clean, clear sound from CDs. In general, there's a tendency for most recordings to sound more 'polite' on CD, and sometimes it can be hard to understand why some tracks were ever regarded as being exciting. There's no absolute rule–sometimes the CD version delivers a presence and warmth that had never been caught on vinyl–but often, CDs fail to recapture the hard-to-describe 'earthy' qualities present on the microgroove pressings."

Should you have a lot of money and time, a large network of collector-oriented stores, magazines, and swap meets still exists that caters to the vinyl collector, even if the market is small potatoes compared to the billions of units shifted at most retail outlets. But even recent CD blues reissues can be hard to find at the store, particularly if you don't live in a big metropolis. For that purpose, there are several mail-order companies that have large catalogs of blues and other roots music, two of the most prominent being Down Home Music and Midnight Records.

For those who want to dive into the world of blues reissues with gusto, but don't know quite where to start, one series can be recommended above all others. Rhino's 15-volume *Blues Masters* provides well-chosen and well-annotated overviews of the most important major blues styles, including Mississippi Delta blues, slide guitar, jump blues, Memphis blues, blues roots, classic blues women, Texas blues, harmonica blues, and Chicago blues. As the cliche goes, it's both informative and enjoyable, for the novice and the well-traveled blues fan alike. The series can serve both as a basic collection of classic blues, and as a port of entry that will help listeners discover their favorite styles and performers.

—*Richie Unterberger*

The Blues on Film

While there's a fair amount of blues on film from the past and present, blues fans have a less bountiful selection of goodies to choose from than rock and jazz lovers. The blues, usually lurking at the commercial margins, get less media exposure than some other forms of popular music. That means fewer cameras whirring at both television studios and live festivals; it also means fewer serious documentaries about the subject.

But the number of blues film clips may surprise you. In the early days of the music business, movie studios occasionally filmed musical shorts (called "soundies" for a time) that would run in theaters, as sort of Stone Age precursors to MTV. One of the first of these was a short film starring Bessie Smith that was built around her performance of the theme song, "St. Louis Blues." The blues revival of the 1960s found many of the rediscovered acoustic bluesmen being filmed for the first time, at folk festivals, by folklorists, or by television companies such as the BBC and PBS. As the blues assumes its rightful place as a pillar of American culture, there will no doubt be more and more historical documentaries of the music.

A trip to the video store (or, for that matter, a large music retail store) often yields a decent selection of blues videos to choose from, especially if you live in an urban area or university town. Those without access to these resources can still, for a larger cash outlay, order the videos themselves via roots music mail-order services such as Down Home Music. There are already so many blues videos that a comprehensive rundown is impossible to complete in a few paragraphs. Here we'll simply point readers to some of the best sources.

The two companies with the largest blues video catalogs are Vestapol and Yazoo. Vestapol's line is oriented toward the guitar player, with entire collections of clips for country blues guitar, Texas blues, and bottleneck guitar. Contrary to the impression you might get from a catalog listing, these are not instructional videos, but actual footage of the bluesmen and blueswomen themselves in performance. The appeal is not limited to guitar players (though they can certainly find much to admire); it's geared toward general blues fans, giving them a chance to watch their heroes in action.

There is an unavoidably inconsistent quality about the compilations, due to the varying nature of the sources. A sterling color clip from the BBC lies shoulder-to-shoulder, for instance, with grainy black-and-white footage in somebody's rundown kitchen (which can have an admitted charm all its own). The performances can vary as well; the elderly blues rediscoveries of the '60s can play as well as they did in their prime or, due to failing health, turn in performances that may have been best withheld from circulation, even given the rarity of clips in the field.

But this shouldn't dissuade blues enthusiasts from picking up Vestapol compilations, which are assembled with care. Each one is selected to ensure a diversity of content, and includes detailed liner notes about the musicians and the clips. Certainly the best of them are riveting, such as a trance-like John Lee Hooker playing solo, for instance, or a Swedish TV clip of Josh White suavely sticking a cigarette behind his ear as he plays. There are also entire compilations devoted to the work of major figures like Hooker, Albert King, and Freddie King. The Freddie King compilation *The Beat!!* is especially sweet, gathering about a dozen vintage color live film clips from a Texas-based R&B/soul TV show of the mid-'60s. (Vestapol also has several videos of jazz guitar players available.)

Yazoo is a name that most blues collectors associate with reissues of ancient country blues from the 1920s and 1930s. Their video line is more diverse than

one might expect; indeed, it almost has to be, as there are few blues clips from the 1920s and 1930s of the kind of performers that Yazoo favors. The accent is still on country blues, with entire videos devoted to Furry Lewis, Son House, Big Joe Williams, and Mississippi Fred McDowell. More modern performers, however, are not ignored; there are also anthologies for Muddy Waters, John Lee Hooker, and Lightnin' Hopkins.

If you're still looking for more vintage film clips after exhausting the Vestapol and Yazoo catalog, you might want to try Rhino's two *Blues Masters* volumes. Companion pieces of sorts to the excellent 15-volume CD series of the same name, this unavoidably comes up short quantity-wise when stacked against the discs. But does offer footage of some of the greats, including Leadbelly, Muddy Waters, Buddy Guy, B.B. King, and less-expected figures like Mamie Smith, Roy Milton, and Jimmy Rushing. There is also BMG's similar *Bluesland*, affiliated with a blues history book of the same name.

Considering that only two photos of Robert Johnson have ever been circulated (and that was only after years of searching), it's ironic that there is now a video based around his work, *Search for Robert Johnson* (SMV). As the title implies, this is not so much a standard documentary (no footage, after all, exists) as a look into his environment, sources, and the few recollections we have been granted by his associates, narrated by John Hammond. Another video that delves into Mississippi deep blues is titled, logically enough, *Deep Blues*. Although critic Robert Palmer authored an excellent book by the name in the early 1980s, and is also involved in the video, this is not really a companion piece, but a look at Mississippi blues as it is played in the early 1990s. Accompanied by, of all people, ex-Eurhythmic Dave Stewart, Palmer spotlights the kind of contemporary, electric jukejoint Delta performers that have surfaced on the Fat Possum label, including Junior Kimbrough and R.L. Burnside.

For modern blues, there are occasional releases of concerts by big names such as B.B. King and Buddy Guy. A mid-1990s PBS history of the blues is also a good bet to make it to the video stores eventually, although the subject merits more than the three parts that the series allotted to it.

The milieu of the blues has yet to translate convincingly into fictional feature-length film treatments, despite the abundant fascinating source material. Maybe that's for the best; *Crossroads*, a mid-'80s Hollywood movie based around some aspects of the Robert Johnson legend, enraged purists even as it helped point some listeners that had been unaware of Mississippi Delta blues to the authentic thing. That film was scored by Ry Cooder, who has ensured that elements of traditional acoustic blues are conveyed to millions via his prolific soundtrack work. One movie worth keeping an eye out for that does not deal with the blues specifically, but does project aspects of the Southern Black experience that the blues details, is *Sounder*, with a soundtrack by Taj Mahal (who also has a small role in the film).

—*Richie Unterberger*

Focus on the Blues Harmonica

The harmonica has secured an enduring place in American music and a very special and central place in the blues.

Its history, as related in *A Brief History of the Harmonica*, distributed by the Hohner Company, and in *America's Harp*, an article by Michael Licht, is as follows. The harmonica, or mouth harp, is one of the family of free reed instruments–those which create a tone by the vibration of reeds which do not strike the frame to which they are attached. This free-reed concept led to the development of the Sheng (sublime voice), said to be invented in 3,000 BCE by the Chinese empress Nyn-Kwa, and brought by a traveler to Western Europe in the seventeenth century. The Sheng is the earliest expression of the principle later applied to such instruments as the concertina and harmonica.

The prototype of the instrument in its present state was invented in 1821 by Christian Friedrich Ludwig Buschmann, a 16-year-old German clockmaker who put 15 pitch pipes together, and called it a "mund-eaoline" (mouth-harp). Another clockmaker, Christian Messner, learned how to make the instruments and sold them on the side to other clockmakers.

In 1857, at 24 years of age, Matthias Hohner bought one and decided to produce it commercially, making 650 of them the first year.

He was made the mayor of his home town of Trossingen, which soon became the harmonica capital of the world. In 1932 his sons founded the State Music College of Trossingen, where harmonica, accordion, piano, and violin are still taught today. This school has graduated 3,000 harmonica players certified to teach the instrument.

Sometime before the outbreak of the Civil War, Hohner sent a few harmonicas to cousins who had emigrated to the United States, and they found the instrument to be extremely popular there. During the Civil War many soldiers on both sides had one and, along with peddlers and immigrants, helped spread the instrument throughout the country.

By the end of the century, America was purchasing more than half of the ten million instruments being manufactured in Germany every year. The Marine Band harmonica, still widely popular today, was introduced in 1896 when it sold for 50 cents. The harmonica was well on its way to becoming the most popular instrument in America's history.

The first steps towards blues stylings on the harmonica must have resulted from attempts at what the nineteenth century classical musician might have termed "programmatic music"–that is, music that attempted to paint a sound-picture. The unique sound potential of the harmonica enabled the more clever players to imitate many of the sounds that surrounded them every day.

Trains, for example, have inspired musicians of all eras. Arthur Honneger, the Swiss composer, created an orchestral train in his *Pacific 231*, while Duke Ellington created one for his orchestra in the "Happy Go Lucky Local." The "Orange Blossom Special" is a standard showcase tune for country fiddlers and banjo pickers, while "Honky Tonk Train Blues" by Meade Lux Lewis remains one of the most famous of all boogie-woogie piano compositions. Singer/guitarist Bukka White got on track with his famous "Panama Limited," which he performed in a bottleneck style.

In the hands of a master, however, the harmonica creates the most vivid portrait of all, due to its capacities for tone-bending and chordal rhythm. Some of the first recorded and best examples available on record are Palmer McAbee's "Railroad Piece," Freeman Stowers' "Railroad Blues," and DeFord Bailey's "Dixie Flyer Blues." Of the many Library of Congress field recordings of train tunes, examples by Ace Johnson and Richard Amerson are extraordinary. Countless numbers of harmonica players must have been expert at imitating trains, but the vast majority of them were never recorded either by folklorists or commercial record companies.

Trains were not the only subjects of these folk tone-poems, however. There were "mama blues," in which the harmonica imitated a baby calling out "mama" or "I want my mama"; "fox chases" that depicted these ritualistic events step-by-step, complete with vocal yelps and descriptive interjections; vignettes of escaped convicts being hunted down by the dogs, as well as pure barnyard scenes with animal sounds of all varieties, fill the harmonica repertory–some with uncanny realism.

The connection between this rural impressionism and the origin of what we recognize as blues-harp style lies in the way in the instrument is constructed and played. The ten-hole diatonic harmonica, the most common of the blues harmonicas, produces a major chord in the key of the harmonica when the holes are blown, and a dominant ninth chord in that same key when the holes are drawn. And, to put it simply, the lower part of the instrument is easier to manipulate when drawn, the upper when blown. That is, when each of the four lowest holes is drawn in a deflected manner, the tone bends and the pitch slides lower; and, when each of the highest four holes is blown in a deflected manner the pitch will also slide lower.

In addition to this, the players discovered that although each harmonica was pitched in a specific key, wherein the tonic or central pitch was located on the number one hole blow, it could be used effectively for other keys by using a different sound hole–blow or draw–as the tonic. Each key created a very different effect or mode that could be used for the purpose of varying the color. These alternative playing modes have become known as positions, of which there are four: straight harp or first position (C harp plays in the key of C); cross-harp or second position (C harp plays in key of G); third position (C Harp plays in key of D); and fourth position (C Harp plays in key of E). Other positions are used–but far less frequently.

Because the players found the lowest registers to be the most expressive, especially for the purposes of mimicry, they found themselves favoring the lowest holes drawn; especially #2, which became the central tone, or tonic. This meant that they were blowing their C Harp in the key of G–a perfect fifth higher than the actual key of the harp. This position produced cross-harp style, or second position.

First position, also known as straight-harp, consists of playing in the actual key of the harmonica, where the lowest hole (#1) when blown becomes tonic, and we play the C harp in the key of C. In this position the expressive high register is exploited. The most well-known master of this position is Jimmy Reed. Straight harp is also used by harmonica players to improvise over ragtime changes and for more folk-style melodies. That familiar, low, wailing sound, however, is an almost certain indication of cross-harp style.

Third position is achieved by making the lowest or first hole draw the tonic or central pitch; the C harp is played in the key of D. Little Walter is a master of third position and used it for a number of his instrumentals. The hallmark of third position is a very unusual and jazzy minor thirteenth chord with added eleventh that is produced when the holes are drawn. This sound is unforgettable.

Most rarely, a fourth position can be achieved by making the #2 hole blow the tonic; that is, playing our C harp in the key of E.

To the beginner this must be confusing, as it must have been for the first

players who discovered these positions as well as for their guitar or piano-playing partners. There is a great example on record of a guitar and harmonica seemingly trying to get into the same key, as the guitar player was playing in the actual key of the harp while the harp player was playing in second position. Not until the very end of the tune were they finally in the same key. ("Just It," *Harmonicas Unlimited*, DLP 503/504.)

Harmonica players of classical and jazz music, however, obtain different keys and foreign tones to the key by using a chromatic harmonica rather than a diatonic one. A chromatic harp has a button on the side that when pushed raises the pitch of every blown or drawn tone one half-step. Larry Adler and John Sebastian, Sr., are two modern-day classic masters, while Toots Thielemans is probably the greatest jazz and pop player who is well known today. Blues players use the chromatic mostly in second or third position, in the same manner as the diatonic, to achieve a deep chordal timbre impossible to get on the smaller diatonic model. Bending is tougher, though, on the more sturdy chromatic type. Blues artists have been known to use two or more harps on the same tune–and, conversely, to use the same key harp for tunes pitched in different keys. Obviously, the players' talent, taste, and creativity are tested here.

The harmonica was for many reasons a very natural choice for the Southern African Americans in the developmental stages of the blues. It was small, inexpensive, durable, portable, and easy for the beginner to approach. Musically, it provided a modern and convenient substitute for the quills, an instrument made of three bound pieces of cane; and it was cheaper and easier to play than the violin–whose place in blues the harmonica usurped. In addition, it had the ability to mimic everything from the human voice to trains, animals, and whistling, as well as the Cajun concertina, and the sophisticated stylings of the jazz-aged clarinet and cornet.

One could get a tremendous variety of tone color, attack, vibrato, tremelo, and glissando, not to mention effects made by manipulating the hand used to cup the harmonica. Moreover, it provided three definite registers, was equally expressive chordally and melodically, and covered the entire dynamic range from a whisper to a shout–quite an arsenal for the size and money.

There must have been an enormous number of African Americans playing the harmonica by the turn of the century, but not until 1924 do we get our first harmonica blues on record. Johnny Watson, known as Daddy Stovepipe, recorded "Sundown Blues" that year–demonstrating a sort of melodic/folky sound using straight or first position harp for fills and solos around his vocals. If various written accounts are true of this amazing performer, born in 1867, we find him touring with the Rabbit Foot Minstrels in the early 1900s, playing for tips in Mexico during the Depression, with zydeco bands in Texas by the end of the '30s, and on Chicago's Maxwell Street from the early '40s until his death in 1963.

Among the very finest players who recorded in or before 1930 were Robert Cooksey, Chuck Darling, and Blues Birdhead. Cooksey was a master of the vaudeville sound which he executed in a unique, virtuosic style. He recorded often with his partner Bobby Leecan through the '20s and '30s. Chuck Darling was a ragtime virtuoso whose complex lines wove effortlessly through all registers. James Simons, known also as Blues Birdhead or Harmonica Tim, is perhaps the best example of how the diatonic harp functioned as a jazz instrument in the early days of that music. His phrasing and timbre are a cross between those of Louis Armstrong and Johnny Dodds, vintage 1928. It is amazing to hear such an advanced jazz concept executed so perfectly on this instrument, and one wonders how it could be that this master recorded only once.

The very first wailing, cross-harp style player to record solo seems to have been the Alabaman, Jaybird Coleman, who made some 20 sides between 1927 and 1930. In his style we hear vestiges of the field holler and work song which were building blocks of the blues; and, through his music, we get an unadulterated and impassioned sense of the meaning of the blues in the South during the '20s. Jaybird entertained the troops during World War I, after which he toured the South with Big Joe Williams as part of the Rabbit Foot Minstrels show. He also toured with the Birmingham Jug Band, but seems to have spent a great deal of his time playing locally in the Birmingham/Bessemer, Alabama, region until he moved to West Memphis in 1949, the year before his death. Jaybird brought his unmistakable style to a large number of major Southern cities, inspiring and influencing many of the harp players of his era. It is perhaps one of blues' greatest ironies that he was managed in 1929 by the Ku Klux Klan.

The seeds of the modern-day blues harp that reached fruition in the golden era of mid-'50s Chicago were sown in the American musical mecca of Memphis, Tennessee. That city, which has played such a crucial role in almost every genre of indigenous American music, boasted the simultaneous presences of Noah Lewis, Jaybird Coleman, Will Shade, Jed Davenport, Hammie Nixon, John Lee Williamson, and Walter Horton, all–off and on–between the years of 1925 and 1930. It must have been a boiling pot of musical ideas as these musicians, some of them not more than children at the time, played on the streets, in Handy Park, in clubs, with jug and jazz bands, and as solo attractions.

As reported in *Memphis Blues and Jug Bands*, by Bengt Olsson, jug bands probably started in Louisville and were active there from around 1915. By the early '30s there were at least six bands in Memphis. The two standout examples were the Memphis Jug Band with Will Shade on harp, and Gus Cannon's Jug Stompers with Noah Lewis on harp.

Noah Lewis was discovered in Ripley, Tennessee, by guitar and banjo player Gus Cannon; it is said that his harmonica playing was unparalleled at the time. As many masters of the day, he was able to play two harps at one time–one with his nose. His style is unique and could be said to represent a consummation of the early chordal-melodic technique being practiced in the South for many years. His playing displays a wealth of ideas, always executed to perfection. His recordings show him to be equally at home as part of a duo, a larger ensemble, or as a soloist. Unfortunately, no recordings seem to be available by the older musicians from whom he learned.

Will Shade, before founding the Memphis Jug Band in 1925, played with Furry Lewis and various medicine shows. After touring with the Memphis Jug Band, he joined the Ma Rainey show in Indiana in 1931, and later recorded under his own name in Chicago as well as with Little Buddy Doyle. Probably his most memorable tune is "Jug Band Waltz," which he recorded with the Memphis Jug Band in 1928. His unique style is in the same general mold as Noah Lewis, but his tone is darker and often he is more melodic.

Jed Davenport, on the other hand, had a distinctively wilder sound than his two contemporaries, often using a "flutter-tongue" technique that lent a metallic edge to his lines. Being flashy and dynamic, he was among the most exciting players of his time. He also recorded with Memphis Minnie, and with some local Memphis jazz bands in the early '30s, and played on the streets of Memphis off and on through the '60s. There can be no doubt that these three players represented the models of excellence for all aspiring bluesmen fortunate enough to have heard them.

If we were to search for one talent that linked this wonderful chordal-melodic style to the horn style pioneered in the 1930s, we might find Hammie Nixon, who actually learned from Noah Lewis and taught John Lee "Sonny Boy" Williamson.

Hammie Nixon was the perfect musical counterpart for the traditional blues guitarist/singer. He had a great talent for filling the sound while never covering it. Perhaps this expertise defeated a possible career as a leader, for he was always the sideman. He became known for his work with Little Buddy Doyle, Son Bonds, Yank Rachell, and especially with Sleepy John Estes, with whom he shared a partnership lasting over 50 years. It could be that Hammie recognized his niche, as did others, and that his career was perfectly suited to his talent. He had a unique sense of how to blow lines behind the singer's verses as sort of an obligato trumpet, spinning a fragile, contrapuntal web that surrounded and enhanced the overall sound.

Before Nixon joined Sleepy John Estes, Noah Lewis was Estes' partner, and Nixon learned much by hearing and watching the master at work. Through the '20s and '30s he practiced his trade on the streets and at parties and picnics, finding just the right riff or chordal touch to complement each song. According to David Evans (notes to High Water LP 1003), Nixon played often in Brownsville, Tennessee, a town that boasted a rich musical life for the blues musician throughout the '30s. There was much work available for a good player, and many travelled there to take advantage of the opportunities–among them Rice Miller (Sonny Boy Williamson II), Big Joe Williams, and John Lee Williamson (Sonny Boy Williamson I). It was perhaps in Brownsville that the next link of the chain was forged, as John Lee Williamson absorbed the style of Hammie Nixon, leaning more heavily on the melodic side, discarding much of the chordal work, and redoing this rural mix into a concept which he was to pioneer in Chicago in just a few years–a concept that was to shape the blues harp style into what it is a half century later.

It is necessary to digress at this point to consider the work of two very special and exceptional virtuosi: DeFord Bailey, and his disciple, Sonny Terry.

Although there were many fine harp players active between the wars, the most influential and widely known was unquestionably DeFord Bailey, the Harmonica Wizard. As told by Bengt Olsson in his May-June 1975 *Living Blues* article, "The Grand Ole Opry's DeFord Bailey," Bailey's story is as unique as any in all of music. In spite of his color, he was a featured performer in the Grand Ole Opry, playing in 48 out of 52 Opry broadcasts–twice as many as any other performer. Between 1925 and 1941, Bailey was heard every Saturday night playing virtuosic train tunes, blues, and all sorts of harmonica showcase instrumentals, inspiring players around the country–White and Black. Although there was more than just a touch of the backwoods influence in DeFord's playing (he was self-taught and learned as a child by imitating all of the animal and train sounds that he knew), his style was polished to the point

of utter perfection–each original tune unique, each a gem. In addition to his astounding appearances on the Opry, Bailey was also the focus of the first major recording project in Nashville, Tennessee. During the years 1927-28 he recorded 11 tunes that were to set the standard for harmonica display pieces in recorded American blues.

Sonny Terry was 11 years younger than DeFord Bailey and was one of his innumerable admirers. Using the fox chases, train tunes, and original blues instrumentals as models, the younger player formed a basis for a personal style that would become world famous.

He began as a young child playing buck dances in his native Georgia, and then moved to the streets of North Carolina. He later toured as soloist with Doc Bizell's Medicine Show, before teaming with Blind Boy Fuller in 1934. His career breakthrough occurred when the great American producer John Hammond engaged him in New York City to participate in the From Spirituals to Swing concert in 1938 at Carnegie Hall.

In 1939 he met Brownie McGhee and there began one of the most famous musical partnerships in all of blues or, for that matter, all of American music. During the next 45 years, Sonny Terry and Brownie McGhee played concerts, clubs, and festivals. They appeared on radio, television, and motion pictures, making countless recordings together with other players, and as solo performers.

Sonny Terry was a tremendously influential player of brilliance whose career and talent could rival almost any other player in the history of blues. He was the finest exponent of the rural, chordal-rhythmic style characterized by whoops and hollers and driving chordal work. The vocal and harp work are so closely knit that one can hardly tell where one starts and the other takes over. He commands a wide variety of tone color and vibrato and an impeccable sense of timing–all of which combine to make his work instantly indentifiable and among the very best examples of this style of blues harp.

Prior to 1925, players were learning primarily by imitating the sounds of their surroundings, from older musicians who played in their area, by the instrumental styles heard on recorings, and from the music heard in the traveling shows such as the Rabbit Foot Minstrels.

However, when DeFord Bailey began his radio career in Nashville, he initiated an entirely new channel through which musicians would be influenced. James Cotton remembers, for example, that Rice Miller (Sonny Boy Williamson II) would talk of hearing DeFord Bailey on the radio. In the early '50s in Memphis, Cotton was able to hear blues on radio from noon until well into the night. And, in fact, he first became seriously interested in the harmonica after hearing Sonny Boy Williamson II on KFFA radio in the mid-'40s.

These beginnings of blues on radio, along with the dissemination of race records featuring contemporary harp styles, and the subsequent invention of the juke box–all in conjunction with the snowballing effects of the first great migration of African-Americans to the north (as detailed by Mike Rowe in his *Chicago Blues: The City and the Music*)–created an environment conducive to the assimilation of all existing styles of blues harp. The stage was set for the next plateau of growth for the instrument, as it would be participating in equal terms with the more urban piano and guitar stylings–and, later, with the full rhythm sections of the bands of the northern cities–especially Chicago.

Perhaps the finest Southern harp player to become an integral part of the modern professional Chicago blues scene was William "Jazz" Gillum, who traveled from Greenwood, Mississippi, to Chicago in 1923, beginning an active career that was to last until his death in 1966. He recorded more than 100 tunes on the Bluebird and Victor labels between 1934 and 1950, using some of the finest sidemen in Chicago including Big Bill Broonzy, Blind John Davis, and Ransom Knowling.

Gillum was at his best in a folksy or ragtime situation when he used the high end of the harmonica in first position (straight harp). Although he was not in the same class as Blues Birdhead or Chuck Darling, he was a respectable singer and player who, nonetheless, enjoyed great success.

Gillum's influence, or lack of it, on the younger players, must be evaluated against the backdrop of the Chicago blues world of the 1920s and 1930s. The Jazz Age placed blues in a collateral position; and, as a result, jazzmen playing in the contemporary ragtime vein were often engaged for blues sessions. The great Ma Rainey, for example, recorded with Tampa Red on some occasions and with jazz bands on others. As with many instrumentalists of the day, these classic blues singers can properly be regarded as belonging to either genre.

Players such as the legendary guitarist/singer Blind Blake found Chicago jazz to be a natural extension of their syncopated East Coast style. Blake often recorded with jazz horn players and singers; and, although it is brilliant work, it is not strictly blues. A real dichotomy of style exists in the work of guitarist/singer/ pianist Lonnie Johnson, who was perhaps the only bluesman who could hold his own with the greatest jazzman of the day, Louis Armstrong, while still functioning as a bluesman on other occasions. Some other startling combinations were downhome Mississippi bluesmen Ishman Bracey and

Tommy Johnson, both of whom were recorded with clarinetist Ernest "Kid" Michall of the Nehi Boys.

Because the vast marjoity of bluesmen lacked either the skill or inclination to play in the demanding contemporary jazz style, some resorted to a sort of comic–or "hokum"–style, replete with nonsense lyrics, kazoos (sometimes called jazzhorns), washboards, and catchy choruses occurring over the same repetitive set of ragtime chord changes. They sounded like jug bands minus jug and soul, and their function was simply to entertain. Although a few exceptionally talented artists such as Tampa Red was able to transcend this limited style, most, including Jazz Gillum, were not. His limitations were most obvious when he played in a "downhome" style using second position (cross-harp), and he seems to have had very little effect–if any–on the subsequent blues harp players in Chicago.

This entertainment-oriented strain of early urban blues in Chicago is documented excellently in Mike Rowe's aforementioned classic. He points out that "the urban blues were altogether more sophisticated–lighter in texture with the emotional power turned down and the beat turned up." And that, "It was probably a reaction to the trauma of the Depression years that the emphasis was more on entertainment." In addition, he describes a scene controlled almost entirely by Lester Melrose, a White businessman who recorded almost every bluesman of note in Chicago. Big Bill Broonzy, Tampa Red, Jazz Gillum, Big Joe Williams, Memphis Minnie, Lonnie Johnson, and John Lee "Sonny Boy" Williamson, among others, formed a remarkable reservoir of talent used over and over again in various combinations throughout the '30s and '40s on the Bluebird label as fodder for innumerable blues hits based on the proven "formula." Although this is a one-sided look at the entrepreneur, it paints a vivid portrait of the same old sound issuing from Chicago during these years.

In spite of the application of this assembly-line production technique, certain talents were of such magnitude that they seemed to jump out of their prescribed setting. One such talent was John Lee "Sonny Boy" Williamson from Jackson, Tennessee–the father of the modern blues harp style. John Lee Williamson's role in the evolution of the style can be compared to that of jazz pianist Earl Hines, who is credited with developing the "trumpet-style" right hand; or later, to pianist Bud Powell who expressed the bop style concepts of Charlie Parker and Dizzy Gillespie through his right-hand work. Like these two great pianists, Williamson created a strongly melodic potential for an instrument bound mostly to a chordal or subordinate role. He transformed the harp into a dynamic lead voice.

Williamson, the original Sonny Boy, played straight and cross-harp styles, ragtime-type tunes, and straight blues–all with enormous conviction and great style. His vocals were equally impressive, employing expressive vibrato and changing timbre. He used formula-like fills and cadence figures to frame his lines, and switched freely from a chordally dominated style to a predominantly single-note style–with all possible graduations between these two stylistic poles. He used sustained tones, short repeated notes and five-six note motives with great intelligence and care and might well have been the first harp player to construct solos consistently in this manner.

One truly amazing characteristic of Williamson's music is that in it, one hears not only the past (shades of Noah Lewis and Hammie Nixon are always present), but also the future. One hears some of the architecture of Little Walter, the vocal and instrumental phrasing of Sonny Boy II (Rice Miller), and the tone of Big Walter Horton–all virtually implied by the older musician's vocal and instrumental innovations. In addition, Williamson was the first of a long and distinguished modern line of accomplished singer/harp players who performed their own tunes.

He began his recording career in Chicago in 1937 with a series of records that featured him fronting his own group and performing as a sideman with Big Joe Williams. He was enormously popular and successful but, tragically, was murdered one night in 1948 while walking home from a performance at the Plantation Club in Chicago. His career must be regarded as one of the most significant phases in the development of blues harp style.

Certain contemporary factors converged to exert a tremendous influence in blues music during the '40s. Perhaps the most significant of these was the so-called Petrillo Ban of 1942. Because James C. Petrillo, president of the Musicians Union, saw recordings and juke boxes as dire threats to the livelihood of musicians, he banned all union members from recording. "This and the strict rationing of shellac" (used for record production), recounts Paul Oliver in his *The Story of the Blues*, "effectively stopped the recording of blues." This two-year ban served to take blues out of the studio and into the clubs and streets where it was infused with new life.

In addition, another peak migration period of Blacks to the north was creating a bigger audience for blues; and a grassroots talent-search by the new independent label-owners in Chicago was providing encouragement and work for the younger players.

From the mid-'40s there collected in Chicago a nucleus of harp players whose work, based at least partially on that of John Lee Williamson, constituted a new style that gained more and more definition as the strictures of the Melrose empire loosened and independent record labels began to appear. Maxwell Street served as the perfect breeding ground for these avant-gardists who jammed there regularly, exchanging ideas and strutting their stuff. In addition, the South side was dotted with small clubs that seemed to unite the Black community, serving as both a sweet reminder of the good side of what many of them had left behind, as well as a musical signpost towards the future. Although the lines of development that these Chicago-based artists were pursuing were very different from the directions being taken by the players based in the South, Junior Wells refuses to think of it as a "city style." Wells is quoted as saying: "We had a country sound, but we also were getting into a different type thing. I wouldn't call it a city-type thing, I would just say we had learned some new riffs to put into the thing and it was more of an uptempo sound. We were listening to different type records."

It was in Chicago that the Brownsville, Helena, and Memphis styles coalesced into what is now regarded as the modern blues harp style and sound. So definitive are its markings, so powerful its effect, that almost one half-a-century later, it has changed hardly at all. Perhaps there is no reason for it to change. Of the many fine harp players practicing today it would be difficult to find many who did not get the basis of their style from players who were fully mature in the '50s.

Snooky Pryor, born in Lambert, Mississippi, moved permanently to Chicago in 1945, and was one of the first of these pioneers to record the new post-war Chicago sound. At his best, he is magnificent, displaying a perfect balance of chordal and melodic style. Using a tenor-range sound, he is capable of contrasting a beautifully smooth tone with a rough-edged compliment. From a stylistic/historical point of view, one hears in his work the infuence of all the major players of the day. He was greatly influenced by his favorite player Rice Miller (Sonny Boy Williamson II) whom he heard on KFFA radio, as well as by the original Sonny Boy, John Lee Williamson, with whom he sat in regularly. An astonishing track, "Boogie," recorded in 1947–48, reveals the note-for-note opening motif of "Juke," the masterpiece recorded by Little Walter in 1952. We will perhaps never know who first developed this classic line, or if, in fact, it was a cliche used by many harp players at the time. Snooky is in great form at the time of this writing–still playing in the style he helped create in the late '40s.

"I had admired the original Sonny Boy, Rice Miller, Big Walter...but when I met Little Walter, then it was an entirely different thing to me. Walter was the best–to me–that I had heard. The different things that he could do on the harmonica was an entirely different thing from what everyone else was doing. John Lee had the blues-type thing–Walter had the blues, but he had that uptempo stuff also...it was the execution that he was getting out of the harmonica." This Junior Wells quotation echoes that of Louis Myers, Walter's guitar player of many years: "All of them cats come along and try to play after John Lee died–but Little Walter was more important than all those cats. He was the best after John Lee...was none of them as good as Walter ... and none of them that have come after [are as good]. He was the best in Chicago ... the baddest." Lester Davenport, a veteran harp player on the Chicago scene since 1944 who recorded with Bo Diddley, says: "I would say that Little Walter was the greatest and most influential that ever played."

Marion "Little Walter" Jacobs was born in Louisiana in 1930. At 12 he was working the small clubs and streets of New Orleans, at 14 he played on Sonny Boy Williamson II's "King of Biscuit Time" of KFFA, at 15 he was in East St. Louis, Illinois, and St. Louis, Missouri–and, at 16 he was in Chicago on Maxwell Street. In 1947 he recorded for Ora-Nelle records and a year later was with Muddy Waters. During the next few years he toured and recorded with the Muddy Waters band and frequently recorded as a sideman with others. His breakthrough occurred with *Juke*, recorded for the Checker label in 1952. As soon as he realized that he had a hit, he left Waters' band to pursue a solo career, backed by the Aces, a band that was at the time fronted by Junior Wells. The band consisted of Louis Myers on guitar, his brother Dave Myers on bass, and Fred Below on drums–arguably the finest band that ever played. Walter's reputation grew throughout the country as well as England and Europe. He was recognized by some of the superstar rock groups of the '60s and recorded as late as 1968, the year he died a violent death.

Little Walter is considered by many peers, harp-playing disciples, blues scholars, and serious fans to be the greatest blues harp player who ever lived. A great musician, songwriter, harmonica player, bandleader–a genius. And, like many productive geniuses, his influences were many and varied. Honeyboy Edwards recalls Walter speaking of the profound effect on him by the musicians he heard in Louisiana as a child. Walter's third-position work, in fact, sounds sometimes like a Cajun concertina. Big Walter spoke of how he taught Walter in Memphis (Edwards introduced them in the '40s). Louis Myers remembers Walter hanging around John Lee Williamson–and how the older player took him under his wing. "John Lee liked Walter because he was young. He was a kid trying to learn," recalls Myers (who remembers this well because Robert Myers, Louis' brother, was playing gigs with John Lee Williamson at this time). On the other hand, Mike Rowe, in his *Chicago Blues: The City and the Music*, tells of Walter playing "all kinds of music" (probably waltzes, pop tunes, and polkas) "until he came under the influence of Big Bill Broonzy and Tampa Red." In addition, Willie Cobbs, Honeyboy Edwards, and Junior Wells all relate stories of Walter learning licks from the jazz horn players of the day–especially Louis Jordan and Bullmoose Jackson. Given the broad range of his style and the marked originality of his concept, it is entirely believable that Walter absorbed all of these influences–that he was learning from everything musical that appealed to him–and that he was capable of assimilating all of this into an original style.

In considering Walter's style, one must admire how masterfully he was able to use every existing technique of blues harp playing, and how easily he was able to shape each of them to his own expressive purpose. He used a rainbow of tone color and sometimes exploited that one facet for a solo ("Mean Old World"). His chordal work is fascinating, especially during his beautiful excursions into the dark choral regions of the chromatic harp or 12-hole diatonic, particulary in third position ("Lights Out"). His "bent" tones are extremely effective, because he was capable both of controlled glissandi (slidings) at any speed ("Blue Midnight") or of merely jumping to the bent tone with perfect intonation at any point in the phrase. His trills, bent or natural, were executed at varying speeds; his numerous types of vibrato; his shifts of tone color; his Monkish gift for playing slightly off the beat (introduction to "I Don't Play"); his jazz-oriented phrasing and overall concept (even Sonny Rollins would have been proud of inserting "A Tisket A Tasket," and then sequencing it in the very next phrase as Walter did in "Crazy Legs")–all of these techniques would have amounted to merely great virtuosity in the hands of a lesser artist. In addition, as a composer and soloist, perhaps Walter's greatest gift was his ability to perfectly balance his lines. He was always the master architect–creating original designs of consummate symmetry.

Walter was equally as creative and virtuosic in a supportive role, never disturbing the solo lines or integrity of the tune. Of the many songs he recorded as a sideman in the Muddy Waters band, "Forty Days and Forty Nights" and "I'm Ready" serve as fine examples of Walter's extraordinary talent in this capacity. In addition to making great tunes even greater, he was also able to make very ordinary ones such as Muddy's "Young Fashioned Ways" positively jump out of their grooves with his use of cross-rhythms and jazzy off-the-beat accents. Clearly, he was not challenged by Muddy's material then, and in fact, was not touring with him at the time–only recording with him at Chess' request.

Among Walter's many contributions to blues music in general, and to harmonica-playing specifically, one must acknowledge as paramount his elevating the amplified harp style to state-of-the-art status. One hears the gradual development in style from the acoustic work in "Louisiana Blues" to the modern amplified masterpiece, "Juke." There are various accounts of John Lee Williamson, Rice Miller, Snooky Pryor, Big Walter Horton, and Little Walter being the first to cup the harp against a microphone, thereby completely altering the timbral attack and overall playing style. One might conclude that this technique was a natural and gradual result of trying to be heard over a rhythm section that grew bigger and louder from the late '40s on.

Like T-Bone Walker and Charlie Parker, Walter redefined for all time the role of his instrument and set standards of excellence that will perhaps never be surpassed.

While the blues was being revolutionized in the northern cities, a complimentary strain was being nurtured and developed by players who remained active in the South throughout the '40s and '50s. The central figure of this activity–Rice Miller or Sonny Boy Williamson II–was perhaps every bit as great and influential as Walter in his own way.

As enigmatic as any character in the blues pantheon, Rice Miller would not divulge his real name or date of birth, although Paul Oliver in his notes to Arhoolie CD 310 fixes his birthplace as Glendora, MS; and the year as either 1894 or 1899. [Reserach of government documents by *Living Blues* has revealed that Sonny Boy Williamson was born in 1910. This information was also confirmed by Williamson's surviving relatives.]

Sonny Boy II's musical achievement is sometimes overshadowed by the enormous humanity, sense of humor, and personality that pervades his work. One of the greatest blues lyricists that ever lived, he recorded relatively few instrumentals and gave equal time to both his highly expressive vocals and his harp-blowing, using both of these talents to underscore the humor, irony, and pathos that infuse his musical poems.

It is important to note that Sonny Boy Williamson was a born entertainer, and that his style was honed for the live, improvisational playing of the juke joints; and, starting regularly in 1941, the live radio broadcasts from KFFA in

Helena, Arkansas. He was 40 years old when he made his first records for the Trumpet label in Jackson, Mississippi. Although there are some gems such as "Might Long Time," some of these early recordings are perhaps too loose to qualify as classics. When he began recording with Chess in Chicago, the change in both producers and sidemen helped to tighten the arrangements and make the tunes more memorable. Talents such as Robert Jr. Lockwood, Otis Spann, Lafayette Leake, and Fred Below helped Williamson turn out lasting works–Chicago classics such as "Help Me," "Trust My Baby," "Nine Below Zero," "Cross My Heart," and many others.

Although he may have lifted the basics of his style from his namesake at some time or another, Rice Miller represents a wholly original style that is the modern epitome of the "downhome blues." He lacks none of the technique that other more "modern" players had. His use of vibrato, sustained tones, trills, glissandi, varying timbral shades, sense of symmetry, along with his impeccable timing, were uniquely developed for his personal, expressive needs. If Walter was abstract perfection, Sonny Boy II was pure natural exuberance.

Rice Miller had many admirers who were greatly influenced by his style. In addition, though, he had a few who were his actual pupils, learning techniques directly from him. Among the first and most famous of these was Chester Burnett, known as the Howlin' Wolf. Williamson and Wolf teamed up and toured the jukes of Tennessee, Arkansas, and Mississippi. Wolf was in no way the virtuosic harp-blower that his teacher was, although he was truly a great bluesman. His playing–expressive and dynamic–was used to create fills and solos around his imposing vocals, and add even more punch and character to his now-classic original tunes.

While Little Walter was in Chicago presiding over the new urban developments, and Sonny Boy II was in Arkansas bringing the rural style into the '50s, there was a very important group of players ruling by committee in Memphis, Tennessee. Once again, this city was to serve as a focal point for the development of the blues in general and of the harp specifically. Howlin' Wolf, both Walters, both Sonny Boys, Jed Davenport, Jaybird Coleman, Sammy Lewis, Junior Parker, James Cotton–all of this talent was in and around Memphis at some time during the late '40s and early '50s. Appearing on radio, in clubs and on the streets and parks, some of these players were to begin their recording career there under the direction of Sam Phillips. Two very influential players who seemed to be always on the move between Chicago, Memphis, and points South were Big Walter Horton and Forrest City Joe Pugh.

"Big Walter was always in and out–a hard person to keep up with... always on the move," relates Junior Wells. Walter Horton was associated with almost all of the great blues scenes since he reputedly recorded as a child with the Memphis Jug Band in 1927. He claimed to have toured with the Ma Rainey Show in Indiana as well as with various bands in the South before settling for a brief time in Memphis in 1935. In 1940 he was on Chicago's Maxwell Street, and seemed to move between there and Memphis off and on from the 1940s to the '60s, playing and recording with many of the great bluesmen of the day including Muddy Waters, Jimmy Rogers, Robert Nighthawk, Howlin' Wolf, and Johnny Shines.

Although he never achieved much fame or fortune for his work, certain masterpieces such as "Easy," "Little Walter's Boogie," "Cotton Patch Hotfoot," and "Walkin' By Myself" (recorded as sideman with the Jimmy Rogers band) assure him a place among the very best players in history.

Sometimes called Mr. Tone, Big Walter played with as rich and deep a color as anyone. He also used various types and speeds of vibrato, trills, and glissandi that he employed with great imagination and flair. His playing bears the shades of Hammie Nixon, Will Shade, and even Jed Davenport; yet he delivers his sculptured lines with such swing that one finds believable his claim to have taught Little Walter.

If Walter Honton's output is uneven in quality it is because his career was interrupted by various bouts with sickness. In addition, he seemed to be teamed often with incompetent or unprepared sidemen and producers who ruined more than just a few of his best efforts. Big Walter, who represents a middle ground between the down-home and uptempo styles, was an exceptionally gifted and personal player, who had an enormous influence on postwar blues harp styles.

The enigmatic Forrest City Joe Pugh seems to have been a man of many parts. From his recordings, he seems little more than an expert imitator of John Lee Williamson; yet, Junior Wells remembers that he had a far deeper tone than Sonny Boy I: "I thought Forrest City Joe was great–but he didn't make it. I admired everything he did because he had such a deep, deep tone. He had a really, really deep tone...and notin' and shakin' the harp." James Cotton used to hear Forrest City Joe play piano while playing harp on a rack, and added that "Forrest City was a boogie-woogie man. First time Big Walter ever heard boogie on the harp was from Forrest City Joe. He was his own man...independent. He had his own style and he influenced me quite a bit. During the late '40s and early '50s, I used to love to hear him play–he used to tell us about Chicago 'cause he'd been there and back. He was very, *very* good." Lester Davenport says: "He was great…I'd put him in the same category as Big Walter. He did a lot of things with the harmonica that other players didn't do. I only remember hearing him outside, playing by himself on the street–never in a club." It is very unfortunate that Joe Pugh died at age 34.

Jimmy Reed began his harp-playing career in the early '50s, recording as a sideman with John Brim, John Lee Hooker, and Eddie Taylor. Often these early recordings showcase his cross-harp style; however, he became a superstar due to his high-end playing in first position over the lay-back shuffle rhythms and fine second guitar work provided by his childhood friend and long-time partner, Eddie Taylor.

Although many of his harp-blowing peers in Chicago did not recognize him as a major talent at first, he was an enormous influence in Louisiana where he affected the work of an entire school of young players such as Silas Hogan, Lazy Lester, Louisiana Red, and the future star Slim Harpo. Reed continued to tour until his death in 1976.

James Cotton and Junior Wells, born within a year of each other, are both brilliant musicians whose careers have intertwined for more than 50 years. Each of their styles, once extremely derivative, have become highly personal ones that are still evolving.

Cotton began imitating trains on the harmonica at age six. Three years later he ran away from home to learn from Rice Miller whom he heard on KFFA radio. A few years later he had taken over Williamson's band when the older master had gone to Jackson, Mississippi, to record. Cotton recorded with Howlin' Wolf in 1952, and two years later recorded the classic "Cotton Crop Blues" for Sun Records in Memphis. When he joined the Muddy Waters band after 1955, he was forced to play in a more urban style in order to fill the shoes of Walter, Junior, and George Smith–all of whom had preceded him. Since then he has toured and recorded with his own groups, being one of the few authentic bluesmen still working full time and one of the greatest harp players alive.

Junior Wells was influenced by all the major players of the day and, in fact, recorded tributes to Rice Miller and Little Walter. His debt to John Lee Williamson is obvious in his recording of a number of the original Sonny Boy tunes, including "Hoodoo Man Blues" and "Cut That Out."

Wells was influenced mostly, however, by Little Walter's "uptempo" sound and remembers being taken to meet him one day in the late '40s when Walter and Waters were playing the Ebony Lounge. Walter let Junior sit in and use his microphone and amplifier. Afterwards, Walter asked him if he played the saxophone. Junior said "Nah" and Walter said "Good, you'll be alright–you got the same ideas about doin' things that I have." About five years later, Wells was to replace Walter in the Muddy Waters band, before going out on his own. Wells' country feel is tempered a great deal by the swing style pioneered by Walter, leaving him with a very dynamic and individual approach to the instrument. He and Cotton are probably the two greatest authentic players alive and working.

–Larry Hoffman

Sources:

February, 1991: quotations from James Cotton, Lester Davenport, Honeyboy Edwards, Louis Myers, and Junior Wells taken from personal interviews with the author.
T.M.W. Dixon and J. Godrich, *Blues and Gospel Records* 1902–1943
David Evans, notes to *Tappin' That Thing*, High Water LP 1003
Sheldon Harris, *Blues Who's Who*
Mike Leadbitter and Neil Slaven, *Blues Records* 1943 to 1979, Volume One
Michael Licht, "Harmonica Magic: Virtuoso Display in American Folk Music," *Ethnomusicology*, Vol. XXIV, No. 2, May 1980
Paul Oliver, *The Story of the Blues*
Bengt Olsson, *Memphis Blues*
"The Grand Ole Opry's DeFord Bailey," *Living Blues*, May-June 1975, No. 21
Mike Rowe, *Chicago Blues: The City and the Music*

Focus on the Slide Guitar

"Then one night at Tutwiler, as I nodded in the railroad station while waiting for a train that had been delayed nine hours, life suddenly took me by the shoulder and wakened me with a start.

"A lean, loose-jointed Negro had commenced plunking a guitar beside me while I slept. His clothes were rags; his feet peeped out of his shoes. His face had on it some of the sadness of the ages. As he played, he pressed a knife on the strings of the guitar in a manner popularized by Hawaiian guitarists who used steel bars. The effect was unforgettable. His song, too, stuck me instantly.

'Goin' where the Southern cross the dog.'"
–W.C. Handy, *Father of the Blues*, 1903

This passage has often been quoted by blues writers who are stunned by the fact that the slide technique has lost none of its "unforgettable effect" despite the passage of nearly 100 years. Perhaps it is because the slide or bottleneck style of guitar playing provides an incomparably personalized approach to this most basic and personal musical idiom that is the blues.

For example, players have chosen from an array of slider materials that has included everything from polished bone; all sorts of knives; all shapes, portions, and sizes of bottles made of plastic or glass; to various types of metal or brass bars or tubes of any chosen diameter of length. A slider can be gripped in any manner desired or "worn" on whatever finger the player chooses. This decision has often been made according to whether the player laid the guitar across his knees, playing lap-style, or whether they held the instrument in the traditional manner. Lap-style players sacrifice the normal methods of chording, committing themselves to chords attacked by the slider.

In addition, the slide style has enlisted a great variety of guitar types over the years, such as the electric steel, played lap-style or on a stand; the National guitar ("bodies have been made of steel, brass, German silver, or wood," wrote Robert F. Gear in "The National Guitar," *Living Blues* 14, 1973); acoustic guitars of all shapes and sizes, with or without a chosen number of resonators (bulbous perforated additions to the front of the body). In fact, this consideration is so involved that is has become the subject of an upcoming book, *The History of National Resonator Instruments*, by Brozman, Centerstream Publications. Metal or steel guitars are particularly effective when played with a slider, of course, because they serve to heighten the sharp percussive effect of the slider on the strings. This was of great importance to the many blues artists who played for dancers in the loud country jukes, as well as for those who used pronounced rhythmic effects in their portrayal of trains.

It is well known that slide players have made extensive if not exclusive use of open tunings–that is, "scordatura" (retuning) of the guitar from "standard tuning" (E-A-D-G-B-E, low to high) to a full major chord. Many variations of open tunings appear on record, but the two most often used and cited are "Spanish" and "Vastopol." The former, often called "G-tuning," actually refers to any tuning with the chord factors 5-1-5-1-3-5 (D-G-D-G-B-D; sol-do-sol-do-mi-sol)–low to high, and often used as open A. The latter is often called "D-tuning," with the arrangement 1-5-1-3-5-1 (D-A-D-F#-A-D; do-sol-do-mi-sol-do)–low to high, and often used as open E. It is the intervallic arrangement of the strings that determines the type of tuning, regardless of concert key–which is often raised or lowered by retuning all of the strings by whole or half step, or by use of a capo. There are other tunings available; and, in fact, players freely invented their own specially-suited ones at will. Bruce Bastin, in *Red River Blues*, quotes Georgia bluesman Son Foster as saying: "I played with a slide too, played Spanish, C-Natural they call it. Vastopol. Tune the guitar in four or five different tunings for different kinds of music."

Analytically, these tunings had a great bearing on the musical qualities of a tune. Vastopol, for example, was the strongest arrangement, in that it presented the tonic as the lowest as well as the highest open string, making possible a dynamic presentation of the tonic chord at the twelfth fret–as heard in the familiar opening riff of "Dust My Broom." The open sixth string, of course, gave a great tonic "anchor" to the chord; and, the bottom pair of strings (five-six) gave easy access to the open fifth (do-sol) needed for the familiar blues shuffle background rhythm. Spanish, on the other hand, is somewhat weaker, perhaps a bit mystical, with its open fifth on the first and sixth open strings.

Open tunings in general were probably derived in the United States from the banjo, an instrument which is always tuned in this manner.

Standard tuning is also an option, especially for players who are primarily interested in using the slide for single-string melodies played on strings one, two, and three. Once the guitar has been tuned to an open chord, all the standard chord shapes and fingerings disappear, and the player either develops new ones or limits himself to the same open chord arrangement "transposed" to higher positions on the neck. That is, barred across the fifth fret produce the IV (sub-dominant) chord; the seventh fret produces the V (dominant) chord; and, the twelfth produces the I (tonic) chord–one octave higher than open. All imaginable varieties of partial chording (triads, diads, etc.) are available in open tuning, as are techniques of slant-barring which provide simultaneous notes on different frets. Still, some of the finest melodic slide players have chosen to stick to standard tuning and chording–using the slider to coax exotic and melodic coloring from the treble strings.

Added to all of these choices, of course, are the usual options of all guitarists–choosing either a six or 12-string instrument, or one of the many number of doctored variants including those with seven or even nine strings. These mutant types were made from either 12-string guitars minus strings or six-string guitars plus any number of added strings. Each variation produced a subtle yet very definite and distinctive alteration of the overall timbral quality. Gus Cannon, in 1927, applied the slide technique to banjo on his recording of "Poor Boy"–achieving a haunting, infectious, and rare timbral quality.

The general concept of changing the sound of an instrument by "tampering" somehow with its make-up or by using a foreign second object to alter the attack or overall tone color is not at all uncommon in music. There is the bow used to stroke the orchestral string instruments which can also be plucked (pizzicato), the various mutes used to shade the timbre and reduce the volume of instruments–most commonly applied to brass but also to some winds and all strings as well. And, in addition, there are certain other techniques that have come about only recently such as the use of the bow to sound instruments such as the electric guitar, vibraphone, and even the timpani. Electric amplification, in fact, provides a dynamic example of the complete transformation of an instrument by an innovation designed originally only to make it somewhat louder.

The uncertain ancestry of the blues slide guitar technique has given rise to two main, divergent schools of thought. One believes the roots to be Hawaiian; the other, African. Although W.C. Handy cites the Hawaiian model in the opening quotation, and though Hawaiian music was recorded, distributed and made widely popular in early 20th-century America, one cannot help but to give the African theory more credence.

Historically, African music has always had a penchant for altering instruments to give them a more percussive edge. Attaching gourds (used as resonators), buzzers, and rattles to stringed instruments is very common there. In addition, one finds instruments with varying numbers of strings and tunings. Species of the harp-lute, for example, can be found with from five to 21 strings; and the kora, played in Guinea and Senegambia, has at least three different tunings used according to the piece. In addition, many of the African stringed instruments, like the two-stringed stopped lute, used a drone string to mark the pulse–not unlike the mesmerizing, open-string tonic that sometimes pulses through every measure of Delta blues.

General Africanisms in blues and jazz have been studied and reported by such leading authorities as Samuel Charters, David Evans, Paul Oliver, and Gunther Schuller. The use of glissandi, "out-of-tune" blue notes, complex cross-rhythms, dropped ends of phrases, underlying drones, timbral contrasts, and call and response patterns all point to the African origin of the blues.

Slide guitar technique heightens the effect of many of these features, especially those dealing with glissandi, percussion, and overall vocal ambience. Evans theorizes, and in fact documents evidence of the slide style originating in the one-string "instruments" improvised by many Mississippi bluesmen out of broom-wire stretched across a wall and played with a small bottle used as a slider. He cites the African musical bow as a probable ancestor to this one-stringed phenomenon (David Evans, "Africa and the Blues," *Living Blues* 10, 1972; David Evans "Afro-American One-Stringed Instruments," *Western Folklore* 29). More modern, portable variations of these one-stringed instruments–called diddley bows–have been recorded in the '50s by One-String Sam (Blues Classics 12, *Detroit Blues*) and in the '80s by contemporary bluesman Lonnie Pitchford (L & R 42.309, *Mississippi Moan*).

Arguments for Hawaiian origin are based on the "slack-key" style of guitar playing that utilizes sliders and open tunings hallmarking the Hawaiian music craze that swept America during the first third of this century. "Even more heavily influenced by the steel guitar than the white country musicians were the black bottleneck guitar playing musicians and singers," writes Robert Armstrong in "The Impact of Hawaiian Music on American Music" (*Encyclopedia of Hawaiian Music and Musicians*; Ed. George Kanahele, University of Hawaii Press). And there is no doubt that it must have had some effect. For one thing, steel sliders were routinely sent by many companies to accompany every guitar purchased by mail order; and, for another, the lap-style technique employed by many bluesmen was undoubtedly of Hawaiian origin. Elmore James recorded a tune entitled "Hawaiian Boogie," and there is more than a taste of the Hawaiian influence in the playing of bluesman Casey Bill Weldon. Although Armstrong considers James' tune to be "a tribute to the origins of the blues slide guitar," it seems far more likely that the African-American banjos and diddley bows, in concert with the concept of a violin-inspired instrumental vocalese, conspired to bring about what is perhaps the most distinctive sound in all of blues.

There does not seem to be a linear development of slide guitar technique; rather, it seems to have burst on the scene–fully formed–somewhere around the turn of the century. It kept pace with developments in blues, adapting to electric amplification in the '40s, and the urban sophistication that was to follow as an inevitable consequence.

The main developmental lines seem to have been drawn regionally instead of chronologically. Schools of influence developed in Georgia, Texas, Louisiana, and Mississippi, and later in urban centers–especially Chicago and certain cities on the West Coast. One must approach such a course with care, however, because so many of the players were making records and traveling throughout the country, that the regional styles became disseminated and, hence, their geo-musical boundaries blurred.

It would be only fitting to begin tracing the slide style with somewhat of an anomaly: the Kentuckian, Sylvester Weaver–"the man who introduced the guitar to blues recording…the first country bluesman to record, and…the first black guitarist in any genre to record extensively." This quote is from an article by Jim O'Neal (*Living Blues* 52, 1982: "Guitar Blues: Sylvester Weaver") that goes on to describe Weaver's accompaniments to classic blues singer Sara Martin's sides as "a radical departure from previous blues recording practice, as blues singers previously had recorded with piano, horns, and jazz bands." Weaver was an excellent musician, a professional conversant with the many forms and idioms of the day, singing and playing in jug bands as well as spiritual quartets. His voice was melodic yet reserved, sharing qualities of old-timey traditional music, minstrelsy, and vaudeville. One can pick out some runs later to be found in the playing of Reverend Gary Davis, earmarking Weaver as an early Piedmont model. Suffice it to say that Sylvester Weaver's "Guitar Blues," recorded in 1923, was the first blues slide guitar ever on record.

Three years later a very enigmatic and accomplished slide player and singer recorded 12 titles–six in Chicago for Paramount as Bo Weavil Jackson and six more in New York, one month later, as Sam Butler–and was never heard from again. Discussed by Paul Oliver in his *Blues Off the Record*, the assumption is that Jackson originally hailed from Alabama, and "was a synthesis of various sources who molded songs…blues…and spirituals … to his own individual way of singing and playing." He had an excellent, unique, and nervous style, using short, dry, staccato notes and chords in juxtaposition with expressive bass runs. He was surely among the most talented of the earliest recorded slide artists.

Atlanta, Georgia, the recording center of the Piedmont region, which can claim probably the greatest giant of the ragtime guitar–Blind Blake–can also claim some of the finest slide players including Blind Willie McTell and Kokomo Arnold, as well as a host of exceptional though now lesser-known talents such as Barbecue Bob, Fred McMullen, and Curley Weaver. Their playing is marked by a certain melodic sweetness, a lighter gait, and a particular elegance of style. Harmonically, there is a leaning toward ragtime changes characterized by chains of borrowed fifths (C-A-D-G-C). This style is further defined by the choice of 12-string guitar used to great effect with slider by McTell and Barbecue Bob. It is worth mentioning that many of the greatest voices in all of the blues have been attracted to the vocal qualities of the slide guitar. And, exceptional even in this select group, is the voice of Blind Willie McTell.

McTell traveled for a time with the slide guitarist/singer/evangelist Blind Willie Johnson, who hailed originally from south of Dallas, Texas. Steven Calt said it best in his notes to Yazoo 1058: "Perhaps no American folk musician ranks as high above his peers from an artistic standpoint as Blind Willie Johnson, whose playing is often so perfect that it cannot be improved upon, even in one's imagination." Indeed, the guitar lines are articulated so organically that he truly sounds like in duet with himself–nowhere has the guitar been used as so real a second voice. And, when he is joined by a female singer, doubled by the slide a full two octaves above Johnson's false bass, there is created a mystical texture so profound and vivid that words become flatly inadequate.

Blind Willie Johnson was a huge popular success as well–a star recording artist for Columbia Records' Race series, as David Evans points out in his notes to Yazoo 1078. His impact on slide guitarists–past and present–has been all-pervasive. Charlie Patton, a contemporary of Johnson, was recording gospel songs in a similar way, while Willie McTell was virtually imitating him, turning out religious slides under the name Blind Willie hoping to capitalize on the singer's popularity. Years later, Fred McDowell sang spirituals in the Johnson mold, while the steel player L.C. Robinson often named Blind Willie Johnson, who was a relative, as his first teacher. Given his genius and the extent of his popularity, few could have fallen outside the sphere of his influence, especially in the area of gospel music or of the slide guitar.

Musically, one can point to various techniques that made Johnson so great: his exceptional use of many notes to one stroke of the slide, his eerie sense of intonation when shading his or his partner's voice at the unison or octave, his mastery of many vibrato speeds, his driving sense of time punctuated by actually beating the body of the guitar or snapping the strings against the neck, his use of glissandi to finish or anticipate a sung line, his alternation of upper and lower strings in a kind of call-and-response pattern, his humming and moaning vocal style that together with the slide created a mesmerizing, hypnotic effect–the list could be longer.

If one endeavors to further define a Texas school of slide, you will come upon the undeservedly obscure singer/guitarist Willard "Ramblin'" Thomas, who might have been a kind of centerpiece to the evolving slide style in the "axis that connects Fort Worth and Dallas with Shreveport and other points east" ("Ramblin' Thomas," Ray Templeton: *Blues and Rhythm*, February 1988). It's difficult to believe that this artist would not have been influenced by Blind Willie Johnson, or that there was not some mutual influence between these two major talents recording and working in the same area during the same period. Thomas sculpted long musical lines on the guitar; he seems to be unique in conceiving of the guitar as an unbroken spectrum of potential three-octave melody. Thomas' penchant for monophonic slide lines coupled with his occasional alteration of treble and bass call-and-response patterns define a style very similar to that of Blind Willie Johnson. Thomas was very much influenced by Blind Lemon Jefferson and, especially, Lonnie Johnson, from whom he gleaned a harmonic sophistication to be found in his non-slide work which is actually far better than that of Blind Willie.

Two slide guitarist/singers associated with Ramblin' Thomas were Cryin' Sam Collins and King Solomon Hill (Chris Smith: notes to Yazoo 1079, *Cryin' Sam Collins*).

Collins, born the same year as Charlie Patton, tuned his third string terribly flat when playing slide in open tuning. On these occasions he was playing and recording on an out-of-tune instrument–a fact which was perhaps due to a lack of musicianship rather than to any Africanism. He did, however, have a distinctively high tenor voice which was well worth hearing. It bore evidence of minstrelsy; and, in fact, Collins' repertoire ranged widely–from spirituals to blues, minstrel songs, and contemporary popular tunes of the day. His slide work was executed very well, mostly on the treble strings, and with good vibrato–alternating sometimes with a plucked or "slide" bass. Lack of good musicianship was demonstrated also in amateurish attempts at more sophisticated harmonies (borrowed dominants and related changes in "Midnight Special") and by simply making a wrong chord change or by not making the appropriate chord changes to suite his vocal line.

King Solomon Hill recorded only six tunes but exhibited a fine guitar style–more sophisticated and musical than Collins. His voice was more similar to Collins' than to that of Willard Thomas, who sang in a lower register and with rather gruff timbre–more like the downhome, narrative kind of bluesman. Hill used short, strummed chords to mark time, and answered his vocals with vibrato-soaked slide lines on the treble strings; or, alternately, with plucked bass lines as a call-and-response pattern. Sometimes he would play interesting bass lines around or in counterpoint to his vocals.

In further tracing the slide lineage to this somewhat obscure and under-recorded area, one discovers two very talented prewar players who played lap-style: Oscar "Buddy" Woods, the Lone Wolf, and his student and partner, B.K. Turner, the Black Ace. Woods had a "good-timey" style and played some hokum numbers that he brought off in a wonderfully infectious style, sometimes as part of various groups such as the Wampus Cats and the Shreveport Home Wreckers. Black Ace, who recorded as late as 1960, adopted his mentor's style, which he executed in a somewhat more downhome manner.

A stunning harmonic twist consistently present in the music of both players is the use of the major flat VI chord (A flat major in the key of C), used often as a subdominant substitute–actually a borrowing from the parallel minor mode. This distinctive sound can also be heard in the work of Black Boy Shine (Harold Holiday), a Texas pianist of the period: and, perhaps the pianists are responsible for its introduction to the chordal vocabulary of these two fine players. Sam Charters reveals in *The Bluesmakers* that both men used "the heavy-necked steel guitar," and that Turner "learned the steel guitar technique from Woods holding the guitar across his lap using a glass medicine bottle as a slide."

Bruce Bastin, in *The Blackwell Guide to Blues Records*, states that "Oscar Woods' slide guitar technique in small-group playing was adapted by Harding 'Hop' Wilson to the flat, electric instument … from the tradition of flat-picking Hawaiian-styled guitarists." Other very important influences on Wilson's playing are noted in Ray Topping's notes to *Hop Wilson and His Buddies* (Ace CHD 240): "… he absorbed the music of Blind Lemon Jefferson, and the steel players of hillbilly and western swing bands who played an important part in Texan music." Wilson, a fine and very expressive musician, used the steel guitar in small group settings and was a fixture in Houston's Third and Fifth Wards from about 1950 until his death in 1975.

Another blues electric steel player who began his career in Texas, eventually to become a part of the San Francisco/Oakland blues scene, starting from about 1940, was L.C. "Good Rockin'" Robinson. In Alan Govenar's *Meeting the Blues*, he states: "I picked up the steel mostly from seeing Leon McAuliffe. He was with Bob Wills [and the Texas Playboys, one of the greatest and most influential of the western swing bands]." Robinson was also influenced, as stated earlier, by his relative Blind Willie Johnson, who used to visit and play at young Robinson's home more often. Robinson was recorded by both Chris Strachwitz and Steve LeVere.

There are at least two steel guitarists active in contemporary blues: Sonny Rhodes and Freddy Roulette. Rhodes makes his home near New York City but hails originally from Texas and was taught by L.C. Robinson, whom he met in California. His phrasing and timing on the instrument bear more than just a

stylistic touch of Mississippians Elmore James and Albert King, and these influences both round off and sweeten some of those hard Texas edges.

Mike Rowe in *Chicago: The City and its Music*, spoke of a particular Freddy Roulette solo as "the most exciting new sound to come out of Chicago in years"; and, indeed, this player–whose records are practically impossible to obtain–has displayed an enormously creative approach to the blues, and has recorded with such hidden giants as Earl Hooker. He also recorded some fascinating background work with the obscure Jackie and Tut and with Bo Diddley. He is perhaps the only guitarist in blues to incorporate the upper partials (9, 11, 13) of the chord by superimposing the appropriate triads in the manner of a modern jazz player, while not sacrificing blues essence in the process. He plays with an incomparable sense of swing and design and is a truly unique artist.

A very interesting electric steel player, Reverend Lonnie Farris, recorded one album in 1962, in Los Angeles, on which he demonstrated a modern, R&B-laden gospel style–dedicated to the service of the church. A performer at heart, the artist played guitar with his feet, behind his back, and in as many other unorthodox ways as he could devise. He began playing the lap steel in the late '40s. Although he refused to sell out to R&B or rock 'n' roll labels, he appeared often on television and even started his own record company in 1962.

One has to wonder what Oscar Woods and Ed Schaffer, the Shreveport Home Wreckers, thought of Memphis when they first recorded there in May 1930, for the Victor label. Did they hear Furry Lewis, Allen Shaw, or any other of the Memphis players who used slide? The stylistic differences would have made for very interesting jam sessions indeed. After all, slider K.C. Weldon had recorded with the Memphis Jug Band three years earlier, and Kokomo Arnold and Bukka White left their mark on the city right around the same time. Everything musical was possible there–and probably occurred on a regular basis.

Because the city of Memphis hosted so many different players and divergent styles of American folk music–especially the blues–since the turn of the twentieth century, it is not surprising that a truly indigenous Memphis style is not quite as apparent as are those of other regions. Charters aptly describes the Memphis vocal style as "rather straight and simple, without melismatic embellishment" and goes on to describe a "wider harmonic range, clear melody, and a sophisticated approach to older material…a softer, talkier blues" (*The Bluesmen*).

Furry Lewis was "almost an archetypal figure in the development of blues in the city," cited Charters, who "rediscovered" him in 1959, and "as a guitarist had few peers in Memphis in the '20s" (*The Bluesmen*). His slide guitar style often displayed an alternating thumb stroke between strings four and six, reminiscent of the Piedmont players or of Mississippi John Hurt, and this characteristic separated him from both the players of Mississippi and Texas. Lewis was not a slide specialist, and one gets the feeling that he made it his business to be able to play all styles well.

The player whose style points to a Hawaiian influence more than any other is Casey Weldon, who was billed as the Hawaiian Guitar Wizard. He is associated with Kansas City (hence his name–K.C.) as well as Chicago, where he recorded in the mid-'30s. He made his first records, however, with the Memphis Jug Band in February 1927. He played lap-style, and his music is hallmarked by a Hawaiian, harp-like sliding tremolo on the treble strings, and a one-octave cadential arpeggio of the tonic chord from the fifth down (5-3-1-5).

A more obscure and impassioned player from the area was Allen Shaw, who recorded only two songs that were issued under his own name, and a very few more as accompanist. On "Moanin' the Blues," he plays an insistent drone bass with his thumb–a characteristic found often in the work of the Mississippi players. Yet his repetitive, fixed treble lines link him more with the songster style of Memphis.

An excellent example of how a "regional" theory of blues categorization can be misleading is demonstrated in the work and life of Kokomo Arnold who, although from Georgia, sounds more like a cross between the Mississippi Delta sliders and the Texas lap-style men. He was a profound influence on Robert Johnson. Paul Oliver traces the original basis for "Dust My Broom" to Arnold's "Sagefield Woman Blues"–adding to the well-known attributions of Johnson's "Sweet Home Chicago" to "Old Original Kokomo Blues," as well as Robert's borrowings from Kokomo's "Milk Cow Blues." Arnold was well-travelled and developed a unique, rhythmically-charged style that retained a sharp melodic emphasis. He was left-handed and often played his metal National guitar lap style, with a bottleneck on his little finger. He favored open-D tuning, sometimes with the use of a capo. He was one of the most popular bluesmen of the '30s–a fixture on the Chicago club scene along with stars such as Tampa Red, Memphis Minnie, and Big Bill Broonzy.

It is a great understatement to mention that there were undoubtedly many slide players of great brilliance and originality who were never recorded–either commercially or as part of any field research. The Library of Congress tapes of field recordings, for example, hold many examples of such nearly-anonymous players. If we were to elect one slide player to represent them, it could be Hambone Willie Newbern who, if not the originator, was indeed the first to record "Rollin' and Tumblin'," one of the greatest and most recorded slide anthems in blues literature. Charley Patton, Robert Johnson, Elmore James, Muddy Waters–these are only a few of the great bluesmen who have worked and reworked this tune during their careers.

Newbern was born in western Tennessee and, according to Paul Oliver, taught Sleepy John Estes in about 1913. He recorded his six titles in 1919 in Atlanta for Okeh, and worked for many years in Memphis. He was reportedly beaten to death in a Marvell, AR, prison sometime in the '40s (Oliver: *The Story of the Blues*).

As trite as it may sound, the blues probably *did* begin in Mississippi–later working its way north, to cities like Chicago where it readapted to its new audience. Whether the magic lay in the soil or the sun, it was potent enough to bring about the deepest and most intense strains of the blues–which still are dominant a century later. The Mississippi blues pantheon is well known to all who listen to the deep blues; the deeper the understanding of the music, the more complex and fascinating become the relationships and influences that shaped the styles of the most influential players.

An unrecorded musician named Henry Sloan is reported to have been the teacher of Charley Patton, perhaps the first great bluesman of the Mississippi Delta. Patton's performances and recordings had an all-pervading influence throughout the South, and he became recognized as the greatest living bluesman of all time. Patton used the slide extremely effectively, as he did many other techniques, such as banging and slapping the guitar and snapping individual strings against the neck. Booker Miller, a contemporary and protégé of Patton, told Steven Calt and Gayle Wardlow that he had a Stella guitar at first, but had to change makes because "it took a Gibson to stand up to him…Charley was rough on boxes" (Calt, Wardlow: *King of the Delta Blues*).

He could play very delicately as well, though, and was adept at shading his vocal lines with the slider either an octave lower, higher, or at the unison over a rhythmic bass/chord pattern–getting a perfect balance between shades of melody and rhythmic drive. As in "Boll Weevil" he sets up an effective call-and-response pattern–sometimes finishing the lyric with sliding notes that function as phrases ("Spoonful"). He used single lines with great expression both on the bass and treble strings–even harmonizing them "organum-style" (in fourths or fifths) using the triads or diads made available by the particular type of open tuning he was using. He often played with Son Sims, a fiddle player whose microtonal shadings and rhythmic syncopations became echoed in Patton's solo slide work (*Devil Sent the Rain*).

Although known for his raucous singing and barrelhousing, some of his greatest slide work surfaced in his gospel songs–especially in "Prayer of Death." One can only imagine what a live performance of this must have been like on an inspired evening. According to Calt and Wardlow, he used the standard open tunings of A and E, tuning his guitar at least one full step above standard tuning in order to achieve a more penetrating sound. His slider was a pipe-like piece of brass, and at times–especially when performing spirituals–he would lay the guitar across his thighs and play lap style.

As with practically all artists of this rare caliber, Patton was the center of a wide constellation of players who emulated and imitated his work and life. Even Bukka White, who was never really influenced by Patton's style of playing, recalled that as a boy he wanted "to come to be a great man like Charley Patton" (Charters: *The Bluesmakers*). The two slide artists most directly influenced by Patton, who were later to become highly influential in their own right, were Eddie "Son" House and Chester Burnett, the Howlin' Wolf. The obvious disparity between these two artists displays the incredible breadth of Patton's influence, which had such deep significance to players of a wide stylistic range who were to be active almost a century after their mentor's style was fully formed.

Son House was a most intense and commanding blues presence. His preacher-like fervor rang out through both his live performances and his recordings. Although perhaps not in the very first rank of guitarists or singers, this artist transcended his limitations, leaving a recorded legacy that rivals any in blues history. In his case the whole was far greater than the sum of the parts; or, as Jim O'Neal put it, "The House was greater than all of the rooms."

House played a steel-bodied National with a brass slider which he wore on his third finger. He sang in the concert keys of D, A, B flat, and E using both Spanish and Sevastopol tunings. His most famous 1930 recordings were "My Black Mama" and "Preachin' Blues." Both of these tunes were learned from James McCoy and reworked later by Robert Johnson. "Preachin' Blues" was perhaps his most successful song artistically, employing a beautifully effective combination of percussive chord-slapping and treble slide work. "Pony Blues," recorded in Robinsonville, MS, by Alan Lomax for the Library of Congress in 1942, reveals the manner in which House reworked Patton's tunes, infusing

them with his own musical personality. Of his 1965 recordings, *Sundown* is memorable for its full-chord octave glissandi, used as both fills and background. For all who saw him, what remains unforgettable is that stern presence, clothed in white shirt and black string tie–that crying, shouting, sliding blues preacher with a message for all time.

Another slider whose roots extended from Charley Patton through the blues revival of the '60s, '70s, and '80s was Big Joe Williams–the archetypal rambling bluesman who heard and played with practically everyone from the Mississippi Delta to St. Louis. His inimitable style, which remained consistently excellent through the years, is made even more personal by his "invention" and use of the nine-string guitar, which he made in the '40s by doubling the first, second, and fourth strings. He sometimes used a Dobro (the trademark name for an acoustic guitar with a metal resonator), as well as a standard six-string, and often capoed as far up the neck as the eleventh fret (From Steven Calt's notes to Mamlish 3810, *Big Joe Williams*). These traits, combined with his intense and very complex, whirlwind-like rhythmic style, punctuated by almost violent bass and treble string snappings in the Patton mold, made him very difficult to imitate (Mark Ryan's notes to Trumpet AA-702, *Delta Blues*). Probably among the first to use amplified slide guitar, Williams was a mentor to both Honeyboy Edwards and Muddy Waters.

Eddie Taylor was a musician who played with both Joe Williams and Howlin' Wolf. His roots stretch from Charley Patton and Son House to the more modern influences of Robert Nighthawk, Elmore James, and Muddy Waters. Although his career was tightly bound to backing Jimmy Reed, he was a very fine and expressive slide guitarist.

As House hung around Patton–learning and working to be accepted as a peer–so too did young Robert Johnson frequent the gigs of Patton, House, and Willie Brown (yearning to be one of these professional Delta bluesmen). Like many other superlative musicians, Johnson was involved in assimilating all of his many influences, a process that was interrupted by his untimely death. This was a time in blues history when the music was on the brink of transforming into an urban electric sound; and Johnson would inevitably have been a key figure in this process. However, as fate had it, his role was to absorb and perfect many of the extant blues styles–both vocal and instrumental–rendering him today the enduring symbol of the prewar blues.

It has been documented that Johnson had a teacher, Ike Zinnerman, who instructed him sometime in 1931–after his initial meetings with Son House, and before he became an accomplished player. Although it is unknown exactly what he taught Johnson (Robert Palmer in *Deep Blues* surmises it to be reflected in the artist's more melodic, non-slide numbers such as "From Four 'til Late"), we do know that Johnson's style closely resembled that of his original mentor Son House and, through him, Charley Patton. The exemplary collection, *The Roots of Robert Johnson* (Yazoo L-1073), with enlightening notes by Steven Calt, presents many of the performances on which Johnson based his style. Well-traveled slide expert Hambone Willie Newbern provided the basis for both "Travellin' Riverside Blues" and "If I Had Possession Over Judgment Day" in his "Rollin' and Tumblin'" (1929), while Son House's "My Black Mama" is the certain protoype of "Walkin' Blues" (Son House recorded a very different "Walkin' Blues" in 1930). Johnson reworked these materials to varying extents, and molded them into lasting monuments to the tradition, infusing them with great power, and delivering them with impeccable taste and flawless execution.

He used a slide on 11 of his 29 recorded titles. It controlled some ("Come On In My Kitchen," "Last Fair Deal Gone Down"), while spicing others ("Stones in My Passway," "Terraplane Blues"). He used it flawlessly, with other-worldly intonation as shading to his vocals ("Come On In My Kitchen"); and regularly as introductions, fills, and even as counterpoint to his vocals ("Crossroads Blues"). He used it chordally ("Last Fair Deal Gone Down"), creating a roaring rhythmic effect; and, even programmatically ("Come On In My Kitchen"), to portray the "howlin'" wind. Ironically, Johnson's most famous and enduring "slide" number, "I Believe I'll Dust My Broom," was performed naturally, without use of a slider.

It is an extraordinary coincidence that the three slide players who were closest to Robert Johnson were all born within months of each other, in 1915–also the year of Muddy Waters' birth. And, even greater fortune finds that two of them are still touring and recording at the time of this writing, over a half-century after Johnson made his records. In fact, the summer of 1991 found Johnny Shines, Robert Lockwood, Jr., and David "Honeyboy" Edwards at the Smithsonian Festival of American Folklife, reminiscing about their mentor along with pianist/guitarist Henry Townsend, who knew Johnson for a time in St. Louis.

Of the three first mentioned, Edwards was probably least affected by Johnson's style. He plays in standard tuning when using a slide–Johnson always used open tunings–and had many other important influences, including non-sliders Tommy McClennan and Tommy Johnson. In addition, he has not recorded many of Johnson's tunes, with the exception of "Sweet Home Chicago," which has been an Edwards mainstay over the years. He is a fine guitarist who has used slide to great advantage.

Robert Jr. Lockwood, was Johnson's only hands-on student. Johnson taught the younger man–then a pianist–his tunes, note-for-note. In fact, Robert Palmer relates in *Deep Blues* that "at the time of Robert's death their repertoires were virtually identical." Lockwood returned the favor by being "the first artist to display Johnson's influence on recordings, and the first to carry his synthesis to Chicago" (Evans: *Blues Records*). These recordings, made in 1941 for the Bluebird label, are masterpieces. Especially on the slide number, "Little Boy Blue," we hear a more swing-oriented style than we associate with Robert Johnson–a style both funkier and jazzier than one might imagine. Although Lockwood has continued throughout his career to be a source of information about his stepfather–as well as a living tribute to his mentor's style, he long ago acquired a preference for the jazzy jump mode being played by Louis Jordan and other horn players of the day. A pioneer and uniquely gifted artist in his own right, Lockwood was one of the first single-string players in the Delta to play the more modern style, and was instrumental in initiating this in Chicago. An innovator at heart, he was soon to tire of the slide technique, preferring his explorations into jazz-oriented styles.

In Johnny Shines, however, we find an unabashed champion of Robert Johnson–perhaps his most staunch and true protege. Although Shines' first mentor was Howlin' Wolf (a Patton protégé), Shines met Johnson in 1933 and was his "running partner"–off and on–for the next five years. Shines' chilling vocal style made him an original, in spite of an almost religious adherence to Johnson's aesthetic. After an unheralded (although stylistically and historically significant) session with Columbia in 1946–on which he played no slide–and two non-slide numbers cut for Chess four years later, Shines finally came into his own in 1952 when he recorded for the JOB label. His first session produced "Fishtail Blues," a direct descendant of Johnson's "Terraplane Blues," and a cover of "Ramblin'" both using slide and played in the concert key of B flat in G tuning. Shines, a distinctive artist with his own musical personality, must always be remembered as one of Johnson's most significant disciples, who brought a very true sound image to Johnson's art to the post-war world.

There are certain rare players in the history of the blues whose enormous influence has been experienced mostly through reflection. Often it is because they were not able or chose not to explore larger avenues of exposure such as recordings, big-city performances, and other trappings of "road to success"–yet without their influence the music would have unfolded differently. Such an artist was Houston Stackhouse, the subject of a lengthy and informative *Living Blues* interview by Jim O'Neal (*Living Blues* 17).

Stackhouse was dubbed a "regional legend" by O'Neal–an artist who preferred the country jukes and houseparties in and around Helena, Arkansas, to the big-city opportunities that were offered to him by his peers and students. He was scheduled at one point to record with Robert Johnson, was part of the KFFA circle of musicians in Helena, and was associated with the greatest players of the day from Tommy Johnson to Little Walter. He played mostly in natural tuning and used a metal guitar until changing to an electric model in the '40s. In his work one hears the rough origins of the slide style later identified with mid-'50s Chicago. The quivers and shakes, the uncanny off-pitches that beg the tone–all of these characteristics make Stackhouse a seminal figure in the blues during its very vital mid-'40s transition.

CeDell "Big G" Davis, like his mentor Houston Stackhouse, has remained an obscure artist. Left with permanently crippled fingers from polio, contracted at age ten, he developed an upside-down and left-handed approach to the instrument, which he plays with a butter knife slider held in his right hand. This unique style, coupled with what sounds like standard tuning, creates a most individual "skewed" sound–distinctive and memorable. His pitches are off-center, as if he is playing the sliding treble lead a microtone flat–the coloration is beautifully dark and fine. In addition, Davis has cultivated, perhaps more than any other player, the ability to maintain a steady shuffle rhythm on the bass strings while simultaneously ringing a contrapuntal slide line. At other times he buoys his slide lines with recurring bass riffs that are often boogie-oriented. His blues are deep, brooding, and forceful–played with a country finesse and Delta intensity.

Davis often played with Houston Stackhouse's cousin and most famous student, Robert Nighthawk. Born Robert McCollum, he later changed his name to McCoy because of some trouble with the law, and finally to Nighthawk after his popular record, "Prowling Night-Hawk." Nighthawk–who had met and heard Charlie Patton–was becoming a professional in the '30s when Elmore James and Robert Jr. Lockwood were just starting out, and Muddy Waters had just switched from harp to guitar. Nighthawk, too, was originally a harp player. He was taught the guitar and slide technique by his mentor, Houston Stackhouse. Robert Palmer describes Nighthawk's notes as "dripping slowly out of the amplifier like thick, oozing oil" (*Deep Blues*). And so they seemed–

each one somehow leaving its own indelible design and coloring–simply unforgettable. Nighthawk recorded on Bluebird in the late '30s but achieved his individual style after switching to electric guitar in the mid-'40s. He was brought back into the studio some ten years later by Muddy Waters, who had received some musical pointers from him early in his career. It was at that time that Nighthawk recorded his masterpiece, "Sweet Black Angel," one of the most magnificent works of electric slide playing–and perhaps of all recorded blues.

Nighthawk's other main influence was the musical giant, Tampa Red, who had been in Chicago since the mid-'20s, and who was for two decades the most famous slide player of them all. In fact, Jim O'Neal reveals in his notes to Blues Classics 25, *Tampa Red, the Guitar Wizard*, that this guitarist released more 78s (over 150) than any other performer in blues history. In addition, his second release, "Tight Like That," was one of the biggest-selling Race records ever. Tampa Red is also credited with writing many blues standards that have been reworked by the most established artists in the field. Elmore James, Robert Nighthawk, Little Walter, B.B. King, Freddie King–all of these artists (and many others) have recorded such Tampa Red originals as "Sweet Little Angel," "Love Her with Feeling," and "It Hurts Me Too." Tampa Red teamed up with the greatest blues pianists in Chicago including "Georgia" Tom Dorsey, Maceo Merriweather, and Blind John Davis, on a series of records and club dates that made him one of the most popular bluesmen of all time. He was also an expressive and sensitive accompanist to such divas as Ma Rainey.

As a slide guitarist, Tampa Red's flawlessly precise style might be described as being melodically elegant; each note seems to follow with a sense of perfection and certainty–each note is delivered in an envelope of fine, mellow timbre. His lines are sculpted, laced with intricate detail, sure attacks, and gentle vibrato. He achieved a beauty of tone with a glass slider worn on his fourth finger, and often used a gold-colored National guitar, a triple-resonator National steel, and a hollow-body Gibson jazz model. Until about 1950, Tampa Red reigned as one of the most influential bluesmen in Chicago–and the most accomplished and famous player of the urban slide-style blues guitar.

Robert Nighthawk fused the homespun Delta intensity of Houston Stackhouse with the more deliberate artfulness of Tampa Red to achieve a most potent and narcotic synthesis–one that was to affect the work of many of the most talented players that were to follow. It should be noted that Nighthawk played in standard tuning, in the key of E (at least at the 1949 session), and relied on the treble strings for his slide lines. Don Kent, who knew Nighthawk in the 1960s, reports that he was using a steel or brass slider on his fourth finger. He is seen in pictures with a solid-body electric, a wooden acoustic, and a full-bodied Gretsch electric jazz model guitar. Nighthawk was surprisingly accomplished in his non-slide work as well, which was solidly in the tradition of Lonnie Johnson and Scrapper Blackwell.

Earl Hooker was a wonderfully gifted and innovative guitarist who learned directly from Robert Nighthawk. His wide-ranging musical palette incorporated genres as diverse as downhome blues (as practiced by his cousin John Lee Hooker), swing, hillbilly, and the bluesy psychedelia of Jimi Hendrix. He used everything he came across including two types of double-necked guitars–one with both six- and 12-string guitar necks, and another with a six-string neck and a (four-string) bass-guitar neck–as well as a variety of tone-altering pedals including a "wah-wah." Reportedly, Hooker was proficient on bass, organ, piano, banjo, harp, and mandolin, as well as guitar.

Praised by Houston Stackhouse, Albert King, B.B. King, Buddy Guy, and T-Bone Walker, Earl Hooker "achieved the reputation of being the finest guitarist in Chicago" before his death in 1975 (Mike Rowe, *Chicago Blues: The City and Its Music*). Not only a great slide player, but a fabulous and complete guitarist by any standard, Hooker's posthumous reputation has been tragically underplayed and overlooked. His influence can be heard in the styles of many of today's greatest players, including non-slide great Otis Rush, who once said, according to Jim O'Neal, that he fashioned the sound of his bends after Hooker's slide work. Veteran bluesman Jimmy Dawkins, who played with Hooker often in Chicago, said that what fascinated him most was the guitarist's ability to switch instantly from slide to natural mode; indeed, Hooker often sounds like two alternating players. Hooker's attraction to country music made him a natural to hook up with Fred Roulette, who was a sideman on many of Hooker's most exciting recordings. Earl Hooker's reputation is kept alive today by many of the greatest living blues musicians, who remember him as the best they ever heard.

Players such as Earl Hooker, and before him Son House and Furry Lewis, were able to feel their personal influence reflected in the work of other talented players. They were able to see their place in the music's history. There were at least two blues musicians, however, whose talents seemed to percolate in a time warp until the blues "revival" of the 1960s: Fred McDowell and Bukka White.

As Bruce Bastin relates in his notes to Flyright CD14, *Fred McDowell*, "

[McDowell] was the perfect example of how much of the finest blues talent failed to be recorded in the 1920s and 1930s...When Alan Lomax discovered him in 1959, he had never recorded before...he was one of the first country bluesmen to carry his music to Europe." McDowell was a master of voice-shading, a device which he employed regularly an octave higher or lower than the sung line. Rhythmically, his playing was direct rather than crossed or contrapuntal. His blues were straightforward and melodic, often controlled by a single riff that dominated the entire musical context ("Kokomo Blues"). He could also be explosively percussive at times ("Shake 'Em on Down"). McDowell had a wonderful talent for making each of his tunes unique–unified in its own special way, like so many musical short stories.

Bukka White, on the other hand, was a continual victim of terribly bad luck. Fear of the worsening Depression caused ten of his 14 tunes recorded in 1930 to be unissued. His next session seven years later was shut down by a sheriff who arrested him for murder (a tale told to Sam Charters by Big Joe Williams, and related in *The Bluesmen*), a charge which eventually sent him to Parchman Prison–where he cut two sides for the Library of Congress. Influential in getting him released, the American Record Company recorded 12 sides which were issued and subsequently described as "folk music" by the *Amsterdam News*, one of the black New York newspapers (Charters: *The Bluesman*). Mostly, these records were simply ignored. It was 1940 and country blues was anachronistic at best; it would take another 23 years before White's time would come, as the taste for blues crossed over to the young, white audiences of the North.

White enjoyed a nice career after being "rediscovered" in 1963–playing concerts, festivals, and television shows, both at home and abroad. As a songwriter, he was known for his ability to create impromptu tunes based on his experiences–he called them "sky songs." As a player, he is remembered for his mosaic-like use of silence, and a thunderous, percussive-chordal style that he used to great advantage in the portrayal of trains (*The Panama Limited*). White sometimes played lap-style, with a knife or screwdriver, used a National steel guitar, a metal ring-like slider on his fourth finger, and preferred the open tunings of G and E.

Charlie Patton, unlike Bukka White, was recorded rather extensively early on, beginning in 1929. While Patton was unusually prolific in the studio, his career had actually started more than 20 years before his first recording session. One can only theorize about the evolutionary stages that might have occurred.

The recordings of Muddy Waters provide a unique opportunity to trace the transition from early country blues to its Northern electric counterpart. Pete Welding, in his notes to *Muddy Waters Down on Stovall Plantation* (Testament T-2210) relates that: "... the singer stated (in 1941) that though his music had been patterned almost totally on that of Robert Johnson, he had never heard him in person. Son House had shown him the essentials of Johnson's remarkable style." Clearly, the slide numbers "Country Blues (Numbers One and Two)," recorded by Alan Lomax for the Library of Congress, are remakes of Johnson's "Walkin' Blues," which Waters learned from Son House (as did Johnson). If not a giant of the country blues tradition, Waters surely is a major architect of the establishment and design of the amplified blues band. Tunes like "I Feel Like Goin' Home" (1948) show him translating his solo country bottleneck guitar style to electric guitar.

Muddy Waters' 1946 Columbia recordings, which were not released until 1971, show that he was already making electric music in an early Chicago ensemble style, with two guitars, piano, bass, and drums. As Robert Palmer points out in the brilliantly annotated *Muddy Waters: The Chess Box* (Chess CHD3-80002): "In the clubs, Muddy and his band were forging their own heavily amplified style. In the studio, Muddy was encouraged to emphasize his Delta roots." Nonetheless, such masterpieces as "Louisiana Blues" and "Long Distance Call" grace the blues repertoire with first-rank artistry. In addition, they brought the sound of slide guitar to a larger audience.

As Chess began to record Muddy Waters with more of a band sound, he played less guitar and concentrated more on his vocals. He always, however, reserved a spot for a solo slide number in his performances and recorded stinging, effective slide guitar on certain later tunes such as "Things That I Used to Do" (1963), "You Can't Lose What You Never Had" (1964), and "Who's Gonna Be Your Sweet Man" (1971).

To quote Mike Rowe: "In 1945 Waters was playing only bottleneck style ... ('Blue') Smitty (Claude Smith) claimed to have taught Muddy how to use his fingers." (*Chicago Blues*). According to Smokey Smothers, early in his career Waters used a short, glass slider and played mostly in G-tuning, shifting later to a slider made of metal and a reliance on standard tuning, mostly in the key of E. Muddy Waters took slide guitar out of the black ghetto and into the larger American musical marketplace. His influence on subsequent slide players–directly and indirectly–as well as on the general language of blues is virtually inestimable.

Another giant of the blues pantheon, Howlin' Wolf, received his training from Charlie Patton and Robert Johnson. He used his slide guitar talent as part of a ferocious, all-imposing musical and physical presence. Beginning his recording career in Memphis for Sam Phillips and Sun Records in 1951, he soon became a fixture on Chicago's South Side. His occasional use of searing slide work on tunes like "Little Red Rooster"–like his effective harp-playing–was only a part of Wolf's magnificent coloration; but its inclusion helped to further embellish slide technique as a permanent characteristic of modern blues.

There is hardly a figure more identifiable with the electric bottleneck guitar sound than Elmore James. James was first inspired to play slide by Robert Johnson, who in 1937, along with Sonny Boy Williamson II (Rice Miller) and Robert Jr. Lockwood, was James' frequent companion. By adding Robert Nighthawk to this roster, we complete the list of ingredients that James needed to cook up his new style–one that still echoes proudly through the corridors of contemporary blues. While Muddy Waters' guitar gradually disappeared into the mix, giving rise to a kind of busy Chicago polyphony, James' became more and more prominent, becoming at last the undisputed lead voice in his tightly-knit groups. He transformed the role of electric slide–not unlike the part John Lee Williamson played in the development of blues harp–making it a dynamic lead instrument, capable of controlling the modern electric blues band. Although he invariably used open-D tuning, James always seemed fresh and exciting. He had a powerfully aggressive sound yet could be gentle when the mood turned subtle, solemn, or romantic. His unvarying excellence throughout most of his career can be attributed, in part, to his fine roster of sidemen–a list that included such luminaries as Johnny Jones, Wayne Bennett, Jimmy Spruill, J. T. Brown, Ike Turner, Maxwell Davis, Odie Payne, and Ransom Knowling. Add to these assets the fact that James' voice was one of the greatest in the history of the music and it becomes easily understandable that so many of his recordings rank among the highest order of blues classics. Although James did not record until 1951, he had been playing in an electric band (that included sax, trumpet, second guitar, and drums) since 1939. "Elmore's position in the Chicago scene is important; for, while Muddy updated Mississippi's blues for an early postwar audience, Elmore followed through the logical development and modernized them for all time" (Mike Rowe: *Chicago Blues: The City and Its Music*).

There are various stories regarding Homesick James Williamson, Elmore James' distant cousin. One finds him with his younger cousin Elmore, as kids, playing a one-string on the wall of a house. Another finds him touring the South with such players as Blind Boy Fuller, Big Walter Horton, Frank Stokes, Buddy Doyle, and, later, Rice Miller, Robert Jr. Lockwood, and Johnny Shines. According to a 1978 interview in *Blues Unlimited*, by Tim Schuller, Homesick James taught the "Dust My Broom" lick to Elmore James–who wasn't even playing at the time Homesick James originally learned it. In this interview he said,: "Elmore was a wonderful slide player for what he *did*. But if a man don't know but one or two runs, I don't call him that *much* of a slide player. But when a guy can play slide and play all the changes, like Earl Hooker, then you can say the man's a slide player. Elmore had a great voice..."

This might sound like jealousy were it not for the fact that Homesick James is an intelligent and superlative musician, secure in his own talents. He plays with an easy, graceful swing in a style more expansive and flexible than Elmore James. He played bass on many of Elmore's sides, and maintained a close personal and professional relationship with him for many years.

In the *Blues Unlimited* interview, Homesick James reports using Fender, Gretsch, and wood-bodied Dobro guitars, as well as every type of slider including a knife, thimble, bottleneck, and metal pipe. In addition, he favors D, C, and B-tunings along with open G. *Blues Unlimited* also quoted him as saying that "... the only worthwhile slide players were Hooker, Nighthawk, and Hound Dog–you can take the rest of these slide players, and put 'em in a paper bag, and throw them in the lake!"

The Hound Dog to whom Homesick referred was Hound Dog Taylor, a native of Natchez, Mississippi, and yet another slide player who claimed to have taught Elmore James the famed *Dust My Broom* lick (Jim O'Neal and R. T. Cuniff, *Living Blues* 4). Taylor claimed that James beat him to Chicago and "stole the stuff" that he heard "the Dog" play in Mississippi (Wesley Race, *Blues Unlimited* 73). Others contend that Taylor learned his style from James. What is important is that Hound Dog Taylor was instrumental in ushering the electric slide into the '70s, helping to rejuvenate its popularity in Chicago. His was a good-time boogie sound that translated to a variety of original instrumentals which found their way into the repertoires of other players, including those of non-sliders Freddie King and Magic Sam (O'Neal, *Living Blues* 4).

J. B. Hutto, however, told *Blues Unlimited* in 1970 that "out of all I've heard, Elmo [James] was the *best*...and would take time out and sit down and explain things to you." Hutto spoke of following James around "just about everywhere he went." Mike Rowe states that: "J. B. blew upon the Chicago scene with one of the noisiest and toughest bands ever...they sounded ready to devour everything in sight!" (Rowe: *Chicago Blues: The City and Its Music*.) Hutto's scream-ing treble strings strained, screeching beyond the octave–testing the limits. This, coupled with the loose-knit arragements held together by his intense and very personal vocals, must have been a wake-up call to those listeners weaned on milkier stuff. Hutto was a powerful presence on the Chicago scene from the '40s through the '70s.

The natural heir to Hutto's style is his nephew, Li'l Ed Williams, who actu-ally uses his late uncle's Gibson. He remembers listening as a child with his grandmother and aunts to Elmore James and Muddy Waters. In an interview (Donald Wilcox, *Living Blues* 95) Williams spoke of learning James' style through Hutto's influence. He is a very talented musician and a dynamic per-former who perhaps has not yet found the key to his fullest artistic success.

The most recent link in the chain of Delta slide guitarists that originated with Charlie Patton is contemporary bluesman Lonnie Pitchford from Lexington, Mississippi. He coaxes complex and stirring rhythms from the one-string diddley bows that he both makes and plays. In addition, he uses a six-string to turn out convincing sets of Robert Johnson material learned directly from his mentor, Robert Jr. Lockwood Pitchford tends to modernize the style somewhat but maintains the character and integrity of his models.

At the time of this writing there are many fine artists who use slide guitar as an appreciable part of their repertoire. Instead of the hoboing, itinerant bluesmen of the past, they are distinguished American folk artists, many of whom tour worldwide, bringing the blues to audiences all over the globe. Adding to the players already mentioned are Big Jack Johnson, who will nor-mally play four or five slide numbers a night, sometimes using a microphone stand; John Primer, who cut his teeth with Sammy Lawhorn in the great Junior Wells bands at Theresa's–and who has been touring with Magic Slim's band while launching a well-deserved and long overdue solo career (he has a CD on Wolf and one on Earwig soon to be released); talented veteran Smokey Smothers, who played and recorded with Howlin' Wolf, Freddie King, and Muddy Waters, and is still active on the club and festival circuits; the multi-tal-ented Louis Myers, who plays everything and all styles so well that (ironically) he rarely receives any attention; Joe Louis Walker, who plays fine, down-home slide; Luther Allison, another multi-talented bluesman who has been living in France; Big Daddy Kinsey, whose silky slide work can be heard regularly in Chicago, along with that of his talented son, Donald Kinsey; the exciting, tough Johnny Littlejohn, one of the fine protégés of Wolf, Waters, and James; R. L. Burnside, whose mesmerizing drone bass and heartfelt vocalese evoke the deep solo tradition of the Delta; and James "Son" Thomas, whose music speaks to the hard life of the South. All of these players appear regularly, along with legions of the even lesser-known–continuing a living tradition that is truly not much changed since W.C. Handy first heard it that day in 1903, and wrote: "It'll take you by the shoulders and waken you with a start–the effect is unforget-table."

–Larry Hoffman

The History of Gospel Music

Gospel praise singing–a combination of joyous spontaneity and earnest supplication–has been around since the dawn of Christianity; although preva-lent through the Old World for centuries, it did not take root in the United States until some time in the nineteenth century, although small numbers of slaves and slave holders worshipped together as far back as 1734. The first published New England collection of hymns were those of Isaac Watts in 1907's *Hymns and Spiritual Songs*. Philip Bliss' publication *Gospel Songs* appeared in 1876 during a period of intense Christian revival: while pulpit-bashing sermons were being preached all over urban North America, Pentecostal black communities of Holiness and Sanctified denomination mul-tiplied.

The black ghettos nurtured small independent churches like the Atlanta Highway sect and Chicago's Widow's Mite Holiness Church, where African-Americans found the freedom to enjoy long-established traditions of improvi-sation in sermon, prayer, music and holiness dance. The continual dialogue and "lining-out" between pastor and flock were formalized in musical patterns of call-and-response. Surviving descriptions and line drawings give a glimpse of the worship at that time, but the informality of this oral form produced no written music, and no concerts were given for fear of change and dilution.

In the early 1870's, George L. White and pianist Ella Sheppard formed the original Fisk Jubilee Singers at Fisk University in Nashville. The basic premise was to demonstrate the potential usefulness of black religious singing in con-ditions of newfound, post-emancipation freedom, elevating the material from folk-liturgy to popular music. The Fisk Singers toured to raise funds for the university, and within a year similar aggregations or choirs had sprung up all over the country. Tours of the U.S. and Europe captured the imaginations of largely Caucasian audiences, and spirituals were written, the best collection of

which was gathered by James Weldon and J. Rosamond Johnson and first pub-lished by Viking in 1925 as *American Negro Spirituals*.

Spirituals have inspired musicians the world over and have been re-absorbed time and again by African-American gospel singers. They were at first adapted from plantation songs, but gradually became formalized, with lyrical arrangement the norm. The music evolved into the expression of the community, a celebration of life in the context of a theology with a strong social and political dimension. As the Azusa Street Revival and the Birth of Pentecostalism came about in California at the turn of the Twentieth century, nightly revival meetings were held to save sinners–choirs were hired, "altar calls" were enacted, "mourners' benches" were provided, and African-Americans became saved, sanctified, and filled with the Holy Ghost. Not only was "speaking in tongues" encouraged, but interracial membership was deemed necessary, and the music produced by the revival reflected African-American religious concerns and heightened sensibilities.

A second attempt to secularize gospel music by taking it out of a church-worship situation and placing it in the modern mainstream came about in the 1920s. The main proponent was Thomas A. Dorsey, the son of an itinerant black Georgian preacher. In spite of a church upbringing and a blues singing career billed as "Georgia Tom," Dorsey reaffirmed his beliefs in Christian music through both personal tragedy and his love for the recorded works of the Rev. A.W. Nix, an extrovert singer and preacher. Dorsey took the simple blues refrain and adapted it for use in the church (the reverse of what later evolved into popular rhythm & blues music during the 1950s); he wrote, pub-lished, performed, and encouraged an artform that later became known as "gospel music."

Dorsey capitalized on his earlier commercial experience and became the first gospel artist to market to a vast audience. He founded his own publish-ing company, printed great numbers of his own gospel songbooks, charged admission to religious concerts, and formed in the early 1930s the first major female gospel quartet, the Roberta Martin Singers. He also discovered and promoted a new generation of singers, including Mahalia Jackson (who dur-ing the Great Depression traveled with one of the first important gospel quar-tets, Prince Johnson and the Johnson Singers). After initial misgivings, church-es absorbed this new gospel music and found a place for it along with the older, traditional forms of worship. The preacher usually opened the service with a sermon, followed by gospel singing.

Of the seminal professional gospel quartets that had sprung up between the two World Wars, the Golden Gate Quartet is perhaps the best remem-bered and certainly the most revered and imitated. The Gates started out as a barbershop quartet in Berkeley, Virginia in 1930, their repertoire including adaptations from Negro spirituals. Buddies A. C. "Eddie" Griffin (tenor) and Robert "Peg" Ford (bass), along with two high school students from Norfolk, Willie Johnson (baritone) and Henry Owens (tenor), formed the original group, and the outfit grew so popular that out-of-town engagements multiplied. As both Griffin and Ford had local commitments, singers free of travel restric-tions had to be found as replacements, so in 1935-36, sixteen-year-old basso Orlandus Wilson and tenor/guitarist William (Bill) "Highpockets" Langford (Landford) stepped in.

With the growth of sell-out live appearances, The Golden Gate Quartet soon found itself a regular weekly radio show singing jubilee over WBT in Charlotte, N.C. By 1937, the singers were being syndicated over NCB airwaves through local affiliates. The group signed with Victor that same year, and ses-sions were conducted from the Charlotte Hotel. With both records and nation-wide radio exposure, the Gates made legions of fans and inspired many a quartet to come up after them. Only the Fairfield Four on WLAC in Nashville were able to exert as much influence, but that was five years down the line.

Jubilee singing by 1952 was fast becoming a thing of the past, but the Trumpeteers stuck to their winning formula of close rhythmic harmony, spe-cial vocal effects and infectious repetition. The presence of a booming basso, call and response, and alternating pitch take us into a more climactic form of quartet. Hard gospel was now replacing the earlier crooning style of the pre-vious decades with an altogether more extravagant delivery, especially from lead and swing lead voices. Theatrical elements like knee drops, thigh slaps, and screaming falsetto ornamentation came to the fore. Quartets such as The Sensational Nightingales, Dixie Hummingbirds, Soul Stirrers, and Harmonizing Four arose to glory.

The beginnings of a real cross-over came in the mid-Fifties when solo artists like Ray Charles, James Brown, and Nappy Brown began to epitomize gospel with a secular, sometimes erotic lyric. Both James and Nappy Brown had begun their careers in gospel quartets. This was also true of many secu-lar vocal groups. The Royal Sons Quartet became The "5" Royales and The Delta Southernaires became The Spiders, to mention just a few. Many black solo artists, in particular those who waxed for major independent labels like Atlantic, Chess, and later Motown, came from gospel backgrounds.

Music Map

Gospel

Roots

Gospel praise singing's beginnings coincide with the dawn of Christianity, and it is prevalent throughout the Old World in the centuries to follow.
• 1734: Slaves and slaveholders in the U.S. worship together for the first time.
• 19th century: Gospel takes root in the U.S. First adapted from plantation songs, hymns gradually become formalized, with lyrical arrangement the norm.
The music evolves into the expression of the community, a celebration of life in the context of a theology with a strong social and political dimension.
• 1876: Philip Bliss' *Gospel Songs* published during a period of intense Christian revival
• 1907: Isaac Watts' *Hymns and Spiritual Songs* published

Fisk Jubilee Singers

Founded in early 1870s in Nashville, the Fisk Jubilee Singers are created to demonstrate the importance of black religious singing in the wake of the Emancipation Proclamation, in the process elevating the material from folk-liturgy to popular music. The group's tours prove profoundly influential–within a year similar choirs had sprung up across the U.S., their live performances captured the imagination–of white audiences, and spirituals were written.

Thomas A. Dorsey

The key figure behind the push to secularize gospel by pushing it out of the context of worship services and into the contemporary mainstream of the 1920s, Dorsey took the simple blues refrain and adapted it for use in church; he wrote, published, performed, and encouraged an artform that later became known as "gospel music." The first gospel artist to market to a vast audience, he founded his own publishing company, printed his own gospel songbooks, charged admission to religious concerts, and in the early 1930s formed the first major female gospel quartet, the Roberta Martin Singers. He also discovered and promoted a new generation of singers, including Mahalia Jackson.

The Rise of the Quartet Style

In the era between the two World Wars, the quartet style became gospel's predominant means of musical expression. Of the period's seminal professional quartets, the Golden Gate Quartet is perhaps the best remembered and certainly the most revered and imitated–with both records and nationwide radio exposure, they made legions of fans across the country, and inspired many a quartet to come up after them.
Other key acts:
The Fairfield Four • The Soul Stirrers • The Dixie Hummingbirds • The Sensational Nightingales • The Harmonizing Four

Hard Gospel

By 1952, the jubilee sound of years past was quickly vanishing, as the crooning style of previous decades gave way to hard gospel, typified by the presence of a booming basso, call and response, and alternating pitch. In addition to an altogether more extravagant delivery, especially from lead and swing lead voices, theatrical elements like knee drops, thigh slaps, and screaming falsetto ornamentation came to the fore.

Crossover

During the mid-1950s, solo pop artists like James Brown began infusing gospel with secular, sometimes erotic lyrics. Many other solo performers and groups originating in gospel found great success as pop acts–for example, the Royal Sons Quartet became the "5" Royales, and the Delta Southernaires became the Spiders.

The Modern Era

The 1960s saw the growth of a soul-based, high-singing gospel quartet movement with proponents like the Violinaires, the Gospelaires and the Mighty Clouds of Joy, whose secular counterparts could be found in the Falcons and the Impressions. Since then, the paths of religious and secular black music became more closely woven together, with gospel itself now drawing most of its input from commercial trends.
• The 1970s saw the growth of choirs, and eventually choirs into mass choirs.

The 1960s saw the growth of a soul-based, high singing gospel quartet movement with proponents like the Violinaires, Gospelaires, and Mighty Clouds whose secular counterparts could be found in The Falcons, Impressions, and Incredibles. Since then, the paths of religious and secular black music have become more closely woven together with gospel itself now drawing most of its input from commercial trends. The 1970s saw the growth of choirs, and choirs into mass choirs whose voices today seem to almost drown out the few remaining professional soldiers still scraping a living on the quartet circuit. – *Opal Louis Nations*

♦♦♦ **The Arrival of B.B. King**, *Charles Sawyer* (Da Capo, 1980) B.B King's authorized biography is a thoughtful and, for the most part, thorough document of his life through the late '70s. Drawing upon conversations with King, as well as early childhood mentors and past and present music/business associates, Sawyer details his rise from poverty in the Mississippi Delta through the chitlin circuit to the top level of American mainstream entertainment. He places a lot of emphasis upon context, which can be both an asset and a hindrance. The extensive passages about his sharecropping roots in the Delta yield an appreciation of the remarkable perseverance and talent King needed to overcome the barriers of prejudice and injustice. At other times Sawyer sets the table with unnecessary elaboration, devoting a bulk of one chapter, for instance, to the mid-'60s blues revival with analysis that will be redundant to many blues fans. He's best when he sticks to his subject, although some phases of King's career (like most of the '60s, prior to his breakthrough to the pop audience) are skimmed over with inappropriate haste. There are also extensive analyses (perhaps too extensive and analytical for general readers) of the unique properties of King's guitar style and compositions, including an appendix devoted solely to one B.B. King guitar solo. —*Richie Unterberger*

♦♦♦ **The Blackwell Guide to Blues Records**, *edited by Paul Oliver* (Blackwell, 1989) The most comprehensive reference book of its sort, not to say that it's even close to perfect, but that there's really not much competition. The Blackwell layout is daunting for the novice: lots of essays of varying quality on regional styles, wads of song listings, and many fine capsule reviews of albums, ranging from famous to very, very obscure. Divided into chapters covering both regions (such as postwar Chicago) and styles (piano blues, "downhome postwar blues"), it also covers subgenres like rhythm and blues and soul blues that some purists would have regarded as too diluted and commercial to include. It's not the kind of thing you can read in a few sittings, but if you have reasonable patience, there's a lot of valuable information here, and the authors are good at pinpointing the best anthologies and starting points. —*Richie Unterberger*

♦♦♦ **Bluesland**, *edited by Pete Welding & Toby Byron* (Dutton, 1991) A large, handsome, near-coffee-table-sized book with essays on twelve blues performers and some fine black-and-white pictures. Perhaps because the volume is well packaged (and a bit on the pricy side), it doesn't fully meet the high expectations readers might bring to the project. Some of the essays are very good, offering a mix of detail and insightful criticism (Robert Palmer on Professor Longhair, Pete Welding on B.B. King). Others are on the slim and perfunctory side, sometimes rehashing biographical material which is presented with greater depth and color elsewhere. The piece on Lonnie Johnson carries special interest, as the author, Chris Albertson, was responsible for rediscovering the guitarist on the eve of the blues/folk revival. Some purists would argue whether Etta James and Chuck Berry belong in a book about blues masters at all. There's some good stuff here, but these studies aren't definitive or, in some cases, even especially detailed. Which means that, considering the hefty ($26.95) price tag, you might want to check it out of the local library. —*Richie Unterberger*

♦♦♦ **The Blues Makers**, *Sam Charters* (Da Capo, 1991) This reprint combines two of Charters' previously published books, *The Bluesmen* (1967) and *Sweet as the Showers of Rain* (1977). In both of these, Charters focused upon profiles of pre-war country bluesmen, as well as devoting some space to overall analysis of regional styles (which includes paragraphs on some of the more obscure singers who didn't merit a chapter of their own). Much of the book is based upon research that Charters, one of the leading pioneers of the field, undertook in the late 1950s and 1960s. Thus, a lot of this is not as fascinating or useful as it once was, since subsequent research has filled out our knowledge of these men (almost every subject, incidentally, is male) and corrected some of Charters' inaccuracies and incomplete deductions. It's important to note, though, that Charters' efforts were among the key foundations of such subsequent research. Read today, it still has considerable value for blues fans, with portraits of Blind Blake, Sleepy John Estes, Furry Lewis, Frank Stokes, Son House, Charley Patton, Skip James, Blind Lemon Jefferson, Henry Thomas, Memphis Minnie, and several other giants of the music's early days. The more

casual fan/reader, however, is better off with histories that are written in a more accessible tone. Charters describes numerous recordings in painstaking detail (remember, hardly anyone else had heard these items when he first wrote about them), and provides musical transcriptions that may bore those without the specialized knowledge to comprehend them. —*Richie Unterberger*

♦♦♦ **Blues: The British Connection**, *Bob Brunning* (Blanford Press, 1986) Brunning is not only an authority on British blues-rock, he was there–he played bass in the first lineup of Fleetwood Mac before John McVie joined, and went on to play with Savoy Brown and other blues-rock groups. This is a good survey of British blues-rock from the days of Alexis Korner through the 1980s, concentrating mostly on the 1960s, when the form was in its heyday. There are chapters devoted to all the major groups: the Yardbirds, John Mayall, Pretty Things, Spencer Davis, Manfred Mann, Graham Bond, Fleetwood Mac, the Groundhogs, Ten Years After, Chicken Shack, Rory Gallagher, and producer Mike Vernon. A lot of them are spiced by first-hand recollections from band members; the ones which aren't are considerably weaker. The sections on minor figures like Dave Kelly, Savoy Brown, and the Blues Band hold considerably less interest than the ones on the more important musicians, but the book does give a pretty complete picture of the scene. —*Richie Unterberger*

♦♦♦ **Bossmen: Bill Monroe & Muddy Waters**, *James Rooney* (Da Capo, 1971) What exactly, you might be wondering, does one have to do with the other? Well, both were responsible for fathering schools of music (bluegrass and electric blues, respectively) that influenced the course of rock and popular music. Both were outstanding bandleaders that schooled many musicians who went on to become innovators in their own right. Structured mostly as oral history, Rooney lets Monroe and Waters (the book is divided into two separate sections) talk at length about their collaborators, songwriting, recordings, and performances, as well as the many changes they witnessed in both music and society during their careers. Quotes by sidemen and other associates flesh out this interesting and very readable work, which should appeal to most readers interested in rock's roots, despite the very different styles that each man pioneered. —*Richie Unterberger*

♦♦♦ **Chicago Blues**, *Mike Rowe* (Da Capo, 1973) Originally published as *Chicago Breakdown*, this is an extremely thorough history of Chicago blues from its beginnings in the 1930s through about 1970, the heart of the volume devoted to the music's peak in the 15 years or so following World War II. Rowe not only accounts for all of the city's major blues artists (and probably all of its minor ones), but also gives detailed histories of all the city's blues labels, from Chess and Vee-Jay through J.O.B. and Cobra, down to outfits that hardly released anything. The text is enlivened by quotes from interviews with many of the major players on the scene, as well as many fine photographs, both of the musicians and the neighborhoods where they lived and played. It must be pointed out that this is too intensely detailed and scholarly for the general fan (though never condescending). Rowe goes on at considerable length about innumerable little-known singles, and even provides tables illustrating migration patterns from the South to Chicago; for those who are unfamiliar with many of the records and performers, some of the information will seem trivial (to the devotees, of course, much of it will be fascinating). Rowe does keep the big picture in mind at all times, though, writing passionately and keeping an eye on the larger trends that enabled the form to thrive, as well as the factors that precipitated its decline. He also reaches the intriguing conclusion, supported by some evidence, that Chicago electric blues did not arise as a result of displaced Southerners demanding the sounds they liked, but because Southern musicians reworked their music to meet the demands of the urban audience. —*Richie Unterberger*

♦♦♦ **The Country Blues**, *Samuel Charters* (Da Capo, 1959) This was one of the first book-length, serious studies of the blues, and perhaps the most influential of its time. Charters, as he admits in his introduction to a revised edition, "was trying to describe Black music and Black culture in a way that would immediately involve a certain kind of younger, middle-class White American." He did a good, straightforward, occasionally dry job of documenting important blues strains from the form's roots through the Delta to Chicago, including chapters devoted to both overall themes/styles and specific performers (such as Leroy Carr, Blind Lemon Jefferson, and Robert Johnson). It's not the first book you'd direct a beginner towards these days, both because it only goes up to the late 1950s, and because subsequent research has built upon Charters' more basic outlines considerably. Indeed, there are some factual errors and incomplete details in the text that Charters chose not to revise for subsequent editions. It also concentrates mostly upon rural guitar blues, largely bypassing developments such as jump blues, honkers and shouters, and West Coast blues. Its chief strengths are its utilization of Charters' own field research in the South (in which he spoke to several surviving bluesmen), and a detailed reconstruction of how major labels recorded the blues before World War II. —*Richie Unterberger*

✦✦✦✦ **Deep Blues**, *Robert Palmer* (Viking Press, 1981) Renowned critic and sometime musician Palmer traces the evolution of a major (perhaps *the* major) strain of blues, from rural Mississippi Delta acoustic forms through its move to the cities, particularly Chicago, where it became amplified and provided a bedrock foundation for rock & roll. There are more comprehensive, scholarly analyses of the blues available, but this is the most readable and accessible by a wide margin, with plenty of first-hand recollections from Muddy Waters, Robert Lockwood, Jr., Sam Phillips, and others. —*Richie Unterberger*

✦✦✦✦ **Elvis: The Illustrated Record**, *Roy Carr and Mick Farren* (Harmony, 1982) At the time this book appeared, there were no serious critical studies of Elvis' work. This remains the volume that, as the authors intended, "set the record straight." Features in-depth criticism, with enthusiastic but considered analysis, of every record Elvis made. Naturally–thankfully, actually–the early Sun and RCA sessions, as well as some isolated later critical triumphs like the late '60s albums, are covered in the most depth, with a scholarship that is both meticulous and compelling. Elvis' relatively brief eras of brilliance were punctuated by long ones of excruciating mediocrity, and the authors do not fail to point out the shortcomings of his many soundtracks and uninspired singles. Indeed, the stretch between 1961 and 1968 can make for pretty thin gruel, and these parts are inevitably much less interesting than the highlights, though the authors do a good job of dismissing, or lightly skipping over, his bad records with curt humor that doesn't waste words. Includes some good essays summarizing specific eras of his career, tons of sleeves and photos, and an exhaustive discography, including bootlegs. —*Richie Unterberger*

✦✦✦✦✦ **Encyclopedia of the Blues**, *Gerard Herzhaft* (The University Of Arkansas Press, 1992) In spite of the fact that this was translated (very ably) from French, this is one of the best blues reference books–perhaps *the* best for someone who wants a comprehensive volume that doesn't become so specialized that novices get lost. Over 500 pages in length, the bulk is devoted to concise profiles of all major (and many minor) blues artists from the beginning of the 20th century to 1990. These are not only passionate and descriptive, but maintain a sense of critical perspective that identifies the performers' chief strengths and weaknesses, their most noteworthy recordings, and their importance within the blues as a whole. The profiles are supplemented by short rundowns of key blues genres such as Delta blues and female blues singers, a selected discography (with brief reviews) of the best blues albums, and a list of popular blues standards and their origins. There's also a list of specific recordings, which demonstrate some of the most characteristic and best uses of blues guitar, harmonica, and piano styles. —*Richie Unterberger*

✦✦✦✦ **Eric Clapton: Lost in the Blues**, *Harry Shapiro* (Da Capo, 1992) There are a few Clapton bios available, and while this one does not have a great deal of first-hand interview material, it does a very good straightforward job of following his musical progression through the Yardbirds and John Mayall to Cream, Blind Faith, Derek & the Dominos, and his lengthy solo career. Every album, as a soloist or group member, is discussed in considerable detail. The author draws upon dozens of previous interviews and press clippings, spanning the mid-'60s to the early '90s, and sheds some light on the several rather mysterious lulls and metamorphoses in the mercurial guitarist's career, especially the decisions to leave all of his groups just when they were peaking or about to launch to stardom, and his years as a secluded heroin addict in the early '70s. Includes meticulous discography, "groupography," and a review of the various guitars Clapton's used over the years. —*Richie Unterberger*

✦✦✦✦✦ **Feel Like Going Home**, *Peter Guralnick* (Vintage, 1971) Guralnick is one of America's premier writers and critics of roots music, and this collection of his early essays is an important work, offering sensitive and in-depth portraits of a gaggle of major early rock and blues stars: Jerry Lee Lewis, Howlin' Wolf, Charlie Rich, Muddy Waters, Skip James, Johnny Shines, Charlie Rich, and the owners of Sun and Chess Records. Guralnick spent a lot of time with each of his subjects, often observing them at home or on stage; in some cases, he was apparently the first journalist to treat the musician as a serious artist. Perhaps

as a result, he landed some poignant and personal material, the kind that publicists have learned to shield from serious but inquisitive writers. Guralnick does tend to romanticize his heroes as artists who have never received their just due, but this is one of the best books of its kind. —*Richie Unterberger*

✦✦✦✦✦ **Good Rockin' Tonight: Sun Records and the Birth of Rock'n'roll**, *Colin Escott with Martin Hawkins* (St. Martin's Press, 1991) Excellent history of what was, in the final estimation, the label most responsible for launching rock & roll, although the contributions of other indies like Atlantic were also immensely important. Includes chapters on all the major Sun stars: Elvis, Johnny Cash, Carl Perkins, Jerry Lee Lewis, and Roy Orbison. Of equal interest, though, are the descriptions of owner/producer Sam Phillips' slap-echo studio sound and distinctive artistic vision, which also encompassed a wealth of blues and country music. Besides first- and second-hand interviews with the most famous characters in the Sun story, you also hear from more obscure performers and sidemen, and get profiles of relatively unheralded artists like Warren Smith and Junior Parker. Fascinating stuff, this is an updated version of a history first published around 1980, and includes a good deal of new information and many great photos. —*Richie Unterberger*

✦✦✦ **The Grove Press Guide to the Blues on CD**, *edited by Frank John Hadley* (Grove Press, 1993) The execution of this handbook was okay; where it really ran into problems was its overall conception. As the title says, it's a guide to blues on compact disc, not blues on record. What this means is that a great many important, essential blues recordings are not discussed because they were out-of-print or had not yet made the leap to the digital format when the book was issued. What's more, some major performers are not included, or, even worse, are represented by one or two of their worst efforts. The reviews and ratings are concise and astute, but simply don't afford reasonable overviews of the artists, or even the blues as a whole (there's a disproportionate amount of bad White blues or bar-band blues). The decision to limit the coverage to digital recordings guaranteed that the book would start to date quickly, as many landmark blues recordings did indeed make their belated way to CD in the years since the guide was printed. —*Richie Unterberger*

✦✦✦ **The History of the Blues**, *Francis Davis* (Hyperion, 1995) With this companion volume to the PBS series, Davis lays out the basic frameworks of the music's development, from its pre-20th century roots to Robert Cray. The major blues styles are covered in reasonable depth: acoustic Delta blues, female-sung vaudeville-blues hybrids of the 1920s, the amplified Chicago sound, the '60s blues revival, and modern soul-influenced blues by Cray, Ted Hawkins, and others. Blues histories tend toward the academic and scholarly more often than not, and Davis gets major points for crafting his text in an accessible, very readable fashion. He also, to his credit, is not content to mouth clichés, but to provide and occasionally champion interpretations that you won't often find elsewhere. His iconoclasm also gets to be a problem, though; he continually backtracks upon himself in a coy, hide-and-seek manner that becomes frustrating (typical sentence: "The blues is dead; the blues will never die. I don't know which it is, though I suspect it's both."). Also, considerable chunks of the story are untold, and some performers (such as Junior Wells, Jimmy Reed, and Son Seals) treated not so much disrespectfully as cursorily. It's not a bad overview, but Robert Palmer's *Deep Blues* still wins out as the best introductory overall study of the blues' evolution, although Palmer's book is not nearly as wide-ranging. —*Richie Unterberger*

✦✦✦✦✦ **I Am the Blues**, *Willie Dixon with Don Snowden* (Da Capo, 1989) If there was ever a man to give the inside story of Chicago blues, Dixon would seem to fit the bill; he wasn't a star, but as a producer, arranger, bass player, and especially songwriter, he did as much as anyone to shape modern electric blues. This autobiography lets Willie do much of the talking, with Snowden filling in other information and quoting from associates of Dixon, including artists and engineers at Chess Records. There are some pretty tasty recollections here, especially Dixon's memories of the groundbreaking '60s tours of Europe by leading blues stars, his disappointment with Chess' exploitative business practices (as a songwriter due many royalties, Dixon was as hurt by these as anyone), and first-hand memories of working out classics like "Hoochie Coochie Man" (with Muddy Waters) and "My Babe" (with Little Walter). There actually aren't as many fascinating stories as one might expect; Dixon doesn't go into great depth about the many legends he worked with (Chuck Berry, Bo Diddley, Howlin' Wolf, and others), doesn't discuss some of his most famous standards, and doesn't introspect heavily on the songwriting or creative processes in general. Worthwhile reading for the rock and blues fan, but not the goldmine of riches for which one might have hoped. —*Richie Unterberger*

✦✦✦ **I Hear You Knockin'**, *Jeff Hannusch* (Swallow, 1983) Portraits of 31 major New Orleans R&B performers, ranging from the famous (Dave Bartholomew, Irma Thomas, Lee Dorsey, Allen Toussaint) to the semi-famous (Smiley Lewis, Guitar Slim, Chris Kenner, Frankie Ford) to the downright unknown (Tuts

Washington, Bill Webb, Dorothy Labostrie). The level of detail is admirable: Hannusch gives the basic facts about the careers and records of his subjects, and usually provides plenty of first-hand quotes and memories as well. But it doesn't make for compelling reading, unless you're a Crescent City specialist. It's not so much that Hannusch is dry (although he's not the most colorful writer), but that he doesn't provide much critical insight into the music, or much of a context for appreciating his subjects' achievements. Peter Guralnick, for instance, manages to excel at describing the music of blues and country performers. Just as vitally, Guralnick lends his portraits a very human dimension by illustrating how environment and experiences help to shape his heroes' music, and assesses the significance of their achievements in the broad canvas of popular music. Hannusch is mostly content to detail who did what and when. Although the occasional colorful anecdote emerges, the tone is closer to a reference book than a volume that helps convey the incredibly rich, important, and colorful history of New Orleans rock and R&B. If you are very interested in the vivacious music of this equally vivacious city, it's still handy to have around, with an appendix/discography of important recordings and chart listings. —*Richie Unterberger*

◆◆◆◆ **Jimi Hendrix: Electric Gypsy**, *Harry Shapiro and Caesar Glebbeek* (St. Martin's, 1991) Hendrix's life story is such a difficult, elusive subject to tackle that a definitive biography may be an impossible goal. Although the memoirs by Mitch Mitchell, Noel Redding, and producer Eddie Kramer all have their value, for my money this is the best overall view of this extraordinarily complicated man's life and music. It's mammoth, weighing in at over 700 pages, but purposefully detailed. The authors examine every stage of his development, and every facet of his musicianship, from his R&B beginnings and his classic studio recordings to his charismatic live performances and innovations in studio technique, amplification equipment, and, of course, guitar playing. It draws upon a staggering mass of archival materials—interviews, letters, press accounts of the period, memories of his many musical colleagues and professional associates. The many rumors and contradictory anecdotes could lead to a quagmire, but the book takes care not to draw uninformed conclusions or pass judgement, presenting many points of view and cautiously offering interpretations to weigh. The large appendix is also quite valuable, offering a lengthy discography (a project in itself, given Hendrix's extraordinarily tangled recorded legacy), list of concerts performed, copious documentation of his equipment and many guitars, and family tree. —*Richie Unterberger*

◆◆◆ **Jimi Hendrix: Inside the Experience**, *Mitch Mitchell with John Platt* (Harmony, 1990) More than almost any other rock superstar, Hendrix has been subjected to different, at times downright wildly varying historical accounts, making it difficult to separate the likely from the unlikely. This book, not a biography but an oral history of sorts from the Experience drummer, is refreshingly straightforward. And, unlike some of the authors and associates who have written about Hendrix, Mitchell was very much there; in fact, he worked with Hendrix more closely than any other musician, although some accounts have painted the Experience (probably inaccurately) as a situation which constrained Hendrix creatively. Mitchell doesn't have axes to grind, or a big ego to inflate, so what you get are detailed, very interesting recollections of the tours, Hendrix's methods of working in the studio, key gigs such as Monterey and Woodstock, Jimi's influences, and the guitarist's innovative use of equipment. With lots of good photos, a good book for those more intereseted in the music than the mystique. —*Richie Unterberger*

◆◆◆◆ **Last Train to Memphis: The Rise of Elvis Presley**, *Peter Guralnick* (Little, Brown & Co., 1994). There are many biographies of Elvis, most of them cheap and shoddy productions that focus on the most sensational and morbid aspects of the King's life (though he did give them a lot to focus on). Guralnick is one of the top authorities on early rock & roll, and the natural candidate to write a biography that is both accurate and focused upon his art and music as much as his personal life. The first volume of a projected multi-part work, this covers what, for the majority of his fans, are his most interesting years, ending just after he leaves the United States in late 1958 to serve as a member of the army in Germany. The early years are thoroughly documented (there are almost 500 footnotes alone): the grinding poverty, the gospel influences, the months of pestering Sun Records to record him, the sculpting of his early rockabilly sound in the Sun Studios, the wild early tours, the early managers, the meteoric rise to fame after his contract was sold to RCA, the hangers-on he felt compelled to surround himself with from Memphis, the induction into the army. Lots of detail and balanced perspective between his personality and his music, only marred by some surprisingly perfunctory appraisals of some of his early sessions, particularly the ones at RCA. —*Richie Unterberger*

◆◆◆ **The Legacy of the Blues**, *Samuel Charters* (Da Capo, 1975) Twelve chapter-length portraits of major and minor bluesmen, including Lightnin' Hopkins, Bukka White, Robert Pete Williams, Juke Boy Booner, Sunnyland Slim, Champion Jack Dupree, Eddie Boyd, Memphis Slim, Big Joe Williams, and

Snooks Eaglin. Charters is neither the best nor worst of interviewers/profilers, and the quality of the pieces is variable, usually according to how loquacious his subjects were. It's not the best project of its sort (Peter Guralnick and Stanley Booth, for instance, are more skilled at this sort of thing), but it will interest most blues fans with a particular curiosity in the featured artists. —*Richie Unterberger*

◆◆◆◆◆ **The Life & Legend of Leadbelly**, *Charles Wolfe & Kip Lornell* (Harper Collins, 1992) Few 20th-century popular musicians had more fascinating lives than Leadbelly's. Even before he was discovered by folklorist John Lomax, he'd lived the typically tough life of a Black southern farmer, played for years with Blind Lemon Jefferson before either of them were well known, been jailed twice for murky murder/manslaughter charges, and sung his way to freedom by composing and delivering a pardon plea directly to the governor of Texas. Then things got even more interesting, as he worked for Lomax as an assistant, became a popular performer at New York high-society gatherings, and eventually fell in with a crowd that included Pete Seeger, the Weavers, Sonny Terry, and Brownie McGhee. To a large degree, many of the details of his life remain a mystery, particularly the years before his discovery at a Louisiana jail by Lomax. Wolfe and Lornell do a good, responsible job of piecing together the facts and the myths, offering speculation (particularly for the shadowy pre-Lomax years) but never unwarranted conclusions. They also provide a wealth of description and criticism of his recordings and songwriting, as well as a great deal of context for understanding both the origins of his music and the harsh social conditions by which they were framed. Leadbelly himself comes across as an extremely guarded, sometimes secretive man, hard to know and judge even for those who knew him best, right up until the end, when he was a renowned international figure. Extensively researched and accessibly written (though some familiarity with Leadbelly's work will enhance its appreciation), it's one of the best biographies of a major folk icon. —*Richie Unterberger*

◆◆◆◆◆ **Lost Highway**, *Peter Guralnick* (Vintage, 1979) Like his previous *Feel Like Going Home*, these are more first-rate, extremely human portrayals of major American roots musicians, going much heavier on the country & western this time around (though blues and early rock musicians are also included). Many musicians of the first echelon and a few more obscure noteworthies are included in this gallery of portraits, including Ernest Tubb, Hank Snow, Rufus Thomas, Bobby Bland, Scotty Moore, Charlie Feathers, Mickey Gilley, Waylon Jennings, Merle Haggard, James Talley, Joe Turner, Howlin' Wolf, and Otis Spann. —*Richie Unterberger*

◆◆◆ **Making Tracks**, *Charlie Gillett* (Souvenir Press, 1974) Gillett is the author of the first comprehensive (and still one of the most acclaimed) rock & roll histories, *The Sound of the City*. This is his history of Atlantic Records, the most successful independent to survive from rock & roll's earliest days. More a history of the music than the business, anyone who's interested in early R&B and rock will find a lot of absorbing reading here. Gillett interviewed Atlantic principals Ahmet Ertegun and (to a significantly greater degree) Jerry Wexler extensively, yielding a lot of first-hand recollections about the early careers of such important artists as Ruth Brown, Clyde McPhatter, Joe Turner, Ray Charles, Solomon Burke, Otis Redding, and Aretha Franklin. Important ancillary figures like Jesse Stone, songwriters Jerry Leiber and Mike Stoller, and Rick Hall of Fame Studios in Muscle Shoals, AL, also get a chance to speak. Gillett is principally an R&B and soul man, so Atlantic's ventures into pop, White rock, and British rock are covered in considerably less depth, although they aren't neglected. —*Richie Unterberger*

◆◆◆ **Peter Green: Founder of Fleetwood Mac**, *Martin Celmins* (Castle Communications, 1995) Like Syd Barrett and Brian Wilson, Peter Green is a figure of such musical talent and personal eccentricity that he holds an ongoing fascination for fans and rock historians. One of the premier late '60s British blues-rockers as the leader of the original incarnation of Fleetwood Mac, and one of the few blues-rockers to expand beyond rocked-up derivations to a more eclectic and personal vision, he turned his back on the music business in 1970. This wasn't a mere temperamental fit; he *really* turned his back, holding a series of low-paying jobs, working on a kibbutz in Israel, giving his money away to charity, and only occasionally playing professionally. This fine, compact bio both documents his musical talents and probes the myths surrounding his mysterious behavior, both at the peak of his stardom and his subsequent departure from the music scene. Most of Green's chief musical associates offer lengthy recollections, including John Mayall (with whom Green first became known, when he filled Eric Clapton's position in the Bluesbreakers), Mick Fleetwood, John McVie, and lesser-knowns such as Bob Brunning (who briefly played bass in Mac's first lineup). Although Green is often thought of as an acid casualty in the manner of Syd Barrett, that judgement is pretty much laid to rest by the fact that Green himself, interviewed in the mid-1990s, offered Celmins quite a few lucid first-hand recollections and comments of his own for this volume. This doesn't negate the tragic dimensions of Green's post-Mac career, which found him at times incarcerated and drugged for psychological problems, and fitfully returning to music with subpar bunches of (by and large) hacks. Those who consider Green one of the finest British rock musicians of his time will find this an even-handed, non-sensationalistic portrait of one of the few stars to refuse to play the music business game, and demonstrate his philosophy via deeds, not just words. Includes a lengthy discography of official and unofficial recordings. —*Richie Unterberger*

✦✦✦ The Rolling Stones: An Illustrated Record, *Roy Carr* (Harmony, 1976) Though flawed, this is the best critical survey of the Stones' work, reviewing every release through *Black and Blue*. That leaves nearly 20 years uncovered, but it could be argued that it nonetheless encompasses just about everything worthwhile. The inconsistency of depth is frustrating; some albums are discussed rather cursorily, and *Between the Buttons* is, unbelievably, dismissed as a trivial affair in the course of several sentences. On the other hand, there are a lot of critical insights and details about the recording and production of masterpieces from "I Wanna Be Your Man" on through "Paint it Black," "Beggar's Banquet," and the rest of their classic material. A running diary of notable incidents and quotes from the band is interspersed throughout, along with photos, a lengthy interview with Mick Jagger, and the most comprehensive discography and tour itineraries (complete with bootlegs and session appearances) of their prime years ever assembled. —*Richie Unterberger*

✦✦✦ The Roots of the Blues, *Samuel Charters* (Da Capo, 1981) No one will be able to pinpoint the origins of the blues with total accuracy. But most can agree that a key root was the indigenous music of Western Africa, from where many of the slaves that were shipped to America came. In 1974, blues scholar Samuel Charters traveled to Gambia, Senegal, and Mali to try to document existing vestiges of African music that may have influenced the development of the blues. This is his narrative of the journey, in which, as he readily admits, he found at least as many questions as answers. While he did get close to the source in some elements of the village griots that he met and recorded, as well as the songs he heard in a Senegalese Creole village, he didn't find a great deal that made explicit connections to blues as it is heard and performed in the United States. It doesn't mean that this isn't interesting reading, not just for the musical analysis (which gets a bit wordy at times), but for Charters' well-related impressions of contemporary African society, and his bracing tale of tracking down traces of present-day slavery in Gambia, generations after the practice had supposedly started to die. —*Richie Unterberger*

✦✦✦ Rhythm Oil, *Stanley Booth*,(Pantheon, 1991) He hasn't written prolifically, and he hasn't written much about music that was performed after the early '70s, but Memphis writer Booth is one of the best chroniclers of blues, soul, and rock that draws upon those influences. This collection of essays, often drawn from first-person experiences with the musicians at recording sessions, concerts, and their homes, includes good pieces on Otis Redding, Furry Lewis, B.B. King, Elvis, Janis Joplin, Al Green, James Brown, and little-known but widely respected Memphis jazz pianist Phineas Newborn. An adept critic, Booth's special skill is drawing upon the cultural ambience of the music–often Memphis, almost always the American South–to give a deeper understanding of how their environment, professional and personal, informs their art. —*Richie Unterberger*

✦✦✦ Searching for Robert Johnson, *Peter Guralnick* (E.P. Dutton, 1989) The life of the most famous Delta bluesman is shrouded in mystery–there's little that can be documented, and although several other blues performers of the time have first-hand memories of Johnson, they can be vague and contradictory. This slim (83-page) volume, in which Guralnick pieces together what is known and critiques Johnson's recordings, is more like a long essay than a book. It's not flimsy, though. The author talked extensively with Johnny Shines and Robert Lockwood, the two musicians who knew Johnson the best, to relate some first-hand perspectives about what the man was like. He also refers often to the research of blues scholar Mack McCormick for details of Johnson's volatile family and personal life, describes Robert's recording sessions thoroughly, and makes intelligent, cautious speculations about the forces that drove the guitarist. Also includes a comprehensive discography (with descriptive reviews) of Johnson's meager body of work, as well as of records by performers that influenced Johnson, and which Johnson influenced. Useful, but ridiculously overpriced (at $14.95) for such a thin book; time to raid the local library again. —*Richie Unterberger*

✦✦✦✦✦ The Sound of the City, *Charlie Gillett* (Da Capo, 1970) Originating as a university thesis, this was the first attempt to write a comprehensive history of rock & roll, dealing with the form primarily in musical terms, not celebrity or popular culture ones. It's still one of the best, although the coverage only extends into the early '70s. Gillett's scholarship, though quite readable, is intensely detailed, accurately describing the cross-fertilization of vocal, instrumental, and production styles from the mid-'40s through the next several decades. He views the struggle of independent labels, as well as the struggle of major labels to come to terms with rock's popularity, as one of the most important undercurrents of rock; hence the performers are often discussed in terms of their labels and producers, as well as their regions or styles. Gillett's tastes run towards R&B and roots rock, and singles rather than album-length statements; some readers may be taken aback by his bluntly clinical, not-wholly-enthusiastic assessments of the Beatles, Jimi Hendrix, Elvis Presley, and other major rock deities. And the focus, concerned with what's in the grooves rather than personality and attitude, may strike some as too detached and analytical. Gillett covered an enormous amount of ground with this volume, though, intelligently and objectively, and this remains an important foundation of rock scholarship. The Da Capo revised edition adds a little material to the 1970 printing, basically just extending the coverage a year or two into the 1970s. —*Richie Unterberger*

✦✦✦✦ The True Adventures of the Rolling Stones, *Stanley Booth* (Vintage, 1984) The Rolling Stones' story is a diffuse and murky one that doesn't lend itself nearly as well to retelling as the Beatles'. This book, originally titled *Dance with the Devil*, is not the most linear of those efforts, but it is the best. Memphis journalist Booth, a friend of the band (particularly Keith Richards), traveled with them through much of their famous late 1969 tour of America. In the account that he finally published 15 years later, he alternates between first-hand reportage of the tour and a history of the band, from their scuffling boues beginnings in the early '60s through their rise to fame and the death of Brian Jones. Not much is spared in either part of the tale; the fierce infighting that resulted in the ouster (which, to a large degree, was self-imposed) of Jones, the backstage groupies and drugs, the violence at Altamont, the pushy businessmen and promoters, the decadent ennui of a megastar touring band are all here, documented entertainingly without undue moralizing. Especially interesting are the sections on Altamont, of course, and the recording of several tracks at Muscle Shoals for Sticky Fingers, to which Booth was an eyewitness. —*Richie Unterberger*

✦✦✦ Unsung Heroes Of Rock'n'roll, *Nick Tosches* (Charles Scribner's Sons, 1984) Brief profiles of 25 pioneers of rock & roll, mostly from the decade before rock & roll was widely known (1945–55). Some are extremely famous (Nat King Cole, Louis Jordan, Big Joe Turner, Bill Haley), but most are known these days to collectors (Stick McGhee, Cecil Gant, Skeets McDonald, Hardrock Gunter); most are early R&B performers, a few are hillbilly C&W singers. Tosches' style is not for everybody, emphasizing lewd and suggestive angles that some may find offensive. He is also of the unequivocal conviction that rock & roll peaked, in essence, before it really started, and his biases can be irritating. Still, this is a handy primer that illustrates how deep rock & roll's roots lie in the most energetic R&B and C&W of the late '40s and '50s, although the mid-'50s are commonly thought of as the music's true starting point. The lengthy final section includes a chronology of the development of rock & roll from 1945 to 1955, and discographies for all of the performers profiled. —*Richie Unterberger*

✦✦✦✦✦ What Was the First Rock'n'roll Record? , *Jim Dawson & Steve Propers* (Faber & Faber, 1992) Everyone can agree that rock & roll came into being sometime in the decade after World War II, but its exact origins can be hard to pinpoint. This is an absolutely fascinating study of 50 key records which pointed the way for rock & roll, or popularized it, between 1944 and 1956. It doesn't so much answer the question posed by the title as illustrate how many divergent strands of music were involved in rock's conception, and what a fascinating and exciting process it was. Major singles by Louis Jordan, John Lee Hooker, Fats Domino, Muddy Waters, Bill Haley, and Elvis are discussed in depth; as are ones by much more obscure artists such as Hardrock Gunter, Big Boy Crudup, Stick McGhee, Jackie Brenston, and Arkie Shibley. Besides explaining the significance of each record with detailed musical analysis, the authors tracked down key artists, session musicians, and producers for their comments, unearthing a wealth of compelling anecdotes. Essential for anyone interested in rock's birth. —*Richie Unterberger*

✦✦✦ Wild Animals, *Andy Blackford* (Sidgwick & Jackson, UK, 1986) The Animals' peak as a truly important group in the mid-'60s was brief, and accordingly, this biography is on the slim side. Appropriately, it focuses almost entirely on the original lineup, before Eric Burdon took the Animals name in 1966 and fronted a variety of psychedelic and hard rock bands for the next few years. For Animals and British Invasion fans, there are a fair number of interesting stories here, including the conception of their classic "House of the Rising Sun," the group's dislike of their more pop-oriented (though excellent) hit singles, and the conflicts between them and producer Mickey Most, and manager Mike Jeffries. There are lots of quotes from members of the band, but in some important respects, it's disappointing. Some of their great singles are barely discussed, and Blackford isn't a top-notch writer, occasionally wandering from the subject into tangents about the era's pop culture. —*Richie Unterberger*

Blues Access

The brainchild of radio show host Cary Wolfson (who won a W.C. Handy Award in 1987 and 1991), Blues Access Magazine was inspired by the Whole Earth Catalog's byline "Access to Tools"–thus, access to blues. It was first published in February of 1990 at 16 pages (all newsprint), but today is almost 100 pages with four-color glossy covers. What you find between these covers is a lot of eye and mind candy for the blues lover.

It contains everything from full-length feature articles to some twenty columns–filled with info (departments). Lots of pictures too. Issues include many well-written reviews, hundreds of new releases (with descriptions), guitar patterns, societies, resources–the works. There is enough information in one issue to seriously tie up your spare time for days. And the ads are just as interesting–major labels, releases, tours, and festivals. When you are done looking at the ads alone, you have a pretty fair idea of what's happening out there in blues world. If you have never seen a copy, go out and get one. You'll not regret it. You can reach them at (303) 443-7245 or write to Blues Access, 1455 Chestnut Place, Boulder, CO 80304-3153. Internet fans can reach them at their web address at http://www.he.net/~blues–*Michael Erlewine*

Blue Suede News

This doesn't deal with the blues exclusively or primarily, concentrating on roots musics of various sorts (blues, R&B, rockabilly, rock & roll, country) past and present (more past than present). The writing and production standards are also closer to fanzine territory than the blues glossies, although they've come a long way over the years. Blues specialists may find it worth picking up for the occasional blues feature and its huge review section, which always covers lots of contemporary blues albums and reissues. (Box 25, Duvall, WA 98019-0025)–*Richie Unterberger*

Blues & Rhythm

Britain's top blues periodical is less comprehensive than its U.S. counterparts, and more devoted to retrospectives and reissue reviews than the contemporary scene. It's a high-quality operation, though, with lively and informed writing, combining interviews/features with an extensive review section. Doesn't limit itself to blues exclusively, also covering some R&B and a little bit of soul. There are also columns for news, live reports, obits, and in-depth examinations of rare recordings. (Byron Foulger, 1 Cliffe Lane, Thornton, Bradford BD13 3DX, UK)–*Richie Unterberger*

Blues Review

Bimonthly glossy is a bit slicker in the production department than the two other major blues mags (*Living Blues* and *Blues Access*). There's a similar concentration of features and new release/reissue reviews, as well as some special-interest columns for live reviews, product surveys, "Cyberblues" (blues on the Internet), and guitar transcriptions. The coverage is perhaps more inclusive of White acts than its peers, and less devoted to historical pieces. That shouldn't be taken as implied criticism–there's room for all three major U.S. blues magazines, which basically cover much of the same thematic ground without duplicating each other too often. (916 Douglas Dr., #101, Endwell, NY 13760)–*Richie Unterberger*

Living Blues

With the establishment of *Blues Access* and *Blues Revue* as class productions in the 1990s, *Living Blues* is no longer as dominant in its field as it once was. But the bimonthly probably remains the best blues publication available, and in fact one of the best specialized music magazines of any kind. Features huge (if occasionally rambling) interviews with major and minor blues performers, a big review section that covers a high percentage of available blues releases and reissues (lots of imports included), news, obituaries, and miscellaneous other features. It's upgraded its production values recently without sacrificing the depth and integrity of the content. Well-written and accessible to the general reader, not just a scholarly publication for blues fanatics. (Hill Hall, Room 301, University, MS 38677-9836)–*Richie Unterberger*

The *All Music Guide* reference books offer just a taste of the wealth of information to be discovered at our website (http://allmusic.com/), the largest and most comprehensive site of its kind on the Internet. Along with the same detailed biographical entries and album reviews found in the books, the AMG website offers much more, touching base with the one-hit wonders, session players, novelty artists, and studio technicians whom, for reasons of space, the book cannot.

Of course, the site doesn't replace the books, it complements them; while the books compile overviews of the superstars, the cult heroes and the true innovators into one handy volume, the AMG homepage fills in the gaps, taking full advantage of the seemingly boundless scope of the web to offer exhaustive coverage of thousands of other, more obscure artists and albums. In addition, it features even more detailed information on music's landmark performers and records, including recording information and hyperlinks to related artists. At the same time, the site affords one luxury that the print format cannot; while published books cannot be updated until the next edition, the AMG website evolves and changes along with the music industry; if your favorite band releases a new album, or their drummer quits, you'll find it noted on-line long before you'll see it mentioned in book form. Information can be accessed through the All Music Guide site in one of three easy ways: to find what you're looking for, simply type the name of the particular artist, album or song in the appropriate space, click on the "search" button, and the available data will appear. You can also click on regular features like our music maps, essays and glossaries, or even help us grow by suggesting new artists and albums to cover.

INDEX

When it comes to music, we wrote the book.

Chasin' That Devil Music
Searching for the Blues

By Gayle Dean Wardlow; Edited with an introduction by Edward Komara

This collection of essays by "bluesfinder" Gayle Dean Wardlow offers a fresh look and listen to the spirited past of the blues and its people. Based on personal interviews with friends and relatives of long-gone bluesmen, and public records research, the author draws lively portraits of legends and unknowns who helped shape the music. Includes a CD of 19 rare recordings by blues pioneers.

Softcover with audio CD, 271pp, 120 B&W photos, 6 x 9, ISBN 0-87930-552-5, $19.95

All Music Guide to Jazz
The Experts' Guide to the Best Jazz Recordings
Third Edition

Edited by Michael Erlewine, Chris Woodstra, Vladimir Bogdanov, and Scott Yanow

Completely updated. A delightful book for both the serious and casual jazz listener, this guide profiles the lives and work of over 1,500 key jazz artists, reviewing and rating each one's best recordings. Also includes essays and music maps that put in context the various jazz styles, key players, and key instruments.

Softcover, 1,378 pp, 7-3/8 x 9-1/4, ISBN 0-87930-530-4, $29.95

Jaco
The Extraordinary and Tragic Life of Jaco Pastorius

By Bill Milkowski

Now in paperback! This is a fitting tribute to the talented but tormented genius who revolutionized the electric bass and single-handedly fused jazz, classical, R&B, rock, reggae, pop, and punk—all before the age of 35, when he met his tragic death.

Softcover with audio CD, 264pp, 6 x 9, ISBN 0-87930-426-X, $14.95

All Music Guide
The Best CDs, Albums & Tapes
Third Edition

Edited by Michael Erlewine, Chris Woodstra, and Vladimir Bogdanov

This fascinating reference leads readers to the best recordings of over 4,000 artists and groups. From rock to rap, blues to bluegrass and everything in between, more than 23,000 recordings in 20 categories are reviewed and rated by 150 top music critics. Includes artist bios, music timelines, and more.

Softcover, 1,500pp, 6-1/8 x 9-1/4, ISBN 0-87930-423-5, $27.95

Tennessee Music
Its People and Places

By Peter Zimmerman

This intriguing book examines how Tennessee's diverse music genres—including country, blues, gospel, bluegrass, soul, and new acoustic—have evolved and influenced one another across the state and over the years. It provides practical site information for visitors exploring this rich musical territory, plus compelling tales of the men and women at the heart of Tennessee's unique musical legacy.

Softcover, 275pp, 30 color and 30 B&W photos, 6 x 9, ISBN 0-87930-533-9, $24.95

The Hammond Organ
Beauty in the B

By Mark Vail

This book salutes the instrumental pairing that has changed the sound of the organ in gospel, blues, jazz, R&B, rock, and pop since the 1950s: the Hammond B-3 and the whirling Leslie speaker. This loving history describes the mechanical innovations and musical influence of this legendary pairing.

Softcover, 239pp, 29 color and 240 B&W photos, 8-1/2 x 11, ISBN 0-87930-459-6, $24.95

Blues Guitar
The Men Who Made the Music
Second Edition

Edited by Jas Obrecht

Readers get a look inside and music of thirty great bluesmen, through interviews, articles, discographies, and rare photographs. Covers Buddy Guy, Robert Johnson, John Lee Hooker, Albert King, B.B. King, Muddy Waters, and more.

Softcover, 278pp, 98 B&W photos, 8-1/2 x 11, ISBN 0-87930-292-5, $22.95

Bass Heroes
Styles, Stories & Secrets of 30 Great Bass Players

Edited by Tom Mulhern

Thirty of the world's greatest bass players in rock, jazz, studio/pop, and blues & funk share their musical influences, playing techniques, and opinions. Inlcudes Jack Bruce, Stanley Clarke, James Jamerson, Paul McCartney, and more.

Softcover, 208pp, 8-1/2 x 11, ISBN 0-87930-274-7, $19.95

All Music Guide to Rock
The Best CDs, Albums & Tapes—Rock, Pop, Soul, R&B and Rap
Second Edition

Edited by Michael Erlewine, Vladimir Bogdanov, Chris Woodstra, Stephen Thomas Erlewine, and Richie Unterberger

Updated and expanded, this ultimate guide to rock now covers over 11,000 recordings and profiles over 1,800 musicians. Recordings are reviewed and rated. Performers are profiled. And major influences and trends are discussed in essays and charted in music maps.

Softcover, 1,234pp, 6-1/8 x 9-1/4, ISBN 0-87930-494-4, $26.95

Secrets from the Masters
40 Great Guitar Players

Edited by Don Menn

Featuring the most influential guitarists of the past 25 years: Jimi Hendrix, Les Paul, Eric Clapton, Eddie Van Halen, Chuck Berry, Andrés Segovia, Pete Townshend and many more. Combines personal biography, career history, and playing techniques.

Softcover, 300pp, 8-1/2 x 11, ISBN 0-87930-260-7, $19.95